ISBN 978-0-666-19016-1
PIBN 10446591

FB &c Ltd, Dalton House, 60 Windsor Avenue, London, SW19 2RR.
Company number 08720141. Registered in England and Wales.

For support please visit www.forgottenbooks.com

DIZIONARIO

DELLE

LINGUE

ITALIANA ed INGLESE

Di GIUSEPPE BARETTI.

Più di dieci mila Vocaboli si sono aggiunti che l' ALTIERI aveva lasciati fuora.

Questa EDIZIONE contiene una GRAMMATICA della due LINGUE.

NOVA EDIZIONE.

VOLUME II.

LONDON:

Printed for W. STRAHAN; J. and F. RIVINGTON; W. JOHNSTON; HAWES, CLARKE, and COLLINS; W. OWEN; G. KEITH; S. CROWDER; T. LONGMAN; B. LAW; T. DAVIES; T. BECKET and Co.; WILSON and NICOL; J. ALMON; ROBINSON and ROBERTS; T. CADELL, and P. ELMSLEY.

MDCCLXXI.

DIZIONARIO

DELLE

LINGUE

ITALIANA ed INGLESE

DI GIUSEPPE BARETTI

[illegible] di dieci mila [illegible] voli si sono aggiunti che l' ALTIERI aveva lasciati fuora.

[illegible] contiene una GRAMMATICA della due Lingue

NOVA [illegible] I NE

VOLUME II.

LONDON:

Printed for W. Strahan, J. and F. Rivington, W. Johnston, Hawes, Clarke and Collins; W. Owen, G. Keith, S. Crowder, T. Longman, B. [illegible] T. [illegible], T. Becket and Co., Wilson and Nicoll, J. Almon, [illegible] and Richardson, T. Cadell, and E. [illegible].

PREFAZIONE.

IN quelle poche righe che vanno in fronte al primo tomo ho già accennate le ragioni per le quali questo mio Dizionario si debbe avere per molto migliore che alcuno di quelli che l' hanno precorso; nè sarebbe cosa bella ripetere quì in Italiano quello che già s' è detto in Inglese. Nulladimeno per non privare questo tomo del solito ornamento d' una Prefazione farò quì quattro parole della lingua di quest' Isola a fine d' incoraggiare i miei Paesani a studiarla a forza, e a farsene bravamente padroni.

Anch' io insieme con molti de' nostri Letterati Italiani m' immaginava un tempo che l' affaticarsi ad apprendere lingue viventi fosse un' opera quasimente perduta, nè mi opponeva troppo volentieri a certe buone persone le quali con più che magistrevole contegno usavano spesso ripetermi, che le due lingue morte insieme con la viva nostra bastavano ad informare gli uomini di tutto quello che agli uomini occorre sapere. Avanzando poscia alquanto con gli anni parevami che l' arricchirsi ancora della Francesse fosse il non plus ultra d' ogni Galantuomo; e dopo d' aver letti Montagne, Pascale, Malebranche, Cornelio, Moliere, la Fontaine, e alcuni altri conosciutissimi Scrittori di quella Nazione, m' era fitto in capo che nulla più si potesse trovare in una moderna Favella veramente meritevole dell' onorate vegghie d' una persona studiosa.

Ma molto piacevolmente m' avveddi essermi ingannato a partito allora che mi trovai mediocremente mastro del Britannico Parlare. Oh quante belle e grandi cose, Paesani miei, ho lette in questi libri che non si leggono in quelli d' altre genti! Passerò in silenzio un Hooker, uno Scot, un Clarke, un Bentley, uno Stillingfleet, un Tillotson, e centinaja d' altri loro teologi e sacri oratori che valorosamente battagliando contra i numerosi Scredenti del loro e d' altri paesi, hanno in mille modi e poco meno che con geometrica evidenza provata la verità della religione rivelata, così che hanno costretti gli Ateisti e i Deisti a rifuggirsi negli sterili deserti dell' ignoranza o a nascon1dersi nelle caliginose cave della mentecattaggine. Non dirò verbo de' loro filosofi e cercatori diligentissimi della natura, come a dire un Bacone, un

Boyle,

Boyle, un Newton, e tant' altri ſcrutinatori dell' uomo e dell' altr' opere della mano onnipotente. Laſcerò indietro i loro tanti moraliſti, i lor politici, gl' iſtorici e cronologiſti loro, i meccanici numeroſiſſimi, e farò ſolamente alcune poche parole de' loro poeti, perché *queſto è l' umore dove io pecco*, per ſervirmi d' un modo di dire del noſtro Berni. Quanta carta però non mi converrebbe ſcarabocchiare per darvi ſolo una malabbozzata idea d' uno Shakeſpeare, d' uno Spenſer, d'un Milton, d' un Dryden, e di molt' altri divini ſpiriti, che accozzando chi più chi meno alla ſchiettezza della poeſia Greca la venuſtà de' Latini, la vaghezza degl' Italiani, e la nitidezza de' Franceſi con la robuſtezza e fantaſticaggine della Saſſonia e delle Gaule, hanno prodotta una maniera di penſar poetico, della quale noi ſucceſſori del Lazio e imitatori di quegli antichi dell' Acaja non ci curiamo ancora quanto dovremmo fare, contentandoci troppo manſuetamente che i noſtri Poeti abbiano con iſcrupoloſa induſtria modellati i penſieri loro e il loro modo di poetare ſugli eſemplari Greci e Latini. Pur troppo è vero. Noi non ſappiamo quaſi che queſti arditi e liberi Iſolani hanno fatto un così maraviglioſo impaſto d' immagini orientali e ſettentrionali, e che hanno creata queſta rara poeſia, alla quale i Verſeggiatori della Senna e i Poeti dell' Arno darebbono molto altiſſimo luogo nel concetto loro ſe da buon ſenno l' apparaſſero. Che non poſs' io tradurre ſoltanto un pajo di Scene di Shakeſpeare o uno ſquarcio ſolo di Milton, e dare una eſatta copia della elevatezza, della baldanza, e della impetuoſa e nobil furia degli originali? Ma o ſia ch' io non abbia baſtevole perizia della lingua noſtra, o ſia che la lingua noſtra non abbia nervi e muſcoli abbaſtanza, io non mi ci ſo arriſchiare. Vedo bene i frutti ſull' albero, e vedo che ſono poma d' oro da far gola a chiunque; ma il terribile Genio di Tramontana che gli guarda non mi laſcia ſtendere la voglioſa mano a ricoglierne pure un panierino, onde quando me ne tornerò alla mia contrada ſarà pur meſtieri che i miei dolci Paeſani ſi contentino d' alcune poche foglie che a ſtento ho ricolte di terra e ripoſte con molta cura fra i pochi regali poetici che ho ſperanza di recar loro quando che ſia.

Voi dunque che ve la godete per quelle benedette ſpiagge d' Italia, ſtudiate un poco il linguaggio degl' Ingleſi, e ſiate certi ſenza ch' io vi dica di più, che da' libri loro apprenderete coſe che non vi poſſono eſſere inſegnate da libri Greci o da libri Latini, e molto meno da libri Franceſi. Valete, e a rivederci preſto.

A

GRAMMAR

OF THE

ITALIAN TONGUE.

GRAMMAR, which is *the art of uſing words properly*, compriſes four parts, Orthography, Etymology, Syntax, and Proſody.

ORTHOGRAPHY.

Orthography is *the art of combining letters into ſyllables, and ſyllables into words.* It therefore teaches previouſly the form and ſound of letters.

The letters of the Italian language are twenty-one.

Rom.—Ital.			Their ſound in compoſition according to the Engliſh pronunciation.
A a	*A a*	pronounce as in	w*a*r, *a*ll
B b	*B b*		*b*ell, a*b*le
C c	*C c*	before *a, o, u, i*, or a conſonant, as in	*c*all, *c*law,
		and before *e* and *i*, as in	ur*ch*in, *ch*ild
D d	*D d*		*d*o, a*dd*er
E e	*E e*		p*e*n, m*e*n
F f	*F f*		*f*ather, *f*lock
G g	*G g*	before *a, o, u, h*, or a conſonant, as in	*g*ame, *g*rant
		before *e* and *i*, as in	*g*in, *g*eometry
I i	*I i*		*i*ndex, *i*diom
J j	*J j*	ſounds like y in	*y*ield, *y*ellow
L l	*L l*		*l*ove, *l*ibel
M m	*M m*		*m*an, wo*m*an
N n	*N n*		a*n*o*n*, *n*u*n*
O o	*O o*		*o*bſure, b*o*rn
P p	*P p*	pronounce as in	*p*am*p*er, *p*e*pp*er
Q q	*Q q*		*q*uack, *q*ueen
R r	*R r*		*r*od, *r*ea*r*
S ſ s	*S ſ s*		*ſ*ea, *ſeſſ*ion
T t	*T t*		*t*i*t*le, *t*o*tt*er
U u	*U u*		f*u*ll, b*u*ll
V v	*V v*		*v*ein, *v*i*v*ify
Z z	*Z z*	The Engliſh have no ſound like any of the two ſounds that this letter has in Italian, of which I ſhall ſay more anon.	

To theſe is to be added

H h *H h*, which is a mere ſign, and has no ſound in compoſition, no more than in the words *h*erb, *h*oneſt, *h*umble.

Obſervations on the Italian Letters.

ALTHOUGH I do not intend this Grammar for the uſe of thoſe that are yet ſo illiterate as not to know which letter is a conſonant and which a vowel; yet, for method's ſake, I ſay that the Italian letters are partly vowels, partly conſonants.

The Vowels are five;

A, E, I, O, U.

Of A.

BESIDES the ſound that I have given this letter in the alphabet, *a*, in compoſition, has another ſharper when it is diſtinguiſhed with an accent, which never happens but at the end of words; as in *calamità* (*cala-*

(*calamity*). In this word the *à* is quicker than in the last *a* of *calamita* (*lodestone*). The whole secret of this difference is, that when a word, ending with any vowel, has such vowel accented, as *città*, *amerà*, *testè*, *avvegnachè*, *aprì*, *comparì*, *vedrò*, *chiamerò*, *perù*, *soprappiù*, the voice makes no stop until it reaches that vowel; but when a word ending with a vowel not accented, as *cara*, *amica*; *vene*, *superbe*; *quanti*, *sostegni*; *primo*, *secondo*; (words ending in *u* not accented we have none throughout the language) then the accent falls on the penultima; excepting the words that we call *sdrùcciole*, as *làgrima*, *bàrbare*, *fùlmini*, *prìstino*; where the accent falls on the antepenultima, as I have marked it.

In poetry, and sometimes in prose, we distinguish some of our vowels with an apostrophe, which generally serves instead of the vowel, or syllable cut off; as *pa'* for *pajo*, *vorre'* for *vorrei*; *fanciu'* for *fanciulli*. Such vowels, thus apostrophised, are pronounced as if they were accented.

Some Grammarians, whom I know not whether to call philosophers or musicians, say that the Italian *a* has six or seven different sounds; and I am not disposed to contradict their opinion. A nice ear will find some shadows of distinction not only in each vowel, but even in each consonant, when placed in different combinations; but as such a minute analysis of sounds would prove endless as well as puzzling, I shall therefore neither trouble myself nor the English reader with such aereal discussions, but follow the common method. It is not difficult to count the elms and oaks in St. James's park; but who will number the branches of each elm, and tell the leaves of each oak?

Of E, I, O, U.

What I have said of *a*, when it is accented, will serve for these four vowels likewise, when they are in the same case. I must only add that E and O have, in some Italian words, two distinct sounds each; one called, by the Italians, *aperto* (*open*); the other *chiuso* (*close*). But I have no infallible rule to give how to find out these differences. A foreigner must find them out by practice, by asking the natives, or by consulting the Crusca and those other Italian books, in which such distinctions are marked.

Our Salvini has printed, if I remember well, his translation from the Greek of Oppian, *On fishing*, with two different E's and O's, and the curious and patient may consult that book.

The Consonants are sixteen;

B, C, D, F, G, J, L, M, N, P, Q, R, S, T, V, Z.

Of the Letter B.

B has no other sound but that which I have given it in the alphabet.

Of C.

C, besides the two alphabetical, has a third sound when it is preceded in a syllable by *s*, and followed by *e* or *i*, as in the words *sciagùra*, *lasciàre*, *esce*; *discèndere*, *sciolgo*, where the *sc* must be pronounced as the English do *sh*. When *sc* is followed by *a*, *o*, *u*, as in the words *esca*, *nascosto*; *trascurato*; pronounce as if it was written *eska*, *naskosto*, *traskurato*.

C, before *h*, has the sound of the English K in *hawk*; *leek*; *kalendar*; or the sound of the English *c* before the vowels *a*, *o*, *u*. Therefore *cheto*, *cherico*, *chiamo*, *chicchera*, must be pronounced as if they were wrote *kéto*, *kérico*, *kiámo*, *kickkera*.

C never comes united with another C in the same syllable. When you see them together, as in the words *occhio*, *bocchèggiare*, *occupare*, *occorso*, *uccidere*, *accetto*, *acclamare*, *ritocca*, you must consider two of the syllables of such words as divided thus, *oc-chio*, *boc-cheggiare*, *oc-cupare*, *oc-corso*, *uc-cidere*, *ac-cetto*, *ac-clamare*, *ritoc-ca*. The second *c*, in such words, always follows the rule that I gave in the alphabet; that is, when preceding *h*, or *a*, *o*, *u*, or a consonant, *c* then is pronounced as hard as *k*; and, when preceding *e* or *i*, is pronounced soft as *ch* in English; and the first *c* always follows the fate of the second. If the second is pronounced soft, the first is soft. If the second is hard, the first is hard likewise; therefore mind the second, and think little about the first.

Of D *and* F.

See the alphabet.

Of

Of G.

G, besides the two alphabetical, has two more sounds that the English have not in their language, and must therefore learn from the voice of an Italian.

The one is when *g* is in the combination of *gli*, and a vowel follows; as in the words *zagaglia*, *veglia*, *vegliando*, *figlia*, *figliastro*, *voglia*, *puglia*, *mugliare*, *battaglieresco*, *veglie*, *figlie*, *moglie*, *battibuglio*, *maglio*, *meglio*, *miglio*, *migliore*, *cespuglio*; or when *gli* stands alone as an article, or when it ends a word, as in *dagli*, *negli*, *figli imbrogli*, *grabugli*.

In this case, I say, the sound of the *g* has a sound that the English have not. The French language has the *l mouillée*, as they call it, which bears much affinity to our *gl* in the abovesaid combination.

Yet you must take notice, that when to that combination a consonant follows, as in the words *negligente*, *negligenza*, *anglicano*, the *g* is pronounced hard as in the words *glimmering*, *glance*, *negligent*, *negligence*, *anglican*; and it is hard likewise in the two poetical words, *Angli (Britons)* and *Anglia (Britain.)*

The other sound of *g*, that the English language has not, is when it is in the combinations *gna*, *gne*, *gni*, *gno*, *gnu*, as in the words *magagna*, *bagnato*, *degne spegnere*, *menzognero*, *incarognito*, *agogni*, *sogno*, *bisognoso*, *ignudo*, *ognuno*. The French have likewise that sound, in their language, in that same combination; as in *besogne*, *lorgner*, *borgne*, and many more.

When two *gg*'s meet together in a word, as in *aggravio*, *tragga*, *spiagge*, *reggere*, *agguerrito*, the first *g* follows the fate of the second; and it is hard if the second is hard, or soft if the second is soft, according to the rule that I gave in speaking of the two *cc*'s.

Of L.

L is pronounced as in English, except in *glia*, *glie*, *gli*, *glio*, *gliu*, where its sound is a little confounded with that of the *g*, and resembles the French *l mouillée*, as I said above.

Of M.

M is pronounced as in English.

Of N.

N is pronounced as in English, except when preceded by *g* in the combinations *gna*, *gne*, *gni*, *gno*, *gnu*, where it is a little confounded with the *g*. I said above, that these combinations are pronounced by the French as by the Italians; but the English have no such sounds, therefore must learn them from the voice of an Italian, or, at worst, by that of a Frenchman.

Of P, Q, R.

Pronounced as in English.

Of S.

S, in some words is pronounced with more and in some with less sibilation. The sibilation is, in general, very forcible when *s* begins a word, as in *sapere*, *santo*, *sarpare*, *sforrere*, *sdrucciolo*. But in many words it has a softer sound, as in *rimaso*, *impresa*, *eseguire*, *caso*, *trasandato*. Yet I think it impossible to give a rule to determine precisely when the *s* is to be pronounced with more, and when with less force. I have even observed, that the Tuscans themselves, and the very inhabitants of Florence, in the rapidity of utterance, do not constantly agree on this particular. Yet before *v* it is always soft, as I shall say anon in speaking of *v*.

I have already said, in speaking of *c*, that when *sc* is followed by *e* or *i*, it is pronounced like *sh* in English, as in the words, *sciagura*, *lasciare*, *esce*, *discendere*, *sciolgo*.

The *s*, when followed by any consonant, is called, by the Italians, an *impure s*, and must never be preceded by a consonant; though, in poetry, some have occasionally neglected this rule. The Tuscans abhor so much the disagreeable sound of an *impure s*, preceded by a consonant, that they say *istante costante*, *coscienza*, *istruire*, *istigare*, instead of *instante*, *constante*, *conscienza*, *instruire*, *instigare*; and those that do not abandon etymology for facility of utterance, are certainly in the wrong, for sweetness is the chief characteristic of the Italian tongue, and the *s impure* preceded by a consonant sounds so harsh in our ears, that we cannot avoid it too much. For the sake of sweetness we disregard sometimes not only etymology, but even grammar, that is *propriety* and *justness of speech*, and use the neuter article instead of the masculine whenever an article is to be prefixed to a name beginning with an *ſ impure*, and we say *lo ſcuolaro*, and not *il ſcuolaro*; we likewise add an *i* to any word that follows the monoſyllables *in*, *con*, *non*, becauſe we cannot change the terminations of theſe monoſyllables, and we ſay *con iſpavento*, *non iſtare*, *in iſtrada*, inſtead of *con ſpavento*, *non ſtare*, *in ſtrada*; and yet it would be ridiculous to ſay *iſpavento*, *iſtare*, *o iſtrada*, in any other caſe throughout the language. In making my Dictionary I have been obliged to peruſe twice that of our Academicians, and I have found but two words *ſolstizio* and *ſuperstizione* that have the *ſ impure*; but I muſt obſerve that the Tuſcans in the rapidity of utterance pronounce the firſt ſometimes *ſoſtizio* and ſometimes *ſoliſtizio*; and the ſecond always *ſupeſtizione*.

Of T.

T is pronounced as in Engliſh.

The ancient Italians uſed to write *ambitione*, *amicitia*, *gratia*, *punitione*, *patienza*, and other ſuch words of Latin derivation, and pronounced the *t* as *z*; but the writers of this as well as of the laſt century, have thought it more convenient and more unequivocal to follow throughout the language pronunciation rather than etymology; and as they wrote and write *ambizione*, *amicizia*, *grazia*, *punizione*, *pazienza*, according to pronunciation, therefore this obſolete *t* has nothing to do in this paragraph.

Of V.

V, when a conſonant, differs not in pronunciation from the Engliſh *v*. Its ſound bearing great ſimilarity with the letter *b*, they are in many words uſed indiſtinctly one for the other; ſo we ſay *ſerbare* and *ſervare*, *nervo* and *nerbo*, *voce* and *boce*. When *ſ* preceeds *v*, it loſes of its natural ſibilation, as in *ſvenire*, *diſviare*, *ſvarione*.

Of Z.

Some Grammarians call the *z* a double letter, but this is not the place to animadvert on their opinion. They ſay that it has many ſounds, and ſay peradventure true; for, as I ſaid in ſpeaking of *A*, nice and muſical ears will find that this is the caſe with every letter. Yet the *z* has but two ſounds eaſily diſtinguiſhed, which are both whizzing and ſibilating, and both much ſtronger than the Engliſh *z*. One of them we call *ſoft*, as in the words *rezzo*, *mezzo*, *orzo*, *zelo*, *zanzara*, where the ſibilation is like *ds*. The other we call *hard* or *ſharp*, as in the words *prezzo*, *carezze*, *zana*, *zio*, *zucca*, *aſtuzia*, *letizia*, *azione*, *ambizione*, *amicizia*, *grazia*, *punizione*, *pazienza*, where the ſibilation is like *ts*. Some good-natured writers have endeavoured to deſerve well of their country, by writing *azzione*, *ambizzione*, *letizzia*. It is pity they did not diſplay their prodigious wit further, and write likewiſe *zzana*, *zzio*, *zzucca*.

I have no rule to give (and it ſeems that the Academicians della Cruſca had none themſelves) for diſtinguiſhing when the *z* is ſoft and when hard.

Gigli, Altieri, Rolli, and other grammatical ſpeculators, although very ignorant of the genius and beauties of their language, and although born and bred in thoſe regions of Italy where the pronunciation is vicious, as Siena, Rome, Piacenza, Venice, and other places diſtant from Florence, have yet preſcribed a multitude of rules, that fixed not only thoſe words in which the *z* is to be pronounced *hard* or *ſoft*, but likewiſe thoſe in which *e* and *o* are *open* or *cloſe*. Their confidence went even ſo far, that their rules leave no perplexity behind, and every word in the Italian language may be pronounced by any Engliſhman, French, Turk, Chineſe, or Californian as well as by the Preſidents of the Florentine Academies. Yet thoſe Engliſh that will be pleaſed to follow my advice, (and who is the preceptor who has not ſome good ſoul that follows his advice?), muſt fling thoſe magiſterial rules into the fire; for it is better not to go a journey than miſs one's way for ever.

Of H.

H is ſo poor a thing in Italy, that it has not the honour of increaſing the ſound of a vowel as it often has in Engliſh; for in Italian we have no ſuch thing as an aſpiration. Its chief uſe is to ſtand erect after *c* and *g*, and inform the reader that thoſe two letters are to be pronounced as hard as when they

they preceed *c*, *o*, *u*. It diſtinguiſhes likewiſe to the eye and not the ear *ha* (he *has*) from the article *a*; and *hanno* (they *have*) from *anno* (year). Some unmerciful people bear ſo great an enmity to this droniſh *h*, that they baniſh it even from theſe two laſt places, and inſtead of *ha* they write *à*, and *ànno* inſtead of *hanno*. In ancient times nevertheleſs *h* was treated with more reſpect, and kept company with all thoſe ſyllables that it was uſed to frequent in the time of the Romans; therefore we find it in all ancient Italian books in the words h*omo*, h*onore*, *dish*o*neſto*, *ab*h*orrire*, h*avere*, h*abitare*, *esh*i*larare*, *arc*h*o*, *patriarc*h*a*, h*ierarchia*, and numberleſs others. Was *h* now ſeen in any ſuch words it would give a very indifferent character to any piece of writing. That I may not therefore give offence to any hot countryman of mine, I have refuſed it the cuſtomary name of *letter*, and even puſhed it out of its place in the alphabet, which uſed to be between *g* and *i*.

Of K, W, X, Y.

K, X, and Y, though uſed by our glorious predeceſſors the Romans, have no place in our alphabet; and of the Engliſh or German W few people in Italy know the exiſtence.

Inſtead of *k* we uſe *c* from the Alps to the Sicilian ſea. The Venetians only write *Kavalier* inſtead of the Tuſcan word *Cavaliere*, and I believe they know not why.

For the *x* we ſometimes ſubſtitute *ſs*; and have changed *Alexander*, *prolixity*, into *Aleſſandro proliſſita*; ſometimes we have metamorphoſed *x* into *ſ*, and ſay *eſempio*, *eſemplare*, for the Latin words *exemplar*, *exemplare*, or *x* into *c*, as *eccelſo*, *ecceſſo*, for *excelſus*, *exceſſus*.

Yet in the beginning of a few proper names that came from Greece, ſome Italians ſtill keep it, as in *Xantippe*, *Xanto*, but pronounce it as a ſoft *s*.

For the *y* we have ſubſtituted the vowel *i*; yet in our old books it generally preſerves its etymological place.

The *w*, we make no ſcruple in tranſlating Engliſh names to change it into *U* when it is a vowel in Engliſh, and into *V* when a conſonant.

ETYMOLOGY.

Etymolgy teaches the deduction of one word from another, and the various modifications by which the ſenſe of the ſame words is diverſified, as *il cavallo*, *i cavalli*; *amo*, *amai*, *buono*, *buoniſſimo*, and ſo forth.

Of the Articles.

The Italians ſtrictly ſpeaking have but three articles, *il*, *lo*, *la*, which precede ſubſtantive and adjective names and pronouns. Theſe articles are declinable, but they want a vocative caſe.

Singular.

Nominative.	Il.	Lo.	La.
Genitive.	Del.	Dello.	Della.
Dative.	Al.	Allo.	Alla.
Accuſative.	Il.	Lo.	La.
Ablative.	Dal.	Dallo.	Dalla.

Plural.

Nom.	I *or* Li.	Gli.	Le
Gen.	Delli.	Degli.	Delle.
Dat.	Alli.	Agli.	Alle.
Accuſ.	I *or* Li.	Gli.	Le.
Abl.	Dalli.	Dagli.	Dalle.

Il and *lo* are maſculine articles. Some call *lo* a neuter article. *La* is feminine.

The article *il* precedes names that begin with a conſonant, except the *impure ſ*. We ſay therefore *il cavallo*, *il ſignore*, *il buono*, *il cattivo*, *il mio*, *il tuo*, *il mangiare*, *il bere*, though our firſt writers ſaid *lo cavallo*, *lo ſignore*, *lo buono*, &c.

The article *lo* precedes names that begin with a vowel or with an *impure ſ*. Grammatically ſpeaking we ought to ſay *lo amore*, *lo ecceſſo*, *lo ingiuſto*, *lo onore*, *lo unico*, *lo ſtudio*, *lo ſchioppo*, *lo ſtare*, *lo ſternutare*; but as the rapidity of utterance has long ago ſunk the vowel of the article before thoſe names that begin with a vowel, we now ſay *l' amore*, *l' ecceſſo*, *l' ingiuſto*, *l' onore*, *l' unico*. Yet in poetry we take ſeveral licenſes, and ſay ſometimes *lo amore*, *lo ecceſſo*, *lo ingiuſto* and *lo 'ngiuſto*; but never *lo onore*, *lo unico*, becauſe the meeting of *o* with *o*, or *o* with *u* make too forcible an hiatus. Some writers ſay

ſay *lo imperadore* in verſe, and *lo 'mperadore* as well as *l' imperadore* in proſe.

The article *la* being, as I ſaid, a feminine one, it precedes feminine names beginning with any conſonant, as *la donna*, *la ſignora*, *la caſa*, *la ſtatua*, *la mia*, *la tua*, *la buona*, *la cattiva*. It ought grammatically to precede likewiſe thoſe that begin with a vowel, but rapidity of utterance has likewiſe deſtroyed its *a*, ſo that inſtead of *la anima*, *la eſca*, *la iniqua*, *la oneſta*, *la ugola*, we ſay *l' anima*, *l' eſca*, *l' iniqua*, *l' oneſta*, *l' ugola*.

It is to be obſerved that in poetry we ſay *lo Dio*, and in the plural, whether proſe or poetry, *gli Dei*, though *Dio* and *Dei* begin with a conſonant. The reaſon of this exception I take to be that *lo* is more ſolemn than *il*, and *gli* than *i* or *li*.

To names beginning with *z*, our acute Grammarian Buonmattei ſays, that we muſt give the article *il* in the ſingular, and *gli* in the plural. I know no reaſon for this irregularity; and though I agree with him in plural, yet (in poetry at leaſt) I ſhould not ſcruple to have *lo* as well as *il* in the ſingular, as I cannot help thinking that *il zecchino*, *il zoccolo*, *il zittello*, ſound harſher than *lo zecchino*, *lo zoccolo*, *lo zittello*. But let the reader take this as an opinion of mine, and not as a rule.

Some of the derivatives of the three articles that I have declined above, that is, thoſe which form two ſyllables, as *delli*, *alli*, *dalli*; *dello*, *allo*, *dallo*; *degli*, *agli*, *dagli*; *della*, *alla*, *dalla*; and *delle*, *alle*, *dalle*, are by ſome Italian Grammarians called *compounded articles*, and I call them *a coalition of the article and the prepoſition*, as they are really a coalition of particles that ſometimes wear the dreſs of the articles, and ſometimes that of the prepoſitions. Our ancient writers both in proſe and verſe generally divided them, and ſaid *de li*, *a li*, *da li*, *de lo*, *a lo*, *da lo*, &c. and in old manuſcripts, and editions of Petrarca's Poems eſpecially, I took notice ſeveral times that this was his practice. Berni, who is looked upon amongſt us as a moſt harmonious and correct poet, has ſaid (if I remember well the lines)

E voi ſtelle lucenti, al lume de le
Quali io cammino al deſtinato ſegno,
Propizio ſia e benigno e fedele
Il favor voſtro a queſto ardito legno.

Arioſto and Taſſo have ſomewhere in rhyme ſplit aſunder the *compounded article*, and both did it, I ſuppoſe, upon good authority; therefore in poetry I ſhould not ſcruple much to do the ſame, as it ſeems to me that ſuch ſeparation produces ſolemnity; though in proſe I would rather uſe the coalition in imitation of the rapidity of diſcourſe.

They call *compounded* likewiſe ſome other articles that abound in our language, as *nello*, *collo*, *ſullo*, *pello*, and their plurals *nelli*, *colli*, *ſulli*, *pelli*; and *nella*, *colla*, *ſulla*, *pella*, and their plurals *nelle*, *colle*, *ſulle pelle*. What I have to obſerve upon theſe articles or coalitions of articles is, that *pello*, *pelli*, *pella*, and *pelle* are obſolete, and we ſay now *per lo*, *per li* or *per gli*, *per la*, and *per le*. *Nello*, *nelli*, *nella* and *nelle* are coalitions of *ne lo*, *ne li* or *ne gli*, *ne la*, and *ne le*; *collo*, *colli*, *colla*, *colle*, coalitions of *con lo*, *con li* or *con gli*, *con la*, and *con le*; and *ſullo*, *ſulli*, *ſulla*, and *ſulle*, coalitions of *ſu lo*, *ſu li* or *ſu gli*, *ſu la*, and *ſu le*.

Nello, *collo*, *ſullo*, *pello*, are much liable to be curtailed of their laſt ſyllables, eſpecially in proſe and in familiar poetry, and become *nel*, *col*, *ſul*, *pel*, when they precede a name or pronoun beginning with a conſonant, provided that ſuch a conſonant be not an *impure ſ*. And *pel* is then obſolete no more, as *pello* is generally reckoned to be, and their plurals *nelli*, *colli*, *ſulli*, *pelli*, become in the ſame caſe *ne'*, *co'*, *ſu'*, or *ſu i*, *pe'*.

Nella, *colla*, *ſulla*, or their plurals, never change and are never curtailed but by caprice, and *pella* is often changed into *per la*, becauſe *pella* has an obſolete look, as I ſaid before.

We have beſides ſix particles in Italian, *di*, *a*, *da*, *con*, *per*, *ſu*, that ſome of our Grammarians call *articles*, ſome *prepoſitions*, and ſome *ſigns for the caſes of a noun* (*ſegnacaſi*). *Di* is genitive; *a* is dative; *da*, *con*, *per*, *ſu*, are ablatives; and from the coalition of theſe with the articles are formed *dello*, *delli*, *della*, *delle*; *allo*, *alli*, *alla*, *alle*; *dallo*, *dalli*, *dalla*, *dalle*; *collo*, *colli*, *colla*, *colle*; *pello*, *pelli*, *pella*, *pelle*; and finally *ſullo*, *ſulli*, *ſulla*, and *ſulle*.

It is to be obſerved, that the three firſt of the abovesaid particles, that is, *a*, *di*, *da*, are often indiſtinctly uſed one for the other. I mean that ſometimes *di* is given to the ablative inſtead of *da*; *a* is given to the genitive inſtead of *di*, or to the ablative inſtead of *da*; *da* is given to the genitive inſtead of *di*, or to the dative inſtead of *a*. Beſides this mutual change of places, they intrude likewiſe in the places of the other three, *in*, *per*, and *con*. *In* is ſometimes given to the dative inſtead of *a*, and *per* drives *da* out of its place; *con* is the only one of the ſix that keeps faithful to its ablative, and though it ſuffers ſometimes to be diſpoſſeſſed of its place, never will intrude into that of another.

I might add a great many more things to this chapter of the articles, but what I have already ſaid I think ſufficient for the inſtruction of an Engliſhman. I am even afraid of having bewildered him by ſaying too much; for I have obſerved that in general the right way to keep a learner backward in his Italian, is to keep him long upon theſe puzzling minuteneſſes. Some of my tongue-teaching Countrymen, have by this art kept a Pupil under their tuition much longer than they would certainly have done, if, inſtead of forcing them to anatomiſe the nature and uſe of articles, they had ſimply pointed them out, and gone onward explaining other parts of ſpeech to them. Therefore let me give this caution to all Engliſh beginners, to ſkim over the moſt difficult parts of Italian Grammar, eſpecially the articles; to treaſure up words and ſentences; and to enable themſelves to read Italian tolerably. When this is done, let them come back to grammar, and carefully read the whole affair of articles, which has been divided by Buonmattei into twenty-two pretty long chapters; and I give them my word that they will be pleaſed at their progreſs. I could name half a dozen young ladies that in a few months read Meteſtaſio and Taſſo by following this method.

The Italian articles are ſtubborn things at a diſtance, and conſidered abſtractedly they will fright foreigners. But by obſerving their different modes and ſituations in ſentences, any body may ſoon be enabled to maſter them.

Of Nouns Subſtantives.

The relations of Italian Nouns to words going before or following, are not expreſſed as in Latin by *caſes* or changes *of termination*, but as in Engliſh and in moſt of the other European languages by *prepoſitions*, *articles*, or *ſegnacaſis*.

There is no noun in Italian but what is either maſculine or feminine.

Thoſe maſculine nouns that in the ſingular end in *a*, *e*, or *o* without accents, end in *i* in the plural; as *poeta*, *padre*, *maeſtro*; plural *poeti*, *padri*, *maeſtri*.

The femine nouns generally end in *a* and in *e*, as *donna*, *ſtella*, *coſa*, *madre*, *moglie*, *torre*. Thoſe in *a* terminate their plurals in *e*, *donne*, *ſtelle*, *caſe*. Thoſe in *e* terminate their plurals in *i*, *madri*, *mogli*, *torri*.

Of thoſe nouns that end their ſingular in *e*, Altieri, who was a laborious, but an ignorant man, ſays that there are only *four* that terminate their plural as their ſingular: *re*, *ſpecie*, *effigie*, and *ſuperficie*. That the number of theſe four is only determined by the article is true; we ſay in the ſingular *il re*, *la ſpecie*, *la effigie*, *la ſuperficie*, and in the plural *i re*, *le ſpecie*, *le effigie*, *le ſuperficie*. I am only apprehenſive that Altieri is miſtaken when he ſays that we have theſe four, and no more, whoſe number does not change the termination. *Requie* at leaſt makes a *fifth*, and there may be a few more that will not come juſt now into my head.

All nouns ending with an accented vowel, whether maſculine or feminine, terminate their plurals with the vowel that they have in the ſingular; as *cittá*, *libertá*, *podeſtá*, *mercé*, *virtú*, *ſervitú*, *Geſú*. The article, the pronoun, or the adjective determine their number.

Almoſt every noun that ends with an accented vowel, had originally a letter or a ſyllable more. *Città* was originally *cittade* or *cittate*, and very anciently *cittae*; *libertà* was *libertade* and *libertate*, or *libertae*; *podeſtà*, when it is maſculine and means *a magiſtrate* ſo called, I ſaw it in our oldeſt writings *podeſtae*, and when it is feminine and means *power*, it was *podeſtate* and *podeſtade*: *Mercé* was *mercede*, *virtú* was *virtue*, *virtude*, or *virtute*, *ſervitú* was *ſervitude* or *ſervitute*, and *Geſú* was *Geſue*.

The

The terminations in *áe*, in *ade*, and in *ate*, ended in the plural in *adi* or *ati*; those in *ede* ended in *edi*, and those in *úe*, *ude*, and *ute*, ended in *udi* and *uti*. Now the terminations in *áe* and in *úe*, as *podestae*, *virtue*, *cesae*, are obsolete; those in *ade*, *ede*, *úde*, are often admitted in prose and in poetry; and those in *ate*, *ete*, and *ute*, are considered as entirely poetical.

Many of our masculine nouns have a double singular, as *console* or *consolo*, *cavaliere* or *cavaliero*, *pensiere* or *pensiero*, *scolare* or *scolaro*. Those ending indistinctly in *ere* and *ero*, as *cavaliere*, *pensiere*, and many others, admit likewise in the singular a third termination in *eri*, as a mere ungrammatical Florentinism, and would never advise any to make use of it but in familiar prose and in rustic poetry, though some of our best ancient writers scrupled not to use it even in solemn prose and in high poetry.

There are a few other nouns that have a double singular, one masculine and the other feminine, as *orecchio* and *orecchia*; the plural of *orecchio* is *orecchi*, and that of *orecchia* is *orecchie*.

There are a few feminine nouns that have a double singular, as *froda* or *frode*, *loda* or *lode*, *arma* or *arme*. These end their plurals in *e* or *i*; *le frode*, *le frodi*, *le lode*, *le lodi*, *le arme*, *le armi*. Generally speaking the plural ending in *i* is for the prose, and that in *e* is more appropriated to poetry.

Some masculine nouns have two plurals, one masculine and the other femine. *Il castello*, *il riso*, *il labbro*, *l' osso*, and others, are plurally *i castelli*, *i risi*, *i labbri*, *gli ossi*, or *le castella*, *le risa*, *le labbra*, *le ossa*.

Our ancients, instead of the regular plural of some masculine nouns, used sometimes one feminine of a very strange termination. They said for instance in the singular *il campo*, *il lato*, *il prato*; and then instead of making the plural *i campi*, *i lati*, *i prati*, they made the feminines *le cámpora*, *le prátora*, *le látora*. Such irregular feminine plurals are now quite obsolete, and we constantly say *i campi*, *i lati*, *i prati*.

Some of our names have no singular, as *le Nozze*, *l' Esequie*, *i Vanni*.

The masculine nouns ending in *co* sometimes end their plurals in *ci* and sometimes in *chi*; as *Monaco*, *Calònaco*, *Medico*, *Porco*, plural *Monaci*, *Calonaci*, *Medici*, *Porci*; *Abbaco*, *Fico*, *Fuoco*, *Giuoco*, plural *Abbachi*, *Fichi*, *Fuochi*, *Giuochi*; and the masculine nouns ending in *go*, sometimes end their plurals in *gi* and sometimes in *ghi*. *Mago*, *Astrologo*, *Sparago*, plural *Magi*, *Astrologi*, *Sparagi*; *Drago*, *Spago*, *Albergo*, *Fungo*, plural *Draghi*, *Spaghi*, *Alberghi*, *Funghi*; but I do not know of any rule that can direct to form properly such plurals, and Buonmattei says, that after long meditation he could find none; that they are therefore to be learned only by practice and observation of the good writers that went before. The feminine nouns in *ca* or *ga* are not subject to such irregularity; but those in *ca* end their plurals in *che*, as *Monaca*, *Medica*, *Porca*; plural *Monache*, *Mediche*, *Porche*; and those in *ga* end their plurals in *ghe*, as *Maga*, *Astrologa*, *Spranga*, *Verga*; plural *Maghe*, *Astrologhe*, *Spranghe*, *Verghe*.

The feminine nouns that end their singular in *cia* or *gia*, end their plurals in *ce* or *cie* and *ge* or *gie*, as *Pancia*, *Francia*, *Caccia*, *Frangia*, *Foggia*, *Franchigia*, plural *Pance* or *Pancie*, *France* or *Francie*, *Cacce* or *Caccie*, *Frange* or *Frangie*, *Fogge* or *Foggie*, *Franchige* or *Franchigie*. Take only notice that the plural terminations in *ce* or *ge* are more used and reckoned more elegant than those in *cie* and *gie*.

The infinitives of our verbs are changed into substantive nouns of the masculine gender; and the article with which they are all accompanied apprises us of their metamorphosis as well as of their cases. *L' andare*, *lo stare*, *il tornare*, *dall' andare*, *allo stare*, *nel tornare*. Some of these substantives admit even of a plural; as *i mangiari*, *i parlari*, *i baciari*, *gli abbracciari*, and others; yet the moderns seem not very fond of using them, and consider them rather as obsolete.

Of ADJECTIVES.

Adjectives in the English language are wholly indeclinable: this is not quite the case in Italian, for the greatest part of them have a masculine and feminine termination in the singular as well as in the plural, which serve to point out their genders as well as their numbers. And we say *caro amico*, *cara amica*,

amica, *cari amici*, and *care amiche*. When therefore adjectives end in *o*, as *caro*, *amoroſo*, *ſtupendo*, *fiero*, they are ſingular and maſculine; when they end in *a*, as *cara*, *amoroſa*, *ſtupenda*, *fiera*, they are ſingular and feminine; when they end in *i*, as *cari*, *amoroſi*, *ſtupendi*, *fieri*, they are plural and maſculine; and when they end in *e*, as *care*, *amoroſe*, *ſtupende*, *fiere*, they are plural and feminine.

Many adjectives end in *e*, as *verde*, *amabile*, *felice*, *facile*, *grande*. Theſe end their plural with *i*, *verdi*, *amabili*, *felici*, *facili*, *grandi*; and both in the ſingular and plural they are common to the maſculine and feminine nouns; as *un prato verde*, *una gonna verde*; *un uomo felice*, *una donna felice*; and in the plural *i prati verdi*, *le gonne verdi*, *gli uomini grandi*, *le donne amabili*.

Of the FORMATION *of* COMPARATIVES.

The adjectives form their comparatives, not by means of a different termination, as it is often the caſe in Engliſh, but by the aſſiſtance of the two adverbs of quantity, *più* and *meno*; as *queſto ſoggiorno mi è* PIU' CARO *di* QUELLO; *gli occhi di Clori ſono* MENO AMOROSI *che que' d' Amarille*; *vedemmo coſe in Italia molto* PIU' STUPENDE *che non le vedute in Francia*; *I prati in Inghilterra mi pajono* PIU' VERDI *che que' del Piemonte: Carlo è molto* PIU' FELICE *di Federigo, e Laura è molto* MENO AMABILE *di Lionora*.

Of the FORMATION *of* SUPERLATIVES.

The ſuperlatives are formed by changing the laſt vowel of the adjective into *iſſimo*, as from *buono*, *buoniſſimo*, *caro*, *cariſſimo*; *fiero*, *fieriſſimo*; *amabile*, *amabiliſſimo*; *verde*, *verdiſſimo*; *grande*, *grandiſſimo*. Superlatives, whether derived from adjectives ending in *o*, as *duono*, *caro*, or from adjectives ending in *e*, as *verde*, *felice*, all end in *o* in the maſculine of the ſingular, as *buoniſſimo*, *feliciſſimo*; in *a* in the feminine of the ſingular, as *buoniſſima*, *feliciſſima*; in *i* in the maſculine of the plural, as *buoniſſimi*, *feliciſſimi*; and in *e* in the feminine of the plural, as *buoniſſime*, *feliciſſime*.

The adjectives *buono*, *cattivo*, *piccolo*, and *grande*, have two comparatives and two ſuperlatives, that may be called regular and irregular.

The regular comparatives and ſuperlatives of *buono* are *più buono* and *buoniſſimo*, and the irregular are *migliore* and *ottimo*. The regular comparative and ſuperlative of *cattivo* are *più cattivo*, *cattiviſſimo*; the irregular are *peggiore* and *peſſimo*. *Piccolo*, regularly *più piccolo*, *piccoliſſimo*; irregularly *minore*, *minimo*, poetically *menomo*; *grande*, regularly *più grande*, *grandiſſimo*; irregularly *maggiore*, *maſſimo*.

Of AUGMENTATIVES *and* DIMINUTIVES.

A great number of our nouns, both ſubſtantive and adjective, are ſuſceptible of ſome augmentation or diminution in their ſignifications by undergoing a change of termination. Theſe changes branch out in ſo many manners, that to point them all out would make a large work by itſelf. They alter not only the ſignification of a primitive word, but ſometimes change even its gender; and make maſculine what is feminine, and feminine what is maſculine.

That I may therefore be ſhort, and give at the ſame time ſome clear idea of this peculiarity in our language, I exhibit here a few primitive words with as many of their augmentatives and diminutives as I could collect.

From UOMO (*a maſc. ſubſt.*) *a* MAN, *we form.*

Uomáccio (*m. s.*) a man both tall and clumſy, *or* wicked and deſpicable.

Uomaccióne (*m. s.*) a man very bulky and clumſy.

Uomináccio (*m. s.*) a very clumſy, ſhameleſs, worthleſs, or inſenſible fellow.

Uomaccíno (*m. s.*) a little active man, *or* a little impudent man, *or* an impertinent little fellow.

Uomicciuólo (*m. s.*) a punny little fellow.

Uomiciátto (*m. s.*) a deſpicable puny fellow.

Uomiciattolo (*m. s.*) a petty fellow, deſpicable punny, and of no conſequence or importance.

From DONNA (*a fem. ſubſt.*) *a* WOMAN, *we form.*

Donnône (*m. s.*) a tall, ſtrong, maſculine woman.

Donnóna, (*f. s.*) a tall, big, and healthful woman.

Donnácia, (*f. s.*) an impudent, deſpicable, *or* ſturdy woman, a tall dirty wench, a ſhameleſs whore.

Donnétta, (*f. s.*) a little or punny woman, an inſignificant woman, a prattling goſſip.

Donnicciuóla, (*f. s.*) a contemptible little woman.

Donnicína, (*f. s.*) a pretty little woman.

Donnúcia, (*f. s.*) a vulgar petty woman.

Donnaccióne, (*f. s.*) a ſtout whore, with a maſculine look.

From CASA, (*a feminine ſubſt.*) *a* HOUSE, *we form.*

Caſóne, (*m. s.*) a very large houſe.

Caſáccia, (*f. s.*) a large ill-contrived houſe.

Caſaménto, (*m. s.*) a well built houſe, and rather large.

Caſalóne, } *Caſoláre*, } (both *m. s.*) a large, rooſleſs, and half-ruined houſe.

Caſolaráccio, (*m. s*) a houſe ſtill worſe than a *caſolare*.

Caſótta, (*f. s.*) a ſnug houſe.

Caſótto, (*m. s.*) a houſe firmly built and ſnug. *It ſignifies alſo*, a dog houſe.

Caſélla, (*f. s.*) a little poor houſe.

Caſellína, (*f. s.*) a very little and pretty houſe.

Caſettíno, (*m. s.*) a pretty and ſnug houſe.

Caſettína, (*f. s.*) a ſnug houſe.

Caſína, (*f. s.*) a very ſmall houſe.

Casíno, (*m. s.*) a ſmall houſe built for the reception and diverſion of a few friends.

Casíle, (*m. s.*) a contemptible houſe, a thatched poor houſe.

Casípola, } *Caſúpola*, } (both *f. s.*) a ſmall contemptible houſe.

Caſúccia, (*f. s.*) a ſmall ill-looking houſe.

Caſúzza, (*f. s.*) a poor, ſmall, contemptible houſe.

Caſucciáccia, (*f. s.*) a poor, ſmall, half-ruined, contemptible houſe.

From LEPRE, (*a maſc. or fem. ſubſtant.*) *a* HARE, *we form*

Lepráccia, (*s. f.*) a very old hare.

Lepróne, (*m. s.*) a young fat hare.

Leproncéllo, (*m. s.*) a young hare, whoſe fleſh is tender eating.

Leprátto } *Leprótto* } (both *m. s.*) a young hare.

Leprétta, (*f. s.*) a hare that has not yet had young.

Leprettína } *Leprottína* } (both *f. s.*) a very ſmall hare.

Leprettíno } *Leprottíno* } (both *m. s.*) a ſmall hare.

From ACQUA, (*a fem. ſub.*) WATER, STREAM, *and* RAIN, *we form*

Acquáccia, (*f. s.*) bad water, large ſhower.

Acquazzóne, (*m. s.*) a large ſhower of long continuance.

Acquétta, (*f. s.*) a ſmall ſtream, ſmall rain.

Acquerélla, (*f. s.*) a very ſmall ſtream, a brook, very ſmall rain.

Acquerúgiola, (*f. s.*) rain ſcarcely perceptible.

Acquicélla, (*f. s.*) a very ſmall brook, very ſmall rain.

Acquitríno, (*m. s.*) water that finds its way out of a wall, dike, rock, or other ſuch place, and falls as in drops.

Acquolína, (*f. s.*) ſmall rain juſt perceptible.

From LUPO, (*a maſc. ſubſt.*) *a* WOLF, *we form*

Lupóne, (*m. s.*) a large wolf.

Lupáccio, (*m. s.*) a large, ugly, or cruel wolf.

Lupacchíno, (*m s.*) a wolf's whelp.

Lupátto, (*m. s.*) a young wolf.

Lupattíno } *Lupottíno* } (both *m. s.*) a very young and ſmall wolf.

Lupicíno, (*m. s.*) a wolf's whelp that juſt begins to wander about.

N. B. The feminine of *lupo* is *lupa*; and from *lupa* as many derivatives may be drawn, ending in *a*, as there are ending in *o* from *lupo*. The difference would only be, that thoſe in *a* would be all feminine, as thoſe in *o* are all maſculine.

From LIBRO, (*a maſc. ſubſt.*) *a* BOOK, *we form*

Libróne, (*m. s.*) a large book, a book materially heavy.

Libráccio, (*m. s.*) a large book of an ugly ſize; a book whoſe contents are wicked or deſpicable.

Li-

Librétto, (*m. s.*) a little book, a pretty book, ſpeaking of the form, and not the contents.

Libriccíno } (both *m. s.*) a very little book, *Libricciuólo* } as to its bulk.

Librettíno, (*m. s.*) a very little and pretty book, as to its bulk and form.

Librícolo } (both *m. s.*) a ſmall contempti- *Libercolo* } ble book, and it is generally ſaid relatively to its ſubject.

From GENTE (*a feminine, collective, and ſubſtantive name*) PEOPLE, FOLKS, *we form*

Gentáccia, (*f. s.*) deſpicable people.

Gentáglia, (*f. s.*) rabble, mob, the contemptible vulgar, wicked people, ſhameleſs people.

Gentagliáccia, (*f. s.*) wretches fit for any thing that is bad.

Gentáme, (*m. s.*) a croud indiſcriminately mixed.

Genterélla, (*f. s.*) people of little worth, of no importance.

Gentúccia, (*f. s.*) low people. *Dante* in this ſignification ſaid *gentúcca*.

Gentucciáccia, (*f. s.*) very deſpicable people.

From BELLO, (*a maſc. adjective*) BEAUTIFUL, *we form*

Bellóne, very beautiful, with the idea of *tightneſs*, or of *heartineſs*, blended with that of *beauty*.

Bellíno, pretty, beautiful without dignity.

Bellóccio, beautiful with compactneſs.

Bellúccio, *ſometimes it means* moderately beautiful, *and ſometimes it mixes the ideas of* beautifulneſs and love.

N. B. End *bello*, and its derivatives, in *a* inſtead of the *o*, and they all become feminine adjectives.

From GRANDE (*a maſculine or a feminine adjective*) *when it means* TALL, *we form*

Grandáccio, tall and clumſy, diſproportionately tall.

Grandétto, rather tall.

Grandicéllo, tall, *relatively to young age*, and it is ſaid of a boy.

Grandicciuólo, ſomething leſs than *grandicello*.

Grandótto, rather tall and ſtout.

Gradúccio, ſomething leſs than *grandétto*.

N. B. Change in *a* the terminations in *o*, and they become feminine.

From RIBA'LDO, (*a maſc. adj.*) INIQUITOUS, *we form*

Ribaldóne, groſsly iniquitous.

Ribaldáccio, groſsly and ſhameleſsly iniquitous

Ribaldonáccio, very groſsly iniquitous.

Ribaldéllo, petty in its iniquity for want of brains.

N. B. End the above words in *a*, and they ſhall be feminine.

From ABRUCIA'TO, (*adj. maſc.*) BURNT, *we form*

Abbruciatíccio, ſinged, ſuperficially or ſcarcely burnt.

Abbruciacchiáto, a little burnt here and there, or very ſuperficially burnt.

Beſides the above augmentatives and diminutives, that may almoſt be reduced to rules, we have ſome that cannot be brought to any analogy, as, from ME'DICO (a phyſician) *medicónzolo* (a punny deſpicable phyſician); from MINISTRO (a miniſter) *miniſtrónzolo* (a ſilly fellow that plays the miniſter of ſtate); from FRATE (a friar) *fratacchióne* (a fat, luſty, greaſy, or ſcandalous friar); from CANE (a dog) *cagnolíno* (a lap dog); from BA'CIO (a kiſs) *baciózzo* (a cordial ſmacking kiſs); and ſeveral other that do not now occur to me.

The general rule to diſtinguiſh the various ſignifications of AUGMENTATIVES is, that terminations in *one* and *ona* indicate *bigneſs* and *ſtoutneſs*; in *otto* and *occio* indicate a *compact and not diſpleaſing bigneſs*. Thoſe in *accio* and *azzo*, indicate *bigneſs as well as wickedneſs and deſpicability*. In *ame* they increaſe indefinitely the number. DIMINUTIVES in *ino*, *etto*, *ello*, and *uccio*, denote *endearment as well as ſmallneſs*; in *uzzo*, *atto*, *iccio*, *àttolo*, *ìpola*, *ùpola*, *uólo*, *anzuólo*, *ónzolo*, indicate *deſpicable pettineſs*; yet all theſe rules have exceptions which nothing but uſe can teach.

Few augmentatives and diminutives are admitted in ſolemn-ſtyle.

Of PRONOUNS.

Pronouns, in the Italian language, are declinable, and, for the greateſt part, admit of of the article. For unity's ſake I divide them into three claſſes only, though I know that a nice diſtinguiſher may parcel them out in many more.

Of the perſonal Pronouns.

Singular.	*Plural.*
Io	Noi
Tu	Voi
Egli	Eglino.

The feminine of Egli is *ella* or *eſſa*; the feminine of Eglino is *elle*, *elleno*, or *eſſe*.

The oblique caſes of Io are, *di me*, *a me*, *me*, *da me*. Thoſe of Tu are, *di te*, *a te*, *te*, *da te*. Thoſe of Egli are, *di lui*, *a lui*, *lui*, *da lui*. Thoſe of Noi are, *di noi*, *a noi*, *noi*, *da noi*. Thoſe of Voi are, *di voi*, *a voi*, *voi*, *da voi*. Thoſe of Eglino are, *di loro*, *a loro*, *loro*, *da loro*, or *d' eſſi*, *ad eſſi*, *eſſi*, *da eſſi*. Some poets, and eſpecially Berni, ſaid likewiſe, *d' elli*, *a elli*, *elli*, *da elli*. Of Elle, Elleno, and Esse, the plural oblique caſes are, *di loro*, *a loro*, *loro*, *da loro*, or *d' eſſe*, *ad eſſe*, *eſſe*, *da eſſe*; and ſome good writers have not ſcrupled to ſay likewiſe, *d' elle*, *ad elle*, *elle*, *da elle*; yet theſe are not ſo frequently uſed as the others, eſpecially in proſe.

The Italians have ſome particles, that ſometimes are uſed indifferently as articles, prepoſitions, adverbs, or expletives. Such particles are likewiſe uſed as pronouns; and they are twelve, *il*, *lo*, *la*, *gli*, *li*, *le*, *ne*, *mi*, *ti*, *ſi*, *ci*, *vi*. *Il* and *lo* are equivalent to *lui*; *la* to *lei*; *gli* and *li* to *loro* and *a lui*; *le* to *eſſe* and *a lei*; *ne* to *noi* and *a noi*; *mi* to *me* and *a me*; *ti* to *te* and *a te*; *ſi* to *ſe* and *a ſe*; *ci* to *noi* and *a noi*; *vi* to *voi* and *a voi*.

Either the *ſenſe*, or the *verb*, or *both*, indicate when any of the above particles is dative or accuſative; for, if the verb requires a dative, then the particle is dative; and, if it requires an accuſative, then the particle is accuſative. Some Grammarians have called ſuch particles *vicepronouns*, becauſe they rather indicate a pronoun than a noun.

They are monoſyllabically admitted in the ſentence, and then they generally precede the verb; as, *mi viene*, *mi mancò*; *lo mangiò*, *lo chiama*, *lo faremo*; *gli avea*, *gli ſcappa*; *ci hai*, *ci vorebbe*; *la domandò*, *la richieſe*; *ne richiedera*, *ne affliggeſti*; *ſi andaſſe*, *ſi andera*, &c.

When they are joined to the verb, it is always at the end, thus, *viénemi*, *mancómmi*, *mangiòllo*, *chiamóllo*, *farémolo*, *avéagli*, *ſcáppagli*, *háici*, *vorrébbeci*, *domandólla*, *richiéſela*, *richiederálla*, *affliggéſtine*, *andáſſeſi*, *anderáſſi*; where it is obſervable that, when any of theſe particles is joined to a word ending with an accented letter, it doubles its conſonant, except the particle *il* becauſe, when joined to the verb, it is changed into *lo*; and the particle *gli*, becauſe it begins with two conſonants; ſo we ſay, *viénemi*, and not *vi némmi*, becauſe *viéne* has not the accent on the ſecond ſyllable; but we ſay, *portómmi*, and not *portómi*, becauſe *portó* has the accent on the ſecond ſyllable.

The final *e* of all our infinitives is deſtroyed by any of the above monoſyllabical pronouns; and we do not ſay, *amárelo*, *vedérela*, *sentíregli*, *guardáreli*, *pagárele*, *fárene*, *laſciáremi*, *diſperáreti*, *bévereſi*, *mangiáreci*, *colcarévi*; but *amárlo*, *vedérlo*, *ſentérgli*, *guardárli*, *pagárle*, *fárne*, *laſciármi*, *diſperárti*, *béverſi*, *mangiárci*, *colcárvi*.

Our other perſonal pronouns are, *coſtui* and *colui*; whoſe feminines are, *coſtei* and *colei*. Of *coſtui* and *coſtei* the common plural is *coſtoro*; of *colui* and *colei* the common plural is *coloro*.

Of the poſſeſſive and relative Pronouns.

The poſſeſſive and relative pronouns, like other adjectives, are declined by the help of particles and articles. *Il mio*, *del mio*, *al mio*, *il mio*, *dal mio*; or *mio*, *di mio*, *a mio*, *mio*, *da mio*: *Il voſtro*, *del voſtro*, *al voſtro*, *il voſtro*, *dal voſtro*; or *voſtro*, *di voſtro*, *a voſtro*, *voſtro*, *da voſtro*, &c. *Il quale*, *del quale*, *al quale*, *il quale*, *dal quale*; or *quale*, *di quale*, *a quale*, *quale*, *da quale*: *L' altrui*, *dell' altrui*, *all' altrui*, *l' altrui*, *dall' altrui*; or *altrui*, *d' altrui*, *ad altrui*, *altrui*, *da altrui*.

If a pronoun ends with an *o* in the maſculine, the feminine is formed by changing only that *o* into an *a*, and the article; as, *il mio*, *la mia*; *il tuo*, *la tua*; *il voſtro*, *la voſtra*.

If a pronoun ends in *e* in the maſculine, as in *tale* and *quale*, the feminine diſtinguiſhes itſelf from the maſculine not by a change of termination, but by the article when the ſentence admits of it; as, *il* Tale *vorrebbe paſſare per buono*; *la* Tale *vorrebbe paſſare per buona*; or by the ſenſe, and by ſome other feminine

in-

included in the sentence when the article is not admitted; as, *quale vorresti esser tu*, TALE *vorrebbe esser Pietro*; *quale è Maddalena*, TALE *credo che sia Francesca*. *Tu* and *Pietro* in the first example indicate that *tale* and *quale* are two masculine pronouns; *Maddalena* and *Francesca* indicate that *tale* and *quale* are two feminine pronouns.

Of the VERB.

Italian verbs, by the generality of our Grammarians, are first divided into personal and impersonal.

The personal verbs, as *amare*, *mangiare*, *bere*, *dormire*, are conjugated by the assistance of the three personal pronouns, *io*, *tu*, *egli*, with their plurals, *noi*, *voi*, *eglino*; as *io amo*, *tu ami*, *egli ama*, *noi amiamo*, *voi amate*, *eglino amano*.

When an active verb is conjugated without the pronoun, as the Italians generally do, the pronoun is supposed.

The impersonal verbs, as *nevicare*, *grandinare*, *piovere*, *balenare*, are conjugated by the third person of the singular only, and without a pronoun; as, *nevica*, *grandina*, *piove*, *balena*.

We say very often *egli nevica*, *egli grandina*, *egli piove*, *egli balena*; and still oftener *e' nevica*, *e' grandina*, *e' piove*, *e' balena*: *E'* is, in this case, a contraction of *egli*; and *egli* is not to be considered, in such a case, as a pronoun, but only as an expletive particle.

Any impersonal verb may, by altering its original nature, become active, and consequently admit of a pronoun; as if a poet was to make Jupiter say, *io tuono su gli erupi*; or, if addressing Juno, he should say, *tu piovi fecondità su i nostri campi*.

Verbs are likewise divided into *active* and *passive*; active, for instance, is *ammazzare*, and passive *morire*.

Every active verb may become passive by the junction of the auxiliary very *essere*, with its participle; *amare* is an active verb; *essere amato* is passive.

No part of the English grammar is so easily learned by an Italian, as that which relates to verbs; because English verbs have very few terminations, and are subject to no irregularity but in the preterite tense. But this part of the Italian grammar is very difficult to an Englishman; because our terminations are numerous, and our irregularities innumerable. That I may not frighten my young readers with a multiplicity of puzzling rules and observations, I will conjugate here the two auxiliary verbs *essere* and *avere*; then I shall speak of our different conjugations of other verbs, and exhibit examples of each of them, accenting each polysyllable, that I may facilitate the pronunciation to learners.

Of the auxiliary Verbs E'ssere *and* Avére.

Conjugation of the Verb

ESSERE.

INDICATIVE.

Present.

Singular	*Plural*
Io sóno	Noi siámo
Tu sei	Voi siéte (a)
Egli è	Eglino sóno.

(a) In familiar or low writings we say likewise *ete*.

Simple

Simple Preterite.

Sing.	*Plur.*
Io éro (*b*)	Noi eravâmo (*c*)
Tu éri	Voi eraváte (*d*)
Egli, *fem.* Ella éra	Eglino, *fem.* Elleno érano.

Determinate Preterite.

Sing.		*Plur.*	
Io ſono	ſtáto; *fe-*	Noi ſiámo	ſtâti;
Tu ſei	*minine*	Voi ſiéte	*fem.*
Egli, *fem.* Ella è	ſtâta.	Eglino, *fem.* Elleno ſóno	ſtâte.

Indeterminate Preterite.

Sing.	*Plur.*
Io fui	Noi fúmmo
Tu fóſti (*e*)	Voi fóſte (*f*)
Egli, *fem.* Ella, fu (*g*)	Eglino, *fem.* Elleno, fúorono. (*h*)

Indeterminate Preterpluperfect.

Sing.		*Plur.*	
Io éra	ſtáto;	Noi eravámo	ſtâti;
Tu éri	*fem.*	Voi eraváte	*fem.*
Egli, *fem.* Ella éra	ſtáta.	Eglino, *fem.* Elleno érano	ſtáte.

Determinate Peeterpluperfect.

Sing.		*Plur.*	
Io fui	ſtato;	Noi fúmmo	ſtâti;
Tu fóſti	*fem.*	Voi fóſte	*fem.*
Egli, *fem.* Ella fu	ſtáta.	Eglino, *fem.* Elleno fúrono	ſtáte.

Imperfect Future.

Sing.	*Plur.*
Io ſarò (*i*)	Noi ſarémo
Tu ſarái	Voi ſaréte
Egli, *fem.* Ella ſará (*k*)	Eglino, *fem.* Elleno ſaránno.

(*b*) (*c*) In familiar or low writings, *erámo:* Some pronounce *erávamo* and *éramo* inſtead of *eravámo* and *erámo*, but I think them wrong.

(*d*) In familiar or low writings *eri.* Some pronounce *erávate* inſtead of *eraváte*, but I think them wrong.

(*e*) (*f*) Some ancient writers ſaid uncorrectly *fuſti* and *fuſte.*

(*g*) Poets ſay likewiſe *fúe.*

(*h*) Poetically *furo.* Some ancients ſaid likewiſe *funno.*

(*i*) (*k*) Our old poets, who ſeem to have been great enemies to accented terminations, ſaid often, *ſaróe* and *ſaráe* for *ſarà.* *Fía,* of two ſyllables, for *ſará,* and *fiéno,* of two ſyllables, for *ſaranno,* are ſtill much uſed in poetry; and, in imitation of ſome few paſſages in Boccaccio, many uſe them in proſe likewiſe; a mere affectation.

Per-

Perfect Future.

Sing.		*Plur.*	
Io ſarò	ſtáto;	Noi ſarémo	ſtáti;
Tu ſarái	*fem.*	Voi ſaréte	*fem.*
Egli, *fem.* Ella ſarà	ſtáta.	Eglino, *fem.* Elleno Sarânno	ſtáte.

IMPERATIVE.

Preſent.

Sing.	*Plur.*
No firſt perſon.	Siámo Noi
Sii Tu, *or* Sia Tù	Siáte Voi
Sia Egli, *fem.* Ella	Siéno Eglino, *fem.* Elleno. (*l*)

Future.

Sing.	*Plur.*
No firſt perſon.	Sarémo Noi
Sarái Tu	Saréte Voi
Sarà Egli, *fem.* Ella	Saránno Eglino, *fem*, Elleno.

OPTATIVE.

Perfect Preſent.

Sing.	*Plur.*
Io fóſſi (*m*)	Noi fóſſimo
Tu fóſſi	Voi fóſte
Egli, *fem.* Ella fóſſe	Eglino, *fem.* Elleno fóſſero. (*n*)

Imperfect Preſent.

Sing.	*Plur.*
Io ſaréi	Noi ſarémmo
Tu ſaréſti	Voi ſaréſte (*p*)
Egli, *fem.* Ella ſarébbe (*o*)	Eglino, *fem.* Elleno ſarébbero. (*q*)

(*l*) Some uncorrectly ſay *síano* for *ſiéno*.

(*m*) The ancients, in proſe and verſe, wrote likewiſe *fuſſi*, *fuſſe*, *fuſſimo*, *fuſte*, *fuſſero*; and modern writers ſtill do ſo in verſe only.

(*n*) In familiar correct language we find likewiſe *fóſſimo*, *fóſſeno*, and *fóſſono*.

(*o*) In poetry, and ſometimes in proſe, we ſay, not without elegance, *ſaria*.

(*p*) In familiar writings *ſareſſi*, as *eri* for *eraváte*.

(*q*) Not inelegantly *ſariéno* and *ſarébbono*. *Sariano* is found likewiſe, but ſeldom in good writers.

Deter-

Determinate Preterite.

Sing.		*Plur.*	
Io sía	ſtáto;	Noi ſiámo	ſtáti;
Tu sii (*r*)	*fem.*	Voi ſiáte	*fem.*
Egli, *fem.* Ella sía	ſtáta.	Eglino, *fem.* Elleno ſiéno	ſtáte.

Indeterminate Preterite.

Sing.		*Plur.*	
Io ſaréi	ſtáto;	Noi ſarémmo	ſtáti;
Tu ſaréſti	*fem.*	Voi ſaréſte	*fem.*
Egli, *fem.* Ella ſarébbe	ſtáta.	Eglino, *fem.* Elleno ſarébbero	ſtáte.

Preterpluperfect.

Sing.		*Plur.*	
Io fóſſi	ſtato;	Noi fóſſimo	ſtáti;
Tu fóſſi	*fem.*	Voi fóſte	*fem.*
Egli, *fem.* Ella fóſſe	ſtata.	Eglino, *fem.* Elleno fóſſero	ſtáte.

Future.

Sing.	*Plur.*
Io sía	Noi ſiámo
Tu sii	Voi ſiáte
Egli, *fem.* Ella sía	Eglino, *fem.* Elleno ſiéno.

CONJUNCTIVE.

Preſent.

Sing.	*Plur.*
Io sía	Noi ſiámo
Tu sii	Voi ſiáte
Egli, *fem.* Ella sía	Eglino, *fem.* Elleno ſiéno.

Simple Preterite.

Sing.	*Plur.*
Io fóſſi	Noi fóſſimo
Tu fóſti (*s*)	Voi fóſte
Egli, *fem.* Ella fóſſe	Eglino, *fem.* Elleno fóſſero.

(*r*) *Sii* is regular, but diſpleaſing to the ear. Poets at leaſt ſay *ſia*, and abhor that ugly jingling of the two *ii*'s in this, as well as in any other word throughout the language.

(*s*) *Foſſi* belongs to the optative; *foſti* to the conjunctive. This is, according to the niceſt grammarians, the moſt material difference between theſe two modes; and ſome of them affirm, that Boccaccio never ſinned againſt this rule. Perhaps he made it himſelf; for I never could diſcover, that either his predeceſſors or ſucceſſors kept very ſtrictly to it.

Com-

Compound Preterite.

Sing.		*Plur.*	
Io sía	ſtáto ;	Noi ſiámo	ſtàti ;
Tu síi	*fem.*	Voi ſiáte	*fem.*
Egli sía	ſtáta.	Eglino ſiéno	ſtáte.

Preterpluperfect.

Sing.		*Plur.*	
Io fóſſi	ſtáto ;	Noi fóſſimo	ſtáti ;
Tu fóſſi	*fem.*	Voi fóſte	*fem.*
Egli fóſſe	ſtáta.	Eglino fóſſero	ſtáte.

Future.

Sing.		*Plur.*	
Io ſaró	ſtáto ;	Noi ſarémo	ſtáti ;
Tu ſarái	*fem.*	Voi ſaréte	*fem.*
Egli ſarà	ſtáta.	Eglino ſaránno	ſtáte.

Infinitive.

Preſent. Eſſere.
Preterite. Eſſere ſtáto.
Future. Eſſere per éſſere, *or* avére a éſſere.

It is obſervable, that this verb, in Italian, is conſtrued by itſelf, except in the future tenſe of the infinitive mood ; whereas, in Engliſh, it is chiefly conſtrued by the aſſiſtance of the other auxiliary *to have* in all compound tenſes.

Conjugation of the Auxiliary Verb A V E R E.

INDICATIVE.

Preſent.

Sing.	*Plur.*
Io ho *(a)*	Noi abbiámo (*c*)
Tu hai	Voi avéte
Egli ha *(b)*	Eglino hánno.

(*a*) (*b*) The ancients ſaid likewiſe, *abbo* and *aggio*. *Aggio* is ſtill uſed ſometimes in poetry. Some modern innovators of orthography, as I have obſerved already, reject the *h* from *ho*, *hai*, *ha*, *hanno*, and ſubſtitute an accent to the next letter, againſt the general ſyſtem of our orthography, that demands accents only on the laſt letter of ſome words, and not on the beginning. They ſave ſome ink by ſo doing.

(c) The ancients wrote likewiſe, *aggiámo* and *avémo*. *Aggiámo* is now grown quite obſolete ; and *avémo*, is ſtill uſed. Some ſay *aviamo*, but it is a barbarous word.

Simple Preterite.

Sing.	*Plur.*
Io avéva (*d*)	Noi avevámo (*e*)
Tu avévi	Voi aveváte
Egli avêva	Eglino avévano.

Determinate Preterite.

Sing.	*Plur.*
Io ho } avúto.	Noi abbiámo } avúto.
Tu hai	Voi avéte
Egli ha	Eglino hanno

Indeterminate Preterite.

Sing.	*Plur.*
Io ébbi (*f*)	Noi avémmo
Tu avésti	Voi avéste (*g*)
Egli ébbe	Eglino ébbero, *or* ebbono.

Indeterminate Preterpluperfect.

Sing.	*Plur.*
Io avéva } avúto.	Noi avevámo } avúto.
Tu avévi	Voi aveváte
Egli avêva	Eglino avévano

Determinate Preterpluperfect.

Sing.	*Plur.*
Io ébbi } avúto.	Noi avémmo } avúto.
Tu avésti	Voi avéste
Egli ébbe	Eglino ébbero

Imperfect Future.

Sing.	*Plur.*
Io avrò (*h*)	Noi avrémo
Tu avrái	Voi avréte
Egli avrá	Eglino avránno.

(*d*) In familiar writings we ſay likewiſe, *avevo* in the firſt perſon, but not in the third. For *aveva*, both in the firſt and third, we ſay poetically *avea*, and often in proſe too.

(*e*) Some pronounce *avévamo*, but they are wrong. Some ſay *avavámo* and *avaváte*, but they are barbarians.

(*f*) For *ebbi*, Dante ſaid once *ei*. No body elſe ever did.

(*g*) In familiar language ſome ſay *aveſti*.

(*h*) The ancients ſaid *avróe*; and, in the third perſon, *avráe*. Now they are obſolete. *Avró*, *avrai*, &c. is contracted from the diſuſed *averó*, *averai*, &c. Negligent folks write, *aró*, *arai*, &c. and think it elegant and poetical. It is clowniſh.

Per-

Perfect Future.

Sing.	*Plur.*
Io avrò } avúto.	Noi avrémo } avúto.
Tu avrâi } avúto.	Voi avréte } avúto.
Egli avrá } avúto.	Eglino avránno } avúto.

IMPERATIVE.

Present.

Sing.	*Plur.*
No first Person.	Abbiámo Noi
Abbi Tu	Abbiáte Voi
Abbia Egli	Abbiano Eglino.

Future.

Sing.	*Plur.*
No first person.	Avrémo
Avrâi	Avréte
Avrá	Avránno.

OPTATIVE.

Perfect Present.

Sing.	*Plur.*
Io avéssi	Noi avéssimo
Tu avéssi	Voi avéste (*k*)
Egli avésse (*i*)	Eglino avéssero. (*l*)

Imperfect Present.

Sing.	*Plur.*
Io avréi (*m*)	Noi avrémmo
Tu avrésti	Voi avréste
Egli avrébbe (*n*)	Eglino avrébbero. (*o*)

(*i*) In familiar, or rather vulgar stile, *avessi.*
(*k*) Vulgarly *avesti.*
(*l*) Or *avéssono.*
(*m*) Or *avre'*, or *avría.*
(*n*) Or *avre'*, or *avría.*
(*o*) Or with as much elegance *avrébbono*; and in poetry *avriéno.*

Determinate Preterite.

Sing.		*Plur.*	
Io ábbia	avúto.	Noi abbiámo	avúto.
Tu ábbi (*p*)		Voi abbiáte	
Egli ábbia		Eglino ábbiano (*q*)	

Indeterminate Preterite.

Sing.		*Plur.*	
Io avréi	avúto.	Noi avrémmo	avúto.
Tu avrésti		Voi avréste	
Egli avrébbe		Eglino avrébbero	

Preterpluperfect.

Sing.		*Plur.*	
Io avéssi	avúto.	Noi avéssimo	avúto.
Tu avéssi		Voi avéste	
Egli avésse		Eglino avéssero	

Future.

Sing.	*Plur.*
Io ábbia	Noi abbiámo
Tu ábbi	Voi abbiáte
Egli ábbia	Eglino ábbiano.

CONJUNCTIVE.

Present.

Sing.	*Plur.*
Io ábbia	Noi abbiámo
Tu ábbi	Voi abbiáte
Egli ábbia	Eglino ábbiano.

(*p*) Buonmatti will have *abbia* by all means, and Boccaccio is his warrant. Other grammarians will have *ábbia*; and they support their opinion with a legion of examples out of the best ancient poets. I say that *abbi* is, perhaps, more regular; but *abbia* is a word of better sound, as I said of *sia*, which is a better word than *sii*.

(*q*) Some clownishly say *ábbino*.

Simple Preterite.

Sing.	*Plur.*
Io avéſſi	Noi avéſſimo (*s*)
Tu avéſſi	Voi avéſte
Egli avéſſe (*r*)	Eglino avéſſero.

Compound Preterite.

Sing.		*Plur.*	
Io ábbia	avúto.	Noi abbiámo	avúto.
Tu ábbi		Voi abbiáte	
Egli ábbia		Eglino ábbiano	

Preterpluperfect.

Sing.		*Plur.*	
Io avéſſi	avúto.	Noi avéſſimo	avúto.
Tu avéſſi		Voi avéſte	
Egli avéſſe		Eglino avéſſero	

Future.

Sing.		*Plur.*	
Io avró	avúto.	Noi avrémo	avúto.
Tu avrài		Voi avréte	
Egli avrá		Eglino avránno	

Infinite.

Preſent. Avére.
Preterite. Avére, avúto.
Future. Avére ad avére, *or* Eſſere per avére.

This verb, as well as the other auxiliary *eſſere*, is conſtrued by itſelf, except in the future tenſe of the infinitive mood; whereas in Engliſh it is chiefly conſtrued by the aſſiſtance of the other auxiliary *to be* in all compound tenſes.

The verb *eſſere* I never ſaw uſed for *avere*; but the verb *avere* is often, and with great propriety, uſed for the verb *eſſere*, as in theſe examples out of Boccaccio.

Quante miglia ci ha? áccene piú di millanta. Ed acci di quelli del popolo noſtro. Come che oggi v' abbia di ricchi uomini, ve n' ebbe già uno il quale fu ricchiſſimo. Ebbevi di quelli che intender vollono alla melaneſe. The French do very often ſubſtitute *avoir* to *être*, but the Engliſh do not.

All our verbs end either in *are*, in *ere*, or in *ire*. Thoſe that end in *arre*, *erre*, or *orre*, muſt be conſidered as contractions of ſome verb that was originally uſed, and is now looked upon either as obſolete or inelegant. *Trarre*, and its compounds, as *protrárre*, *detrárre*, *contrárre*, *ſottrárre*, are contracted from *tráere*, or *trággere*, *protráere*, or *protrággere*, &c. *Scerre* is contracted from *ſcégliere*; *porre* and *torre* from *pónere* and *tóglíere*. *Scégliere* is a word of good uſe ſtill, as well as *tógliere* and *trággere*; but *tráere* and *pónere* are almoſt forgot.

(*r*) In low ſtyle *avéſſi* is ſtill uſed.

(*s*) In low ſtyle *avéſſemo* is to be found in ſome old poets.

 Here

Here I exhibit our three regular Conjugations.

Conjugations of the three regular Verbs

AMA'RE, TEME'RE, SENTI'RE.

INDICATIVE.

Present.

	First Conjug.	*Second Conjug.*	*Third Conjug.*
Sing.	A'mo.	Témo.	Sénto.
	A'mi.	Témi.	Sénti.
	A'ma.	Téme.	Sénte.
Plur.	Amiámo.	Temiámo.	Sentiámo.
	Amáte.	Temète.	Sentíte.
	A'mano.	Témono.	Séntono.

Simple Preterite.

Sing.	Amâva. (*t*)	Teméva.	Sentíva.
	Amâvi.	Temévi.	Sentívi.
	Amâva.	Teméva.	Sentíva.
Plur.	Amavâmo.	Temevâmo.	Sentivâmo.
	Amavâte.	Temevâte.	Sentivâte.
	Amâvano.	Temévano.	Sentívano.

Indeterminate Preterite.

Sing.	Amâi.	Teméi.	Sentj. (*u*)
	Amâsti.	Teméſti.	Sentíſti.
	Amò.	Temé.	Sentí.
Plur.	Amámmo.	Temémmo.	Sentímmo.
	Amáſte.	Teméſte.	Sentíſte.
	Amárono.	Temérono.	Sentírono.

Determinate Preterite.

Sing.	Ho			
	Hai			
	Ha.			
Plur.	Abbiámo.	Amáto.	Temúto.	Sentíto.
	Avéte.			
	Hánno.			

Indeterminate Preterpluperfect.

Sing.	Avéva.			
	Avévi.			
	Avéva.			
Plur.	Avevámo.	Amáto.	Temúto.	Sentúto.
	Avevâte.			
	Avévano.			

Determinate Preterpluperfect.

Sing.	E'bbi.			
	Avêsti.			
	E'bbe.			
Plur.	Avémmo.	Amáto.	Temúto.	Sentíto.
	Avéste.			
	E'bbero.			

Imperfect Future.

Sing.	Ameró. (*)	Temeró.	Sentiró.
	Amerâi.	Temerâi.	Sentirâi.
	Amerá.	Temerá.	Sentirá.
Plur.	Ameremo.	Temerémo.	Sentirémo.
	Amerête.	Temerête.	Sentirête.
	Ameránno.	Temeránno.	Sentiránno.

Perfect Future.

Sing.	Avró.			
	Avrâi.			
	Avrá.			
Plur.	Avrémo.	Amáto.	Temúto.	Sentíto.
	Avrête.			
	Avránno.			

IMPERATIVE.

Present.

Sing.	*No first Person.*	———	———
	A'ma.	Témi.	Sénti.
	A'mi.	Téma.	Sénta.
Plur.	Amiámo.	Temiámo.	Sentiámo.
	Amáte.	Teméte.	Sentíte.
	A'mino.	Témano.	Séntano.

(*) Some write and pronounce *amaro*, *amarâi*, &c. but such is the Tuscan of Venetian gondoliers, Sclavonian sailors, and other such learned people.

Future.

Future.

Sing.	*No first Person.*	——	——
	Amerái.	Temerâi.	Sentirái.
	Amerá.	Temerá.	Sentirá.
Plur.	Ameremo.	Temerémo.	Sentirémo.
	Ameréte.	Temeréte.	Sentiréte.
	Amerànno.	Temerànno.	Sentirànno.

OPTATIVE.

Perfect Present.

Sing.	Amáſſi.	Teméſſi.	Sentíſſi.
	Amáſſi.	Teméſſi.	Sentíſſi.
	Amáſſe.	Teméſſe.	Sentíſſe.
Plur.	Amáſſimo.	Teméſſimo.	Sentíſſimo.
	Amáſte.	Teméſte.	Sentíſte.
	Amáſſero (*y*)	Teméſſero.	Sentíſſero.

Imperfect Present.

Sing.	Ameréi. (*z*)	Temeréi.	Sentiréi.
	Ameréſti.	Temeréſti.	Sentiréſti.
	Amerébbe. (*a*).	Temerébbe.	Sentirébbe.
Plur.	Amerémmo.	Temerémmo.	Sentirémmo.
	Ameréſte.	Temeréſte.	Sentiréſte.
	Amerébbero. (*b*)	Temerébbero.	Sentirébbero.

Determinate Preterite.

Sing.	A'bbia.	Amáto.	Temúto.	Sentíto.
	A'bbi.			
	A'bbia.			
Plur.	Abbiámo.			
	Abbiáte.			
	A'bbiano.			

Indeterminate Preterite.

Sing.	Avréi.	Amáto.	Temúto.	Sentíto.
	Avréſti.			
	Avrébbe.			
Plur.	Avrémmo.			
	Avréſte.			
	Avrébbero.			

(*y*) Some ſay likewiſe, and not inelegantly, *amáſſono, temeſſono, ſentiſſeno.* Thoſe that ſay *amáſſimo, temeſſimo, ſentiſſino,* are not approved.

(*z*) Poets ſaid likewiſe *am.rò', temere' ſentire'*, and *ameria, temeria, ſentiria.*

(*a*) *Ameria, temería,* and *ſentiría,* are likewiſe found in poets as well as *amere', temere', ſentire'*; but theſe laſt in compoſitions of familiar or low ſtyle.

(*b*) Or *amerébbono, temerébbono, ſentirébbono.*

Preter-

Preterpluperfect.

Sing.	Avéſſi.	Amáto.	Temúto.	Sentíto.
	Avéſſi.			
	Avéſſe.			
Plur.	Avéſſimo.			
	Avéſte.			
	Avéſſero.			

Future.

Sing.	A'mi.	Téma.	Sénta.
	A'mi.	Témi.	Sénti.
	A'mi.	Téma.	Sénta.
Plur.	Amiámo.	Temiámo.	Sentiámo.
	Amiáte.	Temiáte.	Sentiáte.
	A'mino.	Témano.	Séntano.

CONJUNCTIVE.

Present.

Sing.	A'mi.	Téma.	Sénta.
	A'mi.	Témi.	Sénti.
	A'mi.	Téma.	Sénta.
Plur.	Amiámo.	Temiámo.	Sénta.
	Amiáte.	Temiáte.	Sentiámo.
	A'mino.	Témano.	Séntano.

Simple Preterite.

Sing.	Amáſſi.	Teméſſi.	Sentíſſi.
	Amáſſi.	Teméſſi.	Sentíſſi.
	Amáſſe.	Teméſſe.	Sentíſſe.
Plur.	Amáſſimo.	Teméſſimo.	Sentíſſimo.
	Amáſte.	Teméſte.	Sentíſte.
	Amáſſero.	Teméſſero.	Sentíſſero.

Compound Preterite.

Sing.	A'bbia.	Amáto.	Temúto.	Sentíto.
	A'bbi.			
	A'bbia.			
Plur.	Abbiámo.			
	Abbiáte.			
	A'bbiano.			

Preterpluperfect.

Sing.	Avéſſi.	Amáto.	Temúto.	Sentito.
	Avéſſi.			
	Avéſſe.			
Plur.	Avéſſimo.			
	Avéſte.			
	Avéſſero.			

Future.

Sing.	Amerò.	Temerò.	Sentirò.
	Amerâi.	Temerâi.	Sentirâi.
	Amerà.	Temerà.	Sentirà.
Plur.	Amerémo.	Temerémo.	Sentirémo.
	Ameréte.	Temeréte.	Sentiréte.
	Amerânno.	Temerânno.	Sentirânno.

Compound Future.

Sing.	Avrò.	Amáto.	Temúto.	Sentito.
	Avrâi.			
	Avrà.			
Plur.	Avrémo.			
	Avréte.			
	Avrânno.			

INFINITIVE.

Present.

Amáre. Temére. Sentíre.

Preterite.

Avére { Amáto. Temúto. Sentíto.

Future.

Avére a { Amáre. Temére. Sentíre.

Dovére { Amáre. Temére. Sentíre.

Eſſere

E'ssere per { Amáre. Temére. Sentíre.

Of Anomalous Verbs.

The Italian language abounds in anomalous verbs, that is, of verbs that deviate from the general rules of analogy or derivation. To point them all out with their irregular conjugations would take up too much room: perhaps a volume in folio would not suffice for such an undertaking. I will therefore conjugate here three of them [one of each conjugation] that occur most frequently in our discourses and writings, and without teazing my reader any longer with rules about verbs, more difficult to be learned than the whole language itself, shall put an end to that part of grammar called Etymology.

Conjugation of the Anomalous Verb

DARE.

INDICATIVE.

Present.

Singular.	*Plural.*
Do.	Diámo.
Dai.	Dáte.
Da.	Dánno.

Simple Preterite.

This tense differs not from the regular of the first conjugation AMARE.

Indeterminate Preterite.

Sing.	*Plur.*
Détti. (*c*)	Démmo.
Désti.	Déste.
Détte. (*d*)	Déssero. (*e*)

(*c*) More commonly *diédi*.
(*d*) More commonly *diéde* and *diè*.
(*e*) More commonly *diédero*, *diédono*, *diérono*; and the poets *diéro* or *dénno*.

Future.

Sing.	*Plur.*
Darò.	Darémo.
Darâi.	Daréte.
Darà.	Daránno.

I M P E R A T I V E.

Preſent.

Sing.	*Plur.*
No firſt perſon.	Diámo.
Da.	Dáte.
Día. (*f*)	Diéno. (*g*)

O P T A T I V E.

Perfect Preſent.

Sing.	*Plur.*
Déſſi. (*h*)	Déſſimo.
Déſſi.	Déſte.
Déſſe.	Déſſero. (*i*)

Imperfect Preſent.

Sing.	*Plur.*
Darêi.	Darémmo.
Daréſti.	Daréſte.
Darébbe. (*k*)	Darébbero. (*l*)

Future.

Sing.	*Plur.*
Día.	Diámo.
Díi. (*m*)	Diáte.
Día.	Diéno. (*n*)

All other tenſes follow the rule of the firſt conjugation.

The verb *Stare* is like the verb *Dare*; change only the *D* into *St*, and even my notes will fit it.

(*f*) The ancients ſaid likewiſe *déa*. Now *déa* is ſcarcely uſed but in poetry, and that ſeldom.

(*g*) Obſolete *déano*, now ſcarcely admitted in poetry.

(*h*) Some clowniſhly ſay *dáſſi*, *dáſſi*, *dáſſe*, *dáſſimo*, *dáſte*, *dáſſero* or *dáſſono*.

(*i*) Or *déſſono*.

(*k*) In poetry we ſay likewiſe *daría*.

(*l*) Or *darébbono*. In poetry we ſay likewiſe *dariéno*.

(*m*) I will ſay it once more that I like better *dia*.

(*n*) Some ſay *diano*. They are not praiſed for it.

Conjugation of the Anomalous Verb

PARERE.

INDICATIVE.

Present.

Sing.	*Plur.*
Pájo.	Pajámo.
Pári. (*o*)	Paréte.
Páre.	Pájono.

Preterite.

Sing.	*Plur.*
Párvi.	Parémmo.
Paréſti.	Paréſte.
Párve.	Párvero.

Future.

Sing.	*Plur.*
Parrò. (*q*)	Parrémo.
Parrái.	Parréte.
Parrà.	Parránno.

IMPERATIVE.

Present.

Sing.	*Plur.*
No firſt perſon.	Pajámo.
Pári. (*r*)	Paréte.
Pája.	Pájano.

The participle is *Parúto* or *Parſo.* The other tenſes are all regular as thoſe of *Temére.*

(*o*) I have ſeen in verſe *paj.*
(*p*) Or *párvono.*

(*q*) Some *parerò.* Wrong.
(*r*) Some *paj.* No bad word.

Conju-

Conjugation of the Anomalous Verb

DIRE. (*ſ*)

INDICATIVE.

Preſent.

Sing.	*Plur.*
Díco.	Diciámo.
Dì. (*t*)	Díte.
Díce.	Dícono.

Preterite.

Sing.	*Plur.*
Díſſi.	Dicémmo.
Dicéſti.	Dicéſte.
Díſſe.	Díſſero. (*u*)

Future.

Sing.	*Plur.*
Dirò. (*x*)	Dirémo.
Dirái.	Diréte.
Dirá.	Diránno.

IMPERATIVE.

Preſent.

Sing.	*Plur.*
No firſt Perſon.	Diciâmo.
Di	Díte.
Díca.	Dícano.

OPTATIVE.

Imperfect Preſent.

Sing.	*Plur.*
Diréi. (*y*)	Dirémmo.
Diréſti.	Diréſte.
Dirébbe.	Dirébbero. (*z*)

(*ſ*) Anciently *dícere.*
(*t*) More frequently *díci.*
(*u*) Or *díſſono.*
(*x*) Anciently *dicerò, dicerái; dicerà, dicerémo, diceréte, diceránno.* None of them is now uſed.
(*y*) Anciently *diceréi, diceréſti, dicerébbe, dicerémmo, diceréſte, dicerébbero,* or *dicerébbono,* All obſolete now.
(*z*) Or *dirébbono.*

Future.

Sing.	*Plur.*
Díca.	Diciámo.
Díchi.	Diciáte.
Díca.	Dícano.

The participle is *Detto*. The other tenses are regular like those of *Sentire*.

Though I have given here a specimen of each of the three conjugations when irregular, the English reader must not think that all other irregular conjugations are to be modelled upon these three; for each anomalous verb differs more or less from all others, and they are only to be learned by use and by observation of the best writers.

The active verbs, as in English, become passive by the junction of the verb *essere* with the participles; as *io sono amato*, *tu sei temuto*, *egli è sentito*. Or, when the speech requires a feminine, *io sono amata*, *tu sei temuta*, *ella è sentita*; in the masculine plural *amati*, *temuti*, *sentiti*, and in the feminine *amate*, *temute*, *sentite*.

SYNTAX.

In respect to concordance and government, the syntax of the Italian tongue has great affinity with that of the Latin. The adjective agrees with the substantive in gender, number, and case; and the verb with the nominative in number and person.

Our adjectives ending in *o* in the masculine undergo four changes in the termination, as *caro*, *cara*, *cari*, *care*; *bello*, *bella*, *belli*, *belle*. Those that end in *e* undergo but two changes, as *felice*, *felici*; *mortale*, *mortali*.

The substantive is placed before or after the adjective, not at pleasure, as some people imagine, but as a judicious ear directs. We may say *donna bella* and *bella donna*; but we say *cavallo bianco*, and not *bianco cavallo*. The shock of *co* and *ca* causes a cackling cacophony.

Collective substantives in the singular never agree with a plural, as they often do in English. We constantly say *il popolo è numeroso*; *la canaglia si levó a romore*; *la gente si lagna*; *l' esercito rimase padrone del campo*.

The personal pronoun is frequently omitted because the termination of the verb determinates the person and number. *Amo il fratello*; *balliamo con queste donne*; *venite a vederci*; *verra domane*.

When the Italians have given the article to a name they give it likewise to all the names of the same sentence, as *il Padre*, *la Madre*, *i Figliuoli*, *e gli Amici loro se ne andarono tutti insieme alla Commedia*. In English *Madre*, *Figliuoli*, and *Amici*, would be deprived of their articles. The reason of this difference in the two languages is that the Italian articles are all different; *il*, *la*, *i*, *gli*; but the English having only one, to repeat it three times would have a bad effect.

None of the modern European languages suffer so many transpositions of words in the sentence as the Italian. We may say, for instance,

Io sono amante di Laura.
Io sono di Laura amante.
Io di Laura sono amante.
Io di Laura amante sono.
Di Laura amante io sono.
Di Laura io sono amante.
Amante io sono di Laura.
Amante di Laura io sono.

Yet transpositions of words and inversions of sentences, in my opinion, are to be sparingly used in prose. The style of Boccaccio abounds in transpositions, but the style of Boccaccio is imitated no more, except by pedants. In poetry, if it be not of the narrative kind, transpositions add grace, vigour, and solemnity; but the art of using them cannot be taught, as it depends on a thorough acquaintance with the language, a nice ear, a refined judgment, and a poetical soul.

PROSODY.

Prosody comprises the rules of pronunciation, and the laws of versification.

Of PRONUNCIATION.

Pronunciation is juſt when every letter has its proper ſound, and when every ſyllable has its proper accent. The ſounds of the letters have been already explained; but rules for the accents are not eaſily given, eſpecially to thoſe that underſtand not the Latin tongue. Such however as are invariable I ſhall give here.

Monoſyllables that ſuffer no accent as *ma*, *ſe*, *mi*, *lo*, are pronounced with no forcible emiſſion of breath; but when they demand an accent as a ſign that a letter or a ſyllable has been cut off, they are pronounced more forcibly, as *sì* when it means *così*; *dì* when it ſignifies *giorno*, becauſe originally it was *díe*; *giù* and *ſù*, becauſe anciently they were *ſuſo* and *giúſo*, or *ſúe* and *giúe*. *Nè* is likewiſe pronounced with more force when it is a negative particle than when it is an expletive or an article.

Monoſyllables ending with a conſonant, as *il*, *per*, *con*, *non*; with an apoſtrophiſed vowel, as *de'*, *ne'*, *pe'*, *vo'*; or with a diphthong, as *mai*, *ſei*, *noi*, *lui*, are languidly pronounced.

Subſtantive nouns, whether diſſylables or polyſyllables, when derived from Latin ſubſtantives ending in *tas* have the accent on the laſt ſyllable, as *bontà*, *povertà*, *iniquità*, *arenoſità*, in Latin *bónitas*, *paupértas*, *iníquitas*, *arenóſitas*. Such nouns in Engliſh end in *ty*, as *bounty*, *poverty*, *iniquity*, *arenoſity*. When it happens that ſuch words are lengthened with a ſyllable, as it often happens, eſpecially in poetry, they ſtill preſerve the accent on the *a*, as *bontáde*, *povertáde*, *iniquitáde*, *arenoſitáde*, or *bontáte*, *povertáte*, *iniquitáte*, *arenoſitáte*.

The accents on the different tenſes of the verbs I have already marked in their conjugations. I ſhall only obſerve, that whenever the laſt letter of a word requires an accent, the Italians mark it, but they never do it in any other place of a word, except it be to avoid an equivoke; as *néttare* (*nectar*) by diligent proſe writers is generally diſtinguiſhed from *nettare* (*to clean*) becauſe in the firſt caſe the ſecond ſyllable is ſhort, and in the ſecond caſe the ſecond ſyllable is long. Few people take this little trouble in poetry, as the quantity generally determines the pronunciation.

The infinitives of our verbs when ending in *are* or in *ire* have the accent on the penultima, as *amare*, *invocare*, *ſentìre*, *diminuìre*; but when they end in *ere* they have it ſometimes on the penultima, as *avére*, *temére*, *volére*, *ſapére*, and ſometimes on the antepenultima, as *éſſere*, *ſcégliere*, *frémere*, *raccógliere*, *conóſcere*, *naſcóndere*. Thoſe that know Latin will eaſily gueſs whence this variety generally proceeds; and thoſe that know it not muſt have recourſe to my dictionary, where they will find every word accented in the alphabetical order.

When a particle is added to a word, whether ſuch word be curtailed or not of its laſt vowel, the accent loſes not its place. Suppoſe, for inſtance, that the ſimple word has the accent on the laſt ſyllable, as *partirà*, or on the penultima, as *parte* and *partiránno*, or on the antepenultima, as *partìrono*; and that the particle *ſi* be added to each of them according to the conſtruction of the language; *partirà* ſhall be turned into *partiraſſi*, *parte* into *parteſi*, *partiranno* into *partirannoſi*, and *partìrono* into *partìronſi*.

All polyſyllables ending in *abile* or in *ibile* from the Latin *abilis* and *ibilis*, in Engliſh *able* or *ible*, have the accent on the antepenultima, as *ſtábile*, *formidábile*, *terríbile poſſíbile*.

All pollyſyllables ending in *evole*, as *colpévole*, *meritévole*, *onorévole*, *pregiudiziévole*, have the accent on the antepenultima likewiſe.

All polyſyllables ending in *énte* have their accents on the penultima.

When the laſt vowel of a polyſyllable is preceded by two conſonants, the accent falls on the penultima.

When a polyſyllable is curtailed of its laſt vowel the accent falls on the laſt vowel remaining.

Of VERSIFICATION.

Verſification is the arrangement of a certain number of ſyllables according to certain laws; and a verſe is a line conſiſting of a particular ſucceſſion of ſounds and a number of ſyllables.

The chief verſe of the Italians conſiſts of eleven ſyllables, and is therefore called *endecaſyllable*.

This verſe, conſidered in itſelf, is moſt harmonious when ſtrong accents fall on each

even

ſyllable, that is on the ſecond, fourth, ſixth, eighth, and tenth;

Che viver piú felice e piú beato
Che ritrovarſi 'n ſervitú d' amore!

Yet a delicate ear would ſoon be cloyed with ſuch accents if they were continued throughout a whole ſtanza, becauſe ſameneſs of ſounds cauſes a diſguſtful inſipidity.

That we may therefore avoid uniformity in our verſification, we place our accents in different manners, ſometimes on even, ſometimes on uneven ſyllables; ſometimes the very firſt ſyllable of the verſe is forcibly accented, and ſometimes the neceſſary rapidity of utterance gives no room at all for accents untill we reach the fourth, fifth, and even ſixth ſyllable. The accents ſometimes are diſtant, ſometimes they meet; now ſtronger, now ſofter, as chance or ſkill direct; as the following verſes will ſhow, in which I have marked the *vowels* or *dipthongs* on which the accents fall.

Signor, nell' altro canto io vi dicea
Che 'l forſennato e furioſo Orlando
Tratteſi l' arme e ſparſe al campo avea,
Squarciati i panni e via gittato il brando,
Svelte le piante, e riſonar facea
I cavi ſaſſi e l' alte ſelve, quando
Alcun Paſtore al ſuon traſſe in quel lato
Lor ſtella o qualche lor grave peccato.
Viſte dell Pazzo l'incredibil prove
Poi piú dappreſſo e la poſſanza eſtrema
Si voltan per fuggir, ma non ſann' ove,
Siccome avviene in ſubitana tema.
Il Pazzo dietro lor ratto ſi muove
Uno ne piglia e del capo lo ſcema
Con la facilità che torria alcuno
Dall' arbor pomo o vago fior dal pruno.
Per una gamba il grave tronco preſe,
E quello uſò per mazza addoſſo il reſto:
In terra un pajo addormentato ſteſe
Ch' al noviſſimo dì forſe fia deſto.
Gli altri ſgombraro ſubito 'l paeſe
Ch' ebbono 'l piede e 'l buono avviſo preſto.
Non ſaria ſtato il Pazzo a ſeguir lento
Se non ch' era già volto al loro armento.
Gli Agricoltori accorti agli altru' eſempli
Laſcian ne' campi aratri e marre e falci;
Chi monta ſulle caſe e chi ſu i templi
Poichè non ſon ſicuri olmi nè ſalci.
Onde l' orrenda furia ſi contempli.
Che a pugni, ad urti, a morſi, a graffi, a calci
Cavalli e buoi rompe, fracaſſa, e ſtrugge,
E ben è corridor chi da lui fugge.
Già potreſte ſentir come rimbombe
L' alto romor nelle propinque ville
D' urli, di corni, e ruſticane trombe,
E più ſpeſſo che d' altro il ſuon di ſquille;
E con ſpuntoni ed archi e ſpiedi e frombe
Veder da' monti ſdrucciolarne mille,
Ed altrettanti andar da baſſo ad alto
Per far al Pazzo un villaneſco aſſalto.
Qual venir ſuol nel ſalſo lito l' onda
Moſſa dall' auſtro che a principio ſcherza
Che maggior della prima è la ſeconda
E con piú forza poi ſiegue la terza,
Ed ogni volta più l' umore abbonda
E nell' arena piú ſtende la ſferza,
Tal contra Orlando l' empia turba creſce
Che giú da balze ſcende e di valli eſce.
Fece morir diece perſone e diece
Che ſenz' ordine alcun gli andaro in mano;
E queſto chiaro eſperimento fece
Ch' era aſſai più ſicur ſtarne lontano.
Trar ſangue da quel corpo a neſſun lece
Che lo fere e percote il ferro in vano.
Al Conte il Re del Ciel tal grazia diede
Per porlo a guardia di ſua ſanta fede.
Era a periglio di morire Orlando
Se foſſe di morir ſtato capace:
Potea imparar ch' era gittare il brando
E poi voler ſenz' arme eſſere audace.
La turba giù s' andava ritirando
Vedendo ogni ſuo colpo uſcir fallace.
Orlando poi che più neſſun l' attende
Verſo un borgo di caſe il cammin prende.
Dentro non vi trovò picciol ne' grande
Che l' borgo ognun per tema avea laſciato;
V' erano in copia povere vivande
Convenienti a paſtorale ſtato.
Senza 'l pane diſcerner dalle ghiande
Dal digiuno e dall' impeto cacciato
Le mani e 'l dente laſciò andar di botto
In quel che trovò prima o crudo o cotto.
E quindi errando per tutto il paeſe
Dava la caccia agli uomini, alle fere,
E ſcorrendo pe' boſchi talor preſe
I capri ſnelli e le damme leggere.
Speſſo con orſi e con cinghiai conteſe,
E con man nude li poſe a giacere,
E di lor carne con tutta la ſpoglia
Piú volte il ventre empì con fera voglia.

By these lines, the reader may easily see that Ariosto was far from thinking that harmony required constant falls of accents on even syllables; and though he lived not long enough to polish all his lines, and augment the musicalness of many whose numbers are none of the best, because sometimes two, and sometimes three vowels clash too hard against one another, yet the generality of the Italians are more pleased with his judicious variety of cadences, than with the almost constant monotony of Tasso, who scarcely dared to place an accent on an uneven syllable, except the third, and carefully avoided the meeting of two accents.

The tenth syllable therefore is the only one that necessarily requires an accent, otherwise the verse would end with a *dactyle* or *slippery word* (*parola sdrucciola*) as we call it, and in this case the metre would be entirely destroyed, and the verse become prose.

Our first versificators frequently interspersed in their poems an endecasyllable by the moderns called *broken* (*scavezzo*), in which the strong accents fall on the fourth, the seventh, and the tenth. Luigi Pulci, in his Morgante, has even whole stanzas consisting of such endecasyllables, and this is one out of the twenty-seventh Canto.

Il mar pur gonfia e coll' onde rinnalza,
E spesso l' una coll' altra s' intoppa,
Tanto che l' acqua in coverta su balza;
Ed or saltava da prora or da poppa;
La nave è vecchia, e pur l' onda la scalza
Tal che comincia ad uscirne la stoppa:
Le grida e 'l mare ogni cosa rimbomba,
Morgante agottà ed ha tolta la tromba.

Dante was not averse to such verses, Petrarca seemed to avoid them carefully, Ariosto has used them sparingly, Berni in his *Orlando Innamorato* has a great many, but Tasso in his *Gerusalemme* has not a single one. Our versificators (poets we scarcely had one since Tasso) have abstained from using *broken verses* from the beginning of the last century; but I see them revived by some living authors, namely Giancarlo Passeroni, the two brothers Carlo and Gasparo Gozzi, and Vittore Vettori, whom I think posterity will rank amongst poets. These gentlemen are not averse to them in those compositions in which they chiefly aim at the style either of Dante in serious, or of Berni in burlesque and satirical poetry; and it is in those two styles that this verse in my opinion has a good effect, if not too lavishly used.

Out of our endecasyllable, two verses are produced, which we, perhaps improperly, call likewise endecasyllables. One of these is made by adding one syllable, the other by cutting off one. The first we call *endecassillabo sdrucciolo*, because it ends with one of those words that we call *parole sdrucciole* or *dactyles*; the other *endecassillabo tronco*, because it ends with a *truncated word*, that is, a word with an accent on its last vowel.

None of these endecasyllables has any great harmony, especially the second, which never has been used by any writer of any name. We find it very scarcely scattered in Epick poetry by Dante, Petrarca, Pulci, Ariosto, and Berni, and, if I remember well, the severe Tasso never employed it once. Some petty rhimers in the last century wrote some contemptible sonnets in this puerile metre, of which, for the satisfaction of the reader, I give here as a specimen the beginning of one which seemed admirable to me when I was a school-boy, and as my memory will not suggest me a better, the reader must have patience, and be contented with this.

Se il libro di Bertoldo il ver narrò,
Questo commando un giorno ebbe dal Rè:
Fa che doman tu torni innanzi a mè
E che insieme io ti veda e insieme nò.
Bertoldo il giorno appresso all Re tornò
Portando un gran Crivello innanzi a se;
Così veder e non veder si fè;
E con la pelle altrui la sua salvò.

I have forgot the remainder of this poor composition.

The *endecassillabo sdrucciolo*, which one may call in English, the *slippery endecasyllable*, though not much better than the *truncated*, has been chiefly used by two writers, whose great names have given it a kind of importance. One was Ariosto in his comedies, the other Sanazzaro in some Eclogues interspersed in his famous book of the Arcadia. Neverthelefs, both Ariosto's Comedies and Sanazzaro's Eclogues were much praised, but seldom reprinted, and seldom read; for, in spight

ſpight of names, nature ſpeaks, and nature tells the *Italians* that of the many metres, in which our poetry has been forced by fanciful writers, ſhe does not approve of this. I ſhall give no ſpecimen out of *Arioſto*'s Comedies, as his verſes, beſides the defect of ending with a *dactyle*, have likewiſe the additional diſagreement of being *blank*; but of the ſlippery verſes of *Sanazzaro* this is a ſpecimen out of the ſixth Eclogue, which is a dialogue between the two ſhepherds, old *Serrano* and young *Opico*.

Serr. *Quantunque, Opico mio, ſii vecchio e carico*
Di ſenno e di penſier che in te ſi covano,
Deh piangi or meco, e prendi il mio rammarico.
Nel mondo oggi gli amici non ſi trovano,
La fede è morta; e regnano le inſidie,
E i mal coſtumi ognor più ſi rinnovano.
Regnan le voglie prave e le perfidie
Per la roba mal nota che li ſtimula,
Tal che il figliuolo al Padre par che inſidie.
Tal ride del mio ben che il riſo ſimula;
Tal piange del mio mal che poi mi lacera
Dietro le ſpalle con acuta limula.
Op. *L' invidia, figliuol mio, ſe ſteſſa macera*
E ſi dilegua come agnel per faſcino.
Che non gli giova ombra di pino o d'acera.
Serr. *Il pur dirò, così gli Dii mi laſcino*
Veder vendetta di chi tanto affondami
Prima che i mietitor le biade affaſcino;
E per l'ira sfogar che al core abbondami,
Così 'l veggia cader d' un olmo e frangaſi
Tal ch' io di gioja o di pietà confondami.
Tu ſai la via che per le piogge affangaſi:
Ivi s' aſcoſe quando a caſa andavamo
Quel, che tal viva, che lui ſteſſo piangaſi.
Neſſun vi riguardò perché cantavamo;
Ma innanzi cena venne un paſtor ſubito
Al noſtro albergo quando al fuoco ſtavamo;
E diſſe a me; Serran, vedi, ch' io dubito
Che tue capre ſian tutte, ond' io per correre
Ne caddi sì che ancor mi duole il cubito.
Deh ſe quì foſſe alcuno a cui ricorrere
Per giuſtizia poteſſi! Or che giuſtizia!
Sol Dio ſel veda che ne può ſoccorrere:
Due capre e due capretti per malizia
Quel ladro traditor dal gregge tolſemi,
Sì ſignoreggia al mondo l' avarizia.
Io gliel direi; ma chi mel diſſe volſemi
Legar per giuramento, ond' eſſer mutolo
Conviemmi, e penſa tu ſe queſta dolſemi.
Del furto ſi vantò poi ch' ebbe avutolo,
Che ſputando tre volte ſu inviſibile
Agli occhi noſtri, ond' io ſaggio riputolo;
Che, ſe il vedea, di certo era impoſſibile
Uſcir vivo da' cani irati e callidi,
Onde non val che l' uom richiami o ſibile
Erbe e pietre moſtroſe e ſughi pallidi,
Oſſa di morti e di ſepolcri polvere,
Magici verſi aſſai poſſenti e validi
Portava indoſſo, che 'l facean riſolvere
In vento, in acqua, in picciol rubo o felice;
Tanto ſi può per arte il mondo involvere.

Next to our verſe of eleven ſyllables, that of ſeven is moſt harmonious; and great uſe has been made of it in lyrick compoſitions, ſparingly mixed with the endecaſyllable; and eſpecially by Petrarca, in thoſe pieces that he called Canzoni, of which this is reckoned one of the beſt.

Che debb' io far? che mi conſigli amore?
Tempo è ben di morire,
Ed ho tradato più ch' i' non vorrei!
Madonna è morta ed ha ſeco il mio core,
E volendol ſeguire
Interromper convien queſt' anni rei!
Perchè mai veder lei.
Di quà non ſpero e l' aſpettar m' è noja,
Poſcia ch' ogni mia gioja
Per lo ſuo dipartire in pianto è volta,
Ogni dolcezza di mia vita è tolta.
Amor, tu 'l ſenti, ond' io teco mi doglio,
Quant' è 'l danno aſpro e grave;
E ſo che del mio mal ti peſa e dole,
Anzi del noſtro; poi ch' ad uno ſcoglio,
Avem rotta la nave,
Ed in un punto n' è ſcurato il ſole.
Qual ingegno a parole
Poria agguagliar il mio doglioſo ſtato?
Ahi orbo mondo ingrato,
Gran cagion hai di dever pianger meco,
Che quel ben, ch' era in te, perdut' hai ſeco!
Caduta è la tua gloria, e tu nol vedi,
Nè degno eri mentr' ella
Viſſe quaggiù d' aver ſua conoſcenza;
Nè d' eſſer tocco da' ſuoi ſanti piedi,
Perchè coſa sì bella
Devea 'l cielo adornar di ſua preſenza.
Ma io laſſo, che ſenza
Lei nè vita mortal nè me ſteſſo amo,
Piangendo la richiamo:
Queſto m' avanza di cotanta ſpene,
E queſto ſolo ancor quì mi mantene.

Oh obimè, terra è fatto il suo bel viso
Che solea far del cielo
E del ben di lassú sede fra noi.
L' invisibil sua forma è in paradiso
Disciolta di quel velo
Che quì fece ombra al fior degli anni suoi,
Per rivestirsen poi
Un' altra volta e mai più non spogliarsi
Quand' alma e bella farsi
Tanto più la vedrem quanto più vale
Sempiterna bellezza che mortale.
Più che mai bella e più leggiadra donna
Tornami innanzi come
La' dove più gradir sua vista sente:
Quest' è del viver mio l' una colonna;
L' altra è 'l suo chiaro nome
Che sona nel mio cor sì dolcemente;
Ma tornandomi a mente
Che pur morta è la mia speranza viva
Allor ch' ella fioriva,
Sa ben amor qual io divento e spero;
Vedel colei che or è sì presso al vero.
Donne, voi che miraste sua beltate,
E l' angelica vita
Con quel celeste portamento in terra,
Di me vi doglia; e vincavi pietate,
Non di lei che è salita
A tanta pace e me ha lasciato in guerra,
Tal che s' altri mi serra
Lungo tempo il cammin da seguitarla,
Quel che amor meco parla
Sol mi ritien ch' i' non recida il nodo:
Ma e' ragiona dentro in cotal modo.
Pon freno al gran dolor che ti trasporta,
Che per soverchie voglie
Si perde il cielo ove il tuo core aspira,
Dov' è viva colei che altrui par morta,
E di sue belle spoglie
Seco sorride, e sol di te sospira;
E sua fama che spira
In molte parti ancor per la tua lingua
Prega che non estingua,
Anzi la voce al nome suo rischiari,
Se gli occhi suoi mai ti fur dolci e cari.
Fuggi 'l sereno e 'l verde;
Non t' appressar ove sia riso o canto
Canzon mia, no, ma pianto!
Non fa per te di star fra gente allegra
Vedova sconsolata in veste negra.

Metastasio, who has brought our musical drama to its perfection, has happily mixed in his recitativos this line of seven syllables with that of eleven, without prefixing to it any determinate place; and simply following the direction of chance, and of his ear, which seems to me the most nice that a poet ever had.

——La Patria è un tutto
Di cui siam parti. All cittadino è fallo
Considerar se stesso
Separato da lei. L' utile o il danno
Ch' ei conoscer dee solo è cio che giova
O nuoce alla sua patria, a cui di tutto
E' debitor. Quando i sudori e il sangue
Sparge per lei, nulla del proprio ei dona
Rende sol ciò che n' ebbe. Ella il produsse,
L' educò, lo nutrì: Colle sue leggi
Dogl' insulti domestici il difende,
Dagli esterni coll' armi. Ella gli presta
Nome, grado, ed onor; ne premia il merto,
Ne vendica le offese; e madre amante
A fabbricar s' affanna
La sua felicità, per quanto lice
Al destin de' mortali esser felice.
Han tanti doni, è vero,
Il peso lor. Chi ne ricusa il peso
Rinunci al beneficio, a far si vada
D' inospite foreste
Mendico abitatore; e là d' irsute
Ferine spoglie avvolto, e là di poche
Misere ghiande e d' un covil contento
Viva libero e solo a suo talento.

By these two compositions it appears, that our verse of seven syllables requires no constant accent, but on the penultima; and that other syllables may, or may not have it, as the poet thinks fit.

The *slippery* verse, that we form from this, consists of eight syllables, and the *truncated* of six; but, that I may not repeat the same thing over again, I must say that every plain Italian verse, whether of eleven, or of less syllables, may be lengthened or shortened at pleasure by a slippery or a truncated word; and I will add further, that, excepting in musical airs and songs, both the slippery and truncated verses, the shorter they are, the more insupportable they are, except when artfully mingled with plain rhimed verses, as we shall shew anon in an hymn of Metastasio; and as of bad things the less one has the better it is, I shall give the reader but two short specimens, out of the Port-Royal Grammar, whose prosody, in my opinion, is so very poor a performance, that one would almost be inclined to think the compilers of it played booty to the Italians,

lians, as their examples seem rather contrived to discredit than to encourage the study of our language and poetry. Their first example of short slippery verses is this:

Limpidi rivoli,
Fertili pascoli,
Frassini e platani
Roveri e salici
Edere e pampini
Satiri e driadi.

In all probability Marino thought himself very cunning in contriving it so, that each of these six verses consists of two slippery words. He might have easily made two lines instead of one, and pass his six verses upon the reader for twelve. The following are less artful, but no less childish:

Poichè vogliono
Stelle perfide
Che in perpetuo
Resti vedovo
D'ogni giubilo,
Siate pregovi
Testimonii
Dell' esequie
Ch'oggi celebro.

Next to the verses of eleven, and of seven syllables, that of eight is the best, whose necessary accent falls on the penultima, the other syllables having it regularly or irregularly as the poet pleases.

Miri pur con ridente occhio
Un signore il suo tesoro;
Pavoneggisi in un cocchio,
Avviluppisi nell' oro,
E con voce altitonante
Sgridi un servo a me davante;
Faccia pur pompa alla mensa
Degli aromati famosi
Che la vasta India dispensa
O fragranti o saporosi,
E sol mangi in creta fina
Del giappone e della cina;
Copra ogni angol d'ogni stanza
D'oro, d'ostro, e marmo eletto,
E di trono abbia sembianza
Ogni seggiola ogni letto,
E nascondan le sue mura
Gran cristalli e gran pittura;
S' io potrò felicemente
Trarre a fine un' oda ardita;
Se una rima ubbidiente
Darà lume, forza, e vita
A un mio nobile pensiero;
Quel signor non curo un zero.

Verses of a shorter measure than seven and eight syllables are not often used by judicious *Italians*, as they are unfit for vigorous poetry. Yet in short songs, or opera-airs, they prove graceful, as it may be seen by this of *Metastasio.*

Come il candore
D'intatta neve
E' d'un bel core
La fedeltà.
Un' orma sola
Che in se riceve
Tutta le invola
La sua beltà.

If *Metastasio*, to the verse of five syllables, has in this air joined the *truncated*, in the following hymn to *Venus*, he has very gracefully joined the *slippery*.

Scendi propizia
Col tuo splendore
O bella Venere
Madre d'amore;
O bella Venere
Che sola sei
Piacer degli uomini
E degli Dei.
Tu, colle lucide
Pupille chiare
Fai lieta e fertile
La terra e il mare.
Presso a' tuoi placidi
Astri ridenti
Le nubi fuggono
Fuggono i venti.
A te fioriscono
Gli erbosi prati,
E i flutti ridono
Nel mar placati.
Per te le tremule
Faci del cielo
Dell' ombre squarciano
L'oscuro velo;

E allor che ſorgono
In lieta ſchiera
I grati zefiri
Di primavera,
Te Dea ſalutano
Gli augei canori
Che in petto accolgono
Tuoi dolci ardori.
Per te le timide
Colombe i figli
In preda laſciano
De' fieri artigli.
Per te abbandonano
Dentro le tane
I parti teneri
Le tigri ircane.
Per te ſi ſpiegano
Le forme aſcoſe,
Per te propagano
Le umane coſe.
Vien dal tuo ſpirito
Dolce e fecondo
Ciò che d' amabile
Racchiude il mondo.
Scendi propizia
Col tuo ſplendore
O bella Venere
Madre d'amore.
O bella Venere
Che ſola ſei
Piacer degli uomini
E degli Dei.

Only ſhort trifles can be written in verſes of three or four ſyllables. *Metaſtaſio* himſelf, who was more than any other *Italian* poet obliged to look often out for all poſſible melodious meaſures, refuſed them a place in his airs and choruſſes, as utterly unmuſical. His predeceſſor *Apoſtolo Zeno*, whoſe verſes ſeem to have been ſcanned on his fingers, wrote many of four, three, and even two ſyllables; but no body can read his dramas without wiſhing that his gift of invention had been the lot of a man furniſhed with an harmonious ſoul. Yet verſes of four ſyllables, when judiciouſly mixed with thoſe of eight, have a pretty effect, as in this canzonet of *Chiabrera*.

Del mio ſol ſon ricciutegli
I capegli,
Non biondetti, ma brunetti:
Son due roſe vermigliuzze
Le gotuzze;
Le due labbra rubinetti
Ma dal dì ch' io la mirai
Fin quì mai
Non mi vidi ora tranquilla;
Che d' amor non miſe amore
In quel core
Neppur picciola favilla.
Laſſo me! quando m' acceſi
Dire inteſi
Ch' egli altrui non affliggea;
Ma che tutto era ſuo foco
Riſo e gioco,
E ch' ei nacque d' una Dea.
Non fu Dea ſua genitrice
Com' uom dice;
Nacque in mar di qualche ſcoglio,
Ed appreſe in quelle ſpume
Il coſtume
Di donar pena e cordoglio.
Ben è ver ch' ei pargoleggia,
Ch' ei vezzeggia
Grazioſo fanciulletto:
Ma così pargoleggiando
Vezzeggiando
Non ci laſcia core in petto.
Oh qual ira! oh quale ſdegno!
Mi fa ſegno
Ch' io non dica, e mi minaccia:
Viperetta, ſerpentello,
Dragoncello
Qual ragion vuol ch' io mi taccia?
Non ſai tu che gravi affanni
Per tant' anni
Ho ſofferto in ſeguitarti?
E che? Dunque lagrimoſo,
Doloroſo,
Angoſcioſo ho da lodarti?

Verſes of nine ſyllables we have none; and thoſe of ten cannot be of any uſe, except in muſical airs: For a ſpecimen I give but this air of *Metaſtaſio*.

Chi mai non vide fuggir le ſponde
La prima volta che va per l' onde,
Crede ogni ſtella per lui funeſta,
Teme ogni zefiro come tempeſta
Un picciol moto tremar lo fa.

Ma

Ma reso esperto sì poco teme
Che dorme al suono del mar che freme,
O sulla prora cantando va.

Besides the metres that I have here exemplified, some of our unskilful *Italians* have tried others that, being not natural to our language, have been universally neglected, *Claudio Tolomei*, of *Siena*, a man of no common parts, who lived in the sixteenth century, and was a cardinal, fancied that our poetry might run better in hexameters and pentamers than in endecasyllables; and here is an epigram writ by *Fabio Benvoglienti*, his friend and follower. For want of types I have marked the *long* syllables with an accent; those that are not accented are all *brieves*, except the second syllable of *empia* in the sixth verse, which makes a strange and harsh coalition with the following *e*; and the four letters, *p*, *i*, *a*, *e*, form the first *cæsura* of that pentameter.

Méntre da' dólci favî fura dêl mél dólce cupídó
Vólt' ál lábbr' un apé púnge la bélla manó.
Súbito pércuóté per acérbo dolóre la térra
E dógliós' ed acró córr' alla mádre suá.
Móstrale piángéndó cómé crudelménte feríva
Quéll' ape quánt' émpia é pícciola féra siá
Vénere dólce ridé; dice vénere: Guárdat' amóré
Pícciolo quánto séi, quánta feríta fai.

Not much less absurd is the following metre, of which I do not know the first *Italian* inventor, but I suppose him some obscure modern; and, for want of a better, I take as a specimen a short piece of *Paolo Rolli*, a harsh versificator, known by his thrice harsh translation of *Milton*'s *Paradise Lost*.

Brillanti limpidi cristalli chiari
Dove pietosa bella e grand' anima
Veggo tralucere, begli occhi cari;
Soavi in tacito ricetto ascoso
Lontan da fiero cipiglio rigido
E da pestifero guardo invidioso,
Vezzosi e placidi e languidetti
Socchiusi in lieto sorriso tremulo
Spirate all' anima tutti gli affetti.
Fin quando s' armano di breve sdegno
Le imperiose ciglia magnanime
Ove ha dispotico l' amor suo regno;
Sempre la candida fronte è serena,
Pietà le dolci pupille spirano,
E il labbro affabile niega e incatena.
In quel che vario più bello crea
Scherzi natura superba o semplice
E industre sieguane l' arte ogn' idea.
D' alma delizia, di gran diletto
Più di sì vaghi occhi non fecero
Né mai far possono lavor perfetto.
Vezzi i più teneri, sensi i più rari
Con voi son nati, da vói s' esprimono,
Inespressibili begli occhi cari.

These verses Rolli called *Catullian endecasyllables*.

One *Pierjacopo Martelli* of *Bologna*, a man of some genius, not many years ago invented a verse of fourteen syllables, and wrote some tragedies in it, pretending that that was the properest verse for the stage. But his tragedies are not read, in spight of one *Goldoni*, a modern comedy-monger, and some other poetasters, who have in my time foolishly endeavoured to revive a metre condemned by the nature of our language to contempt and oblivion. I have not *Martelli*'s works by me, therefore I give no specimen of his odd measures; but no loss to the *English* reader, from whom I take my leave with a wish that his country may for ever be the happy abode of the studious, as it has been for some centuries past.

THE

ENGLISH and *ITALIAN* DICTIONARY:

PART the SECOND.

CONTAINING

The English before the Italian.

DIZIONARIO INGLESE ed ITALIANO:

PARTE SECONDA,

NELLA QUALE

L'INGLESE precede L'ITALIANO.

A.

A *Prima lettera dell' alfabeto in tutte le lingue.*

A, *nella lingua Inglese ha tre differenti suoni. Uno largo, come in* all, wall. *Uno aperto, come in* father, rather. *Uno chiuso e simile a quello dell'* e *in Italiano, e questo è il vero e primario suono della lettera* a *in Inglese, come in* face, place, waste.

A, *articolo posto inanzi a i nomi del numero del meno*; a *man*, a *tree*, a *dog*, a *house*. *Innanzi a porola cominciante con una vocale si converte in* an *per fuggire l' incontro di due vocali che rende suono ingrato*; an *ox*, an *ass*, an *instrument*.

A, *è posto innanzi il participio o gerundio*; a hunting; a begging.

A, *è qualche volta riempitivo, come in* arise, arouse, awake.

A, *qualche volta significa*, per.

So much a man, *tanto per uomo*.

A, *è sovente articolo semplice.*

To wear a sword, *portar la spada.*

Twice a day, *due volte il giorno.*

Once a week, *una volta la settimana*,

Three times a year, *tre volte l' anno*.

A [*in luogo di* in] *a*.

To be a-bed, *essere a letto.*

To go a-foot, *andare a piedi.*

A, *qualche volta è una particella riempitiva.*

Many a time, *molte volte.*

A, *ha un significato dinotante proporzione, come* the landlord has a hundred a year, *il padrone ha cento lire l'anno.*

A, *in poesia piacevole o burlesca serve per allungar una sillaba, come in questo verso di Dryden*,

For cloves and nutmegs to the line-a.

ABA'CK [back, backwards, behind] *dietro, indietro.*

A'BACOT [a cap of ſtate, made like a double crown, worn antiently by the kings of *England*] *ſorta di berretta che i Re d'Inghilterra portavano anticamente.*

ABA'CTED [drawn away by ſtealth or violence] *tolto via per forza.*

ABA'CTION, [the ſtealing or driving away cattle in great number] *il rubare o menar via gran numero di beſtiami.*

ABA'CTOR [he that ſteals or drives away cattle in great numbers] *un ladro di beſtiame.*

A'BACUS, *abaco, arte di far le ragioni e i conti, tavola numeraria.*

ABA'FT, s. *termine marinareſco, per eſprimere una delle parti anteriori d' una nave.*

ABALIENA'TION, s. [alienation, eſtrangement] *alienazione, ſeparazione,* s. f.

To ABA'NDON [to forſake utterly] *abbandonare, laſciar affatto.*

To abandon one's ſelf, *abbandonarſi.*

To abandon one's ſelf to all manner of vices, *abbandonarſi in preda ad ogni ſorta di vizi.*

ABA'NDONED, adj. *abbandonato, laſciato, derelitto. E' anche appellativo d' infamia.*

An abandoned wretch, *uno ſcelerato, un ribaldo, un furfante.*

ABA'NDONING, s. *abbandonamento,* s. m. *lo abbandonare.*

ABAISANCE [a low bow] *una riverenza, un inchino.*

ABAPTI'STON, or ANABAPTI'STON, s. [a ſurgeon's inſtrument or trapan to lay open the ſkull] *trapano, ſtrumento di ferro del quale i chirurghi ſi ſervono per le rotture del cranio.*

To ABA'SE [to lower, to bring down] *abbaſſare, chinare*

To abaſe [to humble] *abbaſſare, deprimere, umiliare, vilipendere, ſpregaire.*

ABA'SED, adj. *abbaſſato, chinato, depreſſo, umiliato.*

ABA'SEMENT, s. *abbaſſamento, abbaſſagione, abbattimento.*

To ABA'SH [to make aſham'd, to confound] *ſcornare, ſvergognare, confondere, far fare il viſo roſſo, fare arroſſire.*

ABA'SHED, adj. *ſcornato, arroſſito, confuſo.*

ABA'SEMENT, s. [confuſion] *ſcorno,* s. m. *vergogna, confuſione,* s. f.

To ABA'TE [to grow leſs] *diminuire, abbaſſare, ſcemare, calare, impicciolire, diffalcare, eſtenuare, ſminuire.*

To abate ſomething of a ſum, *abbattere, detrarre, diffalcare qualche coſa della ſomma.*

I cannot abate a penny of it, *non v' è un ſoldo da levarre.*

To abate one's pride, *deprimere l' altrui arroganza.*

To abate one's courage, *ſcoraggire, ſgomentare.*

To abate one's power, *abbaſſare l' altrui potere.*

To abate ſomething of one's right, *cedere parte di ſua ragione.*

His ſickneſs began to abate, *il ſuo male cominciò a declinare.*

The heat abates, *il caldo s'allenta.*

To abate in one's fleſh, *ſmagrire.*

To abate (in law) [to aboliſh, to beat or pull down, to render of no effect] *abbattere, mandar a terra, rovinare, annullare.*

To abate a caſtle, *demolire un caſtello.*

To abate a writ, *annullare una ſcrittura.*

To abate [to intrude into an eſtate] *uſurparſi i beni di alcuno in pregiudizio del vero erede.*

To abate (in horſemanſhip) [when a horſe working upon curvets puts his two hind-legs to the ground both at once, and obſerves the ſame exactneſs at all times] *affalcarſi.*

ABA'TEMENT, s. *abbaſſamento, ſcemamento, diminuzione.*

An abatement of writ, *derogazione d' una ſcrittura.*

Abatement (in law) [intruding] *l' impoſſeſſarſi dopo la morte d'uno de' ſuoi beni ſenza ragione, in pregiudizio del legittimo erede.*

Abatement of honour (in heraldry) [an accidental mark annexed to a coat of arms, whereby one's dignity is debaſed, by reaſon of ſome diſhonourable quality or ſtain] *ſegno che ſi mette nelle armi di colui che per qualche azione diſonorata ſia degradato dalla ſua dignità.*

ABA'TER [one that intrudes himſelf into houſes or lands after the death of the former poſſeſſor, and not yet taken up by his heir] *uno che s'impoſſeſſa dopo la morte altrui de' ſuoi beni, ſenza avervi veruna ragione, in preguidizio del legittimo erede.*

ABA'TING, s. *abbaſſamento, diminuzione.*

ABATU'RES, s. (among hunters) [the ſprigs or graſs that a ſtag throws down in paſſing by] *traccia d'un cervo.*

ABA'WED [abaſhed] *ſcornato, confuſo, ſvergognato.* Obſol.

A'BBA, s. [a ſcripture word, ſignifying father] *Abba, padre,* s. m.

A'BBACY, s. }
A'BABATHY, s. } [abbey] *abbadia, badia, o dignità d' Abate.*

A'BBAT, v. Abbot.

A'BBATSHIP, s. *abbadia, badia,* s. f.

A'BBESS, s. [governeſs of nuns or of a nunnery] *badeſſa, grado ſupremo tra le monache, abbadeſſa.*

A'BBEY, s. [monaſtery, convent] *badia,* s. f. *ſtanza, o abituro di monachi.*

Abbey-lubber, *poltrone, poltronaccio, fratacchione.*

A'BBOT, s. [chief ruler of an abbey] *abate, ſuperiore e capo d'una badia;* s. m.

Regular abbot, *abate regolare.*

Secular abbot, *abate ſecolare.*

A'BBOTSHIP, s. [abbot's dignity] *dignatà d' abate.*

To ABBRE'VIATE [to abridge, to ſhorten, to make ſhort] *abbreviare, tor via alcuno parte della quantità continua, ſcorciare.*

ABBRE'VIATED, adj. *abbreviato, ſcorciato.*

ABBREVIA'TION, s. *abbreviazione,* s. f. *abbreviamento,* s. m.

ABBREVIA'TOR, s. [that abbreviates or abridges] *abbreviatore,* s. m. *che abbrèvia.*

ABBRE'VIATURE, s. [a ſhortening, as the putting a letter for a word] *abbreviatura,* s. f. *parola abbreviata de' ſuoi caratteri nello ſcriverla.*

ABBREU'VOIR, s. *luogo dove le beſtie vanno o ſon condotte a bere.*

ABBU'TTALS, or ABU'TALS, s. [the butting or bounding of lands, highways] *confine, limite,* s. m.

To A'BDICATE [to renounce, to reſign, to give up] *renunziare, rifiutare, laſciare, rifiutar la propria, ragione a il dominio ſopra che che ſia, abdicare, cedere i ſuoi diritti.*

ABDICA'TING, or ABDICA'TION, s. [the voluntary act of renouncing] *l' atto di ceſſione che uno fa de' ſuoi diritti.*

ABDI'CATIVE, adj. *implicante abdicazione.*

ABDITO'RIUM, s. [a cheſt in which reliques were kept] *reliquiario,* s. m. *vaſo o altra cuſtodia dove ſi tengono a conſervano reliquie.*

Abditórium [a place to hide and keep goods, plate and money] *ripoſtiglio,* s. m. *luogo ritirato da riporvi roba, argenteria, o danari.*

ABDO'MEN, s. *abdóme, cavità comunemente chiamata il baſſo ventre, che contiene lo ſtomaco, le budella, il fégato la milza, e la véſcica.*

ABDO'MINAL }
ABDO'MINOUS } adj. *appartenente all' abdóme.*

To ABDU'CE [to carry away] *menare, condur via.*

ABECEDA'RIAN, s. [one who teaches or learns the ABC] *uno che inſegna o impara l' abbicci.*

ABECE'DARY, adj. [belonging to the letters A, B, C] *appartenente all' abbicci.*

A-BE'D [in bed] *a letto, in letto.*

To be ſick a-bed, *eſſere in letto ammalato.*

To be or lie a-bed, *eſſere, o ſtare a letto.*

To be brought a-bed, *partorire.*

ABE'RRANCE }
ABE'RRANCY }
ABERRA'TION } s. [wandering or going out of the way] *ſviamento, diſviamento, ſmarrimento, errore, deviazione dal cammin dritto.*

ABE'RRANT, s. *uno che s' allontana o che eſce dalla dritta via.*

ABE'RRING, s. *l' uſcire del cammin dritto.*

To ABERU'NCATE, *ſtradicare, ſvellere dalla radice.*

To ABE'T [to encourage, to incite, to ſet on, to uphold, to back, to aſſiſt, to aid] *proteggere, difendere, aſſiſtere, favorire, ſpingere innanzi, ſoſtener uno ne' ſuoi diſegni con arte o con ajuto.*

ABE'TTED, adj. *incoraggiato, incoraggire, animato,* v. To abet.

ABE'TTING, s. *incitamento, iſtigamento,* s. m. *iſtigazione,* s. f. *ſtimolo,* s. m.

ABE'TTER, or ABE'TTOR, s. [one that adviſes or aſſiſts another in doing an unlawful act] *colui che aſſiſte o incoraggiſce*

raggiſce alcuno; e s' intende generalmente nel far male.

To be an abettor of a crime, *eſſer complice d'un delitto.*

To ABHO'R [to loath, to hate] *abhorrire, abbominare, deteſtare, odiare, avere in odio, aver a ſchiſo.*

ABHO'RRED, adj. *abborrito, abbominato, deteſtato, odiato.*

ABHO'RRENCE, or ABHO'RRENCY, s. [averſion from, loathing] *abborrimento,* s. m. *abbominazione, deteſtazione,* s. f. *odio,* s. m.

To have an abhorrence for ſomething, *avere in aborrimento una coſa, odiarla, averla a ſchiſo.*

ABHO'RRENT, adj. *che abboriſce, odia, o deteſta; avverſo, contrario, nemico, che ha a ſchiſo.*

ABHO'RRER, s. [that abhors] *quello che abboriſce o odia, nemico mortale.*

ABHO'RRING, s. [loathing, hating] *abborrimento, orrore, odio,* s. m. *deteſtazione,* s. f.

To ABI'DE [to dwell or live in a place] *abitare, dimorare, ſtare in un luogo (nel preſente* I abode *o* abid.

To abide in the woods, *dimorare fra i boſchi.*

To abide in ſin, *viver in peccato.*

To abide [to endure, to ſuffer] *ſoffrire, compatire, tollerare, ſopportare.*

I will never abide ſuch things, *non ſoffrirò mai tali coſe.*

No body can abide him, *neſſuno puo tollerarlo.*

He can't abide the name of marriage, *il ſolo nome di matrimonio l'inorridiſce.*

If you abide the firſt charge, *ſe farete teſta al primo incontro.*

To abide [to forbear, to refrain] *contenerſi, aſtenerſi, raffrenarſi.*

To abide [to wait for] *aſpettare, attendere.*

To abide [to laſt] *durare, conſervarſi, mantenerſi, continuare.*

To abide [to loiter] *ſtar a bada, indugiare, badaluccare.*

To abide by a thing [to ſtand to it] *ſpalleggian, proteggere.*

ABI'DED, adj. partic. of to abide.

ABI'DING, s. [abode] *dimora, abitazione,* s. f. *abituro,* s. m.

Abiding [enduring to the end] *continuanza, continuazione, perſeveranza,* s. f.

Abiding [ſuffering] *tolleranza, ſofferenza,* s. f.

Abiding [tarrying] *dimora, tardanza,* s. f.

ABJE'CT, adj. [caſt away, mean, baſe, vile] *abietto, vile, baſſo, umile, infimo.*

A man of abject ſpirits, *un uomo di poco cuore.*

An abject, s. [a perſon of no repute or eſteem] *un uomo di baſſa lega, un vile, un uomo da nulla.*

ABJE'CTION, ABJE'CTNESS, s. [abject condition, meanneſs, vileneſs] *viltà, baſſezza, codardia, puſillanimità, dappocaggine,* s. f.

Abjection of mind, *baſſezza d'animo, viltà, codardia, vigliaccheria.*

ABI'LITY, s. [power] *potere,* s. m. *forza, poſſa, capacità, abilità,* s. f.

Every one does according to his ability, *ciaſcuno fa ſecondo la ſua abilità.*

Ability [riches] *facoltà, ricchezza, entrata,* s. f. *avere,* s. m. *beni di fortuna.*

A man of ability may do what he liſts, *un uomo che ha cervello puo far quel che vuole.*

Ability [of body] *robuſtezza, forza, poſſanza, gagliardia.*

Ability [of parts] *abilità, capacità,* s. f. *ſapere, ingegno,* s. m.

ABINTE'STATE, *termine legale. Colui che muore ſenza aver fatto teſtamento quantunque poteſſe farlo.*

To ABJU'DICATE, *ſentenziare, aggiudicare, aſſegnare a qualcuno che che ſia per ſentenzia.*

ABJURA'TION, s. [law term] *abjura.*

To ABJU'RE, *abjurare, giurare di non far una tal coſa, ritrattarſi, negar con giuramento una data coſa.*

To abjure [to renounce] *rinunziare, ſpontaneamente cedere, rifiutare, negare.*

To abjure one's country, *abbandonare la ſua patria.*

ABJU'RING, s. *rinunzia,* s. f. *il rimanziare, l' abjurare.*

ABLACTA'TION, s. [the weaning of a child] *lo ſvezzare o ſpoppare.*

Ablactation (in gardening) [a kind of grafting, when the cyon is cut off by degrees, till it is firmly united to the ſtock] *una della maniere d'inneſtare.*

A'BLATIVE [the laſt of the ſix caſes in nouns and participles] *abblativo, ſeſto caſo de' nomi.*

A'BLE, adj. [capable] *capace, atto, abile, buono, idoneo, che ha poſſa di mente, di mezzi, o di richezza.*

Able [ſtrong] *forte, gagliardo, robuſto.*

Able [wealthy] *ricco, comodo, beneſtante, opulento.*

Able [ſkilful] *eſperto, eſperimentato, pratico, eſercitato, dotto.*

Able to pay, *ſolvente, che puo pagare.*

To be able, *potere.*

I am not able to ſtir, *non poſſo muovermi.*

As far as I am able, *per quanto potrò, o mi ſarà poſſibile.*

None is able to come near him for ſkill, *neſſuno puo agguagliare la ſua deſtrezza, la ſua deſtrezza è ſenza pari.*

He owes more than he is able to pay, *deve più che non ha, più che non poſſiede.*

A'BLENESS, s. *vigore, forza.*

A'BLEPSY, s. [blindneſs] *cecità, mancanza di viſta.*

To A'BLOCATE [to ſet or let out to hire] *affittare, dare ad affitto, allogare.*

A'BLUENT, adj. *abluente, che netta, che puo nettare.*

Abluent medicines (the ſame as aſtergent) *medicine aſterſive.*

ABLU'TION, s. [purgation, waſhing] *abluzione,* s. f. *l' atto del nettare.*

A'BLING, [enabling] *che abilita, o rende abile.*

To A'BNEGATE, *negare.*

ABNEGA'TION [the renouncing one's intereſt, pleaſures, or paſſions, ſelf denial] *rinunzia,* s. f. *rinunziamento, abbandonamento,* s. m.

A'BNODATE [to prune trees] *dibruſcare; dibrucare, levare i ramuſcelli inutili e ſecchicci degli alberi.*

ABO'ARD, adv. *a bordo, in una nave, in un vaſcello.*

To go a-board, *andare a bordo.*

ABO'DE, s. [dwelling-place] *abitazione, dimora,* s. f. *abituro,* s. m.

Abode [delay] *tardanza,* s. f. *indugio,* s. m *lo ſtare, o continuare in un luogo.*

To ABO'DE, v. (bode) *ſervir di pronoſtico, eſſer d' augurio.*

ABO'DEMENT, s. *ſegreta anticipazione di qualche coſa avvenire.*

To ABO'LISH [to deface] *abolire, caſſare, cancellare.*

To aboliſh [to deſtroy] *abolire, annullare, eſtinguere.*

To aboliſh a law, *annullare o rivocare una legge.*

ABO'LISHED, adj. *abolito, caſſato, annullato, cancellato.*

ABO'LISHER, s. *colui che aboliſce.*

ABO'LISHING, or ABO'LISHMENT, s. *annullamento,* s. m. *abolizione, l' annullare.*

ABOLI'TION (in law) [the deſtroying or the abſolute repealing of a law or cuſtom, ſo that it ſhall be of no force] *abolizione, caſſazione, abrogazione,* s. f.

Abolition [a leave given by the king or judges to a criminal accuſer to forbear farther proſecution] *grazia,* s. f. *perdono,* s. m.

ABO'MINABLE, adj. [hateful, hated] *abbominevole, abbominoſo.*

An abominable fact, *un fatto o caſo enorme.*

ABO'MINABLY, adv. *abbominevolmente, con abbominazione.*

To ABO'MINATE [to deteſt, to hate] *abbominare, deteſtare, abborire, avere in odio, odiare.*

ABOMINA'TED, adj. *abbominato, deteſtato, aborrito, odiato.*

ABOMINA'TION, s. [a deteſtable thing] *abbominazione,* s. f. *abominio,* s. m.

Full of abomination, *abbominevole, abbominoſo, odioſo.*

ABORI'GINES, s. *i primi antichi abitanti d'un paeſe.*

To ABO'RT [to miſcarry] *abortire, ſconciarſi.*

ABO'RTION [miſcarriage] *abborto, ſconciatura.*

ABO'RTIVE, adj. *abortivo, nato prima del tempo, imperfetto, informe.*

An abortive child, *un fanciullo abortivo.*

An abortive deſign, *un diſegno immaturo.*

ABO'RTIVELY, adv. *immaturamente, prima del tempo.*

ABO'VE, adv. *ſu, ſopra.*

He is above in my room, *egli è ſu in camera mia.*

Theſe things are above me, *queſte coſe ſono ſuperiori al mio intendimento.*

Above all things, above all, *ſopra tutto, principalmente.*

Above [in greatneſs, excellency, or honour] *maggiore, ſuperiore.*

His liberality is above his ability, *la sua liberalità non corrisponde alle sue facoltà.*
The water scarce reached us above the knee, *l'acqua appena ci arrivava al ginocchio.*
Above [more, longer than] *più.*
I love you above my eyes, *v'amo più degli occhi miei.*
He was not with me above an hour, *non restò meco più d' un' ora.*
She is not above fifteen years old, *ella non ha più di quindici anni.*
A good name is above wealth, *una buona riputazione val più che non le richezze.*
He shall easily get above him, *facilmente lo sopravvanzerà.*
I am above these things, *non bado a queste cose.*
His head was above water, *la sua testa era fuori dell' acqua.*
Over and above, *di più, soprappiù, di più.*
Give that which remains over and above, *datemi il soprappiù.*
Over and above the sum, *più della somma.*
From above, *di sù, dal cielo.*
Gifts from above, *doni del cielo.*
As above, *come sopra.*
Above-mentioned, *sopradetto, sopraccennato.*
Above ground, *espressione usata per significare che uno è vivo, non sotterato.*
Above board, *a vista d' ognuno, senza artifizio, senza inganno.*
To be above [to excel] *avanzare, superare, trapassare, vincere.*
To ABO'UND, *abbondare, avere più che a sufficienza.*
England abounds with all things necessary, *l' Inghilterra abbonda di tutte le cose necessarie.*
ABO'UT, prep. *intorno, indosso, che incerchia, toccante.*
Abóut, adv. *circolarmente in cerchio, in vicinanza, quasi, quasonente, quà e là, dappertutto, col to innanzi al verbo significa, in prozinto.*
About ten of the clock, *in circa le dieci.*
About sun-set, *verso il tramontar del sole.*
I have no money about me, *non ho danari addosso.*
About [near] *intorno, vicino, appresso, all' intorno.*
The army encamped about the town, *l' esercito s'attendò presso la città.*
About, *intorno.*
There are divers opinions about it, *i pareri sono diversi intorno a ciò.*
I come to you about that business, *vengo da voi per quel affare.*
About the latter end of the month, *verso la fine del mese.*
He lives somewhere here about, *sta in qualche parte quì vicino.*
What do they say about the town? *che si dice per la città?*
About ten days, *dieci giorni più o meno.*
He came about the same time, *venne quasi nel medesimo tempo.*

He is about going away, *sta per partire.*
All about, *da per tutto.*
To drink about, *bere in giro.*
Mind what you are about, *badate a quel che fate.*
I am about to do it, *lo farò fra poco.*
Ten leagues about, *per dieci leghe all' intorno.*
To lay about, *esser in disordine.*
All this stir was about you, *tutta questa confusione è nata per conto vostro.*
I don't know what I am about, *non so dove ho la testa, non so quel che mi faccia.*
I am about writing a letter, *sto scrivendo una lettera.*
The farthest way about, is the nearest way home, *chi va piano va sano.*
About a thing, *impegnato in una cosa.*
To ABRA'DE [to shave, to pare off] *radere, nettare, raschiare.*
ABRA'SION, s. [the act of shaving off] *cancellatura, cancellazione, cancellagione,* s. f.
A-BRE'AST, adv. *a canto, vicino, pari.*
To A'BREVIATE [to abridge] *abbreviare.*
ABBREVIA'TION, s. [abridgment] *abbreviamento,* s. m. *abbreviatura,* s. f.
ABREVIA'TOR, s. *abbreviatore,* s. m. *che abbrévia.*
A'BRICK, or A'BRIG, s. [among chymists, sulphur] *solfo, zolfo,* f. m.
To ABRI'DGE [to make shorter in words, still retaining the sense or substance] *abbreviare, tor via alcuna parte della quantità continua, diminuire, scortare, accorciare, compendiare.*
To abridge one's conveniencies, *risparmiarsi, viver con risparmio.*
Christian religion abridges us of no lawful pleasures, *la religione cristiana non ci vieta i piaceri leciti.*
To abridge one's liberty, *dar meno libertà, tirar la briglia.*
To abridge one's charges, *diminuire le spese.*
ABRI'DGED, adj. *abbreviato, diminuito, scortato.*
ABRI'DGMENT, s. *ristretto, compendio,* s. m.
ABRI'DGING, s. *abbreviamento, scemamento,* s. m. *diminuzione,* s. f.
ABRO'ACH, adj. *in atto di scappar fuora.*
To set abroach [to tap] *spillare.*
ABRO'AD, adv. *senza ritegni, a largo, fuor di casa, fuor di paese, da ogni banda, di fuora, non di dentro.*
He laid abroad all night, *è stato tutta la notte fuor di casa.*
To go abroad, *uscire.*
Will you go abroad with me? *volete venire a spasso meco?*
That report runs abroad, *v'è un tal bisbiglio, corre voce.*
There is a wind abroad, *fa vento, il vento soffia.*
'Tis generally talk'd abroad, *non si parla d'altro.*
Abroad [all about] *da per tutto.*
Abroad [in foreign parts] *fuori.*

At home and abroad, *dentro e fuor del regno.*
To set abroad, *divulgare, publicare.*
To A'BROGATE [to make void, to annul, to repeal] *annullare, abolire, rivocare, cassare, cancellare.*
ABROGA'TED, adj. *annullato, abolito, rivocato, cassato.*
ABROGA'TING, or ABROGA'TION, s. [the act of repealing] *rivocazione, rivocagione,* s. f. *rivocamento,* s. m.
ABRO'TANUM, s. [southernwood] *abrótano, abruótino,* s. m. *abruótina,* s. f.
ABRU'PT, adj. *subitáno, repentino, improvviso, unconnesso, rotto, scosceso.*
ABRU'PTION, s. *subita e violenta separazione.*
A'BRUPTLY, adv. *di subito, repente, repentinamente.*
To fall out with one abruptly, *dar nel viso a qualcheduno, offenderlo a torto.*
ABRU'PTNESS, s. f. *subitezza.*
ABSCE'SS, s. [ulceration, imposthume] *postema,* s. f. *absesso,* s. m.
To ABSCI'ND [to cut off] *tagliar via.*
ABSCI'SSION, s. [the act of cutting off] *tagliamento,* s. m.
To ABSCO'ND [to hide one's self]. *nasconderſi, celarsi.*
ABSCO'NDED, adj. *nascosto, celato, ascoso.*
ABSCO'NDING, or ABSCONSION, s. *nascondimento, il nasconderſi.*
A'BSENCE, s. *assenza, lontananza,* s. f.
He did it in my absence, *lo fece in mia assenza.*
A'BSENT, adj. *assente, lontano, discosto.*
Long absent soon forgotten, *lontano dagli occhi lontano dal cuore.*
To ABSE'NT one's self, *assentarsi, allontanarsi, scostarsi.*
To ABSO'LVE [to acquit, to discharge] *assolvere, liberar dalle accuse, liberare, esentare, dispensare.*
ABSO'LVED, adj. *assolto, liberato.*
ABSO'LVING, s. *assoluzione,* s. f. *l'assolvere.*
A'BSOLUTE, adj. *assoluto, libero, non forzato.*
Absolute power, *potere assoluto.*
An absolute prince, *un principe assoluto.*
An absolute knave, *un pretto furbo.*
An absolute fool, *un vero sciocco, un vera baggéo.*
Ablative absolute [a term of Latin grammar] *ablativo assoluto.*
In an absolute manner, *tiberiescamente.*
A'BSOLUTELY, adv. *assolutamente, determinatamente.*
I am absolutely yours, *son tutto vostro.*
ABSOLU'TENESS, s. [absolute power] *un potere assoluto, despotismo.*
ABSOLU'TION [pardon, remission] *assoluzione, remissione,* s. f. *perdono,* s. m.
ABSO'LUTORY, adj. *che assolve.*
A'BSONANT, adj. } [disagreeing from
A'BSONOUS, adj. } the purpose, absurd] *assurdo, discordante, contrario alla ragione.*

Abso-

Abſonous [diſagreeing in ſound] *diſſonante, diſcorde.*

To ABSO'RB [to ſwallow up] *aſſórbere, aſſorbire, inghiottire, ingojare.*

To abſorb [to waſte, to conſume] *conſumare, diſſipare, rovinare, mandare a male.*

ABSO'RBED, adj. *aſſorbito, aſſorto, inghiottito, rovinato, conſumato.*

ABSO'RBENTS, s. pl. *medicine ché hanno qualità di temperare e raſciugare gli umori acidi del corpo.*

To ABSTAI'N [to forbear, to keep from] *aſtenerſi, temperarſi, contenerſi.*

To abſtain from pleaſures, *privarſi de' piaceri.*

To abſtain from meat, *aſtenerſi dalla carne.*

Deſiring they would abſtain from murder and fire, *pregandoli di non mettêr il tutto a fuoco e a ſangue.*

Abſtaining, s. *aſtinenza, l'aſtenerſi.*

ABSTE'MIOUS, adj. [that drinks no wine] *aſtemio, che non bee vino.*

ABSTE'NSION, s. (in law) [the act of with-holding the heir from taking poſſeſſion of his eſtate] *oppoſizione in jure fatta all' erede affinchè non s'impoſſeſſi de' ſuoi beni.*

To ABSTE'RGE [to wipe off, to cleanſe] *nettare, lavare, purgare.*

ABSTE'RGENT, adj. [of a cleanſing or ſcouring quality] *aſterſivo, che ha virtù, facoltà, o potere di nettare, di purgare.*

ABSTE'RGENTS, s. pl. [cleanſing medicines] *medicine aſterſive.*

ABSTE'RSION, s. [the effect produced by abſterſive medicines] *aſterſione,* s. f.

ABSTE'RSIVE, adj. [cleanſing or ſcouring] *aſterſivo, che ha virtù di nettare.*

A'BSTINENCE, s. [temperance, forbearance] *aſtinenza, temperanza, moderazione,* s. f. *temperamento,* s. m.

A'BSTINENT, adj. [temperate] *aſtinente, temperato, ſobrio, moderato.*

ABSTRA'CTS, *quantità minore contemente la virtù o la forza d'un maggiore eſtratto.*

To ABSTRA'CT [to draw away, to ſeparate] *aſtraere o aſtrarre, ſeparare idee, ridurre in compendio.*

ABSTRA'CTED, adj. *ſeparato, eſtratto, aſtratto, aſſente colla mente.*

ABSTRA'CTEDLY, adv. *ſeparatàmente, a parte, independentemente.*

ABSTRA'CTION, s. *aſtrazione, ſeparazione, eſtrazione,* s. f. *non curanzi di mondani oggetti.*

ABSTRA'CTIVE, adj. *che ha poſſa e qualità d'eſtrarre.*

To ABSTRU'DE [to thruſt away from] *ſcacciare, diſcacciare.*

ABSTRU'SE, adj. [dark, obſcure] *aſtruſo, oſcuro, intrigato, difficile ad intendere.*

ABSTRU'SENESS, s. } [darkneſs] *oſ-*
ABSTRU'SITY, s. } *curità,* s. f. *difficolto, avviluppamento,* s. m.

ABSU'RD, adj. [not agreeable to reaſon, ſilly, fooliſh, impertinent] *aſſurdo, impertinente, ſtravagante, incongruo.*

ABSU'RDITY, s. *aſſurdo, ſtravaganza, impertinenza, incongruità.*

A'BSURDLY, adv. *impertinentemente, ſtravagentemente, ſcioccamente.*

ABU'NDANCE, s. [great plenty] *abbondanza, dovizia, copia.*

There is abundance of fruit this year, *v'è grande abbondanza di frutti queſt' anno, queſt' anno i frutti ſono abbondanti.*

He has abundance of books, *ha moltiſſimi libri.*

There was abundance of people, *vi fu un gran concorſo di popolo.*

He has taken abundance of pains to learn Italian, *ha meſſo ogni cura nello ſtudio della lingua Italiana.*

He has abundance of wit, *ha molto ſpirito.*

ABU'NDANT, adj. *abbondante, dovizioſo.*

ABU'NDANTLY, adv. *abbondantemente, in gran copia, in grande abbonaanza.*

I think I have abundantly ſatisfied him, *credo d'averlo appieno ſoddiſfatto.*

His capacity is abundantly ſuperior to yours, *il ſuo engegno è di gran lunga del voſtro.*

ABU'SE, s. [ill uſe] *abuſo, mal uſo,* s. m.

Abuſe [affront] *affronto, ſopruſo,* s. m. *ingiuria,* s. f.

To ABU'SE [to make an ill uſe of, to miſuſe] *abuſarſi, ſervirſi d'una coſa fuor del buon uſo, ſervirſene a male.*

You abuſe my patience, *voi v'abuſate della mia ſofferenza.*

To abuſe [to affront] *ingiuriare, maltrattare, uſar villania, ſvillaneggiare.*

He abuſed him moſt cruelly, *lo maltrattò maliſſimamente.*

To abuſe a virgin, *deflorare una vergine con inganno.*

ABU'SED, adj. *abuſato, maltrattato.*

ABU'SER, s. *colui che maltratta, ingiuriatore, oltraggiatore,* s. m.

ABU'SIVE, adj. *ingiurioſo, oltraggiante.*

Abuſive language, *parole cattive, oltraggioſe, o ingiurioſe.*

ABU'SIVELY, adv. *abuſivamente; ingiurioſamente, malamente.*

ABU'SIVENESS, *ingiuria,* s. f. *oltraggio, maltrattamento,* s. m.

To ABU'T [to border upon] *confinare, riſpondere ad un luogo.*

ABU'TTALS, s. [a law-term] *limiti, termini, confini,* s. m. pl.

ABY'SM. }
ABY'SS. } s. [bottomleſs pit] *abbiſſo,* s. m. *profondità,* s. f. *golfo di gran fondo, coſa in cui un altra ſi perde. Quel corpo d' acque che dicono trovarſi nel centro del noſtro globo, teologicamente inferno.*

ACACI'A, s. f. [a ſort of ſhrub] *acacia o acazia,* s. f. *ſorta d'arbuſto.*

ACADE'MIAL } adj. *accademico d'*
ACADE'MICAL } *accademia.*

ACADE'MIAN } s. *accademico,*
ACADE'MICK } *membro d'un ac-*
ACADEMI'CIAN } *cademia, ſcuolaro*
ACA'DEMIST } *all' univerſità.*

ACA'DEMY, s. [a higher ſchool, or univerſity, alſo a particular ſociety of ingenious perſons, eſtabliſhed for improvement of learning] *accademia,* s. f. *ſtudio publico, univerſità,* s. f. *unione o ſocietà di gente unita per promozione delle belle arte. Luogo dove tal ſocietà s'uniſce.*

Academy [riding-ſchool] *maneggio, luogo deputato per maneggiare i cavalli.*

ACA'ID, s. [a word uſed by ſome chymiſts for vinegar] *aceto.*

To ACCE'LERATE [to haſten] *accelerare, affrettare.*

To accelerate, verb. neut. *accelerarſi, affrettarſi.*

ACCELERA'TED, adj. *accelerato, affrettato.*

ACCELERA'TION, s. *acceleramento, affrettamento,* s. m. *affrettanza, fretta,* s. f.

ACCE'NDED, adj. [lighted, kindled] *acceſo.*

ACCE'NSION, s. [the kindling, or ſetting any thing on fire] *accendimento,* s. m.

ACCE'NT, s. [tone or tenour, the riſing or falling of the voice] *accento, ſuono che ſi fa nel pronunciar la parola.*

He has a good accent, *egli ha buono accento.*

Accent [a mark on a particular ſyllable of any word, to ſhew whether it muſt be pronounced with a ſtronger or a weaker voice] *accento.*

An accent grave, acute, or circumflex, *un accento grave, acuto, o circonfleſſo.*

The muſical accents of birds, *là melodia degli uccelli.*

To ACCE'NT [to mark with an accent] *accentare, notare con accento.*

To ACCE'PT [to receive favourably or kindly] *accettare, aggradire, ricevere benignamente.*

To accept a preſent, *accettare un regalo.*

To accept a bill of exchange, *accettare una lettera di cambio.*

ACCE'PTABLE, adj. [agreeable] *accetto, grato, caro.*

It will be very acceptable to me, *mi ſarà gratiſſimo.*

ACCE'PTABLENESS, s. *accettazione, grazia,* s. f. *accoglimento, favore,* s. m.

ACCE'PTABLY, adv. *gratamente, caramente.*

ACCE'PTANCE, } s. [the act of tak-
ACCEPTA'TION, } ing in good part, the act of receiving kindly] *accettazione,* s. f.

This is not worthy of your acceptance, *non è coſa degna da un par voſtro, non è coſa degna d'eſſervi offerta.*

ACCEPTA'TION [the received meaning of a word, or the ſenſe in which it is uſually taken] *accettazione, ſenſo nel quale una parola è comunemente ricevuta.*

ACCE'PTION, s. *ſignificato d'una parola.*

ACC'EPTING, s. *accetto,* s. m. *accettagione,* s. f.

ACCE'SS, s. [admittance, approach, or paſſage to a place or perſon] *acceſſo,* s. m. *entrata, entratura,* s. f.

No man can have acceſs to him, *neſſuno ha entratura con lui.*

Accefs [fit of ague] *acceffione di febbre.*

ACCE'SSARY, *v.* acceffory.

ACCE'SSIBLE, adj. [that is eafy to be come at, approachable] *acceffibile, da poterfigli accoftare.*

An acceffible place, *un luogo acceffibile.*

Acceffible [affable] *affabile, cortefe, amorevole.*

ACCE'SSION, s. [coming to] *avvenimento,* s. m. *venuta,* s. f.

The acceffion of the king to the crown, *l'avvenimento del re alla corona, al trono.*

ACCE'SSION [addition] *addizione, giunta, aggiunta,* s. f.

ACCE'SSOR, s. [a comer to] *acceffore.*

ACCE'SSORY, adj. [additional] *acceffori o.*

The principal and the acceffory, *il principale e l'acceffori o.*

Acceffory [complice] *complice, confapevole, che è a parte con altri a mettere in efecuzione qualche fatto.*

They thought he was acceffory to that crime, *fu creduto complice di quel delitto.*

ACCE'SSORILY, adv. *acceffori amente, leggiermente, di paffaggio.*

A'CCIDENCE, *libretto che contiene i primi rudimenti della gramatica.*

A'CCIDENT, s. [cafualty, chance, fudden event] *accidente, cafo, avvenimento,* s. m.

Accident [ufed by logicians, in oppofition to fubftance] *accidente.*

ACCIDE'NTAL, adj. [happening by chance] *accidentale, che viene per accidente, cafuale.*

ACCIDE'NTALLY, adv. *accidentalmente, per accidente, cafualmente.*

A'CCIDY, s. [floth, lazinefs, indifpofition to devotion] *accidia, faftidio, tedio del ben fare.*

ACCI'DIOUS, adj. *accidiofo, poco difpofto a lavorare, pigro.*

ACCLAMA'TION, s. [fhouting for joy, applaufe] *acclamazione.* s. f. *applaufo,* s. m.

ACCLI'VITY, s. [the rifing fteepnefs of a hill] *ertezza, erta,* s. f.

ACCLO'YED, adj. [cloyed] *faftidito, fvogliato.*

Accloyed [nailed or prickt in fhooting] *inchiodato.*

A horfe accloyed, *un cavallo inchiodato.*

ACCOLA'DE, s. [the act of embracing about the neck] *abbracciata,* s. f. *abbracciamento,* s. m.

ACCO'MMODATE [to adjuft, to apply] *accomodare, acconciare, adattare, aggiuftare.*

To accommodate one's felf to the times, *accomodarfi al tempo, pigliar il tempo come viene.*

To accommodate [to lend] *accomodare preftare.*

Be fo kind as to accommodate me with your coach, *mi favorifca della fua carrozza.*

To accommodate a difference, *aggiuftare una differenza.*

ACCOMMODA'TED, adj. *accommodato, acconciato, adattato.*

You are mightily accommodated here, *voi fiete molto a voftro agio qui voi ftate molto comodamente qui.*

ACCOMMODA'TING, s. *accommodamento, aggiuftamento, l'accommodare.*

ACCOMMODA'TION, s. [the act of making up a difference] *accomodamento, accordo.*

To come to an accommodation, *reftar d'accordo, accordarfi, convenire.*

ACCO'MMODATELY, adv. *bene acconciamente, comodamente.*

To ACCO'MPANY [to keep company with, to wait on] *accompagnare, andar con uno.*

To accompany a voice, *accompagnare, una voce, fonare alcuno ftrumento col canto.*

Accompanied, adj. *accompagnato.*

ACCO'MPLICE, s. [that has a hand in a bufinefs, that is privy in the fame crime with another] *complice,* s. m. f.

To ACCO'MPLISH [to perform, to finifh, to fulfill] *compire, finire, perfezionare, dar compimento.*

To accomplifh a vow, *fcioglier il voto.*

I will accomplifh what I promife, *atterrò quel che prometto.*

ACCOMPLISHED, adj. *compito, finito, perfezionato.*

A well accomplifhed gentleman, *un gentiluomo molto compito o garbato.*

I have all my wifhes accomplifhed, *ho ottenuto tutto quel che bramavo.*

When ten years were accomplifhed, *finiti i dieci anni.*

ACCO'MPLISHER, s. *un che finifce, che da l'ultima mano, a un lavoro.*

ACCO'MPLISHING, } s. endowment] *compimento, finimento, ornamento,* s. m. *perfezione,* s. f.
ACCO'MPLISHMENT,

ACCO'MPT, *v.* account.

ACCO'RD, s. [agreement, confent] *accordo,* s. m. *convenzione,* s. f.

With one accord, *unanimamente, d'un comun confenfo.*

If the matter may be brought to accord, *fe v' è luogo d'accordare il negozio.*

Of his, her, our, your, or their own accord, *volontariamente, fpontaneamente.*

You did it of your own accord, *l'avete fatto di voftra tefta.*

He gave it to me of his own accord, *mo lo diede fenza che glielo domandaffi.*

They came of their own accord, *vennero da fe, fenza effere invitati.*

By mutual accord, *d'un comune confenfo.*

To ACCO'RD [to agree] *accordarfi, convenire, concordare, effer d'accordo.*

I accord with you in that, *fon del voftro parere in ciò.*

To accord in an opinion, *effer del medefimo parere o fentimento.*

To accord [to adjuft] *aggiuftare, riconciliare, rappacificare, metter d'accordo.*

ACCO'RDANCE, s. [agreement] *accordo,* s. m. *unione, conformità,* s. f.

ACCO'RDED, adj. *accordato,* v. to accord.

ACCO'RDING, adv. *fecondo, fecondo che.*

According as I deferve; *fecondo il mio merito.*

According as there fhall be need, *fecondo il bifogno.*

According to your orders, *fecondo i voftri comandi.*

According to every man's pleafure, *come piacerà a ciafcuno.*

According to my mind, *di mio gufto.*

This is not according to my mind, *quefto non è di mio gufto, non mi piace.*

To act according to reafon, *operare fecondo la ragione.*

To ACCO'ST [to approach, to come up to one] *accoftarfi, avvinarfi, appreffarfi, approdare, fbarcare, accoftare.*

ACCO'STABLE, adj. *benigno, dolce, umano, affabile.*

ACCO'STED, adj. *accoftato, avvicinato.*

ACCO'UNT [reckoning] *conto, càlcolo,* s. m. *ragione,* s. f.

To keep account, *tener conto, notare.*

To caft up an account, *calcolare, fare un calcolo.*

To call to an account, *chiamare a ragione, domandare a' conti.*

To give an account of one's doing, *render conto di quel che fi fa.*

You are out in your accounts, *voi sbagliate, voi non v'apponete.*

You are right in your account, *il voftro conto è giufto.*

Account [efteem] *conto, cafo, pregio,* s. m. *ftima,* s. f.

To make a great account of a thing, *far cafo o conto d'un cofa, ftimarla, pregiarla.*

To make fmall account of a thing, *far poco conto d'una cofa, non la ftimare, difpregiarla.*

Account [relation] *ragguaglio, avvifo,* s. f. *notizia, faputa, relazione,* s. f.

I will give you an account of what I have done, *vi darò un ragguaglio di quel ch' ho fatto.*

No body can give an account how the thing happened, *neffuno fa come fuceffe la cofa, neffun fa come l'andaffe.*

Am I obliged to give you an account of what I do? *fono io obligato di farvi parte di quel che fo?*

I did it upon that account, *lo feci a quefto fine; quefto fu il motivo che ebbi nel fario.*

I'll do it upon your account, *lo farò per amor voftro.*

A man of no account, *un uomo di niente.*

He could not go upon the account of his father's death, *non potette partire per caufa della morte di fuo padre.*

That won't turn to my account, *cotefto non mi tornerà a conto.*

Upon what account do you demand this? *che ragione avete di domandarlo?*

You may command me upon all accounts, *voi potete comandarmi a ogni modo.*

To account [to reckon] *contare, annoverare, computare, calcolare.*

You muſt account to me, *voi avete a réndermene conto.*

To ACCOU'NT [to eſteem] *ſtimare, credere.*

I account it a great folly for a man to be vexed at things when there is no remedy, *ſtimo un gran pazzia il rammaricarſi per quelle coſe alle quali non c' è rimedio.*

ACCOU'NTABLE, adj. *obbligato, tenuto.*

I ſhall be accountable for it, *ne renderò conto io.*

You are accountable for his death, *voi ſiete ſtato cauſa della ſua morte.*

ACCOU'NTANT, s. [one well verſed in caſting up accounts] *abbachiſta, abbachiere*, s. m.

ACCO'UNTED, adj. *ſtimato, conſiderato.*

He is accounted the next man to the king, *è ſtimato la ſeconda perſona dopo il re.*

He is accounted the beſt phyſician in London, *paſſa pel primo medico di Londra.*

To ACCO'UTER [to attire, dreſs, equip] *aggiuſtare, accomodare, ornare, alleſtire, parare.*

ACCO'UTRED, adj. *aggiuſtato, accomodato, ornato, alleſtito, ben in ordine.*

ACCO'UTREMENTS, s. *abiti, veſtiti, arneſi, fornimenti, guernimenti.*

To ACCO'Y [to aſſwage] *mitigare, rallentare, raddolcire, diminuire.*

To ACCRE'W } [to riſe from, to
To ACCRU'E } grow] *derivare, provenire, procedere, redondare.*

What good will accrue to you by it? *che vantaggio ne riceverete voi.*

To ACCRO'ACH [to encroach] *uſurpare.*

ACCRO'ACHMENT, s. *uſurpazione.*

ACCUBA'TION, *la poſitura degli antichi Romani a tavola.*

To ACCU'MB [to lay down at table] *ſtar a tavola come i Romani antichi.*

To ACCU'MULATE [to heap up] *accumulare, ammaſſare, ammonticellare.*

ACCU'MULATED, adj. *accumulato, ammaſſato, ammonticellato.*

Accumulated favours, *ſpeſſiſſimi favori.*

ACCUMULA'TION, s. [the act or ſtate of heaping] *accumulazione*, s. f. *accumulamento, ammaſſamento*, s. m.

A'CCURACY, s. [exactneſs, diligence] *accuratezza, eſattezza, diligenza*, s. f.

A'CCURATE, adj. [exact, curious] *accurato, diligente, eſatto.*

A'CCURATELY, adv. *accuratamente, diligentemente, eſattamente.*

To ACCU'RSE [to excommunicate] *ſcomunicare, maledire, anatematizzare.*

ACCU'RSED, adj. *ſcomunicato, maledetto, anatematizzato.*

ACCUSA'TION, s. [accuſing, charge] *accuſazione, accuſa*, s. f. *rimprovero*, s. m.

ACCUS'ATIVE, s. [a term of grammar] *accuſativo*, s. m. *il caſo accuſativo.*

To ACCU'SE [to charge with a crime] *accuſare, incolpare.*

To accuſe one for, or of a thing, *accuſare, incolpare uno di qualche coſa.*

ACCU'SER, s. m. *accuſatore*, s. m. *che accuſa, accuſatrice*, s. f.

ACCU'SING, s. *accuſamento*, s. m. *l'accuſare.*

To ACCU'STOM [to uſe] *accoſtumare, avvezzare.*

To accuſtom one's ſelf to a thing, *avvezzarſi, aſſuefarſi ad una coſa.*

ACCU'STOMABLY, adv. *ſpeſſo.*

ACCU'STOMARILY, adv. *ordinariamente, comunemente.*

ACCU'STOMED, adj. *avvezzato, avvezzo, aſſuefatto.*

A ſhop well accuſtomed, *una bottega bene avviata o frequentata, una bottega che ha molti avventori.*

ACCU'STOMING, s. *avvezzamento, uſo*, s. m. *conſuetudine*, s. f.

ACE, s. *Aſſo, ſegno unico ne' dadi e nelle carte.*

AMBES-A'CE, *ambaſſi, ambo gli aſſi, nel giuoco de'dadi, quando ambi hanno ſcoperto l'aſſo.*

ACE'PHALOUS, *ſenza la teſta.* An inſect of the acephalous kind; *un inſetto di quelle ſpezie che non han capo.*

ACE'RBITY, s. [ſourneſs, ſharpneſs] *acerbezza, acerbità*, s. f.

Acérbity, *acerbità, aſprezza, durezza, fierezza, crudeltà, ſeverità*, s. f. *rigore*, s. m.

To A'CERVATE, *accumulare, ammaſſare, ammonticellare.*

ACHE, s. *appio*, s. m. *erba di piu maniere.*

Ache, *v.* Ake, *dolore che continua.*

To ACHIE'VE, *v.* to atchieve, *e i ſuoi derivativi.*

A'CHORS, s. [a ſort of cruſted ſcab which makes an itching and ſtink on the ſurface of the head] *tigna*, s. f. *ulcere ſulla cotenna del capo, cagionate da umor viſcoſo che cagiona prurito e puzza.*

A'CID, adj. [tart, ſour, ſharp] *acido, che ha acidità, agro.*

ACI'DITY, s. [ſharpneſs, tartneſs] *acidezza, acidità, agrezza*, s. f.

To ACI'DULATE, *rendere un poco acida la coſa che non lo è punto.*

A'CINUS, s. [a grape ſtone] *àcino, granello d'uva*, s. m.

To ACKNO'WLEDGE [to own, to confeſs] *confeſſare, affermare, concedere, riconoſcere.*

To acknowledge a favour, *riconoſcere un favore.*

To acknowledge one's ſelf guilty, *confeſſarſi colpevole.*

ACKNO'WLEDGED, adj. *confeſſato, affermato, conceſſo, riconoſciuto.*

ACKNO'WLEDGMENT, s. [confeſſion] *confeſſione, affermazione*, s. f.

Acknowledgment [gratitude, thankfulneſs] *riconoſcimento, contraccambio, guiderdone, premio*, s. m. *riconoſcenza, ricompenſa*, s. f.

I give you this in acknowledgment of the favour you have done me, *vido queſto in contraccambio del favore fattomi.*

ACKNO'WLEDGING, s. *il reconoſcere, il confeſſare, riconoſcimento*, s. m.

ACO'LYT, s. [a prieſt's attendant] *accólito*, s. m. *colui che ha il quarto degli ordini minori.*

ACO'NITE, s. [a poiſonous herb, called wolf's or libbard's bane] *acónito*, s. m. *ſorta d'erba.*

A'CORN, s. *ghianda*, s. f. *frutto della quercia, del cerro, del lecce, e ſimili, co' quale s'ingraſſano i porci.*

To ACQUAINT [to make known, to give intelligence] *avvertire, far ſapere, informare, avviſare, dare avviſo, far intendere, ſignificare.*

I will acquaint you with every thing, *vi avviſerò il tutto, v'informerò del tutto.*

This is to acquaint you, *vi faccio ſapere con queſta lettera; queſta ſervira per avviſarvi.*

ACQUAI'NTANCE, s. [familiarity] *conoſcenza, familiarità*, s. f.

Our acquaintance is of no long ſtanding, *non è molto tempo che ci conoſchiamo.*

To get one's acquaintance, *far conoſcenza con uno.*

I have no acquaintance with you, *non vi conoſco; no ſo chi voi ſiate.*

Upon what acquaintance? *per che ragione? in virtù di che?*

Acquaintance [familiar friend] *conoſcente, amico*, s. m.

He is an acquaintance of mine, *è mie conoſcente.*

An intimate acquaintance of mine, *amico mio ſtretto.*

ACQUAINTED, adj. *avviſato, informato, avvertito, ſignificato.*

I am acquainted with it, *ne ho l'avviſo, lo ſo.*

I am very well acquainted with him, *lo conoſco particolarmente.*

We have been acquainted but a very little while, *non è molto tempo che abbiamo fatto conoſcenza inſieme; non è molto che ci conoſciamo.*

To make acquainted, *avviſare, informare, ſignificare, far conſapevole.*

I'll make you acquainted with all, *vi farò conſapevole del tutto.*

I am acquainted by ſome friends of mine, *ricevo avviſo da alcuni amici.*

I will make you acquainted with my deſign, *vi comunicherò o parteciperò il mio diſegno.*

I'll ſee you be made acquainted with all, *procurerò d'informavi del tutto.*

ACQUAI'NTING, s. *informazione, dichiarazione*, s. f. *avviſo*, s. m.

To ACQUIE'SCE [to reſt ſatisfied, to comply with, to conſent] *conſentire, ſommetterſi, contentarſi, ſtare a detta.*

To acquieſce in one's judgment, *ſtare al giudicio d'un altro.*

To acquieſce in one's demand, *condeſcendere ad una dimanda.*

I acquieſce in it, *non ho objezione alcuna; ſon ſoddiſfatto così; ſon d'accordo.*

I cannot acquieſce in your propoſals, *non poſſo venire a' voſtri patti.*

To acquieſce in the will of God, *ſottometterſi alla volontà di Dio.*

ACQUIE'SCED, adj. *conſentito, acconſentito, condeſceſo, contentato.*

ACQUIE'SCENCE, s. } [conſent, com-
ACQUIE'SCENCY, } compliance, con-

condefcenfion] *confenfo, confentimento,* s. m. *condefcendenza, o condifcendenza,* s. f.

ACQUI'RABLE, adj. [that may be acquired] *ricuperabile, che fi puo ricuperare.*

To ACQUI'RE [to get] *acquiftare, guadagnare.*

To acquire [to attain] *arrivare, pervenire, ottenere.*

To acquire [to purchafe] *impoffeffarfi, improdronirfi, fare acquifto.*

To acquire [to learn] *imparare, perfezionarfi.*

ACQUI'RED, adj. *acquiftato, ottenuto,* v. to acquire.

ACQUI'RER, s. *acquiftatore, che acquifta,* s. m. *acquiftatrice, che acquifta,* s. f.

ACQUI'RING, s. *acquiftamento, acquifto,* s. m. *l'acquiftare.*

ACQUISI'TION, s. [an acquiring] *acquiftamento, acquifto,* s. m.

To ACQUI'T [to difcharge or free from] *affolvere, liberare, efentare.*

To acquit a prifoner, *liberare un prigioniero; mandarlo via libero.*

To acquit one's felf of his office, *compire al fuo officio.*

To acquit one's felf of his promife, *tener la fua promeffa.*

To acquit an obligation, *riconofcere un beneficio.*

To acquit a debt, *pagare un debito.*

To acquit a malefactor from his deferved punifhment, *affolvere un reo dal meritato gaftigo.*

ACQUI'TTAL, or ACQUITMENT, s. *affoluzione, liberazione,* s. f. *liberamento,* s. m.

ACQUI'TTANCE, s. [for money received] *ricevuta, confeffione che fi fa per via di fcrittura d'aver ricevuto.*

ACQUI'TTED, adj. *affolto, liberato, efentato.*

ACQUI'TTING, s. *affoluzione, liberazione,* s. f.

ACRE, s. [a meafure of land, containing 40 perches in length, and four in breadth] *bifolca, bubulca,* s. f. *jugero,* s. m.

ACRIMO'NIOUS, adj. [fharp, tart] *agro, acido.*

A'CRIMONY, s. [fharpnefs, tartnefs] *agrezza, acidezza, acidità, acrimonia,* s. f.

ACRO'SS, adv. *a fchiancio, a fgembo, a fghimbefcio.*

To hold one's arms acrofs, *ftar colle braccia in croce.*

ACT, s. [deed, action] *atto,* s. m. *azione,* s. f.

To do a wicked act, *fare una cattiva azione.*

He was taken in the very act, *fu prefo ful fatto.*

Act [decree] *atto, decreto.*

Act of parliament, *atto o decreto de parlamento.*

An act of oblivion, *atto di grazia.*

An act of a play, *atto di comedia.*

Acts regiftered, *atti, fcritture da regiftrarfi, ne' luoghi pubblici.*

To ACT, *fare, operare.*

To act like an honeft man, *trattare da galantuomo.*

To act againft one's confcience, *operare contro il dettame della fua cofcienza.*

To act againft one's own intereft, *far torto al proprio intereffe.*

To act contrary to the law of God, *violare la legge di Dio.*

To act in a play, *rappresentare, recitare.*

He acts in this play, *egli recita in quefta comedia.*

He acts the king, *fa la parte del re.*

A'CTED, adj. *rapprefentato, recitato.*

A'CTING, s. *azione, recitazione,* s. f.

A'CTION, s. *azione, operazione,* s. f. *fatto,* s. m.

Action [gefture] *atto, gefto.*

A man fit for an action, *un uomo di cuore, un uomo rifoluto.*

Action [fuit at law] *caufa, lite,* s. f. *proceffo,* s. m.

An action of trefpafs, *azione criminale.*

To fue one upon an action of trefpafs, *procedere contro alcuno criminalmente.*

To bring or enter an action againft one, *intentare, o far proceffo ad uno.*

To lofe one's action, *perder la caufa.*

An action of covenant, *azione di compromeffo.*

An action upon an appeal, *caufa d'appellazione.*

A'CTIONS [among merchants] *fondi.*

How go actions? *quanto vagliono i fondi?*

Action [fight] *fatto d'armi, combattimento,* s. m. *battaglia,* s. f.

A'CTIVE, adj. [nimble] *agile, fnello, deftro, induftriofo, ingegnofo.*

Active [in grammar] *attivo.*

A'CTIVELY, adj. [nimbly] *agilmente, deftramente, preftamente, prontamente.*

Actively [in an active fenfe] *attivamente, in fenfo attivo.*

ACTI'VITY, s. [brifknefs, nimblenefs] *attività, agilità, prontezza, vivacità,* s. f. *vigore, ftudio,* s. m.

A'CTOR, s. [ftage-player] *attore, recitante, comediante,* s. m.

Actor [one who has an action againft one] *attore, colui che nel litigare domanda.*

A'CTRESS, s. *attrice, comediante,* s. f.

A'CTUAL, adj. [effectual, real] *attuale, effettivo, reale.*

ACTUA'LITY, s. } [perfection of
A'CTUALNESS, s. } being] *attualità,* s. f.

A'CTUALLY, adv. [effectually, really] *attualmente, effettivamente, realmente.*

A'CTUARY, s. [a clerk that regifters the acts and conftitutions of a convocation] *attuario, miniftro deputato dal giudice a ricevere, e regiftrare, e tener cura degli atti pubblici.*

To ACTUA'TE [to bring into act, to move, to quicken] *effettuare, animare, incitare, fpronare.*

ACTUA'TED, adj. *attuato, ridotto all' atto, animato, incitato, fpronato.*

To ACU'MINATE [to fharpen] *agguzzare, fare agguzzo, appuntare.*

ACU'MINOUS, adj. [fharp-edged, pointed] *agguzzato, appuntato, agguzzo, acuto.*

ACU'TE, adj. [fharp, fharp pointed] *acuto, agguzzo, appuntato, pungente.*

Acute [violent] *acuto, violente.*

Acute [fharp-witted, ingenious, fubtil] *acuto, fottile, aftuto, fagace, fcaltrito.*

An acute accent, *accento acuto.*

ACU'TELY, adv. [fharply] *acutamente, fottilmente, aftutamente, fagacemente, fcaltritamente.*

ACU'TENESS, s. [fharpnefs] *acutezza, fottigliezza d' ingegno, aftufia, fagacità,* s. f.

A'DAGE, s. [proverb, old faying] *proverbio, detto proverbiale.*

ADA'GIAL, adj. [proverbial] *proverbiale, di proverbio.*

ADA'IES, adv. ex. NOW ADA'IES, *al giorno d'oggi, adeffo.*

A'DAMANT, s. [diamond; the moft glittering, hard, and valuable of all gems] *adamante, diamante.*

ADAMA'NTINE, adj. [of or belonging to adamant] *adamantino, di qualità d'adamante, diamantino.*

Adamantine [hard, inflexible] *adamantino, crudele, crudo, efferato, afpro, inumano.*

ADAMI'TES, s. [a fort of hereticks in Bohemia, who pretending to be reftored to Adam's innocence, went naked in their affemblies] *Adamiti, razza d'eretici, che fotto colore d'effer ftati reintegrati nell' innocenza d'Adamo, andavano nudi nelle loro adunanze.*

ADAM'S APPLE, s. *pomo d'Adamo; parte della gola.*

To ADA'PT [to make fit, to fuit] *adattare, accommodare una cofa ad un' altra, accommodare, affettare, applicare, proporzionare.*

ADA'PTED, adj. *adattato, accommodato, conveniente, proporzionato.*

ADA'PTING, s. *adattazione, proporzione,* s. f. *aggiuftamento, accommodamento,* s. m.

To ADD [to join or put to] *aggiungere, accrefcere.*

To add one to the number, *aggiungere uno al numero.*

I'll add fomething to it, *vi darò qualche cofa di più.*

Your filence added to my fufpicion, *il voftro filenzio m' , infofpettì maggiormente.*

This added to my misfortune, *quefto accrebbe la mia difgrazia, la refe maggiore.*

That has added to his ruin, *cotefto ha contribuito alla fua rovina.*

To ADDE'CIMATE [to take tithes] *decimare, pigliare la decima.*

A'DDED, adj. *aggiunto, accrefciuto.*

A'DDER, s. [a ferpent, whofe poifon is moft deadly] *bifcia,* s. f. *afpe,* s. m.

Water-adder, *idra.*

Adder's tongue, *briónia.*

Adder's-grafs, *fpezie di fatirion.*

A'DDIBLE, adj. *aggiungibile, che puoffi accrefcere.*

ADDIBI'LITY, s. *la poffibilità d'effer aggiunto, d'effer accrefciuto.*

A'DDICE, or ADZE, s. [an inſtrument generally uſed by coopers] *ſpecie d'aſcia o ſcure.*

To ADDI'CT [to give up one's ſelf wholly to a thing] *addarſi, applicarſi, darſi in preda, abbandonarſi.*

To addict one's ſelf to ſome art, *addarſi, applicarſi ad un' arte.*

To addict one's ſelf to all manner of vices, *darſi in preda ad ogni ſorta di vizi.*

ADDI'CTED, adj. *dedito, inchinato.*

To be addicted to one, *favorire la parte di qualcheduno, aderire ad uno.*

ADDI'CTION, s. *l'eſſer dato in preda, e ſi prende quaſi ſempre in cattivo ſenſo.*

ADDI'TION, *aggiunta, accreſcimento, addizione, raddopiamento.*

To make additions to a book, *fare aggiunte ad un libro, accreſcerlo.*

An addition of favours, *raddoppiamento di favori.*

Her beauty wants no addition, *la ſua bellezza non ha biſogno d'ornamenti.*

ADDI'TIONAL, adj. *di ſoprappiù, che vi è ſtato accreſciuto.*

An additional ſtock, *ſomma di danari accreſciuta al fondo principale.*

A'DDLE, adj. [vain, empty] *vano, vuoto.*

An addle egg, *un uovo ſterile, un uovo ſenza germe.*

Addle headed, *ſcervellato, dicervellato, ſciocco.*

Your brains are addle, *voi non avete cervello; quanto poco cervello avete!*

ADDRE'SS, s. [ſkill; nice or dexterous carriage in the management of an affair] *maniera, arte, ſagacità,* s. f. *modo,* s. m.

A man of good addreſs, *un uomo garbato, di bel garbo.*

Addreſs [epiſtle dedicatory] *lettera dedicatoria.*

The amorous addreſs of a lover to his miſtreſs, *ſollecitazione, iſtanza d'un amante alla ſua amata.*

Addreſs [application, dedication to a perſon] *ricorſo, rifugio.*

You muſt make your addreſs to him, *vi biſogna aver ricorſo a lui.*

Addreſs [a ſhort remonſtrance or petition made to the ſovereign] *ſupplica che ſi preſenta dal parlamento o dalle corporazioni d'Inghilterra al loro re.*

To ADDRE'SS [to make application to, to apply] *ricorrere, aver ricorſo; andare a chiedere ajuto o difeſa ad alcuno; rifuggire, indirizzarſi ad alcuno.*

To addreſs [to preſent a petition to to the king] *preſentare una ſupplica al Re.*

To addreſs a letter, *inviare, mandare una lettera.*

ADDRE'SSED, adj. *ricorſo, rifuggito, preſentato, mandato, ricapitato.*

ADDRE'SSER, s. *quello che preſenta le ſuppliche.*

A'DELING, or A'THELING, s. [a title of honour among the Engliſh Saxons, properly belonging to the heir apparent to the crown] *titolo d'onore fra gli antichi Saſſoni Ingleſi che ſignificava principe o figlio di re.*

ADE'MPTION, s. *privazione,* s. f. *privamento,* s. m.

ADE'PT, (he that is completely ſkilled in the ſecrets of his art) *colui che ſa tutti i ſegreti dell' arte ſua.*

Adept, adj. *dotto, intendente, verſato appieno in una ſcienza.*

A'DEQUATE, adj. [equal, even, proportional] *adequate, proporzionato, conveniente, conforme.*

To ADHE'RE TO [to cleave, to ſtick to] *attaccarſi, appiccarſi, unirſi.*

To adhere [to favour] *aderire, favorire, ſeguitare una parte, inchinarvi.*

ADHE'RED, adj. *attaccato, appiccato, unito, aderito, ſeguitato.*

ADHE'RENCY, s. [a ſticking cloſe to the intereſt or opinions of others] *aderenza,* s. f. *favore.*

ADHE'RENT, s [a ſtickler, a favourer] *aderente, fautore,* s. m.

ADHE'SION, s. [adherency] *aderenza,* s. f. *favore,* s. m. *adeſione,* s. f.

ADJA'CENT, adj. [lying near to, bordering upon] *contiguo, vicino, raſente, circonvicino, adjacente.*

ADIA'PHOROUS, adj. [indifferent] *indifferente, neutrale.*

ADIA'PHORY, s. indifference] *indifferenza, neutralità.*

ADJE'CTIVE, adj. *addiettivo.*

An adjective, s. *un nome addiettivo.*

ADJE'CTIVELY, adv. *addiettivamente, in modo o ſenſo d'addiettivo.*

ADIE'U, s. [farewel] *vale, addio.*

To bid one's friends adieu, *dire addio a' ſuoi amici.*

We bid our dead friend the laſt adieu, *dicemmo l'ultimo vale al morto amico.*

To ADJO'IN [to join to] *aggiugnere, arrogere, accreſcere.*

ADJOI'NED, adj. *aggiunto, accreſciuto.*

ADJO'INING, s. *aggiugnimento, argogimento,* s. m. *l'arrogere.*

Adjoining, adj. [lying next, neighbouring] *contiguo, raſente, vicino, allato, accoſto.*

A'DIT, s. [ſhaft or entrance into] *adito,* s. m. *entrata, apertura,* s. f.

To A'DJOURN [to put off] *differire, rimettere.*

ADJOU'RNED, adj. *differito, rimeſſo.*

To ADJU'DGE, *aggiudicare, condannare.*

ADJU'DGED, adj. *aggiudicato, condannato.*

ADJUDICA'TION, s. *condanna, aggiudicazione,* s. f. *l'aggiudicare, il condannare.*

ADJU'NCT, s. [that which is joined to another thing; a circumſtance] *giunta, particolarità, circonſtanza,* s. f. *acceſſorio,* s. m.

ADJU'NCTION, s. *aggiugnimento, arrogimento,* s. m. *l'arrogere.*

ADJURA'TION, s. *aggiurazione,* s. f. *ſcongiuramento,* s. m.

To ADJU'RE [to charge in God's name, ſtrictly, earneſtly] *ſcongiurare; ricercare uno ſtrettamente di che che ſia; ſtrettamente pregare.*

To adjure [to command an evil ſpirit by the force of an enchantment] *ſcongiurare, coſtringere, violentare i demoni.*

To ADJU'ST [to ſettle or ſtate an account] *aggiuſtare, ſaldare.*

To adjuſt [to determine or make up a difference] *acconciare, accordare, pacificare, metter d'accordo.*

ADJU'STED, adj. *aggiuſtato, ſaldato, acconciato, accordato, pacificato.*

ADJU'STING, s. *aggiuſtamento, accomodamento, acconciamento, ſaldo,* s. m.

A'DJUTANT, s. [an officer in a regiment who aſſiſts the ſuperior officers] *ajutante.*

A'DJUTORY, adj. [aiding, helping] *ajutativo, atto ad ajutare.*

ADJU'VANT, adj. [helping, aiding, aſſiſting] *ajutativo, atto ad ajutare.*

To A'DJUVATE [to help, to aſſiſt] *ajutare, aſſiſtere, ſoccorrere.*

A'DLE, v. Addle.

ADME'ASUREMENT, s. [a writ for the bringing thoſe to reaſon who uſurp more than their part or ſhare] *termine legale, che vuol dire, un atto per obligare uno a reſtituire quel che s'era appropriato ingiuſtamente.*

ADMENSURA'TION, s. [the act of making equal in meaſure] *agguagliamento,* s. m.

A'DMINICLE, s. [help, ſuccour, ſupport] *ajuto, ſoccorſo,* s. m. *aſſiſtenza,* s. f.

ADMINI'CULAR, adj. [helpful] *ajutativo, che ajuta o aſſiſte.*

To ADMINI'STER, [to govern, to manage] *amminiſtrare, reggere, governare.*

To adminiſter [to do ſervice, to aid] *aſſiſtere, ajutare.*

To adminiſter [to give, to diſpence] *amminiſtrare, ſomminiſtrare, porgere.*

To adminiſter the ſacraments, *amminiſtrare i ſacramenti.*

To adminiſter juſtice, *amminiſtrare, o eſercitare la giuſtizia.*

To adminiſter the baptiſm, *dare, amminiſtrare, conferire il batteſimo, battezzare.*

To adminiſter an occaſion, *ſomminiſtare un occaſione, dar occaſione.*

To adminiſter an oath, *dare il giuramento.*

ADMINI'STERED, adj. *amminiſtrato,* v. to adminiſter.

ADMINISTRA'TION, s. [the act of adminiſtering] *amminiſtragione, amminiſtrazione,* s. f. *maneggio,* s. m.

ADMINISTRA'TOR, s. [one that has the management of any affair] *amminiſtratore,* s. m. *che amminiſtra.*

ADMINISTRA'TRIX, s. *amminiſtratrice, quella che amminiſtra.*

A'DMIRABLE, adj. [wonderful, rare, excellent] *ammirando, ammirabile, mirabile, maraviglioſo, buono, eccellente, ſquiſito.*

A'DMIRABLY, adv. *ammirabilmente, mirabilmente, mariviglioſamente, eccellentemente.*

Admirably well, *perfettamente, in ſupremo grado, beniſſimamente.*

A'DMIRAL, s. [a chief commander of a ſquadron of ſhips] *ammiraglio,* s. m.

The Admiral ſhip, *almirante,* s m. *il vaſcello, in cui naviga la perſona dell' ammiraglio.*

The Admiral galley, *la galea capitana.*

The Admiral flag, *lo ſtendardo della galea capitana.*

A'DMIRALSHIP, s. *il comando o il carico dell' ammiraglio.*

A'DMIRALTY, s. [office or court for maintaining maritime affairs] *ammiragliato,* s. m.

ADMIRA'TION, s. [the act of admiring or wondering] *ammirazione, maraviglia,* s. f.

Taken up with admiration, he ſaid, *tutto maravigliato diſſe.*

Note of admiration, *punto ammirativo.*

To A'DMIRE [to look upon with wonder, to be ſurprized at] *ammirare, mirar con maraviglia, maravigliarſi.*

Every body admires him, *tutti l'ammirano.*

I admire how this can be done, *ſtupiſcomi come cio poſſa farſi.*

To admire [to love] *amare.*

I admire England above all the places I have ſeen, *l'Inghilterra mi piace più che qualſivoglia altro luogo ch' ho viſto.*

ADMI'RED, adj. *ammirato, maravigliato.*

ADMI'SSION, s. [admittance] *entrata, entratura,* s. f. *entramento,* s. m.

To ADMI'T [to receive, to allow of, to permit] *ammettere, accettare, ricevere, introdurre.*

To admit one into his familiarity, *ammettere uno nella ſua familiarità.*

To admit to orders, *ammettere, o iniziare negli ordini.*

To admit of one's excuſe, *ricever le ſcuſe, dare orecchio alle altrui ſcuſe.*

To admit of [to permit, to ſuffer] *permettere, comportare.*

The neceſſity we are in admits of no delay, *la neceſſità nella quale ci troviamo non permette indugio, non ſoffre ritardo.*

Admit it was ſo, *dato il caſo; ſuppoſto che foſſe così.*

ADMI'TTANCE, s. *entrata, entratura,* s. f. *entramento,* s. m.

ADMI'TTED, adj. *ammeſſo, introdotto, ricevuto, accettato.*

To ADMI'X [to mix] *miſchiare, meſchiare, meſcolare.*

ADMI'XTION, s. *miſchiamento, miſcuglio,* s. m.

To ADMO'NISH [to warn, to adviſe] *ammonire, eſortare, avvertire, avviſare.*

To admoniſh [to reprove] *ammonire, riprendere, correggere.*

ADMO'NISHED, adj. *ammonito, avvertito, ripreſo, corretto.*

ADMO'NISHER, s. *colui che corregge, colui che riprende la perſona viziosa o incauta.*

ADMO'NISHING, s. } [warning,
ADMO'NISHMENT, s. } advice, in-
ADMONI'TION, s. } ſtruction]
ammonizione, ammonigione, s. f. *avviſo, conſiglio,* s. m. *eſortazione,* s. f.

ADO', s. [ſtir, noiſe] *ſtrepito, romore,* s. m.

What ado he makes, *che ſtrepito che fa.*

With much ado we got rid of him, *ci liberammo da colui con molta fatica; non ce ne ſbrigammo ſenza molta fatica.*

I have much ado to forbear laughing, *appena poſſo contenermi dal ridere.*

They had much ado to get over the river, *con grand difficoltà paſſarona il fiume.*

Without any more ado, *ſenz' altro, ſenza far piu parole.*

ADOLE'SCENCY, s. [youth] *adoleſcenza, gioventù,* s. f.

To ADO'PT, *adottare, prender per figliuolo.*

To adopt another man's works, *arrogarſi, appropriarſi le compoſizioni d'un autore.*

ADO'PTED, adj. *adottato.*

ADO'PTER, s. [he that adopts] *adottatore,* s. m. *che adotta.*

ADO'PTING, s. *adottamento,* s. m. *l'adottare.*

ADO'PTION, s. *adozione, adottazione,* s. f. *adottamento,* s. m.

ADO'PTIVE, adj. [belonging to, or admitted by adoption] *adottivo, che attien per adozione.*

ADO'RABLE, adj. [that which ought to be adored] *adorabile, venerabile.*

ADO'RABLENESS, *merito di eſſer adorato; il meritare divini onori.*

ADORA'TION, s. [the act of adoring] *adorazione,* s. f. *adoramento,* s. m.

To ADO'RE [to pay divine worſhip to] *adorare, riverire con atti pieni d'umiltà, inchinarſi.*

ADO'RED, adj. *adorato, inchinato, riverito.*

ADO'RER, s. *adoratore,* s. m. *che adora.*

ADO'RING, s. *adoramento,* s. m. *l'adorare.*

To ADO'RN [to beautify, to deck, to trim] *adornare, ornare, imbellire, abbellire.*

ADO'RNED, adj. *adornato, ornato imbellito, abbellito.*

The banks adorned with green graſs, *le ripe veſtite di verdi erbette.*

ADORNA'TION, s. [decking, trimming] *adornamento, ornamento, abbellimento,* s. m.

ADO'RNER, s. [that adorns] *adornatore,* s. m. *adornatrice,* s. f. *che adorna.*

ADO'RNING, s. } *adornamento, or-*
ADO'RNMENT, s. } *namento, abbellimento,* s m.

ADVA'NCE, s [a ſtep] *avanzo, avanzamento, paſſo,* s. m.

To ADVA'NCE [lift up] *alzare, inalzare, levare, ſollevare.*

To advance [to ſtep, to go forward] *avanzare, andare avanti.*

To advance [to promote, to further] *avanzare, aggrandire, accreſcere, incoraggire, favorire.*

He is a prince that advances learning very much, *è un principe che favoriſce o incorraggiſce le ſcienze.*

Every body is for advancing his own intereſt, *ognuno cerca d'aggrandire la ſua fortuna.*

He has advanced his family by his noble actions, *ha illuſtrata la ſua famiglia co' ſuoi nobili fatti.*

To advance [to prefer, to raiſe] *innalzare, ſublimare, illuſtrare, promovere.*

His learning advanced him to the firſt dignities of the church, *il ſuo ſapere lo promoſſe alle prime dignità della chieſa.*

To advance [to give before hand] *dare anticipatamente, dare avanti tratto.*

ADVA'NCED, adj. *avanzato,* v. To advance.

ADVA'NCEMENT, s. [preferment, promotion] *avanzamento, aggrandimento,* s. m.

Before his advancement to the Papacy, *prima che aſcendeſſe al Papato.*

ADVA'NCER, s. [promoter, forwarder] *un che promove, che avvanza.*

ADVA'NCING, s. *avanzamento,* s. m.

ADVA'NTAGE, s. [benefit, good, gain, profit] *vantaggio, profitto, utile,* s. m. *utilità, comodità,* s. f. *intereſſe, onore,* s. m.

It will be for your advantage, *cio ſarà per voſtro vantaggio o utile.*

It would be more for your advantage, *ſarebbe meglio per voi; vi tornerebbe più a conto; voi fareſte meglio.*

You ſhall ſay you have laid out that kindneſs to a good advantage, *confeſſerete che i voſtri favori ſono ſtati bene impiegati.*

To make advantage of a thing, *prevalerſi, ſerverſi, approfittarſi d'una coſa.*

We took advantage of the darkneſs of the night to attack the enemy, *col favore delle tenebre della notte aſſaltammo i nemici.*

To let ſlip an advantage, *perdere un' occaſione.*

To give one the advantage, *dar la preferenza ad uno.*

To ſell a thing to the beſt advantage, *vendere una coſa per quanto più ſi puo.*

She dreſſes to the beſt advantage, *coſtei hà una bella maniera d'acconciarſi.*

To ſhow a thing to the beſt advantage, *moſtrare una coſa dal buon verſo per farla ſpiccare di vantaggio.*

Advantage [over meaſure] *vantaggio,* s. m. *ſoprappiu.*

He has advantage a hundred pounds by this, *con queſto ha guadagnato cento lire ſterline di piu.*

To ADVA'NTAGE [to gain, to profit] *aver vantaggio, acquiſtare, guadagnare.*

I am afraid it will not advantage you ſo much, *temo che il profitto non ſarà il grande come voi dite.*

What will it advantage me to deceive you? *di che giovamento ſarammi l'ingannarvi?*

ADVA'NTAGED, adj. *vantaggiato, acquiſtato, guadagnato.*

ADVANTA'GIOUS, adj. [tending to profit or good] *vantaggioſo, utile, profittevole.*

ADVANTA'GIOUSLY, adv. *vantaggioſamente, con vantaggio.*

ADVECTI'TIOUS, adj. [that is brought or carried from another place; foreign] *peregrino, che viene, o è portato da fuori.*

A'DVENT, s. m. [a time appointed by the church before Chriſtmas, to celebrate the coming of our bleſſed Saviour]

viour] *Avvento*, s. m. *il tempo che è dedicato dalla chiesa a celebrare l'avvènimento di Gesù Cristo.*

Advent [coming] *avvento, avvenimento*, s. m. *venuta*, s. f.

ADVENTI'TIOUS, adj. } [that comes
ADVE'NTUAL, adj. } by chance]
avventizzio, accidentale, casuale.

ADVE'NTURE, s. [chance, accident] *ventura, avventura, sorte, fortuna*, s. f. *caso, accidente, avvenimento*, s. m.

Adventure [hazard] *pericolo, rischio, ripentaglio.*

Adventure [enterprise] *impresa*, s. f. *disegno.*

By adventure, *a caso, per accidente.*

At all adventures, *alla ventura.*

To ADVE'NTURE [to venture, to hazard] *avventurare, mettere a rischio, arrischiare, tentar la sorte.*

To adventure his life, *avventurare, o mettere a ripentaglio la vita.*

To adventure the hazard of war, *esporsi a pericoli della guerra.*

To adventure to sea, *mettersi in mare, cimentarsi all' onde.*

I will adventure and seek my fortune, *voglio mettermi nelle mani della fortuua.*

To adventure [to enterprise] *intraprendere, sorprendere.*

ADVE'NTURED, *avventurato, arrischiato.*

ADVE'NTURER, s. *avventuriere, che avventura.*

ADVE'NTUROUS, adj. [bold, daring, hazardous] *audace, ardito, risoluto, coraggioso, animoso, temerario.*

An adventurous act, *un azione temeraria.*

ADVE'NTUROUSLY, adv. *arditamente, risolutamente, temerariamente.*

A'DVERB, s. *avverbio*, s. m.

ADVE'RBIAL, adj. [of or belonging to an adverb] *avverbiale.*

ADVE'RBIALLY, adv. *avverbialmente, a maniera d'avverbio.*

A'DVERSARY, s. *avversario, nemico*, s. m. *la parte avversa, termine legale.*

A'DVERSE, adj. [contrary] *avverso, contrario, nemico.*

Adverse [cross] *avverso, contrario, infelice.*

ADVE'RSITY, s. [affliction, calamity] *avversità, calamità, miseria*, s. f. *infortunio.*

Adversity tries friends, *nei bisogni si conoscon gli amici.*

To help one in his adversity, *assistere uno nelle sue avversità.*

To ADVE'RT [to mark, mind, or take heed] *avvertire, aver l'occhio, considerare, riflettere, stare in cervello, star sull' avviso.*

ADVE'RTENCY, s. [attention, heed] *avvertenza, cura, circospezione.*

To ADVERTI'SE [to give intelligence or advice] *avvisare, dare avviso, fare intendere, significare.*

To advertise [to warn] *avvertire, dare avvertimenti, ammonire.*

ADVERTI'SED, adj. *avvisato, significato, avvertito, ammonito.*

ADVE'RTISEMENT, s. [advice, intelligence, information] *avviso, avvisamento, ragguaglio*, s. m. *intelligenza, informazione*, s. f.

Advertisement [warning] *avvertimento*, s. m. *ammonizione*, s. f.

ADVERTI'SER, s. *avvisatore*, s. m. *che avvertisce.*

ADVERTI'SING, s. *l'avvisare.*

ADVI'CE, s. [counsel] *avviso, consiglio*, s. m.

He will follow no body's advice but his own, *non vuol seguire altro consiglio che'l suo.*

To give one good advice, *dare buon consiglio ad uno.*

To take advice of one, *consultare con alcuno, domandar avviso o consiglio ad alcuno.*

Advice [news] *avviso, ragguaglio*, s. m.

Advice-boat, *nave di procaccio.*

A'DVISABLE, adj. [that may be advised concerning] *da prenderne o domandarne consiglio.*

Advisable [fit to be done] *conveniente, convenevole, necessario.*

It would be advisable that we should consider the matter before we go upon it, *stimerei a proposito che noi esaminassimo bene il negozio prima d'intrappenderlo.*

To ADVI'SE [to give advice] *avvisare, avvertire, ammonire, consigliare.*

I advise you to be quiet, *vi consiglio di darvi pace; vi consiglio di starvene tranquillo.*

I am not to advise you, *voi non avete bisogno del mio consiglio.*

I advise you to it, *vi consiglio di farlo.*

To advise to the contrary, *dissuadere.*

To advise [to take advice] *consultare, consigliarsi con alcuno, seguitare o prendere il consiglio d'alcuno.*

Advise with him before you do it, *consigliatevi con lui prima di farlo.*

To advise [to consider] *considerare, esaminare, deliberare, ponderare.*

He desired a little time to advise what to do, *domandò qualche tempo a deliberare intorno a quanto doveva fare.*

To advise [to give an account, to write] *avvisare, dare avviso, fare intendere, significare.*

ADVI'SED, adj. *avvisato, avvertito.*

Well advised, *avvisato, accorto, cauto, circonspetto, prudente.*

Ill advised, *sconsiderato, incauto, imprudente.*

Be advised by me, *seguite il mio consiglio, credete a me, fate a modo mio.*

I'll do nothing but as I am advised, *non voglio fare che quel che mi verrà consigliato, non voglio far nulla di mia testa.*

It is advised from Rome that, *gli avvisi di Roma portano; abbiamo avviso da Roma, che.*

ADVI'SEDLY, adv. *avvisatamenta, con avviso, con giudicio, cautamente, destramente, prudentemente.*

Whether he did it advisedly, or turned necessity into advice, is doubted, *non si sa se lo facesse a bella posta, o se vi fosse spinto dalla necessità.*

ADVI'SEDNESS, s. *cautela, accortezza, prudenza, sagacità, diligenzia, circospezione*, s. f.

ADVI'SER, s. [one that takes advice] *quello che domanda consiglio o avviso.*

Adviser [he that gives advice] *consigliere, consigliatore, consultatore*, s. m. *consigliatrice*, s. f.

ADVI'SING, s. *avvisamento*, s. m. *l'avvisare.*

ADULA'TION, s. [fawning, flattery] *adulazione*, s. f. *l'adulare, lusinga*, s. f.

ADULA'TOR, s. m. [a fawning fellow, a flatterer] *adulatore, lusinghiere*, s. m. *che adula.*

A'DULATORY, adj. [belonging to, or full of flattery] *lusinghiero.*

ADU'LT, adj. [that is grown to full ripeness of age] *adulto, cresciuto, avvonzato in età.*

ADU'LTERATE, adj. [marred, sophisticated, counterfeit] *adulterato, falsificato, corrotto, imbastardito, tralignato, degenerato.*

To ADU'LTERATE [to corrupt, to counterfeit] *adulterare, falsificare, sofisticare, mischiare.*

To adulterate [to marr or spoil] *adulterare, corrompere, guastare.*

ADULTERA'TED, adj. *adulterato, falsificato.*

ADULTERA'TION, s. *adulterazione, falsificazione, corruzione*, s. f.

ADU'LTERER, s. [a man who commits adultery] *adultero, che commette adultéro.*

ADULTERE'SS, s. [a woman who commits adultery] *adultera, donna che commette adultéro.*

ADU'LTEROUS, adj. [of or belonging, or given to adultery] *adultero.*

ADU'LTERY, s. [the act of defiling the marriage bed] *adultério, adultéro*, s. m. *illecita congiunzion carnale di maritata o d' ammogliato.*

To ADU'MBRATE [to over-shadow] *adombrare, aombrare, coprendo far ombra, offuscare.*

To adumbrate, *schizzare, disegnare alla grossa.*

ADU'MBRATED, adj. [shadowed] *adombrato.*

ADUMBRA'TION, s. [shadowing] *adombrazione*, s. f. *adombramento*, s. m.

Adumbration (in painting) [a sketch or rough draught of a picture] *schizzo; disegno senz' ombra e non terminato.*

ADU'NCITY, s. [crookedness] *curvità, curvezza*, s. f.

ADU'NCOUS, adj. [crooked] *adunco, curvo.*

A'DVOCATE, s. [a man well versed in the civil law] *avvocato*, s. m. *dottore in ragion civile.*

Advocate [intercessor] *avvocato, protettore, intercessore*, s. m.

Advocate [favourer] *favoreggiatore, fautore, difensore*, s. m.

A'DVOCATESHIP, s. *avvocazione*, s. f. *ufficio dell' avvocato.*

ADVOWE'E-PARAMO'UNT [the highest Patron, that is to say, the King] *il primo signore, il Re.*

ADVO'WSON, s. [a right that a Bishop, Dean, and Chapter, or any Laypatron has, to present a Clerk to a benefice] *diritto di padronato.*

ADU'ST, adj. } [burnt] *adusto, ri-*
ADU'STED, adj. } *arso, arido, secco.*

ADU'STIBLE, adj. *adustivo, che puo rimanere adusto.*

ADU'STION, s. [burning, scorching] *adustione*, s. f. *diseccamento per privazion d'umore.*

Il dittongo Æ non è naturale alla lingua Inglese, perciò si usa solo nel principio d'alcuni nomi propri, come Æneas, Enea, e simili, e che derivano dal Latino, o dal Greco.

ÆNI'GMA, s. [a riddle] *enimma*, s. f. *detto oscuro, indovinello*, s. m.

ÆNIGMA'TICAL, adj. [full of dark riddles] *enimmatico.*

ÆQUA'TOR, s. *Equatore, la linea equinoziale.*

ÆQUINOC'TIAL, adj. *equinoziale.*

The Æ'QUINOX, s. *l'equinozio*, s. m.

A'ER, s. [one of the four Elements, the Air] *Aria*, s. f. *uno de' quattro elementi.*

Æ'RA, s. [a particular account and reckoning of time and years, from some remarkable event] *Epoca*, s. f.

AE'RIAL, adj. [belonging to the air] *aereo, d'aria.*

Æ'THER, s. [the firmament, the sky, that part of the heaven that is above the three regions of the air] *etere, la parte più sublime e più sottile dell' aria.*

ÆTHE'REAL, adj. [belonging to the heavens] *etereo.*

A-FAR-OFF, adv. *da lontano.*

AFFABI'LITY, s. [courtesy, kindness] *affabilità, cortesia, gentilezza*, s. f.

A'FFABLE, adj. [civil, courteous] *affabile, benigno, civile, cortese.*

A'FFABLY, adv. *affabilmente, civilmente, cortesemente, benignamente.*

AFFA'IR, s. [business, concern] *affare, negozio, fatto*, s. m. *faccenda*, s. f.

To AFFE'CT [to study, or set one's mind upon] *bramar con ansietà, e oltre al convenevole, usare troppo artificio.*

To affect to speak well, *affettare di parlar bene.*

To affect [to touch, to move] *toccare, muovere, smuovere, penetrare, impressionare, fare impressione.*

His way of preaching could never affect me in the least, *la sua maniera di predicare non m'ha mai tocco.*

To affect [to desire, to hanker after, to endeavour to get] *aspirare, pretendere, cercar d'ottenere.*

AFFECTA'TION [formality, preciseness] *affettazione*, s. f. *soverchio artifizio o squisitezza.*

AFFE'CTED, adj. *affettato, ricercato, studiato.*

Affected, adj. [disposed or inclined to] *portato, inclinato, disposto.*

An affected way of talking, *una maniera affettata nel parlare.*

I was very much affected at her grief, *il suo dolore mi mosse a compassione.*

Every one speaks as he stands affected, *ognuno parla seconda chegli è bene o male affetto.*

To be well or ill affected to the government, *esser bene o male affetto al governo.*

Affected [troubled or seized with a distemper] *travagliato, tormentato da qualche malore o malattia.*

Affected with sadness, *tristo, maninconico, afflitto, mesto.*

AFFE'CTEDLY, adv. *affettatamente, con affettazione.*

AFFE'CTEDNESS, s. [affectation] *affettazione*, s. f.

AFFE'CTION, s. [good-will, love, kindness] *affetto, amore*, s. m. *affezione, benevolenza, benivolenzia, amorevolezza*, s. f.

AFFE'CTIONATE, adj. [well-affected, kind, loving] *affezionato, affettuoso, amorevole.*

AFFE'CTIONATELY, adv. *affettuosamente, amorevolmente, affezionatamente.*

AFFI'ANCE, s. [confidence, trust] *confidenza, fidanza*, s. f.

Affiance (in law) [the plighting of troth between a man and a woman upon agreement of marriage] *sposalizio*, s. f.

To AFFI'ANCE [to betroth] *fidanzare, dar fede di sposo.*

AFFI'ANCED, adj. *fidanzato.*

AFFI'ANCING, s. *sposalizio*, s. m.

AFFIDA'VIT, s. [a deposition, or witnessing a thing upon oath] *deposizione, fatta con giuramento.*

To make an affidavit [to swear to the truth of a thing] *deporre con giuramento.*

A'FFINAGE, s. [the refining of metals] *affinamento*, s. m.

AFFI'NITY, s. [kindred, alliance by marriage] *affinità*, s. f. *parentela che nasce per maritaggio tra i consanguinei della moglie e del marito, e tra i consanguinei del marito e della moglie.*

Affinity [relation, agreeableness between several things] *affinità, convenienza, somiglianza, vicinità, conformità*, s. f.

To AFFI'RM [to assure, to avouch, to maintain] *affermare, confermare.*

AFFIRMA'TION, s. [the act of affirming, the act of assuring] *affermamento*, s. m. *affermazione*, s. f.

AFFI'RMATIVE, adj. [which serves to affirm] *affermativo.*

Affirmative, s. *affermativa*, s. f.

AFFI'RMATIVELY, adv. *affermativamente, con affermazione.*

AFFI'RMED, adj. *affermato, confermato.*

To AFFI'X [to fasten to, to set up] *affiggere, affissare, attaccare, appiccare.*

AFFI'XED, adj. *affisso, affissato, attaccato, appiccato.*

AFFI'XING, s. *attaccamento, appiccamento*, s. m.

AFFLA'TION, s. *afflato, spiramento, infondimento*, s. m. *ispirazione*, s. f.

To AFFLI'CT [to cast down, to grieve, to trouble] *affliggere, dare afflizione, travagliare, donneggiare.*

To afflict one's self, *affliggersi, prendersi afflizione.*

AFFLI'CTED, adj. *afflitto, pien d'afflizione, travagliato, angustiato.*

AFFLI'CTION, s. [anguish, adversity, calamity, distress] *afflizione*, s. f. *dolore, tormento*, s. m. *e dicesi tanto del corpo quanto dell' animo.*

AFFLI'CTIVE, adj. *afflittivo, che affligge, che induce afflizione.*

A'FFLUENCE, s. [abundance, plenty, wealth] *affluenza, soprabbondanza*, s. f.

To AFFO'RD [to give] *dare, fornire, provvedere.*

I can't afford it at that price, *non posso darlo per questo prezzo.*

I can't afford so much money for a hat, *non posso spendere tanto per un cappello.*

I could afford to give him a box on the ear, *gli darei volentieri uno schiaffo.*

To afford [to yield, to produce] *produrre.*

This is the best wine that Italy affords, *questo è il miglior vino che l'Italia ci dia.*

AFFO'RDED, adj. *dato.*

AFFO'RDING, s. *il dare, il fornire.*

To AFFO'REST [to lay a piece of ground waste, and turn it into a forest] *far divenir selva.*

AFFRA'Y, s. [a fray, fight, or skirmish] *leggier combattimento, scaramuccia*, s. f.

Affray (law term) [terror caused in the subjects, by making only an unlawful show of violence] *terrore, spavento causato negli animi de' popoli dalla sola vista d'oppressione.*

To AFFRANCHI'SE [to set at liberty] *affrancare, far franco, render libero, dar la libertà.*

A'FFRICTION, s. [a rubbing upon] *fregagione*, s. f. *fregamento*, s. m. *il fregare una rosa con un' altra.*

To AFFRI'GHT [to put into a fright, or fear] *impaurare, impaurire, far paura, spaventare.*

AFFRI'GHTED, adj. *impaurato, impaurito, spaventato.*

AFFRO'NT, s. [abuse, injury, wrong] *affronto, oltraggio, sopruso*, s. m. *ingiuria*, s. f.

To put a grievous affront upon one, *oltraggiare uno, fare ad uno un grande oltraggio.*

To AFFRO'NT [to offer an affront, to abuse] *affrontare, maltrattare, oltraggiare.*

To affront [to brave, to swagger] *dispregiare, disprezzare, avere o tenere a vile.*

To affront death in the midst of dangers, *incontrar la morte fra i pericoli.*

AFFRO'NTED, adj. *affrontato*, v. To affront.

AFFRO'NTIVE, adj. *oltraggiante, oltraggioso, ingiurioso.*

AFLO'AT, adv. *a galla.*

To set a ship afloat, *mettere un vascello a galla.*

AFO'RE, prep. *avanti, innanzi.*

AFO'REHAND, *innanzi mano, anticipatamente.*

To be aforehand with one, *prevenire uno.*

Afore, adv. *prima, avanti.*

AFOREGO'ING, adj. *precedente.*

AFORESAI'D, adj. *sudetto, predetto, prenominato, già mentovato.*

AFORE-TI'ME, adv. altre volte, tempo fa.

AFRA'ID, adj. che ha paura, che teme.

TO BE AFRA'ID, temere, aver paura.

I am afraid to say it, temo a dirlo.

Are you afraid to do it? non avete l' animo di farlo? temete di farlo?

He is afraid of every thing, ha paura d' ogni cosa, la sua ombra li fa paura.

See how far I am from being afraid, vedi se ho paura.

To make one afraid, far paura a qualcheduno, spaventarlo.

A-FRE'SH, adv. di nuovo, da capo.

To say a thing a-fresh, ridire una cosa.

AFT, s. [in a ship] la poppa d'una nave.

Aft, adv. verso poppa.

Fore and aft, su e giù, innanzi e addietro, per poppa e per prora.

A'FTER, prep. dopo, secondo.

After your coming, dopo la vostra venuta.

One after another, un dopo l'altro.

After the ancient custom, secondo l'uso antico.

After all, in somma.

After the French fashion, alla Francese; alla moda di Francia.

After what manner? in che modo, come? in che maniera?

After this manner, così, in questo modo, in questa maniera.

Presently after I had dined, subito che ebbi pransato.

Half an hour after three, alle tre e mezza.

To call one after his own name, chiamare uno per nome.

We will consider of this after, penseremo a questo a bell' agio.

To put a thing off day after day, differire una cosa d'un giorno all' altro.

To look after [to seek] cercare.

I look after my book, cerco il mio libro.

To look after [to take care of a thing] aver cura d'una cosa.

Pray look after my cloaths, di grazia abbiate l'occhio a' miei abiti.

After, adv. dopo.

A little after, un poco dopo.

The day after, il giorno seguente.

We went to walk in the park, and after that to the opera, andammo a passeggiare nell' parco, e di là all' opera. Quest' averbio s'unisce a molti nomi sostantivi ex.

AFTER-BU'RDEN, AFTER-BI'RTH, seconda.

AFTER-A'GES, AFTER-TI'MES, i secoli futuri, il tempo a venire.

AFTER-NO'ON, il dopo pranzo, dopo nona.

After-noon's nungeon, merenda, s. f. asciolvere.

AFTER-GA'ME, rivincita, s. f.

AFTER-RE'CKONING, secondo conto.

AFTER-SA'ILS, velle maestre.

AFTER-WI'T, senno fuor di stagione.

An after-wit is every body's wit, dopo il fatto le fosse son piene di senno.

AFTER-TA'STE [of any liquor] fasdio, cattivo gusto.

AFTERWA'RDS, adv. dopo, dipoi, dopo ciò.

AGA'N, adv. di nuova, ancora, un' altra volta.

He is sick again, s'è ammalato di nuovo.

Say that again, ditelo un' altra volta.

When will you come again? quando riverrete?

My garden is as big again, il mio giardino è una volta più grande.

Over again, un altra voltra di nuovo.

I must have six-pence back again, mi vengono sei soldi indietro.

He is well again, è guarito, sta bene. Quest' avverbio s'unisce a verbi, per dinotare la reiterazione dell' azione, ex.

To read again, rileggere,

To love again, riamare.

To come again, ritornare.

To write again, rescrivere.

To find again, ritrovare.

To consider again and again, pensare e ripensare.

AGAI'NST, prep. contro.

Against the law, contro la legge.

Over against, dirimpetto, in faccia.

I have not cloaths enough to defend myself against the cold, non ho vestiti sufficienti a difendermi dal freddo.

To do a thing against one's will, fare una cosa contro voglia, o mal volentieri.

To be against a thing, opporsi a qualche cosa, disapprovarla.

I am not against it, v'acconsento.

To dry a thing against the fire, asciugare una cosa al fuoco.

That's against all probability, non è verisimile.

Against the end of the week, verso la fine della settimana.

Be sure you get it done against tomorrow, fate in ogni modo che sia finito per domani.

It shall be ready against you come again, sarà in ordine al vostro ritorno.

Against the hair, against the grain, contra pelo.

Against the hair, against the grain, contro voglia, mal volentieri.

AGA'RICK, s. [a sort of mushroom] agárico, s. m. spezie di fungo medicinale.

AGA'ST, adj. [frighted, amazed] spaventato, stupefatto, atterito.

A'GATE, s. [a precious stone of several colours] ágata, s. f. pietra, transparente, e di vari colori.

A'GE, s. [the whole continuance of a man's life] età, s, f. nome generale, che si da a' gradi del viver dell' uomo.

There is not three days difference between his age and mine, dalla sua età alla mia non vi sono tre giorni di differenza.

At sixteen years of age, all' età di quindici anni.

I remember him when he was ten years of age, lo conosco dall' età di dieci anni.

What age are you of? che età avete? o quanti anni avete? I am thirty years of age, ho trent' anni.

Age [part of a man's life] età, gradi differenti del vivere dell' uomo.

Tender age, tenera età.

Ripe age, età matura.

The prime of one's age, il fior dell' età.

To be of age, esser d'età, non esser più minore.

Age [old age] vecchiaja, età avanzata.

A man of great age, un uomo attempato, un uomo molto vecchio.

He is worn out with age, è carico d' anni, e decrépito.

Age [century] secolo.

After-ages, i secoli futuri.

The golden age, il secolo d'oro.

Full age, adolescenza, s. f.

Non-age, minorità, infanzia, s. f.

A'GED, adj. [of a certain age] vecchio, d'una certa età.

Aged [old] attempato, vecchio, attempatello.

AGE'N, v. again.

A'GENCY, s. azienda, s. f.

A'GENT, s. agente, presidente, ministro d'un principe.

Agent of a regiment, fattore, pagatore, sollecitatore d'un regimento.

Agent, adj. agente, operante, facente.

To AGGLO'MERATE [to gather up in a ball or thread] aggomitolare, far gomitolo ammassare, adunare insieme.

To agglomerate, verb. neut. aggomitolarsi, ammassarsi, adunarsi.

To AGGLU'TINATE [to glue together] conglutinare, unire, attaccare, unire una parte coll' altre.

AGGLU'TINATED, adj. conglutinato, unito, attaccato.

To AGGRANDI'ZE [to make great, to inlarge] aggrandire, accrescere, far grande, aumentare, render più grande.

AGGRANDI'ZED, adj. aggrandito, accresciuto, aumentato.

AGGRANDI'ZEMENT, s. [the act of growing or making great] aggrandimento, s. m.

To A'GGRAVATE [to make heavy or grievous] aggravare, aumentare, far più grave.

AGGRAVA'TED, adj. aggravato, aumentato.

AGGRAVA'TING, s. aggravamento, s. m. l' aggravare.

AGGRAVA'TION, s. aggravazione, s. f. aggravamento, s. m.

To A'GGREGATE [to join together, to unite to the same body] aggregare, unire, aggiungere al numero.

A'GGREGATE, s. [the whole sum or mass that arises from the gathering together] aggregato, accozzamento, misto, s. m. unione, s. f.

AGGREGA'TED, adj. aggregato, unito, aggiunto.

AGGREGA'TION, s. aggregazione, s. f. l'aggregare.

AGGRE'SS, s. } [a setting upon]
AGGRE'SSION, s. } assalimento, assaltamento, s. m. assalita, s. f.

AGGRE'SSOR, s. m. [an assailer, one that first sets upon] assalitore, s. m.

AGGRI'EVANCE, s. dolore, rammarico, s. m. afflizione, s. f.

To AGGRI'EVE [to afflict] affliggere, dare afflizione, travogliare, danneggiare.

AGGRI'EVED, adj. afflitto, addolorato, travogliato.

Ag-

Aggrieved [wronged] *offeso, a chi s'è fatto torto.*
A'GILE, adj [quick, nimble, swift] *agile, snello, destro, sciolto di membra.*
AGI'LITY, s. *agilità, destrezza, prestezza di membra.*
A'GITABLE, adj. [that may be moved] *agitabile, da esser agitato.*
To A'GITATE [to tumble and toss, to stir up] *agitare, perturbare, commuovere.*
To agitate a question, *agitare, trattare, considerare una questione o negozio.*
AGITA'TED, adj. *agitato, perturbato, commosso, trattato, considerato.*
AGITA'TION, s. *agitazione, s. f. movimento, s. m.*
This affair is in agitation, *questo affare si sta maneggiando.*
While these things were in agitation, *nel corso di questo maneggio.*
AGITA'TOR, s. [one who carries on a business or design] *maneggiatore, s. m.*
A'GLET, s. [a little plate of metal] *foglia, s. f. d'oro argento, o rame battuto, e ridotto a sottigliezza di foglia.*
Aglet [tag of a point] *puntale, s. m.*
A'GMINAL, adj. [belonging to a camp] *appartenente a un campo militare.*
AGNA'IL [whitloe] *panereccio, s. m. postema che nasce nella dita delle mani e de' piedi alle radici dell' ugne.*
AGNA'TION, s. [kindred by blood between males descended from the same father] *consanguinità, parentela tra congiunti descendenti dal medesimo padre.*
AGNI'TION, s. [an acknowledgement of some person or thing by some mark or token] *riconoscimento, s. m. parlando di persona o di cosa che si riconosca a qualche segno o indicio.*
To AGNI'SE [to acknowledge, to own] *riconnoscere, confessare.*
AGO', adv. *ex.*
An hour ago, *un' ora fà.*
Long ago, *un pezzo fà.*
Some years ago, *anni sono.*
Three days ago, *tre giorni sono.*
Not long ago, *non è molto tempo.*
A good while ago, *molto tempo fà.*
It is long ago since I saw him, *è un pezzo che non l'ho veduto.*
But a while ago, *poco fà.*
It is but a while ago since he died, *è morto poco fà.*
How long ago? *quanto tempo e?*
AGO'G, adv. *ex.* To set agog [or a-longing] *far venir voglia, o desiderio.*
To set one's curiosity agog, *eccitar la curiosità.*
AGO'NE, adj. [past] *passato.*
A'GONI'STES, s. [a prize-fighter, one that contends at a publick solemnity for a prize] *agonista; una che entra nell' agone a combattere per ottenere una mercede proposta al vincitore in giuochi e feste pubbliche.*
A'GONY, s. [extremity of anguish, the pains of death] *agonia, angoscia, s. f. quel dolore che va innanzi alla morte.*
To be in agony, *agonizzare, esser in agonia di morte.*
AGRA'RIAN LAW [a law made by the old Romans for sharing the lands gotten by conquest] *la legge aggrarai fra gli antichi Romani la quale divideva le terre conquestate.*
AGRE'AT, adv. *all' ingrosso.*
To take a work agreat, *intraprendere un opera all' ingrosso.*
One that takes work agreat, *uno che piglia un opera all' ingrosso.*
To AGRE'E [to make up a difference] *accordare, metter d'accordo, quietare.*
They agree together, *sono d'accordo.*
Let them agree together, *che s'accordino fra di loro.*
I agree with you in this, *sono del vostro parere in cio.*
To agree upon, to, or in, verb. neut. *convenire, far patto, pattuire, esser d'accordo.*
To agree upon a truce, *convenire d'una tregua.*
Authors don't always agree in the same thing, *gli autori discordano alle volte nella medesima cosa.*
His actions and words do not agree, *le sue azioni non corrispondono alle parole.*
They agree very lovingly together, *vivono insieme molto concordamente.*
All things seem to agree to her, *par ch'ogni cosa se le affaccia, le stia bene.*
English and Italians don't agree in their way of living, *gl' Inglesi e gl' Italiani sono differenti nella maniera di vivere.*
To agree for a thing, *pattuire una cosa, convenire del prezzo d'una cosa.*
To make one thing agree with another, *aggiustare, accommodare due cose insieme.*
I could rather agree to write to him than to go myself, *mi contenterei piu tosto di scrivergli che d'andare in persona.*
To agree [to be good] *confarsi.*
Wine does not agree with me, *il vino non mi confà.*
To make to agree [speaking of people] *rappacificare, rappaciare, metter d' accordo.*
They agree like dog and cat, *vivono come cane e gatta, sono sempre in discordia.*
To agree [to resolve] *resolvere, deliberare, determinare, statuire.*
They all agreed to send for him, *tutti risolverono di mandarlo a chiamare.*
AGRE'EABLE, adj. [that agrees or suits with] *convenevole, conveniente, confacente, confacevole, proporzionato, adattato, avvenevole.*
Agreeable [pleasant] *grato, ameno, piacevole, bello.*
An agreeable place, *un luogo ameno, o piacevole.*
Agreeable [charming] *vago, leggiadro, grazioso.*
An agreeable woman, *una vaga donna, una donna piacevole.*
AGRE'EABLENESS, s. *accordo, s. m. unione, conformità, congruità, convenenza, proporzione, s. m.*
Agreeableness [charms] *grazia, bellezza, avvenentezza, avvenevolezza, s. f.*
AGRE'EABLY, adv. *attamente, accomodatamente, convenevolmente, convenientemente, congruamente.*
Agreeably [pleasantly] *gratamente, piacevolmente, deliziosamente, vagamente.*
A house agreeably situated, *una casa vagamente situata.*
AGRE'ED, adj. *stabilito, fisso; convenuto.*
The day is agreed on, *il giorno è stabilito, o fisso.*
A truce is agreed on, *s'è convenuto d'una tregua.*
It is agreed upon by all, *tutti convengono.*
The quarrel is agreed, *la disputa è aggiustata, o accomodata.*
Are you agreed at last? *siete convenuti alla fine?*
I will have them agree, *voglio metterli d'accordo.*
Agreed, adv. *va, toppa.*
AGRE'EING, s. *concordia, unione, corrispondenza, convenenza, s. f. consenso, s. m.*
Agreeing, adj. [conformable] *conforme, conveniente, congruo, atto, simile.*
AGRE'EMENT, s. [covenant] *patto, accordo, s. m. convenzione, s. f.*
To come to an agreement, *convenire, venire a patti.*
To be at agreement, *concordare, esser d'accordo.*
Articles of agreement, *articoli, condizioni, contratto, trattato, s. m.*
Agreement [proportion, sympathy, relation] *proporzione, unione, conformità, relazione, simpatia, s. f.*
Agreement [reconciling] *riconciliazione, pace, amicizia, s. f. accommodamento, aggiustamento, s. m.*
Agreement [in tune] *accordo; concerto, concento, s. m. armonia, consonanza, s. f.*
To bring to an agreement, *accordare, aggiustare, metter d'accordo, riconciliare.*
According to agreement, *secondo 'l patto, il convenuto lo aggiustamento.*
Agreement-maker, *arbitro, mezzano, mediatore, s. m. mezzana, mediatrice, s. f.*
AGRE'STICAL, or AGRE'STICK, adj. *agreste, rustico, selvatico, rustico, rozzo, villesco, da contadino, zotico.*
AGRICU'LTURE, s. [the art of husbandry] *agricoltura, s. f. l' arte del coltivare.*
AGRI'EVANCE, s. *dolore, crucio, travaglio, s. m. afflizione d'animo, mestizia, s. f.*
To AGRI'EVE [to afflict] *affliggere, travaggliare, tormentare, cruciare.*
AGRI'EVED, adj. *afflitto, mesto, sconsolato.*
Agrieved [wronged] *offeso, a chi si è fatto torto.*
AGRI'EVING, s. *afflittivo, che affligge, che induce afflizione.*
Agrieving, s. *dolore, tormento, crucio, travaglio d'animo, s. m. afflizione, mestizia, s. f.*
A-GROUND, adv. *ex.*
To run a-ground, *rimanere sulle secche, il dar in terra d'un vascello.*
To run a ship a-ground (in un senso attivo) *far dare in terra un vascello.*

A'GUE, s. *febbre*, s. f.

A burning ague, *una febbre malig-na.*

A little ague, *una febbricciuola.*

An ague coming by fits, *febbre inter-mittente.*

A quotidian ague, *febbre cotidiana, o quotidiana*, s. f.

A tertian ague, *una terzana, o una febbre terzana.*

A quartan ague, *un quartana, o una febbre quartana.*

Sick of an ague, *febbricitante, tor-mentato di febbre.*

To have an ague, or to be sick of an ague, *aver la febbre.*

Having a quartan ague, *quartanario, che ha la febbre quartana.*

The fit of an ague, *accesso de febbre.*

AGUE-PO'WDER, *febbrifugo*, s. f. *medicamenta per cacciar la febbre.*

A'GUISH, adj. *febbricitante.*

AH, interj. *ah! ahi!*

AID, s. [help] *ajuto, soccorso*, s. m. *aito, assistenza*, s. f.

He desires your aid, *domanda, o im-plora il vostro ajuto.*

The royal aid [tax, subsidy] *sussidio*, s. m. *tassa*, s. f.

To AID, *ajutare, aitare, porgere o dare ajuto.*

A'IDED, adj. *ajutato, aitato, soccorso, assistito.*

AI'DING, s. *l'ajutare, ajuto, soccorso, aita, assistenza.*

To AIL, verb. neut. *aver male.*

What ails you? *che male avete?*

What ails your face? *che avete al viso?*

I ail nothing, *non ho niente, non ho male veruno.*

What ails you to be so ill humour'd? *perchè siete di così cattivo umore?*

What ails the fellow? *che pretende costui? non so quel che si voglia questo sciocco.*

A'ILEMENT, or A'ILMENT, s. *male, leggiera incommodità, indisposizione, indis-posizioncella*, s. f.

A'ILING, adj. *indisposto, incommodato.*

He is always ailing, *è sempre indis-posto, ha sempre qualche indisposizioncella, ha sempre qualche canchero.*

AIM, s. [mark] *segno, berzaglio*, s. m. *mira*, s. f.

Aim [design] *fine, disegno, pensiero*, s. m. *intenzione.*

To take one's aim well, *mirar bene, aggiustar bene il colpo al berzaglio, porre bene la mira.*

To miss one's aim, *mancare il colpo.*

I missed my aim, *il mio disegno è fallito.*

I am quite out of my aim, *sono affatto confuso, non so dove mi sia.*

All my aim was that, *non desideravo altro, se non che questo.*

To aim, to aim at, *mirare, por la mi-ra, imberciare.*

To aim at something, *mirare, volgere il pensiero a che che sia, aspirare, preten-dere, tendere.*

I aim at nothing but your safety, *non cerco che la vostra salute.*

They aimed at his destruction, *con-spirarono la sua rovina.*

I know what you aim at, *so ben quel che cercate, so dove tendono i vostri pen-sieri.*

Aimed at, adj. *mirato, tolto di mira.*

I see I am aimed at, *vedo che son tolto di mira.*

A'IMER, s. *miratore, imberciatore*, s. m. *un che prende la mira.*

A'IMING, s. *il mirare.*

AIR, s. [one of the four elements] *aria*, s. f. Poetically *aere*, s. m.

The birds of the air, *gli uccelli del cielo.*

We have a thick air round about us, *l'aria è molto spessa in torno di noi.*

Our design has taken air, *il nostro di-segno è scoperto.*

In the open air, *nell' aria aperta, al-lo scoperto.*

To build a castle in the air, *far cas-telli in aria, pensare a cose vane e difficili.*

To take the air, *pigliar aria.*

Air [tune] *aria, cantata*, s. f.

Air [looks] *aria, ciera*, s. f. *aspetto.*

Air-hole [a vent] *sfogatojo*, s. m.

To air, *seccare, scaldare.*

To air abroad, *mettere all' aria, sven-tolare.*

To air by the fire, *seccare al fuoco.*

To air a shirt by the fire, *scaldare una camicia al fuoco.*

To air drink, *scaldare un poco una be-vanda.*

To air a house, *dar dell' aria ad una casa.*

To air a room, *aprire le finestre d'una camera.*

AIRE, or AIRY, s. *nido d'uccello di rapina.*

AIRED, adj. *seccato, secco, scaldato.*

Aired abroad, *esposto all' aria.*

Aired by the fire, *seccato al fuoco.*

A'IRINESS, s. [exposure to the air, lightness, gaiety, levity] *l'esporre che si fa all' aria. Leggerezza, letizia, levità.*

A'IRING, s. *l'esporre all' aria, lo scal-dare, o il seccare.*

A'IRLING, s. [a young gay person] *un giovanotto gajo, una giovanotta gaja.*

A'IRLESS, adj. [without communi-cation with free air] *senz' aria.*

A'IRY, adj. [of the air] *aereo, d'a-ria.*

Airy [brisk, full of air and life] *alle-gro, giulivo, festoso, vivace, spiritoso.*

An airy man, *un uomo di bella pre-senza.*

Airy [exposed to the air] *arioso, es-posto all' aria.*

Airy [thin, light] *sottile, fino.*

Airy, s. [hawk's nest] *un nido di falcone.*

AKE, s. *male, dolore*, s. m.

Head-ake, *dolor di testa.*

Tooth-ake, *mal di denti.*

Belly-ake, *mal di ventre.*

To give a woman the tooth-ake, *in-gravidare una donna, fare alzare il grembiule ad una donna. E' parlar furbesco.*

To ake, *far male, dolere.*

My head akes, *mi duole la testa.*

The sun makes my head ake, *il Sole mi fa male alla testa, mi fa doler il capo.*

A'KER, v. Acre.

A'KING, s. *dolore.*

Aking, adj. *doloroso, che fa male.*

I have an aking tooth, *mi duole un dente.*

To have an aking tooth at one, *aver-la con qualcheduno, portar odio ad uno.*

ALABA'STER, s. *alabastro*, s. m.

ALA'CK, interj. *ohimè, o oimè.*

Alack-a-day, *oimè, oh.*

ALA'CRITY, s. *gioja, allegrezza, baldanza, vivezza, vivacità*, s. f.

ALAMO'DE [a sort of silk] *spezie di drappo.*

Alamode, adv. *alla moda, all' usan-za.*

ALA'RM, s. [alarum] *all' arme, spa-vento, terrore*, s. m.

To give an alarm, *gridare all' arme.*

To sound an alarm, *suonare all' arme.*

Alarm-bell, *campana che serve per dar segno al popolo di qualche strano av-venimento.*

Alarm-watch, *sveglia*, s. f.

To ALA'RM, *dare all' arme, toccare all' arme, spaventare, commovere.*

ALA'RMED, adj. *spaventato, com-mosso.*

ALA'RUM, s. v. Alarm.

ALA'S, interj. *ohimè, oimè.*

ALA'TE, adv. [of late] *ultimamente, poco fa.*

ALB, s. [a white vestment or sur-plice, used by the priest, officiating at divine service] *cámice*, s m.

ALBE'IT, adv. *benchè, se bene, none-stante.*

ALBUGI'NEOUS, adj. [resembling an albugo] *bianchiccio*, v. albugo.

ALCA'HEST, s. [an universal dissol-vent] *solvente universale.*

ALCA'ID, s. [the governor of a cas-tle; the judge of a city] *Alcalde, gover-natore d'un castello; giudice d'una città.*

A'LCALIN, adj. *alcalino.*

Alcalin salt, *sale alcalino.*

A'LCHYMIST, s. [one that studies al-chymy] *alchimista*, s. m. *uno che studia l'alchimia.*

A'LCHYMY, s. *alchimia*, s. f. *arte del raffinare, alterare, o mescolare i metalli.*

A'LCORAN, s. *alcorano*, s. m.

ALCO'VE, s. *alcova*, s. f.

ALCY'ON, s. [king fisher] *alcione*, s. m. *sorta d' uccello aquatico simile all' oche.*

Alcyon days, *felici tempi.*

A'LDERMAN, s. *senatore d'una città.*

An alderman of a ward, *caporione.*

To walk an alderman's pace, *cammi-nare a passi contati, camminar grave-mente.*

ALDER-TREE, *ontano*, s. m. *albero noto.*

An alder bed [a bed of alders] *un boschetto d'ontani.*

ALE, s. *cervogia non lupolata, o sen-za lupoli sorta di birra forte.*

New ale, *cervogia novella.*

Strong ale, *cervogia forte.*

Stale ale, *cervogia vecchia.*

An ale-house, *osteria dove si vende la cervogia.*

An ale-house-keeper, *oste che vende della cervogia.*

Ale-draper [an ale-house-keeper] *oste che vende della cervogia.*

A'LEGAR, s. *aceto fatto di cervogia.*

ALE-HO'OF, s. [herb] *edera terrestre.*

A'LEWIFE, s. *donna che tiene un osteria dove si venda cervogia.*

A'LEMBICK, s. [a still] *lambicco, limbicco,* s. m. *vaso da distillare.*

A'LERT, adj. [watchful, vigilant, brisk, pert, petulant] *vigile, vigilante, destro, audace, petulante.*

ALE'RTNESS, s. [the quality of being alert] *vigilanza, destrezza, audacia, petulanza.*

ALEXA'NDERS, s. [herb] *sorta d'erba.*

ALEXANDRI'NE, s. *verso Alessandrino, verso alla maniera de' versi eroici Francesi, così chiamati perchè prima usati in un poema intitolato Alessandro.*

ALEXIPHA'RMICK, adj. [antidotal] *che è contravveleno.*

A'LGEBRA, s. *algebra,* s. f. *sorta d'aritmetica che tratta de' numeri, delle radici, e de' quadrati.*

A'LGID, adj. [cold, chill] *algente, freddo.*

ALGI'DITY, s. [coldness, chillness] *algore, freddo,* s. m.

A'LGUAZIL, s. [a serjeant or officer in Spain, who arrests people] *spezie di sbirro in Ispagna.*

A'LIEN, s. [alien] *forestiero, forestiere.*

A'LIEN, adj. *alieno, contrario.*

To A'LIEN, } *alienare, trasferire in altrui il dominio.*
To A'LIENATE, }

To alienate one from another, *alienare, separare, allontanare.*

He shall never alienate me from you, *non potrà mai fare ch'io mi separi da voi.*

ALIENA'TED, adj. *alienato, separato, allontanato, avverso.*

ALIENA'TING, s. *l'alienare, alienazione,* s. f.

ALIENA'TION, s. [the act of alienating] *alienazione, separazione,* s. f.

Alienation of mind, *alienazione di mente.*

A'LIENABLE, adj. *alienabile, che si può alienare.*

ALI'CANT, s. [sort of wine] *alicante, vino d'alicante.*

To ALI'GHT, *smontare, scendere, metter piè a terra.*

To alight from one's horse, *smontare di cavallo.*

AL'IGHTED, *smontato, sceso di cavallo, o di carozza.*

ALI'KE, adj. *simile, somigliante.*

Those two horses are alike, *questi due cavalli sono simili.*

Alike, adv. *similmente, somigliantemente, parimente.*

If you love me, I love you alike, *se voi amate me, ed io amo pur voi.*

A'LIMENT, s. [food, nourishment] *alimento, cibo,* s. m.

A'LIMONY [that portion or allowance that a married woman may sue for, upon a separation from her husband, when she is not charged with adultery] *alimento, sostentamento che la moglie può richieder del marito nel separarsi da lui, non essendo accusata d'adulterio.*

A'LIQUANT parts [such parts not contained in the number so many times, but some remainder will be left] *aliquanta parte.*

A'LIQUOT part [is such a part as is contained in the number precisely, so many times] *parte aliquota.*

ALI'VE, adj. *vivo, che vive.*

Is he alive still? *è ancor vivo?*

He is the best physician this day alive, *è il meglio medico d'oggidì.*

Hope keeps me alive, *la speranza mi tiene in vita.*

I yield to no man alive, *non la cedo a chi che sia, ad uom che viva.*

A'LKALY, or A'LCALI, s. [a sort of salt extracted from the ashes of calcined herbs] *alcali.*

ALKALI'NE, *v.* Alcaline.

ALL, adj. *tutto, tutta.*

All the kingdom, *tutto il regno.*

All the house, *tutta la casa.*

I have not seen him all this day, *non l'ho visto punto oggi.*

All that while I was at Naples, *tutto quel tempo fui in Napoli.*

When all come to all, *alla fine, in somma, al peggio andare.*

With all speed, *in fretta.*

I would not do it for all the world, *non lo farei per quasivoglia cosa.*

For good and all, *per sempre, affatto.*

When I was busiest of all, *nel colmo delle mie occupazioni.*

To be all in all with one, *esser intimo amico di qualcuno.*

By all means, *certamente, sì per certo, senza dubbio.*

Have her all to yourself, *abbiatevela per voi, sia pur tutta vostra.*

He is all for himself, *non pensa ad altri ch'a se stesso.*

They live all upon bread and water, *non vivono che di pane e d'acqua.*

Make all the haste you can, *sbrigatevi il più presto che potrete.*

He did all he could to ruin me, *ha fatto ogni sforzo per rovinarmi.*

I'll do all that lies in my power, *farò dal canto mio quanto potrò.*

All at one, All under one, *in un fubito, subitamente, in un batter d'occhio.*

All of a sudden, *subitamente, improvvisamente.*

Once for all, *una volta per sempre.*

All over, *da per tutto.*

To travel all over the country, *viaggiare per tutto 'l paese.*

To read a book all over, *legger tutto un libro.*

'Tis all one, *è tutt' uno, è la medesima cosa.*

All and every one, *tutti generalmente.*

Not at all, *no certo.*

To go upon all fours, *andare a quattro piedi, andar carponi.*

All is not gold that glitters, *non è tutto oro quel che luce.*

All is well that ends well, *la vita il fine, e il dì loda la sera.*

I understand not at all, *non intendo nemmeno una parola.*

No where at all, *in nessun luogo.*

Where are you going? No where at all, *dove andate? in nessun luogo.*

I make no doubt at all of it, *non ne dubito punto.*

All the better, *tanto meglio.*

All along, *sempre.*

Without all doubt, *senza dubbio, indubitatamente.*

ALL, *s'unisce spesso co' participi presenti de' verbi.*

All-seeing, *che vede tutto.*

All-knowing, *omnisciente.*

All-saints, *la festa di tutti i santi.*

All-soul's-day, *il giorno de' morti.*

All-fours, *sorta di giuoco di carte.*

ALL-HE'AL (herb) *panacea, erba.*

ALLA'Y, s. [mixture] *mistura,* s. f.

Allay of metal, *lega,* s. f.

Allay [ease, mitigation] *alleggerimento, alleggiamento, sollevamento, alleviamento, refrigerio, conforto,* s. m.

To give one's passion some allay, *alleggerire o mitigare il dolore.*

To ALLA'Y [to mix] *mescolare, mischiare.*

To allay wine with water, *mescolare il vino coll' acqua.*

To allay metals, *far lega de' metalli.*

To allay [to ease] *alleggerire, alleggiare, mitigare, alleviare, sgravare.*

To allay one's grief, *alleviare, mitigare il dolore.*

He allay'd his hunger with roots, *si sfamò con radici d'erbe.*

ALLA'Y'D, adj. *mescolato, mischiato.*

Allay'd [mitigated] *alleggiato, alleggerito. mitigato, alleviato.*

ALLE'CTIVE, adj. [alluring, charming] *lusinghiero, lusinghevole, lusingante.*

To ALLE'DGE [to produce a thing, to proof, to quote] *allegare, citare, produrre l'altrui autorità a corroborazione delle propie opinioni.*

ALLE'DGED, adj. *allegato, citato.*

ALLE'DGING, s. *allegazione, citazione,* s. f. *allegamento,* s. m.

ALLE'DGMENT, or ALLEGATION, s. *allegamento,* s. m. *allegagione, citazione,* s. f.

A false allegation, *una calunnia.*

ALLE'GIANCE, s. [obedience due from subjects to the sovereign] *fedeltà dovuta da' sudditi al principe.*

To pay his allegiance, *giurar fedeltà, riconoscere per suo sovrano.*

ALLEGO'RICAL, adj. *allegorico, che contiene allegoria.*

To ALLEGORI'ZE [to use allegories] *allegorizzare, dire per allegoria.*

ALLE'GORY, s. [a continued metaphor, running through the whole discourse] *allegoria,* s. f. *concetto nascoso sotto velame di parole, che vagliono letteralmente cosa diversa.*

ALLE'GRO, s. [a term in musick, when the movement is quick] *allegro.*

ALLELU'JAH [praise the Lord] *alleluja, voce Ebrea, che significa, lodate il signore.*

To ALLE'VIATE [to ease, to allay] *alleviare, alleggerire, sgravare, alleggiare, raddolcire.*

ALLEVIA'TED, adj. *alleviato, alleggerito, sgravato, raddolcito.*

ALLEVIA'TING, s. *raddolcimento, alleviamento, alleggiamento, conforto,* s. m.

ALLEVIA'TION, s. [allaying, ease] *alleviagione, alleviazione*, s. f. *alleviamento, raddolcimento, conforto*, s. m.

A'LLEY, s. [a narrow lane] *chiasso, chiassolino, chiassuolo*, s. m. *viuzza stretta, viottolo.*

A'LLEYS [walks in a garden] *andari, viottoli bene accommodati ne' giardini.*

ALLI'ANCE [an union of families by marriage] *affinità, parentela, parentesco che nasce per maritaggio tra i consanguinei della moglie e'l marito, e tra i consanguinei del marito e la moglie.*

ALLI'ANCE [league] *alleanza, unione, lega*, s. f.

Alliance [in blood] *consanguinità.*

To ALLI'E, or ALLY', *unire, legare, congiungere, far lega.*

ALLI'ED TO [kin] *parente.*

Allied [joined, united] *alleato, unito, confederato.*

ALLI'SION. s. [the act of dashing against] *lo sbattacchiare; infrangimento, sbattimento*, s. m.

ALLIGA'TOR [a large sort of crocodile] *spezie di cocodrillo grande.*

ALLOCA'TION, s. *allogagione*, s. f. *l'allogare.*

ALLOCU'TION, s. *l' atta del parlare a un altro.*

ALLO'DIAL, adj. [that is free, or for which no rents are due] *franco, libero di dazio e di tasse.*

Allodial lands, *terre libere, che non pagano tasse.*

To ALLO'T [to appoint, to assign] *assegnare, fermare, costituire, prescrivare.*

He allotted me this business, *mi costituì sopra questo affare, assegnò la cura di questo affare a me.*

To ALLO'T [to deliver or share by lot] *aggiudicare, sortire, spartire, o dare in sorte.*

ALLO'TTED, adj. *assegnato, fermato, costituito, prescritto, sortito.*

Allotted unto, *sortito, avuto in sorte.*

I am allotted to punishment, *son destinato al gastigo.*

ALLO'TTING / ALLO'TMENT } s. [appointment, assignation] *assegnazione, distribuzione, divisione fatta per sorte.*

To ALLO'W [to give, to grant] *dare, concedere.*

He won't allow me time to eat my dinner, *non vuol darmi tempo di pranzare.*

To allow a servant ten pounds a year, *dar dieci lire l'anno ad un servo.*

I will allow his expences, *gli farò le spese.*

I am able to allow it, *ho il modo di farlo.*

To allow [to approve of, to permit] *approvare, guidicar per buono, tener per buono, ricevere, concedere, permettere, confessare.*

I allow of your reason, *approvo la vostra ragione, la vostra ragione è buona secondo me.*

It is allowed of in men of your years, *è concesso ad un uomo della vostra età.*

Every body allows him to be a man of learning, *tutti convengono della sua dottrina.*

It is a custom allow'd by every body, *è un costume ricevuto da tutti.*

You must allow, *vi è forza confessare.*

I wont't allow you to go abroad when you have business at home, *non permetterò che voi trascuriate gli affari domestici per andare a' diporti.*

ALLO'WABLE, adj. [that may be allowed or approved of] *da approvarsi, da concedersi, da permittersi, lecito permesso, giusto.*

ALLO'WANCE, s. [maintenance, salary] *mantenimento, sostentamento, salario*, s. m. *paga*, s. f.

Allowance [in reckoning] *detrazione, diminuzione*, s. f. *sbattimento*, s. m.

Allowance [indulgence] *connivenza, licenza*, s. f.

The world makes allowance for some actions in one man, which are condemn'd in another, *la gente chiude gli occhi a certe azione d' alcuni che pur condanna in altri.*

ALLO'WED, adj. *dato, aggiudicato, concesso, approvato, permesso, concesso.*

This is not a thing to be allowed, *questa non è cosa da permettersi.*

If a man may be allowed to say so, *se è permesso il dirlo.*

An author cannot be allowed to be a competent judge of his own works, *non appartiene all'autore d un' opera il giudicarne.*

ALLO'WING, s. [the act of giving] *il dare, il concedere.* v. To allow.

ALLO'Y, *lega che si unisce a' metalli.*

To ALLU'DE [to speak with reference to some other thing or matter] *allùdere.*

ALLU'DED, adj. *alluso.*

ALLU'DING, s. *l'alludere.*

A'LLUM, s. [a kind of mineral] *allume*, s, m. *spezie di minerale.*

Rock allum, *allume di rocca.*

ALLU'MINER, s. [limner] *pittore che dipinge sopra carta o pergamena.*

To ALLU'RE [to decoy, to intice, to draw to the lure or bait] *adescare, aescare, allettare coll' esca, invitare e tirare uno alle voglie sue con lusingle allettamenti e inganni.*

To allure with fair promises, *pascer di belle parole.*

ALLU'RED, adj. *adescato, aescato, allettato.*

ALLU'REMENT, s. [inticement] *allettamento, lacciuólo, vezzo*, s. m. *lusinga*, s. f.

ALLU'RER, s. [inticer] *lusinghiere, lusinghiero, lusingatore*, s. m.

ALLU'RING, s. *l'adescare.*

Alluring, adj. *lusinghevole, pien di lusinghe, attrattivo, fallace.*

Alluring beauties, *lusinghevoli o attrattive bellezze.*

Alluring hopes, *fallaci speranze.*

ALLU'RINGLY, adv. *lusinghevolmente, piacevolmente, con lusinghe, con piacevolezza.*

ALLU'SION, s. *allusione*, s. f.

To ALLY, v. To allie.

ALLY'D, v. Allied.

ALMA'DE, s. *almádia*, s. f. *sorta di barchetta tutta d'un pezzo, usata nelle Indie.*

ALMAIN, s. (in musick) [a certain kind of air that moves in common time] *allemanda*, s. f.

A'LMANACK, s. *almanacco*, s. m. *calendario.*

To make an almanack for the last year, *fantasticare, ghiribizzare, cercar Maria per Ravenna.*

ALMANDI'NE, s. [a coarse sort of ruby] *almandina*, s. f. *pietra rossa simile al rubino, ma di color più scuro.*

ALMI'GHTINESS, s. *onnipotenza*, s. f.

ALMI'GHTY, adj. [all-powerful] *onnipotente.*

The ALMI'GHTY, s. [God] *l'Onnipotente Dio, Iddio.*

A'LMOND, s. [the fruit of the almond-tree] *mándorla*, s. f.

ALMOND TRE'E, *mándorlo*, s. m.

The almond of the ear, *orecchioni*, s. m. *sorta di malattia che viene alle glandule degli orecchi.*

The almonds of the throat [a glandulous substance representing two kernels, placed on each side of the uvula, at the root of the tongue] *glandule*, s. f.

Oil of almonds, *olio manderlino.*

A'LMONER, or A'LMNER s. [a church-officer belonging to a king or prince, who is to take care of the distribution of the alms] *cappellano, elemosiniere*, s. m.

A'LMONRY or A'ULMRY, s. [the office or lodgings of the almner, and the place where the alms are given] *ufficio o stanza del cappellano e dello elemosiniére, e il luogo dove si distribuiscono le limosine.*

ALMS, s. [whatsoever is freely given to the poor for God's sake] *limosina.*

To give alms, *far la limosina.*

To ask alms, *domandar la limosina.*

Alms-giver, s. *elemosiniere, elemosinario*, s. m. *che fa limosina.*

Alms-house, *sorta di spedale.*

A'LNAGE, s. [ell-measure] *misura di lunghezza.*

A'LNAGER, A'LNEGER, or A'ULNEGER, s. [an officer whose business was to look to the assize of woollen cloth, but now is only the collector of the subsidy granted to the king] *officiale regio, che riceve i sussidi concessi al Re per atto di parlamento sopra le manifatture de' panni.*

A'LOES. s. [the juice of a tree that bears the same name] *áloe*, s. m.

Aloes [the tree that bears the aloes] *legno aloe.*

The grosser kind of aloes, *aloe cavallino.*

ALOE'TICK, adj. [of or belonging to aloes] *d'aloe appartenente all' aloe.*

ALOE'TICKS [medicines chiefly consisting of aloes] *medicine composte principalmente d' aloe.*

ALO'FT, adj. *alto, superbo, nobile, magnifico, pomposo.*

Aloft, adv. *su, in alto.*

The boughs grow up aloft, *i rami vanno molto in alto.*

Hoist up this man aloft, *tirate su quest' uomo.*

From aloft, *di su, di sopra.*

To set aloft, *innalzare, sollevare, alzare.*

ALO'NE, adj. *ſolo.*

You are not alone that has done it, *non ſiete voi ſolo che l'abbia fato, vi ſon pur degli altri che l' hanno fatto.*

Let me alone for that, *date a me pur la cura di ciò, laſciate fare a me.*

You may truſt him alone, *laſciate pur fare a lui.*

He is alone in his room, *è ſolo in camera ſua.*

We will do it alone, *lo faremo da noi ſteſſi.*

Let thoſe things alone, *laſciate queſte coſe da banda, non parlate di queſte coſe.*

I think it better to let it alone, *ſtimo molto più ſpediente non farlo.*

Let him alone for that, *laſciate fare a lui.*

It is better to be alone than in bad company, *è meglio eſſere ſolo che male accompagnato.*

All alone, *ſolo.*

To let alone, *abbandonare, laſciare ſtare.*

Let me alone, *non mi toccare, laſciami ſtare, laſciami in pace.* Swift.

Alone, adv. *ſolamente.*

ALO'NG, prep. *lungo.*

Along the ſhore, *lungo la ſpiaggia.*

To go along, *andare, camminare.*

Will you go along with me? *volete venir meco?*

Why don't you go along? *perchè non camminate?*

Come along I ſay, *vien pur via.*

To ſail along the coaſt, *coſteggiare, andar per mare lungo le coſte.*

You are alſo to take this along with you, *voi dovete ricordarvi; fate che ciò vi ſia ſempre avanti gli occhi.*

To lie along, or to lie all along, *coricarſi.*

He was lying all along upon the bed, *era diſteſo ſul letto, s'era coricato ſul letto.*

All along, adv. *ſempre dal principio alla fine.*

ALO'OF, adv. [at a diſtance] *di lungi, da lontano, termine di mare.*

ALO'PECY, s. [a diſeaſe called the fox evil or ſcurf, when the hair falls off from the head by the roots] *alopecia, tigna,* s. f. *infermità che fa cadere i capelli.*

ALO'UD, adv. *ad alta voce, forte.*

To call aloud, *chiamare ad alta voce.*

To talk aloud, *parlar forte.*

A'LPHA [the firſt letter of the Greek alphabet] *alfa, prima lettera dell' alfabeto Greco.*

A'LPHABET, s. [the whole order of the letters in any language] *alfabeto, abbiccì,* s. m. *nome del raccolto degli elementi de' linguaggi.*

ALPHABE'TICAL } adj. [belonging to, or agreeable to the order of the alphabet] *alfabetico.*
ALPHABE'TICK }

ALPHABE'TICALLY, adv. *per ordine alfabetico.*

ALPI'NE, adj. [of or belonging to the Alps] *alpigiano, alpigno, alpino, alpeſtre.*

ALREA'DY, adv. *già, di già.*

Are you come already? *ſete già ritornato?*

A'LSO, conj. *anche, ancóra, anco, eziandio.*

My father is come and my mother alſo, *mio padre è venuto e mia madre anche.*

A'LSO [moreover] *di più, oltre, oltre ciò, oltracciò.*

A'LTAR, s. *altare,* s. m.

Altar wiſe, *a mo' d' altare.*

A'LTARAGE, s. [the free offerings made at the altar by the people, and the profits which ariſe to the prieſt by reaſon of the altar] *offerte fatte volontariamente dal popolo all' altare, e tutti i profitti che i preti ricevono mediante l'altare.*

To A'LTER [to change, to turn, to vary] *alterare, cangiare, rifare.*

To alter one's mind, *cangiar conſiglio.*

To alter a ſuit of cloaths, *rifare un abito.*

To alter a houſe, *rifabbricare una caſa.*

To alter a writing, *correggere, emendare una ſcrittura.*

To alter one's way of living, *mutar vita.*

To alter one's condition, *cangiare ſtato, maritarſi.*

To alter, verb. neut. *cangiare, variare.*

He ſhall never alter, *non cangerà mai, ſarà ſempre quel che è.*

A'LTERABLE, adj. [that may be altered] *alterabile, atto ad alterarſi.*

ALTERA'TION, s. [change] *alterazione, mutazione,* s. f.

ALTERCA'TION, s. [a contentious diſpute, debate] *altercazione, conteſa,* s. f.

A'LTERED, adj. *alterato, mutato, cangiato.*

The cuſtom is ſomewhat altered, *il coſtume è cangiato.*

The caſe is altered, *le coſe vanno altrimente.*

A'LTERING, s. *l'alterare, alterazione, mutazione,* s. f. *cangiamento,* s. m.

Altering medicines [are ſuch as purify and reſtore the due mixture of the blood] *medicine purificative e reſtorative.*

ALTE'RNATELY, adv. *v.* Alternatively.

ALTERNA'TION, s. *alternazione,* s. f. *l'alternare.*

ALTE'RNATIVE, or ALTE'RNATE, adj. [that which is done by turn or courſe, one after another] *alternato, alternativo, vicendevole.*

ALTE'RNATIVELY, or ALTE'RNATELY, adv. *alternativamente, vicendevolmente.*

ALTHO'UGH, or ALTHO', conj. *benchè, ſebbene, anchorchè, quantunque.*

ALTI'METRY, s. [the art of taking and meaſuring heights] *altimetria,* s. f. *arte di miſurare le altezze acceſſibili o inacceſſibili.*

ALTI'SONANT, adj. [high ſounding] *riſonante, rimbombante, altiſonante.*

ALTI'TONANT, adj. [thundering from on high] *altitonante.*

A'LTITUDE, s. [height] *altitudine, altezza,* s. f.

ALTOGE'THER, adv. *affatto, interamente, in tutto e per tutto, ſul totale.*

The report of his being dead is altogether groundleſs, *la fama che s'era ſparſa della ſua morte è in tutto vana.*

He is come to town for altogether, *è venuto per fermarſi in città.*

A'LVEARY, s. [a bee-hive] *alveario, alveare,* s. m. *arnia,* s. f.

A'LUM, s. *allúme,* s. m. *ſpezie di miniera, ſimile al criſtallo.*

Rock-alum, *allume di rocca.*

Full or mixt with alum, *alluminoſo, che tien di qualità d'allume.*

ALU'MINOUS, adj. *che ha dell' allume.*

A'LWAYS, adv. *ſempre, inceſſantemente, continuamente.*

He is always at his books, *non fa altro che leggere, che ſtudiare.*

He is always at his pen, *ſcrive inceſſantemente, non fa che ſcrivere dì e notte.*

AM [I am] *io ſono.* dal verbo to be, *eſſere.*

AMABI'LITY, s. [lovelineſs] *amabilità,* s. f.

A'MABLE adj. [amiable] *amabile.*

AMA'IN (a ſea-term) [when a man of war commands another to yield, ſtrike amain, i. e. lower your ſails] *termine marinareſco, quando una nave da guerra commanda a una nave nemica d' arrenderſi col dirle* ammaina.

Amain, adv. *a voga arrancata, a tutta forza, vigoroſamente, con vigore.*

To row amain, *andare a voga arrancata.*

To AMA'LGAMATE [to mix quickſilver with gold or ſome other metal, ſo as to reduce it into a kind of paſte] *amalgamare.*

AMA'LGAME, s. [any metal that is amalgamated or reduced to a powder or paſte] *amalgame,* s. m.

AMANUE'NSIS, s. [a clerk or ſecretary, one that writes what is dictated by another] *ſegretario, copiatore, copiſta,* s. m.

A'MARANTH, s. [flower gentle] *ſciamito,* s. m. *fiore di color roſſo ſcuro, fatto in forma di pina.*

AMA'SS [heap] *murrhio,* s. m.

To AMA'SS [to heap up] *accumulare, ammucchiare.*

AMA'SSED, adj. *accumulato, ammucchiato.*

To AMA'TE [to diſcourage, to daunt] *ſgomentare, ſbigottire.*

AMA'TED, adj. *ſgomentato, ſbigottito.*

To AMA'ZE [to aſtoniſh] *ſtupire, ſtupidire, ſtupefare, maravigliarſi.*

AMA'ZED, adj. *ſtupito, ſtupidito, ſtupefatto, maravigliato.*

I am amazed at it, *reſto ſtupito di ciò.*

AMA'ZEDNESS, s. } [aſtoniſhment] *ſtupore,* s. m. *maraviglia,* s. f.
AMA'ZEMENT, s. }

AMA'ZING, adj. *ſtupendo, miracoloſo, maraviglioſo.*

AMA'ZINGLY, adv. *maraviglioſamente, con maraviglia o ſtupore.*

AMBA'SSADOR, s. m. *ambaſciadore.*

AMBA'SSADRESS, s. f. *ambaſciadrice, moglie d'uno ambaſciatore.*

A'MBE, s. [a ſuperficial jutting out of bones] *ſporgimento ſuperficiale d'un oſſo,*

A'MBER, s. [a kind of gum] *ambra,* s. f. *bitume di prezioſiſſimo odore.*

A'MBERED, adj. *profumato d'ambra.*

AMBERGREA'SE, or AMBERGRI'S, s. [sweet-scented clammy juice or perfume] *ambracane*, s. f.
AMB-ACE, *ambassi*, v. Ace.
AMBIDE'XTER, adj. [one who uses both his hands alike] *ambidestro, che si serve ugualmente bene d'ambe le mani.*
Ambidexter, s. [a juror who takes money of both parties for giving his verdict] *un furbo, un uomo senza coscienza, che piglia danari da due bande, ma principalmente si dire di quelli da' quali dipende il dare la sentenza.*
AMBIDEXTE'RITY, s. *qualità di quelli che si servono ugualmente d'ambe le mani; furberia, ladroneggiare.*
AMBIDE'XTEROUS, adj. *infame, disonorato.*
Ambidexterous dealings, *azioni infami.*
A'MBIENT, adj. *ambiente.*
The ambient air, *l'aria ambiente.*
AMBIGU'ITY, s. [doubt] *ambiguità*, s. f.
AMBI'GUOUS, adj. *ambiguo, equivoco, che può prendersi in diverso significato.*
AMBI'GUOUSLY, adv. *ambiguamente, equivocamente.*
A'MBIT, s. [the bounds or perimeter of any figure] *ámbito, contorno*, s. m.
AMBI'TION, s. *ambizione*, s. f. *soverchia cupidigia d'onore e di maggioranza.*
AMBI'TIOUS, adj. *ambizioso.*
I am very ambitious to serve you, *ambisco molto di servirvi.*
An ambitious man, *un ambizioso.*
An ambitious woman, *una ambiziosa.*
AMBI'TIOUSLY, adv. *ambiziosamente, con ambizione, ardentemente.*
Ambitiously to seek preferment, *ambire onori, cercare posti lucrativi.*
To A'MBLE [to pace] *andar l'ambio.*
A horse that ambles, *un cavallo che va l'ambio, un cavallo che va di portante.*
An ambling pace, *ambio, portante.*
An ambling nag, *un cavallo che va l'ambio, cavallo che va di portante.*
A'MBLICON, s. [a figure that has an obtuse angle] *amblicone*, s. m. *figura che ha un ángolo ottuso.*
AMBLICO'NIAL, adj. [obtuse angular] *amblicono, d'angoli ottusi.*
AMBRO'SE, s. [a plant] *ambrosia*, s. f. *pianta simile alla ruta.*
AMBRO'SIA, s. [the delicious food, which, as the poets feign, the Gods eat] *ambrosia*, s. f. *cibo degli Dei de gentili.*
A'MBRY, s. [an old-fashioned cupboard] *credenza*, s. f. *armario*, s. m.
AM'BSA'CE, *v.* Ace.
A'MBULATORY, adj. [walking up and down] *ambulatorio, errante.*
A'MBURY, s. [a disease in horses, that causes them to break out in spungy swellings] *malattia ne' cavalli che causa loro tumori spugnosi.*
AMBUSCA'DE, s. } [a body of men
A'MBUSH, s. } who lie hid in a wood, to rush out upon or inclose an enemy unawares] *imboscata*, s. f. *imboscamento, agguato*, s. m.
To lie in ambuscade, *imboscarsi, tender un agguato.*

A'MEL, s. [dal francese *email*] *smalto.*
Amel-corn [a kind of grain, or rice, of which starch is made] *spezie di ségala, della quale si fa l'ámido.*
A'MEN, adv. [verily, so be it] *amen, così sia.*
Amen I say, *molto volontieri, volentiermente.*
AME'ND, s. *ammenda.*
To AME'ND [to reform] *emendare, correggere, purgar dall' errore, rivedere, ammendare.*
To amend a work, *correggere o rivedere un' opera.*
To amend [to grow better] *emendarsi, correggersi, ravvedersi, riconoscere i suoi errori.*
To amend one's life, *cangiar vita, mutar costumi.*
To amend [in health] *riaversi, pigliar vigore, migliorare, guarire, tornar in salute.*
AME'NDED, adj. *emendato, corretto, riavuto.*
AME'NDMENT, s. *emendazione, riforma*, s. f.
AME'NDS, s. *ammenda, ricognizione, ricompensa, ricompensazione*, s. f. *compensamento, compenso, sconto, contraccambio*, s. m.
I'll make myself amends with my own hands, *mi farò giustizia colle mie mani.*
To make amends, *compensare, ricompensare, rimeritare, rimunerare.*
What amends can I make you for so many favours? *come potrò ricompensarvi mai di tanti favori?*
I'll make you amends for the service you have done to me, *saprò riconoscere o rimeritare l'opera mostra.*
You must make me amends for my loss, *bisogna che voi mi risarciate della mia perdita.*
AME'NDER, s *correttore, emendatore, censore, castigatore*, s. m.
AME'NDING, s. *emendazione, correzione*, s. f.
AME'NITY, s. [pleasantness] *amenità, bellezza, piacevolezza di paese*, s. f.
To AME'RCE [to fine] *punire con pena pecuniaria, condannare, all' ammenda.*
AMERCED, adj. *condannato, o punito con pena pecuniaria.*
AME'RCEMENT, s. *ammenda, pena pecuniaria.*
AME'SS, s. [amice] *ammitto*, s. m. *quel panno lino che il sacerdote si pone in capo quando si para.*
AMETHY'ST, s. [a precious stone of a purple colour] *amatista*, s. f. *gioja del colore del fior del pesco.*
AMFRA'CTUOUS, adj. [full of windings or turnings] *serpeggiante.*
A'MIABLE, adj. [courteous] *cortese, affezionato, affabile, benigno.*
Amiable [lovely, worthy to be loved] *amabile, vago, bello, degno d'esser amato.*
A'MIABLENESS, s. *cortesia, benignità, affabilità, bellezza, grazia*, s. f.
A'MIABLY, adv. *amabilmente, affezionatamente, cortesemente, benignamente.*
A'MICABLE, adj. [friendly] *amichevole, piacevole, amorevole, da amico.*

A'MICABLY, adv. *amichevolmente, amicamente, piacevolmente, amorevolmente, da amico.*
AMI'DST, prep. [in the midst] *fra, nel mezzo.*
AMI'CE, or AMICT, *v.* Amess.
AMI'SS, adj. [not rightly] *cattivo, vizioso.*
Amiss, adv. *male, a male, in malo parta, malamente.*
Have I done any thing amiss? *che male ho commesso io? in che ho io peccato?*
He would take it amiss if you did not go to see him, *si offenderebbe se non l'andaste a vedere.*
It won't be amiss to send him a letter, *non sarà fuor di proposito di scrivergli.*
To judge amiss of things, *giudicar male delle cose.*
If any thing should happen amiss, *se arrivasse qualche disgrazia.*
Nothing comes amiss to a hungry stomach, *l'appetito s'accommodata a tutto.*
I think it not amiss to go and take a little walk, *credo che non sarebbe male se andassimo a fare una passeggiata.*
Nothing comes amiss to him, *s'appiglia ad ogni cosa, ogni cosa fa per lui.*
AMI'SSION, s. [loss] *perdita*, s. f.
A'MITY, s. [affection, friendship] *amicizia, amorevolezza, pace, concordia.*
I love to live in amity with all the world, *amo di viver amorevolmente con ognuno, amo di essere amico di tutti.*
AMMO'NIACK, s. *ammoniaco.*
Ammoniac salt, *sale ammoniaco.*
AMMUNI'TION, s. [all sorts of warlike stores and provisions] *munizione*, s. f. *polvere, piombo, e altre cose belliche, provisioni de' soldati.*
Ammunition-bread, *pane di munizione.*
Ammunition [a trull that follows the camp] *bagascia, puttana abjetta che va in traccia de' soldati.*
AMMS-A'CE, s. [where two aces are thrown upon dice] *ambassi.*
A'MNER, s. [almoner] *cappellano.*
A'MNESTY, or A'MNISTY, s. [act of oblivion, general pardon] *indulto*, s. m. *perdono generali concesso dal principe per ogna sorta di delitto.*
A'MNION, or A'MNIOS, s. [a membrane with which the fœtus in the womb is immediately covered] *amnione*, s. m. *membrana, che cuopre immediatamente il feto nel corpo della madre.*
AMO'NG, or AMO'NGST, adv. *fra, infra, tra.*
They divided the booty among themselves, *si spartirono la preda fra di loro.*
Amongst friends all things are common, *fra gli amici non c' è nè mio nè tuo.*
He is not liked among the common sort of people, *non è amato dal volgo.*
A'MORIST, s. *un amante, uno innamorato.*
A'MOROUS, adj. [belonging to love, or apt to fall in love] *amoroso.*
A'MOROUSLY, adv. *amorosamente, con affetto amoroso.*

AMO'RT, adj. *ammortito, ammorzato.*

He is all amort [he is very melancholy] *egli è molto maninconico.*

AMORTIZA'TION, s. (a law-term) *estinzione*, s. f.

To AMORTI'SE, or AMORTI'ZE, *estinguere, parlando d'un feudo.*

To amortise [to kill] *estinguere, uccidere.* Obs.

AMO'TION, s. [removing away] *rimovimento*, s. m. *il rimuovere.*

To AMO'VE [to remove, to take away from] *rimuovere, tor via.*

To AMO'UNT [to rise up in value] *montare, ascendere.*

The sum amounts to ten crowns, *la somma monta a dieci scudi.*

AMO'UR, s. *amore impudico.*

AMO'URS, s. [love intrigues] *amorazzo, innamoramento*, s. m. *intrighi amorosi.*

AMPER, s. [a swelling] *tumore, gonfiamento*, s. m.

Amper [a flaw in cloth] *taglio*, s. m. *squarciatura che si trova in una pezza di panno.*

AMPHI'BIOUS, adj. [that lives both upon land and in the water] *anfibio, che vive sopra la terra e nell' acqua.*

AMPHIBO'LOGICAL, adj. [belonging to amphibology] *anfibologico, che ha anfibologia.*

AMPHIBO'LOGY, s. [a dark speech that has a double meaning] *anfibologia*, s. f. *discorso che ha sentimento doppio ed equivoco.*

AMPHI'BRACHYS, s. [a foot of Latin or Greek verse, having a long syllable in the middle, and a short one on each side] *sorta di piede ne' versi Latini o Grechi che ha una sillaba lunga nel mezzo, e una corta al principio e un' altra alla fine.*

AMPHISBE'NA, s. [a serpent with a head at each end, and goes both ways] *anfesibena*, s. f. *serpente con due teste, una da piè e una da capo, e cammina per ogni verso.* [Favola.]

AMPHI'SCII, s. [inhabitants of the torrid zone, whose shadows at different times of the year fall both ways] *abitatori della zona torrida che hanno in differenti tempi dell' anno l'ombra dalle due bande.*

AMPHITHE'ATRE, s. *anfiteatro*, s. m. *fabbrica di figura tonda o ovale ne' tempi de' Romani, dove si rappresentavano combattimenti ed altri spettacoli.*

A'MPHOR, s. [a measure of liquid things] *ánfora*, s f.

A'MPLE, adj. [large] *ampio, largo, grande per ogni verso.*

An ample testimony, *ampia testimonianza.*

AMPLIA'TION, s. [enlargement] *ampliazione*, s. f.

Ampliation (in law) [deferring of judgment till the cause be better certified] *prolungamento*, s. m. *proroga, prorogazione*, s. f.

AMPLIFICA'TION, s. [enlarging or dilating upon an argument] *amplificazione*, s. f.

A'MPLIER, s. *amplificatore*, s. f.

To AMPLIFY' [to inlarge, to dilate] *amplificare, aggrandire, accrescere.*

AMPLIFY'D, adj. *amplificato, aggrandito, accresciuto.*

AMPLIFY'ING, s. *amplificazione*, s. f. *aggrandimento, accrescimento*, s m.

A'MPLITUDE, s. [largeness of extent, greatness] *ampiezza*, s. f.

A'MPLY, adv. *ampiamente, largamente, copiosamente.*

AMPUTA'TION, s. [the act of cutting or lopping off] *mozzamento, tagliamento*, s. m.

Amputation (in surgery) [the act of cutting off any member of the body] *amputazione, mutilazione*, s. f.

A'MULET, s. [a preservative against witchcraft] *breve, o brieve*, s. m. *piccolo involto entrovi reliquie o orazioni, e portasi al collo dagli scionti superfiziosi contro gl' incantesmi, stregherie, e ammaliamenti.*

To AMU'SE [to hold in play, to keep at bay] *trattenere, tenere a bada, intrattenere.*

To amuse one's self, *badare, attendere, trattenersi, intrattenersi.*

AMU'SED, adj. *trattenuto.*

AMU'SEMENT, s. [a trifling employment to pass away the time] *intrattenimento, passatempo.*

I do it for an amusement, *lo fo per passatempo.*

AMU'SER, s. *quello che tiene a bada gli altri.*

AN, *articolo che significa un, uno, una, ma non si adopra che innanzi a nomi cominciati da vocale. Se un nome comincia con una consonante l'articolo allora è a.*

A'NA, s. [an equal portion or quantity of each ingredient to be taken in compounding the medicine] *ana*, s. f. *ugual quantità d' ingredienti da prendersi nel comporre le medicine (termine medico.)*

ANABA'PTISTS, *anabattisti, sorta d' eretici, che tengono, che uno non deve esser battezzato fin tanto che possa esser instrutto nei punti della sua religione.*

ANACHORE'TAL, or ANACHORE'TICAL, adj. [belonging to an anachoret] *appartenente ad anacoreta.*

ANA'CHORET, s. [a monk who lives by himself] *anacoreta, eremita.*

ANA'CRONISM, s. [an error in chronology] *anacronismo, errore di tempo di cronologia.*

ANAGO'GE, s. [a mystical sense of the holy scriptures] *anagogia*, s. f. *senso mistico.*

ANAGO'GICAL, adj. [mysterious] *anagogico, mistico.*

ANAGO'GICALLY, adv. [mysteriously] *anagogicamente, misticamente.*

A'NAGRAM, s. *anagramma.*

ANALE'PTICK, adj. [restorative] *analettico, ristorativo.*

ANALO'GICAL, adj. [proportional] *analogo, di proporzion simile.*

ANALO'GICALLY, adv. *analogamente, proporzionatamente.*

ANA'LOGOUS, adj. [proportionable] *analogo.*

ANA'LOGY, s. [proportion, relation] *analogìa, proporzione*, s. f.

A'NALYSIS, s. *analisia*, s. f. *esatta divisione delle parti.*

A'NARCHY, s. [want of government in a nation or state] *anarchia, confusione nel governo d' uno stato.*

ANA'THEMA, s. [a curse] *anatema, scomunica, maladizione*, s. f.

To ANATHEMATI'ZE [to excommunicate] *anatematizzare, scommunicare.*

ANATHE'MATIZED, adj. *anatematizzato, scomunicato, maladetto.*

ANATO'MICAL, adj. [of or belonging to anatomy] *anatomico, di anatomia.*

ANATO'MICALLY, adv. *anatomicamente.*

ANA'TOMIST, s. [a person skilled in the art of anatomizing] *anatomista*, s. m. *pratico nell' anatomia, chi esercita la notomia.*

To ANA'TOMIZE [to dissect or cut up the body of a man or beast] *notomizzare, fare l'anatomia d'un corpo.*

ANA'TOMIZED, adj. *notomizzato.*

ANA'TOMY, s. [a dissection or cutting up the body of men or beasts] *anatomia, notomia.*

A'NCESTORS, s. [fore-fathers] *antenati, predecessori.*

A'NCESTREL, adj. [of or belonging to ancestors] *appartenente agli antenati o predecessori.*

A'NCESTRY, s. [race] *prosápia, razza, schiatta*, s. f.

A'NCHOR, s. [an instrument of iron that holds a ship in a place] *áncora*, s. f. *strumento di ferro col quale si fermano i navili. Il CH si pronuncia qui come K.*

To cast anchor, *gittar l'áncora.*

To be, to lie, or to ride at anchor, *stare o esser all' ancora.*

To hoist or weigh anchor, *sarpare, salpare, sciogliere l'ancora.*

To A'NCHOR [to cast anchor] *gittar l'ancora, dar fondo.*

A'NCHORAGE, s. [ground fit to hold the anchor of a ship] *luogo proprio a gittar l'ancora.*

Anchorage [a duty paid to the king for casting an anchor in the pool of an harbour] *dazio che si paga al rè da ogni vascello, che gitta l'ancora nel porto.*

A'NCHORET, s [a monk that leads a solitary life] *anacoreta, eremita. CH, come K.*

ANCHO'VE, s. [a small sea-fish pickled] *acciuga*, s. f. *picciol pesce marino, che per lo più si mangia salato.*

A'NCIENT, adj. [old] *antico, vecchio, anziano.*

An ancient man or woman, *un vecchio, una vecchia.*

The ancient history, *l'istoria antica.*

An ancient custom, *costume invecerato.*

To grow ancient, *invecchiare, divenir vecchio.*

Grown ancient, adj. *invecchiato.*

The ancients, s. *gli antichi, gli antenati.*

A'NCIENTLY, adv. *anticamente, nel tempo antico.*

A'NCIENTNESS, s. *anzianità, antichità, parlando d'una famiglia.*

A'NCIENTY, s. *antichità, anzianità*, s. f.

ANCLE, s. [ankle, the joint between the leg and the foot] *nodo del piede*; *cavicchia*, s. f.

A'NCOME, s. [fellon] *fignolo, cicciolo.*

A'NCON, s. [the turning of the elbow] *il giro che fa il gómito.*

AND, conj. *e, ed.*

You and I, *voi ed io.*

To day and to morrow, *oggi e domani.*

Go and see, *andate a vederè.*

What and if I should do it? *supposto che lo facessi?*

Go and bid him come to me, *andate a dirgli che venga da me.*

A little more and he had been killed, *poco mancò non fosse amazzato.*

I give him what he desires, and yet he is not contented, *gli do quel che desidera, contuttociò non è contento.*

How can you write to him, and not know the place where he is? *come potete scrivergli se non sapete dove è?*

To grow better and better, *migliorare, andare di meglio in meglio.*

To grow worse and worse, *peggiorare, andare di peggio in peggio.*

And therefore, *pereiò, perilchè,*

By and by, *adesso adesso, or ora.*

Now and then, *di quando in quando.*

Two and two, *due a due.*

By little and little, *a poco a poco.*

And so forth, *e così di mano in mano, e va cantando*, e così oltre, *eccetera.*

What's that and please you? *di grazia mi dica che è ciò?*

Without ifs or ands, *senza bilanciare, alla prima.*

A'NDIRON, s. *alare*, s. m. *ferramento che si tiene nel cammino per tenere sospese le legna.*

ANDRO'GYNE, or ANDRO'GYNUS, s. [hermaphrodite] *ermafrodita.*

To A'NEAL [to bake or harden in the fire] *cuocere o indurare al fuoro.* v. To anneal.

To aneal [to paint upon glass] *pingere sul vetro.*

ANE'ALED, adj. *cotto, indurato al fuoco.*

ANE'MONE, or ANE'MONY, s. [a wind-flower] *anémone*, s. m.

ANE'NT, prep. [concerning, relating to] *concernente, toccante.* Obs.

Anent [over-against] *dirincontro, dirimpetto, rincontro.* Obs.

ANE'W, adv. [again] *di nuovo, da capo, ancòra.*

To begin a-new, *ricominciare, cominciar da capo.*

ANGA'RIA, s. [a pressing of men for the publick use] *angheria*, s. f. *sforzamento fatto altrui contro ragione*; *aggravio*, s. m.

A'NGEL, s. *angelo, o angiolo*, s. m. *angiola*, s. f.

Angel [a gold coin] *moneta d'oro antica.*

Angel [a kind of fish] *sorta di pesce.*

ANGE'LICA, s. *angelica*, s. f. *sorta d'erba.*

Angelica water, *acqua d'angelica.*

ANGE'LICAL, adj. [of or belonging to, and partaking of the nature of angels] *angelico, d'angelo.*

A'NGELOT, s. (a kind of French cheese) *spezie di cacio che si fa in Francia.*

A'NGER, s. [wrath, passion] *collera, collora, ira, stizza*, s. f. *si pronuncia col g duro alla tedesca, in Italiano come se fosse scritto* angher.

Extream anger, *ira subitana, collera estrema.*

Aptness to anger, *iracondia.*

He is easily provoked to anger, *è molto iracondo, egli s'adira facilmente.*

To A'NGER, *irritare, stizzare, adirare, far montare in collera.*

A'NGERED, adj. *irritato, adirato, in collera.*

A'NGERLY, adv. *stizzosamente, con istizza, in collera.*

A'NGLE, s. [a corner] *angolo*, s. m. *quello che deriva da due linee concorrenti in un medesimo punto.*

Angle [hook] *amo*, s. m. *strumento d'acciajo da pigliar pesci.*

Angle [angling-rod] *canna da pescare.*

To ANGLE [to fish with an angle] *pescare coll' amo.*

A'NGLER, s. *quello che pesca coll' amo.*

A'NGLICISM, s. [English idiom, manner of speech peculiar to England] *idioma Inglese, maniera di parlare peculiare alla lingua Inglese, anglicismo.*

A'NGLING, s. *il pescare coll' amo.*

An angling line, or rod, *canna da pescare.*

A'NGRED, *v.* Angered.

A'NGRY, adj. *irato, iracondo, collerico, stizzoso.*

Don't make me angry, *non mi fate adirare, non mi fate andare in collera.*

I am so angry that I am not myself, *sono sì transportato dalla collera che non so quel che mi farcia*; *la collora m'acciecca.*

I am very angry with you, *sono in collera con voi.*

Did I ever give you an angry word? *son io mai andato in collera con voi? v' ho io mai detta una parola brusca?*

A'NGRILY, adv. *iracondamente, stizzosamente.*

Angrily [in look] *bieramente, stortamente, travoltamente, con occhio bieco.*

To look angrily at one, *guardar uno con occhio bieco, fare il viso dell' arme ad uno.*

A'NGUISH, s. [excessive pain and grief] *angoscia, afflizione*, s. f. *travaglio, affanno*, s. m.

A'NGULAR, adj. *angolare, che ha angoli.*

ANGULO'SITY, s. [the quality of that which has several angles] *qualità di rosa che ha molti angoli.*

A'NGUST, adj. [narrow] *angusto, stretto.*

ANHELA'TION, s. [a difficulty in fetching one's breath] *auelito, ansamento*, s. m.

ANI'GHTS, adv. *di notte, in tempo di notte.*

ANI'LITY, s. [the old age of a woman] *l'età senile d'una donna, vecchiaja vecchiezza*, s. f.

ANIMADVE'RSION, s. [observations] *osservazioni, attente considerazioni.*

To ANIMADVE'RT [to remark, to observe] *notare, osservare, riflettere, far riflessione, considerare.*

ANIMADVE'RTED, adj. *notato, osservato, riflesso, considerato.*

A'NIMAL, s. [a living creature] *animale*, s. m. *propriamente diciamo di quello che manca della parte razionale.*

Animal, adj. [living, that has life in it] *animale, che ha in se anima.*

Animal spirits, *spiriti animali.*

ANIMA'LITY, s. [the being or quality of an animal) *facoltà o qualità d'un animale.*

To A'NIMATE [to hearten, to encourage] *animare, dare animo*, incitare, *incoraggiare, inanimire.*

To animate, [to enliven, to give life] *animare, dar la vita, infonder l'anima in qualche cosa.*

ANIMA'TED, adj. *animato, che ha anima.*

Animated [heartened] *animato, incitato, incorraggiato, inanimito.*

Animated needle [a needle touch'd with a loadstone] *ago calamitato.*

ANIMA'TING, s. *l'animare, l'infonder l'anima in un corpo.*

Animating, adj. *animante, che anima, che da la vita e l'anima.*

Animating [heartening, encouraging] *incitante, che inrita, incorraggia o inanima.*

ANIMO'SITY, s. [wilfulness] *animosità, bravura*, s. f. *ardire*, s. m.

Animosity [grudge, hatred] *animosità, ira, malizia*, s. f. *odio*, s. m.

ANIMO'SITIES [contentions, quarrels] *animosità, contese, liti.*

A'NIS, s. *anice*, s. m. *pianta simile al finocchio.*

Anis seed, *anici, semi d'anice.*

A'NKLE, or A'NKLE-BO'NE, s. *caviglia nodo del piede.*

A'NNALIST, s. [a writer of annals] *annalista*, s. m. *scrittor d'annali.*

A'NNALS, s. [yearly chronicles] *annali*, s. m. *storia che distingue per ordine d'anni le cose succedute.*

ANNA'TS, or A'NNATES, s. [first fruits paid out of spiritual benefits to the pope] *annata*, s. f. *l'entrata d'un anno di beneficio vacante che si paga al papa.*

To ANNE'AL [to heat glass that the colours laid on it may pierce through] *scaldar un vetro in un forno sì che i colori posti in quello possano passare da banda a banda.*

To anneal [to heat any thing in such a manner as to give it the true temper] *riscaldar una rosa in modo che ne riceva la dovuta* tempra. Johns. Dict.

To ANNE'X [to unite, to join one thing to another] *unire, congiungere, aggiungere.*

ANNE'X, s. *la rosa unessa.* Brown.

ANNEXA'TION, s. *aggiunzione, aggiunta*, s. f. *aggiugnimento*, s. m.

ANNE'XED, adj. *annesso, unito, aggiunto.*

ANNE'XING, s. *aggiugnimento*, s. m. *l'aggiugnere*.

ANNIE'NTED, adj. [made void] *annullato, rivocato, abolito, termine legale*.

To ANNI'HILATE [to destroy utterly] *annichilare, scemare, diminuire, distruggere, ridurre al nulla*.

ANNI'HILATED, adj. *annichilato, distrutto, ridotto al nulla*.

ANNIHILA'TING, s. } [destroying or ANNIHILA'TION, s. } turning to nothing] *annichilazione, distruzione*, s. f. *distruggimento*, s. m.

A'NNIS, *v.* A'NIS.

ANNIVE'RSARY, adj. [that comes every year at a certain time] *anniversario, che torna un tratto ogni anno, che si celebra ogni anno*.

The anniversary of a saint, *la solennità d'un santo, l'anniversario d'un santo*.

The anniversary [the yearly obit of a man] *l'anniversario d'un morto*.

ANNO DO'MINI [the reckoning of time from our Saviour's birth] *Anno Domini, l'anno del Signore, maniera usata nelle scritture pubbliche*.

ANNOTA'TION, s. [note or mark] *annotazione, osservazione*, s. f.

To ANNO'UNCE, *annunziare, pubblicare, far sapere*.

ANNO'UNCED, adj. *annunziato, pubblicato*.

To ANNO'Y [to molest, to hurt, to prejudice] *annojare, apportar noja, molestare, incomodare, scomodare, pregiudicare*.

ANNO'YANCE, s. [prejudice, damage] *danno, pregiudizio, incommodo, scomodo*, s. m. *molestia, noja*, s. f.

ANNOY'D, adj. *annojato, molestato, incommodato*.

ANNO'YER, s. *un molesto, un impertuno*.

A'NNUAL, adj. [yearly] *annuale, o annovale*.

A'NNUALLY, adv. *annualmente, d'anno in anno*.

ANNUI'TY, s. [a yearly rent to be paid for a term of life or years] *rendita annuale*.

To ANNU'LL [to make void, to abolish] *annullare, estinguere, abolire*.

ANNU'LLED, adj. *annullato, estinto, abolito*.

ANNU'LLING, s. *l'annullare, annullazione*, s. f.

ANNU'LET, s. [a little ring which the fifth brother of any family ought to bear in his coat of arms] *annelletto, che il quinto fratello di qualsisia famiglia deve avere nell' arme*.

To ANNU'MERATE [to put into the number] *annoverare, numerare, contare*.

ANNUNCIA'TION, s. [the delivery of a message, but is particularly apply'd to Lady-day] *annunziazione ; festività della madonna, che si celebra a venticinque di marzo*.

ANODY'NE, adj. [softening, speaking of a remedy] *lenitivo, lenificativo*.

ANODY'NES, s. [such remedies as allevia te the pain] *rimedj lenitivi*.

To ANO'INT, *ugnere*.

To anoint a king, *ugnere un re, confermalo*.

ANO'INTED, adj. *unto*.

The anointed of the Lord, *l'unto del Signore, il principe da Dio prescelto*.

ANOI'NTER, s. *quello che ugne*.

ANOI'NTING, s. *ugnimento*, s. m. *l'ugnere, unzione*, s. f.

ANOI'SANCE, *v.* Nuisance.

ANO'MALOUS, or ANO'MALAR, adj. [irregular] *anomalo, fuor di regola*.

ANO'MALY, s. [irregularity in the conjugations of verbs or declensions of nouns] *irregolarità nelle coniugazioni de' verbi o declinazioni de' nomi*.

ANO'N, adv. [by and by] *adesso adesso, fra poco*.

Ever and anon, *ad ogni momento*.

I come anon, *vengo subito*.

ANO'NYMOUS, adj. [nameless, without a name] *anonimo, senza nome*.

ANO'THER, adj. *altro, un altro, l'altro*.

I am of another mind, *io sono d'un altro parere, o sentimento*.

One must not take what is another's, *non bisogna pigliar l'altrui*.

One is better than another, *uno è migliore d'un altro*.

To love one another, *amarsi l'un l'altro*.

I have such another, *ne ho uno simile*.

It costs me ten shillings one with another, *mi costa sotto sopra dieci scellini*.

Three days one after another, *tre giorno continui*.

He is free of another's purse, *è liberale del ben d'altrui*.

One after another, *un dopo l'altro*.

He dispersed them some to one place, some to another, *li disperse chi quà, chi là*.

They differ one from another, *differiscono fra di loro*.

One misfortune comes upon the neck of another, *le disgrazie son come le ciriege, l'una si tira dietro l'altra*.

It is one thing to promise, and another to perform, *altro è promettere, altro mantenere*.

They may be a help to one another, *possono ajutarsi l'un l'altro*.

Another way, *altronde, per altra parte, altrove*.

To ANO'Y, *v.* To annoy, and all its derivatives.

A'NSWER, s. *risposta*, s. f.

To make or give an answer, *fare, o dare risposta*.

To write an answer to a letter, *rispondere ad una lettera*.

To A'NSWER [to give an answer] *rispondere, far risposta*.

To answer a letter, *rispondere ad una lettera*.

To answer [to be answerable to] *rispondere, corrispondere, esser proporzionato*.

The design does not answer my expectations, *il mio disegno è fallito*.

I believe he will do it, but I won't answer for it, *credo che lo farà, ma non ve lo prometto*.

You never can answer that fault, *non potrete mai giustificarvi di questo errore*.

Give him what he wants, and I'll answer for him, *dategli quel che li bisogna, ed io sarò mallevadore*.

This will answer our business, *ciò farà per noi*.

I cannot answer for it in my conscience, *non posso farlo in conscienza*.

To answer a debt, *pagare un debito*.

Money answers all occasions, *il danaro non fallisce mai*.

To answer (in law) *comparire in giustizia per un altro*.

A'NSWERABLE, adj. [accountable] *obligato, mallevadore, che è obligato a render conto di qualche cosa*.

Answerable [proportionable] *proporzionato, conforme, equivalente, uniforme*.

A'NSWERABLENESS, s. *conformità, proporzione, convenenza*, s. f.

A'NSWERABLY, adv. *convenevolmente, proporzionatamente*.

A'NSWERED, adj. *risposto*, *v.* To answer.

A'NSWERER, s. *rispondutore*, s. m. *che risponde*.

A'NSWERING, s. *il rispondere, risposta*, s. f.

ANT, s. [an emet] *formica*, s. f.

A little ant, *formichetta*.

Ant-hill, or nest, *formicajo*, s. m. *luogo dove le formiche si radunano*.

ANTAGO'NIST, s. [an adversary] *avversario, rivale, antagonista*, s. m.

ANTA'RCTICK, adj. *antartico*.

The antarctick pole, *il polo antartico*.

ANTECE'DENT, adj. [foregoing] *antecedente, precedente*.

Antecedent [in grammar, is that word which the relative refers to] *antecedente*, s. m.

Antecedent [in logick, is the former part of the syllogism or argument] *antecedente*.

ANTECE'SSOR, s. [one that goes before] *antecessore*, s. m.

ANTEDA'TE, s. [an older date than ought to be] *antidata*, s. f.

To ANTEDA'TE [to date a letter or any other writing before the time] *antidatare*.

ANTEDILU'VIAN, adj. [whatever was before Noah's flood] *tutto ciò che fu prima del diluvio, antediluviano*.

ANTEDILU'VIANS, s. [those generations from Adam that were before the flood] *popoli che furono prima del diluvio*.

ANTELO'PE, s. [a kind of deer having strait wreathed horns] *spezie di cervo*.

ANTEMERI'DIAN, adj. [belonging to the time before noon] *antimeridiano*.

ANTEME'TICKS, s. [medicines which stop vomiting] *rimedi antimetici, che sono buoni contro'l vomito*.

A'NTEPAST, s. [afore past] *antipasto*, s. m.

ANTEPENU'LTIMA, s. [the third syllable of a word from the last] *antipenultima*, s. f.

To ANTEPO'NE [to set before, to prefer] *antiporre, preferire*.

ANTE'RIOR, adj [that is before the former] *anteriore*.

ANTERIO'RITY, s. [priority of time] *anteriorità, preferenza*, s. f.

A'NTHEM, s. [a sacred song] *antifona*, s. f.

ANTHO'NIANS, s. [an order of monks founded by St. Anthony] *religiosi dell' ordine di Sant' Antonio.*

St. Anthony's fire, *risipola*, s. f. *fuoco di Sant' Antonio.*

ANTICHA'MBER, s. [the chamber next to the bed-chamber] *anticamera.*

A'NTICHRIST, s. [an adversary to Christ, a seducer] *anticristo.*

ANTICHRI'STIAN, adj. [of or belonging to Antichrist] *anticristiano.*

ANTICHRI'STIANISM, s. [the principles or practices of Antichrist] *anticristianismo.*

To ANTI'CIPATE [to do a thing before the proper time comes] *anticipare, vantaggiarsi nel tempo in fare che che si sia.*

ANTICIPA'TED, adj. *anticipato.*

ANTICIPA'TING, s. } [the act of an
ANTICIPA'TION, s. } ticipating] *anticipazione*, s. f. *l'anticipare.*

ANTICIPA'TOR, s. *anticipatore*, s. m. *chi anticipa.*

ANTI'DATE, s. *antidata.*

To ANTIDA'TE [to date a letter or any other writing with an anterior date] *antidatare.*

ANTI'CK, s. *anticaglia*, s. f. *nome generico di cose antiche, come edifici, inscrizioni, statue, medaglie, e loro frammenti.*

A'ntick [a buffoon, a juggler] *buffone, giullare.*

He is a mere antick, *egli è un vero buffone, o un pretto giullare.*

To dance anticks, *ballare con abiti grotteschi.*

Antic work, or antics [several odd figures, or shapes of men, birds, or beasts, rudely done according to the fancy of the artificer] *grottesca, sorta di pittura licenziosa, fatta a capriccio per ornamento di luoghi non rapaci di pittura più bella.*

A'NTICOR, s. [a disease in horses] *anticuore*, s. m.

ANTIDO'TE, [a counter-poison] *antidoto, contravveleno*, s. m.

ANTILO'PE, s. *v.* Antelope.

ANTIMONA'RCHICAL, adj. [that is against monarchy or kingly government] *contrario o avverso al governo d'un solo, antimonarchico, republicano.*

A'NTIMONY, s. [a mineral consisting of a sort of sulphureous and metallick substance] *antimonio*, s. m. *minerale col quale si purga l'oro ; e costa d'una sostanza sulfurea e metallica.*

ANTIPA'THICAL, adj. [belonging to antipathy] *appartenente ad antipatia, antipatico.*

ANTI'PATHY, s. [contrariety of natural qualities betwixt some creatures and things, a natural aversion] *antipatia*, s. f. *avversione o contrarietà che hanno le cose tra di loro.*

ANTIPERI'STASIS, s. [a certain invigoration of any quality by its being environed in by its contrary] *antiperistasis*, s. f.

ANTI'PHONE, s. [anthem] *antifona*, s. f.

ANTI'PHONER, s. [a book of anthems] *antifonario*, s. m. *libro, dove sono scritte le antifone.*

ANTI'PHRASIS, s. [a figure, where a word has a meaning contrary to its original sense] *antifrase*, s. f.

A'NTIPODES, s. [such inhabitants of the earth as live feet to feet, or diametrically opposite one to another] *antipodi*, s. m. *abitatori delle parti della terra, opposte nel globo alle nostre.*

ANTIPO'PE, s. [a false pope chosen by a particular faction against one duly elected] *antipapa ; papa fatto contra'l papa vero e legitimo.*

ANTI'PTOSIS, s. [a figure in grammar, where one case of a noun is put for another] *antiptosi*, s. f. *figura gramaticale per la quale si mette un caso per l'altro.*

A'NTIQUARY, s. [one that is well skilled or applies himself to the study of antiquity, or ancient medals and coins] *antiquario*, s. m. *colui che attende alla cognizione delle cose antiche.*

To A'NTIQUATE [to abolish or repeal] *abolire, annullare.*

ANTIQUA'TED, adj. *abolito, annullato.*

ANTIQUA'TION, s. [an abrogating or leaving off the use of] *abolimento*, s. m. *annullazione*, s. f.

ANTI'QUITY, s. [ancientness] *antichità*, s. f.

ANTISABBATA'RIANS, s. [a sect who deny the sabbath] *settari che negano che si debba osservare il sabbato.*

ANTISCORBU'TICKS, s. [remedies against the scurvy] *rimedi contro lo scorbuto.*

ANTI'THESIS, s. [a rhetorical figure] *antitesi*, s. f.

ANTIVENE'REAL MEDICINES [such as are good against the French pox] *medicine antivenéree, che sono buone contro il mal venereo.*

A'NTLERS, s. [branches of a stag's horn] *corna picciole del cervo, quelle che attraversano le grandi.*

ANTOCO'W, s. [a swelling in the breast of a horse] *anticuore*, s. m. *malattia di cavallo.*

ANTONOMA'SIA, s. [a trope in rhetorick, when the proper name of one thing is applied to several others] *antonomasia*, s. f.

A'NVIL, s. [a tool on which smiths hammer their works] *incude, incudine*, s. f.

A rising anvil [a goldsmith's tool] *incude a due corna.*

The stock of an anvil, *il piede della incudine.*

ANXI'ETY, s. [vexation, trouble of mind] *ansietà, travaglio d'animo*, s. m. *tribolazione*, s. f.

A'NXIOUS, adj. [careful, sorrowful] *ansioso, pieno d'ansietà.*

Anxious cares, *cure mordaci.*

A'NY, adj. or pron. *chiunque, ognuno, qualunque.*

Any thing, *ogni cosa, che che si sia.*

There was never any doubt of it, *non si fatto mai dubbio veruno di cio.*

Have you any thing to say to me? *avete nulla a dirmi?*

He was as much beloved as any man, *era amota al pari di chi si sia.*

If you provoke me any more, *se state a provocarmi di nuovo, se mi provocate ancora.*

Is there any hope of his recovery? *v' è egli luogo da sperare della sua vita?*

In any place, *ovunque si sia.*

Any thing pleases me, *m'appago d'ogni cosa.*

I would do any thing to oblige you, *farei mari e mondi per servirvi ; farei tutto per servirvi.*

Was ever any thing richer than this? *chi vide mai cosa più ricca?*

Any time this week, *un giorno di questa settimana.*

I know not any of them, *non ne conosco nessuno.*

Will you have any? *ne volete?*

Have you any? *ne avete?*

Any thing you shall think fit, *ogni cosa che v'aggradi.*

Command me in any thing rather than this, *da questa cosa in fuori mi comandi a sua posta.*

I love it above any thing, *l'amo sopra modo.*

I would not do it for any man living, *non lo farei per persona vivente.*

Any where, *dovunque.*

I'll go any where, *anderò per tutto.*

Do you know any man that understands it? *conoscere qualcuno che l'intenda?*

Any but you, *ogni altro che voi.*

He must be there, if he be any where, *non puo esser altrove che lì.*

Without any more ado, *senza altra cerimonia.*

If any one asks for me, *se qualcuno domanda di me.*

At any time, *ogni volta che, quando.*

Come at any time, and you shall find me at home, *venite quando volete e mi troverete a casa.*

If at any time I should come to meet him, *se mai l'incontrassi.*

Any thing of a gentleman would scorn to do so, *un uomo onorato avrebbe vergogna di fare una cosa simile.*

If money will do it, I shall not come short of any, *se si potrà fare a forza di danari, non me ne mancheranno.*

Any how, *come si voglia.*

Do it any how, *fatelo come voleto, fatelo come v'aggrada.*

Any more, *più.*

Will you have any more? *ne volete più?*

Any farther, *più oltre.*

Will you go any farther? *volete andare oltre?*

Have you any farther orders for me? *avete altro a comandarmi?*

Any longer, *più lungo tempo.*

I will not stay any longer, *non voglio restar più lungo tempo.*

Without any great trouble, *senza molta fatica.*

In caſe there be any neceſſity for it, *caſo che la neceſſità lo richiegga.*
Any whither, *dovunque*
Are you going any whither? *dove andate?*
Any one, *ognuno, ciaſcheduno.*
His purſe is open to any one, *la ſua borſa è aperta ad ognuno.*
Any while, *qualche tempo.*
Do you ſtay there any while? *ſtarete lì per qualche tempo?*
Any where elſe, *altrove.*
He cannot be any where elſe, *non può eſſer altrove.*
I'll go with you any where elſe but there, *anderò dove volete fuor che là*
APA'CE, adv. *preſto, preſtamente, velocemente, forte.*
To walk apace, *camminar preſto, andar di buon paſſo.*
To read apace, *legger preſto.*
To ſpeak apace, *parlare ſpeditamente, con franchezza.*
The ſhip ſails apace, *il vaſcello va a vele gonfie.*
It rains apace, *piove forte, diluvia.*
The night comes on apace, *la notte s'avvanza,*
APA'RT, adv. *da parte, da canto, in disparte, da banda.*
To ſet or lay apart, *metter da parte, da canto.*
To ſpeak with one apart, *parlare ad uno in disparte.*
To ſtand apart, *ſtare da banda.*
APA'RTMENT, s. [part of a houſe] *appartamento,* s. m. *aggregato di più ſtanze.*
A'PATHY, s. [freedom from all paſſions, indolence] *inſenſibilità, impoſſibilità, indolenza, apatia.*
APE, s. [a monkey] *ſcimia.*
You ape, go, *va via brutta ſcimia.*
A little ape, *uno ſcimiotto,* s. m.
A large ape, *ſcimione,* s. m. *ſcimia grande.*
To APE one, *contraffare uno, imitarlo, far come lui, far la ſcimia ad uno.*
APE'PSIE, s. [bad digeſtion] *cattiva digeſtione, indigeſtione.*
A'PER, s. [a kind of fiſh] *porco marino, ſorta di peſce.*
A'PERTLY, adv. [openly] *apertamente, chiaramente, manifeſtamente, paleſemente, alla ſvelata.*
APE'RITIVE, adj. *apertivo, aperitivo.*
A'PEX, s. [the top, point, or uppermoſt part of any thing] *cima, creſta, ſommità,* s. f. *apice,* s. m.
A'PHORISM, s. [a ſhort ſelect ſentence] *aforiſmo,* s. m. *maſſima, ſentenza,* s. f.
A'PIARY, s. [a place where bees are kept, a bee-hive] *arnia,* s. f. *caſſetta da pecchie.*
A'PISH, adj *che ha della ſcimia.*
An apiſh trick, *giulleria, buffoneria.*
A'PISHLY, adv. *giullereſcamente, buffoneſcamente, da giullare.*
A'PISHNESS, s. *giulleria, azione, giullereſca, buffoneria.*
APOCALY'PSE, s. [a revelation or viſion, the revelation of St. John] *apocaliſſe,* s. f. *uno de libri della ſagra ſcrittura.*
APOCALY'PTICAL, adj. [belonging to a viſion or revelation] *appartenente all' apocaliſſe.*
APO'COPE, s. [a figure in grammar, wherein the laſt letter or ſyllable is cut off] *apocope,* s. f. *figura grammaticale, che toglie via l'ultima lettera o ſillaba.*
APO'CHRYPHA, s. [certain books of doubtful authority, which are not received into the canon of the holy writ] *libri apocrifi.*
APO'CRYPHAL, adj. [doubtful] *apocrifo, non autentico.*
APO'LOGER, s. m. *apologiſta,* s. m. *ſcrittore d'una apologia.*
APOLO'GETICAL } adj. [belonging
APOLOGE'TICK } to an apology] *apologetico, difenſivo.*
An apologetick oration, *diſcorſo apologetico.*
APO'LOGIST, s. [that makes an apology] *apologiſta,* s. m. *ſcrittore di apologie.*
To APOLOGI'SE [to make one's defence] *fare un apologia, difenderſi, ſtolparſi, giuſtificarſi.*
APOLO'GUE [a moral tale, an inſtructive fable] *ſtorietta, favola morale,* s. f. *apologo,* s. m.
APO'LOGY, s. [defence, excuſe] *apologia, difeſa,* s. f.
To make an apology for one, *fare un apologio per uno, giuſtificarlo, defender la ſua opinione o condotta.*
APO'PHTHEGM, s. [a ſhort witty ſentence] *apotemma,* s. f. *detto ſpiritoſo o ſottile.*
APOPLE'CTICAL } adj. [belonging
APOPLE'CTICK } to, or ſubject to an apoplexy] *apopletico, attenente all' apopleſſia, infermo d' apopleſſia.*
APOPLE'XY, s. [a diſeaſe that ſuddenly ſurpriſes the brain, and takes away all manner of ſenſe and motion] *apopleſia,* s. f. *impedimento de' nervi di tutto 'l corpo con privazione del ſenſo e del moto.*
To fall into an apoplexy, *eſſere ſorpreſo d' apopleſſia.*
To die of an apoplexy, *morir d' apopleſſia.*
APO'RIA, s. [a figure by which the ſpeaker doubts where to begin] *figura retorica, e ſi dire quando l'oratore moſtra dubbio del dove abbia a cominciare.*
APOSIO'PESIS, s. [a form of ſpeech by which the ſpeaker, through ſome affection or vehemency, breaks off his ſpeech] *figura retorica, per cui l'oratore ſul caldo del diſcorſo finiſce ſubitanamente di parlare.*
APO'STASY, s. [revolt from the true religion] *apoſtaſia,* s. f. *ſpartimento dalla ſtato, dalla fede, dall' obedienza, e dalla vera religione.*
APO'STATE, s. [one that renounces the true religion, a back-ſlider, a renegado] *apoſtata, quello o quella che laſcia la vera fede e la ſua religione.*
To APOSTATI'ZE [to renounce the true religion] *apoſtatare, laſciare o partire dalla vera religione.*
APOSTE'MA } s. [impoſthume, abſ-
APOSTE'ME } ceſs] *apoſtema, poſtema,* s. f.
APO'STLE, s. *appoſtolo,* s. m. *nome principalmente de' dodici nunzi di Geſù, Criſto.*
APO'STLESHIP } s. [the dignity,
APO'STOLATE } miniſtry or office of an apoſtle] *apoſtolato,* s. m. *dignità, grado o ufficio d'apoſtolo.*
APO'STOLICAL } adj. [belonging
APOSTO'LIC } to, or deriving authority from the apoſtles] *apoſtolico.*
APOSTO'LICALLY, adv. *appoſtolicamente.*
APO'STROPHE, s. [an accent or mark, ſhewing that there is a vowel cut off, expreſſed thus (')], *apoſtrofo,* s. m. *contraſſegno di mancamento di lettera, ſegnato così* (')
APO'STROPHE, s. [in rhetorick, a diverſion of ſpeech to another perſon, than the ſpeech appointed did intend or require] *apoſtrofe, figura retorica, che fa rivolgere ſubitanamente il parlar dell' oratore dalla perſona o coſa a cui era naturalmente diretto ad altra perſona o coſa.*
To APOSTROPHI'ZE, *volgere il diſcorſo improvviſamente e inaſpettamente ad altra perſona.*
APO'THECARY, s. *ſpeziale,* s. m.
An apothecary's ſhop, *bottega di ſpeziale.*
A'POZEM, s. [a medicinal decoction of herbs, flowers, roots, barks, and the like] *decozione medicinale fatta d'erbe, fiori, raddici, ſcorze, e ſimili,*
To APPA'LL [to daunt, to aſtoniſh, to diſcourage] *ſtupefare, atterire, ſpaventare, ſcoraggiare, ſbigottire, ſgomentare.*
APPA'LLED, adj. *ſtupefatto, atterrito, ſpaventato, ſbigottito, ſgomentato.*
APPA'LEMENT, s. [dauntneſs, aſtoniſhment] *ſtupore, ſpavento, terrore, ſbigottimento.*
APPANA'GE, v. Appenage.
APPA'REL, s. [habit, cloathing] *addobbamento, abbigliamento, ornamento, veſtito, veſtimento,* s. m.
To be in a white apparel, *eſſer veſtito di bianco.*
To APPA'REL, *addobbare, ornare, abbigliare.*
APPA'RELLED, adj. *addobbato, ornato, abbigliato.*
Apparelled gallantly, *veſtito o abbigliato di gala.*
Apparelled meanly, *veſtito poveramente.*
Apparelled in mourning, *veſtito di bruno, veſtito a lutto.*
APPA'RELMENT, s. *ex.* Apparelment of war, *preparativi di guerra.*
APPA'RENT, adj. [evident, manifeſt, plain] *apparente, evidente, chiaro, manifeſto.*
The apparent heir of the crown, *l'erede legitimo della corona.*
Apparent tokens of wickedneſs, *ſegni manifeſti di malizia.*
An apparent crime, *un delitto enorme.*
It is apparent, *è chiaro; certa coſa è.*
I'll make it apparent to you, *ve lo farò toccar con mani, ve lo proverò.*

APPA'RENTLY, adv. *apparentemente, evidentemente, chiaramente, manifestamente.*
APPA'RENTNESS, s. *chiarezza, evidenza,* s. f.
APPARI'TION, s. [the appearing of a ſpirit] *apparizione,* s. f.
APPA'RITOR, s. [one that ſummons offenders, and ſerves the proceſs in a ſpiritual court] *bidello, curſore,* s. m. *ſergente che porta altrui le notificazioni de' loro ordini.*
APPA'RTMENT, s. [lodgings] *appartamento,* s. m.
To APPA'Y [to convince] *appagare, ſoddisfare all' altrui volontà, contentare, convincere.*
Well appayed, *ſoddisfatto.*
Ill appayed, *mal ſoddisfatto.*
To APPE'ACH, *v.* to impeach, and all its derivatives.
To APPE'AL [to make an appeal] *appellare, domandare, e chieder nuovo giudicio a giudice ſuperiore.*
I appeal to the parliament, *appello al parlamento.*
I appeal to you, *me ne ſtarò al voſtro parere, ne fo giudice voi.*
To appeal, *appellare, incolpare, accuſare.*
APPE'AL, s. [the act of removing a cauſe from an inferior judge or court to a ſuperiour] *appellagione, appellazione,* s. f.
Without further appeal, *ſenza appellazione.*
Appeal [law term, the act of accuſing an accomplice] *accuſazione,* s. f. *accuſamento, l'incolpare che fa un reo il ſuo complire.*
APPEA'LED, adj. *appellato, incolpato.*
APPEA'LANT, or APPEALER, s. *appellante,* s. m. *chi appella.*
APPEA'LING, s. *appellazione,* s. f. *l'appellare.*
To APPE'AR, [to be in ſight, to ſhow one's ſelf] *apparire, farſi vedere, preſentarſi alla viſta altrui, comparire, moſtrarſi.*
The day begins to appear, *il giorno comincia a ſpuntare.*
The ſun begins to appear, *il ſole ſpunta.*
To appear in publick, *farſi vedere in pubblico.*
To appear in the world, *apparire, far pompa, far figura nel mondo, moſtrarſi al mondo.*
An angel appeared to him in a dream, *un angelo gli apparve in ſogno.*
To appear before the judge, *comparire innanzi al giudice.*
As far as can appear by what is written, *per quel che ſi può vedere dalle ſcritture.*
I'll make it appear to be true, *vi moſtrerò che è vero; farovvi toccar con mano che è la verità; vi proverò ch' è così.*
It appears by this, *da ciò s'argomenta; ſi vede da queſto.*
To appear openly, *eſſer manifeſto o evidente.*
To appear [to peep up] *ſpuntare, cominciare a naſcere, apparire, uſcir fuora, ſpuntare.*

The beard begins to appear in his face, *la barba gli ſpunta.*
You made appear on ſeveral occaſions your good will towards me, *in molte occaſioni ella m'ha dato ſaggio della ſua buona volontà.*
To appear above ground, *ſpuntare, cominciare a creſcere.*
To appear above water, *ſorgere, levarſi ſul l'acqua.*
To appear for another, *comparire per un altro, favorirlo, pigliar la ſua parte.*
To appear againſt one, *opporſi ad uno, eſſer contro lui.*
To appear as through a glaſs, *traſparire, tralúcere.*
To appear [to get over] *ſporgerſi, uſcir del piano o del perpendicolo.*
To begin to appear, *ſpuntare.*
It appears, *pare, è chiaro, è manifeſto, ſi vede.*
To appear [to ſeem, to look] *parere, ſembrare, apparire.*
It appears to me as if it would rain, *mi pare che voglia piovere.*
APPE'ARANCE, s. [outſide, ſhow] *apparenza,* s. f. *eſteriore, aſpetto,* s. m.
A fine woman in appearance, *una bella donna in apparenza.*
Appearance [likelihood] *apparenza, probabilità, veriſimilitudine.*
There's no appearance of truth, *non v' è apparenza di verità, non è veriſimile.*
At firſt appearance, *a prima viſta.*
The appearance of a perſon, *l'apparenza, la preſenza, lo aſpetto d'una perſona.*
Appearance [figure] *sfoggio,* s. m. *compariſcenza.*
He makes great appearance at court, *fa grande sfoggio in corte.*
Appearance [pretence] *preteſto, colore,* s. m. *apparenza, finzione, ſimulazione.*
Appearance [viſion] *apparizione,* s. f. *apparimento,* s. m.
At the firſt appearance of the king, *al ſubito apparir del re.*
Appearance [concourſe of people] *concorſo, moltitudine.*
There was a great appearance at court, *vi fu gran concorſo di gente in corte.*
Appearance in a court of juſtice, *comparſa dinanzi un magiſtrato.*
A day of appearance, *giorno di comparſa.*
The laſt day of appearance, *termine perentorio.*
Default of appearance, *contumacia.*
To make one's appearance at court, *comparire in giuſtizia.*
To be bound for one's appearance, *obligarſi in iſcritto di preſentarſi in giuſtizia.*
Perſonal appearance, *comparſa perſonale.*
APPE'ARED, adj. *apparſo, comparſo.*
APPE'ARING, s. *apparizione,* s. f. *l'apparire.*
To APPE'ASE [to allay, to aſſwage, to pacify] *placare, mitigare, raddolcire, quietare, chetare, aquetare.*
To appeaſe one's wrath, *placare lo ſdegno.*

To appeaſe grief, *raddolcire il dolore.*
To appeaſe a child, *quietare un fanciullo.*
To appeaſe [to expiate] *eſpiare, renderſi proprizio, placare.*
APLEA'SED, adj. *placato, mitigato, raddolcito, quietato.*
APPE'ASABLE, adj. *placabile.*
Not APPE'ASABLE, *implacabile,*
APPE'ASER, s. [he that appeaſes] *quello che placa, interceſſore; colui che acqueta tumulti.*
APPE'ASING, s. *il placare.*
APPE'ASEMENT, s. *il placare, l'acquetare.*
APPELLA'TION, s. [a calling or naming of any thing by a particular name] *nome,* s. m. *appellazione,* s. f. *l'appellare.*
APPE'LLATIVE, adj. *appellativo.*
Noun appellative, *nome appellativo.*
APPE'LLATE, or APPELLE'E, s. [one that is appealed or accuſed] *un accuſato, una perſona accuſata di qualche delitto.*
APPE'LLANT } s. [one who having APPE'LLOUR } confeſſed a crime, appeals, that is, accuſes others that were his accomplices] *uno, che dopo aver confeſſato un delitto, accuſa gli altri complici.*
APPE'LLOUR [challenger, one that challenges another to fight] *sfidatore,* s. m. *colui che sfida a duello.*
APPE'NDAGE, s. [a thing that being conſidered as a leſs principal is added to another] *dipendenza,* s. f. *coſa che dipende.*
APPE'NDANT, adj. [belonging to, acceſſory] *dipendente, che dipende, appartenente ad altra coſa.*
To APPE'NDICATE [to add to another thing] *aggiungere a una coſa, far un appendice.*
APPE'NDIX, s. [a ſupplement to a treatiſe by way of addition or illuſtration] *appendice.* s. f.
Appendix [an addition of itſelf to any thing] *appendice, dipendenza,* s. f.
APPE'NNAGE, s. [appanage; the portion of a ſovereign prince given to his younger children] *piatto,* s. m. *quella porzione che i principi danno di loro ſecondogeniti per il loro mantenimento.*
To APPERTAI'N [to belong] *appartenere, convenirſi, richiederſi.*
APPE'RTENANCE, s. [a thing belonging to another thing that is more principal, as courts, yards, drains to a houſe] *appartenenza, attenenza,* s. f.
APPE'TENCY, s. [earneſt deſire, great inclination] *appetizione, brama,* s. f. *l' appetire, appetito, ardente deſiderio,* s. m.
APPE'TIBLE, adj. [deſirable] *appetibile, da eſſere appetito.*
APPE'TITE, s. [any natural inclination, the affection of the mind, by which we are incited to any thing] *appetito,* s. m. *parte ſenſitiva e concupiſcibile dell' anima, la quale deſidera oggetto che le piaccia.*
Appetite [inordinate deſire, luſt] *appetito,* s. m *deſiderio sfrenato.*
I have loſt my appetite, *ho perſo l'appetito, ſono ſvogliato.*

Gluttonous appetite, *ingordigia.*
APPE'TITIVE, adj. [belonging to the appetite or desire] *appetitoso, appetitivo.*
To APPLA'UD [to commend highly, to approve well] *applaudire, lodare.*
APPLA'UDED, adj. *applaudito, lodato.*
APPLA'USE, s. *applauso,* s. m. *segno di festa e di letizia, e fassi col picchiar le mani, e con simili atti.*
To court popular applause, *andare in traccia dell' aura popolare.*
A'PPLE, s. [all sorts of round fruits, both of trees and herbs] *pomo,* s. m. *il frutto d'ogni albero o pianta quando è tondo.*
Apple [a well known fruit] *mela,* s. f. *frutto del melo.*
A summer or winter-apple, *mela di state o di verno.*
Apple-parings, or parings of apples, *scorze di mele.*
The apple of the eye, *la pupilla dell' occhio.*
An apple core, *il cuore d'una mela.*
Apple-tree, *melo,* s. m. *arbore che produce le mele.*
Apple-monger or seller, *venditore di mele.*
APPLE-WO'MAN, s. *donna che vende mele.*
Apple-loft, s. *luogo dove si conservano le mele.*
Apple-yard, *pometo, pomario,* s. m. *luogo pieno d'alberi pomiferi.*
Bearing apples, *pomifero, che produce mele.*
Mad-apple, *mela salvatica.*
Apple of love [a plant] *sorta di pianta.*
APPLICABI'LITY, s. *facoltà di ricevere applicazione.*
A'PPLICABLE, adj. [that may be apply'd, that has relation, or is conformable] *applicabile, che si puo applicare o appropriare; conforme.*
A'PPLICATE, s. [a right line drawn across a curve, so as to direct the diameter] *applicato, linea retta tirata a traverso una curva onde si divida il diametro in due.*
APPLICA'TION, s. [care, diligence, attention of mind] *applicazione, attenzione,* s. f.
Application [the act of applying or making an address to a person] *ricorso, rifugio,* s. m.
To make one's application to one, *ricorrere, aver ricorso ad uno, rifuggire ad uno.*
To APPLY' [to put, set, or lay one thing to another] *applicare, adattare, porre.*
To apply a plaster, *applicare un impiastro.*
To apply the signification of a word to the meaning of the author, *applicare la significazione d'una parola alla intenzion dell' autore.*
To apply [to have recourse to a thing or person] *ricorrere, aver ricorso, rifuggire, andare a chiedere ajuto o difesa ad alcuno.*
You must apply to him for it, *bisogna ricorriate a lui per questo.*
To apply [to betake one's self] *applicarsi, addarsi, impiegarsi.*

To apply one's mind to philosophy, *applicarsi alla filosofia.*
He apply'd his mind to painting, *era tutto intento alla pittura; si diede a far il pittore.*
APPLY'D, *applicato, intento, addato.*
APPLY'ING, s. *applicazione,* s. f. *l' applicare.*
To APPO'INT [to ordain] *ordinare, commettere, imporre.*
To appoint [to design, to determine] *destinare, deputare, assegnare, constituire, stabilire.*
To appoint a tutor to one's children, *destinare, o assegnare un tutore a' propri figliuoli.*
Do you appoint a place, and I shall be there, *stabilite un luogo ed io mi ci troverò.*
To appoint in another's place, *sostituire, mettere uno in luogo d'altrui o suo.*
To appoint bounds, *terminare, limitare.*
I appointed to meet him to day, *gli ho promesso d'esser con lui oggi, abbiamo stabilito d'essere insieme oggi.*
APPO'INTED, adj. *destinato, deputato, assegnato, constitutio, stabilito.*
It is so appointed by nature, *ha natura così stabilito.*
At the time appointed, *all' ora fissa.*
In God's appointed time, *quando piacerà a Dio, quando Dio vorrà.*
APPO'INTMENT, s. [order] *ordine, mandato,* s. m. *regola,* s. f.
I come to you according to your appointment, *vengo da voi secondo che m' avete comandato.*
Appointment [assignation] *assegnamento, ordine dato.*
They have made an appointment to go out of town together, *hanno deliberato d'andare in villa insieme.*
To APPO'RTION [to divide into convenient portions, to portion] *proporzionare, dividere in parti eguali.*
APPO'RTIONED, adj. *proporzionato, egualmente diviso.*
APPO'RTIONMENT, s. [the act of dividing into parts] *il proporzionare; eguale distribuzione.*
To APPO'SE [to examine] *esaminare, considerare, ventilare.*
APPO'SED, adj. *esaminato, considerato.*
APPO'SER, s. *esaminatore,* s. m.
A'PPOSITE, adj. *addato, atto, congruo, acconcio.*
A'PPOSITELY, adv. *propriamente, congruamente, acconciamente.*
To APPRA'ISE [to rate] *apprezzare, stimare, giudicare il pregio e la valuta d' una cosa, valutare.*
APPRAI'SED, adj. *apprezzato, stimato, valutato.*
APPRAI'SING, s. *il valutare, l'apprezzare la valuta d'una cosa.*
APPRAI'SER, s. *quelli che apprezza, o valuta una cosa.*
To APPREHE'ND [to lay hold of, to seize] *prendere, arrestare, fermar per forza.*
To apprehend unawares, *sorprendere improvvisamente.*
To apprehend a malefactor, *far prigione un malfattore.*

To apprehend [to fear] *temere, aver paura, essere oppresso da timore.*
To apprehend [to conceive] *comprendere, capire, conoscere, intendere.*
APPRE'HENDED, adj. *preso, arrestato, fatto prigione,* v. To apprehend.
APPRE'HENDING, s. *il prendere.*
APPRE'HENSION, s. [understanding, conception] *comprendimento, intendimento, intelletto,* s. m. *intelligenza, sagacità naturale,* s. f.
A boy of a quick or good apprehension, *un giovane d'acuto intendimento.*
He is dull of apprehension, *egli è d'ottuso ingegno.*
According to my apprehension, *a mio parere, in quanto al mio credere.*
Apprehension [fear, jealousy] *timore,* s. m. *paura,* s. f. *sospetto,* s. m.
APPRE'HENSIVE, adj. [quick of apprehension] *atto ad apprendere, d'acuto ingegno.*
I never saw a boy more apprehensive, *non vidi mai un giovane che apprendesse le cose meglio di lui.*
Apprehensive [fearful] *timoroso, timido.*
Apprehensive of danger, *che teme il pericolo*
We were apprehensive of his death, *eravamo in gran timore della sua morte, temevamo morisse.*
APPRE'HENSIVELY, adv. *timorosamente, con timore.*
APPRE'HENSIVENESS, s. [fear] *timore, sospetto,* s. m. *paura,* s. f.
APPRE'NTICE, s. [a learner, one bound by law to learn an art] *garzone, giovane che impara qualche mestiere, ed è obligato di servire il suo maestro per un certo numero d'anni.*
APPRE'NTISHIP, s. *il tempo che un giovane è obbligato di servire il suo padrone coma garzone, garzonato.*
To APPRE'TIATE [to set a high value or esteem upon any thing] *apprezzare, avere in pregio, fare stima, stimare.*
APPRO'ACH, s. [the act of drawing near] *l'atto d'avvicinarsi.*
Appróach [access] *accesso, adito, entrata libera.*
Appróach [hostile advances] *l'avanzarsi d'un nemico.*
Appróach [means of advancing] *modo di avanzarsi.*
To have an approach to one, *aver adito o entrata a qualcheduno.*
To APPRO'ACH [to draw nigh, to come near] *approcciare, approssimarsi, appressarsi, accostarsi.*
The night approaches, *la notte s'avvanza, il giorno s'abbassa.*
APPRO'ACHABLE, adj. *accessibile, da ottersegli, accostare.*
APPRO'ACHED, adj. *approcciato, approssimato, appressato, accostato.*
APPRO'ACHES, s. [all the works, whereby the besiegers approach to the besieged] *approccio,* s. m. *quel ramo di trincea, che si fa per accostarsi coperto alle fortificazioni del nemico.*
APPRO'ACHLESS, adj. *inaccessibile.*
APPROBA'TION, s. [liking, approving] *approbazione,* s. f. *approvamento,* s. m.

To

To Appro'perate [to haften] *affrettare, sollecitare.*

To Appropi'nquate [to draw nigh unto] *appropinquarsi, appressarsi, avvicinarsi.*

To Appro'priate [to ufurp the property of a thing] *appropiare, appropriare, appropriarsi, attribuirsi, far proprio, recare in proprietà.*

Appro'priated, adj. *appropiato appropriato.*

Appropria'tion, s. *appropriazione*, s. f. *l'appropriarsi una cosa.*

To Appro've [to like, to allow of] *approvare, giudicar per buono, tener per buono o per vero, ricevere, accettare, lodare.*

I am glad you approve of what I have done, *godo che voi approviate quel ch' ho fatto; godo che quel ch' ho fatto sia di vostro gusto.*

To approve one's felf to God, *rendersi accetto a Dio.*

To approve one's felf to one, *far cosa grata a qualcheduno, incontrare il genio di qualcuno.*

Not to approve of a thing, *biasimare, avere a male una cosa, non approvarla.*

To approve land [in law, to improve it, to increafe it] *migliorare, coltivare un pezzo di terra.*

Appro'ved, or Appro'ved of, adj. *approvato, ricevuto, accettato, lodato.*

An approved author, *un autore approvato o stimato, un autore d'autorità.*

A man of approved integrity, *un uomo di tutta integrità.*

Appro'vement, s. [in law, is the making the beft advantage of land, by improving and encreafing the rent] *miglioramento*, s. m. *il migliorare o fruttare un pezzo di terra.*

Appro'ver, s. [one that approves or allows of] *approvatore*, s. m. *che approva, che giudica per buona una cosa.*

Approver [in law, one who being guilty of felony, to fave himfelf accufes his accomplices] *un reo che per salvar se stesso accusa i suoi complici.*

Approxima'tion, s. [the act of coming or putting near] *approssimanza, approssimazione*, s. f. *lo avvicinare.*

Appu'rtenance, s. [that which appertains or belongs] *appartenenza, attenenza*, s. f.

Appurtenance of a lamb, *budellame d'un agnello.*

Apri'city, s. [fun-fhine] *luogo aprico.*

A'pricot, s. [a fort of fruit] *albicocco, bericuócolo*, s. m. *abicocca*, s. f.

Apricot-tree, s. *albero d'albicocco.*

A'pril, s. [the fourth month of the year] *Aprile*, s. m. *il quarto mese dell' anno.*

April fhowers bring forth May flowers, *le piogge d'Aprile producono i fiori di Maggio.*

When April blows his horn, 'tis good for hay and corn, *i tuoni d'Aprile pręsagiscono abbondanza.*

A'pron, s. [a garment which women wear before them] *grembiule*, s. m. *pezzo di panno lino o d'altra materia, che tengono dinanzi cinto le donne.*

Apt, adj. [convenient, meet, proper] *atto, proporzionato, acconcio, idoneo, sufficiente.*

Apt to do a thing, *atto o idoneo a fare una cosa.*

He is an apt fcholar, *egli è un uomo letterato.*

Apt to learn, *docile, atto ad apprendere gl' insegnamenti.*

Apt [inclined, bent] *inclinato, dedito, affezionato, inchinato, inchinevole, soggetto.*

Apt to be drunk, *dedito al vino.*

I am apt to fleep after dinner, *sono accostumato dormire dopo pranzo.*

I am apt to belive we fhall have a war, *mi do a credere che averemo la guerra.*

He is apt to commit fuch miftakes, *è molto soggetto a fare questi errori.*

Wine is apt to make me fick, *il vino m'è per lo più nocivo.*

We are too apt to believe thofe things that we ourfelves are guilty of, *noi siamo facili a credere quelle cose delle quali ci conosciamo colpevoli; chi ha sospetto ha difetto.*

Apt to break, *fragile, che agevolmente si rompe.*

A'ptitude, *facilità, attezza, naturale disposizione.*

A'ptly, adv. *attamente, accomodatamente, giustamente, acconciamente.*

A'ptness, s. [fitnefs, a natural difpofition to a thing] *attezza, facilità, dispostezza, disposizione di natura, che rende atto all' operazione.*

Aptnefs to good or evil, *buona, o cattiva indole.*

Aptnefs to learn, *docilità, attitudine ad apprendere.*

Aptnefs [activenefs] *attività, destrezza, accortezza, sagacità*, s. f.

Aqua fortis, *acqua forte.*

Aqua vitæ, *acqua arzente, arqua-vite.*

Aqua'rius, s. [one of the twelve figns of the Zodiack] *acquario*, s. m. *uno de' dodici segni del zodiaco.*

Aqua'tick, Aqua'tical, Aqua'tile } adj. [growing, living, or breeding moftly in or about the water] *aquatico, che cresce, vive, o sta nell' acqua, o presso l'acqua.*

A'queduct, s. [a conduit or pipe to convey water from one place to another] *aquidoccio, aquidotto, condotto*, s. m. *canal murato per lo quale si conduce l'acqua da luogo a luogo.*

A'queous, adj. [like water, waterifh] *acquoso, aqueo.*

Aquili'ne, adj. [refembling an eagle] *somigliante all' aquila. Applicato a naso significa naso a mo' di becco d'acquila, naso inarcato.*

Aquo'se, adj. *acquoso, pieno d'acqua, adacquato.*

A'rabick, s. [the language of Arabia] *l'Arabo*, s. m. *la lingua Araba, l'Arábico. Ariosto nell' Orlando*, Era fcritto in Arábico, *cioè in lingua Araba.*

Arabick, adj. [born in Arabia] *Arabo, nato in Arabia.*

A'rable, adj. [ploughable] *arabile, arconcio ad essere arato.*

Arable land, *terra arabile.*

Ara'neous, adj. [full of fpiders] *pieno di aragni o ragnateli.*

Ara'y, s. v. Array, and all its derivatives.

A'rbiter, s. [an arbitrator] *arbitro*, s. m. *giudice eletto dalle parti al quale volontariamente si sommettono.*

A'rbitrable, adj. [that may be put to arbitration] *da risolversi per arbitrato.*

A'rbitrably, adv. *ad arbitrio.*

Arbitrably punifhable, *da punirsi ad arbitrio del giudice.*

A'rbitrage, s. [the decree or fentence of an arbitrator or umpire] *arbitrato*, s. m. *giudicio d'arbitri.*

Arbitra'rily, adv. *arbitrariamente, ad arbitrio.*

A'rbitrary, adj. [abfolute, free] *arbitrario, assoluto, libero, che depende dall' altrui arbitrio.*

An arbitrary government, *un goverro arbitrario o assoluto.*

To A'rbitrate [to adjudge or act as an arbitrator, to award] *arbitrare, giudicare alcuna cosa ad arbitrio, aggiudicare.*

Arbitra'tion, s. [the act of arbitrating] *arbitrato*, s. m. *giudicio d'arbitri, l'arbitrare.*

To put a thing to arbitration, *compromettere una differenza all' arbitraria decisione d'altrui.*

Arbitra'tor, s. [an extraordinary judge chofen indifferently by mutual confent of two different parties, to decide a controverfy amongft them] *arbitro*, s. m. *giudice eletto dalle parti, per decidere una differenza senza procedere legalmente.*

A'rbitrement, s. [a power granted by the contending parties to the arbitrators to determine the matter in difpute] *arbitrato*, s. m. *giudicio d'arbitri.*

A'rbour, s. [a bower in a garden, a fhady place made by art to fit in] *pergola*, s. f. *pergolato*, s. m.

Arbo'reous, adj. [a term ufed by herbalifts of mufhrooms or moffes, which grow on trees, to diftinguifh them from fuch as grow on the ground] *d'arbore, che nasce d'albero, simile ad un albero, arboreo.*

A'rborist, s. [a perfon well fkilled in the feveral kinds and nature of trees] *uno chè s'intende e che conosce le differenti spezie degli alberi.*

A'rbustine, adj. [fhrubby] *epiteto che si da alla vite salvatica.*

Arbut-Tre'e, or Arbu'te-Tre'e, *rovo*, s. m.

The arbut-fruit, *pruni di rovo.*

A'rch, s. [bow] *arco*, s m. *stromento piegato a guisa di mezzo cerchio per uso di tirar frecce.*

Arch [in architecture, a hollow building raifed with a mould in the form of a femi-circle] *arco, mezzo cerchio*, s. m.

The arch of a bridge, *arco di ponto.*

 A tri-

A triumphant arch, *arco trionfale.*

The ſtarry arch [the ſky] *il cielo, il firmamento.*

Arch, adj. [arrant, or notorious] *aſtuto, deſtro, maliziato, maſcagno, ſcaltrito, ſottile, triſto, furbo, che ha della volpe.*

An arch-rogue, *un guidone, un furfante, un barone, un furbo.*

An arch-traitor, *un gran traditore, un traditoraccio.*

He is an arch blade, *egli è un gran furbaccio.*

E da notarſi, *che la particella* arch, *corriſponde alla noſtra* arci, *e s'aggiugne a molti altri nomi, e da loro forza di ſuperlativo o maggioranza, ex.* Archbiſhop, *Arciveſcovo. Notiſi ancora, che* Arch *quando precede vocale in voce compoſta, ſi pronuncia come ſi farebbe in Italiano* Arcangelo, *cioè colla* ci *dura; quando* Arch *precede conſonante allora ha il ſuono ſchiacciato di* ci *come in* Arciprete.

To ARCH, *archeggiare,* torcere, *piegare che che ſi ſia a guiſa d'arco, volgere; far la volta agli edifici.*

An arch-roof, *teſtuggine, la volta o il cielo della ſtanza.*

ARCHA'NGEL [the prince of angels] *arcangelo, ſpirito dell' ordine primiero degli angeli.*

Archangle [dead nettle] *ſpezie d'erba.*

ARCHBI'SHOP, s. [a chief biſhop] *arciveſcovo o arciveſco.*

ARCHBI'SHOPRICK, s. [the extent of the juriſdiction, and the benefice, dignity of an archbiſhop] *accriveſcovado,* s. m. *dignità ſuprema di chieſa metropolitana, e'l luogo dove l'arciveſcovo ha ſua giuridizione.*

ARCHDE'ACON, s. [a dignified clergyman] *arcidiacono, archidiacono,* s. m.

ARCHDE'ACONRY, s. [the extent of an archdeacon's ſpiritual juriſdiction] *archidiaconato, arcidiaconato,* s. m.

ARCHDU'KE, s. *arciduca,* s. m.

ARCHDU'KEDOM, s. *arciducato,* s. m.

ARCHDU'TCHESS, s. *arciducheſſa,* s. f.

A'RCHED, adj. *archeggiato, volto, fatto a volta.*

The arched ſkies, *il cielo, il firmamento.*

A'RCHER, s. [one ſkilled in archery] *arciere o arciero,* s. m. *tirator d'arco.*

A'RCHERY, s. [the art of ſhooting with the long bow] *l'arte di tirar l'arco.*

Water-archer, s. [herb] *ſagittaria,* s. f.

ARCHETY'PE, s. [the firſt example or pattern] *archetipo,* s. m.

ARCHETY'PAL, adj. [of or belonging to the original] *d'archetipo.*

ARCH-HE'RETICK, s. [a ring-leader of hereticks] *ereſiarca,* s. m. *capo e fondator d'eretica ſetta.*

A'RCHITECT, s. *architetto, architettore,* s. m.

Architect *dal volgo Ingleſe è anche chiamato colui il cui meſtiero è ſoprantendere a' muratori, e quegli che fa fabbricar caſe per proprio o per altrui conto, quantunque nulla ſappia di Barozzio e meno di Vitruvio.*

Architect [the contriver of any thing] *autore, inventore di checcheſſia.*

ARCHITECTO'NICAL, adj. [that belongs to architecture] *architettónico, attenente ad architettura.*

ARCHITE'CTURE, s. [the art of building] *architettura,* s. f. *l'arte dell' inventare e diſporre le forme degli edifici.*

ARCHI'TRAVE, s. m. *quel membro d'architettura che poſa immediatamente ſopra colonne o ſopra ſtipiti; architrave.*

ARCHI'VES, s. [a place where antient records, charters, and evidences are kept] *archivio,* s. m. *luogo dove ſi conſervano le ſcritture pubbliche.*

ARCH-PRIEST, s. [a chief-prieſt] *arciprete,* s. m.

Arch-Prieſt's office, *arcipreſbiterato,* s. m.

ARCHWI'SE, adv. *curvamente, a modo d'arco.*

A'RCTIQUE, or A'RTICK, adj. [northern, northward] *artico.*

The arctick pole and circle, *il polo e il circolo artico.*

ARCTU'RUS, s. [a fixed ſtar of the firſt magnitude in the ſkirt of Arctophylax] *arturo,* s. m. *una dell ſtelle del carro; ſegno celeſte.*

To A'RCUATE [to bend like an arch] *archeggiare,* torcere *o piegare che che ſia a guiſa d'arco.*

ARCUA'TION, s. [the act of ſhaping or faſhioning like an arch] *archeggiamento,* s. m. *l'archeggiare, lo eſſere piegato a mo' d'arco.*

A'RDENCY } s. [heat of paſſion,
A'RDENTNESS } zeal] *ardore, fervore, zelo, calore,* s. m. *violenza, paſſione,* s. f.

A'RDENT, adj. [eager, zealous] *ardente, fervido, fervente, ſollecito, veemente, appaſſionato.*

A'RDENTLY, adv. *ardentemente, con grande ardore, fervidamente, vivamente, veementemente, caldamente, appaſſionatamente.*

A'RDOUR, s. [heat, vehemency, eagerneſs] *ardore, deſiderio, calore,* s. m. *veemenza, paſſione,* s. f.

ARDU'ITY, s. [height, difficulty] *altezza ripida, difficoltà,* s. f.

A'RDUOUS, adj. [hard, difficult] *arduo, importante, difficile, malagevole, pieno di difficoltà, pieno di malagevolezza.*

ARE, *perſona del verbo,* to be, *ex.* we are, *noi ſiamo,* you are, *voi ſiete,* they are, *egline ſono.*

A'REA, s. [the ſuperficial content of any figure, meaſured in inches, feet, yards, &c.] *aja,* s. f. *ſuperficie d'uno ſpazio limitato.*

To ARE'AD [to adviſe, to direct] *dar conſiglio, dirigere.* Parad. Loſt.

ARENA'CEOUS, adj. *ſabbioſo, pien di ſabbia, arenoſo.*

ARENO'SE, adj. *ſabbioſo, arenoſo.*

ARE'NULOUS, adj. *che ha dell' arenoſo, pien di piccoli ſaſſolini come arena.*

AREO'TICK, adj. [ſuch medicines as open the pores] *areotiche medicine chiamanſi quelle che aprono i pori.*

A'RGENT, s. *argento, in aralderia è il color bianco.*

A'rgent [ſilver, bright like ſilver] *argento, lucido come argento.*

ARGENTI'NE, s. [a plant] *argentina,* s. f.

A'RGIL, s. [potters clay] *argilla, ſorte di creta uſata da pentolai.*

ARGILLA'CEOUS } adj. [clayey;
ARGI'LLOUS } conſiſting of argil, or potter's clay] *fatto di quella creta uſata da' pentolaj.*

ARGONA'UTS, s. [Jaſon's companions, who ſailed in the ſhip Argo] *Argonauti,* s. m. pl.

A'RGOSY, s. [from Argo, the name of Jaſon's ſhip; a large veſſel for merchandiſe, a carrack] *carracca,* s. f. *ſorta di vaſcello mercantile.*

To A'RGUE [to diſcourſe, to debate or diſpute] *arguire, argomentare, diſcorrere, diſputare, conteſtare, contraſtare.*

To argue [to ſhow, to make appear] *provare, confermare, moſtrar con ragioni, far vedere, conchiudere, ragionare, aprir ragioni, addur ragioni.*

What does that argue? s. *che volete inferire da ciò?*

That argues nothing, *cio non fa al caſo.*

A'RGUED, adj. *arguito, argomentato, diſcorſo, diſputato, conteſtato, provato, conchiuſo.*

A'RGUING, s. *conteſa, diſputa,* s. f.

Arguing, adj. *l'arguire, il diſputare.*

To ſtand arguing the cauſe, *ſtare a diſputare una cauſa.*

A'RGUMENT, s. [reaſon, proof] *argomento, ſillogiſmo,* s. m. *pruova, ragione,* s. f.

Argument [reaſon] *ragione,* s. f. *ſegno, indizio,* s. m.

A cunning argument, *ſofiſma, ſofiſmo,* s. m. *argomento fallace, caviſlazione,* s. f.

A firm argument, *pruova, dimoſtrazione, chiarezza,* s. f.

Full of arguments, *cavilloſo, ſofiſtico.*

To hold an argument againſt one, *diſputare con qualcheduno.*

Argument [a ſubject to ſpeak or write upon] *ſoggetto, o ſuggetto,* s. m. *materia,* s. f.

Argument [the ſubſtance of a treatiſe or diſcourſe] *argomento, compendio,* s. m, *ſomma,* s. f.

ARGUME'NTATIVE, adj. [convincing in the way of arguing] *che ha forza di convincere, efficace.*

ARGUMENTA'TION, s. *argomentazione,* s. f. *l'argomentare.*

ARGU'TE, adj. [ſubtle, witty] *arguto, aſtuto, pronto, vivace.*

A'RID, adj. [dry] *arido, ſecco.*

ARI'DITY, s. [dryneſs] *aridezza, aridità,* s. f.

ARIE'REBAN, s. [the French king's proclamation to ſummon to the war all that hold of him] *retrobando, bando nel quale il re di Francia commanda a tutti i feudatari di pigliar l'armi per la ſua difeſa.*

A'RIES, s. [one of the twelve celeſtial ſigns] *ariete,* s. m. *uno de' dodici ſegni del zodiaco.*

ARIETA'TION, s. [the act of butting like a ram] *il cozzare de becco.* [The act of battering with an engine called a ram] *il percuotere che facevano gli antichi coll' ariete.*

Arietation [the act of ſtriking or conflicting in general] *il percuotere violento d'una coſa contra un altra.*

ARIE'TTA, s. [in muſick] *aria, arietta, canzone, di una ſtroſe ſola.*

ARI'GHT, adv. *dirittamente, rettamente, ſanamente, ſenza delitto.*

To judge aright of a thing, *giudicare ſanamente d'una coſa.*

To ſet aright, *rettificare, aggiuſtare.*

To ARI'SE [to riſe up] *levarſi, ſollevarſi.*

The vapours that ariſe from the earth, *i vapori che ſi levano dalla terra.*

The ſun ariſes, *il ſole ſi leva.*

To ariſe again, *riſorgere.*

To ariſe [to proceed from] *naſcere, procedere, derivare, venire.*

Our misfortune ariſes from that, *la noſtra diſgrazia ci vien da ciò, procede da ciò.*

Here ariſes a new difficulty, *ecco che ſi preſenta un' altra difficoltà.*

There aroſe ſome words between them] *vennero a parole inſieme.*

ARI'SEN, adj. *levato, nato, proceduto, derivato, venuto.*

ARISTO'CRACY, s. [government by nobles] *ariſtocrazia, s. f. governo degli ottimati.*

ARISTO'CRATICAL, adj. *ariſtocratico.*

ARISTO'LOGY, s. [birth-wort] *ariſtologia, s. f. ſpezie d'erba.*

ARITHME'TICAL, adj. [of, or belong to arithmetick] *arimmetico, d'arimmetica.*

ARITHME'TICALLY, adv. *arimmeticamente.*

ARITHME'TICIAN, s. [one ſkilled in arithmetick] *arimmetico, uno che è verſato nell' arimmetica.*

ARITHME'TICK, s. [a ſcience which teaches the art of accounting, and all the powers and properties of numbers] *arimmetica, s. f. ſcienza di numerare.*

ARK, s. [a large cheſt to put fruit or corn in] *arca, caſſa, s. f.*

Noah's Ark, *l'arca di Noè.*

ARM, s. [a part of man's body] *braccio, s. m. pl. braccia, s. f.*

The right and left arm, *il braccio deſtro e ſiniſtro.*

By ſtrength of arm, *a forza di braccia.*

To take one in his arms, *abbracciare, ſtrigner uno nelle bracccia.*

An armfull, *una bracciata.*

The arm-pit, or arm-hole, *aſcella, s. f. ditello, s. m.* nel plurale fa *ditella e ditelle, s. f.*

An arm of the ſea, *un braccio di mare.*

An arm of a tree, *un ramo.*

The arm of a vine, *ſarmento, ramo della vite.*

An arm-chair [elbow-chair] *una ſedia d' appoggio.*

He is my right arm [he is the perſon I moſt rely on] *egli è la mia man dritta, egli è il mio ſoſtegno.*

A little arm, *bracciolino, s. m.*

A large arm, *braccione, s. m.*

Arm [weapon] *arma, o arme, s. f. ogni arneſe, o ſtrumento di ferro o d'acciajo, per uſo di defender ſe o offendere altrui.*

A fire-arm, *arme da fuoco.*

Offenſive and defenſive arms, *armi offenſive e defenſive.*

To take up arms, *prender l' armi.*

To bear arms, *portar l'armi.*

To be in arms, *eſſer in arme, eſſer ſotto l' armi.*

To continue up in arms, *continuar armato.*

To lay down arms, *metter giu l' armi.*

By force of arms, *a forza d'arme.*

A man of arms, *uomo d'arme, ſoldato.*

Arms [in heraldry] *arme, impreſa, inſegna, s. f.*

To ARM, *armare.*

To arm one's ſelf, *armarſi, veſtir l' armi.*

Arm, arm, interj. *all' armi.*

ARMA'DA, s. [a fleet of men of war] *armata, flotta.*

The Spaniſh armada, *flotta Spagnuola, e s' intende di quella tremenda flotta che Filippo ſecondo mandò contro la regina Eliſabetta.*

A'RMED, adj. *armato.*

Armed cap-a-pe [all over] *armato di tutto punto, da capo a piede.*

A'RMING, s. *armamento, s. m. l'armare.*

ARMADI'LLO, s. [Tatou] *quadrupede Indiano armato di ſcaglie da natura.*

ARMI'LLA, s. [a bracelet or jewel worn on the arm or wriſt] *armilla, s. f. braccialetto, s. m.*

ARMI'LLARY, adj. *armillare, a foggia d'armilla, a guiſa d'armilla.*

Armillary ſphere [amongſt aſtronomers, is the greater and leſſer circles of the ſphere, made of braſs, wood, paſteboard, or the like, put together in their natural order, ſo as to repreſent the true poſition and motion of thoſe circles] *sfera armillare.*

A'RMISTICE, s. [a ceſſation from arms for a time] *armiſtizio, s. m. ceſſazione d'armi.*

A'RMLET, s. [a piece of armour for the arm] *bracciale, s. m. quella parte dell' armatura che arma il braccio.*

Armlet [bracelet] *maniglia, armilla, s. f. braccialetto, s. m.*

ARMO'NIACK, adj. *armenico, armeno.*

Bole armoniack, *bolo armeno.*

ARMO'RIAL, adj. [belonging to armory] *d'armi, attenente all' armi.*

Armorial enſigns, *armi, inſegne, impreſe.*

A'RMORY, s. [heraldry] *aralderia, s. f.*

Armory, s. *armería, ſala d'armi.*

A'RMOUR, s. [defenſive arms that cover the body] *armadura, s. f.*

A coat of armour, *armadura, arme, s. f.*

A'RMOURER, s. [one that makes and ſells arms] *armajuolo, s. m. quegli che fabbrica e vende armi.*

ARMS, *le braccia, o il plurale d'arma.*

A'RMY, *eſercito, s. m.*

A naval army, *armata navale.*

A land army, *eſercito.*

The vanguard of an army, *la vanguardia d' un eſercito.*

The body of an army, *il groſſo o il corpo d'un eſercito.*

The rear of an army, *la retroguardia o retroguardo d'un eſercito.*

The head and wings of an army, *la teſta e le ali d'un eſercito.*

A flying army, *campo volante.*

To draw up an army in battalia [to put an army in array] *ſchierare un eſercito.*

To put an army into winter-quarters, *ſvernare un eſercito, ridurre un eſercito a' quartieri d' inverno.*

To muſter an army, *far la moſtra e la raſſegna d'un eſercito.*

ARO'MATICAL, or AROMA'TICK, adj. [odoriferous, of a ſweet or ſpicy ſmell or taſte] *aromatico, che ha odore o ſapor d'aromato.*

AROMATIZA'TION } s. [a mingle
AROMATI'ZING } of any medicine with a due proportion of aromatick ſpices] *miſtura d'aromati nella compoſizione delle medicine.*

ARO'SE, *è un participio del verbo,* to ariſe.

A ſtorm aroſe, *ſi levò una burraſca.*

ARO'UND, prep. *intorno, all'intorno.*

Around him, *all' intorno di lui.*

ARQUEBU'SE } s. [a large hand-gun]
ARQUEBU'SS } *archibuſo, s. m.*

ARQUEBU'SIER, s. [a ſoldier that bears the arquebuſe] *archibuſiere, s. m. ſoldato armato d'archibuſo.*

ARQUEBUSA'DE, s. [a ſhot of an arquebuſe] *archibuſata, s. f. colpo d'archibuſo.*

Arquebuſade-water, *acqua che gli ſciocchi d'oggidì pretendono abbia molte virtù medicinali.*

To ARRA'IGN [to indict, to bring one to his trial] *accuſare, e anche proceſſare, o fare il proceſſo ad uno.*

To arraign others' judgment [to find fault with it] *condannare il giudicio o il parere altrui.*

ARRAI'GNED, adj. *proceſſato.*

ARRAI'GNING, s. *il proceſſare.*

ARRAI'GNMENT, s. *accuſa, s. f. proceſſo.*

A'RRANT, adj. [mere, downright] *mero, puro, vero, pretto, marcio, cattivo in alto grado.*

An arrant lie, *una mera bugia.*

An arrant knave, *un vero furbo, un furbaccio.*

An arrant raſcal, *un gaglioffáccio, un vero maſcalzóne, un gran briccóne.*

An arrant whore, *una vil puttanaccia.*

An arrant dunce, *un grande ſciocco.*

ARRAS-HA'NGINGS, *arazzi, s. m. panno teſſuto a figure per uſo di parare e adobbare, detto così dal farſi nella città d' Arazzo in Fiandra.*

ARRA'Y, s. [cloaths] *arredo, arneſe veſtito, abbito, abbigliamento, s. m.*

Array [order] *ordine, ſchiera.*

To put an army in array, *schierare un esercito.*

An army in battle-array, *un esercito schierato.*

Out of array, *disordinato, confuso.*

To march in array, *marciare in ordine.*

To ARRA'Y [to clothe] *vestire, abbigliare, addobbare.*

To array [to draw up and dispose an army] *schierare, mettere in ischiera.*

To array a pannel [a law expression, for to impannel a jury] *eleggere i giurati.*

ARRAY'D, adj. *vestito, abbigliato, addobbato.*

ARRA'YERS, s. [certain officers, whose business was to take care of the soldiers armour, and to see them duly accoutred] *provveditori d' un esercito.*

The ARRE'AR of an army, s. [the rear] *la retroguardia d'un esercito.*

ARRE'ARAGES } s. [debts remaining
ARRE'RAGES } of an old account]
ARRE'ARS } *avvanzo de' frutti decorsi.*

To be behind in arrears, *restar debitore.*

To ARRE'ST [to stop, to stay] *arrestare, fermar per forza.*

To arrest one [to seize one] *arrestare uno, metterlo in arresto.*

ARRE'ST [the act of seizing] *arresto.*

To take into arrest, *arrestare, metter in arresto.*

Arrest [sentence of a court] *sentenza,* s. f. *decreto,* s. m. *alto giudiciale.*

ARRE'STED, adj. *arrestato.*

ARRE'STING, s. *arresto,* s. m. *l'arrestare.*

ARRIE'REBAND, v. Ariereban.

ARRIE'RE GUARD, s. [the rear of an army] *retroguardia,* s. f.

ARRI'GHTED, adj. *rettificato.*

ARRI'VAL, s. [coming] *arrivo,* s. m. *venuta,* s. f.

To ARRI'VE [to come to a place] *arrivare, pervenire an un luogo, condursi, giugnere, venire,* pres. *giungo,* pret. *giunsi,* pres. *vengo,* pret. *venni.*

To arrive at a place, *arrivare, giugnere ad un luogo.*

To arrive [to attain to, to compass a thing] *pervenire, arrivare, ottenere,* pres. *ottengo,* pret. *ottenni.*

To arrive at some perfection, *pervenire a qualche grado di perfezione.*

ARRI'VED, adj. *arrivato, giunto, venuto, pervenuto.*

ARRI'VING, s. *l'arrivare, il pervenire.*

A'RROGANCE } s. [haughtiness, pre-
A'RROGANCY } sumption] *arroganza, temerità, insolenza,* s. f. *orgoglio,* s. m.

A'RROGANT, adj. [proud, haughty] *arrogante, superbo, prosontuoso, insolente, orgoglioso, temerario.*

A'RROGANTLY, adv. *arrogantemente, prosontuosamente, orgogliosamente, superbamente, temerariamente.*

To A'RROGATE [to assume too much to one's self, to claim, to challenge] *arrogarsi, attribuirsi, presumere.*

He arrogates too much to himself, *di se tutto presume.*

ARRO'GATED, *arrogato, attribuito.*

A'RROW, s. [dart] *freccia, saetta, verretta,* s. f. *dardo, quadrello, verrettone,* s. m.

To shoot arrows, *frecciare, tirar di freccia.*

Shot or wound by an arrow, *frecciata, colpo o ferita di freccia.*

Shot or wounded with an arrow, *ucciso o ferito di dardo.*

A shower of arrows, *una tempesta di frecce.*

As strait as an arrow, *dritto come un dardo.*

ARROW-HEAD, *punta di freccia.*

Arrow-head [a plant] *quadrello,* s. m. *spezie d'erba.*

A broad-forked-headed arrow, *quadrello, freccia o saetta con punta quadrangolare.*

A'RROWY, adj. *pien di frecce.*

ARSE, s. [the buttocks] *il deretano, le parte con cui si siede.*

To hang an arse [to be tardy, to be sluggish] *esser lento, esser pigro*; *modo di parlar plebeo.*

ARSE-FO'OT [little didapper] *marangone, mergo, smergo,* s. m. *sorta d'uccello aquatico.*

ARSE-SMA'RT [an herb] *persicaria,* s. f.

A'RSENAL, s. [a royal or publick store-house of arms, or warlike ammunition] *arsenale, arzanà, magazino d' armi, darsena.*

A'RSENICK, s. [a mineral body] *arsenico,* s. m.

ART, s. [all that which is performed by the wit and industry of man]] *arte, scienza,* s. f.

The liberal and mechanick arts, *le arti liberali e meccaniche.*

A master of arts, *maestro d' arti.*

A thing done with great art, *una cosa fatta con grand' arte o maestria, cosa maestrevolmente fatta.*

A man of art will live any where, *chi ha arte, ha parte*; *chi sa è ricapitato per tutto.*

Art [cunning, industry] *arte, industria,* s. f. *stratagemma, artificio,* s. m.

The black art, *l' arte magica.*

Art, *seconda persona singolare del verbo,* to be, *ex.* thou art, *tu sei.*

A'RTECHOKE, v. Artichoke.

ARTE'RIAL, adv. [of, or belonging to arteries] *arteriale, d'arteria.*

The arterial blood, *il sangue arteriale, o delle arterie.*

A'RTERY, s. *arteria,* s. f.

The great artery, *la grande arteria.*

A'RTFUL, adj. [from art] *artificioso, fatto con arte, fatto con maestria, maestrevole.*

A'RTFULLY, adv. *artificiosamente, maestrevolmente, con maestria, ingegnosamente.*

A'RTFULNESS, s. *maestria.*

Artfulness, *astuzia.*

ARTHRI'TICAL } adj. [gouty, trou-
ARTHRI'TICK, } bled with the gout] *artetico.*

ARTHRI'TIS, s. [the gout] *gotta artetica,* s. f.

A'RTICHOKE, s. [a plant] *carciofo,* s. m.

Jerusalem artichoke [a plant much of the same nature with potatoes] *sorta di cockearia.*

A'RTICLE, s. [a joint] *articolo, come nervi, giunture, muscoli e simili.*

Article [a condition in a covenant or agreement] *articolo, capo o punto di scritture.*

The articles of an account, *gli articoli o capi d'un conto.*

The articles of a treaty, *gli articoli o punti d'un trattato.*

Article of agreement, *patto, accordo,* s. m.

Article by article, *articolo per articolo.*

To surrender upon articles, *rendersi a patti.*

To A'RTICLE [to make or draw up articles] *pattuire, venire a patti.*

To article [to draw up articles against one for treason] *accusare uno di lesa maestà.*

To article one, *processar uno.*

A'RTICLED, adj. [done by articles] *distinto o diviso in differenti articoli.*

ARTI'CULATE, adj. [distinct] *articolato, distinto.*

Articulate words, *parole articolate e distinte.*

To ARTI'CULATE [to pronounce distinctly] *articolare, pronunciar distintamente.*

ARTI'CULATELY, adv. [distinctly, clearly] *articolatamente, distintamente.*

ARTICULA'TION, s. [joint of the bones of an animal body] *articolazione, giuntura,* s. f.

A'RTIFICE, s. [a cunning fetch, a crafty device] *artificio,* s. m. *arte, sottigliezza, astuzia,* s. f.

ARTI'FICER, s. [a handy-craft's man, an artist] *artefice, artista,* s. m. *esercitator d'arte meccanica.*

ARTIFI'CIAL, adj. [artful, done according to the rules of art] *artificiale, artifiziale, fatto con artificio.*

Artificial day [the time between the sun's rising and setting in any position of the hemisphere] *giorno artificiale.*

ARTIFI'CIALLY, adv. *artificialmente, artifizialmente, con artificio, con arte.*

ARTIFI'CIALNESS, s. [artfulness] *maestria, astuzia, sottigliezza.* Locke.

ARTI'LLERY, s. [all sorts of great fire-arms with their appurtenances] *artiglieria,* s. f.

A train of artillery, *treno d' artiglieria.*

The artillery men, *la milizia.*

A'RTISAN, s. [an artificer or tradesman] *artigiano, artefice, artista,* s. m.

A'RTIST, s. [a master of any art, an ingenious workman] *artista, artefice, artiere,* s. m.

A'RTLESS, adj. [plain, without art] *senz' arte, senz' artificio, schietto, semplice, naturale.*

To A'RTUATE, *sbranare, disfare i membri a pezzi, fare in brani.*

ARUNDI'FEROUS, adj. [bearing reeds] *che produce della canne.*

ARUNDI'NEOUS, adj. [abounding with reeds] *pien di canne, abbondante di canne.*

A'RUSPICE, s. [a divination by looking into the intrails of animals] *aruspicio*, s. m.

As, adv. [implying time of action] *mentre, come.*

As I was writing a letter, *mentre stavo scrivendo una lettera.*

As I was thinking of this, *intanto ch' io pensava a ciò.*

As he was coming into my room, *nell' entrare nella mia camera.*

As, having So answering it, *quale, siccome.*

As you brew, so shall you bake, *qual semini, tal mieterai.*

As it is the duty of a father to love his children, so it is the duty of children to obey their father, *siccome è l'obbligo d'un padre d'amare i suoi figliuoli, così è'l dovere de' figliuoli d'ubbidire illoro padre.*

As [answering to So] *che.*

Who is so bold as to gainsay this? *chi sarà tanto ardito che voglia contraddirlo?*

As [in quality of] *come, da.*

I love you as my own brother, *v'amo come se foste mio proprio fratello.*

He received me as his son, *m'accolse da figlio.*

As [accordingly] *come, secondo.*

As I wrote to you before, *come vi scrissi avanti.*

As occasion requires, *secondo che l'occasione lo richiederà.*

As [which, or which thing] *quel che, quel tanto.*

She did as her mother bid her, *fece quel che la madre le commandò.*

I do as well as I can, *so quel tanto che posso.*

As good as, *così buono quanto.*

As sure as I am alive, *come son sicuro che vivo.*

As I am an honest man I'll do it, *lo farò da galantuomo.*

As sure as can be, *indubitatamente, indubitabilmente.*

As [if] *se.*

As you love me, *se m' amate.*

As you tender your life, be gone, *per quanto v'è cara la vita, andate via.*

Every one as he likes, *ciascheduno a suo modo.*

As big again, *una volta più grande, o una volta più grosso.*

Such as it is, *tale quale è.*

As to, as for, *in quanto, per quanto tocca a.*

As for me, *in quanto a me.*

As for example, *come per esemplo.*

As yet, *ancora.*

He is not come as yet, *non è ancora venuto.*

Are you such a fool as to think that? *siete voi tanto sciocco da crederlo?*

AS SOON AS, *subito che, quanto prima.*

I will come as soon as I can, *verrò subito; verrò quanto prima potrò.*

AS LONG AS, *tanto, fin tanto.*

I shall remember it as long as I live, *me ne ricorderò tanto che vivrò.*

AS FAR AS, *infino, fino, insino.*

I went with him as far as the fields, *l'accompagnai fino ai campi.*

As far as I am able, *per quanto posso, per quanto s'estendono le forze mie.*

AS OFTEN AS, *sempreché, ogni volta che, quando.*

Come as often as you will, *venite sempreché volete, quando v'aggrada.*

AS MANY AS, *tanti quanti, altretanti.*

As many as they are, *tanti quanti sono.*

I have as many as you, *ne ho altretanti che voi.*

AS GREAT AS IT IS, *per grande che sia.*

As little as you please, *sì poco che volete.*

AS MUCH, *tanto.*

Had I known as much, *se avessi saputo tanto.*

I will do as much for you, *farò il medesimo per voi.*

AS MUCH AS, *tanto quanto.*

I have done as much as I promised, *ho fatto quel tanto che ho promesso.*

As if I were not as much concerned in it as you, *come se la cosa non mi concernesse tanto quanto voi.*

As much as lay in you, *per quanto sarà in vostro potere.*

As much as ever, *tanto che mai.*

I love you as much as ever, *v' amo tanto che mai.*

ALTHOUGH [as if] *come se.*

AS WELL AS, *così bene che, quanto.*

I know it as well as you, *lo so tanto bene che voi.*

I love you as well as myself, *v' amo quanto me stesso.*

I'll do it as well as I can, *lo farò il meglio che potrò.*

AS IT WERE, *per così dire, per maniera di dire.*

AS BIG AS A GIANT, *grande come gigante.*

AS WHITE AS SNOW, *bianco come la neve.*

AS CLEAR AS CRYSTAL, *chiaro come il cristallo.*

AS, *dopo* SUCH, *si mette in vere de' pronomé relativó,* WHO, THAT,

I took such as I pleased, *presi quelli che mi piacquero.*

ASAFOE'TIDA, s. [a gum or resin brought from the West Indies, of a sharpe taste and strong offensive smell] *assafetida, sorta di gomma o ragia portata in Europa dalle Indie Occidentali, di gusto forte, e di sorte e cattivissimo odore.*

ASARABA'CCA, s. [a plant] *bàcchera*, s. f. *nome d'una pianta.*

A'SBESTINE, adj. *incombustibile.*

ASBE'STOS, s. [a sort of native fossile stone, which may be split into threads and filaments] *amianto sorte, di fossile che puo filarsi ed è incombustibile.*

ASCA'RIDES, s. [small worms that breed in the strait gut] *ascaridi*, s. m. *vermi che si generano nell' intestino* retto.

To ASCE'ND [to go, get, or climb up] *ascendere, salire.*

To ascend again, *riascendere.*

ASCE'NDANT, s. [in astrology, is that degree of the eclíptick which rises at one's nativity] *ascendente*, s. m. *termine astronomico, quel segno del zodiaco, che spunta dall' orizonte.*

ASCE'NDANT [power or influence over one] *autorità, influenza*, s. f. *potere, credito*, s. m.

He has an ascendant over him, *ha grande autorità sopra di lui, può molto con esso lui.*

Ascendant, *ascendente, uno de' gradi di parentela andando in sù.*

Ascendant, adj. *superiore, predominante, soverchiante.* South.

Ascendant, *termine astrologico* [above the horizon] *sopra l'orrizzonte.* Brown.

ASCE'NDENCY, s. [influence, power] *influenza, potere, facoltà.* Watts.

ASCE'NDING, adj. *ascendente, che ascende.*

ASCE'NSION, s. [the act of ascending, getting or going up] *ascensione, salita*, s. f. *ascendimento*, s. m.

ASCE'NSION-Day [a festival ten days before Whitsuntide] *il giorno dell' ascensione.*

ASCE'NSION right and Ascension oblique of the sun, or of a star [in astronomy] *ascensione* retta, *e ascensione obliqua del sole o d'una stella.*

ASCE'NT, s. [steepness, a rising ground] *montata, salita, costa*, erta, s. f. *colle, poggetto*, s. m.

Ascent [the act of ascending] *ascendimento*, s. m. *ascensione*, s. f. *l'ascendere.*

To ASCERTA'IN [to assert for certain, to assure] *asseverare, avverare*, accertare, *asserire*,

To ascertain [to fix or set a price to a commodity] *tassare o mettere il prezzo ad una mercanzia.*

ASCERTAI'NED, adj. *asseverato, avverato, asserito*, accertato, *tassato.*

ASCERTA'INER, s. *colui che assevera, che avvèra, che tassa.*

ASCERTA'INING, s. *avveramento, l'avverare, certificamento*, s. m.

ASCE'TICK, adj. [employed wholly in exercises of devotion and mortification] *ascettico*, tutto *dato alla divozione. Libro ascettico, libro di divozione.*

Ascétick, s. [he that retires to devotion] *colui che ne va in ritiro o in solitudine per divozione; eremita.*

To ASCRI'BE [to attribute, to impute] *ascrivere*, attribuire, *imputare, incolpare.*

ASCRI'BED, adj. *ascritto*, attribuito, *imputato.*

ASCRI'BING, s. *imputamento*, s. m. *imputazione*, s. f. *attribuimento di colpa.*

ASCRIPTI'TIOUS, adj. [registered, enrolled] *ascritto, registrato, arrolato.*

ASH, or ASH-TREE, s. [a quick thriving tree] *frassino*, s. m.

A wild ash, *orno*, s. m.

A grove of ashes, *frassineto*, s. m. *luogo dove sieno piantati molti frassini.*

ASHA'MED, adj. *vergognoso, confuso, che ha vergogna.*

To be ashamed, *aver vergogna, vergognarsi,*

Are

Are you not aſhamed? *non avete vergogna? non vi vergognate?*

I am aſhamed of him, *mi fa vergogna, ho vergogna di vederlo.*

To make aſhamed, *far vergognare, fare arroſſire, ſvergognare.*

A'SHEN, adj. [made of aſh] *di fraſſino, fatto di legno di fraſſino.*

ASHEN KEYS, *frutti del fraſſino.*

Aſhen-Keys, *lingua d'uccello.*

A'SHES, s. *cenere*, s. f. plural *ceneri.*

To burn to aſhes, *incenerire, ridurre in cenere.*

To lie in aſhes, *eſſer ſepolto nelle ceneri, eſſer incenerito o ridotto in cenere, parlando d'una caſa o d'una città.*

Baked in the aſhes, *ſoccenericcio, cotto ſotto le ceneré.*

Bread baked under the aſhes, *pane ſoccenericcio.*

Pale as aſhes, *pallido come la cenere.*

Lye-aſhes to buck withal, *cenere da bucata.*

ASH COLOUR, *cenerógnolo, di color di cenere.*

ASHO'RE, adv. *a terra, al lido.*

To go aſhore, *prender terra, ſbarcare.*

To get aſhore, *approdare, venire a riva.*

ASH-WEDNESDAY, s. *le ceneri, il mercoledì delle ceneri.*

A'SHY [full of aſhes] *ceneroſo, ſparſo di cenere.*

Aſhy, *del colore della cenere, pallido.*

ASI'DE, adv. *a parte, da banda, da un lato, in diſparte.*

To call aſide, *chiamare in diſparte, o da banda.*

To take a man aſide, *prendere uno a parte.*

To lay aſide [to put apart] *metter da banda.*

To lay aſide [to neglect] *negligere, gittare dietro alle ſpalle, traſcurare.*

To go aſide *andare alla banda.*

AN ASI'DE, s. [that which is ſpoken aſide on the ſtage] *un a parte, quel che un attore dice a parte ſu'l teatro.*

A'SINARY, adj. *aſinevole, aſinario, appartenente a aſino.*

ASINI'NE, adj. *d' aſino, come d' aſino.*

To ASK [to enquire] *chiedere, domandare, ricercare*, pret. *chieſi.*

To aſk one a queſtion, *interrogare uno.*

To aſk buſily, *chiedere inſtantemente.*

I aſk it as a favour, *ve lo dimando in grazia.*

To aſk advice, *domandar conſiglio.*

To aſk pardon, *domandar perdono.*

To aſk the price of a thing, *domandar il prezzo d una coſa.*

I'll aſk him, *glielo domanderò, domanderò a lui.*

To aſk the people in the church, *pubblicare i bandi del matrimonio.*

To aſk after one, *domandar d'uno.*

If any body aſk for me, *ſe alcuno mi domanda.*

To aſk one's aſſiſtance, *implorare l' altrui ajuto.*

You can but aſk and have, *domandate i vi ſarà dato.*

To aſk again, *ridimandare, domandare di nuovo.*

ASKA'UNCE [ſideways, obliquely] *a traverſo, obliquamente, biecamente, di ſchimbeſcio.*

A'SKED, adj. *chieſto, domandato, ricercato.*

A'SKER, s. *dimandatore e domandatore, domandante*, s. m. *dimandatrice, o domandatrice*, s. f.

A ſaucy aſker, *un importuno.*

ASKEW', adv. [on one ſide] *biecamente, ſtortamente, travoltamente.*

To look aſkew, *guardare biecamente.*

To look aſkew [to look diſdainfully] *guardare ſdegnoſamente, o d'una maniera ſchizzinoſa.*

A'SKING, s. *dimanda, domanda, dimandagione, dimandazione*, s. f. *dimandamente e domandamento*, s. m.

A thing not worth aſking, *una coſa che non vale la pena che ſi domandi.*

Shall I give him his aſking? *darogli io quel che domanda?*

You ſhall have your aſking, *averete quel che domandate.*

'Tis not your aſking that will do the buſineſs, *non baſta per ottenerlo che lo domandiate.*

ASLE'EP, adj. *addormentato, ſonnacchioſo.*

Half aſleep, half awake, *mezzo addormentato, tra la vegghia e'l ſonno.*

To be aſleep, *eſſere ſonnacchioſo.*

To make aſleep, *addormentare, far venire il ſono ad uno.*

To fall aſleep, *addormentarſi.*

To lie or to be aſleep, *dormire, ſtare dormendo.*

To be faſt aſleep, *dormire profondamente.*

My foot is aſleep, *ho un piede aſſiderato.*

ASLO'PE, adv. [awry on one ſide] *a traverſo, in traverſo, obliquamente, per obbliquo, a ſgembo, a ſgembeſcio, all'ingiù.*

ASP, or Aſpen-Tree, s. [a kind of white poplar] *ſorta di pioppo*, v. *aſpen.*

Aſp, or Aſpic, s. [a little ſerpent whoſe bite is deadly] *aſpide*, s. m.

ASPA'RAGUS, s. [the plant called by the vulgar ſparrow-graſs] *aſpárago*, s. m.

A'SPECT, s. [look, appearance, countenance] *aſpetto, volto, ſembiante*, s. m. *ſembianza, viſta, apparenza*, s. f.

A man of a good aſpect, *un uomo di bella preſenza*, s. f.

Aſpect [in aſtronomy, the ſituation of the ſtars and planets in reſpect to one another] *aſpetto*, s. m. *configurazione*, s. f. *termine aſtrologico.*

A'SPEN, s. *ſorta d' albero che s'aſſomiglia al pioppo. Credo in Italiano ſi chiami oppio, e lo ſteſſo che* aſp, *o* aſp-tree. *Le foglie di queſto albero ſempre tremano, onde un ſatirico Ingleſe chiama la Donna* aſp-tongued, *che ha la lingua ſempre in motto.*

Aſpen, adj. *d'oppio.*

AS'PER, s. [a Turkiſh coin, in value about three farthings] *aſpro, ſorta di moneta Turcheſca, che vale in circa tre quattrini.*

Aſper, adj. [rough, rugged] *aſpro, rúvido.* Bacon.

ASPE'RITY, s. [roughneſs, ſharpneſs] *aſprezza, durezza, ſeverità, auſterità*, s. f.

To ASPE'RSE [to ſprinkle] *aſpergere, bagnare, ſpruzzare*, pret. *aſperſi.*

To aſperſe [to ſlander, to ſpeak ill of] *diffamare, calunniare, calonniare, infamare, macchiar la fama altrui con maldicenza.*

ASPE'RSED, adj. *aſperſo, bagnato, ſpruzzato; diffamato, infamato, calunniato.*

ASPE'RSING, s. [the act of ſprinkling] *aſperſione*, s. f. *l'aſpergere.*

Aſperſing [ſlander] *diffamazione, calunnia*, s. f. *biaſimo*, s. m.

ASPE'RSION, s. [the act of ſprinkling] *aſperſione*, s. f. *l'aſpergere.*

Aſperſion [ſlander, falſe imputation] *diffamamento, biaſimo*, s. m. *calunnia, macchia, diffamazione*, s. f. *accuſa falſa.*

To caſt an aſperſion upon one, *calunniare uno, diffamare uno, macchiare l'altrui riputazione.*

Malicious aſperſions, *maldicenze, calunnie.*

A'SPICK, s. [a ſort of ſerpent] *aſpide*, s. m.

To A'SPIRATE [to pronounce with an aſpiration] *aſpirare, pronunciare con aſpirazione.*

An aſpirate, s. *un' aſpirazione*, s. f.

ASPIRA'TED, adj. *aſpirato, pronunciato con aſpirazione.*

ASPIRA'TION, s. f. *aſpirazione*, s. f. *aſprezza di fiato colla quale ſi pronunziano talora le lettere, e quel ſegno onde in iſcrivendo ſi dinòta e accenna l'aſprezza di fiato da porſi in pronunziando.*

To ASPI'RE [to breathe] *ſoffiare.*

To aſpire to or after [to pretend to, to aim at] *aſpirare, deſiderare, pretendere di conſeguire*, pret. *preteſi.*

To aſpire to an honour, *aſpirare a qualche onore.*

ASPI'RED to, adj. *aſpirato, deſiderato, preteſo.*

ASPI'RING, s. *l'aſpirare.*

ASPHO'DEL, s. [herb] *aſfodillo*, s. m. *ſpezie d'erba.*

ASQUI'NT, adj. *a traverſo, di traverſo, biecamente, bieco, obliquamente.*

To look aſquint, *guardar bieco, ſtralunare.*

ASS, s. [a well-known beaſt] *aſino*, s. m.

A little aſs, *un aſinello.*

A ſhe aſs, *aſina*, s. f.

A wild aſs, *aſino ſelvatico.*

A young aſs, an aſs-colt, *polledro d' aſino, aſinello.*

Of an aſs, *aſinile, aſinino.*

Aſs-herd, *aſinajo*, s. m. *guidator d'aſini.*

Aſs [coxcomb, fool] *un aſino, un balordo, un minchione.*

He is a great aſs, *egli è un gran pezzo d'aſino.*

He plays the aſs with himſelf, *fa l'ignorante.*

He talks like an aſs, *parla come un aſino, non sà quel che ſi dice.*

ASSAFOETIDA, s. v. *aſafœtida.*

To

To Assa'il [to aſſault] *aſſalire, aſſaltare.*

Assa'ilant, s. [one that aſſaults] *aſſalitore*, s. m.

Assa'iled, adj. *aſſalito, aſſaltato.*

Assa'iling, s. *aſſalimento, aſſaltamento*, s. m. *l'aſſalire.*

Assa'raback, *v.* aſarabacca.

To Assa'rt [to grub up by the roots] *ſterpare, ſbarbare, diradicare, ſvellere.*

Assa'rt, s. [a law term, an offence committed in a foreſt, by plucking up thoſe woods by the roots that are thickets or coverts to the foreſts] termine *legale che ſignifica il delitto di quelli i quali ſterpano le ſelve, che ſervono di nido alle beſtie ſalvatiche sì che non poſſono più imboſcarſi.*

Assa'ssine, s. *aſſaſſino, maſnadiere, omicida improvviſo.*

Assa'ssinate, s. *aſſaſſinamento, aſſaſſinio.*

To Assa'sinate [to murder baſely] *aſſaſſinare, uccidere a tradimento.*

Assa'ssinated, adj. *aſſaſſinato.*

Assassina'tion, s. [the act of aſſaſſinating] *aſſaſſinamento, aſſaſſinio*, s. m.

Assa'ult, s. [attack, onſet] *aſſalto, aſſaltamento*, s. m. *l'aſſaltare.*

A general aſſault, *un aſſalto generale.*

To take a town by aſſault, *prendere d' aſſalto una città, eſpugnare una città*

Aſſault [in law, a violent kind of injury offered to a man's perſon] *aſſalto, attacco*, s. m. *offeſa, ingiuria*, s. f.

To make an aſſault upon one, *aſſalire, attacare uno, batterlo, percuoterlo.*

To aſſault [to attack, to ſet upon] *aſſaltare, aſſalire, attaccare.*

Assa'ulted, adj. *aſſaltato, aſſalito, attaccato.*

Assa'ulter, s. [aſſailer, aſſailant] *aſſalitore, aggreſſore*, s. m.

Assa'ulting, s. *aſſalimento*, s. m. *l'aſſalire.*

Assa'y, s. [proof, trial] *ſaggio*, s. m. *pruova*, s. f. *v.* Eſſay.

To Assa'y [to prove, to try] *provare, pruovare, far pruova, cimentare, eſperimentare, far ſaggio, ſaggiare.*

To aſſay ſilver, *provare, o far ſaggio dell' argento.*

Assa'yed, adj. *provato, cimentato, eſperimentato.*

Assa'yer, s. [officer of the mint for the due trial of ſilver] *ſaggiatore*, s. m. *officiale della zecca che ſaggia la qualità dell' argento.*

Assa'ying, s. *ſperimento, ſaggio*, s. m. *prova*, s. f.

Aſſaying [among muſicians, a flouriſhing before they begin to play] *preludio*, s. m.

Asse'mblage, s. [the ſtate of things joined or united together] *congiugnimento, accozzamento, adunamento*, s. m. *unione, raccolta*, s. f.

To Assemble [to call or get together] *adunare, radunare, ragunare, accozzare, unire.*

To aſſemble [to meet, to come together] *adunarſi, radunarſi, ragunarſi, accozzarſi, unirſi.*

Asse'mbled, adj. *adunato, radunato, ragunato, accozzato, unito.*

Asse'mbling, s. *adunamento, accozzamento, adunazione*, s. f. *l'adunare, l'accozzare, il ragunare.*

Asse'mbly, s. [concourſe or meeting of people] *aſſemblea, aſſembrea*, s. f. *adunanza di gente per diſcorrere inſieme.*

Asse'nt, s. [approbation, conſent] *aſſenſo, conſenſo*, s. m.

The bill has paſſed the royal aſſent, *il re ha dato il ſuo conſenſo all' atto, alla legge.*

To Asse'nt to [to agree] *aſſentire, conſentire, preſtar conſenſo, acconſentire.*

Assenta'tion, s. [flattery, flattering compliance] *adulazione, piacenteria, compiacenza, condeſcendenza, condiſcendenza*, s. f. *compiacimento*, s. m.

Asse'nted to, adj. *aſſentito, conſentito, acconſentito.*

To Asse'rt [to affirm, to maintain] *aſſerire, affermare, tenere, mantenere, ſoſtentare, aſſeverare, difendere con parole o fatti.*

Asse'rted, adj. *aſſerito, affermato, tenuto, mantenuto, difeſo, aſſeverato.*

Asse'rter, s. *aſſeritore*, s. m. *che aſſeriſce.*

Asse'rting, s. *l'aſſerire, l'aſſeverare.*

Asse'rtion, s. [affirmation] *aſſerzióne, affermazione, ſentenza, opinione*, s. f. *detto*, s. m.

This may abundantly ſuffice to vindicate my aſſertion, *baſta queſto per giuſtificare il mio detto.*

Asse'rtor, s. *difenſore, protettore*, s. m.

To Asse'ss [to rate, to tax, to appoint what every one ought to pay] *taſſare.*

Asse'ssed, adj. *taſſato.*

Asse'ssment, s. [the act of aſſeſſing] *taſſagione, taſſa*, s. f. *il taſſare.*

Asse'ssor, s. [one who appoints what proportions every one ſhall pay of the public taxes] *aſſeſſore*, s. m.

Aſſeſſor [an officer in the preſbyterian aſſemblies] *aſſeſſore, ufficiale nelle aſſemblea de' preſbyteriani.*

A'ssets, s [a law word, goods ſufficient for an heir or executor to diſcharge the debts and legacies of an anceſtor or teſtator] termine *legale, che ſignifica beni ſufficienti laſciati all' erede o eſecutore teſtamentario per pagare i debiti ed i legati d'un antenato o teſtatore.*

Assevera'tion, s. [an earneſt affirmation or avouching] *aſſeverazione, proteſtazione, affirmazione*, s. f.

Assidu'ity, s. [continual attendance, conſtant application] *aſſiduità, continuazione, cura, applicazione*, s. f.

Assi'duous, adj. [diligent] *aſſiduo, continuo, applicato, diligente.*

Very aſſiduous, *aſſiduiſſimo.*

Assi'duously, adv. *aſſiduamente, continuamente, ſenza intermiſſione, inceſſantemente.*

Assi'gn, s. [one that is appointed by another to perform any buſineſs] *agente, procuratore, ſoſtituto, ſoſtituito*, s. m.

To Assi'gn [to appoint] *aſſegnare, coſtituire, preſerivere, commettere, delegare.*

To aſſign [to ſhow, to ſet forth] *provare, moſtrare, far vedere.*

To aſſign [to make over a right to another] *aſſegnare, conſegnare.*

He assi'gned part of his eſtate for the payment of his debts, *aſſegnò parte del ſuo avere per pagare i ſuoi debiti.*

Assigna'tion, s. [the act of making over a thing to another] *aſſegnazione, conſegnazione*, s. f.

Aſſignation [appointment] *appuntamento, accordamento*, s. m. *convenzione*, s. f.

To make aſſignation, *reſtare in appuntamento, convenire.*

Assi'gned, adj. *aſſegnato, coſtituito, commeſſo, delegato, provato, conſegnato.*

Assigne'e, s. [he to whom any thing is aſſigned] *agente, procuratore, ſoſtituto*, s. m.

Assi'gnment, s. [the act of aſſigning, the act of ſetting on to another] *aſſegnazione, conſegnazione, condizione, ceſſione*, s. f.

To Assi'milate [to compare] *aſſimigliare, aſſomigliare, comparare, paragonare.*

Assimi'lated, adj. *aſſimigliato, aſſomigliato, paragonato, comparato.*

Assimila'ting }
Assimila'tion } s. *paragone.*

Assi'se, *v.* Aſſize.

To Assi'st [to aid, help, or ſuccour] *aſſiſtere, ſovvenire, ajutare, ſoccorrere.*

I have aſſiſted him in all his neceſſities, *l'ho aſſiſtito in tutti i ſuoi biſogni.*

To aſſiſt [to be preſent at] *aſſiſtere, eſſer preſente, ritrovarſi preſente.*

Assi'stance, s. [help, aid, ſuccour] *aſſiſtenza*, s. f. *ajuto, ſoccorſo, ſovvenimento*, s. m. *ſovvenenza*, s. f.

Assi'stant, s. [helper] *ſovvenitore, ajutatore, ſoccorritore*, s. m. *ſovvenitrice*, s. f.

Aſſiſtant [a ſtander by] *aſſiſtente, uditore*, s. m. *un uomo preſente.*

Aſſiſtant [a colleague, a partner in the management of a buſineſs] *ajutante, collega*, s. m.

Assi'sted, adj. *aſſiſtito, ſovvenuto, ajutato, ſoccorſo.*

Assi'sting, s. *ajuto, ſoccorſo, ſovvenimento*, s. m. *l'aſſiſtere.*

Assi'ze, s. [a ſitting of juſtices, to hear and determine cauſes] certe *corti, alle quali preſiede un giudice, che ſi tengono nelle provincie per decidere cauſe civili e criminali.*

Aſſize of weights and meaſures, *regola o ordine in riguardo a' peſi ed alle miſure.*

The aſſize of commodities, *prezzo o tariffa delle derrate.*

To Assi'ze [to regulate] *regolare, taſſare.*

To aſſize weights and meaſures, *bollare i peſi e le miſure.*

Assi'zed, adj. *regolato, taſſato, bollato.*

Assi'zer of weights and meaſures [an officer who has the care and overſight

ſight of thoſe matters] *officiale che ha cura i peſi e le miſure ſieno giuſte.*

Asso'ciable, adj. [that which may be joined to another] *che puoſſi accompagnare, che puoſſi appajare.*

Asso'ciate, s. [companion, partner] *compagno, collega, ſozio,* s. m.

To Asso'ciate [to bring into ſome ſociety or fellowſhip] *accompagnare, unire, collegare.*

To aſſociate [to keep company with] *converſare, uſare, praticare, bazzicare.*

To aſſociate with one, *accompagnarſi, unirſi, collegarſi, entrare in ſocietà con alcuno.*

Asso'ciated, adj. *accompagnato, unito, collegato,* v. to aſſociate.

Associa'tion, s. [an entering into ſociety with others] *compagnia, unione, confederazione,* s. f.

To Asso'il, or Aſſoyl, [to quit, to pardon] *aſſolvere, liberar dalle accuſe per ſentenza giudiciale, perdonare.*

To aſſoil [in law, ſignifies to ſet free from excommunication] *aſſolvere dalla ſcommunica.*

Asso'iled, or Aſſoyled, adj. *aſſolto, perdonato.*

As so'on as, adv. *ſubito che, toſto che, sì toſto, toſto come.*

As ſoon as he came, *ſubito che venne.*

As ſoon as I ſaw him, *toſto che lo vidi.*

I will be there as ſoon as you, *mi troverò là nel medeſimo tempo che voi.*

As ſoon as he ſaw the danger we were in, *come prima vide il pericolo nel quale ci trovavamo.*

I have my money as ſoon as I want it, *ſecondo il mio biſogno mi vien ſomminiſtrato il danaro.*

To Assua'ge, *mitigare, raddolcire, placare, pacificare, alleggerire, diminuire,* v. aſſwage.

Assua'gement, s. *raddolcimento, diminuzione, mitigazione.*

Assuefa'ction, s. [cuſtom to any thing] *accoſtumanza, coſtumanza, aſſuefazione.*

To Assu'me [to take upon one's ſelf] *arrogarſi, attribuirſi, prendere, preſumere, aſſumere.*

To aſſume a title, *arrogarſi, prendere un titolo.*

He aſſumed the deity to himſelf, *ſi ſpacciò per un nume.*

He aſſumes too much to himſelf, *preſume troppo, ſe l' allaccia vie ſu vie ſu.*

He aſſumes in all companies, *fa del grande da per tutto.*

Our Saviour has aſſumed fleſh, *il noſtre Salvatore s' è incarnato.*

Assu'med, adj. *arrogato, attribuito, preſo, aſſunto.*

Assu'ming, s. *l'arrogarſi, l'attribuirſi.*

Without aſſuming the vain prophetic ſpirit, *ſenza ſpacciarſi per profeta, ſenza attribuirſi lo ſpirito profetico.*

An Assu'mpsit [a law term, a voluntary promiſe made by word of mouth, whereby a man taketh upon him to perform or pay any thing to another] *promeſſa verbale, patto, o contratto, col quale uno s' obbliga di fare una coſa.*

Assu'mption, s. *l'aſſumere ſopra di ſe.*

Aſſumption [in logick, is the minor or ſecond propoſition of a categorical ſyllogiſm] *la minore, o ſeconda prepoſizione d'un ſyllogiſmo.*

Assu'rance, s. [certainty] *certanza, certezza,* s. f.

Aſſurance [ſurety] *ſicuranza, ſicurezza, ſicurtà, fidanza, cauzione,* s. f.

Aſſurance [confidence] *ſicurtà, fidanza, fiducia, fermezza, ſaldezza, coſtanza,* s. f.

Aſſurance [boldneſs, impudence] *arditezza, temerità, audacia, arditanza,* s. f. *ardimento, ardire,* s m.

To Assu're [to affirm, to aſſert] *aſſicurare, render ſicuro, aſſerire, affermare,* preſ. *aſſeriſco.*

To aſſure [to warrant] *aſſicurare, promettere.*

I aſſure you that it is ſo, *v'aſſicuro che è così.*

Aſſure yourſelf, *vivete ſicuro, ſiate ſicuro, aſſicuratevi pure.*

Assu'red, adj. *aſſicurato, certo, ſicuro.*

Assu'redly, adv. *ſicuramente, certamente, per certo, ſenza dubbio.*

To Asswa'ge [to allay, to mitigate] *alleviare, alleggerire, ſgravare, addolcire, mitigare.*

To aſſwage, verb. neut. *alleviarſi, allegerirſi, mitigarſi,* pref. *alleggeriſco, addolciſco.*

To aſſwage, *ſgonfiarſi dopo d' aver gonfiato.*

Asswa'ged, adj. *alleviato, alleggerito, ſgravato, addolcito, mitigato, ſgonfiato.*

Asswa'ger, s. *mitigatore,* s. m. *che mitiga.*

Asswa'ging, s. *mitigazione,* s. f. *mitigamento, alleviamento,* s. m. *alleviagione, alleviazione,* s. f.

A'sterisk, s. [a little mark like a ſtar ſet over a word or ſentence, denoting ſome defect, or ſomething to be noted] *aſteriſco,* s. m. *ſegno a modo di ſtella fatto ſopra una parola o ſentenza.*

A'sterism, s. [a conſtellation of fixed ſtars] *coſtellazione,* s. f.

Aste'rn, adv. *dalla parte deretana d'una nave o vaſcello.*

To Aste'rt [to terrify, to ſtartle, to fright] *ſpaventare, empier di terrore.*

A'sthma, s. [a difficulty in breathing, a ſhort breath] *aſma, o aſima,* s. f.

Asthma'tick, adj. [troubled with an aſthma] *aſmatico, che patiſce d'aſma.*

To Asto'nish [to cauſe an extraordinary ſurprize and admiration] *ſtupire, ſbigottire, ſtordire, far rimanere attonito,* preſ. *ſtupiſco, ſbigottiſco, ſtordiſco.*

To be aſtoniſhed, *reſtare ſtordito, ſbigottito.*

I am aſtoniſhed, *mi ſtupiſco, reſto ſtupito.*

Asto'nished, adj. *ſtupito, ſbigottito, attonito.*

Asto'nishment, s. [extreme ſurprize, admiration] *ſtupore,* s. m. *maraviglia,* s. f.

Astra'dle, adv. *a cavalcioni, con una gamba da una banda e l'altra dall' altra.*

To ſit aſtradle, *ſedere a cavalcioni.*

A'stragal, s. [in gunnery, is the ring of a piece of ordnance] *cordone,* s. m.

A'stral, adj. *aſtrale, di ſtella, d' aſtro.*

The aſtral light, *la luce degli aſtri, la luce delle ſtelle.*

Astra'y, adv. [out of the way] *fuor di mano, fuor di via.*

To go aſtray, *ſmarrirſi, errar la ſtrada.*

To lead aſtray, *ſviare, deviare.*

They were led aſtray from the right worſhip of God, *furono fraſtornati dal vero culto di Dio.*

A going aſtray, s. *ſmarrimento, ſviamento,* s. m.

Astri'ction, s. [a binding] *aſtrignimento,* s. m.

Astri'ctive } adj. [binding, or
Astri'ngent } making coſtive] *ſtitico, ſtringente, aſtringente.*

Astri'de, *colle gambe larghe, allargate, a cavalcione.*

A'strolabe, s. [a mathematical inſtrument to take the altitude of the ſun or ſtars] *aſtrolabio,* s. m. *ſtromento col quale s'oſſerva e ſi conoſce l' altezza e i moti del ſole e delle ſtelle.*

A'stroloġe, s. [hart-wort] *ariſtologia,* s. f. *ſpezie d'erba.*

Astro'loger, s. [one that profeſſes aſtrology] *aſtrologo, aſtrolago,* s. m.

Astrolo'gical, adj. [belonging to aſtrology] *aſtrologico, pertinente ad aſtrologia.*

Astro'logy, s. *aſtrologia,* s. f.

Astro'nomer, s. [one ſkilled in the ſcience of aſtronomy] *aſtronomo,* s. m. *conoſcitore de' corpi celeſti.*

Astrono'mical, adj. [belonging to aſtronomy] *aſtronomico.*

Astro'nomy, s. [the ſcience of heavenly bodies] *aſtronomia,* s. f. *ſcienza che tratta del corſo de' cieli e delle ſtelle.*

Asu'nder, adv. [apart] *ſeparatamente, non inſieme.*

To put aſunder, *dividere, ſeparare.*

To take any thing aſunder, *mettere una coſa in pezzi.*

To examine the witneſſes aſunder, *eſaminare i teſtimoni ſeparatamente.*

To cut aſunder, *tagliare per mezzo.*

Asy'le, or Asy'lum, s. [ſanctuary, place of refuge] *aſilo, rifugio.*

Asympto'tick, adj. [belonging to an aſymptote] *aſintoto.*

Asympto'tes, s. [certain lines which continually approach nearer to each other, but though continued infinitely, can never meet] *aſintote,* s. f. *linee che s' avvicinano ſempre ſenza unirſi mai.*

At, prep. *a, ad, da, in.*

At the, *al, alla, agli, alle.*

At Rome, *a Roma.*

At our houſe, *da noi, in caſa noſtra.*

At home, *in caſa.*

At break of day, *al far del giorno.*

At ſchool, *alla ſcuola.*

At the door, *alla porta.*

At the day appointed, *al giorno deſtinato.*

At the moſt, *al più.*

At laſt, *alla fine.*

To love one at one's heart, *amare uno di tutto cuore.*

At preſent, *adeſſo.*

At leiſure, *a bell' agio.*

To be angry at one, *eſſere in collera con uno.*

To he laughed at, *eſſer burlato, eſſer beffato.*

We are at preſent at peace with every body, *noi ſiamo adeſſo in pace con tutti.*

What would you be at? *che pretendete? che avete in penſiero di fare?*

To be at a thing, *eſſere dietro ad una coſa.*

We are now at it, *ci ſiamo dietro.*

To be at a great deal of charges, *ſpender molto.*

To be at the pains of doing ſomething, *avere l' incommodo di fare una coſa.*

To be at ſea, *eſſere ſul mare.*

To be at a loſs [to be at a ſtand] *non ſaper che fare, eſſere in pena, non ſaper dove dar del capo.*

To be at an end, *eſſer finito.*

To be at odds with one, *eſſer male con uno, aver qualche differenza con uno, non eſſer d' accordo.*

My honour lies at ſtake, *ci va dell' onore.*

To be at leiſure, *ſtare a bell' agio, avere il tempo.*

When you are at leiſure, *quan lo vi ſarà commodo, quando n'avrete l'agio.*

To be at hand, *eſſer vicino.*

At no time, *giammai, non mai.*

At one time or other, *un giorno o l' altro.*

At preſent, *per addeſſo, per ora.*

At firſt, at the very firſt, *alla prima, alla bella prima.*

At unawares, *ſubitamente, improvviſamente.*

At a word, *in una parola.*

At venture, *temerariamente, inconſideratamente.*

At once, *alla prima.*

To be at a word, *eſſer pronto, eſſere apparecchiato.*

To take one at his word, *pigliar uno in parola.*

At all, *punto, in neſſun conto.*

I don't know him at all, *non lo coneſco punto.*

I won't do it at all, *non voglio farlo in conto alcuno.*

To ſet at, *rappacificare, metter d'accordo, riconciliare.*

I did it at your deſire, *lo feci a voſtra richieſta.*

Ready at hand, *vicino.*

At length, *alla fine, finalmente.*

At leaſt, *almeno, almanco.*

To be at work, *lavorare, ſtar lavorando.*

To ATCHIE'VE [ſpeaking of ſome notable enterprize, it ſignifies to execute, to perform, to compaſs] *eſeguire, fare, mettere ad effetto, effettuare*, preſ. *eſeguiſco, effettuo.*

To atchieve [to obtain] *ottenere, acquiſtare, proccaciare.*

ATCHI'EVED, adj. *eſeguito, fatto, effettuato, ottenuto, acquiſtato, procacciato.*

ATCHIE'VEMENT, s. [the performance of ſome exploit] *fatto*, s. m. *prodezza, azione*, s. f.

Atchievement [in heraldry, ſignifies the coat of arms of any gentleman ſet out fully with all that belongs to it] *inſegna, impreſa, arme*, s. f.

ATE, *participio del verbo*, To eat.

A'THEISM, s. [denial or unbelief of the exiſtence or providence of God] *ateiſmo*, s. m.

A'THEIST, s. [a perſon which denies or diſbelieves the exiſtence or providence of God] *ateiſta, áteo.*

ATHEI'STICAL, adj. [belonging to an atheiſt] *ateiſtico, appartenente ad ateiſta.*

An atheiſtical opinion, *un opinione ateiſtica.*

ATHEI'STICALLY, adv. *da ateiſta.*

ATHI'RST, adj. *ſitibondamente.*

A'THLET, s. [wreſtler] *atleta, campione*, s. m.

ATHLE'TICK, adj. [champion-like, luſty, wreſtling, ſtrong] *d'atleta, forte, robuſto, vigoroſo.*

ATHWA'RT, prep. *di traverſo, a ſchimbeſcio, a ſghembo.*

Athwart, adj. [in a manner vexatious and perplexing] *che infaſtidiſce, faſtidioſo, che laſcia in dubbio.*

Athwart [wrong] *ſtorto, obliquo.*

ATI'LT, adj. [with the action of a man making a thruſt] *in atto di dare una ſtoccata.*

Atilt [in the poſture of a barrel raiſed or tilted behind] *alzato di dietro, e diceſi d'une botte, d'un barile.*

ATMOSPHE'RE, s. *atmosfera, l'aria che circonda il noſtro globo per ogni parte.*

ATMOSPHE'RICAL, adj. [belonging to atmoſphere] *atmosfericale, appartenente all' atmosfera.*

A'TOM, s. [a ſmall particle of matter that cannot phyſically be cut or divided into any parts] *atomo*, s. m. *corpo indiviſibile.*

A'TOMICAL, adj. *conſiſtente d'atomi.*

Atomical, *che ha relazione con gli atomi.*

A'TOMY, s. [an atom] *átomo.*

A'TOMIST, s. [one that holds the atomical philoſophy] *uno che ſiegue la filoſofia degli atomi.*

To ATO'NE [to expiate] *eſpiare, purgare.*

To atone [to appeaſe, to make amends for a fault] *placare, mitigare, raddolcire, quietare.*

To atone for a fault, *eſpiare un delitto.*

Virtue atones for bodily defects, *la virtù ſuppliſce ai difetti del corpo.*

ATO'NED, adj. *placato, mitigato, raddolcito, quietato.*

ATO'NEMENT, s. [reconcilement] *propiziazione, eſpiazione*, s. f. *placamento*, s. m.

ATRABILA'RIAN, adj. *pieno di cupa triſtezza, immerſo in profonda malinconia.*

ATRABILA'RIOUS, adj. *malinconico.*

ATRABILA'RIOUSNESS, s. [the ſtate of being melancholy] *malinconia grave.*

ATRABI'LIS, s. [black choler, melancholy] *bile, collera*, s. f.

ATRO'CIOUS, adj. *atroce, orribile, feroce, crudele, ſpaventevole, inumano.*

ATRO'CIOUSNESS, s. [atrocity] *atrocità, inumanità, barbarie, ferocia, orribilità.*

ATRO'CITY, s. [cruelty] *atrocità, crudeltà, inumanità*, s. f.

To ATTA'CH [to ſeize one's goods] *ſequeſtrare i beni altrui.*

To attach [to arreſt one] *arreſtare, far prigione.*

He attached him for debt, *l'arreſto per debiti.*

ATTA'CHED, adj. *ſequeſtrato, arreſtato*, v. To attach.

ATTA'CHMENT, s. [a laying hands on, a ſeizing upon goods, or an arreſt of a perſon] *ſequeſtro, arreſto*, s. m.

ATTA'CK, s. [onſet, aſſault, or charge] *attaccamento, attacco, aſſalto, aſſaltamento*, s. m. *aſſalita*, s. f.

To ATTA'CK [to aſſault, to charge or fall upon] *attaccare, aſſalire, aſſaltare*, preſ. *aſſaliſco.*

ATTA'CKED, adj. *attaccato, aſſalito, aſſaltato.*

A ſore ſickneſs attacked him, *fu sorpreſo da una grave malattia.*

When the peſtilence had attacked one or two, *una volta che la peſtilenza s'appiccava ad uno o a due.*

ANTA'CKING, s. *aſſalimento, attacco*, s. m. *l'aſſalire.*

To ATTA'IN [to obtain, get, or compaſs a thing] *ottenere, conſeguire, pervenire, giugnere, arrivare*, preſ. *ottengo, conſeguiſco.*

He has attained to the thorough underſtanding of the Italian tongue, *s' è perfettamente impoſſeſſato della lingua Italiana.*

They cannot attain to that honour, *non poſſono ſalire a tanto onore.*

Virtue is the ready way to attain a quiet life, *la virtù è il diritto ſentiero ad una vita tranquilla: per la virtù s'arriva ad una vita tranquilla.*

There are ſeveral ways to attain promotions, *vi ſono diverſi mezzi da avanzarſi.*

ATTA'INABLE, adj. [that may be attained] *che ſi può ottenere, o conſegnire.*

ATTA'INDER, s. [a law word, uſed when a man has committed felony or treaſon, and judgment is paſſed upon him] *convinzione, prova evidente d'un delitto.*

ATTA'INED, or attained to, adj *attenuto, conſeguito, pervenuto, giunto, arrivato.*

Things hardly attained are long retained, *quel che s'impara con difficoltà reſta lungo tempo nella memoria.*

ATTA'INING, s. *conſeguimento*, s. m. *il conſeguire, l'ottenere.*

ATTA'INMENT, s. *acquiſto*, s. m.

ATTA'IN, s. [among farriers, is a

knock or hurt on a horſe's leg] *nervo ferito.*

To ATTA'INT [to taint, to corrupt, to ſtain the blood, as high treaſon does] *corrompere, macchiare, imbrattare, infettare.*

To attaint one of ſome crime, *convincere alcuno di qualche delitto.*

ATTA'INTED, adj. *corrotto, macchiato, imbrattato, infetto, convinto.*

Attainted fleſh, *carne corrotta o infetta, carne puzzolente.*

ATTA'INTURE, s. [corruption of blood] *corruzione di ſangue, marcia,* s. f. *umor putrido che ſi genera da ulcere.*

To ATTE'MPER [to temper, to allay] *temperare, moderare, raffrenare, correggere.*

ATTE'MPERED, adj. *temperato, moderato, raffrenato, corretto.*

ATTE'MPT, s. [endeavour] *attentato, tentativo, sforzo, potere,* s. f. *intrapreſa,* s. f.

To make an attempt upon one to take away his life, *inſidiare alla vita di qualcheduno.*

To ATTE'MPT [to endeavour, to undertake, to try] *provare, far pruova, cimentare, eſperimentare, far ſaggio, intraprendere, procurare, tentare.*

To attempt impoſſibilities, *intraprendere coſe impoſſibili.*

To attempt all means, *sforzarſi, fare ogni sforzo, adoperarſi, affaticarſi, impiegarſi.*

To attempt upon a man's life, *inſidiare alla vita altrui.*

ATTE'MPTED, adj. *provato, cimentato, intrapreſo, procurato, tentato.*

ATTE'MPTING, s. *intrapreſa,* s. f. *sforzo, attentato, tantativo,* s. m.

The attempting of that muſt needs be very dangerous, *una tale intrapreſa non può eſſere che molto pericoloſa.*

To ATTE'ND [to bend the mind to] *attendere, ſtare attento, conſiderare, por mente, badare.*

To attend a buſineſs, *attendere, vacare, dare opera ad un affare.*

To attend for one [to wait for one] *attendere, aſpettare.*

I will attend you here, *v'attenderò quì, v'aſpetterò qui.*

To attend upon [to give attendance] *ſervire, ſtar appreſſo ad uno per ſervirlo.*

The like puniſhment attends you, *un ſimile gaſtigo v'aſpetta, un tal gaſtigo non può mancarvi.*

Great misfortunes attend wars, *le guerre ſi tiran dietro grandi calamità.*

Ill luck attend you, *andate in mal ora.*

ATTE'NDANCE, s. [waiting, ſervice] *ſervizio,* s. m. *cura, aſſiduita,* s. f.

To give attendance to one's maſter, *ſervire, eſſer aſſiduo al ſervizio del ſuo padrone.*

He expects great attendance, *vuole eſſer ben ſervito, vuole ch' uno gli ſia ſempre attorno.*

Attendance [retinue, train of ſervants] *corteggio, accompagnamento,* s. m. *comitiva,* s. f.

To dance attendance [to wait long] *fare ſpalliera, aſpettare.*

To make one dance attendance, *fare allungare il collo ad uno, farlo aſpettare.*

He died for want of attendance, *morì per mancanza di ſoccorſo, d'aſſiſtenza.*

ATTE'NDANT, s. [a ſervant] *ſervo, ſervidore, ſeguace,* s. m.

A diſeaſe with its attendants, *una malattia e ſuoi effetti.*

ATTE'NDED, adv. part. of to attend.

ATTE'NTION, s. [an application of the ears and mind to any diſcourſe, and of the eyes and mind to any piece of work] *attenzione, applicazion d'animo,* s. f.

To give attention to ſomething, *fare attenzione a qualche coſa.*

ATTE'NTIVE, adj. [hurtful] *attento, intento, applicato.*

To be attentive on a thing, *ſtare attento, eſſere attento a qualche coſa, badare a qualche coſa.*

Very attentive, *attentiſſimo.*

ATTE'NTIVELY, adv. *attentamente, con attenzione.*

ATTE'NTIVENESS, s. [attention] *attenziône, applicazion d'animo,* s. f. *attendimento,* s. m.

To ATTE'NUATE [to make thin, to weaken, to leſſen] *attenuare, render tenue, diminuire, ſcemare,* preſ. *diminuiſco.*

ATTENUA'TED, adj. *attenuato, diminuito, ſcemato.*

ATTENUA'TION, s. [a leſſening the power or quantity of the morbifick matter] *attenuazione, diminuzione,* s. f. *ſcemamento,* s. m.

A'TTER, s. [corrupt matter] *marcia,* s. m.

To ATTE'ST [to certify, to witneſs] *atteſtare, far teſtimonianza, affermare.*

To atteſt [to aſſure, to vouch] *aſſicurare, certificare.*

ATTESTA'TION, s. [the act of witneſſing, affirming] *atteſtazione, teſtimonianza, pruova,* s. f.

ATTE'STED, adj. *atteſtato, affermato, aſſicurato, certificato.*

ATTI'GUOUS, adj. [hard by, contiguous] *contiguo, raſente, allato, accoſto.*

To ATTI'NGE [to touch lightly] *attingere, toccar leggermente.*

ATTI'RE, s. [apparel, dreſs] *acconciatura,* s. f. *abbigliamento, addobbo, ornamento,* s. m.

Attire [in heraldry, the horns of a ſtag or buck] *rami delle corna d'un cervo o d'un daino.*

To ATTI'RE [to adorn, to dreſs] *acconciare, addobbare, abbellire, ornare.*

ATTI'RED, adj. *acconciato, addobbato, abbellato, abbellito, ornato.*

A'TTITUDE, s. [in painting or ſculpture, the proper poſture of a figure] *attitudine, poſitura,* s. f. *atteggiamento,* s. m.

ATTO'LLENT, adj. [that raiſes or lifts up] *che innalza, che eſtolle, che leva in alto.*

To ATTO'NE, *v.* to atone.

ATTO'RNEY, s. *procuratore,* s. m.

Attorney-General, *procuratore fiſcale.*

A letter of attorney, *procura,* s. f.

To ATTO'RNEY [to perform by proxy] *fare checcheſſia per via di agente minuto di tua carta di procura.* Shakeſp.

To attorney [to employ as a proxy] *coſtituire altrui come tuo agente dandogli carta di procura.*

To ATTRA'CT [to draw to ſomething] *attrarre, tirare.*

To attract [to allure, to entice] *tirar con allettamento, adeſcare, allettare.*

You attract the hearts and love of all the world, *voi rapite i cuori, o sforzate ognuno ad amarvi.*

ATTRA'CTED, adj. *attratto, adeſcato, allettato.*

ATTRA'CTICAL, adj. [having the power to draw] *attraente, attrativo, che ha forza, virtù, o facoltà d'attrarre o di tirare.*

ATTRA'CTION, s. [in natural philoſophy ſignifies that univerſal tendeney which all bodies have toward one another] *attrazione,* s. f. *l'attraere.*

Attraction [the power of alluring, inviting, or enticing] *il tirare, l'allettare, il luſingare, l'adeſcare*; *allettamento,* s. m. *luſinga, eſca,* s. f.

ATTRA'CTIVE, adj. [that attracts or draws to] *attrattivo, atto ad attrarre.*

Attractive [alluring] *attrattivo, grazioſo.*

Attractive, s. *luſinghe,* s. pl. *eſca,* s. f. *allettamento,* s. m.

ATTRA'CTIVELY, adv. *per attrazione, per una virtù attrattiva.*

Attractively, *piacevolmente, con piacevolezza, con luſinghe, con allettamenti.*

A'TTRIBUTE, s. [a property belonging to any ſubſtance or being] *attributo,* s. m. *proprietà, condizione, qualità,* s. f.

To A'TTRIBUTE [to impute, to father upon] *attribuire, imputare, appropriare.*

To attribute to one's ſelf, *attribuirſi, appropriarſi.*

ATTRI'BUTED, adj. *attribuito, imputato, appropriato.*

ATTRI'TION, s. [the act of wearing things by rubbing] *fregamento, ſtrofinamento, ſtropicciamento,* s. m. *fregagione, lo ſtropicciare.*

Attrition [in divinity, a ſlight and imperfect ſorrow for ſin, the loweſt degree of repentance] *attrizione,* s. f. *termine teologico, dolor manco e ſtremo, il qual naſce da ſervil timore, per lo quale l'uomo teme pena o di perder premio.*

To AVA'IL [to be advantageous, profitable, or ſerviceable to] *giovare, valere, ſervire, eſſer utile, eſſer profittevole.*

Good counſels avail nothing when one is not inclined to follow them, *a nulla vagliono i conſigli a chi ſi moſtra alieno dallo abbracciarli.*

AVA'ILABLE, adj. [that may avail or be profitable] *utile, giovevole, vantaggioſo, che giova che contribuiſce, che ajuta.*

AVA'ILMENT, s. [advantage, profit] *vantaggio, profitto, ſervizio, giovamento, utile,* s. m. *utilità,* s. f.

It is of little availment with me, *cio poco mi giova, cio mi è di poco giovamento.*

AVA'NT, interj. [a term of disdain, away, out of my sight] *va via, levamiti d'avanti.*

AVANT-MU'RE, s. [outward wall] *scannafosso, antimuro,* s. m.

AVANT-PE'ACH, s. [a peach that is early ripe] *pesca primaticcia.*

AVANT-WA'RD, s. [the avant-guard, or front of an army] *vanguardia,* s. f.

A'VARICE, s. [covetousness, niggardliness] *avarizia,* s. f.

AVARI'CIOUS, adj. [covetous] *avaro.*

Very avaricious, *avarissimo.*

AVA'ST, interj. [a sea-term, make haste] *presto, via, andate presto.*

A'UBURN, adj. [dark brown, chesnut colour] *bruno, di color nereggiante.*

A'UCTION, s. [any open or publick sale of goods, where he that bids most is the buyer] *incanto,* s. m. *pubblica maniera di vendere o comprare che che sia per la maggiore offerta.*

To sell by auction, *vendere all' incanto.*

AUCTIONE'ER, s. [one that sells, or he that manages a sale by auction] *colui che ha cura dell' incanto.*

AUDA'CIOUS, adj. [confident, overbold, daring] *audace, temerario, baldanzoso, prosuntuoso, ardito.*

AUDA'CIOUSLY, adv. *audacemente, temerariamente, baldanzosamente, prosuntuosamente, arditamente.*

AUDA'CITY, s. } [confidence, AUDA'CIOUSNESS, s. } rashness, saucinefs] *audacia, temerità, arditezza, baldanza, prosunzione,* s. f.

AU'DIBLE, adj. [that may be heard, loud] *che si puo sentire, udibile, alto, sonoro, forte.*

With an audible voice, *ad alta voce.*

A'UDIENCE, s. [hearing] *udienza,* s. f.

To give audience, *dare udienza.*

Audience [assembly of people hearkening to something spoken] *udienza, audienza,* s. f. *auditorio,* s. m.

He had a fine audience at his sermon, *ebbe una bella udienza alla sua predica.*

A'UDIT, s. m. [the hearing and examining an account] *conto, esame,* s. m.

To audit accounts, *esaminare conti.*

A'UDITOR, s. [hearer] *auditore, uditore,* s. m.

Auditor [in law, an officer of the king, or other great person, appointed annually to examine the accounts of all under officers] *auditore, ministro che rende ragione.*

A'UDITORY, s. [the place where lectures, orations, sermons, and the like are heard] *auditorio,* s. m.

Auditory [the assembly of those that hear] *auditorio,* s. m. *audienza, udienza,* s. f.

AVE-MA'RY, s. [a prayer to the Virgin Mary] *Ave Maria, avemmaria,* s. f. *orazione che si fa alla Madonna.*

AVENA'GE, s. [oats paid to a landlord instead of other duties] *biada o avena che si da al padrone della terra.*

To AVE'NGE, *vendicare, far vendetta.*

AVE'NGED, adj. *vendicato.*

To be avenged of one, *vendicarsi, d'uno.*

AVE'NGER, s. *vendicatore,* s. m.

AVE'NGERESS, s. *vendicatrice,* s. f.

AVE'NGING, s. *il vendicarsi, vendetta,* s. f.

A'VENOR, s. [an officer belonging to the king's stables, who provides oats for his horses] *mastro di stalla d'un re.*

A'VENS, s. [an herb] *gariofilata, garofanata,* s. f. *garofanato,* s. m. *sorta d'erba.*

A'VENUE, s. [a passage or way lying open to a place] *passo, adito, passaggio,* s. m.

To stop the avenues, *chiudere i passi.*

Avenue [among gardeners, a walk or row of trees] *viale, viottolo d'albert, o di frasche,* s. m. *spalliera,* s. f.

AVERA'GE, s. [a service which the tenant owes to the Lord by horse or carriage of horse] *lavoro di tante giornate che deve il vassallo al suo signore.*

Average [a certain allowance out of the freight to a master of a ship when he suffers damage] *avaria,* s. f. *termine marinaresco.*

AVE'RMENT, s. [assertion] *avveramento, certificamento,* s. m.

To AVE'R [to assert the truth, to avouch] *avverare, confermare, affermar per vero, verificare, certificare.*

AVE'RRED, adj. *avverato, confermato, affermato, verificato, certificato.*

AVE'RRING, s. *avveramento, certificamento,* s. m. *l'avverare.*

AVERSA'TION [aversion, dislike] *avversione, ripugnanza, contrarietà,* s. f. *odio, disprezzo,* s. m.

AVE'RSE, adj. [that hates, dislikes, or cannot endure a thing] *contrario, nemico.*

Averse from books, *nemico de' libri.*

I am averse to it, *ho della repugnanza per questa cosa, non posso vederla, non posso soffrirla.*

I am averse to physick, *abborrisco le medicine.*

AVE'RSENESS, s. } [a hatred or AVE'RSION, s. } dislike] *avversione, repugnanza, antipatia,* s. f. *odio,* s. m.

To have an aversion to something, *abborrire, o odiare qualche cosa, avere antipatia per qualche cosa.*

To AVE'RT [to turn away] *avvertere, allontanare, alienare, stornare, dissuadere, frastornare.*

AVE'RTED, adj. *allontanato, alienato, stornato, dissuaso.*

AVE'RTING, s. *allontanamento,* s. m. *lo stornare.*

A'VERY, s. [a place where oats or provender are kept for the king's horses] *il granajo dove si conserva il foraggio del Re.*

AUF, s. [a fool, a silly fellow] *uno sciocco, una scioperone, un merendone.*

AU'GAR, or A'uger, s. [a whimble or carpenter's tool for boring] *succhiello, succhio,* s. m. *strumento di ferro da forare.*

To AUGME'NT [to increase or inlarge] *aumentare, accrescere, aggrandire,* pref. *aggrandisco.*

AUGMENTA'TION, s. [growth, increase] *aumentamento, aumento, aggrandimento,* s. m.

AUGME'NTED, adj. *aumentato, accresciuto, aggrandito.*

AUGME'NTER, s. *aumentatore, accrescitore,* s. m. *aumentatrice,* s. f.

AUGME'NTING, s. *aumentamento, accrescimento,* s. m. *l'aumentare.*

A'UGER, *v.* Augar.

A'UGUR, s. [soothsayer, diviner] *auguratore, augure,* s. m. *che dichiara gli auguri.*

To A'UGURATE [to conjecture, to guess] *augurare, fare augurio.*

To augurate [to suppose, to surmise] *conghietturare, presentire, presagire, far presagio,* pref. *presentisco, presagisco.*

A'UGURATED, adj. *augurato, conghietturato, presentito, presagito.*

AUGURA'TION, s. *augurio, presagio, indovinamento,* s. m. *congettura,* s. f.

A'UGURY, s. [divination by singing, flight, or feeding of birds] *augurio,* s. m. *segno, indizio, o presagio,* s. m. *che gli antichi prendevano dal cantare, dal volare, o dal pascersi degli uccelli.*

A'UGUST, adj. [royal, majestick] *augusto, maestoso, venerando.*

August [one of the twelve months of the year] *Agosto,* s. m. *uno de' dodici mesi dell anno.*

AUGU'STIN, or Austin-Friar [Friar of the order of St. Austin] *agostiniano, frate dell' ordine di santo Agostino.*

A'VIARY, s. [a great cage or place where birds are kept] *uccelliera, stia, gabbia,* s. f.

AVI'DITY, s. [greediness, eager desire] *avidità, cupidigia, ingordigia,* s. f.

AUK, *v.* Aukwardly.

A'UKWARD, adj. [unhandy, untoward] *sgarbato, svenevole, sgraziato, sguajato, goffo, inetto, scimunito.*

A'UKWARDLY, adv. *sgarbatamente, svenevolmente, sgraziatamente, goffamente.*

A'UKWARDNESS, s. [untowardness] *sgarbatezza, goffaggine, gofferia, scimunitaggine, scempiaggine, balordaggine,* s. f.

AULN, s. [a vessel that contains forty gallons] *botte,* s. f. *caratello,* s. m.

A'ULNEGER, *v.* Alnager.

A'UMELET, s. [a pancake made of eggs] *frittata,* s. f. *scrivesi anche omelet.*

AUNGEL-WRI'GHT, s. *sorta di stadera altre volte usata in Inghilterra.*

A'UNCESTORS, *v.* Ancestors.

A'UNCIENT, *v.* Ancient, and all its derivatives.

AUNT, s. [a father's or mother's sister] *zia,* s. f. *la sorella del padre o della madre.*

AVOCA'TION, s. *faccenda.*

Avocation, s. *la cosa che uno ha a fare.*

To AVOI'D [to shun, to escape] *evitare, schivare, fuggire, sfuggire, stampare, sforzarsi di fuggire.*
To avoid a danger, *evitare o sfuggire un pericolo.*
To avoid a blow, *parare un colpo.*
He avoids me, *mi fugge, si nasconde da me.*
Impertinent sinners shall not avoid God's vengeance, *i peccatori ostinati non fuggiranno dal gastigo di Dio.*
Avoid my presence, *levatimi d'avanti.*
To avoid the room, *uscire della camera, ritirarsi.*
To avoid [in a physical sense] *scaricare il ventre, andar del corpo.*
Avoid, interj. [be gone] *va via, lungi da me.*
Avoid Satan, *lungi da me, Satanasso.*
AVOI'DANCE, s. [shunning] *scampo, s. m.*
Avoidance [in law, is when a benefice becomes void of any incumbent] *vacanza, s. f. il tempo che un beneficio resta vacante.*
AVOI'DED, adj. *evitato, fuggito, sfuggito, schivato.*
That cannot be avoided, *inevitabile.*
AVO'IDING, s. *scampamento, scampo, s. m. l'evitare, lo scampare.*
AVOIR-DU-PO'IS, s. [a weight of sixteen ounces in the pound] *peso di sedici once per libra.*
To AVO'UCH [to maintain, to justify, to assert] *mantenere, asserire, affermare, accertare, asseverare,* pres. *mantengo, asserisco,* pret. *mantenni.*
AVO'UCHABLE, adj. [that can be avouched] *che si puo asserire, affermare o asseverare.*
AVO'UCHED, adj. *mantenuto, asserito, affermato, accertato, asseverato.*
To AVO'W [to own, to confess, to acknowledge] *confessare, affermare, concedere.*
AVO'WED, adj. *confessato, affermato, concesso.*
AVO'WEDLY, adj. *apertamente, manifestamente.*
AVOWE'E, s. [one that has the right of presenting a benefice in his own name] *padrone, s. m. colui che ha padronato.*
AVO'WER, s. *millantatore, s. m.*
Virgil makes Æneas a bold avower of his own virtues, *Virgilio fa d'Enea un millantatore delle sue virtù.*
AVO'WRY, or Advówry, s. [a law term] *giustificazione, difesa, scusa, s. f.*
AVO'WSAL, s. *confessione, affermazione, s. f.*
AVO'WTRY, s. [adultery] *avolterio, adulterio, s. m.* Obs.
AURI'CULA, s. *spezie di fiore.*
AURI'CULAR, adj. [belonging to, or spoken to the ear] *auriculare.*
The auricular confession, *la confessione auriculare, cosa inventata da' preti per sapere i fatti nostri.*
A'USPICE, s. [a kind of soothsaying among the Romans, by observing the flight, or chirping of birds] *auspicio, auspizio, s. m.*

Auspice [protection, favour] *auspicio, favore, ajuto, s. m. grazia, protezione, s. f.*
AUSPI'CIAL, } adj. [lucky, happy,
AUSPI'CIOUS, } favourable] *felice, favorevole, benigno, fausto, mite.*
AUSTE'RE, adj. [severe, harsh, stern] *austero, severo, rigido, aspro.*
To lead an austere life, *menare una vita austera.*
Austere look, *sembiante severo.*
AUSTE'RELY, adv. *austeramente, severamente, rigidamente, aspramente.*
AUSTE'RITY, s. } [severity, strict-
AUSTERE'NESS, s. } ness, rigour] *austerità, asprezza, rigidezza, severità, s. f. rigore, s. m.*
AUSTIN-FRY'ARS, s. *Agostiniani, frati dell' ordine di santo Agostino.*
AUSTIN-NU'NS, *monache agostiniane.*
A'USTRAL, adj. [southern] *da mezzogiorno, meridionale, australe.*
To AUSTRALI'ZE [to tend towards the south] *tirare verso le parti meridionali; veleggiare verso il mezzogiorno.*
A'USTRINE, *austrino, meridionale.*
AUTHE'NTICAL, adj. [that is of just or good authority] *autentico, valido, autorevole.*
AU'THENTICALLY, adv. *autenticamente, con le circostanze requisite per meritare autorità.*
To make authentical, *autenticare, ratificare.*
Made authentical, *autenticato, ratificato.*
AUTHE'NTICK, *lo stesso che,* authentical.
An authentick witness, *un testimonio degno di fede.*
A'UTHOR, s. } [the inventor, con-
A'UTHOUR, s. } triver or maker of a thing] *autore, s. m. inventore di che che si sia.*
The author of a book, *l'autore d'un libro.*
The author [the head of a party or faction] *capo d'un partito, macchinatore o architetto d'una sedizione.*
AUTHO'RITATIVE, adj. [maintained or done by authority] *autorevole, fatto con autorità, autoritativo.*
AUTHO'RITY, s. [power, credit] *autorità, stima, riputazione, s. f. potere, credito, s. m.*
To be in authority, *esser in autorità, stima, o credito.*
Authority [a passage of a book quoted] *autorità, detto d'autore, passaggio, s. m.*
Authority [leave to do a thing] *autorità, licenza, s. f. privilegio, s. m.*
With authority, *imperiosamente.*
Upon what authority? *con che diritto? in virtù di che? con qual privilegio?*
To exercise his authority, *dominare, signoreggiare.*
Chief authority, *suprema autorità, dominio supremo.*
To put one out of authority, *scavallare alcuno dal suo ufficio; deporre alcuno di qualche carico.*
He does it of his own authority, *lo fa di suo capo.*

To AUTHORI'ZE [to give power or authority, to impower] *autorizzare, dare autorità, autenticare, ratificare.*
AUTHORI'ZED, adj. *autorizzato, autentico, ratificato.*
AUTHORI'ZING, s. *l'autorizzare, l'autenticare.*
AUTOMA'TICAL, adj. [self-moving] *semovente, che si muove da se stesso, automàtico.*
AUTO'MATION, s. [a self-moving instrument, as a clock, a watch, and the like] *automato, ordigno che si muove da se stesso.*
A'UTUMN, s. [the fall of the leaf] *autunno, s. m. una della quattro stagioni dell' anno, che comincia quando il sole entra in libra.*
AUTU'MNAL, adj. [of or belonging to autumn] *autunnale, d'autunno.*
AUXI'LIARY, adj. [helpful, that comes to aid or assist] *ausiliario.*
Auxiliary forces, *milizie ausiliarie.*
The auxiliary verbs, *i verbi ausiliari, il verbo* avere, *ed il verbo* essere.
AUXI'LIARIES, s. [auxiliary troops] *milizie ausiliarie.*
AW, s. [dread, fear, respect] *tema, paura, riverenza, s. f. timore.*
To be in aw, *temere, aver timore.*
To keep in aw, *tenere a segno, reprimere, far che altri non esca de' termini della convenienza o del dovere.*
To stand in aw, *rispettare, portar rispetto, paventare.*
To AW, *fare stare a segno, governar con severità.*
To aw the people into fear and obedience, *tenere i popoli in timore ed obbedienza.*
To AWAI'T [to wait] *aspettare, v.* to wait.
To AWA'KE, *svegliare, destare.*
To awake, *svegliarsi, destarsi.*
I awaked this morning at six o' clock, *mi sono svegliato stammattina alle sei.*
AWA'KE, adj. *destato, desto, svegliato.*
To be awake, *esser desto o svegliato, vegliare.*
To keep awake, *tener desto o svegliato.*
Between sleep and awake, *mezzo addormentato, tra la vigilia e il sonno.*
AWA'KED, adj. *svegliato, destato.*
AWA'RD, s. [a judgment or sentence upon arbitration] *arbitrato, s. m. giudicio d'arbitri.*
To stand to one's award, *starsene alla sentenza d'uno.*
To AWA'RD [to adjudge] *arbitrare, giudicare, sentenziare.*
To award [to beat off] *parare.*
To award a blow, *parare una botta, ribattere un colpo.*
AWA'RDED, adj. *arbitrato, giudicato, sentenziato.*
AWA'RE, adj. *accorto, avveduto, avvertito, cauto.*
To be aware, *antivedere, presentire.*
To be aware of a thing, *stare avvertito, o avvertire ad una cosa, accorgersi,*

gersi, avvedersi d'una cosa, andar cauto.

To be aware of one, *guardarsi da uno.*

I was not aware of you, *non m'era accorto di voi.*

He surprized them before they were aware, *li colse all' improvviso.*

She tasted of it before she was aware, *l'assaggiò senza pensarvi.*

Be aware of her alluring caresses, *guardatevi delle sue carezze lusinghiere, non vi fidate alle lusinghiere carezze di lei.*

Aware, interj. *avvertite, state in cervello.*

AWA'Y, adv. *via.*

To go away, *andar via.*

To send away, *mandar via.*

To slip away, *cógliersela, e córsela, andársene.*

To run away, *fuggirsene.*

To stand away, *scostarsi, allontanarsi.*

Away, interj. *eh via.*

Away for shame! *eh via! che vergogna! deh vergognátevi!*

Away with you, *eh, va via.*

I cannot away with it, *non lo comporterò mai, questo non sarà mai.*

Away with this, *levate via questo.*

Away with him, *menatelo via.*

Away with these compliments, *finiamola con questi complimenti, non più complimenti.*

I'll away hence, *voglio andarmene.*

Time will away, *il tempo passa.*

To make away with one's self, *ammazzarsi, uccidersi, darsi la morte, esser reo di suicidio.*

AWE, *v.* Aw.

To AWE, *v.* to aw.

A'WED, adj. [from to aw] *tenuto a segno o in timore.*

A'WFUL, adj. [terrible, apt to strike a terrour] *terribile, tremendo, spaventevole.*

A'WFULNESS, s. *terrore, spavento,* s. m. *terribilità,* s. f.

A'WKWARD, *v.* Aukward, and its derivatives.

AWL, s. [a sharp-pointed tool] *lésina,* s. f. *strumento di calzolajo.*

A'WME, *v.* Aume.

AWN, s. [scale or husk of any thing] *pula, loppa,* s. f.

AWN [the spire or beard of barley, or any bearded grain] *resta,* s. f.

A'WNING, s. [sea-term, a sail or tarpawlin hung over any part of a ship] *tenda, che cuopre il vascello per ripararsi dal sole.*

AWO'KE, *preterito del verbo,* to awake.

AWRY, adj. *storto, sconvolto, mal fatto, contraffatto, distorto.*

Awry, adv. *storto, di traverso.*

To look awry, *riguardar di traverso, guardar bieco.*

To go awry, *camminare storto.*

The heel of my shoe goes awry, *il calcagno della mia scarpa è storto.*

Ax or AXE, s. [a carpenter's tool] *scure, accia, ascia, accetta,* s. f.

Broad ax, or chip-ax, *accettone, accetta grande.*

Pick-ax, *bipenne,* s. f.

Butcher's ax, *maglio,* s. m.

Battle-ax, or pole-ax, *ascia d'arme.*

An ax for an executioner, *mannaja,* s. f.

AXEL, s. }
AXEL-TRE'E, } *asse,* s. f.

AXEL-PI'N, *ferro in forma di chiodo che serve per ritegno della ruota, ora si scrive* axle, axle-tree, axle-pin.

A'XIOM, s. [a common self-evident principle] *assioma,* s. m. *massima,* s. m.

A'XIS [the axel-tree or diameter of the world] *asse,* s. f.

A'XLE-TRE'E, *v.* Axel-tree.

AY, *adv.* [yes] *sì.*

Ay-Ay, *sì sì.*

Ay, but are you sure of it? *sì, ma ne siete sicuro?*

For ay [for ever] *per sempre.*

AY, interj. *ohimè.*

Ay me, *infelice me! me meschino!*

AYD, *v.* Aid.

AYR, *v.* Air.

A'YRY, *v.* Airy.

A'ZIMUTH, s. [is an arch of the horizon comprehended between the meridian of the place, and any given vertical line] *azimutte, circolo verticale.*

AZU'RE, adj. [sky colour, light blue] *azzurro, azzurrino.*

AZU'RINE, adj. *azzurrino, azzurro.*

B.

B, *Seconda lettera dell' alfabeto Inglese, suona come in Italiano, eccetto quando in fine di parola è preceduta da* m, *come in* dumb, plumb, *che in tal caso è muta.*

BA'A [the cry of a sheep] *il belar della pecora.*

To BA'A [to cry like a sheep] *belare come pecora.*

BABBLE, s. [chat, prattle] *ciarla, chacchiera,* s. f. *cicalamento, cicaleccio,* s. m. *cicalería,* s. f.

To BABBLE [to chat, prate, or talk foolishly] *ciarlare, cicalare, parlar troppo, chiacchierare, cianciare.*

BA'BBLER, s. *ciarlone, cicalone, ciarlatore, ciarliero,* s. m. *ciarlatrice.* s. f.

BA'BBLES, *v.* Bawbles.

BA'BBLING, s. *ciarla,* s. f. *cicalamento, cicaleccio,* s. m.

A babbling hussey, *una chiacchierona, una ciarlona.*

BA'BE, s. [an infant] *bambino, fantolino, bimbo, bambo, bambolino.*

A little babe, *un bambinello.*

BA'BISH, adj. [of or belonging to a babe] *bambinesco, da bambino.*

BABOO'N, s. [a great monkey] *babbuino,* s. m.

BA'BY, s. [a babe] *bambino, fantino, fantolino,* s. m.

Baby [a child's puppet, like a babe] *bàmbola,* s. f. *fantoccio, bamboccio, bambolo,* s. m.

Baby things, *fantocceria, bambocceria, baje, bagattelle, cosa frivola e vana, ciappoleria,* s. f.

BA'CCHANALS, s. [the drunken feasts or revels of Bacchus, the God of Wine] *baccanali, feste in onore di Bacco, Dio del Vino.*

BACCI'FEROUS PLANTS [such herbs, shrubs, and trees as bear berries] *piante o alberi che producono bacche o cóccole.*

Bacciferous animals [creatures which feed upon berries] *animali che si pascono di bacche.*

BA'CHELOR, }
BA'CHELOUR, } s. [a graduate in arms or in the university] *baccellierè,* s. m. *graduato in armi, o in lettere.*

Bachelor [a single or unmarried man] *scapolo, smogliato, celibe,* s. m.

A Knight Bachelour, *un cavalier baccelliere.*

Bachelors buttons, s. [an herb] *piè corvino, erba così detta.*

BA'CHELOURSHIP, s. [the degree of bachelour in the university] *baccelleria,* s. f. *grado d'armi, o di lettere.*

Bachelourship [the state of a single man] *celibato,* s. m.

BACK [the hinder part of the body] *dorso, dosso,* s. m. *tutta la parte posteriore del corpo, dal collo fino a' fianchi.*

The back of a man, horse, or mule, *il dosso d'un uomo, d'un cavallo, o d'un mulo.*

To tie two men back to back, *legare due uomini dosso contro dosso.*

To

To turn one's back to one, *voltar le spalle ad uno.*
To turn one's back to one [to forsake him] *volger le spalle ad uno, abbandonarlo.*
To turn one's back [to be gone, to run away] *volger le spalle, fuggire, prender la fuga.*
To lay all on one's back [to lay all the burden or charge upon him] *addossare una cosa ad uno, lasciargline la cura e la briga.*
To fall on one's back, *cascare all' indietro o alla rovescia, dar delle schiene in terra.*
To rail at one behind his back, *sparlare o beffeggiare dietro dalle spalle.*
He has not a shirt to put to his back, *non ha camicia da mettersi indosso.*
To clap a writ on one's back [to sue him at law] *intentare un processo ad uno.*
Back [hinder part of any thing] *la parte deretana di qualche cosa, dosso.*
The back of a knife, *il dosso d'un coltello.*
The back of a house, *la parte deretana d'una casa.*
The back of the hand, *il dosso della mano, la parte convessa della mano.*
The back of a chair, *l'appoggio d'una sedia.*
A back and breast [a cuirass] *una corazza.*
Back [the reins or loins] *l' a sciena le reni.*
I have a pain in my back, *ho un dolore nella schiena.*
He has a strong back, *ha buona schiena, gli è forte di schiena.*
To break one's back, *sfilar le reni ad uno, romper la schiena ad uno.*
To break one's back [to ruin him] *spiantar uno, rovinarlo.*
He has a strong back [he is a substantial man] *egli ha alto il lardo sull' arnione, egli è molto ricco, gli è forte di schiena e può spendere.*
The back-bone, *la spina, l'osso, il filo delle reni.*
A back sword, *un coltellaccio, uno spadone, s. f.*
A back blow, a back stroke, *rovescione, s. m. colpo dato colla parte convessa della mano.*
Back clouts, *brache, bracoui.*
A back friend, *amico falso.*
The back parts, the back side, *il deretano.*
A back basket, *una sporta.*
On the back side, *per di dietro, dietro.*
Back yard, *cortile di dietro.*
Back room, *camera di dietro.*
The back part of a house, *la parte deretana d'una casa.*
A back door, *porta segreta.*
A back door [a shift] *scusa, s. f. rigiro, s. m.*
Back staff, s. [a sea instrument to take the sun's altitude with one's back towards it] *balestra, strumento marinaresco che serve per conoscere l'altezza del sole.*
Back-stairs, *scala secreta.*
Back, adv. [behind] *dietro in dietro.*
To return back, *ritornare in dietro.*
To go back, *andare in dietro, dietreggiare, dare addietro.*
A pull-back [an obstacle] *impedimento, ostacolo, s. m.*
I shall be back again presently, *ritornerò adesso adesso.*
Back, *s'unisce spesso ad alcuni verbi ma generalmente non significa altro che la reiterazione dell' azione del verbo.*
Ex. To give back [to recoil] *rinculare, arretrarsi, farsi o tirarsi indietro.*
To send back, *rimandare.*
To keep back, *ritenere, trattenere.*
To give back again, *rendere, restituire.*
To cast back, *rispignere, spignere, spingere.*
To draw back, *riterarsi, ritirare.*
To BACK [to mount or get upon a horse] *montare a cavallo, cavalcare.*
To back [to abet, to countenance, to support] *aderire, favorire, spalleggiare, fare spalla, proteggere, pres. aderisco, favorisco.*
BACKBE'ROND, s. [a law term for a thief, taken with the goods about him] *ladro preso sul fatto, ladro col furto addosso.*
To BACKBI'TE [to slander, to revile behind one's back] *calunniare, diffamare, infamare, sparlare, dir male, biasimare, tagliar le legna addosso, e s'intende sempre dietro alle spalle o in assenza di colui al quale si usa tanta villania.*
BACKBI'TER, s. [a slanderer] *calunniatore, maldicente, s. m.*
BACKBI'TING, s. *calunnia, infamia, maldicenza, s. f.*
BA'CKED, adj. [mounted] *cavalcato.*
Backed [abetted, supported] *favorito, spalleggiato, protetto.*
Broken-backed, *dilombato, sfilato.*
BA'CKING, s. [mounting] *il montare, il cavalcare,*
Backing [supporting, countenancing] *appoggio, ajuto, favore, s. m. lo spalleggiare, lo assistere, il proteggere. Assistenza, protezione, s. f.*
To BACKSLI'DE [to turn back, to shuffle] *nicchiare, tergiversare.*
To backslide in religion, *apostatare.*
BACKSLI'DER, s. *colui o colei che tergiversa.*
A backslider in religion, *un apostata.*
BACKSLI'DING, s. *tergiversazione, s. f.*
Backsliding in religion, *apostasia, s. f.*
BA'CKWARD, adj. [slow, negligent] *pigro, lento, tardo nell' operare, neghittoso, infingardo, ritroso.*
How can you be so backward to your own good? *perchè andate così ritenuto, così adagio pel vostro bene? perchè tanta lentezza in una cosa che ridonda in vostro vantaggio?*
I found him a little backward in it, *lo trovai un poco renitente in ciò, un poco restio.*
To be backward in one's duty, *negligere il suo dovere.*
Backward [late] *tardivo, tardo, restio.*
A backward spring, *una primavera tardiva.*
Backward or Backwards, adv. [on the backside] *indietro, dietro, addietro.*
To go backwards, *andare all' indietro, rinculare, dietreggiare.*
To go backward and forward, *andar su, e giù.*
To go backward and forward [not to be in the same story] *contraddirsi, disdirsi.*
BA'CKWARDNESS, s. [slowness] *lentezza, tardità, pigrizia, agiatezza, tardezza, s. f.*
Backwardness [coming late] *tardità, s. f.*
BA'CON, s. [hog's flesh salted and dried] *lardo, s. m.*
Bad bacon, *lardaccio, s. m.*
A flitch of bacon, *costa di lardo.*
A seller of bacon, *pizzicágnolo, s. m.*
A gammon of bacon, *un prosciutto.*
To save one's bacon [to come off unhurt] *uscir salvo d'un affare.*
To save one's bacon [to look to one's self] *aver cura della sua pelle.*
A bacon hog, *un majale.*
Rusty bacon, *lardo rancido.*
Bacon grease, *strutto, s. m.*
BAD, adj. [evil, naught] *cattivo, malo.*
Bad weather, *cattivo tempo.*
Bad wine, *cattivo vino.*
This is bad for the stomach, *questo non è buono per lo stomaco.*
Bad times, *tempi calamitosi.*
Bad fortune [ill luck] *cattiva fortuna, sfortuna, sventura, s. f.*
To be bad [not to be well in health] *star male, esser gravemente ammalato.*
He is very bad, *sta molto male.*
It is very bad with him, *le cose vanno male per lui.*
To keep bad hours, *ritrarsi a casa tardi.*
BAD, } adj. [bidden] *comandato, v.* To bid.
BADE, }
BADGE, s. [sign or token] *segno, contrasegno, indizio, che si porta addosso in forma di medaglia.*
White is the badge of innocence, *il bianco è segno d'innocenza.*
Badge [coat of arms, worn by servants of noblemen] *divisa, s. f.*
To BA'DGE [to mark] *segnare, porre un segno.* Shakesp.
BA'DGER, s. [brock; an animal that eats in the ground, used to be hunted] *Tasso, animale che dorme assai, siccome i Ghirri e simili, e ve ne sono di due spezie, cioè Tasso porco e Tasso cane. Il Tasso porco è buono a mangiare.*
Badger, s. [one that buys corn and victuals in one place, and carries it into another] *uno che compra grano e commestibili in un luogo, e li porta n'un altro.*
BA'DLY, adv. *malamente, cattivamente.*
BA'DNESS, s. *cattiva qualità d'una cosa.*
He was detained by the badness of the roads, *fu ritenuto dalle cattive strade.*

BA'FFLE, s. [sham] *frode*, s. f. *inganno*, s. m.

To BA'FFLE [to sham, to fool] *burlarsi d'uno, deludere, beffare, schermire.*

To baffle [to disappoint] *frustrare, schernire, render vano.*

To baffle one's design, *frustrare o render vano l'altrui disegno.*

To baffle [to confute] *confutare, convincere, riprovare.*

BA'FFLED, adj. *burlato, deluso, beffato, schernito, frustrato, confutato.*

BA'FFLER, s. *un furbo, un ingannatore.*

BA'FFLING, s. *il burlarsi, v.* to baffle.

BAG, s. [sack, pouch] *sacca, borsa*, s. f. *sacchetto, sacco*, s. m.

To put one in a bag [to be stronger than he] *metter la testa nel sacco ad uno, esser più forte di lui.*

A leather bag [a budget] *scarsella di pelle, tasca di pelle.*

A meal bag, *sacco da farina.*

A cloak bag, *valigia*, s. f.

A black bag [woman's hood] *ciarpa, e ffia*, s. f.

To give one the bag to hold [to over-reach one] *ingannare alcuno, calarla ad uno, accoccarla ad uno.*

A bag full of money, *groppo, gruppo, sacchetto pieno di moneta.*

Bag-pudding, *sorta di cibo allesso.*

A bag-pipe, *cornamusa, piva*, s. f.

A bag-piper, *suonator di cornamusa.*

A bag-net, *reticino*, s. m. *reticella*, s. f.

Bag and baggage, *bagaglio*, s. f. *bagaglie*, s. m.

To truss up bag and baggage [at the removal of the camp] *stendare, levar le tende.*

BAGATE'LLE, s. [toy, trifle] *bagattella, cosa frivola e vana, ciappoleria*, s. f.

BA'GGAGE, s. [furniture and necessaries of soldiers, provisions for an army] *bagaglie*, s. f. *bagaglio*, s. m. *masserizie che si portan dietro i soldati nell' esercito.*

Baggage [a camp-whore, a punk] *bagascia*, s. f. *puttana abbietta, puttanella.*

BA'GNIO, s. [a hot house, a place to bathe and sweat in] *bagno artificiale.*

BAIL, s. [surety] *sicurtà, mallevadoria*, s. f.

Bail [the person that bails] *mallevadore*, s. m.

To be bail for one, *essere mallevadore per uno, mallevare, entrare mallevadore per uno.*

To give in bail, to put in bail, *dar sicurtà, dar malleveria.*

Bail [limit, bound within a forest] *limite, termine, confine in una foresta.*

Bail or bale of goods, *balla di mercanzie.*

To BAIL [to be surety for a person arrested] *entrar mallevadore.*

BA'ILABLE, adj. [that may be bailed or set free upon bail] *che si puo mallevare.*

BA'ILED, adj. *mallevato.*

BA'ILIFF, s. [a petty magistrate appointed within a particular province or precinct to maintain the peace] *nome di piccolo magistrato.*

Bailiff [an officer that belongs to a manor to order husbandry] *castaldo, fattore*, s. m. *quegli che è preposto alla cura delle possessioni altrui.*

Bailiff [a person appointed to arrest persons for debt] *birro, soldato di giustizia.*

BA'ILING, s. *malleveria.*

BA'ILIWICK, s. [the precinct of a bailiff's jurisdiction] *dominio o giurisdizione d'un podestà.*

Bailiwick [the office of a bailiff or officer of a manor] *castalderia, fattoria*, s. f. *ufficio del castaldo.*

BA'ILY, or Bum-baily, s. *sbirro, birro.*

BAIN, s. [bath] *bagno*, s. m.

BAIT, s. [to catch fish with] *esca.*

Bait [allurement] *esca, lusinga, allettamento, lacciuolo, vezzo, inganno.*

Bait [meat or collation on one's journey] *rinfresco, ristoro, rifocillamento*, s. m.

To lay a bait, *adescare, aescare, allettar coll' esca, allettare.*

To BAIT [to lay a bait] *aescare, adescare.*

To bait [to allure, to intice] *adescare, lusingare, allettare.*

To bait a bull or bear [to make them fight with dogs] *aizzare, incitare, stimolare un toro o un orso a combattere contro i cani.*

To bait [to teaze] *tormentare, molestare, inquietare, tribolare, importunare.*

To bait, *verb. neut.* [to stop, to take some refreshment on a journey] *rinfrescarsi, ricrearsi, rifocillarsi, prender qualche ristoro.*

The hawk baits [flaps her wings] *il falcone batte l'ali.*

BA'ITED, adj. *adescato, v.* To bait.

BA'ITING, s. *l'adescare, v.* To bait.

A baiting place [an inn] *un' osteria*, s. f. *un alloggio*, s. m.

Bull baiting, *combattimento di tori.*

A baiting place for bulls and bears, *arena, luogo dove i tori e gli orsi combattono co' cani.*

BAI'ZE, s. [baze, coarse cloth] *bajetta*, s. f. *sorta di panno grossolano.*

To BA'KE [to seeth, dress, or roast in an oven] *cuocere, cuocere al forno.*

BAKE-HO'USE, *botegga di fornajo, luogo dove si cuoce il pane.*

BA'KED, adj. *cotto al forno.*

BA'KER, s. *fornajo*, s. m.

A baker's wife, or a woman baker, *fornaja*, s. f.

A baker of spice bread or confectioner, *bericuocolajo, confortinaio*, s. m.

A baker of pies [pastry man] *pasticciere*, s. m.

The baker's trade, *arte o mestiere del fornajo.*

Baker-legg'd, *bilenco, strambo.*

BA'KING, s. *il cuocere.*

Baking [the baker's trade] *l'arte o mestiere del fornajo.*

A baking pan, *tegghia*, s. f.

BA'LAD, *v.* Ballad.

BA'LAIS, s. *ex.* [a ruby balais] *balascio.*

BA'LANCE, *v.* Ballance.

BA'LAST, *v.* Ballast.

BALCO'NY, s. [a frame before the window of a house] *balcone*, s m.

BALD, adj. [without hair] *calvo, spelato.*

Bald-pated, *calvo, che ha il capo senza capelli.*

A bald reason, *una ragione mal fondata.*

Bald [thread-bare] *usato, spelato.*

Bald buzzard, *nibbio*, s. m.

Bald rib, *costa di porco.*

BA'LDERDASH, s. [a mingle-mangle, a mixture] *mescuglio*, s. m. *mescolanza*, s. f.

Balderdash [a confused discourse] *anfanamento, cicaleccio*, s. m.

BA'LDNESS, s. [the state of being bald] *calvezza*, s. f. *calvizie*, s. m.

BA'LE, s. [a pack of any sort of goods] *balla*, s. f.

A bale of silk, *una balla di seta.*

To make up into a bale, *imballare, mettere in una balla.*

A little bale, *ballotta*, s. f. *piccola balla.*

To BALE [to scoop water out of a ship with buckets] *vuotar l'acqua dal vascello con secchio o altro.*

BA'LEFUL, adj. [sorrowful, woeful] *funesto, cordoglioso, lagrimevole, lamentabile, lamentevole, lamentoso.*

BALK, s. [a piece of ground left unploughed] *terreno lasciato incolto.*

Balk [furrow] *solco*, s. m. *quella fossetta, che si lascia dietro l'aratro, fendendo o lavorando la terra.*

Balk [chief beam] *trave.*

Balk [disappointment, baffle] *cilecca, beffa.*

Balk [shame, disgrace] *disonore, vituperio*, s. m. *infamia, vergogna*, s. f.

Balk [prejudice] *pregiudizio, danno, torto*, s. m.

To BALK [to pass by, to omit] *omettere, tralasciare, trapassare.*

Death balks no creature, *la morte non la perdona a nessuno.*

I shall not balk your house, *non mancherò di venir a vedervi in passando.*

To balk one [to disappoint him] *mancar di parola ad uno.*

To balk one [to make a fool of him] *burlarsi d'uno, beffarsi d'uno.*

He balked him not a whit [he told him all] *gli disse tutto, non gli tacque un jota.*

To balk a shop [to hinder its custom] *pregiudicare o far torto ad una bottega, impedire che gli avventori non vi vadano a comprare.*

BA'LKED, adj. *omesso, tralasciato, v.* to balk.

BA'LKERS, s. [persons, who from a high place on the shore show the passage of herrings to fishermen] *persone appostate che dall' alto del lido mostrano a pescatori il passaggio dell' aringhe.*

BA'LKING, s. *omissione, e ommissione*, s. f. *tralasciamento*, s. m.

BALL, s. [any round body] *palla*, s. f. *corpo di figura rotonda.*

A tennis-ball, *palla da giuocare alla corda.*

Foot-ball, *palla da giuocare al calcio.*
Great foot-ball, *pallone*, s. m.
Fire-ball, *palla di fuoco artificiato.*
Wash-ball, or soap-ball, *palla di sapone, saponetta.*
Snow-ball, *palla di neve.*
Wooden ball, *palla di legno.*
Sweet ball, *palla di pastiglia.*
A printer's ink ball, *mazzo*, s. m.
Ball for a gun, *palla di schioppo.*
A round ball on the top of a pillar, *palla.*
The ball of the eye, *la pupilla dell' occhio.*
The ball of the hand, *la palma della mano.*
The ball of the foot, *la pianta del piede.*
The ball [the whirlbone of the knee] *la padella del ginocchio.*
To serve a ball at tennis court, *segnare la caccia al giuoco della pallacorda.*
Ball [dance] *ballo*, s. m.
To BALL, *v.* bawl.
BA'LLAD, s. [a song, commonly sung up and down the streets] *fróttola*, s. f. *canzone che si canta per le strade, balláta.*
BA'LLANCE, s. [a pair of scales] *bilancia*, s. f. *strumento da pesare.*
To bring a thing into the ballance with another [to compare them together] *comparare, paragonare o agguagliare una cosa con un' altra.*
To put one's self into the ballance with another, *compararsi a qualcuno, competere o gareggiare con alcuno, entrare in competenza con alcuno.*
Ballance [even weight] *equilibrio, contrapesamento*, s. m.
To hold the ballance [to stand neuter] *tener l'equilibrio.*
The beam of a ballance, *lo stilo della stadera.*
The tongue of the ballance, *la linguetta della bilancia.*
The scales of a ballance, *i gusci della bilancia, le coppe della bilancia.*
Ballance wheel in a clock, *tempo d'oriuolo.*
The ballance of an account, *il bilancio d'un conto.*
The ballance is right, *il bilancio è eguale.*
While my thoughts were in this ballance, *mentre io ondeggiava in questi pensieri.*
If you weigh these things well, you will find upon the ballance that, *a ben considerare queste cose, al far de' conti troverete che.*
A ballance-maker, *bilanciajo, che fa bilance.*
Ballance [one of the twelve celestial signs] *libra*, s. f. *uno de' dodici segni del zodiaco.*
To BA'LLANCE [to weigh] *bilanciare, pesar con bilancia.*
To ballance [to poize, to make even weight] *bilanciare, aggiustare il peso per l'appunto, bilicare, mettere in bilico.*
To ballance [to counter-ballance] *contrappesare, aggiustare, bilanciare.*
To ballance [to weigh, to consider] *pesare, considerare, diligentemente esaminare.*

His virtue does not ballance his vices, *la sua virtù non contrappesa i suoi vizi.*
To ballance an account, *aggiustare, saldare un conto.*
BA'LLANCED, adj. *bilanciato, pesato*, v. to ballance.
BA'LLANCER, s. *quello, che pesa colla bilancia.*
BA'LLANCING, s. *il bilanciare.*
BA'LLAST, s. [sand, gravel, or stones, laid in the ship-hold to make her sail upright] *stiva, zavorra*, s. f. *quel peso che si mette nel fondo della nave per far ch' ella vada dritta.*
To BA'LLAST [to lade with ballast a ship] *allestire, stivare un vascello.*
BA'LLASTING, s. *lo stivare, l'allestire.*
BA'LLET, v. Ballad.
BA'LLIST, s. [a sort of large cross-bow used by the ancients] *balista*, s. f. *strumento antico da guerra per uso di saettare.*
BA'LLISTER, s. [rail] *balaústro*, s. m. *picciola colonnetta.*
Ballister, or Ballustrade [row of ballisters] *colonnata*, s. f. *balaustro*, s. m.
To BA'LLISTER, *circondar di balaustri.*
BA'LLISTERED, adj. *circondato di balaustri.*
BALLO'ON, s. [a large ball] *pallone*, s. m.
BA'LLOT, s. [a little ball used in giving the votes] *fava*, s. f. *voto*, s. m. *usasi ne' magistrati per confermare il proprio parere di dar fave nere o bianche.*
To BA'LLOT [to vote by ballotting] *palleggiare, pallottare, ballottare.*
BALLOTA'TION, or Balloting, s. *il ballottare, il dare il suo voto.*
BALLUSTRA'DE, s. [ballisters] *colonnata*, s. f. *balaustro.*
BALM, s. [the juice of a tree growing in Palestine] *bálsamo*, s. m. *ragia d'un albero che si chiama anch' esso balsamo.*
Balm-tree, *bálsamo*, s. m. *albero che fa il balsamo.*
Balm [mint, an herb] *menta*, s. f. *erba nota.*
Balm-gentle, *melissa*, s. f. *sorta d'erba.*
Balm-apple, *viticella*, s. f. *sorta d'erba.*
BA'LMY, adj. *balsamico.*
BA'LSAM, s. [the juice of the balm-tree] *balsamo e balsimo*, s. m.
BALSA'MICK, adj. [having the quality of balsam] *balsamico.*
BAMBO'E, s. [a sort of cane] *canna con più nodi.*
To BAMBO'OZLE, *ingannare, minchionare, uccellare, beffare, corbellare.*
BAND, s. [any sort of tie] *legame, vincolo*, s. m. *cosa con che si lega.*
Bands of iron [to cover the fellows of a wheel] *cerchi di ferro.*
The band of a society, *legame o vincolo d'una società.*
A band for a faggot [a faggot-band] *ritorta*, s. f.
A band for a book, *correggia*, s. f.
Head-band, *benda*, s. f.

Hat-band, *cordone del cappello.*
A swaddle, or swathing-band for a child, *fascia*, s. f.
A band of lead to fasten panes of glass-windows, *lamina di piombo.*
Band-dog, *mastino*, s. m.
A band for the neck, *collare, collaretto, collarino*, s. m.
Band-box, *scatola da mettervi biancherie.*
Band [troop, company] *banda*, s. f. *numero o compagnia.*
A band of soldiers, *banda o compagnia di soldati.*
By bands, *in truppe.*
Train bands [trained bands] *bande, le milizie paesane, descritte per servigio pubblico.*
Band roll [muster-roll] *rollo, registro*, s. m. *lista*, s. f.
BA'NDAGE, s. [a binding or tying up] *vincolo, legame, legaccio*, s. m.
Bandage [linen-cloth fitted for binding up wounds or sores] *fascia*, s. f.
BA'NDELET, s. [little band] *legacciolo, legaccio*, s. m.
BA'NDEROL, s. [a little flag or streamer] *banderuola*, s. f. *pennoncello*, s. m.
BANDI'TTI, s. [outlawed persons who are turned robbers or highwaymen] *banditi, ladri di strada.*
BA'NDOG, s. [mastiff] *mastino*, s. m. *spezie di cane.*
BANDOLE'ER, s. [a little wooden case covered with leather, containing charges of powder for a musquet] *bandoliera*, s. f.
BANDO'RE, s. [a musical instrument] *pandora*, s. f. *strumento musicale a corde.*
To BA'NDY [to toss a ball at tennis] *pallare, palleggiare, balzar la palla al giuoco della pallacorda.*
To bandy [to toss about] *scuotere, agitare, muovere, brandire, vibrare.*
To bandy about a business or question, *crivellare, discutere, esaminare, considerar sottilmente un affare, agitare, trattare un punto.*
To bandy [to gather together into a faction] *macchinare, cospirare, far congiura, congiurare.*
To bandy against one, *cospirare contro qualcheduno.*
BANDY, s. [a sort of crooked club or stick to play at ball with] *bastone incurvato da giuocar alla palla.*
Bandy-legg'd, *che ha le gambe torte.*
BANE, s. [poison] *veleno*, s. m.
Rat's-bane [arsenick] *arsenico*, s. m.
Woolf's-bane, *aconito*, s. m.
Ox-bane, *mortalità fra' i buoi.*
Bane-wort [night-shade] *spezie d'erba velenosa.*
Bane [pest] *peste*, s. f.
He was the bane of human kind, *fu la peste del genere umano.*
BA'NEFUL, adj. *pestifero, velenoso.*
BANES, s. [publication of matrimony] *bando, denunziamento, che s'usa ne' matrimoni.*
To bid the banes, *pubblicare i bandi.*
BANG, s. [blow] *colpo*, s. m. *percossa, bastonata*, s. f.

To

To BANG [to beat] *battere, tambussare, tanfanare, zombare, zombolare.*

BA'NGED, adj. *battuto, tambussato, tanfanato, zombato.*

BA'NGING, s. *il battere, zombamento, zombolamento.*

BANGLE-EARED, adj. *che ha gli orecchi pendenti.*

Bangle-ears, or bangling-ears, s. *orecchi pendenti.*

To BA'NISH [to turn out of his native country, to send into exile] *bandire, esiliare, proscrivere,* pres. *bandisco.*

To banish out of the kingdom, *bandire dal regno.*

To banish [to drive or turn away] *scacciare, discacciare.*

Let us banish sorrow, *scacciamo lungi da noi la malinconia.*

BA'NISHED, adj. *bandito, esiliato, proscritto.*

He was banished the court, *fu bandito dalla corte.*

A banished man, *un esule, uno che è in esilio.*

BA'NISHING, s. *il bandire, bando,* s. f.

BA'NISHMENT, s. [exile] *bando, esilio,* s. m.

To recal from banishment, *levare il bando, richiamar dall' esilio.*

BA'NISTERS, *v.* Ballisters.

BANK, s. [little hill, rising ground] *poggio, poggiolino, poggetto,* s. m. *collinetta,* s. f.

A bank of a ditch, *sponda di fosso.*

Bank [side of the sea] *lido, lito,* s. m. *spiaggia,* s. f.

Bank [side of a river] *sponda, ripa, riva,* s. f.

Bank [shelf in the sea] *secca, scoglio.*

A steep bank, *una sponda erta.*

Banks made with turfs to keep water from overflowing, *argine,* s. m. *rialto di terra posticcia, fatto sopra le rive de' fiumi per tener l'acque a segno.*

Bank [a place where there is a great quantity of money taken in and out to use] *banco,* s. m.

The bank of England, *il banco d'Inghilterra.*

To lay money in the bank, *metter danari nel banco.*

The bank at basset, *banco per il giuoco della bassetta.*

To keep the bank, *far banco.*

Bank [the bench or seat of judgment] *banco; tavola alla quale seggono i giudici a render ragione.*

Banks of oars, *banchi dove seggono i galeotti a remare.*

To keep a thing in bank, *conservare, riserbare una cosa.*

To BANK out the sea, *opporsi all' impeto del mare con argini.*

To bank with poles, boards, or the like, to keep off the water from the wharf, *far una travata,* s. f. *far un riparo con travi, per tener l'acqua a segno.*

BA'NKER, s. [he that keeps a bank of money] *banchiere,* s. m. *chi tien banco per prestare e contar danari ad altrui.*

BA'NKET, *v.* Banquet.

BA'NCKUPTCY, s. [the act of turning bankrupt] *fallimento,* s. m. *il mancamento de' danari; a' mercanti per lo quale non possono pagare.*

BA'NKRUPT, s. [one that is run out in trade] *mercante fallito.*

To turn bankrupt, *fallire.*

We conclude them bankrupt to all manner of understanding, *conchiudiamo che hanno perso il cervello.*

To play the bankrupt, *far cedo bonis, essere fallito.*

BANN, s. [publick proclamation] *bando,* s. m. *proclama,* s. f.

BANNS [the publication of marriage contracts] *bando, denunziamento, che s'usa ne' matrimoni.*

To BANN [to exclaim against, to curse] *maledire, maladire.* Obs.

BA'NNED, adj. *maledetto, maladetto.*

BA'NNER, s. [standard, ensign] *bandiera, insegna,* s. f. *stendardo,* s. m.

To display a banner, *spiegar la bandiera.*

A kinght BANNERET [a knight made in the field, with the ceremony of cutting off the point of his standard, and making it as it were a banner] *cavaliere banderese.*

BA'NNING s. [cursing] *maledizione, maladizione, imprecazione.*

To BA'NNISH, *v.* to banish.

BA'NNOCK, s. [oatcake tempered in water, and baked under the embers] *focaccia, schiacciata,* s. f.

BA'NQUET, s. [feast, entertainment] *banchetto, convito, festino.*

To BANQUET [to feast] *banchettare, convitare, far banchetti, scialacquare.*

BA'NQUETING, s. *il banchettare, scialacquamento,* s. f.

Banquetting-house, *sala da banchettare.*

BA'NTER, s. [jest] *burla, beffa, fola,* s. f.

To say a thing in banter, *dire una cosa da scherzo.*

To BANTER [to jest, to jeer] *sojare, dar la soja, burlare, beffare, dileggiare.*

You banter me, *voi mi burlate, voi volete scherzar meco.*

BA'NTERED, adj. *sojato, burlato, beffato, schernito.*

BA'NTERER, s. *beffardo, beffatore,* s. m. *beffatrice,* s. f.

BANTERING, s. *il sojare, il burlare; beffa, burla,* s. f. *scherzo, dileggiamento,* s. m.

BA'NTLING, s. [a child begotten before marriage] *un figliuolo generato prima del matrimonio.*

BA'PTISM, s. [a sacrament of divine appointment in the Christian Church] *battesimo, battesmo,* s. m.

BAPTI'SMAL, adj. [of or belonging to baptism] *battesimale, di battesimo.*

BA'PTISTERY, s. [a bason or font to baptize in] *battisterio, fonte battesimale.*

To BAPTI'ZE [to administer the sacrament of baptism, to christen] *battezzare, dare il battesimo.*

BAPTI'ZER, s. [he that baptizes] *battezzatore,* s. m. *colui che battezza.*

BAPTI'ZED, adj. *battezzato.*

BAPTI'ZING, s. *il battezzare.*

BAR, s. [a long narrow piece of wood or iron] *sbarra, stanga,* s. f.

A bar for a door or window, *una sbarra per una porta o finestra.*

Bar [leaver] *leva, lieva,* s. f.

Bar [in heraldry, a smaller fesse] *sbarra.*

Bar [a sea-term; a rock before a port] *secca,* s. f.

Bar [the place where lawyers stand to plead causes in courts of judicature] *sbarra,* s. f. *il luogo dove siedono gli avvocati piatendo pe' clienti.*

Bar [the lawyers in general] *gli avvocati, i leggisti.*

Bar [in a publick house] *luogo nelle osterie, botteghe, e simili, dove si nota quel che si vende.*

Iron bars before a door, *ferrata, inferrata.*

Cross bars of wood, *gelosia,* s. f. *ingraticolato di legno, il quale si tiene alle finestre per vedere e non esser veduto.*

Bar [hindrance] *ostacolo, impedimento,* s. m.

Bar [cavil] *cavillazione, sofisma,* s. f.

To BAR [to shut or fasten with a bar] *sprangare, stangare, puntellare o serrar con isspranghe, sbarrare, tramezzar con isbarra.*

To bar a door, *sprangare una porta.*

To bar [to keep from] *interdire, vietare, escludere, privare.*

To bar, *parare, al giuoco de' dadi.*

I bar that throw, *paro questo tiro.*

I bar that, *niego cio! m'oppongo a cio.*

Bar wine, England abounds with all necessary things, *dal vino in fuori, l'Inghilterra abbonda d'ogni cosa necessaria.*

BARB, s. [Barbary horse] *barbero,* s. m. *cavallo corridore di Barberia.*

To BARB [to shave, to trim] *tagliare o rader la barba.*

BARBA'RIAN, s. [a barbarous or savage man] *un barbaro.*

BA'RBARISM, s. [a fault in pronunciation, an impropriety of speech] *barbarismo,* s. m. *error di linguaggio, nello scrivere e nel parlare.*

BARBA'RITY, s. [cruelty, inhumanity] *barbarie, inumanità, crudeltà, ferocia,* s. f.

BA'RBAROUS, adj. [cruel, fierce, wild] *barbaro, fiero, crudele, incivile, efferato, d'aspri e rozzi costumi.*

Barbarous speech [improper or broken speech] *lingua barbara, linguaggio corrotto.*

BA'RBAROUSLY, adv. *barbaramente, fieramente, crudelmente.*

BA'RBAROUSNESS, s. [cruelty] *barbarie, crudeltà, inumanità, efferatezza,* s. f.

Barbarousness [clownishness, unpoliteness] *rozzezza, zotichezza, incivilità, salvatichezza,* s. f.

BA'RBED, adj. *raso.*

Barbed [bearded like a fish-hook] *barbato.*

A barbed arrow, *strale pennuto.*

Barbed [covered with barbs] *barbato.*

BA'RBEL, s. [a sort of fish] *barbio,* s. f. *spezie di pesce.*

BA'RBER, s. *barbiere,* s. m. *quegli che rade la barba.*

A barber's shop, *bottega di barbiere.*
A barber's bason, *bacino di barbiere.*
To BA'RBER [to dress out, to powder] *acconciare, ripulire.*
BA'RBER-CHIRU'RGEON, *uno che è a un tratto barbiere e chirurgo.*
BARBER-MONGER, s. *uno attillatuzzo, un zerbinotto, uno che studia d'andar attillato.*
BARBE'RRIES, s. *berberi,* s. m. *frutte del bèrbero.*
BARBERRY-tree, s. [a prickly shrub] *berbero, e berberi,* s. m. *arbuscello spinoso.*
BA'RBES, v. Barbs.
BA'RBICAN, s. [watch tower] *torre di guardia, torrione, merlo.*
Barbican [any outwork belonging to a great building] *antimuro, barbacane,* s. m. *parte della muraglia da basso fatta a scarpa per sicurezza e fortezza.*
BA'RBLES, s. [a disease in black cattle and horses, known by two paps under the tongue] *ulcere che vengono a' cavalli e a' buoi sotto la lingua.*
BARBS, s. [a sort of armour for horses formerly in use] *barda,* s. f. *armadura di cuojo cotto o di ferro, collo quale s'armarva le groppe, il collo, e'l petto a' cavalli.*
BARD, s. [a poet, among the ancient Britons and Gauls] *poeta fra gli antichi Britanni e Galesi, Vate.*
BARE, adj. [naked, uncovered] *nudo, ignudo.*
To stand bare-headed, *stare colla testa scoperta.*
Bare in array, *mal vestito, mal in arnese, pezzente, stracciato.*
Bare [plain] *puro, netto, schietto.*
I tell you the bare truth, *vi dico la pura verità.*
Bare [without hair or glass] *spelato, raso, spianato.*
Threadbare, *usato, spelato.*
Bare of money, *privo di danari, senza danari.*
Bare [simple] *semplice, solo.*
I believe him upon his bare word, *credo alla sua semplice parola.*
He was condemned upon a bare suspicion, *fu condannato per semplice sospetto.*
Bare-faced, *fronte scoperta.*
I can go bare-faced before all the world, *posso andare a fronte scoperta innanzi ad ognuno.*
Bare-footed, *scalzo, a piedi nudi.*
To walk bare-footed, *andare scalzo, andare a piedi nudi.*
Bare-legg'd, *colle gambe nude.*
Bare-headed, *colla testa scoperta.*
To make bare, *nudare, spogliare ignudo.*
Bare [lean] *magro.*
To make bare, *smagrire,* pres. *smagrisco.*
Bare, *è ancora un participio del verbo,* To bear.
To BARB [to uncover] *scoprire, nudare.*
To bare one's arm, *scropire il suo braccio.*
To bare [to strip, to bereave] *spogliare, privare.*

BA'RBONE, s. *un magro.*
BA'RELY, adv. *solamente, semplicemente, unicamente.*
Barely [slenderly, poorly] *poveramente, scarsamente, stentatamente.*
BA'RENESS, s. *nudità,* s. f.
BA'RGAIN, s. [contract] *patto, accordo,* s. m. *convenzione, condizione,* s. f.
I give you this into the bargain, *vi do questo di più, vi do questo per niente.*
To buy a bargain, *fare un accordo, convenire per una cosa.*
To sell one a good bargain, *vender qualche cosa ad alcuno buon patto, a buon mercato.*
To strike up a bargain, *pattuire, patteggiare.*
To meet with a good bargain, *comprare casualmente qualche cosa a buon mercato, fare una buona compra.*
A good bargain is a pick-purse, *il buon mercato vuota la borsa.*
You shall lose nothing by the bargain, *voi non perderete niente nel cambio.*
A bargain is a bargain, *quel che è fatto è fatto, quel che è detto è detto.*
To BA'RGAIN [to beat the price] *convenire, accordarsi, concordare,* pres. *convengo.*
To bargain [to strike up a bargain] *pattuire, patteggiare, far patto,* pres. *pattuisco.*
Did you bargain with him? *avete pattuito insieme, avete fatto il patto con lui?*
BA'RGAINED, adj. *convenuto, accordato, pattuito, patteggiato.*
BARGAINE'E, s. *colui che accetta un partito, un patto fattogli.*
BARGAI'NER, s. *colui o colei che fa o offerisce un patto.*
BARGAI'NING, s. *il patteggiare, patteggiamento.*
BARGE [a boat used for pleasure or state] *navicella che tiensi per pompa o per diletto.*
Barge [a large vessel for carrying of goods on a river] *spezie di barca con fondo piano.*
A barge-man, *un gondoliere, un barcaruolo.*
BARGH-MASTER, s. [a surveyor of mines] *soprantendente delle miniere.*
BARGH-MOTE, s. [a court held concerning the affairs of mines] *magistrato che ha la soprantendenza delle cose appartenenti alle miniere.*
BARK, s. [a small ship that has but one deck] *barca,* s. f.
Bark [the rind or the outermost coat of a tree] *scorza, buccia, corteccia,* s. f.
A thin bark, *cortecciuola, bucciolina,* s. f.
That has a thick bark, *buccioso.*
To BARK [to pill off the bark of trees] *sbucciare, scortecciare, scorzare.*
To bark [like a dog] *abbajare, il mandar fuori che fa il cane la sua voce, latrare.*
To bark like a fox, *gagnolare, mugolare, ringhiare.*
To bark against one, *abbajare ad uno, sparlare, dir male, svillaneggiare.*
BA'RKED, pret. of to bark.
BA'RKER, s. *abbajatore,* s. m. *che abbaja.*
BA'RKING, s. [the baying of a dog] *abbajamento, latrato,* s. m.
Barking [abusive language] *maldicenza, ingiuria,* s. f. *svillaneggiamento,* s. m.
Barking [the taking off the bark] *lo sbucciare, lo scortecciare, lo scorzare.*
BA'RLEY, s. [a sort of corn] *orzo,* s. m. *biada nota.*
Barley-bread, *pan d'orzo.*
Barley-sugar, *zuccherino.*
Barley-water, *orzata,* s. f.
A barley-corn, *un grano d'orzo.*
BARLEY-BRA'KE, s. *sorta di giuoco villereccio.* Sidney.
BARLEY-BR'OTH, s. *birra forte.*
BARM, s. [yest] *feccia di cervogia.*
BARN, s. [a corn-house] *luogo destinato a riporvi il grano in campagna.*
The barn floor, *l'aja, spazio di terra spianato per battervi il grano.*
The barn is full [she is with child] *è gravida, ha mangiate delle fave.*
A barn for hay, *fienile,* s. m. *luogo, dove si ripone il fieno.*
Barn owl, *allocco,* s. m. *uccello notturno, simile quasi al gufo.*
Barn [a child] *un fanciullo, un bambino.*
BA'RNACLE, s. [an instrument to set upon the nose of an unruly horse] *tanaglie, strumento di ferro col quale si stringe il labbro di sopra a' cavalli.*
A barnacle bird, *oca di scozia che dal volgo si dice formarsi da un albero.*
Barnacles, s. plur. *conchiglie che s' attaccano al fondo d'un vascello stato lungo tempo nell' acqua.*
BARO'METER, s. [a machine for measuring the weight of the atmosphere, and the variations in it, in order chiefly to determine the changes of the weather] *barómetro.*
BAROME'TRICAL, adj. *di barometro.*
BA'RON, s. [a degree of nobility, next to a viscount] *barone,* s. m. *grado e titolo di nobiltà.*
A baron or judge, *un giudice.*
Baron of the exchequer, *giudice della tesoreria.*
The lord chief baron, *il primo giudice, della tesoreria.*
Baron and femme [a man and his wife, a law term] *il marito e la moglie.*
BA'RONAGE, s. [the title and dignity of a baron] *baronia,* s. f. *titolo, dignità, e giuridizion di barone.*
BA'RONESS, s. [the wife of a baron] *baronessa,* s. f. *moglie d'un barone.*
BA'RONET, s. [the lowest degree of honour hereditary] *baronetto,* s. m.
A knight baronet, *un cavaliere barone.*
BA'RONY, s. *baronia,* s. f.
BA'ROSCOPE, s. *v.* Barometer.
BARR, *v.* Bar.

BA'RRACAN, s. [a sort of coarse camlet] *barracane*, s. m. *spezie di ciambellotto.*

BA'RRACK, s. [a hut for soldiers to lodge in] *baracca*, s. f. *stanza di legno, per tenere al coperto i soldati.*

To build the barracks, *rizzar le baracche.*

BA'RRATOR, *v.* Barretor.

BA'RREL, s. [a small cask] *barile*, s. m.

Barrel [a measure of liquids] *misura di liquidi.*

The barrel of a gun, *la canna d'un archibuso.*

The barrel of a watch, *tamburo d'oriuolo.*

A little barrel, *bariletto*, s. m. *bariletta*, s. f.

A barrel for to keep pickles, *barigli-one*, s. m.

A barrel-maker, *bottajo*, s. m.

BARREL-BE'LLIED, adj. *che ha il corpo grande a mo' di barile, panciuto.*

To BA'RREL up, *imbottare.*

BA'RRELLED up, *imbottato.*

BA'RREN, s. [unfruitful, sterile] *sterile, infecondo, infruttuoso, che non fruttifica.*

Barren [empty, dry, jejune] *arido, sterile, magro, parlando dell' ingegno.*

BA'RRENLY, adv. *sterilmente, aridamente, brettamente.*

BA'RRENNESS, s. [sterility] *sterilità*, s. f.

BARREN-WORT, s. *sorta d'erba.*

Barren signs [in astronomy, Gemini, Leo, and Virgo] *i tre segni di Gemini, Lione, e Vergine.*

BA'RRESTER, *v.* Barrister.

BA'RRETOR, s. [a wrangler, a stirrer up of quarrels] *brigante, intrigatore, sedizioso, beccalite, litigatore*, s. m.

BARRICA'DE, s. [a sort of intrenchment] *barricata*, s. f. *riparo di legname che si fa attraverso alle vie per impedire il passaggio a' nimici.*

To BARRICA'DE [to shut up with bars] *barricare, fortificare con barricate.*

BARRICA'DED, adj *barricato, fortificato con barricate.*

BARRICA'DO, *pezzo di fortificazione.*

BA'RRIER, s. [a bar to shut a passage] *barra, sbarra*, s. f.

Barriers [a martial exercise of men, fighting with short swords within bars] *barriéra*, s. f. *sorta d'abbattimento, fatto con istocco o picca sottile e corta, tra uomini armati con una sbarra nel mezzo.*

Barriers [in fortification, great stakes planted ten foot one from another] *barriére.*

BA'RRISTER, s. [a pleader at the bar, a lawyer] *un avvocato.*

BA'RROW, s. *barella*, s. f.

A hand-barrow, *una barella.*

A wheel-barrow, *carriuola*, s. f.

To carry in a hand-barrow, *barellare, portar con barella.*

A barrow-hog, *porco castrato.*

Barrow-grease, *sugna*, s. f. *grasso di porco.*

A barrow-maker, *uno che fa barelle*, s. m.

Barrow [a little hill or mount of earth] *monticello*, s. m.

To BA'RTER [to truck, to change one commodity for another] *barattare, cambiar cosa per cosa.*

BA'RTER, *v.* Bartering.

BA'RTERED, adj. *barattato.*

BA'RTERER, s. *uno che fa baratto.*

BA'RTERING, or Barter, s. *baratto*, s. m.

BA'RTON, s. [a coop to keep poultry in] *gallinajo, pollajo*, s. m. *luogo dove stanno le galline.*

BA'RTRAM, s. [wild pellitory] *pilatto*, s. m. *sorta d'erba.*

BASE, s. [the pedestal of a pillar] *base, basa*, s. f. *sostegno e quasi piede, sul quale sta la colonna, e simili.*

The base of a column, *la base d'una colonna.*

Justice is the base of regal authority, *la giustizia è la base dell' autorità regale.*

Base, or Bass [the base part in musick] *il basso, una voce della musica.*

A base viol, *viola da gamba.*

A thorough base, *basso continuato.*

Base [a sea fish] *lupo di mare, sorta di pesce.*

Base, adj. [mean, low, vile] *basso, vile, infimo, abbietto.*

A base spirit, *animo abbietto.*

Base extraction or parentage, *bassa nascita.*

Base born [bastard] *bastardo, vilmente nato.*

A base son, *un bastardo.*

Base [shameful, dishonest, knavish] *infame, indegno, villano, vituperoso.*

A base action, *un' azione infame.*

Base [stant, naught] *scellerato, malvagio, pravo.*

A base rascal, *un disgraziato, un furfantaccio, un vero briccone.*

Base manners, *pravi o malvagi costumi.*

A base trick, *un tiro furbesco, furberia.*

Base [sneaking, cowardly] *vile, codardo, pusillanimo, di poco animo, di poco cuore.*

Base [penurious, niggardly] *mistro, sordido, spilorcio, stremo, stretto, taccagno, gretto, meschino, tanghero.*

Base [counterfeit as metal] *adulterato, falsificato.*

Base coin [money of less value than it ought to be] *moneta bassa, moneta di bassa lega.*

Base coin [small money] *piccola moneta, spicci.*

BA'SELARD, s. [a dagger] *un pugnale.*

BA'SELY, adv. [meanly] *bassamente, abbiettamente, vilmente.*

Basely [shamefully, dishonestly] *infamemente, indegnamente, villanamente, vituperosamente.*

Basely [naughtily, knavishly] *sceleratamente, malvagiamente, pravamente, iniquamente.*

Basely [poorly, pitifully] *miseramente, sordidamente, strettamente, grettamente.*

BA'SENESS, s. [meanness] *viltà, bassezza*, s. f.

Baseness of extraction, *oscurità di natali.*

Baseness [base, dishonest, or knavish action] *infamità, indegnità, furfanteria, bricconeria*, s. f.

Baseness [sneakingness of spirit] *viltà, codardia, pusillanimità*, s. f.

Baseness [penuriousness] *avarizia, grettezza, spilorceria, miseria estrema, strettezza nello spendere.*

BASHA'W, s. *dignità fra Turchi.*

BA'SHFUL, adj. [timorous, modest] *vergognoso, timido, modesto, schivo, peritoso, rispettoso.*

BA'SHFULLY, adv. *vergognosamente, timidamente, modestamente.*

BA'SHFULNESS, s. *vergogna, timidità, modestia, peritanza*, s. f. *rispetto, timore*, s. m. *timidezza*, s. f.

BA'SIL, s. [the herb sweet basil] *bassilico*, s. m. *spezie d'erba odorifera.*

BASI'LICK VEIN [the inner vein of the arm, or liver vein] *basilica, bassilica*, s. f. *una delle vene del braccio, altrimenti detta epatica.*

Basilick, s. [a great church] *basilica*, s. f. *tempio, chiesa principale.*

The basilick of St. Peter's, *la basilica di S. Pietro.*

BA'SILISK, s. [a serpent called cockatrice] *basilischio, basilisco*, s. m.

Basilisk [a great piece of ordnance] *basilisco, pezzo d'artiglieria così chiamato.*

BA'SINETS, s. [an herb] *ranuncolo, ranunculo*, s. f. *sorta d'erba.*

BA'SIS, s. [base, foundation] *base, basa*, s. f. *fondamento, sostegno*, s. m.

To BASK IN THE SUN, *scaldarsi al sole, soleggiarsi, porsi al sole, scherzar al sole come certi uccelletti fanno.*

BA'SKET, s. *canestra*, s. f. *canestro, paniere*, s. m. *paniera*, s. f.

A little basket, *canestrino, canestrello, canestretto, canestruccio, canestruzzo*, s. m.

A hand-basket, *sportella*, s. f.

A basket to carry on the back, *sporta*, s. f.

A bread-basket, *corba da portar il pane.*

A basket for women's work, *paniere, panieruzzo*, s. m.

A wicker-basket, *cestella, zana*, s. f.

A basket-maker, *sportajuolo, cestajuolo*, s. m.

A basket-woman, *zanajuola*, s. f.

A basket-man, *zanajuolo*, s. m.

A basket-full, *zanata*, s. f. *quantità di cose che empiano una zana.*

BA'SON, s. [a vessel to wash hands in] *bacino*, s. m. *vaso di metallo, o di terra, di forma ritonda e rupa, per uso di lavarsi comunemente le mani.*

A small bason, *bacinella*, s. f.

BASS, adj. *vile, spregevole*, vid. *Base.*

Bass, s. [a bed of rushes] *un letto di giunchi.*

BASSA, or Bashaw, s. [an officer of great authority among the Turks] *bascià*, s. m. *officiale de' principali fra Turchi.*

BA'SSET, s. [a sort of game at cards] *bassetta*, s. f. *sorta di giuoco di carte.*

BASSO'ON, s. [a musical instrument] *bassone, fagotto*, s. m.

BAST,

BAST, s. [lime-tree wood made into ropes and masts] *funi o stuoje fatte di tiglio.*
To BAST [to bast soundly] *bastonare, battere, zombare, tambussare.*
To bast flints with butter [to do a thing to no purpose] *far un buco nell' acqua, imbutirrare i sassi.*
To bast meat a-roasting, *spruzzar l' arrosto.*
To bast [to sew with long stitches] *imbastire, unire, insieme i pezzi de' vestimenti con punti grandi o lunghi.*
BA'STARD, adj. [born out of wedlock] *bastardo, nato d'illegitimo congiugnimento.*
A bastard child, *un bastardo.*
Bastard [not true, false] *bastardo, che traligna, falso, tralignante.*
Bastard fruits, *frutti bastardi o tralignanti.*
Bastard Italian, *Italiano corrotto.*
Bastard, s. *un bastardo, una bastarda.*
To BASTARDI'ZE [to corrupt, to mar, to spoil] *imbastardire, far tralignare, far degenerare, adulterare, falsificare, corrompere, convincer uno che gli è bastardo, generar bastardi.*
BASTARDI'ZED, adj. *imbastardito, adulterato, corrotto, falsificato.*
BA'STARDY, s. [the state of a bastard] *bastardigia, s. f. astratto di bastardo.*
To BA'STE, v. To bast.
BA'STED, adj. *battuto, bastonato,* v. To bast.
BA'STEN, adj. *ex.* a basten rope, *fune fatta di scorza di tiglio.*
BASTINA'DO, s. [beating with a cudgel] *bastonata,* s. f. *colpo, o percossa di bastone; bastonatura.*
To BASTINA'DE [to give one the bastinado] *bastonare, percuoter con bastone.*
BASTINADO'D, adj. *bastonato.*
BA'STING, s. [beating] *il bastonare, bastonate, colpi di bastone.*
The basting of meat, *inaffiamento, l'ugner la carne con butirro o lardo mentre si sta arrostendo.*
A basting-ladle, *lardajuolo,* s. m. *strumento di cucina col quale s' inaffia l'arrosto.*
BA'STION, s. [bulwark] *bastione,* s. m. *forte o riparo fatto di muraglia e terrapienato per difesa de' luoghi contra i nemici.*
To fence or fortify with bastions, *bastionare, fortificar con bastioni.*
Fenced or fortified with bastions, *bastionato, fortificato con bastioni.*
BASTO'N, s. [batoon] *bastone,* s. m.
A little baston, *bastoncello,* s. m.
BASTO'N [an officer with the Fleet, who attends the court with a red staff] *bastoniere, mazziere,* s. m. *officiale d'una delle prigioni di Londra, chiamata* Fleet.
BASTONA'DO, v. Bastinado.
BAT, s. [a club to strike a ball with] *mazza, clava,* s. f.
A brick-bat, *un pezzo di mattone.*
Bat-fowling, *l'arramatare, il percuoter con la ramata l'uccelli la notte.*
Bat [reremouse] *pipistrello,* s. m. *nottola,* s. f.

BA'TABLE, adj. *ex.* Batable Ground [ground in debate whether it belongs to England or Scotland, lying between both kingdoms] *campi pe' quali due stati sono in disputa a chi d'essi appartengano.*
BATA'LIA, v. Battalia, and all its derivatives.
BATCH, s. *ex.* a batch of bread, *una fornata di pane.*
BA'TCHELOR, or BA'TCHELOUR, v. Bachelour.
BATE, s. [strife] *lite, contesa, disputa, querela,* s. f.
A make-bate, *un sursurrone, un sursuratore, un facimale.*
To MAKE-BATE, *seminar liti o discenzioni.*
To BATE [to abate or take off from a reckoning] *calare, levare, diffalcare, scontare, trarre o cavar d'una somma, sbattere, detrarre.*
I cannot bate a farthing, *non posso diffalcarne un quattrino, non v' è un quattrino da levare.*
To bate as a hawk does, *svolazzare, calar giù come il falcone.*
BATH, s. [a place to bathe or wash in] *bagno,* s. m. *stufa,* s. f.
A little bath, *bagnuolo,* s. m.
A hot bath, *bagno caldo, stufa,* s. f.
A cold bath, *bagno freddo.*
A knight of the Bath, *un cavaliere del Bagno. Ordine di cavalleria in Inghilterra.*
BATH FLY, *canterella,* s. f.
BATH-KEEPER, *stufajuolo,* s. m.
To BATH, or BATHE [to wash] *bagnare, inaffiare, umettare.*
To bathe one's self, *bagnarsi, entrare in fiume o in altr' acqua.*
BA'THED, adj. *bagnato, inaffiato.*
BA'THING, s. *il bagnare.*
A bathing place, *un bagno, luogo proprio per bagnarsi.*
A bathing tub, *bagno, vaso dentro cui sta acqua o altro liquido per uso di bagnarsi.*
BATING, s. *il calare, levare o diffalcare; disfalco, scemamento,* s. m.
Bating [except some few ones] *eccetto, salvo che.*
BATO'ON, s. [a short thick stick] *bastone,* s. m.
BATTA'ILED, adj. [embattled, having battlements] *merlato, che ha merli.*
Battailed walls, *mura merlate.*
BATTA'LIA, s. [battle-array, order of battle] *battaglia, schiera,* s. f.
To draw up an army in battalia, *schierare, ordinare, un esercito.*
BATTA'LION, s. [a body of foot soldiers] *battaglione,* s. m.
BATTEL, or Battle, s. [an engagement or general fight between two armies] *battaglia,* s. f. *combattimento, fatto d'arme, affrontamento d'eserciti. Oggidì si scrive sempre* BATTLE.
To offer battel, *presentar la battaglia.*
To give battel, *dar battaglia.*
To join battel, *venire alle mani, azzuffarsi, venire a giornata.*
A day of battel, *giornata.*
Battel-array, *schiera, ordinanza,* s. f.

A battel between two, *duello,* s. m.
A sea battel, *battaglia navale.*
Main battel, *il grosso dell' esercito, battaglia.*
To come to a battel, *battagliare, combattere, far battaglia.*
Of a battel, *battaglieresco.*
Fit for a battel, *battaglieroso, atto a battaglia.*
Battel, adj. [fruitful] *fruttifero, fertile, fecondo.*
To BA'TTEL, [to feed as cattle do] *pascere, pasturare, pascolare.*
To battel [to grow fat] *ingrassarsi, divenir grasso.*
To BA'TTEN, [to welter in dung] *voltolarsi nel fango.*
A sow that battens in her own dung] *una scrofa che si voltola nel suo fango.*
To BA'TTEN [to fatten, to get flesh] *ingrassarsi, divenir grasso, impinguarsi.*
BA'TTER, s. [a mixture of water, flower, eggs, &c. to make pancakes] *farina impastata nell' acqua con dell' uova per fare delle frittelle.*
To BA'TTER [to beat down, to demolish] *demolire, atterrare, rovinare,* pres. *demolisco.*
To batter with ordnance, *battere le fortezze o le mura colle artiglierie.*
To batter [to beat, to bruise] *battere percuotere, picchiare, dar percosse.*
To batter one's face, *schiaffeggiare uno.*
BA'TTERED, adj. *demolito, atterrato, rovinato,* v. To batter.
BA'TTERER, s. *battitore,* s. m. *che batte.*
BA'TTERING, s. *battimento,* s. m. *il battere.*
BA'TTERY, s. [a violent beating or striking any person] *battimento,* s. m. *busse, battiture, picchiate, percosse,* s. f. pl.
Battery [a place raised on purpose to plant cannon upon, thence to fire upon the enemy] *batteria,* s. f. *luogo dove sono piantati molti cannoni per battere una piazza, o altra cosa che resista.*
To raise, or set up a battery, *alzare una batteria.*
BATTING STA'FF, s. [a tool made use of by laundresses, to beat washed linen] *battitojo,* s. m. *strumento di legno usato dalle lavandaje per battere le biancherie nel lavarle.*
BATTLE, v. Battel, *scrivi però sempre* BATTLE.
BATTLEDO'RE, s. [an instrument to play at shuttle-cock or tennis] *mestola,* s. f. *strumento di legno col quale si giuoca al volante ed alla palla.*
A battledore [a horn-book] *abbicì, alfabeto,* s. m.
BA'TTLEMENT, s. [a piece of masonry on the top of a building or wall, like a dent] *merlo,* s. m. *parte superiore delle muraglie non continuata, ma interrotta a disuguali distanze.*
BA'TTLER, s. [a young student in the university that battles or scores for his diet] *studente,* s. m.
BATTO'ON, v. Batoon.
BA'TTY. [from Bat; belonging to a Bat] *da nottola, da pipistrello.* Batty wings, *ali da pipistrello.*

BAVARO'Y, s. [a kind of cloak] *sorta di tabarro.*

BAUBE'E, s. [farthing] *un quattrino. E' voce Scozzese.*

BAUD, *v.* Bawd.

BA'VIN, s. [a stick like those bound up in faggots] *flecco, legno,* s. m.

To BAULK, *v.* To balk.

BAULM, *v.* Balm.

To BA'ULTER [to curl] *arricciare, inanellare.*

To baulter one's hair, *arricciarsi, o innanellarsi i capelli.*

BA'WBLE, s. [a plaything] *bagattella, chiappoleria, chiappola,* s. f. *cosa di niuno o di poco pregio.*

A fool's bawble, *baston di matto colla figurina in cima, capocchia,* s. f.

BAWD, s. [a procuress, a lewd woman that makes it her business to debauch others for gain] *ruffiana, mezzana,* s. f.

A bawd [a pimp] *un ruffiano, un mezzano.*

BA'WDRICK, s. [a cord or thong for the clapper of a bell] *fune o nervo di bue col quale si lega il battocchio alla campana.*

Bawdrick [a sword-belt] *bodriere, pendaglio,* s. m.

BA'WDRY, s. [the employment of a bawd] *ruffianeria, ruffiania,* s. f. *ruffianesimo,* s. m.

BA'WDY, adj. [filthy, lewd, smutty] *sporco, osceno, impudico, disonesto, infame, licenzioso, dissoluto.*

Bawdy discourses, *discorsi osceni, parlare disonesto.*

Bawdy words, *parole licenziose.*

Bawdy-house, *bordello, chiasso,* s. m.

To haunt bawdy-houses, *frequentare i bordelli, bordellare, puttaneggiare.*

A haunter of bawdy-houses; *bordelliere,* s. m. *frequentator di bordelli, puttaniere,* s. m.

Bawdy, s. [lewd or filthy discourse, or words] *oscenità; licenza, sfrenatezza, discorsi disonesti, parole licenziose.*

Bawdy, adv. *licenziosamente, sporcamente, oscenamente, impudicamente, disonestamente.*

To talk bawdy, *parlare licenziosamente o sporcamente.*

To BAWL [to bleat as sheep] *belare.*

To bawl [to make a noise] *gridare, strillare, schiamazzare, strepitare.*

To bawl [to proclaim as a crier] *proclamare ad alta voce come fa il banditore.*

BA'WLED, adj. *gridato, strillato, schiamazzato, strepitato.*

BA'WLER, s. *gridatore,* s. m. *che grida, che schiamazza.*

BA'WLING, s. *schiamazzo, schiamazzio, strepito,* s. m.

To keep a bawling, *strillare, schiamazzare.*

Bawling, adj. *strepitoso, che strepita, che schiamazza.*

BA'WSIN, adj. [big, gross] *grosso.*

A great bawsin, *corpulento, grave di corpo, grasso.*

BAY, s. [an arm of the sea coming up into the land, and ending in a nook] *cala, baja,* s. f. *golfo,* s. m. *seno di mare dentro terra.*

Bay [a space left in a wall for a door, gate, or window] *quell' apertura che si lascia nel muro per una finestra o porta.*

A bay window [a round window, a window made archways] *finestra tonda o fatta a volta; occhio,* s. m.

BAYS [holes in a parapet to receive the mouth of a cannon] *cannoniera,* s. f. *quell' apertura donde si scarica da i forti il cannone.*

Bay [dam to stop water] *chiusa,* s. f. *riparo, argine,* s. m.

Bay [joysts betwixt two beams] *travata,* s. f.

To keep one at a bay [to amuse one] *badaluccare uno, tenerlo a bada, trattenerlo.*

Bay, or bay-tree, *lauro,* s. m.

Bay-berry, *bacca di lauro.*

Dwarf bay, *lauro gentile.*

Bay, adj. [a light brown reddish colour in horses and mules] *bajo, mantello di cavallo o di mulo.*

A bay horse, *cavallo bajo.*

Bright bay, *bajo chiaro.*

Dapple bay, *bajo pomellato.*

Bay-salt, *sal nero, sale marino.*

To BAY [to cry like a lamb] *belare.*

To bay [to bark as a dog] *abbajare, latrare.*

To BAY [to follow with barking] *abbajar dietro ad uno.*

BAYA'RD, s. [a bay horse] *un cavallo balzano, un cavallo bajo.*

BA'YING, s. [as a lamb] *belamento,* s. m. *il belare.*

Baying [as a dog] *abbajamento,* s. m. *l'abbajare, il latrare.*

BAYL, *v.* Bail.

BAYLIFF, *v.* Bailiff.

BA'YONNET, s. [a broad dagger to stick on the muzzle of a musket] *bajonetta,* s. f.

BAYZE, or BAZE, s. [a kind of stuff] *bajetta,* s. f.

To BE [to exist] *essere, esistere.*

I am, *sono.*

I have been, *sono stato.*

I should be, *sarei.*

I believe he will be here by and by, *credo che sarà qui fra poco.*

That is true, *è vero.*

You shall be put to your oath, *lo giurerete, vi sarà dato il giuramento.*

It happened as well as could be, *la cosa riuscì felicemente.*

Was I to lose my life I would not do it, *non lo farei se dovessi perdere la vita.*

That's well, *va ben così.*

That will be [will come to pass] *questo sarà, questo succederà.*

Were it not that, *se non fosse che.*

So it is, *così è.*

Who is it? *chi è?*

What's the matter? *che c'è?*

Admit it be so, *supposto che sia così.*

There are some good, some bad, *ve ne sono de' buoni e de' cattivi.*

To be, is often rendered into Italian by the verb *Avere.*

To be hungry, dry, hot, or cold, *aver fame, sete, caldo, o freddo.*

To be ten years old, *aver dieci anni.*

To be of good cheer, *star di buon animo, aver coraggio.*

He is nothing but skin and bones, *non ha che la pelle e l'ossa, non è che pelle ed ossa.*

You are to blame, *avete torto.*

I am to receive money, *ho da ricever danari.*

He is to be hanged, *sarà impiccato.*

You are to play, *tocca a voi a giuocare.*

Who is to deal? *a chi tocca fare.*

He is at dinner, *sta pranzando, è a pranzo.*

I am writing a letter, *sto scrivendo una lettera.*

How is it? *come vanno gli affari?*

How is it with you? *come se la passa? come sta di salute?*

I am very well, *sto molto bene.*

Who are you for? *per chi tenete? con chi tenete?*

Are you for a wing of this capon? *volete un' ala di questo cappone?*

I am for any thing, *amo tutto, m'accomodo a tutto.*

What would you be at? *che volete? che pretendete? che avete disegno di fare? qual è il vostro pensiero.*

This is nothing to you, *cio non v'importa, cio non vi risguarda.*

What is it to me? *che importa a me?*

I will be a father to him, *gli servirò di padre, gli farò in luogo di padre.*

That must be to you instead of a recompence, *ciò deve servirvi di ricompensa, di guiderdone.*

Here he is, *eccolo.*

There she is, *eccola.*

This is the reason why I did not come, *ecco la ragione perchè non venni.*

Thanks be to God, *lodato Iddio.*

If so be that you are resolved to go, *se siete risoluto d'andarvene.*

So it be no trouble to you, *purchè non vi sia incomodo.*

To be in hand with a thing, *aver una cosa fra le mani, star facendo una cosa.*

I cannot be without it, *non posso farne di meno, non posso starne senza.*

I shall be the death of him, *l'amazzerò, gli leverò la vita.*

Gl' Inglesi si servono spesso di questo verbo col participio presente d'un altro verbo.

I am reading, *leggo, o sto leggendo.*

I was reading, *leggevo, o stavo leggendo.*

To be praised. *lodevole, degno di lode.*

Not to be cured, *incurabile.*

That is not to be done, *cio non è fattibile.*

There is good meat eaten in England, *si mangia della buona carne in Inghilterra.*

'Tis great pity, *è gran peccato, gli è peccato.*

'Tis I, *sono io,* 'tis such a one, *è un tale.*

'Tis above an hour since, *è più d'un ora.*

It is day light, *è giorno.*

It is fine weather, *fa bel tempo.*

It is better, *è meglio, val meglio.*
'Tis no matter, *non importa.*
BEACH [shore] *lido, lito,* s. m. *sponda di mare.*
Beach [cape] *capo,* s. m. *punta di terra che sporge in mare.*
Beach [a shrub] *aspalto,* s. m.
BE'ACON, s. [a long pole set upon a rising ground near the sea coasts, on which pitch barrels are fastened ready to be fired, to give notice of invasions, and prevent shipwreck] *faro,* s. m. *lanterna,* s. f.
To watch at a beacon, *star di guardia appresso il faro.*
A watcher at a beacon, *uomo che sta di guardia al faro.*
BE'ACONAGE, s. [money to maintain a beacon] *il dazio che si paga per il mantenimento d'un faro.*
BE'AD, s. *pallottolina bucata, di varie materie e fogge.*
Popish beads to say their prayers over with, *paternostri,* s. m. *avemmarie,* s. f. pl. *quelle pallottoline della filza volgarmente detta corona o rosario.*
A pair of beads, *una corona, un rosario.*
A string of beads or pearls, *un vezzo di perle.*
A necklace of beads, *collana di perle, monile.*
A string of beads for the arms, *armilla, maniglia,* s. f.
To say over one's beads, *dir la corona o il rosario.*
To thread beads, *infilzar paternostri.*
BEAD-RO'LL, or Bed-roll [a list of such who used to be prayed for in the church] *lista o catalogo di quelli pe' quali i preti erano soliti di pregare nelle chiese.*
BEADS-MAN [one who says prayers for his patron] *pregatore,* s. m. *quello, che prega in chiesa per il suo benefattore.*
BE'ADLE, s. [an officer that belongs to a university, to a hall, to a company of citizens, to a ward, or to a parish] *bidello, mazziere,* s. m.
Beadle [crier of a court] *banditore,* s. m.
Beadle, *donzello, sergente, tavolaccino,* s. m.
Beadle [in a corporation to whip beggars] *birro, giustiziere, sbirro,* s. m.
BE'AGLE, s. [a sort of hunting dog] *bracco,* s. m. *sorta di cane da caccia.*
A precious beagle [a rascally fellow] *un uomo da niente, un mascalzone, un birbone, un gaglioffone.*
BEAK, s. [bill of a bird] *becco, rostro,* s. m. *la bocca degli ucelli.*
Beakful, *beccata,* s. f. *quanto può capir nel becco.*
A little beak, *beccuccio,* s. m. *piccolo becco.*
The beak of a ship, *sprone,* s. m. *la punta della prua de' navili.*
The beak head, *beccuccio,* s. m.
The beak of an alembick, *becco, beccuccio,* s. m. *il canaletto adunco del lambicco onde esce l'acqua che vi si stilla.*
BE'AKED, adj. *rostrato, che ha il becco o rostro.*

BE'AKER, s. [a drinking cup] *tazza, ciotola,* s. f.
BEAL, s. [a whelk, a push] *bolla, pustula,* s. f. *enfiatura o bollicella che viene alla pelle.*
To beal [to gather matter] *impostemire, far capo.*
BEAM, s. [a piece of great timber in building] *trave,* s. f.
Beam [the pole or wain of a coach] *timone,* s. m. *quel legno della carozza al quale s'attaccan le bestie per tirare,* Temo lo' disse Dante.
The beam of a ballance, *lo stilo della bilancia.*
The beam [the main horns of a stag's head] *ramo delle corna del cervo.*
A weaver's beam, or yarn beam, *subbio,* s. m.
Beam [ray of light] *raggio,* s. m. *splendore che esce da corpo lucido.*
The beams of the sun, *i raggi del sole.*
A beam [a meteor in the shape of a column] *striscia di fuoco.*
To BEAM [to emit rays or beams] *raggiare, mandar fuora i raggi.*
BE'AMY, adj. [full of beams, radiant] *luminoso, raggiante.*
BEAN, s. [a sort of pulse] *fava,* s. f. *sorta di legume.*
Kidney-beans, or French beans, *fagiuoli,* s. m. *legume, o civaja di diversi colori e varie forme.*
The black of a bean, *viso di fagiuolo, o di fava.*
Every bean has its black, *ognuno ha'l suo impiccato all' uscio, ognuno ha qualche difetto.*
A bean cod, *baccello di fava.*
To shell beans, *diguściare delle fave.*
Bean porridge, *fava,* s. f. *vivanda fatta di fave infrante, macco,* s. m.
Bean bruised, *fave infrante.*
Bean trefoil, *favagello,* s. m. *erba campestre, che nasce nella primavera.*
Bean stalk, *fusta, o gambo di fava.*
A bean flat, *un seminato di fave.*
BEAR, s. [a noted wild beast] *orso,* s. m.
A she bear, *orsa,* s. f.
A bear's club, *orsacchio, orsatto,* s. m.
To sell the bear's skin before one has caught him, *vender la pelle dell' orso; promettere con assegnamenti incerti.*
He goes like a bear to the stake [he goes unwillingly] *va come la biscia all' incanto, vi va mal volentieri.*
A bear dog, *cane che combatte cogli orsi.*
A bear garden, *luogo dove i cani combattono cogli orsi.*
Bear's breech, bear's foot, or brankursine [a plant] *brancorsina,* s. f. *erba medicinale.*
To BEAR [to carry] *portare.*
To bear a burden, *portare una soma.*
These pillars bear all the house, *questi pilastri sostentano tutta la casa.*
To bear [to abide, to suffer] *patire, sopportare, comportare, sofferire.*
I cannot bear the heat, *non posso patire il caldo.*

To bear a thing patiently, *sopportare una cosa con pazienza.*
To bear the enemy's onset, *resistere all' assalto del nemico.*
We must bear what falls to our lot, *bisogna sottometterci alla fortuna, agli eventi della fortuna.*
To be ararms against one, *prendere o portar l'armi contro ad uno.*
To bear [to yield, to bring forth] *produrro, generare, creare.*
This tree bears good fruits, *quest' albero produce buoni frutti.*
To bear children, *generare, fare figliuoli.*
She is so old that she is past bearing, *è sì vecchia che non può più aver figliuoli.*
To bear one company, *accompagnare uno, fare compagnia ad uno.*
To bear one good will [to have a good will for one] *portare amore ad alcuno, amarlo, guardarlo di buon occhio.*
To bear one a grudge, a spite, an ill will, *voler male ad alcuno, odiarlo, averla con alcuno, guardarlo di mal occhio.*
To bear sway [to bear rule] *dominare, governare, signoreggiare, fare alto e basso.*
To bear an office, *esercitare un officio, o carica.*
To bear the charges, *fare le spese, spesare.*
I'll bear your charges, *vi farò le spese.*
I have not one penny to bear my charges, *non ho un soldo per farmi le spese.*
Wine that bears water, *vino che porta l'acqua, che è buono anche dopo averci messa dell' acqua.*
Paper that bears ink, *carta che non beve l'inchiostro.*
This word will hardly bear that sense, *questa parola a malapena si può pigliare in questo senso.*
These two words bear the same sense, *queste due parole hanno il medesimo senso, significano la medesima cosa.*
What date does this letter bear? *di che data è questa lettera? a quanti del mese fu scritta questa lettera?*
To bear witness, *far testimonianza, esser testimonio, testificare.*
Bear witness, *vi prendo per testimonio, siatemi testimonio.*
To bear resemblance [to resemble] *rassomigliarsi, aver somiglianza, esser simile.*
To bear proportion, *aver proporzione, esser proporzionato.*
I shall bear a perpetual memory of his kindness, *conserverò per sempre nella memoria la sua cortesia, mi sarà per sempre impressa nella memoria la sua bontà o amorevolezza.*
To bear a thing in one's mind [to remember it] *avere una cosa nella memoria, ricordarsene.*
Our language will not bear such a stile, *questo stile non si confà colla nostra lingua; l'indole della nostra lingua non soffre questo stile.*

This

This is a subject that would hear a volume, *questo è un sogetto da formarne un volume.*

To bear too hard upon one [to use one too hard] *trattare uno troppo rigrosamente, usar con troppa severità.*

To bear one's self upon one's learning [to glory in it] *vantarsi del proprio sapere, vanagloriársene, pavoneggiársene, farsene bello.*

To behave one's self, *comportarsi, procedere, portarsi.*

To bear one's self as a gentleman, *comportarsi da gentiluomo, da signore, da cavaliere.*

To bear a good price [to sell well, to sell at a good rate] *avere buono spaccio.*

This commodity will bear a good price this year, *questa mercanzia avrà buono spaccio quest' anno.*

It will not bear a better price, *non si venderà a più alto prezzo.*

To bear a little or no price, *vendersi a vil prezzo.*

What price does it bear here? *per quanto si vende quì?*

To bear a good honest mind [to have good principles] *esser d'animo retto, esser leale, aver il cuore integro.*

To bear faith to one, *serbar fede ad alcuno, esser fedele ad alcuno.*

To bear a fair face, *far buona ciera.*

To bear one's age well, *parer più giovane che uno non è, aver salute comechè vecchio.*

He gives more than his estate will bear, *da più di quel che i suoi beni non comportano, da più di quel che la sua condizione non gli permette.*

To bear away [to carry away] *portar via.*

To bear away the prize, *vincere il premio, riportare il premio.*

To bear away, *neut.* [to run away at sea] *prender la fuga, fuggirsene, modo marinaresco.*

To bear out [to make good] *risarcire, ristaurare, racconciare.*

To bear out [to save] *proteggere, difendere, mantenere, sostentare.*

The circumstances will, I hope, bear me out, *le circostanze basteranno a giustificarmi.*

To bear off [to carry away by force] *portar via per forza.*

To bear off a blow, *parare un colpo.*

To bear out [to jut out] *sporgere in fuora.*

To bear with one, *compatire, sopportare, scusare alcuno.*

One may well bear with a little inconvenience for a great deal of convenience, *non è gran fatto che chi ha l'utile s'abbia anche un po' di fastidio, e pazientemente sel porti.*

To bear up, *sostenere, sopportare.*

To bear up, *neut. alzarsi, crescere, avvanzarsi.*

To bear up, *mantenersi.*

To bear up against a person, *resistere, opporsi, far testa ad uno.*

To bear up before the wind [a sea phrase] *andare col vento in poppa.*

To bear up to a ship, *abbordare un vascello.*

To bear towards the coasts, *andare verso le coste.*

To bear down, *abbassare, chinare, abbattere, mandar a terra, mandar giu.*

Love is able to bear down all considerations whatsoever, *l'amore prevale a tutte le considerazioni, l'amore vince tutti i riguardi.*

To bear one down in discourse [to make one yield] *convincere uno col discorso, farlo cedere.*

To bear down [to face down] *mantenere una cosa in faccia ad alcuno.*

A pistole that bears down the weight, *una doppia traboccante.*

To bear off [a sea term] *andar largo.*

To bear respect unto, *rispettare, portar rispetto.*

Beard, s. [the hair about the chin and cheeks of a man] *barba,* s. f. *peli che ha l'uomo nel mento e nelle guance.*

A man's or goat's beard, *la barba d'un uomo, d'una capra.*

Rough beard, *barba ispida.*

The beard of an ear of corn, *barba di spica.*

The beard of roots, *barba; le radici delle piante.*

A little beard, *barbetta,* s. f.

A little beard [speaking of roots] *barbolina, barbuccia,* s. f.

A nasty greasy beard, *barbaccia,* s. f.

Having a great beard, *barbuto, che ha gran barba.*

Having a little beard, *che ha la barba rada e spelazzata.*

To Beard, *strappare la barba.*

To beard wool, *tosare la lana.*

To beard a stuff, *cimare una pezza di panno.*

To beard one [to affront him] *affrontare uno, fargli un affronto.*

Be'arded, adj. *barbato,* v. To beard.

Bearded ears, *spiche barbute.*

A red bearded fellow, *un barbarossa, un uomo che ha la barba rossa.*

A bearded arrow, *una saetta pennuta.*

Be'ardless, adj. *sbarbato, che non ha barba.*

A beardless man, *uno sbarbato.*

There cannot be upon the earth a worse man, than a beardless and pale-coloured one, *poca barba e men colore, sotto'l ciel non e'l peggiore.*

Be'arer, s. [one that bears] *portatore, latore,* s. m. *portatrice,* s. f.

Bearer of dead corps to the grave, *beccamorto, becchino,* s. m.

Bearhe'rd, s. [a man that tends bears] *colui che guarda gli orsi, guardiano degli orsi.*

Bear-wa'rd [Bearherd] *guardiano d'orsi.*

Bea'ring, s. *portamento,* s. m. v. to bear.

There is no bearing of this, *è una cosa insopportabile, da non potersi sopportare.*

A woman past bearing, *una donna frusta, una donna che non genera più per esser troppo attempata.*

A tree past bearing, *un albero sfruttato.*

A field past bearing, *un campo stracco.*

Bearing date, *che ha la data, datato.*

Bearing, s. [suffering] *patimento. dolore,* s. m. *afflizione, angoscia,* s. f.

Beasel, v. Bazil.

Be'asom, s. or besom, *scopa, granata,* s. f.

Beast, s. [a brute] *bestia,* s. f. *nome generico di tutti gli animali bruti, fuorchè gl' insetti.*

A wild beast, *una fera salvatica.*

A tame beast, *una bestia domestica.*

A beast of burden, *una bestia da soma.*

A beast for the saddle, *una cavalcatura, una bestia che si cavalca.*

A little beast, *besticciuola, bestiuola,* s. f.

A great beast, *una bestiaccia,* s. f. *un bestione,* s. m.

A herd of beasts, *un bestiame, una moltitudine di bestie.*

A beast [a filthy creature, a lewd man or woman] *una bestia; un uomo o una donna senza discorso, o che abbia costumi da bestie, azioni da bestie.*

Be'stial, adj. [like a beast] *bestiale, da bestia, simile alla bestia.*

Be'astially, adv. *bestialmente, da bestia, a modo di bestia.*

Be'astliness, s. [brutishness] *bestialità, brutalità, ferità, immanità,* s. f.

Beastliness [filthiness, nastiness] *bestialità, sporchezza, sporcizia, schifezza, laidezza,* s f.

Be'astly, adj. [brutish] *bestiale, bruto.*

A beastly desire, *desiderio bestiale, brutale.*

Beastly [filthy, nasty] *bestiale, sporco, laido, schifo, osceno, impudico.*

Beastly discourses, *discorsi da bestia.*

To Beat [to strike] *battere, dar percosse, bussare, dar busse, picchiare.*

To beat one soundly, *tartassare, malmenare uno, bastonarlo bene.*

To beat one's breast, *battersi il petto.*

To beat the drum, *battere il tamburo.*

To beat time in musick, *tener la battuta.*

To beat down with a pole, *battachiare, sbatter giù con un palo, abbacchiare.*

To beat the hoof, *battere il tacone, andare a piedi.*

To beat [to knock] *picchiare.*

To beat down, *abbattere, mandare a terra.*

To beat [to bruise] *pestare.*

To beat pepper in a mortar, *pestar del pepe in un mortajo.*

To beat flax or hemp, *maciullare del lino o del canape.*

To beat [to get the better of, to overcome] *vincere, superare, sconfiggere.*

To beat the enemies, *vincere o sconfiggere i nemici, rompere il nemico in battaglia.*

I beat him five sets together at piquet, *gli ho guadagnato a picchetto cinque partite alla fila.*

To beat flat, *schiacciare, ammaccare.*

To beat one's head or brains about a thing, *rompersi il capo intorno a qualche cosa, infastidirsi, inquietarsi.*

To beat in, *spingere, cacciare, ficcare con forza.*

To beat a thing into a man's head, brains, mind, or memory, *ficcare una cosa in testa ad uno.*

To beat a thing in one's own head, *ficcarsi una cosa in testa.*

To beat one black and blue, *ammaccare, batter uno a morte, render alcuno livido a forza di battiture.*

To beat back [to beat off] *rispignere, ributtare.*

The wind did beat us back, *il vento ci rispinse.*

To beat down the price, *rincarare il prezzo, offrire piu che non un altro; significa ancora prezzolare, diminuire di prezzo.*

To beat out, *cavare, trarre.*

To beat out one's eyes, *cavar gli occhi ad uno, creparli gli occhi.*

To beat a thing out of one's head, *cavar una cosa di testa ad uno, dissuaderlo.*

To beat one out of his opinion, *smuovere alcuno della sua opinione.*

To beat one out of his reason, *dare a credere ad uno che ha torto.*

To beat one out of countenance, *confondere, far rimaner confuso, imbrogliare, intrigare, avviluppare.*

To beat one's head against the wall, *battersi la testa contro un muro, dar della testa in un muro.*

To beat against, as the waves against the rocks, *sbattere, sbattersi, rompersi contro, parlando dell' onde del mare.*

To beat to powder, *spolverizzare, ridurre in polvere.*

To beat upon, *battere.*

The sun beats upon that place, *il sole batte in questo luogo.*

To beat a thing to make it thinner, *assottigliare una cosa.*

To beat with a hammer, *martellare, percuotere col martello.*

To beat with the fist, *schiaffeggiare.*

To beat as hunters do, *odorare, indagare, andare alla traccia.*

To beat down the seams, *spianar le costure.*

To beat the reveille [to beat the drum at break of day] *batter la diana.*

BE'ATEN, adj. *battuto, bastonato, vinto, guadagnato, spolverizzato,* v. To beat.

An old-beaten soldier, *un soldato vecchio, un soldato veterano.*

Beaten way, *via battuta, via frequentata, via pesta.*

An old beaten argument, *un argomento trito o comune.*

Beaten with rods, *frustato.*

BE'ATER, s. [he that beats] *battitore,* s. m. *che batte.*

Beater [rammer] *strumento di legno col quale si batte o s'assoda il pavimento.*

A printer's beater, *un mazzo.*

BEATIFI'CAL, } adj. [making hap-
BEATIFI'CK, } py or blessed] *beatifico, che fa beato.*

BEATIFICA'TION, s. [the act by which the pope declares a person to be blessed after his death] *beatificazione,* s. f. *il beatificare.*

To BEATIFY' [to make blessed, to enroll among the blessed] *beatificare, beare, mettere o annoverar fra i beati.*

BEATIFY'D, adj. *beatificato, beato.*

BE'ATING, s. *battimento, il battere, percotimento, picchiamento,* s. m.

The beating of him does no good, *il batterlo non giova a nulla.*

The beating of the heart, *palpito, palpitamento,* s. m. *il palpitar del cuore.*

The beating of the pulse, *battimento del polso.*

A beating back, *ripercuotimento,* s. m. *ripercussione,* s. f.

A beating of one thing against another, *dibattimento,* s. m.

BEA'TITUDE, s. [blessedness, bliss, happiness] *beatitudine, felicità,* s. f. *contento,* s. m.

BEAU, s. [a fop, a spark, a spruce gentleman] *un affettatuzzo, un zerbinotto, un parigino, un milordino, un bellimbusto.*

BE'AVER, s. [a beast like an otter] *castoro,* s. m. *animal terrestre e aquatico. I nostri antichi dissero anco bevero.*

Beaver [a hat] *un cappello fatto di pelo di castoro, un castoro.*

Beaver [eating between meals] *merenda,* s. f.

The beaver of a helmet, *v.* Bever.

To BE'AVER, *merendare,*

BEAU'TEOUS, } adj. *bello, leggia-*
BEAU'TIFUL, } *dro, vistoso, vezzoso, vago.*

BEAU'TIFULLY, adv. *bellamente, vezzosamente, vagamente.*

BEAU'TIFULNESS, s. *bellezza, leggiadria, vaghezza,* s. f.

To BEAUTIFY' [to make beautiful, to grace] *abbellire, far bello, ornare, imbellettare,* pref. *abbellisco.*

BEAUTIFY'D, *abbellito, ornato, imbellettato.*

BEAUTIFY'ING, s. *abellimento,* s. m. *l'abbellire, ornamento, belletto,* s. m.

BEAU'TY, s. [comeliness, handsomeness] *bellezza, beltà, vaghezza, leggiadria,* s. f.

Women are mighty fond of their beauty, *le donne sono molto incapriccite dello loro bellezza.*

Beauty water, *acqua della quale le donne si servono per conservare la loro bellezza.*

She is a beauty [she is a very handsome woman] *è la bellezza istessa, è una bellissima donna, è una bellezza.*

To BECA'LM [to make calm, to appease] *calmare, quetare, abbonacciare.*

BECA'LMED, adj. *calmato, quetato, abbonacciato.*

BECA'ME, pret *del verbo,* To become.

BECA'USE, conj. *perchè, perchiocchè.*

I do it because I have a mind to it, *lo fo perchè così mi piace.*

I do it because of you, *lo fo per amor vostro.*

BECCAFI'CO, s. [a fig-eater, a figpecker, a kind of ortolan] *beccafico,* s. m. *uccelletto, che viene in tempo de' fichi e che si pasce di fichi.*

BECK, s. [nod, sign with the head, or with the hand] *cenno, segno, gesto che si fa colla testa, o colla mano.*

To give a beck to one, *far cenno ad alcuno.*

To be at one's beck, *dipendere dai cenni altrui, esser soto la dipendenza d'alcuno, pendere dall' arbitrio di qualcuno.*

He keeps him at his beck, *lo tiene a sua posta, fa di lui quel che gli piace.*

To BE'CKON [to make a sign with the hand or head] *accennare, far cenno.*

BE'CKONED TO, adj. *accennato.*

BE'CKONING, s. *accennamento,* s. m. *l'accennare.*

To BECO'ME, verb. neut. *divenire, diventare.*

The wound became uncurable, *la piaga divenne incurabile.*

He became rich in a little time, *diventò ricco in poco tempo.*

To become [to be fit, fitting, or becoming] *convenire, esser conveniente, affarsi, non disdire, star bene.*

That which becomes one does not become another] *quel che conviene ad uno non conviene ad un altro.*

It does not become a man of your profession, *ciò non è convenevole ad un uomo della vostra professione.*

It becomes not a prudent man to be too angry, *si disdice ad un uomo prudente l'adirarsi soverchiamente.*

You do as becomes you, *voi fate quel che è degno di voi, voi trattate da par vostro.*

This garment becomes you, *questo abito vi stà bene.*

It does not become you to speak so, *non istà bene a voi il parlar in questo modo.*

To become of, *essere.*

What will become of me? *che sarà mai di me?*

Whatsoever becomes of me, *sia di me quel che si voglia.*

You care not what becomes of me, *di me nulla vi cale.*

Become, adj. *divenuto, diventato, v.* to become.

I don't know what's become of him, *non so quel che sia di lui.*

BE'COMING, adj. *convenevole, conveniente, dicevole.*

This is not very becoming of you, *ciò non è convenevole, ciò non istà bene a voi.*

BE'CONAGE, *v.* Beaconage.

BED, s. *letto,* s. m. pl. *letti,* m. e *letta,* f.

To go to bed, *andare a letto, andare a dormire.*

To lie a bed, *stare a letto.*

A bed of state, *un letto di parata.*

A little bed, *un letticciuolo, un letticello, un lettuccio.*

To be brought to bed, *partorire.*

One that has brought to bed, *una partoriente, una donna che ha partorito.*

A truckle bed, } *carriuola,* s. f. *letto,*
A trundle bed, } *che in vere di piedi ha quattro girelle, e tiensi sotto altre letta.*

A feather bed, *coltre,* s. f. *arnese da letto ripieno di piuma sul quale si giace.*

A flock

A flock-bed, *un letto di borra.*
A ſtraw bed, *un pegliariccio, un ſaccone di paglia, un pagliaccio.*
The bed's head, *il capo del letto, il capezzale.*
A bedſtead, *una lettierà, il legname del letto.*
Bed-ſide, *la ſponda del letto.*
The bed poſts, *le colonne del letto.*
Bed-cloaths [bedding] *coperte del letto.*
Bed-chamber, *camera da letto.*
Bed-curtain, *cortinaggio,* s. m. *cortina,* s. f.
Bed-time, *ora d'andare a letto.*
'Tis bed-time, *è ora d'andare a letto.*
Bed-fellow, *compagno o compagna di letto.*
BEDMA'TE, s. [bedfellow] *compagno o compagna di letto.*
Bed [in a garden] *ſolco,* s. m. *ſpazio quadro che ſi fa negli orti.*
A bed of ſtrawberries, *un ſolco di fragole.*
A bed of aſparagus, *un ſolco di ſpáragi.*
A bed of ſnakes, *un gruppo di ſerpentelli.*
The bed of a river, *il letto d'un fiume.*
Ladies bed-ſtraw [an herb] *fioraliſo, mughetto,* s. m. *ſorta di fiore.*
To BED, verb neut. *coricarſi.*
Have they bedded together? [ſpeaking of a new-married couple] *ſi ſono eglino coricati inſieme? hanno eglino giaciuto inſieme?*
To bed a wife, *andare a letto con la ſpoſa.*
To BEDA'GGLE, *zaccherare, macchiar di zácchere.*
BEDA'GGLED, adj. *zaccherato.*
BEDA'GGLING, s. *zaccheramento,* s. m. *lo zaccherare.*
To BEDA'SH, *ſpruzzare, imbrattare.*
BEDA'SHED, adj. *ſpruzzato, imbrattato.*
To BEDA'UB, *ſporcare, bruttare, imbrattare.*
BE'DDED, adj. *coricato.*
BE'DDING, s. [or bed-cloaths] *coperte di letto, quantità di letti.*
BE'DDER, or BEDE'TTER, s. [the nether ſtone of an oil-mill] *màcina del macinatojo, o mulino dove ſi macinano l'ulive.*
To BEDEW', *irrorare, aſperger di rugiada, inaffiare, irrigare, bagnare.*
BEDEW'ED, adj. *irrorato, inaffiato, irrigato, bagnato di rugiada.*
BE'DLAM, s. *i pazzarelli, lo ſpedale de' pazzi.*
A BEDLAMI'TE [a madman] *un pazzo, un matto, un inſenſato, un forſennato.*
BEDLAMLI'KE, adv. *da pazzo, da matto, pazzamente, inſenſatamente, forſennatamente.*
BED-MAKER [a perſon in the univerſities of England whoſe office it is to make the beds] *colui o colei il cui ufficio nelle univerſità d'Inghilterra è di rifar le letta.*
To BEDU'NG, *letamare, ſparger di letame.*

BEDU'NGED, adj. *letamato, aſperſo di letame.*
BE'DUNGING, s. *letamamento,* s. m. *il letamare, lo ſparger letame.*
To BEDU'ST, *impolverare, gettar della polvere ſopra checchè ſia.*
To beduſt [to maul one] *malmenare uno, conciarlo male, tartaſſarlo, tambuſſarlo.*
BEDU'STED, adj. *impolverato, malmenato, tartaſſato, tambuſſato.*
BEE [honey-bee] *ape, pecchia,* s. f.
A ſwarm of bees, *ſciame, ſciamo,* s. m. *quella quantità di pecchie che abitano e vivono inſieme.*
To be as buſy as a bee, *eſſer affaccendato come un' ape, eſſer ſempre in moto.*
Gad-bee, *tafano,* s. m.
A bee-hive, *alveario, alveare,* s. m. *arnia,* s. f. *caſſetta da pecchie.*
Young bees, *cacchioni,* s. m.
To BEE, *v.* to be.
BEECH, s. [a tree] *faggio,* s. m. *albero alpeſtre.*
BEE'CHEN, adj. [of beech] *di faggio.*
BEEF, s. *vaccina,* s. f. *carne di bue.*
Powdered beef [ſalt beef] *vaccina ſalata, bue ſalato.*
Boiled beef, *vaccina leſſa.*
Beef eater, *mangiatore di vaccina.*
Beef eater, *è un ſopranome che ſi da agli alabardieri del Re, per mangiar eſſi communemente della vaccina quando ſono di guardia, detti altrimenti,* the yeomen of the guard.
BEEN, adj. *ſtato.*
I have been, *ſono ſtato.*
BEER, s. [a drink] *birra, cervogia,* s. f. *bevanda fatta di grano, di vena, e d'orzo.*
Strong beer, *birra forte, cervogia forte.*
Small beer, *piccola birra, cervogia piccola.*
Beer [bier to carry dead on] *bara,* s. f. *cataletto,* s. m. *ſtrumento di legname per portare il cadavero alla ſepoltura. Scrivi ſempre* BIER *in queſto ſignificato.*
Thoſe that carry the beer, *beccamorti, becchini,* s. m. pl.
The beer cloth, *panno o drappo da mettere ſopra 'l cadavero nella bara.*
BEE'STINGS, s. [breſtings, the firſt milk of a cow after calving] *primo latte d'una vacca dopo che ha figliato.*
BEET, s. [an herb ſo named] *bietola,* s. f. *erba nota, buona a mangiare.*
Bed-béet, *paſtinaca,* s. f. *ſorta di radice.*
BE'ETLE, s. [a kind of inſect] *ſcarafaggio, ſcarabeo,* s. m.
A dung-beetle, *ſcarafaggio che fa la pallottola dello ſterco.*
The venomous beetle [the long-leg beetle] *ſorta di ſcarafaggio che ſi crede ſia velenoſo.*
Beetle [a wooden inſtrument for driving of piles, ſtakes, wedges, &c.] *maglio,* s. m.
A paving-beetle, *una mezzeranga.*
As blind as a beetle, *affatto cieco, che non può vedere.*
A beetle head, *un bietolone, un dappoco, uno ſciocco.*

Beetle brow'd, *che ha le ciglia folte.*
Beetle brow'd, *che ha il viſo arcigno, di faccia burbera.*
The beetle fiſh, *canterella,* s f.
BEETLEHE'ADED, adj. *vano, ſciocco.*
To BEFA'LL [to happen] *intervenire, avvenire, accadére, ſuccédere,* preſ. *interviene, avviene,* paſſ. *ſucceſſe.*
The ſame things would befall me, *il medeſimo interverebbe a me.*
There has no ſorrow befallen him in his joy, *la ſua allegrezza non fu amareggiata da diſpiacere veruno.*
A very ſtrange accident befell him, *gli avvene uno ſtrano caſo.*
BEFA'LLEN, adj. *intervenuto, avvenuto, accaduto, ſucceſſo.*
To BEFI'T [to ſuit, to be ſuitable to] *convenire, eſſere convenevole, addatto, proprio, acconcio, a propoſito.*
BEFI'TTING, adj. *convenevole, conveniente, proprio.*
To BEFO'OL [to make a fool of, to call fool] *trattare uno da matto, beffarlo, burlarlo.*
BEFO'RE, prep. *and* adv. *avanti, prima, inanzi.*
The day before he went away, *il giorno avanti che partiſſe.*
Before dinner, *prima di pranzo.*
Before all the world, *in preſenza di tutti.*
Before and behind, *inanzi e indietro, dinanzi e didietro.*
Long before [long before now] *molto tempo prima, un pezzo fa.*
An hour before, *un' ora prima.*
I love him before myſelf, *l'amo più di me ſteſſo.*
I'll tell him ſo before his face, *glielo dirò in faccia.*
I'll die before I'll put up the affront, *vorrei più toſto morire che ſopportare un tale ſmacco.*
Before [in the preſence] *in preſenza, al coſpetto, innanzi.*
Before the face of the whole town, *in preſenza di tutto 'l popolo.*
Before one's face, *in faccia.*
To prefer a thing before another, *preferire una coſa ad un' altra.*
To go before, *precedere, andare avanti.*
To know a thing before hand, *antiſapere una coſa, ſapere una coſa avanti tratto.*
To pay money before hand, *pagar danari anticipatamente.*
To be beforehand in the world, *aver più crediti che debiti, aver qualcoſa.*
To be beforehand with one, *prevenire alcuno.*
He has the world before, *è appena entrato nel mondo.*
To get before one, *avanzare alcuno.*
To BEFRIE'ND ONE, *trattar uno da amico, favorirlo.*
To befriend one's ſelf, *penſare a quel che fa per ſe, aver a cuore il proprio intereſſe.*
BEFRIE'NDED, adj. *favorito, aſſiſtito.*
BEFRIE'NDING, s. *favore,* s. m.
To BEG [to aſk alms] *mendicare, andar*

dar mendicando, chieder limosina, limosinare, accattare.

He begs his bread from door to door, *va accattando da uscio a uscio, mendica la sua vita a frusto a frusto.*

To beg [earnestly to desire] *chiedere, ricercare, scongiurare, strettamente pregare.*

Let me beg it of you, *ve ne scongiuro.*

I beg of you that you will do me that kindness, *di grazia fatemi questo favore.*

To beg something of one, *chiedere qualche cosa ad uno.*

I beg your pardon, *vi domando perdono, vi chieggo scusa.*

BEGA'N, *preterito del verbo.* To begin.

I began to speak, *cominciai a parlare.*

Since the world began, *da che il mondo è mondo, dal principio del mondo.*

To BEGE'T [to produce] *generare, produrre, dar l'essere.*

To beget a son or a daughter, *generare un figliuolo o una figliuola.*

To beget [to cause, to procure] *generare, cagionare, produrre, eccitare.*

Plenty begets divisions, *l'abbondanza genera divisioni, cagiona discordia.*

BEGE'TTER, s. *genitore, generatore,* s. m. *genitrice, generatrice,* s. f. *che genera.*

BEGE'TTING, s. *generazione,* s. f. *il generare.*

Begetting, adj. *generante, che genera.*

BE'GGAR, s. *un mendico, un pezzente, un pitocco.*

A beggar woman, *una mendica.*

BEGLERBE'G [the chief governor of a province among the Turks] *beglierbei, governatore d'una provincia fra i Turchi.*

To BEGNA'W [to bite, to eat away] *andar rodendo, roder via.*

BEGO'NE [go away, hence] *vanne via, vattene, parti.*

Sue a beggar and catch a louse, *chi ha da far con pitocchi non aspetti che pidocchi.*

Set a beggar on horseback, and he'll ride to the devil, *metti un pezzente a cavallo e lo vedrai subito galoppare; cioè, non v'è uomo più superbo d'un mendico rifatto.*

I know him as well as the beggar knows his dish, *so ben quanto pesa.*

Beggars bush, *posta di mendici.*

To BE'GGAR, *impoverire, far povero, render povero, mandar allo spedale.*

BE'GGARED, adj. *impoverito.*

BE'GGARLINESS, s. *povertà, miseria, mendicità,* s. f.

BE'GGARLY, adj. *povero, mendico, pezzente.*

A beggarly fellow, *un mendico, un guidone.*

A beggarly thing, *una cosa vile o abbietta.*

Beggarly cloaths, *stracci, cenci.*

Beggarly doings, *azioni infami.*

Beggarly, adv. *poveramente, meschinamente.*

BE'GGARY, s. *mendicità, povertà, miseria, indigenza, necessità,* s. f. *bisogno,* s. m.

Luxury is the highway to beggary, *il lusso mena dritto allo spedale.*

BE'GGED, adj. *mendicato,* v. to beg.

He was begg'd to do it, *fu richiesto di farlo.*

BE'GGER, v. Beggar.

BE'GGING, s. *il mendicare.*

Begging, adj. *mendicando, accattando.*

To go a begging, *andar mendicando, o accattando.*

The begging friars, *i frati mendicanti.*

To BEGI'N [to make a beginning] *cominciare, principiare.*

It begins to rain, *comincia a piovere.*

To begin a discourse, *entrare in parole, cominciare un discorso.*

To begin the war, *entrare in guerra.*

To begin a dance, *entrare in ballo.*

To begin a battle, *venire a battaglia.*

To begin a journey, *mettersi in cammino.*

To begin a loaf, *metter mano ad un pane.*

To begin a picture, *abbozzare un quadro.*

To begin the world, *mettersi in negozio, mettersi in faccende.*

To begin a design, *mettersi in cuore, deliberarsi.*

To begin house-keeping, *pigliar casa, metter su casa.*

To begin to speak of a thing, *metter il becco in molle, entrare a parlare di che che sia.*

To begin afresh, or again, *ricominciare, di nuovo cominciare.*

He begins the old complaints again, *egli rinovella le medesime querele.*

To begin one's journey again, *ripigliare il cammino, ricominciare il viaggio.*

To begin to rain again, *ripiovere.*

To begin [to raise] *nascere, avvenire, levarsi,* pret. *nacqui,* pres. *avvengo.*

There began a quarrel betwixt them, *nacque fra di loro una contesa, vennero a parole insieme.*

To begin to arise, *levarsi, spuntare, cominciar a mostrarsi.*

BEGI'NNER, s. *un principiante.*

The chief beginner, *autore, inventore,* s. m.

A beginner, or learner, *un soro, un novizio, un principiante.*

BEGI'NNING, s. *principio, cominciamento.*

The beginning of the world, *il principio del mondo.*

Beginning [rise] *principio, origine, nascimento,* s. m. *causa,* s. f.

That's it which gave beginning to the report, *questo fu che fece nascere un tal bisbiglio, che cominciò a far creder questo.*

Beginning [first entrance] *introito, ingresso,* s. m. *entrata, entratura,* s. f.

At the beginning, *alla prima.*

To BEGI'RD, *cignere, cingere, circondare,* pret. *cinsi.*

BEGO'T, *preterito del verbo* To beget.

I begot, *io generai.*

BEGO'TTEN, adj. *generato.*

First begotten, *primogenito.*

Only begotten, *unigenito, unico.*

God's only begotten Son, *il Figliuolo unigenito di Dio.*

To BEGREA'SE, *ugnere, ungere, fregar con grasso, sporcare, imbrattare,* pret. *unsi.*

BEGREA'SED, adj. *unto, sucido, sudicio, imbrattato, sporco.*

To BEGRI'ME, *annerare, annerire con fuliggine.*

BEGRI'MED, adj. *annerato, annerito con fuliggine.*

To BEGUI'LE [to couzen, to deceive] *ingannare, truffare, giuntare.*

To beguile the time, *ingannar il tempo, procurare di passar il tempo con qualche occupazione.*

BEGUI'LED, adj. *ingannato, truffato, giuntato.*

BEGUI'LER, s. *ingannatore, truffatore, truffiere, giuntatore, barattiere, furbo,* s. m.

BEGUI'LING, s. *inganno,* s. m. *truffa, giunteria, trufferia, baratteria, marioleria, fraude,* s. f.

BEGUI'NES, s. [an order of nuns of St. Begga] *beghine, pinzocchere,* s. f. *ordine di monache.*

BEGU'N, adj. [from to begin] *cominciato, principiato,* v. to begin.

Begun (*preterito del verbo* to begin) *cominciai.*

BEHA'LF, adv. *per, in favore, per amore, per conto.*

In my behalf, *per me, per amor mio.*

In your behalf, *per voi, per rispetto vostro, per amor vostro.*

I spoke to him in your behalf, *gli ho parlato in vostro favore.*

In his behalf, *per se, in sua difesa, dalla sua parte.*

He said nothing in his behalf, *non disse nulla in sua difesa, in sua discolpa.*

To BEHA'VE, *comportarsi, portarsi, procedere.*

He behaved like a man of courage, *si comportò da uomo valoroso.*

He behaved well in his office, *si portò bene nella sua carica.*

I am resolved so to behave myself, *sono risoluto di procedere in questo modo.*

BEHA'VED, adj. *comportato, portato, proceduto.*

Ill behaved, *mal accostumato, mal creato.*

Well behaved, *ben accostumato, ben creato.*

BEHA'VIOUR, s. *portamento, procedere,* s. m. *modo particolar d'operare.*

Good behaviour, *buon portamento.*

Ill behaviour, *ma' portamenti.*

A man of good behaviour, *un uomo costumato, un uomo di buoni portamenti, che si porta bene, che procede bene.*

To be bound to one's good behaviour, *esser obbligato legalmente a procedere bene, a menare una vita regolata.*

To

To Behea'd [to cut off the head] *decapitare, mozzare il capo, decollare.*

Behe'aded, adj. *decapitato, decollato.*

Behe'ading, s. *decollazione*, s. f. *il decapitare.*

The beheading of St. John the Baptiſt, *la decollazione di ſan Giovanni Battiſta.*

Behe'ld, adj. *and* part. *riguardato, contemplato, oſſervato, v.* to behold.

Behe'sts, s. [promiſe] *promeſſa*, s. f.

To Behest [to promiſe] *promettere.*

Behi'nd, adv. *and* prep. *dietro, indietro, da dietro, addietro, di dietro.*

Behind the wall, *dietro al muro.*

To ſtay behind, *reſtare in dietro.*

He was attacked both before and behind, *fu aſſalito d'avanti e di dietro.*

To leave behind, *laſciare addietro.*

To ride behind one, *cavalcare in groppa.*

He left a ſtink behind him, *ſi laſciò dietro una gran puzza.*

Behind my back, *dietro le ſpalle, in mia aſſenza.*

To rail at one behind his back, *ſparlare d'uno in ſua aſſenza.*

He will be the ſame before your face and behind your back, *ſarà l'iſteſſo preſente ad aſſente voi.*

To ſit behind a hare, *dar la caccia ad un lepre.*

What is behind ſhall be done, *quel che reſta ſi farà.*

I am deſirous to hear what is behind, *ho gran voglia di ſentire il reſtante.*

To be behind in arrears, *reſtar debitore.*

There is ſo much behind [ſo much unpaid] *reſta un tanto a pagare.*

Are you ſo much behind? *dovete voi ancora tanto?*

To be behind hand in the world, *trovarſi in cattivo ſtato, dovere molto danaro, e più che non ſe n' ha.*

I will not be behind hand with him in civility, *non gli cederò in civiltà.*

He comes not behind any in point of learning, *non la cede a neſſuno in ſapere.*

To come behind, *ſeguitare, tener dietro.*

To Beho'ld [to look upon] *riguardare, rimirare, guardare attentamente, contemplare, oſſervare.*

Behold, adv. *ecco.*

Behold him or her, *eccolo, eccola.*

Behold them, *eccoli, eccole.*

Beho'lden, adj. *obbligato, debitore, debitrice.*

I am beholden to you for all your civilities, *vi ſono obbligato di tutte le voſtre corteſie.*

He is beholden to me for his life, *mi deve la vita, m'è debitore della vita.*

I am not at all beholden to him for it, *non gliene ſo nè grado nè grazia.*

We are beholden to God alone for what we have, *da Dio ſolo riconoſciamo quel che abbiamo.*

Beho'lder, s. *ſpettatore, circoſtante, riguardatore*, s. m. *riguardatrice*, s. f.

Beho'lding, s. *riguardamento, ſguardo*, s. m. *il riguardare.*

Beholding, adj. [beholden] *obbligato, debitrore, debitrice.*

Beho'ldingness, s. *obbligo*, s. m. *obbligazione*, s. f.

To Beho'ney, *condire di mele.*

Beho'nied, adj. *condito di mele.*

Beh'oof, s. *profitto, comodo*, s. m. *utilità*, s. f.

Behoo'veable, adj. *profittevole, comodo, utile.*

It is behooveable, *rileva, importa, giova,*

Behoo'veful, adj. *utile, comodo, neceſſario, eſpediente.*

It Behooves, *biſogna, è neceſſario, è d'uopo, fa di meſtiere.*

It behoves us to look before we leap, *ci biſogna ben conſiderare prima d'intraprendere.*

Being, s. [eſſence] *eſſere*, s. m. *eſſenza, eſiſtenza*, s. f.

Action infers being, *l'azione ſuppone l'eſſenza.*

In God we live, move, and have our being, *in Dio abbiamo la vita, il moto, e l'eſſere.*

A thing which is in being, *una coſa che ſuſſiſte, che eſiſte, che è.*

Perhaps my being here may be an hindrance to you, *temo che la mia preſenza non v' incomodi.*

I do no good with being here, *la mia preſenza non vi ſerve non giova nulla ch'io ſtia quì.*

You need not trouble yourſelf at his being gone, *la ſua partenza non vi dia faſtidio.*

There is no being for me here, *queſto non è luogo per me, non poſſo ſtar quì.*

There is no ſuch thing in being, *non v'è tal coſa nel mondo, tal coſa non eſiſte.*

A man's firſt being, *il primo momento della vita.*

Being [participle of the verb, to he] *eſſendo.*

Being ſick, *eſſendo ammalato.*

It being thus, *la coſa andando così.*

Being to come here, *dovendo venir quì.*

He was near being killed, *poco mancò che non foſſe ammazzato.*

To keep a thing from being done, *impedire che una coſa non ſi faccia.*

Your being bound for him will be your ruin, *l'eſſer voi mallevadore per lui ſarà la voſtra rovina.*

To Bela'bour [to beat, to thump] *battere, baſtonare.*

Belabour'd, adj. *battuto, baſtonato.*

Bela'ced, adj. *merlettato, guernito, di merletti.*

To Bela'ge [a ſea term, to faſten any running rope when it is hawled, that it cannot run forth again] *armeggiare, legare, annodare. E' termine marinareſco.*

Bela'gged, adj. [left behind] *laſciato addietro, reſtato addietro.*

To Bela'm, *baſtonare, battere.*

Belami'e, s. [an intimate, a friend] *un' amica intimica, una perſona intrinſeca, è voce non più in uſo.* Obſ.

Bela'mmed, adj. *baſtonato, battuto,*

Bela'mming, s. *il baſtonare.*

To Bela'te, *ritenere uno ſin alla notte.*

Are you not aſhamed to belate us ſo with a trifle, *non avete vergogna di farci annottar quì per una bagattella.*

Bela'ted, adj. *ritenuto troppo tardi annottato.*

To Bela'y [to betray] *tradire, ingannare*, preſ. *tradiſco.*

To belay a man's way, *tendere inſidie ad alcuno.*

Belch, s. [a wind going out upward] *rutto*, s. m. *vento, che dallo ſtomaco ſi manda fuor per bocca.*

To Belch [to break wind upwards] *ruttare, mandar fuora per la bocca il vento che e nello ſtomaco.*

To belch out blaſphemies, *vomitar beſtemmie.*

Be'lcher, s. *quello o quella che rutta.*

Be'lched, adj. *ruttato.*

Be'lching, s. *il ruttare.*

Be'ldam, s [a decrepit, or old ugly woman] *una vecchiaccia.*

To Bele'agure [to beſiege] *aſſediare.* Not much uſed.

Bele'agured, adj. *aſſediato.*

Beleagured with ſickneſs and want, *oppreſſo da malattia e neceſſità.*

Bele'agurer, s. [one that beſieges a place] *il generale che aſſedia una fortezza.* Obſ.

Belfre'y, s. [ſteeple] *companile*, s. m.

Beli'ef, s. [truſt, credit] *fede, credenza, fidanza, fiducia, confidenza*, s. f.

The articles of our belief, *gli articoli della noſtra fede.*

This is my belief, *queſta è la mia credenza.*

It is wrong belief, *è un ſentimento erroneo, è una opinione erronea.*

Light of belief, *credulo.*

Hard of belief, *incredulo.*

Eaſineſs of belief, *credulità*, s. f.

Lack, Hardneſs, } of belief, *incredulità.*

Paſt all belief, *incredibile.*

The belief [the apoſtles creed] *il credo, il ſimbolo degli apoſtoli.*

Beli'evable, adj. [credible] *credibile, degno d'eſſer creduto, non incredibile.*

To Beli'eve [to have faith] *credere, aver fede.*

I believe in God, *credo in Dio.*

I don't believe what you ſay, *non credo a quel che dite, non do fede a quel che dite.*

I cannot believe any ſuch thing, *non poſſo darmi a credere ſimili coſe.*

To believe [to think] *penſare, credere, immaginarſi, perſuaderſi, darſi ad intendere.*

I believe he will come to morrow, *credo che verrà domani.*

I believe ſo, *credo di sì.*

I believe not, *credo di no.*

To believe [to truſt] *credere, fidarſi, confidarſi.*

If you will believe me, *ſe mi volete credere, ſe volete prender il mio conſiglio.*

You

You are a fool to believe him, *pazzo siete a credergli.*
To make one believe, *dare a credere.*
To make one believe that the moon is made of green cheese, *mostrar lucciole per lanterne, dare ad intendere una cosa per un' altra, mostrar la luna nel pozzo.*
BELI'EVED, adj. *creduto.*
It is believed at every hand, *è creduto da ognuno.*
It is not to be believed, *non è da credere, non è credibile.*
If I may be believed, *se volete credere a me.*
A person not to be believed, *una persona a chi non si deve credere o prestar fede.*
BELI'EVER, s. *un fedele, un cristiano.*
BELI'EVING, s. *fede, credenza,* s. f.
BELI'EVINGLY, adv. *in modo credibile, in maniera probabile.*
BELI'EVE, adv. [anon, by and by] *adesso adesso, fra poco.*
BELI'KE, adj. *verisimile.*
Belike, adv. *verisimilmente.*
BELL, s. *campana,* s. f.
A little bell, *campanella, campanello, squilla.*
A bell hung about a cow's neck, *campanaccio,* s. m. *campanello fatto di lama di ferro, e mettesi al collo della bestia che guida l'altre.*
A saint's bell [a sacrificing bell] *campanello,* s. m. *campanella,* s. f.
A hawk's bell, *sonaglio.*
The bell of a clock [whereon the bell clapper strikes] *la squilla d'un oriuolo.*
An alarm bell, *sveglia,* s. f. *la squilla degli oriuoli che suona a tempo determinato per isvegliare.*
To ring the bell, *suonar la campana.*
A ring of bells, *scampanata,* s. f.
A chime of bells, [a ringing of bells] *il suonar le campane a festa, scampanio,* s. m.
To bear away the bell, *riportar la vittoria.*
To cure one with bell, book, and candle, *maledire alcuno, fargli mille imprecazioni.*
A passing bell, *campana a mortorio.*
Bell-founder, *fabbricator di campane.*
Bell-clapper, *battaglio,* s. m.
Bell-man, *uomo destinato a svegliar gli altri, colui che va intorno suonando un campanello.*
Bell-wether, *quella pecora o montone che porta al collo il campanaccio.*
Bell-bit, *campanello,* s. m. *sorta d'imboccatura del morso del cavallo.*
Bell-flower [blue-bell] *campanella,* s. f.
BELLME'TAL, s. [the metal of which bells are made, being a mixture of five parts copper with ore of pewter] *metallo da far campane, nella mistura di cui cinque parti son di rame ed una di stagno.* Newton.
To BE'LLOW [to cry as bulls, oxen, or cows do] *mugghiare, muggire, mugliare, il mandar fuora della voce che fa il bestiame bovino.*

BE'LLOWING, s. *mugghio, muglio, muggito,* s. m.
Bellowing, part. *mugghiante, che mugghia, che muglia.*
BE'LLOWS, s. [an utensil for blowing the fire] *soffietto,* s. m. *strumento col quale si soffia il fuoco.*
BE'LLY, s. [that part of the body which encloses the guts] *ventre,* s. m. *pancia,* s. f.
The belly of a lute, *il fondo o il ventre d'un liuto.*
To be given to one's belly, *esser dedito alla gola.*
A woman with a great belly, *una donna gravida.*
As young as she is, she has had no less than seven great bellies, *con tutto che sia giovane ha avuto sette figliuoli.*
My belly is full, *ho mangiato abbastanza.*
I got my belly full of it, *ne ho fatto una corpacciata, una gran panciata.*
A hungry belly has no ears, *ventre digiuno non ha orecchi.*
Your eyes are bigger than your belly, *voi credete poter mangiare più di quel che non potete.*
A belly full is a belly full, *ogni acqua immolla.*
What is got over the devil's back, is spent under his belly, *beni malamente acquistati non fanno pro.*
Belly-band, *panciera del cavallo.*
Belly-chear, belly-timber, *viveri, provvisioni, cose da mangiare.*
Belly-worm, *verme, vermo,* s. m.
A belly-friend, *un amico interessato, un parasito.*
Belly-ach, *mal di ventre.*
A punch belly, *panciutezza, grossa pancia.*
Belly-cheat [an apron] *un grembiule termine burlesco.*
To BELLY [to grow fat, to get a belly] *divenir panciuto, ingrassare.*
To belly [to bunch out as a wall] *far ventre, parlando d'un muro.*
To BELO'NG [to appertain to] *appartenere, convenirsi, richiedersi, aspettarsi.*
This belongs to me, *questo appartiene a me, questo è mio, questo mi s'aspetta.*
BELO'NGED, adj. *appartenuto.*
BELO'NGING, part. *appartenente, che appartiene.*
BELO'VED, adj. *amato, benvoluto.*
He is beloved of all men, *è amato, è benvoluto da ognuno.*
BELO'W, adv. *giù, a basso.*
He is below, *egli è giù.*
It is below you so to do, *non conviene a voi di farlo.*
He was not below his father for warlike praise, *non fu punto inferiore al padre in onori militari.*
Below, prep. *sotto.*
There is nothing below the moon but what is mortal, *sotto la luna ogni cosa è mortale.*
BELSWA'GGER, s. [a swaggering fellow, a bully, a braggadocio] *un bravo, un rodomonte, un gradasso, un tagliacantoni, uno spacca montagne.*

BELT, s. [a girt to hang a sword by] *pendaglio, brodriere,* s. m.
A shoulder belt, *una ciarpa.*
A belt-maker, *quello che fa pendagli o ciarpe.*
To BELY' [to give the lye] *smentire, dimentire.*
Their actions bely their words, *le loro azioni non corrispondono alle parole loro.*
To bely one's self, *smentirsi, dimentirsi.*
To bely [to calumniate] *calunniare, calonniare, apporre altrui con malignità qualche falsità.*
BELY'D, adj. *smentito, dimentito, colunniato.*
To BEMA'D [to make mad] *far impazzare, far diventar matto.* Shakesp.
To BEMI'RE, *lotare, zaccherare, impillaccherare, imbrattare, sporcare.*
BEMI'RED, adj. *lotato, zaccherato, impillaccherato, imbrattato, sporcato.*
To BEMO'AN [to lament] *deplorare, plorare, compiagnere, compiangere, lamentare, piagnere.*
I bemoan your misfortune, *deploro la vostra sventura.*
To bemoan one's self, *compiagnersi, lamentarsi, condolersi.*
BEMO'ANED, adj. *deplorato, compianto.*
BEMO'ANING, s. *compianto, lamento,* s. m. *condoglienza.*
BEN, s. [an aromatick nut] *noce aromatica.*
BENCH, s. [to sit upon] *scranno, scanno,* s. m. *panca, scranna,* s. f.
A joyner's bench, *una panca di falegname.*
A bench to lean on, *appoggio,* s. m.
Bench [seat of justice] *banco,* s. m. *quella tavola, appresso alla quale seggono i giudici a render ragione.*
BE'NCHER, s. [a lawyer of the first rank in the inns of court] *giurisconsulto, assessore,* s. m.
BEND, s. [in heraldry, one of the eight honourable ordinaries, made by two lines drawn cross ways from the dexter chief to the sinister base point] *sbarra,* s. f.
BEND, [flexure, incurvation] *piegatura, curvità.*
BEND, [the crooked timbers which make the ribs of a ship] *costole d' un vascello, d' una nave. Gran prezzi di legno curvi, che servono di coste al ventre d'un vascello.*
To BEND [to stretch out] *tendere.*
To bend a bow, *tendere un arco.*
To bend a net, *tendere una rete.*
To bend [to bow, to crook] *piegare, curvare, archeggiare, torcere, piegare a guisa d'arco.*
To bend the knee, *piegare il ginocchio.*
To bend the body, *curvare o piegare il corpo.*
To bend a sword, *storcere o piegare una spada.*
To bend, *piegarsi, curvarsi.*
To bend like a bow, *archeggiare.*

To bend forwards, *inclinare, inchinare.*
To bend back, *ritorcere, storcere.*
To bend, or shrink under a burden, *incurvarsi sotto il pondo, sotto un peso.*
To bend one's brows, *inarcar le ciglia.*
To bend the cable to the anchor's ring, *annodare la gomena all' anello dell' áncora.*
To bend one's fist, *serrare il pugno.*
To bend all one's wits about a thing, *fissar l'animo a qualche cosa.*
To bend one's self, or one's mind to, or upon a thing, *volger l'animo, o'l pensiere a che che sia.*
He would have made a good mathematician if he had bent his mind to it, *sarebbe riuscito un buon matematico, se vi si fosse applicato.*
Bend all your wit about this, *mettete ogni studio in questo.*
This is all he bends his mind to, *non bada ad altro che a ciò, tutto l suo animo è rivolto a questo.*
The common people are always bent to new things, *il volgo è sempre portato alle novità.*
The Tiber bends his course towards the sea, *il Tevere piega il suo corso verso il mare.*
BE'NDABLE, adj. *pieghevole, che si può piegare.*
BE'NDED, adj. *piegato, v.* to bend.
With my bended knees, *inginocchione.*
BE'NDER, s. [the person who bends] *colui che piega alcuna cosa che sta dritta o tesa.*
Bender [the instrument with which any thing is bent] *lo strumento con cui si fa piegare una cosa dritta o tesa.*
BE'NDING, s. *piegamento, torcimento,* s. m. *piegatura,* s. f. *il piegare.*
The bending part of a hill, *pendice,* s. f. *fianco di monte, declività,* s. m.
The bending down of a thing, *declinazione,* s. f. *declinamento, declino,* s. m.
Bending [bowing] *curvatura, curvezza, curvità,* s. f.
A bending unto, *inclinazione,* s. f.
Bendings [turnings] *serpeggiamenti,* s. m. plur.
The bending of the elbow, *la piegatura del gomito.*
Bending adj. [shelving] *pendente, declive, che pende.*
Bending unto, *inclinato, dedito.*
Bending archways, *curvo, incurvato.*
Bending as the heavens, *convesso.*
BE'NDLET, s. [a little bend] *piccola sbarra.*
BENDWI'TH, s. [a sort of a plant] *viburno,* s. m. *sorta di pianta.*
BENE'APED, adj [a sea term. A ship is said to be beneaped when the water does not flow high enough to bring the ship off the ground, or over the bar] *a secco termine marinaresco; e si dice quando il vascello giace a terra per non aver acqua sufficiente da tenerlo a galla.*
BENE'ATH, adv. *giù, abbasso.*
Beneath, prep. *sotto, di sotto al di sotto.*

BE'NEDICT, adj. [having mild and salubrious qualities] *benedetto, mite, salubre.*
BENEDICTI'NES, s. [an order of monks founded by St. Benedict] *benedetini, frati dell' ordine di san Benedetto.*
BENEDI'CTION, s. [blessing] *benedizione,* s. f.
BENEFA'CTOR, s. [doer of good offices] *benefattore,* s. m. *che fa bene altrui.*
BENEFA'CTRESS, s. *benefattrice,* s. f.
BENEFA'CTURE, s. *beneficenza, benificenza, amorevolezza, cortesia, utilità,* s. f. *beneficio, servigio, piacere,* s. m.
BE'NEFICE, s. [ecclesiastical living] *beneficio,* s. m.
BE'NEFICED, adj. *ex.* [a beneficed man, one that has a benefice] *un beneficiato, che ha beneficio ecclesiastico.*
He is well beneficed, *egli ha un buon beneficio.*
BENEFI'CENCE, s. [a delight to do good to others] *beneficenza, benificenza,* s. f. *virtù, che consiste in dilettarsi di giovare, e far bene altrui.*
Beneficence [kindness, liberality] *munificenza, liberalità, amorevolezza, benignità,* s. f.
BENE'FICENT, adj. *beneficante, liberale, amorevole, benigno, cortese, benefico.*
BENEFI'CIAL, adj. [advantageous, profitable] *vantaggioso, utile, comodo, buono, profittevole, fruttuoso.*
This will prove very beneficial to you, *questo vi sarà molto vantaggioso.*
If I find it beneficial to me, *se vi troverò vantaggio alcuno, caso che me ne venga bene.*
Beneficial [kind, free] *cortese, amorevole, benigno, liberale.*
BE'NEFIT, s. [kindness, favour] *beneficio, servigio, favore, piacere,* s. m. *amorevolezza, cortesia,* s. f.
Benefit [advantage] *bene, profitto, vantaggio, utile, beneficio,* s. m *utilità,* s. f.
To give God thanks for all his benefits, *ringraziare Iddio di tutti i suoi benefici.*
It will prove much to your benefit, *questo ridonderà a vostro utile o vantaggio.*
Benefit of the clergy, *privilegio del clero.*
It is a privilege formerly allowed, by virtue of which, a man convicted of felony or man-slaughter, was put to read a Latin book of a Gothick black character, and if the ordinary of Newgate said *Legit ut clericus,* " *he reads like a clerk,*" he was only burnt in the hand, and set free, otherwise he suffered death for his crime; *privilegio concesso altre volte, in virtù del quale a un uomo convinto di fellonia o omicidio casuale o involontario, si dava a leggere un libro Latino in lettere Gotiche; e se il capellano della prigione volgarmente detta Newgate, diceva, e' legge come un cherico, era solamente bollato nella mano e messo in libertà, altrimente era posto a morte per quel tal delitto.*
To BE'NEFIT [to profit one] *giovare, far utile, far pro.*
To benefit [to profit] *profittare, far profitto, far progresso, avanzarsi.*

He benefits under his master, *profitta, fa progresso sotto la cura del suo maestro.*
BENE'VOLENCE, s. [good will] *benevolenza, benivolenza,* s. f. *volontà, desiderio del ben del prossimo; affetto, amore,* s. m.
Benevolence [a voluntary gratuity given by the subjects to the sovereign] *dono gratuito; regalo che i sudditi fanno volontariamente al loro principe.*
BENE'VOLENT, adj. [affectionate, kind] *benevolente, benevolo, benigno, affezionato, amico, favorevole, cortese, affabile.*
BE'NJAMIN, s. [a drug much used in perfumes and sweet bags] *bengivì,* s. m. *gomma d'un albero simile al mandorlo molto odorifera.*
Benjamin [a sort of wash for the face] *latte virginale.*
BENI'GHTED, adj. *pernottato, sorpreso dalla notte.*
BENI'GN, adj. courteous, good-natured] *benigno, cortese, affabile, amorevole, favorevole.*
A benign disease, *una malattia benigna.*
BENI'GNITY, s. [goodness, courtesy] *benignità, bontà, umanità, cortesia, affabilità, amorevolezza,* s. f.
BE'NIZON [blessing] *benedizione,* s. f.
BENT, adj. [from to bend] *piegato, teso, storto, v.* to bend.
Bent [inclined, given to] *inclinato, dedito, portato, prono.*
Bent to war, *inclinato, portato alla guerra.*
Bent bloodily against one, *implacabilmente irritato contro ad uno.*
Bent against a thing, *avverso, contrario, nemico, d'una cosa.*
To be stifly bent to something, *appigliarsi a checchessia; ostinarsi in qualche cosa.*
To be obstinately bent against reason, *calcitrare contra la ragione.*
To be cruelly bent against one, *incrudelire contro ad alcuno.*
Earnestly bent, *intenso, intento.*
Easily bent, *flessibile, molto pieghevole, facile a piegarsi.*
Not to be bent, *inflessibile, adro.*
Bent [ply] *piega,* s. f.
Bent [inclination] *inclinazione, propensione, voglia, talento, desiderio.*
Bent [a sort of rush] *giunco,* s. m.
To BENU'MB [to make numb] *assiderare, agghiadare, agghiacciare, intirizzire.*
To benumb [to amaze] *istupidire, stupefare, render torpido,* pref. *istupidisco.*
BENU'MBED, adj. *assiderato, aggiadato, agghiacciato, istupidito, stupefatto.*
To be benumbed with cold, *esser gelato di freddo, essere assiderato.*
BENU'MBEDNESS, s. *intirizzamento, intirizzimento, torpore,* s. m. *assiderazione, torpidezza,* s. f.
BENU'MBING, s. *l'assiderare, l'agghiadare.*
A benumbing, *intirizzimento, addormentamento,* s. m.
To BE'PAINT [to cover with paint] *colorire, far arrossire.*

To

To Bepi'nch [to mark with pinches] *pizzicare, lasciar i segni de' pizzicotti.*
To Bepi'ss, *pisciar sopra, scompisciare.*
To Beque'ath [to give or leave one a legacy by word of mouth, or by the last will] *legare, far legati, lasciare in testamento.*
Beque'athed, adj. *legato, lasciato in testamento.*
A thing bequeathed, *làscito, legáto,* s. m.
The person to whom a thing is bequeathed, *legatario,* s. m. *quegli a cui è fatto il legato.*
Beque'ather, s. *testatore,* s. m.
Beque'athing, s. *il legare, il lasciare in testamento.*
Beque'st, s. [a legacy] *legáto, làscito,* s. m. *termine legale.*
To Bera'ttle [to rattle off, to make a noise at in contempt] *fare strepito in faccia ad uno per dargli segno di disprezzo.*
To Bera'y [to foul] *lordare, sporcare, imbrattare.*
Beray'd, adj. *lordato, sporcato, imbrattato.*
Bera'ying, s. *il lordare, lo sporcare, l'imbrattare.*
To Bere'ave [to deprive or rob one of a thing] *privare, spogliare, togliere, torre.*
Bere'aved, adj. *privo, privato, spogliato.*
Bereaved of sense, *privo di senno.*
Bere'aving, s. *privamento,* s. m. *il privare.*
Bere'ft, adj. *privato, privo, spogliato, destituto.*
Be'rgamot, s. [a pear of a delicious taste] *pera bergamotta.*
Bergamot [a sort of perfume] *bergamotto,* s. m. *spezie di profumo.*
Bergh-Master, s. [the bailiff or chief officer among the Derbyshire miners] *soprintendente a quelli che lavorano nelle mine di Derbyshire, una delle provinces settentrionali dell' Inghilterra.*
Beri'glia, s. *sorta di pietra bianca e lucida che serve a fare il vetro.*
Be'rlin, s. [a coach of a particular form] *berlina, cocchio da viaggio, carrozza di viaggiare.*
To Bero'b [to steal] *rubare.*
Bernardi'nes, s. [a religious order] *frati dell' ordine di san Bernardo.*
Be'rry, s. *baeca, coccola,* s. f. *frutto d'alcuni albert, piante o erbe.*
Juniper-berry, *bacca o coccola di ginepro.*
Ivy-berry, *coccola d'édera.*
Myrtle-berry, *coccola di mirto.*
Elder-berry, *coccola di sambuco.*
Bay-berry, *coccola d'alloro.*
Blackberries, *more.*
Rasberries, *more di rovo, angeliche.*
Service-berry, *sorba,* s. f.
Gooseberries, *uva spina.*
Mulberries, *frutti del gelso, more di gelso.*
Strawberries, *fragole.*
Berry [a borough] *borgo,* s. m. Obs.

To Be'rry [to bear berries] *produr barche.*
Berth, s. [convenient sea room to moor a ship] *luogo comodo dove un vascello possa stare all' àncora.*
Be'rton, s. [farm, barn for barley] *podere,* s. m. *possessione,* s. f.
Be'ryl, s. [a precious stone] *berillo,* s. m. *pietra preziosa.*
Be'sant, s. [a very ancient gold coin at Byzantium] *bisante,* s. m. *moneta antica.*
To Bese'ech [to pray, humbly to intreat] *pregare, supplicare, scongiurare.*
I beseech you heartily, *vi prego, vi supplico istantemente.*
Bese'eching, s. *il pregare; supplicazione, preghiera, istanza,* s. f.
Bese'eched, adj. *pregato, supplicato, scongiurato.*
Bese'echer, s. *pregatore,* s. m.
To Bese'em [to become] *convenire, dirsi, affarsi, esser conforme, esser conveniente, confarsi.*
Bese'eming, adj. [becoming] *conveniente, convenevole, conforme, giusto, ragionevole, dicevole.*
Nothing is more beseeming the nature of a man, *niuna cosa è piu conforme alla natura d'un uomo.*
To Bese't [to encompass] *assediare, circondare, assiepare, attorniare, cignere, intorniare.*
Troubles and fears beset me on all sides, *sono oppresso dalle angustie e da timori; le angustie ed i timori m'ingombrano il cuore, me assediano, mi hanno posto assedio.*
Beset, adj. *assediato, circondato, cinto.*
Hard beset [hard put to it] *angustiato, ridutto in cattivo stato, oppresso.*
A heel beset with nails, *un calcagno guernito di chiodi.*
Beset with diamonds, *tempestato di diamanti.*
To Be'shite [to foul with ordure] *imbrattare di sterco.*
To Beshre'w [to curse, to wish ill to] *maledire, pregar male altrui.*
Beshre'wed, adj. *maladetto.*
Beshre'wing, *maladizione,* e *maledizione,* s. f.
Besi'de, } adv. *oltre, oltre, che*
Besi'des, } *fuorchè.*
Besides, I think you should be moved by the injury, *oltre che dovrebbe muovervi il resentimento dell' ingiuria.*
Except me and few beside, *fuorchè me e pochi altri.*
I ask you no reward besides the eternal remembrance of this day, *non vi domando altra ricompensa che un' eterna memoria di questo giorno.*
Besides, prep. *oltre, eccetto.*
Besides the miseries of war, *oltre le miserie della guerra.*
There was no body besides these two, *non vi furono altri che questi due.*
Besides his age he was also blind, *oltre ch' egli era vecchio era ancor cieco; non era solamente vecchio ma era cieco ancora.*
Besides [near] *vicino, a canto, presso.*
Hannibal encamped besides that village, *Annibale s'attendò presso quel villaggio.*

Two sons lying besides their father, *due figliuoli giacendo a canto del padre.*
Besides one's self [mad] *matto, forsennato, fuor del senno.*
He is besides himself, *egli è matto, egli vaneggia.*
To be besides the mark, *dare in fallo, ingannàrsi.*
Besides the purpose, *four di proposito.*
It is besides my present scope, *questo non fa al mio soggetto.*
These are things quite besides the philosopher's business, *queste son cose che non riguardano il filosofi.*
To Besi'ege [to lay siege] *assediare, metter l'assedio.*
Besi'eged, adj. *assediato.*
The besieged, s. *gli assediati.*
The Besi'egers, s *gli assediatori.*
Besi'eging, s. *assediamento,* s. m. *l'assediare.*
To Besme'ar [to smear over] *imbrattare, sporcare, lordare, sozzare, insudiciare.*
Besme'ared, adj. *imbrattato, sporcato, lordato, macchiato, insudiciato.*
Besme'arer, s. *imbrattatore,* s. m.
Besme'aring, s. *imbrattamento,* s. m. *imbrattatura, sozzura,* s. f.
To Be'smoak, *affumicare, macchiare o tingere col fumo.*
Besmo'aked, adj. *affumato, affumicato, fumicato.*
Besmo'aking, s. *fumicazione,* s. f.
To Besmu't [to blacken with smoke or soot] *imbrattar con fuliggine, o con fumo.*
Besmu'tted, adj. *imbrattato con fuliggine, o con fumo.*
Be'som, s. [an instrument to sweep with] *scopa, strumento da scopare.*
To Beso'rt [to suit, to fit] *quadrare, addattare.*
Beso'rt [company, attendance, train] *campagnia, seguito, accompagnamento.*
To Beso't [to make stupid] *imbalordire, stupidire, stupefare, rendere stupido, stordire, sbalordire,* pres. *stordisco, sbalordisco.*
To besot with drink, *imbriacare.*
Beso'tted, adj. *imbalordito, stupido, sbalordito, senza senso, bolordo, sciocco, besso.*
Beso'tting, s. *stupidezza, balordaggine, bessaggine, sciocchezza,* s. f.
Beso'ught, *preterito del verbo* To beseech, *pregai, supplicai, scongiurai.*
Bespa'ke, *preterito del verbo* To bespeak.
To Bespa'ngle [to adorn with spangles; to besprinkle with something shining] *spruzzare con qualcosa di lucente per mo' d'ornamento.*
To Bespa'tter [to dash with dirt] *spruzzare, spruzzolare, zaccherare, macchiar di zacchere.*
To bespatter [to defame, to slander] *diffamare, macchiar la fama altrui con maledizenza, infamare, calunniare.*
Bespa'ttered, adj. *spruzzato, spruzzolato, zaccherato, diffamato, calunniato.*
Be'spattering, s. *spruzzo,* s. m. *lo zaccherare.*

To BESPA'WL, *sputacchiare, sputare, imbrattar con isputo, scombavare.*

BESPA'WLED, adj. *sputacchiato, sputato, imbrattato con isputo, scombavato.*

To BESPE'AK [to order something before-hand] *ordinare, caparrare, comandare che una cosa si faccia.* I bespoke or bespake; I have bespoken.

To bespeak a pair of shoes, *ordinare un pajo di scarpe.*

To bespeak a coach, *caparrare una carrozza.*

To bespeak some body's good opinion, *cattivarsi l'animo di qualcheduno.*

Let me bespeak your most serious regard to these things, *di grazia considerate attentamente queste cose.*

To bespeak a man [to engage him on one's side] *guadagnar alcuno, farselo amico,* tirarlo *dalla sua, cattivarselo.*

To BESPE'CKLE, *macchiare, tempestare, brizzolare, indanajare, asperger di macchie.*

BESPE'CKLED, adj. *macchiato, tempestato, brizzolato, indanajato, asperso di macchie a guisa di gocciole.*

To BESPE'W, *v.* to bespawl.

To BESPI'T [to bespawl] *sputacchiare, sputare, sporcare con isputo.*

BESPI'TTED, adj. *sputacchiato, sputato, sporcato con isputo.*

BESPO'KE, *preterito del verbo* to bespeak.

BESPO'KEN, adj. *ordinato, caparrato, di comando.*

That hat is bespoken, *quel capello è già venduto.*

Bespoken, *guadagnato.*

These are bespoken thanks, *questi ringraziamenti son fatti contro voglia.*

To BESPO'T, *macchiare, bruttare, imbrattare, sporcare, sozzare, insudiciare.*

BESPO'TTED, adj. *macchiato, imbrattato, sporcato, sozzato.*

To BESPRI'NKLE [to sprinkle upon] *spruzzare, spruzzolare, leggiermente bagnare, aspergere, bagnare gettando minutissime gocciole.*

BESPRI'NKLED, adj. *spruzzato, spruzzolato, leggiermente bagnato, asperso.*

BESPRI'NKLING, s. *spruzzo, sprazzo,* s. m. *lo spruzzare, lo spargere liquore in minutissime gocciole.*

To BESPU'TTER, *scombavare, macchiare, imbrattare, sporcare con isputo.*

BESPU'TTERED, adj. *scombavato, macchiato, imbrattato, sporcato con isputo.*

To BESPU'E, *vomitare.*

To bespue one's cloaths, *vomitare sopra il proprio vestito.*

BESSE, or Besse fish, s. *lupo marino, sorta di pesce.*

BEST, superl. *il migliore, l'ottimo.*

Give me the best you have, *datemi il migliore che abbiate.*

He is the best man alive, *egli è il migliore uomo che viva.*

Authors of the best account, *autori i più stimati, di più gran grido, gli ottimi autori.*

I'll do my best to serve you, *metterò ogni cura o studio in servirvi, vi servirò in tutto quel che potrò.*

We must do the best we can, *bisogna fare come meglio possiamo.*

Do your best to get it done, *fate ogni diligenza che la cosa si faccia.*

Do what is best for yourself, *fate quel che vi vien più in acconcio.*

What had I best to do? *che devo io fare?*

They could not tell what course were best to take, *non sapévano in che modo comportarsi, qual via pigliare ignorávano.*

We strive who shall love her best, *facciamo a gara in amarla.*

The best have their failings, *ognuno ha il suo difetto.*

You had best to do as I bid you, *sarà meglio per voi di fare quel che vi dico.*

He is none of the best, *non è un uomo di grano probità, non è un ottimo uomo.*

To make the best of a thing, trarre *il maggior vantaggio che si puo d'una cosa.*

To make the best of a bad market, *da un cattivo pagatore prendi orzo o paglia.*

He had the best on it, *restò superiore.*

The best is the best cheap, *cosa buona non fu mai cara.*

I have done it for the best, *l'ho fatto credendolo vantaggioso.*

To the best of my remembrance, *per quanto posso ricordarmi.*

Speak to the best of your knowledge, *dite tutto quel che sapete, parlate liberamente.*

Every man likes his own things best, *il suo è caro ad ognuno.*

The devil take the best of the two, *il meglio ricolga il peggio, e si dice quando tra due cose cattive non c'è differenza.*

Best, adv. *meglio.*

I love that best of all, *amo meglio cio che tutto altra cosa, amo questo più che non gli altri.*

To strive who shall do best, *fare a gara, gareggiare.*

To BESTAI'N [to mark with stains] *far macchie, macchiare.*

BE'STIAL [belonging to a beast] *bestiale, di bestia, appartenente a bestia.*

Bestial [brutal, carnal] *bestiale, carnale, lascivo.*

To BESTE'AD, *giovare, dare ajuto, far pro.*

To bestead one [to befriend him] *mostrarsi amico d'uno, servirlo da amico, rendergli qualche servizio.*

To BESTI'NK, *impuzzare, impuzzolire, empiere di puzza.*

To BESTI'R ONE'S SELF, verb. recip. *affaticarsi, ingegnarsi, industriarsi, adoperarsi, impiegarsi.*

To BESTO'W [to give] *dare, presentare.*

To bestow a suit of cloaths upon one, *dare un abito ad uno.*

The booty he bestowed upon soldiers, *diede il bottino a' soldati.*

To bestow [to lay out] *spendere, impiegare, consumare.*

You must bestow some time upon your studies, *bisogna che voi spendiare qualche tempo nello studio.*

Bestow some time upon this consideration, *fate alquanta riflessione a questa.*

To bestow one's time in idle things, *consumare il tempo in cose vane.*

To bestow money upon books, *spender danari in libri.*

To bestow part of one's revenue upon a building, *impiegare parte delle entrate in un edificio.*

To bestow a charity upon an indigent person, *fare la carità ad un bisogno.*

To bestow some favours to one, *compartire favori ad uno, rendergli qualche servizio.*

To bestow cost, *fare grandi spese, spender molto.*

How will you bestow yourself? *che volete fare? in che volete occuparvi?*

To bestow a great deal of pains upon a work, *metter gran fatica in un' opera, affaticarsi assai intorno ad un' opera.*

To bestow a daughter, *maritare, dare in matrimonio una figlia.*

To bestow [to place] *collocare, porre in un luogo, allogare, acconciare.*

BESTO'WED, adj. *dato, speso, impiegato, consumato, collocato, v.* to bestow.

BESTRA'CT, } adj. [mad] *matto,*
BESTRA'UGHT, } *pazzo.* Obs.

BESTRI'D, adj. *cavalcato, v.* to bestride.

This is as good a horse as ever was bestrid, *questo cavallo è buono al pari di qualsissia che abbia mai portato sella.*

To BESTRI'DE, *cavalcare, stare sopra qualsivoglia cosa con una gamba da una banda e l'altra dall' altra.*

BESTRI'DER, s. *cavalcatore,* s. m. *che cavalca.*

To BESTU'D [to adorn with studs] *ornar con borchie, ornar di borchie.*

BET, s. [wager] *scommessa,* s. m.

Name your bet, *quanto volete scommettere.*

To BET [to lay a wager] *scommettere.*

I will bet nothing, *non voglio scommettere niente.*

Bétted, adj. *scommesso.*

Bétter, s. *scommettitore,* s. m. *uno che scommette.*

To BETA'KE ONE'S SELF, verb. recip. [to apply, to addict one's self] *applicarsi, appigliarsi.*

He betakes himself to a very profitable profession, *egli s'impiega in un mestiere molto lucrativo.*

He betakes himself to the study of virtue, *s'applica allo studio della virtù.*

He betook himself to Cæsar for his protector, *ricorse alla protezione di Cesare.*

To betake one's self to one's heels, or to flight, *darla a gambe, darsi alla fuga.*

To betake one's self to one's weapon, *dar di piglio all' armi.*

To betake [to give up, to deliver] *consegnare, dar in guardia, in custudia.*

To BETE'EM [to bring forth] *esser pieno, esser gravido, patorire produrre.*

To BETHI'NK ONE'S SELF, verb. recip. *pensare, considerare, meditare, divisare, riflettere.*

I bethink myself what to do, *sto pensando a quel che dove fare.*

Pray bethink yourself of these things, *di grazia fate un poco di riflessione a queste cose.*

BETHO'UGHT, adj. *pensato, considerato.*

To BETI'DE [to happen, to befall] *accadere, avvenire, succedere, arrivare,* pret. *accadde, avvenne, successe.*

Woe betide thee! *guai a voi!*

BETI'DED, adj. *accaduto, avvenuto, successo, arrivato.*

BETI'MES, adv. [early] *per tempo, di buon' ora, a buon' ora.*

Betimes in the morning, *la mattina per tempo, la mattina a buon' ora, di buon mattino.*

In those countries winter comes betimes, *in quei paesi l'inverno si fa sentire di buon' ora.*

BE'TLE, s. [an Indian plant called water-pepper] *betella, pepe bastardo, foglia d'una pianta che gl' Indiani orientali hanno sempre in bocca, e masticano, e succiano.*

To BETO'KEN [to foreshow] *significare, presagire, pronosticare.*

BETO'KENED, adj. *significato, presagito, pronosticato.*

BETO'KENING, s. *segno, presagio, pronosticamento,* s. m.

BE'TONY, s. [a sort of herb] *bettonica,* s. f. *sorta d'erba.*

BETO'OK, *preterito del verbo* To betake.

I betook myself wholly to the commonwealth, *m'applicai intieramente al bene della repubblica.*

I presently betook me to my heels, *io subito mi diedi alla fuga, io cominciai a fuggire a tutte gambe.*

They quickly betook themselves to their weapons, *subito diedero di piglio all' armi.*

To BETRA'Y [to be false to] *tradire,* pres. *tradisco.*

He has betrayed his country, *egli ha tradita la sua patria.*

To betray [to discover] *palesare, divulgare.*

To betray one's design, *scoprire i disegni altrui.*

He has betrayed my secrets, *ha palesato i mei segreti.*

He has betrayed me into the hands of my enemies, *mi ha dato in mano a' miei nemici.*

To betray one to destruction and ruin, *tramare la perdita e la rovina altrui.*

BETRA'YED, adj. *tradito, palesato, divulgato.*

BETRA'YER, s. *traditore,* s. m.

BETRA'YING, s. *tradimento,* s. m. *il tradire.*

To BETRO'TH [to give or receive a promise of marriage] *fidanzare, promettere e dar fede di sposo.*

To betroth one's daughter to a man, *fidanzare la figlia ad uno.*

To betroth a girl, *impalmare una giovane.*

BETRO'THED, adj. *fidanzato, impalmato.*

BETRO'THING, s. *impalmamento,* s. m. *il fidanzare, l'impalmare.*

To BETRU'ST, *v.* to trust.

BETTE'E, s. [an instrument made use of by house-breakers to break open a door] *strumento di ferro del quale si servono i ladri per rompere le porte.*

BE'TTER, adj. *migliore, meglio.*

Mine is better than yours, *il mio è migliore del vostro.*

This will be the better way, *questo sarà meglio.*

For your better understanding, *perchè l'intendiate meglio, perchè lo veggiate più chiaro.*

What am I the better for this? *che utile me ne viene da cio? che vantaggio ricaverò io da ciò?*

You would do a great deal better, *fareste molto meglio.*

Why should you think one man better than another? *perchè volete voi che un uomo sia migliore d'un altro?*

I can never have a better time, *non mi si presenterà mai una più comoda opportunità.*

To make better, *render migliore, emendare, correggere, riformare, migliorare.*

To grow better in manners, *correggersi, emendarsi, riformarsi.*

To grow better in health, *migliorare, ricuperar le forze, riaversi.*

To give one the better, *ceder l'avvantaggio ad uno.*

To get the better, *restar superiore, rimaner vincitore.*

Our soldiers had the better of them, *i nostri soldati li saperarono.*

Our betters, *i nostri superiori.*

It is better, *è meglio.*

Better be idle than not well employed, *meglio star ozioso che mal impiegato, meglio non far nulla che far male.*

Better be happy than wise, *val più un' oncia di sorte ch' una libbra di sapere.*

I never was in better health, *non ho mai goduto più perfetta salute.*

Better bow than break, *val meglio piegarsi che rompersi.*

I love him better and better, *l'amo di più in più.*

So much the better, *tanto meglio.*

He grows better and better, *sta di meglio in meglio.*

I had better not to have told it, *avrei fatto meglio non dirlo.*

Ten foot high and better, *alto dieci piedi e più.*

As long again and better, *due volte più lungo, e ancora più.*

Better cheap, *a miglior mercato.*

I know better things, *so meglio di voi quel va fatto.*

I thought better of it, *ci ho pensato meglio; ebbi di ciò meglio opinione.*

I love it the better, *l'amo ancora meglio.*

The better I knew him the more I loved him, *quanto più lo conobbi tanto più l'amai.*

The oftener I see her the better I like her, *più l'amo quanto più spesso la vedo.*

To BE'TTER, *migliorare, render migliore, correggere, emendare.*

To better one's fortune, *aggrandirsi, avvanzarsi, farsi strada nel mondo.*

To better one's self [to better one's pennyworth] *comperare a miglior mercato.*

To better one's self, *provvedersi meglio.*

BE'TTERED, adj. *migliorato.*

BE'TTERING, s. *miglioramento,* s. m.

BETWEEN, } prep. *fra, tra.*
BETWIXT, }

There was but one river between the two camps, *fra i due campi non v'era che un fiume.*

She placed herself between them, *si mise fra di loro.*

There was a parcel of ground left between, *v'era un pezzo di terreno tra mezzo.*

Between both, *nel mezzo d'essi due.*

Between both [indifferent] *fra due, irresoluto.*

To put or lay between, *interponere, interporre.*

Between whiles, *fra questo mezzo, di tempo in tempo.*

There is but three days difference between their age, *non differiscono in età che di tre giorni.*

BE'VEL, s. [an instrument made use of by carpenters, bricklayers, and masons, for adjusting the angles] *squadra,* s. f. *strumento col quale si squadra.*

To BE'VEL [to cut to a bevel angle] *tagliare dopo d'aver misurato con quello strumento chiamato da falegnami la squadra.*

BE'VER, s. [a small collation betwixt dinner and supper] *merenda,* s. f.

Béver [the visor or sight of a head-piece] *visiera, buffa,* s. f. *parte dell' elmo che cuopre il viso.*

Béver, *v.* Beaver.

BE'VERAGE, s. [a mingled drink] *beveraggio, beverone,* s. m. *bevanda, beva,* s. f.

Beverage [money given to drink] *beveraggio, mancia da comperar da bere.*

To pay beveragè, *pagar da bere.*

BE'VY, s. [a brood, a flock] *un nuvolo, uno stormo, uno stuolo.*

A bevy of quails, *un nuvolo di quaglie, un volo.*

A bevy of roe-bucks, *un branco di cavriuoli, di daini.*

A bevy of ladies, *uno stuolo di dame. Dicesi da burla.*

Bevy-grease [fat of a roe-deer] *grasso di cervo.*

To BEWA'IL [to lament] *lamentarsi, piagnere, piangere, compiagnere, compiangere, deplorare.*

I bewail your misery and my own, *piango le vostre e le mie miserie.*

If you die I shall bewail my loss, *se morite deplorerò la mia perdita.*

BEWAI'LED, adj. *lamentato, pianto, compianto, deplorato.*

BEWA'ILING, s. *lamento, pianto,* s. m.

To BEWA'RE [to take care of] *guardarsi, avvertire, aver cura, aver l'occhio, stare all' erta.*

Beware of false prophets, *guardatevi da' falsi profeti.*

To beware of a thing [to avoid a thing] *evitare, scansare, fuggire una cosa.*

To BEWE'P [to weep over or upon] piangere, lagrimare su qualche cosa.

To BEWE'T [to wet over] bagnare.

To BEWI'LDER [to lose one's self or others in pathless places; to puzzle] sviare, perdere se o altri in luogo rimoto dalla gente, in luogo solitario.; e metaforicamente, intrigare, imbrogliare.

BEWI'LDERED, adj. [that has a wild look with him] spaventato, stralunato.

Bewildered [that has lost his way] sviato, fuor di strada.

To BEWI'TCH [to infatuate] ammaliare, fare malie.

I think she has bewitched me, credo che m'ha ammaliato.

BEWI'TCHED, adj. ammaliato.

He is bewitched, è stranamente innamorato, è incapriccito come si deve.

Bewitched [out of his wits] ammaliato, stupido, insensato, stupefatto.

I believe you are bewitched, credo v'abbiate perduto il cervello.

BEWI'TCHER, s. ammaliatore, s. m. ammaliatrice, s. f.

BEWI'TCHERY, s. [fascination, charm] fáscino, s. m. stregherìa, s. f.

BEWI'TCHMENT, s. [fascination, charm] fáscino, s. m. stregherìa, malìa, s. f.

BE'WITS, s. [jesses, pieces of leather to which the bells of hawks are fastened and buttoned to their legs] geti, s. m. plur. correggiuoli di cuojo che s' adattano per legame a' piè degli uccelli di rapina, e a cui s'attaccano de' sonaglini.

To BEWRA'Y [to declare, to discover] scoprire, palesare, divulgare, manifestare.

To bewray a secret, palesare, divulgare un secreto.

He bewrays his own cowardliness, si fa vedere codardo, da se stesso si da a conoscere per vigliacco.

Your own knavery will bewray you, la tua stessa furberia di tradirà.

BEWRA'YER, s. [betrayer, discoverer] divulgatore, che divulga, che scopre, che palesa.

BEYO'ND, prep. dilà, oltre, oltra, sopra.

Beyond the Alps, di là delle Alpi.

Beyond sea, di là dal mare.

Beyond my reach, superiore alla mia capacità.

Beyond sea, adj. oltremare, oltramare, di là dal mare.

At that very time I was beyond sea, in quello stesso tempo io era oltremare.

To go beyond, passáre, passare oltre eccedere, sopravanzare, superare.

We are gone beyond the place, abbiamo passato il luogo.

You go beyond your commission, voi eccedete la vostra commissione, i vostri ordini.

He goes beyond all others in learning, egli supera ogni altro in dottrina.

Beyond measure, oltremodo, oltramodo, smoderatamento, fuor di modo, soprammodo.

Beyond what is sufficient, più del bisognevole.

To stay beyond one's time, tardare, indugiare, trattenersi troppo.

To eat beyond digestion, mangiare più di quel che si puo digerire.

To be beyond the reach of the dart, esser fuor di tiro del dardo.

To go beyond one's depth in the watsr, entrar troppo avanti nell' acqua.

BE'ZANT, v. Besant.

BEZA'NTLER, s. [second antler, a second branch of a stag's horn] secondo cornetto del cervo, di que' che attraversano le corna grandi.

BEZEL, or Bezil, s. [the upper part of the collet of a ring that encompasses and fastens the stone] castone, s. m. quella parte dell' annello dove è posta e legata la gemma.

BE'ZOAR, or BE'ZOAR-STONE, s. [a stone taken out of the maw of a Persian goat] bezzuardo, s. m. sorta di pietra verde che nello stomaco d'una capra di Persia crede il volgo si generi.

To BE'ZZLE [to guzzle, to tipple, to drink hard] sbevazzare, bere assai, imbriacarsi.

BIANGULA'TED, } adj. [having two
BIA'NGULOUS, } corners or angles] che ha due canti o angoli.

BIAS, s. [the weight lodged on one side of a bowl, which turns it from the straight line] peso che si mette in una palla o boccia, onde gittata o spinta vada per non dritta via al destinato segno.

Bias [inclination, bent] inclinazione, voglia, s. f. talento.

To go or run bias, pendere da un lato.

To cut bias, tagliare a sghembo, a sghimbescio.

To put one out of his bias, levar di sesto, confondere, imbarazzare, intrigare, imbrogliare alcuno.

You force the natural bias, or sense of the fable, voi stiracchiate il senso naturale della favola.

The bias of interest, la forza dell' interesse.

BIAS, s. quel piombo che si mette nella palla o boccia da giuocare perrhè vada in modo obliquo al destinato segno.

To BIAS [to set a bias upon, to incline] inclinare, volger o piegar l'animo a che che si sia.

To bias one [to prevail with him to do any thing] prevalere con uno, guadagnarlo, indurlo a far le sue voglie.

To bias one [to prepossess one] prevenire, preoccupare alcuno.

BI'ASSED, adj. inclinato, guadagnato, indotto, prevenuto, preocupato.

To be biassed to a party, favorire un partito.

BIB, s. [a small piece of linen put upon the breast of children over their cloaths] bavaglio, s. m.

A bib [a child's sucking bottle] vasetto da bambino.

To BIB [to drink, to sip often] sbevazzare, bere spesso e poco alla volta.

BI'BBED, adj. sbevazzato.

BI'BBER, s. bevitore, s. m.

BI'BBING, s. sbevazzamento, s. m. lo sbevazzare.

To BI'BBLE [to bubble up] bollire, crosciare.

BI'BLE, s. [the holy scripture] Bibbia, s. f. la sacra scrittura.

BIBLIOTHE'CAL, adj. [belonging to a library] appartenente a libreria.

BI'BULOUS, adj. [that which has the quality of drinking moisture] succiante, che succia, che beve, che s'imbeve.

BICA'NE, s. [verjuice grape] agresto, s. m. uva acerba.

BI'CE, s. [a colour used by painters, a blue colour] color turchino, ceruleo, bigio.

To BI'CKER [to quarrel or strive with one] contrastare, contendere, disputare, competere, querelare.

BI'CKERER, s. contenditore, s. m. contenditrice, s. f. riottoso.

BI'CKERING, s. contendimento, s. m. contesa, disputa, querela, contenzione, contestazione, s. f.

BID, adj. comandato, ordinato, v. to bid.

Do as you are bid, fate quel che vi vien comandato.

To BID [to tell, to command] dire, comandare, ordinare, commettere, pret. commisi.

Bid him to come in, ditegli che entri, fatelo entrare.

Bid him to come to me, ditegli che venga da me, fate che venga da me.

Why don't you go when I bid you? perchè non andate quando ve lo comando?

I bid you farewel, andate con dio.

I bid you good night, v'auguro la buona sera.

To bid one welcome, accogliere uno, fargli accoglienza lieta.

To bid the banes of matrimony, pubblicare i bandi del matrimonio.

To bid a holiday, annunciare una festa.

To bid [to invite] invitare, fare un invito.

He bid him to supper, l'invitò a cena.

To bid the enemy battle, presentar la battaglia al nemico, sfidar l'inimico a battaglia.

To bid defiance, sfidare, fare una disfida.

To bid [to offer] offrire, dare.

To bid money for a thing, offrire un prezzo per qualche cosa.

I bid him ten crowns for it, gli ne ho offerto dieci scudi.

What do you bid for it? quanto ne volete dare?

To bid up, incarire, alzar il prezzo, offrir di più.

To bid prayers, pubblicare preghiere pubbliche.

To bid a boon, chiedere un favore.

BID-ALE, } s. [an invitation of
BID-ALL, } friends to drink at a poor man's house, in order to get him their charitable assistance] invito d'amici a bere in casa qualche povero uomo per procurargli da loro qualche caritatevole soccorso.

BI'DDEN, adj. comandato, ordinato, v. to bid.

BI'DDER, s. [commander] comandatore, s. m. comandatrice, s. f.

Goods to be sold to the highest bidder, beni da vendersi all' incanto o al più offerente.

Bidder [inviter] *invitatore*, s. m. *invitatrice*, s. f.

BI'DDING, s. *comandamento, comando*, s. m. *il comandare*.

At your bidding, *ad istanza vostra*.

I shall do it without your bidding, *lo farò senza che me lo comandiate*.

Bidding [inviting] *invito*, s. m.

Bidding [offer of a price] *offerta, profferta*, s. f.

To BI'DE, *v.* to abide.

BIE'NNIAL, adj. [that is of two years' continuance, two years old] *biennio, di due anni*.

BIER, s. [a wooden frame to carry a dead body upon] *bara*, s. f. *strumento di legname fatto a guisa di letto, e mettevisi il cadavero per portarlo alla sepoltura*.

BIG, adj. [large] *grande*.

Big [thick, bulky] *grosso, spesso*.

A woman big with child, *una donna gravida*.

A woman's being big with child, *gravidezza, pregnezza, gravidanza*.

Big in authority, *potente*.

Big with pride, *tumido, superbo, vanaglorioso, vano*.

To talk big, *parlare autorevolmente o altieramente, con superbia, con alterezza*.

Big words, *parole gonfie, parolone, parole superbe*.

To look big, *pavoneggiarsi, avere un aspetto fiero o superbo*.

He looks as big as bull-beef, *egli ha la testa alta, ha un aspetto fiero*.

To look big upon one, *guardare uno con occhi torvi*.

She begins already to look big, *il ventre se le comincia ad ingrossare*.

He has a mind too big for his estate, *vive con troppo fasto, spende più di quel che la sua ricchezza non comporta*.

To be big with expectations, *pascersi di grandi aspettative*.

To go big with projects, *formar gran disegni*.

Big-body'd, *corpacciuto, grosso di corpo*.

Big-belly'd, *panciuto, di grossa pancia*.

To grow big, *ingrossare, divenir grosso*.

BI'GA, s. [a cart with two wheels] *biga*, s. f. *carro con due ruote*.

BI'GAMY, s. [the state of having two wives or husbands at once] *bigamia*, s. f.

BI'GAMIST, s. [one that has two wives or husbands at the same time] *bigamo*, s. m. *bigama*, s. f.

BI'GGER, adj. *più grosso, piu grande*.

This is bigger than yours, *questo è più grande del vostro*.

BI'GGIN, s. [a coif or linen cap for a child] *scuffietta*, s. f.

BI'GNESS, s. *grossezza, spessezza, grandezza*, s. f.

Of the bigness of an egg, *della grossezza d'un uovo, grosso come un uovo*.

BIGHT, or Bite, s. [among sailors, any turn or part of a cable or rope rolled up] *un cerchio di fune*.

BIGHT [of a horse, is the bent of the knees in the fore legs] *la piegatura delle gambe d'avanti del cavallo*.

BI'GOT, s. [a superstitious person] *bacchettone*, s. m. *colui che attende alla vita spirituale superstiziosamente*.

BI'GOTISM, } s. [superstition, hypo-
BI'GOTRY, } crisy] *bacchettoneria*, s. f. *bacchettonismo*, s. m.

BI'GOTTED, adj. [grown bigot] *divenuto bacchettone, dedito al bacchettonismo*.

Bigotted in one's own opinion, *pieno della propria opinione*.

BI'LLANDER, s. [a small sort of ship] *pinco*, s. m. *balandra*, s. f.

BI'LBOES, s. [a sort of punishment at sea] *sorta di castigo usato fra i marinai non molto dissimile dalla corda*.

BILE, s. [boil, sore] *ulcera, bozza, enfiatura*, s. f. *enfiato, ciccione*, s. m.

A venomous or pestilent bile, *ulcera pestilenziale*.

To break into a bile, *ulcerare, pervenire ad ulcera*.

Full of biles, *ulceroso, pieno d'ulcere*.

BILGE, *v.* Bulge.

BILGED, *v.* Bulged.

BI'LIOUS, adj. [cholerick] *bilioso, stizzoso*.

To BILK [to disappoint, to deceive] *ingannare, truffare, fraudare*.

To bilk [to bubble, to gull] *deludere, beffare, schernire*.

BILKED, adj. *ingannato, truffato, fraudato, deluso, beffato, schernito*.

Bilked in his expectations, *deluso nelle sue aspettative*.

BILL, s. [the mouth of a bird] *becco, rostro*, s. m.

A hedging-bill, *falciotto, falcetta*.

A little hedging-bill, *ronciglio, roncone*, s. m.

A bill-man [a lopper of trees] *potatore*, s. m. *quegli che pota i rami inutili e dannosi agli alberi*.

Bill-full, *beccata*, s. f. *quanto puo capire nell becco*.

Bill [note] *biglietto*, s. m. *pólizza*, s. f. *polizzino*, s. m.

A bill of debt, *cedola, pólizza*, s. f. *scrittura privata, che obbliga*.

A bill of exchange, *lettera di cambio*.

A bill of lading, *pólizza di carico*.

A bill [set upon a post, or against a wall] *cartello*, s. m.

Bill of complaint, *querela, lamentanza, doglienza*, s. f.

A bill of indictment, *accusa, accusazione*, s. f. *processo*, s. m.

A bill in chancery, *processo verbale*.

A bill upon a door, *cedola*, s. f.

A bill in parliament, *domanda fatta in iscritto al parlamento o dal publico o da persone private supplicandolo che conoscendo la giustizia della causa voglia concederla*.

Bill [catalogue] *lista*, s. f. *catalogo*, s. m.

The weekly bill, *la lista de' morti che si pubblica in Londra ogni settimana*.

A bill of parcels, *lista o conto particolare che si da dal venditore al compratore, di tutti le sorti e prezzi delle robe comprate*.

Bill of sale, *scrittura colla quale una persona che piglia in prestito una somma di danari da qualcuno obbliga tutti i suoi effetti per sicurtà a quello che impresta il danaro, o da per persa la cosa su cui prese danari in pegno se dopo tanto tempo non la riscuote*.

Bill of store [a license granted at the custom-house to merchants, to carry stores and provisions necessary for their voyage custom-free] *licenza in iscritto concessa per vettovagliare un vascello di tutto quello che gli è necessario per il viaggio senza pagare il dazio*.

Bill of sufferance [is a licence granted to a merchant to trade from one English port to another, without paying custom] *licenza concessa ad un mercante di trafficare da un porto all' altro d'Inghilterra senza pagar dazio*.

BILLBE'RRY, s. *mori di rovo*.

BI'LLEMENTS, s. [ornaments and cloaths of women] *ornamenti femminili, addobbi da donna*.

BI'LLET, s. [a stick or log of wood cut for fewel] *ceppo*, s. m. *pezzo di pedal grosso d'albero per abbruciare*.

Billet [an ingot of gold or silver] *verga d'oro o d'argento*.

Billet [a ticket for quartering of soldiers] *bulletta*, s. f. *bullettino*, s. m.

Billet [a letter or note folded up] *biglietto*, s. m. *letteruccia*, s. f.

Billet-doux [a short love letter] *lettera amorosa breve; pistolotto amoroso*.

To BILLET soldiers [to quarter them in several houses by billet or ticket] *alloggiare soldati col distribuirli per le case dando a ciascuno di loro un bullettino*.

BI'LLIARDS, s. [a sort of game] *trucco*, s. m. *sorta di giuoco, bigliardo*.

To play at billiards, *giuocare al trucco, giuocare al bigliardo*.

Billiard stick, *strumento di legno col quale si giuoco, coda*.

Billiard-ball, *palla colla quale si giuoca al trucco*.

BI'LLINGSGATE LANGUAGE, s. *parlar plebeo; parlar osceno, ingiurioso, e vile come parlano le Pesciajuole e altra bassa gente che vive nelle vicinanze di Billingsgate, che è una parte di Londra abitata da molta bassa gente, e specialmente da venditori e venditrici d'ostriche e di pesce*.

A BI'LLINGSGATE, s. [a scolding impudent slut] *una donna da dozzina, una donna vile e linguacciuta*.

BI'LLOW, s. [a surge of the sea] *onda*, s. f. *cavallone, flutto*, s. m.

BIND, s. [stalk of hops] *sermento, tralcio di lúpoli*.

A bind of eels, *una cordata d' anguille*.

To BIND [to tie] *legare, strignere con fune o altro, attaccare*.

Bind him hand and foot, *legagli le mani e i piedi*.

To bind [to tie, to oblige] *legare, constringere, obbligare*.

To

To bind one with an oath, *legare, obbligare uno con giuramento.*

To bind one by kindness, *cattivarsi l'animo altrui co' benefici, colle cortesie.*

To bind one's self by promise, *impegnarsi con promessa.*

I bound myself with a vow, *feci voto.*

To bind a book, *legare un libro.*

To bind with an earnest, *caparrare, dar la caparra.*

To bind a bargain with earnest, *conchiudere un mercato con caparra.*

To bind the belly, *ristrignere il ventre.*

To bind a servant by giving him earnest, *appostare un servo, dandogli caparra.*

Too much sleep binds up our senses, *il troppo sonno ci lega i sensi.*

To bind with galloon, *orlare con gallone o passamano.*

To bind one apprentice, *mettere uno a servire per imparare un mestiere, metter un giovane per garzone in un negozio.*

To bind one's self, *obbligarsi, impegnarsi, comprometterst.*

To bind one over to the sessions, *obbligare uno a comparire nella sessione, cioè di comparire quando sarà tempo dinanzi al magistrato.*

BI'NDER, s. *legatore*, s. m. *che lega.*

Bookbinder, *legatore di libri.*

BI'NDING, s. *legamento*, s. m. *il legare.*

The binding of stones [in building] *la commessura o commettitura delle pietre.*

Binding of a book, *legatura*, s. f.

Binding, adj. [tying] *che lega.*

Binding by bond, *obbligatorio.*

Binding [costive] *costipativo.*

BIND-WEED, s. [a sort of plant] *smilace, spezie d'erba.*

BIN, s. [a large chest to put corn or bread in] *area, cassa, madia*, s. f.

BIPARTI'TE, adj. [divided in two parts] *bipartito, diviso in due parti.*

BIRCH, s. [a kind of tree] *scopa*, s. f. *nome di pianta.*

BIRCHEN, adj. *di scopa.*

A birchen broom, *granata di scope.*

BIRD, s. *uccello*, s. m.

A little bird, *un uccelletto, un uccellino.*

A bird of game, *uccello da caccia.*

Birds of a feather flock together, *ognuno ama il suo simile.*

There is no catching old birds with straw, *volpe vecchia non cade nella rete.*

A bird in the hand is worth two in the bush, *è meglio oggi l'uovo che domani la gallina, meglio piccione in man che tordo in frasca.*

To hit the bird in the eye, or the nail on the head, *dar nel segno, imberciare, apporsi.*

To kill two birds with one stone, *batter due chiodi ad un caldo.*

A Newgate bird, *uno scelerato, una forca, un mascalzone che merita di essere in Newgate, che è nome d' una prigione, pe' ladri e altra trista gente in Londra.*

You bring up a bird to pick out your eyes, *voi v'allevate la serpe in seno.*

Bird-call, *richiamo*, s. m.

Bird-lime, *vischio*, s. m.

Bird-cage, *gabbia*, s. f.

A large bird-cage, *gabbione*, s. m.

A little bird-cage, *gabbiuola*, s. f.

Birds-nest, *nido d'uccelli.*

Bird-catcher, *uccellatore*, s. m.

To BIRD [to go a birding] *uccellare, tendere insidie agli uccelli per prenderli.*

BI'RDER, s. *uccellatore*, s. m.

BI'RDING, s. *uccellamento*, s. m. *uccellagione*, s. f.

To go a birding, *uccellare, andare a caccia d'uccelli.*

A birding net, *rete da prendere uccelli.*

Birding-piece, *schioppo da uccellare.*

Birding-time, *uccellagione.*

BIRGA'NDER, s. [a sort of wild-goose] *oca salvatica.*

BI'RLED, adj. [studded] *tempestato, biliottato di chiodi, di borchie.*

BIRLET, s. *benda colla quale le donne si conciano la testa.*

BIRT, s. [a fish of the turbot-kind] *sorta di pesce simile al rombo.*

BIRTH, s. [nativity] *nascita, natività*, s. f.

Birth [extraction] *nascita, stirpe, schiatta, condizione.*

He is a gentleman by birth, *è gentiluomo nato.*

Birth [lying in of a woman] *parto*, s. m.

She had two at a birth, *ella ha fatto due figliuoli ad un parto, ella ha partorito di due gemelli.*

Birth [among beasts] *ventrata*, s. f.

A bitch that had four puppies at a birth, *una cagna che ha fatto quattro cagnolini ad una ventrata.*

A new birth, *rigenerazione*, s. f.

Birth is much, but breeding is more, *la vera nobiltà sono i costumi.*

A strange unnatural birth, *un parto contro natura.*

Untimely birth, *abortivo*, s. m. *sconciatura*, s. f.

After-birth, *seconda, secondina*, s. f.

Birth [rise, beginning] *principio, cominciamento, nascimento*, s. m. *origine*, s. f.

This is that which gave birth to such severe laws, *questo fu il motivo, perchè si stabilissero leggi così severe.*

Birth-place, *luogo natio, luogo dove altri è nato.*

Birth-day, *nascita*, s. f. *natale, giorno di nascita.*

The king's birth-day, *il giorno della nascita del re, il dì del natale del re.*

Birth-right, *primogenitura*, s. f. *ragione di succedere negli stati che porta seco l'essere primogenito.*

Birthwort, s. [an herb] *aristologia*, s. f. *spezie d'erba.*

BI'SHOP, s. *vescovo*, s. m.

The bishop, at chess, *alfiere*, s. m. *uno de' pezzi onde si giuoca agli scacchi.*

Bishop's-wort, *nepitella*, s. f. *spezie d'erba.*

Bishop's-leaves [an herb] *bettonica salvatica.*

Bishop's crosier, *pastorale*, s. m. *baston vescovile.*

Of or belonging to a bishop, *vescovile, di vescovo, attenente a vescovo.*

BI'SHOPRICK. *vescovato*, s. m.

BISK, or Bisque, s. [odds at the play of tennis, a stroke allowed to the weaker player] *fallo*, s. m.

Bisk [a rich kind of pottage made of quails, capons, and fat pullets] *piatto alla francese, fatto di quaglie, capponi, e pollastri.*

BI'SKET, s. *biscotto*, s. m. *pane due volte cotto.*

Bisket [sweet bisket] *biscottino*, s. m. *pezzetto di pasta con zucchero e altre cose cotto a modo di biscotto.*

BI'SMUTE, } s. *sorta di marchesetta, sorte di marcassita.*
BI'SMUTH, }

BISSE'XTILE, adj. *bisestile, che ha il bisesto.*

Bissextile, s. [leap year] *bisesto*, s. m. *quell' anno in cui un s'aggiugne al mese di febbrajo, per aggiustar l'anno col sole.*

BI'STORT, s. [the herb snake-weed] *bistorta*, s. f.

BIT, s. [piece] *pezzo, boccone*, s. m.

A bit of bread, *un pezzo di pane, un boccone di pane, un tozzo di pane.*

A tid bit, *un boccon delicato.*

Adam's bit [the protuberance of the throat in some people] *la noce della gola, il pomo d'Adamo.*

Never a bit, *niente affatto.*

It is all nought every bit of it, *tutto questo non val nulla.*

A little bit, *pezzettino, bocconcino, morselletto*, s. m.

Bit of a bridle, *morso, freno*, s. m.

To bite on the bit [in a figurative sense] *rodere il freno, beccarsi i geti.*

A bit and away, *merenda*, s. f.

A poisoned bit, *un boccone.*

WELCH-BIT, *Gl'inglesi chiamano* welch-bit *o* welch-rabbit *(che suona in nostra lingua come* coniglio di Wales) *un po' di pan tostato con un tantin di cacio fresco sopra, per derisione degli abitanti del Principato di Wales. Alcuni per metterli ancora più in ridicolo chiamano quella fetta di pan tostato col cacio* Welch rare-bit, *invece di* Rabbit, *che appo noi suona* Boccone raro.

To tear a thing all to bits, *mettere o stracciare che che si sia in pezzi.*

By bits, *in pezzi.*

To draw bit, *sbrigliare.*

Without drawing bit, *senza sbrigliare.*

The bit of a key, *il buco della chiave.*

Bit, *è un preterito del verbo* To bite.

To BIT, *imboccare.*

To bit a horse, *imboccare un cavallo.*

BITCH, s. [a female dog] *cagna*, s. f. *femmina di cane.*

A proud bitch, *cagna in amore.*

A bitch-fox, *una volpe femmina.*

A bitch, s. *una sgualdrina, una puttanaccia. E' epiteto d'ingiuria dato dalla gente scostumata alle Donne.*

BITE, s. *morso*, s. m. *morsura, morsicatura*, s. f.

I desire but one bite, *non ne voglio più d'un morso.*

To BITE, *mordere, morsicare, morsecchiare.*

I fear

I fear the dog will bite me, *temo che'l cane non mi morda.*

To bite one's nails, *moderſi l'unghie, roderſi l'ugne.*

If you cannot bite, never ſhow your teeth, *a che moſtrar i denti, ſe non potete modere.*

Bite, s. *cilecca, giarda.*

Pepper bites the tongue, *il pepe pizzica la lingua.*

This bites him, *queſto lo pugne, queſto gli diſpiace.*

The froſt bites the graſs, *il gelo ſecca l'erba.*

To bite into little bits, *sbocconcellare.*

To bite off, *portar via il pezzo mordendo.*

To bite on the bridle, *eſſere alle ſtrette, eſſer ridotto a grandi ſtrettezze.*

BI'TING, s. *mordicamento,* s. m. *il mordicare, morſo,* s. m. *morſicatura, morſura,* s. f.

Biting, adj. *mordente, mordace, pungente, pugnente, acuto.*

A biting jeſt, *detto mordace.*

BI'TINGLY, adj. *mordacemente, aſpramente, pungentemente.*

BI'TTACLE, s. [a frame of timber in the ſteerage, where the compaſs ſtands] *buſſola,* s. f. *ſtrumento marinareſco, ove s'aggiuſta l'ago calamitato.*

BI'TTED, adj. [from to bit] *imboccato.*

BI'TTEN, adj. [from to bite] *morſo, morduto, morſicato, morſecchiato,* v. To bite.

A hard bitten dog, *un cane duro di bocca.*

BITTER, adj. [in taſte] *amaro.*

Wormwood is bitter, *l'aſſenzio è amaro.*

As bitter as gall, *amaro come il fiele.*

Bitter [ſharp] *aſpro, bruſco.*

A bitter apple, *una mela bruſca.*

Bitter cold, *freddo acuto, freddo pungente.*

Bitter [biting, ſharp] *mordace, aſpro, crudele, ſatirico, pungente, piccante.*

Bitter words, *parole mordaci.*

A bitter quarrel, *un' aſpra conteſa.*

Bitter-wort, *genziana,* s. f.

To grow bitter, *amareggiare, amarezzare, divenire amaro.*

To make bitter, *rendere amaro.*

BI'TTERLY, adv. *amaramente, aſpramente, acutamente, crudelmente.*

To inveigh bitterly againſt one, *riprender alcuno con aſpre invettive.*

BI'TTERN, or bittour, s. [a kind of bird] *ſorta d'ucello coſì detto.*

BI'TTERNESS, s. *amaro, amarore,* s. m. *amarezza, amaritudine, afflizione,* s. f. *affanno, cordoglio,* s. m.

Bitterneſs [roughneſs] *aſprezza, durezza, rigidezza, rigoroſità,* s. f.

BITTS, s. [in a ſhip, are two main pieces of timber to which the cable is faſtened when ſhe rides at anchor] *bitte, due groſſi pezzi di legno ai quali ſi lega la gomena quando il vaſcello ha gettata l'ancora.*

BITU'MEN, s. [a kind of fat clay or ſlime, clammy like pitch] *bitume,* s. m. *minerale untuoſo, ſimile alla pece.*

BITU'MINOUS, adj. [full of brimſtone, unctuous] *bituminoſo*

BLAB, or Blabber, s. *un ciarlone, un ciarlatore, un ciarliere, un chiacchierone, una ciarlatrice.*

He is a great blab of his tongue, *egli è un gran cicalone.*

To BLAB, *ciarlare, ciaramellare, chiacchierare, cicalare.*

To blab out, *divulgare, ſcoprire, paleſare, parlare inconſideramente.*

To blab out a thing, *divulgare o pubblicare una coſa.*

BLA'BBED, adj. *ciarlato, ciaramellato, cicalato, divulgato, ſcoperto.*

Blabber-lipped, adj. *che ha le labbra groſſe.*

Blabber-lips, s. *groſſe labbra.*

BLACK, adj. *nero, di color nero:*

Somewhat black, *nericcio, che ha del nero, che tende al nero, nereggiante.*

Black [wicked] *cattivo, reo, malvagio, vile, infame, indegno.*

A black action, *un azione cattiva.*

Black day, *un giorno funeſto.*

A black Monday, *giorno nel quale ſi fa giuſtizia.*

The black art, *l'arte magica, negromanzia.*

The black letter, *la lettera Gotica.*

The black friars, *fratti domenicani.*

A black man, *un uomo che ha i capelli neri.*

A black woman, *una donna bruna.*

Black cattle, *beſtiame vaccino.*

To make black, *annerare, annerire, render nero, tinger in nero o di nero.*

To make black [to defame] *annerare, diffamare, macchiar la fama altrui con maledicenza, infamare.*

Blackguard, *birbone, canaglia.*

A black-bird, *un merlo.*

The black-cap [a ſort of bird] *un capinero.*

Blackberries, *mori di rovo.*

Black and blue, *livido.*

To beat black and blue, *ammaccare le carni, far la carne livida con percoſſe.*

Black and blue, *lividezza,* s. f.

Black, s. *color nero.*

Smoke-black, *affumicato.*

To put on black, *veſtirſi di nero.*

Black will take no other hue, *ſopra il nero non vi puo colore.*

Every bean has its black, v. Bean.

To have a thing under black and white, *aver qualche coſa in iſcritto.*

Black brown, *nericcio, fulvo.*

Black-eyed, *che ha gli occhi neri, brunocchiuto.*

Black faced, *brunetto.*

Black mouthed, *che ha la bocca nera.*

Black mouthed [ſatyrical] *ſatirico, maldicente, oſceno.*

BLACKAMO'RE, s. *un moro.*

A ſhe blackamore, *una mora.*

To waſh a blackamore white, *lavar la teſta all' aſino, far un buco nell' acqua.*

To BLA'CKEN, *annerare, annerire, far nero, tinger di nero, render di color nero.*

To blacken, verb neut. *annerire, divenir nero,* pref. *anneriſco.*

BLA'CKENED, adj. *annerato, annerito.*

BLA'CKENING, s. *anneramento,* s. m *l'annerare.*

BLA'CKING, s. [black for ſhoes] *tinta,* s. f.

BLA'CKISH, adj. *nericcio, che tende al nero.*

BLA'CKMORE, v. Blackamore.

BLA'CKSMITH, s. *fabbro,* s. m.

BLA'CKNESS, s. *nerezza,* s. f.

BLA'DDER, s. [a ſkinny bag which receives the urine of living creatures] *veſcica,* s. f. *quella membrana dell' animale che è ricettacolo dell' orina.*

A little bladder, s. *veſcichetta,* s. f.

A large bladder, *veſcicone,* s. m.

A bladder blown, *un otre, un otro, veſcica gonfia.*

A bladder nut, *ſpezie di noce che vien dall' Indie.*

BLADE, s. [of a ſword] *lama di ſpada.*

The blade of an oar, *la paletta d'un remo.*

The ſhoulder blade, *l'aſſo della ſpalla.*

The blade of an herb, *fuſto, gambo, ſtelo d'un' erba.*

The blades of a flower, *le foglie d'un fiore.*

The blade of corn, *lo ſtipite del grano.*

The breaſt blade, *il caſſo o il caſſero del petto.*

A notable young blade, *un furbacciotto, un furbo, uno ſcaltrito, un bravaccio, un giovane beccaſiti.*

An old blade, *una volpe, un volpone.*

A fine blade, *un bell' uomo, un uomo di bella preſenza, un uomo di ſtatura alta e bella.*

A ſtout blade, *un bravo, un bravaccio.*

A cunning blade, *uno ſcaltrito.*

A pair of blades [a pair of yarn-windles] *un naſpo, un aſpo,* s. m.

To blade it, *fare il bravo, procedere con alterigia.*

BLA'DED, adj. *ex.* bladed corn, *biada in erba.*

BLAIN, s. [boil, ulcer] *ulcera,* s. f.

BLA'MABLE, or Blâmeable, adj. *biaſimevole, degno di biaſimo.*

BLAME, s. [imputation, reproach] *biaſimo,* s. m. *colpa, nota, macchia,* s. f.

Let me bear the blame, *datene pur la colpa a me.*

Lay the blame upon him, *incolpate lui, datene la colpa a lui.*

The blame of it will light upon me, *io ne ſarò biaſimato, io ne potererò il biaſimo.*

Blame-worthy, *biaſimevole, degno di biaſimo.*

To blame [to find fault with] *biaſimare, condannare, incolpare.*

I cannot blame you for it, *non poſſo biaſimarvi di cio.*

You are to blame if you do it, *avete torto di farlo.*

I am not to be blamed for this, *non ſon degno di biaſimo.*

You are both to blame for that, *voi ſiete tutti due da biaſimare.*

What do they blame him for? *in che ha peccato egli?*

He blamed me for his death, *m'accuſò d'aver cagionata la ſua morte.*

You

You are more to blame in that than he, *voi siete molto più da biasimare in questo che non esso.*
It is not the use, but the abuse of things which I blame, *io non condanno l'uso, ma l'abuso delle cose.*
Your conduct is to blame, *la vostra condotta è biasimevole.*
BLA'MEABLE, adj. *biasimevole.*
BLAMED, adj. *biasimato, condannato, incolpato.*
BLAMELESS, adj. *innocente, essente d'ogni biasimo o rimprovero.*
BLA'MELESLY, adv. *innocentemente, senza biasimo o rimprovero.*
BLA'MER, s. [fault-finder] *biasimatore, vituperatore, colui o colei che biasima.*
BLA'MING, s. *il biasimare, biasimo,* s. m.
To BLANCH [to whiten] *bianchire, imbiancare, far divenir bianco.*
To blanch [to take off the rind of almonds] *mòndare mándorle.*
To blanch [to palliate] *palliare, ricoprire, dissimulare, colorare.*
They blanched however their answer in handsome words, *vestirono però la risposta loro con parole speziose.*
BLANCHED, adj. *bianchito, imbiancato, imbianchito.*
Blanched almonds, *mándorle monde.*
BLA'NCHER, s. *imbiacatore,* s. m.
BLA'NCHING, s. *imbiancamento,* s. m *imbiancatura,* s. f. *l'imbiancare.*
BLANCKMANGE'R, s. [a kind of jelly made of calves feet, and other ingredients, with powdered almonds] *biancomangiare,* s. m. *sorta di vivanda.*
BLANDI'LOQUENCE, or Blandiloquy, s. [fair and flattering speech] *blandimento, lusinga, piacevolezza, carezze,* s. f.
To BLA'NDISH [to flatter, to sooth with fair speeches] *blandire, adulare, accarezzare, lusingare,* pres. *blandisco.*
BLA'NDISHMENT, s. [alluring caress, wheedle] *blandimento, lusingamento,* s. m. *adulazione, lusinga, carezza,* s. f.
BLANK, adj. [pale, wan] *pallido, smorto, sbiancato.*
Blank [out of countenance] *confuso, stordito, sconcertato.*
Blank verse, *verso sciolto.*
Point blank, adv. [entirely, flap-dash] *di punto in bianco, intieramente, dirittamente, affatto, appunto, per l'appunto.*
This is point blank against the second commandment, *questo è dirittamente contrario al secondo comandamento.*
Blank, s. [a void space in writing] *bianco,* s. m. *spazio vuoto, che si lascia nello scrivere.*
Blank [in a lottery] *bianca.*
Blank [an ancient coin] *un bianco, sorta di moneta antica.*
Blank [a piece of metal in the mint ready for coining] *pezzo di metallo non monetato.*
To grow blank, *impallidire, divenir pallido o smorto,* pres. *impallidisco.*
To have blank [to have no honours at cards] *aver carte bianche.*
To BLANK [to confound] *confondere, sbaldanzire, sgomentare,* pres. *sbaldanzisco.*

BLA'NKET, s. [a coverlet for a bed] *coltre,* s. f. *coperta da letto di lana.*
Blanket for a child, *pannicello di lana col quale s'avviluppano i bambini quando sono in fasce.*
Blanket [of a printing press] *pezzo di panno, di cui si servono stampatori nello stampare.*
To BLARE [as a cow] *muggire, mugghiare,* pres. *muggisco.*
To blare [to melt away as a candle does] *struggersi, liquefarsi.*
To BLASPHE'ME [to curse, to revile, to speak evil of God or holy things] *bestemmiare.*
BLASPHE'MER, s. *bestemmiatore.*
BLASPHE'MOUS, adj. *esecrando, esecrabile, empio.*
Blasphemous words, *parole esecrande.*
BLASPHE'MOUSLY, adv. *con bestemmie, esecrabilmente, empiamente.*
BLA'SPHEMY, s. [cursing and swearing] *bestemmia,* s. f.
BLAST, s. [puff] *soffio,* s. m.
A blast of wind, *un soffio di vento.*
A blast [in corn or trees] *golpe,* s. f.
A blast has spoiled the corn, *la golpe ha guastato il grano.*
To BLAST [to spoil the fruits of the earth] *annebbiare, e dicesi delle frutte, e delle biade quando sono in fiore, che offese dalla nebbia riardono e non allegano, invanire,* pres. *invanisco.*
To blast the corn, *annebbiare il grano.*
To blast another's design [to blast one in his undertakings] *render vano l'altrui disegno, rovinare gli altrui disegni.*
To blast a man's credit or reputation, *far perder il credito ad uno, macchiare l'altrui fama.*
BLA'STED, adj. *annebbiato, invanito,* v. To blast.
BLA'STING, s. *l'annebbiare.*
BLA'TANT, adj. [babling] *ciarliero.*
BLAY, v. Bleak-fish.
BLAZE, s. *fiamma, vampa,* s. f.
To BLAZE [as a fire or torch] *vampeggiare, render vampa.*
The fire blazes, *il fuoco vampeggia.*
To blaze abroad [to publish] *pubblicare, manifestare, divulgare, palesare.*
BLAZED, adj. *vampeggiato, pubblicato, manifestato, divulgato, palesato.*
BLAZER, s. [a publisher of things] *un chiaccherone, un che palesa i fatti altrui.*
BLA'ZING, s. *il vampeggiare,* v. To blaze.
A blazing star, *una stella risplendente, una cometa.*
BLA'ZON, s. [coat of arms] *divisa, arme, impresa,* s. f.
To BLA'ZON [to paint, to express, to display the parts of a coat of arms] *divisare, differenziare, variare l'arme d'una famiglia.*
To blazon [to set out] *dipignere, rappresentare, descrivere.*
BLA'ZONED, adj. *divisato, differenziato, dipinto, rappresentato.*
BLA'ZONING, s. *divisamento,* s. m. *il divisare.*

BLA'ZONRY, s. [the art of heraldry] *l'arte di divisare le armi, aralderia, l'arte araldesca.*
To BLEACH [to whiten abroad in the sun] *bianchire, imbiancare al sole,* pres. *bianchisco.*
To bleach cloth, *bianchire della tela.*
BLEA'CHED, adj. *bianchito, imbiancato.*
BLEA'CHER, s. *imbiancatore,* s. m.
BLEA'CHING, s. *bianchimento,* s. m. *il bianchire.*
BLEAK, adj. [cold] *freddo, aspro, acuto.*
A bleak wind, *un vento freddo.*
Bleak or Bleaky [pale, wan] *pallido, smorto.*
You look very bleak, *voi siete smorto, nel viso.*
The bleak-fish, *laccia, cheppia,* s. f. *pesce di mare che la primavera viene all' acqua dolce.*
BLE'AKY, adv. *pallidamente.*
BLE'AKNESS, s. *pallidezza, pallidità,* s. f. *pallóre,* s. m.
To BLEAR THE SIGHT [to dim it] *offuscar la vista.*
BLE'AREDNESS, s. *cispa, cisposità,* s. f. *umore, che casca dagli occhi, e si risecca intorno alle palpebre.*
BLEAR-E'YED, adj. *cispo, cisposo, lippo.*
To BLEAT [to cry like a sheep or goat] *belare, il mandar fuor la voce che fa la pecora e la capra.*
The sheep bleats, *la pecora bela.*
BLE'ATING, s. *il belare.*
BLEB, s. [bladder] *vescica.*
Bleb [bubble in the water] *bolla, rigonfiamento, che fa l'acqua piovana o bollendo, o gorgogliando.*
BLED, *preterito del verbo* To bleed.
I bled five ounces of blood, *ho perso cinque once di sangue.*
To BLEED, verb neut. *far sangue, gettar sangue.*
To bleed at the nose, *far sangue o gettar sangue del naso.*
My heart bleeds tears for it, *me ne scoppia il cuore.*
To bleed one [to let him blood] *cavar sangue ad uno.*
BLE'EDER, s. *quelli che cava sangue.*
BLEE'DING, s. *il far sangue, il cavar sangue.*
The bleeding at the nose, *il buttar sangue dal naso.*
To stop one's bleeding, *stagnare o ristagnare il sangue.*
Bleeding, adj. *sanguigno, sanguinoso.*
A bleeding condition, *uno stato pericoloso.*
BLE'MISH, s. [stain, spot] *macchia, macula, bruttura,* s. f. *vizio,* s. m.
There was no blemish in his body, *non v'era macchia veruna nel suo corpo.*
Blemish, *macchia, colpo, infamia, nota,* s. f.
This is a great blemish to his reputation, *la sua riputazione resterà da ciò macchiata molto.*
He is the blemish of the family, *egli è il disonore della famiglia.*
BLE'MISHES [in hunting; hunters marks where the deer has gone] *traccia,* s. f.

To BLE'MISH [to ftain] *macchiare bruttar con macchie, magagnare, maculare, imbrattare.*
To blemifh one's reputation, *ofrurare, annerire, difonorare l'altrui riputazione.*
BLE'MISHED, adj. *macchiato, magagnato, maculato, imbrattato.*
BLE'MISHING, s. *il macchiare.*
To BLENCH [to fhrink, to ftart back] *dar indietro per timore, rannicchiarfi.*
To blench [to hinder, to obftruct] *impedire, cagionar impedimento, porre oftacolo.*
To BLEND [to mix] *mefcolare, mifchiare, mefchiare.*
BLE'NDED, adj. *mefcolato, mifchiato, e mefchiato.*
BLENT [the obfolete participle of the verb to blend] *participio del verbo* To blend, *non più in ufo : oggi fi dice,* blended.
To BLESS [to beftow a bleffing] *benedire, dar la benedizione.*
God blefs you, *Dio vi benedira.*
To blefs [to make happy] *rendere o far felice.*
He was bleffed with a numerous iffue, *ebbe la fortuna d'avere una numerofa prole.*
Do but blefs me with your company, *di grazia fate ch'io goda la voftra compagnia.*
To blefs one's felf at a thing, *ricrearfi in qualche cofa.*
To blefs one's felf in a thing, *gloriarfi, glorificarfi in qualche cofa.*
Blefs, interj. *oh dio! dio buono!*
To blefs [to praife] *benedire, lodare.*
To BLESS [to wave, to brandifh] *brandire, ruotare la fpada.* Obf.
BLESSED, adj. *benedetto, felicitato, lodato, felice, refo felice, v.* To blefs.
Bleffed be God, *lodato Iddio.*
Bleffed [holy] *fanto.*
Bleffed [happy] *felice, beato, avventurato.*
The queen of bleffed memory, *la regina di felice memoria.*
The bleffed virgin, *la beata vergine.*
To be bleffed with a good memory, *effer dotato d'una buona memoria, avere una memoria angelica.*
He was bleffed with a long and profperous reign, *ebbe la grazia di godere un lungo e profpero regno.*
I was never bleffed with the fight of her, *non-ho mai avuta la ventura di vederla.*
The bleffed, *I beati.*
BLE'SSEDLY, adv. *beatamente, felicemente.*
BLE'SSEDNESS, s. *beatitudine, felicità,* s. f. *contento,* s. m.
BLE'SSING, s. [benediction] *benedizione,* s. f.
Bleffing [happinefs] *felicità, ventura,* s. f. *contento, piacere,* s. m.
By the bleffing of God, *colla grazia di Dio.*
BLEW, *preterito del verbo* To blow.
What wind blew you hither? *che buon vento v'ha portato qui?*
Blew, *v.* Blue, and all its derivatives.

BLIGHT, s. [blaft] *golpe,* s. f.
BLI'GHTED, adj. *annebbiato.*
Blighted [decayed] *guafto, corrotto, putrido, marcio.*
BLIND, adj. *cieco, che non vede, orbo.*
To be born blind, *effer nato cieco.*
A blind man, *un cieco, un orbo.*
Who fo blind as they that will not fee? *neffuno è fi cieco che quello che finge di non vedere?*
When the devil is blind, *quando il diavolo farà cieco, cioè, mai.*
Blind of one eye, *lofco, cieco d'un occhio.*
The blind gut, *l'inteftino cieco.*
A blind ftory, *una fola pazza, una favolaccia.*
A blind or dark ftair-cafe or clofet, *una fcala o un gabinetto ofcuro.*
A blind or falfe pretence, *un falfo pretefto.*
A blind way, *ftrada cieca, occulta, o coperta.*
Blind nettle, *fcrofularia,* s. f. *forta d'erba.*
Pur-blind [pore-blind] *lippo, di corta vifta.*
Sand-blind [moon-blind] *lippo, lofco.*
Blind worm, *cicigna,* s. f. *piccola ferpe e cieca.*
Blind-born, *cieco nato.*
Stark-blind, *affatto cieco.*
Blind men cannot judge of colours, *il cieco non giudica de' colori.*
As blind as a mole, *cieco come una talpa.*
Stone-blind, *affatto cieco.*
Mole-blind, *cieco davvero.*
A blind or falfe pretence, *velo, pretefto, mantello,* s. m. *fcufa, coperta,* s. f.
His honefty is but a blind for him to cheat the better, *la fua oneftà non è che un mantello da poter più ficuramente ingannare.*
BLINDS. *Quattro pezzi di legno in quadro con una tela dipinta o graticoletta di rame che ne ricopra il vano formano un* blind, *cioè un riparo contro la vifta di chi paffa per la via, onde non poffa vedere per le fineftre a pian* terreno. *Quefti* blinds, *fi ufano moltiffimo in Inghilterra.*
Blind, s. [in fortification, bundles of ofiers bound at both ends, and fet up between ftakes] *fafci,* s. m. *termine di fortificazione.*
To BLIND [to deprive of fight] *accecare, privare della luce degli occhi.*
To blind one's fight, *privar uno della vifta, accecarlo.*
To blind [to deceive] *ingannare, adefcare, buttar polvere negli occhi.*
BLI'NDED, adj. *accecato, ingannato, adefcato.*
BLINDFO'LD, adj. *bendato, che ha gli occhi coperti con benda.*
To BLINDFO'LD, *bendare, coprire gli occhi con benda, imbacuccare, imbavagliare.*
Blindfold [blindly, rafhly] *ciecamente, inconfideratamente, alla cieca.*
BLINDFO'LDED, adj. *bendato.*
BLI'NDLY, adv. *ciecamente, alla, cieca.*
To go blindly to work, *fare le cofe ciecamente, a rompicollo, inconfideratamente.*

Blind-man's buff, *il giuoco della cieca.*
BLI'NDNESS, s. *recità, cechità, cechezza, lo ftato di che è orbo o cieco.*
Blindnefs of mind, *cecità di mente, ignoranza.*
To BLINK [to wink and blink] *ammiccare, accennar cogli occhi, palpebrizzare.*
To blink beer [to keep it unbroached till it grows fharp] *lafciare la cervogia nelle botti finattanto che cominci ad effer piccante.*
BLI'NKARD, } s. [one that winks
BLI'NKER, } or twinkles with his eyes] *lofco, guercio.*
BLINKING CA'NDLES, *candele che non fanno un buon lume.*
BLINKS, s. [among hunters, boughs caft athwart the way, where a deer is likely to pafs] *rami d'alberi meffi a traverfo un viale, per dove fi crede che il daino pafferà, per offervarne poi la traccia.*
BLISS, s. [happinefs] *beatitudine, felicità, contentezza,* s. f.
BLI'SSFUL, adj. *beato, felice, contento.*
BLI'SSFULLY, adv. *beatamente, felicemente, avventurofamente.*
BLI'SSFULNESS, s. *beatitudine, felicità,* s. f.
To BLISSOM [to tup the ewe] *montare, parlando del montone e della pecora.*
BLI'STER, s. [blain, wheal] *bolla, vefcica, púftula,* s. f. *enfiatura o bollicola che viene alla pelle; bolla acquaiuola.*
Blifter, [a fort of plafter] *vefcicatorio,* s. m. *impiaftro, che applicato alla carne vi fa nafcere delle vefciche; vefcicante.*
To BLISTER, *applicare il vefcicante.*
To blifter, verb neut. *levarfi, formarfi delle vefciche.*
BLI'STERED, adj. *a cui è ftato applicato il vefcicante.*
Bliftered, *pieno o coperto di vefciche.*
BLI'STERING, s. *l'atto d'applicare il vefcicante.*
Bliftering, adj. [as bliftering heat] *infiammazione,* s. f.
Bliftering plafter, *un vefcicante.*
BLIT, or Blits, s. [an herb] *bieta, bietola,* s. f.
BLITHE, adj. [merry] *giocondo, allegro, piacevole, dilettofo, lieto, giojofo.*
BLI'THLY, adv. *giocondamente, allegramente, piacevolmente, lietamente, giojofamente.*
BLI'THNESS, } s. *giocondità, le-*
BLI'THSOMNESS, } *tizia, allegrezza, contentezza,* s. f. *giubbilo,* s. m.
BLOACH, s. [blifter] *puftula, vefcica,* s. f.
BLOAT, *v.* Blote.
BLOB-CHEE'KED, adj. *che ha le guance piene.*
BLOBBER [a bubble] *búbbola, palla fatta dal gorgogliar dell' acqua a mo' di vefcica gonfia, e metaforicamente vale fanfaluca, cofa vana.*
BLOBBER-LIPPED, *v.* Blubber-lipped.

BLOCK,

BLOCK, s. [the stem or stump of a tree] *tronco*, s. m. *pedale dell' albero.*

Block [blockhead] *testa di legno che serve per pettinarvi sopra la parrucca.*

The block at the game of bowls, *grillo*, s. m. *quel picciol segno nel giuoco delle pallottole, a cui le palle debbono accostarsi.*

A hatter's block, *forma di capello.*

Block [hindrance, obstacle] *intoppo, ostacolo, impedimento*, s. m.

To cast a block in one's way, *attraversare l'altrui disegno.*

To come to the block [to be beheaded] *esser decapitato.*

A mounting-block, *cavalcatojo*, s. m.

Blockade, s. *bloccata*, s. f. *blocco*, s. m.

BLO'CKHEAD [fool] *pecora, donzellone, pecorone, sciocco, gaglioffo.*

Blockhouse, *un forte, un luogo fortificato.*

To BLOCK UP, *bloccare, assediare alla larga, pigliando i posti acciò non possano entrare i viveri.*

To block up a town, *bloccare una terra.*

BLOCKED UP, adj. *bloccato.*

BLOCKING UP, s. *il bloccare, bloccata*, s. f.

BLO'CKISH, adj. *stupido, balordo, melenso, sciocco, scimunito, besso, balocco, goffo, gaglioffo.*

BLO'CKISHLY, adv *scioccamente, goffamente, scimunitamente.*

BLO'CKISHNESS, s. *sciocchezza, scimunitaggine, scempiaggine, balordaggine, bessagine*, s. f.

BLOCKT UP, adj. *bloccato.*

BLOCKWOOD, *v.* Logwood.

BLOMA'RY, s. [forge of an iron mill] *fornace da fondere il ferro.*

BLOOD, s. *sangue.*

Blood [kindred] *sangue, famiglia, stirpe, progenie.*

Blood [anger] *collera, ira, stizza*, s. f.

Blood [murder] *sangue, omicidio.*

The mass of the blood, *la massa del sangue.*

To let one blood, *cavar sangue ad uno.*

To stanch [to stop the blood] *stagnare, o ristagnare il sangue.*

To whip one till the blood comes, *frustare fino al sangue.*

He killed him in cold blood, *l'ammazzò a sangue freddo, senza essere provocato.*

The blood of the grape, *il sugo dell' uva, il vino.*

Distemper that runs in the blood, *malattia ereditaria, che va di padre in figlio.*

My blood began to rise, *la collera mi cominciò a montare.*

My blood was up, *ella mi fumava, ero tutto acceso d'ira.*

It ought to make your blood rise in your face, *dovreste aver vergogna, dovreste arrossire.*

I cannot for my blood draw a word out of his mouth, *non ho potuto cavarli pur di bocca una parola colle tanagalie.*

They cannot for their bloods keep themselves honest of their fingers, *non possono in conto alcuno astenersi dal rubare.*

To be let blood, *farsi cavar sangue.*

To breed ill blood [to exasperate] *inasprire gli animi.*

Blood-hound, *limiero, can feroce, can corso.*

Blood-shed, *effusione o spargimento di sangue*; *strage*, s. f. *macello*, s. m.

Blood-red, *rosso, sanguigno, sanguineo.*

Blood-warm, *tepido.*

Blood-sucker [leech] *sanguisuga, mignatta*, s. f.

Blood-thirsty, blood-thirster, *sanguinolente, vago di far sangue, crudele.*

Blood-shot eyes, *occhi rubicondi.*

Blood-stone, *pietra ematite.*

Blood-wort [an herb to stanch the blood] *sanguinella, sanguinaria.*

To BLOOD [to let blood] *cavar sangue.*

To blood [to daub with blood] *insanguinare, imbrattare di sangue.*

BLO'ODED, adj. *a chi è stato cavato sangue, insanguinato, imbrattato di sangue.*

BLO'ODILY, adv. *sanguinosamente, sanguinolentemente, crudelmente.*

Bloodily principled, *sanguinolente, vago di far sangue, crudele.*

BLO'ODLESS, adj. *esangue, che non ha sangue, privo di sangue.*

Blood-wit, s. [a law term, a fine or amendment anciently paid for shedding of blood] *amenda che si pagava anticamente per ispargimento di sangue.*

BLO'ODY, adj. [cruel] *sanguinolente, vago di sangue, crudele, sanguinario.*

Bloody [daubed with blood] *sanguinoso, imbrattato di sangue, insanguinato.*

A bloody fight, *una sanguinosa battaglia.*

Bloody-minded, *sanguinolente, crudele, sitibondo di sangue.*

The bloody flux, *il flusso di sangue.*

BLOOM, s. [blossom of trees] *fiore d'alberi.*

She is in the bloom of her years, *ella è nel fiore della sua età.*

To BLOOM, *fiorire*, pres. *fiorisco.*

BLOOMED, adj. *fiorito.*

BLO'OMY, adj. [thick with blossoms] *fiorito, coperto di fiori.*

Bloomy cheeks, *guance di rose.*

BLO'SSOM, s. [the flower of a tree or plant] *fiore d'alberi o di piante.*

To BLO'SSOM, *fiorire*, pres. *fiorisco.*

BLO'SSOMED, adj. *fiorito.*

BLOT, s. [blur] *macchia*, s. f.

A blot with ink, *una macchia d'inchiostro.*

To BLOT, *macchiare, imbrattare.*

To blot a man's reputation, *oscurare, annerire l'altrui riputazione.*

This paper blots, *questa carta spande, non tiene l'inchiostro.*

To blot out, *cancellare, cassare, dare di penna, radere, scancellare.*

To blot a thing out of one's remembrance, *scancellare una cosa della memoria.*

BLOTCH, s. *pustula, enfiatura, vescica*, s. f.

BLOTE, adj. [swelled] *gonfio.*

A blote face, *un viso gonfio.*

To BLOTE, verb. neut. *gonfiarsi.*

To blote, verb. act. [to smoak] *affumicare.*

BLOTED, adj. *gonfio, affumicato.*

A bloted face, *un viso gonfio.*

Bloted lineaments, *fattezze grossolane.*

Bloted herrings, *aringhe affumate.*

BLO'TTED, adj. [from to blot] *macchiato, imbrattato.*

Blotted out, *cancellato, cassato, raso, scancellato.*

BLO'TTING, s. *il macchiare.*

Blotting paper, *carta succiante.*

BLOW, s. [stroke] *colpo*, s. m. *botta*, s. f.

He missed his blow, *egli ha mancato il colpo.*

Blow [misfortune, cross accident] *disastro*, s. m. *disavventura, disgrazia*, s. f.

A slanting blow, *un rovescione.*

He does nothing without blows, *non fa niente senza bastonate.*

To take a town without a blow, without striking a blow, *prendere una terra senza tirar un colpo.*

A blow with a stick, *bastonata*, s. f.

A blow with a stone, *una pietrata.*

A blow [a cuff on the ear] *una guanciata, uno schiaffo.*

To come to blows, *venire alle mani.*

A down right blow, *uno stramazzone.*

It is but a word and a blow with him, *è pronto a menar le mani.*

To BLOW, *soffiare.*

To blow the fire, *soffiare il fuoco.*

The wind blows, *il vento tira, fa vento.*

To blow the trumpet, *suonar la tromba.*

To blow the horn *suonar il corno.*

To blow a bladder, *gonfiare una vescica.*

To blow one's nose, *soffiarsi il naso.*

To blow the candle, *estinguere, spegnere, smorzare la candela.*

To puff and blow, *alenare, alitare, mandar fuor l'alito a bocca aperta, ansare.*

To blow [speaking of flowers] *aprirsi, dilatarsi sbocciando.*

It blew a dreadful storm, *faceva una burrasca terribile.*

To blow up a mine, *far saltare in aria una mina, far volare una mina, far iscoppiare una mina.*

To blow up the city into a tumult, *eccitare un tumulto in una città.*

To blow one up [to make him break] *far fallire uno.*

To blow over a storm, *dissipare una burrasca.*

To blow up, *far saltare in aria.*

To blow down, *rovinare, rovesciare, mandar giù.*

The wind has blowed down many houses, *il vento ha rovinate, o mandate a terra molte case.*

To blow in, *fare entrare soffiando.*

To blow out, *fare uscire soffiando.*

To blow off, *dissipare soffiando, dispergere.*

To blow the coals of sedition, *suscitare il fuoco della sedizione.*

To blow up a thing, *palesare, pubblicare una cosa.*

BLOWED UPON, *screditato.*

A commodity blowed upon, *una mercanzia screditata.*

BLO'WER, s. *soffiatore*, s. m. *che soffia.*

BLO'WING, s. *soffiamento*, s. m. *il soffiare.*

Blowing weather, *tempo ventoso, tempo tempestoso.*

BLOWN, adj. *soffiato*, v. to blow.

Blown [puffed] *gonfio, tumido.*

BLOWTH, s. [bloom or blossom] *l'essere in fiore degli alberi e delle piante.*

BLOWZE, s. [a fat red faced bloted wench] *una femmina che ha le guance gonfie e rosse.*

BLUB, adj. [swollen] *gonfio, gonfiato, tumido.*

BLU'BBER, s. [a sort of sea fish] *polmone marino.*

BLU'BBER [the parts of a whale that contain the oil] *quelle parti della balena che contengono l' olio.*

Blubber-lips, *labbruto, che ha le labbra grosse.*

To BLU'BBER [to weep in such a manner as to swell the cheeks] *piangere in modo forzato e che si faccia gonfiar le guance.*

To BLU'BBER, *gonfiarsi le guance.*

BLUBB-CHE'EKED, *che ha le guance gonfie.*

BLUE, adj. *turchino, azzurro.*

A blue ribbon, *un nastro turchino.*

He looked blue upon it, *restò tutto confuso.*

It will be a blue day for him, *sarà un giorno fatale per lui.*

Blue-bottle [a sort of flower, a flower of the bell shape] *sorta di fiore fatto a mo di campana, campanella.*

Blue bottle [a fly with a large blue belly] *mosca che ha il ventre largo e turchino.*

To BLUE, *tinger turchino.*

To blue one, *fare arrossire uno, farlo restar confuso, farlo rimanere con un palmo di naso.*

He was very much blued, *restò tutto confuso, stupefatto.*

To BLU'FF [to blindfold] *bendare gli occhi.*

BLU'ISH, adj. *azzurriccio, azzurrino.*

BLU'NDER, s. [mistake, oversight] *errore, fallo*, s. m. *strafalcione, marrone, error grande.*

A blunder in chronology, *un anacronismo.*

To BLUNDER, *sbalestrare, strafalciare, operare inconsideratamente.*

To blunder about a thing, *sbagliarsi, ingannarsi in qualche cosa, prender una cosa in isbaglio.*

To blunder a thing out, *parlare inconsideratamente, sbalestratamente, parlare al vento.*

BLU'NDERBUSS, s. [a wide-mouth'd brass gun] *un moschettone, un trombone.*

A meer blunderbuss, or blunderhead, *uno sbalestrato, un tempellone, uno sciocco, uno scimunito.*

BLU'NDERING, s. *l'operar inconsideratamente.*

A blundering fellow, *un balordo, un pecorone, uno sciocco, un minchione.*

To have a blundering look, *avere ciera di balordo.*

BLU'NKET, s. [a light colour] *turchino chiaro.*

BLUNT, adj. *ottuso, rintuzzato, spuntato.*

A blunt knife, *un coltello ottuso o spuntato.*

Blunt [downright in carriage] *pronto, precipitoso.*

A blunt man, *un uomo pronto, uno zotico, un uomo senza artificio.*

A blunt action, *un' azione ardita.*

A blunt invention, *un' invenzione grossolana.*

To BLUNT, *spuntare, levar via, o guastar la punta.*

To blunt a sword, *spuntare una spada.*

To blunt [to allay] *alleggerire, mitigare, temprare.*

BLU'NTED, adj. *spuntato, ottuso.*

BLU'NTLY, adv. *prontamente, arditamente, precipitosamente.*

BLU'NTISH, adj. *alquanto spuntato.*

BLU'NTNESS, s. *ottusità*, s. f. *l'esser una cosa ottusa o spuntata.*

Bluntness [in one's carriage] *rozzezza, zotichezza, prontezza*, s. f.

BLUR, s. [blot] *macchia*, s. f.

Blur [blemish] *macchia, nota, infamia*, s. f. *disonore*, s. m.

This is a blur on his family, *questo è un disonore alla sua famiglia.*

Blurt [tish] *oibò.*

To BLUR, *macchiare, maculare, imbrattare.*

To blur a trumpet, *suonar la sordina.*

BLU'RRED, adj. *macchiato, maculato, imbrattato.*

To BLURT out, *sbalestrare, strafalciare, parlare inconsideratamente, o al vento.*

I blurted out a word which I heartily repent of, *m'è scappata di bocca una parola, di cui mi pento molto.*

BLU'RTED, adj. *sbalestrato, strafalciato.*

BLUSH, s. *rossore*, s. m.

To put one to the blush, *fare arrossire alcuno.*

A blush appears upon his face, *il suo viso si tinge di rossore.*

To get a blush [to obtain a glimpse of a thing] *avere un barlume di qualche cosa, vederla tra lume e bujo.*

At first blush, *a prima vista, subito, in un subito.*

To BLUSH, verb. neut. *arrossire.* pref. *arrossisco.*

She blushed at it, *ella n'ebbe rossore, o arrossì.*

He blushed as red as fire, *egli arrossì come una vampa di fuoco.*

BLU'SHING, s. *l'arrossire, rossore.*

Blushing is virtue's colour, *il rossore è il velo della virtù.*

BLUSHT, adj. *arrossito.*

BLU'SHY [having the colour of a blush] *di quel colore che tinge le guance di bella donna quando arrossisce.*

To BLU'STER, verb. neut. [as the wind] *strepitare, fare strepito, stridere, tempestare, fare come fanno i venti impetuosi, fremere.*

To bluster, *strepitare, imperversare, fare strepito, far fracasso.*

BLU'STERING, s. *strepito, fracasso, rumore, fraccasso*, s. m.

Blustering wind, *vento impetuoso.*

Blustering weather, *tempesta, burrasca, tempo fiero, tempaccio tempestoso.*

A blustering man, *un uomo di spiriti turbulenti.*

A blustering style, *uno stile pomposo, sonante.*

BO, *ex.* he can't say bo to a goose, *non ha una parola a dire in compagnia, sta in compagnia come se fosse muto.*

To BOAD, *v.* to bode.

BOAR, s. [hog] *verro*, s. m. *porco non castrato.*

Wild boar, *cinghiale, cignale.*

BOARD, s. [plank] *asse, tavola*, s. f.

Board [ship] *bordo*, s. m.

To go on board of a ship, *andare a bordo d'un vascello.*

To cast a thing over board, *gittare in mare.*

Board [table] *tavola, mensa*, s. f.

He entertains him at board, *gli da la tavola, gli fa le spese.*

To deal above board [to act openly, frankly] *trattare schiettamente, con ischiettezza.*

I am above board [I fear no body] *sono a cavallo, non temo nessuno.*

Board wages, *quel salario che si da a un servo, acciocchè mangi fuor di casa.*

To put out a child to board, *mettere un fanciullo a dozzina.*

The board [the council board] *la tavola del consiglio del re, il consiglio regio.*

A member of the board, *un membro del consiglio.*

A draught board, *tavola da giuocar a dama, damiere, scacchiere.*

A chess board, *uno scacchiere.*

The side board of a tub, *una doga.*

A falling board [a trap] *una trappola, una schiaccia.*

To BOARD [to cover with boards] *guernire o coprire di tavole, intavolare.*

To board a ship, *abbordare, investire un vascello.*

To board one [to come up with one] *abbordare uno, accostarsi ad uno.*

To board [to keep boarders] *tenere a dozzina.*

To board, verb. neut. [to be a boarder] *stare a dozzina.*

BO'ARDED, adj. *tavolato, guernito o coperto di tavole.*

The boarded bottom of a bed, *una lettiera, il legname del letto.*

BO'ARDER, s. *quello o quella, che sta a dozzina.*

BO'ARDING, s. *l'intavolare.*

The boarding of a ship, *l'abbordo, l'investimento d'un vascello.*

A boarding school, *scuola dove i fanciulli o le fanciulle stanno a dozzina.*

BO'ARISH, adj. [of a boar] *di cinghiale.*

Boarish [clownish, brutal] *zotico, rozzo, villano, rustico, brutale.*

BOAST, s. [vaunt] *vanagloria, millanteria, ostentazione*, s. f. *vanto*, s. m.

Great boast, small roast, *gran vigna e poca uva, molto fumo e poco arrosto.*

To make a boast of something, *vantarsi, gloriarsi, vanagloriarsi di che che si sia.*

To boast of, *vantarsi, gloriarsi, vanagloriarsi.*

He boasts of his learning, *si gloria della sua dottrina, si pregia della sua scienza.*

Women ought to boast more of their virtue than of their beauty, *le donne dovrebbero pregiarsi più della loro virtù che non della loro bellezza.*

BO'ASTED, or boasted of, adj. *millantato, vantato, pregiato.*

BO'ASTING, s. *millanteria, vanaglória, ostentazione, vanità*, s. f.

Boasting expressions, *espressioni vane.*

A boasting fellow, *un vanaglorioso, un millantatore.*

A BO'ASTER, s. *un millantatore.*

BOAT, s. *una barca, un battello, un batello.*

A little boat, *una barchetta.*

A long boat, *una fusta.*

A ship boat, *uno schiffo.*

A ferry boat, *una scafa, una nave destinata a trasportar passaggeri di là da un fiume.*

Packet boat, *vascello che porta il procaccio.*

A fly boat, *un brigantino.*

A boat staff, *palo di barcaruolo.*

BO'ATSWAIN, s. [an officer in a ship] *uno degli ufficiali subalterni d'un vascello.*

BOB, s. [jest] *motto*, s. m. *botta*, s. f. *detto pungente, e satirico.*

Bob [short periwig] *parrucca d'abbate, parrucca tonda e corta.*

Bob [a sort of pendant or ear-ring] *sorta d'orecchino, cióndolo, ciondolino*, s. m. *pendente che s'appicca agli orecchi delle donne.*

To BOB [to strike, to clap] *battere, tartassare, malmenare.*

To bob [to gull] *ingannare, ficcarla o piantarla ad uno.*

To bob, verb. neut. [to hang, to dangle] *pendere, ciondolare, dondolare, penzolare.*

BOBBED, adj. *battuto, part.* di to bob.

BO'BBINS, s. p. *que' cavicchi co' quali si fanno i merletti e le trine.*

A BO'BBING, s. *un cannello.*

Bobbing, s. *il battere, v.* to bob.

Bobbing, adj. [dangling] *dondolone, pendente.*

BOBTA'IL, or bobtailed, adj. *scodato, senza coda. Dicesi d'una sorte di parrucche.*

Bobtail, s. [a kind of short harrow head] *la punta d'una freccia.*

Bobtail [whore] *una puttana, una bagascia.*

BOCCASI'NE, s. [fine buckram] *bucherame fino.*

To BODE [to presage] *presagire, pronosticare*, pref. *presagisco.*

All this bodes nothing good, *tutto questo non indica nulla di buono.*

BO'DED, adj. *presagito, pronosticato.*

BO'DING, s. *presagio, pronostico*, s. m.

To BO'DGE, *v.* to botch.

BO'DICE, s. [a sort of womens stays without whalebone] *corsaletto*, s. m.

BO'DILESS, adj. [without a body] *incorporeo, senza corpo.*

BO'DILY, adj. *corporeo, del corpo, appartenente al corpo.*

Bodily, adv. *corporeamente, secondo il corpo.*

To set bodily upon a thing, *sbracciarsi, impiegare tutte le sue forze in che che si sia.*

BO'DIKINS, or Bodlikins, interj. [a ridiculous oath] *cospetto di bacco.*

BO'DKIN, s. [a pointed iron] *punteruolo*, s. m. *ferro appuntato e sottile, per uso di forar carta, panno, e simili materie.*

A bodkin that women use for their head, *dirizzatojo*, s. m. *strumento sottile ed acuto, del quale si servono le donne per partire e separare i capelli in due parti eguali.*

A printer's bodkin, *punteruolo di stampatore.*

A bodkin [an instrument with a small blade and a sharp point] *stiletto.*

BÓDY, s. [a compound of matter and form] *corpo*, s. m. *materia tangibile e visibile.*

A little body, *corpicciuolo, corpicello, corpicino.*

A natural, physical, simple, or mixt body, *un corpo naturale, fisico, semplice, o misto.*

That wine has a good body, *questo vino è molto pastoso.*

That paper has not body enough, *questa carta è sottile troppo.*

A dead body, *un corpo morto, un cadavere.*

The body of a ship [the hull] *il corpo del naviglio, il guscio d'un vascello.*

The body of a coach, *il guscio d'una carrozza.*

The body of a discourse or of a book, *la sostanza o il contenuto d'un discorso o d'un libro.*

Body [society, company of people] *corpo, società, compagnia.*

A politick body, *un corpo politico.*

The church is a mystical body, *la chiesa è un corpo mistico.*

A great body of men, *un grosso corpo di gente, un buon nervo di gente.*

The army was divided into three bodies, *l'esercito era diviso in tre corpi.*

The parliament waited on the king in a body, *il parlamento andò in corpo ad inchinarsi al re.*

Body [a collection of what relates to an art or science, out of one or several authors] *corpo, l'opere di qualche autore.*

A body of civil law, *un corpo di legge civile.*

The body of a church, *la nave d'una chiesa.*

The body of a tree, *il tronco d'un albero.*

How does your body do? *come state?*

Any body, *chiunque, ciascuno, ognuno, qualcuno.*

He tells every body of it, *lo dice ad ognuno.*

I had sold it for ten shillings to some body else, *l'averei venduto ad un altro dieci scellini più caro.*

He was not seen by any body, *non fu visto da nessuno.*

Can any body know what is the matter with you? *si può sapere che grillo v'è saltato in testa?*

A busy body, *un intrigante, uno che vuol far tutto, uno che vuol aver che fare in ogni cosa, un saccendone.*

Every body, *ognuno, ciascuno.*

No body, *nessuno.*

Some body, *alcuno, qualcuno.*

A pair of womens bodies, *un busto da donna.*

Thick-bodied, *corpulento, grave di corpo, grasso.*

Bigness of body, *corpulenza*, s. f.

BOG, s. *melma, palude, pantano.*

To BO'GGLE, verb. neut. [to be uncertain what to do, to waver] *esitare, star dubbioso, dubitare, bilanciare.*

I did not at all boggle at it, *non esitai punto in ciò.*

BO'GGLER, s. [a doubter, a timorous man] *un uomo dubitativo, che dubita e sta fra due, fra il sì e il no per soverchio timore. E' voce di disprezzo.*

BO'GGY, adj. *paludoso, melmoso.*

Boggy ground, *terreno paludoso.*

BOIL, s. [bile] *ulcera*, s. f. *ciccione*, s. m.

An angry boil, *un ulcera maligna.*

To BOIL, verb. neut. *bollire, cuocere.*

The pot boils, *la pignatta bolle.*

To boil, verb. act. *bollire, lessare.*

To boil meat, *bollire o lessare della carne.*

To boil fast, *bollire in fretta, bollir forte.*

To begin to boil, *grillare, principiare a bollire.*

My blood boiled within me, *il sangue mi bollì nelle vene.*

To boil as the sea, *ondeggiare, muoversi in onde.*

To boil away, *consumarsi a forza di bollire.*

To boil over, *versare pel troppo bollire.*

He began to boil over with rage, *cominciò a bollire di collera.*

BO'ILARY OF SALT, *salina*, s. f. *luogo dove si fa il sale.*

BO'ILED, adj. *bollito, lessato.*

Boiled meat, *lesso, carne lessa.*

BO'ILER, s. *fornello da cucina, caldaja*, s. f.

BO'ILING, s. *bollimento*, s. m. *il bollire.*

Boiling hot, adj. *bollente.*

BO'ISTEROUS, adj. [fierce, stormy] *furioso, impetuoso, tempestoso, violente.*

A boisterous wind, *vento impetuoso.*

Boisterous weather, *burrasca, tempesta.*

BO'ISTEROUSLY, adj. *impetuosamente, violentemente, furiosamente, tempestosamente.*

BO'ISTEROUSNESS, s. *violenza, impetuosità*, s. f. *furore*, s. m.

Bold, adj. [hardy, stout] *ardito, bravo, coraggioso, animoso, prode.*
A bold soldier, *un bravo soldato, un soldato coraggioso.*
Bold [saucy] *ardito, temerario, sfacciato.*
I dare be bold to say, *ardisco dire.*
He was so bold as to call me names, *ebbe l'ardire o la sfacciataggine d'ingiuriarmi con parole.*
If I may be so bold as to say, *se oso dirlo.*
He makes bold with those things to which the greatest reverence is due, *scherza con troppa libertà delle cose piu venerabili.*
How dare you be so bold to do it? *che sfacciataggine è la vostra di farlo?*
I shall make bold to wait upon you, *avrò l'onore di venire a riverirla.*
A bold face, *uno sfacciato, uno sfrontato, uno spavaldo.*
To put on a bold face, *parere ardito, o sfacciato.*
To MAKE BOLD [to take freedoms] *pigliarsi più libertà che non conviene, usar indecenza.*
Bo'ldly, adv. [couragiously] *arditamente, coraggiosamente, animosamente, bravamente, con bravura.*
Boldly [freely] *arditamente, liberamente, francamente, con franchezza.*
To speak boldly, *parlare arditamente, dir l'animo suo liberamente.*
Bo'ldness, s. [stoutness] *arditezza, bravura, intrepidità, s. f. ardire, valore, coraggio, s. m.*
Boldness [sauciness] *temerità, sfacciataggine, s. f.*
Boldness in speech, *libertà, licenza nel parlare.*
Bole, s. *boccale.*
A bole of punch, *un bacino di quella bevanda fatta d'acqua, aquavite, zucchero, e limoni, che gl' Inglesi chiamano* punch. v. bowl.
Bole armoniack, *bolarmenico.*
Boll, s. [stalk, stem] *gambo, stelo, s. m.*
Boll of flax, *gambo di lino.*
Bo'lled, adj. *gambuto, che ha gambo.*
Bolled flax, *lino gambuto.*
Bo'llen, adj. [swollen] *gonfio, gonfiato.*
Bo'lster, s. [for a bed] *capezzale, piumaccio, primaccio, s. m.*
The bolster of a saddle, *cuscinetto di sella.*
A bolster for a wound, *piumaccetto per una piaga.*
To Bolster up [to countenance] *appoggiare, spalleggiare, proteggere, favorire,* 'prei. *favorisco.*
To bolster one up in his wickedness, *favorire altrui nelle iniquità.*
Bo'lstered up, adj. *appoggiato, spalleggiato, protetto, favorito.*
Bolt, s. [of a door] *catenaccio, chiavistello, s. m.*
Bolt [dart] *dardo, s. m.*
Prisoner's bolts, *ferri, catene, ceppi.*
The bolt of a lock, *stanghetta, s. f. ferretto lungo che è nella toppa.*
Thunder-bolt, *fulmine.*

He has shot his bolt, *ha tratto il suo dardo.*
A fool's bolt is soon shot, *un matto dice presto quel che pensa.*
Bolthe'ad, s. [a long strait-necked glass vessel, a matrass, a receiver] *un recipiente di vetro col collo lungo e dritto.*
Bolt upright, *tutto diritto.*
Bolt ropes [those to which the sail of a ship is fastened] *cordelle colle quali si legano le vele all' albero della nave.*
Bolt-sprit, or bow-sprit [the mast in the head of a ship that stoops forwards] *trinchetto, s. m. albero che sta coricato alla prua della nave.*
To Bolt [to fasten with a bolt] *incatenacciare, inchiavistellare, serrare col catenaccio, chiudere col chiavistello.*
To bolt a door, *incatenacciare una porta, chiuderla col chiavistello.*
To bolt [to sift meal] *abburattare, cernere la farina della crusca.*
To bolt [to sift or pump out] *tastare, cavare di bocca altrui alcunu cosa.*
To bolt a coney, *far lemare un coniglio.*
To bolt a case [to argue upon it] *crivellare. discutere un caso, esaminarlo, considerarlo sottilmente.*
Bo'lted, adj. *incatenacciato, inchiavistellato, abburattato, crivellato, discusso.*
Bo'lter, s. [a bolting bag] *burattello, s. m. sacchetto di stamigna per abburattar la farina.*
Bo'lting, s. *l'incatenacciare, o l'abburattare.*
Bolting-Ho'use, *il luogo dove i fornai abburattano la loro farina.*
A bolting hutch [a chest to sift meal in] *frullone, s. m. strumento di legname a guisa di cassone, dove per mezzo d'un burattello si cerne la crusca dalla farina.*
Bo'lus, s. [morsel, gobbet] *boccone, s. m.*
Bolus [in physick, a dose, as much as may be taken at a mouthful] *pillola, s. f. bolo, s. m.*
Bomb, s. [hollow ball of iron, charged with powder, to be shot into besieged towns] *bomba, s. f. palla di ferro piena di polvere, che buttasi nelle città assediate.*
Bomba'rd, s. [a great gun] *bombarda, s. f.*
To Bomba'rd, verb. act. *bombardare.*
Bomba'rded, adj. *bombardato.*
Bomba'rder, s. *bombardiere, s. m. colui, che carica e scarica le bombe e le bombarde.*
Bomba'rding, } s. *bombardamento, s. m. il bombardare.*
Bomba'rdment, }
Bombasi'ne, s. [a sort of stuff] *bambagino, s. m. tela fatta di fil di bambagia.*
Bo'mbast, s. [fustian, big words] *ampollosità, gonfiezza; e dirsi dello stile.*
Bombast, adj. [high-sounding] *gonfio, ampolloso.*
Bomba'stick, adj. *lo stesso che bombast quando è addiettivo.*

Bombula'tion, s. *strepito, romore.*
Bond, s. [obligation] *obbligaanza, obbligazione, polizza, promessa, s. f.*
Bond [tie] *legame, nodo, s. m.*
To enter into a bond of friendship with one, *contrarre amicizia con alcuno.*
A bond-man, *uno schiavo, un mancipio.*
Bond-maid, *schiava.*
Bond-slave, *schiavo.*
Bond-servant, *schiavo.*
Bonda'ge, s. *servitù, schiavitù, s. f.*
To be in bondage, *essere schiavo, o in ischiavitù.*
Bone, s. *osso, s. m. pl. le ossa, f. gli ossi, m.*
The back bone, *spina, s. f. il filo delle rene dove son commesse le costole.*
The shin-bone, *stinco, s. m. osso della gamba.*
The jaw-bone [the cheek-bone] *la mascella, s. f. quell' osso dove son fissi i denti.*
Bone of fishes, *spina di pesce.*
Whale-bone, *osso di balena.*
Bone-lace, *merletto, s. m.*
He is nothing but skin and bones, *non ha che la pelle e l'ossa.*
To give one a bone to pick, *dare che fare ad uno, dar un osso da rodere ad alcuno, dar cosa difficile a farsi.*
To fall upon one's bones, *mettersi addosso ad uno, batterlo ben bene.*
I tremble every bone of me, *tremo da capo a piedi.*
They may as soon take a bone from a dog, *cio sarebbe un pigliar il lupo per le orecchie, sarebbe come un toglier l'osso al cane.*
He made no bones of it, *non ci fece scrupolo veruno.*
Lazy-bones, *un gran poltronaccio, un che dorme troppo.*
The huckle bone, *l'anca, s. f. l'osso, che è tra'l fianco e la coscia.*
To Bone [to pick out the bones] *disossare, trar l'ossa della carne.*
Bo'ned, adj. *disossato.*
Bonefi're, s. *fuoco d'allegrezza.*
Bo'neless, adj. *senz' ossa, che non ha ossa.*
Bo'nespaven, s. [a great crust as hard as a bone, which grows in the inside of the hoof, or on the heels of a horse] *giarda, s. f. giardone, s. m. malattia che viene nella pastoja del cavallo.*
Bona'ta, s. [a fish] *bonitone, s. m. sorta di pesce di mare.*
Bonnet, s. [under cap] *berretta, s. f.*
Bonny, adj. *grata, graziosa, gentile, leggiadra. E' voce Scozzese, e in Inghilterra s' usa per vezzo.*
A bonny lass, *una bella ragazza.*
Bo'ny, adj. *ossuto.*
Bo'ody, s. *uno sciocco, uno sciopeato, balordo, minchione, pecorone, babbuino, babbione.*
Book, s. *libro, s. m.*
Book of accounts, *libro di conti.*
Paper-book, *libro bianco.*
A stitch'd book, *un libro cucito.*

A bound book, *un libro legato.*
A day book, *un diario, un giornale.*
To mind one's book, *applicarsi allo studio, studiare.*
To learn one's book, *imparare la lezione.*
To say one's lesson without book, *dire la sua lezione a mente.*
The book-trade [the trade of books] *il mestiere di librajo.*
To get into one's books, *cattivarsi l'amore d'alcuno.*
To run into one's book, *indebitarsi.*
To get out of one's books, *uscir di debito.*
Bookbinder, *legatore di libri.*
Bookseller, *librajo.*
Book keeper, *quello che tiene ragione de' conti, giovane di negozio.*
Bookworm, *tarlo,* s. m. *tignuóla,* s. f.
To book down, *scrivere nel libro.*
Bo'okish, adj. [given to books] *studioso, applicato a' libri, che ama leggere molto.*
Boom, s. [mast of a ship] *albero di vascello.*
A boom, *una trave.*
Boom [the bar of a haven] *catena che si mette all' entrata d'un porto per chiuderlo.*
Bo'oming, adj. [it is said of a ship, when all the sails are out] *si dice d'un vascello quando veleggia a vele spiegate.*
Boon, s. [favour] *favore,* s. m. *grazia,* s. f.
Boon [request] *richiesta, domanda,* s. f.
I have a boon to ask you, *hò una grazia a domandarvi.*
Will you grant me one boon? *volete farmi un favore?*
Boon, adj. *buono.*
A boon companion, *un buon compagno, un compagnone.*
To do a thing with a boon grace, *fare una cosa di buon cuore.*
Boor, s. [clown] *un rustico, un villano, un zotico.*
He is a meer boor, *egli è un pretto villano.*
Bo'orish, adj. [clownish] *rustico, villano, zotico, villesco.*
Bo'orishness, s. *rusticità, rustichezza, zotichezza,* s. f.
Boot, s. *stivale,* s. m.
A pair of boots, *un pajo di stivali.*
To draw on one's boots, *stivalarsi, mettersi li stivali.*
To pull one's own boots off, *cavarsi li stivali.*
To pull another's boots, *cavar li stivali ad uno.*
Smoak the boots of the fellow, *guarda colui, bade a quel cotale.*
Boot, s. [overplus] *soppra più, vantaggio, guadagno.*
What will you give me to boot? *quanto volete risarmi?*
You shall give this to boot, *voi mi darete questo per soprappiù.*
It is to no boot, *non serve a nulla, è in vano.*
A boot-tree, or boot-last, *forma di stivale.*
To Boot [to profit] *servire, giovare, valere.*

What boots it? *a che serve?*
Bo'oted, adj. *stivalato.*
Booth, s. [small cottage] *capanna,* s. f.
Booth, *palco de' burattini.*
To Boot-ha'le [to go about plundering, to pillage] *predare, rubare, mettere a bottino.*
Boot-ha'ler, s. *predatore,* s. m. *predatrice,* s. f.
Boot-ha'ling, s. *predamento, rubamento,* s. m. *il predare.*
Boot-ho'se, s. *calzetta grossa che serve di stivale.*
Bo'oting, s. [it is a kind of punishment used in Scotland, by putting an iron boot on the offender's leg, and driving an iron peg upon his shin bone] *spànghetta,* s. f. *strumento da tormentare i rei.*
Bo'otless, adj. *inutile, vano.*
Boots, s. [marsh marygold] *fiorancio,* s. m.
Bo'oty, s. [prey] *bottino,* s. m. *preda,* s. f.
To get a great booty, *fare un gran bottino.*
To play booty with one, *intèndersela con alcuno, esser d'accordo con lui, far un mal tiro ad alcuno; giuocar un sottomano ad uno senza che se ne avvegga.*
To write booty, *scrivere alla buona, contraddirsi nello scrivere.*
At Bope'ep, adv. [to play at bopeep] *giuocare al baco, coprirsi il viso ed in un subito scoprirlo, particolarmente per far paura a' bambini.*
To play at bopeep, *guardar sott' occhio, far capolino.*
To Play Bope'ep [to look out and draw back as if frightened] *far capolino e poi dar indietro come se uno fossi spaventato.*
Bora'cchio, s. [a sort of vessel made of skins, wherein wines are brought from the tops of the mountains of Spain] *otre, otro,* s. m. *pelle tratta intera dall' animale, e serve per portarvi entro vino e oglio.*
Bo'rage, s. [an herb] *borraggine, borrana,* s. f.
Bo'rax, s. [a kind of whitish mineral] *borrace,* s. f. *materia, che si trova nelle miniere dell' oro, dell' argento, e del rame.*
Bo'rdel, or Bróthel, s. [a bawdy-house] *bordello, chiasso,* s. m. *la casa o il luogo dove stanno le puttane.*
Bo'rder, s. [extremity] *lembo, orlo,* s m. *margine, estremità,* s. f.
The borders of a garment, *i lembi d'un vestito.*
The borders [the frontiers of a country] *frontiere, limiti, termini, confini d'un paese.*
To Border [to edge, to lace] *orlare, listare.*
To border a garment, *orlare o listare un vestito.*
To border upon, verb. neut. *confinare, esser contigno.*
Lorrain borders upon Alsace, *la Lorena confina colla Alsazia.*
His jests border upon prophaneness, *le sue burle sanno del profano.*

Bo'rderer, s. *confinante, che dimora nelle frontiere.*
They are bórderers, *sono genti delle frontiere.*
Bo'rdering, adj. *confinante, circonvirino, collaterale.*
Bordering countries, *paesi circonvicini.*
Bord-la'nds, s. [lands which lords keep in their hands for the maintenance of their board] *terre, che i signori d'un feudo si riserbano pel mantenimento della loro tavola.*
Bo'rdure, s. [in heraldry, a tract or compass of one metal, colour, or fur, within the escutcheon all round it] *lista, fascia, che è all' intorno l'arme di qualcuno.*
Bore, s. [the hollow in the inside of a piece of ordnance] *la bocca d'un arme a fuoco.*
The bore of a lock, *il pertugio d'una serratura.*
Bore-tree, *sambuco,* s. m.
Bore, *preterito del verbo* To bear.
To Bore, verb act. *forare, bucare, pertugiare.*
To bore a hole, *fare un buco.*
Bo'real, adj. [northern] *boreale.*
Bo'red, adj *forato, bucato, pertugiato.*
Bore'e, s. [a kind of French dance] *borèa, ballo Francese così chiamato.*
Bórer, s. *che pertugia, che fa un buco, un pertugio. Spezie di succhiello.*
Bo'ring, s. *il forare.*
Born, adj. [from to bear] *portato, comportato, sofferto,* part. *di* To bear.
All charges born, *oltre le spese.*
Born [from birth] *nato.*
A man born to great things, *un uomo destinato a cose grandi.*
They are born to slavery, *sono nati per essere schiavi.*
To be well born, *esser ben nato.*
The good sense to which he is born, *il senno del quale è stato dotato della natura.*
A man born of mean parentage, *un uomo di bassa nascita.*
The first born, *il primogenito.*
Born before his time, *abbortivo.*
Base born, *bastardo.*
Born after the death of his father, *póstumo.*
Still-born, *nato morto.*
I never saw the like since I was born, *in vita mia non ho visto il simile.*
To be born, *nascere.*
To be born again, *rinascere.*
Where was you born? *di che paese siete? dove siete nato? in qual luogo nasceste?*
Bo'rough, or Bórow, s. *borgo, villaggio,* s. m.
An inhabitant of a borough, *borghigiano, abitator d'un borgo.*
Bo'rrel, [a mean fellow] *un uomo dappoco.*
To Bo'rrow [to take upon credit] *pigliar in prestito.*
Bo'rrowed, adj. *preso in prestito.*
Bo'rrower, s. *quello o quella, che piglia in prestito.*

Bo'rrowing, s. *prestanza, presta, prestita*, s. f. *prestamento, prestito*, s. m.

Bo'scage, s. [grove, thicket] *boschetto.*

Boscage [a picture that represents much wood and trees] *paesaggio, boschereccia.*

Bo'som, s. *seno, grembo*, s. m.

The bosom of the church, *il grembo della chiesa.*

A bosom friend, *un amico intimo, un amico di cuore.*

A bosom enemy, *un nemico che figne l'amico, un traditore, un perfido.*

The bosom of a shirt, *lo sparato d'una camicia.*

Bosom of the sea, *seno di mare, golfo.*

Bo'son, or Bosen, *v.* Boatswain.

Boss, s. [in the body] *gobba*, s. f. *gobbo, scrigno*, s. m.

The boss of a buckler, *il guscio d'uno scudo.*

Boss [stud of a girdle or bridle] *pomo della briglia o della cinta.*

The boss of a book, *borchia d'un libro.*

Bota'nical, } [belonging to
Bota'nick, adj. } herbs] *appartenente all' erbe ed alle piante, botanico.*

Bota'nicks, s. } [the science of
Bo'tany, s. } simples] *scienza de' semplici, botánica.*

Bo'tanist, s. [herbalist, one skilful in herbs and plants] *semplicista, botanico, quegli che conosce la virtù dell' erbe e delle piante.*

Botano'logy, s. [discourse upon plants] *discorso botanico.*

Bota'rgo, s. [the spawn of a mullet pickled] *bottarga, salcicciotto all' Italiana fatto d'uova e sangue di cefalo e anche d'altri pesci.*

Botch, s. [a piece of cloth stitched to old cloaths] *pezza, toppa*, s. f.

Botch [ulcer, venereous bubo] *un' ulcera*, s. f. *un tincone*, s. m.

To leave a botch behind one, *lasciare una cosa imperfetta.*

To Botch [to piece, to mend] *rappezzare, rattoppare, rabberciare.*

To botch a copy of verses, *rattoppare un sonetto, racconciar un poemetto.*

To botch [to bungle] *racciabattare, fare una cosa alla peggio, ciarpare.*

Bo'tched, adj. *rappezzato, rattoppato, rabberciato.*

Bo'tcher, s. *uno che male racconcia checchessia, mal ciabattino.*

Bo'tching, s. *il racciabattare.*

Bo'tchingly, adv. [bunglingly] *malamente, grossolanamente, alla grossolana, alla peggio.*

Both, adj. *ambo, ambe, l'uno e l'altro, tutti e due, ambedue, ambedui, ambiduo, amendue, amenduni.*

With both my hands, *con ambe mani.*

They went both to see him, *andarono ambedue a vederlo.*

Many were killed on both sides, *molti furono uccisi d'amendue le parti.*

Both handed, *ambidestro, che si serve delle due mani ugualmente.*

A jack on both sides, *un volta casacca, uno che è ora d'una banda ora dell' altra.*

Both, adv. *e, si.*

Both by sea and land, *e per mare, e per terra.*

Both because it is honest, and because I don't think it sure, *si perchè mi pare che sia onesto, come anche perchè non credo che sia sicuro.*

Both in time of peace and war, *in pace ed in guerra.*

He is both poor and saucy, *è povero e insolente.*

Famous both for his father's glory and his own, *famoso tanto per la gloria del padre che per la propria.*

Botryo'id, adj. [having the form of a bunch of grapes] *grappoluto, fatto a mo' di grappol d'uva.*

Bots, s. [small worms in the entrails of horses] *piccioli vermi negl' intestini de' cavalli.*

Bo'ttle, s. *fiasco*, s. m.

A large bottle, *un fiascone.*

A stone bottle, *un orciuolo.*

A bottle of hay, *fastello di fieno.*

Bottle-nosed, *che ha il naso schiacciato.*

To bottle, *infiascare, mettere vino o altro liquore nel fiasco.*

To bottle hay, *affastellare del fieno.*

Bottle-screw, *strumento da cavar il turácciolo d'una bottiglia, cavasughero.*

Bo'ttled, adj. *infiascatò affastellato.*

Bo'ttling, s. *l'infiascare, l'affastellare.*

Bo'ttom, s. [the ground of any thing] *fondo*, s. m. *la parte inferiore di che che si sia.*

The bottom of the sea, *il fondo del mare.*

The bottom of a business, *il fondamento d'un affare.*

The bottom of the heart, *l'intimo del cuore.*

He complained of his acting on a separate bottom, *lamentavasi perchè operasse di sua testa senza l'intervento suo.*

The bottom or settling of a liquor, *fondigliuolo, rimasuglio*, s. m. *posatura di cosa liquida.*

Bottom [end] *fine.*

You will find at the bottom of the account that they are mistaken, *troverete alla fine de' conti, che vi siete ingannato.*

Bottom [valley] *valle*, s. f.

The boarded bottom of a bedstead, *una lettiera.*

The bottom of the stairs, *il fondo delle scale.*

Bottom of thread, *gomitolo di filo.*

The bottom of the belly, *il ventricolo.*

To stand upon a good bottom, *star bene ne' fatti suoi, esser bene in gamba.*

To fix one's bottom upon one, *far capitale d'uno.*

Better spare at the brim than at the bottom, *è meglio risparmiare al principio che alla fine.*

The bottom of a ship, *carena*, s. f. *la parte di sotto del vascello, il suo fondo.*

Bottom [ship] *un legno, un vascello; e dicesi prendendo la parte pel tutto.*

To Bottom, *fondare, far fondo.*

There must be something to bottom on, *bisogno qualche cosa sopra la quale possiamo far fondo.*

To go to the bottom, *andare a fondo, sprofondare, affondare.*

Bo'ttomed, adj. *fondato.*

Flat-bottomed, *piatto di fondo.*

Bo'ttomless, adj. *che non ha fondo.*

Bottomless, *impenetrabile, imperscrutabile.*

A bottomless pit, *un abisso.*

Bo'ttomry, s. [when the master of a ship borrows money upon the keel of his ship, to be paid with interest at the ship's safe return, otherwise the money is all lost, if the ship be lost] *il pigliar in prestito che fa il padrone d'un vascello dando l'istesso vascello per sicurtà, e caso che ritorni a salvamento deve pagare l'interesse del danaro, ma se si perde il danaro si perde ancora.*

Bouge, s. [swelling] *tumore.*

To bouge [to swell] *gonfiarsi.*

Bo'uget, *v.* Budget.

Bough, s. [branch] *ramo*, s. m.

Bought, adj. [from to buy] *comprato.*

Bought [the preter tense of the verb *to buy*] *comprai, ho comprato.*

Boul, *v.* Bowl.

Bo'ulster, *v.* Bolster.

To Boult, *v.* To bolt.

Bounce, s. [great noise] *strepito, fracasso, rumore*, s. m.

To give a bounce, *fare un gran fracasso.*

Bounce [rodomontade] *rodomontata, bravata, millanteria*, s. f.

To Bo'unce [to crack, to make a noise] *crosciare, strepitare, scoppiettare, fare grande strepito.*

To bounce at the door [to knock hard] *picchiar forte alla porta.*

To bounce the door open, *sfondare una porta.*

To bounce [to crack, to boast] *vantarsi, millantarsi.*

To bounce [to bounce up, to leap] *sbolzare, balzare, saltellare, sbalzar su, saltar su repentinamente.*

Bo'unced, adj. *crosciato, strepitato*, *v.* To bounce.

A Bouncer [a boaster, a bully, an empty threatner] *un millantatore, un gradasso, uno smargiasso, un codardo che fa il minaccioso.*

Bouncing, s. *croscio, strepito, fracasso*, s. m.

Bouncing, adj. *ex.*

A bouncing lass, *una ragazza grassotta, una fanciulla vivace, tutta fuoco.*

Bound, adj. [from to bind] *legato, tenuto, obbligato*, *v.* To bind.

Whither are you bound? *dove andate? dove si va?*

Our ship was bound to Leghorn, *il nostro vascello andava a Livorno, era caricato per Livorno.*

We are bound to Cadiz, *noi andiamo a Cadice, cioè la nave nostra è caricata per Cadice.*

Bound, adj. [beholden] *obbligato, tenuto.*
I am bound to you for my life, *vi sono obbligato della vita.*
Bound, s. [limit] *limite, termine,* s. m. *meta,* s. f.
To keep within the bounds of modesty, *ritenersi dentro i termini della modestia.*
To set bounds to one's ambition, *por meta all' altrui ambizione.*
To drink within bounds, *bere moderatamente.*
A bound-stone, *limite, confine, pietra che serve di limite.*
A bound setter, *quello che mette i limiti; colui che segna i confini.*
To BOUND, *limitare, por termine, terminare.*
To bound [to border upon] *confinare, esser contiguo.*
To bound [to rebound] *balzare, sbalzare.*
BO'UNDARY, s. [that which sets out the limits or bounds of a country] *termine, confine,* s. m. *frontiera,* s. f.
The river Tanais was of old the boundary betwixt Europe and Asia, *il fiume Tanai separava altre volte l'Europa dall' Asia.*
BO'UNDED, adj. *limitato, terminato.*
BOUNDEN, adj. *dovuto, convenevole.*
According to my bounden duty, *secondo il mio dovere, secondo il mio dovuto officio.*
BOUNDER, s. *terminatore,* s. m. *quello che termina e stabilisce i limiti.*
BOUNDING, s. *terminamento,* s. m. *il terminare, il limitare, il porre i confini.*
Bounding, adj. [bordering upon] *confinante, che confina, contiguo, vicino, limitrofo.*
BO'UNDLESS, adj. *illimitato, immenso, infinito, non circonscritto, senza confini.*
BO'UNTIFUL, adj. } [generous, liberal] *benigno, generoso, liberale.*
BO'UNTEOUS, adj. }
BO'UNTEOUSNESS, [munificence, liberality] *munificenza, liberalità.*
BO'UNTIFULLY, adv. [*benignamente, generosamente, liberalmente.*
BO'UNTIFULNESS, s. *benignità, liberalità, munificenza, generosità,* s. f.
BO'UNTY, s. [generosity, liberality] *munificenza, liberalità, generosità,* s. f.
BO'UNTIHEAD, } [goodness, virtue] *bontà, virtù,* s. f.
BO'UNTIHOOD, }
BO'URGER, } *borghese, cittadino,* s. m. *cittadina,* s. f.
BO'URGESS, }
To BO'URGEON [to bud] *germinare, germogliare.*
To bourgeon [speaking of olive trees] *mignolare.*
Bourgeon, s. *porro o segno rosso, che viene in faccia spezialmente a' vecchi che beono troppo vino.*
BOURN, s. [brook] *rivoletto, borro, picciolo torrente,* s. m.
Bourn, *confine limite.*
To BOUSE, verb act. *potare.*
BO'USED, adj. *potato.*
BO'USING, s. *potamento,* s. m. *il potare.*
BOUT, s. *volta, fiata,* s. f.
For this bout, *per questa volta.*
Do it all at one bout, *fatelo in una volta, fatelo tutto a un tratto.*
A drinking bout, *bevuta,* s. f.
A merry bout, *un divertimento, un solazzo, un banchetto, una festa, un tripudio, un trebbio.*
Let us have a merry bout to day, *ricreamoci, divertiamoci oggi.*
BOUTEFE'U, s. [an incendiary, a make bate] *un incendiario, un sedizioso, un macchinator di sedizioni.*
Bow, s. [an instrument for shooting arrows] *arco,* s. m.
To have two strings to one's bow, *aver due corde al suo arco.*
A bow long bent at last grows weak, *chi troppo l'assottiglia la spezza.*
He keeps his mind bent like a bow, *sta con l'animo intento.*
Bow [reverence] *riverenza, inchino.*
To make a bow to one, *fare una riverenza o riverire uno.*
A bow for a violin, *archetto,* s. m. *strumento col quale si suona il violino la viola, ed il violoncello.*
Bow [an instrument to take the heighth of any thing] *mezzocerchio, strumento matematico.*
The bow of a sword's hilt, *elsa, else, quel ferro intorno al manico della spada che difende la mano.*
A cross bow, *una balestra.*
To shoot a cross-bow, *balestrare.*
Saddle-bow, *arcione di sella.*
The bow of a ship, *prua di vascello.*
A stone-bow, *mangano,* s. m.
A large stone-bow, *manganone,* s. f.
The rain-bow, *l'arcobaleno,* s. m.
Bowing, *corda d'arco.*
Bow-man, *arciere,* s. m. *tirator d'arco.*
A bow-net, *nassa,* s. f. *rete da pescare che abbia il ritroso.*
Bow-piece [the piece of ordnance which lies in the bow of a ship] *cannone di corsia.*
Bow-legged, *sbilenco, strambo, che ha le gambe arcate.*
To BOW [to bend] *piegare, archeggiare, chinare.*
To bow one's knees, *piegar le ginocchia, inginocchiarsi.*
To bow one's head, *chinar la testa.*
To bow to one [to salute one] *far la riverenza ad uno, salutarlo, riverirlo, inchinarsi ad uno.*
To bow down, *prostrarsi, gittarsi a piedi d'alcuno.*
BOWED, adj. *piegato, chinato, inchinato, archeggiato.*
To BOWEL [to embowel] *sventrare, sbudellare, trarre gl' interiori del corpo altrui.*
BOWELLED, adj. *sventrato, sbudellato.*
BOWELS, s. *budella, viscere,* s. f. *parti interiori dell' animale.*
The bowels of the earth, *le viscere della terra.*
BOWER, s. [an arbour with trees or greens interwoven] *pergola,* s. f.
The celestial bower [the sky] *il cielo. Poetico.*
BO'WET, s. } a young hawk so called, when she draws any thing out of the nest, and covets to clamber on the boughs] *falconcello, falcone giovine.*
BO'WESS, s. }
BOWGE, s. [a rope fastened to the middle of the sail to make it stand closer to the wind] *fune d'una vela per far che prenda piu vento.*
To bowge a ship, *foracchiare, bucacchiare un vascello.*
BO'WING, s. *chinamento, piegamento,* s. m. *il chinare.*
BOWL, s. [a vessel to drink in] *tazzone, tazza grande.*
Bowl [to play with] *boccia, pallottola,* s. f.
To play at bowls, *giuocare alle bocce.*
Bowl [a sea-term, a round space at the head of the mast for the men to stand in] *gabbia,* s. f. *spazio che è in cima all antenna, sulla quale sta la veletta.*
BOWL, *vaso di terra o di porcellana da farvi dento quella bevanda che' gl' Inglesi chiamano* punch; *bacino.*
A bowl of punch, *un vaso di puncio, cioè pieno di quel liquore detto qui sopra.*
Let us have a bowl of punch, *fateci un bacino di puncio.*
The bowl of a spoon, *il concavo del cucchiajo.*
To BOWL, *giuocare alle bocce.*
BOWLED, adj. *ex.* well bowled, *ben giuocato.*
BO'WLING, s. *il giuoco delle bocce.*
Bowling, adj. *ex.* Bowling-green, *giuoco di bocce, luogo piano, dove si giuoca alle bocce, sopra la verdura.*
To BOWSE [to hale to pull the tackle] *tirare, termine marinaresco.*
BO'WSER, s. [the purser or treasurer of a college in a university] *camarlingo, o tesoriero d'un collegio.*
BO'WYER, s. [maker or seller of bows and arrows] *facitore d'archi, quello che vende archi.*
To BOWZE [to drink stoutly] *tracannare, bere fuor di misura.*
BOX, s. [a wooden chest or coffer] *scatola, cassetta,* s. f.
Snuff-box, *scatola da tabacco.*
A little box, *una cassettina.*
An alms box, *cassetta della limosina.*
Christmas-box, *salvadanajo,* s. m.
Christmas-box, *strenna,* s. f. *quel danaro che si da a' servi al natale.*
The box of a screw, *la chiocciola,* s. f. *il cavo della vite.*
The coach-box, *il sedile d'una carrozza, dove sta assiso il cocchiere.*
A box in a play-house, *un palco, un palchetto.*
A box on the ear, *uno schiaffo, un pugno sulla faccia.*
Box-tree, *bosso,* s. m. *arbuscello noto di perpetua verdura.*
A dice box, *bossolo,* s. m. *quel vaso ove si mettono i dadi giuocando.*
A juggler's box, *bossoletto,* s. m.
You are in the wrong box [in a great error] *voi sbagliate, voi scambiate, voi v'ingannate.*
To Box [to inclose in a box] *chiudere in una scatola.*
To Box, *fare a pugni, batterfi alle pugna.*

To Box up, *incassare, mettere nella cassa o nella scatola.*
To box, *schiaffeggiare, dare degli schiaffi; fare alle pugna.*
BOXED, adj. *schiaffeggiato, fatto alle pugna.*
BO'XER, s. *un che si batte e fa alle pugna.*
BO'XEN, adj. *fatto del legno di bosso, che somiglia al bosso, del colore del bosso.*
BO'XING, s. *lo schiaffeggiare, il far alle pugna.*
They have been boxing together, *hanno fatto alle pugna insieme.*
BOY, s. *ragazzo, giovanetto, fanciullo,* s. m.
Boy, s. *ragazzaccio. E' parola di disprezzo a un giovane.*
BOY, s. *adolescente.*
A tall boy, *un giovanaccio, un giovanastro.*
A boy, or servant-boy, *un ragazzo, servo adoperato in vili servizi.*
A singing boy, *un zago, un fanciullo che canta.*
A soldier's boy, *un bagaglione.*
A school-boy, *uno scolare, un fanciullo che va a scuola.*
Boy game, *bambinaggine, azione da bambino, bambineria.*
To do things like a boy, *bamboleggiare, fare cose da bambini, pargoleggiare.*
A boy's trick, *raggazzata,* s. f. *cosa fatta da ragazzo.*
To be past a boy, *esser uomo fatto.*
To BOY [to act apishly or like a boy] *fare il fanciullo, far la scimia.*
BO'YISH, adj. [boy-like] *bambinesco, da bambino, fanciullesco, da fanciullo.*
BO'YISHLY, adv. *fanciullescamente, a guisa di fanciullo.*
BO'YISHNESS, s. *bambineria, bambinaggine, bambocceria, bambolità, ragazzata, fanciullaggine,* s. f.
To BOYL, *v.* To boil.
BO'YSTEROUS, *v.* Boisterous.
BRABBLE, s. [wrangle, dispute] *querela, disputa, contrasto, lite, rissa, riotta.*
To brabble [to wrangle, to dispute] *contendere, contrastare, disputare, litigare, rissare, far risse,* pret. *contesi.*
BRABBLED, adj. *conteso, contrastato, disputato, litigato, rissato.*
BRA'BBLER, s. *contenditore, riottoso, rissoso, litigioso.*
BRA'BBLING, s. *contendimento, contesa, disputa, querela, lite, rissa.*
A brabbling fellow, *un contenditore, un riottoso, un rissoso, un beccalite.*
BRACE, s. [couple] *pajo, paro,* s. m. *coppia,* s. f.
A brace of dogs or hares, *una coppia di cani o di lepri.*
A brace of pistols, *un pajo di pistole.*
A brace of hundred pounds sterling, *dugento lire sterline.*
A brace of iron [to fasten beams in building] *rampicone, rampone,* s. m.
A brace in the art of printing, *abbracciatojo,* s. m. *termine di stampatori.*

The main braces of a coach [thick leather thongs upon which a coach hangs] *le cinghie di cuojo che reggono la carrozza.*
The braces of a ship [ropes to all the yards of a ship except the mizen, two to each yard] *scotte,* s. f. pl. *quelle funi le quali s'attaccano all' antena o alle vele per tirarle a poppa.*
To BRACE [to buckle] *affibbiare, legare, attaccare, unire,* pref. *unisco.*
BRACED, adj. *affibbiato, legato, attaccato, unito.*
BRA'CELET, s. [an ornament for the wrists of women] *armilla, smaniglia, maniglia,* s. f
A bracelet of pearls, *una smaniglia di perle.*
Bracelet [a piece of armour used anciently to defend the arm] *bracciale,* s. m. *quella parte dell' armadura che arma il braccio.*
BRACK, s. [a bitch-hound] *cagna levriera.*
BRA'CKET, s. [a bitch] *cagna,* s. f.
Bracket, s. [a kind of stay in timber work] *beccatello,* s. m. *mensola o peduccio che si pone per sostegno sotto i capi delle travi fitto nel muro e sotto i terrazzini, ballatoi, corridori, e sporti.*
BRA'CHIAL [belonging to the arm] *appartenente alle braccia.*
BRA'CKISH, adj. [somewhat salt] *salmastro, che tien del salso.*
Brackish water, *acqua salmastra.*
BRA'CKISHNESS, s. *salsuggine, salsezza,* s. f.
BRAG, s. *vanto, vantamento,* s. m. *millanteria, vanagloria,* s. f.
To make grievous brags of one's self, *vantarsi, pregiarsi, millantarsi sopra modo.*
To BRAG [to boast] *vantarsi, vanagloriarsi, pregiarsi, darsi vanto, millantarsi.*
He brags at his own exploits, *fa pompa de' suoi fatti, vanta se stesso.*
A wise man never brags nor dispărages himself, *un galantuomo non si vanta nè si biasima da se.*
BRA'GGARD, } s. [a bragging BRAGGADOCHIO } fellow] *un vantatore, un millantatore.*
BRA'GGER, s. *un millantatore.*
BRA'GGET, s. [drink made of honey and spice] *bevanda composta di mele e d' aromati.*
Bragget, *v.* Bracket.
BRA'GGING, s. *vantamento,* s. m. *il vantarsi, millanteria,* s. f.
A bragging fellow, *vantatore, un millantatore, uno smargiasso.*
BRAID, s. [a small lace, or edging] *trina,* s. f. *spezie di merletto.*
Braid of hair, *una treccia di capelli.*
To BRAID [to weave or plait hair properly] *intrecciare i capelli.*
BRA'IDED, adj. *intrecciato.*
BRAILS, s. [small ropes belonging to the courses and the mizen, whose use is, when the sail is furled across, to hale it up or let it fall] *cordicelle che servono ad ammainare o sciorre le vele.*
BRAIN, s. [all the soft substance contained in the scull] *cervello,* s. m. pl. *cervella,* s. f. *quella parte interiore del capo circondata dal cranio, nella quale risiede la virtù dell' animale.*
Brain [wit, judgment] *cervello, giudizio, senno.*
To beat one's brains out, *dicervellare, far saltare le cervella ad uno.*
To have cracked brains, *avere il cervello stravolto, aver del pazzo.*
To have but little brains, *avere poco cervello o giudizio, puzzar di pazzia.*
To beat a thing into one's own brains, *ficcarsi una cosa in testa.*
To beat one's brains about a thing, *stillarsi il cervello in qualche cosa, ghiribizzare, fantasticare, mulinare.*
To break one's brains with studying, *rompersi la testa collo studio.*
Brain-sick [foolish] *sciocco, melenso, milenso, scimunito.*
Brain-sick [mad] *frenetico.*
The brain pan, *il cranio.*
To BRAIN one [to dash out his brains] *dicervellare uno, torgli il cervello.*
BRAINED, adj. *dicervellato.*
Hair-brained, *scervellato, senza cervello, cervel di lepre, cervel d'oca.*
Shuttle brained, *cervel balzano, cervello fatto come oriuolo, incostante, bisbetico, volubile.*
BRA'INLESS, adj. *scervellato, senza cervello pazzo.*
BRAIT, s. [a rough diamond] *diamante non lavorato.*
BRAKE, s. [an instrument used in dressing flax or hemp] *maciulla,* s. f. *strumento col quale si dirompe il lino e la canape.*
Brake [snaffle for horses] *briglione,* s. m. *arnese per maneggiar i cavalli.*
Brake [a baker's kneading trough] *mádia,* s. f. *spezie di cassa per intridervi entrò la pasta da fare il pane.*
Brake [the handle of a ship's pump] *il manico d'una tromba di vascello.*
Brake, *felceto, luogo pieno di felci.*
Brake, preterito *del verbo* to break. *Non è più in uso.* Broke *è il moderno.*
BRAKED, adj. *rotto, maciullato.*
BRA'MBLES, s. [briars, prickly shrubs] *rovo, pruno,* s. m.
A place full of brambles, *roveto, spineto,* s. m.
Bramble-net [a sort of net for catching of birds] *ragna,* s. f. *sorta di rete da uccellare.*
Full of brambles, *pien di pruni.*
BRA'MBLING, s. [a bird so called] *fringuello, pincione,* s. m.
BRAN, s. *crusca,* s. f. *burcia di grano o biade macinate separata dalla farina.*
BRANCH, s. [a bough of a tree] *ramo,* s. m.
A little branch, *ramicello,* s. m.
The branches of a tree, *i rami d'un albero.*
A vine branch, *fermento,* s. m. *ramo della vite.*
The branch of a pedigree, *ramo di genealogia.*
The branch of a candlestick, *i rami d'un candeliere.*
The branch of a stag's head, *le corna d'un cervo.*

To branch out [to divide or ſpread into branches] *ramificare, produr rami, ſpargerſi in rami.*

BRANCHED, adj. *ramificato.*

A branched candleſtick, *candeliere che ha molti lumi, luſtro.*

Branched velvet, *velluto a fogliami.*

Branched [as deer's head in heraldry] *che ha le corna ſparſe.*

Branched out, *diviſo, ſeparato.*

BRA'NCHER, s. [a young hawk or other bird that begins to fly from branch to branch] *falco giovine che comincia a volare, uccello ramace o nidiace, che comincia a ſcappar del nidio.*

Branching out, s. *ramificazione,* s. f. *il ramificare.*

BRAND, s. [a piece of burning wood] *tizzone,* tizzo, s. m. *pezzo di legno abbruciato da un lato.*

Brand [a mark made by a red-hot iron] *ſegno fatto con ferro infuocato.*

Brand [a note of diſgrace or infamy] *nota, macchia,* s. f.

To caſt a brand upon one, *macchiare la riputazione altrui, infamarlo, diffamarlo.*

Brand [a ſword] *vore poetica, brando,* s. m. *ſpada,* s. f. Milton.

Brand-iron [a hot iron to brand or ſet a mark upon a malefactor] *ferro infocato col quale ſi bollano i delinquenti dalla giuſtizia.*

Brand new [fire-new] *nuovo di zecca, affatto nuovo.*

To BRAND [to burn, to mark with a hot iron] *ſuggellare con ferro infocato.*

To brand [to blur, to blemiſh] *macchiare, maculare, diſonorare, vituperare, diffamare.*

To brand with foul names, *macchiare la riputazione, vituperare, diſonorare.*

To brand the throne, *ſparlare del ſuo principe.*

BRA'NDED, adj. *bollato, ſegnato con ferro infocato, macchiato, maculato, diſonorato, vituperato, diffamato.*

To BRA'NDISH [to make ſhine with ſhaking, to ſhake to and fro in the hand] *brandire, vibrare, muovere ſcotendo.*

To brandiſh a ſword, *brandire, vibrare una ſpada.*

BRA'NDISHED, adj. *brandito, vibrato.*

BRA'NDY, s. [a diſtilled ſpirit] *acquavite,* s. f. *vino ſtillato.*

Brandy-ſhop, *bottega dove ſi vende acquavite.*

To BRANGLE [to ſcold, to quarrel, to bicker] *diſputare, contraſtare, contendere, riſſare, far riſſa.*

BRA'NGLING, s. *querela, diſputa, conteſa, riſſa,* s. f. *contraſto, contendimento,* s. m.

BRA'NGLER, s. *riſſoſo, contenditore, riottoſo, beccalite.*

BRANK, s. [a ſort of grain called alſo buck-wheat] *miglio,* s. m. *ſpezie di biada minuta.*

BRANKU'RSIN [bear's breech, the plant] *brancorſina,* s. f. *erba medicinale.*

BRANT-GOO'SE, s. [a ſort of wild fowl] *oca ſalvatica.*

BRA'SIL, s. [braſil-wood] *campéccio,* s. m. *legno che s'adopra a tignere in roſſo.*

BRA'SIER, s. *che lavora coſe di rame.*

Braſier, s. [a pan to hold coals] *caldano, ſtromento di rame da tenervi i carboni dentro.*

BRASS, s. [a ſort of metal] *rame,* s. m.

Yellow braſs, *ottone.*

Braſs money, *moneta di rame.*

A braſs cannon, *un cannone di bronzo.*

Braſs candleſtick, *candeliere d'ottone.*

Braſs kettle, *calderone di rame.*

Braſs ore, *cadmia.*

Braſs [falſe or counterfeit money] *moneta falſa.*

One that makes braſs money, *monetario falſo, uno che falſifica la moneta.*

BRA'SSETS, s. [armour for the arm] *braccialetto, bracciale,* s. m. *armadura, che arma il braccio.*

BRA'SSINESS, s. *qualità o ſomiglianza di rame.*

BRA'SSY, adj. [partaking of braſs] *che ha del rame, che è in parte di rame.*

Braſſy [as hard as braſs] *duro come rame.*

BRAST, adj. [burſt] *crepato.* Obſ.

BRAT, s. [beggarly child] *fanciullo cencioſo, un meſchinello.*

Brat, *voce di diſprezzo per bambino.* Roſcommon.

Brat, *la progenie, la ſtirpe.* South.

BRAVA'DO, s. [rodomontado] *bravata, rodomontata, ſmargiaſſata,* s. f.

BRAVE, adj. [valiant, couragious] *bravo, prode, animoſo, corraggioſo.*

You are a brave man, *voi ſiete un brav' uomo, voi ſiete un galantuomo.*

Brave [fine in cloaths] *attillato, aſſettato, pulito, veſtito di gala.*

Brave [fine, excellent] *bello, eccellente.*

He made a brave ſpeech, *egli fece una bella orazione.*

Brave, s. [a ſwaggerer] *bravo, bravaccio.*

Oh brave! *bravo, viva!*

Brave, s. [challenge] *disfida.*

To BRAVE [to dare, to inſult] *bravare, ſfidare, affrontare, inſultare.*

To brave death, *incontrar la morte.*

He braves me to it, *mi próvoca a ciò.*

To brave [to act the brave] *braveggiare, fare il bravo.*

BRAVED, adj. *bravato, ſfidato, affrontato, inſultato.*

BRA'VELY, adv. *bravamente, animoſamente, coraggioſamente.*

BRA'VERY, s. [courage, valour] *bravura, valentía,* s. f. *coraggio, animo,* s. m.

This I ſpeak not out of bravery, *non dico ciò per braveggiare, per fare il bravo.*

Bravery [finery, gallantry] *magnificenza, ſplendidezza, pompa,* s. f.

BRAVO, s. [a man that murders for hire] *un bravo, un ſatéllite, un briccone che amazza per danari.*

Bravo! interj. *bravo, grido d'applauſo.*

BRAVI'SSIMO! interj. *braviſſimo, grido d'applauſo.*

BRAWL, s. [diſpute, ſquabble] *diſputa, conteſa,* s. f. *contraſto, contendimento,* s. m.

Brawl [a ſort of dance] *carola,* s. f. *ballo tondo.*

To BRAWL [to ſcold, to wrangle] *diſputare, querelare, contendere, ſtrepitare, gridare, ſtrillare, ſchiamazzare, litigare.*

BRAWLED, adj. *diſputato, querelato, conteſo, ſtrepitato, ſtrillato, ſchiamazzato.*

BRA'WLER, s. *litigatore, ſgridatore, garritore, riottoſo,* s. m.

BRA'WLING, s. *garrimento, ſgridamento,* s. *ſchimazzo, ſtrepito,* s. m. *diſputa, conteſa,* s. f.

Brawling, adj. ex. [a brawling woman] *una garritrice.*

BRAWN, s. [hard fleſh] *polpa,* s. f. *parte carnoſa.*

Brawn [the firmeſt part of a boar] *la parte più ſoda e polpoſa d'un verro.*

Brawn, *carne di verro preparata all' Ingleſe.*

Brawn [the arm ſo called from its being muſculous] *braccio, così chiamato dal ſuo eſſere pien di muſcoli.*

The brawn of the arms, *il lacerto delle braccia.*

The brawn of a capon, *la polpa d'un capone.*

BRA'WNINESS, s. *parte carnoſa.*

BRA'WNY, adj. [fleſhy, luſty, ſtrong] *carnoſo, carnuto, membruto, forte, robuſto, polpoſo, polputo.*

BRAY, s. *trincea, braga,* s. f.

Falſe bray [in fortification, a falſe trench made to hide the real one] *trincea falſa, falſabraga.*

BRAY, s. *raglio, ragghio, il ragghiare, il ragliare.*

To BRAY [to bruiſe, to pound] *peſtare, polverizzare acciaccando.*

To bray the ink [among printers] *macinare l'inchioſtro.*

To bray a fool in a mortar [to waſh a blackamoor white] *peſtar l'acqua nel mortajo, perdere il tempo e la fatica in coſa che non ſia per ſortir buono effetto.*

To bray [as an aſs does] *ragghiare, ragliare, il mandar fuòra che fa l'aſino la ſua voce.*

To bray [to cry out] *gridare, ſtridare, alzar la voce, vociferare.*

BRAYED, adj. *peſtato, v.* To bray.

BRA'YER, s. [an inſtrument to temper ink with] *macina,* s. f. *ſtrumento col quale gli ſtampatori marinano l'inchioſtro.*

BRA'YER, s. [one that brays like an aſs] *uno che ragghia come l'aſino.* Pope.

BRA'YING, s. *macinamento, peſtamento.*

The braying of an aſs, *ragghio d'aſino, raglio d'aſino, di ſomiére.*

BRAYL, s. [a piece of leather to bind up a hawk's wing] *bracchiere d'un falcone.*

To BRA'ZE [to cover, to overlay with braſs] *coprire di rame.*

BRAZED OVER, adj. *coperto di rame.*

BRA'ZEN, adj. *di rame, di bronzo.*

A brazen horſe, *un cavallo di bronzo.*

A brazen face, a brazen-faced man, *unosfacciato, uno sfrontato.*

To put on a brazen face, *essere sfacciato, far viso duro.*

To brazen out a thing, *mantenere una cosa con isfacciataggine.*

To brazen one out, *confondere alcuno, farlo restar confuso mantenendogli in faccia alcuna cosa.*

BRA'ZIER, s. [one who makes or sells brass ware] *calderajo,* s. m. *quello che fa o vende vasi di rame.*

Brazier's wife, *calderaja,* s. f. *moglie di calderajo.*

BREACH, s. [the ruin of any part of the works beat down with cannon] *breccia,* s. f. *apertura fatta nelle muraglie con cannone onde si possa penetrare alla parte opposta.*

To make a breach in a wall, *fare una breccia nel muro.*

To enter the breach, *montar la breccia.*

A breach of promise, *mancamento di promessa.*

A breach of faith, *mancanza di fede.*

A breach of peace, *rottura di pace.*

A breach of articles, *violazione di patti.*

A breach of friendship, *inimicizia.*

BREAD, s. [the staff of life] *pane.*

Leavened bread, *pane lievitato.*

Unleavened bread, *pane azzimo, senza fermento.*

White bread, brown bread, *pan bianco, pan bruno.*

Houshold bread, *pan casalingo.*

Crumb of bread, crust of bread, *mica, crosta, o crosticcio di pane.*

Consecrated bread, *pane benedetto, pane consecrato.*

Ginger bread, *confortino,* s. m.

A ginger bread maker, *berricuocolajo, confortinajo,* s. m. *quegli che fa, e vende bericuócoli o confortini.*

The sweet-bread of a breast of veal, *animella di vitella.*

Sow-bread, s. *tartufo,* s. f. *spezie di fungo.*

Bread-basket, *paniere,* s. m. *paniera,* s. f. *canestro pel pane.*

Bread baked under the ashes, *focaccia, cofaccia.*

To BREAD, *ex.* [to bread a porringer for broth] *tagliare del pane per la zuppa.*

BREADTH, s. [from broad] *larghezza, ampiezza,* s. f.

A finger's breadth, *la larghezza d'un dito.*

Cloth breadth, *larghezza o ampiezza del panno, o della tela.*

BREAK, s. *ex.* break of day, *sul far del giorno.*

He rises every morning by break of day, *si leva ogni mattina al far del giorno.*

A break [in the art of printing] *spacio bianco, cioè non istampato.*

To BREAK, *rompere, spezzare,* pret. *ruppi.*

To break a stick, *rompere, spezzare un bastone.*

To break one's own neck, *rompersi il collo.*

To break one's head, *romper la testa ad uno.*

To break asunder, *romper per metà, far due parti d'una cosa.*

To break in pieces, *mettere in pezzi.*

To break one's head with noise or chattering, *stordire, sbalordire, tor la testa altrui, infastidire altrui con soverchio strepito, con troppo cianciare.*

To break a conference, *interrompere una conferenza.*

To break one's sleep, *rompere il sonno, destare, guastare il sonno.*

To break one's word or promise, *mancar di parola, mancare alla promessa.*

To break one's vows, *romper il voto.*

To break one's beauty, *oscurare l'altrui bellezza.*

To break a horse, *scozzonare, domare un cavallo.*

To break one's heart, *spezzare il core, trafiggere il core.*

You break my heart with these expressions, *queste espressioni mi trafiggono il core.*

To break one's oath, *violare il giuramento.*

To break the sabbath, *non osservare il sabbato.*

To break God's laws, *trasgredire, violare la legge di Dio.*

To break one's back, *rompere il dosso ad uno, slombare uno.*

To break a custom, *disusare, divezzare, disviare, lasciar l'uso, svezzare.*

To break company, *lasciar la compagnia, separarsi dalla compagnia.*

To break ground [to open the trenches] *aprir le trincee.*

The strength of the wind that caught them up in the air, broke their fall, *la forza del vento che li portò per l'aria fece la loro caduta meno violenta.*

His debauches have broken his health, *le sue sregolatezze hanno rovinata la sua salute.*

To break a jest upon one, *burlare, beffare, schernire alcuno, motteggiar uno.*

To break a business, *dichiarare, proporre un negozio.*

To break one's mind to one, *svelarsi, palesarsi, dichiarare ad uno, dire il suo sentimento ad alcuno.*

To break friendship, *partir l'amicizia, querelarsi, cessar d'esser amico.*

I'll break with him, *non voglio piu impacciarmi con lui.*

To break, *rompersi, spezzarsi.*

Do you think it will break? *credete che si romperà?*

The ice breaks, *il ghiaccio si rompe.*

To break [as an imposthume] *creparsi.*

I believe the weather will break, *credo che il tempo si romperà, mi pare ch'il tempo sia volto alla pioggia.*

To break [to turn bankrupt] *fallire,* pref. *fallisco.*

He broke for ten thousand pounds, *è fallito di dieci mila lire sterline.*

She begins to break, *ella comincia a perder la sua bellezza, la sua bellezza se ne va.*

To break with sorrow, *consumarsi, struggersi di malinconia, di dolore.*

To break small, *sminuzzare, ridurre in minúzzoli, polverizzare.*

To break silence [to begin to speak] *rompere il silenzio.*

To break one's belly with meat, *creparsi di carne, mangiar troppo carne.*

To break one's sides with laughing, *creparsi scoppiare delle risa.*

To break wind upward, *ruttare, mandar fuora per la bocca il vento che è nello stomaco.*

To break one's fast, *rompere il digiuno, far colezione.*

To break a battalion, *rompere un battaglione, aprire una squadra.*

To break open a door, *rompere una porta.*

To break open a house, *aprire per forza una casa.*

To break open a letter, *aprire una lettera.*

To break loose, *sciorre, sciogliere, scatenare, lasciar andar con émpito.*

My heart is ready to break, *mi scoppia il core.*

To break forth, *sorgere, spuntare.*

He broke forth in tears, *cominciò a piangere.*

To break off, *rompere, spezzare.*

To break off company, *lasciar la campagnia.*

To break off a discourse, *tralasciare un discorso.*

Let us break off here, *finiamola, non ne parliamo più.*

To break off one's work, *tralasciare il lavoro, lasciare di lavorare.*

To break out, verb. neut. *uscire con violenza, crepare, aprirsi, far capo, marcire.*

To break out, as water out of a spring, *sorgere, zampillare.*

To break out as the sea does, *inondare, allagare.*

The war breaks out again, *la guerra s'accende di nuovo.*

To break out of prison, *romper la prigione, scampare, fuggire.*

To break out into an exclamation, *esclamare, sclamare, gridare ad alta voce.*

To break out into tears, *piagner dirottamente.*

To break out into unchast expressions, *prorompere in parole disoneste.*

To break out into wrath, *andare in collera, adirarsi, stizzarsi, infuriare.*

To break in, *entrar dentro impetuosamente, avventarsi, spignersi, gittarsi con impeto a che che si sia.*

To break in upon the enemy, *avventarsi contra i nemici.*

To break in upon other men's business, *impiacciarsi, intromettersi negli affari altrui.*

It is not for one man to break in upon the province of another, *uno non deve pigliarsi briga de' fatti altrui.*

To break in upon the respect a man owes to persons of quality, *mancar di rispetto a' grandi.*

The thieves broke in through the wall, *i ladri entraron per il muro.*

To break into a trench, *sforzare le trincee.*

To

To break into the enemy's camp, *sforzare il campo nemico.*
To break into laughter, *dar nelle risa, sganasciarsi delle risa.*
To break one's self of a thing, *astenersi da qualche cosa.*
To break through, *passare a traverso, passar per il mezzo, farsi strada.*
To break through a squadron, *romper uno squadrone.*
To break through difficulties, *superare le difficoltà, vincere le difficoltà.*
To break up the ground, *rompere il terreno, zappare, vangare il terreno.*
The weather breaks up, *il tempo si schiarisce.*
To break up [to decamp] *stendare, levar le tende.*
To break up [as assemblies do] *separarsi, il separarsi d'un assemblea, andarsene.*
To break up school, *avere vacanza.*
To break down, *abbattere, mandare a terra, rovinare, distruggere.*
BRE'AKER, s. *rompitore,* s. m. *che rompe.*
A house-breaker, *un ladro, uno che t'entra in casa rompendo la porta quando tu dormi o sei assente.*
A breaker of horses, *scozzonatore,* s. m.
Heart-breakers [love-locks] *ricci di capelli.*
BRE'AKFAST, s. *colezione,* s. f. *asciolvere, il mangiare della mattina.*
To eat one's breakfast, *far colezione, asciolvere.*
To BRE'AKFAST, *asciolvere, far colezione.*
BRE'AKING, s. *rompimento,* s. m. *il rompere,* v. to break.
There's no breaking of it, *non si puo rompere.*
A breaking up of school, *vacanze.*
Upon the breaking out of the war, *al principio della guerra.*
A breaking of the belly [burstenness] *crepatura,* s. f.
Break-neck, s. *precipizio, rompicollo,* s. m.
This will prove a breakneck to your designs, *questo rovinèra tutti i vostri disegni.*
BREAM, s. [a fish] *abramo,* s. m. *sorta di pesce.*
BREAST, s. [that part of the body which contains the heart and lungs] *petto, seno,* s. m.
I am wounded in the breast, *sono ferito nel petto.*
To have a sore breast, *aver male al petto.*
She has a fine breast, *ella ha un bel seno, un bel petto.*
To keep a thing in one's breast, *tenere una cosa in petto, tenerla secreta.*
It lies in his breast, *egli solo lo sa.*
A base and dangerous breast, *un anima vile e sordida.*
Back and breast [armour] *corazza.*
Breast-cloth, *gala,* s. f. *striscia di panno lino che portan le donne al petto alquanto fuor del busto.*

Breast-plate, *petto,* s. m. *armadura che cuopre il petto, pettabotta.*
The breast-bone, *l'arco del petto.*
Having a great breast, *pettoruto, alto di petto.*
Breast-work [parapet] *parapetto,* s. m.
Breast-pain [a disease in horses] *anticuore,* s. m. *malattia di ravalli.*
Breast-high, *che arriva al petto, dell' altezza del petto, che aggiunce al petto col suo sommo.*
BREATH, s. [the air received and discharged by the dilatation and compression of the lungs] *lena,* s. f. *alito, fiato,* s. m.
To take, to draw, or to fetch one's breath, *alenare, alitare, respirare, pigliar fiato.*
To run one's self out of breath, *correre fin che si perda, il fiato.*
Stinking breath, *fiato puzzolente.*
To the last breath, *fin all' ultimo sospiro.*
His breath is out of him, *è spirato, ha mandato fuora l'ultimo spirito.*
Shortness of breath, *asma, asima, ambascia,* s. f. *malattia che impedisce la respirazione.*
You spend your breath in vain, *voi parlate al vento, tutto quel che dite non serve a nulla.*
The least breath of commotion, *la minima commozione.*
To BREATHE, verb. neut. *respirare, anelare, alitare, ansare.*
He breathes, he is not dead, *respira, non è ancora morto.*
To breathe a pure air, *respirare un'aria pura.*
He breathes nothing but vengeance, *non brama che vendetta.*
To breathe out, *esalare.*
To breathe through, *perspirare.*
To breathe into, or upon, *spirare, infondere.*
To breathe one's last, *spirare, mandar fuora l'ultimo spirito.*
As long as I breathe, *tanto che viverò.*
To breathe the vein, *aprire una vena, cavar sangue.*
To breathe [to air] *seccare, asciugare, diseccare.*
To breathe one's self with running, *esercitarsi alla corsa.*
To breathe after a thing, *anelare, aspirare a qualche cosa.*
BREATHED, adj. *respirato, anelato, alitato.*
BRE'ATHING, s. *álito, anélito, ansamento, respiro,* s. m.
Breathing casts a mist upon a looking-glass, *il fiato appanna lo specchio.*
Breathing-hole, *spiraglio,* s. m. *fessura per la quale l'aria e il lume trapela.*
Breathing-time, *tempo di riposo.*
BRED, adj. [from to breed] *generato, prodotto, causato.*
Bred [brought up] *allevato, nutrito, ammaestrato, costumato.*
Bred a scholar, *allevato, ammaestrato nelle lettere, letterato.*
There I was bred and born, *lì sono nato ed allevato.*

Obstructions which are bred in the liver, *ostruzioni che si formano nel fegato.*
Our desire of knowledge is bred within us, *il desiderio ch' abbiamo di sapere nasce con noi, ci è naturale.*
That which is bred in the bone will never be out of the flesh, *chi di gallina nasce convien che razzoli.*
To brede, v. to braid.
BREDTH, v. Breadth.
BREE, s. *tafáno,* s. m. *spezie di mosca.*
BREECH, s. [the part on which we sit] *il deretano, le parti deretane.*
Breech [in gunnery, the hinder part of a piece of ordnance] *culatta d'arme da fuoco o di cannone.*
Bear's breech, s. [an herb] *brancorsina,* s. f.
Breeched, adj. *che porta le brache.*
A boy newly breeched, *un ragazzo che comincia a portare le brache.*
BREECHES, s. [a garment worn by men from the waist to the knees] *calzoni,* s. m. p. *brache,* s. f. p. *quella parte del vestito che cuopre dalla cintura al ginocchio.*
To wear breeches, *portar le brache.*
To wear the breeches [to have the mastery] *portar le brache, esser padrone.*
BREED, s. [kind] *razza,* s. f.
Breed of horses, *razza di cavalli.*
A dog of a good breed, *un cane di buono razza.*
To BREED [to engender] *generare, produrre.*
To breed [to cause] *generare, produrre, cagionare, causare.*
To breed [to bring up] *allevare, nutrire, ammaestrare, costumare, educare.*
To breed lice, *generar pidocchi.*
To breed quarrels, *causare, far nascere delle querele.*
To breed youth, *allevare giovani.*
A worm that breeds in the wood, *un verme che si genera nel legno.*
A woman that breeds, *uno donna gravida.*
To breed teeth, *fare i denti.*
BRE'EDER, s. *ex.* a good breeder, *una donna feconda.*
A good breeder of children, *una persona che sa ben allevare i fanciulli.*
A breeder of cattle, *colui che bada ad avere molto bestiame bovino e cavallino, e che si generi ne' suoi poderi.*
BREEDING, s. *generamento,* s. m. *produzione,* s. f. *il generare, il produrre.*
Breeding, s. [civility] *civiltà, costumatezza, buona creanza,* s. f.
Good or bad breeding, *buona o cattiva educazione, buona o mala creanza.*
The breeding of teeth, *il fare i denti.*
A woman that is breeding, *una donna gravida.*
BRE'EZE, s. [a cool wind] *venticello, fresco, aura,* s. f.
Breeze [gad-fly] *tafano.*
BRENT, adj. [burnt] *abbrucciato.*
BRET, or Brut, s. [a fish of the turbot kind] *spezie di rombo,* s. m.
BRE'THREN, s. *plurale di* Brother, *fratelli.—E' parola di bibbia, o da chiesa, o da burla.*

My beloved brethren, *fratelli amatissimi.*

BRE'VET, s. [a brief, a pope's bull] *breve, brieve,* s. m, *bolla,* s. f.

BRE'VIARY, s. [a popish prayer book] *breviario,* s. m. *quel libro ove son registrate l'ore cononiche e tutto l'ufficio divino.*

BRE'VIATE, s. [a short extract, or copy of a process, deed, or writing] *compendio, breve ristretto d'un processo.*

BRE'VIER, s. [a small sort of printing letter one degree smaller than long primer] *garamoncino.*

BRE'VITY, s. *brevità,* s. f.

For brevity-sake, *per brevità, per esser breve, per abbreviare.*

To BREW [to boil ale, &c.] *fare della cervogia, o birra.*

To brew a plot, *ordire o tramare un tradimento.*

As you have brewed so you must drink, *chi la fa la paga.*

BREW, s. [from the verb] *maniera di far la birra.*

BRE'WAGE, s. [from brew] *mistura di varie cose liquide da bere.*

BREWED, adj. *dal v.* To brew.

BRE'WER, s. *quello che cuoce la birra.*

Brew-house, s. *luogo dove si fa la birra.*

BRE'WING, s. *il far la birra.*

BRI'AR, s *pruno, rovo,* s. m.

Sweet-briar, *rovo,* s. m.

To be in the briars, *star fra le spine, essere in augustie.*

He brought me in the briars, *egli m' ha ridotto o tratto in questo perplessità.*

To leave one in the briars, *lasciar uno nelle brighe, in travagli, sulle spine.*

BRIBE, s. *donativo che si da per corrompere altrui.*

Bribes can get in without knocking at the door, *non si chiude porta a' donativi.*

To BRIBE [to corrupt with gifts] *corrompere, indurre uno con donativi a fare quel che non dovrebbe.*

To bribe one's judges, *corrompere i suoi giudici.*

BRIBED, adj. *corrotto.*

To be bribed, *pigliar l'ingoffo, lasciarsi corromper co' presenti.*

BRI'BER, s. *corompitore,* s. m. *quello che corrompe co' donativi.*

BRI'BERY, s. [the art of bribing] *il corrompere co' presenti.*

Guilty of bribery, *ehe s'è lasciato corrompere, che ha preso l'ingoffo.*

Brick, s. [earth moulded into a long square figure, and burnt, for building] *mattone,* s. m. *pezzo di terra cotta per uso di murare.*

To make bricks, *fare de' mattoni.*

Brick wall, *muro di mattoni.*

To make brick walls [to swallow meat greedily] *mangiare ingordamente, inghiottire senza masticare.*

Brick-bat, *pezzo di mattone.*

Brick, *pane d'un soldo, fatto presso a poco come un mattone.*

BRICKCLA'Y, s. [clay used for making brick] *creta adoperata in far mattoni.*

BRICKDU'ST [dust made by pounding bricks] *pólvere di mattoni, polvere fatta fregando mattoni insieme.*

Bricklayer, *fabbricatore di mattoni, o muratore,* s. m.

Brick-maker, *quello ehe fa i mattoni.*

Brick-kiln, *fornace da mattoni.*

To BRICK [to lay bricks] *fabbricar con mattoni.*

BRI'DAL, adj. [of or belonging to a bride] *sposereccio, di sposa, appartenente alla sposa nuziale.*

Bridal, s. [wedding] *sposalizio,* s. m.

BRIDE, s. [a new married woman] *sposa,* s. f. *donna novella, maritata di fresco.*

Bride-bed, *letto sposcereccio.*

Bride-maids, *fanciulle che in Inghilterra accompagnano le spose nel tempo della nozza per onore.*

BRIDECA'KE [a cake distributed to the guests at a wedding] *chicca o foccaccia distribuita alla compagnia in tempo di nezzo.*

Bridegroom, s. [a bride's spouse] *sposo,* s. m. *quegli che novellamente è ammogliato.*

BRI'DEMEN, s. } [the attendants on the bride and bridegroom] *giovanotti e fanciulle che in tempo di nozze stanno servendo la sposa e lo sposo.*
BRI'DEMAIDS, s. }

BRI'DESTAKE, s. [a post set in the ground to dance round] *palo conficcato in terra da ballarvi intorno in tempo di nozze.*

BRI'DEWELL, s. *nome d'una casa di correzione in Londra.*

BRIDGE, s. [a passage made over a river] *ponte,* s. m. *edificio che si fa sopra l'acqua per poterla passare.*

A stone-bridge, *un ponte di pietra.*

A draw-bridge, *un ponte levatojo.*

The bridge of the nose, *il rialto del naso, il soprosso del naso.*

The bridge of a lute, or of a fiddle, *il ponte d'un liuto, il ponticello d'un violino.*

BRIDLE, s. [head-stall] *briglia,* s. f.

The head-stall, the reins and bit of the bridle, *la testiera, la redini, il morso della briglia.*

To give a horse the bridle, *dar la briglia al cavallo, allentargli le redini.*

To bite the bridle, *rodersi i geti.*

To BRIDLE [to keep a horse with a bridle] *imbrigliare, metter la briglia al cavallo.*

To bridle [to curb one's passion] *domare le sue passioni, rintuzzare o mortificare gli affetti.*

BRI'DLEHAND, s. *la mano con cui si tien la briglia cavalcando, la man sinistra.*

BRIDLED, adj. *imbrigliato.*

BRI'DLING, s. *l'imbrigliare.*

BRIEF, adj. [short] *breve, corto, succinto.*

Brief [common, rife] *comune.*

Brief, s. *brieve, breve,* s. m.

Brief [abstract] *compendio, ristretto,* s. m.

BRI'EFLY, adv. [in few words] *brevemente, succintamente, in poche parole.*

BRI'EFNESS, s. *brevità,* s. f.

BRIER, s. *pruno* [*v.* Briar].

BRI'ERY, adj. [rough, full of briars] *pieno di pruni, spinoso.*

BRI'GADE, s. [a considerable party or division of a body of soldiers] *brigata,* s. f.

BRIGADE'ER, s. [an officer who commands a brigade] *brigadiere, capitan di brigata.*

BRIGANTI'NE, s. [an ancient kind of armour] *lorica all' antica.*

Brigantine, s. [a small light pinnace, proper either for giving chace or fighting] *brigantino,* s. m. *picciol naviglio di forma simile alla galea.*

BRIGHT, adj. [lucid, shining] *lucido, lucente, risplendente, luminoso, brillante, scintillante.*

A bright star, *una stella lucente o risplendente.*

A bright night, *una notte chiara e serena.*

Bright pewter, *stagno lucente.*

A bright colour, *un colore vivace.*

Thorough bright, *transparente.*

It is bright, *è giorno, il giorno comincia a spuntare.*

To BRI'GHTEN [to make bright] *pulire, lustrare far lucente.*

BRI'GHTENED, adj. *pulito, lustrato.*

BRI'GHTENING, s. *pulimento,* s. m. *il pulire.*

BRI'GHTLY, adv. *pulitamente, chiaramente, splendidamente.*

BRI'GHTNESS, s. [shiningness] *splendore, chiarezza, lucidezza, lurè.*

Brightness of the stars, *lo splendore delle stelle.*

The brightness of the sun, *la luce del sole.*

BRI'GUE, s. [quarrel] *briga, lite, controversia, nimicizia, contesa,* s. f.

BRI'LLIANCY, s. [lustre, splendour] *lucidezza,* s. f. *splendore,* s. m.

BRI'LLIANT, s. *brillante, diamante ben tagliato.*

BRI'LLIANTNESS, *lucidezza, splendore.*

BRIM, s. *orlo, lembo, margine.*

The brim of a glass, *l'orlo d'un bicchiere.*

The brims of a hat, *le falde d'un cappello.*

To fill a glass to the very brim, *empiere un bicchiere fino all' orlo.*

To BRIM, *empiere fino all orlo, colmare, esser pieno, esser colmo.*

A narrow brimmed hat, *capello che ha la falde strette.*

BRI'MMER, s. *un bicchier trabboccante.*

To drink great brimmers, *bere a bicchieri trabboccanti.*

BRI'MSTONE, s. *solfo, zolfo,* s. m. *minerale.*

Brimstone mine, *solfanai, zolfanaia,* s. f.

Done with brimstone, *solforato, zolforato.*

BRIMSTO'NY, adj. *sulfureo, pien di zolfo.*

BRINDLE, or Brindled, adj. [it is said of the coat of a dog streaked with several colours, especially brown and black] *divisato, vajato, sagginato.*

BRINE,

BRINE, s. [salt liquor] *salamojo, s. f. acqua salata per uso di conservarvi entro pesci, funghi, olive, e simili.*

As salt as brine, *salato come la salamoja.*

Brine [the sea] *il mare. Voce poetica.*

The foaming brine, *il mare ondeggiante, l'onde spumanti.*

BRINE, s. [tears] *lagrime amare.*

BRI'NEPIT, s. *pozzo d' acqua salata.*

To BRING, verb. act. *portare, trasferire una cosa di luogo a luogo, arrecare, recare.*

Bring me my hat and sword, *portami il mio cappello e la mia spada.*

Bring him along with you, *menatelo con esso voi.*

To bring to light, *mettere in luce, produrre alla vista delle genti.*

To bring a child into the world, *mettere al mondo un figliuolo.*

To bring dinner in, *portare in tavola.*

To bring to poverty, *ridurre in miseria o povertà.*

To bring to nought, *annichilare, ridurre al niente.*

To bring to reason, *fare stare a segno, render capace.*

To bring ill luck, *portare mal augurio.*

To bring word to one, *far sapere qualche cosa ad uno, informarlo.*

Bring me word if he is at home, *fatemi sapere s'egli è in casa, sappiatemi dire s'egli è in casa.*

To bring sleep, *far dormire.*

To bring an action against one, *citare in giustizia.*

To bring two persons together, to reconcile them, *metter d'accordo due persone, pacificarle.*

That will bring you to the gallows, *le forche non vi mancheranno se fate cio.*

I shall never bring him to do it, *non potrò mai persuadergliela, non otterrò mai da lui che lo faccia.*

To bring a cause about again, *ricominciare un processo.*

To bring a design about, *venire a fine del suo disegno.*

To bring away, *portar via.*

To bring back again, *riportare, di nuovo portare, ricondurre.*

To bring one back to his duty, *tirare uno al suo dovere, ridurre uno al suo dovere.*

To bring forth a child, *partorire.*

To bring forth before the time, *sconciarsi, abortire.*

To bring forth a prisoner, *presentare un prigioniero.*

To bring forth witnesses, *produrre i testimoni.*

To bring forth fruits, *produrre, portar frutti.*

To bring on, *impegnare, intrigare.*

To bring off, *sbrigare, liberare, cavar d'imbroglio.*

To bring off [to dissuade] *dissuadere, far mutar pensiero.*

To bring over, *portare, recare.*

To bring one over to one's side, *tirar uno dalla sua parte.*

To bring under, *sommettere, sottomettere, sottoporre, soggiogare.*

He has brought the whole country under the king's obedience, *ha sottomesso tutto il paese all' obbedienza del rè.*

To bring in, *fare entrare, introdurre.*

Bring him in, *fatelo entrare.*

To bring one in [to prefer him] *avanzare, ingrandire uno.*

To bring or draw one in, *imbrogliare, intrigare uno in qualche affare.*

To bring a thing cunningly in a discourse, *introdurre con arte qualche cosa nel discorso.*

To bring one in guilty, *condannare alcuno, dichiararlo colpevole, o reo.*

To bring one in not guilty, *assolvere uno, dichiararlo innocente.*

To bring a man in a passion to himself, *addolcire, mitigare, placare l'ira di qualcheduno.*

To bring low, *abbattare, abbassare, umiliare.*

I could not bring myself to it, *non ho potuto risolvermi a cio.*

To bring to perfection, *perfezionare, dar perfezione, finire.*

To bring a thing to pass, *effettuare, mandare ad effetto, seguire, compire, dar compimento.*

The familiarity of dangers brings us to the contempt of them, *la familiarità de' pericoli fa che noi li sprezziamo.*

To bring to agreement, *metter d'accordo, accordare, riconciliare, rapacificare.*

To bring one to his wits again, *far tornare uno in se stesso.*

His age has brought his body to the shape of a bow, *l'età ha reso il suo corpo curvo come un arco.*

He has brought that to a mode, *ne ha fatto venire la moda.*

To bring one into danger, *esporre alcuno a qualche pericolo.*

To bring a man into a fool's paradise, *pascere uno di vane speranze.*

To bring a thing into question, *esaminare una cosa, dibattere una cosa.*

To bring into debt, *indebitare.*

To bring into favour, *mettere in grazia.*

To bring a thing into the ballance with another, *comparare, paragonare, mettere in competenza una cosa non un' altra.*

To bring close to, *avvicinare, accostare.*

To bring one to his death, *causare la morte d'alcuno.*

To bring a thing to one's remembrance, *far ricordare alcuno di che che sia, rimettergliela nella memoria.*

I cannot bring him to learn his lesson by heart, *non posso fargli imparare la sua lezione a mente.*

To bring one out of trouble, *levare uno d'impaccio o di fastidio.*

To bring out a story, *recitare o dire una novella.*

I can't tell how to bring it out, *non saprei raccontárvelo.*

To bring over, *trasportare.*

That farm brings him in an hundred pounds a year, *quel podere gli frutta cento lire sterline all' anno,*

To bring up a child by hand, *allevare un fanciullo colla pappa.*

To bring up a child to good manners, *allevare, accostumare, costumare bene un fanciullo.*

I bring up all my children to my trade, *faccio imparare a tutti i miei figliuoli il mio mestiere.*

To bring up the rear, *comandare la retroguardia.*

I bring up all I eat, *vómito tutto quel che mangio.*

To bring up phlegm, *sputare della bile.*

To bring up to one's hand, *allevare uno alle sue voglie.*

To bring mischief upon one's self, *tirarsi addosso disgrazia.*

To bring down [to humble] *abbattere, abbassare, umiliare, debilitare.*

To bring down the price of a commodity, *far calar di prezzo una mercanzia.*

BRI'NGER, s. *portatore, s. m. portatrice, s. f. che porta.*

A bringer up of children, *quello o quella che alleva i fanciulli.*

BRI'NISH, adj. [from brine] *salmastro, che tien del salso.*

BRI'NISHNESS, s. [saltness] *la qualità dell' acqua salsa.*

BRINK, s. *orlo, lembo, s. m. ripa, s. f.*

The brink of a well, *l'orlo d'un pozzo.*

To be upon the very brink of a precipice, *essere proprio sull' orlo d'un precipizio.*

To be upon the very brink of ruin, *esser in pericolo di rovinarsi.*

BRI'NY, adj. [from brine] *salato.*

The briny depths, *il mare.*

BRI'ONY, s. [a sort of herb] *briónia, s. f. spezie d'erba.*

Briony [the wild vine] *vigna salvatica.*

BRISK, adj. [lively] *vivace, allegro, svegliato, vispo.*

Brisk [jovial, merry] *allegro, giocoso, lieto, allegro, giojoso, festevole.*

BRISK [vigorous] *vigoroso, rigolioso, forte, gagliardo.*

We gave them a brisk charge, *gl' incalzammo vigorosamente.*

A brisk gale of wind, *un vento fresco.*

Brisk wine, *vino frizzante.*

To brisk up [to come up briskly] *avvanzarsi, farsi innanzi con franchezza.*

BRI'SKET, s. *il petto d'un animale.*

BRI'SKLY, adv. *vigorosamente, rigogliosamente, grovialmente, gagliardamente, lietamente.*

We received the enemy briskly, *incontrammo l'inimico animosamente.*

To drink briskly, *bere profusamente.*

To come off briskly, *sbrigarsi d'un affare animosamente.*

BRI'SKNESS, s. [liveliness] *vivacità, s. f. vigore, s. m.*

Briskness [merriness, gaiety] *allegría, gioja, giulività, ilarità, vivezza, giocondità, s. f.*

BRISTLE, s. [strong hair standing on the

the back of a boar] *setola*, s. f. *pelo che ha in sul fil della schiena il porco.*

To **Bristle**, *star su per punta come le setole fanno.* Shakesp.

To bristle a shoemaker's thread, *setolare dello spago, come fa 'l calzolajo o 'l ciabattino.*

Bri'stling, adj. *eretto a mo' di setola.*

Bri'stly, adj. [full of bristles] *setoloso.*

Brit. s. *name d'un pesce.* Carew.

Bri'ttle, adj. [apt to break, frail] *fragile, frale, fievole, che agevolmente si rompe.*

Bri'ttleness, s. *fragilità, fragilezza, fralezza*, s. f.

Bri'ttly, adv. *fragilmente, debolmente.*

Brize, s. [the gadfly] *estro assillo, insetto volante che si ficca nella pelle delle bestie bovine spezialmente, e le fa correre come matte pungendole.*

Broach, s. [spit] *spiedo, schidione, schidone, stidione.* s. m.

To **Broach** [to spit] *mettere nello spiedo, infilzare nello stidione.*

To broach [to tap a vessel] *spillare una botte, metter mano ad una botte.*

To broach a lie, *inventare una bugia.*

To broach, [to spread abroad] *divulgare, pubblicare.*

To broach an heresy, *disseminare un' eresia.*

Bro'ached, adj. [set on the spit] *messo allo spiedo.*

Broached [tapped] *spillato.*

Broached [spread abroad] *divulgato disseminato, inventato.*

Bro'acher, s. [author] *autore, inventore.*

He was the first broacher of that heresy, *egli fu il capo, o fondator di quella eresia.*

Brócher, s. [spit] *spiedo, schidione, schidone, stidione.*

Broad, adj. [wide, extended in breadth] *ampio, esteso in larghezza.*

Broad [large] *largo.*

Broad [clear, open] *chiaro, aperto.* Decay of piety.

Broad, [gross, coarse] *ruvido, grossolano.*

Broad [obscene, fulsom] *osceno, stomachevole.*

Broad [bold, not delicate, reserved] *audace, ardito, baldanzoso, che non ha riguardo, che non ha delicatezza.*

Broad cloth, *panno largo, o ampio.*

Broad day-light, *giorno chiaro.*

At broad noon, *in sul mezzo giorno.*

A broad piece, *una moneta larga.*

Broadside, s. [a discharge of the guns of one side of the ship all at once] s. f. *lo scaricare di tutti i cannoni del fianco d'un vascello alla volta; salva, scarica, sparo.*

We gave them a broadside, *noi tirammo sopra di loro uno sparo di cannonate.*

Bróadside, s. [the side of a ship] *il fianco d'un vascello.*

Broadside, s. [in printing, a sheet of paper printed only on one side] *foglio di carta stampato solamente da una parte.*

To make broad, *slargare allargare, dilatare.*

To grow broad, *slargarsi, allargarsi.*

A broad weaver, *tessitore di drappi.*

The broad of an oar, *la pala del remo.*

Broad, adv. [to speak broad] *parlar goffamente.*

Broad awake, *affato desto, appieno svegliato.*

Broad faced, *che ha una gran faccia.*

To **Bro'aden**, v. n. [to grow broad] *slargarsi allargarsi, crescere in larghezza.*

Bro'adly, adv. *largamente, ampiamente.*

Broadly [in speech] *goffamente, colla bocca piena.*

Bro'adness, s. [breadth, extent from side to side] *larghezza, ampiezza.*

Broadness, s. [coarseness, fulsomness] *rusticità, oscenità.*

Bro'adsword, s. [a cutting sword with a broad blade] *spada tagliente, spada con lama larga.*

Bro'adwise, adv. [according to the direction of the breadth] *seconda la larghezza, a seconda della larghezza.*

Bro'cade, s. [a sort of cloth wrought with gold and silver] *broccato*, s. m.

Broca'ded, adj. [drest in brocade] *vestito di broccato.*

Brocaded [woven in the manner of a brocade] *tessuto a mo' di broccato.*

Broca'ge, s. v. Brokage [the gain gotten by promoting bargains] *guadagno del sensale.*

Brocage [the hire given for any unlawful office] *paga data a un tristo per mal opera fattagli fare.*

Brocage [the trade of dealing in old things] *il mestier del ferravecchio, del rigattiere.*

Bro'ccoli, s. [a species of cabbage] *broccoli, spezie di cavolo.*

Brock, s. [a wild beast also called badger] *tasso* s. m, *animale che dorme assai come i ghiri.*

Brocket, s. [a buck or hart of two years old] *cerviatto, e cervietto*, s. m. *cervo giovene di due anni.*

Brogue, s. [a kind of shoe] *foggia di scarpe usate in Irlanda, per lo più di legno.*

Brogue, [a corrupt dialect] *parlar corrotto, favella cattiva.*

To **Bro'ider** [to adorn with figures of needle-work] *ricamare, adornar di ricamo.*

Bro'idery, s. [embroidery, flower-work] *ricamo, il ricamare*, Tickell.

Broil, s. [tumult] *tumulto, disturbo, romore fracasso di popolo sollevato.*

Broil [quarrel] *querela, disputa, rissa, contesa.* s. f.

To **Broil** [to dress or roast meat on the coals] *arrostire sopra la graticola, o sopra le brace.*

To broil [to be in a heat] *aver caldo.*

Broiled adj. *arrostito sopra la graticola o sopro le brace.*

Broiled meat, *braciuola, carbonata*, s. f.

Bro'iler, s. *quello, o quella che arroste sopra la graticola o sopra le brace.*

Broka'ge, s. [the business or trade of a broker] *il mestiere d'un sensale.*

Brokage or Brokerage [the hire or reward of a broker] *senseria*, s. f. *la mercede dovuta al sensale per le sue fatiche si scrive anco* Brocage.

Broke or Broken, adj. [from to break] *rotto, spezzato, domato, violato.*

A broken spirit, *un animo dimesso.*

A broken week, *una settimana nella quale vi sia qualche festa*

Hell broke loose, *l'inferno si scatenò.*

A broken sleep, *un sonno interrotto.*

A broken or mixt language, *una lingua corotta.*

To speak broken English, *parlare Inglese scorrettamente, alla forestiera, e male.*

Broken winded, *bolso, che respira con difficoltà.*

Broken meat, *minúzzoli, briccioli di carne, avanzi, di carne.*

Broken bellied, *rotto, allentato, crepato.*

Broken handed, *stroppiato dello mano.*

To **Broke** [to contract business for others] *contrattar negozi per altri.*

Bro'kenly, adv. [without any regular series] *interrottamente.*

Bro'ker, [seller of old cloaths] *rigattiere*, s. m. *rivenditor di vestimenti, e di masserizie usate.*

Broker's row, *rigatteria*, s. f. *ghetto*, s. m. *luogo dove si rivendono vestimenti usati.*

Broker [procurer of bargains] *sensale*, s. m.

A pawn-broker, *usuriere, usurajo*, s. m.

Brokera'ge, s. *senseria.* v. Brocage.

Bronchoce'le, s. *tumore che viene in una parte dell' aspera arteria, gozzo*, s. m.

Bro'nchial, }
Bro'nchick, } *appartenente alla gola. Termini medici.*

Broncho'tomy, s. *quella operazione che apre la strozza per incisione onde una persona non rimanga soffocata.*

Brond, s. *brando, parolo poetica, e lo stesso che* brand.

Bronze, s. *bronzo, specie di metallo fatto principalmente di rame.*

Bronze, *medaglia fatta di bronzo.*

Brooch, s. *giojello, ornamento di giogelli.*

To **Brooch**, *adornar di giogelli.*

Brood, s. [a company of chickens hatched by, or going with one hen] *covata.* s. f.

A brood of chickens, *una covata di pulcini.*

A brood-hen, *chioccia*, s. f. *la gallina quando cova l'uova e guida i pulcini.*

Brood [offspring] *prole, prosapia, schiatta, razza, stirpe*, s. f.

To **Brood** [to sit upon the eggs as fowls do to hatch them] *covare, lo star degli uccelli in sull' uova per riscaldarle, acchiochè nascano.*

Bro'oding, s. *covatura*, s. f. *il covare.*

Brooding, adj. *covante. ex.* [a brooding time] *covatura, il tempo del covare.*

A brood-

A brooding pigeon, *columba covante*,
Bro'ody, adj. *che cova, in atto di covare l' uova.*
Brook, s. [rivulet] *ruscello*, s. m. *picciol rivo d'acqua.*
A little brook, *un ruscelletto*,
Bro'oklime, s. *sorta d'acqua.*
To Brook [to hear patiently] *sofferire, tollerare, inghiottire un oltraggio.*
Broom, s. [a plant so called] *ginestra*, s. f.
A broom [a besom] *scopa di ginestra.*
Sweet-broom, *tamarisco*, s. m.
Bro'omland s. [land that bears brooms] *terreno che produce ginestre.*
Bro'omstaff } s. [the staff to Broomstick } which the broom is bound] *il manico della scopa, quel legno a cui è legata la scopa.*
Bro'omy adj. [full of broom] *pieno di ginestre.*
Broom-rape [choke weed] *pisciacane*, s. m. *sorta d'erba.*
A broom-close, *un ginestreto.*
Butchers-broom, *mirto salvatico.*
Brooming of a ship [is the burning off all the filth she has contracted on her sides, with broom, rushes, or straw] *il nettare un vascello bruciando con ginestre, giunchi, o paglia tutte l'immondizie contratte ne' fianchi.*
Broth, s. [the liquor in which flesh is boiled] *brodo*, s. m.
Jelly-broth, *consumato*, s. m. *peverada*, s. f. *acqua nella quale abbiano bollito polli o carne tanto che vi sieno consumati dentro.*
Brothel, s. } [a bawdy-Brothel-House, } house] *chiasso, bordello*, s. m.
He that haunts brothel-houses, *bordelliere, puttaniere.*
Bro'ther, s. *fratello*, s. m. *pl.* brothers *o* brethren.
An elder brother, *fratello primogenito, fratel maggiore.*
A younger brother, *fratello minore.*
Brother in law, *cognato.*
Foster-brother, *fratello di latte.*
A brother of the quill [an author] *un autore.*
A brother of the brush [a painter] *un pittore.*
Brotherho'od, s. [brotherly union] *fratellanza*, s. f. *dimestichezza, intrinsichezza fratellevole.*
Brotherhood, [fraternity] *fraternità, adunanza spirituale, compagnia, confraternita.*
Bro'therly, adj. *fraterno, fraternale; fratellevole.*
Brotherly love, *amore fraterno.*
Brotherly, adv. *fraternamente, fratellevolmente.*
Brought, adj. [from to bring] *portato, condotto, v.* To bring.
Let him be brought to me, *fate che venga da me.*
He was upon their prayers brought to the use of his tongue, *ricoverò la parola per mezzo delle loro preghiere.*
I am now brought to such a pass, *sono adesso ridotto a tal termine.*
See what I am brought to, *vedi a che son giunto.*
I cannot yet be brought to do it, *non posso ancora risolvermi a farlo.*
Brought to bed, *partorita.*
He cannot be brought off from it, *non c'è modo di smuoverlo da cio.*
Brought, è *preterito del verbo* to bring, I brought, *io portai.*
Brow, s. [the part of the face above the eye] *fronte*, s. m. f.
Brow [eye brow] *ciglio*, s. m. pl. *ciglia*, s. f.
To bend or knit the brow, *arricciare o increspar la fronte.*
To clear up the brow [to look merrily] *mostrarsi allegro, fare un viso allegro, o lieto.*
Brow [confidence] *ardire*, s. m. *arditezza, sfacciataggine*, s. f.
He has not brow enough to assert it, *la sua sfacciataggine non è tanta da asserirlo.*
To get one's livelihood by the sweat of one's brow, *vivere delle sue braccia o de' propri sudori.*
The brow of a hill, *ciglio, ciglione*, s. m. *la cima d'un monte.*
The brow of a plain, *l'estremità, d'una pianura.*
Brow-antler [the first start which grows on the head of a stag] *corna picciole d'un cervo.*
To Brow [to be at the edge of] *essere alla somnità d'una cosa.*
To Brow-beat [to look disdainfully or haughtily upon] *fare il viso brusco, fare il viso dell' arme, guardar uno torvamente, con cipiglio di superbia o di superiorità.*
Bro'wbound adj. [crowned] *coronato, cinto di corona.*
Bro'wsick, adj. [dejected] *maninconoso, col viso pieno di maninconia.*
Brown, adj. *bruno.*
Brown hair, *capelli bruni.*
A brown woman, *una bruna, una donna bruna.*
Brown paper, *carta straccia.*
Brown bread, *pan nero.*
Brown blue, *livido.*
Bro'wnbill, s. *arme antica della fantería Inglese.*
To make brown, *imbrunire, imbrunare, far bruno.* pres. *imbrunisco.*
To grow brown, *imbrunire.*
To make the skin of a young pig look brown, *rosolare un porcello.*
Somewhat brown, *crunazzo, brunotto, bruniccio, alquanto bruno.*
To be in a brown study, *star pensieroso o pensoso.*
Bro'wnness, s. [a brown colour] *brunezza, color bruno.*
Bro'wnish, adj. *brunazzo, alquanto bruno, brunetto, bruniccio.*
Bo'wnstudy, s. [gloomy meditations] *il meditare di cose triste, piene di malinconia.*
To Browse [to eat branches or shrubs] *mangiar foglie o erbe, come fan le bestie.*
To Browse, v. n. [to feed] *pascersi, pascolare.*
Browse, or browse wood, s. [young sprouts of trees that shoot early in the spring] *foglie o erbami teneri di cui si pascono le bestie.*
Browsed, adj. *pasciuto.*
Bro'wsing, s. *il pascersi.*
To go a browsing, *andare al pascolo.*
Broyl, *v.* broil.
Bruise, s. *ammaccammento*, s. m. *ammaccatura, schiacciatura*, s. f.
To Bruise [to break small] *ammaccare, schiacciare, rompere, infragnere, pestare.*
To bruise salt, *pestare del sale.*
To bruise nuts and almonds, *schiacciare delle nocciole e delle mandorle.*
To bruise [to beat black and blue] *ammaccare acciaccare, far livido.*
To bruise one's arm by a fall, *ammaccarsi un braccio cascando.*
Bru'ised, adj. *ammaccato, schiacciato, infranto, allividito.*
Bruit, s. [rumour, noise] *romore, strepito.*
To Bruit a thing abroad [to report or spread it abroad] *dar voce, far correr fama di che che si sia.*
'Tis bruited abroad, *corre voce.*
Bru'mal, adj. [winterly, hyemal] *brumale, di verno.*
Brunt; s. [assault, onset, brush] *urto, assalto, impeto, combattimento*, s. m.
If you be able to bide the first brunt, *se potrete far testa al primo impeto.*
Brunt [cross accident] *disastro, accidente*, s. m. *disgrazia*, s. f.
Brush, s. [to brush cloaths withal] *spàzzola, granàta*, s. f. *mazza di scope col quale si spazza.*
A shoe brush, *sètola*, s. f. *spazzola fatta di setole di porco per nettare le scarpe.*
A painter's brush [a pencil] *pennello di pittore.*
A plaisterer's brush, *penello col quale s'imbiancano le mura.*
Brush [faggot of sticks] *fastello di rami secchi.*
Brush [brunt, push, fight] *urto, impeto, combattimento, incontro, cozzo*, s. m.
To give one a brush [to come up to him smartly] *avventarsi, spignersi, gittarsi con impeto sopra ad alcuno.*
Brush maker, *quello che fa • v e granate.*
Brush wood, *stipa*, s. f. *sterpi, tagliati, o legname minuto da far fuoco.*
To Brush, [to cleanse with a brush] *spazzolare, nettare colla spazzola.*
To brush, v. n. [to move with haste] *muoversi in fretta.*
To brush, v. n. [to fly over, to skim lightly] *toccar leggermente nel passar con fretta.*
Brushed, adj. *spazzolato.*
Bru'sher, s. *quello, o quella che spazzola.*
Bru'shy, adj. *setotoso, fatto a mo' di spàzzola.*
Brutal, adj. *brutale.*
Bruta'lity, s. [beastlinesss, brutishness] *brutalità, bestialità*, s. f.
To Brutali'ze, v. n. [to grow brutal or savage] *diventar brutale, diventar salvatico, inselvatichirsi.*
To brutalize, *render brutale, render salvatico.*
Bru'tally, adv. *brutalmente, bestialmente, inumanamente.*

BRUTE, s. *un bruto, una bestia.*
A brute beast, *un bruto, una bestia.*
BRUTE, adj. *insensato, salvatico, irragionevole, aspro, feroce.*
Brúteness, s. [brutality] *brutalità.*
BRU'TISH, adj. *brutale, bestiale, di bruto.*
BRU'TISHLY, adv. *brutalmente, bestialmente.*
BRU'TISHNESS, s. [beastliness] *brutalità, bestialità, salvatichezza, s. f.*
BRY'ONY, s. [an herb] *briònia, s. f. spezie d'erba.*
BUBBLE, s. [a bladder in water] *bolla, búbbola, s. f. sonaglio, s. m. rigonfiamento, che fa l'arqua quando piove o quand' ella bolle.*
Bubble [trifle] *bagatella, s. f. cosa di poco momento.*
Bubble [a silly fellow, a cully] *un gonzo, un goffo, uno sciocco.*
To make a bubble of one, *truffare, ingannare, giuntare alcuno, piantàrla ad alcuno.*
To BUBBLE [to run with a gentle noise] *correndo mormoreggiare.*
To bubble up, *bollire, gorgogliare, crosciare.*
BU'BBLING, s. *il truffare, il giuntare.*
Bubbling up, *bollimento, gorgogliamento, s. m.*
BU'BBY, s. [a woman's breast] *mammella, poppa, s. f.*
BUBO, s. [a tumour in the groin] *tincone, s. m. postema nell' anguinaja.*
BUCE'NTAUR, or Bucentóro, s. [a stately galley in which the Doge and Senate of Venice go annually on Afcension Day to espouse the sea, by throwing a ring into it] *bucentoro.*
BUCK, s. [the male of some wild beasts] *il maschio d'alcune bestie salvatiche, ex.*
A buck goat, *becco, s. m. il maschio della capra domestica.*
A buck, *un daino. Il femminino è* Doe.
A buck coney, *un coniglio.*
A buck [a lye made of ashes] *bucato, s. m.*
Buck ashes, *cenere da bucato.*
BU'CKMAST [the mast of beech] *ghianda di cerro.*
Buck's horn [an herb] *gramigna, caprinella, s f.*
Buck-wheat, *miglio, s. m.*
Buck-stall [a large net to catch deer in] *spezie di rete da pigliar cervi.*
To BUCK, *fare il bucato.*
BU'CKET, s. [a pail made of leather or wood] *secchia, s. f. catino, s. m.*
BU'CKING, s. *fare il bucato.*
Bucking tub, *tinozza da farvi il bucato.*
Bucking cloth, *tela che si mette sopra pannilini quando si fa il bucato.*
BU'CKLE, s. [a four square or round ring with a tongue] *fibbia, s. f.*
The tongue of a buckle, *l' ardiglione d'una fibbia.*
A little buckle, *una fibbietta.*
Buckle [curl] *riccio, s. m. ciocca, s. f. capelli innanellati.*
To BUCKLE [to tie with a buckle] *affibbiare, congiugnere insieme con fibbia.*

To buckle to one's business, *applicarsi o badare a' fatti suoi.*
To buckle [to prepare for war] *prepararsi, accignersi, apparecchiarsi alla guerra. Non è in up in quelpo senso.*
He buckles himself wholly to his study, *s'aplica unicamente allo studio.*
To buckle or yield to one, *cedere, rendersi, o sommetersi a qualcheduno.*
To buckle to one's way, *uniformarsi all' altrui umore.*
To buckle [to put into buckles] *innanellare.*
BU'CKLED, adj. *affibbiato, innanellato.*
BU'CKLER, s. [a piece of defensive armour] *scudo, s. m. arma defensiva.*
A buckle maker, *uno scudajo.*
A buckler of beef, [a piece cut off from the surloin] *pezzo di bue tagliato dal filetto.*
Buckler-thorn, *spinamagna, s. f.*
To Búckler [to support, to defend, to shield] *proteggere, defendere, fare scudo.*
BU'CKRAM, s. [a sort of strong coarse linen cloth stiffened] *bucherame, s. m. sorta di tella.*
BU'CKSOM, *v.* Buxom.
BU'CKSOMNESS, *v.* Buxomness.
BU'CKTHORN, s. [a sort of thorn] *spinamagna, s. f. spinagiudaica, s. m. spezie di pruno.*
Buckthorn-berry, *baco di spinagiudaica.*
BUCO'LICK, s. [pastoral song or poem] *bucolica, s. f.*
VIRGIL'S BUCOLICKS, *le Bucoliche di Virgilio.*
BUD, s. [blossom, young sprout] *bottone, germoglio, pollone, rampollo, sprocco, s. m. boccia, s. f.*
A rose bud, *un bottone di rosa.*
The bud of a vine, *gemma, occhio di vigna.*
Dear bud, *caro mio, voce colla quale le donne accarezzano i loro mariti.*
To BUD [to put forth buds, to burgeon or bloom] *germinare, germogliare, gettare, mettere, mignolare, pullulare.*
To BUDGE, v. n. [to stir] *muoversi.*
BUDGE, s. [lamb's fur] *pelle d'agnello.*
A budge [one that slips privately into a house to steal] *un mariuolo, uno ch' entra secretamente in una casa o altro luogo, e vi s'appiatta per rubare.*
Budge barrel [a little tin powder barrel] *bariletto da mettervi dento della polvere.*
BU'DGET, s. [a bag or pouch] *bolgia, valigia, s. f.*
BU'DGET, s. [store, stock] *provvisione, capitale.*
BUFF, s. [a wild ox] *búfolo, s. m. animal noto da giogo.*
Buff [leather of buff] *cuojo di bufolo.*
Buff-coat, *un abito fatto di cuojo di bufolo.*
Blind-man's-buff, *il giuoco della cieca.*
To BUFF, [to strike] *percuotere.* J.
BUFFALO, [a kind of wild ox] *bufalo.*
BU'FFET, s. [a blow, a box on the ear] *schiaffo, s. m. guanciata, s. f.*

Buffet [cupboard, repository for plate, China ware, &c.] *credenza, credenziera, s. f. armádio, s. m. quel luogo dove si distendon i piatelli e l'argenteria per lo servigio della tavola.*
To BUFEET, verb act. *schiaffeggiare.*
BU'FFETTED, adj. *schiaffeggiato.*
BU'FFLE, *v.* Buffalo.
Buffle-head, *un minchione, un balordo, uno sciocco, un pecorne.*
To BU'FFLE, v. n. [to puzzle] *imbrogliarsi.* Swift.
BUFF'OON, s. [merry jester] *buffone, giullare, s. m. uno che ha a per professione il trattener con buffonerie.*
To play the buffoon, *buffonare, buffoneggiare fare il buffone.*
Buffoon-like, *buffonesco, piacevole, grazioso.*
BUFFOONERY, s. *buffoneria, buffa, burla, beffa, baja, s. f.*
BUG, s. [an insect] *cimice, s. m.*
A may-bug, *bruco, s. m. spezie d'insetto volatile.*
Bug words, *parole fiere.*
Death is a bug word, *la morte è una parola terribile.*
Bugbear, *fantasima, befana, s. f. spaventacchio, s. m.*
To BUGBEAR one, *spaventare alcuno, far paura ad alcuno.*
BU'GGY, adj. [abounding with bugs] *pien di cimici.*
BUGLE [a kind of glass] *una sorta di bigchiere.*
Bugle [an herb] *un' erba che guarisce la piaghe.*
A bugle horn, *corno da caccia.*
BUGLO'SS, s. [a sort of herb] *buglossa, s. f. erba nota.*
To BUILD, verb. act. *fabbricare, edificare.*
Fools build houses, and wise men buy them, *i matti fabbricano le case, e i savi le comprano, casa fatta e vigna posta non si paga quanto costa.*
To build castles in the air, *chimerizzare, ghiribizzare, fantasticare, arzigoglare, fabbricar castelli in aria.*
To build again, *rifabbricare, riedificare.*
To build up, *finire di fabbricare.*
To build a city, *fonaare una città.*
To build upon one, *confidarsi, fidarsi, far capitale di qualcheduno.*
I build upon your word, *mi fido alla vostra parola.*
BUI'LDED, *v.* Built.
BUI'LDER, s. *fabbricatore, s. m. quello che fabbrica.*
A chief, or master builder, *un capomastro di muratori.*
BUI'LDING, s. *fabbricazione, s. f. il fabbricare.*
Building [edifice] *edificio, s. m. casa, fabbrica, s. f.*
The art of building, *l'architettura.*
He hath undone himself by building, *s'è rovinato a fabbricare.*
BUILT [built up] *fabbricato, edificato.*
Dutch built, *malfatto, grossolano fatto all' Olandese.*
BOLB, or bulbe, s. [any root that is round, and wrapped with many skins or

or coats, as onions, tulips, &c.] *bulbo*, s. m. *barba o radice d'alcune piante, la quale diciamo communemente* Cipolla *per la somiglianza che ella ha con essa.*

The bulbe [the apple of the eye] *la pupilla del occhio.*

BULBACEOUS, adj. }
BU'LBOUS } [having a round head in the root] *bulboso, che ha la radice come una cipolla.*

A bulbous plant, *una pianta bulbosa.*

A bulbous root, *una cipolla.*

To BULGE, v. n. [to take in water, to founder] *far acqua, affondarsi, e dicesi delle barche o navi.*

A BU'LIMY, s. [a canine or insatiable appetite] *fame canina o insaziabile, bulima.*

BULK, s. [massiness] *massa, mole*, s. f.

Bulk, s. [bigness] *grandezza, grossezza*, s. f.

To sell one's wares by the bulk, *vendere le sue mercanzie all' ingrosso.*

He has left the bulk of his estate to his son, *egli ha lasciato il grosso de' suoi beni al suo figliuolo.*

A bulk [a stall before a shop] *desco, ceppo*, s. m.

The bulk of a man's body, *tronco, busto*, s. m.

The bulk of a ship, *scaffo, guscio, corpo di naviglio.*

To break bulk, *saccheggiare, o mettere a sacco un vascello.*

Bulk-head, s. [a sea term] *separazione, o spartimento in un vascello fatto di asse.*

To BULK out, *far ventre, piegare innanzi.*

BULKY, adj. [of great size or stature] *grande, grosso, di grande altezza, di grande ampiezza, di statura grande, o grossa.*

Bulky [massy] *massiccio.*

A bulky man [a corpulent man] *un uomo grosso, grasso o corpulento.*

A bulky volume, *un grosso volume.*

Bulky [weighty] *pesante.*

BULL, s. [a beast well known] *toro*, s. m.

Bull's pizzle, *nervo di bue.*

Bull [a pope's brief] *bolla*, s. f.

Bull [an impropriety of speech, a blunder in discourse] *incongruità nel parlare, errore, sbaglio, granchio, granciporro*, s. m.

'Tis a bull to say, *è una sciocchezza il dire.*

To tell one a story of a cock and a bull, *dare della chiacchiere ad uno, dire delle fanfaluche, contar la fola dell' oca, dell' uccellin bel verde.*

Bull-head, *testa di toro.*

Bull-head *piccolo pesce di capo grosso che vive nell' acqua.*

Bull-beef, *carne di toro.*

Bull-beef, [nauseous woman] *befana, donna brutta e contraffatta.*

Bull-beggar, *spaventacchio*, s. m. *fantasma.*

Bull fly or bull-bee, *tafáno*, s. m. *insetto volatile, simile alla mosca, ma alquanto più lungo.*

Bull-finch, *monachino, pincione, nome d' uccelletto.*

Bull-baiting, *combattimento di cani con un toro.*

Bull-dog, *cane allevato apposta per combattere co' tori, cane da torro.*

Bull-feast, *combattimento di tori.*

BULLACE-TREE, *sorta di prugnolo salvatico*, s. m.

BU'LLEN, s. [hemp stalks pilled] *fracidume de lino.*

BU'LLENGER, s. [a small sea vessel or boat] *una filucca.*

BU'LLET, s. [a ball of lead or iron, to be fired out of a musket, pistol, or cannon] *palla di moschetto, pistola, o cannone.*

BU'LLION, s. [uncoined gold or silver in the mass] *oro o argento in verghe, non monetato.*

Bullion of copper [copper plates set on the breast leathers and bridles of horses for ornament] *piastre d'ottone che si mettono per ornamento al pettorale e briglia de' cavalli.*

BULLI'TION, s. *bollimento, il bollire.*

BULLOCK, s. [a young bull] *un torello, un giovenco, un bue giovine.*

BU'LLY, or bully-rock, s. [a hectoring, boisterous fellow] *uno spadaccino, un bravo, uno sgerro, un brigante, un tagliacantoni, un mangiaferro.*

A bully-gamester, *un truffatore.*

To BULLY, [to overbear with noise or menaces] *far il bravaccio, braveggiare, andar addosso ad uno con istrepito e minacce.*

BU'LRUSH, s. *giunco*, s. m.

Bulrush bed, *giuncaja*, s. f. *giuncheto*, s. m.

To cover with bulrushes, *coprir di giunchi.*

Covered with bulrushes, *coperto di giunchi.*

BU'LWARK, s. [a bastion, rampart, or fort] *baluardo, bastione*, s. f.

To BUL'WARK, [to fortify] *fortificare.*

BUM, s. [the part on which we sit] *il sedere, il deretano.*

Bum-bailiff, *uno sbirro.*

BUM'BARD, s. v. Bombard.

BU'MBAST, v. Bombast.

BUMBA'STICK, v. Bombastick.

Bump [swelling, protuberance] *gonfiamento, protuberanza.*

To BUMP, [to make a loud noise] *far un romor grande.*

BU'MPER, s. [brimmer] *un bicchiere pieno o traboccante.*

BUMPKIN, s. [an aukward heavy rustick] *un contadinaccio sciocco.*

BU'MPKINLY, adj. [having the manner or appearance of a clown] *zotico, che ha maniere zotiche e da contadinaccio.*

BUN, s. *spezie di focaccia, o di ciambella*, s. f.

BUNCH, s. [on the back] *gobba*, s. f. *gobbo, scrigno*, s. m.

Bunch [of any thing tied together] *mazzo, fascio*, s. m. *ciocca*, s. f.

A bunch of keys, *un mazzo di chiavi.*

A bunch of radishes, *un mazzo di ravanelli.*

Bunch of grapes, *grappolo d'uva.*

A bunch of cherries, *una ciocca di ciriege.*

A bunch of little sticks, *un fastello.*

A bunch of feathers, *un pennocchio.*

Bunch [knot of a tree] *nodo, nocchio*, s. m.

BU'NCHY, or bunch back'd, *gobbo, che ha lo scrigno.*

To BUNCH out, verb. neut. *gonfiarsi a modo d'una gobba.*

BU'NDLE, s. [a parcel of things bound together] *fagotto, fardello*, s. m. *ravvolto di panni e d' altre materie simili.*

A bundle of cloaths, *un fagotto o fardello di panni.*

A bundle of rods, *un fastello di verghe.*

A little bundle, *un fardelletto, un fardellino.*

To BUNDLE, [to make up into a bundle] *affardellare, affastellare, far fastello.*

BUNG, s. *occhiume*, s. m. *quel turacciolo di legno, che tura la buca donde s'empie la botte.*

To stop with a bung, *turare con cocchiume.*

Bung-hole, *cocchiume, la buca della botte.*

Bung [of a piece of ordnance] *turaccio*, s. m.

BUNGLE, s. *sbaglio*, s. m. *marrone*, s. m.

To BU'NGLE [to do any thing aukwardly, to cobble] *acciabattare, fare che che si sia alla grossa e senza diligenza, abborracciare, acciarpare.*

BU'NGLED, adj. *acciabattato, abborracciato, acciarpato.*

BU'NGLER, s. [an aukward or paltry workman] *un goffo, un balordo, uno sciocco, un minchione.*

A bungler at play, *un gonzo al giuoco.*

BU'NGLINGLY, adv. [bungler like] *goffamente, grossolanamente, scioccamente, alla peggio.*

BUNN, v. Bun.

BUNT, s. [the middle part of the sail, which is purposely formed into a kind of bag, that the sail may receive more wind] *il fondo della vela.*

Bunt lines, s. [a sea term, small ropes in a ship made fast to the bottoms of the sails in the middle part of the belt rope, to hale the bunt of the sail, for the better furling it up] *funicelle che sono legate all' orlo delle vele le quali servono per ammainarle.*

BU'NTER, s. [a gatherer of rags in the streets for the making of paper] *quello che va cogliendo i cenci per le strade per farne della carta.*

A bunter, s. f. *una puttanella, una donnetta sfacciata.*

BU'NTING, s. [a kind of bird] *una calandra.*

BUOY, s. [a log of wood, barrel, or the like tied to an anchor when it is cast in the sea, so as to float over it, and show whereabout the anchor lies] *gavitello*, s. m. *pezzo di legno o altra cosa la quale galleggiando mostri dove s'è gettata l' áncora.*

To Buoy, v. a. [to keep a float] *galleggiare, ſtar a galla.*

To Buoy, v. n. to float, *nuotare, galleggiare.*

To Buoy one up, *ſoſtenere, proteggere, ſpalleggiare alcuno,* preſ. *ſoſtengo,* pret. *ſoſtenni.*

BUOY'D UP, adj. *ſoſtenuto, protetto, ſpalleggiato.*

BU'OYANCY, s. *loſtare a galla, il galleggiare.*

BUO'YANT, adj. [which will not ſink] *galleggiante, che non va al fondo.*

BUR, or Burdock, s. *láppola,* s. f. *erba, che nella ſommità ha certi quaſi ſpini i quali molto s' appiccano alle veſtimenta.*

To ſtick together like burs, *appiccarſi come lappole.*

BU'RBOT, s. *ſorta di peſce pien di ſpine.*

BU'RDEN, s. [or load] *ſoma, ſalma,* s. f. *carico, peſo,* s. m. *ſcriveſi meglio* Burthen.

A heavy burden, *una ſoma peſante.*

His life was a burden to him, *la vita gli era venuta in faſtidio.*

A beaſt of burden, *una beſtia da ſoma, da baſto.*

A ſhip of burden, *una nave da carico.*

The burden of a ſong, *ripetizione nel fine della canzone, chiuſa di canzone o di ſtanza;* ritornello, s. m.

To lay down a burden, *ſcaricare, metter giù il carico.*

To BURDEN [to load] *caricare.*

BU'RDENED, adj. *caricato.*

BU'RDENOUS, adj. [grievous, oppreſſive] *grave, peſante, oppreſſivo.*

Burdenous, adj. [uſeleſs] *di niun uſo.*

BU'RDENSOME, adj. *peſante, grave, incomodo.*

BUREA'U, s. [a cheſt of drawers] *ſegreteria, caſſettone, armário,* according to the different ſorts.

BURG, *v.* Burrow.

BU'RGAMOT, s. *ſpezie di pera.*

BURGANET, s. [a ſort of helmet] *borgognotta,* s. f. *ſorta di celata, che cuopre ſolamente la teſta con un ferro che ſcende poi ſopra'l naſo.*

BURGEO'IS, s. *cittadino, borgheſe.*

BU'RGESS, s. [an inhabitant of a borough] *borgeſe, borgheſe, cittadino,* s. f.

Burgeſs [in the houſe of commons] *membro di parlamento; o deputato d'una cittadinanza.*

Of or belonging to a burgeſs, *cittadineſco, da cittadino.*

BURGH, *v.* Borough.

BU'RGHER, s. *borgeſe, borgheſe, cittadino; che ha certi privilegi.*

BU'RGHERSHIP, s. *cittadinanza.*

BU'RGLARY, s. [robbing a houſe by night, or breaking in with an intent to rob] *il delitto del rubar una caſa in tempo di notte, o d' entrarvi dentro per rottura con intenzione di rubare.*

BURGOMA'STER, s. [a chief magiſtrate in ſome parts beyond ſea] *borgomaſtro,* s. m. *ſpezie di magiſtrato.*

BU'RIAL, s. [from to bury] *ſepoltura, eſequie,* s. f.

To give the dead a chriſtian burial, *ſepellire morti in luogo ſagrato.*

To deny one a chriſtian burial, *privare alcuno della ſepoltura.*

Burial ſolemnities, *eſequie, pompa di mortorio.*

A burial place, *cimiterio, luogo ſagrato dove ſi ſepelliſcono i morti.*

Burial, *mortorio, e mortoro,* s m. *onoranza, o cerimonia nel ſepellire i morti.*

BU'RIED, *v.* Bury'd.

BU'RIER, s. [he that buries] *beccamorto, becchino.*

BU'RIN, s. [a graving tool] *bulino, o bolino,* s. m. *ſorta di ſtrumento colla punta d' acciajo col quale s'intaglia oro, argento, rame, e ſimili metalli.*

BURLE'SQUE, adj. [comical] *burleſco, burlevole.*

A burleſque poet, or ſtyle, *un poeta o ſtile burleſco.*

A burleſque expreſſion, *una eſpreſſione burleſca.*

BU'RLY, adj. [big, fat] *groſſo, graſſo, corpecciuto.*

A burly man, *un uomo groſſo o corpacciuto.*

To BURN [to conſume with fire] *abbruciare, bruciare, ſcottare, ardere.* pret. *arſi.*

To burn wood or coals, *abbruciare delle legna, o del carbone.*

To burn day-light, *accender la candela nel giorno.*

To burn one alive, *abbruciare alcuno vivo.*

To burn one's ſelf, *abbruciarſi, bruciarſi.*

To burn one's fingers, *ſcottarſi le dita.*

To burn away, verb. neut. *bruciarſi, conſumarſi.*

To burn to aſhes, *ridurre in cenere.*

To burn one in the hand, *bruciar uno nella mano per infamia, bollarlo.*

To burn up, *bruciare affatto, conſumare.*

To burn up the graſs, *bruciar le ſtoppie ne' campi.*

To burn faint and dim, *far poco lume, far barlume.*

BURNED, *v.* Burnt.

BU'RNET, s. [a kind of herb] *pimpinella,* s. f.

BU'RNING, s. *ſcottatura,* s. f. *lo ſcottarſi.*

Burning [great fire] *incendio.*

This meat ſmells of burning, *queſta carne ſa nell' abbruſtolato.*

I feel a great burning in my wound, *ſento un grande ſpaſimo nella mia piaga.*

Burning, adj. *abbruciante, caldo.*

A burning heat, *un caldo abbruciante, ardore, caldo eccesſivo.*

A burning iron, *un ferro infocato.*

Burning coals, *brace, carboni acceſi.*

'Tis a burning ſhame, *queſta è una gran vergogna.*

To BU'RNISH [to poliſh] *brunire, dare il luſtro,* preſ. *bruniſco.*

To burniſh a piece of ſilver plate, *brunire dell' argenteria.*

To burniſh [to grow big] *creſcere,* preſ. *creſco.* pret. *crebbi.*

This child begins to burniſh, *queſto fanciullo comincia a creſcere.*

BU'RNISHED, adj. *brunito creſciuto.*

BU'RNISHER, s. *brunitore,* s. m. *quello che bruniſce.*

BU'RNISHING, s. *il brunire.*

A burniſhing ſtick, *pezzo di legno col quale ſi bruniſce.*

BURNT, adj. [from to burn] *abbruciato, bruciato, ſcottato, arſo*

A burnt offering or ſacrifice, *un olocauſto, tutto'l ſacrificio.*

Burnt out, *abbruciato, conſumato, arſo.*

Burnt up, as graſs, *ſecco, arido, inaridito.*

Burnt to aſhes, *ridotto in cenere.*

A burnt dog dreads the fire, *cane ſcottato teme l' acqua fredda.*

Sun-burnt, *abbronzato.*

BURR, s. [the round knob of horn round a deer's head] *la radice delle corna del cervo.*

Burr [burdock] *lappola,* s. f.

A great burr, *lappolone,* s. m.

BU'RREL, s. [a kind of pear] *ſpezie di pero.*

Burrel fly, s. *taſáno,* s. m.

BU'RROUGH, s. [borough] *borgo,* s. m.

Coney-burrough, *tana di coniglio.*

Burrough [covert] *coperta, copertura,* s. f.

To BU'RROUGH, *intanarſi.*

BU'RROW, *v.* Burrough.

BU'RSAR, s. *teſoriere d' un collegio.*

BURSE, s. [exchange] *borſa,* s. f. *luogo dove i mercanti s' adunano per trattare de' loro negozi.*

BU'RSER, s. *teſoriero d' un collegio.*

BURST, adj. *crepato.*

Burſt belly'd, *rotto allentato, crepato.*

To BURST, verb. act. & neut. *crepare, ſcoppiare.*

I am ready to burſt, *mi ſento crepare.*

To burſt one's belly with over eating, *creparſi di mangiare.*

To burſt with envy, *roderſi d' invidia.*

To burſt with laughing, *ſcoppiare o morir delle riſa.*

To burſt forth in tears, *pianger dirottamente, ſtruggerſi in lagrime.*

To burſt out into laughter, *ſmaſcellare delle riſa.*

BU'RSTEN, adj. *rotto, allentato, crepato.*

BU'RSTENESS, s. *ernia, rottura, crepatura,* s. f.

BURT, s. [a flat ſort of fiſh] *linguáttola,* s. f. *ſpezie di peſce piatto.*

BU'RTHEN, *v.* Burden.

BU'RY, s. [a termination added to the names of towns, and is the ſame with borough] *borgo,* s. m.

Bury, s. [a dwelling place] *dimora, abitazione.*

To BURY, *ſeppellire, ſotterare.* preſ. *ſeppelliſco.*

To bury one alive, *ſeppellire uno vivo.*

To bury in oblivion, *mettere in obblio*

If ever I bury him, *caſo che muoia prima di me.*

BU'RY'D, adj. *ſeppellito, ſotterrato, ſepolto.*

Bu'rying, s. *il seppellire.*

A burying place, *sepolcro*, s. m. *sepoltura*, s. f.

Bush, s. *cespuglio*, s. m. *fratta*, s. f.

A gooseberry bush, *ribes*, s. m.

Either a bush or a brake, *passa o s'annega.*

To go about the bush, *menar il can per l'aja.*

A tavern bush, *frasca*, s. f.

Good wine needs no bush, *al buon vino non bisogna frasca.*

A bush of hair, *capellamento, ciuffo di capelli*, s. m. *capellatura*, s. f.

Bush [a fox tail] *coda di volpe.*

One bird in hand is worth two in the bush, *meglio è fringuello in man che in frasca tordo.*

To Bush [to grow thick] *diventar folto, ingrossare.*

Bu'shel, s. [strike; a dry measure] *stajo*, s. m.

To measure another man's corn by one's own bushel, *misurare gli altri col suo passetto.*

Bu'shy, adj. [full of bushes] *cespuglioso, pien di cespugli.*

He has a bushy beard, *egli ha una barba folta, egli è barbuto.*

Bu'sied, *affaccendato.*

Bu'sless, adj. [at leisure] *sfaccendato, scioperato, agiato, che non ha faccende.*

Bu'sily, adv. *sollecitamente, con sollecitudine, accuratamente, diligentemente, ardentemente, foscamente.*

Bu'siness, s. *affare, negozio, fatto, faccenda.*

Mind your business, *badate a' fatte vostre.*

To be full of business, *esser occupato, o affaccendato.*

To be always about some business or other, *aver sempre qualche cosa per le mani, aver sempre che fare.*

A man fit for business, *un uomo d'affare, un uomo pratico o versato negli affari.*

I'll make it my business to serve you, *porrò ogni mio ingegno per servirvi.*

That is not our business, *questo non aspetta a noi.*

Let us come to the business in hand, *torniamo a quel che fa per noi, torniamo al nostro discorso, al fatto di cui discorrevamo prima.*

To manage business, *trattare, o condurre un negozio.*

To do one's business, *andar del corpo.*

He betook himself to the business of a merchant, *s'applicò alla mercatatura.*

The business is done, there is no going back, *il dado è tratto, non è più tempo di dir di no.*

My business is done, I am a dead man, *sono spedito, son morto, è finita per me.*

I have some business in hand, *sono affaccendato, ho un affare per le mani.*

What business have you here? *che avete voi a fare qui?*

To come into business, *avere degli affari, far faccende, essere in voga.*

A hanging business, *un delitto capitale.*

The business will be how to let him know it, *il punto sarà come fare per avvertirnelo.*

Busk, s. [a piece of whalebone, wood, or iron, to keep down the fore part of womens stays] *stecca*, s. f.

Bu'skin, s. [a kind of boots] *borzacchino, stivaletto, coturno*, s. m.

Bu'sky, adj. [woody] *selvoso.*

Buss, s. [kiss] *bacio*, s. m.

Buss [a small sea vessel] *una fusta.*

To Buss [to kiss] *baciare.*

Bussed, adj. *baciato.*

Bu'ssing, s. *il baciare.*

Bust, s [a statue representing only the head, breast, and shoulders of a human body] *busto*, s. m.

Bu'stard, s. [a wild turkey] *gallo d'India salvatico.*

Bu'stle, s. [stir] *strepito, fracasso, rumore*, s. m.

To make a bustle in the world, *esser rinomato nel mondo.*

A man of bustle, *un uomo affaccendato, intrigante, o industrioso.*

To bustle, verb. neut. *strepitare, fare strepito.*

Bu'stler, s. [an active stirring man] *un uomo attivo, un faccendone.*

Bu'stling, s. *fracasso, rumore, strepito*, s. m.

Bu'sy'd, adj. *occupato, affaccendato.*

Bu'sy, adj. *affaccendato, occupato, impegnato.*

I am very busy now, *sono molto affaccendato adesso.*

Busy at work, *assiduo o occupato a lavorare.*

A busy day, *un giorno d'affari.*

A busy body, *un affannone, quegli, che d'ogni cosa si piglia briga, un ser faccenda, uome che volentieri s'intriga in ogni cosa, un ciarpone, un imbroglione.*

To busy one's self, *impacciarsi, pigliarsi briga, travagliarsi, intromettersi.*

But, *ma.*

I went to see him, but he was not at home, *andai per vederlo, ma non era in casa.*

But [except, before, before that] *che, fuorchè.*

He does nothing but cry, *non fa altro che piangere.*

Every body left him but I, *tutti l'abbandonarono fuor ché io.*

England abounds in every thing but wine, *dal vino in fuori l'Inghilterra abbonda d'ogni cosa.*

He is nothing but skin and bones, *non ha che la pelle e l'ossa.*

There's no day almost but he comes to my house, *non passa quasi giorno che non venga da me.*

But that [were it not that] *se non fosse che.*

What ails you but that you may do it? *che v'impedisce di farlo?*

Not but that, *non che.*

But [only] *solamente.*

If you would but take the pains to go thither, *se voleste, solamente darvi l'incommodo d'andarvi.*

Be but ruled by me, *pigliate il mio consiglio.*

But one word, *une parola solamente.*

I do not doubt but he will come to-morrow, *non dubito che non venga domani.*

They all came but you two, *tutti vennero fuor che voi due.*

If we do but reflect upon it, *se vogliamo rifleterre sopra cio.*

Your demand is but reasonable, *la vostra richiesta è ragionevole.*

I cannot but bemoan his misfortune, *non posso far di meno di non compiagnere la sua disgrazia.*

But a while since, *poco fà.*

He is but gone, *è appunto andato via, partì testè.*

But yet, *nientedimeno, però.*

The last but one, *il penultimo.*

There wanted little but he had struck him, *poco mancò che non lo battesse.*

If you do but take my part, *purchè voi pigliate la mia parte.*

You cannot but know, *voi non potete ignorare.*

There's none but is afraid of you, *non v'è nessuno che non abbia paura di voi.*

No question but he will do it, *lo farà senza dubbio.*

There is nothing so good but what may be abused, *non v'è cosa per buona che sia che non sia soggetta ad essere corrotta.*

But if, *se non.*

But rather, *più tosto.*

But, s. [a boundary] *limite, confine.*

But, s. [in sea language, the end of any plank which joins to another] *termine marinaresco, e vale quella morsa che si lascia in un asse onde s'unisca a un' altra.*

But-end, s. [the blunt end of any thing] *la punta piatta d'ogni cosa.*

Bu'tcher, s. *beccajo, macellajo*, s. m.

Butcher's meat, *carne grossa, carne di beccherìa.*

Butcher's broom, *pugnitópo*, s. m. *pianta salvàtica così detta.*

Butcher's shop, *macello*, s. m. *beccheria*, s. f.

To Butcher, verb act. *macellare.*

To butcher [to kill] *assassinare, uccidere, tagliar a pezzi.*

Bu'tchered, adj. *assassinato, ucciso, tagliato a pezzi.*

Bu'tcherly, adj. [cruel, bloody barbarous] *crudèle sanguinário, bárbaro, inumáno.*

Bu'tchery, s. *beccheria, uccisione*, s. f. *macello, ammazzamento.*

Bu'tler, s. *canovajo, dispensiere*, s. m.

Bu'tlerage, s. *dazio sul vino.*

Butt, s. [a large vessel for liquids] *botte*, s. f.

Butt [bound] *limite*, s. m.

Butt [a mark to shoot at] *bersaglio, mira, segno dove li arcieri o altri tiratori dirizzan la mira per aggiustare il tiro.*

To meet one full butt, *incontrare alcuno testa contro testa, cozzare.*

To run full butt at one, *dar della testa contro ad alcuno correndo, dar di cozzo.*

The butt end of a thing, *l'estremità di che che sia.*

The butt end of a musket, *il calcio d' uno schioppo.*

To BUTT [to run against or push with the horns] *cozzare, il percuotere che fanno gli animali cornuti colle corna.*

To butt at one, *cozzare o urtare alcuno.*

BU'TTED, adj. *cozzato.*

BU'TTENS, s. [the burrs or knobs of a deer's head] *le radici delle corna del cervo.*

BU'TTER, s. *butirro, burro,* s. m.

Fresh or new butter, *butirro fresco, burro fresco.*

My money melts like butter against the sun, *la mia borsa non ha fondo, spendo tutto.*

Butter milk, *latte di butirro.*

Butter sawce, *salsa con butirro.*

Butter woman, *donna che fa o vende del butirro.*

Butter-pot, *vaso da butirro.*

Butter-bump [a bird] *grotto,* s. m. *nome d'uccello.*

Butter-burr, s. [an herb] *tignamica,* s. f. *erba salvatica,*

Butter-teeth [great broad fool teeth] *i denti d'avanti.*

Butter-box [a great eater of butter] *un gran mangiatore di butirro.*

To BU'TTER, verb. act. *condire con butirro.*

To butter bread, *ugnere il pane con butirro.*

To butter [to double at play] *truffare al giuoco.*

BU'TTERED, adj. *condito o unto con butirro.*

He knows on which side the bread is buttered, *non è sciocco, non da facilmente nella rete.*

BU'TTERFLY, s. *farfalla, parpaglione, insetto che vola di varie spezie.*

BU'TTERMILK, s. [the whey that is separated from the cream when butter is made] *sero di latte.*

BU'TTERPRINT, s. [a piece of carved wood used to mark butter] *pezzo di legno intagliato che serve a marcare il butirro.*

BU'TTERY, s. [a place where victuals are kept] *dispensa,* s. f. *stanza dove si tengono le cose da mangiare.*

BU'TTOCK, s. [the breech or the haunch] *chiappa nattica,* s. f.

The buttocks of a horse, *la groppa d' un cavallo.*

Buttock of beef, *lombo,* s. m. *la parte carnosa che è sopra la groppa d' un bue.*

Buttock [that part of a ship which makes her breadth right astern from the tuck upwards] *castello di poppa d'un vascello, la parte piu rilevata del vascello verso la poppa.*

That has large butlocks, *naticuto, che ha grosse natiche.*

BU'TTON, s. [a fastening for garments] *bottone,* s. m.

Button [in plants] *bottone,* s. m, *boccia,* s. f.

Handkerchief-buttons, *fiocchi di fazzoletto.*

'Tis not worth a button, *non val nulla, non vale un fico.*

Button-hole, *occhiello,* s. m. *bottoniera,* s. f. *quel piccolo pertugio, che si fa nelle vestimenta e nel quale entra il bottone.*

Button-maker, *bottonajo,* s. m.

A little button, *bottoncello, bottoncino,* s. m.

To BU'TTON [to fasten with buttons] *abbottonare.*

BU'TTONING, s. *abbottonamento,* s. m. *l'abbottonare.*

BU'TTRESS, s. [an arch or mass of stone to bear up a wall, a building, &c.] *barbacane,* s. m. *parte della muraglia fatta a scarpa per sicurezza e fortezza.*

Buttress, s. [support] *appoggio, sostegno, puntello,* s. m.

Buttress [a farrier's tool] *curasnetta,* s. m. *incastro,* s. m. *strumento di ferro tagliente per pareggiare l' unghie alle bestie.*

BU'TWING, s. [a bird] *capinéra,* s. f.

BUTYRA'CEOUS, adj, *butirroso, che ha qualità simili al butirro.*

BU'TYROUS, adj. *butirroso, che ha della natura del butirro.*

BU'XOM, adj. [pliant, obedient] *obbediente, docile, trattabile, benigno, pieghevole, amoroso.*

Buxom [merry] *allegro giocondo. gajo, festoso, giojoso, lieto, gioviale, giulivo.*

Buxom [wanton, amorous] *lascivetto.*

The buxom gales, *l' aure lascivette, l' aurette lascive.*

BU'XOMLY, adv. [wantonly, amorously] *amorosamente, in modo lascivetto.*

BU'XOMNESS, s. [lowliness, submission] *obbedienza, docilità, trattabilità, benignità,* s. f. *l' essere amorosa una donna.*

Buxomness [chearfulness] *allegria, gajezza, gioja, giulività, ilarità,* s. f.

To BUY [to purchase] *comperare e comprare.*

To buy with ready money, *comprare a donari contanti.*

To buy upon trust, *comperar a credito.*

To buy a pig in a poke, *comperar la gatta in sarco, comperar che che si sia senza vederlo.*

To buy a thing at the best hand, *comperar da quelli che vendono a buon mercato, comprar di prima mano.*

To buy one off, *guadagnare alcuno, farselo amico con donativi, corromperlo con donativi.*

To buy and sell, *trafficare, negoziare.*

BU'YER, s. [chapman] *compratore,* s. m. *che compera.*

BUYING, s. *comperamento, e compramento,* s. m. *il comperare.*

To BUZZ [to hum and make a noise as bees, hornets, wasps, and the like] *susurrare, mormorare, bisbigliare, rombare, ronzare come le pecchie, i calabroni, le vespe e simili.*

To buzz into one's ear, *soffiar negli orecchi ad alcuno.*

BUZZ, s. *ronzo, bisbiglio, sussurro, mormorio, come quello che fanno le api, o i calabroni, e le vespe, e per metafora, il cianciare, il bisbigliare.*

BU'ZZARD, s. [a sort of great hawk or kite] *abuzzago, bozzago,* s. m. *uccel di rapina simile al nibbio.*

Buzzard [a senseless fellow, an ignorant fool] *un minchione, un balardo, uno sciocco, uno scioperato.*

To be betwixt a hawk and a buzzard, *esser tra l' incudine e il martello, aver mal fare da tutte le bande.*

BU'ZZER, s. [a secret whisperer] *uno che ti vienne a dir qualche cosa piano all' orecchio.*

BU'ZZING, s. *susurro, ronzo,* s. m.

BY, prep. *per.*

By this place, *per questo luogo, per quà.*

By good luck, *per buona sorte.*

By chance, *per accidente.*

By, *da, dal, di.*

He was slain by Achilles, *fu ucciso da Achille.*

He is beloved by every body, *è amato da ognuno.*

By day, *di giorno.*

By much, *di molto.*

Bigger by two foot, *piu grande di due piedi; due piedi più grande.*

By birth, *di nascita.*

What will you get by that? *che frutto ricavarai da cio.*

By trade a hatter, *del mestiere di cappellajo.*

By, *a, al.*

I shall be back again by one o'clock, *ritornerò a un' ora.*

It is three by my watch, *sono le tre al mio oriuolo.*

By one's self, by itself, by himself, by herself, by themselves, *solo, sola, soli, sole.*

By such a token, *per segnale.*

Turned by the lath, *lavorato al tornio.*

By candle-light, *al lume di candela, alla candela.*

By favour of the night, *col favore della notte.*

By break of day, *sul far del giorno.*

To do by others as we would be done by, *fare ad altri quel che vorresti fatto a te.*

One by one, *uno ad uno.*

I have it by me, *non l'ho meco.*

I have it not by me, *non l'ho addosso, non l'ho, non l'ho qui.*

By, *vicino, appresso, a canto, a lato.*

To sit by one, *sedersi vicino ad uno.*

By the church, *appresso della chiesa.*

Hard by, *quì vicino.*

By the time you come again, *quando ritornerete.*

By the time I got half way thither it was dark; *appena fui a mezza strada, che s' annottò, che si fe bujo.*

He must be back again by Monday, *bisogna che ritorni Lunedì prossimo.*

Doubtless he is dead by this time, *bisogna che sia morto a quest' ora.*

By this time twelve month, *da quì a un anno.*

Be ruled by me, *pigliate il mio consiglio.*

To take example by one, *seguitare l' esempio di qualcheduno.*

I found much good by it, *m'ha giovato molto.*

He went by the name of John, *prese il nome di Giovanni, si spacciò per Giovanni.*

By degrees, *poco a poco.*

Day by day, *di giorno in giorno.*

By all means, *senza dubbio, certamente.*

By no means, *in conto nessuno.*

By reason that, *perchè, a causa che.*

By course, by turns, *in giro.*

He is by himself, *egli è solo.*

By retail, *a minuto.*

We will do the rest by ourselves, *faremo il resto da noi stessi.*

Cæsar got glory by giving, *Cesare si rese glorioso col dare.*

The flame increases by moving the torch, *la fiamma cresce coll' agitar la fiaccola.*

I took my journey by Paris, *presi il cammino per Parigi.*

I shall speak of it only by the by, *parlerò di cio transitoriamente.*

Which things I shall by the way touch in the fifth book, *le quali cose io toccherò, o accennerò nel quinto libro.*

I handled that only by the way, *ho voluto solamente accennarlo.*

By and by, *adesso adesso.*

To be by [to stand by] *essere presente.*

To stand by one, *spalleggiare, proteggere, assistere uno, pigliar le parti d'uno.*

A by street, *una strada fuor di mano, una stradella.*

A by place, *un luogo fuor di mano.*

By stealth, *furtivamente.*

By chance, *a caso, casualmente.*

A by respect, *un secondo fine.*

A by law, *statuto, legge municipale.*

By-stander, *spettatore,* s. m.

By gains, *mancia,* s. m.

A by word, *un motto.*

A by town, *terra, o borgo un poco fuor di strada.*

BYE, s. *abitazione.*

BY'LANDER, s. [a small, swift sailing vessel, so called for its coasting, as it were *by land*] *balandra,* s. f. *spezie di filucca.*

C.

C, *Questa lettera in Inglese ha tre suoni. Il primo duro come la nostra Italiana quando è unita col* A, O, U, *come in* CALL, CLOCK, CORN, CROWN, CUR; *il secondo come una* S *dolcemente pronunziata, come in* CESSATION, CINDER, CYPRESS; *e il terzo stiacciato quasi come la nostra sillabi* ci, *e questo quando è seguita da un* h, *come in* CHARGE, CHEEK, CHILD, CHOICE, CHURCH. *Avvertasi però che questo ultimo suono non lo ritiene costantemente nelle parole derivanti dal Greco e dal Latino, come in* CHARACTER, CHIMERICAL, CHOROGRAPHICAL, CHRONICLE, CHYMISTRY, *o in quelle addottate dal moderno Franzese, come* CHAISE, CAPUCHIN, *che si pronunciano come in Italiano si sarebbe* SCE'S, CAPUSCI'N.

CA'BAL, s. [a secret science which the Rabbins pretend to, by which they unfold all the mysteries in divinity, and expound the scriptures] *cábala,* s. f. *scienza di cose occulte colla quale i Rabbini pretendono interpretare i misteri della teologia e spiegare la scrittura.*

Cabal [private council] *macchinazione, cospirazione, congiura, prattica,* s. f.

Cabal [party, set, gang] *partito,* s. m. *brigata, banda, coorte,* s. f.

To CABAL [to plot together, to make parties] *far cabale, macchinare, cospirare, congiurare, ordir delle prattiche.*

CA'BALIST, s. [one skilled in the tradition of the Hebrews] *cabalista, uomo versato nelle tradizioni Giudaiche.*

CABALI'STICK, } adj. [belonging
CABALI'STICAL, } to the Jewish cabal] *cabalistico, di cabala.*

CABA'LLER, s. [he that engages in close designs; an intriguer] *colui che s'impaccia in faccende segrete, un brigante.*

CABALLI'NE, adj. *cavallino, appartenente a cavallo.*

Caballine aloes [a coarser sort of aloes used by farriers to purge horses] *aloe cavallino, e si usa per medicina de' cavalli.*

CA'BBAGE, s. [a plant] *cávolo.*

Cole cabbage, *una delle spezie del cavolo,* s. m.

Cabbage head, *cesto di cavolo.*

Cabbage lettice, *lattuga capuccia.*

The cabbage of a deer's-head, *la radire delle corna d'un cervo.*

Taylor's cabbage, *ritagli di sarto, que' ritagli che il sarto di ruba.*

To CA'BBAGE [to steal in cutting clothes] *rubare i ritagli del panno, come fanno i garzoni de' sartori che con facezia degna d' essi dicono che il danaro ricavato da que' rubati ritagli serve loro per comprare i cavoli da mangiare col loro bue salato.*

CA'BIN, s. [a little lodging room in a ship] *camorino in un vascello.*

Cabin [cottage, hut] *capanna,* s. f.

Cabin [a small room] *gabinetto,* s. m.

Cabin [a tent] *tenda; barracca da soldati.*

Cabin-boy, s. *un mozzo di vascello.*

CA'BINET, s. [a closet in a palace, or noble-house] *gabinetto,* s. m. *stanza intima.*

The cabinet council, *il gabinetto, i segreti, i misteri della corte.*

Cabinet [a casket to put things of value in] *gabinetto, stipo,* s. m. *cassettina,* s. f.

Cabinet organ [a small portable organ] *organo portatile.*

CABINET-MAKER, s. *falegname che non fa che lavori fini e di prezzo. In alcuni luoghi d'Italia chi fa quel mestiero che gl' Inglesi chiamano* cabinet-maker *è chiamato* ebanista.

CABLE, s. [a great rope] *gómona, gomena,* s. f. *il canapo attaccato all' áncora.*

CA'BURNS, s. [small ropes to bind the cables of a ship] *fila colle quali si legano le gomone.*

CACA'O, s. [an Indian tree like an orange tree, bearing nuts, of which chocolate is made] *cacao,* s. m. *sorta d'albero il di cui frutto serve a fare la ciocolata.*

CACHINNA'TION, s. *cachinno,* s. m. *riso smoderato.*

To CA'CKLE [to cry out as a hen does when she has laid her eggs] *quel gridar delle galline quando hanno fatto l'uovo, crocchiare, crocciare.*

CACHO'MY, s. [depravation of the humours in the blood] *caccocimia,* s. f. *guastamento d'umori nel sangue.*

CACO'PHONY, s. *cacofonia,* s. f. *cattivo suono di parole.*

CA'CKRELL, s. [a sort of fish] *sorta di pesce di mare.*

CADAVE'ROUS, adj. *cadaverico.*

CADE, s. [barrel] *barile,* s. m.

A cade of herring, *un barile d'aringhe.*

Cade, adj. *domestico, ma non si usa che in questo senso.* A cade lamb [a young lamb brought up by hand in a house] *un agnello domestico.*

CA'DENCE, } s. [a just fall of the
CA'DENCY, } tone or voice in a sentence] *cadenza, pausa,* s. f.

CA'DET, s. [a younger brother] *minor nato, ultimogenito, figliuolo minore.*

Cadet [one that serves as a volunteer in a war] *un cadetto.*

CADE'W, s. [the straw worm] *spezie di verme che si genera nella paglia.*

CAG, s. [a vessel containing four or five gallons] *carratello, spezie di botte,* s. m.

CAGE, s. [an inclosure for birds] *gabbia*, s. f.

A great cage, *un gabbione*, s. m.

A little cage, *gabbiuola*, *gabbiolina*, s. f.

Cage [jail] *gabbia*, *prigione*, s. f.

To CAGE, *mettere o chiudere in gabbia*.

To CAJO'LE [to flatter, to sooth] *lusingare*, *vezzeggiare*, *piaggiare*, *adulare*.

To cajole [to beguile] *ingannare*.

CAJO'LED, adj. *lusingato*, *vezzeggiato*, *adulato*, *ingannato*, *piaggiato*.

CAJO'LER, s. *lusingatore*, *lusinghiere*, *adulatore*, s. m. *lusingatrice*, *adulatrice*, s. f.

CAJO'LING, s. *lusingamento*, s. m. *il lusingare*, *lusinga*, *carezza*, s. f.

CAITIFF, [scoundrel] *un furfante*, *un furbo*, *uno scellerato*, *un barattiere*, *un gaglioffaccio*, *un mascalzone*.

CAKE, s. [a flat loaf of bread commonly with spice] *focaccia*, *sfogliatà*, s. f.

Cake of coals, *carboni ammassati insieme dal ca'ore del fuoco*.

A wax cake, *una forma di cera*.

To CAKE [as sea coal does] *rappigliarsi come fa il carbon fossile dopo essere stato alquanto nel fuoco. Questa sorta di carbone di terra è poco conosciuta in Italia*.

CAKED, adj. *preso*, *rappigliato*, *rappreso*.

CA'LABASH-tree, *albero della di cui scorza*, *i negri di alune parti d' Africa formano coppe da bere*, *e stromenti musicali al modo loro*.

CALAMI'NE, s. [lapis calaminaris] *sorta di fossile bituminoso*, *che misto col rame lo fa diventare bronzo*.

CA'LAMINT, s [a sort of plant] *calamento*, s. m. *nepitella*, s. f.

Corn calamint, *calamento salvatico*.

Bush or hoary calamint, *calamento montàno*.

CALA'MITOUS, adj. [unfortunate] *calamitoso*, *infelice*, *sfortunato*, *misero*.

CALA'MITY, [misery, misfortune] *calamità*, *infelicità*, *sfortuna*, *miseria*, s. f.

CA'LAMUS, s. *calamo*, s. m. *pianta che ha similitudine colla canna*.

CA'LASH, s. *calesse*, *sorta di sedia a due ruote*.

CA'LCAR, s. [a calcining furnace used by chemists] *fornello da chimico per calcinare i corpi*.

CALCEDO'NIUS, s. *calcedonia*, *sorta di pierra preziosa*.

CALCINA'TION, s. *maniera di ridurre per mezzo del fuoco ogni sorta di corpi in polvere*, *polverizzamento chimico*.

CALCIN'ATORY, s. *vaso usato nel calcinare*.

To CALCINATE, } [to burn to a
To CALCINE, } calx or friable substance] *calcinare*, *ridurre in calcina*.

CALCINA'TED, adj. *calcinato*.

CALCINA'TING, }
CALCINATION, } s. *calcinazione*, s. f.

CALCINED, ad. *calcinato*.

To CALCULATE, [to cast accounts, to reckon] *calcolare*, *compitare*, *contare*.

To calculate a discourse for the meanest capacity, *adattare un discorso al più basso ingegno*.

Religion is calculated to make us happy, *la religione non tende che a renderci felici*.

CALCULA'TED, adj. *calcolato*, *computato*, *contato*.

CALCULA'TING, }
CALCULATION, } s. *calcolo*, *e calculo*, *compito*, *e computo*, *conto*, s. m.

CALCULATOR, s. *un che fa calcoli*; *computista*.

CA'LCULE, s. [reckoning, compute] *conto*, *compùto*.

CALCULO'SE, }
CALCULOUS, } adj. [stony, gritty] *della natura de' calcoli*; *sassoso*, *arenoso*, *sabbioso*.

CA'LCULUS, s. [the stone in the kidneys or bladder] *calcoli*, s. m. pl. *quelle pietre che si generan nelle rene o nella vescica*.

CA'LDRON, s. [a pot; a boiler; a kettle] *caldaja*, *calderotto di diverse grandezze e forme*.

CALEFA'CTION, s. a heating or warming] *calefazione*, s. f. *riscaldamento*.

To CA'LEFY, v. n. [to grow hot, to be heated] *riscaldarsi violentemente*, *e dicesi di cose poste al fuoco*.

CA'LENDER, s. [almanack] *calendario*, *calendaro*, s. m. *quella scrittura nella quale si distinguono i di festivi dai feriali*.

Calender, s. [day book] *diario*, *giornale*, s. m.

Calender, [an insect] *gorgoglióne*, *gorgóglio*, s. m. *baco che è ne' legumi*, *e li vota*.

Calender [an engine to calender with] *màngano*, s. m.

To CA'LENDER, *lisciare*, *sodare*, *manganare*.

To calender cloth, *sodare del panno*, *lisciarlo col màngano*.

CA'LENDERED, adj. *lisciato*, *sodato*.

CA'LENDS, s. [the first day of every month] *calende*, *calendi*, s. f. *il primo giorno de' mesi*.

CA'LENTURE, s. [a burning fever] *febbre maligna*.

CA'LIBER, s. [the bore; the diameter of the barrel of a gun] *calibro*; *diametro del buco d' ogni ame a fuoco*, *come moschetti*, *cannoni*, *e simili*.

CALF, s. pl. calves, [the young of a cow] *vitello*, s. m. *vitella*, s. f. *il parto della vacca*.

Calf's head, *testa di vitello*.

Calf's leather, *pelli di vitella*.

Calf's foot [an herb] *aro*, s. m.

Sea calf, *foca*, s. f. *vecchio marino*, s. m.

Calf's chaldron, *riccio*, *spinosa*, s. m.

A calf [a hart male of the first year] *un daino d' un anno*.

Calf, *la polpa delle gamba*.

CA'LICO, s. [a sort of cloth made of cotton] *sorta di tela di cottone*.

CALI'DITY, s. [heat] *calidità caldezza*, s. f.

CALIGA'TION, s. [dimness, cloudiness] *abbagliamento*, *oscuramento*.

CALI'GINOUS, adj. [obscure, dim] *scuro*, *nugoloso*.

CALI'GRAPHY, s. *caligrafia*, *il formar bene i carrateri nello scrivere*.

CA'LIVER, s. [a sort of small sea cannon] *piccolo cannone per il mare*.

CA'LIX, s. *càlice*, *coppa*.

To CALK [to drive oakum or spun yarn, into all the seams and rends of a ship to keep out the water] *calafatare*, *calefatare*, *ristoppare i navili*.

CALKED, adj. *calafatto*, *calefatàto*.

CA'LKER, s. [he that calks] *calefato*, *m maestro dà calefatare*.

CA'LKING, s. *il calefatare*.

CALL, s. [calling] *chiamata*, *vocazione*, s. f. *chiamamento*, s. m.

To give one a call, *chiamare uno*, *dare una voce ad uno*.

To be ready at a call, *essere sempre in ordine*.

Call [beat of drum] *chiamata*, *battuta di tamburo che chiama a battaglia*.

The call of partridges, *richiamo di pernici*.

To CALL [to name] *chiamare*, *nominare*, *appellare*.

How do you call that? *come chiamate*, *questa cosa?*

To call one by his name, *chiamare uno per nome*.

To call [to give a call, to desire or bid to come] *chiamare*, *dire ad alcuno che venga a te*, *o nominarlo affine che ti risponda*.

Call my man, *chiamatemi il mio servo*.

I call your conscience to witness, *lo lascio alla vostra coscienza*, *n'appello alla vostra coscienza*.

To call [to assemble] *convocare*, *radunare*.

To call a council, *convocare un concilio*.

To call a parliament, *radunare un parlamento*.

To call one names, *ingiuriare*, *svillaneggiare alcuno*.

To call as a partridge does, *cantare come una pernice*.

To call one's game at cards, *dire il suo giuoco*.

To call one in, *chiamar uno dentro*, *dire ad uno d'entrare*.

To call in or back one's word, *rivocare la sua parola*.

To call in one's money, *ritirare il suo danaro*.

To call in one's debts, *esigere i suoi debiti*, *farsi pagare*.

To call in one's word [to recant] *disdirsi*, *dir contro a quel che s' ha detto prima*, *ritrattarsi*.

To call in a law [to recall a law] *rivocare*, *annullare una legge*.

To call in question or into question, *dubitare*, *mettere in dubbio*.

To call one away, *chiamar fuori uno*, *dirgli d' uscire*.

To call one back, *richiamare alcuno*, *farlo ritornare*.

To call off, *dissuadere*, *distornare*, *stornare*,

ſtornare, ſvolgere, diſtogliere, preſ. *diſtolgo*, preſ. *ſvolſi, diſtolſi*.

To call for, *chiàmare, domandare*.

Did he call for me? *m'ha egli chiamato?*

To call for drink, *domandare a bere*.

To call for dinner, *chiamar pel deſinare*.

To call after one, *chiamare uno ad alta voce*.

To call aſide, *chiamare o prendere uno da parte*.

To call aloud, *eſclamare*.

To call forth, *chiamàr fuori, fare uſcire*.

To call together, *adunare, radunare convocare*.

To call to one [to invoke him] *invocare uno, ricorrere ad uno, chiamarlo in teſtimonio*.

I call God to witneſs, *ne prendo Dio in teſtimonio, Iddio m' è teſtimonio*.

To call a thing to mind, or to remembrance, *ricordarſi, ridurſi a memoria, venire in mente*.

To call one to account, *chiamàre uno à conti*.

To call one out, *chiamar fuori uno*.

To call over an aſſembly, *convocare un' aſſemblea*.

To call one up, *chiamàre uno ſu, dire ad uno di ſalire*.

To call one up in the morning, [to wake him] *ſvegliare uno, fàrlo levàre la mattinà*.

To call up ſpirits, *ſcongiurare, coſtrignere, violentàre, i dèmoni o li ſpiriti; fare incantamento*.

To call one down, *chiamàre uno giu, farlo ſcendere, dir ad uno che ſcenda, chè venga giù*.

To call one on, *eſortare, animare, incitare, ſpronare alcuno*.

To call upon one in one's way, *viſitare, andàre a vedere unò per iſtra:a*.

CA'LLAT, s. [a trull] *una bagaſcia*.

CALLED, adj. *chiamata*, v. To Call.

CA'LLET, v. Callet.

CA'LLICO, v. Calico.

CA'LLID, adj. [crafty, cunning] *aſtuto, ſagace, ſcaltro*.

CALLI'DITY, s. [cunningneſs] *aſtuzia, ſagacità*, s. f. *ſcaltrimento*, s. m.

CALLIMA'NCO, s. [a ſort of woollen ſtuff] *ſciámito*, s. m. *ſpezie di drappo di varie ſorte e colori*.

CA'LLING, s [from to call] *chiamamento*, s. m. *il chiamare*.

Calling [vocation] *vocazione*, s. f.

Calling [trade] *vocazione, àrte*, s. f. *meſtiere, ufficio, impiego, eſercizio*, s. m.

CALLO'SITY, s. [hardneſs] *calloſità*, s. f.

CA'LLOUS, adj. [hardened] *calloſo, pien di calli*.

Callous [inſenſible] *duro, inſenſibile*.

CA'LLOUSNESS s. [induration of fibres] *calloſità, lo indurarſi delle fibre*.

Callouſneſs, s. [inſenſibility] *inſenſibilità, durezza*.

CA'LLOW, adj. unfledged, not covered with feathers] *ſpiumato pelato*.

A callow [a young maid] *una ragàzza*.

A callow [a young boy] *uno ſbarbato, un ragazzo*.

CALM, adj. [quiet, ſtill] *calmo, tranquillo*.

Calm ſea, *mare calmo, o tranquillo*.

Calm weather, *calma bonaccia*.

Calm, s. [tranquility, ſerenity, ſtilneſs] *calma, bonaccia, tranquilità*, s. f.

To CALM [to appeaſe, to quiet, to ſtill] *calmare, abbonacciare, placare, ſedare, quietare, acquetare*.

CALMED, adj. *calmato, abbonacciato, placato, ſedato, quietato, acquetato*.

CA'LMER, s. *la perſona o la coſa che ha poſſa di calmare*.

CA'LMING, s. *il calmare*.

CA'LMLY, adv. *tranquillamente, ſedatamente, pacificamente, quietamente*.

CA'LMNESS, s. *calma, tranquilità, bonaccia*, s. f.

CA'LMY, adj. *calmo, in pace, in tranquilitè, calmato*.

CA'LOMEL, s. *mercurio ſublimato ſei volte*.

CA'LORIFICK, adj. [which has the quality of producing heat] *che produce o cagiona caldo*.

CALOT [a lewd woman, a drab] *bagaſcia, puttana*, s. f.

CALOTTE, s. [a leather cap] *baretta*, s. f.

CA'LTROPS. [irons with four ſpikes, ſo made that which way ſoever they fall, one point ſtill lies upwards, generally thrown in breaches or bridges to annoy the enemy's horſe] *tribolò*, s. m. *ſtrumento con quattro punte di ferro una delle quali ſta ſempre in aria in qualſivoglia poſtura che ſia*.

C'ALTROP, [an herb] *tribolo, capo d' un erba ſalvatica di forma triangolare, che ha gli angoli d' acutiſſime ſpine*.

Water-caltrops, } *tribolo, acquatico*, s. m.
Great caltrops, }

To CALVE, verb. neut. *figliare, fare il vitello, parlando d' una vacca*.

CA'LVES, *il plurale di* calf.

CA'LVINISTS, s. [the followers of Calvin in his principles] *calviniſta, ſettario di Calvino*.

CA'LVINISM, s. [the doctrine and principles of John Calvin] *calviniſmo*, s. m.

To CALU'MNIATE, [to ſlander, to detract] *calunniare, calonniare, oppore altrui con malignità qualche falſa coſa*.

CALU'MNIATED, adj. *calunniato, calonniato*.

CALU'MNIATOR, s. [a ſlanderer] *calunniatore, calonniatore, maldicente*, s. m.

CALU'MNIOUS, adj. [full of calumnies] *calunnioſo, calonnioſo, pien di calunnie, vago di calunniare*.

CA'LUMNY, s. [falſe imputation, aſperſion] *calúnnia, maldicenza*, s. f. *accuſa falſa*.

CALX, s. that powder to which any body is reduced by calcination] *calcina, calce*, s. f. *quella polvere che reſta de' metalli o altri corpi dopo eſſere ſtati calcinati*.

Calx [in anatomy, is the heel or ſecond bone in that part of the foot which ſucceeds the ancle] *tallone*, s. m. *l'oſſo del calcagno*.

CALYCE [the cup of the flower in any plant] *calice, ſommità, incavàta d' ogni fiore*.

CA'MAIL, s. [a biſhop's purple ornament, worn over the rochet] *camaglio di prelato*.

CA'MBER, s. [a piece of timber cut arching] *pezzo di legno tagliato in arco; e ſi uſa nel fabbricar le navi ſpezialmente*.

CA'MBERING, adj. [a ſea term] *incurvato, inarcato, fatto a volta, curvo*.

A ſhip's deck lies cambering, when it does not lie level, but higher in the middle than at the ends, *il ponte del vaſcello è curvo*.

CA'MBRICK, s. [a ſort of fine linen cloth] *cambraja*, s. f. *tela fina che ſi fabbrica in Cambray, città di Fiandra*.

CAME, *preterito del verbo*, to come.

CAMEL, s. *cammello*, s. m. *animal quadrupede, nativo d' Africa e d' Aſia*.

CAME'LOPARD, s. *quadrupede nativo d' Abiſſinia e d' Ethiopia, chiamato da' alcuni viaggatori Cammellopardo perchè ha 'l capo e il collo come il cammello e la pelle roſſa macchiata di macchie bianche quaſi come il pardo. E' beſtia più alta dello elefante, ma non coſi corpacciuta e groſſa e noi Italiani la chiamiamo Giraffa*.

CAMELI'NE, s. [an herb] *camedrio*, s. m. *ſorta d' erba*.

CAME'LION, s. *camaleonte, cameleonte*, s. m. *ſerpentello quadrupede, di fattezze, ſimile alla lucertola*.

CAMELOT, v. Camlet.

CAMER'ADE, s. [a boſom companion] *un amico intrinſeco*.

CAMISA'DO, s. *attacco fatto al bujo colla camicia ſopra l' arme*.

CAMISA'TED, adj. *colla camicia ſopra l' arme onde poter eſſere riconoſciuto in tempo di bujo*.

CA'MLET, s. *ciambellotto*, s. m. *tela fatta di pel di capra*.

CAMMOCK, s. [the herb reſt-harrow] *accutella*, s. f.

CA'MOMILE, s. [a ſweet ſmelling herb] *camomila*, s. f.

CAMO'YS, adj. [flat of the noſe] *ſimo, che ha 'l naſo ſchiacciato ò corto e fatto a ſella*.

CAMP, s. m. [the place where any army lodges in tents or huts] *campo*, s. m.

A flying or running camp, *campo volante*.

Camp fight, *campo di battagglia*.

To CAMP [to pitch a camp] *accamparſi, porre o metter campo, porſi a campo, attendarſi*.

CAMPA'IGN, s. [plain or open country] *campagna*, s. f. *paeſe aperto*.

Campaign [the ſpace of time every year an army continues in the field, during a war] *campagna*, s. m. *quello ſpazio di tempo che un eſercito reſta in campagna in tempo di guerra*.

To open the campaign, *uſcire in campagna*.

CAMPE'CHE, s. [a kind of Indian wood, the ſame with logwood] *campeccio*, s. m. *ſpezie di legno Indiano*.

CAMPED, adj. [from to camp] *accampato, attendato*.

CA'MPHIRE, s. [the gum of an Eaſt-Indian tree] *cánfora*, s. f. *ſpézie di gomma d' un albero, che viene dall' Indie*.

CAMPHORATE, adj. *in cui è stara infusa canfora.*

CAMPING, s. *accampamento*, s. m. *l'accamparsi.*

CAN [to be able] *verbo difettivo, che significa potere.*

I will do it if I can, *lo farò se potrò.*

I cannot, *non posso.*

I will do what I can, *farò quanto potrò.*

Do what you can to save my life, *fate ogni sforzo per camparmi la vita.*

Make all the haste you can, *fate il più presto che potete.*

If I can but see him, *purchè lo veda.*

He can read and write, *sa leggere e scrivere.*

How can you tell? *come lo sapete?*

'Tis more than I can tell, *non ne so nulla.*

No body can tell so well as you, *nessuno lo sa meglio di voi.*

Can you never be satisfied? *non sarete mai contento?*

Every man must do all he can, *ognuno deve fare quel che può.*

He is as like him as can be, *lo rassomiglia molto.*

Can you forsake me? *vi basta l'animo di lasciarmi?*

That's the safest course that can be, *questa è la strada la più sicura, non vedo strada più sicura di questa.*

As sure as can be, *sicuramente, indubitatamente, senza dubbio.*

As soon as can be, *subito che si potrà.*

It cannot be, *ciò non può essere; è impossibile.*

I cannot tell, *non so.*

Cannot you hold your tongue? *debtacete, non potete mo tacere?*

CANA'L, s. [an artificial river in a park] *canale*, s. m.

A little canal, *canaletto*, s. m.

CANA'RY, s. [Canary wine] *vino di Canaria.*

Canary bird, *canario*, s. m.

To CA'NCEL [to raze, to blot out] *cancellare, scancellare.*

To cancel [to make void] *annullare, render nullo, estinguere*, pret. *estinsi.*

To cancel [to stint, to set bounds to] *limitare, ristrignere, por termine*, pret. *ristrinsi.*

CA'NCELLED, adj. *cancellato, scancellato, annullato, estinto, limitato, ristretto.*

CA'NCELLING, s. *l'annullare*, v. to cancel.

CA'NCER, [crab fish] *granchio*, s. m.

A she cancer, *granchiessa*, s. f. *granchio femmina.*

A sea cancer, *grancipporo*, s. m. *granchio femmina.*

A little cancer, *granchiolino*, s. m.

Cancer [ulcer] *canchero*, s. m. *tumore o ulcera cagionata da collera nera.*

Cancer [a celestial sign] *cancro*, s. m. *uno de' dodici segni del zodiaco.*

CA'NDID, adj. [white] *bianco estremamente; candido.*

CA'NDID, adj. [fair, open, ingenuous] *candido, sincero, ingenuo, schietto.*

CA'NDIDATE, s. [one that stands for any place or office] *candidato*, s. m. *quello che concorre a cariche, magistrati, e simili.*

CA'NDIDLY, adv. [sincerely, uprightly] *candidamente, integramente, sinceramente, ingenuamente, schiettamente.*

CA'NDIDNESS, s. [ingenuity; openness of temper] *candidezza, ingenuità.*

To CA'NDIFY, *render candido.*

CA'NDLE, s. *candela*, s. f.

Candle, [light, luminary] *luce, luminario.*

Candle snuffers, *smoccolatojo*, s. m.

Wax candle, *candela di cera.*

Tallow candle, *candela di sevo.*

Rush candle, *candela di giunco, candela che ha il lucignolo di giunco*

CANDLEHO'LDER, s. *un che t'assiste in distanza.*

CA'NDLELIGHT, s. [the light of a candle] *lume di candela.*

To work by CANDLELIGHT, *lavorare alla candela.*

Candlelight, [the necessary candles for use] *le candele di cui s'abbisogna per la famiglia, per farne uso.*

CA'NDLEMAS, or Candlemas day, s. [the festival of the purification of the blessed Virgin, the second of February] *la candelaja, il giorno della festività della purificazion della madonna.*

CA'NDLESTICK, s. *candeliere*, s. m. *strumento dove si ficcano le candele per tenerle accese.*

CA'NDLESTUFF, s. [grease, tallow] *sevo, grasso preparato per uso di far candele.*

CA'NDLEWA'STER, s. [a spendthrift] *uno che butta via i suoi danari in bagatelle.*

CA'NDOCK, s. *spezie di gramigna che nasce ne' fiumi.*

CA'NDOR, or CA'NDOUR, s. [sincerity, uprightness] *candore*, s. m. *sincerità, integrità, schiettezza, ingenuità*, s. f.

To CA'NDY, [to make confectionary ware] *candire, confettare, conciare frutta, o simili, facendoli bollire in zucchero*, pres. *candisco.*

Candy, adj. *candito.*

Sugar candy, *zucchero candito.*

CA'NDY'D, adj. *candito, confetto.*

Candy'd oranges, *melarance condite o confette.*

CANE, s. [an Indian reed] *canna d'India.*

A cane [a stick] *una canna, un bastone.*

Cane, s. [a lance] *lancia.*

The head of a cane, *il pomo d'una canna.*

Cane-bottom chairs, *sedie col fondo di canna.*

To CANE, *bastonare, dare delle bastonate.*

CANED, adj. *bastonato.*

CANI'CULAR, adj. [belonging to the dog-star] *canicolare.*

Canicular days [dog-days] *giorni canicolari.*

CANINE, adj [belonging to, or like a dog] *canino, di cane, attenente a cane.*

Canine appetite, *fame canina.*

CA'NISTER, s. [tea-cannister, a small vessel of silver, tin, &c. to hold tea] *scatola d'argento, latta, o altro metallo da tenervi dentro del Tè.*

Canister, s. [a small basket] *panierina, paniera picciola*

CA'NKER, s. [an eating, spreading sore] *cànchero*, s. m. *tumore o ulcera che rode.*

Canker worm [caterpillar] *bruco*, s. m. *spezie d'insetto, che rode la verdura.*

To CA'NKER, v. n. [to grow corrupt] *incancherirsi, corrompersi*

To Canker, [to corrupt, to corrode] *corrompere, corrodere.*

To Canker, v. a. [to infect, to pollute] *appestare, imbrattare.*

CA'NKERBIT, part. adj. [bitten with an envenomed tooth] *morso da dente avvelenato.*

CA'NKERED, adj. *incancherito.*

CA'NNIBAL, s *Cannibale, antropofago, mangiator di carne umana.*

CA'NNIBALLY, adv. [in the manner of a cannibal] *crudelmente, a mo' di cannibale.*

CA'NNON, s. [a piece of ordnance, a great gun] *cannone*, s. m. *pezzo d'artigliera.*

Cannon bullet, *palla di canone.*

Cannon hole, *cannoniera*, s. f.

To be within cannon shot, *esser a tiro di cannone.*

To CANNONA'DE [to batter with cannon] *cannonare, battere a colpi di cannone.*

CANNONA'DE, s. [cannon shot] *cannonata*, s. f. *tiro di cannone.*

CANNONI'ER, s. [a gunner who discharges the cannon] *cannoniere*, s. m.

CA'NON, s. [church law or decree] *cànone*, s. m. *le leggi pontificie stabilite e ordinate da' papi o da' concili.*

The canon law, *la legge canonica.*

Doctor in the cannon law, *canonista*, s. m.

Canon [a prebendary who enjoys a living in a collegiate church or cathedral] *canònico*, s. m. *che ha canonicato.*

Canon [a printing letter of a large size] *cànone*, s. m. *sorta di lettera majuscola colla quale si stampa.*

Lean or fat canon, *cànone grosso e picciolo.*

Canon [a horse bit] *imboccatura*, s. f. *quella parte della briglia, che va in bocca al cavallo.*

CANO'NICAL, adj. [according to the rule or order] *canonico.*

Canonical book, *libro canonico.*

Canonical hours, *ore canoniche.*

CANO'NICALNESS, s. [agreeable to the canons of the church] *stato canonico o legitimo.*

CA'NONIST, s. [a professor or doctor of the canon law] *canonista*, s. m. *dottor in legge canonica.*

CANONIZATION, s. [the act of canonizing] *canonizzazione*, s. f. *il canonizzare.*

To CANONI'ZE [to declare and pronounce a saint] *canonizzare, atto solenne che fa il pontefice nel dichiarare un defunto degno d'esser annoverato tra i santi.*

CANONI'ZED, adj. *canonizzato.*

CA'NONRY, } s. [the title and be-
CA'NONSHIP, } nefice enjoyed by a canon] *canonicato, canonacato,* s. m.

CA'NOPY, s. [a cloth of state, set or carried over the heads of sovereign princes] *baldacchino,* s. m. *arnese, che si porta o si tiene sopra le cose sacre e sopra i seggi de' principi e gran personaggi in segno d'onore.*

Canopy [a tettern and curtains for a bed] *il cielo del letto.*

The canopy of heaven, *il firmamento.*

To CA'NOPY [to cover with a canopy] *coprir con baldacchino.*

CANO'ROUS, adj. [loud, shrill] *canoro, armonioso.*

CAN'T, *è una abbreviazione della parola* CANNOT, *v.* Can. I can't, *non posso,* he can't, *e' non può.*

CANT, s. [gibberish, or beggars' speech] *gergo,* s. m. *parlare oscuro e sotto metafora usato da birbi.*

Cant, *maniera propria di parlare usata da certe classi di genti.*

Cant, *gergaccio non intelligibile in modo alcuno, parlar del volgo.*

Cant, *ipocrisia, lamentevole e continua protesta che uno è uom dabbene.*

Cant, [auction] *incanto, vendita a suon di tromba.*

To CANT [to talk obscurely after the manner of gypsies and rogues] *parlar in gergo ; parlar furbesco.*

CA'NTAR, s. [a certain weight] *cantaro,* s. m. *peso maggiore o minore secondo la diversità de' paesi.*

CANTHA'RIDES, s. [Spanish fleas] *canterelle; cantaridi,* s. f.

CA'NTHUS, s. [the angle or corner of the eye] *la coda dell' occhio.*

CA'NTICLE, s. [Solomon's song] *cantica,* s. f. *come quella di Salomone.*

CANTILI'VERS, s. [in architecture, a kind of modillions, which are carved] *seggiola,* s. f. *quel legno, che si conficca a traverso sopra l'estremità de' correnti per reggere gli ultimi embrici del tetto detti gronde.*

Canting language, s. *gergo,* s. m. *parlar furbesco.*

CA'NTLE, s. [a piece of any thing] *pezzo, tozzo,* s. m.

A cantle of bread, *un pezzo o un tozzo di pane.*

To CANTLE out [to divide into parcels or parts] *tagliare in pezzi, smembrare, dividere.*

CA'NTLET, s. *frammento, pezzo.*

CA'NTO, s. [a division in any heroick poem] *canto,* s, m. *parte di poema.*

CA'NTON, s. [a division or part of a country in form of a province] *cantone,* s. m.

The thirteen cantons of Swisserland, *i tredici cantoni della Svizzera.*

To Canton [to divide into little parts] *dividere in pezzetti.*

To CANTONI'ZE [to divide into cantons or quarters] *dividere in cantoni.*

CANTONI'ZED, adj. *diviso in cantoni.*

CA'NTRED, adj. [is in Wales what we in England call hundred] *termine di Gallia che significa una certa divisione di provincia.*

CA'NVASS, s. [a sort of coarse linen cloth] *canavaccio,* s. m. *sorta di panno lino grosso e ruvido.*

To CA'NVASS [to sift, to examine, to search diligently into a business] *ventilare, crivellare; consultare, considerare, esaminare, discutere un negozio o una materia,* pret. *discussi.*

CA'NVASSED, adj. *ventilato, crivellato, consultato, considerato, esaminato, discusso.*

CA'NVASSING, s. *il ventilare o discutere un affare.*

CA'NY, adj. *pien di canne; fatto di canne.*

CA'NZONET, s. *canzonetta, canzoncina.*

CAP, s. [a sort of covering for the head] *berretta,* s. f. *copertura del capo fatta in varie fogge e di varie materie.*

A night-cap, *un berettino da notte.*

A cap-maker, *berrettajo,* s. m.

To cast one's cap to one; *darsi per vinto.*

A cardinal's cap or hat, *cappello di cardinale.*

Cap [head] *testa, capo.*

Cap [in a ship, is a square piece of timber over the head of the mast, having a hole to receive the mast or flag staff] *rotella che è in cima dell' albero del vascello.*

Cap of a gun [a piece of lead put over the touch-hole of a great gun] *piastrella di piombo che si mette sopra il focone d'un cannone, perchè la polvere non caschi.*

Cap-case, *sacco,* s. m. *bisaccia,* s. f.

Cap-a-pee, adv. *da capo a piedi.*

He is armed cap-a-pee, *è armato da capo a piedi, di tutto punto.*

Cap-paper [a sort of thick brown paper] *spezie di carta bruna.*

To CAP one [to take off his cap] *sberrettare, levare la berretta ad uno.*

To cap one [to pull off one's hat to one] *sberrettarsi ad uno, far di berretta ad uno, salutare altrui col trarsi la berretta.*

To cap verses, *recitare versi a vicenda ciascuno cominciando il suo verso colla medesima parola con cui l'altro ha finito.*

CA'PABLE, adj. [fit, able] *capace, atto, idoneo, sufficiente, abile, accommodato, disposto.*

Capable of doing a thing, *capace di fare una cosa.*

Capable of discipline, *docile, trattabile.*

Capable of envy, *invidioso.*

A haven capable of four hundred ships, *un porto capace di quattrocento vascelli.*

Very capable, *capacissimo.*

CAPA'CIOUS, adj. [spacious, vast] *capace, spazioso, ampio, vasto.*

CAPA'CIOUSNESS, s. *capacità,* s. f.

To CAPA'CITATE [to make capable] *capacitare, render capace.*

CAPA'CITY, s. [ability, skill, capableness] *capacità, abilità, attitudine, disposizione,* s. f.

A man of great capacity, *un uomo di gran capacità, un uomo di testa.*

CAPA'RISON, s. [a kind of trappings or furniture for a horse] *guarnimento di cavalli.*

To CAPA'RISON [to dress a horse with caparison] *guarnire un cavallo.*

CAPA'RISONED, adj. *guarnito.*

CAPE, s. [a mountain, or other high place, which runs into the sea farther than the rest of the continent] *capo,* s. m. *punta di terra che sporge in mare.*

The Cape of Good Hope, *il capo di buona speranza.*

Cape [the neck piece of a cloak] *bavero,* s. m. *collare del mantello.*

A Spanish cape, *cappa alla Spagnuola.*

CA'PER, s. [a skip or jump] *capriola, e cavriuola,* s. f. *salto che si fa in ballando.*

Cross capers [troubles] *traversie, avversità,* s. f. pl. *infortuni,* s. m. pl.

Caper [a pirate ship, a privateer] *vascello o galea di corso.*

Caper [a sort of fruit] *cappero,* s. m. *frutice noto, e si dice tanto alla pianta quanto al suo frutto.*

To CA'PER [to cut capers] *capriolare, fare delle capriole.*

CA'PILLARY, adj. [belonging to, or like hair] *capillare, simile a capello.*

The capillary veins, *le vene capillari.*

CA'PITAL, adj. [chief, great] *capitale, principale.*

Capital crime, *delitto capitale, o degno di morte.*

A capital, s. [a chief city] *una città capitale, una metropoli.*

A capital ship, *un vascello di linea.*

CA'PITALLY, adv. *capitalmente, di pena della vita.*

To proceed capitally against one, *proceder capitalmente contro uno.*

CAPITA'TION, s. [poll-tax] *capitazione,* s. f. *tassa per testa.*

CA'PITOL, s. [an ancient citadel of Rome] *il campidoglio, cittadella dell' antica Roma.*

CAPI'TULAR, s. [the body of the statutes of a chapter] *libro in cui son registrati gli statuti d'un capitolo.*

Capitular, s. [a member of a chapter] *membro d'un capitolo.*

To CA'PITULATE [to treat upon terms] *capitolare, patteggiare, far convenzioni.*

CAPI'TULATED, adj. *capitolato, patteggiato.*

CAPITULA'TION, s. [the act of capitulating] *capitolazione, convenzione,* s. f. *capitolo,* s. m.

CAPI'VI-TREE, *albero balsamico che nasce nelle Indie occidentali spagnuole.*

CA'PON, s. [a cock cut to be fatted for the spit] *un cappone, un gallo castrato.*

A young capon, *capponcello,* s. m.

To CA'PON, verb act. *capponare, castrare polli.*

CA'PONED, adj. *capponato, castrato.*

CAPONIE'RE, s. [in fortification, is a covered lodgment encompassed with a little parapet, to support planks laden with

with earth] *caponiera*, s. f. *termine di fortificazione.*

CA'POT, s [a term at the game of picket] *cappotto.*

To CAPOT one, *far cappotto.*

CAPO'UCH, *v.* Capuch.

CA'PPER, s. [a cap-maker] *berrettajo*, s. m.

CA'PPING, s. *ex.* a man full of capping and crouching, *un uomo molto umile, un collo torto.*

CAPRI'CE, or CA'PRI'CHIO, s. [a whimsey, a freak, a maggot] *capriccio, ghiribizzio*, s. m. *fantasia, invenzione*, s. f.

CAPRI'CIOUS, adj. [humoursome, fantastical] *capriccioso, fantastico, bisbetico.*

CAPRI'CIOUSLY, adv. *cappricciosamente, fantasticamente, d' una maniera cappricciosa, bisbeticamente.*

CAPRICIOUSNESS, s. [humour, whimsicalness] *cappriccio, fantastichezza, ghiribizzo.*

CA'PRICORN, s. [one of the twelve signs of the Zodiack] *capricorno*, s. m. *uno de' dodici segni del zodiaco.*

CA'PRIOLE, s. *salto di cavallo senza uscire di luogo.*

CA'PSTAN, s. [a great piece of timber in the nature of a windlass, placed next behind the mainmast; its use is to weigh the anchors, to hoist up or strike down top-masts, to heave any weighty thing] *argano di vascello.*

Capstan bars, *le leve d'un argano.*

CA'PTAIN, s. [a head officer of a company of horse or foot, of a ship of war] *capitano, capo*, s. m.

A captain general of an army, *capitan generale d' un esercito.*

A captain of horse, *capitano di cavalleria.*

A captain of foot, *capitano d'infanteria.*

A sea captain, *capitano di vascello.*

CA'PTAINRY, } s. *capitaneria*, s. f.
CAPTAINSHIP, } *ufficio di capitano.*

CA'PTION, s. [a certificate of a commission executed] *certificato*, s. m.

CA'PTIOUS, adj. [apt to take exceptions, quarrelsome] *litigioso, contenzioso.*

A captious fellow, *un litigioso, un accattabrighe.*

Captious [deceitful, crafty, cunning] *cavilloso, ambiguo, dubbioso, sofistico.*

A captious argument, *un sofisma.*

Captious words, *parole, cavillose, ambigue, dubbiose.*

CA'PTIOUSLY, adv. [slily, deceitfully] *argutamente, cavillosamente, ambiguamente, dubbiosamente, sofisticamente.*

CA'PTIOUSNESS, s. [deceit] *fraude, astuzia, furberia*, s. f. *inganno*, s. m.

Captiousness [the being exceptious] *cavillazione, disputa, contesa*, s. f.

To CA'PTIVATE [to enslave, a word applied to the affections of the mind] *cattivare, cattivarsi, rendersi favorevole; si aice degli affetti.*

To captivate, [to charm, to subdue] *incantare, soggiogare.*

CA'PTIVATED, adj. *cattivato.*

CA'PTIVE, s. [a slave or prisoner of war] *cattivo, prigioniero*; s. m. *cattiva, prigioniera*, s. f.

Captive, adj. *prigione, fatto prigione in guerra.*

To CA'PTIVE, *v. a.* [to take a prisoner] *far prigione.*

CA'PTIVITY, s. [slavery] *cattività, schiavitù*, s. f.

CA'PTOR, s. [he that takes a prisoner or a prize] *colui che prende prigione, e colui che fa una preda.*

CA'PTURE, s. [prize, booty] *cattura, presa*, s. f. *bottino*, s. m.

Capture [in law, arrest, seizure] *cattura, presura*, s. f.

CA'PUCH, s. [a monk's hood] *cappuccio*, s. m.

A little capuch, *cappuccetto*, s. m.

CA'PUCHED, adj. *incappucciato.*

CAPUCHI'N, s. *cappuccio, ornamento e parte di veste da donna.*

CA'PUCHINS, s. [friars of the order of St. Francis, having their names from the capouch they wear] *capuccini*, s. m. *frati dell' ordine di san Francesco.*

CAR, s. [a small carriage of burden] *carretta.*

Car [a chariot of war] *carro usato in guerra.*

Car [Charles's wain; a constellation] *il carro di Boote, l' orsa.*

CARABI'NE, s. [a sort of short gun] *carabina*, s. f. *sorta d' archibuso corto.*

CARABINE'ER, s. [a soldier armed with a carabine] *carabina, solidato armato di carabina.*

CA'RACK, s. [a large Portuguese ship] *caracca*, s. f. *spezie di nave Portoghese.*

CA'RACOLE, s. [the half turn, which a horseman makes either to the right or left] *caracollo*, s. m.

To CA'RACOLE, [military term, to wheel about, or cast into a ring] *caracollare.*

CA'RACT, } s. [the weight of one
CA'RAT, } scruple or twenty four grains] *carato*, s. m. *peso, che è il ventiquatresimo dell' oncia, ed è proprio dell' oro.*

CA'RAVAN, s. [a company of merchants travelling together] *caravána*, s. f. *truppa di mercanti che viaggiano in compagnia.*

Caravan [a sea-expedition made by the knights of Malta] *caravana, corsa, che i cavalieri di Malta fanno per mare.*

CARAVA'NSARY, s. [a house built for the reception of travellers] *caravenserà, edifizio orientale per ricetto de' viaggiatori.*

CA'RAVEL, } s. [a light round ship,
CA'RVEL, } with a square poop, rigg'd like a galley] *caravella*, s. f. *vascelletto non molto grande, che cammina velocemente.*

CARAWAY, s. [an herb] *carvi*, s. m. *spezie d' erba medicinale.*

CA'RBINE, *v.* Carabine.

CARBONA'DO, s. [a steak broiled on the coals] *carbonata*, s. f. *carne cotta in su i carboni.*

To CARBONA'DO, *v. a.* [to cut or hack] *tagliar in fette.*

CARBU'NCLE, s. [a precious stone] *carboncello, carbonchio*, s. m. *gioja del colore del carbone acceso, e di maraviglioso splendore.*

Carbuncle [a plague, sore] *carboncello, spezie di fignolo, o di cicione maligno.*

CARBU'NCLED, adj. *adorno o fregiato di carbonchi. Segnato, o guasto da bitorzoli.*

CARCU'NCLAR, adj. *rosso come carbonchio.*

CA'RCANET, s. [a chain or collar of jewels] *collana*, s. f. *monile*, s. m.

CA'RCASS, s. [a dead body] *carcame, scheletro*, s. m. *tutto il corpo d'un animal morto.*

Carcass [a warlike engine] *una carcassa, spezie di bomba.*

CA'RCELLAGE, s. [prison fees] *le spese della prigione.*

CARD, s. [to play with] *carta*, s. f. *da giuocare.*

A pack of cards, *un mazzo di carte.*

A trump card, *un trionfo.*

A mariner's or sea card, *carta da navigare.*

Card [an instrument to comb wool] *cardo*, s. m. *strumento con punte di ferro, da cardare la lana.*

Card-maker, *cartajo*, s. m. *che fa e vende le carte.*

To CARD, verb. act. *cardare.*

To card wool, *cardare della lana.*

CARDAMO'MUM, s. *cardamomo*, s. m. *seme medicinale.*

CA'RDED, adj. *cardato.*

CA'RDER, s. *cardatore*, s. m. *che carda.*

CA'RDIACAL, adj. [good for the heart] *cardiaco.*

CA'RDINAL, s. [one of the chief governors of the Roman Catholick Church] *cardinale*, s. m.

Cardinal's cap, *cappello di cardinale.*

Belonging to a cardinal, *cardinalizio, cardinalesco.*

Cardinal's dignity, *cardinalato*, s. m. *dignità di cardinale.*

Cardinal, adj. *cardinale, principale.*

The four cardinal virtues, Prudence, Temperance, Justice, and Fortitude, *le quattro virtù cardinali, cioè, la Prudenza, la Temperanza, la Giustizia, e la Fortezza.*

Cardinal numbers [one, two, three, *&c.*] *i numeri cardinali, uno, due, tre*, &c.

Cardinal points [of the Zodiack are Aries, Libra, Cancer, and Capricorn] *i punti cardinali del Zodiaco sono Ariete, Libra, Cancro, e Capricorno.*

The four cardinal winds, East, West, South, and North, *i quattro venti cardinali sono Levante, Ponente, Mezzogiorno, e Tramontana.*

CA'DINALSHIP, s. *cardinalato*, s. m. *dignità di cardinale.*

CA'RDING, s. *il cardare.*

CA'RDMATCH, s. *miccia fatta di carte intinte nel solfo liquefatto*

CARDO'ON, or cardoon thistle, s. [an herb] *cardo, cardone*, s. m. *erba spinosa la quale si mangia.*

CARE, s. [heed] *cura*, s. f. *pensiero.*

Leave the care of that to me, *lasciate pur a me la cura di cio.*

I shall

I ſhall take a particular care of your buſineſs, *porrò ogni mia cura ne' voſtri intereſſi.*

Pray let it be your ſpecial care, *vi prego d'averne una cura particolare.*

Take care what you do, *badate a quel che fate.*

Gnawing cares, *cure mordaci.*

To have a care [to take heed] *badare, avvertire.*

To take care for a thing, *provvedere a qualche coſa.*

I ſhall take care never to commit ſuch a fault again, *procurerò di non commettere più un tal fallo.*

To caſt away care, *divertirſi, darſi buon tempo.*

To CARE, *curare, aver cura,* tener *conto, ſtimare, apprezzare.*

I don't care a pin for it, *non me ne curo, me ne burlo, me ne* rido, *non me ne cale un fico.*

He cares for no body, *non iſtima, o non fa conto di neſſuno.*

A man that cares for nothing, *un che non fa conto di niente, uno ſpenſierato.*

What care I? *che importa a me?*

I don't care if I go along with you, *ho voglia d' andare con voi.*

Will you drink a glaſs of wine? I don't care if I do, *volete bere un bicciere di vino? molto volentieri.*

CARED FOR, adj. *curato, ſtimato, apprezzato.*

To CARE'EN [to refit, to trim, to mend a ſhip] *dar carena ad un vaſcello.*

CARE'ER, s. [courſe, race] *carriera,* s. f. *corſo,* s. m.

CA'REFUL, adj. [diligent] *accurato, diligente, ſollecito.*

Careful [heedful] *circoſpetto, cauto, prudente.*

Careful [penſive, full of cares] *penſieroſo, penſoſo, inquieto.*

Very careful, *grandemente ſollecito.*

CA'REFULLY, adv. [diligently] *accuratamente, diligentemente, con ſollecitudine.*

Carefully [heedfully] *cautamente, prudentemente.*

Carefully [penſively] *penſieroſamente.*

CA'REFULNESS, s. [diligence] *diligenza, cura, attenzione, applicazione, eſatezza, aſſiduità,* s. f. *penſiero,* s. m.

Carefulneſs [warineſs] *circoſpezione, prudenza, cautela,* s. f.

Carefulneſs [penſiveneſs] *moleſtia, noja,* s. f. *faſtidio,* s. m.

CA'RELESLY, adv. [negligently] *traſcuratamente, negligentemente, con poca cura, alla ſciamannata, ſpenſieratamente, alla carlona, ſenza diligenza alcuna.*

CA'RELESSNESS, s. *traſcuraggine, traſcurataggine, traſcuranza, negligenza,* s. f.

CA'RELESS, adj. [at eaſe] *ſenza penſiero, ſpenſierato, agiato.*

Careleſs [negligent] *traſcurato, negligente, infingardo.*

He is very careleſs in his buſineſs, *egli è molto traſcurato ne' ſuoi affari.*

CARE'SS, s. *carezza,* s. f. *cordiale amorevolezza.*

To CARESS [to treat obligingly, to make much of] *accarezzare, far carezze, far vezzi, vezzeggiare.*

CARE'SSED, adj. *accarezzato, vezzeggiato.*

CA'RFAX, s. [a place where four ſeveral ſtreets or ways meet together, particularly the market place in Oxford] *crocicchio, quadrivio,* s. m. *luogo dove s'attraverſan le ſtrade.*

CA'RGAISON, } s. [the freight or
CA'RCO, } whole lading of a ſhip] *cárico,* s. m. *ſalma,* s. f. *la mercanzia che ſi carica in un vaſcello.*

CARK, s. [care, anxiety] *cura, anſietà.* Obſ.

To CARK [to take an anxious care] *roderſi, ſtruggerſi, conſumarſi.* Obſ.

Carking cares, *cure mordaci.*

CA'RKNET, or CA'RKANET, s. [a chain of jewels for the neck] *collana, monile.*

CARLE, s. [clown, churl] *un ruſtico, un zotico, un contadino.*

CARL-CAT, s. [a boar cat] *un gatto di una razza poco comune, groſſo e di cattiva natura.*

CARLI'NE, s. [a ſort of flower] *carlina,* s. f.

The carline thiſtle [a plant] *camaleone,* s. m. *carlina nera.*

CAR'MAN, s. *colui che guida il carro.*

CA'RMELITE, s. [a ſort of friars] *carmelitano,* s. m.

Carmelite nuns, *mònache carmelitane.*

CA'RMINATIVE, adj. [a term uſed by phyſicians] *carminativo.*

Carminative remedies [medicines which diſperſe wind, as anniſeed, &c.] *rimedi carminativi, come finocchio, coriandro, anici,* &c.

CARMI'NE, s. [a bright red or crimſon colour] *carmino, ſorta di color roſſo belliſſimo.*

CA'RNAGE, s. [maſſacre, great ſlaughter] *ſtrage, uccíſione, macello.*

Carnage [fleſh that is given to dogs after the chaſe] *carne che ſi da a' cani di caccia.*

CA'RNAL, adj. [belonging to the fleſh, fleſhy, ſenſual] *carnale, ſecondo la carne, ſenſuale, luſſurioſo.*

Carnal ſin, *peccato carnale.*

Carnal pleaſures, *diletti carnali.*

CARNALITY, s. [fleſhly luſt] *carnalità, ſenſualità, concupiſcenza carnale.*

CAR'NALLY, adv. *carnalmente, ſenſualmente, luſſurioſamente, con amor carnale*

To have carnally to do with a woman, *conoſcere una donna carnalmente.*

CARNA'TION, s. [a flower] *garofano, gherofano,* s. f. *ſpezie di fiore.*

Carnation colour [fleſh colour] *colore incarnatino o incarnato.*

Carnation [in painting, are the parts of a human body drawn naked without drapery] *carnagione,* s. f.

CA'RNAVAL, s. [ſhrovetide] *carnaſciale, carnovale,* s. m.

The feaſt in carnaval time, *carnaſcialare, darſi nel carnovale a' paſſatempi e alla crapula.*

CARNE'LION, s. [a precious ſtone] *cornelia, ſpezie di gemma.*

CA'RNEOUS, adj. [fleſhy] *carnoſo, di carne.*

To CA'RNIFY, [to breed fleſh] *far carne, metter carne.* Hale.

CA'RNIVAL, *v.* Carnaval.

CARNI'VOROUS, adj. [fleſh devouring, feeding upon fleſh] *che ama molto la carne, vorace.*

CARNO'SITY, s. [fleſhineſs] *carnoſità,* s. f. *pienezza di carne.*

Carnoſity [a piece of fleſh growing in and obſtructing any part of the body] *carnoſità, creſcenza di carne in qualſiſia parte del corpo.*

CA'ROB, s. [a ſmall weight, being the twenty fourth part of a grain] *ſorta di peſo che è la ventiquattreſima parte d'un grano.*

Carob, or Carob-bean, s. [a fruit whoſe taſte is ſomewhat like cheſnuts] *carroba,* s. f. *carrubbio,* s. m.

Carob-tree, s. *carrubbo e carrubbio,* s. m. *albero che fa la carroba*

CA'ROL, s. [a ſong of joy and exultation] *carola; canto pieno d' allegrezza e di giubilo.*

Carol, s. *carola, canto divoto, inno.*

To CA'ROL, v. n. [to ſing ſongs of joy] *carolare, cantare.*

To carol, v. a. [to praiſe, to celebrate] *laudare, celebrare col canto.*

CA'ROLI, s. [among ſurgeons, venereal excreſcences in the privy parts] *ſorta di malore nella verga.*

CAROLI'NE, adj. *ex.* a caroline hat [a ſort of felt or cloth hat] *cappello di feltro.*

CA'ROLUS, s. [a broad piece of gold of King Charles I.] *cárolo,* s. m. *moneta d'oro del re Carlo primo che vale in circa cinque piaſtre.*

CA'ROT, s. [an eatable root] *carota,* s. f. *radice per lo più di color giallo.*

A carot [a red hair'd man or woman] *un uomo o una donna di pel roſſo.*

CARO'USAL, s. [an extraordinary drinking bout] *crapula,* s. f. *troppo bere.*

To CAROU'SE [to drink hand to fiſt, to quaff] trincare, *bere eccesſivamente.*

CARO'USER, s. [a drinker, a toper] *beone, un che* trinca *di molto.*

CARP, s. [a freſh water fiſh] *carpa.*

To CARP [to blame, to cenſure, to find fault with] *biaſimare, vituperare,* criticare, *avvilire, cenſurare.*

To carp at a thing, *biaſimare, avvilire una coſa, dir male d'una coſa.*

He carps at every body, *egli vitupera ognuno, dice male d'ognuno.*

CARPED AT, adj. *biaſimato, cenſurato, vituperato,* criticato, *avvilito.*

CA'RPENTER, s. *legnajuolo, falegname,* s. m. *arteſice che lavora di legname.*

A ſhip carpenter, *fabbricator di vaſcelli.*

Carpenter's work, *lavoro di legnajuolo.*

CA'RPENTRY, s. [the carpenter's art] *arte di legnajuolo o falegname.*

CA'RPER, s. [from to carp] *critico, maldicente, cenſore,* correttore, *riprenditore,* s. m.

CA'RPET, s. [a covering for a table] *tappeto,* s. m.

A Turky carpet, *un tappeto di Turchia.*

The

The business is upon the carpet, *l'affare è sul tappeto.*

CA'RRIAGE, s. [portage] *porto*, s. m. *vettura*, s. f.

A carriage [a kind of covered waggon] *carriaggio*, s. m.

A beast of carriage or burden, *bestia da soma o da basto.*

A ship of carriage, *nave da carico.*

Carriage [mien] *aria, ciera, presenza*, s. f. *aspetto*, s. m.

Carriage [behaviour] *portamento*, s. m. *modo particolare d'operare e di procedere.*

A carriage for ordnance, *letto di cannone.*

The carriages or luggage of an army, *bagaglie*, s. f. *masserizie, che si portan dietro i soldati dell' esercito.*

CA'RRIER, s. *vetturino, portatore*, s. m.

Carrier-pigeon, *piccione casalingo.*

CA'RRION, *v.* Carion.

To CA'RRY, *portare, menare, condurre.*

To carry a man to another, *menare un uomo in casa d'un altro.*

To carry a thing from one place to another, *portare una cosa d'un luogo ad un altro.*

To carry in a cart, *carreggiare, portare in un carro.*

To carry it high, *far del grande, procedere con alterigia, portarla alta, proceder con fasto, allacciarsela.*

He carries it like a philosopher, *fa del filosofo.*

To carry [to get the better] *vincere, guadagnare, aver l'avantaggio.*

To carry the cause, *guadagnare la causa.*

To carry the day, *ottenere la vittoria, esser vittorioso, riportar la palma.*

To carry it fair, *far buona ciera.*

To carry it fair with one, *trattar bene alcuno, comportarsi bene verso alcuno.*

To carry it cunningly, *usar finezze*, trattare *con politica.*

He carries a mind worthy of praise, *ha un' anima nobile, un animo grande.*

To carry a jest too far, *burlare con troppa libertà.*

To carry one's self well, *portarsi, comportarsi, procedere.*

He knows not how to carry himself, *non sa in che modo acconciarsi, non sa vivere, non sa come comportarsi.*

I know how to carry myself with them, *so ben come trattarli, so come procedere con essi.*

He carries himself like a fool, *si comporta da sciocco.*

To carry away by force, *portar via, rapire*, pres. *rapisco.*

To carry away [to take along with one]. *portar seco.*

To carry back, *rimenare, ricondurre, riportare, portar indietro.*

To carry all before one, *impadronirsi d'ogni cosa, non trovar resistenza.*

His army carries all before it, *il suo esercito non trova veruna resistenza, ogni cosa cede al suo esercito.*

To carry over, *trasportare, trasferire.*

To carry about, *portar quà e là.*

I carry no money about me, *non porto danari addosso.*

To carry out an opinion, *sostenere un' opinione.*

To carry up, *portar su.*

To carry down, *portar giù.*

To carry on, *continuare, andare avanti.*

To carry on a business, *trattare un negozio.*

To carry on a wall, *continuare un muro.*

To carry on the trenches, *avvanzare le trincee.*

To carry on the war, *continuare la guerra.*

To carry on a siege, *proseguire un assedio.*

To carry off, *portar via, dissipare.*

This will carry off the bad humours, *questo dissiperà i cattivi umori.*

To carry off [to kill] *ammazzare.*

This distemper carries men off quickly, *questa malattia ammazza gli uomini presto.*

To carry a thing through, *venire a fine di checchessia.*

To carry good humour through, *esser sempre di buon umore.*

Where's the money that must carry me through? *dov' è 'l danaro che mi bisogna per questo effetto?*

To carry coals to Newcastle, *portare fiasconi a vallombrosa, portare la mercanzia ove se ne abbonda, portare cavoli a legnaja.*

Corn carries a price, *il grano è caro.*

They carry two faces under one hood, *sono piu doppi ch' una cipolla.*

CA'RRY'D, adj. *portato, menato, condotto*, part. *di* To carry.

It was carried at last that—*alla fine fu conchiuso o determinato che*—.

CA'RRY-TALE, s. [a tale-bearer] *spia; colui che ascolta in un luogo, e ridice in un altro.*

CART, s. [to carry any thing in] *carro*, s. m. *carretta*, s. f.

To set the cart before the horses, *mettere il carro innanzi a' buoi.*

A dung cart, *carro da letame.*

Cart-wheel, *ruota di carro.*

Cart-horse, *cavallo di carretta.*

To drive a cart, *carreggiare, guidare il carro.*

A child's cart, *carruccio*, s. m. *strumento di legno con quattro girelle nel quale si mettono i bambini perchè imparino a camminare.*

A dray cart, *un carro da condurre mercanzie grossolane.*

To CART [to expose in a cart] *legar uno sur un carro ed esporlo alla vista del pubblico. E' spezie di castigo come la berlina o fogna.*

To Cart [to use carts for carriage] *condurre col carro.*

CA'RTAGE, *v.* cartouch.

CA'RT-JADE, s. [a vile horse] *cavallaccio, cavallo buono a nulla, pien di guidaleschi e vecchio, carogna.*

CA'RT LOAD, s. [a quantity of any thing piled on a cart] *quantità di checchessia ammucchiata sopra un carro.*

Cart-load [a quantity sufficient to load a cart] *quantità di checchessia bastante a caricare un carro.*

CA'RTWAY, s. [a way through which a carriage may conveniently travel] *strada abbastanza larga perchè un carro ci passi comodamente; la via del carro.*

CA'RTED, adj. *legato ad un carro.*

CA'NTEL, s. [a challenge to a duel, a letter of defiance] *cartello, disfida.*

Cartel, s. [a writing containing stipulations] *cartello; scritto che contiene patti.*

CA'RTER, s. [cart driver] *carrettajo, carrettiere*, s. m.

CARTE'SIAN, s. *cartesiano*, s. m. *filosofo che seguita i sentimenti di Descartes.*

CARTE'SIAN, adj. *ex.* the Cartesian philosophy, *la filosofia di Descartes.*

CARTHU'SIANS, s. [a sort of friars founded by St. Bruno] *Certosini, frati dell' ordine di San Bruno.*

A carthusian friar, *un frate certosino.*

CA'RTILAGE, s. [a gristle, which is a middle substance between a ligament and a bone] *cartilágine*, s. f. *una delle parti del corpo dell' animale dopo l'ossa la più dura.*

CARTILAGI'NEOUS, CARTILA'GINOUS, } adj. [gristly, full of gristles] *cartilaginoso, che ha cartilagine.*

CA'RTOUCH, CA'RTRIDGE, s. [a charge of powder put into a paper case, exactly fitted to the muzzle of the gun or other fire arms] *cartoccio*, s. m. *recipiente fatto di carta ravvolta a mo' di corno nel quale si mette la carica.*

CARVE, CARVAGE, } s. [a certain quantity of land] *cento pertiche di terra.*

To carve [to cut] *trinciare, tagliare le carni cotte che sono in tavola.*

To carve meat, *trinciare della carne.*

To carve wood or stone, *scolpire, intagliare sul legno o sulla pietra*, pres. *scolpisco.*

To carve out one's own satisfaction, *sodisfarsi, contentarsi.*

To carve out one's own fortune, *regolare la sua propria fortuna.*

CA'RVED, adj. *trinciato, tagliato, scolpito, intagliato.*

CA'RVEL, *v.* Caravel.

CA'RVER, s. [from to carve] *scalco, trinciante*, s. m. *quegli che ha l'ufficio del trinciar le vivande.*

We must not pretend to be our own carvers, *noi non dobbiamo pretendere di farci il mondo a modo nostro.*

A carver in wood or stone, *scultore, intagliatore*, s. m.

Carver's work, *scultura*, s. f. *opera o lavoro di scultore.*

CA'RVING, s. *lo scolpire.*

CARU'NCLE, s. [a little excrescency of flesh] *carnosità*, s. f.

CAR'WAY, s. [a sort of plant] *pastricciano*, s. m. *sorta di pastinaca.*

Carway seed, *semenza di pastricciano.*

CARYA'TIDES [an order of pillars in the form of the bodies of women with their

their arms cut off, and clothed down to the feet] *cariatide, termine d'architettura; spezie di pilastri che representano figure di donne senza braccia e coperte di veste fino di piedi.*

CASCA'DE, s. [a fall of waters, either natural or artificial] *cascata*, s. m.

CASE, s [thing, matter, question] *caso, soggetto*, s. m. *cosa, materia*, s. f.

'Tis a strange case indeed, *veramente è un caso strano.*

'Tis a plain case, *è una cosa chiara, è evidente.*

That's another case, *cotesto è un altro affare.*

Put the case it be so, *dato il caso, o supposto che sia così.*

To argue the case pro and con, *disputare pro e contra sopra una materia.*

The case is altered, *le cosa va ora altrimente.*

There's no roguery in the case, *non v'è alcuna furberia costì.*

A case in law, *un punto di legge.*

A case of conscience, *un caso di coscienza.*

Case [occasion] *caso, occasione.*

In such a case, *in tal caso, se ciò fosse.*

Case [in grammar] *caso termine gramaticale.*

The Latin nouns have six cases, *i nomi Latini hanno sei casi.*

Case [condition] *caso, stato*, s. m. *condizione*, s. f.

To be in a sad case, *essere in cattivo stato.*

To be in a good case, *esser in buono stato di salute, star bene.*

You see how my case stands, *voi vedete in che stato sono le cose mie.*

Case [to put any thing in] *astuccio, scátola, fodero, guaina.*

Case of knives, *astuccio per le coltella.*

A hat case, *scatola da cappelli.*

A case for a chair, *una roperta da sedia.*

A rabbet in his case, *un coniglio nella sua pelle.*

As the case stands there is no likelihood of a peace, *nello stato nel quale sono gli affari, non v'è speranza di pace.*

'Tis all a case, *è tutt' uno.*

Were you in my case, *se voi foste nel luogo mio, nel caso mio.*

Case for bottles, *una cantinetta.*

The case for pens in a pocket inkhorn, *pennajuolo*, s. m. *strumento da tenervi dentro le penne da scrivere.*

To CASE [to put in case] *incassare, mettere in una cassa.*

To CASE [to suppose a matter] *supporre una cosa.*

CASEMA'TE, s. [a piece of fortification] *casamatta*, s. f. *sorta di lavoro nelle fortificazioni.*

Casemate [a mason's work in the flank of a bastion next to the curtain] *barbacane*, s. m. *parte della muraglia da basso fatta a scarpa.*

CA'SEMENT, s. [part of a window which opens to let the air in] *finestra*, s. f.

CASE-SHOT, s. [small bullets, nails, pieces of iron, &c. put into cases, to be shot out of murdering pieces] *palle, chiodi, pezzi di ferro, e simili, che si mettono dentro un arme da fuoco per i scaricarli contro il nemico.*

CASH, s. [chest] *cassa*, s. f. *termine mercantile, ogni luogo ove si tengono i danari.*

To have money in cash, *aver danari in cassa.*

Cash [ready money] *danaro contante.*

Running cash, *danaro corrente nel commercio*

To run out of cash, *spender troppo.*

To keep the cash, *tener la cassa.*

CASH-KEEPER, s [a man intrusted with money] *cassiere, tesoriere, colui che ha in cura e in possesso il danaro d'altri o d'un negozio.*

CASHI'ER, s. [cash-keeper] *cassiere*, s. m. *quegli che ha in custodia i danari.*

To cashier [to dismiss from military service ignominiously] *cassare.*

To cashier a soldier, *cassare un soldato.*

CASHI'ERED, adj. *cassato.*

CASHIE'RING, s. *cassazione*, s. f. *il cassare.*

CASHO'O, s. [the juice of an Indian tree] *cascià, gomma d'un albero dell' Indie.*

CA'SINGS, s. [cow-dung dried for fuel] *bovina o sterco di vacca secco per accendere il fuoco.*

CASK [a vessel for liquor] *botte*, s. f. *barile*, s. m.

CASK, or CASQUE, s. *elmo, elmetto.*

CA'SKET, s. [a little chest] *una cassetta.*

To CASKET [to put in a casket] *riporre nella cassetta.*

To CASS [to abrogate] *cassare, cancellare, annullare.*

CASSA'TION, s. [the act of making null or void] *cassazione*, s. f.

CASSIOWA'RY, s. [a large bird of prey] *sorte d'uccellaccio di rapina.*

CA'SSIA, s. *cassia*, s. f. *frutto d'un albero, e serve per medicamento.*

CA'SSOCK, s. [a sort of gown worn commonly by clergymen] *sottana*, s. f.

A short cassock, *casacca*, s. f.

CASSWE'ED, s. [shepherds pouch] *sorta d'erba.*

CAST, s. [throw] *tiro, colpo*, s. m. *tirata*, s. f.

A stone cast, *un tiro di pietra.*

A great cast, *un gran colpo.*

A lucky cast, *un buon colpo.*

A winning cast, *un colpo che guadagna la partita.*

A losing cast, *un colpo che perde la partita.*

A cast of the eyes, *occhiata*, s. f. *sguardo*, s. m.

To have a cast with one's eyes [to squint] *guardar bieco.*

Cast [a couple of hawks] *un pajo di falconi.*

Cast, *getto.*

To be at the last cast [at one's wits end] *esser ridotto all' estremità, non saper che fare, non saper dove dare del capo.*

Cast, adj. *gettato*, v. To cast.

Cast away, *naufragato, che ha fatto naufragio.*

Cast off, s. [refuse] *rifiuto*, s. m.

To CAST [to throw] *gettare, gittare.*

To cast anchor, *gettar l'áncora, dar fondo.*

To cast his rider, *gettar da cavallo.*

To cast lots, *tirar le sorti.*

To cast a mist in one's eyes, *gittare polvere negli occhi, voler mostrar una cosa per un' altra.*

To cast one's self at the feet of another, *prosternarsi a' piedi d' alcuno.*

To cast a dart, *gettare, saettare, lanciare un dardo.*

To cast a lustre, *splendere.*

To cast a bell or a gun, *gettare una campana o un cannone.*

To cast an account, *fare un conto, calcolare, far un càlcolo.*

To cast one's nativity, *fare l'oróscopo di qualcheduno.*

To cast a smell, *aver odore.*

To cast an ill smell, *aver cattivo odore.*

To cast a heat, *render calore.*

To cast [to meditate] *ruminare, riconsiderare, riander col pensiero.*

To cast [in a suit] *guadagnare, vincere.*

To cast one's adversary at the bar, *guadagnare il processo, o la lite.*

The court will cast you, *la corte vi condannerà.*

To cast his coat or skin, *scorzarsi, cangiar di pelle.*

To cast a block in one's way, *attraversare li altrui disegni, metter qualche intoppo all' altrui disegno.*

He begins to cast his teeth, *i denti gli cominciano a cascare.*

To cast [to vomit] *vomitare.*

To cast away, gettar *via, abbandonare, mettere in abbandono.*

To cast away care, *darsi bel tempo, sollazzarsi, divertirsi.*

To cast one's self away, *perdersi, rovinarsi.*

To cast forth, *esalare, mandar fuora.*

To cast forth beams, *scintilare, risplendere.*

To cast about, *spargere, o gettare per ogni parte.*

To cast about [to consider] *considerare, ruminare, riandar col pensiero.*

To cast against, *rimproverare, gettar in volto, rinfacciare.*

To cast headlong, *precipitare.*

To cast into a sleep, *addormentare, far dormire.*

To cast off, *lasciare, abbandonare, rinunciare.*

He has cast off all shame, *ha perduto ogni rossore, ha bandito ogni vergogna.*

To cast off a garment, *spogliarsi d'un abito.*

Some men cast off all to a death-bed repentance, *alcuni procrástinano il pentimento de' loro peccati all' ultimo punto della vita.*

To cast his feathers, *mutar le penne.*

To cast off his skin, *gittar la scoglio, scorzarsi.*

To

To cast off the hounds in hunting, *sciorre i cani.*
To cast in one's dish or teeth, *gettar al volto, rinfacciare, rimproverare.*
To cast the blame upon one, *incolpar uno, dar la colpa ad uno.*
To cast a thing into form, *dar la forma ad una cosa.*
To cast into a fever, *dar la febbre.*
To cast up, *calcolare, fare il calcolo, sommare, computare.*
But upon casting up the whole, *ma a ben considerarla.*
To cast up [to vomit] *vomitare.*
Marshes cast up noisome vapours, *i pantani esalano vapori maligni.*
To cast up a bank, *fare la sponda al fosso, o l'argine al fiume.*
To cast a mist upon one's reputation, *oscurare o macchiare l'altrui riputazione.*
To cast down one's eyes, *abbassare o chinare gli occhi.*
To cast one down [to discourage him] *sgomentare, avvilire, disanimare altrui, fargli perder l'animo.*
To cast down [to afflict] *affliggere, dare afflizione, travagliare, molestare.*
To cast out, *scacciare, mander fuora.*
To cast out devils, *scacciare i diavoli.*
To cast water upon, *spargere dell' acqua sopra qualche cosa.*
To cast up upon a heap, *ammontare, ammonticellare, ammassare.*
To cast up one's eyes, *levare, o alzar su gli orchi.*
To cast a thing behind one's back, *mettersi dietro le spalle che che si sia.*
To cast forth, *gettare, produrre, dar fuori, mettere, rendere.*
To cast a hawk to the pearch [to put her upon it] *posare un falcone sul ramo.*

CA'STANETS, s. [snappers which dancers tie about their fingers] *cemmamelle, castagnette,* s. f. *strumento d'osso o di legno, che si lega alle dita, e si suona percotendolo insieme.*

CA'STAWAY, s. *un réprobo, un malvagio, una persona abbandonata dalla provvidenza.*
Castaway, a. [useless] *inutile, di nessun uso.*

CA'STELLAIN, s. [a constable, or keeper of a castle] *castellano,* s. m. *capitan di castello.*

CA'STELLANY, s. [the manor belonging to a castle] *castellania,* s. f. *ufficio e dignità di castellano.*

CA'STER, s. [a thrower; he that casts] *tiratore; colui che tira o getta.*
Caster, [a calculator; a man that calculates fortunes] *contista; un che fa conti per altri.*

To CA'STIGATE [to correct, to punish] *castigare, gastigare, punire,* pref. *punisco.*

CA'STIGATED, adj. *castigato, gastigato, punito.*

CASTIGA'TION, s. *gastigamento, gastigo, castigamento, castigo,* s. m. *gastigazione, gastigatura, punizione,* s. f.

CA'STIGATORY, adj. *che serve a gastigare.*

CA'STING, s. [from to cast] *il gettare,* v. To cast.
A casting house, *una fonderia.*

CA'STING-NET, s. *nave da buttarsi in acqua.*

CA'STLE, s. [a strong place in a city or country] *castello,* s. m. *fortezza,* s. f.
To build castles in the air, *far castella in aria, fare assegnamenti di cose che non possono riuscire.*
To CA'STLE [a term used at chess play] *roccare, far rocco.*
Castleward, s. *castellania,* s. f.

CA'STLING, s. [the young of any beast brought forth untimely] *un aborto.*

CA'STOR, s. [beaver, a wild-beast] *castoro,* s. m. *animal terrestre, e aquatico.*
A castor [castor hat] *un capello di castoro.*

CASTO'REUM, s. [a medicine made of the liquor contained in the small bags which are next to the beaver's groin] *castorio,* s. m. *medicamento fatto d'un liquore tratto dal castoro.*

To CA'STRATE [to geld] *castrare.*
To castrate a book [to take away some part of it] *castrare un libro.*

CA'STRATED, adj. *castrato.*

CASTRA'TION, s. *il castrare.*

CASTREIL, }
CA'STREL, } s. [kestrel, a sort of hawk] *falcone cattivo.*

CA'SUAL, adj. [accidental] *casuale, accidentale.*
A casual word [a noun] *un nome.*

CA'SUALLY, adv. *casualmente, accidentalmente.*

CA'SUALTY, s. [an unforeseen accident] *caso, accidente,* s. m.

CA'SUIST, s. [a person skilled in resolving cases of conscience] *un casuista, quegli che risolve i casi di coscienza.*

CASUI'STICAL, adj. [relating to cases of conscience] *casuistico.*

CA'SUISTRY, s. *la scienza del casuista.*

CA'SULE, s. [chasuble, a mass priest's vestment] *pianeta,* s. f. *quella veste che porta il prete sopra gli altri paramenti quando célebra la messa.*

CAT, s. [a creature well known] *gatta,* s. f *gatto,* s. m. *ánimal noto.*
A tame cat, *gatto domestica.*
A wild cat, *gatto salvativo.*
When candles are out all cats are grey, *ogni cuffia è buona per la notte.*
Cat to her kind, *ogni simile ama il suo simile.*
A pole cat, *faina,* s. f. *animal rapace, il suo pelo nereggia nel rosso, ed è bianca sotto la gola.*
A cib-cat, *un gatto.*
A civet cat, *gatto del zibetto, animale producente il zibetto.*
A musk-cat, *màrtora,* s. f. *zibellino,* s. m.
Cat-fish, *gatto marino.*
Cat a mountain [a mongrel sort of wild cat] *pardo,* s. m.
Cat's mint [an herb] *pullegio,* s. m. *erba medicinale.*
Cat in the pan, [turning the cat in the pan] *gli è quando quello che uno dice all' altro lo dice come se l' altro l' avesse detto a lui.*
A cat may look upon a king; *noi diciamo, un cane guarda un arcivescovo.*
Cat, *è anche una sorta di nave così chiamata.*

CATACO'MBS, s. [grottoes about Rome, where they say that the primitive Christians hid themselves in time of persecution, and buried the martyrs] *catacombe,* s. f.

CATAGMA'TICK, adj. *che ha virtù di consolidar le parti.*

CATALO'GUE, s. [list] *catálogo, registro,* s. m.

CATAMO'UNTAIN, s. *spezia di gatto salvatico ferocissimo.*

CATAPHRACT, s. *cavaliere armato di tutt' armi.* Milton.

CA'TAPLASM, s. [poultice] *cataplasmo,* s. m.

CA'TARACT, s. [a fall of a river] *caterratta,* s. f. *cascata d'acqua.*
Cataract [a disease in the eyes] *cateratta, certa membrana che toglie all' occhio l'uso del vedere o che il rende appannato.*

CATA'RRH, s. [a defluxion of humours from the head towards the lower parts] *catarro,* s. m. *superfluità d'umore, che stilla dalla testa.*
Full of catarrhs, *catarrale.*
Troubled with catarrhs, *catarroso.*

CATA'STROPHE, s. [the end and issue of a business] *catástrofe,* s. f.
The catastrophe of a tragedy, *la catastrofe d'una tragedia.*

CAT-CA'L, or CATCA'L, s. *fischio usato ne' teari per fischiare il poeta o gli attori.*

CATCH, s. [a booty or prize] *presa,* s. f. *bottino.*
To get a good catch, *fare una buona presa.*
Catch [a kind of swift-sailing ship] *spezie di naviglio.*
A catch [a short witty song] *uno strambotto, un cánone musicale,* s. m.
A catch for a hawk [a hawk's lure] *beccatella,* s. f. *pezzuolo di carne, che si gitta per aria al falcone quando gira sopra la ragnaja.*
A catch of a door, *annello di porta.*
Catchfly, s. [a kind of herb] *sesamoide,* s. f. *sorta d'erba.*
The catch of a latch, *monachetto,* s. m. *quel ferro nel quale entra il saliscendo e l'accavalcia, per serrar l'uscio.*
To be or lie upon the catch, *stare sulle volte, stare all' agguato, tendere insidie.*
To live upon the catch, *viver di rapina.*
A catch bit, *un parasito, un ghiottone, uno scrocco.*
Catchpole [serjeant, bailiff] *zaffo, birro, satellite,* s. m.

To CATCH, *pret.* caught or catched, [to lay hold on] *acchiappare, pigliare, afferrare, aggrappare, carpire, cogliere, incogliere,* pref. *carpisco, colgo.*
To catch [to snatch] *rapire, levar di mano,* pref. *rapisco.*
To catch hold of, *impugnare, afferare.*

To

To catch [to overtake] *arrivare, sopragiungere, e sopragiugnere*, pret. *sopragiunsi.*

To catch a fall, *cascare.*

Catch me in a lye and hang me, *voglio esser impiccato se mi* trovate *mai menzognero.*

To catch a tartar, *v.* Tartar.

To catch cold, *infreddarsi, raffreddarsi.*

To catch a distemper, *prendere una malattia.*

To catch one's death, *causarsi la morte.*

To catch fire, *attaccare il fuoco.*

The bed caught fire, *il fuoco s'attaccò al letto.*

To catch at a thing, cercare, ricercare *una cosa, appetirla, procurare d'ottenerla.*

To catch up, *prendere, impugnare.*

To catch in a net, *accalappiare, irretire, pigliar con* rete.

To catch with a hook, *uncinare, pigliar con uncino.*

To catch with bird-lime, *invischiare, impaniare.*

CATCHED, adj. [caught] *preso, acchiapato, afferrato, aggraffato, v.* To catch.

CA'TCHER, s. *pigliatore*, s. m. *quegli che piglia.*

A bird catcher, *uccellatore*, s. m.

Càtcher, s. [a trap] *schiaccia, trappola, trabbocchetto.*

CA'TCHING, s. *il pigliare, l'afferrare, v.* To catch.

Catching, adj. *contagioso, che si communica.*

A catching distemper, *una malattia contagiosa.*

CATECHE'TICAL, adj. [belonging to catechising] *appartemente a catechismo.*

To CATECHI'SE [to instruct youth in the fundamental articles of the Christian religion] *catechizzare, istruire ne' principi fondamentali della* religione *Cristiana.*

CATECHI'SED, adj. *catechizzàto.*

CATECHI'SING, s. *il catechizzare:*

CA'TECHISM, s. [a short system of instructions of what is to be believed and done] *catechismo*, s. m. *libretto che insegna quello che si deve* credere *e fare dal Cristiano.*

CA'TECHIST, s. [one employed in catechising] *quelli che insegna il catechismo, caterhista.*

CATECHU'MEN, s. [a person some time instructed before he was admitted to baptism] *catecúmeno, e catecumino*, s. m: *cristiano non battezzato.*

CATEGO'RICAL, adj. [affirmative, positive] *categorico, affirmativo, positivo.*

A categorical answer, *una risposta categorica o precisà.*

CA'TEGORY, s. [order, rank] *categoria, disposizione*, s. f. *ordine*, s. m.

CATENA'TION, s. [link, regular connection] *catena in significato metaforico; connessione regolare.*

CA'TER, s. [the number four] *quattro, al giuoco delle carte e de' dadi:*

To CA'TER [to provide victuals] *far le provisioni necessarie per il pranzo.*

A catercousin, s. [a trencher friend] *un parasito, un ghiottone, uno scrocco.*

They are not cater cousins, *non sono d'accordo insieme.*

CA'TERER, s. [a purveyor of victuals in the house of a king or nobleman] *maggiordomo, provveditore*, s. m. *quegli che provvede le cose necessarie.*

CATERPI'LLAR, s. [an insect devouring the leaves of trees and plants] *bruco*, s. m. *insetto che rodè la verdura.*

To CA'TERWAUL, v. n. [to make noise as cats in rutting time] *gnaulare, miagolare, mandar fuori la voce come fanno i gatti quando vanno in amore.*

To càterwaul [to make any offensive or odious noise] *mandar fuori voci e grida fastidiose e spiacevoli.*

CATES, s. pl. *vivanda, cibo.*

CATHA'RTICK, adj. [purging] *purgativo.*

CATHE'DRAL, adj. *cattedrale.*

A cathedral church, *una chiesa* catte*drale.*

CATHEDRA'TICK, s. [a law word, a sum of two shillings paid by the inferior clergy to the bishop in token of subjection and respect] *la somma di due scellini che si paga al vescovo dal'clero in segno di sommessione e rispetto.*

CATHO'LICISM, s. [the Roman catholick profession] *la professione* cattolica *Romana.*

CA'THOLICK, adj. [universal] *cattolico, universale.*

The catholick church, *la chiesa cattolica.*

Catholick [orthodox] *cattolico, ortodosso.*

The catholick faith, *la fede cattolica.*

A catholick, s. *un cattolico, una cattolica.*

A Roman catholick, *un cattolico Romano.*

The Catholic King [a title peculiar to the king of Spain] *il Re Cattolico, titolo appartenente al re di Spagna.*

CATHO'LICON, s. [an universal remedy] *catolico, rimedio universale.*

Catholicon [a plaster for all sores] *rimedio per* tutti *i mali.*

CA'TLING, s. [dismembering knife] *spezie di coltello, coltellaccio.*

Cátling [cat-gut, fiddle-string] *corda da violino.*

CA'TTEL, *v.* Cattle.

To CA'TTERWAUL [to cry as cats do when they are proud] *gnaulare, miagolare.*

CATTERWAUL, or Catterwauling, s. tre*genda di gatti.*

Catterwàuling [noise] *strepito, rumore, fracasso*, s. m.

CA'TTLE, s. *bestiame*, s. m.

Cattle, *bagascie, pettegole, puttane abbiette. Modo basso.*

CAVALCA'DE, s. [a pompous march of persons of quality on horseback upon some solemn occasion] *cavalcata*, s. f.

CAVALI'ER, s. [a knight] *un cavaliere*, s. m. *colui ch' è ornato d'alcuna dignità di cavalleria.*

Càvalier [a soldier on horseback] *cavaliere, soldato a cavallo.*

Cavalier-like, *cavallerescamente, alla cavalleresca, nobilmente, da cavaliere.*

CA'VALRY, s. [horse-troops] *cavalleria*, s. f. *milizia a cavallo.*

CA'UDLE, s. *bevanda stomacale all' Inglese, composta di vino, uova, zucchero, e spezierie.*

CAVE, s. [den, dark hollow place under ground] *grotta, caverna, spelonca*, s. f. *antro*, s. m.

Cave [cellar] *cantina*, s. f.

To CAVE [to dwell in a cave] *dimorare in una spelonca.*

CA'VEAT, s. [a caution, warning, admonition] *avvertenza, ammonizione*, s. f. *avvertimento, avviso*, s. m.

CA'VESON, s. [a false rein to hold or lead a horse] *cavezzone*, s. m. *arnese che si mette alla testa de' cavalli per maneggiarli con facilità.*

CA'VERN, s. [den] *caverna*, s. f.

CA'VERNED, adj. *cavernoso, incavato, fatto a mo' di caverna.*

Caverned [inhabiting a cavern] *che dimora in una caverna.*

CA'VERNOUS, adj. [full of caverns] *cavernoso, pien di caverne.*

CA'VERS, s. [thieves who steal ore out of the mines] *ladri di miniere.*

CAUF, s. [a chest with holes to keep fish under water] *spezie di cassa bucata da tener pesci vivi nell' acqua.*

CAUGHT, adj. [from to catch] *preso, acchiappato, afferrato, v.* To catch.

I am caught, *sono preso.*

CA'VIARE, s. [the eggs of several fishes dried or pickled] *caviale*, s. f. *ovaja del pesce seccata al fumo o al vento, o acconcia in altro mangiabil modo.*

CA'VIL, s. [quirk, shift, captious argument] *cavillazione*, s. f. *cavillo*, s. m. *sofisma, argomento che ha in se fallacia.*

To CA'VIL [to wrangle, to find fault, to argue captiously] *cavillare, gavillare, stiracchiare, sofisticare.*

To cavil at every thing one says, *criticare quel che altri dice.*

CAVILLA'TION, s. [wrangling] *cavillo, cavillazione, gavillazione*, s. f. *il cavillare.*

CAVI'LLER, s. *un cavilloso, un sofista.*

CA'VILLOUS, adj. [full of objections] *cavilloso, sofistico.*

CA'VITY, s. [hollowness] *cavità*, s. f.

CAUL, s. [the net in which women inclose their hair] *rete di cui le donne si servono per raccogliere i lor capelli la notte.*

Caul, *ogni sorta di rete picciola.*

Caul, *l'integumento che contiene le budella.*

CAULIFLO'WER, s. *cavolfiore, spezie di cavolo.*

CA'USAL, adj. [relating to causes] *causale.*

CA'USALITY, s. [the action or power of a cause in producing its effects] *causalità*, s. f.

CA'USE, s. [that which produces its effect] *causa, cagione*, s. f. *principio*, s. m.

A physical or moral cause, *causa fisica o morale.*

He was the cause of my misfortune, *egli fu la causa della mia disgrazia.*

Cause [reason] *ragione, materia, cagione, s. f. motivo, soggetto, luogo, s. m.*

It is not without cause that I complain, *non mi lamento senza ragione.*

I never gave you cause to speak ill of me, *non vi diedi mai soggetto di sparlar di me.*

Cause [party] *partito, s. m.*

To stand for the good cause, *seguitare il buon partito.*

Cause [at law] *causa, s. f. processo, s. m.*

To plead a cause, *difendere una lite.*

A just, or unjust cause, *una causa giusta o ingiusta.*

To plead in one's own cause, *difendere la propria causa.*

I will proceed as I shall see cause, *mi comporterò secondo che meglio mi parrà.*

To give cause of suspicion, *dar luogo o materia di sospettare.*

'Tis for this cause that I will not see him, *per questa ragione non voglio vederlo.*

To CA'USE [to be the cause of] *causare, cagionare, produrre, eccitare, suscitare,* pret. *produssi.*

To cause a rebellion, *eccitare o suscitare una ribellione.*

To cause sleep, *far dormire.*

To cause love, *destar amore, far nascere amore.*

To cause sorrow, *dar dispiacere.*

To cause anger, *concitar ira.*

To cause a thing to be done, *fare o procurare ch' una cosa si faccia.*

CAUSED, adj. *causato, cagionato, prodotto, ecciato, suscitato.*

CA'USELESLY, adv. *senza causa o ragione, a torto.*

CA'USELESS, adj. [without cause] *senza causa, ingiusto.*

CA'USEY, } s. [a highway, a bank CAUSEWAY, } raised in marshy ground for foot passage] *ghiajata, s. f. spandimento di ghiaja per assodare i luoghi fangosi, argine, s. m.*

CAUSTICAL, } adj. [burning] *cau-* CA'USTICK, } *stico, adustivo, corrosivo.*

A caustick, s. *un caustico, sorta di medicamento estrinseco che ha forza adustiva.*

CA'UTEL, s. [caution] *cautéla, scrupolo.*

CA'UTELOUS, adj. [wary, heedful] *cautelosò, accorto, sagace, circospetto.*

To CAUTERI'ZE [to apply a cautery] *cauterizzare, far cauterio.*

To cauterize a horse [to cut a wart, &c. with a sharp hot iron] *incendere un cavallo, cauterizzarlo.*

CAUTERI'ZED, adj. *cauterizzato, inceso.*

CA'UTERY, s. [hot iron] *cauterio,* s. m. *incendimento di carne con ferro rovente o con fuoco morto, rottorio,* s. m.

CA'UTION, s. [heed] *cautela, accortezza, sagacità, circospezione, diligenzia,* s. f.

Caution [warning] *avviso, avvertimento,* s. m.

To CA'UTION [to warn] *avvertire, dare avvertimenti, ammonire, ammaestrare, istruire,* pref. *avvertisco, istruisco.*

CA'UTIONARY, adj. [given in pawn, or pledge] *d'ostaggio.*

Cautionary towns, *città d'ostaggio, città che si danno per istatico di quel che si promette.*

CA'UTIOUS, adj. [heedful, wary] *cauteloso, cauto, circospetto, accorto, sagare.*

CA'UTIOUSLY, adj. *cautelosamente, cautamente, con cautela, accortamente, prudentemente, sagacemente, accortamente.*

CA'UTIOUSNESS, s. *cautela, accortezza, prudenza, sagacità, circospezione,* s. f.

To CAW, [to cry as the rook or crow] *crocitare, come fa il corbo e la cornacchia.*

CAWL, s. *v.* Caul.

CA'YMAN, s. [a sort of crocodile] *spezie di coccodrillo.*

CEASE, s. [extinction, failure] *cessazione, il cessare.*

To CEASE [to leave off, to give over] *cessare, tralasciare, finire, desistere,* pref. *finisco.*

He never ceases to complain, *non cessa mai di lamentarsi.*

To cease from work, *tralasciare il lavoro, finire di lavorare.*

CEASED, adj. *cessato, tralasciato, finito, desistito.*

CE'ASELESS, adj. [incessant, perpetual, continual] *incessante, che non cessa mai, perpetuo, continuo, perenne.*

CE'ASING, s. *cessamento,* s. m. *cessazione,* s. f. *il cessare.*

Without ceasing, *senza cessare, incessabilmente, incessantemente.*

CE'CITY, s. [blindness, privation of sight] *cecità, privazione di vista.*

CE'DAR, s. [cedar tree or wood] *cedro,* s. m. *albero.*

CELANDI'NE, s. [an herb] *celidonia,* s. f. *erba nota.*

To CE'LEBRATE [to solemnize] *celebrare, solennizzare.*

To celebrate a feast, *celebrare una festa.*

To celebrate [to praise] *celebrare, esaltare, lodare.*

CE'LEBRATED, adj. *celebrato, solennizzato, esaltato, lodato.*

Celebrated [famous] *célebre, famoso, rinomato.*

CELEBRA'TING, s. *celebrante,* s. m. *il celebrare.*

CELEBRA'TION, s. *celebramento, celebrazione, solennità,* s. f.

Celebration [praise] *lode,* s. f. *elogio,* s. m.

CELE'BRIOUS, adj. [famous] *celebre, famoso, illustre.*

CELE'BRITY, s. [renown] *celebrità, fama,* s. f.

Celebrity [praise] *lode,* s. f. *elogio,* s. m.

CELE'RITY, s. [swiftness] *celerità, prestezza,* s. f.

CE'LERY, s. [a sort of plant] *selleri.*

CELE'STIAL, adj. [heavenly] *celestiale, celeste.*

The celestial globe, *il globo celeste.*

The twelve celestial signs, *i dodici segni celesti.*

CELE'STIALLY, adv. *celestialmente, in modo celestiale.*

To CELESTIFY', [to give something of heavenly nature to any thing] *dar qualcosa del celeste ad una cosa.*

CELESTI'NES, s. [Celestine monks] *celestini,* s. m. *ordine di frati.*

CE'LIBACY, } s. [single life] *celi-* CE'LIBATE, } *bato,* s. m.

CELL, s. [a small cavity or hollow place] *picciola cava, luogo, incavato.*

Cell [a small and close apartment in a prison] *segreta; prigione stretta e rimota.*

Cell [any small place of residence] *abitazioncella.*

Cell, [the habitation of a monk or nun] *cella,* s. f. *camera dove dormono i frati e le monache.*

CE'LLAR, s. *cantina, cánova,* s. f.

Wine-cellar, *cantina da vino.*

Little cellar, *cantinetta,* s. f.

CELLARA'GE, s. [cellar room] *cantine,* s. f. plural.

There is very good cellarage in that house, *vi sono buone cantine in quella casa.*

Cellarage [duty paid for laying wine in a cellar] *fitto o prezzo che si paga per l'uso d'una cantina.*

CE'LLARIST, s. [the butler in a monastery] *canovajo,* s. m.

CE'LSITUDE, s. [highness] *celsitudine, altezza,* s. f.

CE'MENT, s. [strong cleaving mortar] *smalto,* s. m.

To CEME'NT [to fasten together, to solder] *assodare, fermare, saldare.*

CEME'NTED, adj. *assodato, fermato, saldato.*

CE'METERY, s. [a place where the dead are deposited] *cimitero, cimiterio.*

CE'NCRIS, s. [a green snake] *spezie di serpe brizzolata.*

To CENSE [to perfume with incense] *incensare.* Not in use.

CE'NSER, s. [a vessel to burn incense in, a perfuming pan] *incensiere, turibile o turibolo.*

CE'NSOR, [among the Romans; a magistrate who had the power of correcting manners] *censore.*

Censor, s. [one who is given to censure] *uno che è amante di biasimare i falli altrui.*

CENSO'RIOUS, adj. [apt to find fault with, critical] *critico.*

He is a censorious man, *egli è un censore, un uomo che censura ogni cosa.*

CENSO'RIOUSLY, adj. *da censore.*

CENSO'RIOUSNESS, s. *censura, maldicenza,* s. f.

CE'NSORSHIP, s. *dignità di censore.*

CE'NSURABLE, adj. *che merita censura; degno di biasimo, biasimevole.*

CE'NSURE, s. [correction, reproof] *censura, correzzione, riprensione,* s. f.

To CE'NSURE [to criticise, to find fault with, to check, to reprove] *censurare, criticare, correggere, riprendere,* pret. *corressi, ripresi.*

Ce'nsured, adj. *censurato*, criticato, *corretto, ripreso.*

Cent, s. [a low mercantile word; hundred] *cento*; *termine legale o mercantile.*

To pay intereſt at five per Cent, *pagar l'intereſſe a cinque per cento.*

Ce'ntaur, s. [a fabulous monſter, half man and half horſe] *centauro*, s. m. *moſtro favoloſo mezzo uomo e mezzo cavallo.*

Ce'ntaury, *centáura, ſorta d' erba.*

Ce'ntenary, adj. [belonging to an hundred] *centinario.*

Ce'nter, s. [the middle point of any thing] *centro*, s. m. *punto nel mezzo del cerchio.*

The center of the earth, *il centro della terra.*

Center [in maſonry, a wooden mould to turn an arch] *centina*, s. f. *legno arcato con che s'armano e ſoſtengono le volte.*

To Ce'nter [to meet in a point, to terminate] *terminare, finire.*

Ce'ntinel, *v.* Centry.

Ce'ntory, s. [an herb] *cenáturea*, s. f. *ſorta d'erba.*

Ce'ntry, s. [ſanctuary] *ſantuario*, s. m.

Centry [centinel] *ſentinella, vedetta, veletta*, s. f. *ſoldato che fa la guardia.*

To ſtand centry, *eſſer di ſentinella, far la ſentinella, ſtar alla veletta o vedetta.*

Centry [a mould for an arch] *centina*, s. f.

Ce'ntuple, adj. [an hundred fold] *centuplicato.*

Centu'rion, s. [a captain of an hundred] *centurione*, s. m. *capitano di centa uomini.*

Ce'ntury, s. [company of an hundred among the Romans] *centuria*, s. f. *compagnia di cento fanti fra gli antichi Romani.*

Century [an age containing an hundred years] *centuria*, s. f. *ſecolo*, s. m. *ſpazio di cento anni.*

They lived in the ſame century, *viſſero nel medeſimo ſecolo.*

Cepha'lick, adj. [of or belonging to the head] *ceſalico.*

The cephalick vein, *la vena ceſalica.*

Ce'rate, s. [a medicine made with oil and wax] *cerotto*, s. m. *rompoſto medicinale fatto di cera e olio.*

To Cere, [to wax] *incerare, coprir di cera.*

Ce'rebel, s. [part of the brain] *cervelletto, cerebello.*

Ce're-cloth, s. *incerato*, s. m. *tela incerato.*

Cere'monial, adj. *cerimoniale.*

The ceremonial law, *la legge ceremoniale.*

Ceremonial, s. [a book containing the ceremonies of the Roman church] *ceremoniale e cirimoniale*, s. m. *il libro, dove ſon regiſtrate le cerimonie della chieſa Romana.*

Ceremo'nious, adj. [full of ceremonies] *cerimonioſo, che tratta con cerimonie.*

He is very ceremonious, *è una perſona molto cerimonioſa.*

Ceremo'niously, adv. *ceremonioſamente e crimonioſamente, con cirimonia.*

Ce'remony, s. [formality or formal compliment] *cermonia, cirimonia*, s. f. *complimento*, s. m.

A maſter of ceremonies, *ceremoniere, cirimoniere*, s. m. *maeſtro delle cerimonie.*

A book of ceremonies, *ceremoniale*, s. m.

Ce'rote or Ce'rate, s. [a plaſter made of oil, turpentine, and wax] *cerotto*, s. m.

Ce'rtain, adj. [ſure] *certo, ſicuro, chiaro, evidente, manifeſto.*

Certain [ſettled] *certo, fiſſo, fermo, ſtabile.*

Certain [regular] *certo, regolare.*

Certain [ſome] *certo, alcuno.*

A certain truth, *una verità certa e indubitata.*

'Tis certain, *è certo.*

I am certain of it, *ne ſon certo, ne ſono ſicuro.*

I have no certain abode, *non ho una dimora fiſſa, ſtabile.*

Certain or regular motion, *moto certo o regolare.*

A certain perſon, *una certa perſona.*

Certain others, *alcuni altri.*

Of certain, *per certo, certamente.*

I know it for certain, *lo ſo per certo.*

Ce'rtainly, adv. [aſſuredly] *certamente, ſicuramente, indubitatamente.*

Certainly [in truth] *certo, in vero, per certo.*

Ce'rtainty, s. [ſureneſs] *certezza*, s. f.

For a certainty, *con certezza, certamente, per certo.*

We have now the certainty of his death, *adeſſo ſiamo certi della ſua morte, adeſſo abbiamo novelle ſicura delle ſua morte.*

There is no certainty of any thing, *non v'è nulla di certo.*

I would fain have ſome certainty, *vorrei in qualche modo eſſer ſicuro, vorrei pur avere qualche certezza.*

To leave the certainty and ſtick to chance, *laſciare il certo per l'incerto.*

There is no certainty of him, *non ſi può far capitale di lui.*

Certi'fcate, s. [a teſtimony given in writing of the truth of any thing] *certificato, atteſtato*, s. m.

To Ce'rtify [to aſſure] *certificare, far certo, render certo.*

Ce'rtify'd, adj. *certificato, fatto certo, reſo certo.*

Ce'rtitude, s. [certainly] *certezza, contezza*, s. f.

Ce'rvelas, or Ce'rvelat, s. [a kind of ſauſage] *cervellata*, s. f. *ſorta di ſalſiccia.*

Ceru'lean, } adj. [blue] *ceruleo,*
Ceru'leous, } *turchino, azzurro.*

Ce'ruse, or Ce'russ, s. [white lead, or Spaniſh white] *ceruſſa, biacca.*

Ce'sarian, *Ceſariano*, adj. The Ceſarian ſection of cutting a child out of the womb, *Il taglio Ceſariano è quello che ſi fa per trarre la creatura dell' utero materno.*

Cess, s. [tax] *taſſa, taſſazione*, s. f.

Ceſs, s. [bounds, limits] *limite, confine.*

To Cess [to aſſeſs, to tax] *taſſare.*

Cessa'tion, s. [from to ceaſe] *ceſſagione, ceſſazione*, s. f. *ceſſamento, tralaſciamento*, s. m.

Ceſſation of arms, *ſoſpenſion d'armi.*

Ce'ssed, adj. *taſſato.*

Cessibi'lity, s. [the quality of receding or giving way] *il recedere, il cedere.*

Ce'ssible, adj. [eaſy to give way] *facile a cedere, che cede, non reſiſtente.*

Ce'ssion, s. [the act of reſigning or giving up] *ceſſione*, s. f.

Cessionary, adj. *ex.*

A ceſſionary bankrupt, *un fallito che cede i ſuoi bene a' creditori.*

Ce'ssor, s. [aſſeſſor] *taſſatore*, s. m. *che taſſa.*

Ceſſor, s. [he that ceaſeth or neglecteth ſo long to perform a duty belonging to him, that he incurreth the danger of the law] *colui che tanto tempo traſcura o ceſſa di far il ſuo dovere, che corre poi pericolo da' magiſtrati e dalle leggi.*

Cestus, s. *ceſto*, s. m. *cintura di Venere.*

Ceta'ceous, adj. [of the whale kind] *che tiene della balena, che raſſomiglia alla balena.*

To Chace, *v.* to chaſe.

To Chafe [to make hot] *ſcaldare, riſcaldare.*

To chafe [to rub with one's hand] *fregare, ſtropicciare.*

To chafe [to make angry] *mettere in collera, ſtizzire, far prendere ſtizza.*

To chafe [to fret and fume] *adirarſi, incollorirſi, ſbuffare, arrabbiarſi, andare in collera.*

Chafed, adj. *ſcaldato, fregato, ſtropicciato, ſtizzito, adirato, incollorito, ſbuffato, arrabbiato.*

Chafe, s. [a heat, a rage, a fury] *caldo, rabbia, furore.*

Cha'fer, s. [beetle] *ſorta di ſcarafaggio*, s. m.

Chafer [to warm meat] *ſtromento da riſcaldare le vivande.*

Cha'fery, s. [that part of an iron mill where the iron is wrought into bars] *quella parte del molino da ferro dove ſi mette il ferro in iſbarre.*

Chafe-wax, s. [an officer in Chancery who fits the wax for ſealing of writs] *ſcaldarera, officiale in cancelleria che ſcalda la cera per ſuggellare.*

Chaff, s. [the huſks of corn that are ſeparated by threſhing and winnowing] *pagliuola del grano quando è ſeparata da quello col correggiato o col vaglio.*

Chaff, *per ſimilitudine, coſa ſpregievole e da nulla.*

Cha'ffer, s. [wares] *mercanzia*, s. f.

To Cha'ffer [to buy and ſell, to traffick] *trafficare, negoziare.*

To chaffer [to beat down the price] *diminuire il prezzo.*

CHA'FFWEED, s. *spezie d'erba.*

CHA'FFERING, s. *negozio, traffico, commercio,* s. m.

CHA'FFERN, s. [to heat water in] *caldaja,* s. f.

CHA'FFINCH, s. [a sort of bird] *fringuello, pincione,* s. m. *sorta di uccelletto.*

CHA'FFING, s. *riscaldamento,* s. m. *il riscaldare.*

CHA'FFY, adj. [full of chaff] *paglioso, pieno di paglia.*

A CHAFING-DISH, *uno scaldavivande.*

CHAGRI'N, s. [ill humor, vexation] *malumore, affanno,* s. m. *stizza,* s. f.

CHAIN, s. *catena,* s. f.

A gold, silver, or iron chain, *una catena d'oro, d'argento, o di ferro, una collana.*

To bind one in chains, *mettere alla catena.*

A long chain of hills [a long ridge of hills] *giogaja,* s. f. *una continuazione di monti.*

A little chain, *catenella, catenuzza,* s. f.

A link of a chain, *anello di catena.*

Chain [chain-lace] *catenella,* s. f.

Chains, s. pl. [slavery] *catene, servitù, schiavitù.*

Chain-shot [chain-bullets] *palle incatenate.*

CHAI'N-PUMP, s. [a pump used in large English vessels, which is double, so that one rises as the other falls] *sorte di tromba grande e doppia usata ne' vascelli per cavar loro l'acqua quando occorre.*

To CHAIN [to tie with chains] *incatenare, legare con catena.*

CHA'INED, adj. *incatenato.*

CHA'INING, s. *incatenatura,* s. f. *l'incatenare.*

CHAIR, s. [to sit in] *sedia,* s. f. *strumento da sedervi sopra.*

An arm-chair, *una sedia d'appoggio.*

Chair [sedan] *bussola,* s. f.

To go in a chair, *andar in bussola.*

Privy-chair or stool, *segetta,* s. f. *sedia per uso d'andar del corpo.*

Chairman [one that mends chairs about the town] *un acconciatore di sedie.*

Chairman [one that carries people in a chair] *segettiero, portantino,* s. m.

A chairman in a committee, *il capo o presidente de' commissari eletti per esaminare un negozio.*

CHAISE, s. [a sort of light open chariot with one horse] *calesso,* s. m.

CHA'LCEDONY, s. [a sort of onyx stone] *calcidonio,* s. m. *spezie di pietra preziosa.*

CHA'LCOGRAPHER, s. [engraver in brass] *intagliatore in rame.*

CHA'LDERN, CHA'LDRON, CHAU'LDRON, s. [a measure for coals containing thirty-six bushels] *misura di carbone che dovrebbe pesare due mila libbre.*

CHA'LICE, s. [communion cup] *calice,* s. m.

CHALK, s. [a fossil] *gesso,* s. m. *creta,* s. f.

It is no more like than chalk is like cheese, *è affatto differente.*

To CHALK [to mark with chalk] *segnare o notare col gesso.*

To chalk a picture [to sketch a picture] *schizzare, disegnare un ritratto o quadro.*

To chalk out, *segnare, mostrare, incamminare.*

He has chalk'd us the way to happiness, *egli chi ha segnato la strada alla felicità.*

CHA'LKED, adj. *segnato con gesso, mostrato, istradato.*

CHA'LKING, s. *il segnare col gesso.*

The chalking of a picture [the sketching of a picture] *schizzo fatto col gesso.*

CHA'LKY, adj. *cretoso.*

Chalky clay [marl] *terra grassa e cretosa buona ad ingrassare la terra.*

CHA'LLENGE, s. [defiance, invitation to fight] *disfida,* s. f.

Challenge [claim, pretension] *pretensione.*

Challenge [a law term, an exception against persons and things] *rigettamento, rifiuto,* s. m.

To CHA'LLENGE [to give a challenge to fight] *disfidare, sfidare, chiamare l' avversario a battaglia.*

To challenge [to claim] *pretendere, aver pretensione.*

To challenge [to except against] *rigettare, ributtare, rifiutare.*

To challenge [to accuse] *accusare, incolpare.*

Centries have orders to challenge after ten o'clock, *le sentinelle hanno ordine di gridare chi va là dopo le dieci.*

CHA'LLENGED, adj. *disfidato, sfidato,* v. to challenge.

CHA'LLENGER, s. *sfidatore,* s. m. *che sfida un altro a battaglia.*

Challenge [one that claims superiority] *uno che pretende superiorità.*

Challenger [a claimant] *un che ha domande o pretese sopra chechesia.*

CHA'LLENGING, s. *sfidamento,* s. m. *lo sfidare.*

CHA'LYBEATE, adj. *ex.* Chalybeate water [wherein a hot iron or steel has been quenched] *acqua ferrata.*

CHAMA'DE, s. [the beating of the drum which declares a surrender] *chiamata,* s. f. *quel suonar di tamburo che si fa da una fortezza assediata per dar segno agli assedianti che si vuol rendere.*

CHA'MBER, s. [a room in a house] *camera, stanza.*

A groom of the chamber, *ajutante di camera.*

A bed-chamber, *camera da letto, camera dove si dorme.*

A chamber-maid, *una cameriera.*

A chamber-pot, *un orinale.*

A chamber fellow, *un camerata.*

The chamber of a gun, *camera di cannone, quella parte dell' artiglieria che per maggior fortezza si fa nel voto più stretta vicino al fondo.*

The chamber of London, *la camera di Londra.*

CHA'MBERER, s. [a man of intrigue] *un faccendiere, un uom d'intrighi.*

CHA'MBERING [debauchery] *dissolutezza, disonestà, sfrenatezza,* s. f.

CHA'MBERLAIN, s. *camerlingo, cameriere maggiore,* s. m.

The Lord Great Chamberlain of England, *il gran camerlingo d'Inghilterra.*

The chamberlain of London, *camerlingo o tesoriero di Londra.*

A chamberlain in an inn, *il cameriero d'un albergo, quello che ha cura de' letti e delle camere d'un albergo.*

CHA'MBERLAINSHIP, s. [the office of a chamberlain] *l' officio o dignità del camerlingo.*

CHA'MBERMAID, s. [a maid whose business is to dress a lady] *cameriera, serva destinata a vestir la padrona, e servirla nel suo apartamento.*

To CHA'MBLET, v. a. [to vary, to variegate] *variare, diversificare, render vario.* Not in use.

CHA'MFER, s. [a small furrow or gutter upon a pillar] *scanalatura,* s. f.

To CHA'MFER [to channel or make hollow] *scanalare, incavare legno o pietra per ridurla a guisa di canale.*

To chamfer a pillar, *scanalare una colonna.*

CHA'MFERED, adj. *scanalato.*

CHA'MFRET, *v.* Chamfer.

CHA'MFRING, s. *lo scanalare.*

CHA'MLET, *v.* Camlet.

CHA'IMO'IS, s. [an animal of the goat kind] *camozza, spezie di capra salvatica.*

CHA'MOMILE, s. [the name of an odoriferous plant] *camomilla, nome d'una pianta odorifera.*

To CHAMP [to chew] *masticare.*

A horse that champs the bit, *un cavallo che rode il freno.*

To champ [to devour] *divorare.*

CHAMPAI'GN, s. [large, plain, open field, downs] *pianura,* s. f. *campagna aperta o rasa.*

CHA'MPERTY, s. [a maintenance of any man in his suit depending] *quel che si da al litigante, per farlo sussistere durante il tempo che la sua lite è pendente. E' termine legale.*

CHA'MPED, adj. *masticato.*

CHA'MPERTOR, s. [a barretor] *uno che presta danari ad usura sopra una lite pendente. E' termine legale.*

CHA'MPING, s. *masticamento,* s. m. *il masticare.*

CHA'MPION, s. [one who fights for another] *campione,* s. m.

Champion [a hero, a stout warrior] *un eroe, un combattitor valoroso.*

To CHA'MPION, *v. a.* [to challenge] *isfidare a singolar certame.*

CHANCE, s. [hazard, hap, fortune] *accidente, caso, avvenimento,* s. m. *fortuna, ventura, sorte.*

I met him by chance, *l' incontrai a caso.*

'Tis by mere chance, *è un puro accidente.*

A happy chance, *una buona ventura.*

An unhappy chance, *una sventura, una cattiva fortuna.*

By an unhappy chance, *per mala fortuna.*

To try the chance of war, *tentar la fortuna della guerra.*

The chance of arms is uncertain, *l' esito dell' armi è incerto.*

To

To take one's chance, *arrischiare, arrificare, cimentarsi.*

To look to the main chance, *badare a quel che importa il più, badare a' fatti suoi.*

To bear stoutly the chance of fortune, *sopportar coraggiosamente l'avversa fortuna.*

An ill chance, *disgrazia, sfortuna.*

A chance-customer, *un che compra qualche cosa a caso in una bottega, un avventore casuale.*

A chance-guest, *un che sopraggiugne inaspettamente a casa tua.*

Chance-medley [the casual killing of a man, which is called also man-slaughter] *omicidio casuale o involontario.*

Chance-medley [casualty] *caso fortuito.*

To CHANCE [to happen] *accadere, avvenire, succedere, occorrere, intervenire,* pret. *accadde, avvenne, successe, intervenne, occorse.*

If ever I chance to see him, *se m'avvenisse mai di vederlo, se mi verrà mai fatto di vederlo.*

I may chance to go thither, *può ben essere che io vi vada.*

If any man chance to come in, *se a caso venisse alcuno; caso che alcuno entrasse.*

If my letter should chance to be lost, *se per sorte si perdesse la mia lettera.*

CHA'NCEABLE, adj. [accidental] *casuale, accidentale.*

CHA'NCEL, s. [an enclosed place surrounded with bars to keep judges from the croud] *ruota,* s. f. *quel tribunale dove siedono i giudici che procedono nel giudicare.*

Chancel of a church [the part of a church which is next to the altar, compassed with rails] *il presbiterio, quel luogo innanzi l'altar maggiore circondato di balaustri.*

CHA'NCELLOR, or CHA'NCELLOUR, s. [an officer of very great dignity and power] *cancelliere,* s. m.

The lord high chancellor, *il gran cancelliere d'Inghilterra.*

CHA'NCELLORSHIP, or CHA'NCELLOURSHIP, s. *la carica di cancelliere.*

CHA'NCERY, or CHA'NCERY-COURT, s. *cancelleria,* s. f.

CHA'NDLER, s. [a seller of divers sorts of wares] *pizzicagnolo,* s. m. *che vende salumi, cacio, e altri comangiari.*

A tallow-chandler, *quello che fa o vende candele di sevo.*

A wax-chandler, *quello che vende candele di cera, ceraiuolo.*

A corn-chandler, *quello che vende ogni sorte di biade.*

CHA'NGE, s. [alteration] *cangiamento, cambiamento,* s. m. *mutazione, variazione, alterazione, vicenda,* s. f.

Change [variety] *varietà,* s. f.

To put the change upon one, *rendere il contraccambio ad uno.*

The change of the moon, *interlunio, luna nuova.*

The change of seasons, *il corso delle stagioni.*

England has all along been subject to many changes, *l'Inghilterra è stata sempre soggetta a diverse rivoluzioni.*

Change [conversion] *conversione, il convertirsi.*

'Tis God alone which works our change, *Iddio solo opera la nostra conversione.*

Change [amongst traders] *cambio, il cambiar danari da luogo a luogo per via di lettere.*

The change is very high, *il cambio è molto alto.*

Change [small money] *moneta, quattrini spicci.*

I have no change, *non ho moneta, non ho quattrini spicci.*

To CHANGE [to transform] *cambiare, trasmutare, variare, alterare, mutare.*

To change colour, *cambiarsi nel viso.*

To change one's opinion, *mutar pensiero.*

To change place, *cambiar di luogo.*

To change one's apparel, *mutarsi, cambiarsi di panni.*

To change a piece of gold, *cambiare una moneta d'oro.*

Fortune begins to change, *la fortuna comincia a cangiarsi.*

Will you change your hat with mine? will you change hats? *volete barrattare il vostro cappello col mio?*

The moon will change to-morrow, *la luna farà domani.*

CHA'NGEABLE, adj. *cangiante, mutabile, incostante, variabile, leggero.*

A changeable colour, *un color cangiante.*

A changeable humour, *un umore incostante.*

Changeable weather, *tempo variabile.*

CHA'NGEABLENESS, s. *cambiamento,* s. m. *mutabilità, leggerezza, incostanza,* s. f.

CHA'NGED, adj. *cambiato, cangiato.*

The face of affairs is very much changed, *le cose hanno mutata faccia.*

CHAN'GELING, s. [a child changed] *un parto supposto.*

A changeling [a fool, a silly fellow] *uno sciocco, un minchione, un balocco, un balordo.*

CHA'NGER, s. [money-changer] *cambiatore,* s. m. *mercante che cambia danari.*

CHA'NGING, s. *cambiamento,* s. m. *il cambiare.*

CHA'NNEL, s. *un canale.*

The channel of a river, *il letto d'un fiume.*

The Channel [the narrow seas] *il canale della mancia che divide l'isola d' Inghilterra dal continente.*

The channel of a pillar, *la scanalatura d'una colonna.*

A little channel, *un canaletto.*

To CHA'NNEL [to chamfer] *scanalare.*

CHA'NNELLED, adj. *scanalato.*

To CHANT [to sing] *cantare.*

To chant [to celebrate by song] *celebrar col canto.*

To chant [to sing in the cathedral-service] *cantar in chiesa.*

CHANT, s. [song, melody] *canto melodia.*

CHA'NTER, s. [singer, singster] *cantore,* s. m.

CHANTICLE'ER, s. [a cock] *un gallo.*

CHA'NTRESS, s. [a woman-singer] *donna che canta, cantatrice.*

CHA'OS, s. [confusion] *caos,* s. m. *confusione universale d'ogni cosa.*

CHAP, s. [chink] *fessura, spaccatura, crepatura,* s. f. *fesso,* s. m.

A chap on the ground, *crepaccio,* s. m. *apertura, crepatura nel terreno.*

To CHAP, verb. neut. [to gape, or open as the ground does in a drought] *crepare, spaccarsi, fendersi, screpolarsi, crepolarsi.*

CHAPE [a little thin plate of silver or iron at the point of a scabbard] *puntale di spada.*

CHA'PEL, s. *cappella, parte di chiesa, o chiesetta.*

CHA'PELESS, adj. [without a chape] *senza puntale.*

CHA'PELLANY, s. *cappellania.*

CHA'PERON, s. [a kind of hood worn by the knights of the Garter] *spezie di cappuccio o bacucco propio de' cavalieri della Giartiera ne' loro di solenni.*

CHA'PITER, s. [head or top of a pillar] *capitello,* s. m. *membro, e quasi capo della colonna.*

Chapiters [articles in the sense of the common law] *articoli, capitoli.*

CHA'PLAIN, s. [one who performs divine service in a chapel] *capellano,* s. m.

The living of a chaplain, *cappellania,* s. f. *beneficio che gode il cappellano.*

CHA'PLAINSHIP, s. [the office of a chaplain] *la carica di cappellano.*

CHA'PLESS, adj. [without any flesh about the mouth] *che non ha carne intorno alla bocca.*

CHA'PLET, s. [string of beads] *rosario,* s. m. *corona,* s. f.

A chaplet [a garland] *corona, ghirlanda,* s. f.

Chaplet [tuft of feathers on the peacock's head] *ciuffetto di penne sopra la testa dal paone.*

CHA'PMAN, s. [buyer, customer] *compratore, avventore,* s. m.

He was the chapman for the fish, *egli comprò il pesce.*

He is my chapman, *egli è mio avventore.*

CHAPS, s. [the mouth of a beast of prey] *la bocca d'un animal vorace.*

CHA'PPED, } part. pass. from to chap
CHA'PT, } [cleft, cracked]. *fesso, scoppiato.*

CHA'PTER, s. [a division or part of a book] *capitolo, una delle parti d'un libro.*

A book divided into several chapters, *un libro diviso in diversi capitoli.*

Chapter [the whole body of clergymen belonging to a cathedral, conventual, or collegiate church]. *capitolo, adunanza di preti o frati, o d'altri religiosi.*

To hold a chapter, *tenere un capitolo.*

To have a voice in the chapter, *aver voce in capitolo.*

The chapter house, *capitolo, il luogo ove si rauna il clero.*

CHA'PTREL, s. [the capitals of pilars or pilasters which support arches] *capitelli di pilastri o colonne che sostengono archi.*

CHAR, s. [a fish found only in Winander-meer in Lancashire] *sorta di pesce che non si trova, secondo alcuni, che nella contea di Lancashire in Inghilterra. credo sia quel pesce del lago di garda chiamato carpione.*

To CHAR, v. a. [to burn wood to a black cinder] *arder legno in modo che diventi carbone e non cenere.*

To char, v. n. [to work at other's houses by the day] *lavorar il giorno in casa d' altri per paga.*

CHA'RWOMAN, s. [a woman hired accidentally for odd work] *donna pagata per servire in casa in mancanza o assenza d' altra serva, o per fare i servigi più grossolani solamente.*

CHA'RACTER, s. [letter] *carrattere,* s. m. *lettera,* s. f.

Character [mark] *carattere, segno.*

Character [description] *carattere, descrizione, ritratto.*

Character [dignity] *carattere dignità, qualità.*

A fine character, *un bel carattere, una bella mano.*

An indelible character, *un carattere indelebile.*

To give the true character of people, *dare il vero carattere delle genti.*

The character of an ambassador, *il carattere d'un ambasciadore.*

He has given me a true character of you, *egli m'ha data buona informazione di voi, egli m' ha detto molto bene di voi.*

To give one an ill character, *sparlar d' uno, parlar male d'uno.*

To CHA'RACTER [to inscribe, to engrave] *scolpire, intagliare.*

CHARACTERI'STICK, or CHARACTERI'STICAL, adj. [that which constitutes the character] *caratteristico, che costituisce o segna il carattere.*

To CHARACTERI'ZE [to give the character or description of] *carretterizzare, dare il carattere.*

CHARACTERI'ZED, adj. *caratterizzato.*

CHA'RACTERLESS, adj. [without a character] *senza carattere.*

CHA'RACTERY, s. [impression, mark] *segno impressione.*

CHARCO'AL, s. [coal made of wood burnt] *carbone di legna.*

CHARGE, s. [burden] *carico, peso,* s. m. *carica, soma,* s. f.

Charge [orders] *carico, peso, pensiero,* s. m. *cura,* s. f.

To commit a thing to one's charge, *imporre il carico, o dar la cura di qualche cosa ad uno.*

He delivered what he had in charge, *egli compì le sue pari, egli sodisfece al suo dovere.*

To take the charge of something upon one's self, *pigliarsi l'assunto, o l' incombenza di qualche cosa.*

Charge [conduct, care] *cura, condotta,* s. f.

He committed the whole management of the war to his charge, *egli commise a lui la cura principale della guerra.*

I have had a long time the charge of them, *sono stati lungo tempo sottò la mia condotta.*

Charge [trust] *deposito,* s. m. *incombenza,* s. f.

I give this in charge to you, *vi do questo in deposito.*

This shall be your charge, *questa sarà la vostra incombenza.*

Charge [office, employ] *carica,* s. f. *ufficio, impiego,* s. m.

To perform one's charge well, *comportarsi bene nella sua carica.*

Charge [accusation] *imputazione, colpa, accusa,* s. f.

These are the heads of the charge brought against you, *questi sono i capi d' accusa allegati contro voi.*

Charge [expence, cost] *spesa,* s. f.

I am not able to be at that charge, *non sono atto a fare queste spese.*

I have a great charge, I am at a great charge, *ho molte spese a fare.*

To put one's self to charges, *fare grandi spese.*

To pay one's charges, *spesare altrui, fargli le spese.*

That was not a six-pence charge to him, *cio non gli costò sei soldi.*

All charges borne, *oltro le spese.*

Charge [fight] *carica,* s, f. *assalto,* s. m.

To return to the charge, *ritornare all' assalto.*

To give the enemy a round charge, *incalzare vigorosamente l' inimico, stringerlo.*

To lay a thing to one's charge, *incolpare o dar colpa di qualche cosa ad uno.*

Lay not this sin to their charge, *non imputate loro questo peccato.*

The charge of a gun, *la carica d'uno schioppo, cannone, e simili.*

To CHARGE [to load, to burden] *caricare, por carico addosso.*

To charge a gun, *caricare un arme a fuoco.*

To charge [to command] *commandare, dare ordine, imporre.*

To charge one with a business, *dare l' incombenza di qualche affare ad uno, commettere la cura d' un negozio ad uno.*

He charged me to wait on you from him, *m'ha imposto di venire a voi da sua parte.*

To charge the enemy, *caricar l'inimico, urtarlo con gran forza.*

To charge [to lay to one's charge, to accuse him] *incolpare, accusare, dar la colpa.*

They charge him with a crime, *l'incolpano o l' accusano d' un delitto.*

The witnesses charge him with several crimes, *i testimoni l' accúsano di molti delitti.*

To charge [to trust] *incaricare, commettere alla cura di qualcuno.*

CHA'RGEABLE, adj. [costly] *dispendioso, che porta dispendio.*

'Tis very chargeable living in time of war, *il vivere in tempo di guerra è molto dispendioso.*

To be chargeable to one, *esser d' incommodo ad uno.*

CHA'RGEABLY, adv. [expensively] *con molta spesa, caramente.*

CHA'RGED, adj. *caricato,* v. to charge.

CHA'RGER, s. [a large dish] *un gran piatto.* Obs.

CHA'RILY, adv. [warily, frugally] *cautelosamente, frugalmente.*

To keep a thing charily, *guardar una cosa con molta cautela.*

CHA'RINESS, s. [caution, nicety] *cautela, cura diligente, delicatezza.*

CHA'RIOT, s. [car] *carro,* s. m.

Chariot [a light sort of a coach] *una carrozza per due persone, cocchio.*

To CHA'RIOT [to convey in a chariot] *condurre in carrozza.*

CHARIOTE'ER s. *conduttor del cocchio.*

CHA'RIOT-RACE, s. [a sport where chariots are driven for the prize] *palio di cocchi in uso presso gli antichi.*

CHA'RITABLE, adj. [bountiful] *caritatevole, caritativo.*

Charitable uses, *usi pii, carità.*

CHA'RITABLENESS, s. *disposizione caritativa.*

CHA'RITABLY, adv. *caritatevolmente.*

To be charitably inclined, *esser caritativo.*

CHA'RITY, s. [alms] *carità, limosina,* s. f.

To beg charity of one, *domandar la limosina ad uno.*

To bestow a charity on a poor man, *far la carità ad un povero.*

Charity is the first of christian virtues, *la carità è la prima delle virtù cristiane.*

Charity begins at home, *la prima carità è l'aver cura di se stesso.*

Charity [the love of God and one's neighbour] *carità, diritta affezion d' animo, onde s'ama Iddio per se, ed il prossimo per l' amor di Dio.*

I live in charity with all men, *io vivo in carità con ognuno.*

To CHARK [to burn wood to make charcoal] *far carboni.*

CHA'RLATAN, s. [quack] *cerretano ciarlatano, cantambanco,* s. m.

CHARLES'S WAIN, s. [a northern constellation, the same with Ursa Major] *l' orsa maggiore.*

CHA'RLOCK, s. [a weed growing among the corn, with a yellow flower] *erbaccia che nasce fra'l grano e fa il fiore giallo, zizzania, boglio.*

CHARM, s. [enchantment] *incanto incantesimo,* s. m.

Charms [allurements] *allettamenti, piacevolezze lusinghe.* All plurals.

Charm [beauty] *bellezza, leggiadria, vaghezza,* s. f.

To CHARM [to bewitch] *incantare, fare incanti, ammaliare.*

To charm [to please] *allettare, piacere, rapire, incantare,* pref. *rapisco.*

As musick charms the ear, so does beauty the heart, *la musica alletta gli orecchi e la bellezza rapisca il cuore.*

CHA'RMED, adj. *incantato, allettato, piaciuto, rapito, incatenato.*

CHA'RMER, s. *incantatore,* s. m. *incantatrice,* s. f.

CHA'RMING, s. *incantamento*, s. m. *incantagione*, s. f. *l'incantare*.

Charming, adj. [beautiful] *vezzoso*, *vago*, *leggiadro*, *bello*.

A charming beauty, *beltà vezzosa*.

Charming eyes, *occhi vaghi*.

CHA'RMINGLY, adv. [in such a manner as to please exceedingly] *piacevolmente*, *in modo da piacere estremamente*.

CHA'RMINGNESS, s. [the power of pleasing] *facoltà di piacere*.

CHA'RNEL, adj. [containing flesh or carcases] *che contiene carne morta o cadaveri*.

Charnel-house, s. [a place wherein the skulls and bones of the dead are laid] *luogo dove sono deposte le ossa de' morti*.

CHART, s. [a delineation of coasts] *carta da navigare*.

CHA'RTER, s. [letters patent, wherein privileges are granted] *patente*, *dove sono espressi i privilegi di chicchessia*.

Charter [a written evidence] *testimonianza in iscritto*.

Charter [privilege, immunity, exemption] *privilegio*, s. m. *immunità*, *esenzione*, s. f.

Charter-party [an indenture between merchants or owners and masters of ships, containing the particulars of their covenants and agreements] *contratto fra i mercanti ed i capitani di vascelli*.

CHA'RTERED, adj. [privileged] *privilegiato*, *immune*, *esente*.

CHA'RY, adj. [careful, cautious] *accorto*, *prudente*, *cauteloso*, *cauto*.

CHASE, s. [forest] *bosco*, s. m. *foresta*, s. f.

Chase [at sea] *caccia*, s. f.

To give a ship the chase, *dare la caccia ad un vascello*.

Chase [a sea term] *cannone*, s. m.

Head chase, stern chase, *cannone di poppa*, *cannone di prua*.

Chase [at tennis] *caccia*, s. f. *termine del giuoco della pallacorda*.

To win a chase at tennis, *guadagnare una caccia al giuoco della pallacorda*.

The chase or gutter of a cross-bow, *canale di balestra*.

To CHASE [to hunt] *cacciare*, *andare a caccia*.

To chase or pursue the enemy, *cacciare il nimico*, *dar la caccia al nimico*.

To chase [to drive away] *cacciare*, *scacciare*, *discacciare*, *mandar via*.

To chase [as goldsmiths do] *incastrare*.

CHASED, adj. *cacciato*, *scacciato*, *discacciato*, *incastrato*.

CHA'SE-GUN, s. [a gun in the forepart of the ship fired upon those that are pursued] *cannone da prua con cui si tiran cannonate alla nave che si sta cacciando*.

CHA'SER, s. [hunter, pursuer, driver] *cacciatore*, *che caccia*, *che discacia*, *che ti siegue*.

CHASM, s. [gap, opening] *fessura*, *apertura*, s. f.

Chasm, s. [place unfilled, vacuity] *luogo non riempiuto*; *vacuo*.

CHASTE, adj. [honest] *casto*, *continente*, *pudico onesto*.

A chaste woman, *una donna casta o pudica*.

A chaste flame, *una fiamma pura*.

CHA'STE-TREE, s. *sorta d' albero*.

To CHA'STEN [a Scripture word, to chastise] *castigare e gastigare*.

CHA'STENED, adj. *castegato e gastigato*.

CHA'STENING, s. *gastigamento*, *gastigo*, *castigo*, s. m. *gastigazione*, *punizione*, s. f.

To CHASTISE [to correct to punish] *castigare*, *gastigare*, *punire*, pres. *punisco*.

CHASTISED, adj. *castigato*, *gastigato*, *punito*.

CHA'STISEMENT, s. [punishment] *gastigo*, *gastigamento*, s. m. *punizione*, s. f.

CHASTI'SER, s. *gastigatore*, s. m. *gastigatrice*, s. f.

CHASTI'SING, s. *gastigamento*, s. m. *gastigazione*, s. f. *gastigo*, s. m.

CHASTITY, s. *castità*, *purità*, *pudicizia*, s. f.

To live in chastity, *viver in castità*.

CHASTLY, adv. [honestly] *castamente*, *puramente*, *pudicamente*.

CHASTNESS, s. [chastity] *castità*, *pudicizia*, *purità*, s. f.

CHA'SUBLE, s. [a priest's cape at mass] *pianeta*, s. f.

CHAT, s. [prating] *ciarla*, *vana loquacità*, s. f. *cicaleccio*, *cicalamento*, s. m.

To hold chat with one, *discorrere*, *parlare con alcuno*.

Pray hold your chat, *tacetevi vi dico*.

To CHAT [to prate] *ciarlare*, *cornacchiare*, *cicalare*.

He does nothing but chat, *non fa altro che cicalare*.

CHA'TTELS, s. [a law word, all goods moveable] *i beni mobili*. *Termine legale*.

To CHA'TTER [to make a noise as birds do] *garrire*, *cantare*, *parlando degli uccelli*. pres. *garrisco*.

To chatter [to prate] *ciarlare*, *cicalare*, *cornacchiare*.

To chatter [as the teeth do when a person is shivering with cold] *battere i denti*.

His teeth chatters with cold, *batte i denti*, *trema di freddo*.

CHA'TTER, s. [noise like that of a pye or monkey] *grido o strepito simile a quello d'una gazza o d'una scimia*.

Chatter [idle prate] *il cicalare*, *cicalio*, *il cianciare*, *ciancie*, *il ciarlare*, *ciarle*.

CHA'TTERER, s. [an idle talker] *ciancione*, *ciarlone*, *un che non fa che cianciare*.

CHA'TTERING, s. [the singing of birds] *garrimento*, *canto*, s. m.

Chattering [prate] *cicaleria*, s. m. *cicaleccia*, s. m.

A chattering of teeth, *battimento di denti*.

Chattering, adj. *ex.* chattering birds, *garruli uccelli*.

CHATTER-PYE, s. [a kind of bird] *gazza*, *pica*, s. f. *uccello atto ad imitar la favella umana*.

CHA'TTING, s. [from to chat] *ciarla*, s. f. *cicaleccio*, *cicalamento*, s. m.

Chatting, adj. *ex.* a chatting housewife, *una ciarliera*, *una ciarlatrice*.

To CHAW, *v.* To chew.

CHA'WDRON, *interiora*. plural.

CHEAP, adj. *a buon mercato*.

Meat is very cheap now, *la carne è a buon mercato adesso*.

I can buy it better cheap, *posso comprarlo a miglior merrato*.

Dog-cheap, *a vil prezzo*, *quasi per niente*.

To CHEAPEN [to ask or beat down the price of a commodity] *prezzolare*, *mercatare*, *fare il prezzo della mercanzia*.

To cheapen a piece of cloth, *prezzolare*, *o mercatare una pezza di panno*.

CHEAPENED, adj. *prezzolato*, *mercatato*.

CHEAPENING, s. *il prezzolare*, *o mercantare*.

CHE'APLY, adv. [at a small price, at a low rate] *a buon prezzo*, *a buon mercato*, *per poco*.

CHEAPNESS, s. *buon*, *mercato*.

I admire the cheapness of it, *mi stupisco che si venda a sì buon mercato*.

CHEAR or CHEER, s. *festa*, *pasto*, *convito*.

To make good cheer, *pasteggiare*, *far pasto*, *mangiare e bere bene*.

To make pitiful or coarse chear, *viver malamente*, *farla magra*.

Chear [countenance] *ciera*, *cera*, *sembianza*, *aria di volto*, *volto*, *viso*.

A poor chear, *cattiva ciera*.

A heavy chear, *viso mesto*.

Chear [heart] *animo*.

Be of good chear, *fatevi animo*, *state di buon animo*, *fata buon cuore*.

What chear? *come state*, *come ve la passate*.

To CHEAR, to CHEAR UP [to make chearful] *allegrare*, *rallegrare*, *divertire*, *ricreare*, *confortare*.

I find this wine chears me up, *vedo che questo vino me rallegra*.

To chear up [to encourage] *animare*, *dare animo*, *incitare*.

To chear up, verb. neut. *allegrarsi*, *rallegrarsi*, *divertirsi*, *stare allegramente*.

Chear up, *animo*, *state di buon animo*, *fate buon cuore*.

How chear you? *come state*, *come ve la passate?*

CHEARED UP, adj. *allegrato*, *rallegrato*, *divertito*.

CHEARFUL, adj. [pleasant, lively] *allegro*, *giocondo*, *giojoso*, *festoso*, *lieto*, *ridente*.

A chearful countenance, *un viso lieto o allegro*.

CHEARFULLY, adv. *allegramente*, *di buon aria*, *festevolmente*, *lietamente*, *giocosamente*.

To look chearfully, *aver un viso allegro o ridente*.

To look chearfully on one, *far buon viso ad uno*, *fargli buona cera*, *mostrargli un bel sembiante*.

CHE'ARFULNESS, s. *allegria, giojezza, giulività, ilarità, gioja*, s. f.

CHEAT, s. [deceit, ſhame, knavery] *inganno*, s. m. *fraude, furberia, truffa*, s. m.

To put a cheat upon one, *ingannare, giuntare, o truffare alcuno.*

Cheat, [impoſtor, deceitful man] *un furbo, un barattiere, un truffatore, un truffiere, un baro, un ingannatore, un giuntatore.*

A notorious cheat; *un furbo in chermiſi, un briccone, connoſciuto.*

To CHEAT, [to deceive] *ingannare, far fraude, truffare, giuntare.*

He has cheated me of ten pounds, *mi ha truffato di dieci lire ſterline.*

To cheat one's ſelf, *ingannarſi.*

To cheat at play, *giuntare al giuoco.*

CHE'ATED, adj. *ingannato, truffato, giuntato.*

CHE'ATER, s. *ingannatore, truffatore, truffiere*, s. m. *ingannatrice*, s. f.

CHE'ATINGLY, adv. *ingannevolmente, con inganno.*

CHECK, s. [at cheſs] *ſcacco.*

Check to the King, *ſcacco al Re.*

Check to the King and Queen, *ſcacco a Re e a Regina.*

Check [loſs] *ſcaccomatto, danno*, s. m. *rovina, perdita*, s. f.

This is a great check to him, *queſta è una gran perdita per lui.*

Check [reproof, reprimand] *riprenſione, correzione, rimprovero.*

To give one a check, *fare una riprenſione ad uno.*

To keep a check upon one, *tenere uno in freno, farlo ſtare a ſegno.*

The checks of conſcience [the remorſes of conſcience] *i rimorſi della coſcienza.*

To give one's paſſion a check, *domare, reprimere, raffrenare le ſue paſſioni.*

To take a check at a thing, *offenderſi o crucciarſi de qualche coſa.*

To CHECK [to refrain, to curb] *reprimere, fremare, raffrenare, domare.*

To check one's anger, *frenar l'ira, ritener la collera.*

To check one's talk, *interrompere l'altrui diſcorſo, rompere altrui le parole in bocca.*

To check [to chide, to reprimand] *riprendere, correggere, garrire, ſgridare.* pret. *ripreſi, correſſi.*

I checked him for it, *ne l'ho ripreſo, o ſgridato.*

CHECKED, adj. *repreſſo, frenato, raffrenato, domato, ripreſo, corretto, garrito, ſgridato.*

CHE'CKER-BOARD, s. [cheſs board] *ſcacchiere*, s. m. Cheſs-board, *è meglio detto.*

Checker-wiſe, *a ſcacchi.*

Checker-work, *tarſia*, s. f. *lavoro di minuti pezzuoli di legname di piu colori commeſſi inſieme.*

To CHE'CKER, verb. act. *intarſiare.*

CHE'CKERED, adj. *intarſiato, fatto a ſcacchi.*

Checkered, or checkie [a term of heraldry] *ſcaccato, fatto a ſcacchi.*

CHE'CKMATE, s. [a term uſed at the play of cheſs, when the king is ſhut up ſo cloſe that there is no way left for his eſcape] *ſcaccomato*, s. m.

Checkmate [defeat, overthrow] *ſcaccomatto, danno, perdita rovina.*

To give one a checkmate, *dare uno ſcaccomatto.*

CHE'CKROLL, s. [a book containing the names of all the houſhold ſervants of the king or any other great perſonage] *libro dove ſono ſcritti i nomi de' domeſtici del Re o d'altro perſonnaggio grande.*

CHEEK, s. [a part of the face] *guancia, gota*, s. f.

A roſy cheek, *una guancia vermiglia.*

Blubber-cheeks, *guance paffute.*

A hog's cheek, *una teſta di porco.*

The cheeks of a printer's preſs, *i lati del torchio d'uno ſtampatore.*

The cheeks of a door, *le impoſte d'una porta.*

The cheek piece of an helmet, *viſiera d'elmetto, buffa.*

Cheek by joll, *teſta a teſta, ſola a ſolo. Modo baſſo.*

To go cheek by joll with one, *andar del pari con uno, far frattellanza con uno, eſſer pane e cacio con uno. Modo baſſo.*

The cheek-bone, *la maſcella.*

The cheek-teeth, *maſcellari, denti da lato.*

Cheek varniſh, *belletto*, s. m.

CHEEKED, adj. *guanciuto.* Blub-cheeked, *che ha le guance gonfie, groſſe, o paffute.*

CHE'EKTOOTH, s. [the hinder tooth or tuſk] *dente maſcellare.*

CHEER, or CHEAR, s. [entertainment, proviſion] *paſto, banchetto*, s. m. *mangiari, coſe da mangiare.*

Cheer [invitation to gaiety] *invito a ſtar allegramente.*

Cheer [gaiety, jollity,] *allegrezza, feſta, lo ſtare allegramente.*

Cheer, [air of the countenance] *aſpetto.*

Cheer, [temper of mind] *umore, diſpoſizion d' animo.*

To CHEER, *incitare, incoraggiare, confortare, conſolare, rallegrare.*

To cheer, v. n. *rallegrarſi, divenir lieto.*

CHE'ERER, s. [gladner, giver of gaiety] *un che rallegra, che rende lieto*

CHE'ERFUL, adj. [gay, full of life, full of mirth] *gajo, vivace, allegro, pien di giubbilo, lieto.*

Cheerful, [having an appearance of gaiety] *vaga alla viſta, che appare lieto.*

CHE'ERFULLY, adj. [without dejection, with gaiety] *allegramente, lietamente, coraggioſamente, animoſamente, ſenza timore.*

CHE'ERFULNESS, s. [freedom from dejection, alacrity] *allegrezza vivacità, lieta baldanza.*

CHE'ERLESS, adj. [without gaiety, comfort, gladneſs] *triſto, malinconoſo; il contrario d' allegro è di lieto.*

CHE'ERLY, adj. [gay, cheerful, not gloomy] *gajo, lieto, non triſto.*

Cheerly, adv. [cheerfully] *lietamente, con allegria, con buono animo.*

CHE'ERY, adj. [gay, ſprightly] *gajo, vivace.*

CHEESE, s. [a kind of food made by preſſing the curd of milk] *Cacio, formaggio.*

New cheeſe, *cacio freſco.*

Cream cheeſe, *giuncata*, s. f.

You would make me believe the moon is made of green cheeſe, *voi vorreſte moſtrarmi la luna nel pozzo, voi vorreſte darmi ad intendere una coſa per un' altra.*

Cheeſe curds, *latte rappreſo.*

Cheeſe-cake, *tortelletta*, s. f.

Cheeſe-monger, *formaggiajo, pizzicagnolo.*

CHE'ESELIP, s. [the hog-louſe] *porcellino, inſetto coſi chiamato.*

CHE'ESY, adj. [having the nature or form of cheeſe] *della natura o forma del cacio.*

To CHE'RISH [to make much of] *amare, voler bene.*

To cheriſh one's children, *amar teneramente i ſuoi figliuoli.*

To cheriſh [to maintain] *mantenere, nutrire, allevare,* pref. *mantengo, nutriſco,* pret. *mantenni.*

To cheriſh [to keep warm] *ſcaldare, tener caldo.*

To cheriſh [to ſtroke a horſe] *accarezzare un cavallo.*

To cheriſh one's memory, *conſervar caramente la memoria di qualcheduno.*

CHE'RISHED, adj. *teneramente amato.*

CHE'RISHER, s. *amatore*, s. m.

CHE'RRY, s. [a ſort of fruit] *ciriegia*, s. f. *frutta nota di diverſe ſpezie.*

Black-cherries, *ciriege nere.*

Tart-cherries, *agriotte, amarine.*

Heart-cherry, *marchiane.*

Kentiſh-cherries, *viſciole.*

Cherry-ſtone, *nocciolo di ciriegia.*

Cherry-tree, *ciriego*, s. m. *albero noto che porta le ciriegie.*

Cherry-orchard, *ciriegeto*, s. m. *luogo dove ſieno molti ciriegi.*

Cherry-cheeks, *guance vermiglie.*

Cherry colour, *roſſo.*

CHE'RUB, or CHE'RUBIN, s. [the ſecond of the nine orders of angels] *cherubino*, s. m.

CHE'RVIL, s. [an herb] *cerfoglio*, s. m. *erba nota.*

CHE'SLIP, s. [hog-louſe] *porcellino, inſetto coſi chiamato.*

CHE'SNUT, s. [a fruit] *caſtagna*, s. f.

A great cheſnut, *marrone*, s. m.

Cheſnut-tree, *caſtagno*, s. m. *albero che fa la caſtagna.*

Bread made of cheſnut-meal, *caſtagnaccio*, s. m. *pane fatto di farina di caſtagna.*

Cheſnut-plot, *caſtagneto*, s. m. *boſco di caſtagni.*

Cheſnut-colour, *caſtagnino, mantello di cavallo di color di caſtagna.*

CHESS, s. [a play ſo called] *ſcacchi*, s. m. *giuoco coſi chiamato.*

To play at cheſs, *giuocare agli ſcacchi.*

Cheſs men, *ſcacchi, picciole figure del giuoco degli ſcacchi fatte di legno o d'altra materia.*

Cheſs-

Chess-board, *scacchiere, tavoliere.*

CHEST, s. [a sort of box, coffer or trunk] *cassa*, s. f.

A chest of Florence wine, *una cassa di vino di Firenze.*

A chest of drawers, *uno stipo.*

A man's chest [man's breast] *il cassero o rasso del corpo, la parte concava del corpo circondata dalle costole.*

Chest-foundered [a term of horsemanship] *bolso, parlando d'un cavallo che con difficoltà respira.*

CHE'STED, adj. *ex* hollow chested, full chested, *largo di petto, pettoruto alto di petto.*

CHE'STNUT, s. *v.* chesnut.

CHE'STNUT-TREE, *v.* chesnut-tree.

CHE'VEN, s. [a fish] *muggine*, s. m. *spezie di pesce di mare.*

CHE'VERIL, s. [a kid] *capretto.*

Cheveril, s. [kid leather] *pelle di capretto, cuojo di capretto.*

CHE'VRON, or CHEVERON, s. [in architecture] *travicello*, s. m.

Chevron [in heraldry] *raprone*, s. m.

CHE'VISANCE s. [a law word for an unlawful bargain] *mercato ingiusto e fraudolente.*

To CHEW [to grind food between the teeth] *masticare.*

To chew the meat, *masticare la carne.*

To chew the cud, *ruminare, rugumare, far ritornare alla bocca il cibo mandato nello stomaco non masticato per masticarlo, ed è proprio degli animali dal piè fesso.*

To chew the cud upon a thing, *ruminare, rugumare, riandar nel pensiero, riconsiderare, volger nella mente che che si sia.*

To chew a man's ruin, *tramare, macchinare la ruina d'un uomo.*

CHEWED, adj. *masticato, ruminato, rugumato.*

CHE'WING, s. *masticamento*, s. m. *il masticare.*

A chewing of the cud, *rugumazione*, s. f. *il rugumare.*

CHICA'NE, s. *rigiri, inganni, cavillazioni, e ritardi degli avvocati ed altra simil gente nel trattare le cause per buscar più danari da' clienti.*

Chicane [artifice in general] *artifizio, inganno.*

To CHICA'NE, *prolungare con fraudolente artificio una lite.*

CHICA'NER, s. *sofista, cavillatore.*

CHICA'NERY, s. *sofisticheria, il sofistirare, il cavillare, il cercar il nodo sul giunco.*

CHI'BBOL, s. [a kind of little onion] *cipolletta, cipollina*, s. f. *quella che non ha fatto nè ingrossato il capo, e mangiasi fresca.*

CHICK, or CHICK-PEA, s. *cece*, s. m. *speci di legume.*

Chick } s. [a fowl well known]
CHI'CKEN, } *pollastro*, s. m. *pollo giovane.*

A large chicken, *un pollastrone.*

A little chicken, *un pollastrino.*

Chick, [*pollastrello*] *è voce usata per vezzo a' bambini, giovanotti, e fanciulle.*

Chicken-pox, *morviglioni*, s. m. pl.

Chick-weed, *centonchio*, s. m. *sorta d'erba.*

CHICKENHEA'RTED, adj. *codardo, vigliacco, timido, pauroso, senza coraggio.*

CHID, } adj. *sgridato, ripreso.*
CHI'DDEN, }

To CHIDE [to rebuke] *sgridare, riprendere, biasimare, ammonire, bravare.*

To chide [to quarrel] *disputare, contendere, querelare, venire a parole.*

CHI'DER, s. *riprenditore, riprensore*, s. m.

CHI'DING, s. *riprendimento*, s. m. *riprensione*, s. f. *il riprendere.*

CHIEF, adj. [first, principal] *primo, principale.*

The chief thing, *la cosa principale.*

The chief men of a city, *i principali d'una città.*

He is the chief man of the town, *egli è il primo della città.*

That is our chief happiness, *questa è la nostra suprema felicità.*

The Lord Chief Justice of England, *il primo giudice d'Inghilterra.*

Chief, s. [a commander in chief, a general] *capo, capitan generale, romandante.*

CHI'EFEST, adj. [*superlativo di* chief] *principale, principalissimo.*

My chiefest care will be to serve you, *la mia principal cura sarà di servirvi.*

CHI'EFLESS, adj. [without a head] *senza capo, senza capitano.*

CHI'EFLY, adv. *principalmente, particolarmente, sopra tutto.*

CHI'EFRIE, s. *piccolo tributo che si paga dal vassallo al signore.*

CHIEFTAIN, s. [a captain] *capitano*, s. m.

CHI'EVES, s. pl. [the little threads of flowers] *cestole di fiori, la parte più dura che è nel mezzo delle loro foglie.*

CHI'LBLAIN, s. [a sort of swelling occasioned by cold] *pedignone*, s. m. *male che viene ne' piedi per lo più a' bambini per soverchio freddo.*

CHILD, plur. children, [son or daughter,] *fanciullo, figliuolo*, s. m. *fanciulla, figliuola*, s. f.

A little child [a young child] *un bambino*, s. m. *una bambina*, s. f.

To bring forth a child, *partorire un figliuolo.*

To be past children, *essere sfruttata, non esser più d'età d'aver figliuoli.*

Foster child, *figlio o figlia di latte.*

God child, *figlioccio*, s. m. *figlioccia*, s. f.

A child born before its time, *un aborto, una sconciatura.*

A fatherless child, *un orfano, un'orfana*, s. m.

To get a woman with child, *ingravidare una donna.*

Big with child, *gravida.*

From a child, *dall' infanzia, dalla culla.*

To be past a child, *aver passata l'infanzia.*

Child-bearing, *l' età d'aver figliuoli.*

Child-birth, *parto*, s. m. *la creatura partorita.*

Child-bed, *il letto della partoriente.*

To be in child-bed, *esser in parto.*

To die in child-bed, *morir di parto.*

To play the child, *bamboleggiare, far cose da bambini, pargoleggiare.*

To CHILD [to bring children] *far figliuoli.*

CHI'LDBEARING, s. *il far figliuoli.*

CHI'LDBED, s. [the state of a woman bringing a child] *sopraparto; l' essere d'una donna dopo il partorire.*

CHILDBIRTH, s. [travail, labour] *dolori del parto.*

CHI'LDED, adj. [furnished with a child] *che ha un figlio o una figlia.*

CHILDHOOD, s. *fanciullezza, infanzia, prima età; condizione in cui si trova un fanciullo.*

CHILDERMASS DAY, s. [the feast of the Innocents, being the 28th of December] *la festa degl' innocenti.*

CHILDLIKE, adj. [becoming or beseeming a child] *fanciullesco, bambinesco; da bambino, da fanciullo.*

CHI'LIAD, s. [a thousand] *un migliajo. Non è usato.*

CHILIA'EDRON, s. [a figure of a thousand sides] *figura che ha mille lati.*

CHILDING, s. [child-bearing] *l' età di fare figliuoli.*

CHILDISH, adj. [like a child] *bambinesco, fanciullesco.*

Child-action, *bambinaggine, bambineria, bamboceria, ragazzata*, s. f. *fatto o azion da bambini.*

To have a childish look, *aver il viso di bambino.*

CHI'LDISHLY, adv. *faniullescamente, a guisa e modo di fanciullo.*

CHILDISHNESS, s. *fanciullàggine, bambinàggine, azion da fanciullo, fanciullezza, puerizia, infanzia*, s. f.

CHI'LDLESS, adj. [that has no child] *che non ha figliuoli.*

CHILDREN, s. [the plural of child] *fanciulli, bambini, ragazzi.*

Great many children together, *fanciullaja, ragazzaglia*, s. f.

CHIME'RICALLY, adv. [vainly, wildly] *stranamente, in maniera vana, senza fondamento di verità.*

CHILL, adj. [cold] *freddo, freddoloso, freddoso.*

She is chill, *ella è freddolosa.*

Chill with cold, *tremante di freddo.*

To CHILL, verb act. *freddare, render freddo, agghiacciare, gelare.*

This cold drink chills me, *questa bevanda fredda m' agghiaccia.*

It chills my blood when I think on it, *mi s' agghiaccia il sangue nelle vene al pensarci.*

The snow chills them, *la neve li gela.*

To chill, verb neut. *freddarsi, agghiacciarsi, gelarsi.*

CHILLED, adj. *freddato, agghiacciato, gelato.*

CHI'LLY, adj. [chill] *freddo, freddoloso, freddoso.*

CHI'LLNESS, *freddura*, s. f. *freddo*, s. m.

CHIMB, s. *ex.* a chime of bells, *scampanata*, s. f. *scampanìo*, s. m.

To CHIME, s. *campanare, fare un gran suonar di campane.*

CHIME'RA,

Chimera, s. [a monster feigned by the poets to have the head of a lion, the belly of a goat, and the tail of a serpent, that belches out fire] *chiméra*, s. f. *mostro favoloso.*

Chimera, [a strange fancy, a castle in the air] *chimera, invenzione fantastica.*

All that is but a chimera, *tutto ciò non è che una chimera.*

Chime'rical, adj. [imaginary, whimsical] *chimérico, fantástico, imaginário.*

Chi'nky, adj. [full of holes, gaping] *pien di fessure, tutto fesso, screpolato.*

Chi'mist, *v.* Chymist.

Chi'mmar, s. [a vestment without sleeves, worn by bishops between their gown and rochet] *zimarra*, s. f.

Chi'mney, s [a funnel for the conveyance of the smoak] *camino*, s. m. *quel luogo della casa dove si fa il fuoco.*

A chimney-piece, *quadro o specchio da mettere sopra il cammino.*

A chimney-sweeper, *uno spazzacammino.*

Chimney-money, [hearth-money] *tassa sopra ogni fuoco.*

Chin, s. [the lower part of the face] *mento*, s. m. *parte estrema del viso sotto la bocca.*

Chin-cough, *spezie di tosse molto violenta.*

Chin-cloth, *pezzo di tela col quale si béndano il mento le donne mentre si mettono la cuffia.*

China, or China ware, s. [a fine sort of earthen ware made in China] *porcellana*, s. f. *vasi di terra che vengon dalla China.*

China-orange, *melarancia dolce.*

Chine, s. [back-bone] *schiena, la spina o filo delle reni.*

A chine of pork, *filetto di porco.*

The chine of a horse's back, *il dorso o dosso d'un cavallo.*

To Chine [to break one's back] *sfilare, guastar il filo delle reni.*

Chink, s. *fesso, crepaccio*, s. m. *fessura, spaccatura, crepatura*, s. f.

A little chink, *un fessolino.*

Full of chinks, *crepacciato, pien di crepacci o fessure.*

Chink, s. *il tintinno delle monete o d' altre cose fatte di qualche metallo.*

To Chink, verb neut. [to gape to chap] *crepare, spaccarsi, fendersi.*

To chink [to sound as money does] *tintinnare, tintinnire.*

Chi'nked, adj. *crepato, spaccato, fesso, tintinnato, tintinnito.*

Chi'nky, adj. [full of holes, gaping] *pien di fessure, tutto fesso, screpolato.*

Chi'nned, adj. *mentuto assai*: long-chinned, *che ha un mento molto lungo.*

Chints, s. [cloth of cotton made in India] *tela di cotone o bambagia fatta nell' Indie.*

Chio'ppine, s. [a high shoe formerly worn by ladies] *sorta di scarpa alta usata anticamente dalle donne.*

Chip, s. [of wood] *scheggia*, s. f. *minima particella del legno spiccata, trúciolo, brúciolo*, s. m. *sottil falda che trae la piana nel ripulire il legname.*

Chips of bread, *croste di pane.*

Orange-chips, *scorze di malerance confettate*

'Tis a chip of the old block, *a' segni si conoscon le balle.*

It tastes just like a chip in pottage, *non ha nessun gusto.*

A chip-ax, *piana*, s. f. *strumento de' legnajuoli col quale puliscono e fanno lisci i legnami.*

To Chip, [to cut chips] *truciolare, ridurre in triúcioli o in brúcioli.*

To chip bread, *scrostare del pane.*

Chi'pped, adj. *trucciolato, scrostato, ridotto in trucioli, fatto in brucioli.*

Chipping, s. *il truciolare, lo scrostare, il tagliar un pezzetto.*

Chipping of bread, *crosta di pane, pazzetto di pane.*

Chira'gra, s. [the gout in the hands] *chiragra*, s. f. *gotta delle mani.*

Chira'gricał, adj. [having the hand gout] *chiragroso, che ha gotta nelle mani.*

Chiro'grapher, s. [an officer in the court of Common Pleas who engrosses fines] *registratore delle pene pecuniarie.*

Chiro'graphy, s. [a writing with one's own hand] *chirógrafo*, s. m. *scrittura autèntica, portante, obligazione.*

Chiroma'ncer, s. [a person skilled in the art of chiromancy] *chiromante*, s. m.

Chiroma'ncy, s. [divination by the wrinkles and lines in the hand] *chiromanzìa*, s. f. *indovinamento mediante le linee della mano.*

Chiroma'ntical, adj. [belonging to chiromancy] *attenente a chiromanzia.*

To Chirp, v. n. [to sing, to warble, as birds do] *garrire, cantare, parlando degli uccelli.*

To chirp as a sparrow, *pigolare come fa il pàssero.*

To chirp, v. a. [to make chearful] *rallegrare, far lieto.*

Chi'rping, s. *garrulità*, s. f. *gorgheggio*, s. m. *il garrire, il gorgheggiar degli uccelli, il canto degli uccelli.*

Chirping, adj. *ex.* a chirping cup [a draught of good liquor] *un bicchiere di buon vino.*

To take a chirping cup, *bere lietamente.*

Chiru'rgery, [the art of curing by external application] *l' arte del chirurgo, chirurgìa.*

Chiru'rgical, } adj. [belonging
Chiru'rgick. } to surgery] *appartenente a chirurgia.*

Chi'sel, s. [a carpenter's tool] *scarpello*, s. m. *strumento di ferro tagliente in cima, col quale si lavorano le pietre o i legni.*

To Chi'sel, verb act. *scolpire, lavorar collo scalpello, intagliare.*

Chit, s. [kitling] *gattino, gattuccio*, s. m.

A chit lark, *una calandra.*

Chit [a little boy or girl] *un ragazzo, una ragazza.*

You chit you, *va via balordo.*

Chit-pease, *lenticchia, lente*, s. f.

Chit [freckle in the face] *lentiggine*, s. f. *neo*, s. m. *macchia, simile alle lenti che viene nella persona e particolarmente nel viso.*

That has chits in his face, *lentigginoso, che ha lentiggini pel viso.*

To chit, verb neut. [seed is said to chit when it first shoots its small roots into the earth] *barbare, barbicare, radicare, produr barbe, parlando delle semenze.*

Chit-chat, s. [prattle; idle prate] *cicalío, tattamella, ciancia, il cianciare, il ciancerellare, il ciarlare.*

We had a little chit-chat, *noi canciammo un tantino.*

Chi'tterlings, s. [the guts] *le budella, le minugia.*

Chi'tty, adj. [full of chits] *lentigginoso.*

Chi'tty, adj. [childish like a babe] *bambinesco, fanciullesco; da fanciullo, da bambino.*

Chitty-face, *un viso piccolo, magro, e sparuto.*

Chitty-face [booby] *uno sciocco, un balordo, un minchione.*

Chi'valrous, adj. [relating to chivalry; knightly; warlike] *appartenente alla cavalleria errante; cavalleresco, guerriero, bellicoso, valoroso.*

Chi'valry, s. [knighthood] *cavallerìa*, s. f. *grado e dignità di cavaliere.*

Chivalry, in law [a tenure of lands, where the tenant is bound to perform some military office to his lord] *feudo nobile, che dipende dal Re o da altro signore.*

Chi'ves, *v.* Chieves.

Chloro'sis, s. [the green sickness] *malore che viene alla donne.*

Chi'zel, *v.* Chisel.

To Choak, *v.* To choke.

Chock, or Chuck, s. *sergozzone*, s. m.

To give one a chock under the chin, *dare un sergozzone ad uno.*

Cho'colate, s. [a drink made of the Indian cocoa nut] *cioccolato*, s. f.

To drink chocolate, *bere della cioccolata.*

A chocolate pot, *cioccolatiera, vaso da far la cioccolato.*

A chocolate stick or mill, *frullo*, s. m. *bastone da sbatter la cioccolata.*

Chode, *antico preterito del verbo* to chide, *non più in uso.*

Choice, s. [election] *scelta, elezione*, s. f.

To make choice of a thing, *fare scelta d'una cosa.*

If it were in my choice, *s' io dovessi scegliere.*

To give one the choice, *dare a scegliere ad uno.*

I leave it to your choice, *vi lascio scegliere, scegliete quel che volete.*

The choice of his troops, *il fiore della sua gente.*

Take your choice [do what you think fit] *fate a modo vostro, fate quel che vi piace.*

He may take his choice, *faccia pure quel che vuole, faccia a suo modo.*

Choice [variety] *varietà, diversità*, s. f.

He has great choice of commodities in

In his shop, *egli ha diverse sorti di mercanzie nella sua bottega, la sua bottega è piena di tutte sorte di mercanzie.*

Choice, adj. [rare, chosen] *scelto, eletto, raro, eccellente, squisito.*

Choice men, *gente eletta, fior di gente, gente scelta.*

Choice expressions, *espressioni sublimi.*

Choice commodities, *fior di roba.*

CHO'ICELESS, adj. [without the power of choosing] *indifferente; che non ha potere di scegliere; che non cura scegliere.*

CHO'ICELY, adv. *caramente, preziosamente.*

CHO'ICENESS, s. *cura, delicatezza,* s. f.

CHOIR, s. *il coro d'una chiesa.*

Choir, s. [an assembly or band of singers] *coro di musici; molti musici che cantano insieme o a vicenda.*

Choir [the singers in divine worship] *i musici che cantan salmi, inni, laudi, ed altre cose sacre.*

To CHOKE [to strangle] *strangolare, soffocare, strozzare.*

You choke me, *voi mi strangolate.*

To choke or choke up a pipe, *stoppare un condotto.*

CHO'KED, adj. *strangolato, soffocato, strozzato.*

I was choaked for want of drink, *mi moriva di sete.*

Choked up, *turato.*

CHOKE-PEAR, s. *sorta di pera così chiamata.*

Choke-pear, *sarcasmo che ti chiude la bocca; motto pungente che t' impone silenzio.*

Choke-weed, *orobanche, coda cavallina.*

CHO'KER, s. *cosa che non ha risposta.*

CHO'KING, s. *soffocamento,* s. m. *strozzatura,* s. f.

CHO'KY, adj. *strozzatojo.*

CHO'LER, s. [bile, a yellow humour contained in the gall-bladder] *collera, collora, bile,* s. f.

Choler [anger] *collera, ira, stizza.*

To be in a choler, *aver collera.*

CHO'LERICK, adj. [abounding with choler] *collerico che abbonda di collora.*

Cholerick, [hasty, passionate] *collerico, adiroso, stizzoso, colloroso, bilioso.*

To CHO'OSE, v. a. *pres. I chose, io scelgo; pret.* I have chosen or chose; *Io ho scelto* [to take by way of preference of several things offered] *scegliere. Alcuni scrivono* to chuse.

To choose [to take; not to refuse] *pigliare, non rifiutare.*

To choose [to select; to pick out of a number] *preferire, dar la preferenza.*

To choose [to elect for eternal happiness] *predestinare.*

To choose, *v. n.* [to have the power of choice] *poter scegliere.*

CHOP, s. [slice] *fetta,* s. f.

A mutton chop, *una braciuola di castrato.*

Chops, *la mascella.*

His chops are always going, *il suo mulino sempre macina, non fa altro che mangiare.*

To give one a slap on the chops, *dare uno schiaffo ad uno, dare una ceffata*

To CHOP, [to cut, to cut small, to mince] *tagliare, tritare, sminuzzare, tagliar minuto.*

To chop a piece of meat, *tagliare un pezzo di carne.*

To chop [to make an exchange, to truck] *barattare, cambiar cosa a cosa.*

Will you chop with me? *volete barattar meco?*

To chop logic with one, *disputare, contrastare, contendere con alcuno.*

To chop off, *tagliare, mozzare, troncare.*

To chop off one's head, *tagliar la testa ad uno, decapitare uno, mozzargli il capo.*

To chop in or into [to pop in] *entrare all' improvviso.*

To chop at a thing [to take hold of it] *impugnare, dar di piglio ad una cosa.*

The wind chops about [a sea-term] *il vento si cangia, il vento volta, gira, o va attorno.*

Chop-church, s. *permutazione di benefici. Non in uso.*

CHOPPED, or CHOPPED OFF, adj. *tagliato, tritato, sminuzzato, mozzato, decapitato.*

CHOPPING, s. *l'atto del tagliare.*

A chopping knife, *coltellaccio, coltello da cuoco.*

A chopping board or block, *tagliere, tagliéro,* s. m. *legno a foggio di piattello su cui si taglian le vivande.*

A chopping boy, *un ragazzo robusto.*

CHO'RAL, adj. [belonging to the choir of the church] *di coro.*

A vicar choral, *vicario di coro.*

Cho'ral, adj. [singing in a choir] *cantabile a coro.*

CHORD, s. [the string of a musical instrument] *corda di stromento musicale.*

Chord, [a right line which joins the two ends of any arch of a circle] *linea retta che tocca le due estremità d' ogni arco di cerchio.*

To CHORD, [to furnish with strings] *porre le corde a uno stromento musicale.*

CHORIA'MBICK, s. [a foot in verse consisting of four syllables, two long at each end and two short in the middle] *coriámbo,* s. m. *piede di verso, formato di quattro sillabe, la prima e l'ultima lunga, e le due di mezzo brevi.*

CHO'RIST, or CHO'RISTER, v. Querister.

CHORO'GRAPHER, s. [one skilled in chorography] *corografo,* s. m. *versato in corrografia.*

CHORO'GRAPHY, s. [a part of geography, which treats of the description of particular countries] *corografia,* s. f. *descrizione particolare di qualche paese.*

CHO'RUS, s. [the singing of musick in a play] *coro,* s. m. *adunanza di cantori.*

CHOSE, *un preterito del verbo* to chuse.

CHO'SEN, adj. *participio del verbo* to chuse, *scelto, v.* to chuse.

CHOUGH, s. [a kind of bird] *pola, mulacchia,* s. f.

CHOUSE, s. [cheat, sham, trick] *inganno, tiro,* s. m. *truffa, furberia,* s. f.

To put a chouse upon one, *fare una burla o un tiro ad uno, ingannarlo.*

Chouse [a silly fellow, a bubble] *un gonzo, uno sciocco, un minchione.*

To CHOUSE, [to cozen, to cheat] *ingannare, truffare, giuntare.*

CHOUSED, adj. *ingannato, truffato, giuntato.*

CHOUSING, s. *truffa,* s. f. *inganno,* s. m. *furberia,* s. f.

To CHO'WTER [to mumble and mutter] *brontolare, borbottare.*

That child does nothing but chowter, *questo ragazzo non fa altro che borbottare.*

CHO'WTERING, s. *borbottamento,* s. m. *il borbottare.*

CHRISM, s. [oil and balsam consecrated by a popish bishop to be used in baptism, extreme unction, and coronation of kings] *cresima, cresma,* s. m. *olio santo.*

CHRISMA'TORY, s. [a vessel wherein the chrism is kept] *il vaso dove si conserva la cresima.*

CHRISM or CHRISOM CLOTH, s. *panno lino col quale s'involve la testa d'un bambino novellamente battezzato.*

Chrisoms, s. [infants that die within the month of birth, or at their wearing the chrisom cloth] *nella lista de' morti, che si publica in Londra ogni settimana, si chiamano* Chrisoms *i bambini che muojono prima che abbiano un mese, perchè per lo spazio di questo mese sono soliti portare un panno lino bianco che si chiama* Chrisom-cloth.

Chrisom-calf [a word used in some parts of England to say a calf killed before it is a month old] *parolà usata in alcune parti d'Inghilterra, per dire un vitello ammazzato prima che abbia un mese.*

CHRIST-CROSS-ROW, or CHRISS-CROSS-ROW, s. *abbicci,* s. m. *l'alfabeto.*

To CHRI'STEN [to baptize] *battezzare.*

To christen a child, *battezzare un bambino.*

CHRI'STENDOM, s. [the collective body of Christianity] *christianità,* s. f. *cristianesimo,* s. m.

CHRI'STENED, adj. *battezzato.*

CHRI'STENING, s. *il battezzare battesimo,* s. m.

The christening day, *il giorno di battesimo.*

Christen-name, s. *nome di battesimo, nome che si da al bambino nel battezzarlo.*

CHRI'STIAN, s. *un cristiano, una cristiana.*

To turn or become christian, *farsi cristiano.*

Boon christian pear, *pero buon cristiano, spezie di pera.*

Christian, adj. [of or belonging to Christ or his doctrine] *cristiano.*

The christian religion, *la religione cristiana.*

Christian-name, *nome di battesimo.*

Most Christian, *cristianissimo.*

CHRI'STIANISM, } s. [the doctrine, CHRI'STIANITY, } principles, and religion of Christians] *cristianesimo, cristianità*, s. f. *modo e rito cristiano.*

To CHRISTIANI'ZE [to make christians] *far cristiano, render cristiano.*

CHRI'STANLY, adv. *cristianamente, con modo cristiano.*

CHRI'STMAS, s. *natale*, s. m.

Christmas-day, *il giorno di natale.*

Christmas-holy-days, *le feste di natale.*

Christmas box, s. *salvadanajo, dove si mettono i quattrini che si danno a natale per mancia.*

I gave him a crown for his christmas-box, *gli ho dato uno scudo per istrenna.*

Christ-THORN, s. [a plant] *pruno bianco, spina nazzarena; sorta di pianta.*

CHRO'MA, s. *croma*, s. f. *una delle figure, o note della musica.*

CHROMA'TICK, adj. *cromatico.*

Chromatick musick, *musica cromatica.*

CHRO'NICAL, } adj. *cronico.*
CRO'NICK, }

Chronical diseases [that come at certain times by fits] *malattie croniche.*

CHRO'NICLE, s. [history according to the order of time] *cronica, cronaca*, s. f.

The book of Chronicles in the Old Testament, *il libro delle Croniche del vecchio Testamento*

To CHRO'NICLE [to record in history] *mettere nelle croniche.*

To Chrónicle [to register, to record] *registrare, scrivere ricordi.*

CHRO'NICLED, adj. *messo nelle croniche.*

CHRO'NICLER, s. [he that writes chronicles] *quegli che scrive le croniche.*

CHRO'NOGRAM, s. [an inscription, including the date of any action] *iscrizione fatta per conservar la memoria di qualche gran fatto.*

CHRONOGRA'MMATIST, s. [a writer of a chronogram] *colui che ha composta un'iscrizione che serve per conservar la memoria di qualche gran fatto.*

CHRONO'LOGER, } s. [a person CHRONO'LOGIST, } skill'd in chronology] *cronologista*, s. m. *uno versato nella cronologia.*

CHRONOLO'GICAL, adj. *cronologico, che concerne la cronologia*

A chronological table, *una tavola cronologica.*

CHRONO'LOGY, s. [science teaching how to compute the time from the creation for the use of history] *cronologia*, s. f.

CHRONO'METER, s. [an instrument for the exact mensuration of time] *strumento per misurare il tempo con esattezza.*

CHRO'SOCOL, s. gold-sodder, a mineral somewhat like pumice stone, found chiefly in copper-mines] *crosocollo, borrace*, s. f. *spezie di nitro fossile.*

CHRY'SALIS, s. [aurelia, the first apparent change of the maggot of any species of insects] *crisalide.*

CHRY'SOLITE, s. [a precious stone of gold colour transparent, mixed with green] *crisolito, grisolito*, s. m. *spezie di pietra preziosa di color d'oro, trasparente, mescolata di verde.*

CHUB, s. [a sort of fish, with a great head] *capitone*, s. m. *sorta di pesce.*

Chub [jolt-head] *una testaccia, una testa grossa.*

Chub [clown] *un zotico, un rustico.*

Chub-checked, *che ha le guance paffute.*

CHU'BBED, adj. [big-headed like a chub] *col capo grosso, di capo grosso come il capitone.*

CHUBBY, adj. *paffuto, grasso, nel viso.*

CHUCK, s. [a stroke under the chin] *sorgozzone, sergozzone*, s. m.

To give one a chuck under the chin, *dare un sorgozzone ad uno.*

Chuck-farthing, s. [a boyish play] *fossetta, giuoco fanciullesco.*

To CHUCK [to strike under the chin] *dare un sorgozzone.*

To chuck [to cry like a hen] *stridere come fa la gallina, chiocciare.*

To CHU'CKLE [to burst out ever and anon into a laughter, to laugh by fits] *dar nelle risa di quando in quando.*

To chuckle [to call as a hen] *gridare come fa la chioccia.*

To chuckle [to cocker, to fondle] *accarezzare, vezzeggiare.*

CHUFF, s. [country clown] *un villano, un rustico, un zotico.*

CHU'FFY, adj. *villano, rustico, zotico.*

CHUM, s. [a chamber fellow] *un compagno di camera uno che abita o sta nella stessa stanza.*

CHUMP, s. [a thick, short block, or log] *un pezzo, o un troncho di legno.*

CHURCH, s. [a place set apart for the divine service] *chiesa*, s. f.

A parochial, cathedral, or collegiate church, *chiesa parrocchiale, cattedrale, o collegiata.*

A church [a congegation of christians] *chiesa, congregazion de' fedeli.*

The catholick or universal church, *la chiesa cattolica o universale.*

The Greek church, *la chiesa Greca.*

The reformed church, *la chiesa riformata.*

The nearer the church the farther from God, *vicino alla chiesa lontano da Dio.*

A church man [a clergyman] *un prete, un ecclesiastico.*

CHURCH-ALE, s. [a wake or feast commemoratory of the dedication of a church] *anniversario o festa fatta per celebrare le consecrazione d'una chiesa.*

CHURCH-ATTI'RE, s. [the habits in which men officiate at divine service] *abiti usati dagli ecclesiastici nella chiesa.*

Church-warden, *quello che ha cura degli interessi d'una chiesa.*

Church-yard, *cimiterio, cimitero*, s. m.

A church-yard cough, *tosse che mena al cimitero.*

Church-porch, *portico di chiesa.*

Church-book, *battisterio.*

Church-time, *tempo d'andare alla chiesa.*

Church-robber, *ladro sacrilego*, s. m. *quelli che ruba in chiesa.*

Church-chopper, *un rinnegato.*

To CHURCH, *andare in chiesa, e dicesi per lo più dello andare che fanno le donne in chiesa la prima volta dopo il parto per la benedizione.*

CHURCHED, adj. *entrato in chiesa.*

She is churched, *ella è entrata in chiesa a purificarsi dopo il parto.*

CHURCH-REEVE, *v.* Church-warden.

CHURCH-YARD [the ground adjoining to the church in which the dead are buried, a cemetry] *cimitero, terreno in cui si seppelliscono i morti.*

CHURL, s. [clown] *un zotico, un rustico, un villano.*

Churl, s. [a rude, surly, ill bred man] *un uomo che non ha creanza, un uomo mal costumato.*

A churl [a miser, a niggard] *un taccagno, un misero, un avaro, un cacastecchi.*

CHU'RLISH, adj. [clownish] *rustico, zotico, villano, rozzo, avaro, tanghero, taccagno.*

CHU'RLISHLY, adv. *rusticamente, zoticamente, rozzamente.*

CHU'RLISHNESS, s. *zotichezza, zoticaggine, rusticità, rustichezza*, s. f.

CHURME, s. [a confused sound, a noise] *romore confuso, strepito.*

CHURN, s. [a vessel to make butter in] *vaso di legno da battere il burro.*

To CHURN [to make butter] *fare il burro, fare il butirro.*

Churn-staff, *bastoncello da battere il burro.*

CHUR-WORM, s. [an insect] *spezie d'insetto.*

To CHUSE, v. [to choose, to make a choice, to take one's choice] *scegliere, scerre, eleggere.*

Chuse which you please, *scegliete quello che vi piace.*

To chuse for a captain, *eleggere per capitano.*

Chuse whether you had rather have me your friend than your foe, *vedete se amate meglio avermi per amico o per nemico.*

You may chuse whether you will stay or go, *sta a voi di restare o d'andare.*

You may chuse whether you will or no, *voi siete libero di farlo o di non farlo.*

I cannot chuse but weep, *non posso astenermi dal piangere, non posso far di manco di non piangere.*

He cannot chuse but to be miserable, *non puo esser altro che misero, faccia quel che vuole sarà sempre misero.*

Chuse then, *lasciátelo dunque.*

To chuse king and queen, *far la festa del re.*

To chuse rather, *amare meglio, voler piu tosto.*

To chuse out [to cull] *scegliere, eleggere, cappare.*

CHU'SER, s. *sceglitore*, s. m. *che sceglie.*

Beggars must not be chusers, *chi mendica non sceglie.*

CHU'SING, s. *sceglimento*, s. m. *lo scegliere.*

This was of your own chusing, *questa fu vostro elezione, avete voluto così, la voleste così.*

Chyla'ceous, adj. [belonging to chyle] *di chilo, appartenente al chilo.*

Chyle, s. [the white juice of digested meat, the matter whereof the blood is made] *chilo*, s. m. *quel fugo bianco che lo ftomaco fpreme da' cibi e dalle vivande che poi diventa fangue.*

To change food into chyle, *chilificare, fare il chilo.*

Chylifa'ction, s. [the act or process of making chyle in the body] *il diventar chilo.*

Chy'lous, adj. [confifting of chyle] *chilofo, che ha natura di chilo, che ha fomiglianza col chilo, mefcolato col chilo.*

Chy'mical, } adj. [of or belong-
Chymick, } ing to chymiftry] *chimico, che appartenenente alla chimica.*

A chymical doctor, *un dottor chimico.*

Chy'mist, s. [a perfon fkilful in the art of chymiftry] *chimico*, s. m. *colui che è verfato ed e efercita la chimica.*

Chy'mistry, s. [philofophy by fire] *chimica*, s. f. arte *che col fuoco ed altro fepara le particelle de' mifti.*

Ci'bol, s. [a fmall fort of onion] *fpezie di cipolla picciola.*

Ci'catrice or **Ci'catrix**, s. [a fcar left after a wound or ulcer is healed] *cicatrice*, s. f. *màrgine*, s. m.

Ci'catrice, [a mark, an impreffure] *fegno, impreffione.*

To **Ci'catrize**, [to apply fuch medicine to wounds or ulcers as will fkin them] *applicar tali cerotti e impiaftri alle ferite che le fáldino e fácciano tornarvi sù la pelle, cicatrizzare.*

Cicatri'zed, adj. *cicatrizzato.*

Cich, or **Cich-pease**, [a fort of pulfe] *cece, fpezie di legume. Diceſi anche* Chick *e* Chick-peafe. Not in ufe.

To **Ci'curate** [to tame] *domare.*

Cid, s. [a valiant man, a great captain] *un uomo valorofo, un gran capitano.*

Ci'der, s. [a drink made of apples] *fidro*, s. m. *bevanda fatta del fugo di mele.*

A cider houfe, *cafa dove fi vende fidro.*

A cider-man, *un che vende dal fidro.*

Ci'derist, s. [a maker of cider] *un che fa il fidro.*

Ci'derkin, s. [the liquor made of the grofs matter of apples, after the cider is preffed out] *liquore che fi fa con la pafta de' pomi franti dopo che il fidro ne è ftato fpremuto.*

To **Ciel** with plaifter, *intonacare il cielo d'una camera.*

Ci'eling, s. *foffitto d' una camera.*

Cierge, s. [taper] *cero*, s. f. *candela lunga e groffa fatta di cera.*

C'ilery, s. [work like the tops of leaves on pillars] *fogliame, lavoro a foglie ne' capitegli delle colonne.*

Ci'meter, s [a fort of fword fhort and recurvated] *fcimitarra, forta di fciabla corta.*

Cinca'nter or **Cinca'ter**, s. [a man aged fifty years] *un uomo di cinquant' anni. Non è in ufo.*

Ci'nture, s. [the middle of a pillar, *cintura, fafcia d'una colonna.*

Ci'nders, s. [embers, afhes] *ceneri.* s. f.

Cinder women, *Donne mendiche che vanno cogliendo per le ftrade i carboni che fi trovano fra le ceneri.*

Ci'ngle, s. [a girt for a horfe] *cinghia*, s. f.

Ci'nnabar, s. *cinnabar* is native or factitious; the factitious cinnabar is called *vermillion.* The particles of mercury uniting with the particles of fulphur compofe *cinnobar*] *cinabro.*

Cinnabar of Antimony. *Cinabro, fatto di mercurio, zolfo, ed antimonio.*

Ci'nnamon, s. [the bark of an Indian-tree] *cannella*, s. *cinnamómo*, s. m. *la fcorza d' un albero dell' Indie.*

Cinnamon-tree, *albero di cannella.*

Cinque, s. [at dice or cards] *cinque, dices; al giuoco de' dadi e delle carte.*

Ci'nquefoil, s. [the five-leav'd grafs] *cinquefoglie*, s. f. *erba cofi detta dal fare in cima ad ogni fuo ftelo cinque foglie.*

Ci'nque-pace, s. *fpezie di ballo.*

Ci'nque-spotted, adj. *che ha cinque macchie.*

Ci'on, s. [graft] *nefto, innefto, pollone, germoglio*, s. m.

Ci'pher, s. [number] *fegno d' aritmetica che vale un certo numero.*

Cipher [fecret character] *cifera, fcrittura non intefa fe non da coloro tra i quali s' è convenuto del modo del comporla.*

Cipher [a number expreffed thus (o) and it is of no value, except when it is joined with another figure] *zero*, s. m.

To learn ciphers, *imparar d' abbaco.*

To ftand for a cipher, *fervir per ripieno.*

To **Cipher** [to caft acounts] *calcolare far conti.*

Ci'phered, adj. *calcolato.*

Circle, s. [a compafs, ring] *circolo, cerchio*, s. m.

The circles of a fphere or globe, *circoli d'una sfera o globo.*

The empire of Germany is divided into ten circles, *l' Imperio d' Alemagna è divifo in dieci circoli.*

Circle-wife, *circolarmente, in circolo, a maniera di circolo.*

Circle about the moon, *alone*, s. m. *quella ghirlanda di lume, che vedefi talvolta intorno alla luna.*

A little circle, *circoletto*, s. m. *piccolo circolo.*

The black circle about the eye, *iride*, s. f. *quel cerchio di vari colori, che circonda la pupilla dell' occhio.*

Ci'rclet, s. [an inftrument of metal to fet a difh upon at table] *cerchietto di metallo che ferve a mettervi fopra i piatti in tavola.*

Ci'rcling, adj. [circular, round] *tondo, circolare, che cerchia intorno, che circonda.*

Ci'rcuit, s. [compafs] *circuito, cerchio, giro, contorno*, s. m.

To circuit [to compafs about] *circuire, circondare, andare attorno.*

A guide in a circuit, *giudice ambulante, che va da una provincia in un' altra per amminiftrare la giuftizia.*

Circui'tion, s. [the act of going about] *circuizione, circuimento, circondamento, giramento*, s. m.

Ci'rcular, adj. [round] *circolare, rotondo, tondo.*

A circular motion, *moto circolare.*

Ci'rcularly, adj. [in form of a circle] *a mo' di cerchio.*

Ci'rcularly, adj. [with a circular motion] *circolare che fi muove in cerchio.*

To **Ci'rculate** [to go or move round] *circolare, volgerfi intorno, girare attorno.*

The blood does always circulate, *il fangue circola fempre.*

Money does not circulate, *il danaro non corre.*

Ci'rculated, adj. *circolato.*

Ci'rculation, s. [the motion of that which circulates] *circolazione*, s. f.

The circulation of the blood, *il circolazione del fangue.*

Ci'rculatory, adj. *circolare.*

Circulatory letters, *lettere circolari.*

Circuma'mbient, adj. [encompaffing or flowing about] *che gira attorno, e dicefi propriamente dell' aria ed altri fluidi.*

To **Circumci'se**, *circoncidere*, pret. *circoncifi.*

To circumcife a child, *circoncidere an bambino.*

Circumci'sed, adj. *circoncifo.*

Circumcision, s. *circoncifione.*

Circu'mference, s. [circuit, compafs] *circonferenza*, s. f. *linea, che termina la figura circolare, giro, circuito*, s. m.

Ci'rcumflex, adj, [bowed or bended about] *circonfleffo.*

Circumflex, s. [an accent which being placed over a fyllable, makes it long] *un accento circonfleffo.*

Circumlocu'tion, s. [a compafs, or fetch of words] *circonlocuzione*, s. f. *circuito di parole.*

Circummu'red, adj. [walled round] *murato intorno.*

To **Circumscri'be** [to bound, to limit, to ftint] *circofcrivere, limitare, terminare*, pret. *circofcriffi.*

Circumscri'bed, adj. *circofcritto, limitato, terminato, prefcritto.*

Circumscri'ption, s. *circofcrizione*, s. f. *il circofcrivere.*

Ci'rcumspect, adj. [wary, confiderate] *circofpètto fagace, accorto, confiderato, cauto, prudente.*

Circumspe'ction, s. [warinefs] *circofpezione, fagacità, accortezza, confiderazione, cautela, prudenza*, s. f.

Circumsp'ectively, } adv. *con*
Circumspe'ctly, } *circofpezione, fagacemente, accortamente, confideramente, cautamente, cautelofamente, prudentemente.*

Ci'rcumstance, s. [a particular that accompanies any action, as time, place, &c.] *circoftanza*, s. f. *qualità accompagnante con tempo e luogo.*

One's circumftances, [ftate, condition] *ftato*, s. m. *condizione*, s. f.

Being under thofe circumftances, *effendo in quefto ftato.*

Ci'rcumstanced, adj. [that is attended with circumftances] *accompagnato da circoftanze.*

A fact well circumftanced, *un fatto accompagnato di molte circoftanze.*

Being thus circumſtanced [being thus under thoſe circumſtances] *trovandomi in tale ſtato.*

CI'RCUMSTANT, adj. [ſurrounding] *che accerchia, che intornia, intorniante, circoſtante.*

CIRCUMSTA'NTIAL, adj. [relating to circumſtances] *appartenente a circoſtanza.*

A circumſtantial miſtake, *un errore nelle circoſtanze.*

To circumſtantiate [to deſcribe a thing with its circumſtances] *ſpecificare una coſa colle ſue circoſtanze.*

CIRCUMSTA'NCIATED, adj. *ſpecificato ſecondo le ſue circoſtanze.*

CIRCUMVALLA'TION, s. [in fortification, a trench cut by the beſiegers, and bordered with a breaſt-work, ſo as to encompaſs all their camp] *circonvallazione,* s. f. *termine di fortificazione.*

To CI'RCUMVENT [to over-reach, to deceive] *circonvenire, ingannare, inſidiare, uſare ſoperchierie, deludere, ſoperchiare.*

CI'RCUMVENTED, adj. *ingannato, ſoperchiato.*

CIRCUMVE'NTION, s. [over-reaching, cheating, deceit] *inganno,* s. m. *circonvenzione, frode, inſidia, ſoperchieria,* s. f.

CIRCUMVOLU'TION, s. [the act of rolling or turning about] *circonvoluzione,* s. f. *giro, circuito,* s. m.

CIRQUE, or CI'RCUS, s. [a large theatre in ancient Rome built for ſhows and games] *circo,* s. m. *luogo nell' antica Roma dove ſi facevano gli ſpettacoli nel tempo de' Romani.*

CISTE'RTIAN, adj. *ex.* Ciſtertian Monks, *frati Ciſtercienſi.*

CI'STERN, s. [a place under ground for the keeping of rain water] *ciſterna,* s. f. *ricetto a guiſa di pozzo nel quale ſi raccoglie e conſerva l'acqua piovana.*

Ciſtern [a veſſel of lead to keep water for houſhold uſes] *ciſternetta fatta di piombo nella quale ſi conſerva l'acqua per uſo domeſtico.*

A ciſtern [in a dining-room to put bottles in] *rinfreſcatojo,* s. m. *vaſo di metallo o di terra dove ſi mette acqua freſca per rinfreſcare il vino, e tienſi nella camera dove ſi mangia.*

CIT, s. [citizen] *cittadino. E voce di diſpregio.*

Cit [a pert low townſman] *cittadinello inſolente.*

CI'TADEL, s. *cittadella, fortezza.*

CITA'TION, s. *citazione, allegazione,* s. f.

Citation [ſummons] *citazione,* s. f. *il citare, comandamento.*

To CITE [to quote an authority or paſſage in a book] *citare, addurre, allegare,* preſ. *adduco,* pret. *adduſſi.*

To cite [to ſummon to appear at a court] *citare, chiamare a magiſtrati per mezzo de' miniſtri pubblici.*

CI'TED, adj *citato, addotto, allegato.*

CI'TESS, s. *cittadinella, cittadina di poco affare.*

CI'THERN, *v.* Citern.

CI'TING, s. *il citare, citazione, allegazione,* s. f.

CI'TIZEN, s. [an inhabitant of a city] *cittadino,* s. m. *quegli ch' è capace degli onori e de' benefici della città.*

The citizens of London, *i cittadini di Londra.*

Citizen-like, *cittadineſco, da cittadino.*

CI'TRON, s. [a ſort of lemon] *redrato, cedro,* s. m.

Citron-colour, *di color di cedro.*

CI'TRUL, s. [pumpion] *ſorta di zucca.*

CI'TTERN, s. [a ſort of muſical inſtrument] *cetera,* s. f. *ſtrumento muſicale a corde d'ottone o d'acciajo.*

To play upon the cittern, *ſonar la cetera.*

A player upon the cittern, *ceteriſta,* s. m. *ſonator di cetera.*

CITY, s. [a large walled town] *città,* s. f.

The city of London, *la città di Londra.*

CI'VET, s. [a perfume like muſk, taken out of a civet cat] *zibetto,* s. m.

Civet cat, *zibetto,* s. m. *animale così chiamato.*

CI'VICK, adj. *civico.*

Civick crown [a garland made of the branches of oak, and given as a reward to the Roman ſoldiers who had ſaved a citizen's life in battle] *corona civica che davaſi a que' ſoldati Romani che in battaglia avevano ſalvata la vita d'un cittadino.*

CI'VIL, adj. [courteous, kind] *civile, corteſe, affabile.*

Civil [political, belonging to the citizens, city, or ſtate] *civile, cittadineſco.*

A civil or military life, *una vita civile o militare.*

A civil war, *una guerra civile.*

Civil law [in oppoſition to the canonical law] *la legge civile.*

CIVI'LIAN, s [a doctor, profeſſor or ſtudent in the civil law] *un dottore, un uomo verſato nella legge civile, un giureconſulto, uno ſtudente in legge civile.*

CIVI'LITY, s. [courteſy, obligingneſs] *civiltà, corteſia, affabilità, urbanità, gentilezza, bella creanza,* s. f.

To CIVILI'ZE [to make civil, to poliſh manners] *civilizzare, render civile, coltivare, ringentilire, aggiugner gentilezza.*

CIVILI'ZED, adj. *civilizzato, accoſtumato, ringentilito.*

A civilized nation, *una nazione civile, una nazione colta.*

CI'VILLY, adv. *civilmente, corteſemente, urbanamente.*

CLACK, or MILL-CLACK, s. *batacchio da mulino.*

To ſet one's clack a going, *cominciare a parlare.*

To CLACK [to rattle, to ſnap, to make a ſhrill noiſe] *ſtrepitare, romoreggiare, far romore o ſtrepito, ſchiamazzare.*

To clack wool [to cut off the ſheep's mark, by which it weighs leſs, and yields leſs cuſtom] *tagliare quel ſegno che ſi fa nel doſſo della pecorè con pece, affinchè la lana peſi meno e paghi meno dogana. E' coſtume tutto Ingleſe.*

Clack-gooſe, s. [barnacle] *oca di Scozia.*

CLA'CKING, s. *ſtrepito, romore, ſchiamazzo.*

CLAD, adj. [cloathed] *veſtito, coperto.*

Richly clad, *riccamente veſtito.*

CLAIM, s. [demand, challenge] *pretenſione, ragione,* s. f. *diritto.*

To lay a claim to a thing, *pretendere, aver pretenſione a qualche coſa.*

To CLAIM [to lay a claim to] *pretendere, aver pretenſione o diritto a qualche coſa.*

To claim [to challenge one's promiſe] *pretendere alcuna coſa in virtù dell' altrui promeſſa.*

To claim [to attribute to one's ſelf] *attribuirſi arrogarſi, aſſumere,* pret. *attribuiſco.*

To claim again, *ridomandare, raddomandare.*

CLAIMED, adj. *preteſo, attribuito, arrogato.*

CLA'IMER, *quello o quella che pretende a qualche coſa.*

CLA'IMING, s. *pretenſione, ragione,* s. f. *diritto,* s. m.

To CLA'MBER [to clamber up] *rampicare, arrampicarſi.*

CLA'MBERING, s. *il rampicare, l'arrampicarſi.*

To CLAMM [to clog with any glutinous matter] *impeciare, attaccare una coſa ad un altra con qualche materia viſcoſa.*

CLA'MMINESS, s. *viſcoſità,* s. f.

CLA'MMY, adj. [gluiſh] *tegnente, tenace, viſchioſo, viſcoſo.*

CLA'MOROUS, adj [noiſy] *ſtrepitoſo, che fa ſtrepito, che fa ſchiamazzo.*

CLA'MOUR, s. [noiſe, bawling] *clamore, ſtrepito, ſchiamazzio, ſchiamazzo, baccano, grido,* s. m.

What's all this clamour for? *che vuol dire queſto baccano?*

To CLA'MOUR [to make a noiſe] *gridare, ſtrepitare, ſchiamazzare, romoreggiare.*

To clamour againſt a thing, *richiamarſi contro qualche coſa.*

CLAN, s. [a family, a race] *famiglia numeroſa, razza. Diceſi delle famiglie di Scozia.*

Clan [a body or ſect of perſons] *corpo di perſone, ſetta.*

CLA'NCULAR, } adj. [privy, ſecret,
CLA'NDESTINE, } by ſtealth] *clandeſtino, ſegreto, privato, furtivo, di ſoppiatto.*

Clandeſtine deſigns, *pratiche ſegrete.*

CLANDE'STINELY, adv. *ſegretamente, clandeſtinamente, privatamente, aſcoſamente, ſotto mano, di ſoppiatto.*

To CLANG [to ſound like a trumpet] *ſuonare, parlando d'una tromba.*

CLA'NGOR, s. [ſound of a trumpet] *ſuono di tromba.*

CLAP, s. [crack] *ſtrepito, romore, fracaſſo, ſcoppio;* s. m.

The door gave a great clap, *la porta fece un grande ſcoppio.*

A clap of thunder, *uno ſcoppio di tuono.*

Clap,

Clap [blow] *buſſa*, s. f. *colpo*, s. m. *botta*, s. f.

At one clap [at once] *alla prima, in un colpo*.

A clap [a venereal diſeaſe] *ſcolazione, gonorrèa venerea*.

To Clap [to beat] *battere, percuotere, picchiare, buſſare*, pret. *percoſſi*.

To clap the wings, *ſvollazzare, batter l'ali*.

To clap one's back, *percuotere alcuno nelle ſpalle*.

To clap one's hands [to applaud] *applaudire, picchiar le mani*.

To clap an actor on the ſtage, *applaudire un attore quando rapreſenta la ſua parte ſul* teatro.

To clap [to join on] *appiccare, unire una coſa all' altra*.

To clap a piece to an old ſuit, *applicare, mettere o cucire una pezza ad un veſtito vecchio*.

To clap one's hand upon one's breaſt, *metterſi la mano al petto*.

To clap a lock on the door, *mettere una ſerratura alla porta*.

To clap a horſe on the back, *accarezzare un cavallo battendolo con la mano aperta ſul doſſo*.

To clap [to claſh] *ſcoppiare, ſtridere, ſtrepitare, fare ſtrepito*.

I ſhall clap a writ or action on his back, *gli metterò gli ſbirri addoſſo, lo farò arreſtare*.

To clap one [to give him a clap] *infranciosare, dare una ſcolazione ad uno*.

To clap on all the ſails, *ſpiegar tutte le vele*.

To clap in, *ſpignere, ficcare, cacciare, mettere, ficcare per forza*.

To clap in, *avvanzarſi, cacciarſi, ſpignerſi*.

To clap ſpurs to one's horſe, *ſpronare, dar de' ſproni ad un cavallo*.

To clap up in priſon, *giugner uno alla ſchiaccia, incalappiarlo, farlo imprigionare*.

To clap the door, *chiuder la porta con violenza*.

To clap up a peace, *fare una pace finta, far pace in fretta*.

To clap up an agreement, *fare un accordo*.

To clap up a bargain, *fare un accordo*.

To clap [to wrap up together] *fardellare, far fardello, legare inſieme*.

Cla'pboard, s. [a rib, a board cut ready to make caſks and the like] *doga*, s. f. *una di quelle ſtriſce di legno di che ſi compone il corpo della botte o di ſimili vaſi tondi*.

Clap-bread, s. [thin, hard oaten cakes] *ciambella*, s. f.

Cla'pped, *pret. di* to clap.

Cla'pper, s. [that claps his hands for joy] *colui che applaudiſce, approvatore*, s. m.

The clapper of a bell [bell clapper] *battaglio di campana*.

The clapper of a mill, *battente di mulino*.

The clapper of a door, *il martello d'un porta*.

A clapper of conies, *conigliera*, s. f. *luogo dove ſi tengono rinchiuſi i conigli*.

Cla'pping, s. *battimento*, s. m. *v.* To clap.

A clapping of the wings, *ſvollazzamento*, s. m. *lo ſvolazzare, battimento d'ali*.

A clapping for joy, *applauſo*, s. m.

Clapping [ſtroaking with the hand] *carezza*, s. f. *come ſi fa quando, ſi batte leggiermente il doſſo del cavallo*.

Clapt, adj. *battuto, percoſſo*, *v.* To clap.

Cla'ret, s. [claret wine] *vino roſſo di Francia*.

Cla'richord, s. [a ſort of muſical inſtrument] *ſtromento muſicale che ha ſomiglianza col gravicémbalo*.

To Cla'rify [to make liquor or juices clearer or finer] *chiarificare, chiarire, far chiaro*, preſ. *chiariſco*.

To clarify ſyrup, *chiarificare uno ſciroppo*.

To clarify [to grow clear] *chiarificarſi, chiarirſi*.

It begins to clear, *comincia a chiarificarſi*.

Clarifica'tion, s. [the act of clarifying, or making liquors clear] *chiarificazione*, s. f. *il chiarificare*.

Cla'rified, adj. *chiarificato, chiarito*.

Clarify'ing, s. *chiarificazione*, s. f. *il chiarificare*.

Cla'rion, s. [a ſort of ſhrill trumpet] *chiarione*, s. m. *ſtrumento da fiato, che ha un ſuono acuto*.

Cla'rity, s. [clearneſs, brightneſs] *chiarità, chiarezza, lucidezza, ſplendidezza*, s. f.

Cla'ry, s. [a ſort of herb] *clarea*, s. f. *ſorta d'erba*.

Clash, s. *dibattimento, ſcontramento, romore, fracaſſo, ſtrepito*, s. m.

A claſh of ſwords, *ſtrepito di ſpade*.

Claſh [diſpute, debate] *contraſto, combattimento*, s. m. *diſputa, oppoſizione, differenza, conteſtazione, conteſa*, s. f.

To Clash, verb. neut. [to beat againſt] *urtarſi, ſcontarſi, dibatterſi*.

Their ſwords claſhed againſt one another, *le loro ſpade ſi ſcontrarono*.

To Clash [to diſagree] *contendere, diſputare, contraſtare, contraddire, quiſtionare, contrariare, contradiare*.

Thoſe two parties do ever claſh, *quei due partiti contendono ſempre, ſono ſempre in conteſa inſieme*.

Theſe two laws claſh, *queſte due leggi ſono contrarie, ſono diſcordi fra di loro*.

Your undertakings claſh with mine, *i voſtri diſegni ſono oppoſti a' miei*.

To claſh with one's ſelf, *contraddirſi, variare nel diſcorſo*.

Cla'shing, s. *urto, ſcontro*, s. m. *v.* To claſh.

Claſhing of arms, *ſtrepito d'armi*.

Claſhing [diſpute] *diſputa, conteſa, oppoſizione*, s. f. *contraſto*, s. m.

Clasp, s. [latch] *fermaglio*, s. m. *borchia*, s. f. *ganghero*, s. m.

Claſp [embrace] *ampleſſo, abbracciamento*.

The claſps of a book, *i fermagli d'un libro*.

Claſp [a tendril or ſprig of a tree] *brocco, tenerume*, s. m. *le punte* tenere *de' rami degli alberi*.

To Clasp [to buckle] *affibbiare, congiugnere inſieme con fermaglio*.

To claſp [to embrace] *abbracciare*.

Cla'sped, adj. *affibbiato, abbracciato*.

Two hands claſped and joined together, are the ſymbol of fidelity, *due mani annodate inſieme ſono ſimbolo di fedeltà*.

Cla'sper, s. [tendril] *tenerume, brocco*, s. m. *la punta* tenera *de' rami degli alberi*.

Cla'sping, s. *affibbiamento*, s. m. *l'affibbiare*, *v.* To claſp.

Claſping, adj. *circondante, che abbraccia, che circonda*.

Class [form in ſchools] *claſſe*, s. f.

Claſs [rank] *claſſe, ſfera*, s. f. *ordine*, s. m.

To Class [to range according to ſome ſtated method of diſtribution] *ordinare, diſtribuire per ordine, con metodo*.

Cla'ssical, } Cla'ssick, } adj. *claſſico*.

A claſſick, *un autore claſſico*.

Cla'tter, s. [a rattling noiſe made by frequent colliſion of ſonorous bodies] *ſtrepito cagionato da frequente utarſi di corpi ſonori*.

Clatter [any tumultuous and confuſed noiſe] *ſtrepito confuſo, qualunque romore continuato*.

To Cla'tter [to make a noiſe] *ſtrepitare, fare ſtrepito, romoreggiare, far romore*.

To clatter [to prattle] *cicalare, ciarlare, cornacchiare*.

To clatter [to diſpute] *contendere, diſputare, contraſtare, contraddire, quiſtionare*.

A clatter-coat, *un ciarlone, un cicalone*.

Cla'ttering, s. *ſtrepito, fracaſſo, romore, ſchiamazzo, ſchiamazzio*, s. m.

To Cla'udicate [to halt] *zoppicare, andar zoppo*.

Clave, *preterito del verbo* to cleave.

Cla'ver, *v.* Clover.

Cla'vicles, s. [the channel bones] *clavicule*, s. f. *que' due oſſicelli che chiudono il petto verſo la fontanella*.

Clavicles [young ſhoots of vines] *polloni, ſorcoli di vigna*.

Clause, s. [a condition or proviſo in a contract] *clauſola, clauſula*, s. f.

Clauſe [concluſion] *fine, concluſione*, s. f.

Cla'ustral, adj. [of or belonging to a cloiſter] *clauſtrale, di chioſtro*.

Claw [the nail of a fowl's foot] *artiglio*, s. m. *unghia adunca e pugnente di animali rapaci volatili*.

Claw, *ugna di zampa*, s. f. *unghione*, s. m.

The claws of a lion, *gli unghioni d'un lione*.

The claws of a crab or lobſter, *le forbici de' granchi e de' gamberi*.

The hinder claws of a wild boar, *gli ſproni d'un cinghiale*.

A claw-back [a flatterer] *un adulatore, un' adulatrice*, s. f.

To CLAW [to scratch] *graffiare, sgraffiare.*
To claw [to flatter] *adulare, lusingare.*
Claw me, claw thee, *fatemi un servizio e ve ne farò un altro.*
To claw it off, to claw it away [to fall to it briskly] *spedire, sbrigare.*
I claw'd it off to-day [I work'd very hard] *ho lavorato molto oggi, ho spediti molti affari oggi.*
To claw the victuals off, *mangiar presto e avidamente.*
He had a disease which he could never claw off, *egli aveva una malattia della quale non potette mai liberarsi.*
I have had an ague, and I can't claw it off yet, *ho avuta una febbre la quale non m'ha ancora lasciato affatto.*
CLA'WED, adj. *graffiato, sgraffiato, adulato, lusingato.*
CLAY, s. [potter's clay] *creta, argilla,* s. f. *terra tegnente e densa della quale si fan no le stoviglie.*
Clay [dirt] *fango, loto,* s. m.
Man is but a lump of clay, *l'uomo non è che un pizzico di polvere, un pezzo di terra.*
Clay-land, *terra argillosa.*
Clay-pit, *luogo donde si cava l'argilla.*
To CLAY [to daub with clay] *coprire d'argilla.*
To clay the sugar, *raffinare il zucchero.*
CLEAN, adj. [pure, neat] *puro, netto, pullito, chiaro, bianco, schietto.*
A clean glass, *un bicchiere netto.*
A clean room, *una camera netta, pulita.*
As clean as a penny, *pulito come l'oro.*
Clean water, *acqua chiara.*
A clean shirt, *una camicia bianca.*
Clean sheets, *lenzuola bianche.*
A clean plate, *un tondo netto.*
A clean napkin, *una salvietta netta.*
Quite and clean, *affatto, dell tutto, assolutamente.*
The clean contrary way, *tutto'l contrario, a rovescio.*
To CLE'AN, *nettare, pulire, purgare, lavare.*
CLE'ANLINESS, s. [pureness] *pulizia, pulitezza, nettezza,* s. f.
I love cleanliness, *amo la pulizia.*
CLE'ANLY, adj. *pulito, netto, che ama la pulitezza.*
A cleanly woman, *una donna pulita, che ama la pulitezza.*
Cleanly, adv. *pulitamente, nettamente.*
CLE'ANNESS, s. [pureness] *pulitezza, pulizia, nettezza,* s. f.
Cleanness of mind, *purità di mente, integrità.*
To CLE'ANSE [to make clean] *pulire, nettare, purgare, lavare, mondare,* pres. *pulisco.*
To cleanse a well, *nettare un pozzo.*
To cleanse the blood, *purgare il sangue.*
To cleanse or purge by sacrifice, *espurgare col sacrificio.*
To cleanse one's teeth, *nettarsi i denti.*
CLE'ANSED, adj. *nettato, pulito, purgato, lavato.*

CLE'ANSER, s. *che netta, purga, e lava.*
CLE'ANSING, s. *pulimento, nettamento,* s. m. *il pulire.*
CLEAR, adj. [fair] *chiaro, sereno, puro.*
Clear weather, *tempo chiaro, o sereno.*
Clear water, *acqua pura o limpida.*
A clear style, *uno stile chiaro.*
'Tis a clear case, *è un caso chiaro, o manifesto.*
A clear estate, *beni liquidi.*
A clear reckoning, *un conto chiaro.*
Clear [without mixture] *puro, schietto, netto.*
A clear conscience, *una coscienza pura.*
A clear reason, *una ragione chiara.*
A clear complexion, *una carnagione vivace o delicata.*
Clear [innocent] *innocente.*
I am clear of that crime, *sono innocente di quel delitto.*
A clear reputation, *una riputazione senza macchia.*
A house clear from infection, *una casa che non è infetta.*
To be clear in the world [to be clear from debt] *non dover niente, essere senza debiti.*
A clear countenance, *un viso aperto.*
To make a clear riddance of something, *sbrigarsi, spedirsi di qualchè cosa.*
'Tis all clear gain, *è tutto guadagno.*
To get clear of the port, *uscire del porto.*
Clear, adv. *affatto, del tutto, intieramente.*
I am clear against it, *sono del tutto contrario a cio.*
To come off clear, *uscirsene pel rotto della cuffia, liberarsi dal pericolo senza spesa, o noja.*
He came off clear from all imputation, *s'è giustificato di tutte le calunnie.*
To stand clear, *far ala.*
To leap clear over a ditch, *saltar netto un fosso.*
To have a revenue of a thousand pounds clear, *aver dieci mila lire sterline nette all' anno.*
Clear-sighted, *perspicace, d'acuta vista, che vede perfettamente.*
Clear-spirited, *sincero, candido, integro, franco, libero, ingenuo, aperto.*
Very clear, *chiarissimo.*
To CLEAR [to make clear] *schiarire, nettare, purgare, pulire.*
A water that clears the sight, *un'acqua che schiarisce la vista.*
To clear the ranks of the army, *diradare le fila d'un esercito.*
The sun has cleared the mist, *il sole ha dissipata la nebbia.*
To clear metal, *purificare metallo.*
To clear the trenches, *nettare le trincee.*
To clear the highways of robbers, *tenere libere le strade di ladri.*
To clear a passage, *spacciare un cammino.*
To clear a difficulty, *risolvere, spiegare, sciogliere, schiarire una difficoltà, o un dubbio.*

To clear a prisoner, *assolvere un prigioniere, dichiararlo innocente.*
To clear one's self from a crime, *purgarsi, giustificarsi d'un delitto.*
To clear the table, *sparecchiare la tavola.*
To clear the room, *vuotar la camera.*
To clear the room [to go out] *uscir della camera.*
To clear accounts, *liquidare un conto.*
To clear one's debts, *pagare i suoi debiti.*
To clear a ship at the custom-house, *scaricare un vascello alla dogana e pagar il dazio delle mercanzie che porta.*
To clear up, verb neut. *schiarirsi, rasserenarsi.*
It begins to clear up, *il tempo comincia a schiarirsi.*
CLE'ARED, adj. *schiarito, nettato,* v. To clear.
CLE'ARER, adj. [the comparative of clear] *più chiaro.*
Clearer, s. [brightner, purifier, enlightner] *che rende lucido, che rischiara, che purifica.*
CLE'ARING, s. *schiarimento, nettamento,* s. m. *giustificazione,* s. f.
CLE'ARLY, adv. [plainly] *chiaramente, nettamente, evidentemente, manifestamente.*
Clearly [wholly] *del tutto, affatto, intieramente.*
CLE'ARNESS, s. [brightness] *nettezza, pulitezza, chiarezza, purità,* s. f.
The clearness of the air, *la serenità dell' aria.*
Clearness of voice, *voce netta, nettezza di voce.*
Clearness of sight, *perspicacità, acutezza di vista.*
Clearness of sound, *chiarezza di suono.*
Clearness of mind, *accutezza d'ingegno.*
Clearness from a fault, *innocenza, integrità.*
CLEAR-SI'GHTED, adj. [discerning, judicious] *che discerne bene, giudizioso.*
To CLEA'RSTARCH [to stiffen with starch] *dar l'amido, dar la salda alle biancherie.*
To CLEAVE, v. a. pret. I clove, I clave, I cleft [to cut, to divide] *fendere, dividere, spaccare.*
To cleave, v. n. pret. I clave, part. cloven [to split] *fendersi, dividersi, spaccarsi.*
To cleave [to stick fast to] *attaccarsi, appiccarsi.*
CLE'AVER, s. *quello o quella che fende.*
A wood-cleaver, *uno spaccalegne, un tagliatore di legne.*
A butcher's cleaver, *un coltellaccio di beccajo, una mannaja.*
CLE'AVING, s. *fendimento,* s. m. *il fendere.*
A cleaving [a cleft] *spaccatura, fessura,* s. f.
CLEFT, part. pass. [from to cleave] *fesso, diviso, spaccato.*
Cleft, s. *crepaccio,* s. m. *crepatura, fessura, spaccatura, apertura,* s. f.

CLE-

CLE'MENCY, s. [meekneſs] *clemenza, bontà, benignità,* s. f.
CLE'MENT, adj. [meek, gentle] *clemente, benigno, umano.*
CLEMENTI'NES, s. pl. [the decretals or conſtitutions of pope Clement V.] *clementine,* s. f. *le coſtituzioni di Clemente quinto ſommo pontefice che ſi leggono nel corpo canonico dopo il ſeſto libro delle decretali.*
To CLEPE, v. a. [to call] *chiamare.*
Cleped, *chiamato, nomato.* Obſ.
CLE'RGY, s. [that order of men who are peculiarly devoted to the ſervice of God] *clero,* s. m. *univerſità di cherici, gli eccleſiaſtici.*
A CLE'RGYMAN, *un prete, un eccleſiaſtico.*
CLE'RICAL, adj. [of or belonging to a clergyman] *chericale, di cherico.*
CLERK, s. [a title given to clergymen] *cherico,* s. m. *perſona eccleſiaſtica.*
The clerk of a church, *il cherico o ſagriſtano d'una chieſa.*
A clerk [a man of letters] *un uomo letterato.*
An attorney's clerk, *giovane di procuratore, un briccone in erba.*
A writing clerk, *uno ſcrivano.*
The clerk of a company, *ſegretario d'una communità.*
A clerk of the kitchen, *ſcrivano di cucina.*
The clerk of the king's wardrobe, *il primo cameriere della guardaroba del re.*
CLE'RKSHIP, s. *chericato,* s. m. *dottrina.*
CLE'VER, adj. *abile, deſtro, atto, diſpoſto, ſcaltrito. E' vocabolo plebeo.*
A clever man, *un abil uomo, un uomo da boſco e da riviera.*
CLE'VERLY, adj. *deſtramente, con deſtrezza, pulitamente. Vocabolo plebeo.*
He does it cleverly, *lo fa deſtramente, o pulitamente.*
He cut it off cleverly, *l'ha tagliato netto.*
CLEW, s. [a bottom of yarn or thread] *gomitolo,* s. m. *palla di filo raccolto.*
The clew of a ſail [the lower corner of it] *la punta della vela dove s'attacca la ſcotta.*
CLEW-GA'RNET, s. [a rope made faſt to the clew of a ſail] *ſcotta,* s. f. *quella fune che s'attacca alla punta della vela per tirarla a poppa.*
To CLICK [as a watch does] *tintinnare, parlando del ſuono del bilancino d'un orologio.*
To click [among ſhoemakers to ſtand at the ſhop door to invite cuſtomers] *ſtare alla porta della bottega per invitare gli avventori; e ſi dice de' calzolai quando così fanno.*
CLI'CKET, s. [the knocker of a door] *martello di porta.*
CLI'ENT, s. [a perſon who retains a lawyer or proctor to plead his cauſe] *clientolo, cliente,* s. m.
CLIFF, or CLIFT, s. [a cragged mountain] *dirupo, rupe, luogo ſcoſceſo e dirupato.*

Cliff [the ſide or pitch of a hill] *coſta, ſceſa di monte.*
CLIMACTE'RICAL, adj. *climaterico.*
Climacterical year [every ſeventh year, but the great climacterical is the ſixty third] *anno climaterico, cioè ogni ſette anni, ma l'anno climaterico particolarmente è il ſeſſanteſimo terzo.*
CLI'MATE, s. [a part of the earth between two circles, parallel to the equator] *clima,* s. m. *ſpazio di terra contenuto da due paralelli, tanto lontani fra di loro che il maggior dì dell' uno avanza quel dell' altro d'una mezza ora.*
Climate [country, land] *clima, regione, paeſe.*
To CLI'MATE [to inhabit] *abitare, ſtar in un certo luogo, ſotto un certo clima.*
CLIMATURE, v. Climates.
CLI'MAX, s. [gradation, aſcent; a figure in rhetorick, by which the ſentence raiſes gradually] *figura rettorica per cui la ſentenza aſcende gradatamente.*
To CLIMB, or CLIMB UP [to creep up] *rampicare, andare ad alto con attaccar le zampe al muro.*
To climb up a tree, *rampicare ſopra un albero.*
To climb up a ladder, *ſalire o montare una ſcala.*
To climb up with a ladder, *ſcalare.*
To climb, v. n. *arrampicarſi.*
CLI'MBER, s. *che rampica.*
Haſty climbers have ſudden falls, *ai voli alti e repentini ſogliono i precipizi eſſer vicini.* Taſſo.
CLI'MBING, s. *il rampicare.*
CLIME, s. [climate] *clima,* s. m. *regione,* s. f.
A CLINCH, s. [a pun, an ambiguity] *un biſticcio, un motto ambiguo.*
To clinch [to gripe hard with the fiſt] *ſtrignere, ſerrare con mano, afferrare,* pret. *ſtrinſi.*
To clinch the fiſt, *ſtrignere o ſerrare il pugno.*
To clinch a nail, *ribadire un chiodo.*
CLI'NCHED, adj. *ſtretto, ſerrato, afferrato.*
CLI'NCHING, adj. *ex.*
A clinching witticiſm, *un detto arguto.*
CLI'NCHER, s. [a cramp, a holdfaſt] *coſa che tien ferma un altra con forza.*
To CLING TO, pret. clung, part. clung [to ſtick cloſe to] *attaccarſi, appiccarſi.*
To cling together, *unirſi, attaccarſi inſieme.*
CLI'NGY, adj. [clammy] *tegnente, tenace, viſcoſo.*
CLINK, s. *tintinno,* s. m.
To CLINK [as metal does] *tintinnire, riſuonare, parlando di qualche metallo che ha il ſuono acuto.*
To CLIP [to cut about, to cut ſmall] *tondere, toſare.*
To clip money, *toſar la moneta.*
To clip a bird's wings, *ſpuntare o tarpare le ale agli uccelli.*
To clip a man's wings [to leſſen his power] *abbattere, o levare altrui il potere.*
To clip [to ſhear a ſheep] *tondere o toſare una pecora.*

To clip [to embrace] *abbracciare, ſtrigner colle braccia.* Obſ.
CLI'PPED, adj. *toſo, tonduto, toſato,* v. To clip.
CLI'PPER, s. *quello che toſa.*
A money clipper, *quello che toſa la moneta.*
A clipper [a ſhearer of ſheep] *tonditore di pecore.*
CLI'PPING, s. *tonditura, il toſare, toſatura,* s. f.
Clipping [colling] *abbracciamento, l'accollare.* Obſ.
CLI'PPINGS, *tonditura, toſatura,* s. f. *quel che in tondendo ſi leva.*
CLI'VER, s. [a ſort of herb] s. m. *ſpezie d'erba.*
CLOAK, s. *mantello, ferrajuolo,* s. m.
To CLOAK, *naſcondere, ricoprire, celare.* v. To Cloke
CLO'AKBAG, s. *baule in cui ſi portano li abiti per viaggio.*
CLOCK, s. [a machine to meaſure time with] *orologio, oriuolo,* s. m.
What's o'clock? *che ora è?*
'Tis four o'clock, *ſono le quattro.*
'Tis one o'clock, *è un ora.*
Clock maker, *orologiajo.*
A clock, s. [a beetle] *ſorta di ſcarafaggio, così detto.*
CLO'CK-WORK, s. [movements by weights or ſprings] *movimenti per forza di peſi o ſuſte.*
CLOD, s. [a lump] *zolla,* s. f. *pezzo di terra.*
A field full of clods, *un campo zolloſo.*
To break the clods, *erpicare, tritar coll' erpice la terra lavorata.*
Clods of blood, *grumi di ſangue, maſſa di ſangue quagliato.*
To CLOD [to break clods] *erpicare, tritar coll' erpice la terra.*
To clod [to curd] *quagliarſi, coagularſi, rappigliarſi.*
CLO'DDED, adj. *erpicato, quagliato, coagulato, rappreſo.*
Clodded blood, *ſangue grumoſo.*
Clodded milk, *latte quagliato o rappreſo.*
CLO'DDY, adj. [full of clods] *zolloſo, quagliato, grumoſo.*
CLO'DPATE, *un teſtacciuto, un goffo, un gonzo.*
CLOG, s. [hindrance] *oſtacolo, impedimento, intoppo.*
Clog [a piece of wood faſtened about the legs of beaſts to keep them from running aſtray, and about a dog's neck] *paſtoje che ſi legano ai piedi degli animali affinchè non iſcappino, e quel pezzo di legno che ſi lega al collo de' cani perchè non facciano del male.*
This meat is a clog to one's ſtomach, *queſta carne carica lo ſtomaco.*
To CLOG [to hinder] *confondere, imbarazzare, intrigare, imbrogliare, porre intoppo o oſtacolo.*
You clog me, *voi m'imbarazzate.*
To clog [to load] *caricare.*
This meat clogs my ſtomach, *queſta carne mi peſa ſulla ſtomaco.*
To clog one's belly with meat, *empierſi o impinzarſi il ventre di carne.*
I find this ale clogs my ſtomach, *ſento che queſta cervogia mi gonfia.*

CLO'GGED, adj. *confuso, imbarrazzato*, v. To clog.

Clogged with business, *affaccendato, pien di faccende.*

CLO'GGING, s. *il confondere, l' imbarazzare.*

Clogging, adj. *intricato, imbrogliato, impacciato.*

Ale is clogging, *la cervogia dolce gonfia lo stomaco.*

CLO'ISTER, s. [a place in a monastery with a piazza round it] *chiostro*, s. m. *le logge intorno a' cortili de' conventi.*

Cloister [convent] *chiostro, convento, monastero*, s. m.

To CLO'ISTER up [to shut, to confine in a convent or monastery] *rinchiudere, racchiudere in un convento o monastero.* pret. *rinchiusi, racchiusi.*

CLO'ISTERED, or CLO'ISTERED UP, adj. *rinchiuso, chiuso in un convento.*

CLOKE, or CLOAK, s. [a garment] *mantello, ferrajuolo*, s. m.

Cloke [blind colour] *mantello, velo, pretesto, colore*, s. m. *scusa, coperta*, s. f.

The cloke of religion, *il mantello o il velo della religione.*

Under the cloke, *sotto pretesto.*

To cover one's passion under the cloke of honesty, *ascondere le sue passioni otto il velo d'onestà.*

He made use of that for a cloke of his villany, *si servì di ciò per palliare la sua iniquità.*

A riding-cloke for women, *mantellina*, s. f.

Cloke-bag, *valigia*, s. f.

Cloke bearer, *porta mantello.*

Cloke-loop, *bavero*, s. m.

To CLOKE [to cover, to palliate] *coprire, cuoprire, palliare, ricoprire ingegnosamente.*

He cloked his hatred with a false show of friendship, *cuopre il suo odio con una falsa apparenza d' amicizia.*

He did it only to cloke his crime, *lo fece solamente per palliare il suo delitto.*

To cloke one's ambition, or one's perfidiousness, *dissimulare la sua ambizione o la sua perfidia.*

CLOKED, adj. *ammantellato, coperto di mantello.*

Cloked [palliated] *coperto, palliato, ricoperto.*

CLOSE, adj. [thick, near together] *serrato stretto*

They stood very close to one another, *erano molto serrati o stretti insieme.*

These lines stand mighty close, *queste righe sono troppo strette, troppo vicine.*

A close piece of cloth, *una tela fitta.*

Close [near, as houses are] *contiguo, vicino.*

My house is close to yours, *la mia casa è contigua alla vostra.*

He is a close prisoner, *è strettamente ritenuto prigione.*

To lay close siege to a town, *strignere una terra, assediare strettamente.*

A close discourse, *un discorso conciso, compendioso, succinto, stringato.*

A close room, *una camerina, una picciola camera.*

To keep a close correspondence with one, *tener calde pratiche con uno.*

Close [hidden] *nascosto, celato, segreto.*

A close reserved man, *un uomo riserbato, un musone, un soppiattone.*

Close weather, *un tempo fosco o oscuro.*

A close man, *un uomo stretto, un taccagno, un avaro, un tanghero.*

A close jest, *una burla pugnente.*

A close fight, *una zuffa rabbiosa.*

A close stool, *una seggetta.*

To go to the close-stool, *andare alla seggetta.*

A close mouth catches no flies, *in bocca chiusa non entrò mai mosca.*

Close-fisted [covetous] *avaro, meschino.*

Close-cropt, *tonduto rasente.*

Close, s. [conclusion] *conclusione, fine*, s. f.

Close [a piece of ground hedged about] *chiuso*, s. m. *chiusura*, s. f. *pezzo di terra circondato e serrato da ogni banda.*

Close, adv. *rasente, raso raso.*

To walk close by the wall, *rasentare il muro, camminare rasente il muro.*

Close to the ground, *rasente la terra.*

To live closer *usare economia, viver parcamente, esser buon economo.*

To draw the battalions close, *serrare i battaglioni.*

To write close, *scrivere stretto.*

To pull the bridle close, *tirar la briglia.*

To lye close, *tenersi ben coperto parlando d'una persona che è a letto.*

To stand, to sit, to lye close together, *strignersi insieme.*

Close sits my shirt, but closer is my skin, *mi strigne più la camicia che la gonnella.*

To follow one close, *incalzare uno, seguitarlo di presso.*

My shirt sticks close to my skin, *la mia camicia è appicata alla pelle.*

To stick close to one, *esser sempre accanto ad uno.*

To follow one's work close, *applicarsi al suo lavoro, esser assidue al suo lavoro.*

To study close, *applicarsi allo studio.*

To keep a thing close, *tener segreta una cosa.*

To shut close, *chiuder bene.*

To go close by the wind in failing, *andare a seconda del vento.*

To CLOSE, [to conclude] *conchiudere, terminare, finire.* pret. *conchiusi*, pres. *finisco.*

To close [to shut] *serrare, chiudere.*

To close [to heal up a wound] *saldare una ferita.*

To close in, *rinserrare, rinchiudere, chiudere*, pret. *rinchiusi, chiusi.*

To close an account, *saldare un conto.*

To close, verb neut. [as a wound does] *saldarsi, riunirsi, chiudersi, parlando d'una piaga.*

To close [to agree with one] *accordarsi restar d' accordo con uno.*

To close with the enemy, *venire alle mani o alle stretto col nemico.*

CLOSED, adj *finito, conchiuso, terminato.*

Closed in, *rinserrato, chiuso, rinchiuso.*

Closed up, *saldata, parlando d'una ferita.*

Closed up, *piegata, sigillata, parlando d'una lettera.*

CLO'SELY, adv. [secretly] *segretamente, celatamente, nascosamente.*

CLO'SENESS, s. [thickness] *spessezzà, densità*, s. f.

Closeness [nearness] *vicinità, prossimità, propinquità*, s. f.

Closeness [reservedness] *riserva, circospezione, cautela*, s. f. *riguardo*, s. m.

CLOSES, s. [half a bar in heraldry] *mezza sbarra in un arme di famiglia.*

CLO'SET, s. [a small apartment in a room] *gabinetto*, s. m.

To CLO'SET [to shut up or conceal in r closet] *chiudere o nascondere nel gabinetto.*

To closet [to take into a closet for a secret interview] *condur in gabinetto per discorere in segreto.*

CLO'SETTING, s. [private consultations or intrigues of the cabinet council of a prince] *intrighi, consulte segrete del gabinetto d'un principe.*

CLO'SING, s. *conclusione*, s. f. *il conchiudere*, v. To close.

Closing [inclosure] *chiuso*, s. m. *chiusura*, s. f.

CLO'SURE, v. Inclosure.

CLOT, v. Clod.

Clot, bur, s. [a sort of plant] *lappolone*, s. m. *lappola grande.*

A clot-head [a clot-pated fellow] *un balordo, uno sciocco, un minchione.*

To CLOT, v. To clod.

CLOTH, s. [linen cloth] *tela*, s. f.

Cloth [woollen cloth] *panno*, s. m.

Cloth, *la tovaglia con cui si copre la tavola per mangiare.*

The cloth [the table cloth] *la tovaglia*, s. f.

To lay the cloth, *metter la tovaglia, apparecchiara la tavole.*

To take away the cloth, *sparecchiar la tavola.*

Cotton cloth, *bambagino*, s. m. *tela fatta di fil di bambagia.*

Hair cloth, *cilicio*, s. m.

Tissue cloth, *broccato*, s. m. *tela d' oro o d' argento.*

Sear cloth [cere cloth] *tela incerata.*

Hearse cloth, *panno da morto.*

Horse cloth, *gualdrappa*, s. f.

Scarlet-cloth, *scarlatto*, s. m. *panno lano rosso di nobilissima tintura.*

Cloth-worker, *lanajuolo*, s. m. *che fabbrica panni di lana.*

Cloth-weaver, *tessitore di tele.*

Cloth-trade, *il traffico de' panni e delle tele.*

A cloth of state, *baldacchino*, s. m.

Cloth-beam, *subbio*, s. m.

To CLOTHE [to cover with cloaths, to dress] *vestire, coprire di panni.*

To clothe the soldiers, *vestir di nuovo i soldati.*

CLOTHED, ad. *vestito, coperto.*

Clothed with majesty and honour, *pieno di maestà e di gloria.*

CLOATHS (*si pronuncia clo's*) s. *abito, vestito, vestimento*, s. m.

Men's cloaths, *abiti da uomo.*

Women's

Women's cloaths, *vestimenti da donna.*
A suit of cloaths, *un vestito.*
Cloaths [linen] *panni lini, biancherie.*
To put on one's cloaths, *vestirsi.*
To pull off one's cloaths, *spogliarsi.*
Bed-cloaths, *coperture di letto.*
CLOTHIER, s. *lanajuolo,* s. m. *artefice che fabbrica i panni lani.*
CLO'THING, s. *il vestito, il vestimento,* s. m.
CLO'TTED, v. Clodded.
To CLO'TTER, *coagulare,* v. to clod.
CLO'TTY, adj. *coagulato, grumoso.*
CLOUD, s. *nube, nuvola,* s. f.
To be under a cloud [to be in trouble] *essere nelle avversità.*
To CLOUD [to darken with clouds] *annuvolare, e annugolare.*
To cloud, verb. neut. *annuvolarsi, annugolarsi.*
The sky begins to cloud, *il cielo comincia ad annuvolarsi.*
Cloudcapt, adj. [topped with clouds] *intorniato di nuvoli in vetta.*
CLOUDCOMPE'LLING, adj. *sgombranugoli. E' epiteto dato a Giove.*
CLO'UDED, adj. *annuvolato, annuvolito, offuscato.*
A clouded conutenance, *una ciera maninconosa, un viso mesto.*
CLO'UDINESS, s. *offuscamento,* s. m.
CLO'UDY, adj. *nuvoloso, nugoloso, pien di nuvoli, oscurato, offuscato, ricoperto da nuvoli.*
Cloudy weather, *tempo nuvoloso.*
Cloudy mornings turn to clear evenings, *dopo il cattivo viene il buon tempo.*
Cloudy [sad, melancholy] *accigliato, addolorato, attristato, doloroso, malinconoso, mesto, gramo, tristo, doglioso,*
CLOVE, s. [a sort of spice] *garofano, gherofano, e grofano,* s. m. *aromato noto.*
A clove of garlick, *uno spicchio d'aglio.*
A clove [eight pound of cheese] *un peso di otto libbre di racio.*
Clove [gillyflower] *viola mammola.*
Clove, *pret. del verbo* to cleave.
CLO'VEN, adj. [from to cleave] *fesso, spaccato, spartito.*
A cloven foot, *un piè fesso.*
Cloven-footed, *che ha il piè fesso, piè forcuto.*
CLO'VER, s. [a species of trefoil] *spezie di trifoglio.*
To live in clover [to live luxriously] *vivere nell' abbondanza, menar una vita agiata e da epicureo.*
CLOUT, s. [a piece of cloth, a rag] *straccio, cencio,* s. m. *pezza,* s. f.
Clouts [for children] *pezzi di panno lino che si mettono sotto la camicia a' bambini.*
Iron clouts about cart-wheels, *cerchi di ferro che sono all' intorno d'una ruota.*
To CLOUT [to patch] *rappezzare, rattoppare.*
CLO'UTED, adj. *rappezzato, rattoppato.*
Clouted cream [clotted cream] *fior di latte appreso, mescolatovi zucchero e vin dolce.*
CLO'UTERLY, adj. [stupid] *grossolano, balordo, materiale, rozzo, soro, semplice.*

A clouterly fellow, *un balordo, uno sciocco, un pecorone, un uomo grossolano, di grossa pasta.*
Clouterly, adv. *grossolanamente, rozzamente, alla grossolana.*
CLOWN, s. [a country fellow] *un contadino, un villano.*
He is a very clown, *egli è un vero contadino, egli è un tanghero, un ciompo, un vero villanaccio.*
I got a clown for my husband, *ho un zotico di marito.*
A clown [an unmannerly fellow] *un zotico, un rustico, un mal creato.*
CLO'WNERY, s. *rusticità, rustichezzà, zoticaggine,* s. f.
CLO'WNISH, adj. *rustico, rusticale, zotico, villano, mal creato, incivile.*
A clownish fellow, *un rustico, un villano, un zotico.*
A clownish thing, *una cosa grossolana o fatta alla peggio.*
CLO'WNISHLY, adv. *rusticamente, grossolanamente, zoticamente, villanamente.*
CLO'WNISHNESS, *rustichezza, rusticità, zoticaggine, inciviltà, mala creanza.*
A piece of clownishness, *una mala creanza.*
CLOWN'S-MUSTARD, *spezie d'erba di sapor forte.*
To CLOY [to give one his full, to glutt] *satollare, saziare.*
CLOY'D, adj. *satollato, sazio, saziato.*
I am cloyed with meat, *sono stufo, svogliato, o ristucco di mangiar carne.*
Cloy'd [in gunnery, a piece of ordnance is said to be cloy'd, when any thing is got into the touch-hole] *turato, parlando d'un' arme da fuoco quando il focone è turato.*
Cloy'd [among farriers, a horse is said to be cloy'd when he is pricked with a nail in shoeing] *chiovato, parlando d'un cavallo quando nel ferrarlo si gli pugne al vivo l'ugna col chiodo.*
CLO'YLESS, adj. [that which cannot cause satiety] *che non puo cagionar sazietà.*
CLO'YMENT, s. [satiety, repletion] *sazietà, ripienezza.*
CLUB, s. [a great stick] *mazza, clava,* s. f. *baston pannocchiuto, bastonaccio, bastone grosso e pesante.*
Hercules's club, *la clava d'Ercole.*
Club [at cards] *fiori, bastoni, uno de' quattro semi delle carte da giocare.*
Club [society of friends] *assemblea, compagnia,* s. f. *crocchio,* s. m.
To keep a club, *essere d'una compagnia, d'una società, d'un crocchio.*
A club of wits, *una società d'uomini d'ingegno.*
Club [one's share of a reckoning] *scotto,* s. m. *quella rata che tòrca altrui nel pagar la cena, desinare, o simili.*
To pay one's club, *pagar la sua parte, il suo scotto.*
To be every man his club, *pagar ciascuno la sua parte.*
Club-law, *legge stabilita in una campagnia o società che ognuno paghi la parte sua.*
Club-law, s. [the law of arms] *legge marziale, legge della guerra.*
All things are carried by club-law, *la forza supera ogni cosa.*
Club-footed, *che ha i piedi storti*
Club-fisted, *che ha un gran pugno o le mani grosse.*
To CLUB [to pay one's share] *pagar la sua parte dello scotto, contribuire, andar di metà.*
Will you club with me? *volete andar di metà meco?*
CLU'BBISH, adj. *grossolano, zotico, rustico.*
CLUB-ROOM, s. [the room in which a club or company assembles] *stanza destinata all' assemblea d'una compagnia d'amici.*
To CLUCK [to cry as a hen in calling her chickens together] *chiocciare, crocciare; il mandar fuora della voce che fa la chioccia.*
I'll cluck him over to me, *lo farò ben venire.*
CLU'CKING, s. *il chiocciare.*
CLUMP, s. [a shapeless piece of wood] *pezzaccio di legno, senza forma determinata.*
CLUMPE'RTON, s. [clown] *un rustico, un zotico.*
CLU'MSILY, adv. *grossolanamente, alla grossolana.*
CLU'MSY, adj. [thick and short] *grossolano, tozzo, tozzetto, tangoccio.*
Clumsy, *pesante, greve, disaddatto.*
A clumsy woman, *una donna grossolana, una donnaccia tozza, una donna fatta colle gòmita.*
To have clumsy hands, *aver le mani tozze.*
A clumsy little fellow, *un tozzo d'uomo.*
Clumsy [clownish] *rustico, villano, zotico.*
CLUNG, *pret. e part. del verbo* to cling.
Clung with hunger, *magro, secco, come una persona affamata.*
To CLUNG [to dry as wood does when it is laid up after it is cut] *seccare, parlando del legno dopo che è tagliato.*
CLU'STER, s. [a bunch of grapes] *grappolo d'uva.*
Cluster [heap of several things] *mucchio, gruppo, groppo, viluppo.*
A cluster of bees, *uno sciame di pecchie.*
A cluster of islands, *un aggregato, un accozzamento d'isole.*
To come in a cluster, or by clusters, *venire in folla, in calca.*
To CLU'STER, v. n. [to grow in bunches] *crescere in grappoli.*
To cluster, v. n. [to collect any thing into bodies] *raccogliere insieme, metter insieme, unire insieme strettamente.*
CLU'STERED, adj. *raccolto strettamente insieme in quantità.*
Clustered, *cresciuto in grappoli.*
CLU'STERLY, adj. *ex.* a clusterly vine, *vigna carica di grappoli d'uva.*
To CLUTCH, *chiudere, impugnare, afferrare.*
To clutch the fist, *serrare il pugno o la mano.*

To clutch a thing [to hold it faſt] *afferrare, pigliare, tener per forza una coſa.*

CLUTCH, *artiglio, pl.* CLU'TCHES, *s. artigli, s. m. unghie adunche d'animali rapaci.*

To fall into the enemy's clutches, *caſcar nel poter nel nemico.*

Clutch fiſted [a hold faſt] *uno ſpilorcio, un avaro, un cacaſtecchi, un tanghero.*

CLU'TTER [great noiſe] *ſtrepito, fracaſſo, romore, ſchiamazzo, s. m.*

To make a clutter, *ſtrepitare, fare ſtrepito.*

To CLU'TTER [to make a noiſe or buſtle] *far un grande ſtrepito, ſtrepitare grandemente.*

CLU'TTERING, *s. fracaſſo, ſtrepito, tumulto, romore, s. m.*

To keep a cluttering, *ſtrepitare, romoreggiare, far romore o tumulto.*

CLY'STER, *s. cliſtere, ſerviziale, argomento.*

To COA'CERVATE [to heap together] *accumulare, ammaſſare, ammonticellare.*

COACERVA'TION, s. [the ſtate of being heaped up together] *accumulazione, s. f.*

COACH, s. [a large ſort of chariot] *carrozza, s. f.*

A coach and ſix, *una carrozza a ſei cavalli.*

A hackney coach, *una carrozza d'affitto.*

Coach-horſe, *cavallo da carozza.*

Coach-box, *ſedile dove ſta a ſedere il cocchiero.*

Coachman, *cocchiere, cocchiero, s. m. che guida la carrozza, carrozziere.*

Coach-maker, *carrozzajo, s. m. artefice che fabbrica le carrozze.*

Coach-hire, *affitto di carrozza.*

Coach-houſe, *rimeſſa di carrozza.*

To COACH [to take a coach] *pigliare a affittare una carrozza.*

CO'ACHED, adj. *che ha preſo carrozza.*

I ſaw her coached. *l'ho viſta montare e entrare in carrozza.*

To CO'ACT, [to act together in concert] *operare d'accordo inſieme.*

CO'ACTION, s. [compulſion, force] *forza l' operare di forze riunite.*

COADJU'TOR, s. [aſſiſtant] *coadjutore, aſſiſtente, s. m.*

A biſhop's coadjutor, *un coadjutore d'un veſcovo.*

To CO'AGULATE [to congeal, to curdle] *coagulare, prendere, rappigliare.* pret. *preſi, rappreſi.*

COA'GULATED, adj. *coagulato, preſo, rappreſo.*

COAGULA'TION, s. [curdling] *coagulazione, s. f. coágulo, aſſodamento, s. m.*

COAGULA'TOR, s. [that which cauſes coagulation] *quello che coágula o che cagiona coagulo.*

COAL, s. [an artificial fuel] *carbone, s. m.*

Pit-coal [ſea-coal] *carbone foſſile che ſi arde communemente in Inghilterra in vece di legna.*

Small coal, *carbone minuto.*

Coal-pit [coal mine] *miniera di carbone foſſil.*

Coal-merchant, *mercante di carbone.*

Coal-man, *carbonajo, s. m. che vende, o fa carboni.*

Coal-heaver, *facchino, che ſcarica i vaſcelli di carbone.*

Coal-houſe, or Coal hole, *carbonaja, luogo dove ſi tiene il carbone.*

Coal-baſket, *ceſto del carbone.*

Coal-raker, *forcone, s. m.*

Coal-duſt, *carbone ſpolverizzato.*

Coal-black, *nero come carbone.*

A coal-mouſe s. [a kind of bird] *ſpezie d'uccello piccolo.*

COALE'SENCE, or COALI'TION, [a reunion, or growing together of parts before ſeparated] *riunione, unione, s. f.*

COA'LY, adj. [containing coal] *che contiene carbone, abbondante di carbone, e s'intende del foſſile uſato in Inghilterra.*

COARSE, adj. [not refined] *groſſo, groſſolano; contrario di raffinato.*

Coarſe [not ſoft or fine] *ruvido; contrario di liſcio e di fine.*

Coarſe [rude, uncivil] *groſſolano, rozzo, incivile.*

Coarſe [groſs, not delicate] *groſſotano, non delicato, impuro.*

Coarſe [inelegant, unpoliſhed] *groſſolano, ſenza eleganza, pulitura.*

Coarſe [unaccompliſhed by education] *mal educato, zotico, ſgarbato.*

Coarſe [mean, not nice; vile] *baſſo, vile porco.*

CO'ARSELY, adv. *groſſolamente in tutti i ſignificati dell' addiettivo.*

CO'ARSENESS, s. *impurità, contrario di raffinatezza, ruvidezza, ſporcizia, mala educazione, zotichezza, viltà, baſſezza.*

COAST, s. [a country lying on the ſea, a ſea ſhore] *coſta, ſpiaggia, coſtiera, s. f.*

Coaſt of a country, *paeſe regione.*

From all coaſts, *da ogni parte.*

To COAST along [to ſail along the coaſt] *coſteggiare, andar per mare lungo le coſte.*

CO'ASTED ALONG, adj. *coſteggiato.*

COAT, s. [garment] *veſtito, veſtimento, ſajo, ſajone, s. m.*

To put on one's coat, *metterſi il veſtito.*

A wide coat, *caſacca, s. f.*

A child's coat [an upper coat] *una veſte da fanciullo.*

A coat or petticoat, *una gonnella.*

A waiſtcoat, *una camiciuola.*

A coat of mail, *giaco, s. m. arme di doſſo fatta di maglie di ferro.*

A coat of armour, *veſte militare, paludamento, s. m.*

A coat of arms, *armi, arme, impreſa o inſegna di famiglia.*

To turn coat [to ſhift parties] *voltar caſacca.*

A turn coat, *un volta caſacca, un rinnegato.*

To caſt his coat, *mudare.*

You muſt cut your coat according to your cloath, *biſogna tagliare il veſtito ſecondo il panno, biſogna addattarvi al biſogno; amico mio corteſe ſecondo l'entrate fate le ſpeſe.*

To diſgrace one's coat or gown, *diſonorare o far diſonore alla ſua dignità.*

The coat [hair or ſkin of a horſe] *il pelo o mantello d'un cavallo.*

A hawk of the firſt coat, *un falcone di due anni.*

Coat [cottage] *capanna, s. f.*

A ſheep's coat, *mandra, s. f. ovile, s. m.*

To COAT a child, *veſtire un fanciullo.*

CO'ATED, adj. *che porta una veſte.*

A ſoft coated fiſh, *peſce ſenza ſquame.*

A rough-coated fiſh, *peſce ſquamoſo.*

To COAX [to wheedle, to flatter] *luſingare, adulare, accarezzare, far moine, piaggiare, vezzeggiare.*

CO'AXER, s. *luſinghiero, adulatore.*

COB, s. [a ſea-cob] *ſorta d'uccello di mare.*

A rich cob [a miſer] *un ricco ſpilorcio, un ricco avaro.*

Cob nut [a boyiſh play with nuts] *giuoco fanciulleſco con noci.*

CO'BIRON, s. [an iron whereon the ſpit turns] *alare ſopra'l quale gira lo ſpiedo.*

To CO'BBLE [to botch] *rappezzare, rattoppare.*

To cobble ſhoes, *rappezzare, rattacconare ſcarpe.*

CO'BBLER, s. [one that mends old ſhoes] *ciabattino.*

Cobbler [a bungling woman] *imbrogliatore, avviluppatore.*

The cobbler is not to go beyond his laſt, *biſogna che ciaſcuno guidichi ſecondo la ſua capacità.*

COBWEB, s. *la tela che fa il ragno; e figuratamente, inſidia, trappola.*

COCHINE'AL, s. [*ſorta d'inſetto*] *coccinigla, s. f.*

COCK, s. [a well known fowl] *gallo, s. m.*

The cock crows, *il gallo canta.*

A Turkey-cock, *gallinaccio, s. m.*

The cock of a ſun-dial [the pin of a ſun-dial] *lancetta l'oriuolo.*

The cock of a gun, *il cane d'uno ſchioppo.*

The cock [the needle of a balance] *ago della bilancia.*

The cock of a water pipe, *cannella, doccia, s. f. doccio, doccione, cannoncello di condotti.*

A cock of hay, *un mucchio di fieno.*

To tell the ſtory of a cock and a bull, *dire la canzone o la favola dell' uccellino, novellare a' fanciulli.*

To be cock-a-hoop, or cock-on-hoop, *fare il ſaccente, darſi dell' arie.*

Peacock, *pavone, paone.*

Woodcock, *beccaccia.*

Weather cock, *banderuola, s. f.*

Cockpit, *arena dove ſi fanno combattere i galli.*

Cock-fight, s. [a match of cocks] *battaglia de' galli. Barbaro paſſatempo del popolaccio d'Inghilterra, coſi chiamato dal batterſi inſieme de' galli in un teatro appoſta.*

Cock-

Cock-crowing, *canto di gallo.*
Cock-loft [the room over a garret] *la stanza che è sopra il soffitto, la parte più alta della casa.*
Cock-brained [giddy brained] *scervellato, mentecatto, senza cervello.*
Cock's tread, or cock's treaddle [the sperm of an egg] *seme di gallo.*
Cock-stride, *passo di gallo.*
Cock boat, *sorta di barchetta.*
Cock-swain [cockson] *quello che guida quelle barchetta distinta col nome di cock-boat.*
Cock-shoot or cock-shoot time, *crepuscolo, l'imbrunirsi della sera.*
Cock-sure, *sicuro, certo, che è sicuro di qualche cosa.*
Cock-pigeon, *colombo.*
Cock-sparrow, *passere maschio.*
Cock-broth, s. [broth made by boiling a cock] *brodo di gallo.*
Cockerel, *v.* Cockrel.
To Cock, *montare.*
To cock a gun, *montare il fucile.*
To cock, or to cock up one's hat, *alzar delle tre punte del cappello: quella dinanzi più dell' altre due.*
To cock the match, *mettere la miccia all' archibuso.*
To cock up hay, *ammucchiare il fieno.*
Co'ckal, s. [a sort of play] *giuoco fatto con ossicelli.*
To play at cockal, *giuocare agli ossicelli.*
Cocka'de, s. [a ribband worn in the hat] *nastro a mo' di rosa che si porta sul cappello.*
Co'ckatrice, s. [a sort of serpent, otherwise called a basilisk] *basilischio,* s. m.
To Co'cker [to cade, to fondle] *accarezzare, far carezze, vezzeggiare.*
You cocker your child too much, *voi accarezzate troppo il vostro figliuolo.*
Co'ckered, adj. *accarezzato, vezzeggiato.*
Co'ckering, s. *l'accarezzare, carezza,* s. f. *vezzo,* s. m.
Co'cket, s. [a custom-house seal] *sigillo della dogana.*
Cocket [brisk, malapert] *spavaldo, sfrontato, sfacciato.*
Cocket [an acquittance of the custom-house] *licenza della dogana.*
Cocket-bread, *pane casalingo.*
Co'ckle, s. [a sort of shell fish] *chiocciola,* s. f.
Cockle-shell, *conchiglia, conca,* s. f. *nicchio,* s. m.
Cockle-weed [darnel] *loglio,* s. m. *erba che nasce tra le biade.*
Cockle-stairs, *scala a chiocciola.*
To Co'ckle [to wrinkle as woollen cloth does] *increspar si, raggrinzarsi.*
To cockle [speaking of the sea] *spumare, parlando del mare quando agitato dalla tempesta genera spuma.*
A cockling-sea, *mare spumante.*
Co'ckney, s. [a nickname given to one who is born and bred in the city of London] *sopranome, che si da ad uno nato ed allevato nella città di Londra, e vuol dire un goffo, un gonzo.*

A cockney [a child cockered and tenderly brought up] *un cucco, il figliuolo più amato dal padre e dalla madre, un figliuola allevato nella bambagia, cioè in delizie e morbidezze.*
Cockney [an effeminate low citizen] *un cittadino vile ed effeminato.*
Co'ckrel, or Co'ckerel, s. [a young cock] *galletto,* s. m. *gallo giovine.*
Coco'a, s. [a species of palm tree] *spezie di palma; albero del cacao.*
Co'ction, s. [the act of boiling] *il bollire, bollitura.*
Cod, s. [husk] *baccello, guscio,* s. m.
Pease-cod, *baccello di pisello.*
Cod [a sea-fish] *merluzzo.*
The cod of a silk worm, *bòzzolo,* s. m. *quel gomitolo ovato dove si rinchiude il baco facendo la seta.*
Cod [pillow] *origliere, guanciale,* s. m.
Cod [pin cushion] *torsello,* s. m.
Cod-piece, *brachetta,* s. f.
Co'dded, adj. [as pease] *gusciato, che ha guscio, parlando d'alcuni legumi.*
Code, s. [a volume of the civil law] *códice,* s. m.
Co'dicil, s. [a supplement to a will or other writing] *codicillo,* s. m.
Codi'lle, s. [a term at ombre] *codiglio, termine del giuoco d'ombre o di quadriglio.*
To Co'dle, *bollire, cuocire*
To codle apples, *bollire o lessare delle mele.*
Co'dling, s. [an apple proper to be coddled or boiled, or ready boiled] *mela buona a bollire, o mela lessa.*
Coe'qual, adj. [equal to one another] *coeguale, insieme eguale.*
Coe'rcion, s. [restraint] *raffrenamento, freno,* s. m.
Coe'rcive, adj. [restraining] *che raffrena, che tiene in freno.*
Coesse'ntial, adj. [of the same essence] *della medesima essenza o sostanza.*
Coeta'neous, adj. [of the same age, living together at the same time] *coetaneo, d'una medesima età.*
Coete'rnal, adj. [that is eternal with another] *coeterno, insieme eterno.*
Coe'val, adj. [of the same age] *della stessa età.*
Coexi'stent, adj. [having an existence, or being together existent at the same time] *che esiste nel medesimo tempo.*
Coffe'e, or Coffee-berry, s. *caffè,* s. m.
Coffee [a sort of drink made with coffee-berries] *caffè, sorta di bevanda calda fatta colle bacche dell caffè.*
Coffee-house, *casa dove si vende dell caffè.*
Coffeeman, s. *colui che tiene bottega da caffè.*
Coffee-pot, *vaso dove si bolle il caffè.*
Co'ffer, s. [chest, trunk] *cassa,* s. f. *cófano, forziére,* s. m.
A little coffer, *un forzieretto.*
The king's coffer, *l'erario del re.*
Co'fferer, s. [cofferer of the king's houshold] *tesoriere dell' erario del re.*

Co'ffin, s. [case for a dead body] *cataletto,* s. m. *bara,* s. f. *cassa da morto.*
Coffin [the hollow part of a horse's foot] *quel vuoto che si trova sotto'l piede del cavallo.*
Coffin-maker, *facitor di cataletti.*
To Co'ffin [to enclose in a coffin] *porre il morto nella cassa, nel cataletto.*
Cog, s. [a cog of a wheel] *dente di ruota.*
The cog-wheel, *ruota dentata.*
To Cog [to sooth, to flatter] *adulare, lusingare, lisciare, piaggiare.*
To cog [to cheat at dice] *truffare, barare al giuoco de' dadi, impiombar dadi.*
Co'gency, s. [force, strength] *forza; e si dice generalmente del ragionare, d'un argomento e simili.*
Co'gent, adj. [pressing, enforcing] *potente, urgente.*
A cogent motive, *potente motivo.*
Cogent reason, *ragione urgente.*
Co'gged, adj. [from the verb to cog] *adulato, lusingato, lisciato, piaggiato, truffato, barato.*
Co'gger, s. *adulatore, lusingatore,* s. m. *adulatrice, lusingatrice,* s. f.
Co'gging, s. *lusinga, adulazione,* s. f.
Cogging, adj. *ex.* a cogging gamester, *un furfante, un truffatore, un baro, un che impiomba i dadi per truffare il compagno al giuoco.*
Co'gitabund, adj. [full of thoughts, thoughtful] *pensoso, pien d. pensieri, pensieroso, cogitabondo.*
To Co'gitate [to think] *cogitare, pensare.*
Cogita'tion, s. [the reflection of the mind] *cogitazione,* s. f. *pensiero,* s. m.
Cogna'tion, s. [kindred, alliance] *cognazione,* s. f. *congiunzion di parentado.*
Cognation [affinity] *affinità, somiglianza,* s. f.
Co'gnisance, or Co'gnizance, s. [knowledge] *conoscenza, notizia, contezza,* s. f. *conoscimento,* s. m.
To take cognizance of a thing, *badare, considerare, fare attenzione a qualche cosa.*
Cogno'scitive, adj. [a word used by philosophers] *conoscitivo.*
The cognoscitive faculty, *la facoltà conoscitiva.*
Cog-wa're, s. [coarse cloths made anciently in the north of England] *panni grossi che si fabbricavano un tempo nelle parti settentrionali d' Inghilterra.*
To Coha'bit [to dwell together] *abitare o dimorare insieme, coabitare.*
To cohabit with a woman, *coabitare con una donna.*
Cohabita'tion, s. *l' abitare insieme.*
Cohe'ir, s. [a joint heir with another] *coerede,* s. m. *compagno nell' eredità.*
Cohe'iress, s. *coerede,* s. f. *compagna nell' eredità.*
To Cohe're [to stick or fit together

P 2 well,

well, to agree] *convenire, dirſi, affarſi, eſſer conforme.*

COHE'RENCE, or COHE'RENCY, s. [agreement] *coerenza, congiunzione, conneſſione*, s. f.

There's no coherence in that diſcourſe, *non v'è alcuna conneſſione in quel diſcorſo.*

There's no coherence betwixt thoſe parts, *non v'è conneſſione fra queſte parti.*

COHE'RENT, adj. [that hangs together] *coerente, che ha coerenza o congiunzione.*

A very coherent diſcourſe, *un diſcorſo ben ordinato, di cui le parti coriſpondono bene inſieme.*

CO'HORT, s. [among the Romans, was ordinarily a band of a hundred men] *coorte*, s. f. *banda di cento ſoldati in che erano compartite le legioni Romane.*

COIF, s. [a ſort of cap for women's heads] *cuffia, creſta*, s. f.

CO'IFED, adj. *che ha cuffia.*

COIL, s. [clutter, noiſe, tumult] *rumore, fracaſſo, ſtrepito, garbuglio, battibuglio*, s. m.

To keep a coil, *fare ſtrepito, mettere in garbuglio, ſtrepitare.*

To coil a cable [ſea-term. To wind it about in the form of a ring] *raggomitolare una gomena, raccogliere una gomena.*

COIN, s. [money] *moneta*, s. f. *danaro*, s. m.

Counterfeit coin, *moneta falſa.*

To COIN [to make money] *batter moneta, monetare, coniare.*

To coin [to invent] *fare, inventare.*

To coin new words, *fare e inventare nuove parole.*

CO'INAGE, s. [coining] *il batter moneta, monetaggio*, s. m. *ſpeſa per far la moneta.*

CO'INED, adj. *monetato, coniato, fatto, inventato.*

To COINCI'DE [to fall upon the ſame point] *coincidere, cadere ſullo ſteſſo punto.*

To coincide [to concur] *coincidere, concorrere.*

CO'INCIDENCE, s. [meeting] *rincontro*, s. m.

The coincidence of two lines, *il rincontro di due linee.*

CO'INCIDENT, adj. [happening together] *che accade o ſuccede nel medeſimo tempo.*

COINE [printer's pin to faſten letters in their frames] *bietta di ſtampatore.*

CO'INER, s. *monetario, coniatore*, s. m.

A falſe coiner, *un monetario falſo.*

CO'INING, s. *il coniare monete.*

Coining of new words, *introduzione di nuove parole.*

CO'ISTRIL, s. [a coward hawk] *un falcone codardo.*

COIT, s. [quoite] *morella*, s. f. *laſtruccia colla quale ſi giuoca tirandola al lecco.*

To play at coits, *giuocare alle morelle.*

CO'LANDER, s. [a ſieve through which a mixture is poured, and which retains the thicker parts] *ſtamigna*, s. f. *colatojo*, s. m.

COLA'TION, s. [the art of filtering or ſtraining] *l'arte del filtrare o colare.*

CO'LBERTINE, s. [a kind of lace worn by women] *ſorta di naſtro uſato dalle donne.*

COLD, s. [cold weather] *freddo*, s. m.

Cold [rheum] *catarro*, s. m. *infreddatura.*

I have got a great cold, *ho un gran catarro, ſono molto infreddato.*

To catch cold, *infreddarſi.*

To catch cold upon heat, *aver il cimurro.*

Cold, adj. [contrary of hot] *freddo, di qualità e di natura freddo.*

Cold weather, *tempo freddo.*

A cold wind, *un vento freddo.*

To be of a cold conſtitution, *eſſer d'un temperamento freddo.*

To be cold, *aver freddo.*

To kill one in cold blood, *ammazzare uno a ſangue freddo.*

Cold [reſerved, indifferent] *freddo, pigro, lento, agiato.*

To grow cold, *raffreddarſi.*

A cold comfort, *un triſto conforto.*

To give a cold entertainment, *trattar uno freddamente.*

CO'LDISH, adj. [ſomething cold] *freddiccio, alquanto freddo.*

CO'LDLY, adv. *freddamente, con freddezza, pigramente, lentamente.*

To receive one coldly, *ricever un freddamente.*

He ſpoke it very coldly, *lo diſſe d'una maniera fredda.*

CO'LDNESS, s. *fredezza.*

The coldneſs of water, *la freddezza dell' acqua.*

Coldneſs [reſervedneſs] *freddezza, pigrezza, lentezza*, s. f.

COLE, s. [colewort] *càvolo*, s. m.

CO'LET, s. [that part of a ring where the ſtone is ſet] *quella parte dell' anello dov' è legata la gemma.*

CO'LEWORT, s. *càvolo.*

CO'LICK, or CHO'LICK, s. [a violent griping in the guts] *còlica*, s. f.

The ſtone colick, *il mal di pietra.*

One troubled with the colick, *còlico*, s. m. *colui che ha la colica.*

CO'LLAR, s. *collare, collaretto*, s. m.

The collar of a doublet, *collaretto di giubbone.*

To take one by the collar, *pigliar uno pel collare.*

Dog's collar, *collàre di cane.*

Horſe-collar, *collare di cavallo.*

Collar of eſſes [a collar of ss] *collana de' cavalieri della giartiera.*

Collar-days, *i giorni che i cavalieri della giartiera portano la collana.*

A collar of brawn, *un pezzo di carne ſalata di forma rotonda.*

The collar of a band, *collaretto.*

An iron collar for offenders, *collare di ferro che ſi mette al collo a' malfattori.*

To ſlip one's neck out of the collar [to get out of a bad buſineſs] *uſcirſene pel rotto della cuffia, liberarſi da pericolo ſenza noja, ſpeſa, o danno.*

To COLLA'TE [to beſtow] *conferire, dare.*

To collate a living, *conferire un beneficio.*

To collate [to compare] *comparare, paragonare.*

To collate a book [to ſee by the ſignature of the ſheets whether it be right or no] *collazionare un libro.*

COLLA'TED, adj. *conferito, dato, comparato, paragonato.*

COLLA'TERAL, adj. [not direct] *collaterale.*

The cardinal and collateral winds, *i venti cardinali e collaterali.*

A collateral degree of kindred [as uncles, &c.] *linea collaterale o traverſale.*

COLLA'TION, s. [the act of beſtowing an eccleſiaſtical benefice] *collazione, o conferimente di beneficio.*

Collation [entertainment] *colezione, merenda*, s. f.

Collation [the act of comparing] *collazione, comparazione*, s. f.

To COLLA'UD [to commend] *commendare, lodare.*

COLLE'AGUE, s. [a fellow or companion in an office] *collega*, s. m. *compagno nel magiſtrato o ufficio.*

COLL'ECT, s. [a ſhort prayer appropriated to any particular day or occaſion] *collata, collizione*, s. f.

The collect for the king, *la colletta o preghiera per il rè.*

To COLLE'CT [to gather] *fare una colletta, raccògliere.*

COLLECTA'NEOUS, adj. [gathered up together] *raccolto inſieme.*

COLLE'CTED, adj. *raccolto.*

COLLE'CTION, s. [the act of gathering, the things gathered] *collezione*, s. f. *quell' impoſizione che ſi riſcuote da' collettori.*

A collection of books, *una raccolta di libri.*

COLLECTI'TIOUS, adj. [gathered up] *collettizio, ragunaticcio.*

COLLE'CTIVE, adj. *collettivo.*

A collective noun, *un nome collettivo.*

COLLE'CTIVELY, adv. [in a collective ſenſe] *collettivamente, in modo collettivo.*

COLLE'CTOR, s. *collettore*, s. m. *che raccoglie, che riſcuote.*

CO'LLEGE, s. [a company or ſociety of perſons of the ſame profeſſion] *collegio*, s. m. *congregazione, adunanza d'uomini autorità e di governo.*

A college in a univerſity, *collegio in una univerſità.*

The college of the cardinals, *il collegio de' cardinali.*

COLLE'GIATE, adj. [a ſtudent of a college] *ſtudente d'un collegio, collegiale.*

Collegiate, adj. [belonging to a college] *collegiato.*

A collegiate church, *chieſa collegiata.*

CO'LLET, v. Colet.

CO'LLIERY, s. [a coal-mine] *una miniera di carbone foſſile.*

To COLLI'DE [to beat, knock, or bruiſe together] *dibattere, percuoter inſieme, ſtiacciare, ſchiacciare.*

CO'LLIER,

Co'llier, s. [one who deals in coals] *mercante di carbone di terra, o foſſile.*
Collier, s. *un che cava il carbon foſſile della miniera.*
Collier, s. [a ſhip to carry coals] *baſtimento che carica carbone foſſile.*
Co'lliflower, s. [cauliflower] *cavolfiore.*
To Co'llimate [to level at, or aim at the mark] *avviſare, mirare, tor di mira.*
Collima'tion, s. [the act of aiming at] *l'avviſare, il mirare, il tor di mira.*
Colli'sion, s. [the act of rubbing or ſtriking of one body againſt another] *dibattimento, ſcontro,* s. m.
Colloca'tion, s. [the act of placing or ſetting in order] *collocazione,* s. f. *acconciamento,* s. m.
Co'llock, s. [a pail with one handle] *ſecchia,* s. f.
To Collo'gue [to flatter, to coax, to ſooth] *luſingare, adulare, vezzeggiare, accarezzare, piaggiare.*
Collo'gued, adj. *luſingato, adulato, vezzeggiato, accarezzato, piaggiato.*
Co'llop, s. [a cut or ſlice of meat] *fetta di carne.*
Scotch collops, *fette di vitella acconciate alla Scozzeſe.*
A collop, *un bambino.*
Co'lloquy, s. [talk together, conference] *colloquio, parlamento inſieme,* s. m. *collocuzione,* s. f.
Collucta'tion, s. [ſtruggling together] *diſputa, zuffa,* s. f. *combattimento,* s. m.
To Collu'de [to plead by covin, with intent to deceive] *uſar colluſione, intenderſi inſieme con intento d'ingannare.*
Collu'sion, s. [fraudulent contrivance between two or more parties to bring an action one againſt another for ſome deceitful end] *colluſione,* s. f. *inganno,* s. m. *termine de' leggiſti.*
Co'lly, s. [the black that ſticks to the pots] *fumo che s'attacca alle pignatte o ſimili vaſi.*
To Co'lly [to grime with coal] *tignere o ſporcare col fumo di carbon foſſile.*
To colly [a hawk is ſaid to colly, when ſhe ſtretches out her neck ſtraight forward] *allungare il collo, parlando d'un falcone.*
Co'llyd, adj. *nero, affumicato.*
Colly'rium, s. [any liquid medicine deſigned to cure diſeaſes of the eyes] *collirio,* s. m. *medicamento per gli occhi.*
Co'lon, s. [one of the great guts] *colon,* s. m. *uno degli inteſtini.*
Colon [in grammar, a point which ſhows that the ſentence is imperfect or not entire, but the ſenſe ſtill depending] *due punti.*
Colonna'de, s. [carriage of pillars running round a building] *colonnato,* s. m. *quantità e ordine di colonne diſpoſte ordinatamente.*
Co'lonel, s. [the chief commander of a regiment of horſe or foot] *colonnello,* s. m. *comandante d'un reggimento di cavalleria o fanteria.*
Co'lony, s. [a plantation, a company of people tranſplanted from one place to another] *colónia,* s. f. *popolo mandato ad abitare un paeſe colle ſteſſe leggi della città che lo manda.*
Coloqui'ntida, s. [an herb] *coloquintida,* s. f. *ſpezie d'erba.*
Colo'phony, s. [any pitch or roſin made by extraction of the thinner parts of terebinthinous juices] *colofónia,* s. f.
Colora'tion, s. [colouring] *colorazione,* s. f. *l'atto del colorire.*
Coloration [in chymiſtry, the brightening of gold or ſilver] *il pulimento dell' oro o dell' argento.*
Colo'sse, or Colo'ssus, s. [a large ſtatue] *coloſſo, gigante,* s. m. *ſtatua, che eccede di grandezza.*
Colosse'an, adj. [giant-like] *coloſſeo, giganteſco.*
Co'lour, s. [the ſenſation we perceive when we look upon any coloured body] *colore,* s. m. *quel che è nella ſuperficie dei corpi che gli ci rende viſibili.*
Fine colour, *bel colore.*
Dark colour, *color bruno.*
Colour [complexion] *colore, carnagione.*
She has a fine colour, *ella ha un bel colore, una bella carnagione.*
Colour [at cards] *il ſeme delle carte.*
Colour [pretence] *colore, preteſto,* s. m. *apparenza, finzione, ſimulazione,* s. f.
Rhetorical colours [flouriſhes, ornaments] *colori, ornamenti rettorici.*
Colours [the banner of a company of ſoldiers] *inſegna, bandiera,* s. f.
He is run away from his colours, *egli ha diſertato.*
The colour of a picture, *il colorito d'una pittura.*
To ſet one out in his colours, *rappreſentare uno al vivo o tale quale è.*
When I went to ſpeak to her, her colour roſe preſently, *quando andai per parlarle s'arroſsì tutta nel viſo.*
To change colour, *cangiarſi nel viſo.*
To Co'lour [to give a colour] *colorare, colorire, dar colore, tigner con colore.*
To colour a map, *illuminare una carta.*
To colour the hair, *tignere i capelli.*
To colour [to palliate, to cloke, to excuſe] *colorare, ricoprire, ſimulare, palliare.*
To colour cruelty with the name of juſtice, *coprire la crudeltà col velo della giuſtizia.*
To colour [to bluſh] *arroſſire,* preſ. *arroſſiſco.*
Co'lourable, adj. *ex.* a colourable pretence, *un preteſto ſpezioſo o plauſibile.*
Co'loured, adj. *colorato, colorito.*
Party-coloured, *biſcolore miſchio.*
Coloured [palliated] *colorato, ricoperto, ſimulato, palliato.*
Co'louring, s. *coloramento,* s. m. *il colorare.*
Colt, s. [a young horſe, mare, or aſs] *puledro,* s. m. *ſi dice al cavallo, all' aſino, e al mulo, dalla naſcita al domarſi.*
The colt of an aſs, *un aſinello.*
A ragged colt may make a good horſe, *un cattivo puledro può divenire un buon cavallo, cioè, un fanciullo cattivo può divenire un uomo dabbene.*
Colt's-foot, s. [an herb] *unghia cavallina,* s. f. *ſpezie d'erba.*
Colt's-teeth, *denti di latte, i primi denti che ſpuntano agli animali.*
Colt-ſtaff, s. *curro,* s. m. *legno ritondo, non molto lungo, il quale ſi mette ſotto pietre o ſimili coſe gravi per farle andare e muovere facilmente.*
Co'lumbary, s. [pigeon-houſe] *colombaja,* s. f. *colombajo,* s. m. *ſtanza dove ſtanno i colombi e dove covano.*
Columbi'ne, s. [an herb] *colombina,* s. f. *ſpezie d'erba.*
Columbine, adj. [dove-like] *colombino, di colombo, ſimile al colombo.*
Co'lumn, s. [pillar] *colonna,* s. f.
Column of a book, *colonna di libro.*
Column [in the military art, the long file or row of troops or of baggage of an army] *colonna, fila d'un eſercito.*
Colu'res, s. [two circles which interſect one another at right angles in the poles of the world] *coluri,* s. m. *due cerchi maſſimi della sfera celeſte che diſtinguono i ſolſtizi e li equinozi.*
Coma'te, s. [companion] *ſozio, compagno.*
Comb, s. [an inſtrument to untangle, and trim the hair] *pettine,* s. m.
A box-comb, an ivory-comb, *un pettine di boſſo, un pettine d'avorio.*
The teeth of a comb, *i denti d'un pettine.*
Comb-caſe, *pettiniera,* s. f.
Comb-bruſh, *ſcopetta da nettare il pettine.*
Comb maker, *pettinagnolo,* s. m. *quegli che fa i pettini.*
Comb, *creſta.*
A cock's comb, *creſta di gallo.*
A coxcomb [a fool, a ninny] *uno ſciocco, un balordo, un minchione, un gonzo, un pedante, un milordino, un zerbinotto magro, un bellimbuſto.*
A horſe-comb [a curry comb] *una ſtregghia; ſtrumento di ferro dentato col quale ſi ſtregghiano i cavalli.*
A flax-comb, *un cardo da cardare il lino, uno ſcardaſſo.*
Honey comb, *favo,* s. m. *quella parte di cera dove ſono le celle delle pecchie.*
A comb [a dale betwixt two hills] *una valle, un vallone.*
A comb [a meaſure of dry things holding four buſhels] *una miſura di coſe ſecche che contiene quattro ſtaja.*
To Comb [to untangle the hair] *pettinare.*
To comb a child's head, *pettinare un fanciullo.*
To comb one's head, *pettinarſi.*
To comb a horſe, *ſtregghiare un cavallo.*
To comb wool or flax [to card] *ſcardaſſare della lana, cardarla, pettinarla.*
To comb flax or hemp, *cardare del lino o della canapa.*
Co'mbat, s. [battle, fight] *combattimento,* s. m. *pugna, zuffa, battaglia,* s. f.

A ſingle

A single combat, *un combattimento di solo a solo, un duello.*

To COMBAT [to fight] *combattere, far battaglia insieme.*

To combat an opinion, *oppugnare un' opinione.*

CO'MBATANT, s. [a fighting man] *combattente, guerriero, soldato,* s. m.

Combatant, adj. [in heraldry, two lions are said to be combatant, when they are borne in a coat of arms rampant with their faces towards each other in a fighting posture] *opposto.*

COMBED, adj. *pettinato, cardato.*

CO'MBINATE, adj. [betrothed, promised] *promesso un matrimonio.*

COMBINA'TION, s. [conspiracy] *trama, cospirazione, congiura,* s. f.

Combination [conjunction] *combaciamento, congiugnimento,* s. m.

To COMBI'NE [to join together] *combaciare, combagiare, congiugner bene insieme legno con legno, pietra con pietra, ferro con ferro.*

To combine [to plot together] *tramare, cospirare, insidiare, congiurare.*

CO'MBING, adj. *ex.* a combing cloth [a nightrail] *mantellina,* s. f. *rochetto,* s. m.

CO'MBLESS, adj. [wanting a comb or crest] *screstato, senza cresta, senza cimiero.*

COMBU'RGESS, s. [fellow citizen] *concittadino.*

COMBU'STIBLE, adj. [apt to burn] *combustibile, che facilmente s'abbrucia.*

COMBU'STION, s. [burning] *combustione,* s. f. *incendio, abbruciamento,* s. m.

Combustion [hurly-burly] *confusione,* s. f. *tumulto, disordine, parapiglia,* s. m.

The whole kingdom was in combustion, *tutto 'l regno era sozzopra.*

To COME [to draw nigh, to approach] *venire,* pref. *vengo,* pret. *venni.*

Come hither, *venite qui.*

To come to a place, *arrivare in un luogo.*

To come from a place, *venire da qual che luogo.*

To come to one, *andare o venire da uno.*

Come to me to-morrow, *venite da me dimani.*

I shall come to you, *verrò da voi.*

To come to the crown, *pervenire alla corona.*

To come [to accost, to draw near] *accostarsi, avvicinarsi, presentarsi.*

He came to the king in an insolent manner, *presentossi al re con una maniera insolente.*

To come [to amount] *montare, venire costare.*

The reckoning comes to ten crowns, *il conto monta a dieci scudi.*

The cloth only comes to five pounds, *il panno solamente costa dieci doppie.*

It comes all to the same thing, *è tutt' uno.*

All his discourse comes to this, *questa è la somma o la sostanza del suo discorso.*

To come to end [to have an issue] *finire, terminare.*

We shall see what these things will come to, *vedremo come finiranno queste cose, vedremo dove queste cose andranno a parare.*

See what I am come to! *vedi a che son ridotto!*

To come [as a woman with child] *stare in parto o per partorire.*

To come to a shameful death, *fare una fine ignominiosa.*

To come to an estate, *pervenire ad una eredità.*

When all comes to all, *alla per fine, in somma.*

To come to misery, *esser ridotto a miseria.*

You will come to some mischief or other, *vi accaderà qualche disgrazia.*

To come to good [to succeed] *riuscire, prosperare.*

I desire no more than what comes to my share, *non domando che quel che mi tocca.*

To come to life, *prender vita.*

To come to life again, *riuscitare, rinvenire, ricuperare il sentimento, ritornare in se.*

When it comes to your turn, *quando toccherà a voi.*

What does all his cunning come to? *a che servono tutte le sue astuzie?*

I am more obliged to you than that comes to, *le obbligazioni che vi professo sono vie piu grandi.*

To come to an agreement, *accordarsi, convenire, fare un accordo, venire a patti.*

When I come to die, *quando verrò a morire, quando morrò.*

I would not have him come to any harm, *non vorrei che gli succedesse alcun male.*

To come to one's self again, *rinvenire, ricuperare il sentimento.*

He came to my terms, *abbracciò le condizioni che gli proposi.*

To come to a conclusion, *conchiudere, restar d'accordo, risolvere.*

To come to reasonable terms, *mettersi alla ragione.*

Come the worst that can come, *al peggio de' peggio, il peggio che ne possa succedere.*

They were near coming to hand blows, *poco mancò che non venissero alle mani.*

To come to preferment, *avvanzarsi, far fortuna.*

How should I come to know it? *in che modo potrei io saperlo?*

How came you to do that? *perchè avete fatta cotesta cosa?*

If I can but come to speak with him, *s'io gli posso solamente parlare.*

To come to pass, *arrivare, succedere, avvenire.*

No body thought this would come to pass, *nessuno avrebbe mai creduto che ciò dovesse avvenire.*

To come to and fro, *andare e venire, andar quà e là.*

To come into trouble, *mettersi in imbroglio.*

To come into danger, *esporsi a pericolo.*

Your letter never came into my hands, *la vostra lettera non m' è capitata.*

To come into business, *cominciare a far faccende.*

To come at [to overtake] *arrivare, giugnere.*

To come at [to obtain a thing] *ottenere, pervenire, guadagnare,* pref. *ottengo, pervengo,* pret. *ottenni, pervenni.*

To come in, *entrare.*

The letters which are come in to-day, *le lettere che sono venute oggi.*

'Twill be a good while before dinner comes in, *sarà un pezzo prima che il pranzo sia in ordine.*

If any obstacle comes in the way, *se qualche ostacolo vi s'interponesse, se arrivasse qualche impedimento.*

To come in [to yield and submit] *cedere, rendersi, sottomettersi.*

To come in as an heir, *pretendere l' eredità.*

To come out, *uscire.*

He came out just now, *è uscito in questo punto.*

His teeth begin to come out, *i denti cominciano a spuntargli.*

When shall your book come out? *il vostro libro quando sarà dato alla luce? quando sarà il vostro libro pubblicato?*

To come out [to appear] *apparire, farsi vedere.*

To come out [as blossoms do] *spuntare.*

To come out [as a star does] *spuntare, cominciare a nascere, apparire,* pref. *apparisco.*

To come up, *salire, montare,* pref. *salgo.*

I desire him to come up, *ditegli di salire.*

The corn begins to come up, *il grano comincia a spuntare.*

To come up to one, *accostarsi o avvicinarsi ad uno.*

To come up to a ship, *abbordare, investire un vascello.*

I eat nothing but what comes up, *vòmito tutto quel che mangio.*

The beauties of the body cannot come up to those of the mind, *le bellezze del corpo sono di gran lunga inferiori a quelle dell' animo, le bellezze del corpo non possono agguagliarsi a quelle dell' animo.*

To come down, *scendere, descendere, venire giù, calar giù.*

To come asunder, *disfarsi, andare in pezzi, scollarsi, separarsi, dividersi, in due.*

To come back, } *tornare, ritornare, esser di ritorno.*
To come again, }
To come back again, }

To come about, *girare, fare il giro.*

What do you come about? *che cercate? che volete? che domandate?*

To come together, *unirsi, radunarsi, accozzarsi.*

To come together [to marry] *maritarsi, ammogliarsi.*

To come along, *comminare, andare, venire.*

Will you come along with me? *volete venir meco?*

Come along, *comminate presto, sbrigàtevi, venite via.*

To

To come after, *seguitare.*

To come after one in a place, *succedere, o entrare nell' altrui luogo.*

To come next, *succedere, seguire.*

To come away, *venir via, partire.*

To come on } *avanzare.*
To come forward }

To come forward in one's learning, *profittare nello studio.*

Come on [come away] *sù, via, animo.*

To come of [to descend] *descendere, trarre origine, esser nato.*

He is come of good friends, *egli è nato di buoni parenti, egli discende da una buona famiglia.*

To come off, *cascare.*

All my hair comes off, *tutti i capelli mi cascano.*

To come off with credit, *sbrigarsi d'un negozio con onore.*

Do you think to come off so? *credete di scapparla a sì buon mercato?*

This will make your skin come off, *questo vi scorticherà la pelle.*

You will come off a loser, *voi ci perderete, voi sarete perditore, voi n'avrete la peggio.*

To come off conqueror, *essere vittorioso, aver la vittoria, rimaner vincente.*

To come off with the worst, *aver la peggio.*

What will come of thee? *che sarà di te?*

To come by, *passare.*

How did you come by it? *in che modo l'avete avuto? in che modo l'avete acquistato?*

To come upon, *sorprendere.*

He came upon me when I least thought of him, *mi sorprese quando meno ci pensava.*

To come upon one with force, *avventarsi, spignersi, gittarsi con impeto sopra checchè si sia.*

A sudden fear came upon him, *fu assalito da un subito timore.*

When the fit comes upon me, *quando mi piglia la febbre.*

I never came upon the back of a better nag, *non ho mai cavalcato un miglior cavallo.*

A great war is coming upon us, *una sanguinosa guerra ci viene addosso.*

I shall come upon you for it, *voi me la pagherete, ve la vo' far pagare.*

Before this evil came upon us, *prima che questo male ci arrivasse.*

To come short of a thing, *non riuscire come si voleva o credeva, non venire a fine di che che si sia.*

To come short of [to be inferior to] *essere inferiore, cedere, non arrivare, non aggiungere ad una cosa con un altra cosa.*

To come, adv. *in futuro.*

The time to come, *il futuro, il tempo a venire.*

For the time to come, *in avvenire, d'ora in avanti, quincinnanzi.*

Come, adj. *venuto.*

First come first served, *i primi venuti devono essere primi serviti.*

My design is come to nothing, *il mio disegno è svanito, è ito in nulla, in fumo.*

COMEDIAN, s. [a writer or actor of comedies] *un poeta comico, o un attore, un comico, un commediante, colui che recita in commedia.*

CO'MEDY, s. [a sort of dramatick poesy] *commedia, s. f. poema rappresentativo di private persone.*

CO'MELINESS, s. [beauty, grace] *bellezza, leggiadria, vaghezza, grazia, avvenentezza, gentilezza, s. f.*

CO'MELY, adj. [handsome, beautiful, graceful] *bello, vago, vezzoso, avvenente, gentile, grazioso, di maniere graziose.*

Comely [seemly] *convenevole, onesto, decoro, decoroso, decente.*

Comely, adv. *bellamente, vagamente, vezzosamente, graziosamente, gentilmente, con grazia, avvenentemente.*

Comely [decently] *convenevolmente, onestamente, decentemente, con decoro.*

CO'MER, s. *un che viene.*

To all comers, *a chiunque viene.*

A new comer, *un forestiero.*

For comers and goers, *per que' che vanno e vengono.*

CO'MET, s. [a blazing star] *una cometa, una stella cometa.*

CO'MFITS, s. [sweet-meats] *confetti, s. m. mandorle, pistacchi, e cose simili coperte di zucchero.*

A comfit-maker, *colui che fa e vende i confetti.*

CO'MFORT, s. [consolation] *conforto, ristoro, s. m. consolazione, s. f.*

Comfort [pleasure, enjoyment] *conforto, contento, piacere, s. m. sodisfazione, ricreazione, s. f.*

I have no comfort in this life, *non ho conforto o piacere alcuno in questo mondo.*

To CO'MFORT [to ease] *confortare, alleggerire il dolore altrui con ragioni e parole piacevoli.*

To comfort one in his troubles, *confortare alcuno nelle sue avversità.*

To comfort [to rejoice] *confortare, ristorare, ricreare.*

The very sight of him does comfort me, *mi sento confortare solo in vederlo.*

To comfort one up [to chear him up] *animare uno, fargli animo, incoraggiarlo.*

CO'MFORTABLE, adj. [giving ease] *confortante, confortativo, che ha virtù di confortare, ricreativo, confortevole.*

Comfortable news, *grate novelle.*

To live a comfortable life, *menare una vita contenta.*

CO'MFORTABLENESS, s. [ease] *confortagione, confortazione, s. f. confortamento, conforto, ristoro, s. m.*

CO'MFORTABLY, adv. *contentamente, lietamente, allegramente.*

He lives very comfortably, *e' mena una vita molto contenta.*

CO'MFORTED, adj. *confortato, consolato.*

CO'MFORTER, s. *confortatore, consolatore, s. m.*

God is the great comforter of such as are in trouble, *Iddio è il gran confortatore degli afflitti.*

CO'MFORTING, s. *confortamento, il confortare.*

CO'MFORTLESS, adj. *inconsolabile, che non ha nessun conforto, privo d'ogni consolazione.*

CO'MFREY, or CO'MFRY [a sort of herb] *consolida maggiore, erba.*

CO'MICAL, adj. [fit for comedy] *comico, proprio da commedia.*

Comical [merry, facetious, pleasant] *piacévole, ridicolo, faceto, burlesco, allegro.*

CO'MING, s. [from to come] *venuta, s. f. il venire, arrivo, s. m.*

Since my coming, *dopo la mia venuta.*

At his coming, *al suo arrivo.*

Coming in [income] *entrata, rendita, s f.*

His laying out exceeds his coming in, *le sue spese eccedono le sue entrate.*

Coming, adj. [prone, forward] *inclinato, dedito, disposto, portato.*

A coming stomach, *un buon appetito.*

A coming wench, *una donna tenera di calcagno, donna che facilmente si lascia svolgere, una fanciulla vogliosa.*

CO'MMA, s. [one of the points or stops in writing, and it is marked thus (,)] *una virgola.*

COMMA'ND, s. [order] *comando, comandamento, ordine, s. m.*

I come to receive your commands, *vengo a ricevere i vostri comandi.*

I am ready to observe your commands, *son pronto ad eseguire i vostri ordini.*

Command [charge, government] *comando, governo, s. m.*

To have the command of an army, *aver il comando d'un esercito.*

To have a command in the army, *aver una carica nell' esercito.*

I am at your command, *sono al suo comando, a sua disposizione.*

He has no command of himself, *e' non è padron di se stesso, non sa vincersi, non sa moderarsi.*

He has at command both the French and English, *egli è padrone della lingua Francese egualmente che della Inglese.*

To have the command of his passions, *saper moderare o vincere le sue passioni.*

To command [to order] *comandare, ordinare, dare ordine.*

I command you to do it, *vi comando di farlo.*

To command [to have the command] *comandare, aver il comando, reggere, pret. ressi.*

To command an army, a regiment, a company, *comandare un esercito, un reggimento, una compagnia.*

The citadel commands the city, *la cittadella domina la città.*

To command one's self, *vincer se stesso.*

To command one's passions, *dominare, moderare, raffrenare le sue passioni.*

To command a sum of money, *avere una somma di danari al proprio comando, poter disporre d'una somma di danari.*

To

To command silence, *imporre silenzio.*

Your beauty commands love and respect to every body, *la vostra bellezza ispira amore e rispetto a tutti.*

COMMA'NDED, adj. *comandato, v.* to command.

I am commanded so to do, *così mi vien comandato.*

COMMA'NDER, s [one who has command, a chief officer or general] *comandante, capitano, generale, capo,* s. m.

The commander of an army, *il comandante o generale d'un esercito.*

Commander of a squadron at sea, *il commandante d'una piccola flotta di navi da guerra.*

Commander [governor of a commandry or order of religious knights] *commendatore,* s. f. *quello che gode la commenda.*

A commander [a paving beetle] *mazzeranga,* s. f. *strumento con che si batte il pavimento per renderlo piano.*

CO'MMANDERY, s. [a manor with which lands or tenements are occupied, belonging to the priory of an order of knights] *commenda,* s. f. *rendita ecclesiastica data a godere a un cavaliere.*

COMMA'NDING, s. *comandamento,* s. m. *il comandare.*

COMMA'NDMENT, s. *comandamento, precetto,* s. m. *legge,* s. f.

The ten commandments, *i dieci comandamenti.*

To COMME'MORATE [to celebrate the memory of a worthy person or thing] *commemorare, rammemorare.*

COMMEMORA'TION, s [a solemn remembrance] *commemorazione, memoria, ricordanza,* s. f.

To make a commemoration of a saint, *far commemorazione d'un santo.*

To COMME'NCE, [to begin] *cominciare, dar principio, principiare, incominciare.*

To commence an action against one, *entrare in lite contro ad uno dinanzi a magistrato, cominciare una lite.*

To commence [to take a degree in a university] *prender una matricola o grado in una università, adottorarsi, matricolarsi.*

To commence a doctor, *cominciare a far il medico, il dottore.*

To commence an author, *cominciare ad ergersi o spacciarsi per autore.*

COMME'NCED, adj. *cominciato, principiato, incominciato.*

COMME'NCEMENT, s. [the time when students begin to be masters of arts in the university,] *il tempo nel quale uno studente s'addottora nell' università.*

To COMMEND, [to praise] *commendare, lodare, approvare.*

Every body commends him, *vien commendato da ognuno.*

I commend you for it, *ve ne lodo.*

To commend one's self, *commendarsi, lodarsi, vantarsi.*

A well-bred man never commends nor discommends himself, *un uomo bencreato mai si loda nè si biasima non da se stesso.*

To commend [to recommend] *raccomandare.*

I commend it to your trust, *ve lo raccomando.*

To commend one's spirit to God, *raccomandar l'anima sua a Dio.*

Pray, commend me to him, *di grazia salutatemelo vi prego riverirlo da parte mia.*

To commend highly, *esaltare, magnificare.*

COMME'NDABLE, adj. [praise worthy] *commendabile, degno d'esser commendato, lodevole, laudabile.*

A commendable action, *un' azione commendabile, degna di lode.*

COMME'NDABLY, adv. *lodevolmente, con lode, con onore.*

COMME'NDAM, s. [a void benefice commended to an able clerk, till it be otherwise disposed of] *beneficio in commenda.*

COMMENDA'TION, s. [praise] *commendamento,* s. m. *commendazione,* s. f.

Letters of commendation, *lettere di raccomandazione.*

Commendations [service or respects convey'd to one] *baciamani, saluti, complimenti.*

To send one's commendations, *fare i suoi baciamani ad alcuno.*

To do one's commendations, *riverire uno, fare i suoi baciamani ad alcuno.*

COMME'NDATORY, adj. *di raccomandazione, commendatizio.*

Commendatory letters, *lettere commendatizie.*

Commendatory, adj. [that has a commendam] *commendatorio; che gode una commenda.*

COMME'NDED, adj. *commendato, lodato, v.* To commend.

COMME'NDER, s. [a praiser] *un che loda, lodatore.*

COMME'NDING, s. *commendamento,* s. m. *commendazione,* s. f. *il commendare.*

COMMENSA'LITY, s. [fellowship of table] *compagnia a tavola, lo essere a desco insieme, a tavola insieme.*

COMME'NSURABLE, adj. [equal in measure and proportion] *commensurabile, che puo agguagliarsi o bilanciarsi con l' altro.*

COMME'NSURATE, adj. *commensurato, agguagliato, bilanciato, proporzionato.*

My expences must be commensurate with my revenues, *le mie spese bisogna sieno proporzionate alle mie rendite.*

CO'MMENT, s. [an exposition or interpretation of an author's text, a gloss] *commento,* s. m. *esposizione, interpretazione, chiosa, glosa,* s. f.

To comment [to expound, to write notes upon, to gloss] *commentare, far commento, esporre, spiegare, glosare, far glosa.*

To comment upon [to find fault with] *glosare, criticare.*

COMME'NTARY, s. [an interpretation of an obscure and difficult author] *commento,* s. m. *interpretazione, esposizione, glosa chiosa,* s. f.

COMMENTA'TOR, s. [a maker of commentartes] *commentatore, espositore,* s. m.

COMM'ENTED, adj. *commentato, glosato, esposto, interpretato, criticato.*

COMMENTITIOUS, adj. [forged, counterfeit] *immaginario, inventato, trovato, finto, falso.*

CO'MMERCE, s. [trade, traffick] *commerzio, commercio, traffico,* s. m.

There is no manner of cómmerce in that country, *non v'è commerzio d'alcuna sorte in quel paese.*

Commerce [intercourse, correspondence] *commerzio,* s. m. *corrispondenza, società, comunicazione, pratica,* s. f.

I have no manner of commerce with him, *non ho veruna corrispondenza o pratica con esso lui.*

To COMME'RCE [to hold intercourse] *frequentare, trattare.*

COMME'RCIAL, adj. [relating to commerce or traffick] *appartenente a traffico o commercio.*

COMME'RE, s. [a common mother] *madre comune.*

COMMINA'TION, s. [threatning] *minaccia,* s. f.

To COMMINGLE, v. a. [to mix into one mass, to mix, to blend] *meschiare diverse cose insieme, e far di quelle una, mescolare.*

To Commingle, v. n. [to unite with another thing] *unirsi con un altra cosa.*

COMMINU'TION, s. [division of a thing into very small parts] *sminuzzamento,* s. m. *lo spezzare in minutissime parti.*

To COMMISERATE, [to take pity of] *commiserare, aver pietà, o misericordia.*

COMMI'SERATING, adj. *misericordioso, tenero, sensibile, pieno di compassione, compassionevole.*

COMMISERA'TION, s. [pity, felt] *commiserazione, misericordia,* s. f.

CO'MMISSARY, s. [a church-officer who supplies the bishop's place in remote parts of his diocese, or one who has the distribution of provisions of an army] *commissario d'una chiesa o d'un esercito.*

COMM'ISSION, s. [a power given by one person to another of doing any thing *commissione,* s. f. *ordine, comandamento,* s. m.

To have a commission, *avere una commissione.*

To COMMI'SSION, to COMMI'SSIONATE [to appoint] *commettere, stabilire, dar commissione.*

COMMISSIONED, or COMMI'SSIONATED, adj. *commesso, stabilito, che ha avuto commissione o potere di far qualche cosa.*

COMMI'SSIONER, s. [one who has a commission] *commissario,* s. m.

The commissioners of the custom-house, *i commissari della dogana.*

To COMMI'T [to act, to do] *commettere, fare, operare.*

To commit a sin, *commettere un peccato.*

To commit a fault, *commettere un fallo, fare un errore.*

To commit [to put] *mettere.*

To commit a thing to paper, *metter che che si sia in iscritto.*

To

To commit one to custody, *metter alcuno in arresto o in prigione.*

To commit [to refer or leave business to] *commettere, raccomandare, dare in custodia.*

To commit a business to one, *commettere o raccomandare un negozio ad alcuno.*

To commit a thing to memory, *imprimer che che si sia nella memoria, imparare a mente.*

To commit one's self to God's care and protection, *rimettersi nelle mani di Dio, raccomandarsi alla cura e protezione del signor Dio.*

They commit themselves to be guided, *si lásciano guidare, soffrono d' esser condotti.*

COMMI'TMENT, s. *arresto, imprigionamento,* s. m.

COMMI'TTED, adj. *commesso, v.* To commit.

The care of him was committed to me, *a me fù commessa la cura di lui.*

COMMI'TTEE, s. [several persons committed to examine an affair] *commissari nominati per esaminare un affare.*

A committee of the house of commons, *commissari o esecutori della camera bassa del parlamento deputati a esaminare checchessia.*

COMMI'XION, } s. [mingling
COMMI'XTION, } things together]
COMMI'XTURE, } *miscuglio,* s. m. *mescolanza, mistura,* s. f.

COMMO'DE, s. [a sort of head dress for women] *sorta di cuffia da donne.*

COMMO'DIOUS, adj. [fit, convenient, useful] *cómodo, utile, convenevole opportuno.*

COMMO'DIOUSLY, adv. *comodamente.*

To live very commodiously, *vivere agiatamente, vivere a suo agio, avere i suoi agi.*

COMMO'DIOUSNESS, } s. [advan-
COMMO'DITY, } tage, conveniency] *comodità,* s. f. *comodo,* s. m.

Commodity [profit] *profitto, guadagno, lucro,* s. m. *utilità,* s. f.

Commodity [ware] *roba, mercanzia,* s. f.

Good or bad commodity, *buona o cattiva roba o mercanzia.*

To vent commodities, *vendere, smaltire mercanzie.*

CO'MMODORE, s. [one who commands a squadron at sea] *comandante d'una squadra di navi da guerra.*

CO'MMON, adj. [ordinary] *comune, ordinario, comunale.*

Common [publick] *comune, pubblico, che è di più d'uno, di molti, d' ognuno.*

A common whore, *una puttana pubblica, una bagascia, una cantoniera.*

The common prayers, *le preghiere comuni.*

A common soldier, *un semplice soldato.*

The common people, *il popolo, il popolazzo, il popolaccio, la plebe, la canaglia.*

At the common rate, *al prezzo corrente.*

'Tis a common talk, *è voce comune.*

A commonwealth, *una repubblica.*

A common-wealth's-man, *un repubblicano, un repubblichista.*

Common [common pasture] *pascoli comuni dove tutti li abitanti d'un villaggio hanno ragione di pascolare il lor bestiame.*

To COMMON [to diet] *vivere in comunità.*

CO'MMONALTY, s. [the commons] *comune,* s. m. *comunanza, comunità,* s. f.

CO'MMONER, s. *membro de' comuni, un cittadino, ogni persona che è inferiore ai pari del regno in parlamento.*

A commoner of a college in a university, *un membro d'un collegio.*

Commoner [one of the common people; a man of low rank] *un uomo plebeo, di bassa condizione.*

Commoner, [a prostitute] *una puttanella, una cantoniera, una zambracca, una ciccantona, una briffalda.*

CO'MMONLY, adv. *comunemente, universalmente, generalmente, per l'ordinario, d' ordinario, ordinariamente.*

CO'MMONESS, s. *comunanza,* s. f.

Commonness [frequent occurrence, frequency] *l' occorrere frequente, frequenza.*

To COMMON PLA'CE, [to reduce to general heads] *far un zibaldone metodico.*

COMMON-PLACE-BOOKS, s. *zibaldoni fatti con metodo.*

COMMONS, s. [a proportion of vicuals, especially the regular diet of a college or society] *piatanza,* s. f. *quella vivanda che si da alle mense de' claustrali o de' collegiati.*

The commons of England, *i comuni d' Inghilterra.*

The house of commons, *la camera de' comuni, la camera bassa del parlamento d'Inghilterra o d' Irlanda.*

COMMONWE'AL, } s. *il comune,*
COMMONWEALTH, } *la repubblica, la società.*

COMMO'TION, s. [hurly-burly] *commozione,* s. f. *commovimento,* s. m.

To COMMU'NE [to talk together] *conferire, parlare, discorrere insieme.*

COMMU'NICABLE, adj. *communicabile, da comunicarsi.*

COMMU'NICANT, s. [one who receives the Communion of the Lord's Supper] *comunicante,* s. m. *che comunica.*

There are at least three thousand communicants, *vi sono almeno tre mila comunicanti.*

To COMMU'NICATE [to impart] *comunicare, partecipare, conferire, far partecipe,* pres. *conferisco.*

I did not think fit to communicate it to him, *non ho giudicato spediente di comunicarglielo*

To communicate favour, *compartire, o fare favori.*

To communicate. [to receive the sacrament] *communicarsi, ricever il sacramento.*

He communicates every Sunday, *si comunica ogni domenica.*

COMMU'NICATED, adj. *comunicato, partecipato, conferito.*

COMMUNICA'TION, s. [imparting] *comunicamento,* s. m. *comunicazione, partecipazione,* s. f.

Communication [familiarity, intercourse] *comunicazione, familiarità, conversazione,* s. f. *commercio,* s. m.

Communication [conference] *discorso,* s. m. *conferenza,* s. f.

Evil communication corrupts good manners, *le cattive compagnie corrompono i costumi.*

COMMU'NICATIVE, adj. [free and open] *communicativo, libero, franco, aperto, schietto.*

COMMU'NION, s. [fellowship, union in faith] *comunione, società, comunità,* s. f.

The Roman communion, *la comunione Romana.*

Communion [the Sacrament of the Lord's Supper] *comunione, il sagramento dell' eucaristia.*

To receive the communion, *ricever la comunione, comunicarsi.*

The Protestants receive the communion in both kinds, *i Riformati ricevono la comunione sotto tutte due le specie.*

The communion table, *la tavola della comunione.*

The communion cloth, *la tovaglia che copre la tavola della comunione.*

The communion cup, *il calice.*

COMMU'NITY, s. [partnership of a body of men united in a civil society] *comunità, società, unione, fratellanza,* s. f.

Community of goods, *comunità di beni.*

COMMUTA'TION, s. [exchange] *commutazione,* s. f. *scambiamento,* s. m.

COMMU'TATIVE, adj. [belonging to commutation] *commutativo.*

Commutative justice, *giustizia commutativa.*

To COMMU'TE [to exchange] *commutare, mutare, scambiare.*

To commute a punishment, *commutare una pena.*

COMPA'CT, adj. [close, well joined] *concatenato, saldo, fitto, congiunto, collegato, sodo, stringato, connesso.*

A compact discourse, *un discorso ben concatenato.*

Compact, s. [agreement, bargain] *accordo, patto,* s. m. *convenzione,* s. f.

That was done by compact, *ciò fu fatto d'accordo, di commune accordo.*

The compact of witches with the devil, *il patto delle streghe col diavolo.*

To COMPA'CT [to clap close together] *concatenare, unire insieme, collegare, commettere, stringere insieme.*

COMPA'CTED, adj. *concatenato, unito insieme, collegato, commesso, bene stretto insieme, sodo.*

A well compacted town, *una città ben piena di popolo, piena di popolo come un uovo.*

A compact discourse, *un discorso ben concatenato, stringato, succinto, sodo, pien di pensieri.*

COMPA'CTING, s. *concatenazione, commessura, giuntura,* s. f.

COMPA'CTLY, adj. [close] *compendiosamente, succintamente, stringatamente.*

Compactly [strongly] *fortemente, sodamente.*

Compactly [neatly] *aggiustatamente, con aggiustatezza, attillatamente, con attillatura, pulitamente.*

COMPA'NION, s. [fellow] *compagno, compagnone, socio, sozio,* s. m.

He is my companion, *egli è mio compagno.*

A boon companion [a merry fellow] *un compagnone, un uomo gioviale e piacevole, un uomo di buon tempo, un buon sozio, un uomo compagnevole e alla mano.*

A knight companion of the garter, *un cavaliere compagnone della giartiera.*

A woman companion, *una compagna.*

COMPA'NIONABLE, adj. [fit for good fellowship, social] *compagnevole, di buona compagnia.*

COMPA'NIONSHIP, s. [company, train] *compagnia,* s. f. *séguito,* s. m.

Companionship, [fellowship, association] *compagnevolezza, società,* s. f.

CO'MPANY, s. [assembly of people] *compagnia, unione conversazione assemblea, società, prattica,* s. f. *crocchio,* s. m.

To bear or keep company, *far compagnia, accompagnare.*

I shall be very glad of your company, *la vostra compagnia mi sarà gratissima.*

To keep good or ill company, *frequentare, praticare buona o cattiva compagnia.*

To be good company, *esser buon compagnone, esser gioviale e piacevole in compagnia, esser buon sozio.*

Company [troop] *compagnia,* s. f.

A company of soldiers, *una compagnia di soldati.*

A company of horse or foot, *una compagnia di cavalleria o di fanteria.*

Company [body, society] *compagnia, comunanza d'interessati in un negozio o traffico mercantile, ragione,* s. f.

A company of merchants, *una compagnia di mercanti.*

The East India company, *la compagnia dell' Indie orientali.*

A company of tradesmen, *un corpo d'artigiani.*

Company [herd of wild beasts] *branco d' animali.*

By companies, *a stuolo, in folla, a branchi.*

A company of stage-players, *una compagnia di commedianti.*

A great company of stars, *un gran numero di stelle vicine le une alle altre.*

To keep company, *frequentare, bazzicare.*

To keep women's company, *praticar colle donne.*

To keep a woman company, *donneare, far l'amore con una donna.*

A company keeper, *uno scapestrato, un dissoluto, un licenzioso.*

To CO'MPANY, [to keep company] *praticare, frequentare, bazzicare.*

CO'MPARABLE, adj. [that may be compared] *comparabile, paragonabile, da compararsi, simile, da paragonarsi.*

Is that comparable to this? *è quella una cosa da compararsi a questa?*

CO'MPARABLY, adv. *a comparazione, a petto, a paragone.*

COMPA'RATIVE, adj. [implying comparison] *comparativo.*

Comparative, s. *comparativo,* s. m. *termine gramaticale.*

COMPA'RATIVELY, adv. *a comparazione, a proporzione, proporzionatamente.*

COMPA'RE, s. *comparazione,* s. f. *paragone, agguaglio,* s. m.

Beyond compare, *senza comparozione, incomparabilmente.*

To COMPARE, [to liken, to examine one thing by another] *comparare, paragonare, agguagliare, simigliare, assimigliare, somigliare, assomigliare.*

To compare one thing to another, *comparare una cosa ad un' altra.*

I am not to compare with him, *non v'è comparazione fra me lui, non v'è paragone fra di noi due.*

To compare notes together, *discorrere o ragionare insieme di checche sia.*

COMPA'RED, adj. *comparato, paragonato, agguagliato, simigliato, rassomigliato.*

COMPA'RING, s. *comparazione, il comparare.*

COMPA'RISON, s. [comparing] *comparazione, comparagione,* s. f. *paragone, agguaglio,* s. m.

In comparison of, *a comparazione, a petto, a paragone di.*

Beyond or without comparison, *senza comparazione, senza paragone.*

Comparison, [proportion, analogy] *somiglianza, affinità, analogia,* s.

COMPA'RT, COMPA'RTMENT, or COMPA'RTIMENT, s. [proportionable division in building] *compartimento,* s. m. *il compartire, termine d'architettura.*

Compartment in a garden, *compartimento di giardino.*

COM'PASS, s. [the extent of a thing on all sides or round about] *circuito, giro, contorno, spazio,* s. m. *circonferenza.*

To fetch a great compass, *fare un gran giro.*

The compass of a town, of a house, &c. *il giro o circuito d'una città, d'una casa,* &c.

In the compass of a year, *nello spazio d'un anno, nel giro d'un anno.*

I shall do it within the compass of time, *lo farò in questo tempo, nello spazio di questo tempo, in questo intervallo di tempo.*

A thing not within compass of men's memory, *una cosa immemorabile.*

Both these things are without the compass of any art to teach, *non v'è arte che possa insegnare ad un altro la maniera di fare queste due cose.*

To draw a thing into a narrow compass, *abbreviare, accorciare, sminuire, sorciare che che si sia.*

To keep one within compass, *tenere uno a segno, farlo stare a segno, tenerlo a freno o dentro i limiti del dovere.*

To keep within compass, verb. neut. *contenersi, frenarsi, regolarsi, risparmiare, proporzionar le spese alle sue rendite.*

To speak within compass, *parlare limitamente, dire la cosa come ella stà senza ampliare.*

A compass [a mariner's compass] *bussola,* s. f. *strumento marinaresco ove s'aggiusta l'ago magnètico.*

To CO'MPASS, [to surround] *circondare, girare, intorniare.*

The sea compasses the land, *il mare circonda la terra.*

To compass about the walls of a town, *girare, o fare il giro delle mura d'una città.*

To compass [to gain, to bring about] *spontare, otenere, venire a capo.*

To compass a business, *spuntare un negozio.*

To compass one's desire, *ottenere il suo intento, far si che s'ottenga.*

To compass the death of one, *macchinare la morte d'alcuno.*

CO'MPASSED, adj. *circondato, girato, attorniatto, v.* To compass.

CO'MPASSES, or a pair of compasses, s. *compasso, strumento geometrico che forma il cerchio.*

CO'MPASSING, s. *circondamento, giramento, attorniamento,* s. m.

COMPA'SSION, s. [pity] *compassione, misericordia, pietà,* s. f.

To take compassion of one, *aver compassione o pietà d'uno, muoversi a pietà d' alcuno.*

To raise one's compassion, *muovere a pietà.*

To COMPA'SSION, [to pity] *aver pietà.*

COMPA'SSIONATE, adj. *compassionevole, che ha compassione.*

To compassionate [to pity] *compatire, aver compassione, sentir pietà del male altrui,* pref. *compatisco.*

COMPA'SSIONATELY, adv. *con compassione, pietosamente, con pietà.*

COMPA'TIBLE, adj. [that agrees or suits with another thing] *compatible, che s'accorda o si confà con un' altra cosa.*

Heat is compatible with moisture, *il calore è compatibile coll' umido.*

COMPA'TIBLENESS, s. [consistency] *compatabilità,* s. f.

COMPA'TRIOT, s. [one that is of the same country] *compatriota,* s. m. *d'una medesima patria.*

COMPE'ER, s. [gossip, godfather, companion, fellow] *compare,* s. m. *compagno, compagnone,* s. m.

To COMPE'ER, [to be equal with, to mate] *agguagliare.*

To COMPE'L, [to force, to constrain] *costringere, sforzare,* pret. *costrinsi.*

You shall never compel me to do it, *voi non mi sforzerete mai a farlo, non sarà mai in poter vostro di farmelo fare.*

Poverty compells him to beg, *la povertà lo costrigne a mendicare.*

To compel one to his duty, *sforzare o obbligare altrui a fare il suo dovere.*

COMPE'LLED, adj. *costretto, sforzato.*

COMPE'LLER,

COMPE'LLER, s. [he that forces another] *colui che fa forza ad uno.*

COMPE'LLING, s. *lo sforzare.*

Cloud-compelling, *è aggiunto poetico dato a Giove, e vale sgombranuvoli, scacciatore delle nubi.*

COMPE'NDIOUS, adj. [brief, short, concise] *compendioso, breve, succinto.*

A compendious discourse, *un discorso succinto o compendioso.*

A compendious history, *un' istoria in ristretto, una breve istoria.*

COMPE'NDIOUSLY, adv. *compendiosamente, brevemente, succintamente.*

COMPE'NDIOUSNESS, s. [shortness] *brevità, s. f. compendio, s. m.*

COMPE'NDIUM, s. [abridgement] *compendio, s. m. breve ristretto del trattato.*

To make a compendium, *compendiare, ridurre in compendio.*

To COMPE'NSATE [to make amends for, to recompence] *compensare, contraccambiare, dare l'equivalente contraccambio.*

COMPE'NSATION, s. [recompence] *compensazione, ricompensa, s. f. contraccambio, equivalente, s. m.*

To COMPERE'NDINATE [to delay, to prolong from day to day] *procrastinare, prolungare, prorogare, differire,* pres. *differisco. E' voce legale, e non più in uso.*

CO'MPETENCE, } s. [conveniency,
CO'MPETENCY, } meetness] *competenza, convenevolezza, convenienza,* s. f.

To have a competency to live on, *aver competentemente da vivere.*

To have a competency of learning [to have a competent portion of learning] *esser competentemente dotato di sapere.*

CO'MPETENT, adj. [convenient, meet, sufficient] *competente, convenevole, conveniente.*

He is not a competent man for that employ, *egli non è un uomo competente per questo impiego, questa carica non è una nicchia propria per un tal uomo.*

A competent judge, *giudice competente.*

CO'MPETENTLY, adv. [sufficiently] *competentemente, convenevolmente, convenientemente.*

COMPE'TIBLE, adj. [suitable, agreeable to] *convenévole, conveniente, proporzionato.*

This is a circumstance not competible to any but him, *questa circostanza non può convenire che a lui solo.*

COMPETI'TION, s. [rivalship, canvassing or suing for the same office or thing which another does] *competenza, gara,* s. f.

To stand in competition with another, *stare a competere con un altro, gareggiare con un altro.*

To come in competition [in balance] *entrare in competenza, competere, disputare, gareggiare.*

COMPE'TITOR, s. [a rival, one who sues for the same office or thing with another] *competitore, rivale, pretendente,* s. m.

COMPILA'TION, s. [collection] *compilazione, collezione, s. f. il compilare.*

To COMPI'LE [to collect from several authors] *compilare, comporre.*

To compile a dictionary, *compilare, comporre un dizionario.*

COMPI'LED, adj. *compilato, disposto, composto.*

COMPI'LEMENT, s. *compilazione, s. f. il compilare.*

COMPI'LER, s. *compilatore, s. m. che compila.*

A dictionary compiler, *un compilatore di dizionario.*

COMPI'LING, s. *compilazione, il compilare.*

COMPLA'CENCE, } s. [the act of
COMPLA'CENCY, } taking delight in a thing] *compiacenza, s. f. gusto, diletto che si sente nelle cose.*

To COMPLA'IN [to bewail, to bemoan] *compiagnere, compiangere, lamentarsi, lagnarsi, deplorare.*

I complain of your misfortune, *compiango la vostra disgrazia.*

To complain to one, *lagnarsi con alcuno.*

To complain of one, *lagnarsi, lamentarsi d'uno.*

COMPLA'INANT, s. [plaintiff] *attore, s. m. colui, che nel litigare domanda, il cui avversario si chiama reo.*

COMPLA'INED OF, adj. *lamentato, biasimato.*

He is very much complained of, *molti si lamentano di lui; è vien molto biasimato.*

COMPLA'INER, s. *compiagnitore,* s. m.

COMPLA'INT, s. *querela, doglienza, s. f. lamento, s. m.*

To put a complaint against one, *querelarsi, lagnarsi, lamentarsi d'uno.*

A bill of complaint, *accusa, accusazione che si fa in giustizia contro alcuno.*

Complaint [lamentation] *lamento, dolore, affanno, travaglio, compianto, s. m. condoglienza, s. f.*

COMPLAISA'NCE, s. [obliging carriage, pleasing behaviour] *cortesia, amorevolezza, affabilità, s. f.*

Complaisance [complacency] *compiacenza, s. f. gusto, diletto, che si sente nelle cose.*

COMPLAISA'NT, adj. [civil, courteous] *cortese, amorevole, affabile, civile.*

To COMPLE'AT, *v.* to complete.

CO'MPLEMENT, s. [perfecting that which is wanting] *compimento, finimento, conducimento a fine.*

Complement [kind of expression] *complimento, v.* compliment.

To CO'MPLEMENT, *v.* to compliment.

To COMPLE'TE [to finish] *compiere, compire, finire, dar compimento.*

To complete my misery I heard, *per colmo di miseria intesi.*

COMPLE'TE, adj. [perfect] *compito, compiuto, condotto a fine, perfetto.*

A complete victory, *una vittoria compiuta.*

A complete piece of work, *un' opera perfetta.*

A complete virtue, *una vera virtù.*

He is a complete gentleman, *è un gentiluomo compito.*

COMPLE'TELY, adv. *compitamente, compiutamente, perfettamente.*

COMPLETENESS, s. *perfezione,* s. f.

The completeness of a thing, *la perfezione di che che sia.*

COMPLE'TION, s. [accomplishing, fulfilling, performance] *compimento, adempimento, s. m. esecuzione,* s f.

The completion of our desires, *l'adempimento de' nostri desideri.*

COMPLE'X, adj [compound, consisting of diverse ingredients] *composto.*

Complex ideas [in logick] *idee composte di molte altre idee semplici.*

A complex body of laws, *un corpo di leggi.*

COMPLE'XLY, adv. [jointly] *unitamente, insieme.*

Whether the thing be separately or complexly considered, *se consideriamo la cosa separatamente o unitamente.*

COMPLE'XION, s. [colour of the face] *complessione, carnagione, s. f. colore e qualità di carne.*

A fine complexion, *una bella complessione.*

A lively complexion, *una carnagione vivace.*

Complexion, [temper] *complessione, temperatura, qualità, dispozizione, s. f. stato del corpo.*

COMPLE'XIONAL, adj. *complessionale, di complessione, che viene o deriva da complessione.*

COMPLE'XIONED, adj. *complesso.*

A body well complexioned, *un corpo ben complesso.*

COMPLE'XURE, adj. [joining together] *congiunzione, unione, s. f. assembiamento, assembramento,* s. m.

COMPLI'ANCE, s. [complying, yielding] *compiacenza, condiscendenza, condiscensione, s. f. inchinamento,* s. m.

In compliance to your command, *in esecuzione de' vostri comandi.*

COMPLI'ANT, adj. *cortese, civile, condescendente, obbligante.*

To CO'MPLICATE [to entangle one with another, to join] *intrecciare.*

COMPLICA'TED, adj. [folded, wrapt up together] *ravviluppato, aggregato, aggroppato.*

Complicated diseases, *malattie aggregate.*

COMPLICA'TION, s. [collection or mass of things joined together] *bica, congerie, massa, s. f. aggregato o arcozzamento di più cose.*

A complication of diseases, *un' aggregazione di malattie.*

A complication of miseries, *una sequela di miserie.*

Complication of figures, *un gruppo di figure.*

CO'MPLICE, s. [partner in an ill action, accomplice] *complice, s. m. f. che ha parte in un delitto.*

CO'MPLIMENT, s. [kind obliging words and expressions] *complimento,* s. m. *atto di riverenza, d'ossequio, d' affetto.*

To make a man a compliment, *fare un complimento ad uno.*

Compliments [too many ceremonies] *complimenti, cerimonie.*

To COMPLIME'NT [to use compliments] *complimentare, far complimenti.*

COMPLIME'NTED, adj. *complimentato.*

I complimented him upon his safe return, *mi congratulai con esso del suo salvo arrivo.*

COMPLIME'NTOR, s. *quello, o quella che fa complimento.*

COMPLIME'NTING, s. *il far complimenti.*

I hate complimenting, *odio i complimenti.*

COMPLI'NE, s. [the last prayers, or evening prayers] *compieta,* s. f. *l' ultima delle ore canoniche.*

To CO'MPLOT [to plot together, to combine, to conspire] *cospirare, macchinare, congiurare.*

COMPLO'TTER, s. *cospiratore, congiuratore, machinatore,* s. m. *cospiratrice, congiuratrice, macchinatrice,* s. f.

To COMPLY', [to yield, to submit to] *condescendere, secondare, inclinare, acconsentire.* pret. *condescesi.* pres. *acconsentisco.*

To comply with one, *condescendere all' altrui voleri, secondarli.*

To comply with the will of God, *conformarsi alla volantà di Dio.*

To comply as the church requires, *sottomersi alle ceremonie della chiesa.*

COMPLY'D WITH, adj. *condescesso, secondato, inclinato, aconsentito.*

COMPLY'ING, s. *condescentimento,* s. m. *il condescendere.*

To COMPO'RT [to agree] *accomodarsi, convenire.* pres. *convengo.* pret. *covenni.*

To comport one's self] to behave or demean one's self] *comportarsi, procedere, governarsi, portarsi.*

COMPO'RT, COMPO'RTANCE, COMPO'RTMENT, } s. [carriage behaviour] *portamento; procèdere,* s. m. *modo particolare di procedere.*

To COMPO'SE [to make a composition] *comporre.*

To compose a tune, *comporre un' aria.*

To compose [a term of printing] *comporre, accozzar le lettere insieme. E' termine di stamperia.*

To compose one's self [to put on a serious countenance] *parere grave e serio.*

They compose their faces that they may edify the more, *dimostran maggior compostezza onde più edifichino.*

To compose [to adjust a difference] *decidere una differenza.*

To compose [to quiet a man's passion] *acquetare, calmare lo sdegno.*

To compose [to settle one's affairs] *comporre, assestare, ordinare, accomodare, regolare i suoi affari.*

COMPOSED, adj. *composto,* v. to compose.

A composed countenance, *un' aria grave, un' aria composta.*

He is composed for his end, *egli è preparato o disposto a morire.*

COMPO'SEDLY, adv. [calmly, seriously] *seriamente, compostamente, con compostezza.*

COMPO'SING, s. *componimento,* s. m. *il comporre.*

A composing-stick [a term of printing] *compositore,* s. m. *termine di stampatore.*

COMPO'SITE, adj. [compounded] *composto.*

Composite order [in architecture the fifth order compounded of the other four] *òrdine composto. E' il quinto ordine in architettura, composto delle parti degli altri quattro. Vien anche chiamato òrdine Italico o Romano.*

A composite word, *una parola composta.*

COMPO'SITES, s. [in pharmacy, medicines made up of many simple one's] *composti,* s. m. *in opposizione de' simplici.*

COMPOSI'TION, s. [a mixture of several ingredients] *composizione, mescolanza,* s. f. *accozzamento di cose, miscuglio,* s. m.

Composition [composure] *composizione,* s. f. *poesia o altra simil fattura d' invenzione.*

Composition [agreement] *composizione, convenzione,* s. f. *aggiustamento, accordo patto,* s. m.

COMPO'SITOR, s. [he that ranges and adjusts the types in printing] *compositore, componitore,* s. m. *colui che nelle stamperie trae i caratteri delle cassette e si li acconcia che vengono a formare il disteso e le parole dell' autore.*

CO'MPOST, s. [manure] *letame.*

To COMPOST [to manure] *letamare, spargere il letame pel campo onde s' ingrassi.*

COMPO'STURE, s. [soil, manure] *letame o altra materia da ingrassar il terreno.*

COMPO'SURE, s. [any thing composed] *composizione, combinagione,* s. f.

Composure [calmness of mind] *tranquillità di mente, quiete d' animo.*

COMPOTA'TION, s. [a drinking together] *gozzoviglia,* s. f. *stravizzo e manicamento in allegrezza e in brigata.*

COMPO'UND, adj. *composto, termine grammaticale.*

A compound word, *una parola composta.*

To COMPO'UND [to make up of several ingredients] *comporre,* pres. *compongo,* pret. *composi.*

To compound [to come to an agreement] *comporsi, aggiustarsi, accordarsi, restar d' accordo, convenire.*

To compound with one's creditors, *accordarsi co' suoi creditori.*

The fox was glad to compound for his neck by leaving his tail, *la volpe fu contenta di lasciar la coda per salvar la testa.*

He was fain to compound with his estate to save his life, *fu costretto di dare i suoi bene per salvar la vita.*

COMPO'UNDED, adj. *composto.*

COMPOU'NDER, s. [one who endeavours to bring parties to terms of agreement] *colui che si sforza di amichevolmente accordare due persone di contraria opinione.*

Compounder [mingler; one who mixes bodies] *uno che mesce diverse cose insieme.*

To COMPREH'END, [to contain, to include] *comprendere, contenere, abbracciare.* pret. *compresi.* pres. *contengo.* pret. *contenni.*

To comprehend much in few words, *comprender molto in poche parole.*

This virtue comprehends all others, *questa virtù abbraccia tutte le altre.*

To comprehend [to understand] *comprendere, capire, intendere, conoscere.* pres. *capisco* pret. *compresi, intesi, conobbi.*

COMPREHE'NDED, adj. *compreso, contenuto, capito, inteso, conosciuto, abbracciato.*

COMPREHE'NSIBLE, adj. [that may be comprehended or understood] *comprensibile, intelligibile, che si puo comprendere, intendere o capire.*

COMPREHE'NSION, s. [the understanding of a thing] *comprensione,* s. f. *comprendimento,* s. m. *il comprendere.*

COMPREHE'NSIVE, adj. [containing much, very-significant] *che comprende molto, significativo, succinto.*

COMPREHE'NSIVENESS, s. [the quality of including much in a few words or narrow compass] *il chiudere molto in poche parole, o in poco spazio.*

A COMPR'ESS, s. [a bolster of folded linen to be laid on a wound] *stracci o filacce per le ferite, una benda.*

To compress [to squeeze close together] *comprimere, pigiare, ristrignere* pret. *ristrinsi.*

COMPRE'SSED, adj. *compresso, pigiato, ristretto.*

COMPRE'SSIBLE, adj. [that may be compressed] *compressible, che si puo comprimere.*

COMPRE'SSION, s. [a squeezing or pressing together] *compressione,* s. f. *il comprimere.*

The compression of the air, *la compressione dell' aria.*

To COMPRI'NT [to print a copy or book belonging to another to his prejudice] *stampare segretamente la copia o'l libro d'un altro, contrafferne la stampa.*

To COMPRI'SE, [to contain] *comprendere, contenere, abbracciare.* pret. *compresi* pret. *contengo.* pret. *contenni.*

COMPROBA'TION, s. [mutual allowing or approving] *comprobazione, approvazione,* s. f.

COMPRO'MISE, s. [a promise of two or more parties at difference to refer the deciding their controversies to the decision of arbitrators] *compromesso,* s. m. *atto col quale due o più parti convengono di rimèttere la decisione delle loro differenze al giudicio d' arbitri.*

To COMPROMI'SE, [to stand to arbitrement] *compromettere, rimettere le sue differenze in altrui con piena facultà di deciderle.*

COMPT [account, computation, reckoning] *conto càlcolo,* s. m.

To COMPTRO'L [to controll, to find fault

fault with] *contraddire*, criticare, *sindicare*, *sindacare*, *censurare*, *biasimare*.

COMPTRO'LLED, adj. *contraddetto*, *criticato*, *sindacato*, *censurato*, *biasimato*.

COMPTRO'LLER, s. [overseer] *intendente*, *soprastante*, s. m. *che ha soprastanza in che che sia*.

Comptroller [reformer of manners] *censore*, correttore, *riprenditore*, s. m.

COMPTRO'LLERSHIP, s. [superintendence] *soprintendenza*, *ispezione*, s. f.

COMPTRO'LLING, s. *contraddicimento*, *biasimo*, *sindacato*, s. m. *censura*, s. f.

COMPU'LSION, s. [constraint, force] *costrignimento*, s. m. *forza*, *violenza*, s. f.

COMPU'NCTION, s. [remorse of conscience] *compunzione*, s. f. *compugnimento*, *rimorso*, s. m. *afflizion d'animo con pentimento degli errori commessi*.

A compunction of heart, *compunzione di cuore*.

COMPURGA'TOR, s. [one that by oath justifies the innocence of another] *testimonio che prova con giuramento l'innocenza altrui*.

COMPUTA'TION, s. [a reckoning or casting up accounts] *cómputo*, *calcolo*, *conto*, s. m.

To make a computation, *fare un cómputo*.

COMPU'TE, s. *cálcolo*, *cómputo*, s. m.

To COMPU'TE [to reckon] *computare*, *calcolare*, *contare*.

COMPU'TED, adj. *computato*, *calcolato*, *contato*.

All things rightly computed, *a ben computare il tutto*.

COMPU'TING, s. [reckoning] *computamento*, *il computare*, *cómputo*.

COMPU'TER, } s. [accountant]
CO'MPUTIST, } *computista*, s. m. *che esercita l'arte di tener conti e ragioni*.

COMRA'DE, s. [one who dwells in the same house or chamber] *compagno di casa o di camera*.

Comrade [companion, partner] *socio*, *compagno*.

CON, adv. *contra*.

Pro and con, *pro e contra*.

To CON [to know] *conoscere*.

To con [to study] *studiare*.

To CON THANKS [to thank] *ringraziare*, *render grazie*.

To CONCA'MERATE [to arch over, to vault] *far una volta*, *coprir con un arco*.

CONCATENA'TION, s. [the state of being chained or linked together] *concatenazione*, *connessione*, *sequela*, *seguenza*, s. f.

To CONCA'TENATE [to chain or link together] *concatenare*, *unire insieme*, *collegare*.

CONCA'VE, adj. [hollow] *cóncavo*, *concaváto*.

Concáve, s. [hollowness] *cóncavo*, s. m. *la superficie interiore de corpi piegati in arco*; *concavità*, s. f.

A concave [in gunnery, the bore of a piece of ordnance] *il focone d'un arma a fuoco*.

CONCA'VENESS, } s. [the inside hol-
CONCA'VITY, } lowness of a round or roundish body] *concavita*, *profondità*, s. f.

To CONCE'AL [to keep close or secret] *nascondere*, celare, *occultare*, *tacere*, *tener secreto*, pret. *nascosi*.

To conceal one's grief, *celare il suo dolore*.

To conceal a secret, *tacere un segreto*.

CONCE'ALED, adj. *celato*, *nascosto*, *occultato*, *taciuto*.

CONCE'ALER, s. [he that conceals] *nasconditore*, *occultatore*, s. m. *occultatrice*, s. f.

Concealers [such who find out lands which are privately kept from the king by persons who have nothing to show for them] *così si chiamano coloro che scoprono beni stabili appartenenti al re, ma posseduti da chi non ha ragione di posséderli*.

CONCE'ALING, or CONCE'ALMENT, s. *nascondimento*, *celamente*, s. m. *il nascondere*.

To CONCE'DE [to grant, to yield, to condescend unto] *concedere*, *permettere*, *acconsentire*, *menar buono*.

CONCE'IT, s. [fancy] *concetto*, *pensiero*, *capriccio*, *scherzo*.

A witty conceit, *un concetto bello*, *una fantasia poetica*.

That's a pretty conceit, *è un bel pensiero*.

Conceit [opinion] *fantasía*, *opinione*, s. f. *parere*, *pensiero*, *sentimento*, s. m.

This is my conceit about it, *questo è il mio parere intorno a ciò*, *così l'intendo*.

He has put me out of conceit with it, *me ne ha fatto passar la voglia*.

I am out of conceit with it, *ne sono svogliato*, *me ne scappò la voglia*.

Idle conceits, *concetti vani*, *ghiribizzi*, *capricci*.

To CONCE'IT [to fancy] *immaginarsi*, *figurarsi*, *pensare*, *darsi a credere*.

To conceit a thing, *immaginarsi o figurarsi una cosa*.

They conceit it sovereign against diseases, *viene stimato un rimedio eccellente per ogni sorte di malattia*.

CONCE'ITED, adj. [affected] *affettato*, *mendicato*.

A conceited language, *un linguaggio affettato*, *una dicitura troppo studiata*.

Conceited of himself [proud, puffed up, opinionated] *vano*, *glorioso*, *pien di vento*, *vanaglorioso*.

He is very much conceited of himself, *egli è molto vano*, *egli presume molto di se*.

Conceited [fantastical] *fantastico*, *bisbetico*, *stravagante*, *ridicolo*, *impertinente*.

CONCE'ITEDLY, adv. *vanamente*, *follemente*, *ostinatamente*, *stravagantemente*, *pertinacemente*, *caparbiamente*, *bisbeticamente*.

CONCE'ITEDNESS, s. *affettazione*, s. f.

CONCE'ITLESS, adj. [stupid, without thought] *stupido*, *balordo*, *non atto a pensare*.

CONCE'IVABLE, adj. [that may be conceived] *che si può concepire*.

To CONCE'IVE [to admit into the womb] *concépere*, *concepire*.

To conceive [to imagine, to apprehend] *concepire*, *pensare*, *credere*, *darsi a credere*, *immaginarsi*, *figurarsi*, *comprendere*, *intendere*, pret. *compresi*, *intesi* pres. *concepisco*.

I cannot conceive it, *non posso concepirlo*, *non so comprenderlo*.

I conceived it to be quite another thing, *io m'immaginava che fosse tutt' altro*.

To conceive a jealousy [to entertain a jealousy] *farsi ombra*, *prender sospetto*, *pigliar gelosia*.

CONCE'IVED, adj. *concepito*, v. To conceive.

CONCE'IVING, s. *concepimento*, s. m. *concepigione*, s. f.

CONCE'NT, s. [a consort of voices or instruments] *concento*, s. m. *armonia*, s. f.

Concént [consistency] *fermezza*, *sodezza*.

To CONCE'NTRE [to meet in the same center] *concentrarsi*, *aver un medesimo centro*, *terminare*, *finire*.

All her cares did altogether concenter on her son, *suo figlio era l'unico oggetto delle sue cure*.

CONCE'NTRED, adj. *concentrato*.

CONCE'NTRICK, adj. [that has the same center] *concentrico*, *che ha il medesimo centro*.

CONCE'PT, s. [a set form, a term used in publick acts] *fórmula*, s. f. *maniera e forma usata negli atti pubblici*.

CONCE'PTACLE, s. [that in which any thing is contained; a vessel] *vaso*; *cosa che contiene cose*. *Non in uso*.

CONCE'PTIBLE, adj. [intelligible; capable to be understood] *intelligíbile*; *che si può concepire*; *atto ad esser concepito*.

CONCE'PTION, s. [the act of conceiving] *concezione*, s. f. *concepimento*, s. m. *il concepire*.

The conceptions of the mind, *i pensieri*, *le idee della mente*.

CONCE'PTIOUS, adj. [apt to conceive, pregnant] *atto a concepire*, *grávido*, *pregno*.

CONCE'PTIVE, adj. [capable to conceive] *capace di concepire*.

CONCE'RN, s. [affair, business] *affare*, *interesse*, *negozio che ci concerne*.

To mind one's own concerns, *badare a' fatti suoi*.

To settle one's own concerns, *regolare i suoi affari*, *metter ordine a' suoi negozi*.

To have a great concern for a thing, *interessarsi o pigliar parte in che che si sia*.

A thing of great concern, *una cosa di conseguenza o d'importanza*.

In all the concerns of human life, *in tutti gli avvenimenti della vita umana*.

To CONCE'RN [to belong to, to regard] *concernere*, *risguardare*, *appartenere*.

The public liberty concerns all the world,

World, *la libertà pubblica concerne ognuno.*

That does not concern me neither one way nor the other, *ciò non mi tocca in nessuna maniera*

The thing concerned me very much, *la cosa m'importava molto.*

My life and fortune are concerned, *si tratta della mia vita e de' miei beni.*

To concern [to trouble one's self] *impacciarsi, ingerirsi, intromettersi.*

I won't concern myself with that, *non voglio impacciarmi in ciò.*

It concerns you to do o, *vi debbe premere di far così.*

It concerns me as much as you, *m'importa quanto a voi.*

CONCE'RNED, adj. [interested] *interessato.*

The parties concerned, *le parti interessate.*

Concerned [troubled] *che è in pena, sconsolato.*

He seems very much concerned, *pare molto afflitto, o sconsolato.*

I am very much concerned for his afflictions, *mi pesa molto il sentirlo afflitto.*

What are you concerned? *che importa a voi?*

I will not be concerned with him, *non voglio impacciarmi con esso lui.*

He is concerned in the plot, *egli ha parte nella congiura.*

My heart is concerned for him, *sento nel core un vivo dolore per lui.*

He is not at all concerned at it, *non se ne cura punto.*

CONCE'RNING, prep. *concernente, sopra, circa, intorno.*

Concerning your affairs, *circa i vostri affari.*

CONCE'RNMENT, s. [importance] *importanza, conseguenza, s. f.*

A business of great concernment, *un affare di grande importanza o conseguenza.*

Concernment [interest] *interesse, s. m.*

'Tis a thing of great concernment to us, *questo è un negozio che ci debbe importar molto.*

He has a tender concernment for the publick good, *s'interessa molto pel ben pubblico, ha molto a cuore il ben pubblico.*

CO'NCERT, s. [communication of designs] *concerto, accordo, s. m.*

To act in concert with one, *andar di concerto con uno.*

Concert [a symphony, many performers playing to the same tune] *concerto, s. m. sinfonia, s. f.*

To CO'NCERT [to contrive together] *concertare, ordire, pensatamente, ordinare, risolvere, deliberare.* pref. *ordisco.*

CONCE'RTED, adj. *concertato, ordito, ordinato, risoluto, deliberato.*

CONCE'RTING, s. *il concertare.*

CONCE'SSION, s. [grant] *concessione, s. f. concedimento, s. m.*

By the king's concession, *per concessione del re.*

CONCH, s. *conca, s. f. spezie di pesce.*

To CONCI'LIATE [to reconcile, to make agree] *conciliare, unire, accordare.*

CONCI'LIATED, adj. *conciliato, unito, accordato.*

This single action conciliated to him the love of all good men, *con questa sola azione si cattivò l'amore di tutti gli uomini dabbene.*

CONCI'NNITY, s. [properness, aptness] *proprietà, eleganza, bellezza, concordanza, s. f.*

CONCI'SE, adj. [short, brief] *conciso, corto, succinto.*

A concise discourse, *un discorso conciso, o succinto.*

CONCI'SION, s. [a word used for circumcision] *circoncisione, s. f.*

CO'NCLAVE, s. [the place in the Vatican where the cardinals meet to choose a pope] *conclave, s. m. luogo in Roma dove si racchiúdono i cardinali a creare il pontefice.*

Conclave [the whole assembly of cardinals] *conclave, l'assemblea de' cardinali.*

A CO'NCLAVIST, s. [one who attends a cardinal during his abode in the conclave] *conclavista, s. m. persona che serve un cardinale durante il tempo del conclave.*

To CONCLU'DE [to make an end, to finish] *conchiúdere, conclúdere, venire alla conclusione, venire a capo, finire, terminare.* pret. *conchiusi, conclusi.* pref. *finisco.*

To conclude [to draw a consequence from something said before] *conchiudiere, cavar da quello che s'è detto la sua intenzione, inferire, significare,* pref. *inferisco.*

To conclude a discourse, *conchiudere o finire un discorso.*

To conclude a match, *conchiudere un matrimonio.*

What do you conclude from thence? *che volete inferire da ciò?*

To conclude [to make short] *per finirla, in poche parole, in fine, in conclusione.*

CONCLU'DED, adj. *conchiuso, concluso, finito, terminato, inferito.*

The business is concluded, *l'affare è conchiuso, la faccenda è finita.*

CONCLU'DING, s. *il conchiudere, conchiusione, s. f.*

CONCLU'DENCY, s. [consequence, regular proof] *conchiusione provata, conseguenza dimostrata.*

CONCLU'DENT, adj. [decisive] *conchiudente, decisivo, finale.*

CONCLU'SION, s. [end] *conchiusione, conclusione, s. f. fine, termine, s. m.*

Conclusion [consequence] *conclusione, conseguenza, s. f.*

From thence this conclusion may be made, *dal che si può concludere.*

The conclusion of a play, *la fine d'una commedia.*

To try conclusions, *arrischiare, mettere in rischio.*

In conclusion [to conclude] *in conclusione, finalmente, alla per fine.*

CONCLU'SIVE, adj. [last, which serves to conclude] *ultimo, che conchiude.*

To CONCOA'GULATE [to congeal one thing with another] *congelare una cosa per mezzo d'un altra.*

To CONCO'CT [to purify by heat] *purificare per via di caldo.*

To concoct [to digest] *concuocere. digerire, purificare.* pref. *digerisco.*

To concoct the meat in the stomach, *concuocere o digerire il cibo nello stomaro.*

CONCO'CTED, adj. *concotto, e digerito, purificato.*

A man of a perfect and concocted malice, *un uomo pien di malizia, un tristo.*

CONCO'CTION, s. [digestion] *concozione, digestione, s. f.*

CONCO'MITANCY, or CONCO'MITANCE, s. [the act of accompanying together with] *compagnia.*

CONCO'MITANT, adj. [accompanying] *congiunto, che accompagna.*

Concomitant, s. [companion] *compagno, compagnone.*

CO'NCORD, s. [agreement, union] *concordia, volontà, uniformità, pace, unione, s. f. accordo, s. m.*

Concord [in musick] *concento, concerto, s. m. armonia, s. f.*

To CO'NCORD [to agree together] *concordare, conformare, convenire, esser d'accordo, accordarsi.* pref. *convengo,* pret. *convenni.*

CONCO'RDANCE, s. [agreement] *concordanza, conformità, convenienza, s. f. accordo, s. m.*

Concordance [a general index of the words in the Bible] *concordanza, libro che contiene una tavola esatta delle parole della Bibbia.*

CONCORDANT, adj. [agreeing together] *concordante, che concorda, conforme, simile.*

To CONCOR'PORATE [to mix or mingle together in one body] *incorporare, mescolare e unire piu corpi, confondendoli insieme.*

CONCO'RPORATED, adj. *incorporato, mescolato, unito insieme.*

CONCORPORA'TION, s. [a mixing or tempering in one body] *incorporazione, s. f. incorporamento, s. m.*

CONCO'URSE, s. [a run or resort of a people to a place] *concorso, concorrimento, s. m. calca, moltitudine di gente concorsa.*

There was a great concourse of people, *vi fu un gran concorso di popolo.*

CONCRE'TE, adj. [concreted, grown together] *cresciuto insieme.*

Concrete [in philosophy, made of different principles] *misto.*

Concrete, s. [in logick, is any quality considered with its subject] *concreto.*

CONCRE'TED, adj. [congealed or clotted] *congelato, rappreso, quagliato.*

CONCRE'TION, s. [joining together] *concrezione, s. f. attaccamento, s. m.*

CONCU'BINAGE, s. [the keeping of a concubine] *concubinato, s. m. fornicazione, s. f.*

CO'NCUBINE, s. [an unlawful bedfellow] *una concubina.*

CONCU'BINARY, s. [that keeps a woman] *concubinario, s. m. che tiene la concubina.*

To CONCU'LCATE, [to stamp upon to

to tread under] *conculcare, tener sotto, abbossare, rintuzzare.*

CONCULCA'TION, s. [the act of stamping upon] *conculcamento*, s. m. *il conculcare.*

CONCU'PISCENCE, s. [vehement desire of enjoying any thing, lust] *concupiscenza, concupiscenzia, libidine*, s. f.

CONCU'PISCENT, adj. [libidinous, lecherous] *libidinoso, lussurioso.*

CONCU'PISCIBLE, adj. [that which desires earnestly or naturally] *concupiscibile, che nasce dalla concupiscenza.*

The concupiscible appetite, *l' appetito concupiscibile, quella parte sensitiva dell' anima che desidera oggetto che le piace.*

To CONCU'R [to run together, to conspire, to agree with one] *concorrere, andare insieme, convenire.*

God concurs with the second causes, *Iddio concorre colle cause seconde.*

CONCU'RRENCE, } s. [meeting] *con-*
CONCU'RRENCY, } *corso, concorrimento*, s. m.

Concurrence [agreement in judgment and opinion] *concorrenza, uniformità di parere.*

Concurrence [help] *assistenza, concorrenza*, s. f. *ajuto*, s. m.

God's concurrence with second causes, *la concorrenza di Dio colle cause seconde.*

I want your concurrence therein, *ho bisogno del vostro consenso, della vostra approvazione in questo.*

CONCU'RRENT, s. [rival, competitor] *un concorrente, un pretendente, un competitore, un rivale.*

CONCU'SSION, s. [a shaking or jumbling together] *concussione*, s. f.

Concussion [extortion] *concussione, quando alcuno in uffizio toglie alcuna cosa a' sudditi.*

To COND [to guide a ship in a right course] *guidare o governare un vascello.*

To CONDE'MN [to sentence] *condannare, condennare, sentenziare.*

To condemn one to die, *condannare uno alla morte.*

To condemn [to dislike, to disapprove] *condannare, biasimare, vituperare.*

To condemn one's conduct, *condannare o biasimare l' altrui condotta, disapprovarla.*

CONDE'MNABLE, adj. [which deserves to be condemned] *condannevole, condennevole, degno di condannaggione, biasimevole, degno di biasimo.*

CONDEMNA'TION, s. [sentence of death] *condennagione, condannagione, condannazione, condennazione*, s. f.

Condemnation [blame, disapprobation] *biasimo, vituperio*, s. m.

CONDE'MNED, adj. *condannato, condennato.*

CONDE'MNER, s. [a blamer, a censurer] *un che biasima, un che condanna, che critica.*

CONDE'MNING, s. *il condannare, condennagione.*

CONDE'NSABLE, adj. [that which is capable of condensation] *atto ad esser condensato.*

To CONDE'NSATE [to thicken] *condensare, far denso, spessire, spessare*, pref. *spessisco.*

To condensate [to grow thick] *condensarsi, farsi denso, spessirsi, spessarsi.*

CONDE'NSATE, adj. *condensato, spessito, spessato.*

CONDE'NSATION, s. [thickening] *condensamento*, s. m. *il condensare.*

To CONDE'NSE, v. a. [to make any body more thick, close, and weighty] render *qualsisia materia più densa, più compatta, e più pesante, condensare.*

To condense, v. n. [to grow close and weighty] *condensarsi; divenir più compatto e più grave.*

CO'NDERS, s. [persons who stand upon a high place near the sea coast, at the time of herring fishing, to make signs with houghs in their hands which way the shoal passes] *persone che essendo appostate sopra un' altezza al lido del mare, fanno segno ai pescatori mostrando loro il luogo per dove le aringhe passano.*

To CONDESCE'ND [to comply, to submit, to yield to] *condescendere, condiscendere, concorrere in opinione, secondare, inclinare, acconsentire, conformarsi, uniformarsi all' altrui volontà.*

I'll never condescend to it, *non vi condescenderò mai, non approverò mai tal cosa.*

CONDESCE'NDENCE } s. [compli-
CONDESCE'NSION, } ance] *condescendenza, condiscendenza, compiacenza*, s. f.

CONDI'GN, adj. [worthy, according to merit] *condegno, degno meritato.*

To be brought to condign punishment, *soffrire un meritato gastigo.*

CONDI'MENT, s. [sauce, seasoning] *condimento*, s. m. *conditura*, s. f. *il condire.*

CONDISCI'PLE, s. [school fellow, fellow-student] *condiscepolo*, s. m. *compagno nell' imparare.*

To CONDI'TE [to season] *condire, perfezzionar le vivande co' condimenti*, pref. *condisco.*

CONDI'TION, s. [state] *condizione*, s. f. *stato, essere, affare*, s. m.

Whatever condition you may be in, *in qualunque condizione o stato voi siate.*

Condition [rank, quality] *condizione, qualità*, s. f. *grado*, s. m.

Condition [covenant] *condizione, patto, limitazione, partito.*

Upon condition that—*con questo condizione che— con patto che—*

I grant it you upon condition that your perform your part, *ve lo concedo con condizione che voi facciate la vostra parte, il vostro dovere.*

Condition [nature, disposition] *natura, disposizione, umore.*

He is in a weak condition, *egli è d'una natura debole o inferma.*

To be in a dying condition, *stare per morire.*

He is a good condition'd young man, *egli è un giovane di buona tempra, di buona pasta.*

Where you in my condition, *se voi foste nel luogo mio.*

To CONDI'TION [to make an agreement or bargain with one] *pattuire, convenire con uno.*

CONDI'TIONAL, adj. [implying conditions or terms] *condizionale, condizionato, limitato.*

A conditional proffer, *un' offerta condizionale.*

A conditional licence, *un licenza condizionata.*

CONDI'TIONALLY, adv. *condizionalmente, con condizione, con patto.*

CONDI'TIONED, adj. [endued with certain humours and qualities] *condizionato.*

Goods well conditioned, *robe ben condizionate.*

Good or fair conditioned, *di buona natura di buon umore, di buona pasta.*

He is a good condition'd man, *egli è una buona pasta d' uomo.*

Ill-conditioned, *di cattiva natura, di cattivo umore.*

To CONDO'LE with one [to express some sorrow to one for some misfortune of his] *condolersi con uno, dolersi delle sue sventure.*

I CONDO'LED with him for the death of his father, *mi condolsi con lui, passai seco un ufficio di condoglienza per la morte di suo padre.*

CO'NDOLENCE, s. *condoglienza*, s. f.

A compliment of condolence, *un ufficio di condoglienza.*

CONDO'LER, s. *quello o quella che si condole.*

CONDO'LING, s. *il condolersi.*

To CONDU'CE [to avail, to help, to contribute to] *contribuire, servire, esser utile.*

Do you think that will any ways conduce to your happiness? *credete che ciò contribuirà in alcun modo alla felicità vostra?*

CONDU'CIBLE, } adj. [profitable,
CONDU'CIVE, } good, advantagious] *utile, profittevole, fruttuoso, vantaggioso.*

CO'NDUCT, s. [management] *condotta, direzione, scorta guida, capitaneria*, s. f.

To be under one's conduct, *esser sotto la condotta o direzione d' alcuno.*

To have the conduct of an army, *aver la condotta o il comando d' un esercito.*

Conduct [behaviour] *condotta, procedere, modo di procedere.*

His conduct was very much blamed, *la sua condotta fu molto biasimata.*

A safe conduct, *uno salvocondotto.*

To CONDU'CT [to bring along] *condurre, menare, guidare, essere scorta*, pres. *conduco*, pret. *condussi.*

I conducted him here, *l'ho condotto qui.*

CONDU'CTED, adj. *condotto, menato, guidato.*

CONDU'CTOR, s. [leader, guide] *conduttore, conducitore, guida, maestro*, s. m.

CONDU'CTING, s. *conducimento*, s. m. *il condurre.*

I gave him so much for conducting me here, *gli hò datoun tanto per avermi condotto quà.*

CONDU'CTRESS, s. [she leader] *conducitrice*, s. f.

CO'NDUIT, s. [a pipe for conveying water] *condotto, aquedotto*, s. m.

CONE, s. [a geometrical solid in the form of a sugar-loaf] *cono*, s. m. *corpo solido, la cue base è un cerchio, e che termina in una punta.*

To CONFA'BULATE [to talk together] *confabulare, ragionare, discorrere insieme.*

CONFABULA'TION, s. [familiar discoursing together] *colloquio, discorso, ragionamento*, s. m.

CONFE'CTION, s. [a medicinal composition of gums, powders, syrups, &c. made up into one substance] *confezione*, s. f. *composizione medicinale.*

CONFE'CTIONER, s. [maker or seller of comfits or sweet-meats] *colui che fa o vende i confetti.*

CONFECT, s. [fruit crusted over with dry sugar] *confetto*, s. m.

CONFE'CTION, s. [preparation of fruit with sugar; sweet-meat] *confettura; frutti lavorati collo zúcchero; confetti*, s. m. plur.

Confection [composition, mixture] *un composto, un misto.*

CONFE'CTIONER, s. [one whose trade is to make sweet-meats] *confetturiére.*

CONFE'DERACY, s. [alliance] *confederazione, lega*, s. f. *confederamento*, s. m.

Confederacy [in law, combination] *congiura, cospirazione*, s. f.

CONFE'DERATE, adj. *confederato, che è in confederazione.*

To be confederate in a crime, *esser complice d'un delitto.*

The confederates, s. [the allies] *i confederati, i collegati.*

To CONFE'DERATE [to unite into a confederacy] *confederarsi, collegarsi, unirsi in confederazione o in lega.*

To confederate [to combine, to plot together] *congiurare, conspirare, tramare.*

CONFEDERA'TION, s. [league, alliance] *lega, confederazione.*

To CONFE'R [to compare] *comparare, agguagliare, paragonare, mettere in paragone, assimigliare.*

To confer [to bestow] *conferire, dare*, pres. *conferisco.*

To confer a living upon one, *conferire un benefizio ad uno.*

To confer [to talk or discourse together] *conferire, parlare, discorrere con alcuno*, pret. *discorsi.*

To confer notes [to advise together] *abboccarsi per deliberare qualche cosa, unirsi in consiglio.*

CO'NFERENCE, s. [a discourse held between several persons about particular affairs] *conferenza*, s. f. *discorso, ragionamento, favellamento*, s. m.

CONFE'RRED, adj. *comparato, agguagliato, conferito*, v. To confer.

To CONFE'SS [to acknowledge, to own] *confessare, affermare, concedere*, pret. *concessi.*

To confess [to hear one's confession] *confessare, stare a udire i peccati d'alcuno.*

To confess, verb neut. *confessarsi, dire al sacerdote i suoi falli perchè ne dia l'assoluzione.*

To go to confess, *andare a confessarsi.*

CONFE'SSED, adj. *confessato, affermato.*

It is confessed that, *ognuno sa, ognuno confessa.*

CONFE'SSEDLY, adv. *certamente, indubitatamente.*

CONFE'SSING, s. *il confessare, confessione, affermazione*, s. f.

CONFE'SSION, s. [acknowledgment] *confessione, affermazione*, s. f.

To make a general confession, *fare una confessione generale.*

The auricular confession, *la confessione auricolare.*

CONFESSION CHAIR, } s. [the chair CONFE'SSIONAL, } wherein the priest sits to hear confession] *confessionario, confessionale*, s. m.

CONFE'SSOR, [a priest who hears the confession of penitents and gives them absolution] *confessore*, s. m. *sacerdote, che ascolta i peccati altrui per assolverli.*

Confessor [a person who has adhered to the faith, notwithstanding cruel persecutions and sufferings upon that account] *confessore, ciascuno che abbia confessata la legge di Cristo.*

CONFE'ST, adj. [open; known; not concealed] *chiaro, aperto, noto, non nascosto.*

CO'NFIDANT, s. [a person trusted with private affairs] *confidente; persona, a cui sono confidati affari privati.*

To CONFI'DE [to trust in, to rely upon] *confidare, aver fiducia, fidarsi.*

You may confide in me, *voi potete confidare in me, voi potete far capitale di me.*

CO'NFIDENCE, s. [trust] *confidenza, confidanza, fiducia*, s. f.

I have an intire confidence in him, *ho gran confidenza in lui.*

To commit in confidence a thing to a friend, *confidare, che che si sia ad un amico.*

Confidence [boldness] *audacia, baldanza, arditezza, temerità, arditanza, sfacciataggine, prosunzione, arroganza*, s. f.

CO'NFIDENT, adj. [sure, positive] *sicuro, certo.*

I am confident of the contrary, *sono sicuro del contrario.*

Confident [bold, daring, presumptuous] *ardito, baldanzoso, temerario, sfacciato, prosuntuoso, arrogante.*

A Confident, s. [a trusty friend] *un confidente, un amico*, s. m.

I am the confident of his most secret thoughts, *io sono il depositario de' suoi più occulti pensieri.*

CO'NFIDENTLY, adv. *confidentemente, amichevolmente, sicuramente.*

Confidently [boldly] *arditamente, temerarimente, arrogantemente, sfacciamente, prosontuosamente.*

It is confidently reported, *si dice per certo.*

CONFIGURA'TION, s. [parts adapted to each other] *configurazione*, s. f. *la forma delle diverse parti addattate l'una all' altra.*

A configuration of stars [the conjunction or mutual aspects of stars] *una costellazione, la costituzione de' pianeti, o li aspetti di stelle tra di loro.*

CONFI'NE, s. [common boundary, border, edge] *confine, limite, termine*, s. m. *siepe*, s. f.

To CONFI'NE [to keep in] *reprímere, moderare, ritenere, frenare, raffrenare, rintuzzare, domare*, pres. *ritengo*, pret. *ritenni.*

To confine [to imprison] *imprigionare, mettere in prigione.*

To confine [to banish] *confinare, rilegare, mandare in esilio, sbandire.*

To confine [to border upon] *confinare, esser contiguo, conterminare.*

To confine a wandering lust, *reprimere o frenare una fregolata concupiscenza.*

To confine a man to prison, *imprigionare uno, metterlo in prigione.*

He confined himself to one meal a day, *si ridusse ad un pasto per giorno.*

CONFI'NED, adj. *represso, moderato, confinato*, v. To confine.

To be confined to one room, *non aver che una camera.*

CONFI'NELESS, adj. [boundless, unlimited] *sterminato, non limitato, senza confini.*

CONFI'NEMENT, s. [restraint] *costrignimento*, s. m.

Confinement [prison] *prigione, prigionia*, s. f.

Confinement [slavery] *soggezione, e suggezione, servitù, schiavitù*, s. f.

Confinement [exile] *esilio, bando*, s. m.

CONFI'NER, s. [borderer; one that lives upon confines] *limitrofo; uno che abita alle confine.*

Confiner, [near neighbour] *un vicino, uno che ti abita molto vicino.*

Confiner, [one which touches upon two different regions] *che sta alle confine e sull' orlo di due regioni.*

CONFINES, s. [borders] *confini, termini, limiti.*

Being in the confines of death, *essendo al punto della morte, avendo un piede nella fossa.*

To CONFI'RM [to ratify, to make good] *confermare, mantenere, tener fermo, ratificare*, pres. *mantegno*, pret. *mantenni.*

To confirm one [to give him the confirmation] *confermare uno, amministrargli la confermazione.*

Confirmation, s. [ratification] *confermazione, ratificazione*, s. f. *confermamento*, s. m.

Confirmation [a holy rite or ceremony in the church] *la confermazione, uno de' sette sagramenti della chiesa Romana.*

CONFI'RMED, adj. *confermato, ratificato.*

CONFI'RMING, s. *confermagione*, s. f. *confermamento*, s. m.

To CO'NFISCATE [to seize upon and take away goods, as forfeited to the king's exchequer] *confiscare, applicare al fisco le facoltà de' condannati.*

CO'NFISCATED

Co'nfiscated, adj. *confiscato.*

Confisca'tion, s. *confiscazione*, s. f. *il confiscare.*

Co'nfiture, s. [sweat-meat; confection] *confetture*, s. f. pl. *confetti*, s. m. pl.

To Confi'x [to fix down] *confircare, ficcare, giù.*

Confla'grant, adj. [involved in a general fire] *incendiato, avviluppato in un grande incendio.*

Conflagra'tion, s. [general burning, great fire] *incendio*, s. m.

Co'nflict, s. [fight, combat] *conflitto, combattimento*, s. m.

Co'nfluence, s. [concourse, resort] *concorso, affluenza di popolo, moltitudine, calca, folla di gente.*

Co'nform, adv. *in conformità, conforme.*

Conform to that, *in conformità di cio.*

To Confo'rm, [to make like to, to suit] *conformare, far conforme, concordare.*

To conform, verb neut. [to conform one's self] *conformarsi, uniformarsi.*

Confo'rmable, adj. [agreeable, suitable] *conforme, di simil forma, somigliante, uniformante.*

Their doctrine is not conformable to that of the Fathers, *la loro dottrina non è uniforme a quella de' Padri.*

Co'nformably, adv. *conforme, in conformità.*

Conforma'tion, s. [the form of things as relating to each other] *conformità, somiglianza, di forma, la forma delle cose in quanto corisponde colla forma d' altre cose.*

Conformation [the act of producing suitableness or conformity] *conformità, il produrre addattezza di cosa con cosa.*

Confo'rmed, adj. *conformato.*

Confo'rming, s. *il conformare, o il conformarsi.*

Conf'ormist, s. [one that conforms to any establishment] *conformista*, s. m. *che si conforma al governo ed alle regole prescritte.*

Confo'rmity, s. [compliance] *conformità, simiglianza*, s. f.

In conformity, *conforme, in conformità.*

To Confo'und [to mix together] *confondere, mescolare insieme senza distinzione e senza ordine.* pret. *confusi.*

To confound [to put out of order] *confondere, disordinare, mettere in disordine, sconvolgere.* pret. *sconvolsi.*

To confound [to put out of countenance] *confondere, far restar confuso, mortificare, fare arrossire.*

To confound [to destroy, to waste] *confondere, sconfondere, rovinare, distruggere, mandare a male.* pret. *distrussi.*

To confound one's estate [to spend it prodigally] *mandare a male il suo avere, spenderlo, scialacquarlo.*

Confo'unded, adj. *confuso*, *v.* To confound.

To be confounded, *essere o restar confuso.*

A confounded business, *un maledetto affare.*

Confo'undedly, adv. *malissimamente, terribilmente, orribilmente.*

He swears confoundedly, *giura terribilmente, bestemmia orribilmente.*

Confo'unding, s. *confondimento*, s. m. *il confondere.*

Confrate'rnity, s. [brotherhood or society united together, chiefly upon a religious account] *confraternità*, s. f. *adunanza di persone per opere spirituali.*

Confrica'tion, s. [the act of rubbing against any thing] *fregagione*, s. f. *l' atto del fregare una cosa con un' altra.*

To Confro'nt [to bring face to face, to compare] *confrontare, riscontrare paragonare cosa con cosa.*

Confro'nted, adj. *confrontato, riscontrato, paragonato.*

Confro'nting, s. *il confrontare, riscontro*, s. m.

Confu'sed, adj. [mixt together] *confuso, mescolato, imbrogliato.*

Confused [perplexed] *confuso, perplesso, inviluppato, intrigato, oscuro.*

A confused noise of people, *un confuso strepito di gente.*

A confused style, *uno stile oscuro, uno stile imbrogliato.*

Confu'sedly, adv. *confusamente, disordinatamente, senz' ordine.*

Confu'sion, s. [disorder] *confusione*, s. f. *disordine, scompiglio, perturbamento*, s. m.

Confusion [shame] *confusione, vergogna, perplessità*, s. f.

To bring to confusion, *confondere far restar confuso.*

Confu'table, adj. [possible to be disproved] *che si può confutare.*

Confu'tation, s. [a disproving that which was spoken] *confutazione*, s. f. *confutamento*, s. m.

To Confu'te [to disprove and overthow the reasons and arguments of one's adversary] *confutare, convincere, riprovare*, pret. *convinsi.*

To confute an opinion, *confutare un' opinione.*

To confute a slander, *giustifiarsi una calunnia.*

Confu'ted, adj. *confutato, convinto, riprovato.*

Confu'ting, s. *confutazione*, s. f. *confutamento*, s. m.

Co'nge, s. [leave, licence, permission] *licenza, permissione*, s. f. *congedo*, s. m. *riverenza*, s. f. *saluto*, s. m.

To Conge [to take leave] *congedarsi, accomiatarsi.* Shakesp.

Co'nge d' Eli're [the King's permission to a dean and chapter, in time of vacation to chuse a bishop] *permissione che il Re d' Inghilterra accorda in tempo di sede vacante a un decano e al capitalo di elegger un vescovo.*

Congea'lment, s. [the clot formed by congelation] *grumosità, la cosa congelata.*

To Conge'al, [to freeze] *congelare.*

To congeal, verb neut. *congelarsi, rappigliarsi.*

Conge'aled, adj. *congelato, rappreso.*

Conge'aling, s. *congelamento*, s. m. *congelazione*, s. f.

Congela'tion, s. [freezing] *rongelazione*, s. f. *congelamento*, s. m.

Conge'ner, } adj. [of the Conge'nerous, } same kind] *del medesimo genere, della medesima spezie.*

Conge'nial, adj. [partaking of the same genius; cognate] *che partecipa dello stesso genio.*

Conge'niality, } s. [cognaConge'nialness, } tion of mind] *somiglianza di genio.*

Co'nger, or Conger-E'el, s. [a sort of fish] s. m. *sorta di pesce di mare simile all' anguilla.*

Conge'ries, s. [heap, hoard] *congerie, massa*, s. f. *adunamento*, s. m.

To Conge'st [to heap, to gather together] *amassare, ammonticellare, accumulare, abbiccare.*

Conge'stion, s. [a heaping or gathering together] *bica, congerie, massa, stipa*, s. f. *mucchio, fascio*, s. m.

Congestion [a collection of matter as in abscesses] *ammassamento di materia, come in un assesso o tumore.*

Co'ngiary, s. [a gift distributed to the Roman people or soldiery] *congiario*, s. m. *Dono che veniva distribuito agli antichi soldati o popolo Romano.*

To Congla'ciate [to freeze] *gelarsi, congelarsi.*

Conglatia'tion, s. [act of changing into ice] *congelazione, agghiacciamento.*

To Co'nglobate [to gather into a hard firm ball] *raccogliere a mo' di palla soda e dura.*

Conglobate, adj. [moulded into a firm ball] *raccolto a mo' di palla soda e dura.*

Congloba'tion, s. [a round body] *corpo rotondo, forma di palla.*

To Co'nglobe, v. n. [to coalesce into a round mass] *unirsi in forma rotonda, a mo' di globo.*

To conglobe, v. a. [to gather into a round mass] *unire parti in forma rotonda, a mo' di globo.*

To Con'glu'tinate [to glue, knit, join together] *conglutinare, unire, attaccare*, pref. *unisco.*

To conglutinate, verb neut. *conglutinarsi unirsi, attaccarsi.*

Conglutina'tion, s. [the act of fastening together with glue, or any other glutinous substance] *conglutinazione*, s. f.

To Congra'tulate [to rejoice for some good fortune befallen] *congratulare, congratularsi, rallegrarsi.*

I come to congratulate you upon your marriage, *vengo a congratularmi con esso voi del vostro matrimonio.*

Congra'tultaed, adj. *congratulato.*

Congratula'tion, s. *congratulazione*, s. f. *il congratularsi.*

To Congre'et, to salute reciprocally] *salutarsi reciprocamente.*

To Co'ngregate [to assemble, to gather together] *congregare, raunare, adunare, unire insieme.*

Co'ngregate, adj. *congregato, raccolto, compatto.*

CONGREGA'TION, s. [an assembly or society of people, but more especially for divine service] *congregazione*, s. f.

CO'NGRESS, s. [meeting] *congresso, abboccamento*, s. m. *conferenza*, s. f.

Congress [engagement, fight] *combattimento*, s. m. *battaglia*, s. f.

CO'NGRUENCE, s. [conformity, suitableness] *congruenza, convenienza, conformità*, s. f.

CO'NGRUENT, adj. [agreeable, suitable] *congruente, conveniente, conforme.*

CONGRU'ITY, s. [conformity, agreeableness] *congruenza, convenienza*, s. f.

CO'NGRUOUS, adj. [convenient, meet] *congruo, convenevole.*

CONI'CAL, } adj. belonging to the CO'NICK, } figure of a Cone] *conico, che ha figura di cono.*

To CONJE'CT, [to guess, to conjecture] *conghietturare, congetturare, giudicar per congettura. Non in uso.*

CONJE'CTOR, s. [guesser, conjecturer] *uno che conghiettura, colui che giudica per conghiettura.*

CONJE'CTURAL, adj. [that which is only grounded upon supposition or probability] *conghietturale, di conghiettura.*

Physick is a very conjectural science, *la medicina è una scienza molto conghietturale.*

CONJE'CTURALLY, adv. *per conghiettura.*

CONJE'CTURE, s. [guess, probable opininion] *conghiettura, congettura, conjettura*, s. f. *indizio di cose fondate su qualche apparente ragione.*

A true or false conjecture, *una conghiettura vera o falsa.*

To go upon conjectures, *fondarsi sopra conghietture.*

To CONJE'CTURE [to judge at random, to guess] *conghietturare, far conghietture indovinare.*

To conjecture one thing from another, *conghietturare una cosa da un altra.*

What do you conjecture from thence? *che volete conghietturare da cio?*

CONJE'CTURED, adj. *conghietturato.*

CONJE'CTURER, s. *conghietturatore*, s. m. *che conghiettura.*

CONJE'CTURING, s. [guessing] *il conghietturare, conghiettura*, s. f.

To CONJOBBLE [to concert] *concertare insieme.*

To CONJOI'N [to joint or put together] *congiugnere, congiungere, mettere e attaccare insieme.* pref. *congiungo.* pret. *congiunsi.*

To conjóin, v. n. [to league, to unite] *collegarsi, unirsi in lega far lega.*

CONJO'INED, or CONJO'INT, adj. [joined together] *congiunto, unito, attaccato insieme.*

CONJO'INTLY, adv. [in union, together] *congiuntamente, unitamente, insieme.*

CO'NJUGAL, adj. [belonging to a married couple] *conjugale, congiugale, maritale, matrimoniale.*

To CO'NJUGATE a verb, [to form or vary it, according to its several moods, tenses, and persons] *congiugare un verbo.*

CO'NJUGATE, adj. *congiugato.*

CONJUGA'TING, s. *il congiugare.*

CONJUGA'TION, s. [a term in grammar] *congiugazione*, s. f. *la maniera di congiugare.*

CONJU'NCT, adj. [conjoint; united] *congiunto, unito.*

CONJU'NCTION, s. [union] *congiunzione, unione*, s. f. *congiungimento*, s. m.

Conjunction [a term in grammar] *congiunzione, termine gramaticale.*

COJU'NCTIVE, adj. [that serves to join] *congiuntivo, che congiugne.*

The conjunctive or subjunctive mood of a verb, *il modo congiuntivo o subgiuntivo d' un verbo.*

CONJU'NCTRY, adv. *congiuntamente, unitamente.*

CONJU'NCTURE, s. [the state and circumstance of affairs, *congiuntura, occasione*, s. f. *caso, stato*, s. m.

In this conjuncture of affairs, *nella presente congiuntura, o nella stato nel quale si trovan le cose.*

CONJURA'TION, s. [plot, conspiracy] *congiura, cospirazione, congiurazione*, s. f. *unione di piu contro allo stato o persona di chi domina.*

Conjuration [a personal dealing with the devil or evil spirits] *incanto, incantesimo, scongiuro*, s. m.

To CO'NJURE [earnestly intreat] *scongiurare, strettamente pregare.*

To cónjure [to plot together] *congiurare, cospirare.*

To conjure [to raise or lay spirits] *congiurare, scongiurare, costrignere, e violentare i demoni.*

To conjure as priests do, *esorcizzare.*

CO'NJURED, adj. *scongiurato, v.* To conjure.

CONJU'REMENT, s. [serious injunction] *scongiuro, caldo piego, instanza grande.*

CO'NJURER, s. *scongiuratore, stregone, maliardo, mago*, s. m.

CONJU'RING, s. *stregonneccio, ammaliamento, affatturamento*, s. m. *stregoneria*, s. f.

A conjuring up spirits, *scongiuramento di spiriti.*

To CONN [to learn or get without book] *ricordarsi o imparare a mente.*

To conn one's lesson, *ricordarsi della sua lezione, imparare la sua lezione a mente, studiare la lezione.*

To conn thanks, *ringraziare altrui, rendergli grazie.*

CONNA'TE, adj. [born together with a person] *innato, insieme nato, naturale.*

CONNA'TURAL, adj. [that is natural to several things with others] *connaturale, di somigliante e proporzionata natura.*

CONNE'CTED, adj. *connesso, congiunto, attaccato insieme.*

To CONNE'CT [to knit, to join, to fasten together] *connettere, attaccare, congiugnere, unire insieme*, pret. *connessi, congiunsi.* pref. *unisco.*

CONNED, adj. [from to con] *studiato, imprato a mente.*

To CONNE'X [to join or link together] *connéttere, unire, congiúngere insieme.*

CONNE'XION, s. [dependency of one thing upon another] *connessione, somiglianza*, s. f. *congiugnemento, attaccamento*, s. m.

There's no manner of connexion, *non v' è alcuna connessione.*

CONNE'XITY, s. [that by which one thing is joined to another] *connessità congiungimento.*

CONNE'XIVE, adj. [having the force of connexion] *che puo connettere, che unisce.*

CONNIVA'NCE, s. [winking at] *conniuenza, dissimulazione*, s. f.

To CONNI'VE [to wink at, to take no notice of] *dissimulare, tollerare, chiuder gli occhi, usar, connivenza.*

CONNIVED AT, adj. *dissimulato, tollerato.*

CONNI'VING, s. *il dissimulare il tollerare, connivenza.*

CONNOISE'UR, s. [judge, critick] *buon giudice o buon critico in fatto di lettere, un uomo di gusto raffinatto.* Swift.

CONNU'BIAL, adj. [conjugal *congiugale, maritale.*

To CO'NQUASSATE, [to shake, to agitate] *scuoter forte, agitar con forza, sconquassare, crollare.*

To CONQUER [to bring under, to subdue] *conquistare, acquistare, vincere, domare, soggiogare, rituzzare.* pret. *vinsi.*

To conquer one's passions, *rintuzzare o domare le sue passioni.*

CO'NQUERED, adj. *conquistato, acquistato, vinto, domato, soggiogato, rintuzzato.*

CO'NQUERING, s. *conquista*, s. f. *conquisto*, s. m.

CO'NQUEROR, s. *conquistatore, vincitore*, s. m.

Conqueror [one that subdues and ruins countries] *uno che conquista e rovina li altrui paesi, conquistatore*, s. m.

CO'NQUEST, s. [victory, the thing conquered] *conquista, vittoria*, s. f. *conquesto*, s. m.

There's no conquest like that of our selves, *la piu grande vittoria è di vincer noi stessi.*

CONSANGUI'NEOUS, adj. [near of kin; related by birth] *consanguíneo, parente, dello stesso sangue, della stessa famiglia.*

CONSANGUINI'TY, s. [the relation between persons descended from the same family] *consanguinità, parentela*, s. f.

CO'NSCIENCE, s. [the opinion or judgment which the rational soul passes upon all her actions] *coscienza, constienza*, s. f. *cognizione abituale de principi degli atti morali.*

He makes no conscience of his word, *non ha scrupola di mancare alla promessa.*

To discharge one's conscience, *operare secondo i dettami della coscienza.*

In conscience, *in coscienza.*

Tender consciences, *li scrupolosi, che si fanno scrupolo d' ogni minima cosa.*

CO'NSCIENCED, adj. *ex.* tender conscienced, *scrupoloso.*

CONSCIE'N-

CONSCIE'NTIOUS, adj. [that has a good conſcience] *coſcienzioſe, di buona coſcienza, giuſto ragionevole.*

CONSCIE'NTIOUSLY, adv. *in buona coſcienza, giuſtamente, ragionevolmente.*

CONSCIE'NTIOUSNESS, s. *buona coſcienza.*

CO'NSCIONABLE, adj. [equitable, reaſonable] *ragionevole, giuſto, diſcreto.*

CO'NSCIONABLENESS, s. [juſtice] *giuſtizia, equità*, s. f.

CO'NSCIONABLY, adv. *ragionevolmente, giuſtamente, diſcretamente.*

CO'NSCIOUS, adj [inwardly guilty, privy to one's ſelf of an error] *complice, conſapevole, ſapevole, conſapiente.*

I am conſcious of it, *lo ſo molto bene.*

To be conſcious of one's guilt, *eſſer conſapiente del ſuo delitto, confeſſare il ſuo delitto.*

He made me conſcious of the deſign, *mi fece conſapevole del diſegno.*

CO'NSCIOUSLY, adv. [with knowledge of one's own actions] *ſcientemente.*

CO'NSCIOUSNESS, s. *conoſcenza interiore ch' abbiamo d'una coſa.*

CO'NSCRIPT, adj. [a term uſed in ſpeaking of the Roman Senators who were called *patres conſcripti*] *coſcritto, titolo degli antichi ſenatori Romani, che chiamavanſi Padri coſcritti.*

To CO'NSECRATE [to dedicate, to devote] *conſecrare, e conſegrare, dedicare.*

To conſecrate [to pronounce the ſacramental words] *conſecrare, pronunciare le parole del ſagramento.*

To conſecrate [or offer a thing to one] *conſacrare, offrire, o dedicare che che ſi ſia ad alcuno.*

To conſecrate a church, *conſecrare o benedire una chieſa.*

To conſecrate a biſhop, *conſecrare un veſcovo.*

To conſecrate the bread and wine in the euchariſt, *conſecrare il pane ed il vino nel ſagramento dell' altare.*

To conſecrate a man's memory to poſterity, *immortalizzare l' altrui nome, renderlo immortale, perpetuarlo.*

CO'NSECRATE, } adj. *conſecrato,*
CO'NSECRA'TED, } *e conſacrato, dedicato.*

CONSECRA'TER, s. [one that performs the rites by which any thing is devoted to ſacred purpoſes] *colui che conſagra, che fa l' officio di conſagrare.*

CONSECRA'TION, s. *conſecrazione, e conſacrazione*, s. f. *il conſecrare.*

The conſecration of a church, *la conſecrazione d'una chieſa.*

The conſecration of a biſhop, *la conſacrazione d'un veſcovo.*

CO'NSECTARY, s. [a conſequence or deduction from a foregoing argument or propoſition] *conſeguenza*, s. f. *verità che riſulita d'un' altra che è ſtata provata.*

CONSE'CTARY, adj. [conſequent, conſequential] *che ne viene in conſeguenza.*

CONSECU'TION, s. [train of conſequences; chain of deductions] *conſeguenza, ſeguito di conſeguenze.*

Conſecution, [ſucceſſion] *ſeguito, ſucceſſione.*

CONSE'CUTIVE, adj. [following, ſucceeding, but is always ſaid of things, not of perſons] *conſecutivo, che ſiegue immediatamente, ma diceſi di coſe, e non di perſone.*

CONSE'NT, s. [approbation] *conſenſo, conſentimento*, s. m. *approbazione*, s. f.

To give a man one's conſent, *dare il ſuo conſenſo ad uno, acconſentire a qualche domanda.*

Silence gives conſent, *chi tace acconſente.*

To CONSENT to [to accord or agree] *conſentire, acconſentire, concorrere, condeſcendere nell' altrui opinione*, pret. *condeceſi.*

I conſent to it, *vi conſento.*

CONSENTA'NEOUS, adj. [agreeable, ſuitable] *conforme, conformevole, proporzionale, proporzionato.*

This is not conſentaneous to the word of God, *cio non è in alcun modo conforme alla parola di Dio.*

CONSENTA'NEOUSLY, adv. [agreeably; conſiſtently; ſuitably] *conformente, proporzionatamente, concordemente.*

CONSE'NTED TO, adj. *conſentito, acconſentito, concorſo, condeſceſo.*

CONSE'NTING, adj. *conſcenziente, che conſente.*

CONSE'NTING, s. *conſentimento, conſenſo*, s. m. *il conſentire.*

CO'NSEQUENCE, s. [an orderly following concluſion] *conſeguenza*, s. f. *la coſa, che conſeguita.*

Conſequence [importance, moment] *conſeguenza, importanza*, s. f. *momento, peſo*, s. f.

To draw a conſequence, *tirare una conſeguenza.*

A thing of no conſequence, *una coſa di poco momento.*

A thing of dangerous conſequence, *coſa di pericoloſa conſeguenza.*

By conſequence, *in conſeguenza, per conſeguenza, conſeguentemente.*

CO'NSEQUENT, s. [that which follows upon ſomething] *conſeguenza*, s. f.

Conſequent, adj. [enſuing, following] *conſeguente, che conſegue.*

CO'NSEQUENTLY, adv. *conſeguentemente, per conſeguenza, in conſeguenza.*

CONSE'RVABLE, adj. [that may be kept] *conſervabile, atto a conſervarſi.*

CONSERVA'TION, s. [a keeping or preſerving] *conſervazione, conſervagione*, s. f. *conſervamento*, s. m.

CONSERVA'TOR, s. [a keeper or defender] *conſervatore, che conſerva, difenſore.*

CONSE'RVATORY, s. [a place to keep or lay things up] *conſerva*, s. f. *luogo da conſervare e preſervare alcune coſe.*

Conſervatory, adj. [having a preſervative quality] *che ha facoltà di conſervare, che puo conſervare.*

CONSE'RVE, s. [a compoſition of flowers, roots, or herbs kept together with ſugar] *conſerva*, s. f. *frutti, fiori, erbe, e altre coſe confettate nel zucchero.*

Conſerve of roſes, *conſerva di roſe.*

To CONSE'RVE [to preſerve, to keep] *conſervare, preſervare, ſalvare, mantenere, diſendere.* preſ. *mantengo.* pret. *mantennni, diſeſi.*

To conſerve fruit, *confettare frutti.*

Apt or good to conſerve, *conſervativo.*

CONSE'RVED, adj. *conſervato, preſervato, ſalvato, mantenuto, diſeſo, conſettato.*

CONSE'RVER, s. *conſervatore*, s. m. *conſervatrice*, s. f.

CONSE'RVING, s. *conſervamento*, s. m. *il conſervare, conſervagione, conſervazione*, s. f.

CONSE'SSION, s. [a ſitting together] *il ſedere inſieme; il ſedere a crocchio.*

CONSE'SSOR, s. [one that ſits with others] *chi ſiede con altri, colui che ſta ſeduto a crocchio con altri.*

To CONSI'DER, [to mind, to think of] *conſiderare, attentamente oſſervare, por mente ponderare col diſcorſo, eſaminare, meditare, penſare, reflettere, contemplare.*

To conſider a thing thoroughly, *conſiderar attentamente una coſa, ponderarla, eſaminarla ben bene.*

Take your time to conſider of it, *conſiderate maturamente.*

Conſider what you do, *penſate a quel che fate.*

To conſider [to regard, to have reſpect for] *ſtimare, far ſtima, ſar conto, pregiare.*

Conſider my preſent condition, *abbiata mira al mio ſtato preſente.*

I conſider him much, *lo ſtimo molto, ſo grade ſtima di lui.*

To conſider [to acknowledge] *rimeritare, rimunerare, guiderdonare, render merito, contraccambiare, riconoſcere.* preſ. *riconoſco.* pret. *riconobi.*

I ſhall conſider you for it, *ve ne rimunererò, ve ne renderò il contracambio.*

I ſhall conſider your pains, *ſaprò contraccambiarvi per le voſtre fatiche, ſaprò riconoſcere le voſtre fatiche.*

CONSI'DERABLE, adj. *conſiderabile, da eſſer conſiderato.*

He is a conſiderable man, *egli è un uomo di conto, o di ſtima.*

He has been in England for a conſiderable time, *è ſtato un gran pezzo in Inghilterra.*

CONSI'DERABLENESS, s. [importance, dignity, moment, value, deſert, claim to notice] *importanza, dignità, momento, ſtima, merito, riguardevolezza.*

CONSIDERABLY, adv. *conſiderabilmente, molto.*

CONSI'DERANCE, s. [conſideration, reflection] *conſiderazione, rifleſſione*, s. f. *il conſiderare, il riflettere.*

CONSI'DERATE, adj. [diſcreet] *conſiderato, prudente, diſcreto.*

He is a very conſiderate man, *egli è un uomo molto conſiderato.*

CONSI'DERATELY, adv. [adviſedly] *conſideratamente, con conſiderazione, attentamente, ponderatamente, avviſatamente.*

CONSI'DERATENESS, s. [adviſed neſs] *conſiderazione, prudenza, diſcrezi-*

one, circonspezione, riflessione, attenzione, s. f.

CONSIDERA'TION, s. [a bethinking one's self] *considerazione, riflessione,* s. f. *pensiero,* s. m.

Consideration [motive, reason] *considerazione, causa, ragione,* s. f. *motivo,* s. m.

Consideration [regard, respect] *stima, opinione, mira,* s. f. *pregio, conto,* s. m.

Consideration [requital] *ricompensa, rimunerazione,* s. f. *guiderdone, riconoscimento, premio, contraccambio.*

The consideration of death, *il pensiero della morte.*

I leave it to your consideration, *lo rimetto alla vostra considerazione.*

To do a thing without consideration, *far che che si sia senza considerazione, o inconsideratamente.*

I did it upon your consideration, *l'ho fatto per conto, o rispetto vostro.*

Have a little consideration on me, *abbiate un poco di mira alla mia persona.*

Is this all your consideration for my pains? *è questo il guiderdon che mi date delle mie fatiche?*

To take a thing into consideration, *far considerazione o riflessione sopra che che si sia.*

CONSI'DERER, s. [a man of reflection] *colui che considera bene, che riflette, che pesa le cose.*

CONSI'DERED, adj. *considerato,* v. To consider.

This is a thing to be considered of, *questo merita considerazione.*

CONSI'DERING, s. *consideramento,* s. m. *il considerare.*

Considering, adj. [full of thoughts] *pensoso, pensieroso.*

Considering [thinking, judicious] *considerato, prudente, giudizioso, circospetto, cauteloso.*

To put on one's considering cap, *considerare attentamente, riflettere, ruminare, ponderar il discorso.*

Considering, adv. *atteso, stante.*

Considering the present posture of affairs, *atteso, o considerato lo stato presente degli affari.*

Considering that, *atteso che, perchè, stante che.*

To CONSI'GN [to make over, to deliver] *consegnare, metter nelle mani, dare in custodia, depositare.*

To consign one to punishment, *far punire alcuno.*

CONSI'GNED, adj. *consignato, depositato.*

CONSIGNING, s. *consegnazione,* s. f. *il consegnare.*

CONSI'MILAR, adj. [having one common resemblance] *consimile.*

To CONSI'ST [to be made up of] *consistere, avere il fondamento, l'essere.*

To consist [to agree together] *consistere, accordarsi.*

Our life consists in the union betwixt the body and the soul, *la nostra vita consiste nell' unione del corpo, e dell' anima.*

The enemy's army consisted of fifty thousand men, *l'esercito nemico era composto di cinquanta mila uomini.*

This does not consist with what you said before, *questo non s'accorda con quel che avete detto prima, cio' non corrisponde a quel che avete dià detto.*

This does not consist with equity, *cio ripugna, o è contrario all' equità.*

CONSI'STENCE, } s. [essence, the CONSI'STENCY, } manner of being] *consistenza, e consistenzia,* s. f. *il consistere.*

Consistence, [relation, agreement] *consistenza, somiglianza, conformità, congruenza, convenienza,* s. f.

CONSI'STENCE, s. *densità, spessezza.*

CONSI'STENT WITH, adj. [agreeable or suitable to] *convenevole, conveniente, confacevole, proporzionato adattato.*

This is not consistent with equity, *ciò non è confacevole all' equità, ciò è contrario all' equità.*

Consistent [not fluid] *che ha consistenza, fermo, denso.*

CONSI'STENTLY, adv. [without contradiction, agreeably] *convenevolmente, propriamente, senza che vi sia contraddizione, consequentemente.*

CONSITO'RIAL, adj. [of or belonging to a consistory] *consistoriale, di consistoro.*

A consistorial decree, *un decreto consistoriale.*

CO'NSISTORY, s. [meeting of the pope and cardinals] *concistoro,* s. m. *luogo dove sta il papa co' cardinali a consiglio.*

Consistory [a meeting of the ministers and elders among the French Protestants] *concistoro, assemblea de' ministri ed anziani della chiesa Francese Riformata.*

To CONSO'CIATE, [to join in mutual society] *associarsi, unirsi insieme, far società insieme, unir insieme.*

CONSO'CIATED, adj. *associato, unito in società, unito insieme,*

CONSOCIA'TION, s. [alliance] *lega, alleanza, società.*

Consociation, [union, intimacy, companionship] *unione, l' essere intimo con uno, compagnia.*

CONSO'LABLE, adj. [that may be comforted] *consolabile.*

To CO'NSOLATE [to comfort] *consolare, alleggerire il dolore altrui, dar conforto, e consolazione.*

CONSO'LATION, s. [comfort] *consolazione,* s. f. *conforto, rifrigerio, contento,* s. m.

CONSO'LATORY, adj. [comfortable] *consolativo, confortativo, atto a consolare.*

CONSO'LE, s. [a kind of bracket or shouldering piece, which serves to support a cornice, and bear up figures] *beccatello, peduccio,* s. m. *mensola,* s. f. *serve di sostegno sotto le cornici, statue, vasi, e simili.*

To CONSO'LE [to comfort, to cheer] *confortare, somministrar conforto.*

CONSO'LER, s. [one that gives comfort] *un consolatore, un che conforta.*

To CONSO'LIDATE, [to close, or to make whole] *consolidare, saldare, confermare, assodare, riunire insieme.* pref. *riunisco.*

To consolidate a wound, *consolidare, o saldare una ferita.*

To consolidate, verb. neut. *consolidarsi, saldarsi, confermarsi, assodarsi, riunirsi.*

CONSO'LIDATED, adj. *consolidato, saldato, confermato, assodato, riunito.*

The wound is consolidated, *la piaga è consolidata, o saldata.*

CONSOLIDA'TION, s. [closing up, or hardening of broken bones, or the lips of wounds] *consolidazione,* s. f. *consolidamento,* s. m.

Consolidation [in common law, is a joining of two benefices into one] *la congiunzione, o unione di due benefici.*

Consolidation [in civil law, is the uniting the possession and profits of lands] *la riunione della proprietà, e del usufrutto.*

CO'NSONANCE, s. [conformity] *consonanza, conformità, corrispondenza.*

Consonance [in musick, the agreement of two sounds, the one grave, the other acute] *consonanza, armonia,* s. f.

Consonance of words [is when two words sound alike at the end] *consonanza, rima, armonia, procedente dalla medesima, desinenza, o terminazione di parole.*

CO'NSONANCY, the same as consonance.

CO'NSONANT, adj. [agreeable, conformable] *consonante, consone, conforme, concorde.*

Consonant, s. [in grammar, is a letter which has no sound of itself except it be joined to some vowel] *una consonante, quella lettera dell' alfabeto, che non fa suono, se non unita a qualche vocale.*

Letters are either vowels or consonants, *le lettere sono devise in vocli, e consonanti.*

Consonant, adv. [according] *secondo, conforme.*

To act consonant to reason, *operare secondo la ragione.*

CO'NSONANTLY, adv. [agreeably] *conforme, secondo.*

CO'NSORT, s. [companion] *compagno, socio, consorte, e consorto, partecipe della madesima fortuna, ma propriamente parlando di vascelli che vanno di conserva.*

Consort [a piece of musick consisting of three or more parts] *concerto, o coro di musica.*

Consort [the wife of a sovereign prince, or any other great person] *consorte.*

To CO'NSORT [to keep company, or have society with] *associarsi, frequentare vivere insieme, aver commercio insieme.*

CONSO'UND, s. [the herb comfrey] *consolida maggiore.*

CONSPICTU'ITY, s. [sense of seeing] *il vedere, il censo della vista.*

CONSPE'RSION, s. [a sprinkling] *aspersione,* s. f.

CONSPI'CUOUS, adj. [clear, bright, easy

easy to be seen] *cospicuo, spettabile, splendido.*

CONSPI'CUOUSNESS, s. [exposure to the view] *esposizione alla vista, l'essere cospicuo.*

Conspicuousness, [eminence, fame, celebrity] *eminenza, fama, rinomo.*

CONSPI'CUOUSLY, adv. *notabilmente, splendidamente.*

CONSPI'RACY, s. [plot] *congiura, cospirazione.* s. f.

CONSPI'RATOR, s. [a plotter, one who has conspired for some ill design] *cospiratore, congiuratore,* s. m.

To CONSPI'RE [to plot] *conspirare, e cospirare, congiurare, tramare.*

All things conspire to his advancement, *cogni cosa favorisce il suo avanzamento.*

CONSPI'RED AGAINST, adj. *conspirato, cospirato, congiurato.*

CONSPI'RING, s. *conspirazione, cospirazione, congiura,* s. f.

CO'NSTABLE, s. [petty officer in a parish] *conestabile, o commissario del quartiere.*

Constable of the tower of London, *governatore della torre di Londra.*

Constable of Dover castle, *governatore o castellano dell castello di Dover.*

To over-run the constable [to spend beyond one's estate] *avanzare i piedi fuor del letto, spendere piu che uno ha d' entrata.*

CO'NSTABLESHIP, s. *conestaboleria, grado di conestabile.*

CO'NSTANCY, s. [firmness, stedfastness] *costanza, perseveranza, stabilità, fermezza,* s. f.

Constancy of mind, *costanza, o fermezza d' animo.*

CO'NSTANT, adj. [steady, continuing in the same mind] *costante, stabile, fermo, perseverante.*

He is very constant, *egli è molto costante.*

To be constant in one's resolution, *esser costante, o fermo nella sua risoluzione.*

A constant rain, *una pioggia continua.*

To be constant to one, *esser fedele, o costante ad uno.*

'Tis constant, *certa cosa è.*

He is a constant customer to me, *egli è mio avventore.*

CO'NSTANTLY, adv. *costantemente, fermamente, stabilmente, perseverantemente.*

To CO'NSTELLATE, v. n. [to shine with one general light] *dare splendore o risplendere insieme.*

To constellate, v. a. [to unite several shining bodies in one splendour] *unire molti corpi lucenti in una sola luce.*

CONSTELLA'TION, s. [a cluster of fixed stars] *numero di stelle fisse che vanno insieme, costellazione.*

Constellation [an assemblage of splendours or excellencies] *molte luci unite insieme, o cumulo di buone qualità in senso metaforico.*

To CO'NSTER [to construe] *construire, e costruire.* pres. *construisco, e costruisco.* Obs.

CO'NSTERED, adj. *construito, e costruito.* Obs.

CO'NSTERING, s. *construzione, costruttura,* s. f. Obs.

CONSTERNA'TION, s. [a great fear, or astonishment] *consternazione, paura,* s. f. *timore, dismarrimento, sgomento smarrimento,* s. m.

CO'NSTIPATE [to bind] *costipare, ristrignere.* pres. *ristingo.* pret. *ristrinsi.*

Apt to constipate, *costipativo, atto a costipare.*

CO'NSTIPATED, adj. *constipato, ristretto.*

CONSTIPA'TION, s. *constipazione,* s. f. *rinserramento,* s. m.

CO'NSTITUENT, adj. [which constitutes or makes up] *che costituisce, che compone.*

To CO'NSTITUTE [to appoint] *costituire, e constituire, deliberare, statuire, ordinare.* pres. *costituisco, e constituisco, statuisco.*

CO'NSTITUTED, adj. *costituito, e constituito, deliberato, statuito, ordinato.*

CO'NSTITUTING, s. *constituzione, e costituzione,* s. f.

CONSTITU'TION, s. [settlement, ordinance, decree,] *costituzione, e constituzione, instituzione, legge,* s. f. *ordine, statuto.*

Constitution [temper of the body] *complessione, o temperamento del corpo.*

Constitution [disposition] *stato,* s. m. *disposizione,* s. f.

CONSTITU'TIONAL, adj. [bred in the constitution; radical] *provegnente dalla complessione; che è nel sangue; che nasce dalla radice.*

Constitutional [consistent with the constitution; legal] *che non da di cozzo alla leggi; legale.*

To CONSTRA'IN [to force, to compel] *constringere, costrignere, e constrignere, sforzare, violentare, astrignere.* pres. *costringo.* pret. *constrinsi e costrinsi, astrinsi.*

To constrain [to keep in, to restrain] *costrignere, frenare, tenere a freno.*

CONSTRAI'NED, adj. *constretto, e costretto, sforzato, violentato, astretto.*

CONSTRA'INEDLY, adv. *per forza, di mala voglia.*

CONSTRA'INT, s. [force, violence] *constrignimento,* s. m. *forza, violenza, necessità,* s. f.

To CONSTR'ICT, [to contract, to cause to shrink] *ristringere. rattrarre.*

CONSTRI'CTION, s. [a binding fast, or tying together] *constrignimento, restrignimento, condensamento,* s. m.

CONSTRI'CTOR, s. [that which compresses or contracts] *ciò che comprime o contrae.*

To CONSTRI'NGE, [to compress, to contract to bind] *costringere, comprimere, rattrarre, tener saldo.*

CONSTRI'NGENT, adj. [having the quality of binding or compressing] *costringente.*

To CONSTRU'CT [to build, to form] *costruire, fabbricare, formare.*

CONSTRU'CTION, s. [the act of building or making] *construzione, construttura, fabbricazione,* s. f.

Construction [in grammar] *construzione, ordine di parole secondo le regole gramaticali.*

Construction [interpretation] *interpretazione, spiega,* s. f. *senso,* s. m.

To make the best construction of a thing, *interpretar favorevolmente che che si sia, prendere una cosa in buon senso.*

CONSTRU'CTIVE, adj. [which tends to construction] *costruttivo, che si puo construire.*

CONSTRU'CTURE, s. [pile, edifice, fabrick] *edifizio, fabbrica.*

To CONSTRUE [to expound, to interpret] *construire, spiegare, dichiarare, interpretare.* pres. *construisco.*

CO'NSTRUED, adj. *construito, spiegato, dichiarato, interpretato.*

CONSUBSTA'NTIAL, adj. [of the same substance [*consustanziale, d'una stessa sustanzia.*

CONSUBSTANTIA'LITY, s. [existence of more than one in the same substance] *l'esistere di più d' uno nella stessa sostanza.*

CONSUBSTANTIA'TION, s. [the doctrine of the substantial presence of the body of Christ in the substance of the bread and wine, maintained by the Lutherans] *consustanziazione,* s. f.

CO'NSUL, s. [was the title of a sovereign magistrate among the Romans, whereof there were two in number] *cònsolo, cònsole,* s. m. *sommo magistrato nella repubblica di Roma.*

Consul [a resident for merchants in foreign parts] *cònsolo, cònsole.*

CO'NSULAR, adj. [of, or belonging to a consul] *consolare, di consolo.*

The consular dignity, *la dignità consolare.*

CO'NSULAR man, s. [one who had been consul] *colui che fu un tratto cònsolo.*

CO'NSULATE, } s. [the dignity of
CO'NSULSHIP, } a consul] *consolato,* s. m. *grado e dignità di consolo.*

CO'NSULT, s. [consultation, but commonly taken in an ill sense, for the secret cabals of plotters against the state] *consulta, consultazione,* s. f.

To CONSU'LT [to advise with, to ask advice] *consultare, far consulta, discorrere, esaminare, deliberare.*

To consult [to take care of one's interest] *aver cura dell' altrui interessi, procurare il suo vantaggio, aver a cuore il suo bene.*

He consults nothing but his own interest, *non ha mira o riguardo che al suo proprio interesse, non risguardo ch' il suo comodo.*

To consult [speaking of physicians] *collegiare.*

CONSULTA'TION, s. *consultazione, consulta,* s. f.

A consultation of physicians, *una consultazione di medici.*

CONSU'LTED, adj. *consultato, discorso, esaminato, deliberato, collegiato.*

CONSU'LTER, s. *consultore,* s. m. *che consulta.*

CO'NSULTING, s. *il consultare, consulta, consultazione, deliberazione,* s. f.

CONSU'MABLE, adj. [susceptible of destruction] *che puo esser distrutto, suscettibile di distruzione.*

To CON-

To CONSU'ME [to waste] consumare, logorare, finire, spendere, ridurre al niente. pres. finisco. pret. spesi.
Time consumes all things, il tempo consuma ogni cosa.
He has consumed his estate, egli ha scialaquato o dissipato le sue facultadi.
To consume away, verb. neut. consumarsi, logorarsi.
He consumes away with grief, si consuma di dolore.
CONSU'MED, adj. consumato, logorato, finito, speso, ridotto al niente.
CONSU'MER, s. [one that spends, wastes, or destroys any thing] consumatore, che consuma, che spende, guasta, o distrugge tutto.
CONSU'MING, s. il consumare, consumamento, s. m.
Consuming, adj. [that consumes] consumante, che consuma, consumativo.
To CO'NSUMMATE [to perfect, to finish] perfezionare, dar perfezione e compimento, terminare.
CO'NSUMMATED, adj. perfezionato, terminato.
CONSU'MMATING, or CONSUMMA'TION, s. [finishing, perfecting] perfezione, s. f. compimento, s. m.
CONSU'MPTION, s. [from to consume] consumazione, s. f dissipamento, disfacimento, s. m.
A consumption of commodities, uno spaccio di robe.
Consumption [a disease] etica, s. f. specie di febbre abituata.
CONSU'MPTIVE, adj [that is in, or inclined to a consumption] etico, infermo di febre etica.
CONTA'CT, s. [the touch] contatto, toccamento, s. m.
CONTA'CTION, s. [the act of touching] toccamento, il toccare, l' atto del toccare.
CONTA'GION, s. [pestilence, infection] contagione, infezione, s. f influenza di male che si comunica con altri, contagio, s. m.
CONTA'GIOUS, adj. [infectious, apt to infect] contagioso, appiccaticcio, atto per sua natura ad appiccarsi.
A contagious disease, una malattia contagiosa.
CONTA'GIOUSNESS, s. contagione, peste, s. f. contagio, s. m.
To CONTA'IN [to hold, to comprehend] contenere, tenere, racchiudere dentro di se, comprendere. pres. contengo, tengo, pret. contenni, tenni, racchiusi.
That church contains three thousand souls, quella chiesa contiene tre mila anime.
To contain [to keep back, to refrain] contenire, reprimere, raffrenare, moderare, ritenere.
To contain one's self, contenersi, temperarsi, astenersi, raffrenarsi, moderarsi.
To contain one's anger, raffrenare la collera.
CONTA'INABLE, adj [possible to be contained] che puo esser contenuto, che puo contenersi.
CONTA'INED, adj. contenuto, v. To contain.

CONTA'INING, s. contenimento, s. m. il contenire.
To CONTA'MINATE [to defile, to pollute] contaminare, macchiare, bruttare, corrompere, infettare, pret. corruppi.
CONTA'MINATED, adj. contaminato, macchiato, bruttato, corrotto, infettato.
CONTAMINA'TION, s. [defilement, pollution] contaminazione, il contaminare, macchia, corruzione, polluzione, bruttura, s. f.
To CONTE'MERATE [to violate or pollute] violare, macchiare, bruttare, contaminare, infettare.
CONTE'MERATED, adj. [violated, polluted] violato, polluto.
To CONTE'MN [to despise or slight] dispregiare, sdegnare, vilificare, far poco conto, burlarsi.
CONTE'MNED, adj. dispregiato, sdegnato, vilificato.
CONTE'MNER, s. dispregiatore, e disprezzatore, s. m.
CONTE'MNING, s. dispregio, disprezzo, s. m. il dispregiare.
To CONTE'MPER [to moderate] temperare, moderare.
CONTE'MPERAMENT, s. [the degree of any quality] tempera, grado di qualità.
To CONTE'MPERATE [to moderate, to temper] moderare, temperare.
CONTEMPERA'TION, s. [the act of moderating or tempering] l' atto del moderare o temperare.
Contemperation [proportionate mixture, proportion] mistura proporzionata, proporzione.
To CO'NTEMPLATE [to behold, to muse, to meditate] contemplare, considerare, fissar la mente e'l pensiero.
CO'NTEMPLATED, adj. contemplato, considerato.
CONTEMPLA'TION, s. [meditation, study] contemplazione, attenzione, meditazione, speculazione, s. f.
CONTEMPLATIVE, adj. [given to contemplation] contemplativo, dedito, e acconcio a contemplare.
A contemplative life, vita contemplativa.
CONTE'MPLATIVELY, adv. per contemplazione, d'una maniera contemplativa.
CONTEMPLA'TOR, s. [one who contemplates] contemplatore, s. m. contemplatrice, s f.
CONTE'MPORARY, adj. [of the same time or standing, that lives in the same time or age] contemporaneo, d'un medesimo tempo.
Contemporary, s. [one who lives at the same time with another] un contemporaneo.
To CONTEMPORI'SE, [to make contemporary] far contemporaneo.
CONTE'MPT, s. [despite, disdain, scorn] dispregio, disprezzo, scherno, s. m.
To fall under a general contempt, divenire lo scherno d'ognuno.
The contempt of the court, contumacia, s. f.

CONTE'MPTIBLE, adj. [despisable, base, mean, vile] dispregevole, disprezzabile, vile, disprezzevole.
A contemptible fellow, un uomo vile, un uomo da niente, un vigliacco.
CONTE'MPTIBLY, adv. dispregevolmente e disprezzevolmente, con dispregio.
To think contemptibly of one, aver cattiva opinione d'alcuno.
CONTE'MPTUOUS, adj. [scornful, slighting] dispregiante, e disprezzante, altiero, superbo, fiero, sdegnoso.
A contemptuous word, un termine di dispregio.
CONTE'MPTUOUSLY, adv. con modo dispregiante, altieramente, fieramente, sdegnosamente.
To CONTE'ND [to strive, to dispute] contendere, disputare, contraddire, questionare, mettere in disputa. pret. contesi, contraddissi.
To contend for a trifle, contendere per una bagattella.
To contend for beauty, disputare della bellezza.
To contend [to maintain, or face down] mantenere, pretendere, affermare. pret. mantenni, pretesi.
CONTE'NDED FOR, adj. conteso, disputato, contraddetto, questionato, mantenuto, preteso, affermato.
CONTE'NDENT, s. [antagonist, opponent] che contende, antagonista.
CONTE'NDER, s. [combatant, champion] contenditore, combattiore, campione.
CONTE'NDING, s. contendimento, s. m. il contendere.
Contending, adj. contendente, che contende.
Contending parties, le parti contendenti.
CONTE'NT, adj. [satisfied, well pleased with what one has] contento contentato, soddisfatto.
I am content with it, ne sono contento.
You must be content to do this, bisogna che voi vi contentiate di far questo.
Content, s. [contentedness, satisfaction] contento, piacere, contentamento, soddisfacimento, s. m.
To give content to every body, contentare, o piacere ognuno, dar soddisfazione ad ognuno.
I could give him no content in any thing, non ho potuto piacerli in nulla.
Content [the compass or extent of a thing] contento, contenuto, spazio, s. m. grandezza, s. f.
To CO'NTENT [to please] contentare, soddisfare, piacere, aggradire, adempir l'altrui voglia, pret. soddisfeci, piacqui, pres. aggradisco.
I'll do what I can to content you, farò ogni sforzo per contentarvi.
I shall content you for your pains, vi soddisferò delle vostre fatiche.
Content yourself with what you have, contentatevi di quel che avete.
CONTENTA'TION, v. Contentedness.
CONTE'NTED, adj. [satisfied] contento, soddisfatto.

To be contented with one's small fortune, *esser contento nella sua bassa fortuna.*

A contented mind is a continual feast, *chi è contento è felice.*

I could be contented to live here, *mi piacerebbe molto di dimorar qui.*

He is best contented to go, *ama meglio d'andarsene.*

CONTE'NTEDLY, adv. [with content] *contentamente, con contento, con soddisfazione, lietamente.*

To live contentedly, *viver contento o lietamente.*

I bear with it contentedly, *lo soffro pazientemente.*

CONTE'NTEDNESS, s. *contentezza,* s. f. *contento,* s. m.

CONTE'NTFUL, adj. [full of content] *contento, allegro, lieto, soddisfatto. Non è molto in uso.*

CONTE'NTING, s. *contentamento,* s. m. *il contentare.*

CONTE'NTION, s. [strife, debate] *contenzione, contesa, disputa, querela, differenza,* s. f.

CONTE'NTIOUS, adj. [litigious] *contenzioso, litigioso.*

CONTE'NTIOUSLY, adv. *contenziosamente, litigiosamente.*

CONTE'NTIOUSNESS, s. [contentious humour] *umore contenzioso, o litigioso.*

CONTE'NTLESS, adj. [discontented, dissatisfied, uneasy] *scontento, malsoddisfatto, di mala voglia.* Shakesp.

CONTE'NTMENT, s. [content] *contento, contentamento,* s. m. *contentezza, soddisfazione,* s. f.

Contentment is the greatest wealth, *val più un animo quieto che le ricchezze.*

CONTE'NTS, s. pl. *il contenuto.*

The contents of a letter, *il contenuto, la sostanza d'una lettera.*

The contents of a chapter, *il sommario d'un capitolo.*

The table of contents of a book, *la tavola delle materie d'un libro.*

CONTE'ST, s. [debate] *contesa, disputa, differenza, contenzione,* s. f.

To CONTE'ST [to debate] *contendere, disputare, quistionare.* pref. *contesi.*

CONTESTA'TION, s. [quarrel] *contesa, contenzione, disputa,* s. f.

CONTE'STED, adj. *conteso, quistionato, disputato.*

To CONTE'XT [to weave together] *tessere, intrecciare, intralciare.*

CONTE'XT, s. [a term of divinity, is the series of some passage of scripture that have a coherence one with another] *la tessitura, il tessuto de' passaggi della scrittura sacra fra i quali si trova qualche corrispondenza.*

Context [the general series of a discourse] *il contesto, la serie generale d'un discorso.*

Context, adj. [knit together, firm] *strettamente unito insieme, sodo.*

CONTE'XTURE, s. [interweaving] *tessitura,* s. f. *tessuto,* s. m.

The Jews prayers are but a contexture of places in scripture, *le preghiere degli Ebrei non sono che un tessuto de' passaggi della scrittura sacra.*

CONTIGU'ITY, s. [nearness, closeness] *prossimità, vicinità, propinquità,* s. f.

CONTI'GUOUS, adj. [very near, close, adjoining] *contiguo, rasente, allato, accosto, vicino, prossimo.*

My house and his are contiguous, *la mia casa è contigua alla sua.*

CONTI'GUOUSLY, adv. [without any intervening spaces] *senza intervallo frapposto, contiguamente, vicino, prossimamente.*

CONTI'GUOUSNESS, s. [nearness, closeness] *vicinità, propinquità, prossimità,* s. f.

CO'NTINENCE, } s. [chastity, temperance] *continenza, per la quale l'uomo si fa temperare, e contenere.*
CO'NTINENCY, }

CO'NTINENT, adj. [chaste, temperate] *continente, contenente, casto, temperato, che ha la virtù di continenza.*

Continent fever, *febbre continua.*

Continent, s. [a great extent of land which is not separated by the sea] *continente,* s. m. *terra ferma.*

CO'NTINENTLY, adv. *castamente, moderatamente, con moderazione, temperatamente.*

CONTI'NGENCE, } s. [chance, casualty] *contingenza,* s. f. *caso, accidente,* s. m.
CONTI'NGENCY, }

CONTI'NGENT, adj. [accidental, casual] *contingente, casuale, fortuito.*

Contingent, s. [a thing in the hands of chance] *cosa in balìa della sorte.*

Contingent [a proportion that falls to any person upon any division] *scotto,* s. m. *parte, porzione,* s. f.

CONTI'NGENTLY, adv. *casualmente, accidentalmente, a caso.*

CONTI'NUAL, adj. [that is without intermission] *continuo, non interrotto.*

A continual fever, *una febbre continua.*

CONTI'NUALLY, adv. *continuamente, sempre, del continuo, senza intermissione, senza interrompimento.*

CONTI'NUANCE, s. [lastingness, length of time] *continuanza, continovanza, continuazione,* s. f.

In continuance of time, *in progresso di tempo.*

CONTI'NUATE, adj. [immediately united] *continuato, unito immediatamente.*

Continuate [uninterrupted, unbroken] *non interrotto, senza intervallo frapposto.*

CONTINUA'TION, s. [the lasting of any thing without intermission] *continuazione,* s. f. *il continuare.*

CONTINUA'TOR, s. *quello che continua, o proseguisce un' opera da un altro cominciato.*

To CONTI'NUE [to carry on, to pursue] *continuare, e continovare, proseguire, seguitare avanti, non intermettere.*

To continue [to pursue one's journey] *continuare, o proseguire il suo cammino.*

To continue [to hold on] *continuare, persistere, perseverare.*

To continue in a lewd course of life, *continuare o persistere nelle dissolutezze.*

To continue [to abide] *dimorare, trattenersi, soggiornare.*

I shall not continue long in this place, *non dimorerò, o non mi tratterò lungo tempo in questo luogo.*

To continue [to last] *continuare, durare.*

This rain has continued very long, *questa pioggia ha durato un pezzo.*

To continue a governor in his government, *confermare un governatore nel suo governo.*

I desire you to continue me your friendship, *vi prego di continuarmi la vostra amicizia.*

CO'NTINUED, adj. *continuato, e continovato,* v. To continue.

Continued [continual] *continuato, continuo.*

A continual care, *una cura continua.*

Atoms that are, as it were, a continued body, *atomi, che sono, per così dire, un corpo continuato.*

A continued valley to the very sea, *una valle che continua, o che si stende fino al mare.*

CONTI'NUEDLY, adv. *continuatamente, in modo progressivo, progressivamente senza intermissione.*

CONTI'NUER, s. [having the power of perseverance] *che ha facoltà di perseverare.*

CONTINU'ITY, s. [the connexion or joining together of the several parts of a thing] *continuità, e continovità,* s. f.

CO'NTINUOUS, adj. [joined together without the intervention of any space] *continuo, senza spazi frapposti.*

To CO'NTORT, [to twist, to writhe] *torcere, attorcigliare.*

CONTO'RTION, s. [a wrenching or wresting] *contorsione, convulsione,* s. f.

CONTO'UR, s. [the out-lines of a figure or picture] *contorno,* s. m. *linea che termina una figura, o una pittura.*

CO'NTRABAND, adj. [forbidden] *proibito, illegale.*

Contraband goods, *mercanzie di contrabbando.*

CONTRA'CT, s. [a covenant, agreement, or bargain] *contratto, accordo, strumento,* s. m. *scrittura pubblica che stabilisce le convenzioni, convenzione,* s. f.

To make a contract, *fare un contratto.*

To CONTRA'CT, [to article, to covenant, to make a contract] *contrattare, fare un contratto, convenire,* pref. *convengo.* pret. *convenni.*

To contract [to draw together] *contraere, e contrarre, raggrinzare, ristrignere:* pref. *ristringo.* pret. *ristrinsi.*

To contract one's brows, *inarcar le ciglia.*

It contracts itself little by little, *si raggrinza insensibilmente, si contrae a poco a poco.*

To contract [to get] *contrarre, acquistare, fare.*

To

To contract an ill habit, *fare un cattivo abito.*

To contract debts, *contrarre o far debiti, indebitarsi.*

To contract a disease, *acquistare una malattia.*

To contract [to betroth] *sposare, fidanzare.*

CONTRA'CTION, s. [the act of contracting or shortening] *raccorciamento, l'atto del raccorciare.* Pope.

Contraction [the act of shrinking or shriveling] *l'atto dello impicciolire; il divenir picciolo.*

Contraction [the state of being contracted, drawn into a narrow compass] *ristringimento, l'esser ristretto in poco spazio.*

Contraction [in grammar, the reduction of two vowels or syllables to one] *l'elisione di due vocali o di due sillabe in una.*

Contraction [abbreviation] *abbreviatura.*

Contraction house, s. [a place where agreements or contracts are made for the promotion of trade] *luogo dove si contratta o dove si fanno i contratti.*

CONTRADI'CT, s. [contradiction] *contraddizione, s. f.*

To CONTRADI'CT [to gainsay, to oppose the assertion of another] *contraddire, dir contra, ostare, oppugnare, opporsi,* pres. *contraddico, oppongo.* pret. *contraddissi, opposi.*

To contradict one's self, *contraddirsi, variare o vacillare nel discorso, disdirsi.*

To contradict an inclination, *rintuzzare un' inclinazione.*

CONTRADI'CTED, adj. *contraddetto, ostato, oppugnato, opposto.*

The news is now contradicted, *questa novella non vien confermata.*

CONTRADI'CTER, s. [one that contradicts, an opposer] *uno che contraddice, contraddittore, opponente.*

CONTRADI'CTING, s. *contraddicimento, s. m. il contraddire.*

CONTRADI'CTION, s. [gainsaying] *contraddizione, opposizione, negazione, contrarietà, s. f. ostacolo.*

He is a very learned man without contradiction, *egli è un uomo dottissimo senza dubbio.*

In contradiction to all the ties of honour, *contra tutte le regole alle quali l'onore ci obbliga.*

CONTRADI'CTIOUS, adj. [full of contradictions] *contraddicente, che contraddice, che fa mestiero di contraddire.*

CONTRADI'CTORY, adj. [which contradicts itself] *contraddittorio.*

Contradictory propositions [are such as consist of a universal and particular, of which one affirms, and the other denies] *proposizioni contraddittorie.*

CONTRADISTI'NCTION, s. [a distinction on the other side] *distinzione fatta della parte opposta.*

To CONTRADISTI'NGUISH [to distinguish on the other side] *contraddistinguere, distinguer di nuovo.*

CONTRAPOSI'TION, s. [putting against] *contrapposizione,* s. f. *contrapponimento,* s. m.

CONTRARI'ETY, s. [opposition, disagreement] *contrarietà, opposizione, diversità,* s. f.

CO'NTRARILY, adv. *contrariamente, al contrario, al rovescio.*

CONTRA'RIOUS, adj. [opposite, repugnant] *opposto, ripugnante, contrario.*

CONTRA'RIOUSLY, adv. [oppositely] *contrariamente, oppostamente.*

CO'NTRARIWISE, adv. *altrimente, d'un altra maniera, al contrario.*

CO'NTRARY, adj. [opposite, different] *contrario, opposto.*

Contrary opinions, *opinioni contrarie.*

The wind was contrary to us, *il vento ci era contrario, o disfavorevole.*

That's contrary to reason, *ciò ripugna alla ragione.*

You take every thing in a contrary sense, *voi intendete tutto alla rovescia.*

This is contrary to what ought to be, *questo è tutto il contrario di quel che dovrebbe essere.*

Cóntrary, s. *il contrario.*

This proves the contrary of what you said, *ciò prova il contrario di quel che voi dicevate.*

Contraries are best known by their contraries, *i contrari si conoscon meglio da' loro contrari.*

I will lay ten pounds to the contrary, *scommetto dieci doppie, che la cosa non va così.*

To advise the contrary, *dissuadere,* pret. *dissuasi.*

I can say nothing to the contrary, *non ho che dire in contrario.*

On the contrary, adv. *al contrario.*

It fell out quite contrary, *accadde tutto il contrario.*

It happens with us quite contrary, *le cose ci vanno alla rovescia.*

Contrary, prep. *contra.*

I'll do nothing contrary to my honour and reason, *non farò niente che sia contra al mio onore, ed alla mia ragione.*

Contrary to my expectations, *contra ogni mia speranza, o le mie aspettative.*

Contrary to the general opinion, *contra l'opinione comune.*

It proved contrary to what you thought, *riuscì altrimente che non pensavate.*

To speak contrary to one's thoughts, *dire il contrario di quel ch' altri pensa, fingere, celari i suoi veri sensi.*

To CO'NTRARY, v. To contradict.

CO'NTRAST, s. [a dispute or difference] *contrasto, combattimento,* s. m. *opposizione,* s. f.

Contrast [in painting, is the due placing the different objects and parts of the figures] *contrasto, la diversità nelle debite disposizioni delle figure in un quadro.*

To CONTRA'ST [to place in opposition] *porre all' incontro.*

To contrast [to show another figure to advantage] *collocare una figura contro un' altra in modo che appaja con vantaggio.*

CONTRAVALLA'TION, s. [a trench guarded with a parapet cut round a place by the besiegers] *contravallazione,* s. f. *linea con parapetto tirata dagli assediati intorno ad uno luogo, per impedire le sortite agli assediati.*

To CONTRAVE'NE, [to infringe or break agreement or law] *contravvenire, contraffare, disubbidire,* pres. *contravvengo, disubbidisco,* pret. *contravvenni.*

CONTRAVE'NER, s. [offender] *contravvenente, disubbidiente, quello o quella che contravviene.*

CONTRAVE'NTION, s. [a contravening, or infringement of the agreement] *contravvenzione, inosservanza,* s. f. *rompimento o mancamento di patti e convenzioni.*

CONTRIBU'TARY, adj. [paying tribute to the same sovereign] *contributario, che paga tributo allo stesso sovrano.*

Contributary, s. [that pays contribution] *tributario,* s. m. *che paga contribuzione.*

To CONTRI'BUTE [to assist towards the doing of a thing] *contribuire, concorrere colla speza, colla fatica, cogli uffizi, e simili, a che che si sia,* pres. *contribuisco.*

I contributed towards it, *vi ho contribuito.*

CONTRI'BUTING, s. *il contribuire.*

CONTRIBU'TION, s. *contribuzione,* s. f. *concorrimento, ed adjuto a che che si sia.*

To put a town under contribution, *mettere a contribuzione una città.*

CONTRIBU'TIVE, adj. [that which has the power or quality of promoting any purpose in concurrence with other motives] *che può contribuire.*

CONTRIBU'TOR, s. *chi contribuisce.*

CONTRI'BUTORY, adj. [promoting the same end, bringing assistance to some joint design] *che contribuisce allo stesso fine, che reca ajuto ad una impresa fatta insieme.*

To CO'NTRISTATE [to sadden, to make sorrowful] *contristare, affliggere, render doglioso.*

CONTRISTA'TION, s. *il contristare, doglia.*

CONTRI'TE, adj. [sorrowful, very penitent] *contrito, che ha contrizione, compunto, pentito.*

A contrite heart, *un cuor contrito.*

CONTRI'TION, s. [a true sincere sorrow for sin, proceeding from a love to God, more than fear of punishment] *contrizione,* s. f. *dolor sincero de' peccati commessi procedente dall' amore verso Iddio, non da timore di pena.*

Contrition [the act of grinding, or rubbing to powder] *tritamento, il tritare, il ridurre in polvere.*

CONTRI'VABLE, adj. [possible to be planned by the mind] *trovabile colla mente, col pensiero.*

CONTRI'VANCE, s. [device] *invenzione, inventiva,* s. f. *trovata,* s. m.

A petty contrivance, *una bella invenzione, un bel trovato.*

Contrivance [ingenuity in contriving] *arte,* s. f. *ingegno,* s. m.

Full of contrivances, *ingegnoso, inventore,*

To

To CONTRI'VE [to deceive or invent] *inventare, trovare.*
He contrived that machine, *egli inventò coteſta macchina.*
I contrived a cloſet in my room to put all my things in, *ho trovato modo di fare un gabinetto nella mia camera da potervi mettere tutte le mie robe.*
To contrive [to deſign, to plot] *tramare, macchinare, concertare, ordire.* preſ. *ordiſco.*
To contrive one's ruin, *tramare l'altrui rovina.*
To contrive a deſign, *concertare un diſegno.*
To contrive one's retreat, *trovar il modo di ritirarſi.*
I do what I can to contrive your happineſs, *fo ogni ſforzo per rendervi felice.*
How ſhall we contrive it? *che modo biſogna tenere in queſto negozio? come faremo?*
CONTRI'VED, adj. *inventato, trovato, tramato, macchinato, concertato, ordito.*
An ill contrived houſe, *una caſa male ordinata, mal diſpoſta.*
An ill contrived deſign, *un diſegno mal concertato.*
CONTRI'VEMENT, s. *invenzione,* s. f. *trovato,* s. m.
CONTRI'VER, s. [inventer] *inventore, autore, architetto, macchinatore, artefice,* s. m. *inventrice,* s. f.
CONTRO'L, s [a regiſter or account kept by another officer, that each may be examined by the other] *regiſtro o conto tenuto da un altro onde ambi poſſano eſſere eſaminati dall' altro.*
Control [check, reſtraint] *il tener in dovere, raffrenamento, freno.*
Control [power, authority, ſuperintendence] *potere, poſſa, autorità, ſoprantendenza.*
To CONTRO'L [to keep under check by a counter-reckoning] *tenere a freno, fare ſtar a ſegno con un contraregiſtro.*
To control [to govern, to reſtrain] *raffrenare, reſtringere.*
To control [to overpower, to confute] *ſoverchiare, con ragioni, confutare.*
CONTRO'LABLE, adj. [ſubject to control, ſubject to be over-ruled] *che ſi può frenare, che ſi può fare ſtar a ſegno.*
CONTRO'LLER, s. [one that has the power of governing or reſtraining] *colui che ha la facoltà di raffrenare, di far iſtare a ſegno.*
CONTRO'VER, s. [a law word, a forger of falſe news] *un ſeminatore, un autore, un inventore di falſe novelle.*
CONTROVE'RSIAL, adj. [of, or belonging to controverſy] *di controverſia, che riguarda la controverſia.*
CONTROVE'RSY, s. [debate, diſpute, variance] *controverſia, quiſtione, brigacontesa,* s. f. *litigio, contraſto,* s. m.
To put an end to a controverſy, *terminare una controverſia.*
Without all controverſy, *ſenza contraddizione, indubitatamente, certamente.*
To CONTROVE'RT [to diſpute] *diſputare, contendere, quiſtionare.*

CONTROVE'RTED, adj. *diſputato, conteſo, quiſtionato.*
CONTROVE'RTIBLE, adj. *diſputabile, non certo.*
CONTRO'VERTIST, s. [diſputant] *diſputante, che diſputa*
CONTUMA'CIOUS, adj. [ſelf-willed, ſtubborn] *contumace, oſtinato, caparbio, renitente.*
CO'NTUMACY, s. [ſtubbornneſs] *contumacia, oſtinazione, caparbietà, renitenza,* s. f.
CONTUME'LIOUS, adj. [reproachful, affrontive] *contumelioſo, villano, ſcorteſe, oltraggioſo, rampognoſo, ſtrazievole.*
Contumelious language, *parole ingiurioſe, oltraggi.*
CONTUME'LY, s. [abuſe, affront, reproach] *contumelia, ingiuria, villania,* s. f. *diſprezzo.*
CONTU'SION, s. [bruiſe] *ammaccatura, ſchiacciatura,* s. f. *ammaccamento,* s. m.
CO'NVALESCENCE, } s [recovery of
CO'NVALESCENCY, } health] *convaleſcenza,* s. f. *principio di ricoveramento di ſanità.*
One that is in his convaleſcence, *un convaleſcente.*
CONVALE'SCENT, adj. [recovering] *convaleſcente, che ſi va ricovrando da malattia avuta.*
To CONVE'IGH, *v.* To convey.
CO'NVENABBLE, adj. [law word, convenient, agreeable] *convenevole, conforme, conveniente, giuſto, dicevole.*
To CONVE'NE [to aſſemble, to call together] *convocare, adunare, ragunare.*
To convene [to meet or come together] *adunarſi, ragunarſi.*
CONVE'NED, adj. *convocato, adunato, ragunato.*
CONVE'NIENCE, } [ſuitableneſs, ad-
CONVE'NIENCY, } vantage] *comodità, opportunità,* s. f. *comodo,* s. m.
When it ſhall ſtand with your own conveniency, *quando vi ſarà comodo, quando vi verrà a taglio.*
Convenience [agreeableneſs] *convenienza, proporzione,* s. f.
CONVE'NIENT, adj. [fit, ſuitable] *conveniente, comodo, opportuno, atto.*
A very convenient houſe, *una caſa molto comoda.*
Convenient [agreeable] *conveniente, convenevole, conforme, giuſto, dicevole, ragionevole.*
At time convenient, *in tempo opportuno, opportunamente.*
Do it at your convenient time, *fatelo a voſtro agio.*
Not convenient, *diſdicevole, ſconvenevole.*
It is convenient that you ſhould go and ſpeak to him, *ſarebbe a propoſito o convenevole che voi andaſte a parlargli.*
It is not convenient for a modeſt woman to do this, *diſdice alla modeſtia d'una donna il far queſto.*
CONVE'NIENTLY, adv. *comodamente, bellamente.*
To be very conveniently lodged, *eſſere comodamente alloggiato.*

If you can conveniently, *ſe potrete farlo con voſtro comodo.*
Conveniently [agreeably] *convenientemente, convenevolmente.*
CO'NVENT, s. [monaſtery, religious houſe] *convento, monaſtero,* s. m. *abitazione de' frati, chioſtro,* s. m.
To CONVE'NT [to ſummon, to appear] *citare, chiamare alla ragione, o in giudicio.*
CONVE'NTED, adj. *citato.*
CONVE'NTICLE, s. [a little private aſſembly, an unlawful aſſembly] *conventicolo,* s. m. *combibbia, criocca,* s. f.
CONVE'NTICLER, s. [one that ſupports or frequents private and unlawful aſſemblies] *colui che protegge o frequenta private ed illegali aſſemblee.*
CONVE'NTION, s. [an agreement, or covenant] *convenzione,* s. f. *accordo, trattato,* s. m.
Convention [aſſembly] *aſſemblea,* s. f.
CONVE'NTIONAL, adj. [done by agreement] *fatto per convenzione, o d'accordo.*
CONVE'NTUAL, adj. belonging to a convent] *conventuale.*
A conventual church, *una chieſa conventuale.*
CONVE'NTUALS, s. [friars or nuns, who live in a convent] *religioſi conventuali, frati o monache che abitano in un convento.*
To CONVE'RGE [to tend to one point from different places] *tendere o andare a un punto da differenti luoghi.*
CONVE'RSABLE, adj. [qualified for converſation, fit for company] *qualificato per eſſere o ſtare in converſazione; di buona compagnia.*
CONVE'RSANT, adj. [keeping company with] *converſante, che converſa.*
To be converſant with one [to keep company with him] *converſare, bazzicare, praticare con uno.*
Converſant [well verſed] *verſato, eſperimentato, pratico, eſperto.*
Converſant in ancient hiſtories, *verſato, o pratico nelle iſtorie antiche.*
Converſant about a thing, *che tratta d'una coſa.*
CONVERSA'TION, s. [familiar diſcourſe] *converſazione,* s. f. *diſcorſo familiare.*
To begin the converſation, *entrare in diſcorſo.*
Converſation [intercourſe, ſociety] *commercio,* s. m. *ſocietà, familiarità,* s. f.
Life and converſation, *vita, e coſtumi.*
CONVE'RSATIVE, adj. [relating to publick life, not contemplative] *appartenente al viver comune, non aſtratto o contemplativo.*
CONVE'RSE, s. [familiar intercourſe] *conoſcenza, familiarità, ſocietà, converſazione,* s. f. *commercio,* s. m.
I have no converſe with him, *non ho conoſcenza, o familiarità con lui.*
To CONVE'RSE [to keep company, to be familiar] *converſare, uſare, trattare inſieme, praticare, bazzicare.*
I don't love to converſe with ſuch people;

people, *non amo di conversare con tal sorte di gente.*

CONVE'RSED, adj. *conversato, usato, trattato, praticato, bazzicato.*

CONVE'RSING, s. *conversamento,* s. m. *il conversare.*

CONVE'RSION, s. [alteration, change, especially of manners from bad to good] *conversione,* s. f. *rivolgimento di pensiero e di mente da male a bene.*

CO'NVERT, s. [a person who is turned to the true religion] *un convertito, una persona convertita.*

To CONVE'RT [to bring a person to the profession of the true religion] *convertire, convértere.*

To convért a heathen to the christian religion, *convertire un pagano alla religione cristiana.*

To convért, verb neut. *convertirsi.*

To convért [to turn] *convertire, trasmutare, transformare.*

To convert one substance into another, *convertire una sustanza in un' altra.*

To convért love into hatred, *convertire l'amore in odio.*

To convért a thing to one's own use, *appropriarsi qualche cosa, impiegarla per suo proprio uso.*

CONVE'RTED, adj. *convertito.*

CONVE'RTER, s. *che converte.*

CONVERTIBI'LITY, s. [the quality of being possible to be converted] *convertibilità, il poter esser converso.*

CONVE'RTIBLE, adj. [changeable, that may be turned] *convertibile, atto, ed acconcio a convertirsi.*

CONVE'RTING, s. *convertimento, trasmutamento,* s. m. *conversione,* s. f.

CONVERTI'TE, s. [a convert] *una persona convertita.*

CONVE'X, adj. [bending down on every side] *convesso, concavo.*

Convex, s. [the outside of the globe, or any other round body] *il convesso, il di fuori del concavo.*

CONVE'XED, part. adj. [protuberant in a circular form] *gonfio in cerchio, convesso.*

CONVE'XEDLY, adv. [in a convex form] *convessamente, in modo convesso.*

CONVE'XITY, s. [the bending or bowing of any thing down on the outside] *la parte convessa d'un corpo convesso, convessità.*

CONVE'XLY, adv. [in a convex form] *convessamente, in maniera convessa.*

CONVE'XNESS, s. [spheriodical protuberance, convexity] *gonfiezza sferale, convessità.*

CONVE'XO-CONCAVE, adj. [having the hollow on the inside corresponding to the external protuberance] *la cui concavità quadra colla convessità.*

To CONVE'Y, [to carry] *portare, trasportare, trasferire, condurre.* pref. *trasferisco, conduco.* pret. *condussi.*

To convey [to send] *mandare, far capitare.*

To convey [to make over] *trasferire, trasmettere, cedere.* pref. *trasferisco.*

If you give it me I shall convey it to him, *se voi me lo date glielo manderò, glielo farò capitare.*

To convey a thing over sea, *far trasportare che che si sia per mare.*

To convey commodities by water, *traghettare mercanzie per acqua.*

To convey goods by land, *vetturegiare delle robe.*

How do you convey your letters to him? *in che modo gli fate capitare le vostre lettere?*

To convey one's right to another, *trasmettere o cedere il suo diritto ad un altro.*

He conveys his sense in plain words, *egli si spiega con termini intelligibili, egli ha chiarezza nel dire.*

To convey poison into a thing, *avvelenare che che si sia.*

To convey one's love or respects to a man in a letter, *fare i suoi baciamani, o riverire alcuno per lettere.*

To convey a man out of danger, *salvare alcuno da qualche pericolo, metterlo in luogo sicuro.*

To convey one's self quickly out of a place, *sfilarsela, scappare, fuggirsene, involarsi, andarsine tosto.*

To convey away, *portar via.*

CONVE'YANCE, s. [carrying] *trasporto,* s. m. *vettura,* s. f.

Conveyance [a law word] *cessione,* s. f.

CONVE'YANCER, s. *una notajo.*

CONVE'YER, s. [one who carries or transmits any thing] *colui che porta o trasmette cosa.*

CONVE'YING, s. *il portare o trasportare, trasporto.*

CONVI'CT, s. [one who is found guilty of an offence] *una persona convinta di qualche delitto, un reo.*

Convict, adj. [convicted, detected in guilt] *convinto, provato reo.*

To CONVI'CT [to prove one guilty] *convincere, provare ad altrui il suo delitto.* pret. *convinsi.*

To convict one of high treason, *convincere altrui di delitto di lesa maestà.*

CONVI'CTED, adj. *convinto.*

CONVI'CTION, s. *convinzione,* s. f.

CONVI'CTIVE, adj. *convincente.*

CONVI'CTIVENESS, s. *evidenza, prova,* s. f.

To CONVI'NCE [to make a man sensible of the truth of any thing] *convincere, persuadere, provare, fare, vedere.* pret. *convinsi, persuasi.*

To convince one of his error, *convincere altrui del suo errore.*

To convince you that it is not so, I say—— *per farvi vedere che la cosa non va così, dico——.*

CONVI'NCED, adj. *convinto, persuaso, provato.*

I am convinced of it, *ne sono persuaso.*

CONVI'NCINGLY, adv. *ex.* convincingly true, *evidentemente, d'una maniera evidente.*

To CONVI'VE [to entertain, to feast] *convitare, festeggiare.*

CONU'NDRUM, s. [a low jest] *una facezia plebea.*

To CO'NVOCATE [to call together] *convocare, chiamare insieme, ridurre insieme.*

CONVOCA'TION, s. [a general assembly of the clergy] *convocazonie,* s. f.

To CONVO'KE [to call together] *convocare, chiamare per fare adunanza.*

To CONVO'LVE [to roll together, to roll one part upon another] *ravvolgere una parte intorno a un altra, torcere insieme.*

CONVOLUTED, adj. [twisted, rolled upon itself] *ravvolto, ritorto intorno a se stesso.*

CONVOLU'TION, s. [the act of rolling any thing upon itself] *ravvolgimento, torcimento.*

Convolution [the state of rolling together in company] *lo essere ravvolto insieme a un tratto.*

CO'NVOY, s. [men of war that go along with merchants ships to defend them from the enemies] *convojo, convoglio,* s. m. *scorta,* s. f.

To be a convoy to one, *servir di scorta ad alcuno.*

To CO'NVOY [to guard] *convojare, convogliare, accompagnare, che che si sia per sicurezza, scortare, far la scorta.*

CO'NVOY'D, adj. *convojato, convogliato.*

To CONVU'LSE [to give an irregular and involuntary motion to the parts of any body] *cagionar convulsione, dar un moto irregolare ed involontario a checchessia.*

CONVU'LSION, s. [a shrinking up of the sinews] *convulsione,* s. f. *l'involontario intirizzare e ritrarsi de' nervi e de' muscoli.*

A small convulsion, *convulsioncella.*

Convulsion fits, *convulsione.*

CONVU'LSIVE, adj. [belonging to convulsion] *convulsivo, di convulsione.*

Convulsive motions, *moti convulsivi.*

CO'NY, s. [rabbit] *un coniglio.*

Cony-skin, *pelle di coniglio.*

Cony-burrow, *tana di coniglio.*

A cony-warren, *conigliera,* s. f. *luogo dove stanno i conigli.*

Cony-catcher [cunning cheat] *un furbo, un barattiere, un furfante.*

To CO'NYCATCH [to cheat, to trick] *ingannare con furberia.*

To COO [to cry as a dove or pigeon] *mormorare come fanno le tortorelle, ed i colombi.*

CO'OING, s. [the noise of turtles and pigeons] *mormorìo de' colombi.*

COOK, s. [a man that dresses meat] *un cuoco.*

Cook [woman cook] *una cuoca.*

Cook-maid, s. *fantesca che fa da cuoca.*

A cook [that keeps a cook's shop] *un treccone.*

A cook's shop, *una bettola.*

The cook room in a ship, *la cucina nel vascello.*

To COOK [to prepare victals for the table] *far la cucina, cuocere il mangiare.*

To cook [to prepare for any purpose] *prepararsi a qualche cosa.*

CO'OKERY, s. [the art of dressing victuals] *l'arte del cuoco.*

To understand cookery *intendersi di cucina.*

COOL, adj. [cooling] *fresco di natura, di qualità fresca, freddo temperato.*

'Tis cool, *fa fresco.*

A cool place, *un luogo fresco.*

A cool room, *una camera fresca.*

Little cool, *freschetto.*

To COOL [to make cool] *rinfrescare, far fresco quello che è caldo.*

To cool [to grow cool] *rinfrescarsi, raffreddarsi.*

To cool [to allay] *abbattere, moderare, sminuire, deprimere, conculcare, abbassare.* pres. *sminuisco.*

To cool [to slacken, to relent] *raffreddarsi, minuire, rallentare, divenir lento, scemare il fervore nell' operazione, o nell' affetto.* pres. *minuisco.*

To cool wine, *rinfrescare del vino.*

To cool the cannon, *rinfrescare il cannone.*

This will cool your courage, *questo vi abbatterà o sminuirà il coraggio.*

It begins to cool, *comincia a farsi fresco.*

CO'OLED, adj. *rinfresco, v.* To cool.

CO'OLER, s. *un refrigerativo.*

Verjuice is a cooler, *l' agresto è refrigerativo.*

Cooler [a vessel used by brewers] *tino dove fassi raffreddare la cervogia.*

CO'OLING, s. *il rinfrescare, rinfrescamento.*

Cooling, adj. *refrigerativo, refrigerante, che ha virtù di rinfrescare.*

A cooling liquor, *un liquore rifrigerante.*

CO'OLNESS, s. *freschezza, s. f. fresco, s. m.*

The coolness of the night, *la freschezza, o il fresco della notte.*

CO'OLY, adv. *freddamente, d'un sangue freddo.*

A COOM, or COOMB, of corn, [a measure containing four bushels] *misura di grano.*

COOP, s. [a place where fowls are kept and made fat] *stía, s. f. luogo dove si tengono i polli, per ingrassarli.*

Coop [a barrel, a vessel for the preservation of liquids] *barile, botte, o altro simil vaso da tenervi i liquidi dentro.*

To coop up, *rinchiudere.* pret. *rinchiusi. racchiusi.*

CO'OPED UP, adj. *rinchiuso, racchiuso.*

COOPE'E, s. [a step in dancing] *passo intrecciato, dicesi nel ballare.*

CO'OPER, s. [a person who makes tubs, casks, barrels, &c.] *bottajo,* s. m. *quello che fa, e racconcia le botti.*

A wine cooper, *un mercante di vino.*

To COO'PERATE [to work together, to act with one another in the producing some effect] *coperare, operare insieme.*

COO'PERATED, adj. *cooperato.*

COOPERA'TION, s. [a working together with] *cooperamento,* s. m. *cooperazione,* s. f.

COO'PERATING, adj. [that cooperates] *cooperante, che coopera, che ajuta l' operazione.*

The cooperating grace, *la grazia cooperante.*

CO'OPERATIVE, adj. [promoting the same end jointly] *che coopera, cooperativo.*

COOPERA'TOR, s. [he that cooperates] *cooperatore,* s. m.

COO'RDINATE, adj. [of equal order, degree, or rank] *del medesimo ordine, grado e dignità.*

COOT, s. *smergo,* s. m. *uccello d' acqua così detto.*

A very coot [a fool] *uno sciocco, un balordo, un minchione, un baccello, un' oca, un barbagianni.*

COP, s. [top of any thing] *cima, sommità,* s. f. *il capo di checchessia, il sommo.*

COP [tuft on the heads of birds] *pennacchio, ciuffetto,* s. m.

A cop of hay, *una bica di fieno.*

CO'PAL, s. [a white and bright rosin brought from the West-Indies] *ragia bianca e lucente che ci viene dall' Indie occidentali.*

COPA'RCENER, s. [he that has equal share in the inheritance of his ancestors] *coerede,* s. m. *quello che possiede egualmente l' eredità de' suoi maggiori.*

COPA'RCENY, or COPA'RSENY, [an equal share or division] *parte o divisione eguale.*

To hold an estate in coparceny, *godere un bene congiuntamente con un altro.*

COPA'RTNER, s. [one that has a share in some common stock or affair] *compagno, sozio, uno che ha una parte con un altro in un capitale o in un affare.*

COPA'RTNERSHIP, s. *società, compagnia, egulianza di parte in un capitale o affare.*

COPA'IVA, s. *sorte di gomma.*

COPE, s. [a priest's vestment] *pianeta,* s. f.

'Tis the finest thing under the cope of heaven, *non v' è la piu bella cosa sotto 'l cielo.*

To COPE [to barter, to truck] *barattare, cambiar cosa a cosa.*

To cope right hands [to fight] *venire alle mani, battersi, venire alle strette.*

We are able to cope with him [we may make head against him] *noi siamo capaci di fargli testa, di contrastargli.*

To cope [to jut out] *sporgere, uscir del piano o del perpendicolo, parlando d'un muro.*

COPES-MATE, s. [a partner in merchandizing] *associato, o compagno nel negozio.*

CO'PING, s. [from to cope] *baratto* s. m.

Coping joining together in fight] *combattimento,* s. m. *battaglia,* s. f.

Coping [top in a building] *la cima, la sommità d' un edificio.*

The coping of a wall, *sporto d' uno muraglia.*

Coping-irons [instrument for paring the talons of a hawk] *strumento da rimondare gli sproni del falcone.*

CO'PIOUS, adj. [abounding, plentiful] *copioso, abbondante, abbondevole.*

A copious language, *una lingua copiosa o abbondevole.*

CO'PIOUSLY, adv. *copiosamente, abbondantamente, doviziosamente, ampiamente, largamente.*

CO'PIOUSNESS, s. *copiosità, ropia, abbondanza, ricchezza,* s. f.

CO'PIST, s. [a transcriber] *copista,* s. m. *colui che copia.*

CO'PLAND, s. [a piece of ground which terminates with an acute angle] *pezzo di terreno che termina con un angolo acuto.*

COPP, *v.* COP.

CO'PPED, adj. [as a bird] *crestuto.*

Copped [sharp-pointed] *puntuto, aruto.*

CO'PPEL, s. [a pot in which goldsmiths melt and fine their metal] *coppella,* s. f. *picciol vasetto, nel quale messo nel fuoco si cimenta l'argento.*

CO'PPER, s. *rame,* s. m. *uno de' sei metalli primitivi.*

Red or yellow copper, *rame rosso o giallo.*

Copper, *vaso grande di rame da bollirvi cose dentro.*

Copper-colour [such as many Indians have] *colore di rame, olivastro come molti Indiani.*

Copper-smith, *calderajo,* s. m. *facitor di calderotti, e altri vasi simili di rame.*

Copper-plate, *stampa di rame, lastra di rame sulla quale si scolpiscono le figure che si vogliono stampare.*

Copper-nose, *naso rosso, naso di gallinarcio.*

CO'PPERASS, s. [a sort of mineral] *vitriolo,* s. m. *sorta di minerale.*

CO'PPERSMITH, s. [one that manufactures copper] *fabbro che lavora in rame.*

CO'PPERY, adj. [containing copper] *che contien rame.*

CO'PPICE, s. [a small wood, consisting of underwoods, which may be cut at the growth of twelve or fifteen years] *macchia, bosco folto che si taglia à certi tempi.*

Copple-crowned, adj. *crestato che hà un pennacchio sopra la testa come alcuni uccelli.*

CO'PPLE-DUST, s. [cuple-dust, powder used in purifying metals] *sorta di polvere adoperata nel purificar metalli.*

CO'PPLED, adj. [rising in a conick form] *che s' alza in forma conica o di cono.*

COPSE, s. [short-wood] *bosco tagliato basso.*

To COPSE, s. [to preserve underwoods] *conservare i boschi che sono stati tagliati bassi.*

To CO'PULATE, [to unite, to conjoin] *accoppiare, unire, congiungere.*

To copulate, v. n. [to come together of different sexes] *l' accoppiarsi degli animali di sesso diverso.*

COPULA'TION, s. [a coupling together] *copulazione, copula,* s. f. *rongiugnimento,* s. m.

CO'PULATIVE, adj. [that which serves to couple or join] *copulativo.*

A conjunction copulative, *una congiunzione copulativa.*

Co'py, s. [any writing transcribed] copia, s. f.

Copy, s. [the original of a book] copia originale d'un autore, un manuscritto.

Copy [a pattern to write after] copia, s. f. esemplare, s. m.

Copy [printed book] esemplare, libro stampato.

To compare the copy with the original, collazionare la copia coll' originale.

A copy of verses, un sonetto.

Copy money, la somma che un librajo paga per l'esemplare, o manuscritto d' un libro.

Copyhold [a tenure for which the tenant has nothing to show but the copy of the rolls made by the lord's court] podere che un fittajuolo possiede sotto certe particolari condizioni in virtù della copia d' un ruolo fatta in corte del governatore della provincia.

Copyholder, s. colui che possiede certi beni stabili, che si chiamano Copyhold.

To Co'py [to write after an original] copiare, trascrivere. pret. trascrissi, imitare. pret. imitai.

To copy out a will, copiare un testamento.

Copy'd out, adj. copiato, trascritto.

I must get it copy'd out, bisogna che io lo faccia copiare.

Co'pying out, s. il copiare.

Coque'tte, s. [an amorous, wanton, tattling woman] una civetta, una donna vana e leggiera, che affetta vezzi per allettare.

To play the coquette, civettare, fare atti di vanità e di leggerezza per allettare.

To Coque't, [to treat with an appearance of amorous tenderness] trattare con finta amorosa tenerezza.

Co'quetry, s. [affected carriage to win the love of men] civetteria, vanità, leggerezza, mezzi affettati.

Co'racle, s. [a small boat used by fishermen on the Severn] barchetta usata da' pescatori nella Severna.

Co'ral, s. [a sea plant] corallo, s. m. pianta, quale nasce nel fondo del mare.

Co'ral, s. [a sort of moss sticking to the coral] corallina, s. f. spezie di musco che nasce negli scogli del mare e d' attorno a' coralli.

Cora'line, adj. di corallo, del colore del corallo.

Coralline, s. [a sea plant] corallina, sorta di pianta marina.

Coralloi'd, } adj. [resembling
Corallo'idal, } coral] corallino, che somiglia al corallo.

Co'rant, s. [a nimble sprightly dance] Corrente, sorta di danza vivacissima.

Co'rban, s. [an alms-basket] canestrello della limosina.

Corbe, adj. [crooked] curvo.

Corbe'ils, [little baskets filled with earth, and placed upon the parapets] tonnellate, s. f. corbelli pieni di terra per coprirsi dal nemico nell' andare all' assalto d' una piazza.

Co'rbel, Co'rbet, or Co'rbil, s. [a shouldering piece jutting out into walls to bear up a post, summer, &c. beccatello, peduccio, s. m. mensola, s. f. che si pon per sostegno sotto i terrazzini, ballatoi, corridoi, sporti, &c.

Corbet [places in walls wherein images stand] nicchia, s. f. quel voto o incavato, che fassi nelle muraglie, ad effetto di mettervi statue e simili.

Cord, s. [rope] corda, s. f.

A Cord of wood, catasta di legna.

Cords [the strings of an harp, lute, violin, &c.] corde per uso di sonare, fatte di minugia o di metallo.

Cord [among farriers, is a strait sinew in the fore leg of a horse, which comes from the shackle vein to the gristle of his nose] corda, s. f. téndine, s. m.

Cord-ma'ker, s. cordajo; che fa le corde.

To Cord [to bind with ropes] legar con corde.

Co'rdage, s. [all the ropes belonging to the ringing or tackling of a ship] sartiame, s. m. nome generico di tutte le funi, che si adoperano nelle navi.

Co'rded, adj. [made of ropes] fatto di corde.

Cordeli'er, s. [a grey friar of the order of St. Francis] frate Francescano.

Co'rdial, adj. [good for the heart, comfortable, hearty] cordiale, di cuore.

A cordial julep, giulebbe cordiale.

Cordial [hearty, sincere] cordiale, svisceráto, affettuoso.

Cordial love, amor cordiale.

Cordial friend [hearty friend] amico cordiale, o svisceráto.

A cordial, s. un cordiale.

Co'rdialness, } s. [heartiness,
Cordia'lity, } sincere or hearty love] cordialità, svisceratezza, s. f. affetto, s. m.

Co'rdially, adv. [heartily] cordialmente, svisceratamente, con tutto'l cuore.

Co'rdiner, or Co'rdwainer, s. [a shoemaker] calzolajo, s. m.

Co'rdon, s. [in fortification, a row of stones jutting out between the rampart and the basis of the parapet] cordone, s. m. risalto fatto di sassi in fila, a modo di corda che è fra'l riparo e il parapetto.

Co'rdwain, s. [a sort of leather made of goat skins, in Cordova in Spain] cordovano, s. m. cuojo di pelle di capra.

Cordwainer, s. [a shoemaker] calzolajo.

Core, s. [that part of the fruit wherein the kernel lies] torso, s. m.

The core of a pear or apple, il torso d' una pera o d'una mela, la parte interna.

Core [the matter contained in a sore] materia putrefatta che è n' una piaga.

To be rotten in the core [to have no good principles] esser depravato ne' costumi.

Coria'ceous, adj. [consisting of leather] che è di pelle dura, coriaceo.

Coriaceous, [of a substance resembling leather] coriaceo, d' una sostanza che s' assomiglia alla pelle o al cuojo.

Coria'nder, s. [a kind of plant] coriandro, curiandolo, s. m.

Co'rinth, s. [a small fruit commonly called currant] ribes, pianta nota, il cui frutto è di più colori.

Cori'nthian order, [in architecture] l' ordine Corintio.

Cork, s. [cork-tree] sughero, suvero, s. m.

Cork [the wood or bark of cork tree] sughero, corteccia di sughero.

Cork [stopple] turacciolo, s. m.

To stop a bottle with a cork, turare un fiasco con un turacciolo di sughero.

Co'rkin-pin, s. [a pin of the largest size] ago grande.

Cork, adj. [consisting of cork] che è fatto di sughero.

Co'rmorant, s. [a kind of sea-raven] uccello che vive di pesci.

A cormorant [a glutton] un ghiotto, un goloso, un ghiottone.

Cormu'dgeon, s. [miser] un avaro, uno spilorcio, un cacastecchi.

Corn, s. [the grain of wheat, barley, rice, oats, &c.] grano, frumento, s. m. nome generale di tutti le biade.

Standing corn, biada, s. f. tutte le semente, come grano, orzo, vena e simili ancora in erba.

To give the horses their corn, dar della vena ai cavalli.

A corn of salt, un granello di sale.

A corn on the toe, callo nel piede.

To measure another man's corn by one's own bushel, misurare altrui col suo passetto.

A corn field, un seminato.

Corn-factor, mercante di grano.

A corn-chandler, venditore di grano.

A corn cutter, un che taglia i calli.

A corn-loft, un granajo.

Turkey-corn, grano Turco, s. m.

Corn-rose, nigella, s. f.

To Corn [to powder with salt] aspergerr di sale, salare un poco.

To corn powder, marinare polvere.

Co'rnage, s. [an imposition upon corn] dazio sopra il grano.

Co'rned, adj. salato.

Co'rnel, s. [cornel-berry] corniola, cornia, s. f. frutto del corniolo.

Cornel-tree, s. corniolo, cornio, s. m.

Corne'lian, s. [cornelian stone] cornalina, s. f. sorta di pietra preziosa.

Co'rner, s. [an angle] angolo, canto, cantone, spigolo, s. m.

A corner of a street, una cantonata.

A corner of a room, un canto della camera.

The corner of a wall, cantonata d'un muro.

The corner of the eye, la coda dell' occhio.

A corner-stone, pietra angolare.

A corner-house, casa che fa la cantonata.

Made corner-wise, fatto ad angoli

Corners [windings of rivers] girate, giravolte de' fiumi.

A corner

A corner [lurking-hole] *nascondiglio, ugigattolo*, s. m.

In a corner [privately] *nascosamente, occultamente, celatamente, privatamente, ascosamente, di nascoso.*

CO'RNERED, adj. *angolare, cantonuto, diagonale.*

CO'RNET, s. [a sort of musical instrument made of horn] *cornetta*, s. f. *strumento musicale di fiato.*

Cornet [an ensign of a company of horse] *cornetta, e cornetto*, s. m. *insegna di compagnia di cavalleria.*

Cornet [a linen or lac'd head dress of women] *spezie di cuffia.*

Cornet [a farrier's instrument for letting horses blood] *cornetto*, s. m. *strumento a foggia di coppetta per trar sangue ai cavalli.*

Cornet [coffin of paper] *cartoccio*, s. m.

Cornet [a scarf of black taffety, which doctors of law or physick used to wear on the collar of their robes] *bavero*, s. m.

CO'RNETTER, s. [a blower of the cornet] *colui che suona la cornetta.*

CO'RNICE, or CO'RNISH, s. [the highest part of the entablature, and the uppermost ornament of any wainscot] *cornice*, s. f. *ornamento, e quasi cintura di fabbrica e di edificio, la quale sporge in fuora. Anche l'ornamento di tavolato, di quadri, o simili.*

CO'RNICLE, s. [a small horn] *picciol corno.*

CO'RNMUSE, s. [a bag pipe] *cornamusa, piva*, s. f. *strumento musicale di fiato, composto d'un otro e de tre canne, una per darle fiato, e l'altre due per sonare.*

CO'RNUTE, adj. [horned, having horns] *cornuto, che ha corna.*

Cornute [cuckold] *cornuto.*

To CO'RNUTE [to cuckold] *far le corna, far becco.*

CO'RNUTED, adj. *cornuto.*

CO'RODY, s. [a sum of money, or an allowance of meat, drink, and cloathing, allowed by an abbot out of a monastery to the king for the maintenance of any one of his servants] *spezie di tributo, che un abate pagava altre volte al Re in danari o in vitto e vestimenti per il mantenimento d'alcuni suoi domestici.*

CO'ROLLARY, s. [a consequence drawn from something already proved or demonstrated] *corollario*, s. m. *una conclusione vera che discende dalle cose dei sopra provate.*

CO'RONAL, adj. ex. Coronal suture [is a cleft in the head, made like a comb, and joins as if the teeth of two combs were closely compacted into one another] *sutura coronale, incastratura anteriore del cranio.*

Coronal vien, *la vena coronale, che circonda tutta la sostanza del cuore.*

CORONA'TION, s. [the crowning of a king] *coronamento*, s. m. *coronazione*, s. f.

The coronation of the king of England, *il coronamento de Re d' Inghilterra.*

CO'RONER, s. [an officer, who, with the assistance of a jury of twelve men, enquires in behalf of the crown into all untimely deaths] *officiale deputato, che coll' intervento di dodici giurati ha la cura d'esaminare se un corpo trovato morto sia stato assassinato o morto d'una morte naturale.*

CO'RONET, s. [a little crown] *coronetta*, s. f.

A duke's coronet, *una corona ducale.*

CO'RPORAL, s. [an inferior officer of a company of foot soldiers] *caporale*, s. m.

Corporal [the communion cloth in the church of Rome] *corporale*, s. m. *quel pannicello bianco sul quale posa il prete l'ostia consacrata.*

Corporal, adj. [of, or belonging to the body, bodily] *corporale, di corpo, che ha corpo.*

A corporal punishment, *punizione corporale.*

A corporal oath, *giuramento fatto sopra l'evangelio.*

CORPORA'LITY, s. [the quality of being embodied] *il corpo, l' aver corpo.*

CO'RPORALLY, adv. *corporalmente.*

To punish a man corporally, *punire alcuno corporalmente.*

CO'RPORATE, adj. [united into one body] *unito in un corpo.*

A corporate body, *una comunità, il corpo degli abitanti d'un borgo o d'un villaggio.*

CORPORA'TION, s. [corporate body] *communità.*

A corporation town, *una città municipale.*

CORPO'RATURE, s. [the form, bulk or constitution of the body] *corporatura*, s. f. *tutto il composto del corpo.*

CORPO'REAL, adj. [that is of a bodily substance, or pertaineth to the body] *corporeo, che ha corpo, del corpo.*

The corporeal frame, *la forma corporea.*

To CORPO'RIFY, [to embody] *acquistar corpo.*

CORPS, } s. [dead body] *corpo*
CORPSE, } *morto, cadavere*, s. m.

To accompany the corps to the grave, *accompagnare il corpo del morto alla sepoltura.*

Corps de bataille [the main body of an army drawn up for battle] *il corpo di battaglia.*

Corps de garde, *corpo di guardia.*

COR'PULENCE, } s. [bulkiness of
COR'PULENCY, } body] *corpulenza*, s. f. *grossezza del corpo.*

CO'RPULENT, adj. [big bodied, fat, gross] *corpulento, grave di corpo, grasso, di gran corpo.*

CORPUS CHRISTI-DAY, s [a festival appointed in honour of the Sacrament of the Lord] *Corpus domini*, s. m. *la festa che si celebra in memoria dell' istituzione del sagramento dell' altare dieci giorni dopo la pentecoste.*

CO'RPUSCLE, s. [the smallest part, or physical atom of body] *corpuscolo, piccolo corpo, atomo*, s. m.

CORPU'SCULAR, } adj. [belong-
CORPUSCULA'RIAN, } ing to atoms] *di corpuscolo.*

Corpuscular or corpuscularian philosophy [that which explains natural phænomena, by motions and affections of the minute particles of matter] *filosofia che spiega i fenomeni della natura per mezzo del moto, figura, e qualità degli atomi.*

To CORRA'DE [to scrape together] *accumulare insieme con fatica.*

To Corrade, [to rub off] *rader via.*

CORRADIA'TION, s. [a conjunction of rays in one point] *unione di raggi in un punto.*

CORRE'CT, adj. [without faults] *corretto, senza errore, emendato.*

Correct, adv. *correttamente, emendatamente.*

He writes correct, *egli scrive correttamente.*

To CORRE'CT [to mend the faults] *correggere, emendare, purgare, rimodernare, parlandosi di scritture.* pret. *corressi.*

To correct [to chastise, or punish] *correggere, castigare, punire.* pres. *punisco.*

To correct [to allay or temper] *temperare, moderare, raffrenare, correggere.*

To correct [to reprove or check] *sgridare, riprendere, garrire, improverare.*

To correct a book, *correggere un libro.*

Cinnamon will correct the coldness of it, *la cannella ne modererà la freddezza.*

'Tis your duty to correct your son, *è il vostro dovere di correggere, o castigare vostro figlio.*

My watch corrects the sun, *il mio oriuolo regola il sole.*

To correct the Magnificat [to find fault where there is none] *cercare il pelo nell' uovo.*

CORRE'CTED, adj. *corretto*, v. To correct.

CORRE'CTER, v. Corrector.

CORRE'CTING, s. *correggimento*, s. m. *il correggere.*

CORRE'CTION, s. [correcting, mending] *correzione, emendazione*, s. f. *correggimento*, s. m.

Correction [punishment] *correzione, castigo.*

A house of correction, *una casa di correzione.*

Under correction, *con buona grazia, con rispetto.*

Under correction, gentlemen, he lies, *con vostra buona grazia, signori, egli mente.*

Correction [reproof] *riprensione, ammonizione, sgridata*, s. f.

CORRE'CTIONER, s. [a jayl-bird] *un birbone che è stato in una casa di correzione per qualche bricconeria fatta.*

CORRE'CTIVE, adj. [which serves to correct, to allay or temper] *correttivo.*

A corrective medicine, *una medicina correttiva.*

A corrective, s. *un correttivo, medicamento correttivo.*

CORRE'CTLY, adv. [without fault] *correttamente, emendatamente, senza errore.*

CORRE'CTNESS, s. *esattezza*, s. f.

CORRE'CTOR, s. [one who corrects] *correttore*, s. m. *che corregge*.

A printer's corrector, *correttore di stamperia*.

Corrector of the staple [an officer belonging to the staple who recordeth the bargains of merchants made there] *officiale d'un' magazzino, o mercato, che tiene il registro dei contratti de' mercanti, e delle vendite e delle compre*.

To CO'RRELATE, v. n. [to have a reciprocal relation, as father and son] *aver correlazione*.

CORRE'LATIVE, adj. [relating to another] *correlativo, che ha correlazione*.

To CORRESPO'ND [to answer, to fit, to agree] *corrispondere, confarsi, aver proporzione e convenienza, convenire*. pret. *corrisposi*. pres. *convengo*. pret. *convenni*.

To correspond [to hold mutual commerce and familiarity] *correspondere, far commerzio, negoziare, tener corrispondenza di lettere, trattare*.

CORRESPO'NDENCE, s. [a mutual intelligence, commerce and familiarity] *corrispondenza, familiarità, intrinsichezza*, s. f. *commercio, trattato*, s. m.

To hold correspondence with one, *aver corrispondenza con uno*.

To keep a private correspondence with one, *esser d intelligenza con uno, intenderfela con uno*.

Correspondence [proportion of one thing with another] *corrispondenza, proporzione, convenienza*, s. f.

CORRESPONDENCY, *lo stesso che* correspondence.

CORRESPO'NDENT, adj. [agreeable, suitable] *corrispondente, che corrisponde, proporzionato, che ha proporzione, e convenienza*.

A correspondent, s. [one that holds correspondence, as in trade] *corrispondente*, s. m. *quello col quale siamo soliti di tenere commerzio di lettere, e negoziare*.

He is my correspondent, *egli è mio corrispondente*.

CORRESPO'NSIVE, adj. *che ha esatta corrispondenza, che corrisponde esattamente con un' altra cosa*.

CORRIDO'R, s. [a covered way in fortification] *strada coperta, termine di fortificazione*.

CO'RRIGIBLE, adj. [that may be corrected] *corriggible, docile, che si puo correggere*.

CORRI'VAL, s. [a competitor either in love or business] *competitore, concorrente, rivale*, s. m.

CORRO'BORANT, adj. [having the power to give strength] *che corrobora, che fortifica*.

To CORRO'BORATE [to strengthen, to confirm] *corroborare, confermare, fortificare, dar forza*.

CORRO'BORATED, adj. *corroborato, confermato, fortificato*.

CORROBORA'TION, s. *corroborazione*, s. f.

CORRO'BORATIVE, adj. [serving to strengthen] *corroborativo, confortativo, che corrobora*.

To CORRO'DE [to gnaw or fret] *corrodere, rodere, consumare a poco a poco*.

Aqua fortis corrodes metals, *l'acqua forte corrode i metalli*.

CORRO'DIBLE, adj. [possible to be consumed] *che puo essere corroso o consumato*.

CORROD'ING, s. *corrodimento*, s. m. *il corrodere*.

Corroding, adj. [that corrodes] *corrosivo, che corrode*.

Corroding cares *cure mordaci*.

CO'RRODY, *v.* Corody.

CORRO'SION, s. [a gnawing] *corrosione*, s. f. *rodimento, corrodimento*, s. m.

CO'RROSIVE, adj. [which has a gnawing quality] *corrosivo, che corrode*.

A corrosive, s. [a corroding medicine] *un corrosivo*.

CO'RROSIVENESS, s. [the quality that some liquors have of dissolving bodies] *qualità corrosiva*.

To CO'RRUGATE, [to wrinkle or purse up] *far le grinze, cagionar grinze*.

CORRUGA'TION, s. [contraction into wrinkles] *l' essere ridotto pieno di grinze*.

CORRU'PT, adj. [naught, rotten] *corrotto, guasto, contaminato, cattivo, depravato*.

Corrupt blood, *sangue corrotto*.

Corrupt principles, *cattivi principi*.

A corrupt will or reason, *una volontà, o ragione depravata*.

A corrupt judge, *un giudice corrotto*.

To CORRU'PT [to mar, to spoil] *corrompere, guastare, contaminare, putrefare*. pret. *corruppi*.

To corrupt [to bribe one's judges] *corrompere i suoi giudici*.

To corrupt witnesses, *subornare i testimoni*.

To corrupt [to infect] *corrompere, infettare*.

To corrupt, verb. neut. *corrompersi, guastarsi, putrefarsi, contaminarsi*.

When the blood begins to corrupt, *quando il sangue comincia a corrompersi*.

CORRU'PTED, adj. *corrotto*, *v.* To corrupt.

CORRU'PTER, s. *corruttore, corrompitore*, s. m.

CORRUPTIBI'LITY, s. [aptness to corrupt] *corruttibilità*, s. f.

CORRU'PTIBLE, adj. [subject to corruption] *corruttibile, corruttevole, atto a corrompersi*.

CORRU'PTIBLY, adv. [in such a manner as to be corrupted] *in modo da esser corrotto*.

CORRU'PTION, s. [a corrupting or marring] *corruzione, corrottura, corruttela*, s. f. *corrompimento*, s. m.

Corruption [corrupt matter] *corruzione, putrefazione, marcia*, s. f. *umor putrido che si genera negli enfiati e nelle ulcere*.

CORRU'PTIVE, adj. [apt to corrupt] *corruttivo, pestilenziale*.

CORRU'PTLESS, adj. [insusceptible of corruption, undecaying] *incorrottibile, incorrotto*.

CORRU'PTLY, adv. *corrottamente*.

CORRUPTNESS, s. [the quality of corruption, putrescence, vice] *corruttela, putrefazione, vizio*.

CO'RSAIR, s. [pirate] *corsale, corsare, pirato, pirata*, s. m.

CORSE, s. [a body] *un corpo*.

Corse, [a dead body] *un cadavero, un corpo morto*.

CO'RSLET, or CO'RSELET, s. [an armour for a pike-man] *corsaletto*, s. m. *corazza*, s. f.

Corslets [pike-men] *le pierhe, le picche d'un reggimento*.

CO'RTICAL, adj. [barky, belonging to the rind] *di corteccia, di scorza, appartenente alla corteccia, alla scorza*.

CO'RVET, *v.* Curvet.

CORU'SCANT, adj [shining, bright] *corruscante, risplendente, fiammeggiante*.

CORUSCA'TION, s. [flash] *corruscazione*, s. f. *balenamento, lampeggiamento*, s. m.

COSIER, s. [a botcher] *un che rattoppa, che rattaccona malamente, che fa le cose stracuratamente*.

COSME'TICKS, s. pl. [womens ornaments or washes] *abbigliamenti, ornamenti, addobbi donneschi, o belletti per rendere la carnagione bella*.

COSMO'GRAPHER, s. [one skilled in cosmography] *cosmografo*, s. m. *maestro in cosmografia*.

COSMO'GRAPHY, s. [a science describing the several parts of the visible world] *cosmografia*, s. f. *quella parte della matematica, che ha per oggetto la descrizion delle parti del mondo, dividendolo nelle sfere celesti ed elementari*.

COSMOGRA'PHICAL, adj. [belonging to cosmography] *cosmografico, di cosmografia*.

CO'SSET, s. [a lamb, calf, &c. brought up by hand] *agnello, vitello*, &c. *allevato senza la madre*.

COST, s. [charge, expence] *costo*, s. m. *spesa*, s. f.

I shall do it at your cost, *lo farò a vostro costo*.

To my cost, *a mie spese*.

I have learned it to my cost, *l'ho imparato a' mie spese*.

The cost of a suit, *le spese d'un processo*.

To bestow cost upon something, *fare grandi spese in qualche cosa*.

Cost [price] *prezzo, valore*, s. m.

A horse of great cost, *un cavallo d'un gran prezzo*.

He has lost both his labour and cost, *egli ha pescato pel proconsolo, egli ha perduto il danaro e la fatica*.

It does not quit cost, *non vale la pena, non mi torna a conto, non monta il pregio*.

Much worship much cost, *li onori costano*.

To COST [to stand in] *costare, valere*.

I will do it, let it cost what it will, *voglio farlo, costi quanto si voglia*.

His house cost building above ten thousand pounds, *la sua casa gli costò piu di dieci mila doppie a fabbricarla*.

I fear it will cost him his life, *temo gli costerà la vita*.

It costs me more, *mi costa più.*

The victory costs the Moors much blood, *la vittoria costò ai Mori molto sangue.*

CO'STAL, adj. [belonging to the ribs] *di costa, appartenente alle coste.*

CO'STARD, s. [a head] *una testa.*

Costard, [an apple round and bulky like the head] *sorta di mela tonda e grossa.*

COSTER-MO'NGER, s. [a fruiterer] *fruttajuolo, treccone,* s. m.

CO'STIVE, adj. [binding] *costipativo, ristrignente, atto a costipare.*

To make costive, *costipare, ristrignere.*

CO'STIVENESS, [the being binding] *costipamento,* s. m. *il costipare.*

Costiveness [the being bound] *costipazione,* s. f. *riserramento,* s. m.

CO'STLINESS, s. [sumptuousness, expensiveness] *costo, costo grande, dispendio, spesa grande, magnificenza.*

CO'STLY, adj. [that costs much, dear] *caro, dispendioso, che costa molto.*

Costly [stately] *sontuoso, suntuoso, ricco, superbo, magnifico, splendido.*

Costly, adv. *sontuosamente, suntuosamente, lautamente, splendidamente, magnificamente, con sontuosità.*

COST-MARY, s. *sorta d' erba.*

CO'STREL, s. [a vessel to carry wine in] *fiasco da vino.*

CO'STUS, s. [a sweet root] *costo,* s. m. *sorta di radice medicinale.*

COT, } COTE, } [a cottage] *capanna,* s. f.

Sheep-cot, *una mandra, un ovile.*

COTE, s. [refuse wool clotted together] *lana zaccherosa, lana cattiva.*

To COTE [to leave behind] *lasciar indietro.*

COTE'MPORARY, adj. *coetaneo, contemporaneo, vivente nel medesimo tempo.*

COTQUE'AN, s. [a man who is too busy in meddling with women's affairs] *un uomo che s'impaccia troppo negli affari dell donne.*

CO'TTAGE, s. [a little house in the country] *capanna,* s. f.

A little cottage, *capannella, rapanuccia, capannetta,* s. f.

CO'TTAGER, s. [one who lives in a cottage] *un bifolco che abita in una capanna.*

CO'TTAREL, s. [a cottage] *capanna,* s. f.

CO'TTIER, s. [one who inhabits a cot] *colui che abita in una capanna.*

CO'TTON, s. [a sort of woolly stuff] *cotone,* s. m. *bambagia,* s. f.

The cotton tree, *cotone, l' albero che produce il cotone.*

cotton cloth, *bambagina,* s. f.

To CO'TTON [to frize as some stuffs do] *raggrinzarsi.*

To cotton [to succeed, to hit] *riuscire, aver buon successo.*

Our business will not cotton, *il negozio non ci riuscirà.*

To cotton [to agree] *accomodarsi, adattarsi, accordarsi, convenire, concordare, quadrare.*

COUCH, or COUCH BED, s. [a moveable bed to lie down] *letticciuolo, lettuccio,* s. m.

To lie down upon a couch, *coricarsi sopra un lettuccio.*

To COUCH, [to lie down] *coricare e coricarsi.*

To couch in writing, *mettere in iscritto, mettere in carta.*

To couch the lance, *metter la lancia in resta.*

To couch an eye [to take off the web, as oculists do] *levare la cattarratta o macchia da un occhio.*

COUCH'ANT, adj. [in herald] *giacente.*

COUCHED, *pret. di.* To couh.

A letter well couched, *una lettera bene scritta.*

COUCHER, s. [a low term for a register] *registratore,* s. m.

Coucher [a factor residing in some place for the sake of traffick] *fattore, agente,* s. m. *uno che fa i negozi altrui.*

COUCHFE'LLOW, s. [bedfellow] *compagno di letto, compagno.*

COUCH-GRASS, or COUCH-WEED [quick grass] *gramigna,* s. f.

COVE, s. [a little harbour for boats] *seno di mare.*

CO'VENANT, s. [agreement] *patto, accordo, contratto,* s. m. *convenzione,* s. f.

To make a covenant [to enter into a covenant] *contrattare, fare un contratto con alcuno.*

Covenant [alliance] *confederazione, alleanza, unione, lega,* s. f.

The national covenant, or Scotch covenant] *la confederazione presbiteriana.*

The covenant of grace, *l' alleanza di grazia.*

Covenants of marriage, *sposalizie, sposalizio.*

To agree upon covenant, *pattuire, patteggiare, far patto, convenire.* pres. *pattuisco, convengo.* pret. *convenni.*

To break the covenant, *rompere il patto, mancare alle cose promesse.*

A covenant-breaker, *un violator di contratto, un che non tiene quel che 's è patteggiato.*

To covenant [to make a covenant or agreement] *pattuire, patteggiare, far patto, convenire, stipulare.* pres. *convengo, pattuisco.* pret. *convenni.*

CO'VENANTED, adj. *pattuito, patteggiato, convenuto, stipulato.*

CO'VENANTER, s. [one who took the Presbyterian covenant in the time of the civil wars] *confederato, membro della federazione presbiteriana nel tempo delle guerre civili d' Inghilterra.*

COVER, s. [lid] *coperchio, coverchio,* s. m. *quello con che alcuna cosa si cuopre, coperta, coverta,* s. f.

The cover of a pot, *il coperchio d' un vaso.*

The cover of a book, *la coperta d'un libro.*

The cover of a letter, *l'involto d'una lettera.*

Cover [cloak, pretence] *coperta, scusa, ricoperta,* s. f. *pretesto, colore, mantello,* s. m.

A cover [a plate, napkin, knife, fork, and spoon at table] *una posata, tutti gli strumenti, che si pongono alla mensa davanti a ciascuno de' convivi per uso di prendere la vivanda.*

To CO'VER [to hide] *coprire, porre alcuna cosa sotto che che si sia che l' occulti o che la defenda.*

To cover with earth, *coprire di terra.*

To cover with wax, *incerare, impiastrar con cera.*

To cover with silver, *inargentare, coprire che che si sia con foglia d' argento.*

To cover with gold, *indorare.*

To cover [to conceal] *celare, nascondere, occultare.*

To cover [to disguise, cloke or palliate] *palliare, ricoprire ingegnosamente, velare, coprire, dissimulare.*

To cover [to couple with, speaking of beasts] *coprire, congiugnere il maschio colla femmina per la generazione, ma si dice propriamente delle bestie.*

To cover one's sentiments, *coprire, o dissimulare i suoi veri sentimenti.*

To cover a sin, *palliare un peccato.*

The army covered all the plain, *l' esercito occupava o copriva tutta la pianura.*

To cover one with an eternal shame, *macchiar alcuno d' eterna infamia.*

To cover a mare, *coprire una giumenta.*

To cover over, *coprire.*

To cover [to over-cast] *coprir di nuvole, annuvolare, oscurare.*

To cover the table, *apparecchiare la tavola.*

CO'VERED, adj. *coperto,* v. To cover.

Covered with silver, *inargentato.*

Be covered [put on your hat] *copritevi, mettetevi il cappello.*

Covered with shame, *pieno di vergogna.*

COVER-SHA'ME, s. [some appearance to conceal infamy] *coperta o mantello onde coprire o nasconder l' infamia.*

CO'VERING, s. *coprimento, covrimento,* s. m. *il coprire.*

A covering for a bed, *una copertura da letto.*

CO'VERLET, s. [for a bed] *copertura, coperta, coverta, copertina, covertina,* s. f.

CO'VERT, s. [an umbrage, or shady place, a shelter, a defence] *coperta,* s. f. *coperto e coverto,* s. m. *luogo coperto, tana,* s. f.

To be under the covert, *stare al coperto.*

Covert [hiding place] *nascondiglio, ripostiglio, luogo segreto,* s. m.

Covert [shelter] *asilo, rifugio, ricorso,* s. m. *ala, protezione,* s. f.

A covert [thicket] *boschetto,* s. m.

Covert, adj. [sheltered; not open; not exposed] *ricoperto, non iscoperto, non esposto, guardato.*

Covert, adj. [secret, hidden, private, insidious] *segreto, nascosto, privato, insidioso.*

Covert, adj. [under the power of a husband] *maritata, sotto la podestà del marito.*

Ex. Covert-baron, or Femme covert [in the sense of the law] *una donna maritata.*

COVERT-

Co'VERT-WAY, s. [a space of ground level with the field, three or four fathom broad, ranging quite round the half moons, or other works towards the country] *strada coperta, spazio di terreno incavato al piede e al di fuora delle fortificazioni.*

Co'VERTLY, adv. [secretly, closely] *segretamente, di nascoso, copertamente.*

Co'VERTURE, s. [any thing that covers] *copertura, e covertura, copritūra, e covritura,* s. f.

Coverture [in law, is the state and condition of a married woman, who is under the covert baron, i. e. under the power and protection of her husband, and by law is disabled from making any bargains without her husband's consent] *condizione di donna maritata, che è sotto la dipendezza di suo marito, e secondo la legge, è incapace di far contratti senza il consenso del marito.*

To Co'VET [to desire eagerly, to lust after] *bramare, desiderare ardentemente, appetire, ambire.* pref. *appetisco, ambisco.*

All covet all lose, *chi troppo abbraccia nulla strigne.*

Co'VETABLE, adj. [that which is to be coveted or desired] *desiderabile, appetibile, che marita d' esser bramato e desiderato.*

Co'VETED, adj. *bramato, desiderato, appetito, ambito.*

Co'VETOUS, adj. [very desirous] *avido desideroso, bramoso.*

Covetous of praise, *bramoso di lodi.*

Covetous of glory, *avido di gloria.*

Covetous [avaricious] *avaro interessato, misero, tenace, taccagno, tanghero.*

A very covetous man, *un avarone.*

Co'VETOUSLY, adv. *avaramente, con avarazia, tinacemente.*

Co'VETOUSNESS, s. [desire] *rupidità, cupidigia, disordinato desiderio, passione, ardore.*

Covetousness [avarice, eager desire of of money] *avarizia,* s. f. *appetito disordinato di ricchezze.*

Co'VEY, s. [a hatch, an old bird with her young ones] *una covata, una nidiata di uccellini colla madre.*

Covey [a number of birds together] *uno stormo d' uccelli.*

COUCH, s. [a convulsion of the lungs] *tosse tossa,* s. f.

To COUGH, s. verb neut. *tossire.*

I thought I should cough my heart out, *credevo crepar della tosse.*

COUGHING, s. *il tossire.*

He is always coughing, *non fa altro che tossire.*

Co'VIN, or Co'VINE, s. [a deceitful agreement between two or more, to the prejudice of another] *collusione, fraude* s. f. *inganno,* s. m.

COULD, *questa voce deriva dal verbo difettivo* CAN, *e gl' Inglesi se ne servono in diverse maniere.*

I could not love her, *non potevo amarla.*

He could not do it, *non potette farlo.*

I strived all that I could, *feci ogni mio sforzo mi sforzai quanto potetti.*

I could love her well enough if she was not so whimsical, *potrei ben amarla se non fosse tanto bisbetica.*

I could have done it, *l' avrei potuto fare.*

I could find in my heart, *mi vien voglia.*

Could you do it? *vi basterebbe l' animo di farlo? potreste farlo?*

Co'ULTER, s. [a plough share] *coltro vomero, vomere,* s. m. *strumento di ferro concavo, il qual s' incastra all' aratro, per fendere la terra.*

Co'UNCIL, s. [a general assembly of the clergy of the nation or of a particular province] *concilio,* s. m. *adunanza generale de' prelati di santa chiesa.*

To call a council, *convocare un concilio.*

Council [an assembly of the chief persons of a nation met together to confer about affairs of state] *consiglio,* s. m.

The king's privy council, *il consiglio privato del Re.*

One of his majesty's privy council, *consigliere privato di sua maestà.*

A common council [an assembly of principal citizens chosen of every ward] *il consiglio della città il consiglio della cittadinanza.*

The council chamber, *la camera dove si tien consiglio.*

The council-board, *la tavola del consiglio.*

A great business was debated at the council-board, *s' è trattato un affare di gran momento in consiglio.*

Council [an advocate or counsellor] *un avvocato.*

The king's learned council at law, *l' avvocato fiscale,*

Common council-man [a member of the town council] *membro del consiglio della città.*

Co'UNSEL, s. [advice] *consiglio,* s. m.

To ask counsel of one, *consigliarsi con alcuno, pigliare o domandar il consiglio d' alcuno.*

To give one counsel, *consigliare uno, dargli consiglio.*

To keep one's own counsel, *esser segreto.*

Counsel, or counsellor [he that pleads for his client at the bar] *avvocato,* s. m.

To Co'UNSEL, [to give counsel, to advise] *consigliare dar consiglio.*

To counsel to the contrary, *dissuadere svolgere.*

Co'UNSELLABLE, adj. [willing to receive and follow advice] *volonteroso di ricevere e di seguire il consiglio altrui.*

Co'UNSELLOR, s. *consigliere,* s. m.

A privy counsellor, *consigliere di stato, consigliere privato del Re.*

A counsellor at law, *un avvocato.*

Co'UNSELLORSHIP, s. [the office or post of privy-counsellor] *l' officio o la dignità d' un consigliere privato.*

COUNT, s. [a foreign earl] *un conte. Si da il titolo di* EARL *ai conti d' Inghilterra.*

An Italian count, *un conte Italiano.*

Count [in law, the original declaration in a real action] *termine legale, che significa, domanda.*

Count, s. [number] *numero.*

Count [reckoning] *un conto.*

To COUNT, [to reckon] *contare, annoverare, computare, calcolare.*

Count your money, *contate i vostri danari.*

To count [to account, to esteem] *credere, tenere, stimare, contare, riputare.*

She is counted to be a great beauty, *ella è vantata per una donna bellissima.*

He counts himself a learned man, *egli si stima, o si crede un uomo dottissimo*

A count book, *un libro di conti.*

Co'UNTABLE, adj. [that which may be numbered] *numerabile che può contarsi.*

Co'UNTED, adj. *contato, annoverato, computato, calculato, v.* To count.

He is counted an honest man, *egli è in concetto d' un uomo dabbene.*

He is counted a knave, *egli vien riputato un furbo.*

Co'UNTENANCE, s. [look, visage] *aria, ciera,* s. f. *viso, aspetto, volto.* s. m.

A chearful countenance, *una ciera allegra, o festosa.*

A sober or grave countenance, *un aspetto grave e serioso, un viso contegnoso.*

Countenance [support] *appoggio, ajuto, favore,* s. m. *protezione,* s. f.

To put out of countenance, *confondere, sbalordire, porre fuor di sesto. sconcertare, far fare il viso rosso.* pref. *sbalordisco.*

To be put out of countenance, *restar confuso o fuor di sesto, sbalordire, esser sconcertato, restar fuor di se.*

A sour countenance, *un viso arcigno.*

A courtier is nothing without the countenance of the prince] *un cortigiano non è niente senza il favore o lappoggio o l' aura del principe.*

To Co'UNTENANCE [to favour, to encourage, to abet] *favorire, proteggere, spalleggiare, fare spalle, dare appoggio, sostentare, ajutare, difendere,* pref. *favorisco.* pret. *difesi.*

To countenance vice, *favorire o fomentare i vizi.*

Why does he countenance such a thief? *perche protegge un si gran ladro?*

Co'UNTENANCED, adj. *favorito, protetto, spalleggiato, sostentato, ajutato, difeso.*

She's as pretty a countenanced woman as one can see, *è una donna molto vistosa o avvenente.*

Co'UNTENANCER, s. *fautore, favoreggiatore, favoritore, protettore, partigiano,* s. m.

Co'UNTENANCING, s. *il favorire, lo spalleggiare, favore, appoggio,* s. m.

Co'UNTER, s. [counting board in a shop] *banco,* s. m. *tavola sopra la quale i mercanti contano i danari e scrivono i loro conti.*

Counter, [a piece of brass, silver, &c. to count withal] *un segno di rame, argento, o altro metallo per contare.*

Counters [two prisons of London so called]

called] *nome di due prigioni in Londra così chiamate.*

Counter (against) a particle signifying the opposition, and often used in compounding English words, and sometimes by itself, *questa particola significa opposizione, o contrarietà, e vien spesso usata nel componimento delle voci Inglesi, e spesse volte sola*, ex.

To run counter, *opporsi, ostare, fare ostacolo, contrariare.*

To write counter, *scriver contro.*

Counter-approaches [works made by the besieged to hinder the approach of the enemy, and when they design to attack them in form] *contra approcci, trincee fatte dagli assediati, per accostarsi coperti agli assedianti, per impedire i loro approcci.*

To COUNTERACT, [to hinder any thing from its effect, by contrary agency] *impedire l' effetto di checchessia con opperare oppostamente.*

COUNTERBA'LANCE, s. *contrappeso*, s. m. *cosa che che adegra un' altra nel peso.*

To COUNTERBA'LANCE [to weigh one thing with another, to make equal amends for] *contrappesare, adeguar con peso, aggiustare, balanciare, si usa sovente nel sentimento metaforico.*

That small profit cannot counterbalance the loss I have sustained, *questo piccolo guadagno non può contrappesare la perdita che ò fatto.*

COUNTERBA'LANCED, adj. *contrappesato, aggiustato, bilanciato.*

CO'UNTERBAND, *v.* Contraband.

COUNTER-BATTERY, [a battery raised to play upon another] *contrabatteria*, s. f. *batteria opposta ad un' altra.*

COUNTERBOND, s. [a bond to bear a person harmless who has given bond for another] *cedola che la persona mallevata dà al mallevadore per sua sicurtà.*

To COUNTERBU'FF, [to impel; to strike back] *spignere indietro, rispignere; mandar indietro con urto o percossa.*

COUNTERCA'STER, s. [a book-keeper, a caster of accounts, a reckoner] *un ragioniere, un computista, un che fa conti o tien libro di conti.*

COUNTER-CHA'NGE, s. [a mutual exchange between two parties] *contraccambio*, s. m. *cosa eguale a quella che si da o riceve.*

To COUNTER-CHA'NGE [to exchange one thing with another] *contraccambiare, cambiare una cosa per un' altra.*

COUNTER-CH'ARM, s. [a charm to hinder the force of another] *malia fatta in opposizione d'un altra.*

COUNTER-CHE'CK, s. [a censure made upon a reprover] *censura reciproca.*

To COUNTER-CHE'CK, [to censure again] *censurare o riprendere reciprocamente.*

COUNTER-CU'NNING, s. [subtlety used by the adverse party] *sottiglezza, o astuzia, usata contra la parte avversa.*

COUNTER-CU'RRENT, s. *corrente contraria, o apposta ad un' altra.*

COUNTER-DISTI'NCTION, s. *contraddistinzione, distinzione fatta in rispetto della parte contraria.*

In counter-distinction to that, *in opposizione a cotesto.*

To COUNTER-DRA'W, [to copy a design by means of an oiled paper] *copiar un disegno col mezzo d' una carta prima fregata d'olio, la quale posta su quello tramanda così distintamente le linee che con una matita si possono facilmente toccar tutte.*

COUNTERFEIT, adj. [imitated, feigned, false] *contraffatto, falsificato, falso, imitato.*

A counterfeit writing] *una scrittura contrafatta o imitata.*

Counterfeit coin, *moneta contraffatta o falsa.*

A counterfeit will, *un testamento supposto.*

A counterfeit friendship, *un' amicizia finta.*

A counterfeit devotion or holiness, *una divozione ipocrita, una santità finta dissimulata.*

A counterfeit, s. [a cheat] *un furbo, un ingannatore, un impostore.*

To CO'UNTERFEIT, [to imitate] *contraffare, imitare.*

To counterfeit one's hand, *contraffare l' altrui mano, falsificar l' altrui scrittura.*

To counterfeit the coin, *contraffar la moneta, far moneta falsa.*

To counterfeit [to forge] *contraffare, inventare, trovare.*

To counterfeit [to feign, to dissemble] *contruffare, fingere, far vista.*

To counterfeit a will, *falsificare un testamento.*

He counterfeits being sick, *contraffà l'ammalato, fa vista d' essere ammalato.*

To counterfeit devotion, *fare il divoto, fare il collo torto.*

CO'UNTERFEITED, adj. *contraffatto, v.* To counterfeit.

CO'UNTERFEITER, s. [imitator] *contraffacitore, imitatore*, s. m.

Counterfeiter [forger] *autore, inventore, architetto*, s. m.

A counterfeiter of hands, wills, &c. *un falsario.*

A counterfeiter of coin, *un monetario o monetiere falso.*

COUNTERFE'ITING, s. *contraffacimento*, s. m. *il contraffare, imitazione*, s. f.

COUNTERFE'ILTY, adv. *simulatamente, fintamente.*

COUNTERFE'RMENT, s. [ferment opposed to ferment] *un fermento opposto a un altro.*

COUNTERFO'IL, or COUNTERSTOCK, s. [that part of a tally struck in the exchequer, which is kept by an officer of that court] *contra taglia, quella mezza taglia registrata nell' erario pubblico in custodia d' un ufficiale.*

COUNTER-FORTS, s. [are certain pillars and part of the walls of a place, about fifteen or twenty foot one from another, advanced in the ground, and joined to the height of the cordon by vaults] *contrafforti, sorta di riparo.*

COUNTER-FU'GUE, s. *contrafuga*, s. f. *termine di musica.*

COUNTER-GUARD, s. [in fortification, large heaps of earth in form of a parapet, before the faces and points of the bastions to preserve them] *contra guardia, mucchio di terra in forma di parapetto che si mette di là dal fosso per riparare i bastioni.*

COUNTERMA'ND, s. [a revoking the former command] *contrallettera*, s. f. *contrammandato*, s. m. *rivocamento del mandato.*

To COUNTERMA'ND, [to give contrary orders] *contrammandare, comandare, contro al primo comandamento, rivocar la commissione.*

To countermand a will, *invalidare un testamento.*

COUNTERMA'NDED, adj. *contrammandato, invalido.*

COUNTERMARC'H, s. [or contrary march] *contrammarcia.*

COUNTERMI'NE, s. [a mine made by the besieged in search of the enemy's mine, in order to give air to it, and hinder the effects of it] *contrammina*, s. f. *quella strada che si fa di dentro per rincontrare la mina e darle sfiatatojo per renderla vana.*

To COUNTERMI'NE, [to make countermines] *contramminare, far contrammine.*

To countermine a man's designs, *contramminare, cercar di rompere l' altrui disegni.*

COUNTERMI'NED, adj. *contramminato.*

COUNTERMI'NER, s. *quello che fa le contrammine.*

COUNTERMI'NING, s. *il contramminare, contrammina.*

COUNTERMO'TION, s. [contrary motion] *moto contrario.*

COUNTERMU'RE, s. [a wall made in defence against another] *antimuro*, s. m. *muro fatto in difesa dell' altro.*

COUNTERPA'NE, s. [a coverlet for a bed] *coltre*, s. f. *coperta di letto imbottita*, s. f.

COUNTERPA'RT, s. [in musick, one part opposite to another, as the base is the counterpart of the treble] *contrapparte*, s. f. *termine musicale.*

Counterpart [in law, is the duplicate or copy of any indenture or deed] *copia d' un contratto o d' un atto pubblico.*

COUNTERPLE'A, s. [an answer to an accusation, a recrimination] *replica fatta per giustificarsi d' un accusa.*

COUNTERPLO'T, s. [a plot contrived to overthrow another] *artifizio opposto ad artifizio.*

To COUNTERPLO'T, verb act. *opporre artifizio ad artifizio.*

COUNTERPO'INT, s. [in musick] *contrappunto*, s. m. *termine della musica.*

Counterpoint [counterpain] *coltre*, s. f. *coperta di letto imbottita.*

COUNTERPO'ISE, s. [an equal balance] *contrappeso*, s. m. *cosa che adegua un' altra nel peso.*

To COUNTERPO'ISE [to weigh one thing

thing againſt another] *contrappeſare, adeguar con peſo, aggiuſtare, bilanciare.*

COUNTERPOI'SED, adj. *contrappeſato.*

COUNTER-POI'SON, s. [an antidote to hinder the effect of poiſon] *contraveleno,* s. m. *che che ſi ſia, che abbia virtù contro al veleno.*

COUNTERPRE'SSURE, s. [oppoſite force] *forza contraria, forza oppoſta*

COUNTER-PROJECT, [correſpondent part of a ſcheme] *parte corriſpondente d' un diſegno.*

COUNTER-RA'IL, s. *fila di balauſtri oppoſti ad un' altra fila.*

COUNTER-RO'UND, s. [military term, a number of officers going to viſit the rounds, or the centinels] *contra ronda, termine militare.*

COUNTERSCA'RP, s. [that ſide of the ditch which is next to the camp, or the ſlope of the moat which faces the body of the place] *contraſcarpa,* s. f. *la parte del terreno chiudente il foſſo di contro alla ſcarpa.*

To COUNTERSCA'RP, verb act. *fare una contraſcarpa.*

To counterſcarp a ditch, *fare una contraſcarpa ad un foſſo.*

COUNTER-SECURITY, s. [a ſecurity given to a party who has entered into bonds to another] *polizza o cedula data dalla perſona mallevata al mallevadore per ſua ſicurtà.*

COUNTER-TALLY, s. [a tally to confirm or confute another tally] *contrattaglia,* s. f.

COUNTER-TE'NOR, s. [in muſick, one of the middle parts, ſo called, becauſe it is as it were oppoſite to the tenor] *contra tenore.*

To COUNTERVA'IL [to be of equal value to another thing] *valere altrettanto, eſſere equivalente, equivalere, eſſer di pregio e di valore eguale.*

To COUNTER-WO'RK [to raiſe works in order to oppoſe thoſe of the enemy] *contramminare, far contrammine, cercar di rompere e render vani gli altrui diſegni.*

CO'UNTESS, s. [an earl's lady] *conteſſa,* s. f.

CO'UNTING, s. [from to count] *il contare, contamento,* s. m.

COUNTING-HOUSE, s. [a place where merchants keep their books, and ſettle their accounts] *contorio,* s. m. *ſtanza dove i mercanti tengono i libri e fanno le loro ragioni.*

Counting-houſe of the king's houſhold [the court of the green cloth] *la corte dove ſi regolano tutti gli affari domeſtici e le ſpeſe del Rè.*

CO'UNTLESS, adj. [innumerable, without number] *innumerabile, ſenza numero.*

CO'UNTRY, s. [land or region] *paeſe,* s. m. *regione, provincia,* s. f.

Country [the fields in oppoſition to the town] *la campagna, i campi, il contado.*

A man's own country, *la patria, il paeſe natio.*

A fruitful or barren country, *un paeſe fertile o ſterile.*

A remote country, *una regione remota.*

He ſubdued all the countries of the Eaſt, *ſoggiogò tutto l' oriente.*

So many countries, ſo many cuſtoms, *ogni paeſe ha le ſue uſanze.*

What country was you born in? *di che paeſe ſiete?*

We paſs the winter in town and the ſummer in the country, *il verno ſtiamo in città, e la ſtate in villa.*

A country word, *una parola volgare.*

A country-houſe, *villa, caſa di campagna.*

A country-life, *vita ruſtica o campeſtre.*

A countryman, *un contadino, un villano, un paeſano.*

A countrywoman, *una contadina.*

What countryman are you? *di che paeſe ſiete?*

We are countrymen, *noi ſiamo del medeſimo paeſe, noi ſiamo compatriotti.*

A country-ſquire, *un gentiluomo di provincia o di campagna.*

A country-clown, *un contadino, un paeſano, un ruſtico.*

A country-parſon, *un curato di villaggio.*

Country dance, *contraddanza, ballo tondo.*

CO'UNTY, s. [ſhire] *contea, provincia,* s. f.

England is divided into forty counties, beſides twelve in Wales, *l' Inghilterra è diviſa in quaranta contee, oltre le dodici del principato di Gallia.*

County [earldom] *contea, dominio, e ſtato del conte.*

The county of Burgundy, *la contea di Borgogna.*

To COUP UP, v. To coop up.

COUPE'E, v. Coopee.

COUPED, or COOPED, adj. [in heraldry, that is cut off] *tagliato, fragiato.*

COUPLE, s. [two of a ſort] *coppia,* s. f. *pajo,* s. m. *due inſieme.*

A couple of apples, eggs, &c. *una coppia o un pajo di mele o d' uova.*

A happy couple of lovers, *una felice coppia d' amanti.*

Couple [to couple dogs with] *laccio, guinzaglio,* s. m. *ſtriſcia ſtretta, per lo più di ſovattolo, la quale s' infila nel collar del cane per uſo d' andare alla caccia.*

To COU'PLE, [to join together] *accoppiare, accompagnare o congiugnere inſieme due coſe, far coppia.*

To couple two dogs together with a couple, *accoppiare o legare due cani con un guinzaglio.*

To couple [to copulate] *copularſi, congiugnerſi.*

To couple [to marry] *ammogliarſi parlando dell' uomo, maritarſi parlando della donna.*

COUPLE-BEGGAR, s. [one that makes it his buſineſs to marry beggars to each other] *uno che fa il meſtiere di unire in matrimonio i poveri e i birboni.*

CO'UPLED, adj. *accoppiato, copulato, congiunto.*

CO'UPLET, s. [two verſes; a pair of rhimes] *diſtico; due verſi; due rime.*

Couplet, [a pair; as of doves] *un pajo.*

CO'UPLING, s. *l' accoppiare, copula,* s. f. *congiugnimento,* s. m.

CO'URAGE, s. [mettle, valour] *coraggio, cuore, animo, ardire,* s. m. *bravura,* s. f.

I don't want courage but ſtrength, *l' animo mi baſta, ma le forze mi mancano.*

To put courage into one, *incoraggiare, inanimare alcuno, darli cuore, darli animo, farli cuore.*

Be of good courage, take courage, *fate animo, ſtate di buon cuore.*

To take courage again, *riprender coraggio.*

To loſe one's courage, *perderſi d' animo, caſcare o perdere il cuore, ſgomentarſi, sbigottirſi.*

COURA'GEOUS, adj. [ſtout, full of courage] *corraggioſo, animoſo, intrepido, ardito, bravo.*

CO'URAGEOUSLY, adv. *corraggioſamente, animoſamente. intrepidamente, arditamente, valoroſamente.*

CO'URAGEOUSNESS, s. [bravery; boldneſs; ſpirit; courage] *valore ardimento, fuoco, coraggio.*

COU'RANT, s. [a ſort of dance] *corrente,* s. f. *ſorta di ballo.*

To dance a courant, *ballare una corrente.*

The daily courant, [a news paper] *una gazzetta.*

To COURB [to bend, to bow] *curvare, piegare, archeggiare.*

CO'URIER, s. [a meſſenger] *corriere, e corriero,* s. m.

CO'URSE, s. [running-race] *corſo,* s. m. *corſa,* s. f. *carriera,* s. f.

The courſe of the water, *il corſo dell' acqua.*

The courſe of the ſun, moon, and ſtars, *il corſo del ſole, della luna, e delle ſtelle.*

The courſe of a man's life, *il corſo della vita umana.*

I have finiſhed my courſe, *ho finito il mio corſo, la mia carriera.*

Courſe [in ſailing] *cammino,* s. m.

To appoint a courſe to be ſteered *moſtrar il cammino ai vaſcelli.*

The main courſe [a main ſail in a ſhip] *la vela maeſtra d' un vaſcello.*

Courſe [journey, or voyage] *cammino, viaggio,* s. m.

Courſe [order] *corſo, ordine.*

By the courſe of nature, *ſecondo il corſo o l' ordine della natura.*

I ſhall take a courſe for that, *vi metterò ordine.*

Courſe [turn] *giro,* s. m. *volta, vicenda,* s. f.

Every one in his courſe, *ognuno in giro.*

By courſe, *in giro, a vicenda, per volta.*

Courſe [cuſtom] *conſuetudine, uſanza,* s. f. *rito, coſtume,* s. m.

'Tis our common courſe, *queſta è la noſtra ſolita uſanza.*

According

According to the courſe of the world, *ſecondo il modo di procedere d'oggidì.*

Courſe of life, *maniera di vivere, procedere, condotta.*

To fix upon a courſe of life, *appigliarſi ad una maniera di vivere.*

To lead a bad courſe of life, *menare una cattiva vita.*

Courſe [ways, means] *ſtrada, maniera,* s. f. *mezzo, metodo,* s. m.

This is not the courſe you muſt take to bring your buſineſs about, *queſta non è la ſtrada di venire a capo del voſtro negozio.*

To take a courſe to ruin one, *trovar mezzi per rovinare uno.*

I ſhall take another courſe to bring you to reaſon, *piglierò un altro eſpediente per ridurvi alla ragione.*

Courſe [ſervice of meat] *ſervizio di tavola.*

The firſt, the ſecond, and third courſe, *il primo, il ſecondo, ed il terzo ſervizio.*

A thing of courſe [common] *una coſa ordinaria o comune che accade alla giornata.*

Words of courſe, *maniera di parlare, complimenti.*

In courſe, or of courſe [naturally of one's ſelf, or of itſelf] *naturalmente, ordinariamente, da ſe.*

This follows in, or of courſe, *queſto s'intende.*

Women's monthly courſes, *meſtrui, catamenie, meſi, marcheſe.*

I know not what courſe to take, *non ſo che fare, non ſo che eſpediente pigliare, non ſo in che modo comportarmi, non ſo che partito prendere.*

To take a wiſe courſe, *pigliare buone miſure.*

To take bad courſes, *ſviarſi, darſi ad una vita licenzioſa.*

You muſt take another courſe of life, *biſogna che voi cangiate vita.*

To take a courſe with one in law, *chiamare alcuno alla corte o in giuſtizia.*

I don't fear you, take your courſe, *non ho paura di voi, fate quel che volete.*

Take your courſe, and I will take mine, *prendete voi il voſtro partito, ch' io prenderò il mio.*

To follow the courſe of time, *andar a ſeconda de' tempi, navigar ſeconda il vento, governarſi ſecondo l'opportunità.*

By due courſe of law, *giuridicamente, juridicamente.*

To leave the world to take his courſe, *navigar ſecondo il vento, andar colla corrente, laſciare che il mondo vada come vuole, pigliar il mondo come viene.*

A courſe of eggs, *una covata d'uova.*

To be in a courſe of phyſick, *eſſer nelle mani de' medici.*

To put juſtice into its courſe, *far fare giuſtizia.*

To COURSE [to chace beaſts] *dar la caccia, cacciare.*

To courſe a hare, *cacciar una lepre.*

To courſe over a hill, *trapaſſare un monte, paſſar ſopra una montagna.*

To courſe [to diſpute in the ſchool] *diſputare nelle ſcuole.*

CO'URSER, s. [a diſputant in ſchools] *un diſputante, un diſputatore.*

Courſer [ſteed] *corſiere,* s. m *cavallo bello e nobile.*

CO'URSEY, s. [a ſpace in the middle of a galley about three foot broad, on both ſides whereof the ſeats of the ſlaves are placed] *corſia,* s. f. *lo ſpazio vuoto nelle galee per camminare da poppa a prua.*

COURT, or COURT-YARD, s. [a yard in a houſe] *cortile,* s. m. *corte di caſa.*

Court [before the gate of a church] *il ſacrato d'una chieſa.*

Court [narrow ſtreet] *una ſtradella.*

Court [the palace of a prince] *corte,* s. f. *palazzo de principe.*

Court [the prince and courtiers] *corte, il principe e la famiglia del principe.*

Court [hall of juſtice] *corte, luogo dove ſi tien ragione.*

Court [the judges] *corte, giudici e miniſtri della giuſtizia.*

To go to court. *andare alla corte.*

The court is gone to Kenſington, *la corte è andata a Kenſington.*

The chancery court, *la cancelleria.*

The high court of parliament, *la corte ſovrana del parlamento.*

The court has acquitted him, *la corte l'ha aſſoluto.*

Court party, *il partito della corte.*

Court ladies, *le dame della corte.*

A court viſit, *una viſita di corte, una viſita corta.*

Court holy water [fair and empty words] *belle parole ſenza* fatti.

Court-like, *alla maniera della corte.*

A tennis-court, *giuoco di palla corda.*

Court-card, *carta figurata, figura, come* il Re, la Dama, il Fante.

To COURT [to make love to] *corteggiare, far l'amore.*

To court ladies, *corteggiare dame.*

To court a lady in order to marry her, *far l'amore ad una donzella con intenzione di ſpoſarla.*

To court [to deſire, to ſollicit] *brigare, pigliarſi briga, far diligenza, procurare, ſollecitare.*

To court [to ſtand for a place] *brigare, ſollecitare una carica.*

CO'URTED, adj. *corteggiato, v.* To court.

She is courted by ſuch a one, *un tale le fa l'amore, un tale la corteggia.*

CO'URTEOUS, adj. [civil, affable] *corteſe, civile, affabile, benevolo, benigno.*

Courteous reader, *amico lettore, lettore benevolo.*

To be courteous, *corteſeggiare, uſar corteſia.*

CO'URTEOUSLY, adv. *corteſemente, civilmente, affabilmente, benignamente.*

CO'URTEOUSNESS, s. [civility, kindneſs] *corteſia, civilità, affabilità, benevolenza,* s. f.

To do one a courteouſneſs, *fare altrui una corteſia.*

CO'URTESY, *riverenza di donna.*

Make your courteſy, *fate la riverenza.*

Full of courteſy full of craft, *chi ti fà più carezze che non ſuole, o t'ha gabbato, o che gabbar ti vuole.*

To COURTESY, [to perform an act of reverence] *far un atto di riſpetto.*

To courteſy [to make a reverence in the manner of ladies] *far una riverenza, e ſi dice della donne ſolamente.*

CO'URTEZAN, s. [a lady of pleaſure] *cortigiana, femmina del mondo, puttana, donna da partito.*

COU'RTIER, s. [a man that has a place at court, or that follows the court] *cortigiano,* s. m. *che ſta in corte.*

Courtier [a polite man, full of complaiſance] *un cortigiano, un uomo civile e corteſe.*

Courtier [a court lady] *dama di corte.*

CO'URTIN, s. [in fortification, the front of the wall or rampart lying between two baſtions] *cortina,* s. f. *quella parte di fortificazione che è tra un baſtione e l'altro.*

CO'URTING, s. [from to court] *il corteggiare.*

COURT-LIKE, adj. [elegant, polite] *elegante, civile, cortigianeſco.*

CO'URTLINESS, s. [elegance of manners, complaiſance, civility] *modi elegante, cortigiania, garbatezza, civiltà, nobile* trattare.

COURTLY, adv. *cortigianamente, elegantemente, garbatamente, civilmente.*

CO'URTLY, adj. [airy, gallant, ſpruce] *galante, gentile, grazioſo, gajo, amorevole.*

A Sir Courtly Nice, *un galantino, un zerbino, un cacazibetto, un attillatuzzo.*

CO'URTSHIP, s. [courteſy, or civility] *corteſia, civilità, galanteria,* s. f.

You are mighty full of courtſhip, *voi ſieto molto galante.*

Courtſhip, *quella ſervitù che ſi fa ad una ſignorina prima di ſpoſarla.*

Courtſhip, *il corteggiare chiccheſſia.*

COUSIN, s. *cugino,* s. m. *cugina,* s. f.

Couſin, *cugino, titolo che da il Re a un nobiluomo, e ſpecialmente a' ſuoi conſiglieri privati.*

COW, s. [a beaſt well known] *vacca,* s. f. *la femmina del beſtiame vaccino.*

A great cow, *una vacca groſſa.*

A cow with calf, *un vacra pregna.*

To a cow's thumb [exactly] *eſattamente, per l'appunto, appuntino.*

A cow herd, or cow keeper, *un vaccajo, guardiano di vacche.*

A cow-houſe, *ſtalla da vacche.*

A little cow, *una vacchetta.*

A milk cow, *vacca lattante o da latte.*

Cow blakes [cow dung dryed for fuel] *bovina ſecca per far del fuoco.*

To cow [to put one out of heart] *ſgomentare, ſbigottire, far perder d'animo, intimidire.*

COW-HERD, [one whoſe occupation is to feed cows] *guardiano di vacche.*

COW-HOUSE, [the houſe in which kine are kept] *la ſtalla de' buoi e delle vacche.*

COWLE'ECH, [one who profeſſes to cure diſtempered cows] *uno il cui meſ-*

tiere

tiere è il medicar la vacche quando han qualche male.
To COWLE'ECH, [to profess to cure cows] *far il medico alle vacche malate.*
COW-WEED, s. *sorta di pianta.*
COW-WHEAT, s. *sorta di pianta.*
CO'WARD, s. [one that has no courage, a dastard] *un codardo, un vile, un vigliacco, un pusillanimo.*
To grow a coward, *incodardirsi, avvilirsi.*
CO'WARDICE, or COWARDLINESS, s. *codardia, viltà, vigliaccheria, timore.*
CO'WARDLY, adv. *codardamente, vilmente, vigliaccamente.*
CO'WARDLY, adj. *codardo, timido, vigliacco.*
Cowardly, adj. *propio d'un codardo, d'un vigliacco.*
COWED, adj. [from to cow] *sgomentato, sbigottito, disanimato, intimidito.*
To CO'WER, *dar giù colle ginocchia, piegare.*
CO'WING, s. *sgomentamento, sbigottimento,* s. m.
CO'WISH, adj. *codardo, timido, pauroso.*
COWL, s. [that part of a friar's habit which covers the head] *cappuccio,* s. m.
A capucin's cowl, *il cappuccio d'un cappuccino.*
A little cowl, *un cappuccello.*
To COWR DOWN, [to squat down] *appiattarsi, abbassarsi, chinarsi.*
CO'WSLIP, s. [a flower] *sorta di fiore.*
CO'XCOMB, s *la sommità della testa.*
Coxcomb, s. [a conceited fool, a silly fellow] *uno sciocco, un balordo, un minchione, un goffo, un ferfedocco, un pascibietola.*
A proud coxcomb, *uno stolto.*
An ignorant coxcomb, *un ignorantaccio, un asino.*
CO'XCOMICAL, adj. [foppish, conceited] *superficiale, ignorantello.*
To CO'XE [to flatter] *lusingare, adulare, accarezzare, vezzeggiare, far vezzi.*
CO'XED, adj. *lusingato, adulato, accarezzato, vezzeggiato.*
CO'XER, s. *lusinghiero, adulatore, vezzeggiatore.*
CO'XING, s. *il lusingare, lusinghe, carezze, vezzi.*
By CO'XNOUNS [a comical oath] *al cospetto di bacco.*
COY, adj. [shy] *schifo, ritroso, contegnoso, sdegnoso.*
A coy dame, *una schifa, una ritrosetta.*
Coy [nice, dainty] *delicato.*
Coy [modest, decent] *modesto, vergognoso.*
To COY [to behave with reserve, to reject familiarity] *star in contegno, non soffrir familiarità.*
To coy [not to condescend willingly] *farsi pregare; non acconsentire volentieri.*
CO'YLY, adv. *contegnosamente.*
CO'YNESS, s. [shyness] *schifiltà, ritrosia, ripugnanza, modestia affettata.*
COZ [a cant or familiar word, contracted from *Cousin*] *cugino, ma è parola abbrieviata e usata solo in istile familiare.*
To CO'ZEN [to cheat, chouse] *giuntare, ingannare, truffare, uccellare.*
CO'ZENAGE, or CO'ZENING, s. [cheating] *giunteria, truffa,* s. f. *inganno,* s. m.
CO'ZENED, adj. *giuntato, ingannato, truffato, uccellato.*
CO'ZENER, s. [a cheater, a defrauder] *un baro, un giuntatore, un briccone, un ingannatore.*
CO'ZENING, v. Cozenage.
CRAB, s. [a wild apple] *mela salvatica.*
A crab [crab fish] *granchio,* s. m.
Crab-tree, *melo salvatico.*
Crab louse, *un piattone.*
Crab [an engine with three claws, used by carpenters in launching of ships] *un cane.*
CRA'BBED, adj. [sour as fruit unripe] *acerbo, arcigno.*
Crabbed [rough, uneven] *rozzo, ruvido.*
A crabbed stile, *uno stile rozzo.*
A crabbed look [a sour countenance] *un viso arcigno, burbero, austero o aspro.*
CRA'BBEDLY, adv. *ex.* to look crabbedly, *avere una ciera arcigna, o austera.*
CRA'BBEDNESS, s. [roughness] *rozzezza, ruvidezza,* s. f.
Crabbedness [sourness] *viso arcigno, umor fantastico.*
CRA'BER, s. [a water-rat] *un topo acquatico.*
CRACK, s. [chink] *crepatura, fessura,* s. f.
Crack [a crashing noise] *scoppiata,* s. f. *scoppio, romore, fracasso che nasce dallo scoppiar delle cose.*
The crack of a gun, *lo scoppio d'un' arme da fuoco.*
Crack [whore] *una bagascia, una sgualdrina, una puttanaccia.*
Crack [boaster] *millantatore, ostentatore, mostratore,* s. m. *una salamistra,* s. f.
Crack-brained, *scervellato, mentecatto.*
A crack rope [one that grows for the gallows] *un forca, un gaglioffo, un briccone.*
To CRACK, *fendere, spaccare, crepare, rompere, schiacciare, screpolare.* pret. *ruppi.*
To crack a bell, *crepare una campana.*
To crack a glass, *screpolare un bicchiere.*
To crack a nut, *smallare una noce.*
To crack a louse, *stiacciare un pidocchio.*
He and I have crackt many a bottle together, *egli ed io abbiamo vuotati molti fiaschi insieme.*
To crack, verb neut. [to chink and flaw] *fendersi, creparsi, screpolarsi, aprirsi.*
These boards begin to crack, *queste tavole, o panche cominciano a fendersi, o crepolarsi.*
That glass will crack, *quel bicchiere creperà.*
To crack [as plaistering does] *aprirsi, crepolarsi.*
To crack [to make a noise] *scoppiettare, fare scoppietti, fare romore, e dicesi propriamente delle legne che fanno tale effetto abbruciando.*
To crack [or boast] *vantarsi, millantarsi, vanagloriarsi.*
He does much crack of his kindred, *si vanta molto del suo parentado.*
He eats till his belly is ready to crack, *si crepa di mangiare, mangia a crepa pancia.*
Does he think to crack me out? *crede forse farmi paura?*
CRA'CKED, v. Crackt.
CRA'CKER, s. [squib] *razzo, saltarello,* s. m. *pezzo di carta ripiegata nelle pieghe della quale sia polvere d'archibuso rinchiusa, detto così perchè pigliando fuoco e scoppiando saltella.*
Cracker [to curl hair with] *pezetto di carta nel quale s'involgono i capelli per arricciarli.*
Cracker, s. [a noisy boasting fellow] *un millantatore, un gradasso, uno che fa molto strepito raccontando le sue pretese bravure.*
To CRA'CKLE, verb neut. [as laurel, &c. in the fire] *scoppiettare.*
CRA'CKLING, s. *scoppiamento, lo scoppiettare, scoppio, strepito.*
CRA'CKNEL, s. [a sort of cakes, baked hard, so as to crackle under the teeth] *ciambella,* s. f.
CRA'CKT, adj. *fesso, spaccato, crepato, rotto, screpolato,* v. To crack.
Crackt [crack-brained] *scervellato, senza cervello, mentecatto, stolto.*
Crackt [broken merchant] *mercante fallito.*
CRA'DLE, s. [a sort of bed for a young child] *culla,* s. m. *piccolo letticciuolo per uso de' bambini.*
To rock the cradle, *cullare, dimenar la culla.*
An iron cradle [wherein we used to burn sea-coal] *graticola da fuoco.*
To CRA'DLE [to lay in a cradle] *giacer in culla.*
CRA'DLE CLOATHS, s. pl. [bed-cloaths belonging to a cradle] *panni appartenenti a' bambini in culla.* Shakesp.
CRAFT, or HA'NDYCRAFT, s. [mechanical art or trade] *mestiere,* s. m. *professione, arte,* s. f.
Craft, among mariners [all manner of lines, hooks, nets, &c. for fishing] *tutte le cose necessarie per pescare, come canne, reti, ami,* &c.
Craft [craftiness, cunning] *astuzia, sottiglienza, arte, sagacità,* s. f. *scaltrimento, rigiro, artificio,* s m.
Craft [trick] *inganno, dolo, fallaggio,* s. m. *fallacia, arte, trama, giunteria, trappola,* s. f.
A crafts-man, *artigiano, artefice,* s. m. *un uomo che esercita qualche arte.*
A crafts-master, *maestro, esperto in qualche arte.*
To CRAFT [to play tricks] *fare inganno, far cilecche.*
CRA'FTILY, adv. [by craft, cunningly] *astutamente, con arte, artatamente,*

tamente, avvisatamente, scaltritamente, sottilmente.

CRA'FTINESS, s. [craft] *astuzia, arte, sottigliezza, destrezza,* s. f. *scaltrimento, sottratto,* s. m.

CRA'FTY, adj. [cunning] *accorto, astuto, destro, fino, scaltro, sottile, volpe.*

CRAG, s. [neck, nape of the neck] *collottola, nuca,* s. f.

Crag [rock] *rupe, balza, rocca,* s. f.

The crag [or top of a high rock, *la cima d' una alta rupe.*

CRA'GGED, or CRA'GGY, adj. [rough or steep] *erto, scosceso, chino, dirocato.*

The craggy end of the neck of mutton, *quella parte del collo di castrato ch' è più vicino alla testa.*

CRA'GGINESS, s. [the being craggy] *l' essere scosceso.*

To CRAM [to thrust close] *stivare, ficcare, mettere, cacciare con violenza una cosa in un' altra.*

He crammed it at last in the trunk, *alla fine lo ficcó nel forziere.*

To cram [to stuff] *impinzare, stivare, empire, zeppare.*

To cram one's self with meat, *impinzarsi di carne.*

He crams himself with meat and drink, *si riempie il ventre di carne e di bevanda.*

To cram poultry, *ingrassare il pollame.*

He crams his belly as much as ever he can, *si crepa a forza di mangiare.*

The room is crammed with people, *la camera è stivata di gente.*

CRA'MBE, s. [a repetition of words, or saying the same thing over again] *ripetizione di parole, il ripetere quel che s'è gia detto.*

CRA'MBO, s. [a play in rhiming, in which he that repeats a word that was said before, forfeits something] *giuoco di rima nel quale colui che ripete una parola già usata nella rima perde un tanto.*

CRA'MMED, adj. [from to cram] *stivato, messo, ficcato.* v. To cram.

A crammed capon, *un cappone ingrassato.*

CRAMP, s. [a disease which is caused by a violent distortion of the nerves] *granchio,* s. m. *ritriamento di muscoli.*

Cramp-iron, *graffio, uncino, rampicone, rampino, raffio,* s. m. *strumento di ferro.*

To CRAMP, *aver il granchio.*

To cramp with cramp-irons, *uncinare, attaccare con uncini.*

The cramp or crick in the neck, *torticollo,* s. m.

The cramp-fish, *torpedine,* s. f. *pesce che rattrappa la mano di colui che la tocca.*

To cramp one, verb act. *tirare alcuno fuora del letto con uno spago attaccato al dito dello mano o del piede. Questo verbo significa ancora involgere o inviluppare altrui in qualche affare.*

CRA'MPER, s [cramp-iron] *graffio, uncino, rampicone, rampino, raffio,* s. m.

CRAMPT, adj. *tirato fuora del letto.*

Crampt [that has the cramp] *che è preso dal granchio.*

A crampt word, *vocabolo di minor uso, che non fa autorità.*

CRA'NAGE, s. [money paid for the use of a crane in landing and shipping wares] *dazio che si paga per l' uso dell' argano nello sbarcare e imbarcare mercanzie.*

CRANE, s. [a bird] *gru, grua, grue, e gruga,* s. f. *spezie d' uccello.*

Crane [an engine to draw up burdens] *argano,* s. m. *strumento da tirar pesi che si muove in giro per forza di lieve.*

Crane's bill [a surgeon's instrument, a sort of pincers] *strumento di chirurgo in forma di tanaglie per tirar fuora le schegge d' ossa* rotte.

Crane [a crooked pipe for drawing liquors out of a vessel] *sifone,* s. m.

To crane up, *tirar su per mezzo d' un argano.*

CRA'NIUM, s. [the skull] *il cranio* s. m. *l' osso del capo che ha foggia di volta cuopre e difende il cervello.*

CRANK, s. [the draw-beam of a well] *bùbera,* s. f.

Crank, adj. [brisk, lusty] *vigoroso, robusto, gagliardo, possente, forzuto.*

Crank [merry] *allegro, giojoso, festoso, gajo.*

To CRA'NKLE IN AND OUT [to go winding about] *serpere, andar torto a guisa di serpe, volteggiare.*

CRA'NKLES, s. *giravolte,* s. f. *serpeggiamenti,* s. m.

CRA'NNIED, adj. *fesso, crepato, crepolato.*

CRA'NNY, s. [chink, little crack, crevice] *pelo,* s. m. *piccola, fessura, o crepatura.*

CRAPE, s. [a sort of stuff] *velo,* s. m.

CRASH, s. [great noise] *strepito, fracasso,* s. m.

Crash [contest] *contesa, disputa,* s. f.

To CRASH [to make a noise] *strepitare, fare strepito o romore.*

To crash [to break] *rompere fracassare, conquassare.*

To crash with one's teeth, *stritolare co' denti.*

CRA'SHING, s. *strepito, romore, fracasso, conquasso.*

CRASS, [adj. fat, gross] *grosso, grossolano, spesso.*

CRA'SSITUDE, [thickness] *grassezza, grossezza, gressolanità, spessezza,* s. f.

CRATCH [a rack for hay or straw] *greppia, mangiatoja,* s. f. *dove nella stalla si mette il fieno o la paglia innanzi alla bestie.*

CRA'TCHES, s. [a stinking sore in a horse's heels] *sorta di malattia del cavallo, per lo più nelle postoje.*

CRA'VAT, s. [a sort of neckcloth] *cravatta,* s. f.

To CRAVE [to desire, to demand] *domandare, chiedere instantamente, implorare.* pret. *chiesi.*

May I crave your name? *di grazia mi dica il suo nome?*

To crave a man's help, *domandare, o implorare l' altrui soccorso o ajuto.*

CRA'VED, adj. *domandato, chiesto, implorato.*

CRA'VEN, or CRA'VENT, s. [a coward] *un codarao, un pusillanimo, un poltrone, un vigliacco.*

CRA'VEN, s. [a cock conquered and dispirited] *un gallo che in battaglia contro un altro ha perso il coraggio e si mostra vinto.*

To CRA'VEN [to make recreant or cowardly] *intimidire, render codardo.*

CRA'VENED, adj. *intimidito, sgomentato, sbigottito.*

CRA'VER, s. [from to crave] *domandatore, dimandatore,* s. m.

CRA'VING, s. *il domandare, il chiedere.*

He is always craving, *egli non fa altro che domandare.*

Craving, adj. *domandante, dimandante, che domanda.*

She's a craving woman, *è una donna che domanda sempre, che non è mai contenta o sazia.*

To have a craving stomach, *essere affamato, avere un appetito insaziabile, aver sempre gran fame.*

CRA'VINGNESS, s. *umore insaziabile.*

To CRAUNCH [to crush in the mouth] *schiacciare in bocca, masticare a bocca chiusa.*

CRAW, s. [of a bird] *gozzo,* s. m. *ripostiglio a guisa di vescica che banno gli ucrelli appiè dell collo dove si ferma il loro cibo.*

Craw-fish, s. *gambero.*

To CRAWL [to creep] *andar carpone, rampicare, andar per terra, strascinare.*

A worm that crawls upon the ground, *un verme che si strascina su la terra.*

I am so weak that I can hardly crawl, along, *son sí debole che appena posso strascinarmi.*

To crawl [to wriggle] *serpere, andar serpendo.*

To crawl up to the top of a tree, *rampicare, sur un albero.*

To crawl with lice, *esser coperto o pieno di pidocchi.*

CRA'WLER, s. [crawling creature] *rettile, animal senza piedi, che va colla pancia per terra.*

CRA'YER, s. [a sort of small ship] *spezie di vascello piccolo così chiamato.*

CRAY-FISH, s. [crevice] *gambero,* s. m.

CRA'YON, s. [pastel] *pastello,* s. m.

Designed with crayon, *disegnato col pastello.*

To CRAZE [to break[*fracassare, rompere, schiacciare, sgretolare.* pret. *ruppi.*

CRA'ZED, adj. *fracassato, rotto, schiacciato, sgretolato.*

Crazed [distempered in his brain] *forsennato, stolto, debole di cervello.*

CRA'ZEDNESS, s. [decrepitude, brokeness] *decrepità, vecchiaja,* s. f.

CRA'ZINESS, s. *indisposizione, malsana, mala sanità,* s. f.

CRA'ZY, adj. [distempered, sickly] *malaticcio, malsano, infermo, infermuccio, accasciato, indisposto, che è un po' scemo di cervello, che ha alquanto del matto.*

CREAGHT, s. [herds of catttle] *mandra di bestie bovine. E' vocabolo d' Irlanda.*

To Creak [to make a harſh noiſe] *far un romore acuto e ſpiacevole, ſcricchiolare, cigolare.*

Cream, s. [the thicker and more ſubſtantial part of milk] *fior di latte.*

Cream of tartar [purified tartar] *fior di tartaro.*

Cream [the beſt of a thing] *fiore, la parte più nobile, migliore, e più bella di qualſivoglia coſa.*

The cream of a book, *la midolla d'un libro.*

The cream of a country, *il fiore del paeſe.*

Cream cheeſe, *ſorta di cacio.*

Cream-faced, adj. *codardo, pallido per paura.*

To Cream [to ſkim off the cream] *togliere il fiore dal latte.*

To cream, *togliere il meglio d'una coſa.*

To Cream [to gather into cream] *rappigliarſi, raſſodarſi.*

Cre'amy, adj. [full of cream] *pieno di fior di latte.*

Cre'ancy, s. [truſt] *credenza, confidanza, fede,* s. f.

Crease, s [an impreſſion or fold in a garment] *piega,* s. f. *raddoppiamento di panni, drappi, e ſimili.*

To Create [to make out of nothing] *creare, criare, far qualche coſa dal niente*

God has created the world, *Iddio ha creato il mondo.*

To create [to make, to appoint] *creare, coſtituire, ordinare.* pref. *coſtituiſco.*

To create magiſtrates, *creare, o coſtituire magiſtrati.*

To create [to cauſe] *cauſare, generare, eccitare, ſuſcitare.*

To create ſorrow, *cauſare noja, o dolore.*

To create a ſtomach, *aguzzar l'appetito, provocar la fame.*

To create troubles, *ſuſcitar diſordini.*

To create emulation, *dare emulazione, eccitare emulazione.*

Crea'ted, adj. *creato,* v. To create.

Crea'ting, s. *il creare.*

Cre'ation, s. [the forming ſomething out of nothing] *creazione, criazione,* s. f.

The creation of the world, *la creazione del mondo.*

Creation of magiſtrates, *creazione, elezione, nominazione de' magiſtrati.*

Cre'ator, s. [the perſon who creates] *creatore,* s. m. *colui che crea, e a Dio ſolo s'attribuiſce tal nome.*

Cre'ature, s. [a created being] *creatura,* s. f. *ogni coſa creata.*

A living creature, *una creatura vivente.*

Creature [one who owes his fortune and riſe to the favour of ſome great man] *creatura, colui che è ſtato ſotto la diſciplina d'alcuno* e tirato *innanzi da lui.*

A ſtrange creature, *un moſtro.*

Crea'turely, adj. [having the qualities of a creature] *che ha le qualità d'una creatura. Non è in uſo.*

Cre'dence, s. [belief, credit] *credenza fede,* s. f.

To give credence to a thing, *dare o preſtar fede a che che ſi ſia.*

Credence [name] *nome,* s. m. *fama,* s. f.

He thereby gained a credence of being a good chriſtian, *e con queſto mezzo acquiſtò fama di buon criſtiano.*

Crede'ntials, s. [letters of credit and recommendation, eſpecially ſuch as are given to an ambaſſador, plenipotentiary, &c.] *lettere di credenza che ſi danno ad un ambaſciadore, plenipotenziario,* &c.

Credibi'lity, s. [credibleneſs] *probabilità, veriſimilitudine,* s. f.

Cre'dible, adj. [that which is to be believed] *credibile, da eſſer creduto.*

It is not credible, *non è credibile.*

A credible witneſs, *un teſtimonio degno di fede.*

Cre'dibleness, s. *probabilità, veriſimilitudine,* s. f.

Cre'dibly, adv. *credibilmente, in modo da crederſi.*

I am credibly informed, *mi vien detto per coſa certa.*

Cre'dit, s. [reputation, authority] *credito,* s. m. *ſtima, riputazione, autorità,* s. f.

A man of credit, *un uomo di credito o accredidato, una perſona di ſtima.*

To make uſe of his credit, *ſervirſi del ſuo credito.*

To loſe one's credit, *perdere il credito.*

Credit [honour] *credito, onore,* s. m.

It will be for your credit, *ſarà di voſtro credito o onore.*

Credit [credence, belief] *credito, credenza, fede.*

To give credit to a thing, *dar credito o credenza, preſtar fede a che che ſi ſia.*

Credit [truſt] *credito, credenza.*

To give credit to one [to truſt him] *dare credenza, o fare credenza ad uno, vendergli che che ſi ſia pe' tempi.*

To Cre'dit [to believe] *credere, preſtar fede, dar credenza.*

I am not apt to credit ſuch things, *non poſſo darmi a credere tali coſe.*

That will no ways credit you, *coteſto non vi farà onore alcuno, non ridonderà in voſtro onore.*

Cre'ditable, adj. [which brings honour or credit] *onorevole, vantaggioſo, che fa onore.*

A creditable employment, *un impiego onorevole.*

Cre'ditableness, s. *qualità onorevole, onorevolezza.*

Cre'ditably, adv. [reputably, without diſgrace] *onorevolmente, con molto credito.*

Cre'dited, adj. *creduto.*

He may be credited, *ſe gli può credere, ſi può preſtar fede alle ſue parole.*

Cre'ditor, s. *creditore,* s. m. *colui a che è dovuto.*

To pay his creditors, *pagare i ſuoi creditori.*

Credu'lity, s. [aptneſs to believe] *credulità,* s. f. *facilità a credere.*

He is guilty of too much credulity, *egli ha troppa credulità, egli è troppo credulo.*

Cre'dulous, adj. [apt to believe] *credulo, agevole al credere, che di leggier crede.*

Cre'dulousness, s. [aptneſs to believe; credulity] *facilità a credere, credulità.*

Creed, s. [a ſhort or ſummary account of the chief articles of the chriſtian faith] *il credo, il ſimbolo degli apoſtoli.*

To ſay the creed, *dire il credo.*

Creek, s. [a nook in an harbour, where any thing is landed] *molo,* s. m.

Creek [a little bay] *cala,* s. f. *ſeno di mare dentro al terreno ove poſſa con ſicurezza trattenerſi alcun tempo qualche vaſcello.*

A creek in the neck [a ſmall pain there] *torticollo,* s. m.

I have a creek in my neck, *io ho il torticollo.*

To Creek [to make a harſh noiſe] *croſciare, ſcoppiettare, ſcricciolare,* render *quel romore che fanno talvolta le ſcarpe e le pianelle in andando, o un legno o ghiaccio o vetro nel romperſi.*

Cre'eking, s. *croſcio, ſtrepito,* s. m.

To Creep [to crawl upon all fours] *rampicare, andare ad alto come fanno gli animali attaccando le zampe e i piedi.*

To creep in, *ficcarſi, intrometterſi, introdurſi, inſinuarſi.*

To creep into a corner, *ficcarſi in un cantone.*

To creep into one's favour, *inſinuarſi nelle grazie altrui, cattivarſi la ſua amicizia.*

To creep out, *ſfilare, batterſela.*

To have always a hole to creep out at; *aver ſempre qualche ſutterfugio, qualche ſcampo o modo da ſcampare.*

Old age creeps on [old age comes creeping along] *la vecchiezza s'accoſta inſenſibilmente.*

To creep [to fawn] *adulare, luſingare, accarezzare, far carezze, liſciare, piaggiare.*

He is ready to creep into his mouth, *egli gli liſcia ben la coda.*

Cre'eper, s. [a creeping creature] *una creatura che rampica.*

Creeper [a bird] *un picchio.*

Creeper [a low andiron] *alare,* s. m.

Creep-hole, s. *buco per dove uno può ſcampare. Figurativamente, preteſto, ſcampo, ſutterfugio.*

Cre'eping, s. *il rampicare.*

Creeping and crouching, *viltà, abbiettezza, mancanza d'animo.*

Creeping, adj. *che rampica, che s'inſinua poco a poco.*

A creeping animal, *un rettile.*

Creepingly, adv. *ſtraſcicatamente a mo' di rettile.*

Cre'nated, adj. [notched, indented] *merlato.* Ex. The crenated walls of an old caſtle, *le merlate mura d'un antico caſtello.*

Crept, particip. from to creep, *rampicato.*

Crepu'scle, s. [twilight] *crepuſcolo,* s. m. *l'ora nella quale appariſce il giorno e nella quale ſe ne va.*

Crepu'sculous, adj. [glimmering

ing; in a ftate between light and darkneis] *trà chiaro e bruno, tra'l dì e la notte.*

CRE'SCENT, s. [in heraldry, the figure of a half moon] *luna crefcente, o mezza luna.*

Crefcent [the arms of the Grand Seignior] *la mezza luna, le armi del Gran Signore.*

CRESS, s. [an herb] *crefcione*, s. m. *fpezie d' erba buona da mangiare.*

Garden creffes, *nafturcio*, s. m.

Water-creffes, *crefcione di riviera.*

CRE'SSET, s. [creffet-light for a burning beacon] *lanternone*, s. m.

A creffet to fet a pot on, *un treppiede o treppiè*, s. m.

CREST, s. [of birds] *crefta*, s. f.

Creft in heraldry] *crefta, cimiero.*

The creft of an helmet, *la crefta d' un elmetto, o d'utta celata.*

The creft [the mane of a horfe] *il crine d' un cavallo*

Creft-fallen, adj. [dejected] *fgomentato, sbigottito, perfo d' animo.*

Creft [pride, fpirit, fire] *orgoglio, audacia, boldanza, fuoco.*

CRE'STED, adj. [a term of heraldry] *che ha per cimiero.*

Pallas had a head piece crefted with the head of a horfe, *Pallade aveva per cimiero della fua celata una tefta di cavallo.*

CRE'STLESS, adj. *fcreftato, fenza cimiero, difadorno.*

CRETA'CEOUS, adj. [abounding with chalk, chalky] *abbondante di creta, pien di geffo.*

CRE'VICE, s. [a crack, a cleft, a chink] *una feffura, una crepatura.*

CREW, s. [company, band] *banda, torma, mano.*

A crew of rogues, *una banda ouna man di furbi o di canaglia.*

The crew of a fhip, *la ciurma d'un vaffello.*

CREW, *preterito del verbo* To crow.

CRE'WEL, s. [yarn twifted and wound on a knot or ball] *lana filata avvolta intorno a un nodo o a una palla.*

CRIB, s. [a manger for cattle] *mangiatoja*, s. f.

Crib, s. [a fmall habitation, a cottage] *un piccolo, e povero abituro, una capanna.*

To CRIB [to fhut up in a narrow habitation; to cage] *ferrar fu in un luogo piccolo, ingabbiare, porre in gabbia.*

CRI'BBAGE, s. [a game at cards] *nome di giuoco di carte molto ufato in Inghilterra.*

CRI'BBLE, s. [a corn-fieve] *cribro, vaglio, crivello*, s. m.

CRIBRA'TION, s. [the act of fifting] *cribrare, vagliare, crivellare.*

CRICK, s. *ex.* [a crick in the neck] *un torticolle, incordatura nel collo.*

CRI'CKET, [an infect] *grillo*, s. m.

A fen cricket, *un grillotalpa*

Cricket [low ftool] *forta di feggiola baffa.*

Cricket [a fort of play with a ball] *forta di giuoco che fi fa con una palla che fi fpinge con un baftone.*

To CRIE, *v.* To cry.

CRIED, adj. *gridato, v.* To cry.

Cried unto, *invocato, implorato.*

Cried up, *efultato, vantato.*

Cried down, *fcreditato.*

CRI'ER, s. *gridatore*, s. m. *che grida.*

A publick crier, *banditore*, s. m.

CRIME, s. [offence, fin] *delitto, peccato*, s. m. *offefa, colpa*, s. f.

A heinous crime, *un delitto atroce.*

A capital crime, *un delitto capitale.*

To perpetrate or commit a crime, *fare o commettere qualche delitto.*

CRI'MEFUL, adj. [wicked, criminal] *pieno di peccato, trifto, cattivo, empio, fcellerato.*

CRI'MELESS, adj. [innocent, without crime] *innocente, fenza peccato.*

CRI'MINAL, adj. [guilty] *criminale.*

A criminal caufe, *una caufa criminale.*

A criminal, s. [an offender or malefactor] *un malfattore, un delinquente.*

CRI'MINALLY, adv. *criminalmente, con forma, e maniera criminale.*

CRIMINALTY, s. [a criminal caufe] *caufa criminale.*

CRI'MINOUS, adj. *criminale.*

CRI'MIOUSLY, adv. [enormoufly, very wickedly] *fcelleratamente, triftamente, empiamente.*

CRI'MINOUSNESS, s. [wickednefs, guilt, crime] *peccato, crime, colpa, cattivezza.*

CRI'MOSIN, adj. *cremisí, forta di color roffo.*

CRIMP, adj. [friable, brittle, eafily crumbled] *fragile, che ftiacciando fi riduce agevolmente in polvere.*

To CRIMPLE, [to contract, to corrugate] *ritirarfi, raggrinzirfi, far grinze.*

CRI'MSON, s. [a fine red colour] *chermisì, color roffo nobile.*

Crimfon velvet, *velluto chermisì.*

To CRI'MSON, [to dye with crimfon] *tinger in chermisì, tinger in roffo o in paonazzo.*

CRI'NCUM, s. a cant word [a cramp, a whimfy] *un capriccio, un penfiero negli occhi, una cofa fantaftica.*

CRINGE, s. [bow, fervile, civility] *l' inchinarfi e offequiar troppo altrui, civilità fervile.*

To CRINGE, v. a. [to draw together, to contract] *unire ftrettamente infieme, rattrare.*

To cringe, v. n. [to bow, to pay court, to fawn, to flatter] *inchinarfi troppo, effere vilmente offequiofo, adulare vilmente.*

I hate this cringing, *non poffo patire tante profonde riverenze.*

Full of cringings, *vilmente rifpettofo.*

Cringing, adj. *baffo, abbietto, vile.*

A cringing foul, *un' anima abbietta, un uomo vile.*

To CRINKLE [to go in and out] *ferpede, andar ferpendo.*

CRINKLES, s. *gira volte, finuofità*, s. f. *giri, fpreggiamenti, fvoltamenti*, s. f.

Full of crinkles, *finuofo, fghembo, pieno di finuofità.*

CRI'PLINGS, s. [in architecture, fhort pifes of wood againft the fide of a houfe] *corrente*, s. m. *ciafcun di que' travicelli fottili che fi metton ne' palchi, o ne' tetti, fra trave e trave.*

CRIPPLE, adj. [lame, that has loft the ufe of the limbs] *zoppo ftroppiato, ftorpiato.*

CRI'PPLENESS, s. [lamenefs] *ftorpiatura*, s. f. *ftorpio*, s. m. *lo ftato d' uno che è ftorpiato.*

CRI'SIS, s. [a fudden change in a difeafe either for the better or worfe] *crife, crifi*, s. f.

Crifis, [the point of time at which a any affairs come to the height] *crifi, quel periodo in cui un affare aggiunge al fuo più alto punto.*

CRISP, adj. [curled] *crefpo, ricciuto.*

The fkin of the pig muft be crifp, *la pelle del porcello bifogna che fia crefpa.*

Crifp, [indented, winding] *ferpeggiante, tortuofo.*

Crifp [brittle, friable] *fragile, facile a frantumarfi.*

To crifp [to frizzle, to curl] *increfpare, arricciare, inanellare.*

To crifp hair, *arricciare o inanellare i capelli.*

CRISPED, adj. *crefpo, ricciuto, arricciato, inanellato.*

A CRI'SPIN-PIN, [a curling iron] *calamiftro*, s. m. *ftrumento di ferro ad ufo d' arricciar capelli.*

CRI'SPY, adj. [curled] *crefpo, ricciuto, arricciato.*

CRITE'RION, [a mark by which any thing is judged of, with regard to its goodnefs or badnefs] *fegno per cui fi giudica fe una cofa è buona o mala.*

CRI'TICAL, adj. [cenforious] *critico.*

A critical humour, *un critico, uno che è inclinato a criticare.*

Critical days [among phyficians, are thofe days whereon there happens a fudden change of the difeafe, or on which it comes to its crifis] *giorni critici, fon quelli de' quali il medico giudica dell' infermo.*

Critical times, *tempi pericolofi.*

CRI'TICALLY, adv. like a critick] *da critico.*

CRI'TICISM, s. [the art of judging or cenfuring men's actions, words, or writings] *critica, cenfura*, s. f.

To CRITICI'SE UPON [to find fault with] *criticare, cenfurare, correggere, riprendere.* pret. *correffi, riprefi.*

CRI'TICK, s. [a perfon fkilled in criticifm] *un critico, un cenfore, un riprenditore, un correttore.*

Critick, s. [the art of criticifm] *l'arte del critico, la critica.*

Critick, adj. [critical, relating to criticifm] *critico, appartenente alla critica.*

To CROAK, [to make a hoarfe low noife like a frog] *gracidare, ed è proprio delle rane.*

To croak, [to caw or cry as a raven or crow] *crocitare, ed e' proprio de' corvi e delle cornacchie.*

CROAK, s. [the cry or voice of a frog or raven] *il gracidar della rana o il crocitar de' corvi e delle cornacchie.*

Croceus, adj. *croceo, del colore del zafferano.*

CROCK, s. [a coarse earthen pot] *pignatta,* s. f. *vaso di terra.*

A crock of butter, *una pignatta piena di butirro.*

Crook-butter [salt butter] *butirro salato.*

CROCODI'LE, s. [a very large beast in the shape of a lizard, living both on the land and in the water] *cocodrillo,* s. m.

Crocodile's tears [treacherous tears] *lagrime del cocodrillo, che uccide l' uomo e poi la piagne; e si dice di colui, che a bella posta ti fa male, e poi mostra che gliene rincresca.*

CROCUS, s. [an early flower] *croco, fiore primatticcio giallo così chiamato.*

CROE, s. [a leaver of iron] *una lieva di ferro*

Croe [a notch in the side boards or staves of a cask, where the head-pieces go in] *capruggine,* s. f. *intaccatura delle doghe dentro alla quale si connettono i fondi delle botti o simili.*

CROFT, s. [a little close adjoining to a house for pasture or tillage] *praticello accanto d' una cosa che serve per pascolo, un chiuso.*

CROISA'DE, } s. [a holy war] *crociato,* s. f.
CROISA'DO, }

CROISES, s. [pilgrims who wore a cross on their garments for the sake of religion] *crociati, pellegrini.*

CRONE, [an old ewe] *una pecora vecchia, decrepita.*

CRONE, s. [an old woman] *una vecchiaccia.*

CRO'NY, s [an intimate companion, a good old friend] *un amico vecchio, amico intimo.*

CROOK, s. [hook] *uncino,* s. m.

A little crook, *uncinetto,* s. m.

A shepherd's crook, *rocco,* s. m. *bastone ritorto in cima che portano in mano i pastori.*

By hook and crook, *per ruffa e raffa.*

Crook-back'd, crook-shoulder'd, *gobbo.*

Crook-footed, *che ha i piedi storti.*

Crook-legg'd [that has crooked legs] *che ha le gambe storte.*

To CROOK [to make crooked] *incurvare, far curvo, piegare, archeggiare.*

CR'OOKED, adj. *curvo, piegato in arco, arcato, storto, chinato, chino.*

Grown crooked with age, *curvo per vecchiaja.*

Crooked legs, *gambe storte.*

A crooked line, *una linea curva.*

A crooked mind, *animo curvo, ingiusto, malvagio, bieco.*

To grow crooked, *incurvarsi, piegarsi.*

A crooked nose, *naso adunco.*

CR'OOKEDLY, adv. [not in a strait line] *tortamente, non linea retta.*

Crookedly, adv. [untowardly, not compliantly] *a restio, mal volentieri, a mal in corpo.*

CR'OOKEDNESS, s. *curvatura, curvezza, curvità, chinatura, piegatura,* s. f.

The Crookedness of rivers, *la sinuosità di fiumi, le rivolture, i giri e rigiri de' fiumi.*

CROP, s. [the gathering of hay or corn, or the whole stock which the ground affords] *ricolta, raccolta.*

A crop of corn or hay, *ricolta di grano o di fieno.*

Crop [the handle of a coachman's whip] *la verga della frusta d'un cocchiero.*

Crop [craw of a bird] *gozzo d' uccello.*

Crop [cropped horse] *cavallo scodato.*

Crop-eared, *che ha li orecchi mozzi.*

To CROP [to cut off] *scortare, accorciare, mozzare, tondere, tosare.*

To crop a horse, *scortare la coda o gli orecchi d' un cavallo.*

To crop flowers [to gather flowers] *coglier fiori.*

The goat crops the hedge, *la capra strameggia la siepe, morde l' erba o la mangia intorno alla siepe.*

Cropful, adj. [satiated with a full belly] *sazio, col ventre pieno.*

CROPPED, adj. *scortato, accorciato, mozzato, toso, tosato.*

CRO'PPING, s. *lo sortare.*

CRO'PSICK, adj. [sick with excess and debauchery *malato a forza di gozzovigliar troppo.*

CROPT, v. Cropped.

CRO'SIER, s. [a bishop's staff] *rocco, pastorale,* s. m. *bastone ritorto che si porta davanti a' vescovi.*

Crosiers in astronomy are four stars in the form of a cross, by the help of which, those who sail in the southern hemisphere find the Antarctick pole] *costellazione composta di quattro stelle disposte in croce, per mezzo delle quali quelli che navigano nell' emisphero meridionale, trovano il polo antartico.*

CRO'SLET, s. [forehead-cloth] *frontale,* s. m. *quel panno che si mette sulla fronte.*

CROSS CROSSLETS, [in heraldry] *croci incrociate, vore d' araldería.*

CROSS, s. [a figure of two things crossing one another] *croce,* s. f. *due legni attraverso l' un con altro ad angoli retti.*

Cross [a gibbet on which the ancients used to hang their malefactors] *croce sulla quale gli antichi uccidevano i malfattori.*

Cross [affliction, misfortune, trouble] *croce, pena, afflizzione,* s. f. *tormento, supplizio,* s. m.

To make the sign of the cross, *fare il segno della croce.*

Cross or pile [a sort of play] *croce o testa, sorta di giuoco.*

It was e'en come to cross and pile whether I shou'd go or stay, *si stava in dubbio*

Let him bear his cross and follow me, *porti la sua croce e mi segua.*

He has had many crosses in his life, *egli ha sofferte molte traversie nella sua vita.*

Cross-grained, *dispiacevole, fastidioso, bisbetico, umorista, caparbio, increscevole, nojoso, tedioso, discolo.*

Cross-legge', *che ha le gambe in croce.*

Cross-bow, s. *balestra,* s. f.

A cross-bow man, *balestriere,* s. m. *tirator di balestra.*

Cross-wise, *attraverso, o a traverso, traversamente.*

Cross, adj. [laid cross] *traversato, a traverso.*

Cross [peevish, humoursome] *nojoso, fastidioso, dispiacevole, di cattivo umore, fantastico, bisbetico, discolo.*

A cross wind, *vento contrario.*

A cross answer, *una cattiva risposta.*

Cross words, *parole, ingiuriose.*

A cross business, *affare sinistro.*

A cross wife, *una cattiva moglie.*

A cross child, *un fanciullo nojoso o fastidioso.*

A cross day, *un giorno infelice.*

Cross-path, coss-way, *crocicchio, luogo dove s'incrocicchian le strade.*

Two cross keys, *due chiavi incrocicchiate.*

The cross bars of a window, *la sbarra d'una finestra.*

A cross bar shot, *una palla incatenata.*

Cross-matches, *matrimoni intrecciati, come quando un fratello e una sorella si maritano con due altri che sono altresì fratelli e sorelle.*

A cross fortune, *un rovescio di fortuna, fortuna nemica.*

To have a cross fortune, *aver la fortuna nemica.*

Cross-bite [disappointment] *disgrazia, traversia, sfortuna,* s. f. *malgo,* s. m.

A cross piece of timber, or cross beam, *una trave che traversa.*

Cross lines, *linee traversali.*

Cross, adv. *di traverso, a traverso, traversalmente.*

A thing laid cross, *una cosa messa di traverso o attraverso.*

Every thing goes cross with us, *ogni cosa ci riesce a rovescio, ogni cosa ci va male.*

Cross, prep. *alla traversa, a traverso.*

Cross the fields, *alla traversa de' campi.*

I went cross the wood, *passai a traverso del bosco.*

To CROSS [to go cross] *traversare, passare attraverso, attraversare.*

To cross the street, *traversar la via o la strada.*

To cross the river, *varcare, traghettare, o passare un fiume.*

To cross [to thwart, to be contrary] *attraversare, andare attraverso, impedire, porre ostacolo, contrariare, contraddire, contrastare, opporsi, contravvenire.*

To cross one's designs, *deludere, attraversare o rompere gl' altrui disegni.*

To cross [to vex, to trouble] *tormentare, affliggere, travagliar l' animo, affannare.*

Why do you cross me thus? *perchè volete voi tormentarmi così?*

To cross [to hurt] *nuocere, far male.*

That meat has crossed my stomach, *questa carne m'ha fato male allo stomaco.*

To

To croſs [to lay croſs] *incrocicchiare, attraverſare a guiſa di croce.*
To croſs one's legs, *incrocicchiare le gambe.*
To croſs one's arms, *far delle braccia croce.*
To croſs one's ſelf [to make the ſign of the croſs] *fare il ſegno della croce.*
To croſs one [to make the ſign of the croſs upon him] *crociare alcuno, ſegnarlo col ſegno della croce.*
To croſs again the river, *ripaſſare il fiume.*
To croſs over the way, *attraverſare o traverſare la ſtrada.*
To croſs, or to croſs out, *ſcancellare, cancellare.*
CRO'SSED, adj. *v.* To croſs.
CROSS-BAR-SHOT, s. [a round ſhot or great bullet, with a bar of iron put thro' it] *palla di cannone forata, e attraverſo meſſavi una ſtanga di ferro, uſata ſpecialmente ne' vaſcelli da guerra.*
To CROSS-EXA'MINE [to try the faith of evidence by captious queſtions of the contrary party] *eſaminare i teſtimoni, e ſi fa dagli avvocati della parte avverſa perchè cadano in contradizione con quello che hanno già depoſto.*
CRO'SSBOW, s. *ſorta di dardo o ſaetta.*
CROSSGRA'INED, adj. [having the fibres tranſverſe or irregular] *che trae le fibre irregolari o a traverſo, e ſi dice generalmente del legno.*
Croſsgrained, adj. [perverſe, troubleſome, vexatious] *perverſo, ſtrano, biſbetico, torbido, ſpiacevole.*
CRO'SSLY, adv. [athwart] *attraverſo.*
Croſsly, adv. [oppoſitely, adverſely, in oppoſition to] *al contrario, in modo oppoſto, pel contrario verſo, a contrappelo.*
Croſsly, adv. [unfortunately] *ſventuratamente, diſgraziatamente.*
CRO'SSNESS, s. [tranſverſeneſs, interſection] *ſecamento, coſa che poſſa per traverſo ſopra una coſa dritta onde fa croce.*
Croſsneſs [perverſeneſs, peeviſhneſs] *perverſità, malumore.*
CROSS-ROW, s. *alfabeto.*
CRO'TCHET, s. [a note in muſick, which is half a minim] *croma,* s. f. *una delle figure o note della muſica.*
Crotchet [fancy, whim] *fantaſia,* s. f. *capriccio, ghiribizzo, grillo,* s. m.
His head is full of crotchets, *ha la teſta piena di grilli.*
To be full of crotchets, *ghiribizzare, fantaſticare, eſſere ghiribizzoſo o fantaſtico.*
Crotchet [trick, device] *aſtuzia, furberia,* s. f. *inganno,* s. m.
Crotchet, among printers, a mark expreſſed thus [ ] *ſegno di ſtampatore come due parenteſi in queſto modo* [ ].
CRO'TELS, s. [the ordure or dung of a hare] *ſterco di lepre.*
To CRO'UCH [to lie ſquat] *appiattarſi.*
To creep and crouch, *umiliarſi, proſternarſi.*

CRO'UCHED, adj. *ex.* crouched friars, *frati della crociata.*
CRO'UCHING, s. *l'appiattarſi, umiliazione.*
He got it with much creeping and crouching, *l'ha ottenuto a forza di ſommeſſione.*
CRO'UCHMASS, or CROUCHMASS-DAY, s. *il giorno della ſanta croce.*
CRO'UD, *v.* Crowd.
CRO'W, s. [a ſort of bird] *corvo,* s. m.
To give the crow a pudding [to die] *tirar le calze, morire.*
He has an ill crow to pluck [he has a great difficulty to conquer] *egli tiene l'anguilla per la coda, egli ha per le mani un' impreſa difficile.*
I have a crow to pluck with you, *io ho un calcio in gola con voi, io ho qualche coſa a rimproverarvi.*
Crow's foot [caltrop] *tribolo,* s. m. *capo d'un erba ſalvatica, di forma triangolare, che ha gli angoli d'acutiſſime punte.*
Crow-foot [a ſort of herb] *flamula,* s. f. *erba ſomigliante alla vitalba.*
A crow of iron, *rampino, raffio,* s. m.
Crow-toes [a flower] *giacinto e jacinto,* s. m. *ſpezie di fiore.*
Cock-crow, *il canto del gallo.*
A ſcare-crow, *uno ſpaventacchio o uno ſpauracchio; cencio o ſtraccio che ſi mette ne' campi ſopra una mazza o in ſugli alberi per iſpaventare gli uccelli.*
To CROW [as a cock does] *cantare, come fa il gallo.* preterit, I crew, or crowed; I have crowed.
To crow [to vapour, to brag] *vantarſi, trionfare, millantarſi, gridar vittoria.*
To crow over one, *inſultare altrui, fargli inſulti e ſoperchierie, bravarlo.*
To crow the ſail, *ſpiegar le vele, termine marinareſco.*
CROWD, s. [throng] *calca, folla, folta,* s. f. *moltitudine di gente.*
To get into the crowd, *meſcolarſi nella calca.*
To get through the crowd, *farſi ſtrada tra la folla.*
To get out of the crowd, *ritirarſi dalla folla.*
Crowd [fiddle] *violino,* s. m.
To crowd, verb act. *affollare, calcare, ſtrignere,* pret. *ſtrinſi.*
You crowd me too much, *voi mi ſtate troppo addoſſo.*
To crowd one to death, *affogare alcuno col calcarlo troppo.*
To crowd in, *ſpignerſi nella calca.*
To crowd a thing in, *ſpignere, cacciare, mettere, ficcar che che ſi ſia con forza.*
To crowd the ſail, *ſpiegare tutte le vele al vento.*
CRO'WDED, adj. *affollato, calcato.* *v.* To crowd.
CRO'WDER, s. [fiddler] *ſonator di violino.*
CROW-KE'EPER, s. [ſcarecrow] *ſpauracchio, ſpaventacchio.*
CROWN, s. [a cap of ſtate worn on their heads by ſovereign princes] *corona,* s. f. *ornamento di varie fogge, con che ſi cingono la teſta i re ed altri uomini illuſtri in ſegno d'autorità.*
A golden crown, *una corona d'oro.*
To come to the crown, *pervenire alla corona.*
The crown of the head, *la cima della teſta.*
From the crown of the head to the ſole of the foot, *dalla cima della teſta alla pianta del piede.*
A freak took him in the crown, *gli ſaltò un grillo in teſta.*
A prieſt's ſhaven crown, *corona o cherica di prete.*
Crown [garland] *corona, ghirlanda.*
The crown of a hat, *la forma d'un cappello.*
The crown of a periwig, *la cuffia d'una parurca.*
Crown [a piece of money] *corona,* s. f. *ſorta di moneta, ſcudo,* s. m.
I'll give you a crown for it, *ve ne darò uno ſcudo.*
A crown-piece, *una corona, uno ſcudo.*
Crown [palmer of a deer's head] *le corna piccole del cervo in cima delle grandi a guiſa di corona.*
To CROWN [to ſet a crown on the head] *coronare, mettere o porre altrui la corona.*
To crown [to make perfect, to finiſh with honour] *finire, perfezionare con onore.*
To crown [to reward] *ricompenſare, rimunerare.*
To crown with glory, *coronare di gloria.*
To crown a man at draughts, *damare una pedina al giuoco di dama.*
CRO'WNET, s. [the ſame with coronet] *corona piccola.*
Crownet, s. [chief end, laſt purpoſe] *fine principale, ultima intenzione.*
CRO'WNING, s. *coronamento,* s. m. *coronazione,* s. f. *il coronare.*
To CROYN [to cry as fallow-deer do at rutting time] *quel mugghiare che fa il cervo quando va in frega.*
To CRU'CIATE [to torment] *cruciare, tormentare.*
CRU'CIATED, adj. *cruciato; tormentato.*
CRU'CIBLE, s. [a melting pot made of earth for the melting of metals] *crociuolo, crogiuolo, colatojo,* s. m. *vaſetto di terra cotta ove ſi fondono i metalli.*
CRU'CIFER, s. *boja; colui che mette altri ſulla croce.*
CRUCI'FEROUS, adj. *che porta la croce.*
CRU'CIFIX, s. [a figure of our Saviour hanging upon the croſs] *crociſſo, l'imagine di noſtro Signore confitto in croce.*
CRUCIFI'XION, s. *crociſſione,* s. f. *crocifiggimento,* s. m. *il crocifiggere.*
CRU'CIFORM, adj. [having the form of a croſs] *che ha forma di croce.*
To CRU'CIFY [to faſten or nail to a croſs] *crocifiggere, conficcare in ſulla croce,* pret. *crociſſi.*
To crucify [to torment] *crocifiggere, tormentare.*
CRU'CIFIED, adj. *crociſſo, conficcato in croce, tormentato.*

CRU'CIFYING, s. *crocifiggimento*, s. m. *crocifissione*, s. f. *il crocifiggere*.

CRU'DE, adj. [raw, undigested] *crudo, non cotto, non digerito*.

A crude matter, *materia cruda*.

CRU'DELY, adv. [unripely, without due preparation] *immaturamente, senza precedente preparazione*.

CRU'DENESS, s. [unripeness, indigestion] *immaturità, indigestione*.

CRU'DITY, s. [rawness] *crudità, crudezza, acerbezza, immaturità*, s. f.

CRU'EL, adj. [merciless, inhuman] *crudo, crudele, aspro, efferato, inumano, spietato*.

A cruel tyrant, *un crudel tiranno*.

A cruel death, *una cruda o acerba morte*.

A cruel man, *un crudele*.

A cruel woman, *una crudele*.

'Tis a cruel thing, *è pur una cosa ben cruda*.

Cruel, adv. [for cruelly] *crudelmente, fieramente, terribilmente, estremamente*.

He is cruel-mad, *egli è terribilmente in collera, egli da nelle smanie*.

Cruel-fierce, *terribilmente fiero*.

Cruel-hot, *estremamente caldo*.

CRU'ELLY, adv. *crudelmente, spietatamente, fieramente, inumanamente*.

To use one cruelly, *trattar uno crudelmente*.

CRU'ELTY, s. *crudeltà, atrocità, fierezza, inumanità, barbarie*, s. f.

A great piece of cruelty, *una gran crudeltà o barbarie*.

CRU'ET, s. *guastadetta per l'olio e l'aceto*.

CRUISE, s. [the course of a ship] *corso*, s. m. *il corseggiare*.

The cruise of a ship, *il corso d'un vascello*.

To CRUISE [a sea term, to sail up and down] *corseggiare, andare in corso*.

CRU'ISER, s. [a ship appointed to cruise] *vascello di corso*.

CRU'ISING, s. *il corseggiare, corso*.

To go cruising, *andare in corso*.

CRUM, } s. [the soft part of bread]
CRUMB, } *midolla*, s. f. *quella parte del pane contenuta dalla corteccia*.

A crumb of bread, *una mica di pane*.

To pick up one's crumbs, *v*. To pick.

To CRU'MBLE [to break small or into crumbs] *sminuzzare*, tritare, *stritolare*.

CRU'MBLED, adj. *sminuzzato, tritato, stritolato*.

CRU'MMY, adj. [full of crumb] *midolloso, pien di modolla*.

CRUMP, or CRUMP SHOULDERED, adj. *gobbo, gibboso, gibbuto*.

Crump footed, *che ha i piedi storti*.

CRU'MPED, adj. *curvo, piegato in arco, arcato*.

CRU'MPLE, s. *grinza, ruga, crespa*.

To CRU'MPLE [to ruffle, to rumple] *raggrinzare*.

To crumple, verb neut. *raggrinzarsi*.

CRU'MPLED, adj. *raggrinzato*.

Her skin is all crumpled, *la sua pelle è tutta raggrinzata*.

To CRUNK [to cry like a crane] *gridare come una grue*.

CRU'PPER, s. [the buttocks of a horse, the rump] *groppa*, s. f. *la parte dell' animal quadrupede appiè della schiena sopra i fianchi. Dicesi più propriamente di quelli da cavalcare*; e *degli altri groppone*.

The crupper [a roll of leather under the horse's tail] *groppiera*, s. f. *posolino*, s. m. *posalatura*, s. f. *il cuojo attaccato con una fibbia alla sella, e va per la groppa fino alla coda, nella quale si mette essa coda*.

CRU'RAL, adj. [belonging to the thighs] *crurale*.

Crural artery [the artery of the thigh, which spreads itself among the muscles] *arteria crurale*.

CRUSA'DE, } s. [the expedition of
CRUSA'DO, } the christian princes for the conquest of the holy land] *crociata*, s. f. *lega generale de' cristiani che andava a combattere contro gl' infedeli per la conquista di terra santa*.

CRUSE, s. [a vial for oil or vinegar] *picciol vasetto per uso di tenere olio o aceto per condire*.

To CRUSH [to break or squeeze to pieces] *acciaccare, ammaccare, schiacciare*.

The wheel has crushed him to pieces, *la ruota l'ha tutto acciaccato*.

To crush [to oppress] *opprimere, tener sotto, oppressare, sterminare, rovinare*.

To crush a party down, *sterminare un partito*.

A great building without a good foundation, will crush itself with its own weight, *un grand' edificio, se non è ben fondato, sprofonderà da se stesso*.

CRU'SHED, adj *acciaccato, ammaccato, schiacciato, oppresso, oppressato, rovinato*.

CRU'SHING, s. *acciaccamento, ammaccamento*, s. m. *l'acciaccare, il rovinare*.

CRUST, s. [the shelly part of any thing] *crosta*, s. f.

A crust of bread, *una crosta o corteccia di pane*.

To CRUST, verb neut. *formarsi in crosta, coprirsi di crosta, incrostarsi*.

The bread begins to crust, *il pane comincia ad incrostarsi*.

CRUSTA'CEOUS, adj. [crusty, covered with crust] *crostoso, crostuto, che ha croste*.

Crustaceous fishes [are shelly fishes, such as crabs, lobsters, &c.] *pesci crostacei, come granchi, gamberi di mare, e simili*.

CRU'STED, adj. *crostato, crostuto*.

Crusted with marble, *incrostato di marmo*.

CRU'STY, adj. *crostoso*.

Crusty bread, *pan crostoso*.

CRUTCH, s. [supports for a lame person] *gruccia*, s. f. *bastone commesso in un pezzo di legno incavato, per inforcarvi l'ascelle o mettervi su meglio la mano da chi non può reggersi in sulle gambe*.

To go with crutches, *camminare colle grucce*.

To CRUTCH [to support on crutches] *portar colle grucce, come fanno gli storpiati*.

CRY, s. [noise of the voice] *grido*, s. m. *suono strepitoso, propriamente di voce umana*.

A great cry and a little wool, *assai parole e poche lance rotte*.

Cry [weeping] *pianto*, s. m.

A cry of hounds, *una muta di cani*.

To CRY [to make noise with one's voice] *gridare, mandar fuora la voce con alto suono*.

To cry things about the streets, *vendere che che si sia per le strade*.

To cry mercy, *domandar mercè o misericordia*.

To cry [to call] *chiamare alcuno*.

To cry [to weep] *piangere, e piagnere*.

He does nothing but cry, *non fa altro che piagnere*.

To cry [to bawl] *gridare, strepitare, strillare*.

To cry quittance, *render la pariglia*.

To cry out, *gridare, esclamare, gridare ad alta voce, sclamare*.

To cry out fire, *gridare al fuoco*.

To cry out with all one's strength, *gridare ad alta voce*.

To cry out for help, *domandare ajuto*.

To cry out [as a woman with child] *star per partorire*.

His wife is ready to cry out, *sua moglie è vicina al parto*.

To cry out against one, *esclamare, dolersi, lamentarsi d'uno*.

To cry one's eyes out, *piagner dirottamente*.

To cry unto God, *invocare Iddio*.

To cry aloud, *gridare ad alta voce, alzar la voce*.

To cry up, *esaltare, lodare, vantare*.

To cry up one for a saint, *vantare uno per santo*.

To cry down, *screditare, discreditare*.

To cry down the money, *screditar la moneta, pubblicare ch' ella non avrà più corso, dar il calo alla moneta*.

CRY'D, *v*. Cryed.

CRY'ING, s. *il gridare, il piagnere*.

I could not forbear crying, *non potei ritener le lagrime*.

A crying out, *acclamazione, esclamazione*.

A woman's crying out [labour] *doglie del parto*.

CRY'AL, s. [the heron] *airone, aghirone*; *sorta d'uccello*.

CRY'ER, s. [the falcon gentle] *sorta di falcone*.

CRY'PTICAL, } adj. [hidden, secret,
CRY'PTICK, } occult] *nascosto, segreto, occulto*.

CRY'PTICALLY, adv. [occultly, secretly] *occultamente, segretamente, di nascoso*.

CRY'STAL, s. [a very bright and transparent stone] *cristallo*, s. m.

Rock crystal, *cristallo di rocca*.

Crystal, adj. *cristallino, lucido, trasparente*.

A crystal glass, *un bicchiere di cristallo*.

The

The cryſtal of a watch, *il criſtallo o il vetro d'una moſtra.*

Mineral cryſtal [a compoſition of ſalt-petre well purified, and of flower of brimſtone] *criſtallo minerale.*

CRYSTALI'NE, adj. [like to cryſtal in brightneſs] *criſtallino.*

The cryſtalline humour of the eye, *l'umor criſtallino dell' occhio.*

The cryſtalline heaven, *il cielo criſtallino.*

CUB, s. [bear's whelp, young bear] *orſacchio, orſo giovane.*

A fox-cub, *un volpicino, figliuol piccolo della volpe.*

To CUB [to bring forth] *il partorire de' lupi, delle volpi, delle balene, e di qualch' altro animale.*

CUBE, s. [a ſolid body terminated by ſix equal ſquares, and a dye truly made] *cubo,* s. m. *figura ſolida di ſei facce eguali, e quadrate.*

CUBE-ROOT, } *la radice quadra.*
CUBICK-ROOT, }

CU'BED, s. [a ſmall dried fruit reſembling pepper] *picciol frutto ſecco ſimile al pepe.*

CU'BICAL, or CU'BICK, adj. [belonging to, or having the figure of a cube] *cubico.*

CU'BIT, s. [the length of the arm from the elbow to the middle finger] *cubito, gombito,* s. m.

CU'CKING-STOOL [a machine formerly uſed for the puniſhment of ſcolds and brawling women to duck them over head and ears in the water] *ſpezie di ſedia che ſerviva altre volte di caſtigo alle donne inſolentemente clamoroſe; tuffandole in eſſa nell' acqua.*

CU'CKOLD, s. *un cornuto, un becco.*

He is a true cuckold, *egli è un becco cornuto.*

To CU'CKOLD one, *piantar le corna ad uno, farlo cornuto, piantarli un pajo di corna.*

CU'CKOLDING, s. *il far altrui cornuto.*

CU'CKOLDY, adj. [having the qualities of a cuckold; poor, mean] *povero, abbietto; come chi ha la moglie adultera e non ſa riſentirſene.*

CU'CKOLD-MAKER, s. *colui che fa meſtiero di ſeddurre le mogli altrui.*

CU'CKOLDOM, s. *l'eſſer becco.*

CUCKO'O [a ſort of bird] *cucco, cuculo,* s. m. *uccello coſì detto dal ſuono del ſuo canto.*

To ſing like a cuckoo [to harp always upon the ſame ſtring] *dire la canzone dell' uccellino, dire ſempre la medeſima coſa.*

CU'CUMBER, s. *cetriuolo; ſorta di frutto. v.* CETRIUOLO *e* COCOMERO *nell' altro tomo.*

CUD, s. [the inner part of the throat in beaſts] *la parte interiore della gola degli animali.*

To chew the cud [in a proper ſenſe] *ruminare, far ritornare alla bocca il cibo mandato nello ſtomaco non maſticato per maſticarlo, ed è proprio degli animali di piè feſſo.*

A bull that chews the cud, *un toro che rumina.*

To chew the cud [to think and reflect upon] *ruminare, ponderare, riconſiderare, riandar col penſiero.*

CU'DDEN, or CU'DDY, s. [a changling, a ſilly fellow] *uno ſciocco, uno ſcimunito, uno ſcemo, un minchione, un gaglioffo, un merendone.*

Cudden, adj. [ſilly, fooliſh] *ſciocco, ſcimunito, ſcemo, goffo, cionno.*

To CU'DDLE, v. n. [to lye cloſe, to ſquat] *appiattarſi, giacer appiattato.*

CU'DGEL, s. [a ſtick to fight with] *bacchio, batocchio, baſtone con guardia di giunco col quale la canaglia ſchermiſce in Inghilterra.*

To lay down the cudgels, or to croſs the cudgels [to give over fighting] *metter giu le armi.*

To croſs the cudgels, *darſi per vinto.*

CU'DGEL-PROOF, adj. [able to reſiſt a ſtick] *che ſta ſaldo al baſtone, che non cura eſſer baſtonato.*

To CU'DGEL [to beat] *baſtonare, tartaſſare, batacchiare, zombare.*

To cudgel one's brains about a thing, *beccarſi il cervello intorno a che che ſi ſia.*

CU'DGELLED, adj. *baſtonato, tartaſſato, batacchiato, zombato.*

CU'DGELLING, s. *il baſtonare.*

CU'DWEED, s. [a plant] *ſorta di pianta.*

CUE, s. [an item given to ſtage players, what or when to ſpeak] *ſegno o motto che ſi da a' recitanti di quel che devono dire, e quando devono parlare; e più propriamente quella parola o parte di verſo che il muſico o lo attore ha ſcritta nelle ſua parte, appartenante a un altro che recita o canta ſeco nello ſteſſa ſcena; alla quale parola o parte di verſo toſto che è pronunciata egli deve andar dreto colle ſue parole o verſi,*

To know one's cue, *ſaper ben fare la ſua parte.*

A cue [half a farthing] *mezzo quattrino.*

A merry cue, *un bell' umore.*

IN CUE'RPO, adj. *in camiſcia.*

To walk in cuerpo, *andare in camiſcia.*

CUFF, s. [which men wear] *manichetto,* s. m.

Laced cuffs, *manichini merlettati.*

Cuff [box on the ear] *ſchiaffo o pugno ſulla faccia.*

To go to cuffs, *venire alle mani, batterſi, fare a' pugni.*

To CUFF, *ſchiaffeggiare, dare ſchiaffi o pugni in faccia.*

To cuff one another, *batterſi, fare a' pugni.*

CUFFED, adj. *ſchiaffeggiato.*

CU'FFING, s. *lo ſchiaffeggiare.*

CUI'RASS, s. [armour for the back and breaſt] *corazza,* s. f. *armadura del buſto fatta di lama di ferro.*

CUIRASSI'ER, s. *corazza, ſoldato a cavallo armato di corazza.*

A regiment of cuiraſſiers, *un reggimento di corazze.*

CUISH, s. [armour for the thigh] *coſciale,* s. m. *armadura che cuopre la coſcia.* p. cuiſſes.

CULDE'ES, s. [a ſort of religious people formerly in Scotland] *ſorta di religioſi che erano altre volte in Iſcozia.*

CU'LINARY, adj. [belonging to the kitchen] *di cucina, appartenente alla cucina.*

To CULL [to pick and chuſe, to pick out] *ſcegliere, ſcerre, cappare.*

To cull [to take out] *pigliare, trarre, prendere,* pret. *preſi, traſſi.*

To cull a fine notion out of a book, *pigliare o trarre qualche bel concetto fuor d'un libro.*

CU'LLANDER, s. *cola, calza,* s. f. *colatojo,* s. m. *ſtrumento da colare che che ſi ſia.*

CULLED, adj. *ſcelto, cappato.*

CU'LLION, s. [a ſcoundrel] *un briccone, un triſto, un vile.*

CU'LLIONLY, adj. [mean, baſe] *vile, abbietto.*

CU'LLIS, s. [the ſtrained juice of boiled meat] *conſumato,* s. m. *peverada,* s. f. *brodo nel quale abbino bollito polli o ſimil carne tanto che vi ſieno conſumati dentro.*

CU'LLY, s. [a fool, one who may be eaſily led by the noſe, or put upon] *uno ſciocco, uno ſcemo, un gonzo.*

To CU'LLY one [to make a fool of him] *burlare o ingannare alcuno, uccellarlo, beffarlo, acchiapparlo.*

CU'LPABLE, adj. [guilty] *colpevole, colpabile, che è in colpa, in fallo.*

CU'LPABLY, adj. [blameably, criminally] *reamente, triſtamente.*

CU'LPRIT, s. [a man arraigned before his judge] *perſona accuſata e che ſtà innanzi al giudice.*

CU'LTER, s. *coltro, parte del vomero per arar la terra.*

CULTCH, s. [the bottom of the ſea where oyſters ſpawn] *il fondo del mare dove ſi generano l'oſtriche.*

To CU'LTIVATE [to till or huſband the ground] *coltivare, e caltivare, eſercitar l'agricoltura.*

To cultivate [to improve] *coltivare, conſervare, perfezionare.*

To cultivate one's friendſhip, *coltivarſi l' amicizia di qualcheduno.*

To cultivate one's mind, *coltivare, o perfezionare la mente.*

CU'LTIVATED, adj. *coltivato, cultivato.*

CU'LTIVATING, s. *coltivamento, cultivamento,* s. m. *il coltivare.*

CULTIVA'TION, s. [or improvement] *coltivazione, cultivazione, coltivatura, cultivatura, cultura, cultura,* s. f.

The cultivation of a plant, *la coltura d'una pianta.*

Cultivation, *ammaeſtramento o educazione della gioventù.*

CULTIVA'TOR, s. [one who improves, promotes, or meliorates] *cultore, promotore.*

CU'LTURE, s. *il coltivare, coltura.*

To CULTURE, [to cultivate, to till] *coltivare.*

CU'LVER, s. [pigeon] *colombo, colomba.*

A wood culver, *un colombaccio, un colombo groſſo ſalvatico.*

Culver-tail [for joining pieces together in building] *coda di rondine.*

CU'LVERIN, s. [a piece of ordnance] *colubrina*, s. f. *sorta d'artiglieria.*

CU'LVERKEY, s. *sorta di fiore.*

CU'MBER, s. [trouble] *imbarazzo, impedimento, intrigo*, s. m.

To CU'MBER [to trouble, to stop] *imbarazzare, intrigare, imbrogliare.*

To cumber [to burthen] *caricare, aggravare.*

CU'MBERED, adj. *imbarazzato, intrigato, imbrogliato, aggravato, ingombrato.*

CU'MBERSOM, adj. [troublesome, inconvenient] *molesto, nojoso, annojoso, penoso, incommodo, discaro, grave, rincrescevole.*

CU'MBRANCE, s. [burthen, hindrance, impediment] *peso, soma, impedimento, ingombro.*

C'UMBROUS, adj. *v.* Cumbersome.

CU'MIN, s. [a sort of herb] *comino*, s. m. *spezie d'erba.*

Cumin-seed, *semenza di comino.*

To CU'MULATE [to keep together] *accumulare, ammassare, abbiccare, ammucchiare.*

To CUN, a sea-term, *ex.* to cun a ship [is to direct the person at the helm how to steer her] *mostrare ad un che è al timone del vascello come deve governarlo.*

CUNCTA'TION, s. [delay, prolonging of time] *dimora, tardanza*, s. f. *indugio, tardamento*, s. m.

To CUND [to give notice] *informare, dar notizia.*

CUNNER, s. *sperie d'ostrica.*

CU'NNING, s. [skilfulness, ingenuity] *destrezza, accortezza, sagacità*, s. f.

Cunning [craftiness] *astuzia, sagacità, arte*, s. f. *scaltrimento*, s. m.

Cunning, adj. [expert, skilful] *esperto, esperimentato, astuto, scaltrito, fino, sagace, accorto.*

He is a very cunning man, *egli è un uomo molto esperto o astuto.*

A cunning fetch, *un tiro, una furberia, astuzia.*

Cunning man [diviner] *un indovino.*

A cunning woman, *un' indovina.*

A cunning piece of work, *lavoro fatto con gran maestria.*

A cunning place, *un luogo nascosto, un nascondiglio.*

To cast a cunning look upon one, *occheggiare alcuno, guardarlo con compiacenza.*

CU'NNINGLY, adv. *destramente, accortamente, sagacemente, astutamente, scaltritamente.*

A thing cunningly wrought, *una cosa lavorata con maestria.*

To carry it cunningly, *far l'astuto.*

He brought it about cunningly, *tanto ha fatto che n'è venuto a capo.*

CUP, s. [to drink out of] *coppa, tazza*, s. f. *vaso d'oro, d'argento, o d'altro metallo per uso di bere.*

A silver-cup, *una coppa d'argento.*

The cup of a flower, *la boccia d'un fiore.*

The cup of a rose, *la boccia d'una rosa.*

To take a drinking cup, *bere, divertirsi bevendo.*

To take a cup too much, *bere un poco troppo.*

In one's cups, *nel vino.*

Cup-bearer, *coppiere.*

The communion cup, *il calice.*

A cup-board, *credenza, buffetto, armario.*

Cup-shot, or cup-shotten, *imbriaco, che ha bevuto troppo.*

To CUP [to apply cupping-glasses] *ventosare, appiccar le ventose.*

To CUP-BOARD [to treasure, to hoard up] *tesoreggiare, accumular ricchezze.*

CUPI'DITY, s. [concupiscence, desire] *cupidità, cupidigia*, s. f. *appetito disordinato.*

CU'POLA, s. [an arched tower of a building in form of a bowl turned upside down] *cupola*, s. f. *volta che rigirandosi intorno a un medesimo centro, si regge in se medesima.*

CU'PPED, adj. *ventosato.*

CU'PPING, s. *il ventosare.*

A cupping glass, *ventosa, coppetta*, s f.

CU'PPEL, s. [a small vessel to try gold and silver] *coppella*, s. f. *picciol vasetto fatto di raschiatura di corna, nel quale messo nel fuoco si cimenta l'oro e l'argento.*

CUR, s. [a worthless degenerate dog] *cane buono a nulla, cane degenerato.*

Cur, [a term of reproach for a man] *cane, ingiuria detta ad un uomo.*

CU'RABLE, adj. [that may be cured] *curabile, che si può curare, che non è incurabile.*

CU'RACY, s. [the office of a curate] *carica, ufficio di curato.*

CU'RATE, s. [a parson or vicar of a parish] *curato, parrocchiano, il prete rettor della parrocchia.*

CURA'TOR, s. *curatore*, s. m. *quegli che dalla legge ha podestà d'amministrare i negozi degli adulti, e di tutti coloro che per vizio d'animo o di corpo non possono amministrarli per se stessi.*

CURB, s. [a part of a bridle] *morso, freno*, s. m. *imboccatura*, s. f.

Curb, s. *il raffrenar uno, proibizione fatta ad uno, freno, morso*, s. m.

To CURB, *ritenere il freno, frenare, tener a freno.*

To curb [to restrain, to give a check to] *frenare, raffrenare, tenere a freno, rattenere, reprimere, rintuzzare*, pref. *rattengo*, pret. *rattenni.*

To curb one's passions, *frenare o reprimere le sue passioni.*

To curb a youth, *tener in freno, o tener sotto un giovane.*

CURBED, adj. *frenato, tenuto in freno, raffrenato, rattenuto, represso, intuzzato.*

CURBS [a swelling beneath the elbow of a horse's hoof] *malattia che viene nelle gambe al cavallo.*

CU'RCUMA, s. [an Indian root commonly called turmerick] *cúrcuma*, s. f. *sorta di cippero che nasce nell' Indie simile al gengiovo, e tigne giallo.*

CRRD, or CURDS, s. *latte rappreso, latte quagliato.*

To CU'RDLE, verb neut. *quagliarsi, rappigliarsi.*

To curdle, verb act. *quagliare, rappigliare.*

To curdle milk, *quagliare del latte.*

CU'RDLED, adj. *quagliato, rappigliato, rappreso.*

Curdled milk, *latte rappreso.*

CURE, s. [remedy] *cura*, s. f. *rimedio*, s. m.

An infallible cure for a tertian ague, *un rimedio infallibile per la febbre terzana.*

'Twas the best cure that ever he did, *fu la più bella cura ch' avesse mai fatta.*

Cure [benefice with charge of souls] *cura, parrochia*, s. f.

Cure of souls, *cura d'anime.*

A benefice without cure of souls, *beneficio senza cura.*

I was under his cure when I was sick, *ero sotto la sua cura quando fui ammalato.*

To have a cure for every sore [to have an excuse for every fault] *trovar ritortole ad ogni fascio.*

To CURE [to take care of] *curare, aver cura, tener conto, avere a cuore.*

To cure [to heal] *curare, sanare, medicare, guarire.*

He cured me of that distemper, *egli mi ha curato, o sanato di quella malattia.*

To cure a sick body, *guarire un ammalato.*

CURED, adj. *curato, sanato, guarito, medicato.*

What can't be cured must be indured, *bisogna sofferire pazientemente quel ch'è inevitabile.*

CU'RELESS, adj. [without cure, without remedy] *senza rimedio, irrimediabile.*

CU'RER, s. [a healer, a physician] *un che guarisce, un che medica, un medico.* Harvey.

CU'RFEW, s. [a law made by William the Conqueror, that all persons should put out their fire and lights at the ringing of the eight a clock bell, and go to bed] *legge stabilita da Guglielmo il Conquistatore, che al tocco della campana che suona alle otto delle sera ognuno dovesse estinguere il fuoco e le candele, e andare a dormire.*

Curfew bell [eight o'clock bell] *la campana che suona alle otto delle sera.*

CURIA'LITY, s. [the privileges or retinue of a court] *privelegi o il seguito della curia.* Bacon.

CU'RING, s. *il curare.*

CURIO'SITY, s. [inquisitiveness, desire of knowing] *curiosità*, s. f. *disordinata vaghezza di sapere.*

Curiosity [rarity, curious thing] *curiosità, rarità, cosa rara, pellegrina, e curiosa.*

This is a fine piece of curiosity, *questa è una bella curiosità.*

CU'RIOUS, adj. [desirous of knowing or seeing any thing] *curioso, che ha curiosità.*

Curious [fine, exquisite] *curioso, squisito, eccellente, singolare, bello, pellegrino.*

Curious [nice, delicate] *delicato, morbido.*

You are a little too curious, *voi siete un poco troppo curioso.*

'Tis a curious thing indeed, *per certo che è una cosa molto curiosa.*

Curious meat, *carne delicata, o squisita.*

To be curious in one's diet, *esser delicato nel suo mangiare.*

To be curious in one's dress, *vestire troppo attillatamente.*

A curious piece of work, *una bella struttura.*

A curious author, *un autore esatto, che scrive con esattezza.*

Too curious [hard to please] *difficile a contentare.*

CU'RIOUSLY, adv. *curiosamente, con curiosità.*

Curiously [artfully, exactly] *esattamente, con esatezza, con arte, e maestria, ingegnosamente, perfettamente.*

CU'RIOUSNESS, s. *esattezza, maestria, delicatezza.*

CURL, s. [curling] *riccio,* s. m. *ciocca,* s. f. *capelli crespi, innanellati.*

Curl, s. [undulation, wave, sinuosity, flexure] *piegatura, ondulazione, piega, il piegare, il ripiegarsi.*

A hair curl, *un riccio di capelli.*

To CURL, verb act. *arricciare, innanellare.*

To curl hair, *arricciare, o innanellare i capelli.*

To curl, verb neut. *arricciarsi, innanellarsi.*

CURLED, adj. *arricciato, innanellato.*

CU'RLEW, s. [a sort of bird] *sorta d'uccello acquatico.*

CU'RLING, s. *l'arricciare, l'innanellare.*

A curling iron, *calamistro, strumento di ferro ad uso d'arricciar capelli.*

CURMU'DGEON, s. [a close fisted fellow] *uno spilorcio, un cacastecchi, un tanghero, un avaro.*

CU'RNOCK, s. [a measure of corn containing four bushels] *misura di grano che contiene quatro staja.*

CU'RRANT, s. *ribes.*

Red currant, *ribes rosso.*

CU'RRENCY, s. [course] *corso,* s. m.

Currency of money, *corso della moneta.*

CU'RRENT, adj. [that goes, or is established and received] *corrente, che corre comunemente, che si ha da tutti per tale.*

Current money, *moneta corrente.*

If that part of his history may pass for current, *se si può dar fede a questa parte della sua istoria.*

To take a thing for current payment, *prender che che si sia per danari contanti.*

I am not very current, *non sto molto bene.*

Current, s. [stream] *corrente,* s. f. *acqua che corre.*

A very strong current, *una corrente molto rapida.*

But according to the current of most writers, *ma secondo l'opinione più ricevuta degl' istorici.*

Current, adv. Ex. it is gone current, *è passato.*

CU'RRENTNESS, s. *corso.*

The currentness of money, *il corso della moneta.*

CU'RRIED, *v.* Curry'd.

CU'RRIER, s. [one who dresses tanned leather] *conciatore,* s. m. *colui che concia le pelli.*

CU'RRISH, adj. [having the qualities of a degenerate dog; brutal, sour, quarrelsome] *che ha le qualità d'un can degenerato; brutale, brusco, che accatta brighe, cagnesco.*

A currish look, *una ciera cagnesca.*

Currish [churlish] *brutale, zotico.*

A currish fellow, *un brutale, un zotiro, un malcreato.*

CU'RRISHLY, adv. *brutalmente, zoticamente.*

To CU'RRY [or dress] leather, *conciar pelli.*

To curry a horse, *stregghiare, e strigliare un cavallo.*

To curry one's coat well, *stregghiare alcuno, bastonarlo ben bene, darli un carpiccio di bastonate.*

To curry favour with one, *cercare di cattivarsi l'animo di chicchessia, insinuarsi nelle grazie altrui.*

To curry with one, *corteggiare, adulare, lusingare alcuno.*

CU'RRY-COMB, s. [an iron tool for dressing of horses] *stregghia,* s. f. *strumento di ferro dentato, col quale si ripuliscono i cavalli.*

CU'RRY'D, adj. *conciato, stregghiato, e strigliato.*

CU'RRYING, s. *lo stregghiare, v.* To curry.

CURSE, s. [ill wish] *maledizione, maladizione, imprecazione,* s. f.

To CURSE [to wish ill to] *maledire, e maladire, dar delle maledizioni.*

To curse [to swear] *giurare, bestemmiare.*

CU'RSED, adj. *maledetto, e maladetto, esecrando.*

A cursed business, *un maledetto affare.*

A cursed villain, *uno scelerato.*

CU'RSEDLY, adv. [abominably] *abbominevolmente, cattivissimamente, malissimamente, miseramente, vergognosamente.*

It is cursedly done, *è malissimamente fatto.*

CU'RSITER, or CU'RSITOR, s. [an officer belonging to the chancery, who makes out original writs] *cursore,* s. m. *commissario della cancelleria.*

CU'RSORILY, adv. [slightly, hastily] *alla leggiera, con precipitazione, in fretta, frettolosamente.*

CU'RSORY, adj. [slight, hasty] *leggiero, frettoloso, fatto in fretta.*

A cursory view, *un leggiero esame.*

CURST, adj. [as cursed] *maladetto, cattivo, esecrabile, abbominabile, abbominevole.*

Curst, adj. [forward, peevish, malignant, malicious, snarling] *tristo, di mal umore, maligno, incagnato, malizioso, cagnesco.*

CU'RSTNESS, s. *forza, violenza, cattivezza, rigore.*

Good natures are won rather with entreaty than curstness, *una persona d'una natura affabile si lascia più tosto vincere colle buone che non col rigore.*

CURTA'IL, s. [drab, nasty slut] *una sgualdrina, una sgualdrinella, una puttana sudicia.*

CURTA'IL-Dog, *cane colla coda mozza.*

To CURTA'IL [to cut off, to dismember, to diminish] *mozzare, tagliare, troncare, smembrare, diminuire,* pres. *diminuisco.*

To curtail one of a member, *mozzare un membro ad uno.*

To curtail a horse, *tagliare li orecchi e la coda ad un cavallo.*

To curtail one's wages, *diminuire altrui il suo salario.*

To curtail a kingdom, *smembrare, o dividere un regno.*

CURTA'ILED, adj. *mozzato, tagliato, troncato, smembrato, diminuito.*

CU'RTAIN, s. [a hanging about a bed or window] *cortina,* s. f. *cortinaggio,* s. f.

Bed curtain, *cortinaggio di letto.*

Window curtains, *cortine di finestra.*

Curtain before a door, *portiera.*

To draw the curtain, *abbattere le cortine, tirar le cortine.*

The curtain before a stage, *cortina, tenda che cuopre la scena.*

Curtain [in fortification, is the front of a wall of a fortified place, between two bastions] *cortina, quella parte di fortificazione che è tra un bastione e l'altro.*

Curtain rod, *verga di ferro.*

A curtain lecture, *rabbuffo, bravata che la moglie fa al marito in letto.*

CURTA'NA, s. [king Edward the Confessor's sword, without a point, which is carried before the kings and queens of England at their coronation] *cortana, la spada del rè Edoardo Confessore, senza punta, che si porta innanzi a' re e regine d'Inghilterra il giorno della loro coronazione.*

CU'RTILAGE, s. [a law term, a piece of ground or garden belonging to, and lying near a messuage] *pezzo di terra attenente o contiguo ad una cosa.*

CU'RTLALS, or CU'RTLE-AX, s. [a kind of weapon] *sorta d'arma da taglio.*

CU'RVATURE, s. [crookedness] *curvatura, curvezza,* s. f.

CURVE, adj. [crooked] *curvo, piegato in arco.*

A curve, s. [a crooked line] *linea curva.*

CU'RVET, s. [the prancing of a managed horse] *corvetta,* s. f. *quell' operazion del cavallo, allora che abbassando la groppa e posandosi su piedi di dietro, alza quelli davanti.*

To CU'RVET [to prance] *corvettare, fare le corvette.*

CU'RVETTING, s. *corvette, il corvettare.*

CURVILI'NEAL, } adj. [crooked
CURVILI'NEAR, } lined] *curvilineo, termine di geometria.*

CU'RVITY, s. [crookedness] *curvità, il curvo.*

CU'SHION,

Cu'shion, s. [a sort of pillow to sit or lean on] *cuscino*, s. m.

To be beside the cushion [to be out of the way in discourse] *uscir del seminato, dare nelle scartate.*

Cu'stard, s. [a dish of food made of milk, eggs, &c.] *spezie di torta fatta di latte, uova, &c.*

Cu'stody, s. [keeping] *custodia, cura, guardia*, s. *governo*, s. m.

I leave it in your custody, *lo lascio sotto la vostra custodia.*

Custody [prison] *prigione*, s. f. *arresto*, s. m.

Cu'stom, s. [habit, use] *costuma, e costume, consuetudine, usanza*, s. f. rito, s. m.

A custom [of a tradesman's shop] *avventore.*

A barber that has good custom, *un barbiere che ha molti avventori.*

Custom [a duty paid by the subject to the king, upon the importation or exportation of commodities] *dogana, gabella*, s. f.

To pay custom, *pagar la dogana.*

Cu'stom-house [a building in seaport towns where the king's customs are received] *dogana, luogo dove si scaricano le mercanzie per mostrarle e gabellarle.*

Custom-house officer, *doganiere*, s. m. *ministro della dogana.*

Custom-free, *franco di dogana.*

Cu'stomable, adj. [which is according to custom] *ordinario, usitato, comune.*

Cu'stomably, adv. [usually] *ordinariamente, frequentemente, comunemente.*

Cu'stomary, adj. [usual] *solito, ordinario, frequente, comune.*

The customary laws of a nation, *le leggi comuni d'un paese.*

Cu'stomed, adj. [speaking of a shop] *avviato, che ha molti avventori.*

Cu'stomer, s. [one who buys any thing of another] *avventore*, s. m. *quello o quella che continua a servirsi da qualche bottegajo o mercante.*

To disoblige customers, *sviar la colombaja.*

Customer [or custom-house officer] *doganiere, gabelliere*, s. m.

Cu'strel, s. [a servant to a man of arms, or a prince's life-guard] *bagaglione*, s. m. *scudiere, che porta lo scudo al cavaliere.*

Cu'stler, s. *sorta di vaso da contener vino.*

Cut, adj. *tagliato*, v. To cut.

Cut and long tail [that is, every one] *tutti insieme, gli uni e gli altri.*

Cut [soundly in drink] *cotto, ubbriaco, avvinazzato.*

He is cut out for a mathematician, *egli è nato alle matematiche, egli ha talenti grandi per la matematica.*

They are cut short in their revenues, *le loro entrate sono strette.*

Cut, s. [cutting] *taglio*, s. m. *ferita che si fa nel tagliare.*

Cut [slice] *fetta*, s. f.

Cut [wound] *taglio, ferita.*

Cut [gash in one's face] *sfregio, fendente*, s. m. *taglio fatto nell' altrui viso.*

Cut [misfortune] *disgrazia*, s. f. *disastro*, s. m.

Cut [figure] *figura, stampa.*

The first cut of a loaf, *il primo taglio d'un pane.*

To draw cuts, *giuocare alle buschette.*

He is of the same cut with the rest, *egli è della medesima tempra che gli altri.*

A cut-throat, *uno sgerro, un tagliacantone.*

A cut purse, *un borsajuolo, un tagliaborse.*

To cut [to divide or part with a knife, &c.] *tagliare, dividere, separare, far piu parti d'una quantità continua, mozzare.*

To cut a piece of meat, *tagliare un pezzo di carne.*

Cut me a piece of bread, *tagliatemi una fetta di pane.*

To cut in pieces, *tagliare a pezzi.*

To cut short, *per finirla, per sbrigarmi in poche parole.*

To cut [to prune] *potare, e dicesi delle viti e simili.*

To cut a stone, *tagliare una pietra.*

To cut corn, *mietere il grano.*

Cold weather cuts the lips, *il freddo screpola le labbra.*

To cut one short [to interrupt him when he speaks] *rompere le parole in bocca ad uno, interromperlo nel discorso.*

To cut capers, *far delle capriuole.*

To cut small, *tritare, sminuzzare, sbocconcellare.*

To cut the veins, *tagliar le vene, svenare.*

To cut [to wound] *ferire*, pref. *ferisco.*

To cut [to delve] the ground, *arare la terra, scavarla.*

To cut [to lop] a tree, *scapezzare un albero.*

To cut [to hew] *fendere.*

To cut capons, *capponare, castrare polli.*

To cut lots, *giuocare alle buschette.*

To cut [to shave] the beard, *fare o radere la barba.*

To cut [to slash] one over the face, *sfregiare alcuno, fargli un taglio nel viso.*

To cut [at the game of cards] *alzare.*

To cut off, *tagliare, mozzare.*

To cut off one's head, *tagliare la testa ad uno, decapitarlo.*

To cut off an army, *tagliare a pezzi un esercito.*

To cut one off from an estate [to cut off the entail] *privare alcuno della successione, discreditarlo.*

To cut off the provisions, *chiuder la strada a' viveri.*

To cut off the enemies retreat, *serrar il passo al nemico.*

To cut off their communication, *impedir loro la communicazione.*

To cut off delays, *sbrigarsi, affrettarsi.*

To cut off the ends of hair, *spuntare i capelli.*

To cut asunder, *stracciare, mettere in pezzi, rompere*, pret. *ruppi.*

To cut out work for one, *dar da fare ad uno.*

To cut up, *trinciare.*

To cut up a capon, *trinciare un cappone.*

To cut up a dead body, *notomizzare un corpo.*

To cut down, *segare, secare, mietere, tagliare.*

To cut down the corn, *mietere il grano.*

Cuta'neous, adj. *cutaneo, di cute, di pelle.*

Cute, s. [unfermented wine] *mosto*, s. m. *vin nuovo e non ancor ben purificato.*

Cuth, s. [knowledge or skill] *conoscimento, intendimento, giudizio, cervello.*

Cu'ticle, s. [thin skin] *cute*, s. f. *pelle sottile.*

Cu'tlass, s. *coltellaccio*, s. m. *spadaccia larga.*

Cu'tler, s. [a maker or seller of knives, swords, &c.] *coltellinajo*, s. m. *quello che fa i coltelli.*

A sword cutler, *uno spadajo.*

Cu'tpurse, s. [one who steals by the method of cutting purses] *tagliaborse, ladroncello.*

Cu'tted, adj. [scolding] *brigoso, fazievole, litigioso.*

A cutted housewife, *una donna litigiosa.*

Cu'tter, s. *tagliatore*, s. m.

A corn cutter, *un che taglia calli.*

A stone cutter, *scalpellino*, s. m *quegli che lavora le pietre collo scarpello, uno scultore, uno statuario.*

Cu't-throat, s. [a ruffian, a murderer, an assassin] *un assassino, un masnadiere, un omicida, un brigante.*

Cut-throat, adj. [cruel, inhuman, barbarous] *crudele, inumano, barbaro.*

Cu'tting, s. *il tagliare.*

The cutting of a wood, *le tacca d'un legno.*

Stone cutting, *scultura.*

Cuttings [parings] *ritagli.*

Cutting, adj. [sharp in taste] *piccante, razzente.*

Cutting [biting] *piccante, pugnente, e pungente, acuto, mordace.*

Cutting words, *parole mordaci.*

Cu'ttle, s. [the cuttle fish] *seppia*, s. f. *spezie di pesce, il maschio della quale spezie si chiama calamajo.*

Cuttle, s. [a foul-mouthed fellow] *uno sboccato, uno che è osceno nel parlare. La metafora è tratta dalla seppia che quando è cacciata da qualche pesce vorace dicesi che vomita un liquor nero come inchiostro.*

Cu'vette, s. [in fortification, a trench sunk in the middle of a great dry ditch] *fossatella fatta nel mezzo d'un fosso secco.*

Cycle, s. [revolution] *corso*, s. m. *rivoluzione*, s. f. *spazio di tempo che è periodico.*

The cycle of the sun, *il corso o revoluzione del sole.*

The cycle of the moon, *il corso della luna.*

Cy'cloid, s. [a figure which is made by

by the upper end of the diameter of a circle, turned about the right line] *linea circolare.*

CY'GNET, s. [young swan] *un cigno giovine.*

CY'LINDER, s. a [figure long and round] *cilindro*, s. m. *corpo di figura lunga, e ronda.*

CYLI'NDRICAL, adj. [in form of, or like a cylinder] *cilindrico, che ha figura di cilindro.*

CYMA'TIUM, s. [in architecture, a member whereof the one half is convex, and the other concave] *cimazio, uovolo*, s. m. *membro della cornice composta di due parti, di cui l'una è convessa, e l'altra concava.*

CY'MBAL, s. [a musical instrument] *cembalo*, s. m. *strumento musicale.*

CY'NICAL, adj. [severe or doggish] *severo, austero, cagnesco.*

CYNICK, s. [philosopher of a sect so called] *cinico*, s. m. *nome di filosofo, di setta particolare.*

CY'NOSUYE, s. [the constellation of the Ursa Minor, or of the Lesser Bear] *la costellazione dell' Orsa Minore.*

CY'PHER, *v.* Cipher.

CY'PRESS-TREE, s. *cipresso*, s. m. *albero noto.*

Cypress, or cypress-wood, *cipresso, legname di cipresso.*

CYST, } s. [a bag containing some
CY'STIS, } morbid matter] *borsa o sacchetto nel corpo umano contenente qualche materia cattiva, imputridita, e simili.*

D.

D, *è la quarta lettera dell' alfabeto Inglese, e si pronuncia come in Italiano.*

DAB, s. [a little blow] *una piccola botta, un piccola schiaffo.*

A dab of dirt, *uno schizzo di fango, zacchera.*

A fat dab, *un pezzo di grasso.*

Dab [a sort of fish] *rombo*, s. m.

Dab-chick [a sort of fowl] *sorta d'uccello acquatico.*

To DAB [to strike gently with something soft or moist] *percuotere gentilmente con qualche cosa di molle o d'umido.*

To DA'BBLE [to splash] *zaccherare, macchiar di zacchere.*

To dabble one's cloaths, *zaccherare il vestito ad uno.*

To dabble one's hands in the water, *sguazzare le mani nell' acqua.*

To dabble in the dirt, *dimenarsi nel fango.*

To dabble one's cloaths, *sporcarsi, imbrattarsi gli abiti.*

DA'BBLED, adj. *zaccherato*, *v.* To dabble.

DA'BBLER, s. [one that plays in water] *uno che sta scherzando o giucando nell' acqua.*

Dabbler [one that meddles without mastery; a superficial medler] *uno che vuole impacciarsi di quel che non sa o non intende.* Swift.

DACE, s. [a small river fish] *spezie di pesce di fiume.*

DA'CTYLE, s. [a foot in Latin and Greek, consisting of one long syllable, and two short] *dattilo*, s. m. *sorta di piede ne' versi Latini e Greci, che consiste d'una sillaba lunga, e di due brevi.*

DAD, or DA'DDY, s. [a name whereby young children call the father] *babbo*, s. m. *voce colla quali i fanciulli chiamano il padre.*

DA'DDOCK, s. [the rotten heart or body of a tree] *il trouco marcito d'un albero.*

DA'FFODIL, } s. [a sort of
DA'FFODILY, } plant] *arso-*
DA'FFODOWDILLY, } *dillo*, s. m. *spezie d'erba.*

To DAFT [to toss aside; to throw away slightly] *gittar leggermente da un lato.*

DAG, s. [a hand gun] *uno scoppietto.*

To DAG sheep [to cut off the skirts of the fleece] *tosare la cima della lana delle pecore.*

Dag-locks [the wool slightly cut off] *cimatura di lana.*

To dag. *v.* To daggle.

DA'GGER, s. [a weapon well known] *un pugnale, una daga.*

He held the dagger to his throat, *gli mise il pugnale alla gola.*

To be at daggers drawing, *star sempre in lete.*

To DA'GGLE [to dabble the skirts of one's cloaths with dirt] *zaccherarsi, imbrattarsi, infangarsi.*

DA'GGLED, adj. *zaccherato, imbrattato, infangato.*

Daggled tail, adj. *zaccheroso, pien di zacchere, e di fango.*

DAIES, *il plurale antico di* Day.

To DAIGN [to vouchsafe, to condescend] *degnarsi, compiacersi, condescendere.*

DA'ILY, adj. [every day] *d'ogni giorno, cotidiano, quotidiano, diurno.*

Daily bread, *pane cotidiano.*

Daily experience teaches us, *l'esperienza s'insegna ogni giorno.*

Daily, adv. *giornalmente, ogni giorno, alla giornata.*

Those things happen daily, *queste son cose che accadono giornalmente.*

DA'INTILY, adv. *deliziosamente, delicatamente, con delicatezza, gentilmente.*

DA'INTINESS, s. *delicatezza, e dilicatezza, squisitezza, lecconeria, leccornia, ghiottornia, vivanda da lecconi.*

DA'INTY, adj. [delicate, fine, nice] *delicato, delizioso, esquisito, eccellente, parlando di cose, leccone, ghiotto, goloso, parlando di persone.*

Dainty [costly] *grande, splendido, magnifico, sontuoso, superbo, parlando d'un festino.*

DA'IRY, or DA'IRY HOUSE, s. [a place where milk and milk meats are made and kept] *luogo dove si conserva il latte, e dove si fanno tutte sorte di latticini.*

DA'IRY-MAID, s. [the woman-servant whose business is to manage the milk] *la fante sotto la cui ispezione e cura si fanno le cose di latte alle case di campagna.*

Dairy-woman, *donna che vende del latte.*

DA'ISY, s. [a sort of flower] *margherita, margheritina.* Shakesp.

DAIS, s. [canopy] *baldacchino*, s. m.

DALE, s. [little valley] *valle lunga e stretta, tra poggi alti.*

DALLI'ANCE, s. [wantonness] *scherzo, trastullo, diporto*, s. m. *ciancia*, s. f.

To be at dalliance, *scherzare, trastullare, cianciare.*

DA'LLIER, s. *un che ama a trastullare, o a scherzare, un tentennone, un burlone, un burlatore, un bajone, uno che è irresoluto nell sue operazioni.*

To DA'LLY [to play, to toy] *trastullare, scherzare, diportarsi, giuocare.*

To dally [to play the fool with] *burlarsi, voler la baja, beffare, scherzare.*

You do but dally with me, *voi vi burlate di me, voi mi beffate, voi volete la baja di me.*

To dally [to delay, to trifle] *musare, stare a bada, adagiarsi, baluccare, dimorare, perder il tempo, trastullarsi, indugiare, andare a rilente, stentare, dar tempo, dondolarsi.*

Let us not dally, *non perdiamo il tempo.*

DA'LMATICK,

DA'LMATICK, s. [a certain vestment worn by a priest]. *tonicella, e tonacella*, s. f. *paramento del diacono, e suddiacono.*

DAM, s. [a female beast which brings forth young] *la femmina delle bestie, la madre.*

A calf that sucks his dam, *un vitello che poppa la vacca.*

DAM [a flood-gate or stoppage in a river] *cateratta*, s. f. *sostegno*, s. m. *apertura fatta per pigliare l'acqua, e per mandarla via a sua posta, e si chiude ed apre coll' imposta di legno.*

To DAM up [to stop or shut up] *chiudere, fermare, stoppare, riturare, turare.*

To dam up water, *chiudere, o fermare l'acqua in una cateratta.*

To dam up a window, *stoppare una finestra, murare una finestra.*

To dam up a barrel, *turare un barile.*

DA'MAGE, s. [hurt, loss, detriment] *detrimento, danno, scapito, pregiudicio*, s. m. *perdita.*

Costs and damages, *costo e spese.*

To DA'MAGE, *danneggiare.*

DA'MASCENE, s. [a small black plum; a damson] *sorta di susina picciola e nera, che credesi originalmente portata di Damasco.* Bacon.

DA'MASK, s. [fine silk stuff] *dommasco*, s m. *sorta di drappo.*

A damask bed, *un letto di dommasco.*

Damask linen, *biancherie dommaschine.*

Damask napkins, *salviette dommaschine.*

Damask prunes [or damascenes] *lazzoruola.*

A damask rose, *una rosa damaschina.*

To DA'MASK, ex. to damask wine [to take off the edge of the cold, to make it mantle] *scaldare un poco il vino.*

To dămask, [to form flowers upon stuffs] *fare o ricamar fiori sopra un drappo di seta.*

To damask, [to variegate, to diversify] *variare, diversificare.*

DAME, s. [or mistress] *madonna, donna.*

Dame [a word used instead of lady in law business] *dama, signora.*

A school dame [or school mistress] *maestra di scuola.*

My dame [my wife] *mia moglie, mia donna.*

To DAMN [to condemn, to judge to hell] *dannare.*

To damn one's self, *dannarsi.*

To damn [to explode, to cry down] *dannare, biasimare, incaricare.*

His play was damned, *la sua comedia fu condannata, o fischiata.*

DA'MNABLE, adj. *dannabile, cattivo, pernicioso.*

A damnable doctrine, *una dottrina dannabile.*

DA'MNABLY, adj. *dannabilmente.*

He is damnably angry, *è in collera terribilmente.*

DAMNA'TION, s. *dannazione, perdizione*, s. f. *dannamento*, s. m.

He swore to it upon his damnation, *lo giurò sopra la sua dannazione.*

DAMNED, adj. *dannato.*

The damned, s. *i dannati, quelli che sono dannati.*

To DA'MNIFY, [to damage, to hurt] *danneggiare, far danno, dannificare, apportar detrimento, nuocere.* pret. *nocqui.*

DA'MNIFY'D, adj. *danneggiato, dannificato, nociuto.*

The ship was very much damnify'd, *il vascello rimase molto sdruscito.*

DA'MNINGNESS, s. [tendency to procure damnation] *tendenza all' esser dannato.*

DAMP, s. [moisture, wetness] *umidità, umidezza*, s. f. *umidore, mollore, mollume*, s. m.

A great damp, *una grande umidità.*

To put a damp upon one's spirits, *sgomentare, sbigottire, alcuno, farlo perder d'animo.*

The civil wars have put a damp upon trade, *le guerre civili hanno interrotto il commercio.*

It has put such a damp upon him, *l'ha talmente sbigottito.*

To DAMP [to make moist] *umidire, inumidire, render umido.*

To damp [to dishearten] *sbigottire, sgomentare, disanimare, fare altrui perder l'animo, tor l'animo.*

DA'MPISH, adj. [somewhat moist] *umidiccio, alquanto umido.*

DA'MPISHNESS, s. [tendency to wetness; foggishness, moisture] *principio d' umido; picciola umidità; nebbia leggéra.*

DA'MPNESS, s. *umidità umidezza*, s. f. *umidore, mollore, mollume*, s. m.

DA'MPY, adj. [dejected, gloomy, sorrowful] *depresso, d'animo depresso, tristo, malinconoso.*

DA'MSEL, s. [young maiden] *una zittella, una damigella, una pulzella, una donzella.*

Dámsel, [an attendant of the better rank] *cameriera di non vile condizione.*

Damsel, [a wench, a country lass] *una forosetta, una fanciulla contadinesca.*

DA'MSON, s. [damascen, a small and black plum] *sorta di susina picciola e nera.*

Damson-tree, *spezie di susino che produce il frutto picciolo e nero.*

DAN, s. [the old term of honour for men] *onorifica antica appellazione appropriata solo agli uomini.*

DANCE, s. *ballo*, s. m. *danza*, s. f.

No longer pipe no longer dance, *cessato il guadagno cessa il lavoro.*

To dance [to move in measure] verb neut. *ballare, danzare.*

To dance upon the rope, *ballare sulla corda.*

To dance to every man's pipe, *uniformarsi al volere d'ognuno.*

To dance attendance [to wait] *fare spalliera, aspettare.*

DANCED, adj. *ballato.*

DA'NCER, s. *ballerino*, s. m. *ballerina*, s. f.

DA'NCING, s. *ballo*, s. m. *il ballare.*

To love dancing, *amare il ballo.*

The art of dancing, *l'arte del ballare.*

A dancing room, *sala da ballo.*

A dancing school, *scuola da ballo.*

A dancing master, *un ballerino.*

DA'NCY, adj. [in heraldry, when the out-line of any bordure is largely indented] *dentato.*

DANDELI'ON, s. [lion's tooth, an herb] *spezie di ricorta.*

DA'NDIPRAT, s. [a small coin made by King Henry VII.] *sorta di piccola moneta, ch'era corrente nel tempo d'Enrico settimo.*

Dandiprat [a dwarf, a little fellow] *un nano, un omiciatto.*

To DA'NDLE [to fondle, or make much of] *vezzeggiare, far vezzi, carezzare, far carezze, lusingare, allottare.*

To dandle [to delay, to procrastinate] *diferire, ritardare, procrastinare, posporre a un altro tempo.*

To dandle [to take a child on the knees] *ninare un bambino sulle ginocchia.* Temple.

DA'NDLER, s. [he that dandles or fondles children] *colui che accarezza o ninna i bambini con tenerezza.*

DA'NDLING, s. *vezzeggiamento, vezzo, carezza.*

A dandling child, *il cucco, il figliuol più amato dal padre, e dalla madre.*

D'ANDRAFF, or DA'NDRUFF, or DA'NDRIFF, s. [a scurf sticking to the skin of the head] *forfora, forforaggine*, s. f. *quegli escrementi secchi, bianchi, e sottili, che s'adunano fra' capelli.*

A dandriff comb, *un pettine proprio per levar via la forfora.*

DA'NEGELT, s. [a tribute laid by the Danes, when they lorded it here over the Saxons] *tributo, che i Danesi imposero ai Sassoni, nel tempo che signoreggiavano in Inghilterra.*

DA'NEWORT, s. [an herb] *ebbio, ebulo*, s. m. *erba, o frutice puzzolente, che fa i fiori, e le coccole simili ad sambuco, e anche quasi le foglie.*

DA'NGER, s. [risk, peril, hazard] *pericolo, periglio; rischio*, s. m. *male, e rovina soprastante.*

To be in danger, *pericolare, correr pericolo.*

To run into danger, *esporsi a pericolo.*

To DA'NGER [to put in hazard, to endanger] *arrischiare, avventurare, metter a pericolo, porre a ripentaglio.*

DA'NGERLESS, adj. [without hazard, without risk] *che non ha in se rischio o pericolo.*

DA'NGEROUS, adj. [full of danger] *pericoloso, periglioso.*

Very dangerous, *pericolosissimo.*

DA'NGEROUSLY, adv. *pericolosamente, con pericolo.*

DA'NGEROUSNESS, s. [danger, hazard, peril] *pericolo, rischio, ripentaglio.*

To DA'NGLE [to hang or swim to and fro] *pendere, dondolare.*

To dangle [to hang upon one, to be an humble follower] *corteggiar vilmente, abbiettamente.*

DA'NGLING,

DA'NGLING, adv. *dondoloni, spenzoloni.*
To hang dangling, *pendere dondoloni.*
DA'NGLER, s. [a man that hangs about women] *un effeminato, uno che non sa far altro mestieri che quello di corteggiar femmine.*
DANG-VA'LLET, adv. [abundantly] *abbondantemente, in gran copia, in grande abbondanza, ampiamente.*
DANK, *lo stesso che* Damp.
To DAP [to let fall gently into the water] *lasciar cader pianamente nell' acqua.*
DAPA'TICAL, adj. [sumptuous in cheer] *che tien gran tavola; magnifico alla mensa.*
DA'PING, s. [a way of angling upon the top of the water] *il pescare coll' amo sopra la superficie dell' acqua.*
DA'PPER, adj. [tight and brisk] *rigoglioso, vigoroso, gagliardo, robusto, possente, forzuto.*
A dapper or tight little fellow, *un uomo piccolo di statura, ma gagliardo, e robusto.*
DA'PPERLING, s. [a dwarf] *un nano, un omicciattolo.*
DA'PPLE, or DA'PPLED, adj. [a colour peculiar to horses] *pezzato, pomato, rotato, e dicesi del mantello d'un cavallo.*
Dapple gray, *leardo pomato.*
Dapple bay, *leardo rotato.*
To DA'PPLE [to streak, to vary] *variar le strisce, porle di vari colori a vicenda.*
DAR, or DART, s. [a fish found in the Severn] *sorta di pesce che principalmente si pesca nel fiume Severna.*
To DARE [to hazard, to venture] *ardire, avere ardire, arrischiarsi, osare.*
Do if you dare, *fatelo se vi basta l'animo.*
If I may dare to say so, *se ardisco, o se mi lice dirlo.*
He dared to affront me before all the company, *ebbe l'arditezza d'affrontarmi in presenza di tutta la compagnia.*
I'll lay you what you dare of it, *scommetto quel che volete.*
I dare be bold to tell him, *saprò io ben dirli.*
To DARE [to challenge] *sfidare, invitare a battaglia, disfidare, provocare, irritare.*
Since he dares me to it, *poichè mi provoca a cio.*
To dare death in the middle of dangers, *incontrar la morte nel mezzo de' pericoli.*
I dare to undertake it, *mi basta l'animo di farlo.*
To dare larks [to catch larks by means of a looking-glass] *pigliar le allodole allo specchietto.*
DARE, s. [defiance, challenge] *sfida, disfida, scommessa.*
DA'REFUL, adj. [full of defiance] *baldo; che sfida chicchessia col guardo stesso; burbero.*
DA'RING, adj. *ardito, animoso, coraggioso.*

A daring man, *un uomo ardito, o coraggioso.*
A daring glass [to catch larks with] *una sorta di specchio col quale si va alla caccia delle allodole.*
DA'RINGLY, adv. *arditamente, animosamente, coraggiosamente.*
DA'RINGNESS, s. [boldness] *audacia, ardimento, baldanza.*
DARK, adj. [or obscure] *oscuro, tenebroso, bujo.*
Dark weather, *tempo oscuro, o tenebroso.*
A dark room, *una camera oscura.*
Dark [obscure, hard to be understood] *oscuro, nascoso, difficile ad intendersi, bujo.*
A dark discourse, *un discorso oscuro.*
A dark lanthorn, *lanterna sorda.*
A dark saying, *un' enimma.*
'Tis dark night, *fa molto bujo.*
It grows dark, *s'annota, si rabbuja, si fa notte.*
Dark, s. [darkness] *bujo, scuro,* s. m. *oscurità, tenebre,* s. f.
To be in the dark, *essere al bujo.*
To be in the dark [to know nothing of] *esser al bujo di che che si sia, non saperne nulla, non averne notizia.*
To leave one in the dark, *lasciar nel bujo, o nell' oscurità.*
To live in the dark, *viver nell' oscurità, menare una vita oscura.*
Joan is as good as my lady in the dark, *ogni cuffia è buona per la notte.*
To keep one in the dark [as to business] *lasciar nel bujo, tener nell' ignoranza, tener nascoso.*
Dark-sighted, *di corta vista.*
To DA'RKEN [to make dark] *scurare, oscurare, ottenebrare.*
To darken, verb neut. [to grow dark] *scurarsi, oscurarsi, divenire oscuro.*
DA'RKENED, adj. *scurato, oscurato, ottenebrato.*
DA'RKENING, s. *l'oscurare, oscuramento,* s. m.
DA'RKLING, part. [being in the dark] *oscuramento; l'essere allo scuro.*
DA'RKLY, adv. *oscuramente, con oscurità.*
DA'RKNESS, s. *oscurità, tenebrosità,* s. f. *bujo,* s. m.
Darkness of weather, *tempo scuro, o nuvoloso.*
The land of darkness, *la sepoltura.*
To go to the land of darkness, *morire, passare all' altra vita.*
DA'RKSOME, adj. [gloomy, obscure, not luminous] *scuro, malinconico, non illuminato.*
DA'RLING, s. [beloved, favourite] *un favorito, il cucco, il figliuolo più amato dal padre e dalla madre.*
She is my darling, *ella è la mia favorita.*
Darling, adj. [favoured, dear, beloved] *caro, favorito, diletto, amato.*
DARN, s. *cucitura,* s. f.
To DARN [to mend linen] *rabberciare, rattoppare, racconciare, risarcire, stoppare.* pres. *risarcisco.*
DA'RNED, adj. *rabberciato, rattoppato, racconciato, risarcito, stoppato.*

DA'RNEL, s. [or cockle weed] *loglio,* s. m. *zizzania,* s. f.
DA'RNER, s. [one that darns] *racconciatore, rattoppatore,* s. m. *colui che rabbercia, o risarcisce.*
DA'RNING, s. *il rabberciare, il risarcire.*
DA'RNIX, s. [a sort of stuff] *panno di Turnai.*
DA'RRAIN, adj. [a law word that signifies last] *ultimo, sezzo, sezzajo.*
To DA'RRAIN [to range troops for battle] *disporre l'esercito per la battaglia.*
To darrain [to apply to the fight] *battagliare, entrar in battaglia.*
DART, s. [arrow] *dardo, quadrello, telo, strale,* s. m. *veretta,* s. f. *verettone,* s. m.
To lance a dart, *scoccare o lanciare un dardo.*
To DART [to shoot, to throw] *lanciare, scagliare, scoccare, tirare, dardeggiare.*
To dart a knife, *lanciare, o tirare un coltello.*
The sun darts his beams upon the earth, *il sole vibra i suoi raggi sopra la terra.*
To dart [to fly as a dart] *andar velocemente come un dardo.*
DA'RTER, s. *lanciatore,* s. m. *che lancia.*
DA'RTING, s. *il lanciare, lo scagliare.*
DASH, s. [blow, stroke] *colpo, tratto,* s. m.
At one dash, *in un colpo, in un tratto.*
A dash of the pen, *un tratto, una tirata di penna, una pennata.*
A dash of water or dirt, *schizzo d'acquo o di fango.*
To give one a dash on the teeth, *dare un rovescione, o uno schiaffo ad uno.*
At first dash, *subito, in un subito, ad un tratto.*
Slap-dash, adv. *di punto in bianco.*
To DASH [to hit] *colpire, dare, percuotere, urtare, fracassare.*
To dash one's head against the wall, *sfasciar la testa ad uno, fracassarli la testa contra un muro.*
To dash [to mingle] *mescolare, sbattere insieme.*
To dash one with water, *spruzzare, o bagnare alcuno con acqua.*
To dash one's hopes, *fraudare alcuno delle sue speranze, fare svanire l'altrui speranze.*
To dash a thing in pieces, *spezzare, o mettere che che si sia in pezzi.*
Our ship was like to dash against a rock, *il nostro vascello fu quasi per rompersi contro uno scoglio.*
To dash one in the chaps, *dare un rovescione, o uno schiaffo ad uno.*
To dash a project or design, *rompere, sconcertare l'altrui disegno.*
To dash out, or blot out, *scancellare, cancellare.*
To dash one's confidence, *imbarazzare, confondere, intrigare alcuno, farli perder la tramontana.*

To dash one out of countenance, *stupire, confondere, smarrire, sbalordire alcuno; farlo arrossire, o vergognare, farlo restar confuso.*

To dash one's brain's out, *far saltar le cervella ad uno.*

DA'SHED, adj. *colpito, dato, percosso, urtato, fracassato, v.* To dash.

DA'STARD, s. [coward] *un poltrone, un infingardo, un codardo, un vigliacco.*

To DA'STARD [to terrify, to intimidate] *impaurire, atterrire, spaventare, riempier di paura.*

To DA'STARDISE, *intimidire, render timido, o poltrone, effeminare, render effeminato, render vigliacco.*

DA'STARDLY, adj. *infingardo, codardo, vigliacco.*

DA'STARDLY, adv. *infingardamente, da codardo, da vigliacco, da poltrone.*

DA'STARDY, s. [cowardliness] *codardia, vigliaccheria.*

DA'TARY, s. [the chief officer in the chancery of Rome, thro' whose hands most vacant benefices pass] *Datario, cancelliere in Roma, e anche la dateria ov' è l'officio del Datario.*

DATE, s. [the writing which expresses the day of the month and year when any writing, coin, &c. was made] *data,* s. f.

What date does the letter bear? *di che data è la lettera?*

A thing out of date, *una cosa ch' è fuor d'uso, che non è più in uso.*

A commodity out of date, *una mercanzia che non ha più spaccio.*

To grow out of date, *non esser più in credito, e in istima.*

A date book, *un giornale.*

The date of a coin, *il millesimo, cifera, che mostra il tempo nel quale la moneta fu battuta.*

Date [the fruit of the date tree] *dattero,* s. m. *il frutto della palma.*

Date-tree, s. *palma,* s. f. *albero che produce il dattero.*

To DATE [to set a date to] *metter la data.*

To date a letter, *metter la data ad una lettera.*

DA'TED, adj. *che ha per data.*

My letter was dated the tenth instant, *la mia lettera ha per data li dieci del corrente.*

DA'TELESS, adj. [without any fixed term] *che non ha data, che non ha termine fisso.*

DA'TIVE, adj *dativo.*

The dative case, *il caso dativo.*

The dative, s. *il dativo.*

To DAUB, [to smear with something adhesive] *imbrattare con qualche cosa che s' appicca, con qualche materia viscosa o attaccaticcia.*

To daub, [to paint coarsely] *dipingere grossolanamente, imbrattar le tele.*

To daub, [to cover with something specious or strong] *impiastrare con qualche cosa di particolare o di forte.*

To daub, [to lay on any thing gaudily or ostentatiously] *mettere sopra checchessia cose che sono più d' ostentazione che di bellezza o d' ornamento.*

To daub, [to flatter grosly] *adulare grossamente, senza garbo senza artificio; piaggiare; lusingare senza cortigiania.*

To daub, v. n. [to play the hypocrite] *far l' ipocritone, fingersi santo.*

DA'UBER, s. [a coarse low painter] *un pittoraccio, un pittor di boccali.*

DA'UGHTER, s. [a female child] *figlia, figliuola,* s. f.

A daughter-in-law, *una figliastra.*

A grand-daughter, *una nipote.*

A God-daughter, *una figlioccia.*

To DAUNT [to frighten, to put out of heart] *intimidire, spaventare, disanimare, sgomentare, tor l'animo, far perder d'animo.*

DA'UNTED, adj. *intimidito, spaventato, disanimato, sgomentato, perso d'animo.*

What makes you be so daunted? *di che temete?*

DA'UNTLESS, adj. [intrepid, fearless] *intrepido, animoso, coraggioso.*

DAW, s. [the name of a bird] *nome d' uccello della spezie delle cornacchie.*

DAWK, s. [a hollow or incision in the stuff] *buco, squarcio, incisione, o rottura in checchessia.*

To DAWK, [to mark with an incision] *dar un taglio al panno o altra cosa per segno.*

DAWN, s. [the dawn of the day] *l'alba,* s. f. *ora tra'l mattutino e'l levar del sole.*

Dawn, [beginning, first rise] *il cominciamento, l' alba di qualche cosa; come chi dicesse;* the dawn of life, *l' alba della vita, cioè la puerizia, i primi anni.*

To dawn [to begin to grow light, as the day does] *spuntare, cominciare a nascere, apparire, parlando del giorno.*

It dawns, *il giorno comincia a spuntare.*

DA'WNING, s. *ex.* the dawn of the day, *l'alba, lo spuntare, il far del giorno.*

DAY, s. [that space of time that the sun is in our hemisphere] *giorno, dì,* s. m. *quello spazio di tempo, che il sole sta sopra'l nostro emisfero.*

It is broad day, *fa giorno.*

Night and day, *notte e giorno.*

A day, a whole day, *un giorno, una giornata.*

A holy day, *una festa, un giorno festivo, un giorno di lavoro.*

A work day, *un giorno di lavoro.*

Day by day, *ogni giorno, giornalmente.*

From day to day, *di giorno in giorno.*

The next day, *il giorno seguente, il domani.*

Every day, *ogni giorno.*

Every other day, *ogni secondo giorno, un dì sì, un dì no.*

Every third day, *di tre giorni in tre giorni.*

I have been at work all the day long, *ho lavorato tutto'l giorno.*

Day [battle] *giornata, battaglia,* s. f.

To get the day, *guadagnar la battaglia.*

To lose the day, *perder la battaglia.*

To day [this day] *oggi.*

I never saw him before to day, *non l'ho mai visto prima.*

To this day, *fin al giorno d'oggi.*

From this day, *da qui innanzi.*

The day before yesterday, *avantieri, ierlaltro.*

This many a day, *è un pezzo, molti giorni sono.*

This day se'nnight, or sevennight [that is, a week ago] *otto giorni sono.*

This day se'nnight [a week hence] *da qui, o fra otto giorni, oggi a otto.*

They were two days journey off of this place, *erano a due giornate da qui.*

In those days, *in quei tempi.*

I could have wished that his days had been longer, *averei ben voluto che la sua vita fosse stata più lunga.*

This is the best that ever I saw in my days, *questo è il migliore, che abbia visto in vita mia.*

In the days of old, *anticamente, altre volte.*

Day break, *il fare, lo spuntare del giorno.*

Dog days, *giorni canicolari.*

A day-labourer, *un operajo, un artigiano, un contadino, un che lavora tutto il dì per prezzo.*

A day's work, *una giornata.*

In the day time, *di giorno.*

Fasting days, *giorno di magro.*

Meat day, *giorno grasso.*

Day light, *giorno, giorno chiaro.*

'Tis day light, *è giorno chiaro.*

Broad day light, *giorno chiaro.*

A day book, *un giornale, o diario.*

A day's man, [an umpire] *un arbitro.*

Sabbath day, *giorno di domenica.*

DA'YBED, s. [a bed used for idleness] *letto usato per pigrizia più che per necessità.*

DA'YBOOK, s. [a tradesman's journal] *giornale; libro in cui il mercante registra di dì in dì le sue faccende giornaliere.*

To DAZE [to overpower with light] *abbagliare con soverchia luce.*

DA'ZIED, adj. [besprinkled with daisies] *pieno di que' fiori chiamati margheritine; ed è epiteto dato a zollo, o gleba; e si potrebbe anche darsi a un prato, giardino, o cosa simile.*

To DAZZLE [to hurt the sight with too much light] *abbagliare, offuscare.*

To dazzle, v. n. [to be overpowered with light] *rimaner abbagliato per soverchia luce.*

DA'ZZLED, adj. *abbagliato, offuscato.*

DAZZLING, s. *abbagliamento, abbaglio, abbagliore, offuscamento,* s. m.

Dazzling, adj. *risplendente, lucente, rilucente, lucido, che abbaglia.*

DE'ACON, s. [a minister who is to assist the priest in divine service] *un diacono.*

DE'ACONESS, s. [women of probity, who were chosen to assist those of their own sex in religious concerns] *diaconessa,* s. f. *donna che ha ricevuto l'ordine del diaconato, e che era consacrata al servizio della chiesa.*

DE'ACONRY, } s. *diaconato, diacono,* s. m. *uno degli ordini sacri.*
DE'ACONSHIP, }

DEAD, adj. [from to die] *morto.*

He is dead long fince, *è un pezzo ch' egli è morto.*
He is a dead man, *egli è un uomo spedito.*
Dead flesh, *carne morta.*
Dead pay, *piazza morta.*
Dead drink, *bevanda svaporata.*
A dead coal, *carbone morto, o estinto.*
Dead water, *acqua morta.*
The dead time of the year, *il tempo nel quale si fa poche faccende.*
A dead weight, *peso morto.*
Stand, or you are a dead man, *fermati o che t'amazzo.*
Dead [numb'd as limbs are] *assiderato, addormentato.*
Dead [heavy, dull] *stupido, indormentito.*
Struck dead, *stupito, stupefatto.*
To wish one dead, *desiderar l'altrui morte.*
To fall down dead, *cascar morto.*
He is half dead, *egli è mezzo morto, o egli è più morto che vivo.*
To be in a dead sleep [to be dead asleep] *dormire profondamente, o esser sepolto nel sonno.*
A dead calm, *una gran calma.*
The dead time of the night, *il silenzio della notte.*
Dead pledge [mortgage] *ipoteca.*
A dead wall, *muro che serve di chiusura sopra'l quale non v'è alcuno edificio.*
To help one at a dead lift, *liberare alcuno da qualche imbarazzo, metterlo in piedi.*
To work for a dead horse, *lavorare per pagare un debito vecchio.*
Dead neap [a low tide] *marea bassa.*
Dead, s. *i morti.*
The quick and the dead, *i vivi ed i morti.*
A service for the dead, *ufficio per li morti.*
Dead, adv. *grandemente, molto, affatto.*
He is dead drunk, *egli è molto imbriaco, egli è affatto imbriaco.*
To Dead, } verb act. *rallentare,*
To De'aden, } *allentare.*
A good buff coat deads a bullet, *un buon colletto rallenta un colpo di palla.*
To dead the sound of a musical instrument, *attutire il suono d'un istrumento musicale.*
To dead the spirits, *addormentare, istupidire gli spiriti.*
Dead-do'ing, adj. [destructive, killing, mischievous] *che cagiona morte, distruzione, o mal grande.*
De'adly, adv. [mortal, dangerous] *mortale, che apporta morte, periglioso.*
A deadly sin, *un peccato mortale.*
A deadly disease, *una malattia mortale, o perigliosa.*
'Tis a deadly thing, *è una cosa fatale.*
Deadly [mortal, violent, great] *mortale, violento, acuto, estremo, grande.*
A deadly pain, *un dolore mortale, o acuto.*
A deadly blow, *un gran colpo.*
A deadly deal, *una gran quantità.*

Deadly, adv. *mortalmente, grandissimamente, estremamente, terribilmente.*
I hate him deadly, *l'odio mortalmente, o fin'alla morte.*
He is deadly strong, *egli è estremamente, o molto forte.*
I was deadly angry, *io ero grandissimamente in collera.*
It rains deadly hard, *diluvia.*
De'adness, s. *addormentamento, indormentamento.*
Deadness of spirits, *addormentamento di spiriti.*
Deaf, adj. [not having the sense of hearing] *sordo.*
To make deaf, *assordare.*
To make as if one were deaf, *fare il sordo.*
To Deaf, or De'afen [to make deaf] *assordare, indur sordità.*
De'afish, adj. *alquanto o un poco sordo, sordastro.*
A deafish man, *un sordastro.*
De'afly, adv. *sordamente, alla sorda, chetamente.*
De'afness, s. *sordezza, sordità, sordaggine, s. f.*
Deal, s. [a good deal, a great deal] *molto, quantità, abbondanza.*
Deal [at cards] *la parte di chi tocca a fare le carte.*
Deal [a sort of wood] *abete.*
A deal board, *un pancone d'abete.*
To keep a deal of stir [to make a great ado about something] *fare un grande strepito, un grande schiamazzo per qualche cosa.*
To be in a great deal of trouble, grief, sorrow, *esser in gran pena, dolore, affanno, afflizione, esser molto afflitto.*
To Deal [to trade] *negoziare, trafficare, esercitar la mercatura, o'l traffico.*
He deals in all sorts of commodities, *egli traffica in ogni sorta di mercanzia.*
To deal well or ill with one [to use him well or ill] *trattar uno bene o male, portarsi seco amorevolmente, o villanamente.*
He is a sad man to deal with, *non è terren da porci vigna, non è uomo da farne capitale.*
I shall deal with him well enough, *saprò ben io accomodarmi con lui.*
I know not how to deal with him, *non so in che modo comportarmi con lui.*
I shall let you see who you are to deal with, *vi farò ben vedere con chi avrete a fare.*
You are to deal with one that is not a fool, *voi avete a fare con uno che non è un minchione.*
To deal at cards, *far le carte.*
To De'albate [to whiten, to bleach] *imbiancare, far bianco, render bianco.*
Dealba'tion, s. [the act of bleaching] *l'imbiancare, imbiancatura, il render bianco.*
De'aler, s. [or merchant] *un negoziante, un mercante.*
A plain dealer, *un uomo franco, schietto, un uomo di buona fede, un galantuomo.*
A false dealer, *un uomo di cattiva fede, un uomo doppio, un furfante, un furbo.*
Déaler, s. *colui che fa le carte giuocando.*
De'aling, s. *il negoziare, il trafficare.*
Dealing [trade] *traffico, commercio, negozio, s. m.*
I have no dealings with him, *non ho corrispondenza con lui, non ho niente a fare co' fatti suoi.*
An honest or upright dealing, *un procedere sincero, o franco.*
A false or treacherous dealing, *perfidia, fraude, inganno, furfanteria.*
Dealt with, adj. *trattato.*
Kindly dealt with, *ben trattato.*
Basely dealt with, *maltrattato.*
An easy man to be dealt with, *un uomo ragionevole.*
Hard to be dealt with, *difficile, con chi non si può contrattare.*
Deambula'tion, s. [walk] *spasseggiata, s. f.*
Dean, s. [a church dignitary] *decano, s. m.*
De'anery, s. [the jurisdiction of a dean] *giurisdizione di decano.*
Déanery, *l'entrate d'un decano.*
Déanery, *la carica d'un decano.*
De'anship, s. [the office or dignity of a dean] *ufficio, o dignità di decano, decanato.*
Dear, adj. [costly] *caro, che vale e si stima gran prezzo.*
Dear [beloved] *caro, amato, grato.*
My dear, *mio caro, mia cara, ben mio.*
Dear, adv. *caro, gran prezzo.*
It cost me dear, *caro mi costa.*
Oh dear, interj. *cáppita.*
De'arbought, adj. [purchased at a high price] *comprato a caro prezzo, caro.*
De'arling, s. *in oggi scritto* Darling, *il cucco, il figlio favorito del padre o della madre.*
De'arly, adv. *caramente, amorevolmente, di cuore.*
I love him dearly, *l'amo caramente.*
I love dearly to see him, *piglio gran piacere nel vederlo.*
To Dearn [to mend cloaths] *rattoppare o rabberciare i panni.*
De'arness, s. [from dear] *carestia, scarsità, s. f.*
The dearness of provision, *carestia de' viveri.*
De'arnly, adv. [secretly, privately, unseen] *segretamente, occultamente, di nascoso, non visto.*
De'arning, v. Darning.
Dearth, s. [great scarcity, or want of provisions] *carestia, scarsezza, mancamento delle cose necessarie al vitto.*
Death, s. [the separation of the soul from the body] *la morte.*
To be at the point of death, *essere nel punto, o nell' articolo della morte.*
To be wounded to death, *esser ferito a morte.*
After death comes the physician, *dopo la morte viene il medico, il soccorso viene spesso troppo tardi, il soccorso di Pisa.*

To put one to death, *mettere a morte, far morire.*

To be the death of one, *esser causa dell' altrui morte.*

To catch one's death, *causarsi la morte.*

It is death [it is a capital crime] *è un delitto capitale.*

Death's wound, *piaga mortale.*

He has given me my death's wound, *egli m'ha ferito mortalmente.*

Upon pain of death, *sotto pena della vita.*

To sit upon life and death, *giudicare alcuno per un delitto capitale.*

To threaten one with death, *minacciar alcuno d'ammazzarlo, o di farlo morire.*

To grieve one's self to death, *affliggersi fino alla morte.*

Death bed, *agonia,* s. f.

To be at one's death bed, *agonizzare, essere in agonia.*

He is at his death bed, *egli sta agonizzando.*

DE'ATHFUL, adj. [full of slaughter, destructive, murderous] *mortale, pien di morte, pien di strage, omicida.*

DE'ATHLIKE, adj. [resembling death, still] *che somiglia morte, tacito come morte.*

DEATH'S-DOOR, s. [a near approach to death] *l'esser vicino a morte; agonia, ultima agonia.*

DE'ATHSMAN, s. [executioner, hangman, headsman] *il carnefice, il boja.*

DE'ATHWATCH, s. [an insect that makes a tinckling noise, superstitiously imagined to prognosticate death] *insetto che superstiziosamente si crede predica morte perchè il suo ronzo dicesi somigli a' tocchi d'un campanellino.*

DE'ATHLESS, adj. [immortal, never-dying] *immortale.*

To DEBA'R [to shut out, to keep from] *escludere, privare, vietare, proibire,* pres. *proibisco.*

To debar one's self of pleasures, *astenersi da' piaceri.*

To debar [to hinder] *impedire, contrariare, opporsi,* pres. *impedisco, oppongo,* pret. *opposi.*

To DEBA'RK [to land] *cavare o uscire della barca, sbarcare, trar di barca.*

DEBA'RKED, adj. *sbarcato.*

DEBA'RRED, adj. *escluso, privato, vietato, proibito, impedito, opposto.*

DEBA'RRING, s. *esclusione,* s. f. *l'escludere, viatamento.*

DEBA'SE [to bring down, to humble] *abbassare, deprimere, umiliare, conculcare, avvilire,* pres. *avvilisco.*

To DEBA'SE, *avvilire, avvilirsi.*

To debase [to disparage] *disprezzare, discreditare, screditare, dispregiare, avere o tenere a vile.*

To debase coin, *falsificar la moneta.*

DEBA'SED, adj. *abbassato, depresso, umiliato, conculcato, avvilito, disprezzato, dispregiato.*

DEBA'SEMENT, s. *abbassamento, avvilimento, dispregio, e disprezzo,* s. m.

DEBA'TE, s. [dispute in words] *contesa, contenzione, disputa, discussione,* s. f.

Debate [strife, quarrel] *lite, gara, competenza, tencione, tenzone,* s. f.

To DEBA'TE [to bandy] *discussare, discutere, agitare, trattare, esaminare,* pret. *discussi.*

To debate a question, *discussare, o discutere un dubbio.*

To debate [to quarrel, &c.] *contendere, contrastare, disputare, litigare, gareggiare,* pret. *contesi.*

To debate [to advise with one's self] *deliberare, meditare, pensare a qualche cosa.*

DEBA'TED, adj. *discussato, discusso, agitato, trattato, esaminato, conteso, contrastato, disputato, gareggiato.*

DEBA'TING, s. *discussione,* s. f. *il discutere.*

DEBA'TEMENT, s. [contest, controversy] *disputa, contesa, controversia.*

DEBA'UCH, s. [a riotous banquetting and revelling] *crapula, gozzoviglia,* s. f. *stravizzo.*

To DEBA'UCH [to corrupt, to mar, to spoil] *sviare, sedurre, corrompere, contaminare, sobillare, e subillare, soddurre, subornare, esortare a mal fare,* pres. *seduco, sodduco,* pret. *sedussi, soddussi.*

To debauch a maid, *sedurre, o corrompere una fanciulla.*

DEBAUCHE'E, s. *uno sviato, uno scapestrato, un dissoluto, un licenzioso, un discolo.*

DEBA'UCHER, s. [one who seduces others to intemperance or lewdness] *seduttore.*

DEBA'UCHED, adj. *sviato, sedotto, corrotto, contaminato, sobillato, v.* To debauch.

DEBA'UCHERY, s. [incontinency, licentiousness, lewdness] *dissolutezza, disonestà, sfrenatezza,* s. f.

DEBE'NTUR, or DEBE'NTURE, s. [a bill used in the exchequer, and also at court, and given to the king's houshold servants for the payment of their salaries] *cedule che si danno per assicurare i domestici del rè del loro salario, e della paga delle truppe.*

DE'BILE, adj. [weak, feeble, languid, faint] *debole, debile, languido, fiacco, spossato.*

To DEBI'LITATE [to weaken, to make feeble] *debilitare, affievolire, far divenir debole, scemar le forze,* pres. *affievolisco.*

DEBI'LITATED, adj. *debilitato, affievolito, scemato di forze.*

DEBI'LITATING, s. *debilitamento,* s. m. *il debilitare.*

DEBILITA'TION, s. [a weakening] *debilitazione,* s. f. *debilitamento,* s. m.

DEBI'LITY, s. [weakness] *debilità, e debilità, debolezza, fiacchezza, fievolezza,* s. f.

DEBONA'IR, adj. [courteous, affable] *cortese, affabile, benigno, umano.*

Debonair [airy, brisk] *allegro, giojoso, gajo, festoso, giocondo, giolivo, gioviale.*

DEBONA'IRITY, s. *cortesia, affabilità, benignità, umanità.*

DEBT, s. [what is due from one man to another] *debito,* s. m. *quel che si deve.*

To contract debts [to run into debts] *fare debiti indebitarsi.*

To pay one's debts [to go out of debt] *pagare i suoi debiti.*

To be in debt, *essere indebitato.*

To be deeply in debt [to be in debt over head and ears] *esser infangato ne' debiti.*

I am still something in your debt, *vi devo ancora qualche cosa, vi sono ancora debitore di qualche cosa.*

I am in your debt [or obliged to you] for this, *ve ne resto obligato e con obligo.*

Out of debt, out of danger, *chi non deve niente è fuor di pericolo.*

A little debt, *debituzzo,* s. m.

DE'BTOR, s. [who is indebted to another] *debitore,* s. m.

DE'CADE, s. [the number of ten] *deca,* s. f. *decina, numero di dieci.*

Livy's Decades, *le Deche di Tito Livio.*

DE'CAGON, s. [a figure of ten angles] *decagono,* s. m. *figura solida di dieci angoli.*

DE'CALOGUE, s. [the Ten Commandments of God] *decalogo,* s. m. *il contenuto de' dieci comandamenti di Dio.*

DE'CAMERON, s. [a book of novels, divided into ten books, written by Boccaccio, an Italian] *Decamerone,* s. m. *titolo del libro delle novelle del Boccaccio, diviso in dieci giornate.*

To DECA'MP [to break up the camp, to march off] *levar il campo, levarsi da campo, sfendare, levar le tende.*

DECA'MPED, adj. *levato il campo, sfendato.*

DECA'MPMENT, s. *lo sfendare, il levarsi dal campo.*

To DECA'NT [to pour out of one vessel into another] *trasvasare, travasare, mutare il liquore, o altra cosa di vaso in vaso, termine chimico.*

DECANTA'TION, s. [a chymical term, a pouring the clear part of any liquor by inclination, so that it may be without any sediment or dregs] *il travasare da un vaso in un altro leggiermente i liquori, sicchè la feccia non si confonda col chiarificato.*

DECA'NTED, adj. *trasvasato, travasato.*

DECA'NTER, s. [a flint bottle to hold wine, beer, &c. to be poured off into a drinking glass] *guastada,* s. f.

A small decanter, *guastadetta, guastaduzza,* s. f.

To DECA'PITATE [to behead] *decapitare, mozzare il capo.*

DECA'Y, s. [failure, ruin] *decadenza, diminuzione, declinazione,* s. f. *declinamento, divallamento, declino, fradimento,* s. m.

The decay of trade, *la decadenza del negozio.*

To go to decay, *andare in rovina.*

A beauty gone to decay, *una bellezza sfiorita, che non è piu.*

My memory is gone to decay, *la mia memoria s'è indebolita.*

To

To DECA'Y [to fail, to fall, to decreafe] *decadere, fcadere, declinare, abbaffarfi, calare, diminuire, fcemarfi, mancare.*

To decay [to wither] *appaffirfi, appaffarfi, divenir paffo, o vizzo.*

To decay [to grow worfe] *imbaftardirfi.*

To decay [to wear off] *confumarfi, logorarfi.*

To decay with age, *effer accafciato per vecchiaja.*

To decay in one's eftate, *impoverire, divenir povero.*

DECAY'ED, adj. *decaduto, fcaduto, declinato, abbaffato, calato, diminuito, fcemato, mancato.*

A decayed family, *una famiglia rovinata.*

A decayed merchant, *un mercante fallitto.*

A decayed building, *un edificio rovinofo, che minaccia rovina.*

Decayed with age, *accafciato dall' età.*

Decayed in ftrength, *fpoffato, debole, privo di forze.*

Decayed wine, *vin guafto.*

DECE'ASE, s. [death] *morte,* s. f.

To DECE'ASE [to die] *morire.*

DECE'ASED, adj. *morto.*

DECE'IT, s. [cheat] *inganno, gabbamento, ingannamento,* s. m. *delufione, furberia, fraude, mariuoleria, baratteria,* s. f.

DECE'ITFUL, adj. *ingannatore, giuntatore, falfo, fraudolente, e fraudolento.*

A deceitful man, *un ingannatore, un barattiere, un giuntatore, un mariuolo, un furbo, un ingannatore, un arcadore.*

Deceitful hopes, *fperanze fallaci.*

A deceitful trick, *una furberia, una mariuoleria.*

DECE'ITFULLY, adv. *ingannevolmente, fraudolentemente, con inganno.*

DECE'ITFULNESS, s. *inganno, gabbamento,* s. m. *fraude, furberia, mariuoleria, delufione,* s. f.

DECE'IVABLE, adj. [that may be deceived] *facile ad effer ingannato.*

To DECE'IVE [to beguile, to cheat] *ingannare, gabbare, giuntare, treccare, truffare, foppiattare.*

DECE'IVED, adj. *ingannato, gabbato, giuntato, troccato, truffato, foppiattato.*

He is not eafily deceived, *non fi lafcia facilmente ingannare.*

You are deceived [you are miftaken] *voi sbagliate, voi v'ingannate.*

DECE'IVER, s. *ingannatore, arcadore, avviluppatore, barattiere, giuntatore, fottrattore,* s. m. *ingannatrice,* s. f.

DECE'IVING, s. *delufione,* s. f. *gabbamento,* s m.

DECE'MBER, s. [one of the twelve months of the year] *Dicembre,* s. m. *uno de' dodici mefi dell' anno.*

DECE'MVIRATE, s. the office of the Decemviri, among the Romans, chofen to govern the commonwealth] *Decemvirato, il governo dell' antica Roma dai Decemviri.*

DE'CENCE, } s. [comelinefs, feemli-
DE'CENCY, } nefs] *decenza, modeftia,* s. f. *decoro,* s. m.

DECE'NNIAL, adj. [of ten years continuance] *decennio, di dieci anni.*

DE'CENT, adj. [becoming, feemly] *decente, decorofo, che ha in fe decenza, o decoro, decevole, dicevole.*

That is not at all decent, *quefto non è del tutto decente.*

DE'CENTLY, adv. *decentemente, con decenza, con decoro.*

Decently buried, *onorevolmente, decentemente fepellito.*

DECE'PTION, s. [deceiving] *delufione, fraude, frode,* s. f. *inganno,* s. m.

DECE'PTIOUS, adj. [deceitful] *ingannevole, pien d'inganno.*

DECE'PTIVE, adj. [having the power of deceiving] *ingannevole, che può ingannare.*

To DECHA'RM [to counteract a charm, to difenchant] *difincantare, disfare una malía.*

To DECI'DE [to conclude an affair to bring it to an iffue] *decidere, rifolvere, terminare, difinire, deliberare;* pref. *decifi.*

To decide a bufinefs, *decidere, o rifolvere un negozio.*

To decide a controverfy, *decidere, terminare, difinire una controverfia.*

DECI'DED, adj. *decifo, rifoluto, terminato, definito, deliberato.*

DECI'DER, s. *un che decide, un che determina una cofa; decifore.*

DECI'DING, s. *decifione, determinazione,* s. f. *rifolvimento,* s. m.

DECI'MAL, adj. [numbered by ten] *contato per dieci, decimo.*

To DE'CIMATE [among the Romans, was to take out every tenth foldier by lot, and punifh or put him to death for an example to the reft] *decimare, dicevano i Romani del punire i foldati con ucciderne d'ogni dieci uno, per efempio degli altri*

To decimate [to take tythes] *decimare, levar la decima.*

DECIMA'TION, s. [a punifhing every tenth foldier by lot] *decimazione,* s. f.

Decimation [a gathering tythes] *il pagamento delle derime.*

To DECI'PHER [to find out the meaning of a letter, &c. written in cyphers] *dicifrare, dichiarare, fpiegare le cifere.*

To decypher a letter, *dicifrare, o fpiegare le cifere d'una lettera.*

To decipher [to defcribe] *defcrivere, dipignere, rapprefentare, figurare.*

DECI'PHERED, adj. *defcritto, fpiegato, dichiarato.*

DECI'PHERER, s. *colui che fpiega le cifere.*

DECI'SION, s. [a determining or deciding] *decifione, determinazione,* s. f. *rifolvimento,* s. m.

DE'CISIVE, or DE'CISORY, adj. *decifivo.*

A decifive reafon, *una ragione decifiva.*

DECI'SIVELY, adv. [in a conclufive manner] *decifivamente, ultimatamente.*

DECK, s. [a planked floor in a fhip on which men walk] *bordo, ponte di vafcello.*

The firft deck, *il primo bordo.*

To DECK [to fet out, to adorn] *adornare, acconciare, addobbare, parare, ornare, abbellire,* pref. *abbelifco.*

DE'CKED, adj. *adornato, acconciato, addobbato, parato, ornato, abbellito.*

DE'CKING, s. *ornamento, addobbamento, guernimento, paramento,* s. m.

To DE'CLAIM [to make publick fpeeches] *declamare, arringare, orare, parlamentare.*

To declaim [to inveigh againft] *fparlare, dir male, biafimare.*

DECLAI'MER, s. *arringatore, fparlatore, biafimatore, maldicente,* s. m.

DECLAMA'TION, s. [an oration made upon fome feigned fubject] *arringheria, diceria,* s. f. *parlamento fatto in rhinghiera.*

DECLAMA'TORY, adj. *declamatorio, che concerne l'arringheria.*

In a declamatory way, *in maniera d'arringheria.*

DECLAMA'TOR, *v.* Declaimer.

DECLA'RATION, s. *dichiarazione,* s. f.

Declaration of war, *intimazione di guerra.*

DECLA'RATIVE, adj. [which ferves to declare] *dichiarativo, che dichiara.*

To DECLA'RE [to make known, to publifh, to fhow] *dichiarare, palefare, far chiaro, manifeftare.*

To declare one's mind to a friend, *confidarfi ad un amico, dirli l'animo fuo.*

To declare war, *intimar la guerra.*

To declare [to make plain] *dichiarare, efporre, interpetrare.*

To declare, verb neut. *dichiararfi, moftrarfi, manifeftarfi.*

To declare for or againft one, *dichiararfi per, o contro alcuno.*

I don't like it I declare, *a dirvela fchietta, o vi confeffo che non mi piace.*

DECLA'RED, adj. *dichiarato, palefato, manifeftato, efpofto, interpretato.*

DECLA'RER, s. *dichiaratore,* s. m. *dichiaratrice,* s. f.

DECLA'RING, s. *dichiaramento,* s. m. *dichiarazione.*

DECLE'NSION, s [a term of grammar] *declinazione,* s. f. *termine gramaticale.*

Declenfion [decline] *declinazione,* s. f. *declinamento,* s. m.

Declenfion of manners, *depravazione di coftumi.*

DE'CLINABLE, adj. [having variety of terminations] *declinabile; e dicefi de' nomi. Vocabolo de' grammatici.*

DECLINA'TION, s. [decay] *declinazione,* s. f. *declinamento, declivo,* s. m.

The declination of an empire, *lo fcadimento d'imperio.*

The declination [declenfion] of Greek and Latin nouns, *la declinazione de' nomi Greci, e Latini.*

The declination of the fun, *il declino, o il tramontar del fole.*

DECLI'NE, s. *declinazione,* s. f. *fcadimento,* s. m.

To

To DE'CLINE [a term of grammar] declinare, termine gramaticale, recitar per ordini i casi de' nomi, e i tempi de' verbi.
To decline a noun, declinare un nome.
To decline [to avoid, to shun, to refuse] sfuggire, evitare, schivare, scansare, schisare.
To decline [to decay] declinare, abbassarsi, calare, scadere, venire in peggiore stato.
To decline [to bow downward] declinare, piegare, abbassare, calare.
DECLI'NED, adj. declinato, v. To decline.
He is declined in his credit, il suo credito è scaduto.
DECLI'NING, s. declinamento, scadimento, s. m.
Declining, adj. declinante, scadente.
A declining age, età avanzata, il cader degli anni.
In his declining age, in sul fine della sua vita.
DECLI'VITY, s. [the bending of a hill] pendio, pendente, s. m. declività, s. f.
To DECO'CT, bollire, digerire.
DECO'CTION, s. [a medicinal liquor made of roots, herbs, &c. boiled] decozione, s. f.
DECOLLA'TION, s. [beheading] dicollazione, s. f.
DECO'MPOSITE, s. [a word compounded of another compound] una parola composta d'un altro composto.
DECOMPO'UNDED, adj. doppiamente composto.
To DE'CORATE [to adorn] decorare, ornare, adornare.
DECORA'TOR, s. colui che decora, o adorna, adornatore.
DECORA'TION, s. [ornament] decorazione, s. f. ornamento, adornamento, s. m.
The decorations of the stage, le scene d'un teatro.
DECO'ROUS, adj. decoroso, che ha in se decoro.
DECORTIFICA'TION, s. [the peeling off the outward bark] scorticamento, s. m. lo scorticare, lo scorzare, il dibucciare.
DECO'RUM, s. [decency] decoro, s. m. convenevolezza, convenienza, onestura, s. f.
A DECO'Y, s. [a place fitted for catching of wild fowl] luogo da zimbellare gli uccelli.
A decoy duck, un' anitra che serve di zimbello.
Decoy [lure or wheedle to draw in] allettamento, lacciuolo, zimbello, vezzo, s. m. lusinga, s. f.
To DECO'Y [to draw in] allettare, lusingare, indurre, zimbellare.
DECO'Y'D, adj. allettato, lusingato, indotto, zimbellato.
DECRE'ASE, s. [diminution] scadimento, scemamento, calo, sminuimento, s. m.
The decrease [the wane of the moon] lo scemo della luna.
To DECRE'ASE [to grow less] decrescere, sminuire, diminuire, scemare, calare, declinare, mancare, pref. sminuisco, diminuisco.
My money begins to decrease, il mio danaro comincia a sminuire.
DECRE'ASED, adj. sminuito, diminuito.
DECRE'E, s. [order, statute] decreto, ordine, s. m.
The pope's decrees, i decreti pontificii.
A decree of state, ordine, editto, statuto.
Decree [purpose, resolution] disegno, intento, pensiero, s. m. intenzione, risoluzione, s. f.
To DECRE'E [to appoint, to ordain] decretare, stabilire, statuire, deliberare, ordinare, pref. stabilisco, statuisco.
DECREE'D, adj. decretato, stabilito, statuito, deliberato, ordinato.
What God has decreed we must submit to, bisogna uniformarci a quel che Iddio ha ordinato.
DE'CREMENT, s. [decrease, waste] sminuimento, diminuimento, scemo, scemamento, s. m.
DECRE'PIT, adj. [worn out with age, extreme old] decrepito, d'estrema vecchiezza.
DECRE'PITNESS, } s. [decrepit or
DECRE'PITUDE, } old age] decrepità, estrema vecchiezza.
DECRE'SCENT, s. [the moon decreasing in the last quarter] lo scemo della luna, l'ultimo quarto della luna.
DECRE'TAL, adj. [of or belonging to decrees] decretale, di decreto.
Decretals, s. [the second of the three volumes of the canon-law] le Decretali, una parte delle leggi canoniche.
Decretals [the letters of popes] decretali, s. f. decreto, o statuto canonico.
DECRE'TORY, adj. [which serves to decree, or absolutely to decide] decisivo, definitivo, perentorio.
A decretory, s. [a definitive sentence] una sentenza difinitiva.
To DECRY' [to cry down, to speak ill of] discreditare, screditare, sparlare, dir male, biasimare.
To decry a thing for nought, discreditare una cosa.
To decry a person, parlare d'una persona.
To decry a law or custom, abolire, o annullare una legge, o un costume.
DE'CRY'D, adj. discreditato, screditato, sparlato, biasimato.
To DECU'LCATE [to tread under foot] conculcare, calpestare, oppressare, tener sotto, rintuzzare.
DECU'MBENCE, } s. [the act of lying
DECU'MBENCY, } down; the posture of lying down] decubito, s. m.
DE'CUPLE, adj. [ten-fold] decuplo, dieci volte doppio.
DECU'RION, s. [a captain over ten horses] decurione, s. m.
To DECY'PHER, v. To decipher.
To DE'DICATE [to consecrate] dedicare, offerire, consecrare, e consagrare, presentare, pref. offerisco.
To dedicate a church, dedicare una chiesa.
To dedicate a book to one, dedicare, o presentare un libro ad alcuno.
DE'DICATED, adj. dedicato, offerto, consecrato, e consacrato, presentato.
DE'DICATING, s. dedicamento, s. m. il dedicare.
DEDICA'TION [the act of dedicating or consecrating] dedicazione, s. f. dedicamento, s. m.
DEDICA'TOR, s. [a dedicating author] quegli che dedica un libro.
DE'DICATORY, adj. dedicatorio.
An epistle dedicatory, un lettera dedicatoria, una dedica.
To DEDU'CE [to draw one thing from another, to infer] dedurre, conchiudere, inferire, pref. deduco, inferisco, pret. dedussi, conchiusi.
DEDU'CED, adj. dedotto, conchiuso, inferito.
DEDU'CEMENT, s. [the thing deduced; consequential proposition] conseguenza dedotta; il dedurre una da un' altra cosa.
DEDU'CIBLE, adj che si può dedurre, conchiudere, o inferire.
DEDU'CING, s. deduzione, s. f. il dedurre.
To DEDU'CT [to substract, to take away from] sottrarre, cavar d'una somma maggiore altra minore, pret. sottrassi.
DEDU'CTED, adj. sottratto.
DEDU'CTION, s. sottraimento, s. m. sottrazione, s. f.
Deduction [conclusion, consequence] deduzione, conclusione, conseguenza, inferenza, s. f.
DEED, s. [action, thing done] atto, fatto, s. m. azione, s. f.
Deed [instrument, contract] strumento, contratto, instrumento, s. m.
Deed-poll [a single plain deed unindented] un contratto semplice.
A brave deed, una bella azione.
He was taken in the very deed, egli fu preso su'l fatto, o in flagrante.
I am not satisfied with words, I am for deeds, le parole non mi bastano, voglio fatti.
DE'EDLESS, adj. [unactive] scioperato, che non fa nulla, che non opera.
To DEEM [to judge, to think] credere, stimare, giudicare, pensare, immaginarsi.
DE'EMED, adj. creduto, stimato, giudicato, pensato, immaginato.
DEEM, s. [judgment, surmise, opinion] giudizio che si fa d'una cosa, opinione.
DE'EMSTEER, s. [a kind of judge in the Isle of Man, chosen from among, and by themselves, who, without process, writing or charge, decides controversies there] spezie di giudice o arbitro nell' Isola di Man.
DEEP, adj. [that has a great depth] profondo, alto, cupo.
A deep well, un pozzo profondo.
To be in a deep sleep, essere in un profondo o alto sonno.
To be in a deep study, esser in profonde meditazioni.
A deep scholar, un uomo d'alto sapere.
A deep sorrow, una grande afflizione.

A deep mourning, *un gran bruno.*
A deep coat, *un abito ampio.*
Lace a quarter of a yard deep, *merletto largo un quarto di canna.*
A deep blue, *turchino oscuro.*
Deep [cunning] *astuto, fino, cupo.*
Deep [secret] *segreto, nascosto.*
Deep fetches, *pratiche segrete.*
A deep conspiracy, *una congiura segreta.*
A deep notion, *concetto oscuro.*
A deep way, *un cammino rotto.*
To be deep in debt, *esser pieno di debiti.*
Deep, s. [the sea] *il mare.* Poetical.
Deep, adv. *profondamente, altamente.*
To DEE'PEN [to make deep] *profondare, affondare, render profondo.*
DE'EPLY, adv. *profondamente, altamente.*
Deeply indebted, *molto indebitato, pieno di debiti.*
DE'EPMOUTHED, adj. [having a hoarse and loud voice] *che ha una voce rauca e forte; che hà voce chioccia.*
DEEPMU'SING, adj. [contemplative, lost in thought] *contemplativo, astratto, sprofondato in un pensiero.*
DE'EPNESS, s. *profondità,* s. f.
DE'EPNING, s. *profondamento,* s. m.
The deepnings of a picture, *le lontananze d'una pittura.*
DEER, s. [a wild beast of the forest] *il genere de' cervi.*
Fallow deer, *daino,* s. m. *damma,* s. f.
Red deer, *cervo, cerbio.*
Deer hays, *rete da cervi.*
To DEFA'CE [to mar, to spoil] *guastare, sconciare, rovinare, bruttare.*
To deface a church, *guastare una chiesa.*
To deface a town, *rovinare una città.*
To deface [to disfigure] *sformare, trasformare, disfigurare.*
To deface the coin, *disfigurare la moneta.*
To deface [to blot out] *scancellare, cancellare.*
To deface out of the memory, *scancellare dalla memoria.*
DEFA'CED, adj. *guastato,* v. To deface.
DEFA'CEMENT, s. *lo sconciare, il cancellare.*
DEFA'CING, s. *guasto, guastamento,* s. m. v. To deface.
DEFA'ILLANCE, s. [default] *mancanza,* s. f. *mancamento,* s. m.
DEFALCA'TION, s. [deduction or abatement in accounts] *sottrazione, difalcazione,* s. f.
To DEFA'LK [to deduct] *difalcare, dedurre, trarre, sbattere,* pres. *deduco, traggo,* pret. *dedussi, trassi.*
DEFA'LKED, adj. *difalcato, dedotto, tratto, sbattuto.*
DEFAMA'TION, s. [slander] *diffamazione, calunnia,* s. f. *diffamamento, biasimo, disonore,* s. m.
DEFAMA'TORY, adj. [slanderous, abusive] *diffamatorio, vituperoso, disonorevole.*

To DEFA'ME [to slander, or speak evil of] *diffamare, macchiar la fama altrui con maldicenza, infamare, sparlare, calunniare, calonniare.*
DEFA'MED, adj. *diffamato, infamato, sparlato, calunniato, calonniato.*
DEFA'MING, s. *diffamamento,* s. m. *il diffamare.*
DEFA'MER, s. [one that injures the reputation of another] *diffamatore, che toglie o macchia la riputazione altrui.*
DEFA'TIGABLE, adj. [that may be made weary] *faticabile, faticevole.*
To DEFA'TIGATE [to weary, to tire] *faticare, straccare.*
DEFA'ULT, s. [defect, want] *diffalta, mancanza, falta,* s. f. *mancamento, fallo, vizio, errore,* s. m.
In default whereof, *in diffalta di che.*
Default [in law, is non-appearance in court, without sufficient cause made out] *mancanza, termine legale.*
DEFE'AT, s. [overthrow] *sconfitta, rotta,* s. f.
The defeat of an army, *la sconfitta d'un esercito.*
To DEFE'AT [to overthrow] *sconfiggere, rompere il nemico in battaglia,* pret. *sconfissi, ruppi.*
To defeat an army, *sconfiggere un esercito.*
To defeat [to frustrate] one's design, *rompere, render vano, o deludere l'altrui disegno.*
To defeat [to make void] a thing, *scancellare, cancellare, annullare.*
To defeat one's will, *annullare l'altrui testamento, renderlo invalido.*
DEFE'ATED, adj. *sconfitto, rotto, deluso, scancellato, cancellato, annullato.*
DE'FECATE, adj. [clear from dregs] *raffinato, purificato, chiaro.*
To DE'FECATE [to purge from dregs, to refine] *raffinare, purificare.*
DEFECA'TION, s. [the act of refining or purging from dregs] *raffinamento,* s. m. *purificazione,* s. f.
DEFE'CT, s. [blemish, imperfection] *diffalta, imperfezione, mancanza, colpa,* s. f. *mancamento, difetto, vizio,* s. m.
To DEFE'CT [to be deficient] *mancare, esser manchevole, mancante, difettoso, guasto.*
DEFE'CTION, s. [revolt] *rivolta, rivoltura, rivoluzione,* s. f.
The defection of king James's army, *la rivolta dell' esercito del re Giacomo.*
Defection from the church, *apostasia.*
A general defection, *un' apostasia generale.*
They made a defection to the church of Rome, *abbracciarono la religione Romana, s'accostarono co' cattolici Romani.*
DEFE'CTIVE, adj. [full of defects] *difettivo, manchevole, difettoso, difettuoso.*
A verb defective [that has not all its tenses] *un verbo difettivo.*
DEFE'NCE, s. [guard, protection] *difesa, difensione, guardia, protezione,* s. f. *appoggio, soccorso,* s. m.
To stand in one's own defence [to stand upon one's guard] *star sulla difesa, star sulla sua.*

A place of defence, *una piazza forte, piazza che può far resistenza.*
To undertake one's defence, *abbracciare, impugnare l'altrui difesa.*
What did he say in his own defence? *che disse in sua difesa?*
Defence [opposition, resistance] *difesa, resistenza, opposizione.*
The place has made a very good defence, *la piazza si difese valorosamente.*
Defence [a reply which the defendant makes after the declaration is produced] *difesa, quel che si risponde in giustizia dal reo dopo la dichiarazione fatta dall' attore.*
He has made a very good defence in his trial, *egli s'è difeso bravamente nel suo processo.*
To speak in defence of one, *parlare in difesa altrui, pigliar la sua parte.*
To stand in the defence of one's own life, *difendere la sua vita.*
Defence [in fortification, are all sorts of works which cover and defend the opposite posts, as flanks, parapets, &c.] *difese, ripari, come fianchi, parapetti, trincee, e simili, che difendono i posti opposti.*
DEFE'NCELESS, adj. [naked, unarmed, unguarded] *nudo, disarmato, non in guardia, senza guardia.*
Defenceless, [impotent] *impotente, inabile, incapace.*
To DEFE'ND [to protect, to support] *difendere, guardare, salvare da' pericoli, e dalle ingiurie, proteggere, conservare, preservare,* pret. *difesi, protessi.*
To defend one's self, *difendersi.*
To defend the truth, *difender la verità.*
To defend an opinion, *difendere, mantenere un' opinione.*
To defend one's cause, *difender la sua causa, parlare in suo favore.*
DEFE'NDANT, adj. [defensive, fit for defence] *difensivo, atto a difendere.*
Defendant, s. [he that defends against assailants] *colui che si difende da uno o più assalitori.*
Defendant, s. [the person accused or sued] *la persona che è accusata legalmente, o contro cui s'intenta la lite.*
DEFE'NDED, adj. *difeso, guardato, salvato, protetto, conservato, preservato.*
DEFE'NDER, s. [he that defends] *difenditore, difensore,* s. m.
DEFE'NDING, s. *difendimento,* s. m. *difesa,* s. f. *il defendere.*
DEFE'NDRESS, s. *difenditrice,* s. f. *che difende.*
DEFE'NSATIVES, adj. [medicines which divert humours from a part affected] *unguenti difensivi.*
DEFE'NSIBLE, adj. [that may be defended] *difendevole, atto a difendersi.*
A strong and defensive place, *una piazza forte, e difendevole.*
DEFE'NSIVE, adj. [that serves to defend] *difensivo, che difende.*
To put one's self in a defensive posture, *mettersi in guardia, mettersi in atto difesa.*
A defensive league, *una lega difensiva.*

Defensive arms, *armi difensive.* s. f.

DEFE'NCIVELY, adv. ex. to act defensively, *star sulla difesa.*

To DEFE'R [to put off] *differire, prolungare, porogare, mandare in lungo,* pref. *differisco.*

DE'FERENCE, s. [respect, submission, regard] *rispetto, riguardo,* s. m. *considerazione, stima,* s. f.

DEFE'RRED, adj. *differito, polungato, prorogato.*

DEFE'RRING, s. *il differire, prolungamento,* s. m. *proroga, prorogazione,* s. f.

DEFI'ANCE, s. [challenge] *disfida,* s. f. *chiamata dell' avversario in battaglia.*

To bid one a defiance, *fare una disfida ad uno, sfidarlo.*

To live in open defiance with one, *esser nemico capitale d'uno.*

He lives in open defiance to, or against nature and reason, *egli procede contra le regole della natura e della ragione, egli ha sbanditi da se tutti i dettami della natura e della ragione.*

DEFI'CIENCE, DEFI'CIENCY, s. [defect] *deficenza, diffalta, mancanza,* s. f. *mancamento, difetto,* s. m.

DEFI'CIENT, adj. [wanting] *deficiente, mancante, difettoso, imperfetto.*

I shall not be deficient in any thing that may be agreeable to you, *non mancherò di far cosa che grata vi sia.*

DEFI'ER, s. [a challenger, a contemner] *sfidatore, sprezzatore, smargiasso.*

DEFILE', s. [a narrow passage through which a company of soldiers can pass only in files] *passaggio stretto.*

To DEFI'LE [to pollute] *imbrattare, lordare, sporcare, contaminare, macchiare.*

To defile [to deflower] *disonorare, deflorare.*

To defile [to file off, to march file by file] *sfilare, andare alla sfilata.*

DEFI'LED, adj. *imbrattato, lordato, sporcato, contaminato, macchiato, disonorato.*

DEFI'LEMENT, s. [pollution] *imbrattamento, lordamento, contaminamento,* s. m. *macchia, corruzione, bruttura,* s. f.

DEFI'LER, s. *imbrattore, coruttore,* s. m.

DEFI'LING, s. *imbrattamento, contaminamento,* s. m. *polluzione, macchia, lordura,* s. f.

DEFI'NABLE, adj. [that may be defined] *che si può difinire.*

To DEFI'NE [to explain, to give the definition of] *difinire, dar la difinizione di che che si sia.* pref. *difinisco.*

To define [to determine, to decide] *diffinire, decidere, terminare.* pret. *decisi.*

To define a controversy, *diffinire, o decidere una controversia.*

DEFI'NED, adj. *diffinito, deciso, terminato.*

DE'FINITE, adj. *diffinito, determinato, certo, limitato.*

DEFINI'TION, s. [a short and plain declaration or description of the meaning of a word, or the essential attributes of a thing] *diffinizione,* s. f. *un parlare, il quale brevemente, dichiara la quiddità e natura della cosa che si difinisce.*

DEFI'NITIVE, adj. [decisive, positive] *diffinitivo, che difinisce, termina, e risolve, decisivo.*

A definitive sentence, *una sentenza diffinitiva.*

DEFI'NITIVELY, adv. *diffinitamente, espressamente, precisamente, assolutamente.*

DEFLAGRA'TION, s. [burning] *incendio,* s. m.

To DEFLE'CT, [to turn aside, to deviate from a true course] *deviare del cammin dritto o vero; volgersi da un altro lato.*

DEFLE'XION, DEFLE'XURE, s. [a bending down] *piegamento, torcimento,* s. m.

To DEFLO'UR [to rob a virgin of the flower of her virginity, to ravish her] *deflorare tor la virginità, sverginare, violare.*

To deflour a virgin, *deflorare una vergine, sverginarla.*

DEFLO'URED, adj. *deflorato, disflorato, sverginato, violato.*

DEFLO'URER, s. *colui che deflora, o sverginа una vergine.*

DEFLO'URING, s. *sverginamento,* s. m. *il deflorare, lo sverginare.*

DEFLU'XION, s. [the flowing down of humours to any part of the body] *flussione,* s. f.

DEFO'RCEMENT, s. [a law term, a with-holding lands or tenements by force from the right owner] *usurpazione,* s. f.

DEFO'RCER, DEFO'RCIANT, or DEFO'RSOUR, s. [a law term, one who casts another out of possession by force] *usurpatore,* s. m.

To DEFO'RM [to disfigure, to spoil the form of] *sformare, sfregiare, render brutto.*

To deform one's face, *sfregiare l'altrui viso, far il viso brutto.*

DEFO'RMED, adj. *sformato, sfregiato, reso brutto, brutto, difforme.*

DEFO'RMEDLY, adv. *difformatamente, in modo difforme, con difformità.*

DEFO'RMING, s. *disformamento,* s. m. *il disformare.*

DEFO'RMEDNESS, DEFO'RMITY, s. [ugliness] *difformità, deformità, disformità, bruttezza, laidezza,* s. f.

To DEFRA'UD [to cheat or rob, to cozen or beguile] *defraudare, ingannare, truffare, mariolare, disfrodare, giuntare, fraudare, barattare.*

DEFRA'UDED, adj. *defraudato, ingannato, truffato, mariolato, disfrodato, giuntato, fraudato, barattato.*

DEFRA'UDING, s. *il defraudare, trufferia, baratteria, marioleria, fraude,* s. f. *inganno,* s. m.

To DEFRA'Y [to discharge the expences] *spesare, far le spese.*

To defray one, *spesare uno, darsi le spese.*

DEFRA'Y'D, adj. *spesato.*

DEFRA'YING, s. *lo spesare.*

DEFT, adj. [neat, spruce] *bello, vago, galante, venusto, vezzoso, vistoso.*

Deft [brisk, merry] *allegro, giocondo, gajo, giocoso, scherzevole, sollazzevole.*

Deft [proper, fitting] *proprio, adatto, che quadra appunto.*

Deft [ready, dexterous] *atto, destro, agile, pronto.*

DE'FTLY, adv. [neatly, dexterously] *pulitamente, destramente.*

Deftly [in a skilful manner] *maestrevolmente, accortamente.*

DEFU'NCT, adj. [dead] *defunto, morto.*

Defunct, s. [one that is deceased, a dead man or woman] *un defunto, una defunta, un che è morto, una chè è morta.*

DEFU'NCTION, s. [death] *morte, il morire.*

To DEFY' [to challenge] *sfidare, disfidare, bravare.*

I defy you to do it, *vi disfido di farlo.*

He defied death in the middle of dangers, *sprezzò la morte nel mezzo de' pericoli.*

I defy you, do your worst, *a posta vostra, mi burlo di voi.*

DEFY'D, adj. *sfidato, disfidato, bravato.*

DEFYING, s. *il disfidare, lo sfidare.*

DEFYER, s. [a challenger, one that invites to fight] *uno sfidatore, uno che sfida a battaglia.*

DEGE'NERACY, s. *degenerazione, depravazione, corruzione,* s. f.

To DEGE'NERATE [to grow worse] *degenerare, tralignare, essere o diventare dissimile a' genitori, corrompersi.* pret. *corruppi.*

DEGE'NERATE, adj. *degenerato, tralignato, corrotto.*

DEGE'NERATING, s. *degenerazione, depravazione,* s. f. *il degenerare, il tralignare.*

DEGE'NEROUS, adj. [degenerated] *degenerante, tralignante, che degenera, che traligna.*

Dangerous [base, vile] *basso, abbietto, vile, servile.*

Degenerous practices, *azioni basse, e vili.*

A degenerous soul, *un' anima abbietta, o servile.*

DEGRADA'TION, s. [a degrading] *digradazione,* s. f. *digradamento,* s. m. *il digradare.*

To DEGRA'DE [to put out of office, estate, degree, or dignity] *degradare, e digradare, privar della dignità, officio, grado, o beni.*

To degrade a priest, *degradare un prete, quando per alcun misfatto è privato de' privilegi chericali.*

To degrade one's self, *derogare.*

DEGRA'DED, adj. *degradato.*

DEGRA'DING, s. *digradamento,* s. m. *digradazione,* s. f. *il digradare.*

DEGRE'E, s. [any state which is ascending and descending] *grado,* s. m.

Degree [in mathematicks, is the 360th part of a circle] *grado, termine matematico, ed è la 360 parte d'un circlo.*

A degree of longitude, or of latitude, *grado di longitudine, o di latitudine.*

A degree of kindred [consanguinity] *grado, misura di vicinanza o lontananza di parentado.*

Degree [in physick, is the vehemence or slackness of the hot or cold quality of any mixed body] *grado, secondo i medici, è participazione di caldo o di freddo manifesta nel soggetto nel quale ella opera.*

A degree of heat or cold, *grado di caldezza, o di freddezza.*

To take one's degrees in a university, *prendere i gradi in una università.*

By degrees, *a grado a grado, grado per grado, successivemente, a poro a poro.*

To the highest degree, *in sommo grado.*

To DEHO'RT [to advise to the contrary, to dissuade] *sconsigliare, dissuadere, distorre, svolgere, stornare.* pret. *dissuasi, svolsi.*

DEHORTA'TION, s. *dissuasione,* s. f. *il dissuadere.*

DEHO'RTED, adj. *sconsigliato, dissuaso, svolto, distorto, stornato.*

DE'ICIDE, s. [death of our blessed Saviour] *deicidio, morte del nostro Signore.*

To DEJE'CT [to cast down, to afflict] *abbattere, opprimere, avvilire, sgomentare, sconfortare, affliggere.* pret. *oppressi* pres. *avvilisco.*

To deject one's self, *affliggersi, avvilirsi, sgomentarsi, darsi in preda al dolore.*

DEJE'CTED, adj. *abbattuto, oppresso, mesto, afflitto; sconsolato, amgosciato, sgomentato.*

DEJE'CTEDLY, adv. *afflittamente, sconsolatamente.*

DEJE'CTION, s. *mestizia, afflizione, malinconía,* s. f. *dolore, smarrimento, sgomentamento, sgomento,* s. m.

Dejection [evacuation of the excrements] *evacuazione degli escrementi.*

DEIFY'D, adj. *deificato, annoverato fra gl' Iddii.*

To DEIFY' [to make a God, or adore as a God] *deificare, annoverar fra gl' Iddii.*

DEIFY'ING, s. *deificazione,* s. f. *il deificare.*

To DEIGN, v. n. [to vouchsafe, to think worthy] *degnarsi, creder degno.*

To deign, v. a. [to grant, to permit] *concedere, accordare, permettere.*

DE'ISM, s. [is the belief of those, who denying all revealed religion, acknowledge only natural] *deismo,* s. m. *l'opinione di coloro che non credono che un Dio.*

DE'IST, s. [one who adheres to deism] *deista,* s. m.

DE'ITY, s. [the nature and essence of God, Godhead] *Deità,* s. f. *la divina natura di Dio.*

A deity [a fabulous God] *una Deità, un Nume.*

DELA'TOR, s. [informer, accuser] *delatore,* s. m. *colui, che riferisce in giudizio gli altrui falli, spia.*

DELA'Y, s. [the act of putting off] *indugio, ritardo,* s. m. *dilazione, dimora, tardanza,* s. f.

To use delays, *mandare in lungo.*

To delay [to put off from day to day] *indugiare, tardare, intertenersi, mandar in lungo, prolungare, differire, prorogare, allungare.* pres. *differisco.*

To delay time, *indugiare, dar tempo.*

To delay in judgment, *defferire una sentenza.*

DELA'YED, adj. *indugiato, tardato, trattenuto mandato in lungo, prolungato, differito, allungato.*

DELA'YER, s. *indugiatore, musone, tardante, tentennome,* s. m.

DELAY'ING, s. *irresoluzione, tardanza,* s. f. *tardamento, indugio,* s. m.

DELE'CTABLE, adj. [pleasant] *dilettabile, dilettevole, grato, delizioso, piacevole.*

DELE'CTABLENESS, s. *dilettabilità, dilettanza,* s. f. *dilettamento, diletto,* s. m.

DELE'CTABLY, adv. *dilettábilmente, con diletto, dilettevolmente, piacevolmente.*

DELECTA'TION, s. [delight, pleasure] *dilettazione, dilettanza,* s. f. *dilettamento, diletto, piacere, contento,* s. m.

DE'LEGACY, *v.* Delegation.

DE'LEGATE, adj. *delegato, deputato.*

A judge-delegate, *un giudice delegato.*

Delegate, s. [one to whom authority is committed from another to handle and determine matters] *un delegato, un deputato.*

To DE'LEGATE [to appoint, by extraordinary commission, judges to hear and determine a particular cause] *delegare, deputare.*

DE'LEGATED, adj. *delegato, deputato.*

DELEGA'TION, s. [an appointment of delegates] *delegazione commissione di delegato, deputazione, procura,* s. f.

DELF, or DELVE, s. [a mine] *una mina, una miniera.*

DELIBA'TION, s. [tasting] *delibazione,* s. f. *assaggiamento,* s. m.

Delibation [a ceremony in ancient sacrifices] *sacrificio,* s. m.

DELI'BERATE, adj. [advised, prudent, wary] *avvisato, cauto, destro, accorto, prudente, circospetto, savio.*

To DELI'BERATE [to weigh in the mind, to consult, to debate] *deliberare, risolvere, consultare, esaminare, vedere, pensare, considerare.*

DELI'BERATED, adj. *deliberato, risoluto, consultato, esaminato, visto, pensato, considerato.*

Deliberated [premeditated] *premeditato, a bella posta, pensatamente, a bello studio.*

DELI'BERATELY, adv. [advisedly] *avvisatamonte, con giudicio, maturamente, cautamente, destramente.*

Deliberately [on purpose] *deliberatamente, con deliberazione, con animo risoluto, a bello studio, pensatamente.*

DELIBERA'TION, s. [the act of deliberating] *deliberazione, consulta, risoluzione, determinazione,* s. f.

To take a thing into deliberation, *metter che che si sia in deliberazione o in consulta, deliberare di che che si sia.*

DELI'BERATIVE, adj. *deliberativo.*

DE'LICACY, s. [delicateness] *delicatezza, morbidezza, delizia, pulitezza, nettezza,* s. f.

Delicacy, s. [daintiness] *ghiottornia, cibo o vivanda squisita.*

Delicacy, s. [effeminancy, womanhood] *effemminatezza, far donnesco.*

DE'LICATE, adj. [dainty, neat, nice] *delicato, delizioso, squisito, eccellente.*

Delicate [fine] *bello, grato, ameno, delizioso.*

Delicate weather, *un bel tempo.*

A delicate bird, *un bell' uccello.*

A delicate place to live in, *un soggiorno bello, grato, ameno.*

Delicate [effeminate] *delicato, morbido, voluttuoso, effeminato.*

DE'LICATELY, adv. [curiously] *delicatamente, ingegnosamente, con arte, con maestria.*

Delicately [deliciously] *delicatamente, deliziosamente, amenamente.*

DE'LICATENESS, s. [delicacy] *delicatezza, morbidezza, delizia, nettezza, pulitezza,* s. f.

DE'LICES, s. pl. [pleasures] *piaceri, delizie.*

DELI'CIOUS, adj. [pleasant, sweet, charming] *delizioso, grato, gustoso, ameno, esquisito, delicato.*

DELI'CIOUSLY, adv. *deliziosamente, grata mente, gustosamente, amenamente, delicatamente.*

DELI'CIOUSNESS, s. *delizie, morbidezze, delicatezze, voluttà, piaceri.*

DELI'GHT, s. [pleasure, joy, content] *delizia, vaghezza,* s. f. *contento, gusto, piacere, diletto, divertimento, passatempo,* s. m.

I have no other delight but musick, *non ho altra vaghezza che di musica.*

To take delight in a thing, *dilettarsi, aver diletto, prender diletto in che che si sia.*

To DE'LIGHT [to afford delight] *dilettare, apportar diletto, ricreare, piacere.*

Musick delights me very much, *la musica mi diletta molto.*

To delight [to take pleasure in] *dilettarsi, prender diletto, amare.*

He delights very much in painting, *si diletta molto della pittura.*

I delight in hunting, *amo la caccia.*

The orange tree delights in hot and sunny places, *l'arancio ama i luoghi caldi e aprichi.*

DELI'GHTED, adj. *dilettato.*

I was much delighted with it, *vi presi gran piacere, mi piacque molto.*

DELI'GHTFUL, adj. [agreeable, pleasant] *dilettevole, delizioso, ameno, piacevole, grato, gustoso.*

DELI'GHTFULLY, adv. *dilettevolmente, deliziosamente, amenamente, piacevolmente, gustosamente.*

DELI'GHTFULNESS, s. *delizia, bellezza,* s. f. *contento, piacere,* s. m.

DELI'GHTSOME, *v.* Delightful.

DELI'GHTSOMNESS, *v.* Delightfulness.

To DELI'NEATE [to draw the first draught

draught of a thing] *delineare, disegnar con linee.*

DELI'NEATED, adj. *delineato.*

DELINEA'TION, s. [rough draught] *delineazione*, s. f. *schizzo*, s. m.

DELI'NQUENCY, s. [offence] *delitto, misfatto*, s. m. *colpa, offesa*, s f.

DELI'NQUENT, s. [criminal, offender] *un delinquente, un criminale, un malefattore.*

DELI'QUIUM, s. [swooning] *deliquio, svenimento, mancamento*, s. m.

To DE'LIRATE [to be light-headed] *delirare, esser fuor di se, aver perduto il cervello.*

DELI'RATION, s. [doting, the state of being beside one's self] *delirio*, s. m. *il delirare, l'esser fuor di se.*

DELI'RIOUS, adj. [light-headed, raving, doting] *delirio, pazzo, fuor del senno.*

DELI'RIUM, s. [dotage, raving] *delirio*, s. m.

To DELI'VER [to put into one's hands] *consegnare, dare in guardia o in custodia, dar nelle mani, commettere.* pret. *commisi.*

To deliver something to one, *consegnare che che si sia ad uno.*

Deliver [a word used by highwaymen] *date la borsa.*

To deliver into one's power or possession, *dare in potere o nelle mani.*

He was delivered into the hands of the enemies, *egli fu dato in potere o messo nelle mani degli nemici.*

To deliver [to make restitution] *restituire.* pres. *restituisco.*

To deliver an errand, *fare un messaggio.*

To deliver up, *rassegnare, consegnare, dare in podestà, restituire.* pres. *restituisco.*

To deliver up [to yield] *cedere.*

To deliver up [to betray] *tradire.* pres. *tradisco.*

To deliver [to speak out in discourse] *parlare, discorrere, esprimere, spiegare.*

To deliver a sermon handsomely, *pronunciare una predica con facondia.*

He delivers himself well, *egli parla, o discorre bene, con molta facondia.*

To deliver [to free] *deliberare, e deliverare. liberare, salvare.*

To deliver one from bondage, *deliberare uno di schiavitù, metterlo in libertà.*

To deliver one from an imminent danger, *liberare alcuno da qualche imminente pericolo.*

To deliver a woman in labour, *assistere ad una donna nel parto, levar il parto.*

DELI'VERANCE, s. [setting free, release] *diliveranza, e deliberanza, liberazione, libertà*, s. f.

Deliverance of a woman with child, *parto*, s. m.

To wage deliverance [to give security that a thing shall be delivered] *dar sicurtà per il rendimento di che che si sia.*

DELI'VERED, adj. *consegnato*, v. To deliver.

DELI'VERER, s. *liberatore*, s. m. *liberatrice*, s. f.

DELI'VERY, s. [the act of delivering] *il consegnare, rendere, dare, liberamento*, s. m. *liberazione*, s. f.

Delivery [in speaking] *facondia*, s. f.

To have a handsome delivery, *aver una bella facondia.*

He has no good way of delivery, *egli non s'esprime bene, egli non è facondo nel suo discorso.*

DELL, s. [a pit, a valley] *luogo profondo; valle.*

To DELU'DE [to beguile, to deceive] *deludere, diludere, beffare, schernire, ingannare, truffare.* pret. *delusi, dilusi.* pres. *schernisco.*

DELU'DED, adj. *deluso, diluso, beffato, schernito, ingannato, truffato.*

DELU'DER, s. *ingannatore, truffatore, truffiere, furbo*, s. m.

DELU'DING, s. *delusione, e dilusione, truffa, furberia*, s. f. *inganno*, s. m.

DELVE, s. Ex a delve of coals [a quantity of coals digged in the mine or pit] *la quantità di carbone cavata nella miniera.*

Delve, s. [a ditch, a pitfal, a den] *fosso, cava, caverna, antro, buco profondo e largo nel terreno, in cui la gente corre rischio di cadere.*

To DELVE [to dig] *zappare, vangare.*

DE'LVED, ad. *zappato, vangato.*

DE'LVER, s. *zappatore*, s. m.

DE'LUGE, s. [inundation, general flood] *diluvio*, s. m. *trabocco smisurato di pioggia.*

To DE'LUGE [to drown] *diluviare, piovere trabocchevolmente, inondare.*

DE'LUGED, adj. *diluviato, inondato.*

DE'LVING, s. *il zappare.*

DELUSION, s. [cheat, deceit, imposture] *delusione, dilusione, furberia*, s. f. *inganno*, s. m.

DELU'SIVE, or DE'LUSORY, adj. [apt to delude] *ingannevole, ingannatore, fraudolente.*

DEMAGO'GUE, s. [a ring leader of the rabble] *caporione, capo di molta canaglia, capitano di gentaglia.*

DEMA'INE, or DEME'SNE, s. *dominio, patrimonio*, s. m. *signoria, jurisdizione, proprietà*, s. f.

The king's demaine, *il dominio, o patrimonio del re.*

DEMA'ND, s. [petition, claim] *domanda, e dimanda, richiesta*, s. f.

To yield one's demands, *concedere l'altrui richiesta.*

What's your demand? *che domandate?*

Which I promise to pay upon demand, *che prometto di pagare a sua richiesta.*

In full of all demands, *in saldo.*

Demand [question] *domanda, questione, interrogazione*, s. f.

To DEMA'ND [to ask] *domandare, dimandare, interrogare, chiedere, richiedere.* pret. *richiesi, chiesi.*

To demand a question, *domandare un quesito, fare una domanda.*

To demand one to wife, *domandare una figlia in matrimonio.*

To demand counsel of one, *domandare o chieder consiglio d'uno, consigliarsi con uno.*

To demand [to lay claim to] *richiedere, domandare, addimandare.*

To demand a prisoner of war, *addimandare un prigioniero di guerra.*

To demand [to require] *domandare, esigere.*

To demand a debt, *domandare, o esigere un debito.*

DEMA'NDABLE, adj. [that may be demanded, requested, asked for] *domandabile; che si può domandare.*

DEMA'NDANT, s. [the prosecutor in a real action] *attore*, s. m. *attrice*, s. f. *termine legale.*

DEMA'NDED, adj. *domandato.* v. To demand.

DEMA'NDING, s. *domandagione, e ditmandagione*, s. f. *domandamento, e dimandamento*, s. m. *il domandare.*

To DEMEAN ONE'S SELF [to carry or behave one's self] *comportarsi, portarsi, procedere.*

If you demean yourself well, *se vi porterete bene.*

DEME'ANOUR, s. [behaviour] *portamento, procedere*, s. m.

Good or bad demeanour, *buono, o cattivo partamento, o procedere.*

To DEME'NTATE [to make mad] *far perder il cervello, fare impazzire.*

DEME'NTATED, adj. *impazzito, divenuto pazzo.*

DEME'RIT, s. [that which makes one worthy of blame or punishment] *demerito, misfatto*, s. m. *colpa*, s. f.

He shall be punished according to his demerit, *sarà punito secondo il suo demerito.*

To DEMERIT [to do a thing worthy of punishment] *demeritare, contrario di meritare.*

D'EMI [a word used in composition, which signifies half] *mezzo semi.*

A demi-God, *un semideo.*

A demi-cannon, *un mezzo cannone.*

DEMIGRA'TION, s. [the act of removing or shifting quarters or dwellings] *cangiamento d'abitazione o di luogo.*

DEMI'SE, s. [a law term for the death or decease of a king] *morte, termine legale, dicesi solamente de' re o principi grandi.*

To DEMISE [to farm, to let] *affittare, dare ad affitto, allogare, dare a pigione per un certo numero d'anni.*

To demise by will, *lasciare in testamento.*

DEMISED, *affittato, allogato, lasciato.*

DEMISSION, s. [a letting or casting down]. *calata, inchinata, sommessione*, s. f.

DEMO'CRACY, s. [popular government] *democrazia*, s. f. *governo popolare.*

DEMOCRA'TICAL, adj. [popular] *democratico, popolare.*

To DEMO'LISH [to pull or throw down] *demolire, atterrare, abbattere, smantellare, rovinare, distruggere.* pres. *demolisco.* pret. *distrussi.*

DEMO'LISHED, adj. *demolito, atterrato*

terrato, abbattuto, rovinato, distrutto.

DEMO'LISHER, s. *distruttore*, s. m. *colui che demolisce, o atterra.*

DEMO'LISHING, } s. *il demolire, de-*
DEMOLI'TION, } *molizione, destruzione*, s. f.

DE'MON, s. [an evil spirit, the devil] *demonio, e dimonio, diavolo*, s. m.

DEMONI'ACAL, } s. [a man or wo-
DEMO'NIACK, } man possessed of the devil] *un demoniaco, un indemoniato, una demoniaca, un' indemoniata.*

DEMO'NIAN, adj. [devilish] *diabolico.*

DE'MONSTRABLE, adj. [that may be demonstrated] *dimostrabile, che si può dimostrare.*

DE'MONSTRABLY, adv. *chiaramente, dimostrativamente, visibilmente.*

To DE'MONSTRATE [to show plainly, to prove evidently] *dimostrare, manifestare, far palese, dichiarare, provare.*

DE'MONSTRATED, adj. *dimostrato, manifestato, dichiarato, provato.*

DEMONSTRA'TION, s. [a proof founded on self-evident principles] *dimostrazione, dimostragione*, s. f. *prova evidente.*

DE'MONSTRATIVE, adj. [which serves to demonstrate, evident] *dimostrativo, che dimostra, evidente, convincente.*

DE'MONSRATIVELY, adv. *dimostrativamente, chiaramente, visibilmente.*

DEMONSTRA'TOR, s. *dimostratore*, s. m.

DEMU'LCENT, adj. [softening, mollifying, assuasive] *emolliente, molcente, che molce, che rende morbido, che rammorbidisce.*

DEMU'RE, adj. [affectedly grave, reserved, bashful] *ritroso, contegnoso, grave, serio, serioso, modesto.*

DEMU'RELY, adj. *ritrosamente, gravemente, seriosamente, modestamente.*

DEMU'RENESS, s. *contegno*, s. m. *gravità, serietà, aria grave e contegnosa.*

To DEMU'RR [a law term, to put in objections or doubts to put off a suit] *allegare qualche eccezione per mandare in lungo un processo, termine legale.*

To demurr [to delay] *indugiare, differire, prolungare, mandare in lungo.*

DE'MURRER, DEMU'R, or DEMU'RRAGE, s. [a pause upon a point of difficulty in any action] *dilazione, cunta*, s. f. *indugio, ritardamento*, s. m.

DEN, s. [cave] *tana, cava, caverna, grotta, spelonca*, s. f. *antro*, s. m.

DENA'Y, } s. [denying, refusing]
DENI'AL, } *rifiuto, niego, ricusamento*, s. m. *ripulsa, esclusione, negativa, negazione*, s. f.

DE'NIER, s. [a French copper coin] *un danajo, un picciolo.*

Denier, s. [he that denies] *rifiutatore*, s. m. *rifiutatrice*, s. f. *quello che nega, o rifiuta.*

To DE'NIGRATE [to blacken] *annerire, render nero.*

DENIGRA'TION, s. [a blackening or making black] *l'annerire, il render nero.*

DE'NIZEN, or DE'NISON, s. [a foreigner enfranchised by the king's charter, and made capable of bearing any office, purchasing and enjoying all privileges, except inheriting lands by descent] *un forestiere matricolato per lettere patenti del rè, per mezzo delle quali è reso capace d'esercitare offici, comprare, e godere i privilegi de' nativi del paese, eccetto che non può ereditare beni stabili.*

To DENO'MINATE [to give name to] *denominare, nominare, dar il nome.*

DENOMINATED, adj. *denominato, nominato.*

DENOMINA'TION, s. [name, appellation] *denominazione*, s. f. *nome*, s. m.

DENOMINA'TOR, of a fraction [in arithmetick, is that part of the fraction which stands below the line of separation, which always tells you into how many parts the integer is supposed to be divided] *dinominatore, denominatore*, s. m. *termine aritmetico.*

DENOTA'TION, s. [mark] *segno*, s. m. *nota*, s. f.

To DENO'TE [to mark, to signify] *denotare, e disnotare, significare.*

To DENO'UNCE [to declare] *denunziare, e dinunziare, protestare, notificare, dichiarare, far sapere.*

To denounce war, *denunziare, dichiarare la guerra.*

DENO'UNCED, adj. *denunziato, e dinunziato, protestato, notificato, dichiarato.*

DENOUNCER, s. [one that declares some menace] *colui che dichiara una minaccia.*

DENO'UNCING, or DENUNCIA'TION, s. *denunziazione, e dinunziazione, dichiarazione*, s. f.

DENSE, adj. [thick] *denso, spesso, contrario di raro e poroso.*

DENSITY, s. [thickness] *densità, spessezza*, s. f.

DENT, s. [a notch about the edges] *dente*, s. m. *tacca*, s. f. *dentello*, s. m.

To DENT, verb act. *dentare, intacca.*

DE'NTAL, s. [a kind of fish] *dentice*, s. m. *sorta di pesce.*

DE'NTED, adj. *dentato, intaccato.*

DE'NTELS, or DE'NTICLES, s. in architecture [members of the Ionic cornice square, and cut out at convenient distances, which give it the form of a set of teeth] *dentelli*, s. m. plur. *ornamenti a guisa di denti, che vanno sotto la cornice.*

DE'NTRIFICE, s. [a powder to cleanse the teeth] *polvere da pulire i denti.*

DENTI'TION, s. [the time when children breed their teeth] *il tempo nel quale i fanciulli cominciano a mettere i denti.*

To DENU'DATE [to divest, to strip] *spogliare, snudare.*

To DENU'DE [to strip, to make naked] *spogliare, snudare, render nudo.*

DEUNCIATION, s. [the act of denouncing; a publick menace] *dichiarazione di guerra; minaccia pubblica.*

To DENY' [not to own] *negare, dir di no.*

I deny it, *lo nego.*

To deny [to refuse, not to grant] *negare, rifiutare, ricusare.*

Do not deny me that favour, *non mi negate questo favore.*

To deny [to renounce] *rinunziare, rinegare.*

To deny the faith, *rinegar la fede.*

To deny one's self [when any body comes to speak to, or see one] *far dire che uno non è in casa.*

He denies himself no pleasure, *non si priva di nessun piacere.*

Why should any one deny himself that satisfaction? *perchè non darsi quest a ricreazione?*

DENY'D, adj. *negato, ricusato, rifiutato.* v. To deny.

DENY'ING, s. *negamento*, s. m. *il negare, rifiuto*, s. m. *negativa*, s. f.

To DEOBSTRU'CT [to open, speaking of the pores of the body] *aprire, parlando de' pori del corpo.*

DEOBSTRU'CTED, adj. *aperto.*

DEO'BSTRUENT MEDICINES [are those which open obstructions] *medicine aperitive.*

DE'ODAND, s. a horse, cart, &c. [whereby a man is killed, which being forfeited to the king, belongs to the lord almoner, to bestow in deeds of charity] *così vien chiamato secondo la legge d'Ingilterra, un cavallo, un carro, e simili, che ha ammazzato qualche persona, e che essendo confiscato per il rè, se ne distribuisce il prezzo a' poveri dal suo elemosinario.*

DEOSCULA'TION, s. [the act of kissing] *il baciare, l'atto del baciare; bacio.*

To DEPA'INT [to make the representation of any story, passage, or thing with a pen] *dipignere, rappresentare per via di colori la forma e figura d'una cosa.* pret. *dipinsi.*

DEPA'INTED, adj. *dipinto, rappresentato.*

He depainted Cupid in a net, *dipense Cupido in una rete.*

To DEPA'RT [to go away from a place] *partire, andar via.*

To depart [to go out] *uscire.*

To depart the house, *uscite, o andate via di qui.*

To depart [to quit this life] *uscir di vita, morire.*

To depart from other mens opinions, *dissentire, o discordare dall' opinione degli altri.*

To depart from one's resolution *metter da banda una resoluzione, mutar pensiero, cangiar consiglio.*

To depart from one's religion, *abbandonare la sua religione.*

I am loth to depart from you, *mi rincresce di lasciarvi, non mi basta l'animo di separarmi da voi.*

To depart with a thing, *desistere, o tralasciare un affare.*

DEPA'RT, s. [the act of going away] *partenza, dipartita; l'atto del partire, dell' andar via.*

Depart [death] *morte, il morire, partenza da questa vita.*

Depart, *vocabolo chimico* [an operation so named, because the particles of silver are departed or divided from gold] *separazione*; *il separare chimicamente l'argento dall' oro.*

DEPA'RTED, adj. *partito*, v. To depart.

He is departed this life, *è uscito di vita, è morto.*

DEPA'RTER, s. [an artist who purifies and parts gold and silver from the worse sort] *un affinatore.*

DEPA'RTMENT, s. [separate allotment; business assigned to a particular person] *spartimento*; *affare separato*; *faccenda assegnata particolarmente ad uno.*

DEPA'RTING, } s. [a going away] DEPA'RTURE, } *partenza*, s. f.

Departure [death] *la morte, il transito, l'atto del morire.*

Departure in spite of the court [is when the defendant appears to the action brought against him, and makes default afterwards] *contumacia*, s. f.

To DEPA'STURE, verb neut. *pascolare, pascere.*

To DEPA'UPERATE [to make poor] *render povero, impoverire.*

To DEPE'ACH [to acquit] *assolvere.*

DEPECULA'TION, s. [a robbing of the prince or commonwealth] *ruberia che si fa al principe o ad una repubblica, peculato.*

To DEPE'ND [to have a dependance, or to proceed from] *dipendere, è dependere, derivare, aver l'essere, trar l'origine.*

To depend upon a man, *far capitale, confidarsi, aver confidenza in una persona.*

I depend upon you, *io fo capitale, io mi confido in voi, mi fido a voi.*

I'll do it, you may depend upon it, *assicuratevi, siate pur sicuro, che lo farò.*

He has little to depend upon, *la sua fortuna è ben mediocre, non ha molto da poter sussistere.*

To depend of, *consistere.*

To depend [to hang on, speaking of a suit at law] *esser pendente, parlando d'una lite.*

DEPE'NDANCE, or DEPE'NDENCY, s. [a relation or subjection to] *dependenza, derivazione*, s. f.

My whole dependance is on you, *in voi solo confido, in voi solo ho messo ogni mia fiducia.*

DEPE'NDANT, s. *un dependente, un partigiano, un seguace.*

DEPE'NDENT, adj. [dependent] *dependente, che depende.*

DEPE'NDING, adj. [as a suit at law] *pendente, indeciso, parlando d'una lite.*

It has been long depending, *è un pezzo che dura.*

To DEPI'CT [to paint, to portray] *dipingere, far pitture.*

To depict [to describe to the mind] *descrivere alla mente, dipingere o rappresentare all' imaginazione.*

DEPI'CTED, adj. [represented] *dipinto, rappresentato.*

DE'PILATORY, adj. [that makes the hair fall] *depilatorio, che fa cadere i capelli.*

A depilatory, s. *un depilatorio, medicamento che fa cadere i capelli.*

DEPLO'RABLE, adj. [to be lamented] *deplorabile, degno d'esser deplorato, lagrimevole.*

His condition is deplorable, *egli è in uno stato deplorabile.*

DE'PLORATE, adj. [lamentable, hopeless] *lamentevole, da compiangersi, miserabile.*

DEPLORA'TION, s. [bewailing] *lamentanza, lamentazione*, s. f.

To DE'PLORE [to bewail] *deplorare, plorare, compiangere, lamentare*, pret. *compiansi.*

I deplore your condition, *deploro il vostro stato.*

DEPLO'RED, adj. *deplorato, compianto, lamentato.*

DEPLO'RING, s. *il deplorare, il compiangere.*

To DE'PONE [to give evidence] *deporre, assicurare, avverare, testificare.*

DEPO'NENT, s. [witness] *testimonio*, s. m. *quello, o quella che depone in giudizio.*

Déponent, adj. [term of Latin grammar] *deponente, termine gramaticale.*

A deponent verb, *un verbo deponente.*

To DEPO'PULATE [to unpeople] *dipopolare, votar di popolo le città, e le provincie, spopolare.*

To depopulate [to spoil, to lay waste] *desolare, e disolare, dipopolare, render disabitato, distruggere*, pret. *distrussi.*

DEPO'PULATED, adj. *dipopolato, spopolato, desolato, distrutto.*

DEPO'PULATING, s. *il dipopolare.*

DEPOPULA'TION, s. [laying waste] *disolamento*, s. m. *disolazione, rovina*, s. f.

DEPO'PULATOR, s. [a dispeopler, a destroyer of mankind] *spopolatore*; *distruttore della spezie umana.*

To DE'PORT [to demean] one's self, *comportarsi, portarsi, procedere.*

DE'PORT, } s. [behaviour, carDE'PORTMENT, } riage] *portamento, modo particolar d'operare, condotta*, s. f. *procedere.*

To DEPO'SE [to give evidence as a witness] *deporre, render testimonianza, testificare*, pref. *dipongo, e depongo*, pret. *diposi, e deposi.*

To depose [to turn out of one's office] *deporre, privare alcuno di carica o dignità.*

To depose a king, *deporre un re.*

DEPO'SED, adj. *deposto.*

DEPO'SING, s. *il deporre.*

DEPO'SITARY, s. [one in whose hands a pledge is lodged] *dipositario, e depositario*, s. m. *colui appo'l quale si diposita.*

DEPO'SITE, s. [a thing deposited] *diposito, e deposito*, s. m. *la cosa dipositata.*

To DEPO'SITE [to lay down, or trust a thing with any one] *dipositare, e depositare, porre nelle mani, ed in poter del terzo che che si sia, perch' ei lo salvi e lo custodisca.*

DEPO'SITED, adj. *dipositato, e depositato.*

DEPOSI'TION, s. [what is laid down or deposed by a witness in a court of justice] *diposizione, testimonianza*, s. f.

DEPO'SITORY, s. [the place where any thing is lodged] *deposito*; *luogo dove alcuna cosa è deposta per serbarla a un altro tempo, occasione, e uso.*

DEPRAVA'TION, s. [corruption] *depravazione, e dipravazione, corruzione, alterazione*, s. f.

Depravation of manners, *depravazione di costumi.*

To DEPRA'VE [to spoil, to corrupt] *depravare, guastare, corrompere*, pret. *corruppi.*

DEPRA'VED, adj. *depravato, guastato, corrotto.*

DEPRA'VEDNESS, s. [corruption, taint; vitiated state] *corruttela, depravazione.*

DEPRA'VER, s. *quello che deprava, corruttore, corrompitore*, s. m.

DEPRA'VING, s. *il depravare, depravazione, corruzione*, s. f. *corrompimento*, s. m.

DEPRA'VITY, s. [corruption] *depravità, corruttela, depravazione.*

To DE'PRECATE [to pray against any calamity] *pregare istantemente che una cosa non si faccia o che accada.*

To deprecate God's judgment, *pregar Dio che ci liberi dalla sua ira.*

DEPRECA'TION, s. *preghiera, richiesta, domanda, supplica*, s. f.

To DE'PRECIATE [to cry down the price] *avvilire, abbassare il prezzo, scemar di prezzo.*

DE'PRECIATED, adj. *avvilito.*

To DE'PREDATE [to rob, to pillage] *rubare, mandar a ruba, saccheggiare, depredare, mandare saccomanno.*

To depredate [to spoil, to devour] *guastare, divorare.*

DEPREDA'TION, s. [robbing, spoiling] *depradazione, rovina, preda*, s. f. *guasto*, s. m.

To DEPREHE'ND [to catch one, to take unaware] *sorprendere, pigliar all' improvviso o con violenza.*

To deprehend [to discover, to find out a thing] *scoprire, trovar fuora una cosa.*

DEPREHE'NSIBLE, adj. [that may be conceived] *comprensibile, intelligibile, che si può facilmente comprendere, o capire.*

To DE'PRESS [to press, to weigh down] *coricar per terra, abbassare.*

To depress [to humble] *deprimere, tener sotto, conculcare, abbassare, avvilire*, pref. *avvilisco.*

DEPRE'SSED, adj. *steso per terra, depresso, conculcato, abbassato, avvilito.*

DEPRE'SSION, s. *depressione*, s. f. *conculcamento, avvilimento*, s. m.

The depression of a planet, *la depressione d'un pianeta.*

To DE'PRETIATE, v. To depreciate.

DE'PRIVATION, s. [a bereaving, or taking away] *privazione*, s. f.

To DE'PRIVE [to bereave] *privare, far rimaner senza, dispogliare.*

To deprive one's self of pleasures, *privarsi, astenersi da' piaceri.*

DEPRI'VED, adj. *privato, privo.*

Deprived of sense, *privo di senno.*

DEPRI'VING, s. *privamento*, s. m. *privazione*, s. f.

DEPTH, s. [deepness] *profondità*, s. f.

The depth of the sea, *la profondità del mare.*

The briny depths, *il mare.*

The depth of lace, *la larghezza, o l'ampiezza d'un merletto.*

In the depth of winter, *nel cuor del verno.*

The depth of a battalion or squadron *l'ampiezza d'un battaglione, o d'uno squadrone.*

To DE'PURATE [to purify, to cleanse] *purificare, nettare.*

DEPURA'TION, s. [the cleansing any thing from its excrementitious dregs] *depurazione, purificazione*, s. f.

DEPUTA'TION, s. *deputazione*, s. f.

To DEPU'TE [to send, to appoint] *deputare, e diputare, destinare, ordinare, mandare, delegare.*

DEPU'TED, adj. *deputato, e diputato, destinato, ordinato, mandato, delegato.*

DE'PUTY, s. [a person appointed to represent and act in the place of another] *un deputato, un delegato.*

A lord-deputy [a viceroy] *un viceré.*

A deputy governor, *un luogotenente governatore, un sotto governatore.*

To DERA'CINATE [to pluck or tear up by the roots] *sradicare, sbarbare, svellere dalle radici.*

To DERA'IGN, or DERE'YN [to prove, to justify] *provare, mostrare, far vedere, termine legale.*

To DERE [to hurt] *far del male a qualcuno.*

DE'RELICT, adj. [forsaken] *derelitto, abbandonato.*

DERE'LICTION, s. [a leaving or forsaking] *abbandonamento totale.*

To DERI'DE [to mock] *deridere, schernire, burlare, beffare, dileggiare, dar la soja, berteggiare, beffeggiare*, pres. *schernisco*, pret. *derisi.*

To deride religion, *burlarsi della religione.*

DERI'DED, adj. *deriso, schernito, burlato, beffato.*

DERI'DER, s. *derisore, schernitore*, s. m. *deriditrice, beffatrice, schernitrice*, s. f.

DERI'DING, } s. *derisione, beffa, burla*,
DERI'SION, } s. f. *scherno*, s. m.

DE'RISIVE, adj. [mocking, scoffing] *che beffeggia, che fa beffe, che deride, che burla, che dileggia.*

DE'RIVATION, s. *derivazione*, s. f.

The derivation of a word, *la derivazione, o l'etimologia d'una parola.*

DE'RIVATIVE, adj. [that is derived from another] *derivativo, che deriva d'un altro.*

To DERI'VE [to draw from the original] *derivare, e dirivare, dependere, trarre origine, procedere.*

To derive one thing from another, *far derivare una cosa d'un altra.*

From whence do you derive that word? *donde derivate questa parola?*

DERI'VED, adj. *derivato, proceduto.*

A word derived from a noun, *un verbo derivato d'un nome.*

DERN, adj. [sad, solitary] *mesto, solitario, maninconico.*

Dern [cruel] *crudele, barbaro, inumano, feroce, diro, empio.*

To DE'ROGATE [to lessen, or to take from the worth of any person or thing, to disparage] *derogare, diminuire*, pres. *diminuisco.*

To derogate from one's self, *derogare a se stesso, avvilirsi.*

To derogate from a man's honour or credit, *discreditare un uomo, diminuire la sua riputazione.*

DE'ROGATED, adj. *derogato, diminuito.*

DEROGA'TION, s. *derogazione*, s. f.

DE'ROGATORY, adj. [which tends to derogate] *derogatorio, e dirogatorio, che deroga.*

A derogatory clause, *una clausula derogatoria.*

It is not one jot derogatory to his honour, *ciò non fa torto alcuno alla sua riputazione.*

DE'RVIS, s. [a Turkish priest] *un derviscie, un religioso Turco.*

DE'SART, s. [a wilderness, a large wild part of a country] *deserto, e diserto*, s. m. *luogo solitario, abbondonato per isterilità.*

To live in a desart, *vivere in un deserto.*

DESCA'NT, s. [in musick, the art of composing in several parts] *biscanto*, s. m.

To sing descant, *biscantare, canterellare.*

Descant [a continued discourse] *un lungo discorso, diceria*, s. f.

He made a long descant upon it, *egli fece un lungo discorso sopra ciò, egli si diffuse a lungo sopra ciò.*

Descant [comment] *commento*, s. m. *esposizione, interpretazione, chiosa, glosa*, s. f.

To DESCA'NT [to paraphrase upon words] *commentare, interpretare, glosare.*

To DESCE'ND [to come, to go, to step down] *discendere, e descendere, scendere, calare, venire a basso*, pret. *discesi.*

To descend to particulars, *discendere, o venire alle particularità.*

To descend [to derive one's original from a family] *discendere, trarre origine, e nascimento.*

To descend into one's self, *raccogliersi, ravvedersi.*

I would not descend to speak with him, *non vorrei avvilirmi, o abbassarmi di parlarli.*

DESCE'NDANT, s. [the offspring of an ancestor] *un discendente, colui e colei che discende da un antenato.*

DESCE'NDED, adj. *disceso, descesò, sceso, calato.*

DESCE'NDENT, adj. [falling, sinking, coming down] *che cade, che cala, che vien giù; discendente, che discende.*

Descendent, adj. [proceeding from another of an original or ancestor] *procedere da un antenato, derivante da un altro originale.*

DE'SCENT, adj. [going down] *calata, scesa*, s. f.

To make a descent upon the enemy's country, *fare uno sbarco nel paese nemico.*

Descent, birth, extraction, *nascita, famiglia, schiatta, stirpe*, s. f.

To be of a noble descent, *esser nato di buona famiglia.*

He is of a base descent, *egli è di bassa nascita.*

He came to the crown by lineal course of descent, *pervenne alla corona per diritto di successione.*

To DESCRI'BE [to represent an action or thing in writing or speech] *descrivere, rappresentare, figurare, dipignere*, pret. *descrissi, dipinsi.*

To describe the troubles of the state, *descrivere le agitazioni dello stato.*

I will describe my misery to him, *voglio rappresentargli la mia miseria.*

Pray do you describe him to me, *di grazia vi prego di dipignermelo, o farmi il suo ritratto.*

DESCRI'BED, adj. *descritto, rappresentato, figurato, dipinto.*

DESCRI'BER, s. *quegli che descrive o rappresenta.*

DESCRI'BING, s. *il discrevire.*

DESCRI'ER, s. [a discoverer, a detecter] *scopritore, colui che scorge tosto.*

DE'SCRIPTION, s. *descrizione, rappresentazione*, s. f.

To make an exact description of a country, *fare un' esatta descrizione d'un paese.*

The description of a person, *la descrizione, il ritratto, il carattere d'una persona.*

DESCRY', s. [discovery, thing discovered] *scoperta, cosa scoperta.*

To DESCRY' [to discover afar off, to discover] *scorgere, vedere, discernere, scoprire*, pret. *scorsi, vidi.*

DESCRY'D, adj. *scorto, visto, discernuto, scoperto.*

DESCRY'ING, s. *scoperta, e scoverta*, s. f. *scoprimento, discernimento*, s. m.

DE'SERT, s. [desart, wilderness, solitude, waste country, uninhabited place] *deserto, solitudine, luogo romito, paese sterile, luogo disabitato.*

To DESE'RT [to run away from one's colours] *disertare, parlando de' soldati.*

A great many soldiers deserted, *molti soldati disertarono.*

To desert [to forsake] *lasciare, abbandonare.*

He deserted me in my greatest extremity, *mi lasciò, m'abbandonò nella più grande estremità.*

DESE'RT, s. *merito o demerito.*

Desert [proportional merit, claim to reward] *una certa porzione di merito; pretesa a ricompensa.*

Desert [excellence, right to reward, virtue] *virtù verace.*

DESE'RTED, adj. *disertato, lasciato, abbandonato.*

DESE'RTER, s. [a soldier that goes over to the enemy, or runs away from his colours] *un disertore.*

DE-

il DESE'RTING, s. *disertamento*, s. m. *disertare*.

DESE'RTION, s. *il disertare*.

He was shot for desertion, *egli fu morto per aver disertato*.

DESE'RTLESS, adj. [without merit] *senza merito alcuno*.

DESE'RTOR, *v.* Deserter.

To DESE'RVE [to be worthy either of reward or punishment] *meritare, esser degno di male, o di bene*.

He deserves to be hanged, *merita d'esser impiccato*.

To deserve well of one, *meritar del bene da uno, esser benemerito*.

As every one deserves, *secondo il merito di ciascheduno*.

DESE'RVED, adj. *meritato*.

DESE'RVEDLY, adv. *meritamente, secondo'l merito, a ragione, giustamente, meritevolmente, degnamente*.

DESE'RVING, s. *merito, meritevole di premio*, s. m.

Deserving, adj. *meritevole*; *di merito*.

A very deserving man, *un uomo meritevole, o di merito*.

DESE'RVINGLY, adv. [deservedly] *meritamente, meritevolmente, giustamente*.

To DE'SICCATE [to dry up] *seccare, render secco*.

DE'SICCANTS, s. pl. *medicine o rimedi diseccanti*.

DESICCA'TION, s. [the act of making dry] *seccamento, il seccare*.

DE'SICCATIVE, adj. [of a drying quality] *diseccativo, atto a diseccare*.

DE'SIGN, s. [purpose, project] *disegno, progetto, pensiero*, s. m. *intenzione, intrapresa, volontà*, s. f.

Design [draught] *disegno, disegnamento, termine pittoresco*.

To do a thing through design [or purpose] *fare una cosa a disegno, a posta, a bello studio*.

To have a design upon one, *far disegno sopra uno*.

To DESI'GN [to purpose, to resolve] *disegnare, ordinar nel pensiero, pensare, proporsi, determinare*.

I design to go out of town to-morrow, *disegno, o penso d'andare in villa domani*.

To design [to plot] *macchinare, tramare, insidiare, conspirare*.

To design [to draw] *disegnare, rappresentare, e descrivere con segni e lineamenti*.

To design [to appoint] *disegnare, scegliere, eleggere, destinare*.

DESI'GNED, adj. *disegnato*, *v.* To design.

DESI'GNEDLY, adv. [with design, on purpose] *con disegno, pensatamente, a posta, a bello studio*.

DESI'GNER, s. *disegnatore*, s. m. *disegnatrice*, s. f.

DESI'GNING, s. *disegnamento*, s. m. *il disegnare*.

DESI'GNMENT, s. *disegno, pensiero*, s. m. *intenzione*, s. f.

DESI'RABLE, adj. *desiderevole, desiderabile*.

Desirable [pleasing, delightful] *piacevole, dilettoso*.

DESI'RE, s. [longing, wishing] *desiderio e disiderio, disio, e disio, desire*, s. m. *voglia*, s. f.

I have a great desire to see him, *ho gran desiderio di vederlo*.

He has all things to his heart's desire, *ha tutto quel che desidera*.

Desire [request] *preghiera, domanda, richiesta*, s. f.

My only desire is that you would forbear drinking so much, *non vi domando altro se non che vogliate andar più ritenuto nel bere*.

To DESI'RE [to covet, to wish] *desiderare, e disiderare, aver voglia, appetire*, pref. *appetisco*.

I desire to have the honour to see you, *desidero d'aver l'onore di vedervi*.

To desire a thing earnestly, *desiderare una cosa ardentemente*.

To desire [to pray, to request] *implorare umilmente da uno quel che si desidera, domandare, scongiurare, chiedere*.

I desire you to write to me, *vi prego di scrivermi*.

I desire that kindness of you, *vi domando questo grazia*.

I do not desire it, *non me ne curo*.

To desire [to bid] *ordinare, comandare, dare ordine*.

Did not I desire you to go thither? *non v'ho comandato d'andarvi?*

Desire him to come up, *fatelo salire, diteli che venga su*.

DESI'RED, adj. *desiderato*, *v.* To desire.

DESI'REDLY, adj. *a seconda*.

DESI'RER, s. [one that is eager of any thing] *colui che è molto avido d'alcuna cosa*; *colui che desidera alcuna cosa ardentemente*.

DESI'RING, s. *il desiderare*.

DE'SIROUS, adj. [desiring, wishing for] *desideroso, cupido, avido, vago*.

To be desirous of honour, of riches, *esser desideroso d'onore, di richezze*.

DESI'ROUSLY, adv. *desiderosamente, avidamente, cupidamente*.

To DESI'ST [to leave off] *desistere, tralasciare, lasciare, intermettere, intralasciare*, pret. *intermisi*.

DESI'STANCE, s. [the act of desisting; cessation] *il desistere, il cessare*.

DESI'STING, s. *il desistere, cessamento, tralasciamento*, s. m. *intermissione*, s. f.

DESK, s. *desco, leggio*, s. m.

A quirister's desk, *leggio*, s. m. *strumento di legno sul quale tengono il libro coloro che cantano i divini uffici*.

DE'SOLATE, adj. [forlorn, laid waste] *desolato, rovinato, disabitato, distrutto, rovinato*.

A desolate country, *un paese desolato, o disabitato*.

To make a country desolate, *desolare dipopolare, render disabitato un paese*.

Desolate [solitary] *deserto, abbandonato, solitario*.

Desolate [full of grief] *afflitto, sconsolato*.

To be in a desolate condition, *esser tutto afflitto, o sconsolato*.

To DE'SOLATE [to deprive of i'habitants] *spopolare, desolare*.

DESOLA'TION, s. [ruin] *desolazione, disolazione, rovina, distruzione*, s. f.

Desolation [grief] *afflizione, disperazione; angoscia*, s. f. *dolore, sconforto*, s. m.

DESPA'IR, s. [a passion of the soul which makes it cast off all hopes] *disperazione, e disperagione*, s. f.

To fall into despair, *darsi in preda alla disperazione*.

To DESPA'IR, v. [to be out of all hopes] *disperare; perder la speranza*.

I despair of his life, *dispero, o non ho speranza della sua vita*.

DESPA'IRED OF, adj. *disperato, fuor di speranza*.

DESPA'IRER, s. [one without hope] *colui che dispèra, che ha perduta speranza, che perde speranza*.

DESPA'IRFUL, adj. [hopeless] *disperato, privo di speranza*.

To DESPA'TCH [to send away hastily] *mandar in fretta, spedir via con prestezza*.

To despatch [to send out of the world, to put to death] *ammazzare, uccidere, porre a morte*.

To despatch [to perform a business quickly] *spacciare, terminare con prestezza una faccenda*.

To despatch [to conclude an affair with another] *conchiudere un affare con alcuno*.

DESPA'TCH, s. *fretta*; *condotta, maneggio*; *staffetta*; *messaggier frettoloso*; *messaggio frettoloso*.

DESPERA'DO, s. [a desperate man] *un disperato, un arrabbiato*.

DE'SPERATE, adj. [who is in despair] *disperato, fuor di speranza*.

To be in a desperate condition, *essere in un' estrema disperazione*.

Desperate [dangerous, violent] *disperato, cattivo, pericoloso, furioso, terribile*.

A desperate disease, *una malattia disperata, o pericolosa*.

Desperate diseases require desperate cures, *i mali violenti richiedono non men violenti rimedi*.

A desperate business, *un cattivo negozio*.

A desperate man, *un disperato, un uomo furioso, o violento*.

A desperate attempt, *un colpo da disperato*.

A desperate smoaker, *un gran fumatore di tabacco*.

Desperate, adv. Ex. he is desperate angry, *egli è in grandissima collera*.

DE'SPERATELY, adv. [in despair] *disperatamente, da disperato, da furibondo*.

Desperately [dangerously] *desperatamente, pericolosamente*.

Desperately [madly] *terribilmente, grandemente, in sommo grado*.

He did it despeartely, *lo fece disperatamente, o da disperato*.

To be desperately sick, *esser pericolosamente ammalato, esser in pericolo di morte*.

He

He drinks deſperately, *beve terribil-mente.*

To be deſperately in love with a woman, *eſſer capricciosamente innamorata d'una donna, andar pazzo per una donna.*

De'sperateness, s. [fury] *furia, violenza,* s. f. *ardore,* s m.

Despera'tion, s. [deſpair] *diſperazione,* s. f.

De'spicable, adj. [contemptible] *vile, abbietto, diſprezzabile.*

A deſpicable fellow, *un uomo vile, o abbietto.*

De'spicableness, s. [meanneſs, vileneſs] *viltà, ſpregievolezza.*

De'spicably, adv. *ſordidamente, vilmente.*

Despi'ght, *v.* Deſpite.

Despi'seable, adj [deſpicable] *diſprezzevole, diſprezzabile.*

To Despi'se [to ſlight] *diſprezzare, e diſpregiare, avere o tenere a vile, far poco conto, ſdegnare.*

I deſpiſe all your threatnings, *mi rido delle voſtre minacce.*

Despi'sed, adj. *diſprezzato, diſpregiato, ſdegnato.*

Despi'sing, s. *diſprezzamento, diſpregiamento* s. m.

Despiser, s. *diſpregiatore, diſprezzatore,* s. m.

Despi'te, s. [contempt] *diſprezzo, diſpregio, avvilimento, ſcherno,* s. m.

Deſpite, s. [ſpite] *diſpetto,* s. m. *onta,* s. f.

In deſpite of you, *a diſpetto voſtro, ad onta voſtra.*

In deſpite of me, *mio mal grado.*

Despi'teful, adj. [malicious, full of ſpleen] *diſpettoſo, malizioſo, pien di mal talento.*

Despi'tefully, adv. *diſpettoſamente, con diſpetto, con rabbia, di mal talento, ſdegnoſamente.*

Despi'tefulness, s. [malice, hate, malignity] *triſtizia, odio, malignità, mal talento.*

De'spiteous, adj. [malicious, furious] *pien di diſpettoſa furia.*

To Despo'il [to rob, to ſtrip] *ſpogliare, privare.*

To deſpoil one of his ſubſtance, *ſpogliare uno di tutti i ſuoi beni.*

Despo'iled, adj. *ſpogliato, privato.*

To Despo'nd [to loſe courage, to deſpair, to be dejected] *ſgomentarſi, ſbigottirſi, perderſi d' animo, diſanimarſi.*

He begins to deſpond, *comincia a ſgomentarſi.*

Despo'ndence, or Despo'ndency, s. *ſgomentato, ſbigottimento, ſgomento,* s. m

Despot, s. [a prince or governor in the Ottoman Empire] *deſpoto, o diſpoto principe; o governatore nell' Imperio Ottomano.*

Despo'tical, or Despo'tick, adj. [abſolute, arbitrary] *diſpotico, ſignorile, aſſoluto.*

A deſpotical government, *un governo diſpotico.*

Despo'tically, adv. *diſpoticamente, arbitrariamente, aſſolutamente.*

To rule deſpotically, *governar diſpoticamente.*

Despoticalness, s. [abſolute authority] *autorità aſſoluta*

De'spotism, s. [abſolute power] *potere aſſoluto; deſpotiſmo.*

Despuma'tion, s. in pharmacy, [is the clearing and cleanſing any liquor by letting it boil, ſo as to take off the ſcum] *il chiarificare un liquore col laſciarlo bollire fin tanto che butti fuora la ſchiuma.*

Dese'rt, s. [the laſt courſe at table, as fruits, ſweet meats, &c.] *le frutta.*

To De'stinate, *deſtinare.*

Destination, s. *deſtinazione,* s. f.

To De'stine, [to appoint, to deſign, to order] *deſtinare, deputare, aſſegnare, coſtituire, ſtabilire,* preſ. *coſtituiſco, ſtabiliſco*

Heaven deſtined him for great things, *il cielo ſortillo a gran coſe.*

De'stined, De'stinated, adj. *deſtinato, deputato, aſſegnato, coſtituito, ſtabilito.*

De'stiny, s. [fate] *deſtino, e diſtino, occulto ordinamento d' Iddio, fatto,* s. m. *ſorte,* s. f.

A cruel deſtiny, *crudel deſtino.*

I bewail your deſtiny, *compiango la voſtra ſorte.*

The three deſtinies, *le tre parche, che preſiedono alla vita dell' uomo, ſecondo i poeti.*

De'stiny-Re'aders [fortune tellers] *quelli che predicano la buona, o mala ventura.*

De'stitute, adj. [bereft] *deſtituto, privo, privato.*

Deſtitute of all hopes, *deſtituto, privo d'ogni ſperanza*

Deſtitute [forſaken] *abbandonato, derelitto.*

To leave one deſtitute, *abbandonare, laſciare in naſſo.*

Destitu'tion, s. [leaving, forſaking] *dereliziane,* s. f. *abbandonamento,* s. m.

To Destro'y [to throw down, to ruin, to lay waſte] *diſtruggere, ſtruggere, diſfare, ridurre al niente, conſumare, rovinare.* pret. *diſtruſſi, ſtruſſi, diſfeci.*

To deſtroy a city, *diſtruggere una città.*

To deſtroy one's health, *rovinar la ſalute.*

To deſtroy one's cloaths, *conſumare, logorare, uſare i ſuoi abiti.*

To deſtroy one's ſelf, *ammazzarſi, darſi la morte.*

Destroy'd, adj. *diſtrutto, ſtrutto, diſfatto, conſumato, rovinato, v.* To deſtroy.

Destro'yer, s. *diſtruttore, conſumatore,* s. m.

Destro'ying, s. *diſtruggimento,* s. m. *il diſtruggere, deſtruzione, rovina,* s. f.

Destro'ying, adj. *diſtruttore.*

The deſtroying angel, *l' angelo diſtruttore.*

Destru'ction, s. *diſtruzione, rovina, deſolazione,* s f. *diſfacimento,* s. m.

Destructive, adj. [that which deſtroys; waſteful; cauſing ruin and devaſtation] *diſtruttivo, che cagiona diſtruggimento; ruinoſo; che rovina e diſtrugge.*

Destru'ctor, s. [deſtroyer, conſumer] *diſtruttore; colui che diſtrugge, e rovina*

Desu'etude, s [diſuſe] *diſſuetudine, diſuſanza,* s. f.

Desulto'rious, } adj. [inconſtant,
Desu'ltory, } fickle, mutable] *inconſtante, variabile, mutabile, leggiere, volubile, ſenza metodo o norma.*

To Deta'ch [a term of war, to ſend away a party of ſoldiers upon a particular expedition] *diſtaccare, fare un diſtaccamento di ſoldati.*

Detac'hed, adj. *diſtaccato.*

Detachment, s. *un diſtaccamento di ſoldati*

Deta'il, s. [the particulars, or particular circumſtances of an affair] *particolarità,* s. f.

In detail, *a minuto.*

To Deta'in, [to keep, to withhold] *ritenere, fermare, intrattenere, ſoprattenere.* preſ. *ritengo.* pret. *ritenni.*

To detain one priſoner, *ritenere uno in carcere.*

I will not detain you any longer, *non voglio ritenervi, o trattenervi più lungo tempo.*

To detain [to hinder] *ritenere, impedire.*

You detained me from proceeding any further, *voi m' avete impedito di paſſar oltre.*

Det'ainder, s. [the name of a writ for holding one in cuſtody] *nome d'uno ſcritto con cui ſi continua a tener uno in prigione.*

Deta'ined, adj. *ritenuto, fermato, impedito.*

Deta'iner, s. [he that holds back any one's right; he that detains] *colui che ſi ritiene o ritarda il dritto d' alcuno; colui che ritiene alcuno.*

Deta'ining, s. *ritenimento, ritegno, impedimento,* s. m.

To Dete'ct [to diſcover] *diſcoprire, ſcoprire, diſvelare, ſvelare.*

To detect the fraud, *ſcoprire la ragia o l' inganno.*

Dete'cted, adj. *diſcoperto, ſcoperto, diſvelato, ſvelato.*

Detecting, s. *diſcoprimento, ſcoprimento,* s. m.

Dete'ction, s. [diſcovery] *ſcoperta, e ſcoverta,* s f.

Dete'ntion, s. [detaining, keeping] *ritenzione,* s. f.

To Dete'r [to frighten, to diſcourage one from doing a thing] *ſpaventare, atterrire, ſtornare*

To Dete'rge [to wipe, to rub off] *detergere, mondare, purgare, nettare.*

Detergent, adj. *che netta, che deterge.*

Deteriora'tion, s. [making worſe, ſpoiling] *deteriorazione,* s. f.

Dete'rminable, adj. [which may be determined or decided] *determinabile, che ſi può determinare, ſtabilire, o giudicare.*

To

To DETE'RMINATE, *v.* To determine.

Determinate, adj. [defined, positive] *determinato, preciso.*

DETE'RMINATELY, adv. *determinatamente, precisamente, per l'appunto, positivamente, affirmativamente.*

DETERMINA'TION, s. [a final resolution upon a doing or not doing any action] *determinazione, risoluzione,* s. f. *stabilimento, pensiero,* s. m.

Determination [decision] *determinazione, decisione, conclusione,* s. f.

To DETERMINE [to decide, or judge] *determinare, giudicare, terminare, decidere,* pret. *decisi.*

To determine a business, *terminare un affare.*

To determine a law suit, *terminare un processo o una lite.*

To determine [to design, to purpose] *determinare, disegnare, stabilire, risolvere, far disegno,* pref. *stabilisco.*

DETE'RMINED, adj. *determinato, giudicato, terminato, deciso, v.* To determine.

DETE'RRED, adj. *spaventato, atterrito, sfornato.*

DETE'RSIVE, adj. [of a cleansing nature] *detersivo, astersivo.*

A detersive medicine, *un rimedio detersivo.*

To DETE'ST [to abhor] *detestare, abominare, odiare, abborrire,* pref. *abborrisco.*

To detest vice, *detestare il vizio.*

DETE'STABLE, adj. [to be abhorred] *detestabile, abbominevole, scellerato, da esser detestato.*

DETE'STABLY, adv. *abbominevolmente, d'una maniera detestabile.*

DETESTA'TION, s. [an abhorring, or loathing] *detestazione, abbominazione,* s. f. *orrore,* s. f.

DETE'STING, s. *detestazione,* s. f. *il detestare.*

To DETHRO'NE [to depose a prince, to drive a sovereign prince from his throne] *scacciar dal trono, privar del trono.*

To dethrone a prince, *privare un principe del trono.*

DETHRO'NED, adj. *scacciato, o privato del trono.*

To DETO'RT [to wrest from the original import] *svolgere dal primo volere, dall' intenzione primiera.*

To DETRA'CT [to take from] *detrarre, e detraggere, levare alcuna parte d'un altra, diffalcare.*

To detract [to speak ill, to slander] *detrarre, dir male, offender la fama altrui, mormorare, biasimare.*

To detract of one's neighbour, *mormorare del suo prossimo.*

DETRA'CTED, adj. *detratto, mormorato, biasimato.*

DETRA'CTER, *v.* Detractor.

DETRA'CTING, s. } [slandering] *detrazione, maldicenza, mormorazione,* s. f.
DETRA'CTION, s. }

DETRA'CTOR, s. [slanderer] *detrattore, mormoratore, maldicente,* s. m.

DETRA'CTRESS, s. f. [a censorious woman] *mormoratrice, una donna maldicente.*

DE'TRIMENT, s. [damage, hurt] *detrimento, danno, pregiudizio,* s. m.

DETRIME'NTAL, adj. [hurtful, dangerous] *pregiudicativo, nocivo, pericoloso.*

To DETRU'DE [to thrust down] *detrudere, cacciare in giù,* pret. *detrusi.*

DETRU'DED, adj. *detruso, cacciato in giù.*

DETRU'SION, s. [thrusting down] *il detrudere.*

DEVASTA'TION, s. [a laying waste] *guasto, sarto,* s. m. *rovina, desolazione,* s. f.

DEUCE, s. [two] *due.*

To DEVE'LOP [to disengage from something that enfolds and conceals] *sviluppare, far palese quel che era nascosto.* Pope.

To DEVE'ST [to strip, to deprive of] *svestire, spogliare, privare.*

To devest [to turn out of possession] *spossessare, levar uno dal possesso, termine legale.*

To devest one's self of one's right, *spogliarsi del suo diritto.*

To devest one's self of one's carnal affections, *spogliarsi di tutti gli affetti carnali.*

DEVE'STED, adj. *svestito, spogliato, privato.*

DE'VIATE, adj. [varying from the sense of its primitive] *contrario al senso del suo primitivo, lontano dal senso suo primiero.*

To déviate [to go from, to swerve] *deviare, diviare, traviare, uscir della via, di regola, modo, o ordine.*

To deviate from truth, *allontanarsi dalla verità.*

DEVIA'TION, s. *il deviare.*

DE'VICE, s. [invention, contrivance] *invenzione, maniera,* s. f. *modo, mezzo, spediente,* s. m.

Device [invention, genius] *astuzia, invenzione, sottigliezza,* s. f.

A man full of devices, *un uomo astuto, o arguto.*

DEVICE [the emblem on a shield] *emblema sur uno scudo, divisa.*

DE'VIL, s. [evil spirit] *diavolo,* s. m.

A devil incarnate, *un diavolo incarnato.*

A devil got loose, *un diavolo scatenato.*

Who the devil would have thought it? *chi diavolo l'avrebbe mai creduto?*

To give one's self to the devil, *darsi al diavolo.*

Seldom lies the devil dead in a ditch, *il diavolo non dorme.*

The devil rebukes sin, *il cavallo fa andar la sferza.*

We must needs go when the devil drives, *bisognino fa trottar la vecchia.*

We must give the devil his due, *non bisogna fare il diavolo più nero che non è.*

The devil's bones [dice] *i dadi.*

He is a devil of a man, *egli è un diavolo.*

She is a devil in petticoats, *ella è una vera diavolessa.*

The devil is in him, *egli ha il diavolo addosso.*

DE'VILISH, adj. [of the devil] *diabolico, da diavolo, di diavolo.*

A devilish device, *un' invenzione diabolica.*

A devilish humour, *un umore cattivo o bisbetico.*

A devilish man, *un diavolo, un diavolo incarnato.*

A devilish woman, *una diavola, una diavolessa, una donna riottosa.*

There's some devilish trick or other, *v' è qualche diavoleria nascosta.*

Devilish, adv. *diabolicamente, estremamente, molto.*

He is devilish proud, *è superbo come lucifero.*

Devilish cunning, *astuto come un diavolo.*

DE'VILISHLY, adv. *diabolicamente, perversamente.*

He lies devilishly, *mente come un diavolo.*

DE'VILISHNESS, s. *umore, e azione diabolica.*

DE'VIOUS, adj. [going out of the way, swerving from] *deviante, traviante.*

DE'VISE, s. [motto, conceit] *divisa,* s. f.

Devise [law term, a legacy] *legato, lascio,* s. m.

To DEVISE [to imagine, to invent, to fancy] *divisare, immaginare, disegnare, pensare.*

To devise [to plot, to contrive] *macchinare, tramare, concertare, meditare, formare un disegno.*

To devise [to frame, to fashion] *formare, dar la forma.*

To devise [to consult] *consultare, deliberare.*

To devise [in law, to bequeath, to give or make over lands, &c. by a last will and testament in writing] *legare, lasciare in testamento.*

DEVI'SED, adj. *divisato, concertato, meditato, immaginato, disegnato, pensato, v.* To devise.

DEVI'SER, s. *inventore, autore,* s. m.

DEVI'SING, s. *divisamento,* s. m. *il divisare, v.* To devise.

DEVI'SOR, s. [he that has bequeathed by will his lands to another] *testatore,* s. m. *colui che ha legato ad un' altro i suoi beni per testamento.*

DEVOI'D, adj. [empty, vacant, void] *voto, vacuo, contrario di pieno.* Spenser.

Devoid [without any thing whether good or evil] *senza nulla; che non contien nulla nè ben nè male.*

DEVO'IR, s. [duty] *dovere, debito, obbligo,* s. m.

To pay one's devoirs to one, *riverire, o complimentare alcuno.*

To DEVO'LVE [to fall, to come from one to another, as an estate does] *scadere, cadere, ricadere, venire per via d'eredità,* pret. *caddi, ricaddi.*

The estate devolves to him, *lo stato scade a lui.*

To devolve a trust upon one, *confidare alcuna cosa ad uno, farnelo depositario.*

DEVO'LVED, adj. *scaduto, caduto, ricaduto.*

DEVO'LUTARY, s. [one who claims a benefice becoming void] *devolutario,* s. m.

DEVOLU'TION, s. [passing from one to another] *devoluzione,* s. f.

DEVOTE'E, s. [a bigot, a superstitious hypocrite] *un divoto, un collo torto, un bacchettone, una divota, una spigolistra.*

To DEVO'TE [to vow, to consecrate to God] *votare, botare, dedicare, consacrare.*

To devote one's self to the service of God, *votarsi o consacrarsi al servizio di Dio.*

To devote one's youth to the exercise of arms, *dedicare, applicare, o spendere la sua gioventù al, o nell' esercizio delle armi.*

DEVO'TED, adj. *votato, botato, consarrato, dedicato.*

Devoted [accursed] *maledetto.*

DEVO'TION, s. [piety, religious zeal] *divozione, devozione, pietà,* s. f. *zelo.*

Devotion [service, command, disposal] *divozione, disposizione,* s. f. *cenno, comando,* s m.

He is at my devotion, *egli è a mia disposizione, io ne fo quel che voglio.*

To DEVO'UR [to eat up, to swallow down greedily] *divorare, mangiare con eccessiva ingordigia.*

To devour [to consume, to waste] *divorare, consumare, mangiare, dissipare, spendere, inghiottire,* pret. *spesi,* pres. *inghiottisco.*

DEVO'URED, adj. *divorato, consumato, mangiato, dissipato, speso.*

DEVO'URER, s. *divoratore,* s. m *divoratrice,* s. f.

Devourer [spendthrift] *divoratore, consumatore, scialacquone, scialacquatore.*

DEVO'URING, s. *divoramento,* s. m. *il divorare.*

Devouring, adj. [that devours] *divorante, che divora.*

DEVO'URINGLY, adv. *avidamente, golosamente, ingordamente.*

DEVO'UT, adj. [godly] *divoto, è devoto, che ha divozione, pio, religioso.*

Very devout, *devotissimo, e divotissimo.*

DEVO'UTLY, adv. *divotamente, e devotamente.*

Very devoutly, *divotissimamente, e devotissimamente.*

DEVOU'TNESS, s. [devotion] *divozione, devozione, pietà,* s. f. *zelo,* s. m.

DEUSE, s. [more properly than *deuce,* from *Dusius,* the name of a certain species of evil spirits; devil] *il diáscane, diácine; modo modesto per non nominar il diavolo (molti scrivono* deuce, *in vece di* deuse.)

DEW, s. [vapours of the earth which being exhaled by the heat of the sun, do upon his absence fall down upon the earth again] *rugiada,* s. f. *umore che cade la notte dal cielo.*

DEW-LAP, s. [that part which hangs down the neck of an ox or cow] *giogaja,* s. f. *quella pelle pendente dal collo de' buoi.*

Dew-lap [a lip flaccid with age] *labbro penzolone per soverchia età.*

A dew-snail, *una lumaca.*

Dew-berries, *mori di rovo.*

To DEW [to wet as with dew] *innaffiare o spruzzare leggermente.*

DEWY, adj. [full of dew] *rugiadoso, asperso di rugiada.*

Dewy grass, *erba rugiadosa.*

DE'XTER, adj. [the right, not the left] *il destro; non il sinistro.*

DEXTE'RITY, s. [address, cunning] *destrezza, accortezza, sagacità,* s. f.

DE'XTEROUS, } adj. [cunning, skil-
DE'XTROUS, } ful] *destro, attivo, accorto, sagace.*

DE'XTEROUSLY, adv. *destramente, accortamente, sagacemente.*

DIABE'TES, s. [a disease when one cannot hold one's water] *diabete, diabetica,* s. f.

DIABE'TICAL, adj. [troubled with a diabetes] *diabetico, che patisce di diabete.*

DIABO'LICAL, adj. [devilish, very wicked] *diabolico, da diavolo, di diavolo.*

A diabolical action, *un' azione diabolica.*

DIABO'LICALLY, adv. [devilishly] *diabolicamente, perversamente.*

DIABO'LICK, *v.* Diabolical.

DIACO'DIUM, s. *sciloppo di papaveri.*

DIACO'USTICK, s. [the doctrine of sounds] *la filosofia de' suoni.*

DI'ADEM, s. [an imperial or royal crown] *diadema,* s. m. *era anticamente una fasciuola di tela bianca che portavano in capo i re per contrassegno regio; oggi largamente si piglia per ogni corona reale.*

DIAD'EMED, adj. [adorned with a diadem] *ornato, cinto di diadema.*

DIA'DROM, s. [the time in which any motion is performed] *tempo in cui qualunque moto dura.*

DIA'GONAL, adj. [that goes from corner to corner] *diagonale.*

Diagonal, s. [a line drawn from angle to angle in any figure] *diagonale,* s. f. *linea diagonale.*

DI'AL, or SUN-DI'AL, s. *oriuolo a sole.*

DI'AL-PLATE, s. [that on which hours or lines are marked] *quadrante, quella parte degli oriuoli in cui l'ore o le linee son segnate.*

DIA'LECT, s. [a manner of speaking peculiar to some part of a country] *linguaggio,* s. m. *favella,* s. f.

DIALE'CTICALLY, adv. *dialetticamente.*

DIALE'CTICAL, } adj. [belonging to
DIALE'CTICK, } logick] *dialettico, logicale, loicale.*

Dialectical arguments, *argomenti dialettici o logicali.*

DIALE'CTICK, s. [logick] *dialettica, logica, e loica,* s. f.

DIALECTI'TIAN, s. *dialettico,* s. m. *professor di dialettica.*

DI'ALIST, s. [a constructor of dials] *uno che fa oriuoli da sole.*

DI'ALOGUE, s. [a conference or discourse between two or more parties] *dialogo,* s. m. *discorso di più persone.*

Lucian's Dialogues, *i Dialoghi di Luciano.*

A little, short dialogue, *dialoghetto,* s. m.

To DI'ALOGUE [to make dialogues] *far dialoghi, discorrere insieme.*

DIA'METER, s. [a line which passes through the middle of any figure from one angle to another] *diametro,* s. m. *linea retta che taglia una figura per il mezzo.*

Diameter of a circle [a line which passes through the center of a circle] *diametro, linea che divide il cerchio per mezzo.*

A tree that is six feet diameter, *un albero sei piedi in diametro.*

DIA'METRAL, or DIAME'TRICAL, adj. [belonging to, or that is in the form of a diameter] *diametrale.*

DIAME'TRICALLY, adv. *diametralmente, per diametro.*

Diametrically opposite, *diametralmente opposto.*

DI'AMOND, s. [a precious stone] *diamante,* s. m. *gioja notissima.*

Diamond [at cards] *coppe, cuori, uno de quattro semi del giuoco delle carte.*

To throw or play a diamond, *giuocar coppe, o cuori.*

Diamond cut, *a punta di diamante.*

DI'APASM, s. [a perfumed powder] *diapasme,* s. f. *polvere odorifera.*

DIA'PASON, s. [a term of musick signifying an octave] *diapason,* s. f.

DIAPE'NTE, s. [a fifth in musick] *diapente,* s. f.

DIA'PER, s. [linen cloth wrought with flowers and figures] *biancherie tessute con oro e figure.*

DIAPHANE'ITY, s. [the property of a diaphonous body] *diafanità, trasparenza,* s. f.

DIA'PHANICK, } adj. [transparent,
DIA'PHANOUS, } like glass, that may be seen through] *diafano, trasparente.*

A diaphanous body, *un corpo diafano.*

DIAPAORE'TICK, adj. [causing sweat] *diaforetico, che fa sudare.*

DI'APHRAGM, s. [the midriff] *diaframma, diaflagma, diaflagmate,* s. f. *quel pannicolo che divide per traverso il corpo degli animali, e divide il ventre di mezzo dall' infimo.*

DIARRHOE'A, s. [a flux of the belly] *diarrea,* s. f. *flusso di ventre.*

DI'ARY, s. [journal, day-book] *diario, giornale,* s. m.

DIA'SCORDIUM, s. [an electuary, of which the chief ingredient is the herb Scordium] *diascordio.*

DIATE'SSERON, s. [fourth in musick] *diatesseron.*

DIATRIPI'PERON, s. [a medicine of three sorts of pepper] *sorta di lattovaro dove s'adoprano tutte e tre le maniere de' pepi.*

DIBBLE, s. [a setting tool] *strumento rustico per ficcare i magliuoli o altre piante nella terra.*

DICA'CITY, s. [talkativeness] *ciarleria.*

DIBSTONE, s. [a little stone which children throw at another stone] *sassolino che i fanciulli giuocando gettano ad un altro sasso.*

DICE, s. *dadi, il plurale di.* DIE.

A dice box, *bassolo,* s. m. *quel vaso ove si mettono i dadi in giuocando.*

To set the dice upon one, *ingannare, truffare, mariolare alcuno, farli pagare una cosa più ch' ella non vale.*

To DICE, [to game with dice] *giuocare a' dadi.*

DI'CER, or DICE-PLAYER, s. *giuocator di dadi.*

DI'CKER, s. *ex.* A dicker of leather [a quantity of ten hides] *una decima di cuoi.*

DI'CTATE, s. [rule or maxim delivered with authority] *norma o massima inculcata con autorità.*

To DI'CTATE [to tell another what to write or speak] *dettare, dire a chi scrive le parole appunto ch' egli ha da scrivere.*

To dictate a letter, *dettare una lettera.*

To DI'CTATE, [to deliver to another with authority] *inculcare autorevolmente.*

DICTA'MEN, s. [a thing written by another's instruction] *dettato, dittato, dettame,* s. m.

DI'CTATES, s. [precepts, instructions, rules] *dettami, precetti, insegnamenti, sentimenti, come dell' animo, della coscienza,* &c.

To follow the dictates of reason, *seguitare i dettami, o i precetti della ragione.*

To go contrary to the dictates of one's own conscience, *operare contro i dettami della conscienza.*

DICTA'TOR, s. [a chief ruler among the ancient Romans] *dittatore,* s. m.

DICTA'TORSHIP, s. *dittatura,* s. f. *dignità di dittatore.*

DI'CTIONARY, s. [a book containing a collection of words of a language] *dizionario, vocabolario,* s. m.

DID, *il preterito del verbo,* TO DO.

Did, *serve altresì di segno per l'imperfetto, e preteriti de' verbi inglesi.*

I did love, *amavo, amai, ho amato.*

Did, *è qualchevolta usato per enfasi, come.* I did really love her, *I l'amai veramente, con tutto il cuore.*

DIDA'CTICAL, or DIDA'CTICK, adj. [instructive] *istruttivo.*

DIDA'PPER, s [a dab-chick, a name of a bird] *folaga,* s. f. *uccello aquatico.*

DIDA'SCALICK, adj. [perceptive, didactive] *istruttivo.*

To DI'DDER [to shiver with cold] *tremar di freddo.*

DIE, s. [to play with] *dado,* s. m. *pezzuol d'osso di sei facce quadre con che si giuoca.*

To cog a die, *impiombare un dado, falsificarlo.*

It was within the turn of a die, *poco mancò.*

Die [colour] *tintura, tinta,* s. f. *tinto,* s. m.

A crime of a deeper die, *un delitto atroce, o enorme.*

Die, s. pl. dies, [the stamp used in coinage] *marchio, conio, strumento usato nel coniar monete o medaglie.*

To DIE, verb. neut. *morire, perder la vita, passar all' altra vita.*

Like to die, *vicino a morte, per morire, presso alla morte.*

He was like to die, *fu per morire.*

To die a natural death, *morir di buona morte, o d'una morte naturale.*

To die for love, *morir d'amore.*

Let me die if it be not true, *ch'io possa morire se non è vero.*

When is he to die? [speaking of a malefactor that is to be executed] *quando sarà giustiziato?*

If I was to die for it, *se dovesse costarmi la vita.*

He dies away, *sta morendo, ha la morte in bocca, tien l' anima fra denti.*

To die [speaking of liquors] *sventare, svaporare.*

Don't let your wine die, *non lasciate sventare il vostro vino.*

To DIE [to give a colour] *tignere, e tingere, dar colore.* pret. *tinsi.*

To die black, blue, &c. *tigner nero, turchino,* &c.

DIED, adj. *morto, tinto.*

Died black, *tinto in nero.*

Die-house, *bottega, e luogo dove si tingono i drappi, panni,* &c.

DIER, s. *tintore,* s. m. *che esercita l'arte del tingere.*

A woollen dier, *un tintore di lana.*

A silk dier, *un tintore di seta.*

DIE'SIS, s. [a term in musick, denoting a tone below a semi tone] *diesi,* s. f. *termine musicale.*

DIET, s. [food] *cibo, nutrimento,* s. m.

Diet [strict way of living] *dieta, astinenza di cibo a fine di sanità.*

Diet [an assembly of the States or Princes, or estates] *dieta, assemblea,* s. f.

Diet-drink, *acqua cotta.*

To DIET [to keep to a strict diet] *dietare, tenere a dieta.*

To diet [to provide with diet or food] *nutrire, nutricare uno, darli da mangiare, e da bere.*

To diet [to eat] *mangiare.*

Where do you eat every day? *dove mangiate ogni giorno?*

DI'ETED, adj. *dietato, nutrito, nutricato.*

DI'ETER, s. [one who prescribes rules for eating] *colui che prescrive a un altro i cibi che deve usare.*

DIE'TICK, or DIE'TICAL, adj. [belonging to diet] *di dieta.*

DI'ETING, s. *il dictare, il tenere a dieta.*

To DI'FFER [to be unlike] *differire, variare, esser differente o dissimile.* pres. *differisco.*

This differs very much from that, *questo differisce molto da quello, questo è molto dissimile da quello.*

He often differs from himself, *egli si contraddice spesso.*

They differ a little, *sono alquanto differenti, o dissimili.*

We differ in this, *noi siamo di contrario parere in ciò.*

We shall not differ, *ci aggiusteremo.*

DI'FFERENCE, s. [diversity, disparity] *differenza, diversità, varietà, disparità, disuguaglianza,* s. f.

Difference [dispute, quarrel] *differenza, lite, dissensione, controversia,* s. f.

To DIFFERENCE [to distinguish] *differenziare, distinguere.* pret. *distinsi.*

DI'FFERENT, adj. [unlike, various] *differente, vario dissimile.*

So many different opinions, *tanta diversità di pareri, tanti vari pareri.*

DI'FFERENTLY, adv. *differentemente, variamente.*

It was differently reported, *la cosa fu narrata in diverse maniere.*

DI'FFERING, adj. *differente, dissimile.*

DIFFI'CIL, adj. [difficult, hard, not easy] *difficile, malagevole, non facile.*

Difficil, adj. [scrupulous] *scrupoloso.*

DIFFI'CILNESS, s. [difficulty to be persuaded] *difficoltà ad esser persuaso.*

DI'FFICULT, adj. [hard, uneasy] *difficile, malagevole, faticoso, che ha in se difficoltà, difficultoso.*

Difficult [hard to be understood] *difficile, oscuro, difficile ad intendersi nascoso, scabroso, intrigato.*

DI'FFICULTY, adj. [hardly] *difficilmente, con difficoltà, malagevolmente.*

Difficulty, s. [hardness] *difficoltà, e difficultà, malagevolezza, scabrosità,* s. f.

Difficulty [doubt] *una difficoltà, dubbio.*

To propose a difficulty, *proporre una difficultà, un dubbio.*

To DIFFI'DE [to mistrust] *diffidare, o diffidarsi, non aver fidanza, non fidarsi.*

DI'FFIDENCE, s. [mistrust, suspicion] *diffidenza,* s. f. *timore,* s. m.

DI'FFIDENT, adj. [mistrustful, suspicious] *diffidente, sospettoso, timido.*

DI'FFIDENTLY, adv. *con diffidenza, sospettosamente, timidamente.*

DIFFO'RM, adj. *contrario d' uniforme.*

To DIFFU'SE [to spread here and there] *diffondere, spargere* pret. *diffusi, sparsi.*

The blood diffuses itself all over the body thro' the veins, *il sangue si diffonde nelle vene per tutto' l corpo.*

DIFFU'SE, adj. *diffuso, sparso.*

A diffuse style, *uno stile diffuso o prolisso.*

DIFFU'SED, part. adj. [wild, uncouth, irregular] *strano, fantastico, irregolare.*

DIFFU'SELY, adv. *diffusamente, largamente, copiosamente, ampiamente.*

DIFFU'SION, s. [a scattering abroad] *diffusione,* s. f. *spargimento,* s. m.

DIFFU'SIVE, adj. [of a great extent] *diffusivo.*

A diffusive charity, *una carità grande.*

To DIG [to delve] *zappare, vangare.*

To dig the ground, *zappar la terra.*

To dig a hole in the ground, *fare un buco nella terra.*

To

To dig out, *sterrare, cavar della terra.*

Di'gest, s. [the pandect of the civil law] *il digesto.*

To Dige'st [to dissolve in the stomach] *digerire, smaltire,* pres. *digerisco, smaltisco.*

To digest one's meat, *digerire il cibo.*

To digest [to dispose, to put in order] *disporre, ordinare, accommodare, preparare.*

To digest an affront, *sopportare, o inghiottire un' ingiuria.*

Dige'sted, adj. *degerito,* v. To digest.

Dige'ster, s. *che digerisce.*

Dige'stible, adj. [that is easily digested] *digestibile, facile a digerire.*

Dige'stion, s. *digestimento,* s. m. *digestione,* s. f.

Ill digestion, *indigestione.*

Dige'stive, adj. [that helps the digestion] *digestivo, che ajuta la digestione.*

Dige'stives, s. [medicines which cause digestion] *rimedi digestivi.*

External digestives [are such as dissolve a swelling, or breed good matter in a wound] *rimedi digestivi esterni, che o dissolvono un tumore, o l'ajutano a marcire.*

Dige'sts [the first volume of the civil law] *digesto,* s. m. *le pandette di Giustiniano.*

Digged, adj. [from to dig] *zappato, vangato.*

Digger, s. *zappatore,* s. m.

Di'gging, s. *il zappare, il vangare.*

To Dight [to deck, to set off] *ornare, adornare, abbellire, abbigliare, addobbare.*

Di'git, s. [the quantity of an inch in measure] *dito,* s. m. *misura.*

Digit [in arithmetick, is a character which denotes a figure, as I. for one, V. for five, X. for ten] *figura aritmetica come I. significa uno, V, cinque, X. dieci.*

To Di'gnify [to advance to a dignity, especially an ecclesiastical one] *elevare, innalzare, esaltare a qualche dignità, specialmente ecclesiastica.*

Dignifi'ed, adj. *elevato, innalzato, esaltato a qualche dignità.*

By what title soever dignifyed or distinguished, *di qualunque qualità e condizione si sia.*

Di'gnitary, s. [an ecclesiastical officer, who has not the cure of souls, as a dean, prebend, &c.] *un prelato, colui che possiede dignità ecclesiastica, senza cura d'anime, come un decano, canonico,* &c.

Di'gnity, s. [degree of honour] *dignità, grado d'onore, o d'ufficio.*

Dignity [greatness, nobleness] *dignità, grandezza, nobiltà,* s. f.

Dignity [merit, importance] *dignità, merito, importanza.*

To Digre'ss [to go from the subject in hand] *digredire, far digressione.*

Digre'ssion, s. [a going from the matter in hand] *digressione,* s. f. *tralasciamento del filo principale del discorso.*

To make a digression, *fare una digressione.*

To Diju'dicate [to judge between two parties] *giudicare fra due parti, decidere, determinare,* pret. *decisi,* termine legale.

To Diju'dicate [to distinguish] *discernere, distinguere,* pret. *distinsi.*

Diju'dicated, adj. *deciso, terminato, discernuto, distinto.*

Dike, s. [a ditch] *un fosso.*

Dike [causey] *vallo, argine,* s. m.

Dike-grave, dike reeve, s. [an officer who has the oversight and command of the dikes and banks] *inspettore de' fossi, degli origini, e de' valli.*

To Dila'cerate [to tear in pieces] *sbranare, lacerare, stracciare, mettere in pezzi, dilacerare.*

Dila'cerated, adj. *sbranato, lacerato, stracciato, messo in pezzi, dilacerato.*

Dilacera'tion, s. *lacerazione,* s. f. *laceramento,* s. m.

To Dila'niate [to tear or rend in pieces] *sbranare, rompere in brani, dilaniare.*

To Dila'pidate [to spend wastefully] *dilapidare, mandar male.*

Dilapida'tion, s. [a wasteful spending] *dilapidamento,* s. m.

Dilapidation [a wasteful destroying, or letting of a building run to ruin and decay for want of reparation] *rovina,* s. f. *dilapidamento,* s. m.

A parson guilty of dilapidation, *un prete che lascia andare in rovina la sua cura per mancanza di riparo.*

Dila'table, adj. [that may be dilated] *dilatabile, che si può dilatare.*

Dilata'tion, s. [the act of extending into greater space] *il dilatare, l'estendere.*

Dilatation [the act of being extended] *estesa.*

To Dila'te [to widen] *dilatare, allargare, ampliare.*

To dilate, verb neut. [to enlarge upon a subject] *dilatarsi, diffondersi.*

Dila'tor, s. [a surgeon's instrument to dilate or open the mouth] *un dilatatorio, strumento che serve ad aprire la bocca.*

Dilato'riness, s. [slowness, sluggishness] *lentezza.*

Dila'tory, adj. [full of delays] *dilatorio, che differisce, ehe procrastina.*

Dilatory pleas, or exceptions, *dilazioni, rigiri.*

A dilatory man, *un indugiatore, che indugia, che procrastina, che usa dilazioni.*

Dile'ction, s. [the act of loving] *affetto, amore.*

Dile'mma, s. [an argument consisting of two or more propositions so disposed that neither of them can be well denied] *dilemma,* s. m. *sorta d'argomento composto di due o più proposizioni così ben ordinate che nessuna si può quasi negare.*

Di'ligence, s. [great care, carefulness] *diligenza, cura, accuratezza, esattezza,* s. f.

Di'ligent, adj. [careful] *diligente, esatto, accurato.*

Di'ligently, adv. *diligentemente, esattamente, accuratamente, con accuratezza.*

Dill, s. [a sort of herb] *aneto,* s. m. *pianta, che si coglie negli orti.*

Di'lling, s. [a child born when the parents are old] *fanciullo, o fanciulla nata nell' età avanzata de' genitori.*

Dilling [darling] *mignone, favorito,* s. m.

To Dilu'cidate [to make plain, or clear] *dilucidare, far chiaro, rischiarare, spiegare.*

Dilu'cidated, adj. *dilucidato, rischiarato, spiegato.*

Dilucida'tion, s. [a making clear or plain] *spiega, dichiarazione,* s. f.

Dilu'te, adj. *temperato, mescolato, stemperato.*

To Dilu'te [to mingle with water] *temperare, stemperare.*

To dilute wine, *temperare il vino, mescolarlo con acqua.*

Dilu'ted, adj. *temperato, mescolato, stemperato.*

Dim, adj. [obscure, dark] *oscuro, fosco.*

A dim colour, *un colore oscuro, o fosco.*

Dim-sighted, *che ha la vista affoscata.*

To Dim [to make dim] *offuscare, oscurare, rendere oscuro, abbagliare.*

That dims my sight, *questo m'abbaglia la vista.*

Dime'nsion, s. [the just measure or compass of any thing] *dimensione, misura,* s. f.

Dimica'tion, s. [skirmishing] *combattimento, scaramuccia,* s. m. *scaramuccia,* s. f.

To Dimi'nish [to lessen] *diminuire, scemare, stremare, ridurre a meno,* pres. *diminuisco.*

Dimi'nished, adj. *diminuito, scemato, strèmato.*

Dimi'nishing, s. *diminuimento,* s. m. *il diminuire.*

Dimi'nishment, } s. *diminuzione,*
Diminu'tion, } s. f. *diminuimento,* s. m.

That is no diminution to you, *questo non vi fa torto alcuno.*

Dimi'nutive, adj. [which diminishes or makes less] *diminutivo, che diminuisce.*

A diminutive, s. [in grammar, a word which lessens the original word from whence it is derived] *un diminutivo.*

Di'mish, adj. *alquanto offuscato.*

Dimi'ssory, adj. Ex. dimissory letters [letters sent from one bishop to another, in favour of one who stands candidate for holy orders in another diocese] *una dimissoria, o lettera dimissoria, si dice quella, che si ottiene dal proprio vescovo, ad effetto di poter ricever gli ordini sagri da un altro vescovo.*

Di'mity, s. [a fine sort of fustian] *bombagina,* s. f.

Di'mmed, adj. *offuscato, oscurato, abbagliato.*

Di'mly, adv. *offuscatamente.*

Di'mness, s. [imperfection or weakness of sight] *offuscazione,* s. f. *abbagliamento, bagliore, abbaglio,* s. m.

Di'mple, s. [a little dent in the bottom of the chin or cheeks] *pozzetta,*

s. f. *piccola fossetta nel mento e nelle guance.*

To DI'MPLE, verb neut. *formar delle pozzette nelle guance.*

DI'MPLED, adj. *che ha delle pozzette.*

DIN, s. [a noise] *suono, rumore, frastuono, fracasso*, s. m.

What din is that? *che rumore è cotesto?*

To make a din, *romoreggiare, far romore, strepitare.*

I shall stir your din [I shall make you hold your tongue] *vi farò ben io star zitto.*

To DIN [to stun with noise] *intronare, stordire a forza di strepito.*

To din [to impress with violent and continued noise] *far tintinnire, lasciar un tintinnio negli orecchi.*

To DINE [to eat one's dinner] *desinare, pranzare.*

DI'NED, adj. *desinato, pranzato.*

I have dined, *ho desinato.*

To DING [to dash against, to bruise] *rompere, fragnere, sbattere, sbatacchiare, urtare contra che che si sia.*

To ding one's ear with a thing perpetually, *intronare il capo o gli orecchi ad uno ripetendogli sempre le medesima cosa.*

DING-DONG, s. *voce inventata per esprimer il suono della campana.*

DI'NGLE, s. [a hollow between hills] *luogo profondo fra monti.*

DI'NING, s. *il desinare, il pranzare.*

A dining room, *sala per mangiare, la camera dove si pranza.*

DI'NNER, s. *pranzo*, s. m.

After dinner sit a while, after supper walk a mile, *dopo pranzo riposati, dopo cena passeggia.*

To eat one's dinner, *desinare, pranzare.*

Dinner time, *ora di pranzo.*

DINT, s. [impression, mark] *impressione*, s. f. *segno, vestigio*, s. m.

The dint of a sword, *l'impression o'l segno d'una spada.*

Dint [force] *forza, violenza*, s. f.

To get a thing by dint of sword, *ottener che che si sia colla punta della spada, o a forza d'arme.*

The dint of a discourse, *la forza o la violenza d'un discorso.*

DIO'SCESAN, s. [a bishop who has the care of a diocese committed unto him] *diocesano, o vescovo diocesano.*

Diocesan [an inhabitant within the bounds of a diocese] *diocesano, che è della diocesi.*

DIO'CESS, s. [the circuit or bounds of a bishop's jurisdiction] *diocesi*, s f. *luogo sopra'l quale il vescovo o altro prelato ha spiritual giurisdizione.*

DIO'PTRICKS, s. [a part of opticks, which treat of refracted rays and their union with one another, according as they are received by glasses of this or that figure] *diottica*, s. f. *sorta di prospettiva.*

To DIP [to put into water] *intignere, tuffar leggiermente in cosa liquida, immollare, bagnare.*

To dip one's bread in the sauce, *intignere, o immollar il pane nella salsa.*

To dip into a book [to look casually, or by chance into it] *dare un occhiata in un libro, darvi una scorsa.*

To dip [or engage] one's estate, *impegnare i suoi beni.*

DI'PHTHONG, s. [two vowels sounded together in one syllable] *dittongo*, s. m.

DIPLO'MA, s. [a royal charter, or a prince's letters patents] *diploma, lettera patente*, s. f.

DIPT, adj. [from to dip] *intinto, tuffato, immollato, bagnato.*

DI'PTERON, s. [a building which has a double wing] *ditterio*, s. m. *edificio che ha le ali doppie.*

DIRE, adj. [cruel, unmerciful] *diro, empio, crudele.*

DIRE'CT, adj. [straight, right] *diritto, diretto, dritto, che non ha piega da niuna banda.*

A direct line, *una linea retta.*

In a direct line, *a dirittura, dirittamente, diritto, per diritto.*

To DIRE'CT [to guide, to govern, to rule] *dirigere, ordinare, governare, condurre, regolare, indrizzare, incamminare, addirizzare.*

To direct one's thoughts to gain, *voltare i suoi pensieri al guadagno.*

To direct all one's actions to God's glory, *indrizzare tutte le sue azioni a Dio.*

To direct a letter to one, *dirigere, indirizzare, mandare una lettera ad uno.*

To direct [to show how to do a thing] *mostrare insegnare.*

Pray direct me to such a place, *di grazia mostratemi la strada per andare ad un tal luogo.*

If you do not direct me, I do not know how to do it, *se voi non mi mostrate, non so come farlo.*

To direct one's course towards a place, *prendere il cammino, o incamminarsi verso un luogo.*

To direct [to steer] one's course at sea, *poggiare, o far vela verso un luogo.*

DIRE'CTED, adj. *diretto, ordinato, governato.* v. To direct.

DIRE'CTION, s. [conduct, management] *direzione, cura, incombenza*, s. f. *maneggio*, s. m.

He has the direction of that affair, *egli ha la direzione, la cura, e l'incombenza di questo negozio.*

The direction of a letter, *la soprascritta d'una lettera.*

To follow one's directions, *seguire, o secondare le altrui istruzioni, pigliare gli altrui avvisi.*

The direction word [in printing] *la chiave, termine di stampatore.*

DIRE'CTLY, adv. *direttamente, dirittamente, per linea retta, a dirittura, diritto, per diritto.*

I go directly home, *me ne vo diritto, o a dirittura a casa.*

Directly or indirectly, *direttamente, o indirettamente.*

The sun strikes directly upon their heads, *il sole da a piombo sopra le teste loro.*

Directly against, *dirimpetto.*

DIRE'CTNESS, s. *dirittura, rettitudine*, s. f.

DIRE'CTOR, s. [manager, overseer] *direttore*, s. m.

He was our director, *egli era il nostro direttore.*

DIRE'CTORY, adj. [which serves to direct] *direttivo, che indirizza.*

The directory, s. [a form of publick prayers set forth by the assembly of divines, and used in times past instead of the book of common prayer] *formula di preghiere publiche usate anticamente in luogo della presente liturgia.*

DI'REFUL, adj. [fierce, cruel] *diro, crudele, fiero, empio.*

Direful [hideous] *spaventevole, terribile, orrendo.*

DI'RENESS, s. [dismalness, horror, hideousness] *orrore, cosa spaventevole, cosa orrenda.*

DIRE'PTION, s. [a robbing, or ransacking] *saccheggiamento, ladroneccio, sacco*, s. m. *ruberia, rapina*, s. f.

DIRGE, s. [a service for the dead] *ufficio de' morti.*

Dirge [lamentation] sung at the funeral, *canzone funebre.*

DIRK, s. an Erse word. *Vocabolo della lingua nativa di Scozia* [a kind of dagger] *sorte di daga.*

To DIRKE [to spoil, to ruin] *guastare, rovinare.*

DIRT, s. [mud] *fango, luto*, s. m.

Dirt [filth, nastiness] *sporchezza, sporcheria, sporcizia, porcheria*, s. f.

To throw dirt upon one [to speak slightingly of him] *disprezzare alcuno, parlar di lui con disprezzo, sputarli nel viso.*

His dirt will not stick [his slanders will not take] *le sue ingiurie cascheranno sopra di lui.*

To DIRT [to foul, to bemire] *sporcare, imbrattare.*

DI'RTILY, adv. [basely] *indegnamente, vilmente.*

DI'RTINESS, s. [or dirt] *sporcheria, sporcizia, porcheria*

DI'RTPIE, s. [forms moulded by children of clay] *pezzo di creta molle formata a mo' di pasticcio da' ragazzi.*

DI'RTY, adj. [full of dirt] *fangoso, pieno di fango.*

Dirty [nasty] *sporco, schifo, lordo.*

Dirty [base] *vile, indegno, infame, disonorato.*

To DI'RTY [to make dirty] *sporcare, bruttare, imbrattare.*

DISABI'LITY, s. [a being unable, or uncapable] *inabilità, incapacità, impotenza*, s. f.

To DISA'BLE [to make unable, or uncapable of] *render inabile, o incapace, levar la forza, o 'l potere, metter fuor di stato.*

To disable a ship, *sdruscire, o metter un vascello fuor di servizio.*

DISA'BLED, adj. *inabile, incapace.*

A disabled ship, *un vascello sdruscito.*

To DISABU'SE [to undeceive] *disingannare, sgannare, cavar d'inganno.*

DISABU'SED, adj. *disingannato, sgannato.*

To

To DISACKNOWLEDGE [to disown] *negare.*

To DISACCU'STOM, verb act. *disvezzare, divezzare, disusare.*

DISADVA'NTAGE, s. [damage, prejudice] *svantaggio, pregiudizio, danno,* torto, *detrimento.*

DISADVA'NTAGED, adj. *che ha ricevuto qualche svantaggio, o danno.*

DISADVANTA'GIOUS, adj. [hurtful, prejudicial] *svantaggioso, pregiudizievole.*

DISADVANTA'GIOUSLY, adv. *svantaggiosamente, con isvantaggio.*

DISADVE'NTURE, s. [mischance] *disgrazia, disavventura,* s f.

To DISAFFE'CT [to dislike] *abborrire, odiare.*

DISAFFE'CTED, adj. [bearing no good will to] *mal contento, mal soddisfatto.*

The disaffected to the government, *i malcontenti.*

Disaffected, adj. *malcontento.*

DISAFFECTION, s. *cattiva volontà.*

To DISAGRE'E [not to agree, to fall out, to be at variance] *discordare, non esser concorde, non convenire, differire, esser male.*

We disagree about that, *noi discordiamo in ciò.*

We shall not disagree about the price, *noi non differiremo nel prezzo.*

DISAGRE'EABLE, adj. [contrary] *contrario, opposto, sdicevole, disdicevole.*

Disagreeable [unpleasant] *discaro, odioso, nojoso.*

DISAGRE'ED, adj. *discordato, differito.*

DISAGRE'EMENT, s. [difference] *discordia, dissenzione, divisione, disunione,* s. f.

To DISALLO'W, v. a. [to deny authority to any] *negare autorità ad alcuno.*

To disallow [to consider as unlawful] *considerare come illegale.*

To disallow [to censure by some posterior act] *disapprovare con qualche azione o fatto posteriore.*

To disallow [not to justify] *non giustificare.*

To disallow, v. n. [to refuse permission; not to grant] *rifiutar permissione, non accordare.*

DISALLOWANCE, s. [prohibition] *proibizione.*

DISALLO'WED, adj. from to disallow.

To DISA'NCHOR [to weigh anchor] *sarpar l'ancora.*

To DISA'NIMATE [to dishearten] *disanimare, sbigottire, sgomentare, tor l'animo, far perder d'animo.*

To DISANNU'L [to make void] *annullare, cassare, abolire, rivocare.*

DISANNU'LLED, adj. *annullato, cassato, abolito, rivocato.*

To DISAPPE'AR [to vanish away] *disparire, sparire, svanire.* pref. *disparisco, sparisco, svanisco.*

DISAPPE'ARED, adj. *disparito, sparito, svanito.*

To DISAPPOINT [to break one's word] *mancar di parola, non attenere quel che s'è promesso.*

Pray don't disappoint me, *vi prego, non mi mancate di parola.*

To disappoint [to frustrate] one's design, *deludere l'altrui disegno, o l'altrui aspettativa.*

DISAPPO'INTED, adj. *a chi s'è mancato di parola, deluso.*

He will be disappointed, *egli resterà ingannato, egli non riuscirà nel suo disegno.*

To be disappointed [to miss one's aim] *mancare il colpo.*

I am disappointed in my design, *il mio disegno m'è fallito.*

DISAPPO'INTING, s. *il mancar di parola.*

DISAPPO'INTMENT, s. *mancamento di parola.*

Disappointment [cross] *traversa, traversia,* s. f. *intoppo,* s. m.

This world is full of diappointments, *questo mondo è pieno di traversie.*

His enemy was stark mad for the disappointment, *il suo nemico dava nelle smanie d'aver mancato il colpo.*

DISAPPROBA'TION, s. *biasimo,* s. m.

To DISAPPRO'VE [to dislike] *non approvare, condannare, biasimare.*

DISAPPRO'VED, adj. *non approvato, condannato, biasimato.*

DI'SARD [a prattler, a boasting tatler] *un ciancione, un millantatore.*

To DI'SARM [to take away one's arms] *disarmare, tor via l'armi, spogliar dell' armi.*

DIS'ARMED, adj. *disarmato, senz' armi.*

To DISARRA'Y [to undress any one] *spogliare.*

DISARRA'Y, s. [disorder; confusion] *disordine, confusione.*

DISA'STER, s. [misfortune] *disastro, infortunio,* s. m. *disgrazia, sventura, sciagura,* s. f.

To DISASTER [to blast] *fulminare, coprir di disastro.*

To disaster [to afflict, to mischief] *affliggere, far danno, danneggiare.*

DISA'STROUS, adj. [unfortunate] *disastroso, sventurato, malavventurato, sciagurato.*

To DISAVO'UCH [to retract profession, to disown] *ritrattare, negare quel che s'è fatto o detto, disapprovarlo.*

To DISAVO'W [to disown, to deny] *negare, disdire, non concedere, contraddire,* pret. *disdissi, concessi, contraddissi.*

DISAVO'WED, adj. *negato, disdetto, contraddeto.*

To DISBA'ND [to dismiss out of service] *sbandere, disarmare, licenziare.*

To disband the troops, *sbandar l'esercito.*

To disband, verb neut. *sbandarsi, separarsi.*

To DISBA'RK [to land from a ship] *sbarcare, uscir di nave.*

DISBELI'EF s. [doubt, mistrust] *discredenza, incredulità, diffidenza,* s. f. *dubbio,* s. m.

To DISBELI'EVE, s. [not to believe] *discredere, scredere, non creder più a quel che s'è creduto una volta.*

To disbelieve [to mistrust, to doubt of] *diffidare, non fidarsi, dubitare.*

DISBELI'EVED, adj. *discreduto, screduto, diffidato, dubitato.*

DISBELI'EVER, s. one who refuses belief] *scredente, colui che rifiuta di credere.*

To DISBE'NCH [to drive from a seat] *cavar di seggio per forza o violenza.*

To DISBU'RDEN [to take off a burden, to ease or unload] *scaricare, levare il carico d'addosso, sgravare.*

DISBU'RDENED, adj. *scaricato, sgravato, alleggerito.*

To DISBU'RSE [to lay out money] *sborsare, pagar di contanti.*

DISBU'RSED, adj. *sborsato.*

I have already disbursed a great deal of money, *ho di già sborsato molti danari.*

DISBU'RSEMENT, s. [a disbursing or laying out of money] *sborso, lo sborsare, pagamento,* s. m.

DISCALCEA'TED, adj. [unshod] *scalzo.*

Discalceated friars, *monaci scalzi.*

DISCALE'NDERED adj. [put out of the calendar] *messo fuor del calendario.*

To DISCA'NDY [to dissolve, to melt] *sciogliere, liquefare, fondere.*

To DISCA'RD [to lay out at cards] *scartare, gettare in giocando a monte le carte, che un non vuole.*

To discard [to turn off] *licenziare, accommiatare, dar licenza, mandar via.*

To discard a servant, *licenziare, o mandar via un domestico.*

DISCA'RDED, adj. *scartato, licenziato, accommiatato.*

DISCA'RNATE, adj. [stripped of flesh] *scarnato, privo di carne.*

To DISEA'SE [to strip, to undress] *spogliare, strappar gli abiti d'indosso.*

To DISCE'RN [to perceive; or distinguish one from another] *discernere, ottimamente vedere, distintamente conoscere, differenziare, distinguere.* pret. *vidi, conobbi, distinsi.*

DISCE'RNED, adj. *discernuto, visto, conosciuto, differenziato, distinto.*

DISCE'RNING, s. *discernimento,* s. m. *il discernere.*

To have a discerning spirit, *avere un ingegno perspicace.*

DISCE'RNMENT, s. [discretion, judgment] *discernimento, giudicio, discorso,* s. m. *previdenza,* s. f.

To DISCE'RP [to disjoin, to rent] *separare, stracciare.*

DISCE'RPIBLE, adj. [that may be disjoined, or pulled in pieces] *che si può disceverare, o stracciare.*

DISCHA'RGE, s. [acquittance for money paid, release] *quitanza, ricevuta,* s. f. *atto col quale il creditore confessa aver ricevuto quel se gli doveva.*

Discharge [a dismissing, or sending away] *licenza.*

Discharge [release] *libertà,* s. f.

Discharge [absolution] *assoluzione,* s. f. *perdono,* s. m.

Discharge [firing] of guns, *tiro di cannone.*

To DISCHA'RGE [to ease, free, or release] *liberare, dar libertà, mettere in libertà, scancerare, sprigionare.*

To

To discharge a prisoner, *liberare, scarcerare, o sprigionare un prigioniero.*

To discharge [to acquit] *assolvere, scaricare.*

To discharge one who is charged with a crime, *assolvere uno d'un delitto del quale era accusato, dichiararlo innocente.*

To discharge one's conscience, *scaricar la sua coscienza.*

To discharge one's self from a great obligation, *compire alla sua obbligazione, far le sue parti.*

To discharge one's duty, *fare il suo debito.*

To discharge one's debts, *pagare i suoi debiti.*

To discharge one's promise, *tener la promessa.*

To discharge a business, *spedire un affare.*

To discharge the house, *pagare quel che si deve all' osteria.*

To discharge one from duty, *esentare uno di qualche dovere, o ufficio.*

To discharge a servant, *licenziare un domestico.*

To discharge a soldier, *cassare un soldato.*

A river that discharges itself into the sea, *un fiume che va a scaricarsi nel mare, che mette le sue acque nel mare.*

To discharge a gun, *scaricare, tirare, o sparare un cannone, un archibuso, e simili.*

DISCHA'RGED, adj. *liberato, scarcerato.* v. To discharge.

DISCIPLE, s. [a learner, or scholar] *discepolo, scolare,* s. m.

Our Saviour's disciples, *i discepoli di nostro Signore.*

To DISCI'PLE [to punish, to discipline] *punire, dar disciplina.*

DISCI'PLINABLE, adj. [capable of discipline, teachable] *disciplinabile, atto a ricever disciplina, o a ridursi a disciplina.*

DISCIPLINA'RIANS, s. [sectaries who pretend to a stricter discipline than the established church] *i presbiteriani.*

DI'SCIPLINE, s. [education, instruction, strict order] *disciplina, istituzione, instruzione, educazione,* s. f. *ammaestramento, insegnamento,* s. m.

Military discipline, or discipline of war, *disciplina militare.*

The church discipline, *la disciplina ecclesiastica.*

You are under the discipline of a good master, *voi siete sotto la disciplina d'un buon maestro.*

Discipline [scourge, such as is used by way of pennance in monasteries] *disciplina, mazzo di funicelle o simili, colle quali gli uomini si percuotono per far penitenza.*

To DISCIPLINE [to teach, to instruct] *disciplinare, ammaestrare, instruire, insegnare* pref. *instruisco.*

To discipline an army, *disciplinare un esercito*

To discipline [to correct, to scourge, to whip with a discipline] *disciplinare, dar la disciplina, percuotere con disciplina.*

To discipline, verb neut. *disciplinarsi, darsi la disciplina, percuotere con disciplina.*

DISCIPLI'NED, adj. *disciplinato, ammaestrato, instrutto, insegnato.*

Our soldiers are well disciplined, *i nostri soldati sono ben disciplinati, o agguerriti.*

To be disciplined [to be scourged] *aver la disciplina.*

To DISCLA'IM [to quit claim to, utterly to refuse, to renounce] *rinunciare, cedere, rifiutare.*

DISCLA'IMED, adj. *rinunziato, ceduto, rifiutato.*

To DISCLO'SE [to discover, to reveal] *aprire, palesare, manifestare, scoprire.*

To disclose one's heart to one, *aprire il cuore ad uno, confidarli i suoi sentimenti.*

To disclose a secret, *scoprire, o palesare un segreto.*

To disclose, verb neut. [to blow, to bud, to put forth leaves] *aprirsi, parlando de' fiori, dilatarsi sbocciando.*

DISCLO'SED, adj. *aperto, palesato, manifestato, scoperto.*

DISCLO'SURE, s. [discovery, production into view] *scoperta.*

Disclósure [act of revealing any secret] *l'atto del rivelare una cosa segreta, un segreto.*

To DISCO'LOUR, s. [to alter the colour, to spoil the colour] *scolorare, perder il colore, stignere, scolorire, perder il colore.*

DISCOLOURED, adj. *scolorato, stinto, scolorito.*

To DISCOMFIT [to defeat, to overthrow in battle] *sconfiggere, rompere il nemico in battaglia.*

DISCO'MFITTED, adj. *sconfitto, rotto in battaglia.*

DISCOMFITURE, s. [defeat, overthrow, rout] *sconfitta, rotta, sconfittura,* s. f.

DISCO'MFORT, s. [trouble] *sconforto, travaglio, dolore, dispiacere,* s. m.

To DISCO'MFORT [to afflict, to cast down] *sconfortare, sbigottire, affliggere.* pret. *sbigottisco.* pret. *afflissi.*

DISCOMFORTED, adj. *sconfortato, afflitto, sbigottito.*

To DISCOMME'ND [to dispraise, to blame] *biasimare, condannare, vituperare.*

DISCOMMENDABLE, adj. *biasimevole, degno di biasimo*

DISCOMMENDATION, s. [blame, disgrace, shame] *biasimo, disonore,* s. m. *vergogna, infamia,* s. f.

DISCOMME'NDED, adj. *biasimato, condannato, vituperato.*

DISCOMMO'DE [to incommode] *incomodare, apportare incomodo, scomodare, disagiare.*

DISCOMMO'DED adj. *incomodato.*

DISCOMMODITY, s. [inconveniency] *incomodo, scomodo, disagio,* s. m. *incomodità,* s. f.

To DISCOMPO'SE [to disorder, to disquiet, to trouble] *scomporre, sconcertare, disordinare. mettere in disordine, disturbare, sturbare.* pref. *scompongo,* pret. *scomposi.*

The least thing discomposes me, *la minima cosa mi disordina.*

DISCOMPO'SED, adj. *scomposto, sconcertato, disordinato, disturbato, sturbato*

Discomposed [indisposed] *indisposto, ammalato.*

DISCOMPOSURE, s. [confusion, disorder, trouble] *disordine, travaglio, perturbamento,* s. m. *confusione,* s. f.

DISCO'NSOLATE, adj. [comfortless, afflicted] *sconsolato, travagliato, frontento, afflitto.*

DISCONTE'NT, s. [sorrow, trouble] *scontento, dolore, dispiacere, disgusto,* s. m. *scontentezza, malinconia, afflizione,* s. f.

Discontent, adj. *malcontento.*

To DISCONTE'NT [to displease] *scontentare, dispiacere, affligere, dare scontento.*

DISCONTE'NTED, adj. *malcontento, mal sodisfatto.*

The discontented people, *i malcontenti.*

To have a discontented look, *parere scontento, afflitto o malinconico.*

To bear a thing with a discontented mind, *soffrire che che si sia di mala voglia, o a contro cuore.*

To live a discontented life, *menare una vita infelice, o scontenta.*

DISCONTE'NTEDLY, adv. *con iscontento, con noja, nojosamente, con dispiacere, dispiacevolmente, increscevolmente.*

To look discontentedly, *parer mesto, afflitto, o sconsolato.*

DISCONTE'NTMENT, v. Discontent.

DISCONTI'NUANCE, s. [interruption] *interruzione, intermissione, cessazione,* s. f. *interrompimento, finimento,* s. m.

To DISCONTINUE [to leave, to break off] *cessare, finire, mancare, restare, interrompere.* pref. *finisco.* pret. *interruppi.*

DISCONTI'NUED, adj. *cessato, finito, mancato, restato, interrotto.*

DISCONTINUITY, s. [disunity of parts, want of cohesion] *mancamento di unione, di conformità.*

DI'SCORD, s. [disagreement, strife] *discordia, sconcordia, dissensione, divisione, disunione, discordanza, discrepanza,* s. f. *disparere,* s. m.

To be at discord, *esser in discordia.*

A discord in tunes or voices, *discordanza, dissonanza.*

To DISCO'RD, v. n. [to disagree, not to suit with] *non uniformarsi, non addattarsi l'uno all' altro.*

DISCO'RDANT, adj. [jarring, untunable] *scordante, discordante, dissonante, che non consuona, discrepante.*

A discordant voice, *una voce dissonante.*

To DISCO'VER [to reveal, to make manifest] *scoprire, e scuoprire, manifestare, palesare.* pret. *scoprii, e scopersi.*

To discover a secret, or conspiracy, palesare

palesare un segreto, scoprire una congiura.

To discover one's self [to make one's self known] *scoprirsi, manifestarsi ad alcuno, darsi a conoscere.*

To discover [to find out] *scoprire, trovare, vedere.*

Christopher Columbus discovered first of all the new world, *Cristoforo Colombo fu il primo che scoprì il nuovo mondo.*

To discover the enemies designs, *scoprire, penetrare, indagare i disegni de' nemici.*

To discover a hare [to spy a hare] *scoprir la lepre.*

DISCO'VERABLE, adj. *facile a scoprire, o che si può scoprire o vedere.*

DISCO'VERED, adj. *scoperto, manifestato, palesato. v.* To discover.

DISCO'VERER, s. [he that discovers] *quegli o quella che scopre.*

I am the discoverer, *io l'ho scoperto.*

DISCO'VERY, s. [a discovering, or finding out] *scoperta, e scoverta, s. f. scoprimento, s. m.*

To make the discovery of a country or of a conspiracy, *fare la scoperta d'un paese, scoprire o palesare una congiura.*

He made a full discovery of himself to me, *mi si diede a pieno a conoscere.*

DISCO'UNT, s. *sconto, s. m.*

To DISCO'UNT [to deduct, to abate] *scontare, diminuire, o estinguere il debito, contrapostavi cosa di valuta eguale.*

DISCO'UNTED, adj. *scontato.*

To DISCO'UNTENANCE [to put out of countenance] *fare arrossire.*

To discountenance [to give a check to] *reprimere, raffrenare, rintuzzare.*

To discountenance vice, *disapprovare il vizio.*

DISCO'UNTENANCED, adj. *represso, raffrenato, rintuzzato, disapprovato.*

DISCO'UNTENANCER, s. [one that discourages by a cold treatment] *uno che ti scoraggisce con trattarti freddamente.*

To DISCOU'RAGE [to dishearten] *scoraggiare, togliere altrui il coraggio, disanimare, sgomentare, sbigottire, far perder l'animo.* pres. *sbigottisco.*

DISCO'URAGED, adj. *scoraggiato, disanimato, sgomentato, sbigottito.*

DISCO'URAGEMENT, s. [a putting out of heart] *sgomentamento, sbigottimento, sgomento, s. m.*

DISCO'URAGER, s. [one that impresses diffidence and terror] *colui che imprime diffidenza e terrore; che scoraggisce e sgomenta.*

DISCO'URSE, s. [that rational art of the mind by which we deduce or infer one thing from another] *discorso, s. m. operazione dell' intelletto, colla quale si cerca d'intendere una cosa perfettamente per mezzo di conghietture, o di principj noti.*

Discourse [talk] *discorso, ragionamento, discorrimento.*

To begin a discourse, *cominciare un discorso.*

To turn or change a discourse, *cangiar discorso.*

A discourse of divinity, *un discorso, o trattato teologico.*

Familiar discourse [conversation] *discorso familiare, conversazione.*

To DISCO'URSE [to reason] *discorrere, operar col discorso, discutere, esaminare* pret. *discussi.*

To discourse [to talk] *discorrere, parlare, ragionare.*

To discourse on a subject, *discorrere, o parlare sopra un soggetto.*

To discourse with one, *discorrere, o raggionare con uno.*

To discourse a thing, *discutere, o esaminare una materia.*

To discourse with a man, *intrattenersi, o discorrere con uno, farlo parlare.*

DISCO'URSED, adj. *discorso, parlato, ragionato.*

DISCO'URSIVE, adj. *discorsivo, che appartiene al discorso.*

DISCO'URTEOUS, adj. [unkind, uncivil] *discortese, scortese.*

DISCO'URTEOUSLY, adv. *discortesemente, scortesemente.*

DISCO'URTESY, s. [unkindness, displeasure] *discortesia, scortesia, s. f. dispiacere, s. m.*

You have done me a great discourtesy therein, *voi m'avete fatto in ciò un gran dispiacere.*

DISCRE'DIT, s. [disgrace, reproach] *discredito, scapito nel credito, disonore, torto, s. m. infamia, disistima, s. f.*

It will be much to your discredit, *ciò sarà di vostro discredito, o disonore.*

To discredit [to make one lose his credit, to disgrace] *discreditare, screditare, far perder il credito, disonorare.*

He does what he can to discredit me, *fa ogni sforzo, o tutto quel che può per discreditarmi, o per farmi perdere il credito.*

DISCRE'DITED, adj. *discreditato, screditato, che ha perso il credito, disonorato.*

Discredited [not believed] *screduto.*

DISCRE'ET, adj. [wise, considerate, sober] *discreto, savio, circonspetto, prudente, accorto.*

DISCRE'ETLY, adj. *discretamente, saviamente, prudentemente, accortamente.*

DI'SCREPANT, s. [disagreement] *discrepanza, discordia, s. f. disparere.*

Discrépant, adj. [differing from, repugnant] *discrepante, contrario, differente, opposto.*

DISCRE'TION, s. [discreet management, wisdom] *discrezione, prudenza, circumspezione, buona condotta, s. f.*

The years of discretion, *gli anni della discrezione.*

Discretion [will] *discrezione, volontà.*

I leave it to your discretion, *lo rimetto alla vostra discrezione.*

To surrender at discretion, *rendersi a discrezione.*

Use your discretion in it, *fate come meglio vi parrà a proposito.*

To live at discretion [to have free quarters] *vivere a discrezione.*

DISCRE'TIONARY, ad. [left at large, unlimited, unrestrained] *libero, non ristretto, non limitato.*

DI'SCRETIVE, adj. [that serves to separate] *discreto.*

A conjunction discretive, *una congiunzione discreta.*

To DISCRI'MINATE [to put a difference between, to distinguish] *distinguere, dividere, separare.* pret. *distinsi, divisi.*

DISCRI'MINATED, adj *distinto, diviso, separato.*

DISCRIMINATING, adj. *savio, accorto, perspicace, che sa fare le distinzioni necessarie.*

DISCRIMINATION, s. [a distinction of one thing from another] *distinzione, differenza, s. f.*

DISCRI'MINATIVE, adj. [that which makes the mark of distinction; characteristick] *caratteristico; che è distinto a qualche particolar segno.*

DISCRI'MINATIVE [that which observes distinction] *che osserva distinzione, che distingue.*

DISCU'BITORY, adj. [fitted for the posture of leaning] *propio per appoggiarvisi.*

DISCU'MBENCY, s. [the act of leaning at meat] *lo star appoggiato a tavola.*

To DISCU'MBER [to disengage from any troublesome weight or bulk] *sgombrare, disgombrare, alleggerire.*

DISCU'RE [to discover] *discoprire, scoprire.* Spenser.

DISCU'RSIVE, adj. [running to and fro] *vagante, che vaga, che scorre qua, o là.*

DI'SCUSS, s. among the Romans, was a round quoit used in their exercises] *spezie di morella della quale gli antichi Romani si servivano ne' loro esercizi.*

DIS'CUS, or DISK [in astronomy, is the round phasis of the sun or the moon, which at a great distance appears plain or flat] *disco, il globo del sole o della luna, tale quale pare alla nostra vista.*

To DISCU'SS [to examine, to scan, to sift] *discutere, esaminare, crivellare, ventilare, considerar sottilmente,* pret. *discussi.*

To discuss a matter, *discutere, o esaminare una materia.*

DISCU'SSED, adj. *discusso, esaminato, crivellato, ventilato, considerato.*

DISCU'SSER, s. [he that discusses] *colui che esamina ed argomenta sottilmente e minutamente.*

DISCU'SSION, s. [examination] *discussione, s. esame, s. m.*

DICU'SSIVE, adj. [that can dissolve or disperse humours] *risolutivo, che risolve, o consuma.*

A discussive remedy [a remedy that dissolves humours] *una medicina risolutiva, che risolve, e consuma gli umori.*

DISDA'IN, s. [to scorn] *scorno, disprezzo, sdegno, s. m.*

To DISDA'IN [to despise, to scorn] *sdegnare, avere a sdegno, disprezzare, schifare.*

DISDA'INED, adj. *sdegnato, disprezzato, schifato.*

DISDA'INFUL, adj. [scornful] *sdegnoso, schifo, fiero, altiero, disprezzante.*

DISDA'INFULLY, adv. [scornfully] *sdegnosamente, con sdegno, schifamente, altieramente.*

Disda'infullness, s. *sdegno, scorno, dispregio, o disprezzo*, s. m.

Disda'ining, s. *lo sdegnare, sdegno, scorno, dispregio.*

Dise'ase, s. [distemper] *malattia, infermità, indisposizione*, s. f. *male, morbo*, s. m.

The foul disease, *il mal francese.*

To Dise'ase [to trouble] *inquietare, incomodare, cagionar malattia.*

Dise'ased, adj. [troubled with a disease] *ammalato, indisposto, incomodato, che non sta bene.*

Dise'dged, adj. [blunted, obtunded, dulled] *spuntato, reso ottuso, ribadito, e figurativamente reso melenso, reso stupido.*

To Disemba'rk [to land] *sbarcare.*

To Disemba'rk [to carry to land] *portar in terra*

To Disembogue, *sboccare; e dicesi de' fiumi. v.* Disimbogue.

Disembo'welled, adj. [taken from the bowels] *tratto dalle budella.*

To Disembro'il, adj. [to disentangle, to free from perplexity] *distrigare, sbrogliare.*

To Disena'ble [to deprive of power] *spossare, toglier forza.*

To Disencha'nt [to free from the force of an enchantment] *liberar dall' incantagione.*

To Disenga'ge, *v.* To disingage.

Disestee'm, s. [disrepute] *disprezzo, scorno, sdegno*

To bring one into disesteem, *render uno disprezzabile.*

To disesteém [to have no esteem for] *dispregiare, disprezzare, villipendere, far poca stima, non stimare.*

Disestee'med, *dispregiato, disprezzato, vilipeso.*

Disfa'vour [the state of being out of favour] *disfavore*, s. m. *disgrazia*, s. f.

Disfavour [ill turn, discourtesy] *scortesia*, s. f. *dispiacere, disgusto*, s. m.

Disfavour [disfigurement] *deformità, bruttezza.*

To Disfi'gure [to spoil the shape or figure of] *disfigurare, guastar la figura, render deforme, difformare, e deformare.*

To disfigure one's face, *sfigurare il viso ad uno.*

Dispi'gured, adj *disfigurato, difformato, e deformato.*

He is quite disfigured with the small-pox, *è affatto disfigurato dal vajuolo*

Disfi'gurement, s. [a blemish] *disformamento*, s. m. *bruttura, difformità*, s m.

This will be no disfigurement to her face, *ciò non disfigurerà, o guasterà il suo viso.*

To Disfo'rest [to displant, to cut down the trees of a free forest] *disboscare, e diboscare una foresta.*

To Disfranchi'se [to exclude out of the number of free citizens] *privare, o escludere dalla franchigia o privilegi de' cittadini.*

Disfranchi'sed, adj. *che ha perduto la sua franchigia.*

Disfranchi'sement, s. *privazione della franchigia.*

To Disfu'rnish, *v.* To unfurnish.

To Disgarnish, *sfornire, tor via i fornimenti*, pres. *sfornisco.*

Disg'arnished, adj. *sfornito.*

Disgar'nishing, s. *lo sfornire.*

To Disglo'rify [to deprive of glory; to treat with indignity] *privar di gloria, trattar come vile.*

To Disgo'rge [to cast up] *vomitare, recere.*

To disgorge itself into the sea [as some rivers] *scaricarsi nel mare.*

Disgra'ce, s. [discredit, dishonour] *disonore, vituperio*, s. m. *infamia, vergogna*, s. f.

Disgrace [disfavour] *disgrazia*, s. f.

To be in disgrace at court, *esser in disgrazia, o esser disgraziato in corte.*

To Disgra'ce [to shame] *disonorare, svergognare, far disonore o vergogna, fare onta.*

To disgrace one's self, *disonorarsi, svergognarsi.*

To disgrace [to turn out of favour] *disgraziare.*

Disgra'ced, adj. *disonorato, vergognato.*

Disgraced at court, *disgraziato.*

Disgraceful, adj. [shameful] *disonorevole, vergognoso, vituperevole, ignominioso.*

Nothing can be more disgraceful, *non si può verder cosa più disonorevole.*

Disgra'cefully, adv. *disonorevolmente, senza onore, vergognosamente.*

Disgra'cefulness, s. [disgrace] *disonore, vituperio*, s. m. *infamia, vergogna*, s. f.

Disgra'cer, s. *quegli, o quella che disonora.*

Disgra'cious, adj. [unkind, unfavourable] *spiacevole, scortese, non favorevole.*

Disgui'se, s. [a counterfeit habit] *travestimento*, s. m. *abito mentito.*

Disguise [pretence, colour, cloak] *pretesto, colore*, s. m. *apparenza, finzione, simulazione, finta*, s. f.

To Disgui'se [to put in disguise] *travestire, vestire degli altrui panni.*

To disguise one's self, *travestirsi, vestirsi degli altrui panni.*

To disguise [to dissemble, to conceal] *dissimulare, fingere, nascondere, occultare, far sembiante, far vista.*

Disgui'sed, adj. *travestito, v.* To disguise.

Disgui'sement, s. [dress of concealment] *maschera, l' immascherarsi, l' essere immascherato.*

Disgui'ser, s. [one that puts on a disguise] *colui che s' immaschera, che si traveste.*

Disguiser [one that conceals another by a disguise; one that disfigures] *colui che immaschera, traveste, o sfigura un altro onde non sia più conoscibile.*

Disgu'st, s. [dislike] *disgusto, dispiacere*, s. m.

He took a disgust at me, *mi prese in aversione.*

To take some disgust, *disgustarsi esser mal sodisfatto di qualcheduno o di qualche cosa.*

To Disgu'st [to distaste, to dislike, to be averse from] *disgustarsi, prender disgusto.*

Disgu'sted, adj. *disgustato.*

Disgu'stful, adj. [nauseous] *spiacevole, che fa nausea, disgustoso.*

Dish, s. [a large plate] *piatto grande*, s. m.

A silver, pewter, or earthen dish, *un piatto d' argento, di peltro, o di terra.*

A dish of meat, or fish, *un piatto di carne, o di pesce.*

We had six dishes at dinner, *abbiamo avuto sei piatti a pranzo.*

A dainty dish, *vivande delicate, o esquisite, intingoli.*

A dish [a porringer] *una scodella.*

A dish of coffee, *una tazza di caffè.*

A dish of chocolate, *una chicchera di cioccolata.*

You have done it in a dish [you have done it neatly] *voi l'avete fatto pulitamente.*

To lay a thing in one's dish [to lay the blame of it to him] *dar la colpa ad uno d' una cosa, incolparnelo, rimproverargliela, rovesciar la broda addosso a uno*

A chafing-dish, *uno scaldavivande.*

Dish butter, *burro fresco.*

Dish-clout, *strofinaccio, straccio usato in cucina per nettare*, s. m.

Dish-wash, or dish-water, *broda*, s. f.

Dish meat, [spoon meat] *minestra*, s. f.

To Dish up, *minestrare, metter la minestra nel piatto o nella scodella.*

Di'shclout, s. [the cloth with which the maids rub their dishes] *canovaccio; panno con cui le fanti forbiscono, o nettano o piatti.*

Dishwasher, s. [the name of a bird] *sorta d' uccello.*

Dishabille, s. [undress, home-dress] *l' abito negletto usato dalle gentildonne in casa.*

A woman in her dishabille, *una donna in veste da camera.*

To Disha'bit [to throw out of place] *cacciar fuori uno dalla sua abitazione.*

Disha'rmony, s. [discord, jarring] *dissonanza, discordanza.*

Dished up, adj. *minestrato.*

To Dishe'arten [to put out of heart, to discourage] *discoraggiare, scoraggiare, disanimare, sbigottire, sgomentare* pres. *sbigottisco.*

Dishe'artened, adj. *discoraggiato, scoraggiato, disanimato, sbigottito, sgomentato.*

Why are you so disheartened? *perchè vi perdete d' animo?*

To Dishe'rit, *v.* To disinherit.

Dishe'ritor, s. [one that disherits] *colui che disreda.*

To Dishe'vel, *scapigliare, scompigliare i capelli.*

Dishe'velled, adj. [having the hair hanging loose, or dangling about the shoulders] *scapigliato.*

Dishonest, adj. [base, knavish]

disonesto,

disonesto, ingiusto, fuor del dovere, infame, indegno.

A dishonest man, *un uomo disonesto.*

Dishonest dealings, *azioni indegne, o infami.*

Dishonest [unchaste, lewd] *disonesto, lascivo, impudico.*

Dishonest love, *amore lascivo, o impudico.*

DISHO'NESTLY, adv. *disonestamente, impudicamente.*

DISHO'NESTY, s. [knavery] *disonestà, furberia,* s. f.

Dishonesty [lewdness, impurity] *disonestà, disonestezza, sfacciatezza di costumi, oscenità, impurità, lascivia,* s. f.

DISHO'NOUR, s. [disgrace] *disonore, vituperio,* s. m. *infamia, vergogna,* s. f.

To DISHO'NOUR [to disgrace] *disonorare, tor l' onore, vituperare, svergognare.*

DISHO'NOURABLE, adj. *disonorevole, infame, vituperoso.*

DISHO'NOURABLY, adv. *disonorevolmente, infamemente, vituperosamente.*

DISHO'NOURED, adj. *disonorato, svergognato, vituperato.*

DISHO'NOURER, s. [one that treats another with indignity] *uno che tratta un altro con indegni modi.*

Dishonourer, s. [a violator of chastity] *seduttore di casta donna.*

To DISHO'RN [to strip of horns] *scornare, romper le corna, privar di corna.*

DISHU'MOUR, s. [peevishness, ill humour] *malumore, umor nero.*

To DISIMBA'RK, verb neut. *sbarcare, uscir della barca, approdare.*

To disimbark from an undertaking, *tralasciare, desistere da un intrapresa, metterla da banda.*

DISIMBA'RKED, adj. *sbarcato, approdato.*

DISIMBA'RKING, s. *sbarco,* s. m.

To DISIMBO'GUE, verb neut. *scaricarsi.*

The river Tiber disimbogues itself into the sea, *il Tevere si scarica nel mare.*

To disimbogue [to sail out of a streight at sea] *boccare.*

To DISINCHA'NT [to set free from an inchantment] *romper l'incanto.*

To DISINGA'GE [to revoke from an engagement] *sbrigarsi, liberarsi, svilupparsi, strigarsi, spedirsi.*

DISINGA'GED, adj. *sbrigato, liberato, sviluppato, strigato, libero, in libertà.*

DISINGA'GEMENT, s. *libertà,* s. f.

DISINGENU'ITY, s. *disingenuità,* s. f. *secondo fine, dissimulazione, poca sincerità, doppiezza.*

DISINGE'NUOUS, adj. [unsincere, false-hearted] *disingenuo, doppio, simulato, finto.*

DISINGE'NUOUSLY, adj. *disingenuamente, doppiamente, simulatamente; con doppiezza, dissimulatamente.*

DISINHABITED, adj. *disabitato, deserto, spopolato.*

To DISINHE'RIT, [to deprive one of his inheritance] *diredare, diseredare, disredare, privar dell' eredità.*

DISINHE'RITED, adj. *diredato, diseredato, disredato, privato dell' eredità.*

To DISINTA'NGLE [to unravel] *sviluppare, ravviare, ordinare, strigare.*

To disintangle the hair, *pettinare i capelli.*

To disingtangle one's self from a scurvy business, *svilupparsi, strigarsi d'un cattivo negozio.*

DISINTERESTED, adj. [void of self-interest] *contrario d' interessato, non interessato, imparziale.*

DISI'NTERESTEDNESS, s. *imparzialità,* s. f.

To DISINTE'RR [to dig up, to take a dead body out of the grave] *disotterare, sterrare, cavar di sotterra.*

To DISINTHRO'NE [to put out of the throne] *scacciar dal trono.*

To DISI'NTRICATE [to disintangle] *sviluppare, strigare, avviare.*

To DISINVI'TE [to recal an invitation] *rivocar l'invito.*

To DISJO'IN [to separate, to part, to loosen] *disgiugnere, separare, scommetter le cose congiunte.* pret. *disgiunsi.*

DISJO'INED, adj. *disgiunto, separato, scommesso, segregato.*

DISJO'INING, s. *disgiugnimento,* s. m. *separazione,* s. f.

To DISJO'INT [to put out of joint] *dislogare, e disluogare, disconciare, slogare.*

To disjoint [to divide] an estate, *smembrare uno stato.*

DISJO'INTED, adj. *dislogato, disluogato, disconciato, slogato.*

DISJU'NCTION, s. [separation, division] *disgiunzione, separazione, divisione,* s. f. *disgiugnimento,* s. m.

DISJUNCTIVE, adj. [separating, disjoining] *disgiuntivo.*

A disjunctive particle, *una particola disgiuntiva.*

DISK, s. [the face of the sun or planet as it appears to the eye] *disco; la faccia del sole o d'un pianeta come appare all' occhio.*

Disk [a broad piece of iron thrown in the ancient sports, a quoit] *disco; pezzo di ferro largo rotondo usato dagli antichi ne' loro giuochi.*

DISKI'NDNESS, s. [ill turn] *cattivo ufficio, dispiacere, torto, pregiudizio,* s. m. Not much in use.

DISLI'KE, s. *avversione, ripugnanza.*

To have a dislike for a thing, *avere avversione, o ripugnanza a qualche cosa, non poterla patire.*

To DISLI'KE [to disallow] *dispiacere, non piacere, non aggradire, disamare, odiare, aver a schifo, schifare.*

The chiefest thing I dislike in him, *quel che più mi dispiace in lui.*

DISLI'KED, adj. *che dispiace, che non è aggradito.*

His proceeding is very much disliked, *il suo portamento vien molto biasimato.*

DISLI'KEFUL, adj. [disaffected, malign] *malaffetto, maligno; dispettoso.*

To DISLI'KEN [to make unlike] *guastar la somiglianza.*

DISLI'KENESS, s. [dissimilitude, unlikeness] *dissomiglianza.*

DISLI'KER, s. [a disapprover; one that is not pleased] *disapprovatore; un che non si compiace d'una cosa.*

DISLI'MBED, adj. *smembrato.*

To DISLI'MN [to unpaint; to strike out of a picture] *sdipingere, cancellar da una pittura.*

To DI'SLOCATE [to put out of joint] *dislogare, e disluogare, disconciare, slogare.*

DI'SLOCATED, adj. *dislocato, disluogato, disconciato, slocato.*

To DISLO'DGE [to turn out of house, lodging, &c.] *scacciare; metter fuor di casa.*

To dislodge a stag, *levar un cervo.*

To dislodge a camp, *levar le tende.*

DISLO'DGED, adj. *scacciato, messo fuor di casa,* v. To dislodge.

DISLO'YAL, adj. [unfaithful] *disleale, che manca di lealtà, infido, infedele.*

A subject disloyal to his prince, a wife to her husband, *un soggetto disleale al suo principe, una moglie infedele a suo marito.*

DISLO'YALLY, adv. *deslealmente, infidamente, infedelmente.*

DISLO'YALTY, s. [unfaithfulness] *dislealtà, perfidia, infedeltà,* s. f.

DI'SMAL, adj. [dreadful, hideous, terrible] *orrendo, orribile, terribile, spaventevole, che fa paura, sinestro, funesto.*

A dismal sight, *uno spettacolo orrendo.*

A dismal look, *una ciera cattiva.*

DI'SMALLY, adj. *orribilmente, terribilmente, spaventevolmente.*

To DISMA'NTLE [to beat or pull down the walls or fortifications] *smantellare, diroccare, sfasciare.*

To dismantle a city, *smantellare una città.*

DISMA'NTLED, adj. *smantellato, diroccato, sfasciato.*

DISMA'SK, [to divest of a mask] *smascherare, tor via la maschera.*

To DISMA'Y [to astonish, to terrify] *stupire, stupidire, stupefare, empier di stupore, far restar attonito, spaventare, atterrire.* pret. *stupisco, stupidisco, atterrisco.*

DISMA'YED, adj. *stupito, stupido, stupefatto, attonito, pien di stupore, atterrito.*

DISM'AY, s. [fall of courage; terror felt; desertion of mind] *l' stupidir per terrore, spavento ricevuto.*

DISME, s. [a tenth; the tenth part; tythe] *il decimo, la decima parte.*

To DISME'MBER [to pull in pieces] *smembrare, sbranare, mettere in pezzi.*

DISME'MBERED, adj. *smembrato, sbranato, messo in pezzi.*

DISMES, s. [tithes] *decime,* s. f.

To DISMI'SS [to discharge, to send away] *licenziare, accomiatare, dar licenza, mandar via.*

To dismiss one from his employ, *levar uno di carica.*

To dismiss one's wife, *ripudiar sua moglie.*

DISMI'SSED, adj. *licenziato, accomiatato.*

He was dismissed the court, *fu scacciato, o bandito dalla corte.*

DISMI'SSION, s. [a sending away] *licenziamento*, s. m.

To DISMO'UNT [to unhorse another] *far votar la sella ad uno, scavallarlo.*

To dismount a cannon, to make it unfit for service] *scavallar l' artiglieria.*

To dismount one's prejudices, *capacitare uno, farlo capace.*

To dismount [to alight] *scavalcare, sceNder da cavallo, smontare.*

DISMO'UNTED, adj. *scavallare, scavalcare, smontare.*

DISNA'TURED, adj. [unnatural; wanting natural tenderness] *disamorato, privo di natural tenerezza.*

DISOBE'DIENCE, s. [undutifulness] *disubbidienza, inobbedienza, e inubbidienza, trasgressione*, s. f.

DISOBE'DIENT, adj. [undutiful] *disubbidiente, inobbediente.*

DISOBE'DIENTLY, adv. *disubbidientemente, inobbedientemente.*

To carry one's self disobediently, *esser disubbidiente.*

To DISOBE'Y [to act contrary to order] *disubbidire, trasgredire, non ubbidire.* pres. *disubbidisco, trasgredisco.*

To disobey one's father, *disubbidire a suo padre.*

DISOBE'YED, adj. *disubbidito, trasgresso.*

DISOBE'YING, s. *il disubbidire.*

DISOBLIGA'TION, s. [a disobliging] *disobbligazione*, s. f. *dispiacere*, s. m.

To DISOBLI'GE [to displease, to do an ill office to] *disobbligare, dispiacere, fare un dispiacere, offendere.* pret. *offesi.*

DISOBLI'GED, adj. *disobbligato, dispiaciuto, offeso.*

DISOBLI'GING, s. *scortese, incivile.*

Disobliging ways, *maniere scortesi.*

DISOBLI'GINGLY, adv. *scortesemente, incivilmente.*

DISO'RBED, adv. [thrown out of the proper orbit] *spinto fuora della sua propria orbita o rotaja.*

DISO'RDER, s. [confusion] *disordine, perturbamento*, s. m. *confusione*, s. f.

Every thing was in disorder, *ogni cosa era in disordine.*

Disorder [trouble of mind] *disordine, disturbo*, s. m. *perturbazione, commozione d'animo*, s. f.

He did what he could to hide her disorder, *fece ogni sforzo per celare la commozione del suo animo.*

Disorder of drink [over drinking] *crapula, ubbriachezza*, s. f.

To DISO'RDER [to put out of order, to confound] *disordinare, perturbare, confonder l'ordine.*

Too much drinking disorders the stomach, *il troppo bere disordina, o sconvolge lo stomaco.*

To disorder [to discompose, to vex] *commuovere, agitare, perturbare, scompigliare, disordinare.*

DISO'RDERED, adj. *disordinato.* v. To disorder.

DISO'RDERLY, adj. *disordinato, confuso, in disordine, in confusione, perturbato, scompigliato.*

A disorderly house, *una casa senz' ordine, in confusione, mal regolata.*

A disorderly man, *un uomo sregolato, che mena una vita sregolata.*

I found her in a very disorderly posture, *l'ho travata in una molto sconcia postura.*

Disorderly doings, *disordini, sregolatezze.*

Disorderly, adv. *disordinatamente, senz' ordine, confusamente, in confusione.*

DISO'RDINATE, adj. [in disorder] *disordinato, sregolato, eccessivo, smoderato.*

DISO'RDINATELY, adv. *disordinatamente, sregolatamente.*

DISORIE'NTATED, adj. [turned from the east, turned from the right direction] *svolto dal levante, fuori della vera via.*

To DISO'WN [or deny] *negare, rinunziare, non concedere, non confessare.*

I do not disown my doing of it, *non niego che non l'abbia fatto.*

To disown one for one's son, *non riconoscere, o rinunziare uno per figlio.*

DISO'WNED, adj. *negato, rinunziato.*

To DISPA'RAGE [to slight, to speak ill of] *disprezzare, e dispregiare, avvilire, parlar male, vituperare, mormorare.* pres. *avvilisco.*

To disparage one's commodities, *dispregiare, o avvilire l'altrui mercanzia.*

To disparage one, *sparlar d'uno, parlarne male.*

DISPA'RAGED, adj. *disprezzato, dispregiato, avvilito.*

DISPA'RAGEMENT, s. [undervaluing] *disprezzo, dispregio, scherno, disonore, vituperio*, s. m.

'Tis no disparagement for you to do it, *se fate ciò non sarà vostro disonore.*

A disparagement in marriage, *inegualità di condizione nel matrimonio.*

DISPA'RITY, s. [inequality] *disparità, diseguaglianza, inegualità, differenza*, s. f.

To DISPA'RK [to take away the pales or inclosures of a park] *rompere o tor via i palizzati ehe chiudono un parco.*

To DISPA'RT [to divide into two, to separate, to break] *dividere in due, separare, spartire, rompere.*

DISPA'SSION, s. [freedom from mental perturbation] *tranquillità di mente, il non aver passion d'animo.*

DISPA'SSIONATE, adj. [cool, calm, moderate, temperate] *spassionato, calmo, moderato, disinteressato.*

DISPA'TCH, s. [quick doing] *prestezza, spedizione*, s. f. *spaccio*, s. m.

He is a man of quick dispatch, *egli è un uomo molto speditivo.*

To make a quick dispatch, *spedirsi, spacciarsi, sbrigarsi.*

To DISPA'TCH [to hasten, to speed] *spacciare, spedire, terminare, dar fine con prestezza.* pres. *spedisco.*

To dispatch a business, *spacciare o spedire un negozio.*

To dispatch [to send away in haste] *spacciare, spedire, inviare con prestezza.*

To dispatch a courier, *spacciare o spedire un corriere.*

To dispatch a man, or to dispatch him out of the way, *spedire o spacciare un uomo, ammazzarlo.*

To dispatch, verb neut. [to make haste] *spacciarsi, spedirsi, sbrigarsi, far presto.*

DISPA'TCHED, adj. *spacciato, spedito.* v. To dispatch.

DISPA'TCHER, s. *quegli o quella che spaccia.*

A dispatcher of business, *un uomo speditivo.*

DISPA'TCHES, s. [letters] *dispacci, spacci, lettere, che si danno al corriere o messo che si spaccia.*

To DISPE'L [to drive away] *scacciare, discacciare, espellere.*

DISPE'LLED, adj. *scacciato, discacciato.*

DISPE'NCE, s. [expence, cost, charge] *spesa, costo, carico.*

To DISPE'ND [to spend] *spendere.*

DISPE'NSARY, s. [the place where medicines are dispensed] *luogo in cui si dispensano le medicine.*

DISPENSA'TION, s. [distribution] *dispensa, dispensazione, distribuzione, porzione*, s. f. *scompartimento*, s. m.

Dispensation [a suffering or permitting a man to do a thing contrary to law] *dispensa, dispensazione, il concedere derogando alla legge.*

DISPE'NSATORY, s. [a book which directs apothecaries in ordering every ingredient as to the quantity and manner of making up every physical composition] *farmacopea*, s. f. *libro che insegna la composizione de' rimedi.*

DISPE'NSE, s. [dispensation, exemption] *dispensa, esenzione.*

To DISPE'NSE [to distribute, to dispose of] *dispensare, compartire, distribuire.* pres. *compartisco, distribuisco.*

To dispense with [to bestow] *concedere, permettere, scusare, compatire.*

He shall dispense with me for not believing what he says, *mi compatirà se non credo quel che dice.*

Pray dispense me with it, *vi prego di scusarmi, o di compatirmi.*

DISPE'NSED, adj. *dispensato, compatito, distribuito.* v. To dispense.

DISPE'NSER, s. *dispensatore*, s. m. *dispensatrice*, s. f.

DISPE'NSING, s. *dispensamento*, s. m. *dispensagione*, s. f.

Dispensing, adj. Ex. dispensing power, *facoltà distributiva.*

DISPE'OPLE [to unpeople] *spopolare, dipopolare, disolare, render disabitato, distruggere.* pret. *distrussi.*

DISPE'OPLED, adj. *spopolato, dispopolato, disabitato, distrutto.*

DISPEO'PLER, s. [a depopulator] *spopolatore, colui che spopola.*

To DISPE'RSE [to sprinkle] *spruzzare, inaffiare.*

To DISPE'RSE [to spread abroad, to scatter] *dispergere, spergere, sparpagliare, separare in varie parti.* pret. *dispersi, sparsi.*

To

To disperse the enemy, *dispergere, o sbaragliare il nemico.*

To disperse a rumour, *spargere una novella, far correr voce, dar fuori.*

To disperse, verb neut. *spargersi, sparpagliarsi dispergersi, separarsi qua, e la.*

DISPE'RSED, adj. *disperso, sparso, sparpagliato, separato, sbaragliato.*

DISPE'RSEDLY, adv. *dispersamente, qua e la separatamente, in diverse parti, sparsamente, spartamente.*

DISPE'RSER, s. *dispergitore, s. m.*

A disperser of false news, *seminator di false novelle.*

DISPE'RSING, s. *dispersione, s. f. dispergimento, s. m. il dispergere.*

DISPE'RSION, s. [scattering] *dispersione, s. f.*

The dispersion of the Jews, *la dispersione degli Ebrei.*

To DISPI'RIT [to discourage] *sgomentare, sbigottire, disanimare.* pres. *sbigottisco.*

DISPI'RITED, adj. *sgomentato, sbigottito, disanimato.*

To DISPLA'CE [to put out of place, to remove] *dislogare, levar dal luogo, disordinare.*

To displace [to turn out of an office] *scavallare uno dal suo ufficio.*

DISPLA'CED, adj. *dislogato, disordinato, scavallato.*

To DISPLA'NT [to pluck up what was planted] *spiantare, sbarbar piante, sradicare.*

DISPLA'NTED, adj. *spiantato, sbarbato, sradicato.*

DISPLA'Y, s. [explication] *esplicazione, esposizione, interpretazione, s. f.*

To DISPLA'Y [to spread wide] *spiegare, allargare, aprir le cose ristrette in piega, sbargere, spandere.*

To display one's colours, *spiegar l'insegne.*

To display [to declare] *spiegare, dichiarare, esporre, manifestare.* pres. *espongo.* pret. *esposi.*

To display an intrigue, *scoprire, snodare un intrigo.*

To display one's wit, *mostrare, o far pompa del proprio ingegno.*

DISPLA'YED, adj. *spiegato, allargato, slargato.*

DISPLE'ASANCE, s. [anger, discontent] *collera, scontentezza.*

DISPLE'ASANT, adj. [unpleasing, offending] *spiacevole, offensivo.*

To DISPLE'ASE [not to please, to offend] *dispiacere, offendere, non piacere.*

To displease one, *dispiacere ad uno.*

To displease God, *dispiacere a Dio, offenderlo.*

DISPLE'ASED, adj. *dispiaciuto, scontento, offeso.*

I am displeased with it, *me ne dispiace.*

He was displeased with my writing to him, *si trovò offeso perchè gli scrissi, s'offese che gli scrissi.*

I am utterly displeased with his carriage, *il suo portamento mi dispiace molto.*

DISPLE'ASURE, s. [discontent] *dispiacere, disgusto, dolore, travaglio, s. m. noja, molestia, s. f.*

To do a displeasure to one, *far qualche dispiacere ad uno.*

To incur the king's displeasure, *incorrer la disgrazia, o l'indegnazione del re.*

To DISPLE'ASURE [to displease, not to gain favour] *essere spiacevole, spiacere altrui, perder favore.*

To DISPLO'DE [to disperse with a loud noise; to vent with violence] *dispergere con grande strepito; scoppiare con violenza.*

DISPLO'SION, s. [the act of disploding; a sudden burst with noise] *l'atto del dispergere con gran fracasso; subitano e strepitoso scoppio.*

DI'SPORT, s. [pastime] *diporto, solazzo, spasso, passatempo, s. m. ricreazione, s. f.*

To DI'SPORT, v. n. [to divert, to take pleasure] *diportarsi, solazzarsi, spassarsi, divertirsi.*

To disport, v. a. [to divert] *divertire, dar sollazzo, dare spasso.*

DISPO'SAL, } s. [command, management] *disposizione, balia, s. f. comando, potere, s. m.*
DISPO'SE, }

I left it at his disposal, *l'ho lasciato alla sua disposizione.*

I am not at your disposal, *non sono in vostra balia, non sono sotto la vostra disciplina.*

To DISPO'SE [to prepare] *disporre, accomodare, metter in ordine, preparare.*

To dispose [to set in order] *disporre, ordinare, metter in ordine.*

To dispose of [to do what one pleases with a thing] *disporre, fare quel che si vuole d'una cosa.*

To dispose of one's estate by will, *disporre de' suoi beni in testamento, lasciare i suoi beni in testamento a qualcheduno.*

Man purposes, and God disposes, *l'uomo propone, e Dio dispone.*

I know not how to dispose of it, *non so come disfarmene, non so che farne.*

To dispose of another man's money, *disporre, o servirsi dell' altrui danaro.*

To dispose of a thing [to give it away] *disporre di che che si sia, darla via.*

To dispose of a daughter in marriage, *disporre di sua figlia, maritarla.*

How will you dispose of yourself? *che avete voglia di fare? che pensate di fare?*

To dispose one's time, *spendere il tempo.*

To dispose of a house [to let it] *appigionare una casa.*

To dispose of one [to send him away] *disfarsi d'uno, mandarlo via.*

I am yours to dispose of, *son tutto vostro.*

DISPO'SED, adj. *disposto, d'umore, nella disposizione di.*

Disposed to be merry, *disposto alla gioja, d'umor allegro.*

Disposed to laugh, *d'umor di ridere.*

Well, or ill disposed in health, *bene o mal disposto, in buona o cattiva salute.*

Disposed [prepared] *disposto, pronto, preparato, apparecchiato.*

Disposed [set in order] *disposto, ordinato, in ordine.*

DISPO'SER, s. *dispositore, s. m. che dispone.*

DISPOSI'TION, s. [order] *disposizione, s. f. ordine, s. m.*

Disposition [inclination] *disposizione, intenzione, voglia, volontà, s. f. pensiero, s. m.*

Disposition of body, *disposizione, o stato di salute.*

Disposition of mind, *disposizione, indole, talento.*

To DISPOSSE'SS [to deprive, to put or turn out of possession] *spossessare, privar dal possesso.*

DISPOSSE'SSED, adj. *spossessato.*

DISPO'SURE, s. [disposal] *disposizione, amministrazione, volontà, s. f. potere, maneggio, s. m.*

DISPRA'ISE, s. [blame, reproach] *biasimo, scorno, torto, s. m.*

To DISPRA'ISE [to discommend] *biasimare, vituperare, avvilire condannare, criticare.*

DISPRAISED, adj. *biasimato, vituperato, avvilito, condannato, criticato.*

DISPRA'ISINGLY, adv. [with blame] *biasimevolmente, vituperosamente.*

DISPRO'FIT, s. [loss, prejudice] *perdita, s. f. svantaggio, detrimento, pregiudizio, s. m.*

To DISPRO'FIT [to hurt] *nuocere, apportar nocumento, pregiudicare.*

DISPRO'OF, s. *confutazione, s. f.*

DISPROPO'RTION, s. [inequality] *sproporzione, inegualità.*

To DISPROPO'RTION [to mismatch, to join things unsuitable] *unir cose sproporzionate fra di loro, appajar malamente.*

DISPROPO'RTIONABLE, or DISPROPO'RTIONATE, adj. [unequal] *sproporzionato, che è fuori di proporzione, ineguale.*

DISPROPO'RTIONABLY, adv. *sproporzionatamente.*

To DISPRO'VE [to prove the contrary] *confutare, convincere, riprovare.*

To disprove an argument, *confutare un argomento.*

DISPRO'VED, adj. *confutato, convinto, riprovato.*

DISPRO'VING, s. *confutamento, s. m. il confutare.*

DISPU'NISHABLE, adj. [without penal restraint] *che non ha freno di castigo.*

DISPU'TABLE, adj. [that may be disputed] *disputativo, da disputarsi.*

DI'SPUTANT, s. [a disputer, one who holds a disputation] *un disputante.*

DISPUTA'TION, s. [a debate, dispute] *disputazione, disputa, s. f. il disputare.*

To hold a disputation in philosophy, *mantenere una disputa in filosofia.*

DISPU'TATIVE, adj. [contentious, quarrelsome] *disputativo, che ama a disputare, contenzioso.*

DISPUTAT'IOUS, adj. [inclined to dispute; cavilling] *inclinato a disputare, amico del cavillare.*

DISPU'TE, s. [debate] *disputa, questione, s. f. l'atto del disputare.*

Beyond all diſpute, *ſenza dubbio, ſenza contradizione.*

To DISPU'TE [to agitate, to maintain a queſtion] *diſputare, mantenere una queſtione.*

To diſpute [to conteſt, to debate] *diſputare, contraſtare, conteſtare, contendere.* pret. *conteſi.*

DISPU'TED, adj. *diſputato, contraſtato, conteſtato, conteſo.*

DISPU'TER, s. *diſputatore*, s. m.

DISPU'TING, s. *diſputamento*, s. m. *il diſputare.*

To DISQUA'LIFY [to make unfit; to diſable by ſome natural or legal impediment] *render inetto; diſabilitare per qualche impedimento naturale o legale.*

To diſqualify [to deprive of a right or claim by ſome poſitive reſtriction] *privare d'un diritto o preteſa con qualche preciſa reſtrizione.*

To DISQUI'ET [to trouble] *inquietare, tor la quiete, travagliare, tribolare.*

DISQUI'ET, s. [unquietneſs, trouble] *inquietudine, paſſione, tribolazione*, s. f. *travaglio, tormento*, s. m.

DISQUI'ETED, adj. *inquietato, travagliato, tribolato.*

DISQUI'ETLY, adv. *turbatamente, anſioſamente, ſenza ripoſo.*

DISQUISI'TION, s. [diligent ſearch or inquiry into] *inquiſizione*, s. f. *diligente ricercamento.*

To DISRA'NK [to put out of order] *diſordinare, mettere in diſordine.*

DISRA'NKED, adj. *diſordinato.*

DISREGA'RD, s. [ſlight, neglect] *negglienza, negligenza, traſcuraggine, poco conto, poca ſtima.*

To DISREGA'RD [to have no regard for, to ſlight] *diſprezzare, diſpregiare, traſcurare, negligere, far poco conto, non iſtimare.* pret. *negleſſi.*

DISREGA'RDED, adj. *diſprezzato, diſpregiato, traſcurato, negletto.*

DISRE'LISH, s. [bad taſte, nauſeouſneſs] *nauſea, guſto guaſto.*

Diſreliſh [diſlike, ſqueamiſhneſs] *diſamore, averſione.*

To DISRE'LISH [not to reliſh, to diſlike] *non approvare, non amare, non trovar di ſuo guſto.*

I diſreliſh that, *io non approvo queſto, non lo trovo buono, non mi piace, non è di mio guſto.*

DISREPUTA'TION, } s. [ill name,
DISREPU'TE, } diſcredit] *cattiva riputazione, cattivo nome, infamia*, s. f. *diſcredito, diſonore*, s. m.

To bring one's ſelf into diſrepute, *diſcreditarſi, diſonorarſi.*

To bring a diſrepute upon a thing, *diſcreditare che che ſi ſia, farl perder di credito.*

DISRESPE'CT, s. [incivility] *incivilità, mancanza di riſpetto, malacreanza, irreverenza*, s. f.

To DISRESPE'CT [to ſhow no reſpect, to ſlight, to be uncivil] *diſprezzare, non portar riſpetto, trattar incivilmente.*

DISRESPE'CTFUL, adj. *incivile, malcreato, poco riſpettoſo, irreverente.*

A diſrepectful anſwer, *una riſpoſta incivile, o poco riſpettoſa.*

To DISRO'BE [to pull off the robe] *levar la veſta, ſpogliare della gonna.*

DISRO'BED, adj. *ſpogliato.*

Diſrobed [naked] *nudo.*

DISSATISFA'CTION, s. [diſcontent] *diſguſto, diſpiacere*, s. m.

DISSATISFA'CTORY, adj. [diſpleaſing, offenſive] *ſpiacevole, rincreſcevole, diſpiacevole, diſpiacente.*

To DISSA'TISFY [to diſguſt, to diſpleaſe, to offend] *ſpiacere, diſpiacere, non piacere, diſguſtare, offendere.* pret. *ſpiacqui, diſpiacqui, offeſi.*

DISSATISFY'D, or DISSATISFI'ED, adj. *mal ſoddisfatto, malcontento, diſguſtato.*

To DISSE'CT [to cut open a dead body, to anatomize] *notomizzare, far notomia.*

DISSE'CTED, adj. *notomizzato.*

DISSE'CTING, } s. *notomia, anato-*
DISSE'CTION, } *mia*, s. f.

DISSE'CTOR, s. *notomiſta*, s. m. *colui che eſercita la notomia.*

To DISSE'ISE [to diſpoſſeſs] *ſpoſſeſſare.*

DISSE'ISED, adj. *ſpoſſeſſato.*

DISSEISE'E, s. [a perſon who is put out of his lands] *colui che è ſpoſſeſſato.*

DISSE'ISIN, s. [an unlawful diſpoſſeſſing a man of his land, or tenement] *uſurpazione di beni appartenenti ad altra perſona.*

DISSE'ISOR, } s. [a man or a
DISSE'ISORESS, } woman who puts another out of the poſſeſſion of his land] *quegli, o quella che ſpoſſede, uſurpatore*, s. m. *uſurpatrice*, s. f.

To DISSE'MBLE [to pretend, to feign] *diſſimulare, fingere, naſcondere il ſuo penſiero, far ſembiante, far viſta.* pret. *finſi, naſcoſi.*

To diſſemble [to conceal] *diſſimulare, naſcondere, celare, palliare.*

DISSE'MBLED, adj. *diſſimulato, finto, naſcoſto, celato, palliato.*

DISSE'MBLER, s. [a diſſembling man or woman] *diſſimulatore*, s. m. *un uomo finto o diſſimulato, una donna finta, o ingannatrice.*

DISSE'MBLING, s. *diſſimulazione, il diſſimulare, finzione*, s. f.

Diſſembling, adj. *diſſimulato, finto.*

A diſſembling man, *un uomo finto, o doppio.*

A diſſembling woman, *una donna finta, o doppia.*

DISSE'MBLINGLY, adv. *diſſimulatamente, fintamente.*

To DISSE'MINATE [to ſow, to ſpread abroad] *diſſeminare, ſeminare, ſpargere.* pret. *ſparſi.*

To diſſeminate errors, *diſſeminare errori.*

DISSE'MINATED, adj. *diſſeminato, ſeminato, ſparſo.*

DISSEMINA'TION, s. *il diſſeminare.*

DISSE'NSION, s. [diſagreement, ſtrife] *diſſenſione, diſcordia, controverſia, diviſione*, s. f.

To ſow diſſenſions among friends, *metter la diſcordia fra gli amici.*

DISSE'NT, s. [contrariety of opinions] *contrarietà di pareri, ſentimenti contrari.*

To DISSE'NT [to diſagree, to differ in opinion] *diſſentire, diſcordare, non convenire, non concorrere nel medeſimo parere.*

DISSENTA'NEOUS, adj. [diſagreeing, contrary] *contrario, oppoſto, differente, diſſimile, diſcordante.*

DISSE'NTER, s. [one of a different or contrary opinion] *uno che non concorre nel medeſimo parere.*

Communemente ſi chiamano *diſſenters* i preſbiteriani, e altri, che ricuſano d'uniformarſi alla diſciplina della Chieſa Anglicana.

DISSERTA'TION, s. [a diſcourſe upon any point or ſubject] *diſcorſo, trattato*, s. m. *diſſertazione*, s. f.

To DISSE'RVE [to do a prejudice] *pregiudicare alcuno, farli qualche pregiudizio, o torto, danneggiarlo.*

DISSE'RVED, adj. *pregiudicato, danneggiato.*

DISSE'RVICE, s. [an ill office or turn, prejudice] *torto, danno, pregiudizio, cattivo ufficio*, s. m.

That does great diſſervice to me, *ciò mi fa gran torto.*

DISSE'RVICEABLE, adj. *che fa torto, nocivo, pregiudizievole.*

To DISSE'TTLE [to diſorder] *mettere in diſordine, ſconvolgere, ſregolare, diſordinare, ſcomporre.* pret. *ſconvolſi, ſcompoſi.* preſ. *ſcompongo.*

DISSE'TTLED, adj. *ſconvolto, ſregolato, diſordinato, ſcompoſto.*

To DISSE'VER [to ſeparate, to part] *ſceverare, ſeparare, dividere.* pret. *diviſi.*

DISSE'VERED, adj. *ſceverato, ſcelto, ſeparato, diviſo.*

Two provinces diſſevered by a river, *due provincie ſeparate da un fiume.*

DISSI'MILAR, adj. [of a different kind or nature] *diſſimile, che non ha le medeſime qualità, vario, diverſo.*

DISSIMI'LITUDE, s. [unlikeneſs] *diſſimilitudine, diſſimiglianza*, s. f.

DISSIMULA'TION, s. [diſſembling] *diſſimulazione, il diſſimulare, finzione*, s. f.

DI'SSIPABLE, adj. [that may be diſſipated] *che ſi può diſſipare.*

To DI'SSIPATE [to diſperſe, to ſcatter] *diſſipare, diſfare, diſtruggere, ridurre al nulla, diſſolvere.* preſ. *diſfò.* pret. *diſfeci, diſtruſſi.*

To diſſipate the humours, *diſſipare, o diſſolvere gli umori.*

The heat of the ſun diſſipates the fog, *il calore del ſole diſſipa la nebbia.*

To diſſipate [to conſume, to ſpend, to waſte] *diſſipare, conſumare, ſpendere, mandare a male, prodigalizzare, ſcialacquare.* pret. *ſpeſi.*

To diſſipate one's wealth, *diſſipare, conſumare, ſcialacquare il ſuo avere.*

DI'SSIPATED, adj. *diſſipato, diſfatto, diſtrutto, ridotto al nulla, diſſoluto, conſumato, ſpeſo, prodigalizzato, ſcialacquato.*

DISSIPA'TION, s. [a conſuming, or waſting]

waſting] *diſſipamento, disfacimento,* s. m. *conſumazione, diſtruzione, rovina,* s. f.

DISSO'LVABLE, } adj. [that may be
DISSO'LUBLE, } diſſolved] *diſſolubile, che ſi può diſſolvere.*

To DISSO'LVE [to looſen, to unbind, to penetrate a ſolid body, and divide its parts] *diſſolvere, diſciorre, diſunire, disfare.* preſ. *diſciolgo, diſuniſco, disfò.* pret. *diſciolſi, disfeci.*

Fire diſſolves all bodies, *il fuoco diſſolve ogni corpo.*

To diſſolve [to melt] *diſſolvere, liquefare, fondere.*

To diſſolve metal, *diſſolvere, o liquefare un metallo.*

To diſſolve [to diſſipate] *diſſolvere, diſtemperare, ſtemperare, diſſipare, conſumare.*

To diſſolve humours, *diſſolver gli umori.*

To diſſolve a ſwelling, *diſſipare, mollificare un tumore.*

To diſſolve [to break off] *diſſolvere, rompere, ſeparare, disfare, diſunire,* preſ. *diſuniſco.* pret. *ruppi, disfeci.*

To diſſolve the parliament, *diſſolvere, o ſeparare, o licenziare il parlamento.*

To diſſolve a ſpell, *rompere un incanteſimo.*

To diſſolve, verb neut. [to melt] *diſſolverſi, fonderſi, liquefarſi, diſſiparſi.*

A metal that diſſolves, *un metallo che ſi diſſolve.*

A ſwelling that diſſolves, *un tumore che ſi diſſipa o ſvaniſce.*

To diſſolve in pleaſures, *abbandonarſi, darſi in preda ai piaceri, vivere nelle diſſolutezze.*

DISSO'LVED, adj. *diſſoluto, diſciolto, diſunito, disfatto.* v. To diſſolve.

A thing that cannot be diſſolved, *una coſa indiſſolubile, che non ſi può diſſolvere, o ſeparare.*

To be diſſolved in luxury, *abbandonarſi al luſſo.*

DISSO'LVENT, s. [a medicine fitted to diſperſe collected humours] *medicamento diſſolutivo.*

DISSO'LVING, adj. *diſſolvente, che diſſolve, diſſolutivo, che ha facoltà di diſſolvere.*

DISSO'LVER, s. [that which has the power of diſſolving] *quello che ha il potere di diſſolvere.*

DISSO'LVIBLE, adj. [liable to periſh by diſſolution] *atto a diſſolverſi, diſſoluibile.*

DI'SSOLUTE, adj. [looſe, wanton, lewd] *diſſoluto, licenzioſo, diſoneſto, ſregolato, ſcapeſtrato.*

A diſſolute life, *un vita diſſoluta, o licenzioſa.*

A diſſolute man, *uno ſcapeſtrato.*

DI'SSOLUTELY, adv. [lewdly] *diſſolutamente, licenzioſamente, ſregolatamente.*

DI'SSOLUTENESS, s. [lewdneſs, debauchery] *diſſolutezza, licenza, sfrenatezza, diſoneſtà,* s. f.

DISSOLU'TION, s. [ſeparation of parts] *diſſoluzione, ſeparazione, diviſione,* s. f. *ſpartimento,* s. m.

Diſſolution [breaking off] *diſſoluzione, caſſazione, abolizione, annullazione,* s. f.

The diſſolution of parliament, *la diſſoluzione, o caſſazione del parlamento.*

A diſſolution of marriage, *ſeparazione di matrimonio.*

Diſſolution [lewdneſs] *diſſolutezza, licenza, diſoneſtà, sfrenatezza,* s. f.

DI'SSONANCE, s. [diſagreement in ſound] *diſſonanza, diſcordanza,* s. f.

Diſſonance [a contrariety, or difference in opinion] *diſſonanza, diſcrepanza, diſcordia, differenza,* s. f. *diſparere,* s. m.

DI'SSONANT, adj. [harſh, unharmonious] *aſpro, privo d'armonia.*

Diſſonant [incongruous, diſagreeing] *che non s'accorda, che non ſi confà.*

DISCO'RDANT, adj. [untunable, jarring] *diſſonante, che non conſuona, diſcordante, ſcordante, diſcorde.*

Diſcordant [diſagreeing, contrary] *diſcordante, diſſonante, non corriſpondente, diſſimile, diverſo, diſcrepante, diſcorde, contrario, differente.*

My opinion is different from yours, *la mia opinione è contraria alla voſtra, io ſono d'opinione diſcrepante dalla voſtra.*

To DISSUA'DE [to divert, to adviſe the contrary] *diſſuadere, contrario di perſuadere, ſmovere, ſconſigliare, ſtornare, fraſtornare, rimuovere.* pret. *diſſuaſi, ſmoſſi, rimoſſi.*

DISSUA'DED, adj. *diſſuaſo, ſmoſſo, ſconſigliato, ſtornato, fraſtornato, rimoſſo.*

DISSUA'DER, s. *quegli, o quella che diſſuade.*

DISSUA'DING, adj. *che diſſuade.*

DISSUA'SION, s. *diſſuaſione,* s. f.

DISSUA'SIVE, adj. [apt, or proper to diſſuade] *diſſuaſivo, diſſuaſorio, che ha forza di diſſuadere.*

A diſſuaſive, s. [an argument or diſcourſe proper for diſſuading] *argomento, o diſcorſo diſſuaſorio.*

DISSY'LLABLE, s. [a word of two ſyllables] *parola, o voce di due ſillabe.*

DI'STAFF, s. [an inſtrument uſed in ſpinning] *conocchia, rocca, ſtrumento di canna o ſimile ſopra'l quale le donne pongono lana o lino da filare, e tengonla in cintola.*

A diſtaff-full, s. *roccata, conocchiata,* s. f. *pennecchio,* s. m. *quella quantità di lana o lino che ſi mette in ſulla rocca.*

To ſpin from a diſtaff, *filare con una rocca.*

To DISTA'IN, v. To ſtain.

DI'STANCE, s. [the remoteneſs of one thing from another, whether in point of time, place, or quantity] *diſtanza, e diſtanzia,* s. f. *quello ſpazio che è tra l'un luogo e l'altro, o tra una coſa e l'altra.*

At a diſtance, *da lungi, da lontano.*

He was a great diſtance from hence, *egli era ad una gran diſtanza, o molto diſtante da qui.*

I know my diſtance, *ſo quel che mi ſta bene, o mi conviene.*

To keep one at a diſtance, *tenerſi diſcoſto da uno, guardare il ſuo decoro, non familiarizzarſi troppo con lui.*

To keep one's diſtance, *eſſer riſpetto, o, portar riſpetto.*

To DI'STANCE [to put a diſtance, or ſpace between] *ſcoſtare, diſcoſtare.*

DI'STANCED, adj. *ſcoſtato, diſcoſtato.*

Diſtanced [left behind in a race, outſtripped] *avanzato, laſciato in dietro in una corſa.*

DI'STANT, adj. [far] *diſtante, lontano, diſcoſto.*

Equally diſtant, *in una eguale diſtanza.*

DISTA'STE, s. [diſlike] *averſione, contrarietà, ripugnanza, noja,* s. f. *diſguſto, diſpiacere, faſtidio, tedio, rincreſcimento,* s. m.

To take diſtaſte at ſomething, *odiare, avere a noja o in faſtidio, faſtidiare, faſtidire che che ſi ſia, non poterla patire.*

To give diſtaſte, *diſpiacere, faſtidire, faſtidiare, recar faſtidio o noja.*

To DISTA'STE [to give diſtaſte] *diſpiacere, offendere, faſtidire, faſtidiare, recar noja o faſtidio.* preſ. *faſtidiſco.* pret. *diſpiacqui, offeſi.*

To diſtaſte [to take diſtaſte] *faſtidire, faſtidiare, odiare, aver in faſtidio.*

DISTA'STEFUL, adj. [that gives diſtaſte] *faſtidioſo, nojoſo, rincreſcevole, tedioſo, odioſo, diſcaro, offenſivo, ingrato, ſpiacevole.*

A diſtaſteful expreſſion, *un' eſpreſſione offenſiva o ſpiacevole.*

Diſtaſteful news, *novelle diſcare.*

DISTE'MPER, s. [diſeaſe] *morbo,* s. m. *malattia,* s. f.

Diſtemper [diſorder in a ſtate or kingdom] *diſordine, perturbamento, imbroglio,* s. m. *confuſione,* s. f.

Diſtemper [in painting, colours mixt with white of eggs, or ſuch gluey ſubſtances, inſtead of oil or water] *tempera,* s. f. *guazzo.*

To paint in diſtemper, *dipignere a tempera, o a guazzo.*

To DISTE'MPER [to put out of order] *ſtemperare, diſordinare, far male, nuocere, fare ammalato.*

To diſtemper [to trouble] *intorbidare, diſordinare, metter in diſordine, confondere, diſturbare, diſquietare.*

The leaſt thing diſtempers my ſtomach, *la minima coſa mi guaſta, mi ſconvolge lo ſtomaco.*

DISTE'MPERED, adj. *ſtemperato, diſordinato, ammalato, indiſpoſto.*

A diſtempered ſtomach, *uno ſtomaco ſvogliato.*

DISTE'MPERATURE, s. [being out of order] *indiſpoſizione, diſordine.*

To DISTE'ND [to ſtretch out] *ſtendere, diſtendere, allargare, dilatare.* pret. *ſteſi, diſteſi.*

To diſtend a bladder with wind, *gonfiare una veſcica.*

DISTE'NDED, adj. *ſteſo, diſteſo, allargato, dilatato.*

DISTENTION, s. [a ſtretching out, or enlarging] *diſtendimento, allargamento,* s. m. *diſtenſione, eſtenſione,* s. f.

DISTE'NT, s. [the place through which any thing is ſpread] *diſteſa, eſteſa,* s. f.

To DISTE'RMINATE [to bound place from place, or to ſeparate one place from another] *terminare, limitare, por termini, ſeparare.*

DIS-

Distreminated, adj. *terminato, limitato, separato.*

Di'stich, s. [two verses in a poem making a compleat sense] *distico*, s. m.

To **Disti'l** [to drop, or run down drop by drop] *stillare, uscire a goccia a goccia, scaturire, gocciolare, cascare a gocciole.*

To distil [to draw off some of the particles of a mixt body by fire] *stillare, distillare, cavar l'umor di qualunque cosa per forza di caldo, lambiccare.*

Disti'llable, adj. *che si può distillare.*

Distilla'tion, s. [distilling] *distillazione, stillazione*, s. f.

A distillation of humours, *flussione che casca dal cervello.*

Disti'lled, adj. *stillato, distillato, v.* To distil.

Disti'ller, s. [he that distils] *stillatore*, s. m.

Disti'lment, s. [that which is drawn by distillation] *lo stillato; cosa tratta per distillazione.*

Disti'lling, s. *distillamento, stillamento*, s. m. *distillazione, stillazione*, s. f.

Distilling, adj. [dropping] *stillante, distillante, che gocciola.*

Di'stinct, adj. [clear] *distinto, chiaro, netto.*

A distinct pronunciation, *una pronuncia distinta.*

Distinct [different] *distinto, differente, dissimile.*

Distinct [separate] *distinto, separato, diviso.*

Disti'nction, s. [difference] *distinzione, differenza, diversità*, s. f.

Distinction [separation] *distinzione, separazione*, s. f. *separamento*, s. m.

Distinction by points, *punteggiatura*, s. f.

Disti'nctive, adj. [that makes a distinction] *che fa una distinzione, che distingue.*

A distinctive mark, *un segno di distinzione.*

Disti'nctively, adv. *per distinzione.*

Disti'nctness, s. Ex. the distinctness of pronunciation, *una pronuncia distinta, o chiara.*

To **Disti'nguish** [to discern between, to put a difference between] *distinguere, sceverare, separare, discernere, partitamente considerare*, pret. *distinsi.*

To distinguish one thing from another, *distinguere una cosa da un' altra.*

Disti'nguishable, adj. [which may be distinguished] *che si può discernere o distinguere.*

Disti'nguishableness, s. *differenza, distinzione*, s. f.

Disti'nguished, adj. *distinto, sceverato, seperato, discernuto, considerato.*

Disto'rtion, s. [a wresting or wringing awry] *contorsione, morfia*, s. f. *gesto, rivolgimento di bocca, o di membri.*

To **Disto'rt** [to wrest, or pull awry] *contorcere, ritorcere, rivolgere*, pret. *contorsi, ritorsi, rivolsi.*

To distort one's mouth, *distorcere o storcere la bocca.*

To distort one's eyes, *stralunare gli occhi.*

Disto'rted, adj. *contorto, ritorto, storto, rivolto.*

Distorted eyes, *occhi stralunati.*

Disto'rtion, v. Distorsion.

To **Distra'ct** [to interrupt, to trouble] *distrarre, distraere, e distraggere, diviare, storre*, pref. *distrao e distraggo, stolgo*, pret. *distrassi, stolsi.*

To distract [to make mad] *fare arrabbiare, far dare nelle smanie, far impazzire.*

Distra'cted, adj. *distratto, diviato, stolto.*

Distracted [mad] *pazzo, impazzito, forsennato.*

To run distracted, *smaniare, menar smanie.*

A distracted house, *una casa piena di confusione, e disunione.*

Distracted times [troubles] *tempi imbrogliati, disordini, confusioni nello stato.*

Distra'ctedly, adv. [madly, frantickly] *mattamente, smaniosamente, infuriatamente.*

Distra'ctedness, } s. *distrazione,*
Distra'ction, } *smania*, s. f. *diviamento, svagamento*, s. m.

To **Distra'in** [to seize upon a person's goods for the satisfaction of rent, parish duties, &c.] *staggire, stagginare, sequestrare, fare*, pref. *staggisco.*

Distra'ined, adj. *staggito, sequestrato.*

Distra'ining, s. *staggina*, s. f. *sequestramento, sequestro*, s. m.

Distra'iner, s. *staggitore*, s. m. *colui che staggisce.*

Distra'ught, part. a. [distracted] *impazzato, smaniato.*

Di'stress, s. [the act of distraining] *staggina*, s. f. *sequestro, sequestramento*, s. m.

Distress [misery, calamity, adversity] *miseria, avversità, calamità, necessità, estremità*, s. f. *bisogno, duopo*, s. m.

To **Distre'ss** [to reduce into distress] *ridurre in miseria, angustiare, affannare, tribolare.*

Distre'ssed, adj. *augustiato, affannato, tribolato, ridotto in miseria, o in necessità.*

They were distressed for forage, *si trovavano in grande angustia di viveri.*

To be in a distressed condition, *essere ridotto in grande distretta o miseria, trovarsi in uno stato miserabile.*

Distre'ssful, adj. [miserable, full of trouble, full of misery] *misero, pien d'affanno, colmo di guai.*

To **Distri'bute** [to divide, to share] *distribuire, dispensare, compartire, dare a ciascheduno la sua rata*, pref. *distribuisco, compartisco.*

Distri'buted, adj. *distribuito, dispensato, compartito.*

Distri'buter, s. *distribuitore*, s. m. *che distribuisce.*

Distri'buting, } s. [a dividing, or
Distribu'tion, } sharing] *distribuimento*, s. m. *distribuzione*, s. f. *il distribuire.*

Distri'butive, adj. [which serves to distribute] *distributivo, che distribuisce.*

Distributive justice, *la giustizia distributiva.*

Distri'butively, adj. [by distribution] *distributivamente.*

District, s. [a particular territory, the bounds or extent of a jurisdiction] *distretto, territorio*, s. m. *giurisdizione*, s. f.

Distru'st, s. [or diffidence] *diffidenza, sfidanza*, s. f. *sospetto*, s. m.

To **Distru'st** [to suspect, to be jealous of] *diffidare, non aver fidanza, non fidarsi, sfidare, sospettare, dubitare.*

I distrust him, *mi diffido di lui, non mi fido a lui.*

Distrusted, adj. *diffidato, sfidato.*

Distributing, s. *diffidanza, e diffidenza, sfidanza*, s. f.

To **Distu'rb** [to interrupt, to hinder] *disturbare, sturbare, interrompere, impedire*, pref. *impedisco.*

To disturb [to trouble, to vex] *disturbare, fastidire, molestare, inquietare.*

To disturb [to disorder] *disturbare, metter in disordine, confondere, metter in confusione, imbrogliare.*

To disturb one's rest, *disturbare l'altrui riposo.*

To disturb one that speaks, *interrompere un che parla.*

To disturb one at work, *divertire, impedire, o svolgere uno dal suo lavoro.*

That disturbs me, *ciò mi fa fastidio e mi dispiace.*

To disturb one in his possession, *molestare uno nel suo possesso.*

Why will you disturb your mind about such things? *perchè rompersi la testa, o affannarsi per simile cose?*

Distu'rbance, s. [trouble, disorder] *disturbo, disturbamento, scompiglio, strepito, commovimento, tumulto*, s. m. *disturbanza, molestia, perturbazione, alterazione*, s. f.

There's a great disturbance, *vi è un gran tumulto.*

A disturbance of mind, *inquietudine, cura, pensiero.*

Distu'rbed, adj. *disturbato, v.* To disturb.

Distu'rber, s. *perturbatore, sturbatore*, s. m.

A disturber of the publick peace and quiet, *sturbatore del pubblico riposo.*

Distu'rbing, s. *disturbamento, disturbo*, s. m.

To **Distu'rn** [to turn off] *mandar via, scacciare, cacciar via.*

Disu'nion, s. [discord, disagreement] *disunione, discordia, dissensione, controversia, lite*, s. f.

To **Di'sunite** [to divide, to set at variance] *disunire, mettere in discordia, o in disunione*, pref. *disunisco.*

To disunite [to disjoin, to separate] *disunire, disgiugnere, separare.*

Disuni'ted, adj. *disunito, diviso, separato, disgiunto.*

Disu'nity, s. [a state of actual separation] *disunione, lo essere separato.*

Dis-

DIṢU'SAGE, or DISU'SE, s. [a being out of uſe] *diſuſanza*, s. f. *diſuſo*, s. m.

To DISU'SE [to forbear the uſe of, to break one's ſelf of a uſe or cuſtom] *diſuſare, divezzare, diſviare, laſciar l'uſo.*

To diſuſe wine, *diſuſarſi dal vino, tralaſciare di bere del vino.*

DISU'SED, adj. *diſuſato, divezzato, ſviato.*

DISVO'UCH [to deſtroy the credit of; to contradict] *contraddire, opporſi alle affermazioni altrui.*

DISWI'TTED, adj. [deprived of the witts; made diſtracted] *privo di ſenno, mentecatto, impazzato.*

DIT, s. [a ditty; a poem] *poemetto, compoſizioncella in verſi.*

DITCH, s. [a trench about a field or town] *foſſo*, s. m.

To DITCH [to make a ditch] *fare un foſſo.*

To ditch in or about [to ſurround with a ditch] *affoſſare, vallare, circondare di foſſo.*

To ditch [to cleanſe a ditch] *nettare, o vuotare un foſſo.*

DITCH-DELI'VERED, adj. [brought forth in a ditch] *partorito in un foſſo; nato in un foſſo.*

DI'TCHED, adj. *affoſſato, circondato di foſſo.*

DI'TCHER, s. *uno che affoſſa, o fa foſſi.*

DITHYRA'MBICK, s. [a ſong in honour of Bacchus] *inno o canto in lode di Bacco.*

DITHYRAMBICK, s. [any poem written with wildneſs] *ogni poema ſcritto come in furia e con impeto.*

DI'TONE, s. [a double tone in muſick, or the greater third] *ditono*, s. m. *termine muſicale.*

DI'TANDER, s. [an herb] *lepido*, s. m.

DI'TTANY, s. [a ſort of herb] *dittamo*, s. m. *ſorta d'erba.*

DI'TTIED, adj. [ſung; adapted to muſick] *cantato, accoppiato con muſica.*

DI'TTO [the aforeſaid, the ſame] *ſopraddetto, il meddeſimo.*

DI'TTY, s. [a ſong that has the words ſet to muſick] *un aria, una canzone in muſica.*

DI'VAN, s. [the Grand Seignior's counſel] *il divano, il conſiglio del Gran Turco.*

To DIVA'RICATE [to ſtraddle] *ſlargare, o aprire in due.*

To DIVE [to duck, to go under water] *tuffare, o tuffarſi, immergerſi, andar ſott' acqua, nuotar ſott' acqua.*

To dive [to enquire narrowly into a matter] *eſplorare, conſiderare, eſaminare, crivellare, diſcutere ſottilmente una materia.*

I can't dive into it, *non poſſo capirlo.*

To dive into one's purpoſe, *penetrare gli altrui diſegni o andamenti.*

DIVED, adj. *tuffato, immerſo, eſplorato, conſiderato, eſaminato, crivellato, diſcuſſo, diſcuſſato.*

DI'VER, s. [one who dives] *tuffatore, colui che ſi tuffa nell' acqua, nuotator ſott' acqua.*

Diver, s. [a bird called didapper] *ſmergo*, s. m. *uccello d'acqua.*

To DIVE'RGE [to tend various ways from one point] *andare o tendere per diverſe vie da un punto fiſſo.*

DI'VERS, adj. [different, ſundry] *diverſi, molti, parecchi.*

In divers places, *in diverſi luoghi, in parecchi luoghi.*

Of divers humours, *di diverſi, o molti colori.*

Of divers kinds, *di differenti ſpecie.*

Of divers colours, *biſbetico, fantaſtico.*

DIVE'RSE, adj. *diverſo, differente, in differenti direzioni.*

To DIVERSIFY' [to make divers, to vary] *diverſificare, far diverſo, variare, differenziare.*

DIVERSIFY'D, adj. *diverſificato, variato, differenziato.*

DIVERSIFY'ING, s. *diverſificazione, varietà, differenza*, s. f.

DIVE'RSION, s. [recreation, paſtime] *divertimento, traſtullo, paſſatempo*, s. m. *ricreazione, e recreazione*, s. f.

A little diverſion, *ricreazioncella.*

Diverſion [turning aſide] *diverſione, termine militare.*

To give the enemy a diverſion, *fare una diverſion d'armi al nemico.*

DIVE'RSITY, s. [variety, difference] *diverſità, varietà, differenza, contrarietà, diſtinzione*, s. f.

DI'VERSLY, adv. *diverſamente, con diverſità, differentemente, variamente.*

To DIVE'RT [to entertain, to delight] *divertire, ricreare, ſollazzare, rallegrare, confortare*, preſ. *divertiſco.*

To divert [to lead aſide, to turn aſide, to take off] *divertire, rivolgere altrove, diſtornare, ſtornare, ſvolgere, diſtorre*, pret. *rivolſi, ſvolſi, diſtolſi*, preſ. *diſtolgo.*

To divert to other ſtudies, *volger la mente ad altri ſtudi.*

DIVE'RTED, adj. *divertito*, v. To divert.

DIVE'RTING, adj. [pleaſant] *ſollazzevole, piacevole, guſtoſo, grato.*

To DI'VERTISE [to afford divertiſement, to recreate] *divertire, ricreare, ſollazzare, dar piacere. Non è più in uſo.*

DIVE'RTISEMENT, s. [diverſion, recreation, ſport] *divertimento, ſollazzo, piacère, traſtullo, paſſatempo, intertenimento*, s. m. *ricreazione*, s. f.

DIVERTI'SING, adj. *ſollazzevole, piacevole, guſtoſo.*

DIVES, s. [the name of a rich man in the goſpel] *il ricco epulone, del quale ſi fa menzione nella ſcrittura ſacra.*

To DIVI'DE [to part, to put aſunder] *dividere, ſpartire, ſeparare, diſunire, diſgiugnere l'una parte dall' altra*, preſ. *ſpartiſco, diſuniſco*, pret. *diviſi, diſgiunſi.*

They divided their armies into two bodies, *diviſero il loro eſercita in due corpi.*

To divide [to ſhare, or diſtribute] *dividere, diſtribuire, dar la rata; ſcompartire.*

To divide a thing into four parts, *dividere o ſcompartire una coſa in quattro parti.*

To divide a thing amongſt ſeveral people, *dividere o diſtribuire che che ſi ſia a molti.*

To divide [to ſet at variance] *cagionare diviſione.*

To divide a family, *dividere una famiglia, mettervi la diſcordia.*

To divide, verb neut. *dividerſi, ſepararſi.*

DIVI'DED, adj. *diviſo, ſeparato, ſpartito, diſunito, diſgiunto*, v. To divide.

To be divided in opinion, *eſſer di parere diverſo, o differente.*

DI'VIDEND, s. [in arithmetick, a number given to be divided] *numero dividente, il numero da dividerſi.*

Dividend [in trade, is an equal ſhare of the profits of a joint ſtock] *parte, porzione*, s. f.

DIVI'DER, s. *dividitore*, s. m. *che divide.*

DIVI'DERS [a pair of mathematical compaſſes] *compaſſo matematico.*

DIVI'DING, s. *il dividere, diviſione*, s. f.

DIVI'DUAL, adj. [ſhared or participated in common with others] *diviſo o partecipato in comme con altri.*

DIVINA'TION, s. [a divining, or preſaging things to come] *divinazione*, s. f. *indovinamento, precidimento*, s. m.

DIVI'NE, adj. [belonging to God, heavenly] *divino, che s'appartiene a divinità, o che partecipia di eſſa.*

Divine [excellent] *divino, eccellente, eſquiſito, ottimo, ſublime, ammirabile, ſingolare, ſupremo.*

The divine virtues are faith, hope, and charity, *le virtù* teologali *ſono la fede, la ſperanza, e la carità.*

A divine, s. [a theologian] *un teologo.*

To DIVI'NE [to foretell] *divinare, indovinare, predire, preſagire*, preſ. *preſagiſco*, pret. *prediſſi.*

To divine [to gueſs] *indovinare, congetturare, preſentire, ſoſpettare*, preſ. *preſentiſco.*

DIVI'NED, adj. *divinato, indovinato, predetto, preſagito, congetturato, preſentito, ſoſpettato.*

DIVI'NELY, adv. *divinamente, maraviglioſamente, eccellentemente, ſingolarmente, ottimamente.*

DIVI'NER, s. [conjurer, ſooth-ſayer] *indovino, indovinatore*, s. m.

DIVI'NERESS, s. [propheteſs] *profeteſſa, maga*, s. f.

DIVI'NING, s. *divinazione, indovinazione*, s. f. *divinamento, indovinamento, predicimento*, s. m.

DIVI'NITY, s. [the Divine Nature, the Godhead] *divinità*, s. f. *natura, ed eſſenza di Dio.*

Divinity [deity] *una divinità, una deità.*

Divinity [that ſcience which has for its object God and his revelation] *teologia*, s. f.

To ſtudy divinity, *ſtudiar la teologia.*

DIVISIBI'LITY, s. [the being diviſible] *diviſibilità*, s. f.

Divi'sible, adj. [that may be divided] *diviſibile, atto ad eſſer diviſo.*
Divi'sion, s. [dividing] *diviſione*, s. f. *il dividere, ſpartimento*, s. m.
Diviſion of ſoldiers, *brigata.*
I am not of that diviſion, *non ſono di quella brigata.*
Diviſion [in muſick, is the dividing a tune into many ſmall notes] *trillo*, s. m.
To run diviſions, *gorgheggiare, termine de' muſici, tirar di gorgia.*
Diviſion [variance, diſcord] *diviſione, diſcordia, diſunione*, s. f. *diſturbo, divario*, s. m.
Diviſion [going into parties] *diviſione, fazione, ſedizione*, s. f.
Diviſion [in printing, is a ſmall line betwixt two words, as man-hood] *una diviſione, una virgola fra due parole.*
Divo'rce, s. [a diſſolution of a marriage, or ſeparation of man and wife] *divorzio*, s. m. *ſeparazione, che ſi fa tra marito e moglie.*
A bill of divorce, *una lettera di divorzio.*
To **Divo'rce** [to make a divorce] *ripudiare, fare divorzio, ſeparare.*
To divorce, *ripudiare la moglie, far divorzio con la moglie, ſciogliere il matrimonio.*
Divo'rced, adj. *ripudiato, ſeparato.*
She is divorced from her huſband, *ella è ripudiata, ella ha fatto divorzio con ſuo marito.*
They are divorced, *hanno fatto divorzio, ſono ſeparati.*
Divo'rcer, s. *che ripudia, che fa divorzio.*
Divo'rcing, s. *divorzio, ripudio, e repudio*, s. m.
Diure'tick, adj. [having the power to provoke urine] *diuretico.*
Diu'rnal, adj. [daily] *diurno, del dì.*
The diurnal motion of the heavens, *il moto diurno de' cieli.*
Diurnal, s. [day-book] *un giornale.*
Diutu'rnity, s. [laſtingneſs, or long continuance] *diuturnità*, s. *lunghezza di tempo.*
To **Divu'lge** [to publiſh, to reveal] *divulgare, pubblicare, rivelare, manifeſtare, far noto.*
Divu'lged, adj. *divulgato, pubblicato, rivelato, manifeſtato, pubblico, noto.*
Divu'lger, s. *quegli, o quella che divulga.*
Divu'lging, s. *il divulgare.*
To **Di'zen** [to dreſs, to deck] *veſtire, adornare. Voce plebea.*
Di'zzard, s. [a fool, a filly fellow] *un balordo, uno ſciocco, uno ſcemo, un minchione, uno ſcioperato.*
Di'zziness, s. [giddineſs, or ſwimming of the head] *vertigine*, s. f. *giramento di teſta, offuſcamento di cerebro, che fa parere, che ogni caſa ſi mova in giro, capogiro*, s. m.
I was taken with a dizzineſs, *fui aſſalito da una vertigine.*
Di'zzy, adj. [giddy] *vertiginoſo, che patiſce di vertigine.*

To **Di'zzy** [to whirl round, to make giddy] *cagionar vertigini, aggirare intorno.*
To **Do**, *fare*, pref. *fo*, pret. *feci.*
To do one's buſineſs, *fare i fatti ſuoi.*
To do one's beſt [to endeavour] *fare ogni sforzo, ingegnarſi.*
To have to do with one, *avere a fare ad uno, o con uno.*
Do well, and have well, *chi fa bene, bene aſpetta.*
Self do, ſelf have, *chi la fa la paga, qual aſin da in parete tal riceve.*
To do by others as we would be done by, *fare ad altri quel che noi vorremmo che ci foſſe fatto.*
A man can do no more than he can do, *com' aſino ſape così minuzza rape, ognuno fa quel che ſa.*
When we are at Rome we muſt do as they do at Rome, *vivi in Roma alla Romana.*
To do [to diſpatch] a buſineſs, *ſpedire, o fare un negozio.*
To do [to deal] well with one, *trattar uno bene, portarſi bene con lui.*
He has done very ill by me, *egli s'è portato malamente con me, egli non m'ha trattato come doveva.*
How d'ye? how d'ye do? how do you do? *come ſtate? come ve la paſſate? come ſtate di ſalute?*
How does ſhe do? *come ſta ella?*
How does he do? *come ſta egli?*
To do one a good turn or kindneſs, *rendere qualche ſervizio ad uno.*
To do like for like, *render la pariglia.*
This won't do, this won't do your work [or ſerve your turn] *queſto non baſta, queſto non fa per voi.*
If ever you do ſo again, *ſe mai commettere il medeſimo errore.*
Do but come, and you ſhall ſee, *baſta che veniate, e vedrete.*
Pray do, *ve ne prego.*
That ſuit does very well upon you, *queſto abito vi ſta molto bene.*
Will you do as we do? *queſto è un complimento del quale gl' Ingleſi ſi ſervono comunemente per invitare coloro che vengono a vederli mentre che ſono a tavola, come ſarebbe a dire fra noi Italiani, Volete mangiare un boccone con noi?*
I had much ado to be rid of him, *a gran pena mi ſbrigai di lui.*
But whatever you do, uſe him well, *ma ſopra tutto, trattatelo bene.*
To have ſomething to do with one, *aver da fare con uno.*
What have you to do with it? *ch' importa a voi? di che v'ingerite, v'imbarazzate, v'intrigate?*
I have nothing to do with other mens affairs, *non m'impaccio, o non m'ingeriſco de' fatti altrui.*
I'll have nothing more to do with him, *non voglio più aver niente a ſpartire con lui, non voglio ingerirmi più de' fatti ſuoi.*
I have nothing to do with it, *non me ne impaccio, queſto non mi riguarda.*
What had we beſt do? *che faremo? che partito prenderemo?*

To do as one is bid, *obbedire, ubbidire.*
To ſet one to do, *dare ordine o incombenza a qualcheduno.*
To have carnally to do with a woman, *conoſcere carnalmente una donna.*
Do with me as you ſhall think fit, *diſponete di me a voſtra voglia, fate di me quel che vi pare e piace.*
To do good, *benificare, giovare, far pro.*
To do again, or to do over again, *rifare, far di nuovo.*
To do away, *levare.*
To do away the ruſt, *levare la ruggine.*
To do on [to put on] *mettere*, pref. *miſi.*
To do off, *disfare.*
To do up [to fold up] *piegare, imballare.*
To do over [to daub over] *intonacare.*
To do over with ſilver or gold, *inargentare, indorare.*
è da notare che oltre le precedenti, e altre ſignificazioni, ci ſerviamo di queſto verbo come d'un verbo auſiliare, principalmente quando vogliamo dar più enfaſi al diſcorſo.
Ex. I do love you, *vi amo.*
I do ſee it, *lo vedo.*
Do'cible, } adj. [teachable, apt to
Do'cile, } learn] *docile, trattabile, atto ad apprendere gl' inſegnamenti.*
Do'cibleness, } s. [teachableneſs,
Doci'lity, } tractableneſs] *docilità*, s. f.
Dock, s. [tail] *coda*, s. f. *o più toſto il tronco della coda de' cavalli.*
Dock [breech] *le natiche.*
Dock [leather for a horſe's tail] *borſa di cuojo nella quale s'inviluppa la coda del cavallo.*
Dock [an herb] *ſpezie d'erba così detta.*
Bur-dock, *lappola*, s. f.
Dock, } [a place for ſhips to
Wet-dock, } ride in] *darſena*, s. f.
Dock, } [a place to build and re-
Dry-dock, } pair ſhips] *ridotto dove ſi fabbricano e racconciano i vaſcelli.*
To **Dock** [to cut off the tail] *tagliar la coda.*
Do'cked, adj. *ſcodato, privo di coda.*
Strong docked, *forte, gagliardo, robuſto, forte di ſchiena.*
Do'cket, s. [a bill with direction ty'd to the goods, and directed to the perſon and place they are to be ſent to] *direzione*, s. f. *pezzo di carta nel quale è ſcritto lo indirizzo del luogo dove abita una perſona, legato a quella roba che ſe gli manda.*
Docket [a law term, a ſmall piece of paper or parchment, containing the heads of a large writing] *ſommario, eſtratto*, s. m. *cedola che contiene i capi principali d'una ſcrittura.*
Do'ctor, s. [one who has taken the higheſt degree in any art or ſcience at a univerſity] *dottore*, s. m. *uno che inſegna, o che è ſtato onorato delle inſegne del dottorato.*

Doctor of divinity, law, or physick, *dottore di teologia, di legge, di medicina.*

A paltry doctor, *un dottoraccio.*

To Doctor [to physick, to cure] *medicare, dar medicine.*

Do'ctoral, adj. [belonging to a doctor] *dottorale, di dottore.*

Do'ctorally, adv. [in the manner of a doctor] *a mo' di dottore.*

Do'ctorship, or Do'ctorate, s. *dottorato,* s. m. *grado e dignità del dottore.*

Do'ctress, s. [a she-doctor] *dottoressa,* s. f.

Do'ctrinal, adj. [instructive] *istruttivo, dottrinale.*

Do'ctrine, s. [knowledge, learning] *dottrina, scienza,* s. f. *sapere,* s. m.

Doctrine [precepts, sentiments] *dottrina, istruzione, massima,* s. f. *precetto, insegnamento,* s. m.

Do'cument, s. [lesson, instruction, precept] *documento, insegnamento, precetto, ammaestramento,* s m.

Do'dder, s. [a weed which winds itself about other herbs] *androsace,* s. f.

Do'ddered, adj. [overgrown with dodder] *troppo pieno dell' erba chiamata androsilace.*

To Do'ddle [to daddle] along, *camminar vacillando, come un bambino che comincia a camminare.*

Dode'cagon, s. [a regular polygon consisting of twelve equal sides and twelve angles] *dodecagono,* s. f. *figura che ha dodici angoli, e dodici facciate.*

To Dodge [to use craft, to deal with tergiversation] *usar furberia, usar astuzia nel contrattare.*

To dodge [to shift place as another approaches] *cambiar di luogo quando un altro s'avvicina.*

To dodge [to play fast and loose, to raise expectations and disappoint them] *giuocar presto e perdere; destare speranza in uno e poi deluderlo.*

Do'dkin, s. [a small piece of money about the value of a farthing] *un quattrino.*

Do'dman, s. [the name of a fish] *nome di pesce.*

Doe, s. [the female of a buck] *damma,* s. f.

To doe, *v.* To do.

Doer, s. [he that does any thing] *fattore, facitore,* s. m. *fattrice, facitrice,* s. f.

An evil doer, *un malfattore, una malfattrice.*

Does [the third person from do; for doth] *terza persona singolare del presente del verbo* To do.

To Doff [to put off dress] *spogliare, torre la veste.*

To doff [to strip] *strappar le vesti d' addosso.*

To doff [to put away, to get rid of] *por via, liberarse, alleggerirsi.*

To doff [to delay; to refer to another time] *ritardare, mandare ad altro tempo, differire.*

Dog, s. [a creature well known] *un cane.*

A little dog, *un cagnolino.*

A mastiff dog, or band dog, *un mastino.*

A house dog, *un cane di casa.*

A bull dog, *cane che combatte contro i tori.*

A bear dog, *cane che cambatte contro gli orsi.*

A setting dog, *bracco da ferma.*

A lap dog, *un cagnolino di bologna.*

To be used like a dog, *esser trattato da cane.*

A dog's collar, *collare d'un cane.*

Dog-cheap [a very good pennyworth] *buon mercatissimo, a vil prezzo.*

To play the dog in the manger, *far come il can dell' ortolano, che non mangia la lattuga, nè la lascia mangiare agli altri.*

Love me, and love my dog, *abbi rispetto al cane per amor del padrone.*

What? keep a dog and bark myself? *come? mantenar servi, e poi che mi serva da me stesso?*

A hungry dog will eat dirty pudding, *a chi ha fame ogni cosa par buona.*

A dog [andiron] *alare,* s. m.

A dog of iron [for walls] *catena,* s. f. *quel ferro, che si pone negli edifizi, che gl' incatena, e serra insieme per maggior fortezza.*

To have a dog in one's belly [to be dogged] *aver qualche grillo in testa, esser di cattivo umore.*

A mere dog in a doublet [a sordid fellow] *un gran briccone, un pretto villano.*

An old dog will learn no tricks, *cavallo vecchio non impara l'ambio*

Dog tricks, *furberie, mariolerie, bricconerire.*

Dog-house, *zecca,* s. f.

Dog-berry, *corniuola,* s. f.

Dog-berry tree, *corniuolo,* s. m.

Dog-fish, sea-dog, *can di mare.*

Dog's-grass, *gramigna,* s. f.

Dog's-tongue, *lingua di cane.*

Dog's kennel, *canile,* s. m.

Dog-days, or canicular days, *canicola, o giorni canicolari.*

To Dog [to follow close] *codiare, andar dietro ad uno senza che se ne accorga, spiando con diligenza quel ch' ei fa, e dov' ei va.*

Do'gteeth [the teeth in the human head next to the grinders; the eye-teeth] *quel dente che è vicino al mascellare, e sotto l'occhio.*

Doge, s. *doge,* s. m. *titolo di principato, e di capo di repubblica.*

The doge of Venice, or Genoa, *il doge di Venezia o di Genoa.*

Dogged, adj. [from to dog] *codiato, spiato.*

Dogged [sullen] *cagnesco, arcigno, burbero, austero, aspro.*

A dogged look, *un viso arcigno, o cagnesco.*

Do'ggedly, adv. *d'un' aria austera, o arcigna.*

Doggedly dealt with, *maltrattato.*

Doggedness, s *umor bisbetico, stravaganza, ghiribizzo, capriccio.*

Do'gger, s. [a ship about eighty tons burthen] *spezie di vascelletto, di ottanta tonellate incirca.*

Do'ggerel, s. [pitiful poetry, paltry verses] *versacci, cattiva poesia.*

Dog-hearted, adj. [cruel, pitiless, malicious] *crudele, sanguinario, senza pietà, pieno d'invidia, di malizia, e di dispetto; che ha un cuor di cane.*

Do'ggish, adj. [currish] *brutale, cagnesco, di cane.*

Do'ghole, s. [a vile hole] *un buco da cani, un canile, un luogo infame o cattivo.*

Dogke'nnel, s. [a little house or hut for dogs] *canile, piccola casetta pel cane.*

Do'gma, s. [tenet] *dogma, insegnamento,* s. m.

Dogma'tical, } adj. [instructive]
Dogma'tick, } *dogmatico, di dogma, istruttivo.*

A dogmatical style, *uno stile dogmatico.*

Dogmatical [positive] *assoluto, positivo.*

Do'gmatist, s. [one who is opinionative or bigotted to his own opinion] *un caparbio.*

Dogmatist [one who teaches, or is the author of any new opinion or sect] *autore, inventore di nuove opinioni, fondatore di nuove sette.*

To Do'gmatise [to give instructions or precepts, to instruct] *istruire, ammaestrare, insegnare,* pres. *istruisco.*

Do'gsleep, s. [pretended sleep] *sonno finto, il finger di dormire.*

Do'gsmeat, s. [refuse; vile stuff] *cosa vile, cosa di rifiutarsi; cibo di cani.* Dryden.

Do'gtrot, s. [a gentle trot like that of a dog] *trotto di cane, il trottare soavemente come fanno i cani.*

Dogwe'ary, adj. [tired as a dog] *stracco come un cane, stanchissimo.*

Dolly, s. *sorta di tela fatta di lana.*

Doing [from to do] *il fare, fatto,* s. m. *azione,* s. f.

I blame you for doing that, *vi biasimo d'aver fatto ciò.*

I don't like these doings, *queste cose non mi piaciono.*

To be taken in the deed doing, *esser preso sul fatto, esser colto all' improvviso.*

'Twas your doing that I lost my money, *voi siete causa, ch' io ho perduto i miei danari.*

Doing, adj. *facendo.*

What are you doing? *che state facendo, che fate?*

'Tis a doing, *si sta facendo.*

It has been long a doing, *è un pezzo che vi sono attorno.*

To keep one doing, *dar dell' impiego o dell' occupazione ad uno, tenerlo occupato o impiegato in che che sia.*

Doit, or Doitkin, s. [a small coin in the Low Countries, in value less than our farthing] *un bezzo, un quattrino.*

It is not worth a doit, *non vale un fico.*

Dole, s [a part or pittance] *parte, porzione, pietanza,* s. f.

Dole [a gift of a nobleman to the people]

people] *dono*, s. m. *munificenza, liberalità d'un gran signore al popolo.*

DOLES, or DOOLES [slips of pasture left between the furrows of a ploughed land] *ciglio, ciglione*, s. m. *terreno che resta intiero fra due solchi.*

Dole fish [fish which the fishermen in the north-seas usually receive for their allowance] *porzione di pesce che i pescatori del mare settentrionale ricevono.*

A dole-meadow, wherein divers persons have a share, *un prato, che appartiene a diverse persone.*

To DOLE [to deal, to distribute] *dare, distribuire, scompartire, far liberalità.*

DO'LEFUL, adj. [sad, mournful, lamentable] *tristo, cattivo, lamentevole, deplorabile, dolente, doloroso, mesto.*

A doleful story, *una dolente istoria.*

A doleful voice, *una voce mesta, o lamentevole.*

DO'LEFULLY, adj. *dolentemente, dolorosamente, lamentevolmente.*

DOLL, s. [a little girl's puppet or baby] *la bambola*, s. f. *fantoccino di stracci che serve di trastullo alle fanciulline.*

DO'LLAR, or RIXDOLLAR, s. [a Dutch coin] *un tallaro, uno scudo d' Alemagna.*

DOLO'UR, s. [grief, anguish, sorrow] *dolore, cordoglio*, s. m. *doglia, afflizione*, s. f.

DOLO'ROUS, adj. [grievous, painful] *doloroso, dolente.*

DOLO'ROUSNESS, s. *dolore, cordoglio*, s. m. *doglia*, s. f.

DO'LPHIN, s. f. [a sea-fish] *delfino, e delfino*, s. m. *pesce di mare.*

The Dolphin, or Dauphin of France, *Delfino, titolo di principato in Francia, spettante al primogenito del Re.*

DOLT, s. [a mere sot, a blockhead] *uno sciocco, uno scemo, uno scempiato, un semplice, un minchione, uno sciocco, uno scimunito, un pecorone, un balordo.*

DO'LTISH, adj. *scempio, scempiato, sciocco, semplice, di poco senno, scemo.*

DO'LTISHLY, adj. *scioccamente, semplicemente, da stupido.*

DO'LTISHNESS, s. [sottishness, stupidity] *scempiaggine, scimunitaggine, balordaggine, beffaggine, scempiezza, stupidità, sciocchezza*, s. f.

DOMA'IN, s. [dominion, empire] *sovranità, dominio.*

Domain [possession, estate] *possessione, beni.*

DOME, s. [a vaulted roof or tower of a church; a cupola] *cupola*, s. f. *volta, che rigirandosi intorno ad un medesimo centro si regge in se medesima.*

Dome [among chymists, an arched cover for a reverberatory furnace] *cappello*, s. m.

DO'MESMAN, s. [a judge appointed to hear and determine law suits] *un giudice delegato.*

Domesman [an obsolete word for a confessor] *un confessore.*

DOME'STICK, adj. [belonging to a houshold] *domestico, e dimestico, familiare, di casa.*

A domestick animal, *un animale domestico.*

Domestick affairs, *affare domestici.*

Domestick news, *novelle del paese.*

A domestick, s. [a menial servant] *un domestico, un servo di casa.*

To DOME'STICATE [to withdraw from the publick] *render privato.*

DO'MICIL, s. [a dwelling house, an habitation or abode] *domicilio, ricettacolo, albergo, abituro*, s. m.

To DO'MINATE [to predominate, to prevail over the rest] *predominare, poter più degli altri.*

DOMINA'TION, s. [dominion, empire] *dominazione, signoria*, s. f. *dominio*, s. m.

DOMINA'TIONS, [one of the nine orders of angels] *dominazioni, uno de' nove ordini angelici del paradiso.*

To DOMINE'ER [to bear rule, or authority] *dominare, signoreggiare.*

He domineers wherever he is, *domina dovunque egli è.*

You shall not domineer over me, *voi non mi signoreggerete, voi non avrete mai dominio sopra di me.*

To domineer [to vapour over others] *bravare, braveggiare, fare il bravo.*

DOMINE'ERED, adj. *dominato, signoreggiato, bravato, braveggiato.*

DOMINE'ERING, adj. *insolente, imperioso, borioso, fiero, altiero.*

DOMI'NICAL, adj. *dominicale.*

The dominical letter, *la lettera dominicale.*

DOMI'NICAN, s. [a Dominican friar, of the order of St. Dominick] *un Domenicano, un frate dell' ordine o religione di San Domenico.*

DOMI'NION, s. [government, authority, jurisdiction] *dominio, stato*, s. m. *signoria, giurisdizione, proprietà*, s. f.

The king's dominions, *gli stati del re, il paese, o le terre del suo dominio.*

The dominion of Wales, *il principato di Gallia.*

DON [a Spanish title] *don.*

EX. DON PETER, *don Pietro.*

To DON [to put on] *metter sù.*

DONA'TION, s [a grant, a deed of gift] *donazione*, s. f. *dono*, s. m.

DO'NATISTS, s. [a sort of hereticks] *donatisti, eretici della setta di Donato.*

DO'NATIVE, s. [gift] *donativo, dono*, s. m.

Donative [present] *donativo, regalo, presente*, s. m.

DONE, adj. [from to do] *fatto*, v. To do.

It is done, *è fatto.*

I have done your business, *ho fatto il vostro negozio.*

Done, I yield to it, *va, ci consento, toppa.*

There's no good to be done here for us, *non ci è niente di buono da fare quì per noi.*

When all is done, *in fine, in somma, finalmente.*

'Twill be wisely done of you, *voi farete prudentemente, o saviamente.*

I have done with him, *non voglio più impacciarmi con lui.*

Easy to be done, *facile a fare.*

That may be done, *fattibile, fattevole.*

'Twas kindly done of him, *egli s'è portato molto cortesemente verso di voi.*

It shall be done, *lo farò, si farà.*

The church is done, *il servizio divino è finito.*

This meat is not done enough, *questa carne non è cotta a bastanza.*

DONE'E, s. [a law term, he or she to whom lands or tenements are given] *donatario*, s. m. *donataria*, s. f. *colui, o colei a chi si fa una donazione.*

DO'NJON, s. [in fortification, is a large tower or redoubt of a fortress, where the garrison may retreat in case of necessity, and capitulate with advantage] *il maschio d'una fortezza, torrione nel mezzo d'una rocca, che serve di ritarata alla guarnigione in caso di bisogno.*

DO'NOR, or DO'NOUR, s. [one who gives lands, tenements, &c.] *donatore*, s. m. *donatrice*, s. f.

DON'T, *è una abbreviazione di* DO NOT.

I don't love it, *non l'amo.*

I don't care for it, *non me ne curo.*

DO'ODLE, s. [a trifler, an idler] *uno scioperato, un ozioso.*

DOOM, s. [sentence, judgment] *sentenza*, s. f.

A heavy doom, *una terribile sentenza.*

Doomsman, *un giudice, un arbitro.*

DO'OMSDAY, *finimondo, l'ultimo giorno del giudicio universale.*

Doomsday in the afternoon, *quando pioveranno fichi e uve passe, mai.*

Doomsday, or doomsday book [a tax book] *libro dove son registrati tutti i beni d'Inghilterra, e fu fatto nel tempo di Guglielmo il conquistatore; si conserva nella tesoreria reale.*

To DOOM [to sentence] *sentenziare, giudicare, condannare.*

DO'OMED, adj. *sentenziato, giudicato, condannato.*

DOOR, s. [the entrance into a house] *porta*, s. f. *uscio*, s. m.

A back door, *una porta falsa.*

To knock at the door, *picchiare alla porta.*

Lock the door, *serrate la porta.*

He lives next door to me, *dimora a canto di me, o nella casa contigua alla mia.*

This is next door to madness, *questa è quasi una pazzia.*

He was next door to be being killed, *poco mancò che non fosse ammazzato.*

To go within doors, *entrare in casa.*

To keep within doors, *stare in casa, non uscire.*

To go out of doors, *uscir di casa.*

To turn one out of doors, *scacciar uno fuor di casa.*

A thing out of doors [out of date] *cosa che è fuor d'uso, o non più usitata.*

A door keeper, *un portinajo.*

The door keeper in a prison, *un carceriere.*

A door bar, *sbarra di porta.*

The door-sill, *il limitare, o la soglia della porta.*

Door posts, *imposte, o stipiti della porta.*

Dor, s. [a kind of insect] *sorta d'insetto che ha ali.*

A dor [a term used in Westminster school, for leave to sleep a while] *licenza di dormire.*

Dore'e, or Dora'do, s. [a sea-fish, called also St. Peter's fish] *orata*, s. f. *sorta di pesce, così detta dal colore dell oro.*

Do'rick, adj. *Dorico.*

Dorick order [one of the five orders of architecture; its columns are simple without pilasters] *ordine Dorico.*

Dorick, or Dorian musick [a kind of grave and solemn musick] *musica grave, o patetica.*

Do'rmant, adj. [sleeping] *dormente, che dorme.*

Dormant-tree [a great beam which lies across a house] *una gran trave.*

To lie dormant [not to be put to use] *tener serrato o come morto, non servirsi d'una cosa.*

Money that lies dormant, *danaro morto, che non frutta nulla, del quale non si tira alcuno profitto.*

Dormer Wi'ndow [a window made in the roof of a house] *spiraglio*, s. m. *finestra fatta nel tetto.*

Do'rmitory, or Do'rter, s. [a sleeping place in a monastery] *dormitoro, e dormitorio*, s. m. *luogo dove si dorme, ma è proprio de' monasteri, e de' conventi.*

Do'rmouse, s. [a wild mouse living in hollow trees, and sleeping all the winter] *ghiro*, s. m.

He sleeps like a dormouse, *dorme come un ghiro.*

Dorp, s. [a country town or village] *una terra, un villaggio, un casale.*

Do'rser, s. [a great basket to carry things on horseback] *paniere*, s. m. *paniera*, s. f.

Do'rter, Do'rtoir, Do'rture, s. [the common room where all the friars of a convent sleep] *dormitoro*, s. m.

Dose, s. [the quantity of physick which a physician prescribes to his patient to take at once] *dose*, s. f. *quantità determinata di medicina da prendersi in una volta.*

A dose of physick, *una dose di medicina.*

He has his dose [is fuddled] *egli è cotto, egli è ubriaco.*

A dose of julep, *una presa di giuleppe.*

To Dose, *proporzionar la medicina all' ammalato o al male.*

Do'tage, s. *vaneggiamento, soverchio amore.*

Dotage [loss of understanding, imbecillity of mind] *perdita d'intelletto, imbecillità di mente.*

A Do'tard, s. *un vecchio rimbambito.*

An old dotard, *un povero vecchio che non ha cervello.*

To Dote, *vaneggiare, pargoleggiare, bamboleggiare, far cose da bambini, aver perso il cervello per soverchia età.*

To dote upon one [to be extreme fond of him] *amar molto una persona, amarla soverchiamente.*

Doted, adj. *vaneggiato, pargoleggiato, amato soverchiamente.*

Do'ting, adj. *ex.* An old doting man, *un vecchio rimbambito.*

Do'tingly, adv. [fondly] *con soverchio amore, con soverchia tenerezza.*

Do'ttard, s. [a tree kept low by cutting] *albero tenuto basso col tagliarlo in vetta.*

Do'tterel, s. [the name of a bird] *sorta d'urcello.*

Double, adj. [twofold, twice as much, or twice the value] *doppio, due volte tanto.*

A double sole, *un suolo doppio.*

A double pistole, *un dobblone.*

A double house, *una cosa doppia, che ha due camere in ogni piano.*

To be double [to be married] *esser ammogliato.*

A double man, *un uomo ammogliato, che ha moglie.*

Double [dissembling, treacherous] *doppio, finto.*

A double dealer [a cheat] *un furfante, un furbo, un briccone, un mariuolo.*

Double-hearted, double-tongued, *ingannatore, bugiardo.*

Double-edged, *a due tagli.*

A doubled-edged sword, *una bipenne, una spada a due tagli.*

Double-tongued, *bugiardo, mentitore.*

Double, s. [duplicate, writing] *copia d'una scrittura.*

A horse that carries double, *un cavallo che porta in groppa.*

I gave double the price, *l'ho pagato il doppio.*

To fold double, *piegare in due.*

Doubles [folds] *pieghe.*

Doubles [cunning shifts] *giri, rigiri.*

A double [in printing, a mistake of the compositor in setting the same words twice over] *errore di compositore nel comporre la medesima parola due volte.*

To Double [to make double] *duplicare, raddoppiare, doppiare.*

To double a rank, *raddoppiare le fila.*

To double the soldier's pay, *accrescer la paga a' soldati.*

To double a cape, *trapassare un capo.*

To double the guard, *raddoppiar le guardie.*

To double again, *raddoppiare.*

To double [among hunters, a hare is said to double, when she winds about to deceive the hounds] *volteggiare, dar volta, parlando d'una lepre.*

Do'ubled, adj. *duplicato, addoppiato, raddoppiato, doppiato.*

Do'ubleness, s. [the state of being double] *doppiezza, l'essere doppio.*

Dou'blet, s. [an old sort of garment for men] *giubbetto, giubbone*, s. m.

Do'ublets [at dice, are throws of the same sort, as two fours, two fives, &c.] *pari, due.*

To throw a doublet, *tirar un numero pari.*

To put one in a stone doublet [to cast him into a goal] *mettere uno in prigione.*

Do'ubling, s. *il duplicare*, v. To double.

The doublings of a horse, *le giravolte d'una lepre.*

Do'ubly, adv. *doppiamente.*

Doubt, s. [uncertainty] *dubbio*, s. m. *incertezza*, s. f.

Without doubt, without all doubt, *senza dubbio, indubitatamente.*

No doubt but he will come, *verrà senza dubbio.*

I make no doubt of it, *non ne dubito.*

Do you make a doubt of it? *ne dubitate?*

There's no doubt to be made of it, *non bisogna dubitarne, non c'è luogo da dubitarne.*

To doubt [to make a doubt, to be uncertain] *dubitare, dubbiare, stare in dubbio, esser ambiguo.*

I doubt it very much, *ne dubito molto.*

To doubt [to suspect] *dubitare, sospettare.*

Do'ubted, adj. *dubitato, dubbiato, sospettato.*

It is not to be doubted, *non c'è luogo da dubitare.*

Do'ubtful, adj. [dubious, uncertain] *dubbioso, dubbievole, incerto.*

Doubtful [who is in doubt, or in suspence] *dubbioso, ambiguo, irresoluto.*

Do'ubtfully, adv. *dubbiosamente, con dubbio*

Doubtfulness, s. *dubbio*, s. m. *incertezza*, s. f.

Doubting, s. *dubbio, il dubitare.*

Do'ubtingly, adv. [in a doubting manner, dubiously] *dubbiamente, in modo dubbioso.*

Do'uetless, adj. *certo, indubitabile, sicuro, del quale non si può dubitare.*

Doubtless, adv. [without doubt] *senza dubbio, indubitatamente, sicuramente, certamente.*

Do'ucet, s. [a kind of custard] *spezie di lattajuola.*

Doucets [the testicles of deer] *testicoli di cervo.*

Do'ucker, s. [a bird that digs in the water] *spezie di smergo.*

Dough, s. *pasta*, s. f.

Dough-baked, *mezzo cotto.*

Do'ughy, adj. [unsound, soft, unhardened] *pastoso, molle, non indurito.*

Do'ughty, adj. [valiant, stout] *valoroso, prode, forte, animoso, coraggioso.*

To Douse [to put over head suddenly in the water] *immergere all' improvviso nell' acqua.*

To douse [to fall suddenly into the water] *rastrar nell' arqua improvvisamente.*

Dove, s. [a female pigeon] *una colomba.*

A ring dove, *un colombaccio, un colombo salvatico.*

A turtle dove, *una tortorella.*

A dove-house, } s. *un colombajo, una colombaja, stanza dove stanno i colombi, e dove covano.*
A dove-cot,

Do'wager, s. [a widow who enjoys her dower] *una vedova, ma si dice di principessa, o altra persona grande.*

The queen-dowager, *la regina vedova.*

A countess-dowager, *una contessa vedova.*

DOWDY, s. [a fat, thick, ill dressed, and inelegant woman] *una donnaccia.*

DO'WER, s. [the marriage portion brought by a wife to her husband] *dote, e dota*, s. f. *quello, che la moglie da al marito.*

Dower [that which the wife has with her husband after marriage, or after her husband's decease] *pensione che il marito da dopo la sua morte, e durante la sua vita alla moglie.*

DO'WERED, adj. [supplied with a portion] *dotato, che ha dote.*

DO'WERLESS, adj. [without a portion] *senza dote, che non ha dote, povero.*

DO'WLAS, s. [a sort of linen cloth] *sorta di tela grossolana.*

DOWN, s. [down feather, or down] *piuma*, s. f. *la penna più fina degli uccelli.*

A down bed, *coltrice, arnese da letto pien di piuma su quale si giace.*

Down [soft hair] *lanugine*, s. f. *peli morbidi che cominciano ad apparire a' giovani nelle guance.*

Downs [hilly plains, hills consisting of sands] *luoghi aprichi e sabbiosi.*

Down [hill of sand] *massa d'arena nel mare.*

Down, adv. *giù, a basso.*

To go down, *andar giù.*

To bring down, *calare, o portar giù.*

To lie down, *coricarsi.*

To sit down, *sedersi.*

To set down, *scrivere in carta, mettere in iscritto.*

To fall down, *cascare.*

He fell down stairs, *cascò giù delle scale.*

To pay money down, *pagar danari contanti.*

To drink one down, *imbriacare uno, farlo bere tanto che non possa reggersi in piedi.*

The wind is down, *il vento è cascato.*

He has little down the wind, *egli ha il vento contrario, i suoi affari vanno di male in peggio.*

Down with him, *buttatelo giù, dagli, dagli.*

Up and down, *su e giù, qua e là.*

Upside down, *sozzopra, sotto sopra.*

To turn upside down, *rovesciare, mettere a rovescio.*

Down upon the nail, *danari contanti.*

Down the stream, *a seconda della corrente.*

This will never down with him, *egli non consentirà mai a ciò.*

A down look, *un aria austera.*

To DOWN [to knock, to subdue, to conquer] *buttar in terra con dare un colpo sul capo, buttar giù, vincere, soverchiare.*

DO'WNCAST, adj. [bent down, directed to the ground] *dimesso, che volge a terra, che mira all' ingiù.*

DOWNFALL, s. *traboccamento, disfacimento*, s. m. *rovina, cascata*, s. f.

To have a great downfall, *scadere d'una gran fortuna.*

DOWNFA'LLEN, adj. [ruined, fallen] *rovinato, cascato giù.*

DOWNGY'RED, adj. [let down in circular wrinkles] *calato giù in cerchio.*

DOWNHILL, s. [declivity, descent] *declività, discesa, luogo declive.*

Downhill, adj. [declivous, descending] *declive, che va all' ingiù.*

DOWNLO'OKED, adj. [having a dejected countenance, sullen, melancholy] *tristo, maninconoso, addolorato.*

DOWNRIGHT, adv. *giù a piombo.*

Downright, adj. [plain and clear] *manifesto, evidente, chiaro.*

Downright [plain, open] *franco, schietto, sincero, aperto, puro.*

A downright contradiction, *una contradizione manifesta.*

He is a downright man, *egli è un uomo franco, è sincero.*

A downright truth, *la pura verità.*

A downright rogue, *un pretto villano, un furbo in chermisi.*

DOWNSITTING, s. [rest, repose] *riposo, il riposarsi.*

DOWNWARD, or DOWNWARDS, adv. *giù.*

To look downwards, *guardar giù.*

Downward, adj. *declive, che va all' ingiù.* Dryden.

Downward [melancholy, depressed, dejected] *maninconoso, tristo, afflitto.*

DO'WNY, adj. [full of down] *lanuginoso, che ha lanugine, molle, morbido.*

A downy fruit, *un frutto lanuginoso.*

Downy beard, *lanugine.*

DOWRE, } s. *dota o dote.*
DOWRY, }

DO'XY, s. [a mistress] *l' innamorata quando è peccatrice.*

To DOZE [to grow heavy or sleepy] *addormentarsi, esser sonnacchioso, sonnacchiare.*

To doze [to dull, to stupify] *render stupido, istupidire.*

DOZED, adj. *addormentato, sonnacchioso, che ha gli occhi aggravati di sonno, stupefatto, reso, stupido.*

DOZEL, s. [a tent for a wound without a head] *spezie di testa che si mette in una piaga.*

DO'ZEN, s. [the number of twelve] *dozzina*, s. f.

A dozen of eggs, *una dozzina d'uova.*

A baker's dozen, *tredici per dozzina.*

DO'ZINESS, s. [sleepiness, drousiness] *gravezza d' occhi cagionata dalla voltà di dormire, sonnolenza.*

DO'ZY, adj [sleepy, drousy, sluggish] *sonnacchioso, pigro per sonno.*

DRAB, s. [common whore] *puttanaccia, bagascia.*

To DRAB [to whore] *fare la puttana.*

DRA'BLER, s. [a small top-sail] *piccola vela che s'attacca ad una più grande.*

DRACHM, s. [an old Roman coin] *moneta antica Romana.*

Drachm [an eighth part of an ounce] *ottava parte d'un oncia, dramma.*

DRAD, adj. [terrible, dreaded] *terribile, temuto.*

DRAFF, s. [wash for hogs] *broda che si da a porci, beverone*, s. m.

DRA'FFY, adj. [filthy] *sudicio, sporco.*

DRAG, s. [hook] *uncino, gancio, graffio*, s. m.

A drag-net [tramil, or sweep net] *tramaglio, strascino*, s. m. *sorta di rete.*

Drags [pieces of wood so joined, as swimming upon the water they may bear a burden, or load of wares upon the river] *zatta, e zattera*, s. f.

To DRAG [to draw by force] *tirar per forza, strascinare.*

To drag one to prison, *strascinare uno in prigione.*

To drag [to fish for oysters] *pescare delle ostriche.*

DRA'GANT, adj. *ex.* Gum dragant [a sort of gum] *dragante*, s. m. *lagrima che stilla dalla radice d'una pianta spinosa del medesimo nome, la quale si condensa in gomma.*

DRAGGED, adj. *strascinato.*

To DRA'GGLE [to draw, or trail] *strascinare, strascicare, tirare per terra.*

A woman that draggles her gown, *una donna che strascina la sua gonna pel fango.*

Draggled, adj. *strascinato, strascicato.*

DRA'GGLE-TAIL, *una donna che tira per terra lo strascico.*

DRA'GNET, s. *sorta di rete, che si strascica per terra.*

DRA'GON, s. [a sort of serpent] *drago, dragone*, s. m. *sorta di serpente.*

Sea dragon, *dragone marino, sorta di pesce.*

DRA'GONET, s. [a little dragon] *dragoncello, picciol drago.*

DRA'GON-FLY, s. [a fierce stinging fly] *sorta di mosca che ha un pungiglione molto terribile quando punge.*

DRA'GONISH, adj. [having the form of a dragon] *che ha forma e figura di drago.*

DRA'GONLIKE, adj. [furious, fiery] *furioso, feroce come drago.*

DRA'GONS-BLOOD, s. *sorta di ragia.*

Dragon-wort, *dragontea*, s. f. *erba medicinale.*

DRAGO'ON, or DRAGO'ONERS, s. [a soldier who fights sometimes on horseback, and sometimes on foot] *dragone, soldato che combatte ora a cavallo ora a piedi.*

DRAIN, s. [a water-course, or sink] *fogna*, s. f. *condotto sotterraneo per ricevere e sgorgare acqua, e immondizie.*

To DRAIN [to draw off waters by furrows, ditches, &c.] *fognare, far fogne, e smaltitoi d'acqua.*

To drain a ditch, *scolare, o seccare un fosso.*

To drain a fen, *spadulare, seccare, rasciugare una palude.*

To drain one's purse, *vuotar la borsa.*

DRA'INABLE, adj. [which may be drained] *che si può fognare, scolare, o seccare.*

DRA'INED, adj. *fognato, scolato, seccato.*

DRA'INER, s. *colui che fogna.*

DRAKE, s. [a male duck] *anitra.*

Duck and drake [a sort of play with a flat peeble or stone thrown upon the surface

ſurface of the water] *ſorta di giuoco, che ſi fa col far ſaltare delle pietre ſopra l'acqua.*

To make ducks and drakes with one's money, *ſcialacquare il ſuo danaro, ſpenderlo in vano.*

Drake, s. [a ſmall piece of artillery] *ſorta d' artigliera, drago, cannone piccolo.*

DRAM, s. [a ſort of weight] *dramma*, s. f. *peſo, ch'è l'ottava parte dell' oncia.*

A dram of any liquor, *una dramma, un ſorſo di qualche liquore.*

Not a dram, *nemmeno una goccia, niente affatto.*

To DRAM [to drink diſtilled liquors] *bere liquori diſtillati.*

DRA'MA, s. [a play, either comedy or tragedy] *dramma.*

DRAMA'TICK, adj. [belonging to the ſtage] *drammatico, appartenente a dramma.*

Drammatick poem [a compoſure intended to be acted on the ſtage] *drammatico poema.*

A dramatick poet, *un poeta drammatico.*

DRANK, *è un pretertito del verbo* To drink.

DRAP, or DRAB, s. [a thick cloth] *panno*, s. m.

Drap de Berry [a thick ſort of cloth, ſo called from Berry in France] *panno di Berrì.*

To drape [to make cloth] *fabbricar panni.*

DRA'PER, or WOOLEN DRAPER, s. *un pannajuolo, mercante di panni.*

A linen draper, *un mercante di tele.*

DRA'PERY, s. [a term of painting, or ſculpture, is the cloathing of human figures] *drapperia*, s. m. *termine di pittura e di ſcultura.*

Drapery [a ſort of carvers work] *fogliami.*

DRAPET, s. [cloth, coverlet] *panno, coperta da letto.*

DRAVE, pret. *del verbo*, to drive, *ſi dice più volentieri*, Drove.

DRAUGH, s. corruptly written for DRAFT [refuſe, ſwill] *coſa vile, di neſſun pregio, buona pe' porci.*

DRAUGHT, s. [of drink] *ſorſo*, s. m.

A draught of water, *un ſorſo d'acqua.*

All at one draught, *ad un ſorſo.*

A draught [or bill drawn by a merchant payable by another] *tratta*, s. f.

The draught of a building of a fortreſs, &c. *il piano o la pianta d'un edificio, d'una fortezza*, s. f.

Draught [copy of a writing] *copia d'una ſcrittura.*

The draught of a ſhip [the quantity of water the ſhip draws when afloat, or the number of feet under water when loaden] *il tiro d'acqua d'un vaſcello, un certo numero di piedi d'acqua che un vaſcello peſca quando ſta a galla, e'l numero di piedi d'acqua che ſon neceſſari per tenerlo a galla quando è carica.*

A ſhip of ſmall draught, *un vaſcello che peſca poco a fondo.*

The draught [a houſe of office, neceſſary, or bog-houſe] *il ceſſo, il ſegreto, il neceſſario, il deſtro.*

Mend your draught, *bevete un altro bicchiere.*

To drink one's morning draught, *bere un bichiere la mattina, incantar la nebbia.*

To have a quick draught [to ſell much wine, beer, &c.] *avere buono ſpaccio del liquore che ſi vende.*

Draught [pull] *tratta, ſtratta, ſtrappata*, s. f.

Draught [detachment] of ſoldiers, *un diſtaccamento di ſoldati.*

A rough draught, *abbozzo, abbozzamento*, s. m. *abbozzatura*, s. f.

Draughts [harneſs for horſes to draw with] *tirello, fune o cuojo con che i cavalli tirano carrozze, e ſimili.*

A draught-horſe, *un cavallo da traino.*

Draughts [a ſort of play] *il giuoco delle tavole o delle dame.*

To play at draughts, *giuocare alle tavole, o alle dame.*

DRAUGHT-HOUSE [a houſe in which filth is depoſited] *luogo dove ſi ripongono le immondizie.*

To DRAW [to pull] *tirare, trarre, trainare.*

The horſe draws the cart, *il cavallo tira, o traina il carro.*

To draw [to pull out] *tirare, cavare, trarre.*

To draw ſighs or tears, *trarre ſoſpiri, o lagrime.*

To draw the tongue, *trarre, o moſtrar la lingua.*

To draw the ſword, *cavar la ſpada, metter mano alla ſpada.*

To draw cuts or lots, *tirar a ſorte.*

To draw water out of a well, *attignere, tirar ſu'l acqua dal pozzo.*

To draw wine, *tirare del vino.*

To draw blood, *cavar ſangue, ſalaſſare.*

To draw [to allure] *tirare, allettare, indurre.* preſ. *induco.* pret. *induſſi.*

To draw [to lead on] *indurre, perſuadere alcuno a fare qualche coſa.*

To draw a fowl, *ſventrare un uccello.*

To draw a pond, *peſcare un vivajo.*

To draw a woman's breaſt, *ſucciar le mammelle d'una donna, poppare.*

A plaſter that draws, *un impiaſtro che attrae.*

The ſun draws the vapours, *il ſole attrae i vapori.*

To draw to a head [as an impoſthume] *far capo, aprirſi.*

To draw to a head [to come together] *adunarſi, unirſi inſieme, fare un corpo, far capo.*

To draw to an iſſue, *terminare, finire, metter fine, venire a capo.*

A ſhip that draws ten foot water, *un vaſcello che peſca dieci piedi d'acqua.*

To draw a picture, *fare un ritratto.*

To draw a ſheet at the printing preſs, *ſtampare un foglio.*

To draw, or draw up a writing, *fare una ſcrittura.*

To draw the breviate of the caſe, *iſtruire d'un proceſſo.*

To draw a circle with a pair of compaſſes, *tirare a fare un cerchio con un compaſſo.*

To draw bit, *ſbrigliare, levar la briglia.*

It is time now to draw toward a concluſion of this debate] *è oramai tempo di dar fine, o di finire queſta diſputa.*

To draw a bridge, *fare un ponte.*

To draw breath, *reſpirare, pigliar fiato, rifiatare.*

To draw near to an end, *finirſi, terminarſi.*

To draw nigh, *avvicinarſi, accoſtarſi, approſſimarſi.*

To draw back, *ritirare, tirare indietro.*

To draw back, verb. neut. *ritirarſi, tirarſi indietro.*

To draw again, *ritirare, di nuovo tirare.*

To draw in, *tirare, allettare, indurre.* preſ. *induro.* pret. *induſſi.*

To draw away, *levare, portar via.*

To draw away, *ſtornare, fraſtornare, diſſuadere, rimuovere*, pret. *diſſuaſi, rimoſſi.*

To draw aſunder, *ſeparare, diſunire, dividere.* preſ. *diſuniſco.* pret. *diviſi.*

To draw together, *unire, congregare, aſſembrare.* preſ. *uniſco.*

To draw on, *indurre, perſuadere, portare.*

To draw on, or draw near, verb neut. *avvicinarſi, accoſtarſi.*

To draw on [to be dying] *ſtar per morire, eſſer all' eſtremo.*

The time draws on, *il tempo ci ſtringe.*

The night draws on, *s'annotta, ſi fa notte.*

To draw up, *tirar ſu.*

To draw up water, *attigner dell' acqua.*

To draw up the mouth, *arricciare il muſo.*

To draw up a petition, *fare un memoriale.*

To draw up an account, *ordinare un conto.*

To draw up an army in battalia, *ſchierare uno eſercito, metterlo in battaglia.*

To draw along, *ſtraſcinare, ſtraſcicare, trainare.*

To draw forth, or to draw out, *tirar fuori, metter fuori.*

To draw out a thing in length, *ſtendere, o ſpiegare che che ſi ſia.*

To draw out the time, *differire, mandare alla lunga, procraſtinare.* preſ. *differiſco.*

To draw out a party, *fare un diſtaccamento.*

To draw out a tooth, *cavare un dente.*

To DRAW OUT, *ſtraſcinare, ſtraſcicare.*

To draw out one's words [to ſpeak leiſurely and lazily] *favellare, o parlare collo ſtraſcico.*

Draw-bridge, s. *un ponte levatojo.*

Draw-

Draw-latch, s. *saliscendo*, s. m.

A draw-latch, [one who drawls along his words] *uno che parla con lo strascico.*

A draw-net, *v.* Drag-net.

DRA'WER, s. *tiratore*, s. m. *che tira, ma particolarmente colui che tira il vino nelle taverne.*

A gold drawer, *tirator d'oro.*

A tooth drawer, *un cavadenti.*

A pair of drawers to wear under the breeches, *sottocalzoni, mutande.*

Drawer [a sort of box in a chess table, &c.] *tiratojo*, s. m.

DRA'WING, s. *tiramento*, s. m. *il tirare*, *v.* To draw.

The art of drawing, *il disegno.*

A drawing gargarism, *un gargarismo attrattivo.*

DRAWN, adj. *tirato, tratto*, *v.* To draw.

A drawn sword, *una spada tratta, una spada nuda.*

A drawn game, *una patta.*

A drawn battle, *una battaglia, dove'l vantaggio è stato eguale.*

To be hang'd, drawn, and quarter'd, *esser impiccato, e squartato.*

DRAY, s. [a sort of cart used by brewers] *carro.*

A dray [a sledge] *slitta.*

A dray-man, *un carrettiere.*

DRA'ZEL, s. [a low, mean, worthless wretch] *un povero spregievol birbone.*

DREAD, s. [great fear] *spavento, terrore*, s. m. *paura orribile.*

Dread, adj. *formidabile, terribile.*

To DREAD [to fear] *temere.*

I dread his power, *temo il suo potere.*

He dreads me, *mi teme, ha paura di me.*

DRE'ADED, adj. *temuto.*

DRE'ADER, s. [one that lives in fear] *un che teme, un che vive in timore, un timido.*

DRE'ADFUL, adj. *terribile, spaventevole, spaventoso, orrendo.*

The dreadful judgments of God, *i terribili giudicii di Dio.*

A dreadful fight, *uno spettacolo orrendo.*

DRE'ADFULLY, adv. *terribilmente, spaventevolmente, spaventosamente, orribilmente.*

He looked dreadfully, *fareva paura a vederlo.*

DRE'ADFULNESS, s. *terrore, spavento*, s. m.

DRE'ADLESS, s. [fearless, unaffrighted, intrepid] *intrepido, uno senza timore.*

DRE'ADLESSNESS, s. [fearlessness, intrepidity] *intrepidezza, il non aver alcun timore nel pericolo.*

DREAM, s. [an acting of the imagination in sleep] *sogno*, s. m.

My dream is out, *il mio sogno s' è verificato.*

Dream [idle fancy] *sogni, pazzie, sciocchezze.*

To DREAM, *sognare, far sogni.*

I dream all night, *sogno tutta la notte.*

To dream a dream, *fare un sogno.*

To dream [to rave] *sognare, delirare.*

DREAM'D, adj. *sognato.*

DRE'AMING, s. *il sognare.*

Dreaming, adj. *sonnacchioso, lento, stupido, insensato.*

A dreaming fellow, *un sonnacchioso, uno stupido, un balordo, un pecorone.*

DRE'AMLESS, adj. [without dreams] *senza sogni, senza sognare.*

DREAR, adj. [sad, dismal] *terribile, orribile, spaventevole, spaventoso.*

DRE'ARIHEAD, DRE'ARIMENT, DRE'ARINESS, } s. *terrore, orrore, spavento*, s. m.

DREDGE, s. [a sort of net] *sorta di rete.*

To DREDGE [to gather with a dredge] *raccoglier con una rete.*

DRE'GGY, adj. [full of dregs] *feccioso, pien di feccia.*

DREGS, s. [filth, dross] *feccia*, s. f. *la parte più grossa e peggiore di cose liquide, posatura, fondigliuolo.*

To draw off the dregs, *purificare, chiarificare, levar via la feccia.*

The dregs of the people, *la feccia del popolo, la canaglia, la plebe.*

To DRAIN [to empty] *votare, render vuoto.*

DRENCH, s. [a physical potion for a horse] *beveraggio medicinale per un cavallo.*

To DRENCH [to give a drench] *abbeverare.*

To drench [to bathe] *bagnare, adacquare, innaffiare, inacquare.*

DRENCHED, or DRENCHT, adj. *bagnato, adacquato, innaffiato, inacquato.*

Drencht in tears, *bagnato di lagrime, tutto lagrimoso.*

DRESS, s. [garb] *abito, vestito, vestimento, addobbamento, abbigliamento, ornamento*, s. f.

The dress of a woman's head, *una cuffia da donna.*

A night dress, *una cuffia per la notte.*

To DRESS [to put on one's cloaths] *vestire.*

To dress a lady's head, *acconciare la testa ad una dama.*

To dress one's head, *acconciarsi la testa.*

To dress [to trim] *acconciare, adornare, addobbare, abbigliare, accomodare.*

To dress old cloaths, *rappezzare, acconciare abiti vecchi.*

To dress [to cook meat] *cucinare, cuocer le vivande.*

To dress fish, *accommodare, apparecchiare del pesce.*

To dress a wound, *medicare una ferita.*

To dress a vine, *potare una vigna.*

To dress leather, *conciar della pelle.*

To dress flax, *scotolare il lino.*

DRESSED, adj. *vestito*, *v.* To dress.

DRE'SSER, s. *ex.* A dresser of meat, *un cuoco, una cuoca.*

DRE'SSING, s. *il vestire.*

A dressing cloth, *toeletta, parola corrotta che viene dal francese.*

My lady is at her dressing table, *la signora sta ancora allo specchio.*

DRE'SSING-ROOM, s. [the room in which the clothes are put on] *la camera in cui uno si veste.*

DREST, *v.* Dressed.

DREW, *è un preterito del verbo* to draw.

To DRIB [to crop, to cut off] *cimare, tagliar via.*

To DRI'BBLE [to slabber] *bavare.*

To dribble [to fall in drops] *cascar giù in gocce.*

To dribble [to fall weakly and slowly] *cascar giù con poca forza e adagio.*

To dribble, v. n. [to throw down in drops] *mandar giù a goccie.*

DRI'BLET, s. [a little sum owing] *un debituzzo, un piccol debito.*

DRI'BLING, adj. Ex. a dribling debt, *un debituzzo.*

DRI'ED, adj. *è un preterito del verbo* to dry.

Dried, adj. *secco, seccato.*

Dried to powder, *ridotto in polvere, polverizzato.*

Dried up, *secco, seccato.*

It is all dried up, *è affatto secco.*

The well is dried up, *il pozzo è secco.*

DRI'ER, s. *diseccativo.*

It is a great drier, *è un gran disseccativo.*

DRIFT, s. [aim, scope, purpose] *scopo, segno, disegno, obbietto, fine, maneggio, intrigo*, s. m. *meta, pratica*, s. f.

I understand the whole drift of the business, *io so tutto l'intrigo.*

I know the drift of your discourse, *so dove tende il vostro discorso, so quel che volete dire.*

Drift [a sea term, signifies any thing that floats upon the water] *questa parola significa generalmente ogni cosa che galleggia sopra l'acqua alla discrezione del vento, della marea, o della corrente.*

The boat goes adrift [she has no body to steer her] *la barca galleggia alla discrezione del vento e della marea.*

Drifts of ice, *pezzi di ghiaccio galleggianti.*

Drift of the forest [an exact examination of what cattle are upon the forest] *riviste dei bestiami che pascolano in una foresta.*

DRILL, s. [a tool for boring] *succhiello.*

Drill [a baboon, an overgrown ape] *un babbuino.*

Drill [a small dribbling brook] *ruscelletto, rigagnolo.*

To DRILL [to bore holes with a drill] *forare, bucare, fare un buco, col succhiello.*

To drill a key, *forare, o bucare una chiave.*

To drill [to intice] *tirare, indurre, stimolare uno a far qualche cosa.*

To drill a company of soldiers, *disciplinare una compagnia di soldati, farli fare l'esercizio.*

To drill one on [to amuse one] *tenere uno a bada.*

To drill one's time away, *badaluccare, spender il tempo in vano.*

DRI'LLED, adj. *forato, bucato, succhiellato.*

DRINK, s. [any liquor to be drank] *bevanda*, s. m.

Good or bad drink, *buona o cattiva bevanda*.

To be a little in drink, *esser mezzo cotto, aver bevuto un poco troppo*.

Give me some drink, *datemi a bere*.

Without meat or drink, *senza mangiare, nè bere*.

Physical drink, *pozione medicinale*.

Drink-offering, *aspersione*, s. f.

To DRINK, *bere, e bevere*. pref. *bevo*.

To drink within bounds, *bere moderatamente*.

To drink a good draught, *fare una buona bevuta*.

To drink drunk [to drink hand to fist, to drink hard] *bere smoderatamente, bere in eccesso, trincare*.

To drink one's health, *bere alla salute di qualcheduno*.

To drink round [to drink about] *bere in giro*.

This wine drinks flat, *questo vino è sventato*.

This wine drinks well, *questo vino ha buon gusto*.

To drink off, to drink up [to drink every drop] *bever tutto*.

To drink one down, *imbriacare uno, farlo bere sì che non possa reggersi in piedi*.

To drink out, *bere, vuotare a forza di bere*.

We drank six bottles in three hours, *abbiamo bevuto sei fiaschi in tre ore*.

To drink out of a glass, *bere in un bicchiere*.

To drink in, *bere, imbevere, succiare*.

To drink in an error, *imbevere, succhiare un errore*.

To drink away one's time, *spendere il tempo in bevendo*.

DRI'NKABLE, adj. [good to drink] *buono a bere*.

DRI'NKER, s. *bevitore*, s. m. *bevitrice*, s. f.

DRI'NKING, s. *bevimento*, s. m. *il bere*.

A drinking glass, *un bicchiere*.

A drinking companion, *compagnone in beveria*.

Hard drinking, *beveria*, s. f.

DRINK-MONEY, s. [money given to buy liquor] *mancia, buona mano, danaro dato a uno perchè beva alla tua salute*.

To DRIP [to drop slowly] *gocciolare, cascare a giocciole*.

DRI'PPING, s. [the fat which drops from meat while 'tis roasting] *il grasso che gocciola dall' arrosto*.

A dripping-pan, *una ghiotta*.

To DRIVE, *condurre, menare, guidare*.

To drive a coach, *guidare una carrozza*.

To drive heasts to pasture, *menare il bestiame al pascolo*.

To drive bees, *scacciare, o cacciare le api*.

To drive the country, *dare il guasto ad un paese, scorrerlo, predarlo*.

A ship that drives [when an anchor let fall will not hold her fast] *un vascello che rade*.

The wind drove us ashore, *il vento ci gittò a terra*.

To drive [to put upon, to force] *pignere, spignere, sforzare, obbligare, costrignere*. pret. *pinsi, spinsi, costrinsi*.

He drove me to that necessity, *mi ridusse a questa necessità*.

To drive a great trade, *fare un gran negozio*.

To drive a nail, *ficcare, o caccicare un chiodo*.

To drive to despair, *ridurre alla disperazione*.

He went as fast as he could drive, *andò con ogni prestezza, o celerità*.

A wheel of a cart drove over me, *la ruota d'un carro mi passò sopra il corpo*.

To drive [to aim] at something, *mirare, aver la mira a che che si sia*.

To drive away, *scacciare*.

To drive away the time, *passare il tempo, spassarsi*.

To drive back, *ributtare, rispignere*. pref. *rispingo*. pret. *rispinsi*.

To drive on, *andare avanti, spignere*.

Drive on coachman, *tocca cocchiere*.

To drive on a design, *incamminare un disegno*.

To drive off, *scacciare*.

To drive a player off the stage, *fischiare un attore*.

To drive off time, *indugiare, differire, procrastinare, mandare alla lunga il tempo, prolongare, allungare*.

He drives it from day to day, *mi rimanda da oggi in domani*.

To drive out, *scacciare, cacciare, trarre, cavare*.

One nail drives out another, *un chiodo caccia l'altro*.

To drive in, *cacciare, mettere, ficcar per forza*.

To drive stakes into the ground, *cacciare, o ficcare pali nella terra*.

To drive a nail, *ficcar un chiodo*.

DRI'VEL, s. [that falls out of one's mouth] *bava, spiuma, che esce della bocca*.

Drivel [a fool, an ideot, a driveller] *un besso, uno scemo, uno scioccone*.

To DRI'VEL [to let the spittle fall on one's chin] *bavare, esser bavaso*.

DRI'VELLER, s. [a fool, an ideot] *uno scemo, un idiota, un mentecatto*.

DRI'VEN, particip. *di* To drive.

As white as the driven snow, *bianco come un fiocco di neve*.

DRI'VER, s. *conduttore, giudatore, che spinge, che guida, che conduce*.

A hog-driver, *un porcajo*.

An ass-driver, *un asinaro*.

To DRI'ZZLE, verb neut. *piuviggi-nare, spruzzolare, spruzzare, gocciolare*.

DRI'ZZLING, adj. Ex. a drizzling rain, *spruzzaglia, acquicella, pioggia leggiera*.

Drizzling weather, *tempo umido*.

DRI'ZZLY, adj *piuvigginoso*.

A DROIL, s. [a drudge, a slave] *un garzonaccio, un servo impiegato nei servizi i più vili, un poltroniere buono a nulla*.

To DRÒIL [to work sluggishly and slowly] *lavorar con pigrizia, con fatica, a stento, mal volentieri, per forza*.

DROLL, s. [one whose business is to raise mirth by petty tricks] *un giuocoliere, un buffone di piazza, il cui mestiero è farti ridere con giuochi di mano*.

Droll [a farce; something exhibited to raise mirth] *farsa, cosa rappresentata e che è fatta per muover le risa, per far ridere*.

To DROLL [to play the droll, to jest] *far il buffone, far il zanni*.

DRO'LLERY, s. [idle jokes, buffoonery] *baje, buffonerie sciocche*.

DRO'MEDARY, s. [a sort of camel having two bunches on the back] *dromedario*, s. m. *spezie di cammello*.

DRONE, s. [the bee that makes no honey] *cacchione, fuco*.

A drone [a slothful fellow, a hum-drum fellow] *uno pigro, un infingardo, un poltronaccio buono a nulla*.

To DRONE [to live in idleness] *non far nulla, menar una vita oziosa, marcir nell' ozio e nella pigrizia*.

DRO'NISH, adj. [idle, sluggish] *pigro, inerte, lento, ozioso buono a nulla*.

To DROOP [to fade, as flowers do] *appassarsi, appassirsi, languire*. pref. *appassisco, languisco*.

To droop [to be afflicted] *affliggersi, attristarsi, prendersi affiizione, esser tristo, mesto, o maninconico*.

To droop [to languish, to grow faint] *languire, svenire, perder il vigore, infiebolire*. pref. *languisco, infiebolisco*. pret. *svenni*.

DRO'OPING, s. *afflizione, tristizia, maninconia, languidezza*, s. f. *langore, e languore*, s. m.

Drooping, adj. Ex. to be in a drooping condition, *esser tristo, mesto, maninconico, afflitto, languido*.

DROP, s. [the smallest quantity of any liquor] *gorria, gocciola*, s. f.

By drops, or drop after drop, *a goccia a goccia, una gocciola dopo l'altra*.

Drops [in architecture, is an ornament of pillars of the Dorick order, representing drops or little bells underneath the triglyphs] *gócciole*, s. f. pl. *termine d'architettura*.

He has a drop in his eye [he has drank a little too much] *egli è mezzo cotto, egli è imbriaco*.

A gum drop, *lagrima*.

Speckt with drops, *stellato, pezzato, gocciolato*.

A little drop, *una gocciolina*.

To DROP [to let fall] *lasciar cascare*.

I dropt my watch, *ho lasciato cascare il mio oriuolo*.

I dropt my purse, *m'è cascata la borsa*.

To drop a word, *lasciar andare una parola, scappare una parola*.

I dropt a word, *lasciai andare, o mi scappò di bocca una parola*.

To drop, or let drop [to desist] *desistere*,

ſiſtere, ceſſare, abbandondare, metter da banda.

To drop a deſign, *deſiſtere da un diſegno, abbandonarlo, metterlo da banda.*

To drop one's argument, *non proſeguire il ſuo argomento.*

To drop in, *cacciare, ficcare.*

To drop, verb neut. [to fall by drops] *gocciolare, caſcare a gocciole, grondare.*

The eaves drop, *le gronde gocciolano.*

His noſe drops continually, *il naſò li moccia ſempre.*

To drop with ſweat, *gocciolar di ſudore.*

To drop in, *entrare, cacciarſi dentro, ficcarſi.*

To drop out [to ſteal out] *ſfilarſela, imbolarſi.*

To drop off, or away [to die] *tirar le calze, morire.*

Dro'pped, adj. *v.* Dropt.

Dro'pping, s. *goccia, gocciola.*

The droppings of one's noſe, *cimurro.*

Dropsere'ne, s. [a diſeaſe of the eye, proceeding from an inſpiſſation of the humour] *gottaſerena*, s. f. *ſorta di malore che viene agli orchi.*

Dro'plet, s. [a little drop] *una piccola goccia, una goccetta*, s. f.

Dro'psical, adj. [troubled with the dropſy] *idropico, che patiſce d'idropiſia.*

A dropſical man or woman, *un idropico, un' idropica.*

Dro'psy, s. [a ſort of diſeaſe] *idropiſia*, s. f.

Dropt, adj. [from to drop] *caſcato, gocciolato. v.* To drop.

Dross, s. [the ſcum of metals] *ſcoria*, s. f.

The droſs of lead, *la ſcoria del piombò.*

Dro'ssy, adj. [full of droſs] *pieno di ſcoria, di ſporcizia.*

Dro'ssiness, s. [foulneſs, feculence, ruſt] *feccia, ſporcizia, ruggine.*

Drove, s. [a herd of cattle] *branco*, s. m. *gregge*, s. f.

A drove of cattle, *un branco di beſtiame.*

Drove [a crowd, a tumult] *folla, tumulto.*

Drove, pret. *del verbo*, to drive.

Dro'ven, *è un participio obſoleto del verbo* to drive.

Dro'ver, s. [a man who drives cattle for hire, or for ſale] *conduttore di beſtiame.*

Drought, s. [dryneſs of the earth] *ſiccità, ſecchezza*, s. f. *ſeccóre*, s. m.

We have had a great drought, *abbiamo avuto un gran ſeccore.*

Drought [thirſt] *ſete*, s. f.

I got a great drought upon me, *ho gran ſete.*

Dro'ughty, adj. [wanting rain, ſultry] *che ha biſogno di pioggia, troppo caldo.*

To Drown [to plunge under water] *annegare.*

To drown one's ſelf, *annegarſi.*

To drown [to overflow a country] *inondare un paeſe.*

To drown [to eclipſe, to ſurpaſs] *ecclіſſare, offuſcare, oſcurare, avanzare, ſuperare.*

The light of the ſun drowns the light of the ſtars, *lo ſplendore del ſole eccliſſa il lume delle ſtelle.*

Dro'wned, adj. *annegato.*

Drowned in pleaſures, *immerſo ne' piaceri.*

Dro'wning, s. *l'annegare.*

To Drowse [to ſlumber] *ſonnacchiare, leggiermente dormire, ſonneferare, e ſonniſerare, ſonneggiare.*

Dro'wsily, adv. *lentamente, pigramente, con lentezza, adagio, neghittoſamente, traſcuratamente.*

Dro'wsiness, s. [ſleepineſs] *ſonnolenza*, s. f. *intenſo aggravamento di ſonno.*

I have a great drowſineſs upon me, *ſono in una gran ſonnolenza, ſono tutto ſonnolento, o ſonnacchioſo.*

Drowſineſs [ſluggiſhneſs] *pigrizia, traſcuraggine, traſcurataggine, infingardia, lentezza*, s. f.

Dro'wsy, adj. [ſleepy] *ſonnoglioſo, e ſonniglioſo, ſonnolento, ſonnacchioſo, ſonnoloſo.*

To be drowſy, *eſſer ſonnoglioſo.*

To make drowſy, *addormentare.*

The drowſy diſeaſe, *la letargia, malattia che fa dormire continuamente.*

Drub, s. [a thump, a knock, a blow] *un colpo di baſtione, o d'altra coſa.*

To Drub [to beat] *battere.*

To drub [to cudgel] *baſtonare, dare delle baſtonate.*

Dru'bbing, s. *baſtonatura*, s. f.

Drudge, s. [one who does all mean ſervices] *un garzonaccio, ſervo impiegato ne' ſervigi i più vili, un facchino.*

A drudge in a kitchen, *un guattero di cucina.*

A drudge in a ſhip, *un mozzo di vaſcello.*

To Drudge [to toil and moil] *ſervire, ſtentare, affaticarſi, lavorar come uno ſchiavo, come un facchino.*

To drudge for oyſters, *peſcare delle oſtriche.*

Dru'dger, s. *un facchino.*

Dru'dger, or Dru'dging-box, *quel boſſolotto in cui ſi tien la farina che poi ſi ſbatte ſulla earne mentre ſta al fuoco arroſtendo.*

Dru'dgery, s. [dirty, laborious work, ſlavery] *ſervigio vile, o ſervile.*

To do one's drudgery, *fare i ſervigi i più vili per alcuno.*

Drug, s. [all ſorts of ſimples] *droga*, s. f. *nome generale degli ingredienti medicinali, e particolarmente degli aromai.*

Drugs, *quantità di droghe.*

Drug [a ſorry commodity, which ſticks on hand] *cattiva roba, robaccia, mercanzia di rifiuto.*

Where knavery is in credit, honeſty is ſure to be a drug, *mentre la furberia è in iſtima, l'oneſtà non può non eſſer diſprezzata.*

To Drug [to ſeaſon with medicinal ingredients] *acconciare con ingredienti medicinali.*

To drug [to tincture with ſomething offenſive] *porre in una coſa qualche poco di qualche ingrediente diſpiacevole al guſto.*

Dru'ggist, or Dru'gster, s. [a dealer in drugs] *droghiere, e droghiero*, s. m.

Dru'gget, s. [a kind of ſtuff] *droghetto*, s. m. *ſorta di pannina.*

Dru'ids, s. [certain Pagan learned prieſts among the ancient Britons and Gauls] *Druidi, ſacerdoti pagani fra gli antichi Brettoni, e Galleſi.*

Drum, s. [a muſical warlike inſtrument] *tamburo, ſtrumento militare noto.*

To beat the drum, *battere il tamburo.*

A kettle drum, *un timbalo.*

A drum [a drummer] *tamburino*, s. m. *ſonator di tamburo, tamburo.*

Drum ſticks, *bacchette di tamburo.*

Drum ſtrings, *corde di tamburo.*

To Drum [to beat the drum] *battere il tamburo, batter la caſſa.*

To Dru'mble [to drone, to be ſluggiſh] *poltroneggiare, eſſer pigro.*

Dru'm-fish, s. [the name of a fiſh] *nome d'un peſce.*

Drum-ma'jor, s. [the chief drummer of a regiment] *tamburino maggiore.*

Drum ma'ker, s. [one who deals in drums] *uno che fa o vende tamburi.*

Dru'mmer, s. [he that beats the drum] *tamburino, colui che batte il tamburo.*

Dru'mming, s. *il batter il tamburo, o la caſſa.*

Drunk, adj. [fuddled] *imbriaco, cotto.*

Half drunk, *mezzo imbriaco.*

Dead drunk, *cotto affatto, o del tutto imbriaco.*

To make drunk, *imbriacare.*

Ever drunk ever dry, *più ſi beve più ſi vorrebbe bere.*

Drunk, adj. *bevuto.*

Drunk out, *del tutto bevuto.*

Dru'nkard, s. [a man given to drink] *un imbriaco.*

A great drunkard, *un imbriacone.*

A drunkard [ſpeaking of a woman] *un' imbriaca.*

Dru'nken, adj. *imbriaco, ebrio, briaco.*

A drunken man, *un imbriaco.*

A drunken woman, *un' imbriaca.*

Drunken folks ſeldom come to any harm, *gl' imbriachi iddio gli ajuta.*

Dru'nkenly, adv. [like a drunken man] *da imbriaco.*

Dru'nkenness, s. *imbriachezza, ubbriachezza*, s. f.

Dry, adj. [arid, without wet, without moiſture] *ſecco, arido, privo d'umore, privo d'umido.*

A dry, empty diſcourſe, *un diſcorſo ſecco, di poco ſpirito, duro, inſipido, ſenza ſale, di poco ſapore.*

A dry fountain, *una fontana ſecca.*

Dry [thirſty] *ſitibondo, che ha ſete.*

I am dry, *ho ſete.*

The dry land, *la terra, il continente, terra ferma.*

He went over dry, *paſsò, o traversò a piè ſecco, ſenza bagnarſi.*

A dry nurſe [a nurſe that brings up and feeds a child without the breaſt; or one who takes care of another] *donna*

che

che allieva un bambino ſenza allattarlo, o colei che prende cura d'altri.

A dry jeſt, *botta*, s. f. *motto pungente, e arguto.*

Dry [penurious, ſtingy] *ſecco, ſtretto, abbietto, tapino, avaro, meſchino.*

Dry [reſerved] *riſerbato, grave, contegnoſo.*

Dry-ſhod, *a ſecco, a piè ſecco.*

To dry [to make dry] *ſeccare, tor via l'umido.*

To dry up, *ſeccare, inaridire.*

Dry up your tears, *aſciugate le voſtre lagrime, ceſſate di piagnere.*

To dry, verb neut. *ſeccarſi, inaridirſi, divenir ſecco*, pret. *inaridiſco.*

DRY'ADS, s. [wood nymphs, or fairies] *driade*, s. f. *ninfe de' boſchi.*

DRY'ER, s. [that which has the quality of abſorbing moiſture] *coſa che abſorbe i liquidi, e l'umido.*

DRY-EYED, adj. [without tears, without weeping] *ſenza lagrime, ſenza pianto.*

DRY'LY, adv. [without moiſture] *aridamente, ſenza umidità.*

Dryly [frigidly, coldly, without affection] *freddamente, frigidamente, diſamoratamente.*

Dryly [jejunely, barrenly] *poveramente, ſterilmente.*

DRY'NESS, s. [want of moiſture, ſiccity] *ſiccità, ſeccore, privazion d'umido.*

Dryneſs [want of embelliſhment, want of pathos] *diſadornezza, troppa ſemplicità d'ornamenti.*

Dryneſs [want of ſenſibility in devotion, aridity] *freddezza in divozione.*

DRY'ING, s. *ſeccamento*, s. m. *il ſeccare.*

Drying yard, *luogo fatto a uſo di ſeccare frutti, e d'aſciugare pannilini,* &c.

DU'AL, adj. [belonging to two] *duale, di due.*

The dual number, *numero duale, o ai due.*

To DUB, *fare, creare, armare.*

To dub a knight [to confer the honour of knighthood upon one] *fare, creare, o armar un cavaliere.*

To dub a cock, *capponare un gallo.*

DUB, s. [a blow, a knock] *una percoſſa, un colpo.*

DU'BIOUS, adj. [doubtful] *dubbioſo, ambiguo, irreſoluto, indeterminato, dubbio, indeciſo.*

DU'BIOUSLY, adv. [uncertainly, without any determination] *dubbiamente.*

DUBITA'TION, s. [doubt] *dubitazione, dubitanza*, s. f. *dubitamento, dubbio*, s. m.

DU'CAL, adj. [of, or belonging to a duke] *ducale, di duca, da duca.*

DU'CAT, *v.* Ducket.

DUCK, s. [a water fowl] *anitra*, s. f.

A wild duck, *anitra ſalvatica.*

A tame duck, *anitra domeſtica.*

A young wild duck, *anitraccio, anitrocco, anitroccolo.*

My duck [a word of kindneſs] *ben mio, mio caro, mia cara.*

Duck-weed, *anitrina*, s. f. *erba detta dall' anitra, che volontieri ſe ne paſce.*

To DUCK [to dive under water] *tuffare e tuffarſi, immergere e immergerſi.*

To duck one into the ſea, *tuffare uno nel mare.*

To duck [to ſtoop] *abbaſſarſi, calarſi, inchinarſi.*

To duck with the head, *abbaſſare, o inchinar la teſta.*

DUCKATO'ON, s. [a foreign coin worth about ſix ſhillings and three pence] *ducatone*, s. m. *ſpezie di moneta.*

DU'CKET, s. [a foreign coin of gold or ſilver, of different values, according to the places where current] *ducato*, s. m. *moneta d'oro o d'argento, di differente valuta, ſecondo'l luogo dove corre.*

DU'CKING, s. *il tuffare.*

Ducking [a ſea puniſhment, when a malefactor at ſea, having a rope faſtened about him, is hoiſted up to the end of the yard, and thence violently let fall two or three times into the ſea] *punizione che ſi da ad un malfattore ſul mare, col tuffarlo due o tre volte nel mare.*

A ducking ſtool, *ſedia dove ſono a ſedere quelli che ſono puniti col tuffo.*

DU'CK-LEGGED, adj. [ſhort legged] *che ha gambe corte.*

DU'CK-COY, *v.* Decoy.

To DU'CKOY, *v.* To decoy.

DUCKSFOOT, s. *ſorta d'erba.*

DU'CKLING, s. [a young duck] *anitrocco, anitroccolo*, s. m.

DU'CKSMEAT, s. *ſorta d'erba.*

DUCKT, adj. [from to duck] *tuffato, immerſo.*

DUCT, s. [guidance, direction] *guida; coſa che conduce, che dirige.*

Duct [a paſſage through which any thing is conducted] *paſſaggio per cui alcuna coſa è condotta; canale.*

DU'CTILE, adj. *fleſſibile, pieghevole, facile ad allungarſi.*

Ductile [tractable, obſequious] *di facili coſtumi e pieghevoli; oſſequioſo.*

DU'DGEON, or DUDGEON DAGGER, s. [a ſmall dagger] *daga*, s. f. *pugnale*, s. m.

To take a thing in dudgeon [to take it in bad part, to be diſpleaſed at it] *dar nel cencio, corrucciarſi, e crucciarſi, ſdegnarſi, offenderſi, tenerſi offeſo.*

A dudgeon-haft, *un manico di pugnale.*

DU'DMAN, s. [or dead man, a maulkin] *un' ombra, una fantaſma.*

DUE, *participio paſſivo del verbo* to owe.

Due, adj. [owing] *dovuto, ch' è dovuto.*

Money due, *danaro dovuto, debito.*

A bill of exchange that is due, *lettera di cambio che è ſcorſa.*

I ſhall pay you your bill when it is due, *in iſcadenza onorerò la voſtra tratta.*

There's ſo much due to me, *me è dovuto tanto, mi viene tanto.*

Due, adj. [requiſite] *dovuto, debito, conveniente, acconcio, convenevole, opportuno.*

To do a thing with due reverence, *fare una coſa con dovuta riverenza.*

To aſk a ſum before it is due, *domandare una ſomma prima del tempo.*

To do a thing in due time, in due ſeaſon, *fare una coſa in tempo debito, a tempo e luogo, opportunamente, in tempo opportuno.*

I'll do it in due time, *lo farò a ſuo tempo, o quando il tempo lo richiederà.*

Done in due form, *fatta in tutte le forme.*

DUE, s. *debito.*

To give every one his due, *dare a ciaſcheduno il ſuo debito, o quel che ſe li deve, far giuſtizia ad ognuno.*

We muſt give the devil his due, *non biſogna dipignere il diavolo più brutto che non è.*

To DUE [to pay as due] *pagare com' è dovuto.*

DU'EL, s. [a fight between two perſons] *duello*, s. m. *combattimento tra due a corpo a corpo.*

To fight a duel, *batterſi in duello, duellare.*

DU'ELLIST, or DU'ELLER, s. [a perſon who fights a duel] *un duellante.*

DU'ELLING, s. *il duellare.*

To forbid duelling, *diſendere i duelli.*

DUE'NNA, s. [an old woman kept to guard a younger] *una vecchia pagata per aver cura d'una giovane.*

DUG, s. [the teat of a cow, or other beaſt] *mammella, poppa*, tetta, s. f.

To ſuck a dug, *tettare, poppare.*

Dug, *particip. del verbo* to dig [or digged] *zappato, vangato.*

DUKE, s. [a title of honour] *duca*, s. m. *titolo di principato.*

The grand duke of Tuſcany, *il gran duca di Toſcana.*

DU'KEDOM, s. [the dominion and territories of a duke] *ducato*, s. m. *titolo del principato del duca, e anche del paeſe compreſo ſotto il dominio del duca.*

The dukedom of Parma, *il ducato di Parma.*

DU'LBRAINED, adj. [ſtupid, doltiſh, fooliſh] *ſtupido, ſcempiato, duro di teſta.*

DULCA'RNON, s. [a knotty point or queſtion] *un punto intrigato, ſcabroſo, o difficile a riſolvere.*

I am at dulcarnon [or at my wits end] *ho perſo la tramontana, non ſo dove mi ſia, mi trovo molto imbrogliato.*

DU'LCET, adj. [ſweet to the taſte, luſcious] *dolcigno, dolce al guſto.*

Dulcet [ſweet to the ear, harmonious] *dolce al' udito, armonioſo.*

DULCIFICA'TION, s. [the act of ſweetening; the act of freeing from acidity, ſaltneſs, or acrimony] *il dolcificare, il render dolce, il tor via il ſale, l'acidità, o l' acrimonia.*

To DU'LCIFY [to make ſweet] *addolcire, far dolce, render dolce.*

To dulcify mercury, *raddolcire il mercurio.*

DU'LCIFY'D, adj. *addolcito.*

DU'LCIMER, s. [a muſical inſtrument] *ſtrumento muſicale ſimile al ſalterio.*

DU'LHEAD, s. [a blockhead; a wretch fooliſh and ſtupid] *un baggeo, un baccellone, un birbone ſciocco e ſtupido.*

DULL, adj. [blunt] *ottuſo, ingroſſato, che non taglia.*

A dull razor, *un raſojo ottuſo.*

Dull [heavy, ſtupid, ſluggiſh] *ottuſo, ſtupido, materiale, groſſolano, duro, inſenſato, goffo, balordo, ſciocco, inetto, ſcimunito.*

A dull wit, *un ingegno ottuſo.*

A dull witted man, *un dolcione, un uomo di poco ſenno.*

Dull [lazy, ſlow] *pigro, lento, infingardo.*

Dull [melancholy] *malinconico, meſto, addolorato, triſto.*

A dull piece of work, *un' opera tedioſa, o faticoſa, che tedia.*

A dull noiſe, *un biſbiglio, uno ſtrepito confuſo, un tacito ſuſurro.*

A glaſs that begins to grow dull, *uno ſpecchio che comincia ad appannarſi.*

Dull light, *viſta foſca.*

A candle that burns dull, *una candela che rende poco lume.*

A dull colour, *colore ſmorto.*

There's now but a dull trade, *c'è poco da fare adeſſo.*

Dull of hearing, *duro d'orecchio, che è quaſi ſordo, che non puo appena ſentire.*

Dull of apprehenſion, *duro di teſta, ſtupido, goffo.*

Dull witted, *gaglioffo, capocchio, balordo.*

Dull-pated, *che ha la teſta dura, ſtupido, intormentito, ſenza ſenno, intronato, inſenſato, di dura cervice.*

To DULL [to make one's wit dull] *ſtupidire, intormentire, render ſtupido, o inſenſato,* preſ. *ſtupidiſco.*

To dull [to dazzle with over-much light] *abbagliare, offuſcare.*

To dull a looking-glaſs, *appannare uno ſpecchio.*

To dull the hearing [to deafen] *aſſordare, indur ſordità; far divenir ſordo.*

DU'LLARD, s. [blockhead] *goffo, gaglioffo, ſtupido, balordo, dappoco.*

DU'LLED, adj. *ſtupidito, inotrmentito, inſenſato.*

DU'LLY, adv. *goffamente, ſtupidamente, groſſamente.*

DU'LNESS, s. *goffaggine, goffezza, ſtupidità, groſſezza, materialità, balordaggine,* s. f.

Dulneſs [ſlowneſs] *pigrizia, negligenza, infingardia, lentezza, infingardaggine,* s. f.

DU'LY, adv. *dovutamente, debitamente, con dovere, con ragione, ſecondo le forme, convenevolmente, meritamente.*

Duly [exactly] *eſattamente, preciſamente.*

DUMB, adj. [not having the uſe of ſpeech] *muto, mutolo.*

Dumb ſigns, or mute ſigns, *i ſegni del zodiaco, che hanno il nome di creature mutole.*

A dumb creature, *una beſtia, un uccello.*

To ſtrike one dumb, *ammutare uno, chiudergli la bocca.*

DU'MBLY, adv. *da mutolo, mutamente.*

DU'MBNESS, s. [incapacity to ſpeak] *mutezza, mutolezza, l'eſſer muto.*

Dumbneſs [refuſal to ſpeak, ſilence] *il rifiutar di parlare, il non parlare, taciturnità, ſilenzio.*

To DU'MBFOUND [to confuſe, to ſtrike dumb] *confonder uno, farlo tacere per vergogna.*

DUMP, s. [a ſudden aſtoniſhment] *ſtupore,* s. m. *ſorpreſa,* s. f.

A melancholy dump, *noja, moleſtia, inquietudine,* s. f. *faſtidio.*

To put one in his dumps, *travagliare uno, recarli faſtidio, o noja, darli da penſare, metterlo in travaglio.*

DU'MPISH, adj. [ſad, melancholy, ſorrowful] *triſto, maninconoſo, addolorato, afflitto.*

DU'MPLING, s. [a ſort of pudding] *ſpezie di camangiare all' Ingleſe fatto di paſta e mele leſſe inſieme.*

DUMPS, s. [bits of lead the children play with] *pezzi di piombo con cui i fanciulli giuocano.*

DUN, adj. *bruno, ſcuro, foſco, tanè.*

Dun-neck [a ſort of bird] *ſorta d'uccello.*

Dun-fly, or dun-bee, *tafano,* s. m. *inſetto volatile.*

Dun in the mire, *ridotto in eſtrema povertà.*

DUN, s. [a troubleſome and clamorous creditor] *un creditore importuno.*

To DUN [to demand a debt clamorouſly and preſſingly] *ſollecitare, domandare, riſcuotere inſtantemente il pagamento d'un debito, importunare i ſuoi debitori.*

DUNCE, s. [a blockiſh, ſtupid perſon] *un balordo, un goffo, un gonzo, un minchione, un dolcione, uno ſtupido, uno ſciocco.*

DU'NCERY, s. *goffaggine, ſciocchezza, balordaggine,* s. f.

DUNG, s. [ordure, ſoil] *ſtabbio, concime, ſterco delle beſtie, e letame,* s. m.

Horſe dung, *ſterco di cavallo.*

Cow-dung, *bovina,* s. f. *ſterco di bue.*

A dung farmer, *un votaceſſi, colui che vota i ceſſi.*

A dung-cart, *un plauſtro.*

To DUNG [to manure land with dung] *concimare, letamare.*

DU'NGED, adj. *letamato.*

DU'NGEON, s. [dark priſon] *ſegrete,* s. f. *prigione oſcura.*

DU'NGFORK, s. [a fork to toſs out dung from ſtables] *forcone da rimuovere il letame.*

DU'NGHILL, s. [a heap or accumulation of dung] *letamajo, cumulo di letame.*

Dunghill [a mean or vile abode] *povera, vile, o puttaneſca abitazione.*

Dunghill [any ſituation of meanneſs] *qualunque ſito vile.*

Dunghill [a term of reproach for a man meanly born] *voce ingiurioſa per un uomo di vil naſcita.*

Dunghill, adj. [ſprung from the dunghill; mean, low] *abjetto, vile, nato dal letame, di vil naſcita.*

DU'NGY, adj. [full of dung; mean, vile, baſe] *vile, baſſo, abbieto, pien di letame.*

DUNG-YARD, s. *luogo da riporvi il letame.*

DU'NNED, adj. [from to dun] *eſatto, riſcoſſo, importunato.*

DU'NNER, s. *un eſattore, o riſcuotitore di debiti.*

DU'NCICAL, adj. [from dunce] *ſciocco, ſcimunito, balordo, ſtupido.*

A duncical fellow, *uno ſciocco, un balordo, un minchione, un goffo, un gonzo.*

DUODE'CIMO, *parola preſa dal latino.*

A book in duodecimo [or in twelves] *un libro in duodecimo.*

DUO'DENUM, s. [is the firſt of the inteſtines or guts, in length about twelve fingers breadth] *duodeno,* s. m.

A DUPE, s. [a cully, a fool] *un gonzo, un minchione, uno ſciocco.*

To DUPE [to cozen] *ingannare, truffare.*

DU'PLICATE, s. [a copy, or tranſcript of a writing] *copia d'una ſcrittura.*

To DU'PLICATE [to double] *raddoppiare, piegare in due.*

DUPLICA'TION, s. [in arithmetick, is the multiplying of any number by two] *duplicazione,* s. f. *multiplicazione d'una quantità diſcreta, o continua, per due.*

DURABI'LITY, s. [the power of laſting, endurance] *durevolezza, durabilità.*

DU'RABLE, adj. [laſting] *durabile, atto a durare, permanente.*

A durable peace, *una pace durabile, o permanente.*

DU'RABLENESS, s. *durabilità,* s. f.

DU'RABLY, adv. [in a laſting manner] *durevolmente, da durar molto tempo.*

DU'RANCE, s. [impriſonment, confinement] *prigionia, prigione,* s. f.

To be in durance, *eſſere in prigione.*

DURA'TION, s. [continuance] *durata,* s. f. *il durare, perſeveranza,* s. f.

A thing of long duration, *una coſa di lunga durata.*

To DURE [to endure] *durare, ſoſtenere, ſofferire, tollerare.* preſ. *ſoſtengo.* pret. *ſoſtenni.*

DU'REFUL, adj. [laſting, of long continuance] *durevole, permanente.*

DU'RELESS, adj. [without continuance, fading, *che non dura, che toſto cade.*

DU'RESSE, s. [hardſhip] *durezza, rigidezza, aſprezza, crudeltà, prigionia.*

DU'RGEN, s. [a dwarf, a punching fellow] *un omicciatto, un omicciuolo, un pigmeo,*

Durgen [a little woman] *una donnina, una donnicina, una femminuzza.*

DU'RING, prep. *per, durante, per lo ſpazio.*

During three years, *per tre anni.*

During my ſtay here, *mentre che reſterò qui, tanto che reſterò qui.*

DU'RITY, s. [hardneſs, firmneſs] *durezza, ſodezza, fermezza.*

DURST, *è un preterito del verbo* to dare.

I durſt not ſpeak, *non oſai, non ardii parlare.*

You durſt not do it, *non vi baſterebbe l'animo di farlo.*

DUSK, s. Ex. the dusk of the evening, *l'imbrunir della sera, il far della notte, la sera, il bujore.*
I shall come in the dusk of the evening, *verrò verso la sera, sul far della notte.*
Dusk, adj, *bruno, scuro, bujo.*
To DUSK [to make duskish] *oscurare, render oscuro.*
To dusk [or grow duskish] *imbrunire, e imbrunare, divenir bruno, o bujo.*
It begins to dusk, *comincia ad imbrunire, a far bujo.*
DU'SKISHNESS, s. *bujo, bujore*, s. m. *oscurità*, s. f.
DU'SKY, adj. [somewhat dark] *bujo, oscuro, bruno, fosco.*
DU'SKISH, adj. *che comincia ad oscurarsi, scuretto, brunetto.*
It begins to be duskish, *comincia ad imbrunire, o farsi bujo.*
DUST, s. [earth dried to powder] *polvere*, s. f. *terra arida, e tanto sottile, e minuta, che ell' è volatile.*
To make dust, or to raise dust, *fare o levar della polvere.*
To lay the dust, *abbatter la polvere.*
A cloud of dust, *polverio, quantità di polvere che si lieva in aria, agitata da vento, o da altra cosa.*
The wind blows the dust, *il vento fa volar la polvere.*
We are but dust and ashes, *noi non siamo che polvere, e cenere.*
Saw-dust, *segatura*, s. f. *quella parte del legno, che ridotta quasi in polvere, casca in terra, in segando.*
Pin-dust, or file-dust, *limatura*, s. f.
The dust [or sweepings] of a house, *le immondizie, le sporcizie della casa.*
A dust-man, *quello che scopa la polvere nelle strade.*
A dust basket, *paniere dove si mettono le immondizie.*
A dust box, or sand box, *un polverino.*
To DUST [to cast dust upon] *coprire, o empire di polvere.*
To dust off, *nettar la polvere.*
DU'STINESS, s. *polverio, quantità di polvere.*
DU'STY, adj. [full of dust] *polveroso, asperso, o coperto di polvere.*
A dustry room, *una camera polverosa, o piena di polvere.*
Dusty road, *cammino polveroso.*

To grow dusty, *empirsi, o coprirsi di polvere.*
The roads grow dusty, *il camminare comincia ad esser polveroso.*
DUTCH, or the DUTCH LANGUAGE, *l'Olandese, la favella, o la lingua Olandese.*
To speak Dutch, *parlar Olandese.*
High Dutch, *Alemanno, tedesco.*
To speak high Dutch, *parlar tedesco.*
Dutch, adj. [of Holland] *Olandese, d'Olanda.*
A Dutch man, *un Olandese.*
A Dutch woman, *una Olandese.*
Dutch cloth, *panno d'Olanda.*
DU'TCHESS, s. [a duchess, a duke's wife] *duchessa*, s. f.
DU'TCHY, s. [the territory of a duke] *ducato*, s. m.
The dutchy of Lancaster, *il ducato di Lancastro.*
DU'TEOUS, DU'TIFUL, } adj. *ubbidiente, ufficioso, ossequioso, sommesso, che ubbidisce.*
A dutiful child, *un figliuolo ubbidiente.*
Dutiful to his parents, *ubbidiente a' suoi genitori.*
Dutiful towards God, *pio, religioso; divoto.*
DU'TIFULLY, adv. *sommessamente, ubbidientemente, con sommessione, ufficiosamente, ossequiosamente.*
To carry one's self dutifully, *fare il suo dovere.*
DU'TIFULNESS, s. *ubbidienza, sommessione, osservanza*, s. f.
DU'TY, s. [any thing that one is obliged to do] *dovere, debito*, s. m.
To do one's duty, *fare il suo dovere, compire al suo dovere.*
To pay one's duty to one, *render rispetto ad alcuno, riverirlo, salutarlo.*
The duty of one's place, *l'ufficio, o la funzione della sua carica.*
To present one's duty [or respects] to one, *riverire, o salutare alcuno.*
A soldier upon duty, *un soldato in funzione.*
Hard duty, *fatica.*
Duty [money paid for custom of goods] *dogana, gabella*, s. f.
DWARF, s. [a person of a very low stature] *un nano, una nana, uomo o donna mostruosa per piccolezza.*

A dwarf hen, *gallina nana.*
A dwarf elder, *ebbio, ebulo*, s. m.
To DWARF [to hinder from growing to the natural bulk] *impedire che cheßia dal crescere come naturalmente crescerebbe.*
DWA'RFISH, adj. *piccoletto, piccino.*
DWA'RFISHLY, adv. *piccinamente.*
DWA'RFISHNESS, s. *statura piccola, picciolezza.*
To DWELL [to abide in, to inhabit] *stare, abitare, dimorare, albergare.*
Where does he dwell? *dove sta di casa, dove dimora?*
To dwell [to insist] upon a thing, *diffondersi, dilatarsi, allagarsi, ampliarsi sopra una cosa.*
DWE'LLER, s. *abitatore, abitante*, s. m. *abitatrice*, s. f.
DWE'LLING, adj. *abitante, dimorante.*
A dwelling-house, *stanza, dimora, abitazione*, s. f. *abituro, domicilio, soggiorno*, s. m.
DWELT, adj. *stato, dimorato, abitato, albergato.*
To DWI'NDLE [to decay, to decrease, to waste] *scadere, declinare, venire in peggiore stato, scemare, peggiorare.*
It dwindles away to nothing, *si consuma, o sen va in fumo.*
DWI'NDLED, adj. *scaduto, declinato, scemato, peggiorato.*
DY'ING, s. *tinta*, s. f.
The art of dying, *l'arte del tignere.*
Dying, adj. *moribondo, in termine di morire.*
A dying man, *un moribondo, un uomo che è in termine di morte.*
He is dying, *egli sta per morire.*
The dying words of one, *l'ultime o l'estreme parole di qualcheduno.*
Dying [languishing] eyes, *occhi languidi.*
DY'NASTY, s. [supreme government, or authority] *principato, governo assoluto.*
DY'SENTERY, s. [a looseness accompanied with gripings in the belly] *dissenteria, e disenteria*, s. f.
Troubled or afflicted with the dysentery, *dissenterico, e disenterico, che ha la dissenteria.*
DY'SURY, s. [a difficulty of urine] *stranguria*, s. f. *difficoltà d'orinare.*

E.

E, è la quinta lettera dell' alfabeto Inglese, e la seconda delle vocali. La maniera di pronunciarla è si varia, che non credo si possa imparare che coll' uso.

EACH, adj. and pron. *ciascheduno, ciascheduna, ciascuno, ciascuna, caduno, caduna.*

Each of us, *ciascheduno di noi.*

Each one, *ciascheduno, ciascheduna.*

On each side, *dalle due bande.*

Each one three, *tre per ciascheduno.*

Each other, *l'un l'altro.*

To love each other, *amarsi l'un l'altro, riamarsi.*

EA'GER, adj. [sharp, sour, tart] *agro, aspro, acuto.*

Eager [earnest, vehement] *ardente, fervido, fervente, sollecito, veemente, violento.*

Eager desire, *desire ardente.*

Eager [sharp-set, hungry] *affamato, che ha gran fame.*

Eager, s. Ex. the eager of a river, *la rapidità d'un fiume. Non in uso.*

E'AGERLY, adv. *ardentemente, fervidamente, ferventemente, sollecitamente, veementemente, violentemente, fissamente, intensamente.*

To dispute eagerly, *disputare con ardore.*

To work eagerly, *lavorare gagliardamente, a mazzastanga.*

Eagerly bent on a thing, *applicato, inclinato fissamente, o intensamente ad una cosa.*

E'AGERNESS, s. [sourness] *agrezza, asprezza, acutezza,* s. f.

Eagerness [earnestness] *ardore, calore, desiderio intenso, affetto, fervore,* s. m. *violenza, veemenza, passione, premura, caldezza,* s. f.

E'AGLE, s. [the biggest and strongest of all birds of prey] *aquila,* s. f.

The Roman eagle, *l'aquila Romana, impresa delle insegne de' Romani.*

The Imperial eagle, *l'aquila Imperiale, l'impresa delle insegne dell' Imperio.*

Eagle-eyed, *che ha li occhi d'aquila, acuti come quelli dell' aquila.*

E'AGLESPEED, s. [swiftness like that of an eagle] *velocità come quella dell' aquila.*

E'AGLESTONE, s. *sorta di pietra.*

E'AGLET, s. [a young eagle] *aquilino,* s. f. *aquila piccola.*

E'AGRE, s. [a tide swelling above another tide] *flutto di mare che viene impetuosamente e come a cavallo a un altro flutto.*

EAME, s. [uncle] *zio; fratello del padre o della madre.* Obl.

To EAN [to bring forth young, as female sheep do] *figliare, parlando delle pecore.*

The ewes begin to ean, *le pecore cominciano a figliare.*

EAR, s. [the organ of hearing] *orecchia,* s. f. *orecchio,* s. m. *uno de' membri del corpo dell' animale, che è strumento dell' udito.*

A good, or a quick ear, *orecchia buona, acuta, fina, sottile.*

To have good ears, *aver buon' orecchia.*

To give one a box on the ear, *dare un schiaffo ad uno.*

To whisper something in one's ear, *zufolare, o soffiar negli orecchi ad uno, favellargli di segreto.*

To give ear, *prestare, o dare orecchi, ascoltare attentamente.*

I am undone if that comes to his ears, *sono spedito se ciò perviene alle sue orecchie, se egli ha sentore o notizia di questo.*

To have the prince's ears, *esser ben veduto dal principe, esser ascoltato favorevolmente.*

He is deaf of one ear, *egli è sordo d'un orecchio.*

A hungry belly has no ears, *ventre affamato non ha orecchi.*

He has a flea in his ear, *ha un pulce nell' orecchio.*

In at one ear, and out at the other, *fare orecchie di mercante.*

To fall together by the ears, *venire alle prese, o alle mani, battersi.*

To set together by the ears, *metter male insieme, attizzare, stizzare la discordia.*

To set all the kingdom together by the ears, *seminar la discordia, e la divisione nel regno, mettere il regno sozzopra.*

He was like to have all the rabble about his ears, *poco mancò che la canaglia non gli cascasse addosso.*

To be in love up to the ears, *esser fieramente innamorato.*

To be in debt over head and ears, *esser infangato ne' debiti, esser pieno di debiti.*

Mind your business, I shall be presently about your ears, *badate a' fatti vostri, altrimente vi darò sulla testa.*

To sing by ear, *cantare a orecchio, cioè senza cognizione dell' arte di cantare.*

To open one's ears [to make him mind] *sturar li orecchi ad uno, farlo intender bene.*

I dare not for my ears, *non ardisco farlo.*

The ear of a porringer, *l'orecchio d'una scodella.*

An ear of corn, *una spiga.*

Ear-wax, *cacca o sporcizia che viene all' orecchie.*

Ear-ring, *orecchino.*

Ear-picker, *stuzzicorecchi,* s. m. *strumento, col quale si nettano gli orecchi.*

Ear-witness, *testimonio che attesta una cosa per averla sentita.*

To EAR [to shoot ears, as corn does] *spigare, far la spiga.*

To ear [to till, to plough, or fallow the ground] *arare, lavorra la terra.*

E'ARED, adj. *spigato, arato, lavorato.*

Lap-eared, *che ha gli orecchi pendenti.*

E'ARLESS, adj. [without any ears] *privo d'orecchi, senza orecchi.*

E'AR-RING, s. [jewels set in a ring and worn at the ears] *anelletto che si porta agli orecchi, orecchino, ciondolo, ciondolino.*

E'AR-SHOT, s. [reach of the ear] *tale lontananza quanta l'orecchio v'agiunga per sentire.*

E'AR-WAX, s. [the cerumen or exsudation which smears the inside of the ear] *feccia che si genera negli orecchi.*

E'AR-WIG, s. [a sheath-winged insect] *sorta d'insetto.*

E'AR-WITNESS, s. [one who attests or can attest any thing as heard by himself] *testimonio d'udito.*

EARL, s. [a title of nobility between a marquis and a viscount] *un conte.*

An earl's lady [a countess] *una contessa.*

E'ARLDOM, s. [the dignity and jurisdiction of an earl] *una contea.*

E'ARLY, adj. *mattutino, tempestivo.*

He is an early man, or an early riser, *egli si leva di buon mattino.*

An early spring, *una primavera tempestiva, o avanzata, che comincia di buon' ora.*

Early, adv. [betimes in the morning] *per tempo, di buon' ora, a buon' ora.*

To rise early, *levarsi per tempo, o di buon' ora.*

Early [soon] *a buon' ora, o di buon' ora.*

To go to bed early, *andare a letto a buon' ora.*

Early in the spring, *al principo della primavera.*

Early in the morning, *al far del giorno.*

Very early, *per tempissimo.*

To EARN [to get, to obtain by labour] *guadagnare, procacciarsi, meritare.*

To

To earn one's bread, *guadagnarsi il pane, procacciarsi la vita.*
You earned it very well, *voi l'avete ben meritato.*
My bowels earn, *me ne. dispiace fino alle viscere.*
To earn [to run as new cheese] *filare, come fa il cacio.*
E'ARNED, adj. *guadagnato, procacciato, meritato.*
E'ARNEST, adj. [vehement] *ardente, veemente, fervido, violento, fervente, sollecito, premuroso.*
Earnest [diligent] *accurato, diligente, attento, applicato.*
To be earnest at work, *esser accurato, o applicato al suo lavoro.*
I was not very earnest with him to stay, *non l'ho sollecitato molto di restare.*
An earnest business [a business of concern] *un affare di premura o premuroso, un negozio d'importanza, o di conseguenza.*
An earnest suit, or entreaty, *istanza, e instanza, richiesta, domanda.*
To make earnest suit to one for a thing, *domandare instantemente qualche cosa ad uno.*
Earnest, s. Ex. in good earnest, *in sul serio, in sul sodo, da senno, con serietà, seriamente, da vero, da dovero.*
To be in good earnest, *parlar sul serio, seriamente, o da dovero.*
Earnest, or earnest money [money given in hand to bind a bargain] *caparra, arra,* s. f.
To give earnest, or earnest money, *caparrare, dar la caparra.*
E'ARNESTLY, adv. [vehemently] *vivamente, strettamente, ardentemente, caldamente, con caldezza, efficacemente, fervidamente, premurosamente, istantemente.*
Earnestly to entreat one, *pregare alcuno caldamente, o instantemente.*
Earnestly [diligently] *diligentemente, accuratamente, sollecitamente, attentamente.*
Earnestly to affirm a thing, *asseverare, avverare, asserire una cosa.*
To speak a thing earnestly [or seriously] *dire una cosa in sul serio, seriamente o da dovero.*
To look earnestly upon something, *guardare, o guatar fissamente una cosa.*
Earnestly to strive against, *rintuzzare, resistere pertinacemente, sbracarsi, sforzarsi, fare ogni sforzo contro.*
Earnestly bent, *provano, intestato, fieramente inclinato.*
E'ARNESTNESS, s. [vehemence] *veemenza, instanza, premura, caldezza, promura,* s. f. *ardore, fervore, calore,* s. m.
He spoke it with so much earnestness, *disse ciò con tale veemenza.*
EARSH, s [a plowed field] *un campo arato.*
EARTH, s. [one of the four elements] *la terra.*
The heaven and the earth, *il cielo e la terra.*
Fuller's earth, *terra grascia da nettare gli abiti.*

Potter's earth, *argilla, e argiglia,* s. f.
Earthquake, *terremoto, tremuoto,* s. m.
Earth-worm, *lombrico,* s. m. *baco che nasce nella terra.*
To EARTH [to go into a hole under ground as a fox does] *intanarsi, entrar nella tana, come fa la volpe.*
To earth [to cover with earth] *coprir di terra, nascondere.*
E'ARTHBORN, adj. [born of the earth] *generato dalla terra.*
Earthborn [meanly born] *di vil nascita.*
E'ARTHBOUND, adj. [fastened by the pressure of the earth] *tenuto immobile dal premere o peso della terra.*
E'ARTHEN, adj. [made of earth] *di terra.*
Earthen-ware, *vasellame, o vasellamento di terra.*
Earthen-dish, *un piattello di terra.*
E'ARTHLING, s. [an inhabitant of the earth; a poor frail creature] *abitatore di questa misera terra; misera e frale creatura.*
E'ARTHLY, or E'ARTHY, adj. *terrestre, di terra, che la terra produce.*
Earthly things, *le cose terrestri.*
An earthly man, *un uomo mondano, dedito alle cose del mondo.*
Earthly mindedness, *amor mondano.*
EARTHSHA'KING, adj. [having power to shake the earth, or to raise earthquakes] *che ha possanza di scuoter la terra, di cagionar tremuoto.*
E'ARTHY, adj. [consisting of earth] *fatto di terra, terreno.*
Earthy [not mental, gross, not refined] *grossolano, non raffinato, non intellettuale.*
EASE, s. [rest, pleasure] *agio, comodo, piacere,* s. f.
To live at ease, *vivere comodamente, con sue comodità, a suo agio.*
To love one's ease, *amare i suoi piaceri, o i suoi agi.*
Ease [of pain] *alleggiamento, ristoro, alleggerimento, mitigamento, sollievo,* s. m. *mitigazione,* s. f.
To give one some ease, *prestare, o dare alleggiamento, o sollievo ad uno.*
Ease [comfort] *conforto, ristoro,* s. m. *consolazione,* s. f.
To do a thing with ease, *far che che si sia con facilità, o facilmente, senza pena.*
Do it at your ease, *fatelo a vostro agio. o a bell' agio, a vostro comodo.*
Little ease [a narrow sort of prison] *stretta prigione.*
To have a writ of ease, *esser messo in libertà.*
At heart's ease, *a seconda, prosperamente.*
A chapel of ease, *ajuto di costa.*
To EASE [to give ease, or rest] *alleviare, alleggerire, sgravare, alleggiare, confortare, mitigare, addolcire,* pres. *alleggerisco, addolcisco.*
To ease one's pain, *alleggerire, o mitigare l altrui dolore.*
To ease one of his burden, *alleggiare, o sgravare alcuno del suo peso.*
To ease a ship, *alloggire un vascello;*

To ease a wall of its weights, *sgravare un muro.*
To ease one of all his troubles, *rilevare, o liberare altrui da tutti i suoi fastidi.*
To ease one of his cares, *sgravare alcuno delle sue cure, arrecar sollevamento all' altrui cure.*
To ease one's self, to ease one's belly, *scaricare il ventre, andar del corpo.*
E'ASED, adj. *alleviato, alleggerito,* v. To ease.
E'ASEL, s. [a wooden frame on which a painter sets the cloth to be painted] *telajo di pittore.*
E'ASEFUL, adj. [quiet, peaceable] *tranquillo, calmo, pien di pace, pien di quiete.*
E'ASEMENT, s. [an easing, or refreshment] *alleggerimento, alleggiamento, sollievo, conforto, ristoro, ajuto.*
Easement, s. [a privy, a house of office] *cesso, destro,* s. m.
To go to the easement, *andare al cesso.*
To do one's easement, *andar del corpo, sgravare il ventre.*
E'ASILY, adv. *facilmente, con facilità, agevolmente.*
E'ASINESS, s. *facilità, agevolezza.*
Easiness of belief, *credulità,* s. f.
Easiness of style, *uno stile facile e naturale.*
The easiness [or gentle temper] of a man, *maniera trattabile, benigna, affabile, e pieghevole d'un uomo, condescendenza.*
EAST, s. [that quarter of the earth where the sun rises] *il levante, quella parte, dalla quale spunta, o si lieva il sole.*
East-wind, *levante,* s. m. *nome di vento, sussolano.*
Wind from the east is good neither for man nor beast, *il levante non è buono, nè per gli uomini nè per le bestie.*
E'ASTER, s. *pasqua,* s. f.
Easter day, *il giorno di pasqua.*
Easter-eve, *la viglia di pasqua.*
Easter-week. *la settimana di pasqua.*
Easter-holydays, *le feste di pasqua.*
E'ASTERLINGS, s. [people living in the east of England] *coloro che dimorano nella parte orientale d'Inghilterra.*
E'ASTERLY, or E'ASTERN, adj. *orientale, oriente.*
An easterly, or an eastern wind, *vento orientale, levante, il sussolano.*
The eastern countries, *i paesi orientali.*
The eastern empire, *l'imperio d'oriente.*
E'ASTWARD, adv. *verso levante, verso l'oriente.*
E'ASY, adj. [from to ease] *facile, agevole.*
A thing easy to be done, *una cosa facile a fare, una cosa facile, o agevole.*
Easy [free] *franco, libero, sociabile.*
Easy [gentle, mild] *facile, dolce, di benigna natura, soave, piacevole, trattabile, comodo.*
An easy man to deal withal, *un uomo trattabile, ragionevole, pieghevole, facile a conversare.*

Easy,

Easy to be entreated, *mite, dolce, benigno.*

Easy to be spoken to, *accessibile, affabile, cortese, clemente.*

Easy to be born, *sopportevole, comportevole.*

Easy of belief, *credulo.*

An easy [or clear] style, *uno stile facile, intelligibile, chiaro.*

An easy labour, *un buono, e felice parto.*

As easy as kiss my hand, *facilissimamente, senza veruna difficoltà.*

To EAT, *mangiare.*

To eat one's belly full, *mangiare a crepapelle, o a crepa corpo.*

To eat well [to keep a good table] *trattarsi bene, far buona cera, far gran cera, mangiar bene.*

This meat eats well, *questa carne ha buon gusto.*

To eat a good meal, *fare un buon pasto.*

To eat one's dinner, supper, &c. *desinare, o pranzare, cenare, &c.*

To eat one's words [to disown what one has said] *disdirsi.*

To eat [to feed as cattle do] *mangiare, pascolare, pascere.*

To eat in [or into] *rodere, pret. rosi.*

Rust eats into iron, *la ruggine rode il ferro.*

To eat up a country, *rovinare, divorare un paese, guastarlo.*

E'ATABLE, adj. [good to eat] *buono a mangiare.*

E'ATABLES, s. *camangiari, viveri, vivande.*

EAT-BEE, s. [a small bird that eats bees] *aperuolo, uccelletto che mangia le api.*

E'ATEN, adj. *mangiato.*

E'ATER, s. *mangiatore, s. m. che mangia.*

A great eater, *un mangione.*

E'ATING, s. *il mangiare.*

Eating and drinking, *il mangiare, e'l bere.*

To love good eating and drinking, *amare il mangiar e bere bene, amare di trattarsi bene.*

An eating-house, *bettola, taverna,* s. f.

EAVES, s. [the edges on the top, or sides of a house] *gronda,* s. f. *l'estremità del tetto, ch' esce fuora della parete della casa.*

The eaves drop, *le gronde gocciolano.*

The droppings of the eaves, *le grondaje.*

To EAVES-DROP [to listen under the eaves, or at the window of a house, to hear what the people say] *ascoltare, stare alla finestra per ascoltare quel ch' altri dice.*

EAVES-DRO'PPER, *colui che sta alla finestra per ascoltare quel che si dice.*

EBB, s. [the going out of the tide] *riflusso,* s. m. *il ritorno della marea.*

To be in a low ebb [or in a low condition] *trovarsi in cattivo stato.*

The crown was then reduced to the lowest ebb of its authority, *la corona non riteneva allora, ch' una minima parte della sua autorità.*

To EBB [to flow back, as the tide does] *calare, come fa la marea.*

E'BBING, s. [ebb] *riflusso.*

Ebbing, adj Ex. 'tis ebbing water, *la marea cala.*

Money is ebbing and flowing, *il danaro va e viene come la marea.*

E'BONIST, s. [one who works and deals in ebony] *ebanista,* s. m. *che lavora d'ebano, che traffica in ebano.*

E'BONY, s. [a sort of black wood] *ebano,* s. m. *legno d'ebano.*

Ebony-tree, *ebano, albero che nasce nell' Indie ed in altri luoghi, il cui legno è dentro nero, e fuori del color del bossolo, e di maniera pesante che non galleggia sull' acqua.*

EBRA'ICK, adj. [belonging to the Hebrew tongue] *Ebraico, appartenente alla lingua Ebraica.*

Ebraick, s. [the Hebrew tongue] *la lingua Ebraica.*

EBRI'ETY, s. [drunkenness] *ebreità ebbrezza, ebbriachezza,* s. f.

EBRIO'SITY, *lo stesso che ebriety.*

EBULLI'TION, s. [a boiling or bubbling] *ebollizione,* s. f. *ebollimento, bollimento,* s. m.

A great ebullition of the blood, *una grande ebollizione del sangue.*

The ebullitions [transports] of unruly appetites, *i fervori de' piaceri disordinati.*

ECCENTRICAL, *v.* EXCE'NTRICAL, and all its derivatives.

ECCHO, or E'CHO, s. [the reflection of noise or voice from caves, and hollow places] *echo,* s. m. *voce, che mediante il ripercotimento in alcuni luoghi atti a renderla, ci ritorna all' orecchie.*

To E'CCHO, *echeggiare, risonare, rimbombare.*

E'CCHOED, adj. *risonato, rimbombato.*

E'CCHOING, s. *risuono, rimbombo,* s. m.

ECCLESIA'STES, s. [a title of a book in the holy scriptures] *Ecclesiaste,* s. m.

ECCLESIA'STICAL, or ECCLESIA'STICK, adj. [of, or belonging to the church] *ecclesiastico, di chiesa, appartenente a chiesa.*

An ECCLESIA'STICK, s. [a churchman, or clergyman] *un ecclesiastico, uomo dedicato alla chiesa.*

ECCLESIA'STICUS, s. [a book of apochryphal scripture, written by JESUS the son of SIRACH] *Ecclesiastico,* s. m. *titolo d'uno de' libri del Testamento Vecchio, scritto da* JESU SIRACH.

ECLI'PSE, s. [a defect, or failing of light in the sun, or moon] *ecclissi,* s. m. *oscurazione del sole, o della luna.*

To be in eclipse, *ecclissarsi, esser ecclissato.*

To ECLIPSE [to darken, to obscure] *ecclissare, oscurare.*

To eclipse [to drown, to surpass] *ecclissare, sormontare, avanzare, soprassare.*

ECLI'PSED, adj. *ecclissato, oscurato, v.* To eclipse.

ECLI'PTICK, s. [is a great circle of the heavens, in which the sun moves in its annual motion] *eclittica,* s. f. *quella linea ch' è nel mezzo del zodiaco, intorno alla quale il sole fa il suo corso annuale.*

E'CLOGUE [a pastoral poem] *egloga,* s. f.

ECONOMY, s. *frugalità; economia.*

ECONO'MICAL, ECONO'MICK, adj. *economico; frugale.*

E'CSTACY, *v.* Extasy, and all its derivatives.

EDA'CITY, s. [greedy eating, or devouring] *voracità, ghiottoneria,* s. f.

E'DDY, s. [the running back of the water at any place, contrary to the tide or stream, occasioned by some head of land] *riflusso d'acqua contro la marea o contro la corrente, cagionato da qualche punta di terra, o da vento contrario.*

Eddy, adj. ex. [eddy water, that which falls back as it were on the rudder of a ship under sail] *quell' acqua che spinta dal timone per la violenza del corso del vascello ritorna indietro.*

Eddy wind [is that wind which is reflected from a sail, or any other thing, and so goes contrary to its course] *un vento di rimando.*

EDGE, s. [the sharp point of any weapon] *taglio, filo,* s. f. *parte tagliente d'alcuno strumento che serve a tagliare.*

The edge of a sword, *il taglio, il filo d'una spada.*

The edge [brim] of any thing, *l'orlo, il margine di qualunque cosa.*

The edge [hem] of a garment, *l'orlo d'un vestito.*

The edge [corner] of a stone, a table, &c. *l'angolo, lo spigolo d'una pietra, tavola, &c.*

The edge of a book, *la testa d'un libro.*

I must eat a bit to take off the edge of the stomach, *mi bisogna mangiare un boccone per reprimere l'acutezza del mio appetito.*

Warm my drink to take off the edge of the cold, *scaldate la mia bevanda, per levarle cotesta gran freddezza.*

To take off the edge of wit, *offuscar l'ingegno.*

To put a whole army to the edge of the sword, *mandare, o mettere un esercito a fil di spada.*

To set on edge, *affilare, aguzzare.*

To set the teeth on edge, *allegare i denti.*

Edge-long, or edge-wise, *da canto.*

An edge tool [a cutting tool] *uno strumento tagliente, o di taglio.*

There's no fooling with edge tools, *non bisogna scherzare con istrumento di taglio.*

To EDGE [to make a border, or edge] *orlare, far l'orlo.*

To edge away, or edge off to sea, *andare in alto mare.*

To edge in, *fare entrare.*

E'DGED, adj. *orlato.*

Edged, *acuto, puntuto, affilato, aguzzato.*

A two-edged sword, *una bipenne, una spada a due tagli.*

E'DGELESS, adj. *che non ha taglio, ottuso, sfilato.*

E'DGING,

E'DGING, s. l'orlare.

Edging, or edging lace, *merletto stretto.*

E'DGELESS, adj. [blunt, obtuse, unable to cut] *ottuso, senza taglio, non adatto a tagliare.*

E'DGEWISE, adj [with the edge put in any particular direction] *col taglio volto a qualche precisa parte.*

E'DIBILE, adj. [eatable, that may be eaten] *buono a mangiare.*

E'DICT, s. [decree, proclamation] *editto, bando,* s. m. *legge pubblicata.*

EDIFICA'TION, s. [a building up] *edificazione,* s. f. *edificamento,* s. m.

Edification [improvement in faith] *edificazione,* s. f

E'DIFICE [building] *edificio,* s. m. *la fabbrica, la cosa fabbricata.*

EDIFI'ER, s. *colui che ti edifica colla sua buona e santa vita.*

To E'DIFY [to build] *edificare, fabbricare.*

To edify [to set examples of piety] *edificare, indur buona opinione.*

E'DIFY'D, adj. *edificato fabbricato.*

E'DIFYING, s. *edificamento,* s. m. *l' edificare.*

Edifying, adj. *edificatorio, atto a edificare.*

Edifying words, *parole edificatorie.*

E'DILE, s. *edile,* s. m. *officiale appresso i Romani, che aveva la cura degli edifici pubblici.*

E'DITION, s. [the publication or putting out a book] *edizione,* s. f. *pubblicazione per via di stampa.*

The first edition of a book, *la prima edizione d'un libro.*

E'DITOR, s. [the publisher of a book] *colui che mette, o ha messo alle stampe un libro.*

To E'DUCATE [to bring, or train up] *educare, allevare, istruire.* pres. *istruisco.*

E'DUCATED, adj. *educato, elevato, istrutto.*

A child well educated, *un figliuolo ben allevato.*

E'DUCATING, or EDUCA'TION, s. *educazione,* s. f. *l'educare.*

To EEK [to make bigger by the addition of another piece] *render maggiore con aggiungere un altro pezzo.* s. eke.

To eek [to supply any deficiency] *supplire a quel che manca.*

EEL, s. [a sort of fish] *anguilla,* s. f. *spezie di pesce.*

An eel-pie, *un pasticcio d' anguille.*

An eel-pout, *spezie di pesce simile all' anguilla.*

An eel spear, *una fiocina, una pettinella.*

E'EN, adv. [for even] *quasi, mezzo.*

I was e'en dead when he came, *ero quasi, o mezzo morto quando venne.*

E'en now, *appunto, or' ora, testè, giusto adesso.*

E'en so, *giusto così.*

E'en a little before he died, *un poco prima che morisse.*

We are e'en forward enough of ourselves to wrangle, *noi non siamo che troppo inclinati da noi stessi alle contese.*

E'FFABLE, adj. [that may be uttered or expressed] *che si può esprimere con parole.*

To EFFA'CE [to deface, raze out, or destroy] *cancellare, cassare, radere, scancellare,* pret *rasi.*

EFFA'CED, adj. *cancellato, cassato, raso, scancellato.*

EFFE'CT, s. [any thing done, or brought to pass] *effetto,* s. m. *quello che riceve l' essere dalla cagione.*

Effect [reality] *effetto, realtà, verità.*

'Tis so in effect, *così è in effetto.*

A thing of no effect, *una cosa vana, inutile, che non serve a nulla.*

Effect [end, issue] *effetto, fine, compimento.*

The thing made its effect, *la cosa fece il suo effetto.*

To take effect, *aver effetto, riuscire.* pres. *riesco.*

Effect [execution] *effetto, successo.*

Your counsel has taken its effect, *il vostro consiglio ha operato, o ha fatto il suo effetto.*

Effects [the goods of a merchant] *gli effetti, le sostanze, gli averi, le facultadi.*

To EFFE'CT [to perform, to bring to pass] *effettuare, mandare ad effetto, eseguire.* pres. *eseguisco.*

EFFE'CTED, adj. *effettuato, mandato ad effetto, eseguito.*

EFFE'CTING, s. *esecuzione,* s. f. *l' effettuare, il mandare ad effetto.*

Effecting, adj. [which brings to effect] *effettivo, efficace, efficiente, che fa, che produce.*

Effective [real] *effettivo, che ha effetto, che è in sustanzia, reale.*

An army of fifty thousand men effective, *un esercito di cinquanta mila uomini effettivi.*

EFFE'CTIVELY, adv. [or effectually] *effettivamente, effettualmente, efficacemente.*

Effectively [in effect, or really] *effettivamente, veramente, in effetto, realmente.*

EFFE'CTLESS, adj. [without effect, useless] *inefficace, senza effetto, che non ha successo.*

Effectless words, *parole vane, o inutili.*

EFFE'CTOR, s. m. Effectress, s. f. [the author and performer of a thing] *autore, quello o quella che fa, o che è causa di qualche cosa.*

EFFE'CTUAL, adj. [which necessarily produces its effects] *efficace, che ha gran forza, che fa potentemente il suo effetto nell' opera.*

An effectual virtue, *una virtù efficace.*

The effectual grace, *la grazia efficace.*

EFFE'CTUALLY, adv. *effettualmente, efficacemente.*

To EFFE'CTUATE [to accomplish] *effettuare, compire, mandare, ad effetto, eseguire.* pres. *compisco, eseguisco.*

EFFE'CTUATED, adj. *effettuato, compito, eseguito.*

EFFE'MINANCY, s. [a womanish softness] *effemminatezza,* s. f. *modi, e costumi effemminati.*

EFFE'MINATE, adj. [woman-like, tender, delicate] *effemminato di costumi, modi ed animo femminile, delicato, morbido.*

To EFFE'MINATE [to soften by voluptuousness] *effemminare, far divenire effemminato.*

EFFE'MINATED, adj. *effemminato, delicato, morbido.*

EFFE'MINATELY, adv. *effemminatamente, da femmina, femminilmente.*

EFFERVE'SCENCE, } s. [a great heat]
EFFERVE'SCENCY, } *effervescenza,* s. f. *fervore,* s. m.

EFFICA'CIOUS, adj. [effectual, powerful] *efficace, che ha gran forza, che fa potentemente il suo effetto nell' operare, potente.*

The efficacious grace, *la grazia efficace.*

An efficacious remedy, *un rimedio efficace, o potente.*

EFFICA'CIOUSLY, adv. *efficacemente, con efficacia, con forza, potentemente.*

EFFICA'CIOUSNESS, } s. *efficacia,*
E'FFICACY, } *forza, virtù, potenza,* s. f.

EFFI'CIENCE, } s. [faculty, or power
EFFI'CIENCY, } to do a thing] *la virtù, la forza, la facultà di fare che che si sia.*

EFFI'CIENT, adj. [producing its effect] *efficiente, che fa, che opera.*

An efficient cause, *una causa efficiente.*

EFFI'GIES, } s. the picture, or por-
E'FFIGY, } traiture of a person] *effigie, sembianza, immagine,* s. f. *aspetto.*

To be hanged in effigy, *esser impiccato in effigie.*

EFFLORE'SCENCE, or EFFLORESCENCY, s. [a flowering out as a flower] *fiori, il fiorire.*

The efflorescence of rhetoric, *fiori, abellimenti rettorici.*

The efflorescency of a disease, *segno d' una malattia.*

E'FFLUENCE, EFFLU'VIUM, or EFFLUVIA, s. [a flowering or running out] *effondimento, effluvio,* s. m. *effusione,* s. f.

E'FFORT, s. [a strong endeavour, a forcible attempt] *sforzo, potere, atto violente.*

E'FFRONTERY, s. [boldness, impudence] *sfacciataggine, sfacciatezza, impudenza,* s. f.

EFFU'LGENCE, s. [resplendency] *splendore,* s. m.

EFFU'LGENT, adj. [shining, bright, luminous] *rifulgente, lucido, lucente, splendente, luminoso, chiaro, raggiante.*

To EFFU'SE, s. [waste, effusion] *guasto, effusione.*

EFFU'SION, s. [a pouring out] *effusione,* s. f. *effondimento, versamento, spargimento,* s. m.

A great effusion of blood, *una grande effusione di sangue.*

EFFU'SIVE, adj. [pouring out; dispersing] *che si diffonde, che si spande.*

EFT, s. [a venomous creature in the shape

ſhape of a lizard] *ſtellione*, s. m. *animale velenoſo ſimile alla lucertola.*

EFT, adj. [ſoon, quickly, ſpeedily] *in fretta, preſſo, con preſtezza.*

E'FTSOONS, adv. [ſoon afterwards] *poco dopo.*

To EGE'ST [to throw out food at the natural vents] *evacuare, andar del corpo*

EGE'STION, s. [an evacuation of the excrements, or going to ſtool] *egeſtione*, s. f. *il mandar fuora degli eſcrementi.*

EGESTUO'SITY, s. [extream poverty] *eſtrema povertà.*

EGE'STUOUS, adj. [extream poor] *biſognoſo.*

EGG, s. [the production or ſemen of fowls, inſects, &c.] *uovo*, s. m. pl. *uova*, s. f.

The white, or yolk of an egg, *l' albume, la chiara dell' uovo, il torlo, o'l roſſo dell' uovo.*

A new laid egg, *un uovo freſco.*

A ſtale egg, *uovo ſtantio.*

An addle egg, *un uovo che non è ſtato gallato.*

A reat, or rathe egg, *un uovo morbido, proprio a bere.*

Poched eggs, *uova affogate.*

An egg ſhell, *una ſcorza d'uovo.*

To egg [to provoke, to ſtir up, to ſet on] *incitare, ſtimolare, ſpronare, ſpignere.* ret. *ſpinſi.*

EGGED, adj. *incitato, ſtimolato, ſpronato, ſpinto.*

E'GLANTINE, s. [a flower] *fiore così chiamato.*

EGOTISM, s. [the fault committed in writing by the frequent repetition of the word *Ego* or *I*; too frequent mention of a man's ſelf] *egotiſmo; menzione troppo frequente di ſe ſteſſo nello ſcrivere.*

E'GOTIST, s. [a talker of himſelf] *egotiſta; colui che fa troppo frequente menzione di ſe ſteſſo.*

To E'GOTIZE, *far troppo frequente menzione di ſe ſteſſo, egotizzare.*

EGRE'GIOUS, adj. [rare, excellent, ſingular] *egregio, ſegnalato, eccellente, eccelſo, eſimio.*

An egregious knave, *un furbo in chermisì.*

EGRE'GIOUSLY, adv. *egregiamente, con egregio modo, eccellentemente.*

EGRE'SS, or EGRE'SSION, s. [a going forth] *eſito*, s. m. *uſcita*, s. f.

To have free egreſs and regreſs, *aver il paſſo libero, aver libertà d' andare, e di venire.*

E'GRET, s. [a kind of heron] *ſpezie d' aghirone.*

E'GRIOT, s. [a ſpecies of cherry] *ſpecie di ciriegia.*

To EGRO'TE [to feign himſelf ſick] *fingerſi ammalato, far viſta, e ſembiante d' eſſer ammalato.*

EJACULA'TION, s. [a ſhort and fervent prayer] *corta, e fervente preghiera.*

EJACULA'TION [the act of darting or throwing out] *l' atto del ſaettare.*

To EJE'CT [to caſt or throw out] *gettare, buttare, mandar fuora.*

EJE'CTED, adj. *gettato, buttato, mandato fuora.*

EJE'CTION, s. *emiſſione, evacuazione*, s. f.

EJE'CTMENT, s. [a legal writ, by which any inhabitant of a houſe or tenant of an eſtate is commanded to depart] *ſcritto legale per cui ſi commanda ad uno di uſcire di caſa ſua, o de' ſuoi beni.*

EIGH, interj. [an expreſſion of ſudden delight] *eſpreſſione di ſubito diletto; Ah!*

EIGHT, adj. *otto.*

Eight times, *otto volte.*

Eight hundred, *ottocento.*

EIGHTE'EN, *diciotto.*

EIGHTE'ENTH, *diciotteſimo.*

E'IGHTFOLD, adj. [eight times the number or quantity] *otto volte tanto.*

EIGHTH, adj. *ottavo.*

E'IGHTIETH, adj. *ottanteſimo.*

E'IGHTHLY, adv. *in ottavo luogo.*

E'IGHTSCORE, adj. [eight times twenty] *otto volte venti; centoſeſſanta; otto ventine.*

E'IGHTY, adj. [fourſcore] *ottanta.*

EI'GNE, adj. [the eldeſt or firſt born] *primogenito, primo*, Obſol.

E'ISEL, s. [an old Engliſh word for vinegar] *aceto*, s. m.

E'ITHER, adj. or pron. *ciaſcheduno, o ovvero.*

In either of the banks there are fine gardens, *dalle due ſponde vi ſono bei giardini.*

Either of the two, *o l' uno, o l' altro.*

He is either a fool or a knave, *o egli è pazzo, o furbo*

I am not ſo ſtrong as either of you, *non ſono sì forte che alcuno di voi.*

On either ſide, *dalle due bande.*

'Tis more than either he or you could do, *nè voi nè lui potevate far di più.*

He is always pleaſant, either ſick or well, *egli è ſempre gioviale ſia ammalato, o ſano.*

I will either have two or none, *ne voglio due, o neſſuno.*

In either of the hands he had a ſword, *in ciaſcheduna mano portava una ſpada.*

Theſe things will either profit or delight, *queſte coſe ſaranno utili, o dilettevoli.*

EJULA'TION, s. [a bewailing] *lamento*, s. m. *lamentazione*, s. f. *omei, eſclamazioni di dolore.*

EKE, conj. [alſo, likewiſe] *ancora, anche.* Obſ.

To EKE [to augment] *accreſcere, aumentare.* Obſ.

To eke [to add to, to make larger by adding another piece] *aggiugnere, arrogare, accreſcere, ſlungare, ſlargare.* Obſ.

All ekes [all helps] *tutto è buono, tutto ajuta.* Obſ.

ELA'BORATE, adj. [done with exactneſs and pains] *elaborato, fatto con applicazione, e diligenza, compito, perfetto, limato.*

An elaborate piece of work, *un' opera elaborata.*

An elaborate diſcourſe, *un diſcorſo limato.*

To ELA'BORATE [to produce with labour] *produrre con molta fatica.*

To elaborate [to heighten and improve with ſucceſſive operations] *limare, finire, ritoccare, ripulire con fatica e diligenza.*

ELA'BORATELY, adv. *con applicazione, e diligenza, accuratamente, con eſattezza.*

To ELA'CERATE [to tear in pieces] *lacerare, ſbranare, mettere in pezzi.*

To ELA'NCE [to throw out, to dart] *lanciare, ſaettare, tirar con forza.*

To ELA'PSE [to paſs away, to glide away] *paſſar via, ſcorrer via.*

ELA'PSED, adj. [gone, or paſt] *ſcorſo, paſſato.*

ELA'STICAL, } adj. [ſpringy, or en-
ELA'STICK, } dued with elaſticity] *elaſtico.*

ELASTI'CITY, s. [a power to return to its firſt place and condition, as a ſtick which is forcibly bent] *elaſticità*, s. f. *potere di ritornare nel primo ſtato, come ſono le molle che piegate da una banda, e poi laſciate libere ritornan nel loro primo eſſere.*

ELA'TE, or ELA'TED, adj. [puffed up, haughty, proud] *alto, altiero, orgoglioſo.*

To ELA'TE [to puff up with proſperity] *inſuperbire, imbaldanzire per eventi proſperi.*

To elate [to exalt, to heighten] *eſaltare, innalzare.*

ELATE'RIUM, s. [the juice of wild cucumbers, made up in a thick and hard conſiſtency] *elaterio*, s. m. *ſugo del cocomero aſinino condenſato.*

ELA'TION, s. [haughtineſs proceeding from ſucceſs] *orgoglio procedente da' proſperi ſucceſſi.*

To ELA'XATE [to unlooſe, to make wider] *ſlargare.*

E'LBOW, s. *gomito*, s. m. *è la congiuntura del braccio dalla parte di fuori.*

To lean on one's elbow, *appoggiarſi ſul gomito.*

To be always at one's elbow, *eſſer ſempre accanto ad uno, eſſerli d'appreſſo.*

Elbow-room, *campo, ſpazio, luogo.*

To have elbow-room, *aver campo.*

To give one elbow-room, *far luogo ad uno.*

To ſhake the elbow [to play at dice] *giuocare a' dadi, biſcazzare.*

To be at the elbow, *eſſer vicino.*

An elbow of land, *un gomito di terra.*

E'LBOW-CHAIR, s. *ſedia d'appoggio.*

ELD, s. [old age, decrepitude] *vecchiaja, vecchiezza, decrepità.*

Eld s. [old people, perſons worn out with years] *perſone vecchie, gente decrepita.*

E'LDER adj. [old] *maggiore, maggiore nato.*

An elder brother, *un fratello maggiore.*

In elder years, *in una età provetta.*

Elder, s. [an elder of the church] *un anziano della chieſa.*

The elders [the fathers] *i maggiori, gli antenati.*

Elder

Elder, or elder-tree, s. *sambuco*, s. m. *spezie d'albero.*

Elder-berry, *coccola di sambuco.*

Made of elder, *sambuchino, di sambuco.*

Elder vinegar, *aceto sambuchino.*

Elder syrup, *sciroppo sambuchino.*

E'LDERLY, adj. [no longer young] *attempato, attempatotto, non più giovine.*

E'LDERSHIP, s. [in age] *anzianità, maggioranza*, s. f.

E'LDEST, adj. [the superlative of eld] *maggiore.*

The eldest brother, *il fratello maggiore di tutti, il più vecchio di tutti.*

The eldest at play, *colui che ha la mano nel giuocare alle carte.*

ELECA'MPANE, s. [an herb] *ella, enula, enula campana*, s. f. *erba medicinale aromatica.*

ELE'CT, adj. [chosen, appointed] *eletto, scelto.*

The elect, s. [the faithful, the elected saints] *gli eletti, i predestinati.*

To ELE'CT [to chuse] *eleggere, scegliere.* pref. *scelgo.* pret. *elessi, scelsi.*

ELE'CTED, adj. *eletto, scelto.*

ELE'CTION, s. [a chusing, a choice] *elezione, l'eleggere, scelta*, s. f. *eleggimento*, s. m.

ELE'CTIVE, adj. [pertaining to election, or choice] *elettivo, che può eleggersi, da eleggersi.*

An elective kingdom, *un regno elettivo.*

ELE'CTIVELY, adv. [by choice, with preference of one to another] *elettivamente.*

ELE'CTOR, s. [a chuser] *elettore*, s. m. *che elegge.*

The electors of the empire [certain princes of the empire of Germany, who have a right to chuse the emperors] *gli elettori dell' imperio.*

ELE'CTORAL, adj. [belonging to the electors] *elettorale, ellettore.*

The electoral college, *il collegio elettorale.*

His electoral hignes, *sua altezza elettorale.*

ELE'CTORATE, s. [the dignity, or territories of an elector of the empire] *elettorato.* s. m. *dignità e dominio di elettore.*

ELE'CTRE, s. [amber, which having the quality, when warmed by friction, of attracting bodies, gave to one species of attraction the name of electricity] *elettro, ambra.*

Electre [a mixed metal] *un metallo misto.*

ELE'CTRESS, s. [the wife of an elector] *elettrice, moglie di elettori.*

ELE'CTORSHIP, s. *elettorato*, s. m. *dignità di elettore.*

ELE'CTRICAL, } adj. [that attracts
ELE'CTRICK, } like amber] *ellettrico, di elettro.*

ELE'CTRICITY, s. *qualità elettrica, elettricità.*

ELE'CTUARY, s. [a medicinal composition made to the consistence of a conserve] *elettuario, lattovaro*, s. m. *spezie di composizione medicinale.*

ELEEMO'SINARY, adj. [given by way of alms] *che si da per limosina, caritatevole.*

Eleemósinary, s. [an almoner] *elemosinario, elemosiniere*, s. m. *che fa limosina.*

E'LEGANCE, or E'LEGANCY, s. [fineness of speech, politeness of language] *eleganza, eleganzia*, s. f.

E'LEGANT, adj. [elegant, handsome] *elegante, ben disteso, ben ordinato, ornato, e dicesi di favella, scritura, o simili.*

Elegant [fine] *elegante, bello, vezzoso.*

E'LEGANTLY, adv. *elegantemente, con eleganza.*

Elegantly [or neatly] *elegantemente, pulitamente, con pulizia, con grazia.*

To write elegantly, *scrivere elegantemente.*

ELEGI'ACK, adj. [belonging to an elegy] *elegiaco, di elegia.*

E'LEGY, s. [a mournful poem, a funeral song] *elegia*, s. f.

ELEGIO'GRAPHER, s. [a writer of elegies] *un elegiaco, scrittor d'elegie.*

E'LEMENT, s. [simple body] *elemento*, s. m. *quello, onde si compongono i misti, e nel quale si risolvono.*

Element [ground of a science] *elemento, principio, fondamento d'una scienza.*

Element [what one delights in] *elemento, diletto, piacere*, s. m.

He is in his element, *egli è nel suo elemento.*

Hunting is his element, *la caccia è l'unico suo diletto.*

ELEME'NTARY, adj. [belonging to elements] *elementale, elementare, d'elemento.*

The elementary fire, *il fuoco elementale.*

ELE'NCH, s. [a sophistical argument] *argumento sofistico, sofisma e sofismo*, s. m. *argomento fallace.*

ELE'NCHUS [an index to a book] *elenco, indice, catalogo.*

E'LEPHANT, s. [the biggest and strongest of all four-footed beasts [*elefante*, s. m. *animale il più grande, e'l più forte di tutti gli animali quadrupedi.*

To make a fly an elephant, *fare d'una mosca un elefante.*

Of or belonging to an elephant, *elefantino, d'elefante.*

E'LEPHANTIASIS, s. [the leprosy] *elefantiasi, sorta di lebbra*, s. f.

To E'LEVATE [to lift up, to raise] *elevare, levare in alto, innalzare, esaltare.*

E'LEVATED, adj. *elevato, inalzato, esaltato.*

High elevated thoughts, *pensieri elevati.*

He is elevated in his own conceit, *presume molto di se, è in gran concetto di se.*

He is a little elevated [he has taken a merry cup] *egli è un poco allegro.*

ELEVA'TION, s. *elevazione*, s f. *elevamento.*

The elevation of the host, *l'elevazione dell' ostia.*

The elevation of the pole, *l'altezza del polo.*

ELE'VATORY, s. [a surgeon's instrument] *elevatorio*, s. m. *strumento di cerusico, serve principalmente a levare un pezzo d'osso fiaccato nella pia madre.*

ELE'VEN, adj. *undici.*

Possession is eleven points of the law, *chi è in possesso ha un gran vantaggio.*

ELE'VENTH, adj. *undecimo.*

ELF, s. plural, elves [a wandering spirit, supposed to be seen in wild places] *uno spirito errante, come chi direbbe un folletto, che il volgo superstizioso crede si veda in luoghi silvestri e deserti.*

Elf [a devil] *un demonio.*

To ELF [to intangle] *intricare, come si dice dal volgo sciocco de i folletti i quali fanno le chiome de' cavalli che non si possono poi senza gran fatica districare.*

E'LFLOCK, s. [knots of hair twisted by elves] *ciocche di capelli o di crini intrecciati stranamente dagli spiriti e da' folleti.*

To ELI'DE [to break in pieces] *spezzare, rompere, far in pezzi.*

E'LIGIBLE, adj. [fit to be chosen] *eligibile, da eleggere.*

ELI'SION, s. [or striking off] *troncamento*, s. m.

The elision of a vowel, *il troncamento d'una vocale.*

E'LIXIR, s. [a medicine made by strong infusion] *elisire, elisirvite*, s. m.

ELK, s. [a strong and swift beast, in shape like a hart, and as tall as a horse] *granbestia*, s. f. *sorta d'animale quadrupede del genere de' cervi.*

ELL, s. [a measure containing three foot and nine inches] *nome di misura d'Inghilterra che è circa due braccia alla Fiorentina.*

ELLI'PSIS, s. [in rhetorick, is a figure whereby some part of our discourse is left out or retrenched] *elisse, ellisse*, s. f. *figura rettorica la quale tronca parte del discorso.*

Ellipsis [in geometry, is an oval figure produced from the section of a cone] *elisse, ellisse, figura piana, prodotta da una della sezioni del cono.*

ELLI'PTICAL, } adj. [of or belong-
ELLI'PTICK, } ing to an ellipsis] *elittico, ellitico, di ellisse, che ha figura d'elisse.*

ELM, s. [a tree] *olmo*, s. m. *spezie d'albero.*

An elm-grove, *olmeto*, s. m. *luogo pien d'olmi.*

ELOCU'TION, s. [utterance, delivery] *elocuzione, espressione, facondia nel parlare.*

ELO'GIUM, } s. [a testimonial to
E'LOGY, } one's commendation or praise] *elogio, panegirico*, s. m. *composizione in lode di che che si sia.*

To ELO'IGNE [to remove, or send away to a great distance] *allontanare.*

ELO'IGNED, adj. *allontanato.*

To ELO'PE [to leave a husband, and dwell with an adulterer] *lasciar suo marito, ed abitare con un adultero.*

To elope [to go away by stealth] *fuggire, scappare.*

Elo'ped, adj. *che ha lasciato suo marito, per andar ad abitar con un adultero; fuggito.*

Elo'pement, s. *l'abbandonar una moglie suo marito, per abitare con un adultero; il fuggire d'un servo dal padrone.*

E'loquence, s. [the art of speaking well] *eloquenza,* s. f. *il bene, e facondamente parlare.*

E'loquent, adj. *eloquente, che ha eloquenza.*

Very eloquent, *eloquentissimo*

E'loquently, adv. *eloquentemente, facondamente, con eloquenza.*

Else, adj. *altro, altra.*

No man else, no body else, *nessun altro.*

Some where else, *in qualche altra parte, altrove.*

He minds nothing else but his own interest, *non bada ad altro ch' al suo proprio interesse.*

Else, conj. [otherwise] *altrimente, o.*

Be quiet, else be gone, *tacete o andate via.*

Do as I bid you, else you shall suffer for it, *fate quel che vi comando, altrimente me la pagherete.*

Elsewhere, adv. *altrove, in altro luogo.*

From elsewhere, *altronde, da altro luogo.*

To Elu'cidate [to make clear, or plain] *dilucidare, spiegare, schiarare, manifestare, dichiarare.*

Elu'cidated, adj. *dilucidato, spiegato, schiarato, manifestato, dichiarato.*

Elucida'tion, s. [an explaining, or clearing] *dichiarazione, spiegazione,* s. f.

To Elu'de [to escape any impending trouble or danger, to wave] *schivare, scansare, sfuggire, schifare.*

Elu'ded, adj. *schivato, scansato, sfuggito, schifato.*

Elves, s. pl. *di* elf.

E'lvelock, *v.* elflock.

E'lvish, adj. [relating to elves or wandering spirits] *appartenente a folletto; di folletto, v.* elf.

Elu'sion, s. [fraud] *fraude, fallacia,* s. f. *inganno,* s. m.

Elu'sory, s. [deceitful] *fallace, fraudolente, ingannevole.*

To Elu'te [to wash off] *lavar via, nettare con acqua.*

Ely'sian, adj. *elisio.*

The elysian fields, *i campi elisi.*

'Em, *è una abbreviazione plebea di* Them, *li, le, loro.*

I love 'em, *li amo, o le amo.*

I am not against 'em, *non sono contra di loro.*

To Ema'ciate [to make lean] *smagrare, dimagrare, render magro, emaciare.*

Ema'ciated, adj. *smagrato, dimagrato, emaciato.*

Emacia'tion, s. *macerazione, emaciazione,* s. f. *grande smagrimento.*

E'manant, adj. [issuing from something else] *emanante; che esce d'altra cosa.*

Emana'tion, s. [flowing out] *emanazione,* s. f.

E'manative, or Ema'natory, adj. [that floweth from] *emanato, venuto, proceduto, prodotto.*

To Ema'ncipate [to set at liberty] *emancepare, emancipare, mancepare, liberare, che fa il padre il figliuolo dalla sua podestà.*

Ema'ncipated, adj. *emancepato, emancipato, mancepato.*

Emancipa'tion, s. [a setting at liberty] *emancipazione,* s. f.

To Ema'sculate [to geld] *castrare, tagliare o cavare i testicoli.*

To emasculate [to enfeeble, to enervate] *indebolire, snervare, debilitare, spossare.* pres. *indebolisco.*

Blank verse does but emasculate poetry, *il verso sciolto rende la poesia snervata.*

Ema'sculated, adj. *castrato, snervato, indebolito, debilitato, spossato.*

Emascula'tion, s. *il castrare.*

To Emba'lm, *imbalsimare.*

To Emba'rk, *imbarcare.*

To Emba'rrass [to pester or trouble] *imbarazzare, intrigare, imbrogliare.*

Emba'rrassed, adj. *imbarazzato, intrigato, imbrogliato.*

Emba'rrassment, s. [or trouble] *imbarazzo, impedimento, intrigo,* s. m.

Emba'ssador, s. [one appointed to act for, and represent the person of a prince or state in a foreign country] *ambasciadore, ambasciatore,* s. m.

An ambassador extraordinary, *un ambasciatore straordinario.*

The Welch embassador [the cuckoo] *il cucolo, il barbagianni.*

Emba'ssadress, s. [an embassador's wife] *ambasciatrice,* s. f. *moglie d'un ambasciatore.*

E'mbassage, } s. [the commission
E'mbassy, } given by a prince or state, to an embassador] *ambasciata,* s. f.

To go upon an embassy, *andare in ambasciata.*

To Emba'ttle, *porre in battaglia. v.* To imbattle.

To Embe'llish, *abbellire. v.* to imbellish.

E'mbers, s. [hot embers] *ceneri calde, brage.*

The ember weeks [the first week in Lent, the next after Whitsunday, the 14th of September, and the 13th of December] *le quattro tempora.*

To Embe'zzle, *appropriarsi una cosa, mancando di fede.*

Embe'zzlement, s. *la cosa ch' uno s'è appropriate, mancando di fede; o l' appropriarsi che uno fa una cosa, mancando di fede.*

To Embla'ze, *ornare con lucidi ornamenti.*

To Embla'zon *adornare con adornamenti che rilucono.*

E'mblem, s. [a representation of some moral notion by way of device or picture] *emblema,* s. f. *simbolo.*

Emblema'tical, } adj. [of, or be-
Emblema'tick, } longing to an emblem] *emblematico, di emblema.*

E'mblements, s. [in law, are the profits of lands which have been sowed] *entrate, o usufrutto d'una terra seminata.*

To Embo'ss, *far bernoccolo; alzare o formare in curvo e a mo' di bernoccolo; intagliare.*

Embrasu're, s. [in fortification, the holes in a parapet, through which the cannons are laid to fire into the field] *cannoniera,* s. f. *quella apertura donde si scarica dai forti il cannone.*

Embrasure [in architecture, an enlargement made in a wall to give more light to windows, doors, &c.] *apertura che si fa in un muro per dar più lume alle finestre, ed alle porte.*

To Embro'ider, *v.* to imbroider.

E'mbrio, s. [the fœtus or child in the womb after its members come to be distinctly formed, but before it has its perfect shape] *embrione,* s. m. *il parto concetto nella matrice, avanti che abbia i debiti lineamenti, e dovuta forma.*

A work in embrio, *un lavoro abbozzato, un abbozzo.*

Emenda'tion, s. [a correcting, or amendment] *emendazione, emenda,* s. f. *emendamento,* s. m.

E'merald, s. [a precious stone] *smeraldo,* s. m. *pietra preziosa di color verde.*

Eme'rgence, } s. [a thing which
Eme'rgency, } happens suddenly] *emergenza,* s. f.

Eme'rgent, adj. [accidental, appearing of a sudden] *emergente, che succede accidentalmente.*

An emergent occasion, *un caso emergente.*

E'meril, s. [a sort of stone used in burnishing metals] *smeriglio,* s. m. *sorta di pietra ridotta in polvere colla quale si bruniscono i metalli.*

To burnish with emeril, *smerigliare, brunir collo smeriglio.*

Eme'rsion, s. [in astronomy, is when a star that is so nigh the sun that it cannot be seen, begins to appear again: also the sun or moon's coming out of an eclipse] *emersione,* s. f. *si dire d'una stella, la quale per la sua troppa vicinanza del sole non può vedersi, e apparisce di nuovo col discostarsene; si dire anche del sole e della luna che cominciano ad uscire dell' ecclissi.*

Eme'tick, adj. [that provokes vomiting] *emetico, che ha virtù di far vomitare.*

E'minence, s. [or rising ground] *eminenza, altezza,* s. f. *colle,* s. m.

Eminence, or eminency, s. [qualleney, high degree of quality] *eminenza, eccellenza,* s. f. *qualità eminente.*

A person of eminency, *una persona eminente, di gran qualità, d'un grado eminente.*

Eminency [a title given to cardinals] *eminenza, titolo che si da a' cardinali.*

E'minent, adj. [high] *eminente, alto, elevato.*

Eminent [excellent, high, great] *eminente, eccellente, eccelso, famoso, grande.*

An eminent quality, *una qualità eminente.*

An eminent man in learning and wiſdom, *un uomo eminente in dottrina ed in ſapere.*

Moſt eminent, *eminentiſſimo.*

E'MISSARY, s. [a perſon ſent out to obſerve the motion of an enemy, a ſpy, a ſcout] *emiſſario, ſpia.*

EMI'SSION, s. [a ſending forth, or caſting out] *emiſſione,* s. f. *gittamento,* s. m.

To EMI'T [to ſend forth, or caſt out] *gettare, mandare, metter fuori, ſpicciare.*

EMI'TTED, adj. *gettato, mandato, meſſo fuori, ſpicciato.*

E'MMET, s. [an ant] *una formica.*

To EMME'W, *v.* To mew.

EMO'LLIENT, adj. [making ſoft, pliant] *mollificativo, atto a mollificare, lenificativo, lenitivo.*

An emollient, s. *una medicina leniente, un lenitivo.*

EMO'LUMENT, s. [or profit, advantage] *emolumento, profitto, guadagno.*

E'MONGST, *v.* Amongſt.

EMO'TION, s. [a ſtirring, or moving forth] *ſcoſſa,* s. m.

Emotion [a violent motion of the mind] *emozione,* s. f. *ardore,* s. m.

To EMPA'LE, *far una ſiepe di pali.*

To empale, *fortificare intorno con pali.*

To empale, *chiudere, ſerrare intorno intorno.*

To empale, *impalare, ſorta di ſupplizio turcheſco.*

EMPA'LEMENT, s. [the outward part of the flower of a plant] *boccia,* s. f. *fior ancor non aperto.*

To EMPA'NNEL, *v.* To impannel.

E'MPEROUR, s. [a ſovereign prince of an empire] *imperadore,* s. m.

The eaſtern and weſtern emperors, *gl' imperadori d'oriente e d'occidente.*

E'MPHASIS, s. [a ſtrong and vigorous pronunciation of a word] *enfaſi, energia,* s. f.

To ſpeak with an emphaſis, *parlare con enfaſi.*

EMPHA'TICK, or EMPHA'TICAL, adj. [ſpoken with earneſtneſs] *enfatico.*

An emphatical expreſſion, *un' eſpreſſione enfatica.*

EMPHA'TICALLY, adv. *enfaticamente, con enfaſi.*

E'MPIRE, s. [the dominions of an emperor] *imperio,* s. m. *ſtato, e dominio d'un imperadore.*

The eaſtern empire, *l'imperio d'oriente.*

Empire [power, authority] *imperio, ſupremo dominio, ſignoria.*

EMPI'RICAL, adj. *empirico.*

An empirical doctor, *un empirico, un medico, che ſi ſerve della ſua ſola notizia delle eſperienze.*

An EMPI'RICK, s. [a quack] *un empirico, un ciarlatano, un cantambanco.*

EMPLA'STER, s. [a plaſter] *impiaſtro,* s. m.

To EMPLA'STER [to cover with a plaſter] *coprire con un impiaſtro.*

To EMPLO'Y, *v.* To imploy, *e ſuoi derivativi.*

EMPOI'SON, *v.* To poiſon.

EMPO'RIUM, s. [a market] *emporio,* s. m.

E'MPRESS, s. [the wife of an emperor] *imperatrice,* s. f. *moglie d'imperadore.*

E'MPTINESS, s. *votezza,* s. f.

E'MPTION, s. [a buying] *compra,* s. m.

E'MPTY, adj. [void] *voto, col primo o aperto, contrario di pieno, vano.*

An empty purſe, *una borſa vota.*

An empty veſſel, *un vaſo voto.*

Empty veſſels make the greateſt noiſe, *la più cattiva ruota del carro ſempre cigola.*

Empty [vain] *vano, leggiero, inutile, mal fondato.*

An empty hope, *una vana ſperanza.*

The empty pleaſures of this world, *i vani e momentanei piaceri di queſto mondo.*

An empty [or ſhallow] man, *un uomo di poco ſenno.*

To have but the empty title of a king, *aver il nudo nome di re.*

The town is very empty, *la città è vota di gente, v'è pora gente in città.*

To E'MPTY [to make void] *votare, cavare il contenuto fuor del continente, contrario d'empiere.*

To empty a caſk, *votare un barile.*

To empty out of one veſſel into another, *traſvaſare, travaſare.*

E'MPTY'D, adj. *votato.*

To EMPU'RPLE [to make of a purple colour] *render purpureo.*

EMPY'EMA, s. [a collection of purulent matter in the cavity of the thorax] *empiema,* s. m. *quel malóre, quando nella cavità del petto ſi raccoglie molto marcia.*

Troubled with the empyema, *empiematico, che ha il male dell' empiema.*

EMPY'REAL, adj. [of or belonging to the higheſt heaven] *empireo, epiteto dell' undecimo, e ultimo cielo.*

The empyreal, or higheſt heaven, *il cielo empireo.*

EMPYRE'UMA, s. [that taſte and ſmell of the fire, which in diſtillations happen to ſome oils, ſpirits, &c.] *empireuma,* s. m. *odore, o ſapore d'abbruciato.*

EMPYREUMA'TICK, adj. *empireumatico, che ha odore e ſapore d'abbruciato.*

To E'MULATE [to vie with one, to ſtrive to exceed, or go beyond another in any thing] *emulare, concorrere, gareggiare.*

EMULA'TION, s. [a ſtriving to excel or go beyond another in any thing] *emulazione, gara, conteſa,* s. f.

EMULA'TOR, s. [a rival, a competitor] *rivále, émulo, competitore, gareggiatore.*

E'MULOUSLY, adv. *a gara, con rivalità.*

EMU'LSION, s. [a phyſical drink made of the kernels of ſome ſeeds, infuſed in a convenient liquor] *emulſione,* s. f. *nome de' medicamenti, che ſi colano ſpremendo.*

To ENA'BLE [to make able, or capahle] *abilitare, abbientare, fare abile.*

ENA'BLED, adj. *abilitato, abbientato.*

To ENA'CT [to eſtabliſh an act or law, to ordain or decree] *fare o ſtabilire una legge, ordinare, decretare.*

ENA'CTED, adj. *fatto, ſtabilito, ordinato, decretato.*

ENA'MEL, s. [a compoſition uſed by painters] *ſmalto,* s. m. *compoſto di ghiaja, calcina, e arqua raſſodate inſieme.*

To ENA'MEL [to paint with enamel] *ſmaltare, coprir di ſmalto.*

ENA'MELLED, adj. *ſmaltato.*

ENA'MELLER, s. *artefice che lavora di ſmalto.*

To ENA'MOUR, *innamorare, render innamorato, accender d'amore.*

ENA'MOURED, adj. [in love with] *innamorato.*

ENARRA'TION, s. [recital, rehearſal] *narrazione, narrativa,* s. f. *racconto, ragguaglio,* s. m.

To ENCHA'NT, *incantare. Dar forza ad alruna coſa con qualche incanteſimo. Dilettare in ſommo grado.*

To ENCHA'SE, *incaſſare, fiſſar una coſa dentro ad un' altra.*

ENCO'MIAST, s. [a maker of encomiums] *un panegiriſta, un facitor d'encomi.*

ENCOMIA'STICAL, } ENCOMIA'STICK, } adj. [belonging to an encomium] *appartenente ad encomio.*

ENCO'MIUM, s. [a ſpeech, or copy of verſes in praiſe and commendation of a perſon] *encomio, elogio,* s. m. *lode,* s. f.

To ENCO'MPASS, *v.* To incompaſs.

ENCO'RE, adv. [again, once more] *anrora, un' altra volta, un altro tratte, di nuovo.*

ENCO'UNTER, s. [a fight] *ſcaramuccia, zuffa,* s. f. *ſcaramuccio, badalucco,* s. m.

They had a very hard encounter, *ebbero una grande ſcaramuccia.*

Encounter [meeting] *incontro, riucontro, intoppamento,* s. m.

To ENCO'UNTER [to engage with in fighting] *ſcaramucciare, attaccar la battaglia, azzuffarſi.*

The two armies encountered in the morning, and fought till the evening, *i duoi eſerciti s'azzufforno la mattina, e combatterono fino alla ſera.*

To encounter [to meet] *incentrare, riucontrare.*

ENCO'UNTERED, adj. *ſcaramucciato, badaluccato, azzuffato, incontrato, riucontrato.*

END, s. [the laſt part of any thing] *fine,* s. m. *eſtremità,* s. f. *termine,* s. m.

End [aim, deſign] *fine, diſegno, motivo,* s. m. *cagione, meta,* s. f.

End [iſſue, come off] *fine, ſurceſſo, evento,* s. m.

The end of the world, *la fine del mondo.*

The farther end of the ſtreet, *l'eſtremità della ſtrada.*

To go to the fartheſt end of the world, *andare fino alle parti le più remote del mondo.*

I have it at my tongue's end, *l'ho alla punta della lingua.*

To put an end to a thing [to make an end of it] *mettere o condurre a fine una cosa, finirla, compirla.*

To come to a shameful end, *fare una fine ignominiosa.*

The end of an orator is to persuade, *il fine d'un oratore è di persuadere.*

To compass one's ends, *condurre a fine il suo disegno.*

To what end was man created? *a che fine fu creato l'uomo?*

To the end that, *affinechè, affinchè, acciocchè.*

Who knows what will be the end of all this? *che sa qual sarà la fine di tutto ciò?*

The war is at an end, *è la guerra finita.*

The summer is almost at an end, *la state è quasi passata.*

He will hardly live a day to an end, *appena ha un giorno di vita, appena viverà un giorno intero.*

To make an end of one [to kill him] *spedire, o spacciare uno, ammazzarlo, assassinarlo.*

So there will be an end of him, *così egli sarà spedito.*

To make an end with one [to agree with him] *accordarsi con uno, venire a qualche aggiustamento con lui, finire un conto con lui.*

To have the better end of the staff, *essere, o stare a cavaliere, stare al disopra.*

To no end [to no purpose] *in vane, inutilmente.*

To be at one's wits end, *non saper che fare, essere irresoluto, mettersi il cervello a partito, stillarsi il cervello.*

He cares not which end goes forward, *non si cura di nulla, lascia andar le cose alla peggio.*

It made my hair stand an end, *mi fece raccapricciare.*

There's no end of it, *questo non finirà mai.*

World without end, *per sempre, ne' secoli de' secoli. Questa espressione non è in uso che nella liturgia Anglicana.*

Folks have got it by the end, *si dire.*

He has got it by the end, that I was going to be married, *ha intenso dire, che stavo per ammogliarmi.*

To be all for one's own end, *non riguardar che il suo proprio bene, non badare, non aver mira che al suo vantaggio.*

In the end, *alla fine, alla per fine, in fine.*

An ends-man [a broker that goes about the streets to buy old cloaths] *rivenditore, rivendugliuolo, rigattiere,* s. m.

To END [to make an end of] *finire, terminare, por fine, compire,* pref. *finisco, compisco.*

To end a discourse, *finire un discorso, conchiudere un discorso.*

To end a business, *terminare un affare.*

To end a quarrel, *metter fine ad una contesa, terminare una contesa.*

To end [to have an end] *finire, aver fine.*

When will our troubles end? *quando finiranno i nostri guai?*

All is well that ends well, *la fine corena l'opera.*

E'NDED, adj. *finito.*

E'NDING, s. *fine, conclusione.*

The ending of a controversy, *la decisione d'una controversia.*

E'NDIVE, s. [a sallad herb] *indivia,* s. f. *erba nota.*

E'NDLESS, adj. [without end] *infinito, che non ha fine, senza fine, continuo, perpetuo.*

An endless number, *un numero infinito.*

Endless torments, *pene infinite.*

E'NDLONG, adv. [in a strait line] *dirittamente, in linea retta, non obliquamente.*

E'NDMOST, adj. [remotest, furthest; at the further end] *l'ultimo, il più remoto, il più lontano.*

E'NDWISE, adv. [erectly, uprightly, on end] *erettamente, in modo eretto, in punta.*

E'NEMY, s. [or foe] *nemico, inimico,* s. m. *nemica, inimica,* s. f.

A professed enemy, *un nemico capitale.*

ENERGE'TICK, ENERGE'TICAL, adj. [forcible, efficacious] *energico, forte, efficace.*

E'NERGY, s. [force, efficacy] *energia, efficacia,* s. f.

To E'NERVATE [to weaken or deprive of strength] *snervare, debilitare, spossare.*

E'NERVATED, adj. *snervato, debilitato, spossato.*

ENERVA'TING, or ENERVA'TION, s. *lo snervare, debilitamento,* s. m.

E'NGINE, s. [machine, instrument] *macchina, macchinazione,* s. f. *ordigno, strumento, ingegno,* s. m.

An engine to make sea water fresh, *macchina da dissalare l'acqua del mare.*

Engine [to put out the fire with] *tromba,* s. m.

An engine [or device] *artificio,* s. *astuzia, stratagemma.*

ENGINE'ER, s. [a person skilled in fortifications, both building, attacking and defending forts] *ingegnere,* s. m. *ingegnoso ritrovator d'ingegni e di macchine.*

E'NGLAND, s. *Inghilterra.*

E'NGLISH, s. [the English tongue] *l'Inglese, la lingua Inglese.*

To speak English, *parlare Inglese.*

An English man, *un Inglese.*

An English woman, *una Inglese.*

ENI'GMA, s. [or riddle] *enimma,* s. f. *detto oscuro, che sotto'l velame delle parole nasconde senso allegorico.*

ENIGMA'TICAL, or ENIGMA'TICK, adj. [dark] *enimmatico, di enimma, con enimma.*

To ENLI'VEN [to make brisk or lively] *animare.*

ENLI'VENER, s. [that which animates, that which invigorates] *cosa che anima, che da nuovo vigore, che invigorisce.*

E'NMITY, s. [hatred, grudge] *nemicizia, inimicizia,* s. f. *odio,* s. m.

E'NNEAGON, s. [a regular figure of nine equal sides and nine angles] *enneagono,* s. m. *figura solida di nove angoli eguali, e di nove canti.*

To ENNO'BLE [to make noble] *nobilitare, far nobile.*

ENNO'BLED, adj. *nobilitato, fatto nobile.*

ENNO'BLEMENT, s. *il nobilitare.*

ENODA'TION, s. [an unknotting, in husbandry] *il levare, o tagliare i nodi,* e figur. *lo sciogliere una difficoltà.*

ENO'RMITY, s. [heinousness] *enormità, enormezza, atrocità,* s. f.

Enormity [high misdemeanor] *delitto enorme, o atroce.*

ENO'RMOUS, adj. [heinous] *enorme, nefando, atroce, scellerato.*

An enormous crime, *un delitto enorme.*

ENO'RMOUSLY, adv. *enormemente, atrocemente.*

ENO'UGH, adv. [sufficiently] *assai, a bastanza, a sufficienza.*

I have enough, I have enough of it, *ne ho assai, ne ho a bastanza.*

'Tis enough, *basta.*

This will be enough to live on, *questo basterà per vivere.*

Sure enough, *certamente, sicuramente, senza dubbio.*

'Tis true enough, *è pur troppo vero.*

I know it well enough, *lo so pur troppo bene.*

Enough is as good as a feast, *chi ha assai è ricco.*

ENO'W, *v.* Enough.

ENSA'MPLE, s. [example, pattern] *esemplare, esemplo, modello,* s. m. Obs.

To ENSE'AM a hawk [to bring down his fat by feeding him more soberly] *alenare un falcone.*

ENSI'GN, s. [an officer in a company of foot soldiers, who carries the colours] *alfiere,* s. m. *grado di milizia, ed è quel che porta la'nsegna.*

Ensign [mark] *sopransegna,* s. f. *segno,* s. m.

ENTA'BLATURE, s. [is the architrave, frize, or cornice of a pillar] *architrave,* s. m. *quel membro d'archiettura, che posa immediatamente sopra colonne, o stipiti.*

To E'NTER [to go into] *entrare, andar dentro.*

To enter upon an action, *intentare un' azione.*

To enter a room, *entrare in una camera.*

To enter upon an estate, *entrare in, o prender possesso d'un stato.*

To enter into a league, *entrare in lega, far allianza.*

To enter a thing into a book, *appuntare che che si sia in un libro.*

To enter a scholar in the university, *ricevere, o ammettere uno scolare in una università.*

To enter [or list] one's self a soldier, *arrolarsi, o farsi soldato.*

To enter an action against one, *intentare un' azione contro ad uno.*

To enter one in learning, *dare ad alcuno*

alcuno i principi delle scienze, iniziarlo nelle scienze.

It never entered into my mind, *ciò non m'è venuto mai in pensiero.*

To enter into orders, *prender gli ordini.*

To enter into bond, *mallevare, entrar mallevadore.*

To enter upon a design, *intraprendere, o cominciare un disegno.*

E'NTERED, adj. *entrato, v* To enter.

E'NTERING, s. *l'entrare, entrata*, s. m.

E'NTERPRIZE, s. [design, or attempt] *impresa*, s. f. *disegno, attentato*, s. m.

To E'NTERPRISE [to undertake] *imprendere, intraprendere, pigliare a operare, apparecchiarsi*, pret. *impresi, intrapresi.*

E'NTERPRISED, adj. *impreso, intrapreso, apparecchiato.*

ENTERPRI'SER, s. *imprenditore, intraprenditore*, s. m.

ENTERPRI'SING, s. *imprendimento*, s. m. *l'imprendere.*

ENTHU'SIASM, s. [an inspiration whether real or imaginary; fanaticism] *entusiasmo*, s. m. *vera o pretesa ispirazione.*

ENTHU'SIAST, s. [one who fancies himself inspired with the Divine Spirit] *entusiaste, fanatico, che pretende esser inspirato.*

ENTHUSIA'STICAL, or ENTHUSIA'STICK, adj. [belonging to enthusiasm] *entusiasto, fanatico.*

E'NTHYMEME, s. [an imperfect syllogism in logick, where either the major or minor proposition is wanting] *entimema*, s. f.

E'NTIRE, adj. *v.* Intire.

E'NTITY, s. [a being] *entità*, s. f. *ente*, s. m.

ENTO'MB [to put into a tomb] *metter nella tomba, nel sepolcro.*

E'NTRAILS, s. [the guts or bowels] *gl' intestini, le interiora, le budella, le viscere.*

E'NTRANCE, s. [entry] *entrata*, s. f. *ingresso*, s. m.

He made a solemn entrance, *fare una pomposa entrata.*

At the entrance into the port, *all' entrata del porto.*

Entrance money, *entrata, quel che uno scolare paga al maestro nel cominciare ad imparare.*

Entrance upon a new life, *cangiamento di vita.*

Entrance [admittance] *entratura*, s. f. *accesso*, s. m.

Entrance [beginning] *principio, cominciamento*, s. m.

To ENTRA'NCE [to put into an extasy] *render estatico, mandar in estasi.*

E'NTRY, s. [or passage of a house] *anticorte, antiporto, andito*, s. m.

Entry [entrance] *entrata.*

He made his entry in great pomp and splendor, *fece la sua entrata con gran pompa, e splendore.*

An entry upon an estate, *l'entrare in possesso d'un stato.*

The entry upon the mass, *l'introito della messa.*

To ENTWI'NE [to twist or wind about] *attortigliare, attorcigliare, avvolgere, cignere intorno*, pret. *avvolsi.*

To ENU'CLEATE [to sift and scan] *discussare, discutere, esaminare, considerare, spiegare*, pret. *discussi.*

ENU'CLEATED, adj. [sifted and scanned] *discussato, discusso, esaminato, considerato, spiegato, messo in chiaro.*

E'NVIOUS, adj. *invidioso, invido, macchiato d'invidia.*

An envious man, *un invidioso.*

An envious woman, *un' invidiosa.*

E'NVIOUSLY, adv. *invidiosamente, con invidia.*

To ENU'MERATE [to number or reckon up] *enumerare, numerare, contare, calcolare, sommare.*

ENU'MERATED, adj. *numerate, contato, calcolato, sommato.*

ENU'MERATING, ENUMERA'TION, s. [a numbering or summing up] *enumerazione, numerazione*, s. f. *il numerare, calcolo, e calculo, enumeramento*, s. m.

ENVO'Y, s. [a person sent by a prince to another for the transaction of an affair] *un inviato.*

E'NVY, s. [an uneasy passion of the mind, on beholding the prosperity of others] *invidia*, s. f. *dolore dell' anima dell' altrui utilità.*

To E'NVY, *invidiare, avere invidia.*

To envy one's happiness, *invidiare l'altrui bene.*

I neither envy his wit nor his fortune, *non invidio nè il suo sapere, nè la sua fortuna.*

E'NVYED, adj. *invidiato.*

Better envied than pitied, *è meglio invidia che compassione.*

E'NVYING, s. *l'invidiare.*

To ENWO'MB [to make pregnant] *ingravidare.*

To enwomb [to bury, to hide] *seppellire, nascondere, celare.*

E'PACT, s. [the eleven days which the common solar year has above the common lunar years] *epatta*, s. f. *gli undici giorni che furono aggiunti, per pareggiar l'anno solare, coll' anno comune della luna.*

E'PHA, s. [a kind of measure amongst the ancient Jews] *efa, misura fra gli antichi Ebrei, la quale conteneva incirca una stajo.*

EPHE'MERA, s. [a continual fever which lasts but one day] *febbre continua, che non dura che un giorno.*

EPHE'MERIS, s. [registers or astronomical tables, calculated to show the diurnal motions of the planets through the year] *effemeride*, s. f. *libro dove i calcoli si registrano, contenente i moti, e le apparenze de' corpi superiori.*

Ephémeris [journal] *giornale*, s. m.

EPICE'NE, adj. Ex. the epicene gender [common to both sexes] *il genere comune.*

E'PICK, adj. [heroick] *epico, eroico.*

An epick poem, or poet, *un poema o un poeta epico.*

E'PICKS, s. [epick poetry] *poesia epica.*

E'PICURE, s. [one given to excess of gluttony and voluptuousness] *un epicuro, un uomo dedito alle voluttà, e sensualità.*

EPICURE'AN, s. [a follower of the sect of Epicurus] *un Epicureo, un discepolo d'Epicuro.*

E'PICURISM, s. [the doctrine of Epicurus] *la dottrina d'Epicuro, Epicurismo.*

Epicurism [an Epicure's life] *vita Epicurea, vita licenziosa.*

E'PICYCLE, s. [a little circle, whose center or small orb being fixed in the deferent of a planet, is carried along with its motion] *epiciclo*, s. m. *piccol cerchio, e piccola sfera, che descrive col moto del suo corpo il pianeta, e per sua circonferenza lo muove.*

EPIDE'MICAL, or EPIDEMI'CK, adj. [common among all the people, universal] *epidemico, comune, universale.*

An epidemical disease, *una malattia epidemica, o contagiosa.*

E'PIDEMY, s. *epidemia, o malattia contagiosa.*

EPIGA'STRUM, s. [the forepart of the abdomen, or lower belly] *epigastro*, s. m. *la parte anteriore del ventricolo.*

E'PIGRAM, s. [a short witty poem] *epigramma*, s. m. *spezie di poesia.*

EPIGRA'MMATIST, s. [a maker of epigrams] *compositor di epigrammi.*

EPI'GRAPHE, s. [an inscription] *epigrafio*, s. m.

EPILE'PSY, s. [the falling sickness] *epilessia*, s. m. *mal caduco, mal maestro.*

EPILE'PTICK, } adj. [troubled with EPILE'PTICAL, } an epilepsy] *epiletiro che patisce d'epilessia.*

E'PILOGUE, s. [a conclusion of a speech] *epilogo*, s. m. *breve ricapitolazione delle cose dette.*

E'PINOME, s. [a rhetorical figure, when to move affection the same word is repeated] *epinome*, s. f. *figura rettorica.*

EPI'PHANY, s. [or twelfth day] *epifania*, s. f. *giorno festivo, che si celebra li sei di Gennaro, dicesi con vacobolo corrotto Befania.*

EPI'SCOPACY, s. *episcopato, vescovato*, s. m.

EPI'SCOPAL, adj. [belonging to a bishop] *episcopale, vescovile.*

An episcopal habit, *un abito episcopale.*

The episcopal court, *la corte episcopale.*

EPISCOPA'RIANS, s. [those who are of the episcopal party] *quelli che tengono per i vescovi.*

E'PISODE, s. [a separate story or action which a poet connects in the main plot of his poem, as the story of Dido in Virgil] *episodio*, s. m. *digressione*, s. f.

E'PISTLE, s. [a letter] *epistola, lettera, pistola*, s. f.

The Epistles of the Apostles, *l'Epistole degli Apostoli.*

An epistle dedicatory, *una lettera dedicatoria, una dedicazione.*

A little

A little epistle, *una epistoletta, un pistoletto.*

E'PISTLER, s. [he who reads the epistles in a cathedral church] *colui che legge le epistole in una chiesa cattedrale.*

E'PISTLER, s. [a scribbler of letters] *uno che scarabocchia epistole ; cattivo scrittore ai lettere.*

EPI'STOLAR, or EPI'STOLARY, adj. [belonging to an epistle or letter] *d'epistola, attenente ad epistola.*

EPISTY'LE, s [a mass of timber laid upon the capital of a pillar] *architrave*, s. m.

E'PITAPH, s. [an inscription on a tomb] *epitaffio, e epitafio*, s. m. *iscrizione fatta in onore de' morti.*

EPITHALA'MIUM, s. [a nuptial song] *epitolamio*, s. m. *canzone nuziale.*

E'PITHEM, s. [any outward application, generally of a liquid form, like a fomentation] *epittima, pittima*, s. f.

E'PITHET, s. [a word expressing the nature and quality of another word, to which it is joined] *epiteto*, s. m. *aggiunto che dichiara la qualità, differenza, ed essenza del sustantivo col quale egli è accompagnato.*

EPI'TOME, s. [an abridgment] *epitome*, s. m. *sommario, commento*, s. m.

To EPITOMI'SE [to make an epitome or abridgement of a thing] *fare un epitome, sommare, compendiare, abbreviare.*

EPITOMI'SED, adj. *sommato, compendiato, abbreviato.*

E'POCH, } s. [or date of years]
E'POCHA, } *epoca*, s. f.

E'PODE, s. [a kind of lyrick verse] *un epodo, parte di oda, o poesia lirica.*

EPULA'TION, s. [banquet, feast] *gozzoviglia, banchetto.*

E'PULIS, s. [an excrescence in the gums] *epulide*, s. f. *tumore o escrescenza di carne che viene nelle gingive.*

E'QUAL, adj. [like] *eguale, uguale, pari, simili.*

They are not equal, *non sono eguali.*

Equal [just] *eguale, giusto.*

To be equal to one, *esser eguale con uno.*

Equal, adv. *egualmente, al pari.*

He loves it equal with any other, *l'ama al pari di che che si sia.*

Equal, s. *simili, pari, simigliante.*

He has not his equal, *non ha il simile, o il pari.*

Every body loves his equal, *ogni simile appetisce il suo simile.*

To E'QUAL [to make equal] *agguagliare, fare eguale, pareggiare, aggiustare.*

To equal [or answer] *corrispondere.* pret. *corrisposi.*

His strength equals his courage, *la sua forza corrisponde al suo valore, la sua forza non è inferiore al suo coraggio.*

To equal one's self to, *agguagliarsi, paragonarsi, andar del pari.*

EQUA'LITY, s. [or likeness] *egualità, parità*, s. f.

To be in an equality with one, *andar del pari con uno.*

To EQUALI'SE [to equal] *agguagliare, pareggiare, aggiustare.*

EQUALI'SED, adj. *agguagliato, pareggiato, aggiustato.*

EQUALI'SING, s. *agguagliamento*, s. m. *agguaglianza, egualità, parità, agguagliazione*, s. f.

E'QUALLY, adv. [in the same degree with another; evenly, uniformly, impartially] *egualmente, uniformemente ; senza parzialità.*

EQUANI'MITY, s. [evenness of mind, contentedness] *egualità, serenità, tranquillità di mente.*

EQUA'TION, s. [a making equal, an equal division] *equazione, egualità*, s. f. *aggiustamento, pareggiamento*, s. m.

EQUA'TOR, s. [the equinoctial line] *equatore*, s. m. *la linea equinoziale.*

EQUE'STRIAN, adj. [belonging to a horse-man, or knight] *equestre, di cavaliere.*

An equestrian figure, *una figura equestre.*

The equestrian order among the Romans, *l'ordine equestre fra gli antichi Romani.*

EQUIA'NGULAR, adj. [that has equal angles and corners] *equiangolare, che ha gli angoli eguali.*

EQUIDI'STANT, adj. [that is of an equal distance] *equidistante, egualmente distante.*

EQUILA'TER, or EQUILA'TERAL, adj. [whose sides are all equal] *equilatero, che hà i lati uguali.*

An equilateral triangle, *un triangolo equilatero.*

To EQUILIBRATE [to balance equally] *equilibrare, pesare ugualmente.*

EQUILIBRA'TION, s. [equipoise] *equilibrio, il pesare egualmente.*

EQUILIBRI'OUS, adj. *che è in equilibrio.*

EQUILI'BRIUM, s. [equality of weight and poise] *equilibrio, contrappesamento*, s. m.

To put in equilibrium, *equilibrare, fare equilibrio, mettere in equilibrio.*

EQUINO'CTIAL, adj. *equinoziale.*

The equinoctial line, *la linea equinoziale.*

EQUINOX, s. [when day and night are of equal length] *equinozio*, s. m. *agguaglianza del giorno, e della notte, che è quando'l sole passa sotto l'equinoziale.*

To EQUI'P [to accoutre, to furnish] *apparecchiare, fornire, allestire, preparare, arredare, mettere in punto, munire, provvedere.* pref. *fornisco, munisco, provvidi.*

E'QUIPAGE, s. [the provision of all things necessary for a voyage or journey] *apparecchio, arredo, corredo, fornimento, guernimento*, s. m.

To be in a good or bad equipage, *essere bene, o male alla via, essere in buono, o cattivo stato.*

EQUIPOI'SE, s. [or equal weight] *peso eguale, equilibrio.*

To equipoise, verb. act. *equilibrare, mettere in equilibrio.*

EQUIPO'LLENT, adj. being of equal force] *equipollente, equivalente, di valore, e pregio uguale.*

EQUIPO'LLENCE, s. [being of equal force and value] *equipollenza, equivalenza*, s. f.

EQUIPO'NDEROUS, adj. [of equal weight] *d'ugual peso.*

EQUI'PPED, adj. *apparecchiato fornito, allestito, preparato, arredato, munito, provveduto.*

E'QUITABLE, adj. [just, righteous] *equitabile, giusto, ragionevole.*

E'QUITABLENESS, s. *equità*, s. f.

E'QUITABLE, adv. *con equità, giustamente.*

E'QUITY, s. [the virtue of treating all persons according to the rules of reason and justice] *equità, giustizia*, s. f.

To do things according to equity, *fare le cose in equità.*

The court of equity [the court of chancery] *la corte dell' equità, la cancelleria, che non giudica secondo la legge scritta, ma secondo l'equità.*

EQUI'VALENCE, } s. [equal value]
EQUI'VALENCY, } *equivalenza*, s. f.

EQUI'VALENT, adj. [being of equal might, value or worth] *equivalente, di valore, e di pregio eguale.*

Equivalent, s. *equivalente*, s. m.

To give an equivalent, *dare un equivalente.*

EQUI'VOCAL, adj [which hath a double or doubtful signification] *equivoro, equivosco, dubbio, ambiguo.*

EQUI'VOCALLY, adv. *equivocamente, in modo equivoco.*

To EQUI'VOCATE [to speake ambiguously, to say one thing, and mean another] *equivocare, dare a più cose il medesimo nome.*

EQUIVOCA'TION, } s. [a double
EQUIVO'QUE, } meaning] *equivocazione, ambiguità di parole.*

E'RA, s. [the account of time from any particular date or epoch] *era, conto di tempo da una certa data o epoca.*

To ERA'DICATE [to pull up by the roots] *sradicare, diradicare, estirpare.*

To eradicate a disease, *sradicare una malattia.*

To eradicate a vice, *sradicare, o estirpare un vizio.*

ERA'DICATED, adj. *sradicato. diradicato, estirpato.*

ERA'DICATING, s. *lo sradicare, estirpamento*, s. m.

To ERA'SE [to rub out] *raschiar via, distruggere.*

ERA'SED, adj. [scraped, scratched out] *scancellato, cassato, cancellato.*

ERA'SEMENT, s. [a blotting out] *lo scancellare.*

ERE, adv. [before that, rather than] *prima che, atiche, più tosto.*

Ere I could go, *prima che possa andare.*

Ere I should do it, *più tosto che di farlo.*

Ere long, ere it be long, *frappoco, ben presto.*

Ere while, *qualche volta, delle volte.*

ERE'CT, adj. [raised, upright] *dritte, diritto, ritto, in piedi.*

To ERE'CT [to raise, to set up] *erigere, ergere, innalzare, rizzare, levar su.* pret. *eressi, ersi.*

To

To erect a statue to, or for one, ergere una statua a qualcheduno.

To erect [to build] elevare, fabbricare, costruire, pres. costruisco.

ERE'CTED, adj. eretto, erto, innalzato, rizzato, costruito, fabbricato.

ERE'CTION, s. [a raising] erezione, s. f.

Erection [building] edificio. s. m. struttura, s. f.

E'REMITE v. Hermit.

EREMI'TICAL, adj. romito, religioso, solitario.

E'RMINE, s. [a very rich fur of a weazel, or field-mouse, worn by princesor persons of quality] ermellino, s. m. pelle d'ermellino.

E'RMINED, adj. [lined with ermine] foderato d'ermellino.

To ERO'DE [to eat away] roder via.

To ERR [to mistake] errare, traviare, ingannarsi, deviare, sbagliare.

E'RRAND, s. [message] messaggio, s. m. ambasciata, s. f.

To go on, or upon an errand, fare un messaggio.

To send one on an errand, mandare alcuno per fare un messaggio.

A sleeveless errand, un messaggio impertinente.

To go on a sleeveless errand, tornar colle trombe nel sarco, tornare da qualche impresa, che non sia riuscita.

E'RRANT, adj. [for wandering] errante, erratico, vagabondo.

A knight errant, un cavaliere errante.

Errant justice, giudici erranti.

Errant, or arrant, v. Arrant.

E'RRANTRY, s. [an errant state, the condition of a wanderer] lo errare, l'andar attorno senza saper dove.

Errantry [the employment of a knight errant] cavalleria, l'impiego degli antichi cavalieri erranti.

ERRA'TA, s. [faults or omissions which escape correction in printing] errori di stampa.

ERRA'TICK, or ERRA'TICAL, adj. [wandering] erratico, errante, vagabondo.

Erratick stars [the planets so called in contradistinction to the fixed stars] stelle erranti.

E'RRED, adj. errato.

E'RRING, s. erramento, erorre, s. m.

ERRO'NEOUS, adj. [false] erroneo, erronico, pien d'errori, falso.

An erroneous opinion, un' opinione erronea.

ERRO'NEOUSLY, adv. erroneamente, falsamente.

E'RROUR, s. [or mistake] errore, s. m. l'errare.

To lie under a great errour, ingannarsi di molto.

To fall into an errour, commettere un errore.

Errour of an indictment, nullità in una accusa, o informazione.

ERSE, s. [bitter vetch] legume simile al pisello, ma di sapor men piacevole.

ERST, ERST-WHILE, adv. [long since, formerly] altre volte, tempo fa, anticamente.

ERUDI'TION, s. [learning] erudizione, dottrina, s. f. ammaestramento, s. m.

ERU'PTION, s. [a breaking forth with violence] impetuosità, violenza, sforzo che si fa per uscire.

ERYSIPE'LAS, s. [a disease called St. Antony's fire] risipola, s. f.

ESCA'PE, s. [a getting away from, flight] fuga, s. f. scampo, s. m.

To make an escape, or one's escape, prender la fuga, fuggire.

Escape [fault] errore, inganno, sbaglio, s. m.

He committed a great escape, ha commesso un grand' errore, ha fatto un grande sbaglio.

To ESCAPE [or make one's escape] scampare, liberarsi da pericolo, salvarsi, fuggire, scappare.

You shall not escape, voi non iscapperete.

To escape [to avoid] scampare, scansare, evitare.

To escape one's sight, involarsi dall' altrui vista.

The faults that have escaped the press, gli errori che sono scorsi nella stampa.

ESCA'PED, adj. scampato, salvato, fuggito, scappato.

E'SCHAR, s. [a scar remaining after the healing of a sore] escara, s. f. crosta che viene sopra le piaghe.

To ESCHE'W [to avoid] evitare, schifare, schivare, sfuggire, scansare, fuggire.

To eschew evil, and do good, fuggire il male, e fare il bene.

ESCHE'WED, adj. evitato, schifato, schivato, sfuggito, scansato, fuggito.

ESCHE'WING, s. schifamento, schivamento, s. m.

ESCU'TCHEON, s. l'arme della famiglia; scudo.

E'SNECY, s. [the right of choosing first in a divided inheritance which belongs to the eldest compartner] la prerogativa che il primo de' sozi ha di scegliere il primo quando si fa la divisione d'una eredità.

ESPE'CIAL, adj. speciale, speziale, singolare, particolare.

ESPE'CIALLY, adv. [particularly] specialmente, spezialmente, particolarmente, sopra tutto.

ESPLANA'DE, s. [in fortification, the glacis or slope of the counterscarp] spianata, s. f. termine di fortificazione.

E'SPLEES, s. [a law term, the full profits that the ground or land yieds] l'entrata o il prodotto d'una terra, o campo.

ESPO'USALS, s. [betrothing, the ceremony used upon that occasion] sponsalizio, s. sposalizio, s. m. sponsalizie, s. f. la solennità dello sposarsi.

To ESPO'USE [to betroth, to take in marriage, to wed] sposare, celebrar le sponsalizie, pigliar per moglie, o dar per moglie.

To espouse one's self to one, ammogliarsi con una, maritarsi con uno.

To espouse a man's cause, pigliar la difesa d'uno, abbracciar la sua causa, interessarsi in suo favore.

ESPOU'SED, adj. sposato.

To ESPY' [to perceive] scoprire, scorgere, vedere. pret. scorsi, vidi.

To espy [to observe] spiare, osservare, considerare, investigare.

ESPY'D, adj. scoperto, scorto, visto, veduto, spiato, osservato, considerato, investigato.

ESQUI'RE, s. [a title of dignity next to, and below a knight] scudiere, titolo di nobiltà.

ESQUI'RY, s. [the dignity of an esquire] il titolo di scudiere.

ESSA'Y, s. [attempt, proof, trial] saggio, cimento, s. m.

Essay of a deer, a hunting term [the breast or brisket of a deer] la carne del petto d'un cervo.

To ESSA'Y [to make an essay, to try] saggiare, far il saggio, provare, far pruova.

E'SSENCE, s. [the nature, substance, or being of any thing] essenza, essenzia, s. f. l'essere di tutte le cose, cosa commune alla natura di tutti gli enti.

Essence [in chymistry], a spirit drawn out of certain substances] essenza, sorta di liquore tratto per distillazione da che che si sia.

To ESSE'NCE [to perfume, to scent] profumare, dar odore.

An essenced fop, un zerbino attillato e profumato.

ESSE'NTIAL, adj. [belonging to the essence] essenziale.

The essential part of a thing, la parte essenziale d'una cosa.

An essential, s. l'essenziale d'una cosa.

The essential of religion, l'essenziale della religione.

ESSE'NTIALLY, adv. essenzialmente, con essenza.

ESSO'IA, or ESSO'INE, s. [an excuse alledged for one who is summoned to appear and answer to a real action] scusa legale, o legitima per l'assenza d'una persona citata a comparire in giustizia.

To ESSO'IN [to excuse a person absent] scusare una persona che non comparisce in giustizia.

ESSO'INED, adj. scusato dal comparire legalmente.

To ESTA'BLISH [to settle] stabilire, confirmare, fermare, assodare, render sodo fermo, e stabile.

ESTA'BLISHED, adj. stabilito, confermato, fermato, assodato.

Established [decreed] stabilito, decretato, statuito.

ESTA'BLISHMENT, ESTA'BLISHING, s. stabillimento, s. m. lo stabilire.

Establishment [a settlement concerning a prince's servants or troops, or the account of them] stato, s. m.

ESTA'TE, s. [condizion] stato, s. m. condizione, s. f.

Estate [means, revenues] beni, facoltà.

Estate [degree, rank] stato, ordine, o corpo politico, fra i soggetti d'un regno.

To be in low estate, essere in povero stato, essere in povera fortuna.

A real and personal estate, beni mobili, e immobili.

The

The three estates of the kingdom, *i tre stati del regno.*

To have a great estate, *possedere gran beni, o gran facultadi, esser molto facoltoso.*

An estate left one, *un' eredità.*

Man's estate, *l'età virile.*

Esteem [value, respect one has for a man or his merit] *stima, opinione,* s. f. *pregio, conto,* s. m.

I have a great esteem for him, *l'ho, o lo tengo in grande stima, so gran conto di lui.*

To be in great esteem, *essere in grande stima, esser molto stimato.*

A man of no esteem, *un uomo di poca stima, un uomo da niente, che non è stimato.*

To raise a man's esteem of a thing, *dare buona opinione a qualcheduno di che che si sia.*

To Este'em [to value] *stimare, far conto, fare stima, avere in pregio, pregiare, onorare.*

I esteem honour above life, *stimo più l'onore, che la vita.*

To esteem [or think] *stimare, giudicare, pensare, immaginare.*

Este'emed adj. [valued] *stimato, in istima, pregiato, onorato.*

Esteemed [accounted] *stimato, creduto, giudicato, tenuto, riputato.*

Este'emer, s. *stimatore, assessore, giudice che tassa il prezzo, e che regola il valore delle cose.*

E'stimable, adj. [worthy to be esteemed] *degno di stima.*

E'stimate, s. [the set price or value] *stima, valuta, estimazione,* s. f. *stimo, prezzo,* s. m.

Estimate [value, esteem] *stima,* s. f. *pregio, conto,* s. m.

To E'stimate [to rate, to value] *stimare, dar giudicio della valuta d'una cosa, valutare, apprezzare.*

E'stimated, adj. *stimato, apprezzato, valutato.*

Estima'tion, s. [a valuing or appraising] *estimazione, stima,* s. f. *stimo,* s. m.

E'stival, adj. [belonging to the summer] *estivo, di state*

Esto'pel, or Esto'ple, s. [a law word, is an impediment or bar of an action, which hath, or otherwise might have had his action] *ostacolo, impedimento,* s. m. *opposizione,* s. f.

Esto'ver, s. [a law word, that signifies nourishment or maintenance] *nutrimento, mantenimento, alimento,* s. m. *nutritura,* s. f.

To Estra'nge [to alienate, to draw away the affections] *alienare, stornare, dissuadere, rimuovere.* pret. *dissuasi, rimossi.*

To estrange one from another, *alienare uno da un altro, farli perder l'amore che haveva per lui.*

To estrange one from an agreement, *stornar uno da un patto, rimuovernelo, dissuadernelo.*

Estra'nged, adj. *alienato, stornato, dissuaso, rimosso.*

Estra'ngement, s. *alienazione, separazione,* s. f. *storno,* s. m.

Estra'nger, s. [law term, foreigners, persons born beyond sea] *alieni, stranieri.*

Estrangers [they who are no parties to the levying a fine] *quelli che non hanno parte nel riscuotere le tasse.*

E'streate, s. [the copy of an original writing] *copia vera d'un originale.*

To Estre'pe [to make spoil in lands and woods] *guastare, rovinare, danneggiare, vocabolaccio legale*

Estre'pement, s. [a spoil made in lands and woods by a tenant for term of life, to the damage of the reversioner] *rovina,* s. f. *danno, danneggiamento,* s. m. *gergo della gente di legge.*

To Etch [to grave with aqua-fortis] *scolpire con acqua forte.*

E'tched, adj. *scolpito con acqua forte.*

E'tching, s. f. *scolpitura con acqua forte.*

Ete'rnal, adj. [everlasting] *eterno, eternale, senza fine, e senza principio.*

An eternal happiness, *una felicità eterna.*

Ete'rnalist, s. [one who holds the past existence of the world infinite] *Uno che crede che il mondo sia sempre stato.*

To Eternali'se, v. To eternise.

Ete'rnally, adv. *eternamente, sempre, senza intermissione.*

Ete'rne, adj. v. Eternal.

Ete'rnity, s. [an infinite duration, without being or end] *eternità,* s. f. *misura interminabile e infinita, che non ha principio nè fine.*

God is from all eternity, *Iddio è eterno.*

To Eterni'ze [to make eternal] *eternare, fare eterno, immortalizzare, perpetuare.*

To eternalize one's memory, *eternare l'altrui memoria.*

Eterni'zed, adj. *eternato, immortalizzato, perpetuato.*

E'ther, s. *elemento più sottile dell' aria; aria raffinata o sublimata; ètere.*

Ether, *la materia delle regioni celesti.*

Ethe'real, Ethe'reous, } adj. *etereo, celeste.*

E'thicks, s. [moral philosophy] *etica,* s. f. *scienza de' costumi.*

E'thnick, adj. [heathenish, of or belonging to heathens] *etnico, gentile, pagano; non giudeo e non cristiano.*

Etymolo'gical, adj. [belonging to etymology] *etimologico.*

Etymo'logist, s. [one skilled in searching out the true interpretation of words] *etimologista,* s. m. *uno chè versato nell' etimologia delle parole.*

To Etymologi'ze [to give an account of the derivation of words] *trovare l'etimologia, e l'origine delle parole.*

Etymo'logy, s. [the true origin of a word] *etimologia,* s. f. *ragion della derivazione delle parole.*

E'tymon, s. [origin, primitive word] *origine; parola primitivia.*

To Eva'cuate [to discharge, to empty, to void] *evacuare, votare, cavare, far vacuo, scaricare.*

To evacuate the humours, *evacuare gli umori.*

To evacuate a place, *abbandonare un luogo, uscire d'un luogo.*

Apt to evacuate, *evacuativo.*

Eva'cuated, adj. *evacuato, votato, cavato, scaricato.*

Evacua'tion, s. *evacuazione,* s. f. *l'evacuare.*

To E'vade [to escape, to shift off] *scampare, scappare, sfrattare, fuggire, corsela, battersela, andarsene.*

To evade an argument, *deludere un argomento.*

Eva'ded, adj. *scampato, scappato, sfrattato, fuggito, colto, deluso.*

Evange'lical, adj. [of or belonging to the gospel] *evangelico.*

An evangelical truth, *una verità evangelica.*

Eva'ngelist, s. [a messenger of good tidings] *evangelista,* s. m.

The four evangelists, *i quattro evangelisti.*

To Eva'ngelize [to preach the gospel] *evangelizzare, dichiarare, e predicar il vangelo.*

To Eva'porate [to breathe or steam out] *evaporare, spirare, mandar fuora il vapore, svaporare.*

A liquor that evaporates, *un liquore che s'evapora.*

Eva'porated, adj. *evaporato, spirato, svaporato.*

Evapora'tion, s. *evaporazione,* s. f. *evaporamento,* s. m.

Eva'sion, s. [escape] *scappata, fuga,* s. f.

Evasion [shift] *scampo, sotterfugio, inganno, rigiro, pretesto,* s. m. *scusa,* s. f.

Eva'sive, adj. [crafty, deceitful] *sofistico, astuto, gavilloso.*

Eu'charist, s. [the Sacrament of the Lord's-Supper] *l'eucaristia,* s. f. *il santissimo sagramento dell' altare.*

Eve, s. [the day before a festival or holiday] *vigilia,* s. f. *il giorno avanti alla festa d'alcuni santi, o d'altro giorno festivo.*

Christmas-eve, *la vigilia di natale.*

E'ven, adj. [like, or equal] *eguale, uguale, simile.*

An even weight, *un peso eguale, pari.*

An even number, *un numero pari.*

Even reckonings make long friends, *conto spesso amicizia lunga.*

Even [level, smooth] *piano, uniforme, eguale.*

Now we are even, *adesso siamo pari.*

An even temper, *un' egualità di mente, una tranquillità d'animo.*

To be even with one, *render la pariglia ad uno.*

Even with the ground, *a piana terra.*

To lay a house even with the ground, *demolire una casa a piana terra.*

Even, s. *pari.*

To play at even or odd, *giuocare a pari, o caffo.*

Even [evening] *la sera.*

Even song, *preghiere che si cantano al vespro.*

Even, or e'en, adv. *anche, anzi, ancora.*

It were a shame even to speak of it, *sarebbe vergogna anche di parlarne.*

Even as, *come.*
Even as if, *come se.*
Even he, *egli stesso.*
Even on, *a dirittura, diritto, dirittamente,*
Even down, *diritto giù.*
Even so, *appunto così, giusto così.*
Even now, *appunto, or-ora, in questo punto.*
Even [almost] *quasi, fino.*
To E'VEN [to make even, to level]. *agguagliare, fare eguale, pareggiare, aggiustare, appianare.*
To EVEN [to balance] accounts, *regolare i conti, aggiustare, o saldare i conti.*
To even [to lay even] with the ground, *spianare, rovinare, abbattere a terra.*
E'VENED, adj. *agguagliato, pareggiato, aggiustato, appianato, solidato.*
EVENHA'NDED, adj. [impartial, equitable] *che non ha parzialità, che ha equità.*
E'VENING, s. *la sera.*
Good evening, *buona sera.*
The evening crowns the day, *la fine corona l'opera.*
The evening star, *l'espero, la stella della sera.*
Evening tide, *la sera.*
Morning and evening prayers, *le preghiere della mattina e della sera.*
E'VENLY, adv. *egualmente, ugualmente, uniformemente, parimente.*
E'VENNESS, s. *egualità, parità,* s. f.
Evenness [smoothness] *parità, superficie piana.*
Evenness of temper, *egualità di mente.*
EVENT, s. [the issue or success of things] *evento, caso,* s. m. *riuscita.* s. f.
Event [or accident] *evento, accidente,* s. m.
EVENVI'DE, s. [the time of evening] *la sera.*
To EVE'NTILATE [to winnow or sift] *ventilare, consultare, considerare, discussare, discutere.*
To eventilate [in law, is to estimate or value an estate] *apprezzare, valutare, stimare.*
EVENTILA'TION, s. [a winnowing] *ventilozione,* s. f. *il ventilare.*
Eventilation [a strict examination or sifting into a business] *ventilazione, discussione,* s. f. *esame,* s. m.
E'VER, adv. [without end] *sempre, tuttavia, sempremai, mai sempre.*
It will ever be so, *sarà sempre così.*
If ever I chance to see him, *se m'accadesse mai di vederlo.*
As much as ever, *tanto che mai.*
For ever and ever, *per sempre, eternamente, ne' secoli de' secoli.*
Is there ever a man? *vi fu mai uomo?*
As soon as ever I can, *quanto prima, o subito che potrò.*
Ever since, ever after, *dipoi, dopo, da quel tempo in qua.*
Ever and anon, *di quando in quando, qualche volta.*
Ever [before] *prima, avanti.*
Ever the earth was, *prima che la terra fosse.*

Ever-green, adj. *sempre verde.*
An ever-green, s. [a tree always green] *un albero sempre verde.*
EVERBU'BBLING, adj. [boiling up with perpetual murmurs] *che sempre bolle e mormora.*
EVERLA'STING, adj. [eternal] *eterno, perpetuo.*
The everlasting life or death, *la vita, o la morte eterna.*
EVERLA'STINGLY, adv. *eternamente, perpetuameute.*
EVERLA'STINGNESS, s. *eternità, perpetuità,* s. f.
EVER-LIVING, adj. [immortal] *immortale, che vive sempre.*
EVE'RSION, s. [overthrowing, overturning] *sconvolgimento,* s. m. *rovina,* s. f.
E'VERY, adj. *ogni, ciascheduno.*
It is lawful for every man to do so, *è permesso ad ogni uomo di far così.*
Every man is apt to fall, *ognuno è oggetto a fallire.*
Every way, *da ogni banda.*
Every day, *ogni giorno.*
Every one, every body, *ognuno, ciascheduno.*
Every man for himself, and God for all, *ognuno per se, e Dio per tutti.*
Every other day, *un giorno sì, un giorno nò.*
Every one as he likes, *ognuno a suo modo.*
He drunk every drop, *ha bevuto tutto, ha bevuto fino all' ultima goccia.*
Every whit, every bit, *tutto, affatto, intieramente, del tutto.*
That's every whit as good, *questo è egualmente buono.*
Every where, *da per tutto.*
E'VET, s. [a newt, a lizard] *stellione, animale velenoso simile alla lucertola.*
To EVICT [to prove against one] *provare che che si sia contro ad alcuno, convincernelo.*
EVI'CTION, s. [conviction] *evizione,* s. f. *convincimento,* s. m.
E'VIDENCE, s. [perspicuity, plainness] *evidenza, chiarezza, manifestazione, dimostrazione, apparenza,* s. f. *palesamento,* s. m.
The evidence of a fact, *l'evidenza d'un fatto.*
Evidence [mark, proof] *segno, indizio, saggio,* s. m. *prova,* s. f.
To give singular evidences of one's gratitude, *dar segni evidenti dell altrui gratitudine.*
There are strong evidences against you, *vi sono prove potenti contro di voi.*
A true or false evidence, *un testimonio vero, o falso.*
To give in false evidence, *render falsa testimonianza.*
Evidence [witness in court] *un testimonio.*
Evidences [deeds] *carte, atti, stromenti.*
To E'VIDENCE [to prove] *provare, dimostrare, far vedere.*
E'VIDENCED, adj. *provato, dimostrato.*

E'VIDENCIBLE, adj. *che si può provare.*
E'VIDENT, adj. [apparent, clear, manifest] *evidente, manifesto, chiaro, apparente.*
Very evident, *evidentissimo.*
E'VIDENTLY, adv. *evidentemente, manifestamente, chiaramente, apparentemente.*
E'VIL, adj. [bad] *cattivo, malo, reo, malvagio.*
Evil communications corrupt good manners, *le cattive compagnie corrompono i buoni costumi.*
Evil, s. *male.*
What evil have I done? *che male ho fatto io?*
'Tis a great evil, *questo è un gran male.*
The evil, or the King's evil [a disease so called] *le scrofole.*
Evil, s. *male.*
Evil got, evil spent, *beni malamente acquistati non fanno mai pro, farina del diavolo va tutta in crusca.*
To EVI'NCE [to prove] *convincere, provare, far vedere.* pret. *convinsi.*
To evince [in civil law, to convict and recover by law] *ricuperare in giustizia una cosa comprata da un altro.*
EVI'NCED, adj. *convinto, provato.*
EVI'NCIBLY, adv. *dimonstrativamente, manifestamente, chiaramente.*
To EVI'SCERATE [to unbowel, to take out the bowels] *sviscerare, cavar le viscere.*
E'VITABLE, adj. [that may be avoided] *evitabile, che si può evitare.*
To E'VITATE [to avoid, to shun] *evitare, sfuggire.*]
EU'NUCH, s. [one deprived of the generative parts] *un eunuco.*
To EU'NUCHATE [to geld] *castrare.*
EVOCA'TION, s. [a calling out or upon] *invocazione,* s. f.
Evocation [law term, summons] *citazione, chiamata in giudicio.*
To EVO'LVE [to unfold] *disvolgere, sviluppare, svolgere.* pret. *disvolsi, svolsi.*
EVO'LVED, adj. *disvolto, sviluppato, svolto.*
E'UPHONY, s. [a better sound, a smooth running of words] *eufonia,* s. f. *suono più grato che nasce dallo scontro di certe sillabe.*
EVU'LSION, s. [a plucking, or pulling out] *divellimento, svellimento,* s. m.
Ewe, s. [a female sheep] *una pecora.*
An ewe-lamb, *un mannerino.*
To Ewe [to bring forth lambs] *figliare, parlando delle pecore.*
E'WER, s. [a vessel to hold water] *un boccale.*
A silver ewer, *un boccale d' argento.*
EXACERBA'TION, s. *esacerbazione, irritazione,* s. f. *provoramento,* s. m.
EXA'CT, adj. [strict, punctual] *esatto, puntuale, diligente.*
Exact [accurate] *esatto, giusto, proporzionato.*
To EXA'CT [to demand rigorously] *esigere, domandare, richiedere con autorità o di dritto.* pres. *richieggo,* pret. *richiesi.*

Why should you exact such things? *perchè esigete tali cose?*

To exact upon one, or exact in the price, *domandar troppo, soprafare nel prezzo.*

EXA'CTED, adj. *esatto, domandato, richiesto, sopraffatto.*

EXA'CTION, s. [the taking of an unlawful fee] *esazione.*

EXA'CTLY, adv. *esattamente, accuratamente, diligentemente, con esattezza.*

EXA'CTNESS, s. [care, carefulness] *esattezza, accuratezza, cura, diligenza,* s. f.

EXA'CTOR, s. [a gatherer of taxes] *esattore,* s. m. *riscotitor del pubblico.*

To EXA'GGERATE, [to amplify, to enlarge in words] *esagerare, aggrandire con parole.* pres. *aggrandisco.*

EXA'GGERATED, adj. *esagerato, aggrandito con parole.*

EXAGGERA'TION, s. [amplification] *esagerazione,* s. f.

To EXA'GITATE [to disquiet, to stir up] *agitare, travagliare, tormentare.*

To EXA'LT [to raise, to lift up]. *esaltare, levare in alto, alzare.*

To exalt [to praise highly, to extol] *esaltare, aggrandire, accrescere, lodare.* pres. *aggrandisco,* pret. *accrebbi.*

To exalt a mineral [in chymistry, is to refine it, and increase its strength] *esaltare un minerale, raffinarlo, accrescere la sua virtù.*

EXALTA'TION, s. [or lifting up] *esaltazione,* s. f. *esaltamento,* s. m.

The exaltation of the cross, *l'esaltazione della croce.*

The exaltation of a planet, *l'esaltazione d'un pianeta.*

EXA'LTED, adj. *esaltato, alzato, aggrandito, accresciuto.*

Exalted [sublime, or excellent] *eccellente, sublime, grande, illustre.*

EXA'LTING, s. *esaltazione,* s. f. *esaltamento,* s. m. *l'esaltare.*

EXAMINA'TION, s. [an examining] *esaminazione, esamina, considerazione,* s. f. *esaminamento, discorso,* s. m.

The examination of conscience, *l'esame della coscienza.*

A strict examination, *un' esaminazione rigorosa.*

EXAMINA'TOR, s. *v.* examiner.

To EXA'MINE, [to search, to enquire] *esaminare, interrogare.*

To examine [to weigh] *esaminare, consideratamente, discorrere, ventilare, discussare, discutere.*

To examine a witness, *esaminare un testimonio.*

To examine a business, *esaminare, pensare, considerare un affare.*

EXA'MINED, adj. *esaminato, interrogato, discorso, ventilato, discussato, discusso.*

EXA'MINER, s. *esaminatore,* s. m. *che esamina.*

EXA'MINING, s. *esaminamento,* s. m. *l'esaminare.*

An examining of witnesses, *un' esamina di testimonii.*

EXA'MPLE, s. [pattern, model] *esempio, esemplo, modello, esemplare,* s. m.

To set good or bad example, *da buono, o cattivo esempio.*

Example [instance, precedent] *esempio, uno de' mezzi con che si prova qualche cosa.*

As for example, *come per esempio.*

Example [in logick, the conclusion of one singular point from another] *esempio, uno degli argomenti usati ne' lor discorsi da' filosofi.*

To make one a publick example, *far che uno servi d' esempio, punir alcuno esemplarmente.*

EXA'NGUIOUS, adj. [bloodless, without blood] *esangue.*

To EXA'NIMATE [to deprive of life, to kill] *disanimare, privar d'anima, uccidere.* pret. *uccisi.*

To exanimate [to dispirit, to discourage] *disanimare, sgomentare, scorare, scoraggiare, tor l'animo, far perder altrui l'animo.*

EXA'NIMATED, adj. *disanimato, privato d'anima, ucciso, sgomentato, scorato, scoraggiato.*

EXANIMA'TION, s. *il disanimare.*

EXA'RCH, s. [an officer formerly under the Roman emperors of Constantinople] *esarca, vicerè.*

EXA'RCHATE, } s. [the office of an
E'XARCHY, } exarch] *esarcato, ufficio d'un esarca.*

To EXA'SPERATE [to provoke] *esasperare, aspreggiare, irritare, provocare, innasprire.* pres. *innasprisco.*

EXA'SPERATED, adj. *esasperato, aspreggiato, provocato, irritato, inasprito.*

EXA'SPERATING, s. *esasperamento,* s. m. *l'esasperare.*

EXASPERA'TION, s. *esasperazione,* s. f. *esasperamento,* s. m.

EXCAVA'TION, s. [a making hollow] *lo scavare.*

To E'XCECATE [to blind] *accecare, privar della luce degli occhi.*

E'XCECATED, adj. *accecato, privo della luce degli occhi.*

EXCECA'TION, s. *accecamento,* s. m. *l'accecare.*

To EXCE'ED [to go beyond, to surpass] *eccedere, sopravanzare, passare i dovuti termini, superare, sormontare.*

I will not exceed that sum, *non voglio eccedere questa somma.*

Cicero has exceeded all the orators of his time, *Cicerone ha sormontato tutti gli oratori del suo tempo.*

Our liberality must not exceed our ability, *bisogna che la nostra liberalità non ecceda le nostre forze, bisogna che la nostra liberalità sia adequata alle nostre abilità.*

EXCE'EDED, adj. *ecceduto, sopravanzato, superato, sormontato.*

EXCE'EDING, adj. [excessive] *eccessivo, che eccede.*

Exceeding, or exceedingly, adv [too much] *eccedentemente, eccessivamente, smoderatamente, fuor di misura.*

I am exceeding tired, *sono molto lasso.*

It is exceeding fine, *è bellissimo.*

He writes exceeding fine, *scrive perfettamente bene.*

To be exceeding desirous of praise, *esser avidissimo di gloria.*

So exceeding proud he is, *tanto è altiero.*

EXCE'EDINGLY [extreamly] *molto, estremamente, in sommo grado.*

To EXCE'L [to out do] *eccedere, sormontare, sovranzare, vantaggiare, avanzare, vincere.* pret. *vinsi.*

He excels in every thing, *egli è valente in ogni cosa.*

E'XCELLENCE, or E'XCELLENCY, s. [eminency] *eccellenza, preeminenza,* s. f.

E'XCELLENCY [a title of honour] *eccellenza, titolo d'onore.*

E'XCELLENT, adj. [extraordinary good, rare] *eccellente, eminente, singolare, ottimo, egregio, squisito.*

Excellent wine, *vino eccellente.*

Excellent, adv. *eccellentemente, ottimamente.*

'Tis excellent well done, *questo è fatto eccellentemente, in tutta eccellenza.*

E'XCELLENTLY, adv. *eccellentemente, con eccellenza, ottimamente.*

EXCE'NTRICAL, } adj. [that moves
EXCE'NTRICK, } in a different center] *eccentrico, che non è intorno al medesimo centro.*

The sun runs its course in an excentrick circle, *il sole fa il suo corso in un cerchio eccentrico.*

EXCENTRI'CITY, s. [the distance between the sun and center of the excentrick] *eccentricità, la distanza che è fra i duoi cerchi che non sono eccentrici.*

EXCE'PT, prep. [saving] *eccetto, fuorchè, salvo, se non, trattone, cavatone.*

Except, conj. [unless] *a meno, a meno che.*

To EXCE'PT [to exclude] *eccettare, eccettuare, escludere.* pret. *esclusi.*

I except no body, *non eccettuo nessuno.*

To except [to object against] *escludere, ricusare, rifiutare, non volere.*

To except against the witnesses, *escludere i testimoni.*

EXCE'PTED, adj. *eccettato, eccettuato.*

Excepted against, *ricusato, rifiutato.*

Such a one excepted, *eccetto un tale.*

EXCE'PTION, s. [an exempting from the general rule] *eccezione, eccettuazione,* s. f.

There's no rule without an exception, *non v' è regola generale senza eccezione.*

Exception [in law, is a bar or stop to an action] *eccezione. termine legale, esclusion di pruova o d'altro atto infra i litiganti.*

Exception against a witness, *esclusione d'un testimonio.*

An exception in a contract, *eccezione, limitazione, clausula in un contratto.*

To bring in an exception in law, *allegare qualche eccezione.*

To make an exception against a thing [to find fault with it] *trovar da dire a qualche cosa, farvi qualche objezione.*

To take an exception at a thing, *offendersi, o stimarsi offeso in qualche cosa, prender uggia in qualche cosa.*

EXCE'PTIONABLE, adj. [which may be excepted against] *cosa alla quale si può objettare, o fare objezioni.*

EXCE'PTIOUS, adj. [which is apt to take exception, or to be offended] *discolo, riottoso, uggioso*.

To EXCE'RP [to pick, to cull out] *pigliare, raccogliere, scegliere, chiappare*.

EXCE'RPTION, s. [a picking or culling] *raccolta, collezione*, s. f.

EXCE'SS, s. [superfluity] *eccesso, trapassamento*, s. m.

An excess of love or goodness, *un eccesso d'amore, o di bontà*.

To run out in excess, *andare all' eccesso, peccare nell' eccesso*.

Excess [intemperance, riot] *eccesso, sregolatezza, intemperanza*, s. f.

EXCE'SSIVE, adj. [exceeding] *eccessivo, che eccede, smoderato*.

Excessive heat, *caldo eccessivo*.

Excessive pain, *dolore eccessivo, atroce*.

An excessive love, *amore eccessivo, sregolato*.

EXCE'SSIVELY, adv. *eccessivamente, smoderatamente*.

EXCE'SSIVENESS, s. *eccesso, superfluità*.

EXCHA'NGE, s. [changing, bartering, trucking] *cambio, baratto*, s. m.

To make an exchange, *fare un cambio*.

A bill of exchange, *una lettera di cambio*.

Exchange is no robbery, *il cambio non è ladrocinio, chi cambia non fa torto*.

Exchange [a place where merchants meet] *piazza dove i mercanti si radunano per negoziare*.

The Royal Exchange of the city of London, *la Borsa Reale della città di Londra, luogo in Londra dove i mercanti s'assembrano*.

Exchange [in traffick, is the giving a sum of money in one place for a bill payable in another place] *cambio*.

Exchange-brokers [men who give information to merchants how the exchange of coin goes, and help merchants to chapmen, and chapmen to merchants] *sensali di cambio*.

To EXCHA'NGE [to barter or truck] *cambiare, fare un cambio, barattare*.

To exchange words, *dirsi alcune parole*.

They exchanged some guns [they shot at one another] *si tirarono alcuni colpi di cannone*.

EXCHA'NGED, adj. *cambiato, barattato*.

EXCHA'NGER, s. [he who returns money beyond sea by bills of exchange] *cambiatore*, s. m.

EXCHA'NGING, s. *cambiamento*, s. m. *il cambiare*.

EXCHE'QUER, s. [the place where the king's cash is received and paid] *la camera, il fisco, il luogo dove vanno i danari del re, l'erario*.

The chancellor of the exchequer, *l'avvocato fiscale*.

EXCI'SABLE, adj. *che paga la tassa*.

EXCI'SE, s. [imposition] *tassa, estorsione*.

An excise-man, *un collettore delle tasse*.

EXCI'SION, s. [destroying] *distruzione, rovina, annichilazione, demolizione*, s. f.

To EXCI'TE [to stir-up, to provoke] *eccitare, risvegliare, stimolare, instigare*.

EXCI'TED, adj. *eccitato, risvegliato, stimolato, instigato*.

EXCI'TEMENT, s. [excitation] *eccitamento, provocamento, instigamento, stimolo, aizzamento*, s. m. *eccitazione*, s. m.

EXCI'TER, s. *eccitatore*, s. m. *che eccita*.

EXCI'TING, s. *eccitamento*, s. m. *l'eccitare*.

EXCLA'IM, s. [clamour, outcry] *clamore, strepito, romor di voce. Non in uso*.

To EXCLA'IM [to cry out, to call aloud] *esclamare, gridare ad alta voce, sclamare*.

To exclaim against injustice, *esclamare, sgridare contra l'ingiustizia*.

EXCLA'IMED, adj. *esclamato, sclamato*.

EXCLAMA'TION, s. *esclamazione; strepito di molte voci*.

To EXCLU'DE [to shut out, to except] *escludere, ributtare, privare*. pret. *esclusi*.

To exclude an heir, *escludere un erede, privarlo dell' eredità*.

EXCLU'DED, adj. *escluso, ributtato, privato*.

EXCLU'DING, } s. *esclusione, esclusiva*, s. f.
EXCLU'SION, }

EXCLU'SIONERS, s. *così furono chiamati i membri di parlamento nel regno di Carlo secondo, che volevano escludere suo fratello dalla corona perchè era cattolico*.

EXCLU'SIVE, adj. *esclusivo*.

An exclusive vote, *una voce esclusiva*.

An exclusive particle, *una particola esclusiva*.

EXCLU'SIVELY, adv. *esclusivamente, eccettuato, eccetto*.

'Till Sunday exclusively, *fino a domenica esclusivamente, eccettuato la domenica*.

To EXCO'GITATE [to invent, to devise] *trovare, ghiribbizzare, cercare, inventare*.

EXCO'GITATED, adj. *trovato, ghiribizzato, cercato, inventato*.

EXCO'MMENCEMENT, s. [an old law term for excommunication] *scomunicazione*.

To EXCO'MMUNICATE [to turn or put out of the communion of the church] *scomunicare, imporre scomunica, separare della comunione de' fedeli*.

EXCO'MMUNICATED, adj. *scomunicato*.

EXCO'MMUNICA'TION, s. *scomunicazione, scomunicagione, scomunica*, s f.

To EXCO'RIATE [to flay off the skin] *scorticare*.

EXCO'RIATION, s. [a flaying, or pulling off the skin] *escoriazione*, s. f. *scorticamento*, s. m.

E'XCREMENT, s. [ordure, dregs] *escremento*, s. m. *sporcheria, porcheria, sporcizia*, s. f.

The excrements of the body [whatsoever is separated from the aliment after digestion, and is to be thrown out of the body] *gli escrimenti del corpo*.

EXCREME'NTAL, } adj. *escrementoso*.
EXCREMENTI'TIOUS, }

E'XCRESCENCE, or E'XCRESCENCY, s. [a tumor or superfluous flesh growing upon any part of the body] *escrescenza*, s. f. *tumore, o enfiato che viene nel corpo contra natura*.

EXCRE'TION, s. [separation of animal substance] *separazione di sostanza animale*.

To EXCRUCI'ATE [to torment] *tormentare, affliggere, affannare*, pret. *afflissi*.

EXCRU'CIATED, adj. *tormentato, afflitto, affannato*.

EXCRUCIA'TION, s. *crucio, tormento, affanno*, s. m. *afflizione*, s. f.

To EXCU'LPATE [to excuse] *scolpare, scusare*.

EXCU'LPATED, adj. *scolpato, scusato*.

EXCU'RSION, s [digression] *digressione*, s. f. *tralasciamento del filo principale della narrazione*.

Excursion [invasion, inroad] *scorreria*, s. f. *scorrimento*, s. m.

EXCU'SABLE, adj. [that may be excused] *scusabile, da essere scusato, degno di scusa*

EXCU'SATORY, adj. [which serves to excuse] *che serve a scusare, per iscusarsi*.

EXCU'SE, s. [a reason by which we endeavour to justify some fault or offence committed] *scusa*, s. f.

A bad excuse is better than none, *val meglio servirsi d'una cattiva scusa, che non farne alcuna*.

He alledged for his excuse, *allegò in sua difesa*.

To EXCU'SE [to admit an excuse, to justify] *scusare, scolpare, assolvere*.

To excuse one's self, *scusarsi, scolparsi, addurre ragioni a suo pro*.

To excuse [to dispense with] *scusare, esentare*.

I desire you to excuse me, *vi prego di scusarmi*.

I wish he would excuse me from writing, *vorrei che mi scusasse dallo scrivergli*.

Your indisposition excuses you from fasting, *la vostra indisposizione vi esenta dal digiuno*.

EXCU'SED, adj. *scusato, giustificato, scolpato*.

I desire to be excused, *vi prego di scusarmi*.

EXCU'SER, s. *scusatore*, s. m. *chè scusa*.

EXCU'SING, s. *scusazione*, s. f. *lo scusare*.

E'XECRABLE, adj. [cursed, detestable] *esecrabile, detestabile, scellerato, esecrando*.

An execrable crime or action, *un delitto esecrando, un' azione esecrabile*.

E'XECRABLY, adv. [cursedly, abominably] *esecrabilmente*.

To E'XECRATE [to curse, to detest] *esecrare, detestare, maledire*, pref. *maledico*, pret. *maledissi*.

EXECRA'TION, s. [curse, detestation] *esecrazione, essecrazione, detestazione, maledizione, imprecazione*, s. f.

To E'XECUTE [to do, to effect, to perform] *eseguire, mettere ad effetto, effettuare, fare.*
To execute one's orders, *eseguire gli altrui comandi.*
To execute a design, *effettuare, o mandare ad effetto un disegno.*
To execute a will, *eseguire un testamento.*
To execute a malefactor, *giustiziare un malfattore.*
E'XECUTED, adj. *eseguito, esseguito, effettuato, compito, fatto, giustiziato.*
EXECU'TION, s. [the executing or doing a thing] *esecuzione,* s. f. *compimento, effetto,* s. m.
Execution of a malefactor, *esecuzione, giustizia, punizione d'un reo per le mani del carnefice.*
Execution [the seizing of one's person and goods] *sequestrazione,* s. f. *staggimento,* s. m.
To put a thing in execution, *mettere in esecuzione, o mandare ad effetto che che si sia.*
The execution was declared illegal, *l'esecuzione fu dichiarata non legale.*
The place of execution, *il luogo del supplicio.*
A writ of execution, *mandato.*
The execution day, *il giorno d'esecuzione, il giorno che si fa giustizia.*
EXECU'TIONER, s. [the hangman, the finisher of the law] *giustiziere, e giustiziero, carnefice, manigoldo, boja,* s. m.
EXE'CUTIVE, adj. Ex. executive power, *potere, o autorità d'eseguire.*
EXE'CUTOR, s. [one who executes or performs any thing] *esecutore, eseguitore,* s. m.
Executor, in law [one who is appointed by a person's last will, to dispose of the deceased person's estate or substance] *esecutore testamentario.*
EXE'CUTORSHIP, s. *carica, o impiego d'esecutore testamentario.*
EXE'CUTRIX, s. [a female executor] *esecutrice,* s. f.
She is the sole executrix of his will, *ella è la sola esecutrice del suo testamento.*
EXEGE'TICAL, adj. [explanatory] *espositivo, che espone, dichiara, o interpreta.*
EXE'MPLAR, s. [pattern] *esemplare, esempio, modello,* s. m.
EXE'MPLARILY, adv. *esemplarmente, con esemplarità.*
EXE'MPLARINESS, } s. *esemplarità,*
EXEMPLA'RITY, } s. f.
Exemplarity of life, *esamplarità di vita.*
EXE'MPLARY, adj. [that serves for an example] *esemplare.*
An exemplary life, *una vita esemplare.*
EXEMPLIFICA'TION, s. [a demonstration of a thing by an example] *esemplificazione, similitudine,* s. f. *esempio.*
Exemplification [a copy or draught of an original record] *copia d'una lettera patente.*
EXEMPLIFI'ER, s. *colui che esemplifica.*

To EXEMPLIFY' [to prove or confirm by an example] *esemplificare, apportare esempli, provare, o confirmare con esempli.*
To exemplify [to copy out] *copiare.*
EXEMPLIFY'D, adj. *esemplificato, copiato.*
EXEMPLIFY'ING, s. *esemplificazione,* s. f.
EXE'MPT, adj. [free from] *esente, privilegiato, franco, libero.*
To EXE'MPT [to free, to discharge from] *esentare, fare esente, esenzionare.*
EXE'MPTED, adj. *esentato.*
EXE'MPTION, s. [a freedom from, a privilege] *esenzione,* s. f. *privilegio,* s. m.
To EXE'NTERATE [to draw out the bowels] *sviscerare, sventrare, cavar le viscere.*
EXE'QUIAL, adj. [of or belonging to exequies] *esequiale, appartenente a esequie.*
EXE'QUIES, s. [funeral rites, or solemnities] *esequie,* s. f. *pompa di mortorio.*
EXE'RCENT, adj. [that exercises, or practises] *esercitante, che esercita, che fa esercizio.*
EXERCI'SE, s. [labour, pains, practice] *esercizio, travaglio,* s. m. *fatica.*
Exercise [among physicians, is the motion or stirring of the body in order to health] *esercizio.*
To make or use exercise, *fare, o usare esercizio.*
The military exercise, *l'esercizio delle armi.*
Exercises [the task of a scholar at school, or of a young student in the university] *gli esercizi, il tema, le lezioni che uno scolare deve imparare nella scuola, o uno studente nell' università.*
Exercise [the function or performance of an office] *esercizio, funzione, mestiere, arte.*
To EXERCI'SE [to inure or train up to] *esercitare, accostumare, allevare, provare, operare.*
To exercise soldiers, *esercitare i soldati, disciplinarli.*
To exercise [to practise] *esercitare, fare, professare.*
To exercise an office, *esercitare un ufficio.*
To exercise one's memory, *esercitare la sua memoria.*
To exercise one's self with hunting, *esercitarsi alla caccia.*
To exercise, *far l'esercizio.*
The soldiers exercise, *i soldati fanno l'esercizio.*
EXERCI'SED, adj. *esercitato, v.* To exercise.
EXERCI'SING, s. *esercitamento,* s. m. *l'esercitare.*
EXERCI'SER, s. *esercitatore,* s. m. *esercitatrice,* s. f.
EXERCITA'TION, s. [use, practice] *esercitazione,* s. f. *esercizio, uso,* s. m. *pratica,* s. f.
To EXERT [to put forth, to show] *mostrare, far vedere, dimostrare.*
Now exert your strength and courage, *adesso è tempo di mostrare la vostra forza, e'l vostro coraggio.*
To exert one's self in devotion, *animarsi, infervorarsi alla divozione.*
EXE'RTION, s. [the act of exerting; effort] *l'operare; sforzo.*
EXHA'LABLE, adj. [that may be evaporated] *che può svaporare, esalare, andar in fumo, in nulla.*
EXHALA'TION, s. [steam, vapour] *esalazione,* s. f. *vapore,* s. m.
To EXHA'LE [to breathe, to steam out] *esalare, svaporare, uscir fuori, salendo in alto, ed è proprio de' vapori, e del vigore spiritale.*
To exhale a sweet smell, *esalare un buono odore.*
EXHA'LED, adj. *esalato.*
To EXHA'UST [to waste, spend, or consume] *votare, seccare, consumare, render esausto.*
To exhaust the king's treasure, *votare l'erario del rè.*
EXHA'USTED, adj. *esausto, voto, secco, consumato, estenuato.*
He has exhausted his father's estate, *ha consumato tutte le facultà di suo padre.*
EXHA'USTLESS, adj. [not to be emptied; inexhaustible] *inesausto, da non esser mai esausto; che non si voterà mai.*
To EXHE'REDATE [to disinherit] *diredare, disredare, privar dell' eredità.*
EXHE'REDATED, adj. *diredato, disredato, privo dell' eredità.*
To EXHI'BIT [to produce, to show] *esibire, offerire, produrre, mostrare, presentare,* pres. *esibisco.*
To exhibit [a law term] *esibire, termine de' legisti, presentare le scritture in giudizio.*
To exhibit to God a religious worship, *rendere a Dio un culto religioso.*
EXHI'BITED, adj. *esibito, offerto, prodotto, mostrato, presentato.*
EXHIBI'TION, s. *esibizione,* s. f. *l'esibire.*
To EXHI'LARATE [to cheer up, or make cheerful] *allegrare, rallegrare, render lieto.*
EXI'LARATED, adj. *allegrato, rallegrato, reso lieto.*
EXHILARA'TION, s. *gioja, allegrezza, letizia, giocondità,* s. f. *giubbilo, contento,* s. m.
To EXHO'RT [to encourage, to stir up] *esortare, incoraggiare, animare, incitare, indurre,* pres. *induco,* pret. *indussi.*
EXHORTA'TION, s. [encouraging] *esortazione,* s. f.
EXHO'RTATIVE, or EXHORTATORY, adj. [that serves to exhort] *esortativo, esortatorio, che ha virtù d'esortare.*
EXHO'RTER, s. *quello che esorta.*
EXHO'RTING, s. *l'esortare, esortazione.*
E'XIGENCE, } s. [need, necessity,
E'XIGENCY, } occasion] *esigenza, necessità, occasione,* s. f. *bisogno,* s. m.
According to the exigency of affairs, *secondo lo stato delle cose, secondo che gli affari lo richiederanno.*

Exigency or exigent [pinch, strait] *angustia, miseria, afflizione, strettezza,* s. f. *travaglio, affanno,* s. m.

To bring one to an exigence, *angustiare alcuno, affannarlo, ridurlo in qualche strettezza.*

E'XIGENT, s. [occasion] *bisogno, necessità d'ajuto immediato.*

Upon an exigent, *in un bisogno, in caso di bisogno.*

Exigent [expedient] *espediente,* s. m.

An exigent [a law word, is a writ lying where the defendant in an action personal cannot be found, nor any thing in the country whereby he may be attached or distrained] *citazione fatta allo sceriffe d'una provincia per presentare in giudicio un accusato che non si trova.*

EXI'LE, adj. [thin, subtle] *magro, sottile.*

Exile, s. [banishment] *esilio, sbandeggiamento,* s. m.

An exile [a banished person] *un esule, un bandito.*

To EXI'LE [to banish] *esiliare, mandare in esilio, dar bando, sbandeggiare.*

EXI'LED, adj. *esiliato, mandato in esilio, sbandeggiato.*

EXI'LEMENT, s. *esilio, sbandeggiamento,* s. m.

EXI'LING, s. *l'esiliare.*

EXI'MIOUS, adj. [excellent, notable, singular] *esimio, eccellente, singolare.*

EXINANI'TION, s. *privazione; perdita.*

To EXI'ST [to be, to have a being] *esistere, essere nella natura delle cose, avere esistenza, vivere, aver l'essere.*

EXI'STENCE, } s. [being] *esistenza,*
EXI'STENCY, } *l'essere in atto.*

The existence of natural beings, *l'esistenza degli enti naturali.*

EXI'STIBLE, adj. *che può esistere, che può aver l'essere.*

EXIT, s. [departure] *uscita.*

Exit [death] *morte.*

To make one's exit [to die] *morire, uscir di vita.*

Exit [leave] *congedo.*

They will have their exit, *averanno il loro congedo.*

Exit [in a play] *esce, parte, va via.*

EXI'TIAL, adj. [destructive] *distruttivo, fatale, mortale, che apporta danno, pernizioso, nocivo.*

E'XODUS, s. [the title of the second book of Moses] *Esodo,* s. m. *il secondo libro di Mosè.*

To EXO'NERATE [to unload or unburthen] *alleggerire, alleviare, discaricare, scaricare,* pref. *alleggerisco.*

To exonerate one's belly, *andar del corpo, scaricare il ventre.*

EXO'NERATED, adj. *alleggerito, alleviato, discaricato, scaricato.*

E'XORABLE, adj. [easy to be entreated] *esorabile, persuadevole.*

EXO'RBITANCE, } s. [extravagan-
EXO'RBITANCY, } cy] *esorbitanza,* s. f.

EXO'RBITANT, adj. [extravagant, excessive] *esorbitante, eccessivo.*

An exorbitant price, *un prezzo esorbitante.*

EXO'RBITANTLY, adv. *esorbitantemente, con esorbitanza.*

To EXORCI'SE [to conjure out, or lay evil spirits] *esorcizzare, congiurare, scacciare i demoni del corpo d'un indemoniato.*

To exorcise a demoniack, *esorcizzare un indemoniato.*

EXORCI'SED, adj. *esorcizzato.*

EXORCI'SING, s. *l'esorcizzare.*

E'XORCISM, s. [an abjuration or conjuring] *esorcismo,* s. m.

E'XORCIST, s. [one who casts out devils] *esorcista,* s. m. *colui che fa gli esorcismi.*

EXO'RDIUM, s. [a beginning, a preface or preamble] *esordio, principio, prologo,* s. m.

EXORNA'TION, s. [an adorning] *ornatura,* s. f. *ornamento,* s. m.

To EXOSSATE [to deprive of bones] *disossare.*

EXO'TICK, adj. [foreign, outlandish] *straniere.*

To E'XPAND [to stretch out, to open] *dilatare, distendere, spandere, tendere,* pret. *distesi, espasi, tesi.*

To expand itself, *stendersi, dilatarsi.*

EXPA'NDED, adj. *dilatato, disteso, spaso, teso.*

EXPA'NSE, s. [or extent] *distenzione, dilatazione,* s. f. *spazio,* s. m.

The expanse of heaven, *l'ampiezza, o lo spazio del cielo.*

EXPA'NSION, s. *distensione, dilatazione,* s. f.

An expansion of the heart, *dilatazione del cuore.*

To EXPA'TIATE [to enlarge on a subject] *stendersi, estendersi sopra qualche materia.*

To EXPE'CT [to look for, to stay, to wait for] *aspettare, attendere,* pret. *attesi.*

I have expected you these two hours, *vi ho aspettato due ore.*

Things fall out better than I expected, *le cose sono andate meglio che non speravo.*

What can you expect from such a man? *che altro potevate aspettare da un tal uomo?*

EXPE'CTANCE, EXPE'CTANCY, or EXPECTA'TION, s. *aspettazione, aspettativa, speranza, espettazione,* s. m. *aspettamento,* s. m.

To be in expectation of something, *esser nell' aspettazione, o aspettativa di qualche cosa.*

Contrary to all mens expectation, *contra l'espettazione d'ognuno.*

To answer one's expectation, *riuscire secondo l'altrui desiderio.*

I find my expectation was greater than the enjoyment, *vedo che'l godimento non corrisponde all' aspettativa, vedo che'l piacere non è sì grande che mi pensavo.*

In expectation of a better fortune, *aspettando miglior fortuna.*

EXPE'CTED, adj. *aspettato, atteso.*

He is expected to day, *s'aspetta oggi.*

'Tis not a thing to be expected, *non è cosa da sperare.*

To EXPE'CTORATE [to eject from the breast] *spettorare, sputar feccie catarrose o viscide.*

EXPE'DIENT, adj. [fit, convenient, necessary] *espediente, utile, vantaggioso, necessario, convenevole.*

Expedient [quick, expeditious] *pronto, veloce.*

It is expedient, *è necessario, è convenevole.*

He knows best what is most expedient for us, *egli sa meglio di noi quel che ci è vantaggioso.*

Expedient, s. [means, way] *spediente, modo, mezzo.*

To find out an expedient, *trovar qualche spediente, trovar un mezzo termine.*

E'XPEDITE, adj. [ready, quick, nimble] *spedito, lesto, sollecito, pronto.*

To E'XPEDITE [to dispatch] *spedire, spacciare,* pref. *spedisco.*

EXPEDI'TION, s. [or dispatch] *espedizione,* s. f.

A military expedition, *una espedizione, o impresa militare.*

A famous expedition, *una famosa impresa.*

Expedition [quickness in dispatch of business] *speditezza, celerità, prontezza, sollecitudine,* s. f.

EXPEDI'TIONARY, s. [an officer at the Pope's court for dispatches] *spedizioniere,* s. m. *colui che in Roma procura la spedizione di bolle, brevi, e simili.*

EXPEDI'TIOUS, adj. [quick, nimble] *speditivo, che si spedisce, che si sbriga.*

EXPEDI'TIOUSLY, adv. [quickly] *speditamente, spacciatamente, senza indugio.*

To EXPE'L [to drive out] *espellere, scacciare, mandar fuori.*

EXPELLED, adj. *espulso, scacciato.*

He was expelled Rome, *fu scacciato da Roma.*

EXPE'LLER, s. *quello, o quella ch' espelle, che caccia via.*

An EXPE'NCE, s. [cost, or charges] *spesa,* s. f. *costo, dispendio,* s. m.

To pay one's expences, *far le spese.*

To EXPE'ND [to spend, or lay out money] *spendere,* pret. *spesi.*

EXPE'NDED, adj. *speso.*

EXPE'NDITOR, s. [a steward] *spenditore,* s. m. *colui che ha cura del provvedere per li bisogni della casa.*

EXPE'NSIVE, adj. [chargeable, costly] *dispendioso, che porta dispendio.*

Expensive [that spends lavishly] *spendereccio, che si diletta di spendere, prodigo.*

EXPE'RIENCE, s. [use] *esperienza, sperienza,* s. f.

I have experience of it, *ne ho fatto la sperienza.*

Experience [trial] *esperienza, prova,* s. f. *cimento,* s. m.

A man of great experience, *un uomo di grande esperienza, o esperimentatissimo.*

To EXPERIENCE [to try, or find by experience] *esperimentare, sperimentare, fare sperienza, provare, cimentare, far pruova.*

EXPE-

EXPE'RIENCED, adj. [tried] *esperimentato, sperimentato, provato, rimentato.*

Experienced [skilled] *sperimentato, esperto, versato.*

EXPE'RIMENT, s. [essay, trial, proof] *esperimento, cimento,* s. m. *sperienza, prova,* s. f

To EXPERIMENT [to make an experiment] *sperimentare, esperimentare, fare sperienza, cimentare, provare.*

EXPERIME'NTAL, adj. [grounded upon experience] *esperimentale, sperimentale, di sperienza, di esperimento, fondato sopra l'esperienza.*

Experimental philosophy, *filosofia sperimentale.*

An experimental knowledge, *una conoscenza acquistata coll' esperienza.*

EXPERIME'NTALLY, adv. [by experience] *esperimentalmente, con esperimento.*

EXPERIME'NTED, adj. *sperimentato, esperimentato, provato, cimentato.*

EXPERIME'NTER, s. [a maker of experiments] *esperimentatore,* s. m. *che fa esperimenti.*

EXPE'RT, adj. [skilful, dextrous in his art] *esperto, esperimentato, pratico, versato, sperto.*

Very expert, *espertissimo.*

E'XPERTLY, adv. [skilfully] *espertamente, saviamente.*

E'XPERTNESS, s. [skill] *arte, maestria, saviezza,* s. f.

E'XPIABLE, adj. [that may be atoned for] *che si può espiare.*

To E'XPIATE to atone, or make satisfaction for] *espiare, purgare.*

To expiate a crime, or for a crime, *espiare un delitto.*

E'XPIATED, adj. *espiato, purgato.*

EXPI'ATION, s. [satisfaction or atonement] *espiazione,* s. f.

EXPIRA'TION, s. [the end of an appointed time] *spirazione, o fine di tempo prefisso.*

Expiration [respiration] *respirazione,* s. f.

To EXPI'RE [to be out, or come to an end, as time does] *spirare, terminare, finire, parlandosi di tempo, o di cose ch' abbiano relazione a tempo,* pref. *finisco.*

To expire [to give up the ghost] *spirare, morire, mandar fuori l'ultimo spirito, render lo spirito, basire,* pref. *basisco.*

EXPI'RED, adj. [ended] *spirato, terminato, finito.*

Expired [dead] *spirato, morto, basito, che ha reso l'ultimo spirito.*

To EXPLA'IN [to make plain, or clear] *esplicare, spiegare, dichiarare, esporre, sviluppare, snodare,* pref. *espongo.* pret. *esposi.*

To explain an author, *esplicare, o spiegare un autore.*

EXPLA'INED, adj. *esplicato, spiegato, dichiarato, esposto, sviluppato, snodato.*

EXPLA'INER, s. *dichiaratore, interprete,* s. m.

EXPLA'NATION, s. [an explaining] *esplicazione, spianazione, interpretazione, dichiarazione,* s. m. *spiegamento,* s. m.

EXPLA'NATORY, adj. [which serves to explain] *che esplica, che spiega, che da l'esplicazione di qualche cosa, espositivo.*

E'XPLETIVE, adj. [that fills up] *riempitivo.*

An expletive particle, *particella riempitiva.*

E'XPLICABLE, adj. [that may be explained] *esplicabile, da esplicarsi.*

To E'XPLICATE [to unfold, to expend] *spiegare, spandere, e dicesi dell' ali, delle vele, de panni, e simili.*

To explicate [to explain, to clear] *spiegare, dichiarare, e dicesi d' un libro, d' una scrittura, d' una sentenza oscura o equivoca, e simili.*

EXPLICA'TION, s. [an explaining, exposition] *spiegazione, spianazione, dichiarazione, interpretazione,* s. f.

EXPLI'CIT, adj. [express, formal] *espresso, chiaro, manifesto.*

In explicit terms, *in termini espressi, espressamente.*

EXPLI'CITLY, adv. *in termine espressi, espressamente.*

To EXPLO'DE, *rigettare, ributtare, condannare.*

To explode a vice, *condannare un vizio.*

EXPLO'DED, adj. *rigettato, ributtato, condannato.*

EXPLO'IT [a great act, a noble deed, a brave action] *fatto, fatto d'arme, gesta, impresa, azione.*

To EXPLO'IT [to do some great action] *fare, eseguire qualche gran fatto.*

To EXPLORATE, *v.* To explore.

EXPLORA'TION, s. [a spying, a diligent searching out] *spiamento, investigamento,* s. m. *scoperta,* s. f.

To EPXLO'RE [to find or search out] *esplorare, spiare, investigare.*

An EXPLORA'TOR, s. [a scout or spy] *esploratore, speculatore, spiatore, spia,* s. m.

To EXPO'RT [to carry out, to send abroad over sea] *trasportare, levar con navilio, traghettare.*

To export commodities [to convey them out of one country to another] *trasportare delle mercanzie, traghettarle da un paese in un altro.*

EXPORTA'TION, s. *trasportazione,* s. f. *trasporto,* s m.

An exportation of commodities, *trasporto di mercanzie.*

To pay for the importation and the exportation, *pagare per l'entrata, e l'uscita.*

EXPO'RTED, adj. *trasportato, traghettato.*

EXPO'RTING, s. *trasporto,* s. m. *il trasportare.*

To EXPO'SE [to lay open to the publick view] *esporre, mostrare, far vedere, scoprire.* pref. *espongo.* pret. *esposi.*

To expose a thing to sale, *esporre, o mettere che che si sia in vendita.*

To expose the host, *esporre il sagramento.*

To expose [to venture] one's life, *mettere a ripentaglio la sua vita.*

To expose one's self to danger, *esporsi a qualche pericolo.*

To expose a child, *esporre un fanciullo, metterlo fuori in luogo pubblico, che l'altrui carità gli somministri gli alimenti.*

EXPO'SED, adj. *esposto, mostrato, scoperto.*

EXPOSI'TION, s. [explication] *esposizione, interpretazione, spianazione,* s. f.

EXPOSITOR, s. [expounder] *espositore, interpretatore,* s. m.

To EXPOSTULATE [to argue or reason by way of complaint about an injury received] *lamentarsi, lagnarsi, querelarsi.*

Did you ever expostulate the matter with him? *ve ne siete mai lagnato a lui?*

He began to expostulate with him about it, *cominciò a riscaldarsi contra di lui per questo negozio.*

EXPOSTULA'TION, s. [complaint] *lamentanza, lamentazione, querela, doglienza,* s. f.

EXPO'STULATORY, adj. [serving to expostulate] *pieno di querele, e di rimproveri.*

EXPO'SURE, s. [the act of exposing or setting out to observation] *lo esporre all' osservazione altrui.*

Exposure [the state of being open to observation] *lo essere esposto all' osservazione altrui.*

Exposure [the state of being in danger] *ripentaglio, pericolo, rischio,* s. m.

Exposure [exposition, situation] *sito,* s. m. *esposizione, situazione,* s. f

To EXPO'UND [to explain] *spiegare, esplicare, dichiarare, spinare, interpretare.* pref. *espongo.* pret. *esposi.*

To expound the scripture, *spiegare la scrittura.*

EXPO'UNDED, adj. *spiegato, esplicato, dichiarato, spianato, interpretato, esposto.*

EXPO'UNDER, s. *espositore, interpretatore,* s. m.

EXPO'UNDING, s. *esposizione, interpretazione,* s. f

EXPRESSLY, adv. [plainly] *espressamente, manifestamente, chiaramente spezialmente.*

It is expresly said, *è detto espressamente, o in termini espressi.*

EXPRE'SS, adj. [clear, plain, manifest] *espresso, chiaro, manifesto.*

In express terms, *in termini espressi.*

An express [a messenger, or courier] *uno straordinario, un corriere.*

He sent an express to the King, *mandò un messaggio, una staffetta, un corriere, un uomo apposta al Re.*

To EXPRE'SS [to declare by word or writing] *esprimere, manifestare il suo concetto con chiarezza, e al vivo.*

To express one's self, to express one's mind, *esprimersi, spiegarsi, manifestare il suo concetto.*

To express love to one, *mostrar dell' amore per uno.*

To express [by portraiture or the like] *rappresentare, dipignere, delineare,* pret. *dipinsi.*

EXPRE'SSED, adj. *espresso, manifestato, v.* To express.

It

It cannot be expressed, *non si può esprimere.*

EXPRE'SSION, s. [a word, or phrase] *espressione, parola,* s. f. *maniera d'esprimersi.*

A fine expression, *una bella espressione.*

Expression [in chymistry, is a pressing or squeezing out the juices or oils of plants,] *espressione, l'atto dello spremere i sughi e li oli delle piante.*

EXPRE'SSIVE, adj. [proper to express] *espressivo, che ha espressione, che esprime.*

To use expressive terms, *servirsi di termini espressivi.*

EXPRE'SSIVENESS, s. *forza d'espressione, energia, enfasi.*

EXPRE'SSLY, adv. [in direct terms, plainly, not by implication] *espressamente, con chiarezza, senza equivoco, senza luogo a interpretazione.*

To E'XPROBATE [to reproach] *rimproverare, rinfacciare, biasimare.*

EXPROBA'TION, s. [a reproach] *rimprovero, rimproverio, rinfacciamento, biasimo,* s. m.

ESPUGNATION, s. [a conquering by force] *espugnazione,* s. f.

EXPULSION, s. [a thrusting or driving out] *espulsione,* s. f.

EXPU'LSIVE, adj. [having a power to expel or drive out] *espulsivo, che ha virtù, e forza d'espellere.*

An expulsive medicine, *una medicina espulsiva.*

EXPU'NGED, adj. [blotted out] *scancellato, cancellato, cassato.*

To expunge [to blot, to cross, to wipe out] *scancellare, cassare, cancellare.*

EXPU'RGATORY, adj. [that has the virtue to cleanse, purge, or scour] *purgativo.*

Expurgatory index [a catalogue of books and writings which the Pope has thought fit to censure, and forbid to be read by the Papists] *indice o catalogo di libri proibiti.*

Expurgatory medicines, *medicine purgative.*

E'XQUISITE, adj. [rare, excellent] *squisito, ottimo, eletto, singolare, perfetto.*

Exquisite wine, *vino squisito.*

The most exquisite torments, *i tormenti i più atroci.*

E'XQUISITELY, adv. *squisitamente.*

E'XQUISITENESS, s. [rarity, excellence] *squisitezza,* s. f.

To E'XSICCATE [to dry up] *seccare.*

E'XSICCATED, adj. [dried] *seccato, secco.*

EXSICCA'TION, s. [a drying up] *seccazione, secchezza,* s. f.

E'XTANT, adj. [standing out, that is in being, or to be seen] *che resta, che esiste, che sussiste, che rimane.*

This is the best extant, *questo è il migliore che vi sia.*

The works of Xenophon now extant. *le opere di Zenofonte che ci restano.*

E'XTASY, s. [trance, rapture] *estasi,* s. f. *elevazion dell' anima a contemplar cose che superano la sua condizione.*

To be ravished with extasy, *esser rapito in estasi, andar in estasi.*

To be in an extasy, *restar in estasi, o estatico.*

EXTA'TICAL, adj. *estatico.*

Extatical visions, *visioni estatiche.*

EXTE'MPORAL, } adj. [done, or EXTEMPORARY, } spoke in the very instant of time, without studying or thinking] *extempore, improvviso, che non è premeditato.*

An extemporary composure, *una composizione improvvisa o extempore.*

EXTE'MPORE, adv. *all' improvviso, senza pensarvi su.*

To speak extempore, *parlare senza premeditazione.*

To EXTE'ND, [to stretch out, to enlarge] *estendere, stendere, distendere, dilatare, allargare.* pret. *stesi, distesi.*

To extend one's conquests, *stendere o dilatare le sue conquiste.*

The Russian monarchy extends itself southerly as far as the Caspian sea, *l'imperio di Moscovia si stende verso mezzo giorno fino al mar Caspio.*

To extend [in law; to value lands or tenements] *apprezzare, estimare, valutare.*

EXTE'NDED, adj. *esteso, steso, disteso, dilatato, allargato.*

Extended [valued] *apprezzato, prezzato, stimato, valutato.*

EXTE'NDER, s. [the person or instrument by which any thing is extended] *la persona o lo stromento, che cagiona estensione.*

EXTE'NSIBLE, adj. [that may be extended] *estensivo, atto a stendersi.*

EXTE'NSION, s. [a stretching out, or enlarging] *estensione,* s. f. *l'estendere.*

EXTE'NSIVE, adj. [large, that reaches far] *estensivo.*

EXTE'NT, s. [the compass of a thing in length, breadth, &c.] *ampiezza, larghezza,* s. f. *giro,* s. m.

A country of a large extent, *un paese ampio, di grande ampiezza o giro.*

To see the extent of the ambassador's power, *esaminare quanto il potere dell' ambasciadore si estende.*

Extent [a law word, the valuing of lands and tenements] *estimazione, stima, valuta,* s. f.

To EXTENUATE [to lessen] *sminuire, diminuire, mitigare.* pres. *sminuisco, diminuisco.*

To extenuate a crime, *mitigare o allegerire un delitto.*

EXTE'NUATED, adj. *sminuito, diminuito, mitigato, allegerito.*

EXTENUA'TION, s. [a lessening, or mitigating] *mitigazione,* s. f. *alleggerimento,* s. m.

Extenuation [a leanness of the whole body] *magrezza, macilenza,* s. f.

EXTE'RIOR, adj. [outward] *esteriore, estrinseco.*

On the exterior, *esteriormente, di fuori.*

To EXTE'RMINATE [to destroy] *sterminare, guastare, distruggere, mandare in rovina, in precipizio,* pret. *distrussi.*

EXTE'RMINATED, adj. *sterminato, guastato, distrutto.*

EXTE'RMINATING, or EXTREMINATION, s. *sterminazione, rovina,* s. f. *distruggimento,* s. m.

EXTERMINA'TOR, s. [destroyer] *sterminatore,* s. m.

EXTE'RN, or EXTE'RNAL, adj. [on the outside, outward] *esterno, esteriore, estrinseco.*

EXTE'RNALLY, adv. [outwardly] *esternamente, esteriormente, nell' esterno.*

EXTI'NCT, adj. [dead] *estinto, morto.*

That family is extinct, *questa famiglia è estinta.*

EXTI'NCTION, s. [a quenching or putting out] *estinzione,* s. f.

The extinction of the natural heat, *l'estinzione del calor naturale.*

To EXTI'NGUISH [to quench or put out] *estinguere, spegnere, smorzare* pret. *estinsi, spensi.*

To extinguish the fire, *estinguere o smorzare il fuoco.*

To extinguish the natural heat, *estinguere, o ammorzare il calor naturale.*

To extinguish a rent [to redeem it] *estinguere, o ammorzare una rendita, redimerla.*

To extinguish [to quench] a passion, *ammorzare, o estinguere una passione.*

To extinguish [to abolish, to destroy] *estinguere, ridurre al niente, annichilare, distruggere,* pret. *estinsi, distrussi.*

EXTINGUISHABLE, adj. *che si può estinguere o ammorzare.*

EXTI'NGUSHED, adj. *estinto, spento, smorzato.*

EXTI'NGUISHER, s. [a thing made on purpose to put out a candle] *spegnitojo,* s. m. *arnese da spegner lumi.*

EXTI'NGUISHING, } s. [a quenching or putting out] EXTI'NGUISHMENT, } *estinzione,* s. f. *spegnimento, ammortamento,* s. m.

The extinguishment of a rent, *estinzione, o ammortamento d'una rendita.*

To E'XTIRPATE [to root out] *estirpare, sradicare, distruggere, sterminare.*

To extirpate an heresy, *estirpare un eresia.*

E'XTIRPATED, adj. *estirpato, sradicato, distrutto, sterminato.*

EXTIRPA'TION, s. [a rooting out] *estirpazione,* s. f. *estirpamento,* s. m.

EXTIRPA'TOR, s. *estirpatore,* s. m.

An extirpator of heresies, *un estirpatore d'eresie.*

To EXTO'L [to praise, to cry up] *esaltare, innalzare, lodare sommamente, vantare, commendare.*

To extol one [to raise him up to the sky] *esaltare alcuno, lodarlo, vantarlo.*

EXTO'LLED, adj. *esaltato, innalzato, lodato, vantato, commendato.*

EXTO'RSION, s. [an unlawful and violent wresting of money from any man] *estorzione, esazione violenta oltre al convenevole.*

EXTO'RTIONER, s. [one who practises extortion; a griping usurer] *esattore, che usa estorsione, un infame usurajo.*

To EXTO'RT [to get by force, authority or threats] *strappare, pigliar per forza o per minacce.*

To ex-

To extort a thing from one, *pigliar per forza che che si sia ad uno*

EXTO'RTED, adj. *strappato, preso per forza.*

EXTO'RTION. *v.* Extorsion.

EXTO'RTIONER. *v.* Extortioner.

EXTRA'CT, s. [copy, draught] *copia*, s. f. *sunto*, s. m.

Extract [in chymistry, the pure substance which is separated from the grosser part of bodies] *estratto*, s. m. *essenza*, s. f.

To EXTRA'CT [to draw or pull out] *estrarre, cavar fuori.* pres. *estraggo.* pret. *estrassi.*

To extract [to copy out] *copiare.*

To extract [in chymistry, to draw out, or separate the purer from the grosser parts of any matter] *estrarre, cavare, separare le parti pure dalle impure.*

EXTRA'CTED, adj. *estratto.* *v.* To extract.

Nobly extracted, *di nobil nascita.*

EXTRA'CTION, s. [a drawing out] *estrazione*, s. f. *l'estrarre.*

Extraction [in chymistry, the drawing an essence or tincture from a mixt body] *estrazione, operazione chimica.*

Extraction [birth] *nascita, discendenza, schiatta.*

A man of noble extraction, *un uomo di nobil nascita.*

EXTRAGE'NOUS, adj. [a term used in anatomy and surgery, alien] *estraneo, estranio.*

An extrageneous body, *un corpo estraneo.*

EXTRAJUDI'CIAL, adj. [done out of the ordinary course of law] *quel che è fatto contro il corso ordinario della giustizia.*

EXTRAMUNDA'NE, adj. Ex. extramundane space [the infinite space which is by some supposed to be extended beyond the bounds of the universe.] *li spazi imaginari, che alcuni suppongono essere di la da' limiti dell' universo.*

EXTRA'NEOUS, adj. [from abroad, foreign] *estranio, straniero.*

EXTRAO'RDINARILY, adv. *straordinariamente, fuori dell' ordine.*

EXTRAO'RDINARY, adj. [uncommon] *straordinario.*

An embassador extraordinary, *un ambasciadore straordinario.*

Extraordinaries, s. or extraordinary expences, *spese straordinarie.*

Extraordinary, adv. *straordinariamente, estremamente.*

It is extraordinary cold, *fa estremamente freddo.*

EXTRAPARO'CHIAL, adj. [that belongs to no parish] *che non appartiene a nissuna parrocchia.*

EXTRA'VAGANCE, } s. [lavishness,
EXTRA'VAGANCY, } prodigality] *stravaganza, prodigalità*, s. f.

Extravagance [folly, impertinence] *stravaganza, pazzia, bizzarria, fantasticheria*, s. f.

EXTRA'VAGANT, adj. [excessive, expensive] *stravagante, eccessivo, smoderato, esorbitante.*

Extravagant [foolish, idle, impertinent] *stravagante, fantastico, bizzarro, bisbetico.*

An extravagant man, or woman, *un uomo, o una donna stravagante.*

To do extravagant things, *commettere delle stravaganze.*

Extravagant thoughts, *pensieri vani.*

An extravagant rate, *un prezzo esorbitante.*

Extravagant [lavish, prodigal] *stravagante, spendereccio, prodigo.*

EXTRA'VAGANTLY, adv. *stravagantemente, d'una maniera stravagante.*

EXTRAVA'GANTES, s. [decretal epistles, published after the Clementines by pope John XXII. and some other popes, added to the canon law, so called, because they were not ranged in any order in the body of the common law] *stravaganti*, s. f. *costituzioni pontificie pubblicate de Giovanni XXII. e da altri papi, che non sono raccolte nel corpo canonico.*

To EXTRA'VAGATE [to ramble, to rave, to talk foolishly] *vaneggiare, pargoleggiare, bamboleggiare, dir cose vane.*

To EXTRA'VASATE [to get out of the proper vessels, as blood and humours sometimes do] *stravasarsi, uscire dai propri vasi, parlando del sangue, ed altri umori.*

As soon as the blood begins to extravasate, *subito che il sangue comincia a stravasarsi.*

EXTRA'VASATED, adj. *stravasato.*

Extravasated blood, *sangue stravasato.*

EXTRE'AM. *v.* Extreme.

EXTRE'AMLY. *v.* Extremely.

EXTRE'ME, adj. [very great] *estremo, grandissimo.*

Extreme pain, *dolore estremo.*

Extreme [last] *estremo, ultimo.*

The extreme unction [one of the seven sacraments of the church of Rome, which is a solemn anointing of a sick person at the point of death] *l'estrema unzione, uno de' sette sagramenti della chiesa Romana, che s'amministra a' moribondi coll' olio santo.*

Extreme, adv. *estremamente, in estremo.*

An extreme sharp winter, *un verno estremamente freddo.*

Extreme, s. *estremo*, s. m. *estremità*, s. f.

Prodigality and avarice are the two extremes, *la prodigalità, e l' avarizia sono i due estremi.*

To go from one extreme to another, or to run upon extremes, *passare, o andare da un estremo all' altro.*

EXTRE'MELY, adv. [very, mighty] *estremamente, molto.*

A man extremely poor, *un uomo estremamente povero.*

I am extremely concerned about it, *me ne rincresce, o dispiace molto.*

I love it extremely, *l'amo molto, in sommo grado.*

EXTRE'MITY, s. [the end, edge, brink or border of any thing] *estremità, estrema parte, fine*, s. f.

The extremities of the body, *l'estremità del corpo.*

Extremity [excess, extreme] *estremità, estremo, eccesso.*

Extremity [sad condition, distress, misery] *estremità, calamità, miseria, necessità*, s. f.

He was reduced to such an extremity, that he was forced to beg, *fu ridotto ad una estremità tale, che fu sforzato a mendicare.*

To E'XTRICATE [to disintangle, or disingage] *sviluppare.*

E'XTRICATED, adj. *sviluppato.*

EXTRI'NSECAL, adj. [outward] *estrinseco, di fuora.*

EXTRI'NSECALLY, adv. *estrinsecamente, dalla parte esteriore, esteriormente.*

EXTRINSICK, adj. [outward, external, *estrinseco, esterno.*

EXTRU'SION, s. [thrusting out] *espulsione, il cacciar via.*

EXTU'BERANCE, s. [a swelling] *tumore, enfiato*, s. m.

EXTUME'SCENCE, s. [a swelling] *enfiato, tumore*, s. m.

EXU'BERANCE, s. [abundance, plenty] *abbondanza, pienezza, soprabbondanza*, s. f.

EXU'BERANT, adj. [plentiful] *abbondante, soprabbondevole, soprabbondoso, trabbocante.*

To EXU'BERATE [to abound in the highest degree] *abbondare in supremo grado.*

To EXU'LCERATE [to turn to an ulcer] *ulcerarsi, pervenire ad ulcera.*

EXU'LCERATED, adj. *ulcerato, pervenuto ad ulcera.*

EXULCERA'TION, s. [a turning to an ulcer] *esulcerazione, ulcerazione*, s. f.

To EXU'LT [to rejoice, to leap for joy] *esultare, avere allegrezza.*

EXU'LTANCE, } s. [a leaping for
EXULTA'TION, } joy] *esultazione, gioja, allegrezza*, s. f.

EXUNDA'TION, s. [overflowing] *inondazione*, s. f.

EY'AS, s. [a young hawk just taken from the nest] *un falconcino tolto pur ora del nido.*

EYE, s. [the instrument of the sight] *occhio*, s. m. *strumento della vista.*

A fine eye, *un bell' occhio.*

At the least twinkling of an eye, *in un batter d'occhio, in un instante, in un subito.*

A cast of the eye, *un' occhiata, uno sguardo.*

To look upon one with a good eye, *verder uno di buon occhio.*

To look upon one with an evil eye, *vedere o guardare uno di mal' occhio, non averlo a grado, non-amarlo.*

To have an eye, or to keep a strict eye upon one [to watch him] *aver l'occhio sopra ad uno, osservare i suoi andamenti.*

I have an eye to what he does, *ho un occhio a quel che fa.*

You must have an eye to your family, *bisogna che voi abbiate cura della vostra famiglia.*

To have a thing in one's eye, *uccellare a qualche cosa, desiderarla con avidità.*

The

The eye of a needle, *la cruna, o il foro dell' ago.*

An eye of pheasants, *una covata di fagiani.*

The eye of a plant, *occhio, o gemma d'una pianta.*

To open or shut one's eyes, *aprire o chiudere gli occhi.*

To open one's eyes [to discover an error or cheat] *aprire gli occhi, scoprire un errore o un inganno.*

To shut one's eyes [to wink at a thing] *chiuder gli occhi a che che si sia, passarlo senza considerazione, far vista di non vederlo.*

Eyes [look, sight] *occhi, la vista.*

To cast one's eyes upon a thing, *gettar l'occhio su che che si sia.*

To take off one's eyes from a thing, *staccar l'occhio da che che si sia.*

Every body's eyes are upon you, *ognuno ha gli occhi fissi sopra di voi.*

Two eyes see better than one, *due occhi vedono meglio che uno.*

His eyes are bigger than his belly, *mangia più cogli occhi che con la borra, ha gli occhi più grandi che'l ventre.*

Eyes in bread or cheese, *occhi del pane o del cascio.*

Eyes [spectacles] *occhiali.*

To cast sheeps eyes at one, *guardare uno colla coda dell' occhio, o sott' occhio.*

Eye-sight, *la vista, gli occhi.*

Within eye-sight, *a vista.*

The eye-ball, *la pupilla dell' occhio.*

The eye-lids, *le palpebre.*

The eye-brows, *le ciglia.*

Eye water, *acqua buona per gli occhi.*

Eye-salve, *collirio,* s. m. *medicamento da occhi.*

The eye-teeth, *i denti occhiali.*

Eye-witness, *testimonio oculare.*

The corner of the eye, *la coda dell' occhio.*

Full of eyes, *occhiuto, pien d'occhi.*

Eye-holes, *occhiaje, luogo dove stanno gli occhi.*

Eye-bright [a sort of herb] *eupatorio,* s. m. *spezie d'erba.*

To Eye one, *adocchiare, aocchiare uno, affissar l'occhio verso di lui, guardarlo fisso, occhieggiarlo.*

To eye a thing [to mind it] *aver l'occhio a che che si sia, considerarlo bene.*

To Eye-bite [to bewitch by an evil influence of the eye] *fascinare, ammaliare, far fascinazione.*

Ey'ed, adj. *adocchiato, aocchiato, occhieggiato.*

Black-eyed, *che ha gli occhi neri.*

One eyed [that has but one eye] *losco, lusco, che non ha che un occhio.*

Pink-eyed [that has but little eyes] *che ha gli occhi piccoli.*

Goggle-eyed, *guercio, che ha gli occhi torti.*

Blear-eyed, *cispo, cisposo, lippo.*

Eye-glass, s [spectacles, glass to assist the sight] *occhiali; vetri che ajutan la vista.* Newton.

E'yeless, adj. [without eyes, sightless, deprived of sight] *senz' occhi, cieco, accecato, privo di vista.*

E'ye-shot, s. [sight, glance, view] *occhiata, spazio quanto l'occhio può vedere.*

E'ye-string, s. *il nervo dell' occhio.*

E'yre, s. [the court of justices itinerant or going the circuit] *la corte de' giudici che vanno attorno amministrando la giustizia.*

Justices in eyre [that take care of the king's forests] *giudici ambulanti stabiliti per la conservazione delle foreste reali.*

The chief justice in eyre, *gran mastro delle acque e delle foreste.*

E'yry, s. [the nest where birds of prey sit and hatch their young] *nido d'uccello di rapina.*

F.

F, *è la sesta lettera dell' alfabeto Inglese, e si pronuncia come in Italiano.*

Fa [a musical note] *fa, una delle note della musica.*

Faba'ceous, adj. [having the nature of a bean] *favàceo, della natura delle fave.*

Fa'ble, s. [a story devised for the sake of instruction] *favola,* s. f.

Æsop's fables, *le favole d' Esopo.*

Fable [tale] *favola, falsa narrazione simigliante alla verità.*

To Fa'ble [to tell fables] *favolare, raccontar favole, favoleggiare, dir bugie.*

The poets fabled a great many stories about Jupiter, *i poeti hanno favoleggiato, o inventato molte favole di Giove.*

Fa'bled, adj. [celebrated in fables] *celebrato nelle antiche favole.*

To Fa'bricate [to build] *fabbricare, edificare.*

Fa'bricated, adj. *fabbricato, edificato.*

Fabrica'tion, s. *fabbricazione,* s. f. *magistero.*

Fa'brick, s. [building] *fabbrica,* s. f. *edificio,* s. m.

A stately fabrick, *un superbo edificio.*

Fabrick lands [lands given for building or repairing of churches, colleges, &c.] *beni stabili lasciati per la costruzione, o reparazione delle chiese, collegi, &c.*

Fa'brile, adj. [of or belonging to smiths] *fabbrile, di fabbro, pertinente a fabbro.*

Fa'bulist, s. [a writer of fables] *scrittore di favole.*

Fa'bulator, s. [teller of stories] *favolatore, favoleggiatore,* s. m.

Fa'bulous, adj. [feigned] *fabuloso, favoloso, favolesco.*

A fabulous story, *una narrazione favolosa.*

Fabulous gods, *iddii favolosi.*

Fa'bulously, adv. *d'una maniera favolosa.*

Face, s. [visage] *faccia,* s. f. *viso, volto,* s. m.

To look one in the face, *riguardar alcuno nel viso.*

The face of our Lord, *la faccia del Signore.*

I will justify it to his face, *glielo manterrò in faccia.*

Face [look, countenance] *viso, sembiante,* s. m. *aria, apparenza, vista, sembianza,* s. f.

To put on a new face, *cangiarsi nel viso.*

To carry two faces under a hood, *aver due visi, esser un furbo.*

Face, [presence, sight] *faccia, vista, presenza,* s. f.

Before the face of God, *innanzi la faccia di Dio.*

That was done in the face of the whole town, *ciò fu fatto in presenza, o a vista di tutta la città.*

In the face of the sun [publickly] *apertamente, pubblicamente.*

Before my face, *in presenza mia.*

A letter that has a good face [among printers] *una lettera che ha un bell' occhio.*

Face [or state] of affairs, *faccia, stato, disposizione degli affari.*

The face of affairs is very much altered, *le cose hanno cangiato faccia.*

Face [appearance] *apparenza, il fuori.*

To have a face of religion, *aver qualche apparenza di religione.*

Face [the front or exterior part of a great building] *faccia, facciata,* s. f. *la parte degli edifici, dove per lo più è l'entrata.*

Face [confidence, boldness] *faccia, arditezza, sfacciataggine.*

To lay one on the face, *dare uno schiaffo ad uno.*

I shall see your face no more, *non voglio vedervi più.*

Face to face, *faccia a faccia, a quattr' occhi.*

He dares not show his face, *ha paura di farsi vedere, ha paura degli sbirri.*

A brazen face, or bold face, *uno sfacciato, un sfrontato, una sfacciata, una sfrontata.*

Face, or wry face, *smorfie.*

To make faces, *far delle smorfie.*

To face [to look in the face] *guardar nel viso, affissar gli occhi.*

To face a pair of sleeves, *metter le mostre ad un pajo di maniche.*

To face [to look] *far faccia, esser voltato verso.*

My house faces the sea, *la mia casa fa faccia al mare, o è voltata verso il mare.*

To face the enemy, *far faccia al nemico.*

To face a card [to turn it] *voltare un carta.*

To face about, *voltarsi, girar gli occhi attorno.*

To face one out or down [to outface him] *mantenere una cosa in faccia ad uno.*

To face out a lie, *mantenere una bugia.*

FA'CED, adj. Ex. a pair of sleeves faced with silk, *un pajo di maniche con mostre di seta.*

Fair faced, *di bel viso.*

Ugly faced, *brutto, di brutto viso.*

Boldfaced, or brazenfaced, *sfacciato, sfrontato, impudente.*

Two faced, *che ha due facce.*

Barefaced, *smascherato, a viso scoperto, a fronte levata.*

FACE-PAINTING, s. [the art of drawing portraits] *l'arte del far ritratti.*

FACE'TE, or FACE'TIOUS, adj. [pleasant, witty, merry] *faceto, gioviale, piacevole, burlesco, gajo.*

FACE'TIOUSLY, adv. *facetamente, giovalmente, piacevolmente, burlescamente, gajamente.*

FACE'TIOUSNESS, s. *facezia, piacevolezza, detto arguto, e gioviale.*

FA'CILE, adj. [easy to be done] *facile, agevole.*

Facile [easy of belief] *credulo.*

Facile [of an easy address] *facile, trattabile, benigno, pieghevole.*

To FACI'LITATE [to make easy] *facilitare, levare le difficoltà, render facile o agevole.*

I shall endeavour to facilitate the means to it, *cercherò di facilitarne il modo.*

FACI'LITATED, adj. *facilitato.*

FACILITA'TION, s. *il facilitare.*

For the greater facilitation, *per render la cosa più facile, per fare le cose più facilmente.*

FACI'LITY, s. [easiness] *facilità, agevolezza,* s. f.

FA'CING, s. [from to face] *v.* To face.

The facing of sleeves, *le mostre delle maniche.*

The facing of a building, *la facciata d'un edificio.*

FACI'NOROUS, adj. [villainous, wicked] *facinoroso, scellerato, di mal affare.*

FACT, s. [deed] *fatto, atto,* s. m.

A matter of fact, *uno cosa di fatto.*

'Tis matter of fact, *così va in fatto.*

An heinous fact, *un' azione enorme.*

FA'CTION, s. [party] *fazione, setta, parte,* s. f.

To keep up a faction, *fomentare una fazione.*

FA'CTIOUS, adj. [given to factions, seditious] *fazioso, autore di fazioni, capo di parti.*

A factious man, *un fazioso.*

A factious spirit, *un animo fazioso, o sedizioso.*

FA'CTIOUSNESS, s. *spirito, o animo fazioso*

FACTI'TIOUS, adj. [artificial] *fattizio, fatto a mano, fatto con arte, artifiziale.*

FA'CTOR, s. [agent] *fattore, agente,* s. m. *che fa i negozi altrui.*

FA'CTORSHIP, s. *fattoria,* s. f.

FA'CTORY, s. [any place beyond sea where factors reside] *la residenza del fattore.*

Factory of cloth, *fabrica, o manifattura di panni.*

FACTO'TUM, s. [one who does all sorts of business in a family] *uno che fa tutte le faccende.*

FA'CULTY, s. [ability or power to perform any action] *facoltà, potenza, podestà, possibilità,* s. f.

The faculties of the soul, *la facoltà dell' anima.*

The animal, vital, and neutral faculty, *la facoltà animale, vitale, e naturale.*

His faculty lies totally that way, *egli ha un gran talento per ciò.*

Faculty [privilege, leave, power] *facoltà, licenza, privilegio.*

Faculty [in civil sense, signifies a body of doctors in any science] *facoltà, corpo di dottori.*

FACU'ND, adj. [eloquent] *facondo, eloquente.*

FACU'NDIOUS, adj. [full of eloquence] *facondioso, che ha facondia, eloquente.*

FACU'NDITY, s. [eloquence] *facondità, facondia, eloquenza,* s. f.

To FA'DDLE [to trifle, to toy, to play] *badaluccare, perder il tempo in far nonnulla.*

To faddle a child, *carezzare, o vezzeggiare un fanciullo.*

Fiddle-faddle, s. [trifles] *baje, bagattelle, chiacchiere, ciance, frascherie, chicchibicchiacchi, cianciafruscole, ciaffole.*

FA'DDLED, adj. *carezzato, vezzeggiato, accarezzato.*

FA'DDLER, s. *che accarezza, che vezzeggia.*

To FADE, verb. neut. [to wither] *sfiorire, appassare, appassire, divenir passo, vizzio, parlando de' fiori o della bellezza.* pref. *sfiorisco, appassisco.*

Her beauty begins to fade, *la sua bellezza comincia a sfiorire.*

Great heat fades the flowers, *il gran caldo appassa, o appassisce i fiori.*

To fade [to decay] *abbiosciare, avvilirsi, ricadere, languire, perder la forza e'l vigore.* pref. *languisco.*

FA'DED, or FADED AWAY, adj. *sfiorito, appassato, appassito, abbiosciato, ricaduto, languido, moscio, vizzo, passo.*

A faded flower, *un fiore mosrio, o passo.*

A faded colour, *un colore smorto.*

To FADGE [to agree] *accordarsi, convenire, concordarsi.* pref. *convengo.* pret. *convenni.*

FA'DING, s. ex. excessive heat causes the fading of flowers, *il calore eccessivo appassa i fiori.*

Fading, adj. *languido, che s' appassa, che si sfiorisce.*

A fading colour, *un colore che svanisce.*

FAG-END, s. ex. the fag-end of cloth, *la testa o la coda d'una pezza di panno.*

The fag end of the week, *la fine della settimana.*

FA'GOT, s. [a bundle of sticks or wood for fuel] *fastello, o fascio di legna.*

A fagot band, *una ritorta.*

A fagot man, *uno che vende fastelli.*

A large fagot, *un fastellaccio, un fastellone.*

A little fagot, *un fastellino.*

To FAGOT one [to bind him hand and foot] *legar le mani e i piedi ad uno.*

FA'GOTS, military term [men hired to muster by officers whose company is not full] *paghe morte, passavolanti.*

FAIL, s. *fallo,* s. m.

Without fail, *senza fallo.*

To FAIL [to offend, to do amiss] *fallare, errare, commetter fallo, trasgredire, fallire.* pref. *trasgredisco, fallisco.*

To fail through ignorance, *peccar per ignoranza.*

To fail in one's duty, *mancare al suo dovere.*

To fail of one's word or promise, *mancar di parola, violar la promessa.*

To fail one [to disappoint him] *mancar di parola ad uno.*

My heart fails me, *il cuore mi svenisce.*

My strength fails me, *le forze mi mancano, o m'abbondonano.*

To fail in one's judgment, *ingannarsi, sbagliare.*

To fail in one's hope, *restar deluso nella sua aspettativa.*

To fail [to break as a merchant] *fallire, mancare i danari a' mercanti.*

FAI'LED, adj. *fallato, fallito. v.* To fail.

FAI'LING, s. *fallire, fallo, errore, difetto,* s. m. *mancanza, colpa,* s. f.

To bear with one another's failings, *comportare l'un l'altro i loro difetti.*

Drinking is his great failing, *il suo più gran vizio è il bere.*

FA'ILURE,

FA'ILURE, s. *mancanza.*

Upon failure of which, *in mancanza di che.*

FAIN, adj. [obliged, forced] *sforzato, obbligato, costretto.*

I was fain to do it, *fui sforzato, o costretto di farlo.*

He has ill neighbours that's fain to praise himself, *colui ha cattivi vicini, che è in necessità di lodar se stesso.*

Fain, adv. [willingly] *pur, e pure, volentiermente.*

I would fain see him, *vorrei pur vederlo.*

He would fain persuade me to go along with him, *voleva in ogni modo persuadermi d'andare con lui.*

If I would never so fain, *bench' io il volessi.*

FAINT, adj. [weak] *languido, fiacco, fievole, debole.*

Faint [weary] *fiacco, stracco, lasso.*

Faint heart never won fair lady, *i neghittosi son di rado fortunati in amore.*

Faint-hearted, *timido, vigliacco, vile, poltrone, dappoco, pusillanimo.*

Faint-heartedly, adv. *timidamente, vilmente.*

Faint-heartedness, s. *timidità, vigliaccheria, viltà, poltroneria, dappocaggine, pusillanimità,* s. f.

To FAINT [to faint away, to swoon] *svenire, venir meno, tramortire, perder il sentimento,* pres. *svengo,* pret. *svenni,* pres. *tramortisco.*

To faint [to grow faint] *languire, divenir languido.*

FA'INTED, or FA'INTED AWAY, adj. *svenuto, venuto meno, tramortito.*

FA'INTING, or FA'INTING FIT, s. *svenimento, sfinimento,* s. m.

FA'INTLY, adv. *freddamente, con freddezza, pigramente, lentamente, a malincorpo, languidamente.*

FA'INTNESS, s. [weakness] *debolezza, e debilezza, fievolezza, languidezza, fiacchezza,* s. f. *languidore, languore,* s. m.

FAIR, adj. [beautiful] *bello, vago, vezzoso.*

Fair weather, *bel tempo.*

A fair woman, *una vaga donna.*

Fair words, *belle parole, parolette.*

Fair words butter not parsnips, *le belle parole non danno a mangiare.*

To be in a fair way, *esser bene incamminato.*

Fair hair, *capelli biondi.*

Fair pretence, *un bel pretesto.*

Fair weather, *tempo chiaro, o sereno.*

A fair proposal, *una proposizione ragionevole.*

Fair [honest] *franco, schietto, sincero, candido.*

To play fair play, *giuocar fedelmente, senza inganno.*

To give one fair play, *dar ad uno tempo di difendersi.*

A fair wind, *vento favorevole.*

To give one a fair hearing, *ascoltar uno favorevolmente.*

A fair [or flattering] tongue, *lingua lusinghiera o adulatrice.*

Fair spoken, *lusinghiere, adulatore.*

To use fair means, *trattar colle buone, con piacevolezza, con bello e cortese modo.*

A fair man, *un uomo biondo.*

A fair woman, *una donna bionda.*

Fair dealing, *probità, schiettezza, buona fede, sincerità, ingenuità, candidezza,* s. f. *randore,* s. m.

I shall be very fair with you, *tratterò con sincerità, e candore con voi.*

Fair, s. *il buono, il bello.*

To join together the fair and the good, *unire il bello all' utile.*

Fair, adv. to write a thing fair, *scrivere che che si sia al netto.*

To speak fair to one, *dar buone parole ad uno.*

To play fair, *giuocar fedelmente, senza truffare.*

To stand fair for a good fortune, *essere in istrada di far fortuna.*

He is in a fair way of recovery, *comincia a riaversi.*

Fair and softly goes far, *pian piano si va ben ratto.*

Fair, s. [an annual or general market] *fiera,* s. f. *mercato libero.*

To come a day after the fair [to come too late] *venire allo scorcio della fiera, venire troppo tardi.*

A fair day, *giorno di fiera.*

FA'IRIES, s. *il plurale di* Fairy.

FA'IRING, s. [from fair] *donativo di fiera.*

Pray bring me a fairing, *di grazia portatemi la fiera.*

FA'IRLY, adv. [honestly] *sinceramente, schiettamente, condidamente, di buona fede, ingenuamente.*

FA'IRNESS, s. [beautifulness] *bellezza, vaghezza,* s. f.

Fairness [fair dealing] *probità, schiettezza, sincerità, fedeltà,* s. f. *candore,* s. m.

FA'IRY, s. *fata, maga.*

The fairies of the water, *le ninfe delle arque, le najadi.*

FAITH, s. [belief] *fede e fè, credenza,* s. f.

Faith [doctrine] *fede, religione, dottrina,* s. f.

Faith [fidelity] *fede, lealtà,* s. f.

Faith [a sort of oath] *a fe, per la fede, sorta di giurare.*

I have not faith enough to believe that, *non ho tanta fede da creder ciò.*

I have no faith in miracles, *non presto fede ai miracoli, non credo miracoli.*

Without faith the works are dead, *le opere senza la fede son morte.*

Upon my faith, *affè, a fede mia, alla fe.*

FA'ITHFUL, adj. [or trusty] *fedele, leale.*

A faithful servant, *un servo fedele.*

To give a good and faithful account, *dare un esatto ragguaglio, render un conto esatto.*

The faithful, s. [the elected people of God] *i fedeli, que' che tengono la vera fede.*

FA'ITHFULLY, adv. *fedelmente, con fede, lealmente.*

FA'ITHFULNESS, s. *fedeltà, buona fede, lealtà,* s. f.

I am very well with his faithfulness, *sono molto persuaso della sua fedeltà.*

Faithfulness in love, *fedeltà, costanza.*

FA'ITHLESS, adj. [unbelieving] *incredulo.*

FA'ITHLESNESS, s. *incredulità,* s. f.

Faithlessness [perfidiousness] *infedeltà, perfidia, dislealtà.*

Faithless [perfidious] *infido, disleale, perfido.*

FA'ITOR, s. [an old word used for a vagabond] *un vagabondo, un briccone.*

FA'LCHION, s. [a short sword turning up somewhat like a hook] *coltella,* s. f.

FA'LCON, s. *falcone.*

FA'LCONET, s. [a piece of ordnance] *falconetto,* s. m. *sorta d'artiglieria.*

FA'LDSTOOL, s. [a sort of stool placed on the south side of the altar, at which the kings or queens of England kneel at their coronation] *scabello sul quale i re e le regine d'Inghilterra s'inginocchiano nel lor coronamento.*

FALL, s. *cascata, caduta,* s. f. *radimento, precipizio,* s. m.

A fall of water, *una cascata d'acqua; una cascata.*

Since the fall of the empire, *dopo la caduta o la rovina dell' impero.*

Adam's fall, *la caduta d'Adamo.*

The fall of the leaf [the autumn] *la caduta delle foglie, l'autunno.*

To get a fall, *cadere, cascare,* pret. *caddi.*

You will get a fall, *voi cascherete.*

To give one a fall, *far cascare uno.*

Downfall, *caduta, rovina, precipizio, dirupo.*

A pit-fall, *una trappola, una schiaccia.*

To FALL [to tumble down] *cadere, cascare, venire da alto a basso,* pret. *caddi.*

To fall sick, *cascare ammalato, ammalarsi.*

The waters fall, *le arque s'abbassano.*

To fall a doing something, *mettersi a fare che che si sia, metter le mani a che che si sia.*

To fall a fighting, *cominciare a battersi.*

To fall a crying, *mettersi a piangere.*

To fall to one's share, *scadere, ricadere, radere in sorte.*

To fall [to be cheaper] *calar di prezzo.*

The corn falls, *il grano cala di prezzo.*

My horse fell under me, *il cavallo mi cadde sotto.*

Fall back, fall edge, *comunque si sia, sia come si voglia.*

To fall asleep, *addormentarsi.*

If a man once fall, all will tread on him, *al cane che invecchia la volpe piscia addosso; come mancan le forze l'uomo non è più stimato.*

To fall [to become] *divenire,* pres. *divengo,* pret. *divenni.*

To fall poor, *divenir povero, impoverire,* pres. *impoverisco.*

 To

To fall a facrifice, *effer facrificato.*
He let fall fome hard words to the company, *gli fcapparono di bocca alcune parole ingiuriofe in prefenza della compagnia.*
To let fall the defire of a thing, *paffare, o perder la voglia d'una cofa.*
To fall again, *ricafcare, ricadere,* pret. *ricaddi.*
To fall away [to fall in one's flefh] *fmagrire, divenir magro,* pref. *fmagrifco.*
To fall away from one's religion, *apoftatare, cangiar di religione.*
To fall back, *cafcare indietro, rinculare.*
To fall down, *cadere, cafcare.*
To fall down the ftairs, *cafcar giù delle fcale.*
He fell upon his face, *cadde boccone, o colla faccia innanzi.*
To fall down at one's feet, *proftrarfi, o gettarfi ai piedi di qualcheduno.*
We fell down with the tide, *noi fcendemmo colla marea.*
To fall in love with one, *innamorarfi, invaghirfi d'uno.*
To fall in with one, *metterfi dalla banda d'uno, prender la fua parte.*
To fall in with the enemies, *venire alle mani col nemico, azzuffarfi col nemico, dar la battaglia.*
We fell in at fea with two Englifh men of war, *noi ci abbattemmo in, o incontrammo due navi da guerra Inglefi.*
To fall in hand with a thing, *intraprendere una cofa,* pret. *intraprefi.*
To fall into, *cafcare.*
To fall into a precipice, *cafcare in un precipizio.*
To fall into one's hands, *rafcare o venire nelle mani d'alcuno.*
To fall into a fwoon, *fvenire, venir meno, tramortire,* pref. *fvengo,* pret. *fvenni,* pref. *tramortifco.*
To fall into difcourfe, *entrare in difcorfo.*
We fell into their camp, *noi affaltammo il lor campo.*
To fall into a fweat, *cominciare a fudare.*
To fall into a fleep, *addormentarfi.*
To fall into a paffion, *andare, o metterfi in collera, ftizzarfi, incollerirfi, adirarfi,* pref. *incollerifco.*
To fall into a gallop, *metterfi a galoppare.*
To fall into difcontent, *affliggerfi.*
To fall into a way of doing fomething, *metterfi in iftato di far qualche cofa.*
They fell from their firft heat, *il loro primo ardore fi rallentò.*
To fall off, *cafcare.*
To fall off a horfe, *rafcar da cavallo.*
To fall off one's bargain, *difdirfi d'un contratto.*
To fall off from a difcourfe, *mutar difcorfo.*
To fall out, *caftrare.*
He fell out of a window, *rafcò dalla fineftra.*
My fword fell out of my hand, *la fpada mi cafcò di mano.*
To fall out [to come to pafs] *accadere, avvenire, fuccedere,* pret. *accadde, avvenne, fucceffe.*
It fell out unluckily, *accadde per difgrazia.*
It will fall out better than you expect, *la cofa riufcirà meglio di quel che penfate.*
If things fall out to our minds, *fe gli affari ci favoriranno.*
To fall out with a friend, *inimicarfi con uno, partir l'amicizia con uno, attaccarla con lui, prender gara con lui.*
They fell out moft grievoufly, *vennero alle brutte, vennero a parole infieme.*
To fall to, *metterfi, cominciare.*
To fall to work, *metterfi a lavorare.*
To fall to pieces, *caftrare in pezzi.*
To fall to pieces [to be delivered] *partorire.*
To fall upon, *cafcar fopra, lanciarfi, avventarfi.*
I fell upon the bed, *cafcai fopra il letto.*
We fell upon the rear, *attaccammo, o inveftimmo la retroguardia.*
They fell upon us defperately, *fi lanciarono, o avventarono furiofamente, o a briglia fciolta fopra di noi.*
To fall upon one another [as fhips do in a ftorm] *urtarfi, romperfi.*
That will fall heavy upon you, *quefto vi farà gran torto.*
Before ficknefs fell upon him, *prima che s'ammalaffe.*
To fall upon one's knees, *inginocchiarfi.*
To fall under, *cafcar fotto.*
I fell under him, *rafcai fotto di lui.*
A thing that falls under our fenfes, *una cofa che cafca fotto i fenfi.*
To fall under a burden, *reftar oppreffo dal pefo.*
To fall under one's difpleafure, *incorrere l'indignazione o l'odio di qualcheduno.*
To fall under an accufation, *effer accufato, o proceffato.*
To fall together by the ears, *venire alla prefe, venire alle mani.*
To fall fhort, *reftar delufo, o ingannato.*
We fell fhort of our expectations, *noi reftammo delufi nelle noftre fperanze.*
The enjoyment falls fhort of my expectation, *il godimento è di gran lunga inferiore a quel che m'imaginavo.*
We fell fhort of provifions, *i viveri ci mancarono.*
What I can do for you, will fall fhort of your merit, *qualunque cofa ch'io faccia a voftro vantaggio, farà di gran lunga inferiore al merito.*
Falla'cidus, adj. [deceitful] *fallace, falfo.*
Fa'llacy, s. [cheat, deceit] *fallacia, falfità,* s. f. *inganno,* s. m.
Fa'llen, adj. *caduto.*
Fa'llible, adj. [that may fail or err] *fallibile, che può fallire o errare.*
Fa'lling, s. *cafcamento,* s. m. *il cafcare.*
A falling out, *difputa, querela, contefa,* s. f.
Falling, adj. *cafcante, che cafca.*
The falling ficknefs, *il mal caduco.*
Fa'llow, adj. *rofficcio.*
A fallow deer, *un cervo.*
A fallow field [a land laid up, or that is left untilled for fome time] *maggefe,* s. m. *campo lafciato fodo, per feminarlo l'anno vegnente, maggiatico, novale.*
False, adj. [not true] *falfo, non vero, corrotto, contraffatto.*
Falfe [treacherous] *falfo, perfido, traditore, infedele, difleale, ingannatore.*
A falfe report, *falfe novelle.*
A falfe witnefs, *un teftimonio falfo.*
A falfe prophet, *un falfo profeta.*
Falfe coin, *moneta falfa.*
A falfe coiner, *un monetiere falfo.*
A falfe heart, *un cuore difleale.*
A woman that is falfe to her hufband, *una donna che non è fedele a fuo marito.*
A falfe mufter, *un fagotto, un paga morta.*
Falfe hearted, *perfido, traditore, ingannatore.*
Falfe, adv. *falfamente.*
To fpeak falfe, *parlar falfamente.*
To fwear falfe, *fpergiurare, giurar falfamente.*
To play falfe, *truffare, ingannare al giuoco.*
Fa'lsly, adv. *falfamente, falfo, con falfità.*
To deal falfely with one [to be falfe to him] *trattar falfamente con uno.*
Fa'lseness, Fa'lsehood, s. *falfità, falfezza,* s. f.
Falsifi'able, adj. [which may be falfified] *che fi può falfificare.*
Falsifica'tion, s. [a making faife] *falfificazione,* s. f.
Falsifi'er, s. *falfificatore,* s. m. *falfificatrice,* s. f.
To Fa'lsify [to forge, to counterfeit] *falfificare, falfare, contraffare, corrompere,* pref. *contraffaccio,* pret. *contraffeci, corruppi.*
To falfify a writing, *contraffare una fcrittura.*
To falfify a thruft, *fare un finta, termine di fcherma.*
Fa'lsify'd, adj. *falfificato, falfato, contraffatto, corrotto.*
Fa'lsifying, s. *falfamento,* s. m. *il falfare, falfificazione,* s. f.
Fa'lsity, s. [falfhood] *falfità, falfezza,* s. f.
To Fa'lter, *eftare, mancare, effer mancante.*
To Fa'mble [to falter or ftammer in fpeech] *balbettare, tartagliare, eftare nel parlare.*
Fame, s. [report, reputation] *fama, rinomata, rinomea, nominanza,* s. f. *rinomo, grido, nome,* s. m.
To get a fame, *acquiftar fama.*
Fa'miliar, adj. [intimately acquainted with] *famigliare, e familiare, intrinfeco.*
He is a very familiar man, *egli è un uomo molto familiare.*
To make one's felf familiar, *renderfi familiare.*

To grow too familiar, *prender troppa famigliarità, addimesticarsi troppo.*

A miliar [common] *familiare, comune, ordinario.*

Familiar [plain, easy] *familiare, naturale, facile, parlando d'uno stile.*

A familiar spirit, or a familiar, s. [a spirit] *uno spirito famigliare, un folletto.*

FAMILIA'RITY, s. [a familiar free way] *familiarità, famigliarità, dimestichezza, intrinsichezza,* s. f.

Too much familiarity breeds contempt, *la troppa famigliarità genera disprezzo.*

FAMI'LIARLY, adv. *famigliarmente, familiarmente, dimesticamente, intrinsecamente, familiarescamente.*

To write familiarly, *scriver famigliarmente, d'uno stile familiare, o naturale.*

FA'MILIST, s. [one of the sect of the family of love] *nome che si da a certi eretici, v.* Family of love.

FA'MILY, s. [father, mother, children, and servants] *famiglia, s. f. il padre, la madre, i figliuoli, e i domestici, s. f.*

Family [house, parentage] *famiglia, stirpe, schiatta.*

The royal family, *la famiglia reale.*

He is of a good family, *egli è di buona famiglia.*

The Family of love [a sect which sprang up about the year 1556, followers of one Nicholas, whose chief tenet was, that Christ was already come to judgment] *spezie di eresia, che forse nell' anno 1556, della quale fu l'autore un Nicolao, e i principi fondamentali erano, che Cristo era già venuto al giudicio universale.*

FA'MINE, s. [a general want of provisions] *carestia, fame, s. f.*

To take a town by famine, *espugnare una terra per fame.*

To FA'MISH [to starve] *affamare, far morir di fame, indur fame, e carestia.*

To famish a town, *affamare una città.*

To famish, verb neut. *esser affamato, esser morto di fame.*

I am ready to famish, *sono quasi affamato, mi muojo della fame, vedo la fame in aria.*

FA'MISHED, adj. *affamato, stretto, o morto della fame.*

FA'MISHMENT, s. *fame, carestia.*

FA'MOUS, adj. [renowned] *famoso, chiaro, illustre.*

A famous writer, *un famoso scrittore.*

Very famous, *famosissimo.*

FA'MOUSLY, adv. *famosamente, chiaramente, con fama.*

FA'MOUSNESS, s. *famosità, chiarezza, rinomea, rinomanza, fama, s. f. grido, nome, s. m.*

FAN, s. [an utensil worn by women] *ventaglio, s. m.*

Fan [an instrument to winnow corn] *vaglio, s. m.*

To FAN [to cool or recreate with a fan; to ventilate] *dimenar il ventaglio, ventilare, agitar l'aria scuotendo il ventaglio.*

To fan [to winnow corn] *vagliare del grano.*

FANA'TICAL, adj. [belonging to fanaticism] *spiritato.*

Fanatical conceptions, *concetti, o pensieri stravaganti.*

FA'NATICISM, s. [pretended inspiration, tenets, or opinions of fanaticks] *la setta degli spiritati.*

FA'NATICK, adj. [inspired, possessed] *spiritato, indemoniato.*

A fanatick, s. [one who pretends to inspirations and revelations] *un fanatico, uno che pretende esser inspirato.*

FANCIES, *è il numero del più di* Fancy, *e la terza persona del numero del meno del verbo,* To fancy.

FA'NCIFUL, adj. *fantastico, bizzaro, capriccioso.*

FA'NCIFULNESS, s. *bizzaria, bizzarre fantasie, capriccio.*

FA'NCY, s. [imagination] *fantasia, s. f. una delle facoltà dell' anima.*

Fancy [foolish conceit] *imaginazione, chimera, visione, illusione, s. f.*

Fancy [humour, whim] *fantasia, opinione, s. f. capriccio, pensiero, s. m.*

Fancy is a faculty of the soul, whereby we apprehend sensible things, *la fantasia è una facoltà dell' anima, per mezzo della quale concepiamo le cose sensibili.*

'Tis but a meer fancy, *questa è una mera immaginazione.*

To live according to one's own fancy, *vivere a sua fantasia, a sua modo, a suo talento.*

'Tis my fancy, *così mi piace.*

I had a fancy to see him, *mi venne voglia, o desio di vederlo.*

You have strange fancies in your head, *voi avete strane fantasie in testa.*

To take a fancy to a thing, *pigliar amore ad una cosa.*

I have a great fancy to it, *l'amo molto, mi piace assai.*

His fancy lies extremely to travelling, *egli ha una grande inclinazione di viaggiare.*

To FA'NCY [to think] *immaginarsi, figurarsi, darsi ad intendere, mettersi in testa, credere, pensare.*

To fancy [to like a thing] *amare, piacere.*

To fancy a thing [to let it into one's brains] *immaginarsi, figurarsi una cosa nella mente.*

He fancies himself a great man, *egli s'imniagina, o si crede un grand' uomo.*

That's the thing I fancy, *questo è quel che mi piace.*

I fancy her above all other women, *mi puo più di qualsivoglia altra donna.*

I fancy you are in the wrong, *mi pare che voi abbiate torto.*

FA'NCY'D, adj. *immaginato, v.* To fancy.

FANCY-MONGER, s. [one who delights in tricks of imagination] *uno che ghiribizza, ghiribizzatore, uno che ha il cervello pieno di ghiribizzi.*

FANE, s. *tempio.*

FANG, s. *artiglio o dente acuto.*

To fang [to fong] *afferrare coll'ugne, o co' denti.*

FA'NGLES, s. as new fangles [new whimsies] *nuove invenzioni, capricci.*

FANNED, adj. [from to fan] *vagliato, ventilato.*

FA'NNEL, s. [an ornament like a scarf worn about the left arm of an officiating mass priest] *manipolo,* s. m.

FA'NNER, s. [he that fans] *vagliatore,* s m. *che vaglia, che ventila.*

FA'NNING, s. *il vagliare, il ventilare.*

FA'NTASM, s. [an apparition, or ghost] *una fantasma, una fantasima.*

FANTA'STICAL, } adj. [humourist,
FANTA'STICK, } whimsical] *fantastico, falotico, intrattabile, bisbetico, umorista, cappriccioso.*

A fantastical man, *un uomo fantastico.*

FANTA'STICALLY, adv. *fantasticamente, con modo odioso e fastidioso, capricciosamente.*

FANTA'STICALNESS, or FANTA'STICKNESS, s. *fantasticaggine, fantasticheria, bizzarria, s. f. capriccio, ghiribizzo, s. m.*

FA'NTASY, s. [fancy] *fantasia, s. f.*

FAR, adj. [distant] *lontano, distante, remoto.*

To travel into far countries, *viaggiare in paesi remoti.*

Far [averse] *contrario, opposto, nemico.*

Far [late] *tardi.*

It is far in the day, *è tardi.*

Far, adv. *lontano.*

Far from sea, *lontano dal mare.*

I must go as far as the city, *bisogna che vada fino alla città.*

I am so far from being in love with her, that I almost hate her, *l'odio quasi in vece d'amarla.*

This is far better, *questo è molto migliore.*

Very far from that, *tutto'l contrario.*

By far, *dimolto, di gran lunga.*

Far distant, *molto lontano, o discosto.*

How far is it thither? *quanto è lontano da qui?*

The season is far advanced, *la stagione è molto avanzata.*

So far is my pain from being lessened, that it is increased, *il mio dolore in luogo di mitigarsi via più s'innaspra.*

So far as is possible, *tanto che è possibile.*

You must learn so far, *bisogna che voi impariate tutto questo, o fin qui.*

She is far handsomer than her sister, *elle è via più bella di sua sorella.*

As far as I see, *per quel che vedo, per quanto posso vedere.*

I'll go as far as any man in it, *ci contribuirò tanto ch' un altro.*

I will help you as far as I can, *vi ajuterò per quanto le mie forze si stenderanno.*

As far as I hear, *per quel ch' intendo.*

Far be it from me, *dio me ne guardi, tolga iddio.*

This came as far as from Italy, *questo vien d'Italia.*

It fell out far otherwise, *accadde tutto'l contrario.*

Far and near, or far and wide, *da per tutto, ogni parte.*

Thus far we agree together, *fin qui noi siamo d' accordo, ci accordiamo.*

Thus far of these things, *non parliamo più di queste cose.*

Far fought, *ricercato.*

A far-fetched commodity, *una mercanzia che viene da lontano.*

A far-fetched expression, *un' espressione affettata, o studiata.*

FARCE, s. [mock comedy] *farsa, s. f. comedia mozza, imperfetta.*

Farce [a sort of pudding] *ripieno.*

FA'RCED, adj. [crammed, stuffed] *pieno, riempito.*

FA'RCY, or FA'RCIN, s. [a disease in horses] *lepra de' cavalli.*

FA'RDEL, s. [a bundle or packet] *fardello, s. m. ravvolto di panni, e d' altre materie simili.*

FA'RDINGALE, s. [a whalebone circle or hoop, which ladies wore formerly upon their hips] *guard' infante, cerchio d' osso di balena, che le donne portavano anticamente su i fianchi.*

FARE, s. [cheer] *cera.*

A good or slender fare, *buona o cattiva cera.*

Fare [a watch tower at sea] *faro, s. m.*

The fare of Messina, *il faro di Messina.*

Fare [money paid for passage in a hackney coach, or by water] *vettura, s. f. passaggio, nolo, il prezzo della vettura o del passaggio.*

The fare of four people in a coach, *la vettura di quattre persone in una carrozza.*

To pay the waterman his fare, *pagare il nolo o'l passaggio al barcaruolo.*

To FARE [to live] *vivere, trattarsi, regalarsi.*

To fare deliciously, *viver delicatamente.*

He fares like a prince, *vive da principe, si tratta da principe, fa buona cera.*

He fares very ill, *vive malissimamente.*

To fare [in point of health] *stare.*

How fare ye? [how do ye?] *come state? come ve la passate?*

Fare you well, *conservatevi addio, vale.*

Farewel, adv. *addio, vale.*

To bid one farewel, *dire addio ad uno.*

I shall bid him an eternal farewel, *li dirò addio per sempre*

FARM, s. [a house whereto belongs a considerable estate in land to be employed in husbandry] *podere, s. m. possessione di più campi, con casa da lavoratore.*

To FARM, [to take to farm] *pigliare in appalto.*

To farm the King's revenues, *pigliare in appalto l' entrate del Rè.*

To farm out [to give to farm] *appaltare, dare in appalto, parlando d' entrate pubbliche.*

To farm [to let] *affittare, dare in affitto, locare.*

To farm out land, *affittare, o locare una terra.*

FARMED, adj. *preso in appalto.*

Farmed out, *appaltato, dato in appalto, affittato, dato in affitto, locato.*

FA'RMER, s. [one who occupies a farm] *fattore, gastaldo, s. m. quello che ha cura delle possessioni, fittajuolo.*

A farmer of the King's revenues, *un appaltatore.*

FARRA'GINOUS, adj. [formed of different materials] *confusamente ammucchiato.*

FARRA'GO, s. [a mass formed confusedly of several ingredients, a medley] *farragine, o farraggine, mucchio confuso, e mescolanza di varie robe.*

FA'RRIER, s. [a smith who shoes and doctors horses] *ferratore, maniscalco, s. m.*

FA'RROW, s. [a little pig] *un porchetto.*

To farrow [to bring forth pigs, as a sow does] *figliare, parlando d' una troja.*

The sow has farrowed, *la troja ha figliato.*

FA'RSANG, s. [a Persian word, signifying a league, or the space of three miles] *farsangene, parola Persiana, che vuol dire una lega.*

FA'RSET, s. *un farsetto, vestimento del busto.*

FART, s. [an eruption of wind backward] *coreggia, s. f. il suono del vento che si manda fuora per le parti di sotto.*

To let a fart, *tirare una coreggia.*

He cannot keep a fart, *non terrebbe un cocomero all' erta.*

To FART [to break wind backwards] *tirar corregge.*

To FA'RTHEL [the same as to furl] *ammainare, termine di marina.*

To farthel the sail, *ammainar le vele.*

FA'RTHER, v. Further.

FA'RTHING, s. [the fourth part of a penny] *fardino, s. m. la quarta parte d' un denaro d' Inghilterra.*

I have not a farthing in my pocket, *non ho un picciolo in scarsella.*

FARTHINGALE, v. Fardingale.

FA'SCIA, s. [a swath, or swaddling band] *una fascia.*

To FA'SCINATE [to bewitch] *ammaliare, affatturare, far malie.*

FA'SCINATED, adj. *ammaliato, affatturato.*

FASCINA'TION, s. [a bewitching] *fascinazione, malia, s. f. affatturamento, s. m.*

FASCI'NE, s. [fagot of bavins] *fascina, s. f.*

FA'SHION, s. [way, manner] *maniera, guisa, sorte, s. f. modo.*

In this fashion, *in questa maniera o guisa, in questo modo.*

Fashion [custom] *costume, s. m. moda, usanza, s. f.*

'Tis out of fashion, *è fuor di moda.*

A new or old fashion, *una moda novella o vecchia.*

After the French fashion, *alla moda di Francia, alla Francese.*

'Tis quite out of fashion, *è affatto fuor di moda.*

Fashion [looks, mien, behaviour] *garbo, s. m. avventezza, aria, leggiadria, apparenza, prestanza, s. f.*

People of fashion, *gente di garbo.*

Fashion [form, shape] *forma, figura, s. f.*

To FA'SHION [to form, to shape] *formare, dar la forma, o la figura.*

FA'SHIONABLE, adj. [that is according to the fashion, modish] *alla moda, all' usanza.*

A fashionable suit of cloaths, *un vestito alla moda.*

A fashionable man, *un uomo che segue la moda.*

FA'SHIONABLY, adv. *alla moda.*

FA'SHIONED, adj. *formato, fatto.*

FA'SHIONER, s. ex. the King's fashioner [or taylor] *il sarto del Rè.*

FA'SHIONIST, s. [fashion-monger] *un inventore di nuove mode.*

FAST, adj. [close, tight] *stretto, serrato.*

Fast [swift] *presto, veloce, ratto, spedito.*

Fast [firm] *fermo, stabile, saldo, fisso, immobile, sodo.*

Fast [shut] *serrato.*

A fast knot, *un modo stretto.*

Is the door fast? *è serrata la porta?*

To make the door fast, *serrar la porta.*

Fast, adv. *fermo, stretto.*

Hold it fast, *tenetelo fermo.*

Tie it fast, *legatelo stretto.*

To boil fast, *bollire a ricorsojo.*

Fast [swiftly] *presto, subito, tosto, subitamente, prestamente.*

Don't write so fast, *non iscrivete così presto.*

I'll do it as fast as I can, *lo farò tosto, o quanto prima potrò.*

To stand fast, *star saldo, star fermo, stare alla dura, tener duro.*

To stick fast, *attaccarsi, appiccarsi tenacemente.*

He is fast asleep, *egli dorme profondamente.*

To play fast and loose [to be false in a business] *non esser nè dentro nè fuori, vacillare, trattar con secondo fine.*

Some men make nothing of playing fast and loose with oaths, *vi sono alcuni che non fanno caso di spergiurare.*

A hold fast in a wall, *un anellone.*

I ran away as fast as I could, *mi diedi alla fuga a tutto potere.*

Fast, s. [abstinence from food] *digiuno, s. m.*

To keep a fast, *osservare il digiuno.*

To break one's fast, *rompere il digiuno, asciolvere, far colazione.*

To FAST [to abstain from food] *digiunare.*

I fasted all this day, *ho digiunato tutt' oggi.*

To fast by the church's order, *digiunare per comandamento della chiesa.*

To fast one's self, *lasciarsi morir di fame.*

To fast one's self sharp and hungry, *digiunare per aguzzar l'appetito.*

To fast away a disease, *guarirsi d' una malattia a forza di digiunare.*

To

To Fa'sten [to make fast] *attaccare, legare, appiccare.*
To fasten a thing with a nail, *attaccare che che si sia con un chiodo.*
To fasten a stake in the ground, *ficcar un palo in terra.*
To fasten one's eyes upon a thing, *fissar gl' occhi sopra qualche cosa.*
To fasten a door, *serrare una porta.*
To fasten upon a thing, *afferrare, o afferrarsi, attaccarsi ad una cosa, pigliarla con forza.*
To fasten a crime upon one, *imputare un delitto ad uno.*
To fasten an obligation upon one, *far qualche favore ad uno.*
F'astened, adj. *attaccato, legato,* v. To fasten.
Fa'ster, s. [he or she that fasts] *digiunatore,* s. m. *digiunatrice,* s. f.
Faster, adj. [more fast] *più presto, è il comparativo di* fast.
Fasti'dious, adj. [disdainful, scornful] *fastidioso, sdegnoso, disprezzante, schifo.*
Fastidious [nauseous] *fastidioso, nojoso, importuno, rincrescevole, stomacoso.*
Fa'sting, s. [from to fast] *il digiunare, digiuno.*
A fasting day, *giorno di digiuno.*
Fasting, adv. *a digiuno.*
To go out fasting, *uscire a digiuno.*
Fa'stness, s. *fermezza,* s. f.
Fastness [or strong hold] *un forte.*
Fastness [a place not to be come at for bogs] *luogo inaccessibile, per ragione de' luoghi paludosi che lo circondano.*
Fat, adj. [contrary to lean] *grasso.*
Fat meat, *carne grassa.*
To make fat, *ingrassare, render grasso.*
To grow fat, *ingrassare, divenir grasso.*
Very fat, *grassissimo, grasso.*
Somewhat fat, *grassetto.*
Fat guts, *panciuto, di grossa pancia.*
A fat living, *un buon beneficio.*
Fat, s. *il grasso.*
I don't love fat, *io non amo il grasso.*
A bit of fat, *grassello,* s. m. *pezzuolo di grasso di carne.*
Fat, adv. *grassamente.*
Fat fed, *grassamente nutrito.*
To Fat, v. a. [to make fat, to fatten] *ingrassare, render grasso.*
To fat, v. n. [to grow fat, to grow full-fleshed] *ingrassare, divenir grasso.*
Fa'tal, adj. [belonging to fate] *fatale, cosa che vien dal fato.*
The fatal sisters, *le parche.*
Fata'lity, s. [the state of being liable to fate] *fatalità,* s. f. *fato, destino,* s. m.
Fa'tally, adv. *fatalmente, per fato.*
Fate, s. [destiny] *fato, destino,* s. m. *fatalità,* s. f.
The fates [the fatal sisters] *le parche.*
Fa'ted, adj. *destinato, statuito, determinato.*
Fa'ther, s. [he that has begot a child] *padre, genitore,* s. m.
A father-in-law, *suocero.*
A step-father, *un padrino.*
Such a father, such a son, *qual padre tal figlio.*

The fathers of the church, *i padri del la chiesa.*
A father confessor, *un padre confessore.*
A God-father, *un padrino, un compare.*
A grand-father, *un avo.*
Our fore fathers, *i nostri padri, i nostri antecessori, o antenati.*
Father-like, *da padre, come padre.*
To Fa'ther [to own] *adottare, riconoscere per suo.*
To father a thing upon one [to impute it to him] *imputare, o attribuire che che si sia ad uno.*
Fa'therhood, s. *paternità,* s. f.
Fa'therless, adj. [that has no father] *orfano, privo di padre.*
A fatherless child, *un orfano, un' orfana.*
Fa'therliness, s. *amor paterno.*
Fa'therly, adv. [like a father] *da padre, con amor paterno.*
Fatherly, adj. *paternale, paterno.*
A fatherly care, *cura paternale, o paterna.*
Fa'thom, s. [a measure of length, containing six feet] *misura di sei piedi di lunghezza.*
Fathom [reach, penetration] *acutezza di mente, sagacità.*
To fathom, *misurare la profondità, scandagliare.*
I cannot fathom his design, *non posso indovinare il suo disegno, non lo scandaglio, non ne vedo il fondo.*
Fa'thomless, adj. *che non è misurabile, che non c' è modo di scandagliarlo.*
Fati'dical, adj. [foretelling] *fatidico, indovino.*
To Fa'tigate [to tire] *faticare, travagliare, tediare, tempestare, penare, affannare, straccare.*
Fa'tigated, adj. [tired] *faticato, stracco, affannato.*
Fati'gue, s. [toil] *fatica, pene,* s. f. *travaglio,* s. m.
The fatigues of a long journey, *le fatiche d' un lungo viaggio.*
Fa'tness, s. *grassezza.*
Fa'tted, or Fa'ttened, adj. *ingrassato, grasso.*
To Fa'tten [to fat] *ingrassare, divenir grasso, e render grasso.*
Fa'ttened, adj. *ingrassato.*
Fa'tty, adj. [or unctuous] *grasso, untuoso.*
A fatty substance, *una sostanza grassa, untuosa.*
Fa'ucet, s. [tap] *cannella,* s. f. *legno bucato per il quale s' attigne il vino della botte.*
Faucet [peg] *spillo, cavicchio.*
Faugh [an interjection expressing a dislike] *eh via.*
Fa'ulcon [a great hawk] *un falcone, uccel di rapina.*
Faulcon [a piece of ordnance] *falcone, una sorta d' artiglieria.*
Fa'ulconer, or Fa'ulkner, s. *falconiere,* s. m. *che governa i falconi.*
The King's chief falconer, *il gran falconiere del Re.*
Faulconry, s. [or hawking] *falconeria,* s. *arte del governare i falconi.*

Fault, s. [error, crime, offence] *fallo, errore, mancamento, misfatto,* s. m. *colpa,* s. f.
Fault [mistake] *errore, sbaglio,* s. m.
A fault of the printer, *errore di stampa.*
'Tis your fault, *è vostra colpa.*
It shall not be my fault if I don't learn, *per me non istarà che voi non impariate, sarà vostra colpa se non imparate.*
Fault [defect] *difetto, vizio, mancamento,* s. m. *falta, diffalta,* s. f.
You bear him a grudge only because he tells you of your faults, *voi l' avete in odio, non per altro, se non perchè vi correggè de' vostri difetti.*
To find fault, *riprendere, criticare, vituperare, trovar da dire.*
A fault-finder, *un riprenditore, un censore, un critico.*
To Fault [to find fault] *criticare, riprendere, trovar da dire.* pret. *ripresi.*
To Fault, s. v. n. [to be wrong, to fail] *errare, fallire.*
To Fa'ulter [to stammer in one's speech] *balbettare, cinguettare, linguettare, scilinguare, tartagliare.*
He faulters in his speech, *egli balbetta, o frastaglia.*
To faulter in one's legs [to stumble] *inciampare, vacillare, tempellare, traballare.*
To faulter in one's design, *non riuscire nel suo disegno, mancare il colpo.*
To faulter in one's answer, *contraddirsi nel rispondere.*
To faulter [to mistake] *ingannarsi, sbagliare.*
To faulter [to give over] *desistere, tralasciare, cessare.*
Fa'ultering, s. *il balbettare.*
He has a faultering in his speech, *egli balbetta, o tartaglia quando parla.*
Fa'ultless, adj. *corretto, emandato, senza errori.*
Fa'ulty, adj. [that is in the fault] *colpevole, biasimevole.*
Faulty [full of faults] *scorretto, pieno d' errori.*
Favour, s. [courtesy, service] *favore, servizio,* s. m. *cortesia, grazia,* s. f.
Favour [credit] *favore, credito, stima, riputazione*
Favour [affection] *favore, affetto, dimostrazione di buona volontà.*
Favour [help] *favore, ajuto, protezione, difesa.*
To do one a favour, *fare un favore ad uno, obbligarlo, servirlo in qualche cosa.*
I shall take it as a great favour, *lo terrò a gran favore.*
To be in favour, *esser in grazia, in istima.*
To curry favour with one, *corteggiare alcuno, cercare di mettersi in grazia di qualcheduno.*
By the favour of the night, *col favore della notte.*
Under your favour, *con vostra buona licenza, con vostro rispetto.*
Under your favour, it is not so, *sotto vostra correzione, non è così.*

Favour [countenance] *ajuto, assistenza, favore, spalla.*

To FA'VOUR [to show favour] *favorire, favoreggiare, esser favorevole.* pref *favorisco.*

To favour [to assist, to countenance] *favorire, favoreggiare, ajutare, proteggere, difendere, spalleggiare.* pret. *protessi, difesi.*

You favour him too much, *voi lo favorite troppo.*

To favour an opinion, *favoreggiare, approvare, abbracciare un' opinione.*

To favour [to be like one] *tenere, simigliare, esser simile.*

He favoured his father [he is like his father] *egli patrizza, o padreggia, egli è simile al padre.*

She favours her mother, *ella madreggia, ella è simile alla madre.*

To favour a disease, *palliare un male.*

FA'VOURABLE, adj. [good] *favorevole, prospero, propizio.*

Favourable, wind, *vento favorevole, e prospero.*

A favourable opportunity, *un' opportunità favorevole.*

Favourable [kind] *favorevole, benigno, cortese.*

FA'VOURABLENESS, s. *favore,* s. m. *benignità, bontà, cortesia,* s. f.

FA'VOURABLY, adv. [kindly] *favorevolmente, benignamente, cortesemente, civilmente.*

FA'VOURED, adj. *favorito, trattato favorevolmente.*

Favoured [countenanced] *favorito, assistito, protetto, difeso, ajutato, spalleggiato.*

Well favoured, *bello, grato, vezzoso, vistoso, vago.*

She is a well favoured woman, *è una bella donna, una donna avvenente.*

Ill-favoured, *brutto, deforme, malfatto.*

FA'VOURED, s. *favoreggiatore,* s. m. *che favoreggia.*

FA'VOURITE, s. [one who enjoys the good will or kindness of another] *uno che è in grazia e favore d'un altro.*

Fávourite [one chosen as a companion by his superior] *un favorito, colui che dal suo superiore è scelto per compagno.*

FA'VOURLESS, adj. [unfavoured, not regarded with kindness] *non favorito, non guardato di buon occhio.*

Favourless [unfavouring, unpropitious] *sfavorevole, non propizio, infausto.*

FA'USEN, s. [a sort of large eel] *spezie d'anguilla grossa.*

FA'UTOR, s. [abettor, favourer] *fautore, favoreggiatore, favoritore,* s. m.

FA'UTRESS, s. [a woman that favours or shows countenance] *fautrice, donna che presta favore, che protegge.*

FAWN, s. [a buck or doe of the first year] *un daino giovane.*

To FAWN [speaking of the females of deer] *figliare, parlando delle damme.*

To fawn upon one [to flatter him] *lusingare, adulare, piaggiare, lisciare.*

FAWNED UPON, adj. *lusingato, adulato, piaggiato, lisciato.*

FA'WNING, s. [flattery] *lusinga, adulazione,* s. f. *piaggiamento, lisciamento,* s. m.

Fawning, adj. *adulatore, lusinghiere.*

A fawning man, *un adulatore, un lusinghiere, un piancentiere, un piaggiatore.*

A fawning woman, *un' adulatrice, una lisciatrice.*

FAY, s. [a fairy, an elf] *una fata, una maga.*

Fay, s. [faith] *fè, fede,* s. f.

By my fay, *fe, alla fe.*

To FE'AGUE [to lash, to beat] *frustare o scopare alcuno, scorreggiarlo.*

FE'ALTY, s. [an oath taken at the admittance of every tenant, to be true to the Lord of whom he holds his land] *fede, omaggio, il giuramento, di fedeltà che il vassallo rende al suo signore.*

Fealty [loyalty] *fedeltà, lealtà,* s. f.

FEAR, s. [dread, fright] *timore,* s. m. *paura,* s. f.

To be in fear, *aver paura, temere.*

To stand in fear of one, *temere alcuno.*

To put one in a great fear, *atterire, o spaventare uno.* pref. *atterisco.*

There's fear, *è da temere.*

There's no fear in it, *non c'è paura, non v'è nulla da temere.*

For fear [lest] *per tema che.*

To FEAR [to be in fear of] *temere, aver paura.*

To fear God, *temere Iddio.*

A man that fears God, *un uomo timorato di Dio.*

I fear it is too true, *tem o che la cosa non sia che troppo vera.*

The physician fears for his life, *il medico è in timore per la sua vita.*

To fear [to doubt, to question] *dubitare.*

I don't fear but he will come, *non dubito che non venga.*

To fear [to make afraid] *atterrire, spaventare, far paura.* pref. *atterisco.*

FE'ARED, adj. *temuto.*

To make one's self be feared, *farsi temere.*

Feared [made afraid] *atterrito, spaventato.*

FE'ARFUL, adj. [timorous] *temoroso, timoroso, timido.*

Fearful [frightful] *terribile, spaventoso, orribile.*

A fearful thing, *una cosa terribile.*

A fearful sight, *uno spettacolo orrendo.*

Fearful, ad. *terribilmente, orribilmente, spaventevolmente.*

She is fearful ugly, *ella è brutta da far paura.*

FE'ARFULLY, adv. [dreadfully] *orribilmente, spaventevolmente, orridamente.*

To look fearfully, *avere un cera terribile.*

Fearfully [cowardly] *timidamente, paurosamente, con timore, con paura.*

FE'ARFULNESS, s. *timidità, paura,* s. f. *timore,* s. f.

FE'ARING, s. *timore,* s. m.

FE'ARLESS, adj. *intrepido, ardito, animoso, coraggioso, bravo, che non teme, che non ha paura.*

He is a fearless man, *egli è un bravo, un uomo coraggioso.*

FE'ARLESSLY, adv. *arditamente, animosamente, intrepidamente, senza timore, senza paura, coraggiosamente.*

FE'ARLESSNESS, s. *intrepidità, arditezza, baldanza,* s. f. *animo, coraggio.*

FE'ASIBLE, adj. [which may be done] *fattibile, fattevole, agevole a farsi.*

The thing is feasible, *la cosa è fattibile.*

FE'ASIBLENESS, s. *possibilità, agevolezza,* s. f.

I don't question in the least the feasibleness of the thing, *non dubito punto che la cosa non si possa fare.*

FEAST, s. [banquet] *festino, banchetto, convito,* s. m.

A sumptuous and magnificent feast, *un festino sontuoso e magnifico.*

Feast [holiday] *festività, festa,* s. f.

The feast of Christ's nativity, *la festa di natale.*

A smell-feast, *un parasito.*

To FEAST [to treat] *regalare, trattare magnificamente.*

To feast [to banquet, to revel] *festeggiare, far feste, banchettare, far banchetti.*

He feasts every day, *è ogni giorno in festini.*

To feast like an emperor, *trattarsi, regalarsi da imperadore.*

FE'ASTED, adj. *regalato, festeggiato, banchettato.*

We were highly feasted, *fummo regalati splendidamente.*

FE'ASTER, s. *quello, o quella che fa festini, o banchetti.*

FE'ASTFUL, adj. [festive, joyful] *festoso, lieto.*

Féastful [luxurious, riotous] *romoroso, lussureggiante.*

Féast-rite, s. [custom observed in entertainments] *costume o rito osservato in occasione di feste e banchetti.*

FE'ASTING, s. *festini, banchetti.*

To love feasting, *amare i festini.*

Feasting penny, *caparra che si da ad un servo quando lo prendiamo al nostro servizio.*

FEAT, adj. [fine, spruce] *galante, pulito, attillato, gentile, garbato.*

Feat [odd] *strano, bizzaro, bisbetico, vano.*

A feat man, *un uomo bizzarro, o strano.*

Feat, s. [exploit] *fatti, azioni, gesti.*

Famous feats of war, *fatti d'armi gloriosi, azioni gloriose.*

Feats of activity, *giuochi di mano.*

To do feats, *far cose meravigliose.*

FE'ATHER, s. [a plume of a fowl] *penna, piuma,* s. f.

Light as a feather, *leggiero come una piuma.*

To pluck a bird's feathers off, *spiumare un uccello.*

Birds of a feather flock together, *ogni simile ama il suo simile.*

To cut one's throat with a feather, *nuocere a qualcheduno sotto mano o sotto apparenza d'amicizia, ridere in bocca ad uno, mostrarsi amico d'uno per ingannarlo.*

To

To laugh at a feather [to laugh at the least thing in the world] *ridere per ogni minima cosa.*

A plume of feathers, *un pennacchio, arnese di più penne insieme.*

Down feathers, *piume.*

A feather-bed, *coltrice, letto di piuma.*

Feather footed, *piumato, che ha i piedi piumati.*

To FE'ATHER [to dress in feathers, to fit with feathers] *vestir di piume, acconciar con piume.*

To feather [to tread as a cock] *camminar come un gallo.*

To feather [to enrich, to adorn] *abbellire, ornare.*

To feather one's nest [to heap up riches] *arricchirsi, accumular ricchezze.*

FE'ATHERED, adj. *piumato, pien di piuma.*

He is well feathered, *aver gli arnioni ben coperti di grasso, esser ricco.*

FE'ATHERLESS, adj. *spiumacciato, senza piume.*

FE'ATHERY, adj. [clothes with feathers] *vestito di piume.*

FE'ATLY, adv. *galantemente, pulitamente, attillatamente, gentilmente, garbatamente.*

FE'ATNESS, s. [neatness] *galanteria, gentilezza, garbatezza,* s. f.

FE'ATURE, s. [a lineament of the face] *fattezza,* s. f. *lineamento,* s. m.

She has got excellent features, *ella ha fattezze vaghe.*

To FE'ATURE [to resemble in countenance] *aver somiglianza di fattezze.*

FE'ATURED, adj. [well featured] *che ha belle fattezze.*

FE'AVER, s. *febbre,* s. f. *meglio scritto* Fever.

To be sick of a feaver, *aver la febbre, febbricare.*

A burning feaver, *febbre ardente.*

A continual feaver, *febbre continua.*

A little feaver, *febbretta.*

Intermitting feaver, *febbre intermittente.*

FE'AVERISH, adj. *febbricante, febbricitante, febbricoso.*

To FEAZE [a sea term, that signifies to ravel out at the ends, speaking of any great rope] *sfilarsi.*

FE'AZING, s. *lo sfilarsi.*

To keep the cable from feazing, *far che la gomina non si sfili.*

To FEBRI'CITATE [to fall sick of a fever] *febbricare, febbricitare, esser travagliato dalla febbre.*

FE'BRIFUGE, s. [a medicine which cures an intermitting fever] *febbrifugo,* s. m. *medicamento per cacciar la febbre.*

FE'BRILE, adj. [constituting a fever] *febbrile.*

FE'BRUARY, s. [the second month of the year] *Febbrajo,* s. m. *il secondo mese dell' anno.*

FE'CES, or FE'CULENCE, s. [dregs, lees] *feccia,* s. f.

FE'CULENT, adj. [full of dregs] *fecciosо, pien di feccia.*

Féculent [loathsome] *fecciosо, fastidioso, lezioso, spiacevole, nauseoso.*

FE'CUND, adj. [fruitful] *fecondo, fertile.*

FECUNDA'TION, s. [the act of making prolifick] *il fecondare, il render fecondo.*

FECU'NDITY, s. [fruitfulness] *fecondità, fertilità,* s. f.

FED, adj. [from to feed] *nutrito.*

He is better fed than taught, *e meglio nutrito che instruito.*

To be well fed, *aver il ventre pieno.*

Fed, *è anche un preterito del verbo* to feed.

FE'DERARY, s. [a confederate, an accomplice] *un confederato, un complice.*

FEE, or FEES, s. [reward or wages given to one for the doing of his office] *mercede, paga che si da ad uno nell' esercitar il suo ufficio.*

A physician's fee, *quel che si paga al medico per ogni visita.*

To give a doctor his fee, *pagare il medico.*

Fees [vails] *mancia,* s. f.

Fee [in law, are all such lands which are held by perpetual right] *feudo.*

Fee-simple, or fee-absolute, *feudo assoluto, feudo di condizione feudale.*

Fee-tail [is a conditional estate] *feudo che non appartiene che a noi e a' nostri propri figliuoli.*

Fee-farm [land held of another in fee for ever to himself and his heirs, paying a certain yearly rent out of it] *censo livellario, o enfiteutico.*

To FEE [to pay the fees] *pagare.*

To fee the physician or the lawyer, *pagare il medico o l'avocato.*

To fee [to bribe] *corrompere, guadagnar con donativi, ugner le mani.*

FE'EBLE, adj. [weak] *debile, e debole, di poca forza, di poca possa, fievole, fiacco, fioco.*

To grow feeble, *debilitarsi, affievolirsi, divenir debole.*

FE'EBLENESS, s. [weakness] *debilità, debolezza, fiacchezza, fievolezza,* s. f. *languore,* s. m.

FE'EBLY, adv. *debilmente, e debolmente, fievolmente, fiaccamente.*

FEED, adj. [from to fee] *pagato.*

Feed [bribed] *corrotto, guadagnato con donativi.*

To FEED [to supply with food] *nutrire, nutricare, dare a mangiare, pascere.* pres. *nutrisco.*

He feeds him with nothing but milk, *non lo nutrisce che di latte, non li da a mangiare altro che latte.*

He feeds him with emptiness, *lo pasce di vento.*

To feed the cattle, *pascere il bestiame.*

To feed with vain hopes, *pascer di vane speranze.*

To feed a hawk, *imbeccare un falcone.*

The birds feed their young ones, *gli uccelli imbeccano i loro figliuoli.*

To feed the fire, *conservare il fuoco.*

To feed, *pascersi, nutrirsi, mangiare.*

Cattle feed upon grass, *il bestiame si pasce d'erba.*

He feeds upon nothing but herbs and roots, *non vive che d'erbe e radici, non mangia altro che erbette e radici.*

He feeds like a farmer [he eats with a good stomach] *mangia con buon appetito.*

To feed high, *trattarsi bene, far buona cera.*

'Tis cheaper to feed one's belly than one's eyes, *è più facile di contentare il ventre che gli occhi.*

FE'EDER, s. *mangiatore, quello che mangia.*

Feeder [he that feeds] *nutritore,* s. m. *che nutrisce.*

A dainty feeder, *un delicato, una delicata, che ama le delicatezze o i buoni bocconi.*

A greedy feeder, *un goloso, un ghiottone.*

FE'EDING, s. *nutrimento,* s. m. *il nutrire.*

High feeding, *buona cera.*

Feeding [pasture] *nutrimento, pascolo,* s. m. *nutritura,* s. f.

To FEEL [to be sensible of] *sentire.*

I feel a great pain in my side, *sento un gran dolore nel fianco.*

I feel a great cold in my hands, *sento gran freddo alle mani.*

To feel one beforehand [to feel his pulse about a business, to try him] *tastare, o scandagliar l'animo di qualcheduno.*

To feel [to touch] *toccare, tastare, palpeggiare.*

To feel one's pulse, *toccare il polso.*

To feel, *palpeggiare.*

To feel, verb neut. Ex. to feel soft, *esser morbido al tatto.*

To feel cold, *esser freddo.*

FE'ELING, s. [the sense of feeling] *il tatto.*

Fellow-feeling, *compassione, pietà,* s. f.

FEET, s. *piedi. E' il plurale di* foot.

FE'ETLESS, adj. [without feet] *senza piedi, privo di piedi.*

To FEIGN [to pretend, to make show of] *fingere, simulare, dissimulare, far vista.* pret. *finsi.*

To feign [to devise] *fingere, inventare, ritrovar di fantasia, trovare.*

FE'IGNED, adj. *finto, simulato, dissimulato, inventato, ritrovato, supposto.*

A feigned hatred, *odio coperto.*

A feigned name, *nome finto.*

A feigned treble [in musick] *un falsetto.*

A feigned matter, *una fizione, o finzione.*

Feigned holiness, *ippocrisia.*

FE'IGNEDLY, adv. *fintamente, simulatamente, coloratamente.*

FEINT, s. [disguise, false show] *finzione, simulazione, fizione,* s. f. *fingimento, colore,* s. m.

Feint [in fencing, is when an offer is made at one part, and a real pass at another] *finta, punta falsa, termine di scherma.*

FE'LANDERS [worms in hawks] *vermi che hanno i falconi.*

FE'LDIFARE, s. [a kind of bird] *spezie d'uccello.*

To FELI'CITATE [to greet, and make happy] *felicitare, far felice.*

FELI'CITATED, adj. *felicitato.*

FELI'CITY, s. [happiness] *felicità, prosperità, benavventuranza,* s. f.

FELL, *è un preterito del verbo* To fall.

Fell, adj. [fierce, cruel] *fello, malvagio, ingiusto, empio, crudele, scellerato.*
Fell, s. [skin of a beast] *pelle, pelliccia,* s. f.
Fell monger, *pellicciajo,* s. m.
To FELL [to strike or cut down] *tagliare, abbattere, mandare a terra, buttar giù.*
To fell a tree, *tagliare un albero.*
I shall fell you down, *vi butterò per terra.*
FE'LLABLE, adj. [which may be felled] *buono a tagliare.*
A fellable tree, *un albero buono a tagliare.*
FE'LLED, adj. *tagliato, abbattuto, buttato giù.*
FE'LLER, s. [one that hews down] *uno che taglia gli alberi, i boschi, e le legne.*
FE'LLOW, s. [a companion] *compagno, compagnone,* s. m.
Fellow-wort, *genziana,* s. f.
A fellow servant, *compagno nel servire.*
A fellow soldier, *un camerata, compagno in guerra.*
A good fellow, *un buon compagno, un buon compagnone.*
A bed fellow, *un campagno di letto.*
A fellow [in a college] *un collega, membro d'un collegio.*
A fellow commoner, *un campagno di tavola.*
Fellow subjects, *vassalli d'un medesimo principe.*
The fellows of a wheel [pieces of wood joined together to make the circle of a wheel] *pezzi che fanno il giro della ruota, i cantoni d'una ruota.*
To play the good fellow, *stare allegramente, darsi buon tempo, solazzarsi, far buona cera.*
A school-fellow, *un condiscepolo.*
Fellow [collegue in an office] *un collega*
Fellow [partner] *un sozio.*
He has not his fellow, *egli non ha il simile, o il pari.*
I lost the fellow to this glove, *ho perduto l'altro guanto.*
These shoes are not fellows, *queste scarpe non sono simili.*
Fellow, *è ancora un termine di disprezzo.*
What fellow is that? *che uomo è costui?*
What ails the fellow? *con chi l'ha questo minchione?*
Meddle with your own fellow, *trattate con pari vostri.*
A young fellow, *un giovanastro.*
An old fellow, *un vecchiaccio.*
A sorry fellow, *un uomo vile, un uomo da niente, un briccone.*
A base fellow, *un infame, uno scellerato, un furfante.*
A saucy fellow, *uno sfacciato, uno sfrontato.*
A covetous fellow, *un taccagno, una piattola, un avaro.*
To FE'LLOW. *v.* To match.
FE'LLOWSHIP, s. [company, partnership] *compagnia, società,* s. f.

To join in fellowship with one, *entrare in società con uno, associarsi con uno.*
Fellowship in the university [the place of a member of a college in the university] *il posto d'un membro d'un collegio in una università.*
FE'LLY, s. *ancone di ruota.*
The fellies of a wheel, *gli anconi d'una ruota.*
Felly, adv. *crudelmente, da fellone.*
FELLY-MINDED, adj. [cruel] *fello, crudele, malvagio.*
FE'LLNESS, s. [cruelty] *fellonia, scelleratezza, crudeltà, ferocia,* s. f.
FE'LO DE SE [a law term, one who lays a violent hand upon himself] *uno che si da la morte, o che s'ammazza da se stesso.*
FE'LON, s. [a malefactor, who commits a felony] *un fellone,* s. m. *un malfattore degno di morte fellonesca,* s. f.
Felon [whitlow] *panereccio,* s. m. *una postema che nasce nelle dita delle mani alle radici delle ugne.*
FELO'NIOUS, adj. *fellonesco, di fellonia, pien di fellonia.*
FE'LLONIOUSLY, adv. *fellonescamente, da fellone.*
FE'LONY, s. [an offence that is in degree next to petty-treason, and comprehends several particulars] *fellonia, delitto capitale.*
FELT, *è un preterito del verbo* To feel.
FELT, s. [wool used in making of hats] *feltro,* s. m. *lana da far cappelli.*
Felt [that saddlers use to stuff their saddles with] *borra, cimatura, o tosatura di pelo di panni lani.*
A felt [a hat] *un cappello di lana.*
Felt-maker, *cappellajo,* s. m.
FELU'CCA, s. [a sort of sea vessel] *una filuga.*
FE'MALE, s. *la femmina.*
The male and female, *il maschio e la femmina.*
Female, adj [of the she kind] *femminale, femminino.*
The female sex, *il sesso femminino.*
FEME-CO'VERT, s. [a law word for a married woman] *una donna maritata.*
FE'MININE, adj. [of the female kind] *femmineo, femminino, femminesco.*
The feminine gender, *il genere femminino.*
FE'MORAL, adj. [belonging to the thigh] *appartenente alla coscia.*
FEN, s. [moorish ground] *pantano, lagume, palude, padule,* s. m. *maremma,* s. f.
Fen cricket, s. [an insect] *grillotalpa,* s. m.
FENCE, s. [an hedge or inclosure] *siepe, chiusura,* s. f. *riparo,* s. m.
Fence [defence] *schermo, riparo,* s. m. *difesa,* s. f.
There's no fence against slander, *contro la maldicenza non c'è riparo.*
A fence of pales, *una palificata, palizzata.*
A coat of fence [a coat of mail] *un giaco, arme di dosso fatta di maglie di ferro.*
To FENCE [to inclose or hedge about] *chiudere, circondare, siepare, cigner di siepe.*

To fence [to fortify] *fortificare, munire.* pres. *munisco.*
To fence [to defend] *difendere, proteggere.* pret. *protessi.*
To fence [to fight with swords] *schermire, giuocar di spada, far di scherma.*
FE'NCED, adj. *chiuso, circondato, siepato.*
Fenced [fortified, defended] *munito, fortificato, difeso.*
FENCE MONTH [a month in which it is unlawful to hunt in the forest, because in that month the female deer fawn; it begins fifteen days before Midsummer] *il mese nel quale è proibito di cacciare nella foresta, perchè in quel mese le damme figliano; comincia dai 15 di giugno fin ai 15 di luglio.*
FE'NCER, s. *schermidore, o schermitore, che schermisce.*
FE'NCING, s. *il chiudere con siepe.* v. To fence.
Fencing school, *scuola di scherma.*
Fencing master, *schermidore, mastro di scherma.*
To FEND [to keep off] *parare, impedire, schivare, scansare, sfuggire, schifare.* pres. *impedisco, sfuggo.*
To fend off a blow, *parare un colpo.*
FE'NDER, s. [an iron plate to set before a fire-grate] *arnese di ferro che si mette avanti una graticola da fuoco, per impedire che le ceneri e i carboni non caschino fuor del cammino.*
FE'NNEL, s. [an herb] *finocchio,* s. m. *erba nota.*
Hog's fennel, *finocchio porcino, peucedanno,* s. m.
Fennel-flower, *git, gittajone, gitterone,* s. m. *spezie d'erba.*
FE'NNIGREEK, s. [an herb] *fiengreco,* s. m. *spezie d'erba.*
FE'NNISH, adj. [of or belonging to a fen] *di palude.*
FE'NNY, adj. [full of fens] *paludoso, pantanoso, melmoso.*
FE'ODAL, adj. [of or belonging to a fee] *feudale, di feudo.*
FE'ODARY, or FE'UDARY, s. [an officer belonging to the court of wards and liveries, whose office is to survey and value the land of the wards] *ufficiale della corte nominata* court of wards, *che ha l'incombenza di valutare, e tener conto de' feudi del re.*
FE'ODATARY, s. [a tenant holding his estate by feudal service] *un feudatario.*
To FE'OFF, v. To infeoff.
FEOFFE'E, s. [he to whom a feoffment is made] *colui a chi si fa una donazione per lui e suoi eredi.*
Feoffee in trust, *fidecommessario.*
FE'OFFMENT, s. [any gift or grant in fee simple, that is, to a man and his heirs for ever] *donazione fatta a qualcheduno per lui e suoi eredi.*
Feoffment in trust, *fidecommesso,* s. m.
FE'OFFER, s. [the giver of a feoffment] *donatore.*
FE'RITY, s. [cruelty, fierceness] *ferità, bestialità, crudeltà,* s. f.
FERM, v. Farm.
Ferm [a hole] *un buco, un pertugio.*

FE'RMENT, s. [leaven, yeſt] *liévito, fermento*, s. m.

To FERME'NT [to leaven] *lievitare.*

To fermént [to work, as beer, ale, &c.] *fermentare.*

FERMENTA'TION, s. [a fermenting or working] *fermentazione*, s. f. *il fermentare.*

FERME'NTED, adj. *lievitato, levitato, fermentato, e formentato.*

FERN, s. [a plant] *felce; ſorta di pianta.*

FERO'CIOUS, adj. [ſavage, fierce, ravenous, rapacious [*feroce, ſelvaggio, fiero, fero, crudele, rapace.*

FERO'CITY, s. [fierceneſs, cruelneſs] *ferocità, fierezza, ferocia*, s. f.

FE'RREL, s. [a piece of iron or braſs to be put at the end of a cane] *picciol ferro nel qual ſi mette il piè del baſtone.*

The ferrel of a cane, *il ferro d' una canna d' India.*

FE'RRET, s. [a little creature like a weeſel] *furetto*, s. m. *animaletto poco maggior della donnola; e de' conigli proprio nemico.*

Ferret [a ſort of ribbon] *ſpezie di naſtro metà ſetà e metà filo.*

To FE'RRET [to ſearch out narrowly] *cercare, ricercare, rivilicare, ricercar con diligenza o minutamente.*

To ferret [to vex] one, *moleſtare, tormentare, importunare alcuno.*

FE'RRETTED, adj. *cercato, ricercato, rivilicato, moleſtato, tormentato, importunato.*

FE'RRIAGE, s. *paſſaggio*, s. m. *paſſamento d' un fiume.*

FE'RRY, s. [a place where horſes, coaches, &c. are conveyed over a river] *barca in cui ſi paſſano cavalli, carrozze, &c. ſopra un fiume.*

A ferry boat, *una ſcafa.*

A ferry man, *l' uomo che guida la ſcafa, traghettatore*, s. m.

To FE'RRY over, *traghettare un fiume nella ſcafa.*

To ferry over a horſe, *traghettare un cavallo in una ſcafa.*

FERRY'D OVER, adj. *traghettato.*

FE'RTILE, adj. [fruitful] *fertile, fruttuoſo, fecondo, abbondante.*

A fertile country, *un paeſe fertile.*

FERTI'LENESS, } s. [fruitfulneſs,
FERTI'LITY, } plentifulneſs] *fertilezza, fertilità, fecondità, abbondanza*, s. f.

To FERTI'LISE [to make fruitful] *fecondare, render fecondo, fertile, o abbondante.*

FE'RVENCY, s. [earneſtneſs, vehemency] *ferventezza, caldezza*, s. f. *fervore, zelo*, s. m.

FE'RVENT, adj. [hot, vehement] *fervente, fervido, ſollecito, veemente.*

A fervent prayer, *preghiera fervente.*

Very fervent, *ferventiſſimo, fervidiſſimo.*

FE'RVENTLY, adv. *ferventemente, fervidamente, ardentemente.*

FE'RVID, adj. [fervent] *fervido, fervente, ſollecito, veemente.*

FE'RULA, s. [a flat wooden inſtrument to chaſtiſe boys at ſchool] *ferza, ſferza*, s. f.

FE'RVOUR, s. [fervency, ardour] *fervore, affetto, zelo*, s. m. *ferventezza, caldezza*, s. f.

FE'SCUE, s. [a pointer uſed by children in reading] *fuſcello, fuſcellino, fruſcolo*, s. m.

FE'SSE, s. [one of the honourable ordinaries in heraldry, repreſenting a broad belt or girdle of honour] *faſcia*, s. f.

To FE'STER [to putrify] *infiſtolire, impoſtemire, far poſtema.* pref. *infiſtoliſco, impoſtemiſco.*

FE'STERED, adj. *infiſtolito, impoſtemito.*

FESTINA'TION, s. [haſte, hurry] *fretta, ſollecitudine*, s. f.

FE'STIVAL, adj. [belonging to an holiday] *feſtivo, feſta, di feſta, da feſta.*

A feſtival, s. [a ſolemnity] *feſtività, giorno feſtivo, ſolemnità*, s. f.

FESTI'VITY, s. [mirth, rejoicing] *allegrezza, letizia*, s. f. *gaudio, giubilo*, s. m.

Feſtivity [a feſtival day] *giorno feſtivo, ſolennità.*

FE'STIVONS, adj. [jocund, jovial, merry] *giocondo, feſtoſo, giocoſo, lieto, allegro, feſtevole, dilettoſo, giojoſo.*

FESTO'ON, s. [a garland or border of flowers or leaves, engraven or emboſſed works, or in architecture] *feſtone*, s. m.

FETCH, s. [ſubtlety, ſly pretence, a trick] *ſottigliezza, aſtuzia, induſtria*, s. f. *tiro, giro, rigiro, ſutterfugio, artificio*, s. m.

To FETCH [to go to bring a thing] *andare a cercare, portare.*

Fetch me my ſword, *andate per la mia ſpada, portatemi la mia ſpada.*

To fetch a compaſs, *fare un giro.*

To fetch a walk, *fare una ſpaſſeggiata.*

To fetch one's breath, *reſpirare, ſpirare, prender reſpiro.*

To fetch a blow, *portare un colpo.*

To fetch a ſigh, *ſoſpirare, mandar fuora un ſoſpiro.*

To fetch a leap, *fare un ſalto, ſaltare.*

To fetch away, *portar via.*

To fetch up, *portar ſu.*

To fetch down, *porta giù.*

To fetch in, *portar dentro.*

To fetch out, *portar fuora*

To fetch over [to cheat] *ingannare, mariuolare, acchiappare, fare un tiro.*

To fetch off, *levare, levar via.*

To fetch off the filth, *levar via la ſporcizia.*

To fetch one off of his opinion, *far cangiar conſiglio o parere ad uno.*

To fetch up [to vomit] *recere, vomitare.*

FE'TCHED, adj. *cercato, portato. v.* To fetch.

FE'TID, adj. [ſtinking] *fetido, puzzolento, fetidoſo.*

FE'TLOCK, s. [the hair that grows behind on horſes feet] *quelli peli che naſcono nel garretto dei cavalli.*

Fetlock-joint, *garetto*, s. m.

To FE'TTER [to put in fetters] *inceppare, metter i ferri a' piedi.*

FE'TTERED, adj. *che ha i ferri ai piedi.*

FE'TTERS, s. [irons to chain the legs of malefactors] *ferri, ceppi, catene.*

Fetters for horſes, *paſtoje.*

Fetters [ſlavery] *catene, ſchiavitù.*

To FE'TTLE [to do trifling buſineſs] *badaluccare, far coſe di poca o nulla importanza.*

FE'TUS, s. [any animal in embrio; any thing yet in the womb] *feto.*

FEUD, s. [quarrel, contention] *uggia, nimicizia, riſſa.*

To create fueds in the ſtate, *ſuſcitare diviſioni nello ſtato, ſeminar diſcordie.*

Feud-bote [a recompence for engaging in a fued or faction] *quella mercede che ſi da ad uno che abbraccia, o s'intromette in qualche conteſa.*

FEU'DAL, adj. *v.* Feodal.

FE'VER, s. [a diſeaſe] *febbre.*

To FE'VER [to put into a fever] *cagionar la febbre, dar la febbre.*

FE'VERISH, } adj. [troubled with a
FE'VEROUS, } fever] *che ha febbre.*

FE'VERFEW, s. [an herb good againſt fevers] *matricale*, s. m. *erba nota.*

FEW, adj [ſmall in number] *poco.*

In few words, *in poche parole.*

In few days, *fra pochi giorni.*

A few, s. *un piccolo numero.*

FE'WEL, s. [any thing good to burn] *tutto ciò che ſerve a mantenere il fuoco.*

To add fewel to the fire, *giugner legna al fuoco, arroger male a male.*

FE'WER, adj. *comparativo di* Few, *meno.*

I have fewer than you, *ne ho meno di voi.*

FE'WMETS, or FE'WMISHING, s. [the dung of deer] *ſterco di cervo.*

FE'WNESS, s. [a ſmall number] *piccolo numero.*

FI'ANTS, s. [the dung of a fox or badger] *ſterco di volpe, o di taſſo.*

FIB, s. [lie] *menzogna, cantafavola, finzione bugia*, s. f.

To FIB [to tell a fib; a ſofter expreſſion for to tell a lie] *dire una menzogna, mentire.*

You fib, *voi volete la baja, voi non dite davvero.*

FI'BBER, s. *un bugiardo, una bugiarda.*

FI'BRES, s. [the threads or hair-like ſtrings of muſcles, veins, roots, plants, &c.] *fibra*, s. f. *che ne' muſcoli, e in altre parti dell' animale, ha potenza di naturalmente contraerſi.*

FI'BROUS, adj. [full of fibres] *fibroſo, che ha fibre.*

FI'CKLE, adj. [inconſtant, variable] *variabile, mutabile, inſtabile, incoſtante, mobile, volubile, leggiero.*

FI'CKLENESS, s. *inſtabilità, incoſtanza, volubilità, leggierezza*, s. f.

FI'CTION, s. [a feigned thing] *finzione, invenzione, vanità*, s. f.

FICTI'TIOUS, adj. [feigned, fabulous] *fittizio, finto, inventato, favoloſo*

FI'DDLE, s. [a muſical inſtrument] *violino*, s. m. *ſtrumento muſicale di corde.*

To play upon the fiddle, *suonar il violino.*
Fiddle-ſtring, *corda da violino.*
Fiddle-ſtick, *archetto*, s. m. *ſtrumento col quale ſi ſuona il violino.*
I care not a fiddle-ſtick [or a ſtraw] *non me ne curo punto.*
A fiddle-ſtick [ſpoken by way of contempt] *begattelle, baje.*
A fiddle-faddle, *baje, bagattelle, ciancie, cianciafruſcole, fraſcherie.*
To FI'DDLE [to play upon the fiddle] *ſuonare il violino.*
To fiddle all the day long, *ſuonare il violino dalla mattina fino alla ſera.*
FI'DDLER, s. *ſonator di violino. Vocabolo per lo più di diſprezzo.*
FI'DDLING, s. *il ſuonar il violino.*
Fiddling, s. Ex. a fiddling man [a man that has fiddling ways with him] *un muſone, un perdigiorno, uno ſcioperato.*
A fiddling buſineſs [a buſineſs of nothing] *faccenda frivola, di poca importanza.*
To be fiddling up and down, *andar e venire, andare ſu, e giù, qua e la, per der il tempo.*
FIDE'LITY, s. [faithfulneſs] *fedeltà, lealtà*, s. f.
To FIDGE } [to be continually moving up and down,
To FI'DGET } to ſtir up and down] *dimenarſi, agitarſi, andar qua e la, muoverſi in qua e in là.*
FI'DGING, adj. Ex. to ſit fidging, *dimenarſi, agitarſi, muoverſi.*
FIDU'CIARY, s. [a truſtee] *depoſitario, fidecommiſſario.*
FIEF, s. [a fee] *un feudo.*
FIELD, s. [a piece of ground for tillage] *campo, prato*, s. m.
A fruitful field, *un campo fertile.*
Fields in a city, *piazze*
Fields for armies, *campagna.*
To take the field, *uſcire in campagnà*
Field piece [cannon] *un pezzo di campagna.*
We won the field [we remained maſters of the field] *noi reſtammo padroni del campo di battaglia.*
An army in the field, *oſte campale.*
To challenge one to the field, *sfidare uno a conteſa.*
Field [fight] *combattimento, conteſa, battaglia campale.*
A field was fought, *vennero a giornata.*
A field fight, or field battle, *giornata, o battaglia campale.*
Field mouſe, *ſorcio di campo.*
FIELD [in heraldry] *campo*; *la ſuperficie dello ſcudo. Vocabolo d' araldería.*
Field-marſhal, s. *mareſciallo di campo.*
FIEND, s. [fury, evil ſpirit] *una furia, un demone, uno ſpirito maligno.*
A fiend [foe] *un nemico.*
FIERCE, adj. [cruel, ſtern] *fiero, crudele, fero, efferato, beſtiale, feroce, terribile.*
A tyger is a fierce creature, *la tigre è una beſtia feroce.*
He is a fierce man, *egli è un uomo beſtiale.*
A fierce fight, *un crudel combattimento.*
Fierce [boiſterous] *impetuoſo.*
Fierce [immoderate] *ſmoderato, eceſſivo.*
FI'ERCELY, adv. *fieramente, crudelmente, ferocemente, eceſſivamente.*
FI'ERCENESS, s. *ferità, ferocità, fierezza, crudeltà, ferocia.*
The fierceneſs of a tyger, *la ferocità d' una tigre.*
FI'ERINESS, s. [hot qualities, heat, acrimony] *ardore, qualità ardente, acrimonia.*
FI'ERY, adj. [of fire] *igneo, che ha qualità di fuoco.*
The fiery meteors, *le meteori ignee.*
A fiery man, *un uomo ardente, violento, furioſo.*
Fiery nature, *ardor naturale.*
FIFE, s. [a pipe blown to the drum] *piffero*, s. m. *ſtrumento muſicale di fiato.*
FIFTE'EN, s. *quindici.*
FIFTE'ENTH, adj. *decimo quinto.*
FIFTH, adj. *quinto.*
FI'FTIETH, adj. *cinquanteſimo.*
FI'FTY, s. *cinquanta.*
FIG, s. [a fruit well known] *fico*, s. m. *frutto noto.*
Fig [a diſeaſe in horſes] *fico, malore, che viene nel piede a' cavalli.*
I don't care a fig for him, *non lo ſtimo un fico, mi rido di lui.*
The firſt figs that grow, *fichi fiori.*
A fig-tree, *un fico, albero che produce il fico.*
A wild fig tree, *un fico ſalvatico.*
An orchard of fig-trees, *un fichereto, un ficheto.*
Fig-pecker, s. [a ſort of bird that feeds on figs] *beccafico*, s. m.
Fig wort, s [a ſort of herb] *ſcrofularia*, s. f. *ſpezie d' erba.*
To FIG up and down, *andar qua e la, ſcorrer qua e la, ſu e giù.*
To fig one in the crown with a ſtory, *ficcar qualche coſa in teſta ad uno, metterli un cocomero in corpo.*
FIGARY, s. [freak] *fantaſia*, s. f. *capriccio, ghiribizzo*, s. m.
He took a figary to do it, *gli venne fantaſia di farlo.*
He has many a figary, *egli ha molti grilli in teſta.*
FIGHT, s. [a combat, an engagement] *combattimento, conflitto*, s. m. *pugna, battaglia, miſchia, ruffa*, s. f.
A ſea fight. *combattimento navale.*
A land fight, *una battaglia.*
A cock fight, *combattimento di galli.*
To FIGHT [to combat] *combattere, far battaglia inſieme, batterſi.*
To fight a duel, *batterſi in duello, duellare.*
To fight the enemy, *batter l' inimico, preſentar la battaglia al nemico.*
To fight hand to hand [one man againſt another] *batterſi a corpo a corpo.*
To prepare to fight, *prepararſi alla battaglia.*
To fight one's way to the crown, *farſi ſtrada alla corona*
To fight it out, *decidere una conteſa colle armi.*
FI'GHTER, s. *combattitore*, s. m. *combattitrice*, s. f.
FI'GHTING, s. *il combattere, combattimento.*
I hate fighting, *non amo a battermi.*
Fighting, adj. *combattente.*
A hundred thouſand fighting men, *cento mila combattenti.*
Fights, s. [in a ſhip, are waſte cloths which hang round about a ſhip in a fight, to hinder the men from being ſeen by the enemy] *poſticcia, paveſata*, s. f. *pezzo di tela che circonda una nave da guerra in un combattimento per fare che il nemico non veda gli uomini.*
FI'GMENT, s. [a fiction, a ſtory] *finzione, invenzione*, s. f.
FIGME'NTAL, adj. *immaginario, immaginato.*
FIGURA'TION, s. [imaginary conceit] *figurazione, immaginazione, chimera*, s. f.
FIGU'RATIVE, adj. ſpoken by way of figure] *figurativo, che rappreſenta ſotto figura.*
Figurative expreſſions, *eſpreſſioni figurative.*
FIGU'RATIVELY, adv. [in a figurative ſenſe] *figurativamente, figuralmente, figuratamente.*
FI'GURE, s. [repreſentation] *figura, rappreſentazione*, s. f.
Figure [faſhion, ſhape] *figura, forma, ſembianza, immagine*, s. f. *aſpetto.*
Figure [a ſpace terminated on all parts by lines] *figura, quella che contenuta da più linee, racchiude qualche ſpazio.*
Figure [in arithmetick, one of the nine digits or numerical characters, as 1, 2, 3, &c.] *figura, il ſegno de' numeri dell' abbaco.*
Figure [cut] *figura, immagine, impronta di qualunque coſa ſcolpita, o dipinta.*
Figure [in aſtrology, is a ſcheme or draught of the face of heaven] *figura, coſtituzione del cielo, diſegnata in piano.*
Figure [in diſcourſe, an extraordinary way of ſpeaking, very different from the common and natural] *figura, quel modo di favellare, che s'allontana del comun uſo.*
Grammatical figures, *figure gramaticali.*
Figure [appearance] *figura, apparenza.*
To make ſome figure in the world, *far figura nel mondo, sfeggiare.*
To FI'GURE [to repreſent] *figurare, dar figura, ſcolpire, dipingere.* pref. *ſcolpiſco.* pret. *dipinſi.*
FI'GURED, adj. *figurato, ſcolpito, dipinto.*
Figured velvet, *velluto figurato, con figure.*
A figured dance, *un ballo figurato.*
FILA'CEOUS, adj. [conſiſting of threads] *filaceo, fatto di fila.*
FI'LAMENTS, s. [fibres] *fibre.*
FI'LANDERS, s. [a ſort of worms, ſmall as threads which lie in the reins of hawks] *filandre*, s. f. pl. *vermicciuoli da' quali ſono infeſtati i falconi, e che per aſſomigliarſi ai fili di ſottiliſſimo refe, ſon nominati filandre.*
FI'LBERT, s. [the beſt ſort of ſmall nuts] *avellana, nocciuola*, s. f.

A filbert-tree, s. *nocciuolo*, s. m. *albero che produce le avellane.*

To FILCH [to steal slily] *truffare, mariolare, barattare, fraudare, ingannare.*

FI'LCHER, s. *truffatore, mariuolo, barattiere, baro, giuntatore, furbo*, s. m.

FI'LCHING, s. *truffa, furberia, mariuoleria, baratteria; fraude*, s. f. *inganno*, s. m.

FILE, s. [row] *fila*, s. f.

A file of soldiers, *una fila di soldati.*

File [a tool to work iron, &c. with] *lima*, s. f. *strumento d'acciajo dentato, che serve per assottigliare e pulire ferro, o altre materie.*

A soft or smooth file, *lima dolce, o lima sorda.*

File [a wire upon which loose papers are hung] *filo*, s. m.

File [among fencers, a sort of sword without edges, with a button at the point] *fioretto*, s. m. *spezie di spada per far di scherma.*

File [rank] *fila, linea*, s. f. *ordine*, s. m.

A file of pearls, *filo di perle, vezzo, collana.*

File-dust, *limatura.*

A file leader [the head man of a file] *capo fila.*

File after file, *alla sfilata.*

To FILE [to work with a file] *limare, assottigliare, o pulir colla lima.*

To file up, *infilzare.*

To file off [to file asunder] *tagliare colla lima.*

To file off [a military phrase, to march in length by files] *sfilare, andare alla sfilata,*

The troops begun to file off, *le truppe cominciarono a sfilare.*

FI'LED, adj. *limato*, v. To file.

FI'LEMOT, s. [a brown or yellow-brown colour] *colore che è tra giallo e bruno; giallosçuro, giallonero.*

FI'LER, s. *limatore*, s. m.

FI'LIAL, adj. [belonging to a son] *filiale, di figliuolo, da figliuola.*

FILIA'TION, s. [descent from father to son] *filiazione*, s. f. *l'esser figliuolo.*

FI'LINGS, s. *limatura.*

To FILL [to make full] *empire, riempire.*

To fill a bottle, *empire un fiasco.*

Fill me some drink, *datemi a bere.*

To fill, verb neut. *empirsi, riempirsi.*

The cask fills, *la botte s'empie.*

The town begins to fill, *la città comincia a popolarsi.*

To fill one's belly, *empirsi il ventre, saziarsi, mangiare a crepa pelle, satollarsi.*

I filled my belly with wine, *ho bevuto del vino a crepa pelle.*

To fill up, *empire.*

To fill up the number, *compire il numero.*

To fill up a place with honour, *esercitar una carica con onore.*

FI'LLED, or FI'LLED UP, adj. *empito*, v. To fill.

FYLLER, s. [any thing that fills up room without use] *ogni cosa che occupa un luogo senza esser d'ultile; ingombro.*

Filler, *uno che empie vasi.*

FI'LLET, s. [hair-lace] *intrecciatojo*, s. m.

Fillet of veal, *sfasciatura di vitella.*

FI'LLING, s. *l'empire.*

Filling, adj. *che sazia, che satolla.*

A filling sort of drink, *una bevanda che gonfia.*

FI'LLIP, s. *colpo d'un dito, che scocchi di sotto un altro dito, biscottino.*

To FI'LLIP one, *dare un colpo ad uno con un dito che scocchi di sotto a un altro dito, dar un biscottino.*

FI'LLY, s. [a mare-colt] *una giumenta giovane, una puledra.*

FILM, s. [a fine skin enwrapping the brain, and several other parts of the body] *tunica, membrana*, s. f.

The film of the brain, *pericranio, la membrana che circonda il cranio.*

FI'LMY, adj. *membranoso.*

FILESE'LLA, s. [a kind of coarse silk] *bavella*, s. f.

FI'LTER, s. *un filtro, un colatojo.*

To FI'LTER [to strain through a bag] *colare, filtrare.*

FILTH, s. [dirt] *porcheria, sporcheria, sporcizia, schifezza*, s. f.

FI'LTHILY, adv. *sporcamente, schifamente.*

FI'LTHINESS, s. *schifezza, porcheria, sporcizia, sporcheria*, s. f.

FI'LTHY, adj. *sudicio, sporco, schifo, lordo.*

Filthy discourse, *discorso osceno.*

Filthy lucre, *lucro disonesto*

A filthy deal, *molto, moltissimo.*

To FI'LTRATE, *filtrare, colare.*

FILTRA'TION, s. [a straining a liquor thro' paper] *colamento*, s. m. *il colare.*

FI'LTRED, adj. *colato.*

FIMBLE-HEMP, *quelle piante di canapa che non producon seme.*

FIN, s. [quill or wing of a fish] *pinna, alia de' pesci.*

FI'NABLE, adj. [liable to be fined] *soggetto ad ammenda.*

FI'NAL, adj. [last, that concludes and makes an end] *finale, ultimo, estremo.*

A final cause, *causa finale.*

FI'NALLY, adv. *finalmente, ultimamente, in fine.*

FINA'NCE, s. [the treasures or revenues of the French king] *le finanze, il tesoro del re di Francia.*

FI'NANCER, s. [an officer of the finances] *ufficiale delle finanze.*

FI'NARY, s. [the second forge of an iron mill] *ferriera*, s. f.

FINCH, s. *questa parola significa diverse sorti d'uccelli.*

A gold-finch, *un cardellino.*

A bull-finch, *monachino, monaco*, s. m. *sorta d'uccello col becco rosso.*

A thistle-finch, *calderino, calderugio*, s. m.

A chaff finch, *fringuello, pincione*, s. m.

To FIND [to discover what before laid concealed] *trovare, pervenire a uello che si cerca.*

To find one guilty, *trovar alcuno colpevole, condannarlo.*

To find one's self well or ill, *trovarsi bene, o male.*

To find fault, or to find amiss, *trovar a dire, riprendere, criticare.*

His trade does not find him bread, *il suo mestiere non lo mantiene in pane.*

To find one business, *dar dell' impiego ad uno.*

To find [to see, to perceive] *trovare, conoscere, vedere.*

I find by him, or by his discourse, that, *vedo dal suo discorso, che.*

He found by me that I was not a fool, *li feci conoscere, o vedere, che non ero uno sciocco.*

You shall find by me upon all occasions that I am your friend, *in ogni occasione vi farò conoscere che son vostro amico.*

I shall make you find your legs, *vi farò camminar ben io.*

I can't find in my heart to leave you, *non mi basta l'animo di lasciarvi.*

To find out, *trovare, ritrovare, inventare.*

To find out an expedient, *trovar qualche espediente.*

To find out the truth, *scoprir la verità, venire in cognizione della verità.*

I found out his design, *ho scoperto, ho penetrato il suo disegno.*

FI'NDER, s. *trovatore*, s. m. *trovatrice*, s. f.

A fault finder, *un censore, un critico.*

A gold-finder, *un votacessi.*

FI'NDY, adj. [plump, weighty, firm, solid] *grave, ripieno, pesante, fermo, sodo, solido.*

FINE, adj. [handsome] *bello, vago.*

Fine [spruce] *bello, pulito, attillato.*

Fine [the contrary of coarse] *fino, fine.*

Fine [excellent] *bello, eccellente, ottimo, esquisito, divino.*

A fine man, *un bell' uomo.*

A fine woman, *una bella donna.*

Fine weather, *bel tempo.*

He always goes very fine, *egli è sempre ben vestito*

Fine cloaths, *belli abiti.*

Fine cloth, *panno fino.*

You have a fine time of it, *voi siete molto felice.*

Fine, s. [a penalty, or amends made in money for an offence] *ammenda, multa.*

To pay the fine, *pagar l'ammenda.*

Fine [what a man pays when he takes a lease] *quella somma che si paga da uno per l'affitto.*

In fine, adv. [at last] *in fine, finalmente, alla per fine.*

To FINE [to purge from dregs] *purgare, raffinare, affinare, chiarire*, pres. *chiarisco.*

To fine a liquor, *chiarire un liquore.*

To fine a metal, *raffinare un metallo.*

To fine [to amerce] *condannare all' amenda.*

To fine [to pay a fine] *pagar l'ammenda.*

FINED, adj. *purgato, raffinato, affinato, chiarito; condannato all' ammenda.*

To Fine-draw [to renter] *sarcire*, pref. *sarcisco.*
Fine-drawer, s. *sarcitore*, s. m.
Fine-drawing, s. *sarcitura*; s. f.
Fine-drawn, adj. *sarcito.*
Fi'nely, adv. *bene, molto bene, finamente, finemente, pulitamente, garbatamente, con bella maniera, con bel garbo, ottimamente, per eccellenza.*
Indeed it is finely done, *in vero è ben fatto.*
Fi'neness, s. *finezza, bellezza, vaghezza, leggiadria, garbatezza.*
Finer [comparative of fine] *più bello, più fino.*
Finer, or Finor, *v.* Finor.
Fi'nery, s. [fine attire] *abbigliamento, addobbo, ornamento*, s. m.
Fi'new, s. [mouldiness] *muffa*, s. f.
Fi'newed, adj. *muffato.*
Fi'nger, s. [a member of the hand] *dito*, s. m. *uno de' cinque membretti che derivano dalla mano. Nel numero del più, dita*, s. f.
The fore-finger [the finger next to the thumb] *il dito indice.*
The ring finger, *il dito dove si porta l'annello.*
He has more in his little finger than you have in your whole body, *il suo dito piccolo val più che non tutto il tuo corpo.*
To have, or to know any thing at one's fingers end [to know it perfectly] *avere una cosa su per le dita, saperla a mena dito.*
You will do it with a wet finger, *voi lo farete facilmente.*
To have a finger in the pie [to be concerned in any thing] *aver parte, o esser complice in qualche cosa.*
I'll make you feel my fingers, *vi farò sentire quanto pesano le mie mani, vi bastonerò.*
To Fi'nger [to handle] *maneggiare, toccare, e trattar colle mani.*
You shall finger none of my money, *voi non averete de' miei quattrini.*
He fingers all the king's money, *maneggia tutto'l denaro del re, tutto'l danaro del re gli passa per le mani.*
Fi'ngered, adj. *maneggiato, toccato, o trattato colle mani.*
Light-fingered, *inclinato a rubare.*
To be light fingered, *suonar con leggiadria.*
Fi'nical, adj. [nice, conceited, affected] *affettato, schifo, ritroso, contegnoso.*
Fi'nicalness, s. [niceness] *affettazione, squisitezza, schifiltà, ritrosia*, s. f.
To Fi'nish [to end, to make an end] *finire, terminare, condurre, a fine, dar compimento, compire*, pref. *finisco, compisco.*
To finish a picture [to put the last hand to it] *finire un ritratto, darli l'ultima mano.*
Fini'shed, adj. *finito, terminato, compito.*
Fi'nisher, s. *finitore*, s. m. *che finisce.*
The finisher of law [the hangman] *giustiziere, e giustiziero, carnefice, manigoldo, boja*, s. m.

Fi'nishing, s. *finimento*, s. m. *il finire.*
Fini'te, adj. [which has fixed and determined bounds] *finito, terminato, che ha fine.*
A finite being, *un ente finito.*
Fi'nless, adj. [without fins] *senza pinne, privo di pinne.*
Fi'nlike, adj. *fatto a mo' di pinna.*
Fi'ntoed, adj. [palmipedous; having a membrane between the toes] *di piè membranoso, come l'oche, l'anitre, e simili.*
Fi'nny, adj. *che ha pinne.*
The silver finny race [a poetical expression for fishes] *i pesci, gli abitatori dell' acque.*
Fir, or Fir Tree, s. *abete, e abeto*, s. m.
A forest of fir-trees, *abetajo*, s. f. *selva d'abeti.*
Fire, s. [one of the four elements] *fuoco*, s. m. *uno de' quattro elementi.*
The elementary fire, *il fuoco elementare.*
A wood fire, or a coal fire, *un fuoco di legna, o di carbone.*
A bonefire, *fuoco lavorato, fuoco artificiato.*
To make a fire, *fare del fuoco.*
To set a house on fire, *metter il fuoco ad una casa.*
A great fire, *un gran fuoco, un incendio.*
St. Anthony's fire [a kind of swelling, full of heat and redness] *risipola*, s. f.
St. Helen's fire, *fuoco sant' Elmo, spezie di meteora.*
To take fire, *pigliar fuoco, cominciare ad ardere.*
To strike fire, *batter del fuoco.*
To give fire to a gun, *dar fuoco ad un cannone, spararlo.*
Fire fan, *un parafuoco.*
A fire arm, *arme da fuoco.*
A fire ship, *un brulotto.*
A fire-lock, *un archibuso, uno schioppo.*
The fire-pan, *il focone, quella parte dell' armi da fuoco dove si mette il polverino per dar fuoco.*
A fire brand, *un tizzone, un tizzo.*
A fire-brand of sedition, *autor di sedizione*
The fire-tongs, *le mollette.*
A fire-shovel, *una paletta da fuoco.*
Fire-fork, *un forcone.*
Fire-work, *fuoco lavorato, o artifiziato.*
Fire-wood, *delle legna.*
Fire-drake [a fire sometimes flying in the night like a dragon] *dragon volante, sorta di meteora.*
A fire-ball, *palla di fuoco, una granata.*
Fire-boot, or fire-bote [fuel for necessary occasions, which by common law any tenant may take out of the lands granted to him] *le legna che son concesse dalla legge ad un fittajuolo per suo proprio uso, fuor delle possessioni ch' egli tiene a fitto.*
Fire-kiln, *fornello.*
Wild-fire, *fuoco salvatico.*

To Fire [to set on fire] *metter il fuoco.*
To fire a house, *metter il fuoco ad una casa.*
To fire [to discharge fire-arms] *tirare, sparare, dar fuoco.*
To fire a gun, *tirare, o sparare un cannone.*
To fire upon the enemy, *tirare o sparare sopra'l nemico.*
Fi'red, adj. *messo a fuoco.*
Fi'renew, adj. [new from the forge, new from the melting-house] *giusto uscito del fuoco, giusto uscito della fucina.*
Fi'rer, s. Ex. a firer of houses, *un incendiario.*
Fi'ring, s. [fewel] *legna, carbone, o altra materia da conservar il fuoco.*
To Firk [to beat] *picchiare, dar busse, battere, percuotere, bastonare.*
Fi'rkin, s. [a measure containing eight gallons of ale, and nine of beer] *misura che contiene la quarta parte d'un barile di birra.*
Firm, adj. [hard, solid] *fermo, sodo.*
Firm flesh, *carne ferma.*
The firm land [the continent] *la terra ferma, il continente.*
Firm [constant, steady] *fermo, stabile, costante, saldo.*
To Firm, *fissare, saldare, fermare, render fermo, stabilir sodamente.*
Fi'rmament, s. [the heaven of the fixed stars] *il firmamento, o il firmamento, il cielo stellato.*
Fi'rmly, adv. *fermamente, con fermezza, con istabilità, saldamente, costantemente.*
Fi'rmness, s. [steddiness, constancy] *fermezza, una delle virtù dell' animo, stabilità, saldezza, costanza*, s. f.
Firr, *v.* Fire.
First, adj. [prime, chief] *primo, principale.*
In the first place, *in primo luogo, primieramente.*
The first time I saw him, *la prima volta che lo vidi.*
At the first sight, *a prima vista, subito in un subito.*
First come, first served, *il primo venuto deve esser il primo servito.*
He is the first man of the town, *egli è il primo della città.*
With the first opportunity, *con la primia opportunità.*
First fruits, *primizie*, s. f. *frutti primaticci.*
The first fruits of a benefice, *annata, l'entrata d'un anno d'un benefizio.*
First-born, *primogenito.*
First cousin, *cugino germano.*
At first, at the first, *alla prima, al primo tratto.*
First, adv. [first of all] *primieramente, avanti ogni cosa.*
First or last, *tosto o tardi.*
First and foremost, *primieramente, in primo luogo.*
First-got, First-bego'tten, } s. *il primo nato, il primogenito de' figli.*

FI'RSTLING, s. *primo nato, parlando di bestiame, primizia.*
Firstling, adj. *primaticcio, che è nato o prodotto prima.*
FI'SCAL, adj. [of or belonging to the exchequer] *fiscale, appartenente al fisco.*
Fiscal, s. [an officer of the exchequer] *fiscale,* s. m. *capo e soprantendente del fisco.*
FISH, s. [a water animal] *pesce,* s. m. *nome generale di tutti gli animali che nascono e vivono nell' acqua.*
A small fish, *pescetto, pesciatello, pescatello, pesciolino.*
A large fish, *un pescione.*
The soft and the hard roe of fishes, *le uova de' pesci per le femmine, il latte per i maschi.*
The scales, gills, and fins of a fish, *le squame, le uova, le pinne d'un pesce.*
Fresh water fish, *pesce di fume, o pesce d'acqua dolce.*
Sea fish, *pesce di mare.*
A shell-fish, *conchiglia.*
A cray-fish, *un granchio.*
A fish-pond, *peschiera,* s. f. *vivajo,* s. m. *ricetto d'acqua, per tenervi dentro de' pesci.*
A fish-hook, *un amo.*
Fish-day, *giorno magro.*
Fish-tub, *tinello,* s. m.
Fish-bone, *spina di pesce.*
Fish-market, *pescheria,* s. f. *luogo dove si vende il pesce.*
Fishmonger, *pescajuolo, pescivendolo,* s. m. *che vende il pesce.*
Fish-garth ['tis a dam in a river, made for the taking of fish] *pescaja da pigliar pesci.*
The fish follows the bait, *il cavallo fa andar la sferza, la cosa cammina a rovescio.*
I have other fish to fry, *ho altri pensieri in testa.*
To FISH [to catch fish] *pescare.*
To fish pearls, *pescar delle perle.*
To fish out a thing, *trovare, scoprire che che si sia*
FISHED, adj. *pescato.*
FI'SHER, or FISHER-MAN, s. *pescatore,* s. m.
A poor fisher-man, *un pescatorello.*
A fisher's boat, *barca di pescatore.*
The king's fisher [a bird] *sorte d'uccello aquatico, simile all' oca.*
FI'SHERTOWN, s. [a town inhabited by fishermen] *una città solo abitata da pescatori.*
FI'SHERY, s. [the art or trade of fishing] *pesca, pescagione,* s. f.
FI'SHFUL, adj [abounding with fish] *abbondante di pesci, pien di pesci.*
To FI'SHIFY [to turn fish] *diventar pesce.*
FI'SHING, s. *pesca, pescagione.*
To go a fishing, *andare alla pesca.*
Fishing-line, *canna da pescare, lenza.*
FI'SHY, adj. *pieno di pesci, abbondante di pesce.*
A fishy lake, *un lago pieno di pesci.*
To FISK [to run about hastily] *correr, girar qua e la in fretta.*

To fisk the tail, *scuoter la coda.*
To fisk away, *andarsene, fuggirsene, corsela.*
To fisk [to play fisk] from school, *sfuggire la scuola.*
FISK, s. *il fisco, il tesoro, o l'erario pubblico.*
FI'SSURE, s. [cleft] *fessura, crepatura, fenditura, spaccatura,* s. f. *crepaccio, crepolo, fesso,* s. m.
FIST, s. [the hand clenched] *pugno,* s. m. *la mano serrata,* pl. *pugna,* s. f.
To strike one with the fist, *dare un pugno ad uno.*
To grease one's fist, *ugner la mano ad uno, corromperlo con donativi.*
FI'STED, adj. Ex. club-fisted, *che ha le mani grosse.*
Close-fisted, adj. *spilorcio, avaro, taccagno, stretto, tanghero.*
FI'STICUFFS, s. [battle with the fists] *il fare alla pugna.*
FI'STULA, s. [a narrow callous ulcer hard to cure] *fistola,* s. f. *piaga cavernosa e callosa.*
FI'STULAR, adj. *voto come sono le canne.*
FI'STY, adj. Ex. to fight at fistycuffs, *fare alle pugna.*
A good fistycuff man, *un uomo che si batte bene alle pugna.*
FIT, adj. [apt, meet] *atto, idoneo, capace.*
He is not a fit man for that employment, *non è capace per un tale impiego*
Fit [proportionate] *buono, giusto, proporzionato.*
These shoes are very fit for me, *queste scarpe mi stanno molto bene.*
Fit [convenient, pat] *a proposito, conveniente, comodo.*
If you think fit, *se voi stimate a proposito.*
Fit [ready] *pronto, lesto, in ordine, apparecchiato, parato, preparato.*
Fit to die, *pronto, o preparato a morire.*
A virgin fit for a husband, *una zitella da marito.*
I am not fit to go out, *non sono in istato d'uscire.*
Every thing is fit, *il tutto è in ordine.*
Fit [reasonable] *giusto, ragionevole.*
It is not fit that you should lose by it, *non è ragionevole che voi scapitiate.*
Fit [becoming] *decente, conveniente.*
'Tis not a thing fit to be named, *non è una cosa decente a dire.*
More than was fit, *più che non bisognava.*
To make one's self for fighting, *prepararsi alla battaglia.*
Fit, s. *accesso,* s. m.
A fit of an ague, *accesso di febbre.*
To do a thing by fits and girds, *fare alcuna cosa a spilluzzico, a stento, a poco per volta.*
Fit [freak, whim] *capriccio, ghiribizzo,* s. m. *fantasia,* s. f.
If the fit takes me, *se mi viene in fantasia, se me ne vien voglia.*

To be in a drinking fit, *esser d'umore di bere.*
A fit of disease, *una malattia.*
To be taken with a fit of the gout, *esser sorpreso dalla podagra.*
A mad fit, a fit of madness, *stravaganza, pazzia.*
A fit of the mother, *mal di madre.*
A melancholy fit, *malinconia.*
To FIT [to make fit] *aggiustare, accomodare, preparare, adattare, disporre.* pres. *dispongo.* pret. *disposi.*
To fit every thing for a journey, *preparare, o disporre ogni cosa per un viaggio.*
You must fit his humour, *bisogna incontrare il suo genio.*
This does not fit my turn, *questo non fa per me.*
These shoes fit me, *queste scarpe mi son buone, o mi stanno bene.*
The suit fits you very well, *questo abito vi sta bene alla vita.*
I fitted him [I gave him like for like]; *gli ho reso pan per focaccia, gli ho reso la pariglia.*
To fit out a ship, *allestire un vascello.*
To fit a house] *aggiustare, preparare, addobbare, guarnire una casa.*
I fitted him with every thing he wanted, *l' ho fornito di tutto quel che gli bisognava.*
FITCH, s. [pulse] *veccia,* s. f. *sorta di legume salvatico.*
FI'TCHET, or FITCHE'E, adj. *fitto, puntuto.*
A cross-fitchet [in heraldry, is a cross, the lower part whereof is sharpened into a point] *croceficcata,* s. f. *croce che termina in punta.*
FI'TCHOW, or FI'TCHET, s. [a polecat] *puzzola,* s. f. *sorta d'animale simile alla faina.*
FI'TLY, adv. [from fit] *a proposito, giustamente, convenientemente, aggiustatamente, idoneamente, attamente, opportunamente.*
FI'TNESS, s. [*attitudine, dispostezza, convenenza, convenienza, proporzione, conformità,* s. f.
FITT, *v.* Fit.
FI'TTED, adj. *aggiustato, accommodato, disposto, preparato, adattato.*
A discourse fitted to the meanest capacity, *un discorso adattato alla capacità de' più infimi.*
FI'TTEDNESS, s. *attitudine, dispostezza,* s. f.
FI'TTER, s. [little piece] *fetta,* s. f.
To cut to fitters, *affettare, tagliare in fette.*
FI'TTING, adj. [accommodated] *accomodato, aggiustato, adattato, giusto.*
Fitting [just] *ragionevole, convenevole, giusto.*
Fitting [becoming] *convenevole, decente, decoroso.*
FITZ [a word commonly added to the sirnames of families of this nation, descended of the Norman race, as Fitz-Herbert, Fitz-Williams, Fitzroy, &c.] *parola corrotta dal Francese, che s'unisce ordinariamente ai cognomi di molte famiglie considerabili nella Gran Brettagna:* *che*

che sono di razza Normanna, come Fitz-Herbert, Fitz-Williams, Fitz-Roy, cioe' figlio d' Erberto, figlio di Guglielmo, figlio del Re.

FIVE, adj. *cinque*.

Five hundred, *cinquecento*.

Five thousand, *cinquemila*.

FIVES, s. [a disease of horses] *malattia de' cavalli*.

To FIX [to fasten, to settle] *fissare, affissare, assettare, piantare*.

To fix one's eyes upon something *fissare gli occhi in qualche cosa*.

To fix a gun, *piantare un cannone*.

To fix a business, *conchiudere, terminare un negozio*.

To fix a day, *appuntare, convenire del giorno*.

To fix one's self somewhere, *stabilire la sua dimora in qualche luogo, fermar il piede in qualche luogo*.

To fix upon a resolution, *fermare, deliberare, risolvere*.

FIXED, adj. *fisso, fissato, affissato*, v. To fix.

The fixed stars, *le stelle fisse*.

Fixed upon [made choice of] *scelto, destinato*.

Fixed [intent] *fisso, intento, attento, applicato*.

FI'XEDLY, adv. *fissamente, fisamente, attentamente*.

FI'XEDNESS, [application] *applicazione, attenzione*, s. f.

FI'ZGIG, s. [a dart wherewith mariners strike fish while they swim] *lancia, dardo da ammazzar pesci usato da pescatori di pesci grossi*.

FI'ZZLE, s. [a wind that breaks backward without noise] *loffa*, s. f.

To FI'ZZLE [to break wind backwards without noise] *tirar una loffa*.

FI'ZZLER, s. *che tira delle loffe*.

FLA'BEY, adj. [soft] *frollo, vizzo, moscio*.

Flabby flesh, *carne moscia*.

FLA'CCID, adj. [flagging, withering] *moscio, vizzo, frollo*.

FLAG, s. [banner] *bandiera, insegna*, s. f. *stendardo*, s. m.

Flag-staff, *asta di bandiera*.

Flag [a sort of rush] *spezie di giunco*.

To set up the flag, *inalberare la bandiera*.

A flag-broom, *scopa di giunchi*.

To FLAG [to decay, to grow limber, to wither] *abbiosciarsi, abbandonarsi, avvilirsi, sgomentarsi; e dicesi così dell' animo, come del corpo*.

To flag [to wither] *appassarsi, appassirsi, divenir passo o vizzo, languire*. pref. *appassisco, languisco*.

FLA'GELET, s. [a musical wind instrument] *zufolo, o sufolo*, s. m. *strumento rusticale di fiato, fatto a guisa di flauto*.

FLA'GGING, adj. *abbiosciato, avvilito, languido, moscio, vizzo*.

Flagging ears, *orecchi pendenti*.

To FLA'GELLATE [to whip, to scourge] *flagellare, e fragellare, percuotere con flagello*.

FLAGELLA'TION, s. [whipping, lashing] *flagellazione, e fragellazione*, s. f.

FLA'GGY, adj. *debole, pendente, che dondola, molle insipido, debole al gusto*.

FLAGI'TIOUS, adj. [very wicked, villanous] *furfante, gaglioffo, ribaldo, sciagurato, fellone*.

FLA'GON, s. [a large drinking pot] *un fiasco*.

FLA'GRANCY, s. [burning] *flagranzia*, s. f. *incendio*, s. m.

Flagrancy [ardent desire] *fervore, ardente desiderio*.

FLA'GRANT, adj. [burning, blazing] *cocente, acceso, focace, focoso, fervente, fervido*.

Flagrant [manifest, notorious] *infame, notorio*.

FLAIL, s. [an instrument to thresh corn with] *correggiato*, s. m. *strumento villereccio per uso di battere il grano e le biade*.

To thresh corn with a flail, *battere il grano col correggiato*.

FLAKE, s. [a flake of fire], *una scintilla*.

A flake of snow, *un fiocco di neve*.

The snow falls in flakes, *e' fiocca*.

A flake of ice, *un pezzo di ghiaccio*.

To FLAKE [to peel off] *spelarsi*.

FLAM, s. [an idle story, a sham] *menzogna, favola, chiappola, baja, chiacchiera, ciarla, cantafavola, finzione frivola*, s. f.

To FLAM [to deceive with a lye] *ingannare con una bugia*.

FLA'MBEAU, s. [a sort of torch] *face, fiaccola*.

FLAME, s. [the most subtle part of fire] *fiamma*, s. f.

The flames of love, *le fiamme d' amore*.

To FLAME [to blaze out in flame] *fiammeggiare, esser in fiamme, fiammare*.

The fire begins to flame, *il fuoco comincia a fiammeggiare*.

FLA'MING, } adj. *fiammeggiante, ardente, fiammante*.
FLA'MY, }

FLA'NCONADE, s. [a thrust in the flank] *colpo nel fianco*.

FLANK, s. [side] *fianco*, s. m. *quella parte del corpo che è tra le coste e le cosciole*.

To set upon the enemy in the flank, *assalire l'inimico nel fianco*.

The flank of a bastion, *il fianco d'un bastione*.

To FLANK [to strengthen with flanks] *fiancheggiare*.

FLANKED, adj. *fiancheggiato*.

FLA'NKER, s. *fianco, termine di fortificazione*.

To FLA'NKER [to fortify with bulwarks and countermures] *fiancheggiare, fortificare baloardi*.

FLA'NNEL [a sort of woollen cloth] *spezie di panno rado, e sottile; flanella*.

FLAP, s. [blow, stroke] *botta, percossa*, s. f. *botto, colpo*, s m.

To give one a flap, *dare un colpo ad uno*.

The flaps of a shoe, *le orecchie d' una scarpa*.

The flaps of a coat, *le falde d'un vestito*.

The fore or hind flap of a shift, *la falda d'una camicia*.

A fly flap, *un caccia mosche*.

To give one a flap with a fox's-tail [to gull him] *fare la barba di stoppa ad uno, farli una burla*.

To FLAP [to strike] *battere, percuotere*, pret. *percossi*.

What d'ye flap me for? *perchè mi battete?*

To flap, to flap down [as some hats do] *abbattersi, abbassarsi*.

To FLAPDRA'GON [to swallow, to devour] *divorare, ingojare*.

FLAPPED, adj. *battuto, percosso*.

To FLARE [as a candle does with the wind] *struggersi, consumarsi, come una candela esposta al vento; far barlume*.

To FLARE IN ONE'S EYES, [to stare one in the face] *guatar uno a quattr' occhi, fissarli gli occhi addosso*.

FLASH, s. [a sudden blaze] *vampa, fiamma, baldoria*, s. f.

A flash of fire, *una vampa*.

A flash of lightning, *un baleno, un lampo*.

A flash of water, *spruzzo, o sprazzo d' acqua*.

A flash of the eye, *un' occhiata, uno sguardo*.

A flash of wit, *concetti spiritosi*.

He has fine flashes of wit, *ha belli concetti*.

A man that is but a flash [an empty man] *un uomo vano, o senza cervello*.

To FLASH [to blaze out suddenly] *vampeggiare, balenare, rilucere, risplendere, scintillare*.

To flash as water, *schizzare, zampillare*.

FLA'SHING, s. [of fire] *splendore*, s. m. *luce*, s. f.

Flashing of water, *spruzzo, e sprazzo*, s. m.

FLA'SHY, adj. [sudden, not lasting] *subitaneo, subitano, repentino, improvviso*.

Flashy [fresh tasted] *insipido, che non ha gusto*.

Flask, s. [a box to put gun-powder in] *fiaschetta da mettervi la polvere*.

Flask [a sort of bottle] *fiasco*, s. m.

A flask of Florence wine, *un fiasco di vino di Firenze*.

FLA'SKET, s. [a sort of great basket] *cesto, canestro, paniere*, s. m.

FLAT, adj. [even and level] *piatto, di forma piana, spianato*.

A flat country, *un paese piatto*.

A flat discourse, *un discorso insipido, tedioso*.

A flat taste, *un gusto insipido*.

A flat nose, *un naso schiacciato, o camuso*.

Flat [or dead] drink, *bevanda piccola, che ha perduta la sua forza*.

I told him flat and plain, *li dissi franco, e netto*.

To give one a flat denial, *ricusare nettamente*.

To take one in a flat [or plain] *corre alcuno in una bugia manifesta*.

The flat side of a sword, *il piatto della spada*.

To

To ſtrike one with the flat ſide of a ſword, *dare una piattonata ad uno.*

To lay a thing flat on the ground, *ſtender che che ſi ſia di piatto in terra.*

To lie flat upon the ground, *ſtenderſi per terra.*

To ſound flat, *render un ſuono rauco.*

Flat noſed, *camuſo, rincagnato.*

Flat bottomed, *col fondo piano.*

A flat-bottomed boat, *una piatta, barca con fondo piano.*

Flat, s. [flat country] *pianura, paeſe piano.*

FLATS, [ſhallows at ſea] *ſecche.*

A flat [or ſhelf] *cavello,* s. m. *maſſa di rena nel mare.*

Flat [in muſick] *bimmolle, termine di muſica.*

To FLAT [to make flat] *ſpianare, pianare, appianare, far piano.*

FLA'TLY, adv. [downright] *ſchiettamente, netto.*

He denied it flatly, *lo negò aſſolutamente.*

FLA'TNESS, s. *pianezza, pianura,* s. f. *piano,* s. m.

FLA'TTED, adj. *ſpianato, pianato, appianato.*

FLA'TTER, *è il comparativo di* Flat.

To FLA'TTER [to ſooth up, coax, or wheedle] *luſingare, adulare, piaggiare.*

FLA'TTERED, adj. *luſingato, adulato, piaggiato.*

FLA'TTERER, s. *adulatore, luſingatore, luſinghiere, e luſinghiero,* s. m. *adulatrice, luſinghiera,* s. f.

FLA'TTERING, s. *luſingamento,* s. m. *il luſingare.*

Flattering, adj. *luſinghevole, luſinghiere, luſinghiero, luſingante.*

Flattering hopes, *ſperanze luſinghiere.*

A flattering tongue, *una lingua adulatrice.*

A flattering man, *un adulatore, un luſinghiere.*

A flattering woman, *un' adulatrice, una luſinghiera.*

FLA'TTERINGLY, adv. *luſinghevolmente, con luſinghe, con piacevolezze.*

FLA'TTERY, s. [fawning, wheedling] *adulazione, luſinga, luſingheria,* s. f. *luſingamento,* s. m.

FLA'TTISH, adj. [ſomewhat flat] *alquanto piatto.*

FLA'TULENT, adj. [windy] *flatuoſo, che genera venti, o flati.*

FLATUO'SITY, s. [windineſs] *ventoſità,* s. f. *qualità flatuoſa.*

To FLAUNT [to give one's ſelf airs, to ſtrut or look big, to take ſtate upon one] *pompeggiare, paoneggiarſi, e pavoneggiarſi, sfoggiare, boriare.*

FLAUNTING, adj. *arioſo, borioſo, albagioſo.*

A flaunting woman, *una donna albagioſa, vana nello sfoggio de' ſuoi abbigliamenti.*

A flaunting ſuit of cloaths, *un abito di gala, un abito sfoggiato o pompoſo.*

FLA'VOUR, s. [a pleaſant reliſh, generally applied to wine] *ſapore guſtoſo, che s'applica generalmente al vino.*

FLA'VOUROUS, adj. *guſtoſo, piacevole al guſto o all' odorato.*

FLAW, s. [a defect in precious ſtones] *maglia, o macchia in una pietra prezioſa.*

Flaw [fault] *fallo, difetto, errore,* s. m.

Flaw [chink] *pelo,* s. m. *crepatura, feſſura,* s. f.

A flaw of wind, *un ſoffio, o una folata di vento.*

To FLAW [to break, to crack, to damage with fiſſure] *rompere, crepare, danneggiare cagionando feſſure.*

To flaw [to break, to violate] *rompere, violare.*

FLA'WLESS, adj. [without cracks, without defects] *ſenza feſſure, ſenza difetto.*

FLAWN, s. [a ſort of cuſtard] *lattajuola,* s. f. *ſpezie di torta.*

FLAX, s. [a plant] *lino,* s. m. *erba, della quale ſi fanno i panni lini*

To dreſs flax, *ſcotolare il lino.*

A flax-comb, *ſcotola,* s. f. *ſtrumento di legno a guiſa di coltello, col quale ſi ſcotola il lino.*

FLA'XEN, adj. *fatto di lino.*

Flaxen ſheets, *lenzuola di lino.*

Flaxen hair, *capelli biondi.*

To FLA'Y, *toglier la pelle, ſcorticare, ſpelare.*

FLEA, s. [an inſect well known] *pulce,* s. f. *vermicello noto.*

To catch a flea, *pigliare un pulce.*

To put a flea in one's ear, *mettere un pulce nell' orecchio ad uno, dirgli coſa che glia dia a penſare.*

To have a flea in one's ear, *avere un cocomero in corpo, aver alcun dubbio che faccia ſtare ſoſpeſo e timoroſo.*

Water flea, *pulce di mare, inſetto aquatico.*

Flea-wort, *pulicaria,* s. f. *pſilio, ſilio,* s. m.

Flea-bite, *morſicatura di pulce.*

Flea-bit, *pezzato.*

A flea-bit horſe, *un cavallo pezzato.*

To FLEA [to pull the ſkin off] *ſcorticare.*

To flea one alive, *ſcorticare uno vivo.*

A knife to flea with, *uno ſcorticatojo.*

To flea, *cercar le pulci, nettar delle pulci.*

FLEAD, adj. *ſcorticato.*

FLE'AR, s. *ſcorticatore,* s. m.

Every fox muſt pay his own ſkin to the flear, *tutte le volpi alla fine ſi riveggono in pellicceria.*

FLE'AING, s. *ſcorticamento,* s. m.

A fleaing houſe, *luogo dove ſi ſcorticano gli animali.*

FLEAR, *ciuffo, fiocco.*

FLEAM, s. [flegm] *flemma,* s. f.

Full of fleam, *flemmatico.*

Fleam [a farrier's tool to let a horſe blood] *lancetta, ſaetta, ſtrumento di maniſcalco da cavar ſangue alle beſtie.*

To FLECK } [to ſpot, to ſtreak,
To FLE'CKER } to ſtripe, to dapple, to mark with ſtrokes or touches] *macchiare, ſegnar a macchie, pezzare.*

FLECKT, adj. [ſpeckled, ſpotted] *pezzato, diviſato, vajato, chiazzato, taccato.*

FLED, adj. [from to fly] *volato, v.* To fly.

He is fled, *ſen' è fuggito.*

FLEDGE, } adj. [to be covered
FLEDGED, } with feathers, as young birds are when they begin to fly] *piumato, coperto di piume.*

To FLEDGE, verb neut. *cominciare a metter le piume.*

FLE'ECE, s. [a flock of wool, or ſo much as comes off one ſheep] *vello,* s. m.

The fleece, or the golden fleece, *il toſone, il toſon d'oro.*

To FLE'ECE one, *ſcorticare, o tondere alcuno, trarre di lui tutto quel che ſi può, ſpogliarlo.*

FLE'ECED, adj. *ſcorticato, toſato, ſpogliato.*

FLE'ECY, adj. *lanuto, pien di lana, coperto di lana.*

To FLEER [to caſt a diſdainful, or ſaucy look] *guatar con occhio bieco, o ſott' occhio, far un viſo arcigno, guatar in cagneſco, beffeggiare, fare ſcorno.*

FLE'ERING, s. *occhio bieco, viſo arcigno.*

Fleering, adj. *impudente, sfacciato, sfrontato.*

A fleering fellow, *uno sfacciato.*

FLEET, s. [a number of ſhips together in company] *flotta,* s. f.

To fit out a fleet] *alleſtire, metter in ordine una flotta,*

Fleet, *è il nome d' una prigione di Londra.*

Fleet, adj. [ſwift] *veloce, preſto.*

Fleet dogs, *cani veloci alla corſa.*

Fleet milk, *latte dal quale ſia levato il fiore.*

To FLEET milk, *levare il fior del latte.*

To fleet [to float upon the water] *galleggiare, gallare, ſtare a galla.*

To fleet [to remove from place to place] *cangiar di luogo.*

FLE'ETING, adj. *paſſeggiere, tranſitorio.*

Our fleeting days, *la noſtra vita tranſitoria.*

FLEGM, s. *flemma,* s. f.

FLEGMA'TICK, adj. *flemmattico.*

FLESH, s. *carne.*

A ſoft fleſh, *carne frolla.*

A tough fleſh, *carne dura.*

Raw fleſh, *carne cruda.*

Dead fleſh, *carne morta.*

The fleſh [the carnal part of men] *la carne, la parte ſenſuale dell' uomo.*

The pleaſures of fleſh, *i piaceri della carne, o carnali.*

To gather fleſh [to grow plump] *rimetterſi in carne, ingraſſare.*

To take fleſh, *incarnarſi.*

To go the way of all fleſh [to die] *morire.*

Fleſh colour, *incarnato, incarnatino, color di carne, cioè miſto tra roſſo e bianco.*

Fleſh day, *giorno graſſo.*

The fleſh [among botaniſts, the ſubſtance of any fruit that is between the outer rind and the ſtone] *carne, la polpa di tutte le frutte.*

To FLESH [to encourage] *animare, incorag-*

incoraggiare, inanimire, incorare, incitare, eccitare, pref. *inanimisco.*

To flesh one to a thing, *incoraggiare una a qualche cosa.*

To flesh [to glut, to satiate] *saziare, riempiere uno di carne.*

FLESHED, adj. *animato, incoraggiato, inanimito, incorato, incitato, eccitato.*

Fleshed in roguery, *portato, inclinato al male.*

FLE'SHINESS, s. *carnosità*, s. f.

FLE'SHLESS, adj. *magro, smunto, che non ha che la pelle, e l' ossa.*

FLE'SHLY, adj. [carnal] *carnale, sensuale secondo la carne.*

Fleshly pleasures, *piaceri carnali.*

Fleshly given, *dedito, inclinato ai piaceri carnali, alle sensualità.*

Fleshy, adj. [full of flesh] *carnoso, carnuto.*

The fleshy parts, *le parti carnose.*

FLE'TCHER, s. [a maker of arrows] *colui che fa le frecce.*

FLEW, *è un preterito del verbo* to fly.

FLEXIBI'LITY, s. [aptness to bend] *flessibilità, arrendevolezza*, s. f.

FLE'XIBLE, adj. [apt to bend, limber] *flessibile, pieghevole, arrendevole.*

Flexible [pliant, tractable, easy to be entreated] *flessibile, pieghevole, trattabile, docile, mite, arrendevole.*

FLE'XION, s. [a bending or bowing] *il flettere, il piegare, piegatura, l' arrendersi d' una cosa.*

FLE'XURE, s. [a crooking or bending] *curvatura*, s. f.

To FLI'CKER [to flutter as a bird] *svolazzare.*

FLI'ER [a runaway] *un che fugge, un fuggitivo.*

FLIGHT, s. [a flying] *volo*, s. m. *il volare.*

A flight of birds, *branco, nuvolo, stormo, volata d'uccelli.*

Flight [running away] *fuga*, s. f.

To put to flight, *metter in fuga, fugare.*

To betake one's self to flight, *mettersi in fuga, fuggire.*

Flight [a witticism] *concetti spiritosi.*

Flight-shot, *frecciata*, s. f. *colpo di freccia.*

FLI'GHTY, adj. [fleeting, swift] *veloce, rapido.*

Flighty [wild, full of imagination] *fantastioso, che ha una fantasia che vola.*

FLIM FLAM, s. *baja, bagattella, frascheria, frasche, bajata, scimunitaggine, balordaggine*, s. f.

FLI'MSY, adj. [limber, thin] *abbiosciato, moscio, vizzo, passo, frollo, floscio, vincido.*

Flimsy stuff, *stoffa floscia.*

To FLINCH [to give over, to desist] *tralasciare, desistere, cessare, abbandonare.*

To flinch an undertaking, *abbandonare un' impresa.*

To flinch one basely, *lasciare uno in nasso, lasciarlo in abbandono.*

To flinch the fight, *prendar la fuga, fuggire, voltar le spalle.*

FLINCHING, s. *il desistere, tralasciamento*, s. m. *v.* To flinch.

Without flinching [or fear] *senza spaventarsi.*

FLI'NDERS, s. *pezzi.*

All to flinders, *in pezzi.*

FLING, s. *botta*, s. f. *colpo*, s. m.

Every word he speaks has a fling at some body or other, *non può dire una parola senza sbottoneggiare qualcheduno.*

To FLING [to throw, to hurl] *gettare, gittare, buttare.*

To fling a stone at one, *gettare una pietra ad alcuno.*

To fling a dart, *lanciare, vibrare un dardo.*

To fling from a horse, *gettar da cavallo.*

To fling away one's money, *gettar via, mandar male, sprecare il suo danaro.*

To fling away one's life, *metter a ripentaglio la sua vita.*

To fling [to kick as horses do] *scalceggiare, tirar calci, calcitrare.*

To fling away [to be gone] *involarsi, scantonarsi, svignare, fuggire nascosamente.*

To fling down, *buttar giù.*

To fling out, *gettare, o buttar fuori.*

FLI'NGER, s. *gittatore*, s. m.

FLI'NGING, s. *gettamento, gittamento, gittata*, s. f.

FLINT, or FLINT STONE, s. *selce, o selice*, s. f. *pietra focaja.*

A flint glass, *vetro di rocca.*

Flint [any thing eminently or proverbially hard] *ogni' cosa sommamente dura, come* FLINT-HEARTED, *che ha il cuor più duro che un selce.*

FLI'NTY, adj. [made of flint] *fatto di selce, fortissimo.*

Flinty [full of stones] *pien di sassi, sassoso, scelcioso.*

Flinty [hard of heart, cruel, savage, inexorable] *duro di cuore, crudele, selvaggio, fero, inesorabile.*

FLIP, s. [a sort of sailors drink, made of ale, brandy, and sugar] *bevanda di marinari composta di cevogia dolce, acquavite, e zucchero.*

FLIPPANT, adj. [brisk] *allegro, vivace, giocondo, svegliato.*

To FLIRT, *tirar una cosa con moto celere ed elastico.*

To flirt, *muoversi celeremente, con velocità.*

To flirt, v. n. *bertar uno, beffeggiarlo, farsi scorno di lui.*

FLIRT, s. *moto celere ed elastico.*

Flirt, *beffa subitana, celia*

Flirt, *una sfacciatella, una fanciulla audace e impertinente.*

FLIRTA'TION, s. *moto veloce e di scocco.*

To FLIT, *v.* To fleet.

FLITCH, s. [a side of bacon] *costola di porco salata, costereccio di porco.*

FLI'TTER, s. [a rag or tatter] *straccio, cencio*, s. m.

A suit wore all to flitters, *un abito stracciato.*

Flitter-mouse [bat] *nottola, pipistrello.*

FLIX [down, fur, soft hair] *lanugine, pelle pelosa, pelo morbido.*

FLOAT OF TIMBER, *zatta, zattera*, s. f.

A float to a fishing line [the cork which swims above water] *il sovero o sughero d'una canna da pescare, che sta a galla su l'acqua.*

A ship that is afloat, *un vascello che galleggia, o che sta a galla.*

To FLOAT [to swim upon the water] *galleggiare, stare a galla.*

To float [to be in suspense] *fluttuare, ondeggiare, balenare, barcollare, tentennare, traballare, star sospeso, vacillare.*

To float betwixt hope and fear, *ondeggiar fra la speranza e'l timore.*

FLOA'TING, s. *galleggiare, fluttuamento, ondeggiamento*, s. m.

Floating, adj *fluttuante, ondeggiante.*

A floating bridge, *un ponte di barche.*

FLOCK, s. *gregge, greggia, mandra*, s. f.

A little flock, *greggiuola*, s. f.

A flock of sheep, *una mandra di pecore.*

A flock of geese, *uno stuolo d' oche.*

Flock of wool, *borra.*

A flock bed, *letto di borra.*

A flock of people, *una folla, folta, calca, pressa di gente.*

To FLOCK together, *affollarsi, andar in folla.*

FLO'CKING, s. ex. a flocking of people, *un concorso o folla di popolo.*

To FLOG [to lash, to whip] *frustare, flagellare, battere, percuotere.*

FLOOD, s. *v.* Floud, *ma scrivi sempre* flood [a body of water, the sea, a river] *un corpo d'acque, il mare, un fiume.*

Flood, *un inondazione, un diluvio.*

Flood [flow, flux, not ebb] *il riflusso dell' acque.*

To FLOOD [to deluge, to cover with waters] *diluviare, coprir d' acque.*

FLOOK, s. *la parte dell' ancora che afferra il fondo.*

FLOOR, s. [the surface of a room] *tavolato.*

A house that has two rooms of a floor, *una casa che ha due camere in ogni appartamento.*

The floor of a ship, *il fondo d'un vascello.*

A floor, or barn floor, *aja*, s. f. *il luogo dove si batte il grano.*

The first or the second floor of a house, *il primo o secondo piano, o appartamento d'una casa.*

To FLOOR [to lay a floor] *tavolare, coprir di tavole.*

FLO'OKED, adj. *tavolato, coperto di tavole.*

FLO'RENCES, s. [a sort of cloth] *panno di Firenze.*

FLO'RENTINE, s. [a sort of baked pudding] *torta*, s. f.

FLO'RID, adj [flourishing, adorned with flowers] *fiorito, pomposo.*

A florid discourse, *un discorso fiorito, elegante.*

A florid stile, *uno stile fiorito, o pomposo.*

FLO'RIN, s. [a coin first made in Florence, of several kinds and prices] *fiorino*, s. m. *moneta d' oro battuta nella città*

città di Firenze; così detta dal giglio fiore impresa di detta città, impressovi dentro, e pesava una dramma d' oro fino; fu eziandio moneta Fiorentina d' argento, e' ne furono diverse sorte di vari pesi, e prezzi, e oggidì moneta d' Alemagna, d' Olanda, e Polonia.

FLO'RIST, s. [one who is skilled in flowers] *fiorista*, s. m. *colui che si diletta in fiori.*

To FLOTE, *v.* To skim.

FLO'TSON, or FLO'TZAM, s. [goods which being lost by shipwreck and floating upon the sea, are given to the lord admiral by his letters patent] *ogni sorta di roba perduta in un naufragio, e che galleggia sul mare, che s' aspetta all' ammiraglio d Inghilterra per lettera patente.*

FLO'TTEN, adj. ex. Flotten milk, *latte, dal quale sia levato il fiore.*

FLOUD, s. [deluge of water] *fiotto, flusso, diluvio*, s. m. *v.* Flood, *e scrivi sempre* flood.

The floud of the sea, *il flusso, o la marea del mare.*

Noah's floud, *il diluvio di Noè.*

There's a floud, *v'è un' inondazione.*

To roll on a floud of wealth, *nuotar nelle ricchezze.*

To pour out a floud of tears, *versare un torrente di lagrime, piangere a caldi occhi.*

A floud-gate, *chiusa, chiudenda d' acqua, cateratta*

To FLOUNCE [to jump or plunge in the water] *tuffarsi,*

To flounce into the water, *tuffarsi nell' acqua.*

To flounce [to be in a toss or fume with anger] *soffiare, o sbuffare di sdegno.*

FLOUNDER, s. [a sort of flat sea fish] *pesce passera.*

He lieth as flat as a flounder, *giace disteso per terra.*

To FLO'UNDER [to struggle, with violent and irregular motions] *dibattersi con moto violento ed irregolare.*

FLO'URISH, s. [an ornament in writing] *ghirigoro*, s. m. *intrecciatura di linee fatte a tiro di penna.*

Flourish [in musick] *preludio termine musicale.*

Flourish with a sword, *il brandire la spada.*

Flourish [boast] *spampanata, spampanazione di parole, burbanza, giattanzia, millanteria, ostentazione*, s. f. *ostentamento.*

Flourish [rhetorical flourishes] *fioretti, ornamenti rettorici.*

An idle flourish of words, *una spampanata di parole.*

To FLO'URISH [to beat one's prime] *fiorire, essere in fiore, esser in buono stato, prosperare.* pres. *fiorisco.*

To flourish in discourse, *amplificare, aggrandire, magnificar con parole.*

To flourish in writing, *abbellir uno scritto con frasi scelte.*

To flourish a sword, *brandire la spada.*

FLO'URISHING, s. *il fiorire*, *v.* To flourish.

A flourishing, adj. *fiorente, prospero.*

A flourishing state, *uno stato che prospera.*

FLOUT, s. [jeer] *burla, baja, billera, smorfia*, s. f. *scherno*, s. m.

To FLOUT [to mock, to jeer *giambare, burlare, beffare, scherzare, dar la baja, dar la burla, deridere, schernire.* pret. *schernisco.*

FLO'UTED, adj. *giambato, burlato, scherzato, deriso, schernito.*

FLO'UTER, s. *burlatore, derisore, beffatore*, s. m. *beffatrice, deriditrice*, s. f.

FLO'UTING, s. *burla, ciancia, beffa*, s. f. *scherzo*, s. m.

FLOW, s. *flusso*, s. m.

A flow will have an ebb, *ogni flusso ha il suo riflusso.*

To FLOW [to flow as in water] *scaturire, docciare, colare, scorrere.* pres. *scaturisco*, pret. *scorsi.*

The tears which flow from her eyes, *le lagrime che le scaturiscon dagli occhi.*

All these blessings flow from God, *tutte queste benedizioni ci vengono da Dio.*

The tide flows and ebbs, *la marea monta e scende.*

FLO'WER, s. [the offspring of plants] *fiore*, s. m.

A fine flower, *un bel fiore.*

A sweet-smelling flower, *un fiore odorifero.*

A small flower, *fiorellino*, s. m.

A meadow enamelled with flowers, *un prato smaltato di fiori.*

A flower de luce, *un fiordaliso.*

Flowers of rhetorick, *fiori, concetti rettorici.*

Flower [prime] *fiore, la parte più nobile, più bella, e più scelta di qualsivoglia cosa.*

The flower of the nobility, *il fiore della nobiltà.*

In the flower of his age, *nel fiore dell' età sua.*

Flower [finest meal] *fior di farina.*

Flowers [monthly courses] *mestrui.*

Flowers [in chymistry, that fine mealy water, which in any sublimation is carried up into the head in form of a fine powder] *fiori, appresso i chimici, si dicono quelle più sottili e più leggiere particelle asciutte di qualche corpo, per via della sublimazione separate dalle parti più grosse.*

Flower-gentle, or velvet-flower, *sciamito*, s. m. *spezie di fiore.*

Our ladies-flower, *jacinto, giacinto*, s. m. *fiore odorifero.*

Flower pot, *testo*, s. m. *vaso di terra cotta dove si pongon le piante.*

To FLO'WER [to blossom like trees] *fiorire, far fiori, produr fiori.*

To flower, *ornar di fiori finti o di ricamo, o simili.*

FLO'WRET, s. *fioretto, fiorellino, picciolo fiore.*

FLO'WING, s. *sorgente, scaturiente, colante, rampollante.*

Flowing, s. *flusso*, s. m.

Ebbing and flowing, *il flusso, e riflusso.*

FLOWN, adj. [from to fly] *volato, fuggito, andato via.*

The bird is flown, *l'uccello è volato.*

High-flown, *superbo, altiero, arrogante, borioso.*

FLO'WERED, adj. *fiorito.*

A flowered silk, *drappo fiorito.*

To FLU'CTUATE, [to waver, to be in suspence] *fluttuare, ondeggiare, bilanciare, star sospeso.*

FLUCTUA'TION, s. [a wavering] *agitazione, incertezza, sospension d'animo, irresoluzione.*

FLU'CTUOUS, adj. [unquiet, restless like the waves] *fluttuoso, tempestoso, fluttuante, ondeggiante.*

FLUB, s. [the down or soft hair of a rabbet] *pelo di coniglio.*

Flue [little feathers or flocks which stick to cloaths] *piccole piume, o cose simili, che s'appiccano agli abiti.*

FLU'ELLIN, s. [an herb] *veronica*, s. f. *spezie d'erba.*

FLU'ENCY, *v.* Fluentness.

FLU'ENT, adj. [ready or eloquent in speech] *facondo, facondioso, eloquente.*

FLU'ENTLY, adv. *facondamente, facondiosamente, con facondia, eloquentemente.*

To speak fluently, *parlar facondamente, con facondia.*

FLU'ENTNESS, s. [readiness of speech] *facondia, facondità*, s. f. *copia d'eloquenza.*

FLU'ID, adj. [that easily flows] *fluido, liquido.*

The water is fluid, *l'acqua è fluida.*

FLUI'DITY, } s. [flowingness] *fluidezza, fluidità*, s. f.
FLU'IDNESS, }

The fluidity of water, of the air, *la fluidità dell' acqua, dell' aria, e simili.*

FLU'MMERY, s. [a sort of jelly made of oatmeal] *avena cotta, e condensata.*

FLUNG, adj. *gettato*, *v.* To fling.

Flung, *è anche il preterito del verbo* To fling.

FLURT, s. *meglio è scrivere* Flirt, *capriccio, ghiribizzo*, s. m.

Flurt [banter] *burla, ciancia, beffa*, s. f.

Flurt [a sort of silk] *bavella*, s. f.

Flurt [a jilt flurt, a crack] *una bagascia, una berghinella.*

To FLURT [to banter] *burlare, beffare, schernire*, pres. *schernisco.*

FLU'RTED AT, adj. *burlato, beffato, schernito.*

FLUSH, s. [a term in a game at cards, when they are all of a suit] *flusso*, s. m. *termine del giuoco di carte.*

Flush [red colour in the face] *rossore, che viene nel viso.*

Flush [in musick] *trillo*, s. m.

Flush of money, *copia, dovizia, abbondanza di danari.*

To be flush of money, *esser danajoso, aver molti danari.*

To FLUSH [to redden in the face of a sudden] *arrossire, divenir rosso nel viso.*

FLU'SHED, *v.* Flusht.

FLU'SHING, s. [redness of the face, caused by some sudden apprehension or transport of mind] *rossore*, s. m.

FLUSHT, or FLU'SHED, adj. [encouraged, put in heart with good success] *animato, incorato.*

Flusht with ambition, *pieno, gonfio d'ambizione.*

He is flush enough to think so, *è assai vano per creder ciò.*

FLU'STERED, adj. [somewhat disordered with drink] *mezzo briaco, che ha bevuto un poco troppo; mezzo cotto.*

FLUTE, s. [an instrument of wind musick] *flauto*, s. m. *strumento musicale di fiato.*

To play upon the flute, *suonar il flauto.*

To FLUTE [to channel] *scanalare, termine d'architettura.*

FLU'TED, adj. *scanalato.*

FLU'TINGS, s. [the channels or gutters of pillars] *scanalature*, s. f.

To FLU'TTER [to try to fly, to fly about] *batter l'ali, volitare, svolazzare, cominciare a volare un poco.*

To flutter [to make a fluttering] *dimenarsi, agitarsi, muoversi qua e là.*

FLU'TTERING, s. *dimenamento, dimenio, dimenare*, s. m. *agitazione.*

FLUX, s. [flood, tide] *flusso*, s. m.

The flux and reflux, *il flusso e riflusso.*

Flux [looseness of the belly] *flusso, dissenteria.*

The bloody flux, *flusso di sangue, dissenteria.*

To flux one, *dare il flusso di bocca ad uno, darli il mercurio per provocargli la salivazione pe mal venereo.*

FLU'XING, s. *flusso di bocca, salivazione.*

FLU'XION, s. [flowing of humours] *flussione*, s. f.

FLY, s. [insect] *mosca*, s. f.

A great fly, *un moscone.*

A Spanish fly, *canterella*, s. f.

A gad fly, *un tafano.*

Fly-flap, *ventaglio da scacciar le mosche.*

To FLY [as birds do] *volare.*

To fly [to run away] *scappare, fuggire, andar via.*

To fly from justice, *nascondersi dalla giustizia.*

To fly one's country, *lasciare, abbandonare la sua patria.*

To fly to one for refuge, *rifuggire, ricorrere ad alcuno per salvezza.*

To fly in a battle, *voltar le spalle al nemico.*

To let fly [to shoot] *sparare, tirare.*

To fly top over tail, *cascar col capo all' ingiù.*

To fly out in expences, *spendere, scialacquare il suo avere.*

To fly back [as a horse] *calcitrare, tirar de' calci.*

To fly at one [as a dog does] *lanciarsi, avventarsi ad uno.*

To fly in pieces, *saltare in pezzi.*

To fly into a passion, *montare in collera, adirarsi, stizzirsi.*

To fly abroad, to fly about, *spandersi.*

This news flies about every where, *questa novella s'è sparsa dappertutto.*

To fly away, *involarsi.*

The door flies open, *la porta s'apre da se.*

FLY'BOAT, s. [a sort of swift sea vessel] *brigantino.*

FLYCA'TCHER, s. [one that hunts flies] *cacciator di mosche.*

To FLY'FISH, *pescare con un amo a cui è stata appiccata una mosca; pescare alla lenza o a lenza.*

FLY'ING, adj. *volante.*

Flying fish [a kind of fish] *pesce volante, rondine*, s. f. *pesce di mare.*

A flying camp, *campo volante.*

A flying horse, *un cavallo alato.*

We went out with drums beating, colours flying, *noi uscimmo con tamburo battente, e bandiere spiegate.*

A flying report, *romore, susurro, voce, fama.*

A flying coach, *sorta di carrozza di posta.*

FOAL, s. *parto femminino delle cavalla o dell' asina. Gli antichi lo usarono indistintamente pel maschio e la femmina.*

To FOAL [to bring forth a foal] *figliare ò partorire delle cavalle e delle asine.*

FOAM, s. *schiuma, spuma.*

To FOAM, *schiumare, spumare, fare spuma, generare schiuma.*

To foam, *andar in bestia, aver la schiuma alla bocca di collera.*

FO'AMY, adj. *spumante, coperto di spuma.*

FOB, s. [a small pocket] *scarsella*, s. f.

Fob-dobble, *un gonzo, un goffo.*

I won't be fob-dobbled [or be made an ass of] *non voglio passar per gonzo.*

To FOB one off [to put one off with fair words] *voler la baja d'uno, uccellarlo, beffarlo, burlarlo, tenerlo a bada.*

FO'BBED-OFF, adj. *uccellato, beffato, burlato.*

FO'CIL, s. [the greater bone of the arm or leg] *focile*, s. m. *l'osso del braccio e della gamba.*

The focil bones, *il focile maggiore e minore della gamba e del braccio.*

FO'DDER, s. [any kind of meat for cattle] *foraggio, pascolo, pasco, fodero*, s. m. *pastura, vettovaglia*, s. f.

To FO'DDER cattle [to give them straw, hay, &c.] *pascere, pascolare, pasturare il bestiame con cibo secco.*

FOE, s. [enemy] *nemico, inimico*, s. m. *nemica, inimica*, s. f.

He is my foe, *egli è mio nemico.*

FO'EMAN, s. [an enemy in war] *nemico in guerra.*

FOG, s. [mist] *nebbia*, s. m.

There is a great fog, *fa una gran nebbia.*

FO'GGY, adj. *nebbioso, pien di nebbia.*

Foggy weather, *tempo nebbioso.*

Foggy drink, *bevanda spessa.*

Foggy body, *un corpaccio, un corpo grasso.*

A foggy man, *un uomo carpacciuto, grosso, grasso.*

FOH [an interjection of abhorrence] *oibò.*

FOIL, s. [to learn to fence with] *foretto*, s. m. *col quale s'impara a tirar di scherma.*

To play at foils, *schermire coi fioretti.*

Foil [a sheet of thin tin to be laid on the backside of a looking-glass] *foglia*, s. f. *quello stagno, che si pon dietro alle spere di vetro.*

Foil [for a stone] *foglia, che si mette sotto una pietra per farla rilucere avvantaggio.*

Foil [ornament, set off] *ornamento, abbigliamento*, s. m.

Foil [repulse] *ripulsa, e repulsa, esclusione, negativa*, s. f.

A foil [in wrestling] *stramazzata*, s. f. *stramazzone*, s. m.

To give one a foil [to make him fall] *stramazzare, gettare uno a terra lutando.*

To give a foil, *ripulsare, e repulsare, dare, o far ripulsa.*

To take the foil, *ricevere una repulsa.*

To FOIL [to set off] *abbellire, ornare, adornare, parare*, pref. *abbellisco.*

To foil [to overthrow] *stramazzare, gettare a terra.*

To foil [to overcome] *vincere, superare, sormontare, sopraffare*, pret. *vinsi, sopraffeci.*

To foil [to put to the worst, to defeat] *disfar uno, disfertarlo.*

FO'ILER, s. *colui che ha avuto vantaggio contra un altro.*

FO'ILED, adj. *v.* To foil.

FOIN, s. [push, thrust] *botta*, s. f. *colpo*, s. m.

Foin [a kind of wheezle] *faina*, s. f.

To FOIN [to make a pass or thrust at one in fencing] *dare una botta, un colpo ad uno schermendo.*

FO'ISON, s. [plenty, abundance] *copia, abbondanza, fusone.*

FOIST, s. [a small ship with sails and oars] *fusta*, s. f. *spezie di navilio da remo.*

To FOIST [to forge] *supporre, falsificare.*

To foist [to stuff in] *ficcare, stivare.*

FO'ISTED, adj. *supposto, falsificato, falso.*

FOI'STING, or FOI'STY, adj. *puzzolente, puzzolente.*

FOI'STY, adj. [musty] *mucido, vizzo.*

To taste foisty, *saper di mucido.*

FO'LELAND, or FO'LKLAND, s. [the land of the common people in the time of the Saxons] *terre libere, nel tempo che i Sassoni regnavano in Inghilterra.*

FOLD, s. [a plait] *piega*, s. f.

Two-fold, adj. *doppio, duplicato.*

Two-fold, s. *il doppio, due volte più.*

Three-fold, adj. *triplicato, tre volte più.*

Hundred-fold, *centuplicato.*

Fold, or sheep-fold, s. [a place to put sheep in] *ovile*, s. m. *luogo dove si racchiuggon le pecore.*

To FOLD [to double up, to plait] *piegare.*

To fold up a letter, *piegare una lettera.*

To fold sheep [to get sheep into their fold] *condurre le pecore nell' ovile.*

FO'LDED, or FO'LDED UP, adj. *piegato.*

FO'LDER, s. *quello, o quella che piega i fogli de' libri prima d'esser legati.*

FO'LDING, s. *piegamento.*

A folding stick, *pezzo di legno col quale si piegano i fogli de' libri.*

A folding

A folding chair, *una ciscranna.*
A folding skreen, *un paravento.*
A folding door, *porta a due imposte.*
FO'LIAGE, s. [branched work] *fogliame,* s. m. *lavoro di foglie.*
FO'LIO [a folio book, or a book in folio] *un libro in foglio.*
FOLKS, s. [people] *gente,* s. f. *il popolo,* s. m. *è voce familiare.*
I never saw such folks, *non ho mai visto simile gente.*
The folks say, *si dice.*
To FO'LLOW [to come after] *seguire, seguitare, andare, o venir dietro.*
To follow [to wait upon] *accompagnare.*
To follow one's ear, *seguire una voce, andare verso quella parte dove s'intende la voce.*
To follow [to imitate] *seguire, imitare, seguitare, secondare.*
To follow one's example, *seguire l'altrui esempio.*
Follow your own inclinations, *seguitate il vostro piacere.*
To follow one's books, *applicarsi allo studio.*
To follow a trade, *attendere a qualche mestiere.*
To follow the law [as a student] *studiare la legge.*
To follow one's business, *badare a' fatti suoi.*
To follow one's pleasures, *darsi in preda ai piaceri.*
That does not follow, *ciò non fa al caso.*
To follow [to succeed] *seguire, succedere, accadere, avvenire,* pret. *successe, accadde, avvenne,* pres. *avvengo.*
If you will do so, you must take what follows, *se voi volete far così, vi bisogna soffrire quel che ne verrà.*
Hence it follows that he is so rich, *da questo procede ch' egli è sì ricco.*
FO'LLOWED, adj. *seguito, seguitato,* v. To follow.
FO'LLOWER, s. [adherent] *seguace, aderente,* s. m.
Follower [attendant] *seguito, corteggio,* s. m.
He had a great many followers, *aveva un gran corteggio.*
Follower of an opinion, *settatore.*
FO'LLOWING, s. *seguitamento,* s. m. *il seguitare.*
Following, adj. *seguente, che segue.*
The following chapter, *il capitolo seguente.*
The following year, *l'anno seguente, l'anno d'appresso.*
FO'LLY, s. [madness] *follezza, follia, sciocchezza, pazzia, stoltezza, stoltizia,* s. f.
FOME, s. *scrivi sempre* FOAM [froth] *spuma, schiuma,* s. f.
The fome of a horse, dog, or angry sea, *la spiuma d'un cavallo, d'un cane, del mare irritato.*
The fome of melted lead, *la schiuma del piombo liquefatto.*
To FOME, or FOAM, verb neut. *spumare, schiumare, fare, generare schiuma.*

A horse or dog that foams, *un cavallo o un cane che spuma.*
The sea foams, *il mare è spumoso.*
He fomes at the mouth when he speaks, *fa la schiuma alla bocca quando parla.*
To FOME'NT [to cherish or comfort, by applying warm remedies] *fomentare, applicare il fomento.*
To foment a distempered part of the body, *fomentare qualche parte del corpo offesa.*
To foment [to nourish, to abet, to encourage] *fomentare, nutrire, nutricare,* pres. *nutrisco.*
To foment a sedition, *fomentare una sedizione.*
FOMENTA'TION, s. [a bathing any part of the body with a decoction] *fomentazione,* s. f. *fomento,* s. m. *medicamento composto di vari semplici, il quale scaldato, e applicato alla parte offesa, ha virtù di corroborarla.*
FOME'NTED, adj. *fomentato, nutrito, nutricato.*
FOME'NTER, or FOME'NTOR, s. *fomentatore,* s. m. *fomentatrice,* s. f.
FOME'NTING, s. *il fomentare.*
FO'MING, adj. [foaming] *schiumoso, spumante.*
FON, s. [a fool, an idiot] *uno sciocco, un mentecatto, un idiota.*
FOND, adj. [passionately desirous of, and devoted to] *appassionato, incapriccito, invaghito, matto.*
To be fond of a woman, *esser appassionato per una donna.*
I never saw a man more fond of his wife and children, *non ho mai visto un uomo amare più sua moglie, e i suoi figliuoli.*
Fond [kind, indulgent] *indulgente, buono, benigno.*
To be too fond of one's children, *trattare i suoi figli con troppa indulgenza.*
Fond [idle] *folle, vano, matto.*
A fond conceit, *folle immaginazione.*
A fond humour, *umor fantastico.*
Fond tricks, *piccole pazzie, scappate.*
To FOND } [to coker, to pamper] *accarezzare, far*
To FO'NDLE }
carezze, vezzeggiare.
FO'NDLING, s. [one that we are fond of] *un mignone, un favorito.*
FO'NDLY, adv. *teneramente, appassionatamente.*
I fondly dreamt of it [I mistook the matter] *mi sono ingannato.*
FO'NDNESS, s. *tenerezza,* s. f. *affetto, amore, ardore,* s. m.
Fondness [indulgence] *bontà, indulgenza, connivenza nel permettere e tollerare una cosa.*
FONT, s. [a place or bason in a church, for the administration of baptism] *fonte,* s. m. *il vaso dove si tiene l'acqua battesimale.*
Font [a cast or compleat set of letters for printing] *una compita sequela di lettere da stampare.*
FO'NTANEL, s. [issue] *fontanella,* s. f. *cauterio,* s. m.
FONTA'NGE, s. *sorta di femminile acconciatura di testa.*

FOOD, s. [sustenance, victuals] *pasto, cibo,* s. m. *vivanda,* s. f.
Food and raiment, *la tavola e 'l vestire.*
FOOL, s. [a silly ignorant person, an idiot] *un cionno, uno sciocco, uno stolto, un matto, uno scioperato, uno scimunito.*
To play the fool, *fare il pazzo.*
To play the fool [to jest] *burlare, scherzare.*
You play the fool with me, *voi mi burlate.*
She is a fool, *ella è una sciocca.*
I were a great fool to believe it, *sarei ben pazzo se lo credessi.*
Every man has a fool in his sleeve, *ognuno ha 'l suo impiccato all' uscio, ognuno ha qualche difetto.*
Fools will be meddling, *ogni cencio vuole entrare in bucato, dicesi d'un prosuntuoso, quando e' vuole intromettersi in quello, che la sua condizion non ricerca.*
A fool's bolt is soon shot, *un matto dice subito quel che pensa, e si dice di quelle persone indiscrete che parlano inconsideratamente.*
Fools set stools for wise men to stumble at, *i savi alle volte restano ingannati dai semplici.*
A fool in a play, *un zanni, un buffone.*
'Tis but a fool to it, *è una bagattella a petto di questo.*
Fool-hardy, *temerario, ardito.*
Fool-hardiness, *temerità, arditezza.*
To FOOL one [to make a fool of him] *burlare, beffare, schernire,* pres. *schernisco.*
To fool one of his money, *truffare uno del suo danaro.*
To fool [to play the fool] *burlare, giocare, ridere.*
FO'OLBORN, adj. [foolish from the birth] *pazzo nato ; nato sciocco.*
FO'OLED, adj. *burlato, beffato, schernito.*
FO'OLERY, s. *follia, pazzia, impertinenza, sciocchezza, baggattella, ciancia,* s. f.
FO'OLISH, adj. *folle, pazzo, stolto, vano, sciocco, impertinente, indiscreto.*
Foolish talk, *parole vane, o ciance.*
FO'OLISHLY, adv. *follemente, stoltamente, vanamente, pazzamente, inconsideratamente.*
You have done very foolishly, *voi avete operato indiscretamente, voi avete fatto una gran follia.*
FO'OLISHNESS, s. *follia, pazzia, sciocchezza, semplicità, impertinenza, imprudenza, indiscrezione.*
FOOT, s. [a member of the body] *piede, e piè,* s. m. *membro del corpo dell' animale, sul quale e' si posa, e col qual cammina.*
The right and the left foot, *il piè destro e 'l sinistro.*
To go on foot, *andare a piedi.*
To tread under foot, *calpestare, mettere sotto i piedi.*
The foot of an hill, wall, rock, tree, *il piè d'una montagna, d'un muro, d'una rocca, d'un albero.*
The bed's foot, *i piedi del letto.*
At the foot of the reckoning, *al conto, de' conti.*

Foot [a measure of twelve inches] *piede, misura di dodici dita.*
Foot [foot soldiers] *infanteria, soldatesca a piede.*
To set a thing on foot, *mettere che che si sia in piedi, cominciarla.*
The foot of some beasts, *la zampa d'alcuni animali.*
The foot of a pillar, *la base d'una colonna.*
Foot by foot [by degrees] *piede innanzi piede, poco a poco.*
Do not stir a foot from hence, *non vi movete di qui.*
I have the length of his foot to a hair, *so a quanti punti si calza, conosco perfettamente il suo umore, so quanto pesa.*
Every foot [every moment] and anon, *ad ogni punto, ad ogni momento, ad ogni ora.*
A football, *un pallone.*
To play at football, *giuocare al pallone.*
A foot soldier, *soldato a piede, un fante.*
Footman [lackey] *uno staffiere, un lacchè.*
A footboy, *un lacchè.*
A foot-pad, *un ladro a piedi.*
Foot-pace [slowly] *piede innanzi piede, pian piano.*
To go a foot-pace, *andare di passo.*
Footstep, *traccia, pèdata,* s. f.
To follow one's footsteps, *seguitar le pedate di qualcheduno.*
Foot-stalk, *piede delle piante, la coda de' frutti.*
A foot-race, *corsa di gente a piedi.*
The foot stall of a pillar, *la base, il piedestallo d una colonna.*
The foot of a verse [a certain number of syllables which serve to measure such a verse] *piede di verso, un certo numero di sillable delle quali è composto un verso.*
The foot of a stocking, *pedule di calza.*
To be on the same foot with another [to be under the same circumstances] *esser del pari con alcuno.*
To Foot, *camminare, andare a piedi.*
'Tis but ten miles, I am resolved to foot it, *non vi sono chè dieci miglia, sono risoluto d'andarvi a piede.*
To foot a pair of stockings, *rimpedulare un pajò di calze.*
To foot [to dance, to tread wantonly, to trip] *ballare, camminare con istudiata vaghezza; andar in punta di piedi.*
To foot [to spurn, to kick] *tirar calci, dar calci.*
To foot [to settle, to begin to fix] *stabilirsi, cominciar a fissarsi*
To foot [to tread] *calpestare, porre i piedi su.*
Fo'oted, adj. *rimpedulato.*
Broad-footed, *che ha il piè largo.*
Cloven-footed, *che ha il piè fesso.*
Four-footed, *quadrupede.*
A four-footed beast, *un animale quadrupede.*
Fo'oting, s. *il camminare, l'andare a piedi.*
Footing [print of the foot in treading] *pedata, traccia.*
To get a footing in a place, *fermare il piede in un luogo, farvi la sua dimora.*
The things are on the same footing, *le cose sono nel medesimo stato.*
Footli'cker, s. *un che lecca i piedi, un adulatore, un lusinghiere vilissimo, uno schiavo.*
Fop, s. [a coxcomb; a man of small understanding and much ostentation] *un zerbino, un milordino, un parigino, un cicisbeo, uno scioccherello ben vestito, un bellimbusto, un vagheggino, uno che affetta attillatura.*
A fop-duddle [a fool] *un cionno, un minchione, uno sciocco.*
Fo'ppery, s. *affettazione, soverchia attillatura, sciochezza accompagnata da buona opinione del proprio ingegno.*
Fo'ppish, adj. *attillato, affettato.*
A foppish man, *un damerino, un affettatuzzo.*
Fo'ppishly, adv. *con vanità, con vana ostentazione.*
Fo'ppling, s. [a petty fop] *un affettatuzzo, uno scioccherello.*
For, conj. [because] *perchè.*
Don't speak to me, for I'll have nothing to do with you, *non istate a parlarmi, perchè non voglio aver nulla che fare con voi.*
For, prep. *per, a causa.*
For God's sake, *per l'amor di Dio.*
For my sake, *per l'amor mio.*
For God a-mercy, *per niente, gratis, senza alcuno interesse.*
You deserve to be whipt for doing so, *voi meritereste essere sferzato, per far così.*
She could not come for the bad weather, *ella non ha potuto venire, a causa del cattivo tempo.*
For custom's sake, *perchè è la moda.*
For greater conveniency, *per maggior agio.*
For example, *per esempio.*
For how much? *per quanto?*
For more, for less, *per più, per meno.*
For my part, *in quanto a me.*
I am sorry for it, *me ne dispiace.*
I am sorry for your misfortune, *mi rincresce della vostra disgrazia.*
Take you no care for that, *non vi pigliate fastidio di ciò.*
You are a fool for believing him, *voi siete sciocco di crederlo.*
For the present, *adesso, per adesso, ora com' ora.*
For the time to come, *all' avvenire.*
For ever and ever, *per sempre.*
For a week's time, *per una settimana, per lo spazio d'una settimana.*
I'll not trust him for all his swearing, *non mi fido a lui, non ostante i suoi giuramenti.*
I'll do it for all that, *voglio farlo con tutto ciò.*
I can't speak for grief, *il dolore m'impedisce di parlare.*
You may go for all me, *io non v'impedisco d'andare.*
I'll do it for all you, *lo farò malgrado vostro.*
For all you are my friend, *benchè voi siate mio amico, con tutto che voi siate mio amico.*
Were it not for you, *se non fosse per rispetto vostro.*
'Tis necessary for you to go, *è necessario che voi andiate.*
Are you for wine or beer? *volete vino o birra?*
'Tis not for me to do it, *non appartiene a me di far ciò.*
It is impossible for me to love her, *m'è impossibile amarla.*
What do you cry for? *perchè piangete?*
Is that it you are angry for? *e per questo voi andate in collera?*
For shame don't talk so, *eh via non parlate in questo modo.*
As for me, *in quanto a me, per me.*
As for that, *in quanto a ciò.*
To look for, *cercare.*
I take you for an honest man, *vi stimo un galatuomo.*
To speak for one, *parlare in favore di qualcheduno.*
To be for one, *tenere per alcuno.*
For that end, *a questo fine.*
For what? *perchè, per qual causa?*
To stay, or wait for, *aspettare.*
Fo'rage, s. [provision for horses and cattle in war] *foraggio,* s. m. *vettovaglia,* s. f.
To Fo'rage [to go a foraging] *foraggiare, andar per foraggio.*
Fo'rager, s. *foraggiere,* s. m.
Fo'raging, s. *il foraggiare.*
To go foraging, *andare a foraggiare.*
Forasmu'ch as, *avvegnachè, poichè, perchè, stante chè.*
Forba'd, *è un preterito del verbo,* to forbid.
To Forbe'ar [to spare] *risparmiare, perdonare.*
Pray forbear him a little, *di grazia, risparmiatelo un poco.*
To forbear one, *patire, sopportare, comportare, tollerare.* pres. *patisco.*
I cannot forbear him, *non posso patirlo.*
To forbear [to let alone] *cessare, tralasciare.*
Forbear such expressions, *cessate di parlare in questo modo.*
To forbear [to shun] *fuggire, scansare, evitare.*
Forbear such a man's company, *fuggite la compagnia d'un tal uomo.*
To forbear [to keep one's self from, to abstain] *astenersi, ritenersi, contenersi, raffrenarsi.*
You must forbear drinking wine, *bisogna astenervi dal vino.*
I could hardly forbear crying, *a gran pena ritenni le lagrime.*
I cannot forbear to tell you, *non posso far di manco di dirvi.*
Forbear laughing, *guardatevi di non ridere.*
I shall forbear it as long as I can, *me n' asterrò quanto potrò.*
Forbear, *lasciate stare.*
Forbear doing of that till I come again, *lasciatelo stare fin ch' io ritorni.*

FORBEA'RANCE, s. *pazienza, indulgenza, tolleranza, sofferenza, longanimità*, s. f.

Forbearance is no acquittance, *domeneddio non paga il sabato, cioè, il gastigo può differirsi, ma non si toglie.*

To FORBI'D [to bid not to do, to prohibit] *disendere, proibire, vietare, divietare.* pref. *disesi.* pref. *proibisco.*

Did not I forbid you to do it? *non v'ho proibito di farlo?*

He forbid me his house, *m'ha proibito d'andare a casa sua.*

God forbid, *tolga Iddio, Iddio non voglia.*

FORBI'DDANCE, s. [prohibition] *proibizione, divieto.*

FORBI'DDEN, adj. *proibito, vietato, divietato.*

Forbidden fruit, *frutto vietato.*

FORBI'DDENLY, adv. *in modo illegale.*

FORBI'DDER, s. *vietatore*, s. m. *vietatrice*, s. f

FORBI'DDING, s. *divietamento, vietamento, divieto.*

FORBO'RE, *è un preterito del verbo* to forbear.

FORBO'RN, adj. *risparmiato, tollerato, sopportato, comportato.* v. To forbear.

FORCE, s. [violence] *forza, violenza.*

Force [necessity] *forza, necessità*, s. f.

Force [weight] *forza, peso, pondo.*

Force [vigour, strength] *forza, gagliardia, robustezza, possanza*, s. f. *potere*, s. m.

To repel force by force, *risospigner la forza colla forza.*

The city was under the force of arms, *la città era oppressa della forza delle armi.*

An argument of great force, *un argomento di gran pondo.*

A law still in force, *una legge che sussiste, che è in vigore.*

By open force, *a viva forza.*

FO'RCES [in the plural] *forze, milizia, soldati, soldatesca.*

He got all his forces together, *messe insieme tutte le sue forze.*

With forces much superior to theirs, *con forze via più numerose delle loro.*

To FORCE [to oblige] *forzare, sforzare, violentare, obbligare, far forza, costringnere.* pref. *costringo.* pret. *costrinsi.*

He forced him to do what he would, *lo forzò, lo costrinse di fare quel che voleva*

Who will force me to do it? *chi farà forza al voler mio?*

To force the people to take up arms, *ridurre, sforzare il popolo a prender l'armi.*

To force a post [to take it by force] *forzare, o prender un posto per forza.*

To force a virgin, *sforzare, violare una zittella.*

To force a word, *inventare una parola, e procurare di metterla in uso.*

To force wool [to cut off the upper and most hairy part of it] *diradare la lana, tagliarla dov' ella è più folta.*

To force back, *rispignere, risospignere.*

To force out, *fare uscire per forza, scacciare.*

FO'RCED, adj. *forzato, sforzato, violentato, costretto,* v. To force.

I was forced to do it, *sono stato sforzato a farlo.*

A forced put, *un caso di necessità.*

FO'RCEDLY, adv. *forzatamente, per forza, sforzatamente.*

FO'RCELESS, adj. *debile, o debole, di poca forza, fievole, fiacco.*

FO'RCERS, s. [an instrument to draw teeth] *cane*, s. m. *strumento da cavare i denti.*

FO'RCIBLE, adj. [prevailing, strong, violent] *forte, potente, efficace, violento, nervoso, ponderoso, vigoroso.*

A forcible argument, *un argomento potente convincente.*

Forcible detaining a possession [in law, is a violent act of resistance] *resistenza che si fa a coloro, che vengono con autorità a prender possesso d'un podere, d'una terra, o d'una casa.*

FO'RCIBLENESS, s. *forza, violenza.*

FO'RCIBLY, adv. *forzevolmente, forzatamente, efficacemente, per forza, vigorosamente, poderosamente, potentemente.*

FORD, s [a shallow place in a river] *guado*, s. m *luogo nel fiume, dove può passarsi senza nave.*

To FORD, *guadare, passare fiumi da una ripa all' altra o a cavallo o a piè.*

To ford a river, *guadare un fiume.*

FO'RDABLE, adj. [which may be forded] *guadoso, che si può guadare.*

A fordable river, *un fiume guadoso.*

FORE [a preposition used in compounding words, instead of BEFORE] *è una preposizione usata nel comporre le parole, in vere di* BEFORE.

To fore-appoint, *fissare, determinare, stabilire innanzi.*

Fore-armed, adj. *armato, munito innanzi.*

Fore-warned, fore-armed, *uomo avvertito, mezzo salvato.*

To FORE-BO'DE [to presage] *presagire, fare, dare presagio, indovinare innanzi* tratto, *antivedere.* pref. *presagisco.*

FORE-BODED, *presagito.*

FOREBO'DING, s. *presagio, indovinamento, segno di cosa futura.*

FORE-CAST, s. *antivedere, antivedimento*, s. m.

A man of great forecast, *un uomo antiveduto, cauto, accorto.*

To FO'RECAST [to consider beforehand] *prevedere, antivedere, vedere avanti, considerare innanzi tratto.*

FORECA'STING, s. *antivedere, antivedimento*, s. m.

FORECA'STINGLY, adv. *prudentemente, saviamente, accortamente.*

FORE-CA'STLE, s. [of a ship, that part where the foremast stands] *cassero di vascello.*

FORE-CHO'SEN, adj *eletto primo.*

To FORE-CLO'SE [to bar or exclude for ever] *escluder per sempre, termine legale.*

FORE-CLOSED, adj. *escluso per sempre.*

To FORE-DE'EM, *indovinare, conghietturare.*

FORE-DE'EMED, adj. *indovinato, conghietturato.*

FORE DE'EMING, s. *conghiettura.*

To FO'RE-DO, *derogare.*

FORE-DO'ING, *derogazione*, s. f.

FORE DO'OR, *la porta davanti.*

FORE-FA'THERS, s. [predecessors] *antenati, predecessori.*

FORE-FEET, s. *i piedi d'avanti d'una bestia quadrupede.*

To FO'RE-FEND, or FO'RFEND [to hinder, to keep off] *disendere, impedire, trattenere.* pref. *impedisco, trattengo.* pret. *trattenni.*

FO'RE FLAP, *la falda d'avanti.*

The fore-flap of a shirt, *la falda d'avanti d'una camiscia.*

FO'RE FRONT, s. *frontespizio*, s. m. *facciata*, s. f.

The fore-front of a house, *il frontespizio, la facciata d'una casa.*

To FO'REGO [to part with] *cedere.*

To forego one's right, *cedere il suo diritto.*

To forego a thing [to forsake it] *abbandonare, mettere in abbandono che che si sia.*

FOREGO'ERS, s. [purveyors of the King and Queen] *provveditore del re o della regina.*

FORE'GOING, adj. *precedente.*

The foregoing chapter, *il capitolo precedente.*

To FO'REGUESS, *indovinare, conghietturare.*

FO'REGUESSED, adj. *indovinato, conghietturato.*

FO'REHEAD, s. *fronte*, s m.

A high forehead, *un gran fronte.*

A low forehead, *una piccola fronte.*

In the forehead and the eye, the letter of the mind does lie, *la fronte e gli occhi sono come lo specchio dell' anima.*

FO'REIGN, or FO'REIN, adj. [outlandish] *forestiere, e forestiero, straniero, oltramontano*

Foreign commodities, *mercanzie forestiere.*

Foreign news, *novelle de' paesi stranieri.*

This is foreign to our business, *ciò non fa al nostro proposito.*

FO'REIGNER, or FO'REINER, s. *un forestiere, un forestiero, uno straneiro*, s. m *forestiera, una straniera*, s f.

FO'RE-HORSE, s [the horse that goes before] *il cavallo che va avanti.*

To FO'RE-JUDGE, *giudicare avanti, escludere*, termine *legale.*

FO'RE-JUDGED, adj. *giudicato avanti.*

Fore-judged the court [expelled the court] *escluso.*

FORE-JU'DGING, s. [a judgment whereby a man is deprived of the thing in question] *esclusione*, s. f.

To FO'RE-KNOW, *sapere, conoscere innanzi*

FORE-KNOWLEDGE, s. *prescienza*, s. f.

FO'RE-KNOWN, adj. *saputo, conosciuto innanzi.*

FO'RELAND, s. [a point of land jutting out into the sea] *punta di terra che s'avanza nel mare, capo, promontorio* s. m.

FO'RELOCK, s. [the hair of the head before] *i capelli davanti della testa, ciuffo.*

FO'REMAN, s. *l'uomo che va primo.*

The foreman of a jury, *il capo de' giurati.*

FO'REMAST OF A SHIP, *l'albero di mezzo del vascello.*

The foremast sail, *la mezzana vela, che si spande alla poppa del navilio.*

FO'REMOST, adj. *il primo, che va il primo.*

I went foremost, *io comminavo il primo.*

First and foremost, adv. *primieramente, il primo luogo.*

To FO'RE-NAME, *nominare avanti.*

FO'RE-NAMED, adj. *prenominato.*

FO'RENOON, s. *la mattina.*

FORE-ORDA'INED, adj. *preordinato.*

FO'REPART, s. *la parte d'avanti, la parte anteriore.*

FORERU'NNER, s. *precursore,* s. m.

A forerunner of troubles, *preludio di disturbi.*

FO'RE-SAIL, s. [the sail of the foremast] *la mezzana.*

To FORESEE [to see beforehand] *prevedere, antivedere.* pret. *previddi antividdi.*

To foresee things to come, *preveder l'avvenire.*

FORESE'EING, s. *antivedere, antivedimento,* s. m.

FORESE'ER, s. *antiveditore,* s. m. *che antivede.*

FORESE'EN, adj. *preveduto, antiveduto, antivisto.*

To FO'RESHOW, *mostrare, far vedere avanti.*

FO'RESIGHT, s. [the seeing a thing before it comes to pass] *antivedere, antivedimento,* s. m.

To have a foresight of something, *prevedere qualche cosa.*

FO'RESKIN, s. *il prepuzio.*

To FO'RESLACK [to enervate] *snervare, debilitare, spossare, rallentare.*

To FO'RESLOW [to hinder] *impedire, ritardare, intertenere.* pref. *impedisco, intertengo.* pret. *intertenni.*

To FO'RESPEAK [to bespeak] *comandare, far fare.*

To forespeak [to bewitch, to enchant] *incantare, ammaliare.*

FORE-SPEECH s. *prologo,* s. m.

FORESPU'RRER, s. *colui che galoppa innangi agli altri.*

FO'REST, s. [a large wood] *foresta,* s. m.

Forest-work [a sort of tapestry work] *verdura, spezie di tappezzeria ove vi sono tessuti prati, boschi, alberi, e simili.*

FO'RESTAFF, s. [a sea instrument for observing the sun, moon and stars, and their altitude] *astrolabio,* s. f. *strumento astronomico che serve per misurare l'altezza del sole, della luna, e delle stelle.*

To FO'RESTA'LL, *intercettare, sorprendere.*

To forestall the market [to buy or bargain for corn, cattle, &c. as it is coming to any market or fair to be sold, in order to sell the same at a higher price] *incettare, fare incetta, comprare la roba prima che venga in mercato, per rivenderla poi a più caro prezzo.*

To forestall [to prepossess] *preoccupare, prevenire, antecipare, ovviare.* pref. *prevengo.*

FORESTA'LLER, s. *intercettato, sorpreso.* v. To forestall.

FO'RESTA'LLER, s. *incettatore,* s. m.

FORESTA'LLING, s. *incetta,* s. f.

FO'RESTER, s. *custode della foresta.*

To FORETA'STE [to taste beforehand] *pregustare, gustare, assaggiare avanti.*

FORETA'STED, adj. *pregustato.*

FORETE'ETH, s. *i denti d'avanti.*

To FO'RETEL [to tell beforehand what is to come] *predire, presagire dir quello che ha da essere.* pref. *predico, presagisco,* pret. *predissi.*

To foretell things to come, *predir l'avvenire.*

FORETE'LLER, s. *quello, o quella che predice.*

FORETE'LLING, s. *predicimento,* s. m. *predizione,* s. f.

To FO'RETHINK [to think beforehand] *pensare avanti, premeditare.*

FO'RETHOUGHT, adj. *pensato avanti, premeditato.*

Forethought, s. *premeditazione,* s. f.

FORETO'KEN, s. *presagio, segno,* s. m.

FO'RETOLD, adj. *predetto, profetizzato, presagito.*

To FO'REWARN [to warn beforehand] *avvertire avanti.* pref. *avvertisco.*

I forewarn you of it, *ve ne avvertisco prima.*

FOREWA'RNED, adj. *avvertito prima.*

FOREWA'RNING, s. *avvertimento,* s. m.

FO'RE WHEEL, s. *ruota d'avanti.*

The fore-wheels of a coach, *le ruote d'avanti d'una carrozza.*

FO'RE-WIND, s. *vento in poppa.*

FO'RFEIT, s. [default] *delitto, misfatto, errore,* s. m. *trasgressione, colpa,* s. f.

Forfeit [fine, penalty] *ammenda, pena, multa, condannagione,* s. f.

To pay the forfeit, *pagar l'ammenda.*

To FO'RFEIT [to lose estate, goods, employment, &c. for neglecting doing one's duty, or for some crime committed] *perder per sequestrazione.*

To forfeit one's farm, *perder il suo feudo per sequestrazione.*

To forfeit one's estate, *esserli staggiti i suoi beni.*

To forfeit one's word, *mancar di parola.*

To forfeit one's credit, one's life, *perder il credito, la vita.*

To forfeit one's judgment in a thing, *mancar di giudizio in che che si sia.*

FO'RFEITABLE, adj. *soggetto a confiscazione.*

FO'RFEITED, adj. *confiscato, sequestrato, perduto.*

His estate is forfeited to the king, *i suoi beni sono confiscati per il rè.*

FO'RFEITURE, s. *confiscazione,* s. f.

To FO'RFEND, ex. heaven forfend that, *a Dio non piacria, tolga Iddio, Iddio non voglia.*

FORGA'VE, pret. *del verbo* to forgive.

FORGE, s. [the place where a smith beats his iron] *fucina,* s. f. *luogo dove i fabbri bollono il ferro.*

Forge [a large place where iron ore is melted] *ferriera,* s. f. *fucina dove si raffina il ferro.*

To FORGE [to hammer a work as a smith does] *battere il ferro o altro metallo come fanno i fabbri, per mezzo del fuoco, e del martello.*

To forge iron, *batter del ferro, fabbricare, martellare il ferro.*

To forge [to invent or frame] *inventare, macchinare.*

To forge a lye, *inventare una bugia.*

To forge a deceit, *macchinare un inganno.*

To forge [to counterfeit] *contraffare, falsificare, trovare.*

To forge a will, *contraffare un testamento, fare un testamento falso.*

FORGED, adj. *battuto, fabbricato, martellato.*

Forged [invented] *inventatto, macchinato.*

Forged [counterfeit] *contraffato, falsificato, trovato.*

FO'RGER, s. *fabbro.* s. m.

Forger [inventor] *inventore, macchinatore, fabbricatore,* s. m.

A forger of lyes, *un inventore di bugie, fabbricator di menzogne.*

A forger of false deeds, *un falsario.*

FO'RGING, s. *fabbricazione,* s. f. v. To forge.

FO'RGERY, s. *una falsità.*

To FORGE'T [to let slip out of memory] *dimenticare; e dimenticarsi, scordarsi, sdimenticarsi, dismenticarsi, obliare.*

To forget [to neglect] one, *dimenticarsi d'uno, abbandonarlo.*

To forget that which one has learned, *disimparare, scordarsi le cose imparate.*

You forget yourself, *voi vi scordate chi siete.*

FORGE'TFUL, adj. *dimentichevole, dimentico, irricordevole, oblioso, scordevole, sdimentico.*

Forgetful of benefits received, *sconoscente.*

Forgetful [negligent] *neghittoso, negligente.*

Pray be not forgetful of that business, *vi prego di non iscordarvi di quel negozio.*

FORGE'TFULNESS, s. *dimenticamento, obliamento, oblio, scordamento, smenticamento,* s. m. *oblianza, oblivione, sdimenticanza, smemoraggine, smenticanza, dimenticanza, dimenticagione,* s. f.

To FORGI'VE [to pardon] *perdonare, condonare, rimettere.* pret. *rimisi.*

To

To forgive one's enemies, *perdonare i suoi nemici.*

Forgive me this fault, *perdonatemi quest' errore.*

To forgive a debt, *rimettere un debito.*

FORGI'VEN, adj. *perdonato, rimesso, condonato.*

A fault not to be forgiven, *un errore imperdonabile, irremissibile.*

FORGI'VENESS, s. *remissione, rimissione* s. f. *perdono,* s. m.

To ask God forgiveness of our sins, *domandare a Dio la remissione, il perdono de' nostri peccati.*

FORGI'VER, s. *perdonatore,* s. m. *perdonatrice,* s. f.

FORGI'VING, s. *perdonamento,* s. m. *il perdonare.*

FORGO'T, *è un preterito del verbo* to forget.

FORGO'TTEN, adj. *dimenticato, scordato, sdimenticato, dismenticato, obbliato.*

I had forgotten it, *l'avevo dimenticato, men' ero dimenticato.*

Those things are easily forgotten, *queste cose si dimenticano facilmente.*

FORK, s. [an instrument for several uses] *forca,* s. f.

A fork [to eat with] *forchetta, forcina,* s. f.

A pitch-fork, *un forcone.*

A fire fork, *un ferro dattizzare il fuoco.*

To FORK, *terminare in maniera di forca.*

FO'RKED, FO'RKY, } adj. *forcato, forcuto.*

FORK FISH [a kind of fish] *pastinaca,* s. f. *spezie di pesce di mare.*

FO'RLET, FO'RLORN, } adj. [desperate, cast down] *disperato, sconcertato, sgomentato, che è in disperazione, privo di speranza.*

Forlorn [forsaken] *abbandonato, derelitto.*

The forlorn hope of an army [soldiers who are put upon the most desperate actions] *soldati d'un esercito, che sono impiegati in cose pericolosissime.*

FO'RLORNNESS, s. *misera solitudine, condizione solitaria e infelice; miseria, solitudine.*

FORM, s. [fashion, figure] *forma, figura, foggia,* s. f.

Form [manner] *foggia, maniera, guisa, fazione,* s. f. *moda,* s. m.

FORM [rule] *forma, regola, norma,* s. f. *stile,* s. m.

To give a thing its form, *dare la forma a che che si sia.*

A set form, *formola, e formula.*

To take a new form, *prender nuova forma, o figura.*

A form of government, *forma di governo.*

To do things in due form, *fare che che si sia nelle forme.*

To argue in due form, *argomentare in forma.*

For form sake, *per formalità.*

A set form of prayers, *una formola di preghiere.*

Form of a hare [the seat of a hare] *cavo di lepre.*

The hare forms, *la lepre è a covare.*

Form [bench] *scanno,* s. m. *panca,* s. f.

Form in a school, *classe,* s. f.

The first or the last form, *la prima, o l'ultima classe.*

To set a form [in the art of printing] *comporre una forma.*

To take off a form, *levare una forma.*

To FORM [to fashion] *formare, dar forma, ordinare, creare, comporre.* pref. *compongo.* pret. *composi.*

To form a design, *formare, macchinare un disegno.*

To form a commonwealth, *formare, stabilire una repubblica,* pref. *stabilisco.*

To form the tenses of a verb, *formare i tempi d'un verbo.*

FO'RMAL, adj. [belonging to form] *formale, di forma.*

A formal cause, in logick [is that which gives an internal being or essence to substances and accidents] *una causa formale.*

Formal [affected, precise] *formale, preciso, affettato, puntato.*

A formal man, *un uomo affettato, che usa negli atti, nelle parole, e negli abiti soverchio artificio, e che va composto.*

A formal set speech, *un discorso affettato, puntato, studiato, lerrato; parole superflue, e leziose.*

FO'RMALIST, s. [one who is very punctual or precise in his words and actions *un uomo composto.*

FORMA'LITY, s. [form in law] *forma, formalità,* s. f.

All the formalities of justice were duly observed, *tutte le formalità della giustizia furono affettatamente osservate.*

Formality [ceremony] *formalità, cerimonia,* s. f.

Formality [affectation] *affettazione, maniera affettata.*

Formalities [robes worn by the magistrates of a city or corporation, on solemn occasions] *vesti solenni.*

The mayor and aldermen appeared in their formalities, *il goveruatore, e gli eletti del popolo vi assisterono nelle loro vesti solenni.*

To FO'RMALIZE [to act or play the formal] *trattare con troppa affettazione, comporsi nelle parole, e negli atti.*

FO'RMALLY, adv. *formalmente, con forma.*

Formally [affectedly] *affettatamente, compostamente, con affettazione.*

He doeth things so formally, *fa le cose sì affettatamente, con tanta affettazione.*

Formally [perfunctorily] *pro forma.*

FORMA'TION, s. [a fashioning or framing] *formazione,* s. f. *il formare.*

FORMED, adj. *formato, composto,* v. To form.

FO'RMER, adj. [from fore] *primiero, primo, precedente, passato.*

Let us try to recover our former liberty, *ingegniamoci di ripigliare la nostra primiera libertà.*

In the former chapter, *nel capitolo precedente.*

In former times, *ne' tempi addietro, ne' tempi trascorsi.*

FO'RMERLY, adv. [in former days] *anticamente, altre volte, tempo fu, per l'addietro, già, nel tempo passato.*

FO'RMIDABLE, adj. [dreadful] *formidabile, spaventoso, tremendo.*

A formidable army, *un esercito formidabile, poderoso.*

A formidable prince, *un principe formidabile, o potente.*

FO'RMIDABLENESS, s. *qualità formidabile.*

FO'RMIDABLY, adv. [in a formidable manner] *in una maniera formidabile, poderosamente.*

FO'RMING, s. [from to form] *formamento, componimento,* s. m. *il formare, creazione,* s. f.

FO'RMLESS, adj. [without form] *informe, sformato.*

FORMO'SITY, s. [beauty] *formosità, bellezza,* s. f.

FO'RMULARY, s. [a model for doing any thing] *una formolà, o formula, un formulario.*

FORNICA'TION, s. *fornicazione,* s. f.

To commit fornication, *fornicare.*

FORNICA'TOR, s. *fornicatore* s. m.

FO'RNICATRESS, s. *fornicatrice.*

To FORSAKE, [to leave, to abandon] *abbandonare, lasciare.*

To forsake one's friends, *abbandonare i suoi amici.*

To forsake one's wife, *lasciar sua moglie.*

To forsake sensual pleasures, *rinunziare i piaceri carnali.*

To forsake one's religion, *abbandonare la sua religione, apostatare, fornicare.*

To forsake a vice, *lasciare un vizio, correggersene.*

To forsake the respect which is due to one, *mancare al rispetto dovuto ad una persona.*

To forsake one's colours [to run away from one's colours] *abbandonare la sua compagnia, disertare.*

FORSA'KEN, adj. *abbandonato, lasciato,* v. To forsake.

FORSA'KER, s. *abbandonatore,* s. m. *che abbandona.*

FORSA'KING, s. *abbandonamento,* s. m. *l'abbandonare.*

The forsaking of one's religion, *apostasia,* s. f.

FO'RSET, s. [a little trunk or coffer] *forzieretto, forzierino, forziernolo, forzieruzzo,* s. m.

FORSO'OK, *è un preterito del verbo* to forsake.

FORSO'OTH, adv. *di certo, veramente, da vero, in verità, madiè.*

Yes forsooth, *sì, da vero, sì per certo, madiè sì.*

Forsooth [an interjection of contempt or derision] *parola di disprezzo, o di scorno.*

He goes to Rome to pray, whilst forsooth his family is starving at home, *veramente se ne va a Roma per pregare, e la sua famiglia si muore di fame a casa.*

Yes forsooth, *madonna sì.*

To FORSWE'AR, v. n. [to swear false] *spergiurare, fare uno spergiuro, fare un giuramento falso.*

I'll forswear it to him, *io giurerò il contrario.*

To forswear [to renounce] one's religion, *abbandonare la sua religione, apostatare.*

FORSWE'ARER, s. [perjurer] *spergiuratore, spergiuro.*

FORSWE'ARING, s. *spergiuramento,* s. m. *lo spergiurare.*

FO'RSWORN, adj. *spergiurato.*

FORT, s. [a strong hold] *un forte, un posto fiancheggiato, per guardare un passo, o un sito.*

A little fort, *un fortino.*

FORTE [a term used in musick when the movement is strong and bold] *forte, termine musicale.*

FORTH, adv. ex.

From this time forth, *da qui innanzi, per l' avvenire.*

And so forth, *e così di mano in mano.*

Forth, *è spesse volte unito con un verbo, e partecipa dalla sua significazione,* ex.

To go forth, to come forth, *uscire.* pref. *esco.*

To set forth, *presentare, descrivere, rappresentare.*

To set forth a book, *pubblicare, dare alla luce un libro.*

To set forth on a journey, *incamminarsi, mettersi in cammino.*

Forth coming, s. [appearance in court] *comparigione,* s. f. *il comparire in giudicio.*

To be forth coming in court, *comparire in guidicio.*

FO'RTHWITH, adv. [presently] *incontinente, incontanente, tosto, subito, immantenente.*

FO'RTIETH, adj. [from forty] *quarantesimo.*

FORTIFI'ABLE, adj. [which is capable of being fortified] *che si può fortificare.*

FORTIFICA'TION, s. [an art of fortifying and strengthening a place] *fortificazione,* s. f. *fortificamento,* s. m. *l'arte del fortificare un luogo.*

A fortification, *una fortificazione, un luogo fortificato.*

To FO'RTIFY [to strengthen, or make strong] *fortificare, munire, afforzare, render forte* pref. *munisco.*

To fortify a town, *fortificare, munire una città.*

To fortify one's mind against all temptations, *munirsi contro tutte le tentazioni.*

FO'RTIFIED, adj. *fortificato, munito, afforzato.*

FORTIFY'ING, s. *fortificamento,* s. m. *il fortificare.*

FORTIFI'ER, s. [that fortifies] *fortificatore,* s. m. *fortificatrice,* s. f.

FORTILAGE, } s. *picciol forte.*
FO'RTIN, }

FO'RTITUDE, s. [one of the four cardinal virtues] *fortezza,* s. f. *una delle quatro virtù cardinali.*

FO'RTLET, s. [a little fort] *un fortino.*

FO'RTNIGHT, s. *quindici giorni.*

This day fortnight, or a fortnight hence, *fra quindici giorni, da qui a quindici giorni.*

This day fortnight, or a fortnight ago, *quindici giorni fa, o quindici giorni sono.*

FO'RTRESS, s. [a general name for all places that are fortified] *fortezza, rocca, cittadella,* s. f. *propugnacolo fatto per difender se, e gli altri.*

An impregnable fortress, *una fortezza inespugnabile.*

FORTU'ITOUS, adj. [happening by chance, casual, accidental] *fortuito, di caso, casuale, accidentale, fortunoso, fortunato.*

FORTU'ITOUSLY, adv. *casualmente, a caso, accidentalmente.*

FORTU'ITOUSNESS, s. *accidente, caso, sorte.*

FO'RTUNATE, adj. [happy, lucky] *fortunato, avventuroso.*

He is a fortunate man, *egli è un uomo fortunato.*

Very fortunate, *fortunatissimo.*

FO'RTUNATELY, adv. *fortunatamente, con buona fortuna, avventurosamente.*

FO'RTUNATENESS, s. *buona fortuna.*

FO'RTUNE, s. [adventure, chance, good luck] *fortuna, ventura,* s. f. *avvenimento buono e felice.*

The wheel of fortune, *la ruota della fortuna.*

We are all subject to changes of fortune, *noi siamo tutti soggetti ai capricci della fortuna.*

When once fortune begins to frown, friends will be packing, *subito che la fortuna non ci arride più, tutti gli amici spariscono.*

Fortune [hazard] *fortuna, caso, avvenimento indeterminato.*

To commit a thing to fortune, *rimetter che che si sia alla fortuna.*

To make one's fortune, *far fortuna, ingrandirsi.*

Fortune [estate, goods] *beni di fortuna, richezze, beni.*

To sacrifice one's life and fortune for one's country, *sacrificar la vita e i beni per la patria.*

I was never yet master of any fortune, *non son mai stato possessore di molte ricchezze.*

Fortune [fate] *fortuna, fato, destino.*

To take one's fortune, *rimettersi alla fortuna, mettersi nelle mani del destino.*

She is a great fortune [or rich match] *ella ha una gran dote, ella è una donna molto ricca.*

To marry a fortune, or a great fortune, *sposare una donna ricca.*

Ill fortune, *disgrazia, miseria, malore.*

Fortune [estate, condition] *fortuna, condizione, stato, essere.*

Private fortune, *stato d'uomo privato.*

To FO'RTUNE [to befall, to fall out, to happen, to come casually to pass] *avvenire, accadere.*

FO'RTUNED, adj. [supplied by fortune] *assistito dalla sorte, fortunato.*

FORTUNETELLER, s. [one who cheats common people by pretending to the knowledge of futurity] *un dicitore di buona fortuna; uno che inganna pretendendo di saper l' avvenire.*

FO'RTY, adj. *quaranta.*

FO'RWARD, adj. *avanzato, che comincia presto.*

A forward spring, *una primavera avanzata, che principia a buon' ora.*

A forward fruit, *un frutto primaticcio, che si matura a buon' ora.*

A forward child, *un fanciullo che cresce molto.*

A forward piece of work, *un' opera molto avanzata, che è quasi finita.*

A child that is forward in learning, or forward in his book, *un fanciullo che fa progresso nello studio.*

Forward [free] *libero, ardito.*

You are a little too forward to speak your mind, *voi siete troppo libero nel dire il vostro sentimento.*

Forward [ready, well inclined] *pronto, disposto, inclinato, dedito.*

You will always find me very forward to serve you, *voi mi troverete sempre dispostissimo a servirvi.*

He seems to be forward enough in it, *par che vi sia molto inclinato.*

He is not very forward to pay, *non è molto puntuale nel pagare.*

A forward man in the world, *un uomo benestante, ricco, comodo.*

Forward [on the forepart] *anteriore.*

Forward, or forwards, adv. *avanti.*

To go forward, *andare avanti, inoltrarsi.*

To move forward, *avanzarsi, avanzare.*

The enemy's army moves forward, *l' esercito nemico s'avanza.*

He goes backward instead of going forward, *va indietro in luogo d' andare avanti.*

To go forward in learning, *profittare, far profitto, o progresso nelle scienze.*

To go backwards and forwards, *andare e venire, andare avanti e indietro.*

I walked above two hours backwards and forwards, *sono due ore che cammino.*

To go backwards and forwards [not agree with one's self] *contraddirsi.*

To put forwards, *avanzare, spignere,* pref. *spingo,* pret. *spinsi.*

To put one's self forward, *avanzarsi, ingrandirsi, profittare, approdare, far fortuna.*

To come forward, *avvanzare, avvicinarsi, farsi avanti.*

He is very forward in his work, *la sua opera è molto avanzata.*

Set yourself forward, *avvicinatevi.*

To set one's feet forward, *avanzare, allungare i piedi.*

To set one's hand forward, *stender la mano.*

To set the clock forward, *avanzar l'orologio.*

From this time forward, *d'ora in avanti.*

From

From that time forward, *da quel tempo in qua.*
To egg forward, *spronare, incitare, eccitare, spignere,* pref. *spingo,* pret. *spinsi.*
To FO'RWARD [to set forward] *far fretta, affrettare.*
This will forward your work, *questo accelererà la vostra opera.*
To forward, *ajutare, assistere, promòvere, e promuovere.*
FO'RWARDLY, adv. [eagerly, hastily] *avidamente, con gran fretta.*
FO'RWARDNESS, s. *prontezza, sollecitudine, premura,* s. f.
You cannot blame my forwardness in it, *voi non potrete condannare la mia sollecitudine in ciò.*
I admire the boy's forwardness [or progress] *mi stupisco del gran progresso del giovine.*
A thing which is in good forwardness, *una cosa che è in buon essere, molto avanzata.*
The business is in great forwardness, *il negozio è in buon porto.*
FO'RWARDS, adv. *innanzi e per lo dritto; progressivamente.*
FOSSE, s. [a ditch] *un fosso.*
FOSS-WAY, s. [one of the four principal ways of England made by the Romans] *una delle quatro strade principali d'Inghilterra fatte dai Romani.*
FOSSILE, adj. [that which is or may be digged out of the ground] *fossile.*
A fossile salt, *sale fossile.*
FO'STER FATHER, *balio,* s. m.
Foster son, *pupillo.*
Foster brother, *fratello di latte.*
No longer foster, no longer son, *cessato il guadagno, cessa l'amicizia.*
Foster land [land given or allotted to the finding of victuals for any person] *beni dati, o assegnati per il mantenimento di qualche persona.*
To FO'STER [to nourish, to cherish] *governare, reggere, allevare.*
FO'STERED, adj. *governato, retto, allevato*
FO'STERER, s. *balio,* s. m.
FOUGA'DE, s. [a sort of mine in which are fire-works to blow any thing up] *spezie di mina di fuoco artificiato per far saltar in aria che che si sia.*
FOUGHT, *è un preterito del verbo* to fight.
FO'UGHTEN, *participio passivo del verbo* to fight.
FOUL, adj. [nasty, filthy] *sporco, sezzo, sucido, imbrattato.*
Foul linen, *biancheria sporca.*
Foul water, *acqua sporca.*
Foul stomach, *stomaco in disordine per ripienezza.*
Foul copy, *una copia che non è scritta al netto, piena d'emendazioni.*
'Tis good fishing in foul water, *è molto opportuno di pescare in acqua torbida.*
A foul page [in the art of printing] *una facciata scorretta, piena d'errori.*
A foul action, *un azione indegna.*
The foul disease [the French pox] *il mal Franzese.*
Foul weather [at sea] *fortuna, tempesta, burrasca.*

To play foul play, *truffare, mariuolare nel giuoco.*
Foul papers, *schizzo,* s. m.
To give one foul language, *dire dell' ingiurie ad uno, ingiuriarlo, svillaneggiare uno.*
Foul dealing, or practice, *doppiezza, soperchieria, fraude,* s. f. *inganno,* s. m.
Foul means, *rigore,* s. m. *forza, severità,* s. f.
Never seek that by foul means which thou canst get by fair, *non cercar per forza quel che puoi aver di buona voglia.*
Foul doings [foul work] *strepito, fracasso.*
A foul shame, *una gran vergogna, un' infamia.*
Foul [ill-favoured, ugly] *brutto, malfatto.*
Foul in the cradle, and fair in the saddle, *un brutto bambino, può divenire un bell' uomo.*
A foul deal, *una gran quantità.*
Foul mouthed [apt to give one foul language] *maledico, lingua satirica.*
To fall foul upon one, *avventarsi sopra alcuno, maltrattarlo con bastonate, o con parole.*
To FOUL [to make filthy] *sporcare, imbrattare, bruttare.*
To foul the water, *intorbidar l'acqua.*
FOULED, adj. *sporcato, imbrattato, bruttato.*
FO'ULNESS [filthiness] *sporcizia, sporcheria, porcheria,* s. f.
The foulness of the stomach, *l'impurità dello stomaco.*
Foulness [ugliness] *bruttezza, deformità,* s. f.
FOUND, adj. [from to find] *trovato.*
To FOUND [to settle, to establish] *fondare, collocare, fermare, stabilire, edificare,* pref. *stabilisco.*
To found a college, *fondare un collegio.*
To found [to cast] *fondere, struggere, liquefare i metalli, gettare.*
To found a bell, *gettare una campana.*
FOUNDA'TION, s. [the groundwork of a building] *fondamento,* s. m. *terren sodo, sopra del quale si fondano, e posano edifici.*
To lay the foundation, *piantare, gettare il fondamento.*
FO'UNDED, adj. *fondato, collocato, fermato, stabilito, edificato.*
This hospital was founded by such a one, *questo spedale fu fondato, da un tale.*
A bell new founded or cast, *una campana nuovamente gettata.*
FO'UNDER, s. [one who founds and endows a church, college, &c.] *fonditore,* s. m.
He is the founder of it, *egli n' è il fonditore.*
He is the founder of his own fortune, *egli è il fabbro della sua fortuna.*
A bell-founder, *fonditor di campane.*

The founder of the feast, *colui o colei che regala la compagnia.*
To drink a health to the founder, *bere alla salute di colui che regala la compagnia.*
To FOUNDER a horse [to spoil him with hard working] *stroppiare, rovinare un cavallo colla troppa fatica.*
To founder, *affondare, andar a fondo.*
To founder, *non riuscire, rimaner deluso.*
FO'UNDERED, adj. *stroppiato, rovinato, affondato, deluso.*
A horse foundered in the feet, *un cavallo rappreso.*
A ship foundered, *un vascello sfondato, che sta per andare a fondo.*
FO'UNDING, s. *fondazione,* s. f. *fondamento, stabilimento,* s. m.
The founding of a church, *la fondazione d' una chiesa.*
The founding of a bell, *il gettare una campana.*
FO'UNDLING, s. [an infant exposed or left in any place, and found there] *un fanciullo esposto, un fanciullo trovato.*
FOUNT, s. [a poetical word for fountain] *fonte,* s. m.
FO'UNTAIN, s. [a place where waters break out of the earth, a spring] *fontana,* s. f. *fonte,* s. m.
A little fountain, *una fontanella*
Fountain head, *scaturigine,* s. f. *sorgente,* s. m.
FO'UNTFULL, adj. *pien di sorgenti d'acqua, pien di zampilli.*
FOUR, adj. *quattro.*
Fourscore, *ottanta.*
Four manner of ways, *di quattro differenti maniere.*
Four fold, *quattro volte più.*
Four hundred, *quattrocento.*
Four square, *quadrato, quadro.*
Four cornered, *quadrangolare.*
Four handed, *che ha quattro mani.*
Four footed, *quadrupede, che ha quattro piedi.*
A four-footed beast, *un animale quadrupede.*
Four thousand, *quattromila.*
Fourfold, s. [four times fold] *quattro volte tanto, quadruplo.*
FO'URIER, s. [harbinger] *furiere,* s. m. *colui che va avanti a fare i quartieri.*
FOURTE'EN, adj. *quattordici.*
FOURTE'ENTH, adj. *quattordicesimo, decimo quarto.*
FOURTH, adj. *quarto.*
The fourth part of a thing, *la quarta parte di che che si sia.*
FO'URTHLY, adv. *in quarto luogo.*
FOURWHE'ELED, adj. *che va su quattro ruote.*
FOWL, s. [bird] *uccello,* s. m.
The fowls of the air, *gli uccelli dell' aria.*
A little fowl, *un uccellino.*
A water fowl, *uccello d'acqua.*
Fowl, *pollame, ucellame, polli, galline, oche, e simili.*
To FOWL [to go a fowling] *uccellare, andare alla caccia degli uccelli.*

FO'WLER, s. [that goes a fowling] *uccellatore*, s. m.

Fowler [a piece of artillery] *petriera*, s. f.

FO'WLING, s. *la caccia degli uccelli, l'uccellare.*

To delight in fowling, *amare la caccia degli uccelli.*

To go a fowling, *andare ad uccellare.*

Fowling time, *uccellatura*, s. f. *il tempo dell' uccellare.*

Fowling piece, *scoppietto da uccellare.*

FOX, s. [a beast of chace] *volpe*, s. f.

He is an old fox, *egli è una volpe vecchia, egli è un uomo fine, astuto.*

A cunning fox, *un volpone, un astuto.*

Belonging to a fox, *volpigno, volpino.*

A fox-cub, *un volpicino.*

A little fox, *una volpicella.*

When the fox preaches, beware of your geese, *quando la volpe predica badate alle oche.*

Every fox must pay his own skin to the flear, tutte *le volpi alla fine si riveggono in pellicceria.*

A fox tail, *una coda di volpe.*

Fox tail [an herb] *erba simile alla coda delle volpe.*

Fox case, *pelle di volpe.*

To set the fox to keep his geese, *dar la lattughe in guardia a' paperi.*

To FOX [to make drunk] *imbriacare.*

FOXED, adj. *imbriacato.*

FOY, s. [a treat given to their friends by those who are going a journey] *regalo che si da agli amici da quelli che si mettono in viaggio.*

FOYL, v. Foil.

FOY'LING, s. [the footsteps of a stag upon the grass] *pesta*, s. f. *le pedate d'un cervo che si lascia dietro sull' erba.*

To FRACT [to break, to violate, to infringe] *rompere, violare, oltrepassare.*

FRA'CTION, s. [or breaking] *frangimento, infragnimento, rompimento*, s. m.

Fraction [in arithmetick, a broken number] *numero rotto, termine d'arimetica.*

FRA'CTURE, s. [the breaking of a bone] *frattura*, s. f.

Fracture in the bone, *frattura dell' osso.*

FRA'CTURED, adj. *franto, fratto.*

FRA'GILE, adj. [apt to break, brittle] *fragile, che agevolmente si rompe, frale.*

Glass is very fragile, *il vetro è molto fragile.*

Fragile [weak] *fragile, debole, e debile, frale, fievole.*

FRAGI'LITY, s. [brittleness, weakness] *fragilità, fragilezza, debilità*, s. f.

Human fragility, *la fragilità umana.*

FRA'GMENT, s. [a broken piece, or part of any thing] *frammento*, s. m. *parte di cosa rotta.*

Fragments of meat, *rimasugli, avanzaticci di carne.*

The fragments of a book, *frammenti d'un libro.*

FRA'GRANCE, } s. [sweetness of
FRA'GRANCY, } smell] *fragranzia, e fragranza*, s. f. *odor buono e soave.*

FRA'GRANT, adj. [of a sweet and pleasant smell] *fragrante, odorifero.*

FRAIGHT, s. [money paid for the burden or merchandize a ship carries] *nolo*, s. m. *il pagamento del porto delle mercanzie, o d'altre cose condotte da' navili, è meglio scritto*, FREIGHT.

Fraight [the burden, lading or merchandize a ship carries] *il carico d'un vascello.*

To FRAIGHT [to hire] *noleggiare, prendere a nolo.*

To fraight a ship, *noleggiare un navilio.*

To fraight [to furnish a ship with lading] *caricare un navilio.*

FRA'IGHTED, adj. *noleggiato, caricato.*

FRAIL, adj. [weak] *frale, fragile, debole, fievole.*

Frail, s. [a basket] *sporta*, s. f.

A frail of raisins, *una sporta d'uve passe.*

FRA'ILTY, s. [weakness of nature] *fralezza, fragilità*, s. f.

The frailty of our nature, *la fralezza della nostra natura.*

FRAME, s. [form, structure, composition] *forma, struttura, fabbrica, composizione*, s. f.

Frame [figure] *forma, figura*, s. f.

A frame [an engine to put about any thing] *telajo*, s. m.

The frame of a piece of ordnance, *la cassa d'un cannone.*

The frame of a picture, *la cornice d'un quadro.*

The frame [which some artists, as embroiderers, periwig-makers, &c. work upon] *telajo, del quale si servono alcuni artefici, come ricamatori, parrucchieri, e simili.*

A frame-knitter [one who knits stockings in frames] *calzettajo, colui che fa le calzette al telajo.*

The frame of a clock, *la cassa d'un oriuolo.*

The frame of a table, *i piedi d'una tavola.*

To be out of frame [not well] *esser indisposto.*

The frame wherein farriers put unruly horses when they shoe or dress them, *travaglio*, s. m. *dicono i maniscalchi ad un ordigno nel quale mettono le bestie fastidiose e intrattabili, per ferrarle o medicarle.*

The frame of one's life, *il corso della vita.*

The frame of the mind, *la disposizione, lo stato della mente.*

To FRAME [to form] *formare, fare, dar forma, ordinare, comporre.* pres. *compongo.* pret. *composi.*

To frame a design, *formare un disegno.*

When God framed this universe, *quando Iddio formò, o fece questo universo.*

To frame [to build] *fabbricare, edificare, construire.* pres. *construisco.*

To frame one's life according to God's word, *uniformare la nostra vita alla parola di Dio, regolare la nostra vita secondo la parola di Dio.*

To frame [to contrive] *inventare, fignere, controvare.* pres. *fingo.* pret. *finsi.*

To frame a story, *inventare, fignere un' istoria, una novella.*

To frame one's thoughts into words, *esprimere, dire i suoi pensieri per mezzo delle parole.*

FRA'MED, adj. *formato*, v. To frame.

Ill framed, *informe, deforme, malfatto.*

FRA'MER, s. [maker, former, contriver, schemer] *colui che fa, forma, trova, inventa, disegna, ordina, dispone.*

FRA'MPOLD, adj. [peevish, boisterous, rugged] *di mal umore, romoroso, inquieto, ruvido.*

FRA'NCHISE, s. [liberty, freedom, a particular privilege belonging to a city or corporation] *franchigia, libertà, esenzione, immunità*, s. f. *privilegio*, s. m.

To FRA'NCHISE [to make free] *francare, far franco, esentare, esenzionare.*

FRANCI'SCAN, s. [a Franciscan friar] *un Francescano, religioso dell' ordine di San Francesco.*

FRA'NCOLIN, s. [a sort of bird] *francolino*, s. m. *spezie d'uccello.*

FRA'NGIBLE, adj. [apt to break] *frangibile, agevole a frangersi.*

FRANK, adj. [free, generous, openhearted] *franco, libero, schietto, sincero, candido.*

Frank [liberal] *liberale, generoso.*

Frank almoin [a tenure of lands or tenements bestowed for perpetual alms] *beni stabili dati per distribuirli in limosine perpetue, alle quali il donatore non ha verun dritto.*

FRANK-BANK [copyhold lands, which the wife, being married a virgin, has after the decease of her husband for her dower] *terre assegnate ad una donna per la sua dote dopo la morte di suo marito.*

FRANK-CHASE [a liberty of free chase] *libertà di cacciare.*

FRANK FREE, *feudo franco, o libero.*

FRANK LAW [a free enjoyment of all those privileges which the law permits to a man not found guilty of any heinous crime] *il diritto che un suddito ha per le leggi del paese, non essendo accusato d'alcuno delitto enorme, come sarebbe quello di lesa maestà.*

Frank, s. [a place to feed a boar in] *stia dove s'ingrassano i porci.*

A frank [or French livre] *un franco, una lira di Francia.*

Frank pledge [an ancient custom for the freemen of England at fourteen years of age to find surety for their truth and fidelity to the king, and good behaviour to their fellow subjects] *malleveria che gli uomini liberi in Inghilterra all' età di quattordici anni erano obbligati dare per la loro fedeltà verso' l re, e buona condotta verso i compatriotti.*

To FRANK, *mettere in istia, chiudere in istia.*
To FRANK [to fatten] *ingrassare.*
FRANKI'NCENSE, s. *incenso*, s. m.
FRA'NKLY, adv. [freely] *francamente, liberamente, sinceramente, schiettamente, puramente.*
FRA'NKNESS, s. [openness of heart] *franchezza, libertà, schiettezza, sincerità*, s. f.
FRA'NTICK, adj. [mad, deprived of understanding by violent madness, outragiously mad] *matto, privo d' intelletto da violenta pazzia, ferocemente matto.*
Frantick, *trasportato o agitato da passione violenta e feroce.*
FRA'NTICKLY, adv. [madly, outragiously] *da matto furioso.*
FRA'NTICKNESS, s. *mattezza feroce, mattezza furiosa.*
FRATE'RNAL, adj. [brotherly, belonging to a brother] *fraternale, fraterno, di fratello.*
A fraternal love, *un amor fraternale.*
FRATE'RNALLY, adv. [brotherlike] *fraternalmente, da fratello.*
FRATE'RNITY, s. [brotherhood] *fraternità, fratellanza, campagnia fraternale.*
Fraternity [a company of men enter'd into a firm bond of society] *fraternità, coll' accento sull' antepenultima sillaba, adunanza spirituale, confraternità, compagnia.*
FRA'TRICIDE, s. [the killing of a brother] *fratricidio*, s. m. *uccision di fratello.*
Fratricide [the killer of a brother] *fratricida*, s. m. *ucciditore di fratello.*
FRAUD, s. [deceit, guile, cheat] *fraude, frode, e froda*, s. f. *inganno*, s. m.
FRA'UDULENCE, } s. [deceitfulness] *fraudolenza, fraude*, s. f.
FRA'UDULENCY, }
FRA'UDULENT, adj. [deceitful] *fraudolente, fraudolento, ingannatore.*
A fraudulent contract, *un contratto fraudolente.*
Fraudulent ways, *soperchierie.*
FRAUGHT, adj. [from to fraight] *noleggiato, caricato.*
FRAY, s. [fight] *zuffa, riotta, contesa, baruffa, sciarra, rissa*, s. f. *combattimento, contrasto*, s. m.
To begin the fray, *cominciar la zuffa.*
Better come at the latter end of a feast than the beginning of a fray, *è meglio venire alla fine d'un festino che non al principio d'un zuffa.*
To part the fray, *spartir la baruffa.*
Fray [quarrel] *questione, disputa, contesa*, s. f.
To FRAY [to fret as cloth does by rubbing] *usarsi, parlando del panno.*
To fray [to frighten] *spaventare, intimorire, atterrire, impaurire.* pref. *intimorisco, atterrisco, impaurisco.*
FREAK, s. [a maggot, or whim] *capriccio, ghiribizzo, grillo*, s. m. *fantasia*, s. f.
To be full of freaks, *esser capriccioso, bisbetico, ghiribizzoso, fantastico.*
A freak took him, *li venne fantasia, li saltò il grillo.*

Freak [idle conceit] *sogni, stravaganze.*
To FREAK [to variegate] *divisare a più colori.*
FREA'KISH, adj. [whimsical] *fantastico, capriccioso, bisbetico, ghiribizzoso.*
FRE'CKLE, s. [red spots in the face] *lentiggine*, s. f. *marchia simile alle lenti, che si sparge nella persona, e particolarmente nel viso.*
FRE'CKLED, adj. [full of freckles] *lentigginoso, che ha lentigini per la faccia o pel corpo.*
FREE, adj. [not in bondage or servitude, at liberty] *libero, che non è soggetto, che è in libertà.*
A free nation, *un popolo libero.*
The free-will, *il libero arbitrio.*
You are free to do what you please, *voi siete libero di fare quel che v'aggrada.*
I am free [or at leisure] every morning, *sono libero, disoccupato ogni mattina.*
Free from [exempt] *libero, esente, sgombro, franco.*
Free from debts, *franco di debiti.*
Free from all vices, *esente d'ogni vizio.*
Free from all troubles, *sgombro d'ogni affanno.*
My heart is free from passion, *il mio cuore è libero da passioni.*
Free from love, *disamorato.*
Free [privileged] *libero, franco, pubblico, privilegiato.*
A free town, *una città libera.*
A free chapel *una cappella pubblica.*
A free school, *una scuola pubblica.*
Free [frank, open] *libero, franco, schietto, ingenuo, puro, sincero.*
A free temper, *un animo libero, sincero, schietto.*
A free heart, *un cuor puro, ingenuo, schietto.*
Free [liberal, generous] *liberale, magnifico, genoroso, amorevole, benigno.*
A free gift, *un dono gratuito.*
Free [easy] *libero, snello, agile, disinvolto, naturale.*
She has a free way of dancing, *ella ha un' aria snella nel ballare, ella balla con grande agilità.*
A free stile, *uno stile naturale.*
A free easy shape, *una statura disinvolta.*
He has a free way of delivery, *egli è molto eloquente, o facondo.*
To have free leave to speak, *aver la libertà di parlare.*
It is not free for me to do it, *non m'è permesso, o lecito di farlo.*
It is free for me to do it, or to let it alone, *è in poter mio di farlo, e di non farlo.*
He is a little too free of his tongue, *egli è un poco sboccato, egli parla con troppa libertà.*
To make one free [to relieve him from slavery] *mettere uno in libertà, dargli la libertà, affrancarlo.*
To make one free of a city, *ammettere uno alla cittadinanza.*

To be too free, *arrogarsi troppa licenza.*
To be free from business, *esser disoccupato, non aver niente a fare.*
A free room, *una camera vuota.*
His house is free to every body, *la sua casa è aperta ad ognuno.*
To ride a free horse to death, *abusarsi della bontà, e pazienza altrui.*
Free booter, *scorridore*, s. m.
Free stone, *pietra viva.*
Free born, *nato libero.*
To FREE [to deliver] *liberare, salvare.*
To free [to enfranchise] *affrancare, far franco, dar la libertà.*
To free [to exempt] *esentare, francare, far franco.*
FREED, adj. *liberato, salvato*, v. To free.
Freed-stool, s. *asilo, refugio*, s. m.
FRE'EDOM, s. [liberty] *libertà.*
Every one shall have a freedom to speak his mind, *ognuno avrà la libertà di dire il suo parere.*
Freedom [easiness of doing any thing] *facilità, agilità*, s. f.
The freedom of a pencil, *facilità di pennello.*
Freedom from, *esenzione, immunità*, s. f.
To take one's freedom of a company, *esser ricevuto, o ammesso in una compagnia.*
FRE'ELY, adj. *liberamente, francamente, arditamente, schiettamente.*
To tell one's mind freely, *dire il suo parere liberamente.*
FRE'EMAN, s. [one that is free of a city, corporation, or company] *statuale*, s. m. *che è descritto nel numero de' cittadini, e gode i privilegi d'una città, o compagnia.*
FRE'ENESS, s. [frankness] *franchezza, arditezza*, s. f.
Freeness [sincerity] *franchezza, schiettezza, sincerità.*
Freeness [liberality] *liberalità, generosità*, s. f.
FREETHI'NKER, s. [a libertine, a contemner of religion] *un libertino, uno scapestrato, uno che sprezza ogni religione.*
FRE'EWILL, s. *libero arbitrio, libertà di fare quel che si vuole senza che ci sia usata violenza.*
FREEZE, s. [a term in architecture] *fregio*, s. m. *la parte ch'è fra l'architrave e la cornice, membro d'architettura.*
FREEZE [a kind of stuff] *sorta di panno.*
To FREEZE [to congeal as ice] *gelare, congelare, agghiacciare.*
I was so frightened that the blood freezed almost in my viens, *ebbi una sì gran paura che mi s'agghiacciò quasi il sangue nelle vene.*
It freezes, *gela.*
FREIGHT, s. [any thing with which a ship is loaded] *salma, il carico d'una nave.*
Freight [the money due for transportation of goods] *nolo*; *danaro che si paga*

si paga pel trasporto in nave di mercatanzie.

To FREIGHT, pret. freighted; particip. fraught, freighted [to load a ship or vessel of carriage with goods for transportation] *caricare una nave per trasporto di mercanzie.*

To freight, *noleggiare una nave.*

FREN, s. [a worthless woman] *una donna vile.*

FRENCH, adj. *Franzese, Francese, Francesco.*

The French tongue, *il Francese, la lingua Francese.*

To speak French, *parlar Francese.*

The French fashion, *la moda di Francia.*

The French king, *il re di Francia.*

A French dish, *un manicaretto alla Francese.*

French beans, *fagiuoli.*

French wheat, *miglio*, s. m. *spezie di biada minuta.*

The French pox, or the French distemper, *il mal Franzese.*

A French man, *un Francese.*

A French woman, *una Francese.*

FRE'NCHIFY'D, adj. [that has the French disease] *infranciosato, infetto da mal Franzese.*

Frenchify'd [brought over to the French interest] *che è nell' interesse della Francia.*

FRE'NDLESS MAN, s. [among our Saxon ancestors, an outlaw'd person] *un bandito, un proscritto.*

FRE'NSY, or FRE'NZY, s. [a sort of madness or dotage] *frenesia*, s. f. *male che offende la mente, conducendola al furore, alla pazzia.*

'Tis a meer frensy, *è una mera frenesia.*

FRENE'TICK, adj. [mad] *frenetico, freneticante, insano.*

FRE'QUENCE, } s. [the frequent
FRE'QUENCY, } or often doing of a thing] *frequenza, moltitudine*, s. f. *numero*, s. m.

FRE'QUENT, adj. [often, usual, common] *frequente, spesso, comune, ordinario.*

Frequent visits are troublesome, *le frequenti visite riescono importune.*

To FREQUE'NT [to haunt or visit often, to keep company with] *frequentare, spesseggiare, bazzicare, praticare, conversare.*

To frequent a house, *frequentare, bazzicare una casa.*

To frequent good company, *praticare buona compagnia.*

FREQUE'NTED, adj. *frequentato, spesseggiato, bazzicato, praticato, conversato.*

This part of the town is much frequented, *questa parte della città è molto frequentata.*

FREQUE'NTING, *frequentazione*, s. f. *il frequentare.*

FRE'QUENTLY, adv. [often] *frequentemente, spesso, spessamente.*

FRESCA'DES, s. [shady, cool walks, bowers] *frescura, luoghi freschi.*

FRE'SCO, s. [fresh, cool] *fresco.*

To walk in fresco [to take the fresh air] *spasseggiare nel fresco.*

To drink in fresco [to drink cool liquors] *ber fresco.*

To paint in fresco [to paint upon bare walls newly done, that the colours may sink in, and become more durable] *dipignere a fresco, il dipignere sopra l'intonarato del muro non rasciutto, affinchè i colori vi restino meglio impressi e si conservino più lungo tempo.*

FRESH, s. a sea-term] *corrente d'acqua fresca, termine marinaresco.*

Fresh, adj. [cool] *fresco, che ha in se freschezza.*

Fresh [new] *fresco, contrario di secco o di stantio.*

Fresh [newly done] *fresco, nuovo, novello, di poco tempo.*

Fresh [unsalted] *fresco, contrario di salato.*

Fresh [fine, lively] *fresco, rigoglioso, di buona cera.*

Fresh [not tired] *fresco, non affaticato.*

A fresh air, *un' aria fresca.*

Fresh gale of wind, *vento fresco.*

The wind blows fresh, *il vento rinfresca.*

Fresh beer, *della birra fresca.*

Where the thing is fresh, *mentre la cosa è fresca.*

Fresh meat, *carne fresca.*

A fresh complection, *una carnagione fresca, colorita.*

Fresh men supplied their places, *fu mandata gente fresca in luogo loro.*

To take fresh courage, *riprender animo, rianimarsi.*

To take fresh air, *prender il fresco.*

This beef eats too fresh, *questo manzo non è assai salato.*

He is fresh in my memory, *egli è presente alla mia memoria.*

A fresh water fish, *pesce d'acqua dolce.*

Fresh horses, *cavalli freschi.*

A fresh water soldier [a raw soldier] *soldato d'acqua fresca, non ancora agguerrito.*

A fresh water soldier [the name of an herb] *spezie d'erba.*

To FRE'SHEN [to unsalt] *dissalare.*

To freshen salt meat, *dissalare della carne salata.*

FRE'SHENED, adj. *dissalato.*

FRE'SHET, s. [a pool of fresh water] *un laghetto d'acqua che è fresca.*

FRE'SHLY, adv. [newly] *frescamente, di fresco, nuovamente, novellamente.*

FRE'SHNESS, s. [coolness] *freschezza*, s. f.

Freshness [novelty] *novità*, s. f.

FRET, s. [a stop on a musical instrument] *tasto*, s. m.

Fret [fume, heat of passion] *corruccio, crucio*, s. m. *stizza*, s. f.

To put one in a fret, *corrucciare, crucciare uno, farlo stizzare.*

To be in a fret, *corrucciarsi, crucciarsi, stizzarsi.*

Wine that is upon the fret, *vino che bolle ancora, vino che non è ancora chiaro.*

To FRET [to wear out] *usarsi, logorarsi.*

To fret [to rub one's skin off] *scorticare, levar la pelle.*

To fret [to vex] *corrucciare, crucciare, stizzare.*

To fret one, *corrucciare alcuno, farlo andare in collera.*

My skin frets, *la mia pelle si scortica.*

To fret [as wine does] *ribollire, come fa il vino.*

To fret [to itch] *prudere, pizzicare.*

To fret one's self, or to fret, verb neut. *alterarsi, travagliarsi, inquietarsi, tribolarsi, sdegnarsi.*

To fret at play, *piccarsi al giuoco.*

FRE'TFUL, adj. *iracondo, stizzoso, corrucciosо, crucciosо.*

FRE'TTED, adj. *usato, logorato*, v. To fret.

FRET-WORK, *intaglio.*

FRI'ABLE, adj. [that may be easily crumbled, or rubbed into small parts] *stritolabile, atto a stritolarsi.*

Calcined stones are friable, and easily reduced to powder, *le pietre calcinate sono stritolabili, e facilmente si spolverizzano.*

FRI'AR, s. [monk] *un frate, un monaco, un religioso.*

A friar [a term of a printing-house, a page so ill printed, that it can hardly be read] *un monaco, termine di stampatore, cioè, una facciata sì male stampata, ch' appena si può leggere.*

FRI'ARY, s. *confraternità*, s. f.

FRI'ARY, adj. *fratesco, da frate.*

To FRI'BBLE [to trifle with one, to baffle him] *trattenere alcuno, o tenerlo a bada con baje.*

FRI'BBLING, adj. [captious, impertinent, trifling] *impertinente, frivolo, pien di baje.*

A fribbling question, *una questione impertinente, o frivola.*

FRI'BURG, or FRI'THBURG, s. [a surety for the peace or good behaviour] *malleveria, per mantener la pace, e buoni costumi.*

FRICASSE'E, s. [a dish of fried meat] *fricassea*, s. f.

FRICA'TION, } s. [rubbing] *frega-*
FRICTION, } *mento, frego, stropicciamento*, s. m. *fregatura, frega, fregagione, stropicciagione*, s. f.

FRI'DAY, s. [the sixth day of the week] *Venerdì*, s. m. *il sesto giorno della settimana.*

Good-friday, *il Venerdì Santo.*

To FRI'DGE, or FRIDGE ABOUT, *saltellare, spicciare.*

To fridge one against another, *urtarsi, spignersi.*

FRI'DSTOLE, s. [a sanctuary or place of refuge for malefactors] *asilo, refugio*, s. m.

FRIEND, s. [one who acts kindly towards a person] *amico*, s. m. *amica*, s. f.

He is a good friend of mine, *egli è mio amico.*

A friend in need is a friend indeed, *nel bisogno si conoscon gli amici.*

Friends may meet, but mountains never greet, *talor gli uomini vanno ad incontrarsi e i monti fermi stanno.*

Friends [relations] *parenti.*

He has very good friends, *egli ha buoni parenti, egli è d'un buon parentado.*

To make friends with one, *far pace con uno, riconciliarſi, appaciarſi, rinnovellar l'amicizia.*

To FRIEND [to befriend, to favour] *favorire, aſſiſtere, ſpalleggiare.*

FRIE'NDLESS, adj. [deſtitute of friends] *ſenza amici, che non ha amici, privo d ogni ſoccorſo.*

FRIE'NDLINESS, s. *amicizia, benevolenza, bontà.*

FRIE'NDLY, adj. [kindly] *amichevole, benevolo, amico, favorevole, buono, propizio.*

To do one a friendly turn, *ſervir uno da amico.*

Friendly, adv. *amichevolmente, amorevolmente, affettuoſamente, amicamente.*

To live friendly with one, *vivere amichevolmente con uno.*

The ſmall pox comes out friendly with him, *il vajuolo vien fuora bene.*

FRIE'NDSHIP, s. *amicizia,* s. f. *ſcambievole amore.*

To make a friendſhip, to get into friendſhip with one, *contrattar amicizia, amicarſi, farſi amico con uno.*

To ſcrew one's ſelf into one's friendſhip, *inſinuarſi nell' altrui amicizia, cattivarſi la ſua amicizia.*

To break off friendſhip, *romper l'amicizia, inimicarſi.*

FRI'ER, *v.* Friar.

FRIEZE, s. *ſpezie di panno groſſolano.*

Frieze, or Friſe, s. *termine d'architettura; fregio.*

To FRIG [to leap about] *ſaltare, ſaltellare.*

To frig [to rub] *fregare, ſtropicciare.*

FRI'GA, s. [an idol worſhipped by the ancient Saxons in the form of an hermaphrodite, on the day now called FRIDAY, which thence took its denomination] *ſpezie d'idolo ermafrodito, che gli antichi Saſſoni adoravano il venerdì, donde* FRIDAY *ha preſo il nome.*

FRI'GATE, s. [a ſmall man of war] *fregata,* s. f.

A light frigate, *una ſaettia.*

FRIGHT, s. *paura,* s. f. *timore, ſpavento,* s. m.

You put me in a great fright, *voi m'avete fatto gran paura.*

To be in a terrible fright, *aver gran paura.*

To FRIGHT [to put into a fright] *impaurare, impaurire, intimidire, far paura, ſpaventare, atterrire,* preſ. *impauriſco, atterriſco.*

You will fright him, *voi gli farete paura.*

He does what he can to fright me, *fa ogni sforzo per iſpaventarmi.*

To fright one out of his wits, *ſbalordire, atterrire uno.*

FRI'GHTED, adj. *atterrito, impaurato, impaurito, ſpaventato.*

To FRI'GHTEN, *v.* Fright.

FRI'GHTFUL, adj. [terrible] *ſpaventevole, orrendo, orribile.*

A frightful ſpectacle, *uno ſpettecolo orrendo.*

FRI'GHTFULLY, adv. [in a frightful manner] *terribilmente, ſpaventevolmente, orrendamente, orribilmente.*

FRI'GHTFULNESS, s. *orrore, terrore, ſpavento,* s. m.

The frightfulneſs of death, *gli orrori della morte.*

FRI'GID, adj. [cold] *frigido, freddo.*

The two frigid zones, *le due zone frigide.*

Frigid [cold, impotent] *frigido, impotente.*

FRIGI'DITY, s. [coldneſs, impotency] *frigidità, frigidezza, impotenza,* s. f.

FRI'GIDLY, adv. *freddamente.*

FRIM-FOLKS, s. [ſtrangers, outlandiſh men] *i ſtranieri, i foreſtieri, gli oltramontani.*

FRINGE, s. *frangia.*

A ſilver or gold fringe, *frangia d'argento, o d'oro.*

To FRINGE, *guernire di frangia.*

FRI'NGED, adj. *guernito di frangia.*

FRI'PPERER, s. [a broker that ſells old cloaths] *rigattiere,* s. m. *rivenditor di veſtimenti, e di maſſerizie uſate.*

FRI'PPERY, s. [a ſtreet of brokers] *ſtrada dove abitano i rigattieri.*

Frippery [a thing of ſmall value] *robe vecchie, robe di poco valore, ciarpa, arneſe vile.*

FRISK, s. *ſalto; uno ſcecco d'allegria.*

To FRISK [to leap or jump up and down] *ſaltare, ſaltellare per gioja.*

FRIT, s. [among chymiſts, aſhes and ſalt baked and fryed together in ſand] *ceneri e ſale cotti o fritti inſieme con ſabbia.*

FRITH, s. [a word now uſed in Scotland for an arm of the ſea] *parola uſata in Iſcozia, per uno ſtretto o braccio di mare.*

Frith [among the Saxons, ſignified a wood] *fra gli antichi Saſſoni ſignificava un boſco, o una pianura fra i boſchi.*

FRI'TTER, s. [a ſmall pancake] *frittella,* s. f.

FRI'VOLOUS, adj. [of no account or value] *frivolo, debole, di poca importanza.*

To FRI'ZLE [to curl or criſp the hair] *inanellare, arricciare.*

To frizle the hair, *inanellare i capelli, fare i ricci ai capelli.*

FRI'ZLED, adj. *inanellato, arricciato.*

Frizled hair, *cappelli ricci, o inanellati.*

FRO, adv. Ex. to go to and fro, *andar qua e la, andare e venire.*

FROCK, s. [a kind of dreſs for men] *veſtimento uſato in Inghilterra.*

A child's frock, *veſte da fanciullo.*

A groom's or coachman's frock, *un ſacco di mozzo di ſtalla, o di cocchiere, veſtimento lino che ſi mettono ſopra li abiti per conſervarli netti.*

FROG, s. [an amphibious creature] *ranocchia, rana,* s f. *ranocchio,* s. m. *animal paluſtre, che vive in terra, ed in acqua.*

Frog [the fruſh of a horſe's foot] *paſtoja,* s. f. *la giunta del piè del cavallo.*

FROISE, s. [a ſort of pancake] *ſpezie di frittata con fette di lardo.*

FRO'LICK, s. [a whim] *capriccio, ghiribizzo, grillo,* s. m.

Frolick [merry prank] *fantaſia,* s. f. *ghiribizzo,* s. m.

Frolick, adj. *v.* Frolickſome.

FRO'LICKLY, adv. *gajamente, allegramente.*

FRO'LICKSOME, adj. [full of frolicks] *fantaſtico, capriccioſo, ghiribizzoſo.*

Frolickſome [merry] *gajo, lieto, feſtevole.*

FROM, prep. *da, dal, dallo, dalla, di.*

I come from home, *vengo da caſa mia.*

I come from Rome, *vengo da Roma.*

From top to toe, *da capo a piedi.*

From abroad, *di fuori.*

From my heart, *dal fondo del mio cuore.*

From hence, *da qui.*

From whence, *donde.*

He kept me from writing, *m'impedì di ſcrivere.*

From three a clock to ſix, *dalle tre ſin alle ſei.*

Go from me to tell him, *andate a dirli da parte mia.*

From the king, *da parte del re.*

From my youth, *dalla mia fanciullezza.*

To keep from ſtudying, *ſviare dallo ſtudio.*

From henceforth, *d'or in avanti, da qui innanzi.*

To hide a thing from one, *celare ad uno che che ſi ſia.*

To lie from one another, *far letto a parte.*

Tierce from the king, from the queen [at piquet] *terza al re, terza alla dama al giuoco di picchetto.*

To go from one, *laſciare alcuno.*

FRONT, s. [the fore-part] *fronte, facciata,* s. f. *fronteſpizio,* s. m. *la parte d'avanti di che che ſi ſia.*

The front of an army, *la fronte o frontiera d'un eſercito.*

To charge the enemy in the front, *aſſaltare il nemico alla fronte.*

The front of a building, *la facciata, il fronteſpizio d'un edificio.*

Front [forehead] of a calf, *la fronte d'un vitello.*

To FRONT, *fronteggiare, ſtare a fronte.*

My houſe fronts yours, *la mia caſa fronteggia la voſtra.*

Front-ſtall, s. [a part of a horſe's bridle] *frontale,* s. m.

FRO'NTIER, s. [the limits or borders of a country, or province] *frontiera,* s. f. *luogo ne' confini del dominio a fronte d'altro ſtato.*

The frontiers of a kingdom, *le frontiere d'un regno.*

A frontier town, *una città frontiera.*

FRONTINI'ACK, s. [a ſort of rich French wine, ſo called from the name of the place] *Frontignacco, vino che viene da Frontignacco, villaggio in Provenza.*

FRO'N-

Fro'ntispiece, s. [the fore-front of a house or building] *frontispizio, e frontespizio*, s. m. *facciata*, s. f.

The frontispiece of a book [the title or first page of a book] *il frontespizio d'un libro, la prima facciata d'un libro ove sta scritto il titolo.*

Fro'ntless, adj. [without blushes without shame] *che non arrossisce, sfacciato, sfrontato, senza vergogna.*

Fro'ntlet, s. [an attire for the forehead] *frontale*, s. m. *ornamento che si mette sopra la fronte.*

Fro'nton, s. [in architecture, a member which serves to compose an ornament, raised over doors, cross-works, niches, &c.] *frontone*, s. m. *membro d' architettura, che si mette per ornamento sopra porte, finestre, nicchie, e simili, in forma di cornice.*

Frore, } adj. [from to freeze]
Frorne, } *gelato, agghiacciato.*

Frost, s. *gelata*, s. f.

A hard frost, *una gran gelata.*

Hoar frost, or white frost, *brinata*, s. f.

Frost nail, *chiodo a ghiaccio.*

Frost nailed, *ferrato a ghiaccio.*

Frost-bi'tten, adj. [nipped or withered by the frost] *tocco e offeso dal ghiaccio.*

Fro'stily, adv. *agghiacciatamente, senza caldo d'affetto.*

Fro'sty, adj. *ex.* frosty weather, *tempo di gelata.*

Froth, s. [the spume of fermented things] *schiuma, spuma*, s. f.

The froth of beer, *la schiuma della birra.*

The froth of melted lead, *la spuma del piombo liquefatto.*

To Frorh, *spumare, far la spuma.*

Fro'thy, adj. *spumante, spumoso, pien di spuma.*

Frothy [vain, empty, trifling] *leggiero, vano, voto, di nulla sostanza, pien di baje, di bagattelle, d'inezie.*

To Frounce, *arricciare i capelli.*

Fro'uzy, adj. [dim, fetid, musty] *mucido, fetido.*

Frow, s. [a Dutch word for a woman] *donna.*

A Dutch frow, *una Olandase.*

Fro'ward, adj. [peevish, fretful, surly] *fastidioso, sdegnoso, schifo, incontentabile, ritroso, fantastico, stravagante, aromatico, strano, bizzarro, stizzoso, iracondo, capriccioso, stucchevole.*

A froward master, *un padrone fantastico, bizzarro, e capriccioso.*

A froward man, *un uomo aromatico, o sdegnoso.*

To have a froward look, *avere una cera arcigna.*

Froward [sullen, stubborn] *caparbio, ostinato, perverso, disobediente.*

Froward [malapert] *insolente, arrogante, ardito.*

A froward child, *un fanciullo fastidioso.*

Fro'wardly, adv. *fantasticamente, fastidiosamente, increscevolmente, caparbiamente, ostinatamente, perversamente, insolentemente, arrogantement.*

To look frowardly at one, *guardar uno in cagnesco.*

To speak frowardly at one, *parlare stizzosamente ad alcuno.*

To carry one's self frowardly to one's father, *comportarsi insolentemente verso suo padre.*

Fro'warrness [peevishness] *fantasticaggine, fastidiosaggine, stucchevolezza*, s. f. *modo di proceder fastidioso.*

Frowardness [stubborness] *disobedienza, ostinazione, caparbietà*, s. f.

Frowardness [malapertness] *insolenza, arditezza, ferezza*, s f.

Frown, s. *grugno*, s. m. *ciera arcigna.*

Frown, *cipiglio, sopracciglio, guardatura storta e collerica.*

Frown, *sdegno, disprezzo.*

Frowns of fortune, *colpi di fortuna, disgrazie.*

To Frown [to knit the brows] *increspar la fronte, fare un viso arcigno.*

To frown upon one, *guatar uno con viso arcigno, in cagnesco, biecamente, fare il grugno ad uno.*

The world frowns upon him, *la fortuna li è contraria.*

Fro'wning, adj. *arcigno, burbero, torvo.*

A frowning countenance, *una cera arcigna, burbera, occhi torvi.*

Fro'wningly, adv. *biecamente. stortamente, travoltamente, in cagnesco, austeramente.*

Fro'zen, adj. [from to freeze] *gelato, agghiacciato.*

Frozen water, *acqua agghiacciata.*

My hands are frozen, *le mie mani sono gelate.*

Frozen up, *tutto gelato.*

The river is frozen up, *il fiume è tutto gelato.*

Fructi'ferous, adj. [bearing fruit] *fruttifero, fruttifico, fruttevole, fruttiferoso, che fa frutto, fecondo, fertile.*

Fructiferous trees, *alberi fruttiferi.*

To Fru'ctify [to bear fruit in a figurative sense] *fruttare, far frutto, render frutto.*

To fructify [to make fruitful] *fruttare, coltivare, fecondare.*

Fru'gal, adj. [sparing, thrifty] *frugale, moderato, parco, ritenuto, assegnato.*

Frugal [temperate] *temperato, ritenuto, moderato, sobrio.*

Fruga'lity, s. [thriftyness, good husbandry] *frugalità, moderanza nel vivere, parcità, parsimonia*, s. f.

Frugality [temperance] *temperanza, sobrietà, moderazione*, s. f.

Fru'gally, adv. [thriftily] *frugalmente, parcamente, con risparmio, con parsimonia.*

To live frugally, *vivere frugalmente.*

Frugally [temperately] *temperatamente, sobriamente.*

Frugi'ferous, adj. [bearing fruit] *frugifero, fruttifero.*

Fruit, s. [the product of the earth, trees, plants, &c.] *frutto*, s. m. *frutta*, s. f. *il parto della terra, degli alberi, delle piante.*

The fruits of the earth, *i frutti della terra, tutto quel che la terra produce.*

The fruits of a tree, *il frutto d'un albero.*

Fruit [desert at table] *le frutta.*

Fruit [all manner of eatable fruit] *frutta.*

To live upon fruit, *vivere, o pâscersi di frutta.*

Fruit [profit] *frutto, utile, giovamento, profitto.*

These are the fruits of your rashness, *questi sono i frutti della vostra temerità.*

Fruit [goods, rent, revenue] *frutto, entrata, rendita, profitto annuale.*

The fruits of a living, *i frutti d'un beneficio.*

The first fruits, *le primizie.*

To offer the first fruits to God, *offerire le primizie a Dio.*

The king has the first fruits, *il Rè ha le annate.*

The fruit of the womb, *il parto.*

A fruit tree, *un albero fruttifero, o pomifero.*

Frui'terer, s. [one who deals in fruit] *che vende frutti, fruttajuolo.*

Frui'tery, s. [a fruit house, or fruit loft] *luogo dove si conservan le frutta.*

Frui'tful, adj. [plentiful] *fruttifero, fecondo, fertile.*

Fruitful [profitable] *fruttuoso, utile.*

Fru'itfully. adj. [plentifully] *fecondamente, fertilmente.*

Fru'itfulness, s. [plenty] *fecondità, abbondanza, fertilità*, s. f.

Frui'tion, s. [enjoyment] *fruizione*, s. f. *godimento*, s. m.

Fru'itless, adj. [barren] *sterile, infruttuoso.*

A fruitless country, *un paese sterile.*

Fruitless [vain] *infruttuoso, vano, inutile.*

Fru'itlessly, adv. *senza profitto, senza giovamento, vanamente, invano, per nonnulla.*

Frum, adj. [plump, fat, jolly] *pienotto, grosso, grasso, paffuto.*

Fru'menty, *cibo fatto di frumento, cotto nel latte.*

Frump, s. [jeer] *billera, bischenca, burla, beffa, baja*, s. f, *scherzo*, s. m.

To Frump [to flout or jeer] *burlare, motteggiare, beffare, schernire.* pres. *schernisco.*

Fru'mped, adj. *burlato, motteggiato, beffato, schernito.*

Fru'mper, s. *burlatore, schernitore, motteggiatore, burlone*, s. m.

Frustra'neous, adj. [vain] *vano, inutile.*

Frustra'neously, adv. *in vano, vanamente, inutilmente.*

To Fru'stra'te [to disappoint, make void] *deludere, e diludere, beffare, schernire.* pres. *schernisco.* pret. *delusi, e dilusi.*

To frustrate one's design, *deludere l'altrui disegno.*

To frustrate one of his hopes, *render deluse l'altrui speranze.*

Fru'strated, adj. *deluso, beffato, schernito.*
Frustra'tion, s. *delusione, e dilusione,* s. f. *il deludere.*
Fry, s. [the spawn of young fishes] *frega, fregola di pesci.*
Fry [young fish] *pesciolino,* s. m.
Fry [company] *una camerata, una gran compagnia.*
A fry of little islands, *un numero infinito d'isolette.*
To **Fry** [to dress victuals in a frying pan] *friggere, cuocere che che si sia in padella.* pret.
To fry fish, *frigger del pesce.*
I have other fish to fry, *ho altri pensieri in testa, ho altre cose a pensare.*
Fry'd, adj. *fritto.*
Fry'er, s. [friar] *friere, frate,* s. m.
Fry'ing, s. *il friggere.*
A frying pan, *una padella.*
To fall out of the frying pan into the fire, *cader dalla padella nella brace, schivare un male e incorrere in un peggiore, fuggir da scilla e cadere in cariddi.*
Fu'age, s. [hearth money, an imposition or tax of one shilling for every hearth] *tassa sopra ogni fuoco.*
Fub, s. ex. a fat fub, [a plump chubby boy] *un fanciullo grassotto, o paffuto.*
To **Fub** [to put off] *differire, mandar in lunga.*
Fu'cus, s. [paint for the face] *liscio, belletto.*
To **Fu'ddle** [to make drunk] *imbriacare.*
To fuddle one's self, *imbriacarsi.*
Fuddle-cap [drunkard] *un inbriacone.*
Fu'ddled, adj. *imbriacato, imbricaco, briaco.*
Fu'ddler, s. *un imbriacone, un imbriaco.*
Fu'ddling, s. *imbriacamento,* s. m.
A fuddling bout, *un imbriacatura.*
Fuga, interj. *espressione d'abborrimento, oibò.*
Fu'gitive, s. [a deserter, a runaway] *un fuggitivo, una fuggitiva.*
Fu'gue, s. [in musick, a chace, as when two or more parts chace one another in the same point] *fuga,* s. f. *termine musicale.*
To maintain a fugue, *fare una fuga.*
To **Fu'lfil** [to accomplish or perform] *adempiere, adempire, eseguire, effettuare.* pres. *adempisco, eseguisco.*
To fulfil one's promise, *adempire, attenere, mantenere la promessa.*
Fulfi'lled, adj. *adempito, eseguito, effettuato.*
My desires are fulfilled, *i miei desideri sono adempiti.*
Fulfi'lling, s. *adempimento,* s. m. *effettuazione,* s. f.
Fu'lfraught, adj. [fully stored] *ben provvisto, ben colmo.*
Fu'lgent, adj. [shining, dazzling] *risulgente, lucente, che abbaglia colla molta luce.*
Fu'lgid, adj. [bright, shining] *fulgido, lucido, risplendente, rilucente.*
Fulgi'dity, s. [brightness] *fulgidità, fulgidezza, luce, chiarezza,* s. f.

Fulgura'tion, s. [lightning, or flash of fire in the clouds] *folgore, baleno* s. m. *il folgorare.*
Fu'lham, s. [a cant word for false dice] *voce di gergo che significa dadi falsi, dadi falsificati.*
Fuli'ginous, adj. [sooty, full of smoak] *filigginoso.*
Full, adj. [filled with] *pieno.*
A bottle full of wine, *un fiasco pieno di vino.*
Full of joy, *pieno di gioja, d'allegrezza.*
I am full, *sono sazio, sodisfatto.*
Of full age, *adulto.*
You have a full hour to stay yet, *voi avete ancora un' ora intiera da restare.*
He is full of himself [he is a self-conceited man] *egli è uomo che presume troppo di se, un uomo orgoglioso, pieno d'orgoglio.*
A full power *pieno potere.*
A very full gown, *una gonna ampia.*
This coat is too full, *questo abito è troppo largo.*
To give one a full answer, *dare ad uno un ampia risposta.*
To make a full description of a country, *fare un' ampia, o minuta descrizione d'un paese.*
To eat one's belly full, *satollarsi, mangiare a crepa pelle.*
Is not your belly full yet? *non avete ancora mangiato a bastanza?*
His belly is never full, *egli non è mai sazio, o satollo.*
Full of sorrow, *afflitto, sconsolato, oppresso dal dolore.*
His face is full of the small-pox, *il suo viso è tutto butterato.*
A child full of play, *un ragazzo allegro, giocondo.*
To have one's hand full of business, *aver molti affari per le mani, esser molto affaccendato.*
He is too full of words, *egli chiacchiera, parla troppo.*
To run full speed, *correr a briglia sciolta.*
A full stop, *un punto.*
Full eyes, *occhi grandi.*
A full face, *un viso pienotto.*
A full [or high] sea, *alto mare.*
Full, s. [the full of the moon] *plenilunio,* s. m. *luna piena.*
The moon is in the full, *la luna è piena.*
In full of all demands, *appieno.*
To the full, *pienamente, appieno.*
To pay one to the full, *dare ad uno intiera satisfazione.*
He is satisfied to the full, *egli è pienamente sodisfatto.*
Full, adv. ex. to be full a hundred years old, *aver cent' anni compiti.*
Full forty thousand men, *ben quaranta mila uomini.*
She is full as handsome as her sister, *ella non è punto men bella di sua sorella.*
This is full as big as that, *questo è ben sì grosso che quello.*
He maintained the siege full six months, *egli mantenne l'assedio ben sei mesi intieri.*
My time is not yet full spent, *il mio tempo non è ancora venuto.*

I understand you full well, *v'intendo molto bene.*
Full sore against my will, *a mio marcio dispetto.*
Full enough, *a bastanza.*
Full-faced, *pienotto, paffuto.*
Full bodied, *grosso, corpulento.*
A mouthful, *un boccone.*
A handful, *una manata, un pugno.*
Full nigh, *quasi, appresso a poco.*
To **Full**, verb. act. *sodare.*
To full cloth, *sodare del panno.*
Fu'llage, s. *quel che si paga per sodare i panni.*
Fulle'r, s. *follone,* s. m.
Fuller's earth, *terra, creta usata nel fare i panni.*
Fuller's weed, fuller's thistle, *cardo, a cardare i panni.*
Fuller, *è il comparativo di* Full, *v.* Full, adj.
Fu'llest, *e il superlativo di* Full.
A **Fu'lling Mill**, *gualchiera,* s. f. *edificio, gli ordigni del quale mossi per forza d'acqua sodano i panni lani.*
Fu'lly, adv. [to the full] *pienamente, a pieno, ampiamente.*
I am fully satisfied, *sono pienamente sodisfatto.*
Fu'lness, s. [plenty] *abbondanza, copia,* s. f.
Fu'lsome, adj. [loathsome, luscious] *che stufa, stomacoso, stomachevole, schifo, nauseoso, fastidioso.*
Fulsome meat, *carne che stufa, che viene in fastidio.*
A fulsome favour, *un sapore ingrato, spiacevole.*
A fulsome man, *uno schifo, un uomo spiacevole, fastidioso.*
Fu'lsomely, adv. ex. to be fulsomely fat, *esser molto grasso.*
Fulsomeness, s. *nausea, stomaccagine, schifezza,* s. f. *fastidio,* s. m.
To **Fu'lminate** [to thunder out] *fulminare.*
To fulminate an excommunication, *fulminare una scomunica.*
Fulmina'tion, s. [a clap of thunder] *fulminazione,* s. f.
Fulmination [in chymistry, is when metal heated in crucibles make a great cracking noise] *fulminazione, termine chimico, e vuol dire strepito violento che fanno i metalli infocati nel crociuolo.*
To **Fu'mble** [to handle a thing aukwardly] *malmenare, scompigliare, maneggiar con mala grazia.*
To fumble along, *brancolare, andare al tasto, o a brancolone.*
To fumble [to faulter] in one's speech, *scilinguare, balbettare.*
To fumble up a letter, *piegar male una lettera.*
Fu'mbled, adj *v.* To fumble.
Fu'mbler, s. [aukward fellow] *un bighellone, un bietolone, un dappoco, uno sciocco, uno scempiato, uno scimunito.*
Fume, s. [smoak, steam] *fumo, o fummo, vapore,* s m. *esalazione.*
The glory of mortals is but a fume, *la gloria de' mortali non è ch'un fumo.*
The fumes of wine, *i fumi, i vapori del vino.*

To be in a fume [to be angry] *dar nelle smanie, menare smanie, infuriarsi.*

He is in a fume, *ella gli fuma, l'ira lo rode.*

To FUME [to smoak, to steam] *fumare, e fumare, far fumo, mandar fumo.*

To fume [to chafe, to be in a fret] *smaniare, infuriare, pazzeggiare, dar nelle smanie.*

To fume up, *esalare, mandar su vapori.*

FU'METS, s. [hunting term, the ordure or dung of a hare, hart, &c.] *sterco di lepre, cervo, e simili.*

FUMIGA'TION, s. [a perfuming by smoak] *fumigazione, e fummigazione,* s. f.

FU'MITORY, s. [a plant] *fummosterno,* s. m. *erba nota.*

FU'MOUS, } adj. [apt to fume up]
FU'MY } *fumifero, fummifero, fumoso, fummoso, che fa fummo, che fuma.*

FUN, s. [sport, high merriment] *baja, burla e allegria. Voce bassa.*

FU'NCTION, s. [the exercise, execution or performance of some duty or office] *funzione, operazione,* s. f.

FUND, s. [stock, capital, that by which any expence is supported] *un fondo, un capitale in roba o in danari.*

Fund [stock or bank of money] *banco, monte, deposito di danajo pubblico.*

FU'NDAMENT, s. *il fondamento o la base; quella cosa su cui un' altra viene eretta.*

FU'NDAMENTAL, adj. [principal, chief] *fondamentale, principale, che è come la base, o il fondamento, il sostegno.*

Fundamentals, s. [the fundamental principles, the main points] *il fondamento, la base principale.*

FU'NERAL, s. [burial] *funerale, mortorio,* s. m.

Funeral, adj. [belonging to a burial] *funerale, attenente a mortorio, funereo, funebre.*

A funeral sermon, *un' orazione funebre.*

Funeral pomp, *pompa funerale.*

FU'NGOUS, adj. [spungy, full of holes like a mushroom] *fungoso, spugnoso.*

FU'NGUS, s. [in surgery, soft spungy flesh, which grows upon wounds] *fungo,* s. m. *carne spugnosa, che nasce sulle ferite.*

FUNK, s. [a strong rank smell] *anso,* s. m.

FU'NNEL, s. [an instrument to convey liquors into a vessel] *imbuto,* s. m. *pevera,* s. f. *strumento, che si mette nella bocca de' vasi, per versarvi il liquore, acciò non si sparga.*

Funnel [the upper part of a chimney] *la rocca del cammino, per la quale esce il fumo.*

FUR, *v.* Furr.

FURA'CITY, s. [an inclination to steal] *inclinazione a rubare.*

FU'RBELOW, s. [furr sewed on the lower part of the garment] *falbalà.*

To FU'RBELOW, *adornare, aggiungere un falbalà.*

To FU'RBISH [to polish, to make bright] *forbire, nettare, pulire.* pres. *forbisco, pulisco.*

FU'RBISHED, adj. *forbito, nettato, pulito.*

FU'RBISHER, s. [polisher] *forbitore,* s. m. *che forbisce.*

Furbisher [sword cutler] *spadajo,* s. m.

FU'RBISHING, s. *il forbire.*

A furbishing stick, *forbitoja,* s. m. *strumento con che si forbisce.*

FU'RCHEE, adj. [in heraldry] *forcuto.*

FU'RIOUS, adj. [fierce, mad, raging] *furioso, furibondo, pazzo bestiale, impetuoso.*

A furious storm, *una furiosa tempesta.*

Furious winds, *venti impetuosi.*

FU'RIOUSLY, adv. *furiosamente, con furia, impetuosamente.*

To FURL [a sea term, to wrap up the sail] *ammainare, termine della navigazione, ritirare, piegare le vele.*

To furl the sails, *ammainar le vele.*

FU'RLED, adj. *ammainato.*

FU'RLING LINES [small lines made fast to the topsails, to furl up the sails] *funicelle da ammainar le vele.*

FU'RLONG, s. [the eighth part of a mile] *stadio,* s. m. *ottava parte d'un miglio.*

FU'RLOUGH, s. [a licence granted by a superior officer to be absent for a while] *licenza concessa da un ufficiale generale ad un ufficiale subalterno, o ad un soldato di stare assente per qualche tempo.*

FU'RMENTY, s. [pottage made of wheat] *cibo di fromento e latte.*

FU'RNACE, s. *fornace,* s. f.

A brewing furnace, *un fornello.*

A little furnace, *una fornacella.*

To FU'RNISH [to provide, to supply] *fornire, provvedere,* pret. *provvidi,* pres. *fornisco.*

To furnish a town with victuals, *fornire una terra di vettovaglie, o di viveri.*

To furnish a house, *parare, addobbare una casa.*

FU'RNISHED, adj. *fornito, provveduto, parato, addobbato.*

I am furnished with every thing, *io sono provvisto di tutto.*

A house finely furnished, *una casa riccamente addobbata.*

Rooms ready furnished to let, *camere locande.*

FU'RNITURE, s. [utensils, whatsoever is requisite to furnish a house, or any other place] *fornimento, masserizia di casa, addobbi, mobili.*

A costly furniture, *ricchi fornimenti, superbe masserizie.*

Bad furniture, *masseriziaccia,* s. f.

FURR, or FUR, s. [the skin of several wild beasts used for warmth and ornament] *pelle, pelliccia,* s. f. *pelle che abbia lungo pelo, come di martore, volpi, vai, e simili, oggi si scrive sempre* Fur.

To FURR a coat [to line a coat with furr] *foderare un vestito con pelle.*

FU'RRED, adj. *foderato di pelle.*

A furred coat, *una pelliccia, un pelliccione.*

FU'RRIER, s. *pellicciere, pellicciajo,* s. m.

The streets where furriers live, *pelliceria,* s. f. *la strada dove stanno i pellicciai.*

FU'RROW, s. [a trench cast up by the plow in the fields] *solco,* s. m. *quella fossetta che si lascia dietro l'aratro in lavorando la terra.*

Furrow [a drain for the draining of moist lands] *fosso, gorello,* s. m. *smaltitojo d'acqua.*

To FU'RROW, *solcare; far solchi.*

FU'RRY, adj *vestito di pelliccia, fatto di pelliccia.*

FU'RTHER, adj. [from far] *ulteriore, di là, dall' altra banda.*

The further Calabria, *la Calabria ulteriore.*

On the further side of the Tyber, *di là dal Tevere.*

There's nothing on the further side of those hills, *non v'è niente dall' altra banda di quelle montagne.*

You must go to the further end of the city, *bisogna che voi andiate fino all' ultima parte della città.*

In the further end of the shop, *in fondo della bottega.*

This will be a further obligation, *questo sarà una nuova obbligazione.*

Take no further care of that, *non vi pigliate più fastidio di ciò.*

Till further order, *fino a novell' ordine.*

Further, adv. *più lontano, più avanti, più innanzi, più oltre.*

I went a little further, *andai un poco più lontano, o avanti.*

I cannot go further, *non posso andar più avanti o più oltre.*

'Tis further than my house, *è più in là della mia casa.*

Go a little further that way, *fatevi più in là.*

Further [besides that] *ancora, altro, di più.*

This he said further to me, *di più mi disse ciò.*

Have you any further commands? *avete altro a comandarmi?*

I have nothing further to tell you, *non ho altra cosa a dirvi.*

To FU'RTHER [to assist, to help] *assistere, ajutare, giovare, dare, ajuto.*

He must further you in that, *bisogna che egli vi assista in ciò.*

To further or promote a thing, *proporre, metter in campo che che si sia.*

FU'RTHERANCE, s. [help] *ajuto, appoggio,* s. m. *assistenza,* s. f.

Furtherance [progress] *progresso, avanzamento.*

FU'RTHERER, s. [promoter, advancer] *promotore, uno che fa andare una cosa molto avanti.*

FU'RTHERMORE, conj. [moreover], *oltre, oltre a ciò, di più.*

FU'RTHEST [the superlative of far] *il più lontano.*

I will go to the furthermost part of the world, *voglio andarmene nelle parti le più remote delle terra.*

This

This is the furtheſt way about, *queſta è la ſtrada piu lunga.*

The furtheſt way about is the neareſt way home, *chi va piano, va ſano.*

To morrow at furtheſt, *domani al più tardi.*

FU'RTIVE, adj. [done by ſtealth, ſecret] *furtivo, di furto, occulto, naſcoſo, ſegreto.*

FU'RTIVELY, adv. *furtivamente, di furto, naſcoſamente, ſegretamente, occultamente.*

FU'RY, s. [rage] *furia, ira, ſtizza, pazzia,* s. f. *furore, impeto,* s. m.

To be in a great fury, *dar nelle furie, infuriarſi.*

The furies of hell, *le furie d'inferno, o infernali.*

FURZE, s. [a ſort of prickly broom, uſed for fuel] *ſpezie di gineſtra.*

FUSE'E, s. [a kind of light muſket] *ſcoppietto,* s. m.

Fuſee [a pipe filled with wildfire, and put into the touch-hole of a bomb] *raggio di bomba.*

Fuſee [that part of the watch about which the chain or ſtring is wound] *il rocchello d'un oriuolo.*

Fuſee, s. [the track of a buck] *la traccia o le veſtigia d'un daino.*

FUSELI'ER, s. [a foot ſoldier armed with a fuſee] *fuciliere,* s. m.

FUSIBI'LITY, s. [aptneſs to be melted] *attitudine, e diſpoſizione a fonderſi.*

FU'SIBLE, } adj. [that may be FU'SILE, } melted] *atto a fonderſi.*

FUSILE'ER, } s. [a ſoldier armed FUSILI'ER, } with a fuſil] *ſoldato armato di fucile, fuciliere.*

FU'SION, s. *fuſione, effuſione,* s. f.

FUSS, s. [a tumult, a buſtle] *uno ſtrepito; molto romore e poca lana.*

FUST, s. [the ſhaft of a column from the aſtragal to the capital] *fuſo, o fuſto della colonna.*

Fuſt, s. [a ſtrong ſmell, as that of a mouldy barrel] *tanfo.*

FU'STIAN, s. [a ſort of ſtuff] *ſorta di panno lano.*

Fuſtian, s. [a high ſwelling kind of writing, made up of heterogeneous parts; bombaſt] *ampolloſità, gonfiezza, l'andar ſu i trampani, e diceſi ſolo dello ſcrivere, ſpecialmente in verſi.*

Fuſtian, adj. *ampolloſo, gonfio.*

FU'STILUGS, s. [a woman noiſomly fat] *una donna graſſa e peſſuta, che puzza per la troppa graſſezza.*

FU'STINESS, s. [a rank ſmell] *muffa, mucidezza,* s. f. *tanfo,* s. m.

FUSTY, adj. [that has a rank ſmell] *muffato, mucido.*

To have a fuſty ſmell, *ſaper di mucido.*

FUTI'LITY, s. [lightneſs, vanity] *vanità, leggierezza, loquacità.*

The futility of women, *la vanità delle donne.*

FU'TTOCKS, s. [in a ſhip are the compaſſing timbers which make her breadth] *le coſtole d'un navilio.*

FU'TURE, adj. [that ſhall or will be] *futuro, ſopravegnente, vegnente.*

The future, s. *il futuro.*

FU'TURITY, s. [the time to come] *il tempo futuro.*

To FUZZ [to ravel or run out] *ſfilarſi, ſfilacciarſi.*

A ſtuff that fuzzes, *panno che ſi ſfilaccia.*

FU'ZZBALL, s. *ſpezie di fungo che ſcoppiando quando lo ſtiacci t' empie gli occhi d'una polvere che ha dentro.*

FY [an interjection of abhorring or loathing] *oibò.*

Fy for ſhame, *deh vergognatevi.*

G.

G, *Ha due ſuoni in Ingleſe e non tre come in Italiano. Uno è quello che chiamano* G hard [*G duro*] *che precede* a, o, u, l, r, *e ſomiglia al noſtro in* ga, go, gu, gloria, grazia. *L'altro e quello che chiamano* G ſoft [*G molle*] *è queſto precede generalmente* e, i, *come in* gem gibbet, *pure anche qualche volta innanzi,* e, i, *ſi pronuncia duro, come in* get, geeſe, give, *e in altre voci tanto in principio che in mezzo.*

GA'BARDINE, s. [an old faſhioned coarſe garment] *gabbano, palandrano,* s. m.

To GA'BBLE [to prate or prattle] *cicalare, chiacchierare, cicchirillare. E' voce affatto plebea.*

To gabble [to make an inarticulate noiſe] *articolare confuſamente nel parlare, come verbigrazia fa il pappagallo.*

GABBLE [inarticulate noiſe like that of brute animals] *voci male articolate come quelle de' bruti comparate alla favella umana.*

Gabble [loud talk without meaning] *il cianciare ad alta voce ſenza ſenſo alcuno.*

GA'BBLING, s. *cicalio, cicalamento, cicaleccio,* s. m. *cicaleria,* s. f.

A confuſed gabbling, *un ſuſurro, uno ſtrepito confuſo.*

GA'BEL, s. [a duty paid to the king or lord] *gabella, taſſa.*

GA'BION, s. [baſkets, which being filled with earth or ſtones, are placed upon the batteries] *gabbioni,* s. m. *panieri inteſſuti di vinchi e ripieni di terra o di ſaſſi, uſati in guerra per riparo e difeſa.*

GA'BIONADE, s. [a bulwark made with gabions] *gabbionata,* s. f.

GABLE END OF A HOUSE [the top or front part of a houſe] *gronda,* s. f. *l'eſtremità del tetto, ch'eſce fuora della ſommità della caſa.*

G'ABLOCKS, s. [falſe ſpurs for fighting cocks, of ſteel, ſilver, &c.] *ſproni d'acciajo o d'argento che ſi mettono agli ſproni de' galli quando ſi battono.*

GAD, s. [a ſmall bar of ſteel] *un pezzo d'acciajo.*

A gad-fly, or gad-bee, *un tafano.*

To GAD up and down [to rove, to range or ſtraggle about] *andar ramingo, vagabondare, vagare.*

GA'DDER, s. *un vagabondo, un perdigiorno, uno ſcioperato.*

GA'DDING, s. *vagamento,* s. m. *vagazione,* s. f.

Gadding, adj. ex. a gadding goſſip *una donna che va volentier vagando.*

GAFF, s. [an iron hook to pull great fiſhes into a ſhip] *uncino, col quale ſi tirano ſu peſci groſſi nel navilio.*

GAG, s. [an inſtrument to put in the mouth to keep it from ſhutting] *ſbarra,* s. f. *quello ſtrumento, che ſi mette altrui in bocca, a effetto d'impedirli la favella.*

To GAG, *metter la ſbarra in bocca ad uno.*

GAGE, or GAUGE, s. [a rod to meaſure caſks with] *ſcandaglio, col quale ſi miſurano le botti.*

Gage [a pledge or ſurety] *pegno,* s. m. *ſicurtà,* s. f.

To GAGE, or gauge [to meaſure with a gage, to find what any veſſel contains] *ſcandagliare una botte, per vedere quanto ella contiene.*

To gage a hogſhead of wine, *ſcandagliare una botte di vino.*

To gage a ſhip a-float, *miſurare quanti piedi d'acqua ha un navilio.*

To gage [to wager; to lay down as a wager] *ſcommettere; metter giù quello che ſi ſcommette.*

GAGED, adj. *ſcandagliato.*

To GAGGLE, *gridare come fa un' oca.*

GA'GGLING, s. *grido d'oca.*

GA'ITY, s. [chearfulneſs] *gajezza, allegria, gioja,* s. f.

Gaiety of humour, *gajezza, umor allegro, e gioviale.*

Gaiety of cloths, *abiti sfoggiati, e pompoſi.*

GA'ILY, adv. [airily, chearfully] *gajamente, giojoſamente, allegramente.*

Gaily [ſplendidly, pompouſly] *con magnificenza, con pompa: appariſcentemente.*

GAIN, s. [profit, lucre] *guadagno, lucro, profitto,* s. m.

To make great gains, *far gran guadagno.*

'Tis all clear gain to me, *queſto è tutto guadagno per me.*

To gain [to get, to win] *guadagnare, acquiſtare.*

To gain money, *guadagnar danari.*

To gain one's love, *cattivarſi l'altrui amicizia.*

He has gained a great reputation by it, *egli s' è acquiſtata con ciò una gran reputazione.*

To gain [to carry] *guadagnare,* ri*portare, impadronirſi.*

To gain a battle, *guadagnar la battaglia.*

To gain a breach, *impadronirſi d'una breccia.*

To gain one's end, *ottenere il ſuo intento.*

They gained them over to their religion, *eglino li hanno* tirati *alla loro religione, eglino li hanno convertiti alla loro religione.*

GAINED, adj. *guadagnato, acquiſtato, v.* To gain.

GA'INER, s. *guadagnatore,* s. m. *guadagnatrice,* s. f.

I am neither gainer nor loſer, *non ci guadagno, nè ci perdo.*

GA'INFUL, adj. *lucrativo, profittevole, vantaggioſo.*

A gainful employment, *un impiego lucrativo.*

GA'INING, s. *il guadagnare.*

For the gaining idolaters over to the Chriſtian faith, *per la converſione degli idolatri alla fede Chriſtiana.*

GA'INLY, adv. [eaſily] *facilmente.*

To GA'INSAY [to ſpeak againſt, to deny, to contradict] *contraddire, dir contra, oſtare, opporſi, contradiare, e contrariare, intraverſarſi, contraſtare,* preſ. *contraddico, oppongo.* pret. *contraddiſſi, opposi.*

To gainſay truth, *contraddire la verità.*

GA'INSAY'D, adj. *contraddetto, oſtato, oppoſto, contradiato, contrariato, intraverſato, contraſtato.*

GAINSA'YER, s. *contraddicitore, contraddittore,* s. m.

GAINSA'YING, s. *contraddizione, opposizione, negazione, contrarietà,* s. f. *contraddicimento, contradiamento, contraſto, oſtacolo,* s. m.

'GAINST, *v.* Againſt.

To GA'INSTAND] to reſiſt, to oppoſe] *opporſi, reſiſtere, oſtare.* preſ, *oppongo, opposi.*

GA'IRISH, adj. [gaudy, ſhowy, ſplendid, fine] *pompoſo, viſtoſo, ſplendido, adorno.*

Ga'riſh, *troppo pompoſo, troppo ſplendido, adorno ſtravagantemente.*

GAIRISHNESS, s. [finery, flaunting gaudineſs] *adornezza pompoſa.*

Gairiſhneſs [flighty or extravagant joy] *ſoverchio e ſtravagante gaudio.*

GAIT, s. *il modo, l'andare, il portamento della perſona, l'aria dell' andare, il modo di camminare.*

GA'LANGAL, s. *ſorta di radice medicinale.*

GA'LAXY, s. [a broad white circle in the ſky, called the Milky way] *la via lattea.*

GA'LBANUM, s. [a gum of a ſtrong ſcent] *galbano,* s. m. *liquor d'una pianta.*

GALE, s. [a wind not tempeſtuous] *vento freſco.*

GA'LEASS, s. [a kind of ſea veſſel, chiefly uſed in the Adriatick ſea] *galezza,* s. f. *navilio ſimile alla galea, ma aſſai maggiore.*

GA'LEON, s. [a ſort of ſea veſſel] *galeone,* s. m. *ſorta di nave.*

GA'LINGALE, s. [a ſort of water flag] *ſpezie di giunco angulare.*

GALL, s. [the bile, one of the humours of the body] *fiele,* s. m.

Bitter as gall, *amaro come fiele.*

The gall bladder, *la veſcica del fiele.*

Gall-nut [a fruit which grows on an oak, uſed in dying, and to make ink with] *galla, gallozza, e gallozzola,* s. f. *eſeremento, parto non legittimo d' alcuni alberi di ghiande, che ſerva a tignere e a fare l' inchioſtro.*

To GALL [to fret or rub off the ſkin] *ſcorticare, tor via la pelle.*

To gall the enemy with a continual fire, *infeſtar il nemico con iſpeſſi* tiri *di cannonate, o di moſchettate.*

To gall [to vex, to teaze] *inquietare, infaſtidire, moleſtare, travagliare,* tribo*lare, pugnere, e pungere, offender mordendo con* detti. preſ. *infaſtidiſco, pungo.* pret. *offeſi, punſi.*

GA'LLANT, adj. [civil] *galante, gentile, oneſto, grazioſo, gajo, amorevole.*

Gallant [brave] *bravo, gagliardo, vigoroſo.*

Gallant [fine] *bello, attillato, aggiuſtato, gajo.*

He is very gallant in his behaviour, *egli è ne' ſuoi portamenti molto galante.*

They made a gallant defence, *fecero una gagliarda difeſa.*

A gallant man, *un galantuomo, uomo dabbene.*

GALL'ANT, s. [lover] *un amante, un amoroſo.*

Gallant [ſpark, beau] *amadore, drudo, leggiardo, vago,* s. m.

Gallant to a married woman, *un amico, un ciciſbeo.*

To GALLA'NT [to court a woman in the way of a gallant] *fare il galante appreſſo una donna, corteggiarla.*

To GA'LLANTISE [to play the gallant] *fare il galante, fare il zerbino, il bello, l'attillato.*

GA'LLANTLY, adv. *galantemente, gentilmente, grazioſamente, con belle maniere, corteſemente.*

Gallantly [couragiouſly] *bravamente, con bravura, gagliardamente, vigoroſamente, coraggioſamente.*

GA'LLANTNESS, } s. *galanteria,*
GA'LLANTRY, } *maniera galante, leggiadria, garbatlezza, grazia, grazioſità, lindezza, venuſtà,* s. f. *garbo,* s. m.

Gallantry [ſpirit, bravery] *ſpirito, animo, coraggio, valore,* s. m. *bravura,* s. f.

GA'LLED, adj. [from to gall] *ſcorticato.*

To touch a galled horſe upon the back, *ſolleticar dove ti duole, innaſprire una perſona già irritata.*

GA'LLERY, s. *galleria,* s. f.

An open gallery, *una loggia.*

The galleries of a man of war, *la galleria d'una nave da guerra.*

Gallery [in fortification, is a covered walk croſs the ditch of a beſieged town] *galleria,* ter*mine di fortificazione.*

GA'LLEY, s. [a ſea veſſel much uſed in the Mediterranean] *galea,* s. f. *navilio di remo di forma lunga.*

To be condemned to the galleys, *eſſer condannato in galea, eſſer condannato a remare.*

The admiral galley, *le capitana, la galea capitana.*

A galley ſlave, *un galeotto, quegli che voga in galea.*

Half galley, *una galeotta.*

Galley pot, *alberello,* s. m. *vaſo piccolo di* terra.

A galley foiſt, *un fuſte, un brigantino.*

GA'LLIARD, s. [a kind of merry dance] *gagliarda,* s. f. *ſpezie di ballo.*

GA'LLICAN, adj. [French] *Gallicano.*

The Gallican church, *la chieſa Gallicana.*

GA'LLICISM, s. [French idiom] *Gallicismo,* s. m. *idioma Franceſe, eſpreſſione puramente Franceſe.*

GALLIGA'SKINS, s. [a ſort of wide breeches uſed by the inhabitants of Gaſcoign in France] *calzoni alla maniera de' Guaſroni antichi.*

GALLIMA'WFRY, s. [a hoch-poch made up of ſeveral ſorts of meat] *cibreo,* s. m. *manicaretto compoſto di diverſe ſorte di carne.*

GA'LLION, s. [great ſhip] *galeone,* s. m. *ſorta di nave.*

GALLI-POT, *v.* Galley-pot.

GA'LLON, s. [a meaſure containing four quarts] *miſura di coſe liquide che contiene quattro boccali, o quarte.*

A gallon pot, *un boccale che contiene quattro quarte.*

GALLO'ON, s. [a kind of cloſe lace] *trina,* s. f. *ſpezie di gallone fatto d'oro, d' argento, o di ſeta.*

GA'LLOP, s. [the ſwifteſt pace of a horſe] *galoppo, e gualoppo,* s. m. *il galoppare.*

To fall into a gallop, *prendere il galoppo, metterſi a galoppare.*

To run a full gallop, *andar di buon galoppo, correre a briglia ſciolta.*

To GA'LLOP [to ride faſt] *galoppare, o gualoppare.*

He that gallops, *galoppatore.*

GA'LLOPPING, s. *il galoppare.*

Galloping, adj. Ex. a galloping horse, *un cavallo che galoppa, o che va di galoppo.*

GA'LLO'SHES, s. pl. [a sort of leather cases or clogs worn over shoes, to keep the feet from the wet] *soprascarpe, s. f. pl. sorta di pianelle che servono come di fodera alle scarpe, onde non imbrattino andando per la via quando è sporca.*

GA'LLOWAY, s. *cavallo d'una spezie che è molto piccola, è molto comune nel norte d'Inghilterra.*

GA'LLOW, } s. [a frame of wood
GA'LLOWS, } upon which malefactors are hanged] *forca, s. f. patibolo dove s'impiccano per la gola i malfattori.*

The gallows groans for him, *la forca l'aspetta.*

A gallows [a hang-dog, a Newgate bird] *una forca, uno degna della forca, uno scelerato.*

The gallows of a press, *cavalletto di torchio.*

GAMBA'DOES, s. [a sort of leather boots] *sorta di stivaletti.*

GA'MBLER, s. *un briccone, il cui mestiere è di rubare i malaccorti al giuoco.*

To GA'MBOL [to dance, to skip, to frisk] *ballare, e saltare come fanno verbigrazia le scimie al sole.*

To gambol [to leap, to start] *saltare, spiccar un salto.*

GA'MBOL, s. [a skip, a hop, a leap for joy] *salto fatto per allegrezza.*

Gambol [a frolick, a wild prank] *un moto capriccioso del corpo e delle gambe fatto per far ridere, o che fa ridere.*

GA'MBREL, s. *la gamba d'un cavallo.*

GAME, s. [play, sport] *giuoco, scherzo, trastullo, passatempo, festeggiamento.*

The publick games of the ancient Greeks and Romans, *i giuochi pubblici degli antichi Greci e Romani.*

Game [play] *giuoco, il giuocare.*

A game at cards, *un giuoco di carte.*

Game [a part of a set] *giuoco.*

Five games shall make up the set, *rinque giuochi fanno la partita, la partita sarà di cinque giuochi.*

I want but two games to be up, *non mi bisognano che due giuochi per finire la partita.*

He play'd his game well, *egli ha fatto ben la sua parte.*

He is good at all kind of games, *egli è un uomo da zappa e da vanga, egli è buono ad ogni cosa.*

Game [beasts for hunting, or fowl to shoot at] *caccia, cacciagione, s. f.*

We have had very good game, *abbiamo fatto buona caccia.*

A game-keeper, *guardiano di careia.*

To GAME [to play] *giuocare, e giucare.*

GA'MESOME, adj. [wanton] *giocoso, lieto, festevole, gajo, allegro, giocondo, giojoso.*

GA'MESOMENESS, s. *scherzo giuoco, trastullo, s. m.*

GA'MESTER, s. *giuocatore, biscazziere, s. m.*

GA'MING, s. *giuoco, il giuocare.*

To love gaming [to be given to it] *amare il giuoco, esser dedito al giuoco.*

A gaming house, *bisca, s. f. luogo dove si tien giuoco pubblico.*

GA'MMON, s. [or gammon of bacon] *presciutto, s. m.*

Gammon, *sorta di giuoco che si fa co' dadi e la tavola.*

GA'MUT, s. [the first note in the ordinary scale of musick, and the scale itself] *solfa, e zolfa, s. f. voce colla quale s'esprimono i caratteri e le figure, o note musicali.*

To GANCH [to throw one headlong from a high place upon sharp hooks or iron spikes] *gettare uno da alto a basso sopra uncini di ferro, sorta di supplicio in uso fra i Turchi.*

To ganch [to tear open one's guts] *crepare, sventrare.*

GA'NDER, s. [a male goose] *il maschio dell' oca.*

GANG, s. [company, crew] *banda, frotta, compagnia, s. f. ma si piglia sempre in cattiva parte.*

A gang of thieves, *una banda, una man di ladri.*

Gang-wood, or Rogation-week.

To GANG [to go] *andarsene, colsela, battersela.*

GA'NGREL, s. [a tall ill-shaped fellow] *un uomo mal fatto, una pertica.*

GANGRE'NE, s. [an eating ulcer, that will quickly infect all the body] *cancrena, e cangrena, canrherella, s. f. parte mortificata intorno ad ulceri, o intorno a inflammazioni, che sempre va dilatando.*

To GANGRE'NE [to fall into a gangrene] *incangrenarsi, incancherarsi.*

GANGRE'NED, adj. *incangrenato, incancherito.*

GA'NTLET, s. [an iron glove] *guanto di ferro.*

GA'NTLET, GA'NTLOPE, s. [an usual punishment among soldiers] *bacchette, supplicio militare.*

To run the gantlope, *passar per le bacchette.*

GA'NZA, s. [a kind of wild goose] *sorta d'oca salvatica.*

GOAL, s. [prison] *carrere, prigione, s. f.*

Goal-delivery [the clearing of a prison of prisoners, a law term] *il vuotar le prigioni col giustiziare i colpevoli, e mettere in libertà gl' innocenti.*

GA'OLER, s. *guardiano delle prigioni, carceriere.*

GAP, s. [an open place in a hedge or wall, &c.] *apertura, aperta, crepatura, fenditura, fessura, spaccatura, s. f. crepaccio, screpolo, s. m.*

A gap in a hedge, *apertura in una siepe.*

A gap in the wall, *una crepatura o fessura in un muro, breccia.*

GAP-TOOTHED, adj. *che ha spazi fra un dente e l'altro.*

To GAPE [to yawn] *sbadigliare, e sbavigliare, aprir la bocca.*

To gape after, or for a thing, *uccellare a una cosa, desiderarla con avidità.*

To gape at, *guardar che che si sia collo bocca aperta, baloccare.*

To gape [to open as the ground does] *aprirsi, spaccarsi, creparsi come fa la terra.*

GA'PING, s. *sbadiglio, e sbaviglio, s. m. l'atto dello sbadigliare, v.* To gape.

To stand gaping to the air, *abbajare alla luna.*

Gaping [chink] *una fessura, una crepatura.*

To GAR [to make] *fare, esser ragione.*

GARB, s. [attire, dress] *abito, vestimento, ornamento, s. m.*

To be in a genteel garb, *essere ben vestito.*

Garb [carriage, behaviour] *garbo, s. m. avventezza, leggiadria, s. f.*

A man that has a good garb, *un uomo di bel garbo, un uomo garbato.*

Wine that has a good garb [that has a quick or picquant taste] *vin garbo, vino piccante, e gustoso.*

Of an ill garb, *sgarbato, svenevole.*

Garb [in heraldry, a sheaf of corn] *un manipolo di grano.*

GA'RBAGE, s. [the entrails of cattle] *le budella, le interiora d'un animale.*

Garbage [that hunters give their hounds] *interiora che i cacciatori danno a' cani dell' animale cacciato e preso.*

Garbage [refuse] *mondiglia, spazzatura, s. f.*

To GA'RBLE, *sventrare, sbudellare.*

To garble [to cleanse from dross and dirt, commonly used of spices] *stacciare, vagliare, ed è proprio delle spezierie.*

To garble [to cull out] *scegliere, pret. scelsi.*

GA'RBLED, adj. *stacciato, vagliato, scelto.*

GA'RBLER, s. [an officer that may enter into any shop or ware-house, to view and search drugs, spices, &c.] *ufficiale che ha potere di visitare droghe, spezierie, e simili, in qualunque luogo ch' elle si siano.*

GA'RBLER, *colui che staccia o separa una cosa da un' altra.*

GA'RBLES, s. [the dust or uncleanness that is severed from spice, drugs, &c.] *mondiglie, purgature, vagliature, vagliature di droghe, spezierie, e simili.*

GA'RBOIL, s. [trouble, tumult, uproar] *garbuglio, ravviluppamento, scompiglio, disordine, tumulto, s. m. confusione, s. f.*

GARD, or GUARD, s. [defence] *guardia, custodia, difesa, s. f. oggi però si scrive sempre* Guard, *quantunque si pronunci* Gard.

To stand upon one's gard, *prender guardia, stare in cervello, star rogli occhi aperti, star sulla sua.*

To lie well upon one's gard [a fencing term] *star bene in guardia.*

Gard of soldiers, *guardie, soldati che sono in guardia.*

To be upon the gard, *far la guardia, esser di guardia.*

The king's gard, *le guardie del re.*

The horse gard, *le guardie a cavallo.*

The

The foot gard, *le guardie a piede.*
To come off from gard, *smontar la guardia.*
The gard [or hilt] of a sword, *la guardia o elsa della spada.*
Gard [or hem] of a garment, *l'orlo d'un vestimento.*
A gard-house, *corpo di guardia.*
To GARD, or GUARD [to keep] *guardare, servare, conservare, tener conto.*
To GARD [to protect] *guardare, scampare, liberare, difendere, proteggere, assicurare,* pret. *protessi.*
GA'RDED, adj. *guardato, v.* To gard.
Garded [protected] *guardato, difeso, protetto.*
GA'RDEN, s. *giardino,* s. m.
A kitchen garden, *un orto.*
A nurse-garden, *seminario, semenzajo,* s. m.
A little garden, *un giardinetto.*
A little kitchen garden, *un orticello.*
GA'RDENER, s. *giardiniere, giardiniero,* s. m.
GA'RDENING, s. *erbaggi, ogni sorta d'erba buona a mangiare, ortaggi.*
GA'RDEROBE, *v.* Wardrobe.
GA'RDEVIANT, s. [a wallet for a soldier to put his victuals in] *bisaccia da soldato, dove e' porta le sue provvisioni.*
GA'RDIAN, or GUA'RDIAN, s. [one who has the charge or care of any person or thing] *guardiano, custode.*
The gardian of a pupil, *il tutore, o curatore d'un pupillo.*
The gardian of some religious houses, *guardiano, superiore d'un convento di frati.*
A gardian angel, *angelo custode.*
GA'RDIANSHIP, s. [the office of a gardian to a pupil] *tutela, curatela,* s. f.
Gardianship [the office of a gardian in a religious house] *ufficio di guardiano.*
GARE, s. [a sort of coarse wool, such as grows about the shanks of sheep] *lana zaccherosa, piena di zacchere.*
GA'RGARISM, s. [a liquid medicine to cleanse the throat and mouth] *gargarismo,* s. m. *acqua artificiata colla quale l'uomo si gargarizza.*
To GA'RGARISE [to gargle or wash the mouth] *gargarizzare, risciacquarsi la canna della gola con gargarismo.*
GA'RGLE, s. [the gullet of the throat] *strozza,* s. f. *gorgozzule,* s. m. *la canna della gola.*
Gargle [a liquor with which the throat is washed] *gargarismo.*
To GA'RGLE [to wash the mouth and throat with liquor] *gargarizzare, risciacquare la bocca con alcun liquore.*
To gargle one's mouth, *gargarizzarsi, risciacquarsi la bocca.*
GA'RGLED, adj. *gargarizzato, risciacquato.*
GA'RGLING, s. *il gargarizzare.*
Gargling, adj. Ex. gargling brooks, *mormoranti ruscelli.*
GA'RGOL, s. [a distemper in hogs] *malattia propria de' porci.*
GA'RISH, adj. [gay, gaudy] *pomposo, magnifico, splendido, scrivi anzi,* garish.
A garish dress, *un abito superbo, o pomposo.*
GA'RISHNESS, adj. *pomposità, magnificenza,* s. f. *scrivi anzi* gairishness.
GA'RLAND, s. [an ornament for the head made of flowers] *ghirlanda,* s. f.
GA'RLICK, s. [a plant] *aglio,* s. m.
To smell of garlick, *puzzar d'aglio.*
A clove of garlick, *uno spicchio d'aglio.*
Garlick sauce, *agliata,* s. f.
GA'RMENT, s. [any vestment] *abito, vestimento,* s. m.
A rich garment, *un abito ricco, sfoggiato.*
The wedding garment, *abito di nozze.*
A mourning garment, *il bruno.*
GA'RNET, s. [a tackle in a ship wherewith goods are hoisted in or out] *carrucola,* s. f. *macchina di vascello per mezzo del quale si sbarcano, o s'imbarcano le mercanzie.*
Garnet [granet stone] *granato,* s. m. *gioja del color del vin rosso.*
To GA'RNISH [to furnish] *guarnire, e guernire, munire, corredare, fornire,* pref. *guarnisco, guernisco, munisco, fornisco.*
To garnish a table with sweetmeats, *guarnire una tavola di confetture.*
To garnish [to adorn, to set off] *adornare, ornare, abbellire, abbigliare, addobbare,* pref. *abbellisco.*
GA'RNISH, s. [a fee paid by prisoners to their keepers, at their first entrance into goal] *il benvenuto, danaro che si paga al carceriere da un prigioniere nell' entrare della prigione.*
GA'RNISHES OF DOORS, GATES, or PORCHES, *gli ornamenti, gli abbellimenti d'una porta, d'un portico, e simili.*
GA'RNISHED, adj. *guarnito, guernito, munito, corredato, fornito, v.* To garnish.
GA'RNISHMENT, s. [a warning given to one for his appearance for the better furnishing of the cause and court] *citazione, assegnazione,* s. f. *termine legale.*
GA'RNITURE, s. [the furniture of a chamber] *addobbi, arredi, fornimenti d'una camera.*
GA'RRET, s. [the uppermost floor in a house] *soffitta,* s. f. *stanza a tetto.*
Garret, *legno marcio, tarlato per vecchiezza.*
GA'RRISON, s. [a certain number of soldiers in a strong place for the defence of it] *guarnigione, e guernigione,* s. f. *quella quantità di soldati, che stanno per guardia di fortezza, e altri luoghi muniti, che anche oggi diciamo, presidio,* s. m.
Garrison [a place of defence, into which soldiers are put] *guernigione, luogo ove stanno i presidi.*
A garrison town, *una guarnigione, un presidio.*
To GA'RRISON [to put a garrison in] *presidiare, metter guarnigione, o presidio.*
GA'RRISONED, adj. *presidiato.*
GARRU'LITY, s. [talkativeness, overmuch prating] *garrulità, loquacità,* s. f.
GA'RRULOUS, adj. [full of talk] *garrulo, loquace.*
GA'RTER, s. [a band or ribbon to tie up stockings] *legaccia,* s. f. *legaccio,* s. m.
To tie one's stockings with garters, *legarsi le calzette colle legacce.*
The noble order of the garter, *l'ordine della giartiera.*
Il Davanzati lo chiamò l'ordine della Gerrettiera.
A knight of the garter, *cavaliere della giartiera.*
Garter, *è anche il titolo dello araldo principale d'Inghilterra.*
To GARTER [to tie one's garters] *legarsi le legacce.*
GARTH, s. [a yard in a house] *cortile,* s. m.
Fish-garth [a dam in a river for the catching of fish] *chiusa che si fa ne' fiumi per pigliar pesci.*
Garth-man [fisher-man] *un pescatore.*
Garth, *circonferenza del corpo umano misurato alla cintura.*
GA'SCOINS, s. [the hinder thighs of a horse] *le cosce d'un cavallo.*
GASH, s. [a deep cut] *un taglio, sfregio, fendente,* s. m.
He has a great gash in his face, *egli ha un gran taglio, o sfregio nel viso.*
To GASH [to cut] *tagliare, fendere, sfregiare.*
GASHED, adj. *tagliato, fesso, sfregiato.*
GASP, s. [a panting for breath] *anelito, ansamento, respiro, alito, fiato,* s. m.
To the last gasp, *fin all' ultimo sospiro.*
To give the last gasp, *render l'anima, spirare, mandar fuor l'ultimo spirito.*
To be at the last gasp, *stare per render l'anima.*
To GASP [to gape for breath] *anelare, ansare, respirare con affanno.*
To gasp for life, *esser in punto di morte.*
GA'SPING, s. *respirazione.*
GA'STILINESS, s. [ghastilinefs] *orrore, spavento,* s. m.
Gastilinefs [paleness] *pallidezza, squallidezza,* s. f.
GA'STLY, adj. [ghastly, frightful, like a ghost] *orrido, orrendo, spaventevole, terribile.*
A gastly countenance, *un viso terribile, che fa paura.*
Gastly animals, *animali spaventevoli.*
Gastly [pale] *pallido, squallido, macilente.*
Gate, s. [a great door] *porta,* s. f.
The gates of a city, *le porte d'una città.*
A flood, or water-gate, *una cateratta.*
Gate, *in questo significato scrivesi meglio,* gait [manner of going] *andatura,* s. f. *il modo d'andare.*
To have a portly gate, *avere un' andatura maestosa.*

Gate [presence] *aria, presenza*, s. f. *aspetto, sembiante*, s. m.

Her gate shewed her to be a woman of quality, *la sua aria la fareva conoscere per una persona di qualità.*

GA'THER, s. [plait] *piega*, s. f.

The gathers of a gown, *le pieghe d'una veste.*

A calve's gather, or pluck, *coratella di vitella.*

To GA'THER [to collect, to pick up] *cogliere, e corre.* pres. *colgo.* pret. *colsi.*

To gather flowers, fruits, &c. *coglier fiori, frutti,* &c.

To gather [to get together] *accumulare, ammassare, ammontare.*

To gather wealth, *accumular ricchezze.*

To gather rust [to grow rusty] *irrugginirsi, irrugginirsi, arrugginirsi.*

To gather an army, *mettere insieme un esercito.*

To gather [to plot] *piegare, increspare.*

To gather the sleeves of a shirt, *piegare le maniche d'una camicia.*

To gather [to conclude by discourse] *conchiudere, inferire, argomentare, voler dire, significare.* pres. *inferisco.*

What do you gather from that? *che volete conchiudere, o inferire da ciò? che volete dire per questo?*

To gather the corn, *mietere il grano.*

To gather the grapes, *vendemmiare.*

To gather dust, *cuoprirsi di polvere, impolverarsi.*

To gather strength, *prender forza, ringagliardirsi, rinforzarsi, fortificarsi, rinvigorirsi.* pres. *ringagliardisco, rinvigorisco.*

To gather flesh, *ingrossarsi, ingrassarsi, rimmetersi in carne.*

To gather together, *assembrarsi, unirsi, convenire.* pres. *convengo.* pret. *convenni.*

To gather the matter to a head, *far capo, marcire.*

Now my designs are gathering to a head, *ora sì che i miei disegni cominciano a maturarsi.*

To gather up her gown, *alzarsi la gonnella.*

To gather up a pin, *pigliar di terra uno spilletto.*

GA'THERED, adj. *colto, v.* To gather.

GA'THERER, s. *ricoglitore, raccoglitore*, s. m.

Gatherer of taxes, *riscuotitore, collettore di tasse.*

Gatherer of corn, *mietitore.*

Gatherer of grapes, *vendemmiatore.*

GA'THERERS, s. [the fore teeth of a horse] *scaglioni, i denti d'avanti del cavallo.*

GA'THERING, s. *coglimento*, s. m. *il cogliere.*

To make a gathering, *fare una collezione.*

To GAUDE, *godere, esultare, rallegrasi.*

GA'UDRY, s. *vestir pomposo.*

GA'UDIES, s. [double commons, such as are allowed to students on gaudy days] *pietanza doppia, che si da agli studenti in un collegio in certi giorni festivi.*

GA'UDILY, adv. *fastosamente, sfoggiatamente.*

GA'UDINESS, s. *fasto, sfoggio*, s. m.

GA'UDY, adj. [affectedly gay or fine] *spanto, sfoggiato, troppo fastoso.*

A gaudy suit of cloaths, *un abito spanto, o sfoggiato.*

Gaudy-days, [certain festival days observed in inns of court and colleges] *giorni festivi osservati nelle corti di giudicatura, e collegi.*

GAVE, *è un preterito del verbo* to give.

GA'VEL, s. [tribute, toll, custom, yearly rent, revenue] *spezie di tributo, tassa dogana, rendita, renso.*

GA'VELET, s. *mancanza di pagamento di rendita al padrone del feudo nella provincia di Kent.*

GA'VEL KIND, s. [an equal division of the father's land at his death among all his sons, or of a brother dying without issue among all his brothers] *legge, o costume stabilito in alcuni luoghi d' Inghilterra, e principalmente nella provincia di Kent, per la quale i beni del padre sono dopo la sua morte ugualmente divisi fra i suoi figliuoli, o dopo la morte d'un fratello senza eredi fra i suoi fratelli.*

GAUGE, or GAWGE, *v.* Gage.

GAUNT, adj. [lean] *magro, smunto, gramo.*

GA'UNTLET, s. *Guanto di combattitore, è che si scagliava in terra anticamente per isfida all' avversario o nemico.*

GAUNTRE'E, s. [a frame to set casks upon] *cavalletto da mettervi sopra le botti.*

GAWK, s. *un cucco, uno sciocco.*

GAWZE, s. [a sort of thin silk] *tocca*, s. f. *spezie di drappo di seta sottile.*

GAY, adj. [merry] *gajo, giojoso, festoso, allegro.*

GAY [neat, spruce] *bello, pulito, attillato, galante.*

A gay suit of cloaths, *un abito galante, pulito, gentile.*

Gay colours, *colore vivace.*

GAZE, s. *stupimento, stupore*, s. m. *ammirazione, maraviglia*, s. f.

To be at a gaze, or upon the gaze, *strabiliare, fuor di modo maravigliarsi, stupirsi*, pres. *stupisco.*

To GAZE [to stare, to look earnestly upon] *guardar fissamente che che si sia, specchiarsi, fissamente mirare, affissar gli occhi sopra una cosa.*

GAZED UPON, adj. *fissamente guardato, o mirato, specchiato.*

GAZE-HOUND [a hound that hunts by sight] *levriere*, s. m.

GA'ZEL, s. [an Arabian deer, or antelope of Barbary.] *gazzella*, s. f. *sorta d' animale quadrupede cornuto.*

GAZE'TTE, s. [a news paper] *gazetta*, s. f. *foglio d' avvisi.*

GAZETTE'ER, s. [a writer or publisher of gazettes] *gazzettiere, novellista*, s. m.

GA'ZING, s. *il guardare o mirar fissamente che che si sia.*

A gazing stock, *uno spettacolo; una cosa che tira gli occhi di tutti.*

GEAR, or GEER, s. [stuff, commodity] *roba, mercanzia*, s. f.

GEAR [bauble] *bagattella, ciancrusaglia, frascheria*, s. f.

A woman's night gear, *cuffia di donna per la notte.*

A horse's gears [trappings] *arnesi, fornimenti d'un cavallo.*

To be in one's gears [to be ready] *esser in ordine, in punto, in procinto.*

Gear [putrid matter] *marcia*, s. f.

GE'ARSON, adj. [rare, uncommon] *raro, scarso.*

GEAT, *buco, per cui il metallo fuso può colare.*

GEE-HO, interj. *giò, arri, vore colla quale s' incitano i cavalli da soma a camminare.*

To gee [to succeed] *riuscire.* pres. *riesco.* pret. *riuscii.*

This business won't gee, *questo negozio non reiscerà.*

To geer [to dress] *vestire, abbigliare.*

GEER'D, adj. *vestito, abbigliato.*

Neatly geer'd, *pulitamente vestito*

GEESE, *è il plurale di* Goose.

GEIR, s. [vulture] *avvoltojo, vulture.*

GELD, s. [a Saxon word for money] *danaro.*

To GELD [to castrate] *castrare.*

To geld a horse, *castrare un cavallo.*

GE'LDED, or GELT, adj. *castrato.*

GE'LDER, s. [he that gelds] *norcino*, s. m. *quegli che esercita l'arte del castrare sì gli uomini, che le bestie.*

GE'LDING, s. *il castrare.*

Gelding [cut horse] *ravallo castrato.*

GE'LLY, s. *gelatina.*

GELT, adj. [from to geld] *castrato.*

GEM [jewel, precious stone] *una gemma.*

To adorn with gems, *gemmare, ornare di gemme.*

Adorned with gems, *gemmato.*

To GEM, *adornar di gemme, ingemmare.*

To gem [to put forth the first buds] *germogliare, mandar fuora i primi germogli.*

GE'MINI, s. [one of the twelve signs of the zodiack] *gemini, uno de' dodici segni del zodiaco.*

O gemini, interj. *cappita, capperi, esclamazione, dinotante maraviglia.*

GE'MMOW, or GEMMOW-RING, s. *fede*, s. m. *anello matrimoniale, al quale in cambio di gemma sieno impronte un par di mani congiunte insieme.* Obs.

GE'NDER, s. [the difference of nouns as they are declined with a masculine, feminine, or neutral article] *genere*, s. m.

The masculine and feminine gender, *il genere masculino e femminino.*

To GE'NDER [to engender] *generare.*

GENEA'LOGIST, s. [one skilled in the

the method of deſcribing pedigrees] *genealogiſta*, s. m. *verſato nella genealogia.*

GENEALO'GICAL, adj. [belonging to genealogy] *genealogico, di genealogia.*

GENEA'LOGY, s. [deſcription of the ſtock, lineage or pedigree of any perſon or family] *genealogia, e geneologia*, s. f. *diſcorſo di origine, e diſcendenza di perſona, ſtirpe o famiglia.*

GE'NERAL, adj. [common, univerſal] *generale, univerſale.*

A general maxim, *una maſſima generale.*

A general calamity, *una calamità univerſale.*

A general council, *un concilio univèrſale.*

GE'NERAL, s. [the chief commander of an army] *generale, capitan generale, comandante d'uno eſercito.*

A general of horſe or foot, *un generale di cavalleria, o di fanteria.*

The general of a religious order, *il generale de' frati.*

In general, adv. *in generale, generalmente, comunemente.*

GENERALI'SSIMO, s. [a ſupreme general or commander in chief of an army] *generaliſſimo*, s. m. *ſupremo comandante d' eſercito.*

GENERA'LITY, s. [the whole, or the moſt part] *generalità, univerſalità, la maggior parte.*

The generality of the people, *il popolo in generale.*

The generality of men, *la maggior parte degli uomini.*

GE'NERALLY, adv. [univerſally] *generalmente, univerſalmente.*

Generally [in general] *generalmente, in generale.*

Generally [commonly] *generalmente, comunemente.*

GE'NERALSHIP, s. [the dignity or office of a general] *generalato*, s. m. *la dignità, e carica d'un generale.*

To GE'NERATE, [to ingender or beget] *generare, dare l'eſſere, naturalmente produrre.* pref. *produco.* pret. *produſſi.*

The ſun generates all things, *il ſole produce ogni coſa.*

GE'NERATED, adj. *generato, prodotto.*

GENERA'TION, s. [the production of any thing in a natural way] *generazione*, s. f. *il generare, produzione*, s. f.

Generation [lineage, race] *generazione, razza, genia*, s. f.

From generation to generation, *di generazione in generazione.*

Generation [great many] *moltitudine, gran numero.*

There's a whole generation of them, *ve n' è un gran numero.*

GE'NERATIVE, adj. [that ſerves to beget] *generativo, atto, acconcio a generare, generante.*

The generative faculty, *la facoltà generativa, o generante.*

GE'NERICAL, adj. [belonging to the genus or kind] *generico.*

GENERO'SITY, s. [nobleneſs of mind or ſoul] *generoſità, nobiltà, grandezza d'animo.*

A piece of great generoſity, *una gran generoſità.*

Generoſity [liberality] *generoſità, liberalità*, s. f.

GE'NEROUS, adj. [free, bountiful, of a noble mind] *generoſo, che ha generoſità, magnanimo, liberale.*

GE'NEROUSLY, adv. *generoſamente, liberalmente.*

GE'NEROUSNESS, s. [generoſity] *generoſità, liberalita*, s. f.

GE'NESIS, s. [the firſt book of Moſes] *Geneſi*, s. f. *il primo libro della ſcrittura ſacra, ſcritto da Moisè.*

GE'NET, s. [a kind of Spaniſh horſe] *giannetto*, s. m. *cavallo di Spagna.*

Genet [the white genet which the king of Naples preſents yearly in ceremony to the pope, as a tribute for the kingdom of Naples, which he holds of the pope] *chinea, che il re di Napoli preſenta al papa ogni anno come in tributo per il regno di Napoli.*

Genet, *ſpezie di gatto.*

Genet [the fur of that creature] *la pelle di queſt' animale.*

GENE'VA, s. *ſorta di liquore diſtillato molto uſato dal popolaccio d'Inghilterra, che lo chiama comunemente* Gin.

GE'NIAL, adj. [full of mirth] *giojoſo, feſtoſo, allegro, giocondo.*

Genial [feſtival] days, *giorni di feſta, o feſtivi.*

Genial [natural] *geniale, naturale.*

The genial heat, *il calore naturale.*

The genial bed [or the marriage bed] *letto, o toro geniale.*

GE'NITAL, adj. [ſerving to generation] *genitale, col quale ſi genera.*

The genitals, s. [parts ſerving to generation] *parti che ſervono alla generazione.*

GE'NITIVE, s. [the genitive caſe, one of the ſix caſes] *il genitivo, ò caſo genitivo.*

GE'NITOR, s. [father, begetter] *genitore, padre*, s. m. *che genera.*

GE'NIUS, s. [one's temper, talent, or diſpoſition] *genio*, s. m. *inclinazion d'animo.*

He has a fine genius for poetry, *egli ha un buon genio per la poeſia.*

GENT, adj. [ſpruce, fine, handſomely clad] *faſtoſo, pulito, ben veſtito.*

GENTE'EL, adj. [fine] *gentile, bello, elegante.*

A genteel ſuit of cloaths, *un bell' abito, un abito attillato.*

Genteel [handſomely clad] *pulito, ben veſtito, ben in arneſe.*

He goes very genteel, *egli va ben veſtito.*

Genteel [gallant] *gentile, grazioſo, corteſe, nobile.*

Genteel [that has a genteel carriage] *gentileſco, di bell' aria, di nobili maniere, garbato, leggiadro.*

GENTE'ELNESS, s. [in cloaths] *pulizia d'un abito.*

Genteelneſs [gallantry, agreeableneſs] *gentilezza, grazia, leggiadria, bella maniera, corteſia.*

GENTE'ELY, adv. *gentilmente, con gentilezza, con leggiadria, galantemente, grazioſamente.*

GE'NTIAN, s. [fell-wort] *genziana*, s. f. *radice d'erba.*

GE'NTIL, s. [maggot] *verme che ſi genera nel legno, cacchione*, s. m.

GE'NTILE, s. [heathen] *pagano, gentile.*

The Gentiles, *i gentili, i pagani.*

Gentile [like a gentleman] *v.* Genteel.

GE'NTILISM, s. [heatheniſm] *gentilità*, s. f. *la ſetta de' gentili.*

GENTI'LITY, s. [the quality or degree of a gentleman] *gentilità, gentilezza, nobiltà, qualità di gentiluomo.*

GE'NTLE, adj. [mild, moderate] *moderato, temperato, leggiero.*

A gentle fit of an ague, *un acceſſo di febbre moderato.*

He is very gentle, *egli è molto dolce, o benigno.*

A gentle fall, *una leggiera caſcata.*

Gentle [tame] *domeſtico, manſo, manſueto.*

A lion very gentle, *un leone domeſtico, o manſo.*

A tercel gentle, *falcon gentile.*

Gentle reader [an expreſſion formerly uſed in prefaces] *amico lettore.*

To GE'NTLE [to make gentle] *manſuefare, addomeſticare.*

GE'NTLEFOLKS, s. pl. *gente nobile, nobiltà.*

GE'NTLEMAN, s. [a perſon of good or honourable extraction] *un gentiluomo, uomo nobile, un ſignore, un ricco.*

Gentleman [gallant man] *un galantuomo, un uomo onorato, o dabbene.*

Gentleman-like, *da gentiluomo, da galantuomo.*

GE'NTLENESS, s. [mildneſs] *dolcezza, umanità, benignità, gentilezza, corteſia, bella maniera, leggiadria, amorevolezza.*

GENTLEWO'MAN, s. *una gentildonna, donna nobile.*

A lady's gentlewoman, *damigella, donzella, che ſerve a qualche dama.*

GE'NTLY, adv. [mildly] *gentilmente, con gentilezza, moderatamente, umanamente, benignamente.*

Gently [ſoftly] *dolcemente, pian piano.*

GE'NTRY, s. [the order or rank of gentlemen] *la perſone qualificate, i gentiluomini.*

The nobility and gentry, *i nobili, e le perſone qualificate.*

GENUFLE'XION, s. [a bending of the knee] *genufleſſione, inginocchiazione*, s. f.

GE'NUINE, adj. [natural, true] *vero, naturale, proprio.*

That's the genuine ſenſe of the author, *queſto è il vero ſenſo dell' autore.*

GEO'GRAPHER, s. [one who is ſkilled in geography] *geografo*, s. m. *che eſercita o ſa la geografia.*

GEOGRA'PHICAL, adj. [belonging to geography] *geografico, attenente a geografia.*

GEO'GRAPHY, s. [a deſcription of the whole globe of the earth] *geografia*, s. f. *deſcrizione di tutte le parti della terra.*

GEO'MANCER, s. [one ſkilled in geomancy] *geomante*, s. m. *che fa geomanzia.*

GEO-

GEO'MANCY, s. [a kind of divination by points and circles made on the earth, or by opening the earth] *geomanzia*, s. f. *ſpezie di divinazione che ſia fa per via di figure, e ſegni, o per protrazione di punti.*

GEO'METRAL, adj. *geometrale.*

A geometral draught, *un piano geometrale.*

GEOME'TRICAL, } adj. [belonging
GEOME'TRICK, } to geometry] *geometrico, di geometria.*

A geometrical foot or pace, *un piede, o un paſſo geometrico.*

A geometrical proportion, *una proporzione geometrica.*

GEOME'TRICALLY, adv. *geometricamente, d'una maniera geometrica.*

GEOMETRI'CIAN, s. [one ſkilled in geometry] *un geometra, che ſa la geometria.*

GEO'METRY, s. [the art of meaſuring the earth, or any diſtance or dimenſions on or within it] *geometria*, s. f. *arte del miſurare.*

GEO'RGICKS, s. [books which treat of huſbandry and tillage] *georgica*, s. f. *libro che tratta d'agricoltura.*

GERAH, s. [the laſt ſilver coin among the Hebrews] *l'ultima moneta d'argento fra gli Ebrei.*

GERFA'ULCON, s. [a bird of prey] *girfalco, e girifalco*, s. m. *ſpecie di falcone.*

GE'RMAN, adj. *germano, carnale.*

A couſin german, *un cugino germano, una cugina germana.*

GE'RMANDEL, s. [an herb called otherwiſe Engliſh treacle] *camedrio*, s. m. *ſorta d'erba.*

To GE'RMINATE [to bud, to bloſſom, or ſprout out] *germinare, germogliare.*

GE'RMINATED, adj. *germinato, germogliato.*

GERMINA'TION, s. [a ſprouting or budding forth] *germinazione*, s. f. *germogliamento*, s. m.

GE'RUND s. [a part of a verb] *gerundio*, s. m.

GE'SSAMIN, v. Jeſſamin.

GE'SSES, s. [in falconry, the furniture belonging to a hawk] *geti*, s. m.

GESTS, s. [noble or heroick acts, warlike exploits] *geſti, geſta, impreſe, fatti glorioſi.*

The geſts of the Romans, *i geſti, i fatti glorioſi de' Romani.*

To GESTI'CULATE [to uſe much geſtures] *geſteggiare, far troppi geſti.*

GESTI'CULATION, s. *il geſteggiare.*

GE'STURE, s. [behaviour, the motion of the body] *geſto, atto, movimento delle membra.*

To GET [to obtain, to gain, to attain] *guadagnare, acquiſtare, ottenere.* preſ. *ottengo* pret. *ottenni.*

To get money, *guadagnar danari.*

To get an eſtate, *acquiſtar beni, accumular ricchezze.*

To get one's pardon, *ottenere la ſua grazia.*

What have you got by it? *che avete guadagnato?*

To get the victory, *guadagnar la vittoria.*

To get [or beget] children, *generar figliuoli.*

To get a thing tranſported to another place, *fare traſportare che che ſi ſia in un altro luogo.*

To get a thing done, *far fare una coſa.*

To get [or find out] an invention, *trovare un invenzione.*

To get a good ſervant, *trovare un buon ſervo.*

To get money of one, *cavare o ricever danari da uno.*

To get a place, *trovare un impiego.*

To get the love of all the world, *procacciarſi l'amore d'ognuno.*

To get a wife, *prender moglie.*

To get upon a ladder, *montare ſopra una ſcala.*

To get one's leſſon, *imparare la ſua lezione.*

Get it without book, *imparatelo a mente.*

I got one, *ne ho uno.*

I got it, *l'ho.*

He has got an ague, *egli ha la febbre.*

He has got a great many children, *egli ha molti figliuoli ſopra le ſpalle.*

You got it very cheap, *voi l'avete comprato a buon mercato.*

To get the better, *aver vantaggio.*

To get an ill habit, *prendere un cattivo abito, pigliar mala piega.*

To get a woman with child, *ingravidare una donna.*

To get friends, *farſi amici.*

To get the love of one's hearers, *conciliarſi l'animo de' ſuoi auditori.*

I get nothing by it, *non ci guadagno niente.*

Shall I get you to do this for me? *di grazia degnatevi di far cio per me?*

I will get one made for you, *ve ne farò fare uno.*

I ſhall get it done by to-morrow, *avrò cura che ſia fatto per domani.*

To get a fall, *caſcare, fare una caduta.*

To get a thing ready, *preparare, apparecchiare, mettere in ordine che che ſi ſia.*

Get you ready [dreſs yourſelf] *veſtitevi, alleſtitevi.*

Get you gone, *andate via, ſfrattate da qui.*

To get home, *venire, o arrivare a caſa.*

By the time I got half way thither, *quando fui a mezza ſtrada.*

Get you that way a little, *fatevi un poco in là.*

To get a name, *metterſi in credito, acquiſtar fama, renderſi famoſo.*

He always comes to get money of me, *viene ſempre per iſcroccarmi del danaro.*

To get one's money, *ricever il ſuo danaro.*

To get together, *radunare, adunare, accozzare, unire, mettere inſieme.* preſ. *uniſco.*

To get together, verb neut. *radunarſi, adunarſi, accozzarſi, unirſi.*

To get clear, *ſtrigarſi, ſbrigarſi, liberarſi, ſvilupparſi di qualche impaccio.*

To get well again, *riaverſi, pigliar vigore, ricuperar la ſalute.*

To get abroad, *fare uſcire.*

To get above one, *ſuperare alcuno.*

To get before one, *prevenire alcuno, andare avanti.* preſ. *prevengo.* pret. *prevenni.*

To get [or take] away, *portar via.*

To get away, verb neut. *andarſene, ritirarſi.*

To get in, *entrare.*

To get in with one [to ſcrew one's ſelf into his friendſhip] *cattivarſi l'amicizia di qualcheduno.*

I ſhall get you in, *vi farò entrare.*

To get in one's debts, *farſi pagare.*

To get out, *uſcire*, preſ. *eſco.* pret. *uſcii.*

Get you out, *uſcite di quì.*

I can't get him out, *non poſſo farlo uſcire.*

To get one out of priſon, *liberare uno di prigione.*

To get a nail out, *cavare un chiodo.*

To get a thing out of one, *ſcalzare, uno, cavarli di bocca artatamente quello, che ſi vorrebbe ſapere.*

To get on one's feet, *levarſi in piedi.*

To get out of bed, *levarſi da letto.*

To get to a place, *arrivare, giugnere a qualche luogo.*

To get to ſhore, *andare a terra, ſbarcare.*

As ſoon as I got home, *ſubito arrivato a caſa.*

To get [or put] on, *metterſi.*

To get one's coat on, *metterſi il ſuo giuſtacore.*

To get one's ſhoes and ſtockings on, *calzarſi.*

To get off, *tirare.*

To get one's coat off, *tirare il ſuo giuſtacore.*

To get off [to get out of trouble] *cavar d'impaccio, ſtrigare, ſviluppare.*

I will do what I can to get him off, *farò ogni ſforzo per cavarlo d'impaccio.*

I don't know how to get off, *non ſo come farò per iſtrigarmi.*

To get off from one's horſe [to alight] *ſcavalcare, ſcendere, o ſmontar da cavallo.*

To get from, *togliere e torre, levare, cavare.*

I had much ado to get from him, *ebbi che fare per ſtrigarmi da lui.*

To get through, *paſſare per mezzo.*

To get through the crowd, *paſſare per il mezzo della calca, farſi ſtrada fra la calca.*

To get over, *paſſare, attraverſare, traghettare.*

To get over the river, *paſſare, o attraverſare un fiume.*

To get over a bridge, *paſſare ſopra un ponte.*

To get up, *levare, alzare.*

I can't get it up, *non poſſo levarlo.*

To get up [to get out of bed] *levarſi da letto*

It is time to get up, *è tempo di levarſi da letto.*

To get up on horseback, *montare, o saltare a cavallo.*
To get up a ladder, *montare una scala.*
To get up stairs, *salire, montare le scale.*
I am so much a loser, I must get it up another way, *ho perduto tanto, bisogna che trovi il modo di rimborsarmi, o di riparare la perdita per qualch' altra via.*
To get up again, *rilevare, rilevarsi, levare, alzare di nuovo.*
To get down, *scendere, andar giù.*
To get down stairs, *andar giù, scendere.*
This meat is too hard, I cannot get it down, *questa carne è troppo dura, non posso inghiottirla.*
GE'TTER, s. [a getter of children] *un uomo o una donna, che fa molti figliuoli.*
GE'TTING, s. *il guadagnare, v.* To get
This is all of my getting, *io ho guadagnato tutto ciò.*
This child is not of your getting, *questo fanciullo non è vostro.*
One's getting [that which one has got by his labour] *quel ch'una persona ha guadagnato colla sua industria, o fatica.*
GEU'LES, s. [in heraldry, a vermillion colour] *color vermiglio.*
GEWGAW, s. [a showy trifle, a toy, a bauble] *una cianciafruscola, una bubbola, una cosa di molta apparenza e poca sostanza.*
GEWGA'W, adj. [splendidly trifling, showy without value] *che ha splendida apparenza e nulla sostanza.*
GHA'STFUL, adj. [dreary, dismal, melancholy, fit for walking spirits] *spaventevole, squallido, orribile, tristo, solitario, dicesi dell' ombre, degli spiriti, e dell' anime de' morti.*
GHA'STLINESS, s. *orrore, spaventosa vista, solitudine che spira tristezza e spavento, squallidezza.*
GHA'STLY, adj. *di faccia orrenda; di spaventevole aspetto o vista, squallido.*
GHA'STNESS, s. [horror of look] *aspetto spaventevole, squallido aspetto; come verbigrazia quello d'un morto che apparisce ad un vivo.*
GHE'RKIN, s. [pickled cucumber] *cetriuolo confettato con sale e aceto.*
To GHESS, *v.* To guess.
GHITA'R, s. [a musical instrument] *chitarra, s. f. strumento musicale da corde.*
GHOST, s. [the spirit of a person deceased] *ombra, anima, spirito de' morti.*
To give up the ghost, *render l'anima, o lo spirito, spirare.*
The Holy Ghost, *lo Spirito Santo.*
GHO'STLY, adj. *spirituale, di spirito.*
Ghostly comforts, *conforti spirituali.*
A ghostly father, *un padre spirituale, un confessore.*
GI'ANT, s. [a man of a prodigious stature and bigness] *un gigante, uomo grande oltre al naturale uso.*
GI'ANT LIKE, } *giganteo, gigantesco, di gigante.*
GI'ANTLY, }
GI'ANTESS, s. *gigantessa, s. f. femmina di gigante.*

GI'BBE, s. *un animale quand' è vecchio e buono a nulla.*
GI'BBERISH, s. [nonsensical talk, pedlar's French] *gergo, garamuffa.*
To talk gibberish, *parlare in garamuffa.*
GI'BBET, s. [a great cudgel, such as they throw up the trees to beat down the fruit] *bacchio, battacchio, s. m.*
Gibbet [gallows] *la forca.*
To go to the gibbet, *andare alle forche.*
To GI'BBET, *impiccare, appendere.*
GI'BBIER, s. *selvaggiume, uccelli presi o morti dal cacciatore.*
GIBBO'SITY, [a bunching out, most commonly of the back] *gobba, s. f. scrigno, s. m.*
GI'BBOUS, adj. [bunched on the back] *gibboso, gobbo, scrignuto, soprossuto.*
GI'B-CAT, s. *un povero vecchio gatto.*
GIBE, s. [jeer] *beffa, s. f. scorno disprezzo.*
To GIBE [to jeer] *beffare, schernire, disprezzare.*
GI'BER, s. *colui che disprezza.*
GI'BING, s. *scherno, disprezzo.*
GI'BLETS, s. [the offals or entrails of birds] *le frattaglie, le interiora, le ale, e il collo de pollami.*
GI'DDINESS, s. [dizziness of the head] *vertigine, s. f. capogirlo, capogiro, s. m.*
To be troubled with a giddiness, *esser soggetto alle vertigini.*
GI'DDY, adj. [vertiginous, dizzy] *che ha vertigini, soggetto alle vertigini.*
My head is giddy, *mi gira la testa.*
Giddy-headed, giddy-brained, *cervellato, mentecatto, leggiere, incostante, bisbetico, balordo, stordito.*
A giddy pate, *un cionnò, un minchione, uno sciocco, un balordo, uno stordito.*
GIFT, s. [a present] *dono, regalo, donativo, s. m.*
A free-gift, *un dono gratuito, una liberalità gratuita.*
A deed of gift, *un contratto di donazione.*
A new years gift, *capo d'anno, strenna.*
Gift [talent] *dono, talento, favore, s. m. grazia, s. f.*
To have the gift of speaking well, *avere il dono di ben parlare.*
He has an admirable gift that way, *egli ha un talento marivaglioso in ciò.*
Infused gifts, *grazie infuse.*
These gifts come from above, *questi favori ci vengono dal cielo.*
This living is in the king's gift, *questo beneficio è alla nominazione del re, o alla collazione del re.*
One must not look a gift horse in the mouth, *a cavallo dato non si guarda in borra.*
GI'FTED, adj. *dotato di qualche talento, o vantaggio.*
The gifted men and women of our age [the enthusiasts] *quelli che pretendono esser inspirati.*
GIG, s. [a turning top] *ruzzola, trottola, s. f. paleo, s. m.*
GIG [a wanton woman] *una donna lasciva, una berghinella, una bagascia.*
GIGA'NTICK, adj. [giant like] *gigantesco, giganteo.*
GIG-MILL [a sort of fulling-mill] *gualchiera, s. m. mulino da sodare i panni.*
To GI'GGLE [to laugh wantonly] *sghignazzare, ridere strepitosamente.*
GI'GGLING, s. *sghignazamento, sghignazzio, s. m. sghignazzata, s. f.*
GI'GOT, s. [a leg of mutton] *coscia di castrato.*
To GILD [from gold] *indorare, dorare.*
To gild a picture frame, *indorare una cornice.*
GI'LDED, adj. *indorato, dorato.*
GI'LDING, s. *doramento, indoramento, s. m. il dorare.*
GI'LDER, s. *doratore, indoratore, s. m.*
GILL, s. *chiamansi* gills, *que' buchi come narici che hanno i pesci sopra l'estrema punta del capo.*
Gill, *quella carne che pende sotto il becco a' volatili di certe spezie.*
Gill, *la carne di sotto al mento.*
Gill, *misura Inglese di certi liquidi, poco più d'un bicchiere de' nostri comuni.*
Gill, *nome dato scherzosamente alle donne.*
Gill, *spezie d'edera che serpe per terra, ed è anche nome d'una bevanda medicinale in cui ellera è stata infusa.*
GILLIFLO'WER, s. [a flower of a grateful scent] *viuuolo, s. m. fiore odorifero.*
A stock-gilliflower, *garofano, s. m.*
GILT, adj. *dorato, indorato.*
Gilt-head [a sort of sea fish] *orata, s. f. sorta di pesce, detta così dal suo colore.*
GIM, adj. [pretty, neat] *bello, pulito.*
GI'MLET, s. [a piercer to make holes with] *succhiello.*
GIN, s. [trap] *trappola, s. f.*
Gin [snare] *tagliuola, s. f.*
Gin, *liquore. v.* Geneva.
GI'NGEMBER, } s. [a sort of spice]
GI'NGER, } *zenzero, zenzevero, gengiovo, s. m.*
Ginger-bread, *bericuocolo, confortino, s. m. pane intriso con mele, entrovi spezierie.*
Ginger-bread maker, *bericuocolajo, confortinajo, s. m.*
GI'NGERLY, adv. [softly] *pianamente, pian piano.*
To tread gingerly, *camminar pian piano.*
GI'NGLE, s. *tintinno, tintinnio s. m.*
To GI'NGLE [to make a tinkling noise] *tintinnire, risonare.*
He loves to hear his money gingle in his pocket, *ha piacere di sentire i suoi danari tintinnire nella scarsella.*
To gingle in words [to use words that have an affected sound] *servirsi di parole sonore con affettazione.*
GI'NGLING, s. *tintinno, tintinnio, s. m.*
The gingling of glasses, *il tintinnio de' bicchieri.*

GI'PSY, s. [a rambling woman, who under pretence of being an Egyptian, pretends to tell people their fortune] *una zingara.*

A cunning gipsy, *una volpaccia, una furbaccia.*

GI'RASOL, s. [a sort of precious stone] *girasole, spezie di pietra preziosa, è anche nome d'un erba.*

GIRD, s. [taunt] *beffa, burla, baja,* s. f. *scherno,* s. m.

By shifts and by girds, *a spilluzzico, a poco per volta.*

By girds and snatches, *alla sfuggita, con poco agio, quasi furtivamente.*

To GIRD [to bind round about] *cignere, e cingere.* pret. *cinsi.*

To gird [to twinge] *pizzicare.*

To gird [to taunt] *ghignare, burlare, schernire.*

GI'RDER, s. [main beam going across a floor of a house] *trave,* s. f.

GI'RDLE, s. [a band or ribbon] *cintolo, cintolino,* s. m. *cintura,* s. f. *nastro che cigne.*

To have one's head under one's girdle, *aver l'avvantaggio sopra qualcheduno, tenerlo soggetto.*

GIRL, s. [a young woman or child] *una fanciulla, una ragazza, una donzella, una zitella, una bambina.*

A pretty girl, *una bella ragazza.*

Girl, among hunters [the roe buck of two years old] *damma, o cervatta di due anni.*

GI'RLISH, adj. *di ragazza, fanciullesco, donzellesco.*

GI'RLISHLY, adv. *da ragazza, fanciullescamente, donzellescamente.*

GIRT, adj. [from to gird] *cinto.*

To girt [to gird, to encompass, to incircle]. *cingere, cerchiare, circondare.*

GIRTH, s. [a girdle buckled under a horse's belly] *cinghia,* s. f.

A horse's girth, *cinghia di cavallo.*

The girths are too strait, *le cinghie sono troppo strette.*

Girth-leather, *sopraccigna,* s. f.

To GIRTH, *cinghiare, cingere.*

To girth a horse, *cinghiare un cavallo.*

You girth him too hard, *voi lo cignete troppo stretto.*

GI'RTHED, adj. *cinghiato, cinto, legato con cintura.*

GI'SARD, s. [the bag under the throat or craw of a fowl] *ventriglio, o ventre degli uccelli.*

To have a grumbling in the gisard, *gorgogliare, borbottare, non esser contento.*

GITH, s. [an herb growing amongst corn] *nigella,* s. f.

To GIVE [to bestow] *dare, donare.* pres. *do.* pret. *diedi.*

To give one something, *dar qualche cosa ad uno.*

Give me some drink, *datemi a bere.*

To give every one his due, *dare ad ognuno quel che se gli deve.*

To give orders, *dar gli ordini.*

To give battle, *dar la battaglia.*

To give thanks, *render grazie, ringraziare.*

I give God thanks for it, *ne rendo grazie a Dio.*

To give like for like, *render la pariglia.*

To give evidence, *render testimonianza.*

My father gives his services to you, *mio padre vi saluta.*

To give ground, *rinculare, arretrarsi, ritrarsi indietro.*

To give way, *cedere, dar luogo.*

To give one the way, *cedere a qualcheduno.*

The ground gives way under me, *la terra sfonda sotto i miei piedi.*

To give way to melancholy, *abbandonarsi, darsi in preda alla malinconia.*

They gave us forty guns, *ci fecero una salva di quaranta cannonate.*

To give joy, *felicitare, congratularsi.*

To give alms, *fare limosine.*

To give one content, *contentare, soddisfare alcuno.*

To give credit, *prestar fede, credere.*

To give one credit [to trust him] *far credito ad uno.*

To give ear, *dare orecchio, stare attento, ascoltare.*

To give leave, *permettere, dar licenza.*

Give me leave to do it, *mi permetta ch' io lo faccia.*

To give a guess, *indovinare.*

To give fire, tirare, *separare, parlando d'un' arma da fuoco.*

To give one a call, *dare una voce ad uno, chiamarlo.*

To give place, *cedere, dar luogo.*

He gave not a word, *non disse una parola.*

To give judgment, *pronunciar la sentenza.*

To give it for one [to give it on his side] *deridere in favore di qualcheduno.*

My mind gives me, *io prevedo, mi dice il core.*

To give a good price for a thing, *pagar una cosa molto cara.*

To give one trouble, *incomodare, dare incomodo.*

To give one the slip, *svignare, sfilare, piantare alcuno, fuggirsene.*

To give warning, or notice, *avvertire.* pres. *avvertisco.*

To give suck, *allattare.*

To give one a fall, *far cascare alcuno.*

The door gave a great clap, *la porta fece grande strepito.*

To give one's mind to a thing, *affezionarsi a qualche cosa, applicarsi, mettervi ogni studio.*

To give one the hearing, *dare orecchio ad uno, ascoltarlo.*

To give one a look, *guardare, riguardare alcuno, darli un' occhiata.*

To give heed, *badare, stare attento.*

To give again, *rendere, restituire.* pret. *resi.* pres. *restituisco.*

To give way, *dar via.*

He gives all away, *da tutto quel che ha.*

To give away for lost, *tener per perduto.*

We all gave you over for dead, *noi tutti vi credevamo morto, o spedito.*

To give back [to give ground] *rinculare, arretrarsi, tirarsi indietro.*

To give back again, *rendere, restituire.* pres. *restituisco.* pret. *resi.*

To give in one's account, *render conto.*

To give in one's name, *dare il suo nome.*

To give in one's verdict, *dar la sua voce, o suffragio.*

To give in an information, *fare un' informazione, processare.*

To give in charge, *incaricare, ingiugnere, commettere, ordinare, comandare.*

To give out, *dare, distribuire.* pret. *distribuisco.*

To give out commissions, *dar delle commissioni.*

To give out [to report, to spread abroad] *spargar voce, divulgare, promulgare, dire.*

He gave out himself to be such a man, *si spacciava per un tale.*

To give out, or to give off, *cessare, desistere.*

To give over, *finire, cessare, lasciare, tralasciare, desistere.*

The physicians have given him over, *i medici l'hanno abbandonato, egli è disperato da' medici.*

To give over one's right, *cedere, dare il suo diritto.*

To give a thing over for lost, *tenere, o creder una cosa perduta.*

To give one's self over to all manner of vices, *abbandonarsi, darsi in preda ad ogni sorta di vizi.*

To give up, *rendere.* pret. *resi.*

To give up one's accounts, *render conto.*

To give up one's commission, *rendere, restituire, rassegnare la sua commissione.*

To give up the ghost, *render l'anima o lo spirito, spirare.*

To give up [or over] one's right, *cedere al suo diritto.*

He was forced to give it up, *fu costretto di cedere, o darla per vinta.*

GI'VER, s. *donatore,* s. m. *donatrice,* s. f.

Law-giver, *legislatore,* s. m.

GI'VING, s. *donamento, dono,* s. m. *il donare.*

Giving is dead, *il dare è morto oggidì, il donare è una virtù morta.*

GI'ZZARD, } s. *v.* Gisard.
GI'ZZERN, }

He frets his gizzard [he harrasses his imagination] *e' si tormenta il cervello; e' si da la tortura al cervello; e' va studiando come fare.*

GLA'CIAL, adj. [belonging to ice] *glaciale, agghiacciato.*

The glacial sea, *il mare glaciale.*

GLACIA'TION, s. *agghiacciamento,* s. m. *congelazione,* s. f.

GLACI'S, s. [a gentle steepness, or an easy sloping bank, in fortification] *pendio,* s. m. *scoscesa,* s. f.

The glacis of a counterscarp, *il pendio d'una contrascarpa.*

GLAD, adj. *allegro, giojoso, contento.*

I am

I am glad of it, *ne godo, ne sento gran contento.*

I am very glad to see you in good health, *mi rallegro di vedervi in buona salute.*

To make one glad, *rallegrare, indurre allegrezza e contento in altrui.*

This makes me glad at the heart, *questo mi rallegra molto, o m'empie il cuore d'allegrezza.*

Glad-tidings, *liete novelle.*

To GLAD, } [to make glad]
To GLA'DDEN, } *rallegrare.*

Wine glads the heart of man, *il vine rallegra il cuore dell' uomo.*

GLA'DDER, s. *un che rallegra, che ti caccia la malinconia d' addosso.*

GLADE, s. [an open and light passage made through a wood, by lopping off the branches of trees] *passo fatto nel mezzo d'un bosco.*

To make a glade in a wood, *fare un passo in un bosco, tagliando gli alberi.*

GLA'DER, s. [sword grass] *ghiaggiuolo,* s. m. *pianta, le cui barbe secche sono odorifere, e fa i fiori paonazzi.*

GLADIA'TOR, s. [a fencer, a sword-player] *gladiatore,* s. m.

GLA'DLY, adv. *volentieri, volentiermente, con gusto, con piacere.*

GLA'DFULNESS, } s. *gioja, allegria,*
GLA'DNESS, } *allegrezza,* s. f. *contento, piacere,* s. m.

GLA'DSOME, adj. [joyful] *giojoso, allegro, contento.*

GLAIRE, s. [the white of an egg] *chiara,* s. f. *albume d'uovo.*

GLAIRE [a kind of halbert] *sorte d' alabarda usata anticamente.*

To GLAIRE [to smear with the white of an egg] *spandere e impiastricciare con la chiara d'uovo, vocabolo ancora usato da' legatori di libri.*

GLANCE, s. *occhiata,* s. f. *sguardo,* s. m.

Glance [allusion] *allusione,* s. f.

At the first glance, *a prima vista, in un subito.*

Glance [a sudden shot of light or splendor] *baleno; scocco repentino di splendore; raggio di luce improvviso.*

To Glance [to view with a quick cast of the eye] *dar un occhiata.*

To GLANCE upon [to graze] *scalfire, calterire.* pres. *scalfisco, calterisco.*

The bullet did but glance upon the skin, *la palla non fece che scalfire la pelle.*

To glance upon a thing [to give a hint of it] *menzionare una cosa, toccare, accenare una cosa, discorrere brevemente.*

To glance over a page, *scorrere una facciata coll' occhio.*

GLAND, s. [flesh kernel] *glandula,* s. f.

GLA'NDERS, s. [a disease in horses, a running at the nose] *stranguglione,* s. m. *malattia di cavallo.*

GLA'NDULE, s. [a kernel in the flesh] *glandula,* s. f. *corpo molle e soffice, che si trova in più parti dell' animale.*

GLA'NDULOUS, adj. [full of kernels] *glanduloso.*

GLARE, s. [overpowering lustre; splendor, such as dazzles the eye] *luce soverchia; splendore che abbaglia.*

Glare [a fierce piercing look] *occhiata di fuoco; occhiata che penetra, che entra nel midollo, occhiata feroce.*

To GLARE [to over blaze, to dazzle] *fiammeggiare, scintillare, offuscare la vista, abbagliare.*

GLA'RING, s. [a glaring light] *splendore che abbaglia la vista.*

A glaring crime, *un delitto troppo patente.*

GLA'SIER, *v.* Glazier.

GLASS, s. [a transparent substance] *vetro;* s. m.

A drinking glass, *un bicchiere.*

To drink out of a glass, *bere in un bicchiere.*

A looking-glass, *uno specchio.*

The glass of a coach, *i vetri d'una carrozza.*

The glass of a looking-glass, *bambola,* s. f. *lo vetro dello specchio.*

A prospective glass, *un cannocchiale.*

Glass [sand glass] *ampolletta,* s. f. *un oriuolo a polvere.*

Glass [varnish] *vernice,* s. f.

A glass bottle, *un fiasco.*

A glass window, *un invetriata.*

A glass coach, *carrozza con vetri.*

A glass maker, *un vetrajo, quegli che fa la vasella di vetro.*

Glass-house, *luogo dove si fabbricano i vetri.*

Glass-shop, *bottega di vetrajo.*

To GLASS [to see as in a glass, to represent as in a mirrour] *vedere come si vede n'uno specchio, rappresentare come in uno specchio.*

To glass [to case in glass] *incassar in vetro.*

To glass [to cover with glass, to glaze] *inverniciare.*

GLASSGA'ZING, adj. *sciocco, vano, leggiere, contemplator di se stesso, che per vanità e troppa opinione di se stesso si guarda nello specchio come le donne vane.*

GLA'SSY, adj. [transparent like glass] *invetriato, lisciato, lucido come vetro.*

To GLA'VER [to sooth up, or flatter] *accarezzare, vezzeggiare, adulare, lusingare, piaggiare.*

GLA'VERING, s. [fawning] *lusinga, adulazione, carezze,* s. f. *vezzo,* s. m.

Glavering, adj. *adulatore, lusinghiere.*

Glavering words, *parole lusinghiere.*

A glavering fellow, *un adulatore, un lusinghiero.*

GLAUNCE, *v.* Glance.

To GLAZE [to set up with glass] *invetrare, chiudere con invetriate.*

To glaze a room, *chiuder una camera con invetriate.*

To glaze earthen vessels, *inverniciare vasi di terra.*

To glaze gloves, *lisciare de' guanti.*

GLAZED, adj. *invetriato, inverniciato, lisciato.*

A room well glazed, *una camera chiusa da buona invetriate.*

A vessel well glazed, *vasi di terra ben invetriati.*

Glazed frost, *brina,* s. f.

GLA'ZIER, s. [an artificer who works glass windows] *un vetrajo.*

GLA'ZING, s. *il chiudere con invetriate.*

The glazing of my room costs me so much, *l' invetriate della mia camera mi costano tanto.*

GLEAD, s. *sorta d'uccel di rapina, un nibbio.*

GLEAM, s. [a beam of the sun] *un raggio di sole improvviso.*

To GLEAM [to shine, or to cast beams of light] *rilucere, risplendere, scintillare.*

To GLEAN [to pick up the scattered ears of corn after reaping] *spigolare, coglier le spighe.*

To glean grapes after vintage, *raspollare, andar cercando i raspolli dopo la vendemmia.*

GLE'ANED, adj. *spigolato, raspollato.*

GLEA'NER, s. *spigolatore,* s. m. *spigolatrice,* s. f.

GLE'ANING, s. *lo spigolare, il raspollare.*

To go a-gleaning, *andare a spigolare, o raspollare.*

GLEBE, s. [a clod or lump of earth] *zolla,* s. f.

Glebe-land [that land belonging to a parsonage, besides the tythes] *terre che appartengono ad una cura.*

A GLEDE [a kite] *un nibbio.*

GLEE, s. [joy, mirth] *gioja, allegrezza, festa, allegria,* s. f. *giubilo,* s. m.

GLEED, s. [a hot glowing coal] *un carbone acceso.*

GLE'EFUL, adj. [gay, merry cheerful] *gajo, allegro, giovilae.*

GLEEK, s. [musick, or musician] *la musica, o un musico.*

To GLEEK [to gibe; to sneer, to droll upon] *burlare, beffare.*

To GLEEN [to shine with heat or polish] *rilucere per calore o per brunitura.*

GLEET, s. [a thin ichor running from a sore] *scolagione, gonorrea; umor che cola da una o più ulcere.*

GLIB, adj. [slippery, smooth] *sdrucciolante, sdrucciolevole, lubrico, liscio.*

His tongue runs very glib, *egli ha la lingua ben affilata.*

GLI'BLY, adv. *correntemente, a corsa, spacciatamente.*

He went on glibly in his discourse, *egli continuò il suo discorso con grand' eloquenza.*

GLI'BNESS, s. *volubilità, prestezza, facilità,* s. f.

The glibness of the tongue, *volubilità, prestezza di lingua.*

To GLIDE [to slip down easily, or gently] *correre, scorrere.*

A river that glides smoothly along, *un fiume la di cui acqua lambe dolcemente.*

GLIKE, s. *beffa, burla, celia.*

To GLIMMER [to begin to appear by degrees, as the light does at break of day] *spuntare, come fa il giorno la mattina.*

The day-light begins to glimmer, *il giorno comincia a spuntare.*

GLI'MMERING, adj. Ex. a glimmering light [such as peep of day] *barlume*, s. m. *quasi vario lume, tra lume e bujo.*

Glimmering, s. *luce*, s. f. *lume, splendore*, s. m.

GLI'MPSE, s. [a flash or beam of light] *lampo, balenamento, barlume*, s. m.

To have but a glimpse of a thing, *avere un barlume di che che si sia, veder che che si sia alla sfuggita.*

GLI'STER, s. *serviziale, argomento*, s. m.

To give a glister, *dare, o mettere un serviziale.*

Glister-pipe, *una siringa.*

To glister [to shine] *brillare, lucere, risplendere, scintillare.*

All is not gold that glisters, *non è tutt' oro quel che luce.*

GLI'STERING, s. *brillamento*, s. m. *il brillare.*

Glistering, adj. [shining] *brillante, lucente, risplendente, scintillante.*

GLI'STERINGLY, adv. *risplendentemente.*

To GLI'TTER [to glister] *lucere, rilucere, risplendere, scintillare.*

GLI'TTERING, adj. *lucente, scintillante, risplendente, brillante.*

GLOAR, adj. Ex. gloar fat [fulsomely fat] *eccessivamente grasso, grasso a far isvogliare lo stomaco.*

To GLOAR [to look a-skew] *guardare in cagnesco, fare il viso arcigno, guardare con mal' occhio.*

To GLOAT [to cast side-glances as a timorous lover] *guardare colla coda dell' occhio, guardar sottecchi come timido amante.*

GLOBE, s. [a round solid body] *globo*, s. m. *corpo rotondo per tutti i versi.*

Globe, celestial or terrestrial, *la sfera celeste, e terrestre.*

A little globe, *un globetto.*

GLOBO'SE, GLOBOUS, GLOBULAR, } adj. [round like a globe] *sferico, sperico, rotondo come un globo.*

GLOBO'SITY, s. [roundness] *globosità, ritondezza, rotondezza*, s. f.

GLO'BULE, s. [a little globe] *globetto*, s. m.

GLO'OMINESS, s. [darkness] *oscurità, tenebrosità*, s. f.

GLO'OMY, adj. [dusky, dark, cloudy] *bujo, oscuro, tenebroso, nuvoloso.*

Gloomy weather, *un tempo oscuro, o nuvoloso.*

GLO'RIED, adj. [illustrious, honourable] *illustre, orrevole.*

GLORIFICA'TION, s. [a glorifying] *glorificazione*, s. f. *glorificamento*, s. m.

To GLO'RIFY [to give glory, to praise] *glorificare, lodare, dar gloria.*

To glorify God, *glorificare Iddio.*

To glorify one's self, *glorificarsi, lodarsi, vantarsi, millantarsi, paoneggiarsi.*

GLO'RIFY'D, adj. *glorificato, lodato.*

GLORIFY'ING, s. *glorificamento*, s. m. *il glorificare.*

GLO'RIOUS, adj. [full of glory, famous] *glorioso, pien di gloria, illustre, famoso.*

A bright and glorious day, *un bel giorno.*

Vainglorious, *glorioso, pien di vanto, vanaglorioso.*

GLO'RIOUSLY, adv. [honourably] *gloriosamente, con gloria, onoratamente.*

GLO'RY, s. [honour, renown, reputation] *gloria, nominanza, lode*, s. f. *onore*, s. m.

Glory [in painting, those beams of light which are usually drawn round about the head of our Saviour, saints, &c.] *corona*, s. f.

To GLO'RY [to brag, to boast] *gloriarsi, vantarsi, pregiarsi.*

To glory of a thing, *gloriarsi di che che si sia.*

To GLOSE, v. To gloze.

GLOSS, s. [comment, exposition] *glosa, chiosa*, s. f.

Gloss [lustre, brightness, set upon silk, cloth, &c.] *lustro, liscio*, s. m.

To GLOSS [to comment, to make notes upon] *glosare, far glose.*

GLO'SSARY, s. [a dictionary to explain words] *dizionario, che serve alla spiegazione delle parole le più oscure d'una lingua.*

GLOSSA'TOR, s. [interpreter] *chiosatore, interprete*, s. m.

GLOSSO'GRAPHER, s. [a writer of a glossary] *colui che scrive un dizionario il quale serve alla spiegazione delle parole ofcure d'una lingua.*

GLO'SSY, adj. *lustrato, liscio, lucido.*

GLOVE, s. [a covering for the hand] *guanto*, s. m.

A pair of gloves, *un pajo di guanti.*

Glove-silver [money given to servants to buy gloves] *mancia, buona mano.*

Fox gloves, our ladies gloves [a sort of herb] *bacchera*, s. f. *spezie d'erba.*

To be hand and glove with one, *esser come pane e cacio, essere amicissimi.*

To give one his glove [to challenge him] *sfidare uno, chiamarlo a duello.*

GLO'VER, s. *guantajo*, s. m.

To GLOUT, v. To Glowt.

To GLOW [to be hot and red] *rosseggiare, esser rosso, e infocato.*

GLO'WING, adj. *ardente, infocato, rosseggiante, rovente.*

A glowing coal, *un carbone infocato.*

A glowing envy, *un' invidia che arde.*

GLOW-WORM [an insect that shines in the night] *lucciola*, s. f.

To GLOWT [to look doggedly] *guardare in cagnesco, fare viso arcigno, guardar con mal' occhio.*

GLOW'TING, s. [glowting look] *un viso arcigno, una ciera brusca.*

To GLOZE [to flatter] *lusingare, adulare, piaggiare.*

GLO'ZED, adj. *lusingato, adulato, piaggiato.*

GLO'ZER, s. *lusingatore, lusinghiere, adulatore*, s. m. *lusingatrice, adulatrice*, s. f.

GLOZING, s. *lusingheria, lusinga, adulazione*, s. f. *lusingamento*, s. m.

Glozing, adj. *lusingante, lusinghiere, e lusinghiero.*

A glozing tongue, *una lingua lusinghiera.*

GLUE, s. [a sticky composition to join things together] *colla*, s. f.

Glue made of fish skins, *colla di pesce.*

To GLUE, *incollare, appiccare insieme con colla.*

GLUED, adj. *incollato.*

GLU'ER, s. *colui che incolla.*

GLU'ING, s. *l'incollare.*

GLU'ISH, adj. *tenace, viscoso, tegnente.*

GLUM, adj. [sullen, sour in countenance] *arcigno, cagnesco, brusco.*

To be glum [or of a sour countenance] *fare il viso arcigno, guardar in cagnesco, fare il viso dell' arme.*

GLU'MMING, adj. [sullen] *torbido, conturbato, aspro, brusco.*

GLUT, s. [a great quantity] *abbondanza, gran quantità.*

A great glut of rain, *una gran pioggia.*

A glut of corn, *una grand' abbondanza di grano.*

Glut [satiety] *satollezza, sattollità, sazietà*, s. f.

To GLUT [to overcharge] *satollare, saziare, empire.*

I am glutted with things, *sono stufo di questa cosa.*

To glut one with meat, *satollare uno di carne.*

To glut one's self with a thing, *satollarsi, saziarsi di che che si sia, mangiarne a erepa pelle.*

GLU'TINOUS, adj. [gluish, clammy] *viscoso, tegnente, tenace.*

GLU'TTED, adj. *sazio, saziato, satollo, pieno.*

I am glutted with meat, *sono stufo, o svogliato di carne.*

GLU'TTON, s. [a greedy eater] *un ghiotto, un goloso, un pacchione, un ingordo, un arlotto, un lurcone.*

To GLU'TTONIZE [to be given to gluttony] *morsire, mangiare, e bere assai, esser dedito alla gola.*

GLU'TTONOUS, adj. [greedy] *ghiotto, goloso, ingordo, leccardo.*

GLU'TTONOUSLY, adv. *ghiottamente, avidamente, golosamente, ingordamente.*

GLU'TTONY, s. [immoderate eating and drinking] *ghiottornia, leccornia, ingordigia*, s. f.

GLYN, s. [valley, dale] *una valle, un fondo tra due montagne.*

GLYSTER, v. Glister.

GNAR, s. [a knot in a tree] *nodo di legno.*

To GNASH WITH THE TEETH, *battere i denti come fanno verbigrazia le scimie quando sono in collera, digrignare i denti, stridere.*

GNASHING WITH THE TEETH, *stridore di denti.*

GNAT, s. [a sort of insect] *zanzara*, s. f.

Gnat-snapper, s. [a bird] *monaco, monachino*, s. m.

To GNAW [to bite off] *rodere*, pret. *rosi.*

To gnaw a bone, *rodere un osso.*

GNAWED,

GNAWED, adj. *roso.*

GNA'WER, s. *roditore*, s. m. *che rode.*

GNA'WING, s. *rodimento*, s. m. *di rodere.*

Gnawing, adj. *rodente, che rode, mordace.*

Gnawing cares, *cure mordari.*

GNO'MON, s. [the needle of a dial] *gnomone*, s. m. *l'ago degli oriuoli a sole.*

Gnomon [a geometrical figure, like a carpenter's square] *gnomone, figura geometrica.*

GNOMO'NICK, s. [the art of dialling] *l'arte di fare oriuoli a sole.*

GNO'STICKS, s. [a sort of hereticks, who held the soul of men to be of the same substance with God; that there were two Gods, the one good, the other bad, and denied the future judgment] *Gnostici; nome di certi eretici che credevano l'anima dell' uomo esser dalla medesima sustanza che quella d'Iddio, che asserivano esservi due Iddii, l'uno buono e l'altro cattivo, e niegavano il giudicio universale.*

To Go [to walk, to move] *andare, camminare*, pres. *vada* or *vo, vai, va, andiamo, andate, vanno.*

To go a foot, *andare a piedi.*

You go too fast, *voi andate, voi caminate troppo presto.*

How goes it with you? how goes the world with you? *come ve la passate? come vanno i vostri negozi?*

To go [speaking of money] *correre, o non correre, esser ricevuta, o non esser ricevuta, parlando della moneta.*

This coin does not go here, *questa moneta non corre qui.*

To go [to be accounted, to pass] *passare, esser tenuto o stimato, esser in concetto.*

He goes for a man of learning, *egli passa per, egli è in concetto d'uomo dotto.*

A mare goes twelve months with foal, *una giumenta porta dodici mesi.*

The bitch goes a salt, *la cagna è in frega.*

To go a journey, to go a voyage, *fare un viaggio, mettersi in cammino.*

To go four miles in an hour, *fare quattro miglia in un' ora.*

To go halves with one, *andare di metà, o spartire con uno.*

The bell goes, *la campana suona.*

As the things go now, *secondo lo stato presente delle cose.*

To go ashore, *sbarcare, approdare.*

She has three months yet to go, *ella ha ancora tre mesi di gravidanza.*

So the report goes, *così porta la fama.*

To go to service, *mettersi a servire.*

We will go another way to work, *noi troveremo un altro mezzo termine.*

To go according to the times, *temporeggiare, accomodarsi al tempo.*

To let go the anchor, *gettar l'ancora, dar fondo.*

To go about, *fare il giro.*

To go about a thing [to undertake it] *dar di mano a qualche cosa, mettersi a fare qualche cosa.*

To go about the bush, *andar per ambage, cerrar giri e rigiri.*

Go about your business, *andate a fare i fatti vostri.*

To go round the world, *fare il giro del mondo.*

To go abroad, *uscire*, pres. *esco.*

Such report goes abroad, *così si dice, così porta la fama.*

To go against, *opporsi, contrariare, esser contrario.*

This meat goes against my stomach, *questa carne mi svoglia lo stomaco.*

To go along, *proseguire il suo rammino, andare avanti.*

To go along with one, *andare con uno, accompagnarlo.*

To go astray, *sviarsi, uscir di via.*

To go away, *andarsene, partire.*

He is gone away, *egli sen' è andato.*

To go away with a thing, *portar via che che si sia.*

You shall not go away with it so, *voi me la pagerete.*

A great deal of money goes away in the maintaining of a family, *il mantenimento d'una famiglia consuma gran danari.*

To go back [to retire] *rinculare, ritirarsi, tirarsi indietro.*

To go back [to return] *ritornarsene.*

To go before, *andare avanti, precedere.*

To go between, *andar nel mezzo.*

To go behind, or after one, *seguitare alcuno, andargli appresso, o dietro.*

To go beyond, *trapassare, passar oltre.*

To go beyond [to excel] *passare avanti, eccellere.*

To go by, *passare per, o vicino.*

Let us go to see the king go by, *andiamo a veder passare il re.*

He goes by that name, *egli si fa chiamare così.*

That's it we go by, *questa è la norma con la quale dobbiamo regolarci.*

To go down, *scendere, andar giù.*

To go down stairs, *scender le scale.*

To go down the stream, *andare a seconda del fiume.*

To go with the worst, *aver la peggio.*

To go by a thing [to take it for a rule] *regolarsi sopra qualche cosa.*

The sun goes down, *il sole tramonta.*

No meat will go down with him, *non può mangiar niente.*

That will never go down with him [he will never like it] *egli non approverà mai ciò, egli non consentirà mai a questo.*

Any thing will go down with him, *egli s'appaga d'ogni cosa.*

To go down the wind, *declinare, andar declinando, o diminuendo.*

To go for [to fetch] *andare a cercare.*

Go for your books, *andate a cercare i vostri libri.*

To go for a virgin, *passare per zittella.*

The verdict went for him, *egli guadagnò il processo.*

To go forth, *uscire, mostrarsi.*

To go forward, *avanzare.*

To forward with a business, *continovare, proseguire un negozio.*

To go forward in learning, *far progresso nelle scienze.*

To go from, *lasciare, abbandonare.*

To go from the company, *lasciar la compagnia.*

I went from thence to Rome, *di là men' andai a Roma.*

To go from one's word, *disdirsi, mancar di parola.*

To go from the matter in hand, *tralasciare il filo del discorso, digredire dal soggetto.*

To go in, *entrare.*

To go in slippers, *portar pianelle.*

He always goes in very good cloaths, *egli va sempre ben vestito.*

To go near, *avvicinarsi.*

He will go near to lose it, *egli corre rischio di perderlo.*

Nothing went so near the heart of him in his distress, *niente le trafisse più il cuore nella sua disgrazia.*

I go as near as I can with you [I'll sell it as cheap as I can] *vi farò tutte quelle cortesie che potrò.*

To go off, *lasciare.*

To go off the stage, *lasciare il mestiere di comediante.*

He is gone off [he is broke] *egli è fallito.*

This commodity will never go off, *questa mercanzia non si spaccerà, o non si venderà mai.*

Did you hear the guns go off? *avete inteso sparare i cannoni?*

To go on, *avanzare, continovare, andare avanti.*

Go on with your discourse, *proseguite, continuate il vostro discorso.*

To go over, *traversare, attraversare, traghettare, passare.*

To go over sea, *traversare, passare il mare.*

To go out, *uscire*, pres. *esco.*

He is gone out, *egli è uscito.*

To go out of tune, *cantare, o sonare fuor di tuono.*

To go out of one's way [to go astray] *smarrire la strada, uscir di strada, sviarsi.*

The fleet went out, *la flotta ha messo alla vela.*

The fire goes out, *il fuoco si smorza.*

To go out her time, *finire la gravidanza, arrivare al termine della gravidanza.*

To go out doctor [to take the degree of a doctor] *addottorarsi.*

To go through, *passare.*

To go through a bridge, *passare un ponte.*

To go through the fields, *passare per i campi.*

To go through stitch with a business, *terminare, finire un negozio.*

To go through all the formalities, *fare tutte le formalità.*

To go through many dangers, *esporsi a molti pericoli.*

To go through many hardships, *soffrire molti inconvenienti.*

I won't go to the price of it, *io non voglio spender tanto.*

Go to [an old interjection] *orsù animo.*

To go up, *salire, montare.* pres. *salgo.*

To go up and down [to ramble about] *andar qua e la, vagare, vagabondare.*

To go upon a business, *intraprendere un negozio.*

To go upon a tick [to run a score] *pigliare a credito, o a credenza.*

To go with child, *esser gravida, o grossa.*

To go with the tide, *scendere colla marea, andare a seconda della marea.*

To go with the wind, *andare a seconda del vento.*

To go without a thing [to make shift without it] *star senza di che che si sia, farne di meno.*

Go, s. ex. this horse has a good go with him [he goes well] *questo cavallo ha un buon passo.*

GOAD, s. [a pointed stick to prick oxen forward] *pungiglione,* s. m.

To GOAD, *punzecchiare, pungere.*

GOAL, s. [a prison or jail] *carcere, prigione,* s. f.

Goal [the land-mark set up to bound a race] *il segno che indica dove un palio o corsa di cavalli deve finire.*

Goal, *il segno dove il palio o corsa di cavalli deve cominciare.*

Goal, *il termine ch'uno s'è prefisso.*

GOAR, *v.* Gore.

GOAT, s. [a beast] *capra,* s. f.

A he goat, *un becco.*

A wild goat, *una camozza.*

A goat-herd, or keeper of goats, *un caprajo.*

A goat-milker, *un mungi-capra.*

Goats-bread, *caprifoglio,* s. m.

A goat-herd, *un caprajo.*

Belonging to a goat, *caprino, di capra.*

GOA'TISH, adj. [stinking like a goat] *che sa di berco.*

Goatish [lecherous] *lascivo.*

GOB, } s. [a mouthful, or GO'BBET, } piece] *un boccone, un pezzo.*

To swallow a great gob of meat, *inghiottire un grosso pezzo di carne.*

To GO'BBET, *inghiottire a grossi bocconi.*

To GO'BBLE [to swallow hastily and with noise] *inghiottire in fretta e con romore.*

GO'BELET, s. [cup] *tazza, coppa,* f. f.

GO'ELING, s. [evil spirit] *un fantasma spaventevole.*

Goblin [a fairy, an elf] *un folletto, uno spirito.*

GOD, s. [the supreme Being] *Dio, Iddio.*

God be thanked, or thanks be to God, *lodato Iddio, grazie a Dio.*

God save you, *Iddio vi guardi, o vi conservi.*

God be with you, *Iddio v' accompagni, andate con Dio.*

God forbid, *tolga Iddio, Iddio non voglia.*

God save the king, *viva il re.*

God-like, *divino.*

God-father, *patrino, compare,* s. m.

God-mother, *comare,* s. f.

To be God-father or God-mother to a child, *tenere un fanciullo a battesimo.*

God-child, *figlioccio, figlioccia.*

God-son, *figlioccio,* s. m.

God-daughter, *figlioccia,* s. f.

God a-mercy, *Iddio ve lo renda.*

GO'DDESS, s. *dea,* s. f.

GO'DHEAD, s. *divinità,* s. f.

The godhead of Christ, *la divinità di Cristo.*

GO'DLESS, adj. *ateo, empio.*

A godless man, *un ateo, un empio.*

GO'DLILY, adj. *piamente, divotamente, religiosamente.*

GO'DLINESS, s. *pietà, divozione,* s. f.

GO'DLY, adj. *pio, divoto, religioso.*

He is a godly man, *egli è un uomo pio.*

Godly, adv. *piamente, divotamente, religiosamente.*

GO-DOWN, s. *sorso.*

He drunk a bottle of wine at two godowns, *ha bevuto un fiasco di vino in due sorsi.*

GOD-WIT, s. [a delicate sort of bird] *francolino,* s. m.

To GOE, *v.* To go.

GOEL, adj. [yellow] *giallo.*

GOER, s. [from to go] *andante.*

Comers and goers, *andanti e vegnenti, quelli che vengono, e vanno.*

GOFF, s. [a sort of play at ball] *sorta di giuoco di palla.*

GOG, s. ex. to be a-gog for a thing [to desire it earnestly] *aver gran voglia d' una cosa, desiderarla, appetirla ardentemente, essere in fregola, o in uzzolo.*

To set a-gog, *toccar la fregola, toccar l' uzzolo, far venir la voglia.*

To GO'GGLE, *stralunare, guardare storto o bieco.*

GO'GLE, adj. a gogle eye [a full rolling eye] *occhio di bue, occhio stralunato.*

Gogle-eyed, *stralunato, che ha li occhi stralunati.*

GO'ING, s. *l'andare, v.* To go.

The going down of the sun, *il tramontar del sole.*

Going, *andando.*

Where are you going? *dove andate?*

I am a-going, *me ne vo.*

I was a-going to tell it you, *stavo per dirvelo.*

I am going in my forty-four, *tocco de quaranta quattro.*

She is now going on four months, *elle è gravida quasi di quattro mesi*

Going [gait] *andatura, camminatura.*

The going of a horse, *il passo d'un cavallo.*

GO'LA [cymaticum] *gola. Voce d' architettura.*

GOLD, s. [the most weighty and most valuable of all metals] *oro,* s. m.

Leaf-gold, *foglia d' oro.*

Gold-beater, *battiloro,* s. m. *quegli che riduce l' oro in foglia.*

Gold-mine, *miniera d' oro.*

Gold-ore, *miniera d' oro, materia della quale s' estrae l' oro.*

A gold-ring, *un anello d' oro.*

Goldfinch, s. [a singing bird] *calderello, calderino,* s. m.

Gold finder, *votacessi,* s. m.

A gold-finer, *affinator d' oro.*

Gold-weight, *peso d' oro.*

The gold-flower, *capelvenere,* s. m.

Gold hammer, s. [a sort of bird] *rigogolo,* s. m. *uccello della grandezza del pappagallo.*

GO'LDEN, adj. *d' oro.*

A golden cup, *una coppa d' oro.*

The golden rule [the rule of three] *la regola d' oro, la regola del tre.*

The golden number, *il numero d' oro.*

The golden fleece, *il toson d' oro.*

GO'LDING, adj. ex. a golding apple, *appiuolo,* s. m. *sorta di mela.*

GO'LDSMITH, s. *orefice,* s. f.

A goldsmith's shop, *bottega d' orefice*

GOLLS, s. [hands] *le mani.*

See what dirty golls she has, *vedete un poco che sporche mani ha.*

GOME, s. [the black and oily grease of a cart-wheel, printing-press, &c.] *untume, che si forma nella ruota d' un carro o carrozza, nel torchio d'uno stampatore, e simili.*

GO'MER, s. [an Hebrew measure] *gomer, misura fra gli Ebrei.*

GO'NDOLA, s. [a Venetian boat] *gondola,* s. f.

GONE, adj. [from to go] *andato, v.* To go.

He is gone, *egli sen' è andato, egli è partito.*

Get you gone, *andatevene, andate via da qui.*

I must be gone, *bisogna che me ne vada.*

If you will not be gone presently, *se voi non ve ne andate subito.*

Gone with child, *gravida.*

Gone [undone] *perduto, rovinato.*

I will give it all for gone, *tengo tutto per perduto.*

He is dead and gone, *egli è morto.*

Gone in drink, *cotto, imbriaco.*

Far gone in years, *attempato, avanzato in età.*

This is gone so far, that there's no remedy, *le cose sono ridotte a tale stato, che non vi è più rimedio.*

Before a year was gone, *avanti la fine dell' anno.*

As soon as the soul is gone from the body, *subito che l' anima è separata dal corpo.*

GONORRHOE'A, s. [running of the reins] *gonorrea,* s. f.

GOOD, adj. *buono.*

Good bread, good meat, *buon pane, buona carne.*

A good man, *un buon uomo, un uomo dabbene.*

A good prince, *un principe buono, benigno, clemente.*

A good action, *una buona azione.*

Good will, *buona volontà, benevolenza.*

Good [wholesome] *buono, salutare, giovevole.*
A good advice, *un buon consiglio.*
Good for the health, *buono per la salute.*
He knows what is good for him, *egli sa quel che li è giovevole.*
He is very good at it [he is skill'd in it] *egli è molto destro, esperto, esperimentato in questo.*
I count myself as good as he, *mi stimo al pari di lui.*
He is as good a man as you, *egli è un uomo che non vi cede in nulla.*
I left him as good as I found him, *l' ho lasciato nel medesimo stato che l' ho trovato.*
I gave him as good as he gave me, or as he brought, *li ho reso pan per focaccia.*
'Tis as good as done, *la cosa è quasi fatta.*
'Twill be as good as money to me, *questo mi servirà in luogo di danaro.*
Good for nothing, *che non val niente.*
A thing good in law, *una cosa valida.*
All in good time, *ogni cosa a suo tempo.*
To come in good time, *venire opportunamente.*
And reason good, *e con ragione.*
He is come to town for good and all, *egli è venuto in città per soggiornarvi.*
A good while, *lungo tempo, un pezzo.*
A good while ago, *un pezzo fa.*
A good deal, *molto.*
Good many things, *molte cose.*
We were a good many men and women, *noi eramo molti fra uomini e donne.*
A man of good parts, *un uomo di garbo, di mente, di cervello, d' ingegno.*
A good understanding man, *un uomo dotto, un uomo di spirito, un uomo di testa.*
He is as good a man as lives, *egli è il miglior uomo del mondo.*
I have a good mind to do it, *averei quasi voglia di farlo.*
To be as good as one's word, *esser uomo di parola.*
Will you be as good as your word? *mel atterrete? volete mantenermi la parola?*
To make good, *provare, giustificare, tenere, mantenere, far conto, stimare, reparare.*
I'll make good what I have said, *proverò quel ch' ho detto.*
To make one's word good, *tenere, mantenere la promessa.*
I'll make it good, *io vene terrò conto, io m' obbligo.*
To make good a loss, *riparare una perdita.*
To make good one thing with another, *riparare, risarcire una cosa con un' altra.*
Take care to make good the door, *badate di chiuder bene la porta.*
There's no good to be done with him, *non c' è niente da guadagnare con esso.*

If you think good, *se voi lo giudicate a proposito.*
Good liking, *approbazione*, s. f.
A good turn, *un favore, un servizio*, s. m.
Good luck, *ventura, fortuna.*
Good-Friday, *il Venerdì santo.*
In good earnest, *seriamente, da senno, davero, in verità.*
Good natured, good conditioned, good humoured, *di buon cuore, che ha un buon cuore, di buon umore, gioviale.*
The good man of the house, *il padron della casa.*
Good, s. *bene, vantaggio, profitto, utile*, s. m.
I did it for your good, *l' ho fatto per vostro bene.*
Much good may it do you, *buon pro vi faccia.*
I found much good by it, *trovo che m' ha giovato, m' ha fatto del bene.*
What good will it do you? *a che vi servirà? a che vi gioverà? che vantaggio ne ricaverete?*
Very good, *buonissimo, molto bene.*
Goods, *beni, effetti, mercanzie, masserizie.*
Ill gotten goods seldom thrive, *beni mal' acquistati non fanno mai prò.*
The goods [or furniture] of a house, *le masserizie d' una casa.*
These goods are not good, *queste mercanzie non sono buone.*
Go'odliness, s. *bellezza*, s. f.
Go'odly, adj. *bello.*
Goodly, interj. *cappità, capperi.*
Goo'dness, s. *bontà*, s. f.
The goodness of God is infinite, *la bontà d' Iddio è infinita.*
Go'ody, s. [a title usually given to a country woman] *madonna, buona donna.*
Go'oge, s. [a tool used by carpenters] *gurgio*, s. m.
Go'ose, s. [a fowl well known] *un' oca. plurale*, Geese.
Goose [the play of the goose] *il giuoco dell' oca.*
A green goose, *un papero.*
A taylor's goose, *ferro di sartore, per appianare le costole.*
A goose pen [wherein geese are fatted] *luogo dove s' ingrassano l' oche.*
Goose gibblets, *regali d' oca.*
A goose cap, *uno sciocco, un minchione, un cionno, un balocco, un balordo.*
A Winchester goose [a swelling in the groin] *un tincone, un bubone Gallico.*
Go'oseberry, *uva spina.*
Gooseberry-bush, *pianta d' uva spina.*
Gorbe'llied, *v.* Gore-bellied.
Gore, s. [a piece sowed into a garment to widen it] *punta*, s. f.
A gore of a woman's shift, *punta di camicia da donna.*
Gore, *sangue quagliato, o corrotto.*
To Gore [to prick] *punzecchiare aprire con cosa puntuta.*
To gore an ox, *punzecchiare un bue.*
A bull that gores with his horns, *un toro che da delle cornate, che tira di corna.*

Gore-bellied, adj. [that has a great belly] *panciuto, di grossa pancia.*
Gore-belly, s. *una pancia grossa.*
Gore blood, s. *sangue quagliato, o sangue corrotto.*
He is all of a gore-blood, *egli è tutto coperto di sangue.*
Go'red, adj. *punzecchiato.*
Gored with a horn, *che ha rice vuto una cornata.*
Gorge, s. [or crop of a bird] *gozzo*, s. m.
To cast gorge [as a hawk does] *vomitare.*
Gorge, [gullet] *gorgia, gorga*, s. f.
To Gorge [to feed and fill] *empire, saziare, satollare.*
To gorge one's self with meat, *empirsi la pancia di carne.*
Gorged, adj. *empito, satollato, saziato.*
Go'rgeous, adj. [costly, stately] *superbo, magnifico, suntuoso, splendido.*
Go'rgeously, adv. *superbamente, magnificamente, suntuosamente, splendidamente.*
Go'rgeousness, adj. *pompa magnificenza.*
Go'rget, s. [a woman's neck dress] *gorgiera*, s. f. *collaretto di bisso, o d' altra tela fina, che le donne portano intorno alla gorgia.*
Go'rget, s. [a neck piece of plate worn by the officers of foot-soldiers] *gorgiera; quell' armadura che arma la gola.*
To Go'rmandize [to eat, to devour greedily, or gluttonously] *esser dedito alla gola, mangiare da ghiottone.*
Gormandi'zer, s. *un uomo dedito alla gola, un ghiotto, goloso, avido di cibi.*
Gormandi'zing, s. *ghiottornia*, s. f.
Gorse, s. [a shrub called furz] *spezie di ginestra.*
Go'sling, s. [a young goose] *un pápero.*
Gosling upon a nut-tree, *fior di noce.*
Go'spel, s. *Evangelo, vangelo*, s. m.
'Tis not all gospel what he says, *non è vangelo tutto quel che dice, cioè, tutto quel che dice non è vero.*
A gospel truth, *una verità evangelica.*
To preach the gospel, *evangelizzare.*
Go'speller, s. [he that reads the gospel in a cathedral or collegiate church] *colui che legge l' evangelo in una chiesa catedrale, o collegiata.*
Go'sshawk, s. [goss hawk] *astore*, s. m. *uccello della natura degli sparvieri.*
Go'ssip, s. [a god father, or mother] *un compare, una commare.*
A gadding gossip, *una berghinella.*
A drinking gossip, *una buona commare, un' imbriaca.*
A prating gossip, *una taccola, una ciarliera.*
To Go'ssip [to play the gossip] *divertirsi,*

vertirsi, stare allegramente le comari insieme.

Go'ssipping, s. [a merry meeting of gossips] *allegria, divertimento, conversazione di comari che bevono e mangiano insieme.*

Got, Go'tten, adj. [from to get] *guadagnato, acquistato, ottenuto, v.* To get.

Gotten [begotten] *generato.*

Go'tham, ex. as wise as a man of Gotham [a fool] *un matto, uno sciocco, un insensato, uno che ha bevuto a Fontebranda.*

Go'thick, adj. [belonging to the Goths] *Gotico.*

Gothick building [such an one which is built after the manner of the Goths] *un edificio Gotico, fabbricato alla maniera de' Goti.*

To Go'vern [to rule] *governare, reggere.* pret. *ressi.*

To govern a kingdom, *governare un regno.*

To govern a case [a grammatical phrase] *governare, o reggere un caso, termine gramaticale.*

Go'verna'ble, adj. [that may be governed] *che può esser governato.*

Go'vernance, s. *governamento,* s. m. *condotta, amministrazione,* s. f.

Go'vernante, s. [governess] *governatrice,* s. f.

Go'verned, adj. *governato, retto.*

A commonwealth well governed [or ordered] *una republica ben governata, ben regolata.*

A well governed man, *un uomo savio, moderato, ritenuto.*

Go'verness, s. [or governante] *governatrice, colei che ha cura dell' educazione de' figliuoli di persone ricche.*

Go'verning, s. *il governare, governamento,* s. m.

Go'vernment, s. *governo, maneggio,* s. m. *amministrazione,* s. f. *potere, o maniera di governare.*

Government [rule, dominion] *governo, podesteria, e altri simili uffici.*

To have the government of a province, *avere il governo d' una provincia.*

To be under one's government, *essere sotto' l governo, o giurisdizione di qualcheduno.*

One that has no government of himself, *una persona che non sa governarsi, o condursi, che si lascia andare alle sue passioni.*

A man of government [a sober man] *un uomo savio, discreto, moderato.*

Go'vernour, s. [or ruler] *governatore,* s. m.

The governour of a province, *il governatore d' una provincia.*

A governour of a young prince, or of a young gentleman, *tutore, o balio d'un giovine principe o gentiluomo, colui che ha cura della sua educazione.*

Gourd, s. [a plant of the nature of a melon] *zucca,* s. f. *pianta.*

Go'urdy, adj. *grosso.*

Go'urnet, s. [a fish] *nome di pesce.*

Gout, s. [a painful disease in the legs, feet, &c.] *gotta, podagra,* s. f.

The gout in the hips, *la sciatica.*

Gout [a drop] *una goccia.*

Gout [a taste] *gusto.*

Go'utiness, s. *lo stato d' un gottoso.*

Go'uty, adj. *gottoso, podagroso.*

The gouty disease, *la gotta.*

Gown, s. [long garment] *una gonna, una veste o vesta, toga, veste religiosa.*

A night gown, *una vesta da camera.*

The gown men, *le persone togate.*

Go'wned, adj. [that wears a gown] *togato.*

Go'wnman, s. *uomo intento solo all' arti di pace.*

To Gra'bble [to handle untowardly] *palpare, palpeggiare sgarbatamente. Vocabolo affatto del volgo.*

To grabble a wench, *palpare o palpeggiare una femmina.*

To grabble [to feel in the mud] *frugare nel loto.*

Gra'bbled, adj. *palpato, palpeggiato, frugato.*

Grace, s. [favour, mercy] *grazia, bontà, misericordia,* s. f. *favore,* s. m.

I am well through God's grace, *io sto bene per la grazia di Dio.*

If God gives grace, *se Iddio mi fa la grazia.*

The state of Grace, *lo stato della grazia.*

Grace [agreeableness] *grazia, bellezza, avvenentezza, leggiadria,* s. f.

To have a good grace, *aver buona grazia.*

To say grace before meat, *benedire la tavola.*

To say grace after meal, *render grazie, dir l' agimus.*

The three Graces, feigned by poets to be the daughters of Jupiter and Venus, *le tre Grazie, finte dai poeti, essere le figlie di Giove, e di Venere.*

Grace, *titolo che si da ai duchi e alle duchesse d' Inghilterra, che appresso noi si direbbe eccellenza.*

To Grace [to set out] *abbellire, ornare, adornare.* pres. *abbellisco.*

This will grace it very much, *questo l' abbelirà molto.*

To grace [to behave with a grace] *comportarsi, fare che che si sia con grazia, con avvenentezza.*

Graced, adj. *abbellito, ornato, adornato.*

To be graced with admirable eloquence, *avere il dono dell' eloquenza, esser dotato d'una maravigliosa eloquenza.*

Gra'ceful, adj. [handsome, comely] *grazioso, gentile, avvenente, leggiadro, graziato, vezzoso.*

Gra'cefully, adv. *graziosamente, con grazia, gentilmente, avvenentemente, leggiadramente, vezzosamente.*

Gra'cefulness, s. *graziosità, gentilezza, venustà, avvenentezza, leggiadria,* s. f.

Gra'celess, adj. [without grace] *sgraziato, sgarbato, senza grazia, svenevole, senza avvenentezza.*

Graceless [brazen face] *sfacciato, sfrontato.*

Graceless [impious] *empio, scelerato.*

Graceless [that has not said grace] *che non ha reso grazie.*

Gra'cious, adj. [full of grace] *grazioso, avvenente, garbato.*

Gracious [courteous, favourable] *grazioso, benigno, favorevole, cortese, affabile.*

He is a most gracious prince, *egli è un principe molto grazioso, o benigno.*

To be under the King's most gracious protection, *esser sotto la protezione favorevole del re.*

Our most gracious sovereign, *il nostro serenissimo re.*

Most gracious Lord [a title given to God in our prayers] *Dio benignissimo.*

Gra'ciously, adv. *graziosamente, benignamente, favorevolmente, affabilmente, cortesemente.*

He received me very graciously, *m'accolse molto benignamente.*

The king was graciously pleased to grant it, *il re s' è compiaciuto di concederlo.*

Gra'ciousness, s. *bontà, benignità, cortesia,* s. f.

Gra'dual, adj. [that is done or comes by degrees] *graduale, di grado.*

Gradual, s. [that part of the mass which is said or sung between the epistle and the gospel] *graduale,* s. m. *que versetti che si recitano o che si contano nella messa avanti l' evangelio.*

Gradual, or Grail [a book containing certain offices and ceremonies of the Roman church] *graduale, libro nel quale si contengono le ceremonie e riti de la chiesa Romana.*

Gradual psalms [fifteen psalms from the 118th to 133d. or from the 119th. to the 134th, which were wont to be sung by the Levites, as they went up the fifteen steps of Solomon's temple, a psalm on each step] *salmi graduali.*

Gra'dually, adv. [by degrees] *gradualmente, in grado, poco a poco, passo a passo, successivamente.*

Gra'duate, s. [one who has taken a degree in the university] *graduato,* s. m. *che ha grado, dignità, o carica.*

Graff, s. [a graft or scion] *innesto.*

Graff, s. *una fossa, un fosso fangoso.*

Gra'ffer, s. [an obsolete word for scrivener] *un notajo.*

Graft, s. [graff, scion] *innesto, nesto,* s. m.

To Graft [to inoculate or plant a graft in another stock] *innestare.*

Gra'fter, s. *innestatore,* s. m. *che innesta.*

Gra'fting, s. *innestamento,* s. m. *innestatura,* s. f.

Grail, s. *picciole parti di chicchessia.*

Grain, s. [all sorts of corn] *grano, seme,* s. m. *semenza, biada,* s. f.

A grain of mustard-seed, *un grano, o granello di mostarda.*

A grain of salt, *un grano di sale.*
Grain [the twentieth part of a scruple] *un grano.*
Grain of leather, *grano di cuoja.*
Grain of wood, *tiglio di legno, quelle vene o fila, che sono le parti più dure del legname.*
Grain [wherewith scarlet is dyed] *grana,* s. f. *colore col quale si tingono i panni rossi.*
To dye in grain, *tigner in grana.*
A rogue in grain, *un furbo in chermisi, cioè in estremo grado.*
Against the grain, *a contrappelo.*
Against the grain [against one's will] *mal volentieri, di mala voglia, per forza.*
A grain of allowance, *una minima connivenza.*
GRA'INED, adj. *granoso, pien di granella, ben granito.*
GRA'INER, v. Granary.
GRA'MERCY [I thank you] *vi ringrazio.*
GRA'MINEOUS, GRA'MINOUS, } adj. [grassy] *gramignoso.*
Graminous plants [such which have a long narrow leaf of grass and no footstalk] *piante gramignose, sono quelle che hanno le foglie lunghe e strette, senza piede.*
GRA'MMAR, s. [the art of speaking any language truly] *grammatica,* s. f. *arte che insegna a correttamente parlare, e scrivere.*
Grammar [a book containing the rules of that art] *grammatica, libro nel quale si contengono le regole grammaticali.*
A grammar school, *una scuola dove s' insegna la grammatica.*
GRA'MMARIAN, s. [one that is skilled in, or teaches grammar] *grammatico,* s. m. *professor di grammatica.*
GRA'MMATICAL, adj. [belonging to the art of grammar] *grammaticale, di grammatica, attenente a grammatica.*
A grammatical word, *un termine grammaticale.*
GRAMMATICA'STER, s. [a bad grammarian] *un grammaticastro, un grammatico ignorante.*
GRANARY, s. [the place where corn is kept] *granajo,* s. m. *stanza, o luogo dove si ripone il grano.*
GRA'NATE, adj. ex. granate marble, *granito,* s. m. *nome d' un durissimo marmo.*
Granate, s. [a shining transparent gem of a yellow red] *granato,* s. m. *gioja del color del vin rosso.*
GRAND, adj. [great] *grande.*
GRAND [chief] *grande, principale.*
This was their grand design, *questo era il loro principale disegno.*
GRAND-SIRE, GRAND-FATHER, } *avo, avolo.*
GRAND-MOTHER, *ava, avola.*
GRAND-SON, *nipotino.*
GRAND-DAUGHTER, *nipotina.*
GRAND-CHILD, *nipote,* s. m. f.
GRA'NDAM, s. [grandmother] *ava, avola,* s. f.
To teach one's grandam to give suck, *i paperi voglion menare a bere l' oche.*
Great grand-father, *bisavo,* s. m.
Great grand-mother, *bisava,* s. f.
GRANDE'E, s. *grande.*
A grandee of Spain, *un grande di Spagna.*
The grandees of the realm, *i grandi, i primi del regno.*
GRANGE, s. [farm house] *casa da lavoratore.*
GRANI'FEROUS, adj. [bearing grains] *granito, granoso.*
GRA'NITE, s. [a sort of marble, and very hard] *granito,* s. m. *nome d' un durissimo marmo.*
GRANI'VOROUS, adj. [feeding on grain] *che si pasce di grano.*
GRANT, s. [a gift in writing of such a thing which cannot be passed or conveyed by word of mouth] *concessione, permissione,* s. f. *privilegio,* s. m.
To get a grant, *ottenere una concessione.*
To GRANT, [to give, to bestow, to allow] *concedere, dare, cedere, permettere,* pret. *diedi, concessi, permessi.*
To grant [or acknowledge] *concedere, acconsentire, menar buono.*
Grant it be so, *dato il caso che sia così, supposto che sia come voi dite.*
GRA'NTABLE, adj. [that may be granted] *accordabile; che si può accordare.*
GRA'NTED, adj. *concesso, dato, ceduto, permesso.*
I take it for granted, *io mi suppongo, o io mi presuppongo.*
GRANTE'E, s. [he or she to whom the grant is made] *quello, o quella che ha ottenuta una permissione, o privilegio.*
GRA'NTING, s. *il concedere.*
The granting of that is of dangerous consequence, *il concederlo sarebbe molto pericoloso.*
GRA'NTOR, s. [he or she that makes, or has made such a grant] *colui, o colei, che fa una concessione, o da un privilegio.*
GRANULA'TION, s. [the art of reducing metals into grains] *granulazione,* s. f. *termine chimico, l' arte di ridurre i metalli in granelli, il che si fa col gettarli gorria a gorria nell' acqua fredda.*
GRA'NULE, s. [a small grain] *granello,* s. m.
GRAPE, s. [the fruit of the vine] *uva,* s. f.
A bunch of grapes, *un grappolo d' uva.*
To gather the grapes in order to make wine, *far le vendemmie, vendemmiare.*
To glean grapes, *raspollare, andar cercando i raspolli.*
A grape stone [or kernel in the grape] *granello, vinacciolo,* s. m.
GRA'PHICAL, adj. [perfect, exact] *compito, perfetto, esatto.*
A graphical description, *una descrizione esatta.*
GRA'PNEL ANCHOR, s. [a sort of anchor for a small ship or boat to ride by] *spezie d' ancoretta.*
Grapnels [in men of war, are instruments of iron to be thrown into an enemy's ship to catch hold of her] *uncini di ferro che sono nelle navi da guerra per uso di gettarli nel vascello nemico ed arrampinarlo.*
To GRA'PPLE [to grasp and lay hold of] *arraffare, afferrare, arrampinare.*
To grapple a ship, *arraffare, arrampinare un vascello.*
To grapple with the enemy, *venire alle prese, o alle mani col nemico.*
To grapple with one's stubbornness, *combattere l' altrui pertinacia.*
To GRASE, v. To graze.
GRASHO'PPER, s. [a sort of insect] *grillo,* s. m.
GRASP, s. *una brancata, una manata.*
To GRASP [to take hold of] *abbrancare, acchiappare, afferrare, abbracciare.*
All grasp, all lose, *chi troppo abbraccia nulla stringe.*
GRASPED, adj. *brancato, acchiappato, afferrato, abbracciato.*
GRASS [herbage for cattle] *erba,* s. f.
To turn or put a horse to grass, *metter un cavallo all' erba.*
Grass of the second crop, *guaime,* s. m. *l' erba tenera che rinasce ne' campi dopo la prima segatura.*
Grass-plantane, [an herb] *serpentaria,* s. f.
Grass-week, *le rogazioni.*
GRATE, s. [to make a sea coal fire] *graticola di ferro, nella quale si fa il fuoco di carbone.*
Grate [a sort of iron lattice] *grata, gelosia,* s. f.
One cannot speak to the nuns but through a grate, *non si può parlare alle monache, se non da una grata.*
To GRATE [to scrape or crumble to powder by rubbing on a grater] *grattugiare, sbriciolare, fregare che che si sia alla grattugia,*
To grate cheese, *grattugiare del cacio.*
That grates my ear, *ciò m' offende gli orecchi.*
To grate the teeth, *raggrinzare, stridere co' denti.*
To grate upon, *urtare.*
To grate upon one another, *urtarsi.*
GRA'TEFUL, adj. [pleasant] *grato, piacevole, ameno.*
Grateful [thankful] *riconoscente, grato, che riconosce i benefici.*
Grateful [acceptable] *grato, caro, apprezzato, accetto.*
GRA'TEFULLY, adv. [thankfully] *gratamente, con gratitudine, caramente.*
GRA'TEFULNESS, s. [thankfulness] *gratitudine, riconoscenza.*
Gratefulness [pleasantness] *vaghezza, amenità.*
GRA'TER, s. [an instrument to grate with] *grattugia,* s. f. *arnese, che serve a grattugiare.*
GRATIFICA'TION, s. [free gift] *gratificazione, dono gratuito, riconoscimento, regalo.*

To GRA'TIFY [to oblige one] *gratificare, piacere, fare qualche gratificazione, render qualche servizio ad alcuno.*

I shall gratify your desires, *compiacerò a'vostri desideri.*

To gratify one's passion, *contentare le sue passioni, darsi in preda alle sue passioni.*

To gratify one's resentment, *risentirsi, far risentimento, sfogare il suo risentimento.*

GRA'TIFY'D, adj. *gratificato, v.* To gratify.

GRA'TING, s. [from to grate] *il grattugiare.*

The grating remembrance of a thing, *l'acerba memoria di che che si sia.*

GRA'TINGLY, adv. ex. An oath sounds gratingly, *un giuramento offende li orecchi.*

GRA'TIS, adv. [freely, for nothing] *gratis, in dono, per niente.*

GRA'TITUDE, s. [thankfulness] *gratitudine, riconoscenza, riconoscimento di beneficio ricevuto.*

GRATU'ITOUS, adj. [freely done] *gratuito, dato per grazia.*

GRATU'ITOUSLY, adv. *gratuitamente, per nulla.*

Gratuitously, adv. [without proof] *senza prove.*

GRA'TUITY, s. [free gift] *dono gratuito, liberalità, dono, presente,* s. m.

To GRA'TULATE [to congratulate] *gratularsi, congratularsi, rallegrarsi con altrui delle sue, o delle proprie felicità.*

GRATULA'TION, s. [a rejoicing on another's behalf] *congratulazione,* s. f. *il congratularsi.*

GRA'TULATORY, adj. *di congratulazione.*

A gratulatory letter, *una lettera di congratulazione.*

GRAVE, adj. [soher, serious] *grave, serioso, composto.*

A grave look or countenance, *un aria grave e composta.*

A grave discourse, *un discorso serioso.*

A grave suit of cloaths, *un abito modesto.*

An accent grave [a term of grammar] *accento grave.*

Grave [relating to sounds, low, deep] *basso.*

Grave, s. [a hole dug in the earth to bury the dead in] *fossa, tomba,* s. f. *sepolcro.*

GRAVECLOATHS, s. pl. [the dress of the dead] *l'abito che hanno addosso i morti.*

To have one foot in the grave, *aver un piede nella fossa.*

To wish one in the grave, *desiderare la morte d'alcuno.*

To lay one in his grave, *seppellire alcuno, sotterrarlo.*

Grave-makers, *beccamorti.*

A grave stone, *lapida, lapide,* s. f. *quella pietra che cuopre le sepoltura.*

To GRAVE [to ingrave] *scolpire, intagliare,* pres. *scolpisco.*

To grave an image, *scolpire un' imagine.*

To grave a seal, *intagliare un suggello.*

To grave a ship [to daub it with tallow and train oil mixed together] *insegare un vascello, uguerlo con sego, spalmarlo.*

To grave a galley, *spalmare una galea.*

GRAVED, adj. *intagliato, scolpito.*

A ship newly graved, *un vascello novamente spalmato.*

GRA'VEL, s. [the larger and stony sort of sand] *ghiaja,* s. f. *rena grossa, entrovi mescolati sassatelli.*

A place full of gravel, *un luogo ghiajoso, pieno di ghiaja.*

Gravel [in the kidnies] *renella,* s. f. *malattia che viene nelle reni.*

To be troubled with the gravel, *aver la gravella.*

A gravel pit, *luogo dove si scava la ghiaja.*

A gravel walk, *un viale ghiajato.*

To GRAVEL, verb active *coprir di ghiaja.*

To gravel a walk, *coprire un viale di ghiaja.*

To gravel [to perplex] one, *disturbare, imbarazzare, inquietare alcuno.*

GRA'VELESS, adj. [without a tomb, unburied] *senza onor di tomba; insepolto.*

GRA'VELLED, adj. *coperto di ghiaja.*

GRA'VELLING, s. *il coprir di ghiaja.*

GRA'VELLY, adj. [full of gravel] *ghiajoso, che abbia della ghiaja.*

A gravelly urine, *urina arenosa.*

GRA'VELY, adj. [from grave] *gravemente, con gravità.*

GRA'VEN, adj. [from to grave] *intagliato, scolpito.*

GRA'VER, s. [or engraver] *scultore, intagliatore,* s. m.

Graver [a tool to grave with] *bulino,* s. m.

GRAVI'DITY, s. [pregnancy] *gravidanza.*

GRA'VING, s. *scultura,* s. f. *l'arte dello scolpire.*

A graving tool, *un bulino.*

To GRA'VITATE [to weigh] *pesare, gravitare.*

GRAVITA'TION, s. [or weighing] *peso,* s. m.

GRA'VITY, s. [or weight] *gravità,* s. f. *peso,* s. m.

Gravity [the being grave] *gravità, maestrevole e autorevole presenza.*

GRAVY of MEAT, *sugo che esce della carne, nel tagliarla dopo cotta.*

Gravy of beef or mutton, *sugo di manzo o di castrato.*

Meat full of gravy, *carne sugosa.*

GRAY, adj. [ash-coloured] *bigio, color simile al cenerognolo, grigio.*

GREYBEARD, s. [an old man] *un vecchio; un barbabianca; un uom canuto.*

Gray cloth, *panno bigio.*

A gray horse, *cavallo leardo.*

Gray hair, *capelli canuti.*

To grow gray, *incanutire, divenir canuto.* pres. *incanutisco.*

Gray-brock [badger] *tasso,* s. m. *spezie d'animale.*

A gray hound, *un levriero.*

Gray hound bitch, *una levriera.*

Gray eyes, *occhi grigi.*

Gray-haired, *canuto, che ha i capelli canuti.*

GRA'YISH, adj. *che tira sul bigio.*

GRA'YLING, s. [a fish] *ombrina,* s. f. *spezie di pesce.*

GRA'YNESS, s. *color bigio, o grigio.*

Grayness of hair, *canizie, canutezza,* s. f.

To GRAZE [to feed] *pascere, pascolare.*

The sheep graze on the hills, *le pecore pascolano sopra le colline.*

To graze [to glance, as a bullet does] *rasentare, passare, accostarsi tanto alla cosa, che quasi ella si tocchi.*

A horse that slightly grazes upon the ground, *un cavallo che rasenta il suolo, che galoppa leggiermente sopra la terra.*

The bullet grazed the ground, *la palla rasentò la terra.*

GRA'ZIER, s. [one that deals in cattle, that feeds and fattens them for sale] *un uomo che traffica in bestiame, che ingrassa il bestiame per venderlo.*

GRA'ZING, s. *il pascere, il pascolare.*

The art of grazing, *l'arte d'ingrassare il bestiame per venderlo.*

To turn one to grazing, to send one a-grazing, *licenziare alcuno, mandarlo a fare i fatti suoi.*

GREASE, s. [fat] *grasso, sucidume,* s. m.

A spot of grease, *una macchia di grasso.*

Hog's grease, *strutto.*

To GREASE [to daub or smear with grease] *ungere, ugnere, fregare o aspergere con grasso, olio, o altra cosa che abbia dell' untuoso.*

To grease a wheel, *ugnere una ruota.*

To grease one's cloaths, *macchiare, sporcarsi gli abiti con grasso.*

To grease one in the fist, *ugner la mano ad uno, corromperlo con donativi.*

To grease a fat sow in the tail [to give to those that don't want it] *portar acqua al mare, dare a quelli che non ne hanno di bisogno.*

GRE'ASED, adj. *unto bisunto.*

GRE'ASILY, adv. *sporcamente, sucidamente.*

GRE'ASINESS, s. *sucidume, untume, grassume,* s. m.

GRE'ASY, adj. *sucido, imbrattato, sporco, sporcato, untuoso.*

A greasy suit of cloaths, *un àbito sucido, o sporeo, macchiato d'untume.*

This table is greasy all over, *questa tavola è tutta piena di grassume.*

GREAT, adj. [big, large, huge, mighty] *grande.*

A great house, *una gran casa.*

A great hat, *un gran cappello.*

A great garden, *un gran giordino.*

A great wind, *un gran vento, un vento impetuoso.*

A great friend, *un grand' amico, un amico intimo.*

A great silence, *un grande, un profondo silenzio.*
A great estate, *gran beni.*
Great [noble] *grande, nobile, illustre, generoso.*
A great soul, *un anima grande, un' anima nobile, e generosa.*
A great general, *un gran generale.*
A great while, *lungo tempo.*
A woman great with child, *una donna gravida*
To be great with one, *esser famigliare, o intimo con alcuno.*
'Tis no great matter, *non importa, non fa caso.*
A great deal, *molto.*
'Tis a great way thither, *v'è un buon pezzo di strada.*
His recommendation goes a great way with him, *la sua raccommandazione può molto con lui.*
A great many, *molti.*
To ride the great horse, *cavalcare un cavallo di maneggio.*
To sell by the great, *vendere all' ingrosso.*
To take work at the great, *pigliare a lavorare a staglio.*
To GRE'ATEN [to make greater] *aggrandire, accrescere, far grande.*
GRE'ATER [is the comparative of great] *più grande.*
My house is greater than yours, *la mia casa è più grande della vostra.*
The greater excommunication, *la scomunica maggiore.*
GRE'ATEST [is the superlative of great] *il più grande.*
A business of the greatest consequence *un affare di grandissima importanza.*
GRE'ATLY, adv. *grandemente, molto, estremamente, in sommo grado.*
GRE'ATNESS, s. *grandezza, eccellenza, grandigia, eccellenza,* s. f.
Greatness of soul, *grandezza d'animo.*
The greatness of sin, *la grandezza o l'enormità del peccato.*
GRE'AVES, s. [a sort of armour for the legs] *gamberuolo,* s. m. *gambiera,* s. f. *armadura di gamba.*
GRE'CIAN, s. *un Greco, una Greca.*
A good Grecian, *un uomo versato nella lingua Greca.*
GREGISM, s. [the idiom or propriety of the Greek language] *il Greco, l'idioma della lingua Greca.*
GREE, s. [law term, satisfaction] *sodisfazione, riparazione,* s. f.
GREE'DILY, adv. *avidamente, golosamente, ingordamente, con avidità, con ardore.*
GRE'EDINESS, s. *avidità, ingordigia, ghiottornia, golosità,* s. f.
Greediness [heat] *avidità, calore, ardore, gran desiderio d'avere.*
GRE'EDY, adj. [very covetous] *avido, ingordo, ghiotto, goloso.*
A greedy man, or a greedy gut, *un ghiotto, un goloso.*
Greedy [eager after] *avido, cupido, desideroso, bramoso.*
Greedy of glory, *avido di gloria.*
Greedy of praise, *bramoso di lode.*
Greedy of money, *avaro.*
Greedy of honours, *ambiziosa.*
GREEK, adj. [belonging to Greece] *Greco di Grecia.*
Greek wine, *vin Greco, o Greco,* s. m.
A Greek book, *un libro Greco.*
Greek, s. [the language of the Grecians] *il Greco, la lingua Greca.*
To understand Greek, *intendere il Greco, o la lingua Greca.*
GREEN, adj. [the colour given by nature to leaves and herbs] *verde, quel colore ch' hanno le foglie e l'erbe quando son fresche.*
Green [not ripe] *verde, non maturo.*
Green [fresh] *verde, fresco, verdeggiante.*
Green [not dry] *verde, fresco, contrario di secco.*
Green [raw] *soro, semplice, inesperto.*
Green as grass, *verde come l'erba.*
A green ribbon, *un nastro verde.*
Green cloth, *panno verde.*
Green fruit [that is not ripe] *frutti verdi, non maturi.*
Green fish, *merluzzo fresco.*
Green wood [in opposition to dry wood] *legno verde.*
To be green [or raw] in a business, *esser soro, essere inesperto in qualche affare.*
The green sickness, *itterizia,* s. f.
A green goose, *un papero.*
Green-finch [a sort of bird] *verdone,* s. m.
Green corn, *biada.*
To grow green, *verdeggiare, verdicare.*
To make one believe the moon is made of green cheese, *mostrar lucciole per lanterne ad uno, mostrar la luna nel pozzo, dare ad intendere una cosa per un' altra.*
Green, s. [green colour] *verde, color verde.*
Sea-green, *verdemare.*
GRE'ENISH, adj. *verdiccio, alquanto verde, verdagnolo.*
GRE'ENLY, adv. *verde, con un color verde; frescamente, nuovamente, novellamente; immaturamente.*
Greenly [wanly, timidly] *timorosamente, timidamente, paurosamente.*
GRE'ENESS, s. *verdume,* s. m. *verdura, verzura,* s. f.
GRE'ENSICKNESS, s. *malore donzellesco.*
GREESE, s. [a step] *un grado, uno scaglione.*
To GREET [to salute] *salutare, riverire.* pres. *riverisco.*
To greet, *mandar salute, mandar salutazione.*
GRE'ETING, s. *saluto,* s. m.
GREGA'RIOUS, adj. [going in droves] *gregario.*
GRE'NADIER, s. [a soldier which throws grenadoes] *granatiero,* s. m. *soldato che getta delle granate.*
GRE'NADO, s. [a little hollow globe of iron filled with fine powder] *granata,* s. f.
To throw grenadoes, *gettar delle granate.*
GRE'YHOUND, s. *levriere, veltro; cane sottile ed altro.*
GRICE, s. [a little pig] *porchetto.*
GRI'DELIN, s. [a changeable colour of white and red] *fior di lino, sorta di colore tra bianco e rosso.*
GRI'DIRON, s. [an utensil for broiling of meat] *graticola,* s. f.
To broil a thing upon a gridiron, *arrostire che che si sia sopra la graticola.*
GRIEF, s. [sorrow, affliction] *dolore, rammarico, dispiacere, cordoglio, affanno,* s. m. *afflizione, angoscia, doglia,* s f.
It is a great grief to me, *me ne rincresce, me ne dispiace molto.*
I did it to my great grief, *lo feci contro mia voglia.*
To be full of grief, *esser addolorato, mesto, afflitto.*
GRI'EVANCE, s. [wrong] *gravame, querele, torto.*
The grievances of the nation, *i gravami della nazione.*
To redress the grievances, *riparare i danni, riformare gli abusi.*
To GRIEVE [to afflict] *affliggere, attristare, travagliare, angustiare, affannare.*
To grieve, or grieve one's self, *affliggersi, attristarsi, affannarsi, prendersi afflizione.*
That grieves my heart, *questo mi trafigge il cuore.*
To grieve for one's death, *compiagnere l'altrui morte.*
It grieves me that I cannot serve you, *mi dispiace, mi rincresce di non potervi servire.*
GRI'EVED, adj. *afflitto, attristato, travagliato,* v. To grieve.
I am grieved to see him in that condition, *mi dispiace, sento gran dolore di vederlo in tale stato.*
I have been extremely grieved for his death, *la sua morte m'ha rincresciuto molto.*
GRI'EVINGLY, adv. *cordogliosamente, con gran dolore di cuore, affannosamente.*
GRI'EVOUS, adj. *cordoglioso, doloroso, grave, aspro, crudele, greve, nojoso, affannoso.*
Under grievous penalties, *sotto gravi pene.*
This is grievous weather, *fa un cattivo tempo.*
A grievous crime, *un delitto enorme, o atroce.*
To be in a grievous fright, *aver gran paura.*
Grievous angry, *molto adirato.*
GRI'EVOUSLY, adv. [peevishly, painfully] *gravemente, duramente, acerbamente, aspramente, atrocemente, rigorosamente, severamente.*
He will be grievously punished, *sarà gravemente punito.*
We suffered grievously in that voyage, *noi abbiamo sofferto molto in quel viaggio.*
I am grievously concerned for your misfortune, *mi rincresce fino all' anima della vostra disgrazia.*

To be grievously sick or wounded, *esser gravemente ammalato o ferito.*

To beat one grievously, *battare alcuno spietatamente.*

To take a thing grievously, *soffrire impazientemente qualche cosa.*

GRI'EVOUSNESS, s. *enormità, atrocità.*

The grievousness of a crime, *l'enormità d'un delitto.*

The grievousness of one's condition, *lo stato infelice d'una persona.*

GRI'FFIN, } s. [a fabulous crea-
GRI'FFON, } ture] *grifone*, s. m. *animal favoloso alato, e quadrupede, aquila la parte anteriore, e lione la posteriore.*

GRIG, s. [the smallest sort of eel] *anguilla piccicla*, s. f.

A merry grig, *un buon compagno, un uomo gioviale, e festevole.*

GRILLA'DE, s. [or broiled meat] *braciuola*, s. f. *sottil fetta di carne arrostita sopra la graticola.*

GRIM, adj. [fierce; crabbed, sour in countenance] *arcigno, austero, rigido, burbero, minaccioso, torvo.*

A grim look, *una ciera arcigna, un viso burbero.*

To look grim at one, *fare il viso arcigno ad uno.*

The grim-ferry-man [a poetical expression] *Caronte.*

Grim-faced, *austero, arcigno.*

GRIMA'CE, s. [or wry mouth] *smorfia, morfia, bocca.*

To make grimaces at one, *fare morfie, far bocche ad uno, aguzzar le labbra inverso uno in segno di dispregio.*

Grimace [hypocrisy, dissimulation] *finta, apparenza, dissimulazione*, s. f.

GRIMALKIN, s. [an old cat] *un gatto vecchio.*

GRIME, s. [dirt, deeply insinuated] *sporchezza, sudiciume che è entrato molto dentro.*

GRI'MLY, adv. [from grim] *austeramente, rigidamente, in cagnesco, con viso burbero.*

GRI'MNESS, s. *severità, austerità, viso torvo, o burbero, guardatura arcigna.*

To GRIN [to show the teeth, to laugh contemptuously] *ghignare, rider per beffe, digrignare i denti.*

To GRIND, *macinare.*

To grind with the teeth, *masticare.*

To grind a knife, *affilare, aguzzare un coltello.*

To grind the teeth together, *raggrinzare i denti.*

To grind the poor [to oppress them] *opprimere i poveri.*

GRI'NED, adj. *macinato*, v. To grind.

GRI'NDER, s. [he that grinds knives] *arrotino*, s. m.

GRI'NDERS [the side teeth] *mascellari*, s. m. *denti da lato.*

GRI'NDING, s. *macinamento*, s. m. *il macinare.*

GRIND-STONE, s. *mola* s. f.

GRI'NNING, s. [from to grin] *lo sgrignare, ringhio*, s. m.

GRIPE, s. [handful] *una manata*, s. *un pugno*, s. m.

GRIPES [the gripping in the guts] *dolori colici.*

The gripes of avarice, and twinges of ambition, *le cure mordaci dell' avarizia, e i tormenti dell' ambizione.*

A gripe money, *un avaro, un taccagno, un misero, uno spilorcio, un cacastecchi.*

To gripe [to seize] *abbrancare, afferrare, prendere.* pret. *presi.*

To gripe [to cause gripings in the guts] *dare, o causare dolori colici.*

GRIPED, adj. *abbrancato, afferrato, preso.*

GRIPED [troubled with gripes] *che ha dolori colici.*

GRI'PING, s. *l'afferrare, l'abbrancare.*

Gripings of the guts, *dolori colici, la colica.*

GRI'PING, adj. [a griping man] *un avaro, un misero, uno spilorcio, un taccagno, un cacastecchi.*

GRI'SLY, adj. [hideous, frightful] *deforme, orrido, spaventevole, orribile.*

A grisly hue [a frightful aspect] *un aspetto orribile.*

GRIST, s. [corn ground] *farina*, s. f.

To bring grist to one's own mill, *tirar l'acqua al suo mulino.*

GRI'STLE, s. [a cartilage] *cartilagine.*

GRI'STLY, adj. [full of gristles] *cartilaginoso, che ha cartilagine.*

GRIT, s. [the dust of stones or metals] *polvere di pietra, limatura di metallo.*

GRITH, s. [an old Saxon word for peace] *pace.*

Grith-breach, *violazione di pace.*

GRI'TTY, adj. ex. gritty bread, *pane pieno di sabbia.*

Grizle, s. [gray] *canutezza, color bigio.*

GRI'ZLED, adj. [hoary] *canuto, bianco di pelo per vecchiezza.*

GROAN, s. [deep sigh] *gemito, sospiro*, s. m.

To GROAN [to fetch deep and hard sighs] *gemere, e gemire, sospirare, piangere, lamentarsi.* pret. *piansi.*

The gallows groans for him, *la forca l'aspetta.*

GRO'ANING, s. *gemito, il gemere.*

GROAT, s. [a coin in value four pence] *moneta che val quattro soldi.*

He is not worth a groat, *non ha quattro soldi al suo comando.*

Groats, or oatmeal groats, *farina di vena.*

GRO'BIAN, s. [a slovenly fellow] *uno sporco, un uomo sudicio, un porco.*

GROCE, s. [twelve dozen] *grossa*, s. f. *dodici dozzine.*

A groce of strings for a violin, *una grossa di corde de minugia.*

GRO'CER, s. *droghiere, droghiero*, s. m.

A grocer's shop, *bottega di droghiere.*

Grocery ware, *drogheria*, s. f. *quantità di droghe.*

GRO'GRAM, s. [stuff made of silk and hair] *grossagrana.* s. f. *sorta di panno fatto di seta e di pelo di capra.*

GROIN, s. [the part between the belly and the thighs] *anguinaja*, s. f. *quella parte del corpo umano ch' è tra la coscia e'l ventre.*

A swelling in the groin, *un tincone, una postema nell' anguinaja.*

GROOM, s. [one who looks after horses] *mozzo di stalla, palafreniere.*

Groom of the stole, *gentiluomo della camera del re d'Inghilterra.*

A groom of the king's bed-chamber, *cameriero del re.*

The groom porter, *il primo portiere della corte.*

GROOVE, s. [a channel cut in wood, or stone] *scannellatura*, s. f.

GROOVE [a deep cavern or hollow] *fondo*; *caverna profonda.*

To GROOVE [to make a groove] *scannellare.*

To GROPE [to feel] *palpare, tastare, maneggiare, toccare dove uno non può vedere.*

GRO'PED, adj. *palpato, tastato, maneggiato, toccato.*

GROPER, s. *uno che palpa, che tocca, che tasta.*

GRO'PING, s. *il palpare, il tastare.*

To go groping along, *andare al tasto, o a tastone, andar brancolando.*

GROSS, adj. [or thick] *grossiere, grosso, materiale, rozzo.*

A gross air, *un' aria grossa, e spessa.*

A gross error, *un errore palpabile, un grand errore, un errore manifesto.*

A gross knave, *un pretto villano.*

To give one gross language, *parlare incivilmente ad uno, ingiuriarlo, svillaneggiarlo.*

A gross lye, *una gran bugia.*

Gross [lumpish, dull] *grossiere, semplice, ignorante, stolto, stupido.*

Gross, s. *grosso*, s. m. *la parte maggiore, e migliore di che che si sia.*

The gross of an army, *il grosso dell' esercito, il nervo dell' esercito, la parte maggiore dell' esercito.*

Gross [groce] v. Groce.

GRO'SSLY, adv. *grossamente, rozzamente, zoticamente, con poca arte, grossolanamente, alla grossolana.*

You are grossly mistaken, *voi v'ingannate a partito.*

GRO'SSNESS, s. *grossezza, materialità, rozzezza*, s. f.

GROT, } s. [cave, den] *grotta,*
GRO'TTO, } *spelonca, caverna*, s. f. *antro*, s. m.

GROTE'SK-WORK, [rude figures made at the pleasure of the artist] *grottesca*, s. f. *pittura fatta a capriccio.*

GROVE, s. [a little wood] *un boschetto.*

To GRO'VEL [to lie prone, to creep low on the ground] *giacer bocconi, strisciar per terra.*

To grovel [to be mean, to be without dignity] *esser vile, mostrarsi vile.*

GRO'VELING, adj. [lying on the face, or with the face to the ground] *boccone, colla pancia verso terra.*

To lay groveling, *giacer boccone.*

To GROUL [to grumble, to mutter]

brontolare, borbottare, borbogliare, mormorare.

He does nothing but groul all the day, *non fa altro che brontolare tutto'l giorno.*

GRO'ULING, s. *borbottamento, borbotto*, s. m. *il borbottare.*

GROUND, s. [the earth] *la terra.*

To fall upon the ground, *cascare a terra.*

To lay in the ground [to bury] *sotterrare, seppellire, mettere sotterra.*

Ground [land belonging to one] *terreno, territorio, beni stabili, terra, campi.*

These are his grounds, *queste sono sue terre, o possessioni.*

To gain ground, *avanzar terreno.*

To give or lose ground, *rinculare, arretrarsi, trarsi indietro.*

To stand or keep one's ground, *stare alla dura, star saldo, costante, non si lasciar' andare, tener duro.*

To quit one's ground, *ritirarsi.*

The grounds of an art, *i fondamenti, i principi d'un arte.*

The ground of a flower'd silk, *fondo, campo d'un drappo fiorito.*

The grounds of the Italian language, *i principj della favella Italiana.*

Ground [reason] *fondamento, soggetto, campo.* s. m. *ragione*, s. f.

It is not without ground, *non è senza fondamento.*

What ground have you to believe it? *che ragione avete per creder ciò?*

I have ground to hope for a better fortune, *ho campo di sperare una più prospera fortuna.*

A fine plot of ground, *un bel luogo.*

Marshy grounds, *luoghi pantanosi, paludosi.*

To break ground [to open the trenches] *aprir le trinciere.*

To go upon sure ground, *esser sicuro del suo negozio, giuocare a carte scoperte.*

To overthrow a city to the ground, *smantellare, rovinare, distruggere una città.*

The grounds [or dregs] of a liquor, *sendigliuolo, o feccia di qualche liquore.*

Ground-work, *fondo, piano.*

Ground-plot, *la pianta d'un edificio.*

Ground-plot [principles] *principio, base, fondamento.*

Ground-ivy, *edera terrestre.*

Ground-worm, *ombrico*, s. m.

A ground room, *camera terrena.*

Ground rent, *terratico*, s. m.

Ground tackle, *l'ancora, sartiame, e tutto quello che è necessario per l'armamento d'un vascello.*

Ground, adj. [from to grind] *macinato, affilato, arruotato.*

To GROUND upon, *fondare, stabilire appoggiare.* pref. *stabilisco.*

To ground one's opinion upon reason and authority, *fondare la sua opinione sopra la ragione, e l'autorità.*

To ground a young man in a science, *insegnare ad un giovine i principi e rudimenti d'una scienza.*

To ground a ship [a sea term] *mettere un vascello a secco per calafatarlo.*

GRO'UNDED, adj. *fondato, stabilito, appoggiato.*

Well grounded in any art, *fondato, bene instrutto in qualche arte.*

GRO'UNDING, s. *il fondare.*

GRO'UNDLESS, adj. [void of reason] *senza ragione, senza fondamento.*

GROUNDLESSLY, adv. *senza fondamento, in aria.*

GRO'UNDLING, s. [a fish] *spezie di pesce.*

GRO'UNDSEL } [the threshold of
GROUNSIL, } a door] *limitare, soglia*, s. f.

Groundsel [an herb] *crescione*, s. m. *spezie d'erba.*

To GROUNDSEL a house, *gettare i fondamenti d'una casa.*

GRO'UNDSELLING, s. *fondazione*, s. f. *fondamento d'una casa.*

GROUP, s. [a term of painting, a knot or separate collection of figures] *gruppo*, s. m.

GROUSE, s. [a kind of fowl, a heath-cock] *spezie d'uccello salvatico buono a mangiare.*

GROUT, s. [the grout of oatmeal] *farina di vena.*

Grout-head [one that has a huge head] *inteschiato, testuto, che ha una grossa testa.*

To GROW [to thrive] *crescere.* pret. *crebbi.*

To grow [to become, to prove] *divenire, diventare, farsi.*

To grow apace, *crescer molto.*

To grow tall, *crescere in altezza, divenire, o farsi alto.*

To grow thick, *ingrossare, divenir grosso.*

To grow fat, *ingrassare, divenir grasso.*

To grow thin, *smagrire, divenir magro smilzo.*

To grow strong, *invigorirsi, divenir forte.*

To grow old [to grow in years] *invecchiare, avanzarsi in età, entrar negli anni.*

To grow lean, *smagrire, divenir magro.* pref. *smagrisco.*

To grow little, *impiccolirsi.*

To grow heavy, *divenir pesante.*

To grow rich, *arricchirsi, divenir ricco*, pref. *arricchisco.*

To grow poor, *impoverire, divenir povero* pref. *impoverisco.*

To grow handsome, *abbellire, divenir bello.* pref. *smagrisco.*

To grow ugly, *divenir brutto.*

To grow proud, *insuperbirsi, divenir superbo:* pref. *insuperbisco.*

To grow obstinate or stubborn, *ostinarsi, divenir ostinato.*

To grow humble, *umiliarsi, divenir umile.*

To grow weary, *infastidire, svogliarsi, venire a noja.*

It grows late, *si fa tardi, annotta, si fa notte.*

To grow little, lesser, or short, *diminuire, scemare, divenir corto.*

The days begin to grow short, *i giorni cominciano a diminuire.*

To grow young again, *ringiovenire.*

To grow weary, *tediarsi, faticarsi.*

To grow dear, *incarire, divenir caro.* pref. *incarisco.*

To grow tame, *addimesticarsi, ammansarsi.*

To grow into a fashion, *venire alla moda.*

To grow into a proverb, *passare in proverbio.*

To grow into favour with one, *cattivarsi l'amorevolezza di qualche persona.*

To grow out of favour with one, *esser disgraziato.*

To grow up, *crescere.*

This rain will make the corn grow up, *questa pioggia farà crescere il grano.*

To grow up again, *rinascere.*

To grow upon one, *divenir troppo forte per uno.*

It grows near harvest, *il tempo della raccolta s'avvicina.*

The night grows apace, *la notte s'avanza a gran passi.*

It grows out of fashion, *comincia a non esser più alla moda.*

To grow out of use, *divenir fuor d'uso.*

To grow out of credit, *perder il credito.*

To grow towards an end, *finirsi, avvicinarsi alla fina.*

It grows towards morning, *comincia a farsi giorno.*

It grows near day, *il giorno comincia a spuntare.*

GRO'WING, s. *il crescere.*

That will hinder his growing, *questo l'impedirà di crescere.*

Growing, adj. *nascente.*

A fine growing weather, *un buon tempo per i frutti della terra.*

GRO'WER, s. ex. A slow grower [a tree that does not grow fast] *un albero che è lungo tempo a crescere.*

To GROWL. v. To groul.

GROWN, adj. *cresciuto, divenuto*, v. To grow.

He is a grown man, *egli è un uomo fatto.*

Grown weary of all things, *svogliato, infastidito, stufo d'ogni cosa.*

GROWTH, s. ex. This wine is out of my own growth, *questo vino è del mio proprio terreno.*

This is not out of your own growth [not out of your own head] *questa non è erba del tuo orto.*

Growth [increase] *accrescimento, aggrandimento, avanzamento.*

He is not come to his full growth, *egli non ha finito ancora di crescere.*

Growth-half-penny [a rate paid in some places for tithe of every fat beast] *dazio che si paga in certi luoghi, per la decima delle bestie grasse.*

GRO'WTHEAD, } s. [a kind of fish]
GRO'WTNOL } *sorta di pesce che ha l'capo grosso.*

Grouthead [an idle lazy fellow] *un ozioso, un poltronaccio.*

GRUB, s. [maggot] *lombrico, baco*, s. m.

His head is full of grubs, *la sua testa è piena di grilli, di ghiribizzi, egli è mol-*

to capricciofo, bifbetico, ghiribizzofo, fantaftico.

Grub [dwarf] un nano, un uomicciatto, un pigmeo.

To GRUB up [to delve or dig up trees] fradicare, fvellere.

To grub up bufhes, fradicare arbufcelli.

To grub up a wood, fbofcare un bofco.

To grub up weeds, farchiare l'erbe falvatiche.

GRUBBED UP, adj. fradicato, fvelto, farchiato.

GRU'BBING, adj. Ex. a grubbing ax, farchio, farchiello, s. m. piccola marra, per ufo di farchiare.

The grubbing of a cock [the cutting off his feathers under the wings] il tagliare al gallo le penne che fono fotto le ali.

To grubble [to feel in the dark] palpare, andar taftoni.

GRU'BSTREET, nome d'una ftrada in Londra; in cui abitano molti autori per lo più di poco nome e valore, onde è che ogni cattiva o povera fcrittura è in Inglefe chiamata Grubftreet-writing.

GRUDGE, s. [fecret hatred, ill-will] odio coperto, rancore, odio, livore, s. m.

To bear a grudge to one, tener rancore contro, o ad uno.

A grudge of confcience, ftimolo di cofcienza.

To GRUDGE, } [to envy] invidiare, portare invidia.
To GRUDGE AT, }

I don't grudge him his happinefs at all, io non gl' invidio la fua fortuna.

I don't grudge my pains, non mi lagno delle mie fatiche.

He grudges his men their victuals, gli difpiace di veder mangiare i fuoi domeftici.

GRUDGED, adj. invidiato.

GRU'DGING, s. invidia, s. f. l'invidiare.

To have a grudging to a thing, aver defiderio, aver voglia o uzzolo di qualche cofa.

GRU'DGINGLY, adv. [with an ill-will] di mala voglia, con pena, con iftento, a mal' incorpo.

GRUEL, or WATER GRUEL, bevanda all' Inglefe, fatta di farina d'orzo bollita nell' acqua.

GRUFF, adj. [grim-faced, four looked] faftidiofo, oftico, arcigno, fdegnofo, fpiacevole, burbero, rigido, auftero, afpro.

GRU'FFLY, adv. aufteramente, ruvidamente, afpramente, burberamente.

GRUM, adj. lo fteffo che gruff.

To GRU'MBLE [to mutter between the teeth] borbottare, brontolare, borbogliare, mormorare.

To grumble at one, mormorare, lamentarfi, lagnarfi d'uno.

GRU'MBLED, adj. borbottato, brontolato, borbogliato, mormorato.

GRU'MBLING, s. borbottamento, borbottio, borboglio, borbogliamento, s. m.

To have a grumbling in the gizard, mormorare, brontolare, lamentarfi, non effer contento, lagnarfi.

GRUMPO'RTERS, s. [heavy dice] dadi groffi.

GRU'MOUS, adj. [full of clods or lumps] grumofo.

GRUNSEL, s. [groundfil, the lower part of a building] le fondamenta, il fondamento, la parte più baffa d'una cafa.

To GRUNT [to cry like a hog] grugnare, grugnire, lo ftridere del porco.

GRU'NTING, s. grugnito, s. m. ftrepito del porco nel mandar fuori la voce.

To GRU'NTLE, lo fteffo che to grunt.

To GRUTCH, v. To grudge.

GRUTCH, v. Grudge.

GRY, s. [a meafure containing one tenth of a line] è una mifura che contiene la decima parte d'una linea.

GUAIA'CUM, s. [the wood of an Indian tree, ufed in decoctions to provoke fweat] legno fanto, guaiaco.

GUARANTE'E, s. [a perfon agreed on to fee articles performed in treaties between princes] ficurtà, mallevadore.

GUARD, v. Gard.

To GUARD, v. To gard, con i derivativi, però fcrivi fempre GUARD, to GUARD, GUARDIAN, &c.

GUDDS-BOB, s. [a comical oath] cofpetto di bacco.

GU'DGEON, s. [a fort of fifh] ghiozzo, s. m.

To fwallow a gudgeon [to bear an affront] bere un affronto.

GUE'RDON, s. [reward] guidèrdone, guidardone, premio, merito, s. m.

GUESS, s. [conjecture] conghiettura, conjettura.

To read by guefs, leggere fenza compitare.

To GUESS [to conjecture] conghietturare, indovinare.

Gueffed, adj. conghietturato, indovinato.

GUE'SSER, s. conghietturatore, indovinatore, s. m. indovinatrice, s. f.

GUE'SSING, s. conghiettura, s. f. il conghietturare.

Gueffing, adj. conghietturale.

Phyfick is but a gueffing fcience, la medicina è una fcienza conghietturale.

GUEST, s. [a perfon invited to, or received at a feaft] un convitato.

Gueft [a ftranger that lodges with one] ofpite, s. m. il foreftiere ch' è alloggiato in cafa di qualcheduno.

A troublefome gueft, un importuno, un' importuna.

GU'GAWS, or GEW-GAWS, s. [trifles] cianciafrufcole, baje, bagattelle, frafcherie, cofe di poco valore.

To GU'GLE [to make a noife as a narrow-mouth'd bottle does while it is emptying] gorgogliare, il romoreggiar de' liquori ufcenti di luogo ftretto.

GU'GGLING, s. gorgogliamento, gorgoglio, s. m.

GUI'DANCE, s. [a guiding or leading] guida, fcorta, condotta.

Under your guidance, fotto la voftra guida, o fcorta.

GUIDE, s. [or leader] guida, fcorta, s. f. conduttore, duce, s. m.

To GUIDE [to direct, to conduct in the way] guidare, fcorgere, moftrare altrui avanti il cammino, condurre, menare, pret. fcorfi, conduffi.

GUI'DED, adj. guidato, fcorto, condotto, menato.

GUI'DING, s. il guidare.

GUI'DON, s. [the ftandard of a troop] ftendardo, s. m.

Guidon [the ftandard bearer] quello che porta lo ftendardo.

GUILE, s. [a tax, or tribute] taffa, s. f. dazio, tributo.

Guild [fine] ammenda, s. f.

Guild [a company or fociety of men] compagnia, focietà, s. f.

Guild-Hall [the chief hall of a city] la cafa della città.

GUI'LDER, s. [a Dutch coin] fiorino, s. m. moneta Olandefe.

GUILE, s. [fraud, deceit] frode, e fraude, furberia, furfanteria, baratteria, mariuoleria, guidoneria, s. f. inganno, s. m. aftuzia, s. f.

Full of guile, ingannatore, furbo, guidone, furfante, barone, s. m.

GUI'LEFUL, adj. [deceitful] ingannatore, furbo.

GUI'LEFULNESS, s. fraude, furberia, guidoneria, s. f. inganno, s. m.

GUI'LEFULLY, adv. ingannevolmente, da traditore.

GUI'LER, s. [one that betrays into danger by infidious practices] colui che ti conduce in pericolo infidiofamente.

GUILT, s. [crime] delitto, s. m. colpa, s. f. peccato, s. m.

To avouch one's guilt, confeffare la fua colpa, il fuo peccato.

GUI'LTINESS, s. delitto; confapovolezza del proprio delitto.

GUI'LTLESS, adj. innocente.

He is found guiltlefs, è ftato dichiarato innocente.

GUI'LTLESSNESS, s. innocenza, s. f.

GUI'LTY, adj. colpevole, reo.

He is guilty of that crime, egli è reo di tal delitto.

To find one guilty, trovar reo.

GUI'NEA, s. [a gold coin] una ghinea; moneta d'Inghilterra, che vale quattro piaftre, e più.

A guinea-pig, un porcello d'India.

GUISE, s. [fafhion] guifa, maniera, s. f. modo, s. m.

GUITA'R, s. [a kind of mufical inftrument] chitarra, s. f. ftrumento muficale da corde.

To play upon the guitar, fuonar della chitarra.

GULCH, } s. [a little glutton] un ghiottoncello, un leccardo.
GU'LCHING, }

GULE OF AUGUST [the day of St. Peter in Vincula, celebrated on the firft of Auguft] il primo giorno d'Agofto, nel quale fi celebra la fefta di San Pietro in Vincula.

GULES, s. [in heraldry, the red or vermillion colour in a coat of arms] il roffo dello fcudo, vocabolo araldefco.

GULF, s. [a part of the fea that is between two lands] golfo, s. m.

The gulf of Venice, il golfo di Venezia.

Gulf [abyfs] abiffo.

GULL, s. [a fea gull, a fea-bird] gabbiano, s. m. forta d'uccello di mare.

A gull [a cheat] *un furbo, un mariuolo, un guidone.*

A gull [one who is easily cheated] *un gonzo, un minchione, un bietolone.*

To Gull [to deceive, to cheat] *ingannare, truffare, frodare, acchiappare.*

Gu'lled, adj. *ingannato, truffato, frodato, acchiappato.*

Gu'llet, s. [the wind-pipe] *gorgozzule,* s. m. *gola,* s. f. *strozza,* s. f.

Gu'lling, s. *inganno,* s. m. *truferia, guidoneria,* s. f.

Gu'ller, s. [cheat] *ingannatore, truffiere, guidone,* s. m.

Gu'lleries, s. [stories] *ciancia-frusćole, baje, bagattelle, ciance, frasche-rie,* s. f.

Gully gut, s. [glutton] *un ghiotto, un ghiottone, un goloso.*

Gulp, s. *tratto, sorso,* s. m.

To take a gulp of wine, *prendere un sorso di vino.*

To swallow a glass of wine at one gulp, *bere un bicchiere di vino in un tratto.*

To Gulp down [to swallow down] *inghiottire, trangugiare, tranghiottire,* pref. *tranghiottisco.*

To gulp down a glass of wine, *trangugiare un bicchiere di vino.*

To gulp [to pant] *palpitare, battere.*

Gum, s. [a concealed tough juice, issuing out of trees] *gomma,* s. f. *umor viscoso, ch'esce dagli alberi per la scorza; al quale si dice anche ricchico.*

Gum of the eyes, *cispa che casca dagli occhi.*

The gums [the flesh covering the jaw-bone] *gengia, gengiva,* s. f. *la carne che ricuopre gli ossi delle mascelle.*

To Gum [to stiffen with gum] *intridere con gomma,* part. *intriso.*

Gum-copal-elemy [a sort of gum] *gommaelemi.*

Gu'mmy, adj. [full of gum] *gommoso.*

Gun, s. [a fire-arm of several sorts] *arme da fuoco.*

To let off a gun, *spirare, tirare un' arme da fuoco.*

A great gun, *un cannone.*

Gun-powder, *polvere da cannone.*

Gun-room [in a ship] *la santa Barbera, luogo nel vascello dove si conserva la polvere.*

Gúnshot, Ex. to be within gunshot, *essere a tiro di cannone, esser alla portata d'una palla di cannone.*

A gun-stick, *una bacchetta.*

A gun-smith, *un armajuolo.*

Gu'nner, s. *cannoniere,* s. m.

Gu'nnery, s. [the art how to charge, level, mount, and discharge great guns] *l'arte del cannoniere.*

Gurge, s. [whirlpool, gulf] *golfo, abbisso.*

Gu'rgians, s. [coarse-meal] *semola, crusca,* s. f.

To Gu'rgle [*lo stesso che* to gugle] *gorgogliare, il romoreggiare che fa un liquore uscendo di luogo stretto, come d'un fiasco o simili.*

Gu'rnard, } s. *sorta di pesce di*
Gu'rnet, } *mare.*

To Gush [to pour out suddenly, and with force] *sgorgare, sboccare, traboccare, scannellare; schizzare.*

To gush out in tears, *sgorgare in lagrime.*

The blood did gush out of his wound, *il sangue sboccò dalla ferita.*

A spring of water that gushes out, *una sorgente che schizza, o zampilla.*

Gush, s. *lo sboccare impetuoso, o d un tratto, di qualche liquore fuori di checchessia.*

Gu'sset, s. [a piece of cloth put to shirts in order to strengthen them] *gherone,* s. m.

The gusset of a shirt, *il gherone d'una camicia.*

Gust, s. [taste] *gusto,* s. m.

To have a good gust, *aver buon gusto.*

Gust [desire] *desiderio,* s. m. *inclinazione,* s. f.

A sudden gust of wind, *bufera, nodo, groppo di vento.*

Gu'stable, } adj. [pleasant to the
Gu'stful, } taste] *gustoso, grato al gusto.*

Gu'sto, s. [intellectual taste] *gusto, buon discernimento, buon gusto.*

Gu'sty, adj. [stormy, tempestuous] *tempestoso, burrascoso, procelloso.*

To Gut, *sventrare, sbudellare, trarre gl' interiori del corpo.*

Guts, s. [the bowels] *budello, intestino,* s. m. pl. *budella,* s. f.

A greedy gut [one that loves his guts] *un ghiotto, un ghiottone, un goloso, un uomo dedito al ventre.*

A fat guts, *un panciuto, una pancia grossa.*

Gut tide [shrove-tide] *carnasciale, il martedì grasso.*

Gu'tter, s. [a canal or rain spout for water] *gronda,* s. f.

A gutter tile, *tegola,* s. f.

A hollow gutter in rebating of pillars, *scanalatura.*

To Gu'tter [as a candle does] *scolare, parlando d'una candela,*

To Guttle [to feed luxuriously, to gormandise] *crapulare, empiersi la panciaccia di buoni bocconi.*

To guttle [to swallow] *ingojare, trangugiare.*

Gu'ttural, adj. [belonging to the throat] *gutturale.*

Guttural letters [in grammar, which are pronounced in the throat] *lettere gutturali, che si pronuncian in gola.*

Guy, s. in a ship [any rope used to keep off things from beating or falling against the ship's side, when they are to be hoisted in] *corde che servono di difesa ad un vascello, appiccate lungesso per difenderlo dagli urti che potrebbe ricevere nell' imbarcare le mercanzie.*

To Gu'zzle [to drink greedily, to tipple] *mangiare, crapulare, bere, trincare, bere smoderatamente.*

Gu'zzler, s. *un bevitore, un imbriacone, un epulone, crapulone.*

Gybe, s. [a sneer, a taunt, a sarcasm] *una botta, un motto di scorno, un sarcasmo.*

To gybe [to sneer, to taunt] *scornare, mostrar dispregio per quel che un altro dice.*

Gymna'siarch, s. [a chief schoolmaster, the governor of a college] *il principale, il rettore, il capo d'un collegio.*

Gy'mnick, adj. *atletico, ginnastico.*

Gy'ron, s. [in heraldry, an ordinary consisting of two strait lines, issuing from diverse parts of the escutcheon, and meeting in the fesse's point] *girone.*

Gy'ves, s. [gives] *ferri, ceppi,* s. m. *catene,* s. f.

To Gyve [to fetter, to shackle] *porre in ceppi; incatenare.*

H.

H.

H, Questa lettera in Inglese, come in alcune altre lingue, si fa spesso sentire, e principalmente in principio di parola, mandando fuora il fiato con una certa forza, e non adoperando quasimente quegli organi della voce, che servono a distinguere ogni altro suono dell' alfabeto. In Italiano l' acca non ha alcun suono, onde bisogna che gl' Italiani sentano l'acca Inglese pronunziata per imitarla bene.

HAAK, s. [a fish] *nome di un certo pesce.*

HABERDAS'HER, s. *merciajo.*

Haberdasher's shop, *bottega di merciajo.*

HABERDI'NE, s. [a sort of salt fish] *merluzzo salato.*

HABE'RGEON, or HABE'RGION, s. [a little coat of mail, covering the neck and breast] *usbergo, corsaletto,* s. m.

HABI'LEMENT, HABI'LIMENT, HABI'LLIMENT, s. [apparel, attire] *abbigliamento, abito vestito,* s. m.

To HABI'LITATE [to qualify, to entitle] *abilitare, conferir diritto.*

HA'BIT, s. [dress, attire] *abito, vestimento,* s. m.

Habit [custom] *abito, costume,* s. m. *qualità acquistata per frequente uso d'operazioni.*

Habit of the body [constitution or temper of the mind or body] *complessione, costituzione, disposizione di corpo.*

To HA'BIT [to dress, to accoutre, to array] *vestir le truppe, provvedere i soldati d'abiti.*

HA'BITABLE, adj. [which may be inhabited] *abitabile, da potersi abitare.*

HA'BITABLENESS, s. *lo stato d'una casa abitabile.*

HA'BITANCE, s. [dwelling place] *abitacolo, abituro,* s. m.

HA'BITANT, s. [inhabitant, dweller] *abitante; uno che sta, che dimora in un certo luogo.*

HABITA'TION, s. [dwelling-place] *abitazione, dimora.* s. f. *luogo da abitare.*

HA'BITED, adj. [clad] *vestito.*

Well habited, *ben vestito.*

HABI'TUAL, adj. [grown to a habit by long use, customary] *abituale, che procede da abito, e disposizione.*

To HABI'TUATE [to accustom] *abituarsi, accostumarsi, avvezzarsi.*

HABI'TUATED, adj. [that has got an habit of, or is accustomed to a thing] *abituato, che ha fatto l'abito, accostumato, avvezzato.*

To be habituated in a sin, *esser abituato a qualche peccato.*

HA'BITUDE, s. [or habit] *abitudine,* s. f. *modo, e disposizion dell' essere, costume,* s. m.

HAB'NAB, s. *accidente.*

'Tis a meer hab-nab whether it succeeds or not, *è un puro accidente se la cosa riesce.*

Hab-nab, adv. [rashly, at a venture] *temerariamente, inconsideratamente, a caso.* v. Hob-nob, *e la nota che vi ho fatta.*

HACK, s. [a cratch for hay] *rastrelliera,* s. f.

Hack [a hackney-horse] *un cavallo d'affitto.*

To HACK [to hue or cut] *tritare, sminuzzare, tagliare.*

To hack in pieces, *tagliare a pezzi.*

To Hack [to speak unreadily or with hesitation] *parlare adagio e malamente, senza la dovuta prontezza di parole.*

To Hack, v. n. [to turn hackney or prostitute] *divenire meretrice.*

HA'CKED, adj. *tritato, sminuzzato, tagliato.*

HA'CKLE, s. [raw silk, or any filmy substance unspun] *seta greggia, o qualunque altra fibrosa sostanza non filata.*

To Hackle [to cut small] *sminuzzare, tagliuzzare, tritare.*

HA'CKLED, adj. *sminuzzato, tagliuzzato, tritato.*

HA'CKNEY, adj. *d'affitto.*

HAD, *preterito, e participio del verbo* to have.

I had very good weather, *io ebbi bellissimo tempo.*

Had we but time, *se avessimo almeno il tempo.*

After I had it, *avuto che l'ebbi.*

Before I had it, *prima ch' io l' avessi.*

He had like to have been lost, *poco mancò che non perisse.*

If I had it now, *s'io l'avessi adesso.*

Had not I been a fool, *s' io non fossi stato un sciocco.*

I had been there before, *v' ero stato prima.*

He had me with him, *mi prese con lui.*

I had rather, *amerei meglio, vorrei più tosto.*

HA'DDOCK, s. [a sort of codfish] *specie di baccalà.*

HA'EMATITES, s. [a kind of stone] *ematita, amatita, matita,* s. f. *sorta di pietra.*

HAFT, s. [handle] *manico.*

The haft of a knife, *il manico d'un coltello.*

To HAFT, [to set a haft on] *metter il manico a qualche strumento.*

To haft a knife, *metter il manico ad un coltello.*

HA'FTER, s. *un beccalite.*

HAG, s. [a witch] *una strega.*

An old hag, *una strega vecchia, una vecchia sdentata.*

A hag [a night mare] *una fantasma, una furia, un mostro.*

To HAG [to torment, to harrass with terrour] *spaventare empire di spavento, atterrire, tormentar con larve e fantasmi.*

HA'GGARD, adj. [that has a fierce or wild look] *selvaggio, austero, aspro, brusco, ritroso, magro, brutto, deforme.*

HAGAR-HAWK [a wild hawk which prey'd for herself before she was taken] *un falcone salvatico.*

HA'GGARD, s. *cosa selvaggia e da non mai mansuefarsi.*

HA'GGESS, s. [a sheep's maw filled with minced meat] *spezie di sanguinaccio.*

HA'GGISH, adj. *deforme, orrido, spaventevole.*

To HA'GGLE, v. a. [to cut, to chop, to mangle] *tagliare, sminuzzare tagliando, guastare con molti tagli.*

To HA'GGLE [to stand hard in buying] *stiracchiare nel prezzo, andar troppo stirato, stare in su'l prezzo.*

HA'GGLER, s. *stiracchiatore, che va troppo stirato nel prezzo.*

Haggler, s. *uno che taglia e sminuzza tagliando.*

HA'GGLING, s. *lo stiracchiare nel prezzo.*

To what purpose is all this haggling, *a che serve tanto stiracchiare nel prezzo.*

HAIL, s. *grandine,* s. f.

Hail shot, *pallini, treggea.*

Hail [all health, an old way of saluting] *ave, Iddio vi salvi.*

To be hail fellow well met, *vivere in buona società, esser familiare, trattare alla buona.*

Hail, adj. [healthful] *sano, che sta bene, in buona salute.*

To HAIL, verb neut. *grandinare.*

It hails, *grandina.*

To HAIL, v. n. *dir Ave, salutare.*

HA'INOUS, adj. [odious, hateful, horrid]

horrid] *odioso, atroce, abbominevole, esecrando, orribile, enorme.*

HA'INOUSLY, adv. *odiosamente, atrocemente, abbominevolmente, orribilmente.*

HA'INOUSNESS, s. [odiousness] *enormità, atrocità,* s. f. *errore,* s. m.

The hainousness of the crime, *l'enormità del delitto.*

HAIR, s. *capello, pelo,* s. m.

The hair of the head, *i capelli del capo.*

'Twas within a hair's breadth, *poco mancò.*

The hair of the body, *i peli del corpo.*

Soft downy hair, *lanugine,* s. f.

The hair of a dog, or any other beast, *i peli d'un cane, o d'altra bestia.*

Against the hair, *a contrappelo.*

The hair of a horse, *i crini d'un cavallo.*

The hair of a boar, or wild boar, *le setole d'un porco, o d'un cinghiale.*

False hair, *capelli posticci.*

Against the hair [or against the grain] *di mala voglia, a mal in corpo, mal volentieri.*

To a hair, *per l'appunto.*

I understand him to a hair, *l'intendo perfettamente.*

A fine head of hair, *una bella capellatura, una bella zazzera.*

I shall not love him a hair the worse, *non l'amerò meno.*

Hair shirt, or hair fillet, *cilicio,* s. m.

Hair lace, or hair fillet, to tie up hair with, *intrecciatojo,* s. m.

Hair buttons, *bottoni di pelo.*

Hair brained, *mentecatto, scervellato.*

A hair-brained youth, *un giovane scervellato, di poco cervello.*

HA'IRED, adj. *capelluto.*

Red-haired, *che ha i capelli rossi.*

Curl-haired, *che ha i capelli ricci.*

HA'IRINESS, s. *capellamento,* s. m. *quantità di capelli.*

HA'IRLESS, adj. [without hair] *senza capelli, pelato, calvo.*

HA'IRY, adj. *capelluto, peloso.*

A hair star, *una stella comata.*

To HAKE after, *uccellare, desiderare con avidità.*

HALBERD, s. [a weapon well known] *alabarda,* s. f. *sorta d'arme in asta.*

HA'LBERDIER, s. [one who carries an halberd] *alabardiere, soldato armato d'alabarda.*

HALCY'ON, s. [a sea-fowl] *alcione,* s. m. *sorta d'uccello aquatico.*

Halcyon, adj. [placid, quiet, still] *placido, quieto, tranquillo; dalla supposta placidezza e calma che si suppone in mare nel tempo che le alcione covano.*

To HALE [to pull, to drag] *rimurchiare, e rimorchiare, tirare, strascinare.*

To hale a ship, *rimurchiare una nave.*

HA'LED, adj. *rimurchiato, rimorchiato, tirato, strascinato.*

HALF, adj. *mezzo.*

Half-man, half woman, *mezzo uomo, mezza donna.*

Lesser by half, *la metà più piccolo.*

Half an hour, *una mezz'ora.*

Half-moon, *mezza luna.*

A pound and a half, *una libbra e mezza.*

Half-dead, *mezzo morto, più morto che vivo.*

We went half way, *andammo fino a mezza strada.*

Half-moon [in fortification] *mezza luna,* s. f. *termine di fortificazione.*

Half-brother, *fratello dalla parte del padre, o della madre.*

Half-tongue [a jury impanelled in a cause where a foreigner is a party] *giurati spartiti, per giudicare degli affari de' forestieri.*

Half, s. plur. halves [moiety] *la metà.*

To go halves with one, *andar di metà, o spartire con uno.*

To do things by halves, *fare che che si sia imperfettamente, negligentemente, alla carlona.*

HA'LIBUT, s. *sorta di pesce.*

HA'LIDOM, s. [our blessed Lady] *la Madonna, la santissima Vergine.*

HA'LMASS, s. [the fast of All Souls] *il giorno de' morti, la vigilia dell' ognissanti.*

HALL, s. [a large room at the entrance of a house] *sala,* s. f.

Hall [a public building belonging to a society] *sala.*

Westminster hall, *la sala di Westminster.*

Hall-days, *giorni curiali.*

Guild-hall at London, *la casa della città di Londra.*

A hall [for tradesmen] *fondaco.*

Grocers hall, *il fondaco de' droghieri.*

A hall wherein all the servants of a great family dine and sup, *tinello,* s. m. *nelle corti de' signori è il luogo dove mangiano i cortigiani.*

HALLE'LUJAH, s. [a song of thanksgiving] *alleluja, sia laudato il Signore, laudate il Signore.*

HA'LLIBUT, s. [a kind of fish] *sorta di pesce,* s. m.

HALLO'O, interj. [a word of encouragement] *voce che si usa per incoraggire i cani nella caccia.*

To HA'LLOO, *incoraggire i cani in caccia, gridando Halloo, Halloo.*

To HA'LLOW [to make holy, to consecrate] *santificare, consacrare, dedicare, riverir come sacro.*

HA'LLOWED, adj. *santificato consacrato, dedicato, riverito come sacro.*

HA'LLOWING, s. *il santificare, il consacrare, il riverire come sacro.*

To HA'LLUCINATE [to mistake, to blunder] *sbagliare, ingannarsi.*

HALLUCINA'TION, s. [a blunder or oversight] *sbaglio, errore,* s. m. *colpa,* s. f.

HALM [the stem or stalk of corn from the root to the ear] *stoppia,* s. f.

HALO, s. [a certain meteor in form of a bright circle that surrounds the sun, moon, or stars] *alone,* s. m. *quella ghirlanda di lume non suo, che vedesi intorno al sole, alla luna, o altro pianeta.*

HA'LSER, s. [a cable to hale a ship or barge along a river or channel] *fune da rimurchiare navi, alzana.*

HA'LSONG, s. [or pillory] *berlina,* s. f.

HA'LSIER, s. [he that hales or draws a ship or barge along the river] *colui che rimurchia un vascello tirando l'alzana.*

HALT, s. [or stand] *alto, termine militare.*

To make a halt, *fare alto, fermarsi, ed è proprio degli eserciti.*

To halt [to stop] *far alto, fermarsi.*

To halt [to go lame] *zoppicare, andar zoppo.*

You halt before you are lame, *vo'gridate prima che vi si faccia del male.*

Don't halt before a cripple, *non zoppicare avanti un zoppo; non nomina la corda a chi è stato impiccato il padre.*

HA'LTER, s. [a rope to tie about the neck of a horse] *cavezza,* s. f.

Halter [a rope to tie about the neck of a malefactor] *capestro,* s. m. *corda,* s. f.

Halter-sick [that deserves to be hanged] *una forca, uno scellerato.*

To HA'LTER, *legare con una corda.*

HA'LTERED, adj. *legato con una corda.*

HALVES, *plurale di* half.

HAM, s. [the part behind the knee] *garretto, e garetto,* s. m.

Ham [the leg and thigh of a hog] *presciutto.*

A Westphalia ham, *un presciutto di Vestfalia.*

HAMES, s. [the two crooked pieces of wood which encompass a horse collar] *asticelle che circondano il collare d'un cavallo.*

HA'MKIN, s. [a pudding made in a shoulder of mutton] *ripieno, fatto in una spalla di castrato.*

HA'MLET, s. [a little town] *un casale, un picciol villaggio.*

HA'MMER, s. *martello.*

To drive a nail with a hammer, *ficcare un chiodo con un martello.*

To HA'MMER [to beat with a hammer] *martellare, percuotere col martello.*

To hammer a dish, *martellare un piatto, batterlo ben bene.*

To hammer in one's speech, *balbettare, balbetticare, pronunziar male, e con difficoltà la parole.*

To hammer upon a thing [to be in a quandary] *esitare, star dubbioso, dubitare, non saper a che risolversi, esser nell' incertezza.*

To hammer out one's own fortune, *esser fabbro della sua propria fortuna, avanzarsi, aggrandirsi colla sua industria.*

To hammer a thing into one's head, *ficcare che che sia in testa ad uno.*

To HA'MMER, *essere affaccendato, aver molte cose a fare, e farle.*

HA'MMERED, adj. *martellato,* v. To hammer.

Hammered money, *moneta battuta.*

HAMMERING, s. *il martellare.*

I hear

I hear a great hammering, *odo un grande strepito di martelli.*

A hammering upon a thing, *dubbio, irresoluzione, incertezza.*

HA'MMOCK, s. [a little hanging bed on ship-board] *piccolo letticciuolo sospeso in un vascello.*

HA'MPER, s. [a sort of strong basket] *paniere, cesto,* s. m.

To HA'MPER [to entangle to perplex] *imbrogliare, intrigare, confondere, imbarazzare,* pret. *confusi.*

HA'MPERED, adj. *imbrogliato, intrigato, confuso, imbarazzato.*

HA'MSEL [hamlet] *un casale, un picciolo villaggio.*

HAMSO'KEN, } s. [the crime of vio-
HOMESOKEN, } lently assaulting a man in his own house] *il delitto d'assaltare un uomo nella sua propria casa.*

To HAM-STRING, *tagliare i garretti.*

HA'NAPER, s. *il tesoro; la tesoreria, l'erario.*

HAND, s. [a member of the body] *mano,* s. f.

The right or the left hand, *la man dritta, la man manca.*

Lend me your hand a little, *datemi la mano un poco.*

To fall into one's hands, *venir nelle mani altrui.*

I have a note under his hand, *io ho una cedula scritta di sua mano.*

To have a business in hand, or to be in hand with a business, *avere un negozio fra le mani.*

To give one the upper hand, *dar la man dritta ad uno.*

To fight hand to hand, *venire alle prese.*

Under hand, *sotto mano, segretamente.*

To go hand in hand, *tenersi per la mano, andar del pari.*

He is my right hand [or my best help] *egli è la mia man dritta, il mio gran sostegno.*

To have one's hands full [to have work enough upon one's hands] *aver molti affari nelle mani.*

Hand [writing] *mano, scrittura.*

I know his hand, *conosco la sua mano, o la sua scrittura.*

A horse fifteen hands high, *un cavallo che ha quindici palmi d' altezza.*

On the one hand, *da una parte.*

On the other hand, *dall' altra parte.*

I have it from very good hands, *lo so da persona di fede.*

We have it from several hands, *ne abbiamo l'avviso da molte parti.*

To have a thing from the best hand, *saper una cosa originariamente.*

A hand in hand ring, *una fede.*

Near at hand, *quì vicino, non molto lontano da quì.*

To pay money in hand, *dar danari per caparra.*

To buy things at the best hand or at the first hand, *comprare una cosa a buon mercato, di prima mano.*

You buy always at the worst hand, *voi comprate da quelli che vendono il più caro, o da quelli che vendono le peggio cose.*

To take in hand, *intraprendere, impegnarsi in qualche cosa.*

That's the business now in hand, *questo è l' affare del quale si tratta.*

To go from the business in hand, *digredire dal suo soggetto.*

To be in hand with a business, *esser attorno a qualche cosa, averla fra le mani.*

I have been long in hand with it, *è un pezzo che vi sono attorno.*

To be in hand with one, *esser in trattato con uno, negoziare con lui.*

To have a good hand at cards, *aver buon giuoco.*

To make a hand of a thing, *far durare una cosa con fine di profittarne più, tirarla alla lunga.*

To have a hand in a business, *aver parte in un negozio.*

He had a hand in the plot, *egli era complice della congiura.*

To get the upper hand or the better of it, *restar superiore, aver l' avvantaggio.*

Keep off your hands, *non lo toccate.*

To lay violent hands on one's self, *ammazzarsi, darsi la morte.*

To live from hand to mouth, *vivere alla giornata.*

To bring up a child by hand, *allevare un bambino colla pappa.*

They are hand and glove one with another, *eglino sono come pane e cacio insieme, due anime in un nocciolo.*

To drink hand to fist, *bere leccessivamente.*

To go hand in hand in a business, *fare una cosa di concerto.*

To be on the mending hand, *star meglio, cominciare a riaversi.*

To part even hands, *separarsi senza alcuno vantaggio, nè dall' una parte, nè dall' altra.*

Out of hand, *subito, presto, speditamente.*

To bear one in hand [to make him believe the thing will be done] *far credere, dare ad intendere che una cosa si farà.*

Hand over head, *inconsideratamente, temerariamente, a caso, a catafascio, a vanvera.*

To take one in hand, *volerla con alcuno, pigliarla con alcuno.*

We want more hands to do this, *abbiamo bisogno d' altra gente per far ciò.*

To be heart and hand for a thing, *esser incapricciato d'una cosa.*

The hand of a watch, *l'ago d'un oriuolo.*

Under hand dealings, *pratiche sorde o segrete.*

Hand-basket, *paniere con manico, sporta.*

A hand-bell, *un campanello.*

Hands-breath, *la larghezza della mano.*

Hand-writing, *mano, scrittura.*

Hand-fetters, *manette,* s. f.

Hand-gun, *schioppo,* s. m.

Hand-gallop, *piccolo galoppo.*

Hand-mill, *mulinello,* s. m.

Hand-strokes, *colpi di mano.*

To come to hand-strokes, *venire alle prese, o alle mani.*

Hand-cloth [handkerchief] *fazzoletto,* s. m.

Hand-saw, *seghetta,* s f.

To HAND, *dar la mano.*

To hand a thing to one [to convey it to him from hand to hand] *dare una cosa ad uno da mano a mano.*

To hand a lady into a coach, *menare per la mano una dama alla carrozza.*

HA'NDED, adj. *dato di mano in mano.*

A two-handed fellow [a strong lusty fellow] *un uomo forte, gagliardo, robusto.*

Right-handed, *manritto, che adopera la man dritta.*

Left-handed, *mancino, che adopera la man sinistra.*

HA'NDFUL, s. *manata,* s. f. *pugno,* s. m.

HA'NDKERCHIEF, s. *fazzoletto, moccichino,* s. m. *pezzuola,* s. f.

To blow one's nose with a handkerchief, *soffiarsi il naso. con un fazzoletto.*

A neck-handkerchief, *un fazzoletto pel collo.*

The holy handkerchief, *il santo sudario.*

HA'NDLE, s. *manico, orecchio,* s. m.

The handle of a knife, *il manico d'un coltello.*

The handle of a pot, pail, or basket, *l' orecchio d'una pignatta, d'una secchia, o d'un paniere.*

The handle of a sword, *l' impugnatura d'una spada.*

To HA'NDLE [to feel with the hand] *maneggiare, toccare, trattare colle mani.*

To handle a business, *maneggiare, governare un negozio.*

To handle a subject, *trattare, discorrere, parlare d'un soggetto.*

HA'NDLED, adj. *maneggiato, toccato, trattato.*

Very ill handled [ill used] *ben maltrattato.*

HA'NDLING, s. *il maneggiare.*

The handling of a business, *il maneggio d'un affare.*

HA'NDMAID, or HANDMA'IDEN, s. *una serva.*

HANDS OFF, *frase volgare equivalente a quelle nostre, Non toccate; tenete le mani a voi; lasciate stare.*

HA'NDSAILS, s. *vele che si maneggiano colle mani.*

To HA'NDSELL, *far uso d'una cosa per la prima volta.*

HA'NDSOME, adj. [beautiful] *bello, leggiadro, vezzoso.*

A handsome woman, *una bella donna.*

A handsome present, *una bel regalo.*

A handsome treat, *un pasto nobile.*

It is not handsome for you to say so, *non vi sta bene, non vi conviene di parlare in questo modo.*

HA'NDSOMLY, adv. *bellamente, con bel modo, acconciamente, pulitamente, vezzosamente*

vezzosamente, piacevolmente, molto bene, ornatamente, garbatamente.

She is handsomely drest, *ella è acconciamente, pulitamente vestita.*

He writes very handsomely, *scrive molto pulito, o molto bene.*

HA'NDSOMENESS, s. *bellezza, beltà, leggiadria*, s. f.

HA'NDY, adj. [ready with the hand] *destro, accommodato a operare, abile.*

That thing lies very handy, *quella cosa sta bene a mano.*

Handy-blows, or handy-strokes, *colpi di mano.*

Handy-craft, *mestiere, arte meccanica.*

A handy craft's-man, *un uomo di mestiere, un artigiano.*

Handy-work, *opera manuale.*

To HANG, *appiccare, attaccare, impiccare.*

To hang one's hat to a nail, *appiccare il capello ad un chiodo.*

To hang a malefactor, *impiccare un criminale, giustiziarlo.*

Go hang yourself, *andate a farvi impiccare, andate alla forca.*

To hang a room, *tappezzare una camera, pararla con tappezzerie, e simili.*

To hang, verb neut. *pendere, star sospeso, appiccato a che che si sia.*

To hang in the air, *pendere, star sospeso in aria.*

It hangs too much that way, *pende troppo inverso quella parte.*

These things don't hang well together, *queste cose non s'accordano, non convengono bene insieme.*

To hang up, *appiccare, attaccare, impiccare.*

To hang up, *pendere, star sospeso.*

To hang down one's head, *abbassare, chinare la testa.*

To hang by, *appendere.*

To hang loose, to hang dangling, *pendere, star pendolone.*

To hang about one's neck, *tenere le braccia al collo ad uno.*

To hang back [to lag in a thing] *tirarsi indietro, rinculare.*

They hung out a white flag, *innalberarono bandiera bianca.*

HA'NGED, adj. *appiccato, attaccato, impiccato.*

He deserves to be hanged, *egli merita la forca.*

Go and be hanged, *andate a farvi impiccare, andate alle forche, andate in tanta malora.*

HA'NGER, s. [a short crooked sword] *coltellacrio*, s. m.

A hanger on [or spunger] *uno scrocco, uno scroccone, un parasito.*

Pot hanger, *catena del cammino.*

HA'NGING, s. *l' appiccare, v.* To hang.

Marriage and hanging go by destiny, *il matrimonio, e la forca son cose del destino.*

Hangings [for a room] *tappezzerie, arazzi.*

A hanging look, *viso d'impiccato.*

HA'NGMAN, s. [executioner] *carnefice, boja*, s. m.

A HANK OF THREAD, *una matassa di filo.*

Hank [fondness, or great inclination] *inclinazione, propensione, voglia, volontà*, s. m. *talento, desiderio*, s. m.

To have a great hank upon one, *aver grande autorità o potere sopra una persona, essere in credito o in autorità con uno.*

To HA'NKER, *ansiare, ambire, desiderare ansiosamente.*

HA'NKERING, s. *inclinazione, propensione, voglia, desidero, ansietà.*

HANS-TOWNS [certain free towns in Germany, in number twenty-seven, as Hamburg, Lubeck, Magdenbourg, &c. joining in league offensive and defensive against all enemies whatsoever] *città ansiatiche, certe città libere in Germania, ventisette in numero come Amburgo, Lubec, Magdebourg, le quali sono collegate insieme in lega offensiva, e defensiva, contro qualsivoglia nemico.*

HANS-EN KELDER, s. *vocabolo Olandese* [jack in a cellar, a child in the mother's belly] *bambino che è nell' utero della madre.*

Here's, madam, a health to the hansen kelder, *signora, alla salute del bambino del quale siete gravida.*

HANSEA'TICK, adj. [belonging to hans-town] *ansiatico.*

HA'NSEL, s. *strenna*, s. f. *termine di mercante, o di bottegajo.*

To take a hansel, *cominciare a vendere.*

To HA'NSEL [to give a hansel] *esser il primo a comprare, v.* To handsel.

I have hanselled your shop, *io sono stato il primo a comprare nella vostra bottega.*

To hansel a thing [to use it the first time] *servirsi d'una cosa per la prima volta.*

HAN'T, *è una abbreviazione volgare per* have not, *e* has not.

I han't seen him, *non l'ho veduto.*

HAP, s. [chance] *accidente, caso.*

By good hap, *per buona fortuna.*

To HAP, *arrivare, accadere, succedere.*

Hap what hap can, *arrivi, o accada quel che si voglia.*

If he should hap to come, *dato il caso che venisse, se per fortuna venisse.*

Should I hap to discourse, *se per accidente venissi a parlarne.*

HA'PLESS, adj. [unhappy, unfortunate, luckless] *sfortunato, disgraziato, sventurato, malavventurato.*

HA'PLY, adv. *forse, può essere, per accidente, a caso.*

HA'PNEO, adj. *arrivato, accaduto, successo.*

To HA'PPEN [to fall out] *arrivare, accadere, succedere, avvenire*, pret. *accadde, successe, avvenne.*

I happened to speak of it, *m'accadde di parlarne.*

Whatever happens, *succeda quel che si voglia, in ogni modo.*

It happened well for you, *questa fu una buona fortuna per voi.*

I happened unfortunately that I was not there, *intervenne per disgrazia ch'io non mi trovai presente.*

As it happens, *ad ogni caso, in ogni modo, come vien viene.*

HA'PPENED, *succeduto, accaduto.*

HA'PPIER, } *sono il comparativo,*
HA'PPIEST, } *e il superlativo di* Happy.

HA'PPILY, adv. *felicemente, fortunatamente, per fortuna.*

HA'PPINESS, s. *felicità, ventura, sorte, fortuna*, s. f.

HA'PPY, adj. [blessed] *felice, avventuroso, venturoso, prospero, benavventurato.*

To lead a happy life, *menare una vita felice.*

Happy had it been for me if he had not died, *felice me se non fosse morto.*

Happy be lucky [let it go how it will] *arcada quel che si voglia.*

To make happy, *felicitare, render felice.*

HAPSE, s. [a catch or bolt of a door] *catenaccio, chiavistello*, s. m.

To hapse, verb act. *incatenacciare, fermare con catenaccio.*

HA'PSED, adj. *incatenacciato.*

HA'QUETON, s. *pezzo d'armatura, usato anticamente.*

HA'RANGUE, s. [an oration or speech made in publick] *arringa, orazione*, s. f. *ragionamento pubblico.*

He began to harangue with these words, *diede principio alla sua arringa con queste parole.*

To HA'RANGUE [to make a speech in publick] *arringare, far publica diceria, parlar in pubblico.*

HA'RANGUED, adj. *arringato.*

To HA'RASS [to tire, to weary out] *straccare, stancare, faticare.*

To harass an army, *straccare un esercito.*

To harass a country [to ruin it with continual inroads] *rovinare, distruggere, scorrere, dare il guasto ad un paese con continue scorrerie.*

HA'RASSED, adj. *straccato, stancato, faticato.*

HA'RBINGER, s. [an officer belonging to the court, who provides lodgings in a prince's progress] *furiere*, s. m. *ufficiale che va avanti a preparare i quartieri.*

HA'RBOUR, s. [a station where ships may ride safely at anchor] *porto*, s. m.

To get into a harbour, *entrare in un porto.*

Harbour [shelter, place of safety] *porto, ricovero, riparo, rifugio*, s. m.

To HA'RBOUR [to receive, to entertain, to lodge] *accogliere, e accorre, albergare, alloggiare, ricevere in casa ad albergo*. pret. *accolsi.*

No body would harbour us, *nessuno volle accoglierci, o albergarci.*

To harbour prophane thoughts, *concepire profani pensieri.*

This place harbours a great deal of dust, *questo luogo è pieno di molta polvere.*

To harbour a stag, *avere il cervo a cavaliere, termine di cacciatore, quando vedono il cervo u covo.*

HA'RBOURED, adj. *accolto, albergato, alloggiato, v.* To harbour.

HA'RBOURLESS, adj. [that has no harbour] *che non ha porto, senza porto.*

An harbourless coast, *una spiaggia senza porto.*

Harbourless [that has no shelter or abode] *che non ha ricetto o domicilio, vagabondo.*

HARD, adj. [not soft] *duro, sodo, che resiste al tatto contrario di tenero.*

A hard and solid body, *un corpo duro, e sodo.*

A hard capon, *un cappone duro, che non se ne può masticare la carne.*

Hard [sad] *duro, nojoso, spiacevole, aspro, faticoso.*

'Tis a hard case, *questo è pur ben duro.*

Hard [ill] *cattivo.*

Hard face, *cattiva ciera.*

Hard [not easy] *duro, faticoso, difficile.*

A hard lesson, *una lezione difficile.*

A hard word, *parola dura, difficile a pronunciare.*

Hard to be understood, *difficile ad intendere, oscuro.*

Hard to be pleased, *difficile a contentare, incomodo, bizzarro, fantastico.*

Hard to come at, *difficile ad ottenersi.*

Hard to come at, *di difficile accesso, parlando d'un luogo.*

Hard to get, *raro.*

Hard [rigorous] *duro, rigoroso, crudele, severo, aspro, inesorabile.*

A hard battle, *un duro combattimento.*

A hard master, *un padrone, o maestro severo.*

A hard winter, *un aspro, o rigoroso verno.*

Hard of taste, *aspro, arcigno.*

Hard wine, *vino aspro.*

These are hard times, *questo è un tempo duro, o infelice.*

A hard stile, *uno stile aspro, che non è facile.*

He is a very hard [or covetous] man, *egli è un uomo che sta troppo in sul tirato.*

You are too hard [you ask too much for your commodities] *voi siete troppo caro, voi angariate troppo per le vostre mercanzie.*

As cunning as he is, I was too hard for him, *per astuto ch' egli si sia, io l' ho acchiappato.*

Hard-witted, *duro di testa, di dura cervice.*

Hard of hearing, *sordastro, quasi sordo.*

Hard-hearted, *di duro cuore, crudele, efferato.*

Hard-heartedness, *crudeltà, efferatezza.*

It is hard for me to conceive, *a gran pena posso concepire.*

Hard of belief, *incredulo.*

A hard student, *una persona che studia molto, troppo applicata allo studio.*

Hard drinking, *eccesso nel bere.*

To entertain hard thoughts of one, *avere cattiva opinione d'una persona.*

Hard to deal withall, *intrattabile, fiero, feroce.*

The fever is hard upon him, *ha una febbre acuta, o violenta.*

There passed some hard words betwixt them, *ebbero qualche parole insieme.*

Hard frost, *gran gelo.*

To make hard, *indurare, indurire, fare divenir duro.*

To strike hard, *batter forte.*

The wind blows hard, *fa gran vento.*

It freezes hard, *gela forte.*

Hard [roughly] *rozzamente, stizzosamente, aspramente, bruscamente.*

To speak hard to one, *parlar bruscamente ad uno, con maniera rozza e brusca.*

To follow one hard, *seguitare uno d'appresso, incalzarlo.*

To be hard put to it for a livelihood, *stentare a vivere.*

He works very hard, *lavora notte e giorno, lavora come un forzato.*

It rains very hard, *piove strabocchevolmente, diluvia.*

To found a letter hard, *pronunciare una lettera aspramente.*

To drink hard, *bere eccessivamente, trincare.*

It goes hard with him, *le sue cose vanno male.*

Hard by, *qui vicino.*

He lodges hard by, *dimora qui vicido.*

Hard-mouthed horse, *cavallo duro di bocca.*

Hard-roed herring, *una aringa che ha delle uova.*

Hard-witted [dull witted] *stupido, intormentito, insensato, goffo, melenso, sciocco, scimunito.*

To HA'RDEN [to make hard] *indurare, indurire, far divenir duro, pres. indurisco.*

To harden one's self to hardship, *farsi, incallirsi, assuefarsi, fare il callo alla fatica.*

HA'RDENED, adj. *indurato, indurito, incallito.*

HA'RDILY, adv. *arditamente, animosamente, con ardire, coraggiosamente.*

HA'RDINESS, s. *arditezza, s. f. ardire, animo, coraggio, s. m.*

Hardiness of constitution, *temperamento, complessione robusta.*

HA'RDISH, adj. *duriccio, alquanto duro.*

HA'RDLY, adv. [with much ado] *appena, a pena, a grande stento, difficilmente.*

I can hardly believe it, *stento a crederlo.*

He will hardly compass it, *stenterà molto a finirlo.*

Hardly [severely] *duramente, aspramente, crudelmente, severamente, rigorosamente.*

To live hardly [to live poorly] *menare una vita stentata, vivere miseramente.*

Things hardly attained, are long retained, *quelle cose che difficilmente s'imparano, difficilmente si scordano.*

To be hardly put to it, *esser maltrattato.*

HA'RDNESS, s. *durezza, fermezza, solidità, quel che rende un corpo duro.*

The hardness of stones, *la durezza delle pietre.*

Hardness [cruelty] *durezza, rigidezza, asprezza, barbarie, inumanità, crudeltà, s. f. rigore, s. m.*

Hardness of heart [insensibility] *durezza di cuore, insensibilità.*

Hardness [difficulty] *difficoltà, s. f.*

Hardness [covetousness] *avarizia, ingordigia, umore avaro, e interessato.*

HARDS, s. [hards of flax or tow] *capecchio, s. m. quella materia grossa e liscosa che si trae della prima pettinatura del lino avanti alla stoppa, e simile anche alla canapa.*

HA'RDSHIP, s. *pena, fatica, s. f. affanno, travaglio, s. m.*

Inured to hardship, *fatto, assuefatto, incallito alla fatica.*

HARDWARE, s. [manufactures of metal] *cose di metallo, manifatture di metallo.*

HARDWA'REMAN, s. *uno che fabbrica o vende cose di metallo, come bottoni, fibbie, catenelle d'orologio e simili.*

HA'RDY, adj. [inured to hardship] *fatto, indurito alla fatica, robusto, forte.*

Hardy [bold] *ardito, valoroso, prode, coraggioso.*

Fool-hardy, *temerario.*

HARE, s. [an animal well known] *lepre, s. m.*

To start a hare, *levar una lepre.*

A young hare, *un leprone, un leprettino, leprottino, leproncello, leprattò.*

Of or belonging to a hare, *leporino.*

Hare-foot [an herb] *piè di lepre.*

Hare-lip, *labbro leprino, labbro fesso che si vede qualche volta alle persone.*

Hare-brained, adj. *leggiero di cervello, pazzesco.*

Hare-hearted [timorous] *timoroso, pauroso, timido, che ha poco cuore.*

To HARE, *spaventare.*

You hare me so that I don't know what I do, *voi mi stordite talmente, ch'io non so quel che mi faccia.*

HA'RED, adj. *spaventato, stordito.*

HA'RIER, s. [a sort of hunting dog] *spezie di levriere.*

To HARK [to listen] *ascoltare, star attento a udire.*

HARK, interj. [list! hear! listen!] *odi! senti! sta attento!*

HARL, s. *le fibre della canapa.*

Harl [any filamentous substance] *qualunque materia fibrosa.*

HA'RLEQUIN, s. *arlecchino, trossaldino; buffone.*

HA'RLOT, s. [a proud whore] *una puttana, una zambracca, una bagascia.*

HA'RLOTRY, s. [whoring] *puttanesimo.*

Harlotry, *voce di disprezzo per una donna.*

HARM, s. [hurt, damage] *danno, pregiudizio, torto, male, s. m.*

To do one harm [to hurt him] *far del male ad uno, offenderlo.*

It is no harm to try, *non sarà gran fatto se proviamo, il tentar non nore.*

Harm [disaster] *disgrazia,* s. f. *disastro,* s. m.

To keep out of harm's way, *mettersi in sicurtà, in luogo sicuro, fuor di pericolo.*

Harm watch, harm catch, *anche delle volpi si piglia; e anche gli astuti talora sono ingannati.*

To HARM [to do harm] *far male.*

HA'RMFUL, adj. *nocivo, contrario, che fa male, dannoso.*

HA'RMLESS, adj. [that does no harm] *innocente, che non può far male.*

He is a poor harmless man, *egli è un uomo di buona pasta, che non fa male a nessuno.*

He came off harmless, *egli n' è uscito salvo, senza alcun male.*

To save one harmless, *risarcire, rifare i danni altrui.*

HA'RMLESSLY, adv. *innocentemente, semplicemente, senza malizia.*

HA'RMLESSNESS, s. *qualità di cosa che non può far male.*

Harmlessness [innocence] *innocenza, semplicità.*

HARMO'NICAL, } adj. [full of
HARMO'NICK, } harmony] *ar-*
HA'RMONIOUS, } *monioso, armonico, che ha, o rende armonia.*

HARMO'NIOUSLY, adv. *armoniosamente, dolcemente, con armonia.*

HA'RMONY, s. [or m lod] *armonia, consonanza, e concento sì di voci, sì di strumenti, melodia.*

HA'RNESS, s [all the accoutrements of an armed horseman] *arnese, arme di soldato a cavallo.*

Horse-harness, *arnesi, arredi, fornimenti di cavallo.*

Coach-harness, *arnesi, guernimenti di carrozza.*

To HA'RNESS [to accoutre, to dress with harness] *arredare, fornire, mettere in arnese.*

To harness a horse, *arredare un cavallo.*

HARP, s. [a musical instrument] *arpa,* s. m. *strumento musicale di corde di minugia.*

To HARP [to play upon the harp] *suonar dell' arpa.*

To harp always upon the same string, *cantar la canzone dell' uccellino, cantar sempre la medesima cosa, ripetere il medesimo soggetto.*

What do you harp at? [what do you mean?] *che volete dire? chè intendente dire per questo?*

HA'RPER, s. *suonator d'arpa.*

HA'RPING-IRON, s. [irons to strike great fish with] *uncino di ferro, il quale serve alla pesca delle balene e altri pesci grossi.*

HARPONE'ERS, s. [they who catch fish with harping-irons] *quelli che pigliano pesci cogli uncini di ferro.*

HA'RPSICORD, s. [a musical instrument] *arpicordo, buonaccordo,* s. m.

HA'RPY, s. [a fabulous monster] *arpia,* s. f. *mostro favoloso alato.*

A harpy [a griping woman] *un' arpia, una donna avara.*

HA'RQUEBUSS, s. [a sort of hand-gun] *archibuso,* s. m.

HA'RRIDAN, s. *cavallo pieno di guidaleschi, vecchio e buon a nulla; rozza, rozzone, rozzaccia.*

HA'RROW, s. [a drag with iron teeth to break the clods of earth after ploughing] *erpice,* s. f. *strumento di legname con denti di ferro, che tirato da' buoi, e calcato dal bifolco, spiana, e trita la terra de' campi.*

To HA'RROW [to break the clods with the harrow] *erpicare, spianare, e tritar coll' erpice la terra de' campi lavorati.*

To harrow a field, *erpicare un campo.*

HA'RROWED, adj. *erpicato.*

HA'RROWER, s. *erpicatore,* s. m. *bifolco che erpica.*

To HA'RRY [to hare or hurry] *tempestare, affannare, faticare, tormentare, straccare.*

HA'RRIED, adj. *tempestato, affannato, faticato, tormentato, straccato.*

HARSH, adj. [of taste] *aspro, lazzo, afro, rozzo.*

This is a harsh sort of wine, *questo vino è afro.*

A harsh word, *una parola dura, aspra, che offende l'orecchie.*

A harsh master, *un maestro austero, severo, rigido.*

HA'RSHLY, adv. *aspramente, agramente, rozzamente, severamente, rigorosamente, duramente.*

HA'RSHNESS, s. [of taste] *asprezza, rozzezza, afrezza.*

Harshness of sound, *durezza che offende l'orecchie, suono dispiacevole, suono ingrato.*

Harshness [severity] *asprezza, severità, durezza, rigidezza,* s. f.

HA'RSLETS, or HOGS-HARSLETS, [entrails] *interiora di porca.*

HART, s. [a stag of five years compleat] *cervo,* s. m.

A hart-royal, *cervo che è stato cacciato dal re, e che è scampato.*

Hart's horn, *corno di cervo.*

Hart's tongue [a plant] *scolopendria,* s. f.

Hart-wort, *aristologia,* s. f. *spezie d'erba.*

Harts-trefoil, *melilofo,* s. m.

HA'RVEST, s. [the time of reaping] *mietitura, ricolta,* s. f.

To make harvest, *far la ricolta, mietere.*

He sows for harvest [he spends in order to get] *e' semina per ricogliere o mietere.*

Harvest-time, *la mietitura, il tempo del mietere.*

Harvest man, *mietitore, segatore.*

To HA'RVEST, *mietere.*

HAS [the third person singular of the verb to have] *ha.*

He or she has, *egli, o ella ha.*

HA'SEL, *v.* Hazel.

HASH, s. [a dish of minced meat] *guazzetto all' Inglese.*

HASP, s. [a reel to wind yarn on] *aspo, naspo,* s. m.

HA'SSOCK, s. [a bass or cushion made of rushes, to kneel upon in churches] *spezie d'inginocchiatoja fatta di giunchi sopra 'l quale s'inginocchiano nelle chiese in Inghilterra.*

HAST, *è la seconda persona del presente dell' indicativo del verbo* To have. Ex. Thou hast, *tu hai.*

HASTE, s. [nimbleness, speed, hurry] *fretta, prescia, prestezza, sollecitudine,* s f.

To do a thing in haste, *fare che che si sia in fretta.*

With all the haste that may be, in all haste, in post haste, *in gran fretta, con tutta la sollecitudine possibile.*

Make all the haste you can, *fate con tutta prestezza, affrettatevi quanto potete.*

To make haste, *affrettarsi, avacciarsi, sbrigarsi.*

Make haste thither, *andatevi presto.*

What haste you are in, *perchè così affrettato.*

The more haste the worse speed, *chi troppo s'affretta meno avanza.*

To haste [to make haste] *affrettarsi, avacciarsi, spacciarsi, sbrigarsi.*

To HA'STEN [to quicken, to push] *affrettare, avacciare, sollecitare.*

To hasten one's death, *affrettare, precipitare l'altrui morte.*

To HA'STEN, verb neut. *affrettarsi, avacciarsi, spacciarsi, sbrigarsi.*

He hastened home, *sen' andò a dirittura a casa.*

HA'STENED, adj. *affrettato, avacciato, spacciato, sbrigato.*

HA'STILY, adv. [in haste] *in fretta, affrettatamente, festinatamente, frettolosamente.*

Hastily [in a passion] *in collera, stizzosamente.*

HA'STINESS, s. *prestezza, prontezza, sollecitudine.*

Hastiness [passion] *collera, stizza, passione,* s. f.

HA'STINGS, s. [fruit early ripe] *frutti primaticci.*

Green hastings, *piselli primaticci.*

HA'STY, adj. [done in haste] *affrettato, precipitato, avacciato, fatto in fretta, frettoloso, avaccioso.*

Hasty [impatient] *frettoloso, impaziente.*

Hasty [soon angry] *pronto, violento, stizzoso, bilioso, che si mette facilmente in collera, rollerico.*

Hasty-pudding, *sorta di cibo all' Inglese.*

HAT, s. [a covering for the head] *cappello,* s. m.

A beaver hat, *un castoro.*

A hat band, *un cordone di cappello.*

To put on or pull off one's hat, *mettersi, e levarsi il cappello.*

To put on one's hat, *mettersi il cappello, coprirsi.*

Hat-maker, *cappellajo,* s. m.

An old hat, *un cappellaccio.*

HATCH, s. [a sort of half door frequently grated and spiked with iron spikes] *cancello,* s. m. *spezie di mezza*

porta

porta guernita dalle parte di sopra con punte di ferro.

Hatch [brood of young birds] *covata*, s. f. *quella quantità d' uova che in una volta cova l' uccello.*

To HATCH [to breed young by sitting upon eggs] *covare; nascere; parlando degli uccelli, quando escono dall' uova.*

To hatch [to contrive or plot] *covare, macchinare, tramare, far tratti, e pratiche.*

To hatch some mischief, *covare, tramare qualche male.*

HA'TCHED, adj. *covato, nato, macchinato, tramato.*

You count your chickens before they be hatched, *voi contate senza l' oste.*

You must not count your chickens before they be hatched, *non bisogna dir quattro prima che tu l' abbi nel sacco.*

HA'TCHELL, s. [a tool to dress flax, hemp, &c] *cardo, scardasso, pettine*, s. m. *strumento con denti di ferro da scardassare lino, canapa, e simili.*

To HA'TCHELL [to dress flax, hamp, &c.] *pettinare, scardassare.*

HA'TCHELLED, adj. *pettinato, scardassato.*

HA'TCHELLER, s. *pettinatore.*

HA'TCHES, s. [in a ship, the coverings in the midship, as it were trap-doors, by which any goods of bulk are let down into the hold] *sportelli che sono nel cassero del vascello, per dove si fanno calare le mercanzie sotto 'l ponte.*

To be under hatches [in a low condition] *condursi, trovarsi in estrema necessità; essere in cattivo stato.*

HA'TCHET, s. [a little ax] *azza, scure*, s. f.

Hatchet-helve, *manico di scure.*

Hatchet faced, *sfregiato, che ha il viso sfigurato.*

HATE, v. Hatred.

To HATE [to bear ill-will to] *odiare, abbominare, detestare, voler male, avere in odio.*

He hates me mortally, *m' odia alla morte.*

I hate a lye; *io sono nemico della bugia.*

To hate each other, *odiarsi.*

HA'TED, adj. *odiato, abbomminato, detestato.*

HA'TEFUL, adj. *odioso, spiacevole, abbominevole, detestabile, odiabile, odievole.*

HA'TEFULLY, adv. *odiosamente, abbominevolmente.*

HA'TEFULNESS, s. *qualità odiosa, e spiacevole.*

HA'TER, s. *odiatore, nemico*, s. m.

A hater of women, *un nemico del sesso.*

A man hater, *un misantroppo.*

HATH, ex. he or she hath, *egli, o ella ha.*

HA'TING, s. *l' odiare, l' avere in odio.*

HA'TRED, s. [ill-will] *odio*, s. m.

To bear an hatred against one, *avere in odio una persona, non poterla patire.*

HA'TTER, s. [hat-maker] *cappellajo*, s. m.

To HA'TTER, *tormentare, stancare.*

HA'UBERG, s. [a coat of mail] *usbergo, armatura.*

To HAVE [to possess] *avere.*

He has a fine house, *egli ha una bella casa.*

I have it at my tongue's end, *l' ho alla punta della lingua.*

What would you have? *che volete, che pretendete?*

I have it from a good author, *lo so da buona parte.*

I have it from him, *l'ho inteso da lui.*

To have a thing by heart, *sapere che che si sia a mente.*

Have a care of it, *abbiatene cura.*

Have a care of yourself, *badate a voi, state in cervello.*

I must have it with me, *bisogna che lo porti meco.*

To have a foresight, *prevedere*, pret. *previddi.*

God have you in his keeping, *Iddio vi conservi.*

He won't do as I would have him, *non vuol fare quel che li dico, non vuol pigliare il mio consiglio.*

I will have it so, *voglio che sia così.*

I would have you know that I am not a fool, *sappiate ch' io non sono un gonzo.*

As fortune would have, *per buona fortuna.*

Let have his desert, *che sia trattato come merita.*

Do well and have well, *chi fa bene, bene as petti.*

When will you let me have my book? *quando volete restituirmi il mio libro?*

I would have you write to me every week, *vorrei che mi scriveste ogni settimana.*

Have me excused, *scusatemi, perdonatemi.*

Have your wits about you, *state in cervello.*

Have him away, *menatelo, portatelo via.*

HA'VEN, s. [harbour] *porto.*

HA'VENER, s. [an overseer of a port] *un ispettore o custode d'un porto di mare.*

HA'VER, s. *un che ha, che possiede, che tiene.*

HA'UGHT, adj. *v.* Haughty.

HA'UGHTILY, adv. *fieramente, alteramente, superbamente, orgogliosamente, arrogantemente.*

HA'UGHTINESS, s. *fierezza, alterigia, arroganza*, s. f. *orgoglio*, s. m.

HA'UGHTY, adj. *fiero, arrogante, altiero, superbo, orgoglioso, prosuntuoso*, s. m.

HA'VIOUR, s. [behaviour, conduct of manners] *maniera, modo di condursi, modo di vivere; condotta.*

To HAUL A SHIP, *rimurchiare un vascello.*

HAUL, s. *sforzo nel tirare a se.*

HAUNT, s. [hold of some beasts] *covolo, covile.*

Haunt [of habit, or custom, of being often in a certain place] *costume che uno ha di essere spesso in certo luogo.*

A haunt [place of meeting] *bazzica, conversazione, compagnia.*

To HAUNT [to frequent] *frequentare, bazzicare, conversare, praticare, usare in un luogo.*

To haunt bawdy houses, *bordellare, praticare i bordelli*

HA'UNTED, adj. *frequentato, bazzicato, conversato, praticato.*

A house haunted with spirits, *una casa infestata dagli spiriti.*

HA'UNTER, s. *quello che bazzica, o frequenta.*

A haunter of bawdy houses, *bordelliere, frequentator di bordelli, puttaniere.*

HA'UNTING, s. *bazzica, pratica, conversazione*, s. f.

HA'VOCK, s. [waste, destruction] *guasto, danno*, s. m. *rovina, strage*, s. f.

To make havock, *sconquassare, fare strage.*

To make havock of an estate, *dissipare, distruggere, spendere, scialacquare, mandare a male i suoi beni.*

HA'UTBOY, s. *oboè; stromento musicale da fiato.*

HAW, s. [the fruit of the white-thorn shrub] *moro di spinalba.*

Haw-thorn, *spinalba.*

Haw [a web or spot in the eye] *maglia negli occhi.*

Haw [a gristle growing between the eye-lid and eye of a horse] *unghia nell' occhio d' un cavallo.*

Haw [a close or small piece of land near a house] *camperello vicino ad una casa.*

To HAW, ex. To hum and haw, *esitare, star dubbioso, dubitare.*

HAWK, s. [a bird of prey] *falcone*, s. m.

A hawk's nose, *naso aquillino.*

To be between hawk and buzzard, *esser tra l' incudine e'l martello.*

To HAWK [to go fowling with hawks] *uccellare col falcone, falconare, andare a caccia col falcone.*

To hawk [to spit, to spawl] *fornacchiare, sputar fornacchi.*

HA'WKED, adj. *fornacchiato.*

A hawked nose, *un naso acquilino.*

HA'WKERS, s. [pedlars who go about the town or country selling wares] *merciai, che vanno attorno per la città, e per la campagna vendendo mercanziuole.*

HA'WKING, s. *falconeria, caccia di falcone.*

HAY, s. [grass cut and dry'd] *fieno*, s. m.

To make hay, *segar l' erba per far del fieno.*

Make hay whilst the sun shines, *bisogna battere il ferro mentre è caldo.*

Hay-maker, *segator d' erba da far il fieno.*

Hay-

Hay-cock, *bica di fieno.*

Hay-ſtack, or Hay-rick, *un gran mucchio di fieno.*

Hay-loft, *fienile,* s. m. *luogo dove ſi ripone il fieno.*

Hay [a net to catch conies in] *galappio, lacciulo; rete da prender conigli.*

Hay [a ſort of dance] *ballo tondo, carola.*

Hay-boot [a permiſſion to take thorns to make or repair hedges] *licenza di prender pruni, per fare, o racomodare le ſiepi.*

Hay-ward, s. [a keeper of the common herd or cattle of a town] *il paſtore pubblico d'una città.*

HA'ZARD, s. [chance, peril] *riſchio, pericolo,* s. m. *ventura, incertezza,* s. f.

To run the hazard of a battle, *arriſchiar la battaglia.*

To ſtand at all hazards, *ſtarſene alla fortuna.*

To HA'ZARD [to venture] *arriſchiare, mettere in pericolo, mettere in cimento, a ripentaglio, cimentare.*

To hazard one's life, *arriſchiare o mettere a cimento la vita.*

HA'ZARDER, adj. *arriſchiato, meſſo in pericolo, in cimento, o ripentaglio, cimentato.*

HA'ZARDOUS, adj. *arriſchievole, pericolſo, dubbioſo, incerto.*

HA'ZARDOUSLY, adv. *pericoloſamente.*

HAZE, s. *nebbia,* s. f.

To HAZE, *ſpaventare.*

To haze [to be foggy or miſty] *eſſer l'aria piena di ſpeſſa nebbia.*

It hazes [it miſles ſmall rain] *piuviggina; la nebbia è foltiſſima.*

HA'ZEL, or HA'ZEL-NUT, s. *nocciuola,* s. f. *frutta nota.*

Hazel-tree, *nocciuolo,* s. m.

HA'ZY, adj. [foggy, miſty] *pien di nebbia, foltiſſima.*

He, pron. m. *egli, eſſo, colui.*

He learns very well, *egli impara molto bene,*

He that keeps God's commandments will be ſaved, *colui che oſſerva i comandamenti di Dio ſarà ſalvo.*

HE, is ſometimes uſed for a diſtinction of the male from the female, before nouns that imply both genders, *ci ſerviamo del medeſimo pronome per diſtinguere il maſchio dalla femmina nei nomi che comprendono i due generi.*

A he couſin, *un cugino.*

A he goat, *un becco.*

This pronoun is alſo thus rendered in Italian.

Here he comes, *eccolo che viene.*

If I was he, *s'io foſſi in ſuo luogo.*

HEAD, s. [that part of the body which contains the brains] *teſta,* s. f. *capo,* s. m.

The head of a man, horſe, &c. *la teſta d'un uomo, d'un cavallo,* &c.

He loſt his head, *egli ha perduto la teſta, egli è ſtato decapitato.*

A crowned head [a king or an emperor] *una teſta coronata, un re, un imperadore.*

To put a thing into one's head [to fancy a thing] *metterſi una coſa in teſta.*

I can't beat it out of his head, *non poſſo levargliedo di teſta.*

The head of a nail, pin, garlick, &c. *la teſta d'un chiodo, il capo d'uno ſpillo, d'aglio,* &c.

The bed's head, *la teſta del letto.*

The head of an army, *la teſta d'un eſercito.*

To give ſo much head, *dare un tanto per teſta a ciaſcheduno.*

To make head againſt one [to withſtand him] *far teſta ad uno, reſiſterli.*

Head to head, *a quattr' occhi.*

A fine head of hair, *una bella capelliera.*

Head [or chief] *capo.*

The pope ſtiles himſelf the head of the church, *il papa ſi dice capo della chieſa.*

The heads of a diſcourſe, *i capi, i punti principali d' un diſcorſo.*

The head of a wild boar, *il teſchio d'un cinghiale.*

The head of a river, *la ſorgente d'un fiume.*

The head of a college, *il capo, il rettore d'un collegio.*

The head of a book, *il titolo, la prima facciata d'un libro.*

The head of a lute, *il manico d'un liuto.*

The head of a ſhip, *la prua d'un vaſcello.*

The head of a cane, *il pomo d'una canna d'India.*

The head of an arrow, *la punta d' uno ſtrale.*

To draw to a head [as an impoſthume] *far capo, marcire, parlando di poſtema.*

To draw to a head [to ſum up] *ſommare, raccogliere ſommariamente i punti principali d'un diſcorſo.*

To bring a wound to a head, *far chiudere una piaga.*

Te bring a buſineſs to a head, *conchiudere, terminare un negozio.*

To hit the nail on the head, *apporſi, indovinare, dar nel ſegno, imberciare.*

To be dipt over head and ears in water, *eſſer ſommerſo nell' acqua.*

To be in love over head and ears, *eſſer eſtremamente innamorato.*

To be in debt over head and ears, *aver più debiti che non ha la lepre, eſſer molto indebitato.*

'Tis quite gone out of my head, *m'è affatto uſcito di mente.*

Hand over head, *inconſideratamente, ciecamente, temerariamente.*

To give a horſe the head, *dar la mano ad un cavallo.*

Head ache, *mal di teſta.*

The head-board of a bed, *il capezzale d'un letto.*

The head-piece of a bridle, *frontale di briglia.*

Head-piece [helmet] *cimiero, elmo, celata.*

The head-pieces of a caſk, *le doghe d'una botte.*

The head ſtall of a bridle, *la teſtiera d'una briglia,*

HE'ADSTRONG, adj. [obſtinate] *caparbio, oſtinato.*

A headſtrong horſe, *un cavallo vizioſo.*

Head quarters of an army, *i quartieri del re.*

The head man of a city, *i principali, i capi d'una città.*

HEAD LAND, *capo, promontorio.*

To HEAD [to command, to be at the head] *comandare, eſſer il primo a comandare.*

To head, *tagliar il capo, decollare.*

To head, *porre un principio ad una coſa che ne è ſenza.*

To head trees, *potar alberi.*

HE'ADACH, s. *mal di capo, dolor di teſta.*

HE'ADED, adj. [commanded] *comandato.*

Headed with iron, *che ha una punta di ferro.*

Hot-headed, *collerico, adiroſo, ſtizzoſo, bilioſo, che ſi mette facilmente in collera.*

Giddy-headed, *ſtordito, mentecatto, ſcimunito, ſcervellato, temerario.*

HE'ADILY, adv. *inconſideramente, a caſo, a vanvera, follemente, temerariamente, diſavvedutamente.*

HE'ADLESS, adj. *ſenza teſta, che non ha teſta, ſenza capo, che non ha capo.*

HE'ADLONG, adv. [with the head foremoſt] *alla impazzata, a caſo, inconſideratamente, a taſtone.*

To run headlong to ruin, *correre al precipizio, correre alla ſua rovina.*

To caſt down headlong, *precipitare.*

HE'ADSMAN, s. *il boja, il giuſtiziere, il carnefice; colui che taglia il capo a' condannati rei.*

HE'ADY, adj. [headſtrong, ſtubborn] *oſtinato, caparbio.*

Heady wine [ſtrong wine, which is apt to fly up into the head] *vino forte, fumoſo, che monta alla teſta.*

To HE'AL [to cure] *guarire, rimarginare, ſaldare, chiudere.* pref. *guariſco* pret. *chiuſi.*

To heal up a wound, *guarire, o rimarginare una ferita.*

HE'ALED, adj. *guarito, rimarginato, ſaldato, chiuſo.*

HE'ALING, s. [from to heal] *cura, guarigione, e guerigione,* s. f.

Healing, adj. *conſolidativo, atto, e buono a conſolidare.*

A healing plaiſter, *un impiaſtro conſolidativo.*

HEALTH, s. [ſoundneſs of body] *ſalute, ſanità,* s. f.

To be in health, or have one's health, *ſtar bene di ſalute, eſſer in buona ſalute.*

To drink a health, *bere alla ſalute di qualcheduno.*

HE'ALTHFUL, adj. [or wholeſome] *ſano, che ha ſanità, parlando delle perſone, ſano, ſalutifero, che conferiſce alla ſanità, parlando delle coſe.*

A healthful man, *un uomo ſano, che gode una perfetta ſalute.*

A healthful place, *un luogo ſano, ſalutifero.*

HE'ALTHFULLY, adv. *sanamente, con sanità.*

HE'ALTHFULNESS, *salute, sanità, salubrità,* s. f.

The healthfulness of the air, *la salubrità dell aria.*

HE'ALTHY, adj. *v.* Healthful.

HEAP, s. [a pile of things laid one upon another] *mucchio, fascio,* s. m. *bica, congerie, massa, catasta,* s. f.

To put in an heap, *abbicare, accumulare, aggroppare, ammassare, ammontare.*

To HEAP, } [to lay or pile one
To HEAP UP, } upon another] *ammontare, ammonticare, ammonticellare, ammonzicchiare, accumulare, abbicare, ammassare.*

To heap up riches, *tesaurizzare, accumular ricchezze.*

HEAPED, or HEAPED UP, adj. *ammontato, v.* To heap.

HE'APER, s. *quello, o quella che accumula, che ammassa.*

To HEAR [to receive a sound or voice by the ear] *udire, sentire, ascoltare, dare orecchio, stare attento.*

To hear [to be informed] *intendere, avere avviso, esser informato, sentir dire.*

I hear he is come to town, *intendo, o mi vien detto, ch' egli sia giunto in città.*

To hear ill [to have an ill fame] *essere in cattiva riputazione, essere in cattivo concetto.*

Pray, let me hear of you now and then, *di grazia datemi parte di quando in quando della vostra salute.*

I hear of your carriage, *sono informato del vostro procedere.*

HEARED, adj. *udito, sentito, ascoltato, v.* To hear.

HE'ARER, s. *uditore, auditore,* s. m.

HE'ARING, s. *l'ascoltare, audienza, udienza.*

He would not give me the hearing, *non m'ha voluto ascoltare, non ha voluto darmi udienza.*

To have a fair hearing, *avere una favorevole udienza.*

To condemn one without hearing, *condannare alcuno senza ascoltarlo.*

Hearing [one of the five senses] *l'udito.*

To be hard of hearing, *esser sordastro, esser quasi sordo.*

To HEARKEN [to give ear to] *ascoltare, dare orecchio.*

To hearken to an accommodation, *dare orecchio ad un aggiustamento.*

HE'ARKENED TO, adj. *ascoltato, dato orecchio.*

HE'ARKENER, s. *ascoltante,* s. m. f.

HE'ARSAY, s. [report, rumour] *fama, romore, quel che si dice.*

HEARSE, s. *bara da riporvi i morti.*

HEART, s. [the most noble part of the body] *cuore,* s. m.

It makes my heart ach, *questo mi ferisce il cuore.*

With an open heart, *con cuore aperto, apertamente, schiettamente, francamente.*

To learn a thing by heart, *imparare una cosa a mente.*

My dear heart, *cuor mio, ben mio: espressione di tenerezza.*

With all my heart, *di tutto cuore, molto volentieri.*

To have a good heart, to be of good heart, to pluck up a good heart, *star di buon cuore, pigliar animo.*

These expressions break my heart, *queste espressioni mi spezzano, mi strappano, mi passano il cuore.*

The heart of Italy, *il cuore, il mezzo d'Italia.*

To take a thing to heart, *avere a cuore, prendere a cuore.*

I am vexed at the heart, I am sorry at my very heart, *me ne dispiace fin' al cuore, o fin' all' anima.*

The heart of coals, *la sostanza del carbone, quel che vi si trova di combustibile.*

To keep a field in good heart, *coltivare bene un campo.*

A piece of ground out of heart, *terra stanca.*

To put one out of heart, *far cascare il cuore ad uno, disanimarlo, sgomentarlo.*

To put one in good heart, *mettere in cuore, incorare, dar cuore, dar animo, far cuore.*

To have one's heart to one's mouth [to be frighted] *essere spaventato, aver gran paura.*

My heart is set upon him, *l'amo appassionatamente.*

I could not find in my heart to leave him, *non mi sofferì, non mi bastò il cuore di lasciarlo.*

To win one's heart, *cattivarsi l'altrui benevolenza.*

A man's sweatheart [a mistress] *l'amanza, l'innamorata.*

A woman's sweatheart, *amante, innamorato.*

Heart-ach, s. [sorrow, pang, anguish] *tristezza, dolore, cordoglio, crepacuore, ed è anche usato per pene amorose, dolori degli amanti.*

Heart breaking, *cordoglio, crepacuore.*

Heart-case [a sort of strong water] *acqua distillata, che conforta il cuore, conforto, consolazione.*

Heart-wort [an herb] *siler, silermontano,* s. m. *spezie d'erba.*

HE'ARTED, adj. [stout-hearted] *ardito, coraggioso, prode.*

Faint-hearted, adj. *vile, codardo, vigliacco, poltrone.*

Light-hearted, *gajo, allegro, festoso, gioviale.*

Hard-hearted, *duro, crudele, efferato, inumano, barbaro.*

To HE'ARTEN [to animate, to encourage] *incorare, animare, dare animo.*

To hearten up, *fortificare, dar nuove forze.*

HE'ARTENED, adj. *animato, incorato.*

HE'ARTENING, adj. *nutritivo, che ha virtù di nutrire.*

Heartening wheat, *carne nutritiva.*

HEARTH, or HEARTH-PIES, s. [the paving before the chimney] *focolare,* s. m.

Hearth-money, *fuoco, danaro che si paga per ciaschedun fuoco.*

HE'ARTILY, adv. [from heart] *cordialmente, interamente, con tutto'l cuore, con tutto l'animo, svisceratamente.*

I love her heartily, *l'amo cordialmente, o svisceratamente.*

I thank you heartily, *vi ringrazio di tutto cuore.*

He made me laugh heartily, *mi ha fatto sganasciar dalle risa.*

To eat heartily, *mangiare a crepa pelle.*

HE'ARTINESS, s. [sincerity] *cordialità, svisceratezza, sincerità,* s. f. *affetto,* s. m.

HE'ARTLESSNESS, s. *codardia, viltà, vigliaccheria, poltroneria.*

HE'ARTLESS, adj. [that has no heart] *codardo, pusillanimo, vigliacco, poltrone.*

HE'ARTY, adj. [well in health] *sano, che sta bene, gagliardo.*

Hearty [chearful] *gajo, allegro, giojoso, festoso.*

Hearty [sincere] *cordiale, sviscerato, sincero, affezionato.*

To eat a hearty meal, *mangiare con buono appetito.*

HEARTY-HALE, adj. [good for the heart] *che conforta il cuore, confortevole, buono a guarire le angoscie dell' animo. Non in uso.*

HEAT, s. *calore, caldo,* s. m.

Heat [ardour, vehemence] *calore, ardore, amor fervente, zelo, fervore, desiderio, intento,* s. m. *veemenza,* s. f.

In the heat of the fight, *nel più fervido della battaglia.*

In the heat of my business, *nel bel mezzo de' miei affari.*

In the heat of the day, *nel fitto meriggio.*

Heat [passion] *calore, collera, ira, stizza, furia.*

The heat of youth, *i bollori della gioventù.*

With great heat, *ardentemente, con grande ardore.*

Heat [pimple] *cosso, riscaldamento,* s. m.

A race horse that has run a heat, *un cavallo che ha fatto una corsa, che ha corso una carriera.*

To be in a great heat, *aver molto caldo.*

To be in a great heat or passion, *esser in gran collera, esser molto adirato.*

To put one in a great heat, *metter uno in collera, farlo andare in collera, eccitare, provocar la sua collera.*

To HEAT, *scaldare, riscaldare.*

To heat the oven, *scaldare il forno.*

To heat one's blood, *scaldare il sangue.*

To heat cold meat, *riscaldare della carne fredda.*

To heat, verb neut. *scaldarsi, riscaldarsi.*

HE'ATED, adj. *scaldato, riscaldato.*

HE'ATER, s. [a piece of iron to smooth linen with] *ferro da sopressare panni lini.*

HEATH, s. [a sort of wild shrub] *scopa.* s. m. *arbuscello molto picciolo, quasi simigliante al ginepro.*

Heath [a plain covered with heath] *luogo aprico coperto di scope.*

Heath-cock, or heath-powt, *francolino*, s. m.

HE'ATHEN, s. [pagan] *pagano, idolatro.*

The heathens, *i pagani, i gentili.*

Heathen, Heathenish, adj. *pagano, di pagano, gentile.*

The heathen gods, *gli Dei de' pagani, i numi de' gentili.*

HE'ATHENISHLY, adv. *paganamente, paganicamente, da pagano.*

HE'ATHENISM, s. *paganesimo*, s. m. *gentilità*, s. f.

HE'ATING, s. [from to heat] *lo scaldare, il riscaldare, l' infuocare.*

HEAVE OFFERINGS, s. [the first fruits given to the priests of the Jews] *le primizie.*

Heave, s. [lift; effort upwards] *alzata con forza.*

Heave [rising of the breast] *l' alzarsi del petto per palpito e ansietà.*

Heave, *sforzo nel recere.*

Heave, *sforzo per alzarsi quand' uno è in terra.*

To HEAVE [to heave up, to lift up] *alzare, levare con isforzo.*

To heave a thing overboard, *gittare che che si sia in mare.*

To heave [to swell as dough] *lievitarsi.*

HE'AVED UP, adj. *alzato, levato.*

HE'AVEN, s. [the sky] *il cielo, il firmamento, o il fermamento.*

Heaven [paradise] *il cielo, il paradiso.*

The Lord of heaven, *Dio, Iddio.*

HE'AVENLY, adj. *celeste, di cielo, celestiale.*

The heavenly spirits, *gli spiriti celesti.*

HE'AVILY, adv. [from heavy] *pesantemente, lentamente, con lentezza.*

To go on heavily, *camminare, avanzare lentamente.*

To complain heavily, *lamentarsi grandemente.*

To go on heavily with a business, *andare, o mandare in lunga un negozio, procrastinarlo.*

HE'AVINESS, s. [weight] *pesanza, gravezza*, s. f. *peso*, s. m.

Heaviness [drowsiness] *addormentamento*, s. m. *sonnolenza*, s. f.

Heaviness [dulness] *stupidezza, balordaggine*, s. f.

Heaviness [sadness] *pesanza*, s. f. *affanno, travaglio d'animo*, s. m.

HE'AVY, adj. [weighty] *pesante, grave.*

A heavy burden, *una soma pesante.*

Heavy [dull] *stupido, insensato, balocco, scimunito.*

Heavy way, *cammino fangoso e aspro.*

Heavy [drowsy] *sonnacchioso, stupido.*

Heavy [sad] *tristo, addolorato, affannoso, maninconico, mesto.*

A heavy piece of work [that goes on heavily] *un' opera laboriosa, che avanza poco a poco.*

A heavy book, *un libro che annoja ancorchè buono.*

HE'BRAISM, s. [an idiom of the Hebrew language] *Ebraismo*, s. m. *maniera di parlare Ebracia.*

HE'BREW, adj. *Ebraico.*

The Hebrew tongue, *la lingua Ebraica.*

Hebrew, s. [the Hebrew tongue] *l'Ebraico, la lingua Ebraica.*

HE'CATOMB, s. [a sacrifice, wherein an hundred oxen were sacrificed at one time] *ecatombe, sacrifizio di cento buoi.*

HE'CTICK, adj. *etico.*

A hectick fever, *febbre etica.*

HE'CTOR, s. [bully, braggadochio] *sgherro, tagliacantoni, brigante, mangiaferro, che fa il bravo.*

To HE'CTOR [to play the hector, to insult, to bully] *bravare, fare il bravo, insultare, oltraggiare, braveggiare.*

HE'CTORED, adj. *bravato, insultato, oltraggiato.*

HEDGE, s. [a fence about lands] *siepe.*

A quick-set hedge, *siepaglia, siepone.*

A hedge-row of fruit trees set close together, *un filare d'alberi fruttiferi.*

A hedge-hog, *riccio, spinosa*, s. m.

A hedge-creeper, *un vagabondo, un perdigiorno.*

To be on the wrong side of the hedge [to mistake] *sbagliare, ingannarsi a partito.*

Hedge-marriage, *matrimonio clandestino.*

To HEDGE, } [to encompass
To HEDGE IN, } with a hedge] *siepare, cigner di siepe.*

HE'DGED, } adj. *siepato, cinto di*
HE'DGED IN, } *siepe.*

HE'DGER, s. [one that makes hedges] *colui che fa delle siepi.*

HE'DGING, s. *il siepare, il cinger di siepe.*

Hedging-bill, *roncone*, s. m.

HEED, s. [care, caution] *cura, guardia, cautela.*

Take heed what you do, *abbiate cura, o badate a quel che fate.*

To HEED [to mind] *badare, osservare, curare, attendere, stare attento, o accurato.*

HE'EDFUL, adj. [attentive] *attento, accurato.*

Heedful [cautious] *avvisato, accorto, circospetto, prudente, cauteloso.*

HE'EDFULLY, adv. *accuratamente, con cura, accortamente, avvisatamente, prudentemente, con circonspezione, cautelosamente.*

HE'EDFULNESS, s. *attenzione, applicazione*, s. f.

HE'EDLESSLY, adv. [negligently] *negligentemente, neghittosamente, con negligenza.*

Heedlesly [inconsiderately] *inconsideratamente, senza considerazione, trascuratamente.*

HE'EDLESSNESS, s. [negligence] *negligenza, inconsiderazione, inavvertenza, trascuraggine*, s. f.

HE'EDLESS, adj. *negligente, inavvertito, inconsiderato, trascurato.*

HEEL, s. [the back part of the foot] *calcagno, tallone*, s. m.

The heel of the foot, *il calcagno del piede.*

The heel of a shoe or boot, *il tallone d'una scarpa, d'uno stivale.*

To trip up one's heels, *dare il gambetto ad uno, farlo cascare.*

To trip one's heels [to supplant him] *piantarla ad uno, farlo restar ingannato, soppiantarlo, giuntarlo.*

He is at the heels of us with his army, *egli ci è alle spalle col suo esercito.*

To have one's heart at one's heels, *mostrar la pianta de' piedi, darsi alla fuga.*

He is always at my heels, *egli m'è sempre allato, egli mi seguita da per tutto.*

To betake one's self to one's heels, *calcagnare, voltar le calcagna, andarsene, fuggire, darsi alla fuga.*

To show a pair of heels, *fuggire, darla a gambe.*

In the heel of the evening, *sullo imbrunir della sera.*

To heel a ship, *metter un vascello alla banda per calafatarlo.*

To make a ladder heel, *appoggiare una scala.*

To heel [to dance] *ballare, danzare, menar le calcagna al ballo.*

HEFT, s. [the evenness or weight of any thing] *peso*, s. m. *gravezza*, s. f.

Heft, s. [effort up] *isforzo all' insù.*

Heft [haft, handle] *manico.*

HEGI'RA, s. [the epoca or account of time used by the Arabians and Turks] *egira, l'epoca della quale si servono i Turchi, e gli Arabi.*

HE'GLER, s. [a forestaller, or huckster, one that brings provisions out of the country, to sell at people's doors] *spezie d'incettore, che porta delle provisioni dalla campagna, per venderle poi alle porte de' cittadini.*

HE'IFER, s. [a young cow] *una giovenca*, s. f.

HEIGH, interj. *olà.*

HEIGH HO! *espressione di languidezza.*

HEIGHT, s. *altezza*, s. f.

A steeple of a prodigious height, *un campanile d'una maravigliosa altezza.*

Height [greatness] of courage, *grandezza d'animo.*

Height [the highest pitch] *colmo*, s. m. *cima, sommità*, s. f.

In the height of his happiness, *nel colmo della sua felicità.*

To HE'IGHTEN [to increase] *aggrandire,*

grandire, accrescere, agumentare, e aumentare. pres. aggrandisco, pret. accrebbi.

To heighten the soldiers courage, accrescer l'animo ne' soldati, animare i soldati.

To heighten a tapestry with gold and silver, ricamare una tappezzeria con oro e argento.

HE'IGHTENED, adj. aggrandito, accresciuto, aumentato.

Being heightened with that victory, pigliando ardire, o reso ardito da quella vittoria.

HE'INOUS, adj. atroce, cattivo in alto grado.

HEIR, s. [he that by will succeeds in the right of the testator] erede, s. m.

He is the next heir to the crown, egli è il primo erede della corona.

Joint-heir, coerede.

Heir-loom, mobili, suppellettili, beni mobili.

To HEIR [to inherit] eredare, ereditare.

HE'IRESS, s. [the female heir] erede, s. f.

HE'LL, è un' abbreviazione di He will.

He'll do it, egli lo farà.

HELD, adj. [from to hold] tenuto, v. To hold.

HELL, s. [the residence of damned spirits] inferno, s. m.

HELL-BLACK, adj. [black as hell] nero o scuro come l'inferno.

Hell-fire, il fuoco dell' inferno.

Hell-hound [the dog of hell] cerbero, s. m.

Hell-hound [a cruel man] un uomo crudele, barbaro, spietato.

HE'LLOTROPE, s. [the plant turnsol, or waterwort] clizia, elitropia, girasole, s. f.

HE'LLEBORE, s. [a physical herb] elleboro, s. m. erba nota medicinale.

White or black hellebore, elleboro bianco o nero.

HE'LLISH, adj. [of hell] infernale, d'inferno.

HELLISHLY, adv. diabolicamente, iniquissimamente.

HELM, timone, s. m. quel legno col quale si guida e regge la nave.

To sit at the helm [to govern] esser al timone; aver in mano le redini del governo, governare, reggere lo stato.

Helm [among chymists, is the head of a still or alembick] campana di lambicco.

Helm, s. celata, elmo, elmetto.

To HELM [to guide, to conduct] guidare, condurre.

HELMED, adj. coperto di celata; coll' elmo in capo.

HE'LMET, s. [a head-piece, or armour for the head] celata, s. f. elmo, elmetto, s. m.

HELP, s. [aid, assistance] ajuto, soccorso, ajutorio, appoggio, sovvenimento, s. m. sovvenenza, s. f.

To call for help, domandare ajuto, gridar a corr' uomo.

To bring help to one, portare, o dare soccorso ad uno.

Help [means] ajuto, mezzo.

All this he did by the help of a little money, egli fece tutto ciò coll' ajuto, o col mezzo d'una piccola somma di danari.

Help [remedy] rimedio.

There's no remedy for it, non v'è rimedio, è un male irremediabile.

He was a great help to me, mi fu d'un grande appoggio, o ajuto.

To help [to assist, to aid] ajutare, porgere o dare ajuto, soccorrere, sovvenire, assistere, favorire, servire. pres. sovvengo, favorisco. pret. porsi, soccorsi, sovvenni.

To help one another, ajutarsi l'un l'altro.

I cannot help myself with my right hand, non posso ajutarmi, valermi, o servirmi della man dritta.

To help one at table to a thing, servire uno a tavola di qualche cosa.

Shall I help you to a wing of this partridge, volete che vi serva un' ala di questa pernice.

Help yourself, si serva, o servitevi.

To help one to money, assistere uno con danari.

To help one to employment, procurare un impiego a qualcheduno.

We have not a penny to help ourselves withal, noi non abbiamo un soldo per vivere.

I can't help it, non so che farci, non è mia colpa.

Who can help it? non si può far di meno?

To help a lady into a coach, dar la mano ad una dama ch' entra in carrozza.

To help one in [to get him in] fare entrare alcuno.

To help one out, fare uscire uno, ajutarlo ad uscire.

To help one up, ajutare alcuno a salire, o a rilevarsi, dargli la mano.

To help one down, ajutare uno a scendere.

To help a business on, avanzare, sollecitare, condurre a fine un negozio.

HELPED, adj ajutato, soccorso, assistito, v. To help.

I could not help it, non ho potuto far di meno, non v'era rimedio, non è stata mia colpa.

HE'LPER, s. ajutatore, s. m, ajutatrice, s. f.

HE'LPLESS, adj. [that cannot help himself] che non può ajutarsi, che non ha nessun soccorso, disagiato, necessitoso, povero.

To be helpless [to be left without help] esser destituto d'ogni soccorso, esser abbandonato.

Helpless [that has no use of his limbs] stroppiato.

HE'LTER-SKE'LTER, adv. [confusedly] confusamente, senz' ordine, disordinatamente, in gran fretta.

HELVE, s. [the handle of a hatchet, ax, &c.] manico.

To throw the helve after the hatchet, trarre il manico dietro alla zoppa.

To HELVE, porre il manico.

To helve an ax, porre il manico ad un accia.

HEM, s. [hedge or outmost part of cloth] orlo, s. m.

Hem, interj. em, voce colla quale si chiama una persona.

To HEM [to make a hem] orlare, fare un orlo.

To hem in [to enclose or surround] cignere, rinchiudere, circondare. pret. cinsi, rinchiusi.

To hem a person [to call him by crying hem] chiamare una persona con un em.

HE'MICRANY, s. [a pain in either half part of the head] emicrania, s. f.

HE'MISPHERE, s. [half of the compass of the visible heavens] emisfero, emisperio, s. m. la metà della macchina mondiale terminata dall' orrizzonte.

The upper and lower hemisphere, l' emisfero superiore, e inferiore.

HE'MISTICK, s. [half a verse] mezzo verso, la metà d' un verso.

HE'MLOCK, s. [a venomous plant] cicuta, s. f. pianta velenosa.

HEMMED, adj. [from to hem] orlato, v. To hem.

Hemmed in, cinto, rinchiuso, circondato.

HE'MORRHOIDS, s. [emrods, piles] emorroidi, morici.

HEMP, s. [coarse flax] canapa, e canape, s. f.

A hemp cord, fune fatta di canape.

HE'MPEN, adj. [of hemp] di canapa, fatto di canapa.

A hempen rogue, una forca, un furfante, un guidone, un che merita il capestro.

HEN, s. [a female fowl] una gallina.

A Turkey hen, una gallina d'India.

A pea-hen, una paonessa, pagonessa, e pavonessa.

A moor-hen, folaga, s. f. uccello noto.

A brood-hen, una chioccia.

To cluck as a hen, gracidare, il gridare della gallina.

A hen-house, gallinajo, s. m.

A hen-roost, pollajo, s. m.

Of a hen, gallinacio, di gallina.

Hen hearted, pusillanimo.

Gl' Inglesi si servono spesso di Hen coi nomi degli uccelli, per esprimere la femmina. ex.

A hen sparrow, un passero femmina, una passera.

HENCE, adv. da qui.

He is gone from hence but just now, è appunto andato via di qui.

Ten years hence, da qui a dieci anni.

Hence it came to pass, that——donde accadde, che——

Not many days hence, fra pochi giorni.

HE'NCEFORTH, } adv. da qui in-
HENCEFORWARD, } nanzi, da ora in-

innanzi, per innanzi, da quinci innanzi.

HE'NCH-MAN, s. [a foot-man] *uno staffiere, un servo.*

Henchman [a page of honour] *un paggio d'onore.*

To HEND [to seize, to lay hold on] *acchiappare, afferrare, prendere strettamente.*

To hend [to croud, to surround] *affollarsi, circondare.*

HENT, ad. [caught] *acchiappato, preso.*

HEN-PECK'D, adj. [commonly applied to a man who is governed by his wife] *governato dalla moglie, e dicesi d'un marito.*

HEP, s. [the fruit of the hep-tree] *il frutto della spinalba.* s. f.

Hep-tree, *spinalba.* s. f.

HEPA'TICAL, } adj. [belonging
HEPA'TICK, } to the liver] *epatico, che appartiene al fegato.*

Hepatick vein [or the liver-vein] *la vena epatica.*

HE'PTAGON, s. [a figure of seven sides, and as many angles] *ettagono,* s. m. *figura solida di sette angoli.*

HER, *caso obliquo del pronome relativo* SHE, *lei, la, le.*

I remember her, *mi ricordo di lei.*

I see her, *la vedo.*

I had this present from her, *ho ricevuto questo regalo da lei.*

I told her, *le dissi.*

Her, *è anche pronome possessivo del genere femminino, suo, sua, suoi, sue.*

She is like her father, *ella rassomiglia a suo padre.*

She has married her daughter, *ella ha maritata sua figlia.*

She is very kind to her sons, *ella è molto amante de' suoi figliuoli.*

Her daughters are not so handsome as she, *le sue figliuole non sono sì belle che lei.*

'Tis she herself, *è ella stessa.*

She thinks herself very handsome, *ella si crede molto bella.*

She is by herself, *ella è sola.*

She knows what's good for herself, *ella sa quel che le sta bene.*

She lives like herself, *ella vive da pari sua.*

'Tis like herself, *è il suo umore.*

HE'RALD, s. [an officer at arms] *araldo,* s. m.

HE'RALDRY, s. [the art of blasoning] *araldería.*

HE'RALDSHIP, s. *l'ufficio, o la carica d'un araldo.*

Herb, s. *erba,* s. f.

Pot-herbs, *erbaggi,* s. m. *ogni sorta d'erba da mangiare, erbacce.*

Physick-herbs, *erbe medicinali.*

Herb of grace, *ruta,* s. f.

An herb woman, *un' erbajuola, un' erbolaja.*

Bad herbs, *erbacce.*

HE'RBAGE, s. [or pasture] *erbaggio, erba, pascolo.*

HE'RBAL, s. [a book treating of herbs] *libro che tratta dell' erbe.*

HE'RBELET, s. [diminutive of herb] *erbetta.*

HE'RBALIST, } s. [one that has
HE'RBARIST, } skill in physical herbs] *erbajuolo, erbolajo, colui che s'intende d'erbe medicinali.*

HE'RBID, } adj. [full of herbs]
HE'RBOUS, } *erboso, pien d'erba, che*
HE'RBY, } *ha sapor d'erba.*

HERD, s. [great company] *branco, armento, greggia.*

A herd of cattle, *un branco di bestiame.*

A herd of deer, *una frotta di cervi.*

Herds-man, s. [one that looks after the herd] *un pastore.*

A cow-herd, *un vaccaro.*

A swine herd, *un porcaro.*

A shepherd, *un pecorajo.*

To HERD, *andare in truppa.*

HE'RDSMAN, s. *colui che guarda il bestiame.*

HERE, adv. [in this place] *qui.*

I am here, *sono qui.*

Here he comes, *eccolo che viene.*

Come here, *venite qua.*

Here [take it] *prendetelo, eccolo qui.*

Here's your money, *ecco il vostri o danaro.*

Here and there, *qua e la.*

Here is to you, *brindisi.*

HE'REABOUTS, adv. *qui vicino, qui all' intorno.*

HEREA'FTER, adv. *da qui innanzi, da ora innanzi.*

HE'RETOFORE, adv. *per l'addietro.*

HE'REBY, adv. *per questo mezzo, così.*

HERE'DITABLE, adj. [whatever may be occupied by inheritance] *che si può ereditare, che si può avere per eredità.*

HERE'DITAMENTS, s. [a law word] *eredità,* s. f.

HERE'DITARY, adj. [that comes by inheritance] *ereditario.*

HERE'FROM, adv. [from hence] *da qui.*

HE'REIN, adv. [in this] *in questo, in ciò.*

HE'REOF, adv. [of this] *di questo, di quello.*

HERE'ON, adv. [upon this] *su questo.*

HEREO'UT, adv. [out of this place] *fuor di qui.*

HE'RESIARCH, s. [the chief of a sect of hereticks] *un eresiarca, capo, e fondator d'eretica setta.*

HE'RESY, s. [an opinion contrary to the fundamental points of religion] *eresia,* s. f. *opinione erronea, intorno a religione.*

HERE'TICAL, adj. [belonging to heresy] *eretico, che ha eresia.*

HE'RETICK, s. [one who holds heretical opinions] *un eretico, che ha opinion d' eresia.*

HERETO', adv. [to this] *a ciò.*

What can a man say hereto? *che si può dire contro a ciò?*

HERETOFO'RE, adv. *altre, volte, per l'addietro, per il passato.*

HEREU'NTO, adv. [to this] *a ciò.*

Hereunto I shall add, *aggiugnerò a questo.*

HEREUPO'N, adv. *in questo mezzo, in questo mentre.*

HE'REWI'TH, adv. *con ciò.*

HE'RITAGE, s. [inheritance] *eredita.*

HERMA'PHRODITE, s. [one who has the genital parts of both sexes] *ermafrodito, dell' uno e dell' altro sesso.*

HERME'TICAL, } adj. *ermetico.*
HERME'TICK, }

HERME'TICALLY, adv. *ermeticamente, col figlio d' ermete.*

HE'RMIT, s. [a solitary person, given to a religious life] *eremita, romito,* s. m.

HE'RMITAGE, s. [the place where a hermit lives] *eremitaggio, eremo,* s. m.

HE'RMITESS, s. [a woman hermit] *una eremita, una romita.*

HERN, s. [a large fowl] *airone, e aghirone,* s. m.

Hern-shaw, s. *luogo pieno d'aironi.*

HE'RNIA, s. [a rupture] *ernia, crepatura, allentatura.*

HE'RO, s. [a great illustrious person] *eroe,* s. m. *uomo illustre.*

HERO'ICAL, } adj. [great, noble,
HERO'ICK, } sublime] *eroico, grande, nobile, sublime, illustre, famoso.*

Heroick poem, or verse, *poema, o verso eroico.*

HERO'ICALLY, adj. *d'una maniera eroica.*

HE'ROINE, s. [a woman hero] *una eroina.*

HE'RON, s. [a sort of bird] *airone, e aghirone,* s. m.

HE'RRING, s. [a fish well known] *aringa,* s. f.

HERS, from her, [one of the pronouns possessive, absolute] *suo, sua, suoi, sue.*

This is hers, *questo, e questa, o suo, o sua.*

This book is hers, *questo libro è suo.*

I have no money of hers, *io non ho del suo danaro.*

HERSE, s. *una bara.*

To HERSE, *metter in una bara.*

HE'RSELIKE, adj. *funero, conveniente a funerale.*

To HE'RY, *custodir come sacro.*

HE'SITANCY, s. [uncertainty] *incertezza, irresoluzione, dubbiezza, dubbietà,* s. f.

To HE'SITATE [to doubt, to be uncertain what to do or say] *esitare, star dubbioso, dubitare, star sospeso.*

HESITA'TION, s. [a doubting, an uncertainty, a faultering in speech] *maniera di parlare in balbettando.*

Without hesitation, *senza pensare.*

HEST, s. [commands or decrees] *comando, decreto, ordine.*

HETERO'CLITE, adj. [a term in grammar, irregular] *eteroclito, irregolare, che non seguita regola generale* [*termine grammaticale.*]

HE'TERODOX, adj. [differing in sentiments or opinion from the generality of the church] *eterodosso, contrario ai ſentimenti, e opinione ricevuta nella vera religione.*

HETEROGE'NEOUS, adj. [of different kind, nature, or quality] *eterogeneo, di differente ſpezie, natura, o qualità.*

HEW, s. [colour] *colore, v.* Hue.

To HEW [to cut ſtones or timber] *tagliare delle pietre, o del legname, minuzzare, tritare.*

To hew down, *tagliare, abbattere.*

To rough hew, *ſchizzare, abbozzare.*

HEWED, or HEWN, adj. *tagliato.*

Hewed down, *tagliato, abbattuto.*

HE'WER, s. *tagliatore,* s. m.

A hewer of ſtones, *tagliatore di pietre.*

HEWN, *v.* HE'WED.

Rough-hewed, *abbozzato, ſchizzato.*

HEXA'GONAL, adj. [that has ſix angles or corners] *eſagono.*

HE'XAGONE, s. [a figure of ſix angles] *eſagono,* s. m. *figura piana di ſei lati.*

HE'XAMETER, s. [a verſe of ſix feet] *eſametro,* s. m. *ſorta di verſo, che ha ſei piedi.*

HEY, interj. *eſpreſſion di gioja, di giubbilo.*

HEY-DAY, interj. *eſpreſſione di gaudio e d'allegria.*

HIBE'RNAL, adj. *invernale, d'inverno.*

HICCIUS-DOCCIUS, s. *fraſaccia di gergo per dir che uno giuoca preſto per fraudare.*

HI'CKET, } s. *ſinghiozzo,* s. m.
HICC-UP, }

HI'CKWELL, s. [a bird, called otherwiſe a wood-pecker] *picchio,* s. m.

HID, } adj. [from to hide] *naſcoſto, v.* To hide.
HI'DDEN, }

HI'DDENLY, adv. [privately] *naſcoſamente, celatamente, di naſcoſo.*

HIDE, s. [the ſkin of a beaſt] *pelle, cuojo,* s. m.

To dreſs a hide, *conciare una pelle.*

To warm one's hide [to bang or maul him] *ſpianar le coſture ad uno, baſtonarlo, tartaſſarlo, batterlo ben bene.*

Hide of land [as much land as one plough could cultivate in a year] *tanta terra che un pajo di buoj potevan lavorare in un giorno.*

Hide-bound [among huſbandmen, trees are ſaid to be ſo when the bark ſticks too cloſe] *duriccio, parlando degli alberi quando hanno la corteccia troppo tegnente al tronco.*

Hide-bound [niggardly] *ſtretto, ſerrato, miſero, ſpilorcio, avariſſimo.*

To HIDE [to cover, to conceal] *naſcondere, celare, occultare.*

To hide one's ſelf ſomewhere, *naſconderſi, appiattarſi in qualche luogo.*

To hide [to keep ſecret] *naſcondere, celare, tener celato.*

Hide and ſeek [a ſort of play] *moſcacieca, ſpezie di giuoco fanciulleſco.*

HI'DEOUS, adj. [dreadful, frightful, terrible] *orrido, orribile, ſpaventevole, tremendo, terribile.*

HI'DEOUSLY, adv. *orridamente, orribilmente, ſpaventevolmente, terribilmente.*

HI'DEOUSNESS, s. *orribilità, coſa orribile, ſpaventevolezza.*

HI'DING, s. *naſcondimento,* s. m. *il naſcondere.*

Hiding-place, *naſcondiglio, luogo ſegreto.*

To HIE [to haſten] *affrettare, verbo difettivo, che non è in uſo ſe non nel preſente.* ex.

Hie thee, *affrettatevi.*

HIE'RARCH, s. [the chief of a ſacred order] *gerarca, capo d'un ordine ſacro.*

HIERA'RCHICAL, adj. [belonging to the government of the church] *gerarchico, appartenente al governo eccleſiaſtico.*

HIE'RARCHY, s. [church government] *gerarchia,* s. f. *governo eccleſiaſtico.*

Hierarchy [the holy orders of angels, which conſiſts of nine] *gerarchia.*

HIEROGLY'PHICAL, } adj. [belonging to hieroglyphicks] *geroglifico, appartenente al geroglifico.*
HIEROGLY'PHICK, }

Hieroglyphicks, s. [were certain myſterious characters of creatures, or letters uſed among the Egyptians, whereby they kept their policy and ethicks ſecret] *geroglifico, caratteri miſterioſi d'animali, o di lettere in uſo fragli Egizij per mezzo de' quali naſcondevano gli affari di ſtato.*

To HI'GGLE [to chaffer, to be penurious in a bargain] *andar a ſpizzico nel comprare, eſſer lento nell' aggiungere qualche poco di più alla ſomma da primo offerta.*

To higgle [to go ſelling proviſions from door to door] *andar vendendo commeſtibili di porta in porta.*

HI'GGLER, s. *un che vende commeſtibili al minuto.*

HIGH, adj. [tall, lofty] *alto, eminente, ſublime.*

A very high ſteeple, *un campanile molto alto.*

High water, *alta marea.*

The high Dutch, *il tedeſco, la lingua tedeſca o Alemanna.*

The ſun is very high, *il ſole è molto alto.*

The Moſt High, *l'Altiſſimo, Iddio.*

High-treaſon, *delitto di leſa maeſtà.*

A high place, *un luogo eminente.*

High [tall, or great] *grande.*

A high tree, *un grand' albero.*

The high way, *la ſtrada maeſtra, la ſtrada battuta.*

A high forehead, *una fronte alta.*

A high-day, *una gran feſta.*

High maſs, *la meſſa cantata.*

High wind, *gran vento.*

High compliment, *un gran complimento.*

To aim too high, or at great matters, *aſpirare a coſe grandi, fiſſar la viſta troppo in alto.*

High notions or expreſſions, *penſieri o eſpreſſioni ſublimi.*

A high ſpirit, *uno ſpirito fiero, altiero, orgoglioſo.*

The high prieſt, *il ſommo ſacerdote.*

High altar, *altare maggiore.*

At high noon, *di mezzo dì.*

'Tis high time, *è già tempo.*

High born, *d'alta naſcita.*

High minded, *ambizioſo, orgoglioſo, albagioſo.*

High flown, *fiero, altiero, ſuperbo, orgoglioſo, gonfio, affatto gonfio.*

A high flown ſtile, *uno ſtile elevato, gonfio, affettato.*

High ſpirited, *fiero, orgoglioſo.*

Highway-man, *malandrino, rubator di ſtrada.*

HI'GHLANDS, *paeſe montagnoſo.*

HI'GHLANDER, *un montanaro.*

High, adv. *alto.*

You go too high, *voi andate troppo alto.*

On high, *in ſu, in alto.*

From on high, *da ſopra.*

To ſpend high, *far gran di ſpeſe.*

To feed high, *trattarſi bene, viver l'autamente, far buona cera.*

His pulſe beats very high, *il ſuo polſo è molto agitato.*

To play high [to play deep] *giuocar gran giuoco.*

The wind blows very high, *fa gran vento.*

High-tapper [a plant] *taſſobaſſo, verbaſco,* s. m.

HIGHER, *è il comparativo di* High, *più alto.*

The higheſt office of the kingdom, *le prime cariche del regno.*

HI'GHLY, adv. *grandemente, molto, infinitamente.*

He has highly obliged me, *egli m'ha obbligato infinitamente.*

Highly commendable, *molto lodevole, o commendabile.*

I am highly obliged to you, *vi reſto ſommamente obbligato.*

HI'GHMOST, adj. [higheſt, topmoſt] *che è il più alto, che ſta in ſulla eſtrema vetta.*

HI'GHNESS, s. *altezza.*

His royal highneſs, *ſua altezza reale.*

His highneſs [ſpeaking of the grand Seignor] *ſua altezza, parlando del gran Turco.*

HIGHT, adj. [called] *nominato, chiamato.*

HILL, s. [either a mountain or a little riſing ground] *monte, colle,* s. m. *montagna, collina, altezza, eminenza,* s. f.

The top, the cliff, the foot of a hill, *la cima, il pendio, il piede d'una montagna.*

To write up hill, *ſcrivere a ſchimbeſcio.*

Mole-hill, *monticello di terra, che le talpe fanno nella terra.*

To make a mountain of a mole-hill, *far d'una moſca un elefante.*

An ant-hill, *formicajo.*

HI'LLOCK, s. [a little hill] *una collinetta, un monticello.*

HI'LLY, adj. [full of hills] *montuoso, montagnoso.*
HILT, s. [the handle of a sword] *elsa, else,* s. f. *la guardia della spada.*
A silver hilt, *una guardia d'argento.*
HIM, *caso obliquo del pronome* He, *lui, li, lo.*
You have no reason to complain of him, *voi non avete ragione di lamentarvi di lui.*
Tell him from me, *diteli da parte mia.*
Give it him, *dateglielo.*
I shall see him to morrow, *lo vedrò domani.*
This is for him, *questo è per lui.*
To HI'MPLE [to halt] *zoppicare, andar zoppo.*
HIMSE'LF, pron. *istesso, egli stesso, se stesso.*
He will go himself, *egli vuole andare in persona.*
He did that for himself, *egli ha fatto questo per se stesso.*
He thinks himself a great man, *egli si stima un grand' uomo.*
He dresses himself, *egli si veste.*
He is gone away by himself, *egli sen' è andato solo.*
HIN, s. *misura di cose liquide presso i Giudei antichi.*
HIND, s. [the female of a stag] *damma, cerva,* s. f.
Hind-calf, or fawn, *cerbiatto.*
Hind, adj. *posteriore, deretano, della parte di dietro.* Hinder, *comparat.* Hindmost, *superlativo.*
The hind part of the brain, *la parte deretanta del cervello.*
The hind feet, *il piede di dietro.*
The hind part of a ship, *la poppa d' un vascello.*
HI'NDER, adj. *comparativo di* Hind.
To HI'NDER [to keep from] *impedire, stornare, frastornare, interrompere.* pref. *impedisco,* pret. *interruppi.*
You hinder me from working, *voi m'impedite di lavorare, voi mi stornate dal mio lavoro.*
To hinder one's time [to lose his time] *far perder il tempo ad uno.*
What hinders me from beating you, *mi vien voglia di darvi cento bastonate.*
HI'NDERANCE, s. [impediment] *impedimento, stormo, interrompimento, ostacolo, impaccio,* s. m.
Hinderance [prejudice] *torto, pregiudizio, danno,* s. m.
Without hinderance of time, *senza perdita di tempo.*
HI'NDERED, adj. *impedito, stornato, frastornato, interrotto.*
HI'NDERER, s. *colui o quella cosa che impedisce, che frastorna, che interrompe.*
HI'NDERING, s. *impedimento,* s. m. *l'impedire.*
HINDERMOST, } adj. *superlativo di*
HINDMOST, } Hind [the last] *'ultimo.*
He is the hindermost of all, *egli è l' ultimo di tutti.*
HINE, s. [servant] *un servo, un servo di campagna.*
HINE-FARE, *licenza, congedo, permissione di ritirarsi, e di lasciare di fare i servizi ch'era solito di fare.*
HINGE, s. [an iron device on which a door turns] *cardine, arpione, ganghero,* s. m.
The hinges of a door, *i cardini, gli arpioni d'una porta.*
These are the two hinges of the controversy, *questi sono i due punti principali della controversia.*
To be off the hinges [to be out of humour] *esser fuor di sesto; esser di cattivo umore, esser fuor de' gangheri.*
HINT, s. [or notice] *vento, sentore, indizio, avviso, cenno, barlume, sospetto, allusione, tocco.*
I had a hint of it, *io ne ebbi un cenno, n'ebbi qualche sentore.*
To give one a hint of a thing, *dare indizio, o cenno ad uno di qualche cosa, avvertirgliela.*
I have got a hint of it, *ne ho qualche barlume.*
You gave me that hint, *voi me lo avete leggermente tocco.*
To HINT [to give a slight notice of a thing] *dare un leggiero indizio, suggerire, menzionare, intimare.* pref. *suggerisco.*
To hint, *alludere, toccar una cosa leggiermente; accennare.*
HINTED, adj. *suggerito, menzionato, intimato.*
HIP, s. [or huckle bone, the upper part of the thigh] *anca,* s. f. *l'osso ch' è tra'l fianco, e la coscia.*
The hip-gout, *la sciatica.*
Hip [the fruit of the briar] *sorta di frutto salvatico.*
To have on the hip [a low phrase] *aver vantaggio sopra un altro.*
To HIP, *sciancare, guastar l'anca.*
HI'PPED, adj. [whose hip is out of joint] *sciancato.*
HIP, } adj. *ipocondriaco, sono*
HI'PPISH, } *voci basse.*
HI'PPOCRAS, s. [a rich sort of liquor made of wine, cinnamon and sugar] *ippocras, spezie di liquore delizioso.*
HIPPO'CRATES' SLEEVE, s. *chiamasi così un certo sacchetto fatto di lana usato nel filtrare sciloppi e simili.*
HIRE, s. [wages] *salario, stipendio,* s. m.
The hire of a house, *l'affitto, o la pigione d'una casa.*
Coach-hire, *affitto di carrozza.*
To HIRE [to take to hire] *affittare, pigliare a fitto, ad affitto.*
To hire a servant, *pigliare un servo.*
To hire a house, *appigionare, pigliare a pigione una casa.*
To hire [to let to hire] *affittare, dare affitto, allogare.*
To hire out one's self, *allogarsi, mettersi a servire.*
HI'RED, adj. *affittato, allogato, appigionato.*
HI'RELING, s. *un mercenario, colui che serve per danaro, venale.*
Hireling, adj. *che è venale; che si prostituisce per danaro; che serve per mercede pecuniaria.*
HIRSE, s. [millet] *miglio,* s. m. *spezie di biada minuta.*
HIS, pron. pos. *suo, sua, suoi, sue.*
His father, *suo padre.*
His mother, *sua madre.*
His children, *i suoi figliuoli.*
His coach, *la sua carrozza.*
This is his book, *questo libro è il suo.*
To HISS [to make a hissing noise, as serpents and winds do] *fischiare, sibilare.*
To hiss at one, *fischiar uno, ridersi, burlarsi di lui.*
HI'SSED, } adj. *fischiato, sibi-*
HISSED AT, } *lato.*
HI'SSING, s. *fischiata,* s. f. *il fischiare.*
HIST, interj. [silence] *zitto.*
HISTO'RIAN, s. [a writer of histories] *istorico,* s. m. *scrittor d'istoria.*
HISTO'RICAL, adj. [belonging to history] *istorico, d'istoria.*
HISTO'RICALLY, adv. *istoricamente, a modo d'istoria.*
HISTORIO'GRAPHER, s. [a writer of histories] *istoriografo, istorico,* s. m. *scrittor d'istoria.*
HI'STORY, s. [a narration or relation of things as they are, or of actions as they did pass] *istoria, storia,* s. f.
To understand history, *sapea l'istoria.*
Truth is the life of history, *la verità è l'anima dell' istoria.*
A history book, *un libro d'istoria.*
HISTRIO'NICK, adj. [belonging to an actor, player-like] *d'istrione, di commediante, teatrale.*
HIT, s. [stroke, blow] *colpo,* s. m. *percossa, botta,* s. f.
He has given me a deadly hit, *egli m'ha dato un colpo mortale.*
A lucky hit, *un colpo di fortuna.*
He has had a lucky hit, *egli l'ha incontrata bene.*
Look to your hits, *badate a' fatti vostri, state in cervello, aprite gli occhi.*
Hit, adj. [from to hit] *battuto, percosso.*
To HIT [to strike] *battere, percuotere, bastonare.*
To hit one stick with another, *battere un bastone contro un altro.*
To hit one a box on the ear, *applicare uno schiaffo ad uno.*
To hit the mark, *imberciare, dar nel segno.*
I could not hit the door for my life, *non m' è stato possibile di trovar la porta.*
You hit the nail on the head, *voi vi siete apposto, voi l'avete indovinata, voi avete dato nel segno.*
To hit [to succeed, to happen] *accadere, riuscire, succedere.* pret. *accadde, successe.*
It hit pretty luckily, *la cosa accadde assai felicemente.*

To hit one in the teeth with a thing, rimproverare qualche cosa ad uno, gettargliela in volto.

To hit on him [to do the business] fare il colpo.

To hit on him [to sharp with him] sbottoneggiare alcuno.

To hit one's head against the wall, sbatter la testa contro al muro.

A ship that hits against a rock, un vascello che si rompe contro uno scoglio.

To hit together, incontrarsi.

To hit upon, incontrare, abbattersi.

I chanced to hit upon him, a caso m' abattei in lui.

I can't hit off his name, non posso ricordarmi del suo nome.

To HITCH [to riggle] muoversi, dimenarsi.

To hitch a little farther, avanzarsi, un poco più.

HITHE, s. [a little port for landing, loading, and unloading goods] piccolo porto che non ammette navi grosse.

HI'THER, adv. [in this place] qui, qua.

Come hither, venite qua, o qui.

Call him hither, diteli che venga qui.

Hither, adj. Ex. when Pompey fled into the hither Spain, quando Pompeo se ne fuggì nella Spagna citeriore.

HI'THERMOST, adj. il più vicino, che è da questa banda.

HI'THERTO, adv. fin' adesso, fino a quest' ora.

HI'THERWARD, } adv. da questa
HI'THERWARDS, } banda.

HIVE, s. [the cell or habitation of bees] alveario, arnia; cassetta da pecchie.

Hive [the bees inhabiting a hive] quella famiglia di pecchie contenuta da un' arnia.

Hive [a company being together] un crocchio di persone.

To HIVE [to put into hives, to harbour] far entrar nell' arnia; dar ricetto.

To hive [to take shelter together] ricovrarsi insieme con altri al coperto; rifugiarsi con altri in qualche luogo a similitudine delle pecchie nell' arnia.

Ho, } interj. oh!
HOA, }

HOARD, s. [a store laid up in secret; a hidden stock; a treasure] un mucchio fatto in segreto; un capitale nascosto; un tesoro.

To HOARD, v. n. tesaurizare, accumular danari.

To hoard, v. n. far economia, accumular in segreto.

HO'ARDER, s. colui che accumula in segreto roba o danari.

HOAR-FROST, brina, s. f.

HO'ARINESS, s. i capelli canuti, canizie.

Hoariness [mouldiness] muffa, mucidezza, s. f.

HOARSE, adj. [having a rough voice] rauco.

To grow hoarse, divenir rauco.

To speak hoarse, parlar con voce rauca; Dante disse, voce chioccia.

HOA'RSELY, adv. [with a hoarse voice] con voce rauca.

HO'ARSENESS, s. raucedine, fiochezza, s. f.

HO'ARY, adj. [gray headed, as old men commonly are] canuto, che ha i capelli bianchi.

Hoary [covered with hoar-frost] bianco, brinoso, coperto di brino.

Hoary [mouldy] muffato, mucido.

To grow hoary with age, incanutire, divenir canuto, imbiancare il pelo per vecchiezza.

To grow hoary [to grow mouldy] muffarsi.

HOB, s. [a country hob, a clown] un rustico, un villano, un contadino.

HOB-NOB, corrotto da HAB-NAB [give it or take it] prendi o lascia. Gl' Inglesi a tavola quando sono allegri hanno questo costume, che uno dice a un altro, hob or nob. Se colui risponde hob, tocca ad esso a scegliere di qual vino essi due hanno a votar un bicchiere per ciascuno, se risponde nob, tocca all' altro, cioè a quello che fece l'invito dicendogli hob or nob.

Will you hob or nob with me? volete che beviamo insieme un bicchiere?

To HO'BBLE [to limp, to go lame] zoppicare, ire, andar zoppo.

A verse that hobbles, or a hobbling verse, un verso zoppo.

HO'BBLE, s. zoppicamento, o mala grazia nel camminare.

HO'BBY, s. [a sort of Irish horse] spezie di cavallo d'Irlanda.

Hobby-horse, s. quel legno o bastone che i fanciulli si mettono fra gambe e chiamano il loro cavallo.

HOBGO'BLIN, s. spirito, folletto.

HO'BLERS, s. [certain Irish knights, who used to serve as light horsemen] cavalieri Irlandesi che servivano altre volte da cavalli leggieri.

Hoblers [men who by their tenure were obliged to maintain a little light nag, for certifying an invasion toward the sea-side] spezie di scorridori.

HO'BNAIL, s. que' chiodi che servono a tener saldi i ferri de' cavalli.

HO'BOY, s. [a musical instrument, or he that plays upon that instrument] oboè, s. m. strumento musicale di fiato, così si dice anche quello che suona l' oboè. Scrivesi meglio Haut-boy.

HOCK, s. parte della coscia.

A hock of bacon [or a little gammon] un prosciutto.

HOCK, } s. vino del reno
HO'CKAMORE, } quand' è vecchio e buono.

To HO'CKLE [to cut the joints towards the hough] tagliare il garetto.

HOCUS-POCUS, s. [a jugler, one who shows tricks by slight of hand] un giocolare, un bagattelliere, colui che fa leggierezze di mano; un giuntatore, un gabbatore.

HOD, s. [a sort of tray for carrying mortar] truogolo, s. m. per portar la calce sopra le spalle.

HO'DMAN, s. manovale, s. m. quegl che serve il muratore col portagli le materie per murare.

HODGE-PODGE, s. mescuglio di varie cose bollite insieme.

HOE, s. [an instrument to cut up the earth] strumento da scavare il terreno.

HOG, s. [a swine] porco, s. m.

A barrow hog, un verro.

A hog-badger, tasso porco, s. m.

A sea-hog, porco marino.

A hedge-hog, un riccio.

I brought my hogs to a fine market, io sto fresco.

Hog's-flesh, carne di porco.

Hog's-skin, cuojo di porco.

Hog-wash, broda.

Hog's-cheek, teschio di porco.

Hog's-greese, sugna, s. f. grasso di porco.

Hog-sty, } porcile, s. m.
Hog cote, }

HO'GGISH, adj. porcino, di porco.

To lead a hoggish kind of life, menare una vita di porco, viver da porco.

HO'GSBEANS, }
HO'GSBREAD, } s. nomi di
HO'GSMUSHROOMS, } piante.
HO'GSFENNEL, }

HOGO'O, s. [a strong smell] tanfo, fetore, odore ingrato.

This meat has a deadly hogoo, questa carne ha del tanfo, ha un odore ingrato.

HO'GSHEAD, s. botte, s. m.

A hogshead of wine, una botte di vino.

HO'IDON, } s. [a clownish, rusti-
HO'IDEN, } cal woman] una contadina, una rustica, una donna grossolana.

To HO'IDEN [to romp indecently] far giuochi grossolani e indecenti, come fanno le contadine quando vogliono star allegre.

To HOISE, } [to heave up] alza-
To HOIST, } re, levare.

To hoise the sail, spiegar le vele, mettere alla vela, far vela.

To hoise up the price of any thing, incarire, alzar il prezzo.

HOISED, } adj. alzato, levato,
HOISED UP, } v. To hoise.

HOLD, s. [the place by which one holds a thing] presa.

To let go one's hold, lasciare andare, lasciar la presa.

The hold of a ship, il fondo della nave.

To lay or take hold of a thing, aggrapparsi, dar di piglio, appigliarsi, impugnare, prendere, pigliare qualche cosa.

To lay hold of a favourable opportunity, abbracciare un' occasione favorevole.

He thinks no law can lay hold of him, egli si crede esente d'ogni legge.

They could not take hold of his words, non ebbero niente a dire in contrario alle sue parole.

A strong hold, un forte, un fortino, una fortezza.

HO'LDFAST [in a wall] *una catena, quel ferro che si pone negli edifizi, che li incatena, e serra insieme.*

A joiner's holdfast, *granchio*, s. m. *quel ferro, ch'è conficcato sur una panca per appuntellarvi il legno ch' e' vogliono piallare, perch' è non iscorra.*

A holdfast, *un cacastecchi, un meschino, un taccagno, uno spilorcio, un tanghero.*

The condemned hold, *camerotto*, s. m. *segrete*, s. f. *luogo nella prigione dove sono rinchiusi i malfattori che devono esser giustiziati.*

To hold [to lay hold on, to keep] *tenere, pigliare, prendere*, pres. *tengo*, pret. *tenni, presi.*

Hold him fast, *tenetelo fermo.*

To hold [to stick fast] *prendere, rappigliarsi, attaccarsi, tenere insieme.*

It holds very fast, *tien forte.*

To hold one's opinion [or to hold in one's opinion, to continue in it] *tener duro, stare nella opinione di prima, persistere nella sua opinione.*

To hold [to stop] *fermare, fermarsi.*

Hold coachman, *alto cocchiere.*

To hold [to contain] *capire, contenere*, pres. *capisco, contengo*, pret. *contenni.*

The room was so small that it could not hold them, *la camera era si stretta, che non vi potettero capire.*

To hold [to believe] *tenere, stimare, giudicare, reputare, far conto, credere, esser d'opinione*, pres. *tengo*, pret. *tenni.*

To hold [to maintain] *mantenere*, pres. *mantengo*, pret. *mantenni.*

To hold a thing to be true, *mantenere una cosa per vera.*

To hold a wager, *fare una scommessa, scommettere.*

What will you hold on't? *quanto volete scommettere?*

To hold [to last] *durare, continovare.*

This way of living of yours won't hold long, *questra vostra maniera di vivere non durerà lungo tempo.*

To hold people in suspence, *tener la gente sospesa, o in sospensione.*

To hold one's eyes open, *star cogli occhi aperti.*

To hold [to call] *chiamare, adunare, congregare, tenere.*

To hold a council of war, *tener un consiglio di guerra.*

To hold a senate, *adunare il senato.*

To hold a consultation, *tener consulta.*

To hold a consultation [speaking of physicians] *collegiare.*

To hold an honour for life, *godere, o possedere qualche onore, o dignità durante la sua vita.*

To hold of one [as a tenant does of his lord] *dipendere da qualcheduno, come un vassallo dal suo padrone.*

He holds his land of the emperor, *le sue terre dipendono dall' imperadore.*

To hold a thing at a great rate [to make much of it] *far grande stima di qualche cosa, stimarla, apprezzarla molto.*

He held the dagger to his throat, *teneva il pugnale alzato per trafiggerli il petto.*

To hold one's tongue, to hold one's peace, *tacersi.*

To hold one's breath, *ritenere il fiato.*

I am scarce able to hold my legs, *appena posso reggermi in piedi.*

This argument holds good on my side, *questo argomento fa per me, è a mio vantaggio.*

To hold with one, *tener per uno, esser dalla sua parte, pigliar la sua parte.*

To hold on, *continovare, persistere, tener duro.*

To hold on one's design, *persistere nel suo disegno.*

To hold off. Ex. Hold off your hands, *non toccate, levate via le mani.*

To hold forth [to preach] *predicare.*

To hold in, *tener corto, ritenere, tener in freno.*

To hold in the reins, *tener la briglia corta.*

To hold in one's breath, *ritenere il fiato.*

To hold one in hand, *tenere uno a bada.*

To hold out, *tener duro, star saldo, o fermo, mantenersi.*

The place cannot hold out if it be besieged, *la piazza non può mantenersi, se viene assediata.*

I held it out against them all, *io solo feci testa a tutti.*

To hold out a long siege, *mantenere un lungo assedio.*

This law suit holds out too long, *questo processo tira alla lunga.*

To hold up, *levare, alzare.*

To hold up one's hands, *levar le mani.*

To hold up [to bear up] *appoggiare, appuntellare, puntellare, sostenere, proteggere*, pres. *sostengo*, pret. *sostenni, protessi.*

To hold back, *ritenere*, pres. *ritengo*, pret. *ritenni.*

HO'LDEN, adj. *tenuto*, v. To hold.

HO'LDER, s. *un che tiene.*

HO'LDFAST, v. Hold.

HO'LDING, s. *il tenere*, v. To hold.

HOLE, s. [a hollow place] *buco, pertugio, foro*, s. m.

To make a hole, *bucare, bucherare, foracchiare.*

Arm-hole [arm-pit] *ascella*, s. f.

The touch-hole of a gun, *focone d' arme da fuoco.*

Hole [vent, out of which air, smoke, &c. comes out] *spiraglio*, s. m.

Lurking hole, *un nascondiglio.*

To grow full of holes, *bucarsi, bucherarsi.*

To have a hole to creep out, *trovar qualche scusa, pretesto, sotterfugio.*

HO'LIDAM, s. [blessed Lady] *nostra donna; la beatissima Vergine.*

HO'LILY, adv. [from holy] *santamente, religiosamente, piamente.*

HO'LINESS, s. *santità*, s. f.

His holiness [a title given to the pope] *sua santità, sua beatudine.*

To pretend to much holiness, *voler passare, o esser tenuto per santo.*

HO'LLAND [or Holland cloth] *tela d'Olanda.*

HO'LLOW, adj. *concavo, vuoto, cavo, profondo, cavernoso, cupo.*

The cane is hollow, *la canna è vuota, o concava.*

Hollow eyes, *occhi incavati.*

A hollow noise, *susurro, bisbiglio.*

A hollow heart, *un cor doppio, o finto.*

Hollow hearted, *doppio, finto, dissimulato.*

Hollow, s. [a hollow place] *una fossa.*

Hollow [crying out] *grido*, s. m.

To give a hollow, *fare un grido, gridare.*

To HO'LLOW [to make a hollow] *cavare, zoppare, vuotare, far vuoto, scavare.*

To hollow, v. n. [to shout, to hoot] *gridare oh! gridar dietro a qualcheduno, acclamare.*

HO'LLOWNESS, s. *cavità, concavità*, s. f.

HO'LLY, or HOLLY-OAK, s. *sorta di pianta.*

Holly-wand, *bacchetta.*

HOLME, or HOLME-TREE, s. *olmo*, s. m.

HO'LOCAUST, s. [or burnt-offering] *olocausto*, s. m.

HOLP, *antico preterito di* to help.

HO'LPEN, *antico participio passivo del verbo* to help.

HO'LSTER, s. [leather case for a pistol] *fonda della pistola, quell' arnese fatto per custodia della pistola.*

HOLT, s. [a small wood] *boschetto*, s. m.

HO'LY, adj. *santo, sacrato, pio.*

The holy writ, *la scrittura sacra.*

A holy place, *un luogo sacrato, o sacro.*

The Holy Ghost, *lo Spirito Santo.*

Holy water, *aqua santa.*

Court holy water [fair empty words] *belle parole, parole di corte.*

Holy thistle, *cardo santo.*

To make holy, *santificare.*

A holy day, *giorno di festa, festa, festività.*

Set holy days, *feste immobili.*

Moveable holy days, *feste mobili.*

Holy Thursday [Ascension-day] *il giorno dell' Ascensione.*

A holy water pot or stock, *acquasantaro, pila.*

Holy-rood day, *l'esaltazione della croce.*

Holy, s. Ex. The holy of holies, *il santa santorum, il santuario.*

HO'MAGE, s. *omaggio*, s. m.

To do homage to one's lord, *render omaggio al suo signore.*

HO'MAGER, s. [one that pays homage, or is bound so to do] *vassallo*, s. m.

HOME, s. [house, place of abode] *casa, dimora, stanza*, s. f.

To go home, *ritirarsi o andare a casa*.

To return home [into one's own country, *ritornarsene alla patria*.

Home is home, let it be ever so homely, *una capanna ci pare un palagio, quando sia nostra*.

I Fiorentini dicono con molto garbo e semplicità.

Casa mia, casa mia.
Per piccina che tu sia
Tu mi pari una badia.

To go to one's long home [to die] *andare a babbori-veggoli, morire*.

Home bred, *del paese*.

Home bred commodities, *mercanzia del paese*.

Home bred wars, *guerre civili*.

Home spun, *casalingo, casereccio*.

A home spun woman, *una donna fatta col gomito, o mal fatta*.

Home, adv. ex. To speak home [to the purpose] *parlar al proposito*.

To hit one home, *sbottoneggiare alcuno*.

Your crimes will come home to you, *voi farete la penitenza de' vostri misfatti*.

HO'MEFELT, adj. [inward, private] *interno, segreto, privato, che torca sul vivo*.

HO'MELINESS, s. [coarseness] *grossezza, materialità, semplicità, rozzezza*, s. f.

HO'MELY, adj. [mean, coarse] *grossolano, rozzo, materiale*.

A homely woman, *una donna grossolana*.

Homely, adv. [plainly] *grossolanamente, semplicemente, rozzamente*.

HO'MEWARD, adv. *verso casa*.

To go homeward, *andar verso casa*.

A ship homeward bound, *un vascello di ritorno*.

HO'MICIDE, s. [manslayer] *un omicida*.

Homicide [manslaughter] *omicidio*, s. m.

HO'MILIST, s. [a writer of homilies] *un autor d'omelie*.

HO'MILY, s. [a discourse made upon the gospel] *omelia*, s. f. *ragionamento sagro sopra i vangeli*.

HOMOGE'NEAL, } adj. [having the
HOMOGE'NEOUS, } nature or principles] *omogeneo*.

HONE, s. [a fine sort of whetstone for razors] *cote*, s. f. *pietra da affilar rasoi*.

HO'NEST, adj. [good, just, righteous] *onesto, virtuoso, dicevole, convenevole*.

A down right honest man, *un uomo onestissimo, un uomo dabbene*.

Honest [chaste] *onesto, onorato, casto, pudico*.

She is an honest woman, *ella è una donna onesta, onorata*.

She kept herself honest, *ella si conservò casta*.

A honest soul, *un galantuomo, un uomo sincero, franco, schietto*.

HO'NESTLY, adv. *onestamente, con onore, onoratamente, castamente*.

To deal honestly, *trattare con onestà, trafficare e procedere onestamente*.

HO'NESTLY, s. *onestà, virtù, modestia*, s. f. *onore*, s. m.

I don't question your honesty, *non dubito della vostra probità*.

HO'NEY, s. *miele, mele; produzione dell' api*.

HO'NEY [sweetness, lusciousness] *dolcezza, cosa dolce*.

Honey, *espressione amorosa; dolce amor mio*.

To HO'NEY [to talk fondly] *parlar con piacere; sentir dolcezza parlando; parlar amorosamente*.

HO'NEY-BAG, s. *stomaco, lo stomaco*.

HONEY-COMB, s. *favo, quelle cellette di cera in cui le pecchie ripongono il lor mele*.

HONEY-DEW, s. *rugiada dolce; manna*.

HONEY-FLOWER, s. *nome di pianta*.

HONEY-GNAT, s. *nome d'insetto*.

HONEY-MOON, s. *il primo mese di matrimonio*.

HONEY-SUCKLE, s. [woodbine] *succiamele; nome d'una pianta*.

HO'NEYLESS, adj. [without honey] *senza miele, privo di mele*.

HONEY-WORT, s. *nome di pianta*.

HO'NORARY, adj. [done in honour] *fatto in onore, onorario*.

HO'NOUR, s. [respect, reverence] *onore, rispetto*, s. m. *stima, venerazione*, s. f.

To pay or give one the honour due to him, *render ad uno l'onore che se li deve*.

I take it as a great honour, *lo tengo a grand' onore*.

I have a great honour for him, *so grande stima di lui*.

Honour [honesty] *onore, probità, integrità, fedeltà*, s. f.

A man of honour, *un uomo onorato*.

The point of honour, *puntiglio d'onore*.

You are bound in honour to do it, *voi siete in onore obbligato di farlo*.

Honour [glory, reputation] *onore, gloria, riputazione, fama*.

Honour [chastity] *onore, castità, pudicizia*.

A woman that has lost her honour, *un donna disonorata, che ha perduto il suo onore*.

Honours [dignities, preferments] *onore, grado, dignità*.

To be raised to great honours, *esser innalzato a grandi onori*.

A lady of honour to the princess, *dama d'onore della principessa*.

Your honour, *titolo che si da in Inghilterra ai titolati e dame di qualche qualità: si da anche a' semplici gentiluomini e gentildonne. Non s'usa più troppo.*

Honour, in law [the most noble part of seigniories, upon which other inferior lordships or manors depend] *signoria*, s. f.

Honour [coat card] *figura, testa*.

Honour [courtesy] *riverenza di donna. Non è più in uso in questo senso.*

To pay honour to a bill of exchange [among merchants] *fare onore ad una lettera di cambio*.

I shall pay honour to your bill when due, *in scadenza farò onore alla vostra tratta*.

To HO'NOUR [to respect, to reverence] *onorare, far onore, rispettare, portar rispetto, riverire*.

Fear God and honour the king, *temi Dio e onora il re*.

Honour me with your commands, *fatemi l'onore de' vostri comandi*.

To honour a bill of exchange, *fare onore ad una lettera di cambio*.

HO'NOURABLE, adj. [worthy of honour] *onorabile, degno d'onore, stimabile, onorevole, onorato*.

Honourable person, *una persona onorabile, degna d'onore*.

An honourable action, *un' azione onorevole, onorata*.

Right honourable [a title given to persons of quality] *eccellentissimo*.

HO'NORABLY, adv. *onorevolmente, onoratamente*.

HO'NORARY, adj. [or titular] *titolare*.

An honorary officer, *un ufficiale titolare*.

HO'NOURED, adj. *onorato, stimato, riverito*.

Honoured Sir, *stimatissimo Signore*.

HO'NOURER, s. *colui che onora, che rispetta, che stima, che venera*.

HOOD, s. [a covering for the head] *cappuccio, bavaglio, bacucco*, s. m.

The hood of a cloak, *cappuccio di mantello*.

A hawk's hood, *cappello di falcone, quella coperta di cuojo, che si mette in capo al falcone*.

A monk's hood, *cappuccio di frate*.

A woman's riding-hood, s. f. *veste da donna per cavalcare*.

A woman's hood, *cuffia da donna*.

HO'ODED, adj. *incappucciato*.

She went out hooded and scarfed, *ella uscì colla cuffia, e colla ciarpa*.

To HO'ODWINK [to blindfold] *bendar gli occhi, imbacuccare, imbavagliare*.

To hoodwink the mind, *accieear la mente*.

Hoodwinked [or hoodwinkt] adj. *che ha gli occhi bendati, imbacuccato, imbavagliato*.

HOOF, s. *unghia*, s. f.

A horse's hoof, *unghia di cavallo*.

To beat the hoof [to travel a foot] *batter la strada, viaggiare a piedi*.

Hoof-bound, *incastellato, si dice del piè del cavallo, quando è troppo stretto, e alto*.

HOOK, s. [a bended iron to hang things upon] *uncino*, s. m. *strumento di ferro adunco*.

Hang it upon the hook, *appiccatelo, all' uncino*.

A tenter-hook, *pendaglio*, s. m.

A fishing-hook, *amo*, s. m.

A sheep-hook, *baston di pastore*.

A pot-hook, *catena da cammino*.

A flesh-hook, *una forcina*.

To get a thing by hook or by crook, *guadagnar che che si sia di ruffa in ruffa*.

To be off the hooks [or out of humour] *esser di cattivo umore*.

To put one off the hook, *fare andare in collera alcuno*.

To HOOK, or to hook in, *arrampinare, uncinare*.

To hook a thing out of one, *scalzare alcuno, sottrarre, e cavare altrui di bocca artatamente quello che si vorrebbe sapere*.

HO'OKED, adj. [or made like a hook] *uncinato, storto, curbo*.

HOOP, s. [a circle to bind a barrel, &c.] *cerchio*, s. m. *quello che cigne e circonda la botte, e simili*.

Hoop, *quel coso d'osso di balena o d' altro, fatto a cerchi, che le donne portan sotto le vesti che le fa somigliare in qualche modo alle campane*.

A hoop [a bird called a lap-wing] *upupa*, s. f. *uccello con una cresta in capo*.

Hoop-ring, *anello*, s. m.

A hoop [a measure of a peck] *stioro*, s. m. *la quarta porta dello stajo*.

To HOOP [to bind with hoops] *cerchiare, legare con cerchi*.

To hoop a barrel, *cerchiare un barile*.

To hoop, or whoop [to cry out inarticularly] *gridare, vociferare*.

HO'OPER, s. [cooper] *bottajo*, s. m.

Hooper [wild swan] *cigno selvatico*.

HO'OPING COUGH, s. *spezie di tosse convulsiva*.

To HOOT, *gridar dietro per disprezzo*.

To hoot, *gridare come fa il cucco, o barbagianni*.

HOOT, s. *il gridar dietro con romore; grido di molte voci insieme*.

HOP, s. [a plant] *lupolo*.

A hop yard, *luogo dove si piantano i lupoli*.

Hop, s. [or hopping] *salto*, s. m.

To HOP [to leap with one leg] *arrancare, salterellare; saltar sur un piè solo*.

To hop beer, *metter lupoli nella birra*.

HOPE, s. [expectation] *speranza*, s. f. *aspettazione, credenza di futuro bene*.

God is my only hope, *Iddio solo è la mia speranza; io spero in Dio solo*.

To be in great hopes, *aver buona speranza*.

To answer one's hopes, *riuscire secondo le nostre speranze*.

There's no hope of his life, *non v' è speranza della sua vita; egli è spedito*.

'Tis past hope [there's no hope] *non c' è più rimedio, non c' è più luogo da sperare*.

I have great hopes in him, *confido, o spero molto in lui*.

To HOPE, *sperare*.

I hope he will live, *spero, che viverà*.

To hope for a thing, *sperare, aspettare, attendere*. pret. *attesi*.

To hope in God, *sperare, confidare, in Dio*.

HO'PED, adj. *sperato*.

Hoped for, *sperato, aspettato, atteso*.

A thing not to be hoped for, *una cosa da non sperare*.

HO'PEFUL, adj. *di grande aspettazione, che da di se buona speranza*.

A hopeful youth, *un giovine di grande aspettazione*.

HO'PEFULNESS, s. *aspettazione, espettazione*, s. f.

The hopefulness of a child, *la buona indole d'un fanciullo*.

HO'PELESS, adj. [without hope] *disperato, senza speranza*.

HO'PER, s. *colui che spera cose piacevoli*.

HO'PPER, s. [from to hop] *saltatore, che salta*.

A mill-hopper, *tramoggia*, s. f.

Hopper-horsed, *che cammina come uno sciancato*.

He went hopper-hors'd in that business [he was disappointed] *egli ritornò colla tromba nel sacco; riuscì male in quel negozio*.

HO'RAL, } adj. [belonging to
HO'RARY, } hours] *orario, d'ora, appartenente ad ora*.

An horary circle, *un cerchio orario, dove son comprese le ore*.

To say one's horary prayers, *recitare l'ufficio divino*.

HORDE, s. [a clan; a migratory crew of people] *truppa di gente che non sta troppo tempo in un luogo, ma passa e va in altri*.

HO'RIZON, s. [that great circle of the sphere, which in that place divides the upper hemisphere from the lower hemisphere that is under us] *orizzonte*, s. m. *linea, o cerchio celeste, che divide l'uno e l'altro emisperio, e termina la nostra vista*.

HO'RIZONTAL, adj. *orrizontale, d' orizzonte*.

HO'RIZONTALLY, adv. *orizzontalmente*.

HORN, s. *corno*, s. m. pl. *corna*, s. f.

The horns of an ox, *le corna d'un bue*.

The horns of a snail, *le corna d'una lumaca*.

Hart's horn, *corno di cervo*.

The horns of the moon in her increase, *le corna della luna nuova*.

Horn-mad [jealous] *geloso*.

A bugle horn, or hunter's horn, *corno da caccia*.

To wind, or blow a horn, *sonar il corno*.

An ink-horn, *calamajo*, s. m.

A horn-book, *un abbicci, un libretto pe' ragazzi in cui è l'alfabeto*.

Horn-howl, or horn-coot [a bird of prey] *un gufo*.

Horn-work [a piece of fortification] *opera a corno*.

A shoe-horn, *calzatojo*, s. m. *quello strumento, col quale si calzan le scarpe*.

Horn-back [a fish] *spezie di pesce simile all' anguilla*.

HORNED, adj. *cornuto, che ha corna*.

HORNET, s. [a sort of fly] *calabrone*, s. m.

HO'RNY, adj. *fatto di corno*.

Horny, *somigliante al corno*.

Horny, *calloso; duro come corno*.

HO'ROLOGE, s. [clock, dial, watch] *orologio, oriuolo*, s. m.

HO'ROSCOPE, s. [the degree of the ascendant, or the star ascending above the horizon, at the moment an astrological figure or scheme is made] *oroscopo*, s. m. *il punto natale di qualche persona*.

HO'RRIBLE, adj. [frightful] *orribile, spaventevole*.

Horrible [excessive] *orribile, grande, eccessivo*.

HO'RRIBLENESS, s. *orribilità*, s. m. *orrore, spavento*, s. m.

HO'RRIBLY, adv. *orribilmente, con orrore, spaventevolmente*.

HO'RRID, adj. [dreadful] *orrido, orribile, spaventevole*.

A horrid monster, *un mostro orribile*.

A horrid crime, *un delitto enorme*.

HO'RROUR, s. [dread, fright] *orrore, spavento*, s. m. *eccessiva paura*.

HORSE, s. [a beast well known] *cavallo*, s. m.

The head, neck, main, tail, and feet of a horse, *la testa, il collo, i crini, là coda, e i piedi d'un cavallo*.

A saddle, pack, post, race, and cart horse, *cavallo di sella, basto, posta, corso, e carro*.

The fore horse of a coach, *il cavallo che è a destra del cocchiere*.

The near horse, *il cavallo che è alla man manca del cocchiere*.

Hackney horse, *cavallo d'affitto*.

Stage horse, *cavallo di posta*.

Double horse, *cavallo che porta in groppa*.

A winged horse, *un cavallo alato*.

A pacing or trotting horse, *un cavallo che va l'ambio, o che trotta*.

A horse of state, *un cavallo a manco*.

The great horse, *cavallo di maneggio*.

A Barb-horse, *un barbero, cavallo corridore di Barberia*.

A Spanish-horse, *un cavallo di Spagna.*
A sea horse, *un cavallo marino.*
A wooden horse, *un cavallo di legno.*
To get upon a horse, *montare a cavallo.*
To ride a horse, *cavalrare un cavallo.*
To give a horse the head, *dar la mano, o la briglia ad un cavallo.*
To come off one's horse, *scavalcare, smontare, scendar di cavallo.*
He has a horse that never stumbles, *gli è uno che sta sodo al macchione.*
I'll win the horse, or lose the saddle, *voglio guadagnar tutto, o perder tutto.*
A gentleman of the horse to a nobleman, or the master of the horse to a prince, *un cavallerizzo.*
Horse, or horsemen, *cavalleria.*
A troop of horse, *una compagnia di cavalleria.*
Light-horse, *cavalli leggieri.*
A stalking horse [such as is used in fowling] *un cavallo fatto alla caccia.*
Horseback, *a cavallo.*
To get up on horseback, *montare a cavallo.*
To ride a horseback, *cavalcare, andare a cavallo.*
A horse block, *un cavalcatojo, luogo rialto fatto per comodità di montare a cavallo.*
Horse trappings, *arnesi di cavallo.*
Horse lock, *pastoje di cavallo.*
Horse guard, *gardie a cavallo.*
Horse litter, *lettiga,* s. f.
Horse dung, *sterco di cavallo.*
Horse colt, *puledro.*
Horse meat, *quel che si da a mangiare a' cavalli.*
Horse-shoe, *ferro di cavallo.*
Horse-comb, *stregghia,* s. f.
Horse-tail, *coda di cavallo.*
Horse-load, *soma,* s. f.
Horse race, *corsa di cavalli.*
Horse leech, or horse doctor [a farrier] *maniscalco.*
Horse fly, *tafano,* s. m.
Wooden horse, *cavalletto,* s. m.
Horse radish, *rafano,* s. m.
To horse a mare [as a stallion does] *montare una cavalla.*
To horse one at school [to hold him up while he is whipt] *alzare uno a cavallo, o dare un cavallo ad uno, sferzare un fanciullo alla scuola.*
HO'RSED, adj. *montato.*
To be well horsed, *esser ben montato, aver buon cavallo sotto.*
HO'RSEMAN, s. *cavaliere,* s. m. *colui che cavalca.*
HO'RSEMANSHIP, s. [the art of riding or managing horses] *maneggio,* s. m. *l'arte di maneggiare un cavallo.*
HOSA'NNA [an Hebrew word for, save us we beseech you] *osanna, vocabolo Ebreo, che è interpretato deh facci salvi.*
HOSE, s. [stocking] *calzetta,* s. f.
HO'SED, adj. *calzato.*
HO'SEN, *è il numero del più di* Hose.

HO'SIER, s. [one who sells stockings] *calzettajo,* s. m.
HO'SPITABLY, adj. [that uses hospitality, friendly] *ospitale, che usa ospitalità.*
HO'SPITAL, s. [a house erected out of charity for the entertainment or relief of the poor, sick, impotent, or aged people] *spedale,* s. m.
HO'SPITALLERS, s. [an order of knights who built an hospital at Jerusalem, for entertainment of pilgrims, whom they protected in their travels] *spedaliere, cavaliere dello spedale Gerosolimitano.*
HOSPITA'LITY, s. [the entertaining and receiving strangers] *ospitalità,* s. f. *liberalità nel ricevere i forestieri.*
To keep hospitality, *usare ospitalità.*
HOST, s. [the consecrated wafer at the communion among the Roman catholicks] *ostia,* s. f. *quel pane che si consacra alla messa.*
Host [an innkeeper or landlord] *oste,* s. m. *quegli che da bere e mangiare, e alberga altrui per danari.*
To reckon without one's host, *fare il conto senza l'oste.*
Host [an army] *oste, esercito.*
The Lord of hosts [an expression used in the Old Testament] *il Dio degli eserciti.*
To HOST, *mangiare in casa d'un altro.*
To Host [to encounter in battle] *venir a battaglia.*
To Host [to review a body of men, to muster] *dar la rivista a' soldati.*
HO'STAGE, s. [a person left as a surety for the performance of the articles of a treaty] *ostaggio, statico,* s. m. *quella persona, che si dà in potere altrui per sicurtà dell' osservanza del convenuto.*
HO'STESS, s. [landlady] *ostessa,* s. f. *la moglie dell' oste.*
HO'STESS-SHIP, s. *grado di ostessa.*
Your hostess-ship, *vossignoria signora ostessa, modo da burla.*
HO'STILE, adj. [enemy like] *ostile, nemico, da nemico.*
In an hostile manner, *ostilmente.*
They set upon us in an hostile manner, *ci assalirono ostilmente.*
HO'STILITY, s. [enmity] *ostilità, atto da nemico.*
HO'STLER, s. [a groom who looks to the stables in an inn] *mozzo di stalla.*
HO'STRY, s. [the stables in an inn] *stalla,* s. f.
HOT, adj. [contrary to cold] *caldo, ardente, contrario di freddo.*
The fire is hot, *il fuoco è caldo.*
A very hot fire, *un fuoco ardente.*
Hot weather, *tempo caldo.*
To be of a hot constitution, *esser d'un temperamento caldo.*
Hot [eager, passionate] *caldo, veemente, violento.*
A hot man, *un uomo caldo, o violento.*

To be hot, *aver caldo.*
To grow hot, *scaldarsi.*
To drink hot, *ber caldo.*
To make a thing hot, *scaldare che che si sia.*
Hot-bed, s. *pezzo di terreno scaldato con molto letame o altra cosa che fermenti molto.*
Hot-house, or bath, *stufa, bagno caldo.*
To be hot upon a thing, *infervorirsi in che che si sia, farlo con caldezza, con veemenza.*
Hot-headed, *violento, caldo di testa, veemente.*
Hot-shot, *ex.* he is a meer hot-shot [a pitiful, or impotent fellow] *un povero uomo, uno scarno.*
HOTCH-POTCH, or HODGE-PODGE, *zibaldone, miscuglio,* s. m.
HO'TLY, adv. *caldamente, con ardore, ardentemente, vivamente.*
HOT-SPUR, s. *un uomo caldo di testa, precipitoso, violento, veemente nelle sue passioni, ostinato, caparbio.*
Hot-spur, s. *spezie di pisello che cresce presto.*
HOT-SPURRED, *violento, caldo di testa, temerario.*
HOVE, pret. *del verbo* to heave.
HO'VEL, s. [a covering or shelter for cattle] *capanna fatta in campagna per il bestiame.*
To HO'VEL, *dar ricovero in una capanna.*
HO'VEN, part. pass. *alzato, gonfio, tumido, tumefatto.*
To HO'VER [to flutter, to fly over] *svolazzare, bilanciarsi sull' ali.*
To hover a fire, *covar il fuoco, star di continuo presso al fuoco.*
The dangers which hover over our heads, *i pericoli che ci soprastanno, che pendono sopra di noi.*
To hover [or shiver] for cold, *battere i denti di freddo.*
HOUGH, s. [the joint of the hinder leg of a beast] *garretto,* s. m.
To HOUGH [to cut the houghs] *tagliare il garretto.*
HOULT, s. [a small wood] *boschetto.*
HOUND, s. [a hunting dog] *bracco,* s. m. *can da caccia.*
A grey hound, *veltro, can da giungere, levriere.*
A blood-hound, *bracco da sangue.*
Hell hound, s. *cane infernale, cerbero.*
Hound-grass [an herb] *sorta d'erba.*
To HOUND, *ex.* to hound a stag, *lasciare i cani al cervo, cacciare il cervo.*
HOUP, s. [puet] *upupa; sorta d'uccello.*
HOUR, s. [the 24th part of a natural day] *ora,* s. f.
Half an hour, *mezz' ora.*
A quarter of an hour, *un quarto d' ora.*
An hour and an half, *un' ora e mezzo.*
An hour ago, *un' ora fa.*
Within an hour, *fra un' ora.*

Within two hours, *fra due ore.*
To the last hour, *fin all' ultimo.*
In a good hour, *alla buon' ora.*
In an ill hour, *alla mal' ora.*
To keep good hours, *ritirarsi a casa di buon' ora, per tempo.*
To keep bad hours, *ritirarsi a casa tardi.*
Hour-glass, *oriuolo a polvere.*
Hour-plate, *mostra d'oriuolo.*
HO'URLY, adv. *ad ogni momento, d'ora in ora.*
HOUSE, s. [a place of abode] *casa,* s. f. *edificio da abitare.*
A town house, *casa della città.*
A country house, *villa,* s. f.
To keep a house, *tener casa.*
House [family] *rasa, schiatta, famiglia, stirpe,* s. f. *legnaggio,* s. m.
The house of Austria, *la casa d'Austria.*
The two houses of parliament, *le due camere del parlamento.*
The house of lords, *la camera de' signori.*
The house of commons, *la camera de' comuni, o la camera bassa.*
An ale house, *un' osteria di birra.*
To keep a good house, *tener buona tavola, trattarsi bene.*
To keep open house, *tener corte bandita.*
A house of office, *il privato, agiamento, o cesso.*
A coffee-house, *un caffè, una bottega da caffè.*
A pigeon house, *una colombaja.*
A wash house, *luogo dove si lavan le biancherie.*
A work house, *il luogo dove l'artigiano fa i suoi lavori.*
A store house, *un magazzino.*
An ice house, *una ghiacciaia, o diaeciaria.*
House room, *luogo, spazio.*
To give one house room, *alloggiare uno in casa sua.*
House eaves, *gronde,* s. f.
House top, *tetto,* s. m.
Housekeeper, *uomo o donna che tien casa.*
Housekeeper [a man that looks to a great house] *cesiere, casiero, guardiano della casa.*
Housekeeper [a sort of woman servant] *cesiera, guardiana della casa.*
Housekeeping, *masserizie.*
To go to housekeeping, *aprir casa.*
Good housekeeping [good table] *buona tavola.*
House breed, *pan casereccio.*
House leek [an herb] *sempreviva,* s. f.
House rent, *la pigione della casa.*
Housemaid, *serva, che fa i letti, e spazza le camere.*
House [in astrology, is a twelfth part of the heavens] *casa, in astrologia è la dodicesima parte dei cieli.*
Victualling house, *bettola, osteria,* s. f.
To HOUSE, *ricever in casa.*
To house cattle, *stallare del bestiame.*
To house corn, *rigorre il grano.*

HO'USHOLD, s. *famiglia, casa, domestici.*
The king's houshold, *la famiglia del re.*
Houshold government, *economia, governo d'una famiglia.*
Houshold-stuff, *masserizie di casa.*
HO'USING, s. [a horse cloth worn behind the saddle] *gualdrappa, coverta da cavalli.*
Housing, *quantità di case abitate, gruppo di case.*
To HOUT, verb. neut. *esclamare, gridare. E' meglio* hoot.
To hout [or hiss] at one, *fischiare ad uno.*
HO'UTED, adj. *esclamato, gridato, fischiato.*
HOW, s. [a tool used by gardeners] *marra.*
How, ad. [before an adjective] *quanto.*
How much? *quanto?*
How well? *quanto bene?*
How great? *quanto grande?*
To how much? *per quanto?*
How many? *quanti?*
How many times? *quante volte?*
How far? *quanto lontano, discosto, o distante?*
How long? *quanto tempo?*
How long have you been here? *quanto tempo siete stato qui? quanto tempo è cho siete qui?*
How old is he? *quanti anni ha? di che età è?*
You cannot think how pleased I was, *non potete credere quanto restassi sodisfatto.*
They say so, how truly I cannot tell, *si dire così, ma se sia vero non lo so.*
Give us an account how it was, *diteci come andò la cosa.*
He told how he travelled from one country to another, *ci diede un pieno ragguaglio del suo viaggio in diversi paesi.*
How [after what manner] *come, in che modo.*
How do you do? *come state?*
How goes the world? *come va il mondo?*
I don't know how to do it? *non saprei in che modo farlo.*
How think you? *che ve ne pare?*
How now? *cosa è questa, che vuol dir questo, dove siamo?*
How soon will you come? *quando verrete, quanto tempo sarete a venire?*
How near is it, *è molto vicino?*
When I consider how near I was being killed, *quando considero quanto poco mancò che non fossi ammazzato.*
How so? *perchè, per che causa?*
How great soever, *per grande che sia.*
How small soever, *per piccolo che sia.*
How many soever, *per molti che sieno, benchè sieno in gran numero.*
HOWBE, HOWBEIT, } *v.* However.
HOWDYE, [how do ye] *come state? come va la salute?*
HO'WEVER, conj. *però, nulla di meno, con tutto ciò, pure.*

I am not disposed to go, however to oblige you I will, *non ho gran voglia d'andarvi, però per obbligarvi v'anderò.*
However the matter stands, *in qualunque stato sieno le cose.*
However desirous I was to see it, *benchè avessi gran desiderio di vedero.*
To HOWL [to cry like a dog or wolf] *urlare, mandar fuori urli, gagnolare, mugolare, squittire.* pres. *squittisco.*
HOWL, s. *urlo, mugghio.*
HO'WLET, s. [a night bird] *allocco,* s. m. *uccello notturno.*
HO'WLING, s. *urlamento, urlo,* s. m.
HOWP, s. [a bird] *upupa,* s. f. *spezie d'uccello.*
HOWSOE'VER, adv. [nevertheless] *però, pure, con tutto ciò, nulladimeno.*
To HOX [to hamstring] *tagliare garetti.*
HOY, s. [a kind of bark] *sorta di barra assai grande.*
HU'BBUB, s. [great tumult, uproar] *tumulto, fracasso, frastuono; strepito,* s. m.
HUCKLE-BONE, s. [the hip bone] *anca,* s. f. *l'osso che è tra'l fianco, e la coscia.*
HUCK-SHO'ULDERED, adj. *gobbo, scrignuto.*
HU'CKSTER, s. [a seller of provisions by retail] *rivenditore, rivendugliolo, rigattiere,* s. m. *rivendugliola,* s. f.
To fall into the huckster's hands, *esser acchiappato, esser truffato.*
HU'DDLE, s. [a bustle, disorder, confusion] *strepito, tumulto, disordine,* s. m. *confusione,* s. f.
All in a huddle, *confusamente, in confusione, disordinatamente, in disordine.*
To HU'DDLE [to put up things in a confused manner] *rimescolare, confonder insieme, mescolare, confondere.* pret. *confusi.*
To Huddle [to come in a croud or hurry] *venir in folta e in fretta.*
HU'DDLED, adj. *rimescolato, mescolato, confuso.*
HU'DDLING, s. *rimescolamento, mescuglio,* s. m. *confusione,* s. f.
HUE, s. [colour] *colore.*
Black hue, *nero, color nero.*
Hue [countenance] *cera,* s. f. *sembiante,* s. m.
Hue and cry, *schiamazzo, grido di molte persone.*
To make hue and cry after one, *perseguitar alcuno con grida, correr dietro ad alcuno gridando.*
HUFF, s. [a swaggering fellow, a bully] *un millantatore, un tagliacantoni, uno sgherro, un bravo, un bravaccio.*
To be upon the huff about a thing, *vantarsi, vanagloriarsi di qualche cosa.*
To be in a huff, *esser in collera, saltar la mosca, incollerirsi.*
To HUFF [to puff, to blow] *soffiare, mandar fuor l'alito con impeto, soffiare.*
To huff a man at draughts, *soffiare una pedina al giuoco delle tavole.*

To huff [to swagger, to rant, to vapour] *bravare, fare il bravo, minacciare altieramente, e imperiosamente, braveggiare.*

HU'FFER, *v.* Huff.

HU'FFING, s. *bravata,* s. f. *il bravare.*

HU'FFISH, adj. *insolente, fiero, arrogante, imperioso, petulante.*

HU'FFISHNESS, s. *petulanza, insolenza, falsa bravura.*

To HUG [to embrace] *abbracciare, prender nelle braccia, strigner nelle braccia.*

To hug one's self, *ammirarsi, applaudirsi.*

HUGE, adj. [great, large, vast] *grande, smisurato, vasto, grande fuor di modo.*

A huge man, *un uomo grande, un omaccio.*

Huge strong, *fortissimo, molto forte.*

HU'GELY, adv. *molto, grandemente.*

HU'GENESS, s. *grandezza, vastità, smisuratezza,* s. f.

HU'GGED, adj. [from to hug] *abbracciato, stretto nelle braccia.*

HU'GGER-MUGGER, adv. [privately, clandestinely] *segretamente, sordamente, di nascosto, di soppiatto, nascosamente.*

To do a thing in hugger-mugger, *fare che che si sia nascosamente, di nascosto, sotto mano, di soppiatto.*

HU'GGING, s. [from to hug] *abbracciamento,* s. m. *l'abbracciare.*

HU'GY, adv. *v.* Huge.

HUKE, s. [a cloak] *un mantello, un ferrajuolo.*

HULCH, s. [bunch] *gobba,* s. m. *scrigno,* s. m.

HULK, s. [a sort of a ship] *piatta,* s. f. *spezie di barca Olandese con fondo piano.*

Hulk [the body of a ship] *il corpo d' una nave.*

Hulk [any thing bulky and unwieldy] *ogni cosa di molta grandezza, e da non potersi agevolmente maneggiare.*

To HULK, *sviscerare; e dicesi per lo più del cavar l'interiora a una lepre.*

HULL, s. [the chaff of corn, the cod of pulse] *guscio, baccello,* s. m.

Hull [the main body or hulk of a ship without rigging] *il guscio, il corpo d'un vascello senza arredi.*

To HULL [to float] *galleggiare, stare a galla.*

To hull [or to lye a hull, to ride to and fro upon the water, as a ship does] *andare o onde, barcollare, come fa il vascello che ha le vele ammainate.*

To hull beans, *sgranar delle fave.*

HU'LLING, adj. *galleggiante.*

HU'LLY, adj. *che ha baccello, che ha guscio.*

To HUM, verb neut. [as bees do] *rombare, ronzare, e dicesi delle pecchie, vespe, mosconi, e simili.*

To hum and haw, *esitare, star dubbioso, dubitare.*

To hum a tune, *cantarellare un aria.*

To hum one [to applaud him] *applaudire a qualcheduno, approvarlo, farli applauso.*

HUMA'NE, adj. [belonging to mankind] *umano, di uomo, attenente a uomo.*

Human nature, *la natura umana.*

Human [affable, courteous, mild] *umano, affabile, benigno, mansueto, cortese, trattabile.*

Human learning, *lettere umane, belle lettere.*

HUMA'NELY, adv. *umanamente, a modo d'uomo.*

Humanely speaking, *umanamente parlando.*

Humanely [kindly] *umanamente, con umanità, cortesemente, benignamente.*

HU'MANIST, s. [one who is skilled in human learning] *umanista,* s. m. *che professa belle lettere.*

HUMA'NITY, s. [human nature] *umanità,* s. f. *la natura umana.*

Humanity [kindness] *umanità, benignità, cortesia,* s. f.

To HUMANI'ZE [to make humane and kind] *umanare, render umano, trattabile.*

HUMANI'ZED, adj. *umanato.*

HU'MBLE, adj. [lowly minded, modest] *umile, modesto, dimesso.*

To HU'MBLE [to make humble] *umiliare, fare umile, rintuzzar l'orgoglio, abbassare, mortificare.*

To humble one's self, *umiliarsi, divenire umile, abbassarsi.*

HU'MBLED, adj. *umiliato, abbassato, mortificato.*

HU'MBLENESS, s. [or humility] *umiltà, sommessione.*

HU'MBLES, s. [a part of the entrails of a deer] *coratella di cervo.*

HU'MBLY, adv. *umilmente, con umiltà.*

Most humbly, *umilissimamente.*

A HUM-DRUM, *un alocco, un gonzo, un minchione, un babbuasso, uno scimocco.*

To HU'MECT, } [to moisten] *umettare, inumidire,* pres. *inumidisco.*
To HU'MECTATE, }

HUMECTA'TION, s. [moistening] *umettazione,* s. f. *l'umettare.*

HU'MID, adj. [damp, moist, wet] *umido, che ha in se umidità.*

HUMIDI'TY, s. [dampness, moistness] *umidità, umidezza,* s. f. *umido, umidore,* s. m.

To HU'MILITATE [to make low, to humble] *umiliare, fare umile, abbassare, mortificare.*

HUMILIA'TION, s. [the state of being humbled] *umiliazione, l'umiliarsi, sommessione,* s. f.

HUMI'LITY, s. [humbleness] *umiltà, sommessione,* s. f.

HU'MMER, s. *uno che applaude.*

HU'MMING, s. [from to hum] *ronzio, ronzo, ronzamento, rombo,* s. m.

The humming of bees, *il ronzo, il rombo delle pecchie.*

The humming of several people together, *sussurro, bisbiglio,* s. m.

The humming bird, *spezie d'uccello.*

HU'MOR, *v.* Humour.

HU'MORIST, s. [one who is full of humours, or whimsies] *umorista, uomo fantastico e incostante.*

HU'MOROUS, *v.* Humoursome.

HU'MOUROUSLY, adv. *fantasticamente, da fantastico, cappricciosamente.*

HU'MOUR, s. [moisture] *umore,* s. m. *materia umida, e liquida.*

The humours of the body, *gli umori del corpo.*

Humour [disposition of the mind] *umore, disposizione dell' animo.*

A good humour'd man, *un uomo di buon umore.*

To put one in good humour, *mettere alcuno in buon umore.*

Take him in the humour, *pigliatelo quando sta di vena.*

To be out of humour, to be in an ill humour, *esser di cattivo umore.*

Humour [fancy] *umore, capriccio,* s. m. *fantasia,* s. f.

If the humour takes me, *se mi vien voglia.*

'Tis a meer humour, *è una pura fantasia.*

To please one's own humour, *piacersi, compiacersi, divertirsi, secondare le sue inclinazioni.*

What is the humour of this? *che vuol dir ciò?*

He has a great deal of wit and humour, *egli ha delle specie singolari; ha una sorta d'ingegno bisbetica e singolare; è faceto e bizarro insieme.*

A man of humour, *uomo faceto, ma d'una foggia sua particolare, e che pizzica del disbeticamente acuto.*

To HU'MOUR, *piacere, compiacere, contentare, andare a seconda, secondare.*

I'll do what I can to humour him, *farò ogni possibile per compiacerlo.*

You humour him too much, *voi gli andate troppo a versi, voi avete troppa condescendenza per lui.*

He humours him in every thing, *egli lo seconda in ogni cosa.*

To humour the tune that one sings, *dar delle grazie ad un' aria.*

HU'MOUR'D, adj. *compiaciuto, contentato, secondato.*

HU'MOURSOME, adj. [fantastical, whimsical] *umorista, fantastico, capriccioso, bisbetico, ritroso.*

A humoursome man, *un fantastico.*

HUMP, s. [a crooked back] *gobba, scrigno.*

HU'MPBACK, s. [crooked back; high shoulders] *un gobbo, che ha larghe e curve spalle.*

HU'MPBACKED, adj. [having a crooked back] *gobbo, scrignuto.*

HUNCH, s. [a thrust with the elbow] *gomitata,* s. f. *percossa col gomito.*

Hunch-back'd, adj. [crooked back'd] *gobbo, scrignuto.*

To HUNCH [to give a thruſt with the elbow] *dare una gomitata.*
HU'NCHED, adj. *percoſſo col gomito.*
HU'NDRED, adj. *cento.*
A hundred, *un centinajo.*
By hun'reds, *a centinaja.*
Hundred [a part of a ſhire] *cantone,* s. m. *parte d'una provincia.*
Hundred weight, *cantàro,* s. m. *cento libbre, un quintale.*
Hundredfold, adj. *centuplo, cento doppio.*
HU'NDREDTH, adj. *centeſimo.*
HUNG, adj. [from to hang] *appiccato, impiccato, appeſo.*
Hung-beef, *del bue affumicato.*
A room hung with rich tapeſtry, *una camera riccamente tappezzata.*
HU'NGER, s. *fame,* s. f. *grande appetito, voglia grande di mangiare.*
Pinched with hunger, *affamato, morto di fame.*
Hunger is the beſt ſauce, *appetito non vuol ſalſa.*
Starved with hunger, *affamato, morto di fame, che ha gran fame.*
To HU'NGER [to ſuffer hunger] *morir di fame.*
To hunger [to deſire with great eagerneſs] *bramare con molta anſietà.*
HU'NGERBIT, HU'NGERBITTEN, } adj. *tormentato dalla fame.*
HU'NGERLY, adv. [greedily] *avidamente, ingordamente, goloſamente, da ghiotto.*
HU'NGERLY, adj. *affamato.*
HU'NGERSTARVED, adj. *affamato; morto di fame; che ha gran fame; magro per lunga fame.*
HU'NGRILY, adv. *con molto appetito, con gran fame, affamatamente.*
HU'NGRY, adj. [craving after food] *affamato, che ha gran fame.*
To be hungry, *aver fame.*
To be deadly hungry, *morir di fame.*
Hungry dogs will eat dirty pudding, *a tempo di careſtia pan veccioſo; ad uno che ha fame ogni coſa par buona.*
A hungry ſtomach, *un grand' appetito, una gran fame.*
The hungry evil [the canine appetite] *la fame canina.*
A hungry table [a table that does not afford victuals enough] *tavola famelica, o ſcarſa dove c' è poco da mangiare.*
HUNKS, s. a meer hunks [a ſordid miſer] *un miſero, un avaro, uno ſpilorcio.*
To HUNT [to chaſe wild beaſts] *cacciare, perſeguitare le fiere ſalvatiche per pigliarle, andare alla caccia.*
To hunt a wild boar, *cacciare i cinghiali, andare alla caccia de' ringhiali.*
To hunt after one [to look for one up and down] *andare in traccia d'uno, cercarlo da per tutto.*
To hunt after riches, *andare in traccia delle ricchezze, eſſer avido di ricchezze.*
To hunt out, *ſcoprire, trovare.*

HU'NTED, adj. *cacciato,* v. To hunt.
HU'NTER, s. *cacciatore,* s. m.
Hunter [a horſe for hunting] *corſiero, cavallo da caccia,*
HU'NTING, s. *caccia,* s. f.
To go a hunting, *andare alla caccia.*
A hunting-nag, *un cavallo da caccia.*
HU'NTRESS, s. *cacciatrice.*
HU'NTSMAN, s. *capocaccia,* s. m. *ſoprantendente della caccia, cacciatore.*
HU'RDLE, s. [a frame of hazel-rods wattled together] *graticcio gruticcio,* s. m. *ſtrumento di varie forme, fatto per lo più di vimini teſſuti.*
To HU'RDLE, *cerchiare di graticci, graticolare.*
HURDS, s. *il capecchio, la ſtoppa.*
To HURL [to fling, to caſt] *ſcagliare, tirare, lanciare, geſtare, rotolar giù.*
To hurl a dart, *lanciare un dardo.*
To hurl one's ſelf into inevitable ruin, *rovinarſi affatto, precipitarſi in qualche diſgrazia.*
HURL, s. [tumult, riot, commotion] *tumulto, riotta, ſollevamento.*
HU'RLED, adj. *ſcagliato, tirato, lanciato, rotolato giù.*
HURLY-BURLY, s. [confuſion] *ſcompiglio, diſordine, tumulto, garbuglio, perturbamento,* s. m. *confuſione,* s. f.
Hurly-bury [crowd of people] *calca, folla,* s. f. *concorſo di popolo.*
HU'RRICANE, HU'RRICANO, } s. [a violent ſtorm, or wind] *tempeſta di venti contrari.*
HU'RRY, s. [confuſion] *ſcompiglio, diſordine, garbuglio,* s. m. *confuſione,* s. f.
Hurry [great haſte] *fretta, preſcia, precipitazione.*
To do things in a hurry, *fare che che ſi ſia in fretta.*
You are in a great hurry, *voi ſiete ben frettoloſo.*
To HU'RRY [to precipitate] *precipitare, affrettare con ſomma ſollecitudine.*
To hurry a buſineſs, *precipitare, affrettar troppo un negozio.*
To hurry one along to deſtruction, *precipitare alcuno in qualche diſgrazia.*
To hurry [to haſten over much] *affrettare, far fretta, ſollecitare.*
To hurry one on, *affrettare, ſollecitare alcuno, eccitarlo, ſpronarlo.*
HU'RRY'D, adj. *precipitato, affrettato, ſollecitato.*
HURST [a grove or thicket of trees] *un boſchetto.*
HURT, s. [prejudice, damage] *male, pregiudizio, torto, danno,* s. m.
To do one a great deal of hurt, *far gran male ad uno.*
To my hurt, *a mio danno, a pregiudizio.*
Hurt [ſore] *male, ferita.*
Take heed, you will do yourſelf ſome hurt, *avertite che non vi facciate del male.*
To receive a hurt in any part of the body, *eſſer ferito in qualche parte del corpo.*
What hurt is there in that? *che male c' è in ciò?*
Hurt, adj. *ferito, ſtroppiato, che c' è fatto male.*
I am ſadly hurt in the leg, *mi ſon fatto gran male alla gamba, mi ſono ſtroppiato una gamba.*
You are more afraid than hurt, *voi avete più paura che male.*
To HURT, *ferire, ſtroppiare, far male.*
You hurt my hand, *voi m' avete ſtroppiato una mano.*
You hurt me, *voi mi fate male.*
To hurt [to damage] *nuocere, pregiudicare, arrecar pregiudicio.*
HU'RTFUL, adj. [miſchievous] *nocevole, nocivo, dannoſo, pernicioſo, pericoloſo.*
HU'RTFULLY, adv. *pernicioſamente, nocivamente, pericoloſamente.*
HU'RTFULNESS, s. *pregiudicio, danno, nocumento,* s. m.
To HU'RTLE [to ſkirmiſh; to run againſt any thing; to joſtle] *ſcaramucciare, gioſtrare, correr colla lancia contro checcheſſia.*
To hurtle [to move with violence and impetuoſity] *urtare, muovere con violenza ed impeto.*
HUR'TLESS, adj. [innocent, harmleſs, innoxious, doing no harm] *innocente; che non fa male; che non cagiona danno.*
Hurtleſs [receiving no hurt] *che non ſoffre danno; illeſo.*
HU'RTLE-BERRY, s. *ſorta di pianta.*
HU'SBAND, s. [a wife's conſort] *marito.*
They live together like huſband and wife, *vivono inſieme come marito e moglie.*
A virgin ready for a huſband, *una zitella da marito.*
A good huſband, *un buon maſſajo, un uomo da far roba, e da mantenerla.*
To HU'SBAND [to manage in the ſpending] *riſparmiare, far maſſerizia.*
To huſband one's purſe, *riſparmiare la borſa, andar riſtretto nello ſpendere.*
To huſband one's time well, *ſpender bene il tempo.*
To huſband the ground, *coltivar la terra.*
HU'SBANDED, adj. *riſparmiato, coltivato.*
Ill huſbanded, *male ſpeſo.*
HUSBANDMAN, s. *agricoltore,* s. m. *che eſercita l' agricoltura.*
HU'SBANDRY, s. [the art of tilling and improving land] *agricoltura,* s. f. *l'arte del coltivare la terra.*
Huſbandry [management of expences] *economia,* s. f. *riſparmio, riſparmiamento,* s. m. *agricoltura,* s. f.
HUSCARLE, s. [a houſhold ſervant] *un domeſtico.*
HUSH, interj. [ſilence] *zitto; ſilenzio; tacete; non parlare.*

To

To hush [or keep silence] *tacere, stare zitto.*

To hush a thing [not to speak a word on't] *tacere una cosa, tenerla segreta, non parlarne.*

To HUSH, v. a. [to still; to silence; to quiet; to appease] *acquietare; far tacere; placare; calmare.*

HUSHMO'NEY, s. *danaro dato ad alcuno perchè si taccia; perchè non riveli una cosa; perchè non ne farcia testimonianza.*

HUSK, s. [the coat of corn, grain, seed, &c.] *pula, lolla, loppa,* s. f. *guscio,* s. m.

The husk of corn, *pullo di grano.*

The husk of a walnut, *guscio di noce.*

HUSKY, adj. *che ha guscio.*

HU'SSEL, s. [an old Saxon word for the holy sacrament] *la santa cena, il sagramento dell' altare.*

HU'SSELLING PEOPLE [communicants] *communicanti.*

HU'SSY, s. *corrotto da* Housewife [a sorry or bad woman] *una femminella, una femminaccia.*

HU'STINGS, s. [a principal court in London] *nome d'una delle principali corti della città di Londra.*

HU'SWIFE, s. [a manager of houshold affairs] *una massaja.*

She is an excellent huswife, *ella è una eccellente massaja.*

Huswife, *si servono qualche volta di questa parola come d'un termine di disprezzo, che vuol dire appresso di noi, una pettegola, una impertinente.*

Huswife, *è anche quella come cartella, in cui le donne pongono gli aghi, il filo, e altre loro coserelle.*

To HU'SWIFE [to manage with œconomy and frugality] *usar con economia e frugalmente; e dicesi di donna e non d'uomo.*

HU'SWIVELY, adj. *economa, parlando d'una donna.*

HU'SWIFRY, s. *masserizia, economia,* s. f. *risparmio,* s. m.

HUT, s. [a small cottage] *una capanna.*

A soldier's hut [a barrack] *baracca di soldato.*

HUTCH, s. [bin] *mádia,* s. f. *spezie di cassa, per uso d' intridervi entro la pasta da fare il pane.*

Hutch [to keep bread in] *cassa,* s. f.

HUZZ [to bum as bees do] *rombare, ronzare.*

To huzz [or keep a noise] *susurrare, bisbigliare.*

HU'ZZA, interj. *acclamazione,* s. f.

To HY, *v.* To hie.

HY'ACINTH, s. [a flower of a purple colour] *giacinto,* s. m. *spezie di fiore.*

HY'ADES, s. [seven stars in the head of the bull] *jade,* s. f. *sette stelle che sono alla testa del toro, che nel loro nascimento crede il volgo che cagionino pioggia.*

HY'DRA, s. [a monstrous and fabulous serpent] *idra,* s. f. *serpente favoloso.*

HYDROGRA'PHICAL, adj. *idrografico.*

HYDRO'GRAPHY, s. [the description of the waters] *idrografia,* s. f. *descrizione delle acque.*

HYDRO'MANCY, s. [divination by water] *idromanzia,* s. f. *arte dello indovinare, per via delle arque.*

HYDRO'PICAL, adj. [belonging to the dropsy, or troubled with the dropsy] *idropico.*

HYE'MAL, adj. [winterly] *iemale, del verno.*

The hyemal solstice, *il solstizio iemale.*

HY'EN, } s. [a sort of heast] *iena.*
HY'ENA, } s. f. *animal quadrupede che ha somiglianza col lupo.*

HYM, s. *spezie di cane.*

HY'MEN, s. [the god of wedlock] *Imeno,* s. m.

Hymen [marriage] *imeneo, matrimonio.*

HYMENE'AL, } adj. *nuziale, ma-*
HYMENE'AN, } *trimoniale.*

HYMN, s. [a spiritual song] *inno,* s. m.

HYPE'RBOLA [a section of a cone made by a planet] *iperbole, figura piana, generata da una delle sezioni del cono.*

HYPE'RBOLE, s. [a figure in rhetorick, which in expression exceeds truth] *iperbole, figura rettorica.*

HYPERBO'LICAL, adj. *iperbolico.*

HYPERBO'LICALLY, adj. *iperbolicamente.*

To HYPE'RBOLIZE [to use hyperboles] *iperboleggiare, usare iperbole, aggrandire con parole.*

HYPOCO'NDRIA, s. [the lateral parts of the belly about the short ribs, where lies the liver, stomach, and spleen] *ipocondria.*

HYPOCHONDRI'ACAL, } adj. be-
HYPOCHO'NDRIACK, } longing to the hypochondria] *impocondriaco, d' ipocondria.*

HYPOCHO'NDRIACK, s. [troubled with the hypochondria] *ipocondriaco,* s. m.

HYPO'CRISY, s. *ipocrisia,* s. f.

HY'POCRITE, s. [a false pretender to honesty or holiness] *ipocrito, e ipocrita,* s. m. f.

A great hypocrite, *un ipocritone.*

HYPOCRI'TICAL, adj. *ipocrito.*

HYPO'STASIS, s. [the substance or person of the Trinity] *ipostasi,* s. f.

HYPOSTAT'ICAL, adj. [belonging to an hypostasis] *ipostatico.*

HYPOTHE'SIS, s. [a supposition] *ipotesi, supposizione.*

HYPOTHE'TICAL, adj. [supposed] *supposto.*

HYPOTHE'TICALLY, adv. *per supposizione.*

HYRST, } s. [a wood, a grove, a
HURST, } thicket] *un bosco, un*
HERST, } *boschetto, un pianetto.*
Non molto in uso.

HY'SSOP, s. [a sort of herb] *isapo, isopo,* s. m. *erba nota.*

HYSTE'RICAL, } adj. [belonging
HYSTE'RICK, } to the womb] *isterico, uterino.*

HYTH, } s. [a little haven to load
HYTHE, } and unload wares at] *molo,* s. m.

I.

I, *che nell' alfabeto e in molte voci si legge come si leggerebbe in Italiano* ei, *e quando è consonante come il nostro* G.

I *pronome della prima persona, io.*

I walk, *io cammino.* I eat, *io mangio.*

Shakespeare ha scritto molte volte I *per* ay *e per* yes.

To JA'BBER, *parlar presto, e confusamente, cianciare, tattamellare.*

JA'BBERER, s. *uno che pronuncia male e non intelligibilmente.*

JA'BBERING, s. *maniera di parlar presto e imbrogliatamente, ciancia, ciarla, tattamella.*

JA'CENT, adj. [lying at length] *giacente, disteso giù. E' vocabolo araldesco.*

JA'CINTH, s. *lo stesso che* Hyacinth; *ed è anche nome d'una gemma chiamata da noi giacinto.*

JACK [turn-spit] *menarrosto,* s. m.

Jack [in bowling] *grillo,* s. m. *quel picciol segno nel giuoco delle pallottole, a cui le palle debbono accostarsi.*

Jack [the male of birds of sport] *il maschio degli uccelli di cacciagione.*

Jack [a coat used formerly in war] *giaco,* s. m. *arme di dosso fatta di maglie di ferro concatenate insieme.*

Jack [a diminutive of John] *Giannotto, Gianni, Giannino, Giannozzo.*

The jacks of a virginal, *salterelli di spinetta.*

Jack [a fish] *luccio,* s. m. *sorta di pesce.*

To be Jack of all sides [to be a turn-coat] *voltar casacca, tenere ora con uno, ora con un altro.*

Jack-an-apes, *una scimia, un babbuino, uno sciocco, un impertinente.*

To be Jack of all trades, *fare ogni mestiere.*

Jack-catch, *il boja.*

Jack-pudding, *un buffone, un pulcinella, un zanni.*

Jack-daw, *gracchia, cornacchia, putta,* s. f.

Jack-boots, *stivali grossi.*

JA'CK-A-LENT, s. [a simple sheepish fellow] *un sempliciotto, un sempliciaccio, una pecora, un besso, un cionno.*

JACKA'L, s. *animaletto che si suppone insegni al lione dove può trovare da far preda.*

JA'CKET, s. [a sort of garment] *sajo, sajone, saltambarco,* s. m.

Jacket [jack of mail] *giaco,* s. m.

JA'COBIN, s. [Jacobin friar] *domenicano, un religioso dell' ordine di San Domenico.*

JACOB'S STAFF [astrolabe] *astrolabio,* s. m. *significa anche un bastone da pellegrino.*

JA'COBUS, s. [a broad piece of gold] *un Giacobus, moneta d'oro d'Inghilterra.*

JA'COBINE, s. [a pigeon with a high tuft] *sorta di piccione che ha un ciuffo sul capo.*

JACULA'TION, s. *l'atto dello scagliar un arme.*

JADE, s. [a sorry horse, or mare] *rozza, carogna, un cattivo cavallo.*

Jade [sorry base woman, leud wench] *baldracca, sgualdrina, pettegola, puttana, scanfarda, cantoniera.*

JA'DISH, adj. *cattivo, vizioso come un cavallo.*

Jadish, *impudico, incontinente.*

JAG, s. [notch] *tacca,* s. f.

To JAG [to notch] *intaccare, far tacca.*

JAGGED, adj. *intaccato, dentato.*

JAIL, s. [or goal] *carcere, prigione,* s. f.

To go to jail, *andare in prigione.*

JAI'LBIRD, s. [one who has been in a jail] *uno che è stato in prigione.*

JA'ILER, s. *carceriere,* s. m. *custode della prigione.*

JAKES, s. [house of office] *privato, cesso,* s. m.

A jakes-farmer, *un votacessi.*

IAMBICK, adj. Ex. Iambick verse, *verso iambo.*

JAMES [the side posts of a door] *stipite di porta.*

To JA'NGLE [to be at variance, to contend in words] *contendere, contrastare, disputare, garrire, questionare.*

To JA'NGLE, v. a. *cagionar suono spiacevole, far garrire o scricchiolare una cosa.*

JA'NGLER, s. *contenditore, riottoso, garritore.*

JA'NGLING, s. *contesa, disputa, riotta,* s. f. *contrasto, garrimento,* s. m.

JA'NIZARY [a Turkish foot soldier] *giannizzaro, fantaccino Turco.*

JA'NNOCK, s. [a loaf made of oats] *un pane di vena.*

JA'NSENISM, s. [the doctrine of Jansenius] *Giansenismo, la dottrina di Giansenio.*

JA'NSENIST, s. *un Giansenista, colui che seguita la dottrina di Giansenio.*

JA'NTY, adj. *gentile, giulivo, belloccio, vago.*

JA'NUARY, s. [the first month of the year] *Gennajo,* s. m. *il primo mese dell' anno.*

JAPAN, s. [work varnished and raised in gold and colours] *sorta di lavoro fatto con una certa vernice nera e lucida così chiamato perchè dapprima recato, a quel che si pretende, dal giappone in Inghilterra.*

To JAPA'N [to varnish or draw figures on wood, metal, &c. after the manner of the artificers in Japan] *verniciare alla maniera del Giappone.*

JAPA'NNER, s. *forbitore di scarpe, così chiamato con giocosa similitudine.*

JAPE, s. [a tale] *novella,* s. f.

JAR, s. [difference, quarrel, contention] *discrepanza, discordia, contenzione, contesa, disputa,* s. m. *disparere, contendimento,* s. m.

To make a jar, *venire a contesa.*

Jar [an earthen vessel for oil] *giara,* s. f.

A jar of oil, *una giara d'olio.*

To JAR [to quarrel, to fall out] *discordare, variare, contendere, garrire, disputare,* pres. *garrisco.*

To jar [in musick, to disagree, to be out of tune] *scordare, dissonare, non accordare.*

JA'RGON, s. [gibberish] *gergo,* s. m.

JA'RGONELLE, s. *sorta di pera.*

JA'RRING, adj. *scordante, scordevole, discordante, dissonante.*

A jarring voice, *una voce dissonante.*

JA'SMIN, s. [a shrub] *gelsomino,* s. m. *pianta nota.*

Jasmin, or jasmin-flower, *fiore di gelsomino.*

JA'SPER, JA'SPER-STONE, } s. [a precious stone of a green colour] *diaspro,* s. m. *pietra dura, che s'annovera tra le gioje di minor pregio, e trovasene di diversi colori.*

JASS-HAWK, s. [a young hawk, newly

newly taken out of the neſt] *un falcone ſoro, un falcone giovane, che non ha ancora mudato.*

JA'VELIN, s. [a ſort of weapon] *giavellotto*, s. m. *ſpezie di dardo.*

JA'UNDICE, s. [a diſeaſe cauſed by the overflowing of gall] *itterizia*, s. f. *malattia, che procede da ſpargimento di fiele.*

Sick of the jaundice, *itterico, che patiſce d'itterizia.*

JAUNT, s. [the fellows of a wheel] *gavelle di ruota.*

Jaunt [ramble] *ſcorſa, camminata, girata*, s. f.

I made many a jaunt, *io ho fatto molte ſcorſe.*

To JAUNT [to trot, to trudge up and down] *ſcorrere, andar qua e la, vagare, vagabondare, andare attorno. è uſatto da' moderni ſempre per diſprezzo.*

JA'UNTINESS, s. *leggerezza; e s' applica alla mente.*

JAW, s. [the bone wherein the teeth are ſet] *maſcella, ganaſcia.*

The jaw bones, *le maſcelle.*

The jaw teeth, *i maſcellari, denti laterali.*

JAY, s. [a bird] *ghiandaja*, s. f. *uccello noto di piuma varia.*

ICE, s. [water congealed by a freezing wind] *ghiaccio*, s. m.

To drink with ice, *ber freſco.*

She is all ice to me, *ella è di ghiaccio per me.*

Ice-houſe, *conſerva di ghiaccio, luogo dove ſi conſerva il ghiaccio per la ſtate.*

Ice bound [ſpeaking of a ſhip] *ſerrato, o circondato di ghiaccio, parlando d'un vaſcello.*

ICED, adj. *agghiacciato.*

ICH [for I in the weſt] *io.*

Ich dien [the motto belonging to the deviſe of the Prince of Wales, which ſignifies I ſerve] *motto della diviſa de' principi di Galles, che ſignifica*, io ſervo.

I'CHOR, s. *umor ſottile e acqueo che s'aſſomiglia al ſero.*

I'CICLE, s. [from ice] *ghiacciuolo*, s. m. *umore che agghiaccia nel grondare.*

I'CINGLASS, s. [a mineral] *talco*, s. m. *ſorta di minerale.*

ICY, adj. [from ice] *glaciale, agghiacciato.*

I'D, *è abbreviazione di* I would.

IDE'A, s. [the image or repreſentation of any thing conceived in the mind] *idéa*, s. f. *immagine d'una coſa che ſi forma nell'immaginazione.*

To have an idea of ſomething, *aver un idea di qualche coſa.*

To form to one's ſelf an idea of a thing, *formarſi un' idea di che che ſi ſia.*

IDE'AL, adj. [of or belonging to an idea] *ideale, dell' idea.*

IDE'NTICAL, } adj. [that is the
IDE'NTICK, } ſame] *identico, che è il medeſimo.*

IDE'NTITY, s. [the ſameneſs of a thing] *identità, medeſimezza*, s. f.

IDES, s. [eight days, reckoned backwards, to the end of the noones, in every month] *idi*, s. m. *quelli otto giorni in ogni meſe dopo le none.*

I'DIOM, s. [the peculiar phraſe or manner of expreſſion in any language, a propriety of ſpeech] *idioma*, s. m. *fraſe*, s. f.

I'DIOT, s. [an unlearned man] *idiota, ignorante, illetterato.*

Idiot, in law [a natural fool, a changeling] *un idiota, uno ſciocco, un beſſo.*

I'DIOTISM, s. [a propriety of ſpeech belonging to any language] *idiotiſmo*, s. m. *proprietà, maniera particolare di favellare.*

Idiotiſm [natural folly or ſimplicity] *idiotaggine*, s. m. *ignoranza di letteratura.*

I'DLE, adj. [at leiſure] *ozioſo, che ſta in ozio, che non ha nulla a fare, sfaccendato.*

An idle life, *una vita ozioſa.*

To be idle, *ſtar ozioſo, o ſtar in ozio.*

Idle [ſlothful] *ozioſo, pigro, infingardo, ſcioperato.*

Idle [lazy] *negligente, traſcurato.*

Idle [ſimple, impertinent] *vano, inutile, frivolo, di poco momento.*

Idle thoughts, *vani penſieri, penſieri ozioſi.*

An idle ſtory, *baja, fraſcheria, ſciocchezza.*

Idle expences, *ſpeſe inutili.*

Idle thing, *baja, bagatella, fraſcheria.*

To IDLE, *poltroneggiare; buttar via il tempo; perder l'ore in ozio ed in fare coſe da nulla.*

I'DLENESS, s. [ſluggiſhneſs] *ozio*, s. m. *negligenza, traſcurataggine, traſcuraggine, traſcuranza, infingardaggine*, s. f.

I'DLER, s. *un ozioſo, un pigro, un traſcurato, un buono a nulla, uno sfaccendato, un fuggifatica, un poltrone, un poltroniere.*

IDLY, adv. *ozioſamente, negligentemente, traſcuratamente.*

To live idly, *viver nell' ozio, viver ozioſamente, menare una vita ozioſa.*

Idly [ſimply, ſillily] *ſcioccamente, ſpropoſitatamente, da ſciocco.*

To talk idly, *vaneggiare, dir coſe vane, pargoleggiare.*

See how idly you talk, *vedi come vaneggi.*

I'DOL, s. [an image or ſtatue for repreſenting ſome falſe diety] *idolo*, s. m. *immagine d'iddei falſi.*

Gold is the idol of covetous men, *l' oro è l'idolo degli avari.*

Idol-worſhip, *idolatria*, s. f.

IDO'LATER, s. [one that worſhips idols] *idolatro, idolatra*, s. m.

IDO'LATRESS, s. *un' idolatra.*

To IDO'LATRIZE [to commit idolatry] *idolatrare, adorare, e onorare gl' idoli.*

IDO'LATROUS, adj. [guilty of idolatry] *idolatro.*

IDO'LATRY, s. [idol worſhip] *idolatria*, s. f. *coltura, e adorazion degli idoli.*

I'DOLET, s. [a little idol] *idoletto*, s. m.

I'DOLIST, s. [a worſhipper of images] *un idolatra, un adoratore degl' idoli.*

To IDOLI'ZE [to be extremely fond of, to doat upon] *aver troppa venerazione per qualche coſa, idolatrare, portar troppo amore a qualche coſa, farne il ſuo idolo.*

IDOLI'ZED, adj. *idolatrato, avuto in troppa venerazione, o ſtima.*

IDO'NEOUS, adj. [fit, proper, convenient] *idoneo, adatto, proprio, convenevole.*

I'DYL, s. [a ſmall ſhort poem] *idilio, poemetto per lo più paſtorale.*

JE'ALOUS, adj. [afraid of having a rival] *geloſo, travagliato da geloſia.*

To make one jealous, *render alcuno geloſo, darli della geloſia.*

To grow jealous, *ingeloſire, divenir geloſo, pigliar geloſia.*

Jealous [tender, nice] *geloſo, delicato.*

Every body ought to be jealous of his reputation, *ognuno dovrebbe eſſer geloſo della ſua riputazione.*

A jealous man or woman, *un geloſo, una geloſa.*

JE'ALOUSY, adv. *geloſamente, con geloſia.*

JE'ALOUSIE, } s. [a being jealous]
JE'ALOUSY, } *geloſia*, s. f. *paſſione, e travaglio degli amanti, per timor che altri non goda la coſa da loro amata.*

Jealouſie [ſuſpicion] *geloſia, ombra*, s. f. *ſoſpetto, timore*, s. m.

To conceive a jealouſy of ſomething, *pigliar geloſia, inſoſpettirſi di qualche coſa.*

Full of jealouſies, *ſoſpettoſo.*

JEAT, s. [a black, light, and brittle ſtone] *ſpezie di pietra nera.*

JEER, s. [banter] *ſoja, burla, beffa* s. f.

To paſs a jeer upon one, *dar la baja, ad'uno, beffarlo, ſchernirlo, burlarlo.*

To JEER [to laugh at, to ridicule] *beffare, dar la baja, ſchernire, burlarſi, ſojare.*

JE'ERED, adj. *beffato, ſchernito, burlato, ſojato.*

JE'ERER, s. *ſchernitore, beffardo, beffatore*. s. m. *beffatrice, ſchernitrice*, s. f.

JE'ERING, s. *beffa, burla*, s. f.

Jeering, adj. *beffardo, ſchernitore.*

A Jeering man, *un beffardo.*

A jeering woman, *una beffarda.*

JE'ERINGLY, adv. [ſcornfully, contemptuouſly] *ſprezzantemente, con iſcorno.*

JE'GGET, s. *ſorta di ſalſicciotto.*

JE'HOVAH, s. *il ſantiſſimo nome di Dio in Ebraico.*

JEJU'NE, adj. [barren, dry, empty] *ſterile, arido, voto, vano, inſipido.*

A jejune ſtile, *uno ſtile ſecco, inſipido.*

JEJU'NUM, s. [the ſecond part of the inteſtines] *jejuno*, s. m.

JEJU'NENESS, s. *penuria, ſcarſezza, povertà.*

JE'LLIED, adj. *viſcoſo, glutinoſo, attaccaticcio.*

JE'LLY, s. [a juice of fruit or meat congealed] *gelatina*, s. f. *brodo rappreſo.*

A jelly of calves feet, *gelatina di piedi di vitella.*
Jelly broth, *consumato*, s. m.
Jelly of fruit, *sugo di frutti rappreso.*
JE'NNET, *v.* Gennet.
To JE'OPARD [to hazard] *avventurare, arrischiare, cimentare, mettere al cimento, sparimentare, provare.*
JE'OPARDED, adj. *avventurato, arrischiato, cimentato, sperimentato, provato.*
JE'OPARDY, s. [danger, hazard, risk] *pericolo, cimento, rischio*, s. m. *prova*, s. f.
JE'QUER, s. [an officer belonging to the custom-house, who oversees the waiters] *ufficiale della dogana che soprantende a' doganieri.*
JERK, s. [pull, twitch] *colpo*, s. m. *scossa, spinta*, s. f.
To give one a jerk, *spignere alcuno, darli una spinta.*
At one jerk, *in un colpo, in un subito.*
Jerk of a horse man, *sbrigliata, strappata di briglia, sbrigliatura, sbarbazzata.*
To give a jerk [to start] *balzare, sbalzare, fare un balzo.*
Jerk [lash, or whip] *sferzata, frustata*, s f.
To JERK [to lash] *sferzare, frustare, scopare.*
To jerk [to pull, to twitch] *strappare, dare una strappata.*
To jerk [to whince as a horse does] *calcitrare, trar calci.*
JERKED, adj. *sferzato, frustato, scopato.*
JERKIN, s. [jacket] *casacca*, s. f. *giubbone*, s. m.
Jerken of leather, *colletto*, s. m. *casacca di cuojo, che veste il petto e la schiena.*
JE'RKIN, s. [a kind of hawk] *sorta di falcone.*
JE'RKING, s. [from to jerk] *lo sferzare, sferzata*, s. f.
JESS, s. [short straps of leather tied about the legs of a hawk, with which she is held on the fist] *geti*, s. m. plur.
JE'SSAMINE, *v.* Jasmin.
JEST, s. [joke or banter] *burla, baja, beffa*, s. m. *scherzo, trastullo*, s. m.
A biting or nipping jest, *motto pungente, bettu, bottone.*
To be full of jests, *essere scherzoso, burliero.*
In jest, *da burla, per ischerzo.*
I spoke it in jest, *l'ho detto in burla, o per ischerzo.*
To put a jest upon one, *burlarsi, beffarsi d'uno.*
That's a jest, *bagattella, voi burlate.*
To JEST, *burlarsi, beffarsi*, ridere, *motteggiare, scherzare.*
You jest, *voi burlate.*
He loves to jest, *egli ama a scherzare.*
JE'STER, s. *burlatore, schernitore, burlone, motteggiatore, buffone.*
JE'STING, s. *burla, beffa*, s. f. *scherzo*, s. m.

Without jesting, *seriosamente, da vero.*
Jesting, adj. *burlevole, scherzevole, scherzoso.*
A jesting man, *un burlone, un motteggiatore.*
JE'STINGLY, adv. *scherzevolmente, scherzosamente, con ischerzo, da scherzo.*
JESUA'TI, s. pl. [an order of monks] *gesuati, ordine di religiosi.*
JE'SUITS, s. [of the society of Jesus] *gesuiti*, s. m. *frati della compagnia di Gesù.*
Jesuits bark or powder [quinquina] *la china.*
JESUI'TICAL, adj. *di gesuita.*
JET [*da alcuni scritto* jeat] *sorta di fossile nero, duro, e lucido.*
To JET [to run up and down] *vagare, vagabondare, andar girando, andar qua e là, andare attorno.*
To jet along [to carry the body stately and proudly] *pavoneggiarsi, e paoneggiarsi, comminare con albagia, boriosamente.*
JEW, s. *un Giudeo, un Ebreo.*
A woman Jew, or Jewess, *una Giudea, un' Ebrea.*
The Jews doctrine, or religion, *Giudaismo, legge o rito giudaico.*
JE'WEL, s. [a precious stone] *Gioja*, s. f. *pietra preziosa.*
Jewel [a term of kindness] *gioja mia, tesoro mio.*
JE'WELLER, s. [one who deals in jewels] *giojelliere*, s. m. *quegli che conosce le qualità delle gioje, e ne fa mercanzia.*
A jeweller's wife, *giojelliera*, s. f.
JE'WESS, s. [a woman Jew] *una Giudea, un' Ebrea.*
JE'WISH, adj. [belonging to the nation of the Jews] *Giudaico, Ebraico.*
IF, conj. *se.*
If it pleases God, *se piace a Dio, a Dio piacendo.*
If I can, *s'io posso.*
If [provided] *purchè.*
If you do but come, *purchè veniate.*
If [tho', altho'] *benchè, se, quantunque, quando.*
I will do it, if I should die for it, *voglio farlo, quando anche dovessi morire.*
I must have it if it cost ever so much, *voglio averlo, costi quanto si voglia.*
As if one should say, *come chi dicesse.*
He made as if he were dead, *fece le viste d'esser morto.*
I'GNEOUS, adj. [fiery] *igneo, che ha qualità di fuoco.*
IGNO'BLE, adj. [of mean birth] *ignobile, di bassa nascita.*
IGNO'BLY, adv. [basely] *vilmente, bassamente.*
IGNOMI'NIOUS, adj. [disgraceful, dishonourable] *ignominioso, svergognato, infame, disonorato.*
IGNOMI'NIOUSLY, adv. *ignominiosamente, con ignominia, svergognatamente, disonoratamente.*
IGNO'MINY [infamy, disgrace] *ignominia, infamia*, s. f. *vituperio, disonore*, s. m.

I'GNORANCE, s. [want of knowledge] *ignoranza*, s. f. *mancanza di sapere.*
To do a thing through ignorance, *far che che si sia per ignoranza.*
I'GNORANT, adj. [unlearned, illiterate] *ignorante, privo di sapere.*
An ignorant man, *un ignorante.*
An ignorant woman, *una ignorante.*
An ignorant coxcomb, *un ignorantone.*
To be ignorant of a thing [to know nothing of it] *ignorare che che si sia.*
You cannot be ignorant of it, *non potete ignorarlo.*
I'GNORANTLY, adv. *ignorantemente, con ignoranza, per ignoranza, senza saperlo.*
JIG, s. [a sort of dance] *giga*, s. f. *sorta di ballo.*
To JIG, *battar la giga.*
JI'GMAKER, s. *un ballerino allegro.*
JILT, s. [a woman who cheats or disappoints one] *una ingannatrice in amore.*
To JILT [to cheat, to disappoint one's expectations, especially in love] *ingannare, giuntare, dileggiare, beffare, mancar di parola, e dicesi principalmente in amore.*
To JI'NGLE, [to chink, to sound correspondently] *tintinnare, rendere suono consimile, come è verbigrazia quello di due rime.*
JI'NGLE, s. *tintinno, suono simile a un altro suono.*
ILE, s. *lo spazio in mezzo a una chiesa o edificio pubblico, per cui la gente passa.*
I'LL, contraction of I will, ex. I'll do it, *io lo farò.*
ILL, s. [harm] *male*
To return ill for good, *render il male per il bene.*
Ill [woe, misfortune] *male, infortunio*, s. m. *disgrazia, miseria*, s. f.
Ill, adj. [bad] *malo, cattivo.*
Ill man, *mal' uomo.*
Ill woman, *mala donna.*
Ill taste, *cattivo sapore.*
Ill news, *cattive novelle.*
Ill will, *mala volontà, odio, maltalento.*
To bear an ill will to one, *voler male ad uno, odiarlo.*
To do a thing with an ill will, *fare che che si sia contro voglia, a mal' in corpo, mal volentieri.*
Ill luck, *disgrazia, sventura.*
Ill, adv. *male.*
A suit ill made, *un abito mal fatto.*
You have done very ill, *voi avete fatto male.*
To speak ill of one, *sparlar d'uno, dirne male.*
I am ill, *io sto male, io sono ammalato.*
He is fallen very ill, *egli s' è ammalato, egli è cascato ammalato.*
Ill of the gout, *ammalato della gotta.*
You must not take it ill, *non l'abbiate a male.*
To think ill of one, *aver cattiva opinione di qualcheduno.*

Ill natured man, *un uomo di cattivo umore.*

Ill minded [ill affected] *mal' intenzionato, mal contento.*

Ill grounded, *mal fondato.*

Ill boding, *ſiniſtro.*

Ill fated, *sfortunato, ſventurato, fatale.*

Ill favoured, *brutto, deforme, ſgraziato, ſvenevole.*

Ill favouredly, adv. *ſgraziatamente, ſvenevolmente.*

Ill ſhaped, *mal fatto.*

Ill pleaſed, *malcontento.*

Ill gotten, *mal' acquiſtato.*

To ILLA'QUEATE [to enſnare] *illaqueare, adeſcare, accalappiare.*

ILLA'TION, s. [an inference, or concluſion] *inferenza, concluſione, conſeguenza,* s. f.

ILLA'UDABLE, adj. [not worthy of praiſe] *indegno di lode.*

ILLE'CTIVE, s. [allurement, enticement] *allettamento, lacciuolo, vezzo,* s. m. *luſinga, luſingheria,* s. f.

ILLE'GAL, adj. [contrary to law] *illecito, non legale, contro la legge.*

This is an illegal proceeding, *queſto procedere è contro la legge.*

ILLEGA'LITY, s. [unlawfulneſs] *ingiuſtizia,* s. f.

ILLE'GALITY, adv. *ingiuſtamente.*

ILLEGI'TIMATE, adj. [unlawfully begotten] *illegittimo, naturale, baſtardo.*

An illegitimate ſon or daughter, *un figliuolo illegittimo o naturale, un baſtardo, una figliuola illegittima, o naturale, una baſtarda.*

ILLI'CERAL, adj. [baſe, niggardly] *meccanico, miſero, ſordido, ſtretto, taccagno, vile, ignobile, non da gentiluomo.*

ILLIBERA'LITY, s. *ſordidezza, ſtrettezza, miſeria, avarizia,* s. f. *modo di parlare, di ſcrivere, o di procedere vile e plebeo.*

ILLI'BERALLY, adv. *ſordidamente, ſtrettamente, tenacemente, avaramente.*

ILLI'CIT, adj. [unlawful] *illecito, che non è permeſſo.*

ILLI'MITABLE, adj. [that cannot be limited] *illimitato, che non ſi può limitare.*

ILLI'MITABLY, adv. *illimitatamente, ſfrenatamente, illecitamente.*

ILLI'TERATE, adj. [that has little or no knowledge of letters, unlearned] *illetterato, ignorante, ſenza lettere.*

I'LLNESS, s. [diſeaſe] *malattia, indiſpozione,* s. f.

To ILLU'ME, } [or to en-
To ILLU'MINATE, } lighten] *illuminare, dar lume, luce, ſplendore, ſchiarire.* pref. *ſchiariſco.*

To illuminate the mind, *illuminare, ſchiarire la mente.*

To illuminate [to lay colours on maps, or prints] *colorire.*

To illuminate [to gild and colour the initial letters of manuſcripts] *colorire, indorare.*

ILLU'MINATED, adj. *illuminato, colorito, indorato.*

ILLUMINA'TION, s. *illuminazione,* s. f. *illuminamento,* s. m.

ILLU'SION, s. [deceit, falſe repreſentation] *illuſione, fantaſma,* s. f. *falſo, finto, ingannevole rappreſentamento.*

ILLU'SORY, adj. [deceitful] *fallace, finto, falſo, ingannevole.*

Illuſory arguments, *argomenti fallaci.*

To ILLU'STRATE [to make clear and evident, to explain] *illuſtrare, far chiaro, ſchiarire, ſpiegare, dar luſtro, luce, chiarezza, ſplendore.*

ILLU'STRATED, adj. *illuſtráto, ſchiarito, ſpiegato.*

ILLUSTRA'TION, s. *illuſtrazione, dichiarazione,* s. f. *ſvelamento,* s. m.

ILLU'STRIOUS, adj. [eminent, famous, noble, renowned] *illuſtre, chiaro, famoſo, celebre.*

Moſt illuſtrious, *illuſtriſſimo.*

ILLU'STRIOUSNESS, s. *qualità illuſtre.*

I'MAGE, s. [a natural or artificial repreſentation, or reſemblance of a thing] *immagine,* s. f. *figura di rilievo, o dipinta, ritratto,* s. m. *ſimiglianza, ſembianza, idea; coſa rappreſentata alla mente.*

To IMAGE, *immaginare.*

I'MAGERY, s. [painted or carved work of images] *immagini, figure di rilievo, o dipinte.*

I'MAGERY [ſhow, appearance] *moſtra, apparenza.*

Imagery [copies of the fancy; falſe ideas; imaginary phantaſms] *forme immaginate; falſe idee; fantaſmi creati dall' immaginazione.*

IMA'GINABLE, adj. [that may be imagined or conceived with the mind] *immaginabile, che ſi può immaginare.*

IMA'GINARY, adj. [not real, fantaſtick] *immaginario, immaginato, che non è reale.*

IMAGINA'TION, s. [fancy] *immaginazione,* s. f.

Imagination [thought] *immaginazione, penſiero.*

IMA'GINATIVE, adj. [of or belonging to the imagination] *immaginativo.*

The imaginative faculty, *la facoltà immaginativa, l'immaginativa, potenza dell' anima, la quale dalla rappreſentazion dell' obbietto cava molte conſiderazioni oltre al rappreſentato.*

To IMA'GINE [to fancy] *immaginare, figurarſi nella mente, penſare, concepir coll' intelletto.*

What greater thing can one imagine? *che ſi può mai immaginar di più grande?*

I cannot imagine any ſuch thing, *non poſſo immaginarmi tal coſa.*

To imagine [to invent] *immaginare, inventare. trovare.*

To imagine [to think] *immaginarſi, rappreſentarſi nella mente, concepire, comprendere, perſuaderſi, credere.*

IMA'GINED, adj. *immaginato,* v. To imagine.

It is not to be imagined, *non ſi può immaginare, o comprendere.*

IMA'GINING, s. *immaginamento, penſiero, concetto.*

To IMBA'LM, *imbalſamare, ugner con balſamo, imbalſimare.*

IMBA'LMED, adj. *imbalſamato, imbalſimato.*

IMBA'RGO, s. [a ſtop or ſtay of ſhipping by publick authority] s. m. *proibizione ai vaſcelli d' uſcir del porto.*

To IMBA'RGO [to ſtop] *impedire* pref. *impediſco.*

To imbargo all traffick by ſea, *impedire ogni traffico per mare.*

To IMBARK [to take ſhip] *imbarcarſi, montar ſulla nave.*

We imbarked at Leghorn, *noi c'imbarcammo a Livorno.*

To imbark [to put on ſhipboard] *imbarcare, metter nella nave.*

To imbark in a buſineſs, *imbarcarſi, entrare, metterſi in qualche impreſa.*

IMBARKA'TION, s. *imbarco,* s. m.

IMBA'RKED, adj. *imbarcato.*

To IMBA'SE [to mix with baſer metals] *falſificare.*

To imbaſe gold or ſilver, *falſificar l'oro o l'argento.*

IMBA'SED, adj. *falſificato.*

To IMBA'TTLE [to put into battle array] *ſchierare, ordinare.*

To imbattle an army, *ſchierare un eſercito.*

IMBA'TTLED, adj. *ſchierato, ordinato.*

IMBECI'LLITY, s. [weakneſs, feebleneſs] *imbecillità, debolezza,* s. f.

To IMBE'LLISH [to adorn, to beautify, to ſet off] *abbellire, far bello, ornare.* pref. *abbelliſco.*

IMBELLISHED, adj. *abbellito, adornato.*

IMBE'LLISHMENT, s. [a ſet off, or ornament] *abbellimento, ornamento,* s. m.

To IMBE'SIL, } to conſume or
To IMBE'ZEL, } waſte things com-
To IMBE'ZLE, } mitted to one's truſt] *guaſtare, diſſipare, mandare a male le robe commeſſe alla noſtra cura.*

To imbezle the coin, *alterare, diminuire la moneta.*

To imbezle the king's treaſure, *rubare il danaro del re, frodare il danaro del re.*

IMBE'ZELLED, } adj. *guaſtato, diſſi-*
IMBEZLED, } *pato.*

IMBE'ZELMENT, s. [a waſting] *guaſto, diſſipamento.*

To IMBI'BE [to ſoke in] *imbevere, attrarre, ſucciare, riempirſi.* pref. *attrao, e attraggo.* pret. *attraſſi.*

To imbibe good principles, *eſſer imbevuto di buone iſtituzioni.*

IMBI'BED, adj. *imbevuto, attratto, ſucciato, riempito.*

To IMBI'TTER [to make bitter] *amareggiare. far amaro.*

The fear of death imbitters all the ſweets of life, *il timor della morte amareggia tutte le dolcezze della vita.*

To imbitter [to exaſperate, to provoke] *irritare, provocare, eſaſperare, inaſprire, aſpreggiare.* pref. *inaſpriſco.*

IMBI'TTERED, adj. *amareggiato,* v. To imbitter.

An imbittered enemy, *un nemico capitale, o giurato.*

IMBO'DIED, adj. *incorporato.*

To IMBO'DY [to incorporate] *incorporare.*

To IMBO'LDEN [to make bold, to encourage] *inanimare, animare, dar animo, inanimire, incoraggiare, dar coraggio.* pref. *inanimiſco.*

IMBO'LDENED, adj. *inanimato, animato, inanimito, incorraggiato.*
To IMBO'SOM [to hold on the bosom; to cover fondly with the folds of one's garment] *tener sul petto; coprire il petto amorosamente colle falde della veste a un altra persona. Non usato più in questo senso.*
To imbosom, *ammettere nel seno, nel petto, nel cuore, nell' affetto.*
To IMBO'SS [to raise with bosses or bunches] *rilevare, far di rilievo.*
IMBO'SSED, adj. *rilevato.*
Imbossed work, *lavoro di rilievo.*
IMBO'WED, adj. *areato, piegato in arro, curvo.*
To IMBO'WEL [to take out the bowels] *sbudellare, cavar fuora le budella.*
IMBO'WELED, adj. *sbudellato.*
Imbowelled [impregnated] *pieno, che rinchiude nelle viscere.*
Mountains imbowelled with rich mines, *montagne che rinchiudono nelle loro viscere ricche miniere.*
IMBRA'CE, s. *abbracciamento, l'abbracciare,* s. m.
To receive one's imbraces, *sostener gli altrui abbracciamenti.*
To IMBRA'CE, *abbracciare, circondare, e strigner colle braccia.*
To imbrace an opinion, *abbracciare un' opinione.*
To imbrace an opportunity, *abbracciare una opportunità, servirsi d'un opportunità.*
IMBRA'CED, adj. *abbracciato.*
IMBRA'CING, s. *abbracciamento,* s. m. *l'abbracciare.*
To IMBRO'IDER [to make flowers, and other curious work with a needle upon cloth, silk, &c.] *ricamare.*
IMBRO'IDERED, adj. *ricamato.*
IMBROI'DERER, s. *ricamatore,* s. m. *ricamatrice,* s. f.
IMBRO'IDERING, } s. *ricamatura,*
IMBRO'IDERY, } s. f. *il ricamare.*
To IMBRO'IL [to cause broils and quarrels, to put into confusion] *imbrogliare, intrigare, confondere, avviluppare.* pret. *confusi.*
IMBRO'ILED, adj. *imbrogliato, intrigato, confuso, avviluppato.*
IMBRO'ILING, s. *imbroglio, intrigo, viluppo,* s. m.
To IMBRO'WN [to make brown; to darken; to obscure; to cloud] *imbrunire, oscurare, abbujare, rannugolare.*
To IMBRU'E [to soak, to steep] *intridere, inzuppare, stemperare.* pret. *intrisi.*
To imbrue one's hands in blood [to commit murder] *imbrattarsi le mani nel sangue, commettere un omicidio.*
IMBRU'ED, adj. *intriso, inzuppato, stemperato.*
Imbrued with blood, *insanguinato.*
To IMBU'E [to season the mind with good principles, virtue, learning] *imbevere, insegnare, inspirare, infondere.* pret. *infusi.*
To imbue one with learning, *istruire alcuno nelle scienze.*
To imbue one with virtue, *ispirare virtù ad alcuno.*
To imbue a child with good principles, *allevare un fanciullo in sani documenti.*
IMBU'ED, adj. *insegnato, ispirato, infuso.*
I'MITABLE, adj. [that may be imitated] *imitabile, che si può imitare.*
To I'MITATE [to follow the example of another] *imitare, prender l'altrui esempio.*
To imitate [to do the like, according to a pattern] *imitare, fare a somiglianza, contraffare.*
I'MITATED, adj. *imitato, contraffatto.*
Not to be imitated, *inimitabile.*
IMITA'TION, s. *imitazione,* s. f. *l' imitare.*
IMITA'TOR, s. [a man who imitates] *imitatore,* s. m.
IMITA'TRIX, s. [a woman who imitates] *imitatrice,* s. f.
IMMA'CULATE, adj. [without spot or stain, unspotted] *immaculato, senza marula, senza peccato originale. Questa parola non è in uso, se non quando si parla della concezione della santissima Vergine.*
To IMMA'NACLE [to fetter, to confine] *inceppare, metter in ceppi, incatene, in ischiavitù, in prigione.*
IMMA'NITY, s. [fierceness, wildness] *bestialità, ferità, fierezza,* s. f.
Immanity [vastness, hugeness] *smisuratezza, sfrenatezza, enormità, grandezza,* s. f.
IMMARCE'SSIBLE, adj. [that cannot wither or decay] *incorruttibile, che non può marcire o corrompersi.*
IMMATE'RIAL, adj. [that consists not of matter or body] *non materiale.*
It is very immaterial whether it is so or no, *non importa che cio sia o no.*
IMMATERIA'LITY, s. [an immaterial quality or nature] *immaterialità, qualità o natura immateriale.*
IMMA'TURE, adj. [unripe] *immaturo, non maturo.*
Immature [hasty, done before the time] *immaturo, prima del tempo, fuor di stagione.*
IMMATU'RITY, s. [unripeness] *immaturità,* s. f.
Immaturity [too great haste, precipitation] *immaturità, precipitazione.*
IMME'DIATE, adj. [that follows without any thing coming between] *immediato, senza altro di mezzo.*
IMME'DIATELY, *immediatamente, immediate.*
Immediately [presently] *immediatamente, subitamente, subito, in un subito.*
IMME'DICABLE, adj. [which cannot be healed, incurable] *immedicabile, da non potersi medicare, incurabile.*
IMME'MORABLE, adj. [not worth remembrance] *immemorabile, indegno della memoria degli uomini.*
Immemorable [past memory] *immemorabile.*
IMMEMO'RIAL, adj. [which is out of mind, or beyond the memory of man] *immemorabile, da non poter conservarsi nella memoria.*
IMME'NSE, adj. [vast, exceeding great] *immenso, di smisurata grandezza, vasto, grande.*
IMME'NSELY, adv. *d'una maniera immensa infinitamente.*
IMME'NSITY, s. [unmeasurableness, vastness] *immensità.*
To IMMERGE, } [to plunge or dip
To IMME'RSE, } over head and ears] *immergere, tuffare, attuffare.*
IMME'RGED, } adj. [dipt in] *immerso.*
IMMERSED, }
To immerge one's self in all manner of vices, *immergersi in ogni sorta di vizj.*
IMME'RSION, s. [a dipping or plunging] *immersione,* s. f. *l'immergere.*
IMMETHO'DICAL, adj. [that is without any method or order, confus'd] *confuso, senza metodo, ordine, o regola.*
IMMETHO'DICALLY, adv. *confusamente, senza metodo, ordine, o regola, disordinatamente.*
I'MMINENT, adj. [approaching, at hand, hanging over our head] *imminente, che soprasta,*
An imminent danger, *un imminente pericolo.*
IMMI'SSION, s. [a putting or letting into] *injezione.*
Immission of seed, *spargimento di seme.*
To IMMI'T [to let into] *gettare, spicciare.*
To IMMI'X [to mingle] *mescere, mescolare, mischiare.*
IMMOBI'LITY, s. [unmoveableness, stedfastness] *immobilità, fermezza,* s. f.
IMMO'DERATE, adj. [unseasonable, excessive] *immoderato, senza modo, smoderato, eccessivo, sregolato.*
Immoderate desires, *immoderati affetti.*
Immoderate expences, *spese eccessive.*
IMMO'DERATELY, adv. *immoderamente, smoderatamente, eccessivamente, sregolatamente.*
IMMODERA'TION, s. [excess, intemperance] *immoderanza, sregolatezza, intemperanza,* s. f. *eccesso,* s. m.
IMMO'DEST, adj. [that has no modesty, wanton] *immodesto, che non ha modestia o vergogna, sfacciato.*
IMMO'DESTY, s. [wantonness, unmannerliness] *immodestia, sfacciataggine,* s. f.
To I'MMOLATE [to offer sacrifice] *immolare, sacrificare.*
I'MMOLATED, adj. *immolato, sacrificato.*
IMMOLA'TION, s. *immolazione,* s. f. *sacrificio,* s. m.
IMMO'RAL, adj. [of depraved morals] *sregolato ne' costumi, contrario a' buoni costumi, depravato.*
IMMORA'LITY, s. [corruption of manners, lewdness] *sfrenatezza, sregolatezza,* s. f.
IMMO'RTAL, adj. [that never dies, everlasting] *immortale, non sottoposto alla morte, eterno.*
The soul is immortal, *l'anima è immortale.*
An immortal glory, *una gloria immortale.*

IMMORTA'LITY, s. *immortalità*, s. f.

To IMMORTA'LIZE [to make immortal] *immortalare, fare immortale.*

To immortalize one's self, *immortalarsi, segnalarsi.*

IMMO'RTALIZED, adj. *immortalato, segnalato.*

IMMO'RTALLY, adv. [eternally] *immortalmente, sempiternamente, eternamente.*

IMMO'VEABLE, adj. [which cannot be moved] *immobile, senza moto, che non può moversi.*

Immoveable feasts [which constantly fall upon the same day of the month] *feste immobili.*

IMMU'NITY, s. [exemption from any office, duty or charge, freedom, liberty] *immunità, esenzione*, s. f.

To IMMU'RE [to shut up between walls] *murare, serrar fra muri.*

IMMU'RED, adj. *murato, serrato fra due muri.*

IMMUTABI'LITY, s. [unchangeableness, constancy] *immutabilità*, s. f.

IMMU'TABLE, adj. [unchangeable, constant] *immutabile, che in nulla guisa si muta, costante.*

IMMUTA'TION, s. [a changing or altering] *cangiamento*, s. m. *mutazione, alterazione*, s. f.

IMP, s. [familiar spirit] *folletto, spirito folletto.*

Imp [graft] *innesto*, s. m.

To IMP a feather in a hawk's wing, [to add a new piece upon an old broken stump] *mettere una penna all' ala del falcone.*

To IMPA'IR [to diminish, to make worse] *scemare, diminuire, sminuire, peggiorare*, pres. *diminuisco, sminuisco.*

To impair one's estate, *scemare il suo patrimonio.*

To impair one's health, *debilitar la sua salute.*

IMPA'IRED, adj. *scemato, diminuito, sminuito, peggiorato.*

IMPA'IRING, *scemamento, diminuimento, sminuimento*, s. m. *diminuzione*, s. f.

To IMPA'LE [to set pales about, to fence with pales] *chiuder con pali, palificare, ficcar pali in terra a riparo.*

To impale a piece of ground, *palificare un pezzo di terra*

To impale [to drive a stake thro' the body of a malefactor] *impalare, cacciare nella parte posteriore d'un criminale un polo e farlo uscire di sopra.*

IMPA'LED, adj. *palificato, impalato.*

IMPA'LPABLE, adj. *impalpabile, da non esser conosciuto per mezzo del tatto.*

To IMPA'NNEL [to set down the names of the jury into a roll called the pannel] *scrivere sopra un pezzo di carta o di pergamena i nomi de giurati eletti, o per parlar più distintamente, nominare, costituire i giurati per giudicare un processo civile o criminale.*

IMPA'NNELLED, adj. Ex. [an impannelled jury] *un corpo di giurati nominati, eletti, o costituti dall' intendente della provincia per la decisione d'una causa civile o criminale.*

To IMPA'RADISE, *imparadisare, beatificare, colmar di somma gioja e beatitudine.*

IMPA'RITY, s. [inequality] *disparità, disuguaglianza*, s. f.

To IMPA'RK [to inclose, to fence in a piece of ground for a park] *siepare, palificare un pozzo di terra per parco.*

IMPA'RKED, adj. *siepato, palificato.*

To IMPA'RT [to communicate] *comunicare, conferire, far partecipe, dar parte*, pres. *conferisco.*

To impart one's mind to a friend, *comunicare i suoi pensieri ad un amico, svelargli i suoi segreti.*

IMPA'RTED, adj. *comunicato, conferito.*

IMPA'RTIAL, adj. [void of partiality] *imparziale, sincero, schietto, giusto.*

IMPA'RTIALITY, s. [disinterestedness] *imparzialità*, s. f.

IMPA'RTIALLY, adv. *imparzialmente.*

IMPA'RTIALNESS, s. *imparzialità.*

IMPA'RTING, s. *il comunicare, partecipazione*, s. f.

Without imparting me with it, *senza farmene partecipe, senza la mia saputa.*

IMPA'SSABLE, adj. *che non ammette passaggio ; che non si può varcare.*

Impassable ways, *strade impraticabili.*

IMPA'SSIBLENESS, } s. [uncapableness of suffering] *impassibilità*, s. f.
IMPASSIBI'LITY, }

IMPA'SSIBLE, adj. [incapable of suffering] *impassibile ; che non può sentir dolore o pena.*

IMPA'TIENCE, s. [uneasiness of mind] *impazienza*, s. f.

IMPA'TIENT, adj. [that has no patience] *impaziente, che non ha pazienza, iroso, sdegnoso.*

I am impatient to see him, *mi par mille anni di vederlo.*

IMPA'TIENTLY, adv. *impazientemente.*

To IMPE'ACH [to accuse and prosecute for treason and felony] *inquisire, processare, accusare un reo in causa criminale*, pres. *inquisisco.*

To impeach one of high treason, *inquisire, accusare alcuno di delitto di lesa maestà.*

IMPE'ACHABLE, adj. *che merita d' esser inquisito.*

IMPE'ACHED, adj. *processato, accusato.*

IMPE'ACHER, *accusatore, delatore, denunciatore.*

IMPE'ACHMENT, s. *accusa, informazione*, s. f.

IMPECCABI'LITY, s. [a being uncapable of sinning] *impeccabilità*, s. f.

IMPE'CCABLE, adj. [that cannot sin] *impeccabile, che non può peccare.*

To IMPE'DE [to hinder] *impedire, opporsi*, pres. *impedisco, oppongo*, pret. *opposi.*

IMPE'DED, adj. *impedito, opposto.*

IMPE'DIMENT, s. [hindrance, obstruction] *impedimento, ostacolo*, s. m. *opposizione*, s. f.

To have an impediment in one's speech, *aver un difetto di lingua, tartagliare, balbettare.*

To IMPE'L [to force] *impellere, spignere, incitare, sforzare, costrignere, obbligare*, pres. *spingo, costringo*, pret. *spinsi, costrinsi.*

IMPE'LLED, adj. *spinto, incitato, sforzato, costretto, obbligato.*

To IMPE'ND [to hang over] *soprastare.*

IMPE'NDENT, } adj. [hanging over] *soprastante, che soprasta, imminente.*
IMPENDING, }

A danger impending over us, *un pericolo che ci soprasta.*

IMPENETRABI'LITY, s. *impenetrabilità*, s. f.

IMPE'NETRABLE, adj. [that cannot be pierced through] *impenetrabile, che non può esser penetrato.*

IMPE'NITENCE, } s. [continuance in sinful courses] *impenitenza*, s. f. *ostinazione nel peccato.*
IMPE'NITENCY, }

IMPE'NITENT, adj. [who does not repent] *impenitente, ostinato nel peccato.*

IMPE'RATIVE, adj. [commanding] *imperativo, che comanda.*

The imperative mood, *il modo imperativo.*

IMPERCE'PTIBLE, adj. [that is not to be perceived] *impercettibile, che non si può comprendere da senso.*

IMPERCE'PTIBLENESS, s. *qualità impercettibile.*

IMPERCE'PTIBLY, adv. *impercettibilmente.*

IMPE'RFECT, adj. [not perfect or compleat] *imperfetto, che non è finito.*

An imperfect piece of work, *un' opera imperfetta.*

An imperfect book, *un libro imperfetto, dove manchi qualche cosa.*

IMPERFE'CTION, s. [defect] *imperfezione*, s. f. *difetto*, s. m.

IMPE'RFECTLY, adv. *imperfettamente, d'una maniera imperfetta.*

IMPE'RIAL, adj. [belonging to an emperor or empire] *imperiale, d'imperadore, d'imperio.*

The imperial crown, *la corona imperiale.*

The imperial army, *l'esercito imperiale, gl' imperialisti.*

The imperial lilly [a flower] *il fiore imperiale.*

IMPE'RIALISTS, s. *gl' imperialisti.*

IMPE'RIOUS, adj. [haughty] *imperioso, altiero, orgoglioso, fiero, arrogante.*

IMPE'RIOUSLY, adv. *imperiosamente, altieramente, orgogliosamente, arrogantemente.*

IMPE'RIOUSNESS, s. [haughtiness] *imperiosità, alterezza, soprastanza, superbia.*

IMPE'RISHABLE, adj. *immarcessibile ; che non può perire.*

IMPE'RSONAL, adj. Ex. [impersonal verbs in grammar, are such as are used in the third person singular only] *verbi impersonali.*

IMPE'RSONALLY, adv. *impersonalmente.*

IMPE'RTINENCE, } s. [foolery, non-
IMPE'RTINENCY, } sense] *impertinenza, cosa indecente, cosa baldanzosa oltre al dovere, scioccagine, sciocchezza*, s.f.

IMPE'RTINENT, adj. [not to the purpose, absurd, silly] *impertinente, incongruo, indecente, sciocco, stolto, fuor di proposito*.

It would not be impertinent here to speak something of it, *non sarebbe fuor di proposito di farne una piccola menzione qui*.

An impertinent, s. [a troublesome man] *un impertinente*.

IMPE'RTINENTLY, adv. [idly, sillily, *impertinentemente, spropositatamente, vanamente, scioccamente*.

IMPE'RVIOUS, adj. *inaccessibile*.

IMPE'TRABLE, adj. [that may be obtained by entreaty] *impetrabile, che si può impetrare*.

To I'MPERATE [to obtain] *impetrare, ottenere quel che si domanda*, pref. *ottengo*, pret. *ottenni*.

I'MPETRATED, adj. *impetrato, ottenuto*.

IMPETRA'TION, s. *impetragione, impetrazione*, s. f.

IMPETUO'SITY, s. [vehemency] *impetuosità, violenza*, s. f. *impeto*, s m.

IMPE'TUOUS, adj. [violent, rapid, boisterous] *impetuoso, furioso, precipitoso, violento, rapido*.

An impetuous motion, *un moto impetuoso, o furioso*.

An impetuous river, *un fiume rapido*.

Impetuous winds, *venti impetuosi*.

An impetuous person, *uno spirito impetuoso, ó precipitoso*.

IMPE'TUOUSLY, adv. *impetuosamente, con impetuosità, rapidamente*.

IMPE'TUOUSNESS, *v*. Impetuosity.

IMPI'ETY, s. [ungodliness] *empietà*, s. f.

I'MPIOUS, adj. [ungodly, profane, lewd] *empio, malvagio, tristo*.

An impious man, *un empio, un malvagio*.

An impious woman, *un' empia, una malvagia*.

I'MPIOUSLY, adv. *empiamente, con empietà, malvagiamente*.

IMPLACABI'LITY, } s. [unrecon-
IMPLA'CABLENESS, } cileableness] *odio implacabile*.

IMPLA'CABLE, adj. [not to be appeased] *implacabile, mortale*.

An implacable hatred, *un odio implacabile*

To IMPLA'NT [to fix, to fasten in] *piantare, fissare, scolpire, imprimere*, pref. *scolpisco*.

IMPLA'NTED, adj. *piantato, fisso, scolpito, impresso*.

To IMPLE'AD [to sue, or prosecute by course of law] *litigare, piatire, muover lite*.

I'MPLEMENTS, s. [all things necessary in trade, tools] *ordigni, stromenti*.

The implements [or furniture] of a house. *mobili, masserizie di casa*.

IMPLE'X, adj. [intricate, entangled, complicated] *imbrogliato, intrigato, confuso*.

To I'MPLICATE [to entangle, to embarrass, to infold] *intrigare, imbrogliare, confondere*.

IMPLI'CIT, adj. [tacitly understood] *implicato che non è espresso, ma si comprende per necessità*.

Implicit terms, *termini impliciti*.

IMPLI'CITLY, adv. *implicitamente, non direttamente, ma per altra maniera*.

To IMPLO'RE [to be earnestly with prayers, to beseech] *implorare, domandare, chiedere*, pret. *chiesi*

IMPLO'RING, s. *l'implorare, domanda, richiesta*, s. f.

IMPLO'Y, s. [office] *impiego*, s. m. *carica*, s. f.

To IMPLO'Y, *impiegare, porre, collocare*, pref. *pongo*, pret. *posi*.

To imploy one about a business, *impiegare alcuno in qualche negozio*.

I don't know what to imploy myself about, *non so in che impiegarmi, o occuparmi*.

IMPLOY'D, adj. *impiegato, posto, collocato*.

To keep one imploy'd, *dar dell' impiego ad uno*.

IMPLO'YMENT, s. *impiego*, s. m. *carica*.

To IMPLY' [to contain, to denote, to signify] *implicare, intrigare, avviluppare, contenere*, pref. *contengo*, pret. *contenni*.

That implies contradiction, *ciò implica contradizione*.

A word that implies two genders, *una parola che comprende due generi*.

To imply one thing from another, *inferire una cosa da un' altra*.

IMPLY'D, adj. *implicato, intrigato, avviluppato, inferito*.

IMPOLITE, adj. [unpolish'd, rude, coarse] *rozzo, grossolano, zotico, scortese*.

IMPOLI'TICAL, } adj. [imprudent,
IMPO'LITICK, } unwise] *imprudente, poco saggio*.

IMPO'LITICALLY, } adv. *impru-
IMPO'LITICKLY, } dentemente*.

IMPO'RT, s. [sense, meaning] *il senso, la significazione d'una cosa*.

Import [use] *uso*, s. m. *utilità*, s. f.

To IMPO'RT [to signify] *importare, dinotare, significare*.

To import [to bring into a port] *portare, trasportare*.

To import commodities into the country, *portare, traspottare delle robe in un paese*.

IMPO'RTANCE, s. [moment, weight] *importanza, conseguenza*, s. f. *momento*, s. m.

Importance [import, meaning] *il senso, la significazione d'una cosa*.

IMPO'RTANT, adj. [of great concern, weight, or moment] *importante, che importa, considerabile, di conseguenza, di momento*.

IMPORTA'TION, s. [the bringing in of merchandizes from foreign countries] *entrata delle robe che vengono da' paesi stranieri*.

To prohibit the importation and exportation, *proibire l'entrata, e l'uscita*.

IMPO'RTED, adj. *portato, trasportato*.

IMPO'RTER, s. [one that brings in from abroad] *colui che reca mercanzie d'altro paese*.

IMPO'RTLESS, adj. *di niun momento, che non è d'alcuna importanza*.

IMPO'RTUNACY, s. *importunità*, s. f.

To prevail with importunacy, *ottenere per importunità*.

IMPO'RTUNATE, adj. [troublesome] *importuno, incomodo, fastidioso, nojoso, rincrescevole*.

To be very importunate with one about a thing, *sollecitar importunamente alcuno per qualche cosa*.

IMPO'RTUNATELY, adv. *importunamente, incomodamente, fastidiosamente*.

To IMPORTU'NE [to press or sue for with great earnestness, to trouble] *importunare, domandare istantemente, con importunità*.

IMPORTU'NED, adj. *importunato*.

IMPORTU'NITY, s. *l'importunare, importunanza, importunezza, importunità*, s. f.

IMPO'SE, s. *romando, ordine*.

To IMPO'SE [to enjoin] *imporre, precisamente comandare, commettere*, pref. *impongo*, pret. *imposi, commisi*.

To impose [to give] *imporre, porre, dare*.

To impose a name, *imporre, dare un nome*.

To impose a tax, *imporre, mettere imposizioni, imposte, porre aggravi*.

To impose a form [in printing, is to set the pages in due order in the frame or chase, and make them ready for the press] *imporre una forma, termine di stampatore*.

To impose upon [to cheat] *infinocchiare, inzampognare, far cornamusa, ingannare, gabbare, giuntare*.

IMPO'SED, adj. *imposto*, *v*. To impose.

Imposed upon, *infinocchiato, inzampognato, ingannato, gabbato, giuntato*.

IMPOSI'TION, s. [a laying an injunction] *comando*, s. m. *imposizione*, s. f.

Imposition [assessment] *imposizione, gravezza, imposta, gabella*, s. f. *dazio, balzello*, s. m.

Imposition [cheat] *inganno*, s. m. *truffa, giunteria*, s. f.

IMPOSSIBI'LITY, s. [that which cannot be done] *impossibilità*, s. f. *cosa impossibile*.

IMPO'SSIBLE, adj. [that is not possible] *impossibile, contrario di possibile*.

Impossible, s. *l'impossibile*.

IMPO'ST, s. [tax, custom] *imposta, imposizione, gravezza*, s. f. *dazio*, s. m.

To IMPO'STHUMATE [to grow into an imposthume] *impostemire, far postema*, pref. *impostemisco*.

IMPO'STHUMATED, adj. *impostemito*.

IMPOSTHUMA'TION, s. *l'impostemire*

IMPO'STHUME, s. [a swelling of humours

humours of corrupted matter in any part of the body] *poſtema*, s. f.

IMPO'STOR, s. [cheat] *impoſtore*, *furbo*, *ingannatore*, s. m.

IMPO'STURE, s. [cheat, deceit] *impoſtura*, *furberia*, *giunteria*, s. f. *inganno*, s. m.

I'MPOTENCE, } s. [want of power
I'MPOTENCY, } or ſtrength, weakneſs] *impotenza*, *incapacità*, s. f.

A huſband's impotence, *l'impotenza d'un marito*.

I'MPOTENT, adj. [infirm] *impotente*, *infermo*.

Impotent [lame] *impotente*, *ſtroppiato*.

I'MPOTENTLY, adv. *debilmente*, *con debilità e impotenza*.

To IMPO'VERISH [to make poor] *impoverire*, *fare*, *o render povero*. preſ. *impoveriſco*.

To impoveriſh [to grow poor] *impoverire*, *divenir povero*.

IMPO'VERISHED, adj. *impoverito*.

IMPO'VERISHING, or IMPOVERISHMENT, s. *l'impoverire*.

To IMPO'UND, *v*. To pound.

To IMPO'WER [to veſt one with power, to enable him to act] *dar potere*, *abilitare*.

IMPO'WERED, adj. *che ha potere*, *abilitato*.

IMPRA'CTICABLE, adj. [which cannot be done] *impraticabile*, *che non ſi può*, *nè ſi deve fare*.

To I'MPRECATE [to curſe] *maledire*. preſ. *maledico*. pret. *malediſſi*

IMPRECA'TION, s. [curſe] *imprecazione*, *maledizione*, s. f.

To IMPRE'GN, *riempiere*, *impregnare*.

IMPREGNABLE, adj. [that cannot be taken by force] *ineſpugnabile*, *che non ſi può eſpugnare*.

IMPRE'GNATE, adj. *impregnato*, *gravido*, *pieno*.

To IMPRE'GNATE, *impregnare*, *ingravidare*, *riempiere*.

To impregnate [to imbibe, to incorporate] *impregnarſi*, *incorporarſi*, *imbevere*, *ſucciare*, *riempirſi*.

Whilſt the powder imbibes the water, the water impregnates the powder, *nel tempo che la polvere imbeve l'acqua*, *l'acqua s'impregna della polvere*.

IMPRE'GNATED, adj. *impregnato*, *imbevuto*, *incorporato*, *ſucciato*, *riempito*.

IMPREGNA'TION, s. *l'impregnare*.

IMPRE'SS, s. [a print, ſtamp, or image] *impreſſione*, *impronta*, s. f.

To IMPRE'SS [to print, or make impreſſion upon] *improntare*, *imprimere*, *formare effigie*, *effigiare*, *formare*, *figurare*.

Objects impreſs their own images upon the organs, *gli oggetti improntano le loro immagini ſopra gli organi*.

To impreſs [to compel men to enter into the publick ſervice] *levar gente per forza*.

IMPRE'SSED, *v*. To impreſs.

IMPRE'SSION, s. *impreſſione*, s. f.

The impreſſion of a ſeal, *l'impreſſione d'un ſigillo*.

The impreſſion of a book, *l'impreſſione*, *o l'impreſſo d'un libro*.

The impreſſion of an object upon the mind, *l'impreſſione d'un oggetto nella mente*.

IMPREST, adj. *improntato*, *impreſſo*, *effigiato*, *formato*, *figurato*.

Impreſt money [money paid to ſoldiers, &c compelled into the publick ſervice] *danaro che ſi da alla gente levata per forza per il ſervizio dello ſtato*.

To IMPRI'ME [hunting term, to rouſe or diſlodge a wild beaſt] *levare*.

IMPRI'MED, adj. *levato*.

IMPRI'MERY, s. [law term, a printing houſe, or the art of printing] *ſtamperia*, s. f. *luogo dove ſi ſtampa*, *e l'arte dello ſtampare*. *Voce del foro*.

To IMPRI'NT [to impreſs] *improntare*, *imprimere*, *effigiare*, *formare*.

To imprint a thing in one's mind, *imprimere*, *ſcolpire che che ſi ſia nella memoria*.

IMPRI'NTED, adj. *improntato*, *impreſſo*, *effigiato*, *formato*.

To IMPRI'SON [to put in priſon] *imprigionare*, *mettere in prigione*.

IMPRI'SONED, adj. *imprigionato*.

IMPRI'SONMENT, s. *imprigionamento*, s. m. *l'imprigionare*, *prigionia*, s. f.

To be condemned to perpetual impriſonment, *eſſer condannato ad una prigione perpetua*.

IMPROBABI'LITY, s. [an unlikelineſs of being true] *improbabilità*, *poca verſimilitudine*.

IMPRO'BABLE, adj. [unlikely] *improbabile*, *che non è verſimile*.

To I'MPROBATE [to diſallow, or diſlike] *diſapprovare*, *riprovare*, *ributtare*, *rigettare*, *ſcartare*, *condannare*.

IMPRO'BATION, s. *ributtamento*, *rigettamento*.

IMPRO'BITY, s. [wickedneſs] *cattivezza*, *cattività*, *furfanteria*, *malignità*, *malvagità*, s. f.

IMPRO'PER, adj. [unfit, inconvenient] *improprio*, *che non è proprio*, *indecente*.

Improper words, *termini impropri*.

IMPRO'PERLY, adv. *impropriamente*, *e impropiamente*.

To IMPRO'PRIATE [to employ the revenues of a church living to one's own uſe] *appropiarſi*, *appropriarſi*.

IMPRO'PRIATED, adj. *appropiato*, *e appropriato*.

IMPROPIA'TION, s. *l'appropriarſi*.

IMPROPRI'ETY, *improprietà*, *maniera impropria*.

IMPRO'VEABLE, adj. [that may be improved] *che ſi può migliorare*.

To IMPRO'VE [to better, to cultivate, to promote, to advance] *migliorare*, *avanzare*, *accreſcere*, *aumentare*, *coltivare*, *perfezionare*.

To improve one's eſtate, *migliorare*, *aumentare*, *accreſcere i ſuoi beni*.

To improve arts and ſciences, *coltivare*, *perfezionare le arti*, *e le ſcienze*.

To improve lands, *coltivare la terra*.

To improve one's mind, *coltivar l'ingegno*.

To improve, verb neut. [to make a progreſs in arts and ſciences] *profittare*, *far profitto progreſſo nelle arti e nelle ſcienze*.

Improved, adj. *migliorato*, *v*. to improve.

Improved in knowledge, *avanzato in ſapere*.

Improved in health, *migliorato in ſalute*.

IMPRO'VEMENT, s. [bettering] *miglioramento*, s. m. *il migliorare*.

Improvement [progreſs, advancement] *profitto*, *progreſſo*, *avanzamento*, s. m.

The improvements of arts and ſciences, *la cultura delle arti*, *e delle ſcienze*.

IMPRO'VER, s. *cultivatore*, s. m. *che coltiva*.

IMPRO'VIDENCE, s. [want of forecaſt] *improvidezza*, *improvidenza*, *inconſiderazione*, *imprudenza*, s. f.

IMPRO'VIDENT, adj [that has no forecaſt, imprudent] *improvido*, *inconſiderato*, *imprudente*.

IMPRO'VIDENTLY, adv. *improvvedentemente*, *inconſideratamente*, *imprudentemente*.

IMPRU'DENCE, s. [indiſcretion, unadviſedneſs] *imprudenza*, *inavvertenza*, *inconſideratezza*, s. f.

IMPRU'DENT, adj. [inconſiderate, unwiſe] *imprudente*, *inconſiderato*, *indiſcreto*.

IMPRU'DENTLY, adv. *imprudentemente*, *inconſideratamente*.

I'MPUDENCE, s. [ſhameleſſneſs ſaucineſs] *sfacciataggine*, *sfacciatezza*, *impudenza*, s. f.

Thou impudence! *impudente che tu ſei!*

IMPUDENT, adj. [ſhameleſs, ſaucy.] *impudente*, *sfacciato*, *ſenza vergogna*, *sfrontato*.

I'MPUDENTLY, adv. *impudentemente*, *sfacciatamente*, *ſenza vergogna*, *sfrontatamente*.

To IMPU'GN [to oppoſe, to withſtand] *impugnare*, *oppugnare*, *contrariare*, *reſiſtere*.

IMPU'GNED, adj. *impugnato*, *oppugnato*, *contrariato*, *reſiſtito*.

IMPU'GNER, s. *impugnatore*, s. m. *che impugna*.

IMPU'GNING, s. *impugnamento*, s. m. *impugnazione*, s. f.

IMPUI'SSANCE, s. *impotenza*, *incapacità*, *inabilità debolezza*.

IMPU'LSE, s. [motion, perſuaſion] *impulſo*, *incitamento*, *inſtigamento*, *ſtimolo*, s. m. *forza*, s. f.

IMPU'LSION, s. *impulſo*, s. m.

Impulſion [impulſe] *impulſo*, *incitamento*, *inſtigamento*, *ſtimolo*, s. m.

IMPU'LSIVE, adj. [that drives or thruſts forward] *impulſivo*.

IMPU'NELY, adv. *impunemente*, *ſenza punizione*.

IMPU'NITY, s. [a being free, or exempt from puniſhment] *impunità*, s. f.

IMPURE, adj. [unclean, filthy] *impuro*, *non puro*, *ſporco*, *diſoneſto*, *impudico*, *laſcivo*, *immondo*.

IMPU'RENESS, } s. [uncleanneſs]
IMPU'RITY, } *impurità*, *ſporchezza*, *immondizia*, s. f.

To IMPU'RPLE, *imporporare, tignere di color di propora.*
IMPU'RPLED, adj. [dyed with a purple colour] *purpureo.*
IMPUTA'TION, s. [charge] *imputazione*, s. f. *attribuimento di colpa.*
To IMPU'TE [to attribute or ascribe the merit to one] *imputare, incolpare, attribuire la colpa.*
IMPU'TED, adj. *imputato, incolpato, attribuito.*
IMPU'TING, s. *imputamento*, s. m. *l'imputare.*
IN, prep. *in, nel, nello, nella.*
He is in Italy, *egli è in Italia.*
She is in her chamber, *ella è nella sua camera.*
I did it in three days, *l'ho fatta in tre giorni.*
To go in, *entrare.*
In my opinion, *a mio parere, a mio giudizio.*
In respect to him, *per rispetto suo.*
Instead of, *in luogo di.*
In comparison, *a petto, a paragone.*
In the, *nel, nello, nella.*
In the garden, *nel giardino.*
In the city, *nella città.*
In the times past, *per il passato.*
In order, *per ordine, ordinatamente.*
In contempt, *per disprezzo.*
In obedience to you, *per obbedirvi.*
In short, in fine, *alla per fine, finalmente.*
In the day time, *di giorno.*
To be in, *esser impegnato.*
INABI'LITY, s. [incapacity] *inabilità, incapacità*, s. f.
To INA'BLE, *abilitare, render abile, o capace, mettere in istato di fare qualche cosa.*
INA'BLED, adj. *abilitato.*
INACCE'SSIBLE, adj. [not to be come at] *inaccessibile.*
INA'DEQUATE, adj. [disproportionate] *sproporzionato.*
Inadequate ideas, *idee incomplete, termine filosofico.*
INADVE'RTENCE, } s. [a want of
INADVE'RTENCY, } heed or care] *inavvertenza, imprudenza, trascuraggine, inconsiderazione*, s. f.
INA'FFABLE, adj. [not courteous] *incivile, scortese, non affabile.*
INA'LIENABLE, adj. [that cannot be alienated] *inalienable, che non si può alienare.*
INA'MOUR'D, adj. [in love] *innamorato.*
INA'NE, adj. *voto, vacuo.*
INA'NIMATE, adj. [lifeless, without life or soul] *inanimato, senz' anima.*
INA'NITY, s. [emptiness] *vanità, inutilità*, s. f.
INA'PPETENCY, s. [want of appetite] *inappetenza*, s. f. *mancanza d'appetito.*
To INA'RCH, *innestare in un certo modo.*
INARTI'CULATE, adj. [indistinct, confused, not articulate] *indistinto, confuso, non chiaro.*
INARTIFI'CIAL, adj. [without art] *senza arte, o artificio, naturale, schietto, puro.*
INARTIFI'CIALLY, adv. *senz' arte, senz' artificio, naturalmente.*
INASMU'CH AS, *perchè, a causa chè, poichè.*
INA'UDIBLE, adj [not to be heard] *inaudibile, inaudito, che non si può sentire.*
To INA'UGURATE [to instal, to invest with an office or dignity] *inaugurare, mettere in possesso, installare.*
INA'UGURATED, adj. *inaugurato, installato.*
INAUGURA'TION, s. *inaugurazione, installazione*, s. f.
INAUSPI'CIOUS, adj. [unlucky] *infelice, malaguroso, malagurato sciagurato.*
I'NBORN, adj. [innate, natural] *innato, nato con noi, naturale.*
An inborn vice, *un vizio innato, vizio che ci è naturale.*
INBRE'D, adj. *prodotto, o generato dentro.*
To INCA'GE *ingabbiare, chiudere in gabbia, o in ristretto luogo.*
To INCA'MP [to pitch tents] *accamparsi porsi a campo.*
INCA'MPED, adj. *accampato.*
INCA'MPMENT, s. *l'accamparsi.*
INCANTA'TION, s. [charm] *incantesimo*, s. m. *incantagione, incantazione*, s. f.
INCANTA'TOR, s. [charmer] *incantatore*, s. m. *incantatrice*, s. f.
INCAPABLE'NESS, } s. *incapacità,*
INCAPABILI'TY, } s. f.
INCA'PABLE, adj. [not capable, unable, unfit] *incapace, che non è capace.*
To INCAPA'CITATE [to render incapable] *rendere incapace.*
INCAPA'CITATED, adj. *reso incapace.*
INCAPA'CITY, s. [inability] *incapacità*, s. f.
To INCA'RCERATE [to imprison] *incarcerare, carcerare, imprigionare, mettere in carcere.*
To INCA'RN, v. a. [to cover with flesh] *coprir di carne.*
To INCA'RN [to breed flesh] *incarnarsi, generar carne, produr carne.*
INCA'RNADINE, adj. [of a bright carnation or flesh colour] *incarnatino, incarnato.*
INCA'RNATE, adj. [that has taken flesh] *incarnato, che ha preso carne, divenuto carne.*
Incarnate devil [a devil in man's shape, a devilish person] *un diavolo incarnato.*
INCARNA'TION, s. [an assuming or taking flesh] *incarnazione*, s. f. *il prender carne.*
Incarnation [a certain salve that makes flesh to grow] *unguento incarnativo.*
Incarnation [a deep bright carnation colour] *color incarnato.*
An INCA'RNATIVE, s. [a medicine causing flesh to grow] *rimedio incarnativo, che fa crescer la carne.*
INCA'STELLED, adj. [spoken of beasts, narrow heeled or hoof-bound] *incastellato, stretto e alto.*
An incastelled horse, *un cavallo incastellato.*
INCE'NDIARY, s. [a setter of houses on fire] *incendiario*, s. m.
An incendiary [a sower of divisions] *un incendiario, un seminator di discordie.*
I'NCENSE, s. [frankincense] *incenso*, s. m.
To I'NCENSE [to inflame, to stir up to anger] *provocare, innasprire, infiammare, irritare.* pref. *innaspro.*
INCE'NSED, adj. *provocato, innasprito, infiammato, irritato.*
INCE'NSING, s. *irritamento, provocamento*, s. m. *irritazione, provocazione*, s f.
INCE'NSOR, s. [a kindler of anger, an inflamer of passions] *che accende collera; che infiamma le passioni.*
INCE'NSORY, s. [a perfuming-pan] *incensiere, turibile*, s. m.
INCE'NTIVE, s. [motive] *incentivo, motivo.*
INCE'SSANT, adj. [continual] *continuo, costante, incessabile.*
INCE'SSANTLY, adv. *incessantemente, incessabilmente.*
I'NCEST, s. [a carnal copulation with one who is too near akin] *incesto*, s. m.
INCE'STUOUS, adj. *incestuoso; colpevole d'incesto.*
INCH, s. [the twelfth part of a foot] *dito*, s. m. *la duodecima parte d'un piee.*
An inch breaks no squares, *non bisogna badare a poca cosa, non bisogna andar troppo stirato.*
To sell a thing by inch of candle, *vendere che che si sia all' incanto.*
He is a gentleman every inch of him, *egli è gentiluomo davvero.*
I won't bate an inch of it, *non voglio abbatterne un picciolo.*
To INCH out [to measure by inches] *misurare a dita.*
To inch out [to make the best of a thing] *far servire una cosa quanto si può.*
To inch out [to measure by inches] *misurare a dita.*
INCHA'INED, adj. *incatenato.*
To INCHA'IN [to put in chains] *incatenare.*
To INCHA'NT [to bewitch, to charm] *incantare, fare incanti, ammaliare.*
INCHA'NTED, adj. *incantato, ammaliato.*
INCHA'NTER, s. *incantatore, mago*, s. m.
INCHA'NTING, s. *incantamento, incanto*, s. m. *incantagione, incantazione*, s. f.
INCHA'NTMENT, s. [charm] *incanto, incantamento* s. m. *malia*, s. f.
INCHANTRESS, s. *incantatrice, maga*, s. f.
INCHA'SE [to set in gold, silver, &c.] *incastrare, congegnare, commettere una cosa dentro dell' altra.*
INCHA'SED, adj. *incastrato, congegnato, commesso.*
To INCHA'UNT, v. To inchant.

To

To I'NCHOATE [to begin] *rominciare, principiare, dar principio.*

I'NCIDENCE, I'NCIDENCY, } s. [the place where two lines or rays meet] *incidenza*, s. f. *termine geometrico.*

I'NCIDENT, adj. [happening to, or falling out occasionally] *incidente, ordinario, comune, che accade romunemente.*

These things are incident to mankind, *queste son cose ordinarie, o frequenti all' uomo, o alle quali gli uomini sono soggetti.*

Incident, s. [circumstance] *circostanza.*

Incident [event] *accidente, evento*, s. m.

I'NCIDENTLY, adv. *incidentemente.*

To INCI'RCLE [to incompass, to surround] *cerchiare, circondare, intorniare.*

INCI'RCLED, adj. *cerchiato, circondato, intorniato.*

INCI'SED, adj. *inciso, tagliato.*

INCI'SION, INCI'SURE, } s. [a cutting] *incisione*, s. f. *taglio*, s. m.

INCITA'TION, s. [stitring up, provoking] *incitazione*, s. f. *incitamento*, s. m.

To INCI'TE [to stir up] *incitare, stimolare, spronare, sollecitare, animare, spignere.* pres. *spingo.* pret. *spinsi.*

INCI'TED, adj. *incitato, stimolato, spronato, sollecitato, animato, spinto.*

INCI'TEMENT, s. *incitamento, stimolo, motivo*, s. m.

INCI'TER, s. *incitatore*, s. m. *incitatrice*, s. f.

INCI'TING, s. *incitamento*, s. m. *l' incitare.*

INCI'VIL, adj. [unmannerly, rude] *incivile, malcreato, zotico.*

INCIVI'LITY, s. *inciviltà, malacreanza, zotichezza*, s. f.

INCI'VILLY, adv. *incivilmente.*

INCLE'MENCY, s. [unmercifulness, severity] *inclemenza, severità*, s. f. *rigore*, s. m.

INCLI'NABLE, adj. [inclining to, prone, apt] *inclinato, inclinevole, dedito, prono.*

INCLINA'TION, s. [a natural disposition to a thing] *inclinazione, attitudine, naturale disposizione a qualche cosa.*

Of one's own inclination, *di sua propria volontà.*

To INCLI'NE [to bow, to bend to, to lean towards] *inclinare, inchinare, piegare.*

To incline, *inclinare, aver attitudine, o inclinazione a qualche cosa.*

Victory inclined sometimes to one side, and sometimes to another, *la vittoria piegava ora da una banda, ora dall' altra.*

This flower inclines to red, *questo fiore tira al rosso.*

INCLI'NED, adj. *inclinato, inchinato, piegato, prono, dedito.*

INCLI'NING, s. *inchinamento, l' inchinare, inclinazione, disposizione.*

Inclining, adj. *inclinante, che inclina.*

Fortune inclining to his side, *arridendoli la fortuna.*

The day inclining towards the evening, *già s' inchinava il sole al vespro, già cominciava ad annottarsi.*

To INCLI'P, *abbracciare, cingere, circondare.*

To INCLO'ISTER [to shut up in a cloister or monastery] *mettere, o rinchiudere in un monastero.*

To INCLO'SE [to shut in, to fence about] *chiudere, rinchiudere, inchiudere, circondare, attorniare.* pret. *chiusi, rinchiusi.*

To inclose [to contain] *rinchiudere, contenere, comprendere, capire.* pres. *contengo, capisco.* pret. *contenni.*

To inclose a letter within another, *ravvolgere una lettera dentro un' altra.*

INCLO'SED, adj. *chiuso, rinchiuso, circondato, attorniato, contenuto, compreso.*

The inclosed [speaking of a letter inclosed within another] *l'inclusa.*

To INCLU'DE [to comprehend] *comprendere, abbracciare, inchiudere, contendere.*

INCLU'DED, adj. *compreso, abbracciato, inchiuso, contenuto.*

INCLU'SIVE, adj. [that comprehends or takes in] *inclusivo, che rinchiude, che comprende.*

Justice is inclusive of all other virtues, *la giustizia comprende tutte le altre virtù.*

INCLU'SIVELY, adj. *inclusivamente.*

INCO'G, adj. [mutilated from incognito] *incognito, sconosciuto.*

INCO'GITANCY, s. [want of thought, inconsideratenes, rashness] *inconsiderazione, imprudenza, improvedenza, temerità, sconsideranza*, s. f.

INCO'GITANT, adj. [heedless, thoughtless] *inconsiderato, imprudente, sconsiderato.*

INCO'GNITO, adj. [unknown] *incognito, non conusciuto, sconosciuto.*

He travelled incognito, *egli viaggiava incognitamente.*

INCOHE'RENCE, INCOHE'RENCY, } s. [want of connection; incongruity; inconsequence; want of dependance of one part upon another] *improprietà; incoerenza; assenza di connessione; incongruità; conseguenza mala o nulla; nulla relazione e attaccamento d'una con un' altra parte.*

INCO'HERENT, adj. [that does not suit or agree well together] *sconcordante, che sconcorda, che non si confà, dissonante.*

INCOMBU'STIBLE, adj. [that cannot be burnt or consumed by fire] *che non è combustibile, che non si può abbruciare.*

I'NCOME, s. [revenue] *rendita, entrata*, s. f.

INCOMME'NSURABLE, adj. [that cannot be measured] *incommensurabile, che non si può misurare.*

To INCOMMO'DE [to trouble] *incomodare, apportare incomodo, scomodare.*

INCOMMO'DED, adj. *incomodo, scomodato.*

INCOMMO'DIOUS, adj. [troublesome] *incomodo, scomodo, importuno, fastidioso, che apporta incomodo.*

INCOMMO'DIOUSLY, adv. *incomodamente, scomodamente, con incomodità.*

INCOMMO'DITY, s. [trouble] *incomodità, scomodità*, s. f. *incomodo, scomodo*, s. m.

INCOMMU'NICABLE, adj. [that cannot be common, or imparted to others] *incomunicabile, che non si può comunicare, e partecipare.*

INCOMPARABLE, adj. [matchless] *incomparabile, che non si può comparare, senza paragone.*

INCO'MPARABLY, adv. *incomparabilmente, senza comparazione.*

To INCO'MPASS [to surround] *circondare, attorniare.*

INCO'MPASSED, adj. *circondato, attorniato.*

INCOMPA'SSIONATE, adj. [void of pity, that has no compassion] *crudele, spietato.*

INCOMPATIBI'LITY, s. [contrariety] *incompatibilità, contrarietà*, s. f.

INCO'MPATIBLE, adj. [disagreeing, not consisting one with another] *incompatibile, contrario, che non può sussistere con un altro.*

INCOMPE'NSABLE, adj. [incapable of being recompensed] *incompensabile, da non si poter compensare.*

INCO'MPETENCY, s. [insufficiency] *incompetenza*, s. f. *inabilità per mancanza di giuridizione.*

INCO'MPETENT, adj. [incapable, not duly qualified, unfit] *incompetente, incapace.*

INCO'MPETENTLY, adv. *incompetentemente.*

INCO'MPETIBLE, adj. [unsuitable, that agrees not] *che non conviene, che non si confà.*

INCOMPLE'TE, adj. [not complete] *che non è compiuto, imperfetto.*

INCOMPLI'ANCE, s. *poca compiacenza.*

INCOMPO'SED, adj. [uncouth, neglected, ill favoured] *disadorno, mal in ordine, scompigliato, sgraziato, sconcio.*

INCOMPO'SEDNESS, s. *disordine, scompiglio*, s. m.

INCOMPO'SURE, s. [confusion, disorder] *confusione*, s. f. *scompiglio, disordine*, s. m.

INCOMPREHE'NSIBLE, adj. [that cannot be comprehended] *incomprensibile, da non potersi comprendere.*

INCOMPREHENSIBI'LITY, INCOMPREHE'NSIBLENESS, } s. *incomprensibilità*, s. f.

INCONCE'IVABLE, adj. [not to be conceived, or imagined] *da non potersi concepire o comprendere.*

INCONGRU'ITY, s. [disagreeableness] *incongruità, sconvenevolezza*, s. f.

Incongruity of speech, *un incongruità di discorso, un solecismo, un barbarismo.*

INCO'NGRUOUS, adj. [unfit, disagreeable] *incongruo, improprio.*

An incongruous expression, *un' espressione incongrua, o impropria.*

It is incongruous for a man that pretends to so much honesty, to——*non istà bene, non conviene ad un uomo che affetta tanta lealtà, di——*

INCO'NGRUOUSLY, adv. *incongruamente, impropriamente.*

INCO'NSEQUENCE, } s. weakness
INCO'NSEQUENCY, } of arguing, when the conclusion follows not from the premises] *discorso, o conseguenza mal fondata.*

INCO'NSEQUENT, adj. [that does not follow, or result from] *improprio, mal fondate, falso.*

INCONSI'DERABLE, adj. [of small account, not worthy of regard] *inconsiderabile, di poco momento, di poca considerazione.*

He is an inconsiderable fellow, *egli è una persona dozzinale, di poca considerazione, un uomo da niente.*

INCONSI'DERATE, adj. [unadvised, rash] *inconsiderato, senza considerazione, senza discorso, indiscreto, imprudente, poco giudizioso.*

INCONSI'DERATELY, adv. *inconsideratamente, senza considerazione, imprudentemente, indiscretamente.*

INCONSI'DERATENESS, s. *inconsiderazione, imprudenza, mancanza di giudizio.*

INCONSI'STENCE, } s. *incompati-*
INCONSI'STENCY, } *bilità, sconvenevolezza,* s. f.

INCONSI'STENT, adj. [that is not consistent, agreeable, or suitable to] *contrario, opposto.*

This is inconsistent with reason, *questo è contrario alla ragione.*

INCONSO'LABLE, adj. [that cannot be comforted] *inconsolabile, che non può consolarsi.*

INCO'NSTANCY, s. [unsteadiness, changeableness] *incostanza, leggierezza mutabilità,* s. f.

INCO'NSTANT, adj. [fickle, changeable] *incostante, leggiero, volubile, mutabile.*

INCO'NSTANTLY, adv. *incostantemente, leggiermente.*

INCONTE'STABLE, adj. [indisputable, undoubted] *incontestabile.*

INCO'NTINENCE, } s. [intemper-
INCO'NTINENCY, } ance] *incontinenza, sfrenatezza, licenziosità, intemperanza,* s. f.

INCO'NTINENT, adj. [that has no government of himself, unchaste] *incontinente, sfrenato, licenziose, impudico, lascivo, dedito a' piaceri, sensuale.*

INCO'NTINENTLY, adv. *sfrenatamente, licenziosamente, impudicamente.*

Incontinently [immediately, presently] *incontinente, incontanente, tosto, subito, immantinente. Non è più in uso in tal senso.*

INCONVE'NIENCE, v. [inconveniency, trouble, disturbance] *inconvenienza,* s. f. *scomodo,* s. m.

INCONVE'NIENCED, adj. *incomodo, scomodo.*

INCONVE'NIENT, adj. [troublesome] *inconveniente, incomodo, scomodo.*

INCONVE'NIENTLY, adv. *inconvenientemente.*

INCONVE'RSABLE, adj. [unsociable, unfit for conversation] *insociabile, che non è sociabile.*

INCONVE'RTIBLE, adj. [that cannot be altered, or converted] *inconvertibile.*

Inconvertible terms, *termini inconvertibili.*

INCORPO'RATE, adj. [imbodied together] *incorporato.*

A body incorporate [a corporation] *una comunità, una società.*

To INCOR'PORATE [to imbody, to admit into a society] *incorporare, ammettere in una società, o campagnia.*

To incorporate [to mix or unite the particles of one body with another] *incorporare, mescolare, e unire più corpi.*

INCO'RPORATED, adj. *incorporato.*

INCORPORA'TION, s. *incorporazione,* s. f. *incorporamento,* s. m.

INCORPO'REAL, adj. [having no body, bodiless] *incorporeo, che non ha corpo.*

INCORPO'REITY, s. [the condition or state of that which has no body] *incorporalità,* s. f. *stato incorporeo.*

INCO'RRECT, adj. [not correct, faulty] *scorretto, pieno d'errori, incorretto.*

INCO'RRECTLY, adv. *scorrettamente, d'una maniera scorretta.*

INCORRECTNESS, s. *scorrezione,* s. f. *errore di stampa.*

INCO'RRIGIBLE, adj. [past correction, obstinate] *incorrigibile, da non potere essere corretto, che non riceve correzione.*

INCO'RRIGIBLENESS, s. [hopeless depravity, badness beyond all means of amendment] *cattivezza o malvagità che non lascia speranza di correzione.*

INCORRU'PT, adj. [untainted] *incorrotte, che non soggiace a corruzione, che non si lascia corrompere.*

INCORRU'PTIBLE, adj. [not subject to corruption or decay] *incorruttibile, non corruttibile, che non soggiace a corruzione.*

INCORRU'PTIBLENESS, s. *incorruttibilità,* s. f. *qualità incorruttibile.*

INCORRU'PTIBLY, adv. *incorruttibilmente, senza corruzione.*

INCORRU'PTION, s. *incorruzione,* s. f.

INCO'UNTER, s. [meeting] *incontro,* s m. *l'incontrare.*

Incounter [brunt, fright] *assalto, conflitto,* s. m. *baruffa, mischia; zuffa,* s. f.

It was a very sharp encounter, *fu una fiera zuffa, o un fiero conflitto.*

A good opportunity for an incounter, *un occasione favorevole per battersi.*

To INCO'UNTER [to meet] *incontrare, riscontrare, abbattersi in camminando.*

To incounter [to fight, to join in battle] *azzuffarsi, dar battaglia, venire a battaglia, attaccare, assalire, combattere, venire alle armi, venire alle mani col nemico.*

INCO'UNTRED, adj. *attaccato, assalito, v.* To incounter.

To INCO'URAGE [to incite] *incoraggiare, inanimire, incorare, dar cuore, dar animo.*

To encourage [to countenance] *favorire, appoggiare, spalleggiare,* pres. *favorisco.*

To incourage trade, *far fiorire il commercio.*

To incourage learned men, *avanzare, portare avanti, proteggere, gratificare gli uomini letterati.*

INCO'URAGED, adj. *incoraggiato, inanimito, incorato, v.* To incourage.

INCO'URAGEMENT, s. [incentive] *stimolo, motivo,* s. m.

Incouragement [gift, recompence] *gratificazione, ricompensa,* s. f. *regalo, presente,* s. m.

A book that meets with incouragement, *un libro che ha buono spaccio.*

INCO'URAGER, s. *quello, o quella che incoraggia.*

He is a great incourager of learning, *egli è un gran promotore delle scienze.*

To INCRA'SSATE [to thicken or make thick] *ingrossare, far grosso.*

INCRE'ASE, s. *accrescimento,* s. m. *augumentazione,* s. f.

An increase of a family, *un accrescimento di famiglia.*

An increase of children, *un più gran numero di figliuoli.*

The increase of trade, *l'avanzamento del negozio.*

The increase of three years, *l'entrata di tre anni.*

To increase, verb neut. *crescere, augumentarsi, aggrandirsi.*

INCRE'ASED, adj. *cresciuto, aumentato, aggrandito.*

His estate is very much increased, *i suoi beni sono molto migliorati, aumentati.*

INCRE'ASER, s. *secondatore, quello, o quella che accresce, che aumenta.*

INCRE'ASING, s. *accrescimento,* s. m.

INCREDIBI'LITY, } s. *l'esser in-*
INCRE'DIBLENESS, } *credibile.*

INCRE'DIBLE, adj. [past all belief] *incredibile, da non credersi.*

INCRE'DIBLY, adv. *incredibilmente, d'una maniera incredibile.*

Incredibly large, *d'una grandezza incredibile.*

INCREDU'LITY, s. [unbelief] *incredulità, miscredenza,* s. f.

INCRE'DULOUS, adj. [hard of belief] *incredulo, che non crede, miscredente.*

An incredulous man, *un incredulo.*

An incredulous woman, *un' incredula.*

I'NCREMENT, s. [increase, improvement] *accrescimento,* s. m.

To I'NCREPATE [to chide, or rebuke] *increpare, riprendere, sgridare.*

INCREPA'TION, s. [rebuke] *increpazione,* s. f. *biasimo,* s. m.

To

To INCRO'ACH [to usurp] *usurpare, occupare ingiustamente l'altrui.*

To incroach upon [to abuse] *abusare, usar male.*

To incroach upon one's kindness, *abusare dell' altrui cortesia.*

INCRO'ACHED UPON, *usurpato, abusato.*

INCRO'ACHER, s. *usurpatore,* s. m. *usurpatrice,* s. f.

INCRO'ACHING, } s. *usurpa-*
INCRO'ACHMENT, } *mento,* s. m. *usurpazione,* s. f.

To INCRU'ST, } [to parget] *incrostare,*
To INCRU'STATE, } *intonacare.*

INCRUSTA'TION, s. [a pargetting] *incrostatura,* s. f. *l'incrostare, intonaco, intonacato,* s. m.

To I'NCUBATE, *giacer sull' uova, covare.*

I'NCUBUS, s. [night-mare] *sorta di malattia, che si genera dormendo supino.*

To INCU'LCATE [to beat into one's head] *inculcare, ripetere, ridire una cosa ad uno affine d' imprimergliela nella memoria.*

INCU'LCATED, adj. *inculcato.*

INCU'LPABLE, adj. [unblameable] *incolpabile, incolpevole, che non può incolparsi.*

INCU'MBENT, s. [one that is in present possession of a benefice] *un beneficiato, colui che è in possesso di qualche beneficio.*

Incumbent, adj. ex. I have a great business incumbent upon me, *ho un gran negozio appoggiato a me.*

This is a duty now incumbent upon me, *questo è un' dovere al quale mi bisogna compire.*

To INCU'MBER [to croud, or clog] *ingombrare, occupare, impedire,* pres. *impedisco.*

A great fear incumbers my heart, *un gran timore m' ingombra il cuore.*

INCU'MBRANCE, s. [hindrance] *ingombro, ingombramento, occupamento, impacciamento,* s. m.

INCU'MBERED, adj. *ingombrato, occupato, impedito.*

To INCU'R [to run upon, to fall under] *incorrere, cascare.* pret. *incorsi.*

To incur one's displeasure, *incorrere nell' altrui dispiacere.*

To incur a mischief, *esporsi a qualche disgrazia.*

INCU'RABLE, adj. [that cannot be cured] *incurabile, da non potersi curare, senza rimedio.*

INCU'RABLENESS, s. *qualità incurabile.*

INCU'RABLY, adv. *d'una maniera incurabile.*

To be incurably sick, *esser ammalato d'una infermità incurabile.*

INCU'RRED, adj. *incorso.*

INCU'RSION, s. [an inroad of soldiers into an enemy's country] *scorreria,* s. f.

INCU'SSION, s. [a violent shaking against, or into] *scossa,* s. f. *scuotimento,* s. m.

To I'NDAGATE [to search, to enquire diligently] *indagare, ricercare.*

INDAGA'TION, s. [a diligent searching or enquiring into] *indagazione, ricerca,* s. f.

INDA'MAGE [to bring damage, to hurt] *danneggiare, nuocere,* pret. *nocqui, offesi.*

INDA'MAGED, adj. *danneggiato, nociuto, offeso.*

To INDA'NGER [to expose to danger] *arrischiare, esporre a pericolo o rischio, mettere a ripentaglio o cimento, cimentare.*

INDA'NGERED, adj. *arrischiato, esposto a pericolo, cimentato.*

To INDE'AR [to gain, or to cause affection] *cattivare, rendersi favorevole, obbligare.*

A genteel and civil carriage will indear you to all, *il vostro portamento affabile e civile vi cattiverà l' amore di ciascuno.*

INDE'ARMENT, s. [that which gains love] *grazia, maniera graziosa e cortese che ci fa esser ben veduto da ognuno.*

INDE'AVOUR, s. *sforzo,* s. m.

To do one's endeavour, *fare ogni suo sforzo, porre ogni suo ingegno.*

To INDE'AVOUR [to strive] *sforzarsi, fare ogni sforzo, procurare, ingegnarsi, porre ogni studio, cercare.*

To indeavour after a thing, *sforzarsi, procurare di fare qualche cosa.*

Indeavour to do it, *cerrate di farlo.*

He indeavours what he can to undo me, *cerca, fa ogni sforzo di rovinarmi.*

INDE'AVOURED, adj. *sforzato, procurato, ingegnato, cercato.*

INDE'BTED, adj. [in debt] *indebitato, che ha debiti.*

To be indebted to one for something, *esser obbligato, o tenuto a qualcheduno per che che si sia.*

INDE'CENCY, s. [unbecomingness] *indecenza,* s. f.

INDE'CENT, adj. [unbecoming] *indecente, immodesto.*

INDE'CENTLY, adv. *indecentemente, immodestamente,*

INDE'CIMABLE, adj. [not liable to pay tithes] *che non è obbligato di pagar le decime.*

INDE'CLINABLE, adj. [a grammatical term used of nouns that do not vary the cases] *indeclinable, che non si declina.*

INDE'CLINABLY, adv. *indeclinabilmente, senza declinare.*

INDECO'RUM, s. [unhandsome carriage] *indecenza,* s. f.

INDE'ED, adv. *in verità, in vero, da vero, per certo.*

INDEFA'TIGABLE, adj. [that cannot or will not be wearied] *infaticabile, indefesso, che non si stanca.*

INDEFA'TIGABLY, adv. *infaticabilmente, indefessamente.*

A man indefatigably laborious, *un uomo infaticabile, indefesso.*

INDEFE'ASIBLE, } adj. [that can-
INDEFE'SIBLE, } not be made void] *inviolabile, irrevocabile, che non si può rivocare o scancellare.*

INDE'FINITE, adj. [unlimited, undefined] *indefinito, indeterminato, termine grammaticale.*

INDE'FINITELY, adv. *indefinitamente, d'una maniera indefinita.*

INDE'LIBLE, adj. [that cannot be cancelled or blotted out] *indelebile, che non si può cancellare.*

INDE'LICACY, s. *grossezza di costumi, privazione o mancanza di elegante decenza.*

To INDE'MNIFY [to bear, or save harmless] *render indenne, assicurare.*

INDE'MNIFY'D, adj. *indenne.*

INDE'MNITY, s. [being saved harmless] *indennità,* s. f. *sfuggimento di danno.*

INDEMO'NSTRABLE, adj. [that cannot be proved or demonstrated] *che non si può dimostrare o provare.*

To INDE'NT [to jag, or notch] *intaccare, far tacca.*

INDENTED, adj. *intaccato.*

INDE'NTURE, s. [a contract indented at the top, containing an agreement between two or more persons] *patto, contratto, accordo,* s. m.

INDEPE'NDENCY, s. *independenza,* s. f.

INDE'PENDENT, adj. [that has no dependency upon any one] *independente, che non dipende da nissuno, assoluto.*

INDEPE'NDENTS [dissenters who manage all things relating to church discipline, and do not allow any dependance on a national church] *independenti, setta d'eretici in Inghilterra.*

INDEPE'NDENTLY, adv. *independentemente, assolutamente.*

INDETE'RMINATE, adj. [undecided] *indeterminato, indeciso, che non é determinato, o deciso.*

INDETE'RMINATELY, adv. *indeterminatamente, d'una maniera indeterminata.*

INDEVO'TION, s. [want of devotion] *indevozione, irreligione, mancanza di religione.*

I'NDEX, s. [table of contents of a book] *indice,* s. m. *tavola,* s. f.

To I'NDICATE [to discover or show] *indicare, accennare, dinotare, mostrare.*

INDICA'TION, s. [a showing, a sign] *indicazione,* s. f. *l indicare, indice, segno,* s. m.

INDI'CATIVE, adj. [a term of grammar] *indicativo, termine gramaticale*

The indictive mood of a verb, *il modo indicativo d'un verbo.*

To INDI'CT, *v.* To Indite.

INDI'CTION, s. [in chronology, is the space of fifteen years, a way of reckoning appointed by the emperor Constantine in the room of the Olympiade] *indizione,* s. f. *termine cronologico, esprimente distinzion di tempo, e ogni tanto si muta, e cammina dall' uno infino al numere 15, e poi si torna all' uno.*

INDI'CTMENT, *v.* Inditement.

INDI'FFERENCE, } s. [uncon-
INDI'FFERENCY, } cernedness] *indif-*

indifferenza, tepidezza, freddezza, s. f.

INDI'FFERENT, adj. [little, not material] *indifferente, di poca importanza.*

'Tis indifferent to me ['tis all one] *ciò m' è indifferente, ciò poco m'importa.*

Indifferent [cold, that has no affection or love for] *indifferente, poco curante, tepido, freddo.*

Indifferent [pretty good, tolerable] *indifferente, tollerabile, mediocre, passabile.*

Indifferent [common, ordinary] *comune, triviale, ordinario.*

To put a thing into the hands of an indifferent person, *metter che che si sia nelle mani d'un terzo.*

I am indifferent whether he comes or not, *che venga o non venga, poco mi cale*; *poco m'importa.*

Indifferent, adv. *indifferentemente, assai, così così, assai bene.*

I am indifferent well, *sto assai bene, e così così,*

INDI'FFERENTLY, adv. [with indifference] *indifferentemente, freddamente, con indifferenza.*

Indifferently [without distinction] *indifferentemente, senza differenza, egualmente.*

INDIGENCE, s. [need, want] *indigenza, necessità, povertà*, s. f. *bisogno*, s. m.

I'NDIGENT, adj. [needy, poor, wanting] *indigente, necessitoso, povero, bisognoso.*

INDIGE'STED, adj. [not digested] *indigesto, non digesto.*

INDIGE'STIBLE, adj. [that cannot be digested] *indigestibile, non digestibile.*

INDIGE'STION, s. [a want of digestion] *indigestione*, s. f. *contrario di digestione.*

To INDI'GITATE [to show plainly, as it were with the finger] *mostrare, provare, far vedere chiaramente, far toccar con mano, far toccar col dito.*

INDIGITA'TION, s. [a plain demonstration] *dimostrazione, prova evidente.*

INDIGNA'TION, s. [anger] *indignazione, e indegnazione, ira*, s. f. *sdegno*, s. m.

I'NDIGNITY, s. [affront, infamy, disgrace] *indegnità.*

I'NDIGO, s. [a plant brought out of the Indies, us'd in dying, painting, &c.] *indico*, s. m.

INDIRE'CT, adj. [unfair, unhandsome] *indiretto.*

Indirect means, *vie indirette.*

INDIRE'CTLY, adv. *indirettamente, per modo indiretto.*

Directly or indirectly, *direttamente, o indirettamente.*

INDISCE'RNABLE, adj. [that cannot be discerned or perceived] *che non si può discernere.*

INDISCE'RPABLE, adj. [that cannot be rent, divided or separated] *indivisibile, inseparabile, che non si può dividere o separare.*

INDISCERPIBI'LITY, s. [a being inseparable] *indivisibilità, qualità inseparabile, o indivisibile.*

INDISCRE'ET, adj. [unwise] *indiscreto, imprudente, inconsiderato, poco savio o giudizioso.*

INDISCRE'ETLY, adv. [unwisely] *indiscretamente, senza discrezione, imprudentemente.*

INDISCRE'TION, s. [want of discretion] *indiscrezione, imprudenza, indiscretezza,*

INDISPE'NSABLE, adj. [that cannot be dispensed with] *indispensabile, che non si può dispensare.*

INDISPE'NSABLENESS, s. *cosa indispensabile, necessità.*

To INDISPO'SE [to make unfit or incapable] *render incapace.*

INDISPO'SED, adj. [sick, out of order] *indisposto, ammalato.*

Indisposed [not willing to do any thing] *che non è disposto a fare qualche cosa.*

INDISPO'SEDNESS, s. *avversione, repugnanza*, s. f.

INDISPOSI'TION, s. [illness] *indisposizione, mala sanità.*

INDISPU'TABLE, adj. [not to be questioned or disputed] *incontestabile, indisputabile.*

INDI'SPUTABLY, adv. *incontestabilmente, indubitatamente.*

INDISSO'LVABLE, adj. [that cannot be dissolved] *indissolubile.*

INDI'SSOLUBLE, adj. [that cannot be loosened, broken or undone] *indissolubile, che non si può sciorre.*

INDI'SSOLUBLY, adv. *indissolubilmente, d'una maniera indissolubile.*

INDISTI'NCT, adj. [confused, disordered] *indistinto, confuso, disordinato.*

INDISTI'NCTLY, adv. *indistintamente, non distintamente, confusamente.*

INDISTI'NGUISHABLE, adj. [not to be distinguished] *che non si può distinguere, generale.*

To INDI'TE [in the sense of the law, to accuse] *accusare, processare, denunciare in guidicio.*

To indite [to compose or deliver the matter of a letter or other writing] *comporre, dettare, o scrivere una lettera, o altra scrittura.*

INDI'TED, adj. [accused] *accusato, processato.*

Indited [composed] *composto, scritto, dettato.*

INDITE'E, s. *l'accusato, quello, o quella che è accusata.*

INDI'TEMENT, s. *accusa*, s. f.

INDI'TER, s. [he that indites one] *accusatore, denunciatore, delatore*, s. m.

INDI'TING, s. *l'accusare, v.* To indite.

INDIVI'DUAL, adj. [the same only, not to be divided] *individuo, indivisibile.*

Every individual man, *ciascheduno individuo.*

An individual, or individuum [an individual thing or person] *un individuo, cosa particolare compresa sotto la spezie.*

INDIVISIBI'LITY, s. [the quality of that which is not divisible] *indivisibilità*, s. f. *astratto d'indivisibile.*

INDIVI'SIBLE, adj. [that cannot be divided] *indivisible, non divisibile, che non si può dividere.*

INDI'VISIBLENESS, s. *indivisibilità, qualità indivisibile.*

INDI'VISABLY, adv. *indivisibilmente, inseparabilmente.*

INDO'CIBLE, } adj. [not to be taught, unapt to learn] *indocile, che non è docile, che non è trattabile.*
INDO'CILE,

INDOCI'LITY, s. *indocilità*, s. f.

To INDO'CTRINATE [to instruct, to teach] *dottrinare, ammaestrare, insegnare.*

INDO'CTRINATED, adj. *indottrinato, ammaestrato, insegnato.*

I'NDOLENCE, } s. [insensibility] *indolenza, insensibilità*, s. f. *privazione di dolore.*
I'NDOLENCY,

I'NDOLENT, adj. [insensible, careless, supine] *indolente, pigro, infingardo, insensibile.*

I'NDOLENTLY, adv. [carelesly, lazily, inattentively, listlesly] *indolentemente, negligentemente, pigramente, senza cura, senza attenzione, senza gusto, senza pigliar piacere o interesse.*

INDO'MABLE, adj. [untameable] *indomabile, indomito, da non potersi domare.*

To INDO'RSE [to write on the back] *indossare, termine mercantile.*

To indorse a bill of exchange, *indossare una lettera di cambio,*

INDO'RSED, adj. *indossato.*

INDOR'SEMENT, s. *indossamento*, s. m.

INDO'RSING, s. *l'indossare.*

To INDO'W [to settle rents or revenues upon] *dotare, assegnare una rendita, fondare.*

To indow an hospital, *dotare uno spedale.*

INDO'WED, adj. *dotato.*

A man endowed with excellent qualities, *un uomo dotato di belle qualità.*

INDO'WMENT, s. [a natural gift] *talento, dono di natura.*

INDRAUGHT, s. [a gulph or bay running in between two lands] *golfo, braccio di mare fra due terre.*

To INDRENCH, *impregnar d'acqua, imbevere, tuffare, immergere.*

INDU'BITABLE, } adj. [not to be questioned] *indubitabile, indubitato, che non è da mettersi in dubbio, certo.*
INDU'BITATE,

INDU'BITABLY, adv. *indubitatamente, senza dubitazione, certamente.*

To INDU'CE [to lead, to persuade] *indurre, e inducere, persuadere, muovere a fare.* pref. *induco.* pret. *indussi, persuasi.*

INDU'CED, adj. *indotto, persuaso.*

INDUCEMENT, s. [a motive to a thing] *persuasione*, s. f. *inducimento, motivo*, s. m.

INDU'CING, s. *inducimento*, s. m. *l'indurre.*

To INDU'CT [to give induction] *mettere in possesso.*

INDU'CTED,

INDU'CTED, adj. *meſſo in poſſeſſo.*

INDU'CTION, s. [a leading into] *induzione*, s. f. *inducimento*, s. m.

Induction [in the ſenſe of the law, a putting a clerk in poſſeſſion of his church] *preſa di poſſeſſo.*

To receive induction [to take poſſeſſion of a living] *prender poſſeſſo d'un beneficio.*

To give induction, *metter in poſſeſſo.*

Induction [in logick, a kind of argumentation or imperfect ſyllogiſm] *induzione, ſpezie d'argomento.*

To INDU'E [to qualify, to ſupply, to furniſh] *dotare, privilegiare, ed è proprio di Dio e della natura.*

INDU'ED, adj. *dotato, privilegiato.*

Indued with excellent natural gifts, *dotato d'eccellenti doni da natura.*

To INDU'LGE [to cocker, to humour, to be fond or make much of] *eſſer indulgente, vezzeggiare, favorire, trattar benignamente.*

To indulge one's paſſions, *darſi in preda alle paſſioni, contentare le ſue paſſioni.*

To indulge [to allow] *dare, concedere*, pret. *diedi, conceſſi.*

INDU'LGENCE, s. *indulgenza*, s. f. *l'eſſere indulgente.*

Indulgence [forgiveneſs] *indulgenza, perdono.*

A plenary indulgence, *indulgenza plenaria.*

INDU'LGENT, adj. [gentle, kind] *indulgente, mite, affabile, corteſe, buona.*

INDU'LGENTLY, adv. *con indulgenza, con maniera dolce e benigna, benignamente.*

To uſe one indulgently, *trattar uno con indulgenza.*

INDU'LT, } s. [a ſpecial grant of
INDU'LTO, } a prince, or of the pope] *indulto*, s. m.

I'NDUMENTS, s. pl. [properties] *proprietà*, s. f. pl.

INDU'RABLE, adj. [that may be indured] *ſopportabile, tollerabile, che ſi può ſopportare.*

To INDU'RATE [to harden, to make hard] *indurare, indurire, divenir duro.*

Indurate, or indured, adj. *indurato, indurito.*

INDU'RATION, s. *induramento*, s. m. *l'indurare.*

To INDU'RE [to bear, to ſuffer] *patire, tollerare, comportare, ſofferire, è ſoffrire*, preſ. *patiſco.*

I can't indure him, *non poſſo patirlo.*

To indure [to laſt] *durare, ſoſſiſtere.*

INDU'RED, adj. *patito, tollerato, comportato, ſofferto.*

Not to be indured, *inſopportabile.*

INDU'STRIOUS, adj. [laborious, pains taking] *induſtrioſo, ingegnoſo, laborioſo, accurato, diligente.*

INDU'STRIOUSLY, adv. *induſtrioſamente, con induſtria.*

I'NDUSTRY, s. [labour, diligence] *induſtria, diligenza ingegnoſa.*

To INE'BRIATE [to intoxicate] *innebbriare.*

INE'BRIATED, adj. *innebbriato.*

INEBRIA'TION, s. *innebbriazione.*

INEFFABI'LITY, s. [unſpeakableneſs] *ineffabilità, indicibilità*, s. f.

INE'FFABLE, adj. [unſpeakable, not to be expreſſed] *ineffabile, innarrabile, indicibile, che non ſi può con parole eſprimere.*

INEFFE'CTIVE, } adj. [that has no
INEFFE'CTUAL, } effect, vain] *inefficace, inutile, vano.*

INEFFE'CTUALLY, adv. *ſenza frutto, inutilmente, vanamente, in vano.*

INEFFICA'CIOUS, adj. [of no efficacy, force, or virtue] *inefficace, vano, inutile.*

INENA'RRABLE, adj. [that cannot be related] *innarrabile, da non poterſi narrare.*

INE'PT, adj. [unfit, meek, ſilly] *inetto, non atto, ſciocco, ſcioperato.*

INE'PTITUDE, s. [unaptneſs, incapacity] *impoſſanza, incapacità*, s. f.

Ineptitude [defect] *imperfezione, mancanza*, s. f.

INEQU'ALITY, s. *inegualita*, s. f.

INERRABI'LITY, s. *infallibilità*, s. f.

INE'RRABLE, adj. *infallibile, che non può errare.*

INE'RT, adj. [ſluggiſh, unfit for action] *inerte, pigro, dappoco, infingardo.*

INE'STIMABLE, adj. [not to be valued] *ineſtimabile, imprezzabile, da non poterſi ſtimare.*

INE'VITABLE, [adj. [not to be ſhunned or avoided] *inevitabile, da non poterſi evitare, ſfuggire, o ſcampare.*

INE'VITABLY, adv. [infallibly] *inevitabilmente, infallibilmente, certamente, ſicuramente.*

INEXCU'SABLE, adj. [not to be excuſed] *ineſcuſabile.*

INEXHAU'STED, adj. [unemptied, not poſſible to be emptied] *ineſauſto, che non ſi può votare.*

INEXHA'USTIBLE, adj. [which cannot be ſpent or emptied] *ineſauſto, che non manca, che non vien meno.*

INE'XORABLE, adj. [not to be prevailed upon with prayers] *ineſorabile, implacabile, che non ſi laſcia ſvolgere da' preghi.*

INEXPE'DIENT, adj. [not convenient, not fit] *che non è ſpediente, o neceſſario.*

INEXPE'RIENCE, s. [want of experience or ſkill] *ineſperienza, mancanza d'eſperienza.*

INEXPE'RIENCED, adj. [that has no experience] *ineſperto, che non ha ſperienza, o pratica.*

INE'XPIABLE, adj. [not to be expiated or atoned for] *che non ſi può eſpiare.*

INE'XPLICABLE, adj. [which cannot be unfolded or explained] *ineſplicabile, che non ſi può eſplicare.*

INEXPRE'SSIBLE, adj. [that cannot be expreſſed] *ineffabile, innarrabile, indicibile, che non ſi può con parole eſprimere.*

INE'XPUGNABLE, adj. [not to be taken or won by force, impregnable] *inſepugnabile, che non ſi può eſpugnare.*

INE'XTINGUISHABLE, adj. [not to be put out or quenched] *ineſtinguibile, da non poterſi eſtinguere.*

INE'XTIRPABLE, adj. [that cannot be extirpated] *che non ſi può eſtirpare, diſtruggere, o ſradicare.*

INE'XTRICABLE, adj. [not to be diſentangled] *ineſtricabile, da non ſi potere ſtrigare, imbrogliato.*

An inextricable caſe, *un negozio ineſtricabile, o imbrogliato.*

INEXU'PERABLE, adj. [that cannot be ſurpaſſed or overcome] *inſuperabile, da non poterſi ſuperare.*

INFALLIBI'LITY, s. [a faculty or gift of never erring] *infallibilità*, s. f.

INFA'LLIBLE, adj. [that cannot err or be deceived] *infallibile, che non può fallire.*

Infallible [certain, ſure] *infallibile, certo, ſicuro.*

INFA'LLIBLY, adv. [certainly, without fail] *infallibilmente, ſenza fallo, certamente, ſicuramente.*

I'NFAMOUS, adj. [baſe, villainous, ſhameful] *infame, vituperoſo, ignominioſo, di mala ſama, vergognoſo.*

An infamous death, *una morte ignominioſa.*

An infamous perſon, *un infame, un diſonorato, un uomo infame, ſenza onore.*

I'NFAMOUSLY, adv. *d'una maniera infame, vituperoſamente, ignominioſamente.*

I'NFAMY, s. [diſgrace, diſcredit, ſhame] *infamia, cattiva fama, ignominia, vergogna*, s. f. *diſonore, vituperio*, s. m.

I'NFANCY, s. [childhood, the firſt ſtate of human lite] *infantilità, infanzia*, s. f. *la prima etade dell' uomo.*

I'NFANT, s. [a young child] *infante, bambino*, s. m.

Infants [all the ſons of the kings of Spain and Portugal] *infante, nome anneſſo ai figliuoli de' re di Spagna e di Portogallo.*

INFA'NTA, s. [all the daughters of the kings of Spain and Portugal] *infanta, titolo dato a tutte le figliuole de' re di Spagna e di Portogallo.*

I'NFANTRY, s. [the foot ſoldiers of an army] *fanteria*, s. f. *ſoldateſca a piede.*

INFA'TIGABLE, adj. [not to be tired or wearied] *infaticabile, che non cura fatica, indefeſſo, che non ſi ſtanca.*

INFA'TIGABLENESS, s. *qualità infaticabile.*

INFA'TIGABLY, adv. *infaticabilmente, ſenza eſſer vinto dalla fatica.*

To INFA'TUATE [to bewitch] *infatuare, ammaliare, preoccupare.*

INFA'TUATED, adj. *infatuato, ammaliato, preoccupato, oſtinato.*

INFATUATION, s. *ammaliamento, oſtinazione, caparbietà.*

To INFE'CT [to communicate to another corruption or peſtilence, to corrupt, to taint] *infettare, guaſtare, corrompere, render infetto*, pret. *corruppi.*

INFE'CTED,

INFE'CTED, adj. *infettato, infetto, compreso da infermità, da corruzione, maculato, guasto.*

INFE'CTION, s. *infezione, corruzione, contagione,* s. f.

INFE'CTIOUS, adj. [apt to infect, tainting, catching] *infetto, contagioso.*

An infectious breath, *un fiato infetto.*

An infectious disease, *una malattia contagiosa.*

INFECU'ND, adj. [unfruitful, infertile] *infecondo ; non fertile.*

To INFE'EBLE [to weaken, to make feeble] *infiebolire, e infievolire, indebolire, debilitare, snervare,* pref. *infiebolisco, infievolisco, indebolisco.*

INFELI'CITY, adj [unhappiness, misery, calamity] *infelicità, sventura, disavventura, miseria, calamità, disgrazia.*

To INFE'OFF [to unite, or join the fee] *unire, incorporare al feudo.*

INFE'OFFED, adj. *unito, incorporato al feudo.*

INFE'OFFMENT, s. [a settling in fee] *l'unire, l'incorporare al feudo.*

To INFE'R [to conclude, to draw a consequence] *inferire, voler dire, significare, conchiudere,* pret. *conchiusi.*

What do you infer from that? *che inferite da ciò? che volete dire per questo?*

I'NFERENCE, s. [conclusion, consequence] *conseguenza, conclusione,* s. f.

INFERIO'RITY, s. [lower rank, or degree] *inferiorità, grado inferiore.*

INFE'RIOUR, adj. [of a lower degree or rank] *inferiore, che è meno d'un altro in dignità, in merito, in forza, &c.*

An inferiour judge, *un giudice inferiore.*

An inferiour officer, *un ufficiale subalterno.*

He is inferiour to none, *egli non la cede a nessuno.*

A town of an inferiour note, *una città di poca considerazione.*

Inferiour, s. [a person of lower rank, or meaner quality] *un inferiore.*

INFE'RNAL, adj. [belonging to hell, hellish] *infernale, d'inferno.*

The infernal Gods, *gli Dei, o le Deità infernali, o d'inferno.*

The infernal stone, *la pietra infernale.*

INFE'RTILE, adj. [barren] *infertile, sterile.*

INFE'RTILENESS, } s. [barrenness]
INFE'RTILITY, } *infertilità, sterilità,* s. f.

To INFE'ST [to annoy, to trouble] *infestare, importunare, nojare, travagliare, tribolare, molestare.*

To infest the seas, *infestare i mari, fare scorrerie per mare.*

INFE'STED, adj. *infestato,* v. To infest.

His reign was infested by many new troubles, *il suo regno fu travagliato da molti nuovi tumulti.*

I'NFIDEL, s. [a heathen, a Turk] *infedele.*

INFIDE'LITY, s. [unbelief] *infedeltà, incredulità,* s. f.

Infidelity [unfaithfulness, disloyalty] *infedeltà, dislealtà, perfidia,* s. f. *tradimento,* s. m.

I'NFINITE, adj. [boundless, endless] *infinito, che non ha fine.*

God is an infinite being, *Iddio è un essere infinito.*

An infinite number of people, *un numero infinito di gente, un' infinità di gente.*

I'NFINITELY, adv. [exceedingly] *infinitamente, molto, sommamente, senza misura.*

I am infinitely obliged to you, *vi resto infinitamente obbligato.*

God is infinitely good, *Iddio è sommamente buono.*

I'NFINITENESS, s. *infinità,* s. f.

I'NFINITIVE, adj. *infinito.* Ex. The infinitive mood of a verb, *l'infinito d'un verbo.*

INFI'NITUDE, } s. *infinità.*
INFI'NITY, }

INFI'RM, adj. [weak, feeble, sickly] *infermo, malsano, infermiccio, malaticcio, debile.*

To INFI'RM [to weaken, to shake, to enfeeble] *indebolire, render fiacco.*

INFI'RMARY, s. [an apartment for sick people in a monastery] *infermeria,* s. f. *luogo ne' conventi, dove si curano gl' infermi.*

The overseer of an infirmary, *infermiere.*

INFI'RMITY, s. [sickness, weakness] *infermità, malattia.*

INFI'STULATED, adj. [turned to, or full of fistula's] *infistolito, pieno di fistole.*

To INFI'X [to fix in the mind] *imprimere, scolpire nella mente.*

INFI'XED, or INFI'XT, adj. *impresso, scolpito nella mente.*

To INFLA'ME [to set on fire] *infiammare, accendere, appiccar fiamma a che che si sia, abbruciare.*

To inflame one's anger, *infiammare, accendere, eccitar l'ira.*

To inflame a reckoning, *arrendere, accrescere un conto.*

INFLA'MED, adj. *infiammato, abbruciato,* v. To inflame.

INFLA'MING, s. *infiammamento,* s. m. *l'infiammare.*

INFLA'MMABLE, adj. *infiammabile, atto ad infiammarsi.*

INFLAMMA'TION, s. *infiammagione, infiammazione,* s. f. *rossore, che apparisce nelle parti del corpo per soverchio calore.*

INFLA'MMATIVE, adj. [which setteth in a flame] *infiammativo, che infiamma.*

To INFLA'TE [to blow up, to puff] *gonfiare.*

Inflate, adj. [swollen, or puffed up with wind] *gonfio, gonfiato.*

INFLA'TION, s. [a blowing, or puffing up] *gonfiamento.*

Inflation [a windy swelling] *gonfiatura,* s. f. *tumore.*

INFLEXIBI'LITY, s. [obstinacy, stiffness] *inflessibilità, ostinazione, pertinacia, caparbietà,* s. f.

INFLE'XIBLE, adj. [not to be prevailed upon] *inflessibile, rigido, pertinace, ostinato, caparbio.*

INFLE'XIBLY, adv. *inflessibilmente, gagliardamente, rigidamente, poderosamente, ostinatamente, pertinacemente.*

To INFLI'CT [to lay a punishment upon] *infliggere.*

To inflict a punishment upon one, *infliggere una pena ad alcuno, punirlo, castigarlo.*

INFLI'CTED, adj. *inflitto*

He deserves to have a punishment inflicted upon him, *merita di esser castigato.*

INFLI'CTION, s. *inflizione,* s. f. *l' infliggere.*

I'NFLUENCE, s. [power] *influenza,* s. f. *influsso,* s. m. *infondimento di sua qualità sopra che che si sia.*

The influence of the stars, *l'influenza degli astri.*

To have a great influence over one's mind, *avere grande influenza, o potere sopra qualcheduno.*

To I'NFLUENCE [to have influence upon] *influere, e influire, l'operar de' corpi celesti ne' corpi inferiori.*

To influence [to produce] *causare, produrre,* pref. *produco,* pret. *produssi.*

I'NFLUENCED, adj. *influsso, causato, prodotto.*

INFLUE'NTIAL, adj. Ex. [an influential operation] *un' operazione che si fa per influenza.*

INFLU'X, s. [flowing, running into] *sboccamento d'un fiume in un altro.*

To INFO'LD [to fold, to wrap up] *inviluppare, avviluppare.*

INFO'LDED, adj. *inviluppato, avviluppato.*

To INFO'RCE [to force, to oblige] *forzare, sforzare, costrignere, obbligare,* pref. *costringo,* pret. *costrinsi.*

Reason cannot oblige me to believe any such thing, *la ragione non può darmi a credere una tal cosa.*

INFO'RCED, adj. *forzato, sforzato, costretto, obbligato.*

INFO'RCEMENT, s. *forza,* s. f. *sforzamento,* s. m.

To INFO'RM [to give notice, to tell] *informare, dare notizia, notificare, ragguagliare.*

To inform [to teach, to instruct] *informare, disporre, render atto, istruire, insegnare, ammaestrare,* pret. *disposi,* pref. *instruisco.*

One soul informs them, *una medesima anima gl'informa ; non hanno che una medesima anima.*

To inform against one, *informare, fare un' informazione contro qualcheduno.*

INFORMA'TION, s. [advice] *informazione, istruzione, contezza,* s. f. *avviso, ragguaglio,* s. m.

Information [accusation] *informazione, accusa, accusazione,* s. f.

To give in an information against one, *fare un' informazione contro qualcheduno, accusarlo, processarlo.*

Information [instruction] *informazione, insegnamento, ammaestramento,* s. m.

INFO'RMED, adj. *informato,* v. To inform.

If you have the curiosity to be better informed, *se voi avete la curiosità d'esser meglio informato.*

I am informed so, *così mi vien riferito.*

Informed against, *processato, accusato.*

INFO'RMER, s. *informatore, accusatore, delatore, denunciatore.*

INFO'RMOUS, adj. [that is without form, shape, or fashion] *informe, sformato, senza forma.*

INFO'RTUNATE, adj. [unhappy] *infortunato, sfortunato, sgraziato, sventurato.*

To INFRA'NCHISE [a law word, to give one his liberty] *affrançare, far franco, libero, dar libertà.*

To infranchise [to incorporate into a society, or body politick] *aggregare, ricevere alcuno in corpo, o società.*

To infranchise [to make a freeman] *ricever uno statuale di qualche communità.*

INFRA'NCHISED, adj. *affrancato, v.* To infranchise.

INFRA'NCHISEMENT, s. *l'affrancare.*

INFRE'QUENT, adj. [rare, uncommon] *raro, non comune, non frequente.*

To INFRINGE [to break a law, custom, or privilege] *trasgredire, rompere, violare.* pref. *trasgredisco.* pret. *ruppi.*

To infringe a law, *trasgredire una legge.*

INFRI'NGED, adj. *trasgredito, rotto, violato.*

INFRI'NGEMENT, s. *transgressione, violazione,* s. f.

INFRI'NGER, s. *transgressione, violatore,* s. m.

INFU'RIATE, adj. [enraged, raging] *infuriato, furioso, arrabbiato, rabbioso.*

To INFU'SE [to pour in or into, to steep] *infondere, inzuppare, mettere che che si sia dentro ad alcun liquore.* pret. *infusi.*

To INFU'SE [to inspire] *infondere, inspirare.*

To infuse good principles into one, *infondere, dare buoni precetti a qualcheduno.*

INFU'SED, adj. *infuso, inspirato.*

Infused gifts, *grazie infuse.*

INFU'SING, } s. *infusione,* s. f. *l'atto dello infondere.*
INFU'SION, }

To INGA'GE [to pawn] *impegnare, dare, o mettere una cosa in pegno.*

To engage [to bind] *impegnare; obbligare.*

To ingage one's word] *impegnar la fede, dar la fede in pegno, impegnarsi di parola.*

To ingage one's self in a business, *impegnarsi, intrigarsi, intromettersi, imbarcarsi in qualche negozio.*

To ingage one's self to do a thing, *impegnarsi, obbligarsi di fare una cosa.*

To ingage one's word, *promettere, entrar mallevadore, obbligarsi, impegnarsi di parola.*

I'll ingage he shall not do it, *vi prometto, v'assicuro, vi so dir io che non lo farà.*

To ingage [as armies do] *attaccar la battaglia, venire alle armi, venire alle mani, battersi, venire a giornata.*

To ingage the enemy, *attaccar l'inimico, investirlo, attaccare o appiccar la battaglia.*

INGA'GEMENT, s. [obligation] *obbligazione, promessa,* s. f. *impegno,* s. m.

I am under such ingagements that I cannot recede, *mi trovo talmente impegnato, che non posso dir di no.*

Ingagement [fight] *conflitto,* s. m. *battaglia, zuffa, mischia,* s. f.

INGA'GING, adj. [alluring] *attrattivo, avvenente, gentile, di maniere graziose.*

INGA'THERING, s. [the act of getting in the harvest] *ricolta; l'atto del far la ricolta.*

To INGE'MINATE [to double, or repeat often] *geminare, raddoppiare.*

INGE'MINATED, adj. *geminato, raddoppiato*

To INGE'NDER [to breed] *ingenerare, generare, produrre, fare.* pref. *produco, fo.* pret. *produssi, feci.*

INGE'NDERED, adj. *generato, prodotto, fatto, ingenerato.*

INGE'NDERING, s. *generamento,* s. m. *il generare.*

INGE'NERATED, adj. [not produced by generation, bred in one naturally] *non generato, innato.*

INGE'NIO, s. [a house or mill where sugar is made] *una casa, o un mulino da zucchero, dove si fa il zucchero.*

INGE'NIOUS, adj. [witty] *ingegnoso, spiritoso, dotato d'ingegno.*

Ingenious [industrious] *ingegnoso, industrioso, laborioso, intrigante.*

An ingenious piece of work, *un opera ingegnosa.*

INGE'NIOUSLY, adv. *ingegnosamente, con ingegno.*

Ingeniously [industriously] *ingegnosamente, industriosamente.*

INGE'NIOUSNESS, s. [or wit] *ingegno, genio,* s. m.

INGE'NITE, adj. [inbred, innate] *ingenito, naturale, innato.*

INGENU'ITY, s. [wit] *ingegno, genio, spirito,* s. m. *destrezza,* s. f.

Ingenuity [freedom, frankness, sincerity] *ingenuità, sincerità; franchezza, schiettezza;* s. f. *candore,* s. m.

INGE'NUOUS, adj. [frank, free, open, sincere] *ingenuo, sincero, schietto, aperto, franco.*

INGE'NUOUSLY, adv. *ingenuamente, sinceramente, schiettamente, apertamente, francamente.*

INGE'NUOUSNESS, s. [ingenuity, candor] *ingenuità, schiettezza, sincerità,* s. f. *candore,* s. m.

I'NGENY, s. [genius, natural disposition] *genio, umore,* s. m. *inclinazione d'animo, affetto. Non è più in uso.*

INGINE'EK, *v.* Engineer.

INGLE, s. [a Scotch word for fire] *fuoco,* s. m. *E' vocabolo scozzese.*

INGLO'RIOUS, adj. [that is of no repute, dishonourable] *disonorato, senza gloria, disonorevole, infame.*

INGLO'RIOUSBY, adv. *disonorevolmente, con disonore.*

INGOT, s. [a wedge of gold and silver] *verga d'oro o d'argento.*

To INGRA'FT [to graft] *innestare.*

To ingraft [to imprint] *imprimere, scolpire.* pref. *scolpisco.* pret. *impressi.*

INGRA'FTED, adj. *innestato.*

INGRA'FTING, s. *innestazione,* s. f. *innestamento,* s. m.

To INGRA'IL [to notch about] *intaccare.*

INGRA'ILED, adj. *intaccato.*

INGRA'TE } *v.* Ungrateful.
INGRA'TEFUL, }

To INGRA'TIATE one's self [to endeavour to gain the good will of another] *cattivarsi l'amore, la benevolenza di qualcheduno, insinuarsi nelle altrui grazie, ingraziarsi.*

INGRA'TITUDE, s. [ungratefulness] *ingratitudine,* s. f. *dimenticanza di benefici ricevuti.*

To INGRA'VE, *scolpire, intagliare,* pref. *scolpisco.*

INGRA'VED, or INGRA'VEN, adj. *scolpito, intagliato.*

INGRA'VER, s. *scultore, intagliatore,* s. m.

INGRE'DIENT, s. [one of the simples put into a compound medicine] *ingrediente,* s. m. *quello che entra ne' medicamenti, o simile, e li compone.*

INGRE'SS, s. [an entrance upon, or going into] *ingresso,* s. m. *entrata, entratura,* s. m.

Ingress and regress, *l'entrata, ol'uscita.*

To INGRO'SS [to write over the draught of a deed in fair and large characters] *scrivere al netto, copiare al netto.*

To ingross a commodity, *incettare una mercanzia con disegno d'esser solo a venderla.*

They ingross all the trade to themselves, *si rendon padroni assoluti di tutto'l negozio, hanno in mano tutto'l negozio.*

INGRO'SSED, adj. *scritto, copiato al netto.*

INGRO'SSER, s. *colui che scrive al netto.*

Ingrosser [one who buys up corn or victuals to sell again] *incettore.*

INGRO'SSING, s. *il copiare, o scrivere a netto.*

Ingrossing [forestalling] *incetta,* s. f.

To INGU'LPH [to swallow down, to devour] *inghiottire, ingojare avidamente.*

INGURGITA'TION, s. [a swallowing greedily] *ghiottornia; voracità,* s. f.

To INHA'BIT [to live, to dwell] *abitare, dimorare.*

INHAB'ITABLE, adj. [habitable, that may be inhabited] *abitabile, dove si può abitare.*

Inhabitable [not habitable] *inabitabile, non abitabile.*

INHA'BITAT, s. *abitante, abitatore,* s. m.

A country without inhabitants, *un paese senza abitanti, un paese spopolato, o deserto.*

INHABITA'TION, s. *abitazione, dimora.*

INHA'BITED, adj. *abitato.*
A place much inhabited, *un paese molto abitato, pieno d'abitanti, popolato, frequentato.*
INHA'BITER, s. *abitatore, abitante,* s. m.
To INHA'NCE [to raise the price] *incarire, alzare il prezzo.*
INHA'NCED, adj. *incarito.*
INHA'NCER, s. *incaritore,* s. m.
INHA'NCING, s. *incarimento,* s. m. *l'incarire.*
INHE'RENCY, } s. *inerenza,* s. f.
INHE'SION, }
INHE'RENT, adj. [sticking, cleaving in] *inerente.*
An inherent quality, *una qualità inerente.*
To INHE'RIT [to get by inheritance] *ereditare.*
Inheritance, s. [a perpetuity of lands and tenements to a man and his heirs] *eredità,* s. f. *ereditaggio,* s. m.
INHE'RITED, adj. *ereditato.*
INHE'RITER, s. *erede,* s. m. f.
INHE'RITING, *l'ereditare.*
INHE'RITRESS, } *erede,* s. f.
INHE'RITRIX, }
INHE'SION, *v.* Inherency.
To INHI'BIT [to prohibit, to forbid] *inibire, proibire,* pref. *inibisco, proibisco.*
INHI'BITED, adj. *inibito, proibito.*
INHIBI'TION, s. [prohibition] *inibizione, proibizione,* s. f.
To INHOLD [to have inherent; to contain in itself] *avere in se, contenere in se.*
INHO'SPITABLE, adj. [discourteous, unkind] *scortese, barbaro, crudele, senza ospitalità.*
INHO'SPITABLY, adv. [unkindly to strangers] *inospitabilmente, senza amore al forestiere.*
INHOSPITA'LITY, s. *barbarie, scortesia, crudeltà verso i forastieri.*
INHUMAN, adj. [cruel, barbarous] *inumano, barbaro, crudele, efferato.*
INHUMA'NLY, adv. *inumanamente, barbaramente, crudelmente, efferatamente.*
INHUMA'NITY, s. [barbarity, cruelty] *inumanità, barbarie, crudeltà, efferatezza,* s. f.
To INHU'ME [to bury, to enter] *interrare, seppellire, sotterrare,* pref. *seppellisco.*
INHUM'ED, adj. *interrato, seppellito, sotterrato.*
INHUMA'TION, s. *l'interrare, il seppellire, il sotterrare.*
To INJE'CT [to cast in, to throw in] *gettar dentro.*
To Inject [to cast up, to throw up] *gettar su, gettar fuori per di su.*
INJE'CTED, adj. *gettato dentro.*
INJE'CTION, s. *injezione,* s. f.
INI'MITABLE, adj. [that cannot be imitated] *inimitabile, che non si puo imitare.*
INIMA'GINABLE, adj. [not to be imagined] *non immaginabile.*
To INJO'IN [to command] *ingiugnere, commettere, ordinare, comandare,* pret. *ingiunsi, commisi.*
INJO'INED, adj. *ingiunto, commesso, ordinato, comandato.*
To INJO'Y [to possess] *godere, possedere, aver il possesso, gioire.* pref. *gioisco.*
To injoy the comforts of this life, *godere i piaceri di questa vita.*
To injoy a woman, *gioire d'una donna, possederla.*
To injoy one's self, *godere, gioire, stare in gioja, in festa, rallegrarsi, prender contento, darsi buon tempo.*
INJO'YED, adj. *goduto, gioito.*
INJO'YMENT, s. *godimento, possesso,* s. m.
Injoyment [pleasure] *godimento, piacere, contento,* s. m. *gioja, allegrezza,* s. f.
INI'QUITY, s. [injustice, wickedness] *iniquità, malvagità, nequizia, ingiustizia,* s. f.
INI'TIAL, adj. [beginning] *iniziante, che principia.*
An initial letter, *lettera majuscola.*
To INI'TIATE [to instruct in the first principles of any art or science] *iniziare, dar principio, cominciare, instruire, ammaestrare ne' primi principj d'un arte o scienza.*
INI'TIATED, adj. *iniziato.*
INITIA'TION, s. *iniziazine,* s. f.
INJUDI'CIOUS, adj. [void of judgment or discretion] *poco giudizioso, imprudente, indiscreto.*
INJUDI'CIOUSLY, adv. *senza giudizio, imprudentemente, indiscretamente.*
INJU'NCTION, s. [command] *comando, ordine,* s. m.
To I'NJURE [to wrong, to abuse] *ingiuriare, fare ingiuria, far torto, oltraggiare, nuocere, offendere.* pret. *nocqui, offesi.*
I'NJURED, adj. *ingiuriato, offeso, oltraggiato.*
The injured party, *la parte offesa.*
I'NJURER, s. *ingiuriatore, offensore,* s. m.
INJU'RIOUS, adj. [offensive] *inguriosò, contumelioso, oltraggiante, oltraggioso.*
INJU'RIOUSLY, adv. *ingiuriosamente, oltraggiosamente, ingiustamente.*
INJU'RIOUSNESS, s. *lo essere inguriosò; disposizione o prontezza a ingiuriare.*
I'NJURY, s. [wrong] *ingiuria, offesa,* s. f. *torto, oltraggio, pregiudicio, danno,* s. m.
INJU'STICE, s. [an unjust act] *ingiustizia,* s. f.
INK, s. [liquor to write with] *inchiostro.*
To daub with ink, *schiccherare, imbrattar con inchiostro, scarabocchiare.*
INKHORN, *calamajo,* s. m.
To INKI'NDLE [to catch fire] *accendersi, infiammersi, attaccarsi il fuoco.* pret. *accesi.*
Inkindled, adj. *acceso, infiammato.*
His zeal inkindled, *il suo zelo s'accese.*
I'NKLING, s. [a hint, or intimation] *sentore, odore, indizio, avviso.* s. m.
To have an inkling of a business, *avere odore, o sentore d'un trattato.*
INKMA'KER [he who makes ink] *facitor d'inchiostro.*
INKY, adj. *che consiste d'inchiostro, che è fatto d'inchiostro; che somiglia all' inchiostro; che è nero come inchiostro.*
INLA'ID, adj. *intarsiato.*
Inlaid work, *tarsia,* s. f. *lavoro di minuti pezzuoli di legname di più colori, commessi insieme.*
I'NLAND, adj. [situate upon the main land, or in the heart of a country] *che è dentro terra, o nel mezzo del continente, lontano dal mare.*
An inland province, *una provincia dentro terra, lontana dal mare, una provincia mediterranea.*
Inland country, *terra ferma.*
To INLA'RGE [to discourse at large upon a subject] *ampliare, amplificare, aggrandire con parole, diffondersi, accrescere, dilatare.* pref. *aggrandisco.* pret. *diffusi, accrebbi.*
To inlarge a discourse, *amplificare un discorso, diffondersi nel discorso.*
To inlarge one's dominions, *ampliare, accrescere, dilatare il suo dominio, allargarlo.*
To inlarge a close prisoner [to allow him some liberty] *dar qualche libertà ad un prigioniero, più di quel che non aveva prima.*
To inlarge upon a subject, *diffondersi sopra un soggetto.*
INLA'RGED, adj. *ampliate, amplificato, diffuso, accresciuto, dilatato, allargato.*
INLA'RGEMENT, s. *ampliazione, dilatazione, amplificazione, agumentazione,* s. f. *aggrandimento, dilatamento,* s. m.
To INLA'Y [to work in wood or metal with several pieces of different colours] *intarsiare, connettere insieme diversi pezzuoli di legname o metallo di più colori.*
INLA'Y'D, *v.* Inlaid.
INLE'ASED, adj. [intangled] *inviluppato, imbrogliato.*
I'NLET, s. [entrance, passage into] *entrata,* s. f. *passaggio,* s. m.
An inlet into the sea, *un' entrata nel mare.*
To INLI'GHTEN [to give light to] *illuminare, dar lume, schiarire.* pref. *schiarisco.*
INLI'GHTENED, adj. *illuminato, schiarito.*
INLI'GHTENER, s. *illuminatore,* s. m. *illuminatrice,* s. f.
INLI'GHTENING, s. *illuminamento,* s. m. *illuminazione,* s. f.
I'NMATE, s. [a law word for a lodger] *pigionale, quello o quella che tiene qualche appartamento o camera a pigione; chi sta dentro, chi allogia dentro.*
I'NMOST, adj. *interiore, remoto.*
Inmost [secret] *segreto, nascosto, recondito.*
God knows our inmost thoughts, *Iddio sa i più reconditi nostri pensieri.*
INN, s. [a publick house for the enter-

tertainment of travellers] *oſteria*, s. f. *albergo*, *oſtello*, s. m.

To keep an inn, *tenere oſteria.*

The inns of Chancery, *collegi per gli ſtudenti di legge.*

The inns of court, *i collegi degli avvocati.*

Innkeeper, *oſte.*

Innkeeper's wife, *oſteſſa, la padrona dell' oſteria.*

To INN [to lodge at an inn] *albergare, alloggiare in un' oſteria.*

To inn corn [to lay it up] *metter il grano nel granajo.*

I'NNATE, adj. [inbred, natural] *innato, nato con noi, naturale.*

Innate faculty, *facoltà innata o naturale.*

INNA'VIGABLE, adj. [that cannot be ſailed upon] *che non è navigabile.*

An innavigable river, *un fiume che non è navigabile.*

I'NNER, adj. [inward] *interiore, avanzato.*

The inner part of a thing, *la parte interiore di che che ſi ſia.*

An inner room in a great houſe, *una camera avanzata, che è nel mezzo di molte altre camere.*

Inner [ſecret] *ſegreto, naſcoſto, recondito.*

God knows the inner thoughts of our heart, *Iddio ſa i più reconditi penſieri del noſtro cuore.*

I'NNOCENCE, } s. [purity of ſoul]
I'NNOCENCY, } *innocenza, nettezza di colpa, purità di coſcienza.*

I'NNOCENT, adj. [guiltleſs, harmleſs] *innocente, puro, ſenza peccato.*

Innocent, s. *innocente*, s. m. f. *una creatura innocente.*

The Innocents day, or Childermas day, *gl' innocenti, la feſta, o il giorno degl' innocenti, che viene in Dicembre.*

An innocent [idiot, or ninny] *innocente, un idiota, un ſemplicione.*

I'NNOCENTLY, adv. *innocentemente, ſenza peccato.*

INNO'CUOUS, adj. [harmleſs, doing no hurt] *che non è nocivo, che non fa male, che non nuoce.*

INNO'MINATE, adj. [nameleſs] *innominato, ſenza nome.*

To I'NNOVATE [to change, or alter] *innovare, introdurre delle novità, fare delle innovazioni.*

I'NNOVATED, adj. *innovato.*

INNOVA'TION, s. [change, alteration] *innovazione, novità*, s. f.

INNOVA'TOR, s. *innovatore*, s. m.

INNO'XIOUS, adj. [harmleſs] *innocente, che non è nocivo.*

INNU'MERABLE, adj. [not to be numbered] *innumerabile, innumerevole, che non ſi può numerare.*

INNU'MERABLENESS, s. *un' infinità, un numero infinito, o innumerabile.*

INNU'MERABLY, adv. *innumerabilmente, ſenza numero, in infinito.*

INNU'MEROUS, adj. *innumerabile, che non ſi può numerare.*

To INO'CULATE [to graft in the bud] *anneſtare a occhio, ingemmare.*

To inoculate [to propagate the ſmall-pox by inoculation] *far venire il vajuolo con artifieio.*

INO'CULATED, adj. *anneſtato a occhio.*

Inoculated, *che ha avuto il vajuolo artificialmente.*

INNO'CULATION, s. *l'anneſtare a occhio.*

Innoculation [the act of procuring the ſmall-pox] *l'operazione che fa venire il vajuolo.*

INODO'ROUS, adj. [without ſcent] *ſenza odore.*

INOFFE'NSIVE, adj. [that gives no offence, harmleſs] *innocente, che non fa male, che non è nocivo.*

INOFFE'NSIVELY, adv. *innocentemente, ſenza offendere.*

INOFFE'NSIVENESS, s. *innocenza*, s. f.

INOFFI'CIOUS, adj. [backward in doing one any good office or turn, diſcourteous] *ſcorteſe, incivile.*

INOFFI'CIOUSNESS, s. *ſcorteſia*, s. f.

INO'PINATE, adj. [unexpected] *inopinato, non penſato, non immaginato.*

INO'PINATELY, adv. *inopinatamente, non penſatamente, all' improvviſo.*

INO'RDINATE, adj. [extravagant, immoderate] *inordinato, diſordinato, ſregolato, ſmiſurato.*

INO'RDINATELY, adv. *inordinatamente, diſordinatamente; ſregolatamente, ſmiſuratamente.*

INO'RDINATENESS, s. *inordinatezza, ſregolatezza*, s. f. *eceſſo*, s. m.

INORGA'NICAL, adj. [wanting organs or inſtruments proper for any motion or operation] *ſenza organi.*

An inorganical body, *un corpo ſenza organi, che non è organizzato.*

INORGA'NITY, s. *privazion d'organi.*

I'NQUEST, s. [inquiry, ſearch] *inchieſta*, s. f. *ricercamento*, s. m.

Inqueſt [thoſe of the inqueſt, the jury] *i commiſſari deputati a fare inchieſta.*

INQUI'ETUDE, s. [diſquiet, unquietneſs] *inquietudine, paſſione, tribolazione*, s. f. *travaglio*, s. m.

To I'NQUINATE [to defile, to foul] *contaminare, imbrattare, lordare, macchiare, ſozzare. Non in uſo.*

I'NQUINATED, adj. *contaminato, imbrattato, lordato, macchiato, ſozzato.*

INQUINA'TION, s. [a defiling, or fouling] *contaminamento*, s. m. *maculazione, ſozzura, bruttura*, s. f.

INQUI'RABLE, adj. [that may he inquired about or ſearched about] *del quale ſi può far inchieſta.*

To INQUI'RE [to aſk, to demand] *minutamente dimandare, informarſi, cercare, ricercare.*

To inquire of one, or about one, *dimandar d'uno.*

Inquire about it. *informatevene.*

To inquire after one, *demandar d' uno.*

To inquire after news, *domandar delle novelle.*

I'll inquire no further about it, *non voglio ſaperne altro.*

To inquire into a thing, *eſaminare che che ſi ſia.*

INQUI'RED of, about, or after, adj. *inchieſto, dimandato.*

Inquired into, *eſaminato.*

INQUI'RER, s *ricercatore*, s. m.

INQUI'RY, s. [ſearch] *inchieſta*, s. f. *ricercamento*, s. m.

To make a ſtrict inquiry, *fare un' eſatta inchieſta.*

INQUISI'TION, s. [a diligent ſearch, or inquiry] *inquiſizione*, s. f. *diligente ricercamento.*

The inquiſition [a tribunal, or great council of matters of religion] *l'inquiſizione, il ſanto ufficio, dove s'inquiſiſcono quelli, che differiſcono dai* riti e *iſtituti della chieſa Romana.*

INQUI'SITIVE, adj. [deſirous to know every thing, curious] *curioſo, che s'informa d'ogni coſa, che vuol ſapere ogni coſa.*

An inquiſitive body, *un uomo curioſo di ſaper i fatti altrui.*

INQUI'SITOR, s. [a ſheriff, or coroner] *inquiſitore*, s. m. *perſona che ha il potere di fare inchieſte.*

Inquiſitor [a judge of the inquiſition] *inquiſitore, giudice del ſanto ufficio.*

To INRA'GE [to put to a rage, to make mad] *fare arrabbiare, far dare alle ſmanie, fare ſmaniare, infuriare.*

INRA'GED, adj. *arrabbiato, furibondo, ſmaniante*, irritato, *ſtizzato.*

To INRA'IL [to incloſe with rails] *circondare o chiudere con cancelli.*

To INRA'VISH [to raviſh] *rapire*, preſ. *rapiſco.*

INRA'VISHED, adj. *rapito.*

INRA'VISHING, adj. *che rapiſce.*

INRA'VISHMENT, s. *rapimento, ratto*, s. m.

To INRI'CH [to make rich] *arricchire, render ricco*, preſ. *arricchiſco.*

INRI'CHED, adj. *arricchito.*

INRI'CHING, s. *l'arricchire.*

INROA'D, } s. [invaſion] *incurſione,*
INRODE, } *ſcorreria*, s. f. *ſcorrimento*, s. m.

To INRO'LL [to ſet down in a roll, to record or regiſter] *arrolare, ſcrivere nel ruolo, regiſtrare.*

To inroll one's ſelf a ſoldier, *arrolarſi per ſoldato.*

INROLLED, adj. *arrolato, regiſtrato.*

INRO'LLMENT, s. *regiſtramento, il regiſtrare.*

INSA'NE, adj. *inſano, matto, pazzo.*

INSA'NITY, s. [madneſs, frenzy] *inſania, pazzia, ſtoltizia*, s. f.

INSATIABI'LITY, s [unſatisfiedneſs] *inſaziabilità*, e *inſaziabiltà*, e, s. m. *ſmoderato appetito.*

INSA'TIABLE, adj. [that cannot be ſatisfied] *inſaziabile, che non ſi può ſaziare.*

INSA'TIABLENESS, s. *inſaziabilità*, s. f.

INSA'TIABLY, adv. *inſaziabilmente, ſenza ſaziarſi.*

INSA'TIATE, } adj. *v.* Inſatiable.
INSA'TURATE, }

To INSCRI'BE [to write in, or upon] in

inscrivere, e iscrivere, porre iscrizione. pret. *inscrissi o iscrissi.*

To INSCRIBE [to mark any thing with writing] *segnare una cosa con iscrittura.*

To inscribe [to assign to a patron without a formal dedication] *indirizzare un opera d'ingegno ad uno senza far dedicatoria in forma.*

To inscribe [to draw a figure within another] *disegnare una figura dentro ad un' altra figura.*

INSCRI'BED, adj. *v.* To inscribe.

INSCRI'PTION, s. [a title, name, character, written or engraved over a thing] *inscrizione, e iscrizione.*

INSCRU'TABLE, adj. [unsearchable, unfathomable] *imperscrutabile, impenetrabile.*

To INSCU'LP [to engrave, to carve, to cut] *scolpire, intagliare.*

INCU'LPED, adj *scolpito, intagliato.*

To INSE'AM [to impress or mark any thing by a seam or cicatrix] *imprimere o segnare checchessia con un taglio o altro simil segno.*

I'NSECT, s. [any small living creature that creeps or flies] *insetto, bacherozzolo, entomato,* s. m. pl. *entomati.*

INSECU'RE, adj. [that is not secure] *che non è sicuro.*

We are continually insecure of life, *noi siamo ad ogni momento in pericolo di perder la vita.*

INSE'NSATE, adj. [senseless, foolish] *insensato, stupido, stolto, sciocco.*

INSENSIBI'LITY, s. [senselessness] *insensibilità,* s. f.

INSE'NSIBLE, adj. [void of sense, that has no feeling] *insensibile, che non sente, che non ha sentimento.*

Insensible of pain, *insensibile al dolore.*

Insensible [not to be perceived] *insensibile, che non apparisce al senso, impercettibile.*

INSE'NSIBLENESS, s. *insensibilità.*

The insensibleness of stones, *l'insensibilità delle pietre.*

An insensibleness of heart, *insensibilità, durezza di cuore.*

INSE'NSIBLY, adv. [by degrees] *insensibilmente, senz' apparire al senso, a poco a poco, senza avvedersene.*

INSE'PARABLE, adj. [not to be parted] *inseparabile, non separabile, incapace di separazione.*

INSE'PARABLY, adv. *inseparabilmente, senza separazione.*

INSE'PARATELY, adv. [jointly] *unitamente, insiememente.*

To INSE'RT [to put or bring in] *inserire, metter l'una cosa nell' altra, metter dentro,* pref. *inserisco.*

INSE'RTED, adj. *inserito, inserto.*

INSE'RTION, s. *addizione, inserzione, l'inserire.*

To INSE'RVE [to bear part in, or promote] *aver parte, partecipare.*

INSE'RVICEABLE, *v.* Unserviceable.

INSI'DE, s. *il di dentro, l'interiore.*

The inside of a house, *il di dentro d' una casa.*

To look into the inside of a thing, *penetrare l'interiore d'una cosa.*

INSIDIOUS, adj. [insnaring, treacherous] *insidioso, pien d'insidie.*

INSIGHT, s. [hint, knowledge] *indizio, sentore,* s. m. *conoscenza, cognizione, notizia,* s. f.

To give one an insight into a thing, *dare ad uno indizio, e conoscenza di qualche cosa.*

INSIGNI'FICANCY, s. [unprofitableness] *vanità, cosa vana, e inutile.*

INSIGNIFICANT, adj. [inconsiderable] *inutile, vano, di veruna considerazione.*

He is a pitiful insignificant fellow, *egli è un uomo da niente, di nessuna considerazione, un dappoco.*

INSIGNIFICANTLY, adv. [in vain, to little porpose] *inutilmente, in vano.*

INSINCE'RE, adj. *non sincero, falso; non cordiale; che dissimula; infedele.*

Insincere [not found, corrupted] *non sano, corrotto, guasto.*

INSINCE'RITY, s. *il contrario di sincerità, falsità, dissimulazione, infedeltà.*

To INSI'NEW [to strengthen, to confirm] *fortificare, aggiunger forza, confermare.*

To INSI'NUATE [to intimate, to gave a hint of] *insinuare, intimare, far sapere, fare intendere.*

To insinuate one's self, *insinuarsi, introdursi.*

To insinuate one's self into one's favour] *cattivarsi l'altrui amicizia, o benevolenza.*

INSI'NUATED, adj. *insinuato.*

INSINUA'TION, s. *insinuazione,* s. f. *l'insinuare.*

INSI'NUATIVE, adj. [engaging] *insinuante, attrattivo.*

INSI'PID, adj. [that has no taste, unsavory] *insipido, scipito, senza sapore, sciocco.*

An insipid food, *ribi insipidi.*

An insipid discourse, *un discorso insipido o sciocco.*

INSIPI'DITY, s. [unsavourableness] *scipidezza, insipienza,* s. f.

INSI'PIENCE, s. [want of knowledge] *insipidezza, sciocchezza,* s. f.

To INSI'ST [to stand much upon, to urge] *insistere, star fermo e ostinato in alcuna cosa, persistere, fare instanza.*

You must chiefly insist upon that, *bisogna, che voi insistiate principalmente in questo.*

To insist upon trifles, *badare a cose frivole.*

INSI'STED upon, adj. *insistito, persistito.*

To INSLA'VE [to make a slave of] *cattivare, far servo, o schiavo, ridurre in schiavitù.*

INSLA'VED, adj. *cattivato, ridotto, o fatto schiavo.*

To INSNA'RE [to draw into a snare] *allacciare, adescare, accalappiare, inlacciare, irretire.*

INSNARED, adj. *allacciato, adescato, accalappiato, inlacciato, irretito, insidiato.*

INSNA'RER, s. *insidiatore, che insidia, che tende insidie.*

INSO'CIABLE, adj. [not sociable, unfit for society] *che non è sociabile, che non ama la società.*

INSOCIABLENESS, s. *umore poco sociabile.*

I'NSOLENCE, }
I'NSOLENCY, } s. [impudence, sauciness] *insolenza, arroganza, arditezza, sfacciataggine,* s. f. *orgoglio,* s. m.

To I'NSOLENCE [to insult] *insultare, far ingiuria, offendere.*

I'NSOLENT, adj. [saucy, bold] *insolente, arrogante, orgoglioso, ardito, sfacciato.*

INSO'LUBLE, *v.* Indissoluble.

INSO'LVENCY, s. [not being able to pay one's creditors] *incapacità di pagare i suoi creditori.*

INSO'LVENT, adj. [not able to pay] *che non è in istato di poter pagare.*

INSO'MINOUS, adj. [troubled with dreams, full of dreams] *che ha sogni.*

INSOMU'CH as or that, adv. *talmente che, di maniera che, onde.*

Insomuch that I know not what to do with it, *talmente che non so che farne.*

To INSPE'CT [to look narrowly into, to oversee] *mirare, guardare, aver l'inspezione, aver l'occhio, vegliare, esaminare.*

INSPEC'TED, adj. *mirato, guardato, esaminato.*

INSPE'CTION, s. [overseeing, insight] *inspezione, e ispezione, considerazione, cura,* s. f.

INSPEC'TOR, s. [an overseer] *inspettore, soprantenditore, soprantendente,* s. m.

INSPE'RSION, s. *aspersione.*

To INSPHE'RE, *collocare in un orbe, in una sfera.*

INSPIRA'TION, s. [an inspiring into] *inspirazione,* s. f.

To INSPI'RE [to put into one's head, to prompt, to suggest] *inspirare, spirare, infondere.* pret. *infusi.*

INSPI'RED, adj. *inspirato, spirato, infuso.*

To INSPI'RIT [to put life or spirit into] *inspirare del coraggio, animare, dare animo, incoraggire,* pref. *incoraggisco.*

To inspirit one with boldness, *dar del coraggio ad uno, incoraggiarlo, animarlo.*

INSPI'RITED, adj. *animato, incoraggiato.*

INSTABI'LITY, s. [unsteadfastness] *instabilità, incostanza.*

I'NSTABLE, adj. [inconstant, unsteady] *instabile, incostante.*

A man of an instable temper, *un uomo instabile, incostante.*

To INSTA'LL [to put in possession of an office, order, or benefice] *installare, metter in possesso d'un ufficio, ordine, o benefcio, promuovere.* pret. *promossi.*

INSTALLA'TION, s. *installazione, promozione,* s. f.

Installation of a bishop, *promozione d'un vescovo.*

INSTA'LLED, adj. *installato, promosso.*

INSTA'LLING, }
INSTALMENT, } s. *installazione, promozione,* s. f.

I'NSTANCE, s. [example, proof] *prova*, s. f. *esempio*, s. m.

Instance [entreaty, sollicitation] *istanza, premura, sollecitazione, richiesta*, s. f.

To INSTANCE [to bring or produce some instances] *citare, produrre, addurre esempi, o prove*.

I'NSTANCED, adj. *citato, prodotto, addotto in prova*.

I'NSTANT, adj. [eager upon a thing, earnest, pressing] *che insiste in una cosa, che sta fermo e ostinato nel domandarla*.

An instant business, *un negozio urgente*.

Instant [present] *corrente, presente*.

The letter is dated the tenth instant, *la lettera è datata ai dieci del corrente*.

At this very instant time, *in questo punto*.

Instant, s [a moment of time] *istante, momento di tempo*.

I'NSTANTLY, adv. [earnestly] *istantemente, con istanzia*.

Instantly [presently] *in un istante, adesso, in questo punto, or ora*.

INSTAURA'TION, *istaurazione*, s. f.

INST'EAD, adv. [for] *in luogo*.

He gave me gold instead of silver, *mi diede dell' oro in vece d'argento*.

I'NSTEP, s. *il collo del piede*.

To be high in the instep [to be proud] *esser fiero, orgoglioso, altiero*.

To INSTIGATE [to egg, or set on] *istigare, incitare, stimolare*.

I'NSTIGATED, adj. *istigato, incitato, stimolato*.

I'NSTIGATING, s. *istigamento*, s. m.

INSTIGA'TION, s. [a stirring up to, incitement] *istigazione, stimolo, incitamento*, s. m.

Such a thing was of a great instigation to him, *cio li servì di potente motivo*.

INSTIGA'TOR, s. [an encourager, or abetter] *sollecitatore, inducitore, istigatore*, s. m.

To INSTI'L [to pour in by drops, or by little and little] *istillare, stillare, infondere a stilla a stilla*.

To instil good principles into one's mind, *istillare buoni principi nell' animo altrui*.

INSTILLA'TIO N s. *stillazione*, s. f. *l'instillare*.

INSTI'LLED, adj. *istillato, stillato*.

INSTI'NCT, s. [a natural bent or inclination to a thing] *istinto*, s. m. *inclinazione*, s. f.

To I'NSTITUTE [to enact, to decree, to ordain] *istituire, ordinare, stabilire*, pref. *istituisco, stabilisco*.

I'NSTITUTED, adj. *istituito, ordinato, stabilito*.

I'NSTITUTES, s. [principles, precepts, ordinances] *istituti, principi, precetti*, s. m. *istituzioni*, s. f.

INSTITU'TION, s. [establishment] *instituzione*, s. f. *ordine, modo, stabilimento*, s. m.

Institution [instruction, education] *istruzione, educazione*, s. f. *ammaestramento*, s. m.

INSTITU'TOR, s. [an instructor] *ammaestratore*, s. m.

Institutor [founder] *institutore, e istitutore, fondatore*, s. f.

To INSTRUC'T [to teach, train, or bring up] *istruire, ammaestrare, insegnare*, pref. *istruisco*.

INSTRU'CTED, adj *istruito, istrutto, insegnato, ammaestrato*, s. m.

INSTRU'CTOR, s. [or teacher] *istruttore, ammaestratore, maestro, mastro, precettore*.

INSTRU'CTION, s. [teaching, education] *istruzione, educazione*, s. f. *ammaestramento, insegnamento*, s. m.

Instructions [directions in an affair of moment] *istruzioni, direzioni nel maneggiare un negozio*.

INSTRU'CTIVE, adj. [apt to instruct] *istruttivo, che istruisce*.

I'NSTRUMENT, s. [tool to do any thing with] *istrumento, strumento, ordigno*, s. m.

Mathematical or musical instruments, *instrumenti di matematica, o musicale*.

A case of instruments, *astuccio da tenervi stromenti*.

He was the instrument of my ruin, *egli fu lo stromento della mia rovina*.

Instrument [publick act] *strumento, contratto, istromento*, s. m. *scritura publica*.

INSTRUME'NTAL, adj. *istrumentale, e strumentale*.

To INSUE [to follow] *nascere*.

INSUFFI'CIENCY, s. [inability, incapacity] *insufficienza, impotenza, incapacità*, s. f.

INSUFFI'CIENT, adj. [not sufficient, uncapable] *insufficiente, insofficiente, impotente, incapace*.

INSU'ING, adj. [following] *seguente, che segue*.

In the times ensuing, *in progresso di tempo*.

I'NSULAR, INSULARY, } adj. [belonging to an island] *isolano, d' isola*.

I'NSULT, s. [abuse, affront] *insulto*, s. m. *ingiuria, superchieria*, s. f.

To INSU'LT [to affront, to abuse] *insultare, fare insulto, bravare, oltraggiare*.

To insult one, or over one, *insultare, oltraggiar alcuno*.

INSU'LTED, adj. *insultato, bravato, oltraggiato*..

INSU'LTING, s. *l'insultare*.

INSU'PERABLE, adj. [not to be overcome] *insuperabile, invincibile*.

INSU'PERABLENESS, s. *qualità insuperabile, invincibile*.

INSU'PPORTABLE, adj. [not to be endured] *insopportabile, da non poter sopportarsi, intollerabile, insoffribile*.

INSU'RANCE, s. [security given to make good the loss of ships, merchandize, houses, &c. in consideration of a sum of money paid in hand] *afsicuranza, sicurtà*, s. f.

An insurance office, *ufficio dove si fanno le sicurtà*.

Insurance money, *il danaro che si da nell' assicurare vascelli, mercanzie, case, e simili da ogni perdita o danno*.

To INSU'RE [to engage to make good any thing that is in danger of being lost] *assicurare, obbligarsi a qualcheduno (mediante una somma di danari) di riparare la perdita ch' egli potrebbe fare*.

INSU'RED, adj. *assicurato*.

INSU'RER, s. *assicuratore*, s. m.

INSU'RING, s. *l'assicurare*.

INSU'RMOUTABLE, adj. [that cannot be overcome by labour or industry. *insormontabile, insuperabile*.

INSURRE'CTION, s. [a rising against, a popular tumult, or uproar] *sollevazione, ribellione, sedizione, rivolta*, s. f.

INTA'IL, s. [a fee tail, by which means the heir is limited, and tied up to certain conditions] *sostituzione*, s. f. *termine legale*.

To cut off the intail, *annullare, cassare, cancellare una sostituzione*.

To INTA'IL an estate [to make it over by intail] *sostituire un bene, fare una sostituzione*.

To intail [to cut, to grave] *scolpire, intagliare*. pref. *scolpisco*.

INTA'ILED, adj. *sostituito, scolpito, intagliato*.

INTA'ILER, s. *colui che ha sostituito i suoi beni*.

INTA'NGIBLE, adj. [that cannot be touched] *che non si può toccare*.

To INTA'NGLE [to twist together] *intrigare, avviluppare, intralciare, ingarbullare, e ingarbugliare, confondere, disordinare, imbrogliare*. pret. *confusi*.

To intangle a skain of thread, *intrigare, disordinare, imbrogliare una matassa di filo*.

To intangle [to perplex, to confound] *imbrogliare, intrigare; confondere, imbarazzare*.

To intangle one's self in a business, *imbrogliarsi, imbarazzarsi in qualche affare*.

INTA'NGLED, adj. *intrigato, avviluppato, intralciato, ingarbugliato*, v. to intangle.

INTA'NGLEMENT, s. *imbarazzo, imbroglio, intrigo*, s. m. *confusione*, s. f.

I'NTEGRAL, adj. [whole, intire] *integrale, essenziale, principale*.

Integral parts [the parts that constitute the whole] *parti integrali*.

INTE'GRITY, adj. [honesty, uprightness] *integrità, onestà, probità*, s. f. *candore, onore*, s. m.

I'NTELLECT, s. [the faculty of the soul, which is commonly call'd the understanding] *intelletto*, s. m. *potenza dell' anima, colla quale l'uomo è atto ad intendere tutte le cose*.

INTELLE'CTUAL, adj. [belonging to the understanding] *intellettuale, intellettivo*.

Intellectuals, s. [the powers and properties of the understanding] *intelletto, intendimento*, s. m.

INTELLIGENCE, s. [knowledge, underftanding] *intelligenza, cognizione,* s. f. *intelletto, intendimento, fapere,* s. m.

Intelligence [the correfpondence that ftatefmen and merchants hold in foreign countries] *intelligenza, corrifpondenza, comunicazione.*

Intelligence [advice, news] *avvifo,* s. m. *novella,* s. f.

To fend out a party for intelligence, *mandare un diftaccamento a far la fcoperta.*

Intelligences [angels, fpiritual beings] *intelligenze, foftanze incorporee, angioli.*

INTE'LLIGENCER, s. [one who makes it his bufinefs to inquire into, and fpread news] *novellifta, uno ch' è vago di fapere e di raccontare delle novelle.*

INTE'LLIGIBLE, adj. [capable of being underftood] *intelligibile, atto ad effer intefo, chiaro.*

INTE'LLIGIBLY, adv. *intelligibilmente, con intelligenza, chiaramente.*

INTE'MERATE, adj. [pure, uncorrupted] *puro, pretto, intiero, incorrotto.*

INTE'MPERANCE, s. [immoderate defires, excefs] *intemperanza,* s. f. *difordine, eccefso,* s. m.

INTE'MPERATE, adj. [immoderate, that has no command of himfelf] *intemperato, difordinato, fregolato.*

An intemperate courfe of life, *una vita fregolata.*

Intemperate weather [either too hot or too cold] *tempo intemperato, che non è temperato, o troppo caldo, o troppo freddo.*

INTE'MPERATELY, adv. *intemperatamente, fenza temperanza, difordinatamente, fregolatamente, diffolutamente.*

To live intemperately, *viver intemperatamente, fregolatamente, menare una vita fregolata.*

INTE'MPERATENESS, } s. [intem-
INTE'MPERATURE, } perance] *intemperanza,* s. f.

Intemperatenefs, } [a diforder in the
Intemperature, } air or humours of the body] *intemperie,* s. f. *cattiva compleffione.*

The temperature of the air, *l'intemperie dell' aere.*

INTE'MPESTIVE, adj. [unfeafonable] *intempeftivo, fuor di tempo.*

To INTE'ND [to defign, to purpofe] *intendere, aver intenzione, far penfiero, difegnare, far difegno, proporfi, far conto,* pret. *intefi.*

What do you intend to do? *che avete in penfiero di fare?*

I did not intend it, *ciò non era il mio difegno.*

You fhall know what I intend, *voi faprete quel che mi propongo, che lo difegno di fare.*

I intend to go out of town to morrow, *io ho intenzione, io fo conto d'andare in campagna domani.*

What d'ye intend by that? *che volete dire per quefto?*

To intend a bufinefs, *intendere, attendere, badare ad un affare.*

INTE'NDANT, s. [the governor of a province in France] *intendente, capo, governatore d'una provincia in Francia.*

INTE'NDED, adj. *intefo, propofto, difegnato.*

It was fo intended by me, *quefto era il mio penfiero, la mia intenzione, il mio difegno.*

INTE'NDMENT, s. [intention, purpofe] *intendimento, difegno, proponimento,* s. m. *intenzione,* s. f.

Intendment [fenfe, meaning] *intendimento, fenfo, concetto,* s. m.

To INTE'NERATE [to make tender, to foften] *intenerire, far divenir tenero, ammollire.*

INTE'NERATED, adj. *intenerito, ammollito.*

INTENERA'TION, s [a making tender] *l'intenerire, l'ammollire.*

INTENSE, adj. [very great, or exceffive] *intenfo, eccefsivo, veemente.*

An intenfe defire, *un intenfo defiderio.*

INTE'NIBLE, adj. [that cannot hold] *che non iftà faldo; che non può ftar faldo; che non è fufcettibile di difefa o di foftegno.*

INTE'NSENESS [excefs] *eccefso,* s. m. *immenfità,* s. f.

INTE'NSION, s. [in philofophy, is the increafe of the power or energy of any quality, as heat, and cold] *intenfione,* s. f. *termine filofofico, fi dice la forza, la violenza delle qualità, degli umori, e de' corpi naturali.*

INTE'NSELY, adv. *intenfamente; in un alto grado.*

INTE'NSIVELY, adv. *infinitamente, eccefsivamente.*

INTE'NT, adj. [fixed or clofely bent upon a bufinefs] *intento, attento, fifso.*

To be intent upon a thing, *effer intento a qualche cofa.*

His eyes were intent upon you, *i fuoi occhi erano fitti in voi.*

To be intent at prayer, *pregare attentamente.*

Intent, s. [intention] *intento, defiderio, intendimento, proponimento, penfiero,* s. m. *intenzione,* s. f.

That was my intent, *quefto era il mio intento, o la mia intenzione.*

To the intent that I might fee him, *affinchè poteffi vederlo.*

To all intents and purpofes, *in tutte le maniere, intieramente, affatto, del tutto.*

To be ruined to all intents and purpofes, *dar l'ultima fcoffa; effer del tutto rovinato.*

INTE'NTIONAL, adj. [belonging to the intention] *intenzionale, d'intenzione.*

INTE'NTIONALLY, adv. *intenzionalmente, con intenzione.*

INTE'NTIVE, adj. [fixed, clofe bent] *intento, attento, fifso.*

INTE'NTIVELY, adv. *intentivamente, con attenzione, intentamente, attentamente.*

To INTE'R, v. To interr.

INTE'RCALAR, adj. *intercalare.*

Intercalar day [the odd day of the leap-year inferted in February] *il giorno intercalare, il ventinovefimo di Febbrajo.*

INTERCALATION, s. [the inferting a day in February every fourth year] *intercalazione,* s. f.

To INTERCE'DE [to ufe one's intereft on the behalf of another] *intercedere, effer mediatore a ottener grazie per altrui.*

INTERCE'DED, adj. *interceduto.*

INTER'CEDER, s. *interceffore,* s. m. *che intercede.*

INTERCE'DING, s. *interceffione,* s. f. *l'intercedere.*

To INTERCE'PT [to take up by the way] *intercettare.*

To intercept letters, *intercettar lettere.*

To intercept one's return, *impedire il ritorno ad uno.*

To intercept the trade of a company, *fare il meftiere di contrabbandiere.*

INTERCE'PTED, adj. *intercetto.*

INTERCEPTION, s. [ftoppage in courfe; hindrance; obftruction] *oftacolo, impedimento, intoppo.*

INTERCE'SSION, s. [an entreating in behalf of another] *interceffione,* s. f. *l' intercedere.*

INTERCE'SSOR, s. [a mediator] *interceffore, mediatore,* s. m.

To INTERCHA'NGE [to exchange between parties] *cambiare, fcambiare, cangiare.*

To interchange fome compliments, *farfi complimenti reciprocamente.*

INTERCHA'NGEABLY, adv. *mutuamente, reciprocamente, vicendevolmente, fcambievolmente.*

INTERCHA'NGED, adj. *cambiato, fcambiato, cangiato.*

To INTERCLU'DE, *impedire, far intoppo, effer d'intoppo.*

To INTERCOMMU'NICATE [to communicate mutually, or one with another] *comunicarfi reciprocamente, o l'una all' altro.*

INTERCO'URSE, s. [commerce, correfpondence] *commercio,* s. m. *corrifpondenza, communicazione,* s. f.

INTERCU'RRENT, adj. [running between] *che paffa per mezzo.*

To INTERDI'CT [to prohibit, to forbid] *interdire, proibire, vietare,* pref. *interdico, proibifco,* pret. *interdiffi.*

To interdict [to fufpend, to exclude from partaking of the facraments] *interdire, punire d'interdetto.*

INTERDI'CTED, adj. *interdetto, proibito, vietato, punito d'interdetto.*

INTERDI'CTION, s. [prohibition] *interdizione, proibizione,* s. f. *interdetto, vietamento,* s. m.

Interdiction [in law, is an ecclefiaftical cenfure, forbidding the exercife of the minifterial function] *interdetto, cenfura, o pena ecclefiaftica, per la quale fi vieta il celebrare, feppellire, e alcuni facramenti.*

To INTERE'SS, or to INTERE'ST [to concern, or engage] *intereffare, mefcolare, impacciare.*

To interess one's self in something, *intereſſarſi, meſcolarſi, impacciarſi in qualche coſa.*

INTERE'STED, adj. *intereſſato, meſcolato, impacciato.*

I'NTEREST, s. [uſe money, paid for the loan of a principal ſum, lent for a certain time] *intereſſe,* s. m. *utile, o merito, che ſi riſcuote de' danari preſtati, o ſi paga degli accattati.*

Intereſt [concern, advantage] *intereſſe, vantaggio, utile,* s. m. *utilità,* s. f.

Intereſt [right] *diritto, parte,* s. m. *pretendenza,* s. f.

I have an intereſt in it, *io ho diritto e pretendenza in ciò, vi ſono intereſſato.*

Intereſt [credit, power] *credito, potere,* s. m.

To make uſe of one's intereſt, *ſervirſi del potere, o del credito altrui.*

To get or make an intereſt with one, *guadagnare alcuno, tirarlo dalla ſua, farſelo amico, renderſelo favorevole.*

There is great intereſt made for that place, *vi ſono molti competitori per queſta carica, molti brigano o s'ingegnano d'aver queſta carica.*

Self-intereſt, *intereſſe, l'intereſſe, l'utile proprio, amor proprio, utile privato.*

INTERE'STED, adj. *intereſſato.*

To INTERFE'RE [to knock and rub one heel againſt another, as ſome horſes do] *tagliarſi le gambe in andando, come fanno alcuni cavalli.*

To interfere [to fall on one another] *urtarſi, acceczzarſi.*

To interfere [to claſh] *ripugnare, eſſer oppoſto, eſſer contrario.*

To interfere with one, *competere, eſſer in competenza, contraſtare con alcuno.*

INTE'RFLUENT, adj. [flowing between] *che ſcorre o paſſa ſcorrendo in mezzo.*

INTERFU'LGENT, adj. [ſhining between] *che ſplende, che riſulge in mezzo.*

INTERFU'SED, adj. [poured or ſcattered between] *verſato in mezzo.*

INTERJA'CENT, adj. [lying between] *che è nel mezzo, o fra due.*

INTERJE'CTION, s. [one of the eight parts of ſpeech] *interjezione,* s. f. *una delle otto parti dell' orazione.*

I'NTERIM, adj. [in the mean while] *frattanto, in quel mentre.*

In the interim, *mentre, in quel mentre.*

INTE'RIOR, adj. [in the inſide] *interiore, che è di dentro.*

To INTERLA'CE [to twiſt one with another] *intralciare, attrocigliare, avvolgere, intrecciare,* pret. *avvolſi.*

INTERLA'CED, adj. *intralciato, attorcigliato, avvolto, intrecciato.*

To INTERLA'RD [to lard or ſtuff meat with fat] *interporre o metter del lardo in mezzo, meſcolare con graſſo.*

INTERLA'RDED, adj. *tramezzato con graſſo.*

To INTERLE'AVE [to put blank paper between the leaves of a book] *mettere o frapporre della carta bianca fra i fogli d'un libro.*

To INTERLI'NE [to write between two lines] *interlineare, ſcrivere tra linea e linea, o tra verſo e verſo.*

INTERLINED, adj. *interlineato.*

INTERLOCU'TION, s. [an intermediate ſentence before a final deciſion] *interlocuzione,* s. f. *termine legale.*

INTERLO'CUTORY, adj. *interlocutorio.*

An interlocutory order [is that which decides not the cauſe, but only ſettles ſome intervening matter relating to the cauſe] *ſentenza interlocutoria.*

To INTERLO'PE [to intercept or diſturb the trade] *far contrabbandi, fare il meſtiere di contrabbandiere.*

INTERLO'PER, s. [he that without legal authority intercepts the trade of a company] *contrabbandiere.*

INTERLU'DE, s. [a part of a ſtage play, that which is ſung or repreſented between the ſeveral acts] *intermedio,* s. m *quell' azione che tramezza nell' opera o nella commedia gli atti, ed è ſeparata da eſſa.*

To INTERME'DDLE [to concern one's ſelf in another's buſineſs] *intrometterſi, e intrametterſi, intrigarſi, impacciarſi, ingerirſi,* pret. *intromiſſi, intramiſi,* preſ. *ingeriſco.*

INTERME'DLER, s. *mezzano,* s. m. *mezzana,* s. f.

INTERME'DIATE, adj. [that lies between] *intermediato, che ſta nel mezzo.*

An intermediate ſpace, *intervallo, ſpazio, diſtanza fra due coſe.*

INTERME'DIUM, s. [ſpace or diſtance between] *intervallo, ſpazio,* s. m. *diſtanza,* s. f.

To INTERME'LL [to mix, to mingle] *miſchiars, frammiſchiare, meſcolare.*

INTERMENT, s. [from to inter] *eſequie,* s. f.

INTERME'SS, s. [certain courſes ſet on the table between other diſhes] *trameſſo,* s m. *vivanda, che ſi mette tra l'un ſervizio e l'altro.*

INTE'RMINABLE, } adj. [boundleſs,
INTE'RMINATE, } endleſs] *interminabile, ſterminato, da non poterſi terminare, che non ha termine.*

To INTERMI'NGLE [to mingle among or with] *frammiſchiare, meſcolare, trameſtare.*

INTERMI'NGLED, adj. *frammiſchiato, trameſcolato, trameſtato.*

INTERMI'SSION, s. [diſcontinuance, ceaſing] *intermiſſione,* s. f. *tralaſciamento,* s. m.

Without intermiſſion, *ſenz' intermiſſione, inceſſantemente, continuamente.*

To INTERMI'T [to leave off for a while] *intermettere, intralaſciare, tralaſciare, ceſſare.*

INTERMI'TTENT, or INTERMITTING, adj. [diſcontinuing] *intermittente, che intermette.*

An intermittent fever, *febbre intermittente.*

An intermittent pulſe [that which is held up by the fit for a while, and then beats again] *polſo intermittente.*

To INTERMI'X [to mingle between or among] *frammiſchiare, meſcolare.*

INTERMI'XED, } adj. *frammiſchiato,*
INTERMI'XT, } *meſcolato.*

INTERMI'XTURE, s. *miſcuglio,* s. m.

INTE'RNAL, adj. [that is within, inward] *interno, interiore, di dentro.*

INTE'RNALLY, adv. *internamente, dalla parte interna.*

INTERNO'DIUM, s. [is the ſpace contained between any two knots or joints of the ſtalk of a plant] *internodo,* s. m. *ſpazio tra nodo e nodo.*

INTERN'UNCIO, s. [an agent for the court of Rome, in the courts of foreign princes, where there is no expreſs nuncio] *internunzio,* s. m.

To INTERPLE'AD [to diſcuſs or try a point which incidentally falls out before the main cauſe be determined] *diſcutere, eſaminare un punto che riguarda qualche cauſa, prima che detta cauſa ſia terminata.*

INTERPLE'ADER, s. *competitore d'un eredità.*

To INTE'RPOLATE [to alter, to falſify] *falſificare.*

To interpolate an original, *falſificare un originale.*

INTE'RPOLATED, adj. *falſificato.*

INTERPOLA'TION, s. *falſificazione,* s. f.

INTERPOLA'TOR, s. *falſificatore,* s. m.

To INTERPO'SE [to put in, or between] *interporre, tramezzare, inframmettere, porre tra l'una coſa, e l' altra,* preſ. *interpongo,* pret. *interpoſi, intrammiſi.*

To interpoſe one's authority, *interporre la ſua autorità.*

To interpoſe [to intermeddle in a buſineſs] *interporſi, entrar di mezzo, trammetterſi, ingerirſi, intrigarſi, impacciarſi.*

INTERPO'SED, adj. *interpoſto,* v. To interpoſe.

INTERPO'SING, s. *interponimento,* s. f. *l'interporre.*

INTERPOSI'TION, s. *interpoſizione,* s. m. *interponimento,* s. m.

To INTE'RPRET [to expound, to explain] *interpretare, eſporre, dichiarare, ſpiegare,* preſ. *eſpongo,* pret. *eſpoſi.*

To interpret an author, *interpretare, eſporre un autore.*

INTERPRETA'TION, s. [explanation] *interpretazione,* s. f. *interpretamento,* s. m.

INTE'RPRETATIVELY, adv. Ex. Interpretatively ſpoken, *detto per maniera d'interpretazione.*

INTE'RPRETED, adj. *interpretato, eſpoſto, dichiarato, ſpiegato.*

INTE'RPRETER, s. [an expounder] *interpretatore, interprete, interpreto;* s. m.

INTE'RPRETING, s. *interpretamento,* s. m. *l'interpretare.*

INTERPU'NCTION, s. [a diſtinction by pricks or points ſet between] *puntteggiatura,* s f. *diſtinzione che ſi fa per via di punti.*

To INTE'RR [to bury, to lay under ground] *ſotterrare, metter ſotterra, ſeppellire, interrare,* preſ. *ſeppelliſco.*

INTE'RRED, adj. *sotterrato, seppellito.*

INTE'RREIGN, } s. [the space of time between INTE'RREGNUM, } the death or deposition of a king, and the successiou of another] *interregno,* s. m.

To INTE'RROGATE [to ask a question] *interrogare, domandare, ricercare.*

INTE'RROGATED, adj. *interrogato, domandato, ricercato.*

INTERROGA'TION, s. [question or demand] *interrogazione, domanda, richiesta,* s. f.

An interrogation, or a note of interrogation [a point of interrogation thus expressed ?] *un punto interrogativo* (?)

INTE'RROGATIVE, adj. [that interrogates] *interrogativo.*

INTE'RROGATORY, adj. [belonging to questioning or asking] *interrogatorio, d'interrogazione.*

An interrogatory, s. [an interrogation] *un interrogatorio, un' interrogazione.*

INTE'RROGATORIES [in law, are questions put to witnesses brought to be examined] *interrogatori, interrogazioni, questioni, domande.*

To INTERRU'PT [to hinder, to stop] *interrompere, impedire la continuazione,* pret. *interruppi.*

To interrupt one when he speaks, *interrompere l'altrui discorso.*

INTERRU'PTED, adj. *interrotto.*

INTERRU'PTER, s. *quello, o quella che interrompe.*

INTE'RRUPTING, s. *interrompimento,* s. m. *l'interrompere.*

INTERRU'PTION, s. *interruzione,* s. f. *interrompimento,* s. m.

INTERSE'CTION, s. [mutual cutting off] *intersezione, intersecazione,* s. f.

To INTERSERT, *v.* To insert.

INTERSHO'CK, s. [a clashing or hitting one thing against another] *urto,* s. m.

To INTERSHO'CK, *urtarsi l'un l'altro.*

INTERSPE'RSED, adj. [scattered or sprinkled here and there] *tempestato, biliottato, sparso, seminato.*

INTE'RSTICE, s. [distance or space between] *interstizio spazio, intervallo,* s. m. *distanza,* s. f.

To INTERTA'IN [to lodge] *ricevere, accogliere in casa sua,* pret. *accolsi.*

To intertain a great many servants, *mantenere gran numero di servitori.*

To intertain [to treat] *trattare, regalare.*

To intertain a principle, an opinion, &c. *ricevere, ammettere un' opinione, crederla.*

To intertain [to accept of, to receive] *ricevere, accettare.*

To intertain ill thoughts, or an ill opinion of one, *concepire, o avere una cattiva opinione, o un cattivo concetto d'uno.*

I am not apt to intertain any suspicions of my friends, *io non sono atto, o solito d'aver ombra o sospetto de' miei amici.*

INTERTA'INED, adj. *ricevuto, accolto, v.* To intertain.

INTERTAINING, adj. [pleasant] *grato, piacevole, gustoso, gioviale.*

INTERTA'ININGLY, adv. *giovialmente, piacevolmente.*

INTERTA'INMENT, s. *trattamento, accoglimento,* s. m. *accoglienza,* s. f.

There we met with very good intertainment, *noi fummo molto ben accolti, ci fecero grandissime accoglienze.*

We had a princely intertainment, *noi fummo trattati, o regalati da principi.*

INTE'RTWISTED, adj. [interwoven] *attorto, ritorto, intralciato, avvinto, avviticchiato.*

I'NTERVAL, adj. [a space between] *intervallo, spazio,* s. m. *distanza,* s. f.

To INTERVE'NE [to come between, to come unlook'd for] *intervenire, avvenire, accadere, succedere,* pret. *intervenne, avvenne, accadde, successe.*

And nothing to intervene [an expression used in the votes of parliament] *ogni altro affare cessante.*

If the grace of God do not intervene, *se la grazia di Dio non ci ajuta.*

INTERVI'EW, s. [meeting] *abboccamento, congresso,* s. m. *conversazione, conferenza,* s. f.

To INTERVO'LVE [to involve one within another] *involgere una cosa in un altra.*

To INTERWE'AVE, s. [to weave with, or mingle among] *intessere, intrecciare insieme tessendo.*

INTERWO'VEN, adj. *intrecciato, intessuto.*

INTE'STABLE, adj. [incapable by law to make any will, or to be taken for a witness] *incapare di testare, o di servir per testimonio.*

INTE'STATE, adj. [that has made no will] *intestato, senza testamento.*

He died intestate, *egli morì intestato.*

INTE'STINAL, adj. [belonging to the guts] *appartenente agl' intestini, alle interiora, alle budella.*

INTE'STINE, adj. [inward, within] *intestino, interno.*

Intestine war [a civil war] *una guerra intestina, o una guerra civile.*

INTE'STINE, s. [entrails] *intestini,* s. m. *interiora, budella,* s. f.

To INTHRA'L [to enslave, to bring into bondage] *render schiavo, ridurre in schiavitù, cattivare, far servo.*

INTHRA'LLED, adj. *reso schiavo, ridotto in ischiavitù, cattivato.*

To INTHRO'NE [to set upon the throne] *metter sul trono.*

INTHRO'NED, adj. *messo sul trono.*

To INTI'CE [to allure, or set on] *allettare, indurre, adescare, descare, incitare, invitare, tirare, sollecitare,* pres. *induco,* pret. *indussi.*

To intice away, *sodurre, sedurre.*

INTI'CED, adj. *allettato, indutto, adescato, descato, incitato, invitato, tirato, sollecitato, soddotto, sedotto.*

INTI'CEMENT, s. [instigation, allurement] *allettamento, vezzo, lacriuolo, instigamento, stimolo,* s. m. *lusinga, instigazione, sollecituzione,* s. m.

Full of inticements, *lusinghevole, allettatrice.*

INTI'CER, s. *lusinghiere, incitatore, instigatore,* s. m.

INTI'CING, adj. *allettatrice, lusinghevole, lusinghiero.*

INTIMA'CY, s. [strict friendship, great familiarity] *intrinsichezza, dimestichezza, famigliarità, fratellanza.*

I'NTIMATE, adj. [most dear or familiar, hearty] *intimo, confidente, famigliare, dimestico, svisceraro, intrinseco.*

An intimate friend, *un amico intimo o sviscerato.*

To I'NTIMATE [to give to understand] *intimare, far sapere, fare intendere.*

I'NTIMATED, adj. *intimato.*

INTIMA'TION, s. [a hint] *intimazione, notizia,* s. f. *sentore,* s. m.

I have had some intimation of it, *ne ho avuto qualche sentore.*

Intimation [in law] *intimazione, citazione,* s. f.

I'NTIME, adj. [inward, being within the mass, internal] *intérno, intimo.*

To INTI'MIDATE [to put in fear, to frighten] *intimorire, recar timore, intimidire, spaventare,* pres. *intimorisco, intimidisco.*

INTI'MIDATED, adj. *intimorito, intimidito, spaventato.*

INTIMIDA'TION, s. [a frighting] *spavento, timore,* s. m. *minaccia,* s. f.

INTI'RE, adj. [whole] *intero, che non gli manca alcuna delle sue parti.*

Intire [perfect] *intero, sincero, puro, leale.*

I have an intire love for him, *io gli porto un intero amore, io l'amo interamente.*

INTI'RELY, adv. *interamentè, sinceramente, puramente, lealmente.*

INTI'RENESS, s. *lo stato d'una cosa che è intera.*

Intireness [perfection] *integrità, perfezione.*

To INTI'TLE [to give a title] *intitolare, appellare, dare il titolo.*

To intitle a book, *intitolare un libro.*

To intitle [to give a title or claim] *dar diritto di pretendere.*

Your valour intitles you to the admiration of mankind, *il vostro valore vi rende degno d'esser ammirato da tutto'l mondo.*

INTI'TLED, adj. *intitolato.*

INTITULA'TION, s. *intitolazione, inscrizione,* s. f.

INTO, prep. [used instead of IN, after a verb signifies a local motion] *in, nel, nella.*

I went into the city, *andai in città.*

He paid the money into my hands, *il danaro fu pagato nelle mie mani.*

I had that into the bargain, *ho avuto questo per saprappiù.*

INTO'LERABLE, adj. [not to be born or indured] *intollerabile, da non tollerarsi, incomportabile.*

INTO'LERABLENESS, s. *qualità intollerabile.*

INTO'LERABLY, adv. *intollerabilmente, incomportabilmente.*

INTO'LERANT, adj. *intollerante, impaziente, non capace di ſoffrire.*

To INTO'MB [to put into a tomb, to bury] *mettere in una tomba, ſeppellire,* pref. *ſeppelliſco.*

INTONA'TION, s. [the giving the tone or key by the chanter to the reſt of the choir in a cathedral] *l'intonare, il dar principio al canto, dando il tuono della voce.*

To INTO'NE, *intuonare.*

To INTO'RT [to twiſt, to wreath, to wring] *torcere, attorcigliare.*

To INTO'XICATE [to poiſon, to bewitch, in a figurative ſenſe] *toſſicare, avvelenare, incantare, ammaliare, ubbriacare.*

INTO'XICATED, adj. *toſſicato, avvelenato, incantato, ammaliato, ubbiacato.*

INTRA'CTABLE, adj. [ungovernable, unruly] *intrattabile, fantaſtico, indomito, violento, oſtinato, caparbio.*

INTRA'CTABLENESS, s. *umore o qualità intrattabile, o biſbetica.*

INTRA'DO, s. [a Spaniſh word for a ſolemn entry] *entrata pubblica.*

To INTRAP [to catch in a trap, to inſnare] *acchiappare, allacciare, ingannare.*

INTRA'PPED, adj. *acchiappato, ingannato.*

To INTRE'AT [to beg earneſtly] *ſupplicare, chiedere iſtantemente, ſtrettamente pregare, ſcongiurare.*

To intreat [to diſcourſe of a thing] *trattare, diſcorrere, parlare, ragionare.* pret. *diſcorſi.*

INTRE'ATED, adj. *ſupplicato, pregato, ſcongiurato.*

Not to be intreated, *ineſorabile.*

INTRE'ATING, s. *preghiera, ſupplica, iſtanza,* s. f. *ſcongiuro,* s. m.

There's no intreating of him, *egli è ineſorabile.*

INTRE'ATY, s. *preghiera, iſtanza, domanda, richieſta, ſupplica,* s. f. *ſcongiuro, ſtretto prego,* s. m.

To INTRE'NCH [to fortify with intrenchments] *trincierare, fortificare con trincee.*

To intrench upon another man's right, *uſurpare l'altrui diritto.*

INTRE'NCHED, adj. *trincierato, fortificato con trincee.*

Intrenched upon, *uſurpato.*

INTRE'NCHMENT, s. *trincea,* s. f.

INTRE'PID, s. [fearleſs] *intrepido, di gran cuore; forte, ardito, coraggioſo, prode.*

INTREPI'DITY, s. [undauntedneſs, courage] *intrepidità, intrepidezza, fermezza, prodezza,* s. f. *animo valore, coraggio,* s. m.

INTRE'PIDLY, adv. *intrepidamente, con intrepidezza.*

I'NTRICACY, s. *intrigo, imbarazzo,* s. m. *difficoltà,* s. f.

A buſineſs of great intricacy, *un negozio molto intrigato.*

I'NTRICATE, adj. [intangled, perplexed] *intrigato, imbrogliato, imbarazzato.*

An intricate buſineſs, *un negozio intrigato, o imbrogliato.*

To I'NTRICATE [to perplex, to darken] *metter in dubbio, oſcurare.*

I'NTRICATELY, adv. *intrigatamente, imbrogliatamente, con intrigo.*

INTRI'GUE, s. [a cunning deſign, plot, or ſecret conſpiracy] *intrigo, maneggio,* s. m. *pratica,* s. f.

INTRI'NSICAL, v. Intrinſick.

INTRI'NSICALLY, adv. [inwardly] *intrinſicamente, interiormente.*

INTRI'NSICK, adj. [inward, occult] *intrinſico, e intrinſeco, racchiuſo, interno, di dentro.*

To INTRODU'CE [to bring, or lead in] *introdurre, condurre,* pref. *introduco; conduco.* pret. *introduſſi, conduſſi.*

To introduce a new opinion, *introdurre, ſtabilire una nuova opinione.*

INTRODU'CED, adj. *introdotto, condotto.*

INTRODU'CING, s. *introducimento, l'introdurre,* s. m. *entratura, entrata,* s. f.

INTRODU'CTION, s. *introduzione,* s. f.

The introduction of ambaſſadors, *l' introduzione degli ambaſciadori.*

An introduction to hiſtory, *un' introduzione all' iſtoria.*

INTRODU'CTOR, s. *introduttore,* s. m. *che introduce.*

INTRODU'CTORY, adj. *che ſerve d' introduzione.*

To INTROM'IT [to let in, to admit, to allow to enter] *laſciar entrare, ammettere.*

To Intromit [to ſend in] *far entrare; metter dentro.*

To INTRU'DE [to intermeddle] *intruderſi, intrometterſi, ingerirſi, impacciarſi, intramet terſi,* pref. *ingeriſco,* pret. *intromiſi, intramiſi.*

To intrude one's ſelf into a buſineſs, *intrometterſi, ingerirſi in qualche affare.*

To intrude one's ſelf into a company, *ficcarſi, intrometterſi in una compagnia.*

To intrude into an eſtate, *impoſſeſſarſi d'un bene, uſurpare un bene.*

INTRU'DED, adj. *intromeſſo, ingerito, impacciato, intrameſſo.*

INTRU'DER, s. *quello, o quella, che s'ingeriſce, s'impaccia di che che ſi ſia.*

Intruder, in law [one who gets poſſeſſion of lands, void by the death of a tenant for life, or years] *colui che s'impoſſeſſa degli altrui beni, un uſurpatore.*

INTRU'SION, s. [an intruding or thruſting one's ſelf into company] *intruſione,* s. f. *l'intruderſi, il ficcarſi in compagnia*

Intruſion [in law, a violent or unlawful entrance upon lands, tenements, &c.] *intruſione, uſurpazione,* s. f.

To INTRU'ST [to put in truſt with] *depoſitare, metter nelle mani, confidare.*

To intruſt one with a thing, *depoſitare che che ſi ſia nell' altrui mani.*

INTRU'STED, adj. *depoſitato, confidato.*

To be intruſted with a thing, *aver che che ſi ſia in depoſito.*

INTRU'STING, s. *il confidare.*

INTU'ITION, s. [ſudden comprehenſion of any thing, immediate knowledge] *ſubitano conoſcimento, di che che ſſia, intuito ſapere o conoſcimento dedotto da ragionamento improvviſo.*

INTU'ITIVE, adj. *veduto immediate dalla mente.*

INTU'NABLE, adj. [that cannot be tuned] *che non ſi può accordare.*

To INTWI'NE [to twiſt, or wreath together] *torcere due o più coſe inſieme, attorcigliare.*

To INVA'DE [to ſeize violently, to uſurp] *invadere, uſurpare, fare un' invaſione, pigliar per forza, violentare.*

To invade a kingdom, *invadere un regno.*

To invade one's right, *uſurpare l'altrui diritto.*

To invade the privileges of a city, *violare i privilegi d'una città.*

INVA'DED, adj. *invaſo, uſurpato.*

To be invaded with fear, *eſſer aſſalito da timore.*

INVA'DER, s. *uſurpatore,* s. m. *uſurpatrice,* s. f.

INVA'DING, s. *invaſione, l'uſurpare.*

INVA'LID, adj. [of no force, not good in law] *invalido, debole, infermo, che non vale nulla.*

To INVA'LID, } [to annul] *invalidare, render invalido.*
To INVA'LIDATE, }

INVA'LIDATED, adj. *invalidato, annullato.*

INVA'LIDATING, s. *l'invalidare, l' annullare.*

INVALI'DITY, s. *invalidità, nullità.* s. f.

INVA'LUABLE, adj. *ineſtimabile, prezioſo oltra ogni ſtima.*

INVA'RIABLE, v. Unvariable.

INVA'SION, s. *invaſione, uſurpazione,* s. f.

INVA'SIVE, adj. *che entra oſtilmente in quello che appartiene altrui.*

INVE'CTIVE, adj. [a railing] *invettivo, che contiene invettiva.*

An invective ſpeech, *un diſcorſo pieno d'invettive.*

Invective, s. *un' invettiva.*

To INVE'IGH againſt [to ſpeak bitterly againſt one, to rail] *ſparlare, calunniare, villaneggiare, ingiuriare, declamar contro.*

INVE'IGHED againſt, adj. *ſparlato, calunniato, ſvillaneggiato, ingiuriato.*

To INVE'IGLE [to allure, entice, or deceive by fair words] *attrarre, allettare, luſingare, adeſcare, invitare, tirare uno alle voglie ſue con luſinghe o allettamenti, mariuolare, truffare, piaggiare, ingannare.*

INVE'IGLED, adj. *allettato, attratto, luſingato, adeſcato.*

INVE'IGLER, s. *un ingannatore.*

To INVE'LOPE [to wrap up, to infold] *inviluppare, involgere, avviluppare,* pret. *involſi.*

INVE'LOPED, adj. *inviluppato, involto, avviluppato.*

To INVE'NOM [to poiſon, to infect] *avvelenare, intoſſicare.*

INVE'NOMED, adj. *avvelenato, intoſſicato.*

To INVE'NT [to find out, to contriv

or devise] *inventare, esser il primo autore di che che si sia.*

To invent [to forge] *inventare, supporre, macchinare, ordire,* pret. *ordisco.*

INVE'NTED, adj. *inventato, v.* To invent.

INVE'NTER, s. *inventatore, inventore, macchinatore,* s. m.

INVE'NTING, s. *l' inventare.*

INVE'NTION, s. [a finding out] *invenzione,* s. f. *ritrovamento,* s. m.

Invention [trick, deceit] *invenzione,* s. f. *ritrovamento,* s. m.

Invention [in rhetorick, is that part which consists in finding out proper means to persuade] *invenzione, una delle cinque parti della rettorica.*

INVE'NTIVE, adj [apt to invent] *inventivo, proprio a inventare.*

INVE'NTOR, *v.* Inventer.

INVE'NTORY, s. [a catalogue of the goods and chattels of a party deceased] *inventario,* s. m.

To INVE'NTORY [to put into an inventory] *inventariare, fare inventario.*

INVE'NTORY'D, adj. *inventariato.*

INVE'NTRESS, s. [a woman that invents] *inventrice,* s. f.

INVE'RSION, s. *inversione,* s. f. *cangiamento,* s. m.

To make an inversion, *invertere, rivoltare, arrovesciare.*

To INVE'RT [to turn upside down, or inside out] *invertere, rivoltare, arrovesciare.*

INVE'RTED, adj. *inverso, inversato, rivoltato, arrovesciato.*

To INVE'ST [to put into possession of lands, tenements, &c.] *investire, concedere il dominio.*

To invest one with an estate, *investire uno di qualche bene, metterlo in possesso di qualche bene.*

To invest a place [military term] *investire una piazza.*

INVE'STED, adj. *investito.*

To INVE'STIGATE [to trace or find out, to search or enquire diligently] *investigare, diligentemente cercare.*

INVE'STIGATED, adj. *investigato.*

INVE'STIGATION, s. [a strict search] *investigazione,* s. f. *investigamento,* s. m.

INVE'STITURE, s. [a putting into possession of an estate] *investitura, investità,* s. m.

INVE'TERACY, s. *lunga continuazione in cosa mala.*

INVE'TERATE, adj. [confirmed by long use, grown into custom] *inveterato, invecchiato.*

An inveterate hatred, *un odio inveterato.*

To inveterate, *indurarsi, ostinarsi, invecchiare in cosa mala.*

INVI'DIOUS, adj. *invidioso, invido.*

INVI'DIOUSLY, adv. *invidamente, invidiosamente, malignamente.*

INVI'GILANCY, s. [carelessness] *negligenza, trascuraggine, infingardaggine,* s. f.

To INVI'GORATE, [to give vigour] *invigorire, dar vigore, inanimire,* pref. *invigorisco, inanimisco.*

INVIGORA'TION, s. *vigore, forza.*

INVI'NCIBLE, adj. [not to be overcome] *invincibile, che non può esser vinto, insuperabile.*

An invincible army, *un esercito invincibile.*

An invincible ignorance, *un' ignoranza crassa.*

INVI'NCIBLENESS, s. *qualità invincibile.*

INVI'NCIBLY, adv. *invincibilmente, d'una maniera invincibile.*

INVI'OLABLE, adj. [not to be violated or broken] *inviolabile, che non si può violare.*

INVI'OLABLY, adv. *inviolabilmente, con intera fede.*

INVI'OLATE, adj. [not violated] *inviolato, non corrotto, intero.*

I'NVIOUS, adj. *senza via, che non si passa.*

To INVI'RON [to surround, or compass about] *intorniare, circondare.*

INVI'RONED, adj. *intorniato, circondato.*

INVI'SIBLE, adj. [not to be seen] *invisibile, non visibile, che non può vedersi, impercettibile.*

INVI'SIBLENESS, s. *qualità invisibile, invisibilità.*

INVI'SIBLY, adv. *invisibilmente, impercettibilmente.*

INVITA'TION, s. *invitamento, invito,* s. m.

To INVI'TE [to desire, or bid one to come] *invitare, dire, o far dire altrui di venire.*

He has invited me to dinner, *egli m' ha invitato a pranzo.*

The weather invites us to go abroad, *il tempo c'invita a passeggiare.*

He invited me to be godfather to his child, *egli m'ha pregato di tenere suo figliuolo a battesimo.*

INVI'TED, adv. *invitato, pregato.*

INVI'TER, s. *invitatore,* s. m. *invitatrice,* s. f.

INVI'TING, s. *invitamento, invito,* s. m.

Inviting, adj. *attrattivo, grazioso.*

INVI'TINGLY, adv. *ex.* To look invitingly upon one, *guardar uno con occhio attrattivo, vezzeggiarlo.*

INUNDA'TION, s. [flood] *inondazione,* s. f.

To I'NVOCATE [to call upon] *invocare, chiamare in ajuto pregando.*

I'NVOCATED, adj. *invocato.*

INVOCA'TION, s. *invocazione,* s. f.

INVO'ICE, s. [a particular account of any goods sent by a merchant to his correspondent in another country] *polizza di carico.*

To INVO'KE, *v.* To invocate.

To INVO'LVE [to wrap, to fold] *involvere, inviluppare, involgere,* pret. *involsi.*

To involve [to ingage, to intangle] *avviluppare, imbarazzare, imbrigare, imbrogliare, impacciare, intrigare, inviluppare, implicare.*

To involve one's self in troubles, *imbrogliarsi in qualche disordine.*

INVO'LVED, adj. *involto, inviluppato, v.* To involve.

INVOLU'NTARY, adj. [contrary to one's will] *involontario, contra volontà.*

INVOLU'NTARILY, adj. [against one's will] *involontariamente, contra voglia.*

INVOLU'TION, s. *involgimento, avvolgimento,* s. m. *involtura,* s. f.

To INU'RE [to use, to accustom] *assuefare, accostumare, avvezzare, usare,* pret. *assuefeci.*

To inure one's self to hardship, *assuefarsi, accostumarsi alla fatica.*

INU'RED, adj. *assuefatto, accostumato, avvezzato, usato.*

INU'REMENT, s. *pratica, costume, abito, frequenza.*

To INU'RN, *metter nell' urna sepolcrale.*

INU'SITATE, adj. [not in use] *inusitato, che non è in uso, fuor d'uso.*

INUTI'LITY, s. [unusefulness] *inutilità,* s. f.

INVU'LNERABLE, adj. [that cannot be wounded] *invulnerabile.*

To INWA'LL, *circondar di mura, cingere con un muro.*

I'NWARD, adj. [on the inside] *interiore, interno, intimo.*

An inward evil, *un male interno.*

An inward friend, *un amico intimo, o stretto.*

I'NWARDLY, adv. *interiormente, internamente.*

I'NWARDS, s. [intrails] *le interiera, le viscere.*

The inwards of a beast, *le interiora d'un animale.*

Inward, } adv. *al di dentro, interiormente.*
Inwards, }

To INWE'AVE, *tessere, attorcigliare,* pret. inweaved or inwove; *part. pass.* inwove or inwoven.

To INWO'OD [to hide in woods] *nasconder ne' boschi.*

To INWRA'P [to wrap up] *inviluppare, avvolgere,* pret. *avvolsi.*

INWRA'PPED, adj. *inviluppato, avvolto.*

To INWRE'ATHE, *ringer d' un serto, incoronare, inghirlandare.*

JOB, s. [a small piece of work] *lavoro,* s. m. *operetta,* s f.

I did a job for him once, *feci qualche cosa per lui una volta; lavorai una volta un poco per lui.*

He has done many a good job for me, *egli ha spesse volte lavorato per me.*

Job [blow] *un colpo con uno stromento acuto.*

JO'BBER, *ex.* A stock-jobber, *un sensale.*

JO'BBERNOWL, s. [a blockhead] *uno sciocco, un gonzo.*

JO'CKEY, s. [one who deals in horses] *mezzano o sensale di cavalli.*

Jockey, *colui che corre il palio a cavallo.*

JOCO'SE, adj. [merry, pleasant] *giocoso, motteggioso, scherzoso, lieto, allegro, festevole, giocolare, gioviale, piacevole.*

A jocose man, *un uomo allegro, o giocolare.*

A jocose humour, *umore allegro.*

In

In a jocose sense, *in un senso burlesco.*

JOCO'SELY, adv. [in a jocose sense] *giocosamente, da giuoco, in un senso burlesco.*

JO'CULAR, adj. [pleasant, merry] *giocolare, giocoso, giocondo, allegro, festevole, lieto, giojoso, burlesco, scherzoso, piacevole.*

JO'CUND, v. Jocose.

JOG, s. *scossa*, s. f. *scotimento, crollo, crollamento*, s. m.

A jog of a cart or a coach, *scossa di carro o di carrozza.*

To jog [to push, to shake] *spignere, urtare, scuotere, crollare, balzare*, pret. *spinsi, scossi.*

This coach jogs horribly, *questa carrozza balza terribilmente.*

To jog one on, *spignere qualcheduno avanti, farlo andare avanti.*

JO'GGED, adj. *spinto, urtato, scosso, crollato, balzato.*

To JO'GGLE, verb. neut. *muoversi, agitarsi, dimenarsi.*

JO'GGLING, s. *agitazione*, s. f. *movimento*, s. m.

To JOIN, v. To joyn, and all its derivatives.

JOIST, v. Joyst.

JOKE, s. [jest] *burla, beffa*, s. f. *scherzo, giuoco*, s. m.

To put a joke upon one, *burlarsi, ridersi d'uno, beffarlo, schernirlo.*

In joke, *da burla, per ischerzo, da giuoco.*

To JOKE [to jest] *burlare, beffare, scherzare.*

JO'KED, adj. *burlato, beffato, scherzato.*

JO'LLILY, adv. *allegramente, gajamente, festevolmente, piacevolmente, giojosamente.*

JO'LLITY, s. [gaity, mirth] *gajezza, allegria, festa, allegrezza, giulività*, s. f.

JO'LLY, adv. [brisk, merry, lively] *giulivo, allegro, festevole, piacevole, giojoso, gajo.*

A jolly blade, *un buon compagnone, un uomo allegro e piacevole, d'umor allegro.*

JOLT, v. Joult.

IO'NIAN, } adj. *Jonico.*
IO'NICK, }

Ionick order, *ordine Ionico, uno de' cinque ordini dell' architettura.*

JO'NQUIL, s. [a sort of flower] *giunchiglia*, s. f. *sorta di fiore.*

JO'RDEN, s. *orinale.*

JO'SSING-BLOCK, s. [a block to get up on horseback] *cavalcatojo*, s. m.

JOT, s. [a title, a point] *jota, niente, punto, mica, acca.*

Not a jot, *non un jota, punto.*

He won't stir a jot, *non vuol muoversi un jota.*

Every jot, *tutto, affatto.*

JO'VIAL, adj. [pleasant, merry] *gioviale, piacevole, giocondo, festevole, allegro, gajo, giojoso.*

JOULT, s. *balzo, scrollo*, s. m. *scossa*, s. f. *è meglio scritto* Jolt.

A Joult head [a clumsy pate] *un gonzo, uno sciocco.*

To JOULT [to shake, to toss] *scuotere, crollare, scrollare, balzare*, pret. *scossi.*

JO'ULTED, adj. *scosso, crollato, scrollato, balzato.*

JO'URNAL, s. [a diary, or day-book] *giornale, diario*, s. m. *libro, nel quale dì per dì si nota ciò che si fa nelle botteghe o nelle case.*

JO'URNEY, s. [travel by land] *viaggio*, s. m.

To take a journey, *fare un viaggio.*

To go a long journey, *fare un lungo viaggio.*

Journey [a day's march] *giornata*, s. f. *cammino, che si fa in un giorno.*

To come long or short journeys, *venire a gran giornate, o corte giornate.*

A JO'URNEY-MAN [one that works by the day] *un lavorante, un uomo che lavora a giornate.*

Journey's work [or day's work] *giornata, lavoro d'un giorno.*

To JO'URNEY [to travel by land] *viaggiare.*

JO'URNEYINGS, s. *viaggi.*

To JOUST [to run in the tilt] *giostrare.*

JOUST, s. *giostra, torniamento.*

JOWL, s. [a head] *testa*, s. f.

A jowl of salmon, *una testa di pesce salmone.*

JO'WLER, s. *sorta di cane da caccia.*

JOY, s. [mirth, pleasure] *gioja, allegrezza, letizia, giocondità, contentezza*, s. f. *giubilo, contento*, s. m.

To leap for joy, *gioire, rallegrarsi.*

To wish you joy, *mi rallegro con voi, mi congratulo con voi.*

To JOY [to rejoice] *rallegrare, indurre allegrezza e piacere in altrui.*

It joys my heart to see you well, *mi rallegro, godo sommamente di vederla in buona salute.*

JO'YFUL, adj. [joyous] *giojoso, contento, gajo, allegro.*

To make one joyful, *rallegrare alcuno.*

JO'YFULLY, adv. *giojosamente, con gioja, giocondamente, festevolmente.*

JO'YFULNESS, s. *gioja, allegrezza, allegria*, s. f. *contento, giubilo, piacere*, s. m.

To JOYN [to put together] *congiungere, mettere, attaccare insieme, unire*, pret. *congiunsi*, pres. *unisco.*

To join a thing to another, *congiungere, attaccare, unire una cosa con un' altra.*

To joyn with one [to bear half the charges] *accomunarsi, unirsi con uno, fare a metà con esso lui.*

To joyn [to come together] *accozzarsi, accompagnarsi, unirsi.*

The armies are ready to joyn, *gli eserciti sono in punto d' accozzarsi.*

To joyn battle [to engage] *venire a giornata, far giornata, venire a battaglia.*

To joyn interest with one, *associarsi con alcuno.*

There I joyn with you, *in ciò io sono del vostro parere.*

JO'YNDER, s. [the joyning of two in a suit or action against one] *l'associazione di due persone in processo contro un' altro.*

JO'YNED, adj. *congiunto, giunto, messo, attaccato insieme, unito.*

When the battle was joyned, *principiata che fu la battaglia.*

JO'YNER, s. *falegname.*

JOYNT, s. [a place where one thing or member is added to another] *giuntura, congiuntura, commessura, commettitura.*

A joynt of veal, or mutton, *lacchetta di vitella, o di castrato.*

A joynt of meat, *un pezzo di carne.*

To put one's arm out of joynt, *disluogarsi un braccio.*

A bone out of joynt, *un osso disluogato.*

To put one's nose out of joynt, [to supplant him] *soppiantare, ingannare, alcuno, darli il gambetto.*

A turning joynt, *vertebra, spezzatura*, s. f. *nodo*, s. m.

The joynts of stones in walling, *commessure.*

The joynt of a snuff-box, *l'incastratura d'una tabacchiera.*

Joynt, adj. ex. joynt-heir [or coheir] *coerede, compagno nell' eredità.*

Joynt-tenants, *molti fittuali, che tengono terre, o case per indoviso, in compagnia.*

With joynt consent, *d'un comune consenso, unanimamente.*

To JOYNT, ex. To joynt a piece of meat [to part it by cutting the joynts] *tagliare un pezzo di carne per le giunture.*

JO'YNTED, adj. *tagliato per le giunture.*

JO'YNTLY, adv. *unitamente, congiuntamente.*

JO'YNTURE, s. [a maintenance allotted or joined to the wife in consideration of the dowry she brought her husband] *dote*, s. f. *mantenimento che il marito da alla moglie, in considerazione della sua dote, durante la sua vita.*

To make a woman a joynture, *assegnare la dote ad una donna, dotarla.*

To JOYNTURE a wife [to make her a joynture or settlement] *dotare una moglie.*

JO'YOUS, adj. [merry] *giojoso, allegro, contento.*

JOYSTS, s. [pieces of timber which are framed into the girders or sommers of a house] *travicello, corrente*, s. m. *que' travicelli sottili, che si metton ne' palchi, o ne' tetti fra trave, e trave.*

IPECACUA'NHA, s. *nome d'una pianta medicinale Indiana.*

IRA'SCIBLE, adj. [capable of anger, apt to be angry] *irascibile, iracondo, inchinato all' ira, che agevolmente s'adira.*

IRE, s. [anger, wrath] *ira, stizza, collera*, s. f.

I'REFUL, adj. *irato, adirato, colmo d'ira.*

I'RIS, s. [the rainbow] *iri, iride, arcobaleno.*

Iris [in anatomy, the fibrous circle next the pupil of the eye, distinguished with variety of colours] *iride, quel cerchio di vari colori, che circonda la pupilla dell' occhio.*

To IRK, *dispiacere, riuscire spiacevole, nauseoso.*

It irketh me to do it, *mi dispiace, mi rincresce, mi duole di farlo.*

I'RKSOME, adj. [troublesome, displeasing] *increscevole, rincrescevole, tedioso, fastidioso, nojoso, molesto, affannoso.*

I'RON, s. [a sort of metal] *ferro*, s. m. *sorta di metallo.*

White Iron, *ferro bianco.*

A smoothing iron, *un ferro da lisciare i panni lini.*

Old iron, *ferri vecchi, sferre.*

Iron gray, *grigio, bigio.*

Iron tool, *ferramento*, s. m. *strumenti di ferro da lavorare.*

Iron bar, *sbarra di ferro.*

Iron wire, *ferro filato.*

To beat the iron whilst 'tis hot, *batter il ferro mentre è caldo.*

A cramp iron, *un rampino, un rampicone.*

Iron-plate, *piastra di ferro.*

An iron mine, *una ferriera, una mina di ferro.*

Iron mill, *ferriera, il luogo e la fucina dove si raffina il ferro.*

Ironmonger, *ferrajo, mercante di ferro.*

The iron age, *il secol di ferro.*

Iron sick, sea phrase [a ship is said to be iron sick, when her spikes, bolts, nails, &c. are so worn out, that they make hollows in the planks, whereby the ship leaks] *che ha chiodi consumati dalla ruggine, parlando d'un vascello.*

To I'RON, *lisciare con ferro caldo.*

IRO'NICAL, adj. [spoken in jest] *ironico.*

IRO'NICALLY, adv. [in an ironical sense] *ironicamente, con ironia.*

I'RONY, s. [a figure in rhetorick] *ironia*, s. f. *contrario senso a quello che suonano le parole.*

To IRRA'DIATE [to shine upon] *irradiare, inradiare, raggiare.*

To irradiate [to cast forth beams] *irradiare, brillare, scintillare, risplendere.*

IRRADIA'TION, s. *raggio, splendore*, s. m.

IRRA'TIONAL, adj. [void of reason] *irrazionale, privo di ragione.*

IRRECO'NCILEABLE, adj. [not to be reconciled] *irreconciliabile.*

IRRECO'VERABLE, adj. [not to be recovered] *irreparabile, a che non si può dar riparo.*

IRRECO'VERABLY, adv. *senza riparo.*

IRRECU'PARABLE, adj. [irrecoverable] *irrecuperabile, che non si può recuperare.*

IRREFRA'GABLE, adj. [undeniable] *irrefragabile, incontestabile, da non potersi confutare.*

IRREFU'TABLE, adj. [that cannot be confuted] *che non si può confutare.*

IRRE'GULAR, adj. [not regular, without rule] *irregolare, che non è secondo le regole.*

An irregular verb, *un verbo irregolare.*

Irregular [disorderly, unruly] *sregolato, sfrenato.*

Irregular appetites, *appetiti sregolati.*

IRREGULA'RITY, s. [going out of rule] *irregolarità*, s. f.

Irregularity [disorderlineſs] *sregolatezza, sfrenatezza*, s. f.

Irregularity [in canon law, an incapacity of taking holy orders] *irregolarità, impedimento canonico per ricevere, o esercitare gli ordini sacri.*

IRRE'GULARLY, adv. *irregolarmente.*

IRRELI'GION, s. [want of religion, ungodlineſs] *irreligione, irreligiosità, empietà*, s. f. *mancanza di religione.*

IRRELI'GIOUS, adj. [without, or having but little religion] *irreligioso, che non ha religione, empio.*

IRRELI'GIOUSLY, adv. *irreligiosamente, senza religione.*

IRREME'DIABLE, adj. [that cannot be remedied] *irremediabile, inremediévole, e irremedievole, senza rimedio.*

IRRE'MISSIBLE, adj. [not to be remitted or forgiven] *irremissibile, da non si poter perdonare.*

IRRE'MISSIBLY, adv. *irremissibilmente.*

IRREMO'VEABLY, adj. *immovibile, che non si può muovere.*

IRREMU'NERABLE, adj. [not to be rewarded] *irremunerabile.*

IRRE'PARABLE, adj. [which cannot be repaired or recovered] *irreparabile, senza riparo.*

IRRE'PARABLY, adv. *irreparabilmente.*

IRREPREHE'NSIBLE, adj. [not to be reprehended, or blamed] *irreprensibile, che non può esser ripreso.*

IRREPREHE'NSIBLY, adv. *d'una maniera irreprensibile.*

IRRE'PROACHABLE, adj. *che non se gli può apporre, che non si può biasimare, netto di fallo.*

IRREPRO'VEABLE, adj. [not to be reproved, blameleſs] *irreprobabile, che non si può riprovare.*

IRRE'SISTIBLE, adj. [that cannot be resisted or withstood] *al quale non si può resistere.*

An irresistible power, *un potere al quale non si può resistere.*

IRRE'SISTIBLY, adv. *d'una maniera alla quale non si può resistere.*

IRRE'SOLUTE, adj. [or wavering] *irresoluto, dubbioso, sospeso.*

IRRE'SOLUTELY, adv. *irresolutamente, dubbiosamente, in sospeso.*

IRRESOLU'TION, s. [unresolvedneſs, suspense] *irresoluzione, dubbiezza, sospension d'animo.*

IRRETRIE'VABLE, adj. [not to be retrieved or recovered] *irreparabile, senza rimedio.*

IRRETRI'EVABLY, adv. *irreparabilmente, senza riparo.*

IRRE'VERENCE, s. [want of reverence for sacred things and holy persons] *irreverenza*, s. f. *mancanza di reverenza, o di rispetto.*

IRRE'VERENT, adj. [that shows no reverence or respect] *irreverente, poco rispettoso, che manca di rispetto.*

IRRE'VERENTLY, adv. [without due reverence] *irreverentemente, senza reverenza, o rispetto.*

IRREVERSIBLE, adj. [that cannot be reversed, repealed, or made void] *irrevocabile.*

IRRE'VOCABLE, adj. [not to be revoked] *irrevocabile, che non si può revocare.*

IRRE'VOCABLY, adv. *irrevocabilmente.*

To I'RRIGATE [to water] *irrigare, e inrigare, innaffiare.*

I'RRIGATED, adj. *irrigato, innaffiato.*

IRRI'GUOUS, adj. [moist, wet] *irriguo, inaffiato, umido.*

IRRI'SION, [laughing to scorn] *irrisione, e inrisione, derisione*, s. f.

To I'RRITATE [to provoke to anger, to incense or urge] *irritare, provocare.*

I'RRITATED, adj. *irritato, provocato.*

I'RRITATING, s. *irritamento*, s. m. *irritazione*, s. f.

IRRITA'TION, s. [provocation] *irritazione*, s. f. *irritamento*, s. m.

IRRORATE [to bedew, to besprinkle] *irrorare, aspergere di rugiada, irrugiadare.*

IRRU'PTION, s. [inroad] *incursione*, s. f. *scorrimento, scorreria di nemici nel paese.*

Is [a person of the verb, to be] *è.*

He is, *egli è.*

She is beloved, *ella è amata.*

ISABE'LLA, s. [a sort of colour] *Isabella, spezie di colore, che partecipa del bianco e del giallo.*

I'SICLE, s. *iciolo*; *goccia di ghiaccio pendente.*

I'SLAND, s. [a tract of land surrounded with water] *un' isola, paese racchiuso d'ogni intorno d'acqua.*

ISLANDER, s. *abitator d'isola.*

ISLE, s. [island] *isola.*

Isle, in architecture [the sides or wings of a building] *le ali d'un edificio.*

The isles of a church, *le ali della nave d'una chiesa.*

ISO'SCELES, adj. [that has only two sides equal] *isoscele, che ha solo due lati uguali.*

Isosceles triangle, *triangolo isoscele.*

I'SSUE, s. [end, event] *fine, evento, successo*, s. m.

Who knows what will be the issue of all this? *chi sa qual fine avrà tutto questo?*

A good issue, *evento felice.*

The issues of war are uncertain, *i successi della guerra sono incerti.*

An issue [in one's arm, leg, &c.] cauterio, rottorio, s. m. fontanella, s. f.

Issue [offspring] prole, progenie, prosapia, schiatta, razza, s. f. figliuoli.

To die without issue, morire senza figliuoli.

Issue male, figliuoli maschi.

The issues growing from fines, or of lands, profitti.

Issues [expences] spese.

The matter in issue is this, questa è la questione della quale si tratta.

To issue out, or forth [to publish] pubblicare.

The king has issued out a proclamation, il re ha pubblicato una proclamazione.

The money must not be issued out without order, non si deve sborsare il danaro senz' ordine.

To I'SSUE, uscire, pres. esce.

The sun seems to issue from the sea, pare che il sole esca dal mare.

The veins that issue from the heart, le vene che vengono dal core.

I'SSUED, adj. pubblicato, uscito.

I'SSUELESS, adj. [that has no issue] che non ha prole, o figliuoli, senza prole.

ISTHMUS, s. [a little neck or part of land joining a peninsula to the continent] istmo, s. f. braccio di terra fra due mari.

IT [pronoun] egli, lo, la.

It is the custom, egli è il costume.

That's it I fear, questo è quel che temo.

It rains, it snows, piove, nevica.

Give it him, dateglielo.

I see it, lo, o la vedo.

It is my father, or my mother, è mio padre, è mia madre.

I got sixpence by it, ne ho avuto sei soldi.

I got nothing by it, non ci ho guadagnato niente.

It is nothing to me, ciò non m'importa.

The inhabitants of it, i suoi abitanti.

ITA'LIAN, s. [one born in Italy] un Italiano, un nativo d'Italia.

Italian, adj. [the Italian language] l'Italiano, la lingua Italiana.

The italick letter, la lettera italica.

ITCH, s. rogna, scabbia, s. f.

Itch [itching] prurito, pizzicore, mordicamento, s. m.

Itch [itching desire] uzzola, fregola, appetito intenso.

To ITCH, verb neut. prudere, pizzicare.

My arm itches, mi prude il braccio.

My fingers itch to be at him, mi vien voglio o gran voglia di bastonarlo.

I'TCHING, s prurito, pizzicore, formicolamento.

An itching powder, polvere che causa prurito.

Itching desire, fregola, frega, s. f. uzzolo, s. m. appetito intenso.

I'TCHY, adj. rognoso, scabbioso, che ha pizzicore, o la rogiona.

I'TEM, adv. item, di più.

Item [I bequeath to such a one] item, di più lascio ad un tale.

Item, s. [an article of an account] articolo, capo d'un conto.

To examine the several items of disbursements, esaminare i differenti articoli di quel che s'è sborsato.

Item [caution, warning] avviso, consiglio.

This is a fair item for you, questo è un buon avviso per voi.

To I'TERATE, ripetere, ridire, dir di nuovo il già detto.

To iterate, far di nuovo il già fatto, rifare.

ITI'NERANT, adj. [travelling] che viaggia, che è in viaggio.

Itinerant justices [justices formerly sent into diverse countries to hear and determine causes] giudici ambulanti.

ITI'NERARY, s. [journal, account of the occurrences in a journey or voyage] itinerario, s. m. libro, nel quale si notano le cose le più principali che accadono pel viaggio.

ITS [pronoun from IT] suo, sua, suoi, sue.

To put a sword in its scabbard, mettere una spada nel suo fodero.

A primitive with its derivatives, un primitivo co' suoi derivativi.

ITSELF. Il pronome neutro reciproco applicato a cose.

JU'BILANT, adj. che canta inni trionfali.

JU'BILATE, s. [a monk in the Romish church, who has been fifty years a professor] un giubilato, un religioso che ha cinquant' anni di professione.

JUBILA'TION, s. [a solemn rejoicing] giubilazione, giubbilazione, allegrezza pubblica.

JU'BILE, } s. [a solemnity first in-
JU'BILEE, } stituted by pope Boniface VIII. in the year 1300, who ordained it to be kept every hundredth year; afterwards Clement IV. ordered it to be kept every fiftieth year; and Sextus IV. every twenty-fifth year] giubbileo, s. m.

The year of jubilee, l'anno del giubbileo.

JUCU'NDITY, s. [pleasantness] giocondezza, giocondità, s. f.

JUDA'ICK, adj. [of or belonging to the Jews] Giudaico.

JU'DAISM, s. [the religion or customs, or religious rites of the Jews] Giudaismo, s. m.

To JU'DAIZE [to hold the customs, or religious rites of the Jews] Giudaizzare, imitare i riti Giudaici.

JUDGE, s. [an officer appointed to execute justice in civil or military causes] giudice, s. m.

A judge in civil or military causes, un giudice civile, o criminale.

Let any body be judge, ne sia giudice alcuno di voi.

A judge lateral, un assessore.

To JUDGE [to try or determine causes] giudicare, risolvere, determinare per via di ragione, dando sentenza.

To judge [to make judgment of, to tell one's opinion] giudicare, pensare, stimare.

To judge of colours, giudicare de' colori.

To judge of one by his actions, giudicar d'uno dalle sue azioni.

JUDGED, adj. giudicato, pensato, stimato.

JU'DGMENT, s. [the discerning faculty] giudicio, discernimento, discorso, s. m. facoltà dell' anima, colla quale si giudica delle cose.

Judgment [prudence, discretion] giudicio, prudenza, condotta, discrezione.

Judgment [opinion] giudicio, parere, sentimento, opinione.

Judgment [sentence] giudicio, determinazione del giusto e dell' ingiusto, sentenza.

Judgment [punishment] giudicio, gastigo.

A man of great judgment, un uomo di gran giudicio, un uomo molto giudicioso.

In my judgment he is greatly mistaken, a mio giudicio, egli s'inganna a partito.

There's no judgment to be given upon accidents, non si può giudicare degli accidenti.

To stand to the judgment of the court, stare o rimettersi al giudicio della corte.

To prevent God's judgment, prevenire i giudici di Dio.

This judgment upon us is just, noi meritiamo questo gastigo.

The great day of judgment [the last day] l'ultimo giorno del giudicio, il giudicio universale.

To give one's judgment upon a thing, far giudicio, giudicare di qualche cosa.

Judgment seat, giudicio, tribunale.

JU'DGING, s. giudicamento, giudicio, il giudicare.

JU'DICATURE, s. giudicatura, giustizia, s. f.

A court of judicature, una corte di giudicatura.

JUDI'CIAL, adj. [belonging to a cause, tryal, or judgment] giudiciale, e giudiziale, pertinente a giudicio, giudiciario, e giudiziario.

To do a thing in a judicial way, fare che che si sia secondo l'ordine giudiciale.

JUDI'CIALLY, adv. giudicialmente, giudiciariamente.

JUDI'CIARY, adj. [judicial] giudiciario, e giudiziario, giudiciale, e giudiziale.

JUDI'CIOUS, adj. [indued with good judgment or reason] giudicioso, e giudizioso, che ha giudizio, prudente, savio, discreto.

JUDI'CIOUSLY, adv. giudiciosamente, e giudiziosamente, con giudicio, prudentemente, saviamente, discretamente.

JUG, s. [an earthen pot or pitcher to hold drink] boccale di terra.

A jug [a common pasture, or meadow] un prato, un campo.

Jug [nightingale] usignuolo, s. m.

JU'GGLE, s. [juggling trick, legerdemain] gherminella, s. f. giuoco di mano, baratteria, inganno.

To JU'GGLE [to shew tricks with flight of hand, to play legerdemain] giocolare, far giuochi di mano.

To juggle [to cheat] ingannare, mariuolare, truffare.

JU'GGLER, s giocolatore, bagattelliere, giocolare, travagliatore.

Juggler [cheat] un bagattelliere, un ciarlatano, un furbo, un mariuolo, un guidone.

JU'GGLING, s. il fare giuochi di mano.

Juggling trick, gherminella, giuoco di mano, baratteria, inganno.

JU'GGLINGLY, adv. [deceitfully] con inganno, da furbo, da bagattelliere.

JU'GULAR, adj. appartenente alla gola, al gorgozzule, alla strozza.

JU'ICE, s. [moisture] sugo, succo, sostanza fluida.

The juice [or gravy] of meat, il sugo della carne quando è cotta.

The juice of an orange, il sugo d'un melangolo, d'un arancio.

JU'ICELESS, adj. senza sugo, che non ha sugo.

JU'ICINESS, s. sugosità, abbondanza di sugo.

JU'ICY, adj. [full of juice] sugoso, e succoso, pien di sugo.

A juicy fruit, un frutto sugoso, pien di sugo.

JU'JUBE, s. [a sort of fruit] zizzibbo, frutta nota.

To JUKE [to pearch, to rooft, as birds do] appollajarsi, andare a dormire come fanno gli uccelli.

JU'LAP, s. [a liquid medicine of a pleasant taste] giulebbo, e giulebbe, s. m.

JU'LIAN, adj. Giuliano.

Julian law, la legge Giuliana, la quale condannava l'adultero alla morte.

JU'LIO, s. [an Italian coin worth about five pence] giulio, s. m.

JU'LY, s. [the seventh month in the year] Luglio, s. m. quinto mese dell' anno.

JU'MART, s. spezie di mulo nato d'un cavallo e d'una vacca, o d'un toro e d' una giumenta. Sull' alpi li chiamano Giamerri. Da poco in quà si è voluto che non vi sieno tali animali, e che sia error popolare il credere che ve ne sieno.

JU'MBLE, s. miscuglio, s. m. mescolanza, confusione, s. f.

To JU'MBLE [to mingle, to confound] mescolare, confondere, mettere insieme, pret. confusi.

JU'MBLED, adj. confuso, mescolato.

JU'MBLING, s. mescolamento, s. m. mescolanza, s. f.

JU'MENT, s. [a labouring beast; any sort of beast used for tillage or carriage] giumento, s. m. cavallo, o altra bestia da soma, e da traina.

JUMP, adv. [exactly, nicely] esattamente, con dilicatezza.

Jump, s. [leap] salto, s. m.

To give a jump, fare un salto.

Jump [for a woman] giubba da donna.

To JUMP [to leap] saltare, fare un salto.

To jump over a ditch, saltare un fosso.

To jump [as a coach does in a rugged way] balzare, sbalzare.

To jump [to agree] accordarsi, convenire, confarsi, pret. convenni.

Their opinions jump much with ours, le loro opinioni s'accordano colle nostre.

JU'MPER, s. saltatore, s. m. saltatrice, s. f.

JU'MPING, s. il saltare.

JU'NCATE, s. cosa dilicata a mangiare.

JU'NCTION, s. unione, accoppiamento.

JU'NCTO, s. [cabal, private faction] cabala, fazione, s. f. pratica secreta.

Juncto [a meeting of men to sit in council] assemblea de' consiglieri, consiglio, s. m.

JU'NCTURE, s. [the present state, or posture of affairs] congiuntura, s. f. stato, s. m.

JUNE, s. Giugno; nome del sesto mese cominciando a contare da gennajo.

JU'NIOR, adj. uno più giovine d'un altro.

JU'NIPER, } s. ginepro,
JUNIPER BERRY, } s. m.

The juniper berry, ginepro, arbore noto.

A juniper lecture, ripassata, riprensione, bravata.

To give one a juniper lecture, fare una ripassata, fare una buona riprensione ad uno.

JUNK, s. nome di picciola nave Indiana.

Junk, s. [among sailors, a piece of old cable] un pezzo di gomena vecchia.

To JU'NKET [to entertain one another with banquets, or treats] banchettare, far banchetti, gozzovigliare, far gozzoviglia, stare in gozzoviglia, stare allegramente, far buona cera.

Junkets, s. [any sorts of delicious fare to feast and make merry with] gozzoviglia, s. f. cibi delicati.

JU'NKETTING, s. buona cera, gozzoviglia.

I'VORY, s. [the elephant's teeth] avorio, s. m. dente di lionfante.

Ivory teeth, denti d'avorio.

An ivory comb, un pettine d'avorio.

JU'PPON, s. giubbone, sorta di vestimento.

JU'RAT, s. [a magistrate in some corporations in the nature of an alderman] giurato, s. m. spezie di magistrato.

JURI'DICAL, adj. [belonging to the law] giuridico, juridico, secondo la legge.

JURISDI'CTION, s. [power and authority to minister justice] giuridizione, e jurisdizione, s. f. podestà di render altrui ragione.

Jurisdiction [a court of judicature] giurisdizione, giustizia, tribunale.

Jurisdiction [the extent of one's jurisdiction] giurisdizione.

JURISPRU'DENCE, s. [the knowledge of the law] jurisprudenza, scienza della legge.

JU'RIST, s. [civilian lawyer] giurista, s. m. dottore di legge.

JU'ROR, s. [one of the jury sworn] uno de dodici, o de' vintiquatro giurati.

JU'RY, s. [either twelve or twenty four men, sworn to enquire of the matter of fact, and declare the truth upon such evidence as shall be delivered them, touching the matter in question] giurati, dodici, o vintiquattro uomini, scelti per giudicare d'un fatto, seconda la deposizione de' testimoni, ai quali si da il giuramento per quest' effetto.

JU'RYMEN, uno de' dodici o de' ventiquattro giurati.

JU'RIMAST, s. albero messo alla nave in vece di quello perduto in burrasca o in battaglia.

JU'SSEL, s. [a dish made of several meats mixed together] manicaretto, s. m. vivanda composta di più carni e cose appetitose.

JUST, adj. [righteous] giusto, leale, diritto, buono.

A just man, un uomo giusto, o leale.

A just cause, una causa giusta.

I have just cause to complain, io ho giusta ragion di lamentarmi.

Just design, buon fine, sincerità, probità.

Just, s. il giusto.

The just shall live by faith, il giusto viverà di fede.

Just, adv. appunto, giusto, precisamente, appuntino.

To come just at the time appointed, venire appunto al tempo prescritto.

Just as, come se.

Just so, appunto così.

Just now, appunto, or'ora, teste, in questo punto.

He is just now gone, egli è appunto partito.

To just [to run a tilt] giostrare.

JUSTS, s. [tiltings or combats on horseback] giostre.

JU'STICE, s. [equity] giustizia, equità, s. f.

To administer justice, amministrare la giustizia.

To do justice, render giustizia.

To do justice upon one, punire alcuno.

A justice, or justicer, un giudice, un giustiziere.

A justice of peace, un giudice di pace.

To JU'STICE, amministrar giustizia.

JU'STICIARY, s. [an administrator of justice] giudice, mantenitor della giustizia.

JUSTIFI'ABLE, adj. [that may be justified] che si può giustificare.

JUSTIFI'ABLY, adv. con ragione, con giustizia.

JUSTIFICA'TION, s. [a clearing or justifying] giustificazione, s. f. provamento di ragione, scolpamento, scusa.

Justification [in divinity, is a clearing of transgressors of the divine laws, by the imputation of Christ's righteousness] giustificazione, termine teologico.

To JU'STIFY [to make appear one's innocency] giustificare, provare, mostrare con ragioni la verità del fatto, far capace, sincerare;

To justify [in divinity, to make or declare innocent] *giustificare, far giusto.*
JU'STIFY'D, adj. *giustificato.*
JU'STIFYING, s. *il giustificare.*
Justifying, adj. *giustificante, che giustifica.*
The justifying grace, *la grazia giustificante.*
JU'STING, s. [from to just] *il giostrare, giostra.*
Justing-place, *aringo,* s. m. *lizza,* s. f.
To JU'STLE [to push] *urtare.*
To justle one another, *urtarsi.*
JU'STLED, adj. *urtato.*
JU'STLER, s. *quello, o quella che urta.*
JU'STLING, s. *l'urtare, urto,* s. m.
JUSTLY, adv. *giustamente, con giustizia, con ragione.*
JU'STNESS, s. [justice] *giustizia, equità,* s. f.
JUSTS, s. [tournaments] *giostre, tornei.*
To JUT out, *sporgere, sporgere in fuori, uscir del piano, o del perpendicolo.*
JU'TTY, s. [a part of a building which juts out farther than the rest] *sporto, risalto,* s. m. *muraglia che sporge in fuora dalla dirittura della parete principale.*
JU'VENILE, adj. [youthful] *giovanile, o fanciullesco.*
Juvenile years, *anni giovanili.*
JUVENI'LITY, s. [youthfulness] *giovanezza, ardore di gioventù.*
I'VY, s. [a plant which twines about trees, and fastens upon walls] *ellera, edera,* s. f.

K.

K, *è la decima lettera dell' alfabeto Inglese, e ha il suono della nostra lettera C dinanzi a A, O, U, ma quando precede la N non ha suono.*
KA, ex. ka me, ka thee [that is, one good turn for another] *una mano lava l'altra, amor con amor si paga.*
KA'LENDAR, s. *calendario.*
KAM, adj. [crooked] *torto, gobbo, curvo.*
KAW, s. *il crocito del corvo o della cornacchia.*
To KAW [to cry as a jack daw does] *cornacchiare, gracchiare.*
To kaw for breath [to fetch one's breath with much ado] *respirare con difficoltà.*
KAYLE, s. [ninepin, kettlepin] *sorta di giuoco.*
To KECK [or make a noise in the throat, as one does when something sticks to it] *sforzarsi di gettare per la bocca quel che s'attacca alla gola.*
KECKS, s. [dry stalks and sticks] *frasche,* s. f.
To KE'CKLE, *vestire una gomena di corde con attorcigliarle intorno ad essa.*
KEDGE, adj. [brisk, lively] *allegro, spiritoso, vivace.*
To KEDGE [to set up the foresail, foretopsail, and mizen, and to let a ship drive with the tide, when in a narrow river they could bring her up and down, the wind being contrary to the tide] *ammainare.*
KE'DGER, s. [a small anchor us'd in calm weather] *ancoretta,* s. f.
KEE [plurale di Cow] *vacche; ma è vocabolo contadinesco. Il proprio è* COWS, *l'antico era* Kine.
KEEL, s. [the lowest piece of timber in a ship in the bottom of her hull] *carena,* s. f. *la parte di sotto del navilio.*
Keel [a vessel for liquor to stand and cool in] *tino da rinfrescarvi dentro qualche liquore.*
To KEEL, *rinfrescare.*
KE'ELING, s. [a kind of fish] *nascilo,* s. m. *sorta di pesce.*
KEEN, adj. [sharp, that cuts well] *affilato, acuto, aguzzo, che taglia bene.*
Keen, adj. [sharp, or subtle] *acuto, sottile.*
A keen air, *aria sottile, o serena.*
A keen style, *uno stile acuto, mordente, satirico.*
Keen appetite, *buono appetito, appetito aguzzato.*
Keen-sighted, *perspicace.*
To KEEN [to sharpen] *aguzzare, auzzare.*
KE'ENLY, adv. [sharply] *sottilmente, acutamente.*
Keenly [eagerly] *ardentemente con ardore, aspramente.*
KE'ENNESS, s. *sottigliezza, acutezza.*
Keenness, *asprezza, veemenza.*
Keeness, *amarezza di mente.*
The keenness of the air, or sight, *sottigliezza d'aria, o bontà della vista.*
To KEEP [to preserve, to defend, to maintain, &c.] *tenere, mantenere, difendere, conservare.*
To keep a place, *tenere un luogo.*
To keep one's own, to keep one's own estate, *mantenere il suo.*
To keep to the cattle, *guardare il bestiame.*
To keep one's chamber, *tenersi in camera.*
To keep one's money, *conservare il suo danaro.*
To keep one's bed, *stare in letto.*
To keep [to observe] *tenere, mantenere, osservare.*
To keep one's promise, *tener patto, mantenere, attenere la promessa.*
To keep God's commandements, *osservare i comandamenti di Dio.*
To keep holy days *guardar le feste.*
To keep silence, *osservare il silenzio.*
To keep house, *tener casa.*
To keep shop, *tener bottega.*
To keep a good table, *tener buona tavola, trattarsi bene, far buona cera.*
To keep a good retinue, *mantenere un gran corteggio.*
To keep one's word, or to keep touch, *tener patto, mantenere, attenere la promessa.*
He did not keep his word to me, *egli non m'ha attenuto la promessa, egli m'ha mancato di parola.*
To keep in suspence, *tenere in forse, tener sospeso, fare stare in dubbio.*
Keep that way, *pigliate quella strada.*
To keep [to maintain] *mantenere, allevare.*
To keep a family, *mantenere una famiglia.*
To keep an army, *mantenere un esercito.*
To keep a child, *allevare un ragazzo.*

To keep a whore, *tener puttana, tener la puttana.*

To keep fair together, *vivere in buona intelligenza, in amistà.*

To keep from a thing [to forbear it] *astenersi di qualche cosa.*

To keep from wine, *astenersi dal vino.*

To keep one from the rain, *mettere alcuno a coperto della pioggia.*

To keep from ill company, *sfuggire, schivare la cattiva compagnia.*

He kept me in his house, *mi ritenne in casa sua.*

He has left her nothing that he could keep from her, *non le ha lasciato che quel che non le poteva levare.*

To keep a thing from one [to conceal it from him] *celare, nascondere che che si sia ad alcuno.*

He shall not keep me from it, *per lui non istarà che io non lo faccia.*

To keep a feast, *celebrare una festa.*

To keep one's birth day, *celebrare l' altrui natività.*

To keep [to continue, to live] *dimorare, stare.*

Keep where you are, *restate dove siete.*

To keep at home, or within doors, *dimorare, starsene a casa.*

To keep a thing from one, *tenere una cosa d'uno, riconoscerla da lui.*

To keep in the fields, *esser in campagna.*

To keep counsel, *tenere il segreto, esser segreto, non palesare il segreto.*

To keep company with one, *bazzicare, conversare, praticare, aver pratica con alcuno.*

To keep an eye upon a thing, *osservare qualche cosa.*

To keep a strict guard, *stare attento.*

To keep one doing, employed, or at work, *trovare, o dar dell' impiego ad uno, darli da lavorare, occuparlo, impiegarlo.*

To keep a thing to one's self, *tener segreto che che si sia.*

To keep Lent, *far quaresima, osservare la quaresima.*

To keep one short of money, *tener uno corto a danari.*

To keep one hungry, or dry, *far morire di fame o di sete.*

To keep watch and ward, *far la guardia.*

To keep to a diet, *fare dieta.*

To keep going, *avanzare, andar avanti.*

To keep a house in repair, *ristaurare una casa, fare tutte le ristaurazioni d'una casa.*

To keep good hours, *ritirarsi a casa a buon'ora.*

To keep bad hours, *ritirarsi a casa tardi.*

To keep one to a thing, *occupare, impiegare uno in qualche cosa.*

To keep one to his work, *far lavorare alcuno.*

To keep a thing, *addarsi, applicarsi a che che si sia.*

To keep to a bargain, *mantenere il contratto.*

To keep away [to keep out of the way] *allontanare, tener lontano.*

To keep out of the way, verb neut. *assentarsi, allontanarsi.*

To keep asunder, *separare, tener separato.*

To keep asunder, *separarsi, viver separatamente.*

To keep back, *tener indietro.*

To keep in, *reprimere, rintuzzare, ritenere, tener in freno, moderare.*

To keep in one's grief, *nascondere, celare il suo dolore.*

To keep one in a room, *tener uno rinchiuso in una camera.*

To keep one in, *tener altrui corto, legarlo corto.*

To keep in the house, verb neut. *tenersi in casa, non uscir di casa.*

To keep off, *ributtare, rispignere.*

Keep off your hands, *non toccate.*

To keep off, *non avanzare, tenersi in dietro, o in disparte.*

To keep out, *impedire d'entrare.*

To keep out, verb neut. *star di fuori, non entrare.*

To keep up, *mantenere, sostenere, conservare*, pres. *mantengo, sostengo*, pret. *mantenni, sostenni.*

To keep up, verb neut. *mantenersi, sostenersi, conservarsi.*

To keep down, *abbassare, umiliare, deprimere.*

To keep from [to restrain, to hinder] *ritenere, impedire*, pres. *ritengo, impedisco*, pret. *ritenni.*

To keep from [to conceal] *celare, nascondere, occultare*, pret. *nascosi.*

To keep from [to forbear] *astenersi, guardarsi*, pres. *astengo*, pret. *astenni.*

To keep from [to avoid] *sfuggire, evitare, scampare, schivare.*

To keep under, *tener corto, legar corto, tenere in soggezione, tener in freno.*

To keep the shore aboard [a sea expression] *andare terra terra, costeggiare.*

KE'EPER, s. *guardiano, custode*, s. m.

The keeper of a park, *il guardiano d'un parco.*

The keeper of a woman of pleasure, *drudo.*

The keeper of a prison, *carceriere.*

A company keeper, *uno scapestrato.*

KE'EPING, s. *guardia, custodia*, s. f.

To have a thing in one's keeping, *aver che che si sia nella sua cura, o custodia*

KE'EVER, s. [a brewing vessel] *tino*, s. m.

KEG, s. *sorta di barile.*

KELL, s. [cawl or membrane that covers the bowels] *rete*, s. f.

Kell, *sorta di minestra.*

KELP, s. *sale prodotto da piante marine calcinate.*

KE'LSON, s. *nome d' uno de' legni di sotto una nave.*

KE'LTER, ex. To be in kelter [to be ready] *essere in ordine, o in punto.*

To be in kelter [in good health] *star bene, essere in buona salute.*

To KEMP, *v.* To comb.

KEN, s. [sight] *vista*, s. f.

A thing within ken, *una cosa che è in vista, che può vedersi.*

This is quite out of my ken [beyond my capacity] *ciò è fuor della mia portata, o della mia capacità.*

To KEN [to spy at a distance] *scoprire, veder da lontano.*

To ken [to know] *conoscere, riconoscere*, pres. *conosco, riconosco*, pret. *conobbi, riconobbi.*

KE'NNEL, s. [in a street] *canale*, s. m.

Kennel [a hut for a dog] *canile*, s. m.

Kennel [a pack, or cry of hounds] *muta di cani.*

Kennel [the hole of a fox, or other beast] *tana di volpe o d'altro animale.*

To KE'NNEL *abitare; e dicesi propriamente delle bestie, e per dispregio d'un uomo.*

KE'NNETS, s. [a sort of coarse cloth] *spezie di panno grossolano.*

KEPT, adj. [from to keep] *tenuto*, *v.* To keep.

KE'RCHIEF, s. [a sort of linen dress formerly worn by women on their heads] *spezie di cuffia.*

KE'RCHIEFED, KE'RCHIEFT, } adj [dressed, hooded] *col capo acconcio; col capo coperto.*

KERB-STONE, s. [a stone laid round the brim of a wall] *quella pietra che è alla sponda d'un pozzo.*

KERF, s. [a notch in wood] *tacca*, s. f.

KERN, s. [a country bumkin] *un villano, un contadino, un rustico.*

Kern [an Irish foot soldier, lightly armed] *spezie di fantaccino Irlandese armato alla leggiera.*

Kern [vagrant fellow] *un vagabondo, un guidone.*

Kern, *sorta di mulino da macinar grano.*

To KERN [to corn, to grain] *granare, fare il granello, granire*, pres. *granisco.*

To kern, *indurire come fa il grano.*

To kern [to salt, to powder] *salare.*

KE'RNEL [any eatable part of a nut, or almond] *noce, mandorla, tutta quella parte della noce, o della mandorla che è buona a mangiare; nocciolo.*

The kernels of grapes, *vinacciuoli d'uva.*

Kernel of a pine, *pinnochio, seme della pina.*

The kernels of a pear, apple, &c. *granella di pere, mele, e simili.*

A kernel of the body [a fleshy and porous substance] *glandula*, s. f.

To KE'RNEL [to grain, as corn does] *granare, granire.*

KE'RNELLY, adj. *glanduloso.*

KE'STREL, s. [a kind of hawk] *gheppio*, s. m.

KE'RSEY, s. [coarse woollen cloth] *spezie di panno grossolano.*

KE'ST, *preterito del verbo* To cast, *non più in uso.*

KE'TCH, s. [a sort of ship] *tartana*, s. f.

KE'TTLE, s. *una caldaja.*

A large kettle, *un calderone.*

A

A ſmall kettle, *un calderotto, un calderino.*

Kettle drum, *timpano, taballo,* s. m.

KEW, s. [cue, humour] *umore, genio,* s. m.

To be in a good kew, *eſſer di buono umore.*

This wine is in a good kew, *queſto vino è nelle ſua beva.*

KEY, s. [an inſtrument to open a lock] *chiave,* s. f.

Key [in muſick, a certain tone whereunto every compoſition ought to be fitted] *chiave, figura muſicale, che inſegna a variare i tuoni.*

The key [or middle] ſtone of an arch, *la chiave d' una volta.*

Calais is one of the keys of France, *Calais è una delle chiavi della Francia.*

The keys of organs or virginals, *taſtiera d'organo, o di gravicembalo.*

Key [ſtraight] *ſtretto,* s. m.

A key [or pin to run into the eye of another pin] *chiavello,* s. m. *chiavetta,* s. f.

Key-hole, *il buco della chiave.*

KIBE, s. [a chilblain with inflammation upon the heels] *pedignone,* s. m. *male che viene ne' calcagni per ſoverchio freddo.*

Kibe-heels [in horſes] *ſorta di malattia ne' cavalli, per lo più ne' piedi.*

KI'BRIET, s. [a chymical term; ſulphur] *zolfo,* s. m.

KI'BSEY, s. [a kind of wicker baſket] *paniere di vinchi.*

KICK, s. calcio, s. m. *percoſſa che ſi da col piede.*

To give one a kick, *dare un calcio ad uno.*

To KICK [to ſtrike with the foot] *calcitrare, trar de' calci, dar de' calci.*

A horſe that kicks, *un cavallo càlcitroſo, che tira calci.*

To kick at or againſt a thing, *calcitrare contro qualche coſa.*

To kick one out of the houſe, *ſcacciare alcuno di caſa a calci.*

To kick up one's heels, *inalberarſi.*

To kick up one's heels [to die] *tirar le calze, morire.*

KI'CKED, or KICKT, adj. *calcitrato,* v. To kick.

KI'CKSHAW, s. [French ragoo] *manicaretto alla Franceſe.*

Kickſhaws [ſlight buſineſs] *bagattelle, baje, cianciafruſcole.*

KI'CKSEY-WICKSEY, s. *voce inventata per mettere in ridicolo, e per moſtrar un pò di ſdegno a una moglie.*

KID, s. [young goat] *capretto,* s. m. *figliuolo della capra.*

Kid-leather, *pelle di capretto.*

To KID [to bring forth kids] *figliare, parlando d' una capra.*

KIDDER, s. *un che compra biade per farle rincarare.*

To KI'DNAP [to ſteal away children] *trafugare figliuoli.*

KI'DNAPPER, s. [a perſon who makes it his buſineſs to decoy children or young perſons to ſend them to the Engliſh plantations in America] *colui che fa il meſtiere di trafugare figliuoli per mandarli in America.*

KI'DNEY, s. *arnione,* s. m.

Kidney, *per iſcherzo, razza, progenie.*

He knows my kidney, *egli ſa il mio parentado.*

KI'DNEY-BEANS [French beans] *fagiuoli,* s. m.

KI'DNEYWETCH } s. *nomi di piante.*
KI'DNEYWORT }

KI'LDERKIN, s. [a liquid meaſure] *un mezzo barile, un barlotto.*

To KILL [to ſlay] *ammazzare, uccidere.* pret. *uccisi.*

To kill one's ſelf [to take too much pains] *ammazzarſi, affaticarſi troppo.*

To kill, *privare delle facoltà vegetative; come chi direbbe, il troppo freddo uccide o fa morire le piante.*

A kill-cow [a braggadochio] *un tagliacantoni, un mangiaferrò, uno ſgherro.*

KI'LLED, adj. *ammazzato, ucciſo.*

KI'LLER, s. *ammazzatore, ucciſore, omicida,* s. m.

KI'LLING, s. *l' ammazzare, ucciſione.*

Killing, adj. *che ammazza, mortale, che cauſa la morte.*

KI'LLOW, s. *ſorta di terra di color bruno o turchinoſcuro.*

KILN, s. [a furnace to burn chalk for making lime] *fornace,* s. f. *edificio murato nel quale ſi cuoce la calcina, ed altre coſe ancora.*

Kiln-cloth [hair-cloth] *cilicio,* s. m.

To KI'LNDRY, *ſeccare al fuoco d' una fornace.*

KILT for KILLED, adj. *ammazzato, morto, ucciſo.*

KI'MBO, adj. [crooked, bent, arched] *curvo, incurvato, piegato, arcato.*

KIN, adj. [related] *parente, congiunto di parentado.*

Next to kin, *parente ſtretto.*

Are you any kin to him? *ſiete voi ſuo parente?*

He is no kin to me, *egli non è mio parente.*

Kin [like] *ſimile, che ha qualche ſimilitudine, o ſomiglianza.*

KIND, adj. [benevolent, good, courteous] *corteſe, affabile, benigno, buono, favorevole, civile, umano, grazioſo, benevolo.*

She is very kind to me, *ella mi è molto corteſe, ella mi tratta con gran benignità.*

A kind reception, *benigna accoglienza.*

Will you be ſo kind as to come to ſee me? *volete compiacervi di venire a vedermi?*

Be ſo kind as to do it for me, *mi favoriſca, o favoritemi di farlo per me.*

KIND, s. [ſort] *ſorta, ſpezie, qualità,* s. f *genere,* s. m.

Fruits of all kinds, *frutti di tutte le ſorte.*

A thing admirable in its kind, *una coſa ammirabile nel ſuo genere.*

To receive the ſacrament in both kinds, *ricevere il ſagramento nelle due ſpezie.*

Kind [or ſex] *ſeſſo.*

The female kind, *il ſeſſo femminino.*

Kind [manner] *ſorta, maniera,* s. f. *modo,* s. m.

I took him to be another kind of man, *lo credevo un altro uomo.*

I ſuppoſe you know by this time what kind of woman ſhe is, *io mi ſuppongo che voi ſapete adeſſo che donna ella ſi ſia.*

What kind of life is that of your's? *che vita è mai queſta che voi menate?*

To grow out of kind [to degenerate] *tralignare, degenerare.*

KI'NDER [the comparative of kind] *più dolce, più umano,* v. Kind, adj.

Kinder, s. [or company of cats] *uno ſtuolo di gatti.*

KI'NDEST [the ſuperlative of kind] *il più corteſe, il più umano,* v. Kind, adj.

To KI'NDLE [to ſet on fire] *accendere.* pret. *acceſi.*

To kindle [to take fire] *accenderſi.*

To kindle [to bring forth young] *figliare.*

KI'NDLED, adj. *acceſo.*

KI'NDLER, s. [one that lights, one who inflames] *uno che alluma, che accende, che infiamma.*

KI'NDLING, s. *accendimento,* s. m. *l' accendere.*

KI'NDLY, adj. [lovingly, courteouſly] *amorevolmente, corteſemente, umanamente, benevolmente, civilmente, benignamente, affabilmente.*

To take a thing kindly [or in good part] *prendere che che ſi ſia in buona parte, prendere in grado, aggradire.* preſ. *aggradiſco.*

I thank you kindly, *vi ringrazio di buon cuore.*

KI'NDNESS, s. [love, affection] *amore, affetto,* s. m. *umanità, corteſia, affabilità, benignità, bontà,* s. f.

Kindneſs, [courteſy, favour] *favore, piacere, ſervizio,* s. m. *grazia,* s. f.

Do me the kindneſs, *fatemi il favore, o la grazia.*

KI'NDRED, s. [perſons of the ſame blood or deſcent] *parenti, congiunti.*

He has many good kindred, *egli ha molti buoni parenti*

KINE, s. [all ſorts of cows] *vacche.*

KING, s. [a ſovereign Prince] *Re.*

The King of England, *il Re d' Inghilterra.*

The King at cheſs or cards, *il Re al giuoco degli ſcacchi o delle carte.*

A King at draughts, *dama.*

The King's evil, *ſcrofola,* s. f.

King's fiſher [a ſort of ſea fowl] *alcione,* s. m. *ſorta d'uccello aquatico.*

King-like, *da Re, realmente, regalmente.*

To King, ex. To king a man at draughts, *damare una pedina.*

KI'NGDOM, s. [one or more countries ſubject to a King] *regno,* s. m.

The kingdom of England, *il regno d' Inghilterra.*

KI'NGLY, adj. *reale, di re, monarchico.*

KI'NSMAN, s. *parente, congiunto.*

KI'NSWOMAN, s. *parente, congiunta.*

KI'NTAL, s. [a hundred pound weight] *cantaro,* s. m.

KIRK, s. [church] *voce Scozzeſe per church, chieſa,* s. f. *e' voce ſovente di ſcherno quando uſata degl' Ingleſi.*

KIRTLE, s. [a sort of short jacket] *sorta di vestimento antico.*

KISS, s. *bacio,* s. m.

Give me a kiss, *datemi un bacio.*

A treacherous kiss, *un bacio di Giuda.*

To KISS, verb. act. *baciare.*

To kiss one another, *baciarsi.*

To kiss again, *ribaciare.*

KI'SSED, adj. *baciato.*

KI'SSER, s. *quello, o quella che bacia.*

KI'SSING, s. *baciare,* s. m. *il baciare.*

A kissing [or kiss] *un bacio.*

Kissing, adj. ex. A kissing man or woman, *un uomo, o una donna che ama baciare.*

Kissing-crust, *orliccio di pane.*

KIT, s. [pocket violin] *un violino da portar in tasca.*

Kit [pail] *secchia.*

One that has neither kit nor kin, *uno che non ha parenti.*

He is neither kit nor kin to me, *egli non è mio parente.*

Kit keys [the fruit of the ash-tree] *il frutto del frassino.*

KI'TCHEN, s. [a room where meat is dress'd] *cucina,* s. f. *luogo dove la vivanda si cuoce.*

Kitchen tackling, *ordigni di cucina.*

Kitchen stuff, *grascio di cucina.*

A kitchen maid, or a kitchen wench, *una serva da cucina.*

A kitchen boy, *guattero di cucina.*

Kitchen garden, *un orto.*

KITE, s. [a bird of prey] *nibbio,* s. m. *uccello di rapina.*

A kite [or paper kite] *una cometa.*

KITESFOOT, s. *sorta di pianta.*

KI'TLING, s. [or little cat] *un gattuccio, un gattino, una mucina, un mucino.*

To KI'TTEN, or to KITTLE [to bring forth kittens] *figliare, parlando d' una gatta.*

KI'TTEN, s. [a little cat] *un gattino, un gattucio.*

A young kitten, *una mucina, un mucino.*

To KLICK [to make a small sharp noise] *far un picciolo ma acuto romore, come quando qualcosa di duro casca o batte su qualche cosa dura.*

To KNAB, ex. To knab upon grass, *pascer l' erba; mordere.*

KNACK, s. [toy] *bagattella.*

Knack [skill, faculty] *arte, destrezza, abilità.*

He has got a peculiar knack that way, *egli ha una destrezza particolare in ciò.*

To KNACK [or crack] *rompere.*

To knack a nut, *rompere una noce.*

To Knack with one's fingers, *fare scoppiare le dita.*

KNA'CKER, s. *un che fa lavori minuti.*

Knacker [a rope-maker] *un cordajo, un che fa corde.*

KNAG, s. [or knot in wood] *nodo d' albero, nocchio.*

KNA'GGY, adj. [full of knots] *nodoroso, noderoso, nodoso, nocchiuto.*

KNAP, s. [or top] *cima, sommità,* s. f.

The knap of a hill, *la cima d'una montagna.*

To KNAP [to snap] *strappare.*

To knap, *scoppiare, scoppiettare, crocchiare, cricchiolare.*

To knap at [or pick at] *prendere, acchiappare, scroccare.*

To knap [among hunters, to feed upon the tops of leaves, shrubs, &c.] *mangiar le punte delle foglie e d' ogni verde cosa.*

To KNA'PPLE [to gnaw off] *rodere.* pret. *rosi.*

To knapple, *far crocchiare rompendo.*

KNA'PSACK, s. *bisacchia che i soldati portano col loro pane e arnesi dentrovi.*

KNA'PWEED, s. *sorta di pianta.*

KNARE, s. *nocchio, nodo duro d'un albero.*

KNAVE, s. [a deceitful fellow, a cheat] *un furbo, un guidone, un mariuolo, un furfante, un ribaldo.*

An arrant knave, *un furbo in chermisi.*

Knave [at cards] *il fante, al giuoco delle carte.*

Knave, *anticamente significava un figlio maschio, e anche un servo.*

KNA'VERY, s. *furfanteria, furberia, malvagità, cattività, ribalderia,* s. f.

KNA'VISH, adj. *cattivo, fello, fellonesco, furbesco, reo, ribaldo, malvagio, tristo.*

A knavish trick, *un tiro di furfante, una furfanteria.*

KNA'VISHLY, adv. *da furbo, da furfante, fellonescamente, malvagiamente.*

KNA'VISHNESS, s. [knavery] *furfanteria, furberia, malvagità,* s. f.

To KNEAD [to work meal into dough] *impastare, intridere.* pret. *intrisi.*

To knead the dough, *intridere la pasta.*

KNE'ADED, adj. *intriso, impastato.*

KNE'ADING, s. *l'intridere.*

A kneading trough, *madia,* s. f.

KNEE, s. [the upper part of the joint-ture of the leg and thigh] *ginocchio,* s. m. plur. *ginocchia,* s. f.

To fall upon one's knees, *inginocchiarsi, mettersi inginocchioni.*

Knee-holm, *pugnitopo,* s. m.

The knee-pan, *la padella del ginocchio.*

To bow the knee, *genuflettersi, inginocchiarsi.*

A bowing the knee, *genuflessione,* s. f.

The knees [or ribs] of a ship, *le coste d'un vascello.*

Armour for the knees, *ginocchiello,* s. m. *arme difensiva del ginocchio.*

Knee-grass, s. *gramigna,* s. f.

To KNEEL [to lay down upon one's knees] *inginocchiarsi, mettersi inginocchioni.*

KNE'ELING, adv. *inginocchioni.*

I found him kneeling, *lo trovai inginocchioni.*

KNEL, s. [a passing bell; the ringing of a bell at the departure of a dying person] *campana a mortorio.*

KNEW, *preterito del verbo* To know.

KNIE, s. [hough] *ramo,* s. m.

KNIFE, s. *coltello,* s. m.

A table knife, *coltello da tavola.*

A pruning knife, *roncone, falcetto,* s. m.

A pen-knife, *un temperino.*

A shoemaker's paring knife, *coltello da calzolajo.*

KNIGHT, s. [a degree of honour] *cavaliere.*

A knight of the garter, *un cavaliere della giartiera.*

Knight baronet, *cavaliere baronetto.*

A knight banneret, *cavaliere dello stendardo.*

Knight of the Bath, *cavaliere del Bagno.*

Knights of the Temple, or Templars, *cavalieri Templari, Tempieri.*

A knight errant, *un cavaliere errante.*

Knight-errantry, s. *l' officio o mestiere degli antichi cavalieri erranti; cavalleria.*

A knight of the round table, *cavaliere della tavola rotonda.*

Knight of the shire, *un rappresentante in parlamento d' una provincia.*

KNI'GHTLY, adv. *signorilmente, cavallerescamente.*

A knight of the post [a false hired witness] *un testimonio falso.*

To KNIGHT [to dub a knight] *fare, o creare cavaliere.*

KNI'GHTED, adj. *fatto, o creato cavaliere.*

KNI'GHTHOOD, s. *cavalleria,* s. f. *grado e dignità di cavaliere.*

KNIT, s. *lendine,* s. f. *uovo di pidocchio.*

Full of knits, *lendinoso.*

Knit, adj. [or tied] *nodato, legato, attaccato.*

Knit-stockings, *calzetti fatti all' aguchia.*

To KNIT [to tie] *legare, annodare, legar con nodo, unire.*

To knit stockings, *lavorare calzette all' ago.*

To knit the brows, *increspar la fronte.*

KNI'TTER, s. *quello, o quella che lavora calzette all' ago.*

KNITTINGNE'EDLE, s. *ago da far calzette.*

KNI'TTLE, s. *cordicella, o cordoncino d' una borsa.*

KNOB, s. [tuft] *fiocco,* s. m.

A knob of wood, *un nodo, un nocchio, un gruppo che è nel legno.*

To KNOB [to grow into knobs] *annodarsi, formarsi in nodi, o nocchi.*

KNO'BBY, adj. [knobbed] *noderoso, nodoso, e nocchieroso, nocchieruto, nocchiuto.*

KNOCK, s. *un colpo.*

A good knock on the pate, *un gran colpo sulla testa.*

Knock [knocking at the door] *picchio, il picchiare alla porta.*

To KNOCK [to hit, to strike upon] *battere, picchiare.*

To knock at the door, *picchiare alla porta.*

To knock one's head against a wall, *batter or dar la testa contra un muro.*

To knock one about the pate, *percuoter sulla testa.*

To knock one down, *picchiare alcuno e stramazzarlo per terra.*
To knock in, *ficcare, cacciar dentro per forza.*
To knock out, *cacciar fuori per forza.*
To knock off, *rompere, far saltare in aria.*
KNO'CKED, adj. *percosso, picchiato, v.* To knock.
KNO'CKER, s. *martello di porta.*
KNO'CKING, s. *picchio, il picchiare.*
Knocking [noise] *strepito, romore, fracasso.*
KNOLL, s. [the top of a hill] *la cima d'un monte.*
To KNOLL, *suonar la campana de' morti.*
KNOP, *v.* Knap.
A knop of flower, *un bottone di fiore.*
KNOT, s. *nodo,* s. m.
To make or tie a knot, *fare un nodo.*
A running knot, *nodo scorsojo.*
A knot [or difficulty] *nodo, gruppo, e groppo,* s. m. *difficoltà,* s. f.
The knots of a tree, *i nodi, i nocchi d' un albero.*
A knot, or leaf knot, *bottone di fiore.*
Knot [company, crew] *banda, stormo, stuolo, cricca, criocca, brigata.*
Knot-grass [a plant] *sanguinaria,* s. f.
To KNOT [to grow into knots] *annodarsi, formarsi in nodi.*
To knot, *intrigare, imbrogliare.*
To knot [to bud as trees do] *germogliare; gemmare.*
KNO'TTED, adj. *annodato, aggroppato.*
KNO'TTINESS, s. *nodosità,* s. f.
KNO'TTY, adj. *nodoso, noderoso, nocchieruto, nocchiuto.*
To KNOW [to be acquainted with] *sapere, conoscere,* pres. *so.* pret. *seppi, conobbi.*
To know what one says, *saper quel che si dice.*
I know nothing of it, *non ne so niente.*
I know not what to do, *non so che fare.*
To let one know, *far sapere, avvisare, dar avviso, partecipare.*
Let me know first, *ditemi prima.*
To know a man, *conoscere un uomo.*
To know one by sight, *conoscere alcuno di vista.*
I shall make him know who I am, *gli farò vedere chi io mi sia, chi io sono.*
To know one's self, *conoscersi.*
I know better things, *non sono tanto sciocco.*
I have more than I know what to do withal, *ne ho più che non mi bisogna.*
He knows not what is good and what is bad, *egli non sa discernere il buono dal cattivo.*
You cannot but know it, *voi non potete ignorarlo.*
KNO'WABLE, adj. *che si può sapere.*
KNO'WER, s. *sapiente; conoscitore.*
KNO'WING, s. *il sapere.*
A thing worth knowing, *una cosa degna di sapersi, che merita che si sappia.*
Knowing, adj. *saputo, sapiente, intelligente, saccente, dotto.*
KNO'WINGLY, adv. [on purpose] *a posta, a bello studio, a posta fatta, a caso pensato; scientemente.*
To KNOWL [to ring a bell] *sonare la campana a mortorio.*
KNO'WLEDGE, s. *scienza, dottrina, conoscenza, saputa, notizia,* s. f. *sapere,* s. m.
The knowledge of things to come, *la conoscenza delle cose future.*
He has some knowledge of the Italian tongue, *egli ha qualche conoscenza o tintura della lingua Italiana.*
A man of great knowledge, *un uomo di gran sapere, un uomo molto dotto, o scienziato.*
As soon as that came to my knowledge, *subito che ciò mi venne a notizia.*
He did it without my knowledge, *lo fece senza la mai saputa.*
No body is gone in to my knowledge, *nessuno è entrato per quel che ne so.*
How came you to the knowledge of it? *come l' avete saputo?*
To have a carnal knowledge of a woman, *conoscere carnalmente una donna.*
KNOWN, adj. *conosciuto, saputo.*
He is known by every body, *egli è conosciuto da ognuno.*
A thing well known, *una cosa cognita, palese, che ognuno sa.*
It is well known, *ciascheduno sa.*
A thing easy to be known, *una cosa facile a sapere.*
To make a thing known, *far sapere una cosa, pubblicarla, manifestarla.*
The like was never known, *non si vide mai il simile.*
To KNU'BBLE [to beat with the fist] *batter con pugna, schiaffeggiare.*
I shall knubble your chops, *ti darò degli schiaffi.*
KNU'CKLE, s. [knot, or joint] *nodo, congiuntura delle dita; le nocca, plur.*
The knuckles of the fingers, *le nocca delle dita.*
The knuckle of a leg of veal, *garetto di vitella.*
Knuckle, s. *nodo o nocchio d' una pianta.*
To KNU'CKLE, *sottomettersi.*
KNU'CKLED, adj. *nocchiute, nocchieruto.*
KNUR } s. [knot in wood] *nodo,*
KNURLE } *nocchio.*
KNU'RLED, adj. *nodoso, nocchiuto.*
KO'NED, part. [knew] *seppe, conobbe.* Obs.
To KYD, v. n. *sapere, conoscere.* Obs.

L.

L, *Undecima lettera dell' alfabeto Inglese. Ha lo stesso suono che in Italiano.*
LA, interj. [see, look, behold] *là, ecco, guarda, ve', vendi, mira.*
LA'BEL, s. [a narrow slip of parchment fastened to deeeds or writings] *striscia di cartapecora che pende da uno strumento, o scrittura.*
Label [a term in heraldry, lines which hang down from the file in the top of an escutcheon, and make a distinction for an elder brother] *fascia,* s. f.
LA'BIAL, adj. ex. [The labial letters] *le lettere labiali, che si pronunciano colle labbra.*
LABIODE'NTAL, adj. *formato o pronun-*

nunciato colle labbra e co' denti a un tratto.

LA'BOR, *v.* Labour.

LA'BORANT, s. *un chimista, un chimico.* Obs.

LA'BORATORY, s. [a chymist's work-house] *fonderia,* s. f. *il luogo dove i chimici fanno i loro lavori.*

LABO'RIOUS, adj. [that takes pains] *laborioso, che s'affatica molto, che lavora molto, industrioso.*

Laborious [painful, difficult] *laborioso, faticoso, difficile a farsi.*

LABO'RIOUSLY, adv. *laboriosamente, con fatica.*

LABO'RIOUSNESS, s. [pains, difficulty] *fatica,* s. f.

LA'BOUR, s. [pains] *fatica, opera, pena,* s. f. *travaglio,* s. m.

To enjoy the fruits of one's labour, *godere de' frutti delle sue fatiche.*

You will lose your labour, *voi perderete la vostra opera.*

He lives upon his labour, *vive del suo travaglio.*

A woman's labour, *doglie, dolori del parto.*

To be in labour, *aver le doglie.*

To LA'BOUR [to take pains, and to endeavour earnestly] *lavorare, operare, affaticarsi, faticare.*

To labour in vain, *lavorare in vano.*

To labour might and main, *lavorare a mazza stanca, fare ogni sforzo.*

To labour [sea term, a ship is said to labour, when she is very unsteady, and rolls and tumbles] *barcollare, traballare, ondeggiare.*

To labour under great difficulties, *aver molte difficoltà a sormontare.*

To labour for an office, *cercare un ufficio o una carica, far diligenza per ottenere una carica.*

To labour one [to practice upon him] *guadagnare, corrompere, sedurre alcuno.*

LA'BOURED, adj. *lavorato, operato, faticato.*

LA'BOURER, s. [one that lives by hand labour] *un operajo, un lavoratore, un lavorante.*

LA'BOURING, s. *il lavorare, lavoro, stento, sforzo, fatica.*

Labouring, adj. ex. [A labouring beast] *una bestia da soma, di carico, di traino, di vettura*

LA'BOURSOME, adj. [toilsome, troublesome] *faticoso, penoso, difficile.*

LABRA, s. [the lips] *le labbra.*

LA'BYRINTH, s. [maze] *laberinto,* s. m. *luogo pien di vie, tanto dubbie, e tanto intrigate, che chi vi entra non trova modo a uscirne.*

To be in a labyrinth of trouble, *esser in un gran laberinto di guai.*

LAC, s. [a sort of red gum] *lacca,* s. f. *spezie di gomma rossa.*

LACE, s. *merletto,* s. m. *trina,* s. f.

Gold or silver lace, *merletto d'oro, o d'argento.*

A lace [to lace a suit] *gallone, passamano.*

A twisted lace, *cordellina, cordella,* s. f.

A lace [to lace a woman's stays with] *stringa.*

Bone lace, *merletto.*

Tape lace, *nastro di refe.*

A hair lace, *intrecciatojo,* s. m.

A necklace, *collana,* s. f. *monile,* s. m.

To LACE [to set off with lace] *gallonare, trinare, guarnire di merletto, o di gallone.*

To lace a livery suit, *gallonare una livrea.*

To lace a petticoat with gold lace, *guarnire una gonna con gallone d'oro.*

To lace a coat with gold lace, *gallonare un vestito.*

To lace [to tie] *legare, attaccare, allacciare.*

To lace a woman's stays, *allacciare un busto.*

To lace coffee, *mettere del zucchero in una tazza di caffè.*

To lace one, to lace his coat [to lash him] *spianar le costure ad uno, bastonarlo, malmenarlo, dirne un mondo di male.*

LACED, adj. *gallonato, merlettato, trinato.*

LACED-MUTTON, s. *una puttana, una bagascia. E' voce antica.*

LA'CEMAN, s. *uno che traffica, o uno che fabbrica merletti, o galloni.*

LA'CERABLE, adj. *lacerabile, che può esser lacero o lacerato, che può essere stracciato a pezzi.*

To LA'CERATE [to tear, or pull to pieces] *lacerare, sbranare, stracciare.*

LACERA'TION, s. *lacerazione,* s. f. *laceramento,* s. m.

LA'CHRYMABLE, adj. [to be lamented, or wept for] *lagrimabile, lagrimevole.*

LA'CHRYMAL, adj. *lagrimale.*

A lachrymal fistula, *una fistola lagrimale.*

LACK, s. [want] *mancanza, falta, diffalta,* s. f. *bisogno, mancamento,* s. m.

Lack of money, *mancanza di danari.*

To LACK [to want] *faltare, mancare, aver bisogno abbisognare.*

What d'ye lack? *che vi manca, che v'abbisogna?*

I lack to see him, *mi par mill' anni di vederlo, ho gran desiderio, di vederlo.*

Lack-a-day, interj. *capperi, cappita.*

LA'CKBRAIN, s. *uno sciocco, un pazzerello; uno che ha bisogno d'aver più cervello.*

LA'CKER, s. a [sort of varnish] *sorta di vernice tra giallo e oro.*

A lacker-hat [without stiffening] *cappello senza colla.*

To LA'CKER, *inverniciare, dar la vernice.*

LA'CKEY, s. [footman, footboy] *lacchè,* s. m.

To LACKEY after one, *seguitare alcuno come suo lacchè.*

LACKLI'NEN, adj. *che non ha neppure una camicia da mutarsi.*

LACKLU'STRE, adj. *che non ha splendore, luce, o chiarezza.*

LACO'NICK, adj. [concise, brief] *laconico, breve, compendioso.*

LA'CONISM, s. [a brief, concise way of speaking] *laconismo, maniera di parlare breve e compendiosa.*

LA'CTARY, } adj. [milky] *latteo.*
LA'CTEAL,

Lacteal veins, *vene lattee.*

LACTI'FICAL, adj. [that breeds milk] *lattifero, che genere del latte.*

LAD, s. [boy] *un giovanetto, un garzone, un ragazzo.*

LA'DDER, s. [a machine for getting up to high places] *scala,* s. f. *strumento per salire.*

The round of a ladder, *staglione, grado.*

To LADE [to load] *caricare.*

To lade a ship, *caricare un vascello.*

LA'DEN, adj. *caricato, carico.*

Laden with honours and rewards, *carico d'onori, e di regali.*

LA'DING, s. *il caricare, caricamento.*

Lading [cargo] *carico.*

A bill of lading, *una polizza di carico.*

LA'DLE, s. [a kitchen utensil] *mestola,* s. f. *romajuolo,* s. m.

Ladle [in gunnery, a long staff with a hollow plate at the end of it, which will hold as much as is the due charge of the piece it belongs to] *romajuolo da cannone.*

LA'DY, s. [a person of quality's wife or daughter] *dama, signora.*

My lady, *madama, signora.*

The gentleman and his lady, *il signore con la signora sua.*

Our Lady, *la Madonna.*

Lady, *preso assolutamente vale una donna illustre, una donna eminente.*

LADY-BE'DSTRAW, s. *sorta di pianta.*

LADY-BIRD, } s. *nome d'un picciolo insetto.*
LADY-COW,
LADY-FLY,

LADY-DAY, *la festa della Madonna, l'Annunziazione.*

LADY-LIKE, adj. *donnesco, molle, dolce, gentile, elegante, delicato.*

LADY-MANTLE, s. *nome di pianta.*

LA'DYSHIP, s. *qualità di dama.*

When your ladyship pleases, *quando piacerà a vostra eccellenza.*

LADY'S-SLIPPER, } s. *nomi di fiori.*
LADY'S SMOCK,

LAG, s. [a school word for last] *ultimo.*

The lag of a form, *l' ultimo d'una classe.*

Lag, s. *l'ultima classe in una scuola.*

Lag, adj. *ultimo; che vien dietro, che vien dopo.*

Lag, *pigro, tardo, negligente.*

Lag, *differito, ritardato.*

To LAG [to stay behind] *restare indietro.*

To lag, *muoversi pigramente, poltroneggiare.*

LA'GGER, s. [one that lags] *quello che resta indietro, che sta a bada.*

LA'GAN, } s. [such goods which the seaman cast overboard in danger of shipwreck] *getto, mercanzie che si gettano in mare in tempo di qualche tempesta.*
LA'GON,

LA'ICK, adj. [or secular] *laico, secolare.*

LAID, *pret. particip. del verbo* To lay.

A design well laid, *un disegno ben concertato.*

LAIN, *preterito e part. del verbo* To lay.

I have lain in bed all this morning, *sono stato in letto tutta questa mattina.*

LAIR, s. [the place where deer harbour by day] *ricettatolo di cervo nel giorno.*

LAIRD, s. *il signore d'un feudo. Vocabolo Scozzese.*

LAITY, s. [or the people, as distinguished from the clergy] *i laici, i secolari.*

LAKE, s. [a place full of water, encompassed with dry land] *lago,* s. m.

Lake [lacca] *lacca.*

To LAM [to beat] *bastonare, tartassare, malmenare, battere.*

LAMB, s. [a sheep under a year old] *agnello.*

Lamb, or lamb's flesh, *agnello, carne d'agnello.*

LA'MBENT, adj. ex. A lambent medicine, *sorta di medicamento che si lambisce.*

LA'MBKIN, s. [a young, or little lamb] *un agnelletto, un agnellino.*

LAME, adj. [maimed in the members] *stroppiato, zoppo, storpiato*

Lame of one leg, *stroppiato d'una gamba.*

Lame of one hand, *monco.*

A man lame of one hand, *un moncherino.*

To go lame, *zoppicare, andar zoppo.*

Lame [imperfect, faulty] *storpiato, imperfetto, difettoso, zoppo.*

A lame expression, *un espressione storpiata.*

A lame account, *un ragguaglio imperfetto.*

A lame comparison, *una comparazione zoppa.*

To LAME [to make lame] *stroppiare, e storpiare.*

LAMED, adj, *stroppiato, e storpiato.*

LA'MELY, adv. [against one's will, or one's grain] *mal volentieri, contro voglia.*

Lamely [imperfectly] *imperfettamente, d' una maniera imperfetta.*

LA'MENESS, s. *storpio,* s. m. *storpiatura, stroppiatura,* s. f.

To LAME'NT [to mourn, or bewail] *lamentare, deplorare, piagnere, compiangere.* pret. *piansi, compiansi.*

LAME'NT, s. [lamentation] *lamento, pianto,* s. m. *lamentazione, doglienza,* s. f.

LA'MENTABLE, adj. [to be lamented, doleful] *lamentabile, lamentevole, deplorabile, doloroso, compassionevole, degno di compassione, lagrimevole.*

LA'MENTABLY, adv. *lamentabilmente, lamentevolmente, con lamentanze.*

LAMENTA'TION, s. [complaint] *lamentazione, lamentanza,* s. f. *lamento, pianto,* s. m.

LAME'NTED, adj. *lamentato, pianto, compianto, deplorato, plorato.*

LAME'NTER, s. *un che deplora, che compiange.*

LA'MENTINE, s. *sorta di pesce di mare molto grande.*

LA'MIERS, s. [a sort of ship ropes] *corde da amarrare lo sperone.*

LA'MINA, s. [a plate, or thin piece of metal] *lama, lamina, piastra di metallo.*

LA'MMAS } s. [the first day of
LAMMAS-DAY } August] *il primo giorno d' Agosto.*

A latter lammas [never] *mai.*

LAMP, s. *lampana, lampada, e lampade,* s. f.

A lamp maker, *un lampanajo.*

LA'MPASS, s. [a disease in horses, when the throat is swelled] *lampasco,* s. m. *malattia che viene nella gola del cavallo.*

LA'MPERN, s. [a little lamprey] *lampredotto,* s. m. *lampreda piccola.*

LA'MPERS, *v.* Lampass.

LAMPO'ON, s. [a drolling poem or pamphlet, in which some person is treated with abusive language] *satira, versi satirici.*

To LAMPO'ON one [to ridicule him in a lampoon] *satireggiare alcuno, fare una satira contro a qualcheduno.*

LAMPO'ONED, adj. *satireggiato.*

LA'MPREY, s. [a kind of fish] *lampreda,* s. f.

LA'MPRIL, s. [lamper] *lampredotto,* s. m.

LANCE, s. [a kind of weapon] *lancia,* s. f.

To couch the lance, *arrestar la lancia.*

Lance, or lance-man, or lancier [a soldier armed with a lance] *lancia, cavaliero armato di lancia.*

To LANCE [to cut with a lancet] *aprire con lancetta, dar un colpo di lancetta.*

LANCEPESA'DO, s. [one who has command of ten soldiers, an under corporal] *lancia spezzata.*

LA'NCET, s. [a surgeon's instrument to let blood] *lancetta.* s. f.

To LANCH [to put a ship or boat afloat out of a dock] *varare, tirar di terra in acqua la nave. E' meglio scrivere* launch, *v.* To launch.

To lanch a ship, *varare un vascello.*

To lanch, verb. neut. *lanciarsi, gettarsi con impeto, scagliarsi, avventarsi.*

To lanch into the water, *lanciarsi nell' acqua.*

To lanch out into the recital or history of something, *entrare nella narrativa, intraprendere istoria di che che si sia.*

LA'NCHED, adj. *varato.*

LAND, s. [ground, in opposition to water] *terra,* s. f.

To travel by land, *viaggiare per terra.*

Land [country] *terra, provincia, paese, regione.*

A fruitful land, *una terra, un paese fertile.*

Land [ground] *terra, terreno, suolo.*

Arable land, *terra arabile.*

Land [possession] *terra, podere, possessione.*

To buy land, *comprar delle terre.*

Land of inheritance, *patrimonio.*

Land forces, or land men, *forze terrestri.*

A land captain, *capitano che serve per terra.*

Land flood, *inondazione.*

Land mark, *limite.*

Land cape, *un capo, un promontorio.*

Land tax, *taglia, imposizione, gravezza che si pone sopra le terre e case.*

Land loper [a vagabond] *un vagabondo, un perdigiorno.*

A land steward, *un gastaldo.*

Lay-land, *maggese, maggiatica, campo lasciato sodo per seminarlo l'anno vegnente.*

To LAND [to come or set on land from on board of a ship, or boat] *sbarcare, pigliare o mettere a terra, approdare.*

LA'NDED, adj. *sbarcato, pigliato e messo a terra, approdato.*

A landed man [a man rich in land] *un uomo ricco in terre, in possessioni, in poderi.*

LA'NDING, s. *sbarco,* s. m. *lo sbarcare.*

LA'NDLADY, s. *la propietaria d' un fondo di terra, o d'una casa.*

LA'NDLORD, s. [the owner or proprietor of lands or tenements] *proprietario di terre o poderi, padron di casa.*

Landlord [host] *oste.*

LA'NDRESS, s. [a washer-woman] *lavandaja,* s. f.

LA'NDRY, s. [a place where linen is washed] *il luogo dove si lava la biancheria.*

LA'NDSCAPE, } s. [a description of
LA'NDSKIP, } the land, by hills, valleys, woods, rivers, &c. in a mixt picture, or drawing] *paesaggio, paese in pittura.*

LA'NDWARDS, adv. *verso terra.*

LANE, s. [a narrow street or passage] *vico, chiasso,* s. f. *strada stretta.*

A lane [a way hedged about] *viottola,* s. f. *viottolo,* s. m.

A lane [or defile] *sfilata.*

Soldiers making a lane, *soldati ordinati in ispalliera.*

LA'NGNEL-SHOT, s. [a sort of shot which runs loose, with a shackle or joint in the middle] *palla incatenata.*

LA'NGUAGE, s. [tongue, or speech] *lingua, idioma, favella, linguaggio.*

The English language, *il linguaggio, la lingua Inglese.*

To give one good language [to speak civilly to one] *dar delle buone parole, o parlar colle buone ad uno.*

To give one ill or rude language, *maltrattar uno di parole, ingiuriarlo, svillaneggiarlo.*

LA'NGUAGED, adj. *che possiede varie lingue.*

LA'NGUAGE-MASTER, s. *un maestro di lingua.*

LA'NGUID, adj. [languishing, faint] *languido, senza forze, debole, fiacco.*

LA'NGUIDLY, adv. *languidamente, fiaccamente, debolmente.*

To LA'NGUISH [to consume, or pine away] *languire, svenire, mancar di forze, infiebolire, perdere il vigore, divenire afflitto.* pres. *languisco, infiebolisco.*

To languish in misery, *languire nella miseria,*

To languish one's days in sorrow, *menare una vita penosa.*

LA'NGUISH, s. [soft appearance] *languore affettato.*

LA'NGUISHING, s. *languore, mancamento di forze, malattia, debilitamento, afflizione, languidezza.*

Languishing, adj. [faint] *languente, languido, senza forze, debole, fiacco, afflitto.*

Languishing eyes, *occhi languidi.*

LA'NGUISHINGLY, adv. *d'una maniera languida.*

LA'NGUISHMENT, } s. [faintness,
LA'NGUOR, } weakness] *languidezza, fiacchezza, s. f. languore, languidore, mancamento di forze, debilitamento, s. m.*

To LA'NIATE [to butcher, to tear in pieces] *laniare, sbranare, lacerare.*

LA'NIATED, adj. *laniato, sbranato, lacerato.*

LA'NIFICE, s. [woollen manufacture] *manifattura di lana.*

LANI'GEROUS, adj. [bearing wool, or down] *velloso, peloso, lanuto, lanifero.*

LANK, adj [slender] *minuto, sfentato, delicato, sottile, magro, macilente.*

Lank [limber] *fiacco, debole, languido, frollo.*

LANKNESS, s. *magrezza, macilenza, s. f.*

LA'NNER, } s. *laniere, s. m.*
LA'NNER-HAWK, } *spezie di falcone.*

LA'NNIER, } s. [small ropes in a
LA'NNIARD, } ship, which serve to slacken or make stiff the shrouds] *scotta, s. f. quella fune che s'attacca alle vele per mollarle o distenderle.*

LANSQUENET, adj. [a German foot soldier, also a game at cards] *lanzo, s. m. soldato tedesco a piedi; giuoco di carte.*

LA'NTERN, s. *lanterna, s. f.*

Magical lantern [a small optical instrument, which shows by a gloomy light upon a white wall monsters so hideous, that those who are ignorant of the secret, believe it to be performed by magick art] *lanterna magica.*

A dark lantern, *lanterna sorda.*

To turn one's lantern to one, *lanternare, volgere la lanterna accesa verso alcuno.*

A small lantern, *lanternetta, s. f. lanternino, s. m.*

A large lantern, *lanternone, s. m.*

The lantern of a ship, or galley, *fanale, s. m.*

A lantern maker, *lanternajo, s. m. colui che fabbrica e vende le lanterne.*

LANTERN-JAWS, s. [a thin visage] *faccia secca; viso asciutto, muso magro.*

LANTHORN, *malamente scritto da molti per* lantern.

LAP, s. [the knees of a person sitting] *grembo, s. m. quella parte del corpo umano dal bellico insino alle ginocchia, in quanto o piegata o sedendo ella è accon cia a ricevere che che si sia.*

To hold a child upon one's lap, *tenere un bambino in grembo, sulle ginocchia.*

The lap of the ear, *la punta dell' orecchio.*

The lap of a garment, *le falde, le pieghe d' un abito.*

A Lap dog, *un cagnolino.*

Lap ear'd, *che ha gli orecchi pendenti.*

To LAP [to lick up with the tongue, as dogs, foxes, and some other creatures do when they drink] *leccare, come fanno i cani, le volpi, e altri animali quando bevono, lambire.*

To lap up [to wrap up] *involgere, avviluppare, pret. involsi.*

To lap [to cover] *coprire, invogliare.*

To lap something about a commodity, *invogliare della mercanzia.*

LA'PIDARY, s. [one that polishes or works stones] *lapidario, giojelliere, s. m.*

Lapidary, adj. [belonging to stones] *lapideo.*

Lapidary verses [epitaphs, verses cut on stone monuments] *versi d' epitaffio.*

To LA'PIDATE [to stone to death] *lapidare, percuotere con sassi.*

He that lapidates, *lapidatore.*

LAPIDA'TION, s. [a stoning to death] *lapidazione, s. f. il lapidare.*

LAPIS-LA'ZULI, s. [a stone of a sky colour] *lapislazzalo, s. m. pietra preziosa di color azzurro.*

LA'PPET, s. [a skirt, or hanging part of a garment] *falda, s. f.*

The lappet of a gown, *la falda d'una gonna.*

LAPSE, s. [slip, fall] *cascata.*

Lapse [or omission] *errore, s. m. mancanza, colpa, s. f.*

LA'PSED, adj. [fallen] *cascato.*

LAPT, adj. [from to lap] *involto, inviluppato, avvolto.*

He was lapt in his mother's smock, *egli è nato vestito.*

LA'PWING, s. [a bird] *pavoncella, s f. sorta d'uccello.*

LA'RBOARD, s. [the left hand side of a ship, or boat, when one stands with his face towards the stern] *il lato manco d'un vascello, quando uno sta rivolto verso la prua.*

LA'RCENY, s. [a law word for theft] *ladroneccio, furto, s. m.*

LARCH-TREE, s. [a lofty kind of tree] *larice, s. f. albero di grand' altezza.*

LARD, s. [the fat of a hog beaten or melted] *lardo, s. m.*

To LARD [to stick little slices of fat bacon] *lardare, metter lardelli in quello che si debbe arrostire.*

To lard a hare, *lardare una lepre.*

LA'RDED, adj. *lardato.*

LA'RDER, s. [a place where victuals are kept] *dispensa, s. f. la stanza dove si tengono le cose da mangiare.*

LA'RDING, s. *il lardare.*

Larding-pin, *strumento da lardare.*

LA'RDON, s. [a small slip of bacon proper for larding] *lardello, s. m. pezzuol di lardo.*

LARE, s. [a turner's wheel] *tornio, s. m.*

LARGS, s. *larve, s. f. pl.*

LARGE, adj. [great, ample] *grande, spazioso, vasto, ampio, d'una grand' ampiezza, largo.*

A large house, *una gran casa.*

A large conscience, *coscienza larga.*

You have been too large [or prolix] in that point; *voi vi siete troppo diffuso sopra questo punto.*

Large [bountiful] *liberale, largo, magnifico.*

At large, adv. [fully] *distesamente, alla distesa, minutamente, ampiamente, largamente, diffusamente.*

Large, in musick [the greatest measure, containing two longs, one long two briefs, one brief, two semibriefs] *largo, termine musicale.*

To go large [sea-phrase, when a ship goes right before the wind] *aver il vento alla prua.*

To LARGE [a ship is said to large, when she goes neither before the wind nor upon the wind, but, as it were, quartered between both] *volteggiare, aver il vento alla banda.*

LA'RGELY, adv. [or amply] *largamente, ampiamente, molto.*

He spoke largely upon that subject, *egli parlò largamente sopra questo soggetto.*

Largely [abundantly] *largamente, copiosamente, abbondantemente.*

LA'RGENESS, s. *larghezza, grandezza, ampiezza, s. f.*

LA'RGESS, s. [gift, liberality] *larghezza, liberalità, s. f.*

LA'RING-TREE, s. *larice, s. f.*

LARK, s. [a singing bird] *allodola, lodola, s. f.*

LA'RYNX, s. [the top of the wind pipe] *laringe, s. f. principio, o bocca della canna de' polmoni.*

LASCI'VIOUS, adj. [wanton, lustful] *lascivo, impudico.*

LASCI'VIOUSLY, adv. *lascivamente, con lascivia, impudicamente.*

LASCI'VIOUSNESS, s. *lascivia, lascivanza, lascività.*

LASH, s. *scorreggiata, sferzata, scudisciata, frustata, s f.*

To be under the lash, *esser sotto la disciplina.*

I shall bring him under the lash, *lo gastigherò ben io.*

To be under the lash of an evil tongue, *esser esposto ad una cattiva lingua.*

To LASH [to whip] *sferzare, frustare.*

To lash out into expences [to be lavish] *fare spese eccessive, prodigare, scialacquare i suoi beni.*

To lash out into expression [to speak more than one should] *parlar troppo.*

To lash out into sensuality, *abbandonarsi, darsi in preda alle sensualità.*

LA'SHED, adj. *frustrato, sferzato.*

LASK, s. [looseness] *uscita, cacajuola, s. f. flusso di ventre.*

LASS, s. [or girl] *una ragazza, una zittella, una fanciulla.*

A pretty lass, *una bella ragazza.*

LA'SSITUDE, s. [weariness] *lassezza, stracchezza, stanchezza, s. f.*

LA'SSLORN, adj. [forsaken by his mistress]

mistress] *abbandonato dalla sua ragazza, della sua innamorata, della sua bella.*

LAST, adj. *ultimo.*

The last but one, *il penultimo.*

The last but two, *l'antipenultimo.*

The last week, *la settimana passata.*

He is brought upon his last legs, *egli è ridotto in cattivo stato, egli non sa che fare per vivere.*

Last night, *jersera.*

At last, adv. *alla fine, in fine, finalmente.*

Last of all, *l'ultima volta, ultimamente.*

Last, adv. ex. How long is it since you saw him last? *quanto tempo è che non l'avete veduto?*

When I had last the honour to see you, *l'ultima volta ch' ebbi l'onore di vedervi.*

Last, s. ex. He has breathed his last, *egli è spirato, egli ha reso lo spirito, o l'anima.*

To the last, *fino alla fine.*

They are resolved to hold out to the last, *sono risoluti di tener fermo fino all' estremità.*

At last, *finalmente, alla fine, infine, in conchiusione.*

Last, s. [the shoemaker's last] *forma,* s. f.

To put a shoe upon the last, *mettere una scarpa alla forma.*

Last [a weight or measure so called] *sorta di peso o di misura così detta.*

To LAST [to enquire, to continue] *durare, continuare, sussistere.*

LA'STAGE, s. [duty paid for wares sold by the last] *tassa, che si paga per tutte le mercanzie che si vendono al peso o misura chiamata* last.

Lastage [or ballast] *v.* Ballast.

LA'STING, adj. [durable, permanent] *durabile, di lunga durata, permanente.*

A lasting cloth [a cloth that wears well] *buon panno, panno di lunga durata.*

LA'STINGLY, adv. *durevolmente.*

LA'STINGNESS, s. *durevolezza, continuazione.*

LA'STLY, adv. *finalmente, alla fine, in fine.*

LATCH, s. [a fastening of a door] *saliscendo, e saliscendi,* s. m.

To LATCH, *chiudere con saliscendo.*

To latch, *chiudere, serrare.*

LA'TCHES, s. [laskets] *nome di certe corde di cui si servono nelle navi.*

LA'TCHES, s. *cordicella da legar le scarpe in vece di fibbia.*

LATE, adj. *ultimo.*

In the late times, *negli ultimi tempi.*

In the late storm, *nell' ultima tempesta.*

Late [deceased] *defunto.*

The late king, *il re defunto.*

Of late years, *da qualche anno in qua.*

Late, adv. *tardi, tardo.*

It is late, *è tardi.*

Better late then never, *è meglio tardi che mai.*

It was late in the night, *la notte era molto avanzata.*

Of late [not long since] *ultimamente, non ha guari, poco fa.*

Late [ripe] *tardivo, serotine, che viene allo scorcio della stagione.*

LA'TED, adj. *sorpreso dalla notte.*

LA'TELY, adv. *ultimamente, poco tempo fa, non ha guari.*

LA'TENT, adj. [hid] *latente, oscuro, nascoso.*

LA'TER, adj. [the comparative of late] *posteriore, il più ultimo.*

The later math [or after pasture] *guaime, fieno dopo la prima segatura.*

Later, adv. *più tardi.*

We came later than you, *noi arrivammo più tardi di voi.*

LA'TERAL, adj. [belonging to the sides of any thing] *laterale, de' fianchi.*

LA'TEST, adj. [the superlative of late] *l'ultimo, il più tardo.*

I was the latest of all, *io fui l'ultimo di tutti, o il più tardo di tutti.*

LA'TEWARD, adj. [that is of the later season] *tardivo, che viene allo scorcio della stagione.*

Lateward hay, *guaime, fieno dopo la prima segatura.*

LATH, s. [a thin piece of cleft wood] *assicella,* s. f.

Lath [a turner's instrument] *tornio,* s. m.

To LATH [to cover with laths] *coprir di assicelle.*

LATHE, s. [a great part or division of a country] *un cantone, divisione di provincia.*

LA'THER, s. [water well mixed with soap till it froth] *saponata,* s. f. *quella schiuma che fa l'acqua dove sia disfatto il sapone.*

To LATHER, verb neut. *schiumare, parlando dell' acqua dove sia disfatto il sapone.*

To lather, verb act. *insaponare.*

LA'TIN, adj. *Latino.*

The Latin tongue, *la lingua Latina.*

Latin, s. [the language antiently spoken at Rome] *il Latino, la lingua Latina.*

The Latins [the Latin people] *i Latini; i popoli del Lazio.*

LA'TINED, adj. [made Latin] *tradotto in Latino.*

LA'TINISM, s. [a Latin expression] *latinismo, espressione Latina.*

LA'TINIST, s. [one skilled in Latin] *un latinista, uno versato nella lingua Latina.*

LATI'NITY, s. *Latinità,* s. f.

To LA'TINIZE, verb act. *latinizzare, dire in Latino; terminar le voci latinamente.*

LA'TINIZED, adj. *latinizzato.*

LA'TITANT, *v.* Latin.

LA'TISH, adj. [somewhat late] *tardetto, alquanto tardi.*

It is latish, *è tardetto; comincia a farsi tardi.*

LA'TITUDE, s. [breadth] *latitudine, larghezza,* s. f.

Latitude of a place [in geography, is the distance of that place, either North or South, from the equinoctial] *la latitudine d'un luogo, l'arco del meridiano, da un luogo tra esso e l'equinoziale.*

Too great a latitude [too much liberty] *troppa libertà, o licenza.*

LATITUDINA'RIAN, s. [one who takes too great a liberty in point of religion] *una persona che si da troppa libertà in punto di religione.*

Latitudinarian, adj. [not confined, not restrained] *non limitato, non ristretto.*

LA'TRANT, adj. [barking] *che latra.*

A latrant writer [an author who snarls at others] *un autore che non fa che latrare o gracchiare.*

LA'TTEN, s. [iron tinned over] *latta,* s. f.

LA'TTER, adj. ex. The latter end, *il fine, o la fine.*

The latter end of the month, *la fine del mese.*

To think of one's latter end, *pensare alla morte, pensare alla fine della vita.*

A latter spring, *una primavera tardiva.*

LA'TTICE, s. *graticcio,* s. m.

A lattice window, *una gelosia.*

To LA'TTICE up, *ingraticolare, chiudere un apertura con cosa a guisa di graticola.*

LATTICED, adj. *ingraticolato.*

LAVA'TION, s. [the act of washing] *l'atto del lavare, lavatura.*

LAUD, s. [praise] *laude, commendazione, lode,* s. f.

To LAUD [to praise] *laudare, commendare, dar lode, lodare, celebrare con lodi.*

LA'UDABLE, adj. [praise worthy] *laudabile, lodevole, degno di lode.*

LA'UDABLY, adv. *laudabilmente, lodevolmente, con modo laudabile.*

LA'UDANUM, s. [a sort of gum] *laudano,* s. m.

LA'UDES, s. [praises, read or sung: last, either at morning or evening service] *laude, laudi.*

To LAVE [to throw out] *vuotare, o gettare tutta l'acqua d'un luogo.*

To lave, *lavare.*

To LAVEER, *non andar dritto in correndo.*

LA'VENDER, s. [a sweet smelling herb] *spiga,* s. f. *spezie d'erba odorifera.*

To lay up in lavender [to pawn] *impegnare, mettere in pegno.*

LA'VER, s. [a vessel to wash in] *lavatojo,* s. m. *vaso da lavare.*

To LA'VER, *lavare.*

To LAUGH, *ridere.* pret. *risi.*

Let him laugh that wins, *chi ha dentro amaro non può sputar dolce.*

To laugh at [to jeer] *ridersi, burlarsi, farsi beffe, beffare, schernire,* pres. *schernisco.*

I laugh at you, *mi rido di voi.*

I laugh at your threatnings, *mi rido, mi burlo, fo poco conto delle vostre minacce.*

If you do such a thing you will be laugh'd at, *se voi fate una tal cosa si burleranno di voi.*

To

To laugh in one's sleeve, *rider di nascoso.*

Laugh, s. *v.* Laughter.

LA'UGHED, adj. *riso.*

Laughed at, *riso, burlato, beffato, schernito.*

LA'UGHER, s. *un che ride.*

LA'UGHING, s. *riso, il ridere.*

He fell a laughing, *si mise a ridere.*

Laughing is proper to man, *il ridere è proprio dell' uomo.*

Laughing, adj. [a laughing stock, a thing to be laughed at] *zimbello, trastullo, ludibrio, soggetto o oggetto degno di riso.*

To make one's self a laughing stock, *servire per zimbello.*

LA'UGHTER, s. [laugh, or laughing] *riso*, s. m.

To break out into laughter, *scoppiar delle risa.*

Immoderate laughter, *cachinno*, s. m. *riso smoderato.*

LA'VIH, adj. [prodigal] *prodigo, che spende eccessivamente, profuso.*

Lavish [extravagant] expences, *spese eccessive, o immense.*

To LA'VISH [to waste, to squander away] *scialacquare, spender profusamente, buttar via le sue facultà.*

LA'VISHING, s. *scialacquamento, scialacquo*, s. m.

LA'VISHLY, adv. *prodigamente, profusamente, scialacquatamente.*

LA'VISHNESS, s. *prodigalità*, s. f. *scialacquo*, s. m.

To LAUNCH, *v.* To lanch.

LAUND, s. *pianura che s'estende fra' boschi.*

LA'UNDRESS, s. [landress, washer-woman] *lavandaja.*

LA'UNDRY, s. *luogo dove si lavano i panni.*

LAVO'LTA, s. *sorta di danza antica. Vocabolo non più in uso.*

LA'UREATE, adj. [crowned ith laurel] *laureato, coronato d'alloro.*

A poet laureat, *un poeta laureato.*

LA'UREL, s. [a shrub that is always green] *alloro, lauro*, s. m.

A crown of laurel, *laurea*, s. f. *corona d'alloro.*

A laurel tree, *lauro, alloro.*

LA'URELLED, adj. *coronàto d'alloro.*

LAW, s. *legge*, s. f.

The law of nature, *la legge della natura.*

The divine and human laws, *legge divine o umane.*

To give laws, *dar la legge.*

The law of arms, *la legge della guerra.*

The law of merchants, or the law of staple, *le leggi del commercio.*

Law [common right] of nations, *diritto delle genti.*

Law [jurisprudence] *legge.*

The civil law, *la legge civile.*

The cannon law, *la legge canonica.*

To follow the law, *studiar la legge.*

To go to law, *processare, formar processo, litigare.*

A man learned in the law, *un giurisconsulto, un giureconsulto*

A thing good in law, *una cosa valida.*

A father in law, *un patrigno, un suocero.*

A mother in law, *una matrigna, una suocera.*

A son in law, *un figliastro.*

A daughter in law, *una figliastra.*

A brother in law, *un cognato.*

A sister in law, *una cognata.*

A law suit, or suit of law, *un processo.*

LA'WFUL, adj. *permesso, legittimo che è secondo la legge.*

'Tis lawful, *ciò è permesso.*

A lawful match, *un matrimonio legittimo.*

Lawful issue, *figli legittimi.*

A good and lawful excuse, *una buona scusa, una scusa valida.*

LA'WFULLY, adv. *legittimamente, secondo la legge, giustamente, convenientemente.*

Lawfully [good in law] *valido, con validità.*

A child lawfully begotten, *un figlio legittimo.*

LA'WFULNESS, s. *equità, giustizia*, s. f.

LAWGI'VER, s. *legislatore.*

LAWGI'VING, ad. *legislativo.*

LA'WLESS, adj. [that is without law] *che non ha legge, che è senza legge, sregolato, scapestrato.*

A lawless man [one that has no benefit of the law, an out-law] *un bandito.*

LA'WLESLY, adv. *in maniera contraria alle leggi.*

LAWMA'KER, s. *legislatore.*

LAWN, s. *una gran pianura.*

Lawn [a sort of fine linen cloth] *renso*, s. m. *sorta di tela finissima.*

LA'WYER, s. *un avvocato, un legista, un dottor di legge, un giurista.*

LAX, adj. [loose, flack] *molle, non teso.*

Lax [weak] *molle, debole, fiacco.*

LA'XATIVE, adj. [that is of a loosening or opening quality] *lassativo, che ha virtù di lenire, mollificare, o purgare.*

LAY, adj. [secular, not religious] *laico, secolare, del secolo.*

Lay man [one who follows a secular employment] *un laico.*

A lay brother [in a monastery] *un frate laico.*

A lay prince, *un principe secolare.*

A lay priest, *un prete secolare.*

A lay habit, *un abito secolare.*

Lay, *preterito del verbo* to lye.

Lay, s. *letto*, s. m.

A lay of mortar, *un letto di calcina.*

Lay [wager] *scommessa.*

'Tis an even lay whether it be so or no, *sista in dubbio se ciò sia o no.*

Lay [song] *una canzone.*

To LAY [to put, to place] *mettere, porre, posare, disporre, ordinare.* pret. *misi.* pres. *pongo, dispongo.* pret. *posi, disposi.*

To lay in order, *metter in ordine, ordinare.*

To lay every thing in its place, *mettere o disporre ogni cosa nel suo luogo.*

To lay siege to a place, *metter l'assedio ad una piazza, assediarla.*

To lay taxes, *imporre delle tasse.*

To lay the cloth, *apparecchiar la tavola.*

To lay [to deliver] a woman *assistere a partorire una donna.*

To lay the foundations, *gettar i fondamenti.*

To lay the land [a sea term, to sail from it just as far as they can see] *perder di vista la terra.*

To lay, or to lay a wager, *scommettere, fare una scommessa.*

To lay a net, *tendere una rete.*

To lay snares, *tender insidie, insidiare.*

To lay a plot, *fare, concertare, tramare una congiura.*

To lay eggs, *fare dell' uova.*

To lay the dust, *abbattere la polvere.*

The rain has laid the corn, *la pioggia ha coricato il grano.*

To lay [to allay] the heat, *diminuire, o scemare il calore.*

To lay one's self at one's mercy, *rimettersi alla mercè altrui, al suo arbitrio, nelle sue braccia.*

To lay hold of one, *afferrare, prendere alcuno.*

He thinks no law can lay hold of him, *egli si crede esente d'ogni legge.*

To lay a charge against one, *incolpare, accusare alcuno.*

To lay the fault to one, *dar la colpa ad uno.*

To lay asleep, to lay to sleep, *addormentare, far dormire.*

To lay waste, *desolare, e disolare, distruggere, rovinare, saccheggiare, depredare, predare.*

To lay open, *scoprire, spiegare, dichiarare, dire, rivelare, manifestare.*

To lay hands on, *metter le mani addosso ad uno, acchiapparlo, afferrarlo.*

To lay by, *metter da banda, guardare, conservare.*

To lay off a garment, *lasciare un abito.*

To lay over, *coprire.*

To lay about one's self [to use one's endeavours] *sforzarsi, fare ogni sforzo, sbracciarsi, sudar sangue.*

To lay about one [to beat him] *battere, bastonare, malmenare alcuno.*

To lay along upon the ground, *stendersi, coricarsi per terra.*

To lay aside, *metter da banda, o da parte.*

To lay aside [to neglect, not to mind] *omettere, negligere.*

To lay aside [to depose] *deporre, metter giù.*

To lay aside [to renounce] *rinunciare, lasciare, tralasciare, abbandonare.*

To lay a thing before one, *rappresentare, esporre che si sia ad uno.*

To lay in provisions, *fare le sue provvisioni, provvedersi.*

To lay out money, *sborsare, impiegare, pagare del danaro.*

To lay out in expences [to bela ish] ia-

scialacquare, spender profusamente le sue facultadi.

To lay out one's cards, *scartare.*

To lay violent hands upon one's self, *ammazzarsi, uccidersi, darsi la morte.*

To lay a command or charge upon one, *commandare, imporre, ordinare a qualcheduno.*

To lay on heaps, *ammassare, ammucchiare, incatastare.*

To lay an obligation on, or upon one, *obbligare qualcheduno.*

To lay one on the face, *dare uno schiaffo ad uno.*

To lay a punishment on one, *punire alcuno.*

To lay [to apply to] *applicare.*

To lay a thing to one's charge, *accusare, incolpare alcuno di qualche cosa.*

To lay a thing to heart, *prender una cosa a cuore.*

To lay an injury to heart, *risentire un' ingiuria, farne risentimento.*

To lay a claim to a thing, *pretendere, aver pretensione a qualche cosa.*

To lay up, *accumulare, ammucchiare, ammassare, adunare.*

To lay up money, *accumular danari.*

To lay up provisions, *far le sue provvisioni.*

Lay that up for another time, *riserbate questo per un' altra volta.*

To lay one up [to make him fall sick, so as to keep his bed] *far cascare ammalato alcuno.*

To lay one up [to lay him up by the heels] *far mettere alcuno in prigione.*

To lay up land, *lasciar riposare una terra.*

To lay down one's commission, *consegnare, rendere la sua commissione.*

To lay down one's life, *lasciare o perdere la vita, morire.*

I laid him down ready money for what I had, *gli ho pagato tutto quel che ho avuto in danari contanti.*

To lay one's self upon the bed, *coricarsi sul letto.*

To lay together, *ammassare, adunare, mettere insieme.*

To lay heads together, *consultare insieme.*

To lay under, *sottomettere, sottoporre.*

LA'YER, s. *strato che si sparge sopra un altro strato, o suolo che giace sopra un altro suolo.*

LA'YING, s. *il mettere, v.* To lay.

A hen past laying, *una gallina che non fa più uova.*

A laying on of the hands, *l'imposizione delle mani.*

LAY-MAN, s. *un laico, v.* Lay, adj.

LA'Y-STALL, s. [a place to lay dung or soil in] *letamajo,* s. m.

LA'ZAR, s. [a leprous person] *un lebroso.*

LA'ZAR-HOUSE, } s. [a pest-house]
LAZARE'TTO, } *lazzaretto,* s. m. *spedale d'appestati.*

LA'ZILY, adv. *pigramente, lentamente, neghittosamente, tardamente.*

LA'ZINESS, s. [slothfulness] *pigrizia, freddezza, infingardia, neghiezza, infingardaggine, tardezza, tiepidezza,* s. f.

LA'ZING, adj. [sluggish, idle] *pigro, neghittoso.*

LA'ZULE, } s. [a stone of a
LAPIS LAZULI, } sky colour] *lapislazzolo,* s. m.

LA'ZY, adj. [slouthful, sluggish] *pigro, infingardo, neghittoso, lento, tardo.*

A lazy man, *un pigro, uno scioperato, un infingardo.*

A lazy-bones, *uno scioperato, un infingardo.*

LEA, s. [ground inclosed; not open] *terreno chiuso intorno.*

LEACH, *v.* Leech.

LE'ACHER, *v.* Lecher.

LEAD, s. [a sort of metal] *piombo,* s. m.

Lead-mine. *miniera di piombo.*

Red-lead, *minio,* s. m. *piombo, che precipitato per calcinazione di riverbero acquista colore tra'l rosso e'l giallo, e serve per dipignere.*

To LEAD [to do over with lead] *impiombare.*

To lead [to guide] *menare, guidare, condurre,* pres. *conduco,* prét. *condussi.*

To lead one by the hand, *menare uno per la mano.*

This way leads to the town, *questa strada va alla città.*

To lead a good life, *menare buona vita, viver da uomo dabbene.*

To lead [to be chief, to command] *menare, condurre, comandare, esser il capo.*

To lead along, *condurre.*

To lead off, *stornare, sviare.*

To lead away, *menar via.*

To lead out, *menar fuora.*

To lead one out of the way, *sviare alcuno, stornarlo dal suo cammino.*

To lead back, *ricondurre,* pres. *riconduco,* pret. *ricondussi.*

To lead in, or into, *introdurre,* pres. *introduco,* pret. *introdussi.*

LE'ADED, adj. *impiombato, v.* To lead.

LE'ADEN, adj. [made of lead] *di piombo, piombino.*

LE'ADER, s. [guide] *conduttore, guida, duce, capitano.*

The leader [at cards] *colui che ha la mano.*

A ring-leader, *il capo d'un partito.*

LE'ADING, adj. Ex. a leading man, *un capo.*

The leading men of the town, *i principali della città.*

A leading word, *la prima parola, la parola dalla quale dipendono le altre.*

The leading card, *la prima carta, la carta di colui che ha giuocato il primo.*

To have the leading hand at cards, *aver la mano, esser il primo a giuocare.*

Leading strings, *stringhe o nastri, che servono a sostenere un bambino allora che comincia a camminare.*

LEAF, s. *foglia,* s. f.

The leaves of a tree or flower, *le foglie d'un albero, o d'un fiore.*

The fall of the leaf, *l'autunno.*

A leaf of gold or silver, *foglia d'oro, o d'argento.*

Leaf gold, *oro in foglia.*

A leaf of a book, *un foglio, due facce.*

To turn over the leaves of a book, *voltar i fogli d'un libro.*

I shall make him turn over a new leaf, *li farò ben io mutar discorso.*

To LEAF, *produr foglie, germogliar frondi, rinverdirsi.*

LE'AFLESS, adj. *sfrondato, senza foglie, senza fronde.*

LE'AFY, adj. *fronzuto, pien di frondi, frondoso, carico di foglie.*

LEAGUE, s. [alliance] *lega,* s. f. *compagnia, unione formata con patto solenne tra principi e tra repubbliche di difender se o offender altri.*

To enter into a league, *legarsi, far lega.*

League [the space of three miles] *lega, numero di tre o più miglia.*

LE'AGUED, adj. *alleato, confederato.*

LE'AGUER, s. *colui che è della lega, confederato.*

Leaguer [a siege] *assedio,* s. m.

LEAK, s. [chink] *apertura per la quale l'acqua trapela.*

To LEAK [to spring a leak, to take in water, speaking of a ship] *fare acqua, trapelare.*

This vessel leaks [this vessel runs] *questo vaso trapela.*

LE'AKY, adj. *che trapela, pieno di crepature, di fessure, fesso, screpolato.*

LEAM [among hunters, a lash] *guinzaglio,* s. m.

LEAN, adj. [poor in flesh] *magro.*

Lean meat, *carne magra.*

A lean soil, *terra magra.*

Lean [slender] *magro, macilente, smilzo.*

To make lean, *smagrare, dimagrare.*

To grow lean, *smagrire, divenir magro.*

Lean, s. *del magro.*

I love lean, *amo del magro.*

To LEAN [to rest against, to stay upon] *appoggiarsi, posare, reggersi su.*

To lean upon a stick, *appoggiarsi ad un bastone.*

To lean upon one's arm, *reggersi sull' altrui braccio.*

A beam that leans upon a column, *una trave che posa sopra una colonna.*

A thing to lean upon, *un appoggiatojo, cosa a che l'uomo s'appoggia.*

To lean [to incline] *pendere*

A wall that leans on one side, *un muro che pende da una parte.*

To lean over [to stand out] *sporgere.*

LE'ANING, s. *l'appoggiarsi.*

A leaning staff, *un bastone per appoggiarsi.*

A leaning stock, *un appoggiatojo.*

LE'ANNESS, s. *magrezza,* s. f.

LEAP, s. [jump] *un salto.*

To take a leap, *fare un salto.*

Leap [weal to take fish in] *una nassa.*

The leap year [that has a day more than

than any other, which falls out every fourth year] *anno bisestile.*

To LEAP [to jump] *saltare.*

To leap over a ditch, *saltare un fosso.*

To leap for joy, *far galloria, galluzzare, ringalluzzare, giubbilare, brillare.*

He is ready to leap out of his skin, *egli non cape nella pelle dall' allegrezza.*

To leap [as the heart does] *palpitare, battere.*

To leap [as the horse does the mare] *montare, coprire, parlando d'un cavallo.*

LE'APER, s. *saltatore,* s. m. *saltatrice,* s. f.

LE'APING, s. *il saltare.*

LEAPT, *preterito del verbo* To leap.

To LEARN [to receive instructions in arts or sciences, to get the knowledge of] *imparare, apprendere,* pret. *appresi.*

To learn by heart, *imparare a mente.*

To learn with [to grow cunning] *scozzonarsi, dirozzarsi.*

To learn [to hear] *apprendere, sapere, esser informato,* pret. *appresi, seppi.*

To learn [to teach] *apprendere, insegnare.*

To learn, v. n. [to take pattern] *pigliar una mostra di checchessia.*

LE'ARNED, adj. *dotto, saputo, intelligente.*

A very learned man, *un uomo dottissimo.*

A learned discourse, *un discorso dotto.*

The learned, s. [or scholars] *i dotti, gli uomini dotti.*

LE'ARNEDLY, adv. *dottamente, saputamente, scientemente, con sapere.*

LE'ARNER, s. *quello, o quella che impara, un principiante, uno scolare.*

LE'ARNING, s. *l'imparare.*

Learning, s. [scholarship] *sapere,* s. f. *dottrina, erudizione, scienza,* s. f.

A man of great learning, *un uomo di gran sapere, un uomo dottissimo.*

The commonwealth of learning, *la repubblica delle scienze.*

LEARNT, *è un preterito del verbo* To learn.

LEASE, s. [a demise, or letting of lands or tenements to another for a rent reserved] *affitto,* s. m.

To take a lease of a house, *pigliare una casa in affitto.*

To LEASE [to let a lease] *dare in affitto, a pigione.*

To lease [to glean] *spigolare.*

LE'ASER, s. [gleaner] *spigolatore,* s. m. *quello o quella che va spigolando.*

LEASH, s. [a small thong of leather to hold a dog in] *guinzaglio,* s. m. *lassa,* s. f.

A leash of hounds, *tre cani agguinzagliati insieme.*

Leash [a small thong of leather, by which the falconer holds his hawk fast] *geto,* s. m.

LE'ASING, s. [lie] *una menzogna, una bugia.*

LE'ASOUR, } s. [the person who
LEASOR, } grants or lets a lease] *quello o quella che da in affitto.*

LEAST, adj. [the smallest] *il minimo, il più piccolo.*

I am the least of all, *io sono il minimo, o il più piccolo di tutti.*

You have not the least cause of complaint, *voi non avete la minima causa di lamentarvi.*

There's not the least difference, *non c'è differenza alcuna.*

I don't fear him in the least [or at all] *non lo temo punto.*

I have not wrong'd him in the least, *non gli ho fatto torto alcuno.*

That I may say the least, *per non dire troppo.*

Least, adv. *meno.*

I love him least of all, *l'amo meno d'ogni altro.*

At least, at the least, *almeno, almanco.*

Least, *per dubbio, per tema, per paura.*

Least he should come, *per dubbio, per paura che non venisse.*

LE'ATHER, s. [hides of beasts dressed] *cuojo,* s. m.

Leather bag, *sacchetto di cuojo.*

Leather dresser, *conciatore,* s. m. *colui che concia le pelli.*

A leather seller, *un pellicciajo.*

The upper leather of a shoe, *tomajo,* s. m. *la pelle di sopra della scarpa.*

To lose leather, *scorticarsi, levare un poco di pelle.*

A leather bottle, *otre, o otro,* s. m. *pelle tratta intera dall' animale, per lo più di becchi e di capre, e serve per portarvi entro olio, vino, e simili liquori.*

LE'ATHERN, adj. [made of leather] *di pelle.*

LE'AVE, s. [permission or licence] *libertà, licenza, permissione,* s. f.

To give one leave to go out, *dar licenza o permettere ad uno d'uscire.*

By your leave, *con licenza vostra.*

To have free leave to do any thing, *aver la libertà di fare che che si sia.*

By your leave it is not so, *con vostra licenza, con vostra pace, la cosa non va così.*

Give me leave to answer you, *permettetemi di rispondervi.*

If you give me leave [if you please] *se vi piace, se volete.*

Leave [farewel] *congedo, commiato,* s. m.

To take leave of one, *prender congedo, accommiatarsi d'uno.*

To LE'AVE [to forsake] *lasciare, abbandonare.*

I left him a bed, *l'ho lasciato in letto.*

I leave you to think, *lascio pensare a voi.*

To leave the door open, *lasciar la porta aperta.*

I left word with the maid that I should be at home to night, *ho lasciato detto alla serva, che sarei a casa stasera.*

Why will you leave me? *perchè volete lasciarmi, o abbandonarmi.*

To leave one's work, *tralasciare di lavorare.*

To leave one to the wide world, *lasciare uno in abbandono, o in nasso.*

To leave one's wife, *ripudiare la moglie.*

To leave off crying, *cessar di piagnere.*

I never leave exhorting him to a sober life, *non cesso mai d'esortarlo a viver sobriamente.*

I leave it to your judgment, *io me ne sto al vostro parere.*

To leave off, or over, *tralasciare, lasciare, cessare, finire.*

To leave off writing, *tralasciar di scrivere.*

To leave off trade, *lasciare il negozio.*

To leave off an ill habit, *lasciare un cattivo costume.*

Leave off your prating, *finitela con queste vostre chiacchiere.*

Leave that to me, *lasciate fare a me.*

To leave out [to take out] *levare, scancellare.*

To leave out [to omit, to forget] *ommettere, dimenticare.*

To leave out [not to admit] *escludere, non ammettere.*

LE'AVED, adj. Ex. Broad leaved, *che ha le foglie larghe.*

Narrow leaved, *che ha le foglie strette.*

LE'AVEN, s. [a piece of dough soured to ferment] *fermento,* s. m.

To LE'AVEN, *lievitare, fermentare.*

LE'AVENED, adj. *lievitato, fermentato.*

LE'AVER, s. [a bar of wood or iron to lift or bear up a weight] *leva,* s. f.

LE'AVES, *il plurale di* Leaf.

LE'AVING, s. [from to leave] *lasciamento,* s. m. *il lasciare.*

LE'AVINGS, *rimasuglio, avanzaticci.*

I won't eat your leavings, *non voglio mangiare i vostri rimasugli.*

LE'AVY, adj. [full of leaves] *figlioso, fogliuto, frondoso.*

To LECH [to lick over] *leccare.*

LE'CHER, s. [a lecherous man] *un' uomo lascivo.*

LE'CHEROUS, adj. *lascivo, impudico, lussurioso.*

LE'CHEROUSLY, adv. *lascivamente, impudicamente, lussuriosamente.*

LE'CHERY, s. *lascivia, impudicizia, lussuria,* s. f.

LE'CTERN, s. [a reading desk in a church] *leggio, lettorile,* s. m. *strumento di legno sul quale tengono il libro coloro che cantano i divini uffici.*

LE'CTURE, s. [a discourse upon any art or science] *lettura, lezione,* s. f.

A lecture in divinity, *una lettura in teologia.*

A reader of lectures, *un professore, un lettore.*

In the forehead and in the eye, the lecture of the mind doth lie, *la fronte egli occhi sono interpreti dell' animo.*

Lecture [reprimand] *bravata, ripassata, correzione, ammonizione,* s.

LE'CTURER, s. [a minister who preaches in the afternoon] *propriamente un ajutante di ministro d'una parrocchia,*

chia, che predica ordinariamente il dopo pranso.

LED, adj. [from to lead] *menato, condutto, v.* To lead.

A led horse, *un cavallo a mano.*

LEDGE, s. *orlo,* s. m.

A ledge of rocks, *una giogaja, una continuazione di monti.*

Ledge, s. *strato, suolo; v.* Layer.

LEE, s. [that part the wind blows upon, or that part which is opposite to the wind] *la parte dove da il vento, o la parte opposta al vento.*

The lee bow of a ship, *il canto d'un vascello opposto al vento.*

To lee the helm [to put the helm to the leeward side of the ship] *spignere il timone verso la banda del vascello opposto al vento.*

Lee-shore [is that on which the wind blows] *la costa, o la spiaggia alla quale da il vento.*

To go by the lee [to come off a loser] *restar perditore.*

Lee [dregs, sediment, refuse] *feccia, fondacchio, rimasuglio di liquor fecciosо.*

LEECH, or LEECHWORM, s. *sanguisuga, mignatta.*

Leech [an old word for a physician] *un medico.*

A horse leech [or horse doctor] *un maniscalco, quegli che medica i cavalli.*

LEECH-CRAFT, s. *l' arte del medicare.*

LEEF, adj. [kind, fond] *amante, affezionato.*

LEEK, s. [a pot-herb] *porro,* s. m.

Leek-pottage, *della zuppa con porri.*

LEER, s. [or leering look] *sguardo bieco, occhiata obliqua.*

To LEER upon [to cast a cunning, or wishly look] *occhieggiare, guardar sott' occhio, colla coda dell' occhio.*

LE'BRING, adj. ex. A leering look, *uno sguardo bieco, un occhiata.*

LE'ERO, a LEERO VIOL, s. [a kind of musical instrument] *lira,* s. f. *strumento musicale.*

LEES, s. [dregs] *feccie.*

LEEWARD SHIP, s. [sea term, one which is not fast by wind, or which doth not sail so near the wind, to make her way so good as she could] *un vascello che non va a seconda del vento.*

A leeward tide [when the tide and the wind go both one way] *vento e marea.*

LEFT, adj. [the contrary of right] *manco, sinistro, opposto a destro.*

The left hand, or foot, *la man manca, il pie manco, o sinistro.*

A left-handed man, *un mancino, che adopera naturalmente da la sinistra mano, in cambio della destra.*

LEFT [from to leave] *lasciato, v.* To leave.

If there be yet any hope left, *se vi resta ancora qualche speranza.*

LEG, s. [a part of the body] *gamba,* s. f.

The leg of a fowl, *la coscia d'un uccello.*

A leg of mutton, *una lacchetta di castrato.*

To make a leg [or a bow] *far la riverenza.*

A leg of wood, to put in a stocking, *forma, per informare le calzette.*

LE'GACY, s. [a gift bequeathed by a testator in his will] *legato, lascio, lascito,* s. m.

A pious legacy, *un legato piò.*

LE'GAL, adj. [according to the law, lawful] *legale, legitimo, secondo la legge.*

LEGA'LITY, s. [lawfulness] *conformità alle leggi, equità,* s. f.

LE'GALLY, adv. [according to the law] *legalmente, legitimamente, secondo la legge.*

LE'GATARY, or LE'GATEE, s. [a person who has a legacy left him in a will] *legatario,* s. m. *quegli in chi è fatto il legato.*

LE'GATE, s. [the Pope's ambassador] *legato,* s. m. *ambasciadore del Papa.*

LE'GATEE, *v.* Legatary.

LE'GATESHIP, or LEGA'TION, s. [the place or function of a legate] *legazione, ambasceria,* s. f.

LE'GATINE, adj. *del legato.*

The legatine power, *il potere del legato.*

Legatine, s. Legateship.

LEGA'TOR, s. *testatore, colui che fa testamento, o lascia legati.*

LE'GEND, s. [a book containing a particular account of the lives of the saints] *leggenda.*

Legend [or fabulous story] *leggenda favola.*

Legend [the words that are about the edge of a piece of coin or metal] *le parole scolpite intorno ad una moneta o medaglia.*

LE'GENDARY, adj. *di leggenda.*

Legendary stories, *legende, favole.*

LE'GERDEMAIN, s. [slight of hand, juggling tricks] *ghermінella,* s. f.

LE'GIBLE, adj. [easy to be read] *leggibile, agevole a potersi leggere.*

LE'GION, s. [a body of foot soldiers among the Romans] *legione,* s. f. *squadra, schiera di soldati fra gli antichi Romani.*

LE'GIONARY, adj. [of or belonging to a Roman legion] *legionario, di legione.*

LEGISLA'TION, s. *il far leggi; lo instituir leggi.*

LE'GISLATIVE, adj. ex. A legislative power, *il potere di far le leggi.*

LEGISLA'TOR, s. [a law-giver, or law-maker] *legislatore, colui che fa le leggi.*

LEGISLATURE, s. *legislatura; quel potere che fa le leggi.*

LEGI'TIMACY, s. [the being a lawful child] *legittimità,* s. f.

LEGI'TIMATE, s. [a lawful child] *un figlio legittimo.*

To LEGI'TIMATE, [to make or declare legitimate] *legittimare, far legittimo.*

LEGI'TIMATED, adj. *legittimato.*

LEGITIMA'TION, s. *legittimazione.*

LE'GUME, LEGU'MEN, } s. *legume.*

LE'IGER, or LEIGER Book, s. *gran libro di mercante.*

LE'ISURABLE, adj. [made at leisure] *fatto ad agio.*

LE'ISURE, s. [time to spare] *agio, tempo,* s. m. *comodità.*

To be at leisure, *avere agio, aver il tempo.*

When I am at leisure, *quando averò il tempo.*

LE'ISURELY, adv. [at leisure] *a bell' agio.*

Do it leisurely, *fatelo a bell' agio, a vostra comodità.*

Leisurely [by little and little] *lentamente, a poco a poco.*

LE'MAN, s. *un innamorato, un damo.*

LE'MBICK, *v.* Alembick.

LEMMA, s. [in geometry, a proposition which serves previously to prepare the way for the demonstration of some theorem, or for the construction of some problem] *lemma,* s. m. *dicono i geometri quella preposizione che serve loro per dimostrare alcun problema o teorema immediatamente.*

LE'MNIAN, adj. [of Lemnos, an island] as Lemnian earth, *terra sigillata.*

LE'MON, s. *limone, limoncello,* s. m.

Lemon tree, *limone albero.*

Lemon colour, *color di limone.*

LE'MONADE, s. *limonata; bevanda fatta d' acqua, zucchero, e sugo di limoni.*

To LEND [to grant the use of to another] *improntare, accomodare, prestare.*

To lend one money, *improntare, prestare del danaro ad uno.*

To lend out, *prestare.*

Lend me your hand, *datemi porgetemi la mano.*

LE'NDER, s. *prestatore,* s. m. *che presta.*

LE'NDED, adj. *improntato, accomodato, prestato.*

LE'NDING, s. *presta, prestita, prestanza,* s. f. *presto, prestito,* s. m.

LENGTH, s. [is the first dimension of bodies] *lunghezza.*

The length [or duration] of time, *lunghezza, durazione, continuazione di tempo.*

In length of time, *a lungo andare, in processo di tempo.*

Length of time will not waste it away, *il tempo, e l' età non lo consumeranno.*

To lye at one's length, *esser coricato, tutto disteso.*

To have the length of one's foot [to know his ways and humour] *conoscer l' umore di qualcheduno.*

At length [at last] in fine, *alla fine, finalmente.*

A picture in full length, *un ritratto in grande.*

Length-wise, *in lungo.*

To LE'NGTHEN, verb act. *allungare, accrescere una cosa, farla più lunga, che ella non è.*

To lengthen a petticoat, *allungare una gonnella.*

To lengthen a discourse, *allungare un discorso.*

LE'NGTHENED, adj. *allungato.*

LE'NGTHENING, s. allungamento, s. m. l'allungare.

LE'NIENT, adj. [assuasive, softening, mitigating] molcente, dolcificante, mitigante.

Lenient [laxative, emollient] che scioglie, emolliente.

To LE'NIFY [to allay, to soften, to give ease to] lenificare, addolcire, rammorbidare, pref. addolcisco.

LE'NIFY'D, adj. lenificato, addolcito, rammorbidato.

LE'NIFYING, s. lenificamento, s. m. il lenificare.

LE'NITIVE, adj. [that is of a softning and asswaging quality] lenitivo, lenificativo, che ha virtù, e forza di lenificare.

LE'NITY, s. [softness, mildness, gentleness] dolcezza, amorevolezza, affabilità, s. f.

LENS, s. [a glass spherically convex, that is made to throw the rays of vision into a point] lente, s. f. vetro o cristallo di figura simile alla lente civaja.

LENT, s. [a set time for fasting, and an abstinence of forty days next before Easter] quaresima, s. f. digiuno di quaranta giorni.

To keep Lent, osservare le quaresima, far quaresima.

Lent, adj. [from to lend] imprestato, dato in prestito.

LE'NTEN, adj. [belonging to Lent] quaresimale, di quaresima, da quaresima.

Lenticular, adj. [of the form of a lens; doubly convex] a foggia di lente; convesso doppiamente.

LE'NTIL, s. [a kind of pulse] lente, lenticchia, lentiggine, s. f.

LE'NTISK, s. [the lentisk, or mastick tree] lentischio, e lentisco, s. m. albero.

LE'NTNER, s. [a kind of hawk] spezie di falcone.

LE'NTOR, s. [tenacity, viscosity] viscosità, tenacità.

Lentor [slowness, delay] lentezza, ritardo.

LE'O, s. [one of the twelve signs of the Zodiack] leone, s. m. uno de' dodici segni del Zodiaco.

LE'ONINE, adj. [belonging to a lion, of a lion-like nature] leonino, lionino, di lione.

Leonine verses [a sort of Latin verses which rhime in the middle and at the end] versi leonini, sorta di versi Latini che rimano nel mezzo e nel fine.

LE'OPARD, s. [an African wild beast] leopardo, s. m.

LE'PER, s. [a leprous man or woman] un lebbroso, una lebbrosa.

LE'PID, adj. [pleasant, jocose, smart, witty] scherzevole, sollazzevole, gajo, galante, giocoso, spiritoso, allegro, festoso, lepido.

LE'PIDITY, s. [pleasantness] garbo, s. m. gajezza, grazia, lepidezza.

LEPRO'SITY, } s. [a dry white scab
LE'PROSY, } or scurf] lebbra, s. f. spezie di scabbia.

LE'PROUS, adj. [afflicted with leprosy] lebbroso, infetto di lebbra.

The leprous disease, la lebbra.

LERE, s. lezione, dottrina.

LERRY, s. lettura.

LESS, adj. minore, più piccolo.

He is less than I, egli è più piccolo di me.

To make less, appiccolare, far piccolo, diminuire, scemare, pref. diminuisco.

To grow less, impiccolire, divenir piccolo, pref. impiccolisco.

Less, adv. meno.

Much less, molto meno.

More or less, più o meno.

In less than an hour, in meno d' un' ora.

To make less of one friend than another, far meno conto d'un amico, che d' un altro.

LESSE'E, s. [he that taketh a lease] colui che piglia in affitto.

To LE'SSEN [to make less] impicciolire, scemare, diminuire, sminuire, render più piccolo, pref. diminuisco, sminuisco.

To lessen [to derogate to] one's self, abbassarsi, umiliarsi.

To lessen, v. n. [to grow less] impiccolire, divenir piccolo, pref. impiccolisco.

LE'SSENED, adj. scemato, diminuito, sminuito, impicciolito.

LE'SSING, s. diminuimento, s. m.

LE'SSER, adj. [a barbarous corruption of less] più piccolo, minore.

The lesser Asia, l'Asia minore.

Lesser, adv. formato corrottamente da less avverbio.

LE'SSES, s. [the dung of a ravenous beast, such as wolf, boar, bear] lo sterco d'un lupo, cinghiale, orso, e altri animali rapaci.

LE'SSON, s. [a task for one to learn] lezione, s. f. quelle parte di cose insegnare dal maestro da impararsi dallo scolare.

Lesson [of scripture read in churches] lezione.

Lesson [instruction] lezione, instruzione, s. f. precetto, insegnamento, s. m.

To give one his lesson [to scold at him] fare una bravata, o una ripassata ad uno, bravarlo, ammonirlo.

To LE'SSON [to instruct] instruire, ammaestrare, addottrinare.

LE'SSOR, s. colui che da a pigione o in affitto.

LEST, conj. per paura, per tema, per dubbio.

Lest he go away, per paura, che non sene vada via.

LET, adj. affittato, appigionato.

Let, s. [hinderance] ostacolo, intoppo, impedimento, s. m.

To LET [to suffer, or give leave] permettere, lasciare, dar licenza.

Let me go out, permettetemi ch'io esca, lasciatemi uscire.

Let me alone, lasciatemi stare.

To let blood, cavar sangue.

To let, or let out [to lease] affittare, appigionare, allogare, dare ad affitto, o a ferma.

To let see, far vedere, mostrare.

To let a fart, fare, o tirare una coreggia.

To let [to hinder] impedire, ritenere, trattenere, ritardare, intertenere, pref. impedisco, ritengo, trattengo, intertengo, pret. ritenni, trattenni, intertenni.

Let, è anche una spezie di verbo ausiliare, che serve all' imperativo.

Let us go, andiamo.

Let him speak, che parli.

Let him come, che venghino.

Let me die if it be not true, che possa morire se non è vero.

He let fall a word, li scappò di bocca una parola.

To let off, tirare, sparare.

To let off a pistol, tirare, sparare una pistola.

To let down, calare, abbattere, abbassare.

To let down a bridge, calare, abbassare un ponte.

To let down the strings of a lute, allentare le corde d'un liuto.

To let in or into, lasciare, o fare entrare, introdurre, pref. introduco, pret. introdussi.

To let one in [to open the door, to let him in] aprir la porta ad uno.

To let [or farm] out, affittare, appiggionare.

To let out [to let go out], fare, lasciare uscire.

To let out money to use, metter danaro all' interesse.

LE'TANY, v. Litany.

LE'THAL, adj. [mortal] letale, mortale.

LE'THARGICK, s. [sick of the lethargy] letargico, che ha letargo.

LE'THARGY, s. [the drowsy disease] letargo, s. m.

LE'TTER, s. [a character, such as those of the alphabet] lettera, s. f. carattere dell' alfabeto.

A capital letter, lettera majuscola, lettera grande.

Letter [an epistle sent to one] lettera, quella scrittura che si manda agli assenti, pistola.

To write, seal, or direct a letter, scrivere, sigillare, indrizzare una lettera.

Letters patents, una patente.

Latter of attorney, una procura.

To LE'TTER a book [to write the title of it on the back with golden letters] mettere il titolo sul dosso d'un libro.

LE'TTERED, adj. ex. A lettered book, un libro che ha il titolo sul dosso.

Lettered [or learned] letterato, scienziato, dotto.

A well lettered man, un uomo letterato.

A man slenderly-lettered, un uomo di poco sapere.

LE'TTICE, } s. [a sallad herb] lattu-
LE'TTUCE, } ga, s. f. erba nota.

Headed lettuce, lattuga cappuccia.

LE'TTING, s. [from to let] il lasciare, v. To let.

Letting of blood, il cavar sangue.

LEVA'NT, s. [East] il Levante, l'Oriente.

LE'VANTINE, adj. [of or belonging to the eastern countries] del levante, orientale.

A Levantine wind, Levante, s. m.

LE'VANTINES, s. [inhabitants of the eastern countries or Levant] I Levantini, gli orientali, le nazioni orientali.

LEVE'E, s. [the time of one's rising] levata, il levarsi, il tempo nel quale uno si leva la mattina.

He was at the King's levee, egli era alla levata del Re.

LE'VEL, adj. [even, plain, flat] livello piano.

A level ground, terreno piano.

To lie level, esser a livello.

To make level, livellare, spianare, mettere a livello.

This knowledge lies level to human understanding, questa cognizione è proporzionata, o accomodata alla portata dell' ingegno umano.

Level, s. [a carpenter's instrument] livella, s. f. strumento col quale s' aggiustan le cose al medesimo piano.

Level [or even ground] livello, piano, s. m.

To be upon the level, esser a livello, esser del pari.

Level-coil [is when he who has lost the game sits out, and gives another his place] a vicenda, termine di giuocatore, quando uno ha perduto la partita fa luogo ad un altro.

To LE'VEL [to make level] livellare, mettere, aggiustare le cose al medesimo piano.

To level a house with the ground, spianare una casa.

To level [to aim] at, mirare, aver la mira, por la mira, fissamente volgere il pensiero.

To level [to compare] ugualare, comparare, metter del pari, pareggiare.

To level a cannon, mirare, aggiustare un cannone, porlo in mira.

LE'VELLED, adj. livellato, piano, v. To level.

LE'VELLER, s. colui che livella.

LE'VEN, v. Leaven.

LE'VER, v. Leaver.

LE'VERET, s. [young hare] lepretti-no, lepratino, lepratto, s. m. lepre giovane.

LE'VERHOOK, s. [lark] allodola, lodola. E' voce antica, e solo ritenuta in Iscazia.

LE'VET, s. un soffio solo di tromba.

LE'VIABLE, adj. che si può levare.

LE'VIATHAN, s. [whale] balena.

LEVI'TE, s. [one of the tribe of Levi] un Levita.

LEVI'TICAL, adj. [of or belonging to the Levites] Levitico.

LEVI'TICUS, s. [one of the five books of Moses] il Levitico, uno di cinque libri di Moisè.

LE'VITY, s. [lightness, fickleness] levità, leggerezza, incostanza, volubilità, s. f.

LE'VY, s. [raising, collection] leva, levata.

A levy of taxes, una levata di tasse.

Levy of soldiers, leva di genti, o soldati.

To LE'VY [to raise] levare.

To levy a tax, levare una tassa.

To levy soldiers, levar soldati, o gente, far gente.

LE'VY'D, adj. levato.

LEWD, adj. [wicked, wanton, riotous] dissoluto, scostumato, cattivo, tristo, infame, disonesto, vituperoso, impudico, osceno, licenzioso.

A lewd life, una vita dissoluta.

A lewd discourse, un discorso osceno.

A lewd man, un dissoluto, uno scapestrato, un uomo scostumato.

A lewd woman, una prostituta, una donna infame.

LEW'DLY, adv. dissolutamente, scostumatamente, infamemente, cattivamente, disonestamente, impudicamente, licenziosamente.

LEW'DNESS, s. dissolutezza, licenza, disonestà, dissoluzione, sfrenatezza, oscenità, infamità, s. f.

LE'WDSTER, s. colui che s' abbandona intermente alla lussuria.

LEXICO'GRAPHER, s. vocabolista; un che fa dizionari.

LE'XICON, s. [or dictionary] un dizionario.

LI'ABLE, adj. [subject] soggetto, e suggetto, esposto.

We are all liable to fail, noi siamo tutti soggetti ad errare.

This expression is liable to misconstruction, questa espressione può pigliarsi in cattivo senso.

To make one's self liable to an inconveniency, esporsi a qualche inconvenienza.

LI'AR, s. un bugiardo, un mentitore, un menzognero, o menzognere.

LI'ARD, adj. leardo; colore di pelo di cavallo.

To LIB [to geld] castrare.

LIBA'TION, s. [a light casting of a drink offering] libazione, s. f.

LI'BBARD, s. [leopard] leopardo, s. m.

Libbard's bane [an herb] aconito, s. m.

LI'BBED, adj. [from to lib] castrato.

LI'BEL, s. [a little book] libello, libretto, s. m.

Libel [a scandalous and invective pamphlet] libello famoso, o infamatorio, cartello.

Libel, in law [is an original declaration of an action] libello, domanda giudiciaria, fatta per iscrittura.

To LIBEL one [to set forth libels against him] scriver libelli infami contro, a qualcheduno, diffamarlo, infamarlo, screditarlo.

LI'BELLED, adj. diffamato, infamato, screditato.

LI'BELLER, s. un diffamatore, un calunniatore.

LI'BELLOUS, adj. [defamatory] diffamatorio, infamatorio.

LI'BERAL, adj. [free, generous] liberale, generoso, che usa liberalità, magnanimo.

The liberal arts, le arti liberali.

A liberal education, una nobile, o buona educazione.

LIBERA'LITY, s. [generosity] liberalità, magnanimità, generosità, s. f.

LI'BERALLY, adv. liberalmente, largamente, generosamente.

LI'BERTINE, s. [a dissolute and lewd liver] uno scapestrato, uno sviato.

Libertine, adj. scapestrato, licenzioso, sviato.

LI'BERTINISM, s. [licentiousness] licenza, sfrenatezza, vita licenziosa.

LI'BERTY, s. [freedom] libertà. s. f.

To give a slave his liberty, dar la libertà ad uno schiavo.

To set at liberty, mettere in libertà.

The liberties of a city, le franchigie, le immunità d' una città.

Liberty [leave] libertà, licenza, permissione, s. f.

Liberty of will, libero arbitrio.

LIBI'DINOUS, adj. [voluptuous] libidinoso, voluttuoso, impudico, lascivo.

LIB'LONG, s. [a sort of herb] aloe cicotrino, s. m.

LI'BRA, s. [one of the twelve celestial signs] Libra, s. f. uno de' dodici segni celesti.

LIBRA'RIAN, s. [one who has the care of a library] bibliotecario.

LI'BRARY, s. [a study or place where books are kept] libreria, biblioteca.

A library keeper, bibliotecario, s. m.

LIBRA'TION, s. [a weighing, or balance] libramento, s. m.

LICE, s. [the plural of louse] pidocchi.

LI'CENCE, s. [liberty, permission] licenza, libertà, permissione, s. f.

A poetical licence, licenza poetica.

A licence [to print or publish a book] licenza, privilegio di stampare, o di pubblicare un libro.

Licence [leave] licenza, permissione.

To LI'CENCE [to give leave, or power] dar licenza, conceder privilegio.

To licence a book, dar licenza di stampare, o pubblicare un libro.

LI'CENCED, adj. ex. A book licenced, un libro stampato con privilegio.

LICE'NTIATE, s. [one who has a full licence to practise in any art or faculty] un licenziato.

LICE'NTIOUS, adj. [loose, lewd, disorderly] licenzioso, dissoluto, fregolato, scapestrato, sfrenato.

A licentious life, una vita licenziosa, o fregolata.

Licentious talking, discorsi licenziosi.

LICE'NTIOUSLY, adv. licenziosamente, sfrenatamente, fregolatamente.

LICE'NTIOUSNESS, s. licenza, troppa libertà di costumi, sfrenatezza, fregolatezza, dissolutezza, scostumatezza.

LICH, s. cadavere, corpo morto.

LI'CH-OWL, s. spezie di barbagianni, o di civetta, quel lich vi è aggiunto per dinotare che è uccello di mal augurio, e che predice morte.

Lich-gate [a gate in church-yards, thro' which the corps of the dead are carried] porta di cimeterio.

LI'CH-WAKE, s. quel tempo in cui si veglia accanto a' morti.

Lichwale, s. [an herb] spezie d'erba vetensia.

LICITA'TION, s. [an auction] incanto, s. m.

LICK, s. [a gentle stroke] un piccol colpo, una botta.

He gave him a lick over the shoulders, gli diede una botta sulle spalle.

A lick-dish, un leccapiatti, un ghiottone, un leccardo.

A lick-stone, s. [a fish] *murena*, s. f. *sorta di pesce di mare.*

To LICK, or to lick up [to take up with the tongue] *leccare.*

To lick one's fingers, *leccarsi le dita.*

LI'CKERISH, } adj. [that loves tid LI'CKEROUS, } bits, or sweet things] *leccardo, ghiotto, goloso.*

LI'CKERISHNESS, s. *golosità, ghiotternia*, s. f.

LI'CORICE, s. [a shrub which has a sweet root] *liquorizia, regolizia*, s. f. *erba nota*

LI'CTORS, s. [Roman officers who carried the axes and rods before the magistrates] *littori.*

LID, s. [cover] *coperchio, e coverchio*, s. m.

The lid of a pot or box, *il coperchio d'una pignatta o d'una scatola.*

The eye-lid, *la palpebra*, s. f.

LIE, s. [untruth] *bugia, menzogna*, s. f.

To tell lies, *dire delle bugie, delle menzogne, mentire.*

Lie [story] *menzogna, favola, finzione.*

I tell you no lie, *non vi dico menzogna, non vi burlo.*

To give one the lie, *smentire, dismentire alcuno.*

Lie [made of ashes] *v.* Ly.

To LIE, v. a. *dir bugia, mentire.*

To lie, v. n. *pr.* I lay; I have lain or lien, *v.* to ly, *che così scrive l'Altieri, e non senza esempio, ma si dove scrivere* to lie.

LIEF, adv. [rather] *più tosto, più presto.*

I had as lief go as stay, *è tutt'uno per me d'andare o di restare.*

I had as lief die as do any such thing, *vorrei più tosto morire, che fare una tal cosa.*

Lief, adj. *caro, diletto, v.* Leef.

LIEGE, adj. *ligio, suddito.*

A liege lord, *un signore ligio.*

A liege lord [a sovereign prince] *un principe sovrano.*

A liege man [he who owes allegiance or homage to the liege lord] *uomo ligio, un vassallo.*

LI'EGES [liege people, people that owe allegiance to their liege lord] *un popolo sogetto ad un principe, vassalli suggetti.*

LI'EGEANCY, *v.* Ligeancy.

LI'EGER, s. *ambasciatore che risiede.*

LIENTE'RY, s [a kind of looseness wherein the food presses so suddenly thro' the stomach and guts, as to be thrown out by stool with little or no alteration] *lienteria*, s. f. *spezie di flusso.*

LI'EN [*participio del verbo* to lie] *giaciuto.*

LI'ER, s. *un che giace giù.*

LIEU, s. [stead] *luogo, vece.*

In lieu of, *in luogo, in vere.*

Lieu, adv. *volentieri.*

LIEUTE'NANCY, s. [a lieutenant's place] *carica di luogotenente.*

LIEUTE'NANT, s. *luogotenente*, s. m.

The lieutenant of a company of foot, or troop of horse, *il luogotenente d'una campagnia di fanteria, o di cavalleria.*

A lieutenant colonel, *un luogotenente colonnello.*

A lieutenant general, *un luogotenente generale.*

A lord lieutenant of a county, *un governatore di provincio.*

The lord lieutenant of Ireland, *il vicerè d' Irlanda.*

LIEUTE'NANTSHIP, *v.* Lieutenancy.

LIFE, s. [the union of the soul with the body] *vita*, s. f. *l'unione dell' anima col corpo.*

To have a life [to be alive] *aver vita, essere in vita.*

To lose one's life [to die] *perder la vita, morire.*

To spend one's life in pleasures, *passar la vita in piaceri.*

The lives of the fathers, *le vite de' santi padri.*

Life [mettle, sprightliness] *vivacità, vigore.*

To be full of life, *esser pieno di vivarità, esser vivace.*

To give life, *animare, vivificare.*

If God give me life, *se Dio mi da vita.*

To draw one's picture to the life, *fare l'altrui ritratto al naturale.*

I will beg his life, *io domanderò la sua grazia.*

As you tender your life don't do it, *per vita vostra non lo fate.*

To depart this life [to die] *uscir di vita, morire.*

To be weary of one's life, *esser lasso di vivere.*

There's life in him still, *egli respira ancora, egli non è ancor morto.*

To steep life and soul together, *vivere meschinamente.*

To sit upon life and death [to try one for his life] *fare il processo ad uno.*

A pension for life, *una pensione vitalizia.*

Life [manner of living] *vita, maniera di vivere.*

To live a religious life, *menare una vita religiosa, viver religiosamente.*

For life, *a vita.*

A life-guard, or a life-guard man, *un soldato di guardia.*

Life-time, *vita, il tempo della vita.*

To pass one s life-time in the country, *passar la vita in campagna.*

In his life-time, *nella sua vita.*

Life-rent, *pensione a vita.*

LI'FELESS, adj. *che non ha vita, che non è animato.*

LIFT, s. *sforzo che si fa per levar su una cosa.*

To give one a lift [to help him] *ajutare alcuno, assisterlo.*

To give one a lift [to supplant him] *soppiantare alcuno, dargli il gambetto.*

At one lift [at once] *in un colpo, in un subito, alla prima.*

To help one at a dead lift, *trarre alcuno d'impaccio.*

To LIFT, or to lift up, *alzare, inalzare, sollevare, levare, ergere. pret. ersi.*

To lift up a piece of timber, *alzare un pezzo di legno.*

To lift up a stone, *levar su una pietra.*

To lift up [or to raise] one's voice, *alzar la voce.*

To lift up one's hands to heaven, *alzare, levare le mani al ciele.*

To lift [or to cut] for deal at cards, *alzare le carte.*

LI'FTED UP, adj. *alzato, innalzato, sollevato, levato.*

Lifted up with pride, *gonfio d'orgoglio.*

A lifter up, s. *colui che alza, o leva.*

To LIG, v. n. [to lie] *giacere, starsi giù.*

LI'GAMENT, s. [a part of the body of a middle-substance betwixt a cartilage and a membrane, appointed for the tying of the parts together] *ligamento*, s. m.

LI'GATURE, s. [a tie, or band] *legatura*, s. f. *legame*, s. m.

The ligatures of the nerves, *le legature de' nervi.*

LI'GEANCE, } s. [the dominion of LIEGEANCE, } a liege lord] *vassallaggio*, s. m.

LIGHT, adj. [the contrary of heavy] *leggiere, leggieri, leggiero, contrario di grave.*

A light burden, *una soma leggera.*

Light [that is not full weight] *leggiero, che non è di peso.*

This guinea is light, *questa ghinea è leggiera, o non di peso.*

Light [nimble] *leggiero, agile, snello, veloce, presto.*

Light [small, trifling] *leggiero, di poco momento, frivolo, picolo, di poco importanza.*

A light wound, *una leggiera ferita.*

A light penance, *una penitenza leggiera.*

Light gains make a heavy purse, *i guadagni mediocri empiono la borsa.*

A light meal, *pasto leggiero.*

Light, or light-armed, *armato alla leggiera.*

Light [inconstant] *leggiero, incostante, volubile.*

Light bread, *pan buffetto.*

Light [superficial] knowledge, *conoscenza leggiera, che non è profonda.*

Light [bright] *chiaro, risplendente, luminoso.*

A light room, *una camera chiara.*

Light [of a flaxen colour] *biondo.*

Light hair, *capelli biondi.*

Light of belief, *credulo, che crede volentieri.*

To make light of a thing [to make light account of it, to set light by it] *dispregiare, tenere, o avere a vile una cosa, farne poca stima o poco conto, vilipenderla.*

If you don't think light of it, *se voi lo stimate a proposito.*

Light-armed, *armato alla leggiera.*

Light-heeled, or light-footed, *leggiere alla corsa.*

Light-coloured, *chiaro.*

Light-headed, *gajo, allegro, festoso.*

Light-headed, *delirante, pazzo, fuor del senno.*

Light, s. [brightness, *splendore, lume,* s. m. *chiarezza,* s. f.

The light of the sun, *lo splendore del sole.*

The light of the moon, *il lume della luna.*

Light, or day light, *giorno.*

It begins to be light, *comincia a far giorno.*

To stand in one's light, *impedire in lume ad uno.*

To stand in one's light [to hurt him] *far torto ad uno, daneggiarlo.*

To stand in one's own light [to prejudice one's self] *farsi torto, pregiudicarsi.*

Light [candle, torch] *lume, candela.*

Bring a light hither, *portate del lume, portate una candela qui.*

The lights of a church, *i lumi, le candele, le lampada d'una chiesa.*

A wax light, *una candela di cera.*

A watch light [in a ship, or on land] *fanale.*

A light house, *faro,* s. m. *lanterna,* s. f.

Light [knowledge] *lumiera, lume, intelligenza, conoscenza.*

The light of nature, *la lumiera, il lume della natura.*

Light [a person of great knowledge and worth] *lume, persona illustre, celebre, gloriosa per il suo proprio merito.*

Light [insight, hint] *indizio, barlume.*

The lights of a picture, *i lumi, i chiari d'una pittura.*

The lights of a house, *le finestre d'una casa.*

The lights [lungs] of a beast, *i polmoni d'un animale.*

To carry a light before one, *far lume ad uno.*

To give light to things that are obscure, *schiarire, sviluppare, dichiarare le cose oscure.*

To bring to light, *metter in chiaro, scoprire.*

To LIGHT [to give light] *far lume.*

To light [or kindle] *accendere.*

To light a candle, *accendere una candela.*

To light a fire, *accendere il fuoco, far del fuoco.*

To light on, or upon [to meet by chance] *imbattersi, abbattersi, avvenirsi a caso, incontrare.*

To light on one, *imbattersi in uno, incontrarlo a caso.*

If I can light with such a thing, *se una tal cosa mi capitasse, o mi venisse nelle mani.*

To light [to happen] *arrivare, succedere, venire per accidente.*

Some mischief or other will light on him, *gli arriverà qualche disgrazia.*

To light [to alight] off one's horse, *scendere, o smontar di cavallo, scavalcare.*

To light [to settle as birds do] *poggiarsi, posarsi.*

LI'GHTED, adj. *o chi si fa lume.*

Lighted [set out with glass windows] *vitriato.*

To LI'GHTEN [to make light or easy of weight] *alleggerire, sgravare, render leggieri.*

To lighten one's burden, *alleggerire l' altrui soma.*

To lighten a ship, *alleggerire un vascello.*

To lighten, *lampeggiare.*

It lightens, *lampeggia.*

To lighten [to give light to] *illuminare, schiarire.*

LI'GHTENED, adj. *alleggerito, v.* To lighten.

LI'GHTNING, s. *alleggerimento,* s. m.

A lightning, or flash of lightning, *un lampo, un baleno.*

A lightning before death, *nunzio di morte.*

LI'GHTER, s. [a kind of boat] *piana,* s. f. *sorta di barca.*

LI'GHTLESS, adj. [or without light] *scuro, oscuro, che non ha chiarezza.*

LI'GHTLY, adv. [inconsiderately, slenderly] *alla leggiera, leggiermente, un poco*

Lightly [inconsiderately] *leggiermente, imprudentemente.*

Lightly [or easily] *facilmente, di leggieri.*

Lightly come, lightly go, *quel che viene di ruffa, se ne va in raffa.*

To believe lightly, *creder di leggieri, o facilmente.*

To take lightly, *voi delirate*

Lightly [swiftly] *presto, prestamente.*

LI'GHTNED, *v.* Lightened.

LI'GHTNESS, s. [the contrary of being heavy] *larghezza,* s. f.

Lightness of the head, *delirio,* s. m.

Lightness [nimbleness] *leggierezza, agilità, prestezza,* s. f.

Lightness of belief, *credulità,* s. f.

LI'GHTSOME, s. *luminoso, chiaro.*

A lightsome room, *una camera chiara.*

Lightsome [cheerful] *gajo, giojoso, allegro.*

LI'GNEOUS, adj. [woody] *ligneo di legno.*

LIGNA'LOES, s. [aloes wood] *legno aloè.*

Lignum vitæ, *spezie di legno che viene dall' Indie.*

LI'GURE, s. [a precious stone] *sorta di pietra preziosa.*

LIKE, adj. *simile, somigliante, pari.*

He is like his father, *egli è simile a suo padre, egli rassomiglia a suo padre, egli patrizza.*

Like will to like, or like loves like, *ognuno ama il suo simile.*

I never saw the like, *non hò mai visto cosa simile.*

Like master, like man, *qual padrone, tal servo.*

Like [the same] *medesimo.*

To be of like force, *essere della medesima forza.*

In the like manner, *parimente, similmente.*

Like [likely] *verisimile, probabile, credibile.*

'Tis like enough, *è molto verisimile.*

Such like things, *tali cose, simili cose.*

This is something like, *questo qui è mediocre.*

No, nothing like it, *non c' è tal cosa.*

'Tis like we shall have a good harvest, *secondo l'apparenza noi avremo una buona raccolta.*

'Tis very like so, *è molto verisimile.*

He is like to do well, *secondo ogni apparenza egli riuscirà ne' suoi affari.*

He is like to do well [or to live to recover] *per quel che si può vedere non morirà.*

You are not like to see me any more, *forse che non mi vedrete più.*

He was like to die, *egli fu in punto di morte, poco mancò che non morisse.*

He was like to be drowned, *egli fu per annegarsi, poco mancò che non s'annegasse.*

He is like to lose his money, *egli corre rischio di perdere il suo danaro.*

I had like to have forgot it, *l'avevo quasi dimenticato.*

We are like to have war, *in ogni apparenza noi averemo la guerra.*

You are like to stay while I come back, *bisogna che voi aspettiate fin ch' io ritorni.*

Like, s. *la pariglia, la medesima cosa.*

To give like for like, *render la pariglia, render pan per focaccia.*

The like was never heard, *non s' è mai udita una cosa simile.*

He has not his like [he is without a match] *non c'è il simile a lui.*

Like, adv. *come, da.*

To do like another, *fare come un altro.*

Like a mad man, *come un matto, da matto.*

He carried himself like a man, *egli si comportò da bravo uomo.*

They looked like dead men, *parevano come morti.*

He did like himself, *è un' azione degna d'un par suo.*

To live like one's self, *viver seconda la sua qualità.*

He acted like an honest man, *egli trattò da galantuomo.*

To like [to love, to be pleased with, to approve] *amare, gradire, piacere, essere a grado, andare a gusto, a genio,* pret. *piacqui.*

I like her very well, *io l'amo molto, ella mi va a genio.*

How do you like it? *come vi piace, che ne dite?*

I like your advice, *io gradisco il vostro consiglio, il vostro consiglio mi piace, e è buono.*

As you like yourself, *come vi piacerà.*

LI'KED, adj. *amato, piaciuto.*

That is not well liked, *ciò non viene approvato, o gradito.*

LI'KELINESS, *v.* Likelihood.

LI'KELIHOOD, s. *apparenza, verisimilitudine, probabilità.*

LI'KELY, adj. [probable] *verisimile, probabile, credibile, apparente.*

It is not likely, *ciò non è verisimile.*

A good likely man, *un uomo ben fatto, un uomo di bella apparenza.*

Very likely it might be so, *questo è molto verisimile.*

To Li'ken [or compare] *rassomigliare, paragonare, comparare, uguagliare.*

Li'kened, adj. *rassomigliato, paragonato, comparato, uguagliato.*

Likeness, s. [resemblance] *somiglianza, e simiglianza, conformità.*

Li'kewise, adv. *parimente, similmente.*

Li'king, s. *genio, gusto,* s. m. *scelta,* s. f.

This is not to my liking, *questo non è di mio gusto, non m' aggrada.*

To create a liking, *rendersi amabile, o grato.*

Good liking [approbation] *approvazione, consenso.*

Good liking [good plight of the body] *buono stato di salute.*

Li'lach, s. *nome di pianta.*

Li'lied, adj. [embellished with lilies] *abbellito di gigli, ornato di gigli.*

Li'ly, s. [a flower] *giglio,* s. m.

The wild, or mountain lily, the lily of the valley, *fioraliso, mughetto.*

To adorn with lilies, *ingigliare, adornare di gigli.*

She looked all roses and lilies, *ella aveva una carnagione di gigli e di rose.*

Li'mation, s. [a filing] *limatura,* s. f. *il limare.*

Limatu're, s. [powder or dust which comes off filings] *limatura, quella polvere che cade della cosa che si lima.*

Limb, s. [a part of the body, a member] *membro,* s. m. *parte del corpo.* pl. *i membri,* m. *le membra,* f.

Lime-meal, *membro a membro, in pezzi, a brani.*

To tear one limb-meal, or limb from limb, *sbranare alcuno, metterlo in pezzi.*

To Limb [to supply with limbs] *dar membra, somministrar membra.*

To limb [to tear asunder, to dismember] *smembrare, sbranare, disfare a membro a membro, a brano a brano.*

Li'mbeck, s. *lambicco.*

Li'mbed, ex. strong limbed, *tarchiato, di buone membra.*

Li'mber, adj. [supple, pliable] *pieghevole, arrendevole, flessibile.*

Li'mberness, s. *flessibilità.*

Li'mbo, s. [the place where the deceased patriarchs, and other good men stood waiting for Christ's coming, and where lie those who die without baptism] *limbo,* s. m.

Limbo, *luogo di miseria.*

In limbo [in prison] *in prigione.*

Lime, s. [chalk burnt for mortar] *calcina,* s. f. *pietra cotta la quale s'adopera a murare.*

Quick lime, *calcina viva.*

Lime-kiln, *fornace.*

Lime [mud] *limo, fango,* s. m. *poltiglia, mota,* s. f.

Lime [bird lime] *vischio,* s. m. *pania,* s. f.

Lime twigs, *paniuzzola,* s. f. *paniuzzo,* s. m. *fuscello impaniato.*

A lime-hound, or limmer [a bloodhound] *bracco da sangue.*

Lime, *sorta di limone.*

To Lime [to couple] *annodarsi, accoppiarsi come fanno i bracchi.*

To lime, *invischiare, pigliar col vischio; incolappiare.*

To lime, *sparger di vischio.*

To lime, *incalcinare, cimentare.*

To lime, *ingrassar il terreno spargendolo di calce.*

Li'mit, s. [bound] *limite, termine, confine,* s. m.

To set a limit, *limitare, por termine.*

To Li'mit [to set bounds to] *limitare, restringuere, por termine, terminare, confinare.*

To limit [to appoint] *limitare, assegnare, determinare, accordare, convenire.* pres. *convegno.* pret. *convenni.*

Limita'tion, s. [stinting] *limitazione, determinazione, riserva,* s. f.

Li'mited, adj. *limitato, ristretto, terminato.*

Limited [appointed] *limitato, assegnato, determinato, accordato, convenuto.*

Li'mmer [a mongrel] *spezie di cane.*

To Limn [to paint in water-colours] *miniare, dipignere con acquerelli.*

Limned, adj. *miniato.*

Li'mner, s. [painter] *miniatore, pittore in miniatura, o pittore in generale. Non è vocabolo molto in uso.*

Li'mon, v. Lemon.

Li'monade, s. [a cooling liquor made of lemons, water and sugar] *sorta di bevanda fatta con acqua, zucchero, e agro di limone, limonata.*

Li'mose, adj. [muddy] *limoso, melmoso, fangoso.*

Li'mosity, s. [muddiness] *limosità,* s. f. *astratto di limoso.*

Li'mous, adj. [muddy] *limoso, fangoso, melmoso, limaccioso.*

To Limp [to halt] *zoppicare, esser zoppo.*

Li'mpid, adj. [clear, fair] *limpido, chiaro.*

Limpid water, *acqua limpida.*

Limpi'dity, } s. [clearness] *limpidezza, chiarezza,* s. f.
Li'mpitude, }

Li'mpin, s. [a shell fish otherwise call'd a muscle] *tellina,* s. f.

Li'mping, s. [from to limp] *il zoppicare.*

Limping, adj. ex. A limping man, *un zoppo.*

Limping woman, *una zoppa.*

To Lin [to cease] *cessare, desistere.*

Li'nage, s. [stock] *lignaggio, e legnaggio,* s. m. *stirpe, schiatta, famiglia,* s. f.

Li'nament, s. [or thread] s. f. pl. *filaccia.*

Li'nament [lint for a wound or tint] *filaccia.*

Linch pin, s. [the pin that keeps in the wheel to the axle tree] *palicello o chiodo di ruota.*

Li'nden Tree, s. *nome d' albero.*

Line, s. *una linea.*

Line [a row of words in writing, or printing] *linea, riga.*

A page that contains so many lines, *una facciata che contiene tante linee.*

To draw a strait and parallel line, *tirare una linea dritta, e paralella.*

A line of circumvallation, *una linea de circonvallazione.*

He drew up his army into two lines, *egli dispose il suo esercito in due linee.*

The equinoctial line, *linea equinoziale, si dice quella, che ugualmente distante da' poli, divide la sfera in parti uguali.*

Line [descent] *linea, descendenza,* s. f. *lignaggio,* s. m.

Line [small cord] *cordellina, cordicella.*

To Line [to put a lining to] *foderare, soppannare.*

To line a coat, *foderare un vestito.*

To line with fur, *soppanare con pelliccia.*

To line a brick wall with free stone, *incrostare un muro di pietre di taglio.*

To line [to couple as a dog does] *annodarsi, accoppiarsi.*

Li'neage, v. Linage.

Li'neal, adj. [that goes in a right line] *lineale, che va per linea diretta.*

A succession in a lineal descent, *una successione per linea diretta.*

Li'neament, s. [the feature or proportion of the face] *lineamento,* s. m. *fattezza,* s. f.

Li'ned, adj. *foderato, soppannato.*

Li'nen, s. *tela; tessuto di canape o di lino.*

Linen, adj. *fatto di tela, somigliante a tela.*

Li'nendraper, s. *mercante di tela.*

Ling, s. [a sort of salt fish] *baccalà,* s. m. *sorta di pesce salato.*

Ling [heath] *tamerice, tamarisco.*

Ling-wort [an herb] *angelica,* s. f. *erba medicinale.*

To Li'nger [to languish] *languire, menare una vita languida.*

To linger [to be long a doing] *tardare, prolongare, differire, tirare in lungo.*

To linger about a business, *tirare in lungo un negozio.*

Li'ngerer, s. *un uomo lento, tardo, pigro.*

Li'ngering, adj. [long, tedious] *lungo, tardo, lento, pigro.*

Lingering [languishing] *languido, fievole.*

To go a lingering pace, *camminare a passi lenti.*

Lingering, s. [delay] *ritardamento, indugio,* s. m. *dilazione,* s. f.

Li'ngeringly, adv. [slowly] *lentamente, lento, pigramente, adagio.*

Li'nget, v. Ingot.

Li'ngo, s. [language, tongue, speech] *linguaggio, la lingua, il parlare.*

Lingua'city, s. [talkativeness] *loquacità, garrulità,* s. f. *cicaleccio, cicalio,* s. m.

Li'nguist, s. [a person skilful in languages] *dotto, versato nelle lingue, che sa molte lingue.*

Li'ngworth, } s. [an herb] *angelica.*
Lo'ngwort, }

Li'niment, s. [an external medicine of a middle conſiſtence between an oil and an ointment] *linimento*, s. m. *ſpezie di medicamento eſterno.*

LI'NING, s. [from to line] *il foderare.*

The lining of a garment, *fodera*, s. f. *ſoppanno*, s. m.

The lining of a hat, *la cuffia d'un cappello.*

LINK, s. [a ring of a chain] *anello di catena.*

A link of ſauſages, *ſalſicciuolo, pezzo di ſalſiccia, rocchio*, s. m.

LINK [torch] *fiaccola, torcia a vento.*

To link [to join or tie together] *incatenare, legare, unire inſieme.*

LI'NKBOY, s. *ragazzo che porta una torcia in mano di notte tempo per le vie, e fa lume alla gente per mercede.*

LI'NKED, adj. *incatenato, legato, unito inſieme.*

To be linked in conſanguinity with one, *eſſer parente, o congiunto d'uno.*

LI'NEN, s. [or linen cloths] *biancheria, panni lini.*

Linen cloth, *tela.*

Linen-draper, *mercante di tela.*

LI'NNET, s. [a ſinging bird] *fanello*, s. m.

LI'NSEED, s. [the ſeed of flax] *ſementa di lino.*

Linſeed-oil, *olio di lino.*

LINSEY-WOOLSEY, s. [any ſtuff made of thread and wool] *mezzalana*, s. f. *ſorta di panno fatto di lana e lino.*

Linſey-woolſey, adj *vile, abbietto.*

LI'NSTOCK, s. *baſtone in punta al quale gli artiglieri appiccano un pezzo di miccia per uſo di dar fuoco a' cannoni.*

LINT, s. [linen threads, or filament to put on a wound] *fila di panno lino, filaticcio.*

Lint ſtock [a ſhort ſtaff of wood, uſed by gunners in firing cannon] *baſtone che contiene alla punta la miccia colla quale il cannoniere da fuoco al cannone.*

LI'NTEL, s. *quella parte della cornice della porta che ſta appunto ſovra i colonnati che ſoſtengonla.*

LI'ON, s. [a beaſt of prey] *leone, lione*, s. m.

A ſhe lion, or a lioneſs, *una leoneſſa, lioneſſa.*

A young lion, or a lion's whelp, *leoncello, lioncello.*

A LI'ONCEL, *un leoncello, un lioncello.*

LI'ONESS, s. [a ſhe lion] *leoneſſa, lioneſſa*, s. f.

LI'ONLEAF,
LI'ONSMOUTH,
LI'ONSPAW,
LI'ONSTAIL,
LI'ONSTOOTH, } s. *nomi di piante.*

LIP, s. [the upper or nether part of the mouth] *labbro*, s. m. *eſtremità della bocca.*

To part with dry lips [or without kiſſing] *ſepararſi ſenza baciarſi.*

A little lip, *labbricciuolo*, s. m.

Hare lip, *labbro di lepre, o leporino.*

Lip [the edge of any thing] *labbro, e orlo di checcheſſia.*

To make a lip [to hang the lip in ſullenneſs and contempt] *ciondolar il labbro per moſtrar diſprezzo, o per caparbietà.*

To LIP [to kiſs] *baciare. Non è in uſo.*

LIPLA'BOUR, s. *ciarla che non finiſce mai. Il cianciar molto ſenza che la mente l'affatichi a dirigger le parole.*

LI'PPED, adj Ex. Hare-lipped, *che ha un labbro leporino.*

LI'PPITUDE, s. [bleer-eyedneſs] *lippitudine, ciſpoſità*, s. f.

LIPWI'SDOM, s. *ipocriſia; ſaviezza in parole ſenza fatti.*

LIQUA'TION,
LIQUEFA'CTION, } s. [melting, or diſſolving] *liquefazione*, s. f. *il liquefare.*

To LI'QUATE, } [to melt] *liquefare,*
To LI'QUEFY, } *far liquido, ſtruggere, fondere.*

To liquefy, verb neut. *liquefarſi, ſtruggerſi, fonderſi.*

LIQUE'SCENCY, s. [a melting or growing ſoft] *liquefazione.*

LIQUID, adj. [that has its parts fluid] *liquido, che cede al tatto, fleſſibile.*

A liquid body, *un corpo liquido.*

Liquid, s. *coſa liquida, liquore.*

The liquids [five letters ſo called] *le lettere liquide, cioè*, l, m, n, r, s.

To LI'QUIDATE [to make liquid] *liquidare, far divenir liquido.*

LIQUIDE'SCENCY, s. *diſpoſizione d'un corpo a liquefarſi.*

LIQUI'DITY, s. [ſubtilty] *liquidità*, s. f.

LI'QUORISH, s. *liquorizia.*

LIQUOR,
LIQUOUR, } s. [any liquid thing] *liquore*, s. m. *tutte quelle coſe che ſi ſpargono e traſcorrono.*

Liquor [drink] *liquore, bevanda.*

Liquor [juice] *ſugo, zugo.*

A thing full of liquor, *una coſa ſugoſa.*

To LI'QUOR, *ugnere, umettare.*

To liquor boots, *ugnere gli ſtivali.*

LI'QUORED, adj. *unto, umettato.*

LIRICO'FANCY, s. [the lily of the valley] *mughetto*, s. m.

LISNE, s. [a cavity, a hollow] *una cavità, un buco.*

To LISP [to falter in the ſpeech, to clip words] *ſcilinguare, balbettare.*

Liſp, s. *difetto nella lingua o nelle labbra che cagiona il balbettare.*

LI'SPER, s. [a liſping man or woman] *uno ſcilinguato, una ſcilinguata.*

LISPING, adj. Ex. a liſping man, *uno ſcilinguato.*

LI'SPONED, s. [a foreign weight of fifteen or ſixteen, and ſometimes twenty pounds] *peſo di quindici o ſedici libbre, e qualche volta di venti.*

LIST, s. [catalogue] *liſta*, s. f. *catalogo*, s. m.

To make a liſt, *fare una liſta.*

The liſt [edge] of cloth, *cimoſa*, s. m.

Liſt, or liſts [a place incloſed with rails, for tournaments, races, wreſtlings, and other exerciſes] *lizza, gioſtra*, s. f.

To enter the liſt or liſts, *entrare in liſta, o entrare in gioſtra.*

Liſt [will] *voglia, volontà*, s. f.

To LIST, *arrolare, ſcrivere al ruolo.*

To liſt ſoldiers, *arrolare, far ſoldati, levar ſoldati.*

To liſt one's ſelf a ſoldier, *arrolarſi, farſi ſoldato.*

To liſt, verb neut. [to be willing] *volere.*

Let him do what he liſts, *faccia quel che vuole.*

When I liſt, *quando mi piacerà.*

Let him live as he liſts, *viva à modo ſuo.*

LI'STED, adj. *v.* To liſt.

To LI'STEN [to hearken] *aſcoltare, ſtare ad udire con attenzione; udire.*

LI'STNER, s. *quello, o quella che aſcolta.*

LI'STNING, s. *l'aſcoltare, aſcolta*, s. f.

LI'STLESS, adj. [regardleſs, careleſs] *che non ſi cura di niente, pigro, infingardo, ſvogliato.*

LISTLESSLY, adv. [without thought, without attention] *ſenza penſiero, diſattentamente, ſtraccuratamente, ſvogliatamente.*

LI'STLESSNESS, s. [inattention; want of deſire] *diſattenzione; noja; totale abſenza di deſiderio, ſvogliatezza perfetta.*

LIT, *preter. del verbo* To light.

LI'TANY, s. [a general ſupplication, or prayer] *Litania, Letane*, s. f.

LI'TERAL, adj. [according to the letter] *letterale.*

A literal ſenſe, *il ſenſo letterale.*

A literal fault [in printing] *errore di ſtampa.*

LITERA'LITY, s. *ſenſo primiero, ſenſo originale.*

LI'TERALLY, adv. [in a literal ſenſe] *letteralmente.*

LI'TERATE, adj. [learned] *letterato, dotto, ſcienziato.*

A literate man, *un uomo litterato.*

LI'TERATURE, s. [knowledge in letters, learning] *letteratura*, s. f.

LI'THARGE of gold, *letargo d'oro.*

LI'THARGIC,
LI'THARGE, } s. [the ſcum of lead, ſilver, or gold] *letargo*, s. f.

LITHE, s. [ſupple, limber] *pieghevole, arrendevole.*

LI'THENESS, s. [limberneſs] *qualità pieghevole, o arrendevole.*

LI'THER, adj. [lazy] *molle, pieghevole.*

Lither, s. [lazineſs] *pigrizia, lentezza, tardezza, infingardaggine*, s. f.

LI'THY, adj. [lithe] *arrendevole, pieghevole.*

LITIGA'TION [quarrelling] *litigamento*, s. m. *il litigare, lite, conteſa*, s. f.

LITI'GIOUS, adj. [that delights in going to law, quarrelſome] *litigioſo, che volentieri litiga.*

A litigious man, *un uomo litigioſo, un litigatore.*

A litigious woman, *una donna litigioſa, una litigatrice.*

A litigious thing [a thing contended for] *una coſa litigioſa, che è in lite.*

LITI'GIOUSLY, adv. [contentiouſly] *litigioſamente, contenzioſamente.*

LITI-

LITI'GIOUSNESS, adv. [or contentious humour] *umore litigioso.*

LITISPE'NDENCE, s. [the time during which a law suit is depending] *lite pendente.*

LI'TTER, s. [a sedan carried by two horses, or mules] *lettiga,* s. f. *arnese da far viaggio, portato per lo più da due muli.*

Litter [straw spread under cattle to lie down upon] *letto, paglia che si mette sotto le bestie per riposarvisi sopra.*

Litter [the brood of a bear brought forth at once] *ventrata,* s. f.

A litter of pigs, *una ventrata di porcelli.*

To make a litter in a room, *metter ogni cosa in disordine, in iscompiglio, sozzopra in una camera.*

LI'TTERINGS, s. [small sticks which keep the webb stretched on a weaver's loom] *croci di tessitore.*

LI'TTLE, adj. *piccolo, o picciolo.*

A little horse, *un piccolo cavallo.*

A little house, *una piccola casa.*

A little man, *un piccol uomo.*

For so little a matter, *per si poca cosa.*

A little, s. *un poco.*

Stay a little, stay a little while, *aspettate un poco.*

A little more, *un poco più.*

A little less, *un poco meno.*

A little one [or a child] *un fanciullo, un bambino.*

How many little ones have you? *quanti figliuoli avete?*

Many a little makes a mickle, *a quattrino a quattrino si fa'l soldo, spesseggiando a poco a poco si fa l'assai.*

Little, adv. *poco, un poco.*

To have but little money, *aver poco danaro.*

By little and little, *a poco a poco.*

He has but little wit, *egli non ha molto spirito.*

Too little, *troppo poco.*

Never so little, *un pochettino.*

LI'TTLENESS, s. *picciolezza,* s. f.

LI'TURGY, s. [a form of ceremonies, or common prayers] *liturgia,* s. f. *formulario di preghiere, e di ceremonie nel servizio divino.*

Live, adj. [alive] *vivo, che ha vita; attivo, non estinto.*

To LIVE [to be alive] *vivere, stare in vita,* pret. *vissi.*

In God we live, move, and have our being, *in Dio abbiamo la vita, il moto, e l'essere.*

To live [to enjoy life] *vivere, aver vita.*

As long as I live, *tanto che viverò.*

To live [to pass one's life] *vivere, passar la vita.*

To live in solitude, *viver nella solitudine, menare una vita solitaria.*

To live [to agree] well together, *vivere insieme, esser d accordo insieme.*

To live [to feed, to subsist] *vivere, nutrirsi, cibarsi.*

To live from hand to mouth, *vivere di per dì.*

To live upon one's income, *viver d'entrata.*

To live by one's work, *viver delle sue fatiche.*

To live upon herbs and roots, *vivere o pascersi d'erbe, e di radici.*

To live [to endure, to subsist] *vivere, soffrire, sussistere.*

I can live no longer at this rate, *non posso viver più di questa maniera.*

The Latin tongue will live for ever, *la lingua Latina viverà per sempre.*

To live [to dwell] *dimorare, far la sua dimora.*

Where do you live? *dove dimorate, dove state di casa?*

He lives in the country, *egli dimora in campagna.*

He is as good a man as lives [or the best man in the world] *egli è il miglior uomo del mondo.*

If ever you live to see him again, *se mai lo rivedrete.*

As I leave and breathe, *per vita mia.*

To live a country life, *menare una vita campestre.*

Would I might never live if it be so, *che possa morire, se ciò è vero.*

I shall never live to see it, *sarò morto prima di questo tempo.*

This will be enough for me to live on, *questo mi basterà a vivere, a mantenermi.*

To live up to the height of religion, *conformarsi alle regole della religione, vivere conforme alle regole della religione.*

No man can live up to the law, *non c'è nessuno che possa compire appieno la legge.*

To live upon one's estate, *consumare le sue entrate.*

LI'VED, adj. *vissuto,* v. To live.

Long lived, *che è di lunga vita, di lunga durata, che dura lungo tempo.*

Short lived, *di corta vita, che non vive lungo tempo.*

LI'VELESS, adj. [dead] *che non ha vita, senza vita, morto.*

Liveless [without strength] *languido, spossato, fievole, debole, senza forze.*

LI'VELIHOOD, s. [maintenance] *vitto, mantenimento,* s. m. *vita,* s. f.

To get one's livelihood, *guadagnarsi il vitto, la vita.*

Livelihood [estate] *bene, patrimonio,* s. m. *facultà,* s. f.

Livelihood [trade] *arte,* s. f. *mestiere.*

LI'VELINESS, s. [briskness, vivacity] *vivacità,* s. f. *spirito,* s. m.

LI'VE-LONG, adj. *durevole troppo.*

LI'VELY, adj. [brisk, sprightly] *vivace, spiritoso.*

A lively young man, *un giovane vivace.*

A lively complexion, *una carnagione vivace.*

A lively resentment, *un vivo risentimento.*

A lively faith, *viva fede.*

He is a lively image of his father, *egli è l'imagine viva di suo padre.*

Lively, adv. *vivamente, con modo vivace, con veemenza.*

LI'VER, s. *vivente.*

A good liver, *un buon vivente, un uomo di buona vita.*

A bad liver, *un uomo di cattiva vita.*

Liver, s. [one of the noblest parts of the body] *fegato,* s. m.

Liver coloured, *di color di fegato, bruno.*

Liverwort, s. [an herb] *epatita,* s. f. *sorta d'erba.*

LI'VERED, adj. ex. A white livered fellow, *uno stupido, un insensato, un melenso, uno sciocco, uno scimunito, un minchione, un gonzo.*

LI'VERY, s. *livrea,* s. f.

To wear a livery, *portar la livrea.*

Livery men, *gente di livrea.*

Livery men, *son chiamati in Londra certi per lo più mercanti e mercidj, che sono aggregati a certe compagnie.*

Livery lace, *gallone di livrea.*

To keep horses at livery, *tener cavalli d'affitto.*

Livery of seisin [law phrase, is a delivery of possession of lands, tenements, &c. unto one who hath right to them] *il mettere qualcheduno in possesso.*

To receive livery, *esser messo in possesso.*

LIVES, *è plurale di* life.

LI'VID, adj. [black and blue] *livido.*

LI'VIDITY, s. [a being livid] *lividezza,* s f. *lividore,* s m.

LI'VING, s. [from to live] *vita,* s. f. *vivere,* s. m.

A good living, *buona vita.*

To be weary of living, *esser lasso di vivere.*

Living [food, livelihood] *vita, vitto, nutrimento.*

Living [substance, estate] *bene, avere, facultà.*

Living [church benefice] *beneficio.*

Living, adj. [alive] *vivente, vivo, che ha vita.*

A living creature, *una creatura vivente.*

Living, s. [one alive] *vivente, vivo.*

The living and the dead, *i vivi, ed i morti.*

The land of living, *la terra de' viventi.*

LI'VRE, s. [a sort of coin] *lira,* s. f. *e s'intende per lo più di Francia.*

LIXI'VIAL, adj. *di ranno; di lisciva; ottenuto per mezzo d'una rannata, d'una lisciva.*

LI'ZARD, s. [a green sort of serpent] *lucerta, lucertola,* s. f.

Lizard point [the outmost south west point of the Land's End in Cornwal] *il capo di san Michele, la punta la più meridionale del paese di Cornovaglia, in Inghilterra.*

LO, interj. *ecco.*

Lo him, lo her, *eccolo.*

LOACH, s. [a fresh water fish] *ghiozzo,* s. m. *picciolo pescatello senza lische.*

LOAD, s. [burden] *soma, carica,* s. f. *peso.*

A heavy load, *una soma pesante.*

He has his load, or he has taken his load

load [he is drunk] *egli ha bevuto troppo, egli è cotto.*
A cart load, *una carrettata, tanta materia, quanto contiene una carretta.*
LOADS [trenches to drain fenny places] *fossata,* s. f. *fossato,* s. m.
A loads-man, *guida, conduttore.*
The load-stone [the magnet] *calamita, magnete,* s. f.
Rubbed with a load stone, *calamitato.*
Load star [the North star that guides mariners] *l' orsa minore.*
To LOAD [to lay on a load or burthen] *caricare.*
To load a cart, *caricare una carretta.*
To load a pistol, *caricare una pistola.*
LO'ADED, adj. *caricato, carico.*
LOAF, s. *un pane, una pagnotta.*
A penny loaf, *un pan d' un soldo, una pagnotta.*
Half a loaf is better than no bread, *chi spelluzzica non digiuna.*
A sugar loaf, *un pane di zucchero.*
LOAM, s. [grafting clay] *terra grassa, creta.*
LOAN, s. [a thing lent] *presta, prestanza,* s. f. *prestito,* s. m.
To put out to loan, *prestare, dar in presto.*
LOATH, s. *disgusto; nausea per ehecchessia; aborrimento.*
To LOATH [to nauseate] *aborrire, schifare, avere a schifo, aver a noja, nauseare, svogliare, aver in fastidio, stomacare.*
LO'ATHED, adj. *aborrito, schifato, nauseato, svogliato, stomacato.*
LO'ATHFUL, adj. *che stomaca, che reca nausea.*
Loathful, *che aborre, che soffre nausea, che ha schifo d'una cosa.*
LO'ATHING, s. *aborimento, fastidio, schifamento,* s. m. *schifanza, nausea,* s. f.
LO'ATHLY, } adj. *schifo, lordo, stomachevole, sporco,*
LO'ATHSOME, } *stucchevole.*
LO'ATHSOMNESS, s. *schifezza, laidezza, sporcizia, stucchevolezza,* s. f.
LO'AVES, *plurali di* Loaf.
LOB, } s. [a country clown] *uno zotico, rustico, un*
LO'BCOCK, } *villano, un contadino, un balordo, un melenso.*
Lob-lolly, s. [a hotch-potch, or mingle mangle] *miscuglio di diverse carni insieme; un manicaretto.*
Lob-worm, *spezie di verme col quale si pescan le trote.*
To LOB [to toss] *scuotere, scrollare.*
To lob, *lasciar cadere in pigra o sconcia maniera.*
LO'BBY, s. [a kind of passage room] *un portico, una galleria.*
LO'BES [the several divisions of the lungs or liver] *lobo,* s. m. *particella del polmone, o fegato dell' animale.*
LO'BSTER, s. [a fish] *gambero di mare.*
LO'CAL, adj. [of or belonging to a place] *locale, di luogo.*
A local motion, *un moto locale.*
Local medicaments [those medicines which are applied outwardly] *medicamenti esterni.*
LOCA'LITY, s. [the being of a thing in a place] *presenza, esistenza locale.*
LO'CALLY, adv. *localmente, in luogo.*
LOCA'TION, s. [a letting out to hire] *allogagione,* s. f.
LOCH, s. [a lake] *lago; voce scozzese.*
LOCK, s. [an instrument to make fast a door or the like] *serratura, toppa,* s. f.
To pick a lock, *aprire una serratura.*
A spring lock, *serratura a molla.*
The lock or firelock of an harquebuss, *rotella d' archibugio.*
Lock [for horses legs] *pastoje.*
The lock of a pond, *chiusa di stagno.*
A lock in a river, *cateratta,* s. f.
A lock of hair, *ciuffetto, ciuffo di capelli.*
A lock of wool, *un fiocco di lana.*
To be underlock and key, *esser serrato a chiave.*
Lock-smith, *magnano, facitor di toppe, e di chiavi.*
To LOCK [to shut up, to fasten with a lock and key] *serrare con serratura.*
Lock the door, *serrare la porta.*
To lock in, *rinchiudere.* pret. *rinchiusi.*
To lock one out, *serrar la porta ad uno.*
To lock up, *serrare.*
To lock up money, *serrar del danaro.*
LOCKED, adj. *serrato.*
LO'CKER, s. [or pigeon hole] *colombajo,* s. m. *buchi dove i colombi covano.*
LO'CKET, s. [a set of diamonds, or other jewels] *giojello,* s. m. *più gioje legate insieme.*
LO'CKRAM, s. [a coarse sort of linen cloth] *sorta di tela grossa.*
LOCKT, *v.* Locked.
LO'CUST, s. [a kind of grasshopper] *locusta,* s. f. *spezie d' animaletto simile al grillo.*
Locust [a kind of tree] *sorta d' albero.*
LOCU'TION, s. [way of speaking] *locuzione,* s. f. *maniera di dire, loquela, favella.*
LODE-SHIP, s. [a small fishing vessel] *spezie di barca di pescatore.*
LODEMA'NAGE, s. the hire of a pilot for conducting a ship] *quel prezzo che si da ad un piloto per condurre un vascello.*
LO'DESMAN, s. [pilot] *un piloto.*
L'ODESTAR, *v.* Loadstar.
LO'DESTONE, *v.* Loadstone.
LODGE, s. [little room] *loggia,* s. f. *alloggiamento, ostello, tugurio,* s. m. *cameretta,* s. f.
The lodge of a stag, *il covo d' un cervo.*
To LODGE [to give lodging] *alloggiare, dar l' alloggio, albergare.*
The rain lodges [or lays] the corn, *la pioggia carica le biade.*
To lodge [to live] *alloggiare, albergare, dimorare, star di casa.*
LODGED, adj. *alloggiato, albergato.*
The supreme power is lodged in the King, *il supremo potere risiede nella persona del Re.*
LO'DGMENT, s. *alloggiamento, alloggio,* s. m.
Lodgment [militia term, the place where the soldiers quarter among the townsmen in huts and tents, also a retrenchment dug for shelter, when the counterscarp or some other post is gained] *alloggiamento, termine militare.*
LO'DGER, s. [one who lives in a room or apartment in another person's house] *un pigionale, colui che sta a camera locanda.*
LO'DGING, s. [room, apartment] *alloggiamento, alloggio, camera locanda.*
Where's your lodging? *dove alloggiate?*
Have you any lodging to let? *avete delle camere ad affittare?*
To give one a night's lodging, *alloggiare uno per una notte, dargli l' alloggio per una notte.*
LOE, *v.* Lo.
LOFT, s. ex. [a corn loft] *un granajo.*
A hay loft, *un fienile, luogo dove si ripone il fieno.*
LO'FTILY, adv. *magnificamente, superbamente, maestosamente, alla grande.*
LO'FTINESS, s. [or height] *altezza, grandezza.*
The loftiness of a tree, *l' atezza d' un albero.*
Loftiness [sublimity, majesty] *elevazione, sublimità, maestà,* s. f.
A loftiness of stile, *sublimità di stile.*
Loftiness [haughtiness] *fierezza, albagia, altierezza, superbia,* s. f. *orgoglio,* s. m.
His loftiness [the title of the grand Signior] *sua altezza.*
L'FTY, adj. [tall, high] *grande, alto.*
A lofty tree, *un grand' albero.*
Lofty [great, majestick] *grande, nobile, superbo, sublime, eccelso.*
A lofty stile, *uno stile elevato, o sublime.*
Lofty [haughty] *fiero, albagioso, altiero, superbo, borioso.*
LOG, s. [the trunk of a tree, or stump of wood or fuel] *toppo, ceppo,* s. m. *pezzo di pedal d' albero reciso, proprio ad abbruciare.*
Log-line, *v.* Minute line.
Log-wood, s. [a sort of wood used by dyers] *legno indico.*
LO'GGARS, s. *sorta di giuoco.*
LO'GGERHEAD, s. [a blockhead, a foolish person] *un balordo, uno sciocco, un minchione.*
To fall to loggerheads [to go together by the ears, to fight] *venire alle mani, venire alle prese.*
LO'GICAL, adj. [belonging or agreeing to the rules of logick] *logicale, di logica, loicale.*
LO'GICALLY, adv. *secondo le regole della logica.*
LOGI'CIAN, s. [one who is skilled in logick] *logico, e loico,* s. m. *che sa la logica,*

LO'GICK, s. [the art of thinking, reasoning, or making a right use of the rational faculty] *logica, loica, s. f. arte onde s' apprendono i modi del disputare per discernere il vero dal falso.*

LO'HOCK, s. *sorta di medicina.*

LOIN, s. *l'arnione, le rene.*

To LO'ITER, s. *spender il tempo neghittosamente.*

LO'ITERER, *un infingardo, un pigro.*

To LOLL [to lean] *appoggiarsi, reggersi.*

To loll [to lye] upon the bed, *stendersi, coricarsi sul letto.*

To loll one's tongue, *stender la lingua.*

LOME, *v.* Loam.

LO'MBAR, } s. [a bank for usury or LO'MBARD, } pawns] *lombardo, luogo dove si presta del danaro per scurtà.*

LO'NDON, s. [the metropolis of Great Britain] *Londra.*

LONE, adj. [solitary] *solitario.*

Lone [single, without company] *solo, senza compagnia.*

LO'NELINESS, s. [solitude, want of company] *solitudine, privazione di compagnia.*

LO'NELY, } adj. [solitary] *solita-* LO'NESOM, } *rio.*

LO'NENESS, s. *solitudine, disamore di compagnia.*

Lonesom, adj. [solitary, dismal] *solitariamente bujo e solenne, solitario, remoto.*

LONG, adj. [of great extent in length] *lungo.*

Long street, *strada lunga.*

Long boat, *barca lunga.*

Long [that lasts long] *lungo, che dura molto.*

A long reign, *un regno lungo.*

The days are long, *i giorni sono lunghi.*

Long [speaking of the quantity of syllables] *lungo.*

A long syllable, *una syllaba lunga.*

Long [tedious] *lungo tedioso.*

Long [that lingers about a thing] *lungo, lento, tardo.*

A long mile, *un miglio lungo.*

'Tis a long way thither, *è molto lontano di qui.*

To go to one's long home, *andare a babborivegoli, morire.*

'Tis as broad as 'tis long [it is all one] *è tutt' uno, non c' è differenza.*

A long way about, *un gran giro.*

Long-legged, *che ha le gambe lunghe.*

Long-necked, *che ha il collo lungo.*

Long-wasted, *che ha la vita lunga.*

Long-winded, *che ha buon fiato.*

A long winded discourse, *un discorso lungo e tedioso.*

A long winded story, *una fola da veglia.*

Long lived, *longevo, di lunga età, vecchio.*

Long wort [angelica] *angelica, s. f.*

Long sufferance, or long suffering, *pazienza.*

He knows the long and the short of that business, *egli sa come va questo affare.*

It is long of you not of me, *è vostra colpa, non mia.*

It was long of you that he died, *voi siete la causa della sua morte.*

Long, adv. *lungo tempo.*

Long after, *lungo tempo dopo.*

Long since, long ago, *molto, o lungo tempo fa.*

Not long before, *non molto prima.*

Not long before day, *un poco prima del giorno.*

How long is it since? *quanto tempo fa?*

So long, or as long as I live, *tanto che viverò.*

So long as I do my duty I think myself safe, *io so il mio dovere, e così non temo nessuno.*

I think it long till I see him, *mi par mill' anni di vederlo.*

All my life long, *tutta la mia vita.*

All this day long, *tutto questo giorno, tutt' oggi.*

E're long, *in breve, fra poco.*

To LONG [to desire very earnestly] *aver voglia, desiderare, appetire, pres. appetisco.*

She longs for a glass of wine, *ella ha gran voglia di bere un bicchier di vino.*

I long to go, *mi par mill' anni d'andare.*

LONGANI'MITY, s. [long sufferance, forbearance, great patience] *longanimità, tolleranza, sofferenza, perseveranza con animo paziente, voce della scrittura.*

LO'NGER [the comparative of long] *più lungo.*

Longer, adv. *più lungo tempo.*

LO'NGEST, s. [the superlative of long] *il più lungo.*

LONGE'VITY, s. [long life] *lunga vita.*

LO'NGING, s. [an earnestly desiring] *voglia, s. f. desiderio intenso.*

To save one's longing, *far passar la voglia di qualche cosa ad uno.*

Longing, adj. *bramoso.*

The longing expectation we are in, *l' impazienza nella quale siamo.*

LO'NGINGLY, adv. *bramosamente, con intensa brama.*

LONGI'NQUITY, s. [distance] *lontananza, distanza.*

Longinquity [length of time] *lungo spazio di tempo.*

LO'NGISH, adj. [pretty long] *lunghetto, alquanto lungo.*

LO'NGITUDE, s. [length] *longitudine, lunghezza, s. f.*

Longitude [in geography, is the difference either East or West, between the meridians of any two places counted on the equator] *longitudine appresso i geografi è l' arco dell' equinoziale, e d' ogni cerchio paralello ad esso da Ponente a Levante tra'l primo meridiano e qualunque altro.*

Longitude [in the heavens, is an arch of the eclipticK, counted from the beginning of Aries, to the place where the stars circle or longitude crosses the ecliptick] *longitudine, appresso gli astronomi, arco dell' eclittica dal principio d' Ariete verso levante fino al cerchio di latitudine di qualche stella.*

LONGITU'DINAL, adj. *longitudinale.*

LONGITU'DINALLY, adv. [in length, long-ways] *in lungo.*

LO'NGLY, adv. *bramosamente, con brama intensa.*

LO'NGSOME, adj. [tedious, wearisome by its length] *nojosamente lungo, nojoso per soverchia lunghezza.*

LO'NGWAYS, adv. *pel lungo.*

LOO, s. *giuoco di carte.*

To LOO [to set on a dog] *aizzare i cani.*

LO'OBILY, adj. ex. A loobily fellow, [a looby] *uno sciocco, un cionno, uno scimunito.*

LO'OBY, s. [loggerhead] *un balordo, un minchione, un bietolone, un cionno, un gonzo.*

Loo'd, adj. *aizzato.*

LOOF, s. [that part of a ship aloft, that lies just before the timber, call'd chess-trees, as far as the bulk head of the fore-castle] *lunghezza del vascello dall' albero fino alla sponda.*

To spring the loof [is when a ship which was going large before the wind is brought close by the wind] *andare vicino al vento.*

To loof up [to keep the ship nearer to the wind] *bordeggiare, serrare il vento.*

LO'OFED, adj. *andato distante.*

LOOK, s. [a glance of the eye] *guardo, sguardo, s m. guardatura.*

Look, } [aspect, mien, countenance] Looks, } *guardo, aspetto, viso, s. m. guardatura, vista, cera, s. f.*

A modest look, *un guardo modesto.*

To have an honest look, *aver cera d'uomo dabbene.*

By his looks you would take him to be a saint, *a vederlo lo crederesti un santo.*

One may see it in his looks, *si può discernere nel suo viso.*

A look-out [a watch tower] *veletta, s. f.*

To LOOK [to see] *vedere, mirare, guardare.*

To look, *andate a vedere.*

Look there, *mirate lì.*

To look askew, or awry, *guardar bieco.*

To look one in the face, *guardar uno nel viso, o a quattr' occhi.*

To look [to take heed] *guardare, badare, aver cura, stare in cervello, considerare, prender guardia.*

To look [to seek] *cercare.*

To look [to be situated] *guardare, esser volto colla faccia verso una parte, rispondere, riuscire.*

His house looks in the garden, *la sua casa guarda verso il giardino, è volta verso il giardino.*

To look [to have the look or looks of] *aver l'aria, aver la cera, parere.*

He looks like an honest man, *egli ha la cera d'uomo dabbene.*

To look great, *aver l'aria grande, esser nobile.*

This cloth looks very fine, *questo panno pare molto fino.*

She looks very pretty, *ella pare molto bella.*

To look well [in point of health] *egli ha buon viso, egli ha buona cera.*

You look very ill, *mi pare che voi non stiate bene.*

This looks as if she had no love at all for me, *pare che ella non m' ami.*

My thoughts don't look at all that way, *io non penso a queste cose.*

It won't look well on you to do it, *non vi sta bene di far ciò.*

To look like, *rassomigliare, esser simile.*

To look down upon one with scorn, *guardar uno con isdegno, con disprezzo.*

To look big, *braveggiare.*

To look to one [to take care of him] *aver l' occhio sopra a qualcheduno, averne cura.*

To look to [to watch, to observe] *codiare alcuno, osservare i suoi andamenti.*

Look to it, *badate, abbiate l' occhio a ciò.*

To look on, or upon, *mirare, vedere, considerare, badare.*

To look on, or upon [to esteem] *tenere, stimare, considerare.*

To look upon it as a great honour, *lo tengo a grand' onore.*

Do not look upon me as your equal, *non mi trattate da par vostro.*

To look about one [to mind one's business] *badare a' fatti suoi.*

To look after a thing [to take care of it] *aver cura di qualche cosa, aver l' occhio sopra a qualche cosa.*

To look after a thing [to seek it] *cercare qualche cosa.*

To look back [to reflect] upon a thing, *riflettere, far riflessione sopra qualche cosa, ruminarla nel pensiero.*

To look for [to seek] *cercare.*

To look, or to look for [to expect] *aspettare.*

When do you look for him? *quando l' aspettate?*

Those who have liv'd wickedly must look to meet with punishment in the other world, *quei che hanno vissuto male devono aspettare d' esser puniti nell' altro mondo.*

To look into a thing [to examine it] *esaminare, considerare, ventilare una cosa.*

To look out [to seek] *cercare.*

To look out of a window, *affacciarsi alla finestra.*

LOOKED, *v.* Lookt.

A LO'OKER ON, s. [a spectator] *un riguardante, uno spettatore, un circostante; uno che guarda quando gli altri operano.*

LO'OKING, s. *il vedere, il mirare.*

LO'OKING-GLASS, *uno specchio.*

A looking-glass maker, *uno specchiajo.*

LOOKT, adj. *visto, mirato, v.* To look, *è meglio scrivere* looked.

Well lookt on, or well lookt after, *ben servato, ben custodito.*

Ill lookt on, or ill lookt after, *negletto, mal custodito.*

Not lookt for, *inaspettato.*

A well lookt man [a man of good aspect] *un uomo di bella presenza.*

An ill lookt man, *un uomo mal fatto, che ha una cattiva cera.*

LOOM, s [the frame a weaver works upon] *telajo,* s. m.

Loom-gale [a fresh gale at sea] *vento fresco, vento di terra.*

To LOOM [a sea-term, to appear] *parere.*

That ship looms a great deal, *quel vascello pare molto grande.*

LO'OMING, s. ex. The looming of a ship [that is her shew or prospective] *l' apparenza, il di fuori d' un vascello, la sua forma.*

LOON, s. [a sorry fellow; a scoundrel] *un birbone, un briccone.*

LOOP, s. [an ornament for a button hole] *alamare, affibbiaglio,* s. m.

Loop hole, s. *la bottoniera,* s. f.

Loop holes [in fortification, are little holes in the walls of a castle or fort, to shoot thro'] *i finestrini d'una casamatta,* s. f.

A loop hole [that one can peep thro'] *buco, spiraglio,* s. m.

Loop hole [evasion] *sotterfugio, scampo, giro, rigiro,* s. m.

LOOSE, adj. [not fast] *che si move, che non istà fermo.*

A loose tooth, *un dente che crolla, che non istà fermo.*

Loose [united] *sciolto, slegato.*

Loose [slack] *lento, molle, contrario di teso.*

This cord is too loose, *questa corda è troppo lenta.*

Loose [in one's body] *che ha il flusso di ventre.*

Loose [lewd, debauched] *dissoluto, sviato, licenzioso, disonesto, scapestrato.*

A loose young fellow, *un giovane dissoluto, uno sviato, uno scapestrato.*

Loose verses, *versi lascivi.*

To make the belly loose, *solvere il ventre.*

A loose gown, *una veste da camera.*

To be in a loose condition [as a man pleases himself] *vivere a suo modo, esser libero.*

A loose liver, *uno sviato, uno scapestrato.*

To hang loose, *essere scinto, strascinare per terra.*

Your gown hangs loose, *la vostra gonna è scinta.*

To grow loose, *allentarsi, sciorsi, slegarsi.*

To get loose, *scatenarsi.*

To get loose from one, *strigarsi di qualcheduno, levarselo d' attorno.*

To let loose, *scatenare.*

To LOOSE, *allentare, sciogliere, strignere, lasciar ire, sprigionare, slegare, disimpegnare dall' obbligo.*

To loose [a sea term, to get away] *partire, uscir dal porto.*

LO'OSED } adj. *sciolto, slegato, allentato, molle, lento.*
LO'OSENED }

LO'OSELY, adv. [lewdly] *dissolutamente, sfrenatamente, licenziosamente.*

To LO'OSEN [to make loose] *allentare, render lento, rallentare.*

To loosen one's girdle, *rallentarsi la cintura.*

To loosen the belly, *solvere il ventre.*

To loosen [to unite] *sciorre, sciogliere, slegare,*

LO'OSENED, adj. *allentato, rallentato, v.* To loosen.

LO'OSENESS, s. [the being loose] *allentamento, rallentamento,* s. m.

Looseness [lask] *flusso di corpo.*

LO'OSENING, s. *allentamento,* s. m.

Loosening, adj. [apt to make one loose] *lassativo, che solve il ventre.*

To LOP [to cut off the top of trees] *scapezzare, diramare, tagliare a corona, stralciare.*

LO'PPED, adj. *scapezzato, diramato, stralciato.*

A LO'PPER OF TRESS, *un potatore, colui che scapezza o dirama gli alberi.*

LO'PPING, s. *lo scapezzare, o diramare.*

The loppings of trees, *i rami tagliati d' un albero.*

LOQUA'CIOUS, adj. [talkative] *loquace, che parla assai.*

LOQUA'CITY, s. [talkativeness] *loquarità,* s. f. *cicaleccio, cicalio,* s. m.

LORD, s. [an appellation of honour] *un signore.*

A great lord, *un gran signore.*

An English lord, *un Milordo.*

The Lord President, *il Presidente del consiglio.*

My Lord, *Milordo.*

Lord-like, *da gran signore.*

In the year of our Lord, *l' anno di nostro Signore.*

To LORD [to domineer] *far il signore, fare il grande, dominare, signoreggiare.*

LO'RDANT } s. [a lazy lubber] *uno scioperato, un cionno, un minchione, un bietolone.*
LO'RDANE }

LO'RDLY, adj. [or stately] *che fa il grande, magnifico, signorile.*

LO'RDSHIP, s. [the dominion of a lord] *signoria,* s. f. *dominio e podestà di signore.*

Lordship [a title given to lords] *eccellenza.*

Your lordship, *vostra eccellenza.*

To have the lordship [or the dominion] of the sea, *aver il dominio del mare, esser padrone del mare.*

LORE, s. [lesson, doctrine, instruction] *lezione, insegnamento, istruzione.*

Lore, adj. [lost, destroyed] *perduto, distrutto.*

LO'REL, s. [an abandoned scoundrel] *un grandissimo furfante, un gran briccone, un bricconaccio.*

LO'RIMERS } s. a company of artificers in London, who make bits for bridles, spurs, and such like iron ware for horses] *una compagnia d' artefici in Londra, che fanno briglie, sproni, e simili strumenti per i cavalli.*
LO'RINERS }

LO'RIOT, s. [wit-wall, a bird] *nome d' uccello.*

LORN, adj. [forsaken, lost] *derelitto, abbandonato, perduto.*

To LOSE [to be at the loss of] *perdere, far perdita.*

Lose one's money, time, and reputation, *perder il suo danaro, il suo tempo, la sua riputazione.*

I lost sight of him, *lo perdei di vista.*

I lose more than ten pounds by it, *io ci scapito più di dieci doppie.*

To lose [to forget] *scordare, dimenticare.*

To lose ground [to give way in battle] *rinculare, piegare.*

He lost his life in the wars, *egli perdè la vita in guerra, egli fu ammazzato in guerra.*

To lose one's head, *perder la testa, esser decapitato.*

To lose one's way, *smarrire la strada.*

To lose leather, *scorticarsi le natiche.*

LO'SEL, s. [a scoundrel, a sorry worthless fellow] *un gaglioffaccio, un birbonaccio, un furfante.*

LO'SENGER, s. [a flatterer] *un adulatore, un lusingatore.*

LO'SER, s. [from to lose] *perditore,* s. m. *che perde.*

You shall be no loser by it, *non ci perderete, non iscapiterete niente.*

LO'SING, s. *il perdere.*

LO'SINGS, s. *perdita,* s. f.

Losing, adj. ex. A losing bargain, *un cattivo patto, o contratto.*

LOSS, s. *perdita,* s. f. *danno, scapito, discapito,* s. m.

To suffer, to sustain, or to receive a great loss, *fare una gran perdita.*

You'll come by the loss, *voi scapiterete.*

He has had a great loss in his wife, *la perdita di sua moglie li è stata di gran discapito.*

I am at loss [at my wits end] *non so quel che devo fare, sono confuso.*

They are at a loss what to do, *non sanno che fare.*

LOST, adj. *perduto, perso.*

All is not lost that is delay'd, *quel che è differito non è perduto.*

All was like to be lost, *ogni cosa era in pericolo di perdersi.*

There's no love lost betwixt us, *v' amo altrettanto che voi m' amate.*

LOT, s. [chance, fortune] *sorte,* s. f. *destino,* s. m.

To draw lots, *tirare alla sorte.*

By lots, *per sorte, alla sorte.*

It fell to my lot, *mi cadde in sorte.*

Lot [portion of a thing] *parte, porzione.*

To pay scot and lot [to pay such charges and parish duties as housekeepers are liable to] *pagare i diritti della parrocchia.*

It is not every one's lot to be learned, *non è concesso ad ognuno d' esser dotto.*

LOTE-TREE, s. *loto,* s. m. *albero.*

LOTH, adj. [unwilling] *avverso, opposto, contrario, nemico, che non si cura, che non ha voglia di fare che che si sia.*

I am loth to do it, *mi rincresce di farlo.*

He is very loth to fight, *egli non ha voglia di battersi.*

I was loth to tell you on't before him, *non voleva dirvelo in presenza sua.*

LO'TION, s. [a washing] *lozione, lavatura,* s. f.

LO'TTERY, s. [a sharing of lots by chance] *lotto,* s. m. *giuoco, dove per polizze beneficiate o bianche, si trae o non si trae il premio.*

LO'VAGE, s. [an herb] *nome di pianta.*

LOUD, adj. [sounding] *alto, forte.*

A loud voice, *una voce alta, o forte.*

A loud fame, *una gran fama, un gran rinomo.*

Loud, adv. ex. [to speak loud] *parlar forte, ad alta voce.*

LO'UDLY, adv. *ad altra voce.*

LO'UDNESS, s. *forza di suono, strepito.*

The loudness of the voice, *la forza della voce.*

LOVE, s. [kindness, affection] *amore, affetto,* s. m. *benevolenza,* s. f.

Paternal love, *amor paterno.*

The love of God, *l' amor di Dio.*

The love of riches, *l' amore delle ricchezze.*

Self-love, *amor proprio.*

To die for love, *morir d' amore.*

To make love, *far l'amore, amoreggiare, vagheggiare.*

Love [Cupid the God of love] *l' amore, Cupido, il Dio d' amore.*

To be in love with one, *esser innamorato d' una persona.*

To fall in love, *innamorarsi.*

To get every body's love, *cattivarsi l' amore d' ognuno, farsi amare da ognuno.*

That makes me in love with him, *questo mi sforza ad amarlo.*

I did it out of love, *l' ho fatto con buon fine.*

To be out of love with a thing, *essere stufo, o svogliato di qualche cosa.*

For the love of God [for God's sake] *per l' amor di Dio.*

Love flames, *le fiamme d' amore.*

A love wound, *piaga amorosa.*

A love knot, *laccio amoroso.*

To LOVE [to have an affection for] *amare, portare amore.*

I love her better than myself, *l' amo più che me stesso.*

I love you with all my heart, *io v' amo di tutto cuore.*

Love me, love my dog, *abbi rispetto al cane per amor del padrone.*

Love me little, and love me long, *amami poco, ed amami sempre.*

LO'VED, adj. *amato.*

LO'VELETTER, s. *pistolotto, amoroso, lettera amorosa.*

LO'VELINES, s. *bellezza, grazia, amorevolezza.*

LO'VELORN, adj. [forsaken of one's love] *abbandonato dall' oggetto amato.*

LO'VELY, adj. *amabile, degno d'esser amato, bello, grazioso.*

Lovely, adv. *amabilmente, con amorevolezza, con amore.*

LO'VER, s. *amatore,* s. m. *amatrice,* s. f.

I am a great lover of musick, *io amo molto la musica.*

Lover [gallant, spark] *amadore, drudo, leggiadro, vago,* s. m.

Lovers [a lover and a mistress] *amanti.*

LO'VESOME, adj. [lovely] *amabile, degno d' amore.*

LO'VESONG, s. *canzone amorosa.*

LO'VESUIT, s. [courtship] *il corteggiare una bella.*

LO'VETOY, s. *donativo, presente di poco valore alla innamorata.*

LOUGH [an Irish word, for a lake] *lago.*

LO'VING, s. *l' amore.*

Loving, adj. [good, kind] *amabile, affezionato, cortese, buono.*

A loving wife, *una moglie amabile.*

LO'VINGLY, adv. *amabilmente, con amorevolezza, affettuosamente.*

To LOUNGE, *impigrirsi, viver da pigro, da neghittoso.*

LOUSE, s. [a small insect which infests human kind] *pidocchio,* s. m.

Full of lice, *pidocchioso, pieno di pidocchi.*

A crab louse, *una piattola.*

To LOUSE, *spidocchiare, levar via i pidocchi.*

To louse one's self, *spidocchiarsi.*

LO'USINESS, s. *abbondanza i pidocchi, lo stato d' una persona pidocchiosa.*

LO'USILY, adv. [in a paltry, mean, and scurvy way] *bricconescamente, vilmente, vigliaccamente, avaramente, da pidocchioso, da tanghero.*

LO'USY, adj. *pidocchioso, pieno di pidocchi.*

A lousy rascal, *un bricconaccio, un mendico, un birbone pien di pidocchi.*

LOUT, s. [a mean aukward fellow, a bumkin, a clown] *uno sguajataccio, un villanaccio.*

To LOUT, *render omaggio, inchinarsi.*

LOW, adj. [the contrary of high] *basso, piccolo, che non è alto.*

A low house, *una casa bassa.*

Low water, *marea bassa.*

Low [mean] *basso, vile, abbietto, umile, infimo.*

Low extraction, *bassa nascita, umil parentaggio*

At a low rate, *a vil prezzo.*

Low [humble] *basso, umile.*

Low [under, inferior] *basso, inferiore.*

Low [the contrary of loud] *bassa.*

A low voice, *una voce bassa.*

A low pulse, *un polso profondo.*

To bring low, *abbassare, abbattere.*

To bring low [to humble] *abbattere, umiliare.*

To be low, or in a low condition [in point of health] *star molto male, esser abbattuto, o debole.*

To be in a low condition [to be low in the world] *esser in cattivo stato, esser povero.*

Low, adv. *basso, bassamente.*
To speak low, *parlar basso.*
To bow very low, *salutar profondamente, fare una profonda riverenza.*
His house stands low [or in a bottom] *la sua casa è situata in luogo basso.*
I cannot find him high nor low, *non posso trovarlo in nissun luogo.*
A low built ship, *un vascello di basso fondo.*
A low masted ship, *un vascello che ha gli alberi troppo corti.*
To Low [to bellow] *muggire, mugghiare,* pref. *muggisco.*
To low, *abbassare, metter giù.*
Lo'wer [the comparative of low] *più basso.*
The lower house, or the house of commons, *la camera bassa, la camera de' comuni del parlamento d'Inghilterra.*
To Lo'wer [to bring down] *abbassare.*
To lower the price, *diminuire il prezzo.*
Lo'wermost, } [the superlative of Lo'west, } low] *il più basso.*
'Tis the lowest price, *questo è il più basso prezzo, non posso venderlo a minor prezzo.*
Lo'wing, s. [from to low] *muggito,* s. m.
Lo'wliness, s. [humbleness] *mansuetudine, umiltà, bassezza,* s. f.
Lo'wly, adj. [humble, lowly minded] *mansueto, umile, sommesso.*
Lown, s. [a scoundrel, a rascal] *un briccone, uno sciagurato, un gaglioffo.*
Lo'wness, s. *bassezza, poca distanza dal suolo.*
Lowness, *viltà o di natali o di mente o di cuore.*
Lowness, *sommissione, ubbidienza abbietta.*
Lowness, *abbiettezza, depressione.*
Lowtho'ughted, adj. *di pensieri mondani e vili.*
To Lowt [to overpower] *soperchiare, soverchiare, opprimere, o abbassare con soverchieria.*
Lo'yal, adj. [faithful] *leale, fedele.*
Lo'yally, adv. [faithfully] *lealmente, fedelmente.*
Lo'yalty, s. [fidelity] *lealtà, fedeltà,* s. f.
Loyn, s. ex. [A loyn of veal] *un filetto di vitella.*
Loyn [the lower part of one's back] *i lombi, le reni.*
To Lo'yter [to tarry, or stand trifling] *tentennare, stare a bada, badare, tardare, intertenersi, musare,* pref. *intertengo,* pret. *intertenni.*
Lo'yterer, s. *un pigro, un infingardo, un musone.*
Lo'ytering, f. *pigrizia, infingardia, infingardaggine, negligenza.*
Loytering, adj. [a loytering fellow] *un infingardo.*
Lo'zel, s. [a lazy booby] *un perdigiorno, uno scioperato, un neghittoso, un pigro, un infingardo.*

Lo'zenge, s. [a figure whose opposite angles are acute, and the other two obtuse, and the four sides equal] *rombo,* s. m.
Lozenge [a little square cake of preserved flowers, herbs, &c.] *pasticca, pastiglia,* s. f.
Lu, s. *sorta di giuoco di carte.*
Lu'bber, s. [a drudge] *un facchino, un servo che s'impiega intorno ad uffizi vili.*
A long lubber, *un uomo mal fatto.*
A lubber [a lazy drone] *un poltrone, un pigro, un infingardo.*
Lu'bberly, adj. *ozioso, pigro, frioperato, infingardo.*
Lu'bberly, adv. *grossamente, sconciamente, senza bello artificio.*
Lubric, adj. [slippery, uncertain] *lubrico, vano, fallace.*
A lubric hope, *speranza vana, o fallace.*
Lubric [fickle, inconstant] *leggiero, volubile, incostante.*
A lubric [inconclusive] argument, *un argomento mal fondato.*
Lubric [wanton] *lascivo.*
Lubri'city, s. [uncertainty, fickleness] *leggierezza, inconstanza, incertezza, volubiltà,* s. m.
Lubricity [wantonness] *lascivia, lascività,* s. f.
Luce, s. ex. A flower de luce, *fiordaliso,* s. m.
Luce, s. [a pike full grown] *luccio, pesce noto.*
Lu'cent, adj. [bright, shining] *lucente, luminoso.*
Lu'cern, s. [a sort of Russian beast near the bigness of a wolf] *sorta di lupo cerviero.*
Lu'cid, adj. [bright, shining] *lucido, lucente.*
Lucid interval, *lucido intervallo, quello spazio di tempo, nel quale il pazzo ricupera l'uso della ragione.*
Lu'cifer, s. [the chief of the devils] *Lucifero,* s. m. *nome del maggior diavolo.*
Lucifer [the morning star] *lucifero, la stella di venere, la stella mattutina.*
Luck, s. [chance, fortune] *ventura, fortuna,* s. f. *caso, accidente,* s. m.
By good luck, *per buona ventura, o per buona fortuna.*
I wish you good luck, *vi auguro buon successo.*
Ill luck, *sventura, disgrazia, sfortuna.*
Lu'ckiness, s. [good fortune, good hap, casual happiness] *buona fortuna, buon incontro, felicità venuta inaspettatamente.*
Lu'ckless, adj. [unfortunate, unhappy] *sventurato, mal arrivato, infelice.*
Lu'ckily, adv. [by good luck] *fortunatamente, avventurosamente, per fortuna*
Lu'cky, adj. *fortunato, avventuroso, buon auguroso.*
Lu'crative, adj. [gainful] *lucrativo, da guadagno.*
Lu'cre, s. [gain] *lucro, guadagno, profitto,* s. m.

Lucri'ferous, } adj. *che produce lu-* Lucri'fick, } *cro, che apporta guadagno, profittevole.*
Lu'crous, *v.* Lucrative.
To Lu'cubrate, *studiare di notte; vegliare studiando.*
Lucubra'tion, s. [night study] *vigilie, studio notturno.*
Lu'cubratory, adj. *composto a lume di candela o di lucerna.*
Lu'culent, adj. [clear] *luculento, lucente, luminoso, evidente.*
Luculent proof, *prova chiara, o evidente.*
Lu'dicral, } adj. [burlesque, Lu'dicrous, } comical] *burlesco, comico.*
Ludicrous [pleasant] *piacevole, gustoso, divertente.*
Luff, or Lough, s. [light, or frame to fowl with, a bow-bell] *fuoco, o lume per andare alla caccia degli uccelli col campanaccio.*
To Luff, *tenersi contra il vento; vore marinaresca.*
Lug, s. [the lug of the ear] *la punta dell' orecchio.*
To give one a lug, *tirar l'orecchio ad uno.*
A lug [a pole to measure land with] *pertica.*
To Lug [to pull] *tirare.*
To lug one by the ear, *tirar gli orecchi ad uno.*
To lug out, *cavar la spada, metter fuora fuserta.*
To lug, *strascinarsi a fatica.*
Lu'ggage, s. [heavy weight, or burden] *imbroglio, arredo, bagaglio,* s. m. *salmeria, bagaglie,* s. f.
Lu'gged, adj. *tirato.*
Lugu'brous, } adj. [mournful] *lu-* Lugu'brious, } *gubre.*
Lu'kewarm, adj. [between hot and cold] *tepido, tra caldo e freddo.*
Lukewarm [cold, indifferent] *tepido, pigro, lento.*
Lukewa'rmness, s. *tepidezza, tiepidità,* s. f.
Lukewarmness [indifference] *tiepidezza, pigrizia, freddezza,* s. f.
To Lull [to entice to sleep by singing, as a nurse does her child] *cullare, ninnare, accarezzare, cantare per addormentare un fanciullo.*
To lull asleep, *addormentare, ninnare.*
Lu'llaby, } s. *ninna, can-* Lu'llaby Songs, } *zone per addormentar bambini.*
Lu'lled, adj. *cullato, ninnato.*
Lulled asleep *addormentato.*
Lu'mbar, } adj. [belonging to the Lu'mbary, } reins] *lombare, dei lombi.*
Lu'mber, s. [old houshold stuff] *masseriziaccia,* s. f. *masserizia o arnesi usati.*
Lu'mbrical, adj. As lumbrical muscles, *muscoli lombart.*
Lu'minary, s. [or light lamp] *luminare, lume,* s. m. *corpo luminoso.*
The sun and the moon are the two great luminaries, *il sole, e la luna sono i duoi gran luminari.*

LU'MINOUS, adj. [bright] *luminoso, lucente, risplendente.*

LUMP, s. [mass] *massa,* s. f. *pezzo,* s. m.

A lump of flesh, *una massa di carne.*

To sell by the lump, *vender all' ingrosso.*

Lump.[heap] *mucchio.*

To lump, *informarsi all' ingrosso, senza badare a circostanze minute.*

LU'MPFISH, s *nome di pesce.*

LU'MPING, adj, *grosso, grave, massiccio, pesante.*

LU'MPISH, adj. [heavy] *pesante, massiccio.*

Lumpish [heavy, dull] *massiccio, materiale, semplice, rozzo.*

LU'MPISHNESS, s. *materialità, sciocchezza, balordaggine.* s f.

LU'MPY, adj. *massiccio, grave.*

LU'NACY, s. [frenzy, or madness] *frenesia, follia, pazzia,* s. f.

To be smitten with lunacy, *esser lunatico.*

LU'NAR, adj. [of or belonging to the moon] *lunare, della luna.*

Lunar months, *mesi lunari.*

LU'NATICK, adj. [smitten with lunacy] *lunatico, che patisce al cervello secondo il variar della luna.*

Lunatick, s. *lunatico,* s. m.

LUNA'TION, s. [the space of time between one new moon and another] *lunazione,* s. f. *lunare,* s. m.

LUNCH, s. *pezzo, tozzo.* s. m.

A great lunch of bread, *un gran pezzo di pane.*

LU'NCHION, s. *merenda,* s. f.

LUNCH, s. [lowings, leashes, or long lines to call in hawks] *lunga,* s. f. *quella striscia di cuojo, colla quale gli strozzieri annodatala a'geti de' falconi li tengon legati.*

LUNE, *v.* Lunacy.

LUNE'TTE, s. *mezzaluna* termine *di fortificazione.*

LUNG, s. [that part of an animal which is the instrument of respiration] *polmone,* s. m.

The pipe of the lungs, *la canna della gola.*

LU'NG-WORT [white hellebore] *polmonaria,* s. f. *sorta d'erba.*

LUNT, s. [match to fire guns with] *miccia,* s. f.

LU'PINE, s. [a sort of pulse] *lupino.* s. m. *sorta di legume noto.*

LU'PUS, s. [a sort of canker in the thighs and legs] *ulcere che vengono alle ginocchia, ed alle gambe.*

LURCH, *marrio,* s. m. *termine del giuoco, posta doppia.*

To leave one in the lurch, *lasciare uno in nasso, dare il gambetto ad uno, abbandonarlo.*

To lye upon the lurch [or upon the catch] *stare agli agguati, tendere insidie, insidiare.*

To lurch one at play, *guadagnar il marcio, guadagnar posta doppia.*

To lurch [to lye upon the lurch] *insidiare, tender insidie, stare agli agguati.*

LU'RCHED, adj. *a chi si è guadagnato il marcio, v.* To lurch.

LU'RCHER, s. [a kind of dog] *un bassetto,* s. m.

LU'RCHING, s. *il guadagnar il marcio.*

A lurching, or lying upon the lurch, *agguato, aguato, inganno,* s. m. *insidia,* s. f.

LURE, s. [a hawk's lure, a device of leather to call back a hawk] *logoro,* s. m. *il logoro fatto di cuojo e di penne a modo d'un alia, con che lo falconiere suol richiamare il falcone.*

Lure [decoy] *esca,* s. f. *adescamento,* s. m.

To LURE a hawk, *richiamare un falcone col logoro.*

To lure [to allure, to decoy] *adescare, allettare.*

LU'RID, adj. [pale, wan] *livido, pallido, macilente.*

LU'RING, s. *il nasconderst, l'appiattarsi.*

To LURK [to lye hid] *nasconderst, appiattarsi, celarsi.*

Lurking, adj. ex. A lurking hole, or lurking place, *un nascondiglio.*

A lurking fellow, *un uomo che si nasconde.*

LU'SCIOUS, adj. [over sweet] *melato, troppo dolce.*

Luscious, *piacevole, delizioso.*

Luscious wines, *vino melato, vin dolce.*

Luscious meat, *carne che stufa, che viene a fastidio.*

LU'SCIOUSNESS, s. *dolcezza,* s. f.

LU'SCIOUSLY, adv. *dolcemente.*

LUSH, adj. *vivo, ben colorito*; *e dicesi in opposizione di pallido, smorto.*

LUSK, adj. *pigro, neghittoso, buono a nulla.*

A LUSK, s. [a slug, a slothful fellow] *un pigro, un poltrone, un infingardo, un dappoco, uno scioperato.*

LU'SKISHNESS, s. [laziness] *pigrizia, lentezza, infingardia, infingardaggine,* s. f.

LUST [concupiscence, unlawful passion or desire] *appetito, senso,* s. m. *concupiscenza, sensualità, incontinenza,* s. f.

Lust [among sailors, a ship is said to have a lust to one side or other, when she is inclined to heel, or lean more to one side than another] *andare alla banda, parlando d'un vascello.*

To lust [to desire, to have an inclination to] *concupiscere, desiderare.*

To lust after a woman, *concupiscere, desiderare una donna.*

LU'STED AFTER, adj. *desiderato.*

LU'STER, } s. [brightness] *lustro,*
LUSTRE, } *splendore, lume,* s. m.

LU'STFUL, adj. [full of lust, lecherous] *sensuale, lascivo, impudico.*

LU'STFULLY, adv. *sensualmente, lascivamente, impudicamente.*

To look lustfully upon a woman, *guardare una donna con occhi lascivi.*

LU'STFULNESS, s. *concupiscenza, lascività, sensualità,* s. f. *appetito, desiderio,* s. m.

LU'STIHED, } s. *vigore, forza di*
LU'STIHOOD, } *membra.*

LU'STILY, adv. [stoutly] *vigorosamente, gagliardamente.*

To eat and drink lustily, *mangiare, e bere con appetito.*

LU'STINESS, s. *forza, gagliardia,* s. f. *vigore,* s. m.

LU'STLESS, adj. *che non ha concupiscenza.*

LU'STRAL, adj. [purging] *lustrale.*

Lustral water, *acqua lustrale.*

LUSTRA'TION, s. [a purging sacrifice among the ancients] *lustrazione,* s. f. *specie di sacrificio in uso fra gli antichi.*

LU'STRE, *v.* Luster.

Lustre, } s. [the space of five
Lustrum, } years] *lustro,* s. m. *spazio di cinque anni.*

LU'STRING, s. [a sort of glossy silk called lutestring] *lustrino* s. m. *sorta di drappo.*

LU'STROUS, adj. *lucido, splendente, luminoso.*

LU'STWORT, s. *nome d'erba.*

LU'STY, adj. [strong, stout] *robusto, gagliardo, rigoglioso, forte vigoroso.*

LU'TANIST, s. [a player on the lute] *sonator di liuto.*

LUTA'RIOUS, adj. *che sta nel loto, nel fango, nella mota.*

LUTE, s. [a musical instrument] *leuto, e liuto,* s. m. *strumento musicale da corde.*

To play upon the lute, *suonar del liuto.*

Lute-string, *corda di liuto.*

A lute player, *un sonator di liuto.*

Lute [among the chymists, a compound paste made of clay, mortar, sand, potters earth, &c. to join together the necks of retorts and receivers] *loto,* s. m.

To LUTE [to cover or stop up with such a loam or clay] *lotare, termine chimico.*

LU'TED, } adj. *lotato, chiuso con*
LU'TEOUS, } *loto.*

LU'THERANISM, s. [the sect or religion of the Lutherans] *il Luteranismo.*

Lutherans, s. [those who follow the tenets of Luther, one of the reformers] *Luterani.*

LU'TULENT, adj. [miry, dirty] *lotoso, fangoso.*

To LUX, } [to put out of joint]
To LU'XATE, } *disconciare, dislogare, slogare, sforcere,* pret. *sforsi.*

LUXA'TION, s. [a dislocation, a putting out of joint] *slogamento, lo slogare.*

LUXE, s. *lussuria, voluttà, lusso.*

LUXU'RIANCY, } s. [abundance]
LUXU'RIANCE, } *abbondanza, copia,* s. f.

LUXU'RIANT, adj. [growing to excess, growing rank] ex. Luxuriant plants, *piante che gettano troppe foglie o rami, piante lussuriose.*

A luxuriant way of speaking, *un' eloquenza pomposa.*

Luxuriant flesh, *carne grossolana,*

To LUXU'RIATE [to abound, to exceed, or grow rank] *esser troppo fertile, troppo abbondante.*

LUXU'RIOUS, adj. [that lives in luxury, wanton] *lussurioso, libidinoso, incontinente, lascivo.*

Luxurious [extravagant in one's diet or

or garb] *lussuriante, che vive nel lusso, pomposo.*

Luxurious [luxuriant, exuberant] *lussureggiante, esuberante.*

Luxurious, *amante di ben mangiare, d'aver buona tavola, di buoni bocconi.*

LUXURI'OUSNESS, } s. [excess, riot, riotness]
LU'XURY, } *lusso, fasto, superfluità nel mangiare, vestire, o altro.*

LU'XURY [lust, incontinence] *lussuria, smoderato appetito carnale, incontinenza, lascivia.*

Luxury [voluptuousness; addictness to pleasure] *voluttà; l'esser dedito a' piaceri.*

Luxury, *esuberanza, soverchia abbondanza, troppa ricchezza nel produrre.*

Luxury [delicious fare] *mangiar delizioso; buona cucina; buona tavola; buoni bocconi.*

To be given to luxury, *lussuriare.*

To LY, *è meglio scrivere* to lie, *v.* To lie [to be] *essere, stare.*

To ly open, *essere o stare allo scoperto.*

To ly sick, or ill of a fever, *esser ammalato della febbre, aver la febbre.*

To ly sick a-bed, *stare in letto ammalato.*

To ly a-bed, *stare a letto.*

To ly [to lodge] *alloggiare, dimorare.*

Where do you ly? *dove dimorate?*

To ly [to be situated] *giacere, essere situato.*

Rome lyes in a plain, *Roma giace in una pianura.*

To ly lurking, *tenersi nascosto, appiattarsi.*

To ly idle, *star neghittoso, ozioso.*

Herein lyes our happiness, *in ciò consiste la nostra felicità.*

It lyes all upon you, *dipende in tutto e per tutto da voi.*

The fault lyes at your door, *voi ne porterete la pena.*

Those commodities will ly a great while upon your hands, *voi sarete lungo tempo a disfarvi di queste mercanzie.*

To ly under a great ignominy, *esser coperto d'infamia.*

To ly under an imputation, *esser accusato, o incolpato di qualche fallo.*

To ly under a mistake, *ingannarsi, sbagliare.*

To ly under a distemper, *esser ammalato.*

To ly under a great affliction, *esser molto afflitto.*

To ly under an obligation, *esser obbligato a qualche cosa.*

To ly down, *coricarsi.*

To ly down [to be brought to bed] *partorire.*

To ly about [to ly up and down] *esser disperso qua e là, esser in disordine.*

To ly in, *partorire.*

It lyes me in a great deal of money, *mi costa molti danari.*

If ever it lyes in my way to serve you, *se mai sarà in mio potere di servirvi.*

I'll do it if it lyes in my way, *se mi vien fatta lo farò.*

That lyes in my way [that is an hindrance to me] *ciò m'è d'un grande ostacolo.*

To ly in wait for one, *stare in agguato, tender insidie, insidiare qualcheduno.*

I'll do what lyes in me, or what lyes in my power, *farò ogni mio sforzo.*

To ly out [to lye out of doors] *dormire fuor di casa.*

LYE s. [to wash with] *bucato,* s. m.

To wash with lye, *fare il bucato.*

Lye-washed, *bianco di bucato.*

LYE'KE, adj. [like] *simile.* Obs.

LY'ING, s. [a woman's lying in] *parto, il partorire.*

Lying, *menzogna, bugia,* s. f.

LYMPH, s. [transparent, colourless liquor; water] *linfa; acqua; liquor trasparente senza colore.*

LYMPHATICK, adj. *linfatico, che contiene linfa,*

LYNCE'AN, } adj. [quick sighted]
LY'NCEOUS, } *linceo, d'acuta vista, che ha occhi di lince.*

LYNX, s. [a sort of quick-sighted beast] *lince, lupo cerviere,* s. m.

To have a lynx-like eye, *aver li occhi di lince, aver occhi lincei.*

LYRE, s. [a musical instrument] *lira* s. f. *strumento musicale.*

LY'RICK, } adj. [belonging to the
LY'RICAL, } lyre] *lirico.*

Lyrick poet, *poeta lirico.*

LY'RIST, s. he that plays on [or sings to the lyre] *sonatore di lira, quello che canta al suono della lira.*

M.

M, *Duodecima lettera dell' alfabeto Inglese, si pronuncia come in Italiano.*

MAC, s. [son] *parola Irlandese, che significa, figlio.*

Mac William, *il figlio di Guglielmo.*

MACARO'NICK, adj. only used in this expression, a macaronick poem [a sort of burlesque poetry, wherein the native words of a language are made to end with a Latin termination] *un poema maccheronico.*

MACARO'ONS, s. *maccheroni.*

MA'CAW, s. *sorta d'uccello dell' Indie orientali.*

MACAW-TREE, s. *sorta d'albero del genere delle Palme.*

MACE, s. [a sort of spice] *mace,* s. f. *maris,* s. m.

Mace [a known ensign of honour carried before a magistrate] *mazza,* s. f.

Mace-bearer, s. *mazziere,* s. m.

To MA'CERATE [to steep, or soak] *inzuppare, macerare.*

To macerate [to make lean; or bring down in flesh] *macerare, affievolire, infiacchire,* pres. *affievolisco, infiacchisco.*

MA'CERATED, adj. *inzuppato, macerato, affievolito, infiacchito.*

MACERA'TION, s. [or soaking] *macerazione,* s. f.

Maceration [mortification] *macerazione, mortificazione.*

To MA'CHINATE [to contrive, to devise]

deviſe] macchinare, ordinare, apparecchiare, tramare.

MACHINA'TION, s. [device, plot] macchinazione, trama, invenzione, s. f. artifizio, s. m

MACHINA'TOR, s. [deviſer, contriver, or plotter] macchinatore, inventore, s. m.

MACHI'NE, s. [an engine, or inſtrument] macchina, macchinazione, s. f. ordigno, ſtrumento, s. m.

MA'CHINIST, s. [an inventor, or manager of engines] macchiniſta, s. m.

MA'CILENT, adj. [lean, thin, lank] macilente, ſtenuato, magro.

MA'CKEREL, s. [a ſea fiſh] ſgombro, s. m.

MACKEREL-GALE, s. vento che ſoffia forte.

To MA'CULATE [to ſtain, to ſpot] maculare, macolare, macchiare, magagnare, imbrattare.

MA'CULATED, adj. maculato, macolato, macchiato, magagnato, imbrattato.

MAD, adj. [deprived of reaſon, furious] arrabbiato, furioſo, furibondo, privo di ſenno, inſenſato, matto, pazzo, forſennato.

A mad man, un pazzo, un matto.

A mad dog, un cane arrabbiato.

He is ſtark ſtaring mad, egli è un pezzo da catena.

To make one mad, far arrabbiare uno, farlo dare nelle ſmanie.

I am mad at it, queſto mi fa arrabbiare, o ſmaniare.

He is mad at me, egli è in gran collera con me.

Mad fond of [that has a great paſſion for a thing] appaſſionato, incapricciato.

To be mad for a thing, eſſer appaſſionato per qualche coſa, deſiderarla ardentemente.

Mad fit [whimſy, caprice] capriccio, ghiribizzo, s. f. fantaſia, invenzione, s. f.

Mad [hare brain'd, giddy brain'd] matto, ſtordito, ſcervellato.

A mad thing, or a mad trick, una gran pazzia.

A mad cap [one full of play] un pazzerello.

A mad cap [giddy-brain'd] uno ſtordito, uno ſcervellato.

Mad houſe [bedlam] ſpedale pe' matti.

To MAD [to make mad] fare arrabbiare, fare ſmaniare, far dare nelle ſmanie.

To mad, v. n. dar nel matto, dar nelle furie, impazzar per rabbia, infuriare.

MA'DAM, s. [a title of honour given to women] Madama, Signora.

MADBRAIN, } adj. matto, im-
MADBRAINED, } pazzato, caldo di teſta.

MADCAP, s. teſta matta, uno ſcapeſtrataccio, un pazzaccio.

To MA'DDEN [to make mad] far impazzare.

MA'DDER, s. [a plant uſed in dying] robbia, s f. erba la cui radice s'adopera a tignere i panni.

Madder, comparativo di mad, più pazzo.

MA'DDING, s. ex. To run a madding after a thing, andare appreſſo a qualche coſa con grande ardore.

He runs a madding after that woman, egli è incapricciato di quella donna.

MADE, preterito, e participio del verbo to make, v. To make.

A made word, una parola inventata.

MADEFA'CTION, s. [a moiſtening or wetting] bagnamento, immollamento, s. m.

MADGE HOWLET, s. [an out] un cucco, un barbagiani.

To MA'DEFY [to wet] ammollire, bagnare.

MADLY, adv. [like a mad man] pazzamente, da pazzo, forſennatamente, ſtoltamente, follemente, da matto.

Madly [raſhly] follemente, ſtorditamente, da ſtordito.

MA'DNESS, s. [the being mad] rabbia, pazzia, s. f.

Madneſs [fury, paſſion] pazzia, follezza, follia, furia, s. f.

MA'DRIGAL, s. [a ſort of poem] madriale, e madrigale, s. m. poeſia lirica breve, e non ſoggetta a ordine di rime.

To MA'FFLE [to ſtammer or ſtutter] ſcilinguare, balbettare, tartagliare.

MA'FFLER, s. ſcilinguato, balbo, tartaglione, s. m. ſcilinguata, s. f.

MA'FFLING, s. lo ſcilinguare, il balbettare.

MA'GAZINE, s. [ſtore houſe] fondaco, magazzino, s. m. ſtanza dove ſi ripongon le mercanzie.

MAGE, s. [a magician] un mago, un negromante.

MA'GGOT, s. [a kind of worm] cacchione, s. m. quelle uova che generano le moſche o nella carne o in altro, che poi diventano vermicciuoli.

Maggot [whimſy] capriccio, ghiribizzo, fantaſia, s. f.

I ſhall do it when the maggot bites [or when I have a mind to it] la farò quando mi verrà in fantaſia.

Maggot-headed, maggot-pated, or maggotty, adj. [whimſical, full of whims] capriccioſo, fantaſtico, ghiribizzoſo.

MA'GICAL, adj. magicale, magico.

MA'GICALLY, adv. magicamente, con magia, per magia.

MAGI'CIAN, s. [a wizard, ſorcerer, or conjurer] un mago, uno ſtregone.

MA'GICK, s. [the black art] magia, s. f. l'arte magica.

Natural magick [the ſcience of nature] la magia naturale.

Magick, adj. [magical] magico, mago, magicale.

Magick lantern, lanterna magica.

MAGISTE'RIAL, } adj. [maſter-
MAGISTE'RIOUS, } like, imperious] magiſtrale, di maeſtro, imperioſo, borioſo, fiero.

MAGISTE'RIALLY, } adv. magi-
MAGISTE'RIOUSLY, } ſtralmente, da maeſtro, imperioſamente, borioſamente, fieramente.

To command magiſterially, comandare magiſtralmente, da maeſtro, a bacchetta.

MA'GISTERY, s. [maſterſhip] magiſtero, e magiſterio, s. m. opera di maeſtro.

MA'GISTRACY, s. [the office and dignity of a magiſtrate] magiſtrato, s. m.

MA'GISTRATE, s. [an officer of juſtice, or civil government] magiſtrato.

MAGNANI'MITY, s. [greatneſs of mind, great ſpirit] magnanimità, s. f. grandezza d'animo.

MAGNANI'MOUS, adj. [of great courage, or ſpirit, generous] magnanimo, di grande animo.

MAGNANIMOUSLY, adv. con magnanimità, con grandezza d'animo, coraggioſamente.

MA'GNET, s. [loadſtone] magnete, calamita, s. f.

MAGNE'TICAL, } adj. magnetico, di
MAGNE'TICK, } magnete.

A magnetick ſtone, una magnete, una calamita.

MA'GNETISM, s. virtù magnetica.

MAGNI'FICAT, s. [the ſong of the bleſſed Virgin] il Magnificat, il cantico della beata Virgine.

MAGNI'FICENCE, s. [largeneſs of ſoul, ſtatelineſs, ſumptuouſneſs] magnificenza, pompa, s. f. ſplendore, faſto, s. m.

MAGNI'FICENT, adj. [ſtately, ſumptuous] magnificente, magnifico, pompoſo, faſtoſo, ſuperbo, grande, ſplendido.

Magnificent words, parole gonfie, o pompoſe.

MAGNI'FICENTLY, adv. magnificamente, con magnificenza, ſplendidamente, pompoſamente, ſuperbamente.

MAGNI'FICO, s. [a noble Venetian] un magnifico, un nobile Veneziano.

To MA'GNIFY [to command praiſe, to cry up] magnificare, aggrandir con parole, eſaltare, ſublimare.

MA'GNIFY'D, adj. magnificato, aggrandito, eſaltato, ſublimato.

MA'GNIFYING, adj. che aggrandiſce.

A magnifying glaſs, lente, s. f. microſcopio, s. m.

MA'GNITUDE, s [bigneſs] magnitudine, grandezza, s. f.

MAG-PYE, s. [a bird] pica, gazza, s. f.

MAHO'METAN, s. [one that follows the doctrine of Mahomet] un Maomettano, uno della ſetta e religione di Maometto.

MA'HONE, s. [a Turkiſh veſſel] maona, galeazza Turca.

MAID, s. [a virgin] una vergine, una zittella, una pulzella, una donzella, una fanciulla.

A pouring maid, una pulzelletta, una fanciullina.

A chamber maid, una cameriera.

Maid [ſerving maid] una ſerva.

The queen's maid of honour, le damigelle delle regina.

A maid ſervant, una ſerva.

A maid [a fort of fea fifh] *forta di pefce di mare.*

MA'IDEN, s. [maid, virgin] *fanciulla, vergine, pulzella, zittella.*

MA'IDENHEAD, s. [virginity] *pulcellaggio, virginità, verginità,* s. f.

To get a virgin's maidenhead, *fverginare, fpulcellare, fpulzellare una vergine.*

MA'IDENHEAD, s. [an herb] *capelvenere,* s. m. *erba medicinale.*

MA'IDENLY, } adj. *verginale,*
MA'IDEN-LIKE, } *di vergine, modefto, pudico.*

MA'IDENLY, adv. *da vergine, modeftamente, con modeftia.*

MAJES'TATIVE, } adj. [noble,
MAJE'STICAL, } ftately] *maeftofo, pieno di*
MAJE'STICK, } *maeftà.*

Majeftick [great, lofty, fublime] *maeftofo, grande, fublime, fuperbo.*

MAJE'STICALLY, adv. *maeftofamente, con maeftà.*

MA'JESTY, s. [a title given to emperors and kings only] *maeftà,* s. f. *titolo d' imperadore e di rè.*

Majefty [ftatelinefs, greatnefs] *maeftà, apparenza, fembianza, che apporti feco venerazione.*

MAIL, s. [a little iron ring] *maglia,* s. f. *piccolo cerchietto di ferro.*

A coat of mail, *giaco,* s. m. *armadura di maglia.*

Mail[a kind of portmanteau or trunk to travel with] *valigia,* s. f.

We want two mails from Holland, *ci mancano due pofte d'Olanda.*

MAILE, s. [a fort of bafe coin] *fpezie di moneta baffa.*

MA'ILED, adj. [fpeckled] *maculato, chiazzato, macchiato di vari colori.*

MAIM, adj. [curtailed of any member] *ftroppiato, e ftorpiato.*

Maim, adj. *privo di qualche neceffaria parte.*

Maim, s. *privazione di qualche effenzial parte del corpo.*

Maim, s. *ingiuria, offefa grande.*

Maim, s. *diffetto effenziale.*

To MAIM [to cut off any member, to hurt] *ftorpiare, e ftroppiare.*

MA'IMED, adj. *ftorpiato, e ftroppiato.*

MAIN, adj. [principal] *principale, effenziale.*

The main point of a bufinefs, *il punto principale d'un negozio.*

The main maft, *il grand' albero.*

The main fail, *la gran vela.*

The main guard, *la gran guardia.*

A main [full] gallop, *un gran galoppo.*

The main land, *la terra ferma, il continente.*

The main fea, *l'alto mare.*

The main body of an army, *il groffo d'un efercito.*

A river that runs with a main ftream, *un fiume molto rapido.*

To look to the main chance, *badare a' fatti fuoi.*

I did it by main ftrength, *l'ho fatto a viva forza.*

Main, s. [the main fea] *alto mare.*

The main [the main land] *il continente, terra ferma.*

With might and main, *a tutto potere, a viva forza.*

He is honeft in the main, *nel refto è un uomo dabbene.*

Upon the main [after all] *in fomma.*

MA'INLY, adv. [chiefly] *principalmente, fopra tutto.*

MAINPE'RNABLE, adj. [bailable, that may be bailed] *che fi può mallevare.*

MAINPE'RNOR, s. *ficuratore, mallevadore.*

MA'INPRISE, } s. [the bailing of a
MA'INPRIZE, } man] *malleveria,* s. f.

To MA'INPRISE, } [to bail] *mal-*
To MA'INPRIZE, } *levare.*

MAINPRISED, } adj. *mallevato.*
MAINPRIZED, }

MAINPRI'SER, s. [one who gives fecurity for another] *mallevadore,* s. m.

MA'INSWORN, s. [a northern word for perjured] *fpergiuro.*

To MAINTA'IN [to defend, or preferve] *mantenere, difendere, prefervare, confervare,* pref. *mantengo,* pret. *mantenni, difefi.*

To maintain [to plead] a caufe, *difendere una caufa.*

To maintain [to keep] *mantenere, foftentare, dare il vitto.*

To maintain [to affirm] *mantenere, affirmare.*

I'll maintain it [I'll prove it] *lo proverò.*

MA'INTAINABLE, adj. *che fi può mantenere, o foftenere.*

MAINTA'INED, adj. *mantenuto, difefo, prefervato, confervato,* v. To maintain.

MAINTA'INER, s. [defender, preferver] *mantenitore, difenfore,* s. m.

MA'INTENANCE, s. [upholding, defence] *mantenimento,* s. m. *difefa, protezione, confervazione,* s. f.

Maintenance [food, living, things neceffary to live] *mantenimento, foftentamento, cibo, vitto.*

MA'JOR, adj. [great, bigger] *maggiore.*

The major part, *la magior parte.*

The major propofition, or the major, s. [the firft part of a fyllogifm] *la maggiore d'un fillogifmo.*

A tierce major [at picket] *terza maggiore.*

Major [an officer in the army] *un maggiore.*

Major-domo [the fteward of a great man's houfe] *maggiordomo,* s. m.

MAJO'RITY, s. [the greater number or part] *la maggior parte, pluralità.*

The majority of votes, *la pluralità delle voci.*

Majority [a man's being of age] *maggiorità, lo ftato di colui che è maggiore.*

MAIZE [Weft Indian corn] *miglio Indiano, frumento dell' Indie.*

MAKE, s. [making] *fattura, manifattura.*

Make [fhape] *forma, figura,* s. f.

Make, s. [companion] *compagno, fozio.*

To MAKE [to execute, to perform] *fare.* pref. *fo,* pret. *feci.*

To make a pair of fhoes, *fare un pajo di fcarpe.*

To make a law, *fare una legge.*

To make [to create] *fare, creare.*

To make war, *far la guerra, guerreggiare.*

To make water, *fare acqua.*

To make way, } *far luogo.*
To make room, }

To make [to force] *fare, obbligare, coftrignere, violentare, sforzare.*

To make one do a thing, *far fare, obbligare, coftrignere, uno a fare una cofa.*

To make one acquainted with a thing, *far fapere ad uno qualche cofa, fargliela fapere, avifargliela.*

To make one mad, *fare arrabbiare uno, farlo dare nelle fmanie.*

To make account [to intend] *far conto, proporfi, difegnare, aver difegno.*

To make as if, to make as tho' one were fick, *fingere, e fignere, far vifta, infingerfi, farle vifte d'effer ammalato.*

To make one happy, *render uno felice.*

To make one's felf miferable, *renderfi mifero, o infelice.*

To make hafte, *affrettarfi, far prefto, fpedirfi, fbrigarfi.*

To make ready, *apparecchiare, preparare, metter in ordine.*

To make one's efcape, *fcampare, falvarfi, girfene.*

To make angry, *fare andare in collera.*

To make hot, *fcaldare.*

To make clean, *nettare, pulire,* pref. *pulifco.*

To make a requeft, *domandare, fupplicare, pregare.*

To make a doubt or queftion, *dubitare, ftare in dubbio.*

To make known, *notificare, avertire.*

To make anfwer, *rifpondere.* pret. *rifpofi.*

To make a ftand, *far paufa, paufare.*

To make trial, *far la prova, provare, fperimentare, far la fperienza.*

To make free, *liberare, dar la libertà.*

To make an excufe, *fcufarfi, fcolparfi.*

To make a fool of one, *beffare, fchernire, burlare uno.*

I made a very good dinner, *ho pranfato molto bene.*

To make ufe of a thing [to ufe it] *fervirfi di che che fi fia.*

To make a wonder of a thing, *maravigliarfi, farfi maraviglia d'un cofa.*

I make no queftion of it, *non ne dubito.*

This makes for me, *quefto fa per me.*

To make one [to make his fortune] *far la fortuna ad uno, arrichir uno.*

To make friends, *pacificare, appaciare, far pace.*

I will make her my wife, *io la prenderò per moglie.*
To make gain of, *guadagnare.*
To make a virtue of a neceſſity, *far della neceſſità virtù.*
To make much of one, *accarezzare, vezzeggiare alcuno,* trattarlo *bene, amarlo.*
To make a pen, temperare *una penna.*
To make the beſt of a bad market, *trarſi d' impaccio il meglio che ſi può.*
I don't know what to make of it, *io non comprendo, io non ſo quel che ſignifica, quel che ſi voglia dire.*
To make one [to be one among the reſt] *eſſer del numero.*
To make a blow at one, tirare *un colpo ad uno.*
To make a ſhoot at one, *ſparare ad uno.*
To make money of a thing [to ſell it] *far danari d'una coſa, venderla.*
He makes a thouſand pounds a year of his poſt, *egli tira mille lire ſterline l' anno del ſuo impiego.*
To make many words about a trifle, *diſputare, contraſtare per una bagattella.*
I won't make many words with you, *non voglio andar* tirato *con voi.*
I will not meddle nor make with it, *non voglio impacciarmene.*
To make a paſs at one, tirare *una botta ad uno.*
To make it one's boaſt, *vantarſi, vanagloriarſi d'una qualche coſa.*
To make a thing another man's, *alienare una coſa.*
To make [to prove, to become] *divenire, eſſere.* pref. *divengo.* pret. *divenni.*
He'll never make a good ſcholar, *egli non ſarà mai un uomo dotto.*
I'll make [to warrant] it good, *ve lo do per buono.*
I'll make it good to you, *io ve lo farò buono.*
To make good one's ground [to maintain it] *difendere il ſuo poſto.*
To make good a ſiege, *mantenere un aſſedio.*
To make good [to prove] *provare, giuſtificare.*
To make [or give] an aſſignation, *fare un appuntamento.*
To make [to run] after one, *ſeguitare, correr dietro ad uno.*
To make again, *riſare, far di nuovo.*
To make aſhamed, *fare arroſſire.*
To make afraid, *atterrire, ſpaventare, far paura.* pref. *atterriſco.*
To make blind, *acciecare.*
To make better, *migliorare.*
To make an end, *finire,* pref. *finiſco.*
To make for a place, *incamminarſi ve ſo un luogo.*
To make head againſt one, *far teſta ad uno, contraſtarlo opporſi.*
To make one away [to kill him] *ammazzarè uno.*
To make one's ſelf away, or to make away with one's ſelf, *darſi la morte, ucciderſi, ammazzarſi.*
To make leſs, *ſminuire, ſcemare, diminuire,* pref. *ſminuiſco, diminuiſco.*
To make away with one's eſtate [to ſquander it away] *ſpendere, ſcialacquare i ſuoi beni, mandare a male il ſuo avere.*
To mark for land, *approdare, pigliar terra, ſbarcare.*
To make off [to go away] *andar via, ſalvarſi, fuggire.*
To make towards one, *avvicinarſi ad uno, andar verſo lui.*
To make a noiſe, *ſtrepitare, fare ſtrepito, o romore.*
To make nothing of, *far poco conto, far poca ſtima, villipendere, diſpregiare.*
To make large promiſes, *prometter mari e mondi.*
To make a ſtand, *fermarſi.*
To make over one's right or eſtate to another, *traſferire, cedere, il ſuo diritto o i ſuoi beni, il ſuo avere ad uno.*
To make out a thing [to prove, or juſtify it] *provare una coſa, farla vedere con prove, giuſtificare.*
This will never make me out of love with her, *non laſcerò per queſto d' amarla.*
To make up [to finiſh, to conclude] *fare, conchiudere, terminare, finire.*
To make up a ſhirt, *finire una camicia.*
To make up an account, *ſaldare un conto.*
To make up a letter, *piegare una lettera.*
To make up [to repair] a breach, *riparare una breccia.*
To make up one's loſſes, *riparare le ſue perdite.*
To make up one's want of parts by diligence, *ſupplire alle mancanze dell' ingegno colla diligenza.*
To make up [to make amends] *ricompenſare.*
To make up a quarrel, or difference, *accomodare una querela, o conteſa.*
To make up to one [to draw near him] *avvicinarſi ad uno, accoſtarſegli.*
To make five games up, *giuocare a cinque giuochi la partita.*
MA'KEBATE, s. [a cauſer or promoter of quarrels] *un ſeminatore di diſcordie, un attizzabrighe, un brigante, un ſedizioſo.*
MA'KER, s. *facitore, fattore,* s. m. *facitrice,* s. f.
God is the maker of heaven and earth, *Iddio è 'l fattore del cielo,* e *della terra.*
A ſhoe-maker, *un calzolajo.*
MA'KING, s. *facimento,* s. m. *il fare,* v. To make.
Making [make] *fattura, manifattura,* s. f.
Is this of your making? *è queſta opera voſtra?*
I have a new ſuit of cloaths making, *mi fo fare un abito nuovo.*
It is now making, *ſi ſta facendo adeſſo.*
This was the making of him, *queſto è ſtata la ſua fortuna queſto l' ha arricchito.*
MA'KEPEACE, s. [peacemaker, reconciler] *pacificatore; colui che ha far pace.*
MA'KEWEIGHT, s. *qualche coſuccia che ſi mette ſulla bilancia onde ſi compia il peſo.*
MA'LACHITE, s. [a precious ſtone] *malachite, pietra prezioſa.*
MAL-ADMINISTRA'TION, s. [miſdemeanor in publick employment] *mal procedere, cattiva condotta nell' amminiſtrazione d'una carica.*
MA'LADY, s. [diſeaſe] *malattia,* s. f.
MA'LAGA } s. *vino di Malaga.*
MA'LAGA WINE, }
MA'LANDRES, s. [a horſe diſeaſe] *malandre, malattia che viene alla giuntura del ginocchio d'un cavallo.*
MA'LAPERT, adj. [ſaucy] *impertinente, inſolente, sfrontato, sfacciato.*
MA'LAPERTLY, adv. *inſolentemente, impertinentemente, sfrontatamente, sfacciatamente.*
MA'LAPERTNESS, s. *inſolenza, impertinenza, sfacciataggine,* s. f.
MALE, s. [the he of any kind] *il maſchio.*
Male and female, *il maſchio, e la femmina.*
Male, adj. *maſchio.*
Iſſue male, *figliuoli maſchi.*
MA'LECONTENT, s. [one that is diſcontented] *malcontento.*
MALEDI'CTION, s. [curſe] *maladizione, e maledizione,* s. f.
MALEFA'CTOR, s. [offender] *malfattore,* s. m.
MA'LEFICE, s. [evil deed, ſhrewd turn] *maleficio, malfacimento, delitto, torto,* s. m. *ingiuria,* s. f.
MALE'FICENCE, s [miſchievouſneſs] *qualità malfacente, malignità,* s. f.
MALE'FICK, adj. [miſchievous] *malefico, maligno, malfacente.*
MA'LETENT, } s. [a toll of forty
MA'LETOLTE, } ſhillings, formerly paid for every ſack of wool] *dazio di quaranta ſcellini per ogni ſacco di lana.*
MALE'VOLENCE, s. [ſpight, ill will] *malavoglienza, e malevoglienza, cattiva volontà, malizia, malignità,* s. f. *odio,* s. m.
MALE'VOLENT, adj. [that has an ill-will, or ſpight againſt one] *malevolente, che vuol male a qualcheduno, male intenzionato, invidioſo, maligno.*
MA'LICE, s. [malignity] *malizia, aſtuzia, triſtizia, cattivezza, malignità,* s. f.
Malice [grudge, ſpight] *malizia, perfidia, malevoglienza,* s. f. *odio,* s. m.
To bear malice [or ill-will] to one, *voler male ad uno.*
To MA'LICE, *eſſer pieno di maltalento, uſar malignità.*
MALI'CIOUS, adj. [miſchievous, unlucky] *malizioſo, cattivo, maligno.*
Malicious [malevolent] *malvolente, che vuol male.*
MALI'CIOUSLY, adv. *malizioſamente, con malizia.*

MALI'GN, adj. [mischievous] *maligno, malfacente, nocivo.*

To MALI'GN [to envy] *invidiare, portar invidia.*

MALI'GNANCY, s *malignità*, s. f. *qualità, e natura maligna.*

MALI'GNANT, adj. *maligno, malignoso.*

A malignant diſtemper, *una malattia maligna.*

Malignant, s. [ill affected perſon] *una perſona male intenzionata.*

MALI'GNED, adj. *invidiato.*

MALI'GNER, s. [one who regards another with an ill-will] *colui che guarda di mal occhio un altro; che ha maltalento, che invidioſamente biaſima e trova fallo.*

MALI'GNITY, s. [or malignancy] *malignità mala natura*, s. f. *mal talento.*

Malignity [ill will, grudge] *malignità, malvagità d'animo, malevoglienza*, s. f. *odio*, s. m.

MA'LKIN, *una bagaſcia.*

MALL, s. [a ſort of play] *maglio*, s. m. *ſpezie di giuoco.*

Mall-ſtick, *maglio, ſtrumento da giuocare.*

MA'LLARD, s. [a wild drake] *anitra ſalvatica.*

MA'LLEABLE, adj. [that might be hammered out, and will ſpread, being beaten] *che ſi può martellare, o che ſi può ſtender col martello.*

Malleable [flexible, ſupple, pliant] *pieghevole, arrendevole, fleſſibile, docile, trattabile.*

MALLEABI'LITY, } s. *dolcezza.pieghevolezza,*
MA'LLEABLENESS, } *paſtoſità, fleſſibilità ſotto il martello; e dicesi de' metalli.*

To MA'LLEATE [to hammer] *battere col martello.*

MA'LLET, s. [a wooden hammer] *maglio, martello di legno.*

MA'LLOWS, s. [an herb] *malva*, s. f. *erba nota.*

MA'LMSEY, s. [a ſort of luſcious wine] *malvagia*, s. m. *ſpezie di vin dolce.*

MALT, s. [barley ſoak'd and dry'd, in order to make drink] *orzo franto per fare della birra.*

A malt mill, *un mulinello.*

A malt kiln, *un forno, una fornace.*

Malt long, or malt worm, s. [a cancerous ſore about the hoof of a horſe] *rappa*, s. f. *malattia del cavallo.*

To MALT, *macerar orzo per far la birra.*

MALSTER, } s. *mercante d'orzo.*
MALT-MAN, }

MALVERSA'TION, s. [prevarication, miſdemeanor in an office] *pravaricazione, traſgreſſione*, s. f.

MAM, } s. [mother] *mamma, voce*
MAMMA, } *fanciulleſca, e vale madre.*

MA'MMALUCKS, s. [light horſe men, an order of ſoldiers, who were the chief military ſupport of the Saracens in Egypt] *mammalucchi nome che avevano certi ſoldati in Egitto nel tempo de' Califfi.*

MA'MMET, s. *fantoccio, marmocchio, mattaccino, burattino.*

MA'MMOCK, s. [a fragment, piece, or ſcrap] *frammento, pezzaccio, pezzo groſſo.*

MA'MMON, s. [the god of wealth] *mammona, e mammone*, s. m.

MAMMONIST, s. [a worldling] *un mondano.*

MAN, s. [a creature endowed with reaſon] *uomo*, s. m. *creatura ragionevole.*

An honeſt man, *un uomo dabbene.*

An old man, *un vecchio.*

A grown man, *un uomo fatto.*

A man [one, ſomebody] *qualcheduno.*

To do a man a kindneſs, *fare un ſervizio a qualcheduno*

Where's my man [or ſervant] *dov' è il mio ſervo.*

A coal-man, *un venditor, di carbone.*

Man [ſhip] *nave, vaſcello.*

A man of war, *una nave da guerra.*

A merchant-man, *un vaſcello mercantile, una nave da carico.*

A man [at cheſs] *pedina, pedona*, s. f.

To be one's own man [to depend upon no body] *eſſer padrone di ſe ſteſſo, non dipender da neſſuno.*

So much a man [ſo much a head] *tanto per teſta.*

But what ſhall a man do in ſuch a caſe? *ma che biſogna fare in tal caſo?*

Can a man know? *ſi può mai ſapere?*

I love him beyond any man, *l'amo più di qualunque ſi ſia.*

There's no man alive that will undertake it, *non c' è neſſuno che voglia intraprenderlo.*

I am the man that did it, *io ſon quello, che l'ho fatto.*

I like the man well enough, *io l'amo aſſai.*

The good man of the houſe, *il padron di caſa.*

An ungrateful man, *un ingrato.*

A perfidious man, *un perfido.*

A man ſervant, *un ſervo.*

A man or a mouſe, *o tutto o niente, ceſare o niccolò.*

Every man, *ciaſcheduno, ognuno.*

Every man has his humour, *ognuno ha il ſuo umore.*

No man *neſſuno.*

There's no man that knows him better than I, *neſſuno lo conoſce meglio di me.*

To play the man, *trattare da uomo coraggioſo.*

Like a man, *da uomo, virilmente, coraggioſamente.*

A man hater, *un miſantropo.*

A man ſlayer, *un omicida.*

Manſlaughter, *omicidio*, s. m.

To MAN [to furniſh with men] *armare, fornire d'uomini.*

To man a ſhip, *armare, o fornire un vaſcello d'uomini.*

To man [to garriſon] a town, *preſidiare una città.*

To man a hawk [to make her gentle, tame, or tractable] *addimeſticare un falcone.*

To MA'NACLE [to bind with hand-cuffs, or fetters] *metter le manette.*

MA'NACLED, adj. *che ha le manette.*

MA'NACLES, s. [hand fetters, cuffs] *manette*, s. f. *ſtrumento di ferro, col quale ſi legano le mani giunte a' malfattori.*

MA'NAGE, s. [a riding academy, or riding horſe] *maneggio*, s m. *luogo deputato per maneggiare i cavalli.*

The MA'NAGE of a concern, *il maneggio d'un negozio.*

To MA'NAGE [to order, to handle, to rule, to govern] *maneggiare, condurre, ordinare, governare*, pres. *conduco*, pret. *conduſſi*

To manage a buſineſs, *maneggiare un negozio.*

To manage [to govern] one, *maneggiare, governare alcuno.*

To manage a horſe, *maneggiare un cavallo, ammaeſtrarlo, eſercitarlo.*

MA'NAGED, adj. *maneggiato, condotto, ordinato, governato.*

A horſe well managed, *un cavallo ben maneggiato, bene ammaeſtrato.*

MA'NAGEMENT, s. [ordering or conduct] *maneggio*, s. m. *condotta*, s. f

MA'NAGER, s. *maneggiatore, direttore, conduttore, amminiſtratore*, s. m. *quello che maneggia qualche affare.*

A good manager, *un uomo frugale, un amante d'economia.*

MA'NAGERY, s. [management] *condotta, manneggio.*

MA'NCA, s. [a ſquare piece of gold in ancient times] *ſpezie di moneta d'orò antica.*

MA'NCHE, s. [a ſleeve in heraldry] *manica.*

MA'NCHET, s. [a fine ſort of ſmall bread] *pan buffetto.*

A manchet loaf, *una pagnotta bianca.*

MA'NCHINEEL-TREE, s. *albero nativo dell' Indie occidentali che non cede in grandezza alla quercia; il legno de' eſſo ridotto in panconi e in aſſe è di buon uſo, che prende un bel lucido e colore; il frutto all' incontro è corroſivo e per lo più da morte a chi ne mangia.*

MANCIPA'TION, *v.* Emancipation.

MA'NCIPLE, s. [a caterer, one who buys victuals and common proviſions for a college, or monaſtery] *diſpenſiere, e diſpenſiero, provveditore*, s. m.

MANCU'SA, s. [an ancient cion] *ſpezie di moneta antica.*

MANDA'MUS, s. [a writ ſent by the King to the heads of a college, &c. for the admittance of a fellow or member into the ſociety; alſo ſeveral others, by which any thing is commanded] *un ordine, un mandato.*

MA'NDARIN, s. *mandarino; magiſtrato o nobiluomo Chineſe.*

MA'NDATARY, s. [he to whom a charge

charge

charge is given] *mandato, colui che viene col mandato.*

Mandatary [he who obtains a benefice by a mandamus] *mandatario*, s. m.

MA'NDATE, s. [a commandment, or writ] *mandato, ordine*, s. m.

A Pope's mandate, *un mandato del Papa.*

MA'NDIBLE, s. [the jaw] *mascella*, s. f.

MANDI'LION, s. [a soldier's garment] *mandiglione*, s. m. *spezie di casacca.*

MA'NDRAKE, s. [a sort of plant] *mandragola*, s. f. *spezie d'erba.*

MA'NDY, } s. [the next
MAUNDY THURSDAY, } Thursday before Easter] *il Giovedì santo.*

MANE, s. [the long hair hanging down on a horse's neck] *chioma*, s. f. *crine*, s. m. *pelo lungo che pende al cavallo dal fil del collo.*

MANES, s. [the souls departed] *le anime de' morti.*

MA'NFUL, adj. [stout] *bravo, coraggioso, valoroso, prode, generoso, ardito, animoso.*

MA'NFULLY, adv. *da bravo, animosamente, valorosamente, coraggiosamente.*

MA'NFULNESS, s. [courage, stoutness] *bravùra, prodezza, valentìa*, s. f. *valore, coraggio*, s. m.

MA'NGANESE, s. [a sort of stone used in making glass] *manganese, spezie di pietra.*

MANGE s. [a kind of scab on dogs] *sizza, scabbia*, s. f. *male simile alla rogna, il quale è proprio de' cani.*

MA'NGER, s. [a sort of a trough for horses to feed in] *mangiatoja*, s. m.

To leave all at rack and manger [at random] *lasciar tutto in abbandono.*

To live at rack and manger, *viver prodigalmente, scialacquare.*

MA'NGINESS, s. [from mange] *prurito causato dalla sizza.*

To MA'NGLE [to cut, to rend, to tear in pieces] *stracciare, mettere in pezzi, minuzzare, sbranare.*

To Mangle [to maim] *storpiare, e stroppiare.*

MA'NGLED, adj. *stracciato, messo in pezzi, minuzzato, sbranato.*

MA'NGLER, s. *quello, o quella che straccia, che minuzza, che mette in pezzi.*

MA'NGO, s. [an East Indian fruit] *spezie di frutto che viene dall' Indie orientali.*

MA'NGON, } s. [an engine used
MA'NGONEL, } anciently for casting stones] *mangano*, s. m. *antico strumento da guerra da tirare o scagliare e sassi.*

MA'NGY, adj. [from mange] *rognoso, che ha la sizza, scabbioso.*

MA'NHOOD, s. [man's estate] *virilità l' età virile.*

Manhood [courage] *valore, coraggio*, s. m. *bravura*, s. f.

MA'NIA, s. [a sort of madness] *mania, pazzia*, s. f.

MA'NIACK, adj. [troubled with the mania] *maniaco, furibondo.*

MA'NIFEST, adj. [or plain] *manifesto, palese, pubblico, noto.*

To make manifest, *manifestare.*

To MA'NIFEST [to make manifest] *manifestare, far manifesto, scoprire, palesare far vedere.*

MANIFESTA'TION, s. *manifestazione.*

MA'NIFESTED, adj. *manifestato, scoperto, palesato.*

MA'NIFESTLY, adv. *manifestamente, chiaramente, apertamente, evidentemente.*

MANIFE'STO, s. [a publick declaration of a prince or state] *manifesto.*

MA'NIFOLD, adj. [from many] *di molte maniere o sorti, molti.*

MA'NIPLE, s. [a handful of herbs, or any other thing] *manipolo*, s. m. *manata*, s. f.

Maniple [a kind of ornament, like a scarf, worn about the wrists, by Roman mass priests] *manipolo, striscia di drappo o altro, che tiene al braccio manco il sacerdote nel celebrar la messa.*

Roman maniple [company of foot soldiers] *compagnia di fanti Romani.*

MA'NKIND, s. *il genere umano.*

MA'NLINESS, s. [or manly look] *aspetto maschile, maschiezza.*

MA'NLY, adj. [of a man] *maschio, maschile.*

Manly [stout] *maschio, nobile, generoso, coraggioso, prode, animoso.*

MA'NNA, s. [honey dew] *manna*, s. m.

MA'NNED, adj. [from to mañ] *armato, fornito*, v. To man.

MA'NNER, s. [fashion, way] *maniera, guisa, forma*, s. f. *modo*, s. m.

In or after this manner, *in questa maniera, in tal guisa, in questo modo.*

Manner [sort, kind] *maniera, spezie, sorta*, s. f.

What manner of man is he? *che sorta d'uomo è?*

Manner [condition] *maniera, natura, inclinazione*, s. m. *umore*, s. m.

This is the manner of the man, *questa è la sua maniera, il suo umore.*

In a manner [almost, as it were] *quasi, per così dire, per maniera di parlare.*

We were in a manner lost, *noi eramo quasi perduti.*

In like manner [likewise] *similmente, parimente.*

Manner [custom] *maniera, usanza*, s. f. *costume*, s. m.

According to our accustomed manner, *secondo il nostro costume, come noi siamo accostumati, o soliti di fare.*

Manners [in the plural] *maniere, costumi, qualità di procedere.*

To corrupt or reform manners, *corrompere o riformare i costumi.*

Manners, } [civility, good
Good manners, } breeding] *civiltà, buona creanza.*

He has no manners, *egli non ha civiltà.*

I shall teach you better manners, *v' insegnerò ben io a vivere.*

MA'NNERED, v. Mannerly.

MA'NNERLINESS, s. *civiltà, buona creanza.*

MA'NNERLY, adj. [civil, well bred] *civile, manieroso, che ha bel modo di procedere.*

MA'NNIKIN, s. [a little man] *un uomicciato, un uomicciuolo.*

MA'NNING, s. [from to man] *armamento*, v. To man.

Manning [day's work] *giornata, il lavoro d'un giorno.*

MA'NOR, } s. [a Lordship] *feudo,*
MA'NOUR, } *signoria.*

The manor house, *castello, casa del signore d'un feudo, casa signorile.*

Manor [house without the city] *villa signorile, podere.*

MAN'SION, s. [or manor house, or capital messuage] *villa*, s. f. *podere*, s. m.

Mansion [abode, dwelling place] *soggiorno*, s. m. *dimora*, s. f.

The mansion of the blessed is in heaven, *il soggiorno de' beati è nel cielo.*

MANSLA'UGHTER, s. [the unlawful killing of a man, without prepensed malice] *omicidio*, s. m.

MA'NSUETE, adj. [courteous, gentle, meek] *mansueto, benigno, affabile, cortese.*

MA'NSUETUDE, s. [gentleness, courtesy] *mansuetudine, gentilezza, benignità, cortesia, affabilità.*

MANTI'GER, s. [a large monkey or baboon] *manticora, babbuino, scimmione.*

MA'NTLE, s. [a cloak or long robe] *manto*, s. m.

A royal mantle, *il manto reale, o mantelletta.*

A lady's mantle, *mantellina da donna.*

A child's mantle [used at a christening] *to vagliuola.*

The mantle-tree of a chimney, *la cappa del cammino.*

To MA'NTLE [to flower, to smile like drink] *fare una piccola spuma.*

Ale that mantles, *cervogia che fa una piccola spuma.*

To mantle [as a hawk does, when she spreads her wings] *stender l'ali, párlando d' un falcone.*

To mantle [to joy, to revel] *far allegria, gozzovigliare.*

To mantle [to be expanded, to spread luxuriantly] *allargarsi, spandersi esuberantemente; e dicesi per lo più delle piante nate in terreno ricco secondo l'indole loro.*

To mantle, *esser in agitazione grande, in gran fermento.*

MA'NTLET, s. [a penthouse to shroud soldiers under] *tavolato da soldati da stare a coperto.*

MA'NTUA, s. [a sort of woman's gown] *manto da donna.*

MA'NTUA-MAKER, s. *sarta da donne.*

MA'NUAL, adj. [of the hand] *manuale, fatto con mano.*

A sign manual, *segno manuale, segno, segnatura.*

A

A manual, s. [a book portable in the hand] *un manuale, un libretto.*

MA'NUALIST, s. [or handicraftſman] *un artegiano, un operajo, un manifattore.*

MANDU'CTION, s. [a guiding or leading by the hand; a help] *guida, ſcorta,* s. f. *ajuto, ſoccorſo,* s. m.

MANUFA'CTURE, } s. [the making
MANUFA'CTORY, } of ſome handy-works] *manifattura, fabbrica.*

A manufacture of cloth, or ſilks, *fabbrica di panni, o di drappi.*

To MANUFA'CTURE [to work, or make] *fabbricare.*

MANUFA'CTURED, adj. *fabbricato.*

MANUFA'CTURER, s. *manifattore, fabbricatore.*

MANUFA'CTURING, s. *manifattura, fabbricatura,* s. f.

MANUMI'SSION, [a making of a ſervant free] *il metter in libertà.*

To MANUMI'T [to ſet free] *porre in libertà, dar la libertà.*

MANUMI'TTED, adj. *meſſo in libertà.*

MANU'RANCE, s. *agricoltura, cultura.*

MANU'RE, s. [dung, marl, &c.] tutto *quello che ſerve a letamare la terra, letame, concime, concio.*

To MANU'RE [to fatten] the ground, *letamare, concimare la terra.*

To manure [to till] the ground, *coltivare, lavorare la terra.*

MANU'RED, adj. *letamato, concimato, coltivato, lavorato.*

MANU'RER OF GROUND, s. *agricoltore, lavoratore.*

MA'NUSCRIPT, s. [a book or copy written with the hand] *un manoſcritto, e manuſcritto.*

MA'NY, adj. [a great number] *molti.*

Good many, great many, *molti, un gran numero.*

Many a man, *molti uomini.*

Many a time, *molte volte.*

So many, *tanti.*

How many, *quanti.*

As many as, *quanti.*

Too many, *troppi.*

He is too many [too ſtrong] for me, *egli è troppo forte per me.*

Twice as many, *due volte più.*

So many men, ſo many minds, *quanti uomini, tanti conſigli.*

Many feet, s. [the fiſh pourcontrel] *polpo, ſpezie di peſce.*

MANI'LANGUAGED, adj. *che ſa molte lingue.*

MANYTIMES, *fraſe avverbiale* [often, frequently] *molte volte, ſpeſſe volte, parecchie volte, ſpeſſo, ſovente, frequentemente.*

MAP, s. [a repreſentation of the earth, or ſome particular part thereof, upon a plain ſuperficies] *carta geografica.*

A general map, *carta generale del mondo, mappamondo.*

To MAP, *delineare, deſcrivere.*

MA'PLE, } s. *acero,* s. m. *ſpe-*
MA'PLE TREE, } *zie d'albero.*

MA'PPERY, s. *l'arte topografica, e l'arte del diſegnare.*

To MAR, *v.* To marr.

MA'RA, s. [meer, marſh, bog] *pantano, lagune,* s. m. *laguna,* s. f. *acqua ſtagnante che fa palude.*

MARANA'THA, s. *la ſcomunica degli antichi giudei, o la formola del loro ſcomunicare.*

MARA'SMUS, s. *malattia che conſuma parte del corpo umano.*

MA'RBLE, s. [a ſort of fine ſtone] *marmo,* s. m.

Of, or made of marble, *marmoreo, marmorino, di marmo.*

MA'RBLES, s. pl. [round fine clay nickers for children to play with] *pallottole di creta.*

To MA'RBLE [to do marble-like] *ſcreziare a guiſa di marmo.*

To marble paper, *ſcreziare la carta a guiſa di marmo.*

MA'RBLED, adj. *ſcreziato a guiſa di marmo.*

Marbled paper, *carta marmorata.*

MA'RCASITE, s. [a kind of mineral ſtone] *marcaſſita,* s. f. *ſorta di minerale.*

MARCH, s. [the third month of the year] *Marzo,* s. m. *il terzo meſe dell' anno.*

March [marching, going] *marcia,* s. f. *il marciare degli eſerciti.*

To begin one's march, *metterſi in marcia*

To MARCH [to go, to ſet forwards, as an army does] *marciare, il camminare degli eſerciti.*

To march in, *entrare.*

To march out, *uſcire,* pref. *eſco.*

To march off, *andarſene, ritirarſi, piegar le tende, ſfendare, fuggire.*

To march an army, *far marciare un eſercito.*

To march off [to die] *morire, andare a babboriveggoli.*

MA'RCHES, s. [bounds, limits] *limite, termine,* s. m. *le frontiere d'uno ſtato.*

MA'RCHING, s. *marcia, il marciare.*

MA'RCHIONESS, s. [a marquiſs's lady] *marcheſana, marcheſa,* s. f. *femmina di marcheſe.*

MA'RCHPANE, s. [a ſort of ſweet bread] *marzapane,* s. m. *paſta fatta di mandorle, e di zucchero, infuſovi un po' d'acqua roſa.*

MA'RCID, adj. *gretto, miſerello, marcio, magro.*

MARE, s. [a female horſe] *cavalla, giumenta,* s. f.

The night-mare, s. *ſorta di malattia.*

A mare colt, *un puledro.*

MA'RESHALL, *v.* Marſhall.

MA'RGIN, s. [the edge or brim of any thing] *margine,* s. f. *orlo,* s. m.

The margin of a book, *il margine d'un libro.*

MA'RGINAL, adj. *marginale, che è in margine.*

Marginal notes, *annotazioni che ſono nel margine; note in margine.*

MA'RJORAM, s. [a plant] *majorana, perſa,* s. f. *erba nota.*

Baſtard or wild marjoram, *majorana ſalvatica, origano,* s. m.

MARI'GOLD, s. [a flower] *ſorta di fiore giallo.*

MA'RINADE, s. [pickled meat, either fleſh or fiſh] *marinata,* s. f.

To MA'RINATE [to fry in oil, and then to pickle] *marinare, friggere del peſce e altri cibi, e mettervi poi ſu dell' aceto per conſervarlo.*

MA'RINATED, adj. *marinato.*

MARI'NE, s. [or navy] *marina,* s. f.

The officers of the marine, *gli uffiziali della marina.*

Marine, adj. *marino.*

A trump marine, *una tromba marina.*

MA'RINER, s. [ſeaman] *marinaro, e marinajo.*

Of or belonging to marines, *marinareſco, di marinajo.*

MA'RJOROM, *v.* Marjoram.

MA'RISH, s. [a bog, a fen, a ſwamp, a watry ground] *un pantano; una palude.*

Mariſh, adj. *paludoſo, limaccioſo, pantanoſo.*

MA'RITAL, adj. [of the huſband] *maritale.*

MA'RITIMAL, } adj. [near the ſea]
MA'RITIME, } *marittimo, marino.*

MARK, s. [ſign, token] *ſegno, indizio, ſegnale.*

Mark [proof] *prova,* s. f. *atteſtato, contraſſegno, teſtimonio,* s. m.

Mark [print] *traccia,* s. f. *veſtigio,* s. m.

Mark [boundary of land] *limite, termine,* s. m.

Mark [a weight of eight ounces] *marco,* s. m. *peſo d'ott' once.*

Mark [a ſilver coin, anciently valued at thirty ſhillings, but now generally taken for the ſum of thirteen ſhillings and four pence ſterling] *marco, marca, pezzo di moneta che valeva altre volte trenta ſrellini preſo adeſſo comunemente per la ſomma di tredici ſcellini e quattro ſoldi.*

Mark [white aim to ſhoot at] *berſaglio, berzaglio, ſegno,* s. m.

To ſhoot above the mark, *tirar troppo alto.*

To ſhoot below the mark, *tirar troppo baſſo.*

To miſs one's mark, *mancar il colpo.*

A good or bad mark's-man, *un buono, o un cattivo tiratore.*

To MARK [to put a mark to a thing in order to know it again] *marchiare, contraſegnare.*

To mark with a red-hot iron, *ſuggellare.*

To mark [to take notice, to mind] *oſſervare, badare, ſtare attento.*

To mark out [to ſhow] *moſtrare, far vedere.*

MA'RKED, adj. *marchiato, contraſſegnato, v.* To mark.

MA'RKER, s. *ſegnatore,* s. m. Ex. The marker at tennis, *il ſegnatore al giuoco della pallacorda.*

MA'R-

MA'RKET, } s. [a place where MA'RKET PLACE, } provisions, or any manner of goods are set to sale] *mercato*, s. m. *luogo dove si rompera e vende.*

Hay-market, *mercato di fieno.*

Fish-market, *pescheria, luogo dove si vende il pesce.*

Market-folks, s. *gente che bazzica continuamente in mercato.*

To make one's market [or gain] of a thing, *far mercato di che che si sia, guadagnarvi.*

I'll make the best market I can, *farò il miglior mercato che potrò, venderò la mia mercanzia per quanto potrò.*

Good ware makes quick markets, *buona mercanzia ha buono spaccio.*

You brought your hogs to a fine market, *voi avete fatto un buon negozio, in senso ironico.*

A market town, *una terra, un borgo.*

The price of the market, *il prezzo corrente.*

MA'RKET-PRICE, } s. *il prezzo cor-* MA'RKET-RATE, } *rente di checchessia.*

A market-man, or market-woman, *un uomo, o una donna che frequenta il mercato.*

MA'RKETABLE, adj. [that is fit to be sold in a market] *buono, ben condizionato.*

Marketable wine, *vino buono.*

MA'RKING, s. [from to mark] *il marcare, v.* To mark.

Marking-iron, *marchio, marco*, s. m.

MA'RKMAN, } s. [a man skilful to MA'RKSMAN, } hit a mark] *uno che tira al segno bene.*

MARL, s. [a kind of earth which is cast upon the earth to fertilize it] *terra grassa.*

To MARL [to spread land over with marl] *concimare, letamare con terra grassa.*

MA'RLED, adj. *concimato, letamato.*

MA'RLINE, s. *canape impeciata e avvolta intorno alle gomene d'una nave per conservarle.*

MA'RLPIT, s. *cava onde la terra grassa si scava.*

MA'RLY, adj. *produttivo o abbondante di terra grassa.*

MA'RMELADE, } s. [a confection MA'RMALET, } made of quinces, or other fruits] *cotognato*, s. m. *confettura di mele cotogne, o altri frutti*

MA'RMOSET, s. [a kind of grotesque figure in building] *mascherone*, s. m. *figura grottesca.*

Marmoset [a kind of black monkey] *bertuccia, scimia, monna*, s. f.

MA'RMOT, } s. [or mountain rat] MA'RMOTTO, } *marmotta*, s. f. *spezie di topo.*

MA'RQUE, *v* Mark.

MA'RQUESS, *v.* Marquis.

MA'RQUETRY, s. [inlaid work] *tarsia*, s. f.

MA'RQUIS, s. [a title of honour, next before an earl, and next after a duke] *marchese*, s. m. titolo *di signoria.*

MA'RQUISATE, or MA'RQUISDOM, s. *marchesato*, s. m. *stato, e dominio di marchese.*

MA'RQUISHIP, s. titolo, *qualità di marchese.*

MA'RRER, s. *uno che guasta, che danneggia.*

To MARR [to spoil] *guastare, sconciarr, rovinare, corrompere*, pres. *corruppi.*

To marr [to deprave] manners, *corrompere i costumi.*

MA'RRED, adj. *guastato, sconciato, rovinato, corrotto.*

MA'RRIAGE, s. [wedlock] *matrimonio*, s. m.

Marriage [wedding] *matrimonio, sposalizio*, s m. *nozze*, s. f.

He married my sister in second marriage, *egli sposò mia sorella in seconde nozze.*

MA'RRIGEABLE, adj. [that is of age, fit to be married] *da marito.*

MA'RRIAGEABLENESS, s. *età da marito.*

MA'RROW, s. [a soft fat substance contain'd in the hollow of the bones] *midolla*, s. f.

The marrow of a bone, *la midolla d'un osso.*

Marrow [quintessence] *midolla, sustanza*, s. f. *concetto*, s. m.

A marrow bone [a bone full of marrow] *un osso midolloso, pieno di midolla.*

Marrow-bone, s. *E' vore burlesca per ginocchio.*

MA'RROWLESS, adj. *senza midolla.*

To MA'RRY [to join by wedlock] *sposare, maritare.*

He has married a handsome woman, *egli ha sposato una bella donna.*

To marry, verb neut. [to take a wife, or husband] *sposarsi, maritarsi.*

Marry in haste and repent at leisure, *chi erra in fretta, a bell' agio si pente.*

Marry again, *rimaritarsi.*

Marry, ay, marry, adv. [yes forsooth] *veramente, sì per certo.*

MA'RRY'D, adj. *sposato, maritato.*

A marry'd life, *matrimonio, vita congiugale.*

MARS, s. [one of the seven planets] *Marte*, s. m, *nome del pianeta del quinto cielo.*

Mars, s. [the heathen God of war] *Marte, il Dio della guerra.*

MARSH, s. [a fen or boggy ground] *pantano, lagume*, s. m. *palude*, s. f.

MARSHA'L, s. [the name of several officers] *maresciallo*, s. m.

The Lord or Earl Marshal of England, *il Gran Maresciallo d' Inghilterra.*

A camp marshal, *maresciallo di campo.*

A marshal of France, *un maresciallo di Francia.*

To MA'RSHAL [to put in order] *schierare, ordinare, regolare.*

To marshal an army, *schierare un esercito.*

MA'RSHALLED, adj. *schierato, ordinato, regolato.*

MA'RSHALLER, s. *uno che ordina, che regola, che mette in ordinanza.*

MA'RSHALSEA, *nome d'una prigione vicina a Londra.*

MA'RSHALSHIP, s. *la carica o l'ufizio di maresciallo.*

MA'RSHY, adj. [fenny] *paludoso, pantanoso.*

MART, s. [great fair] *fiera*, s. f.

To MART, *trafficare, mercanteggiare.*

MA'RTEN, or MA'RTERN, s. [a wild beast, like a ferret] *martora*, s. f. *animale salvatico simile alla faina.*

MA'RTIAL, adj. [warlike] *marziale, guerriero, militare.*

A court martial, *consiglio di guerra.*

MA'RTIALLED, adj. [used to war] *agguerrito.*

MA'RTIALIST, s. [warrior] *un guerriero, un uomo di guerra.*

MA'RTIN, s. [a bird] *rondone*, s. m.

MA'RTINGAL, s. [a thong of leather fastened at one end to the girts under the belly, and at the other to the mussroll, to prevent a horse's rearing] *martingalla*, s. f.

MA'RTINMASS, s. [the festival of St. Martin] *festa di San Martino.*

MA'RTINET, } s. [a kind of bird] MA'RTLET, } *rondone, uccello pescatore*, s. m.

MA'RTYR, s. [one that suffers death for truth] *martire*, s. m.

To MA'RTYR [to make one suffer martyrdom] *martirizzare, martirare.*

MA'RTYRED, adj. *martirizzato, martirato.*

MA'RTYRDOM, s. *martirio, e martiro*, s. m.

MA'RTYROLOGY, s. [a book treating of the acts, names, and sufferings of martyrs] *martirologio*, s. m. *storia, e leggendario de' martiri.*

MA'RVEL, s. [wonder] *maraviglia*, s. f. *cosa maravigliosa, stupore*, s. m.

Marvel of Peru [a sort of nightshade, with flowers of such variety, that it is called the wonder of the world] *maraviglia, erba colle foglie di diversi colori.*

To MA'RVEL [to wonder] *maravigliarsi, prendersi maraviglia, stupirsi*, pres. *mi stupisco.*

MA'RVELLED AT, adj. *maravigliato, stupito.*

MA'RVELLOUS, adj. [wonderful] *maraviglioso, che apporta maraviglia, maraviglievole, stupendo.*

MA'RVELLOUSLY, adv. [wonderfully] *maravigliosamente, con maraviglia, a maraviglia.*

MA'SCARADE, s. *mascherata*, s. f. *quantità di gente in maschera.*

To go in mascarade, *mascherarsi, andare in maschera.*

MASCARA'DING, s. Ex. To go a mascarading, *andare in maschera.*

MA'SCULINE, adj. [of the male kind] *mascolino, e masculino, di maschio sesso.*

The

The masculine gender, *il genere mascolino.*
A masculine courage, *un coraggio maschile.*
MASH, s. [mixture] *miscuglio*, s. m. *mescolanza*, s. f.
A mash [or drench] for a horse, *beverone*, s m. *bevanda composta d'acqua e di farina, che si da a' cavalli.*
To MASH [to mingle] *mescolare, fare un mescuglio.*
MA'SHED, adj. *mescolato.*
MASK, s. [or vizor] *maschera*, s. f.
To put on, or wear a mask, *mettere una maschera, mascherarsi.*
She had a mask on, *ella era in maschera, o era mascherata.*
Mask [pretence, colour] *maschera, pretesto, colore, mantello.*
To take off the mask, *cavarsi la maschera, dire il suo parere alla libera.*
To MASK, verb act. *mascherare.*
To mask, verb neut. *mascherarsi.*
MA'SKED, adj. *mascherato.*
A MA'SKER, s. *una maschera*; *colui che porta la maschera sul volto.*
MA'SKING, adj. ex. A masking habit, *un abito da mascherata.*
MA'SON, s. [bricklayer] *muratore, fabbricatore.*
A master mason, *un architetto.*
A journeyman mason, *un manovale.*
To do mason's work, *murare, fabbricare.*
MA'SONRY, s. [mason's work] *fabbrica*, s. f. *lavoro di fabbricatore.*
MA'SQUERADE, v. Mascarade.
To MA'SQUERADE, *andar in maschera.*
To masquerade, *far ridotto in maschera.*
MASQUERA'DER, s. *una maschera, colui che va in maschera.*
MASS, s. [lump] *massa*, s. f.
The mass of the blood, *la massa del sangue.*
Mass [a church service among the Roman Catholicks] *messa*, s. f.
To say, or sing mass, *dire, o cantare la messa.*
A mass book, *messale*, s. m.
To MASS [to celebrate mass] *celebrar la messa, dir la messa.*
MA'SSACRE, s. [a general slaughter] *macello*, s. m. *uccisione, strage*, s. f.
To MA'SSACRE [to butcher after a barbarous manner] *uccidere, fare strage, far macello.*
MA'SSACRED, adj. *ucciso, fatto strage.*
MA'SSACRING, s. *uccisione, strage*, s. m. *macello*, s. m.
MA'SSICOT, *sorta di colore usato da' pittori.*
MA'SSINESS, } s. [weight, bulk,
MA'SSIVENESS, } ponderousness] *peso, gravezza, qualità d' esser massiccio e grave insieme.*
MA'SSIVE, } adj. [solid] *massiccio,*
MA'SSY, } *grasso, tutto solido.*
MAST, s. [one of the sound pieces of timber in a ship, to which the yards, sails, tackle, &c. are made fast] *albero*, s. m. *lo stile, che regge le vele delle navi.*
The main mast, *il grand' albero.*
Misen, } *l' albero mezzano.*
Misen mast, }
The fore mast, *l' albero dell' artimone.*
Mast [the fruit of wild trees, as oak, beech, wild chesnut, &c.] *ghianda*, s. f. *frutto della quercia, del cerro, del leccio, e simili.*
MA'STER, s. [the governor or head] *padrone*, s. m.
The master of the house, *il padron di casa.*
Master [or teacher] *maestro.*
A master of arts, *maestro d'arti.*
A school master, *un maestro di scuola.*
A dancing master, *un ballerino, un maestro di ballo.*
A writing master, *un maestro di scrivere.*
Master [a title given to any gentleman] *signore.*
Master such one, *il signor tale.*
Master [a title belonging to some places] *maestro, o mastro.*
The master of a ship, *il padrone d'un vascello.*
The master of the posts, *il maestro delle poste.*
The master of the ordnance, *il gran maestro dell' artiglieria.*
Master [one well skill'd in a thing] *maestro, titolo d'uomo perito in qualche professione.*
A master of the horse, *un cavallerizzo, colui che esercita o insegna i cavalli, ed insegna altrui a cavalcare.*
The king's master of the horse, *cavallerizzo maggiore del rè.*
To be master of a thing [to possess it, to have it at one's command] *esser padrone d'una cosa, possederla.*
To be master of a language, *esser perfetto in una lingua, intenderla bene.*
To make one's self master of a thing, *impossessarsi d'una cosa, impradonirsene.*
A master piece, *magistero, magisterio, opera di maestro.*
Master like, *magistralmente, da maestro.*
Master stroke, *colpo da maestro.*
To MA'STER [to get the better of one] *vincere, superare, sormontare, soprassare.* pret. *vinsi.*
To master [to make one's self master of a thing] *impossessarsi, impadronirsi d'una cosa.* pres. *impadronisco.*
You will soon master the language, *voi v' impossesserete ben presto della lingua.*
To master [to govern] *dominare, governare, signoreggiare.*
To master [to keep under] *reprimere, raffrenare, rintuzzare.*
To master one's passions, *reprimere, le sue passioni.*
MA'STERLESS, adj. [without master] *senza maestro, o padrone.*
Masterless [froward, obstinate, headstrong] *ostinato, caparbio, di sua testa.*
MA'STERLY, adv. [or master like] *magistralmente, da maestro.*
MA'STERSHIP, } s. [power, autho-
MA'STERY, } rity] *potere, dominio*, s. m. *autorità, maestria, maggioranza*, s. f.
To try masteries with one, *fare a gara con qualcheduno.*
To get the mastery of a thing [to master it] *venire a fine di qualche cosa.*
He has a perfect mastery of the English tongue, *egli possiede, o intende perfettamente la lingua Inglese.*
MA'STERSHIP [the dignity of a master] *maestria, arte, eccellenza d'arte.*
MASTICA'TION, s. [chewing] *masticazione*, s. f. *masticamento*, s. m.
MA'STICATORY, s. [a medicine to be chewed to provoke spitting] *masticatorio*, s. m. *medicina da masticare.*
MA'STICINE, adj. [belonging to mastick] *masticino, di mastice.*
MA'STICK, s. [the gum of the lentisk tree] *mastice, mastrice*, s. f. *mastico*, s. m. *ragia di lentischio.*
The mastick tree [the lentisk tree] *lentischio.*
MA'STICOT, s. v. Massicot.
MA'STIFF, s. *mastino*, s. m. *spezie di cane.*
MA'STLESS, adj. [without masts] *senz' alberi*; *e dicesi d'un navilio.*
MA'STLING, s. [mixed corn, as, wheat and rye] *mistura di grani, come frumento e riso.*
MAT, s. [contexture of rushes] *stuoja*, s. f. *cosa tessuta di giunchi, o dell' erba sala.*
A mat [flock bed] *materasso*, s. m. *materassa*, s. f. *arneje da letto, ripieno por lo più di lana.*
A mat maker, *un materassajo.*
Mat weed [a sort of rush] *sala*, s. f.
To MAT [to cover with a mat] *coprire con istuoja.*
MA'TTADORE, s. *mattadore*; *e sono propriamente tre al giuoco dell' ombre, cioè spadiglia, maniglia, e basto. Così chiamate per la loro efficacia contro qualsia altra carta.*
MA'TACHIN, } s. *i mattac-*
MATACHIN DANCE, } *cini.*
MATCH, s. [a piece of cord to keep in fire] *miccia*, s. f.
The match of a lamp, *il lucignolo d' una lucerna.*
Match [a piece of wood, card, &c. tinged in brimstone] *zolfanello*, s. m.
Match [an agreement for several persons to meet, &c.] *partita*, s. f.
To make a match for hunting, *fare una partita di caccia.*
A match for playing, *una partita di giuoco.*
An equal match, *una partita eguale.*
Match [marriage] *un matrimonio.*
To make a match [to marry] *fare un matrimonio, maritare.*
'Twill be a match, *si mariteranno.*
A match maker, *un mezzano di matrimoni, un sensale d' matrimoni.*
A rich match [a fortune] *un ricco partito.*

Match.

Match [equal] *pariglia, simile, uguale.*

He has not his match, *egli non ha il simile, o il pari.*

You have met with your match, *voi avete trovato carne da vostri denti, o voi avete trovato scarpa al vostra piede.*

The wolf goes to match [desires copulation] *il lupo è in frega.*

To Match [to be like] *assortire, rassomigliare, uguagliare, esser simile.*

To match [to pair] *agguagliare, pareggiare, aggiustare.*

To match a glove, *agguagliare un guanto.*

To match [to couple] *accoppiare, accompagnare.*

To match [to marry] *maritare.*

You cannot match him, *voi non potrete trovare il suo pari.*

He alone is able to match them all, *egli solo è capace di resistere, o di far testa a tutti.*

Ma'tchable, adj. [that may be matched] *che si può agguagliare, pareggiare.*

Ma'tched, adj. *agguagliato, pareggiato, assortito, aggiustato, accoppiato, v.* To match.

Not to be matched, *che non ha il suo pari, incomparabile.*

Ma'tchless, adj. *incomparabile, che non ha il suo pari.*

Mate, s. [companion] *compagno,* s. m. *compagna,* s. f.

The mate of a ship, *sottopadrone d'un vascello.*

Mate, or check mate [at the play of chess, is when the game is brought to that pass, that there's no way left for the king to escape] *scaccomatto, termine del giuoco degli scacchi, che segue quando s' è chiusa l'andata al re.*

To give check-mate, *dare scaccomatto.*

To Mate [to amaze, to astonish] *stupidire, stupire.* pres. *stupidisco, stupisco.*

To mate [to dash, to mortify] *mortificare.*

To mate [to match] *agguagliare, pareggiare, aggiustare.*

To mate [to equal] *uguagliare.*

Mateo, adj. *stupidito, stupito, v.* To mate.

Mate'rial, adj. [consisting of matter or substance] *materiale, di materia.*

Material [principal, main] *principale, essenziale.*

Material [important] *importante, che importa, d'importanza.*

Mate'rials, s. pl. [stuff proper for the making or doing any thing] *materiali,* s. m. pl. *materia preparata per far che che si sia.*

Materia'lity, s. [the being material] *materialità,* s. f. *parte materiale.*

Mate'rnal, adj. [belonging to a mother, motherly] *materiale, materno, di madre.*

Mate'rnity, s. [motherhood] *maternità,* s. f. *qualità di madre.*

Math, or After Math, *tarda ricolta di fieno.*

Mathema'tical, adj. [of mathematicks] *matematico.*

Mathema'tically, adv. *matematicamente, secondo le regole della matematica.*

Mathemati'cian, s. *matematico,* s. m. *che sa matematica.*

Mathema'ticks, s. [sciences exercised about magnitude and numbers, or of quantity continued or discrete] *matematica,* s. f. *scienza intorno alla quantità.*

Ma'thurins, s. [an order of friars founded by pope Innocent] *ordine di religiosi.*

Ma'tin, adj. *usato la mattina.*

Ma'tin, s. [morning] *la mattina.*

Ma'tins, s. [one of the canonical hours for prayer in the Roman church] *mattutino,* s. m. *l'ora canonica, che si dice la mattina innanzi giorno da' preti.*

Ma'trass, s. *materasso, o materazzo.*

Matrass, *nome di un vaso usato da' chimici.*

Ma'trice, } s. [the womb] *matrice,* s. f. *parte dove il feto si forma.*
Ma'trix,

Matrice [a mould wherein printed letters are cast] *forma di lettere.*

Ma'tricide, s. [a killer of one's own mother] *matricida,* s. m. *che uccide la madre.*

Matricide [the killing of one's own mother] *matricidio,* s. m. *uccision della madre.*

Matri'cious, adj. [belonging to the matrix] *matricale.*

Matri'cular, adj. ex A matricular book, *una matricola, il libro dove si registran que' che si metton alla tassa.*

To Matri'culate, [to set down in the matricular book] *matricolare, registrare alla matricola.*

Matri'culate, adj. *matricolato.*

Matricula'tion, s. [the being matriculated] *il matricolare.*

Matrimo'nial, adj. [of matrimony] *matrimoniale, di matrimonio.*

Matrimonial articles agreed on, *contratto matrimoniale.*

Ma'trimony, s. [wedlock] *matrimonio,* s. m.

To commit matrimony, *ammogliarsi, maritarsi.*

Ma'trix, *v.* Matrice.

Ma'tron, s. [a grave and motherly woman] *una matrona, donna autorevole per età.*

Matron [midwife] *mammana, levatrice.*

Ma'tted, adj. [from to mat] *coperto di stuoja.*

Matted hair [intangled hair] *capelli sconpigliati.*

Matter, s. [the stuff any thing is made of, or consists] *materia,* s. f. *soggetto di qualunque componimento.*

Matter [substance] *materia, sostanza.*

Matter, or subject matter [theme] *materia, soggetto.*

To enter upon the matter, *entrar in materia, o soggetto.*

To go from the matter in hand, *digredire, far digressione dal suo soggetto, tralasciare il filo principale della narrazione.*

Matter [cause, occasion] *materia, cagione, causa, occasione,* s. f. *soggetto,* s. m.

There's no matter of complaint, *non c' è materia, o cogione da lamentarsi.*

Matter [thing, business] *cosa, affare, negozio, fatto.*

'Tis no great matter, *non importa molto, non è gran fatto.*

In matters of religion, *in materia di religione, per quel che concerne alla religione.*

He confessed the matter of fact, *egli confessò il fatto.*

Matter [such as runs out of a sore] *marcia,* s. f.

To resolve or gather into matter, *far capo, marcire.*

'Tis matter of fact, *fatto sta, è certo.*

What is the matter? *che c' è, che vuol dir ciò?*

What is the matter that you are so sad? *perche siete così maninconico?*

What is the matter with you? *che avete?*

Something is the matter that he is not yet come, *qualche cosa gli è sopraggiunta che l'ha impedito di venire.*

I'll tell you what the matter was, *vi dirò tutto il fatto.*

It is not a likely matter, *non è verisimile.*

'Tis all a matter to me ['tis all one to me] *m' è tutt' uno.*

I make no matter of it [I don't trouble my head about it] *non me ne curo, non me ne piglio fastidio.*

He spoke much to the matter, *egli parlò molto a proposito.*

'Tis no matter, *non importa.*

A matter [about] *incirca quasi.*

I spent a matter of twenty crowns, *ho speso incirca venti scudi.*

I walk'd a matter of ten miles, *ho camminato quasi dieci miglia.*

No such matter, *non c' è tal cosa.*

Upon the whole matter, *in fatti.*

To Matter [to care] *curare, aver cura, stimare.*

I matter it not, *non me ne curo.*

He matters not his dying, *non si cura di morire, non li rincresce di morire.*

To matter, verb imperf. ex. What matters it?, *che importa?*

It matters not, *non importa.*

It matters much, *importa molto, è di gran conseguenza.*

Ma'ttery, adj. *marcioso, pien di marcia, marcio.*

Ma'ttins, *v.* Matins.

Ma'ttock, s. [a tool of husbandry] *marra, zappa.* s. f. *zappone,* s. m.

Ma'ttress, s. [mat, flock bed] *materasso,* s. m. *materassa,* s. f.

Mattress-maker, s. *materassajo,* s. m. *quegli che fa le materasse.*

Matura'tion, s. [ripening] *maturazione,* s. f. *il maturare.*

Matu're, adj. [or ripe] *maturo.*

To grow mature, *maturare.*

Upon mature deliberation, *dopo matura deliberazione.*

To MATU'RE [to ripen] *maturare.*

MATU'RELY, adv. [with deliberation] *maturamente, con maturità, consideratamente, con consiglio.*

MATU'RING, adj. *maturativo, che matura.*

MATU'RITY, s. [ripeness] *maturità, maturezza.*

Maturity of age, *maturità, età matura, età perfetta.*

To MA'UDLE [to besot, to put out of order, as drinking does in the morning] *stupidire, render stupido,* pres. *stupidisco.*

MA'UDLED, adj. *stupidito.*

MA'UDLIN, adj. [half drunk, maudled] *cotto, stupidito.*

Maudling [contracted of Magdalen] *Maddalena, nome proprio di donna.*

MA'UGRE, prep. [in spight of, notwithstanding] *malgrado, a dispetto.*

MA'VIS [a kind of thrush] *spezie di tordo; malvezzo, parola napoletana.*

To MAUL [to beat soundly] *tartassare, malmenare, battere.*

MAUL, s. [a heavy hammer] *martello pesante.*

MAULKIN, s. [oven mop] *spazzatojo,* s. m. *arnese per ispazzare il forno.*

MA'ULKIN [a scarecrow, to fright birds] *spaventacchio,* s. m.

MAUL-STICK, s. [a painter's stick upon which he leans his hand when he is at work] *bacchetta, alla quale il pittore appoggia la mano quando dipigne.*

MAUND, s. [a hamper or basket with handles] *cesto,* s. m. *sporta,* s. f.

To MA'UNDER [to grumble, to mutter] *borbottare.*

MA'UNDERER, s. *borbottatore,* s. m.

MA'UNDERING, s. *borbottamento, borbottío,* s. m.

MA'UNDY-THURSDAY, s. [the last Thursday in Lent] *il Giovedì santo.*

MAUSOLE'UM, s. [a pompous funeral monument] *mausoleo,* s. m.

MA'UTHER, s. [a word in Norfolk for a little girl] *una fanciullina.*

MAW, s. [the stomach of animals] *lo stomaco delle bestie, e degli uccelli.*

The maw of a calf, *lo stomaco d'un vitello.*

MA'WKISH, adj. [sick at the stomach, squeamish] *svogliato.*

Mawkish [nauseous] *nauseoso, nauseante, stomachevole, stomacoso, che fa nausea.*

MA'WKISHNESS, s. [aptness to cause loathing] *facoltà di cagionar nausea.*

MAWKS, s. [a nasty, dirty slut] *una porca, una sporca.*

MA'WMET, s. [an idol] *un idolo.*

Mawmet [a little puppet] *un fantoccio di stracci.*

MAW-WORMS, s. *vermi che si generano nel corpo umano, e che intanto che si stanno nelle bubella e nel ventre sono da' medici Inglesi chiamati* gut-worms, *ma quando poi montano su, e si cacciano nello stomaco, acquistano il nome di* maw-worms.

MAXI'LLAR, adj. [belonging to the jaw bone] *attenente alla mascella, mascellare.*

MA'XIM, s. [principle, general rule] *massima,* s. f. *detto communemente approvato, regola, principio, assioma.*

MAY, s. [one of the twelve months of the year] *Maggio,* s. m. *uno de' dodici mesi dell' anno.*

May-day, *il primo giorno di Maggio.*

To make a may-game [to mock, or play the fool with one] *burlarsi, ridersi, beffarsi d'uno.*

A May-bug, s. [an insect] *bruco,* s. m.

A May-pole, *un majo.*

May-lily [liricon-fancy] *fioraliso, mughetto.*

May [a defective verb, used only in few tenses] *è un verbo difettivo, che significa, potere.*

You may if you will, *voi potete farlo se volete.*

That you may do it with more ease, *affinchè possiate farlo più comodamente.*

If I may say so, *se mi lice dirlo.*

It may be, *può essere.*

You may do it for all me, *io non v' impedisco di farlo.*

As much as may be, *tanto che si può.*

As little as may be, *pochissimo, molto poco.*

As like as may be, *simile quanto si può essere.*

Do it as fast as may be, *fatelo il più presto che potete.*

That I may not say his foolishness, *per non dire la sua sciocchezza.*

MA'YOR, s. [the chief magistrate of a city or corporation] *supremo magistrato d'una città non molto dissimile dal governatore.*

The lord mayor of London, *il governatore di Londra.*

MA'YORALTY, s. *la carica, e la dignità di governatore.*

MA'YORESS, s. [the mayor's lady] *la moglie del governatore.*

MAZE, s. [labyrinth] *laberinto,* s. m.

Maze [astonishment] *stupore,* s. m. *maraviglia.*

To be in a maze, *stupirsi, maravigliarsi.*

MA'ZER, s. [a broad drinking cup] *una ciotola, un vaso in cui si beve.*

ME [a pronoun used instead of I, in all its oblique cases] *me, mi.*

This is for me, *questo è per me.*

He told me, *mi disse.*

ME'ACOCK, s. [an effeminate fellow] *un effeminato.*

A meacock [an uxorious man] *un uomo che ama troppo la moglie.*

MEAD, s. [a drink made of honey and water] *idromele,* s. m. *bevanda composta di mele, e d'acqua.*

Mead [meadow] *un prato.*

ME'ADOW, s. [a land that yields store of grass for hay and pasture] *prato,* s. m.

ME'AGER, adj. [lean, thin] *magro, macilente, stenuato, sparuto.*

ME'AGERLY, adv. *magramente.*

To look meagerly, *aver il viso magro.*

ME'AGERNESS, s. *magrezza, macilenza,* s. f.

MEAL, s. [repast] *pasto,* s. m.

To eat a good meal, *fare un buon pasto.*

A meal's meat, *uno pasto.*

Meal [any corn ground] *farina,* s. f.

A meal man, *un venditor di farina.*

A meal sieve, *un frullone.*

ME'ALY, adj. *farinoso.*

Mealy-mouthed, adj [bashful] *contegnoso, ritroso, vergognoso, schifo, timoroso.*

MEAN, adj. [middle, between two extreams] *mezzano, mediocre.*

Mean [poor, pitiful] *povero, misero, di poca stima.*

Mean [low, pitiful, poor] *basso, vile, disprezzabile.*

He is of a mean descent, *egli è di bassa nascita.*

Mean spirited, *che ha l'animo basso o vile.*

Meanwhile [in the mean while] *frattanto, in questo mentre.*

Mean [mean part in musick, is the tenor] *il tenore.*

MEANS, s. [method, ways, devices] *mezzo, via, maniera.*

By that means, *con questo mezzo.*

By some means or other, *d'una maniera, o d'altra,*

By lawful or unlawful means, *per vie dirette o indirette.*

By all means, *in ogni modo, necessariamente, assolutamente.*

I desire you by all means to come, *vi prego in ogni conto di venire.*

By no means, *in conto nessuno.*

By foul means, *per forza.*

He was a means of my ruin, *egli è stato la causa della mia rovina.*

That was the only means [way, or expedient] *ciò era il solo mezzo, o espediente.*

Means [estate, riches] *beni, facultadi, ricchezze.*

To MEAN [to intend, to resolve, to design, to purpose] *intendere, aver intenzione, o pensiero, proporsi, disegnare, far disegno, far conto.*

He means to go tomorrow, *egli intende o fa conto di partire domani.*

They meant no harm to each other, *il loro disegno era di non offendersi.*

I don't mean to do it, *non mi propongo di farlo.*

To mean [to signify] *significare, voler dire.*

What does this word mean? *che vuol dire questa parola? che significa questa parola?*

To mean [to understand] *intendere, voler dire,* pret. *intesi.*

I mean so, *io l'intendo così; questo è il mio pensiero.*

You know what I mean, *voi sapete quel che voglio dire.*

What d'ye mean to do so? *che modo di procedere è il vostro?*

To mean one ill, *voler del male ad uno.*

ME'ANDERS, s. pl. [intricate turnings and windings] *giri, rigiri, e dicesi d'acque correnti.*

MEA'NDROUS, adj. [full of meanders] *pieno di giri e di rigiri; intrigato, avviluppato, imbrogliato.*

ME'ANER, adj. [the comparative of mean] *minore, più povero, più vile.*

The meaner fort of people, *il popolo più comune, il volgo, la plebe, il popolazzo.*

To think the meaner of one, *stimar meno una persona.*

ME'ANEST, adj. [the superlative of mean] *il più vile, il più infimo, il più povero.*

ME'ANING, s. [intention, sentiment] *intenzione, volontà, s. f. pensiero, sentimento, disegno, s. m.*

With an ill meaning, *con cattiva intenzione, con cattivo disegno, maliziosamente, per malizia.*

Meaning [fenfe, fignification] *senso, s. m. significazione, s. f.*

Meaning, adj. ex. A well meaning man] *un uomo dabbene, un uomo di buona fede, sincero, leale, schietto, candido, sincero.*

ME'ANLY, adv. *mediocremente, mezzanamente.*

Meanly [poorly] *poveramente, malamente, cattivamente.*

Meanly born, *di bassa nascita, di nascita oscura.*

ME'ANNESS, s. [mediocrity] *mediocrità, mezzanità.*

Meannefs [poornefs] *viltà, bassezza, povertà, s. f.*

Meannefs [low condition] *bassezza, oscurità di natali.*

MEANT, *preterito del verbo*, To mean.

Meant, adj. *significato.*

MEASE, s. [a meafure of herrings, containing five hundred] *misura di cinquecento aringhe.*

ME'ASLES, s. *rosellia, e oggi più comunemente rosolia; sorta d'infermità che viene alla pelle, coprendola di macchie rosse con piccola elevazione e con febbre continua.*

Meafles, *malore che viene a' porci.*

Meafles, *malore che viene agli alberi.*

ME'ASURE, s. [that which ferves to determine the extent of any quantity, length, breadth, thicknefs, or capacity of other things by] *misura, s. f. distinguimento determinato di quantità.*

To cheat in the meafure, *fognare la misura.*

Meafure [or dimenfion] of a body, *misura o dimensione d'un corpo.*

To take a man's meafure for a fuit of cloaths, *pigliare la misura d'un' abito.*

Meafure [cadence in verfes] *misura, numero.*

Meafure [in mufick, a fpace of time, fet out by a conftant equal motion of the hand or foot, up and down fucceffively] *battuta, s. f. quella misura di tempo che da il maestro della musica in battendo a' cantori e sonatori.*

Meafures [ways, defigns] *misure, disegni.*

He has broke all my meafures, *egli ha attraversato tutti i miei disegni, egli ha rese vane tutte le mie misure.*

In fome meafure [in a manner] *in qualche modo, in qualche maniera.*

In a great meafure [very much] *molto, grandemente.*

He has had hard meafure, *egli è stato molto maltrattato.*

Meafure [mean] *misura, mediocrità.*

Beyond meafure, *oltre misura, fuor di misura, smisuratamente, eccessivamente.*

To MEASURE, *misurare.*

To meafure corn, *misurare del grano.*

To meafure every one's corn by one's own bufhel, *misurare gli altri al suo passetto.*

To meafure a thing by one's own profit, *non istimare una cosa, che per il profitto che se ne tira.*

ME'ASURED, adj *misurato.*

A meafured mile, *un miglio misurato, o geometrico.*

ME'ASURELESS, adj. [immenfe, immeafurable] *smisurato, eccedente ogni misura.*

ME'ASURER, s. *misuratore, s. m.*

ME'ASURING, adj. *misuramento, s. m. il misurare.*

MEAT, s. [flefh, provifion of any fort] *cibo, nutrimento, alimento, s. m. vivanda, s. f.*

This is very good meat, *questo è un buon alimento, o un buon mangiare.*

A difh of meat, *un piatto di carne.*

Meat [flefh] *carne.*

To forbear meat, *astenersi dalla carne.*

Horfe meat, *cibo da cavalli, come fieno, biada.*

Roaft meat, *dell' arrosto.*

Boiled meat, *del lesso.*

Minced meat, *manicaretto.*

Spoon meat, *tutto quel che si mangia col cucchiajo.*

Sweet meats, *confetture.*

White meats, *latticini.*

To fit down at meat, *mettersi a tavola.*

Without meat or drink, *senza mangiare, nè bere.*

This is meat and drink to him, *l'arma sopra ogn' altra cosa.*

ME'ADED, adj. [fed] *pasciuto; che ha mangiato.*

ME'ATHE, s. [drink] *bevanda.*

ME'AZELS, s. [a difeafe fomewhat like the fmall pox] *rossellia, e rosolia, s. f. sorta d'infermità che viene alla pelle, empiendola di macchie rosse, scrivi* meafles, *che è meglio.*

MECHA'NICAL, } adj. [belonging MECHA'NICK, } to the mechanicks] *meccanico.*

MECHA'NICALLY, adv. *meccanicamente.*

MECHA'NICK, [mean, fordid] *meccanico, vile, abbietto.*

A mechanick, s. [a tradefman] *un meccanico, un artigiano.*

MECHA'NICKS, s. [that part of the mathematicks which is converfant about machines] *meccanica, s. f.*

MECHO'ACAN, s. [a white purging root like briony, brought from the Weft-Indies] *mecioacan, s. m. pianta purgativa, chiamata così dal luogo ove nasce, detto mecioacan.*

MECO'NIUM, s. [expreffed juice of poppy] *sugo spremuto da' papaveri.*

Meconium, *primo escremento de' bambini.*

ME'DAL, s. [a piece of mettle like money, ftamp'd upon fome extraordinary occafion] *medaglia, s. f.*

ME'DALLICK, adj. *medallico, appartenente a medaglie.*

ME'DALLION, s. [a large medal] *medaglione, s. m. medaglia grande.*

ME'DALLIST, s. [a man fkilled or curious in medals] *uomo che studia, conosce, o raccoglie medaglie antiche.*

To ME'DDLE WITH [to intermeddle, to concern one's felf] *mescolarsi, impacciarsi, pigliar briga, travagliarsi, intromettersi, pret. intromisi.*

Meddle with your own bufinefs, *impacciatevi de' fatti vostri, badate à fatti vostri.*

To meddle with [to touch, to handle] *toccare, maneggiare.*

Don't meddle with it, *non lo toccate.*

To meddle with one [to have to do with him] *avere a fare con uno, mescolarsi con lui.*

I'll not meddle nor make with him, *non voglio aver niente a fare con lui, non voglio impacciarmi con lui.*

I neither meddle nor make, *non voglio impacciarmente nè in bene nè in male.*

MEDDLED with, adj. *impacciato, mescolato, intromesso.*

This is not to be meddled with, *non bisogna impacciarsene.*

ME'DDLER, s. [bufy body] *una persona che s'intromette negli affari altrui.*

ME'DDLESOME, adj. *che si vuole intromettere ne' fatti altrui.*

ME'DLEY, s. [mixture] *un miscuglio, una mescolanza.*

A confufed medley, *un fracasso, un frastuono, una confusione.*

Medley colour, *un color mescolato.*

ME'DDLING, s. *mescolamento, s. m. il mescolare.*

It is not good to meddle with it, *non bisogna impacciarvisi.*

Meddling, adj. ex. You will always be meddling, *voi volete sempre impacciarvi in quel che non vi tocca.*

ME'DIAN, adj. [which is in the middle] *mediano.*

The median vein [the middle vein in the bending of the elbow betwixt the cephalick and bafilick] *la vena mediana.*

To ME'DIATE [to procure by one's means, to act the part of a mediator] *procurare, esser mediatore.*

To mediate the peace, *procurare la pace.*

ME'DIATE, adj. *interposto; che sta in mezzo fra due estremi.*

Mediate, adj *che agisce come mezzo.*

ME'DIATELY, adv. *mediatamente.*

MEDIA'TION, s. *mediazione, intercessione, s. f.*

MEDIA'TOR, s. *mediatore, mezzano, intercessore, s. m.*

MEDIA'TRIX, s. *mediatrice, intercedItrice, mezzana.*
ME'DICABLE, adj. [that may be cured] *che si può medicare.*
ME'DICAMENT, s. [a medicinal composition] *medicamento,* s. m. *medicina,* s. f.
MEDICAME'NTAL, adj. *medicinale.*
MEDICA'STER, s. [a peddling physician, a quack] *medicastro, medico di poco valore, medicastronzolo, mediconzolo.*
ME'DICATED, adj. mixed with medicinal ingredients] *preparato, mescolato secondo la medicina.*
MEDICA'TION, s. [curing] *medicamento,* s. m. *medicazione,* s. f. *il medicare.*
ME'DICINABLE, adj. [curable] *medichevole, atto a medicare.*
MEDI'CINAL, adj. [medicamental, able to heal] *medicinale.*
ME'DICINE, s. [the art of physick] *medicina,* s. f. *la scienza, e l'arte del medicare.*
Medicine [a physical remedy] *medicina,* s. f. *medicamento,* s. m. *tutto quel che s'adopera a pro del s' infermo per fargli ricoverare la sanità.*
To MEDICINE [to give physick in order to cure] *medicare, curare le infermità, medicinare.*
MEDICK-FODDER, s. [an herb] *trifoglio di spagna.*
ME'DIETY, s. [the moiety, or half of a thing] *la metà.*
MEDIO'CRITY, s. [competency, moderation] *mediocrità, mezzanità, moderazione,* s. f.
To ME'DITATE [to think, to muse, to reflect] *meditare, pensare, riflettere, far riflessione.*
To meditate upon a subject, *meditare sopra un soggetto.*
To meditate [to devise beforehand] *meditare, premeditare.*
ME'DITATED, adj. *meditato, premeditato.*
ME'DITATING, s. *il meditare.*
MEDITA'TION, s. *meditazione,* s. f. *il meditare.*
ME'DITATIVE, adj. *meditante, che medita.*
A meditative posture, *una positura pensierosa, o d'un uomo che medita.*
MEDITERRANEAN, adj. [shut up between the lands] *mediterraneo, posto dentro terra.*
The Mediterranean sea, *il Mare mediterraneo, o il Mediterraneo.*
ME'DIUM, s. [mean] *mezzanità, mediocrità,* s. f.
Medium [expedient, way, device] *mezzo, modo, spediente, mezzo termine,* s. m. *invenzione,* s. f.
ME'DLAR, s. [a sort of fruit] *nespola,* s. f. *frutta nota.*
A medlar-tree, *nespolo,* s. m. *albero, che produce la nespola.*
To ME'DLE, *v.* To meddle.
ME'DOW, *v.* Meadow.
ME'DULLAR, } adj. [belonging to
ME'DULLARY, } the marrow] *della midolla.*
MEED, s. [reward] *guiderdone, premio,* s. m. *ricompensa,* s. f.
Meed [merit] *merito,* s. m.
Meed, s. *regalo, dono.*
MEEK, adj. [mild] *piacevole, mansuete, moderato, trattabile, benigno, mite, affabile, mansueto, buono, umano, placido.*
Meek [humble] *umile sommesso.*
ME'EKLY, adv. [mildly] *piacevolmente, moderatamente, benignamente, umanamente, affabilmente, cortesemente.*
Meekly [humbly] *umilmente, con umiltà.*
MEEKNESS, s. [gentleness] *mansuetudine, clemenza, trattabilità, piacevolezza, affabilità, cortesia, umanità,* s. f.
Meekness [humility] *umiltà,* s. f.
MEEN, s. [presence] *cera, sembianza, aria,* s. f.
MEER, adj. [downright, arrant] *puro, pretto, vero, franco.*
He is a meer dunce, *egli è un vero sciocco.*
A meer knave, *un pretto furbo.*
Meer, s. [bound] *limite, confine, termine,* s. m.
A meer stone, *meta, pietra che serve di termine.*
Meer [a pool, a low marshy ground] *palude,* s. f. *pantano,* s. m.
Meer sauce [brine] *salamoja,* s. f.
ME'ERED, adj. [bounded] *limitato, terminato.*
ME'ERLY, adv. [purely] *meramente, puramente, semplicemente, solamente.*
MEET, adj. [fit, convenient] *atto, idoneo, acconcio, buono, convenevole.*
It is very meet, *è molto a proposito.*
To MEET, } [to find] *incon-*
To MEET WITH, } *trare, riscontrare, abbattersi in camminando.*
I met him, or I met with him by chance, *l'ho incontrato a caso.*
The parliament will meet next week, *il parlamento si radunerà la settimana prossima.*
The king intends to meet his parliament, *il re ha risoluto di convocare il suo parlamento.*
To meet with one [to be even with him] *vendicarsi d'uno, rendergli la pariglia.*
I shall meet with him, *me la pagherà.*
To go to meet one, *andare all' incontro d'uno.*
He promised to meet me to day, *ha promesso di venire a trovarmi oggi.*
He met with a very kind reception, *li fu fatta una grande accoglienza, fu accolto con molta benignità.*
To meet with a storm, *esser sorpreso da una tempesta.*
To meet with a repulse, *esser ributtato.*
His project meets with no success, *il suo progetto non ebbe successo.*
To meet, verb neut. [to assemble, or come together] *adunarsi, radunarsi, incontrarsi, trovarsi.*
ME'ETER, s. *uno che s'avvicina a un altro.*
ME'ETING, s. [coming together, Interview] *incontro, riscontro,* s. m.
A great meeting [concourse] of people, *un gran concorso, una gran calca, e moltitudine di gente.*
A meeting [assembly] *assemblea, adunanza, radunanza,* s. f.
A meeting of sectaries, *un conventicolo di settari.*
A meeting house, *conventicolo; luogo dove si radunano gli settari.*
ME'ETLY, *propriamente, adottatamente, a proposito.*
ME'ARIM, s. [a distemper causing great pain in the temples] *migrana,* s. f. *dolor di testa che viene in una tempia.*
To MEINE [to mingle] *mischiare, mescere.* Obs.
ME'INY, s. [a retinue; domestick servants] *seguito; numero di servitori e gente al tuo soldo.* Obs.
MELANCHO'LICK, adj. [troubled with melancholy] *malinconico, e maninconico, malinconoso.*
MELANCHO'LILY, adv. *maninconicamente, d'una maniera maninconica.*
MELANCHO'LIST, or MELANCHO'LY, s. *un malinconico.*
MELANCHO'LY, s. [black choler] *malinconia, e maninconia,* s. f. *collera nera.*
Melancholy [madness, pensiveness] *malinconia; tristezza, afflizione, passion d'animo.*
Melancholy, adj. [sad, pensive] *malinconoso, tristo, afflitto, travagliato, pensieroso.*
A melancholy man or woman, *un malinconico, una malinconica.*
Melancholy [sad, that causes melancholy] *maninconoso, tristo, infelice, dolente.*
A melancholy story, *una dolente istoria.*
MELICO'TONY, s. [a sort of peach] *meliaca,* s. f.
Melicotony tree, s. *meliaco,* s. m.
ME'LILOT, s. [an herb] *meliloto,* s. m.
To ME'LIORATE [to mend, or make better] *migliorare, render migliore.*
ME'LIORATED, adj. *migliorato.*
MELIORA'TION, s. *miglioramento,* s. m. *il migliorare.*
MELIO'RITY, s. [betterness] *miglioranza,* s. f. *l'esser migliore.*
MELLE'AN, } adj. [of, or like
ME'LLEOUS, } honey] *melato, di mele.*
MELLI'FEROUS, adj. [bringing honey] *mellifluo, ond'esce mele.*
MELLI'FICK, adj. [that makes honey] *che fa, che produce del mele.*
MELLI'FLUENT, } adj. [flowing
MELLIFLUOUS, } with honey] *mellifluo, ond'esce mele.*
ME'LLICISM, s. [honey'd wine] *melichino,* s. m. *vino con mele.*
ME'LLOW, adj. [ripe, soft] *maturo, molle, tenero.*
Mellow [pretty well in drink] *cotto, mezzo briaco, avvinazzato.*
To ME'LLOW [to ripen] *maturare.*
ME'LLOWNESS, s. *maturità,* s. f.
MELO'COTON, s. [a quince] *mela cotogna.*

Melo'dious, adj. [harmonious] *melodico, melodioso, armonioso, armonico.*

Melo'diously, adv. *melodiosamente, amonidsamente, con melodia.*

Melo'diousness, s. *melodia, dolcezza di cantare.*

Me'lody, s. [harmony] *melodia, armonia, soavità di canto o di suono,* s. f. *concento,* s. m.

Me'lon, s. [a sort of fruit] *popone,* s. m.

Water melon, *mellone.*

Me'lon-thistle, s. [a plant] *nome di pianta.*

To Melt [to make liquid, or fluid] *colare, fondere, liquefare, squagliare, struggere,* pret. *fusi, liquefeci, strussi.*

To melt gold, *fondere liquefare dell' oro.*

To melt God's anger into mercy, *placare l' ira di Dio, renderselo propizio.*

To melt one down [to make his heart relent] *intenerire alcuno.*

To melt, verb neut. *fondersi, liquefarsi, struggersi, squagliarsi.*

To melt into tears, *fondere, struggersi in lagrime.*

Me'lted, adj. *fonduto, strutto, liquefatto, squagliato.*

Me'lter, s. *fonditore,* s. m. *colui che fonde.*

Me'lting, s. *il fondere, liquefazione,* s. f.

A melting-house, *fonderia,* s. f.

Melting, adj. *che si fonde.*

A melting pear, *una pera che si fonde.*

A melting discourse, *un discorso patetico, che muove, che eccita le passioni.*

Melting language, *parole melate, carezze, vezzi, lusinghe.*

Me'ltingly, adv. *con istruggimento; in mo' come se si liquefacesse.*

Me'lwell, s. [a sort of codfish] *merluzzo,* s. m.

Me'mber, s. [a part of a body natural, or politick] *membro,* s. m. *parte d' un corpo naturale, o politico.*

A member of parliament, *un membro di parlamento.*

A little member, *membretto, membricciuolo.*

Membra'neous } adj. [full of
Me'mbranous } membranes] *membranoso.*

Me'mbrane, s. [the upermost thin skin in any part of the body] *membrana, tunica, buccia, pellicola,* s. f.

Memo'irs, s. [remarkable observations] *memorie, ricordi, annotazioni, istorie.*

Me'morative, adj. of or belonging to memory] *memorativo, della, memoria.*

Me'morable, adj. [worthy of remembrance] *memorabile, da rammemorarsene, degno di memoria.*

Me'morably, adv. *memorabilmente; in modo memorabile o degno di memoria.*

Memora'ndum, s. *ricordo,* s. m. *annotazione, memoria.*

A memorandum book, *un taccuino.*

Memo'rial, s. [that which puts one in mind] *memoriale,* s. m. *contrassegno per ricordare.*

Memorial [a note of something to be remembered]. *memoriale, memoria.*

Memorial [a writing delivered by a publick minister of state about part of his negotiation] *memoriale, supplica,* s. f.

Memo'rialist, s. *uno che scrive memorie.*

Me'mory, s. [that faculty of the soul that preserves the remembrance of known and past things] *memoria,* s. f. *una delle potenze dell' anima, la quale ci ripete le cose conosciute, e passate.*

'Tis out of my memory, *m' è uscito dalla memoria, me ne sono scordato.*

Memory [or remembrance] *memoria, ricordanza.*

To call to memory, *richiamare alla memoria, ricordarsi.*

To have, or keep a thing in memory [to remember it] *conservar la memoria, ricordarsene.*

The memory of great men, *la memoria, il rinomo, il grido de' grandi uomini.*

Men [the plural of man] *gli uomini.* v. Man.

To Me'nace [to threaten] *minacciare.*

Me'naced, adj. *minacciato.*

Me'naces, s. [threats] *minacce.*

Me'nacing, s. *il minacciare, minacce.*

Menacing, adj. *minacciante.*

To Mend [to vamp, to patch] *racconciare, accommodare, rappezzare.*

To mend a suit of cloaths, *racconciare un abito.*

To mend a fault, *correggere un errore.*

To mend one's life, *emendarsi, riformarsi, correggersi.*

To mend a structure, *ristaurare, riparare una fabbrica.*

To mend one's pace [to go faster] *affrettare i passi, camminar più presto.*

To mend one's draught, *bere un altro bicchiere.*

To mend one's market, *comprare a miglior mercato, o vender più caro.*

Where will you mend your self? *dove potrete esser meglio?*

To mend one's fortune, *migliorare la sua condizione.*

To mend [to grow better, to reform] *emendarsi, correggersi, riformarsi.*

To mend [to be on the mending hand after a sickness], *migliorare, ricuperar le forze, alleggerirsi dalla malattia.*

Me'nded, adj. *racconciato,* v. To mend.

Me'nder, s. *acconciatore, racconciatore,* s. m.

Me'ndicant, adj. [begging] *mendicante, che mendica.*

A mendican tfriar, *un frate mendicante.*

A mendicant, s. [a begging friar] *un mendicante, un frate mendicante.*

Mendi'city, [want, beggary] *mendicità, mendicanza, estrema povertà,* s. f.

Me'nding, s. [from to mend] *racconciamento,* s. m. *il racconciare.*

Mending, adj. ex. To be on the mending hand, or in a mending condition, *migliorare, andar migliorando, essere convalescente, ricoverar la sanità.*

Mends for amends, v. Amend, *sustantivo.*

Me'nial, adj. [or domestick] *domestico, di casa.*

A menial servant, *un servo, un domestico.*

Me'nials [or menial servants] *domestici.*

Me'now, s. commonly Minow [a little fresh water fish] *spezie di pesce d' acqua dolce.*

Me'nsal, adj. *appartenente alla mensa, alla tavola.*

Me'nstrual } adj. [monthly]
Me'nstruous } *mestruale, di mestruo.*

Me'nstruum, s. [chymical term, a dissolving liquor, which eats thro' metals, and melts stones] *mestruo,* s. m. *da chimici si dice ad ogni liquore proporzionato nel quale si infonde che che si sia o per cavarne tintura o per render liquido.*

Mensurabi'lity, s. [capableness of being measured] *qualità di cosa che si può misurare.*

Me'nsurable, adj. [capable, or that may be measured] *misurabile, misurevole, che si può misurare.*

To Me'nsurate [to measure] *misurare.*

Mensura'tion, s. [measuring] *misuramento,* s. m. *il misurare.*

Me'ntal, adj. [of the mind] *mentale di mente.*

To pray God with a mental devotion, *pregar Iddio mentalmente.*

Me'ntally, adv. *mentalmente.*

Me'ntion, s. [commemoration] *menzione, nominazione, memoria, commemorazione,* s. f.

To make mention of a thing, *far menzione, d' una cosa.*

To Me'ntion [to make mention of] *menzionare, mentovare, far menzione.*

To mention the receit of a letter, *accusare la ricevuta d' una lettera.*

Me'ntioned, adj. *menzionato, mentovato.*

Me'ntioning, s. *menzione,* s. f. *il menzionare.*

Me'nuet, s. [a sort of tune and dance] *minuetto,* s. m. *sorta di suono e di ballo.*

Me'rcantile, adj. [belonging to mercature] *mercantile, mercatantile.*

A mercantile town, *una città mercantile.*

ME'RCATURE, s. [merchandize] *mercanzia, traffico, negozio, commercio.*

MERCENA'RINESS, s. *venalità.*

ME'RCENARY, adj. [greedy of gain] *mercenario, interessato, che serve a prezzo.*

Mercenary s. [hireling] *un mercenario, un interessato.*

ME'RCER, s. [one who deals in silks] *merciajo, setajuolo,* s. m.

Mercer [haberdasher of small wares] *merciajulo, merciajo di poche merci.*

ME'RCERY, s. [mercers goods or wares] *il mestier de' merciaj.*

ME'RCHANDISE, s. [commodities or goods to trade with] *mercanzia, mercatanzia,* s. f.

Merchandise [mercature, trade] *mercanzia, traffico, negozio, commercio.*

To ME'RCHANDISE [to deal as a merchant, to traffick, to trade] *trafficare, negoziare, far commercio.*

ME'RCHANDISING, s. [traffick] *la mercatura, il traffico, il negozio, il commercio.*

ME'RCHANT, s. [trader] *mercante, mercatante,* s. m.

A woman merchant, *una mercatantessa.*

A great or rich merchant, *un mercantone.*

A petty merchant, *un mercantuzzo.*

A timber merchant, *un mercante di legname.*

A merchant man, *un vascello mercante.*

ME'RCHANTABLE, adj. *ben condizionata.*

ME'RCHANTLY } adj. *mercantesco, mercatantesco.*
ME'RCHANT-LIKE }

Merchantly } adv. *mercantilmente, mercantescamente.*
Merchant-like }

ME'RCIABLE, adj. *pietoso, misericordioso, compassionevole. E' vocabolo improprio usato in voce di* merciful.

ME'RCIFUL, adj. [full of mercy] *misericordioso, benigno, pietoso, compassionevole.*

To be merciful to one, *aver pietà, o compassione d' uno.*

Merciful [humane, kind] *umano, cortese, affabile, buono, clemente.*

ME'RCIFULLY, adv. *misericordiosamente, benignamente, pietosamente, compassionevolmente.*

ME'RCIFULNESS, s. [compassion] *misericordia, pietà, compassione,* s. f.

Mercifulness [humanity, clemency] *umanità, bontà, clemenza, benignità,* s. f.

ME'RCILESS, adj. *spietato, crudele, inumano, che non ha compassione.*

MERCU'RIAL, adj. [full of mercury] *mercuriale, allegro, spiritoso, vivace.*

ME'RCURY, s. [a heathenish God] *Mercurio,* s. m. *Dio favoloso.*

Mercury [one of the planets] *mercurio, uno de' pianeti.*

Mercury [quick silver] *mercurio, argento vivo.*

The London mercury [a news paper] *il mercurio di Londra, sorta di gazzetta.*

Mercury [a purging plant] *mercorella,* s. f. *sorta d' erba.*

ME'RCY, s. [compassion] *mercè, misericordia, pietà, compassione,* s. f.

Mercy [pardon] *mercè, grazia,* s. f. *perdono,* s. m.

To cry mercy, *gridar mercè, domandar perdono.*

To deliver one to the mercy of his enemies, *rimetter uno alla mercè, in arbitrio, alla discrezione de' suoi nemici.*

Mercy seat, *propiziatorio.*

We cast ourselves down before thy mercy seat, *noi ci prosterniamo innanzi il trono della tua grazia.*

MERE, *v.* Meer.

ME'RELY, *v.* Meerly.

MERETRI'CIOUS, adj. [whorish] *meretricio, di meretrice, puttanesco.*

MERETRI'CIOUSLY, adv. *da meretrice, da bagascia, da donnaccia che si prostituisce, puttanescamente.*

MERI'DIAN, s. [a great circle passing thro' the poles of the world, and both the Zenith and Nadir] *meridiano,* s. m.

Meridian, *mezzo dì, mezzo giorno.*

Meridian, adj. ex. The meridian altitude of the sun or star, *l' altezza meridiana del sole, o d' una stella.*

Meridian line, *linea meridiana.*

Meridian, *figurativamente, il più alto grado, l' altezza più cospicua, il centro dell' altezza.*

MERI'DIONAL, adj. [southern] *meridionale, di mezzo dì.*

MERI'DIONALLY, adv. [with a southern aspect] *con un aspetto da mezzogiorno.*

ME'RIT, s. [desert, worth] *merito, prezzo, valore.*

A man of merit, *un uomo di merito.*

The merits of our Saviour, *i meriti del nostro Salvatore.*

The merit of a cause, *il merito, le ragioni d' una causa.*

To ME'RIT [to deserve] *meritare, esser degno di male o di bene secondo le operazioni.*

ME'RITED, adj. *meritato.*

MERITO'RIOUS, adj. *meritorio, degno di merito, di premio.*

MERITO'RIOUSLY, adv. *meritevolmente.*

ME'RITOT, s. [a sort of play used by children, by swinging on ropes] *alcalena,* s. m. *giuoco fanciullesco, sedendo sopra una tavola tra due funi che la fanno, ondeggiare.*

ME'RLIN, s. [a kind of hawk] *smeriglio,* s. m. *uccel di rapina.*

ME'RMAID, s. [Syren] *sirena,* s. f.

ME'RMAID'S-TRUMPET, s. *sorta di pesce.*

ME'RRILY, adv. *allegramente, festevolmente, festeggevolmente, giocosamente, lietamente.*

ME'RRIMAKE, s. [a festival, a meeting for mirth] *festa; crocchio dove si sta allegria.*

To ME'RRIMAKE, *star in festa, star in allegria.*

ME'RRIMENT, s. [or merry making] *galloria, allegria,* s. f. *festeggiamento, buona cera.*

ME'RRINESS, s. [mirth] *festa, allegria; inclinazione all' allegria; natura allegra.*

ME'RRY, adj. [gay, frolick, cheerful, jocund] *allegro, giocoso, giocondo, festevole, festoso, gajo, giojoso.*

Merry [pleasant, diverting] *gustoso, gustevole, grato, ameno, gradevole, sollazzoso.*

We have been mighty merry, *noi ci siamo divertiti molto bene.*

A merry countenance, *un viso allegro.*

Be merry, *state allegramente.*

It is good to be merry and wise, *bisogna divertirsi, ma con moderazione.*

To live a merry life, *passar la vita in festa, in allegria.*

To make one merry, *divertire, rallegrare, sollazzare alcuno.*

To make merry, *divertirsi, sollazzarsi, pigliarsi piacere e buon tempo, far galloria.*

To make merry with one [to banter him] *burlarsi, beffarsi d' uno.*

A merry grig, *un uomo gioviale, o gustoso.*

A merry Andrew, *un buffone, un giocoliere.*

To be set on the merry pin, *essere di buon umore, esser allegro.*

ME'RRYTHOUGHT, s. [a forked bone in the body of fowls] *osso forcuto del petto del pollame.*

ME'RSION, s. [ducking] *tuffo,* s. m. *immersione,* s. f.

MESARA'ICK, adj. [belonging to the mesentery] *mesaraico.*

The mesaraick veins [the right branches of the venæ portæ] *le vene mesaraiche.*

MESE'EMS, *verbo impersonale* [I think; it appears to me] *io penso; pare a me.*

MESENTE'RICK, adj. [belonging to the mesentery] *mesenterico.*

MESENTE'RIUM } s. [a membranous part, situate in the middle of the lower belly, which fastens the bowels to the back, and one to another] *mesenterio,* s. m. *corpo membranoso intorno a' lombi, nel quale sono attaccati gl' intestini.*
MESENTE'RY }

MESH, s. [the interstice of a net; the space between the threads of a net] *maglia, buco di rete.*

To MESH [to catch in a net; to insnare] *prendere nella rete; incalappiare.*

ME'SLIN, s. [wheat mixt with rye] *frumento misto con riso.*

Meslin bread, *pan misto.*

ME'SNALTY, s. [the right of a mesne] *diritto, o dominio signoresco, che dipende da un altro signore.*

ME'SNE } s. [a Lord of a manour who holds
ME'SNE LORD }

of

of a superior lord, tho' he has tenants under himself] *signore d' un feudo servile; colui che tiene un feudo d' un altro signore.*

MESOLA'BIUM, s. [a mathematical instrument, for finding mean proportionals between any two lines given] *mesolabio.*

MESS, s. [dish of any thing served up at table] *vivanda, s. f. piatto, s. m.*

A good mess, *una buona vivanda.*

A mess of meat, *un piatto di carne.*

A mess of soup, *un piatto di minestra.*

Mess [share of meat] *porzione di carne, pietanza.*

We are four of a mess, *noi siamo quattro che mangiamo insieme.*

ME'SSAGE, s. [errand] *messaggio, s. m. ambasciata, s. f.*

To deliver one's message, *fare il suo messaggio.*

ME'SSENGER, s. [that goes on an errand] *messaggiere, messaggiero, messaggio. s. m.*

King's messenger [an officer who attends the secretary of state to carry dispatches] *messaggiere, corriero.*

MESSI'AH, s. [the name and title of or Lord and Saviour Jesus Christ] *il Messia, Gesù Cristo.*

ME'SSIEURS, s. plur. [sirs, gentlemen] *signori.*

Gl' Inglesi fanno uso di questo vocabolo Francese mercantilmente, dicendo, verbigrazia messieurs Drummond and company, *e non* masters Drummond and company, *quantunque nominando poi ciascuno in particolare della società di* Drummond, *lo chiamino* master *e non* monsieur; *cosicchè si può dire che in questo caso* messieurs *è un plurale irregolare o capriccioso di* master *anzi che di* monsieur.

MESS-MATE, s. *uno che mangia alla stessa tavola.*

ME'SSUAGE, s. [a dwelling house with some land adjoining and all other conveniencies belonging to it] *podere, s. m. possessione di più campi con casa da lavoratore.*

MET, *preterito del verbo* to meet, *v.* To meet.

Met, adj. [from to meet] *incontrato.*

He is not to be met, *non si può trovare.*

They are well met [or well matched] *eglino sono bene accoppiati.*

ME'TAL, s. *metallo, s. m. materia, che si cava dalle viscere delle terra, atta a fondersi.*

META'LLICK } adj. [belonging to,
ME'TALLINE } or partaking of the nature of metals] *metallico, metallino, di metallo, che attiene a metallo.*

ME'TALLIST, s. [one who is skill'd in the knowledge of metals] *metallista, s. m. conoscitor di metalli.*

METAMO'RPHOSIS, s. [transformation] *metamorfosi, trasformazione, s. f.*

ME'TAPHOR, s. [a rhetorical figure] *metafora, s. f. figura rettorica.*

METAPHO'RICAL, adj. [or figurative] *metaforico, figurativo.*

METAPHO'RICALLY, adj. *metaforicamente, figurativamente.*

To speak metaphorically, *metaforizzare, parlare metaforicamente.*

To METAMORPHO'SE [to change from one form to another] *trasformare.*

METAMORPHO'SED, adj. *trasformato.*

ME'TAPHRASE, s. [a turning word for word] *metafrase, traduzione parola per parola.*

METAPHY'SICAL, adj. [of metaphysicks] *metafisico, di metafisica.*

METAPHY'SICKS, s. [a part of philosophy which treats of immaterial beings] *la metafisica.*

To METE [to measure] *misurare.*

ME'TED, adj. *misurato.*

ME'TEOR, s. [a body imperfectly mixt of vapours, drawn up into the middle region of the air] *meteore.*

METE-WAND } *una misura, una can-*
METE-YARD } *na, un' alla.*

ME'TER, s. *colui che misura colla canna e coll' alla.*

ME'THEGLIN, s. [drink made of honey boiled with water and fermented] *bevanda fatta di miele bollito con acqua e fermentato.*

METHI'NKS [I think] *mi pare, io penso.*

ME'THOD, s. [an apt disposition of things, so as to be easiest understood or retained] *metodo, ordine, s. m.*

To put things in a right method, *mettere le cose in ordine.*

Method [way] *metodo, maniera.*

METHO'DICAL, adj. [orderly] *metodico, ordinato in ordine.*

METHO'DICALLY, adv. *metodicamente, con metodo, con ordine.*

METHO'UGHT [the preter tense of the impersonal verb METHI'NKS] *mi pareva, mi parve, credevo, credei.*

METONY'MICAL, adj. *metonimico.*

METO'NYMY, s. [a figure in rhetorick which implies a changing or the putting one name or thing for another, as when the cause is put for the effect, the subject for the adjunct, or the contrary] *metonimia, s. f.*

ME'TRE, s. [speech confined to a certain number and harmonick disposition of syllables] *metro; parlare ristretto da certe misure e da certa armoniosa disposizione di sillabe.*

ME'TRICAL, adj. [belonging to meter or verse] *metrico, di verso, appartenente a verso.*

METRO'POLIS, s. [the chief city of a province or kingdom] *metropoli, s. f. città principale.*

METROPO'LITAN, adj. [belonging to a metropolis] *metropolitano, di metropoli.*

A metropolitan city, *una città metropolitana, una metropoli.*

A metropolitan church, *una chiesa metropolitana.*

A metropolitan, s. [an archbishop] *un metropolitano, un arcivescovo.*

METROPO'LITANSHIP, s. [a metropolitan's dignity] *dignità di metropolitano, o arcivescovo.*

ME'TTLE, s. [vigour, life, sprightliness] *vivacità, s. f. spirito, s. m.*

That horse has too much mettle, *quel cavallo è troppo furioso, o ha troppa foga.*

Mettle [stoutness, courage] *animo, ardire, coraggio, cuore.*

ME'TTLED } adj. [lively spright-
ME'TTLESOME } ly] *vivace, allegro, spiritoso, vivo.*

Mettled } [stout] *vigoroso, corag-*
Mettlesome } *gioso, ardito*

MEW, or SEA MEW, s. [a sort of bird] *gabbiano, s. m. uccello acquatico.*

A hawk's mew [a kind of cage where hawks are kept when they mew] *muda, s. f. gabbia, dove si rinchiude l' uccello di rapina quando vuol mudare.*

To MEW [to cry like a cat] *miagolare, il mandar fuor la voce che fa la gatta.*

To mew [to molt, to cast the feathers as birds do, to shed the horns, as a stag does] *mudare, rinnovar le penne come fanno gli ucelli, o le corna come fanno i cervi.*

To mew [to shut up] *rinchiudere. pret. rinchiusi.*

To mew one's self up from the world, *ritirarsi dal mondo, entrare in una vita solitaria.*

MEWED, adj. *mudato.*

Mewed up, *rinchiuso.*

MEW'ING, s. *muda, s. f. il mudare.*

The mewing of a cat, *il miagolare d' una gatta.*

Mewing up, *il rinchiudere*

To MEWL [to squall as a child] *piagnere e gridare come fanno i bambini.*

MEZE'REON, s. *spezie d' alloro.*

MEYNT, adj. [mixed] *mischiato.*

MEZZOTI'NTO, s. [a particular way of engraving pictures on copper plates, by punging and scraping] *mezzo tinto.*

MI'ASM, s. *atomi supposti uscire da corpi malati, putrefatti, o velenosi.*

MICE, s. *sorci, s. m. pl. è il plurale di* Mouse.

MI'CHAELMASS, s. *la festa di san Michele Arcangelo, che si celebra li 29 di Settembre.*

To MICHE [to lie hid, to skulk in a corner] *nascondersi, appiattarsi.*

MI'CHER, s. [a covetous, sordid fellow] *un avaro, un taccagno, un misero, uno spilorcio.*

Micher [a lazy loiterer, who skulks about in corners and by-places; hedge-creeper] *un furfante che ama star in ozio.*

MI'CHES [white loaves paid as a rent to some manors] *pagnotte bianche.*

MI'CKLE, s. [it is only used in this pro-

proverbial expression] Many a little make a mickle, *molti pochi fanno un molto.*

MI'CROCOSM, s. [little world] *microcosmo, picciol mondo.*

MICROCO'SMICAL, adj. *appartenente a microcosmo.*

MI'CROSCOPE, s. [a magnifying glass] *microscopio,* s. m.

MID, adj. [middle; equally between two extremes] *mezzo; equalmente distante da' due estremi.*

MID-COURSE, s. *mezza via, mezza strada.*

MID-DAY, s. [noon, meridian] *mezzogiorno, mezzodì, meridiano.*

MI'DDEST, *superlativo di* mid *che è nel bel mezzo, che sta proprio in mezzo.*

MIDDAY, s. [noon] *mezzodì, mezzogiorno,* s. m.

MI'DDLE, adj. *mezzano, mediocre, mezzo.*

In the middle way from London, *a mezza strada da Londra.*

Middle, s. [the midst] *il mezzo.*

The middle of a town, of a discourse, &c. *il mezzo d'una città, d'un discorso, &c.*

The middle of the week, *mezzedima.*

The middle of one's body, *la cintura.*

Middle-sized, *di mezzana statura.*

A middle aged man, *un uomo di mezzana età.*

MI'DDLEMOST, *che è nel mezzo, del mezzo.*

MI'DDLING, adj. *mezzano, mediocre.*

MIDGE, s. [gnat] *zanzara,* s. f.

MID-HEAVEN, s. *centro de' cieli.*

MI'DLAND, adj. *mediterraneo, che è dentro terra.*

MIDLEG, s. *mezza gamba.*

MIDLENT, s. *la metà della quaresima.*

MI'DMOST, adj. [the middle] *che è in mezzo.*

MI'DNIGHT, s. *mezza notte.*

MI'DRIFF, s. [a skin or membrane which separates the heart and lungs from the lower belly] *diafragma, e diaframma,* s. f. *quel pannicolo, che divide per traverso il corpo degli animali, e divide il ventre di mezzo dall' infimo.*

MIDST, s. *mezzo,* s. m.

In the midst of the croud, *nel mezzo della folla.*

Midst, prep. [a contraction of amidst] *nel mezzo, fra.*

MI'DSTREAM, s. [the middle of the stream] *corrente; il mezzo dell' acqua.*

MIDSU'MMER, s. *il mezzo della state.*

Midsummer day, *la festa di San Giovanni.*

MIDWALL, s. [a bird that eats bees] *uccello che mangia l'api.*

MI'DWAY, s. *mezza strada.*

MI'DWIFE, s. *mammana, levatrice,* s. f.

A man midwife, *chirurgo che fa il mestière di levatrice.*

MI'DWIFERY, s. *l'arte, o'l mestiere di levatrice.*

MIDWI'NTER, s. *il cuore, il mezzo del verno.*

MIEN, s. [air, look, manner] *l'aria, l'aspetto, il portamento.*

MIGHT, s. [power] *potere,* s. m. *potenza, possa, possanza, forza,* s. f.

He cried out with all his might, *egli gridò ad alta voce.*

With might and main, *con ogni forza, a tutto potere.*

He did it with might and main, *vi si sbracciò, vi adoperò ogni forza e sapere.*

To fight with might and main, *combattere vigorosamente.*

Might, *è un tempo del verbo difettivo* May, *&c.* She might possibly love him, *forse ch' ella l'amava.*

If it might be, *se fosse possibile, se si potesse fare.*

I might do it with ease, *potrei farlo facilmente.*

You might have gone thither, *voi avreste potuto andarvi.*

MI'GHTILY, adv. [very much] *molto.*

MI'GHTINESS, s. *potenza, possanza,* s. f. *potere,* s. m.

MI'GHTY, adj. [powerful] *potente.*

Mighty, adv. [very] *molto.*

Mighty rich, *molto ricco, ricchissimo.*

Mighty little, *molto piccolo, piccolissimo.*

MIOKA'TION, s. [act of changing place] *l' andar da un luogo all' altro.*

MILCH, adj. [giving milk] *che da latte, che allatta.*

MILD, adj. [gentle] *dolce, piacevole, affabile, moderato, mite.*

Mild [to the taste] *dolce, che non è forte al palato.*

Mild weather, *tempo moderato.*

MI'LDERNIX, s. [a sort of canvas for sail-cloth] *sorta di canavaccio, del quale si fanno le vele de' vascelli.*

MI'LDEW, s. [a sort of dew] *brina, golpe,* s. f.

To MI'LDEW, *sparger di brina.*

MI'LDEWED, adj. [blasted] *golpato.*

MI'LDLY, adv. *placidamente, benignamente, clementemente, mitemente.*

MI'LDNESS, s. [the being mild] *dolcezza, piacevolezza, benignità, clemenza, umanità,* s. f.

MILE, s. [the distance of a thousand paces] *miglio,* s. m. *lunghezza di mille passi.* pl. *miglia,* s. f.

MI'LESTONE, s. *sasso messo nella strada pubblica per segnar la distanza delle miglia; pietra migliaria.*

MI'LFOIL, s. [an herb] *mille foglie, spezie d'erba.*

MI'LITANT, adj. [combating, fighting] *militante, che milita.*

The church militant, *la chiesa militante.*

MI'LITARY, adj. [belonging to soldiers, or war, warlike] *militare, di milizia, da soldato.*

Military discipline, *disciplina militare, milizia.*

Military execution [a ravaging and destroying the country by the soldiers] *esecuzione militare.*

MILI'TIA, s. [a certain number of the inhabitants of a city or country form'd into companies and regiments, for the defence of it] *milizia, soldati del paese.*

Militia [or implements of war] *apparecchi di guerra.*

MILK, s. *latte,* s. m.

A woman's, or cow's milk, *latte di donna, o di vacca.*

Butter milk, *latte di butirro.*

Thick milk, *latte quagliato.*

A milk cow, *vacca lattante.*

A milk maid, or milk woman, *una lattaja.*

A milk pail, *una secchia da latte.*

Milk house [dairy] *una cascina.*

MILKSOP [a man that is ruled by his wife] *un' uomo che si lascia governare da sua moglie.*

Milk weed, or wolves milk, s. *nome di pianta.*

Milk thistle, *titimaglio,* s. m.

To MILK [to press out milk from the cow's udder] *mugnere, spremere le poppe agli animali, per trarne il latte,* pres. *mungo,* pret. *munsi.*

To milk a cow, *mugnere una vacca.*

To milk the bull, *fare cosa sciorcamente vana.*

MI'LKED, adj. *munto.*

MI'LKNESS, s. *qualità che tiene della natura del latte.*

MI'LKING, s. *il mugnere.*

MI'LKY, adj. *latteo, di latte.*

A milky substance, *una sostanza lattea.*

The milky way [galaxy] *la via lattea.*

MILL, s. [an engine for grinding, &c.] *mulino,* s. m. *edificio dove si macina.*

A water, or wind mill, *un mulino d'acqua, o da vento.*

A hand mill, *un mulinello.*

A paper mill, *una cartiera, fabbrica dove si fa la carta.*

A mill to coin money, *un mulinello.*

To bring grist to the mill, *trar l'acqua al suo mulino.*

A mill stone, *macine, e macina,* s. f.

An oil mill, *macinatojo,* s. m. *mulino dove si macinan l'ulive.*

Mill clap, } *battagliuola di mulino.*
Mill clapper, }

Mill dam, *chiusa di mulino.*

Mill leat, *gora,* s. f.

A mill horse, *cavallo da mulino.*

To MILL, *macinare.*

To mill chocolate, *frullar la cioccolata.*

To mill [to stamp coin in the mints] *coniare, stampar la moneta.*

MILL-COGS, s. *denti intorno a una ruota che entrano ne' denti d'un altra ruota.*

MILLENARIAN, or MILLENARY, s. *millenario*, s. m. *ſetta d'eretici.*

MI'LLENER, s. [a ſeller of ribbons, gloves, &c.] *merciaja, creſtaja*, s. f.

MI'LLER, s. [one who grinds corn, &c.] *mugnajo*, s. m. *quegli che macina grano o biade.*

Every miller draws water to his mill, *ognuno tira l'acqua al ſuo mulino.*

A miller's wife, *una mugnaja.*

A miller's thumb [a gull] *capitone*, s. m. *ſpezie di peſce.*

MI'LLET, s. [hirſe] *miglio*, s. m. *ſpezie di biada minuta.*

MI'LLION, s. [the number of ten hundred thouſand] *milione*, s. m. *ſomma di mille migliaja.*

MILT, s. [ſpleen] *la milza.*

Milt [ſoft roe of fiſhes] *latte di peſci.*

MI'LTER, s. *il maſchio de' peſci. La femmina ſi chiama* ſpawner.

MIME, } s. [a buffoon, that imi-
MI'MICK, } tates and ridicule other people] *un buffone, un mimo.*

MI'MICAL, } adj. [apiſh] *buffoneſco,*
MI'MICK, } *giullareſco*; *imitativo.*

MI'MER, *un mimo, un buffone.*

To MIME [to play the mime] *far il buffone.*

MI'MICK, s. *imitatore per beffa*; *mimo*; *buffone che imita i moti, la voce, o i modi altrui per muovere altri a riſo.*

Mimick, s. [imitator] *ſervile.*

To MI'MICK [to imitate in order to expoſe] *imitare, contraffare.*

MI'MICKRY, s. [burleſque, imitation] *imitazione burleſca, buffoneria imitando.*

MINA'CIOUS, } adj. *minaccioſo.*
MI'NATORY, }

To MINCE [to cut ſmall] *ſbriciolare, ſbrizzare, minuzzare, tagliuzzare, tritare.*

To mince it, *fare il contegnoſo, ſtare in contegno.*

MINCED, adj. *ſbricciolato, ſbrizzato, minuzzato, tagliuzzatto, tritato.*

Minced meat, *manicaretto.*

A minced pie, *ſorta di paſticcio all' Ingleſe.*

MI'NCING, s. *il minuzzare, il tritare.*

Mincing, adj. [affected] *affettato, contegnoſo.*

MI'NCINGLY, adv. *a minuzzoli, ſminuzzatamente, contegnoſamente, con affettazione.*

MIND, s. [the reaſon, or rational part of the ſoul] *mente*, s. f. *la parte la più eccellente dell' anima, colla quale l'uomo intende e conoſce, intelletto*, s. m.

To give one's mind to a thing, *applicar la mente a che che ſi ſia.*

Mind [memory] *mente, memoria*, s. f.

To call to mind, *richiamare, tornare nella memoria.*

Mind [affection] *mente, volontà, affetto, ſpirito, animo.*

To exaſperate the minds of the people, *inaſprire gli animi de' popoli.*

Mind [ſentiment, opinion] *ſentimento, penſiero, parere*, s. m. *opinione.*

To ſpeak one's mind, *dire il ſuo ſentimento.*

I am of your mind, *io ſono del voſtro parere.*

So many men, ſo many minds, *quanti uomini, tanti cervelli.*

Mind [will, or deſire] *mente voglia, inclinazione*, s. f *deſiderio*, s. m.

I have a mind to learn Italian, *ho in mente d'imparare l'Italiano.*

I have a great mind to go, *ho gran voglia d'andarvi.*

To fulfil one's mind, *fare, adempire, l'altrui volontà.*

To have a woman to one's mind, *avere a grado, aggradire, gradire, trovar di ſuo genio una donna.*

Mind [reſolution] *penſiero, diſegno*, s. m. *riſoluzione.*

My mind is altered, *io ho cangiato penſiero.*

It comes now to my mind, *ora mi viene in mente, ora me ne ricordo.*

A thing out of mind, *una coſa immemorabile.*

Time out of mind, *di tempo immemorabile.*

To put in mind, *far ricordare.*

'Tis now out of mind, *non me ne ricordo più, m' è affatto uſcito della mente.*

To do a thing of one's own mind [or accord] *far che che ſi ſia di ſua teſta, o di ſua propria volontà, di proprio moto.*

It was my mind that he ſhould go, *è ſtato il mio piacere ch' egli ſene andaſſe.*

To be all of one mind, *eſſer d'accordo, convenire.*

My mind gives me that——*il cuore mi dice, prevedo, che——*

Every thing falls to his mind, *ogni coſa gli rieſce.*

To be of a great many minds, *eſſer irreſoluto, ſoſpeſo, o dubbioſo, non ſaper a che riſolverſi.*

I have my mind, *io ſon ſodisfatto.*

As they had a mind, *come volevano.*

To MIND [to obſerve, to take notice of] *notare, oſſervare, badare, por mente, fare attenzione o rifleſſione, riflettere.*

Mind well what I ſay, *oſſervate bene le mie parole.*

To mind own's buſineſs, *badare a fatti ſuoi.*

He minds me no more than if—— *non ſi cura più di me che ſe——*

To mind one's health, *aver cura della ſua ſalute.*

To mind [to put in mind] *far ricordare, avvertire*, pref. *avvertiſco.*

Mind me of it, *fatemene ricordare.*

This is all he minds, he minds nothing elſe but this, *queſta è tutta la ſua cura.*

To mind one's book, *ſtudiare, applicarſi allo ſtudio.*

To mind one's work, *lavorare, applicarſi, eſſer aſſiduo al ſuo lavoro.*

MI'NDED, adj. *notato, oſſervato, badato*, v. To mind.

As every one is minded, *ciaſcheduno a ſuo modo.*

To be minded [to purpoſe, or deſign] *proporre, deliberare, ſtatuire, far conto, eſſer riſoluto.*

High minded [ambitious, proud] *ambizioſo, altiero, orgoglioſo, ſuperbo.*

Well minded [well affected] *ben affetto, ben diſpoſto, bene impreſſionato.*

Ill minded, *male affetto, mal diſpoſto, male impreſſionato.*

MI'NDFUL, adj. [careful] *accurato, diligente, vigilante.*

Mindful [that remembers] *ricordevole.*

MI'NDFULNESS, s. [care, diligence] *cura, diligenza, attenzione*, s. f.

MI'NDLESS, adj. [inattentive, regardleſs] *che non ha attenzione, che non ha riguardo, diſattento, traſcurato.*

Mindleſs [not endued with a mind; having no intellectual powers] *non dotato di buona mente*; *ſciocco*; *ſenza teſta*; *ſcervellato.*

MI'ND-STRICKEN, adj. *commoſſo ferte nella mente.*

MINE, pron. [poſſeſſive] *mio, mia, miei, mie.*

This book is mine, *queſto libro è mio.*

Mine, s. [my friends, my relations] *miei.*

Mine [the place where metals are digged] *mina, miniera*, s. f.

Mine [in military affairs, a hole dug to be filled with gun powder, in order to blow it up] *mina, quella ſtrada ſotterranea che ſi fa per andare a trovare i fondamenti delle muraglie per mandarle in aria, con polvere d'artiglieria.*

To MINE [to dig the earth hollow, and fill it with gun powder] *minare, far mine.*

MI'NER, s. [a man who works in mines] *quello che è impiegato nelle mine.*

MINDED, adj. *minato.*

MI'NERAL, adj. [belonging to, or partaking of the nature of minerals] *minerale, che è di mina.*

Mineral waters, *acque minerali.*

A mineral, s. [a metallick ſubſtance dug out of a mine] *minerale*, s. m. *materia di miniera.*

MI'NERALIST, s. [one ſkilled in the knowledge of minerals and metals] *una perſona che s' intende di minerali.*

MI'NEVER, s. [a ſort of fur] *pelle di vajo.*

A MI'NGLE, s. [or mixture] *miſcuglio*, s. m. *meſcolanza*, s. f.

To MI'NGLE [to mix] *meſcolare, meſchiare, miſchiare, confondere inſieme*, pret. *confuſi.*

MI'NGLED, adj. *meſcolato, meſchiato, o miſchiato, confuſo.*

MI'NGLE-

MINGLE-MANGLE, s. [a confused mixture] *mescuglio, mischiamento, garbuglio*, s. m. *mischianza*, s. f.

MINGLING, adv. *mescolamento*, s. m. *il mescolare.*

MI'NIATURE, s. [the art of drawing pictures in water colours] *miniatura*, s. f.

MI'NIKIN, s. [a small sort of pins] *sorta di spille picciolissime.*

Minikin, adj. [small, diminutive] *picciolo, diminutivo, minuto.*

MI'NIM, } s. [in musick, half a MI'NIME, } semibreve] *minima*, s. f. *nota musicale.*

MI'NIMES [minim friars, a religious order] *minimi, ordine di religiosi.*

MI'NIMUS, s. *un ente de più piccoli.*

MI'NION, s. [darling, favourite] *mignone, favorito, cucco.*

To MI'NISH, *v.* To diminish.

MI'NISTER, s. [parson] *prete protestante.*

Minister, s. [attendant, assistant] *ministro.*

A minster of state, *un ministro di stato.*

To MI'NISTER [to officiate, to serve] *ministrare, servire.*

To minister [to give] *ministrare, somministrare, dare, porgere*, pret. *diedi, porsi.*

MINISTRA'TION, s. [ministry] *ministerio, ministero*, s. m.

Ministration [administration] *amministrazione.*

MI'NISTRY, s. [priestly function, or that of a minister of state] *ministero*, s. m. *ufficio o carica di ministro.*

MI'NIUM, s. [red lead] *minio*, s. m.

MINKS, } s. *una figliuolina, una* MI'NNEKIN, } *ragazzina.*

MI'NNEKIN [little pin] *spilletto*, s. m.

MI'NNING DAYS, s. [commemoration days, or anniversary feasts, on which the souls of the deceased were had in special remembrance] *anniversario*, s. m.

MI'NNOW, s. [menow, pink] *sorta di pesciolino d'acqua dolce.*

MI'NOR, adj. [less] *minore, più piccolo.*

Asia minor, *l'Asia minore.*

Minor [younger] *più giovane.*

Minor, s. [one under age] *minore che è nella sua minorità.*

Minor, s. [the minor proposition of a syllogism] *la minore d'un sillogismo.*

MI'NORS, [friar minors] *frati minori.*

MINO'RITY, s. [non-age] *minorità*, s. f.

MI'NOTAUR, s. [a poetical monster, half a man and half a bull] *minotauro*, s. m.

MI'NSTER, s. [a monastery, or conventual church] *monastero, chiesa conventuale.*

The minster of York, *la chiesa cattedrale di York.*

MI'NSTREL, s. [a fiddler] *un sonator di violino o d'altro strumento.*

MI'NSTRELSEY, s. [musick, instrumental harmony] *musica stromentale.*

Minstrelsey [a number of musicians] *truppa di musici.*

MINT, s. [an herb] *menta*, s. f. *erba nota.*

Wild mint, or horse mint, *mentastro*, s. m. *menta salvatica.*

Spear mint, *menta Romana, erba santamaria.*

Mint [the place where the King's coin is made] *zecca*, s. f. *luogo dove si battono le monete.*

To MINT [to coin money] *monetare, batter moneta.*

MI'NTAGE, s. [that which is coined or stamped] *conio.*

Mintage [the duty paid for coining] *quel che si paga per il privilegio di batter moneta.*

MI'NTER, s. [coiner] *zecchiere.*

MI'NTMAN, s. *colui che intende l'arte del coniare, o che è impiegato nella zecca.*

MINTMA'STER, s. *il soprantendente della zecca.*

Mintmaster, s. *un inventore, un che conia vocaboli, frasi, o cose a capriccio.*

MI'NTED, adj. *monetato.*

Money ready minted, *danaro monetato.*

MI'NUET, s. *minuetto, sorta di ballo in due o in tre.*

MINU'TE, adj. [small, little] *minuto, picciolissimo.*

Minute, s. [the sixtieth part of an hour] *minuto*, s. m. *la sessantesima parte d'un ora.*

Minute [moment] *un minuto, un momento.*

A minute watch, *oriuolo che mostra i minuti.*

Minute [the first draught of a writing] *minuta*, s. f. *bozza di scrittura.*

Minute [the sixtieth part of a degree] *minuto, la sessantesima parte d'un grado.*

To MI'NUTE down [to draw a rough draught, or to enter short notes for memorandum] *abozzare.*

MI'NUTELY, adj. *che accade ogni minuto.*

MINX, s. [a pert girl] *una sfacciatella, una ragazza baldanzosetta.*

MI'RACLE, s. [a work perform'd by the almighty power of God] *miracolo*, s. m.

Miracle [wonder] *miracola, maraviglia.*

MIRA'CULOUS, adj. [done by a miracle] *miracoloso.*

Miraculous [wonderful, surprising] *miracoloso, maraviglioso, stupendo.*

MI'RACULOUSLY, adv. *miracolosamente, per miracolo, d'una maniera miracolosa.*

MIRADO'R, s. [a balcony] *un verrone un balcone.*

MIRE, s. [dirt, mud] *fango, limaccio, limo*, s. m. *fanghiglia, mota, melma*, s. f.

A mire, or quag-mire, *fango, luogo, fangoso.*

To be deep in the mire [to be put to hard shifts] *esser ridotto in povero stato.*

To MIRE, *imbrattar di fango.*

MI'RKSOME, adj. [dark, obscure] *bujo, scuro, tenebroso.*

MI'RIFICAL, adj. [wonderful] *mirifico maraviglioso.*

MI'ROUR, } s. [a looking glass] MI'RROUR, } *specchio*, s. m.

Mirrour, [pattern] *modello, esempio*, s. m.

MIRTH, s. [joy, merriment] *gioja, allegria*, s. f. *giubilo, gaudio, contento*, s. m.

Full of mirth, *giojoso, festoso, allegro.*

MIRTHFUL, adj. *giojoso, gajo, allegro, pieno, d'allegria.*

MI'RTHLESS, adj. [joyless, cheerless] *privo di gioja, privo d'allegria, tristo, dolente, pien di guai.*

MI'RY, adj. [from mire] *fangoso, melmoso*, s. m.

MISADVE'NTURE, s. *una disgrazia*, s. f. *un accidente sinistro.*

Misadventure, s. [the killing of a man, partly by negligence, and partly by chance] *omicidio che si commette per accidente.*

MISADVI'SE, s. *un cattivo consiglio.*

To MISADVI'SE [to advise ill] *mal avisare.*

MISADVI'SED, adj. *mal avisato.*

MISAI'MED, adj. *non ben preso di mira, mal preso di mira, mal diretto.*

MI'SANTHROPE, s. [a man-hater] *un misantropo, odiator degli uomini.*

MI'SANTHROPY, s. [the hating of men] *qualità di misantropo.*

To MI'SAPPLY [to apply ill] *applicar male.*

MISAPPLY'D, adj. *male applicato.*

To MISAPPREHE'ND [not to understand right] *intender male, o non intendere.*

MISAPPREHE'NDED, adj. *mal inteso.*

To MISBECO'ME, *disdire, sconvenire, non esser dicevole.*

It very much misbecomes him, *ciò gli disdice molto.*

MISBECO'MING, adj. *disdicevole, sconvenevole, indecente.*

MISBEGO'T, adj. *nato d'una donna prostituta, bastardo.*

To MISBEHA'VE, verb recip. *comportarsi male.*

MISBEHA'VIOUR, s. *cattivo portamento, cattiva condotta, imprudenza.*

MISBELI'EF, s. *miscredenza, mala credenza*, s. f. *errar nella fede.*

To MISBELI'EVE, verb act. *esser miscredente, discredere.*

MISBELI'EVER, s. *un miscredente, un discredente.*

To MISCA'LL [to give a wrong name] *ingannarsi, sbagliare chiamando una cosa con un nome che non le apparti ene.*

MISCA'RRIAGE, s. [folly, ill behaviour] *fallo mancamento, errore*, s. m. *mancanza, cattiva, condotta.*

Miscarriage of a business, *cattivo successo in un negozio.*

Miscarriage [the untimely bringing forth of a child] *sconciatura*, s. f. *aborto*, s. m.

To MISCA'RRY [to bring forth a child before the time] *sconciarsi, disperder la creatura le femmine gravide.*

To miscarry [not to succeed] *fallire, fallare, mancare, non riuscire, aver cattivo successo.*
To miscarry [to be lost] *perdersi.*
The letter miscarry'd, *la lettera s'è perduta.*
To miscarry [as a ship at sea] *perdersi, naufragare, far naufragio.*
MISCA'RRYING, s. [disappointment in any undertaking] *cattivo successo.*
Miscarrying [speaking of woman] *sconciatura, abortivo.*
MISCELLA'NEOUS, adj. [mixt together] *misto, mescolato, miscellaneo.*
MISCE'LLANY, s. [a collection of several different matters] *opere miste, opere diverse.*
MISCHA'NCE, s. [disaster, a cross accident] *disgrazia, s. f. disastro, infortunio, s. m.*
MISCHIEF, s. [hurt, damage] *male, danno, torto, s. m. malignità, malizia, s. f.*
To delight in mischief, to be full of mischief, *esser cattivo, malizioso, tristo, pernizioso.*
Mischief [misfortune] *disgrazia, infortunio, disastro,*
To MI'SCHIEF [to do mischief] *offendere, far del male.*
MI'SCHIEF-MAKER, s. *seminator di mali, di zizzania, di discordia.*
MI'SCHIEVOUS, adj. [hurtful] *maligno, tristo, cattivo, pernizioso, pericoloso.*
Mischievous [unlucky, full of malice, *malizioso, maligno, cattivo, tristo.*
MI'SCHIEVOUSLY, adv. *cattivamente, maliziosamente, malignamente, per malizia.*
MI'SCHIEVOUSNESS, s. [malice] *malizia, cattivezza, cattivanza, ribalderia, tristizia, malvagità, cattività, s. f.*
Mischievousness [mischievous quality] *malignità, s. f.*
MISCLA'IM, s. [mistaken claim] *domanda mal fondata.*
MISCONCE'IT, s. [false opinion, wrong notion] *opinione falsa, idea torta.*
MISCONCE'IVED, adj. *mal inteso, falso.*
MISCONJE'CTURE, s. *una falsa congettura.*
To MISCONJE'CTURE, verb act. *fare false congetture.*
MISCONSTRU'CTION, s. *cattiva interpretazione.*
To MISCO'NSTRUE [to interpret amiss, to put an ill meaning upon] *interpretare male, o in mala parte, storcere il senso di qualche cosa.*
MISCO'NSTRUED, adj. *male interpretato.*
MISCONTI'NUANCE [discontinuance] *tralasciamento, s. m.*
MI'SCREANCY, s. [the state or condition of a miscreant] *miscredanza, mala credenza, s. f. l'errar nella fede.*
MI'SCREANT [an infidel, an unbeliever] *un miscredente, an infedele.*
MISDE'ED, s. [trespass] *trasgressione, s. f. misfatto, peccato, fallo, s. m.*

To MISDE'EM, *giudicar male, sbagliare.*
To MISDEME'AN one's self, verb recip. *portarsi male, governarsi, condursi male.*
MISDEME'ANOUR, s. [an offence, or fault] *misfatto, delitto, s. m. offesa, s. f.*
To MISDO'UBT, *dubitar male a proposito.*
MISE, s. [expence, charges] *spesa, s. f.*
Mise [a gift, or customary present of five thousand pounds paid by the inhabitants of Wales to every new prince at his entrance into that principality] *tributo, o sia regalo di cinque mila lire sterline, che gli abitanti del paese di Gallia hanno costume di fare ad ogni nuovo principe, che entra nel possesso di cotesto principato.*
Mise [tax] *tassa.*
MI'SER, s. [covetous wretch] *un avaro, un taccagno, un misero.*
MI'SERABLE, adj. [wretched, unfortunate] *miserabile, meschino, infelice, sfortunato.*
Miserable [sordid, niggardly] *misero, stretto, avaro, spilorcio, sordido, taccagno.*
MI'SERABLENESS, s. [covetousness] *miseria, avarizia, grettezza, spilorceria, sordidezza, s. f.*
MI'SERABLY, adv. [poorly, unfortunately] *miserabilmente, miserevolmente, con miseria.*
Miserably [like a miser] *grettamente, meschinamente, avaramente, sordidamente.*
MISERE'RE, s. [one of the penitential psalms] *il miserere, uno de' salmi penitenziali.*
MI'SERY, s. [calamity] *miseria, infelicità, calamità, s. f.*
To live in great misery, *vivere in gran miseria, viver miseramente.*
Misery [poverty] *miseria, povertà.*
Misery [sad condition] *miseria, pena, dolore.*
MISFO'RTUNE, s. *disgrazia, disavventura, sventura, s. f. infortunio, accidente sinistro.*
To MISGI'VE, *dar timore,* ex. My mind misgives me that—*il cuore mi dice che*—*io temo che*—
A MISGI'VING, s. [or doubt] *timore, s. m. temenza, s. f.*
To MISGO'VERN, *governar male.*
MISGO'VERNED, adj. *mal governato.*
MISGO'VERNMENT, s. *cattivo governo.*
MISHA'P, s. [mischance] *disgrazia, sventura, accidente sinistro, infortunio.*
To MISHA'PPEN, *intravenir male.*
To MISHE'AR, *frantendere, non bene intendere, intendere al contrario di quel che s'è detto.*
MI'SHMASH, s. [hotch potch] *miscuglio, mescolanza, confusione, garbuglio.*
To MISIMPLOY, *impiegar male, servirsi male, spender male.*
MI'SIMPLOY'D, adj. *mal impiegato, male speso.*

To MI'SINFORM, *informar male, dare falsi avvisi.*
MISINFORMA'TION, s. *cattiva informazione.*
MI'SINFORMED, adj. *malamente informato.*
To MISINTE'RPRET [to interpret amiss] *interpetrar male, storcere il senso.*
MISINTE'RPRETED, adj. *interpretato male, male inteso.*
To MI'SJUDGE, *giudicar male, fare un giudicio temerario.*
MISKE'NNING, s. [a law term, a varying or changing one's speech in court] *il contraddirsi innanzi al giudice.*
To MISLE'AD [to seduce] *sviare, sedurre, pres. seduco, pret. sedussi.*
MISLE'ADER, s. *seduttore, s. m.*
MISLE'ADING, s. *seduzione, s. f. il sedurre.*
MISLE'D, adj. *sviato sedotto.*
To MISLI'KE, v. To dislike.
To MISMA'NAGE, verb act. *maneggiar male.*
MISMA'NAGED, adj. *malamente maneggiato.*
MISMA'NAGEMENT, s. *cattivo maneggio.*
MISO'GAMIST, s. [a marriage-hater] *colui che ha in odio il matrimonio.*
MISO'GAMY, s. [hating marriage] *odio al matrimonio.*
MISO'GYNIST, s. [a woman-hater], *colui che odia le donne.*
MISO'GINY, s. [misogamy] *l'odiar il sesso donnesco.*
To MISPE'ND, pret. and part. pass. mispent [to spend ill to waste, to consume to no purpose] *spender male, buttar, via, consumare il suo.*
MISPE'NDER, s. *un prodigo; un che butta via il suo senza giudizio.*
MISPERSUA'SION, s. *errore, s. m.*
To MISPLA'CE, *slogare, metter fuora del suo luogo.*
MISPLA'CED, adj. *slogato.*
To MISPRI'NT, *fare errore nella stampa.*
To misprint one word for another, *stampare una parola per un' altra.*
MISPRI'NTED, adj. *malamente stampato.*
MISPRISION, s. [oversight, neglect] *errore.*
To MISPROPO'RTION, *proporzionare malamente.*
MISPROPO'RTIONED, adj. *mal proporzionato, sproporzionato.*
MISQUOTA'TION, s. *falsa citazione.*
To MISQUO'TE, *citar falsamente.*
MISQUO'TED, adj. *citato malamente,*
To MISRECKON, *errare nel conto, sbagliare nel calcolo.*
MISRE'CKONED, adj. *mal contato.*
MISRE'CKONING, s. *error nel conto.*
To MISREME'MBER, *ricordarsi male, non ricordarsi bene d'una cosa.*
If I misremember not, *non m'inganno, se la memoria non m'inganna.*
To MISREPRESENT [not to represent fairly, to give a false character of] *rap-*

rappresentare male, dare una falsa relazione di qualcheduno, o di qualche cosa.

MISREPRESENTA'TION, s. *falsa relazione.*

MISREPRESE'NTED, adj. *malamente, o falsamente rappresentato.*

MISS, s. [a young lady] *una giovane signora nubile.*

Miss, s. *una puttanella, una concubina, una prostituta.*

Miss [mistake, error] *sbaglio errore, marrone, granchio, a secco, granciporro.*

To MISS [to fail] *mancare, fallire,* errare, pres. *fallisco.*

To miss [not to hit] *mancare.*

To miss the mark [in shooting] *mancare il colpo.*

To miss one's aim [in an undertaking] *mancare il colpo, non colpire, non riuscire.*

To miss fire [as a gun] *mancare.*

To miss [to slip, to omit] *saltare, omettere.*

To miss [to want, not to find] *mancare, aver perduto.*

I miss a book, *mi manca un libro, ho perduto il libro.*

To miss one [to want one's company] *desiderare, aver desiderio.*

All his friends miss him, *è desiderato da* tutti *i suoi amici.*

MI'SSAL, s. [mass-book] *messale,* s. m.

MI'SSED, adj. *mancato, v.* To miss.

To MI'S-SHAPE, *disfigurare, render deforme.*

MI'S-SHAPED, } adj. *disfigurato,*
MIS-SHA'PEN, } *deforme.*

MI'S-SHAPE, s. *deformità,* s. f.

MI'SSILE, adj. *che si trae di lontano, che si può gittare da lontano.*

MI'SSING, adj. [from to miss] *perduto.* Something is missing here, *qui ci manca qualche cosa.*

He has been missing these two days, *sono due giorni che non s'è veduto.*

MI'SSION, s. [sending] *missione,* s. f.

The mission of the apostles, *la missione degli apostoli.*

Mission [dismission, discharge] *congedo, comiato, l'accomiatare, il mandar via, il licenziare.*

Mission, s. *fazione. partito. E' vore fuor d'uso in questo significato.*

MI'SSIONARY, s. [one that is sent to preach the gospel] *missionario,* s. m.

MI'SSIVE, s. [a letter] *un lettera. Vocabolo Scozzese.*

Missive, adj. *missivo, che si può mandare.*

Missive, *adoperato in distanza; come* missive weapons, *arme adoperate da lontano, che si gettano da una certa distanza.*

To MI'S-SPEL, verb act. *compitar male.*

MI'S-SPELT, adj. *mal compitato.*

To MI'S-SPEND, *spendere male a proposito, scialacquare, buttar via il suo.*

MI'S-SPENT, adj. *male speso, scialacquato.*

MIST, s. [fog] *nebbia,* s. f.

To go away in a mist [to steal away] *corsela, battersela, andersene via nascosamente.*

To be in a mist, *esser al bujo, non saper che si fare.*

To cast a mist before one's eyes, *gittar polvere negli occhi ad uno.*

Breathing casts a mist upon the looking glass, *il fiato appanna lo specchio.*

A Scotch mist [a good shower] *acquazzone, gran pioggia.*

MISTA'KE, s. [oversight, blunder] *sbaglio, errore, fallo,* s. m.

To be, or lie under a mistake, *sbagliare, ingannarsi.*

To MISTA'KE [to be out] *ingannarsi, sbagliare,* errare.

To mistake [to take one thing for another] *scambiare, pigliare una cosa in cambio d'un' altra, prendere in iscambio.*

You mistake me [you don't know me] *voi non mi conoscete.*

He mistook me [he did not understand me] *egli non ha ben inteso quel che volevo dire.*

To mistake the way, *smarrire la strada.*

MISTA'KEN, adj. *ingannato, sbagliato, errato, v.* To mistake.

He is greatly mistaken, *egli s'inganna di molto, egli s'inganna a partito.*

If I be not mistaken, *se non m'inganno.*

MI'STER, } s. [trade] *mestiero,*
MI'STERY, } s. m.

To MISTI'ME to do a thing out of season] *fare un cosa a contrattempo, fuor di tempo.*

MISTI'MED, adj. *fatto a contrattempo.*

MI'STLE-TOW, s. [a sort of shrub that grows in an oak, apple tree, &c.] *vischio,* s. m. *frutice che cresce sopra le querce, peri, e simili.*

MI'STLE-BIRD, s. [a thrush which feeds on mistle-tow] *tordo,* s. m.

MI'STLIKE, adj. [resembling a mist] *che par nebbia; folto come nebbia.*

MISTO'OK, *è preterito del verbo* to mistake.

MI'STRESS, } s. *padrona.*
MI'STRISS, }

The mistress of the house, *la padrona della casa.*

A school mistress, *una maestra di scuola.*

Mistress [sweet heart] *innamorata, amata, amanza,* s. f.

Mistress [a title given to gentlewomen, and others] *signora.*

Mistress such a one, *la signora una tale.*

She is mistress of the Italian, *ella intende perfettamente la lingua Italiano.*

MISTRU'ST, s. [distrust] *diffidenza, sconfidanza,* s. f.

To MI'STRUST, *diffidare, dubbiare, dubitare, sospettare.*

MISTRU'STED, adj. *diffidato, dubitato, sospettato.*

MISTRUSTFUL, adj. *sospettoso, diffidente, dubitoso.*

MISTRUSTLESS, adj. *che non si diffida, che non è sospettoso.*

MISTY, adj. *nebbioso.*

To MISU'NDERSTAND, *intender male, non intendere, non comprendere,* pret. *intesi, compresi.*

You misunderstand me, *voi non m' intendete.*

MIS'UNDERSTANDING, s. *discordia, poca buona intelligenza.*

There's a misunderstanding between them, *sono in discordia fra di loro, passa poca buona intelligenza fra di loro.*

MISU'NDERSTOOD, adj. *male inteso.*

MISU'SAGE, s. [abuse, ill usuage] *abuso, mal uso.*

Misusage [ill treatment] *cattivo trattamento, villania.*

MISU'SE, s. *maltrattamento; mal uso.*

To MISU'SE [to make an ill use of] *abusare, servirsi a male, fare un cattivo uso.*

To misuse [to abuse, to treat ill] *maltrattare, trattar male, usar villania, svillaneggiare, bistrattare.*

MISU'SED, adj. *abusato, v.* to misuse.

MISWO'MAN, s. [whore] *una puttana.*

MITE, s. [an ancient coin, about the third part of a farthing] *spezie di moneta antica bassa.*

Mite [a worm breeding in cheese or meat] *tonchio, gorgoglione.*

Full of mites, *intonchiato.*

Mite [a worm eating corn] *gorgoglio, gorgoglione,* s. m. *baco ch' è ne' legumi, e li vota.*

Mite [the fourteenth part of a grain in weight] *la decima quarta parte d'un grano.*

MI'TER, s. [a bishop's crown] *mitra,* s. f.

MI'THRIDATE, s. [a preservative against poison] *mitridate,* s. m. *sorta di medicamento contra i veleni.*

To MITIGATE [to pacify or appease] *placare, mitigare, raddolcire, quietare,* pres. *raddolcisco.*

To mitigate God's anger, *placare l'ira di Dio*

To mitigate the severity of the law, *mitigare la severità delle leggi.*

MI'TIGATED, adj. *mitigato, placato, raddolcito, quietato.*

MITIGA'TING, } s. *mitigazione,* s.
MITIGA'TION, } f. *placamento, raddolcimento,* s. m.

MI'TRAL, adj. [belonging to a mitre] *di mitra, appartenente a mitra.*

MI'TRE, s. *mitra,* s. f.

MI'TRED, adj. [wearing a mitre] *mitrato.*

Mitred abbots, *abbati mitrati.*

MI'TTENS, s. [gloves without fingers] *guanti senza dita.*

MI'TTIMUS, s. [a warrant from a justice of peace, sending an offender to prison] *ordine, in virtù del quale uno è mandato in prigione.*

MI'VA, s. [is the flesh or pulp of a quince, boiled up with sugar into a thick consistence] *medicamento, fatto per lo più di mele cotogne mescolate con zucchero.*

To MIX [to mingle] *mischiare, meschiare, mescolare.*

To mix colours together, *mescolare i colori insieme.*

To mix, *mischiarsi, mescolarsi.*
MI'XED, *v.* Mixt.
MI'XEN, s. [dunghill] *letamajo*, s. m.
MI'XING, s. *mischiamento, mescuglio, mescolamento*, s. m. *mischianza, mischiatura*, s. f.
MIXT, adj. *mischiato, meschiato, mescolato.*
A mixt body [in philosophy] *un misto, un composto, un corpo misto.*
A mixt tense [in grammar] *un tempo misto.*
MI'XTION, } s. *mistione, mescolanza, mistura*, s. f.
MIXTURE, }
MI'XTLY, adv. *mischiatamente, mescolatamente, confusamente.*
MI'ZMAZZLE, s. *laberinto, luogo intrigato. Non in uso.*
MI'ZZEN, s. [a sea term] *mezzana*, s. f. *vela che si spande alla poppa del naviglio.*
The mizen mast, *l'albero di poppa.*
Mizzen top sail, *trinchetto*, s. m.
To MI'ZZLE [to rain in very small drops] *piovigginare, piovere leggiermente, spruzzolare.*
MI'ZZLING, adj. ex. mizzling rain, *spruzzaglia, acquicella, pocca pioggia e minuta.*
MI'ZZY, s. [a bog, a quagmire] *pantano, luogo limaccioso.*
MO, adv. [for more] *più, v.* More.
MOAN, s. *gemito, lamento, pianto*, s. m.
To MOAN [to make moan] *gemere, piagnere, lamentarsi, querelarsi, lagnarsi, gagnolare.*
MO'ANFUL, adj. *querulo, dolente, lamentevole, dolente.*
MO'ANFULLY, adv. *lamentevolmente, con lamento.*
MOAT, s. [a small invisible body, such as play in the beams of the sun] *atomo*, s. m. *corpo indivisible, festuca.*
MOAT, *canale d'acqua intorno a una casa o castello per difesa.*
To MOAT [to surround with canals by way of defence] *far un canale intorno per difesa.*
MOB, s. [the giddy multitude, rabble] *il popolazzo, la canaglia, la plebe, il popolo minuto.*
Mob, s. *sorta d' acconciatura pel capo delle donne.*
To MOB [to harrass or overbear by tumult] *tumultuare, o assaltar tumultuosamente, come fa il popolaccio troppo spesso in Londra e in altre parti d' Inghilterra.*
MO'BBISH, adj. *appartenente al popolaccio, da canaglia, canagliesco.*
MO'BBY, s. [a sort of drink made of the roots of potatoes] *bevanda fatta delle radici d'una pianta chiamata potatoes.*
MO'BILE, } s. [mob, rabble] *la plebe, il popolazzo, la parte ignobile del popolo.*
MOBI'LITY, }
Mobility [power, or aptness to move] *mobilità*, s. f. *facilità a muoversi.*
Mobility [changeableness] *incostanza*, s. f.

To MO'BLE, *vestir grossolanamente, o judiciamente.*
MO'CHO-STONE, s. *sorta di pietra fine che si rassomiglia alquanto all' agata.*
MOCK, s. [a laughing stock] *ludibrio, zimbello, scorno, strazio*, s. m.
To make a mock of one, *beffare, burlarsi, schernire alcuno.*
A mock stick, *uno stile comico, o burlesco.*
A mock poem, *un poema burlesco.*
A mock prophet, *un falso profeta.*
Mock shade, *l'imbrunire, il far della sera.*
To MOCK [to laugh at] *burlare, schernire, beffare, beffeggiare, deridere.*
To mock [to deceive] *ingannare, burlarsi.*
MO'CKABLE, adj. *esposto, alla derisione o besiggiamento altrui.*
MO'CKADEES, } s. [a kind of woollen stuff] *spezie di panno lano.*
MO'CKADOES, }
MO'CKED, adj. [scoffed] *beffato, schernito, dileggiato, deriso.*
Mocked [deceived] *deluso, ingannato.*
MO'CKEL, adj. [many, much] *molti, di molti*
MO'CKER, s. *beffardo, beffatore, irrisore, schernitore*, s. m. *beffarda, schernitrice*, s. f.
MO'CKERY, s. *gabbo, scherno*, s. m. *burla, baja*, s. f.
He made a mockery of me, *egli s' è burlato, o beffato di me.*
MO'CKING, s. *il dileggiare, uccellamento, scherno*, s. m.
MO'CKINGLY, adv. *per baja, schernevolmente, per ischerno.*
MODE, s. [fashion] *usanza, moda, foggia*, s. f.
Mode [way, manner] *maniera, guisa, forma*, s. f. *modo*, s. m.
A mode of speech, *una maniera di parlare.*
MO'DEL, s. [pattern] *modello*, s. m.
To MODEL [to frame according to a model] *modellare, far modello, architettare.*
MO'DELLED, adj. *modellato, architettato.*
MO'DELLING, s. *il modellare.*
MO'DERATE, adj. [temperate, sober] *moderato, temperato, savio, ritenuto.*
Moderate [that exceeds not] *moderato, mediocre, temperato.*
To MO'DERATE [to allay, to qualify, to temper] *moderare, modificare, temperare.*
To moderate [to diminish] *moderare, diminuire, sminuire.*
To moderate [to govern] *governare, regolare.*
MODERATELY, adv. [with moderation] *moderatamente, con moderanza, temperatamente.*
MODERA'TION, s. [temperance, discretion] *moderazione, moderanza, temperanza, discrezione*, s. f.
MODERA'TOR, s. [a decider of a controversy] *moderatore*, s. m.

MODERA'TRIX, s. *moderatrice*, s. f.
MO'DERN, adj. [of this time] *moderno, secundo l'uso presente.*
The MODERNS, s. [in opposition to the ancients] *i moderni.*
To MO'DERNISE [to make modern] *render moderno.*
MO'DEST, adj. [bashful, sober] *modesto, moderato, contegnoso, vergognoso.*
Modest [honest] *modesto, onesto, casto.*
MO'DESTLY, adv. *modestamente, con modestia.*
MO'DESTY, s. [soberness] *modestia, moderazione*, s. m.
Modesty [honesty] *modestia, onestà*, s. f. *pudore*, s. f.
MO'DICUM, s. [a small pittance, a mouthful] *un pezzo, un tozzo, un poco, un boccone.*
MO'DIFICABLE, adj. [capable of heing modified] *che si può modificare.*
MODIFICA'TION, s. [restriction] *modificazione, limitazione*, s. f.
To MO'DIFY [to moderate, or qualify] *modificare, moderare, temperare.*
MO'DIFY'D, adj. *modificato, moderato, temperato.*
MODI'LLON, s. [little brackets which are often set under the corners, and serve to support the projecture of the drip] *modiglione*, s. f.
MODISH, adj. [fashionable] *alla moda, secondo la moda.*
MODULA'TION, s. [tuning, agreeable harmony] *modulazione*, s. f. *misura armonica.*
MO'DULE, s. [in architecture, a measure, commonly half the diameter of the pillar at the lower end in the Tuscan and Dorick order] *modulo.*
MO'DWALL, s. [or wood-pecker] *picchio; sorta d'uccello.*
MOHA'IR, s. [a sort of stuff] *panno tessuto con peli di camello.*
MO'HOCK, s. *nome d'una nazione crudele in America, e dato a certi sgherani, che un tempo infestavano le vie di Londra.*
MOI'DORE, s. *moneta Portoghese a' tempi nostri* [1757] *valutata a ventisette scellini moneta di Londra.*
MO'IETY, s. [half] *metà*, s. f.
To MOIL [to work with might and main, to drudge] *affaticarsi, sudare, stentare.*
To moil [to daub with dirt] *infangare, involvere nel fango.*
To moil in the dirt, *infangarsi.*
MOIST, adj. [wettish, damp] *umido, bagnato.*
To MOIST, } verb act. *umettare, inumidire*, pres. *inumidisco.*
To MO'ISTEN, }
MO'ISTENED, adj. *umettato, inumidito.*
MO'ISTNESS, } s. [wetness, dampness] *umidezza, umidità*, s. f. *umidore, umido*, s. m.
MOISTURE, }
The radical moisture, *l'umido radicale.*
The moisture of plants, *succhio, sugo, umore delle piante.*
MO'KES, s. [the meshes of a net] *le maglie d'una rete.*

MO'KY,

Mo'KY, adj. *nuvoloſo, oſcuro, bujo.*
Moky weather, *tempo nuvoloſo.*

Mo'LAR, adj. *maſcellare.* The molar teeth [the five outmoſt teeth on either ſide of the mouth] *i maſcellari, i denti da lato.*

MOLE, s. [a peer, or fence againſt the ſea] *molo,* s. m. *riparo di muraglia contro all' impeto del mare.*

MOLE, s. [a ſpot on the ſkin] *neo,* s. m. *certa piccola macchia nericcia che naſce naturalmente ſopra la pelle.*

Mole, s. *talpa,* s. f.

MOLE-HILL, *topinaja.*
To make mountains of mole-hills, *fare d'una moſca un elefante.*

To MOLE'ST [to vex, to trouble] *moleſtare, dar moleſtia, faſtidio, infaſtidire, importunare.* pref. *infaſtidiſco.*

MOLESTA'TION, s. [trouble, vexation] *moleſtia, noja, importunità,* s. f. *faſtidio,* s. m.

MOLE'STED, adj. *moleſtato, faſtidito, importunato.*

MOLE'STING, s. *moleſtamento,* s. m. *il moleſtare.*

MO'LETRACK, s. *via che la talpa ſi fa ſotto terra.*

MO'LEWARE, s. [mole] *una talpa.*

MO'LINISTS, s. [Jeſuits] *i Moliniſti, i Geſuiti.*

MOLLIFICA'TION, s. *mollificazione,* s. f. *il mollificare.*
Mollification [alleviation] *alleviagione, alleviazione, alleggerimento.*

MO'LLIFICATIVE, adj. [ſoftening] *mollificativo, atto a mollificare.*

To MO'LLIFY [to ſoften] *mollificare, far molle, render molle,* metaph. *rammorbidire, addolcire, alleviare.*

MO'LLIFY'D, adj. *mollificato, rammorbidito, addolcito, alleviato.*

MOLLIFY'ING, s. *mollificamento,* s. m. *il mollificare.*

MOLO'SSES, s. [dregs of ſugar] *fondigliuoli di zucchero.*

To MOLT, v. To moult.

MO'LTEN, adj. [from to melt] *fonduto, liquefatto, ſquagliato.*
Molten greaſe [a diſeaſe in horſes] *malattia di cavallo.*

MO'LY, s. *ſorta d' eglio ſalvatico.*

MOME, s. [drone, dull, blockiſh fellow] *un minchione, un pecorone, uno ſciocco, un melenſo.*

MO'MENT, s. [the leaſt part of time that can be aſſigned] *momento,* s. m. *breviſſimo ſpazio di tempo.*
Moment [importance, weight] *momento, importanza, conſeguenza.*

MOMENTA'NEOUS, } adj. [that
MO'MENTARY, } laſts as it
MOME'NTOUS, } were but for a moment] *momentaneo, di breve momento, caduco.*

MO'NACHAL, adj. [belonging to a monk, monkiſh] *monacale, di monaco.*

MO'NACHISM, s. [the ſtate and condition of monks] *ſtato monacale, monacato, monachiſmo,* s. m.
Monachiſm [the monks] *i monaci.*

MO'NAD, } s. [an indiviſible
MO'NADE, } thing] *coſa indiviſibile.*

MO'NARCH, s. [a ſingle governor] *monarca,* s. m. *ſupremo ſignore.*
Monarch-like, *da monarca.*

MONA'RCHAL, adj. *grande, da principe, da gran re.*

MONA'RCHICAL, adj. [belonging to a monarch] *monarchico, monarcale, di monarca.*
A monarchical government, *un governo monarchico, o monarcale.*

To MO'NARCHISE, *farla da re; commandare a bacchetta.*

MO'NARCHY, s. [the government of a ſtate by a ſingle perſon] *monarchia,* s. f. *ſignoria ſuprema d' un ſolo.*

MONASTE'RIAL, adj. [belonging to a monaſtery] *di monaſtero, monaſtico.*

MO'NASTERY, s. [a convent, or cloyſter] *monaſtero, convento,* s. m.

MONA'STICAL, } adj. [belonging
MONASTICK, } to a monk] *monaſtico, di monaco, da monaco.*
A monaſtick life, *vita monaſtica.*

MONA'STICALLY, adv. *monaſticamente, romitamente.*

MOND, s. [a golden globe, being one of the enſigns of an emperor or king] *pomo,* s. m. *quella palla che ha ſopra una crocetta, che ſi porta in mano dagli imperadori e da' re.*

MO'NDAY, *Lunedì, il ſecondo dì del'a ſettimana.*

MO'NEY, *moneta; metallo, coniato, danaro.*

MO'NEYBAG, s. *il ſacco de' denari.*

MO'NEYCHANGER, s. *ſenſale di denaro.*

MO'NEYED, adj. *che poſſiede in contanti anzi che in terreni.*

MO'NEYLESS, adj. [pennyleſs] *povero, ſenza danari.*

MO'NEYMATTER, s. *conto fra creditore e debitore.*

MO'NGER, s. a merchant, now added to ſeveral mercantile traders, ex.
A cheeſemonger, *formaggiajo, pizzicagnolo.*
A fiſhmonger, *peſciajuolo, peſcivendolo,* s. m.
A woodmonger, *un mercante di legna.*
An ironmonger, *mercante di ferro.*
A fellmonger, *un pellicciajo.*
A news monger, *un novelliſta.*
A whore monger, *un puttaniere.*
Monger [fiſher boat] *barca da peſcatore.*

MO'NGREL, adj. [got by two kinds] *generato da due ſpezie.*
A mongrel, s. [one that is born of parents of ſeveral countries] *un mulatto.*

MO'NIER, s. [mint man] *monetiere,* s. m. *che batte la moneta.*
Monier [banker] *un banchiero.*

To MO'NISH, v. To admoniſh.

MO'NISHER, v. Monitor.

MONI'TION, s. [exhortation, warning] *ammonizione, eſortazione,* s. f. *avertimento,* s. m.

MO'NITOR, s. [admoniſher, warner] *ammonitore,* s. m. *che ammoniſce, che conſiglia.*

MO'NITORY, adj. *monitorio, che ammoniſce.*
Monitory letters, *lettere monitorie.*

MONK, s. [one that lives in a monaſtery] *monaco,* s. m.
Monk's hood [an herb] *aconito,* s. m.

MO'NKERY, s. *monachiſmo, monacato,* s. m.

MO'NKEY, s. *ſcimia, bertuccia,* s. f.
A little monkey, *un bertuccino.*
A large monkey, *un ſcimmione, un bertuccione.*

MO'NKLY, adj. *monacale, monachile, monaſtico.*
A monkly habit, *abito monacale.*

MO'NOCHORD, s. [a muſical inſtrument] *monocordo,* s. m. *ſtrumento muſicale.*

MONO'CULAR, adj. [one ey'd] *loſco, cieco d' un occhio.*

MONO'GAMY, s. [the marrying of one only wife] *monogamia,* s. f.

MONO'GRAM, s. [a cypher or character conſiſting of one or more letters interwoven together, alſo a ſentence in one line, or epigram in one verſe] *monogramma,* s. m.

MONO'LOGY, } s. [ſoliloquy] *ſo-*
MONOLOGUE, } *liloquio,* s. m.

MONO'MACHY, s. [a ſingle combat, or fighting a duel] *un duello.*

MONO'POLIST, } s. [one that in-
MONOPOLI'ZER, } groſſes all commodity or trade to himſelf] *un monopoliſta, incettatore.*

To MONO'POLIZE [to ingroſs all a commodity, or trade, into one's own hands] *monopolizzare, incettare.*

MONO'POLY, s. [an ingroſſing of commodities] *monipolio, e monopolio,* s. m. *quella incetta che ſi fa comprando tutta una mercanzia per eſſer ſolo a venderla.*

MONOSY'LLABLE, s. [a word of one ſyllable] *monoſillaba,* s. f. *parola d' una ſillaba.*

MO'NSTER, s. [a miſhapen living creature] *moſtro,* s. m. *animale generato con membra fuor dell' uſo della natura.*
A ſea monſter, *un moſtro marino.*
A monſter [in morality] *moſtro, coſa moſtruoſa.*
A monſter of pride, *un moſtro di ſuperbia.*

MONSTROSITY, } s. [monſtruouſ-
MONSTRUOSITY, } neſs] *monſtruoſità,* s. f. *coſa moſtruoſa.*

MO'NSTRUOUS, adj. [like a monſter] *moſtruoſo, che ha del moſtro.*
Monſtruous [prodigious] *moſtruoſo, prodigioſo.*

MO'NSTRUOUSLY, adv. *moſtruoſamente, prodigioſamente.*

MO'NSTRUOUSNESS, s. *moſtruoſità,* s. f. *coſa moſtruoſa.*

MONTEFIA'SCO, s. [a rich wine made at Montefiaſcone in Italy] *Montefiaſcone,* s. m. *ſpezie di vino.*

MONTE'RO, s. [a ſort of cap uſed by ſeamen and hunters] *montiera,* s. f.

MONTE'TH, s. [a baſon to cool glaſſes in] *ſpezie di bacile del quale ſi ſervono in Inghilterra per infreſcare i bicchieri.*

MONTH, s. [a part of the year] *meſe,* s. m.

A twelve month [a year] *un anno.*
To have a month's mind to a thing, *desiderare ardentemente una cosa, averne gran voglia o desiderio.*
Women's months [monthly flowers] *mesi, mestrui.*
MO'NTHLY, adj. *che accade ogni mese; che si fa ogni mese; una volta il mese.*
MO'NUMENT, s. [remembrance, memorial] *monumento,* s. m.
Monument [tomb] *monumento, sepolcro,* s. m.
MOOD [humour] *umore, capriccio,* s. m. *fantasia,* s. f.
To be in a good mood, *esser di buon umore.*
To be in a drinking mood, *esser d'umore di bere.*
A mood of a verb [in grammar] *modo d' un verbo.*
MO'ODY, adj. [humoursome] *capriccioso, fantastico.*
MOON, s. [one of the seven planets] *la luna, uno de' sette pianeti.*
Full moon, *plenilunio, luna piena.*
New moon, *luna nuova.*
He would make me believe that the moon is made of green cheese, *egli vorrebbe mostrarmi lucciole per lanterne.*
Moon-shine, *chiaro di luna.*
Moon-shiny-night, *notte serena, che fa chiaro di luna.*
Moon-ey'd, adj. *che vede meglio al chiaro della luna che non nel giorno.*
A moon-ey'd-horse, *un cavallo lunatico.*
Moon-calf [a false conception] *mola,* s. f. *bugiarda pregnezza.*
Moon-struck, adj. *lunatico, matto, imparrato.*
MOOR, s. [fen] *pantano, stagno,* s. m. *palude, melma.*
Moor, or black moor, *un moro, una mora.*
Moor's head [the head of a still] *campana di lambicco.*
Moor hen, *folaga,* s. f. *uccello aquatico noto.*
To MOOR [to lay out the anchor] *gettar l' ancora, dar fondo.*
To moor a ship, *fermare un vascello con l' ancora.*
MO'ORED, adj. *fermato con ancora.*
MO'ORISH, adj. *pantanoso, paludoso, melmoso.*
Moorish [Moor like] *Moresco.*
MOOT, s. [a disputation in law] *disputa in legge su qualche punto supposto.*
Moot hall, *la sala dove si disputa in legge.*
Moot case, *questione legale.*
Moot man, *disputante in legge.*
To MOOT [as lawyers do] *disputare di qualche materia legale.*
MOP, s. [utensil for washing of houses] *spazzatojo per lavare le camere.*
To MOP, ex. To mop and mow, *fare il grugno.*
MOPE, s. [a dull blockish fellow] *uno sciocco, un cionno, un minchione.*
To MOPE [to become stupid, or sottish] *divenir stupido, stupidire,* pres. *stupidisco.*

MO'PED, adj. *stupidito, stupido, insensato.*
MO'PE-EY'D, } adj. [dim sighted]
MO'PSICAL } *losco, di corta vista.*
MO'PPET, } s. *fantoccio di stracci*
MOPSEY, } *con cui le bambine si divertono.*
MO'PUS, s. [a drone, a dreamer] *uno che vive sempre chiribizzando per soverchio ozio.*
MO'RA, s. [a sort of play with the fingers] *mora,* s. f. *giuoco, che si fa alzando le dita d' una delle manie chiamando il numero.*
MO'RAL, adj. [belonging to manners] *morale, appartenente a costume.*
The moral-philosophy, *la filosofia morale.*
A good moral man, *un uomo che vive moralmente.*
Moral, ex. The moral of a fable, *la morale d' una favola.*
MO'RALIST, s. *colui che dà, o spiega i precetti della morale.*
MO'RALITY, s. [moral principles] *moralità,* s. f.
A man of morality, *un uomo dabbene.*
Morality [moral sense] *moralità, senso morale.*
To MO'RALIZE [to give the moral sense, or to make moral reflections] *moralizzare, ridurre a moralità.*
To moralize a fable, *moralizzare sopra una favola.*
To moralize [to discourse of morality] *moralizzare, discorrere di morale.*
MO'RALIZED, adj. *moralizzato.*
MO'RALLY, adv. [in a moral sense] *moralmente, con moralità.*
Morally [likely] *moralmente verisimilmente.*
Morally speaking, *moralmente parlando.*
Morally [according to the dictates of natural reason] *moralmente, secondo i dettami della ragione naturale.*
MO'RALS, s. [moral philosophy] *la morale.*
A man of good morals, *un uomo dabbene, un uomo di probità, un uomo costumato, di buoni costumi.*
MORASS. s. [moorish ground, marsh, a fen] *un pantano, una palude, un luogo pantanoso, o paludoso.*
MO'RBID, adj. *ammalato, morboso, non sano.*
MO'RBIDNESS, s. *male, malore, morbo.*
MORBI'FICAL, } adj. [that causes
MORBI'FICK, } diseases] *che causa, o genera delle malattie, o morbi.*
MORBO'SE, adj. *malato, che ha morbo, non sano.*
MORDA'CIOUS, adj. *mordace, che morde.*
MORDA'CITY, s. [sharpness of speech] *mordacità, maldicenza,* s. f.
MORE, adj. [the comparative of much and of many] *più di vantaggio.*
Much more, a great deal more, *molto più, via più.*

More and more, *di più in più.*
More than enough, *più che non bisogna.*
Give me some more, *datemente più.*
If you provoke me any more, *se mi fate andare in collera.*
I attribute it more to his good luck, than to his wisdom, *l'attribuisco più tosto alla sua fortuna, che al suo sapere.*
I spoke to him no more but once, *non li ho parlato più d' una volta.*
There's nothing that I love more, *l' amo sopra ogn' altra cosa.*
'Tis more than I knew, *non lo sapevo.*
'Tis more than every one will believe, *non tutti crederanno ciò facilmente.*
He robbed him, and more than that, he kill'd him, *lo rubò, e non contento di questo l'ammazzò.*
He made no more of it [he proceeded no further] *non ne parlò più.*
A little more and he had been drown'd, *poco mancò che non s'annegasse.*
To make more of a thing than it is, *esaggerare, aggrandire una cosa.*
Once more, *ancora una volta, un' altra volta.*
The more haste the worst speed, *più uno s'affretta meno avanza.*
So much the more, *tanto più.*
MO'REL, s. [a sort of plant] *spezie d'erba.*
Morel [a kind of cherry] *sorte di ciriegia.*
MOREO'VER, conj. *di più, ol tre a ciò.*
MO'RESK, adj. ex. moresk work [antick painting or carving] *lavoro moresco.*
MORI'GEROUS, adj. [obedient, dutiful] *obbediente, sommesso.*
MO'RIL, s. [a sort of mushroom] *spezie di fungo.*
MO'RION, s. [a sort of steel cap, or head-piece] *morione,* s. m. *armadura del capo.*
MORI'SCO, s. [a morris, or moorish dance] *moresca,* s. f. *sorta di ballo.*
MO'RISH [from more] ex. It tastes morish, *è si buono che mi fa venire la voglia d'averne di più.*
MO'RKING, s. [a wild beast dead by sickness or mischance] *bestia salvatica morta di malattia, o per accidente.*
MORLING, } s. [the wool of a
MO'RTLING, } dead sheep] *la lana d'una pecora morta.*
MORN, s. [the first part of the day] *l' alba, l'aurora.*
MO'RNING, s. *la mattina.*
To rise early in the morning, *levarsi per tempo, a buon' ora.*
'Tis something cold now in the morning, *fa un poco freddo la mattina adesso.*
The morning star, *lucifero,* s. m. *la stella di venere quando è mattutina.*
The morning prayers, *le preghiere della mattina, mattutino,* s. m.
Morning's draught, *quel che si beve la mattina a digiuno.*

To

To wish one a good morning, *dare il buon giorno ad uno.*

A morning gown, *una vesta de camera.*

Moro'se, adj. [sullen] *aromatico, rematico, fastidioso, fantastico, bisbetico, ostico, sdegnoso, ritroso.*

Moro'seness, } s. *fantasticaggine,*
Moro'sity, } *sdegnosità,* s. f. *capriccio, fastidio,* s. m.

Mo'rphew, s. [a kind of white scurf upon the body, or tawny spots on the face] *morfia,* s. f. *macchie bianche e ruvide che vengono sopra la pelle.*

Mo'rris-Dance, s. [morisco] *moresca,* s. f. *spezie di ballo.*

Nine mens morris [a kind of play with nine holes in the ground] *sorta di giuoco.*

Mo'rrow, adj. *dimane, domane, il giorno vegnente.*

After to morrow, *posdomane, posdomani.*

The morrow, *il giorno seguente.*

Good morrow, *buon dì, buon giorno.*

Morse, s. *un cavallo marino.*

Mo'rsel, s. [a bit] *un pezzo, un tozzo, un boccone, un bocconcino.*

A morsel of bread, *un tozzo di pane.*

To be brought to a morsel of bread, *esser ridotto a mendicare.*

Mo'rtal, adj. [liable to death] *mortale, che è soggetto a morte.*

Mortal [deadly, dangerous] *mortale, pericoloso.*

A mortal hatred, *un odio mortale.*

Mo'rtals, s. [men] *i mortali, gli uomini.*

Morta'lity, s. [mortal condition or nature] *mortalità, stato, o natura mortale.*

Mortality, s. [great sickness] *mortalità,* s. f.

Mortality, s. [death] *morte, morte subita.*

Mo'rtally, adv. [deadly] *mortalmente, che apporta morte, a morte.*

He was mortally wounded, *egli fu ferito a morte.*

Mortally [grievously] *mortalmente, gravemente, molto, estremamente.*

Mo'rtar, s. [a vessel wherein things are pounded] *mortajo,* s. m. *vaso nel quale si pestan le materie.*

Mortar } s. [lime and sand mixt to-
Morter } gether] *calcina,* s. f. *gesso, smalto,* s. m.

A mortar, or mortar-piece [to shoot off bombs] *mortajo,* s. m. *strumento militare.*

Mo'rtgage, s. [a pawn of lands and tenements, or any thing moveable, laid or bound for money borrowed] *pegno, ipoteca di cose mobili e immobili.*

To Mo'rtgage, *ingaggiare ad usura, ipotecare.*

Mo'rtgaged, adj. *ingaggiato, ipotecato.*

Mo'rtgagee, s. [the party to whom any thing is pawned or mortgaged] *quello, o quella che ha un ipoteca.*

Mortga'ger, s. [the party who has made a mortgage] *quello, o quella che ha ingaggiato.*

Mortife'rous, adj. [deadly] *mortifero, mortale, che apporta morte.*

Mortifica'tion, s. *mortificazione,* s. f.

Mortification [in surgery, loss of life, or of nature, heat and sense in any member] *mortificazione, appresso i medici significa una totale estinzione del calor nativo in qualche membro, come avviene nelle cancrene.*

To Mo'rtify [to afflict] *mortificare, affliggere,* pret. *afflissi.*

To mortify [to subdue] *mortificare, reprimere, rintuzzare.*

To mortify one's passions, *mortificare, reprimere le sue passioni.*

To mortify [to vex, to humble] *mortificare, umiliare.*

To mortify [in cookery, to make flesh grow tender, to keep it till has a hogo] *mortificare la carne.*

Mo'rtify'd, adj. *mortificato, afflitto,* v. To mortify.

Mortify'ing, s. *mortificamento, il mortificare.*

Mo'rtise, s. [the hole which is cut in a piece of wood or rafter, to let in another] *scavo,* s. m. *tacca,* s. f.

To Mo'rtise [to put in, or join by mortise] *incastrare, congegnare, commettere l'una cosa dentro dell' altra.*

Mo'rtised, adj. *incastrato, congegnato, commesso.*

Mo'rtling, s. [morling] *lana di pecora morta.*

Mo'rtpay, s. [dead pay, payment not made] *paga morta, pagamento non fatto.*

Mo'rtress [a dish of meat of various kinds beaten together] *cibi di varie sorte pesti insieme.*

Mo'rtuary, s. [a gift left by a man at his death to the church] *legato, o donazione fatta da alcuno alla chiesa poco prima di morire, nell' agonia.*

Mo'rtuum Caput, s. [the gross or earthly substance which is left of any mix'd body, when the moisture is drawn out] *testa morta, termine chimico.*

Mosa'ical, } adj. [belonging to
Mosa'ick, } Moses] *Mosaico, di Mosè,* Ex. The Mosaical law, *la legge Mosaica.*

Mosaick work [a curious work wrought with stones of all colours, artificially set together upon a wall or floor] *Mosaico, pitture fatte di pietruzze, o di pezzuoli di smalto colorati, e commessi.*

Mosche'to [a kind of gnat] *moscherino,* s. m.

Mo'sque, s. [a temple or church among the Turks] *moschea, meschita,* s. f. *tempio de' Turchi.*

Moss, s. [a kind of plant growing upon trees, stones, and some earths] *muschio, musco, erba nota che nasce sopra i pedali degli alberi, e altrove.*

A rolling stone never gathers moss, *pietra che rotola non fa muffa.*

Moss-troopers, *una banda di ladri nella Scozia settentrionale, come erano un tempo i banditi nel regno di Napoli.*

Mo'sses [moorish or boggy places in Lancashire] *pantani, paludi, luoghi paludosi.*

Mo'ssiness, s. [in fruits and herbs] *lanugine, che viene a certi frutti ed a certe erbe.*

Mossiness [downy hair] *lanugine, peli morbidi che cominciano ad apparire a' giovani nelle guance.*

Mossiness, s. [the state of being covered or overgrown with moss] *lo essere ricoperto di muschio, o musco.*

Mo'ssy, adj. [full of moss] *pieno, o coperto di muschio, o di mosco.*

Most [the superlative of much] *il più, le più, le più molto.*

The most beautiful, *il più bello.*

Most often, most commonly, most usually, *il più spesso, ordinariamente, comunemente.*

The most agreeable woman, *la più leggiadra donna.*

A most learned man, *un uomo molto dotto, o dottissimo.*

When the most part of the night was spent, *la notte essendo molto avanzata.*

Most are of your opinion, *la più gran parte è del vostro parere.*

The most part, *la maggior parte.*

Most of us, *la maggior parte di noi.*

At the most, *al più.*

To live most upon fruits, *viver per lo più di frutti, non mangiar quasi che frutti.*

Most of all, *principalmente.*

Mo'stick, s. [a painter's staff] *la canna o bastoncino su cui il pittore appoggia la mano nel dipingere.*

Mo'stly, adj. [generally] *generalmente, ordinariamente, per ordinario, communemente.*

Mote, s. *una briciola, ogni cosa picciolissima.*

Moth, s. [a vermin that eats cloaths] *tignuola,* s. f. *tarlo,* s. m.

Moth eaten, *roso dalle tignuole, tarlato.*

Mo'ther, s. [she that has brought forth a child] *madre,* s. f.

A mother in law, *suocera.*

A grandmother, *ava.*

A mother in law, or step-mother, *matrigna.*

Mother of pearl, *madreperla.*

Diffidence is the mother of safety, *la diffidenza è la madre della sicurtà.*

Every mother's child, *ognuno, ciascheduno.*

A mother city, *una città capitale, o metropoli.*

Mother tongue, *lingua materna.*

Mother [womb] *madre, matrice.*

A fit of the mother, *un dolore della matrice.*

Mother-wort, *matricale,* s. m. *erba nota.*

Mo'therhood, s. *qualità di madre.*

Mo'therless, adj. *che non ha madre, senza madre.*

MO'THERLY, adj. [of a mother] *maternale, materno, di madre.*
Motherly love, *amor materno.*
A motherly woman, *una matrona, una donna autorevole per età o per dignità.*
Motherly, adv. *da madre, come una madre.*
MO'THY, adj. *pien di tignuole, roso dalle tignuole, tarlato.*
MO'TION, s. [the act of a natural body, which moves or stirs itself] *moto, movimento,* s. m.
Motion [inclination, disposition] *movimento, inclinazione, voglia, disposizione.*
Motion [request] *richiesta, preghiera, istanza, sollecitazione.*
Motion [proposal, overture] *proposizione, apertura.*
Motion [will, accord] *moto, movimento, volontà.*
He did it of his own motion, *lo fece di suo proprio moto.*
To MO'TION [to propose] *proporre far una proposizione.*
MO'TIONED, adj. *mosso, proposto.*
MO'TIONER, s. *quegli che propone una cosa.*
MO'TIONLESS, adj. *immobile, senza moto.*
MO'TIVE, adj. [or moving] *motrice, movitrice.*
The motive faculty, *la facoltà motrice.*
Motive, s. [inducement, reason moving] *motivo, causa, ragione, ragione, occasione,* s. f. *impulso,* s. m.
MO'TLEY, adj. [mixt] *maculato, chiazzato.*
A motley colour, *un color chiazzato.*
MO'TOR, s. [mover] *motore, colui che muove, o la facoltà che muove.*
MO'TORY, adj. *movente, che da moto, che mette in moto.*
MO'TTO, s. [a word, or short sentence put to an emblem, device, or coat of arms] *motto,* s. m.
MO'VABLE, } adj. [that may be MO'VEABLE, } moved] *mobile, atto a muoversi.*
A moveable feast, *festa mobile.*
Moveable goods, *beni mobili.*
MO'VABLENESS, } s. [aptness to MO'VEABLENESS, } move] *mobilità,* s. f.
MOVE, s. [a move at chess or draughts] *mossa,* s. f.
To MOVE [to stir, to shake] *movere, e muovere, scuotere, agitare,* pret. *mossi, scossi.*
To move a thing [to propose it, to speak for it] *muovere, proporre una cosa.*
To move [to stir up, to egg on, to persuade] *muovere, indurre, persuadere, commuovere, esortare, sollecitare.*
To move to sedition, *muovere, eccitare alla sedizione.*
What could move him to do so? *che cosa l'ha mai mosso a far ciò?*
To move one to do good, *eccitare, persuadere, muovere alcuno a ben fare.*
To move [to affect] *movere, toccare, intenerire,* pres. *intenerisco.*
To move to compassion, *muovere a pietà, o compassione.*
To move one to anger, *fare andare in collera alcuno, irritarlo, provocarlo all' ira.*
To move laughter, *muover le risa.*
MOVE'ABLE, v. Movable.
MO'VED, adj. *mosso,* v. To move.
MO'VELESS, adj. [unmoved, not to be put out of the place] *immobile, da non esser mosso.*
MO'VEMENT, s. [or motion] *movimento, moto,* s. m.
MO'VENT, } s. *motore, movitore,* s. MOVER, } m. *motrice, movitrice,* s. f.
MO'VING, s. *movimento, il movere.*
Moving, adj. [affective, touching] *che move a compassione, che intenerisce.*
Moving [forcible, powerful] *forte, potente, persuasivo, patetico, che tocca.*
A moving reason, *motivo.*
MO'VINGLY, adv. [pathetically; in such a manner as to seize the passions] *in modo patetico, e atto a muover il cuore.*
MOULD, s. [a form wherein any thing is cast] *forma,* s. f. *modello,* s. m.
A mould cannon, *un cannone di getto.*
Mould [earth mixt with dung] *terra,* s. f.
To MOULD [to cast into a mould] *gettare.*
To mould a figure, *gettare una figura.*
To mould bread, *far del pane, impastare.*
To mould [to fashion] *formare, fare.*
To mould, verb neut. [to grow mouldy] *muffare divenir muffato.*
MO'ULDABLE, adj. *che si può formare.*
MO'ULDED, adj. *gettato, formato, fatto.*
Moulded [mouldy] *muffato.*
To MO'ULDER, } [to fall to To MO'ULDER AWAY, } dust] *ridursi, o andare in polvere.*
To moulder [to be consumed, to be wasted] *fondersi, struggersi, consumarsi.*
MO'ULDERED, adj. *ridotto in polvere.*
MO'ULDINESS, s. [from mouldy] *muffa,* s. f.
MO'ULDING, s. [in architecture, ornaments either of wood or stone] *modanatura,* s. f. *termine degli architetti. Foggia, componimento di membretti, come di cornici, base, e simili membri.*
Moulding [that which bears up an arch] *imposta,* s. f.
MO'ULDWARP, s. [mole] *talpa, animaletto noto.*
MO'ULDY, adj. [hoary with mouldiness] *muffato.*
To MOULT [to cast the feathers, as birds do] *mudare, dicesi degli uccelli, quando rinnuovan le penne.*
MO'ULTER, s. [a young moulting duck] *anitrino, che è in muda.*
To MOUNCH [to eat] *mangiare, rodere.*
MOUND, s. [hedge, bank] *una siepe, una ripa, un argine.*
Mound [fence, rampier] *terrapieno, baluardo.*
To MOUND [to fence] *munire, fortificare, terrapienare.*
MOUNT, s. [hill] *monte,* s. m. *montagna,* s. f.
Mount Ætna, *il Monte Etna.*
To MOUNT [to go up, to get up] *montare, andare, salire ad alto.*
To mount a horseback, *montare a cavallo.*
To mount the breach, *montare la breccia.*
To mount the guard, *montar la guardia.*
To mount a trooper [to give him a horse] *montare un cavaliere.*
To mount a cannon [to lay it on the carriage] *montare un cannone.*
MO'UNTAIN, s. [hill] *montagna,* s. f. *monte,* s. m.
To make mountains of mole hills, *fare d'una mosca un elefante.*
A little mountain, *una montagnetta, una montagnuola.*
MO'UTAINEER, s. [an inhabitant of the mountains] *abitatore di monti; un che abita ne' monti.*
Mountaineer [a savage, a free-booter, a rustick] *un selvaggio, un rustico, un ladrone che stiasi appiattato ne' monti.*
MO'UNTAINET, s. [a hillock] *una collinetta, una montagnuola.*
MO'UNTAINOUS, adj. [hilly] *montagnoso.*
MO'UNTEBANK, s. [a juggling, quacking pretender to physick] *montinbanco, cerretano,* s. m.
MO'UNTED, adj. *montato.*
Our ship had seventy guns mounted, *il nostro vascello portava settanta cannoni.*
MO'UNTING, s. *montamento,* s. m. *il montare.*
MOUNTS, adj. [the raising of a hawk] *l'alzarsi d'un falcone.*
To MOURN [to lament, to bewail] *piagnere, lamentare, compiagnere,* pret. *piansi, compiansi.*
To mourn for a dead friend, *piagner la morte d'un amico.*
To mourn for one, *portar bruno per uno.*
To mourn for one's sins, *piagnere i suoi peccati.*
MO'URNED [mourned for] adj. *pianto, lamentato, lagrimato, compianto.*
MO'URNER, s. *piagnone,* s. m. *quegli che in gramaglia accompagna il morto.*
MO'URNFUL, adj. *piagnevole, e piangevole, lugubre, dolente, tristo.*

Mo'URNFULLY, adv. *cordogliosamente, dogliosamente.*

Mo'URNING, s. [affliction] *duolo, dolore,* s. m. *passione, doglia, afflizione, pena,* s. f.

Mourning [black cloaths] *bruno,* s. m. *gramaglia,* s. f. *abito lugubre, abito di lutto, di scorruccio.*

MOUSE, s. [a domestick creature well known] *sorcio, topo,* s. m.

A little, or young mouse, *un topolino.*

A mouse trap, *una trappola.*

Mouse-ear [a sort of herb] *pelosella,* s. f. *spezie d'erba.*

A field mouse, *sorcio campestre.*

A dormouse, *un ghiro.*

A flitter mouse, *una nottola.*

To MOUSE [to catch mice] *prender sorci.*

Mo'USER, s. [*che piglia topi*] ex. This cat is a good mouser, *questa gatta piglia molti sorci.*

MOUTH, s. [a part of the body] *bocca,* s. f.

The mouth of the stomach, *la bocca dello stomaco.*

The mouth of an oven, of a cannon, *la bocca d'un forno, d'un cannone.*

To stop one's mouth [to make him hold his tongue] *chiuder la bocca ad uno, farlo tacere.*

To tell a thing by word of mouth, *dire una cosa a bocca, o di viva voce.*

The mouth of a haven, *l'entratura, o l'entrata d'un porto.*

The mouth of a river, *l'imboccatura d'un fiume.*

To live from hand to mouth, *vivere alla giornata.*

They take our bread out of our mouths, *ci levano il pane della bocca.*

He that sends mouths sends meat, *Iddio provede a tutti, se ci manda figliuoli ci da anrora il modo da mantenerli.*

He is ready to creep into his mouth, *egli l'ama appassionatamente.*

To have one's mouth out of taste, *aver il gusto corrotto.*

To have one's heart in one's mouth [to be possessed with a sudden fear] *aver gran paura.*

'Tis in every body's mouth, *è nelle lingue d'ognuno, ognuno ne parla.*

To make mouths, *fare smorfie.*

A mouthful, *un boccone, una boccata.*

To MOUTH [to catch with the mouth, as a dog, &c.] *afferrare, acchiappare colla bocca.*

MOUTHED, adj. ex. wide mouthed, *che ha una gran bocca.*

Wry-mouthed, *che ha bocca storta.*

Foul-mouthed, *che ha una cattiva lingua, maldicente; osceno.*

Mo'UTHLESS, adj. *senza bocca, che non ha bocca.*

MOW, s. [heap] *mucchio, cumulo,* s. m. *bica,* s. f.

A mow of hay, *una bica di fieno.*

To MOW [to cut down with a scythe] *segare, mietere.*

To mow [to make mouths] *fare il grugno.*

To mow at one, *far il grugno ad uno.*

Mo'WED, } adj. *segato, mietuto.*
Mo'WEN, }

MO'WER, s. *segatore, mietitore,* s. m.

Mo'WING, s. *il segare, segamento.*

Mowing time, *segatura, mietitura, ricolta,* s. f.

Mowing [making wry mouths] *grugno,* s. m.

MUCH, adv. *molto.*

He is much older than I, *egli è molto più vecchio di me.*

By much, *di molto, via più.*

Much more, *molto più, via più.*

Much good may it d'ye, *buon pro vi faccia.*

With much ado, *a grande stento, a mala pena.*

You are much mistaken, *voi v' ingannate di molto.*

This is much the same thing, *è quasi la medesima cosa.*

To make much of one, *far mille carezze ad uno, accoglierlo benignamente farsi mille accoglienze, far grande stima d'alcuno.*

To make much of one's self, *trattarsi bene, o delicatamente.*

To make much of one another, *riamarsi.*

To make much of one's time, *impiegar bene il suo tempo, spender bene il suo tempo.*

She can make much of him, *ella può molto con lui.*

He thinks much to come to me, *egli fa difficoltà, o scrupolo di venirmi a vedere.*

How much, *quanto.*

As much, *tanto, altrettanto.*

As much as you will, *quanto vi piacerà.*

As much as you, *al par di voi, altrettanto che voi.*

I did as much as laid in my power, *ho fatto quanto ho potuto.*

Had I known as much, *se avessi saputo questo, se l'avessi saputo.*

I'll do as much for you, *farò altrettanto per voi.*

As much again, or as much more, *una volta più.*

It is much that you won't mind your own business, *strana cosa in vero, che voi non vogliate aver cura de' vostri interessi.*

So much *tanto.*

If she be ever so handsome, *per bella ch' ella sia.*

He has not spared so much as his own son, *non l'ha perdonata nè meno al suo proprio figliuolo.*

If you you should desire it never so much, *per grandi che fossero le vostre istanze.*

Will you do so much as to write this letter for me? *volete favorirmi di scrivere questa lettera?*

So much for this time, *tanto basti per adesso.*

Thus much, *tanto.*

But thus much of these things, *ma non più di queste cose.*

Very much, *molto.*

Too much of any thing is good for nothing, *il soverchio rompe il coperchio.*

MU'CILAGE, s. [a viscous extraction made of seeds, roots, gums, &c. with water] *mucilagine, mucellagine,* s. f. *sugo viscoso premuto da' semi, radici, erbe, o pomi.*

MUCILA'GINOUS, adj. [slimy] *mucilaginoso, e mucellaginoso.*

MUCK, s. [dung] *letame, stabbio, concime, sterco delle bestie.*

Muck and pelf [what an usurer scrapes up] *guadagno sordido.*

A muck hill, *letamajo,* s. m.

A muck worm, *un verme di letamajo; un avaro.*

He is a mere muck worm, *egli è un vero spilorcio.*

Muck, adj. [moist, wet] *umido, bagnato, molle.*

To be in a muck sweat, *esser molle di sudore.*

To run a muck [to run madly and attack what we meet] *correre all' impazzata ad attaccarla con chiunque s'incontra per via.*

To MUCK [to dung] *letamare, concimare.*

MU'CKED, adj. *letamato, concimato.*

MU'CKENDER, s. [a child's handkerchief] *moccichino da fanciulli.*

MU'COUS, adj. [slimy] *viscoso, attaccaticcio.*

MU'CUS, s. *mucco, cimurro, escremento del naso.*

Mucus, s. *ogni cosa di natura viscosa e attaccaticcia.*

MUD, s. [slime, mire] *fango, luto,* s. m. *belletta, melma,* s. f.

To fall into the mud, *infangarsi, cascar nel fango.*

A mud wall, *muro fatto di paglia e fango.*

To MUD, *sotterrare nel fango o nella mota.*

To mud, *intorbidar l'acqua movendone il fango che è al fondo.*

MU'DDILY, adv. *fangosamente, torbidamente, con mistura sporca.*

MU'DDINESS, s. *feccia, sedimento, fondacchio, fangosità.*

To MU'DDLE [as geese and ducks do] *sguazzare, render l' acqua torbida.*

To muddle, *render mezzo briaco, far vacillar la testa con troppo vino.*

MU'DDY, adj. *fangoso, melmoso.*

Muddy water, *acqua torbida.*

A muddy look, *ciera brusca.*

To MU'DDY [to make muddy] *intorbidare, render torbido.*

To muddy water, *intorbidare l' acqua.*

To MUE [to moult, to change feathers] *mudare, cangiar le penne.*

MUFF, s. [a case of fur to put the hands in] *manicotto,* s. m.

To MU'FFLE, } [to wrap up the
To MU'FFLE UP, } mouth and face in

in cloaths] *camuffare, imbacuccare, imbavagliare, incaperucciare.*

MU'FFLED, } adj. *camuffato, im-*
MU'FFLED UP, } *bacuccato, imbavagliato, incaperucciato.*

MU'FFLER, s. *benda di tela che s'attacca al mento.*

MU'FTY, s. [the high prieſt of the Mahometans] *mufti.*

MUG, s. *brocca,* s. f. *vaſo di terra cotta da portare liquori.*

Mug-wort [an herb] *artemiſia,* s. f. *erba.*

MU'GGY, } adj. [moiſt, damp,
MU'GGISH, } mouldy] *umido, bagnato, muffato.*

MU'GHOUSE, s. [an alehouſe, a low houſe of entertainment] *una bettola, un oſteria da birbe.*

MULA'TTO, s. [one born of parents of whom one is a Moor, and the other of another nation] *mulatto.*

MU'LBERRY, s. [a fruit well known] *mora,* s. f. *frutto del moro.*

Mulberry tree, *moro, gelſo,* s. m.

MULCT, s. [penalty] *multa, condannagione, pena, ammenda,* s. f.

A pecuniary mulct, *pena pecuniaria.*

To MULCT [to fine] *condannare all' ammenda.*

To mulct [to puniſh] *punire, caſtigare,* pret. *puniſco.*

MU'LCTED, adj. *condannato all' ammenda, punito caſtigato.*

MU'LCTUARY, adj. ex. A mulctuary puniſhment, *multa, pena, ammenda.*

MULE, s. [a beaſt ingender'd between an aſs and a mare] *mulo,* s. m. *mula,* s. f. *animal nato d'aſino e di cavalla, o di cavallo e d'aſina.*

MU'LE-DRIVER, } *mulattiere,* s. m.
MU'LETEER, } *quegli che guida i muli.*

To MULL WINE [to burn and ſeaſon it with ſpice, ſugar, &c.] *abbruciare del vino, meſcolandovi ſpezierie, zucchero, &c.*

MU'LLED, adj. *abbruciato.*

MU'LLEIN, s. [an herb] *verbena,* s. f.

MU'LLER, s. [a ſtone to grind colours] *macinetta, marinella,* s. f.

MU'LLET, s. [a ſort of fiſh] *muggine,* s. m. *ſpezie di peſce di mare.*

MULSE, s. [wine mingled and boiled up with honey] *vino ed acqua con miele.*

MULTIFA'RIOUS, adj. [frequent] *frequente, comune.*

Multifarious [of diverſe or ſundry ſorts] *di diverſe maniere, differente.*

MU'LTIPLE, adj. *moltiplice.*

MU'LTIPLIABLE, } adj. *moltiplica-*
MU'LTIPLICABLE, } *bile, che ſi può moltiplicare.*

MULTI'PLICAND, s. [a term of arithmetick, number to be multiply'd] *il numero da moltiplicare.*

MULTIPLICA'TION, s. [one of the principal rules in arithmetick] *moltiplicazione.*

MULTIPLICA'TOR, *v.* Multiplier.

MULTIPLI'CITY, s. [multitude, great deal] *moltiplicità, moltitudine, quantità, numero grande.*

MU'LTIPLI'ER, s. *moltiplicatore,* s. m.

To MU'LTIPLY [to increaſe] *moltiplicare, accreſcer di numero e di quantità.*

To multiply [in arithmetick, to proceed according to the rule of multiplication] *moltiplicare, termine aritmètico.*

MU'LTIPLY'D, adj. *moltiplicato.*

MU'LTIPLYING, s. *moltiplicamento,* s. m. *moltiplicazione,* s. f. *il moltiplicare.*

MU'LTITUDE, s. [great number] *moltitudine,* s. f. *copioſo numero.*

The multitude [the vulgar, or mobile] *la moltitudine, il volgo, il popolo minuto, la plebe.*

MU'LTURE, s. [a law word, for the miller's fee for grinding] *molenda, mulenda,* s. f. *il prezzo, che ſi paga della marinatura al mugnajo o in farina o in danari.*

MUM, s. [a ſort of thick beer] *mum, ſpezie di birra.*

MUM, interj. [ſilence] *ſta zitto.*

To MU'MBLE [to mutter] *mormorare, borbottare.*

To mumble [to chew] *maſticare a bocca chiuſa.*

MU'MBLED, adj. *mormorato, borbottato, maſticato a bocca chiuſa.*

MU'MBLER, s. *borbottatore, borbottone,* s. m.

MU'MBLING, s. *borbottamente, borbottio,* s. m. *il borbottare.*

MU'MMER, s. [maſk] *una maſchera, una perſona maſcherata.*

MU'MMERY, s. *maſcherata,* s. f.

MU'MMING, adj. ex. To go a mumming to a ball, *andare ad un ballo in maſchera.*

MU'MMY [an embalmed corpſe] *mummia, cadavero ſecco, corpo imbalſamato.*

To beat one to mummy [to bruiſe him all over] *ammaccare il viſo ad uno a forza di pugni, batterlo, baſtonarlo ben bene.*

To MUMP [to diſappoint] *acchiappare, ingannare.*

I ſhall mump ye, *v'acchiapperò.*

To mump [to ſpunge] *ſcroccare.*

To mump [to beg] *mendicare, andar accattando.*

To mump [to nibble; to bite quick; to chew with a continued motion] *mangiare, mordere, o rodere il cibo digrignando i denti e movendoli preſto preſto, come fanno verbigrazia le ſcimie, e i conigli, dentìcchiare.*

MU'MPED, adj. *acchiappato, ingannato.*

MU'MPER, s. [ſpunger] *ſcroccone,* s. m.

Mumper [beggar] *un pezzente, un' mendico.*

MUMPS, s. [a ſort of quinſey, or ſwelling of the chaps] *ſchinanzia, ſquinanzia,* s. f. *ſtranguglioni.*

To be troubled with the mumps [to be out of humour] *eſſer di cattivo umore.*

To MUNCH [to chew] *maſticare a gran bocconi.*

MU'NCHED, adj. *maſticato.*

MU'NCHER, s. *quello, o quella che maſtica a gran bocconi.*

MU'NCHING, s. *maſticatura,* s. f. *il maſticare.*

MU'NDANE, adj. [worldly] *mondano.*

MUNDA'NITY, s. [worldlineſs] *mondanità.*

MU'NDATORY, adj. [cleanſing] *mondificativo, che ha virtù, e forza di mondificare.*

MUNDIFICA'TION, s. *mondificazione, il mondificare.*

MUNDIFICATIVE, adj. *mondificativo.*

To MU'NDIFY [to cleanſe] *mondificare, nettare, purgare.*

MU'NDIFY'D, adj. *mondificato, nettato, purgato.*

MU'NGREL, *v.* Mongrel.

MUNI'CIPAL, adj. [of or belonging to a corporation] *municipale,* ex. municipal laws, *leggi municipali.*

MUNI'FICENCE, s. [liberality] *munificenza, liberalità.*

MUNI'FICENT, adj. [liberal] *munificente, liberale.*

MUNI'FICENTLY, adv. *liberalmente, con munificenza.*

MU'NIMENT, s. [authentick deeds or writings, by which a man is enabled to defend his title to his eſtate] *titolo,* s. m.

MUNI'TION, s. *munizione, fortificazione,* s. f.

MU'RAGE, s. [a tribute to be paid for the building or repairing of publick walls] *danaro che ſi paga per la coſtruzione, o riſarcimento delle mura pubbliche.*

MU'RAL, adj. [belonging to a wall] *murale, di muro.*

Mural crown [a reward given by the ancient Romans to thoſe ſoldiers who firſt ſcal'd the walls, and firſt entered the enemy's city] *corona murale.*

MU'RDER, } s. [a wilful and felo-
MUR'THER, } nious killing one] *omicidio, aſſaſſinio,* s. m.

To MU'RDER [to kill with malice] *ammazzare, aſſaſſinare.*

To murder a thing [to do it aukwardly] *ſtroppiare una coſa, farla male.*

MU'RDERED, adj. *ammazzato, aſſaſſinato.*

MU'RDERER, s. *aſſaſſino, ſgherano, omicida.*

A ſhe murderer, *un' aſſaſſina.*

A murderer [a ſmall cannon] *mezzo cannone.*

MU'RDERING, s. *omicidio, aſſaſſinamento, aſſaſſinio.*

Murdering, adj. ex. A murdering piece, *una bomba.*

MU'RDEROUS, adj. *crudele, ſanguinolente.*

To MURE UP [to wall up] *murare.*

MU'RED UP, adj. *murato.*

MU'RING, or muring up, s. *muramento,* s. m. *il murare.*

MURK.

Mu'rk, s. [darkneſs, want of light] *bujo, oſcurità, tenebre.*

Murk, s. *la pelle o la ſcorza de' frutti; il mallo.*

Mu'rky, adj. [dark, wanting light] *oſcuro, bujo, tenebroſo, privo di luce.*

Mu'rmur, s. [a humming noiſe] *mormorio, ſuſurro, biſbiglio,* s. m.

To Mu'rmur [to grumble] *mormorare, brontolare, borbottare, ſuſſurrare, biſbigliare.*

Mu'rmured, adj. *mormorato, brontolato, borbottato, ſuſſurrato, biſbigliato.*

Mu'rmurer, s. *mormoratore,* s. m. *mormoratrice,* s. f.

Mu'rmuring, s. *mormoramento, mormorio, biſbiglio, ſuſſurro.*

Mu'rmuringly, adv. *mormorando, borbottando.*

Mu'rnival, s. [four cards of the ſame ſuit, at the game called gleek] *quattro carte del medeſimo grado, come quattro rè, quattro dame, &c.*

A murnival of aces, *quattro aſſi.*

Mu'rrain, s. [rot amongſt cattle] *moria,* s. f. *mortalità peſtilenziale fra'l beſtiame.*

Mu'rrey, s. [a dark red colour] *color roſſo che inclina al nero.*

Mu'rrion, *v.* Morion.

Murth of Corn, *abbondanza di grano.*

Mu'scadel, } s. [a ſort of ſweet
Mu'scadine, } and rich wine] *moſcadello, o vin moſcadello,* s. m.

Muſcadine grapes, *moſcadello, nome d'uva, detta così dal ſuo ſapore, che tien di moſcado.*

Muſcadine, s. *ſorta di pera molto dolce.*

Mu'scle, s. [an inſtrument of voluntary motion, made of fibres and fleſh] *muſcolo, e muſculo,* s. m. *parte carnoſa del corpo dell' animale, compoſta di nervi, carne, e fibre, che ſervi principalmente al moto.*

Muſcle [a ſhell fiſh] *nicchio,* s. m.

Musco'sity, s. [moſſineſs] *l'eſſer pieno o abbondante di quell' erba chiamata muſchio o muſco.*

Mu'scular, adj. [belonging to the muſcles] *muſcolare.*

Mu'sculous, adj. [full of muſcles] *muſcoloſo, e muſculoſo, pien di muſcoli.*

Muse, s. [a goddeſs of poetry] *muſa,* s. f. *nome di deità prepoſta alla poeſia.*

Muſe, s. [deep thought, cloſe attention] *penſiero profondo, contemplazione o meditazione profonda.*

To be in a muſe [in a melancholy fit] *muſare, ſtar penſieroſo.*

To Muse upon [to ſtudy, to think upon] *ruminare, penſare, rifletter, muſare.*

Mu'sed upon, adj. *ruminato, penſato, muſato.*

Mu'shroom, s. *fungo,* s. m.

Muſhroom [an upſtart, a wretch riſen from the dunghill] *un birbone pien d'orgoglio, venuto dal nulla, e ſuperbo perchè ricco.*

Mu'sical, adj. [of muſick] *muſicale, muſico.*

Mu'sically, adv. *da muſico, ſecondo le regole della muſica.*

Musi'cian, s. [a minſtrel, a profeſſor or practitioner of muſick] *un muſico.*

Mu'sick, s. [one of the ſeven liberal ſciences, which conſiders the number, time, and tune of ſounds, in order to make delightful harmony] *muſica,* s. f. *ſcienza della proporzion della voce e de' ſuoni.*

Muſick [harmony] *muſica, melodia, armonia.*

A concert of muſick, *un concerto di muſica.*

A paultry muſick, *muſicaccia, muſica cattiva.*

The muſick room in a play-houſe, *orcheſtra.*

Musk, s. [a ſort of perfume] *muſchio,* s. m.

Perfumed with muſk, *muſcato, e muſchiato.*

Muſk ball, *paſtiglia,* s. f.

A muſk cat, *zibetto, ſpezie d'animale.*

A muſk pear, *pero moſcadello.*

Muſk roſe, *roſa muſcata.*

Mu'sked, adj. *muſcato, muſchiato.*

Mu'sket, s. [a ſort of gun] *moſchetto,* s. m.

A muſket-ſhot, *una moſchettata, colpo di moſchetto.*

Muſket-baſket, *gabbione,* s. m.

Muſket-proof, *a prova di moſchetto.*

A volley of muſket-ſhot, *una ſalva di moſchettate.*

Muſket [a male hawk] *il maſchio dello ſparviere.*

Mu'sketeer, s. *moſchettiero.*

Mu'sketoon, s. [a blunderbuſs] *un moſchettone.*

Mu'skin, s. [titmouſe] *cingallegra,* s. f.

Mu'schy, adj. [fragrant, ſweet of ſcent] *fragrante, di piacevole odore.*

Mu'slin, s. [a thin ſort of cloth made of cotton] *moſſelina,* s. f. *ſpezie di tela finiſſima fatta di bambagia.*

Mu'srol, s. [the noſe band of the bridle of a horſe] *muſeruola, muſoliera,* s. f. *quella parte della brilia che puſſa ſopra i portamorſi per la teſtiera e la guancia per iſtrigner la bocca al cavallo.*

Muss, s. [a ſcramble; an eager conteſt for ſomething] *baruffa; conteſa violente per qualche coſa.*

Mu'ssulman, s. [or Mahometan] *Muſulmano, Maomettano,* s. m.

Must, s. [ſweet wine newly preſs'd from the grape] *moſto,* s. m. *vin nuovo, non ancor ben purificato.*

Muſt, verb imperfect, *biſogna.*

I muſt do it, *biſogna ch' io lo faccia.*

You muſt ſtudy, *vi biſogna ſtudiare.*

It muſt be ſo, *biſogna che ſia così.*

You muſt conſider, *voi dovete conſiderare.*

To Must [to mould, to make mouldy] *marcire, diventar rancido, muffo, o putrido, guaſtarſi.*

Mu'staches, s. [whiſkers] *muſtacchi,* s. m. *baſette.*

Mu'stard, s. *ſenapa,* s. f.

Mu'ster, s. [a review of military forces] *moſtra, raſſegna di ſoldati.*

To paſs muſter, *far la moſtra, o la raſſegna.*

Paſs muſter [faggot] *una paga morta, un paſſavolante.*

A muſter of peacocks [a flock of them] *uno ſtuolo di pavoni.*

A muſter-maſter, *raſſegnatore,* s. m.

To Mu'ster [to review] *raſſegnare, far la raſſegna de' ſoldati.*

To muſter [to ſhow] *moſtrare, far vedere.*

To muſter [to gather together] *adunare, radunare.*

Mu'stiness, s. *rancidezza, muffa,* s. f.

Mu'sty, adj. *rancido, muffato.*

To have a muſty ſmell, *ſentir di muffa.*

Muſty [out of humour] *di cattivo umore.*

Muſty [dull, heavy, wanting activity, wanting practice in the occurrences of life] *ſtupido, pigro, che non ha attività ne eſperienza o pratica delle faccende del mondo.*

Mutabi'lity, s. [changeableneſs] *mutabilità, leggerezza, incoſtanza,* s. f.

Mu'table, adj. [apt to change] *mutabile, leggiero, incoſtante, volubile.*

Mu'tableness, s. *mutabilità, incoſtanza.*

Muta'tion, s. *mutazione, variazione,* s. f.

Mute, adj. [ſpeechleſs] *muto, mutolo, che non parla.*

Mute [not pronounced] *muto, che non ſi pronuncia.*

A mute letter, *una lettera muta, che non ſi pronuncia.*

A mute, s. *un muto.*

Mute [dung] *ſterco.*

To Mute [to dung as hawks do] *ſtallare, parlando degli uccelli.*

To Mu'tilate [to maim] *ſtorpiare, mozzare, troncare.*

Mu'tilated, adj. *ſtorpiato, mozzato, troncato.*

Mutila'tion, s. *ſtorpiatura; ſtroppiatura,* s. f. *ſtorpio, e ſtroppio,* s. m.

Mu'tine, } s. *un ammutinato, un*
Mu'tineer, } *ſedizioſo.*

Mu'tinous, adj. [factious] *ſedizioſo, tumultuoſo, fazioſo.*

A mutinous fellow, *un fazioſo, un ſedizioſo.*

Mu'tinously, adv. *tumultuoſamente, ſedizioſamente.*

Mu'tiny, s. [commotion, ſedition] *ſollevazione, ribellione, ſedizione, rivolta,* s. f.

To Mu'tiny [to raiſe a mutiny] *am-*

ammutinarsi, rivoltarsi, ribellarsi, sollevarsi, abbottinarsi, tumultuare.

To MU'TTER [to speak confusedly between the teeth] *brontolare, borbottare, mormorare.*

To mutter at heaven, *mormorare contro'l cielo.*

What do you mutter? *che borbottate?*

MU'TTERED, adj. *brontolato, borbottato, mormorato.*

MU'TTERER, s. *borbottatore, che borbotta.*

MU'TTERING, s. *borbottare, borbottio,* s. m.

MU'TTON, s. *castrato, carne di castrato.*

MU'TTONFIST, s. *una mano grande, grossa, e rossa.*

MU'TUAL, adj. [reciprocal] *mutuo, scambievole, reciproco.*

MU'TUALLY, adv. *mutuamente, scambievolmente, reciprocamente.*

MUTU'ALITY, s. [reciprocation] *mutualità, cosa reciproca.*

MU'ZZLE, s. [of an ox or a bull] *il muso d'un bue o d'un toro.*

Muzzle [a device of leather to put about the mouth of a dog, &c.] *musoliera, museruola,* s. f. *strumento, che si mette al muso de' cani e d'altri animali che mordono.*

The muzzle of a gun, *la bocca d'una schioppo.*

To MU'ZZLE [to cover or secure the mouth with a muzzle] *mettere una musoliera.*

To muzzle [to fondle with the mouth close] *stroppicciar con tenerezza col viso e a bocca chiusa.*

MU'ZZLED, adj. *che ha una musoliera.*

MY, pron. poss. *mio, mia, miei, mie.*

My father, my mother, *mio padre, mia madre.*

My children, *i miei figliuoli.*

My sisters, *le mie sorelle.*

This is my book, *questo libro è il mio.*

MYNCHEN, s. [a nun] *una monaca.*

MYO'GRAPHY, s. *descrizioni de' muscoli.*

MY'OPY, s. *vista corta.*

MY'RIAD, adj. [ten thousand] *dieci mila.*

MY'RMIDON, s. *uno sgherano, un briccone che insulta e maltratta a torto.*

MYRRH, s. *mirra, sorta di vegetabile odorifissimo.*

MY'RRHINE, adj. *di mirra, odoroso come mirra.*

MY'RTLE, } s. *mirto,* s. m.
MY'RTLE TREE, } *mortella,* s. f.

A myrtle grove, *mirteto, luogo pieno di mirti.*

Myrtle berry, *mirtillo,* s. m. *coccola della mortella.*

Of myrtle, *mirtino, di mirto.*

MYSTE'RIOUS, adj. [secret, obscure] *misterioso, segreto, oscuro.*

MY'STERY, s. [a thing hard to apprehend] *misterio,* s. m. *segreto sacro.*

The mysteries of religion, *i misteri della religione*

Mystery [secret] *mistero, segreto.*

The mysteries of trade, *i segreti del negozio.*

The mysteries of state, *gl' intrighi di stato.*

MY'STICAL, } adj. *mistico, pieno d'o-*
MY'STICK, } *scurità sacra.*

MY'STICALLY, adj. [secret] *mistico, misterioso.*

Mystically, adv. *misticamente, misteriosamente.*

MYTHOLO'GICAL, adj. [belonging to mythology] *mitologico.*

MYTHOLO'GIST, s. [an expounder of fables] *mitologista, espositore di favole.*

To MYTHO'LOGIZE [to expound fables] *spiegare le favole.*

MYTHO'LOGY, s. [a system of fables, or poetical fictions] *mitologia,* s. f. *sistema delle antiche favole.*

N.

N, *decimaterza lettera dell' alfabeto Inglese, pronunciasi come in Italiano.*

No. [signifies number] *numero,* Ex. at No. 5, *al numero cinque.*

NA'DIR, s. [that point of the heavens, which is directly under the feet, and is diametrically opposite to the Zenith] *Nadir,* s. m. *punto astronomico sotto di noi a piombo, opposto al Zenit, che si finge sopra il nostro capo.*

A NAG, s. [a young or little horse] *cavallo di primo morso, cavallino,* s. m.

A little nag, *un ronzino.*

NA'IADES, s. [false Goddesses, believ'd by the Heathens to preside over fountains and rivers] *Najade, ninfe de' fonti e de' fiumi.*

NA'IF, adj. [natural] *naturale.*

A naif stone [a stone perfect in its properties] *una pietra naturale.*

A NAIL, s. [an iron pin] *chiodo, chiavello,* s. m.

The head of a nail, *la testa d'un chiodo.*

The nails of the fingers or toes, *le unghie delle dita della mano o del piede.*

A nail [the eighth part of an ell] *l'ottava parte d'un' alla, che è una misura d'Inghilterra.*

One nail drives out another, *un chiodo caccia l'altro.*

To hit the nail on the head [to guess right] *dar nel segno, dar nel brocco, indovinare, apporsi.*

To pay down money upon the nail [to pay ready money] *pagar danari contanti.*

To labour tooth and nail [to use all one's utmost endeavours] *sbracciarsi, adoperare ogni forza, fare ogni sforzo.*

A nail-piercer, *foratojo,* s. m.

A nail-smith, *chiodajo,* s. m. *fabro che fa chiodi.*

To NAIL [to fasten with nails] *inchiodare, conficcare con chiodi.*

To nail a cannon [to drive an iron spike into the touch-hole, by which means the cannon is rendered unserviceable for the present] *inchiodare un cannone, metter un chiodo nel focone, e così renderlo inabile ad essere adoperato.*

To

To nail a horſe, *chiovare un cavallo, pugnere un cavallo col chiodo nel vivo dell' unghia.*

To nail up, *inchiodare.*

NA'ILED, adj. *inchiodato, chiovato.*

Nailed up, adj. *inchiodato.*

NA'KED, adj. [that has no cloaths on] *nudo, ignudo.*

To ſtrip a man ſtark naked, *nudare, ſpogliar nudo.*

A naked ſword [out of its ſcabbard] *una ſpada ignuda, ſenza fodero.*

The naked truth, *la pura verità.*

NA'KEDLY, adv. *nudamente, ignudamente.*

NA'KEDNESS, s. *nudità*, s. f.

NA'KER, s. [mother of pearl] *madere perla.*

A NAME, s. *nome*, s. m. *vocabolo, col quale propriamente s' appella ciaſcuna coſa.*

A proper name, *nome proprio.*

A chriſtian name, *nome di batteſimo.*

In God's name [or for God's ſake] *in nome di Dio, per l' amor di Dio.*

Salute him in my name, *ſalutatelo in nome mio, o da parte mia.*

A name [pretence, colour] *nome, preteſto, colore*, s. m. *ombra, ſcuſa, coperchiella*, s. f.

A name [reputation or renown] *nome, credito, grido*, s. m. *fama, rinomo, rinomanza*, s. f.

He has the name of a very honeſt man, *è in credito d' uomo onorato, egli paſſa per un uomo dabbene.*

To get a great name, *acquiſtarſi gran fama.*

To get a good or ill name, *metterſi in buono o cattivo credito.*

One had as good be hang'd as have an ill name, *val meglio morire, che avere una cattiva riputazione.*

If one's name be up, he may lie a bed, *fortuna è dormi.*

What is your name? *come vi chiamate, o nomate?*

My name is Peter, *mi chiamo Pietro.*

A rich man, John by name, *un uomo ricco nomato Giovanni.*

To call one names [to abuſe him] *ingiuriare, maltrattare, trattar male alcuno.*

One's name-ſake, *una perſona che ha il medeſimo nome.*

He is my name-ſake, *egli ed io abbiamo il medeſimo nome.*

To NAME [to give a name] *nomare, nominare, chiamare.*

To name one, *nomare o nominare alcuno.*

How do you name him? *come lo chiamate, come ſi chiama?*

The king has named him for that office, *il rè l' ha deſtinato, o eletto a queſta carica.*

To name [to mention] *nomare, nominare, menzionare, far mezione, mentovare.*

NA'MED, adj. *nomato, nominato, chiamato, detto, mentovato.*

NA'MELESS, adj. *ſenza nome, anonimo.*

A nameleſs author, *un autore anonimo.*

By a friend of yours, who ſhall be nameleſs, *da un voſtro amico, che non voglio nomare.*

NA'MELY, adv. *cioè.*

NA'MING, s. *il nomare.*

NAME-SAKE, s. *colui che ha lo ſteſſo nome d' un altro.*

NAP, s. [the hairy or ſhaggy part of woollen cloth] *pelo*, s. m. *cima di panno.*

The nap of cloth or a hat, *il pelo del panno o d' un cappello.*

Nap [ſhort ſleep] *ſonnicello*, s. m.

To take a nap after dinner, *fare un ſonnicello dopo pranzo.*

The nap [the edge of a hill] *la ſommità d' un colle.*

To NAP [to ſleep] *dormicchiare, dormire leggiermente, ſonnecchiare, ſonneferare.*

To nap, *cardare* [to nap cloth] *cardare del panno, cavar fuora il pelo a panni col cardo.*

The NAPE, s. [the hinder part of the neck] *nuca, coppa*, s. f. *la parte di dietro dol capo.*

NA'PERY, s. [table linen] *biancheria da tavola.*

NA'PHEW, s. [a French turnep] *rapa*, s. f.

NA'PKIN, s. *ſalvietta*, s. f. *tovagliuolo*, s. m.

NA'PTHA, s. [Babyloniſh bitumen] *napta*, s. f. *ſpezie di bitume che facilmente s' aerende, ma difficilmente s' eſtingue.*

NA'PPED, adj. *cardato.*

NA'PPING, s. *cardatura*, s. f. *il cardare.*

To take one napping [to ſurprize him] *cogliere all' improviſo, ſorprendere alcuno.*

NA'PPY, adj. *velloſo, velluto, peloſo.*

Cloth that wears nappy, *panno che moſtra il pelo nel portarlo.*

Nappy ale, *cervogia gagliarda o forte.*

NARCI'SSUS, s. [daffodil] *narciſſo, narciſo*, s. m. *fiore noto.*

NARCO'TICAL, } adj. [ſtupifying,
NARCO'TICK, } beaumbing, taking away the ſenſes] *narcotico, ſonniſero, che induce ſonno.*

A narcotick, s. *medicina narcotica.*

NARD, } s. [an Indian plant]
SPIKENARD, } *nardo*, s. m. *la vanda*, s. f. *pianta odorifera.*

NARE, s. [noſtril] *narice, buco del naſo.*

To NA'RRATE [to relate] *narrare, raccontare.*

NARRA'TION, s. [relation of any particular actions or circumſtances] *narrativa, narrazione, relazione*, s. f. *racconto*, s. m.

Narration [in rhetorick, that part of an oration in which an account is given of matter of fact] *narrazione*, s. f. *ragguaglio*, s. m.

NA'RRATIVE, s. [relation, recital] *narrativa, narrazione, relazione*, s. f.

Narrative, adj. [declarative, expreſſive] *narrativo, narratorio.*

NARRA'TOR, s. [relator] *narratore*, s. m. *che narra.*

To NA'RRIFY [to relate, to give account of] *narrare, raccontare.*

NA'RROW, adj. [of ſmall breadth] *ſtretto, anguſto, breve.*

Narrow cloth, *panno ſtretto.*

A narrow paſſage, *varco o paſſo ſtretto.*

A narrow place, *uno ſtretto, un luogo anguſto.*

A narrow fortune, *ſtretta baſſa o ſcarſa fortuna.*

A narrow ſoul, *un' anima vile e baſſa.*

To make narrow, *ſtringere, riſtringere, rendere ſtretto o anguſto.* pret. *ſtrinſi, riſtrinſi.*

To bring into a narrow compaſs, *abbreviare, riſtringere.*

To be lodged in a narrow compaſs, *eſſer alloggiato in luogo anguſto.*

We made a narrow eſcape out of that danger, *a grande ſtento ci liberammo da quel pericolo; poco mancò che non perimmo in quel pericolo.*

Narrow heeled, *che ha il tallone ſtretto.*

A narrow heeled horſe, *un cavallo incaſtellato, un cavallo che ha il piè ſtretto e alto.*

Narrow breaſted, *che ha il petto ſtretto.*

To NA'RROW [to make narrow] *ſtringere, riſtringere.* pret. *ſtrinſi, riſtrinſi.*

NA'RROWED, adj. *ſtretto, riſtretto.*

NA'RROWING, s. *ſtrignimento*, s. m. *lo ſtrignere.*

NA'RROWLY, adj. *ſtrettamente, anguſtamente.*

To look narrowly into an affair, *eſaminare, minutamente un negozio.*

We narrowly eſcaped being drowned, *poco mancò che non ci annegammo.*

NA'RROWNESS, s. *ſtrettezza, anguſtia*, s. f.

NAS, contracted from *ne has* [has not] *non ha.*

NA'SAL, adj. *naſale, appartenente al naſo.*

The naſal vein, *la vena del naſo.*

Naſal, s. [the noſe-piece of an helmet] *naſale*, s. m. *parte dell' elmo, che cuopre il naſo.*

NA'STILY, adv. *ſporcamente, ſchifamente, lordamente.*

NA'STINESS, s. *ſporchezza, ſporcizia*, s. f.

NA'STY, adj. *ſporco, ſchifo, lordo, ſudicio.*

Naſty [obſcene] diſcourſes, *diſcorſi oſceni.*

Very naſty, *ſporchiſſimo.*

NA'TAL, } adj. [belonging
NATALI'TIOUS, } to nativity] *natale, natalizio.*

NATA'TION, s. [ſwimming] *il nuotare, nuoto.*

NA'THLESS, adv. [nevertheleſs] *nulladimeno, nondimeno, nondimanco, tuttavia, con tutto ciò.*

NA'THMORE [never the more] *nulla più, nulla di più.*

NA'TION, s. [the people of a country] *nazione*, s. f. *generazione d' uomini nati in una medeſima provincia.*

NA'TIONAL, adj. [of a whole nation] *nazionale, della stessa nazione.*
A national synod, *un sinodo nazionale.*
NA'TIVE, adj. [belonging to the place of one's birth] *natio, nativo.*
My native country, *il mio paese natio.*
Native [natural, inbred] *naturale.*
A native, s. [one born in a certain place] *un nativo, uno nato in qualche luogo.*
He is a native of Florence, *egli è nativo di Firenza.*
A native [one who lives in the country where he was born] *un originario.*
NATI'VITY, s. [birth] *natività,* s. f. *natale, nascimento,* s. m.
NA'TURAL, adj. [belonging to, or proceeding from nature] *naturale, di natura, secondo natura.*
Natural [not counterfeit, such as nature made it] *naturale, semplice, senz' arte.*
The natural and artificial day, *il giorno naturale ed artificiale.*
A natural son [a bastard] *un figlio naturale, un bastardo.*
The natural sense of a passage, *il vero, senso d' un passaggio.*
Natural moisture, *umido radicale.*
The natural philosophy, *la filosofia naturale.*
A natural philosopher, *fisico, un filosofo naturale.*
To have good natural parts, *aver buone doti dalla natura, esser dotato d'un ingegno grande.*
Natural [free, easy] *naturale, semplice, facile, non affettato.*
To have an easy way of writing, *avere una maniera naturale o corrente nello scrivere.*
A natural, s. [a fool] *un idiota, uno sciocco.*
NA'TURALIST, s. [one skill'd in natural philosophy] *un naturale, maestro e scrittore di cose naturali.*
NATURALIZA'TION, s. [when an alien is made a natural subject by act of parliament] *naturalizzazione,* s. f. *quando un forestiero è annoverato fra i nativi per atto di parlamento.*
To NA'TURALIZE [to admit into the number of natural subjects] *naturalizzare, ammettere nel numero de' nativi.*
To naturalize a word, *adottare una parola forestiera.*
NA'TURALIZED, adj. *naturalizzato.*
NA'TURALLY, adv. *naturalmente, per natura, secondo la natura.*
He is naturally fearful, *è naturalmente timido.*
Naturally [without art] *naturalmente, semplicemente, schiettamente.*
NA'TURALNESS, s. [natural affection] *naturalità, naturalezza,* s. f.
NA'TURE, s. [the world, the universe] *la natura, il mondo, l' universo.*
God is the author of nature, *Iddio è l' autore della natura.*
There is no such thing in nature, *non v' è tal cosa nella natura.*

Nature [a particular disposition of parts in some particular body] *natura, quiddità, proprietà, essenza,* s. f.
The nature of fire, *la natura del fuoco.*
Nature [condition, disposition] *natura,* s. f. *genio, costume, umore,* s. m.
A good or bad nature, *una buona, o cattiva natura.*
A very sweet nature, *un umore, ungenio molto affabile.*
He has good nature in him, *egli ha un buon naturale.*
By nature, *seconda natura, naturalmente.*
Beyond nature, *sopranaturale.*
Nature [sort, manner] *natura maniera, sorte, specie,* s. f.
NA'TUR'D, adj. ex. good natur'd, *d' un buon naturale, affabile, umano, cortese, benigno.*
Ill natur'd, *d' un cattivo naturale, maligno, scortese.*
NA'VAL, adj. [belonging to a ship or navy] *navale, di nave, attenente a nave.*
Naval forces, *forze navali.*
NAVE, s. [that part in the middle of a wheel where the spokes are fixed] *quel pezzo della ruota dove son fitti i raggi.*
The nave of a church, *la nava d'una chiesa.*
NA'VEL, s. [a part on the middle of the belly] *bellico, umbilico,* s. m. *quella parte del corpo donde prima è preso il nostro alimento.*
The navel-string, *budello del bellico che hanno i bambini quando nascono.*
Navel-wort, *bellico di venere, sorta d' erba.*
Navel gall [a horse's disease] *guidalesco,* s. m. *ulcera, che si fa nel dosso del cavallo, o altre bestie da soma.*
The navel-timber [the ribs or futtocks of a ship] *le costole d' un vascello.*
NA'VET, s. [censer-box] *navicella di turibile.*
NA'UFRAGE, s. [ship-wreck] *naufragio,* s. m.
NAUGHT, adj. [bad, wicked] *cattivo, reo, malvagio.*
You are very naught, *voi siete molto cattivo.*
Naught for the eyes, *nocivo agli occhi.*
Naught money, *moneta falsa.*
Naught [lewd] *scostumato, disonesto.*
Naught, adv. *nulla.*
NA'UGHTY, adv. *male, maldmente, scostumatamente.*
NAUGHTINESS, s. [badness, wickedness] *cattivezza, ribalderia, tristizia.*
NA'UGHTY, adj. [not good, wicked] *cattivo, malvagio, ribaldo, tristo.*
A naughty boy, *un cattivo ragazzo.*
A naughty trick, *cattività, tiro di ribaldo.*
A naughty woman, *un donna disonesta, una donna di cattiva vita.*

NA'VIGABLE, adj. [where ships may pass] *navigabile, che si può navigare.*
A navigable river, *un fiume navigabile.*
To NA'VIGATE [to sail on the sea] *navigare, andar con nave per acqua.*
NAVIGA'TION, s. [the art of sailing] *navigazione,* s. f. *il navigare.*
NAVIGA'TOR, s. [sailor, sea traveller] *navigatore,* s. m. *che fa l' esercizio del navigare, marinajo,* s. m.
NA'ULAGE, s. [the freight or passage money for goods by sea] *nolo,* s. m. *il pagamento del porto delle mercanzie o d' altre cose condotte da navili l'Ariosto in rima disse* naulo.
NA'UMACHY, s. [a sea-fight represented on the stage] *combattimento navale rappresentato su teatro.*
To NA'USEATE [to grow squeamish; to turn away with disgust] *ricever nausea; voltar via disgustato, andarsene come in atto di recere.*
To nauseate [to loath, to reject with disgust] *abborrire, recere.*
To nauseate [to strike with disgust] *far nausea, cagionar nausea.*
NA'USEATIVE, } adj. [going a-
NA'USEOUS, } gainst one's stomach, loathsome] *nauseoso, che fa nausea.*
NA'USEOUSNESS, s. [loathsomeness] *nausea, abbominazione,* s. f.
NA'USEATING, adj. *nauseante, che nausea.*
NA'UTICAL, } adj. [belonging to
NA'UTICK, } ships or mariners] *nautico, di nave.*
NA'UTICAL chart, *carta nautica, carta del navigare.*
NA'UTILUS, s. *nautilo, sorta di lumaca marina.*
NA'VY, s. [a fleet] *flotta, armata,* s. f.
The royal navy, *l' armata regia.*
A commissioner of the navy, *commissario della marina.*
The navy-office, *ammiragliato,* s. m.
NAY, adv. [no] *no.*
To say nay, *dir di no, negare.*
Nay, he is a covetous man, *anzi, è molto avaro.*
Nay [refusal] *ripulsa, e repulsa, esclusione, negativa,* s. f.
I will have no nay, *non ammetto ripulse, non voglio che mi si dica di no.*
NA'YWARD, s. *negativa.*
NEAP, s. [a fist] *quella parte del braccio che s'unisce alla mano.*
To NEAL, *ricuocere, cuocer di nuovo.*
To neal glass or metals, *ricuocere del vetro o de' metalli.*
NE'ALED, adj. *ricotto.*
NE'ALING, s. *ricuocimento,* s. m. *il ricuocere.*
NE'AP-TIDES, s. [low tides, not high, not so swift as the spring tides] *marea bassa.*
NEAR, prep. & adv. [nigh at hand] *vicino, appresso, accanto, allato, presso.*
Near the church, *vicino alla chiesa.*
Near the prince, *presso il principe.*

You

You muſt come near to ſee it, *biſogna vederlo da vicino.*

Sit near me, *ſedete accanto di me.*

Very near, *viciniſſimo, vicin vicino.*

Very near [almoſt] *quaſi, preſſo, intorno, circa.*

He has near a thouſand pounds a year, *egli ha preſſo mille lire ſterline all' anno.*

He was very near being drowned, *fu per annegarſi, fu in pericolo d' annegarſi.*

The ſtanding corn is near ripe, *le biade ſono quaſi matare.*

She is near twenty years old, *ella tocca li venti anni.*

A woman near her reckoning, *una donna che s'avvicina al parto.*

Near at hand, *a mano, vicino, in pronto, in ordine.*

The kingdom of heaven is near at hand, *il regno de' cieli è vicino.*

He is nothing near ſo bad, *egli ſta molto meglio.*

He is nothing near ſo ſevere as he was, *egli non è molto meno ſovero di prima.*

They were very near coming to handy blows, *poco mancò che non veniſſero alle mani.*

As near as I can remember, *per quanto mi recordo.*

To come, or to go near, *avvicinarſi, accoſtarſi, approſſimarſi.*

Come near, *avvicinatevi.*

To draw near, *avvicinare, accoſtare, approſſimare.*

He will go near to do it, *è probabile che lo faccia, è da temerſi che non lo faccia.*

He will go near to have me do it, *vorrebbe forſe ch' io lo faceſſi.*

To go as near the wind as one can [to be very ſaving] *riſparmiare quanto ſi può.*

Near, adj. *vicino.*

My houſe is near yours, *la mia caſa è vicina alla voſtra.*

He is my near kinſman, *è mio ſtretto parente.*

A near concern, *un affare che ci tocca al vivo.*

Near [niggardly] *ſtretto, abbietto, tapino.*

A near, or ſaving man, *un uomo ſtretto, un tapino, un cacaſtecchi, uno ſpilorcio.*

Near is my coat, but nearer is my ſkin, *mi ſtrigne più la camicia, che la gonnella.*

The near or left foot of a horſe, *il piè della ſtaffa, o il piè ſiniſtro del cavallo.*

NE'ARER, adj. [the comparative of near] *più vicino.*

NE'AREST [the ſuperlative of near] *il più vicino, la più vicina.*

This is the neareſt way, *queſto è il più corto cammino, queſta è la ſtrada più corta.*

NE'ARLY, adv. *da vicino.*

That nearly concerns me, *queſto mi tocca al vivo.*

Nearly [niggardly] *meſchinamente, tenacemente, avaramente, ſtrettamente, da ſpilorcio.*

NE'ARNESS, s. [vicinity] *vicinità, proſſimità, propinquità,* s. f.

Nearneſs of kin, *affinità, proſſimità, attenenza, parentela.*

Nearneſs [niggardlineſs] *ſtrettezza, parſimonia, miſeria,* s. f.

NEAT, adj. [clean, cleanly] *netto, pulito.*

A neat man, *un uomo pulito.*

A neat ſuit of cloaths, *un abito pulito.*

To be neat in one's cloaths, *veſtir pulitamente.*

A neat ſnuff-box, *una tabacchiera pulita, bella, ben fatta.*

Neat [cunning, ſubtile] *aſtuto, ſcaltro.*

Neat handed, *deſtro, attivo, abile, ſagace, ingegnoſo.*

Neat-handedneſs, s. *deſtrezza, abilità; e figurativamente, ſagacità,* s. f. *ingegno,* s. m.

Neat, s. [an ox or cow] *bue,* s. m. *vacca,* s. f. *beſtiame vaccino.*

Of neat, *vaccino.*

Neat's leather, *vacchetta,* s. f. *cuojo di beſtiame vaccino.*

A neat's tongue, *lingua di bue.*

Neat's herd, *vaccajo, biſolco,* s. m.

Neat houſe, *ſtalla da buoi.*

NE'ATLY, adv. *deſtramente, pulitamente, ingegnoſamente.*

To manage buſineſs neatly, *trattare un negozio con deſtrezza.*

To ſpeak or write neatly, *parlare o ſcrivere giudizioſamente, con giudizio, con ſapere.*

NE'ATNESS, s. [cleanlineſs] *pulizia, pulitezza, nettezza,* s. f.

Neatneſs [ſpruceneſs, beauty] *leggiadria, pulitezza, delicatezza, garbatezza,* s. f. *garbo,* s. m.

Neatneſs of ſtyle, *purità di ſtile.*

NEB, s. [the bill or beak of any thing] *cuſpide, punta,* s. f. *eſtremità acuta di qualunque ſi voglia coſa.*

The neb of a pen, *la punta d'una penna.*

NE'BULA [films upon the eyes] *panno,* s. m. *macchia o maglia a guiſa di nugola che ſi genera nella luce dell' occhio.*

NE'BULOUS, adj. [cloudy] *nugoloſo, e nuvoloſo.*

NE'CESSARIES, s. pl. [things not only convenient but needful] *coſe non ſolamente commode, ma neceſſarie; il neceſſario, le coſe neceſſarie alla vita umana.*

NE'CESSARILY, adv. *neceſſariamente, aſſolutamente, di neceſſità.*

Neceſſarily [inevitably] *neceſſariamente, inevitabilmente.*

NE'CESSARY, adj. *neceſſario, che è di neceſſità.*

Neceſſary [inevitable] *neceſſario, inevitabile.*

A neceſſary effect, *un effetto neceſſario.*

A neceſſary-houſe, *neceſſario, ceſſo, agiamento,* s. m.

To NE'CESSITATE [to force, to compel] *neceſſitare, sforzare, violentare, mettere in neceſſità.*

NE'CESSITATED, adj. *neceſſitato, sforzato, violentato.*

NE'CESSITOUS [indigent, needy, poor] *neceſſitoſo, ch' è in neceſſità, biſognoſo.*

NE'CESSITY, s. [indiſpenſableneſs, the ſtate of a thing that needs muſt be] *neceſſità,* s. f. *tutto ciò ch' neceſſario.*

Of neceſſity, *di neceſſità, neceſſariamente, indiſpenſabilmente.*

Neceſſity has no law, *la neceſſità non ha legge.*

To conſult with neceſſity, to make virtue of neceſſity, *far della neceſſità virtù.*

Neceſſity [conſtraint, force] *neceſſità, violenza, forza,* s. f.

Neceſſity [indigence, poverty] *neceſſità, eſtremo biſogno, povertà, indigenza,* s. f.

NECK, s. [a part of the body between the head and the ſhoulders] *collo,* s. m. *quella parte del corpo ch' è tra le ſpalle e la nuca.*

To take one about the neck, or to fall about one's neck, *gittar le braccia al collo ad uno, abbracciarlo.*

Woman's neck [boſom] *il petto d'una donna.*

Neck of land [iſthmus] *braccio di terra fra due mari.*

A neck of mutton, *un collo di caſtrato.*

The neck of a violin and other muſical inſtruments, *il manico d'un violino e d' altri ſtrumenti muſicali.*

The neck of a bottle, *il collo d'un fiaſco.*

The neck lock of a wig, *il riccio di dietro d'una parrucca.*

To ſlip one's neck out of the collar, *mancar di parola.*

One miſchief comes on the neck of another, *una diſgrazia non vien mai ſola; I malanni ſono come le ciriege, uno tira l' altro.*

On the neck of theſe miſchiefs, this alſo comes, *queſt' altra diſgrazia ci mancava; queſto ancora per colmo di diſgrazie.*

NE'CK-PIECE [part of the armour] *gorgiera,* s. f. *quell' armadura che arma il collo.*

The neck band of a ſhirt, *collare d' una camicia.*

NE'CKLA[illegible] *[illegible]ile, vezzo,* s. m.

NE'CKCLOTH, s. [that which men wear on their neck] *cravatta; fazzoletto, o pezzuola di turbante o d'altro panno finiſſimo che ſi porta al collo.*

Neckweed [hemp] *canape, canapa,* s. f.

NE'CKERCHIEF, NE'CKABOUT, s. [a woman's neck linen] *fazzoletto di tela che le donne portano al collo.*

NECROMA'NCER, s. [magician, wizzard] *un negromante,* s. m.

NECROMA'NCY, s. [a divination by calling up dead mens ghoſts, or the devil] *negromanzia,* s. f.

NECROMA'NTICK, adj. [belonging to necromancy] *negromantico, di negromanzia.*

NE'CTAR, s. [a pleaſant liquor, feigned by the poets to be the liquor of the gods] *nèttare,* s. m. *bevanda degli dei ſecondo li antichi.*

NEC-

NECTA'REAN, } adj. *di néttare.*
NECTA'REOUS, }

NE'CTARINE, adj. *dolce come néttare.*

NEED, s. [want, neceffity, or occafion] *bifogna, uopo,* s. m. *occorrenza, neceffità,* s. f.

To ftand in need of a thing, to have need of it, *aver bifogno di qualche cofa.*

What need is there to do it? *che neceffità c' è di farlo?*

There is no need of it, *ciò non e neceffario.*

Need [want, poverty] *bifogno, mancamento,* s. m. *neceffità, povertà, indigenza,* s. f.

To be in great need, *trovarfi in neceffità, o ftrettezza.*

A friend in need, is a friend indeed, *al bifogna fi conofcon gli amici.*

Need makes the naked man run, the naked quean fpin, and the old wife trot, *il bifogno fa trottar la vecchia.*

If need be, *fe farà neceffario, fe la neceffità lo richiederà.*

You had need to mind that bufinefs, *voi farefte bene di badare a queft' affare.*

To do one's needs [to go to ftool] *andar del corpo, fcaricare il ventre.*

To NEED [to want] *aver bifogno, bifognare.*

I do not need it, *non ne ho di bifogna.*

He needs neceffaries, *gli manca il neceffario.*

I may fee him need, but I will not fee him bleed, *voglio che foffra, ma non voglio abbandona lo.*

You need not come, *non occorre, non è uopo che veniate.*

You need not fear, *non temete, non abbiate paura.*

You need but tell him, *ditegli folàmente.*

There is nothing yet that you need be afraid of, *non avete ancora ragione di temere.*

What need you care? *che importa a voi?*

What need fo many words? *a che tante parole? a che fervon tante parole?*

It needs not, *non è neceffario, non occorre.*

There needs no difpute about the matter, *non è una cofa di difputare.*

He needs to carry himfelf well, *bafta che fi comporti bene.*

It muft needs be fo, *bifogna che fia così, la cofa non può effer altrimente.*

NE'EDFUL, adj. [neceffary] *neceffario, opportuno.*

It is needful, *bifogna, è neceffario.*

Very needful, *neceffariffimo.*

NE'EDFULNESS, } s. [neceffity, indigence] *neceffità, occorrenza, ftrettezza, indigenza, povertà,* s. f. *bifogno, mancamento,* s. m.
NE'EDINESS, }

NE'EDLE, s. [a fmall tool to few withal] *ago,* s. m.

A fewing needle, *ago da cucire.*

The needle of a dial, *ago dell' oriuolo a fole.*

A mariner's needle, *ago, ful quale s' accomoda la calamita della buffola.*

Needle-work, *lavoro d' ago.*

To work needle work, *lavorare coll' ago.*

A needle full, *agugliata,* s. f.

A needle-cafe, *ftrumento da tenervi dentro gli aghi.*

A needle maker, s. *colui che fa gli aghi.*

The needle fifh, *aguglia,* s. f. *fpezie di pefce.*

NE'EDLESS, adj. [unneceffary, fuperfluous] *inutile, fuperfluo, che non è neceffario,*

It is needlefs to ufe words, *le parola non vagliono a nulla, è vano il far tante parole.*

It is needlefs for me to fay any thing, *non occorre ch' io dica nulla.*

NE'EDLESSLY, adv. [without neceffity] *inutilmente, fenza neceffità.*

NEEDS, adv [of neceffity] *neceffariamente, affolutamente, di neceffità.*

It muft needs be fo, *bifogna neceffariamente che fia così.*

If you will needs be gone, *fe volete andarvene affolutamente, fe fiete rifoluto d' andarvene.*

I muft needs tell you, *non poffo far di meno di non dirvi, m' è forza dirvi.*

NE'EDY, adj. [poor, indigent] *bifognofo, neceffitojo, povero.*

NE'ER, *v.* Never.

To NEESE, *ftarnutare, fternutare.*

NEF, s. *nave d' una chiefa.*

NEFA'NDOUS, adj. [horrible, heinous] *nefando, empio, fcellerato.*

NEFA'RIOUS, adj. [wicked, curfed, villainous] *nefario, fcellerato, abbominevole.*

NE'CATION, s. [a denying] *negamento,* s. m. *negazione,* s. f. *negare.*

NE'GATIVE, adj. [belonging to negation] *negativo, che nega.*

The negative voice, *vore negativa.*

Negative, s. [a denying propofition] *negativa,* s. f.

Negative pregnant [in common law, is a negative implying an affirmative] *una negativa che comprende un affirmativa.*

NE'GATORY, adj. [belonging to a denial] *negativo che nega.*

NEGLE'CT, s. [omiffion, difregard] *negligenza, trafcuraggine,* s. f.

To NEGLE'CT [to difregard, to flight] *negligere, trafcurare, trafandare, mettere in non cale.*

To neglect one's duty, *mancare al fuo dovere.*

To neglect an opportunity, *perdere un opportunità.*

NEGLE'CTED, adj. *negletto, trafcurato, trafandato.*

NEGLE'CTER, s. *un negligente, un trafcurato, un infingardo.*

NEGLE'CTING, s. *negligenza, trafcuraggine, trafcuratagine,* s. f.

NE'GLIGENCE, s. [carelefsnefs] *negligenza, trafcuratagine, trafcuraggine,* s. f.

NE'GLIGENT, adj. *negligente, trafcurato, infingardo.*

NE'GLIGENTLY, adv. *negligentemente, trafcuratamente.*

To NEGO'TIATE [to tranfact, to manage] *negoziare, trattare.*

To negociate a bufinefs, *negoziare, o trattare un negozio.*

To negotiate [to traffick, to trade] *negoziare, trafficare, efercitar la mercatura.*

To negotiate a bill of exchange, *negoziare una lettera di cambio.*

NEGO'TIATED, adj. *negoziato, trattatò, traficato.*

NEGO'TIATING, s. *il negoziare.*

NEGOTIA'TION, s. [managing of bufinefs] *negoziazione,* s. f. *negozio,* s. m.

A negotiation [a merchandizing or trafficking] *negozio, traffico, affare,* s. m. *faccenda,* s. f.

NEGO'TIATOR, s. [a manager of affairs] *negoziatore, mediatore,* s. m.

NEGOTIATRIX, s. [a woman manager of affairs] *negoziatrice, mediatrice,* s. f. *quella che negozia qualche affare d'importanza.*

NE'GRO, s. [black-moor] *un Moro, un Negro, un Nero.*

NEIFE, s. [a law word, a bondwoman] *una fchiava.*

NEIGH, s. [the voice of a horfe] *nitrito.*

To NEIGH [to cry as a horfe does] *nitrire, annitrire,* pref. *nitrifco, annitrifco.*

NE'IGHBOUR, s. [one that lives by another] *vicino,* s. m. *vicina,* s. f.

A good lawyer, an ill neighbour, *buon avocato, cattivo vicino.*

Neighbour [in terms of fcripture] *proffimo.*

To love one's neighbour, *amare il fuo proffimo.*

To NE'IGHBOUR, *abitar vicino, confinare.*

NE'IGHBOURHOOD, s. [a place near to that one lives in] *vicinato,* s. m. *vicinanza,* s. f.

Neighbourhood [the neighbours] *i vicini.*

Neighbourhood [nearnefs] *vicinanza proffimità,* s. f.

NE'IGHBOURING, adj. [bordering or adjoining] *vicino, circonvino.*

The neighbouring parts of a place, *i contorni o le parti circonvicine d' un luogo.*

NE'IGHBOURLY, adj. ex. a neighbourly man, *un buon vicino.*

A neighbourly office, *un buon officio.*

Neighbourly, adv. *amichevolmente, amicamente, da amico.*

To compound neighbourly with one, *accordarfi, convenire amichevolmente con uno.*

NE'IGHING, s. [from to neigh] *nitrito,* s. m. *il nitrire.*

A neighing-bird, s. [a little bird which imitates the neighing of a horfe] *fpezie d'uccellino che imita il nitrito del cavallo, in Latino fi chiama* Anthus.

NE'ITHER, conj. *nè.*

He is neither covetous nor prodigal, *non è nè avaro, nè prodigo.*

Neither more nor less, *nè più, nè meno.*
Neither is he so bad as you speak of, *non è però così cattivo come dite.*
Neither, pron. *nè l'uno nè l' altro.*
To be on neither side [to stand neuter] *non tener con nessuno.*
NE'NUFAR, } s. [a water-lilly] NE'NUPHAR, } *sorta d'erba.*
NE'OPHYTE, s. [new convert] *neofito,* s. m. *cristiano novellamente battezzato.*
NEOTE'RICK, adj. [modern, of late times] *moderno.*
NEP, or NIP, s. [cat-mint, an herb] *nepitella,* s. f.
NE'PHEW, s. [the son of a brother or sister] *nipote, e nepote,* s. m. *figliuolo del fratello o della sorella.*
A young nephew, *un nipotino.*
NEPHRITICK, s. [a pain of the reins] *nefritico,* s. m. *dolore di renella.*
NE'POTISM, s. [a word chiefly used in respect to the power given by some popes to their nephews] *nipotismo,* s. m.
NERE'IDES, s. [the nymphs or fairies of the sea] *nereidi,* s. f. *le ninfe del mare.*
NE'ROLY, s. [a sort of perfume] *spezie di profumo.*
NERVE, s. [sinew] *nervo,* s. m.
Money is the nerve of war, *il nervo della guerra è il danaro.*
A man of great nerves [a strong or lusty man] *un uomo di buon nervo, un uomo forte, gagliardo.*
NERVO'SITY, s. [fulness of nerves] *nervosità,* s. f.
Nervosity [strength, vigour] *forza,* s. f. *vigore,* s. m.
NE'RVOUS, } adj. [full of nerves] NE'RVY, } *nervoso, nerboso, pien di nervi.*
Very nervous *nervosissimo.*
Nervous [strong] *nervoso, forte, robusto, gagliardo.*
Nervous [solid, weighty] *sodo, solido, forte, di pondo, convincente.*
A nervous argument, *un argumento fondato o convincente.*
NESS, s. [a point of land running into the sea] *capo, promontorio,* s. m. *braccio di terra, che sporge in mare.*
NEST, s. *nido, nidio.*
To build or make his nest, *annidarsi, fare il nido, nidificare.*
A nest of birds, *nidata, nidiata* s. f.
A nest of thieves, *nidio, ricetto, ricettacolo, asilo di ladri.*
A nest-cock, a man that never was from home, *un nidiace, un cova cenere, un uomo che non è mai uscito del paese.*
A nest-egg, *endice, guardanidio,* s. m.
To NEST, } [to make a nest] *ni-* To NESTLE, } *dificare, far nido.*
To nestle [to settle any where] *annidarsi, eleggersi luogo per abitare, posarsi, fermar sua stanza, stanziarsi.*
To NE'STLE [to shift and shuffle up and down] *dimenarsi, agitarsi, muoversi qua e là.*
NE'STLING, s. [a young bird newly fledg'd, and taken from the nest] *un uccello nidiace, un uccello tolto del nidio e allevato.*

NET, s. rete, *ragna,* s. f. *strumento da pigliar pesci, e uccelli.*
To lay or spread a net, *spiegare o tendere una rete.*
A birding-net, *una ragna.*
A fishing-net, rete *da pescare.*
To fall into the net, *cascar nella* rete.
A drag-net, *un tramaglio.*
A little net, *reticella, reticina,* s. f. *piccola* rete.
A hunter's net, *calappio,* s. m. *trappola,* s. f.
A net [wherein apples, wallnuts, pears, &c. are put to be sold] *reticella,* s. f.
Net-wise, *reticolato, intrecciato a guisa di* rete.
A net of wire, *gelosia, o grata di fil di ferro.*
A net-maker, *un facitor di* reti.
A place fit to spread nets, *luogo acconcio per tendervi la ragna.*
NE'THER, adj. [lower] *basso, inferiore.*
The Nether-lands, *i paesi bassi, la Fiandra.*
NE'THERMOST, adj. *il più basso, il più inferiore.*
NE'TTLE, s. [an herb well known] *ortica,* s. f. *erba nota.*
Blind nettle, *scrofularia,* s. f.
A nettle-tree, *aliso,* s. m.
To NE'TTLE [to sting with nettles] *percuotere, e pugnere altrui con ortiche.*
To nettle [to nip, to bite, to teaze, to vex] *esasperare, aspreggiare, inasprire, pugnere, provocare, irritare.*
NE'TTLED, adj. *esasperato, aspreggiato, punto, provocato, inasprito.*
NE'TTLING, s. *v.* To nettle.
NE'TWORK, *reticella,* s. f.
NE'VER, adv. [at no time] *mai, giammai.*
Never since, *mai dopo.*
I never saw him, *non l'ho mai visto.*
Never [not] *non, no.*
Never deny him so small a kindness, *non li negare un così piccolo favore.*
Never a one, *nè meno uno.*
Never a whit, *niente affatto.*
He never durst say a word to him, *non ardì dirli la minima parola.*
I am never the better for it, *non mi giova a nulla.*
Never a word came from him, *non disse la minima parola.*
Never-ceasing [incessant] *che non cessa, che non finisce.*
Never-failing [infallible] *che non fallisce mai, infallibile.*
NE'VERTHELESS, conj. *nientedimeno, nondimeno, non pertanto, però, pure, tuttavia.*
NEUTER, adj. [a term of grammar] *neutro, termine gramaticale.*
A verb neuter, *un verbo neutro.*
The neuter gender, *il genere neutro.*
Neuter [of never party or side] *neutro, neutrale, che non si dichiara per alcuna parte, indifferente.*
NEU'TRAL, adj. *neutro, neutrale, indifferente.*
In a neutral sense, *in un senso neutro*

To stand neutral, *esser neutrale, non dichiarsi per alcuna parte.*
NEUTRA'LITY, s. [indifferency] *neutralità, indifferenza,* s. f.
NEU'TRALLY, adv. [in a neutral sense] *neutralmente, in un senso neutro.*
NEW, adj. [never used or worn before] *nuovo, non adoperato.*
A new hat, *un cappello nuovo.*
Spick and span new, *nuovo di zecca.*
New, fresh [of late days, of little standing] *nuovo, che è fatto novellamente, di fresco, novello.*
New wine, *vin nuovo.*
A new mode, *una moda novella.*
A new year, *un nuovo anno.*
A new moon, *luna nuova, novilunio,* s. m.
A new-year's gift, *strenna,* s. f.
New bread, or butter, *del pane, o del butirro fresco.*
A new thing, *una cosa novella, novità,* s. f.
This is something new to me, *ciò m' è nuovo.*
That is no new thing to him, *ciò non gli è nuovo, ciò gli è molto comune.*
To put on a new face, *cangiarsi in viso.*
A new beginner, *un principiante, un novizio.*
New-year's day, *il capo d'anno.*
New, adv. [newly] *nuovamente, di fresco, novellamente.*
New married, *novellamente maritato, maritato di fresco.*
New found, *trovato di fresco.*
Anew, adv. *di nuovo, da capo, ancora.*
To begin anew, *ricominciare, cominciar da capo.*
To new-vamp, *raccomodare, racconciare.*
A new laid egg, *un uovo fresco.*
To new mould, *rifondere, di nuovo, fondere.*
To new dress, *rivestire, di nuovo vestire.*
A new comer, *venuto di fresco, un forestiero.*
NE'WING, s. [barm, yeast] *fercia di cervogia.*
NE'WISH, adj. [something new] *alquanto nuovo.*
NE'WLY, adv. *nuovamente, novellamente, di fresco.*
NEW'NESS, s. *novità, cosa nuova.*
NEWS, s. [tidings, new intelligence of affairs] *novella, nuova, notizia,* s. f. *avviso,* s. m.
Is there any news stirring? *si dice qualche cosa di nuovo?*
What news? *che si dice di nuovo?*
This is news to me, *ciò m' è nuovo.*
Printed news, *avvisi stampati, una gazzetta.*
A news maker, *novellatore,* s. m. *raccontator di novelle.*
A news monger, a news writer, *un novellista, un gazzettante.*
I have news, *mi viene avvisato.*
NEWT, s. [a small sort of lizard] *ramarro,* s. m. *spezie di lucertola.*
NEXT, adj. [near, contiguous] *vicino, contiguo.*

The next houſe, *la caſa vicina o contigua.*

The very next houſe to mine, *la caſa contigua alla mia o a canto della mia.*

He is my next neighbour, *egli è mio vicino.*

The next month, *il meſe proſſimo.*

The next day, *il giorno ſeguente.*

He is the next man to the King, *egli è il primo appreſſo il Re.*

Next time we ſhall meet together, *la prima volta che ci rivedremo.*

The next town you come to, *la prima terra che troverete.*

I'll do better next time, *farò meglio all' avvenire.*

I was the next man to him, *io li ſtavo a canto.*

Next before me, *immediatamente avanti di me.*

That part of France which is next to Germany, *quella parte della Francia, che più s'avvicina alla Germania.*

Next [in the next place] *ſecondariamente, in ſecondo luogo.*

NIAS, adj. ex. a nias hawk [a young hawk juſt taken out of the neſt, and not yet taught] *un falcone nidiace.*

NIB, s. [a bill] *becco, s. m. la bocca degli uccelli.*

The nib of a bird, *il becco d'un uccello.*

The nib of a pen, *la punta d'una penna.*

NI'BBED, adj. ex. a hard nibbed pen, *una penna che ha la punta troppo dura.*

To NIBBLE [to bite a little by degrees] *morſecchiare, mangiar morſecchiando, denticchiare, mangiucchiare.*

The mice have nibbled all the cheeſe, *i ſorci hanno morſicato tutto 'l caſcio.*

NI'BBLER, s. *un morditore, un riprenſore.*

NI'BBLING, s. *il morſecchiare.*

NI'BBLINGS, s. pl. [things nibbled] *morſecchiature, s. f.*

NICE, adj. [curious, tender] *delirato, dilicato, tenero, morbido.*

A nice man in his diet, *un uomo delicato nel mangiare.*

Nice [ticklish, touchy] *delicato, zeloſo, curante, geloſo.*

A perſon nice of his reputation, *una perſona zeloſa della ſua riputazione.*

A very nice buſineſs, *un negozio molto geloſo.*

Nice [ſly, ſcrupulous] *delicato, ſcrupoloſo, circoſpetto.*

He is more nice than wiſe, *egli è troppo circoſpetto.*

Nice [dainty] *delirato, delizioſo, eſquiſito.*

Nice [exactly] *eſatto, accurato, diligente.*

A nice examination, *un eſame eſatto.*

Nice [difficult] *delicato, difficile, geloſo.*

A nice point, *una materia dilicata, o geloſa.*

To be nice in ſomething, *aſſottigliarſi in qualche coſa.*

Nice [fooliſh, ſilly] *ſciocco, ſciaperato, ſtolto, ſcimunito.*

NI'CELY, adv. *delicatatamente, dilicatamente, teneramente, morbidamente.*

Nicely [exactly] *eſattamente, accuratamente, con eſattezza.*

Nicely [curiouſly] *perfettamente, eſquiſitamente, ottimamente.*

NICE'AN, } adj. [belonging to Nice,
NICE'NE, } a city in Bithynia] *Niceno.*

The Nicene council, *il concilio Niceno.*

NI'CENESS, s. [coyneſs, daintineſs] *delicatezza, morbidezza, delizia, s. f.*

Niceneſs [exactneſs, curiouſneſs] *eſattezza, cura, diligenza, accuratezza, s. f.*

Niceneſs [ſubtility] *ſottigliezza, induſtria, ſinezza, acutezza, s. f.*

The NI'CETIES of politicks, *le ſottigliezze de' politici.*

The niceties of honour, *le finezze, o i puntigli d'onore.*

The niceties of logick, *le ſottigliezze della logica.*

NI'CHAR, s. [a plant] *nome di pianta.*

NI'CHE, s. [a cavity in a wall to place a ſtatue in] *nicchia, s. f. quel voto che faſſi nelle muraglie ad effetto di mettervi ſtatue, o ſimili.*

NICK, s. [notch] *tacca, s. f. piccolo taglio, v.* To notch.

In the very nick of time, *appunto, opportunamente.*

Old nick [the devil] *il diavolo.*

To NICK [to notch] *intaccare, v.* To notch.

To nick [to do in the very point of time] *incontrare, riſcontrare, cogliere.*

He has nicked the buſineſs, *egli ha incontrato bene.*

To nick the time, *incontrare il tempo, o corre il tempo.*

I nicked you, *vi ho incontrato opportunamente, o molto a propoſito.*

NI'CKNAME, s. *ſoprannome, s. m.*

To NI'CKNAME one, *ſoprannomare altrui.*

How many do we nickname friends, that prove but ſtrangers at a pinch, *quanti vi ſono di quelli che chiamiamo amici, che nel biſogno ci volterebbero le ſpalle.*

NI'CKNAMED, adj. *ſoprannomato.*

To NI'CTATE [to twinkle the eyes] *ammiccare, occhieggiare.*

NIDE, s. ex. A nide of pheaſants *una nidiata, o nidiata di fagiani*

NIDGERIES, s. [fooleries] *bagattelle, coſe frivole, chiappolerie.*

NI'GET, s. [a fool, a ninny] *un goffo, un gonzo.*

NI'DING, adj. *voce antica. Baſſo, abbietto, di mente vile.*

NIECE, s. *la nipote, la figliuola d'un fratello o d'una ſorella.*

NI'FFLE, s. [an old law term, a thing of little or no value] *bagattella, coſa frivola, chiappoleria.*

NIGE'LLA, s. [a plant] *nigella, s. f.*

NI'GGARD, s. [a covetous ſordid man] *uno ſpilorcio, un migneca, uno ſpizzeca, un leſinante, un cacaſtecchi, un taccagno, un miſero, un avaro.*

NI'GGARLINESS, s. [ſtingineſs] *grettezza, ſordidezza, miſeria, leſina, avarizia, ſpilorceria, s. f.*

NI'GGARDLY, adj. *avaro, leſinante, ſpilorcio, miſero, ſordido, ſtretto, taccagno.*

A niggardly man, *un avaro, uno ſpilorcio, un taccagno.*

Niggardly doings, *baſſezze, ſordidezze, grettezze*

Niggardly, adv. *avaramente, grettamente ſordidamente, miſeramente.*

NICH, adj. [near] *vicino.*

To be nigh, *eſſer vicino.*

To draw nigh, *avvicinarſi, accoſtarſi.*

Winter is nigh at hand, *il verno s' avanza.*

Nigh of kin, *parente ſtretto.*

Nigh [or almoſt] *quaſi.*

It is nigh twelve o'clock, *ſono quaſi le dodici.*

Nigh, prep. [by] *vicino, allato, a canto, accoſto.*

The gardens nigh the river, *i giardini vicini al fiume.*

Set you nigh me, *ſedetevi allato di me.*

To write too nigh together, *ſcriver troppo ſerrato.*

Nigh at hand, *vicino, proſſimo.*

Too nigh a thing, *avvicinarſi, o accoſtarſi ad una coſa.*

NI'GHER, adj. [nearer] *più vicino.*

Come nigher, *avvicinatevi più, fatevi più in qua.*

You ſhall be never the nigher, *ciò non vi varrà a nulla.*

NIGHNESS, s. [nearneſs] *vicinità, proſſimità, s. f.*

NIGHT, s. [the time while the ſun is below the horizon] *notte, s. f.*

By night, *di notte tempo.*

In the dead time of the night, *nelle ore più tacite delle notte.*

To tarry all night, *pernottare.*

To ſet up all night, *vegliare tutta la notte.*

It grows night, *s' annotta, ſi fa notte.*

Night [the latter part of the day before one goes to bed] *ſera.*

He will come back to night, *ritornerà ſtaſera.*

Laſt night, *iernotte, ierſera.*

Night ſtudies, *vigilie.*

A night-gown, *veſte da camera, zimarra, s. f.*

A night-cap, *un tocco, una berretta da notte.*

A night-dreſs, *una cuffia da notte.*

A night-rail, or combing-cloth, *rocchetto, s. m. mantellina, s. f.*

Night-ſhade, *ſolatro, s. m. erba nota.*

A night-raven, *guſaccio, guſo, s. m. uccel notturno.*

The night-mare [a diſtemper cauſed by undigeſted humours ſtopping the paſſage of the animal ſpirits, ſo that the body cannot move] *fantaſima, s. f. ſorta di malattia, cagionata da indigeſtione che priva il corpo d'ogni operazione.*

Night revellings, *divertimenti notturni.*

In the night-time, *di notte tempo, nel tempo della notte.*

NI'GHTINGALE, s. [a fine ſinging bird]

bird] *rusignuolo, usignuolo*, s. m. *uccelletto noto per la dolcezza del canto.*

Ni'ghtly, adj. [that happens in the night] *notturno*, *di notte, che appartiene a notte.*

Nightly, adv. [every night] *ogni notte, ogni sera.*

Nihily, s. [nothingness] *nulla.*

Nill, s. [the sparkles or ashes that come off brass tried in a furnace] *le scintille o la cenere che esce del rame nella fornace.*

To Nill [to be unwilling] *non volere.*

Will he, nill he, *per forza, malgrado, voglia non voglia.*

To Nim [to take by stealth, to filch] *furare, rubare, imbolare, involare.*

Ni'mble, adj. [agile, quick, ready] *agile, snello, lesto, destro, leggiero, sciolto di membra.*

Nimbleness, s. *agilità. snellezza, destrezza, leggierezza, snellezza*, s. f.

Ni'mble-witted, adj. *dotato di mente pronta, d' ingegno veloce; volonteroso di parlare.*

Ni'mbly, adv. *agilmente, prestamente, destramente, snellamente, leggiermente.*

Ni'mmer, s. *truffatore, ladro.*

Nine, adj. *nove.*

Nine times, *nove volte.*

The sacred nine [the muses] *le nove sorelle, le muse.*

Nine-fold, adj. *nove volte più.*

Ninete'en, adj. *diecinove.*

Nineteenth, adj. *decimo nono.*

Ni'netieth, adj. *nonantesimo.*

Ni'nety, adj. *novanta.*

Nine score, adj. *centottanta.*

Nine-hundred, adj. *novecento.*

Ni'nny, s. or ninny-hammer [a silly fellow, a dolt] *uno sciocco, uno scimunito, un melenso, uno scioperato, un gonzo, un uccellaccio, uno squasimodeo.*

Ninth, adj. *nono.*

Ni'nthly, adv. *in nono luogo.*

Nip [a pinch with the nail or teeth] *pizzico, pizzicotto.*

Nip [a small cut] *tagliuzzo, taglio piccolo, taglio di poco momento.*

Nip [a blast] *golpe; soffio di vento cattivo che manda in malora i frutti della terra.*

Nip [a taunt, a sarcasm] *botta, motto satirico, motto acuto e pungente.*

To nip [to pinch] *pizzicare.*

The winter nips the flowers, *il verno guasta i fiori.*

To nip off, *tagliare.*

To nip [to taunt] *pugnere con sarcasmi, motteggiare.*

Nipped, adj. *pizzicato, punto.*

Ni'ppers, s. [tweezers] *mollette*, s. f.

Ni'pping, s. *il pizzicare*, v. To nip.

Nipping, adj. [biting, cutting] *mordace, mordente, pungente.*

A nipping jest, *un detto mordace, una botta.*

Ni'pple [the teat of a breast] *capezzolo*, s. m. *quella punta della poppa ond' esce il latte.*

She has a sore nipple, *ella ha male a un capezzolo.*

Nit, s. *lendine*, s. f. *uovo di pidocchio.*

Nithing, s [a coward, a villain] *un codardo, un pusillanimo, un vigliacco, un poltrone, un furbo.*

Nitre, s [a salt impregnated with abundance of spirits out of the air] *nitro*, s. m. *spezie di sale, salnitro*, s. m.

Ni'trous, adj. *nitroso, che tien del nitro, o ha qualità del nitro.*

Ni'tty, adj. [full of nits] *lendinoso, pien di lendini.*

Ni'zy, s. [a fool, or silly fellow] *uno sciocco, uno scimunito, uno allocco, un gonzo.*

No, adv. [not] *no, non.*

Will you do it, or no? *volete farlo o no?*

No, I will not, *no, non voglio.*

No, not if I were to die, *no, quando anche dovessi morire.*

You shall come to no harm, *non ve ne verrà male alcuno.*

I have no money, *non ho danari.*

I have no reason to doubt of it, *non ho ragione alcuna da dubitarne.*

To no purpose, *invano, inutilmente.*

No where, *in nessun luogo.*

By no means, by no manner of means, *in conto alcuno, in nessun modo.*

No body, *nessuno, veruno.*

It is no matter, *non importa.*

No such matter, *niente affatto.*

No such thing, *non c' è tal cosa.*

I have no time now, *non ho tempo adesso.*

To Nobi'litate [to make noble or famous] *nobilitare, far nobile, render chiaro e famoso.*

Nobi'litate, adj. *nobilitato.*

Nobi'lity, s. [the quality or degree of a nobleman] *nobiltà, chiarezza di nascita*, s. f.

The nobility [the whole body of noblemen] *la nobiltà.*

Nobility [fame, reputation] *nobiltà, fama, riputazione*, s. f.

To forfeit one's nobility, *degradare della sua nobiltà.*

Noble, adj. [raised above the commonalty and gentry] *nobile, di chiara e illustre schiatta.*

Noble [great, renowned] *nobile, riguardevole, grande, illustre, insigne.*

A noble action, *un azione nobile, o grande.*

A noble soul, *un anima illustre.*

A noble style, *uno stile sublime.*

The noble parts of the body, *viz.* the liver, heart, and brain, *le parti nobili del corpo, cioè il fegato, il cuore, ed il cervello.*

A noble entertainment, *un festino magnifico.*

A noble building, *un edificio superbo.*

A noble, or nobleman, s. [a person of honour, as a duke, marquiss, earl, &c.] *un nobile, una persona titolata, come un duca, un marchese, un conte.*

The noblemen of the kingdom, *i nobili d' un regno, i pari del regno.*

A noble [an ancient coin] *un nobile, moneta d' oro, che valeva in circa sei scillini ed otto soldi.*

No'bleness, s. [nobility] *nobiltà, chiarezza di natali.*

Nobleness [greatness, sublimity of mind or expressions] *nobiltà, grandezza, eccellenza, sublimità.*

No'bly, adv. *nobilmente, splendidamente, magnificamente.*

He has treated us nobly, *ci ha regalato nobilmente o splendidamente.*

Nobly born, *nobilmente nato, di nascita illustre.*

No'cent, adj. [guilty, criminal] *colpevole, criminale.*

Nocent, adj. [hurtful, mischievous] *nocente, dannoso.*

No'ctive, adj. [hurtful] *nocivo, nocevole, che nuoce.*

No'ctulabe, s. [an instrument to find the motion of the north star about the pole] *nottolabio*, s. *strumento marinaresco per trovare l' altezza della stella di tramontana intorno al polo.*

No'cturn, adj. [nightly] *notturno, di notte, che appartiene a notte.*

Nocturn, s. [part of church service for the night] *notturno*, s. m. *parte del mattutino, che si recita nelle chiese.*

Noctu'rnal, s. [a mathematical instrument for taking the height or depression of the pole-star] *nottolabio, strumento matematico per misurare l' altezza o la bassezza della stella polare.*

Nocturnal, adj. [nightly] *notturno.*

Nod, s. [a motion or sign with one's head] *cenno, segno, o gesto che si fa colla testa.*

To give a nod for refusal, *far cenno di no.*

To Nod [to give a sign by moving the head] *far cenno, accennare.*

To nod [to sleep with a motion of the head] *dormicchiare.*

To nod, *tentennare.*

No'dding, s. *accennamento*, s. m. *l' accennare; cenno, o segno di testa.*

No'ddle, s. [the head] *la testa.*

No'ddy, s. [ninny] *un allocco, un minchione, uno sciocco, un pecorone.*

Node, s. [knot, noose] *nodo*, s. m.

Nodo'sity, s. [a being nodous] *nodosità*, s. f.

No'dous, adj. [knotty, full of knots] *nodoso, nodoruto, pien di nodi, nocchiuto, nocchieruto.*

Nodous [knotty, difficult] *difficile, scabroso, intrigato.*

No'ggin, s. [a little mug] *boccaletto*, s. m. *foglietta*, s. f.

No'iance, s. [nusance] *nocumento, nocimento*, s. m.

Noise, s. [a strife or squabble] *strepito, romore, fracasso, schiamazzo*, s m.

To make a noise, *strepitare, fare strepito, far remore.*

The noise of trumpets and drums, *lo strepito delle trombette, e de' tamburi.*

That makes a great noise in the world, *questo fa grande strepito nel mondo.*

A noise in one's ears, *ronzo, susurro, rombo*, s. m.

A noise of water running, *mormorio*, s. m.

A shrill noise, *stridore, strido*, s. m.

A hum-

A humming noiſe, ſuch as bees make, *ronzio, rombo*, s. m.
A noiſe with the feet, *calpeſtio*, s. m.
To NOISE abroad, *divulgare, publicare, manifeſtare, far paleſe.*
Noiſed abroad, adj. *divulgato, publicato.*
It is noiſed abroad, *corre voce, è fama, ſi dice.*
NO'ISOME, adj. [naſty, ſtinking] *nojoſo, ſtomachevole, che fa nauſea, puzzolente, nauſeoſo.*
NO'ISOMLY, adj. *ſporcamente, nojoſamente, ſtomachevolmente.*
NO'ISOMNESS, s. *ſporchezza, nauſea*, s. f.
NOLI ME TANGERE, s. [a ſort of canker in the face] *malattia cancrenoſa che viene nel viſo.*
NOMENCLA'TOR, s. [remembrancer among the Romans] *nomenclatore fra gli antichi Romani.*
NO'MENCLATURE, s. [a ſet of names, or vocabulary] *nomenclatura*, s. f. *vocabolario*, s. m.
NO'MINAL, adj. [only in name, not real] *di nome, non reale.*
A nominal king, *un rè di nome.*
NO'MINALLY, adv. *nominalmente, a nome, per nome, ſpecialmente.*
To NO'MINATE [to name, to appoint] *nomare, nominare, deſtinare, eleggere*, pret. *eleſſi.*
NO'MINATED, adj. *nomato, nominato, deſtinato, eletto.*
NO'MINATING, s. *il nomare.*
NOMINA'TION, s. *nominazione*, s. f.
He has the nomination of that living, *quel beneficio è alla ſua nominazione.*
NO'MINATIVE, ex. The nominative caſe [or only the nominative] *il nominativo, o caſo retto.*
NO'MPAREL } s. one of the leaſt
NO'NPAREIL } ſorts of printing letters] *ſorta di lettera piccoliſſima di ſtamperia.*
Nomparel [a kind of pear] *ſpezie di pero.*
Nomparel [a ſort of ſugar-plumbs] *confetti piccioli.*
NON-ABI'LITY, s. [an exception againſt a perſon that diſables him to commence a ſuit] *inabilità*, s. f. *termine legale, eccezione contro una perſona che lo rende inabile di principiare un proceſſo.*
NO'NAGE, s. [all the time that a man is under age] *minorità*, s. f.
NONCE, s. ex. for the nonce [or deſignedly] *a poſta, a bello ſtudio.*
NON-CO'NFORMIST, s. [one who does not conform to the church of England, with reſpect to its diſcipline and ceremonies] *nome che ſi da a quelli che non ſi conformano alla diſciplina e cerimonie della chieſa Anglicana.*
NONE, adj. or pron. [not one] *neſſuno, veruno.*
There's none of us that will do it, *non v' è neſſuno fra noi che voglia farlo.*
None of e'm, *neſſuno di loro.*
It is none of my fault, *non è mia colpa.*
It is none of the beſt, *non è molto buono.*
There is none but knows, *non v' è neſſuno che non ſappia, ognuno ſa.*
I have none, *non ne ho.*
I will have none of it, *io non ne voglio.*
Let there be none put in, *che non ve ſe ne metta niente.*
'Tis none of ours, *non è noſtro.*
It could be none elſe, *non poteva eſſere altri che lui.*
Such an artiſt, as none is able to compare with him, *un tale arteſice, che neſſuno altro può paragonarſi a lui.*
You are none of our company, *voi non ſiete della noſtra compagnia.*
I love none but you, *non amo altri che voi.*
NONE, s. [a canonical hour in the Roman church] *nona*, s. f. *nome della quinta ora canonica.*
NON-E'NTITY, s. [a thing that is not in being] *nichilità, un nonnulla.*
NO'NES, s. [among the Romans, are the next days after the calends, or firſt days of every month] *le none de' meſi.*
NON-PA'YMENT, s. *mancanza di pagamento.*
NO'N-PLUS, s. ex. [to put one to a non-plus] *confondere altrui, farlo reſtar confuſo.*
To be at a non-plus, *reſtar confuſo o ſorpreſo.*
NON-RESIDENCE, s. [when the ſpiritual lords are not reſident upon their benefices] *aſſenza*, s. f.
NON-RE'SIDENT, adj. [abſent from his ſpiritual charge] *che non fa la ſua reſidenza, aſſente.*
NO'NSENSE, s. [impertinence, abſurdity] *ſvarioni, ſpropoſiti, detti ſpropoſitati, parlare ſciocco, irragionevolezza.*
'Tis nonſenſe to believe this, *è una ſciochezza credere tal coſa.*
NONSE'NSICAL, adj [impertinent] *ſpropoſitato, ſcedato, impertinente.*
A nonſenſical diſcourſe, *un diſcorſo ſpropoſitato, pien di ſpropoſiti.*
NONSE'NSICALLY, adv. *ſpropoſitatamente, ſciccamente.*
NON-SOLVENT, adj. [not able to pay] *che non può pagare, inſolvente.*
NO'NSUIT, s. [a renouncing or letting fall the ſuit] *tralaſciamento, o deſiſtimento di lite.*
To NO'NSUIT, *condannare per deſiſtimento di lite.*
Non-ſuited, adj. *condannato per deſiſtimento di lite.*
NO'N-TERM, s. [a vacation-time between term and term] *vacanze, ferie.*
NOOK, s. [corner] *cantone, angolo*, s. m.
The nook of the neck, *la noce del collo.*
NOON, s. [mid-day] *mezzodì, mezzogiorno*, s. m.
At noon day, *ſul mezzodì.*
At laſt, the night advancing to her noon, *alla fine nell' avvanzarſi della mezza notte.*
The forenoon, *la mattina.*
The afternoon, *il dopo pranzo.*
To ſleep at noon, *dormire di meriggiana.*
NO'ONING, s. [noon ſleep] *meriggiana*, s. f.
NOOSE, s. [a ſliding knot] *nodo, o cappio ſcorſojo.*
The nooſe of matrimony, *il nodo matrimoniale.*
Nooſe [ſnare] *laccia, inganno*, s. m. *inſidia*, s. f.
To NO'OSE [to inſnare] *accalappiare, allacciare, inſidiare, tendere inſidie.*
NO'OSED, adj. *accalappiato, allacciato, inſidiato.*
NOR, conj. *nè.*
Neither fortunate, nor wiſe, *nè fortunato, nè ſavio.*
NORTH, s. [one of the four corners of the world] *il ſettentrione, tramontana.*
The north of England, *la parte ſettentriouale d'Inghilterra.*
North, adj. *ſettentrionale, di ſettentrione.*
A north wind, *vento ſettentrionale, tramontana, ventavolo.*
The north-ſtar, *la ſtella di tramontana.*
The north pole, *il polo artico.*
North eaſt, or Nord-eaſt, *volturno, vento greco.*
North-weſt, *quarta di maeſtro verſo ponente.*
A north-weſt wind, *vento maeſtro verſo ponente.*
NO'RTHELY, adj. *ſettentrionale, di ſettentrione.*
A northerly-wind, *vento ſettentrionale.*
NO'RTHERN, adj. *ſettentrionale.*
NOSE, s. [part of the face] *naſo*, s. m.
A flat noſe, *un naſo ſchiacchiato.*
A large noſe, *un naſaccio.*
A little noſe, *naſello, naſetto.*
A high-mounted noſe, *un naſo ſchiacciato.*
A hawk-noſe, *naſo acquilino.*
To ſpeak in the noſe, *parlar col naſo.*
The noſe, or nozel of a pair of bellows, *il cannoncello d'un ſoffietto.*
To lead one by the noſe [to govern him intirely] *menar altrui pel naſo, governarlo.*
To thruſt one's noſe into every corner [to concern one's ſelf with every thing] *ingerirſi, intrometterſi, impacciarſi in ogni coſa.*
To put out one's noſe out of joint [to ſupplant him] *far rimanere altrui con un palmo di naſo, ingannarlo, deluderlo.*
To make one pay through the noſe, [or very dear] *far pagare caro altrui qualche coſa.*
There will be many bloody noſes, *vi ſarà un gran conflitto.*
He did it under my noſe [or before my

my face] *lo fece alla barba mia, sotto i miei occhi, in presenza mia.*

To tell noses [to tell how many there are to pay the reckoning] *contare le persone che devono pagar lo scotto.*

Nose-band [for a horse] *musoliera, s. f. strumento che si mette al muso a' cavalli acciocchè non possan mordere.*

Nose-bleed, s. [a plant] *millefoglie, s. f. spezie di pianta.*

To NOSE [to scent, to smell] *fiutare, odorare.*

To nose, *volger la faccia, mostrar il viso, mostrare che non s' ha paura.*

To nose, v. n. [to look big, to bluster] *pavoneggiarsi, braveggiare, vantarsi.*

NO'SED, adj. *nasuto, che ha naso grande.*

Nosed, part. *nasuto.*

Flat-nosed, *che ha il naso schiacciato.*

Well-nosed, *nasuto, che ha gran naso.*

NO'SEGAY, s. *mazzetto di fiori.*

NO'STOCK, s. *stella errante.*

NO'STRIL, s. [the breathing holes of the nose] *nare*, pl. *nari*, s. f. *i buchi del naso.*

His memory will stink in the nostrils of men, *la sua memoria sarà odiosa alla posterità.*

NOT, adv. *non, no.*

I will not, *non voglio.*

Why not? *perchè no?*

Not a drop, *nem meno una goccia.*

Not at all, not in the least, *niente affatto.*

Not yet, not as yet. *non ancora.*

Not that I doubt him an honest man, *non ch' io dubiti della sua onestà.*

Not long after, *poco dopo, da lì a poco, non molto tempo dopo.*

I shall not do it, *non lo farò.*

Not one, *nemmeno uno.*

If not, *se non.*

Not that I know of, *non ch' io sappia.*

NO'TABLE, adj. [remarkable, considerable] *notabile, considerabile.*

Notable [great, extraordinary] *notabile, grande, segnalato, straordinario.*

A notable rogue, *un pretto villano.*

A notable sum of money, *una somma grande di danaro.*

A notable favour, *un favore segnalato.*

NO'TABLY, adv. *notabilmente, considerabilmente, grandemente.*

NO'TARY, s. [scrivener] *notajo*, s. m.

A publick notary, *un notajo pubblico.*

NOTCH, s. [dent, jag] *tacca*, s. f. *picciol taglio.*

The notch of a cross-bow, *cecca*, s. f. *tacca della freccia, nella quale entra la corda dell' arco.*

Notch-weed, *sorta d'erba.*

To NOTCH [to make a notch] *intaccare, far tacca.*

To notch the hair, *tagliar i capelli a scala, o malamente.*

NO'TCHED, adj. *intaccato.*

NO'TCHING, s. *tacca*, s. f. *taglio*, s. m.

NOTE, s. [mark] *nota*, s. f. *segno, ricordo*, s. m.

Note [remark] *nota, annotazione, osservazione*, s. f.

Note [merit, consideration, credit] *distinzione, considerazione, stima*, s. f. *merito, conto*, s. m.

A man of great note, *un uomo di gran considerazione o stima, un uomo di conto.*

A town of note, *una città considerabile.*

Note [in musick] *nota.*

To sing the notes, *cantar le note.*

To prick down the notes in a musick book, *notare un libro di musica.*

Note [point, in grammar] *punto*, s. m.

A note of interrogation, *punto interrogativo.*

A note of admiration, *punto ammirativo.*

Note [bill under one's hand] *biglietto*, s. m. *cedola*, s. f.

To confer notes [to consult, to confer] together, *consultare, concertare, ordire insieme.*

To NOTE [to observe] *notare, considerare, osservare, fare attenzione.*

NO'TED, adj. *notato, considerato, osservato.*

Noted [notable, famous] *notabile, considerabile, famoso, illustre, particolare, rinomato.*

Noted [notorious, arrant] *famoso, insigne.*

NO'TEDLY, adv. *notevolmente, con modo da notarsi.*

NO'THING, s. [a word made of no and thing] *niente, nulla.*

I have nothing, *non ho niente.*

I know nothing of it, *non ne so niente o nulla.*

God made the world out of nothing, *Iddio creò il mondo d'un niente.*

Of nothing, nothing comes, *d'un niente non si può far nulla.*

That is nothing [no matter] *non importa.*

Nothing venture, nothing have, *chi non arrischia, non guadagna.*

That is nothing to me, *ciò non m' importa, o concerne, ciò non mi risguarda.*

He is nothing but skin and bones, *non ha che la pelle e l'ossa.*

To live upon nothing but herbs and roots, *non pascersi d'altro che d'erbe, o radici.*

He does nothing but eat and sleep, *non fa altro che mangiare e dormire.*

Prodigality is nothing near so much blamed as covetousness, *la prodigalità è molto meno da basiarme che non l'avarizia.*

This is nothing near so good as the other, *questo non è sì buono quanto l'altro.*

To make nothing of one [to slight him] *disprezzare, burlarsi, non far conto d'uno.*

He makes nothing of drinking two bottles of wine, *stima un nulla il bere due fiaschi di vino.*

I can make nothing of it [I do not understand it] *non comprendo, o non intendo niente di ciò, io non so quel che significa, o quel che si voglia dire.*

He could make nothing of it, *non ne ha potuto venire a capo.*

That business will come to nothing, *questo negozio svanirà, o anderà in fumo.*

He is nothing taller than he was, *non è punto più alto che era.*

Nothing doubting, but if he came, *non dubitando punto, che se fosse venuto.*

Little or nothing, *quasi niente.*

It is good for nothing, *non val niente.*

I will have nothing to do with you, *non voglio impacciarmi co' fatti vostri.*

I desire nothing more, *altro non desidero.*

NO'THINGNESS, s. *nichilità*, s. f. *un nonnulla*, s. m.

NO'TICE, s. [knowledge] *notizia, cognizione, conoscenza, contezza*, s. f.

Notice [observation] *osservazione, attenzione*, s. f.

To take notice of a thing, *osservare, por mente, fare attenzione a qualche cosa.*

Take notice of that, *badate a ciò.*

Take no notice of any thing, *non fate sembiante, o vista di niente.*

He took no notice of me, *finse, o fece sembiante di non vedermi.*

Notice [advice] *notizia, contezza*, s. f. *avviso, ragguaglio*, s. m.

To have notice of a thing, *aver contezza, o notizia di che che si sia.*

To give notice, *avvisare, dare avviso, fare intendere, significare, avvertire*, pref. *avvertisco.*

This is the second time I give you notice, *questa è la seconda volta che ve ne avvertisco.*

Take notice, that it is not good meddling with him, *sappiate, o avvertite che non è di vostro vantaggio impacciarvi con lui.*

NOTIFICA'TION, s. *notificazione, notificagione*, s. f.

To NO'TIFY [to make known, to give to understand] *notificare, far noto, significare.*

NO'TIFIED, adj. *notificato, significato.*

NO'TIFYING, s. *notificazione, notificagione*, s. f.

NO'TION, s. [a conception or idea in the mind] *concetto, pensiero*, s. m. *concezione, idea*, s. f.

To have a confused notion of a thing, *aver qualche idea confusa di qualche cosa.*

Airy notions, *pensieri vani.*

A silly notion, *un concetto mal' fondato.*

I have no notion how this can be done, *non posso capire o darmi ad intendere come ciò possa farsi.*

NO'TIONAL, adj. *ideale, imaginativo*

A notional property, *una proprietà ideale, o imaginativa.*

NOTORI'ETY, *v.* Notoriousness.

NOTO'RIOUS, adj. [publickly known, manifest] *notorio, manifesto, evidente, chiaro.*

Notorious [arrant] *insigne, famoso, grande.*

A notorious lie, *una gran bugia.*

A notorious rogue, *un puro e pretto furbo.*

NOTO'RIOUSLY, adv. *notoriamente, pubblicamente, manifestamente, evidentemente.*

NOTO'RIOUSNESS, s. [plain evidence of the matter of fact] *evidenza, chiarezza,* s. f.

To NOTT [to shear] *tagliar la lana al'e pecore, tosare.*

NO'TWITHSTANDING, prep. and adv. *non ostante, benché, con tutto che, mal grado.*

Notwithstanding all your endeavours, *non ostante tutti i vostri sforzi.*

NOVA'TION, s. [a making new] *innovazione, rinnovazione,* s. f.

NOVA'TOR, s. [he that makes any thing new] *innovatore,* s. m. *che innova.*

NO'VEL, s. [an ingenious relation of a pleasant adventure or intrigue] *novella,* s. f. *narrazion favolosa.*

To tell a novel, *novellare, raccontar novelle.*

A little short novel, *novelletta, novelluzza,* s. f.

A ridiculous novel, *una novellozza, una novella ridicola.*

A teller of novels, *novellatore, novelliere, novelliero,* s. m. *raccontator di novelle.*

Novel, adj. [new] *nuovo, novello.*

A novel party, *un nuovo partito.*

A novel assignment [in law terms] *una novella assegnazione, un novello assegnamento.*

NO'VELTY, s. [innovation, change] *novità,* s. f.

NOVE'MBER, s. [the ninth month from March] *Novembre,* s. m. *uno de' dodici mesi dell' anno.*

NO'VENARY, adj. [belonging to the number nine] *che appartiene al numero di nove.*

NOUGHT, s. [nothing] *niente, nulla,* s. m.

You shall not make a fool of me for nought, *non vi burlerete di me per nulla.*

To set at nought, *disprezzare, vilipendere, non far conto.*

To come to nought, *ridursi a niente, svanire, andare in fumo.*

NOUGHT [cypher] *zero.*

NO'VICE, s. [a new beginner in any art or profession] *un novizio, un principiante.*

Novice [a monk or nun, newly entered into the order] *un novizio, una novizia.*

NO'VITIATE, } s. [the time during
NO'VICESHIP, } which one is a novice] *noviziato,* s. m.

To pass a long novitiate, *fare un lungo noviziato.*

NOVILU'NIUM, s. [the new moon] *novilunio,* s. m. *il tempo della luna nuova.*

NO'VITY, s. [newness, a new thing] *novità,* s. f.

NOUN, s. [a part of speech in grammar] *nome,* s. m. *termine grammaticale.*

To NO'URISH [to feed, to keep, to maintain] *nutricare, nutrire, alimentare, sostenere,* pref. *sostengo,* pret. *sostenni,* pref. *nutrisco.*

To nourish [to cherish] *nutrire, allevare, fomentare.*

NO'URISHED, adj. *nutricato, nutrito, alimentato, sostenuto, fomentato.*

NO'URISHING, s. *nutrimento,* s. m. *nutritura, nutrizione,* s. f.

Nourishing, adj. *nutritivo, nutrichevole, nutrimentale.*

NO'URISHMENT, s. [food] *nutrimento,* s. m. *nutritura, nutrizione,* s. f.

Now, adv. [at present, at this time] *adesso, ora.*

Just now, *appunto, or ora, testè, poco fa*

Till now, *fin adesso.*

He came even now, *in questo momento venuto.*

Nowadays, *al giorno d'oggi.*

Now and then, *di quando in quando.*

They stand now on one foot and then on the other, *stanno ora sopra un piede, ora sopra l'altro.*

Before now, *prima, avanti, altre volte.*

This happened before now, *ciò è occorso prima o altre volte.*

How now? *eh bene?*

The now King, *il Re regnante.*

Now at length, *alla fine.*

Now, conj. *ora.*

Now, as I was telling you, *ora, come avo dicendovi.*

NO'WED, adj. [knotted] *annodato.* Obf.

NOWL, s. [the top of the head] *cocuzzolo,* s. m. *la cima della testa.*

NO'XIOUS, adj [hurtful, offensive] *nocivo, nocente, nocevole, offensivo.*

The NOZLE, s. [the upper part of a candlestick] *il cannone d' un candeliere.*

The nozle of a pair of bellows, *il cannoncello d'un soffietto.*

The nozle of a leather bag, *la bocca d'un sacco di pelle.*

To NU'BBLE, *rompere o amaccare co' pugni. Non in uso.*

NU'BILOUS, adj. [cloudy] *nuvoloso, oscuro, fosco.*

To NU'DATE [to make bare or naked] *nudare, spogliare ignudo.*

To NU'DDLE along [to go carelesly, and in haste] *camminar presto e trascuratamente.*

NUDE, adj. [naked, bare] *nudo.*

A nude contract [a bare promise of a thing without any consideration] *una semplice promessa.*

NU'DITY, s. [nakedness] *nudità,* s. f.

A nudity [in painting, a picture representing a naked person] *una figura ignuda.*

NUEL, s. [the spindle of a winding stair-case] *chiocciola di scala.*

NU'ISANCE, s. *cosa nociva.*

Nuisance, s. *cosa che incommoda o nuoce al vicino. Vocabolo legale.*

NUKE, s. [the hinder part of the head, the noddle] *nuca,* s. f. *la parte deretana del capo.*

NULL, adj. [void] *invalido, nullo.*

To NULL [to make null] *annullare, cassare, abolire,* pref. *abolisco.*

NU'LLED, adj. *annullato, cassato, abolito.*

To NU'LLIFY [to make null] *annullare, rassare.*

NU'LLITY, s. [the being null, invalidity] *nullità, invalidità,* s. f.

NUMB, adj. *torpido, stupefatto, intirizzito.*

To NUMB, *v.* To benumb.

NU'MBER, s. [collection of units] *numero,* s. m.

An even or odd number, *numero pari, o impari.*

A broken number, *un numero rotto.*

The singular or plural number, *il numero singolare o del meno, il numero plurale o del più.*

Number [cadence of words] *numero, cadenza o desinenza di parole.*

The golden number [among the astrologers, a period of nineteen years] *numero d'oro.*

The Numbers [a book in the Old Testament] *i Numeri, libro del Vecchio Testamento.*

To number [to count] *numerare, annoverare, contare.*

The NU'MBLES, s. [the entrails of a deer] *le interiora d'un cervo.*

NU'MBERED, adj. *numerato, annoverato, contato.*

NU'MBERABLE, adj. *numerabile, che si può numerare.*

NU'MERAL, adj. *numerale.*

To NU'MERATE [to count or number] *numerare, contare, annoverare.*

NUMERA'TION, s. [the art of reading or expressing any number set down in figures] *numerazione,* s. f. *il numerare.*

NUMERA'TOR, s. [one who numbers or counts, an arithmetician] *numeratore, aritmetico,* s. m.

NUME'RICAL, adj. *numerico.*

A numerical difference [in logick] *una differenza numerica.*

NU'MERO, s. [a term prefix'd by merchants, or others, to a certain number of things marked thus: No.] *numero.*

NUMEROSITY, s. [numerousness] *numerosità*, s. f.
NU'MEROUS, adj. [manifold] *numeroso, di molto numero*.
Numerous [harmonious] *armonioso*.
NU'MEROUSNESS, s. [numerosity] *numerosità*, s. f.
The numerousness of verses, *la desinenza de' versi*.
NUN, s. [a virgin that has bound herself by vow to a single and chaste life in a monastery] *una monaca*.
A nun, s. [a bird] *monachino*, s. m. *sorta d'uccelletto*.
NU'NCHION, s. [an afternoon's repast] *merenda*, s. f.
NU'NCIATURE, s. [the office of a nuncio] *nunziatura*, s. f.
NU'NCIO, s. [the Pope's ambassador] *nunzio*, s. m. *ambasciadore del Papa*.
NU'NCUPATIVE, } adj. [declar-
NUNCUPATORY, } ed by word of mouth] *verbale*.
A nuncupative will, *testamento verbale*.
NU'NNERY, s. [a cloister of nuns] *convento di monache*.
To go into a nunnery, *monacarsi, farsi monaca*.
NU'PTIAL, adj. [of a wedding] *nuziale, che appartiene a nozze*.
NURSE, s. [a wet nurse] *bái a*, s. f.
A nurse [one who takes care of a sick body] *una guardia d' ammalati*.
A nurse-child, *un bambino di latte*.
A nurse's pay, *balliatico*, s. m. *prezzo che si da per allattare il fanciullo*.
A nurse's husband, *balio*, s. m. *marito della balia*.
To NURSE [to take care of, to nourish, to feed] *nutrire, nutricare, allevare*.
To nurse a child, *allattare un fanciullo*.
To nurse a sick body, *curare, o aver cura d'un ammalato*.
To NURSE [to encourage or uphold] *fomentare, incorraggiare, animare, spalleggiare*.
To nurse one in his vicious courses, *fomentare in altrui i vizi*.
NU'RSED, adj. *nutrito, nutricato, allevato, fomentato, incoraggito*.
NU'RSERY, s. [the nurse s chamber] *la camera della balia*.
A nursery of trees, *semenzajo*, s. m. *luogo dove si pongono i semi di piante o d' erbe per trapiantare*.
A nursery of young people design'd for priesthood, *seminario, luogo dove si pongono in educazione i fanciulli destinati alla vita ecclesiastica*.
Nursing, s. *nutrizione*, s. m. *il nutrire*.
NURST, *v*. Nursed.
NU'RTURE, s. [education] *educazione*, s. f.
Nurture, s. [food, diet] *cibo, mangiare*.
NU'SANCE, s. [annoyance] *pregiudizio, torto, danno, nocumento*, s. m.
He is a publick nusance, *è la peste del paese*.
NUT, s. [a sort of fruit] *noce*, s. f. *frutto*.
A wall nut, *una noce*.
A wall-nut tree, *un albero di noce*.
A hasel-nut, or small nut, *nocella, nocciuola*, s. f.
A hasel-nut tree, *nocciuolo*, s. m.
The nut of a cross-bow, *noce*, s. f. *quella parte della balestra dove s'appicca la corda quando si scarica*.
A nut-shell, *scorza di noce*.
A nut-cracker, *un acciaccanoci, un ammaccanoci*.
Nut-gall, *galla*, s. f.
Nut-peach, *noce persira*.
Nut-brown [of the colour of ripe nuts] *castagnino*.
NU'TMEG, s. [a well known spice] *noce moscada*, s. f.
NU'TRIMENT, s. [nourishment] *nutrimento*, s. m. *nutritura*, s. f.
NUTRI'TION, s. [a nourishing] *nutrizione*, s. f. *nutrimento*, s. m.
NU'TRITIVE, adj. [apt to nourish] *nutritivo, che hà virtù di nutrire*.
NU'TTING, part. ex. to go a nutting, *andar a coglier delle noci o delle nocciuole*.
To NUZZLE [to hide the head, as a young child does in its mother's bosom] *nasconder si*.
To nuzzle [to nurse, to foster] *allattare, nutrire*.
To nuzzle [to go with the nose down like a dog] *andar col naso per terra fiutando come fa il cane*.
NYE, s. [a flight or great company of pheasants] *nuvolo di fagiani, stormo di fagiani*.
NY'MPHAL, } adj. *di ninfa*.
NYMPHOUS, }
NIS, *corrotto, da* none is *e da* not is.

O.

O [An interjection of calling]. *o*.
O! [an intejection of sorrow] *oh!*
O God, *oh Dio*.
O sad, *oh che disgrazia*.
O brave, *viva*.
O, *Shakespeare l'ha usato in vece di cerchio*. Within this wooden O, *in questo cerchio di legno*.
OAF, s. [a changeling; a foolish child left by the fairies] *bambino sciocco lasciato da una fata invece d'uno spiritoso da lei rubato*.
Oaf, s. *uno sciocco, un baccellone*.
O'AFISH, adj. *sciocco, stupido*.
O'AFISHNESS, s. *stupidezza*.
OAK, s. [a tree] *quercia, querce*, s. f. *albero noto*.
A stone-oak, *elce*, s. f. *leccio*, s. m.
The bitter-oak, *cerro*, s m.
A grove of bitter oaks, *cerreto*, s. m. *bosco di cerri*.
Holme-oak, *elce*, s. m.
Oak of Cappadocia, s. f. *pianta simile alla ruta*.
A mast oak, *eschio, ischio*, s. m.
The gall-bearing oak, *quercia che porta delle galle*.
An oak-apple, *galla*, s. f.
An oak-grove, *querceto*, s. m. *bosco di querce*.
A young oak, *querciuola*, s. f. *querciuolo*, s. m.
Oak of Jerusalem, *querciuola*, s. f. *sorta d'erba*.
OA'KEN, adj. [made of oak] *di quercia*.
OAR, s. [metal unrefin'd, as it is mixed with the oar of the mine] *miniera*,

ra, s. f. materia della quale s' estraggono i metalli. Scrivi ORE, che è meglio.

Oar of gold or silver, miniera d' oro o d' argento.

Brass-oar, miniera di rame.

Oar [a long stick to row with] remo, s. m. strumento di legno da remare.

The blade of an oar, la paletta d' un remo.

To have an oar in another man's boat, darsi gl' impacci del rosso, pigliarsi le brighe che non gli toccano.

An oar handle, manico di remo, s. m.

Oars [a boat with two water-men to row] barchetta a due remi.

To OAR, vògare, andar a remi, remare.

OARY, adj. che ha forma o uso di remi.

OAT-CAKE, focaccia di vena.

OA'TEN, adj. [of oats] di vena.

An OATH, s. [a swearing, lawful or unlawful] giuramento, s. m.

To take one's oath, pigliare il giuramento.

To put one to his oath, dare il giuramento ad alcuno.

He said he was under an oath of secresy not to tell any body, disse aver promesso sotto sigillo di confessione di non dirlo a nessuno.

A false oath, spergiuro.

To take a false oath, spergiurare.

An oath [a curse] un giuramento, bestemmia.

O'AT-MEAL, s. paniro, s. m. biada minutissima.

Oat-meal, farina di vena.

Oat-meal grout, farina di panico.

OATS, s. [a sort of corn] vena, s. f. biada nota.

O'BDURATE, adj. [hardened] indurito, indurato, ostinato, intrattabile, inesorabile, inflessibile.

An obdurate sinner, un peccatore ostinato.

To O'BDURATE [to harden] indurare, indurire, pres. indurisco.

O'BDURATENESS, } s. induramento,
OBDURA'TION, } s. m. ostinazione, s. f.

OBE'DIENCE, s. [dutifulness, submission] obbedienza, ubbidienza, s. f.

I did it in obedience to you, l'ho fatto per obbedirvi.

OBE'DIENT, adj. [dutiful] obbediente, sommesso.

To be obedient to one's father, esser obbediente a suo padre, obbedire a suo padre.

Very obedient, obbedientissimo.

OBE'DIENTLY, adv. obbedientemente.

To carry one's self obediently, essere obbediente.

OBE'ISANCE, s. [a congee, or low bow] riverenza, s. f. saluto, s. m.

O'BELISK, s. [a solid piece of marble, or rather stone, four-square, and all of one piece, ending in a point at the top, like a pyramid] obelisco, s. m. guglia, aguglia, s. f.

To OBE'Y, obbedire, ubbidire, pres. obbedisco, ubbidisco.

To obey God's commandments, ubbidire a' comandamenti di Dio.

OBE'Y'D, adj. obbedito, ubbidito.

I will be obey'd, voglio esser obbedito.

He must be obey'd, bisogna ubbidirli.

An O'BJECT, s. [any thing which is opposed to our sight, or any other senses] oggetto, abbietto, s. m. quello in che s' affissa la vista, o l' intelletto.

A pleasant object to the sight, un obbietto grato agli occhi.

The object of my love, l' oggetto dell' amor mio.

The object [subject, matter] suggetto, s. m. materia, s. f.

To OBJE'CT [to make an objection, to oppose, to argue against] obbiettare, opporre, dare obbiezione, pres. oppongo, pret. opposi.

What have you to object against it? che potete obbiettarvi in contrario?

To object [to reproach] obbiettare, rimproverare, incolpare, dar colpa.

OBJE'CTED, adj. obbiettato, opposto, rimproverato, incolpato.

O'BJECT-GLASS, s. [glass remotest from the eye] il vetro più lontano dall' occhio. Dicesi de' cannocchiali e simili.

OBJE'CTION, s. [difficulty rais'd against a proposition] obbiezione, opposizione, s. f. opponimento, che si fa all' altrui opinione, o ragione.

To raise, start, or to make an objection, fare un obbiezione.

Objection [reproach] rimprovero, s. m. accusa, s. f.

OBJE'CTOR, s. [one who opposes or brings an argument against] quegli che fa un obbiezione.

O'BIT, s. [funeral solemnity, office for the dead] esequie, s. f. mortorio, e mortoro, s. m. onoranza nel seppellire i morti.

Obit [anniversary appointed in remembrance of the death of any person] anniversario, s. m.

O'BITUARY, s. [a register book, in which the friers enter the obits of their benefactors] libro nel quale i frati scrivono gli anniversari de' loro benefattori.

To O'BJURGATE [to chide or reprove] bravare, garrire, gridare, sgridare, riprendere.

OBJURGA'TION, s. [a chiding or reproving] bravata, riprensione, s. f. sgridamento, sgrido, garrimento, s. m.

O'BJURGATORY, adj. garrevole, che garrisce, o rimprovera minacciando.

O'BLATE, adj. [flatted at the poles] oblato, cipollare, piatto dal canto de' poli.

OBLA'TION, s. [offering] obblazione, offerta, s. f.

OBLECTA'TION, s. [recreation] diporto, spasso, trastullo, solazzo, s. m.

To OBLIGATE [to bind, to tie] obbligare, costrignere, legare o per parola o per iscrittura.

OBLIGA'TION, s. [duty, engagement] obbligagione, obbligazione, s. f. obbligo, dovere, s. m.

I am under no such obligation, io non son tenuto o obbligato a ciò.

An obligation [a bond or writing obligatory] obbligazione, contratto.

O'BLIGATORY, adj. [that is of force to oblige, binding] obbligatorio, che contiene obbligo.

To OBLI'GE [to bind, to constrain, to engage] obbligare, costrignere, sforzare, impegnare.

What reason obliges you to do it? qual motivo vi muove a farlo?

To oblige one [to do him a kindness] obbligare altrui, fare qualche servizio, o favore ad alcuno.

You will oblige me very much, m' obbligherete molto, mi farete un gran favore.

OBLI'GED, adj. obbligato, forzato, costretto.

I am obliged to you, vi resto obbligato.

He was obliged to leave the country, fu forzato d' abbandonare il suo paese.

OBLIGE'E, s. [a person to whom the bond is made] la persona alla quale l' obbligazione è fatta.

O'BLIGEMENT, s. [obligation] obbligazione, obbligagione, obbliganza, s. f. obbligo, s. m.

OBLI'GOR, s. [one that enters into a bond for payment of money] mallevadore, s. m. quegli che s' obbliga, o s' è obbligato, di pagare una somma di danari per un altro.

OBLI'GING, s. obbligamento, s. m. obbliganza, s. f.

Obliging, adj. [kind, complaisant] obbligante, cortese, affabile.

You are very obliging, voi siete molto cortese.

OBLI'GINGLY, adv. obbligantemente, con maniera obbligante.

OBLIQUA'TION, s. [declination from perpendicularity; obliquity] obliquità.

OBLI'QUE, adj. [crooked, awry] obbliquo, non retto, torto.

Oblique case [in terms of grammar, all but the nominative] i casi obbliqui, tutti i casi de' nomi eccetto il retto.

An oblique angle, angolo ottuso.

Oblique dealings, trattamenti pravi, maniere di procedere fraudulenti.

OBLI'QUELY, adv. obbliquamente.

OBLI'QUITY, s. [crookedness] obbliquità, s. f.

To OBLI'TERATE [to blot out, to raze out of memory] scancellare, o cancellare della memoria, dimenticare, obbliare.

OBLI'TERATED, adv. scancellato, cancellato dalla memoria, dimenticato.

OBLITERA'TION, s. dimenticanza, s. f. il dimenticare.

OBLI'VION [forgetfulneſs] *oblio*, s. m. *dimenticanza*, s. f.

An act of oblivion [an amneſty] *indulto, perdono generale*.

OBLI'VIOUS, adj. *che cagiona dimenticanza*.

OBLOCU'TION, s. [ill report, ſlander] *maledicenza, garrulità, detrazione*, s. f. *ſparlamento*, s. m.

OBLOCU'TOR, s. [a backbiter, or ſlanderer] *maldicente, maldicitore, detrattore, mormoratore, ſparlatore*, s. m.

OBLONG, adj. [more long than ſquare] *biſlungo, che tende più al lungo che al quadro*.

OBLO'QUIOUS, adj. [ſlandering] *maldicente, maledico*.

O'BLOQUY, s. [ſlander] *detrazione, maldicenza, garrulità*, s. m.

To lie under ſome obloquy, *eſſer diffamato*.

OBNO'XIOUSNESS, s. [the being liable to puniſhment] *il ſoggiacere a qualche pena*.

OBNO'XIOUS, adj. [liable, ſubject to] *ſoggetto, ſoggiacente*.

Obnoxious to puniſhment, *colpabile, colpevole di qualche delitto, criminale*.

An obnoxious conſcience, *una coſcienza leſa, o macchiata*.

To OBNU'BILATE [to make dark with clouds] *annebbiare, annuvolare*.

OBNU'BILATED, adj. *annebbiato, annuvolato*.

OBNUBILA'TION, s. [a darkening with clouds] *l'annebbiare, oſcuramento*, s. m.

O'BOLE, s. [an old ſmall coin worth a halfpenny] *obolo*, s. m. *ſpezie di moneta, e due valevano un danajo*.

OBRE'PTION, s. [a creeping or ſtealing in] *il ficcarſi innanzi, l'intrometterſi proſuntuoſamente*.

OBREPTI'TIOUS, adj. *orrettizio*.

OBSCE'NE, adj. [unclean, bawdy, lewd] *oſceno, diſoneſto, ſporco, impudico, impuro*.

OBSCE'NELY, adv. *diſoneſtamente, impudicamente, ſporcamente, impuramente*.

OBSCE'NITY, s. [an unclean ſpeech or action] *oſcenità, diſoneſtà, impudicizia*, s. f.

OBSCURA'TION, s. *oſcuramento*, s. m. *oſcurazione*, s. f.

OBSCU'RE, adj. [dark, without light] *oſcuro, tenebroſo, privo di lume*.

Obſcure [dark, difficult to underſtand] *oſcuro, difficile ad intenderſi, naſcoſo*.

An obſcure birth, *una naſcita oſcura, o ignobile*.

Obſcure [ſecret, little known] *oſcuro, privato, naſcoſto*.

To live in an obſcure condition, *vivere in uno ſtato oſcuro, o oſcuramente, menare una vita privata*.

To OBSCU'RE [to darken] *oſcurare, fare oſcurare, ottenebrare, offuſcare*.

To obſcure another man's merit, *oſcurare, denigrare, eccliſſare l' altrui merito*.

OBSCU'RED, adj. *oſcurato, offuſcato, intenebrato*.

OBSCU'RELY, adv. *oſcuramente*.

OBSCU'RING, s. *oſcuramento*, s. m. *l'oſcurare*.

OBSCU'RITY, s. [darkneſs] *oſcurità, tenebroſità*, s. f. *bujo*, s. m.

To O'BSECRATE [to entreat earneſtly] *pregare, ſupplicare, ſcongiurare, chiedere iſtantemente*.

OBSECRA'TION, s. [an earneſt entreaty] *preghiera*, s. f. *ſcongiuro ſtretto, prego*, s. m.

O'BSEQUIES, s. [funeral ſolemnities] *eſequie*, s. f. *pompa di mortorio*.

OBSE'QUIOUS, adj. [complaiſant] *oſſequioſo, obbligante, corteſe, affabile*.

Obſequious [dutiful] *oſſequioſo, obbediente, ſommeſſo*.

OBSE'QUIOUSLY, adv. *oſſequioſamente, riverentemente, corteſemente, obbedientemente*.

OBSE'QUIOUSNESS, s. [complaiſance] *oſſequio*, s. m. *ſervitù, oſſervanza, riverenza*, s. f.

Obſequiouſneſs [dutifulneſs] *obbedienza*.

O'BSERVABLE, adj. [fit, eaſy, or worthy to be obſerved] *oſſervabile, da oſſervarſi*.

Obſervable [remarkable] *notabile, conſiderabile*.

OBSE'RVANCE, s. [performance] *oſſervagione, oſſervanza, mantenimento*, s. m.

For the obſervance of his word, *per il mantenimento della parola data*.

Obſervance [reſpect, regard] *oſſervanza, riverenza, conſiderazione, ſommiſſione*, s. f. *riſpetto, riguardo*, s. m.

OBSERVANCES [the rules or cuſtoms of a monaſtery] *oſſervanze, regole, ordini d'un monaſtero*.

OBSE'RVANT, adj. [having regard to, reſpectful] *oſſervante, obbediente, ſommeſſo, riſpettoſo*.

Obſervant of his word, *eſatto ad attendere o mantenere la promeſſa*.

OBSE'RVANT, } s. pl. [a branch
OBSE'RVANTINES, } of the order of the Franciſcans] *zoccolanti*.

OBSERVA'TION, s. [a note or remark] *oſſervazione, oſſervagione, attenta conſiderazione*, s. f.

OBSERVA'TOR, s. [an obſerver of people's manners] *oſſervatore*, s. m. *oſſervatrice*, s. f.

OBSE'RVATORY, s. [a building erected to make natural and aſtronomical obſervations] *oſſervatorio*, s. m.

To OBSE'RVE [to keep, to follow a rule, law, &c.] *oſſervare, ſervare, mantenere*.

To obſerve the laws, *oſſervare, ſervare le leggi*.

To obſerve [to mark] *oſſervare, notare, diligentemente conſiderare*.

To obſerve [to watch] *oſſervare, por mente, ſpiar gli altrui andamenti*.

To obſerve one's maſter, *aſcoltare gli ammaeſtramenti del maeſtro*.

OBSE'RVED, adj. *oſſervato, ſervato, mantenuto, notato, conſiderato*.

Fit to be obſerved, *oſſervabile, notabile*.

OBSE'RVER, s. *oſſervatore*, s. m. *oſſervatrice*, s. f.

OBSE'RVING, s. *oſſervamento*, s. m. *l'oſſervare*.

OBSE'SSION, s. [a beſieging or compaſſing about] *aſſedio, circondamento, ſteccato*, s. m.

OBSE'T, adj. [beſet, haunted by an evil ſpirit] *ſpiritato, indemoniato*.

O'BSOLETE, adj. [grown old, or out of uſe] *vecchio, fuor d'uſo, non più in uſo, vieto, obſoleto*.

An obſolete word, *parola di minor uſo*.

O'BSTACLE, s. [hindrance, let, rub] *oſtacolo, ritegno, impedimento*, s. m. *oppoſizione*, s. f.

O'BSTINACY, s. [wilfulneſs, ſtubbornneſs] *oſtinazione, pertinacia*, s. f.

O'BSTINATE, adj. [wilful, ſtubborn] *oſtinato, pertinace, perfidioſo, protervo, caparbio, teſtereccio, capone*.

An obſtinate man or woman, *un caparbio, un teſtereccio, una caparbia, una teſtereccia*.

To be or grow obſtinate in a thing, *oſtinarſi, ſtare oſtinato in che che ſi ſia*.

O'BSTINATELY, adv. *oſtinatamente, con oſtinazione, pertinacemente*.

They are obſtinately reſolved either to vanquiſh or to die] *ſono riſoluti in ogni modo di vincere, o di morire*.

He perſiſts obſtinately in it, *egli è ben fermo in ciò*.

OBSTRE'PEROUS, adj. [making a loud noiſe, troubleſome] *ſtrepitoſo, incomodo, nojoſo*.

To OBSTRU'CT [to ſtop up, to hinder] *ſtoppare, riturare, turare*.

This will not obſtruct [not hinder] your deſign, *ciò non impedirà il voſtro diſegno*.

OBSTRU'CTED, adj. *ſtoppato, riturato, turato*.

OBSTRU'CTER, s. *quegli o quella che ſtoppa*.

OBSTRU'CTING, s. *lo ſtoppare, turamento*, s. m.

OBSTRU'CTION, s. [ſtoppage] *oppilazione*, s. f. *rituramento, rinſerramento de' meati del corpo*.

An obſtruction [hindrance] *oſtacolo, impedimento*, s. m.

OBSTRU'CTIVE, adj. [apt to ſtop up, ſtopping] *oppilativo, che riſtrigne il corpo*.

To OBTA'IN [to get, to gain] *ottenere, conſeguire, acquiſtare*, preſ. *ottengo*, pret. *ottenni*.

To obtain one's pardon, *ottenere il ſuo perdono*.

To obtain the victory, *guadagnar la vittoria*.

I cannot obtain of myſelf to do it, *non poſſo indurmi a farlo*.

OBTA'INED, adj. *ottenuto, conſeguito, acquiſtato*.

OBTA'INING, s. *l'ottenere, acquiſto*, s. m.

To OBTE'MPERATE, [to obey] *obbedire*, preſ. *obbediſco*.

OBTEMPERA'TION, s. *obbedienza, ubbidienza*, s. f.

To OBTE'NEBRATE [to darken, to make dark] *ottenebrare, oscurare, offuscare.*

OBTE'NTION, s. *opposizione.*

OBTESTA'TION, s. [an earnest or pressing request] *istanza, preghiera, supplica*, s. f.

OBTRECTA'TION, s. [back-biting, slander] *maledicenza, calunnia*, s. f.

To OBTRU'DE [to thrust or force in or upon, to impose] *intrudere, spinger dentro, introdurre, imporre*, pres. *impongo*, pret. *imposi.*

To obtrude new laws upon the people, *imporre nuove leggi al popolo.*

He would fain obtrude these his wild conceits upon the world, *vorrebbe in ogni modo farci approvare questi suoi vani concetti.*

To obtrude one's self every where, *ficcarsi, intromettersi per tutto.*

OBTRU'DED, adj. *intruso, introdotto, imposto, ficcato.*

OBTRU'DER, s. *quegli che intrude.*

OBTU'SE, adj. [blunt] *ottuso.*

An obtuse angle [any angle which is greater than a right one] *angolo ottuso.*

An obtuse wit, *un ingegno ottuso.*

OBVE'NTIONS, s. [church revenues] *rendite ecclesiastiche.*

To OBVE'RT [to turn back or against] *volgere indietro o contro.*

To O'BVIATE [to prevent to hinder] *ovviare, opporsi, impedire, rimuovere*, pres. *oppongo, impedisco.*

To obviate a danger, *ovviare, fransare un pericolo.*

O'BVIATED, adj. *ovviato, opposto, impedito, rimosso.*

O'BVIOUS, adj. [easy to be understood, plain, common] *facile, triviale, comune, facile a comprendersi, chiaro.*

I'll make it obvious by an example, *lo renderò chiaro con un esempio.*

This is obvious to all the Christian world, *ciò è noto a tutta la Cristianità.*

This is not obvious to every common understanding, *non ogni intendimento è sufficiente a capirlo.*

It is obvious to the eye [one cannot but see it] *non si può far di manco di non vederlo, è molto visibile.*

O'BVIOUSNESS, s. [state of being evident or apparent] *evidenza, chiarezza.*

To O'BUMBRATE [to overshadow] *adombrare.*

OBUMBRA'TION, s. [an overshadowing] *adombramento, obbombramento*, s. m. *adombrazione, obbombrazione*, s. f.

OCCA'SION, s. [season, convenient, time, opportunity] *occasione, congiuntura, occorenza, opportunità*, s. f.

To take the occasion, *prender cagione, pigliare occasione.*

Occasion [cause, reason, motive] *occasione, cagione, causa, ragione, materia*, s. f. *motivo, luogo, soggètto*, s. m.

To give an occasion of complaint, *dar materia da lamentarsi.*

He was the occasion of, *egli ne fu la causa.*

Occasion [want, necessity] *bisogno*, s. m. *necessità*, s. f.

I have occasion for it, *ne ho di bisogno.*

Have you occasion for money? *vi mancan danari? avete di bisogno di danari?*

If occasion serves, *se mi viene il taglio, se mi vien fatta.*

If my occasions give me leave, *se i miei affari me lo permetteranno.*

To OCCA'SION [to cause] *causare, cagionare, esser la causa.*

OCCA'SIONAL, adj. ex. an occasional cause [in philosopy] *una causa occasionale.*

Occasional [done by chance, casual] *casuale, accidentale.*

OCCA'SIONALLY, adv. *casualmente, accidentalmente.*

OCCA'SIONED, adj. *causato, cagionato.*

This was occasioned through inadvertency, *ciò accade per inavvertenza.*

OCCA'SIONER, s. *cagionatore; colui che è cagione; la cosa che cagiona.*

O'CCIDENT, s. [west] *occaso, occidente*, s. m. *la parte dove il sole va sotto.*

OCCIDE'NTAL, adj. [western] *occidentale, d'occidente.*

OCCI'SION, s. [a killing] *occisione, uccisione*, s. f.

OCCU'LT, adj. [secret] *occulto, celato nascoso.*

O'CCUPANT, s. [possessor] *occupatore, possessore*, s. m. *occupatrice*, s. f.

OCCUPA'TION, s. [business or employment] *occupazione, faccenda, briga*, s. f. *negozio, impiego, affare*, s. m.

Occupation [trade] *mestiere, impiego*, s. m.

Occupation [in law, tenure of land] *occupazione, possessione*, s. f.

O'CCUPATIVE, adj. ex. an occupative field [a field, which being left by its proper owner, is possessed by another] *un campo abbandonato, del quale un altro s' è impossessato.*

To O'CCUPY [to fill or take up a space] *occupare, ingombrare spazio, tener luogo.*

To occupy [to be in possession of] *occupare, possedere.*

To occupy [to employ] *impiegare, esercitare.*

To occupy husbandry, *esercitare l'agricoltura.*

To occupy a woman, *godere d'una donna.*

To occupy [to trade] *trafficare, negoziare.*

O'CCUPIED, adj. *occupato*, v. To occupy.

To OCCU'R [to meet, to come in the way, to offer itself] *occorrere, accadere, avvenire.*

OCCU'RRENCE, s. [occasion] *occorrenza, occasione*, s. f. *bisogno*, s. m.

Occurrence [event, news] *evento, caso*, s. m. *novelle*, s. f.

OCCU'RRING, s. *occorrimento*, s. m.

OCCU'RSION, s. [an occurring or meeting] *occorimento*, s. m.

The occursion of a ghost, *l'apparizione d'uno spirito.*

Various is the occursion of thought in man's sleep, *varie sono le immagini che si presentano all' uomo mentre dorme.*

O'CEAN, s. [the vast collection of waters, or main sea, which surrounds the whole globe of the earth] *l' oceano.*

OCTAE'DRON, s. [a solid geometrical figure, consisting of eight equal sides] *figura geometrica d' otto angoli uguali, ottaedro*, s. m.

O'CTAGON, s. [a figure consisting of eight angles] *ottangolo*, s. m. *figura di otto angoli.*

OCTA'NGULAR, adj. [having eight angles] *ottangolare, di otto angoli.*

O'CTAVE, s. [the eighth day after some peculiar festivals of the year] *ottava*, s. f.

An octave [or eighth in musick] *un ottava.*

OCTA'VO, s. ex. an octavo book, having eight leaves in a sheet] *un ottavo, un libro in ottavo.*

OCTE'NNIAL, adj. [of eight years] *ottennio, di otto anni.*

OCTO'BER, s. [the eighth month from March] *ottobre*, s. m. *il secondo mese dell' autunno.*

O'CTOGONE, s. [a figure of eight angles] *Ottangolo*, s. m. *figura di otto angoli.*

O'CTOGENARY, adj. [that is eighty years old] *ottuagenario, vecchio d'ottant' anni.*

O'CTONARY, adj. [belonging to the number eight] *ottonario, d'otto.*

O'CULAR, adj. [belonging to the eyes of sight] *oculare, di veduta.*

Ocular witness, *un testimonio oculare, o di veduta.*

O'CULATE, adj. [quick sighted] *oculato, cauto, avvertente.*

O'CULIST, s. [one skill'd in curing the diseases of the eyes] *un oculista.*

O'CULUS CHRISTI, s. [an herb] *clarea*, s. f.

ODD, adj. [not even] *casso, dispari, impari.*

An odd number, *numero casso.*

To play at even and odd, *giuocare a pari, o casso.*

An odd shoe, *una scarpa spajata.*

Odd [strange] *strano, straordinario, bizzarro, capriccioso.*

An odd kind of man, *un uomo strano, capriccioso, o bisbetico.*

I saw her in an odd kind of dress, *la vide bizzarramente vestita.*

An odd expression, *una espressione non comune o strana.*

Odd

Odd [ill] *cattivo, male.*
An odd kind of fmell, *un cattivo odore.*
An odd kind of bufinefs, *un cattivo negozio.*
It is odd if I don't do it, *è un miracolo fe non lo faccio.*
There is fome odd money, *v' è qualche danaro d' avanzo.*
The bill comes to ten pounds odd money, *il conto viene a dieci doppie, e più.*
He is fourfcore and odd, *egli ha ottanta e più anni.*
O'DDLY, adv. [ftrangely; particularly, unaccountably, uncouthly] *bisbeticamente, fantafticamente, ftranamente.*
O'DDNESS, s. *fantaftichezza, capriccio, ftranezza, bizzarria, ftravaganza, bisbetichezza*
I could not help fmiling at the oddnefs of his drefs, *non potetti trattenere le rifa veggendolo così fantafticamente veftito.*
ODDS, s. [difference, difparity] *difparità, difuguaglianza, differenza, s. f.*
See what odds there is between man and man, *vedete un poco che differenza o difpartità c' è fra un uomo ed un altro.*
Odds [advantage] *avvantaggio, vantaggio, s. m.*
You muft give me fome odds, *bifogna darmi qualche avantaggio.*
To have the odds of one, *aver l' avantaggio fopra d' uno, reftar fuperiore.*
To lay odds with one, *fare una fcommeffa ineguale con uno, cioè due o tre contro uno.*
To fight againft odds, *combattere con difavvantaggio, combattere con uno più forte di fe.*
Two againft one is odds, *due contro uno è troppo.*
Odds [difference, quarrel] *contefa, difputa, differenza, s. f. contrafto.*
To be at odds with one, *contendere, contraftare con uno, ftar punta punta, effer mal d' accordo.*
To fet at odds, *mettere in difcordia, metter male infieme.*
Odds-bobs [a comical oath] *cofpetto di bacco, gnaffe.*
ODE, s. [a fong, or lyrick poem] *ode, oda, s. f. forta di componimento poetico.*
O'DIOUS, adj. [hateful, deteftable] *odiofo, molefto, odievole, nojofo.*
An odious crime, *un delitto enorme, o atroce.*
Very odious, *odiofiffimo.*
O'DIOUSLY, adv. *odiofamente, con odio.*
O'DIOUSNESS, s. *qualità odiofa, enormità.*
The odioufnefs of the fact, *l' enormità del fatto.*
O'DIUM [fault] *colpa, s. f.*
To caft the odium upon one, *dar la colpa ad uno.*
ODORI'FEROUS, adj. [fweet-fmelling] *odorifero, odorifico, che getta odore.*
O'DOUR, s. [fmell] *odore, s. m.*

OECONO'MICAL, } adj. [belonging
OECONO'MICK, } to œconomy, or family government] *economo.*
OECONOMIST, s. [one who governs or rules a family] *un economo.*
OECO'NOMY, s. [thriftinefs, good hufbandry] *economica, economia, s. f. arte di ben amminiftrare gli affari domeftici.*
OECUME'NICAL, adj. [general, univerfal] *ecumenico, generale, univerfale.*
OEDE'MA, s. [a tumour or fwelling but more ftrictly any infenfible tumour, proceeding from pituitous matter] *edema, s. f. tumore procedente da materia biliofa.*
OF [prep. which generally denotes the genitive cafe] *di, del, della, dei, de', delle.*
A man worthy of praife, *un uomo degno di lode.*
The duty of man, *il dovere dell' uomo.*
I am of your opinion, *fono del voftro parere.*
They repent of their follies, *fi pentono delle loro pazzie.*
I will make an end of fpeaking, *finirò di parlare*
This friend of mine, *quefto mio amico.*
That life of yours, as it is called, is a death, *quefta voftra vita, come voi la chiamate, non è che morte.*
We were brought up together of little ones, *fiamo ftati allevati infieme dalla gioventù.*
I will write to you of this matter, *vi fcriverò intorno a quefta materia.*
He is ten years of age, *ha dieci anni.*
Of a tradefman he is pretty honeft, *per un artigiano è affai onefto.*
A man ill fpoken of, *un uomo di cattiva riputazione, o fama.*
It is cheap of twenty pounds, *è buon mercato a venti doppie.*
Out of hand, *fubito, immantinente.*
Of late, *ultimamente, di frefco, teftè, poco fa.*
Of old, *anticamente, già, altre volte.*
A friend of old, *un amico vecchio.*
It would not be well done of you, *voi non farefte bene.*
It will be wifely done of him, *farà faviamente.*
He is a friend of mine, *è un amico mio.*
I have never a horfe of my own, *non ho un cavallo che fia mio.*
I never faw the like of him, *non ho mai vifto un uomo fimile a lui.*
To make a fool of one, *burlarfi d' uno.*
OFF, *avverbio, che quando è unito co' verbi equivale generalmente al noftro* via; ex.
He got off, *e' fcappò via.*
Far off, *lontano, lunge, e lungi.*
A great way off, *molto lontano.*
How far is it off? *quanto è lontano?*
It is ten miles off, *è diftante dieci miglia.*
My cloaths are off, *fono fpogliato.*

To fpeak to one with one's hat off, *parlare ad uno col capello in mano.*
Off with your hat, *mettete giù il cappello.*
To have all the fkin off, *effer tutto fcorticato.*
To be off and on, *effere irrefoluto, effer in bilancia, bilanciare.*
To keep one off and on, *tenere uno a bada.*
Off-hand [prefently] *fubito, immediatamente.*
To be off with a thing, *non penfar più ad una cofa, lafciarla dar bando a che che fi fia.*
To be off with one, *non aver più a fare con uno, romper l' amicizia con uno.*
To be off from one's youthful pranks, *emendarfi o correggerfi delle pazzie giovanili.*
To go off, *v.* To go.
To leave off, *v.* To leave.
Off-fpring, s. *defcendenti, pofteri, s. m.*
Off-fets, s. [young fhoots which fpring and grow from others] *rampolli, polloni, s. m.*
O'FFAL, s. [refufe, dro's] *rimafuglio, avanzaticcio, s. m.*
Offals of meat, *rimafugli di carne.*
OFFE'NCE, s. [fault, trefpafs] *offefa, colpa, s. f. peccato, delitto, s. m.*
Offence [injury, wrong] *offefa, ingiuria, s. f. danno, oltraggio, affronto, s. m.*
To give an offence, *fare un' offefa, offendere.*
To take an offence at fomething, *tenerfi offefo di che che fi fia.*
Offence [fcandal] *fcandalo, s. m.*
To give an offence, *dare fcandalo, fcandalizzare.*
To OFFE'ND [to injure, to hurt] *offendere, far danno o ingiuria, nuocere.* pret. *offefi.*
To offend [to difpleafe] *offendere, difpiacere.*
The fmell of tobacco offends me, *l' odore del tabacco mi fa male, m' offende.*
To offend the laws, *trafgredire le leggi.*
To offend [to commit a fault] *fallire, peccare,* pref. *fallifco.*
OFFE'NDED, adj. *offefo, v.* To offend
Pray, Sir, be not offended, *di grazia fignore non vi difpiaccia.*
He is offended at every thing, *ogni cofa li fa noja, o l' infaftidifce.*
To be offended at, or with one, *effer in collera o adirato contro una perfona.*
OFFE'NDER, s. *offenditore, delinquente, malfattore, s. m.*
OFFE'NDING, s. *offendimento, s. m. l' offendere.*
OFFE'NSIVE, adj. [hurtful] *offenfivo, nocivo.*
Offenfive [difpleafing, injurious] *offenfivo, ingiuriofo, difpiacente.*
Offenfive [fit to attack the enemy] *offenfivo.*
Offenfive arms, *armè offenfive.*
OFFE'NSIVELY, adv. *offenfivamente,*

 ingiu-

ingiuriosamente, d' una maniera offensiva.

O'FFER, s. [profer] *offerta, proferta*, s. f.

To make an offer at a thing [to attempt it] *tentare, provare, cimentarsi.*

To O'FFER [to prefer, to tender] *offerire, offerere, proferire, presentare, esibire.* pret. *proferisco, esibisco.*

I offer myself to do you that service, *m' offro o m' esibisco a farvi questo piacere.*

To offer battle, *presentar la battaglia.*

To offer [to bid] *proferire.*

You offer less than it is worth, *voi proferite meno di quel che vale.*

To offer [to dedicate] *offerire, dare, dedicare, sacrificare.*

To offer up requests, *porger preghiere.*

To offer to abuse a maiden, *attentare alla pudicizia d' una zittella, tentare di spulzellarla.*

To offer one's self to danger, *esporsi a qualche pericolo.*

To offer in sacrifice, *immolare, sacrificare.*

To offer one's self to die for another, *offerirsi a morte per un altro.*

To offer a thing to one's consideration, *rimetter che che si sia all' altrui considerazione.*

To offer violence to one, *far violenze ad altrui.*

To offer a blow to one, *portare un colpo ad uno.*

To offer an abuse to one, *maltrattare alcuno.*

To offer [to undertake, to take upon one's self] *offerirsi, impegnarsi, obbligarsi, intraprendere.*

To offer [to dare] *ardire, aver ardire, osare.*

Would you offer to do such a thing? *ardireste, avreste l' ardire di farlo?*

He offered to clap his hand to his sword, *fece sembiante di metter mano alla spada.*

I offered him to lie with me, *l' ho invitato a dormire meco.*

Do not offer to do it, *guardatevi di farlo.*

O'FFERED, adj. *offerto*, v. To offer.

O'FFERING, s. *offerta, proferta*, s. f.

O'FFERTORY, s. [that part of the mass where the offering is made] *offertorio*, s. m.

O'FFICE, s. [place, employment] *officio, ufficio, impiego, carico*, s. m.

Office [the place where a man does the business belonging to his office] *officio.*

The treasury office, *la tesoreria.*

The secretary's office, *la secreteria.*

The post-office, *la posta.*

Office [turn, service] *officio, servizio, piacere*, s. m.

To do one a good or bad office, *fare un buono o cattivo ufficio, o servizio ad alcuno.*

Office [duty, part] *ufficio, dovere*, s. m. *carica*, s.

It is my office to do it, *è mio ufficio il farlo, s' aspetta a me di farlo.*

Office [divine service] *ufficio.*

A house of office, *cesso*, s. m.

O'FFICER, s. [one that is in an office] *ufficiale*, s. m. *quegli che ha ufficio.*

O'FFICERED, adj. [provided with a competent number of officers] *capitanato.*

An army well officered, *un esercito ben capitanato.*

OFFI'CIAL, s. [the chancellor of an episcopal court] *ufiziale o cancelliere d' una corte episcopale.*

Official [an arch-deacon's deputy] *deputato d' un arcidiacono.*

To O'FFICIATE [to do the duty belonging to one's office] *ufficiare, e uffiziare, fare il servizio divino.*

OFFI'CIOUS, adj. [serviceable, obliging] *ufficioso, uffizioso, amorevole, affabile, affettuoso.*

OFFI'CIOUSLY, adv. *officiosamente, cortesemente, benignamente, affettuosamente, amorevolmente, affabilmente.*

OFFI'CIOUSNESS, s. *cortesia, amorevolezza, affabilità*, s. f. *ossequio, affetto*, s. m.

O'FFING, s. [a sea term, the open sea] *alto mare ma in vista.*

To keep in the offing [a ship is said so to do, when she keeps in the middle of the channel] *tenersi in alto.*

O'FFSPRING, s. *descendenti, posteri*, s. m. pl.

To O'FFUSCATE [to make dark or cloudy] *offuscare, oscurare, adombrare.*

O'FFUSCATED, adj. *offuscato, oscurato, adombrato.*

OFFUSCA'TION, s. [a making dark or cloudy] *offuscazione, oscurazione*, s. f. *offuscamento, adombramento*, s. m.

OFT, } adv. *spesso, sovente, frequentemente, spesse volte.*
OFTEN, }

How often? *quante volte?*

Not often, *rare volte, non ispesso, di rado.*

As often as I please, *ogni volta che, o quando voglio.*

Very often, *spessissime volte, spessissimamente.*

O'FTENTIMES, *spesse volte.*

O'FTWARD, s. [a sea term, toward the sea] *alto, alto mare.*

To sail to the oftward, *tenersi in alto.*

OGE'E, } s. [in architecture, member of a moulding, consisting of a round and a hollow] *sestone, sporto*, s. m.
O'GIVE, }

O'GLE, s. *occhiata*, s. f. *sguardo*, s. m.

To O'GLE [to look at, to look amourously at] *occhieggiare, guardare, dar occhio, guardare con compiacenza, vagheggiare.*

O'GLER, s. *quegli o quella che occhieggia, vagheggino, gaveggino.*

O'GLIA, v. *olio.*

OH, interj. *oh.*

OIL, s. [the juice of olives] *olio*, s. m. *liquore che si cava dall' uliva*, v. Oyl.

Oil of bays, *olio laurino.*

Oil of roses, *olio rosato.*

Oil-jar, *giara da olio.*

Oil-man, *oliandolo, che rivende olio.*

Oil-mill, } s. *macinatojo*, s. m. *mulino dove si macinan l' ulive.*
Oil-press, }

O'ILET-HOLE, s. *occhiella*, s. m.

To OIL, verb. act. *oliare, condire con olio.*

O'ILED, adj. *oliato, condito con olio.*

O'ILINESS, s. *qualità oleosa, grassa, o untuosa.*

O'ILY, adj. [full of oil] *olioso, che ha in se olio.*

O'INTMENT, s. [unguent] *unguento*, s. m.

An ointment maker or seller, *unguentario, unguentiere*, s. m.

O'ISTER, s. [oyster] *ostrica*, s. f.

Oister-bed, *luogo dove si pescano l' ostriche.*

Oister-man, *uomo che vende ostriche.*

Oister-woman, *donna che vende ostriche.*

Oister-shell, *conchiglia d' ostrica.*

Oister-green, s. [an herb] *titimaglio*, s. m.

O'ISTER-WENCH, *donna che vende ostriche; donnuzza, puttanella vile.*

O'KER, s. [a mineral] *ocra*, s. f. *certa terra di color giallo, che si trova nelle miniere de' metalli.*

Oker-de-lace, or yellow-oker, *ocra gialla.*

Red-oker, *ocra rossa.*

OLD, adj. [ancient, aged] *vecchio, antico, annoso.*

An old man, *un vecchio.*

An old woman, *una vecchia.*

A little old man or woman, *un vecchietto, una vecchierella.*

He died, being old, *morì di vecchiaja.*

Old [worn] *vecchio, usato.*

An old sute, *un abito vecchio o usato.*

Old [obsolete] *vecchio, fuor d' uso.*

An old castle, *un castello antico.*

An old oak, *una quercia annosa.*

How old is he? *quanti anni ha?*

He is thirty years old, *ha trent' anni.*

To grow old, *invecchiare, diventar vecchio.*

Old age, *la vecchiaja.*

Of old, or in old time, *altre volte, anticamente,*

A friend of old, *un amico vecchio.*

In the time of old, *ne' tempi addietro.*

An old fox, *un volpone.*

O'LDER [comparative of old] *più vecchio.*

He is older than you, *egli è più vecchio di voi.*

To grow older, *invecchiare.*

O'LDEST, adj. [the superlative of old] *il più vecchio.*

Who is the oldest of you two? *chi è il più vecchio di voi due?*

O'LDISH, adj. [somewhat old] *vecchietto, vicino alla vecchiaja, vecchiccio, che ha del vecchio*

O'LDNESS, s. [old age] *vecchiaja*, s. f. *età avanzata.*

OLEA'GINOUS, adj. [oily] *olioso, untuoso, grasso, oliginoso.*

Oli'ander, s. [a shrub] *oleandro*, s. m. *spezie d'arbuscello.*
Oli'banum, s. [tree] *olibano*, s. m. *albero che produce l'olibano, o l'incenso.*
Oliga'rchical, adj. [governed by few men] *oligarchico, governato da pochi.*
O'ligarchy, s. [a government in the hands of a few men] *oligarchia*, s. f. *governo di pochi.*
O'lio, s. [a rich pottage made of beef, veal, mutton, and gammon of bacon, ducks, partridges, pigeons, &c.] *manicaretto, composto di diverse sorti di carne.*
Oliva'ster, s. [a wild olive-tree] *oleastro*, s. m. *ulivo salvatico.*
Olivaster, adj. [olive coloured] *oleastro, ulivastro.*
O'live, s. [the fruit of the olive-tree] *uliva*, s. f. *frutta dell' ulivo.*
Olive-tree, *ulivo*, s. m.
Olive-tree, *ulivastro, di color d'uliva.*
An olive-grove, *uliveto*, s. m. *luogo piantato d'ulivi.*
Oly'mpiad, s. [the space of four compleat years] *Olimpiade, spazio di quattro anni.*
Oly'mpian, or Olympick, adj. *Olimpico.*
Oly'mpus, s. [a high hill in Thessaly, used by the poets for heaven] *Olimpo*, s. m.
O'mbre, s. [a Spanish game at cards] *ombre*, s. f. *giuoco di carte.*
Omelet, s. [a pancake of eggs] *una frittata.*
O'men, s. [a sign or token of good or bad luck] *augurio, segno, presagio, pronostico*, s. m.
A bad omen, *ubbia*, s. f. *opinione malagurosa.*
Ome'ntum, s. [the caul] *omento*, s. m. *rete che cuopre gl' intestini degli animali.*
O'mer, s. *sorta di misura di liquidi presso gli antichi Ebrei.*
To O'minate [to forebode, foretell, or presage] *augurare, predire, presagire, pronosticare*, pref. *predissi*, pref. *presagisco.*
O'minated, adj. *augurato, predetto, presagito, pronosticato.*
O'minous, adj. [ill-boding, or portending ill luck] *malaguroso, malagurato, di male augurio, sinistro, fatale.*
Omi'ssion, s. [neglect] *lasciamento, tralasciamento*, s. m. *omissione, e ommissione*, s. f.
To Omi't [to leave out, to pass by, to neglect] *omettere, e ommettere, tralasciare, negligere, mancare.*
I omit to tell you that, *passo sotto silenzio, che.*
He omits no opportunity, *non lascia passare opportunità.*
Omi'tted, adj. *omesso, tralasciato, negletto, mancato.*
Omi'tting, s. *omissione, tralasciamento.*
An omitting for a time, *intermissione*, s. f.
Omni'potence, } s. *omnipotenza*,
Omni'potency, } s. f.

Omni'potent, adj. [almighty] *onnipotente, che può tutto.*
Omnipre'sence, s. [a being present in all parts] *ubiquità*, s. f. *attributo per il quale Iddio si trova presente in ogni luogo.*
Omnipre'sent, adj. [that is every where present] *presente in ogni luogo.*
Omnisci'ence, s. [the knowledge of all things] *conoscenza, scienza infinita.*
Omnisci'ent, adj. [knowing all things] *che sa tutto.*
On, prep. [upon] *sopra, al, alla, a.*
You may rely on me, *potete riposarvi sopra di me, potete starvene a me.*
On the right hand, *alla man dritta.*
On the left hand, *alla man manca.*
On foot, on horseback, *a piedi, a cavallo.*
On purpose, *a posta, a bello studio.*
On the contrary, *al contrario.*
I thought on you, *ho pensato a voi.*
On my part, on my side, *dal canto mio, dalla parte mia.*
On the one side, *d'un canto.*
On the other side, *dall' altro canto, dall' altra banda.*
On a sudden, *in un subito, in un batter d'occhio.*
On the east, *dalla parte d'oriente.*
To play on the harp, *suonar l'arpa.*
I laid hold on him, *l'afferrai.*
To go on, *passare avanti.*
I am going on my twenty-four, *arriverò fra poco a ventiquattro anni.*
Put on your hat, *mettetevi il cappello, copritevi.*
I have got my cloaths on, *sono vestito.*
I have my hat on, *ho il cappello in testa.*
My shoes are on, *sono calzato.*
To get one's boots on, *mettersi gli stivali.*
Having a scarlet cloak on, *avendo addosso un mantello di scarlatto.*
On that day, *in quel giorno.*
To be on one's way, *esser in cammino.*
He looks merrily on't, *pare molto allegro, ha la ciera molto allegra.*
Lay not the blame on me, *non date la colpa a me.*
He has a fine ring on his finger, *egli ha un bell' anello nel dito.*
On pain of death, *sotto pena di morte.*
She kept her eyes fixed on the ground, *tenne gli occhi fissi in terra.*
On these terms you may have her, *con questi patti voi potete averla.*
On the first opportunity, *colla prima opportunità.*
On't [of it] Ex. I don't believe a word on't, *non ci credo punto.*
On [go on] *via, su, avanti.*
Questa particola si trova unita spesso coi verbi Inglesi, ed allora fa una parte principale della loro significazione; è da notarsi però, che esprime sempre la continuazione dell' azione del verbo. Ex. Play on, *giuocate pure, continuate a giuocare.*
Once, adv. [one time] *una volta.*

Once for all, *una volta per sempre.*
At once, *alla prima, in un colpo, in una volta.*
All at once, *in un subito.*
Once [formerly] *altre volte, già, tempo fà.*
I used once to go there, *altre volte ero solito d'andarvi.*
If it would but once come to that, *se mai ciò avvenisse.*
One, adj. [that is singular in number] *un, uno, una.*
There was not so much as one, *non ve ne fu nemmeno uno.*
Here is one, *eccone uno o una.*
It is all one to me, *è tutto uno a me, ciò poco m'importa.*
It is all one [no matter] *è tutt' uno, non importa, non fa caso.*
One with another, *fra l'uno e l'altro.*
Such a one, *un tale, una tale.*
There is no such one here, *non c'è un tale uomo qui.*
What shall one do with such folk? *che bisogna fare con tale gente?*
They differ from one another, *differiscono fra di loro.*
To love one another, *amarsi l'un l' altro, riamarsi.*
It is one thing to come late, and another not to come at all, *altro è venir tardi, altro non venir mai.*
As if one should say, *come sarebbe a dire.*
With one accord, *d'un comune consenso, unanimamente.*
There is but this one shift, *non vedo altro rimedio.*
To put in for one, *mettersi nel numero.*
To make one, *esser del numero.*
Will you make one of us? *volete esser del numero, volete venir con noi?*
But one word, *in una sola parola.*
To have two strings to one's bow, *aver due corde al suo arco.*
To live according to one's estate, *viver secondo le sue forze.*
Words that have one and the same signification, *parole, che hanno una medesima significazione.*
One's self, *se stesso, si.*
Every one, *ciascheduno, ognuno.*
Any one, *chiunque, chi si sia.*
There is a good one, *eccone un buono, o una buona.*
They are but little ones, *sono molto piccoli.*
The little and the great ones, *i piccoli, ed i grandi.*
One man's meat is another man's poison, *quel che giova ad uno nuoce ad un altro.*
As being one that understood the business, *come un uomo ch' era pratico in questi affari.*
But that one thing was wanting, *non ci mancava altro.*
One by one, *uno ad uno.*
One-ey'd, *guercio, che non ha che un occhio.*
O'nely, v. Only.
O'nerary, adj. [serving for burden] *di carico.*

To O'NERATE [to burden, to load] *caricare.*
O'NION, s. [a well known root] *cipolla*, s. f.
Young onions, *cipollette.*
O'NLY, adj. *solo, sola.*
You are the only man I can trust my self to, *voi siete il solo a chi possa fidarmi.*
She is the only woman I love, *fra tutte le donne amo lei sola.*
My only desire is, *tutto quel che domando è.*
Only, adv. *solamente, solo.*
Once only, *solo una volta.*
Not only, *non solo, non solamente.*
O'NSET, s. [an attack or assault] *assalto.*
To give a fresh onset, *ritornare all' assalto.*
O'NWARD, adv. [forward] *avanti.*
To come onward, *avvicinarsi.*
To go onward, *avanzarsi, inoltrarsi.*
O'NYX, s. *onice*, s. f. *nome d'una gemma così chiamata.*
OPA'CITY, s. [the contrary to transparency] *opacità*, s. f.
OPA'COUS, } adj. [obscure, that is OPA'QUE, } not transparent] *opaco, ombroso.*
O'PAL, s. [a gem] *opalo*, s. m. *sorta di pietra preziosa.*
OPEN, adj. [not shut] *aperto.*
Wide open, *spalancato.*
A little open, *mezzo aperto.*
To keep open table, *tener corte bandita.*
To lye open to some danger, *esser esposto a qualche pericolo.*
Open [not covered] *aperto, scoperto.*
His breast is opened, *il suo petto è scoperto.*
An open country, *una campagna aperta.*
Open [evident] *aperto, palese, chiaro, manifesto.*
With open force, *a viva forza.*
Open war, *guerra aperta.*
An open theatre, *un teatro pubblico.*
A man of an open temper, *un uomo franco libero, sincero.*
An open town, *una terra aperta, senza mura.*
To keep one's body open [or one's belly loose] *tenere il ventre sciolto.*
Open weather, *un tempo moderato, temperato, sereno, chiaro.*
In the open air, *all' aria scoperta.*
To lie in the open air, *dormire a cielo scoperto.*
To lay open, *palesare, scoprire, far vedere, dichiarare, far noto.*
To set open, *aprire.*
In the open field, *in campagna aperta.*
In the open streets, *nelle pubbliche strade.*
In open court, *in piena udienza.*
As long as my eyes are open, *tanto che vivrò.*
Open handed, *liberale, generoso, magnifico*
Open-hearted, *franco, sincero.*
Open-heartedness, *franchezza, sincerità.*
To OPEN [the contrary to shut] *aprire.*
Open the door or the window, *aprire la porta o la finestra.*
To open a bundle, *sciogliere un fascio.*
To open the trenches, *aprire le trincee.*
To open a letter, *aprire una lettera.*
To open one's heart to a friend, *scoprirsi con alcuno, manifestargli il suo segreto.*
To open [that which was stop'd] *sturare.*
Open that bottle, *sturate quel fiasco.*
To open trees at the root, *scalzare gli alberi, levar la terra intorno alla barba degli alberi, e delle piante.*
To open [to lay open, to make plain or manifest] *scoprire, manifestare, palesare.*
To open the campaign, *uscire in campagna.*
To open the body [to loosen the belly] *sciorre il ventre, disoppilare.*
To open, verb neut. *aprirsi.*
To open [as a flower does] *aprirsi, dilatarsi sbocciando, parlando de' fiori.*
To open an assembly, *tenere un assemblea.*
To open [to bark as a dog does] *abbaiare.*
O'PENED, adj. *aperto. v.* To open.
O'PENING, s. *aprimento*, s. m. *l'aprire, apertura, aperta*, s. f.
The opening of a campaign, *il principio d'una campagna.*
Opening, adj. [that opens the body] *aperitivo, apritivo.*
O'PENLY, adv. [publickly] *apertamente, pubblicamente.*
Openly [plainly, evidently] *apertamente, chiaramente, evidentemente, manifestamente, liberamente.*
To speak openly, *parlar apertamente, o liberamente.*
O'PENNESS, s. [freedom] *franchezza, libertà, sincerità, schiettezza*, s. f.
Openness of temper, *franchezza, schiettezza d'animo.*
O'PERA, s. [a play in musick] *opera*, s. f. *dramma in musica.*
To O'PERATE [to work] *operare, fare effetto.*
The medicine begins to operate, *la medicina comincia ad operare, a fare effetto.*
OPERA'TION, s. [a working] *operazione*, s. f.
O'PERATIVE, adj. [apt to work] *operativo, che fa operazione, che ha virtù d'operare.*
OPERA'TOR, s. [a workman] *operatore*, s. m.
Operator [mountebank] *cerretano, cantambanco*, s. m.
An operator for the teeth, *un cavadenti.*
OPERO'SE, adj. [laborious, hard] *laborioso, faticoso, difficile.*
Operose [busy, active] *attivo, diligente, industrioso, operoso.*
O'PIATE, s. [a medicine made of opium, to cause sleep] *laudano*, s. m.
OPINA'TION, s. [opening] *opinazione, immaginazione*, s. f. *divisamento, pensiero*, s. m.
OPINA'TOR, s. *opinante*, s. *che pensa, che s'immagina.*
To OPI'NE [to think, to be of opinion] *opinare, pensare, immaginarsi.*
To O'PINATE [to give in one's opinion or judgment about a matter] *giudicare, credere, essere di parere, sentire, tenere opinione.*
OPI'NER, s. [he that gives in his opinion] *opinante*, s. m.
OPI'NIATIVE, } adj. [wedded to his OPINIATRE, } own humour] *ostinato, perfidioso, protervo, che sta troppo pertinacemente nel suo proposito, caparbio, testereccio, pertinace, capone.*
OPI'NIATIVENESS, [obstinacy, self-willedness] *ostinazione, caparbieria, pertinacia, caparbietà*, s. f.
OPI'NION, s. [judgment, sentiment] *opinione*, s. f. *sentimento, parere*, s. m.
If I were to speak my opinion, *a dirvi la mia opinione, a dirvi quel che ne sento.*
To my opinion, *secondo il mio parere.*
I am of a contrary opinion, *sono di parere contrario.*
Opinion [belief] *opinione, credenza*, s. f.
To broach new opinions, *seminare, stabilire novelle opinioni.*
Opinion [esteem] *opinione, stima*, s. f.
He has a pretty good opinion of himself, *ha una assai buona opinione di se stesso, presume molto di se stesso.*
OPI'NIATE, } adj. [obstinate, wed-OPI'NIATED, } ded to his own opi-OPI'NIATIVE, } nion] *ostinato, perfidioso, pertinace, caparbio.*
OPI'NIATIVENESS, s. *ostinazione, caparbietà, pertinacia*, s. f.
OPI'NIATIVELY, adv. *ostinatamente, pertinacemente.*
O'PIUM, s. *oppio*, s. f.
To give an opium, *adoppiare, dar l' oppio.*
O'PLE-TREE, *sorta d'albero.*
OPOBA'LSAM, } s. [the gum dis-OPOBALSAMUM, } tilling from the balm-tree] *balsamo*, s. m.
To O'PPILATE [to cause a stoppage] *oppilare, fare oppilazione, costipare.*
This is apt to oppilate, *questo è costipativo.*
O'PPILATED, adj. *oppilato, costipato.*
OPPILA'TION, s. [an obstruction or stoppage] *oppilazione*, s. f. *rituramento, riserramento*, s. m.
O'PILATIVE, adj. [obstructive] *ristrignente, costipativo.*
To OPPO'NE [to oppose] *opporre, contrariare, ripugnare, contrastare, contraddire*, pret. *contraddico*, pret. *contraddissi.*
OPPO'NENT, s. [one who maintains a contrary argument in a school] *un opponente.*
O'PPORTUNE, adj. [convenient, seasonable] *opportuno, comodo, a tempo, conveniente.*

He came in an opportune time, *venne opportunamente, a tempo.*

OPPORTU'NELY, adv. *opportunamente, opportunatamente, comodamente, a tempo.*

OPPORTUNITY, s. [convenient time or occaſion] *opportunità, comodità, occaſione,* s. f.

Opportunity makes the thief, *all' arca aperta il giuſto vi pecca, la comodità fa l'uomo ladro.*

To OPPO'SE [to ſet againſt, to withſtand, to thwart] *opporre, contrariare, ripugnare, contraſtare, contraddire,* preſ. *contraddico,* pret. *contraddiſſi.*

To oppoſe [to withſtand] *opporſi.*

To oppoſe one's ſelf to a thing, *opporſi a qualche coſa.*

He oppoſes all my deſigns, *egli ſconcia tutti i miei diſegni.*

OPPO'SED, adj. *oppoſto.*

OPPO'SER, s. [adverſary] *avverſario.*

O'PPOSITE, adj. [over againſt] *oppoſito, che è dirimpetto.*

Oppoſite [contrary] *oppoſto, contrario.*

Oppoſite, adv. [over againſt] *dirimpetto, rincontro, di rincontro.*

OPPOSI'TION, s. [the being oppoſed or contrary] *opponimento,* s. m. *oppoſizione,* s. f.

Oppoſition [obſtacle, hindrance] *oppoſizione, ripugnanza, reſiſtenza,* s. f. *contraſto, oſtacolo, impedimento,* s. m.

The oppoſition of the ſtars [in aſtronomy] *l'oppoſizione degli aſtri, termine d'aſtronomia.*

To OPPRE'SS [to be heavy upon, to over-lay] *opprimere, oppreſſare, ſoffocare.*

The night mare oppreſſes one's breaſt, *la fantaſima opprime lo ſtomaco.*

To oppreſs [to over-burden, to cruſh by authority and violence] *opprimere, tener ſotto, oppreſſare, angariare, tiranneggiare.*

To oppreſs the innocent, *opprimer gl' innocenti.*

OPPRE'SSED, adj. *oppreſſo, oppreſſato.*

My heart is oppreſſed with grief, *il mio cuore è oppreſſo di dolore.*

OPPRE'SSING, } s. [over-burden-
OPPRE'SSION, } ing] *oppreſſione,* s. f.

An oppreſſion of the heart, *oppreſſione, ſoffocamento di cuore.*

OPPRE'SSIVE, adj. *che opprime, che oppreſſa.*

OPPRE'SSOR, s. [he that oppreſſes] *oppreſſore,* s. m.

OPPRO'BRIOUS, adj. [reproachful, injurious] *obbrobrioſo, diſonorevole, vituperoſo.*

OPPRO'BRIUM, s. [infamy, diſgrace] *obbrobrio, diſonore, ſcorno, vituperio,* s. m. *infamia, vergogna,* s. f.

To OPPU'GN [to oppoſe, to reject, to confute] an opinion, *oppugnare, impugnare, contrariare un' opinione.*

OPPU'GNED, adj. *oppugnato, impugnato, contrariato.*

OPPU'GNER, s. *impugnatore,* s. m. *che impugna.*

O'PTATIVE, s. [the optative mood] *l'ottativo.*

O'PTICAL, } adj. [belonging to the
O'PTICK, } ſight] *ottico, appartenente alla viſta.*

O'PTICKS, s. [a ſcience which treats of the ſight in general] *ottica,* s. f. *ſcienza che tratta della viſta.*

O'PTIMACY, s. [the government of a commonwealth by the nobles] *ottimato,* s. m.

O'PTION, s. [a choice or liberty of accepting or refuſing a thing] *arbitrio,* s. m. *volontà, ſcelta,* s. f.

He had his option, *ebbe quel che deſiderava.*

O'PULENCY, s. [wealth] *opulènza, ricchezza,* s. f.

A man of great opulency, *un uomo molto opulente, o ricco.*

O'PULENT, adj. [wealthy] *opulènte, ricco.*

O'PULENTLY, adv. *opulentemente, riccamente, ſplendidamente.*

O'PUSCULE, } s. [a ſhort work] *o-*
O'PUSCLE, } *peretta, opericciuola,* s. f.

OR, conj. [either] *o.*

To day or to morrow, *oggi o domani.*

More or leſs, *più o meno.*

Or ever, *prima che.*

Whether you will or no, *vogli o non vogli, tuo mal grado, a tuo marcio diſpetto.*

Or, s. [gold colour in heraldry] *oro, color giallo.*

O'RACHE, s. [a pot herb] *erba che ſi mangia cotta.*

O'RACLE, s. [an ambiguous and obſcure anſwer, which the heathen prieſts gave to people about things to come] *oracolo,* s. m. *riſpoſta degli Dei.*

Oracle [the god which delivered the oracles] *oracolo, il dio che dava l'oracolo.*

ORA'CULAR, adj. [belonging to an oracle] *appartenente ad oracolo.*

O'RAL, adj. [delivered by the mouth or voice] *vocale.*

Oral prayer, *preghiera vocale.*

O'RANGE, s. [a well known fruit] *arancia, melarancia,* s. f.

An orange tree, *un arancio, un melarancio,* s. m.

Orange colour, *color d'arancia.*

Orange water, *aqua lanfa.*

An orange houſe, *luogo dove ſi conſervano i melaranci per difenderli dal freddo.*

An orange woman, *una donna che vende melarance.*

O'RANGERY, s. [a ſort of perfume] *odore di melarancia.*

Orangery ſnuff, *tabacco che ha l'odore di melarancia.*

ORA'TION, s. [ſpeech] *orazione,* s. f. *diſcorſo detto in pubblico.*

Oration [prayer] *orazione, preghiera,* s. f.

ORA'TOR, s. [an eloquent ſpeaker or pleader] *oratore,* s. m.

ORATO'RIANS, s. [a religious fraternity or order] *i frati del' oratorio.*

O'RATORY, adj. [pertaining to an orator] *oratorio, appartenente all' oratore.*

Oratory, s. [eloquence or the art of making publick ſpeeches] *l'arte oratoria, eloquenza.*

Oratory [a private chapel or place ſet apart for prayers] *oratorio,* s. m. *luogo ſagro dove ſi fa orazione.*

ORB, s. *sfera, ſpera,* s. f. *orbe,* s. m.

ORBI'CULAR, adj. [round like a ball or globe] *tondo, ritondo, rotondo.*

ORBI'CULARLY, adv. *ritondamente.*

O'RBIT, s. [in aſtronomy, the courſe in which any planet moves] *il corſo d' un pianeta.*

O'RCHANET, s. [a plant] *ſorta di pianta.*

O'RCHARD, s. [a place planted with fruit trees] *pometo,* s. m. *luogo piantato d'alberi pomiferi.*

O'RCHESTRA, } s. [the place where
O'RCHESTRE, } the muſicians ſit, a muſick room] *orcheſtra,* s. f. *quel luogo a piedi del teatro dove ſiedono i muſici.*

ORDE'AL, s. [an old Saxon word, which ſignifies certain particular ways of trial, by which perſons accus'd of crimes were to clear themſelves] *prova, cimento.*

Ordeal by combat [when the perſon accus'd of murder was obliged to fight the next relation of the perſon deceaſed] *purgar gl' indizi combattendo.*

Ordeal by fire [when the party accuſed undertook to prove his innocence, by walking blindfold and barefoot, over nine red hot plough ſhares, or by holding a red hot iron in his hand] *purgar gl' indizi col fuoco.*

Ordeal by cold water [being bound and thrown into a river or pond] *purgar gl' indizi coll' acqua fredda.*

Ordeal by hot water [by putting the hands or feet into ſcalding water] *purgar gl' indizi coll' acqua bollente.*

To ORDA'IN [to command] *ordinare, comandare, commettere, imporre,* pret. *commiſi,* preſ. *impongo,* pret. *impoſi.*

To ordain [to confer holy orders] *ordinare, dar gli ordini eccleſiaſtici.*

ORDA'INED, adj. *ordinato, comandato, commeſſo, impoſto.*

ORDA'INER, s. *ordinatore,* s. m. *che ordina.*

ORDA'INING, s. *ordinamento,* s. m. *l'ordinare.*

O'RDER, s. [a diſpoſing things in their places] *ordine,* s. m. *diſpoſizione, e collocamento di ciaſcuna coſa a ſuo luogo.*

Will you never give over? *non la finirete mai?*
To give over one's work, *tralasciare di lavorare.*
Indebted over head and ears, *indebitato fino ai capelli, oppresso di debiti.*
To be over [or remain, to be left] *avanzare, restare.*
There is nothing over, *non ci resta niente, non c' è niente d' avanzo.*
To mourn over a dead friend, *affliggersi, attristarsi per la morte d' un amico.*
Over and over, *cento volte.*
Over-against, *dirimpetto.*
Over and besides, *oltre.*
Over and above, *oltre, d' avantaggio, più.*
I give you this over and above what I owe you, *vi do questo oltre quel che vi devo.*
To boil over, *traboccare bollendo.*
To carry over, *trasportare.*
To ferry over, *traghettare.*
To give over, *cedere, rassegnare, restituire.*
To give over one's office, *rassegnare il suo officio.*
To make over an estate to one, *dare o cedere un bene ad uno.*
To make over an estate [to mortgage it] *pignorare, o impegnare un bene.*
To say over, *ridire, dire di nuovo.*
To turn over, *voltare.*
To OVER-ACT [to act beyond one's commission] *eccedere, sopravanzare, passare i dovuti termini.*
To O'VER-AWE, *frenare, raffrenare, tenere in timore, o in freno.*
Over-awed, adj. *frenato, raffrenato.*
To OVER-BA'LANCE [to exceed in weight] *tracollare, o dare il tracollo alla bilancia.*
To O'VER-BEAR [to overcome] *vincere, formontare, avanzare, soprassare, prevalere.*
To over-bear [to oppress] *opprimere, oppressare.*
To O'VER-BID [to bid too much] *offerire troppo, alzar il prezzo.*
O'VER-BIG, adj. *troppo grosso.*
O'VER-BOLD, adj. *troppo ardito, temerario, tracotato, prosuntuoso.*
O'VER-BORN, adj. [from over-bear] *vinto, formontato, avanzato, sopraffatto, oppresso, oppressato.*
To O'VER-BOIL, *bollire troppo.*
Over boiled, adj. *troppo cotto.*
To O'VER BURDEN, *caricar troppo, aggravare, opprimere.*
O'VER-BURDENED, adj. *caricato troppo, aggravato, oppresso.*
O'VER-CAST, adj. [dark, cloudy] *offuscato, oscurato, adombrato, tenebroso.*
The weather begins to be over-cast, *il tempo comincia ad annuvolarsi.*
He is over-cast with melancholy, *egli è oppresso da malinconia.*
A wall over cast with stone, *un muro incrostato di pietre.*

To O'VER-CAST [to cover, to cloud] *annuvolare, offuscare, adombrare.*
To over-cast [to grow dark or cloudy] *annuvolarsi, offuscarsi, adombrarsi.*
To over-cast a wall with stone, *incrostare un muro con pietre o macigni spianati.*
To over-cast the jack at bowls, *trapassare il lecco, al giuoco delle pallottole.*
O'VER-CAUTIOUS, adj. *troppo cauteloso.*
To O'VER-CHARGE, *caricar troppo, opprimere.*
To over-charge the stomach with eating, *mangiar troppo, caricar lo stomaco con troppo mangiare.*
To O'VER-CLOUD, *annuvolare, oscurare, offuscare.*
Over-clouded, adj. *annuvolato, oscurato, offuscato.*
To O'VERCOME [to get the better of] *vincere, superare, formontare,* pret. *vinsi.*
She overcomes me with civilities, *ella mi confonde con tante civiltà.*
This smell overcomes me, *questo odore m' offende, o mi fa male.*
O'VERCOME, adj. *vinto, superato, formontato.*
O'VERCOMER, s. *vincitore,* s. m. *vincitrice,* s. f.
O'VERCOMING, s. *il vincere, superamento.*
OVER-CO'NFIDENT, adj. *temerario, troppo ardito, tracotato, prosuntuoso.*
OVER-CORNED, adj, *troppo salato.*
Beef over-corned, *del bue troppo salato.*
Over-curious, adj. *troppo curioso.*
Over-curious [too nice] *troppo delicato.*
To O'VERDO [to do too much] *eccedere, fare con eccesso, fare o dire più di quel si deve.*
To overdo [to make one work too hard] *faticar troppo, opprimere di fatica.*
To overdo one's self, *faticarsi troppo, far più che le sue forze non li permettono.*
Over-done, adj. *ecceduto,* v. To overdo.
This meat is over-done, *questa carne è troppo cotta, è stracotta.*
To OVER-DRINK one's self, *bere troppo.*
OVER-EARNEST, adj. *troppo ardente, o intento.*
OVER-E'ARNESTNESS, s. *troppo grande ardore, desiderio intenso.*
To OVER-EAT one's self, *mangiar troppo, creparsi di mangiare.*
OVER-FI'ERCE, adj. [too bold] *troppo fiero o troppo ardito.*
Over-fierce [too eager] *troppo intenso, intento, o attento.*
OVER-FI'ERCELY, adv. *troppo fieramente, o intensamente.*
To OVER-FILL, *empier troppo.*

OVER-FINE, adj. *strafino.*
To OVER-FLOW, verb act. *inondare, allagare, traboccare.*
The rivers over-flow the land, *i fiumi inondano la terra.*
OVER-FLOWED, adj. *inondato, allagato, traboccato.*
OVER-FLOWING, s. *inondazione,* s. f. *allagamento, traboccamento,* s. m.
To OVER-FLY, *volar oltre.*
OVER-FOND, adj. *che ama troppo, che ama troppo teneramente.*
OVER-FO'RWARD, adj. *troppo ardente, troppò frettoloso, troppo ardito.*
To OVER-FRE'IGHT, *caricar troppo.*
OVER-FRE'IGHTED, adj. *troppo carico.*
OVER-FULL, adj. *troppo pieno.*
To OVER-GO, *passar troppo oltre, trapassare.*
OVER-GRE'AT, *troppo grande.*
To OVER-GROW, *crescere in troppo grande abbondanza.*
OVER-GROWN, adj *che è cresciuto troppo, o che è troppo grande.*
A garden over-grown with weeds *un giardino tutto pieno d' erbe.*
OVER-HAPPY, adj. *troppo felice.*
To OVER-HASTEN, *affrettar troppo, precipitar gl' indugi.*
OVER HA'STENED, adj. *troppo affrettato, o frettoloso.*
OVER-HA'STILY, adv. *troppo frettolosamente, precipitosamente, con troppa precipitazione*
OVER-HA'STINESS, s. *precipitazione, fretta,* s. f.
OVER-HA'STY, adj. *frettoloso, troppo affrettato, troppo intenso, precipitoso.*
Over-hasty fruits, *frutti prematuri.*
To OVER-HEAR, *sentire, intendere.*
Over-heard, adj. *sentito, inteso.*
To OVER-HEAT, *scaldare.*
OVER-HE'AVY, adj. *troppo pesante.*
OVER-JOY'D, adj. *allegro, contento, giojoso, pieno di gioja, contento.*
I am over-joy'd to see you, *mi rallegro sommamente di vedervi.*
OVER-KIND, adj. *troppo appassionato, troppo tenero, che ama troppo.*
OVER-LAID, adj. [stifled] *affogato.*
To OVER-LAY [to stifle] *affogare, suffocare.*
She has over-laid her nurse child, *ella ha affogato il suo bambino.*
OVER-LAYING, s. *affogamento,* s. m.
To OVER-LIVE, *sopravvivere,* pret. *sopravvissi.*
OVER-LIVED, adj. *sopravvissuto.*
OVER-LIVING, adj. *sopravvivente.*
To OVER-LOAD, *caricar troppo,*

Over-

Over-loaded, adj. *troppo carico.*
OVER-LONG, adj. *troppo lungo.*
To OVER-LOOK [to have an eye upon, or look after] *aver l' occhio sopra, aver l' ispezione, la soprantendenza.*
To over-look a piece of work, *aver la soprantendenza d'un edificio.*
To over-look [to over-top] *dominare, essere a cavaliere, soprastare.*
A high hill over-looks the town, *un alto monte domina la città.*
To over-look [to connive, to wink at] *dissimulare, tollerare, chiudere gli occhi.*
To over-look [to scorn, to look upon with contempt] *sdegnare, disprezzare, avere, o tenere a sdegno.*
To over-look [to pass by a fault] *omettere un errore.*
OVER-LOOKED, *part. di* to over-look.
OVER-LO'OKER, s. *soprantendente, soprastante,* s. m.
OVER-LO'OKING, s. *ispezione, e inspezione, soprantendenza,* s. f. *v.* To over-look.
OVER-MA'TCH, s. [unequal match] *partita ineguale.*
OVER-MA'TCHED, adj. *vinto, sormontato.*
OVER ME'ASURE, s. *soprappiù,* s. m. *quel che si da più della misura.*
OVER-MUCH, adj. *troppo, troppo grande, superfluo.*
This is over-much, *questo è troppo, o superfluo.*
Over-much, adv. *troppo.*
OVER-OFFI'CIOUS, adj. *troppo officioso.*
OVER-OLD, adj. *troppo vecchio.*
OVER-PAID, adj. *strapagato.*
To OVER-PASS [to surpass] *sorpassare, avanzare, eccedere, vincere.*
To over-pass [to let slip] *preterire, omettere, lasciare.*
To over-pass [to go beyond] *trapassare, trascorrere, passar oltre,* pret. *trascorsi.*
OVER-PAST, adj. *sorpassato, v.* To over-pass.
The time is over-past, *il tempo è passato.*
To OVER-PAY, *strapagare, pagare più del dovere.*
To OVER-PE'RSUADE, *persuadere male a proposito.*
OVER-PE'RSUADED, adj. *persuaso male a proposito.*
O'VERPLUS, s. *soprappiù, soperchio,* s. m.
To O'VERPOISE [to over-weigh] *contrabilanciare.*
O'VERPOISED, adj. *contrabilanciato.*
To O'VER-POWER, *vincere, superare, sormontare.*
To O'VER-PRIZE, *mettere un prezzo grande, estimar troppo.*
O'VER-PRODIGAL, adj. *troppo prodigo.*
O'VER-RATE, s. [an excessive rate] *prezzo eccessivo, o esorbitante.*
To O'VER-RATE [to over-prize] *stimare troppo caro, mettere un prezzo eccessivo.*
To over-rate a commodity [to ask too high for it] *domandar troppo per una mercanzia, sopravvenderla.*
To over-rate [to assess too high] *tassar troppo.*
Over-rated, adj. *estimato troppo, v.* To over-rate.
OVER-REACH, s. [a strain, swelling of a master sinew of a horse] *malattia di cavallo.*
To OVER-REACH [to couzen] *acchiappare, ingannare, giuntare, deludere.*
He has over-reached me, *m'ha acchiappato.*
To over-reach [to hurt one's self] *farsi torto.*
To over-reach one's self [to hurt one's self with reaching] *scavallarsi qualche nervo a forza di stender il braccio.*
To over-reach [to prevent] *prevenire.*
To over-reach [speaking of a horse, to hit the fore-feet with the hinder] *tagliarsi, parlando de' cavalli, quando in camminando avanzano tanto i piedi di dietro, che vengono a tagliarsi quei d' avanti.*
OVER-REACHED, adj. *acchiappato, ingannato, giuntato, deluso, v.* To over-reach.
OVER-REACHING, adj. ex. an over-reaching horse, *un cavallo che si taglia.*
To OVER-READ one's self, *legger troppo, offendersi col legger troppo.*
To O'VER-RECKON, *contar troppo.*
To O'VER-RIDE, *straccare il cavallo cavalcando, cavalcar troppo.*
O'VER-RIGID, adj. *troppo rigido, o severo.*
O'VER-RIGIDNESS, s. *troppa rigidezza, o severità.*
O'VER-RIPE, adj. *troppo maturo.*
To O'VER-ROAST, *arrostire troppo.*
O'VER-ROASTED, adj. *arrostito troppo.*
To O'VER-RULE [to domineer, to bear sway] *dominare, signoreggiare, governare, predominare.*
She over rules my policy, *ella è più astuta di me.*
To over-rule an objection [a law term, not to allow it, to reject it] *rigettare, o ributtare un obbiezione.*
O'VER-RULED, adj. *dominato, signoreggiato, governato, v.* To over-rule.
O'VER-RULING, adj. *che governa tutto.*
To believe an over-ruling providence, *credere ad una providenza che governa tutto.*
To O'VER-RUN [to out-run, to run beyond] *stracorrere, correre più presto.*
To over-run [to cover all over] *coprire, empiere.*
To over-run [to invade every where] *trascorrere, inondare, depredare, predare.*
To over-run the enemies country, *trascorrere il paese nemico.*
To over-run a page [to run it over again, to dispose the lines after another manner] *maneggiare di nuovo una pagina, riordinarla in altra maniera.*
OVER-SCRUPULOUS, adj. *troppo scrupoloso.*
O'VER-SEA, adj. *oltramarino, d'oltre mare.*
To O'VER-SEE [to have the management of] *aver il maneggio, soprantendenza, o inspezione di che si sia.*
To over-see [to over-look, to let pass] *omettere, preterire,* pref. *preterisco,* pret. *omisi.*
How could you over-see that mistake? *come avete potuto omettere un tale errore?*
O'VERSEEN, adj. *ch' è sotto il maneggio soprantendenza o ispezione di qualcheduno, omesso, preterito.*
Over-seen [blinded] *cieco, acciecato.*
Overseen [mistaken] *ingannato, sbagliato, errato.*
Overseen in drink, *cotto, ubbriaco, avvinazzato.*
O'VERSEER, s. *soprantendente,* s. m.
To OVERSEETH, verb neut. *cuocersi troppo.*
To O'VER-SELL, *stravendere, vendere più del dovere.*
To O'VER SET [to over-turn] *rovesciare, voltar sozzopra, ribaltare.*
To over-set a coach, *rovesciare una carrozza.*
O'VER-SET, adj. *rovesciato, arrovesciato, ribaltato.*
To O'VER-SHADOW, *adombrare, ombreggiare, ombrare, offuscare.*
O'VER-SHADOWED, adj. *adombrato, ombreggiato, ombrato, offuscato.*
To O'VER-SHOOT, [to shoot beyond the mark] *tirar di là del segno.*
To over-shoot one's self [to go too far in any business] *inoltrarsi troppo in qualche negozio, avventurarsi troppo in qualche affare.*
O'VERSHOT, } adj. *che s' è inol-*
O'VERSHOTTEN, } *trato o avventurato troppo.*
O'VERSIGHT, s. [inspection, conduct] *ispezione, e inspezione, soprantendenza, cura, condotta,* s. f. *maneggio,* s. m.
Oversight [mistake] *colpa, inavvertenza,* s. f. *errore,* s. m.
To O'VER-SKIP, *v.* To over-slip.
To O'VER-SLEEP one's self, *dormir troppo.*
To O'VER-SLIP, *omettere, lasciare, preterire, trascurare.*
Over-slip, s. *omissione, trascuraggine,* s. f.
O'VER-SLIPT, adj. *omesso, preterito, lasciato, trascurato.*
O'VER-SODDEN, adj. *bollito troppo.*
O'VER-SOLD, adj. *stravenduto.*

To O'VERSPREAD, *cuoprire, spandere, slargare, dilatare.*
To O'VER-STOCK one's self, *fare troppo larghe provvisioni.*
To O'VER-STRAIN, *forzare, sforzare, affettare.*
To over-strain one's voice, *forzar la voce.*
To over-strain one's self, *slogarsi qualche nerbo.*
Over-strained, adj. *forzato, sforzato, affettato.*
To O'VER STRETCH, *stender o tender troppo.*
To over-stretch a matter, *stiracchiare una materia.*
Over-stretched, adj. *steso, teso troppo, stiracchiato.*
O'VERT, adj. [open, manifest] *chiaro, manifesto.*
O'VERT-ACT [in law, a plain matter of fact, serving to prove a design] *azione notoria o manifesta, che basta a provare qualche disegno.*
To O'VERTAKE [to catch] *arrivare, giugnere, sopraggiugnere, acchiappare, cogliere.*
We overtook them upon the road, *gli arrivammo per istrada.*
The night overtook us, *la notte ci colse.*
The storm overtook them, *furono sopraggiunti dalla tempesta.*
This punishment at last overtook him, *non potè alla fine evitare questo gastigo.*
OVERTAKEN, adj. *arrivato, giunto, sopraggiunto, acchiappato, colto.*
We were overtaken on the road with a terrible tempest, *fummo colti per istrada da una terribile burrasca.*
Overtaken in drink, *cotto dal vino, ubbriaco, avvinazzato.*
OVERTA'KER, s. *quello che arriva giugne e coglie.*
To OVER-TALK one's self, *parlar troppo.*
To OVER-TAX, *tassare troppo, opprimere con tasse o imposizioni.*
O'VERTHROW, s. [defeat] *rotta, sconfitta,* s f.
To O'VERTHROW [to overturn, to destroy] *abbattere, sovvertire, mettere sozzopra, alterare, rovesciare, rovinare, sconvolgere.*
To overthrow the laws, *sovvertire le leggi.*
To overthrow [to defeat, to disappoint, to frustrate the designs of one's enemy] *attraversare, rompere, o render vani i disegni del nemico.*
To overthrow one at law [to cast him] *aver la sentenza in favore contro la parte contraria.*
OVERTHRO'WER, s. *attraversatore,* s. m.
OVERTHRO'WING, s. *abbattimento, sconvolgimento,* s. m. *rovina, alterazione,* s. f.
O'VERTHWART, adj. [a cross, or from side to side] *a traverso, bieco, bistorto, obbliquo, sghimbescio, sghembo, sgancio.*
Overthwart [forward] *ostinato, caparbio.*
Overthwart [out of order] *di traverso, male in ordine, disordinato.*
Overthwart, adv. [a-cross] *a traverso, biecamente, indirittamente,, per traverso, obbliquamente, tortamente.*
To overthwart [to cross] *attraversare, porre a traverso.*
To overthwart [to contradict] *contradire, repugnare, opporsi, contrariare.*
To overthwart with words [to give cross answers] *svillaneggiare, dire altrui villanie.*
OVERTHWA'RTED, adj. *attraversato, contradetto, repugnato, opposto, contrariato.*
OVERTHWA'RTLY, adv. *a traverso, indirettamente, per traverso, obbliquamente, tortamente.*
OVERTHWA'RTNESS, s. *caparbieria, ostinazione, pertinacia,* s. f.
O'VERTOOK, pret. *e* part. *passivo del verbo* To overtake.
To OVER-TIRE, *faticar troppo.*
OVER-TIRED, adj. *troppo faticato.*
O'VERTLY, adv. [from overt] *apertamente, chiaramente, manifestamente.*
To O'VER-TOIL, verb recip. *faticarsi, o affannarsi troppo.*
O'VER-TOILED, adj. *troppo faticato, o affannato.*
To O'VER-TOP [to be taller] *essere più grande, o più alto.*
He over-tops me already, *è di già più grande, o più alto di me.*
To over-top [to surpass] *sormontare, avanzare, sopraffare,* pref. *sopraffaccio,* pret. *sopraffeci.*
OVER-TOPPED, adj. *che è più alto o più grande, sormontato, avanzato, soprafatto.*
O'VERTURE, s. [proposal] *proposizione, apertura,* s. f.
To make an overture, *fare una proposizione.*
Overture [a flourish of musick before the scenes are opened in an opera] *sinfonia,* s. f.
To OVERTURN, *sovvertere, rovesciare, sconvolgere, rovinare, mandar sozzopra, metter in rotta,* pret. *sconvolsi.*
O'VERTURNED, adj. *sovvertito, sconvolto, rovinato, rovesciato.*
O'VERTURNING, s. *sovvertimento, sconvolgimento.*
To OVER-TWA'TTLE one, *stordire, sbalordire, intronare il capo ad uno a forza di parlare.*
OVER-TWA'TTLED, adj. *stordito, sbalordito.*
OVER-TWA'TTLING, s. *stordimento, sbalordimento, rompimento di testa a forza di parlare.*
To OVER-VALUE [to over-prize] *stravendere, estimar troppo.*
To over-value one's self, *stimarsi troppo, aver troppa buona stima di se stesso*
OVER-VALUED, adj. *stravenduto, estimato troppo.*
OVER-VIOLENT, adj. *troppo violento.*
To OVER-VOTE, *aver la pluralità delle voci.*
To OVER-WEEN, *lusingarsi, aver troppo buona opinione di se stesso.*
OVER-WEENING, adj. *prosuntuoso, arrogante, tracotato, insolente.*
Over weening, s. *prosunzione, arroganza, tracotanza, insolenza,* s. f.
OVER-WINNINGLY, adv. *insolentemente, arrogantemente, prosuntuosamente.*
To OVER-WEIGH, *pesa più, esser più pesante.*
OVER WELL, adj. *troppo bene.*
To OVER-WHELM [to cover over] *sommergere, inondare.*
To overwhelm in water, *sommergere nell' acqua.*
To overwhelm with grief, *opprimere di dolore.*
OVER-WHELMED, adj. *sommerso, inondato.*
OVER-WHELMING, s. *sommergimento, inondazione,*
OVER-WORN, adj. *oppresso, roso.*
Over-worn with grief, *oppresso dal dolore, roso dall' affanno.*
OVER-YE'ARED, adj. [to old] *troppo invecchiato, troppo vecchio.*
OUGHT, s. [somewhat] *qualche cosa.*
If I had ought to do with him, *se avessi nulla a fare con lui.*
It may be so for ought I know, *ciò può essere benchè non ne sappia nulla.*
For ought I see, *a quel che vedo; per quanto posso vedere.*
Ought [a preter-imperfect of the verb to OWE] ex. I ought to go thither, *devo, sono obbligato, è mio dovere d'andarvi.*
You ought to have done it, *voi dovevate averlo fatto.*
It ought to be so, *deve esser così.*
You ought to love him, *dovreste amarlo.*
OVI'PAROUS, adj. [that breeds by eggs or spawn] *che si genera o moltiplica per mezzo delle uova.*
O'VIFORM, adj. [having the shape of an egg] *ovale, che ha forma d'uovo.*
OUNCE, s. [a sort of weight] *oncia,* s. f.
Half an ounce, *mezz' oncia.*
Ounce [a kind of beast] *sorta di pantera; leonza.*
O'UPHE, s. [a fairy, a gobbling] *un folletto, uno spirito aereo.*
O'UPHEN, adj. [eel fish] *di folletto, di spirito aereo.*
O'URSELF, *pronome reciproco è solamente usato da' principi sovrani nel singolare.*
OURSE'LVES [*plurale di* ourself] *noi, noi in persona, noi stessi.*
OUR [a pron. possessive] *nostro, nostra, nostri, nostre.*
Our country, *il nostro paese, la nostra patria.*
Our books, *i nostri libri.*
Our letters, *le nostre lettere.*
Our father, our mother, *nostro padre, nostra madre.*
This is ours, *questo è nostro.*
That's none of ours, *questo non è nostro.*
A friend of ours, *un amico nostro.*
OUSE, s. [tanner's bark] *scorza di querica*

quercia adoperata nell' acconciar le pelli; concia, v. Owse.

O'USEL, s. [a black bird] *un merlo, uccello noto.*

OUT, prep. *fuori, fuora, fuore.*

Out of the house, *fuor di casa.*

Out of danger, *fuor di pericolo.*

To be out of his wits, *esser fuor di se stesso, aver perduto il cervello.*

Out of doors, *fuor di casa.*

Out of desire of glory, *per desio di gloria.*

Out of friendship, *per amicizia.*

To be out of hope, *esser senza speranza.*

Out of measure, *sopra modo.*

Out of hand [forthwith] *subito, subitamente, immantenente, incontanente, in un subito*

Out of sight, *che non si vede più, perso di vista.*

Out of sight, out of mind, *lontano dagli occhi, lontano dal cuore.*

I did it out of design, *l'ho fatto a posta.*

The fire is out, *il fuoco è spento.*

The candle is out, *la candela è estinta.*

The barrel is out, *il barile è vuoto.*

The time is out [or expired] *il tempo è scorso, passato, o scaduto.*

The cherries are quite out, *le ciriege sono finite, non vi sono più ciriege.*

To speak out [to speak aloud] *parlar forte, o ad alta voce.*

My dream is out, *il mio sogno è arrivato.*

Out of favour, *in disgrazia.*

To be out of favour, *venire, o entrare in disgrazia.*

Out of place, *che ha perduto il suo impiego, senza impiego.*

Out of fashion, *fuor di moda.*

A book out of print, *un libro che scarsamente si trova, fuor di stampa.*

Out at the elbow, *rotto al gomito.*

Out of order [in a confusion] *in disordine, in confusione, disordinato, confuso.*

Out of order [to be indisposed] *indisposto, ammalato.*

To drink out of a glass, *bere in un bicchiere.*

A way out, *un' uscita, escita, apertura da uscire.*

To be out of the way [to be absent] *essere assente.*

To go out of the way, *assentarsi, allontanarsi, discostarsi.*

That's out of my way, *questo non è della mia portata; non m'intendo di questo.*

To ask out of the way, *domandar troppo, stravendere.*

To bid out of the way, *offrire troppo poco.*

To be out [to be mistaken] *sbagliare, errare, scambiare.*

He is grievously out, *egli si sbaglia di molto.*

To be out [as when a man's memory fails him in a discourse] *perder la tramontana; rimanere in secco, entrar nel pecoreccio, non saper che dire, perdere il filo del discorso.*

'Tis out of my head; or, 'tis out of my mind, *l'ho dimenticato, me ne sono scordato, m'è uscito di mente o di testa.*

To be out of taste, *essere svogliato.*

To be out of humour, *esser di cattivo umore.*

I am so much out of pocket, *ho sborsato tanto.*

To be out of stock, *non aver il capital di bottega o magazino pienamente assortito.*

I am out of my wine, *non ho più vino.*

Out of patience, *che ha perduto la pazienza.*

Time out of mind, *tempo immemorabile.*

An instrument out of tune, *uno stromento scordato.*

To be out of tune [to be out of humour] *esser di cattivo umore.*

I am out with him [I am done with him] *non ho più niente a fare con lui, non voglio più impacciarmi con lui.*

Out with him, *scacciatelo fuori.*

Out with you, *eh va via.*

Get thee out of my sight, *levatimi della presenza.*

Get you out of doors, *uscite di qui.*

Shut him out, *chiudetegli la porta in faccia.*

Let him out, *lasciatelo uscire.*

To read a book out, *leggere un libro dal principio alla fine.*

Pray hear me out, *di grazia ascoltatemi, lasciatemi parlare.*

Out upon you, *deh vergognatevi.*

Out with it [speak it] *via su parlate, o dite quel che avete a dire.*

To whip a child out of his tricks, *sculacciare un ragazzo finchè si corregga de' suoi vizietti.*

To physick one out of his life, *ammazzare uno a forza di medicine.*

To OUT [to put out, to turn out] *spogliare, privare.*

To out one of his estate, *spogliare uno de' suoi beni.*

To out one of his office, *scavallare uno dal suo officio.*

To OUT-BID, *incarire, alzar il prezzo.*

OUT-BIDDER, s. *che incarisce.*

OUT-CASE, *fodero.*

OUT-CAST, s. [refuse] *rifiuto,* s. m.

OUT-CRY, s. [a cry or noise] *strepito, romore, schiamazzo,* s. m.

An out-cry [portsale] *incanto,* s. m.

To sell at an out-cry, *vendere all' incanto.*

To OUT-DO [to surpass] *superare, avanzare.*

He has out-done me, *egli m'ha superato, o vinto.*

OUT-DOER, s. *superatore,* s. m.

OUT-DOING, s. *superamento,* s. m.

OUT-DONE, adj. *superato, vinto, avanzato.*

OUTED, adj. *spogliato, privato.*

OUTER, adj. *esteriore, di fuori.*

OUTER-DARKNESS, *le tenebre esteriori.*

To OUT-FACE, *mantenere in faccia, negare in faccia.*

This is to out-face the sun at noonday, *ciò sarebbe negare che non fa giorno a mezzodì.*

OUT-GUARD, s. *guardia avanzata.*

To out-go one, *andar più presto che un altro, avanzare uno camminando, precedere.*

OUT-GONE, adj. *avanzato.*

OUT-GOING, s. [a way out] *uscita, escita,* s. f.

OUT-LANDISH, adj. [foreign] *forestiero, che è d'un altro paese.*

An outlandish man or woman, *un forestiero, una forestiera.*

To OUT-LAST, *durare più.*

OUT-LAW, s [a person deprived of the benefit of the law, and the king's protection] *un bandito.*

To OUT-LAW one [to deprive him of the benefit of the law] *proscrivere uno, condannarlo ad esilio.*

OUT-LAWED, adj. *proscritto, condannato ad esilio.*

OUT-LAWRY, s. [is the loss of the benefit of a subject, and the king's protection] *proscrizione,* s. f. *esilio, bando,* s. m.

To OUT LEARN another, *avanzare, o superare uno nell' imparare, far più gran progresso d'un altro nell' imparare qualche cosa.*

OUT-LET, s. *uscita, escita, apertura,* s. f.

To OUT LIVE, verb act. & neut. *sopravvivere, viver più,* pret. *sopravvissi.*

OUT-LIVED, adj. *soppravvissuto.*

OUT-LIVER, s. *sopravvivente,* s. m.

OUT-LIVING, s. *il sopravvivere.*

OUT-MOST, adj. *l'estremo, che è più in fuori.*

OUT-PARISH, s. *parrocchia ne' borghi d'una città.*

O'UTRAGE, s. [injury] *oltraggio,* s. m. *soperchieria, villania, ingiuria,* s. f.

OUTRA'GIOUS, adj. [abusive, injurious] *oltraggioso, ingiurioso.*

Outragious [cruel, fierce] *oltraggioso, crudele, fiero, violento.*

OUTRA'GIOUSLY, adv. *oltraggiosamente, ingiuriosamente.*

Outragiously [fiercely] *oltraggiosamente, crudelmente, fieramente, violentemente.*

OUTRA'GIOUSNESS, s. [violence or cruelty] *oltraggio,* s. m. *villania, soperchieria, violenza,* s. f.

OUTREMA'RIN, } s. *oltramarino.*
ULTRAMARINE, }

To OUT-RIDE, *avanzare a cavallo, andar più presto a cavallo.*

OUT-RIDERS, s. [bayliffs-errant imployed by the sheriffs, or their deputies] *sbirri,* s. m.

O'UTRIGHT, adv. [forthwith] *subito, subitamente, incontanente, in un subito, immantenente.*

To laugh out-right, *smascellarsi delle risa.*

To O'UT-RUN one, *avanzare uno nel correre, correr meglio di lui.*

To out-run the constable [to run out of expences] *far l'agresto, avanzar nello spendere.*

To

To O'UT-SHINE, *esser più risplendente.*
To O'UT-SHOOT, *portar il colpo più lontano.*
OUT-SIDE, s. [the outward part] *superficie*, s. f. *il di fuori di che che si sia.*
The out-side of a coat, *la parte esteriore d'un abito.*
Out-side [appearance] *apparenza*, s. f. *aspetto*, s. m.
The out-side of an action, *azione apparente.*
To affect a grave out-side, *affettare un aspetto grave.*
'Tis the out-side, *questo è il più.*
OUT-STANDING, s. [or projecture in architecture] *sporto*, s. m. *muraglia che sporge in fuora della dirittura della parete principale.*
O'UT-STREET, s. *strada che è quasi fuori della città.*
To O'UT-STRIP [to out-run] *precorrere, andare avanti, prevenire*, pret. *precorsi.*
To out strip [to surpass] *avanzare, superare.*
O'UT-STRIPPED, adj. *precorso, prevenuto, avanzato, superato.*
To O'UT-WALK one, *camminar più presto d' un altro, lasciarsi addietro uno in camminando.*
O'UT-WALL, *antimuro*, s. m. *muro avanti all' altro.*
O'UTWARD, adj. [to the out-side] *esteriore, della parte di fuori, superficiale.*
An outward friendship, *un' amicizia esteriore, o finta.*
An outward appearance, *esteriormente, apparentemente.*
The outward laws [in opposition to the laws of nature] *le leggi umane.*
An outward court, *un cortile.*
An outward show, *pretesto, sembiante, colore*, s. m. *apparenza*, s. f.
Outward show [parade, ostentation] *ostentazione, pomposa mostra, ambiziosa dimostrazione.*
Outward, adv. *esternamente, di fuora.*
Outward [to the outer parts] *fuor del paese; in parti forestiere.*
To laugh but from the teeth outward [to make a faint show of laughing] *ridere in bocca, ridere esteriormente.*
A ship outward bound, *un vascello caricato per qualche paese forestiero.*
O'UTWARDLY, adv. *esteriormente apparentemente, in apparenza, di fuori.*
O'UTWARDS, adv. *lo stesso che outward avverbio.*
To O'UT-WEIGH, *pesar più, dar il tracollo alla bilancia.*
O'UT-WEIGHED, adj. *che pesa meno.*
To O'UT-WIT one, verb act. *esser più astuto o accorto d' un altro, acchiapparlo.*
O'UT-WITTED, adj. *acchiappato.*
O'UT-WORK, s. *edificio esteriore.*
The out-works of a place, *gli edifici esteriori d' un luogo.*
OUZE, s. [moist ground] *terra umida o melmosa; pantano*, s. m.
Ouse [miry sedge] *acoro*, s. m.
O'UZLE, v. Owsel.
O'UZY, adj. [moist, wet, plashy] *umido, melmoso, pantanoso.*
To Ow, } [to be in debt] *dovere,*
To Owe, } *esser debitore.*
You owe me ten crowns, *voi mi dovete dieci scudi.*
He owes more than he is worth, *deve più che non ha.*
I owe my life to you, *vi son tenuto della vita.*
To owe one a spite [to have a grudge against him] *dare un calcio in gola altrui, aver da rimproverarli qualche cosa.*
O'WING, s. *il dovere, l' esser debitore.*
Owing, adj. *dovuto.*
A great deal of money is owing to me, *m' è dovuta una gran somma di danari.*
To pay what is owing, *pagare quel che dobbiamo.*
These advantages are owing to their own courage, *riconoscono questi vantaggi dal loro proprio valore, questi vantaggi sono gli effetti del loro valore.*
OWL, s. [a night bird] *civetta*, s. f. *barbagianni, alocco*, s. m.
To make an owl of one, *burlarsi d' uno.*
OWLER, s. [a master of a ship who conveys wool or other prohibited goods, by night, to the sea-side to be shipp'd off, contrary to the law] *contrabbandiere*, s. m. *che fa contrabbandi; e' vocabolo burlesco.*
OWN, adj. *proprio.*
He is my own brother, *egli è mio proprio fratello.*
Of his own accord, *di sua propria testa.*
My own self, *io medesimo, io stesso.*
Our own selves, *noi stessi, noi medesimi.*
It is your own fault, *è vostra colpa.*
It is your own choice, *sta in vostra libertà.*
You do not know your own mind, *voi non sapete quel che volete fare.*
To be one's own man, *esser in libertà, non dipendere da nessuno.*
My own, *il mio.*
Every one likes his own best, *ognuno ama meglio il suo.*
He has nothing of his own, *non ha niente del suo.*
I told him his own, *gli ho detto il fatto suo.*
To OWN [to confess, to acknowledge] *confessare, affermare, concedere.*
To own one's own fault, *confessare la sua propria colpa.*
His father would never own him for his son, *suo padre non volle mai riconoscerlo per figlio.*
To own [to claim, to challenge as his own] *attribuirsi, arrogarsi, appropriarsi.*
To own [to possess] *possedere, esser padrone, aver in suo potere.*
Who owns that house? *di chi è quella casa? chi è il padrone di quella casa?*
O'WNED, adj. *confessato, affermato, concesso*, v. To own.
O'WNER, s. *proprietario*, s. m.
OWSE, s. [the bark of a young oak beaten small, and used by tanners] *concia*, s. m. *scorza di quercia colla quale si conciano le pelli*, v. Ouse.
O'WSEL, s. [black bird] *merlo, uccello noto.*
OX, s. [a well known beast] *un bue, animal da giogo*, plur. OXEN.
A wild ox, *un bue salvatico.*
A sea ox, *un bue marino.*
Pertaining to an ox, *bovino.*
An ox-gang [as much land as may be ploughed by one team or gang of oxen in one day] *bubulca*, s. f. *jugero*, s. m. *tanta terra quanta due buoi possono lavorare in un giorno.*
Ox-heal, *la radice dell' elleboro.*
Ox-house, or ox stall, *stalla da buoi.*
Ox-fly, *tafano*, s. m.
Ox-eye [an herb] *occhio di bue, erba.*
Ox-tongue [an herb] *buglossa*, s. f.
O'XICRATE, s. [a mixture of fair water and vinegar] *ossizzocchera*, s. f. *bevanda fatta d'acqua, ed aceto.*
O'XIMEL, s. [a syrup made of honey, vinegar, and water boiled together] *ossimele*, s. m. *bevanda fatta d' aceto mele, ed acqua.*
O'YER, s. a law word, anciently used for what we now call assizes, ex. OYER and TERMINER, a special commission, granted by the King to certain judges, to hear and determine criminal causes, *commissione speciale concessa dal Rè a certi giudici per giudicare alcune cause criminali.*
A justice of oyer and terminer, *un giudice delegato per giudicare cause in virtù di questa commissione.*
O YES [or hear ye, from the French OYEZ, a word used by publick criers, when they make proclamation of any thing] *parola che significa ascoltate, usata da' banditori, nel proclamare qualche cosa.*
OYL, s. *olio, ed oglio*, s. m. *oggi si scrive anzi* OIL.
Pure olive oyl, *olio vergine.*
Oyl of roses, *olio rosato.*
The holy oyl used in the church of Rome, *olio santo.*
To throw oil into the fire, *aggiugner legna al fuoco.*
He could get oyl out of a flint, *potrebbe tirar sugo d'una pietra.*
An oyl-man, *un oliandolo, un che rivende olio.*
An oyl case, *tela incerata.*
To OYL, *condire con olio.*
O'YLED, adj. *oliato, condito d' olio.*

O'YLI-

O'YLINESS, s. [the ftate or quality of being oyly] *qualità oliofa.*
O'YLY, adj. *oliofo, che ha in fe olio.*
O'YSTER, s. [a fort of fhell-fifh] *oftrica,* s. f.
An oyfter-fhell, *conchiglia d' oftrica.*
An oyfter-man, *un uomo che vende delle oftriche.*
O'YSTER-WOMAN } s. [a woman
O'YSTER-WENCH } whofe bufinefs is to fell oyfters] *donna il cui meftiere è vender oftriche.*
OZE'NA, s. [an ulcer in the infide of the noftrils] *ozena,* s. f. *ulcera che fi genera dentro al nafo.*
O'ZIES, s. [a fort of willow-tree] *falce, falcio,* s. m. *albero noto, che nafce ne' luoghi umidi e paludofi. Oggi fi fcrive* ofier.
An ozier-bed, *falceto,* s. m. *luogo pien di falci.*
Ozier, adj. [of oziers] *fatto di falci.*

P.

P *Decimaquarta lettera dell' alfabeto Inglefe, e fi pronuncia come in Italiano.*
PACE, s. [ftep, manner of going] *paffo,* s. m. *quel moto de' piedi che fi fa in andando; e pigliafi anche per ifpazio comprefo dell' uno all' altro piede, in andando.*
A geometrical pace, *un paffo geometrico.*
To go a great pace, *andar a gran paffi, camminar prefto.*
To go a flow pace, *andar a pian paffi, camminar pian piano.*
To go a main pace [at fea] *andare a vele gonfie.*
To mend one's pace, *raddoppiare i paffi.*
To keep always one pace, *camminar fempre d' un paffo.*
A horfe that goes a good pace, *un cavallo che va bene all' ambio.*
To keep or hold pace with one [to go as faft as he] *camminar del pari con uno.*
A pace [or herd] of affes, *un truppa d' afini.*
To PACE [as a horfe does] *andar l' ambio, o portante.*
PACIFICA'TION, s. [peace making] *pacifcazione,* s. f. *il far pace.*
PA'CIFICATORY } adj. *pacifico, quie-*
PACI'FICK } *to amator di pace.*
The pacifick ocean, *il mar pacifico.*
PA'CIFIER, s. [a maker of peace] *pacificatore,* s. m.
To PA'CIFY [to make peace or appeafe] *pacificare, rappacificare, far pace, metter pace, quietare, rappattumare.*
PA'CIFY'D, adj. *pacificato, rappacificato, quietato, rappattumato.*
PA'CIFYING, s. *il pacificare.*
PA'CING, adj. [from to pace] ex. A pacing horfe, *un cavallo portante o ambiante.*
Pacing, s. ex. The pacing of a horfe, *il portante o l' ambio d' un cavallo.*
PACK, s. [bale] *balla,* s. f. *ballotto,* s. m.
A pack of wool, *una balla di lana.*
A pack of hounds, *una muta di cani.*
A pack of knaves, *una man di canaglia.*
A pack of cards, *un mazzo di carte.*
A pack-cloth, *tela di facco.*
A pack-needle, *ago per cucire facchi.*
A pack-horfe, *cavallo da bafto o da foma.*
A pack-faddle, *bafto,* s. m.
Pack-thread, *fpago,* s. m.
To PACK up [to bundle up] *imballare.*
To pack up, *corfela, batterfela, andarfene, o fuggirfene via.*
To pack off [to die] *tirar le calze, morire.*
PA'CKER, s. *imballatore,* s. m.
PA'CKET, s. [bundle] *fafcio, faftello, fardello,* s. m.
A packet of letters, *un piego di lettere.*
A packet of goods, *un ballotto a fardello di mercanzie.*
A packet-boat, *nave che porta il procaccio.*
PA'CKING up, s. *l' imballare.*
A packing away, *il corfela, il batterfela, l' andarfene via.*
Get thee packing, *vattene via.*
To fend one packing, *mandar uno pe fatti fuoi, mandarlo via.*
Packing-whites [a fort of cloth] *tela da facco.*
PACT } s. [a bargain, covenant,
PA'CTION } agreement] *patto, accordo,* s. m. *convenzione.*
PACTI'TIOUS, adj. [done upon condition, agreed] *pattuito, patteggiato.*
PAD, s. [a foft faddle for a horfe to carry a portmantle] *cuscinetto da cavallo per portarvi fopra una valigia.*
A pad of ftraw, *un pagliaccio.*
A pad way, *una ftrada battuta.*
A pad, or a pad nag, s. [a nag that goes eafy] *un cavallo portante, una chinea.*
A foot-pad [one who robs upon the road on foot] *ladro di ftrada che ruba a piedi.*
To PAD [to rob upon the highway] *gettarfi o andare alla ftrada, rubar le ftrade.*
PA'DDER, v. Foot-pad.
PA'DDING, s. *il rubar alla ftrada.*
To PA'DDLE [to move the water with hands or feet] *guazzare, dimenar l' acqua colle mani o co' piedi.*
To paddle in the dirt, *dimenarfi nel fango.*
A paddle-ftaff [a long ftaff with an iron fpike at the end of it, ufed by mole-catchers] *raftrello,* s. m.
PA'DDOCK, s. [great toad] *botta,* s. f.

f. *animal velenoso, di forma simile al ranocchio.*

Paddock-stool, *fungo*, s. m.

Paddock-course [a place in a park paled in for hounds to run matches] *luogo chiuso in un parco dove si esercitano, i cani alla caccia del cervo.*

PA'DDOW-PIPE, s. [an herb] *sorta d' erba.*

PA'DLOCK, *catenaccio, chiavistello*, s. m.

To PA'DLOCK, *chiudere col catenaccio.*

PA'GAN, s. [heathen] *un pagano, una pagana.*

Pagan, adj. [belonging to an heathen] *pagano, idolatra.*

PA'GANISM, s. [the principles of the Pagans] *paganesimo*, s. m. *religion pagana.*

PAGE, s. [a youth of honour in the service of a prince, or some great personage] *paggio*, s. m.

Page [one side of the leaf of a book] *pagina, facciata*, s. f.

To PAGE, *segnar le facciate d'un libro con numeri.*

To Page [to attend as a page] *servire come fa un paggio.*

PA'GEANT, s. [a triumphal chariot, or arch] *carro, o arco trionfante.*

Pageant [great show] *spettacolo*, s. m. *pompa*, s. f.

He is but the pageant of a friend [or a friend in show] *non è amico che in vista.*

Pageant, adj. *pomposo, di molta ostantazione.*

PA'GEANTRY, s. [great show] *fasto*, s. m. *pompa*, s. f.

It is but mere pageantry, *non è che un mero pretesto.*

PA'GOD, s. [an image worshipped by the Indians and Chinese] *Pagode, idolo pagano.*

Pagod [the temple belonging to such an idol] *pagode, tempio dove s' adora l' idolo.*

Pagod [an Indian piece of gold] *pagode, moneta d' oro Indiana.*

PAID, *preterito e participio passivo del verbo* to pay.

PAIL, s. [vessel to hold liquid things] *secchia*, s. f.

A pail full of water, *una secchia piena d' acqua.*

PAIN, s. [punishment] *pena, punizione*, s. f. *castigo, supplizio.*

Upon pain of death, *sotto pena di morte.*

Pain [torment] *pena, afflizione*, s. f. *travaglio, dolore*, s. m.

Pain [ach] *male, dolore*, s. m.

A pain in the head, *mal di testa.*

The pains of a woman in labour, *dolori del parto*

You put me to much pain, *voi mi fate penar troppo.*

To be full of pain, *soffrir gran dolori.*

Pain [grief, uneasiness] *pena, afflizione*, s. f. *dolore*, s. m.

Pain [labour, toil] *pena, fatica*, s. f. *travaglio, stento, lavoro*, s. m.

With much pains, *a gran pena, con grande stento.*

To take pains, *porre ogni pena, affaticarsi.*

Without pains, no gains, *non v' è rosa senza spine.*

He must take that for his pains, *egli l' ha ben meritato.*

He had his labour for his pains, *ecco quel che n' ha guadagnato.*

He is an ass for his pains, *egli ha trattato da asino.*

A pains taker, *laborioso, industrioso, diligente.*

To PAIN [to put to pain] *dolere, dar della pena, sentir dolore.*

It pains me horribly, *mi fa gran male, mi duole molto.*

To pain [to trouble] *penare, patir pene, tormentare, dar pena.*

PA'INFUL, adj. [full of pain] *doloroso, pien di dolore, che duole.*

My wound is very painful, *la mia piaga è molto dolorosa, o mi duole molto.*

Painful [hard, difficult] *penoso, faticoso, difficile, laborioso.*

A painful man, *un uomo laborioso, industrioso, diligente, faticoso.*

PA'INFULLY, adv. *penosamente, faticosamente, con pena.*

PA'INFULNESS, s. *difficoltà, pena*, s. f.

PAINT, s. [counterfeiting colour] *belletto, liscio*, s. m. *materia colla quale le donne procurano di farsi colorite, e belle le carni.*

White paint, *biacca*, s. f.

To paint [to draw pictures] *dipignere.*

To paint in oil, in fresco, &c. *dipignere in olio, in fresco*, &c. pret. *dipinsi.*

To paint [to beautify the face] *lisciare, porre il liscio o l' belletto, imbellettare.*

To paint, *lisciarsi, imbellettarsi.*

PA'INTED, adj. *dipinto, lisciato, imbellettato.*

PA'INTER, s. [one that paints in oyl] *dipintore, pittore.*

Painters gold, *oro macinato.*

PA'INTING, s. *pittura, dipintura*, s. f. *il dipignere.*

Painting in oyl, *pittura in olio.*

The art of painting, *la pittura, l' arte di dipignere.*

Painting [paint for one's face] *liscio, belletto*, s. m.

PAIR, s. [couple] *un pajo*, s. m. *due d' una stessa cosa, coppia*, s. f.

A pair of pigeons, *un pajo di piccioni.*

A pair of shoes, gloves, stockings, *un pajo di scarpe, guanti, calze.*

A pair of scissers, *un pajo di forbici.*

A pair of bellows, *un soffietto.*

A pair of tables, *un tavoliere.*

To PAIR [to match] *appajare, accoppiare, accompagnare*

PA'IRED, adj. *appajato, accoppiato, accompagnato.*

PA'LACE, s. [a court or mansion house of a prince] *palagio, e palazzo*, s. m.

PALA'CIOUS, adj. *reale, nobile, maestoso, magnifico.*

PA'LADIN [a knight of the round table] *paladino*, s. m. *cavaliero della tavola rotonda.*

PALANKA, s. [a defence made of great poles or stakes] *palanca*, s. f. *forte fatto di pali.*

PA'LANQUIN, s. [a kind of covered carriage, used in the eastern countries, that is supported on the shoulders of slaves] *Palanchino, sorta di seggiola usata in alcune parti d' oriente portata dagli schiavi in ispalla.*

PA'LATABLE, adj. [agreeable to the palate] *grato o gustoso al palato.*

PA'LATE, s. [the roof of the mouth] *palato*, s. m. *parte superiore di dentro, quasi cielo della bocca.*

To have a dainty palate, *esser d' un gusto delicato.*

PALA'TINATE, s. [the country of a count Palatine] *palatinato*, s. m.

PALATINE, s. [the name of a certain dignity] *palatino*, s. m.

A count Palatine, *un conte Palatino.*

An electoral Palatine, *elettore Palatino,*

PALE, adj. [wan, whitely look'd] *pallido, smorto, sbiancato.*

Somewhat pale, *pallidetto, pallidiccio, alquanto pallido.*

To grow or change pale, *impallidire, e impallidare, divenir pallido.*

Pale, s. [stake] *palo*, s. m. *legno ritondo e lungo.*

A fence or enclosure with pales, *palata, palafitta.*

To be within the pale [or the communion] of the church, *esser nel grembo della chiesa.*

To PALE [to fence with pales] *palificcare, ficcar i pali in terra, o sostenimento de' frutti.*

To pale a vine, *palificcare una vigna.*

PALED, adj. *palificcato.*

PA'LENESS, s. [whiteness, wanness of countenance] *pallidezza*, s f.

PA'LFREY, s. [a horse for ladies] *palafreno*, s. m.

PA'LINDROM, } s. [a verse or sen-
PA'LINDROME, } tence which is the same read backwards as forwards] *verso o sentenza di cui le lettere sono le medesime, lette da sinistra a dritta o da dritta a sinistra, come* madam, *come questa sentenza,* subi dura a rudibus.

PA'LINODY, s. [recantation] *palinodia*, s. f.

A PALISA'DO, s [a fence of pales] *palificata, palizzata, palicciata*, s. f.

To PALISA'DE [to fence with pallisadoes] *palificare.*

PALISA'DED, adj. *palificato.*

PALL, s. [cloth or velvet that covers a coffin at a funeral] *panno di morto.*

Pall [a long robe or mantle worn upon solemn occasions by the knights of the garter] *palio, manto che portano in alcune solennità i cavalieri della giartiera.*

Pall [an ornament made of lambs wool, which the Pope bestows on archbishops] *palio, ornamento del sommo Pontefice concesso a' Metropolitani, portato da loro sopra gli abiti sagri in giorni determinati, tessuto di luna.*

Pall, adj. [dead, inſipid] *mucido, inſipido.*

You let your wine pall, *il voſtro vino ſarà inſipido.*

To Pall [to cloak, to inveſt] *metterſi il palio.*

To pall [to grow vapid; to become inſipid] *diventar mucido; perdere il ſapore.*

Pa'lled, adj. *mucido.*

Pa'llet, s. [the painter's thin oval piece of wood that holds his colours] *tavolozza, s. f.*

A pallet bed, *un pagliaccio.*

To Pa'lliate [to diſguiſe, to colour, to cloak] *palliare, ricoprire ingegnoſamente.*

Pa'lliated, adj. *palliato, ricoperto.*

Pa'lliating, } s. *palliamento,* s. m.
Pallia'tion, } *il palliare.*

Pa'lliative, adj. *palliativo.*

Palliative cure, *cura palliativa, ed è differente dalla cura curativa, che la palliativa ſolamente addolciſce il male, ma non lo ſana.*

Pa'llid, adj. [a poetical word, pale] *pallido, ſmorto.*

Palli'dity, s. [paleneſs] *pallidità, pallidezza,* s. f.

Palm, s. [the inward part of the hand] *palma,* s. f. *il concavo della mano.*

Palm [a hand's breadth] *palmo,* s. m. *ſpazio, di quanto ſi diſtende la mano, dall' eſtremità del pollice a quella del mignolo.*

Palm, } *palma, l'albero che fa i*
Palm-tree, } *datteri.*

The branch of a palm-tree, *una palma, un ramo di palma.*

Palm-berries, or palm-fruits, *datteri, il frutto della palma.*

A grove of palm-trees, *palmeto,* s. m.

Palm-ſunday, *Domenica degli olivi.*

To Palm [to handle] *maneggiare, toccare, trattar colle mani.*

To palm [to cog, to cheat at dice] *truffare al giuoco de' dadi.*

Palm-chri'sti, s. [a plant] *nome di pianta.*

Palmer [among hunters, the crown of a deer's head] *le corna piccole del cervo in cima delle grandi a guiſa di corona.*

Palmer, } s. [a caterpillar]
Palmer-worm, } *centogambe,* s. m. *vermicello che ha moltiſſime gambe.*

Palmer [pilgrim] *palmiere, pellegrino,* s. m.

Pa'lmestry, s. ex. [one ſkill'd in the art of palmeſtry] *chiromanzia,* s. f. *indovinamento mediante le linee della mano.*

Pa'lmister, s. [one ſkill'd in the art of palmeſtry] *chiromante,* s. m. *che eſercita la chiromanzia.*

Pa'lpable, adj. [that may be eaſily felt] *palpabile, che ha corpo, che può toccarſi.*

Palpable [manifeſt, plain, evident] *palpabile, chiaro, aperto, manifeſto, che ſi tocca con mano.*

Pa'lpableness, s. *qualità palpativa, o ſenſitiva.*

Pa'lpably, adv. *manifeſtamente, apertamente, chiaramente.*

Palpita'tion, s. [a panting] *palpitazione,* s. f. *il palpitare.*

To Pa'lpitate [to pant, to beat quick, like the heart] *palpitare, frequentemente muoverſi, ed è proprio quel battere che fa il cuore per qualche paſſione.*

Pa'lsgrave, s. [a count or earl who has the over-ſeeing of a palace] *conte palatino, un palatino.*

Pa'lsey, s. [a diſeaſe which cauſes a ſlackening of the nerves] *paraliſia,* s. f. *ſorta di malattia nota.*

A man or woman ſick of the palſey, *un paralitico, una paralitica.*

To Pa'lter [to prevaricate, to play faſt and looſe] *cianciare, fraſcheggiare, voler la baja, dire ora di sì ora di no, trattar con doppiezza, anſanare, auſaneggiare.*

To palter [to ſquander away] *diſſipare, mandare a male.*

Pa'lterer, s. *un uomo doppio, uno che non tratta ſchiettamente con una perſona.*

Pa'ltry, adj. [pitiful, ſorry, bad, vile] *povero, meſchino, di poco ſtima, abbietto, diſpregievole.*

A paltry book, *un libraccio.*

A little paltry houſe, *una caſaccia.*

A paltry fellow [a baſe, ſordid fellow] *un poltroniere, un 'infame, un furfantaccio.*

A paltry quean, *un bagaſcia, una puttanaccia.*

Pam, s. *il fante di fiori in un giuoco di carte.*

To Pa'mper [to feed high, to indulge] *impinguare, ingraſſare, trattar delicatamente, tenere nella bambagia, in delizie, o in morbidezze, allevar morbidamente.*

To pamper one's ſelf, *trattarſi bene, darſi buon tempo.*

To pamper a horſe for ſale, *impinguare, o ingraſſare un cavallo.*

Pa'mpered, adj. *impinguato, ingraſſato, trattato, delicatamente.*

Pa'mphlet, s. [a little ſtitch'd book] *libretto di pochi fogli di ſtampa.*

A ſcandalous pamphlet, *un libello, ſcandaloſo, o infamatorio.*

Pa'mphleteer, s. [a pamphlet writer] *ſcrittore di libretti, d'opere brevi. Talvolta è in cattivo ſenſo, e vale autore d'uno o più libelli infamatori.*

Pan, s. [a general name for many utenſils] *termine generale per eſprimere per lo più arneſi di cucina.*

Pan [frying-pan] *una padella.*

A dripping-pan, *una ghiotta.*

A warming-pan, *uno ſcaldaletto.*

A baking-pan, *una tegghia, un tegame.*

A cloſe-ſtool pan, *un pitale.*

The fire pan of a gun, *il focone d'un arma da fuoco.*

The brain-pan [the ſcull] *il cranio,*

The knee-pan, *la padella del ginocchio.*

A pan-pudding, *una torta.*

A fire-pan, *un braciere.*

To ſtand on one's pan pudding [to ſtand to what he has promiſed, or ſaid] *mantenere la promeſſa, ſtar fermo a quello che s'è detto.*

Pan-tile, *tegola,* s. f. *tegolo,* s. m.

To Pan [to cloſe, to join together] *giugnere, unire inſieme.*

Panace'a, s. [an univerſal medicine good for all diſeaſes] *panacea,* s. f. *medicamento univerſale.*

Pana'do, s. [a kind of food made of bread] *panata,* s. f.

Pa'n-cake, s. [a cake made in a pan] *fritella,* s. f. *vivanda di paſta, tenera, fretta nella padella con olio o altro.*

Pa'ncreas, s. [the ſweet-bread of an animal] *pancreas,* s. m. *una delle principali glandule del ventre degli animalati.*

Pancrea'tick, adj. [belonging to the ſweet-bread] *pancreatico, attenente al pancreas.*

Pa'ndects, s. [a treatiſe that comprehends the whole of a ſcience] *pandette; trattato che tocca tutti i punti d'una ſcienza.*

Pandects [a volume of the civil law] *pandette.*

Pa'nder, s. [a pimp] *un ruffiano.*

To Pander, *far il ruffiano, ruffianeggiare, far il mezzano infame in coſe d'illecito amore e di laſcivia.*

Panderly, adj. [pimping, pimplike] *ruffianeſco, da ruffiano.*

Pane, s. [a ſquare of wood or glaſs] *un pezzo quadro di legno o di vetro.*

A pane of glaſs, *un vetro di fineſtra.*

Panegyr'ical, adj. [belonging to a panegyrick] *attenente a panegirico.*

Panegy'rick, s. [a ſpeech made in praiſe of one] *un panegirico, un elogio,* s. m.

Pane'gyrist, s. [a maker of panegyricks] *un panegiriſta, che fa panegirici.*

Panel, s. *pezzo quadro di metro o d'altra materia che ſi commette in altre materie, verbigrazia un vetro di fineſtra.*

Panel, *ſi chiama così quello ſcritto che contiene i nomi de' giurati ſcelti dallo ſceriffe a giudicar una cauſa in Inghilterra.*

A panel [a ſaddle for carrying burdens on horſe-back] *bardella,* s. f.

A panel [in falconry, the ſtomach of a hawk] *lo ſtomaco del falcone.*

Pang, s. [violent pain] *affanno grande; eſtremo dolore,* s. m. *angoſcia, doglia eſtrema,* s. f.

Pangs of death, *le angoſce delle morte.*

Pangs of a woman in labour, *i dolori del parto.*

Pangs of ſenſual luſt, *le violenze e gl' impeti del ſenſo.*

Pa'ngutts, s. [gorbelly'd fellow; fat-guts] *un panciuto, un uomo di groſſa pancia.*

Pa'nick, s. [a ſort of millet] *panico,* s. m.

Panick, adj. *panicc.*

Panick fear, *terrore panico, coſternazione.*

PA'NNIER, s. [a baſket to carry bread, fruit, &c.] *paniera*, s. f. *paniere*, s. f. *ceſta fatta di vinchi da portarvi pane.*

A pannier-man [one who winds the horn, or rings the bell at the inns of court] *officiale ſubalterno nelle corti civili, che ſuona il corno o il campanello.*

To PANT [to fetch one's breath ſhort, or breathe quick] *anelare, anſare, reſpirar con affanno.*

To pant after a thing [to deſire it earneſtly] *deſiderare anſioſamente una coſa.*

To pant [to beat quick] *palpitare, battere.*

To pant for fear, *anſar di paura.*

PANTALO'ON, s. [a ſort of garment worn anciently, conſiſting of breeches and ſtockings faſtened together, and both of the ſame ſtuff] *calzoni alla pantaloneſca.*

PA'NTESS, s. [a hawk's hard fetching of wind] *anſamento di falcone.*

To have the panteſs [to be ſhort winded] *anſare, reſpirar con affanno.*

PA'NTERS, s. [among hunters, nets or toils to catch deer in] *rete da pigliar cervi o daini.*

PA'NTHEON, s. [an ancient temple at Rome] *il Panteon, oggi detto la Rotonda.*

PA'NTHER, [a fierce beaſt] *pantera*, s. f.

PANTING, adj. [that pants] *anſante che anſa.*

Panting, s. [beating] *palpitante, che pa'pita.*

Panting, s. [the fetching one's breath ſhort] *anſamento*, s. m. *l'anſare.*

Panting [beating of the heart] *palpitazione di cuore.*

PA'NTLER, s. [an officer who keeps the bread in a king's court, or houſe of a nobleman] *panettiere*, s. m.

PA'NTOFLE, } s. [a flipper] *pianella*, s. f. *calzamento de' piedi, che non ha calcagno.*
PA'NTOUFLE, }

To ſtand upon one's pantofles, *fare il fiero, alzar le corna, inſuperbirſi.*

PANTO'METER, s. [a mathematical inſtrument for meaſuring all ſorts of angles, heights, lengths, &c.] *pantometro*, s. m. *ſtrumento matematico per miſurare ogni ſorta d'angoli, altezze, larghezze, &c.*

PA'NTOMIME, s. [a player that can repreſent the geſture, and counterfeit the ſpeech of any man] *un pantomino, un buffone, un che imita i geſti e la voce d'ogni uomo.*

PA'NTRY, s. [a room or cloſet where bread and meat are kept] *diſpenſa*, s. f. *ſtanza dove ſi tengono le coſe da mangiare.*

The yeoman of the pantry [at the king's court] *diſpenſiero, e diſpenſiere*, s. m. *propoſto alla cura della diſpenſa.*

PAP [a ſort of ſpoon-meat for children] *pappa*, s. f. *pane cotto in acqua pura, che ſi da a' bambini quando ſi allattano.*

Pap [teat] *mammella, poppa*, s. f.

PAPA', s. [a child's name for father] *babbo*, s m. *padre, e diceſi ſolo da piccioli fanciulli.*

PA'PACY, s. [the dignity of a pope, or time of his government] *papato, pontificato*, s. m. *dignità papale, e 'l tempo del ſuo governo.*

PA'PAL, adj. [belonging to the pope] *papale, di papa.*

PAPA'VEROUS, adj. [belonging to poppy] *di papavero, attenente o ſimile al papavero.*

PA'PER, s. [a ſubſtance made of rags, to write upon, and for other uſes] *carta*, s. f.

Paper-royal, *carta reale.*

Writing-paper, *carta da ſcrivere.*

Blotting paper, *carta ſugante.*

Waſte-paper, *carta di niun uſo.*

A ſheet of paper, *un foglio di carta.*

A paper mill, *una cartiera, luogo dove ſi fabbrica la carta.*

A paper ſeller, *cartajo*, s. m.

A paper book, *un libro di carta bianca.*

Paper windows, *impannate*, s. f.

Bad paper, *cartaccia*, s. f. *carta cattiva.*

PA'PERS, [writings] *ſcritti, ſcritture.*

Old papers, *ſcartafacci, ſcartabelli.*

PA'PIST [one that profeſſes the popiſh religion] *papiſta, nome di diſpregio dato a un cattolico Romano.*

PA'PISM, } s. [popery] *il papiſmo, la religione Romana.*
PAPISTRY, }

PAR, adj. [equal] *pari, uguale, eguale.*

To be at par, *eſſer del pari, eſſere uguale.*

PA'RABLE, s. [a continued ſimilitude] *parabola, ſimilitudine*, s. f.

Parable, adj. [eaſy to be had, which may be got] *che ſi può ottenere facilmente.*

PARA'BOLA, s. [one of the ſections ariſing from a cone] *parabola, figura prodotta da una delle ſezioni del cono.*

PARABO'LICAL, } adj. [belonging to a parable, or a parabola] *parabolico, di parabola a ſimiglianza di parabola.*
PARABO'LICK, }

PARACLE'TE, s. [advocate, comforter] *conſolatore*, s. m. *lo ſpirito ſanto.*

PARA'DE [great ſhow, ſtate] *parata, moſtra, oſtentazione*, s. f. *ſoggio*, s. m.

To keep up a parade in town, *fare gran figura in città, ſfoggiare.*

Parade [in military affairs, the place where troops aſſemble or draw together] *parata, piazza d'arme, luogo dove i ſoldati ſi radunano.*

PA'RADISE, s. [a place of pleaſure, the garden of Eden] *paradiſo, giardino delizioſo.*

Paradiſe [the place of bliſs in heaven] *paradiſo*, s. m. *luogo de' beati.*

To bring one into a fool's paradiſe [to give him a falſe joy] *paſcere alcuno di vana ſperanze, paſcerlo di vento, promettergli mari e mondi, dargli un' allegrezza di pan caldo.*

The bird of Paradiſe, *l'uccello Paradiſo.*

PARA'DOX, s. [a ſtrange ſentiment, contrary to the common opinion] *paradoſſo*, s. m. *coſa fuori della comune opinione.*

PARADO'XAL, } adj. [belonging to a paradox] *attenente a paradoſſo, ſtrano, ſtupendo.*
PARADO'XICAL, }

PA'RAGON, s. [a complete model or pattern] *un paragone, modello, perfetto.*

She is a paragon of beauty, *ella è un paragon di bellezza.*

To PARA'GON [to match or compare] *paragonare, far paragone, aſſimigliare, comparare, uguagliare.*

PA'RAGRAPH, s. [a ſmaller ſection, of a book, where the line breaks off, or what is comprehended between one break and another] *paragrafo*, s. m.

PARA'KITE, s. *pappagallo verde.*

PA'RALLEL, adj. [equally diſtant aſunder] *paralello, parallelo, equidiſtante, termine geometrico.*

Parallel, s. [a parallel line] *una linea paralella.*

Parallel [compariſon of things] *competenza, comparazione*, s. f.

Would you put yourſelf in a parallel with me? *vorreſte forſe venire in competenza meco?*

To PA'RALLEL [to compare] *paragonare, far paragone, aſſimigliare, comparare.*

PA'RALLEL'D, adj. *paragonato, aſſimigliato, comparato.*

Thoſe things are not to be parallel'd, *queſte coſe non hanno veruna comparazione fra di loro, non v'è paragone fra queſte coſe.*

PA'RALLELISM, s. [parallel, compariſon] *paragone*, s. m. *comparazione, egualità*, s. f.

PA'RALLELOGRAM, s. [a plane figure drawn with four parallel lines] *paralellogrammo*, s. m. *figura di quattro lati paralelli.*

PARALELLOPE'PID, s. [is a ſolid figure contained under ſix parallelograms] *paralellepipedo*, s. m. *figura ſolida geometrica, compoſta ne' lati oppoſti di ſuperficie paralelle.*

PA'RALOGISM, s. [a fallacious way of arguing] *paralogiſmo, ſofiſmo*, s. m.

To PA'RALOGIZE [to reaſon ſophiſtically] *ſofiſticare, far ſofiſmi, ſottilizzare, cavillare.*

PA'RALOGY, s. [falſe reaſoning] *falſo ragionare; ragionamento fondato ſu falſe ſuppoſizioni.*

PARALY'TICAL, adj. [belonging to, or ſick of a palſy] *paralitico, infermo di paraliſia.*

PARALY'TICK, s. [one troubled with the palſy] *un paralitico.*

PA'RAMENTS, s. [robes of ſtate] *paramenti, robe, o veſti di cerimonia.*

PA'RAMOUNT, adj. [ſovereign or abſolute lord] *ſignore aſſoluto.*

The king is patron paramount to all the benefices of England, *il rè è padrone aſſoluto di tutti i benefici d'Inghilterra.*

PA'RAMOUR [or lover, he or ſhe that loveth or is loved] *amatore, drudo, vago*, s. m. *amanza, dama*, s. f.

PA'RANYMPH, s. [a brideman or bridemaid] *paraninfo, quello che conduce* va la sposa, ed aveva la cura delle nozze.

Paranymph [one who makes a speech in commendation of one who commences doctor in an university] paraninfo, quello che fa l' elogio di qualche licenziato in una università.

PA'RAPET, s. [a breast-work on a rampier] parapetto, s. m.

PARAPHARNA'LIA, s. [those goods which a wife brings her husband over and above her dower] paraferna, sopradotte, s. f.

PA'RAPHRASE, s. [the expressing of a text in plainer words, and somewhat more largely and accommodated to the reader's capacity] parafrasi, s. f. traduzione ampliata.

To PA'RAPHRASE [to make a paraphrase of, to comment upon] commentare, esporre con parafrasi.

PA'RAPHRASED, adj. commentato, esposto con parafrasi.

PA'RAPHRAST, s. [one who paraphrases] commentatore, quello che commenta, o spiega una materia con parafrasi.

PARAPHRA'STICAL, adj. spiegato con parafrasi.

PARAPHRE'NITIS, s. [a madness accompanied with a continual fever] frenesia, con febbre continua.

PARAQUITO, s. [the lesser sort of parrots] pappagallo piccolo.

PA'RASANG, s. misura di lunghezza usata in Persia.

PA'RASITE, s. [a smell-feast, a spunger] parasito, ghiottone, pappalardo, bacchettone, s. m.

A vile parasite, un parasitaccio.

PARASI'TICAL, adj. [belonging to a parasite] di parasito.

Parasitical plants [those that are nourished by the stock of others] piante che pigliano il loro nutrimento dalle altre piante.

PA'RASOL, s. [umbrello] parasole, ombrella.

PA'RAVAIL, s. [he who is tenant to one who holds his fee of another] quello che tiene un feudo da uno che lo tiene dal signore del feudo.

To PA'RBOIL [to boil but in part] sobbollire, mezzo bollire.

PA'RBOILED, adj. sobbollito, mezzo bollito.

To PA'RBREAK [to vomit] vomitare.

PARBRE'AKING, s. vomito, s. m. il vomitare.

PARCEL, s. [part, portion] parte, porzione, particella, s. f.

Parcel [sum] una somma.

Parcel [or bundle] of linen, un fardello di biancherie.

A pretty good parcel, una buona quantità.

I have a pretty good parcel of books to sell, io ho un buon numero di libri a vendere.

This is a good parcel of books, questa roba è molto buona.

By parcel, a minuto.

To PA'RCEL [to divide into parcels] dividere, sminuzzare, partire, far parti, separare, pret. divisi.

To parcel a seam [a sea term] is after the ship is caulked, to lay over it a narrow piece of canvass, and to pour on it hotch pitch and tar, mettere una pezza di canavaccio intrisa nella pece sopra le fessure d'un vascello, dopo d' averle turate.

PA'RCELLED, adj. diviso, sminuzzato, partito, separato.

PA'RCELLING, s. partimento, s. m. il partire, divisione, s. f.

PA'RCENERS, s. [joint-heirs or tenants] coeredi, s. m.

To PARCH [to burn, to dry up] abbruciare, seccare, arsicciare.

PA'RCHED, adj. abbruciato, secco, adusto, arsiccio.

PA'RCHING, s. l'abbruciare, adustione, s. f.

PA'RCHMENT, s. pergamena, cartapecora, s. f.

Virgin-parchment, carta fatta di pelle d' animale tratto dal ventre della madre inanzi che nasca.

PA'RDON, s. [forgiveness] perdono, s. m. perdonanza, remissione, grazia, s. f.

The pardon of sins, il perdono, o remissione de' peccati.

To obtain the king's pardon, ottenere la grazia del rè.

The pope's pardons [or indulgencies] le indulgenze del papa.

I beg your pardon, vi domando perdono.

To PA'RDON [to forgive] perdonare.

Pardon me, mi perdoni.

To pardon a malefactor, perdonare, far grazia ad un malfattore.

To pardon sins, assolvere o rimettere peccati.

PA'RDONABLE, adj. [that may be pardoned] perdonabile, scusabile, remissibile.

PA'RDONED, adj. perdonato, assoluto, rimesso.

A crime not to be pardoned, un delitto da non perdonarsi.

PA'RDONING, s. perdonamento, s. m. perdonanza, s. f. il perdonare.

To PARE [to clip, to cut] affilare, pareggiare.

To pare the nails, tagliare le unghie.

To pare a horse's hoof, pareggiare le unghie al cavallo.

To pare bread, scrostare il pane.

To pare a little the end of a cloak, raffilare un mantello.

To pare an apple or pear, scortecciare una mela o una pera.

PA'RED, adj. raffilato, pareggiato.

PA'REMENTS, s. [the ornaments of an altar] paramenti, ornamenti d'altare.

PA'RENT, s. parente, genitore, padre, e madre.

God is the great parent of the world, Iddio è il grand' architetto o creatore del mondo.

Plenty is the parent of luxury, l' abbondanza è la madre del lusso.

PA'RENTAGE, s. [kindred, stock, family] parentado, legnaggio, s. m. stirpe, prosapia, parentela, s. f.

PARE'NTALS, s. [feasts performed by the Romans at the funerals of their relations and friends] festini che i Romani facevano all' esequie de' loro parenti ed amici.

PARE'NTHESIS, s. [a clause put into the middle of a sentence] parentesi, s. f.

PA'RENTICIDE, s. [one that kills father and mother] un patricida, un matricida.

PA'RGET, s. [the plaister of a wall] intonicato, intonacato, s. m. coperta liscia che si fa al muro colla calcina.

To PA'RGET [to plaister] intonicare, e intonacare, dar l' ultima coperta di calcina sopra l' arricciato del muro.

PA'RGETTED, adj. intonicato, e intonacato.

PA'RGETTING, s. l' intonicare, intonicato, s. m.

PARHE'LION, s. [a mock sun] parelio, s. m.

PA'RIETARY, s. [an herb] parietaria, s. f.

PA'RING, s. [from to pare] il pareggiare, v. To pare.

The parings [things pared off, as off nails] tonditure, s. f. quel che in pareggiando si leva, ritagli, s. m.

The parings of an apple or cheese, scorza di mela, o di formaggio

A paring knife [for a shoemaker] trinco, s. m. coltello trinciante di calzolajo.

A paring shovel, un orso, strumento con che si puliscono i pavimenti.

PA'RISH, s. parrocchia, s. f. chiesa che ha cura d'anime e tutto quel luogo che è suggetto alla parrocchia.

A parish church, una parrocchia, o chiesa parrochiale.

The parish priest, il parrocchiano, il prete rettor della parrocchia.

PARI'SHIONER, s. un parrocchiano, chè è della parrocchia.

PARISYLLA'BICAL, PARISYLLABICK, } adj. del medesimo numero di sillabe.

PA'RITY, s. [equality, evenness] parità, egualità, similitudine, somiglianza, s. f.

PARK, s. [a piece of ground enclosed, and stock'd with wild beasts of chase] parco, serraglio, s. m. luogo dove si racchiuggon le bestie cinto di muro o d' altro riparo.

Park of artillery in a camp [is the place appointed for the artillery] luogo destinato per mettervi l'artigliera e altre munizioni da guerra.

Park of provisions [in a camp, a place in the rear of every regiment, with all sorts of provisions] luogo del campo dove sono le provisioni da bocca, o i viveri.

PA'RKED, adj. murato, circondato di muro, di pali, o simili.

PA'RK LEAVES, s. [an herb] ruta salvatica.

PA'RLEY, s. [conference with an enemy] parlamento, s. m. conferenza, s. f.

To desire a parley, domandare a parlamentare.

 To

To beat or sound a parley, *suonar la chiamata.*

To Pa'rley [to come to a parley] *parlamentare, conferire insieme,* pret. *conferisco.*

Pa'rliament, s. [the chief assembly and council of the nation met together, to make or alter laws] *parlamento, senato,* s. m.

The parliament of England, *il parlamento d' Inghilterra.*

The parliament-house, *parlagio,* s. m. *luogo dove si fa il parlamento.*

A parliament man, *un membro di parlamento.*

Parlia'mentary, adj. ex. to do things in a parliamentary way, *far le cose regolarmente, o con libertà conveniente al parlamento.*

Pa'rlour, s [a low room to receive company in] *sala bassa, o sala.*

Parlour [in a monastery of nuns] *parlatorio,* s. m. *luogo, dove si favella alle monache.*

Pa'rlous, adj. [keen, shrewd, subtle] *astuto, accorto.*

Pa'rmesan, s. [a sort of cheese] *parmigiano,* s. m. *sorta di cacio che si fa in Lombardia.*

Pa'rnel, s. ex. a pretty parnel, *una bella ragazzina.*

Paro'chial, adj. [of the parish] *parrocchiale.*

Paro'le, s. [word, promise] *parola,* s. f.

Upon his parole, *sopra la sua parola.*

Paro'tides, s. [the glandules behind the ear] *noccioletti che sono appiccati sotto gli orecchi, glandule,* s. f.

Parotides [the swelling of those glandules] *parotide,* s. f. *enfiato che viene sotto, gli orecci, tumore intorno agli orecchi.*

Pa'roxysm, s. [the access or fit of an ague, fever, or other distemper] *parossismo, e parosismo,* s. m. *termine de' medici, il corso d' una febbre.*

Pa'rracoot, s. [parrot fish] *sorta di pesce.*

Pa'rricide, s. [a murtherer of his father or mother, or any of his near kindred] *parricida,* s. m. *uccisore del padre o della madre, o altro stretto parente.*

Parricide [the crime or offence of parricide] *parricidio,* s. m.

Pa'rrot, s. [a sort of bird] *pappagallo,* s. m. *uccello che viene dall' Indie, di più colori, e grandezze, ed impara ad imitar la favella umana.*

To Pa'rry, *parare, termine di scherma.*

To parry and thrust, *parare e rispondere.*

To Parse [to expound a lesson according to the rules of grammar] *spiegare la sua lezione secondo le regole della gramatica.*

Parsimo'nious, adj. [saving, thrifty] *moderato, frugale, risparmiante, economo, e iconomo.*

Parsimo'niously, adv. *frugalmente, moderatamente, con parsimonia ed economia.*

Pa'rsimony, s. [savingness] *parsimonia, frugalità, economia,* s. f. *risparmio,* s. m.

Pa'rsley, Pa'rsly, } s. [a pot-herb] *persemolo.*

Pa'rsnep, Pa'rsnip, } s. [a well-known root] *pastinaca,* s. m. *spezie di radice d' acuto sapore, e si mangia cotta.*

Wild parsnep, *sisaro,* s. m.

Yellow parsnep, *carota,* s. f.

Pa'rson, s. [the rector of a parish church] *piovano, ministro, o curato d'una parrocchia.*

Pa'rsonage, s. [a parson's cure, or spiritual living for the maintenance of the minister of a church] *beneficio,* s. m.

Parsonage [the parson's house] *la casa del piovano.*

Part, s. [a piece of any thing, share, portion] *parte,* s. f. *quello di che è composto il tutto, e nel quale il tutto si divide.*

The parts of the body, *le parti, o le membra del corpo.*

The parts of speech, *le parti del favellare.*

To sing one's part, *cantare la sua parte.*

Part [share] *parte, porzione,* s. f.

Pray let the company take part with you, *di grazia, fatene, parte alla compagnia.*

In what part of the town do you live? *in qual parte della città dimorate?*

Part [side] *parte.*

To to take one's part, *pigliar le parti d' uno, pigliar la sua difesa.*

Part [duty] *dovere, debito,* s. m.

'Tis your part to do it, *è vostro dovere di farlo, s' aspetta a voi di farlo.*

To exercise all the parts of a good husband, *fare tutte le funzioni d'un buon marito.*

He discharges his part well, *soddisfare in tutto al suo dovere.*

Part [of a player] *parte.*

Parts [natural endowments] *parti, costumi buoni, o cattivi.*

He has all the parts requisite for a commander, *egli ha tutte le qualità requisite per un capitano.*

A man of parts, *un uomo dotto o di garbo, un uomo garbato, o costumato.*

I take part in your concerns, *piglio a cuore, m' interesso in tutto quel che vi risguarda.*

To take in good part, *pigliare in buona parte.*

To take in ill part, *pigliare in cattiva parte.*

The greatest part of mankind, *la maggior parte degli uomini.*

Men are for the most part ignorant, *la maggior parte degli uomini sono ignoranti, gli uomini sono per la maggior parte ignoranti.*

For the most part [or most times] *la maggior parte del tempo, ordinariamente.*

For my part, or for my own part, *per me, in quanto a me, dal canto mio.*

To do the part of one, *tenere la vice d' uno.*

Part by part, or by part, *partitamente, a parte a parte, a uno per uno, distintamente, particolarmente.*

In some part, *in qualche parte, o luogo.*

On the other part, *dall' altra parte, dall' altra banda, dall' altro canto.*

On all parts, *da per tutto.*

To put a-part, *metter da parte.*

To Part [to divide] *partire, far parti, separare, dividere.*

To part a difference, *spartire una differenza*

To part [to put asunder] *separare.*

To part the gold and silver, *partire l' oro, e l' argento, scioglierli l' uno dall' altro con aqua forte.*

To part a fray, *spartire una contesa.*

To part with a thing, *disfarsi d' una cosa, alienarla da se.*

Will you part with your horse? *volete disfarvi del vostro cavallo?*

To part with one's right, *cedere, o rinunciare alle sue ragioni.*

I will part with my life first, *perderò prima la vita.*

To part [to distribute] *distribuire, compartire.*

To part with a thing to the poor, *distribuire o dare qualche cosa a i poveri.*

To part in the midst, *spartire per mezzo.*

To part with or from one [to leave him] *separarsi d' uno, licenziarsi d' uno, lasciarlo.*

I parted from him an hour ago, *mi son separato, o licenziato da lui un' ora fa.*

To part [to go away] *partirsi, andar via.*

Pa'rtage, s. [partition, sharing, dividing] *partizione, divisione,* s. f. *partimento,* s. m.

To Parta'ke [to take part of] *participare, aver parte, o porzione in che che si sia.*

Will you partake of a bottle of wine? *volete aver parte d' un fiasco di vino?*

Parta'ker, s. *participatore,* s. m. *che participa.*

To be partaker with one in a crime, *esser complice d'un delitto con uno.*

Parta'king, s. *participamento,* s. m. *participazione,* s. f.

Pa'rted, adj. [from to part] *partito, separato, diviso.*

Pa'rterre, s. [a flower-garden] *un giardino da fiori.*

Pa'rtial, adj. [inclining to one party more than another] *parziale, appassionato, favorevole verso una delle parti.*

A partial judge, *un giudice parziale o iniquo.*

Partia'lity, s. [a siding too much with a party] *parzialità,* s. f.

To

To PA'RTIALIZE [to use partiality] *parteggiare, esser parziale.*

PA'RTIALLY, adv. *parzialmente, con parzialità.*

PA'RTIBLE, adj. [that may be parted] *divisibile.*

To PARTI'CIPATE [to partake of] *participare, aver parte o porzione in che che si sia.*

PARTI'CIPATING, } s. [a taking part PARTICIPA'TION, } of] *participamento*, s. m. *participazione*, s. f.

PARTICI'PIAL, adj. [belonging to a participle] *attenente a participio, di participio.*

PARTICI'PIALLY, adv. *a modo di participio.*

PA'RTICIPLE, s. [one of the eight parts of speech, so named from its partaking both of the noun and of the verb] *participio*, s. m.

PA'RTICLE, s. [an undeclined word] *particola*, s. f.

Particle [small parcel, little part] *particella, piccola parte o porzione.*

PARTI'CULAR, adj. [singular, proper, peculiar] *particolare, speziale, singolare, peculiare, proprio.*

He answered me in these particular words, *mi rispose queste precise parole.*

I shall give you a particular account of the whole business, *vi darò un conto esatto, un ragguaglio preciso di tutto l' negozio.*

To be particular or singular in a thing, *esser particolare o singolare in che che sia, esser solo in far una cosa.*

A particular way, *una maniera particolare.*

A particular friend, *amico stretto o intimo.*

PARTI'CULAR, s. [a particular circumstance] *particolarità*, s. f.

Tell me the particulars, *ditemi le particolarità.*

To come to the particulars, *scendere alle particolarità.*

You missed in that particular, *voi avete sbagliato in questa particolarità, in questo particolare.*

A particular of one's estate, *l'inventario de' beni di qualche persona.*

To PA'RTICULARIZE [to enlarge upon particulars, to give a particular account of] *particolarizzare, distinguere con particolarità, narrar minutamente, venire al particolare.*

PA'RTICULARISED, adj. *particolarizzato.*

PARTI'CULARLY, adv. *particolarmente, con particolarità, distintamente, minutamente.*

PA'RTING, s. [from to part] *partimento*, s. m. *il partire, divisione*, s. f. *spartimento*, s. m.

Parting [separation] *separazione*, s. f.

Parting [going away] *partenza, partita*, s. f. *il partire.*

The parting cup, *la mancia, la buona mano.*

PA'RTISAN, *v.* Partizan.

PARTI'TION, s. [division] *partizione*, s. f. *partimento*, s. m.

The rule of partition, *la regola di partizione.*

An equal partition of lands, *una eguale partizione di terre.*

A partition, or partition-wall [betwixt two rooms] *tramezzo*, s. m. *tramezza, separazione*, s. f.

A partition-wall [betwixt two houses] *muro di mezzo.*

PA'RTIZAN, s. [a weapon much like an halberd] *partigiana*, s. f. *spezie d' arme in asta.*

A little partizan, *una partigianetta.*

Partizan [favourer, abettor of a party] *partigiano, fautore*, s. m.

Partizan [in military affairs, a commander of a party] *partigiano, comandante d'una banda di soldati.*

PA'RTLET, s. [ruffs or bands for women] *goletta*, s. f.

Partlet, s. *femmina d' ogni pennuto.*

PA'RTLY, adv. *in parte, in qualche modo.*

PA'RTNER, s. [one who is joined with another in some concern] *sozio, compagno*, s. m.

PA'RTNERSHIP, s. *ragione, compagnia di traffico.*

To enter into partnership, *creare una ragione, mettersi in compagnia.*

PARTO'OK, *preterito del verbo* To partake.

PA'RTRIDGE, s. [a dainty fowl] *pernice, coturnice*, s. f.

PA'RTY, s. [a person] *una persona.*

Party [one that is at law with another] *parte*, s. f. *l' un de' due littiganti.*

We are too much parties in that affair, *noi siamo troppo interessati o parziali, in questo affare.*

Party [side, faction] *parte, fazione, setta*, s. f.

To draw one to his own party, *tirar uno dalla sua parte.*

To make one's self party in a thing, *intraprendere, interessarsi, prender parte in qualche cosa.*

Party [a body of men sent out upon some expedition] *distaccamento di soldati.*

To go upon a party, *andare in distaccamento.*

To make one's party good, *difendersi bene, vendicarsi.*

Party-coloured [a term of heraldry] *biscolore.*

Party-jury [a jury consisting of half English and half foreigners] *giurati spartiti, cioè la metà Inglesi e l'altra metà forestieri.*

Party-wall, s. *muro divisorio.*

PA'RVIS, s. [porch] *portico*, s. m.

PA'RVITUDE, } s. [littleness, small-PA'RVITY, } ness] *picciolezza, piccolezza*, s. f.

PA'SCHAL, adj. [of the passover] *pasquale, di pasqua.*

The paschal lamb, *l' agnello pasquale.*

Pascal rents [annual duties paid by the inferior clergy to the bishop, at their Easter visitations] *diritti annuali che il clero paga al vescovo che va in visita nella Pasqua.*

PASH, s. [a kiss] *un bacio.*

To PASH [to dash together] *schiacciare, ammaccare, infragnere*, pret. *infransi.*

PA'SHED, adj. *schiacciato, ammaccato, infranto.*

PA'SHING, s. *schiacciamento, ammaccamento, infragnimento*, s. m.

Pash-flower, s. [a plant] *spezie di pianta.*

PA'SQUIL, } s. [a statue in Rome; a PA'SQUIN, } slanderous libel posted up for publick view] *pasquinata*, s. f. *libello famoso.*

PA'SQUINADE, *v.* Pasquil.

PASS, s. [a licence to travel] *passaporto, salvocondotto*, s. m.

Pass [passage] *passaggio.*

Pass [state, condition] *stato, grado*, s. m. *condizione, situazione*, s. f.

My business is come to a bad pass, *i miei affari sono ridotti a mal partito.*

Things are come to that pass, *nello stato nel quale son le cose.*

I am indeed at a fine pass, *per certo che sono acconciato per le feste, ecco a che son ridotto.*

A pass by hawk, *un falcone di passaggio.*

A pass [in fencing] *botta*, s. f. *colpo*, s. m.

To make a pass at one, *portare una botta ad uno.*

To PASS [to go from one place to another by crossing a middle place] *passare, verbo che significa moto per luogo.*

This morning I passed by your door, *questa mattina son passato davanti la vostra porta.*

To pass [to cross] *passare, trapassare.*

To pass the sea, *passare il mare.*

To pass [to go beyond] *trasandare, trapassare molto avanti, trascorrere.*

To pass one's troops over a river, *far traversare un fiume alle sue truppe.*

To pass the time, *passare, consumare il tempo.*

To pass the winter in town, *passar il verno in città.*

To pass an act, *passare, o fare una legge.*

That will never pass, *ciò non sarà mai approvato, o ricevuto.*

To pass a judgment upon one, *sentenziare uno.*

To pass a compliment upon one, *complimentare uno, fare un complimento ad uno.*

To pass one's word for one, *impegnare, o dar la sua parola per alcuno.*

To pass a trick upon one, *fare una burla ad uno.*

To pass one's approbation upon a thing, *approvare una cosa.*

To pass one's verdict, *giudicare, dire*

dire il suo sentimento, o la sua opinione.

To pass sentence, *pronunciar la sentenza.*

I shall tell you what passed, *vi dirò quel che è successo.*

The thing passed thus, *la cosa arrivò in questa maniera.*

There passed some hard words betwixt them, *vennero insieme a parole ingiuriose.*

To come to pass, *avvenire, accadere, occorrere.*

It came to pass, *avvenne, accadde, occorse.*

To bring a thing to pass, *effettuare, eseguire una cosa, metterla in effetto.*

To be well to pass, *esser benestante, esser comodo, aver di che passarsela bene.*

To let pass [to omit] *lasciar passare, omettere, trulasciare.*

He is in a passion, but that will pass, *è in collera, ma gli passerà.*

Let us let that pass for this time, *per questa volta non ne parliamo.*

To pass along, *passare per.*

As I passed along, *nel passare.*

To pass by [to take no notice of, to omit, or to forget] *passar sotto silenzio, omettere, non curare.*

To pass by injuries, *dimenticare le ingiurie.*

To pass over in silence, *passar sotto silenzio.*

To pass over a word in reading, *omettere una parola nel leggere.*

It is better to pass over those things, *il meglio è di non far più menzione di queste cose.*

To pass for [to be reputed] *esser in concetto, essere stimato.*

He passes for an honest man, *è in concetto d'uomo dabbene.*

To pass away the time, *passar il tempo.*

While that passed on, *in questo mentre.*

I have said nothing but what passes about in common discourse, *non ho detto altro che quel che comunemente si discorre.*

To pass the bounds, *passare i termini.*

PA'SSABLE, adj. [that may be passed over] *per dove si può passare, praticabile.*

Money that is passable [that will go] *moneta corrente, che corre.*

Passable [indifferent] *mediocre, mezzano.*

PA'SSADE, s. [alms given to passengers] *passata, s. f. limosina che si da a' poveri che passano.* Obs.

Passade [in fencing, a pass or thrust] *botta, s. f.*

Passade [the manage of a horse forward and backward upon the same plot of ground] *passo, termine di maneggio.*

PA'SSAGE, s. [a going from one to another] *passaggio, s. m. il passare.*

Passage [the place through which one goes] *passaggio, luogo onde si passa.*

I took a passage with him for France, *passai in Franzia con lui.*

Passage [the fare for passing] *passaggio, dazio, che si paga in passando.*

Passage [a place in a book] *passo, s. m. luogo di scrittura.*

The passage of the urine, *il passaggio dell' urina.*

Passage [event, transaction] *evento, caso, accidente, s. m.*

Passage [a game with three dice] *zara, s. f. giuoco, che si fa con tre dadi.*

PA'SSED, adj. *passato, v.* To pass.

PA'SSENGER, s. [traveller] *un viandante, un passeggiere, e passeggiero, s. m.*

A passenger hawk, *un falcone di passo.*

PASSI'BILITY, } s. [capacity to
PA'SSIBLENESS, } suffer] *passibilità, s. f.*

PA'SSIBLE, adj. [capable of suffering] *passibile, atto a patire.*

PA'SSING, s. *passamento, s. m. il passare.*

In passing [by the way] *passando, nel passare, di passaggio.*

Passing, adj. [a passing-bell] *campana a mortorio.*

A passing beauty, *una estrema bellezza, un paragon di bellezza, una bellezza senza pari.*

Passing, adv. *grandemente, in sommo grado.*

That's passing fine, *questo è bellissimo.*

PA'SSION, s. [affection, transport of the mind] *passione, s. f. affetto d'animo.*

Passion [strong inclination] *passione, inclinazione, attitudine, s. f. talento, incentivo, s. m.*

Passion [love] *amore, affetto, zelo, ardore, s. m.*

Passion [transport] *passione, furia, s. m.*

Passion [anger] *collera, stizza, ira, s. f.*

To be in a passion, *essere in collera.*

To put one in a passion, *mettere in collera, stizzare.*

To vent one's passion, *sfogare la collera.*

Passion [suffering] *passione, pena, s. f. patimento, travaglio, s. m.*

Our Saviour's Passion, *la Passione di nostro Signore.*

The Passion Week, *la Settimana della Passione, quella che precede la Settimana Santa.*

PA'SSIONATE, adj. [soon angry] *collerico, stizzoso, bilioso, impetuoso.*

Passionate for a thing [that has a strong inclination for it] *appassionato, ansioso, inclinato, dedito a qualche cosa.*

Passionate [full of love] *appassionato, tenero, amoroso.*

PA'SSIONATELY, adv. [or angrily] *stizzosamente, con stizza, ira condamente, iratamente.*

Passionately [with a strong love] *passionatamente, capricciosamente, smisuratamente, svisceratamente.*

To be passionately in love with, *essere smisuratamente, passionatamente, esviscoratamente innamorato, andar pazzo o perduto.*

PA'SSIONATENESS, s. [state of being subject to passion] *disposizione alla collera, alla stizza, allo sdegno.*

Passionateness [vehemence of mind] *veemenza di mente; forza impetuosa di mente.*

PA'SSIVE, adj. [the contrary of active] *passivo.*

A passive verb, *un verbo passivo.*

Passive principles [among chymists, are earth and water] *principi passivi, sono sono in chimica, la terra e l'acqua.*

PA'SSIVELY, adv. *passivamente.*

PA'SSIVENESS, } s. *qualità passi-*
PA'SSIVITY, } *va.*

PA'SSOVER, *Pasqua.*

PA'SS-PORT, s. [pass] *passaporto, salvocondotto, s. m.*

PA'SS-ROSE, s. [a flower] *spezie di fiore.*

PA'SS-VOLANT, s. [a faggot in mustering of soldiers] *passavolante.*

PAST, adj. [from to pass] *passato, v.* To pass.

When we were past the town, *passata che avemmo la città.*

The time past, *il tempo passato.*

In times past [formerly] *per l'addietro, altre volte.*

Past the best, *attempato, vecchio.*

A woman past child bearing, *una donna fuor d'età d'aver figliuoli.*

Past marrying, *che non è più d'età di prender marito.*

Past all dangers, *fuor di pericolo.*

Meat past eating, *carne guasta, che non è più buona a mangiare, infradiciaticcia.*

Past cure [incurable] *incurabile.*

A thing past cure, *una cosa dove non v' è più rimedio, o irremediabile.*

He is past recovery, *egli è disperato da' medici.*

Past dispute [not to be disputed] *incontrastabile, da non gli poter far contrasto, indubitabile.*

To be past shame, *aver bandito ogni pudore, sfacciato, sfrontato.*

It is a thing past and done, *è una cosa stabilita, o conchiusa.*

It is past ten, *sono sonate le dieci.*

Half an hour past nine, *nove ore, e mezza.*

About four months last past, *sono quattro mesi in circa.*

These four months last past, *per questi quattro mesi, da quattro mesi.*

I have not seen him these four months last past, *non l'ho visto per quattro mesi, o da quattro mesi.*

PASTE,

PASTE, s. [dough] *pasta*, s. f.
Paste, to glue things together with, *pasta*, *colla*.
To paste up, *appiccare*.
To PASTE [to glue with paste] *impastare*, *appiccare insieme con pasta*.
PA'STED, adj. *impastato*, *appiccato con pasta*.
Pasted up, *appiccato*, *affisso*.
PA'STEL, s. [a plant] *spezie d' erba*.
PA'STERN, s. [the hollow of a beast's heel] *garretto*, s. m.
PA'STIL, s. [a composition of sweet paste] *pastiglia*, s. f.
PA'STIME, s. [sport, recreation] *passatempo*, *divertimento*, *diporto*, s. m. *ricreazione*, s. f.
By way of pastime, *per passatempo*, *per diporto*.
PA'STING, s. *impastamento*, s. m. *l' impastare*.
PA'STOR, s. [a shepherd, and figuratively, a church-minister] *pastore*, s. m. *ministro della chiesa*.
PA'STORAL, adj. [belonging to a shepherd, or church-minister] *pastorale*, *di pastore*, *da pastore*, *attenente a pastore*.
PASTORAL, s. [a sort of poem relating to affairs between shepherds and shepherdesses] *pastorale*, s. f. *spezie di poema*.
PA'STRY, s. [work made of paste and dough] *pasticceria*, s. f. *pastume*, s. m.
A Pastry-cook, s. *un pasticciere*, *un pastelliere*, *che fa i pasticci*, *che lavora di pasta*.
A pastry-cook's wife, *una pasticciera*, *moglie di pasticciere*.
PA'STURABLE, adj. [that is fit, or serves for pasture] *che serve di pastura*, *o proprio a pasturare*.
PA'STURAGE, PA'STURE, PA'STURE GROUNDS } s. [land reserved for the feeding of cattle] *pastura*, s. f. *luogo dove le bestie si pascono*, *pascolo*, s. m.
Pasture [fodder, food for cattle] *pastura*, s. f. *pasto*, s. m.
The pasture or viands of deer, *pastura*, *pascolo per cervi*.
To PA'STURE [to put into pasture, to feed cattle] *pasturare*, *pascolare*, *pascere*.
PA'STURED, adj. *pasturato*, *pascolato*, *pasciuto*.
PA'STURING, s. [fodder for cattle] *pascolo*, s. m. *pastura*, s. f.
PA'STY, s. [pie] *pasticcio*, s. m.
A venison pasty, *un pasticcio di salvaggina*.
PAT, s. [a small blow, a little stroke] *botta*, *percossa*, s. f. *picchio*, *colpo*, s. m.
To PAT one [to give one a pat] *dare una botta o una percossa ad uno*, *picchiarlo*, *percuoterlo*.
To pat at the door, *picchiare alla porta*.
Pat, adj. [fit, suitable, or to the purpose] *opportuno*, *comodo*, *atto*, *proporzionato*, *acconcio*.
PA'TACOON, s. [a Spanish coin] *pataccone*, s. m. *sorta di moneta Spagnuola*.
PA'TCH, s. [piece] *pezza*, *toppa*, s. f.
Patch [a black patch to wear on one's face] *neo*, s. m. *piccole pezzette nere di seta che le donne si mettono sul viso*.
A patch of cleared ground, *un pezzo di terra lavorata*.
You are a cross-patch, *voi siete capriccioso*, *o bisbetico*.
To PAT'CH [to mend with patches] *rappezzare*, *rattoppare*.
To patch up a wall, *stuccare un muro*.
To patch up a disease, *nascondere*, *o palliare un male*.
To patch [to put patches upon one's face] *metter nei sul viso*.
PA'TCHED, adj. *rappezzato*, *rattoppato*.
Patched [full of patches on the face] *che porta nei sul viso*.
PA'TCHER, s. *quello che rappezza*, *o rattoppa*.
PATE, s. [the head] *la testa*.
How came that into your pate? *in che modo ciò v' è saltato in testa*.
To break one's pate, *romper la testa ad uno*.
PA'TED, adj ex. a long pated fellow [a cunning fellow] *un uomo astuto*, *o scaltrito*.
PA'TEE, s. *pasticcio*, s. m.
Petty patees, *pasticcetti*.
PATEFA'CTION, s. [a laying open] *palesamento*, *manifestamento*, s. m *manifestazione*, *dichiarazione*, *notizia*, s. f.
PA'TENT, adj. [lying open] *patente*, *aperto*, *manifesto*.
Patent, s. [letters patent] *patente*, s. f. *lettera segnata col sigillo del principe*, *che fa nota a' ciascuno la sua volontà*.
PA'TENTEE, s. [a person to whom the king has granted his letters patent] *colui o colei a chi il principe ha concesso la patente*.
PATER-GUARDIAN, s. [the head of a Franciscan convent] *il padre guardiano*.
PATE'RNAL, adj. [fatherly, belonging to a father] *paternale*, *paterno*, *di padre*, *attenente a padre*.
PATE'RNITY, s. [fatherhood] *paternità*, s. f. *l' esser padre*.
PATER-NOSTER, s. [the Lord's prayer, so called from the first two words of it in Latin] *paternostro*, s. m. *orazione domenicale*, *così detta*, *perchè il Latino concincia* pater noster.
PATER NO'STERS [the great beads of a chaplet] *paternostri*; *quelle pallottoline grandi della corona*, *in segno che si dove dire un paternostro*.
PATH, s. [track, by-way] *sentiero*, s. m.
PA'THLESS, adj. *privo di sentiero*; *che non ha sentiero nè via*.
PATHE'TICAL, PATHE'TICK } adj. [moving the passions or affections] *patetico*, *affettuoso*, *pieno d' affetti*.
PATHE'TICALLY, adv. *pateticamente*, *affettuosamente*.
PA'TIBLE, adj. [sufferable] *passibile*, *atto a patire*.
PATI'BULARY, adj. [belonging to a gallows] *di patibolo*, *attenente a patibolo*.
PA'TIENCE, s. [a virtue enabling to bear afflictions and pains with calmness of mind] *pazienza*, *sofferenza*, *tolleranza*, s. f.
To take patience, *prender o pigliar pazienza*.
You wear out my patience, *voi mi farete scappar la pazienza*.
To be out of patience, *rinnegar la pazienza*, *perder la pazienza*.
Long patience, *tolleranza*, *perseveranza*, *animo paziente*.
PA'TIENT, adj. [enduring, suffering] *paziente*, *che ha pazienza*, *sofferente*, *tolerante*.
A patient, s. [a doctor's patient, a sick body] *un ammalato*.
Very patient, *pazientissimo*.
PA'TIENTLY, adv. *pazientemente*, *con pazienza*.
Very patiently, *pazientissimamente*.
PA'TINE, s [a sort of plate with which the chalice is covered] *patena*, s. f. *il coperchio del calice*.
PA'TLY, adv. [commodiously, fitly] *commodamente*, *addattatamente*.
PA'TRIARCH, s. [a chief father, or the first father of a family or nation] *patriarca*, s. m. *primo de' padri*.
Patriarch [among ecclesiasticks, is a dignity above an archbishop] *patriarca*, *titolo di dignità ecclesiastica*, *un grado più alto degli arcivescovi*.
PATRIA'RCHAL, adj. [belonging to a patriarch] *patriarcale*, *di patriarca*.
PA'TRIARCHATE, s. [the state, dignity, or jurisdiction of a patriarch] *patriarcato*, s. m.
PATRI'CIAN, s. [among the Romans, a nobleman, descended of senators, and the founders of their commonwealth] *patrizio*, s. m. *uomo nobile*, *de' primi della città*.
PATRIMO'NIAL, adj. [belonging to patrimony] *patrimoniale*, *di patrimonio*.
PA'TRIMONY, s. [inheritance or estate left by a father to his son] *patrimonio*, s. m. *beni pervenuti per eredità del padre*.
The patrimony of St. Peter [a province in Italy belonging to the pope] *il Patrimonio di San Pietro*.
PA'TRIOT, s. [one whose ruling passion is the love of his country] *un vero amante della sua patria*.
To PATRO'CINATE [to protect, to defend] *patrocinare*, *tener protezione*, *proteggere*, *difendere*.
PATROCINA'TION, PA'TROCINY, } s. [a protecting or defending] *patrocinio*, s. m. *protezione*, s. f.
PATRO'L, s. [a night-watch of about five or six men, commanded by a serjeant] *ronda*, s. f. *la guardia che va attorno la notte*.
To PATRO'L, *far la ronda*.

PA'TRON, s. [protector, advocate] mecenate, protettore, s. m.

Patron [in law, one who has the right of presentation to a benefice], padrone, quello che ha padronato.

A patron [in civil law, one who has made his slave or servant free] padrone, colui che da la libertà al suo schiavo.

A patron [the saint or advocate of a kingdom, town, &c.] padrone o protettore d' un regno, città, &c.

PA'TRONAGE, s. [the right of presentation to a benefice] padronaggio, padronato, s. m. ragione, che s' ha sopra benefici ecclesiastici, di potergli conferire.

Patronage [defence, protection] padronato, protettorato, s. m. protezione, s. f.

PA'TRONAL, adj. [belonging to a patron] di padrone, che appartiene ad un padrone.

PA'TRONESS, s. padronessa, padrona, protettrice, avvocata, s. f.

To PA'TRONISE [to protect, to defend] proteggere, diffendere, patrocinare, pret. protessi, difesi.

PA'TRONIZED, adj. protetto, difeso, patrocinato.

PA'TTEN, } s [a sort of wooden
PA'TTIN, } shoes, with a support of iron] zoccolo, s. m. calzare di legno come pianella con ferramento intaccato nella parte di sotto.

Patten-maker, zoccolajo, s. m. che fa li zoccoli.

The patten of a pillar, whereon the base is set, zoccolo d' una colonna.

To PA'TTER [to beat thick] dibattere un liquore, tanto, che si vegga spessire.

They came pattering down like hail, cascavan giu come la grandine.

To patter out prayers [to mumble prayers] masticar paternostri.

PA'TTERN, s. [model] modello, esempio, s. m.

A pattern [a piece of cloth, &c.] mostra, s. f. saggio di lavorio.

PA'VAN, } s. [a light Spanish dance]
PA'VIN, } spezie di ballo alla Spagnuola.

PA'UCITY, s. [fewness] piccolo numero.

To PAVÉ [to lay a way with stones] lastricare, coprire il suolo della terra con lastre.

To pave with bricks, ammattonare.

PA'VED, adj. lastricato.

Paved with bricks, ammattonato.

PA'VEMENT, s. [cause-way, paved floor] pavimento, lastricato, smalto, s. m.

A pavement of bricks, un ammattonato.

A pavement-beater, un perdigiorno un vagabondo, uno scioperato.

PA'VER, } s. un lastricatore.
PA'VIER, }

PA'VESE, } s. [a large shield which
PA'VICE, } covers the whole body] pavese, s. m. arma difensiva, come targa che cuopre tutto l' corpo.

A soldier armed with pavese, un pavesato.

PA'VESADE, } [a target defence in
PA'VOISADE, } a gallery to cover the slaves which row on the benches] palvesata, s. f. coperta, e difesa di palvesi fatta sopra le galee per difender i galeotti che stanno a remare.

PA'VIAGE, s. [toll, contribution towards repairing or maintaining pavements] dazio, o gabella che si paga, per il mantenimento del lastricato.

PA'VICE, v. Pavese.

PAVI'LION, s [tent] padiglione, s. m. arnese fatto di panno o di drappo, tenda, s. f.

Pavilion [in architecture] padiglione, termine d' architettura.

Pavilion [the flag of a general officer in a fleet] stendardo, s. m.

To PAVI'LION [to furnish with tents] fornir di tende e di paviglioni.

To pavilion [to be sheltered by a tent] esser al comperto sotto un paviglione.

PA'VING, s. il lastricare.

To PA'ULTER, v. To palter.

PA'ULTRY, v. Paltry.

PAUNCH [belly] pancia.

Paunch [belly'd] panciuto, di grossa pancia.

To PAUNCH, sventrare, sbudellare.

PA'UNCHED, adj. sventrato, sbudellato.

PAUSE, s. [stop] pausa, fermata, s. f.

A pause in a verse, pausa d' un verso.

To PAUSE [to make a pause] pausare, far pausa, fermarsi.

To pause upon a thing [to consider of it] riflettere sopra una cosa, farci riflessione, considerarla bene.

PA'USING, s. pausa.

PAW, s. [the foot of a beast of prey] zampa, s. f. piede d' animale quadrupede.

A little paw, una zampetta.

Paw-paw, interj. via, via.

A paw thing, una sporcizia, sporcheria, o porcheria, s. f.

To PAW, zampettare, dimenar le zampe.

A dog that paws his master, un cane che zampetta, o accarezza il suo padrone colle zampe.

To paw [to fumble] stazzonare, malmenare, maneggiare, toccare, trattare colle mani.

PA'WED, adj. zampettato, stazzonato, malmenato, maneggiato.

Pawed [broad-footed] zamputo, che ha le zampe grandi.

PAWN, s. [pledge] pegno, s. m.

To lend upon pawn, prestare con pegno.

Pawn [at chess] pedona, s. f. quel pezzo che nel giuoco degli scacchi s' alluoga inanzi agli altri pezzi.

A pawn-broker, prestatore, usuraio, s. m.

To PAWN [to give in pawn] impegnare, dare alcuna cosa per sicurtà a chi ti presta danari.

PA'WNED, adj. impegnato.

PA'WNING, s. l' impegnare.

PAX, s. [an image given to be kiss'd when they go to the offering] pace, s. f.

PAY, s. [satisfaction] paga, s. f.

His pay is very good, egli è un buon pagatore, egli paga puntualmente.

A soldier's pay, la paga, o soldo di soldato.

A pay-master, pagatore, s. m.

A pay-mistress, pagatrice, s. f.

A bad pay-master, un pagatoraccio, che paga debolmente, e a poco per volta.

To PAY [to discharge a debt] pagare, uscir di debito.

To rob Peter to pay Paul, scoprire un altare per ricoprirne un altro; fare un debito nuovo per pagarne un vecchio.

To pay a visit, rendere una visita.

To pay one's respects to another, riverire o salutare uno.

I pay'd him his own, or in the same coin, li ho reso pan per focaccia, o frasche per foglie, o la pariglia.

I shall pay him [I shall be revenged of him] me la pagherà, me ne vendicherò.

To pay for one's folly, pagar la pena della sua pazzia.

To pay a rope, impeciare una fune.

To pay a ship [to lay the seams of a ship with hot pitch] impeciare, o turare le fessure d' un vascello con pece.

To pay one's debts, pagare i suoi debiti.

To pay off [to beat soundly] bastonare uno ben bene, malmenarlo, maltrattarlo con bastonate, tartassarlo, zombarlo.

To pay back, pagar indietro, restituire.

To pay away money, pagare una somma di danari.

To pay down, pagar contanti, pagar di buona moneta.

PA'YABLE, adj. [to be pay'd] pagabile, da pagarsi.

A bill of exchange payable at sight, una lettera di cambio pagabile a vista.

PAY'D, adj. pagato, v. To pay.

PA'YER, s. pagatore, s. m. pagatrice, s. f.

PA'YING, } s. pagamento, s. m.
PA'YMENT, }

PEA, s. [a well known pulse] piselio, s. m.

PEACE, s. [rest, quietness] pace, s. f. riposo, s. m. tranquillità, s. f.

The peace of the soul, la pace o la tranquillità dell' anima.

Peace [concord, good intelligence] pace, concordia, unione, s. f. accordo.

To live in peace, vivere in pace o in concordia, viver d' accordo.

A justice of the peace, un giudice di pace, commissario stabilito per mantenere la pace e punire quelli che disturbano il riposo pubblico.

To bind one to the peace, obbligare alcuno nelle forme e con malleveria di non far alcuna violenza ad altra persona.

To make peace, far la pace.

A treaty of peace, or peace, un trattato di pace.

Peace [reconciliation] pace, riconciliazione.

To make one's peace with one, far

pace

pace con uno, rappaciarſi, pacificarſi, riconciliarſi con uno.

Peace [ſilence] *ſilenzio.*

To hold one's peace, *far ſilenzio, ſtare zitto.*

Hold your peace, *tacete.*

Peace there, *ſilenzio zitto.*

Peace with your impertinent queſtion, *eh andate via con queſte voſtre ſciocche domande.*

He that would live in peace and reſt, muſt hear and ſee and ſay the beſt, *odi, vedi e taci, ſe vuoi viver in pace.*

A peace-maker, *paciere, mediatore, mezzano per trattare, e conchiuder la pace, paciale, paciaro,* s m.

PE'ACEABLE, adj. [quiet] *pacifico, quieto, tranquillo, amator di pace.*

PE'ACEABLENESS, s. *umor pacifico, natura quieta e pacifica.*

PE'ACEABLY, adv. *pacificamente, tranquillamente, con pace.*

PE'ACEFUL, adj. [quiet] *pacifico, quieto, tranquillo.*

PE'ACEFULLY, adv. *pacificamente, con pace, tranquillamente.*

PE'ACEFULNESS, s. *ſtato pacifico e tranquillo, pace, tranquilità,* s. f.

PEACH, s. [a delicious fruit] *perſica, peſca,* s. f.

A peach-tree, s. *perſico, peſco,* s. m.

To PEACH [to impeach] *accuſare, ſervir di teſtimonio contro alcuno.*

PE'ACHED, adj. *accuſato.*

PE'ACHER, s. *accuſatore,* s. m. *accuſatrice,* s. f.

PEA'CHICK, s. [the chicken of a peacock] *pavone appena nato.*

PE'ACHING, s. *accuſazione, accuſa,* s. f.

PE'ACOCK, s. [a very fine bird] *pavone, e paone,* s. m.

A young peacock, *pavoncello.*

The ſpots in a peacock's tail, *gli occhi della coda del paone.*

PEA-HEN, s. *paoneſſa, pagoneſſa, pavoneſſa,* s. f. *la femmina del paone.*

PEAK, s. [the ſharp point of any thing] *punta,* s. f. *eſtremità acuta di qualunque ſi voglia coſa.*

The peak of a hill, *la cima, la ſommità d 'un monte.*

The peak of a mourning coif, *la punta d' una cuffia da bruno.*

PE'AKING, adj. [of a puny ſickly conſtitution] *malaticcio, infermiccio di mala ſanità.*

PEAL, s. [a great noiſe, particularly of bells] *ſcampanata,* s. f. *ſcampanio,* s. m. *un gran ſonar di campane.*

To ring the bells in peals, *ſcampanare le campane.*

Peal [a great noiſe in general] *ſtrepito, fracaſſo, rumore, ſchiamazzo, rombazzo, fraſtuono.*

A peal of rain [as when it rattles down] *una burraſca, un diluvio, trabocco ſmiſurato di pioggia.*

A peal of hail, *una burraſca di gragnuola.*

To ring one a peal [to ſcold at him ſoundly] *lavar il capo ad uno, farli una ripaſſata, ſgridarlo.*

PEAR, s. [a ſort of fruit] *pera,* s. f. *frutta nota.*

Winter pear, *pera d' inverno.*

Pear-tree, s. *pero,* s. m. *albero noto.*

Pear-pye, *paſticcio, torta di pere.*

PEARCH, s. [rod or pole to meaſure land with] *pertica,* s. f. *da miſurar la terra.*

A pearch [a freſh water fiſh] *perchiao,* s. f.

A ſea pearch, *perchia marina.*

To PEARCH [to light, to ſit upon as birds does] *poſarſi ſopra un ramo o altro come fanno gli uccelli.*

PE'ARCHED, adj. *poſato ſopra un ramo.*

PEARCHING-STICK, *ſtecco ſul quale ſi poſa l' uccello nella gabbia.*

PEARL, s. [a precious ſtone, that is bred in a ſhell-fiſh] *perla,* s. f.

A ragged pearl, *una perla tonda e bernoccoluta.*

Mother of pearl, *madreperla,* s. f. *ſpezie di conchiglia.*

A croſs ſet out with pearls, *una croce imperlata.*

A pearl on the eye, *maglia nell' occhio, macchia generata nell' occhio.*

Pearl [the ſmalleſt kind of printing letters] *ſorta di lettera picciolíſſima da ſtampare.*

PEASANT, s. [country-man] *un contadino.*

PE'ASANTRY, s. [a collective for country-people] *i contadini, l' ordine contadineſco.*

PEASE, s. [the plural number of pea] *piſelli.*

Peaſe-porridge, *zuppa di piſelli.*

PE'BBLE, s. [a ſort of ſtones for paving] *ſelce, o ſelice, pietra viva,* s. f.

PECCADI'LIO, s. [a ſmall fault or crime, a pardonable ſin] *peccatuzzo,* s. m. *un peccato veniale.*

PE'CCANT, adj. [offending] *peccante.*

Peccant humours [ſuch humours of the body that contain ſome malignity, or elſe abound too much] *umori peccanti.*

PE'CCAVI [a Latin word uſed in this vulgar expreſſion] I'll make him cry, peccavi, *li farò ben io domandar perdono.*

PECK, s. [a ſort of meaſure] *ſorta di miſura Ingleſe.*

I am in a peck of troubles, *mi trovo in un mar di guai.*

To PECK [to ſtrike with the bill, as birds do] *beccare, picchiare col becco.*

To peck down one's head, *chinare la teſta.*

PE'CTORAL, adj. [belonging to the breaſt, or ſtomachick] *pettorale, ſtomacale.*

Pectoral ſyrup, *uno ſciroppo pettorale.*

Pectoral, s. [breaſt-plate] *un pettorale.*

PECU'LIAR, adj. [particular, ſingular] *peculiare, ſpeziale, ſignolare, particolare.*

He is my peculiar friend, *egli è mio intimo, intrinſeco o ſtretto amico.*

PECU'LIARS, s. [pariſhes exempt from other ordinaries and biſhops courts and peculiarly belonging to the ſee of Canterbury] *cappelle o parrocchie privilegiate, che dipendono immediatamente dall' arciveſcovo di Cantorberi.*

Regal peculiar [the king's chapel] *la cappella del rè.*

PECULIA'RITY, s. *ſingolarità, particolarità,* s. f.

PECU'LIARLY, adv. *particolarmente, ſingolarmente.*

PECUNIARY, adj [of or belonging to money] *pecuniario, pecuniale, di pecunia, attenente a pecunia.*

PECU'NIOUS, adj. [monied, full of money] *pecunioſo, abbondante di pecunia, danajoſo, ricco.*

PED, s. [ſmall packſaddle] *ſorta di baſto piccolo per le beſtie da ſoma.*

Ped [baſket, hamper] *un paniere, un canceſtro.*

PE'DAGE, s. [money given for paſſing] *pedaggio,* s. m. *dazio, che ſi paga per il paſſare di qualche luogo.*

PEDAGO'GICAL, adj. *da pedante, da pedagogo, da maeſtro di ſcuola.*

PE'DAGOGISM, s. [the office of a pedagogue] *offizio di pedagogo.*

PEDAGO'GUE, s. [inſtructor, teacher of youth] *pedagogo, pedante,* s. m.

To PE'DAGOGUE [to teach with ſupercilíouſneſs] *inſegnare come fanno i pedanti e i pedagoghi, con ciera arcigna, parlar bruſco, e ſferzate crudeli.*

PE'DAGOGY, s. [inſtruction, diſcipline] *pedagogia, iſtruzione,* s. f. *ammaeſtramento,* s. m.

PE'DAL, adj. [belonging to a foot in meaſure] *lungo d' un piede.*

PEDALS, s. [low keys of ſome organs to be touch'd with the foot] *pedali, i cannoni groſſi d' un organo, che ſi fanno ſuonar col piede.*

PEDA'NEOUS, adj. [going a-foot] *pedaneo, che va a piedi.*

A pedaneous judge, *un giudice pedaneo, che giudica in piedi.*

PE'DANT, s. [a paltry ſchool-maſter] *pedante, pedagogo,* s. m.

A pedant [a conceited pretender to ſcholarſhip] *un pedante, un pedantuzzo, un ſaccentone, un ſer ſaccente.*

Pedant-like, adv. *pedanteſcamente, da pedante.*

PEDA'NTICAL, } adj *pedanteſco, di*
PEDA'NTICK, } *pedante.*

PE'DANTISM, s. [the profeſſion or practice of a pedant] *profeſſione, o maniera di pedante.*

To PEDANTI'ZE [to play or act the pedant's part] *fare il pedante.*

PE'DANTRY, s. [awkward oſtentation of needleſs learning] *pedanteria, ſciocca pompa di letteratura inutile.*

PE'DDLAR, *v.* Pedlar.

To PEDDLE [to be buſy about trifles] *affaccendarſi intorno a coſe da nulla, far il cecco ſuda.*

PE'DEE, s. [foot-boy] *uno ſtaffiere, un ſaccardo.*

PEDE'RERO, } s. [a ſort of gun]
PETERERO, } *ſtrumento militare da fuoco per gittar pietre.*

PE'DESTAL, s. [that part of a pillar which ſerves to ſupport it] *piedeſtallo,* s. m. *quella pietra che è ſotto al dado, ſul quale poſa la colonna.*

PE'DICLE, s. [the little ſtalk of leaves of fruit] *picciuolo*, s. m. *gambo di foglie o di frutti.*

PE'DICULAR, } adj. [louſy] *pi-*
PE'DICULOUS, } *docchioſo.*

The pedicular diſeaſe, *la malattia pediculare.*

PE'DIGREE, s. [ſtock, race] *genealogia, diſcendenza, ſtirpe*, s. f.

PE'DIMENT, s. [fronton] *frontone*, s. m. *ornamento d'architettura.*

PE'DLAR, } s. [one who ſells ſmall
PE'DLER, } wares about the country] *un merciajuolo, un mercantuzzo*, s. m. *un che porta intorno dello mercanziuole a vendere.*

Pedlars ware, *mercanziuole.*

Pedlar's French [gibberiſh] *gergo, lingua corotta.*

To PE'DDLE [to ſell things of ſmall value] *fare il meſtiere di ciurmadone, e di bagatelliere, vender per le ſtrade delle mercanziuole.*

PE'DLERY, s. [wares ſold by pedlers] *mercanziuole, bagatelle.*

PE'DLING, adj. ex. to go pedling about, *andare attorno vendendo delle bagattelle, e delle mercanziuole.*

A pedling or ſmall ſum, *una piccola ſomma.*

PEDOBA'PTISM, s. [infant baptiſm] *il batteſimo de' bambini.*

PEEK, s. [pique, grudge] *rancore, ſdegno, livore*, s. m. *picca, gara*, s. f.

There is a peek betwixt them, *c' è qualche rancore fra di loro.*

I have no other peek of honour in proſpect, than—*non ambiſco che al gloria di—non ha altro deſiderio, che di—*

PEEL, s. [the rind or coat of fruits] *ſcorza*, s. f.

Orange-peel, *ſcorza di melarancia.*

An oven peel, *pala da forno.*

To PEEL [to pull or take off the rind] *ſcortecciare, ſcorzare, mondare, ſbucciare.*

To peel barley, *mondare del orzo.*

To peel a pear, *ſbucciare una pera.*

To peel hemp, *maciullare della canapa.*

To peel off, *ſcortecciarſi, ſcorticarſi, ſbucciarſi.*

PE'ELED, adj. *ſcortecciato, ſcorzato, mondato, ſbucciato.*

PEEP, s. [break of day] *il fare, o lo ſpuntar del giorno.*

To PEEP [to look through a hole] *ſpiare guardar di ſegreto, far capolino.*

To peep in, *guardar dentro.*

To peep out, *guardar fuora.*

The day begins to peep out, *il giorno comincia a ſpuntare.*

To peep over [to die] *tirar le calze, morire.*

To peep [as chickens do] *pigolare, il mandar fuora la voce, che fanno i pulcini e li altri uccelli piccoli.*

PE'EPING, s. *lo ſpiare, lo guardar di ſegreto.*

You ſhall pay for your peeping, *la voſtra curioſità vi coſterà cara.*

PE'EPHOLE, } s. [hole through
PE'EPINGHOLE, } which one may peep without being diſcovered] *buco da cui ſi poſſono ſpiare i fatti d' altri ſenza eſſere ſcoperto.*

PEER, s. [nobleman] *un pari, un ottimato.*

A peer of the realm, *un pari del regno.*

Peer [equal] *pari, eguale.*

To be try'd by one's peers, *eſſer giudicato da ſuoi pari, o da' ſuoi eguali.*

To peer upon or at a thing [to leer at a thing] *rimirar biecamente una coſa, guardarla ſottecchi.*

PE'ERAGE, s. [a peer's dignity] *dignità di pari.*

PE'ERDOM, s. [the dignity of a peer] *dignità d'un pari.*

PE'ERLESS, adj. [that has no peer, incomparable] *ſenza pari, incomparabile.*

PE'EVISH, adj. [croſs, moroſs] *fantaſtico, diſpettoſo, faſtidioſo, ſtrano, capriccioſo, ritroſo, oſtico.*

PE'EVISHLY, adv. *fantaſticamente, increſcevolmente, rincreſcevolmente, capriccioſamente, ritroſamente.*

PE'EVISHNESS, s. *fantaſticaggine, ſdegno, umore ſtrano e faſtidioſo, capriccio, faſtidio.*

PEG, s. [a ſmall pointed piece of wood] *pivolo, brocco, ſtecco, fuſcello, cavicchio*, s. m. *cavicchia, caviglia*, s. f.

Peg [for Margaret] *Margherità.*

A peg of muſical inſtrument, *biſchero*, s. m. *legnetto congegnato nel manico del liuto o d' altro ſtrumento per attaccarvi le corde.*

To PEG, *incavigliare, attaccare inſieme con caviglie.*

To peg the door, *ſtangare la porta.*

PELF, s. [riches] *ricchezze, beni di fortuna, ma ce ne ſerviamo parlandone con diſprezzo.*

PE'LICAN, s. [a ſort of bird] *pellicano*, s. m.

Pelican [a blind alembick] *pellicano, ſorta di lambicco.*

PE'LLET, s. [a little ball] *pallottola, piccicla palla.*

Pellets of paſte, *pallotta di paſta.*

PE'LLICLE, s. [a thin ſkin] *pellicina, pellicella*, s. f.

PE'LLITORY [an herb] *parietaria, ſorta d' erba.*

Pellitory of Spain, *pilatro*, s. m. *erba medicinale.*

PELL-MELL, adv. [confuſedly] *confuſamente, meſcolatamente.*

PELLU'CID, adj. [tranſparent] *lucido, traſparente.*

PELLU'CIDNESS, s. *traſparenza, diafanità*, s. f.

PELT, s. [the ſkin or hide of a beaſt] *pelle*, s. f. *cuojo*, s. m.

A ſhepherd's pelt, *pelliccione di paſtore.*

A pelt-monger, *colui che traffica in cuojo.*

The ſtreet where they ſell pelts, *ſtrada dove ſi trafficano i cuoi.*

Pelt-wool, *lana tratta da una pecora morta.*

Pelt [a target of ſkins] *targa*, s. f. *ſpezie di ſcudo di cuojo.*

To PELT [to ſtrike by ſomething thrown] *tirare, lanciare ſopra.*

They pelted us with their ſmall ſhot as we croſſed the river, *ci ſpararono ad doſſo una tempeſta di tiri nel traverſare il fiume.*

To pelt with ſtones, *lapidare, percuotere con ſaſſi.*

PE'LTED, adj. *tirato, lapidato.*

PEN, s. [a quill cut to write with] *una penna da ſcrivere.*

To make or cut a pen *temperare una penna.*

To ſet pen to paper, *metter mano alla penna.*

Pen, or a pen-man [one that writes well or ill] *ſcrittore, colui che ſcrive bene o male.*

Pen [writer, author] *una penna, un autore.*

A pen full, *una pennata.*

A pen-knife, *un temperino.*

A pen-caſe, *un pennajuolo, ſtrumento da tenervi dentro le penne.*

Pen [coop for fowl] *pollajo*, s. m. *luogo dove ſi tengono i polli.*

A pen [or fold for ſheep] *mandra*, s. f. *covile*, s. m.

A pen [the top of a mountain] *penna, cima, ſommità di monte.*

To PEN [to write down] *ſcrivere, mettere in carta*; *participio* penned.

To pen, *rinchiudere*; *participio* pent.

To pen up ſheep, *rinchiuder delle pecore in mandra, o parco, o altro luogo.*

PE'NAL, adj. [belonging to, or inflicting penalty] *penale, di pena, per gaſtigo.*

PE'NALTY, s. [a fine impoſed by way of puniſhment] *pena pecuniaria, penalità.*

PE'NANCE, s. [a mortification] *penitenza*, s. f.

To do penance, *far penitenza.*

PE'NATES, s. [houſhold gods] *i Dei penati.*

PENCE, s. [the plural of penny] *ſoldi.*

Three-half-pence, *un ſoldo e mezzo.*

PE'NCIL, s. [a ſmall inſtrument uſed in drawing and painting] *penello*, s. m. *ſtrumento, che adoperano i dipintori a dipignere.*

PE'NDANT, s. [jewels which women hang on their ears] *orrecchino*, s. m. *quel pendente, che s' appicca agli orecchi delle donne, ciondolino, ciondolo.*

The pendants or ſtreamers of a ſhip, *pennoni di vaſcelli.*

Pendant, adj. [left undecided] *pendente, non deciſo.*

Pendant, adj. [hanging down] *pendente, che pende.*

PE'NDULOUS, adj. [hanging down] *pendolone, ſpenzolone, pendente.*

PE'NDULUM, s. [a weight hanging at the end of a ſtring, wire, or chain, by the vibrations or ſwings of which, to and fro, the parts or differences of time are meaſured] *pendolo*, s. m. *peſo pendente da filo, a uſo di miſurare il tempo colle ſue vibrazioni.*

A pendulum watch] *un oriuolo a pendolo.*

PENETRABI'LITY, s. [aptneſs to be penetrated] *qualità penetrabile.*

PE'NETRANT, adj. [ſubtil, quick] *penetrante, che penetra.*

To PE'NETRATE [to get or pierce into

into or through] *penetrare, passare addentro, alle parti interiori.*

To penetrate into, *penetrare, indagare.*

I cannot penetrate into that mystery, *non posso penetrare questo segreto.*

To penetrate with love, *penetrare d' amore.*

PE'NETRATED, adj. *penetrato.*

PE'NETRATING, s. *penetramento,* s. m. *penetrazione,* s. f.

PENETRA'TION, s. [a penetrating or piercing into] *penetrazione,* s. f. *penetramento,* s. m.

Penetration [quickness of wit] *penetrazione, sottigliezza o acutezza d' ingegno.*

PE'NETRATIVE, adj. [which easily penetrates] *penetrevole, penetrativo, che penetra, che ha virtù di penetrare.*

PENI'NSULA, s. [a track of land surrounded with water, except in one place] *penisola,* s. f. *luogo quasi in isola.*

PENI'SSONS, s. [a sort of coarse woollen cloth] *spezie di panno grossolano.*

PE'NITENCE, s. [repentance] *pentimento,* s. m. *penitenza,* s. f.

PE'NITENT, adj. [repenting, being sorrowful for having committed any sin] *penitente, contrito, che si pente, che ha contrizione de' suoi peccati.*

Penitent, s. *un penitente, una penitente.*

PENITE'NTIAL, adj. [belonging to repentance] *penitenziale, di penitenza.*

The penitential psalms, *i salmi penitenziali.*

Penitential, s. [a book which directs priests how to enjoin penance] *penitenziale,* s. m. *libro che regola le penitenze secondo la natura de' peccati.*

PENITE'NTIARY, s. [a priest who imposes penance on an offender] *penitenziere,* s. m. *confessore, che ha autorità d' assolvere ne' casi riservati.*

Penitentiary [a place in Rome to hear confession, and absolve some particular sins] *penitenzieria,* s. f. *residenza de' penitenzieri in Roma.*

PE'NNANCE, *v.* Penance.

PE'NNANT, s. [a rope to hoise up a boat or merchandize into or out of a ship] *fune che serve a tirar su pesi o mercanzie dal vascello o nel vascello.*

PE'NNED, adj. *scritto vergato con penna.*

PE'NNILESS, adj. [moneyless, poor, wanting money] *senza denari; povero; che ha bisogno di denari.*

PE'NNON, s. [a flag or banner ending in a point] *pennone,* s. f.

PE'NNY, s. *soldo; picciola moneta Inglese, di cui dodici fanno uno scellino. Il plurale di* penny *è* pence.

PE'NNYWISE, adj. *è aggiunto di persona che arrischia scioccamente l' assai per salvar il poco.*

PE'NNYWORTH, s. *quanto si compra per un soldo.*

Pennyworth, s. *ogni compra; ogni cosa comprata o venduta per denaro.*

Pennyworth, s. *cosa comprata con vantaggio; compra, o acquisto fatto con meno danaro di quel che vale.*

Pennyworth, s. *picciola quantità di checchessia.*

Penny-post, s. *la posta d'un soldo che va per Londra e per alcune miglia intorno.*

Penny-father, s. *un taccagno, un avaro, un tanghero, uno spilorcio.*

PE'NSILE, adj. [hanging] *pendente, sospeso, pensile.*

PE'NSION, s. [a yearly allowance] *pensione,* s. f. *salario, stipendio,* s. m.

Pension of Gray's Inn [an assembly of the members of that society, who meet to consult about the affairs of the house] *consiglio, o assemblea de' membri del collegio chiamato Gray's-Inn, per consultare degli affari appartenti ad esso collegio.*

PE'NSIONER, s. [one who receives a pension] *uno stipendiato, o salariato, che riceve stipendio, o pensione.*

The gentlemen pensioners, or the king's pensioners [a band of gentlemen] who, armed with partizans, attend as a guard upon the king's person in the palace] *banda di gentiluomini stipendiati, che servono di guardia alla persona del re, nel palazzo.*

PE'NSIVE, adj. [thoughtful] *pensoso, pensieroso, pensivo.*

PE'NSIVELY, s. *pensierosamente, mestamente.*

PE'NSIVENESS, s. [thoughtfulness] *pensiero, pensamento,* s. m.

Pensiveness [sorrow] *pensiero, inquietudine di mente, affizion d' animo, mestizia, affizione, melanconia,* s. f.

PENT, adj. [from to pen] *quando vale rinchiudere rinchiuso, rinserrato.*

PENTA'GONAL, adj. [of five angles] *pentagonale, di cinque canti.*

PE'NTAGON, s. [a figure of five angles] *pentagono, quinquangolo,* s. m. *figura di cinque lati.*

PE'NTAMETER, s. [a Greek or Latin verse which consists of five feet] *pentametro, verso che consiste di cinque piedi.*

PENTAPE'TALOUS, adj. ex. pentapetalous plants [are such as have a flower consisting of five leaves] *piante che fanno il fiore di cinque foglie.*

PENTA'STICK, s. [a stanza, or division in a poem consisting of five verses] *stanza composta di cinque versi. In architettura, portico di cinque ordini di colonne.*

PE'NTECOST, s. [the festival of Whitsuntide] *la Pencecoste, la festa dello Spirito Santo.*

PENTECO'STALS, s. [offerings made on Whitsunday, by the parishioners to their priest] *offerte, che i parrocchiani facevano al loro parroco il giorno della Pentecoste.*

PE'NTHOUSE, s. [eves, by which the water slides from the wall] *gronda, grondaja,* s. m. *estremità del tetto che esce fuora della parete della casa.*

PENUL'TIMA, s. [the last syllable but one] *la penultima.*

PENU'MBRA, s. [an imperfect shadow] *ombra imperfetta; una quasi ombra.*

PENU'RIOUS, adj. [niggardly, stingy] *avaro, tirato, stitico, spilorcio, stretto, taccagno, misero.*

Penurious [very poor] *povero, misero, meschino, bisognoso, indigente.*

PENU'RIOUSLY, adv. *avaramente, da spilorcio.*

PENU'RIOUSNESS, s. [niggardliness] *avarizia, stitichezza, strettezza nello spendere, miseria estrema, spilorceria.*

PE'NURY, s. [want] *bisogno, disagio,* s. m. *povertà, stremità, miseria; indigenza,* s. f.

PE'ONY, s. [an herb] *peonia,* s. f. *erba nota.*

PE'OPLE, s. [the whole body of persons who live in a country] *popolo,* s. m. *nazione,* s. f.

The people of Israel, *il popolo d' Israele.*

The English people, *il popolo d' Inghilterra, la nazione Inglese, gl' Inglesi.*

The people, or the common people, or the common sort of people, *il popolo, il popolo minuto, la gente bassa, la plebe, il volgo.*

People [men in general] *gente, persone.*

They are good people, *sono buone persone.*

I met with a great many people, *ho incontrata molta gente.*

What will the people say, if you do it? *che si dirà di voi, se fate ciò?*

Before all the people, *a pien popolo.*

People will talk sometimes, *ognuno vuol dir la sua.*

A town very full of people, *una città molto popolata.*

A throng of people, *una calca di gente.*

The favour of the people, *l' aura popolare.*

Pertaining to the people, *popolano.*

To PE'OPLE [to stock with people] *popolare, metter popolo in un luogo che l' abiti.*

PE'OPLED, adj. *popolato.*

PE'OPLING, s. *il popolare.*

PE'PPER, s. [a sort of spice] *pepe,* s. m. *aromato noto.*

PEPPER-BOX, s. *il bossolo del pepe.*

To take pepper in the nose [to be angry] *saltare in collera, entrare in valigia, adirarsi, stizzarsi.*

The pepper plant or tree, *albero di pepe.*

Pepper-wort, *nome d' erba.*

PEPPER-MINT, s. *nome d' erba.*

Wall-pepper, *sempreviva,* s. f.

Pepper-proof, *che è accostumato al pepe.*

To PE'PPER [to season with pepper] *impepare, condir con pepe.*

To Pepper [to pox] *infranciosare, dare il mal Francese,*

To pepper [to beat; to mangle with shot or blows] *tirar molte moschettate, dar molte busse.*

PE'PPERED, adj. *impepato.*

PE'PTICK, adj. *che ajuta la digestione.*

PER [a preposition borrowed from the Latin, used instead of BY] *per.*

Per force, *per forza.*

Per annum, *per anno.*

PERACU'TE, adj. [very sharp] *acutissimo.*

PERADVE'NTURE, adv. [perhaps] *forse, può essere, per avventura.*

Without peradventure [without question] *senza dubbio, indubitatamente, sicuramente, senza fallo.*

PERAGRA'TION, s. [travelling or wandering about] *corso,* s. m. *peragrazione.*

Peragration month [the space of the moon's course, from any point of the zodiack, to the same again] *il mese di peragrazione, il corso che fa la luna ogni mese.*

To PERA'MBULATE [to walk about] *girare, andare attorno, vagare, andare errando.*

PERAMBULA'TION, s. *giro, viaggio,* s. m. *vagazione,* s. f.

PERCE'IVABLE, adj. [that may be perceived] *percettibile, che si può vedere o scuoprire.*

PERCE'IVABLY, adv. *visibilmente, percettibilmente.*

To PERCE'IVE [to discover] *scoprire, vedere, osservare, accorgersi,* pret. *vidi, veddi,* pret. *m' accorsi.*

To perceive [to understand, to apprehend] *concepire, comprendere, intendere, capire,* pret. *compresi, intesi,* pref. *capisco.*

To perceive before hand, *presentire,* pref. *presentisco.*

PERCEI'VED, adj. *scoperto, visto osservuto, accorto, concepito, compreso, inteso, capito.*

PERCE'PTIBLE, adj. [that may be perceived] *percettibile, visibile, che si può vedere o scoprire.*

PERCE'PTION, s. [clear and distinct apprehension of objects] *percezione, intelligenza, capacità,* s. f. *il comprendere, o capire qualche cosa.*

PERCH, s. *nome d' un pesce di natura vorace.*

Perch, s. *pertica, sorte di misura.*

Perch, s. *pertica o ramo, su cui li uccelli o i pollami s' adagiano.*

To PERCH, *adagiarsi sopra una pertica o ramo, come fanno gli uccelli o i polli.*

To perch, *collocare sur una pertica, ramo, o palo.*

PERCHA'NCE, adv. [perhaps] *forse, per avventura, per caso.*

PERCU'SSION, s. [striking] *percussione, percuotitura, percossa,* s. f. *porcotimento,* s. m.

PERDI'TION, s. [utter ruin or destruction] *perdizione, dannazione, rovina,* s. f. *perdimento, danno,* s. m.

PE'RDUE, adj. [lost, forlorn] *perduto.*

To lie perdue [to lie flat upon the belly] *giacere boccone, o a boccone, giacere colla pancia per terra, e in aguato.*

A perdue [a soldier placed in a dangerous post] *sentinella avvanzata.*

PERDU'RABLE, adj. [continuing, lasting long] *perdurabile, durabile, permanente, perdurevole.*

PERDURA'TION, s. [lasting very long] *perdurabilità,* s. f. *lunga durata.*

PEREGRINA'TION, s. [travelling in foreign countries] *peregrinazione, pellegrinazione,* s. f.

PE'REGRINE, adj. [foreign, outlandish] *peregrino, straniero, forestiero.*

A peregrine hawk, *un falcone pellegrino.*

PEREMPTO'RILY, adv. *perentoriamente, assolutamente, decisivamente, definitivamente.*

He stood peremptorily in what he first affirmed, *stette fermo in quel che prima aveva affermato.*

PEREMPTO'RINESS, s. *maniera decisiva.*

PE'REMPTORY, adj. [final, determinate] *perentorio, definitivo, decisivo.*

A peremptory action [a determinate and final act, which cannot be renewed] *atto perentorio.*

Peremptory [positive, absolute, pragmatical] *assoluto, decisivo, determinato, risoluto, ardito, temerario.*

To play a peremptory game, *giocare l' ultima partita, o una partita e non più.*

PERE'NNIAL, adj. [lasting all the year] *perenne, che dura tutto l' anno.*

Perennial [everlasting] *perenne, continuo, perpetuo.*

PERE'NNITY, s. [long continuance, perpetuity] *perpetuità,* s. f.

PE'RFECT, adj. [compleat, intire] *perfetto, compito, intiero, compito, condotto a perfezione.*

Perfect [accomplished, well skill'd] *versato, consumato, perfetto.*

He is a perfect master of the Italian tongue, *egli è versatissimo nella lingua Italiana.*

A perfect beauty, *una bellezza consumata.*

To be perfect in a thing [to know it by heart] *saper a mente che che si sia, saperla a menadito.*

Perfect [arrant] *vero, pretto, puro.*

He is a perfect cheat, *egli è un pretto furbo, un furbo, bagnato o cimato.*

To PERFE'CT [to make perfect, to finish] *perfezionare, dar perfezione, finire, compire,* pref. *finisco, compisco.*

PE'RFECTED, adj. *perfezionato, finito, compito.*

Very perfect, *perfettissimo.*

PERFE'CTING, s. *finimento, compimento,* s. m.

PERFE'CTION, s. [accomplishment] *perfezione,* s. f. *fine, compimento,* s. m.

Perfection [excellency] *perfezione, eccellenza,* s. f.

PE'RFECTLY, adv. *perfettamente, interamente, compitamente.*

Very perfectly, *perfettissimamente.*

PE'RFECTNESS, s. [perfection] *perfezione,* s. f. *fine, compimento,* s. m.

PERFI'DIOUS, adj. [false, treacherous] *perfido, disleale, infido, malvagio.*

A perfidious man, *un perfido, un disleale.*

A perfidious woman, *una perfida, una malvagia.*

PERFI'DIOUSLY, adv. *perfidamente, deslealmente, malvagiamente.*

PERFI'DIOUSNESS, s. [falseness, treachery] *perfidia, dislealtà, malvagità,* s. f.

To PE'RFORATE [to pierce through] *perforare, forare, trafiggere,* pret. *trafissi.*

PE'RFORATED, adj. *perforato, forato, trafitto.*

PERFORA'TION, s. [a boring through] *perforazione,* s. f. *perforamento,* s. m. *il perforare.*

Perforation [hole] *buco, pertugio,* s. m.

PER-FORCE, adv. *perforza, forzatamente, di viva forza.*

To PERFO'RM [to accomplish] *effettuare, compiere, e compire, eseguire, mettere ad effetto, fare,* pref. *compisco, eseguisco, faccio o fo,* pret. *feci.*

To perform one's word or promise, *effettuare, o mandare ad affetto la promessa, mantener la parola.*

To perform a design, *effettuare, o eseguire un disegno.*

I have performed your orders, *ho compito a' vostri ordini.*

To perform well upon an instrument, *sonar bene d' un instromento.*

To perform wonders, *far miracoli.*

To perform one's devotion, *dire le sue divozioni.*

PERFO'RMANCE, s. [performing] *effezione,* s. f. *fatto, effetto, compimento,* s. m.

Performance [work] *opera,* s. f.

An ingenious performance, *un opera ingegnosa.*

Military performances, *fatti militari.*

I had rather performances without promises, than promises without performances, *vorrei più fatti, e meno promesse.*

PERFO'RMED, adj. *effettuato.*

PERFO'RMER, s. *quello o quella che effettua, o manda ad effetto, eseguitore, esecutore,* s. m.

PERFO'RMING, s. *l' effettuare, effezione,* s. f. *effetto, compimento,* s. m.

PERFU'ME, s. [sweet scent] *profumo,* s. m. *odore grato.*

To PERFU'ME [to give a sweet scent to] *profumare, dare odore, spirare odore di profumo.*

To perfume one's self, *profumarsi.*

PERFU'MED, adj. *profumato.*

PERFU'MER, s. [one who makes and sells perfumes] *profumiere, unguentario,* s. m.

PERFU'MING, s. *il profumare.*

Perfuming, adj. ex. a perfuming pan or pot, *profumiera,* s. f. *vaso nel quale si fa il profumo, turibile,* s. m.

PERFUN'CTORILY, adv. [slightly, care-

careleſſy] *negligentemente, leggiermente, alla peggio.*

PERFU'NCTORY, adj. [done careleſly, ſlightly] *acciabbattato, abborracciato, fatto alla groſſa e ſenza diligenza.*

PE'RHAPS, adv. [it may be ſo] *forſe.*

PERICA'RDIUM, s. [a membrane which ſurrounds the heart] *pericardio,* s. m. *quella borſa dove ſta chiuſo il cuore dell' animale.*

PERICA'RDIAN, } adj. ex. the peri-
PERICA'RDICK, } cardian, or pericardick vein, *la vena del pericardio.*

PERICLITA'TION, s. [hazard, jeopardy] *pericolamento,* s. m. *il pericolare, pericolo,* s. m.

PERICRA'NIUM, s. [a membrane which infolds the ſcull, and covers it all, except where the temporal muſcles are] *pericranio,* s. m.

PE'RIGEE, } s. *perigéo; quel punto*
PERICE'UM, } *nel cielo in cui un pianeta è conſiderato come vicino tanto al noſtro globo quanto può mai eſſere.*

PE'RIL, s. [danger] *pericolo, riſchio,* s. m.

As they will anſwer the contrary at their own perils, *in mancanza ne renderanno conto a loro riſchio.*

PE'RILOUS, adj. [dangerous] *pericoloſo, periglioſo.*

PE'RILOUSLY, adv. *pericoloſamente, periglioſamente.*

PERI'METER, s. [the utmoſt line of any ſolid body] *perimetro,* s. m.

PE'RIOD, s. [revolution of a ſtar] *periodo,* s. m. *rivoluzione d' un aſtro.*

Period, in phyſick [the ſpace between the coming of fits in intermitting diſeaſes] *intermiſſione di febbre.*

In the laſt period of his life, *nell' ultimo punto della ſua vita.*

In the higheſt period of glory, *nel colmo della ſua gloria.*

To bring to a period, or to an end, *terminare, finire.*

Period [among chronologers, a revolution of a certain number of years] *periodo, ſpazio di tempo.*

The Julian period, *il periodo Giuliano.*

Period [a perfect ſentence or cloſe] *periodo, parte d'un diſcorſo.*

PERIO'DICAL, adj. [that has its periods] *periodico.*

PERIO'DICALLY, adv. *periodicamente.*

PERIO'STEUM, s. [a membrane that incloſes immediately the greateſt part of the bones] *il perioſte.*

A PERIPATE'TICK, s. [a follower of Ariſtotle] *peripatetico, diſcepolo d'Ariſtotile.*

PE'RIPHERY, s. [circumference] *circonferenza,* s. f. *contorno,* s. m.

PE'RIPHRASE, or PERIPHRASIS, s. [circumlocution] *parafraſi,* s. f. *traduzione ampliata.*

To PE'RIPHRASE [to uſe circumlocution] *uſar parafraſi.*

PE'RIPHRASED, adj. *ſpiegato con parafraſi.*

PERIPHRA'STICAL, adj. [belonging to periphraſis] *parafraſtico.*

To PE'RISH [to go to ruin, to decay] *perire, mancare, capitar male,* pref. *periſco.*

To periſh [to be caſt away] *perire, naufragare.*

To periſh with hunger, *morir di fame.*

PE'RISHABLE, adj. [apt to periſh, or come to ruin] *caduco, cadevole.*

Periſhable goods, *beni caduchi.*

PE'RISHABLENESS, s. *caducità.*

PE'RISHED, adj. *perito, mancato, naufragato, morto.*

PE'RISHING, s. *il perire.*

Periſhing, adj. [periſhable] *caduco, cadevole.*

PE'RISTYLE, s. [a place encompaſſed with pillars ſtanding round about on the inſide] *colonnato, portico,* s. m. *luogo circondato di colonne.*

PE'RIT, s. [a ſmall ſort of weight leſſer than a grain] *ſcropolo,* s. m. *peſo che vale la vigeſima quarta parte dell' oncia.*

PE'RJUER, s. [a perjured or forſworn perſon] *una perſona che ha ſpergiurato, uno ſpergiuro.*

To PE'RJURE one's ſelf, *ſpergiurare, fare ſpergiuro.*

PE'RJURED, adj. *ſpergiurato.*

A perjured man, *uno ſpergiuro.*

A perjured woman, *una ſpergiura.*

PE'RJURER, s. *ſpergiuro, ſpergiuratore,* s. m. *un che ha giurato il falſo.*

PE'RJURY, s. [falſe oath] *ſpergiuro,* s. m. *giuramento falſo.*

PE'RIWIG, s. *parrucca, capelli poſticci.*

To PE'RIWIG, *ornare o coprire di capelli poſticci o di parrucca.*

PE'RIWINCLE, s. *pervinca, nome di pianta.*

Periwincle, *nome di certa piccola lumaca di mare.*

To PERK up [to lift up the head, to appear lively] *alzar la teſta, ingalluzzarſi.*

PERK, adj. *lieto, baldo, feſtevole, allegro.*

PE'RKED up, adj. *ingalluzzato.*

PE'RMANENT, adj. [durable, continuing] *permanente ſtabile, permanevole, durabile.*

PERMA'NSION, s. [durableneſs] *permanenza, perſeveranza, ſtabilità,* s. f.

PERMI'SSIBLE, adj. [which may be permitted] *che può eſſer permeſſo.*

PERMI'SSION, s. [leave] *permiſſione, licenza,* s. f.

To PERMI'T [to allow, to give leave, to ſuffer] *permettere, concedere, laſciar fare,* pret. *permiſi, conceſſi.*

Permit me to tell you, *con voſtra buona grazia ſia detto.*

PERMI'TTED, adj. *permeſſo, conceſſo.*

PERMI'TTING, s. *permiſſione, il permettere.*

PERMI'XTION, s. [a thorough mingling together] *permiſtione, meſcolanza,* s. f. *meſcuglio, meſcolamento,* s. m.

PERMUTA'TION, s. [exchanging] *permutazione, permutanza,* s. f. *permutamento,* s. m.

To PERMU'TE [to exchange] *permutare, cambiare.*

PERMU'TED, adj. *permutato, cambiato.*

PERMU'TER, s. *permutatore, cambiatore,* s. m. *permutatrice,* s. f.

PER'NICIOUS, adj. [miſchievous, or very hurtful] *pernizioſo, nocivo, dannoſo.*

Very pernicious, *pernizioſiſſimo.*

PERNI'CIOUSLY, adv. *pernizioſamente, dannoſamente.*

PERNI'CIOUSNESS, s. *qualità pernizioſa, nocumento.*

PERORA'TION, s. [the cloſe of an oration or ſpeech] *perorazione,* s. f.

To PERPE'ND [to ponder thoroughly in the mind, to weigh, to examine] *librare, ponderare, rifletter, bilanciare, contrapeſare, peſare, diligentemente conſiderare, ruminare.*

PERPE'NDED, adj. *librato, ponderato, riſleſſo, bilanciato, peſato, ruminato.*

PREPE'NDER, } s. [a ſtone fitted
PERPE'ND STONE, } to the thickneſs of a wall, ſo as to ſhow its ſmoothed ends on both ſides] *pietra che è per l' appunto della larghezza del muro.*

PERPE'NDICLE, s. [a plumb-line] *perpendicolo,* s. m. *piombino, o pietruzza, legata all' archipenzolo con un filo, col quale i muratori aggiuſtano il piano.*

PERPENDI'CULAR, adj. *perpendicolare, che pende a piombo.*

A perpendicular line, *una linea perpendicolare.*

Perpendicular, s. [plumb-line] *perpendicolo,* s. m.

PERPENDI'CULARLY, adv. *perpendicolarmente, a piombo, a perpendicolo.*

To PE'RPETRATE [to effect, to perform] *perpetrare, effettuare, mandare ad effetto, eſeguire, fare.*

To perpetrate [to commit] a crime, *commettere un delitto.*

PE'RPETRATED, adj *perpetrato, effettuato, eſeguito, fatto, commeſſo.*

PE'RPETRATING, s. *il perpetrare, o mandar ad effetto.*

PERPE'TUAL, adj. [everlaſting, endleſs] *perpetuo, continuo, continovo.*

PERPE'TUALLY, adv. *perpetuamente, e perpetualmente, continuamente.*

To PERPE'TUATE [to make perpetual, to eternize] *perpetuare, far perpetuo, immortalizzare.*

To perpetuate one's name, *perpetuare l'altrui nome.*

PERPE'TUATED, adj. *perpetuato.*

PERPE'TUATING, } s. *perpetuan-*
PERPETUA'TION, } *za, perpetuità,* s. f.

PERPETU'ITY, s. [everlastingness] *perpetuità, perpetualità*, s. f.

To PERPLE'X [to confound, to puzzle, to trouble] *intrigare, imbrogliare, ingarbugliare, confondere, scompigliare*, pret. *confusi*.

To perplex [to disquiet] *inquietare, travagliare, tribolare, disturbare*.

To perplex a business, *intrigare, o imbrogliare un affare*.

PERPLE'X, adj. [doubtful, full of perplexity] *intrigato, imbrogliato, confuso, perplesso*.

PERPLE'XED, adj. *perplesso, ambiguo, intrigato, imbrogliato, confuso*.

A perplexed business, *un negozio imbrogliato*.

A perplexed style, *uno stile confuso, o oscuro*.

PERPLE'XEDLY, adv. *confusamente, ambiguamente, intrigatamente*.

PERPLE'XITY, } s. [doubtfulness, trouble]
PERPLE'XIVENESS, } *perplessità, ambiguità*, s. f. *dubbi, intrigo, imbroglio*, s. m.

PE'RQUISITES, s. [any thing that a man gets over and above his wages] *emolumento, profitto, guadagno, soprappiù*.

PERQUISI'TION, s. [a strict enquiry] *perquisizione, inquisizione*, s. f. *diligente, ricerca*.

PERQUI'SITOR, s. [inquisitor, searcher] *inquisitore*, s. m. *diligente ricercatore*.

PERRY, s. [a drink made of pears] *bevanda fatta di pere, cidro, fatto di pere*.

To PE'RSECUTE [to oppress, to trouble, to torment] *perseguitare, opprimere, tormentare*.

To persecute [to importune] *perseguitare, importunare*.

PE'RSECUTED, adj. *perseguitato oppresso, tormentato, importunato*.

PE'RSECUTING, s. *il perseguitare*.

PERSECU'TION, s. *persecuzione*, s. f. *l'atto del perseguitare*.

PERSECU'TOR, s. *persecutore, perseguitore*, s. m.

PERSEVE'RANCE, s. [constancy firmness] *perseveranza, costanza*, s. f.

PERSEVE'RANT, adj. [constant] *perseverante, costante*.

To PERSEVE'RE [to continue, to be steadfast] *perseverare, aver perseveranza, continuare*.

PERSEVE'RED, adj. *perseverato, continuato*.

PERSEVE'RING, s. *il perseverare, perseveranza*.

PERSEVERINGLY, adv. *perseverantemente, con perseveranza*.

To PERSI'ST [to continue, to hold, to abide] *persistere, perseverare*.

PERSI'STANCE, } s. [continuance]
PERSI'STING, } *persistenza, perseveranza, fermezza*, s. f.

PE'RSON, s. [a man or woman] *persona*, s. f. *vale uomo o donna*.

A publick or private person, *una persona pubblica, o privata*.

To appear in person [personally] *comparire in persona, personalmente*.

Person [the outward form or shape of one's body] *persona, corpo umano*.

I am extremely pleased with his person, *la sua persona mi piace molto*.

Person [a term used in divinity] *persona, termine teologale*.

The three persons of the blessed Trinity, *le tre persone della santissima Trinità*.

The persons of a verb, *le persone d'un verbo*.

PE'RSONABLE, adj. [having a good presence, or air, comely] *vistoso, ben fatto, di bella presenza*.

A personable woman, *una donna vistosa, ben fatta, di bella presenza*.

Personable [a law term, enabling to maintain a plea in court] *che ha libertà o diritto d'entrare in processo*.

PE'RSONAGE, s. [the same with person, but especially an honourable person] *personaggio*, s. m. *uomo di grande affare*.

PE'RSONAL, adj. [belonging to a person] *personale, attenente alla persona*.

Personal appearance, *comparigione personale*.

He has good personal valour, *egli è un uomo prode, o un uomo coraggioso*.

Personal goods, *beni mobili*.

A personal verb, *un verbo personale*.

PERSONA'LITY, } s. [the property of
PE'RSONALTY, } being a distinct person] *personalità*, s. f.

An action in personality [when it is brought against the right person] *azione personale*.

To PE'RSONATE [to represent a person] *rappresentare la persona d'un altro*.

He personates the fop admirably well, *rappresenta la parte del damerino, perfettamente*.

PE'RSONATED, adj. *rappresentato*.

PE'RSONATING, s. *il rappresentare*.

PERSPE'CTIVE, s. [a part of the opticks] *perspettiva, e prospettiva*, s. f.

Perspective [landskip] *prospettiva, persaggio*.

Perspective [respect] *prospettiva, vista*.

Perspective, adj. *visuale; appartenente alla scienza della vista; visivo; ottico*.

PERSPICA'CIOUS, adj. [quick-sighted, quick-witted] *perspicace, d'acuta vista, d'acuto ingegno*.

PERSPICA'CITY, s. [quickness of sight, or apprehension] *perspicacità, acutezza di vista o d'ingegno*.

PERSPICU'ITY, s. [clearness or plainness in writing or speaking] *chiarezza e purezza nello scrivere e nel parlare*.

PERSPI'CUOUS, adj. [clear, plain, easy to be apprehended] *apparente, chiaro, puro, netto, evidente*.

PERSPI'CUOUSLY, adv. *chiaramente, evidentemente, con nettezza; con oscuramente*.

PERSPIRA'TION, s. [a breathing or steaming through] *perspirazione*.

To PERSPI'RE [to emit by the cuticular pores] *perspirare*.

To PERSTRI'NGE [to touch lightly, or to glance upon a thing in discourse] *toccare, discorrere brevemente, superficialmente accennare*.

To PE'RSUADE [to convince, to make believe] *persuadere, dare ad intendere, far credere*, pret. *persuasi*.

To persuade one's self, *persuadersi, darsi a credere, imaginarsi*.

PERSUA'DED, adj. *persuaso*.

I cannot, or I am not to be persuaded, that it is so, *non posso persuadermi, o non posso darmi a credere che ciò sia vero*.

Men are easily persuaded of what they desire, *gli uomini facilmente credono quello che desiderano*.

He was easily persuaded to it, *vi si lasciò facilmente indurre*.

PERSUA'DER, *colui o colei che persuade*.

PERSUA'DING, s. *il persuadere*.

PERSUA'DINGLY, adv. *d'una maniera persuasiva*.

PERSUA'SION, s. [sollicitation] *persuasione, sollicitazione, istanza, richiesta, istigazione*, s. f.

Persuasion [belief] *persuasione, opinione, credenza*, s. f.

Persuasion [religion] *credenza, religione*.

PERSUA'SIVE, } adj. *persuasivo,*
PERSUA'SORY, } *suasivo, atto a persuadere*.

PERSUA'SIVELY, adv. *in mo' da persuadere*.

To PERSWA'DE, *v.* To persuade.

PERT, adj. [brisk, lively] *losto, presto, agile, destro, vivace*.

Pert [talkative] *ciarliero, che ciarla troppo*.

Pert [saucy] *impertinente, malcreato*.

Pert in discourse, *troppo vivace nel discorrere*.

To PERTA'IN [to belong to, to concern] *appartenere, convenirsi, concernere, ragguardare, spettare, toccare*.

PERTINA'CIOUS, adj. [obstinate, stubborn] *pertinace, capitoso, ostinato, caparbio*.

PERTINA'CIOUSLY, adv. *pertinacemente, ostinatamente*.

PERTINA'CITY, } s. [stubbornness]
PE'RTINACY, } *pertinacia, ostinazione, caparbieria, durezza*, s. f.

PE'RTINENCE, s. [fitness or suitableness] *pertinenza, appartenenza, attenenza, convenenza, proporzione, convenevolezza*, s. f.

PE'RTINENT, adj. [fit, pat, suitable] *pertinente, convenevole, conveniente, giusto, ragionevole, proporzionato, dicevole*.

A per-

A pertinent excuse, *una scusa pertinente.*

This is pertinent to my purpose, *ciò fa per me.*

PE'RTINENTLY, adv. *convenevolmente, convenientemente, con convenevolezza.*

PERTI'NGENCY, s. [a reaching to] *il battere o ferire.*

The pertingency of the object, to the sensitive organ, *il battere o ferire che fa un oggetto l'organo sensitivo.*

PERTI'NGENT, adj. [reaching to, touching] *che batte, o ferisce.*

PE'RTNESS, s. [briskness, liveliness] *vivacità, destrezza,* s. f.

Pertness [talkativeness] *cicalamento, cicaleccio, cicalio,* s. m.

Pertness [sauciness] *impertinenza, malacreanza,* s. f.

To PE'RTURBATE [to disquiet or disturb] *perturbare, scompigliare, turbare.*

PE'RTURBATED, adj. *perturbato, scompigliato, turbato.*

PERTURBA'TION, s. [disquiet, disorder, trouble of mind] *perturbazione, alterazione,* s. f. *commovimento, scompiglio, perturbamento,* s. m.

PERTURBA'TOR, s. [disturber] *perturbatore,* s. m.

To PERVA'DE [to go over or through] *penetrare, trapassare, passare oltre.*

PE'RVERSE, s. [froward, cross, untoward] *perverso, iniquo, malvagio, maligno, pessimo, iniquitoso.*

PERVE'RSELY, adv. *perversamente, malvagiamente, pessimamente, iniquamente.*

PERVE'RSENESS, } s. [frowardness,
PERVE'RSITY, } crossness] *perversità, iniquità, malvagità,* s. f.

The perversity of manners, *la depravazione de' costumi.*

PERVE'RSION, s. [perverting] *pervertimento, sconvolgimento,* s. m.

To PERVE'RT [to turn upside down, to debauch, to seduce] *pervertere, sconvolgere, metter sozzopra, depravare, corrompere, contaminare,* pret. *sconvolsi, corruppi.*

To pervert manners, *pervertere, corrompere i costumi.*

To pervert a thing to a wrong end, *misurare di che che si sia, servirsene a male.*

To pervert the order of things, *pervertere, o sconvolgere l'ordine delle cose.*

PERVE'RTED, adj. *pervertito, sconvolto, depravato, corrotto.*

PERVE'RTER, s. [debaucher] *corruttore, corrompitore,* s. m.

PERVE'RTING, s. *il pervertere.*

PERVICA'CIOUS, adj. [wilful, stubborn] *ostinato, caparbio, pertinace.*

PERVICA'CITY, } s. [stubbornness,
PE'RVICACY, } wilfulness] *ostinazione, pertinacia, caparbieria,* s. f.

PE'RVIOUS, adj. [passable, easy to be passed] *per cui si può passare, passabile.*

PERU'KE, s. [a cap of false hair, a periwig] *parrucca, capelli posticci.*

PERU'KE-MAKER, s. *parrucchiere; colui che fa parrucche, che impropriamente chiamiamo anche barbiere.*

PERU'SAL, s. [a perusing or reading over] *lettura,* s. f. *il rileggere, o rivedere una scrittura.*

The perusal of a book, *la lettura d' un libro.*

After your perusal of it, *dopo che l' avrete riletto.*

To PERU'SE [to look or read over] *rileggere, leggere, rivedere, esaminare,* pret. *rilessi, lessi.*

To PERU'SE a book, *rileggere, o esaminare un libro.*

PERU'SED, adj. *riletto, letto, riveduto, esaminato.*

PERU'SER, s. *lettore, quello che legge e rivede qualche scrittura.*

PERU'SING, s. *lettura, il rilegger, o rivedere.*

PERU'VIAN, adj. *che è del Perù.*

The Peruvian bark [a drug commonly called Jesuits bark, or powder] *china,* s. f. *scorza d'un albero che viene d'America, ed è buona contro la febbre.*

PERWIG, or PERIWIG, s. [a cap of false hair] *parrucca,* s. f.

To wear a perwig, *portar parrucca.*

A perwig-maker, *un parrucchiere.*

PERWI'NKLE, s. [a sort of herb] *pervinca,* s. f. *sorta d'erba.*

Perwinkle [sea-snail] *lumaca di mare.*

PE'SAGE, s. [a common custom, or duty paid for the weighing of goods] *diritto che si paga per il peso delle mercanzie.*

PE'SSARY, s. [any oblong medicine to be thrust into the neck of the womb] *pessario,* s. m. *sorta di medicamento.*

PEST, s. [plague, pestilence] *peste, pestilenza,* s. f.

A pest-house, *spedale degli appestati.*

He is the pest of the commonwealth, *egli è la peste della repubblica.*

To PE'STER [to plague, to trouble] *angosciare, balestrare, travagliare, affliggere, affannare, dare affanno, inquietare, importunare, nojare, turbare, disturbare.*

The pirates pester our coasts, *i corsari infestano le nostre coste.*

PE'STERED, adj. *angosciato, travagliato, afflitto, affannato, importunato, nojato.*

PESTI'FEROUS, adj. [bringing the plague] *pestifero, che apporta peste, pestilenziale.*

Pestiferous [pernicious] *pestifero, perniciosa, malvagio.*

PE'STILENCE, s. [plague] *pestilenza, e pestilenzia,* s. f. *male contagioso.*

PE'STILENT, } adj. *pestilenziale,*
PE'STILENTIAL, } *pestifero.*

PE'STLE, s. [an instrument to pound with in a mortar] *pestello,* s. m. *strumento col quale si pesta*

A pestle of pork [the very end of the leg] *l'osso del presciutto.*

PET, s. [a fit of anger] *collera, sdegno, sdegnuzzo improvviso.*

To take pet at a thing, *offendersi o sdegnarsi di qualche cosa.*

He is in a great pet, *egli è in gran collera.*

PE'TAR, } s. [a mortar-like engine
PE'TARD, } to break open gates] *petardo,* s. m. *strumento militare da fuoco, per romper porte e simili.*

PE'TARDER, s. [one who manages a petard] *petardiere,* s. m.

PE'TER-PENCE, s. [a tribute of a penny for every house, given to the pope by Ina king of the West Saxons] *tributo d'un soldo, che ogni casa pagava al papa, concessogli da Ina re delli Sassoni occidentali.*

PE'TIT, s. *piccolo, inconsiderabile.*

PETI'TION, s. [request to a superior] *petitione, supplica, domanda, supplicazione,* s. f. *memoriale,* s. m

To put up a petition to the king, *presentare una supplica al re.*

To PETI'TION one [to request, to put up a petition] *presentare una supplica ad uno, supplicarlo, pregarlo.*

PETI'TIONED, adj. *a chi s' è presentata una supplica, supplicato, pregato.*

Petitioned against, *contro chi s' è presentata una supplica.*

PETI'TIONER, s. [he or she that puts up a petition] *supplicante,* s. m. f.

PETI'TIONING, s. *il supplicare.*

PE'TITORY, adj. [belonging to a petition] *petitorio.*

PE'TRARY, s. [mangonel, an engine of old to cast stones] *mangano,* s. m. *strumento militare antico, per tirare o scagliar pietre.*

PE'TREL, s. [breast-plate] *pettorale,* s. m.

PETRI'FICK, adj. *petrifico, che ha virtù di cambiar una cosa e farla divenir sasso.*

PETRIFICA'TION, s. [a changing any body into a stony substance] *petrificazione,* s. f.

To PE'TRIFY [to turn into a stone] *impietrare, impietrire, convertire in pietra,* pres. *impietrisco.*

To petrify [to become a stone] *impietrare, impietrire, divenir pietra.*

PE'TRIFY'D, adj. *convertito in pietra, impietrito, impietrato.*

PE'TROL, } s. [rock-oyl, a cer-
PETROLEUM, } tain liquor that flows out of a rock] *petrolio,* s. m. *olio petroso.*

PE'TRONEL, s. [a sort of hand-gun] *sorta d'archibuso.*

PE'TTICOAT, s. *sottana, sottoveste da donna della cintura in giù.*

PETTIFO'GGER, s. [an ignorant and troublesome lawyer, or attorney] *un avvocato o procuratore ignorante, un procuratorello, un beccalite, uno sforcileggi,*

dot-

dottoretto di grande audacia, di poco sapere, e di molta voglia di rubare a' clienti.

PETTIFO'GGING, s. [the practice of a pettifogger] *briga, lite, controversia,* s. f.

PE'TTINESS, s. *picciolezza, poca pregievolezza di checchessia.*

PE'TTISH, adj. [peevish, touchy] *umorisia, fantastico, di cattivo umore, stravagante, fastidioso, un bell' umore.*

PETTITO'ES, s. [pigs feet] *piedi di porcello.*

Pettitoes, s. pl. *piedi piccoli; e dicesi per disprezzo.*

PE'TTO, s. Ex. to keep a thing in petto [to keep a thing in one's own breast] *tener in petto che che si sia, tenere scritto nella memoria.*

PE'TTY, adj. [little] *piccolo, picciolo, dispregievole, di poco valore o importanza.*

A petty king, *un regolo, un piccolo re.*

Petty-pattees, *pasticetti.*

Petty-larceny [small theft] *ladroncelleria, piccolo ladroneccio.*

Petty-treason, *v.* Treason.

PE'TULANCE, PE'TULANCY, s. [saucinefs, malapertnefs] *petulanza, protervia, arroganza, prosunzione,* s. f.

PE'TULANT, adj. [saucy, malapert] *petulante, protervo, arrogante, prosuntuoso, superbo, spavaldo, sfacciato.*

Petulant [wanton] *lascivo, amoroso.*

PE'TULANTLY, adv. *petulantemente, sfacciatamente, arrogantemente.*

PEW, s. [church-seat] *banco di chiesa con uno steccato intorno, dove si sta per pregare e ascoltar le prediche.*

PEW'TER, s. [a white mixed metal] *stagno, peltro,* s. m.

Pewter-dishes, plates, &c. *piatti o tondi di stagno o di peltro.*

PEW'TERER, s. *quello che lavora di stagno.*

PHÆNO'MENA, *il plurale di* phænomenon.

PHÆNO'MENON, s. [an appearance in nature] *fenomeno.*

PHALANX, s. [a body of foot amongst the Macedonians] *falange,* s. f. *corpo d' infanteria fra i Macedoni.*

PHANA'TICK, *v.* Fanatick.

PHA'NCY, *v.* Fancy.

PHA'NTASM, PHANTA'SMA, s. *vana e aerea apparizione; cosa che non ha esistenga che nell' imaginazione.*

PHANTA'STICAL, PHANTA'STICK, adj. *fantastico, cappricciosо.*

PHA'NTASTRY, s. [whimsies] *fantasia,* s. f. *capriccio, pensiero, ghiribizzo,* s m.

PHA'NTOM, s. *fantasma,* s. m. *fantasima, larva,* s. f. *spettro, apparizione.*

Phantom, s. *visione imaginata.*

PHARE, s. [fare, a light-house, a watch-tower to guide ships to haven] *faro,* s. m. *la torre de' porti dove la notte per uso de' naviganti s'accende il lume, altrimente detta lanterna.*

The phare of Messina in Sicily, *il faro di Messina in Sicilia.*

PHARISA'ICAL, adj. [belonging to the Pharisees] *di Farisei.*

PHARI'SAISM, s. [the religion of the Pharisees] *la religione de' Farisei.*

PHA'RISEE, s. [a sect of Jews] *Fariseo,* s. m. *setta d' Ebrei.*

PHARMACE'UTICAL, PHARMACE'UTICK, [belonging to pharmacy] *di farmazia.*

PHARMACE'UTY, PHA'RMACY, s. [the apothecary's trade] *farmazia,* s. f. *l'arte di comporre i rimedi.*

PHA'SIS, pl. phases, s. [appearance] *fase, apparenza,* s. f.

The phasis of the moon, *la fase, o apparenza della luna.*

PHASM, s. *lo stesso che* Phantom.

PHE'ASANT, s. [a dainty fowl] *fagiano,* s. m.

A hen pheasant, *una fagiana.*

A pheasant powt [a young pheasant] *un fagianotto.*

PHI'AL, s. *fiala, caraffa.*

PHI'LANTHROPAL, adj. [courteous] *cortese, umano, benigno, amorevole.*

PHILA'NTHROPY, s. [humanity, courtesy] *cortesia, umanità, benignità, amorevolezza,* s f.

PHILA'UTY, s. [self-love] *filautia,* s. f. *amor proprio.*

PHI'LEMOT, adj. [dead leaf colour] *foglia morta.*

PHI'LOLOGER, s. [a humanist, a lover of letters] *filologo,* s. m. *amator del parlare, che fa studio nelle parole, erudito.*

PHILOLO'GICAL, adj. *di filologia, attenente alla filologia.*

PHILO'LOGIST, *v.* Philologer.

PHILO'LOGY, s. [the study of humanity, or skill in the liberal arts and sciences] *filologia,* s. f. *studio di belle lettere.*

PHI'LOMEL, s. [nightingale] *filomena,* s. f. *rosignuolo,* s. m.

PHILOSOPHA'STER, s. [a paltry philosopher] *filosofastro,* s. m. *filosofo di poco valore, filosofo cattivo.*

PHILO'SOPHER, s. [one skill'd in the study of philosophy] *filosofo,* s. m. *professor di filosofia.*

Philosopher like, *da filosofo.*

The philosopher's stone, *la pietra filosofale.*

A natural philosopher, *un fisico, un naturalista.*

A moral philosopher, *un moralista.*

PHILOSO'PHICAL, adj. [belonging to philosophy] *filosofico, di filosofia.*

PHILOSO'PHICALLY, adv. *filosoficamente, da filosofo.*

To PHILO'SOPHIZE [to play the philosopher] *filosofeggiare, filosofare.*

PHILO'SOPHY, s. [the knowledge of things natural and moral] *filosofia,* s. f. *conoscimento delle cose naturali, delle divine, e delle umane.*

Natural philosophy, *la fisica.*

Moral philosophy, *la morale.*

PHI'LTER, PHI'LTRUM, s. [a medicine, or charm, to procure love, a love potion] *filtro,* s. m. *malia, bevanda amorosa.*

Philter charmed [inchanted with love potions] *ammaliato.*

PHLEBO'TOMY, s [the art of letting blood] *flobotomia, e flebotomia,* s. f. *il cavar sangue.*

PHLEGM, s. *flemma.*

PHOE'NIX, s. [an imaginary bird in Arabia, about the bigness of an eagle] *fenice,* s. f.

PHO'SPHORUS, s. [the morning-star] *lucifero,* s. m. *la stella di venere quando mattutina.*

Phosphorus [a sort of stone, or chymical composition, which burns like fire] *sorta di pietra, detta pietra di Bologna, o composizione chimica.*

PHRASE, s. [expression, or manner of speech] *frase,* s. f. *maniera particolare di parlare.*

To PHRASE it [to express a thing after a particular manner] *esprimere.*

PHRA'SED, adj. *espresso.*

PHRASEO'LOGY, s. [a collection of phrases] *un libro, o collezione di frasi.*

PHRE'NSY, s. *frenesia, mattezza spericata.*

PHTHI'SICAL, adj. [troubled with the phthisick] *tisico, infermo di tisichezza.*

PHTHI'SICK, s. [a consumption of the whole body, accompanied with a slow continual fever] *tisichezza,* s. f.

PHY'SICAL, adj. [belonging to natural philosophy] *fisico, di fisica.*

A physical motion, *moto fisico o naturale.*

Physical [medicinal] *fisico, fiscale, medicinale.*

A physical remedy, *un rimedio, una medicina.*

PHY'SICALLY, adv. *fisicamente, naturalmente.*

Physically [according to physick] *secondo i precetti della fisica o medicina.*

PHYSI'CIAN, s. [one skilled in natural philosophy] *un fisico, scienziato di fisica.*

Physician [doctor of physick] *un fisico, un medico.*

PHY'SICK, s. [the science of all material beings] *fisica,* s. f. *scienza della natura delle cose.*

Physick [the art of curing diseases] *la professione della medicina.*

Physick [medicine, remedy] *una medicina, un rimedio.*

Averse from physick, *nemico di medicine.*

To PHY'SICK [to give physick] *medicinare, medicare, dar delle medicine.*

PHY'SICKED, adj. *medicinato, medicato.*

PHY'SICKS, s. [natural philosophy] *fisica, la filosofia naturale.*

Physicks [books treating of physick] *libri di medicina, libri che trattano della medicina.*

PHYSIO'GNOMER, } s. [one skilled
PHYSIO'GNOMIST, } in physiognomy] *fisonomista,* s. m. *uno che è versato nella fisonomia.*

PHYSIO'GNOMY, s. [an art which teaches to guess the natures, conditions, or fortunes of persons by a view of their face, body, &c.] *fisonomia,* s. f. *arte, per la quale dalle fattezze del corpo e da' lineamenti e aria del volto si pretende conoscere la natura degli uomini.*

Physiognomy [looks] *fisonomia, aria, effigie,* s. f.

PHYSIO'LOGER, s. [one who is versed in physiology] *colui ch' è versato nella fisiologia.*

PHYSIOLO'GICAL, adj. [belonging to physiology] *fisiologico.*

PHYSIO'LOGY, s. [that part of physick which treats of the constitution and structure of a human body, and its several parts] *fisiologia,* s. f.

PHYTO'LOGY, s. [a discourse or treatise of plants] *fitologia,* s. f. *discorso o trattato sopra le piante.*

PHYZ, s. [the face] *il viso, la faccia, il muso, la fisonomia.*

PIA'CULAR, adj. [serving for an atonement, or that has power to atone for] *che serve ad espiare una colpa o un errore.*

The PIA MA'TER, s. [the inmost skin which incloses the brain] *dura madre, pia madre, le tuniche o membrane che cuoprono il cervello.*

PI'ANNET, s. [the lesser wood-pecker, a bird] *spezie di picchio.*

PIA'STER, s. [a foreign coin, about the value of a crown English] *piastra,* s. f. *moneta che vale incirca uno scudo d' Inghilterra.*

PIA'ZZA, s. [a walk under a roof supported by pillars] *portico da passeggiarvi sotto; voce pretta Italiana, adattata stranamente dagl' Inglesi.*

PIBBLE, } s. *v.* Pebble.
PIBBLE-STONE, }

PICA, s. [a longing, as] of women with child] *voglia di donna gravida.*

Pica [a printing-letter, of which there are three sorts, small, great, and double] *spezie di lettera per istampare.*

PICARO'ON, s. [a robber, a plunderer] *ladro, rubatore, saccheggiatore.*

PICK [a tool used by carvers] *mazzuolo,* s. m. *martello di ferro col quale gli scalpellini lavorano.*

A pick-ax, *una vanga.*

A pick-lock [an instrument to pick locks with] *grimaldello,* s. m. *strumento di ferro ritorto da uno de' capi, e serve per aprir le serrature senza chiave.*

A pick-lock [one that picks locks] *quello che apre le serratura col grimaldello.*

He is a pick-lock of the law [he is an excellent lawyer] *egli è un grande avvocato.*

Pick-pocket, } *un borsajuolo, un ta-*
Pick-purse, } *gliaborse, un pelamantelli.*

A pick-thanks [one that tells stories to curry favour, a tale-bearer] *un palpatore, un adulatore, un lusinghiere, uno scrocco.*

To PICK [to cleanse] *mondare, nettare, cappare.*

To pick a sallad, *nettare un' insalata.*

To pick one's teeth, *nettarsi i denti.*

To pick a bone, *rosicchiare, rosecchiare un osso.*

To pick [to proin, as a bird does] *spiumacciarsi.*

To give one a bone to pick, *dar che pensare ad uno, metterlo in travaglio.*

To pick a bird or fowl [to pull off his feathers] *spennare un uccello.*

To pick a quarrel with one, *attaccarla con alcuno, attaccar lite con alcuno, prender gara con lui.*

To pick [to gather] *cogliere,* pret. *colsi.*

To pick and chuse, *scegliere, cappare.*

To pick a lock, *aprire una serratura col grimaldello.*

To pick and steal, *rubare, ciuffare, imbolare.*

To pick one's pockets, *truffare, giuntare alcuno.*

To pick an acquaintance with one, *fare, o contrarre amicizia con alcuno.*

The pigeons pick up all the corn, *i piccioni mangiano tutto 'l grano.*

To pick up one's crumbs, *riaversi, pigliar vigore.*

To pick thanks, *adulare, lusingare, piaggiare.*

To pick a dart, *tirare, o lanciare un dardo.*

To pick wool, *spillaccherare, o levar le pillacchere dalla lana.*

To pick out, *scegliere, cappare.*

Where have you picked that out? *dove avete trovato, o preso cio?*

To pick out a corn, *sradicare un callo.*

To pick out a livelihood, *guadagnar la vita, guadagnarsi il vitto.*

To pick up, *accogliere, e raccorre, pigliar che che si sia, levandolo di terra.*

To pick up a wench, *pigliar su una puttana, pigliarsela in compagnia per la strada.*

To pick a hole in one's coat [to find fault with another] *trovar di che apporre ad alcuno.*

PI'CKAGE, s. [money paid at fairs, for breaking ground to set up booths or stalls] *diritto che si paga alle fiere da quelli che piantano botteghe.*

PI'CAROON, s. [a sort of pirate ship] *legno sottile da corseggiare.*

Pickaroon [pirate] *corsale, pirata,* s. m. *ladro di mare.*

To PI'CKAROON [to go robbing and plundering] *corseggiare, andar in corso.*

PI'CKED, adj. [from to pick] *mondato, nettato, v.* To pick.

Picked [sharp] *puntuto.*

A picked hat, *un cappello puntuto.*

PI'CKER, s. ex. a picker of quarrels, *un accatta lite, uno struzzicatore, un brigante.*

An ear-picker, *uno stuzzicorecchi, strumento col quale si nettano gli orecchi.*

A tooth-picker, *uno stuzzicadenti.*

A purse or pocket picker, *un borsajuolo, un tagliaborse.*

A lock picker, *colui che apre le serrature col grimaldello.*

PI'CKET, s. [a game at cards] *picchetto,* s. m. *sorta di giuoco di carte.*

Picket, a stake sharp at one end, and pointed with iron, to mark out the ground and angles of a fortification] *picchetto, baston puntuto e ferrato che si ficca in terra per notare gli angoli e le misure della pianta d' una fortezza.*

To stand upon the picket [is when a horse-man is sentenced for some offence to stand on the point of a stake with one toe, having the contrary hand ty'd up as high as it can reach] *stare al picchetto.*

PI'CKING, s. *il mondare o nettare, v.* To pick.

Picking of thanks, *adulamento, lusinga.*

PI'CKLE, s. [a seasoning with brine, vinegar, salt, spices, &c.] *salamoja,* s. f. *salsa composta d' aceto, sale, e spezierie.*

To be in a sad pickle, *esser mal' acconciato, essere sporco, o sciamannato.*

To PI'CKLE [to season or preserve in pickles] *confettare, salare, marinare.*

To pickle cucumbers, *confettare dei cocomeri.*

To pickle fish, *marinare del pesce.*

To pickle herrings, *salare delle aringhe.*

PI'CKLED, adj. *confettato, salato, marinato.*

Pickled herrings, *aringhe salate.*

A pickled rogue, *un furbo in chermisi, un gran furbaccio.*

PI'CKLES, s. [fruits or plants pickled for sauces] *frutti, o piante confettate.*

PI'CKREL, s. [a young pike-fish] *un piccolo luccio.*

PICT, s. *una persona imbellettata.*

PI'CTURE, s. [the image or representation of a person or thing, made in painting or graving] *pittura, dipintura, effigie, imagine,* s. f. *quadro, ritratto,* s. m.

A fine picture, *un bella pittura, un bel quadro.*

Your picture is very much like you, *il vostro ritratto vi rassomiglia molto.*

He is the picture of his father, *egli rassomiglia molto a suo padre, è molto somigliante a suo padre.*

Picture-drawing, *pittura,* s. f. *l' arte del dipignere.*

A picture-drawer, *un pittore.*

To PI'CTURE [to describe] *dipigne-re.*

re, delineare, rappresentare, descrivere, pret. *dipinsi, descrissi.*

PI'CTURED, adj. *dipinto, delineato, rappresentato, descritto.*

To PI'DDLE [to eat here and there a bit] *spilluzzicare, levare pochissimo dalla cosa che si mangia, mangiar contro voglia, denticchiare.*

To piddle [to stand trifling] *badaluccare, stare a bada, trattenersi intorno a cose piccole, e trascurar le importanti.*

PI'DDLED, adj. *spilluzzicato, v.* To piddle.

PI'DDLER, s. [at his victuals] *quello, o quella che spilluzzica*; *uno svogliato.*

Pidler [trifler] *un perditempo, un badalucco.*

PI'DDLING, s. *badaluccare, badalucco.*

To stand piddling, *badaluccare, stare a bada.*

Piddling, adj. ex. a piddling business, *una bagattella, chiappoleria, cosa frivola.*

PI'DGEON, *v.* Pigeon.

PIE, s. [a dish of meat or fruit baked in paste] *pasticcio,* s. m.

Pie [mag-pie] a bird, *una pica, una gazza, sorta d' uccello.*

A sea pie, *gabbiano,* s. m. *spezie d' uccello.*

Pie-bald, or pied, adj. [black and white, as a mag pie] *pezzato, vajato.*

Pie bald, s. [a pie-bald horse] *cavallo pezzato.*

PIECE, s. [a part of a whole] *pezzo,* s. m. *parte di un tutto.*

A piece of wood, *un pezzo di legno.*

A piece of bread, *un tozzo di pane.*

Piece-meal, *pezzo a pezzo, poco a poco.*

To do a thing by piece-meal, *fare che che si sia a spilluzzico, o a poco per volta.*

To tear a thing by piece-meal, *stracciare, mettere, o tagliare che che si sia a pezzi.*

A broken piece of a lance, *un tronco di lancia.*

A piece [a pound sterling, twenty shillings] *una lira sterlina, cioè venti scellini.*

A piece [a certain number of ells, or yards, of cloth or stuff] *pezza,* s. f. *panno, o tela intera.*

A piece of cloth, *una pezza di panno.*

A birding or a fowling-piece, *uno schioppetto.*

A soldier's piece or musket, *uno schioppo, un moschetto.*

A piece of ordnance [a cannon] *un pezzo d' artiglieria, un cannone.*

A piece of gold or silver, *una pezza d' oro, o d' argento*

A chimney-piece, *un quadro da metter sopra 'l cammino.*

Piece is sometimes only used for emphasis sake. *Qualche volta la parola* Piece *è usata solo per dar enfasi al discorso, come nel seguente esempio.*

A piece of good-counsel [a good counsel] *un buon consiglio.*

It is a great piece of folly, *è una gran pazzia.*

A piece, or each piece, *ciascuno, ciascuna, ciascheduno, ciascheduna.*

These horses cost me thirty pounds a-piece, *questi cavalli mi costano trenta doppie ciascheduno*; *ciascheduno di questi cavalli mi costa trenta doppie.*

To PIECE [to patch] *rappezzare, racconciare, rattoppare, mettervi un pezzo.*

To piece a gown, *rappezzare una gonna.*

We PI'ECED up the matter as well as we could, *racconciammo, o rappatumammo l' affare il meglio che seppamo.*

Pieced, adj. *rappezzato, racconciato, rattoppato.*

PI'ECING, adj. *il rappezzare.*

PIED, adj. [black and white, or white and bay] *pezzato.*

A pied-horse, *un cavallo pezzato.*

Pied-powder, s. [a vagabond] *un vagabondo, un perditempo.*

PI'EDNESS, s. *varietà di colori.*

PIE-POWDER court, s. [a court held in fairs, to do justice to buyers and sellers, and to redress disorders committed in them] *corte che si tiene nelle fiere per far giustizia ai compratori e venditori, e per acquietare i disordini che potrebbon nascervi.*

PIER, s. *pilastro su cui s' alza l' arco d' un ponte sopra un fiume.*

In one of the piers of London bridge there is a chapel. *Nell' interno d'uno de' pilastri del ponte di Londra v' è una cappella.*

To PI'ERCE [to bore through] *foracchiare, forare, perforare, pertugiare, straforare.*

To pierce [to penetrate] *penetrare, trapassare, trafiggere,* pret. *trafissi.*

That pierced my heart, *ciò mi trafisse il cuore.*

To pierce or broach a hogshead of wine, *spillare una botte di vino, metter mano ad una botte di vino.*

PI'ERCED, adj. *foracchiato, v.* To pierce.

PI'ERCER, s. [an instrument to pierce or broach a vessel] *ferro col quale si foran le botti*; *succhiello.*

PI'ERCING, s *il foracchiare, o pertugiare.*

Piercing, adj. [sharp, acute] *penetrante*; *pugnente, pungente*; *acuto*; *sottile.*

Piercing eyes, *occhi vivi, vivaci.*

A piercing look, *uno sguardo brusco.*

A piercing winter, *uno verno aspro.*

Piercing words, *parole pugnenti.*

PI'ERCINGLY, adv. *sottilmente, acutamente.*

PI'ERCINGNESS, s. [power of piercing] *acutezza, sottigliezza.*

PI'ETY, s. [godliness, devotion] *pietà, devozione, religione,* s. f.

Piety [natural affection] *pietà, amorevolezza,* s. f. *amore,* s. m.

PIG, s. [young swine] *porcello, porcastro, porchetto.*

A barrow-pig, *un verro.*

A sucking-pig, *un porcello lattante.*

A little sow-pig, *una porcella, una porcelletta.*

A pig-badger, *un tasso porco.*

A guinea-pig, *porcellino d' India.*

A pig-sty, *porcile,* s. m. *stanza dove si tengono i porci.*

A pig-nut, *tartufo,* s. m. *spezie di fungo.*

Pignut [which falls from the beech] *ghianda di faggio.*

A pig of lead, *una forma di piombo.*

He sleeps like a pig, *dorme come un ghiro.*

Pig-eyed [that has little eyes] *che ha gli occhi piccoli.*

To PIG [to farrow, to bring pigs] *figliare, parlando d' una troja.*

PI'GEON, s. [a fowl well known] *colombo,* s. m. *colomba,* s. f. *uccello noto.*

A young pigeon, *un piccione, pippione, un piccioncello, un piccioncino.*

A wild pigeon, *un colombaccio, colombo salvatico.*

A pigeon-house, *una colombaja, un colombajo*; *stanza dove stanno i colombi.*

A rock-pigeon, *un colombo terrajuolo.*

A pigeon-hole, *cestino,* s. m. *luogo dove covano i colombi.*

A pigeon-pie, *un pasticcio di piccioni.*

Pigeons herb, *verbena*; *erba colombaja.*

Pigeon's-foot [an herb] *piede colombino, e piede di colombino, sorta d' erba.*

PI'GEONLIVERED, adj. *mite, affabile, innocente.*

PI'GGIN, s. [a wooden vessel to milk in] *una secchia.*

PI'GMENT, s. [a sort of plant wherewith women colour their faces] *belletto,* s. m.

PI'GMY, s. *un pigmeo, un pimmeo, un nano.*

PI'GSNEY, s. [a fond title given to a girl] *una bella bambina*; *nome dato alle fanciulle per amorevolezza.*

PIKE, s. [a fish] *luccio,* s. m. *pesce noto.*

A pike [a long weapon for a foot-soldier, arm'd at the end with a little spear] *picca,* s. f. *sorta d' arme.*

To pass many pikes [to endure much hardship] *soffrir molti travagli.*

A pike-man, *soldato armato di picca.*

Pike-staff, *baston puntuto.*

It is as plain as a pike staff, *è chiaro come il sole nel mezzo dì.*

PI'KED, adj. [sharp, ending in a point] *acuto, puntuto.*

PI'LASTER, s. [a kind of square pillar made to jut out of a wall] *pilastro,* s. m. *parte dell' edificio, sul quale si reggono gli archi.*

PILCHARD, s. *v.* Pilcher, *quando significa pesce.*

PI'LCHER, s. [a covering for a saddle] *copertura da sella.*

A pilcher [a piece of flannel to wrap about a young child] *panno lano che serve per avvilupparvi i bambini.*

Pilcher, s. [a sea-fish somewhat like a her-

herring] *ſaracca*, s. f. *ſorta di peſce di mare, ſcriveſi anche* pilchard.

PILE, s. [heap] *mucchio, monte, faſcio*, s. m. *cataſta, bica, maſſa, ſtipa*, s. f.

A pile of wood, *una cataſta di legna*.

A ſtately pile of buildings, *un ſuperbo edificio*.

A pile [a great ſtake rammed into the earth for a foundation to build upon in marſhy grounds] *palo*, s. m.

To build upon piles, *fabbricar ſopra pali*.

To ſtrengthen with piles, *palificare, ficcar pali in terra a riparo*.

Croſs or pile [a ſort of game] *croce o teſta*.

Piles [a diſeaſes in the fundament, hemorrhoides] *emorroide, morice*, s. f.

Pilewort, s. [a plant] *ſcrofularia*, s. f.

Small pile-wort, *celidonia*, s. f.

To PILE up, *ammaſſare, ammonticchiare, ammucchiare, ammonticellare, accataſtare*.

To pile up wood, *accataſtare delle legna*.

Pile up, adj. *ammaſſato, ammonticchiato, ammonticellato, accataſtato*.

To PI'LFER [to ſteal things of ſmall value] *furare, rubare, e ſi dice di coſe frivole*.

PI'LFERED, adj. *furato, rubato*.

PI'LFERER, s. *ladro, ladroncello*, s. m.

PI'LFERING, s. *ladroneccio*, s. m. *ladroncelleria*, s. f.

PI'LGRIM, s. [one who travels through foreign countries to viſit holy places] *un pellegrino, un peregrino*.

To PI'LGRIM, *peregrinare, andar errando, andar in pellegrinaggio*.

PI'LGRIMAGE, s. *pellegrinaggio*, s. m. *pellegrinazione*, s. f.

PILL, s. [a medicine made up in a little ball] *pillola*, s. f. *piccola pallottolina medicinale*.

I was fain to ſwallow that pill, *mi fu forza inghiottire queſta pillola, o ſopportar queſto affronto*.

To PILL, } v. To pillage.
PI'LLAGE, }

To pill and poll [to uſe extortions] *ſcorticare, uſar violenza, diſtruggere con troppe gravezze*.

PI'LLAGE, s [plundering, plunder] *ſacco*, s. m. *preda*, s. f.

To PI'LLAGE [to plunder] *ſaccheggiare, dare il ſacco; porre o mettere a ſacco; predare*.

PI'LLAGED, adj. *ſaccheggiato*.

To give up a town to be pillaged, *mettere una città a ſacco, a ſaccomanno*.

PI'LLAGER, s. *ſaccheggiatore, ſaccheggiante*.

PI'LLAGING, s. *ſaccheggiamento, ſacco*, s. m. *il ſaccheggiare*.

PI'LLAR, s. [column] *pilaſtro*, s. m. *colonna*, s. f.

Pillar [ſupport] *colonna, appoggio, ſoſtegno*.

He is a pillar of the church, *egli è una colonna della chieſa*.

PI'LLING, s. [extortion] *eſtorſione, eſazione violenta, ruberia*, s. f. *ladroneccio*, s. m.

PI'LLION, s. [a kind of ſoft ſaddle for women to ride on] *ſella da donna*.

PI'LLORY, s. [an engine on which offenders ſtand to be examples of publick ſhame] *berlina*, s. f. *ſorta di gaſtigo che ſi da a' malfattori con eſporli al pubblico ſcherno*.

To PI'LLORY, *mettere alcuno alla berlina*.

PI'LLOW, s. [a ſort of cuſhion to lay one's head on] *guanciale, origliere*, s. m.

To adviſe with one's pillow, *conſigliarſi col guanciale*.

A little pillow, *un guancialetto*.

A PILLOW-BEER, } *fodera di guanciale*.
PI'LLOW-CASE, }

To PI'LLOW [to reſt any thing on a pillow] *poſare checcheſſia ſur un guanciale*.

PI'LOT, s. [ſteerſman] *piloto, nocchiere, e nocchiero*, s. m. *governator della nave*.

To PI'LOT a ſhip, *reggere, guidare, o governare una nave*.

PI'LOTAGE, s. [the office of a pilot] *l' ufizio del piloto; e talvolta il ſuo ſalario*.

PIMP, s. [procurer] *ruffiano, mezzano*.

To PIMP [to play the pimp] *fare il ruffiano*.

PI'MPERNEL, s. [an herb] *pimpinella*, s. f. *erba*.

PI'MPING, s. *ruffianeria*, s. f. *ruffianeſimo*, s. m.

Pimping, adj. [pitiful] *povero, meſchino, vile, di poco pregio, di poca ſtima*.

A pimping-fellow, *un uomo vile*.

PI'MPLE, s. [a little wheal] *picciolo, enfiatello, e viene comunemente nel viſo; puſtuletta*, s. f.

A face full of pimples, *un viſo pieno di puſtulette*.

A pimpled face, *un viſo pieno di puſtulette*.

PIN, s. [a ſmall braſs utenſil for faſtning on cloaths in dreſſing] *ſpilla*, s. f.

A pin of wood, nine of which make up a ſort of play, *ſbriglio*.

To play at nine-pins, *giuocare agli ſbrigli*.

Pin [peg] *caviglia, e cavicchia*, s. f. *cavicchio, piuolo*, s. m.

A pin to make a door faſt, *chiaviſtello*, s. m.

The pin of a ſun-dial, *ſtile, o ago d' oriuolo a ſole, lancetta*, s. f.

A pin in the eye, *cateratta, maglia*, s. m. *membrana che toglie all' occhio l' uſo del vedere, o il rende appannato*.

Axel-pin, or linch-pin of a wheel, *chiodo di ruota*.

A larding-pin, *lardaruola*, s. f. *ſtrumento da lardare*.

A rolling-pin [to make pye-cruſt] *matterello di paſticciere*.

A criſping-pin, *calamiſtro*, s. m. *ſtrumento di ferro ad uſo d' arricciar capelli*.

A pin [or peg] of a muſical inſtrument, *biſchero*, s. m. *legnetto congegnato nel manico d'uno ſtrumento muſicale, per attaccarvi le corde*.

'Tis not worth a pin *non vale una ſpilla, non vale un frullo*.

I care not a pin, I don't care a pin's head, *non me ne curo niente, me ne burlo; me ne rido*.

To be in a merry pin, *eſſe in zurlo, eſſer allegro e feſtoſo*.

A pin maker, *ſpillettajo*, s. m. *colui che fa, e vende gli ſpilletti*.

Pin duſt, *limatura*, s. f.

Pin fold [pen for ſheep] *parco da pecore*.

To PIN [to tie with a pin] *appuntare con degli ſpilletti*.

Pin in my gown, *appuntatemi la gonna*.

A dog that pins a bull [that faſtens at his noſe] *cane che afferra il toro pel muſo*.

To pin one's opinion upon another man's ſleeve, *ſtarſene al ſentimento d'alcuno, ſeguitare l'altrui parere*.

To pin one's reaſon to a woman's petticoat, *ſottometterſi in tutto e per tutto ad una donna*.

To pin a window [to make it faſt with an iron-pin] *ſerrare una fineſtra con caviglia*.

To pin up a gown, *ſuccignere una gonnella*.

To pin cattle [to pen up cattle] *rinchiudere il beſtiame*.

PI'NACLE, *v.* Pinnacle.

PI'NCER, s. [a ſurgeon's inſtrument to draw teeth] *cane*, s. m. *ſtrumento col quale i barbieri cavano i denti*.

PI'NCERS, s. [an iron tool for various uſes, as to pull out nails] *tanaglie*, s. f. *ſtrumento di ferro per uſo di ſtrignere, e di ſconficcare*.

Small pincers, *tanagliette*, s. f.

PINCH, s. *un pizzico un pizzicotto*.

To give one a pinch, *dar un pizzicotto ad uno*.

A pinch of ſnuff, *una preſa di tabacco*.

Pinch [ſtreight, great neceſſity] *ſtrettezza, anguſtia, neceſſità, miſeria*, s. f. *biſogno*, s m.

To be under the pinch of preſſing neceſſity, *trovarſi in grande anguſtia, eſſer ridotto all' eſtremo, eſſer coſtretto dal biſogno*.

His courage failed him upon the very pinch, *l' animo gli mancò quando più ne aveva di biſogno*.

To be at a pinch, *eſſer in pena e faſtidio, trovarſi all' eſtremità*.

To leave one in the lurch at a pinch, *laſciare uno in aſſo o in naſſo, abbandonarlo nel biſogno*.

Pinch-penny, } [a penny-father] *un avaro, uno ſpilorcio, un taccagno, un tanghero*.
A pinch-fiſt, }

A pinch-gut, } *un avaro che ſi rimprovera quel che mangia, un uomo che ſi laſcia morir di fame per non iſpendere*.
Pinch-belly, }

To PINCH [to nip hard with the fingers] *pizzicare, ſtrignere altrui le carni colle dita*.

My ſhoes pinch me, *le mie ſcarpe mi ſtringono troppo, mi fanno male*.

To pinch [to reduce to a pinch or neceſſity] *ſtrignere, ridurre in iſtrettezza, o neceſſità.*

I am now and then pinched for money, *mi trovo ſpeſſe volte in iſtrettezza per danari.*

To pinch [nip or taunt] *pugnere, offendere altrui mordendo con detti.*

To pinch one of meat, *fare ſtare, o tenere a ſtecchetto, tenere altrui col poco, magramente, e con iſcarſità di vitto.*

To pinch one's guts, verb neut. *riſparmiare, privarſi del neceſſario, laſciarſi patire, o morir di fame.*

To pinch ſomewhat from one's ſelf, *privarſi, o aſtenerſi di qualche coſa.*

To pinch the hair off, *ſtrappare il pelo.*

To pinch [to ſuffer, to be at a pinch] *patire, ſoffrire, ſtentare, trovarſi nel biſogno.*

PI'NCHED, adj. *pizzicato, v.* To pinch.

Pinched with hunger, *affamato, morto di fame.*

PINCUSHION, s. [pincaſe] *cuſcinetto ripieno di cruſca, di lana, o di altra coſa da tenervi le ſpille fitte dentro per uſo quotidiano.*

PINDA'RICAL, } adj. *pindarico.*
PINDA'RICK, }

A pindarick ode, *un' ode pindarica.*

PI'NDUST, s. [ſmall particles of metal made by cutting pins] *limatura; particelle di metallo che ſi fanno quando ſannoſi le ſpille.*

PINE, } s. *pino,* s. m. *albero noto.*
PINE-TREE, }

Wild pine, *pino ſalvatico.*

Pine grove, *pineta,* s. f. *pineto,* s. m. *ſelva di pini.*

Pine-apple, s. *pina,* s. f. *frutto del pino.*

The kernel of a pine-apple, *pinocchio,* s. m. *ſeme del pino.*

PINE-APPLE, *è anche chiamato l'ananaſſo per qualche eſterior ſomiglianza che ha colla pina, quantunque non ſia frutto d' albero alcuno, ma d' una poca di pianticella quaſi tutta foglie poco più alta di due palmi.*

To PI'NE, to pine away [to languiſh, to conſume and waſte away] *ſtruggerſi, languire, ſvenire, mancar di forze, infiebolire, perder il vigore, immortire,* pref. *languiſco, ſvengo, infieboliſco, immortiſco,* pret. *mi ſtruſſi.*

To pine one's ſelf to death, *morire di dolore.*

Pined away, adj. *ſtrutto, languito, ſvenuto, infiebolito, immortito.*

PI'NEAL, adj. *pineale.*

The pineal gland, *la glandula pineale, che Carteſio ſognò foſſe la ſede dell' anima noſtra.*

PINE'FEATHERED, adj. [not fledged, having the feathers yet only beginning to ſhoot] *che non ha ancor meſſo le penne; le cui penne cominciano appena a ſpuntare; e diceſi degli uccelli.*

PI'NFOLD, s. *luogo in cui ſi rinchiudono gli animali.*

Pining, } s. *languidore, languore,* s. m. *languidezza,* s. f.
Pining away, }

Pining, adj. *languente, che languiſce.*

PI'NION, s. [the nut or leſſer wheel of a clock or watch, that plays in the teeth of another] *rocchetto d' oriuolo, la ruota più piccola d' un' oriuolo.*

Pinions of a fowl, *l' ali d' un uccello, i vanni.*

To PI'NION, *inchiodare, attaccar con chiodo o con caviglia.*

To pinion one [to bind his arms faſt] *legar le braccia ad alcuno.*

PI'NIONED, adj. *che ha le braccia legate.*

PINK, s. [a flower] *garofano,* s. m. *ſpezie di fiore.*

Pink-ey'd, adj. *che ha gli occhi piccoli.*

Pink, s. [a ſort of little ſwift ſailing ſhip] *pinco,* s. m. *fuſta,* s. f.

Pink-colour, *color di carne.*

A pink [a ſea-fiſh] *gobbio,* s. m. *peſce di mare.*

To PINK [to wink with the eye] *batter gli occhi, palpebrizzare.*

To pink [to cut cloth, or ſilk, with variety of figures, in round holes] *tagliuzzare, minutamente tagliare.*

PI'NKED, adj. *tagliuzzato.*

PI'NKER, s. *tagliuzzatore,* s. m.

PI'NKING, s. *tagliuzzamento,* s. m. *il tagliuzzare.*

PI'NMONEY, s. [money allowed to a wife for her private expences without account] *ſpille,* f. f. pl. *danaro che ha una moglie per ſuo uſo proprio, e di cui non ha a render conto.*

PI'NNACE, s. [a ſmall veſſel going with ſails and oars] *ſorta di barca.*

PI'NNACLE, s. [or battlement] *pinacolo, e pinnacolo, comignolo,* s. m. *la parte più alta de' tetti.*

The pinnacle of glory, *il colmo della gloria.*

Pinnacles of walls, *merli,* s. m.

PI'NNED, adj. [from to pin] *appuntato, v.* To pin.

PI'NNER, s. [a maker of pins] *ſpillettajo,* s. m.

Pinner, s. [a ſort of dreſs for women's heads] *ſorta di cuffia.*

PI'NNOCK, s. [a bird, called alſo tom-tit] *ſorta d' uccello.*

PI'NSON, s. [a ſort of ſhoe without heels, a pump] *ſcarpetta,* s. f.

PINT, s. [a ſort of meaſure] *foglietta,* s. f.

Half a pint, *mezza foglietta.*

PIONE'ER, s. [a labourer taken up for the uſe of an army] *guaſtatore,* s. m. *colui, che ſeguita l' eſercito, a fine d' accomodar le ſtrade, far fortificazione, e ſimili.*

PI'ONY, *v.* Peony.

PI'OUS, adj. [godly] *pio, religioſo, divoto.*

A pious man, *un uomo pio.*

PI'OUSLY, adv. *piamente, religioſamente, divotamente.*

PIP, s. [a diſeaſe in the tongue of poultry] *pipita,* s. f. *malore, che viene a' polli ſulla punta della lingua.*

Pip [any ſpot, or mark upon cards] *macchia nelle carte.*

To PIP [to take away the pip] *levar via la pipita.*

To pip, v. n. [to chirp or cry as a bird] *garrire o piare come fanno gli augelletti e i polli.*

PIPE, s. [any long hollow body; a tube] *ogni coſa tonda, lunga, e vuota dentro; un tubo.*

Pipe, s. [to ſmoak tobacco with] *pippa,* s. f.

Pipe [conduit] *condotto, aquidotto,* s. m.

Water-pipe, *condotto d' acqua.*

The wind-pipe [the pipe of the lungs] *gorgozzule, gola, eſofago, la canna della gola.*

To have a fine pip [or voice] *avere una bella voce.*

A pipe of wine, *una botte di vino.*

Pipe [flute] *zampogna,* s. f.

To play upon the pipe, *zampognare.*

Pipe [in the Exchequer, a roll] *ruolo,* s. m.

A bag-pipe, *una cornamuſa, una piva.*

A gliſter-pipe, *cannella di ſerviziale.*

To PIPE [to play on the pipe] *zampognare, ſuonar la zampogna.*

To pipe [to have a ſhrill ſound] *aver un ſuono ſottile o acuto.*

PI'PER, s. [a player on a pipe] *zampognatore.*

Bag-piper, *un ſonator di zampogna.*

PI'PING, *il zampognare.*

Piping, adj. ex. piping hot, *caldo caldo.*

PI'PKIN, s. [earthen-pot] *pignatta, pentola,* s. f.

PI'PPIN, s. [an excellent ſort of apple] *mela appia.*

PI'QUANT, adj. [quick, ſharp] *piccante.*

Piquant wine, *vino piccante.*

Piquant ſatyr, *una ſatira pugnente.*

PI'QUE, s. [an ill-will; an offence taken; petty malevolence] *picca; mal talento; offeſa preſa; picciola malevolenza.*

Pique [a ſtrong paſſion] *collera veemente.*

Pique [point, nicety, punctilio] *puntiglio, puntigliuzzo.*

To PIQUE, *piccare, deſtar collera e ſtizza.*

To pique, *offendere, irritare.*

To pique, *piccarſi, farſi un punto di checcheſſia.*

To PIQUE'ER [to ſkirmiſh] *ſcaramucciare.*

To piqueer [to ogle] *guardare ſott' occhio, occhieggiare.*

PIQUE'ERER, s. *un rubatore, un ſaccommanno.*

PIQUE'ERING, s. *ſcaramuccia,* s. f.

PI'QUET, s. *giuoco di carte, picchetto.*

PI'RACY, s. [the trade of a pirate] *corſo,* s. m. *il corſeggiare.*

To exerciſe piracy, *corſeggiare, andare in corſo, fare il corſale.*

PI'RATE, s. [ſea robber] *corſale, corſaro, pirato,* s. m.

To drive a pirate's trade, *corſeggiare, andare in corſo, fare il corſale.*

PIRA'TICAL, adj. *di pirato, o corſale.*

PI'RA-

PISCARY, [in law, a liberty of fiſhing] *il privilegio della peſca, la libertà di peſcare.*

PI'SCES, s. [one of the twelve ſigns of the zodiack] *peſce,* s. m. *uno de' dodici ſegno del zodiaco.*

PI'SMIRE, s. [ant] *formica.*

PISS, s. [urine] *orina,* s. f.

To piſs [to make water] *orinare.*

PISTA'CHIO, s. fiſtich-nut [a kind of ſmall nut] *piſtacchio,* s. m. *frutto noto.*

PISTOL, s. [a ſort of ſmall gun] *piſtola,* s. f. *arme da fuoco.*

Piſtol-caſe, *fonda di piſtola.*

Piſtol-ſhot, *piſtolettata, colpa di piſtola.*

A ſmall piſtol, *una piſtoletta.*

A large piſtol, *un piſtolottò.*

To PI'STOL [to ſhoot with a piſtol] *tirar piſtolettate.*

PI'STOLE, s. [a French or Spaniſh piece of gold] *doppia di Francia, o di Spagna.*

PIT, s. [a hole in the ground] *foſſa,* s. f. *ſpazio di terreno cavato.*

To be at the pit's brink [to be very old] *avere un piede nella foſſa, eſſer molto vecchio.*

The pit of the ſtomach, *la bocca dello ſtomaco.*

A little pit to keep fiſh in, *un vivajo.*

The arm-pit, *l'aſcella,* s. f. *il concavo dell' appiccatura del braccio colla ſpalla.*

A bottomleſs pit, *un abbiſſo.*

The pit in a play-houſe, *la platéa, il pianterreno d'un teatro.*

A coal-pit, *una miniera di carbone.*

A ſand-pit, *un renajo, una zavorra, bolgia di terreno arenoſo.*

A clay-pit, *luogo argilloſo.*

A pit-fall [a gin to catch birds] *ſchiaccia,* s. f. *ſorta di ſtrumento por prendere uccelli.*

PI'TAPAT [a word expreſſing the frequent beating of the heart] *parola inventata per eſprimere il frequente palpitamento del cuore per ſubita paura.*

My heart goes pitapat [pit to pat] *tremo di paura, il cuore mi palpita.*

PITCH, s. [a gluiſh black ſubſtance] *pece,* s. f. *ragia di pino.*

Stone-pitch, *pece dura.*

Pitch-tree, *pino, zampino,* s. m. *albero, che fa la pece.*

Pitch-fork, *forca,* s. f. *forcone,* s. m.

Pitch [ſtature, height] *altezza,* s. f.

The higheſt pitch [or top] of a thing, *il più alto grado, la cima, la ſommità.*

To ſtrain one's ſkill to the higheſt pitch, *sforzarſi, fare ogni sforzo, adoperare tutto il ſuo ingegno.*

Birds that fly to a very high pitch, *uccelli che volano molto alto.*

The pitch of a hill, *la cima d'un monte.*

To PITCH [to do over with pitch] *impeciare, impegolare, impiaſtrar di pece.*

To pitch a wheel, *impeciare una ruota.*

To pitch a ſhip, *ſpalmare un vaſcello.*

To pitch a tent, *piantare una tenda.*

To pitch a net, *ſpiegare una rete.*

To pitch a camp, *accampare, porſi a campo, porre gli alloggiamenti alla compagna, attendarſi.*

To pitch [to pave] *laſtricare.*

To pitch upon a thing [to chuſe it] *appigliarſi, o attenerſi a che che ſi ſia, ſtarſi a che che ſi ſia, ſceglierla.*

I pitch upon this hat, *io ſcelgo queſto cappello, o queſto cappello fa per me.*

To pitch [or fall] upon one's head, *caſcare colla teſta all' ingiù.*

PI'TCHED, adj. *impeciato, impegolato,* v. To pitch.

A pitched fight or battle, *battaglia ſchierata.*

PI'TCHER, s. [an earthen water-pot] *brocca,* s. f. *vaſo di terra cotta da portare acqua.*

The pitcher goes ſo often to the well, that it comes home broken at laſt, *tanto va la ſecchia al pozzo che vi laſcia il manico; tanto va la capra zoppa che nel lupo alfin s'intoppa; tanto torna la gatta al lardo ch' alla fine vi laſcia la zampa.*

PI'TCHFORK, *forca,* s. f. *forcone,* s. m.

PI'TCHING, s. *l'impeciare,* v. To pitch.

Pitching-pence [a duty paid in fairs and markets for the ſelling of commodities] *dazio che ſi paga nei mercati, e nelle fiere per vendere le mercanzie.*

PI'TCHY, adj. [of pitch] *di pece.*

PI'TIOUS, adj. [pitiful, wretched] *miſero, povero, meſchino.*

'Tis very piteous with him, *egli è in un miſero, o povero ſtato.*

PI'TEOUSLY, adv. *miſeramente, poveramente, meſchinamente.*

PI'TFAL, s. *abbiſſo, fondo cupo, precipizio.*

PITH, s. [marrow] *midolla,* s. f. *midollo,* s. m.

Pith of a tree, *il midollo d'un albero.*

To take the pith out, *ſmidollare, tor via la midolla.*

The pith of a quill [the light ſtuff that is within it] *anima della penna.*

PI'THILY, adv. *fortemente, vigoroſamente, energicamente, nervoſamente, virilmente.*

PI'THINESS, s. *midolla, forza, nervoſità, energia,* s. f. *vigore,* s. m.

PITHY, adj. *midolloſo, pien di midollo.*

PI'THLESS, adj. *ſmidollato, ſenza midolla.*

PI'TIED, v. Pity'd.

PI'TIFUL, adj. [that deſerves to be pitied] *compaſſionevole, che muove a compaſſione, miſerabile, meſchino.*

A pitiful fellow, *un barone, un uomo da niente, un uomo dozzinale.*

Pitiful [compaſſionate] *pietoſo, pieno di pietà.*

PI'TIFULLY, adj. [wretchedly ill] *miſeramente, poveramente, meſchinamente.*

Pitifully [with pity] *compaſſionevolmente, pietoſamente, con pietà.*

PI'TIFULNESS, s. *miſericordia, pietà,* s. f.

Let the pitifulneſs of thy great mercy help us [an expreſſion uſed in the common prayer] *la tua gran miſericordia ci liberi da queſti lacci.*

PI'TILESS, adj [unmerciful] *ſpietato, ſenza pietà, crudele, inumano, fiero.*

PI'TTANCE, s. [the ſmall portion of victuals given to monks in colleges] *pietanza,* s. f. *quel ſervizio di vivandà, che ſi da alle menſe de' clauſtrali.*

Small pittance of any thing, *particella, piccola parte, porzioncella,* s. f.

PITU'ITOUS, adj. [full of phlegm] *pituitoſo, che abbonda di pituita.*

PI'TTED, adj. ex. pitted with ſmall-pox, *butterato.*

PI'TUITE, s. [phlegm] *pituita, flemma,* s. f.

PI'TY, s. [compaſſion] *pietà, compaſſione,* s. f.

To move to pity, *muovere a pietà o a compaſſione.*

Pity [ſad thing, misfortune] *peccato,* s. m.

It is pity he is not bigger, *è un peccato, che non ſia più grande.*

To PI'TY [to take pity of] *compatire, aver compaſſione, compiagnere, e compiangere, lamentare,* preſ. *compatiſco, compiango,* pret. *compianſi.*

I pity your misfortune, *compatiſco, o compiango la voſtra diſgrazia.*

PI'TYABLE, adj [to be pity'd] *compaſſionevole, degno di compaſſione.*

PI'TYED, adj. *compianto, pianto, lamentato.*

It is better to be envy'd than pity'd, *è meglio far invidia che non compaſſione.*

PI'VOT, s. [a piece of iron like a top, ſet into the ſole or ring at the bottom of a gate] *perno,* s. m. *ferro ritondo, ſul qual ſi reggono le porte, o altre coſe che ſi volgono in giro.*

PIX, s. *piſſide, in cui ſi tengono l' oſtie conſecrate.*

PLACABI'LITY, s. [eaſineſs of being pacified or appeaſed] *facilità a placarſi.*

PLA'CABLE, adj. [eaſy to be pacified or appeaſed] *placabile, atto ad eſſer placato.*

PLA'CARD, } s. [a proclamation or
PLA'CART, } ordinance] *proclamazione, bando, editto.*

Placard, in law [a particular licenſe, by which a man is allowed to ſhoot with a gun, or uſe guns] *licenza ſpeziale conceſſa a qualcheduno di poterſi ſervire d' arme da fuoco a caccia.*

PLACE, s. [ſpace or room in which a perſon or thing is] *luogo, poſto,* s. m. *termine contenente i corpi.*

To yield one's place, *ceder il ſuo luogo.*

A pleaſant place, *un luogo ameno.*

A trading place, *una piazza di negozio, o mercantile.*

In ſome place, *in qualche luogo.*

From what place, *donde, da qual luogo.*

In what place, *dove, in qual luogo.*

In another place, *altrove, in un altro luogo.*

To put one in another's place, *mettere uno nel luogo d' un altro.*

Were I in your place, *s' io foſſi voi, s' io foſſi nel luogo voſtro; s' io foſſi ne' voſtri piedi.*

A place of scripture, *luogo o passo di scrittura.*
Place [town, hold] *piazza, fortezza*, s. f.
Turin is a strong place, *Torino è una piazza forte.*
Place [employment] *impiego*, s. m. *carica*, s. f.
To give place [to yield] *cedere, dar luogo.*
This must give place to that, *ciò non è da paragonarsi con questo.*
To take place of one, *precedere, andare avanti ad uno, avere il luogo, tenere il luogo, seder nel primo luogo.*
A fore place, *parte offesa.*
A shady place, *luogo ombroso.*
A place of arms [a strong city or town which is pitched upon for the chief magazine of any army] *piazza d'arme.*
To PLACE [to put away] *mettere, locare, allogare, assegnare il luogo, collocare*, pret. *misi.*
Where have you placed your books? *dove avete messi i vostri libri?*
Place it to my account, *mettetelo a mio conto.*
To place one [to put him to service] *allogare uno, acconciarlo al servizio d'altri, metterlo a servire.*
PLA'CED, adj. *messo, locato, allogato, collocato.*
PLA'CKET, s. [the fore-part of a woman's petticoat] *la parte d'avanti d'un abito da donna.*
PLAD, s. a Scotch plad [a kind of cloak] *striscia di panno lungo in circa tre braccia che gli abitanti della parte settentrionale di Scozia portano in luogo di mantello.*
Plad [a sort of Irish or Scotch stuff] *spezie di sargia che si fabbrica in Irlanda, e in Iscozia.*
PLAGIA'RIAN, adj. Ex. the plagiarian law [against plagiaries] *le legge contro plagiarj, o contro quelli che rubano i fanciulli.*
PLA'GIARISM, s. [theft; literary adoption of the thoughts or works of another] *ladrocinio letterario; l'appropriarsi i pensieri o le opere letterarie altrui.*
PLA'GIARY, s. [kidnapper] *un ladro di fanciulli.*
Plagiary [a book thief] *un plagiario, un che s'arroga le opere, o gli scritti d'un altro.*
PLAGUE, s. [a pestilential disease] *la peste.*
Those sort of people are the plague of human kind, *questa sorta di gente è la peste del genere umano.*
A plague sore, *gavocciolo*, s. m. *quell' enfiato che fa la peste.*
Plague [troublesome man] *un fastidioso, un importuno.*
Plague [punishment] *flagello, tormento, gastigo*, s. m.
To PLAGUE [to infest with pestilence] *infettar di peste, appestare, ammorbare.*
To plague [to vex, to teaze, to torment] *fastidire, tormentare, importunare, tribolare, affliggere, travagliare*, pref. *fastidisco.*

PLA'GUED, adj. *fastidito, tormentato, importunato, afflitto, travagliato.*
PLA'GUILY, adv. *fortemente, grandemente, gagliardamente.*
PLA'GUING, adj. *fastidio*, s. m.
PLAGUY, adj. *cattivo, pernicioso, pericoloso.*
PLAICE, s. [a sea-fish] *sorta di pesce di mare.*
PLAI'D, s. *v.* Plad.
PLAIN, adj [even, or smooth] *piano eguale in ogni sua parte.*
A plain superficies, *una superficie piana*
Plain song [in musick] *canto fermo.*
Plain [without ornament] *semplice, senza ornamento, schietto, uniforme.*
A plain suit of cloaths, *un abito schietto, ordinario, modesto.*
Plain linen, *biancheria ordinaria, senza merletti.*
A plain man, a man that goes plain, *un uomo semplicemente vestito.*
Plain [clear] *piano, chiaro, intelligibile.*
A plain man, *un uomo alla buona.*
A plain [downright, sincere, honest] man, *un uomo franco, sincero, ingenuo, schietto.*
The plain truth, *la pura verità.*
Plain [homely] *comunale, dozzinale, volgare.*
Plain dealing [fair and honest dealing] *equità, sincerità, schiettezza, franchezza, probità, buona fede.*
A plain dealer, *un galantuomo, un uomo dabbene, franco, schietto, sincero.*
In plain terms, *chiaramente, schiettamente, spiattellatamente.*
To be plain with you, *per dirvela liberamente, schiettamente, o francamente.*
Plain, adv. Ex. to speak plain [or distinctly] *parlar chiaramente, o distintamente.*
To go plain [to wear plain cloaths] *andar semplicemente vestito, andar vestito alla buona.*
PLAIN, s. [a level extent of country] *pianura*, s. f. *campagna rasa.*
To PLAIN [to lament, to wail] *compiangere, mostar compassione d'altrui con lamenti.*
To plain [to level, to make even] *livellare, uguagliare, render a livello; piallare.*
PLA'INER, PLA'INEST [the comparative and superlative of plain] *più piano, pianissimo.*
PLA'INLY, adv. [freely] *francamente, spiattellatamente, ingenuamente, liberamente, sinceramente, schiettamente.*
Plainly [manifestly] *pianamente, chiaramente, evidentemente.*
Plainly [without ornament] *semplicemente, schiettamente, senza ornamento.*
PLA'INNESS, s. [evenness] *egualità, parità*, s. f.
The plainness [or clearness] of a discourse, *la chiarezza d'un discorso.*
The plainness of one's cloaths, *la semplicità nel vestire.*
PLAINT, s. [complaint, lamentation] *querela, lamentanza, doglienza*, s. f.
PLA'INTFUL, adj. *querulo, dolente.*
PLA'INTIF, s [he that commences a suit in law against another] *colui che chiama in giudizio un altro per danno o ingiuria che ha o pretende aver ricevuta; e la sua parte contraria si chiama* DEFENDANT; *l'uno dal lagnarsi, l'altro dal difendersi.*
Plaintiff, adj. for plaintive; *voce non più usata.*
Plaintive, adj. [complaining, lamenting, expressive of sorrow] *dolente, mesto, che si lagna.*
PLA'INWORK, s. *ricamo di filo sopra la semplice tela.*
PLAIT, s. [fold] *piega*, s. f.
A plait of hair, *una treccia di capelli.*
To PLAIT [to fold] *piegare.*
To plait the hair, *intrecciare i capelli.*
PLA'ITED, adj. *piegato, intrecciato.*
PLAITING, s. *piegamento*, s. m. *il piegare, l'intrecciare.*
PLAN, s. [draught] *pianta*, s. f. *il piano d'un edifizio.*
The plan of a city, *la pianta d'una città.*
Plan [scheme or draught of a project] *disegno, projetto*, s m.
PLA'NCHED, adj. *fatto d'asse, fatto di tavola.*
PLA'NCHER, s. [plank, board] *pancone*, s. m. *asse, tavola*, s. f.
PLANE, s. [a joiner's tool to smooth boards with] *pialla*, s. f. *strumento di legnajuoli col quale puliscono, e fanno lisci i legnami.*
Plane [in geometry, a plane surface] *piano*, s. m. *che ha nella superficie egualità in ogni sua parte.*
To PLANE [to make smooth with a joiner's plane] *piallare, pulire, e far lisci i legnami colla pialla*, pref. *pulisco.*
To plane [as a bird that flies or hovers without moving her wings] *librarsi sopra l'ali, volare senza quasi muover l'ali.*
The plane-tree, s. [a tall sort of tree] *platano*, s. m. *sorta d'albero introdotto in Inghilterra dal celebre Bacone di Verulamio.*
PLA'NED, adj. *piallato, pulito, lasciato.*
PLA'NER, s. *piallatore*, s. m.
PLA'NET, s. [a wandering star] *pianeta*, s. f. *stella errante.*
To be born under a lucky planet, *esser nato sotto una benigna stella.*
Planet-struck [blasted] *golpato, guasto dalla golpe.*
Planet struck [astonished, amazed] *attonito, stupito, stupefatto, stordito.*
PLA'NETARY, adj. [belonging to the planets] *di pianeta, attenente a pianeta.*
PLA'NIMETRY, s. [the art of measuring all sorts of plain surfaces] *arte di misurare ogni superficie piana.*
To PLA'NISH, s. [to make plain as silver-smiths and pewterers do] *adeguare, far piano, ripulire, lisciare.*
To planish a dish, *rendere un piatto liscio.*
PLA'NISPHERE, s. [a sphere or globe described upon a plain surface] *sfera piana, o planisfera.*
PLANK, s. [a piece of timber sawed] *piana, asse, tavola*, s. f. *pancone*, s. m.
To

To PLANK, *tavolare, coprir con tavole.*

PLA'NKED, adj. *tavolato.*

PLANT, s. [an herb, or young tree to set] *pianta*, s. f. *nome generico d' alberi e d' erbe.*

A plant of fruit, *una pianta fruttifera.*

The plant of the foot, *la pianta del piede.*

Plant [young tree to set] *ramicello, o rampollo tolto dall albero per piantarlo.*

A young or small plant, *pianterella, pianticella.*

Plant animal, *piantanimale, zoofito*, s. m. *sorta di vivente che ha la natura mezzana tra le piante, e gli animali.*

To PLANT [to set trees or herbs] *piantare, porre dentro alla terra i rami degli alberi e delle piante.*

To plant the christian faith in a country] *piantare la fede cristiana in un paese.*

To plant the cannon, *piantare l' artiglierie.*

To plant colonies [to make plantations] *stabilire colonie.*

To plant, verb neut. *piantarsi, stabilirsi.*

PLA'NTAIN, s. [an herb] *piantaggine*, s. f. *spezie d' erba.*

PLA'NTAL, adj. [vegetative] *vegetativo, appartenente a pianta.*

PLA'NTAR, adj. [belonging to the sole of the foot] *attenente alla pianta del piede.*

The plantar arteries or muscles, *le arterie o muscoli della pianta del piede.*

PLANTA'TION, s. [a colony or settlement of people in a foreign country] *piantazione, colonia*, s. f.

PLA'NTED, adj. *piantato*, v. To plant.

PLA'NTER, s. [one that plants or sets] *piantatore*, s. m. *che pianta.*

Planter [one that has a plantation] *il padrone d' una colonia.*

PLA'NTING, s. *il piantare.*

PLASH, s. [a place full of standing water, a puddle] *pantano*, s. m. *palude*, s f.

To PLASH [to dash with water] *sprazzare, bagnare gettando minutissime gocce d' acqua, spruzzare.*

To plash [among gardeners, to bend] *piegare.*

To plash trees, *dibruscare li alberi.*

To plash mortar, *rimescolare la calcina.*

PLA'SHED, adj. *sprazzato, bagnato, spruzzato*, v. To plash.

PLA'SHY, adj. *pantanoso, melmoso.*

PLA'STER, s. [an outward remedy for sores] *impiastro*, s. m.

Plaster, s. *stucco*; *sorta di pasta fatta di calce o di gesso polverizzato; con cui s' intonacan le mura e si fanno altri lavori.*

To PLA'STER [to overlay as with plaster] *intonacare, coprire l' arricciato del muro con calce o gesso ridotto in pasta*; *e si prende anche figurativamente per impiastricciare, o coprire la superficie di checchessia.*

To plaster, *porre un impiastro medicinale.*

PLA'STERER, s. *muratore, la cui principal faccenda è intonacar le mura.*

Plasterer, s. *statuario in gesso, o stuccatore.*

PLA'STICAL, } adj. [skilful in mak-
PLA'STICK, } ing statues of earth] *pratico, esperto nell' arte di fare figure di gesso.*

Plastick, adj. *atto a dar forma.*

Plastick, s. [the art of making figures in clay or earth] *arte di fare figure di getto, o di gesso.*

PLA'STRON, s. [a fencing-master's breast-leather, for his scholars to push at] *piastrone*, s. m.

PLAT, s. [plot of ground] *campicello, camperello*, s. m.

PLAT, adj. ex. the plat-veins of a horse, *le vene ove si salassano i cavalli.*

PLATE, s. [all vessels made of silver or gold] *argenteria*, s. m. *vasellamento d' argento o d' oro.*

A plate to be run for, *pezzo d' argenteria che si da per premio d' una corsa.*

A plate to eat upon, *un tondo.*

A plate [a flat piece of metal] *piastra, lama, lamina*, s. f. *metallo ridotto a sottigliezza.*

A copper-plate, *una stampa di rame.*

Plate-buttons, *bottoni d' oro, o d' argento.*

A plate-candlestick, *candeliere con manico.*

To PLATE [to cover with a thin plate of gold or silver] *inargentare, indorare.*

To plate brass money, *inargentare, o indorare della moneta falsa.*

To plate a metal [to bring it into plates] *ridurre il metallo a sottigliezza, in piastre.*

PLATED, adj. *inargentato, o indorato, coperto con foglie d' oro o d' argento.*

A plated half crown, *un mezzo scudo inargentato.*

Plated metal, *metallo ridotto in piastre.*

PLA'TEN, s. [the plate of a printer's press] *piastretta di stampatore.*

PLA'TFORM, s. [in fortification a raising of earth made level on the rampart on which the cannon is planted] *piattaforma*, s. f.

Platform, s. [a kind of terrass-walk on the top of a building] *terrazzo*, s. m.

PLA'TTER, s. [a wooden dish] *tafferia*, s. f. *vaso di legno di forma simile al bacino.*

PLA'USIBLE, adj. [seemingly fair and honest] *plausibile, spezioso.*

PLA'USIBLENESS, } s. *qualità plau-*
PLAUSIBI'LITY, } *sibile, o che renda una cosa plausibile.*

PLA'USIBLY, adj. [with applause] *con applauso.*

PLAY, s. [divertisement] *giuoco, divertimento, passatempo*, s. m. *ricreazione*, s. f.

Publick plays [shows and spectacles] *giuochi, spettacoli.*

Play [stage-play, comedy] *una commedia, o tragedia*, s. f. *poema rappresentativo.*

To go to a play, *andare alla commedia.*

To beat one at his own play, *battere alcuno colle sue proprie arme.*

I fear some false play from, *temo che non ci faccia qualche burla, o qualche tiro.*

To give one fair play [to let him do his worst] *lasciar fare ad uno, dargli ogni vantaggio che desidera.*

To hold or to keep one in play [to amuse him] *tenere uno à bada.*

A play fellow, *compagno di giuoco.*

A play-day, *giorno di festa.*

A play-house, *un teatro.*

To PLAY [to divert by play] *giocare, giuocare.*

To play at cards, *giuocare alle carte.*

To play or set a game, *giuocare una partita.*

To play sure [to go on sure grounds] *giuocare a giuoco sicuro.*

To play the fool [to be full of game or mad tricks] *trastullare, scherzare, burlare.*

To play fair, *giuocare alla scoperta, o francamente.*

To play foul, *truffare, giuntare, ingannare.*

To play upon a musical instrument, *sonare d' uno strumento.*

To play a play, *rappresentare una commedia.*

To play the knave, *fare delle furberie, o delle furfanterie.*

To play the whore, *far la puttana, prostituirsi.*

To play the truant, *fuggir la scuola, spender il tempo in vano.*

To play one a trick, *fare una burla, o un tiro ad alcuno.*

To play the wanton, *trastullare, vezzeggiare.*

To play the hypocrite, *far l' ippocrita, fare il collo torto, far il graffiasanti, graffiare il santi; far il leccamarmi e il baciapile, far il barchettone, il santinfilza; masticar paternostri.*

To play the engines [to set them a going] *mettere in opera le macchine.*

To play upon a bastion with great guns, *battere un bastione con cannoni grossi.*

Our cannon plaid upon the enemies, *la nostra artiglieria faceva fuoco sopra i nemici.*

To play with a man at his own weapons, *battere alcuno colle sue proprie arme.*

To play pranks, *far delle sue; dare negli spropositi, far de' soprusi.*

To play the thief, *fare il ladro, rubare.*

To play away, *giuocare, perdere al giuoco.*

To play the child, *dar nelle ragazzate.*

To play upon [to jeer, to banter] *burlarsi d' uno, beffarsi di lui.*

PLAY'D, or PLAID, adj. *giucato, giuocato.*

PLA'YER, s. *giucatore, giuocatore*, s. m.

A player upon an instrument, *sonator di qualche strumento.*

Player [one that acts in a playhouse] *un commediante, una commediante.*

PLA'YING, s. *il giuocare.*

PLEA, s. [that which either party alledgeth for himself at court] *ragioni, o pruove che sono allegate per la difesa d' una causa, piate,* s. m.

Plea [excuse] *scusa,* s. f. *pretesto, colore,* s. m.

To PLEAD [to put in plea at law] *litigare, piatire, cimentare, esperimentare le sue ragioni in giudicio.*

To plead guilty or not guilty, *confessare o ributtare l' accusa, rispondere se uno è colpevole o innocente.*

To plead [to alledge or pretend] *allegare, pretendere, scusarsi,* pret. *pretesi.*

To plead ignorance, *allegar causa d' ignoranza.*

He pleaded poverty, *si scusò sopra la sua povertà.*

I answer to that I can plead for myself, *in risposta di ciò posso dire per mia difesa.*

Pleaded, adj. *piatito, litigato.*

A PLE'ADER, s. [a counsellor at law, a barrister] *un causidico, un avvocato.*

PLE'ADING, s. *piato,* s. m. *il piatire.*

PLE'ASANT, adj. [agreeable] *piacevole, grato, affabile, cortese, trattabile, gioviale, allegro.*

He is a pleasant man, *egli è un uomo molto piacevole o gioviale.*

Pleasant [delightful] *piacevole, grato, ameno, dilettevole.*

That house stands upon a pleasant place, *quella casa è fabbricata in luogo molto piacevole o ameno.*

Pleasant [impertinent, ridiculous] *impertinente, ridicolo.*

PLE'ASANTLY, adv. *piacevolmente, cortesemente, giovialmente, allegramente.*

PLE'ASANTNESS, } s. *piacevolezza, gentilezza, affabilità, cortesia.*
PLE'ASANTRY,

To PLEASE [to content, to satisfy] *piacere, esser grato, aggradire, soddisfare,* pret. *piacqui, soddisfeci,* pres. *aggradisco.*

That wine pleases me, *questo vino mi piace o m' aggradisce.*

To please one [to oblige him] *far piacere ad alcuno, servirlo in qualche cosa.*

To please one [to be complaisant to him] *compiacere, far la voglia altrui, far servigio, far cosa grata.*

To please [to be pleased] *compiacersi, dilettarsi, prender gusto e piacere in una cosa o d' una cosa.*

Will you please to drink, *si compiaccia di bere, abbia la bontà di bere.*

As you please, *come vi piacerà, voi siete padrone.*

You are pleased to say so, *voi dite ciò per divertirvi, o per burla.*

If you please, *se volete, se v' è grato, se ciò è di vostro gusto.*

If God pleases, *piacendo o Dio, se piace a Dio.*

Let him please himself, *faccia quel che vuole.*

Please yourself, *fate come vi piace.*

PLE'ASED, adj. *contento, soddisfatto.*

Hard to be pleased, *difficile a contentare, bisbetico, fantastico.*

The devil himself is good when he is pleased, *il diavolo stesso è buono quando li pare e piace.*

To be pleased with a thing, *rimaner soddisfatto, e contento d' una cosa.*

I never was more pleased with any thing, *non vi fu mai cosa che mi piacesse tanto.*

I am pleased to do so, *così mi pare e piace.*

PLE'ASING, adj. acceptable agreeable] *piacevole, grato, gustoso, accetto.*

PLE'ASURABLE, adj. *piacevole, ameno.*

PLE'ASURE, s. [content, joy, delight] *piacere, contento, diletto, gusto,* s. m.

Pleasure [diversion] *piacere, divertimento, diporto, trastullo, passatempo,* s. m.

Pleasure [good turn] *piacere, servigio, favore,* s. m.

Pleasure [will] *piacere,* s. m. *volontà, voglia,* s. f.

Such is our will and pleasure, *così vogliamo, così ci piace.*

At his own pleasure, *a sua voglia.*

Your pleasure madam? *che comanda signora?*

Do it at your pleasure, *fatelo col vostro agio, o col vostro comodo.*

To PLE'ASURE [to give content] *piacere, aggradire, soddisfare,* pret. *piacqui.*

To pleasure [to humour] *compiacere, far la voglia altrui, far cosa grata,* pret. *compiacqui.*

To pleasure [to oblige] *piacere, soddisfare, far piacere.*

PLE'ASURED, adj. *piaciuto.*

PLEBE'IAN, s. [one of the commonalty, a mean person] *un plebeo, un uomo volgare.*

PLEDGE, s. [surety, pawn] *pegno,* s. m. *sicurtà,* s. f.

PLEDGE [surety] *sicurtà, mallevadore.*

He is my pledge, *egli è mio mallevadore.*

Pledge [proof] *pruova, prova, testimonianza,* s. f.

This is a sufficient proof of the truth I assert, *questa è prova sufficiente della verità che mantengo.*

Pledges in war, *ostaggi, statichi.*

To PLEDGE [to pawn] *impegnare, dare in pegno, o per sicurtà.*

To pledge one [in drinking] *far ragione ad uno in bere.*

PLE'DGED, adj. *impegnato.*

PLE'DGET, s. [a small mass of lint to be laid upon a wound, as after letting blood] *piumaccetto,* s. m. *pezza,* s. f.

PLE'IADES, s. [the seven stars in the neck of the bull] *pleiadi, gallinelle,* s. f. *le sette stelle, che si veggono tra'l toro e l'ariete.*

PLE'NARY, adj. [full] *penario.*

Plenary [indulgence] *indulgenza plenaria.*

PLE'NIPOTENCY, s. [full power] *pieno potere.*

PLENIPOTE'NTIAL, adj. [belonging to a plenipotentiary] *plenipotenziario.*

PLENIPOTE'NTIARY, s. [an ambassador, or commissioner, who has full power and authority from his prince or state to treat with others about peace, or conclude upon all points contained in his commission] *plenipotenziario,* s. m.

PLE'NITUDE, s. [fullness] *plenitudine, pienezza,* s. f.

PLE'NTEOUS, } adj. [abundant, fertile] *abbondante, abbondevole, copioso.*
PLE'NTIFUL,

A plentiful estate, *gran beni, immense ricchezze.*

A plentiful dinner, *un lauto, o magnifico pranzo.*

Very plentiful, *abbondantissimo.*

PLE'NTIFULLY, adv. *abbondantemente, abbondevolmente, copiosamente.*

PLE'NTIFULNESS, } s. [abundance, great store] *abbondanza, dovizia, copia,* s. f.
PLE'NTY,

To have plenty of all things, *abbondare d' ogni cosa, aver dovizia d' ogni cosa.*

Money is very plenty with him, *egli abbonda molto di danari.*

PLE'ONASM, s. [a figure in grammar, where a letter or syllable is added either to the beginning, middle, or end of a word] *pleonasmo.*

PLE'URA, s. [a double membrane which covers all the inward cavity of the thorax] *pleura,* s. f.

PLE'URISY, s. [a disease caused by the inflammation of the pleura] *plurisia,* s. f. *infermità cagionata dal riscaldarsi, o raffreddarsi.*

PLEURI'TICK, adj. [subject to the pleurisy] *che patisce di plurisia.*

PLI'ABLE, adj. [flexible] *flessibile, pieghevole, trattabile.*

PLI'ABLENESS, } s. *flessibilità,* s. f.
PLI'ANCY,

PLI'ANT, adj. [or yielding, in a proper and figurative sense] *pieghevole, atto ad esser piegato, arrendevole, flessibile, agevole a lasciarsi persuadere, trattabile, umile, sommesso, docile.*

PLI'ANTNESS, s. *flessibilità,* s. f.

PLI'CA, s. [a disease among the Polanders, which causes their hair to cling together like a cow's tail] *malattia che regna fra i Pollacchi.*

PLIGHT, s. [state and condition of body] *abitudine, stato, condizione, disposizione del corpo.*

Plight, s. [pledge, gage] *pegno.*

Plight, s. [plait, fold] *piega, piegatura.*

To PLIGHT [to engage, to promise solemnly] *promettere, impegnare, dare,* pret. *promisi.*

To plight one's faith or troth, *dare la sua fede, impegnare la sua parola.*

PLINTH, s. [the lowermost part of the foot of a pillar, being in the form of a tile or square brick] *zoccolo,* s. m.

PLITE, s. [an ancient sort of measure, such as a yard or an ell] *misura antica che corrisponde al braccio o canna d'oggidì.*

To PLOD, ex. to plod upon a business [to have one's head full of it] *aver l' animo intento, attento, o fisso a qualche affare,*

To

To plod at one's books, *ſtudiar notte giorno, darſi allo ſtudio, affaticarſi.*

PLO'DDING, adj. he went plodding about, *ſe ne andava* tutto *penſieroſo.*

A plodding head, *una mente penſieroſa.*

PLOT, s. [conſpiracy] *congiura, congiurazione, coſpirazione, trama,* s. m.

To lay a plot, *fare una congiura, congiurare, tramare.*

The plot of a play, *l' intreccio d' una commedia o tragedia.*

A plot of ground, *un pezzo di terra.*

The ground-plot of a building, *lapianta d' un edificio.*

To PLOT [to conſpire, to combine] *congiurare, coſpirare, tramare, ordire,* preſ. *ordiſco.*

To plot againſt the ſtate, *congiurare, o coſpirare contra lo ſtato.*

They have plotted his ruin, *hanno tramato, o ordito la ſua rovina.*

They plot againſt your life, *inſidiano la voſtra vita.*

To plot [to adviſe, to conſult] *concertare, pigliar miſure.*

PLO'TTED, adj. *congiurato, coſpirato, tramato, ordito.*

PLO'TTER, s. *coſpiratore,* s. m. *coſpiratrice,* s. f.

PLO'TTING, s. *il congiurare, o coſpirare.*

PLO'VER, s. [a ſort of wild fowl] *ſorta d' uccello.*

PLOUGH } s. [an inſtrument to till
PLOW } the ground] *aratro, aratolo, vomero, e vomere,* s. m.

The plough-tail } s. *il manico dell'*
Plough-handle } *aratro.*

The plough-ſhare, *il coltro dell' aratro.*

A plough-man } s. *un biſolco, un la-*
Plow-man } *voratore, un aratore.*

A plow-wright, *un facitor d' aratri.*

Plow-Monday [is the next Monday after Twelfth day, when the plow-men in the north country draw a plow from door to door, and beg plow-money to drink] *il Lunedì degli aratri, il primo Lunedì dopo l' Epifania, quando i biſolchi nelle parti ſettentrionali d' Inghilterra ſtraſcinano un aratro di porta in porta e domandano danari per bere.*

To PLOUGH } [to till] *arare, rom-*
To PLOW } *pere, e lavorare la terra coll' aratro.*

PLO'UGHED } adj. *arato.*
PLO'WED }

PLO'UGHING, *aramento,* s. m. *aratura,* s. f. *l' arare.*

PLOW, *v.* To Plough.

To PLOW, *v.* Plough.

PLUCK, s. [the entrails of a calf or ſheep] *coratella di vitella e di càſtrato.*

Pluck, s. [a pull, a draw, a ſingle act of plucking] *tirata, ſtrappata;* s. f. *lo ſtrappar via ad un tratto ſolo un fiore un frutto, o checcheſſia più colle dita che colla mano. Di qui forſe venne il noſtro verbo* piluccare.

To PLUCK [to pull away by force] *tirare per forza, ſtrappare, ſvellere,* pret. *ſvelſi.*

To pluck up by the root, *ſradicare, ſvellere dalle radici.*

To pluck up one's ſpirits, to pluck up a good heart, *ſtar di buon cuore, farſi animo.*

To pluck up a bird's feathers, *ſpiumare un uccello.*

PLU'CKED } adj. *tirato, ſtrappato,*
PLU'CKT } *ſveltoi.*

Plum, adv. [or perpendicularly] *a piombo, penpendicolarmente.*

Down plum, *giù a piombo.*

Plum over, *ſu a dirittura.*

PLU'MAGE, s. [feathers of a bird] *le piume degli uccelli.*

Plumage [a bunch of feathers] *un ciuffo di piume.*

PLUMB, s. [prune, damſon] *ſuſina, prugna,* s. f.

A wild plumb, *prugnolo,* s. m. *ſuſina ſalvatica.*

Damaſk plumb } *ſuſina damaſcena.*
Damſon }

A plumb-tree, *prugno, ſuſino,* s. m.

Plumbs [raiſins] *paſſo,* s. m. *uva paſſa.*

A plumb-pudding, *una torta con paſſi.*

Plumb-porridge, *brodo con uva paſſo.*

A plumb-cake, *paſticetto di ſuſine.*

Plumbs, or ſugar-plumbs, *confetti.*

A PLUMB, *chiamano anche gl' Ingleſi la ſomma di cento mila lire ſterline.*

PLUMB, s. *ſorta di giuoco fanciulleſco, in cui fanciulli ſi domandano l' un l' altro* how many plumbs for a penny? *quante ſuſine date per un ſoldo?*

To PLUMB [to work by a plumb-line] *piombare, far corriſpondere col diſopra il diſſotto a linea retta perpendicolare, adoperare il piombo per corriſpondenza.*

Plumb, adv. ex. to fall down plumb, *piombare, cadere giù a dirittura, o a piombo.*

A plumb-line } s. [a plummet] *pi-*
A plumb-rule } *ombino,* s. m. *ſtrumento di piombo il quale s' appicca ad una cordicella col quale i muratori, e legnajuoli aggiuſtan le dirittüre.*

PLU'MBAGIN, s. [lead naturally mingled with ſilver] *piombagine,* s. f. *minerale di piombo ed argento inſieme.*

PLU'MBEOUS, adj. [like lead] *di piombo, ſimile o del color del piombo.*

PLU'MBER, *v.* Plummer.

PLUME, s. [a ſet of oſtrich feathers prepared for ornament, or any bunch of feathers] *pennacchio,* s. m. *arneſe di più penne inſieme.*

A plume-ſtriker [a flatterer] *un adulatore, un luſingatore.*

To PLUME [to pluck the feathers off] *ſpiumare, levar le piume, pelare.*

PLU'MED, adj. *ſpiumato.*

PLU'MING, s. *lo ſpiumare.*

PLU'MMER, s. [one that works or deals in lead] *piombajo,* s. m. *colui che lavora di piombo.*

PLU'MMET, s. [a plumb-line uſed by carpenters and maſons] *piombino,* s. m. *ſtrumento di piombo, il quale s' appicca a una cordicella per trovar le dirittüre.*

Plummet [an inſtrument to ſound the depth of the ſea] *piombino, ſtrumento per trovar l' altezza de' fondi.*

PLUMP, adj. [full and round in fleſh] *pienotto, tondo, graſſotto, paffuto, carnacciuto.*

A plump face, *un viſo pienotto, un viſo tondo.*

Plump faced, *che ha il viſo pienotto.*

To PLUMP [to ſwell] *gonfiare.*

To plump [to fall plump into] *piombare, caſcare a piombo.*

To plump in the water, *piombare, o caſcare a piombo nell' acqua.*

PLU'MPED, adj. *gonfiato, e gonfio.*

PLU'MPNESS, s. *buono ſtato di ſalute, graſſezza.*

PLU'NDER, s. [booty got by plundering] *bottino, ſacco,* s. m. *preda propriamente de' ſoldati.*

To PLU'NDER [to rob, ſpoil, or take away by violence] *predare, ſaccheggiare, mettere a ſacco.*

To plunder one of his cloaths, *ſpogliare alcuno de' ſuoi abiti.*

PLU'NDERED, adj. *predato, ſaccheggiato.*

To give up a town to be plundered, *mettere a ſacco, porre a ſacco una città, dare il ſacco ad una città.*

PLU'NDERER, s. *ſaccheggiante, predatore,* s. m.

PLU'NDERING, s. *ſaccheggiamento, ſacco,* s. m. *il ſaccheggiare.*

PLUNGE, s. [trouble] *pena, noja,* s. f. *faſtidio, imbarazzo, impedimento, intrigo,* s. m.

To be put to a plunge, to be in a great plunge, *trovarſi in guai, eſſer in gran perpleſſità, eſſere imbarazzato.*

To PLUNGE [to dip over head and ears] *tuffare, ſommergere, immergere,* pret. *ſommerſi, immerſi.*

To plunge one's ſelf, *tuffarſi, immergerſi.*

He has plunged himſelf into all manner of lewdneſs, *s' è immerſo s' è dato in preda ad ogni ſorte di diſſolutezze.*

PLU'NGED, adj. *tuffato, ſommerſo, immerſo.*

PLU'NGEON, s. [a ducker, a water-fowl] *ſmergo, ſorta d' uccello d' acqua.*

A PLU'NGER, s. *tuffatore, che ſi tuffa, peſcatore di perle.*

PLU'NGING, s. *tuffo,* s. m. *il tuffare.*

PLU'NKET colour [a ſort of blue colour] *colore azzurro o ceruleo.*

PLU'RAL, adj. [belonging to many] *plurale, del numero del più.*

Plural, s. [the plural number] *il plurale, il numero del più.*

PLURA'LITY, s. [greater part, or greater number] *pluralità, più gran numero, multiplicità.*

Plurality of benefices, *la pluralità de' benefici.*

Plurality, adv. *pluralmente, al numero plurale.*

PLUSH, s. [a kind of cloth made in imitation of velvet] *felpa,* s. f. *drappo di ſeta o di lana, col pelo più lungo del velluto.*

PLU'VIAL, s. [a priest's vestment or cope] piviale, s. m. paramento sacerdotale.

PLU'VIOUS, adj. [rainy] piovoso.

PLY, s. piega, s. f.

He has taken a bad ply, egli ha preso una cattiva piega.

To ply [to bend or give one's mind to a thing] applicarsi, attendere, dare opera, impiegarsi in che che si sia.

To ply one's books or studies, studiar molto, dare opera alla studio.

To ply one's oars, vogare, remare di forza, remare a voga arrancata.

A dog that plies his feet, un cane che corre con gran velocità.

To ply one hard [to make him work hard] far lavorare uno incessantemente.

To ply at a place [as porters, watermen, coachmen, &c. in order to get a fare] avere il suo posto.

Waterman, where do you ply? barcaruolo, dove è il vostro posto?

To ply to the south, west, &c. [as a ship does] tirare verso mezzodì, ponente, &c.

To ply off and on [to keep plying off and on] bordeggiare, star su le volte, dicesi d' un vascello, allora che senza vento favorevole, pur cerca d' acquistar cammino.

PLY'D, adj. applicato, v. To ply.

To POACH [to beat one's eyes black and blue] far gli occhi ad uno come un calamajo.

To poach eggs, bollire delle uova.

To poach [to destroy game by unlawful means] ammazzare, o acchiappare qualche bestia da caccia con istrumenti dises' della legge.

PO'ACHED, adj. livido.

A poached eye, un occhio gonfio.

Poached eggs, uova affogate.

POCK, s. [a scab or dent of the small pox] crosta di vajuolo.

A pock hole, buttero, s. m. quel segno o margine che resta altrui dopo il vajuolo.

His face is full of pock-holes, il suo viso è tutto butterato.

PO'CKET, s. [a little bag commonly worn in a garment] scarsella, taschetta, s. f. borsa di cuojo che è cucita ad un abito.

A pocket of wool [half a sack] un mezzo sacco di lana.

A pocket-book, libretto da portare in iscarsella.

A pocket-dagger, uno stilo, o stiletto.

A pocket-handkerchief, uno pezzuola, un fazzoletto.

Pocket-money, danari che si portano in iscarsella per ispendere in divertimenti o simili.

To PO'CKET [to pocket up, to put in one's pocket] imborsare, metter nella borsa.

To pocket up money, imborsar del danaro.

To pocket up an affront, bere o inghiottire un' ingiuria.

PO'CIFY'D } adj. [that has got the
PO'CKY } French-pox] infranciosato.

POD, s. [the husk of any pulse] pula, lolla, loppa, s. f. guscio, s. m.

PODA'GRICAL, adj. [gouty] podagrico, gottoso, che patisce di podagra.

PO'DDERS, s. [poor people employ'd to gather peas] così chiamano in Londra quella povera gente che colgono i piselli.

PO'DESTA } s. [a kind of magi-
PO'DESTAT } strate in the state of Venice] podestà, s. m. magistrato nello stato Veneto.

PO'EM, s. [a composition in verse] poema, s. m.

PO'ESY, s. [or poem] poesia, s. f. componimento poetico.

Poesy [the art of making verses] poesia, arte del poeta, poetica, s. f.

PO'ET, s. [one that makes poetry] un poeta.

POETA'STER, s. [a paltry poet] un poetastro, un poetaccio, un poetuzzo.

PO'ETESS, s. [a she poet] poetessa, s. f.

POE'TICAL } adj. [belonging to poe-
POE'TICK } try] poetico, di poesia,

POE'TICALLY, adv. poeticamente, con modo poetico.

To PO'ETIZE [to make verses, or play the poet] poetare, compor poemi, e poesie.

PO'ETRESS, s. poetessa.

PO'ETRY, s. [the art of making verses] poesia, poetica, s. f. arte del poetare.

The pastoral poetry, la poesia pastorale.

PO'IGNANCY, s. [the power of stimulating the palate, sharpness] acutezza; forza che si fa sentire come una puntura al palato.

PO'IGNANT, adj. [sharp, tart, biting, in a proper and figurative sense] pugnente, e pungente, acuto, aspro.

POINT, s. [the sharp end of any thing] la punta.

The point of a sword, knife, &c. la punta d' una spada, d' un coltello, &c.

The point of a rock, la cima d' un sasso; o d' uno scoglio.

A point of land [a cape or promontory] una punta di terra, un capo, o promontorio.

The point of a dial, gnomone, o ago d' oriuolo a sole.

The points of a compass, i punti della calamita, i trentadue venti segnati nella bussola.

Point [such as men wore about their breeches] stringa, s. f.

A mathematical point [which is considered as having no parts] punto matematico, punto indivisibile.

The point [head or chief matter] punto, materia, passo

The difficulty lies in this point, la difficoltà consiste in questo punto.

Whether he should die or not was the point, il caso era s' egli morirebbe o no.

The point of honour, punto, o puntiglio,

Point [issue, pass] punto, termine, stato.

The matter was brought to that point, la cosa era ridotta a tal punto, termine, o stato.

To pursue one's point [or design] seguir l' impresa.

Point of time, punto, momento.

To be upon the point of going away, star sul punto di partire, star per partire.

To be upon the point of death, stare sul punto, o sull' articolo della morte.

Point [full stop] punto, quel segno di posa, che si mette nella scrittura, al fin del periodo.

Point [a sort of needle-work] punto in aria, s. m.

The point [at cards] il punto, nel giuoco delle carte.

Tell your point, accusate il vostro punto.

Point at dice, ex. the ace-point, l' asso.

The deux-point, il due.

The tray-point, il tre.

The quater-point, il quattro.

The cinque point, il cinque.

The six-point, il sei.

In point of controversy, in materia di controversia.

In point of conscience, in caso di coscienza parlando secondo la coscienza.

In point of religion, in materia di religione, in quanto alla religione.

It is a material point, è un caso d' importanza, è un affare d' importanza.

At all points [intirely] intieramente, totalmente.

Point wise, in punta, a punta.

To hit point-blank, dar nel punto in bianco.

Point-blank, nettamente, schiettamente, positivamente, di punto in bianco.

He told me point-blank that he would not do it, mi disse nettamente, positivamente che non lo farebbe.

Point-blank contrary, direttamente, affatto, contrario.

To POINT [to make sharp at the end], appuntare, aguzzare, fare aguzzo, fare la punta.

To point [to mark with points or stops] puntare, fare i punti è i segni nelle scritture.

To point at one, mostrare alcuno col dito.

To point at a thing, mostrare, indicare una cosa.

To point the cannon against the town, voltare o piantar l' artiglieria contro la città.

PO'INTED, adj. aguzzo, acuto, v. To point.

Pointed at, mostrato a dito, indicato, mostrato.

PO'INTEDLY, adv. ex. he writes too pointedly, la sua scrittura è troppo piena di punti.

PO'INTING, s. l' aguzzare, o puntare.

Pointing, adj. ex. his discourse was still pointing that way, il suo discorso tendeva sempre a questo, non aveva altra mira che questo.

PO'INTLESS, adj. senza punta, spuntato.

POISE, s. [weight] peso, s. m. gravezza.

A water-poiſe, *peſo da peſar l'acqua.*
Equal poiſe, *equilibrio.*
To POISE [to weigh with the hand] *peſare colla mano, ponderare.*
To poiſe [to bring in an equal balance] *peſare, contrappeſare, bilanciare.*
PO'ISED, adj. *peſato, ponderato, contrappeſato, bilanciato.*
The balance ſtands poiſed, *la bilancia è ben contrappeſata.*
A well poiſed body, *un corpo ben proporzionato.*
Poiſed [grave, ſober] *poſato, quieto, ſedato.*
PO'ISER, s. *peſatore,* s. m. *che peſa.*
PO'ISING, s. *il peſare, ponderare, e contrappeſare, contrappeſo,* s. m.
PO'ISON, s. [venom] *veleno, e veneno, toſſiro,* s. m.
To PO'ISON [to give poiſon in order to kill] *avvelenare, attoſſicare,* e *attoſcare.*
To poiſon ſomething [to put poiſon in it] *avvelenare che che ſi ſia, porvi del veleno.*
To poiſon [to infect with an ill ſmell] *appeſtare, fieramente putire, infettare.*
To poiſon [to corrupt or vitiate] *appeſtare, corrompere, guaſtare, contaminare.*
To poiſon a woman [to get her with child] *ingravidare una donna, o piuttoſto corromperne la virtù, e ſedurla.*
PO'ISONED, adj. *avvelenato, attoſſicato.*
PO'ISONER, s. *avvelenatore,* s. m. *che avvelena.*
PO'ISONING, s. *l' avvelenare, l' attoſſicare.*
PO'ISONOUS, adj. [full of poiſon] *avvelenato, attoſſicato, velenoſo.*
Poiſonous [dangerous] *peſtifero, mortale, pericoloſo, pernicioſo.*
PO'ITRAL, s. [or breaſt-plate] *pettorale,* s. m.
POIZE, *v.* Poiſe.
To poize, *v.* To poiſe.
POKE, s. [a bag] *taſca,* s. f. *ſacco, ſacchetto,* s. m.
To buy a pig in a poke, *comprare gatta in ſacco.*
To POKE [to feel in the dark] *cercare al taſto.*
To poke up, *inſaccare, mettere in ſacco.*
To poke in, *frugare, frugolare, frugacchiare.*
To poke in the fire, *frugare, o attizzare il fuoco.*
To poke in with a ſtick, *frugacchiare con un baſtone.*
PO'KER, s. *fercone, ſtrumento di ferro aguzzo per attizzare il fuoco.*
PO'KING, s. *frugata,* s. f. *il frugare.*
You are always poking in the fire, *voi non fate che frugare il fuoco.*
POL, s. [a diminutive of parrot] *pappagallo.*
PO'LAR, adj. [belonging to the poles of the world] *polare.*
The two polar circles, *i duoi circoli polari.*
POLA'RITY, s. [tendency to the pole] *polarità; natura della calamita di volgerſi verſo il polo.*
POLE, s [the end of the imagined axle-tree of the world] *polo,* s. m. *i poli ſon due punti terminati dall' aſſe, intorno al quale ſi volgon le ſfere.*
The pole arctick and antarctick, *il polo artico ed antartico.*
Pole-ſtar, s. [lodeſtar; cynoſure] *ſtella vicina al polo, dalla quale i naviganti calcolano la loro ſettentrional latitudine.*
POLE-ſtar, s. *guida, direttore, conduttore, maeſtro.*
Pole [long ſtick] *pertica,* s. f. *palo,* s. m.
A barber's pole, *inſegna di barbiere.*
The pole-bolt of a coach, *timone di carrozza.*
A waterman's pole, *palo da barcaiuolo.*
A pole [to dance on the rope] *contrappeſo.*
Pole-ax, or battle-ax, *ſcure.*
Pole-edge, or pole-arbour, *pergolato*
To bear down with a pole, *batacchiare.*
PO'LECAT, s. [a ſort of wild cat] *puzzola,* s. f. *ſorta d' animale ſimile alla faina.*
POLIDA'VIS, s. [a ſort of coarſe canvas] *ſpezie di canavaccio groſſolano, tela di ſacco.*
PO'LEME, s. [a ſort of ſhoe, pick'd and turn'd up at the toe] *ſorta di ſcarpe fatte colla punta, che ſi portavan altre volte in Inghilterra.*
PO'LICY, s. [the art of governing a kingdom or commonwealth] *politica,* s. f. *facultà che inſegna il governo publico.*
Policy [conduct, addreſs, cunning way] *politica, arte, maeſtria, aſtuzia,* s. f. *artificio,* s. m.
Policy goes beyond ſtrength, *l' arte può più che la forza.*
Policy of inſurance [an inſtrument or writing given by inſurers, to make good the thing inſured] *polizza di ſicurtà.*
To PO'LISH [to make ſmooth] *pulire, liſciare, luſtrare, far liſcio,* pref. *puliſco.*
PO'LISHABLE, adj. *che ſi può pulire.*
PO'LISHED, adj. *pulito, liſciato, lurato.*
PO'LISHER, s. *colui, o colei che puliſce.*
PO'LISHING, s. *pulimento,* s. m. *il pulire.*
Poliſhing, adj. ex. a poliſhing iron, *ferro da pulire.*
PO'LITE, adj. [well poliſhed, genteel, accompliſhed] *pulito, garbato, civile, corteſe, grazioſo, leggiadro.*
A polite man, *un uomo garbato, un uomo di garbo.*
A polite ſtyle, *uno ſtile pulito.*
POLI'TELY, adv. *pulitamente, garbatamente.*
POLI'TENESS, s. *civiltà, bellacreanza, pulitezza, garbatezza, corteſia, gentilezza,* s. f. *garbo,* s. m.
POLI'TICAL, adj. [belonging to policy] *politico, civile, che è ſecondo la politica.*
A POLITI'CIAN, s. [a ſtateſman] *un politico.*
POLI'TICK, adj. [of, or belonging to politicks] *politico, civile, che è ſecondo la politica.*
Politick [cunning] *politico, accorto, fine, ſagace, aſtuto.*
To have a politick fit of ſickneſs, *far l' ammalato, fingerſi ammalato.*
A Sir politick, *un miſterioſo, un che fa un miſtero di nonnulla.*
PO'LITICKLY, adv. *politicamente.*
PO'LITICKS, s [the art of governing] *politica,* s. f. *l' arte del governare.*
Politicks [the book which treats about politicks] *politica, libri, come quelli d' Ariſtotile che trattano dell' amminiſtrazione della città.*
Politicks, [police, addreſs] *politica, arte, aſtuzia, maeſtria,* s. f. *artificio,* s. m.
He is out in his politicks, *la ſua arte non ha avuto luogo, egli ſ' è ſbagliato, ha dato in fallo.*
PO'LITURE, s. [a poliſhing] *pulimento,* s. m *pulitura,* s. f.
PO'LITY, s. [government] *pulitezza, ordine, governo.*
The eccleſiaſtical polity, *il governo eccleſiaſtico.*
PO'LIUM, s. [an ingredient in the Theriaca Andromachi] *polio,* s. m. *ſerta d' erba.*
POLL, s. [the head] *teſta,* s. f.
A poll of ling, *teſta di merluzzo ſecco.*
POLL [in elections, a ſetting down the name of thoſe who have right to vote in chuſing a publick magiſtrate] *ſquittino,* s. m. *adunanza di cittadini per creare i magiſtrati.*
To demand a poll, *domandare uno ſquittino.*
Poll-tax, or poll money [a tax when every ſubject is aſſeſſed by the head or poll, to pay a certain ſum of money] *capitazione, taſſa, impoſizione di danari tanto per teſta.*
To POLL [to ſhave the head] *tondere, radere la teſta,* pret. *toſi.*
To poll [at an election, to give in the names, and reckon up the number of the votes] *ſquittinare, mandare a partito, rendere il voto per l' elezione de' magiſtrati.*
PO'LLARD. s. [chevin, chub fiſh] *muggine, ſpezie di peſce.*
Pollard [among hunters, a ſtag or male deer, which has caſt his head] *cervo, che ha ſpuntato le corna.*
Pollard [among gardeners, an old tree which has been often lopp'd] *albero che è ſtato ſcapezzato di quando in quando.*
Pollard [an ancient coin in England] *ſorta di moneta Ingleſe antica maltagliata.*
PO'LLED, adj. *toſato, raſo.*
PO'LLER, s. *toſatore,* s. m.
Poller [he that polls] *ſquittinatore,* s. m.
PO'LLING, s. *lo ſquittinare.*
To POLLU'TE [to defile] *imbrattare.*

 im-

imbruttare, lerciare, spercare, violare, sozzare.

POLLU'TED, adj. *imbrattato, lercio, sozzato, sporcato, violato.*

POLLU'TION, s. [uncleanness, defilement] *sozzura, bruttura, laidezza, polluzione,* s. f.

PO'LTRON, } s. [a coward] *un poltrone, un codardo, un*
POLTRO'ON, } *infingardo, un dappoco.*

POLTRO'ONERY, s. [cowardice] *poltroneria, codardia, dappocaggine, infingardia, infingardaggine,* s. f.

PO'LYGAMY, s. [the having more wives than one] *poligamia,* s. f.

PO'LYGARCHY, s. [a government which is in the hands of many] *poligarchia,* s. f.

PO'LYGON, s. [a figure consisting of many angles and sides] *poligono,* s. m. *figura che ha molti angoli.*

PO'LYGONY, s. [a plant] *poligone,* s. m. *erba.*

PO'LYPODY, s. [oak fern] *polipodio,* s. m. *erba simigliante alla felce.*

PO'LYPUS, s. [a lump of spungy flesh arising in the hollow of the nostrils] *polipo,* s. m. *malattia, che viene per lo più dentro 'l naso.*

Polypus [a fish that has many feet, a pourcontrel] *polpo,* s. m. *spezie di pesce.*

POMA'DA, s. [an exercise of vaulting the wooden horse, laying only one hand over the pommel of the saddle] *pomata,* s. f. *esercizio nel maneggiare un cavallo tenendo una mano sola sul pomo della sella.*

POMA'NDER, s. [a little round ball made of several fragrant perfumes] *pastiglia,* s. f. *palla fatta di pastiglia.*

POMA'TUM, s. [an ointment] *pomata,* s. f. *sorta d' unguento.*

To POME [to grow into a round head, as a cabbage which begins to pome] *cestire, fare il cesto come i ravoli e le lattughe.*

A cabbage that begins to pome, *un cavolo che comincia a cestire.*

POMECI'TRON, s. [a fruit somewhat like a lemon, but much larger] *redro,* s. m. *frutto.*

Pomecitron-tree, *cedro albero.*

Pome royal, *mela appiuola.*

POMED, adj. [headed] *cestito, cestuto.*

PO'MEGRANATE, } s. [a round fruit
PO'MGRANATE, } full of grains and kernels] *melagranà, melagranata,* s. f. *granato,* s. m. *frutta nota.*

Pomegranate-tree, *melagrano,* s. m. *albero che produce la melagrana.*

PO'MEROY, } s. *sorta di mela.*
POMERO'YAL, }

PO'MMEL, s. [the round knob on a saddle bow, or on the hilt of a sword] *pomo,* s. m.

The pommel of a sword or saddle, *il pomo d' una spada o d' una sella.*

To PO'MMEL [to beat or bang soundly] *battere, stregghiare, zombare.*

PO'MMELLED, adj. *battuto, streggkiato, zombato.*

POMP, s. [state or glory] *pompa, magnificenza, grandezza,* s. f.

PO'MPETS, s. [printer's ink-balls] *mazzi di stampatore, colle quali mettono l' inchiostro sopra le lettere.*

PO'MPION, } s. [a sort of large fruit
PU'MKIN, } of the nature of melons, *zucca,* s. f.

PO'MPOUS, adj. [stately, glorious] *pomposo, magnifico, grande.*

Very pompous, *pomposissimo.*

PO'MPOUSLY, adv. *pomposamente, magnificamente, con modo pomposo.*

PO'MPOUSNESS, s. *pompa, magnificenza, splendore; ostentazione.*

POND, s. [pool, standing water] *stagno,* s. m. *ricettacolo d' acqua che sbocca da' fiumi, e quivi si ferma e muore.*

To water one's horse in a pond, *abbeverare un cavallo in uno stagno.*

A fish-pond, *un vivajo.*

To POND, *v.* To ponder.

To PO'NDER [to weigh in the mind, to consider] *ponderare, pesare, diligentemente esaminare, considerare.*

PO'NDERED, adj. *ponderato, pesato, esaminato, considerato.*

PO'NDERER, s. *un uomo considerato, un uomo giudicioso o di giudicio, un uomo che va col passo di piombo.*

PO'NDERING, s. *il ponderare.*

PONDERO'SITY, s. [weightiness] *pondo, peso,* s. m. *gravezza,* s. f.

PO'NDEROUS, adj. [weighty] *ponderoso, pesante, di gran pondo.*

PO'NDEROUSNESS, s. [ponderosity] *pondo, peso,* s. m. *gravezza,* s. f

PO'ND-WEED, s. *nome di pianta.*

PO'NENT, adj. [western] *occidente, ponente.*

PO'NIARD, s. [or dagger] *pugnale,* s. m.

A blow with a poniard, *pugnalata,* s. f. *ferita di pugnale.*

To PO'NIARD [to stab] *pugnalare, dar delle pugnalate.*

PO'NIARDED, adj. *pugnalato.*

PONK, s. [a nocturnal spirit, a hag] *un folletto, uno spirito notturno.*

PO'NTAGE, s. [a contribution for the repairing and re-edifying of bridges, also a bridge-toll] *contribuzione che si paga per riparare e riedificare i ponti.*

PO'NTIFF, s. [bishop, prelate] *pontefice.*

PONTI'FICAL, adj. [belonging to a pontiff] *pontificale.*

A pontifical habit, *abito pontificale.*

The book of pontifical rites, *il pontificale.*

PONTIFICA'LIBUS, s. ex. the Pope was in his pontificalibus [or pontifical ornaments] *il Papa era vestito ne' suoi paramenti pontificali.*

PONTI'FICATE, s. *pontificato, papato.*

PO'NTON, s. [a bridge of boats] *ponte di barche.*

PO'NY, s. [a small horse] *un cavallo piccolo, un cavallino, un cavalluccio.*

POOL, s. [pond] *stagno,* s. m.

The pool of Jerusalem, *la piscina di Gerusalemme.*

POOP, s. [the stern of a ship] *poppa,* s. f. *parte deretana della nave.*

POOR, adj. [needy, indigent] *povero, necessitoso, bisognoso.*

Poor man [beggar] *un povero, un pezzente.*

Poor people, *i poveri.*

Poor [is often used out of pity or kindness] *povero, si usa bene spesso in segno di pietà e compassione.*

Poor me, what must I do? *misero me, che debbo io fare?*

Poor [mean, pitiful] *povero, scarso, cattivo.*

He is in a poor condition, *egli si trova in povero stato.*

Poor land, *terra povera, o sterile.*

Poor [lean] *magro.*

A poor horse, *un cavallo magro, una rozza.*

This is but a poor shift, *questo è un ripiego che giova poco.*

Poor man, *poveraccio.*

Poor woman, *poveraccia.*

The poor, *la poveraglia, i poveri.*

PO'ORJOHN, s. *nome di pesce.*

PO'ORLY, adv. [wretchedly] *poveramente, poverettamente, meschinamente.*

Poorly clad, *poveramente vestito.*

PO'ORNESS, s. [meanness] *povertà, povetezza,* s. f.

POORSPI'RITED, adj. *senza spirito, vigliacco, codardo.*

POORSPI'RITEDNESS, s. *viltà, codardia.*

POP, s. [a small smart quick sound] *picciol romore ma presto e acuto.*

To POP in, *entrare, sorvenire, sopravvenire all' improvviso.*

To pop out [or steal away] *uscire, sfilarsela, corsela.*

To pop out a word [to blurt it out] *lasciare andare una parola.*

He popped out a word that spoiled all, *gli scappò una parola che guastò tutto l' intrigo.*

To pop off a pistol, *sparare una pistola.*

A pop gun, *un buffo, un buffetto.*

POPE, s. *il Papa.*

The Pope's dignity, *il papato.*

PO'PEDOM, s. [or papacy] *il papato.*

PO'PERY, s. *papismo. Gl' Inglesi Protestanti per derisione chiamano Papismo la religione Cattolica Romana, per rifarsi di quell' Eretico che noi diam loro tanto continuamente pel capo. Carità cristiana da ambidue i lati.*

PO'PISH, adj. [or Roman Catholick] *Cattolico Romano.*

The popish religion, *la religione Romana.*

PO'PINJAY, s. [a parrot of a greenish colour] *pappagallo,* s. m.

Popinjay, s. *uccello chiamato picchio.*

Popinjay, s. *un zerbinotto, un parigino.*

PO'PLAR, s. [the poplar-tree] *pioppo,* s. m.

PO'PPET, *v.* Puppet.

POPPY, s. [a sort of plant and flower] *papavero,* s. m. *erba sonnifera nota.*

PO'PULACE, s. [the common or the meaner

meaner sort of people] *il popolo, la moltitudine popolare, le plebe, la parte ignobile del popolo.*

PO'PULAR, adj. [the common people] *popolare, popolano.*

A popular government, *un governo popolare.*

A popular [or epidemical] disease, *una malattia commune.*

Popular [that courts the favour of the people] *popolare, che cerca di cattivarsi l'animo de' popoli.*

Popular [beloved of the people] *popolare, e popolano, amato del popolo.*

POPULA'RITY, s. [the populace, the mobile] *popolazzo,* s. m. *plebe,* s f.

PO'PULARLY, adv. *popolarescamente.*

To PO'PULATE [to depopulate, to lay waste a country] *spopolare, dipopolare, privar un paese d'abitanti, distruggere, desolare, rovinare,* pret. *distrussi.*

To populate [used by some to stock a country with people] *popolare, metter popolo in un luogo che l'abiti.*

PO'PULATED, adj. *spopolato, dipopolato, distrutto, rovinato, popolato.*

PO'PULATING, s. *lo spopolare, il dipopolare, il popolare.*

POPULA'TION, s. [or devastation] *distruzione, rovina, desolazione,* s. f.

PO'PULOUS, adj. [full of people] *popolato, popoloso, pien di popolo.*

PO'PULOUSNESS, s. *abbondanza, o frequenza di popolo.*

PO'RCELAIN, s. [the chalky earth of which China ware is made] *porcellana,* s. f. *terra preziosa della quale se ne fanno stoviglie di molto pregio.*

Porcelain [vessels or ware made of Chinese earth] *porcellana, vasi di porcellana.*

Porcelain, s. *nome d'erba anche da noi chiamata porcellana.*

PORCH, s. [the entrance of an house] *portico,* s. m.

PO'RCUPINE, s. [a kind of hedgehog armed with sharp darts and prickles, which resemble pens] *istrice, porco spinoso,* s. m. *animal noto.*

PORE, s. [a spiracle in the skin, through which sweat or vapours pass insensibly out of the body] *poro,* s. m. *picciol meato della pelle e della cotenna, donde svapora il corpo.*

To PORE [to look close to] *riguardar fissamente, fissar la vista.*

To pore upon a book, *aver li occhi fissi sopra un libro, leggerlo con attenzione.*

Pore blind, adj. *di corta vista.*

FORK, s. [swine's flesh] *carne di porco.*

PO'RKER, s. [a hog, a pig] *porco, porcello, porchetto, porcastro.*

PORKE'ATER, s. *uno che mangia carne di porco, uno che non è giudeo.*

PO'RKET, s. [a young hog] *porcello, porcelletto, porcellino,* s. m.

PO'RKLING, s. *porcello, porchetto, porcelletto, porco di latte.*

PORO'SE, } adj. [full of pores] *po-*
PO'ROUS, } *roso, pien di pori.*

PORO'SITY, s. [a being porous, or full of pores] *porosità,* s. f. *astrato di poroso.*

PO'ROUS, *v.* Porose.

PO'RPHIRE, } s. [a kind of fine
PO'RPHYRY, } marble] *porfido,* s. m. *marmo noto durissimo.*

PO'RPOISE, } s. [a sea-hog] *porco*
PORPUS, } *pesce, porco di mare.*

PO'RRENGER, s. [a kitchen utensil] *scodella,* s. f. *vasetto cupo, e serve per lo più a mettervi dentro minestre.*

A little porrenger, *uno scodellino.*

To put broth or porridge in the porringer, *scodellare, metter la minestra nelle scodelle.*

A surgeon's porringer [to receive blood in] *scodellino di chirurgo.*

PO'RRIDGE, s. [soop, pottage] *minestra, zuppa,* s. f.

Milk porridge, *minestra, o zuppa di latte.*

A porridge dish, *piatto di minestra.*

PO'RRINGER, *v.* Porrenger.

PORT, s. [haven] *porto,* s. m. *luogo nel lito del mare, dove per sicurezza ricovrano le navi.*

The port of a billiard, *porta di trucco.*

Port, or port-holes in a ship [square holes through which the great guns are thrust out] *cannoniera di vascello.*

Port-clearing, *partenza d'un vascello.*

Port [red wine from Oporto] *vin rosso d'Oporto in Portogallo.*

Port [the court of the grand Signior] *la Porta Ottomana, la corte del gran Signore.*

To port [to carry] *portare.*

PO'RTABLE, adj. [that may be carried] *portabile, portatile, da potersi portare.*

PO'RTABLE, adj. [supportable] *sopportevole, che si può sopportare o soffrire.*

PO'RTAGE, } s. [the price of car-
PO'RTERAGE, } riage] *il porto, la portatura, il prezzo che paghi per cosa che t' è stata portata.*

Portage, s. [port-hole] *portello.*

PO'RTAL, s. [a gate; the arch under which the gate opens] *una porta, o l'arco sotto cui la porta s'apre.*

PO'RTCULLIS, s. [a falling gate or door like a harrow, hung over the gates of fortified places, and let down to keep the enemy out of a city] *saracinesca, seracinesca,* s. f. *serratura di legname, o simile, che si fa calare da alto a basso per impedire il passaggio a' nemici che non entrino nella città.*

PO'RTED, adj. *portato.*

To PO'RTEND [to forebode, to foreshow, to betoken] *predire, prevedere, pronosticare, prevedendo annunziare il futuro,* pret. *predissi, previdi.*

PO'RTENDED, adj. *predetto, pronosticato, previsto.*

PORTE'NT, s. [omen, prodigy] *portento, prodigio,* s. m.

PORTE'NTOUS, adj. [ominous] *portentoso, prodigioso.*

PO'RTER, s. [one who keeps the door] *portinajo,* s. m. *custode della porta.*

The porter of the verge [that carries a white rode before the judges] *bidello,* s. m.

The porter [or carrier] *portatore, facchino,* s. m. *quegli che porta pesi addosso prezzolato.*

PO'RTGLAIVE, s. [one who carries the sword before a prince or magistrate] *colui che porta la spada avanti un principe o magistrato.*

PO'RTGREVE, s. [the title of the governor of some sea-port towns] *nome di magistrato in alcune terre maritime d'Inghilterra.*

PO'RTICO, s. [porch] *portico,* s. m.

PO'RTION, s. [share] *porzione, parte,* s. f.

A small portion, *porzioncella,* s. f.

A woman's portion [that which she brings her husband in marriage] *dote,* s. f.

She had ten thousand pounds to her portion, *ella ha avuto dieci mila lire sterline di dote.*

PO'RTIONERS, s. [ministers which serve a parsonage alternately] *ministri o preti che fanno le funzioni del loro ministero alternamente, e così vengono tutti à partecipare delle decime.*

PO'RTLINESS, s. [majestick gate] *aria maestosa, vago portamento.*

PO'RTLY, adj. [majestick, stately] *maestoso, grande, nobile, vago.*

A portly mien, *un' andatura maestosa, o nobile.*

PO'RTMAN, s. *borghese, borgese, cittadino.*

The twelve portmen of Ipswich, *i dodici borghesi d'Ipswich.*

The portmen [or inhabitants] of the cinque ports, *i cittadini de' cinque porti.*

PORTMA'NTEAU, s. [a cloak-bag to carry necessaries on a journey] *portamantello,* s. m.

PO'RTMOTE, s. [a court kept in seaport towns] *corte che si tiene nelle città o terre maritime.*

To PO'RTRAIT, *dipignere ritratti, far ritratti.*

PO'RTRAITURE, s. [picture] *ritratto,* s. m. *pittura,* s. f. *quadro,* s. m.

To PO'RTRAY [to draw] *dipignere,* pret. *dipinsi.*

PO'RTRAYED, adj. *dipinto.*

PO'RTRESS, s. [a female guardian of a gate] *portinaja; guardiana della porta.*

PO'RTSALE, s. [outcry or publick sale of any commodity] *incanto,* s. m.

Portsale [a sale of fish presently after a return into the haven] *la vendita del pesce nell' arrivare nel porto.*

PO'RY, adj. [full of pores] *poroso; pieno di pori.*

POSE, s. [a physical term for rheum in the head] *catarro,* s. m. *gravedine,* s. f.

To POSE [to puzzle, to put to a nonplus] *imbarazzare, intrigare, imbrogliare.*

PO'SED, adj. *imbarazzato, intrigato, imbrogliato.*

A PO'SER, s. *quello che imbarazza.*

PO'SING, s. *imbarazzo, intrigo, imbroglio,* s. m.

POSI'TION, s. [situation] *positura, proposizione,* s. f.

Poſition [theſis] *poſizione, propoſta, propoſizione*, s. f.

Po'sitive, adj [abſolute, certain] *poſitivo, aſſoluto, certo.*

Poſitive [real, neither relative nor arbitrary] *poſitivo, che non è relativo nè arbitrario.*

Poſitive divinity [that which is according to the poſitions and tenets of the fathers of the church] *teologia poſitiva.*

The poſitive degree [the firſt degree of compariſon] *grado poſitivo, il poſitivo.*

To be poſitive in a thing [to ſtand to it] *eſſer certo o ſicuro di che ſi ſia.*

I am poſitive of it, *ne ſon certo, ne ſono ſicuro.*

Po'sitively, adv. *poſitivamente, aſſolutamente, certamente.*

Po'siture, s. [diſpoſition] *poſitura, ſituazione, diſpoſizione.* s. f.

To Posse'ss [to enjoy, to be maſter of] *poſſedere, aver in podeſtà, in podere, in potere*

The devil poſſeſſes him, *egli ha il diavolo in corpo.*

To poſſeſs one with an opinion, *preoccupare altrui di qualche opinione.*

To poſſeſs one's ſelf of a thing, *impoſſeſſarſi di che che ſi ſia.*

To poſſeſs one's ſelf of a town, *impadronirſi d'una città o d'una terra.*

Posse'ssed, adj. *poſſeduto.*

To be poſſeſſed by the devil, *eſſer indemoniato, o tormentato dal diavolo.*

Poſſeſſed with a pannick fear, *aſſalito d'un timor panico.*

Poſſeſſed [prepoſſeſſed] *preoccupato.*

To be lively poſſeſſed with God's grace, *eſſer vivamente penetrato dalla grazia di Dio.*

Poſſeſſed with buſineſs, *occupato, che ha molti affari affaccendato.*

Posse'ssion, s. [actual enjoyment] *poſſeſſione*, s. f. *il poſſedere, poſſeſſo*, s. m.

To be in poſſeſſion of a thing, *eſſer in poſſeſſione, o poſſeſſo di che che ſi ſia.*

Posse'ssions [demeſnes, lands, or tenements] *poſſeſſione, poderi.*

Possessive, adj. *poſſeſſivo.*

Poſſeſſive pronoun, *pronome poſſeſſivo.*

A Posse'ssor, s. [he that poſſeſſes] *poſſeſſore, poſſeditore*, s. m. *che poſſiede.*

Po'sset, s. [milk turn'd with ale] *ſorta di bevanda molto comune in Inghilterra compoſta di latte e cervogia dolce.*

Sack poſſet, *bevanda compoſta di vin dolce, di latte, nocemoſcata, uova ſbattute, e zucchero.*

To Po'sset [to turn, to curdle, as milk with acids] *divenir agro e rappreſo, come fa il latte inſuſovi degli acidi*

Possibi'lity, s. [likelihood] *poſſibilità*, s f. *aſtratto di poſſibile.*

There's no poſſibility of it, *non è poſſibile.*

Po'ssible, adj. [that may be done, or may happen, likely] *poſſibile, che può farſi, che può eſſere.*

Po'ssibly, adv. [perhaps] *poſſibile, forſe.*

Poſſibly you'll ſay, *forſe voi mi direte.*

I will do it if I poſſibly can, *lo farò, ſe potrò, o ſe ſarà in poter mio.*

Post, s. [a term of war, a ſtation or place that is capable of lodging ſoldiers] *poſta*, s. f. *poſto, luogo*, s m.

Advanced poſt [a ſpot of ground before the other poſts, to ſecure thoſe behind] *poſto avanzato.*

Poſt [place, employment] *carica*, s. f. *impiego*, s. m.

He has a poſt of a hundred a year, *egli ha una carica di cento lire ſterline l'anno.*

Poſt [an expeditious way of travelling] *poſta*, s. f.

To ride poſt, *andare per le poſte, correr la poſta.*

Poſt horſes, *cavalli di poſta.*

He that keeps poſt horſes, *poſtiere*, s. m.

He rid poſt hither, *venne quà per le poſte.*

Poſt [the meſſenger that carries letters] *poſta, il corriere, procaccio, che porta le lettere.*

The poſt is not come, *la poſta non è ancora arrivata.*

A foot poſt, *corriere a piedi.*

Poſt-houſe, *la poſta, il luogo dove ſi danno, e portano le lettere.*

Poſt-houſe, *la poſta.*

Poſt-maſter, *il maeſtro della poſta.*

Poſt-boy, *poſtiglione, guida de' cavalli di poſta.*

Pe'nny-post, *poſta che va per Londra e poche miglia intorno ſolamente.*

In poſt-haſte, *in fretta.*

To make poſt-haſte, *andar per le poſte, fare ogni diligenza poſſibile.*

Poſt-ſtage, *poſta, ſpazio di cammino, dove muta i cavalli chi corre la poſta.*

Poſt [a ſtake, or ſmall wooden pillar driven into the ground] *palo fitto in terra.*

To tie a malefactor to a poſt, *legare un malfattore ad un palo.*

To be toſſed from poſt to pillar, *eſſer grandemente agitato, o ſbattuto.*

A knight of the poſt [a falſe witneſs] *un teſtimonio falſo.*

Poſt-doctor [mountebank] *cerretano, montimbanco, ciarlatano.*

To Post [to ride poſt] *andare in poſta, o per le poſte.*

To poſt away with a thing, *ſpedire o ſpacciare che che ſi ſia.*

To poſt one for a coward [to make his cowardice publick] *ſpacciare uno per codardo, far nota la ſua codardia.*

To poſt, among merchants [is to put an account forward from one book to another] *traſcrivere un conto d'un libro di conti in un altro.*

Po'stage, s. [money paid for the carriage of letters and packets] *porto*, s. m. *il danaro che ſi paga per la portatura delle lettere.*

Post-commu'nion, s. [the office ſaid at church after the communion] *il poſtcommunio, preghiere dopo la comunione.*

Po'st-date, *data falſa.*

To Po'st-date [to ſet a new or falſe date upon it] *metter una data falſa, cioè qualche tempo dopo la vera data.*

Po'st-dated, *che ha la data falſa.*

Po'ster, s. [a courier; one that travels haſtily] *corriere; uno che viaggia in fretta, e correndo la poſta.*

Posterio'rity, s. [a being after or behind] *poſteriorità.*

Poste'riour, adj [that comes after] *poſteriore, che ſegue.*

Poſteriours, s. [hinder parts] *le parti deretane, il deretano.*

Poste'rity, s. [off-ſpring, iſſue, children] *poſterità, diſcendenza*, s. f.

Po'stern, s. [a back-door, or poſtern gate] *poſtierla, porticciuola*, s. f.

Po'sthume, } adj. [born after
Po'sthumous, } the father's death] *poſtumo, nato dopo la morte del padre.*

A poſthumous child, *un poſtumo.*

An author's poſthumous works [publiſhed after his death] *opere poſtume d'un autore, date alla luce dopo la ſua morte.*

Po'stil, s. [a ſhort note or explication upon any text] *poſtilla*, s. f. *parole brevi, che ſi pongono in margine a' libri, in dichiarazion d'eſſi.*

To Po'stil, *poſtillare, far poſtille.*

A Posti'llion, s. [he that rides on one of the foremoſt of the coach-horſes when there is a ſet; or he that guides a poſt-chaiſe] *poſtiglione.*

Po'stiller, s [he that writes poſtils] *comentatore*, s. m. *colui che fa poſtille.*

Postme'ridian, adj. [done in the afternoon] *del dopo mezzogiorno, fatto dopo mezzogiorno.*

To Po'stpone, s. [to make leſs account of, to leave or neglect] *far poco conto, diſprezzare, diſpregiare, avere a vile, tenere a vile.*

To poſtpone [to ſet behind] *poſporre, metter dopo, negligere*, pres. *poſpongo*, pret. *poſpoſi, negleſſi.*

Po'stponed, adj. *diſprezzoto, diſpregiato, avuto o tenuto a vile, poſpoſto, neglctto.*

Po'stcript, s. [an addition at the end of a writing] *poſcritto*, s. m.

Po'stulate, s. [poſition ſuppoſed or aſſumed without proof] *punto ſuppoſto vero, da cui un argomento diriva, e ſu cui ſi regge.*

To Po'stulate, s. [to demand] *domandare, richiedere*, pret. *richieſi.*

Postula'tion, s. *richieſta, domanda*, s. m.

Po'stulatory, adj. [belonging to a poſtulate] *che ſerve a domandare.*

Po'sture, s [a certain ſituation of the body] *poſtura, poſitura*, s. f.

Poſture [condition, ſtate] *ſtato*, s. m. *condizione*, s. f.

Poſture [order] *ordine*, s m.

Posy, s [device, motto] *motto*, s. m. *parole ſcolpite in un anello.*

Poſy [noſegay] *un mazzetto di fiori.*

Pot, s. [a veſſel to hold liquor or any other thing in] *boccale, vaſo*, s. m.

Drinking pot, *boccale.*

Flower-pot, *teſto, vaſo di terra cotta dove ſi pongon le piante.*

Watering-pot, *annaffiatojo.*

Gally

Gally-pot, *vaso di majolica, boccia*, s. f.

Seething-pot, *pentola, pignatta*.

Pot [a measure] *boccale, misura*.

A pot of beer, *un boccale di cervogia*.

A pot [a sort of head-piece] *morione*, s. m. *armadura del capo del soldato appiè*.

A pot-lid, *un coperchio d' un vaso, un testo*.

Pot-hook, *manico d' un vaso*.

A pot-hanger, *catena del cammino*.

Pot-sherd, *coccio*, s. m. *pezzo di vaso di terra cotta, rotto*.

Pot-gun, *cannoniera*, s. f.

Pot-ashes [to make soap] *ceneri di sermenti da fare il sapone*.

Pot-butter, *butirro salato*.

Pot-herb, *erba buona a mangiare, erbaggio*.

Pot-belly'd, *panciuto, di grossa pancia*.

A pot companion, *uno scialacquatore, un gran bevitore*.

To go to pot [to be destroyed or devoured] *esser divorato o distrutto*.

To Pot [to put in the pot] *mettere in vaso*.

Po'table, adj. [drinkable] *potabile, che si può bere*.

Po'targo, s. [a West-Indian pickle] *cosa mangiativa che viene dall' Indie Occidentali*.

A Pota'toe, s. [a sort of eatable root] *pomo di terra*.

Po'tency, s. [power] *potenza, e potenzia, possanza, forza*, s. f. *potere*, s. m.

Po'tent, adj. [mighty] *potente, possente*.

Po'tentate, s. [a sovereign prince] *potentato*, s. m. *che ha signoria, e dominio*.

Pote'ntial, adj. [having a power or possibility of acting or being] *potenziale, che ha potenza di fare*.

Pote'ntially, adv. [a philosophical word, opposite to actually] *potenzialmente, con virtù potenziale, termine scientifico*.

Po'tently, adv. *potentemente, con gran possanza, con molto vigore*.

Po'thecary, s. [*abbreviato da* apothecary] *speziale; compositore o venditore di medicine e di droghe e cose medicinali*.

Po'ther, s. [bustle, tumult, flutter] *scompiglio, tumulto, confuso, strepito*.

Pother [suffocating cloud] *nube o nuvola che soffoca*.

To Po'ther [to make a blustering ineffectual effort] *far molto strepito e molto gridare e schiamazzare senza che ne segua effetto alcuno*.

Po'tion, s. [a physical mixture to drink] *pozione, bevanda*, s. f. *beveraggio*, s. m.

Love-potion, *bevanda amorosa*.

Po'tsherd, s. *coccio*, s. m. *pezzo di vaso rotto, di terra cotta*.

Po'ttage, s. [porridge] *minestra, zuppa*, s. f.

French pottage, *minestra alla Francese*.

Po'tter, s. [a maker or seller of earthen ware] *pentolajo*, s. m. *quegli che fa e vende le pentole*.

Potter's ware, *ogni sorta di vasi di terra, vasellamenti di terra*.

Potter's clay, *argilla*, s. f. *terra tegnente, dalla quale si fan le stoviglie*.

Po'ttle, s. *misura Inglese di fragole e altre cose*.

Pot-valliant, adj. *valoroso, pien di coraggio dopo d' aver bevuto*.

Pouch, s. [bag, purse] *tasca, scarsella, borsa*, s. f.

A shepherd's pouch, *un zaino*.

A pouch-mouth, *labbruto, che ha grosse labbra*.

To Pouch, verb neut. *arricciare il viso, fare il grugno*.

To pouch, *intascare, riporsi in tasca; e anche inghiottire, ingojare*.

Po'verty, s. [the being poor] *povertà, mancanza, necessità*, s. f. *bisogno*, s. m.

Po'uldavis, s. [a sort of sail cloth] *sorta di tela grossolana da far vele*.

Poult, s. [a young chicken] *pulcino; pollastrello*.

Po'ulterer, s. [he that sells poultry] *pollajuolo*, s. m. *mercante di polli*.

Po'ultice, s. [a medicine made of several ingredients boiled together, and apply'd hot to the part afflicted, to asswage a swelling, &c.] *cataplasmo*, s. m.

Po'ultry, s. [all sorts of domestick fowls] *pollame*, s. m.

Pounce, s. [the talon or claw of a bird of prey] *artiglio*, s. m. *unghia adunca, e pugnente d' animali volatili rapaci*.

The pounces of an eagle, *gli artigli d' un acquila*.

Pounce [a sort of powder] *polvere di pietra pumice*.

To Pounce [to grasp with pounces] *artigliare, prendere e tener coll' artiglio, sforacchiare*.

Po'unced, adj. *artigliato, preso coll' artiglio, sforacchiato*.

Po'uncetbox, s. *scatoletta sforacchiata, cioè col coperchio pieno di buchi, onde scuotendola n' esca quel che v' è dentro*.

A Pound, s. [a place where cattle, distrain'd for a trespass, are detain'd till they are deemed] *spezie di prigione per le bestie che sono sequestrate quando son trovate mangiando l' erba o le biade altrui*.

A pound, s. [a sort of weight] *libbra*, s. f.

A pound sterling [twenty shillings] *una lira sterlina, cioè venti scellini; è moneta imaginaria*.

A pound Scots [twenty-pence] *lira Scozzese, venti soldi*.

A pound weight, *il peso d' una libbra*.

To Pound [or beat in a mortar] *pestare*.

To pound [to shut up cattle in a pound] *rinchiudere il bestiame in un pound*, v. Pound, *nel primo significato*.

Po'undage, s. [a shilling in the pound] *uno scillino per lira*.

Poundage, s. [a duty of one shilling for every twenty shillings value of merchandize, imported or exported, paid to the king] *dazio d' uno scillino per lira sopra tutte le mercanzie che sono portate e trasportate*.

To pay poundage, *pagare uno scillino per lira*.

Po'under, s. [from pound] ex. a ten pounder, *un cannone di dieci libbre di portata*.

Po'unding, s. *pestamento*, s. m. *il pestare*.

To Pour, to pour out [to empty out of one vessel into another] *versare*.

To pour water into a sieve, *versar dell' acqua in un vaglio; lavare il capo all' asino; far beneficio a chi no 'l conosce, e non ne fa capitale*.

To pour one's forces into the enemy's country, *inondare il paese nemico*.

To pour down [to rain deadly fast] *diluviare, piovere strabocchevolmente*.

Po'urcontrel, s. [a fish] *polpo*, s. m. *spezie di pesce*.

Po'ured, adj. *versato*, v. To pour.

Pouring, s. *il versare*.

Pout, v. Powt.

To Pout, v. To powt.

Po'wder, s. *polvere*, s. f.

Sweet powder, *polvere di cipro*.

Gun-powder, *polvere d' archibuso*.

To do a thing with powder [or in great haste] *far che che si sia in gran fretta*.

Powder sugar, *zucchero polverizzato*.

A powder-box, *polverino*.

A powder-mill, *mulino da polvere*.

Powder-ink, *polvere per far l' inchiostro*.

He that makes the powder, *polverista*.

To Po'wder, *spolverizzare, coprire di polvere*.

To powder a perriwig, *dar la polvere a una parrucca*.

To powder [or bring to powder] *polverizzare, ridurre in polvere*.

To powder beef [to salt it] *salare del manzo*.

Po'wdered, adj. *polverizzato, spolverizzato*, v. To powder.

Powdered with spots, *maculato, macchiato di più e varj colori; chiazzato*.

Powdering, s. *il polverizzare*, v. To powder.

Powdering, adj. ex. a powdering tub, *un tinello*.

Po'wer, s. [ability, force] *potere, vigore*, s. m. *forza, potenza, possanza*, s. f.

Power [authority] *potere, autorità*.

Power [influence] *potere, influsso, influenza*.

Power [puissance, a sovereign prince, or state] *potentato, principe o stato sovrano*.

The powers of the soul, *le potenze dell' anima, le facoltà dell' anima*.

Powers [in divinity, are the third order of the hierarchy of angels] *podestadi, potestadi, nome del terzo ordine della gerarchia degli angeli*.

A power [or a great deal] *una gran quantità, un gran numero, molto*.

He has a power of flowers in his' garden, *egli ha una gran quantità di fiori nel suo giardino.*

Po'WERFUL, adj. [that has power or authority] *potente, possente.*

Powerful [efficacious] *potente, efficace.*

Very powerfully, *potentissimo.*

Po'WERFULLY, adv. *potentemente, possentemente.*

POWT, s. [a sea-lamprey] *lampreda di mare.*

Eel-powt [small eel] *ciecolina, anguilla piccolissima.*

Powt [a sort of bird] *francolino*, s. m.

Pheasant-powt [young pheasant] *un fagianotto, fagiano giovine.*

To POWT [to look surly or gruff] *fare il grugno, guardare in cagnesco, fare il viso arcigno.*

Po'WTING, s. *viso torvo, o arcigno.*

Powting fellow, *un uomo burbero, d' aspetto torvo, austero o rigido.*

Po'WTINGLY, adv. *con viso torvo, arcigno, austero, burbero, cagnesco.*

Pox [venereal disease] *malfranzese*, s. m. *sorta di malattia contagiosa.*

The small-pox, *vajuolo*, s. m. *le vajuola*, s. f.

The chicken-pox, *morviglione, rovaglione*, s. m.

POY, s. [the pole used by rope dancers, to stay themselves with] *contrappeso di ballerino di corda.*

Po'YNANT, v. Poinant.

Po'YSON, v. Poison.

PRA'CTICABLE, adj. [that may be practised or done] *praticable, da esser praticato.*

PRA'CTICAL, } adj. [belonging to
PRA'CTICK, } practice, the contrary of speculative] *pratico, contrario di speculativo.*

The practical part of a thing, *l' uso pratico, la pratica.*

Practical divinity, *la teologia pratica, la morale.*

PRA'CTICE, s. [actual exercise, especially that of the profession of a physician, surgeon, or lawyer] *pratica*, s. f.

That physician hath a great deal of practice, *quel medico ha gran pratica.*

Practice [custom, usage] *pratica, uso, conversazione.*

You want but some practice, *non vi manca che un poco di pratica.*

To put in practice, *porre, mettere in pratica.*

To bring into practice, *ridurre in uso pratico.*

Practice [device, intrigue, way of proceeding] *pratica, negozio, trattato.*

By foul practice, *con mezzi indiretti.*

Secret practice, *pratiche segrete.*

He entered into new practice with several English noblemen, *entrò in nuove pratiche con diversi signori Inglesi; cominciò di nuovo a praticare con molti signori Inglesi.*

To PRA'CTISE [to put into practice] *praticare, mettere in pratica.*

To practise [to profess, to exercise a profession] *praticare, esercitare, professare, far professione.*

To practise physick, *praticare, professare, o esercitare la medicina.*

To practise upon one [to endeavour to draw him into one's interest] *praticare alcuno, tastarlo, sollecitarlo, cercare di tirarlo dalla sua banda, guadagnarlo, tirarlo dalla sua.*

PRA'CTISED, adv. *praticato, versato, pratico, esperto, esercitato*, v. To practise.

He is well practised in the law, *egli è ben versato nella legge.*

PRACTI'TIONER, s. [one that practises in the law, physick, surgery, &c.] *uno studente, o studiante.*

PRAGMA'TICAL, } adj. *prammati-*
PRAGMA'TICK, } *co.*

Pragmatical [over busy in other mens affairs, saucy, arrogant] *spavaldo, protervo, arrogante, sfacciato.*

A pragmatical fellow, *un ser faccenda, un uomo che volentieri s' intriga in ogni cosa; un affannone; quegli che d' ogni cosa si piglia soverchia briga; un imbroglione, un arcifanfano, un tuttesalle.*

PRAGMA'TICALNESS, s. *protervia, arroganza*, s. f.

PRAGMA'TICK, s. [an ordinance about ecclesiastical affairs] *prammatica*, s. f.

PRAISE, s. [commendation] *lode, laude, laudazione, lodo*, s. f. *vanto*, s. m.

Praise worthy, adj. [or worthy of praise] *laudabile, laudevole, lodevole, commendabile.*

To PRAISE [to give praise to, to commend] *laudare, lodare, commendare, dar lode.*

Praise the sea, but keep on land, *loda il mare e tienti alla terra; cioè lodare l' util grande e pericoloso, e tenersi al piccolo e sicuro.*

To praise God [to give him thanks] *lodare, o ringraziare Iddio.*

To praise [to prize, to appraise, to value goods] *apprezzare, stimare, valutare.*

PRA'ISED, adj. *laudato, commendato, apprezzato, stimato, valutato.*

PRA'ISER, s. [a praiser of goods] *stimatore, estimatore, avvisatore*, s. m. *avvisatrice*, s. f.

A praiser [he that praises, or gives praises] *lodatore*, s. m. *lodatrice*, s. f.

PRA'ISING, s. *lodamento*, s. m. *il lodare*, v. To praise.

PRAME, s. [a flat-bottomed boat] *battello o barca col fondo piatto.*

To PRANCE [to throw up the forelegs, as horses do] *inalberarsi, impennarsi, alzarsi i cavalli su i piedi di dietro.*

PRA'NCER, s. *un cavallo a mano.*

PRA'NCING, adj. *che s' inalbera, o s' impenna.*

A prancing horse, *un cavallo che s' inalbera.*

PRANK, s. [a shrewd or unlucky trick] *tiro*, s. m. *burla, giarda*, s. f.

To play one a lewd prank, *fare un tiro, o una giarda ad uno.*

A prank, *pazzia, stravaganza, fraschería frasche, bojata, bagattella.*

To PRANK [to set off, to deck, to trim] *ornare, adornare, abbigliare, abbellire*, pres. *abbellisco.*

To prank one's self up, *ornarsi, adornarsi, abbellirsi per ostentazione.*

PRA'NKED, adj. *ornato, adornato, abbellito, abbigliato.*

PRA'NKING up, s. *ornamento, abbellimento.*

PRATE, s. [tattle, slight talk, unmeaning loquacity] *ciarla, ciancia, tattamella, cicalio, cicaleccio, cicalamento, il ciaramellare; vana loquacità.*

To PRATE [to talk very much, to prattle] *ciarlare, parlare assai e vanamente, cornacchiare, cicalare, ciaramellare.*

PRA'TER, s. *ciarlatore, ciarliero, cicalone, ciarlone*, s. m. *ciarlatrice*, s. f.

PRA'TING, s. *ciarla, vana loquacità, cicaleria, cicalata*, s. f. *cicaleccio, cicalio*, s. m.

Prating, adj. *ciarlante, cicalante, che ciarla, che cicala.*

A prating man or woman, *un ciarlone, un ciarliero, una ciarlatrice.*

PRA'TIQUE, } s. [a licence to traffick
PRA'TICK, } or trade, granted to masters of ships in the ports of Italy] *pratica, commercio, negozio, traffico.*

To PRA'TTLE [to talk or chat] *ciarlare, essere vanamente loquace.*

PRATTLER, s. *cicalone, ciarlone, ciarliero*, s. m. *ciarlatrice*, s. f.

PRA'TTLING, s. *ciarla, ciarleria*, s. f. *cicaleccio, cicalio*, s. m.

PRA'VITY, s. [corruption of manners, lewdness] *pravità, malignità, malvagità*, s. f.

PRAWN, s. [a little sort of sea-fish] *squilla*, s. f. *spezie di gambero piccolo di mare.*

To PRAY [to entreat, to beseech] *pregare, supplicare, domandare in grazia, scongiurare.*

Pray do it, *ve ne prego, ve ne supplico.*

Pray tell me what it is, *ditemi di grazia quel che è.*

To pray to God [to call upon God] *pregare, o invocare Iddio.*

To pray to the saints, *pregare i santi.*

PRA'YER, adj. *pregato, supplicato, scongiurato.*

Prayer, s. [desire, request] *priego, prego*, s. m. *richiesta, domanda, preghiera*, s. f.

Prayer [a supplication to God] *preghiera, orazione*, s. f.

To say one's prayers, *dire le sue divozioni.*

The common prayers, *le preghiere comuni che si dicono in chiesa secondo 'l rito della chiesa Anglicana.*

To be at prayers, *stare in orazione.*

A prayer book, *libro di preghiere.*

The Lord's prayer, *l'orazione dominicale, il paternostro.*

PRA'YING, s. *il pregare.*

To PREACH [to deliver a sermon] *predicare, fare una predica.*

To preach [to publish, to proclaim] *pre-*

predicare, annunziare, dichiarare pubblicamente.

To preach [to read a lecture to one] garrire *riprendere, fare una predica ad uno, fargli una riprensione.*

To preach up [to cry up] *predicare, lodare, vantare, esaltare, magnificare, sublimare.*

To preach one's self up, *lodarsi, vantarsi.*

PRE'ACHED, adj. *predicato, v.* To preach.

PRE'ACHER, s. [one who preaches] *un predicatore.*

A mean or sorry preacher, *un predicatorello.*

PRE'ACHING, s. *predicazione, predica,* s. f.

PRE'ACHMENT, s. [sermon] *predica,* s. f.

Leave off your preachments, *deh finitela con queste vostre prediche.*

PRE-A'DAMITES, s. [people fancied by some to have lived before Adam] *preadamiti, quelli, che alcuni credono essere stati prima d' Adamo.*

PREA'MBLE, s. [the introduction or beginning of any discourse] *preambolo, e preambulo,* s. m. *prefazione,* s. f.

A long preamble [a tedious discourse] *un lungo preambolo, un discorso lungo e tedioso.*

PRE'BEND, s. [a canon's place or revenue] *prebenda,* s. f. *prebendato, prebendatico,* s. m. *rendita ferma di canonicato.*

Prebend, } [he that has a prebend]
Prebendary } *un cherico prebendato.*

PRECA'RIOUS, adj. [got by favour, or held upon courtesy, at another's will and pleasure] *ottenuto per favore, incerto, mendicato.*

A precarious government, *un governo incerto, ottenuto per favore.*

Precarious praises, *lodi mendicate.*

A precarious king, *un Re che non ha ch' una autorità mendicata.*

I will not have it in a precarious way, *non voglio mendicarlo.*

PRECA'RIOUSLY, adv. *per preghiera, per favore.*

PRECA'UTION, s. [fore-warning, caution, or heed given or taken beforehand] *cautela, cauzione,* s. f. *avvedimento, avvertimento,* s. m.

To use great precautions, *andar cauteloso, o circonspetto.*

Take your precaution, *pigliate le vostre misure.*

To PRECE'DE [to go before] *precedere, andare avanti, aver la precedenza.*

To precede [to excel] *eccedere, sopravanzare, superare, sormontare, avanzare, soprafare.*

PRECE'DED, adj. *preceduto.*

PRECE'DENCE } s. *precedenza,* s. f.
PRECE'DENCY } *il precedere.*

To give one the precedency, *dar la precedenza ad uno, cedergli il luogo.*

PRECE'DENT, adj. [foregoing] *precedente, che è avanti, che precede.*

Precedent [example] *esempio,* s. m. *instanza, e istanza,* s. f.

A precedent, in law [an original writing or deed, to draw others by] *scrittura originale.*

A precedent-book [a book containing precedents or draughts of deeds for attornies] *protocollo,* s. m. *libro dove i notai mettono i testamenti, e i contratti ch' essi rogano.*

PRECEDE'NTIAL, adj. [belonging to precedency] *che concerne la precedenza.*

PRECE'DENTLY, adv. *precedentemente, innanzi.*

PRECE'LLENCE } s. [excellency a-
PRECE'LLENCY } bove another thing] *eccellenza, preminenza,* s. f. *vantaggio d' onoranza, che ha più un che un altro.*

To give a thing the precellency above another, *preferire, o preporre una cosa ad un' altra.*

PRECE'NTOR, s. [the chanter that begins the tune in a cathedral] *intonatore, e intuonatore,* s. m. *che intuona, che da principio al canto.*

PRE'CEPT, s. [rule, instruction] *precetto, ammaestramento,* s. m. *istruzione, regola, norma,* s. f.

Precept [commandment] *precetto, comandamento, ordine,* s. m.

PRE'CEPTOR, s. [tutor, master, *precettore, maestro, ajo,* s. m.

PRECE'PTORIES, s. [benefices anciently possess'd by the more eminent Templars, whom the chief masters created] *benefici che altre volte possedevano i Templari.*

PRECI'NCT, s. [a particular jurisdiction, within which several parishes are comprehended] *precinto, circuito, territorio, limite,* s. m.

PRE'CIOUS, adj. [that is of great price or value] *prezioso, di gran pregio di gran valore, di grande stima.*

PRE'CIOUSLY, adv. *preziosamente.*

PRE'CIOUSNESS, s. [the being precious] *preziosità,* s. f. *astratto di prezioso.*

PRE'CIPICE, s. [a steep place dangerous to go upon] *precipizio, luogo dirupato.*

Precipice [danger] *precipizio, pericolo.*

Precipice [misfortune] *precipizio, disgrazia, rovina.*

PRECI'PITANCE } s. [rash, haste,
PRECI'PITANCY } headlong, hurry] *fretta temeraria, precipitoso correre capitombolando.*

PRECI'PITANT, adj. [dangerous, rash] *precipitoso, pericoloso, inconsiderato.*

A precipitant conceit, *precipitoso giudizio.*

PRECI'PITATE, adj. [over hasty] *precipitoso, inconsiderato, senza ritegno.*

Precipitate mercury [mercury dissolved in spirit of nitre] *mercurio precipitato.*

To PRECI'PITATE [to throw or cast down headlong] *precipitare, gittare una cosa con furia e rovinosamente da alto a basso.*

To precipitate [to hurry, to overhasten] *precipitare, affrettare.*

To precipitate a business, *precipitare o affrettare un negozio.*

To precipitate [among chymists, is to separate a matter which is dissolved, so as to make it settle at bottom] *precipitare, termine proprio de' chimici, ed è il cadere de' metalli o altro in fondo del vajo quando corrosi dall' acqua forte vi s' infonde altra cosa appropriata a ciò.*

To precipitate mercury, *precipitar del mercurio.*

PRECI'PITATE, adj. *precipitato.*

PRECIPITA'TION, s. [hurry, too great haste] *precipitazione, troppo gran fretta, inconsiderazione,* s. f.

Precipitation [a chymical preparation] *precipitazione, preparazione chimica.*

PRECI'PITOUS, adj. [over hasty, rash] *precipitoso, inconsiderato, senza ritegno frettoloso.*

PRECI'SE, adj. [exact, particular] *preciso, distinto, particolare, esatto.*

Precise [scrupulous] *scrupoloso, superstizioso.*

A precise man, *un uomo scrupoloso.*

Precise [finical, affected] *affettato, che negli atti e nelle parole usa soverchio artificio, e che va composto, e riservato.*

A precise woman, *una donna affettata, o riservata.*

PRECI'SELY, adv. *precisamente, succintamente, risolutamente, distintamente, esattamente, particolarmente.*

PRECI'SIAN, s. [one who is overscrupulous in points of religion] *uno scrupoloso, un superstizioso, un bacchettone.*

To PRECLU'DE [to shut out or hinder by some anticipation] *chiuder fuora o escludere giungendo o facendo prima.*

PRECO'CITY, s. *maturità prima del tempo.*

To PRECO'GITATE [to think of before-hand] *premeditare.*

PRECO'GITATED, adj. *premeditato.*

PRECOGNI'TION, s. [foreknowledge] *preconoscenza, e precognoscenza,* s. f.

PRECONCE'ITED, adj. ex. a preconceited opinion, *un concetto, una concezione.*

To PRECONCE'IVE, ex. this is an opinion which he has preconceived, *questa è un opinione che s' è formata nell' idea.*

PRECONCE'PTION, s. [prejudice or notion taken up before-hand] *idea o concetto formato nella mente innanzi tratto.*

To PRECONCI'SE [to make a report in the pope's consistory, that the party presented to a benefice is qualified for the same] *preconizzare.*

PRECO'NTRACT, s. [a bargain made before another] *contratto anteriore.*

PRECU'RSOR, s. [fore-runner] *precursore,* s. m.

PRE'DATORY, adj. *predatorio.*

PREDECE'SSOR, s. [one who was in the employment before] *predecessore, antecessore,* s. m.

PREDECE'SSORS, s. pl. [ancestors, fore-ſore-fathers] *antenati, progenitori, predeceſſori.*

To PREDE'STINATE [to decree or ordain what ſhall come hereafter] *predeſtinare, il prevedere che fa Iddio della ſalvazione degli uomini; ſtatuire, deliberare, deſtinare avanti.*

PREDE'STINATED, adj. *predeſtinato.*

PREDESTINA'TION, s. [a fore-ordaining or appointing] *predeſtinazione,* s. f. *il predeſtinare, ed è quando Dio prevede che alcuno ſarà ſalvato, che non può eſſere che non ſia.*

To PREDETE'RMINE [to determine before-hand] *determinare, ſtatuire, deliberare, deſtinare avanti.*

PREDETE'RMINATED, adj. *determinato, ſtatuito, deliberato, deſtinato avanti.*

PRE'DIAL, adj. ex. predial tithes, law term [are thoſe which are paid of things ariſing and growing from the ground only] *decime che provengono dalla terra ſolamente, come grano, fieno, e ſimili.*

PREDICABLE, adj. [in logick, is a common word or term, which may be attributed to more than one thing] *predicabile, termine di logica.*

PRE'DICABLES, s. [are called UNIVERSALS, and are five in number, *viz. genus, ſpecies, proprium, differentia, and accidens*] *univerſali, termine di logica.*

PRE'DICAMENT, s. [a certain claſs or determinate ſeries or order in which ſimple terms or words are ranged] *predicamento,* s. m. *termine logicale, che vale uno de' dieci generi ſupremi a' quali ſi riducono tutte le coſe.*

PRE'DICANT, adj. [preaching] *predicante.*

The predicant friars, *i padri predicatori dell' ordine de' predicatori, i frati Domenicani, o dell' ordine di ſan Domenico.*

PRE'DICATE, s. [the latter part of a logical propoſition] *predicato,* s. m. *termine l g.co.*

To PRE'DICATE [to publiſh, to cry to preach up] *predicare, annunziare, dichiarare, pubblicare, manifeſtare, divolgare.*

To predicate, a term of logick; ex. Theſe two terms predicate one upon another] *queſti due termini ſono predicabili l' uno dell' altro.*

PRE'DICATED, adj. *predicato, annunziato, dichiarato, pubblicato, manifeſtato, divolgato.*

PREDICA'TION, s. [preaching, crying up] *predicazione,* s. f. *il predicare.*

PREDI'CTION, s. [foretelling] *predizione,* s. f. *predicimento,* s. m. *il predire.*

To PRE'DISPOSE [to diſpoſe before-hand] *diſporre, o ordinare avanti.*

PRE'DISPOSED, adj. *diſpoſto, ordinato avanti.*

PREDO'MINANCY, s. [a being predominant] *qualità o virtù predominante, che predomina.*

PREDO'MINANT, adj. [bearing chief ſway, over-ruling] *predominante, dominante, che predomina.*

To PREDO'MINATE [to over-rule, to bear ſway, or rule] *predominare, dominare.*

PREDY, adj. [a ſea word for ready] *pronto, in ordine.*

Make the ſhip ready for a fight, *alleſtite il vaſcello per la battaglia.*

To PRE-ELECT [to chuſe before] *eleggere avanti.*

PRE'-ELECTED, adj. *eletto avanti.*

PRE'-ELECTION, s. [an election made before-hand] *elezione fatta avanti.*

PRE-E'MINENCE, s. [an advantageous quality or degree above others] *preminenza, eminenza, prerogativa,* s. f. *vantaggio,* s. m.

PRE-E'MINENT, adj. [advanced above the reſt] *ſopraeminente, vantaggioſo, che tiene il primo luogo.*

PRE-E'MPTION, s. [a firſt buying, or buying before-hand] *compra antecipata.*

To PRE-'ENGAGE, *impegnare anticipatamente.*

To PRE'-EXIST [to exiſt, to have being before-hand] *preeſiſtere, eſiſtere, o aver l' eſſere avanti.*

PRE-EXI'STENCE, s. *preeſiſtenza,* s. f.

PRE-EXI'STENT, adj. *preeſiſtente, che eſiſte, o hà l' eſſere avanti.*

To PREEN [to proin, to dreſs] *aggiuſtare, accommodare, ordinare, mettere in ordine.*

The birds preen and dreſs their feathers, *gli uccelli s' aggiuſtano le penne.*

PRE'FACE, s. [a ſpeech preparatory to a diſcourſe or treatiſe] *prefazione,* s. f. *prefazio, preambulo,* s. m.

To PRE'FACE [to tell before-hand] *dire avanti.*

He prefaces his diſcourſe with theſe words, *ecco quel che dice al principio del ſuo diſcorſo.*

PRE'FATORY, adj. [that is in form of, or by way of preface] *in forma di prefazio.*

A prefatory diſcourſe, *un diſcorſo in forma di prefazio.*

PRE'FECT, s. [a magiſtrate among the Romans] *prefetto, prepoſto,* s. m. *magiſtrato fra i Romani.*

PREFE'CTURE, s. [the government or chief rule of a city or province] *prefettura,* s. f. *carica, e officio di prefetto.*

To PREFE'R, [to eſteem above, to ſet more by] *preferire, preporre,* preſ. *preferiſco, prepongo.*

To prefer one [to advance, to promote him] *avanzare, aggrandire, promuovere alcuno,* preſ. *aggrandiſco.*

To prefer a law, *proporre una legge.*

To prefer a bill againſt one in chancery, *proſeguire contro alcuno in cancelleria.*

PRE'FERABLE, adj. [that is to be preferred] *preferibile, da preferire.*

PRE'FERENCE, s. *preferenza,* s. f.

PRE'FERIBLE } adj. *preferibile, da*
PRE'FERABLE } *preferire.*

PREFE'RMENT, s. [advancement] *avanzamento, aggrandimento,* s. m. *promozione,* s. f.

To come to preferment, *avanzarſi, aggrandirſi.*

Preferment [place, or employ] *carica,* s. f. *impiego, ufficio,* s. m.

Preferment in the church, *promozione,* s. f.

PREFE'RRED, adj. *preferito.*

PREFE'RRER, s. ex. a preferrer of an indictment, *un accuſatore, delatore, denunciatore,* s. m.

PREFE'RRING, s. *il preferire, v.* To prefer.

To PREFI'GURATE } [to ſignify be-
To PRE'FIGURE } fore] *dar ad intendere, ſignificare avanti.*

To PREFI'X [to put before] *preporre, mettere avanti.*

To prefix a time, *prefiggere, ſtabilire, o determinare, ſtatuire, appuntare il tempo, convenire del tempo,* preſ. *ſtabiliſco, ſtatuiſco, convengo,* pret. *prefiſſi, convenni.*

PREFI'XED, adj. *prefiſſo, v.* To prefix.

PRE'GNANCY, s. [the ſtate of being pregnant or big with child] *pregnezza, gravidanza,* s. f

She pleaded pregnancy, *allegò ch' era gravida.*

Pregnancy [ſharpneſs of wit] *ſottigliezza d' ingegno.*

PRE'GNANT, adj. [big with child] *pregno, gravido.*

A pregnant wit, *un ingegno ſottile, acuto.*

A pregnant reaſon, *una ragione convincente.*

A pregnant token, *un ſegno infallibile.*

PRE'GNANTLY, adv. *molto, grandemente.*

The crime whereof he is pregnantly ſuſpected, *il delitto del quale è grandemente ſoſpettato.*

PREGUSTA'TION, s. [a taſting before-hand] *guſto, aſſaggiamento anteriore.*

To PRE-INGA'GE [to ingage before-hand] *impegnare anteriormente.*

PRE-INGA'GED, adj. *impegnato avanti.*

To PRE-JU'DGE [to judge before] *giudicar prima.*

To pre-judge [to gueſs] *indovinare, preſentire,* preſ. *preſentiſco.*

PREJU'DICATE, adj. ex. a prejudicate opinion, *prevenzione,* s. f. *pregiudicio,* s. m.

A PREJU'DICATE ſtiffneſs, *una mera oſtinazione.*

PREJUDICA'TION, s. [a judging before-hand] *pregiudicio,* s. m.

PRE'JUDICE, s. [a raſh judgment before the matter is duly weigh'd, conſidered, and heard] *pregiudicio,* s. m. *prevenzione, preoccupazione,* s. f.

Prejudice [damage, injury] *pregiudicio, danno, torto, detrimento,* s. m.

To PRE'JUDICE [to injure, to hurt] *pregiudicare, arrecar pregiudicio, nuocere,* pret. *nocqui.*

This will prejudice your health, *ciò pregiudicherà alla voſtra ſalute.*

I

I shall not prejudice you in the least, *non vi farò torto alcuno.*

PRE'JUDICED, adj. *pregiudicato, nociuto.*

PREJUDI'CIAL, adj. [hurtful] *pregiudicativo, nocivo.*

PRE'LACY, s. [a prelate's dignity] *prelatura,* s. f. *dignità di prelato.*

PRE'LATE, s. [one who has a great dignity in the church] *prelato,* s. m. *che ha dignità ecclesiastica.*

PRE'LATESHIP, } s [prelacy] *prelatura.*
PRE'LATURE,

PRELA'TICAL, adj. *di prelato.*

PRELIBA'TION, s. [foretaste] *prelibazione,* s. f. *il prelibare.*

PRE'LIMINARY, adj. [that goes before] *preliminare.*

Preliminary, s. [the first step in a negociation, treaty, or important business] *preliminare,* s. m. *prima disposizione delle cose attenenti al trattato da farsi*

PRE'LUDE, s. [a flourish of musick before the playing of a tune, or entrance into any business] *preludio, principio, preemio,* s. m.

To PRE'LUDE [to play a prelude] *suonare un preludio.*

PRELU'DIOUS, adj. [preparatory] *che prepara, che dispone, che serve di preludio.*

These are preludious suspicions to further evidence, *questi sospetti servon di preludio a prove maggiori.*

PRE'MATURE, adj. [ripe before due time and season] *prematuro, maturo avanti il tempo.*

Premature [untimely] *intempestivo.*

PREMATU'RITY, s. [the condition of that which is premature] *qualità di cosa prematura.*

To PREME'DITATE [to think upon before hand] *premeditare, pensare avanti.*

PREME'DITATED, adj. *premeditato, pensato avanti.*

PREMEDITA'TION, s. *premeditazione,* s. f.

To PRE'MISE [to speak or treat of before, by way of preface or introduction] *dire una cosa, trattare d' una cosa per via di prefazio.*

PRE'MISED, adj. *del quale s' è parlato o trattato avanti per via di prefazio.*

PRE'MISSES, s. [propositions antecedently supposed or proved] *premesse; proposizioni già provate, o supposte vere.*

Premesses [in low language] *case, terreni, beni.*

PRE'MISS, s. [antecedent proposition] *proposizione antecedente.*

PRE'MIUM, s. [reward] *premio,* s. m. *mercede, ricompenza,* s. f.

Premium [among merchants, that sum of money which is given for the insuring of ships, goods, houses, &c.] *premio, mercede.*

To PREMO'NISH [to forewarn] *ammonire, avvertire avanti,* pres. *ammonisco, avvertisco.*

PREMO'NISHED, adj. *ammonito, avvertito avanti.*

PREMONI'TION, s. *ammonizione, avvertimento dato avanti.*

PREMUNI'RE, s. [imprisonment and loss of goods] *imprigionamento, e confiscazione di beni. Termine legale.*

Premunire [trouble] *inconvenienza,* s. f. *inconveniente, disordine, piato,* s. m.

To run one's self into a premunire, *esporsi a qualche inconveniente.*

PRE'NDER, s. [a law word, is the power or right of taking a thing before it is offered] *diritto, o potere d' impadronirsi di che che si sia prima che ci sia offerto.*

To PRENO'MINATE, *nominare avanti.*

PRENO'MINATED, adj. *prenominato, detto avanti.*

PRENOMINA'TION, s. [a naming before] *nominazione fatta avanti.*

PRENO'TION, s. [fore-knowledge] *prescienza,* s. f.

PRE'NTICE, s. [one who is bound to a master for a certain term of years, to learn his trade] *novizio, garzone, principiante, giovane che s' obbliga di servire a qualche maestro per un certo numero d' anni per imparare il suo mestiere.*

PRE'NTISHIP, s. *il tempo che un giovane s' obbliga di servire ad un maestro per imparare la sua arte, garzonaggio.*

PREO'CCUPATE, adj. [taken beforehand] *preoccupato, occupato avanti.*

PREOCCUPA'TION, s. [a possession or enjoying before] *preoccupazione.*

That land was in his preoccupation, *aveva prima la possessione di questa terra, ne era in possessione.*

To PREO'CCUPY [to possess before another] *preoccupare, occupare avanti.*

To PREO'MINATE [to presage] *presagire, far presagio, dar presagio.*

To PREO'RDAIN [to ordain beforehand] *ordinare avanti.*

PREO'RDAINED, adj. [fore-ordained] *ordinato avanti.*

PREPARA'TION, s. [a preparing or making ready before-hand] *preparazione,* s. f. *preparamento, preparativo,* s. m.

Preparations of war, *preparativi di guerra.*

The preparation [or composition] of remedies, *la preparazione o composizione de' rimedi.*

PREPA'RATIVE, } adj. *preparativo,*
PREPA'RATORY, } *preparatorio, che serve a preparare.*

Preparative, s. [preparation] *preparativo, preparamento,* s. m.

To PREPA'RE [to make read] *preparare, apparecchiare, mettere in ordine, allestire.*

To prepare, verb neut. [or prepare one's self] *prepararsi, apparecchiarsi, mettersi in ordine, allestirsi.*

To prepare one's self for death, *acconciarsi dell' anima, prepararsi a morire.*

He prepares for a long journey, *si prepara, si mette in punto per un lungo viaggio.*

PREPA'RED, adj. *preparato, apparecchiato, messo in ordine, allestito.*

PREPA'REDNESS, s. *preparazione,* s. f. *preparamento,* s. m.

PREPE'NSE, adj. [or fore-thought] *premeditato.*

Malice prepense, *malizia premeditata.*

To PREPO'NDER, } to outweigh, to
To PREPO'NDERATE, } be of greater importance] *esser di più gran peso, esser di più grande importanza, o momento.*

To preponderate a business [to weigh it before hand] *esaminare, considerare, ponderare un negozio avanti.*

PREPO'NDERATED, adj. *esaminato, considerato, ponderato prima.*

To PREPO'SE [to set before] *preporre, porre avanti, mettere innanzi,* pres. *prepongo,* pret. *preposi.*

PREPO'SITION, s. [one of the eight parts of speech in grammar] *preposizione,* s. f.

PREPO'SITIVE, adj. *che si prepone, o va innanzi.*

PREPO'SITOR, s. [a scholar appointed by the master to oversee the rest] *un preposto, o proposto,* s. m. *capo di scuola.*

To PREPO'SSESS [to fill one's mind before-hand with prejudice] *preoccupare, prevenire,* pres. *prevengo,* pret. *prevenni.*

PREPO'SSESSED, adj. *preoccupato, prevenuto.*

PREPO'SSESSING, s. *il preoccupare.*

PREPO'SSESSION, s. [prejudice] *pregiudicio,* s. m. *preoccupazione, prevenzione,* s. f.

PREPO'STEROUS, adj. [done the wrong way] *fatto a rovescio, tutto 'l contrario, contrario al dritto, fuor di stagione.*

PREPO'STEROUSLY, adv. *a rovescio, al contrario, fuor di stagione.*

PREPUCE, s. [the fore-skin; that which covers the glans] *il prepuzio,* s. m.

PRERO'GATIVE, s. [a peculiar preeminence or authority above others] *preminenza, e preminenzia,* s. f. *quel vantaggio d' onoranza, o d' altra cosa simile, che ha più un che un altro.*

Prerogative-court [a court wherein wills are proved, and all administrations taken out, that belongs to the archbishop of Canterbury by his prerogative] *corte della prerogativa, così vien chiamata la corte dell' arcivescovo di Cantorberi, dove si provano i testamenti e si stabiliscono gli amministratori.*

PRE'SAGE, s. [a sign or token shewing what will happen] *presagio, indovinamento, augurio, pronostico,* s. m. *segno di cosa futura.*

To PRESA'GE [to divine, to foretell, to betoken] *presagire, fare, o dar presagio, predire, congetturare, pronosticare,* pres. *presagisco,* pret. *predissi.*

To presage [to signify before-hand] *presagire, indicare.*

PRE'SBYTER, s. *un prete.*

PRE'SBYTER, } s. [abettor, pro-
PRESBYTE'RIAN, } fessor, or follower of presbytery or calvinistical discipline] *calvinista, presbiteriano; un che sostiene, professa, o segue la dottrina e la di-*

disciplina Calviniſtica o Preſbiteriana. In Iſcozia v' hanno molti di coteſta ſetta.

Presbyterian, adj. *Preſbiteriano, Calviniſtico.*

Pre'sbitery, s. *il preſbitero; il corpo degli anziani preti, o laici, della romunione Calviniſtica.*

Presci'ence, s. [foreknowledge] *preſcienza, s. f. notizia del futuro.*

To Prescri'be [to order, to appoint] *preſcrivere, ſtatuire, ordinare, ſtabilire,* pref. *ſtatuiſco, ſtabiliſco,* pret. *preſcriſſi.*

To preſcribe a medicine, *ordinare una medicina.*

Prescri'bed, adj. *preſcritto, ſtatuito, ordinato, ſtabilito.*

Prescri'bing, s. *il preſcrivere.*

Pre'script, *v.* Preſcribed.

A preſcript of divine ſervice, *una formula di preghiere.*

Prescri'ption, s. [an appointing or preſcribing] *preſcrizione, s. f. il preſcrivere.*

A phyſician's preſcription, *ricetta di medico.*

Preſcription [in law, is a right or title to any thing grounded upon a continued poſſeſſion of it beyond the memory of man] *preſcrizione, ragione acquiſtata per paſſamento di tempo.*

Pre'sence, s. [the contrary of abſence] *preſenza, s. f. l' eſſer preſente.*

Preſence [mien, looks] *preſenza, cera, ſembianza, aria, s. f. aſpetto, coſpetto, s. m.*

A man of a good preſence, *un uomo di bella preſenza, che ha buon' aria, o buona cera.*

Preſence of mind [readineſs of wit] *accortezza, vivacità d' ingegno.*

Pre'sent, adj. [not abſent] *preſente, che è al coſpetto, avanti, nello ſteſſo tempo, nel qual ſi parla.*

Preſent [in the time wherein we live] *preſente, che è nel tempo nel quale viviamo.*

The preſent ſtate of things, *lo ſtato preſente degli affari.*

A preſent poiſon [that kills preſently] *veleno violento, che ammazza ſubito.*

A preſent remedy [that operates preſently] *un rimedio efficace.*

This preſent year, *l' anno preſente, l' anno corrente.*

The preſent tenſe of a verb, *il tempo preſente d' un verbo.*

Preſent, s. [gift] *preſente, dono, regalo,* s. m.

Theſe preſents, *le preſenti, o la preſente.*

At preſent, } [now] *preſentemente, in queſto punto, addeſſo, ora, al preſente.*
For the preſent, }

To Pre'sent [to offer] *preſentare, offerire,* pref. *offeriſco.*

To preſent a child at the font, *preſentare un bambino al ſacro fonte del batteſimo.*

To preſent the arms [a military term] *preſentare le armi.*

To preſent [or name] to a benefice, *conferire un beneficio.*

To preſent [to make a preſent] *preſentare, regalare, far donativo, far un preſente.*

To preſent one with a horſe, *preſentare un cavallo ad uno.*

To preſent an offender to the jury, *preſentare, conſegnare, condurre un malfattore ai giurati, accuſarlo.*

Presenta'nious, adj. [preſent, effectual] *preſentaneo, che opera di preſente.*

Presenta'tion, s. [the act of preſenting] *preſentazione, s. f. il preſentare.*

Preſentation [the preſenting one to a benefice] *preſentazione.*

The preſentation of a play, *la rappreſentazione d' un poema teatrale.*

Prese'nted, adj. *preſentato, v.* To preſent.

Pre'sentee, s. [the clerk who is preſented by the patron] *colui ch' è preſentato dal padrone al veſcovo.*

To Prese'ntiate, *rappreſentarſi, figurarſi.*

Pre'sently, adv. [juſt now, in a moment] *adeſſo, ora, in queſto punto, ſubito.*

I will come preſently, *verò adeſſo adeſſo.*

Prese'ntment, s. [a meer denunciation of the jurors, or ſome other officer, concerning an offence] *ſemplice denuncia o accuſa.*

Preserva'tion, s. [a preſerving] *preſervazione, s. f. preſervamento, s. m. il preſervare.*

Self-preſervation, *la ſua conſervazione, o preſervazione.*

Prese'rvative, s. [a remedy made uſe of to keep off a diſeaſe] *un preſervativo, o rimedio preſervativo.*

Prese'rve, s. [conſerve] *confettura, conſerva,* s. f.

To Prese'rve [or keep] *preſervare, difendere, conſervare,* pret. *difeſi.*

To preſerve fruits, *confettare frutti.*

Pre'served, adj. *preſervato, difeſo, conſervato.*

Fruits preſerved, *confetture, frutti confettati.*

Prese'rver, s. [he that preſerves] *conſervatore, difenſore,* s. m.

This is a great preſerver of health, *queſto è eccellente per conſervare la ſalute.*

Prese'rves [a ſort of ſpectacles] *occhiali per conſervare la viſta.*

Prese'rving, s. *preſervamento,* s. m. *il preſervare.*

The preſerving of fruits, *il confettar frutti.*

To Presi'de [to be the chief in an aſſembly] *preſidere, aver il maneggio, o la direzione.*

Presi'dency, s. [the place or office of a preſident] *dignità di preſidente, prefettura,* s. f.

Pre'sident, s. [chief, governor, overſeer] *preſidente, prefetto,* s. m.

The lord preſident of the king's moſt honourable privy-council, *il preſidente del conſiglio privato di ſua maeſtà.*

The preſident of a college, *il preſidente, prefetto, o rettore d' un collegio.*

The preſident's lady, *la preſidente.*

The preſident of Wales, York, and Berwick, *il governatore o luogotenente del re del paeſe di Wales, di York, o di Berwick.*

Pre'sidentship, s. *ſtato o officio di preſidente.*

Pre'ss, s. [an engine to preſs, to print, &c.] *ſtrettojo, torchio,* s. m. *ſtrumento di legno, che ſtringe per forza di vite, per uſo di premere.*

A printer's preſs, *torchio,* s. m. *ſtrumento da ſtampare.*

A wine preſs, *torcolo,* s. m.

A preſs for clothes, *una guardaroba.*

Preſs [croud] *perſſa, calca, folla, moltitudine,* s. f.

A preſs-man [among printers] *ſtampatore, colui che attende al torchio.*

Preſs-work [a printer's preſs-work] *torchio.*

A preſs bed, *letto che ſi rinchiude in un armario, in forma di guardaroba.*

To Press [to ſqueeze] *premere, incalzare, ſtrignere.*

To preſs the grapes, *pigiar l' uve.*

To preſs [to haſten] *affrettare, far fretta, ſollecitare.*

To preſs [to ſolicit, to be earneſt] *ſollecitare, ſtimolare, fare inſtanza, importunare, affrettare.*

To preſs ſoldiers, *levar ſoldati, far ſoldati.*

To preſs ſea-men for the fleet, *forzare i marinari a ſervire il re nell' armata, pigliarli per forza.*

To preſs eagerly for a thing, *ricercar che che ſi ſia con premura.*

To preſs upon a man's table, *ficcarſi innanzi ad uno perchè li dia da pranzare.*

To preſs upon dangers, *eſporſi a' pericoli.*

To preſs a benefit upon one, *far ſervizio ad uno contro ſua voglia.*

To preſs in upon one to help him, *ccrrere al ſoccorſo d' uno.*

Pre'ssed, adj. *premuto, preſſato, incalzato, ſtretto, v.* To preſs.

Pressing, s. *il premere.*

Pre'ssion, s. [the art of preſſing] *preſſione, l' atto del premere.*

Prest, s. [a duty in money to be paid by the ſheriff, upon his account in the Exchequer, or for money left in his hands] *ſomma di danari che lo ſceriffe paga all' erario del re.*

Preſs-money [money given commonly to a ſoldier or ſailor when preſſed] *il danaro che ſi da al ſoldato o al marinajo quando è arrolato, per forza.*

Pre'stiges [illuſions, impoſtures] *preſtigi, illuſioni, impoſture.*

Prestigia'tion, s. [a deceit] *preſtigio, inganno, giunteria.*

Presti'gious, adj. [deceitful] *preſtigioſo, ingannevole.*

Presto, s. [an Italian word among fiddlers, and ſignifies quickly] *preſto.*

To Presu'me [to imagine, to think, or ſuppoſe] *ſupporre, preſumere, far conghiettura, immaginare, preſuppore,* pref.

pref. *suppongo, presuppongo*, pret. *supposi, presupposi.*

To presume [to have a good opinion of] *presumere, pretendere oltre al convenevole, arrogarsi.*

He presumes too much of himself, *presume troppo di se medesimo.*

PRESU'MER, s. *un prosuntuoso, un arrogante.*

PRESU'MPTION, s. [conjecture] *presunzione, prosunzione, dubitazione, opinione, conghiettura*, s. f.

Presumption [arrogance, pride] *presunzione, arroganza, baldanza*, s. f.

PRESU'MPTIVE, adj. *presuntivo, supposto.*

PRESU'MPTUOUS, adj. [proud, arrogant] *presuntuoso, e prosuntuoso, arrogante, baldanzoso, di sfacciato ardire.*

PRESUMPTUOUSLY, s. *presuntuosamente, e prosuntuosamente.*

PRESU'MPTUOUSNESS, s. *presuntuosità, e prosuntuosità, presunzione, arroganza*, s. f.

To PRESUPPO'SE [to suppose beforehand] *presupporre, supporre, mettere, e formar che che si sia per vero*, pref. *presuppongo, suppongo*, pret. *presupposi, supposi.*

PRESUPPO'SED, adj. *presupposto, supposto.*

PRESUPPO'SITION, s. *presupposizione, supposizione*, s. f. *il presupporre.*

PRETE'NCE, s. [opinion, conceit] *opinione, concetto parere.*

So strong is their pretence of infallibility, *tanto grande è il concetto che hanno della loro infallibilità.*

Pretence [pretext, colour, appearance] *pretesto, colore*, s. m. *ombra, ragione, apparenza*, s. f.

To PRE'TEND [to imagine, to believe] *pretendere, supporre, imaginarsi, credere, persuadersi.*

To pretend [to use a pretence, to make as if] *pretendere, pigliar pretesto, fingere, far vista.*

To pretend ignorance, *pretender causa d'ignoranza.*

He pretends love to me, *e' finge d'amarmi, e' fa vista d'amarmi.*

Some men pretend fair, *vi sono alcuni che sono buoni in apparenza.*

He pretended poverty, *si scusò allegando povertà.*

To pretend business, *far l'affacendato.*

To pretend one thing and do another, *fare una finta*; *prometter danari e dar bastoni.*

I'll pretend to be his brother, *dirò che sono suo fratello*; *mi spaccerò per suo fratello.*

To pretend to a thing, *piccarsi di che che si sia.*

To pretend to learning, *piccarsi d'esser dotto, fare il dotto.*

PRETE'NDED, *preteso*, v. To pretend.

A pretended title or right, *un titolo supposto.*

PRE'TENDER, s. *quello o quella che pretende.*

PRETE'NDING, s. *il pretendere.*

PRETE'NSION, s. [claim] *pretensione*, s. f. *il pretendere.*

To set a pretension to a thing, *pretendere, o aver pretensione a che si sia.*

PRETE'R, s. and adj. *preterito*, adj. Ex.

Preter imperfect, *preterito imperfetto.*

The preter tense, *il preterito.*

PRETERI'TION, s. [a passing by] *il preterire, omissione.*

PRETERMI'SSION, s. [or omitting] *il preterire, omissione, negligenza*, s. f.

To PRETERMI'T [to omit, to pass by, to neglect] *preterire, lasciare, tralasciare, ommettere, negligere*, pref. *preterisco*, pret. *ommisi, neglessi.*

PRETERMI'TTED, adj. *pretermesso, lasciato, ommesso, neglette.*

PRETERMI'TTING, s. *il pretermettere, tralasciamento*, s. m. *ommissione, negligenza*, s. f.

PRETERNA'TURAL, adj. [besides nature] *sopranaturale, che è contra il corso della natura, straordinario.*

PRETERNA'TURALLY, adv. *sopranaturalmente, d'una maniera sopranaturale.*

PRE'TEXT, s. [pretence] *pretesto, colore*, s. m. *scusa, ombra*, s. f.

PRE'THEE, *è abbreviazione di* pray thee, *di grazia, ti prego.*

PRE'TOR, s. *pretore*; *giudice Romano*; *dignità fra gli antichi Romani. Alcuni scrittori Inglesi chiamarono talvolta* Pretor *con parlar sublime quello che in volgare chiamano* Mayor.

PRE'TTILY, adv. *bellamente, con bel modo, piacevolmente, acconciamente.*

PRE'TTINESS, s. [handsomeness] *bellezza, leggiadria.*

PRE'TTY, s. [handsome] *bello, leggiadro, vago, grazioso.*

Pretty [spoken by way of contempt, or ironically] *bello.*

A pretty thing indeed, *oh la bella cosa.*

You are a pretty man indeed [by way of irony] *a dirvi il vero voi siete un uomo che non si può far di più.*

For a pretty while, *per un gran pezzo.*

Pretty, adv. [so, so, indifferent] *assai, così così.*

A pretty handsome woman, *una donna assai bella.*

This picture is pretty like you, *questo ritratto vi rassomiglia assai bene.*

Pretty well, *così così, assai bene, poco.*

Pretty near [thereabouts] *in circa, presso, quasi.*

He is pretty near as tall as you, *è quasi tanto grande quanto voi.*

To PRE'VAIL [to have the advantage over, to be of greater force] *prevalere, esser di più valore, eccedere*, pref. *prevaglio*, pret. *prevalsi.*

Virtue ought to prevail over, or above riches, *la virtù deve prevalere, o andare innanzi alle richezze.*

To prevail with one [to have a power over him] *prevalere ad uno, esser gli superiore.*

Gold and silver shall never prevail with me, *il danaro non avrà mai forza sopra di me*; *non mi lascerò mai vincere dall' interesse.*

To prevail with one for a thing [to obtain it] *ottenere, impetrare che che si sia d'uno.*

To prevail with one by intreaties, *guadagnare, o piegare altrui con preghiere.*

To prevail with by bribes, *guadagnare o corrompere altrui con donativi.*

To prevail with one to do a thing, *disporre alcuno a fare qualche cosa, ottenere d'alcuno che faccia una tal cosa.*

Prevailed with, adj. *prevaluto*, v. To prevail.

Easy to be prevailed with, *facile a smuovere o a persuadere.*

PREVA'ILING, s. *il prevalere.*

Prevailing [powerful, efficacious] *potente, efficace.*

A prevailing sin, *un peccato dominante.*

PRE'VALENCE, } s. [a being prevalent] *forza, efficacia*, s. f.
PRE'VALENCY, }

PRE'VALENT, adj. [powerful, prevailing] *potente, efficace.*

To PREVA'RICATE [to shuffle and cut, to play fast and loose] *prevaricare.*

PREVARICA'TION, s. [deceit, double dealing] *prevaricazione.*

PREVARICA'TOR, s. [one who prevaricates] *prevaricatore*, s. m.

PREVE'NIENT, adj. [that prevents] *che previene.*

To PRE'VENT [to come before, to be before-hand with] *prevenire, venire, avanti, anticipare*, pref *prevengo*, pret. *prevenni.*

To prevent dangers, *prevenire, ovviare, scansare i pericoli.*

To prevent one [to get the start of him] *prevenire alcuno, esser il primo a fare che che si sia.*

PREVE'NTED, adj. *prevenuto, anticipato.*

PRE'VENTING, } s. *prevenzione, anticipazione*, s. f.
PREVE'NTION, }

Prevention [prepossession] *prevenzione, preoccupazione, ostinazione*, s. f.

PREVE'NTIVE, s. [that serves to prevent] *preservativo, rimedio che serve à prevenire il male.*

Preventive, or preventing, adj. [prevenient] *preveniente, che previene.*

PRE'VIDENCE, s. [a fore-seeing] *antivedere, antivedimento*, s. m.

PRE'VIOUS, adj. [that goes before] *che precede, che va avanti.*

PREVI'SION, s. [foresight] *antivedere, antivedimento*, s. m.

PREY, s. [that which is caught by wild beasts, or men by violence, craft, or injustice] *preda, rapina*, s. f.

A bird of prey [a ravenous bird] *uccello di rapina.*

He became the prey of his enemies, *fu preda de' suoi nemici.*

He makes a prey of me, *mi scortica, mi succia il sangue.*

To prey upon, verb neut. *predare, far preda.*

Some beasts prey upon their own kind, *alcune bestie si mangiano l'una l' altra.*

Prey'd upon, adj. *predato.*

PRE'YER, s. *un predatore.*

Prey

Preying upon, s. *predamento*, s. m. *il predare*.

PRI'APISM, s. [a preternatural tension] *priapismo*, s. m.

PRICE, s. [the estimation, value, or rate of any thing] *prezzo*, s. m. *valuta*, s. f.

The market price, *il prezzo corrente*.

A set price, *un prezzo fisso o stabilito*.

Tell me the lowest price, *ditemi l'ultimo prezzo*.

What's your price? what's the price of it? *di che prezzo è questa cosa? quanto vale questa cosa?*

What price did you give for it? *a che prezzo l'avete comprato? quanto v' è costato?*

I gave a great price for it, *l'ho comprato a gran prezzo, m' è costato molto caro*.

I had it for a small price, *l'ho comprato a vil prezzo, a buon mercato*.

To PRICE [to pay for] *pagare, dar il giusto prezzo*.

PRICH, s. [thin drink] *bevanda molto tenue*.

PRICK [a point, a wound with a pointed weapon] *puntura*, s. f. *ferita che fa la punta di che si sia*.

Prick [mark to shoot at] *bersaglio*, s. m.

A prick of conscience, *rimorsi di coscienza*.

The prick and praise of a thing, *la gloria d'aver fatto che che si sia*.

Prick-wood, s. *nome di pianta*.

To PRICK [to make a hole with a point] *pugnere, e pungere, leggiermente forar con cosa puntuta, foracchiare*, pret. *punsi*.

To prick with a needle, *pugnere con un ago*.

To prick [among hunters, to trace the steps of a hare] *seguitar la lepre alla pesta*.

To prick a tune or a song, *notare un aria, o una canzone*.

To prick a cask of wine, *spillare una botte*.

To prick a horse to the quick, *chiovare un cavallo*.

To prick on, or forward, *spignere, spronare, stimolare, eccitare, istigare*.

To prick up one's ears, *star cogli orecchi tesi*.

To prick down the notes in a musick-book, *notare un libro di musica*.

PRI'CKED, *participio del verbo* To prick.

PRI'CKER, s. [a huntsman on horseback] *cacciatore a cavallo*, s. m.

PRI'CKET, s. [a young male deer of two years old] *cerbiatto*, s. m. *cerbio di due anni*.

PRI'CKING, s. *pugnimento, pungimento*, s. m. *il pugnere*.

PRI'CKLE, s. [a sharp pointed thing, as a thorn] *spina*, s. f.

PRICKLES of a porcupine, *le penne d'un istrice*.

PRI'CKLY, adv. *spinoso, pieno di spine*.

PRIDE, s. [presumption, vanity] *orgoglio*, s. m. *alterigia, superbia, grandigia, boria, vanità*, s. f.

To take a pride in a thing, *piccarsi, vanagloriarsi, vantarsi di che che si sia*.

To PRIDE [to take pride in, or to be proud of] *vantarsi, vanagloriarsi, glorificarsi, tener maggioranza o gloria; pregiarsi*.

PRI'ER, s. [spy] *spia*, s. m. *ricercatore*, s. m.

PRIEST, s. [a clergyman] *un prete*.

A priest of the church of England, *un prete*, s. m. *un ministro della chiesa Anglicana*.

PRIEST CRAFT, s. [religious frauds] *fraudi ecclesiastiche*.

PRIEST'S-PINTLE, s. [an herb] *spezie d'erba*.

PRIEST-RIDDEN, *che si lascia governare da' preti*.

PRI'ESTESS, s. [a woman priest] *sacerdotessa*.

PRI'ESTHOOD, s. [the office or dignity of a priest] *sacerdozio*, s. m.

PRI'ESTLY, adj. *sacerdotale, di prete, pretesco*.

The priestly habits, *gli abiti sacerdotali*.

To PRIG [to filch] *truffare, mariolare*.

PRIG, s. [a pert, conceited, saucy, pragmatical fellow] *uno sguajatello prosontuoso*.

PRILL, s. [birt, turbot] *pesce simile al rombo*.

To PRIM [to have affected ways] *civettare, far la civetta*.

To prim [to deck up precisely; to form to an affected nicety] *ornarsi con affettata leggiadria*.

PRIM, adj. [formal, precise, affectedly nice] *pieno d'affettazione, studiato, leccato*.

PRI'MACY, s. [a primate's dignity] *primato*, s. m. *dignità di primato*.

PRI'MAGE, s. [a duty paid to the mariners for loading a ship] *quel che si paga ai marinari per caricare il vascello*.

PRI'MARILY, adv. *primieramente, principalmente*.

PRI'MARY, adj. [first] *primiero, primo*.

A primary substance, *una sostanza primiera*.

Primary [chief] *primario, principale, essenziale*.

PRI'MATE, s. [the first or chief archbishop] *primato, metropolitano, il primo arcivescovo*.

PRIME, adj. [first chief, sovereign] *primo, principale, grande*.

A thing of prime use, *una cosa di grand' uso*.

Prime [excellent, exquisite] *eccellente, esquisito, insigne*.

A prime rogue, *un furbo in chermisi*.

Prime, s. [the chief, the flower, or choice] *il primo, il fiore, il principale*.

The prime of the nobility, *il primo, il fiore delle nobiltà*.

He died in the prime of his age, *morì nel fior dell' età*.

The prime of a gun, *il polverino d' un' arme da fuoco, quella polvere che si mette sul focone dell' archibuso per darli fuoco*.

Prime [the first of the canonical hours] *prima*, s. f. *una delle ore canoniche*.

Prime-print, s. [or privet] *ligustro, rovistico*, s. m.

To PRIME [to put powder into the pan or touch-hole of a gun or piece of ordnance] *mettere la polvere sul focone*.

To prime [among painters, is to lay the first colour] *preparare la tela d'una pittura*.

PRI'MER, } s. [a little book in PRI'MMER, } which children are first taught to read] *un salterio, piccolo libretto nel quale i fanciulli imparano a leggere*.

A primer [a Roman catholick prayer-book] *breviario*, s. m. *quel libro dove son registrate l'ore canoniche, e tutto l'officio divino*.

Primer [among printers, printing letter of divers sorts] *romano*.

The long primer, *piccolo romano*.

The great primer, *romano grande*.

PRIME'RO, s. [a game at cards] *primiera*, s. f. *sorta di giuoco di carte*.

PRIME'VAL, adj. *primo, antico, originale; come fu dapprima*.

PRI'MING, s. *il mettere la polvere sul focone dell' archibuso*.

Priming-iron [an iron made use of in the priming of a great gun] *uno spillo*.

PRIMI'TIAL, adj. [belonging to the primitiæ] *che appartiene, o concerne le primizie*.

PRI'MITIVE, adj. [of or belonging to the first age, ancient] *primitivo, primo, primiero, che non ha origine da alcuno*.

A primitive word [an original word] *una parola primitiva*.

A primitive cause, *una causa primitiva*.

The primitive church, *la chiesa primitiva*

PRIMOGE'NITURE, s. [the title and privilege of an elder brother, in right of his birth] *primogenitura*, s. f. *ragione di succedere negli stati che porta seco l'esser primogenito*.

PRIMO'RDIAL, adj. [primitive, original] *primitivo*.

PRI'MROSE, s. [a sort of flower] *fior di primavera*.

Primrose, adj. [gay, flowery] *gajo, florido*.

PRI'NCE, s. [one who governs a state in chief] *principe*, s. m. *signore assoluto*.

The prince of Wales, *il principe di Galles*.

Prince [the chief, first, or most excellent] *principe, principale, primo*.

Aristotle is the prince of philosophers, *Aristotile è il principe de' filosofi*.

Prince-like, *da principe*.

To PRINCE [to play the prince] *farla da principe, far il gran signore*.

PRI'NCEDOM, s. [the rank, estate, or power of the prince; sovereignty] *principato, sovranità*.

PRI'NCELY, adj. *di principe, degno d'un principe, principesco*.

A princely look, *un' aria maestosa, un principesco aspetto*.

A princely soul, *un' anima grande*.

He

He has given us a princely entertainment, *ci ha regalati da principe.*

Princes feather, s. [a flower] *amaranto*, s. m. *forta di fiore.*

PRINCE'SS, s. [a prince's lady] *principessa*, s. f.

PRI'NCIPAL, adj. [chief, main.] *principale, foprano, maggiore.*

Principal, s. [the principal fum of money borrowed or lent, diftinct from intereft] *il capitale, il principale.*

The principal of a college, *il rettore d' un collegio.*

PRINCIPA'LITY, s. [the dominions or jurifdiction of a prince] *principato*, s. m. *titolo del dominio, e grado del principe.*

PRI'NCIPALLY, adv. [chiefly] *principalmente, fopra tutto, particolarmente.*

PRI'NCIPLE, s. [the firft caufe of the being or production of any thing] *principio*, s. m. *caufa, origine*, s. f.

The principles of an art or fcience, *i principi, le regole, i cominciamenti, i fondamenti d' un' arte, o d' una fcienza.*

Principle [motive] *principio, motivo.*

Out of a principle of honour, *per un motivo d' onore.*

Principle [fentiment] *principio, fentimento, maffima.*

A man of good principles, *un uomo onorato, un uomo dabbene.*

Principle [in philofophy] *un affioma.*

To PRI'NCIPLE, *dari i principi.*

To principle one well, *imbever uno di buoni fentimenti.*

PRI'NCIPLED, adj. ex. A man well principled, *un uomo onorato, un uomo dabbene.*

PRI'NCOCK, } s. [a youngfter too
PRI'NCOX, } foon ripe-headed] *un giovane che fa il faccente, un faccentino.*

PRINT, s. [mark, fign] *fegno*, s. m. *impreffione*, s. f.

The prints of the foot, *pedate.*

The print of a nail, *unghiata.*

A print [a cut] *una ftampa.*

Print [letter] *impreffione, lettera, carattere.*

A fine print, *una bella impreffione, un bel carattere.*

To put in print, *mandare alle ftampe.*

To come out in print, *venire alla luce.*

A book out of print, *un libro che non fi trova più a comprare.*

I faw his name in print, *ho vifto il fuo nome ftampato.*

To fet one's cloaths in print, *veftire attillato.*

To PRINT [to practife the art of printing] *ftampare, imprimere, pubblitare colle ftampe.*

To print a book, *ftampare un libro.*

PRI'NTED, adj. *ftampato.*

To caufe to be printed, *fare ftampare.*

PRI'NTER, s. [he that prints] *ftampatore.*

PRI'NTING, s. [the art of printing books] *lo ftampare, impreffione, ftampa.*

A printing-houfe, *ftamperia, luogo dove fi ftampa.*

PRI'NTLESS, adj. *che non lafcia impreffione, orma, o veftigio.*

PRI'OR, s. [the head of a priory] *priore*, s. m.

PRI'ORESS, s. *prioreffa*, s. f.

PRI'ORSHIP, s. [a prior's dignity] *priorato*; s. m. *dignità di priore.*

PRI'ORITY, s. [advantage of place] *priorità*, s. f.

PRI'ORY, s. [a religious community under the direction of a prior, or priorefs] *priorato.*

PRISM, s. [a prifm of glafs is a glafs bounded with two equal and parallel ends, and three plain and well polifhed fides, which meet in three parallel lines, running from the three angles of one end to the three angles in the other end] *prifma*, s. m. pl. *prifmi.*

PRI'SON, s. [jail] *prigione, carcere*, s. f.

The keeper of a prifon, *un prigioniero, quello che fta a guardia della prigione.*

PRI'SONER, s. [one in cuftody] *prigioniere, e prigoniero, prigione*, s. m. *prigiona*, s. f.

PRI'STINE, adj. [ancient, former] *priftino, prifco, antico.*

PRI'TTLE PRA'TTLE, s. [talk, prating] *cicaleria, ciarla, ciarleria*, s. f. *cicaleccio*, s. m.

To PRI'TTLE-PRA'TTLE [to prate] *cicalare, ciarlare, cianciare come fanno le donnicciuole.*

PRI'VACY, s. [familiarity] *fegretezza, dimeftichezza, familiarità, e famigliarità*, s. f.

Privacy [retirement] *ritiratezza, folitudine*, s. f.

With great privacy [fecretly] *fegretiffimamente.*

PRI'VADO, s. [private friend, favourite] *un favorito, un confidente, un amico intimo.*

PRI'VATE, adj. [fecret, retired] *privato, fegreto, nafcofto, ripofto.*

A private houfe, *una cafa privata, o particolare.*

A private place, *un luogo privato, un ripoftiglio, un nafcondiglio.*

I defire to be private, *voglio effer folo, o da me.*

A private man, *un uomo privato.*

To make a private purfe, *far borfa a parte.*

A private chapel, *una cappelletta.*

A private ftair-cafe, *una fcala fegreta.*

In private, *privatamente, in privato, in particolare.*

PRIVATE'ER, s. *una nave corfara.*

PRI'VATELY, adv. [in private] *privatamente, in privato, fegretamente, in particolare, in fegreto.*

PRI'VATION, s. [depriving] *privazione*, s. f.

PRI'VATIVE, adj. [that deprives] *privativo, che priva.*

PRI'VET, s. *nome d'erba.*

Barren privet [ever green privet] *fempreviva.*

PRI'VILEGE, s. [prerogative, advantage] *privilegio, vantaggio*, s. m. *immunità, prerogativa*, s. f.

To PRI'VILEGE [to inveft with rights or immunities; to grant a privilege] *privilegiare; accordar diritti o immunità; concedere un privilegio.*

To privilege [to exempt from cenfure or danger] *efimere da biafimo o pericolo.*

To privilege [to exempt from paying tax or impoft] *efentar da una taffa o gabella.*

PRI'VILEGED, adj. *privilegiato, che ha privilegio.*

A privileged place, *un luogo privilegiato.*

PRI'VILY, adv. [fecretly] *privatamente, in privato, fegretamente, in particolare, in fegreto.*

PRI'VITY, s. [private knowledge] *partecipazione, faputa, notizia*, s. f.

She did it without her hufband's privity, *ella l' ha fatto fenza faputa di fuo marito.*

PRI'VITIES, s. [the privy parts] *le parti fegrete.*

PRI'VY, adj. [fecret] *fegreto, nafcofto.*

The privy parts, *le parti fegrete.*

Privy-ftairs, *fcala fegreta.*

Privy [particular] *privato, particolare.*

The privy-council, *il configlio privato.*

Privy-feal, *il fuggello privato.*

The privy purfe, *borfa privata.*

Privy to [acquainted with] a thing, *confapevole, fciente, di che che fi fia.*

Privy to a crime, *complire d' un delitto.*

Privy, s. [houfe of office] *privato, ceffo, deftro.*

PRIZE, s. [that which is taken, any kind of booty] *prefa, cattura*, s. f. *bottino*, s. m.

He made prize of the whole town, *egli mife tutta la città a facco.*

Prize [a benefit ticket in a lottery] *beneficio*, s. m. *grazia*, s. f.

Prize [a reward propofed to him that fhall do any thing beft] *guiderdone*, s. m. *ricompenfa*, s. f.

To PRIZE [to prife, to value] *apprezzare, ftimare, valutare, dar la valuta d' una cofa.*

PRI'ZED, adj. *apprezzato, ftimato, valutato.*

PRIZEFI'GHTER, s. [one that fights publickly for a reward] *uno che combatte in pubblico per ottenere un premio.*

PRI'ZER, s. *ftimatore*, s. m.

PRI'ZING, s. *l' apprezzare, il valutare.*

PRO, prep. [for; in defence of] *pro.*

Pro and con, *pro e contra.*

To know the pro and the con, *fapere il pro e contra.*

PRO'BABILITY, s. [likelihood] *probabilità, verifimilitudine*, s. f.

PRO'BABLE, adj. [likely] *probabile, verfimile.*

PRO'BABLY, adv. *probabilmente, verifimilmente.*

It is very probably fo, *è probabile; può effere; probabilmente è così.*

PRO'BATE, s. ex. The probate of teftaments [the proving of wills in the fpiritual court] *la verificazione de' teftamenti.*

PRO-

PROBA'TION, s. [proof, trial] *prova, pruova,* s. f. *esperimento, cimento,* s. m.

Probation [in the university, the trial of a student who is about to take his degrees] *proba,* s. f.

Probation [a trial of one before he be admitted to profess a religious life] *prova, noviziato.*

PROBA'TIONARY, adj. ex. probationary laws, *leggi fatte solamente per prova.*

PROBA'TIONER, s. [in the university, a scholar who undergoes a probation] *una scolare o studente che fa la sua prova*

A probationer in a religious house, *un novizio.*

PROBE, s. [a surgeon's instrument to search the depth, windings, &c. of a wound] *tenta,* s. f. *quello istrumento, onde il cerusico conosce la profondità della ferita.*

To PROBE a wound [to search it with a probe] *cercar con una tenta la profondità d' una ferita.*

PRO'BITY, s. [uprightness, integrity] *probità, bontà, integrità,* s. f.

PRO'BLEM, s. [a proposition relating to practice, or which proposes something to be done] *problema,* pl. *problemi,* s. m. *proposta, questione,* s. f.

PROBLEMA'TICAL, } adj. [belonging to a problem] *problematico.*
PROBLEMATICK, }

PROBO'SCIS, s. [an elephant's trunk] *proboscide,* s. f. *naso dell' elefante.*

PROCA'CIOUS, adj. [malapert, saucy] *insolente, arrogante, sfacciato, sfrontato.*

PROCA'CITY, s. [sauciness, malapertness] *insolenza, arroganza, sfacciataggine, sfacciatezza,* s. f.

PROCE'DURE, s. [a course of pleading] *il procedere in giustizia, l' ordine giudiciario.*

PROCE'ED, s. [what arises from a thing] *prodotto,* s. m.

The neat proceeds [among merchants] *il netto prodotto.*

To PROCE'ED [to come from, to be derived, to spring, to have its rise from] *procedere, derivare, nascere, venire,* pret. *nacqui, venni,* pref. *vengo.*

From whence does that proceed? *donde procede, donde viene questo?*

Proceed, or go on, *continuate, andate, o seguitate avanti.*

He proceeded to that height of impiety, *la sua empietà giunse a tal segno.*

To proceed [to act, to deal] *procedere, comportarsi.*

To proceed against one, *procedere contro alcuno.*

To proceed doctor, *esser ammesso dottore.*

PROCE'EDED, adj. *proceduto,* v. To proceed.

The malefactor shall be proceeded against, *si procederà contro 'l reo.*

PROCE'EDING, s. *procedimento,* s. m. *il procedere.*

Proceeding [action, dealing] *procedere, comportamento, portamento,* s. m.

The proceedings at law, *la forma di procedere in giustizia, l' ordine giudiciario.*

PROCE'EDER, s. one who goes forward; one who makes a progress] *colui che tira inanzi molto; colui che fa progresso.*

PRO'CESS, s. [the manner of proceeding in any cause, or the beginning or principal part of it] *processo,* s. m. *tutte le scritture degli atti, che si fanno nelle cause sì civili, che criminali.*

A verbal process, *un processo verbale,*

A criminal process, *un processo criminale.*

To take out a process against one, *fare il processo ad uno, procedere contro alcuno in giustizia.*

A process of things, *un processo, procedimento, continuazione di cose, una serie di cose.*

In process of time, *in progresso di tempo.*

PROCE'SSION, s. [a solemn march of the clergy and people in their ornamental habits] *processione,* s. f.

PROCE'SSIONAL, adj. [belonging to a procession] *di processione.*

PRO'CINCT, adj. [ready, at hand] *lesto, apparecchiato, in ordine.*

In procinct, *in procinto, apparecchiato.*

To PROCLA'IM [to publish, to declare solemnly] *proclamare, pubblicare, bandire, dichiarare, solennemente.*

To proclaim one king, *proclamare uno per re.*

To proclaim war, *dichiarare, intimare la guerra.*

PROCLA'IMED, adj. *proclamato, pubblicato, bandito, dichiarato.*

PROCLA'IMER, s. *proclamatore, banditore,* s. m.

PROCLA'IMING, s. *il proclamare, il bandire.*

PROCLAMA'TION, s. *proclamazione, dichiarazione,* s. f. *bando,* s. m.

A proclamation of war, *dichiarazione, o intimazione di guerra.*

To make a proclamation of a thing, *pubblicare, divulgare, palesare, che che si sia.*

PRO'CLIVE, adj. [inclined, hanging downward] *proclive.*

Proclive [ready, bent to, apt, prone] *proclive, arclino, disposto, inchinevole, prono, dedito, inclinato.*

PROCLI'VITY, s. [aptness, propensity, inclination] *inclinazione, attitudine, dispostezza,* s. f.

PROCO'NSUL, s. [a Roman magistrate of old, to govern a province with consular power] *proconsolo,* s. m.

PROCO'NSULAR, adj. *proconsolare.*

PROCO'NSULSHIP, s. *proconsolato,* s. m.

To PROCRA'STINATE [to put off from day to day, to delay or defer] *procrastinare, indugiare, d' oggi in domane, dar tempo, differire, prolungare,* pref. *differisco.*

PROCRA'STINATED, adj. *procrastinato, indugiato, differito, prolungato.*

PROCRASTINA'TION, s. *procrastinazione,* s. f. *il procrastinare.*

PROCRASTINA'TOR, s. [a dilatory person] *un che procrastina, che aspetta fare domane quello che potrebbe far aggi.*

To PRO'CREATE [to beget] *procreare, generare.*

PRO'CREATED, adj. *procreato, generato.*

PRO'CREATING, s. *procreamento,* s. m. *il procreare.*

PROCREA'TOR, s. *procreatore,* s. m.

A PROCREA'TRIX, s. *procreatrice,* s. f.

PRO'CTOR, s. [one who undertakes to manage a cause in the ecclesiastical court] *procuratore,* s. m.

PRO'CTORS [in the university, two persons chosen from among the students, to see good orders and exercises duly performed there] *moderatori in una università.*

Proctors of the clergy, *i procuratori, o deputati d'un assemblea ecclesiastica.*

To PRO'CTOR [to manage] *fare, operare, diriggere.*

PRO'CTORSHIP, s. *ufficio di procuratore.*

PROCU'RABLE, adj. *procurabile, che si può procurare, o ottenere.*

PROCU'RACY, s. [the writing or deed whereby one is made a procurator] *proccura, procura,* s. f. *strumento di scrittura fatto per pubblica persona, col quale si da autorità a uno di fare in nome e vere di se medesimo.*

PROCURA'TION, s. [a power by which one is entrusted to act for another] *procura, proccura,* s. f.

Procuration [a composition paid by the parish priest to the bishop or archdeacon, to commute for the entertainment which was otherwise to have been procured for them at their visitation] *proccurazione, certa somma di danari che paga il parrocchiano al vescovo o all' arcidiacono in vece del vitto che è obbligato di dar loro nel tempo che sono in vista.*

PROCURA'TOR, s. [factor, sollicitor, one who looks after another man's affairs, *procuratore,* s. m. *fattore, agente,* s. m. *che fa i fatti e negozi altrui.*

Procurator of St. Mark [at Venice, a magistrate who is next in dignity to the Doge] *procurator di San Marco.*

A procurator [one who gathers the fruits of a benefice for the parson] *colui che, in virtu di proccura, ha potere d' esigere i frutti d'un beneficio per il beneficiato.*

To PROCU'RE [to get for another, to help] *procurare, cercare, procacciare, ingegnarsi.*

To procure [to act as a pimp or bawd] *fare il ruffiano, e la ruffiana.*

PROCU'RED, adj. *procurato, procacciato, cercato.*

PROCU'REMENT, s. *intrapresa,* s. f.

PROCU'RER, s. [a mediator] *proccuratore, procacciatore, mediatore, mezzano,* s. m.

Procurer [pimp, bawd] *un ruffiano, una ruffiana.*

PROCU'RESS, s. [a bawd] *una ruffiana.*

PROCU'RING, s. *procuragione*, s. f. *il procurare.*

PRO'DICAL, adj. [lavish, profuse, wasteful, riotous] *prodigo, che da e spende eccessivamente.*

A prodigal man, *un prodigo, un scialacquone.*

A prodigal woman, *una prodiga.*

To be prodigal, *usar prodigalità, esser prodigo.*

PRODIGA'LITY, s. [profuseness, lavishness] *prodigalità*, s. f. *eccesso nello spendere e nel donare*; *scialacquo*, s. m.

PRO'DIGALLY, adv. *prodigalmente, prodigamente, con prodigalità.*

To spend prodigally, *spendere prodigamente, prodigalizzare, usar prodigalità nello spendere.*

PRODI'GIOUS, adj. [monstrous, wonderful] *prodigioso, mostruoso, stupendo.*

Prodigious [extraordinary] *prodigioso, insolito, straordinario.*

Prodigious [excessive] *prodigioso, eccessivo, smisurato.*

PRODI'GIOUSLY, adv. *prodigiosamente, eccessivamente.*

PRO'DIGY, s. [monstrous or preternatural thing] *prodigio*, s. m. *cosa insolita.*

PRODI'TION, s. [treason] *tradimento*, s. m.

PRODI'TOR, s. [traitor] *traditore*, s. m.

PRODITO'RIOUS, adj. [traitor-like, treacherous] *traditoresco, da traditore.*

PRO'DROME, s. [fore-runner] *presagio*, s. m.

To PRODU'CE [to bring forth] *producere, produrre, generare, creare*, pres. *produco*, pret. *produssi.*

To produce [to expose to the view, to show] *produrre, mostrare, addurre, mettere in campo.*

To produce [to cause] *produrre, causare, esser causa.*

PRODU'CED, adj. *prodotto*, v. To produce.

PRODU'CING, s. *producimento*, s. m. *il produrre.*

PRO'DUCT, s. [fruit] *produzione*, s. f. *frutto*, s. m.

The product of the earth, *i frutti della terra.*

The product of one's wit, *parto dell' ingegno.*

This is a mere product of his fancy, *questo è un mero effetto della sua fantasia.*

The product of two sums, or numbers, *il prodotto di due somme o di due numeri.*

PRODU'CTION, s. [product, fruit] *produzione*, s. f. *frutto.*

Productions of the brain [ingenious works] *produzioni, o parti dell' ingegno.*

Productions of nature, *produzioni, o effetti della natura.*

PRODU'CTIVE, adj. [apt to produce or bring forth] *produttivo, che produce, atto a produrre.*

PRO'EM, s. [a preface or an entrance into a discourse] *proemio*, s. *la prima parte d' orazione, o d' altra opera, ove principalmente si propone quel che s' ha a trattare.*

PROFANA'TION, s. [the act of violating any thing sacred] *profanazione*; *il profanare*; *il violare cosa sacra.*

Profanation [irreverence to holy things or persons] *dispregio o irriverenza per cose a persone sacra.*

PRO'FANE, adj. *profano*; *non sacro*; *laico*; *secolare*; *polluto*; *impuro*; *non purificato da' riti sacri.*

To PROFA'NE, *profanare*; *violare*; *far cattivo uso.*

PROFA'NELY, adv. *profanamente*; *con profanazione.*

PROFA'NER, s. *profanatore, violatore di cosa sacra.*

PROFA'NENESS, s. *profanità*; *irriverenza a cosa sacra.*

PRO'FER, v. Proffer.

To PROFE'SS [to practise, to exercise openly] *professare, far professione, esercitare.*

To profess christianity [to profess one's self to be a christian] *far professione del cristianesimo, professare la religione cristiana.*

To profess a doctrine, *seguitare, o mantenere una dottrina.*

To profess [to swear, to protest] *giurare, protestare, dichiarare.*

PROFE'SSED, adj. *professato.*

A professed monk [one who having made his vow, is admitted to he of a religious order] *un frate professo, un professo.*

A professed nun, *una monaca professa, una professa.*

A professed enemy, *un nemico giurato.*

He is a professed eye-witness of it, *dice d' averlo visto co suoi propri occhi.*

PROFE'SSEDLY, adv. [openly] *pubblicamente, manifestamente, apertamente.*

He was professedly his friend, *egli professava d' esser suo amico, ei si diceva pubblicamente suo amico.*

PROFE'SSION, s. [trade, calling] *professione, arte*, s. f. *esercizio, mestiere*, s. m.

Profession [publick confession] *professione.*

Profession [entering into a religious order] *professione, solenne promessa che' fanno i regolari.*

Profession [protestation] *protesto*, s. m. *protestazione, testimonianza, sicurtà*, s. f.

PROFE'SSOR, s. [one who professes any religion or persuasion] *professore*, s. m. *che professa qualche religione o credenza.*

Professor, in an university [lecturer, reader of any art or science in the publick schools] *professore, lettore pubblico.*

PROFE'SSORSHIP, s. [the office of a professor] *carico di professore.*

PRO'FFER [offer] *profferta, offerta*, s. f.

Proffer [attempt] *tentativo*; *sforzo*, s. m. *tentativa, prova*, s. f.

He made a proffer at it, *egli ha fatto la profferta.*

To PRO'FFER [to offer] *profferire, offerire, fare offerta*, pres. *profferisco.*

To proffer [to try, to venture] *provare, cercare, tentare, far prova.*

PRO'FFERED, adj. *profferto, offerto, provato, cercato, tentato.*

Proffered service stinks, *chi si offerisce è peggio il terzo.*

PRO'FFERING, s. *profferta, offerta*, s. f.

PROFI'CIENCY, s. [progress] *progresso, processo, profitto, avanzamento*, s. m.

PROFI'CIENT, adj. [forward in learning] *avanzato, che ha fatto qualche progresso.*

He is a great proficient in the Italian tongue, *egli è molto avanzato, o egli ha fatto gran progresso nella lingua Italiana.*

PRO'FILE, s. [a term of drawing, a design which shews the side with the rising and falling of any work] *profilo*, s. m. *una delle parti che è delle bande.*

The profile of a face, *il profilo d' una faccia.*

The profile of a picture, *il profilo d' una pittura.*

A face drawn in profile, *un viso o una faccia disegnata in profilo.*

The profile of a building or fortification, *il profilo d' un edificio, o d' una fortezza.*

PRO'FIT, s. [advantage, gain] *profitto, utile, guadagno, giovamento*, s. m.

A place of profit, *un impiego lucrativo.*

An estate that yields but small profit, *uno stato di poco emolumento, o che porta poco frutto.*

To PRO'FIT [to make a progress, to improve] *profittare, far profitto, far progresso, avanzarsi.*

To profit [to be useful] *profittare, acquistare, guadagnare, trar profitto, utile, o vantaggio.*

To profit by [to make a benefit of] *trar vantaggio, utile, o giovamento.*

PRO'FITABLE, adj. [beneficial, useful, advantageous] *profittevole, profittabile, fruttuoso, utile, vantaggioso, giovevole.*

PRO'FITABLENESS, s. [advantage, profit] *profitto, utile, guadagno, giovamento*, s. m.

PRO'FITABLY, adv. *profittevolmente, con profitto, vantaggiosamente.*

PRO'FITLESS, adj. [void of gain or advantage] *che non da profitto*; *che non procura vantaggio.*

PRO'FLIGATE, adj. [wicked, lewd, debauch'd to the highest degree] *scellerato, malvagio, sviato.*

A profligate man or woman, *uno scellerato, una scellerata, uno sviato, una sviata.*

Profligate doings, *azioni enormi, scelleratezze.*

To PRO'FLIGATE, *abbandonarsi, darsi in preda alle scelleratezze.*

PRO'FLIGATELY, adv. [shamelessly] *sfacciatamente, senza punta di vergogna, con dissolutezza.*

PRO'FLIGATENESS, s. *ſcellerataggine, ſcellerità, ſcelleratezza*, s. f.

PROFO'UND, adj. [deep] *profondo, cupo*.

A profound reverence, *una profonda riverenza*.

Profound [great, immenſe] *profondo, grande, eminente, inſigne*.

Profound learning, *ſcienza profonda*.

Profound ſleep, *profondo ſonno*.

PROFO'UNDLY, adv. [or deeply] *profondamente*.

Profoundly learned, *d' una profonda ſcienza*.

PROFO'UNDNESS, s. [or depth, in a figurative ſenſe] *profondità, penetrazione*, s. f.

Profoundneſs of learning, *profondo ſapere*.

PROFU'NDITY, s. [depth] *profondità*, s. f.

PROFU'SE, adj. [laviſh] *ſcialacquato, prodigo*.

Profuſe [overabounding, exuberant] *troppo abbondante, eſuberante*.

PROFU'SELY, adv. *ſcialacquatamente, prodigamente*.

Profuſely [with exuberance] *con ſoverchia abbondanza o profuſione; uſuberantemente*.

PROFU'SENESS, } s. [laviſhneſs] *ſcia*
PROFU'SION, } *lacquo, ſcialacquamento*, s. m. *prodigalità*, s. f.

Profuſion [abundance; exuberant plenty] *abbondanza ſoverchia, eſuberanza*.

To PROG [to uſe all endeavours to get or gain] *ingegnarſi, induſtriarſi, affaticarſi, cercare, uſar ogni mezzo per guadagnare*.

To prog [to rob, to ſteal] *rubare, rapire involare*.

To prog for victuals, to prog for one's belly, *cercar da mangiare*.

To prog for riches, *andar dietro alle ricchezze, affannarſi dietro alle ricchezze*.

PROG, s. victuals; proviſion of any kind] *vettovaglia; provviſione di checcheſſia*.

PROGE'NITOR, s. [a fore-father] *progenitore, antenato*, s. m.

PRO'GENY, s. [offspring, iſſue] *progenie, ſtirpe, ſchiatta, generazione*, s. f.

To PROGNO'STICATE [to foretel, to conjecture] *pronoſticare, prevedere, antivedere*, pret. *previdi, antiveddi*.

PROGNO'STICATED, adj. *pronoſticato, previſto, antiviſto*.

PROGNO'STICATING, } s. [a fore
PROGNOSTICA'TION, } telling] *pronoſticamento, pronoſtico*, s. m. *pronoſticazione*, s. f.

PROGNOSTICA'TOR, s. *quello, che pronoſtica*.

PROGNO'STICK, s. [a boding ſign, or token of ſome thing to come] *pronoſtico, preſagio*, s. m.

Prognoſtick, adj. ex. [a prognoſtick ſign, *un pronoſtico*.

PRO'GRESS, s. [proficiency] *progreſſo, proceſſo, profitto*, s. m.

A progreſs [a journey taken by a Prince or King] *viaggio*, s. m. *andata*, s. f.

PROGRE'SSION, s. [going on] *progreſſione*, s. f.

Arithmetical progreſſion, *progreſſione d' aritmetica*.

The month of progreſſion [the lunar month, which contains twenty-nine days and a half] *il meſe lunare*.

PROGRE'SSIONAL, } adj. [which
PROGRE'SSIVE, } proceeds or goes on] *progreſſivo, che ha virtù d' andare avanti*.

Progreſſional or progreſſive motion, *un moto progreſſivo*.

To PROHI'BIT [to forbid] *proibire, vietare, difendere*, pref. *proibiſco*.

PROHI'BITED, adj. *proibito, vietato, difeſo*.

A prohibited commodity, *una mercanzia di contrabbando*.

PROHI'BITING, s. *il proibire*.

PROHIBI'TION, s. [a forbidding] *proibizione*, s. f. *il proibire*.

PROHI'BITORY, adj. [that prohibits] *proibitivo, che proibiſce*.

A prohibitory edict, *un editto proibitivo, che proibiſce*.

A PRO'JECT, s. [deſign, purpoſe, contrivance] *progetto, diſegno*, s. m.

To PROJE'CT [to deſign, to contrive] *far progetti, intraprendere, diſegnare, macchinare, formar diſegni*.

PROJE'CTED, adj. *intrapreſo, diſegnato, machinato*.

PROJE'CTING, s. *il far progetti*.

Projecting, adj. *macchinatore*.

A projecting head, *un gran macchinatore, un formator di progetti*.

PROJE'CTION, s. [the art of projecting] *diſegno, penſiero, diſegnamento*, s. m. *macchinazione*, s. f.

PROJE'CTOR, s. [one who projects or contrives any deſign] *macchinatore, inventore*, s. m.

PROJE'CTURE, s. [the jutting or leaning out of any part of a building] *ſporto*, s. m. *muraglia, che ſparge in fuora dalla dirittura della parete principale*.

To PROIN, *v.* To prune.

PROLEGO'MENA, s. [previous diſcourſe; introductory obſervations] *prolegomeni, diſcorſo previo, oſſervazioni introduttorie*.

PROLETA'RIAN, adj. [mean, wretched, vulgar] *vile, baſſo, abbjetto, plebeo*.

PROLI'FICAL, } adj. [fit for genera
PROLI'FICK, } tion] *prolifico, proprio alla generazione, fecondo*.

PROLI'X, adj. [long, tedious] *proliſſo, lungo, tedioſo, non conciſo*.

PROLI'XITY, s. [tediouſneſs, or length of a diſcourſe] *proliſſità, lunghezza*, s. f.

PROLI'XLY, adv. *proliſſamente, lungamente, diſteſamente*.

PROLOCU'TOR, s. [chairman or ſpeaker of either houſe of convocation, or of a ſynod] *l' oratore ò il preſidente dell' aſſemblea eccleſiaſtica in Inghilterra*.

PRO'LOGUE, s. [a preface, properly a ſpeech before a ſtage play] *prologo, prolago*, s. m. *quel ragionamento poſto avanti a' poemi rappreſentativi*.

Prologue, s. *introduzione a un diſcorſo o altra opera d' ingegno*.

To PROLO'NG [to lengthen out] *prolungare, allungare, differire, prorogare, mandare in lungo*.

To prolong one's life, *prolungare, o allungare la vita*.

PROLONGA'TION, s. [a lengthening *prolungamento*, s. m. *prolungazione*, s. f.

PROLO'NGED, adj. *prolungato, allungato, differito, prorogato, madato in lungo*.

PROLO'NGER, s. [ſave-all] *pivolo di metallo ſul quale ſi ficca la candela*.

PROLO'NGING, s. *prolungamento*, s. m. *il prolungare*.

PRO'MINENCE, s. [jutting out, ſtanding forward] *prominenza*, s. f. *ſporto*, s. m.

PRO'MINENT, adj. [jutting out, ſtanding forward] *prominente che ha prominenza*.

Prominent paunch, *una groſſa pancia*.

PROMI'SCUOUS, adj. [mingled together, confuſed] *confuſo, meſcolato*.

In a promiſcuous ſenſe, *nell' uno e nell' altro ſenſo*.

PROMI'SCUOUSLY, adv. *confuſamente, meſcolatamente*.

PRO'MISE, s. [an aſſurance by word of mouth to do any thing] *promeſſa, impromeſſa*, s. f. *quel che s' è promeſſo*.

To keep one's promiſe, *attener la promeſſa*.

To PRO'MISE [to make a promiſe, to engage or give one's word] *promettere, obbligare altrui la ſua fede*, pret. *promiſi*.

A young man that promiſes much [a hopeful young man] *un giovine di buona indole*.

To promiſe [to undertake] *promettere, affermare, accertare*.

To promiſe in marriage, *promettere, promettere in moglie*.

To promiſe one's ſelf [to hope] *prometterſi, darſi ad intendere di poter fare, ſperare*.

To promiſe a great deal, *promettere mari e mondi*.

PRO'MISED, adj. *promeſſo*.

PRO'MISER, s. [he or ſhe that promiſes] *promettitore*, s. m. *promettitrice*, s. f.

PRO'MISING, s. *promiſſione, promeſſa*, s. f.

Promiſing, adj. [hopeful] *di buona indole*.

A promiſing youth, *un giovane di buona indole*.

A promiſing couutenance, *una bella fiſonomia*.

PRO'MISSARY, s. [he to whom a promiſe is made] *colui a chi s' è fatta qualche promeſſa*.

PROMI'SSION, s. *promiſſione*, s. f.

The land of promiſſion, *la terra di promiſſione*.

PRO'MISSORY, adj. [belonging to promiſe] *che contiene in ſe promeſſa*.

A promiſſory note, *una promeſſa in iſcritto, una redola, un obbligo*.

PRO'

PRO'MONTORY, s. [a mountain or hill, or any high ground running out a great way into the sea] *promontorio*, s. m. *monte lungo la marina*.

To PRO'MOTE [to advance, to extend, to carry further] *promovere, e promuovere, crescere, stendere*, pret. *promossi*.

To promote [to carry on] a design, *promovere, portare avanti un disegno*.

To promote trade, *accrescere, far fiorire il traffico*.

To promote a book, *mettere un libro in credito o in istima*.

To promote God's glory, *cercar l'avanzamento della gloria di Dio*.

PROMO'TED, adj. *promosso*, v. To promote.

PROMO'TER, s. *promotore*, s. m.

I have been a great promoter of it, *io ne sono stato il principal promotore, io vi ho contribuito molto*.

Promoter [one who complains of offenders in a spiritual court] *procurator generale in una corte ecclesiastica*.

Promoters [in law, informers, who, for prosecuting such as offend, have part of the fines for a reward] *delatori, informatori*.

PROMO'TING, s *avanzamento, aggrandimento*, s. m. *il promovere, promovimento*, s. m.

PROMO'TION, s. [preferment, advancement] *promozione, esaltazione*, s. f. *promovimento, avanzamento, aggrandimento*, s. m.

To seek for promotion, *attendere ad innalzarsi, o avanzarsi, cercar di tirarsi innanzi, cercar di far fortuna*.

PROMPT, adj. [ready, quick, nimble] *pronto, lesto, presto, apparecchiato*.

Prompt payment [ready money] *danari contanti*.

Prompt, adj. [quick, petulant] *petulante, baldanzoso*.

To PROMPT [to tell or whisper to one] *suggerire soffiare negli orecchi, dar notizia o avvertimento segretamente*.

To prompt one to a thing [to put him upon it] *sollecitare, instigare, importunare, insinuare, suggerire, indurre* pres. *induco*, pret. *indussi*.

PROMPTED, adj. *soffiato, prontato, sollecitato, istigato, importunato, insinuato, suggerito, indotto*.

PRO'MPTER, s. [one that prompts another] *suggeritore*.

PRO'MPTING, s. *il suggerire*.

Prompting [instigation] *istigazione, sollecitazione, istanza*, s. f.

PRO'MPTITUDE, } s. [readiness]
PRO'MPTNESS, } *prontezza, sollecitudine, speditezza, lestezza, diligenza*, s f.

PRO'MPTLY, adv. [readily] *prontamente, sollecitamente, speditamente, spacciatamente, lestamente, senza indugio*.

PRO'MPTUARY, s. [a store house] *magazzino, fondaco*, s. f.

Promptuary [buttery] *dispensa*, s. f.

To PRO'MULGATE, } [to publish or
To PROMU'LGE, } proclaim] *promulgare, pubblicare, divolgare*.

To promulge a law, *promulgare una legge*.

PROMULGA'TION, s. [a publishing] *promulgazione*, s. f.

PRO'MULGATED, } adj. *promulgato*,
PROMU'LGED, } *pubblicato, divolgato*.

PRONE, adj. [inclined to a thing] *prono, inclinato, dedito, volto per natura, a che che si sia*.

PRO'NENESS, s. [inclination] *propensione, inclinazione, disposizione*, s. f.

PRONG, s. [pitch fork] *bidente*, s. m. *forca, forchetta*, s. f.

PRO'NOMINAL, adj. [belonging to a pronoun] *di pronome*.

A pronominal particle, *una particola che ha il senso d' un pronome*.

A PRO'NOUN, s. [a personal noun, one of the parts of speech] *pronome*, s. m. *termine gramaticale, così detto, perchè esercita la voce del nome, come* IO, TU, EGLI, *&c.*

To PRO'NOUNCE [to utter, to speak] *pronunziare, profferire le parole*.

To pronounce a discourse, *pronunciare o fare un discorso*.

To pronounce [to judge, to decide, or declare] *pronunziare, pubblicare, dichiarare, giudicare*.

I will pronounce any man a traytor that shall say so, *io dichiaro traditore chiunque dirà tal cosa*.

PRONOU'NCED, adj. *pronunziato*, v. To pronounce.

PRONOU'NCING, s. *il pronunziare, pronunzia*, s. f.

PRONUNCIA'TION, s. [utterance of speech] *pronunziazione, pronunzia*, s. f.

PROOF, s. [tryal, essay] *prova, e pruova*, s. f. *esperimento, cimento*, s. m.

Proof [a printed sheet sent to the author or corrector of the press, in order to be corrected] *pruova, prima prova, termine di stampatore*.

Proof [reason, argument of truth] *prova, testimonianza, ragion confermativa*.

An authentick proof, *una prova autentica*.

Proof [mark, testimony] *prova, testimonianza, segno, indizio*, s. m.

Proof, adj. *che è a pruova*.

Ex. Musket-proof, *che è alla pruova del moschetto*.

Heaven cannot be proof against his petition, *il cielo non può non condescendere alla sua preghiera*.

PROP, s. [a support] *puntello, sostegno*, s. m.

A vine-prop, *un palo*.

A prop, *appoggio, sostegno, ajuto, favore*.

To PROP [to stay, to support, or bear up] *appuntellare, puntellare, rincalzare, sorreggere*, pret. *sorressi*.

To prop one up [to support him] *reggere, sostenere, spalleggiare, favorire, alcuno*, pret. *ressi, sostenni*, pres. *favorisco*.

PRO'PAGABLE, adj. [such as may be spread] *che si può propagare*.

To PRO'PAGATE [to multiply, to increase] *propagare, allargare, dilatare*.

To propagate the gospel, *propagar l' evangelo*.

To propagate mankind, *multiplicare il genere umano*.

To propagate a vine, *propagginare una vigna*.

To propagate [to spread abroad] *spargere, divulgare, seminare*.

To propagate a false doctrine, *seminare una falsa dottrina*.

PRO'PAGATED, adj. *propagato*, v. To propagate.

PRO'PAGATING, } s. [a spreading a-
PROPAGA'TION, } broad or increasing] *propagazione*, s. f. *il propagare*.

Propagation [the generation and multiplication of creatures] *generazione, multiplicazione*, s. f.

PROPAGA'TOR, s. *propagatore*, s. m. *quello che propaga*.

To PROPE'ND [to incline to a thing] *inclinare, avere attitudine, o inclinazione a che che si sia*.

PROPE'NDENCY, s. *propensione, inclinazione*.

Propendency, s. [pre-consideration, attentive consideration] *esame anteriore*.

PROPE'NSE, adj. [prone] *prono, inclinato, dedito*.

PROPE'NSION, } s. [inclination,
PROPE'NSITY, } proneness] *inclinazione, attitudine, e naturale disposizione a cosa particolare*.

PRO'PER, adj. [peculiar] *proprio, propio, che attiene, conviene, ed è solamente di colui, di cui si dice esser proprio*.

A proper name, *un nome proprio*.

A proper judge, *un giudice competente*.

Proper [fit] *conveniente, convenevole, dicevole*.

It is not proper for you to do it, *non è convenevole o dicevole, che voi facciate ciò*.

It is proper for an orator to speak eloquently, *è proprio dell' oratore di discorrere con eloquenza*.

A fine proper man, *un uomo ben fatto, di bella statura*.

A proper owner, *un proprietario*.

Proper, adv. *propriamente, e propiamente, acconciamente, correttamente, congruamente*.

To speak proper, *parlar correttamente, o congruamente, secondo le regole*.

PRO'PERLY, adj. *propriamente, giustamente, congruamente, correttamente*.

To speak properly, *parlar correttamente*.

PRO'PERNESS, s. [tallness] *una bella vita, una bella statura*.

PRO'PERTY, s. [natural quality or disposition] *proprietà*, s. f *la natura, la qualità propria e naturale di ciascheduna cosa*.

Property [a right of possession of a thing] *proprietà, tutto quel che si possiede in proprio*.

Pro'phecy, s. [prediction] *profezia*, s. f. *cosa predetta da profeta*; *predizione*.

To Pro'phesy [to foretel things to come] *profetare, profeteggiare profetizzare, predire*, pres. *predico*, pret. *predissi*.

Pro'phesied, adj. *profetato, profeteggiato, profetizzato, predetto*.

Pro'phet, s. [one who foretels future events, but properly a person inspired by God to reveal his will] *profeta*, s. m.

Pro'phetess, s. [a woman who prophesies] *profetessa*.

Pro'phetical, } adj. [belonging to
Pro'phetick, } a prophet, or prophecy] *profetico, di profeta*.

Prophe'tically, adv. *profeticamente, da profeta, in modo profetico*.

To Pro'phetize, *profetizzare, profeteggiare, predire il futuro*.

Propi'nquity, s. [nearness, nighness] *propinquità, vicinità, prossimità*, s. f.

Propinquity of blood, *affinità, prossimità, parentela*, s. f.

To Propi'tiate [to atone for] *espiare*.

His charity propitiated for his sins, *la sua carità ha espiato i suoi peccati*.

To Propi'tiate [to atone or make propitious] *placare, render propizio rendere favorevole*.

Propitia'tion, s. [atonement] *propiziazione*, s. f.

Propi'tiatory, adj. [that serves, or is of force to propitiate or atone] *propiziatorio*.

Propi'tious, adj. [favourable, kind, merciful] *propizio, favorevole, benigno*.

Propi'tiously, adv. [favourably, kindly] *propiziamente, favorevolmente, amorevolmente*.

Propo'rtion, s. [agreement, agreeableness] *proporzione, convenenza, conformità*, s. f.

Proportion [rule, measure] *proporzione, regola, misura*, s. f.

Beyond all proportions of reason, *contro tutte le regole della ragione*.

Proportion [portion] *parte, porzione*, s. f.

To Propo'rtion [to make answerable, or proportionable] *proporzionare, adattare*.

Propo'rtionable, adj. [answerable] *proporzionale, proporzionato, porzionevole*.

Propo'rtionably, adv. *proporzionalmente, proporzionevolmente, proporzionatamente*.

Propo'rtional, adj. [answerable in mathematicks] *proporzionale, proporzionato*.

Propo'rtionally, adv. *proporzionalmente, con proporzione, proporzionatamente*.

Propo'rtioned, adj. *proporzionato*.

Propo'rtioning, s. *il proporzionare*.

Propo'sal, s. [proposition, offer] *proposizione, offerta*, s. f.

To Propo'se [to offer] *proporre, e proponere, offerire, proferire*, pres. *propongo, offerisco, proferisco*, pret. *proposi*.

To propose a thing to one's self [to design to do it] *proponere, deliberare, statuire, intendere, aver intenzione, o pensiero*.

What do you propose to do? *che proponete, deliberate, o intendete di fare?*

Propo'sed, adj. *proposto, offerto, proferto, deliberato, statuito, inteso*.

Propo'ser, s. *quello, o quella che propone una cosa*.

Propo'sing, *il proporre*.

Proposi'tion [proposal] *proposizione, proposta, deliberazione*, s. f.

Proposition [a sentence upon any subject] *proposizione*.

To Propo'und [to propose, to set on foot some discourse or some question] *proporre, porre avanti, mettere in campo il soggetto del quale, o sopra' quale si vuol discorrere*.

Propo'unded, adj. *proposto*.

Propo'under, s. [one who propounds a matter] *colui che propone una questione*.

Propounder [in law, a monopolizer, or ingrosser of commodities] *incettatore*, s. m.

Propo'unding, s. *il proporre*.

Pro'pped, adj. [from to prop] *puntellato*, v. To prop.

Propri'etor, s. [an owner, one who has a property in any thing] *proprietario*, s. m. *che tiene in proprietà*.

Propri'ety, s. [proper sense] *proprietà, il senso naturale*.

The proprieties of speech, *le proprietà del discorso*; *l'idioma d' una lingua*.

In propriety of speaking, *propriamente parlando*.

Proroga'tion, s. [a deferring or putting off] *proroga, prorogazione*, s. f.

The prorogation of the parliament, *la proroga del parlamento*.

To Pro'rogue [to put off till another time, to prolong] *prorogare, allungare, differire*, pres. *differisco*.

Proro'gued, adj. *prorogato, allungato, differito*.

Proro'guing, s. *prorogazione*, s. f. *il prorogare*.

Prosa'ick, adj. [being in, or belonging to prose] *prosaico, in prosa*.

A prosaick composition, *composizione prosaica*.

To Pro'scribe [to out-law, to banish] *proscrivere, condennare ad esilio, esiliare*, pret. *proscrissi*.

Pro'scribed, adj. *proscritto, esiliato*.

Pro'script, s. [an out-law] *un bandito*.

Proscri'ption, s. [exilement, or making one an out-law] *proscrizione*, s. f. *esilio*, s. m.

Proscription [a confiscation of goods, and setting them to open sale] *il confiscare i beni del debitore, e venderli all' incanto per pagare i suoi creditori*.

Prose, s. [the plain usual way of expression, opposed to verse] *prosa*, s. f. *favellare sciolto, a distinzione de' versi*.

He that writes in prose, *un prosatore*.

To Pro'secute [to carry on, or go on with] *proseguire, seguitare avanti, continuare, proseguitare*, pres. *proseguisco*.

To prosecute a design, *proseguire un disegno*.

To prosecute one at law, *proseguire uno in giustizia*.

To prosecute a story in all its circumstances, *narrare, dire, o scrivere un' istoria minutamente*.

Pro'secuted, adj. *proseguito, continuato, proseguitato*.

Many expedients have been prosecuted, *si sono tentati molti espedienti*.

Pro'secuting, s. *proseguimento*, s. m. *prosecuzione*, s. f.

Prosecu'tion, s. [continuance] *prosecuzione, continuazione*, s. f.

To dispose things for a vigorous prosecution of war, *far i preparativi necessari per continuare vigorosamente la guerra*.

Prosecu'tor, s. [one who sues at law in another's name] *attore*, s. m. *colui che nel litigare domanda*.

Pro'selyte, s. [a stranger converted to any religion] *un proselita, un nuovo convertito a qualche religione*.

Proso'dian, s. [one skilled in prosody] *uno che è versato nella prosodia, ne' metri*.

Pro'sody, s. [that part of grammar which teaches to accent right, or rightly to distinguish syllables and the measures of verse] *prosodia*, s. f.

Prosopope'ia, s. [a rhetorical figure, wherein the speaker addresses himself to things inanimate, as if they were living, and makes them speak as if they had rational souls] *prosopopea*, s. f. *figura rettorica*.

Pro'spect, s. [a view or sight afar off] *perspettiva, vista*, s. f.

These houses yield a fine prospect, *queste case fanno una bella vista, o un bell' effetto*.

The prospect of torments, *la vista de' tormenti*.

Prospect [view, design, aim] *fine, disegno, intento*, s. m. *meta*.

He has nothing but his private interest in prospect, *non risguarda che il suo proprio interesse, non ha altro in mira che il suo proprio interesse*.

The diversity of cases cannot be brought within the prospect of one law, *una sola legge non può comprendere o abbracciare la diversità de' casi*.

Prospec'tive, adj. *di lunga vista*.

Prospec'tive-glass, *un cannocchiale*.

To Pro'sper [to give success, to make prosperous] *prosperare felicitare, mandar di bene in meglio*.

To prosper [to succeed, to be successful] *prosperare, avanzarsi in felicità, andar di bene in meglio*.

To prosper [to thrive, to have a fair gale

gale of fortune] *prosperare, aver la fortuna favorevole.*

PROSPE'RITY, s. [happiness or good fortune] *prosperità, felicità*, s. f.

PRO'SPEROUS, adj. [favourable] *prospero, felice, favorevole, secondo.*

Prosperous fortune, *fortuna prospera.*

Prosperous wind, *vento favorevole, o secondo.*

PRO'SPEROUSLY, adv. *prosperamente, felicemente, favorevolmente.*

PROSPI'CIENCE, s. [foresight] *antivedimento*, s. m.

PROSTERNA'TION, s. [a bowing down] *prosternazione*, s. f.

PRO'STITUTE, adj. [base, lewd] *impudico, lascivo.*

Prostitute, s. [a common harlot] *una prostituta, una meretrice, una puttanaccia, una bagascia.*

To PRO'STITUTE [to yield up one's honour or body to lust, and sensual pleasures] *prostituirsi, abbandonarsi, darsi in preda alle lascivie e piaceri carnali.*

To prostitute one's self to a man's ambition, *sottomettersi all' ambizione di qualcheduno.*

PRO'STITUTED, adj. *prostituito, abbandonato, dato in preda.*

PRO'STITUTING } s. *il prostituirsi.*
PROSTITU'TION }

PRO'STRATE, adj. [laid flat along] *prostrato, disteso a terra, disteso.*

To prostrate one's self [to throw one's self down] *prostrarsi, distendersi a terra.*

PRO'STRATING } s. [a lying flat along, a falling to one's feet] *prosternazione*, s. f.
PROSTRA'TION }

PRO'TASIS, s. [the first part of a play] *argomento*, s. m.

To PROTE'CT [to defend, to maintain] *proteggere, difendere*, pret. *protessi, difesi.*

PROTE'CTED, adj. *protetto, mantenuto, difeso.*

PROTE'CTING } s. *protezione, difensione, cura, difesa*, s. f.
PROTE'CTION }

To take one into protection, *avere uno in protezione.*

PROTE'CTOR, s. [defender] *proteggitore, protettore, difensore*, s. m.

He betook himself to Cæsar for his protector, *ricorse alla protezione di Cesare; prese Cesare per suo protettore.*

Protector of a kingdom [one made choice of to govern it, during the minority of a prince] *protettore, reggente, amministratore d' uno stato.*

PROTE'CTRESS, s. *protettrice*, s. f.

PROTE'CTORSHIP, s. *protettorato*; s m. *ufficio del protettore.*

To PROTE'ND [to hold out, to stretch forth] *porgere.*

PROTE'ST, s. [a declaration against a person charged with the payment of a bill of exchange, for refusing to pay it] *protesto*, s. m.

To protest [to vow, to assure, to swear] *protestare, confessare, assicurare, giurare.*

To protest a bill of exchange, *protestare una lettera di cambio.*

To protest against the proceeding of a judge [to oppose it, to declare it unlawful] *protestare contro il procedimento d' un giudice.*

PRO'TESTANTISM, s. [the principles and doctrine of Protestants] *la religione protestante.*

PRO'TESTANT, s. [one of the reformed religion, according to Luther, Calvin, or the Church of England] *un protestante, un riformato.*

Protestant, adj. *protestante.*

The Protestant religion, *la religione protestante.*

PROTESTA'TION, s. [a protesting against, a solemn vow or assurance] *protesto*, s. m. *protestazione*, s. f.

A protestation at law, *un protesto in forma giudiciaria.*

PROTE'STED against, adj. *protestato.*

PROTE'STER, s. *quegli, o quella che protesta o solennemente dichiara.*

PRO'TOCOL, s. [the first draught of a deed, contract, or instrument] *protocollo*, s. m.

PROTOMA'RTYR, s. [the first witness or martyr, who suffered death in testimony of truth] *protomartire, primo martire.*

St. Stephen the protomartyr, *Santo Stefano il protomartire.*

PROTHONO'TARY, s. [a chief clerk of the King's Bench and Common Pleas] *protonotajo*, s. m.

The prothonotary of the court of Rome, *il protonotajo della corte di Roma.*

PRO'TOTYPE, s. [an original type, the first pattern or model of a thing] *prototipo*, s. m. *il primo modello.*

To PROTRA'CT [to prolong, to delay] *protrarre, prolungare, allungare, differire, prorogare, mandare in lunga*, pret. *protrassi.*

PROTRA'CTED, adj. *protratto, prolungato, allungato, differito, prorogato.*

PROTRA'CTING, s. *protrazione*, s. f. *il protrarre.*

PROTRA'CTOR, s. *quello o quella che protrae.*

To PROTRU'DE [to thrust, to push forward] *spignere, ficcare, cacciare*, pret. *spinsi.*

PROTU'BERANCE, s. [rising, swelling] *tumore, gonfiamento*, s. m. *gonfiagione*, s. f.

PROTU'BERANT, adj. [bunching out] *gonfio, gonfiato, tumido.*

A protuberant sore, *un tumore, una enfiagione.*

To PROTU'BERATE [to swell forward; to swell out beyond the parts adjacent] *gonfiare, gonfiarsi.*

PROUD, adj. [haughty, puffed up with pride] *superbo, altiero, arrogante, orgoglioso.*

A proud man, *un superbo, un uomo altiero.*

To be proud of a thing [to take pride in it] *vantarsi, vanagloriarsi di che che si sia.*

A proud [stately] horse, *un cavallo fiero.*

A proud bitch, *una cagna in fucchio.*

I will speak a proud word for myself, *dirò questo in mia lode.*

Proud flesh [excrescency] *carne morta.*

PRO'UDLY, adv. *superbamente, altieramente, arrogantemente, orgogliosamente.*

To carry one's self proudly, *comportarsi altieramente, alzar le corna.*

To PROVE [to make out, to make good] *provare, confermare, mostrar con ragioni, e autorità.*

To prove [to try, to make an experiment] *provare, pruovare, far pruova cimentare, esperimentare, far saggio.*

To prove [to come to be, to come to pass] *divenire, succedere, accadere, riuscire*, pret. *divengo, riuscisco*, pret. *divenne, successe, accadde.*

He will prove an honest man, *diverrà, o sarà un galantuomo.*

If what you say prove true, *se quel che dite sarà vero, o si verificherà.*

I am afraid it will prove otherwise, *temo che non succeda o non arcada tutto 'l contrario.*

PROVED, adj. *provato*, v. To prove.

PROVE'DITOR, s. [a military officer among the Venetians]. *proveditore*, s. m.

PROVE'DITOR } s. [one that engages to provide, one that provides] *provveditore, e proveditore.*
PRO'VEDORE }

PROVE'NDER, s. [food for cattle] *pastura, pascolo*, s. m.

PRO'VERB, s. [a common or old pithy saying] *un proverbio, breve e arguto detto ricevuto comunemente.*

To PRO'VERB [to mention in a proverb] *far menzione in un proverbio.*

To proverb [to provide with a proverb] *somministrare un proverbio.*

PROVE'RBIAL, adj. [belonging to a proverb] *proverbiale.*

PROVE'RBIALLY, adv. *proverbialmente, in proverbio, per proverbio.*

To PROVI'DE [to furnish with] *provedere, provvedere, procacciare, trovar quello che bisogna, munire.*

To provide a town with ammunition, *provvedere, supplire, o munire una città di munizione.*

To provide what to say, *provvedere, prevedere, antivedere, o pensare a quel che si dice.*

To provide one of a benefice, *conferire un beneficio ad uno.*

He has provided for all his children, *egli ha provvisto tutti i suoi figliuoli.*

I shall provide for you, *averò cura di voi, farò qualche cosa per voi, provvedere a' vostri bisogni.*

To provide one's self, *provvedersi, munirsi.*

To provide for one's self, *provvedirsi, impiegarsi, prender qualche partito.*

To provide against, *metter ordine, disporsi.*

PROVI'DED, adj. *provvisto*, v. To provide.

Provided of necessaries, *provvisto delle cose necessarie.*

I am provided for it, *sono preparato.*

He was provided of an answer, *aveva la risposta in ordine.*

Provided, or provided that, adv. [on condition that] *purchè, a condizione.*

PRO'VIDENCE, s. [the foresight or supreme intelligence of God, and his government of all created things] *providenza, provvidenza,* s. f.

It is a great providence that he was not drowned, *fu un effetto particolare della provvidenza che non s' annegasse.*

Providence [wariness, foresight] *antivedimento,* s. m. *circonspezione, cautela,* s. f.

Providence [husbandry] *economia,* s. f. *risparmio,* s. m.

PRO'VIDENT, adj. [wary] *proveduto, e provveduto, cauto, accorto, provido.*

Provident [thrifty, saving] *economo, risparmiante.*

A provident man [a good husband] *un buon economo.*

PROVIDE'NTIAL, adj. [belonging to divine providence] *della provvidenza.*

PROVIDE'NTIALLY, adv. [by the case of providence] *per disposizione della divina provvidenza.*

PRO'VIDENTLY, adj. [warily] *prudentemente, cautamente, con circonspezione e cautela, cautelosamente.*

PROVI'DER, s. [provedóre, provisor] *proveditore, e provveditore.*

PRO'VINCE, s. [a considerable part of a country or kingdom] *provincia,* s. f. *spazio di paese contenuto sotto un nome.*

The province of Canterbury or York [the circuit of each archbishop's jurisdiction] *la provincia o la giurisdizione degli arcivescovi di Cantorberi e di York.*

Province [business] *affare, assunto, carico,* s. m. *incombenza, cura,* s. f.

It is in his province to do it, *è suo assunto, o sta incombenza di farlo.*

It is not within my province [or sphere] *non è della mia portata.*

PROVI'NCIAL, adj. [belonging to a province] *provinciale, di provincia.*

A provincial synod, *un sinodo provinciale.*

A provincial, s. [a chief governor of all the religious houses of the same order in a province] *un provinciale, dicono i frati a quello, che tra loro è il primo capo nella provincia.*

PROVI'SION, s. [necessaries of life] *provvisione, provvedimento di cose necessarie.*

Provisions for an army, *viveri per un esercito*

Till further provision be made, *per provvisione.*

To make a provision for one [to provide for him] *provvedere alcuno, provvedere ai bisogni d' uno.*

PROVI'SIONAL, adj. *provvisionale.*

PROVI'SO [a clause, a caveat or condition] *condizione, clausula,* s. f. *patto,* s. m.

With a proviso, *condizionalmente, con condizione.*

PROVI'SOR, s. [the chief governor in some colleges] *rettore d' un collegio.*

A provisor of a religious house, *provveditore, o spenditore d' un monastero.*

PROVOCA'TION, s. [increasing, stirring up] *provocamento,* s. m. *provocazione,* s. f.

PRO'VOCATIVE, adj. [apt to provoke or stir up] *provocativo, che ha forza di provocare.*

To PROVO'KE [to anger, to move, to stir up] *provocare, incitare, commuovere,* pret. *commossi.*

To provoke one, *provocare alcuno, irritarlo.*

That provokes vomiting [makes one vomit] *ciò provoca il vomito, o fa vomitare.*

To provoke urine, *far urinare.*

PROVO'KED, adj. *provocato, incitato, commosso, irritato.*

PROVO'KER, s. *provocatore, incitatore,* s. m.

PROVO'KING, s. *il provocare, provocamento,* s. m. *provocazione,* s. f.

Provoking, adj. *che provoca, che irrita.*

That is very provoking, *questa è una cosa da far ismaniare, o dar nelle smanie.*

PRO'VOST, s [a chief magistrate of a city] *proposto,* s. m. *magistrato che tiene il primo luogo.*

A provost-marshal, or land [an officer whose business is to seize and secure deserters and other criminals] *proposto della milizia.*

The provost of a college, *il rettore d' un collegio.*

PRO'VOSTSHIP, s. [the office or dignity of a provost] *propositura, propostato,* s. m. *dignità di proposto.*

PROW, s. [the fore part of a ship] *prora, prua,* s. f. *la parte dinanzi del navilio, col quale si fende l' acqua.*

Prow, adj. [valiant] *prode, valente, animoso.*

PRO'WESS, s. [valour, a valiant or mighty act] *prodezza, valenzia, valenteria, valoria,* s. f. *valore,* s. m.

PRO'WEST, adj. [bravest, most valiant] *valentissimo, il più prode, il più valoroso.*

To PROWL [to go about for pelf] *andar in busca; cercar di rubare; rubare, saccheggiare, truffare.*

PRO'WLING, adj. ex. a prowling fellow, *un furbo, un barattiere, un mariuolo.*

PROXI'MITY, s. [nearness] *prossimità, vicinità, vicinanza,* s. f.

Proximity of blood, *prossimità, attenenza, parentela,* s. f.

PRO'XY, s. [a deputy, one who does the part of another, or acts for him in his absence] *procuratore, deputato, colui che fa le parti d' un altro in sua assenza.*

Proxy [procuration] *procura,* s. f.

They were married by proxies, *furono maritati per procura.*

PRUCE, s. *cuojo di prussia.*

PRUDE, s. [a woman over-nice and scrupulous, and with false affectation] *un' affettatuzza, una sputasenno, una spigolistra.*

PRU'DENCE. s. [wisdom] *prudenza, saviezza,* s. f.

PRU'DENT, adj. [wise] *prudente, savio, accorto.*

PRUDE'NTIAL, adj. *prudenziale, di prudenza.*

PRUDE'NTIALLY, adv. *prudentemente.*

PRU'DENTLY, adv. *prudentemente, con prudenza.*

PRUNE, s. [plumb] *susina secca.*

To PRUNE trees [to lop them] *dibruscare, o dibrucare, rimondare alberi.*

To prune a vine, *potare una vigna.*

PRUNED, adj. *dibruscato, dibrucato, rimondato, potato.*

PRU'NEL, s. [an herb] *prunella,* s. f. *spezie d' erba.*

PRUNE'LLO, s. [a sort of plumb] *susina,* s. f.

Prunello [wild plumb] *prugnola,* s. f. *susina salvatica.*

PRU'NER, s. [he that prunes] *potatore,* s. m.

PRU'NING, *potamento,* s. m. *potagione,* s. f.

A pruning knife, *un falcetto.*

PRU'RIENCE, PRU'RIENCY, s. [an itching or a great desire or appetite to any thing] *prudore, pizzicore,* s. m. *prudura,* s. f. *desiderio, o appetito grande di chechessia.*

PRU'RIENT, adj. [itching] *che prude, che pizzica.*

To PRY into [to search, enquire, or dive into] *spiare, investigare, andare investigando, diligentemente cercare.*

To pry into other men's concerns, *spiare, o investigare i fatti altrui.*

PRYED into, adj. *spiato, investigato, diligentemente cercato.*

PRY'ING, into, s. *investigamento, lo spiare, l' investigare.*

PSALM, s. [an hymn upon some sacred subject] *salmo,* s. m. *canzone sacra.*

To sing psalms, *cantar salmi, salmeggiare.*

He that sings psalms, *salmeggiatore,* s. m.

PSA'LMIST, s. [one who makes psalms] *salmista,* s. m. *componitor di salmi.*

A psalmist [one who sings psalms] *salmeggiatore,* s. m. *che salmeggia.*

PSA'LMODY, s. [a singing of psalms] *salmodia,* s. f. *canto di salmi.*

PSA'LTER, s. [a book of psalms] *saltero, e salterio,* s. m. *libro di salmi.*

PSA'LTERY, s. [a kind of musical instrument] *saltero, salterio,* s. m. *strumento musicale.*

PSHAW, interj. [an expression of contempt] *via. via. Espressione di disprezzo.*

PTI'SANE, s. [tisane] *acqua cotta. bevanda medicinale.*

PU'BERTY, s. *pubertà, adolescenza.*

A Pu'blican, s. [a farmer of publick rents and revenues] *pubblicano, gabelliere, ricoglitore de' dazi, e gabelle.*

Publica'tion, s. [the act of making publick] *pubblicazione,* s. f. *pubblicamento,* s. m.

Pu'blick, adj. [manifest, known by every body] *pubblico, noto, manifesto.*

Publick [common, belonging to every one] *pubblico, che è comune ad ognuno.*

The publick-good, *il ben pubblico.*

A publick place [as a church or market place] *un luogo pubblico.*

A publick person [one that serves the publick] *una persona pubblica.*

A publick house, *una casa pubblica, un osteria.*

To make a book publick [to publish it] *pubblicare un libro, darlo alla luce.*

A publick concern, *un affare che concerne il pubblico.*

Publick spirited, *che è portato per il ben pubblico.*

The publick, s. [every body in general] *il pubblico, la comunità, il comune.*

In publick, adv. [publickly] *pubblicamente, in pubblico.*

Pu'blickly, adv. *pubblicamente, ad occhi veggenti d' ognuno, in pubblico.*

To Pu'blish [to make publick] *pubblicare, manifestare, divolgare.*

To publish a book, *pubblicare, o dar alla luce un libro.*

Pu'blished, adj. *pubblicato, manifestato, divolgato.*

Pu'blisher, s. *pubblicatore,* s. m. *che pubblica.*

Pu'blishing, *publicamento,* s. m. *pubblicazione,* s. f.

Pu'celage, s. [maidenhead] *pulcellaggio,* s. m. *virginità,* s. f.

Puck, s. *folletto, spirito, spiritello, un ente immaginario negli antichi Romanzi Inglesi.*

Pu'ckball, s. *sorta di fungo pieno di polvere.*

To Pu'cker [to shrink up or lie uneven, not to lie close to the body, speaking of a suit of clothes] *raggrinzarsi, empirsi di grinze, non esser attillato alla vita, parlando de' vestimenti.*

Pu'ckered, adj. *raggrinzato.*

Puck-fist, s. [fuz-ball] *spezie di fungo.*

Pu'dder, s. [noise, bustle] *strepito, fracasso, schiamazzo, rumore,* s. m.

To Pu'dder, *agitar la polvere.*

To pudder [to make a tumult, to make a bustle] *tumultuare, strepitare, schiamazzare.*

To pudder in, *dimenarsi, agitarsi, muoversi in qua e 'n là.*

Pu'ddering, s. *dimenamento, dimenio,* v. To pudder.

Pu'dding, s. [a dish of food, well known] *spezie di torta all' Inglese, delle quali ven' hanno di differentissime maniere.*

Pudding [or hog's pudding] *sanguinaccio,* s. m.

To come in pudding time, *venire a tempo, giungere a tempissimo.*

Better some of a pudding than none of a pie, *chi spilluzzica non digiuna.*

Pudding [in the belly of any beast that is dressed] *ripieno.*

A pudding about a child's head, *ravvolto di panno che si mette in capo a fanciulli per salvar loro il capo quando cascano.*

Pu'ddle, s. *picciolo spazio fangoso, limarcio, limo, fango,* s. f.

Puddle water, *acqua fangosa.*

To Pu'ddle, *sguazzare, o dimenare nell' acqua, e nel fango.*

Pu'dency, s. *pudore,* s. m. *modestia,* s. f.

Pudi'city, s. [chastity, modesty] *pudicizia, castità,* s. f.

Pu'efellow, s. [a partner] *un sozio, un compagno.*

Pu'erile, adj. [childish] *puerile, di fanciullo, fanciullesco.*

Pueri'lity, s. [childhood] *puerizia, età puerile, fanciullezza,* s. f.

Pu'et, s. [a kind of bird] *upupa,* s. f. *uccello con una cresta in capo, e vive di cose putride.*

Puff of wind, *soffio di vento.*

Puff [utensil for powdering the hair] *un fiocco.*

Puff-paste, *pasta a sfoglie.*

An earth-puff [truffle] *tartufo,* s. m. *spezie di fungo.*

Puff-ball, puff-fist, or puck-fist, *vescia,* s. m. *spezie di fungo.*

To Puff [to blow] *soffiare.*

To puff, verb neut. [to swell] *sbuffare gonfiarsi.*

He buffs and puffs [he is in a fume] *egli sbuffa, egli freme d' ira.*

To huff and puff [as one out of breath] *anelare, ansare, sbuffare.*

To puff up one with pride, *fare insuperbire uno.*

Pu'ffed up, adj. *gonfio, paffuto.*

Pu'ffin, s. [the sharp-snouted ray, a sea-fish] *spezie di pesce.*

Puffin [a sea fowl] *sorta d' uccello marino.*

Pu'ffingly, adv. *tumidamente, in modo gonfio.*

Pu'ffy, adj. [or puffed up] *gonfio, paffuto, tumido.*

A swelling puffy stile, *stile gonfio, o ampolloso.*

Pug, s. [a little monkey] *uno scimiotto.*

Dear pug, *ben mio, cuor mio. Modo plebeamente burlesco.*

Pugil, s. [a term used by physicians and apothecaries] *pugillo,* s. m. *quanto si può prendere con tre dita.*

Pui'ssance, s. [power] *potenza, possanza, forza,* s. f.

Pui'ssant, s. [powerful] *potente, possente.*

Mighty puissant, *potentissimo, possentissimo.*

Pui'ssantly, adv. *potentemente, possentemente.*

To Puke [to be ready to spue, or vomit] *aver voglia di vomitare, star per vomitare.*

Pu'ker, s. *vomitivo; medicina da provocar il vomito.*

Pu'king, s. *voglia di vomitare.*

Pucking, adj. ex. to have a puking stomach, *essere svogliato.*

Pu'lcritude, s. [beauty] *bellezza,* s. f.

To Pule [as chickens and young birds do] *piare, pigolare, il mandar fuor la voce che fanno i pulcini e gli altri uccelli piccoli.*

To pule [to whimper] *il rammaricarsi che fanno i fanciulli desiderando checchessia, o che avendo assai sempre si dolgon d' aver poco.*

Pu'ling, adj. [sickly, crazy] *malaticcio, infermiccio.*

Pu'liol, s. [puliol royal, the same as penny-royal] *puleggio,* s. m. *erba medicinale.*

Pull, s. [pluck] *strappata, tirata, scossa,* s. f. tratto, s. m.

To give one a pull, *dare una scossa ad uno,* tirar *via uno per forza.*

Give your patience another pull, *abbiate ancora un poco di pazienza.*

Pull-back [hindrance] *ostacolo, impedimento,* intoppo, s. m.

To Pull [to pluck, to drag] tirare, *or* trarre, *cavare,* pres. trao, traggo, pret. *trassi.*

To pull money out of one's pocket, *tirar fuora danari dalla scarsella.*

To pull a fowl, *spiumare un uccello.*

To pull away, *tirar via.*

Pull away [drink about] *su bevete.*

To pull asunder, *svellere, sconficcare.*

To pull back, *tirar in dietro, far rinculare.*

To pull down, *abbattere, mandare a terra, atterrare.*

To pull down a wall or a house, *demolire un muro o una casa.*

To pull down one's spirits [to humble him] *abbatter alcuno, umiliarlo.*

To pull in, tirare *a se.*

Pull in the bridle, tirate *la briglia.*

To pull in pieces, *sbranare, stracciare, metter in pezzi.*

To pull to, *tirar a se.*

To pull off, tirare, *cavare, levare.*

To pull off one's clothes, *svestirsi, spogliarsi.*

To pull off one's shoes and stockings, *scalzarsi.*

To pull off one's boots, *cavar gli stivali.*

To pull one's hair off, *strappare* i *capelli.*

To pull off one's hat to one; *levar il cappello ad uno, salutarlo.*

To pull off one's mask, *cavarsi la maschera.*

To pull out, *cavare, tirare, levare.*

To pull out one's eyes, *cavar gli occhi ad uno.*

To pull up, *tirar su, alzare.*

To pull up by the roots, *svellere, sradicare.*

To pull up a good heart, *farsi animo.*

To pull along, *strascinare.*

To pull up that which was set, *spiantare.*

Pu'lled, adj. *tirato, tratto,* v. To pull.

Pu'llen, s. [poultry] *pollame,* s. m.

Pu'ller, s. [one that pulls] *uno che tira o spinge con forza.*

Pu'llet, s. [young hen] *un pollastro.*

Pu'lley, s [a little wheel used to pull up and let down burdens] *girella, carrucola, che gira intorno a un perno.*

A little pulley, *una carrucoletta.*

A pulley piece [an armour for the knee] *ginocchiello, s. m. arme difensiva del ginocchio.*

The pulley-piece of a boot, *ginocchiello d' uno stivale.*

A pulley-door, *porta che si serra da se per mezzo d' una carrucola.*

To Pu'llulate [to spring or come up young, to bud forth] *pullulare, mandar le piante e arbori fiori e germogli dalle radici, o dal seme, germogliare.*

Pulmona'rious, adj. [diseased in the lungs] *tisico.*

Pu'lmonary, s. [or lung-wort] *polmonaria, s. f. sorta d' erba.*

Pu'lmonary, } adj. [belonging to
Pulmo'nick, } the lungs] *attenente ai polmoni.*

Pulp, s. [the fleshy part of a thing] *polpa, s. f. carne senz' osso.*

The pulp of any fruit, *la polpa d' un frutto.*

Pu'lpit, s. [a desk to preach or make an oration in] *pulpito, pergamo, s. m.*

Pu'lpous, } adj. [fleshy] *polposo,*
Pu'lpy, } *polputo*

Pulse, s. [the beating of the arteries] *polso, s. m. moto dell' arterie.*

To feel one's pulse, *toccare il polso.*

To feel one's pulse [to see how he stands affected] *toccare il polso ad uno, scandagliare il suo valore, o la sua intenzione, tastar l' animo di qualcheduno.*

Pulse [all sorts of grain, contained in cods, husks, or shells] *legume, s. m. tutte quelle granella che seminate nascono co' baccelli.*

To Pulse [to beat as the pulse] *battere come batte polso.*

Pu'lverable, adj. [possible to be reduced to dust] *che si puo ridurre in polvere.*

Pulveriza'tion, s. [a reducing to powder] *polverizzamento, s. m. il polverizzare.*

To Pu'lverize [to reduce any body into a fine powder] *polverizzare; fare o ridurre in polvere che che si sia.*

Pu'lverized, adj. *polverizzato, ridotto in polvere.*

Pu'lvil, s. [sweet scents] *odori piacevoli; cose fragranti fatte dall' arte; profumi.*

To pulvil [to sprinkle with perfumes in powder] *spargere checchessia con profumi polverizzati.*

Pu'mice, s. [a spungy, crumbling stone] *pomice, s. f. sorta di pietra.*

To Pu'mmel, *v.* to pommel.

Pump, s. an engine for drawing water] *tromba, s. f. strumento con che si sollevano i liquidi a forza di pressione.*

Pump brake [a sea-term, the pump-handle] *manovella di tromba.*

Pump-water, *acqua di tromba.*

Pumps, s. [a sort of light shoes] *scarpe, sottili.*

To Pump [to draw water with a pump] *sollevar l' acqua colla tromba, cavarla.*

To pump one [to wash one under the pump] *lavare o bagnare uno sotto la tromba. E' castigo tumultuariamente dato dalla canaglia d' Inghilterra a i ladri di fazzoletti quando sono acchiappati sul fatti.*

To pump one [to sift one by a sly enquiry] *scalzare uno, cavare altrui di bocca artatamente quello che si vorrebbe sapere.*

I have pumped him so, that he told me all at last, *ho fatto tanto che alla fine m' ha scoperto il tutto.*

Pu'mped, adj. *sollevato colla tromba, v.* To pump.

Pu'mpion, s. [a plant] *spezie di zucca.*

Pun, s. [quibble] *bisticcio, bisticchio, s. m. scherzo, che risulta da vicinanza di parole, differenti di significato e simili di suono; giuoco o giochetto di parole.*

To Pun [to quibble] *bisticciare, scherzare con bisticci.*

Punch, s. [a shoemaker's tool to make holes with] *punteruolo, s. m.*

Punch [a sort of strong drink, made of brandy, water, sugar, and juice of lemons] *sorta di bevanda composta d' acquavite, acqua, zucchero, e sugo di limone.*

Punch, } s. *pulicinella,* s. m.
Punchinello, }

To Punch [to bore with a punch] *forar con punteruolo.*

To punch [to thrust one with the fist or elbow] *spignere alcuno col pugno, o col gomito.*

Pu'nched, adj. *forato.*

Punchine'llo, s. [a stage puppet] *pulicinella, s. m.*

Pu'nchion, s. [a sort of chizzel] *succhio, s. m.*

A punchion [a vessel of wine] *botte da vino.*

Punctilio, s. [a little point or trifle] *puntiglio, s. m.*

To stand upon punctilios, *star sul puntiglio, star in sul punto.*

The punctilio of honour, *puntiglio, punto d' onore.*

Puncti'lious, adj. [trifling] *puntiglioso, che sta sul puntiglio.*

Pu'nctual, adj. [exact] *puntuale, molto diligente.*

Very punctual, *puntualissimo.*

Punctua'lity, s. [exactness] *puntualità, esattezza, s. f.*

Pu'nctually, adv. *puntualmente, minutamente.*

Punctua'tion, s. [the method of pointing, or making stops in writing] *punteggiatura, s. f.*

Pu'ncture, s. *puntuare, il pungere con cosa aguzza.*

Pu'ndle, s. ex. [she is a very pundle, an ill-shap'd and ill-dress'd creature] *ella è una vera baldracca.*

Pu'ngar, s. *nome d' un pesce.*

Pu'ngency, s. [pricking, sharpness] *punta, s. f. qualità pungente, acutezza, s. f.*

Pu'ngent, adj. [pricking, sharp] *pugnente, e pungente, acuto.*

Pu'nger, s. [a sea crab-fish] *granciporro, s. m. spezie di granchio marino.*

Pu'nice, s. [bug] *cimice, cimicione; sorta d' insetto fetente.*

Pu'niness, s. [pettiness, smallness] *grettitudine, magrezza d' una persona malaticcia, sparutezza.*

To Pu'nish, [to inflict bodily pain upon one, to chastise] *punire, dar pena convenevole al peccato, gastigare,* pres. *punisco.*

Pu'nishable, adj. [fit to be punished] *da esser punito, o gastigato, degno di punizione.*

Pu'nished, adj. *punito, gastigato.*

Pu'nisher, s. *punitore, gastigatore.*

Pu'nishing, s. *punigione, punizione, gastigazione, s. f. punimento, gastigo, s. m.*

Pu'nishment, s. [chastisement] *punimento, gastigo, castigo, s. m. punizione, s. f.*

To bring one to an exemplary punishment, *punire alcuno esemplarmente.*

Puni'tion, s. [punishment] *punizione, s. f. gastigo, s. m.*

Punk, s. [an ugly strumpet] *una bagascia.*

Pu'nster, s. [a quibbler; a low wit who endeavours at reputation by double meaning] *un bisticciere, uno che vuol far il bell' ingegno con bisticci e giuochetti di parole.*

Puny, adj. [little, small] *piccolo, piccino, malsano, infermiccio, malaticcio, sparuto, sparutello; inferiore, spregevole,*

Pu'pil, s. [one under age, or ward] *pupillo, s. m. quegli che rimane, dopo la morte del padre minore di quattordici anni.*

A pupil [a disciple of a tutor] *allievo, discepolo, scolare.*

The pupil of the eye, *la pupilla dell' occhio.*

Pu'pilage, s. *minor età, minorità.*

Pu'ppet, s. [poppet] *burattino, s. m.*

Puppet-play, } *commedia di burat-*
Puppet-show, } *tini.*

To go to a puppet-show, *andar a vedere i burattini.*

Puppet [a word of contempt] *fantoccio di stracci, barattino; è vore di dispregio.*

A puppet-player, } *un ciarlatano.*
Puppet-man, }

Pu'ppy, s. [a bitch's whelp] *cagnolino, cagnuolo, s. m.*

Puppy [an abusive word] *minchione, balordo, sciocco.*

To Pu'ppy [to bring forth puppies, as a bitch] *figliare, parlando d' una cagna.*

To Pur, *v.* to purr.

Pu'rblind, adj. [short-sighted] *di corta vista, che ha la vista corta.*

Purbli'ndness, s. *corta vista.*

Pu'rchase, s. [bargain] *acquisto, s. m. compra, s. f.*

Purchase [booty] *bottino, s. m. preda, s. f.*

To Pu'rchase [to get] *comprare, acquistare, ottenere,* pres. *ottengo,* pret. *ottenni.*

To purchaſe lands or houſes, *comprar terre, o caſe.*

PU'RCHASED, adj. *comprato, acquiſtato, ottenuto.*

PU'RCHASER, s. *compratore, acquiſtatore,* s. m. *acquiſtatrice,* s. f.

PURE, adj. [ſimple, uncompounded] *puro, ſemplice, ſchietto, pretto.*

Pure wine, *vin puro, ſchietto, o pretto.*

Pure [unſpotted, chaſte] *puro, mondo, immaculato, netto.*

A pure virgin, *una vergine pura o caſta.*

Pure [clear, abſolute, without any condition] *puro, ſemplice, aſſoluto, non condizionato.*

A pure gift, *un dono puro o ſemplice.*

A pure air, *aria pura, o ſottile.*

Pure [mere, downright] *puro, mero, ſchietto.*

Pure malice, *pura, mera malizia.*

He is a pure knave, *egli è un pretto villano.*

Pure [very good, agreeable, or excellent] *molto buono, eccellente, ſquiſito, ammirabile.*

This is pure bread, *queſto pane è molto buono.*

You lead a pure [or happy] life, *voi menate una vita felice.*

You lead a pure life [ſpoken by way of irony] *voi menate una bella vita.*

He is a pure youth, *egli è un gran furfante.*

Pure, adv. [very] *molto,* ex. This is pure good, *queſto è molto buono.*

Pure clean *molto netto, o pulito.*

PU'RELY, adj. [exactly] *puramente, correttamente, ſchiettamente.*

Purely [very well] *beniſſimamente, molto bene.*

Purely [merely, only] *puramente, ſemplicemente, ſolamente.*

I did it purely out of love, *l'ho fatto per puro amore.*

To look purely, *avere buona ciera.*

PU'RENESS, s. *purità,* s. f.

PU'RFLE, s. [bodkin-work, made of tinſel or gold thread] *profilo,* s. m. *ornamento della parte eſtrema de' veſtimenti.*

To PU'RFLE, *profilare.*

PU'RFLED, adj. *profilato.*

PURGA'TION, s. [a cleanſing] *purgazione, purgagione,* s. f.

Purgation [in law, is the clearing one's ſelf of a crime] *purgazione d' un delitto.*

Canonical purgation [is when the party ſuſpected makes an oath in the ſpiritual court, that he is clear of the crime laid to his charge] *purgazione canonica, o per giuramento.*

Vulgar purgation [was either by combat, or trial by fire or water] *purgazione ſecolareſca, come quella del combattimento, del ferro rovente, e dell' acqua bollente.*

PU'RGATIVE, adj. [that is of a purging quality] *purgativo, che ha virtù di purgare.*

Purgative, s. [a purging medicine] *una purga, un medicamento purgativo.*

PU'RGATORY, s. [a place of purgation for the ſouls of the faithful, according to the Roman Catholicks] *purgatorio,* s. m. *luogo dove ſi ſuppone che l' anime patiſcan pena temporale per purgarſi de' lor peccati.*

PURGE, s. [a cleanſing medicine] *purga, medicina,* s. f. *rimedio, che purga.*

To PURGE [to cleanſe the body from ill humours] *purgare, dare una medicina.*

To purge one's ſelf, *purgarſi, pigliar medicina.*

To purge one's ſelf of a crime, *purgarſi, diſcolparſi, giuſtificarſi d' un delitto.*

PU'RGED, adj. *purgato.*

PU'RGING, s. *purgamento,* s. m. *il purgare.*

Purging, adj. *purgativo, che purga.*

PURIFICA'TION, s. [the act of purifying] *purificazione,* s. f. *il purificare.*

The feaſt of the purification of the bleſſed Virgin Mary, commonly called Candlemaſs-day, *il giorno feſtivo della Purificazione della Madonna, comunemente detto Candelaja.*

PU'RIFICATIVE, } PU'RIFICATORY, } s. [the little linen cloth with which the prieſt wipes the chalice and his fingers after the conſecration] *purificatorio,* s. m.

To PU'RIFY [to make pure and clean] *purificare, far puro, nettare, purgare da ogni macchia, e da ogni vizio.*

PU'RIFY'D, *purificato, nettato, purgato.*

PU'RIFYING, s. *purificazione,* s. f. *il purificare.*

PU'RIM, s. [a feaſt among the Jews, appointed by MORDECAI, in memory of their deliverance from HAMAN'S conſpiracy] *Purime, feſta fra gli Ebrei, inſtituita da Mordecai, in memoria dalla loro liberazione dalla congiura di Haman.*

PU'RIST, s. [one who affects to ſpeak neatly and properly] *uno che affetta di parlare pulitamente, e propriamente.*

PU'RITAN, s. [a nick name given to the diſſenters from the church of England] *un Puritano, ſoprannome dato dalla Chieſa Anglicana ai Calviniſti, e Preſbiteriani.*

Puritan [hypocrite] *ipocrita, ipocrito, picchiapetto, graffiaſanti.*

PU'RITY, s. [honeſty, innocence] *purità, mondizia, nettezza, ſincerità, ſchiettezza.*

PURL, s. [a kind of edging for bone lace] *dentello,* s. m. *merletto ſtretto.*

Purl [a ſort of drink] *cervogia con aſſenzio.*

To PURL, [to turn with a murmuring noiſe, as a ſtream does] *gorgogliare, lo ſtrepitare che fa l' acqua correndo, mormorare.*

To purl [to decorate with fringe or embroidery] *ornar di frange e ricami.*

PU'RLIEU, s. [the grounds on the borders of a foreſt] *terreni confinanti con una foreſta.*

PU'RLING, adj. *mormorante.*

The pleaſant noiſe of purling ſtreams, *il grato mormorio de' ruſcelli.*

To PU'RLOIN [to pilfer, to filch] *rubare, involare naſcoſtamente.*

PU'RLOINED, adj. *rubato, involato.*

PURLOINER, s. *rubatore, ladro, involatore di naſcoſo.*

PU'RPLE, } PURPLE-FISH, } s. [a kind of ſhell-fiſh] *polpo,* s. m. *ſpezie di peſce.*

PURPLE [the dye anciently taken out of the purple fiſh] *porpora,* s. f. *liquore, che ſi cava delle fauci del peſce polpo col quale ſi tingeva roſſo.*

Purple [a ſort of colour] *pavonazzo.*

Purple [cloth died in purple] *porpora, panno tinto di porpora.*

The purple [a dignity or dignitary in the church, as a cardinal, and of kings] *la porpora, la dignità cardinalizia o de' re.*

The purple-fever [the ſpotted-fever] *febbre maligna.*

Purple, adj. *pavonazzo, porporino.*

A purple ribbon, *un naſtro pavonazzo.*

To wax purple, *porporeggiare, tirare al colore della porpora.*

Of purple, *porporino, di color di porpora.*

PU'RPLISH, adj. *porporeggiante, che tira al color della porpora.*

PU'RPORT, s. [meaning] *ſenſo,* s. m. *ſignificazione,* s. f.

Purport [the tenor or ſubſtance of a writing] *il tenore, il contenuto d' una ſcrittura.*

PU'RPOSE, s. [deſign, reſolution] *propoſito, proponimento, penſiero, diſegno, conſiglio,* s. m. *intenzione, riſoluzione, deliberazione,* s. f.

To change one's purpoſe, *mutar propoſito, cangiar conſiglio.*

I come with a firm purpoſe not to drink, *vengo con fermo propoſito di non bere.*

For that purpoſe, *a queſto effetto.*

A thing done on purpoſe, *una coſa fatta a bella poſta, a bello ſtudio, penſatamente.*

This is for my purpoſe, *queſto fa per me.*

Purpoſe [ſubject, matter of diſcourſe] *propoſito, ſoggetto,* s. m. *propoſta,* s. f.

To ſpeak much to the purpoſe, *parlare molto a propoſito.*

To be all for croſs-purpoſes [or be of a contradicting humour] *eſſere d' un umore biſbetico.*

To no purpoſe [in vain] *inutilmente, in vano.*

It will be to no purpoſe for you to go, *non vi gioverà, non vi ſervirà a nulla.*

To no purpoſe [uſeleſs] *inutile, di neſſun giovamento.*

All thoſe remedies will be to no purpoſe, *tutti queſti rimedj ſaranno inutili, o di neſſun giovamento.*

For what purpoſe? *a che fine? a che ſerve?*

For what purpoſe to make ſo many words? *a che ſervono tante parole?*

What can be ſaid more to the purpoſe? *che ſi può dire di più?*

This is nothing to the purpoſe, *tutto ciò non fa al propoſito.*

To all intents and purpoſes, *intieramente, affatto.*

He is ruined to all intents and purposes] *egli ha dato l' ultimo tuffo, è andato affatto in rovina.*

That is nothing to my purpose, *questo non fa al mio proposito.*

It will be to as much purpose, *sarà tutt' uno, sarà la medesima cosa.*

He spoke much to the same purpose, *disse presso a poco la medesima cosa.*

To PU'RPOSE [to design, to intend, to resolve] *proporre, deliberare, statuire,* pres. *propongo, stabilisco,* pret. *proposi.*

He purposes to be gone very speedily, *egli si propone di partir ben presto.*

Man purposes and God disposes, *l' uomo propone, e Dio dispone.*

PU'RPOSED, adj. *proposto, deliberato, statuito, risoluto.*

PU'RPOSELY, adv. *a posta, a bella posta, a bello studio, deliberatamente, pensatamente, appostatamente.*

PURR, s. [a bird] *allodola di mare.*

To PURR [to murmur as a cat or leopard in pleasure] *far quel mormorio che fa il gatto quando gli si stroppiccia la schiena, o che fa il leopardo quando sente piacere.*

A PURSE, s. [a little bag to put money in] *borsa,* s. f. *sacchetto di varie fogge, grandezze, e materie, per uso di tener danari.*

Purse [a gratification of a thousand crowns given by the Grand Signior] *borsa, donativo di mille scudi fatto dal Gran Signore.*

PURSE-NET [a sort of net to take hares and rabbets in] *tagliuola,* s. f. *sorta di rete da prender lepri e conigli.*

A cut-purse, *un borsajuolo, un tagliaborse.*

To PURSE, *imborsare, metter nella borsa.*

PU'RSER, s. of a ship [an officer who has the charge of the victuals, and is to see that they be good, well laid up and stored] *provveditore d'un vascello.*

PU'RSLAIN, } s. [an herb] *porcellana,* s. f. *erba nota.*
PU'RSLANE,

PURSU'ANCE, s. [what follows, consequence] *conseguenza,* s. f.

In pursuance of what, *onde che, donde che, quindi, indi, dopo questo.*

In pursuance of the orders he received from court, *conforme, o secondo gli ordini ricevuti dalla corte.*

PU'RSUANT, prep. [according, or agreeable to] *conforme, secondo.*

To PURSU'E [to follow, to run after] *seguitare, seguire, andare o correr dietro, perseguitare, incalzare.*

To pursue the enemy, *incalzare il nemico.*

To pursue [to go on with, to carry on] *seguitare, continuare, seguire, proseguire, andare avanti.*

To pursue an enterprize, *seguitare, continuare un' intrapresa.*

To pursue one's point, *proseguire il suo intento.*

PURSU'ED, adj. *seguitato, seguito, incalzato, v.* To pursue.

PURSU'ER, s. *fugatore, seguitore, persecutore,* s. m.

PURSU'IT, s. [a running after] *caccia, fuga,* s. f. *incalzo,* s. m.

He was engaged in the pursuit of the enemy, *s' era occupato o intento ad incalzar il nemico.*

The enemy were always in the pursuit of us, *il nemico non lasciava d' incalzarci.*

Pursuit [sollicitation] *sollecitazione, instanza, richiesta,* s. f.

PURSUI'VANT, s. *messaggier di stato che accompagna l' araldo.*

PU'RSY, adj. [short or broken winded] *bolso, che con difficoltà respira.*

PU'RSINESS, s. [shortness of breath] *bolsuggine,* s. f.

To PU'RVEIGH, } [to provide] *provedere, procacciare,* pret. *proveddi.*
To PURVEY,

He purvey'd all necessaries, *egli si providde, o fece provisione di tutte le cose necessarie.*

PURVE'YANCE, s. [the providing of corn, fewel, victuals, &c. for the king's house] *provisione di grano, di legna, viveri,* &c. *per la famiglia del re.*

PURVE'YOR, s. [an officer to whom is committed the purveyance] *provveditore,* s. m. *officiale che ha l' incombenza della provisione.*

PU'RVIEW, s. [law term, the body of an act of parliament beginning with, Be it enacted] *il disponimento d'un atto di parlamento.*

PU'RULENCE, } s. [generation of pus or matter] *marcia, marcidume, il marcire d'una ferita o cosa simile.*
PU'RULENCY,

PU'RULENT, adj. [full of corrupted matter, mattery] *marcioso, pien di marcia, marcio, putrido.*

Purulent matter, *marcia, marciume.*

PUS, s. [the matter of a well digested sore] *marcia, materia,* s. f.

PUSH, s. [shove] *pinta, sospinta, spinta,* s. f. *urto,* s. m.

To give one a push, *dare una spinta ad uno, spignerlo, urtarlo.*

Push-pin, *giuoco di spilli fra i fanciulli.*

Push [effort to do a thing] *sforzo, potere,* s. m. *possibilità,* s. f.

We had best make a push at it, *sarebbe meglio che noi facessimo ogni sforzo.*

The business is come to the last push, *il negozio è giunto all' ultimo termine.*

To bring a thing to the last push, *condurre a fine un negozio.*

A push [blister] *pustula, enfiatura, bollicola, vescica,* s. f.

To PUSH [to thrust] *spignere, sospignere, urtare,* pret. *spinsi, sospinsi.*

To push back, *rispignere, spignere indietro.*

To push back the enemy, *rispigner l' inimico.*

They push'd him headlong from the rock, *lo precipitorno dalla cima d' un precipizio.*

To push on, *seguitare, continuare, portare avanti.*

To push on the war, *seguitare, o continuare la guerra.*

To push on a horse, *spronare o toccare un cavallo.*

PU'SHED, adj. *spinto, pinto, sospinto, urtato.*

PUSILLANI'MITY, s. [faint-heartedness] *pusillanimità, debolezza d' animo, timidità, codardia,* s. f.

PUSSILA'NIMOUS, adj. [faint-hearted, cowardly] *pusillanimo, di poco animo, timido, rimesso.*

PUSS, s. [a name given to a cat] *un gatto, una gatta.*

A dirty puss, *una sporca, una schifa.*

An ugly puss [an ugly woman] *una brutta.*

PU'STULE, s. [a little wheal or bladder in the skin] *pustula, vescichetta, bolla, bollicina,* s. f.

PUT, s. [a game at cards] *sorta di giuoco di carte usato in Inghilterra.*

Upon a forced put, *in raso di necessità.*

A put [a fool] *uno sciocco, un goffo, un minchione.*

Put off [delay] *indugio,* s. m. *dimora, tardanza,* s. f.

Put, adj. [from to put] *messo, v.* To put.

To PUT [to lay, to set, to place] *mettere, porre, collocare,* pret. *misi,* pres. *pongo,* pret. *posi.*

To put by or aside; to put apart, *metter da banda, metter da canto.*

To put up, down, under, in, out, before, after, between, *metter giù, sotto, dentro, fuori, avanti, dopo, fra.*

To put upon the table, *metter su, o sopra la tavola.*

To put one in a passion, *mettere alcuno in collera, farlo andare in collera, farlo adirare.*

To put one's self in a passion, *mettersi, o andare in collera, arrabbiarsi.*

To put one's arms about one's neck, *gettare le braccia al collo ad uno, abbracciarlo.*

To put cases, *supporre, fare supposizioni.*

Put the case it was so, *supposto, o data il caso che sia così.*

To put [to propose] *proporre,* pres. *propongo,* pret. *proposi.*

To put a question, *proporre un dubbio.*

He put the case to me, *egli m' ha proposto il punto, egli m' ha fatto questa dimanda.*

He put fair to be a great man, *egli è messo in istrada di far gran fortuna.*

To put again, *rimettere,* pret. *rimisi.*

To put away, *levare.*

Put that away, *levate questo.*

To put away cards [at play] *scartare.*

To put away a servant [to turn him out of service] *licenziare un domestico, mandarlo via.*

To put away one's wife, *ripudiare la moglie.*

To put about, *fare andare in giro.*

Put the glass about, *bevete.*

To put back, *rinculare, arretrare, tirare indietro.*

Put back your coach, *arrestate, tirate indietro la vostra carrozza.*

To put by, *parare, schivare, evitare.*

To

To put by a blow, *parare, o schivare un colpo.*

To put by a jest, *pigliare a giuoco.*

I put by his argument, *io ho confutato il suo argomento.*

He put me by [he refused to admit me] *egli m' ha negato l' entrata.*

To put down [to suppress] *sopprimere.*

To put forth [to produce] *produrre, mostrare,* pres. *produro,* pret. *produssi.*

To put forth [to propose] *proporre, porre avanti, mettere in campo il soggetto.*

To put forth one's hand, *stender la mano.*

To put forth a book, *pubblicare, o dare alla luce un libro.*

A tree that puts forth [that shoots] leaves, *un albero che spunta le foglie.*

To put forward, *avanzare, aggrandire, accrescere,* pres. *aggrandisco, accresco,* pret. *accrebbi.*

To put one's self forward, *avanzarsi, aggrandirsi.*

To put forward [to hasten] *sollecitare.*

To put in for a place, *brigare un impiego, studiarsi, ingegnarsi d'ottenerlo.*

To put in for one, *mettersi nel numero.*

To put in bail, *dar mallevadoria.*

To put in some hope, *dar qualche speranza.*

To put in an answer in writing, *dar la sua risposta in scritto.*

To put in a word for one, *dire una parola, o parlare in favore di qualcheduno.*

To put in for an harbour, *cercare d' entrare nel porto.*

To put in mind, *avvertire, mettere in pensiere, far ricordare,* pres. *avvertisco.*

To put in print, *stampare.*

To put in fear, *far paura, impaurire, intimidire,* pres. *impaurisco, intimidisco.*

To put into a fright, *far paura, atterrire,* pres. *atterisco.*

He put himself into the habit of a shepherd, *egli prese l' abito di pastore.*

To put into an harbour, *entrare in un porto.*

To put off, *spogliare, levare.*

To put off one's cloathes, *spogliarsi.*

To put off one's hat, *levarsi il cappello.*

To put off [to delay] *differire, prolongare, mandare in lungo, procrastinare.*

He puts me off from day to day, *egli mi manda da oggi in dimane.*

He did not long put off his punishment, *egli non tardò molto a punirlo.*

To put off a business, *differire, mandare in lungo un negozio.*

To put off a commodity, *vendere, o spacciare una mercanzia.*

To put off one's shoes or stockings, *scalzarsi.*

To put off one's boots, *cavarsi gli stivali.*

You must not think to put me off so, *non crediate ch' io voglia contentarmi di questo.*

To put on, *mettere.*

Put on your hat, *mettetevi il cappello, copritevi.*

To put on one's shoes and stockings, *calzarsi.*

To put on a smiling countenance, *far buona ciera.*

To put out, *scacciare, scavalcare, scavallare.*

To put one out of his place, *scavallare uno dal suo impiego.*

Put out that word, *cancellate quella parola.*

To put out the fire, the candle, *estinguere, smorzare, spegnere la candela, il fuoco.*

To put out one's eyes, *cavar gli occhi ad uno.*

You put me out, *voi mi fate sbagliare.*

To put out a proclamation, *fare un bando.*

To put out a book, *pubblicare, o mandare alla luce un libro.*

To put out money, *metter danari all' interesse.*

To put out to sea, *mettere in mare, far vela, partire.*

To put out the flag, *inalberare lo stendardo.*

To put out of one vessel into another, *travasare.*

To put one out of his biass, *disturbare alcuno, rompere la sue misure.*

To put out of order, *disordinare, metter in disordine.*

This meat has put my stomach out of order, *questa carne m' ha sconvolto lo stomaco.*

To put one out of doors, *metter uno fuor di casa.*

To put one out of heart, *sgomentare, sbigottire, disanimare alcuno, farlo perder d'animo.*

To put one out of conceit with a thing, *svogliare alcuno di che che sia, fargliene passar la voglia.*

He has put me out of all hope, *egli m' ha tolto ogni speranza.*

To put a thing out of one's head, *tor che che si sia di testa ad uno.*

To put out of joint, *slogare, dislogare.*

To put one's nose out of joint, *acchiappare uno, ingannarlo.*

To put one out to service, *allogare uno, metterlo al servizio di qualcheduno.*

To put out a thing to do, *dare a fare che che si sia.*

To put to, *aggiugnere, arrogere,* pres. *aggiungo,* pret. *aggiunsi.*

Since you put me to it, *piochè voi mi costrignete, o m' obbligate a ciò; poichè volete così.*

To put a question to one, *fare una questione, o una domanda ad uno.*

I won't put you to that expence, *non voglio che voi facciate questa spesa.*

I won't put you to that trouble, *non voglio incomodarvi tanto, non voglio darvi questo fastidio.*

To be put to one's last shifts, *non saper dove dar la testa, trovarsi in cattivo stato.*

To put all to the sword, *metter tutti a fil di spada.*

To put one to his oath, *dare il giuramento ad uno.*

To put all to him [I leave it all to his judgment] *lascio fare a lui.*

To put one to silence, *fare ammutolire uno, imporli silenzio, confonderlo.*

To put one to the blush, *fare arrossire uno, farli fare la faccia rossa.*

To put one to shame, *svergognare alcuno.*

To put a thing to the test, *esaminare una cosa.*

To put to venture, *arrischiare, cimentare, mettere in cimento.*

To put one to charges, *fare spender del danaro ad uno.*

To put a stop to a thing, *opporsi a che che si sia, impedire che non vada avanti.*

To put up, *tendere.*

To put up a suit of hangings, *tendere una tappezzeria.*

To put up a prayer to God, *porger preghiere a Dio.*

To put up a petition to the king, *presentare una supplica, o un memoriale al re.*

To put up a motion, *proporre una cosa; metterla in campo.*

To put up a thing [to lay it up] *guardare o conservare che che si sia.*

To put up an affront, *inghiottire un' ingiuria, sopportarla.*

To put up one's sword, *rimetter la spada nel fodero.*

To put up a claim to a thing, *formar pretensione sopra che che si sia, pretendervi.*

To put up a hare [to start it] *levare una lepre.*

To put a trick upon one, *fare una burla ad uno, acchiapparlo.*

To put a joke upon one, *burlarsi, o ridersi d' uno.*

To put a bad commodity upon one, *vender della cattiva roba ad uno.*

To put upon [to cheat, to impose upon] *tirarla giù, far un tiro, ingannare.*

To put one upon a thing, *impegnare uno in che che si sia.*

He put me to it, *me l' ha fatto fare, m' ha instigato a farlo.*

To put up a horse on a gallop, *mettere un cavallo al galoppo.*

To put to death, *mettere a morte, ammazzare.*

PU'TAGE, s. [a law term, for fornication on the woman's side] *fornicazione dalla parte della donna.*

PU'TATIVE, adj. [reputed, supposed] *putativo, tenuto e riputato.*

PU'TID, adj. [stinking] *puzzolente, che puzza, vile, abbietto, spregevole.*

PU'TLOG, s. [a short piece of timber to be put into a hole in building of scaffolds] *capra,* s. f. *dicono i muratori a que' legni confitti ne' buchi del muro su i quali fanno i ponti per fabbricare.*

PUTRE'DINOUS, adj. *putrefatto, pien di putredine.*

PUTREFA'CTION, s. [corruption, rottenness] *putrefazione, corruzione,* s. f.

To PU'TREFY [to corrupt, to rot] *putrefare, corrompere,* pret. *putrefeci, corruppi.*

To putrefy [to rot, to grow rotten] *putrefarsi, corrompersi.*

PU'TREFIED, adj. *putrefatto, corrotto.*

PU'TREFYING, s. *putrefazione,* s. f.

PU'TRID, adj. [corrupt, rotten] *putrido, corrotto.*

A putrid fever, *una febbre putrida.*

PU'TTER, s. [one who puts] *mettitore, un che mette.*

PUTTER on, s. [inciter, instigator] *incitatore, istigatore.*

PU'TTINGSTONE, s. *in alcune parti di scozia alcuni mettono de' gran pezzi di sasso onde far prova di forza sollevandoli o rimuovendoli, e questi chiamansi* puttingstones.

PU'TTOCK, s. [a kind of long winded kite] *abbuzzago,* s. m.

PU'TTY, s. [powder of calcined tin] *polvere di stagno calcinato.*

Putty, *sorta di cimento usato da' vetraj.*

PU'ZZLE, s. [difficulty] *garbuglio, ravviluppamento, imbarazzo, intrigo,* s. m. *difficoltà, confusione,* s. f.

To put to a puzzle, *confondere, mettere in confusione, garbugliare.*

A dirty puzzle [a dirty slut] *una sporcaccia.*

To PU'ZZLE [to confound] *confondere, imbarazzare, intrigare, imbrogliare,* pret. *confusi.*

PU'ZZLED, adj. *confuso, imbarazzato, intrigato, imbrogliato.*

PU'ZZLING, s. *imbarazzo, intrigo.*

PYE, *v.* Pie.

PY'EGARG, s. [a bird] *nome d' uccello.*

PIGME'AN, adj. *pimmeo, nano, piccolo, appartenente a pimmeo.*

PY'GMY, s. [dwarf] *pimmeo, pigmeo,* s m. *uomo piccolo, detto così da' pigmei, popoli supposti piccini piccini.*

A Pygmy, *un pimmeo, un nano.*

PYLO'RUS, s. [the lower orifice of the ventricle which lets the meat out of the stomach into the intestines] *piloro,* s. m. *il destro o inferiore orifizio dello stomaco dal quale la roba contenuta rala nelle budella.*

PY'RAMID, s. [an obelisk] *piramide,* s. f.

PYRAMIDAL, or PYRAMIDICAL, [in the form of a pyramid] *piramidale, piramidato, fatto a foggia di piramide.*

PYRAMI'DICALLY, adv. [in form of a pyramid] *in forma di piramide, piramidalmente.*

PY'RAMIS, s. [pyramid] *piramide.*

PYRE, s. [a pile to be burnt] *pira,* s. f. *rogo,* s. m.

PYROMANCY, s. [or divination by fire] *piromanzia,* s. f. *indovinamento per via di fuoco.*

PY'RRHONISM, s. *pironismo; il dubitar di tutto.*

PYTHON, s. [a familiar or prophesying spirit, or one possessed with it] *pitone.*

PYTHONESS, s. [a prophetess, a sorceress] *pitonessa maga.*

PYX, s. [a vessel in which the host is p by Roman Catholicks] *pisside,* s. f. e t

Q.

Q *Sedicesima lettera dell' alfabeto Inglese. Suona come in Italiano.*

QUACK, QUACKSALVER, s. [mountebank] *un medicastro, un ciarlatano, un cerretano, un cantambanco, un ciurmadore in medicina.*

To QUACK, *fare il mestiere di ciarlatano in medicina.*

To quack [to make a noise like a duck] *gracchiare, voce che manda fuora l'anitra.*

QUA'CKERY, s. *ciarlatanesimo medicinale; lo spacciarla da medico e non esser che ciarlatano.*

QUACKSALVER, s. *un medicastro, un ciarlatano.*

QUADRAGENA'RIOUS, adj. [of forty years] *quadragenario, che ha quarant' anni*

QUADRAGE'SIMA, s. ex. Quadragesima-sunday [the first Sunday in Lent] *la prima Domenica di Quaresima.*

QUADRAGE'SIMAL, adj. [belonging to Lent] *quaresimale, di quaresima, da quaresima.*

QUADRA'NGLE, s. [a figure of four angles] *quadrangolo,* s. m. *figura di quattro canti.*

QUADRA'NGULAR, adj. [belonging to, or in the form of a quadrangle] *quadrangolare, figura di quadrangolo.*

QUA'DRANT, s [a fourth part] *quadrante,* s. m. *la quarta parte.*

Quadrant [in mathematicks, is an arch containing the fourth part of a circle, or ninety degrees] *quadrante, una quarta parte d' un tondo piano, o novanta gradi.*

Quadrant, s. *quadrante; strumento matematico da pigliar l'altitudini.*

QUA'DRATE, s. [a four square figure] *quadrato,* s. m. *figura di quattro lati, che ha tutti quattro gli angoli e lati uguali.*

Quadrate [a piece of metal used by printers] *quadrato, termine di stampatore.*

Quadrate, adj. [four-square] *quadrato, quadro; ridotto in forma quadra*

To QUAD'RATE [to agree or suit] *quadrare, accomodarsi, piacere, soddisfare,* pret. *piacqui, soddisfeci.*

The answer does not quadrate with the question, *la risposta non quadra alla domanda.*

QUA'DRATURE, s. [the squaring of any thing] *quadratura,* s. f. *il ridurre in figura quadra.*

QUADRIE'NNIAL, adj. [belonging to the space of four years] *quadriennio, lo spazio di quattro anni.*

QUADRILA'TERAL, adj. [having four sides] *quadrilatero.*

A quadrilateral figure, *un quadrilatero, figura di quattro lati.*

QUA'DRILLE, s. *quadriglio; giuoco di carte derivante dal giuoco dell' ombre.*

QUA'RIPARTITE, adj. [divided into four parts] *quadripartito, diviſo in quattro parti.*

QUADRISY'LLABLE, s. [a word of four ſyllables] *una parola di quattro ſillabe.*

QUADRI'VIAL, adj. [conſiſting of four ways] *quadrivio.*

QUA'DRUPED, s. [a four-footed beaſt] *un quadrupede, animale a quattro piedi.*

QUADRU'PEDAL, adj. [having four feet] *quadrupede, e quadrupedo, che ha quattro piedi.*

QUA'DRUPLE, adj. [or four-fold] *quadruplo, quattre volte maggiore, o più.*

QUADRU'PLICATE, adj. [folded four times] *quadruplicato.*

To QUADRU'PLICATE [to encreaſe four times as much] *quadruplicare, augumentare o accreſcere quattro volte più.*

QUADRUPLICA'TION, s. *il quadruplicare.*

To QUAFF [to drink hard] *zizzolare, ſbevazzare, trincare, bere aſſai.*

QUA'FFER, s. *un beone, un gran bevitore.*

To QUA'FFER [to feel out] *toccare.*

QUA'FFING, s. *ubbriachezza, bere ſmoderato.*

To QUAG [to provoke to lechery] *provocare, eccitare, ſtimolare alla luſſuria.*

QUA'GGY, adj. [marſhy, boggy] *pantanoſo, paludoſo, melmoſo.*

QUA'GMIRE, s. [a marſhy or boggy place] *pantano,* s. m. *palude,* s. f.

QUAIL, s. [a bird] *quaglia,* s. f.

Quail-pipe, *richiamo.*

To QUAIL [to curdle] *quagliare, rapprendere.*

To quail [to cruſh] *acciaccare.*

To quail [to languiſh] *languire, ſvenire, mancar di forze, infiebolire, perdere il vigore.*

QUA'ILING, s. *languore, debilitamento,* s. m. *mancamento di forze.*

QUAINT, adj. [ſcrupulouſly, neat, fine, accompliſh'd] *eſtremamente pulito, bello, leggiadro, ſquiſito.*

A quaint diſcourſe, *un diſcorſo ricercatamente elegante, troppo ſtudiatamente fatto.*

A quaint fellow, *un zerbino attillatiſſimo.*

Quaint [odd, ſtrange] *ſtrano, ſtravagante, biſbetico.*

To make quaint, *abbellire, adornare quanto ſi può, ma ſtranamente e con eceſſo.*

QUA'INTLY, adv. *pulitamente, bellamente, leggiadramente, delicatamente, eſquiſitamente, attillatamente.*

QUA'INTNESS, s. *minuta e ſtudiata pulitezza, delicatezza, eleganza, leggiadria, grazia,* s. f.

To QUAKE [to tremble] *tremare.*

To quake for fear, *tremar di paura.*

QUA'KER, s. *che trema.*

Quakers [a modern ſect, who took their name firſt from their ſtrange geſtures and quaking fits] *ſetta di fanatici in Inghilterra, così detti per li ſtrani geſti che fanno tremando.*

QUA'KING, s. *tremore, tremito,* s. m. *il tremore.*

Quaking, adj. *tremante.*

QUALIFICATION, s. [a particular faculty or endowment] *qualità,* s. f. *talento, dono, vantaggio,* s. m.

To QUA'LIFY [to make fit] *qualificare, dar qualità.*

To qualify [to temper] *temperare, moderare, mitigare, raddolcire, quietare.*

To qualify anger, *placare, raddolcire la collera.*

To qualify one's ſelf, *capacitarſi, renderſi capace.*

QUA'LIFIED, adj. *qualificato, atto, idoneo, capace.*

A man well qualified, *un uomo qualificato, un uomo di merito.*

He is not qualified for ſuch an employment, *egli non è capace d' un tale impiego.*

QUA'LITY. s. [condition, nature] *qualità, natura, condizione,* s. f. *ſtato,* s. m.

The qualities of meats, *la qualità de' cibi.*

Quality [inclination, habit] *qualità, inclinazione.*

Good or ill qualities, *buone, o cattive qualità.*

Quality [noble birth] *qualità, la condizione d' una perſona nobile.*

A man of quality, *un nobiluomo.*

To take upon one the quality of an earl, *aſſumere il titolo di conte.*

QUALM, s. [fainting fit] *ſvenimento, languore,* s. m.

QUA'LMISH, adj. [troubled with, or ſubject to qualms] *che ſviene.*

QUA'NDARY, s. [a ſtudy or doubt what to do, ſuſpence of mind] *dubbio,* s. m. *irreſoluzione, ſoſpenſion d' animo.*

To be in a quandary, *ſtar ſoſpeſo, eſſer irreſoluto, non ſaper che fare.*

QUA'NTITY, s. [bigneſs, extent] *quantità, grandezza,* s. f.

Quantity [number, abundance] *quantità, abbondanza,* s. f *numero,* s. m.

In great quantity, *in gran quantità, in gran numero.*

The quantity of ſyllables, *la quantità o miſura delle ſillabe.*

QUA'RANTAIN } s [a denying of en-
QUA'RANTINE } trance into a healthful place for forty days, to thoſe perſons who are ſuppoſed to come from any infected place] *quarantena,* s. f.

To perform the quarantine, *far la quarantena.*

QUA'RREL, s. [ſtrife, diſpute, difference] *querela, lite, controverſia, diſcordia, diſſenſione, riſſa,* s. f.

To make a quarrel betwixt two perſons, *metter due perſone in diſcordia, metter l' inimicizia fra due perſone.*

To pick a quarrel with one, *appiccar lite con uno.*

To eſpouſe one's quarrel, *prender le parti d' alcuno, difenderlo, proteggerlo.*

To make up a quarrel between two perſons, *racconciare, rappacificare, rappattumare due perſone, metterle d' accordo.*

To breed a quarrel, *eccitare, o ſuſcitare lite, diſcordie, o diſſenſioni.*

A quarrel of glaſs, *quadro di vetro.*

A quarrel of a croſs-bow, *quadrello,* s. m. *freccia, ſaetta,* s. f. *detto così dalla punta quadrangolare.*

An unfeathered quarrel, *un quadrello diſarmato di vanni.*

To QUA'RREL [to fall out, to diſpute] *litigare, contraſtare, contendere, piatire,* preſ. *piatiſco,* pret. *conteſi.*

To quarrel with one, *litigare o contendere con uno, appiccar lite con lui.*

To quarrel with, *querelarſi, lamentarſi, trovar a ridire.*

QUA'RRELLED, adj. *litigato, contraſtato, conteſo, piatito.*

QUA'RRELLER, s. [he that picks quarrels] *litigatore,* s. m. *litigatrice,* s. f. *che litiga.*

QUA'RRELLING, s. *lite, il litigare.*

QUA'RRELSOME, adj. [apt to quarrel] *litigioſo, che volentieri litiga.*

QUA'RRELSOMENESS, s. *umore litigioſo.*

QUA'RRY, s. [a place where ſtones are digged out] *petraja,* s f. *miniera di pietre.*

A quarry man, *un uomo che lavora nelle petraje.*

A quarry [among falconers, any fowl flown and killed] *la preda degli uccelli di rapina.*

Quarry [among hunters, the reward given to hounds after they have taken the game] *la mancia.*

Quarry [fat man] *un uomo groſſo, e repleto.*

To QUA'RRY [a hunting term, to feed upon the quarry] *viver di rapina.*

QUART, s. [an Engliſh meaſure, the fourth part of a gallon] *miſura Ingleſe di liquidi, che contiene quaſi un boccale.*

A quart pot, or quart bottle, *un boccale, un fiaſco che contiene la miſura d' un boccale.*

A quart [a ſequence of four cards at picket] *quarta al giuoco di picchetto.*

QUA'RTAN, adj. ex. a quartan ague, *quartana,* s. f. *febbre che viene de' tre di l' uno.*

He or ſhe that has a quartan ague, *quartanario,* s. m. *quartanaria,* s. f. *colui o colei che ha la febbre quartana.*

QUA'RTER, s. [the fourth part] *quarto,* s. m. *la quarta parte.*

A quarter of an hour, *un quarto d' ora.*

A quarter of a pound, *un quarto di libbra.*

A quarter of mutton, or lamb, *un quarto di caſtrato o d' agnello.*

A quarter of a year, *un quarto d' anno, tre meſi, un trimeſtre.*

The quarters of the moon, *i quarti della luna.*

A quarter of corn, *un ſacco di grano, miſura d' Inghilterra.*

A quarter [a piece of timber] *travicello quadrato.*

Quarter [is the sparing of the lives and giving good treatment to a conquered enemy] *quartiere, la vita.*

To cry quarter, to call for quarter, *chieder quartiere, domandar la vita.*

To take quarter, *pigliar quartiere.*

To give quarter, *dar quartiere.*

The four quarters of the world, *le quattro parti del mondo.*

From all quarters, *da ogni parte.*

Quarters for soldiers, *quartieri, le stanze pe' soldati nelle guarnigioni e nell' accampare.*

Winter-quarters, *quartieri d' inverno*

To go to winter quarters, *svernare andare in quartieri d' inverno.*

The King's quarters, *i quartieri del Re.*

To beat up the enemies quarters, *assalire i quartieri del nemico.*

To have free quarters, *esser alloggiato a discrezione*

Quarter-day, *l' ultimo giorno del quartiere.*

A quarter-master, *quartiermastro, colui che fra i soldati soprintende alla distribuzione de' quartieri, e anche quello che ha l' incarico di fazarsi.*

Quarter-deck, *il cassero d' un vascello.*

Quarter-staff, *mezza picca, bastone a due punte.*

To QUA'RTER [to break or cut into quarters] *squartare, dividere in quarti.*

To quarter soldiers, *mettere i soldati ne' quartieri.*

To quarter soldiers for the winter, *svernare i soldati.*

To quarter, verb neut. [to be quartered, or to lodge] *essere in quartiere, esser alloggiato.*

QUA'RTERED, adj. *squartato, v.* To quarter.

QUA'RTERAGE, s. [money paid quarterly] *quartiere, il salario o danaro che si paga ogni quarto d' anno.*

QUA'RTERLY, adv. *per quartiere, ogni tre mesi.*

The quarterly seasons of devotion the Ember-weeks] *le quattro tempora.*

QUA'RTERN, s. [a gill, the fourth part of a pint] *una mezza foglietta.*

QUA'RTO, s. [a book whereof four leaves make a sheet] *un libro in quarto.*

To QUASH [to overthrow, to spoil, to bring to nothing] *guastare, dissipare, conquassare, mettere in rovina, fracassare, rovinare, opprimere.*

To quash [to annul, to nullify, to make void] *annullare, render nullo.*

To quash [to defeat] *disfare, rompere, sbaragliare, mettere in rotta, sconfiggere,* pret. *sconfissi.*

To quash, v. n. [to be shaken with a noise] *essere scosso da improvviso strepito scuotersi.*

QUA'SHED, adj. *guastato, dissipato, conquassato, fracassato, rovinato, disfatto, rotto, sconfitto.*

QUA'TER-COUSINS [good friends] *buoni amici.*

They are not quater-cousins, *non sono buoni amici.*

QUA'TERNARY, adj. [belonging to a quaternion] *quadernario, di quattro.*

QUA'TERNION, s. [the number four] *quattro, il numero di quattro.*

QUA'TRAIN, s. [a stanza of four verses] *quadernario,* s. m. *strofe di quattro versi.*

QUA'VER, s. [half a crotchet in musick] *semicroma.*

Quaver [a shake or trill in singing] *trillo,* s. m.

To QUA'VER [to tremble, to vibrate] *tremolare per effetto di vibrazione.*

To quaver [to run a division with the voice] *gorgheggiare, termine de' musici, quando cantando pare, per così dire, che increspino la voce.*

QUA'VERING, s. *il gorgheggiare, trillo,* s. m.

QUEAN, s. [whore, drab, jade] *una bagascia, una sgualdrina, una puttana vile.*

QUE'ASINESS of stomach [aptness to vomit] *nausea,* s. f. *turbamento di stomaco, e voglia di vomitare.*

QUE'ASY, adj. [sickish at the stomach, apt to vomit] *schifo, nauseoso.*

QUEEN, s. [the wife or consort of a King] *regina,* s. f.

The queen [at cards or chess] *la dama, al giuoco delle carte, e degli scacchi*

To QUEEN [to play the queen] *farla da regina, operar da regina.*

QUEEN-APPLE, s. *sorta di mela.*

QUEER, adj. [odd, fantastical] *strano, ridicolo, stravagante, bisbetico.*

A queer fellow, *un uomo strano, o bisbetico.*

QUE'ERNESS, s. *stranezza, fantastiraggine, bisbetichezza, stravaganza d' umore.*

QUEEST, s. [a ring dove] *colombaccio, colombo salvatico.*

To QUELL [to restrain or keep under, to depress] *reprimere, raffrenare, rintuzzare, domare.*

QUELL, s. [murder] *omicidio, ammazzamento. Non è usato più.*

QUE'LLED, adj. *raffrenato, rintuzzato, domato, represso.*

QUE'LLER, s. [one that crushes or subdues] *oppressore, soggiogatore.*

To QUENCH [to put out, to extinguish, *estinguere, smorzare, spegnere,* pret. *estinsi, spensi.*

To quench one's thirst, *estinguer la sete.*

To quench a sedition, *sedare una sedizione.*

QUE'NCHED, adj *estinto, smorzato, spento.*

QUE'NTIN, s. [a sort of linen cloth] *sorta di tela.*

QUERIMO'NIOUS, adj. [complaining] *dolente, mesto, querulo, lamentevole.*

QUE'RIST, s. *interrogatore.*

QUERK, s. [quirk, cavil, shift, fetch] *cavillo,* s. m. *cavillazione, sottigliezza* s. f. *puntiglio, giro,* s. m.

The quirks and cavils of the law, *i giri e rigiri della legge.*

QUERN, s. [a hand-mill] *un mulinello.*

QUERPO, s. *abito stretto alla vita.*

QUE'RRY, s. [a Prince's stables] *le stalle d' un Principe.*

Querry [or a gentleman of the querry to the Prince] *sotto scudiero d' un Principe.*

QUE'RRIES, s. [grooms of the King's stables] *mozzi di stalla del Re.*

QUE'RULOUS, adj. [moanful, doleful] *querulo, dolente, mesto, lamentevole.*

QUE'RY, s. [question] *quesito,* s. m. *domanda,* s. f.

QUEST, s. [inquest, inquiry] *inchiesta,* s. f. *ricercamento,* s. m.

Quest [search] *traccia,* s. f.

To go in quest of one, *andare in traccia d' uno.*

I was in quest of you, *vi cercavo.*

To QUEST [to seek out as a dog, to go in quest of] *tracciare, intracciare, seguitar la traccia, cercare.*

QUE'STION, s. [demand] *questione, domanda, interrogazione,* s. f.

To ask one a question, *fare una questione ad uno, proporli un dubbio, muoverli una questione.*

The question was put to me, *fui domandato.*

To beg the question, *supporre per vero quello di che si dubita.*

To give up the question, *concedere quel che si domanda.*

That is now the matter in question, *questa è la materia della quale si tratta.*

When was the question, *quando si venne al punto.*

QUE'STION [doubt] *questione, dubbio.*

To call into question, *dubitare, far dubbio.*

I make no question of it, *non ne dubito punto.*

There is no question to be made of it, *non bisogna dubitarne.*

Question [account] *conto, sindicato.*

To call one in, or into question, *chiamare a' conti, chiamare a sindicato.*

To question [to ask a question] *questionare e quistionare, interrogare, domandare.*

To question [to call into question] *chiamare a' conti o a sindicato, far render conto.*

To question [to doubt] *dubitare.*

I question his honesty, *dubito della sua fedeltà.*

QUE'STIONABLE, adj, [that may be called in question, doubtful] *questionabile, questionevole, dubbioso, incerto.*

QUE'STIONED, adj. *questionato, quistionato, v.* To question.

QUE'STIONER, *questionatore, e quistionatore,* s. m.

QUE'STIONLESS, adv. [doubtless] *indubitatamente, senza dubbio, certamente.*

QUIB,

QUIB, s. [a farcasm, a bitter taunt] *botta sul vivo* ; *sarcasmo*.

QUI'BBLE, s. [pun] *bisticcio*, s. m. *scherzo che risulta da vicinanza di parole, differenti di significato e simili di suono*.

To QUI'BBLE [to pun, or to play with words] *bisticciare, scherzare bisticciando*.

QUI'BBLER, s. [punster] *sciocco bisticciere*.

QUICK, adj. [alive] *vivo, che ha vita*.

To be quick, or to be quick with child, *esser gravida, ma propriamente esser avanzata nella gravidanza tanto che il bambino habbia preso vita*.

Quick [agile, nimble] *agile, lesto, snello, presto*.

Quick [sprightly, lively] *allegro; vivace, vivo*.

Quick [subtle] *astuto, fine, sottile, sagace, accorto*.

A quick wit, *perspicacità, ingegno svegliato, vivo, o acuto*.

A quick apprehension, *sagacità, vivezza d'ingegno*.

A quick ear, *orecchio fine*.

A quick fire, *fuoco vivo, o ardente*.

To make a quick return [to sell well, as a commodity] *esser di buono spaccio*.

A quick motion, *un moto presto, o veloce*.

A quick sand, *rena movente, che non è ferma*.

This wine has a fine quick taste, *questo vino ha un sapore piccante*.

Quick of scent, *che ha l'odorato fine*.

To have a quick eye, *aver la vista acuta*.

Quick, quick, *presto*.

Be quick [make haste] *fate presto, sbrigatevi*.

Quick, s. [live flesh] *vivo*, s. m. *la carne viva*.

To cut to the quick, *tagliare fin al vivo, fino alle carne viva*.

To cut or touch one to the quick, *toccare uno al vivo*.

Quick, adv. *presto, subito, tosto, subitamente, prestamente*.

Quick-beam, or quick-tree, *sorbo, albero noto*.

Quick-sand, *secca*, s. f. *luogo infra mare, che per la poca acqua è pericoloso a' naviganti*.

Quick-sighted, *di vista acuta*.

Quick-sighted, *perspicace, accorto, oculato, cauto, avvertito, scaltrito*.

Quick sightedness, s. *perspicacità, vista acuta, accortezza, oculatezza, sottigliezza, sagacità*.

Quick witted, *d'acuto ingegno*.

A quick-set hedge, *siepaglia*, s. f. *siepone*, s. m.

Quick-silver [mercury] *argento vivo*.

To QUI'CKEN [to vivify, to enliven] *animare, vivificare, dare vita*.

To quicken [to encourage, to excite] *animare, dare animo, eccitare, risvegliare, stimolare, istigare*.

To quicken [as a woman with child does] *esser gravida d'un bambino che già ha preso vita*.

She was very well before she came to quicken, *ella stava molto bene nei primi mesi della sua gravidanza, o prima che sentisse movere la creatura*.

QUI'CKENED, adj. *animato, eccitato, risvegliato, stimolato, istigato*.

QUI'CKENING, adj. *vivificante, che vivifica*.

Quickening grace, *grazia vivificante*.

QUICKLY, adv. [readily] *subitamente, prestamente*.

Quickly [soon] *presto, subito, tosto*.

I'll come quickly, *verrà ben presto, o subito*.

QUI'CKNESS, s. [swiftness] *agilità, prestezza, velocità*, s. f.

Quickness of wit, *sagacità, sottigliezza, sottilità, acutezza d'ingegno*.

Quickness of understanding, *perspicacità, vivacità, ingegno penetrativo*.

QUI'DDANY, } s. [a conserve of quin-
QUI'DDENY, } ces] *cotognato*, s. m. *conserva, e confettura di mele, o pere cotogne*.

QUI'DDITY, s. [the essence or being of a thing] *quiddità, o essenza d'una cosa*.

Quiddity [querk, subtle question] *fiuezza, sottiglieżza*, s. f. *giro, rigiro*, s. m.

QUIE'SCENCE, s. *quiete, riposo*.

QUIET, s. [rest, peace] *quiete, pace, tranquillità*, s. f. *riposo*, s. m.

Quiet, adj. [or peaceable] *quieto, pacifico, tranquillo, calmo, cheto*.

A quiet life, *una vita tranquilla*.

A quiet mind, *un animo calmo, o tranquillo*.

Let me be quiet [let me alone] *lasciatemi stare, lasciatemi in pace*.

To be quiet [to hold one's peace] *tacere*.

To QUIET [to make quiet, or to appease] *quetare, chiamare, placare, sedare, acchetare, acquetare*.

QUI'ETED, adj. *quetato, calmato, placato, acchetato, acquetato*.

QUI'ETING, adj. *che addormenta, che fa dormire, soporativo*.

A quieting bolus, *una pillula che addormenta*.

QUI'ETLY, adv. *chetamente, senza romore, pian piano, quietamente, pacificamente, tranquillamente*.

QUI'ETNESS, s. *quiete, tranquillità, pace*, s. f. *riposo*, s. m.

QUI'ETSOME, adj. *queto, tranquillo, senza disturbo, senza agitazione*.

QUI'ETUDE, s. [rest, repose] *quiete, riposo*.

QUI'ETUS EST [an expression used in the Exchequer for an acquittance given to an accomptant] *chetanza*, s. f.

He has his quietus est [he is put out of his place] *ha perduto il suo posto, gli è stato tolto l'ufficio*.

QUILL, s. [a stalk-feather pull'd from the wing of a fowl] *penna*, s. f.

A heroe of the quill, *un autore. è frase di dispregio*.

The quill of a barrel, *la cannella d'una botte*.

QUI'LLET, s. [subtilty, nicety] *sottigliezza, delicatezza*.

Quilt [to lie on] *materasso*, s. m. *materassa*, s. f. *arnese da letto, pieno per lo più di lana per dormirvi sopra*.

A quilt-maker, *materassajo*, s. m. *quegli che fa le materasse*.

A quilt [a covering for a bed] *coltre, sargia*, s. f. *coperta da letto imbottita*.

To QUILT, *trapuntare, imbottire*, pref. *imbottisco*.

QUI'LTED, adj. *trapuntato, imbottito*.

QUINCE, s. [a sort of fruit] *mela cotogna*.

A quince-tree, *cotogno*, s. m. *arbore noto che fa le mele cotogne*.

QUINQUAGE'SIMA-SUNDAY [Shrove Sunday] *la Domenica della Quinquagesima*.

QUINQUE'NNIAL, adj. [of five years continuance] *quinquennio, di cinque anni*.

QUI'NQUINA, s. [a drug called the Jesuit's bark] *la china*.

QUI'NSY, s. [a disease in the throat] *squinanzia*, s. f. *male, che riserra le fauci e soffoca*.

QUINT, s. [a set of five cards of the same colour, at the game called picket] *una quinta, al giuoco di picchetto*.

QUI'NTAIN, } s. [a sport, in which,
QUINTIN, } running a tilt on horseback with poles against a thick post fixt in the ground, he who breaks most poles has the prize] *il giuoco della quintana*.

To run at quintain, *correr la quintana*.

A QUI'NTAL, s. [a hundred pound weight] *cantaro*, s. m. *peso di cento libbre*.

QUINTE'SSENCE, s. [the purest substance extracted out of any thing] *quintessenza, o secondo 'l Boccaccio, essenzia quinta*, s. f. *l'estratto il più puro delle cose*.

QUINTESSE'NTIAL, adj. [belonging to quintessence] *che riguarda la quintessenza*.

QUI'NTIN, s. [a thick plank set fast in the highway] *quintana*, s. f. *il segno o uomo di legno ove vanno a ferire i giostratori*.

QUIP, s. [a jeer or flout] *burla, beffa*, s. f. *scherzo, motteggiamento, motto*, s. m.

He gave him a notable quip, *li diede una buona botta* ; *lo motteggiò molto argutamente*.

To QUIP [to rally with bitter sarcasm] *esser sarcastico* ; *motteggiar aspramente*.

QUIRE, s. [that part of the church where divine service is performed] *coro*, s. m. *quella parte dove stanno i preti a cantare il divino ufficio*.

A quire of paper [consisting of 24 or 25 sheets] *un quinterno di carta*.

A

A book in quires [a book unbound] *un libro ſcielto, non ancora legato.*

To QUI'RE, *cantar in coro; cantar molti inſieme.*

QUIRK, s. *cavillo, cavillazione.*

Quirk [looſe, light tune] *canzoncina o ſuonatina ſenza impiego.*

QUIT, adj. [ſafe, free from] *libero, liberato.*

I am not quit of my fever yet, *non ſono ancora libero della mia febbre, la mia febbre non mi ha ancora laſciato.*

You and I are quits, or we are quits, *noi ſiamo pare.*

I ſhall be quit, or quits with you, *ti renderò la pariglia, me la pagherai.*

To go quit [to come off ſcot-free] *eſſer fuor d'impaccio.*

Quit-rent, s. [a ſmall rent or acknowledgment, payable by the tenant of moſt manors] *cenſo*, s. m.

To QUIT [to leave or forſake] *laſciare, abbandonare.*

I quitted him juſt now, *l' ho laſciato appunto.*

To quit [to leave off] *tralaſciare, ceſſare, finire.*

To quit an employment, *metter giù, o rinunciare ad un impiego.*

To quit [to yield, to give up] *quitare, far quitanza, ceder le ragioni.*

I quit you from all the debt, *vi rilaſcio tutto 'l debito.*

I quit you for half the money, *vi aſſolvo per la metà del danaro, vi rendo la metà del danaro.*

To quit a deſign, *abbandonare un' impreſa, deſiſtere da un' impreſa.*

To quit the ſiege, *levar l'aſſedio.*

To quit [to free, to diſpenſe with] *ſcuſare, eſentare, diſpenſare.*

To quit one's ſelf like a man, *portarſi da galant' uomo, far le ſue parti come ſi deve.*

To quit one's ſelf of one, *liberarſi o ſbrigarſi d' uno, levarſelo d' attorno.*

To quit one's ground, *batterſela, andar via.*

It will never quit coſt, *non val la pena.*

To quit ſcores with one [to pay him what one owes him] *pareggiar le taglie con uno, pagargli quel che ſi li deve.*

A quit-claim [a law word, is the releaſing a man from any action one has or might have againſt him] *ceſſione, o rinuncia a qualche ragione che uno ha di muover lite ad un' altro.*

QUI'TCH-GRASS, s. [an herb] *gramigna*, s. f.

QUITE, adv. [wholly, entirely] *affatto, del tutto, intieramente.*

I have quite forgot it, *l'ho affatto dimenticato.*

It is quite another thing, *è tutto un' altra coſa, è affatto differente.*

The fire is quite out, *il fuoco è tutto ſpento.*

I am quite of another mind, *ſono di contrario parere.*

Quite and clean, *affatto, intieramente, del tutto.*

Quite contrary, *al contrario, tutto 'l contrario.*

You are quit out [or groſsly miſtaken] *voi v' ingannate a partito.*

Quits [even] *pace.*

We are quits, *ſiamo pace.*

QUI'TTANCE, s. *ricevuta in iſcritto di denari o roba avuta.*

Quittance, *premio, guiderdone, mercede, ricompenſa.*

To QUI'TTANCE [to repay, to recompence] *premiare, rimunerare, guiderdonare, rimunerare, ricompenſare.*

QUI'TTED, adj [from to quit] *laſciato, abbandonato*, v. To quit.

QUI'TTER, s. [the matter of a ſore or ulcer] *marcia*, s. f. *materia corrotta che eſce da una piaga.*

QUI'VER, s. [a caſe for arrows] *faretra*, s. f. *turcaſſo*, s. m. *guaina dove ſi portan le freccc.*

Wearing or bearing a quiver, *faretrato.*

Quiver, adj. [nimble] *ſnello, agile, leſto.*

To QUI'VER [to ſhiver, to ſhake] *tremare.*

To quiver with cold, *tremare di freddo.*

To quiver through fear, *raccapricciarſi.*

To QUOB [to move as the child in the belly] *muoverſi, parlando d'una creatura nell' utero della madre.*

To quob [to beat as the heart] *battere, palpitare.*

QUO'DLIBET, s. [quirk, quibble] *ſottigliezza, finezza*, s. f. *giro, rigiro*, s. m.

QUODLIBE'TICAL, adj. ex. a quodlibetical queſtion [a quodlibet] *una ſottigliezza, una queſtione ſottile.*

QUOIF, s. [coif] *cuffia; berretta.*

To QUOIF [to dreſs with a headdreſs] *acconciare il capo.*

QUOIFFURE, s. *acconciatura di capo.*

QUOIL, v. Coil.

QUOIT, s. *quel pezzo che ſi tira primo giuocando alle morelle.*

To QUOIT, *giuocare alle morelle.*

To quoit, *tirare, gittare.*

QUO'RUM, a word borrowed from the Latin, ſignifying OF WHICH, ex. a juſtice of the quorum [one of the judges] *uno de' giudici.*

In a company of twenty men, eleven make a quorum [that is, eleven of the twenty is enough to do buſineſs] *in una ſocietà di venti perſone, undici baſtano per terminare un affare.*

QUO'TA, s. [ſhate, contribution] *parte, porzione*, s. f.

QUOTA'TION, s. [quoting, citing] *allegazione, citazione*, s. f.

To QUOTE [to alledge, to bring in] *allegare, citare, addurre*, pref. *adduco*, pret. *addusſi.*

QUO'TED, adj. *allegato, citato, addotto.*

QUOTH-I [ſay I] *dico io, o diſſi io.*

QUOTH-HE, *dice egli, o diſſe egli.*

QUOTH-SHE, *dice ella, o diſſe ella.*

QUOTI'DIAN, adj. [daily] *quotidiano, cotidiano.*

Quotidian, s. *febbre quotidiana.*

QUO'TIENT, s [is that number that ſhews quoties, or how many times the diviſor is contained in the dividend] *quotiènte*, s. m. *termine d' aritmetica.*

QUO'TING, s. [from to quote] *citazione, il citare, l' allegare.*

R.

R, *diciasettesima* lettera *dell' alfabeto Inglese. Si pronuncia come in Italiano.*

To RA'BATE, in falconry [to recover a hawk on the fist] *ricovrare il falcone, farselo tornar sul pugno.*

RA'BBET, s. [a joint made by paring two pieces so that they may wrap over one another] *scanalatura fatta incavando in guisa due pezzi di legno o d'altra materia che si combacino bene insieme.*

To RA'BBET [to pare down pieces of wood so as to fit one another] *incavare e lisciare due o più legni in modo che si rombacino bene insieme.*

RA'BBI, } s. [a doctor or teacher of
RA'BBIN, } the Jewish law] *Rabbino,* s. m. *dottore nella legge Ebraira.*

RABBI'NICAL, adj. [belonging to the Rabbies] *attenente a Rabbino.*

RA'BBINIST, s. [one who follows the doctrines or opinions of the Rabbins] *colui chè siegue la dottrina e opinione de' Rabbini.*

RA'BBIT, s. *coniglio, animal noto.*

Welch-rabbit, *chiamano gl' Inglesi una fetta di pane con su del cacio, e poi abbrustolita e mangiata con un po' di senapa sparsavi sopra leggermente.*

RA'BBLE, s. [the dregs of the people] *la canaglia, il popolaccio, la plebe, la fercia del popolo che tumultua e fa fracasso.*

RA'BBLEMENT, s. *folla di popolaccio tumultuante.*

RA'BINET, s. [a kind of smaller ordnance] *pezzo d'artiglieria molto piccolo.*

RACE, s. [stock, family] *razza, stirpe, schiatta, generazione, progenie,* s. f.

The first of all human race, *il primo uomo.*

Race [the course or running of persons on foot or horseback] *rorsa,* s. f. *palio,* s. m.

A horse-race, *corsa di cavalli; palio.*

A foot race, *corsa di gente a piedi, palio.*

There is a race to be run to-morrow, *domani si deve fare una corsa, o un palio.*

A race-horse, *un corsiere, e corsiero, un corridore, un barbero.*

RA'CER, s. [one that contends in speed] *corridore.*

RACK, s. [wooden engine for several uses] *rastrello,* s. m.

Rack [manger] *mangiatoja,* s. f.

Kitchen rack, *rastrello di cucina.*

Rack [crib for beasts fodder] *rastrelliera,* s. f.

A rack to lay the spit on, *strumento di ferro sul quale si posa lo spiedo nell' arrostire che che si sia.*

Rack of mutton, *un collo di rastrato.*

Rack [torture] *tortura, corda, colla,* s. f. *tormento che si da a' pretesi rei.*

To put to rack, *dar la corda, collare.*

To put one's brains to the rack, *limarsi il cervello, becrarsi il cervello, fantasticare, ghiribizzare.*

The rack of a cart, *le stanghe d'un carro.*

Rack [to put bottles in] *rastrelliera.*

A rack [for a cross-bow] *lieva,* s. f. *martinetto,* s. m. *strumento con che si caricano le grandi balestre.*

To set up a cross-bow with a rack, *caricare una balestra col martinetto.*

To leave all at rack and manger, *lasciar tutto in abbandono.*

To RACK [to torture offenders upon a rack] *collare, tormentare con fune, colle braccia legate dietro sospendendo e dando de' tratti, dar la corda.*

To rack [to torment] *tormentare.*

To rack wine [to draw it off the lees] *tramutare del vino.*

RA'CKET, s. [an instrument to beat the ball with at tennis-play] *racchetta,* s. f.

Racket [a stir, a hurly-burly, a noise] *strepito, fracasso, romore, schiamazzo,* s. m.

RA'CKING, s. [from to rack] *tortura.*

RA'CK-RENT, s. [rent raised to the uttermost] *affitto di rasa o beni alzato quanto si può alzare.*

RACKO'ON, s. *quadrupede molto peloso che abita nella Nuova Inghilterra.*

RAD, *antico preterito del verbo* To read.

RA'DDOCK, s. *nome d'uccello.*

RA'DIANCE, } s. [brightness] *splen-*
RA'DIANCY, } *dore, splendimento,* s. m.

RA'DIANT, adj. [casting forth rays, shining, sparkling] *scintillante, risplendente, lurido, splendente, splendido, rilucente.*

RADIA'TION, s. [a casting forth beams] *splendore,* s. m.

RA'DICAL, adj. [belonging to the root, inbred] *radicale, che deriva della radice.*

Radical moisture [the fundamental juice of the body, said to nourish and preserve the natural heat, as oil does a lamp] *umido radicale.*

A radical word, *parola radicale, una parola primitiva.*

RADICA'LITY, s. [a being radical] *stato di quel ch' è radicale, sorgente, principio.*

RA'DICALLY, adv. *radicalmente, colla radice.*

Love radically is in the heart, *l'amore radicalmente sta nel cuore.*

RADICATE, } adj. *radicato.*
RA'DICATED, }

To RA'DICATE [to take root, in a proper and figurative sense] *radicare, appigliarsi, alla terra colle radici, abbarbicare, appiccarsi.*

RA'DICATED, adj. *radicato, abbarbicato, appiccato.*

Radicated [old, inveterate] *radicato, invecchiato, inveterato.*

RA'DICLE, s. [a term among botanists, that part of the seed of a plant which upon its vegetation becomes its root] *radice, quella parte della semenza, che essendo seminata, getta le prime radici.*

RA'DISH, s. [a well-known root] *ravanello.*

Horse-radish, *rafano, ramolaccio,* s. m.

RA'FFLE, s. [a game with three dice] *zara,* s. f. *giuoco che si fa con tre dadi.*

To RA'FFLE [to play at raffle] *giuocare a zara.*

RA'FFLE-NET [a fort of fishing-net] *forta di rete da pefcare.*

RAFT, s. [a frame or float made by laying pieces of timber crofs each other] *zatta, zattera,* s. f.

RA'FTER, s. [a piece of timber for building] *corrente,* s. m. *travicello fottile che fi mette ne' palchi o ne'* tetti.

To RA'FTER, verb act. *impalcare, mettere il palco.*

RA'FTERING, s. *l'impalcare.*

RAG, s. [a tatter, an old piece of cloth] *cencio, ftraccio.*

His cloths are worn out to rags, *il fuo veftito è tutto ftracciato.*

Meat boiled to rags, *carne troppo bollita.*

RAGAMU'FFIN, s. [a paltry mean fellow] *un birbone, un cenciofo, un guidone, un furfante.*

RAG-BOLT, *cavicchia di ferro, che ferve per la coftruzione d'un vafcello.*

RAGE, s. [fury, madnefs] *rabbia, ira,* s. f. *furore,* s. m.

Rage [cruelty] *rabbia, gran crudeltà.*

To RAGE [to be in a rage] *arrabbiare, ftizzirfi, incollorirfi, fmaniare, dar nelle fmanie, furiare.*

To rage [as the fea does] *tempeftare.*

RA'GGED, adj. [torn to pieces] *ftracciato, lacero, tutto ftrarci.*

A ragged fellow, *uno ftracciato.*

RA'GGEDNESS, s. *ftracci, cenci.*

RA'GING, adj. *furibondo, adirato, furiofo, violento, corrucciato, corrucciofo, iracondo, fdegnofo.*

A raging fea, *mar tempeftofo.*

Raging, s. *rabbia, furia, ira, ftizza,* s. f. *furore, corruccio, cruccio,* s. m.

RA'GINGLY, adv. *furiofamente, con furia, fdegnofamente, rabbiofamente, con furore, con ifdegno.*

RAGO'O, } s. [a high feafoned difh
RAGO'UT, } of meat] *guazzetto, intingolo alla Francefa,* s. m.

RA'GWORT, s. [a plant] *nome di pianta.*

RA'GSTONE, s. [a ftone fo named from its breaking in a ragged manner] *nome di pietra.*

Ragftone, *quel faffo con cui fi pulifce un arme da taglio dopo che è ftata arrotata.*

RAILS, s. [a wooden fence to enclofe a place] *cancello, fteccato,* s. m.

Rails on the fide of a gallery, *balauftri.*

Iron rails before a houfe, *ferrata,* s. f.

The rails of a bridge, *le fponde d'un ponte.*

The rails of a cart, *fteconi di carro.*

NIGHT-RAIL, *mantellina,* s. f.

To RAIL, *difporre in fila, in ordinanza.*

To rail [to enclofe with rails] *circondare o chiudere con cancelli, o balauftri.*

To rail [to banter, to mock] *beffare, corbellare, dar la feja.*

RA'ILED-IN, adj. *circondato, o chiufo con cancelli, o balauftri.*

Railed at, adj. *corbellato, fojato.*

Railed, adj. *meffo in fila, in ordinanza.*

RA'ILER, s. *corbellatore, colui che minchiona, che beffa, che da la foja.*

RA'ILINGLY, adv. [in a railing manner] *corbellevolmente, con modo ironico.*

RA'ILLERY, *fatira leggiera, fcherzo pungente, corbellatura, foja.*

RA'IMENT, s. [attire, garment] *veftimento, addobbo, abbigliamento, veftito, abito,* s. m.

RAIN, s. *pioggia,* s. f.

Small rain, *fpruzzaglia, acquicella,* s. f.

Rain water, *acqua piovana.*

A fudden fhower of rain, *un acquazzone.*

The rain bow, *l'arcobaleno, l'arco celefte, l'iri, l'iride.*

Rain-deer [a fort of ftag] *animale fimile al cervo, ma alquanto minore.*

To rain, *piovere.*

It rains, *piove.*

It is going to rain, *pioverà adeffo adeffo.*

To rain very fmall, *piovigginare.*

To rain ftones, blood, &c. *piover pietre, fangue, &c.*

To rain down a fhower of arrows upon the enemy, *far piovere, o fragliare una grandine di frecce fopra 'l nemico.*

RA'INY, adj. *piovofo.*

RAIP, s. [a rod to meafure ground] *pertica da mifurar il terreno.*

To RAISE [to lift, to lift up, to fet higher] *levare, alzare, mandare in fù, follevare, innalzare.*

To raife fomething from the ground, *levare, o tor fu che che fi fia di terra.*

To raife a wall [to make it higher] *alzare un muro, farlo più alto.*

To raife a monument, *ergere un monumento.*

To raife from the dead, *rifufcitare da morte.*

He will raife us out of our graves, *ci farà ufcire dalle noftre fepolture.*

To raife men, or an army, *levar genti, levar milizie, far foldati.*

To raife taxes, *efigere, o rifcuotere le gabelle.*

To raife the fiege, *levar l'affedio.*

To raife money, *trovar danari.*

The fun raifes the vapours, *il fole attrae i vapori.*

To raife one's voice [to fpeak louder] *alzar la voce, parlar più forte.*

To raife the price, *alzare, o augumentare, crefcer di prezzo.*

To raife [to prefer, to advance] *innalzare, fublimare, aggrandire, elevare, efaltare.*

To raife one's felf, *innalzarfi, fublimarfi, aggrandirfi, elevarfi, efaltarfi.*

To raife [to excite, to caufe] *eccitare, rifvegliare, ftimolare, iftigare, fufcitare, caufare.*

To raife a ftorm, *fufcitare una tempefta.*

To raife a fedition, *eccitare, o caufare una fedizione.*

To raife quarrels, *caufare, o far nafcer querele, o diffenfioni.*

To raife pride in one, *levare in fuperbia altrui, dargli occafione d'infuperbirfi.*

To raife the devil, *fcongiurare il diavolo.*

To raife plants [to make them grow] *coltiva piante.*

To raife the duft, *far della polvere, far volare la polvere.*

To raife a man's paffion, *mettere alcuno in collera, farlo andare in collera, farlo adirare, infiammar la fua collera.*

Don't raife my paffion, *non mi fate venir la bile.*

To raife the country, *far pigliar l'armi ad una provincia.*

To raife a report, *fparger voce, divulgare, dar fuora.*

To raife up, *levare, alzare, rilevare, fcufcitare.*

To raife up [to prefer] *avanzare, aggrandire,* pref. *aggrandifco.*

To raife a family, *aggrandire una famiglia.*

To raife war, *muover guerra.*

To raife a doubt where there is none, *cercare il pelo nell' uovo.*

To raife a doubt, *muovere un dubbio.*

To raife a bank, *fare o alzare un argine.*

RA'ISED, adj. *levato, alzato,* v. To raife.

RA'ISEDLY, adv. *pateticamente, d'una maniera compaffionevole.*

RA'ISIN, s. [dry grapes] *uva paffa.*

RAKE, s. [a tool for hufbandry] *raftrello, raftro,* s. m.

As lean as a rake, *magro come uno fcheletro.*

A little rake, *raftrellino,* s. m.

A rake to pull up weeds by the root, *farchio,* s. m.

An oven-rake or coal rake, *fpazzaforno, fpazzatojo,* s. m.

Rake [a profligate man] *uno fcapeftrato, uno fviato, un diffoluto, un viziofo.*

RAKE-SHAME [a bafe rafcally fellow] *un uomo indegno, un uomo di cattiva vita, un furfante.*

The rake of a fhip, *becco di naviglio.*

To RAKE [to gather with a rake] *raftrellare.*

To rake weeds by the root, *farchiare, farchiellare.*

To rake the fire, *attizzare il fuoco.*

To rake and fcrape for an eftate, *fudar fangue per accumulare o aquiftare ricchezze; cercare di diventar ricco a qualunque prezzo.*

Rake hell and fkin the devil, you cannot find fuch another man, *cercate pure per mare e per terra, non troverete un simil furfante.*

To rake into, *frugare, frugolare, cercar accuratamente, esaminare, andar tentando.*

To rake [to play the rake] *menare una vita sregolata, viziosa, sviata*

RA'KED, adj. *rastrellato, sarchiato.*

RA'KER, s. [a man employed for cleansing the streets] *colui che netta le strade.*

RA'KING, adj. *avaro, meschino.*

A raking fellow, *un avaro, un uomo stretto, un che cerca sempre d' accumulare e teme di spendere.*

RA'KEHELL, s. *un furfantaccio, uno scellerato, un briccone infame.*

RAKEHELL, adj. [wild, dissolute] *scapestrato, sviato, scostumato.*

RA'KISH, adj. [loose, lewd, dissolute] *lascivo, scostumato, dissoluto.*

RA'LLERY, s. [jest] *burla, beffa, baja,* s. f. *scherzo,* s. m.

In rallery, *in burla, da giuoco.*

To RA'LLY [to re-unite, to gather together dispersed troops] *riunire, raccogliere, mettere insieme,* pres. *riunisco.*

To rally, *unirsi, riunirsi, raccoglierſi, mettersi insieme.*

To rally [to jeer, to banter] *burlare, beffare, dar la baja, scherzare.*

RA'LLYED, adj. *riunito, raccolto, messo insieme; burlato, beffato.*

RAM, s. [a male sheep] *montone,* s. m. *il maschio della pecora.*

Ram [a warlike engine made use of anciently to batter walls] *ariete, montone, strumento militare antico da batter muraglie.*

RAM'S-HEAD [an iron leaver to heave up great stones with] *lieva di ferro da levar pietre.*

To RAM [to beat or drive in] *arietare, ficcare, mettere, e cacciar dentro per forza.*

To ram in stones or piles, *ficcare pietre, e pali.*

To ram down a paving, *mazzerangare un pavimento.*

To ram down the powder in a gun, *batter la polvere nel cannone, nello schioppo, e simili.*

RA'MAGE, s. [boughs or branches of trees] *rami d'albero.*

A ramage hawk [one that is wild and coy] *falcone ramingo.*

To have a ramage taste, *puzzar di salvaggiume.*

To RA'MAGE [to ramble] *scorrere, andar qua e la, andare attorno.*

RA'MBLE, s. *scorsa,* s. f. *l'andar qua e la, l'andare attorno.*

To be all upon the ramble, *andar sempre attorno, andar battendo le strade.*

To RA'MBLE [to go up and down] *scorrer la cavallina, andar qua e la, andar attorno, andar ramingo, vagare, andare errando, trascorrere, vagabondare.*

To ramble in one's discourse, *trapassare da un discorso in un altro, cambiar di soggetto all' impazzata.*

RA'MBLED, adj. *trascorso, scorso, vagato, vagabondato, ramingo.*

RAMBLER, s. [rover, wanderer] *un vagabondo, un perdigiornate.*

RA'MBLING, s. *scorsa, il trascorrere, l'andar vagabondo.*

Rambling, adj. *vagando.*

To go a rambling, *andar vagando, scorrer la cavallina, vagabondare.*

A rambling man or woman, *un vagabondo, una vagabonda.*

A rambling head, *un cervello fatto a oriuoli, un cervel balzano.*

Rammed in, adj. [from to ram] *ficcato,* v. To ram.

RA'MMER, s. [an instrument for driving stones or piles into the ground] *mazzeranga,* s. m.

Rammer [or gun-stick] *una bacchetta da schioppo.*

RA'MMISH, adj. [that smells rank like a ram or goat] *che sa del becco.*

To smell rammish, *sentir del becco.*

RA'MMISHNESS, s. *odore che sente del becco.*

RA'MOUS, adj. [branchy] *ramoso, pien di rami.*

RAMP, s. [a great ramp, or ramping girl] *una ragazza che va volentieri vagando e correndo qua e la.*

Ramp, s. [leap, spring] *salto, srocco.*

To ramp [to get up] *rampicare.*

To ramp [to rove, to frisk, to jump about] *girare, andare attorno, saltellare, andar intorno saltellando.*

To ramp, *scoccare con violenza.*

RAMPA'LLIAN, s. [a mean wretch] *un abbietto furfante, un birbo, un briccomacrio.*

RA'MPANT, adj. [in heraldry, is when a beast of prey is reared on his hinder legs in a fighting posture] *rampante.*

A lion rampant, *un lione rampante.*

To RA'MPART, } [to fortify with
To RA'MPIRE, } ramparts] *fortificar con ripari o con bastioni.*

RA'MPART, } s. [a great massy bank
RA'MPIRE, } of earth raised about the body of a place] *riparo, terrapieno,* s. m.

To fence with ramparts, *terrapienare, circondar di terrapieni.*

RA'MPION, s. [a sallad root] *raperonzo, e raperonzolo,* s. m.

RA'MPIRE, *riparo, terrapieno.*

RA'MPIRED, adj. [fenced with ramparts] *terrapienato.*

RAN, *è un preterito del verbo* To run.

To RANCH [to sprain; to injure with violent contorsion] *storcere; slogare storcendo fortemente.*

RA'NCID, adj. [mouldy, musty] *rancido, stantio, mucido.*

RANCI'DITY, } s. [mouldiness, mus-
RA'NCIDNESS, } tiness] *rancidezza,* s. f.

RA'NCOUR, s. [a concealed or secret grudge, spite, or spleen] *rancore, sdegno, odio coperto,* s. m. *malignità,* s. f.

RAND, s. [the seam of a shoe] *la cucitura delle scarpe.*

Rand of beef [a long fleshy piece cut out between the flank and buttock] *pezzo di carne di bue tagliata tra 'l fianco e la coscia; la sfasciatura.*

RA'NDOM, s. [chance] *caso, accidente,* s. m.

To run at random, *vagare, andare senza saper dove.*

To leave all at random, *lasciar tutto in abbandono.*

A random-shot, *un colpo a caso.*

At random, adv. [without aim, rashly, inconsiderately] *a caso, a tastone, inconsideratamente, alla cieca, senza pensare.*

To speak at random, *tirare in arcata, parlar alla cieca, e senza fondamento, parlare al barchio*

Rang, *è un preterito del verbo* To ring, *sonare.*

RANGE, s. [row, rank] *graticola per la cucina.*

Range [coach beam] *timone di carrozza.*

Range [ramble, jaunt] *giro,* s. m. *girata, corsa,* s. f.

They took a great range, *fecero un gran giro.*

Women that love to take their free range abroad, *donne che amano scorrer la cavallina.*

To give one's fancy its free range, *dar campo alla sua fantasia.*

Range [sieve] *burattello,* s. m. *sacchetto da abburattar la farina.*

To RANGE [to ramble] *andare attorno, andar ramingo, vagare, vagabondare, scorrer la cavallina.*

To range up and down, *andare attorno, andar qua e la.*

To range [to sift through a sieve] *abburattare.*

To range [to set in order] *ordinare, schierare.*

To range an army, *schierare un esercito.*

RA'NGED, adj. *vagato, vagabondato, ordinato, schierato, abburattato.*

RA'NGER, s. [an officer of a park or forest] *maestro di caccia.*

RANK, s. [order, disposition of several persons or things] *ordine, grado,* s. m. *sfera, fila,* s. f.

A rank of soldiers, *una fila di soldati.*

A lord of the first rank, *un signore della prima sfera.*

To keep his rank, *mantenere la sua dignità.*

Rank, adj. [that shoots forth too many branches or leaves, over fruitful] *che produre troppi rami e foglie.*

To grow rank [as plants do] *pullulare in troppa abbondanza.*

Rank, adj. [stinking, smelling strong] *rancido, vieto, puzzolente, stantio, lezzoso, nauseoso.*

A rank smell, *cattivo odore, puzzura, lezzo, fetore.*

To smell rank, *sentire del rancido, aver cattivo odore, lezzare, saper del lezzo.*

'Tis rank poison, *questo è veleno del più perfetto.*

To RANK [to put in the rank] *mettere nel numero, annoverare; metter in ordinanza.*

To RA'NKLE [to fester] *putrefarsi, corrompersi, infistolirsi.*

To

To rankle [to putrefy] *putrefare, corrompere, guastare, infracidare, e infradiciare.*

Ra'nkness, s. [superfluity of leaves and branches] *troppo abbondanza di foglie e di rami.*

Rankness [strong smell] *puzza, rancidezza,* s. f. *puzzo,* s. m.

Rankly, adv. [coarsely, grossly] *grossolanamente, rozzamente.*

To Ra'nsack [to plunder, to rifle] *saccheggiare, predare, mettere a guasto, o a sacco, rovinare.*

To ransack [to search narrowly] *cercare accuratamente, esaminare minutamente.*

To ransack [to violate, to deflower] *violare, sfiorare, sverginare.*

Ra'nsacked, adj. *saccheggiato, predato, messo a guasto, rovinato, v.* To ransack.

Ra'nsacker, s. *predatore, guastatore, dissipatore,* s. m. *guastatrice,* s. f. *v.* To ransack.

Ra'nsacking, s. *saccheggiamento, guasto, sacco,* s. m. *preda, rovina,* s. f. *v.* To ransack.

Ra'nsom, s. [money paid for redeeming a captive] *riscatto,* s. m. *taglia,* s. f. *prezzo, che s'impone agli schiavi per riscattarsi*

Ransom [money paid for the pardoning some notorious offenders] *taglia, quel prezzo che si paga per il perdonare un criminale.*

To Ra'nsom [to pay ransom for, to redeem] *riscattare.*

Rant, s. [high-sounding language] *il parlare troppo gonfio, troppo ampolloso, troppo romoroso che alcuni poeti usano in tragedia, e il far dare nelle smanie un personaggio più del bisogno.*

To Rant, *smaniare parlando in tragedia, o sonoramente e ampollosamente parlare.*

Ra'ntipole, adj. [wild, roving, rakish] *sviato, scapestrato.*

To Ra'ntipole [to run about wildly] *andar intorno vagabondando, e dicesi delle femmine rivettine.*

Rap, s. [a quick smart blow] *picchio; colpo forte e presto.*

To Rap [or knock] *bussare, battere, picchiare,*

To rap at the door, *bussare, o picchiare alla porta*

To rap, *rapire con violenza, strappar per forza.*

To rap, *rapire in estasi, far andar in estasi.*

To rap out a great oath. *fare un gran giuramento.*

To rap and rend, *acchiappare tutto quel che si può.*

Rapa'cious, adj. [ravenous, greedy] *rapace, ingordo, avido, ardente di preda.*

Rapa'city, } s. [ravenousness] *rapacità, ingordigia,* s. f.
Rapa'ciousness, }

Rape, s. [the act of violence committed on the body of a woman] *stupro, ratto,* s. m.

To commit a rape, *commettere uno stupro, stuprare.*

One that has committed a rape, *stupratore,* s. m. *colui che commette ratto, o stupro.*

Rape of the forest [a trespass committed in the forest] *delitto commesso in una foresta appartenente al Rè.*

Rape [a farrier's tool] *raspa,* s. f.

Rape [a wild radish] *rapa salvatira.*

Rape [the stalks of grapes dry'd] *raspi d'uva secchi.*

Rapes [in Suffex, certain divisions of the county] *certe divisioni della provincia di Suffex.*

Rape-wine, *acquerello, vinello,* s. m. *bevanda fatta d' acqua messa in sulle vinacce, cavatone prima il vino.*

Ra'peries, s. [Irish robbers] *ladri Irlandesi.*

Ra'pid, adj. [swift] *rapido, velocissimo, prestissimo.*

Rapi'dity, s. [swiftness] *rapidità, velocità,* s. f.

Ra'pidly, adv. *rapidamente, velocemente.*

Ra'pier, s. [a small sword made only for thrusting] *stocco,* s. m. *arme simile alla spada, ma più acuta.*

Ra'pine, s. [robbery, pillage] *rapina, forza, violenza,* s. f.

Ra'per, s. [great oath] *un gran giuramento.*

Ra'psody, s. [a tedious and impertinent spinning out of a discourse to no purpose or benefit to the reader] *congerie lunga e tediosa di parole.*

To Rapt, *mandare o rapire in estasi.*

Ra'pture, s. [a taking away] *rapimento, ratto,* s. m.

Rapture [extasy, transport] *estasi, eccesso di gioja o d'allegrezza, ratto.*

A poetical rapture [the heat of a poet's fancy] *furia poetica, furor poetico.*

Ra'ptured, adj. [transported, ravished] *rapito, trasportato, estatico.*

To be raptured in bliss, *esser tutto giojoso, tutto giocondo, esser pieno di gioja.*

Ra'pturous, adj. *che rapisce, estatico.*

Rare, adj. [that happens but seldom, uncommon] *raro, non comune.*

Rare [scarce] *raro, scarso, difficile a trovare.*

Rare [excellent] *raro, singolare, eccellente.*

A rare man in his profession, *un uomo raro, o eccellente nel suo mestiere.*

Rare [in the physical sense, thin, not compact] *raro, rado, non denso.*

Rare, adv. [or very] *molto.*

This is rare good, *questo è molto buono.*

Rarefa'ction, s. *rarefazione,* s. f. *il rarefare.*

To Ra'refy, *v. a.* [to make thin] *rarefare, far divenir raro, indur rarefazione, rarificare,* pret. *rarefeci.*

To rarity, *v.* n. [to grow thin] *rarefarsi divenir raro, rarificarsi.*

Ra'rified, adj. *rarefatto; rarificato.*

Ra'refying, s. *il rarefare, rarefazione.*

Ra'rely, adv. [seldom] *radamente, raramente, di rado, non sovente.*

Rarely, } [very well] *benissimamente, perfettamente, ottimamente.*
Rarely well, }

Ra'reness, s. [uncommonness] *rarezza, radezza,* s. f.

To Ra'rify, *v.* To rarefy.

Ra'rity, s. [a rare thing, a curiosity] *rarità, cosa rara, curiosità;* s. f.

Rarity [thinness, opposite to density] *rarità, contrario di densità.*

Ra'sberry, s. [raspberry, a sort of fruit] *mora di rovo.*

A rasberry tree, *rogo, rovo.*

Ra'scal, s. [rogue, paltry fellow] *un furfante, un briccone, un uomo vile, originalmente significava un uomo castrato.*

Rascal deer [lean deer] *un cervo magro.*

Rasca'lion, s. *un birbone, uno del più abbietto popolo.*

Rasca'lity, s. [the base rabble, the scum or dregs of the people] *la canaglia, gente vile e abbietta, la plebe, il popolazzo, la feccia del popolo.*

Ra'scally, adj. *furfante, barone.*

A rascally servant, *un furfante di servo.*

Rascally, adv. *da furfante, bricconescamente.*

To Rase [to skin, to strike on the surface] *percuotere leggermente sulla superficie.*

To rase [to overthrow, to destroy, to root up] *rovinar affatto, distruggere dalle fondamenta, mandar sozzopra.*

To rase [to erase] *raschiar via, cancellare raschiando.*

Rash, adj. [over-hasty, unthinking, unadvised] *temerario, precipitoso, sconsiderato, imprudente, inconsiderato, troppo ardito.*

He is very rash in all his undertakings, *è troppo inconsiderato in tutte le sue imprese.*

A rash word, or rash expression, *parola, o espressione inconsiderata*

Rash-headed *sconsiderato inavvertente, inavvertito, precipitoso, precipite.*

Ra'sher, s. [a thin slice] of bacon, *una fetta di prosciutto sottilissima.*

A rasher on the coals, *una carbonata.*

Ra'shly, adv. *temerariamente, inavvedutamente, disavvedutamente, imprudentemente, precipitosamente, inavvertentemente, sconsideratamente, inavvertitamente.*

Ra'shness, s. [hastiness] *temerità, inavvertenza, imprudenza, sconsideranza, precipitazione,* s. f.

Rasp, s. [a kind of file] *raschia,* s. f.

To Rasp [to file, to pare into shavings] *raschiare, raspare.*

To rasp bread, *scrostare del pane.*

Ra'spatory [a surgeon's instrument to scrape foul and scaly bones] *raspatojo,* s. m. *strumento di chirurgo.*

Ra'sped, adj. *raschiato, rastiato.*

Ra'spberry, s *mora di rovo.*

Ra'sure, s. [a shaving or scraping] *raschiatura*, s. f.

Rasure, *una pennata, o colpo di penna raschiato via.*

Rat, s. [an animal which infests houses] *topo, sorcio.*

A house rat, *un topo domestico.*

I smell a rat [I distrust something] *io non mi fido, mi dubito di qualche furberia.*

Rat-trap, *trappola*, s. f.

Rats-bane, *tossico.*

Ra'teably, adv. [by equal portion] *ugualmente, per rata.*

Rate, s. [price, value] *prezzo, valore* s. m. *assisa, tassa*, s. f.

An extravagant rate, *un prezzo esorbitante.*

At low rate, *a vil prezzo, a buon mercato.*

To set rates upon provisions, *metter l' assisa sopra le provvisioni.*

Corn is at a great rate, it bears or yields a great rate [it is dear] *il grano è molto caro, il grano si vende molto caro.*

To give a great price for a thing [to pay dear for it] *comprar caro che che si sia, pagarla raro.*

To hold it at a great rate, *venderla caro.*

To spend at a huge rate [to spend high] *fare grandi spese, spender molto.*

To drink at a great rate [or with excess] *ber molto, bere terribilmente.*

He lives at an extravagant rate, *vive prodigalmente, o da prodigo.*

Rate [tax, assessment] *tassa, imposizione*, s. f.

A moderate rate, *una tassa ragionevole, o moderata.*

Rate [rank, order] *rata, sfera*, s. f. *ordine.*

A man of war of the first rate, *una nave di guerra di prima rata.*

An author of the first rate, *un autore di prima sfera.*

Rate [interest for money lent] *ragione.*

To lend money at the rate of five per cent, *imprestar danari a ragione di cinque per cento.*

I bought at the rate of ten shillings a yard, *l' ho comprato a ragione di dieci scellini il braccio.*

At that or this rate [if it be so] *a questo modo, in questa maniera, se la cosa va così.*

I cannot live any longer at this rate, *non posso più vivere in questa maniera.*

You talk at a high rate, *voi parlate troppo arditamente.*

At a strange rate, *stranamente.*

At the old rate, at the usual rate [as formerly] *all' ordinario, secondo il costume, al solito.*

Rate tythe [for cattle kept in a parish less than a year] *certa decima che si paga per i bestiami.*

To **Rate** [to value] *stimare, apprezzare, valutare.*

To rate [to assess, to tax] *tassare, ordinare, e fermar la tassa.*

To rate [to chide] *censurare, riprendere, biasimare, bravare.*

Ra'ted, adj. *stimato, apprezzato, valutato*, v. To rate.

Ra'ter, s. *stimatore, estimatore*, s. m.

Rath } adj. [early ripe] *primaticcio, che si matura a buon ora.*
Rathe }

Rath fruits, *frutti primaticci.*

A rath egg, *uovo morbido, che si può bere.*

Rath, s. [a hill] *un colle, una collinetta, un luogo elevato, un poggio.*

Ra'ther, adv. *più presto, più tosto, meglio.*

I had rather, *vorrei più presto.*

To have rather, *amar meglio.*

She had rather, *ella vorrebbe più tosto.*

You should do it rather for that, *per questa ragione voi dovreste farlo.*

Ratifica'tion, s. [a ratifying or confirming] *ratificamento*, s. m. *ratificazione*, s. f.

Ra'tifier, s. [the person or thing that ratifies] *la persona o la cosa che ratifica.*

To **Ra'tify** [to confirm, to establish] *ratificare, confirmare quello, che altri ha promesso per te.*

Ra'tified, adj. *ratificato, confirmato.*

Ra'tifying, s. *ratificamento*, s. m. *il ratificare.*

Ra'ting, s. *estimazione*, v. To rate.

Ratiocina'tion, s. [or reasoning] *il raziocinare, ragionamento, discorso*, s. m.

To **Ratio'cinate**, s. [to reason] *raziocinare, discorrere per via di ragione.*

Ratio'cinative, adj. [belonging to ratiocination] *discorsivo.*

Ra'tional, adj. [endowed with reason] *razionale, ragionevole, razionabile.*

A very rational discourse, *un discorso molto ragionevole.*

The rational horizon, *l' orizonte razionale.*

Ra'tionalist, s. [one who proceeds in his disquisitions and practice wholly upon reason] *uno che in ogni cosa procede secondo i più stretti dettami della ragione.*

Rationa'lity, s. *facolta di usare della ragione.*

Rationality, s. [reasonableness] *ragionevolezza.*

Ra'tionally, adv. *razionalmente, ragionevolmente.*

Ra'tsbane, s. *arsenico, veleno pe' topi.*

Ratte'en, s. [a kind of stuff] *sorta di panno lano.*

Ra'ttle, s. [a child's toy] *sonaglio*, s. m.

A cock's rattles [waddles] *cresta che il gallo ha sotto' l becco, i pendenti.*

Yellow rattle [a plant] *cresta di gallo (pianta.)*

Rattle-headed [shuttle-headed] *uno stordito, un menteratto, uno scervellato, un cervello scemo.*

To **Ra'ttle** [to make a noise as a rattle] *scricchiolare, strepitare, romoreggiare, fare strepito.*

Do you hear how it rattles? *sentite come strepita? sentite che strepito?*

To rattle at the door, *bussare alla porta.*

To rattle in the throat, *gorgogliare, gargarizzare.*

To rattle [to scold at, to quarrel with] *bravare; sgridare, garrire, riprendere, rimbrottare, lavar il capo ad uno, farli una ripassata.*

To rattle a great oath, *fare un gran giuramento.*

To rattle [to speak fast] *parlar presto.*

Ra'ttlesnake, s. *caudisona, codisona*, s. f. *sorta di serpe velenosissima.*

Rattlesnake-root, s. *pianta della Virginia usata dagl' Indiani per rimedio contra il morso della caudisona.*

Ra'ttling, s. [noise] *strepito, romore, fracasso*, s. m.

The rattling of a coach, *lo strepito d' una carrozza.*

The empty rattling of words, *parole vane e pompose.*

Rattling in the throat, *gorgogliamento*, s. m. *il gorgogliare.*

Rattlings } [those lines which make
Rat-lines } the ladder-steps to get up the shrouds and puttocks] *funicelle*, s. f.

Ratto'on, s. [a West-Indian fox] *volpe dell' Indie occidentali.*

Ra'vage, s. [havock, spoil] *strage, rovina*, s. f. *disordine, guasto, strazio*, s. m.

To **Ra'vage** [to lay waste] *predare, saccheggiare, rovinare, distruggere, guastare, dissipare, mettere a guasto, e a sacco.*

Ra'vaged, adj. *predato, saccheggiato, rovinato, distrutto, guastato, dissipato, messo a guasto.*

To **Rave** [to be light-headed] *delirare, farneticare, esser fuori di se, aver perduto il cervello.*

To **Ra'vel** [to snarl up as hard twisted thread] *imbrogliare, intrigare, confondere, avviluppare*, pret. *confusi.*

To ravel out, *sfilarsi, sfilacciarsi.*

Ra'velin, s. [a piece of fortification] *rivellino*, s. m. *sorta di fortificazione.*

Ra'ven, s. [a well known bird] *un corbo.*

To **Ra'ven**, *divorare con grande avidità e rapacità.*

To raven, *rapacemente predare.*

Ra'venous, adj. [greedy, gluttonous] *rapace, avido, goloso, ghiotto, ghiottone, ingordo.*

Ra'venously, adv. *avidamente, con rapacità, ingordamente*

Ra'vin, s. [prey, food gotten by violence] *preda; ribo rapito violentemente.*

Ravin, *rapina, rapacità.*

Ra'ving, s. [from to rave] *delirio.*

Raving, adj. *delirante, freneticante, frenetico.*
RA'VINGLY, adv. *mattamente, freneticamente.*
To RA'VISH [to take away by force] *rapire*, torre *con violenza*, pref. *rapisco.*
To ravish [to commit a rape] *sforzare una donna, stuprare, commettere stupro.*
To ravish [to please exceedingly, to charm] *rapire, incantare.*
You ravish me with joy, *voi mi rapite d' allegrezza.*
I am ravished with pleasure, *son quasi fuor di me di contento.*
RA'VISHED, adj. *rapito, strupato, e stuprato.*
She has ravished my heart, *ella m' ha imbolato il cuore.*
RA'VISHER, s. *rapitore*, s. m *rapitrice*, s. f.
RA'VISHING, s. *rapimento, ratto*, s. m
Ravishing, adj. [charming] *che rapisce, che incanta.*
RA'VISHMENT, s. [rapture, great joy, transport] *ratto*, s m. *estasi, gran piacere, gran contento.*
Ravishment [rape] *ratto, stupro*, s. m.
RAW, adj. [neither boiled, roasted, nor baked, uncooked] *crudo, non cotto.*
Raw meat, *carne cruda.*
Raw fruit, *un frutto crudo.*
Raw meat in the stomach, *carne indigesta.*
Raw silk, *seta cruda.*
Raw leather, *pelle cruda, non conciata.*
Raw [unskilled] *ignorante, soro, semplice, inesperto.*
Raw weather [cold and moist weather] *tempo freddo e umido.*
To have a raw stomach, *avere uno stomaco indigesto.*
A raw-bon'd fellow [lusty lean fellow] *un uomo magro e ossuto, un uomo robusto e magro.*
RA'WNESS, s. [crudity] *crudità, astratto di crudo.*
Rawness [unskilfulness] *inesperienza, semplicità.*
Rawness of weather, *tempo freddo, e umido.*
RAY, s. [a beam of light] *raggio*, s. m. *splendore che esce di corpo lucido.*
The rays of the sun, *i raggi del sole.*
Ray [the fish thornback] *razza*, s. f. *sorta di pesce.*
A ray [a thin leaf] of gold, *una foglia d' oro.*
Ray-cloth [cloth that was never coloured or dyed] *panno che non è stato mai tinto.*
To RAY out [to cast forth rays] *raggiare, splendere, fare lunghe strisce.*
RAZE, s. [a measure of corn now disused] *certa misura di grano non più in uso.*
Raze, s. *nome d' una radice aromatica.*
To RAZE [to lay even with the ground] *spianare, rovinare, distruggere, mandare a terra, abbattere, atterrare* pret. *distrussi.*
RA'ZED, adj. *spianato, rovinato, distrutto, abbattuto, atterrato.*
RA'ZOR, s. *rasojo, coltello taglientissimo col quale si rade il pelo.*
REACH, s. [the distance as far as a line can be extended, as a bow, as a gun, &c. can carry, or as a man can carry] *tiro*, s. m.
Within the reach of a gun-shot, *ad un tiro di cannone.*
It is out of my reach, *non posso arrivarci.*
Reach [capacity] *sufficienza, capacità*, s. f.
Reach of thought, *sagacità, perspicacità, acutezza d' ingegno.*
Reach [power] *possa*, s. f. *potere*, s. m.
It is not in my reach, *non è in poter mio, io non son da tale, io non mi stimo capace.*
A reach [or fetch] *astuzia, sottigliezza*, s. f.
A man of deep reach, *un uomo astuto fine, o sottile.*
A reach [the distance between any two points of land that lie in a right line one from the other] *la larghezza o distanza d' un braccio di mare, o di fiume d' un canto all' altro in linea retta.*
Reach [vomit] *sforzo che si fa per vomitare o recere.*
To REACH [to come at] *arrivare, giugnere*, pret. *giunsi.*
I cannot reach it, *non posso arrivarci.*
To reach [or over-reach] *arrivare, raggiugnere in camminando.*
To reach a place, *arrivare, giugnere, pervenire ad un luogo*, pret. *giunsi, pervenni*, pres. *pervengo.*
To reach [to give] *dare, porgere*, pret. *porsi.*
Reach me my sword, *datemi, o porgetemi la mia spada.*
To reach the meaning of a thing, *arrivare, intendere, o capire il senso d' una cosa.*
To reach [to concern] *toccare, spettare, concernere.*
It is not possible for the law to reach or comprehend all the various cases, *la legge non può comprendere in se tutte le diversità de' casi.*
It costs too dear, I cannot reach the price of it, *è troppo caro, non posso spender tanto.*
To reach at a thing, *arrivare ad una cosa.*
To reach [to be extended] *stendersi, distendersi.*
The town reaches two miles along the river, *la città si stende due miglia lungo il fiume.*
The noise of this action has reached our ears, *la fama di quest' azione ci è giunta all' orecchie.*
To reach [to strain, to vomit] *sforzarsi per vomitare, cercar di vomitare, recere.*
REACHED, adj. *arrivato, giunto*, v. To reach.
RE'ACTION, s. [a reciprocal motion of one part of matter against another] *azione reciproca.*
READ, s. [counsel, advice] *consiglio, avviso*, s. m.
Read, *è un preterito del verbo* to read, *lessi.*
I read, *io lessi.*
Read, adj. *letto.*
To READ, *leggere*, pret. *lessi.*
To read a book, *leggere un libro.*
To read on, *continuare a leggere.*
To read out or loud, *legger forte, o ad alta voce.*
To read out } *legger tutto, leggere*
To read all } *dal principio alla fine.*
To read over, *legger tutto, trascorrere.*
To read about, *legger quà e là.*
To read again, to read over again, *rileggere, tornare a leggere, legger di nuovo o da capo.*
To read [to guess, to divine] *congetturare, indovinare.*
I read in his countenance that he is a rogue, *posso indovinare dal suo volto ch' egli è un furbo.*
To read [to teach in publick] *leggere, far letture.*
To read divinity, *leggere, o far letture in teologia.*
RE'ADER, s. *lettore*, s. m.
A reader in a college, *un lettore o professore in un collegio.*
A great reader [one that reads much] *uno che ama a leggere, o legge molto.*
RE'ADILY, adv. [quickly] *prestamente, subitamente, prontamente, in un subito.*
Readily [gladly, chearfully] *volontiermente, di buon animo, con sollecitudine.*
Readily [or without book] *a mente.*
RE'ADINESS, s. [diligence] *prontezza, diligenza, sollecitudine*, s. f.
Readiness of wit, *acutezza, o sublimità d' ingegno.*
RE'ADING, s. *lettura*, s. f. *il leggere.*
Reading, adj. the reading part, *quello che deve esser letto.*
To READJO'URN [to adjourn again] *differire, o prorogare di nuovo.*
READJOU'RNED, adj. *differito, o prorogato di nuovo.*
READMI'SSION, s. [the action of readmitting] *il riammetter l' ammettere di nuovo.*
To READMI'T [to admit, to receive again] *riammettere, ammettere, o ricever di nuovo.*
RE'ADY, adv. [prepared, at hand, in readiness] *apparecchiato, preparato, lesto, in ordine, in procinto.*
Ready at hand, *apparecchiato, in ordine.*
Is the dinner ready? *il pranzo è in ordine?*
I am ready to go, *son pronto, o in ordine d' andare.*
Ready [inclined, prone] *prono, disposto, dedito, pronto, inclinato.*

To

To have a ready wit, *avere uno spirito vivace.*

To have a ready tongue, *avere una gran facilità in esprimersi, aver la lingua ben affilata.*

Ready money [money down on the nail] *danari contanti.*

To make or get ready, *metter in ordine, preparare, allestire, apparecchiare, mettere in punto.*

To get one's self ready, *prepararsi, apparecchiarsi, mettersi in ordine, o in punto.*

To get one's self ready [or to put one's clothes on] *vestirsi.*

This is a ready way to honour, *questa è la dritta strada agli onori.*

Ready, adv. [already] *gia, di già, oramai.*

The time was ready come, *il tempo era già, o oramai giunto.*

Rooms let ready furnished, *camere locande.*

REAFO'RESTED, adj. a law term [made forest again] *rimboscato.*

REAKS, s. ex. to play reaks, to domineer, to hector, *braveggiare, fare il bravo, lo smargiasso.*

REAL, adj. [that is indeed, true] *reale, che è in effetto, o in realità, effetivo, vero.*

Real estate, *beni immobili.*

RE'AL, s. [a Spanish coin] *reale,* s. m. *spezie di moneta di Spagna.*

REA'LGAR, s. [among chymists, red arsenick] *realgale,* s. m. *sorta d' arsenico.*

REA'LITY, s. [real essence, the truth of the matter] *realtà, verità.*

The reality of my friendship, *la sincerità della mia amicizia.*

I cannot conceive what reality there is in greatness, *non posso capire che cosa abbi la grandezza di reale.*

In reality, } adv. [indeed, in effect] RE'ALLY, } *realmente, effettivamente, in effetto, in vero.*

Really [in earnest, truly] *veramente, certamente, sicuramente, da dovero.*

REALM, s. [kingdom] *reame, regno,* s. m.

REAM, s. [a quantity of twenty quires of paper] *risma,* s. f. *venti quaderni.*

To REA'NIMATE [to revive, to put in heart again] *rianimare, rincorare, dare nuovo animo.*

REA'NIMATED, adj. *rianimato, rincorato.*

To REA'NNEX [to annex again] *riunire di nuovo; commetter di nuovo insieme.*

To REAP [to cut down corn] *mietere, segar le biade.*

To reap the fruits of one's labour, *mietere il frutto delle sue fatiche.*

The benefit you shall reap by it, *il vantaggio che ne ricaverete.*

RE'APED, adj. *mietuto.*

RE'APER, s. *mietitore,* s. m.

RE'APING, s. *mietitura,* s. f. *il mietere.*

Reaping-time [harvest-time] *la mietitura, il tempo del mietere.*

A reaping sickle, *una falce.*

REAR [the hindermost part of an army] *retroguardia.*

To bring up the rear, *andar di retroguardia.*

A rear admiral, *vice ammiraglio.*

The rear guard, *la retroguardia.*

A rear-mouse [reremouse] *una nottola.*

To REAR [to raise or set up] *levare, ergere, innalzare, levar in alto, rizzare,* pret. *ersi.*

To rear a boar [a hunting term to dislodge him] *levar un cinghiale, farlo uscir dal suo covo.*

A horse that rears himself up, *un cavallo che s'innalbera.*

To rear up a building, *rizzare un edificio.*

To rear [to bring up] *allevare, ammaestrare, nutrire,* pref. *nutrisco.*

To rear up a child, *allevare o nutrire un fanciullo.*

To rear one up [to raise him] *allevare, levare, innalzare uno agli onori, aggrandirlo.*

RE'ARED, adj. *levato, erto, innalzato, rizzato,* v. To rear.

RE'ARWARD, s. [the last troop] *l' ultima schiera, la schiera di retroguardia.*

Rearward, s. [the end, the tail; a train behind] *strascico, coda, quel che vien dopo.*

Rearward, s. [the latter part] *l' ultima parte, la sezzajo parte.*

To REA'SCEND [to ascend, to get up again] *rimontare, montar di nuovo, risalire,* pref. *risalgo.*

RE'ASON, s. [that faculty of the soul whereby we judge of a thing] *ragione,* s. f. *potenza dell' anima, che sceglie il vero dal falso.*

Sound reason, *diritta ragione.*

To speak reason, *parlar sensatamente, o con senno.*

Reason [cause] *ragione, cagione, causa,* s. f. *motivo.*

What is the reason that you did not come? *per che ragione non siete venuto?*

By reason of, *a causa di.*

By reason that, *perchè, a causa che.*

Reason [consideration] *ragione, considerazione,* s. f. *riguardo, rispetto,* s. m.

Reason [justice, right, duty] *ragione, il giusto, il convenevole, il dovere, equità, giustizia.*

To bring one to reason, *mettere uno alla ragione.*

To have reason [to be in the right] *aver ragione.*

To yield or submit to reason, *sottomettersi alla ragione.*

That is all the reason in the world, *è ben dritto, è ragionevole.*

A thing contrary to reason, *una cosa irragionevole, o contraria alla ragione.*

It were more reason, *sarebbe più giusto, o ragionevole.*

Good reason too, *con ragione.*

To do one reason [to give him satisfaction] *far ragione ad uno, aggiudicare altrui quel che gli si convien per giustizia.*

To RE'ASON [to discourse] *ragionare, discorrere,* pret. *discorsi.*

To reason [to dispute] *ragionare, disputare.*

To reason with one's self, *meditare, considerare, disporrer fra se stesso.*

RE'ASONABLE, adj. [agreeable to the rules of reason, just] *ragionevole, conforme alla ragione, giusto.*

Reasonable [moderate] *ragionevole, moderato.*

Reasonable [competent, convenient] *ragionevole, competente, convenevole, non esorbitante.*

At a reasonable rate, *a un prezzo ragionevole.*

Reasonable [rational] *razionale, ragionevole.*

RE'ASONABLENESS, s. *giustizia, ragione, equità,* s. f.

RE'ASONABLY, adv. *ragionevolmente, con ragione, giustamente, moderatamente.*

RE'ASONER, s. *colui che ragiona.*

RE'ASONING, s. *ragionamento,* s. m. *il ragionare.*

RE'ASONLESS, adj. [void of reason] *irragionevole, senza ragione.*

To REASSE'MBLE [to meet together again] *radunarsi di nuovo, radunare.*

Reassembled, adj. *radunato.*

To REASSE'RT [to assert anew] *asserir di nuovo, di nuovo affermare.*

To REASSU'ME [to take upon one's self again] *riassumere, assumer di nuovo;* pret. *riassunsi.*

REASSU'MED, adj. *riassunto.*

REASSU'MING, s. *il riassumere.*

To RE'AVE [to take away by stealth or violence] *portar via di furto o con violenza.*

REBAPTIZA'TION, s. *ribattezzamento, nuovo battezzare.*

To REBAPTI'ZE [to baptize again] *ribattezzare, di nuovo battezzare.*

REBAPTI'ZED, adj. *ribattezzato.*

REBA'TE, s. [chamfering] *scanalatura,* s. f.

To REBA'TE [to chamfer] *scanalare.*

To rebate [to blunt] *spuntáre.*

To rebate [to check] *abbáttere, abbassáre, rintuzzare, ribáttere.*

To rebate one's pride, *abbattere, o rintuzzare l'altrui orgoglio.*

To rebate [to deduct] *ribattere, dedurre.*

REBA'TED, adj. *scanalato,* v. To rebate.

REBA'TEMENT, s. [a discount upon the payment of ready money] *deduzione; difalcazione,* s. f.

Rebatement [diminution of figures] *diminuzione di figure.*

REBE'CK, s. [a musical instrument having three strings] *ribeca,* s. f. *strumento musicale a tre corde.*

A rebeck [an old trot] *una vecchiaccia.*

RE'BEL, s. [one who rebels against his sovereign] *un ribello, un rubello.*

To RE'BEL [to rise up in arms, to revolt.

revolt againſt lawful authority] *ribellarſi.*

REBE'LLION, s. [a riſing againſt, or taking up arms againſt the ſupreme power] *ribellione*, s. f.

REBE'LLIOUS, adj. [apt to rebel, diſobedient] *ribello, rubello.*

A rebellious child, *un figlio diſobediente.*

To REBE'LLOW [to bellow in return; to eccho back a loud noiſe] *rimugghiare*; *ribattere un gran ſuono o un muglio indietro, come fa l' eco.*

REBOUND, s. *rimbalzo, balzo*, s. m.

To REBO'UND [to leap back again, or bounce back again as a ball does] *rimbalzare, ſaltare in alto balzare.*

REBO'UNDED, adj. *rimbalzato, balzato.*

REBU'FF, s. [repulſe, rough denial] *rabbuffo*, s. m.

To REBUI'LD [to build up again] *riſabbricare, fabbricar di nuovo.*

REBUI'LT, adj. *riſabbricato.*

REBU'KABLE, adj. [worthy of reprehenſion] *riprenſibile, meritevole di riprenſione.*

REBU'KE, s. [check, reproof] *riprenſione, bravata, ripreſa ammonizione, ripaſſata*, s. f.

To REBU'KE [to reprove, to check] *riprendere, bravare. ſgridare.*

The devil rebukes ſin, *la padella dice al pajuolo, fatti in là che tu mi tingi.*

REBU'KED, adj. *ripreſo, bravato, ſgridato.*

REBU'KEFUL, adj. *agro, ſevero, pungente.*

Rebukeful language, *parole agre o pungenti.*

REBU'KEFULLY, adv. *agramente, ſeveramente, aſpramente.*

REBU'KER, s. *riprenditore, riprenſore, garritore*, s m. *garritrice*, s. f.

REBU'KING, s. *riprendimento, garrimento*, s. m. *il garrire.*

Rebuking, adj. ex. a rebuking letter, *una lettera di reprenſione.*

RE'BUS, s. [a word repreſented by a picture] *parola rappreſentata con una coſa dipinta.*

To RECA'LL [to call back, to call home] *richiamare, far ritornare, dar ordine di ritornare, rivocare.*

RECA'LLED, adj. *richiamato.*

RECA'LL, s. *richiamo*; *il rivocare.*

RECA'LLING, s. *richiamo*, s. m. *ordine di ritornare.*

To RECA'NT [to recall what one has ſaid or written before, to unſay] *ritrattare, ritrattarſi, diſdirſi, dir contro a quel che s' è detto prima, rivocare, negare*, pret. *diſdiſſi.*

RECANTA'TION, s. [a revoking or unſaying] *ritrattazione, diſdetta, negazione, rivocazione*, s. f.

RECA'NTED, adj. *ritrattato, diſdetto, rivocate, negato.*

RECA'NTING, s. *ritrattazione, diſdetta*, s. f.

To RECA'PITULATE [to rehearſe briefly, or ſum up the heads of a former diſcourſe] *ricapitolare, tornare a ridire, replicare, dir di nuovo.*

RECA'PITULATED, adj. *ricapitolato, tornato a dire, replicato, detto di nuovo.*

RECAPITULA'TION, s. *ricapitolazione*, s. f. *il ricapitolare.*

To RECE'DE [to go back or retire] *rincalzare, tornare indietro, retrogradare.*

To recede [to depart from] *partire, andar via.*

I am under ſuch engagements that I cannot recede, *mi trovo talmente impegnato, che non poſſo dare indietro.*

RECE'IPT, s. [acquittance for money received] *ricevuta*, s. f. *confeſſione per via di ſcrittura d' aver ricevuto.*

Receipt [medicine preſcribed for the cure of diſeaſes] *ricetta*, s. f. *regola e modo di compor le medicine e di uſarle.*

Receipt [the act of receiving] *ricevimento*, s. m. *il ricevere.*

RECE'IVABLE, adj. [that may be received] *ricevevole, atto a ricevere.*

To RECEI'VE [to take what is given] *ricevere, pigliare, accettare per amore, o per forza quello che è dato o preſentato.*

To receive money, *ricever danari.*

To receive great honours, *ricever grandi onori.*

The tree receives its nouriſhment from the root, *l' albero riceve o piglia il ſuo nutrimento dalla radice.*

To receive [to gather] taxes, *riſcuoter le taſſe.*

To receive [to entertain] one at one's houſe, *ricevere, accogliere uno in caſa ſua.*

To receive one into an office, *ricevere, e ammettere uno a qualche ofizio.*

To receive an opinion, *ricevere o abbracciare un' opinione.*

To receive a great loſs, *fare una gran perdita.*

To receive ſtolen goods, *celare, o naſcondere beni maltolti.*

RECE'IVED, adj. *ricevuto*, v. To receive.

RECE'IVER, s. *ricevitore*, s. m. *ricevitrice*, s. f.

A receiver of rents, *ricevitore di rendite.*

RECE'IVING, s. *ricevimento*, s. m. *il ricevere.*

RE'CENT, adj. [new, freſh, lately done or happened] *recente, nuovo, novello, di poco tempo fa, di freſco.*

RE'CENTLY, adv. *recentemente, nuovamente, freſcamente, di freſco.*

RECE'PTACLE, s. [ſhelter or place to receive or keep things in] *ricettaccolo, ricetto, ricovero*, s. m.

RECE'PTION, s. *ricevimento, accoglimento*, s. m. *accoglienza*, s. f.

RECE'PTIVE, adj. [apt or fit to receive] *ricettivo, atto a ricevere, che ha virtù di ricevere.*

RECE'SS, s. [a retreating or withdrawing] *receſſo*, s. f. *ritiro*, s. m.

A private receſs [a by-place, a ſolitude] *una ſolitudine, un luogo ritirato, un naſcondiglio.*

The moſt ſecret receſs of our ſoul, *i più intimi ſegreti, arcani, o penſieri del cuor noſtro.*

To RECHA'NGE [to change again] *cangiar di nuovo.*

To RECHA'RGE [to accuſe in return] *accuſar l' accuſatore.*

To recharge [to attack anew] *riazzuffarſi, ricominciar l' attacco.*

RECHE'AT, s. [among hunters, a leſſon which the huntſman winds on the horn when the hounds have loſt their game] *chiamata che il cacciatore fa col corno ai cani che hanno ſmarrito l' animale a cui correvano dietro.*

To RECI'DIVATE [to relapſe] *ricaſcare, rinciampare, caſcare di nuovo (ſi dice particolamente degli errori.) Non è vocabolo in uſo.*

RECIDIVA'TION, s. [a relapſing or falling again] *ricidiva, ricaſcata*, s. f.

RE'CIPE, s. [medical preſcription] *ricetta*, s. f. *preſcrizione medica.*

RECI'PIENT, s. [the veſſel that receives what comes out of the lembick] *recipiente*, s. m. *vaſo da ſtillare, che riceve la materia ſtillata.*

RECI'PROCAL, adj. [mutual] *reciproco, mutuo, vicendevole, ſcambievole.*

A pronoun, or verb reciprocal, *un pronome o verbo reciproco.*

RE'CIPROCALLY, adv. *reciprocamente, mutuamente, ſcambievolmente, vicendevolmente.*

RE'CIPROCALNESS, s. [mutual return, alternateneſs] *vicendevolezza, cambio, alternamento, contraccambio.*

To RECI'PROCATE [to requite, to be even with] *render la pariglia, contraccambiare, ricompenſare.*

RECIPROCA'TION, s. [an interchange, a return, like for like] *reciprocazione, pariglia*, s. f. *contraccambio*, s. m.

Reciprocation of love, *amor vicendevole.*

RECI'SION, s [cutting off] *reciſione, mutilazione*, s. f. *tagliamento, troncamento, mozzamento*, s. m.

RECI'TAL, s. [relation, account] *narrativa, relazione, narrazione*, s. f. *ragguaglio, narramento*, s. m.

RECITA'TION, s. [rehearſing] *recitazione*, s. f. *il recitare.*

RECI'TATIVE, adj. [belonging to recitation] *recitativo, che ſi recita.*

RECI'TATIVE } s. [ſinging that
RECITATI'VO } comes near to plain pronunciation] *recitativo*, s. m.

To RECI'TE [to ſay without book] *recitare, dire a mente.*

To recite [to relate, to rehearſe] *recitare, raccontare, narrare.*

RECITE, s. *uſato in vere di recital.*

RECI'TED, adj. *recitato, raccontato, narrato.*

RECI'TING, s. *recitazione*, s. f. *narramento, racconto*, s. m.

To RECK [to heed, to care for] *por mente, badare, curarſene, penſarci.*

To reck, *pigliar cura, aſſumere.*

RE'CKLESS, adj. [carelefs, heedlefs, mindlefs] *ftraccurato, che non fi cura, che non fi da penfiero, indifferente, negligente, trafcurato.*

RE'CKLESNESS, s. [carelefnefs, negligence] *indifferenza, negligenza, trafcuratezza, trafcuraggine, trafcuratag-gine.*

To REC'KON [to count, to compute] *contare, computare, calcolare.*

To reckon [to efteem, to believe, to think] *contare, ftimare, riputare, tenere, credere.*

I fhall reckon it a favour, *lo terrò a favore.*

I reckon him a dead man, *lo conto come un uomo morto.*

To reckon [to defign] *difegnare, far difegno, proporfi.*

I reckon to fee him to-morrow, *difegno d'andarlo a vedere domani.*

To reckon [to rely, to depend] *afficurarfi, dipendere, far capitale, fidarfi.*

To reckon upon a thing [to expect it] *far conto fu qualche cofa, farvi capitale fopra.*

I reckon little on it, *ne afpetto poco vantaggio.*

He that reckons without his hoft, muft reckon again, *chi fa il conto fenza l'ofte, conta due volte.*

Reckon not your chickens before they are hatched, *non dir quattro fe tu non l'hai nel facco; e vale che non bifogna far affegnamento d' una cofa in fin che non l' abbiamo in noftra balia.*

RE'CKONED, adj. *contato, computato, calcolato, v.* To reckon.

RE'CKONER, s. *contatore,* s. m. *che conta.*

RE'CKONING, s. *il contare, conto,* s. m.

Even reckoning makes long friends, *conto fpeffo amicizia lunga.*

To come to a reckoning with one, *venire a' conti con uno.*

Reckoning [in a publick houfe] *fcotto,* s. m.

Let us pay our reckoning and be gone, *paghiamo lo fcotto, e andiamocene.*

He makes no reckoning [or account] of it, *non ne fa conto di ciò, non fe ne cura.*

We make more reckoning of our liberty, than of our friendfhip, *noi ftimiamo più la noftra libertà che la voftra amicizia.*

Reckoning of a woman with child, *termine d' una donna gravida.*

She went to her reckoning, *ella partorì alla fine del fuo termine.*

She is near her reckoning, *ella è vicina al parto.*

Off reckoning, *difconto.*

To RECLA'IM [to reduce to amendment of life, to call back from ill courfes] *correggere, emendare, mettere alla ragione, far cangiar vita, convertire, riformare,* pref. *convertifco.*

To reclaim, verb neut. [to leave off vices] *correggerfi, emendarfi, riformarfi, cangiar vita.*

To reclaim [a term of hunting] *richiamare.*

The partridge reclaims [is faid when fhe calls her young ones] *la pernice richiama.*

To reclaim a hawk [is to tame or make it gentle] *addomefticare un falcone.*

RECLA'IMED, adj. *corretto, emendato, richiamato.*

RECLA'IMLESS, adj. *incorrigibile, abbandonato, perduto.*

RECLU'SE, adj. [fhut up or fecret] *privato, fegreto, ritirato.*

A reclufe, s. [a monk or nun fhut up in a cloyfter] *un monaco, o una monaca.*

RECO'GNISANCE, s. [a bond or obligation, acknowledged in fome court of record, or before fome judge] *malleveria, o obbligazione fatta in corte.*

To RECOGNI'ZE [to acknowledge] *confeffare, dichiarare in ifcritto d' effer obbligato a pagare, o fare qualunque altra cofa.*

To RE'COGNISE [to acknowledge] *riconofcere.*

To recognife, *rivedere, efaminar di nuovo.*

RECOGNI'SEE, s. [he to whom one is bound] *colui a chi folenne malleveria, o obbligazione è fatta in ifcritto.*

RECOGNI'TION, s. [acknowledgment] *ricognizione, riconofcenza,* s. f.

Recognition [examination, review] *efame, efaminamento,* s. m.

RECO'IL, s. [or giving back] *rinculamento,* s. m. *ritirata,* s. f.

To RECO'IL [to fly, or draw back as a gun does] *rinculare, farfi indietro, come l'armi da fuoco fparandole.*

To recoil of one's promife, *venir meno, o mancare alla fua promeffa.*

To RECO'IN [tò coin over again] *battere, o ftampare di nuovo.*

To recoin money, *batter la moneta di nuovo, rifarla.*

RECO'INED, adj. *battuto, o ftampato di nuovo.*

To RECOLLE'CT [to reflect in one's mind] *riflettere, penfare, rivolger nella mente, ruminar nel penfiero.*

To recollect [to call a thing to mind] *ricordarfi, fovvenirfi, rammentarfi, ridurfi a memoria.*

Pray recollect yourfelf well, *rifletteteci o penfateci bene, fateci ben rifleffione fopra.*

I cannot recollect his name, *non poffo ricordarmi, o ridurmi a memoria il fuo nome.*

RECOLLE'CTION, s. [reflection of the mind] *rifleffione,* s. f.

RECOLLE'CTS, s. [a branch of the Francifcan fryars] *zoccolanti,* s. m. *ordine di religiofi di San Francefco.*

To RECOMME'NCE [to commence or begin again, or anew] *ricominciare, di nuovo cominciare.*

RECOMME'NCED, adj. *ricominciato.*

To RECOMME'ND [to commit to one's favour, protection, or care] *raccomandare, pregare altrui, che voglia avere a cuore quello che fe gli propone, dare in protezione, cura, e cuftòdia.*

If you will recommend yourfelf to the efteem of men, *fe volete cattivarvi la ftima degli uomini, fe volete effere in iftima fra gli uomini.*

RECOMME'NDABLE, adj. [to deferve to be, or may be recommendable] *ftimabile, lodevole, degno di lode, o di ftima.*

RECOMME'NDATORY, adj. [which deferves to be recommended] *raccomandatorio, di raccomandazione.*

A recommendatory letter, *una lettera di raccomandazione, o di favore.*

RECOMME'NDED, adj. *raccomandato.*

RECOMME'NDER, s. *quello o quella che raccomanda.*

RE'COMPENCE, s. [requital or reward] *ricompenza, rimunerazione,* s. f. *contraccambio,* s. m.

To RE'COMPENCE [to requite, to make amends] *ricompenfare, contraccambiare, rimunerare, dare il contraccambio.*

RE'COMPENSED, adj. *ricompenfato, contraccambiato, rimunerato.*

RE'COMPENSER, s. *quello o quella, che ricompenfa, rimuneratore,* s. m. *rimuneratrice,* s. f.

RE'COMPENSING, s. *ricompenfamento,* s. m. *il ricompenfare.*

To RE'COMPOSE [to compofe again] *ricomporre, comporre di nuovo,* pret. *ricompofi, compofi.*

To RE'CONCILE [to make thofe friends again who were at variance] *riconciliare, metter d' accordo, far ritornare amiro, metter pace.*

To reconcile [to make agree what feems to be contrary] *conciliare, unire, accordare,* pref. *unifco.*

To reconcile the principles of feveral fects, *conciliare, o accordare i principi di fette differenti.*

To reconcile, *difporfi, rifolverfi, indurfi.*

He could not reconcile himfelf to do it, *non potè rifolverfi a farlo.*

RE'CONCILED, adj. *riconciliato, unito, accordato, v.* To reconcile.

Thefe things cannot be reconciled, *quefte fon cofe che non fi poffon conciliare.*

He won't be reconciled to her, *egli non vuole riconciliarfi, o far pace con lei.*

I cannot be reconciled with ale, *non poffo patire la birra dolce.*

RECONCI'LEMENT, } s. *riconciliamento,* s. m.
RECONCILIA'TION, } *riconciliazione,* s. f.

RECONCI'LER, s. *conciliatore,* s. m.

RECONCI'LING, s. *riconciliamento,* s. m. *il riconciliare.*

RECO'NDITE, adj. [fecret, hidden] *recondito, nafcofo, fegreto.*

To RECONDU'CT [to conduct or lead back again] *ricondurre, di nuovo condurre, rimenare, riportare,* pret. *ricondussi.*

RECONDU'CTED, adj. *ricondotto, rimenato, riportato.*

RE'CORD, s. [a publick act enrolled] atto pubblico registrato.

A court of records, *corte dove son registrati gli atti.*

It is upon record, *questo è registrato.*

Record [authentick testimony] *testimonio autentico.*

To bear record, *far testimonianza.*

The records of the Tower, *gli archivi d'Inghilterra.*

Records of time, *istoria.*

Of whom there is so much record in the ancient poets, *tanto vantato fra gli antichi poeti.*

To REC'ORD [to sing, or tune notes as birds do] *cantare a vicenda, rispondersi nel cantare come fanno alcuni uccelli.*

To record [to register, to enroll] *registrare, arrolare.*

To record a thing in history, *metter che che si sia nell' istoria.*

RECORDA'TION, } s. *il registrare,*
RECO'RDING, } *menzione fatta nell' istoria.*

RECO'RDED, adj. *registrato, arrolato.*

You will find it recorded in history, *voi troverete nell' istoria.*

RECO'RDER, s. [he that keeps the records] *attuario,* s. m. *ministro deputato dal giudice a ricevere, registrare, e tener cura degli atti pubblici.*

Recorder [flute] *un flauto.*

To RECO'UCH [to lie down again] *ricolcarsi, colcarsi di nuovo, ricoricarsi, di nuovo coricarsi.*

To RECO'VER [to get again] *ricoverare, ricovrare, racquistare, recuperare.*

To recover one's health, *ricoverar la salute.*

To recover breath, *pigliar fiato, rifiatare, ricovrare il fiato.*

To recover one's money, *riavere, racquistare il suo danaro.*

To recover [to retrieve] a loss, *riparare una perdita.*

To recover one's self [to come to one's self again] *ritornare in se, ricuperar gli spiriti.*

To recover from a sickness, *riaversi, ricuperar la salute, rimettersi in piedi, ripigliar le forze, cominciare a star bene, esser in convalescenza.*

To recover a hare, *rilevare una lepre.*

RECO'VERABLE, adj. [that may be recovered] *ricuperabile, che si può ricuperare.*

RECO'VERER, adj. *ricuperato,* v. To recover.

He is not yet recovered of his losses, *egli non ha risarcito le sue perdite.*

RECO'VERY, s. [a regaining, or getting again] *ricoveramento, e ricovramento, ricovero,* s. m.

The recovery of our liberty, *il ricoveramento della nostra libertà.*

Recovery of health, *ricovramento di salute, convalescenza, guarigione,* s. f.

He is past recovery, or past hope of recovery, *egli è spedito, egli è disperato da' medici.*

I have no hope of his recovery, *dispero della sua salute o guarigione.*

I am lost without hopes of recovery, *sono affatto perduto, o rovinato.*

'Tis a thing past recovery, *non c' è più rimedio.*

To RECO'UNT [to tell or relate] *raccontare, narrare.*

RECO'UNTED, adj. *raccontato, narrato.*

RECO'URSE, s. [application, refuge, address] *ricorso, rifugio, ricovero,* s. m.

To have recourse to justice, *aver ricorso alla giustizia, andar per giustizia.*

Recourse [passage, return] *passo, passaggio,* s. m.

When the blood has a free recourse, *quando il sangue ha il passo libero.*

The recourse of spirits, *il ricovero degli spiriti.*

Recourse [resort, concourse] *concorso,* s. m.

RE'CREANT, adj. [faint-hearted, cowardly] *codardo, poltrone, vigliacco.*

Recreant [apostate, false] *apostata, falso, miscredente, scredente.*

To RE'CREATE [to refresh, to divert or delight] *ricreare, divertire, dilettare, spassare.*

RECREA'TION, s. [refreshment, pastime] *ricreazione, recreazione, divertimento, spasso, sollazzo, passatempo,* s. m.

RE'CREATIVE, adj. [diverting, pleasant] *ricreativo, gustoso, piacevole, che divertisce.*

RECREDE'NTIALS, s. [an answer to the credential letters of an ambassador] *lettere di credenza.*

RE'CREMENT, s. [dross, spume, superfluous or useless parts] *feccia, spuma, parti superflue o inutili.*

To RECRI'MINATE [to return an accusation or reproach] *rinfacciare, rimproverare, incolpare uno che incolpa te.*

RECRIMINA'TION, s. [return of an accusation or reproach] *rimprovero,* s. m. *accusa reciproca.*

RECRU'IT, s. [new or fresh supply of soldiers] *recluta*

Recruit of provisions, *rinforza di viveri.*

To RECRU'IT [to supply, to fill up] *reclutare, supplire, rinforzare,* pres. *supplisco.*

To recruit a regiment, *reclutare un reggimento.*

To recruit the fire [to add fuel to it] *metter nuove legne o nuovo carbone al fuoco.*

To recruit one's self [to refresh one's self, to gather strength] *ristorarsi, prender qualche ristoro, ricoverar le forze, rimettersi in piedi.*

RECRU'ITED, adj. *reclutato,* v. To recruit.

RECTA'NGLE, s. [a figure of four right angles] *rettangolo,* s. m. *figura piana di quattro lati con tutti gli angoli retti.*

RECTA'NGULAR, adj. [having one or more right angles] *rettangolo, che ha uno, o più angoli retti.*

RECTIFICA'TION, s. [a rectifying or making right] *rettificazione,* s. m. *il rettificare.*

RECTIFI'ER, s. *rettificatore,* s. m. *che rettifica.*

RE'CTIFIABLE, adj. [capable to be set right] *rettificabile; capace d' emendazione; che si può rettificare.*

To RE'CTIFY [to set to rights again, to correct or mend] *rettificare, aggiustare, accomodare, correggere,* pret. *corressi.*

To rectify a globe [to bring the sun's place in the eclipick on the globe to the brass meridian] *rettificare una sfera.*

You have rectify'd my thoughts as to that, *voi m' avete sgannato in ciò.*

RE'CTIFIED, adj. *rettificato.*

RE'CTIFYING, s. *rettificazione* s. f.

RECTILINEAL, } adj. [that consists
RECTILI'NEAR, } of right lines] *rettilineo, che ha le linee rette.*

RE'CTITUDE, s. [rightness, uprightness] *rettitudine, giustizia, dirittura, bontà,* s. f.

RE'CTOR, s. [a governor or principal] of a college, *rettore d' un collegio.*

The rector of a parish church, *il piovano d' una parrocchia.*

RE'CTORSHIP, s. *dignità o ufficio di rettore.*

RE'CTORY, s. [a spiritual living] *rettoria, beneficio, terre beneficiali.*

RE'CTUM, s. [the straight gut] *l' intestino retto.*

RECUBA'TION, } s. [the act of lying
RE'CUMBENCY, } or leaning] *l' atto del giacere o dell' appoggiarsi.*

RECU'MBENT, adj. [in a lying posture] *giacente.*

RECU'PERABLE, adj. [recoverable]. *che si può ricuperare.*

To RECU'PERATE [to recover] *ricuperare, ricoverare, ricovrare.*

RECUPERA'TION, s. [recovery] *ricovero, ricovro, ricuperamento,* s. m.

To RECU'R [to run back, to return] *ricorrere, correre indietro, ritornare.*

To recur [to have recourse to] *ricorrere, rifuggire, andare a chiedere ajuto, aver ricorso.*

RECU'RRENTS, s. or recurrent verses [verses that are read the same backward and forward] *versi che si leggono a dritto e a rovescio.*

RECU'RSION, s. [a running back] *ricorso,* s. m.

RECU'RVATED, adj. [bending backwards] *curvo, incurvato.*

RECURVA'TION, } s. [a bending
RECU'RVITY, } back] *curvità, curvatura, curvezza,* s. f.

RECU'SANTS, s. *setta di gente in Inghilterra che rifiutava comunanza con gente d' altre sette in fatto di religione.*

To RECU'SE, a juridical word [to re-

refuſe] ricuſare, rifiutare, è vocabolo uſato ſolo in coſe legali.

RED, adj. roſſo.

Red wine, vin roſſo.

Red cloth, panno roſſo.

Red lips, labbra vermiglie.

To make, or grow red, arroſſire, far divenir roſſo.

Red-hot, infocato.

Red-herring, aringhe ſalate.

Red-deer, il genere de' cervi.

The red-letter tribe, ſoprannome che ſi dava altre volte ai cattolici Romani.

Red-ſtreak [a ſort of apple] ſorta di pomo.

Red-faced, rubicondo, che ha il viſo roſſo.

Red-hair'd, che ha i cappelli roſſi.

Robin-red-breaſt, un pettiroſſo.

Red-ocre, rubrica.

Red, s. [or red colour] roſſo, color roſſo.

I love red, amo il roſſo.

Red [or red paint] roſſo, ſorta di belletto, liſcio.

She paints red, ella s' imbelletta di roſſo.

To REDA'RGUE [to refute] rifiutare, ritorcere l' argomento.

RE'DBREAST, s. [a ſmall bird] pettiroſſo.

RE'DCOAT, s. ſoldato. È voce di diſprezzo.

To RE'DDEN [to make or grow red] arroſſire, far arroſſire.

RE'DDISH, adj. [ſomewhat red] roſſiccio, alquanto roſſo.

REDDI'TION, s. [the act of giving again, or reſtoring] rendimento, s. m. reſtituzione, s. f.

RE'DDLE, s. nome di minerale.

REDE, s. [counſel, advice] conſiglio, avvertimento, avviſo. Obſ.

To REDE [to adviſe] dar conſiglio, dar buoni avvertimenti, conſigliare. Obſ.

To REDE'EM [to buy off, to recover] redimere, ricomprare, riſcattare.

To redeem goods out of pawn, riſcattare o riſcuotere delle robe impegnate.

To redeem time, riparar la perdita del tempo.

REDE'EMABLE, adj. [that may be redeemed] che ſi può redimere, riſcattare.

REDE'EMED, adj. redento, ricomprato, riſcattato.

REDE'EMER, s. [deliverer] redentore, ſalvatore.

Chriſt the redeemer of mankind, Criſto il redentore del genere umano.

REDELI'VERED, adj. [delivered again] liberato di nuovo.

To RE'DEMAND [to aſk again] ridomandare, domandare di nuovo.

REDEMA'NDED, adj. ridomandato.

REDE'MPTION, s. [ranſom] redenzione, s. f.

RE'DEVABLE, adj. [obliged] obbligato, tenuto.

RE'DHOT, adj. [heated to redneſs] infocato.

To REDI'NTEGRATE [to reſtore, to make new] reintegrare, e rintegrare, rinnovare, ritornar ne' primi termini.

REDI'NTEGRATED, adj. reintegrato, e rintegrato, rinnovato.

REDINTEGRA'TION, s. reintegrazione, s. f. rinnovamento, s. m. il reintegrare, riſtabilimento.

RE'DLEAD, s. [minium] minio.

RE'DNESS, s. [red colour] roſſezza, s. f. roſſore, s. m.

RE'DOLENT, adj. [fragrant, perfumed] odorifero.

To REDO'UBLE [to double again, to encreaſe] raddoppiare, addoppiare, creſcere, aumentare, pret. crebbi.

His fever redoubles upon him by night, la febbre gli ſi raddoppia la notte.

REDO'UBLED, adj. raddoppiato, addoppiato, creſciuto, aumentato.

REDO'UBLING, s. raddoppiamento, aumento, s. m.

REDO'UBT, s. [a ſmall ſort of a ſquare figure, which hath no defence but in the front] ridotto, s. m.

REDO'UBTED, adj. [feared] temuto, formidabile, tremendo.

To REDO'UND [to abound over and above] ridondare, traboccare, ſovrabbondare, avanzare, ſoperchiare.

To redound, ridondare, riſultare, tornare.

That will redound to your honour, queſto ridonderà in voſtro onore.

REDRE'SS, s. [amends] rimedio, s. m. riformazione, correzione, emendazione.

To REDRE'SS [to ſet to rights, to reform] riordinare, rimediare, riformare, correggere, pret. correſſi.

To redreſs grievances, rimediare abuſi.

To redreſs the faults of an author, correggere gli errori d' un autore.

To redreſs one's ſelf [to do one's ſelf juſtice] farſi giuſtizia.

REDRE'SSED, adj. riordinato, riformato, corretto.

REDRE'SSER, s. riformatore, s. m. riformatrice, s. f.

REDRE'SSLESS, adj. irremediabile, incorrigibile, ſenza rimedio.

To RE'DSEAR, romperſi al batter del martello, ex. if iron be too hot, it will redſear; that is, break under the hammer. Se il ferro è troppo rovente, ſi rompe al picchio del martello; non regge al battere del martello.

REDU'BBERS, s. [a law term, are ſuch as buy ſtolen cloth, knowing it to be ſo ſtolen, and turn it to ſome other form or colour, that it may not be known] coſì ſon chiamati con termine legale coloro, che comprano del panno che è ſtato rubato, ſapendo eſſer tale, e poi lo traſformano o tingono d' un altro colore per non eſſere ſcoperti.

To REDU'CE [to bring] ridurre, pret. riduſſi.

To reduce into powder, ridurre in polvere.

To reduce to an extremity, ridurre all' eſtremità.

To reduce a town [to bring it into ſubjection] ridurre, debellare, o eſpugnare una terra, una città.

To reduce one to his former health, riſtorare uno nella priſtina ſalute.

REDU'CED, adj. ridotto.

REDU'CIBLE, adj. [that may be reduced] reducibile, che ſi può ridurre.

REDU'CING, } s. riduzione, s. f. riducimento, s. m.
REDU'CTION, }

REDU'CTIVE, adj. [that ſerves to reduce] riduttivo, che ajuta a ridurre.

Reductive ſalt [in chemiſtry] ſale riduttivo.

REDU'NDANCE, } s. [ſuperabundance] colmatura, ſoprabbondanza, ſuperfluità, s. f.
REDU'NDANCY, }

REDU'NDANT, adj. [overflowing, abounding, ſuperfluous] avanzante, ſoprabbondante, ſoprabbondevole, ſopravanzante, ſuperfluo.

To REDU'PLICATE [or redouble] raddoppiare, addoppiare, creſcere, aumentare, pret. crebbi.

REDU'PLICATED, adj. raddoppiato, addoppiato, creſciuto, aumentato.

REDUPLICA'TION, s. raddoppiamento, aumento, s. m.

REDU'PLICATIVE, adj. [that redoubles] riduplicativo, aumentativo.

RE'DWING, s. [a bird] nome d' un uccelletto.

To REE'CHO [to echo back] echeggiare.

RE'ECHY, adj. [ſmoky, ſooty] calginoſo, affumicato.

REED, s. [a plant growing in fenny or watry places] canna, s. m.

Reed mace, canna ſalvatica.

Reed-plot, or reed-bank, un canneto; luogo dove ſon piantate le canne.

RE'EDY, adj. [full of reeds] cannoſo, adj. pien di canne.

REEK, s. [mow, heap of corn or hay] un covone di grano o di fieno.

Reek [ſteam, vapour] fumo, vapore, s. m.

To REEK [to caſt a ſteam or ſmoke] fumare, far del fumo.

His body reeked with ſweat, il ſuo corpo fumava di ſudore.

RE'EKING, adj. fumante, che fuma.

REEL, s. [a device to ſkain yarn] aſpo, naſpo, arcolajo.

To REEL [to wind] aggomitolare.

To reel thread, aggomitolar filo o accia.

To reel [to ſtagger] traballare, vacillare, barcollare.

RE'ELED, adj. aggomitolato, v. To reel.

RE'ELER, s. quello, o quella che aggomitola.

RE'ELING, s. barcollamento, vacillamento, s. m.

To REE'NTER [to enter again, to take poſſeſſion again] rientrare in poſſeſſo, ripigliare il poſſeſſo, eſſer reintegrato.

To REESTA'BLISH [to eſtabliſh or ſettle again] riſtabilire, riordinare, preſ. riſtabiliſco.

REESTABLISHED, adj. riſtabilito, riordinato.

REESTA'BLISHING, s. *riſtabilimento*, s. m.

RE'EVE, s. [the bailiff of a franchiſe or manor] *guardiano d' un feudo.*

To RE'EVE [a term uſed by ſailors, for to put in or pull through] *tirare una corda.*

REEXAMINA'TION, s. [a ſecond examination] *una ſeconda eſaminazione.*

To REEXA'MINE [to examine again] *eſaminare di nuovo, eſaminare un' altra volta.*

To reexamine an account, *rivedere un conto, riſcontrarlo.*

REEXA'MINED, adj. *eſaminato di nuovo.*

REFE'CTION, s. [repaſt, meal] *refezione*, s. f. *paſto*, s. m.

REFE'CTORY, s. [a room wherein friers and nuns eat together] *refettorio*, s. m. *luogo dove i religioſi clauſtrali ſi riducono inſieme a mangiare.*

To REFE'L [to confute] *confutare, riprovare.*

REFE'LLED, adj. *confutato, riprovato.*

REFE'LLING, s. *confutamento*, s. m. *il confutare.*

To REFE'R [to ſend back, to direct to a paſſage in a book] *riferire, rimandare, rimettere.*

He refers me to a paſſage of the ſcripture, *mi riferiſce ad un paſſo della ſcrittura.*

The court has referred the parties to their proper judge, *il magiſtrato ha rimandate le parti al loro giudice competente.*

I refer it to you, *lo riferiſco, lo rimetto a voi, mi ſto al voſtro parere.*

To refer a difference to arbitration, *ſtarſene al giudicio degli arbitri, rimettere una differenza all' arbitrio degli arbitri.*

REFERE'E, s [arbitrator] *arbitro.*

RE'FERENCE, s. [a mark in a book, directing the reader to the margin, or ſome other place] *riferenza, poſtilla*, s. f.

Reference [arbitration] *arbitrato*, s. m. *giudicio d' arbitri.*

In reference to that, *in quanto a ciò.*

RE'FERENDARY, s. [an office in the court of chancery] *riferendario*, s. m.

REFE'RRED, adj. *riferito, v.* To refer.

To REFINE [to make finer, to purge, to purify] *raffinare, affinare, purgare, purificare.*

To refine gold, *raffinare, o affinare dell' oro.*

To refine a liquor, *raffinare, purificare, chiarificare un liquore.*

REFI'NED, adj. *raffinato, v.* To refine.

Refined language, *lingua pura, parlar forbito.*

REFI'NEDLY, adv. [with affected elegance] *con eleganza troppo ſtudiata; raffinatamente.*

REFI'NER, s. *affinatore*, s. m.

REF'INING, s. *affinamento*, s. m. *l' affinare.*

To REFI'T a ſhip [to fit it out again] *racconciare un vaſcello, ammannarlo.*

REFI'TTED, adj. *racconciato, ammannato.*

REFI'TTING, s. *ammannamento, racconcio, racconciamento*, s. m.

REFLECTED, adj. *rifleſſo.*

To REFLE'CT [to beat or ſend back light or heat] *riflettere, ribattere, ripercuotere, rimandare indietro, e diceſi propriamente de' raggi e del calore.*

To reflect upon [to ſpeak ill, to cenſure or reproach] *parlar male, calunniare, eſſer ſatirico o pungente.*

To reflect upon a thing [to think ſeriouſly of it] *riflettere ſur una coſa, farci rifleſſione, conſiderarla, peſarla bene.*

To reflect, *riflettere, ruminar nella mente.*

To reflect [to return, to redound] *ritornare, caſcare.*

This reflects upon you, *queſto caſca ſopra di voi.*

REFLE'CTED, adj. *rifleſſo, v.* To reflect.

REFLE'CTING, s. *rifleſſione*, s. f.

Reflecting, adj. [that reflects upon one] *ingiurioſo, offenſivo, oltraggioſo.*

REFLE'CTION, } s. [a beating back]
REFLE'XION, } *rifleſſione, e rifleſſione*, s. f. *riverbero, riverberamento*, s. m. *il riflettere.*

REFLE'XIBILITY, s. [the quality of that which reflects] *qualità rifleſſiva.*

REFLE'XION [conſideration, meditation] *rifleſſione, conſiderazione, meditazione*, s. f.

Reflexion [reproach, abuſe, cenſure] *rifleſſione, ingiurioſa cenſura, ingiuria, nota d' infamia.*

To caſt a reflexion upon, *ſparlar d' uno, infamarlo, dir male di lui, cenſurarlo.*

REFLE'XIVE, adj. [capable of reflecting] *rifleſſivo, che riflette.*

To REFLO'W [to flow back] *ritornare, rimontare verſo la ſorgente, parlando delle acque.*

REFLU'X, s. [a flowing back, the ebbing of the ſea or tide] *rifluſſo*, s. m. *il ritorno della marea.*

REFO'RM, s. [reformation, mending] *riforma, riformagione, riformazione*, s. f.

Reform [diſbanding of ſome part of the army] *riforma, il licenziare parte delle truppe.*

To REFO'RM [to mend, to put in a better form] *riformare, riordinare, dar nuova, e miglior forma.*

To reform [in military affairs, is to reduce a body of men, either by diſbanding the whole, or only breaking a part, and retaining the reſt] *riformare, licenziare; ſbandare parlando de' ſoldati.*

To reform an officer [to bring him lower as to his pay] *riformare un ufficiale, metterlo a mezza paga.*

To reform troops, *riformare, o licenziar delle truppe.*

REFORMA'TION, s. [the act of reforming] *riformazione, riformagione*, s. f.

REFO'RMED, adj. *riformato, v.* To reform.

The reformed religion, *la religione riformata, o proteſtante.*

REFO'RMER, s. [a perſon who reforms] *riformatore*, s. m. *riformatrice*, s. f.

REFO'RMING, s. *riformagione, riformazione*, s. f. *il riformare.*

REFO'RMIST, s. [a monk whoſe diſcipline or rules have been reformed] *un frate riformato.*

To REFRA'CT [to break back again] *refrangere*, pret. *refranſi.*

REFRA'CTED, adj. [a philoſophical term] ex. a refracted beam, *un raggio refratto.*

REFRA'CTEDNESS, } s. [a term uſed
REFRA'CTION, } in natural philoſophy] *refrazione*, s. f.

REFRACTORILY, adv. [or ſtubbornly] *caparbiamente, oſtinatamente.*

REFRACTORINESS, s. [or unrulineſs] *caparbieria, caparbietà, oſtinazione*, s. f.

REFRA'CTORY, adj. [obſtinate, unruly, headſtrong] *caparbio, oſtinato, pertinace, diſubbidiente.*

Refractory child, *fanciullo diſubbidiente.*

To REFRA'IN [to bridle, to curb] *raffrenare, reprimere, moderare, tenere a ſegno.*

To refrain [to forbear] *raffrenarſi, reprimerſi, contenerſi, moderarſi, attenerſi*, pref. *mi contengo, mi aſtengo*, pret. *mi contenni, mi aſtenni.*

REFRA'INING, s. *raffrenamento*, s. m. *il raffrenare.*

REFRA'NE, s. [a Spaniſh proverb] *un proverbio Spagnuolo.*

To REFRE'SH [to recreate] *rinfreſcare, ricreare, riſtorare, prender riſtoro, rifocillare.*

To refreſh [to renew] *rinfreſcare, rinnovare, rinnovellare.*

To refreſh the memory of a thing, *rinfreſcare la memoria di qualche coſa, richiamar a mente qualche coſa, riandarla col penſiero, ricordarſene.*

To refreſh one's ſelf, *rinfreſcarſi, ricrearſi, ripoſarſi, riſtorarſi, rifocillarſi, prender riſtoro.*

To refreſh the hair, *ſpuntare i capelli.*

REFRE'SHED, adj. *rinfreſcato, ricreato, riſtorato, rifocillato; v.* To refreſh.

REFRE'SHER, s. *ricreatore, che rinfreſca, che ricrea.*

REFRE'SHING, s. *rinfreſcamento, ripoſo, refocillamento.*

Refreſhing, adj. [that refreſhes] *che rinfreſca, che rinnova.*

REFRE'SHMENT, s. [*rinfreſcamento, rinfreſco, riſtoro, ripoſo, rifocillamento*, s. m.

To REFRI'GERATE [to cool] *refrigerare, e rifrigerare, rinfreſcare.*

REFRI'GERATED, adj. *refrigerato, e rifrigerato, rinfreſcato.*

REFRI'GERATIVE, adj. [cooling]

ing] *refrigerativo, che ha virtù di refrigerare.*

REFRI'GERATORY, s. [that part of an alembick which is placed about the head of a still, and filled with water to cool it] *rinfrescatojo*, s. m.

REFT, pret. and part. of to reave [took away, taken away, deprived] *privato, privo, tolto, tolto via.*

RE'FUGE, s. [a place of safety, a sanctuary] *refugio, rifugio, scampo, santuario, asilo*, s. m.

He is fled to me for refuge, *è ricorso a me per refugio, è rifuggito da me.*

A refuge [a protector] *rifugio, protettore, appoggio, sostegno*, s. m.

To RE'FUGE [to shelter, to protect] *dar asilo, dar rifugio, proteggere.*

REFU'GED, adj. *rifuggito.*

REFUGE'E, s. [a French protestant, fled for refuge from France] *un rifuggito, un protestante Francese che è fuggito di Francia.*

REFU'LGENCE } s. [brightness,
REFU'LGENCY } splendor] *lustro, splendore.*

REFU'LGENT, adj. [shining] *risulgente, risplendente, lurido.*

To REFU'ND [to pay, to give back money that has been paid] *rifondere, rendere, restituire.*

REFU'SAL, s. [denial] *rifiuto, ricusamento*, s. m. *ripulsa, rinunzia*, s. f.

He met with a refusal, *fu rifiutato, ricusato, ributtato.*

To have the refusal of a thing, *aver la preferenza di scegliere, aver la libertà di prender o di lasciare una cosa.*

REFU'SE, s. [outcast] *resto, rimasuglio, avanzaticcio*, s. m. *fercia*, s. f.

I will not have another man's refuse, *non voglio il resto, il rimasuglio degli altri.*

She is the refuse of the sex, *ella è l' obbrobrio del suo sesso.*

To REFU'SE [to deny, to reject] *rifiutare, ricusare, rigettare, ributtare.*

I will refuse no pains, *non issuggirò fatica alcuna.*

REFU'SED, adj. *rifiutato, ricusato, rigettato, ributtato.*

REFU'SER, s. *rifiutatore*, s. m. *rifiutatrice*, s. f.

REFU'SING, s. *rifiuto, rifiutamento*, s. m.

REFUTA'TION, s. *confutazione*, s. f. *confutamento*, s. m.

To REFU'TE [to confute with reasons] *confutare, convincere, riprovare*, pret. *convinsi.*

REFU'TED, adj. *confutato.*

To REGA'IN [to get again] *riguadagnare, di nuovo guadagnare, riacquistare, ricuperare.*

REGA'INED, adj. *riguadagnato, riacquistato, ricuperato.*

RE'GAL, adj. [royal] *reale, regale di Rè, da Rè.*

The regal fishes, such fishes as by the King's perogative belong to him, as whales, sturgeons, &c. *pesci reali, come la balena, lo storione*, &c.

REGA'LE, s. [a noble treat or entertainment] *regalo, festino*, s. m.

Regale [the prerogative of monarchy] *preragativa reale.*

To REGA'LE [to treat nobly] *regalare, fare un gran regalo, o festino.*

REGA'LIA, s. [the ensigns of the royal dignity] *le insegne reali.*

Regalia [the rights of a King] *le prerogative del Re.*

REGA'LITY, s. [royalness, sovereignty] *realtà, sovranità*, s. f.

REGA'LED, adj. *regalato.*

RE'GALLY, adv. *realmente, regalmente, da Rè.*

REGA'RD, s. [consideration, respect, account] *riguardo, rispetto, conto*, s. m. *considerazione, stima, circospezione*, s. f.

She has a great regard for him, *ella ha un gran riguardo per lui, ella fa grande stima di lui.*

In regard [in consideration] *in riguardo, per riguardo, per rispetto.*

In regard [in comparison] *per rispetto, in quanto a, in paragone di.*

So great regard there was among the ancients in making of war, *tale era la circospezione degli antichi nel far la guerra.*

The regard of the forest [the overseeing and viewing of it] *l' ispezione della foresta.*

To REGA'RD [to heed or consider, to have respect to] *riguardare, avere o portar rispetto, rispettare, aver riguardo, o considerazione.*

You ought to regard his merit, *dovreste riguardare al suo merito, dovreste aver riguardo al suo merito.*

He does not regard what any man says to him, *non si cura, o non si piglia fastidio di quel che altri dice di lui.*

REGA'RDABLE, adj. *riguardevole, da esser riguardato, degno d' esser riguardato.*

REGA'RDANT, adj. [in heraldry, a lion, or such a kind of beast of prey, painted looking behind him] *riguardante.*

REGA'RDED, adj. *riguardato, rispettato.*

REGA'RDER, s. [an officer, whose business is to make the regard of the forest, and overlook all other officers] *ufficiale che ha l' inspezione della foresta.*

REGA'RDLESS, adj. *che non ha riguardo, o considerazione.*

They are so regardless of their liberty, *hanno sì poco riguardo alla loro libertà, fanno sì poco conto della lora libertà.*

REGA'RDLESSLY, adv. [without heed.] *senza riguardo, trascuratamente.*

RE'GENCY, s. [the government of a kingdom during the minority or absence of a prince, by one or more of the subjects] *reggenza*, s. f.

REGE'NERATE, adj. [new born] *rigenerato.*

To REGE'NERATE [to beget again, to cause to be born again] *rigenerare, di nuovo generare.*

REGE'NERATE, s. *rigenerato, di nuovo generato, prodotto di nuovo.*

REGENERA'TION, s. [a new and spiritual birth] *rigenerazione*, s. f.

RE'GENT, s. [one who governs a kingdom during the minority of a Prince] *reggente*, s. m. f.

RE'GICIDE, s. [a king-killer, or the murderer of a King] *regicida, colui che ammazza un Re, o il delitto d' ammazzare un Re.*

REGI'MEN [with physicians, the method to be observed by a patient, with respect to his diet] *reggime, o maniera di vivere prescritta dal medico ad un ammalato.*

RE'GIMENT, s. [government, rule] *reggimento, governo*, s. m.

The regiment of a religious house, *il reggimento, o la regola d' un monastero.*

The regiment of the church, *il governo ecclesiastico.*

Regiment [a body of several companies of soldiers] *reggimento.*

The regiment of our actions, *il reggimento, o la condotta delle nostre azioni.*

RE'GION, s. [country] *regione, provincia*, s. f. *paese*, s. m.

The three regions of the air, *le tre regioni dell' aria.*

The region of the heart, *la sedia del cuore.*

RE'GISTER, s. [a memorial, or book of publick records] *registro*, s. m. *libro, ove sono scritti e registrati gli atti pubblici.*

To enter a thing into a register, *scrivere, o mettere che che si sia nel registro.*

Register [an officer who keeps registers] *ministro che ha cura di registrare, e tener cura degli atti pubblici.*

Register [in printing] *registro.*

Register [in chymistry, a contrivance in furnaces to make the heat more intense or remiss, by letting more or less air come to the fire] *registro, turaccio che chiude la bocca delle fornaci per fare il fuoco più intenso o più mite secondo la quantità dell' aria che vi entra.*

To RE'GISTER [to record, to enter into a register] *registrare, scrivere, notare nel registro.*

To register a thing in one's memory, *scrivere, o imprimere che che si sia nella mente, o nella memoria.*

RE'GISTERED, adj. *registrato, scritto, o notato nel registro.*

REGI'STRY, s. [the office where records are kept, and also the books and rolls are kept] *il luogo dove si tengono i registri.*

RE'GNANT, adj. [principal, chief] *regnante, principale, predominante*

To REGO'RGE [to bring, or cast up, to vomit] *recere, vomitare.*

REGRA'NTED, adj. *di nuovo concesso.*

To REGRA'TE [to drive a huckster's trade] *fare il mestiere di treccone.*

To

To regrate [to offend, to shock] *offendere, far offesa.*
REGRA'TER } s. [a huckster] *rigattiere,* s. m. *rivenditor di vestimenti, di masserizie usate, e più di commestibili*
REGRA'TOR }
REGRE'SS, s. [returning, coming back] *uscita,* s. f. *ritorno,* s. m.
To have a free egress and regress, *avere l' entrata e l' uscita libera, aver il passo franco, o libero.*
To REGRE'SS [to go back, to return] *tornare indietro, dar indietro.*
REGRE'SSION, s. *l' atto del tornar indietro.*
REGRE'T, s. [grief, sorrow, reluctancy] *dispiacere, disgusto, rincrescimento, dolore.*
To do a thing with regret, *fare una cosa contro voglia, di mala voglia, a stento, malvolentieri.*
To REGRE'T [to lament, to grieve for] *rincrescere, aver dolore, compiagnere, lamentare, sentir dispiacere.*
REGRE'TTED, adj. *compianto, lamentato.*
REGU'ERDON, s. [reward, recompence] *guiderdone, premio, ricompensa.*
To REGU'ERDON, *guiderdonare, premiare, ricompensare.*
RE'GULAR, adj. [according to rule, orderly] *regolare, regolato, fatto secondo le regole.*
Regular building, *edificio regolare, fatto con simetria.*
Regular motion, *moto regolare.*
To live a regular life, *menare una vita regolata.*
To do things in a regular way, *fare le cose regolarmente, secondo le regole.*
Regular [exact, punctual] *regolare, esatto, puntuale.*
Regular [not lay nor secular] *regolare, che vive sotto una regola, che non è secolare.*
A regular canon, *un canonico regolare.*
The regular clergy, or the regulars [such as live under some rule or obedience, and lead a monastick life] *i regolari, i monachi, o religiosi claustrali.*
REGULA'RITY, s. [exactness, strict order] *regolarità, puntualità, esattezza,* s. f. *ordine,* s. m.
RE'GULARLY, adv. [according to rule] *regolarmente, secondo le regole.*
Regularly [constantly, precisely] *regolarmente, regolatamente, costantemente, precisamente.*
To RE'GULATE [to set in order, to govern, to direct, to judge] *regolare, dar regola, ordinare, governare, guidare, dirigere,* pret. *diressi.*
To regulate [to frame, to square] *regolare, squadrare.*
To regulate one's expences, *regolare, o ridurre le sue spese.*
To regulate [to decide, to determine] *regolare, decidere; determinare, stabilire,* pret. *decisi,* pref. *stabilisco.*
RE'GULATED, adj. *regolato, v.* To regulate.

REGULA'TION, s. *regola,* s. f.
REGULA'TOR, s. [one who regulates] *regolatore,* s. m.
RE'GULUS, s. [among chymists, is the purest part of any metal or mineral, when the dregs are separated or taken away] *ogni sorta di metallo o di minerale purificato.*
Regulus antimonii, *antimonio purificato.*
To REGU'RGITATE, [to be poured back] *regurgitare, sgorgar indietro.*
To RE'HEAR [to hear again] *udir di nuovo.*
REHE'ARSAL, s. [relation, report] *narrazione, relazione,* s. f.
Rehearsal [a private practice] *prova, ripetizione, recitazione,* s. f.
The rehearsal of an opera, *la prova, o la ripetizione d' un' opera.*
To REHE'ARSE [to tell, to relate] *recitare, narrare, raccontare, referire, contare, dire,* pref. *riferisco, dico,* pret. *dissi.*
To rehearse [to repeat] *ripetere, ridire.*
To rehearse [to practise in private, in order to publick performance] *ripetere.*
To rehearse a play, *ripetere una commedia.*
REHE'ARSED, adj. *raccontato, riferito, contato, narrato, detto, v.* To rehearse.
To REJE'CT [to cast off, to slight, to refuse] *rigettare, ributtare, ricusare, dispregnare.*
REJE'CTABLE, adj. [that may be rejected] *che si deve rigettare, da rigettare.*
REJE'CTED, adj. *rigettato, ributtato, ricusato, dispregiato.*
REJE'CTION, s. *rigettamento,* s. m. *il rigettare.*
REIGN, s. [government by a sovereign prince] *regno,* s. m. *autorità regia.*
To REIGN [to rule as a king or sovereign prince] *regnare, dominare da Rè.*
To reign [to have the sway] *regnare, dominare, signoreggiare.*
To reign [to be in vogue] *regnare, esser in credito, esser in voga, o in istima.*
RE'IGNING, adj. [predominant] *regnante, dominante.*
To REIMBA'RK [to take shipping again] *imbarcarsi di nuovo.*
REIMBA'RKED, adj. *imbarcato di nuovo.*
REIMBA'RKING } s. *nuovo imbarco.*
REIMBA'RKMENT }
To REIMBU'RSE [to pay back again, to repay] *rimborsare.*
REIMBU'RSED, adj. *rimborsato.*
REIMPRE'SSION, s. [a second edition of a book] *seconda edizione d' un libro.*
REIN, s. [a thong of leather for a bridle] *redine,* s. f. *una delle due strisce di cuojo attaccate al morso del cavallo per reggerlo.*
To let loose the reins, *allargar la mano, scior la briglia.*

To hold the reins of the empire [to reign, to sit at the helm] *aver in mano le redini dell' imperio, governare lo stato.*
Reins [kidneys] *reni, arnioni.*
The running of the reins [the gonorrhea] *la gonorrea.*
RE'INARD, s. [a fox] *una volpe.*
To REINFO'RCE [to add new force or strength] *rinforzare, aggiugnere, e accrescer forze, fortificare.*
REINFO'RCED, adj. *rinforzato, fortificato.*
REINFO'RCEMENT, s. [recruit, supply] *rinforzata,* s. f. *rinforzamento, accrescimento di forze.*
To REINGA'GE [to engage again] *attaccar di nuovo la battaglia.*
To REINGRA'TIATE one's self [to get into favour again] *rimettersi nella buona grazia di qualcheduno.*
To RE'INSTATE [to restore to the former state and condition] *ristabilire, rimettere nel primo stato,* pref. *ristabilisco.*
RE'INSTATED, adj. *ristabilito, rimesso nel primo stato.*
RE'INSTATING, s. *ristabilimento,* s. m.
To RE'INTEGRATE [to return one to his own] *reintegrare, e integrare, rimetter nel primo stato.*
REI'NTEGRATED, adj. *reintegrato, e rintegrato.*
To RE'INVERT, verb act. *ristabilire, rimettere nel primo stato, rimettere in possesso.*
To REJO'ICE [to fill with joy, to delight] *rallegrare, indurre allegrezza, e piacere.*
To rejoice, verb neut. [to be merry or glad] *rallegrarsi, prender allegrezza, godere.*
REJO'ICED, adj. *rallegrato.*
REJO'ICING, s. *allegrezza,* s. f. *allegramento,* s. m.
To REJO'IN [to join again, to get together again] *riunire, di nuovo unire,* pref. *riunisco.*
To REJOIN [to reply] *replicare, rispondere,* pret. *risposi.*
REJO'INER, s. [an answer or exception to a replication, a second answer] *seconda risposta, termine legale.*
REJO'LT, s. [shock, succession] *crollo, scossa.*
REIT, s. [sea weed] *pianta marina così chiamata.*
To REI'TERATE [to repeat] *reiterare, ricominciare.*
REI'TERATED, adj. *reiterato.*
REITERA'TION, s. *reiterazione,* s. f.
RELA'PSE, s. [the return of a disease] *ricadimento,* s. m. *ricaduta, recidiva, ricascata,* s. f.
To RELA'PSE [to fall sick again] *riammalarsi, ricascare, o ricadere ammalato.*
To relapse in the same fault, *ricadere in qualche errore, ritornare al medesimo errore, commettere il medesimo errore, ritornare al vomito.*

RELA'PSED, adj. *riammalato*, *v.* To relapse.

To RELA'TE [to tell, to give an account of] *recitare, raccontare, rapportare, riferire, narrare, dire*, pret. *riferisco, dico*, pret. *dissi*.

To relate [to belong to, to be agreeable or answerable] *rassomigliarsi, rassembrarsi, somigliare, esser simile, aver somiglianza*.

RELA'TED, adj. *recitato, raccontato, rapportato, riferito, narrato, detto*.

Related [akin] *parente, cogiunto*.

RELA'TER, s. [he that relates a thing] *relatore*, s m. *che riferisce*.

RELA'TION, s. [account] *relazione, narrazione*, s. f. *ragguaglio*, s. m.

By relation, *per quel che si dice*.

Relation [affinity] *affinità, convenienza, somiglianza, connessione*, s. f.

Relation [kinsman, kinswoman] *un parente, una parente*.

RE'LATIVE, adj. [having relation to] *relativo*.

Pronoun relative, *pronome relativo*.

Relative, s. *relativo*.

RE'LATIVELY, adv. *relativamente*.

To RELA'X [to loosen, to slacken] *rilassare, indebolire, rilasciare*, pref. *indebolisco*.

To relax [to yield, to give way] *cedere, sbattere, detrarre, disalcare*.

To relax one's government, *moderare il rigore o andar più moderato nel rigore del suo governo*.

RELAXA'TION, s. [slackening] *rilassazione*, s. f. *prosciogliment*o, *scioglimento, debilitamento*, s. m.

Relaxation, s. [slackening] *rilassazione*, s. f. *scioglimento, scioglimento, debilitamento*, s. m.

Relaxation [breathing time] *riposo, ristoro*, s. m. *ricreazione*, s. f.

To give now and then some relaxation to one's mind, *dare di quando in quando qualche alleggiamento allo spirito*.

RELA'XED, adj. *rilassato, indebolito*, *v.* To relax.

RELA'Y, s. [the place where the dogs are in readiness to be cast off when the game passes that way] *posta*.

To be in relay, *stare alla posta*.

Relay [fresh hounds] *muta di cani da posta*.

Relays [fresh horses] *cavalli freschi*.

RELE'ASE, s. [a discharge, a setting at liberty] *libertà*, s. f. *scarico*, s. m.

The release of prisoners, *la libertà de' prigioni*.

To RELE'ASE [to set at liberty, to let go] *liberare, mettere in libertà*.

To release [to free] *esentare, fare esente, dispensare*.

To release one from his oath, *sciogliere uno dal giuramento*.

To release one from his promise, *dispensare altrui della sua promessa*.

RELE'ASED, adj. *liberato, messo in libertà*.

RELE'ASEMENT, s. [a releasing or discharging] *libertà*, s. f.

Orders are come for the releasement of ships, *son venuti ordini di lasciar partire i vascelli*.

To RE'LEGATE [to banish to a certain place for a time] *rilegare, mandare in esilio in luogo particolare*.

RE'LEGATED, adj. *rilegato, esiliato*.

RELEGA'TION, s. [a banishment for a time] *rilegamento, esilio*, s. m.

To RELE'NT [to sweat] *sudare, trapelare, distillare*.

The marble relents, *il marmo suda, o trapela*.

The ice relents [melts] *il ghiaccio si fonde, o comincia a fondersi*.

The heat relents [abates, grow less] *il caldo si rallenta, si mitiga, si scema*.

To relent [to grow tender or compassionate] *intenerirsi, muoversi a pietà*.

To relent [to yield] *cedere*.

RELE'NTED, adj. *sudato, trapelato*, *v.* To relent.

RELE'NTING, s. *rallentamento*.

Relenting, adj. *pietoso, tenero, pieno di pietà e di tenerezza*.

RELE'NTLESS, adj. [unpitying, unmoved by kindness or tenderness] *duro, crudele, spietato, tiranno, che non vuole intenerirsi, che non sente compassione*.

RELI'ANCE, s. [trust, dependance, confidence] *fede, fiducia, speranza*.

RE'LICK, s. [certain remains of the bodies or clothes of saints] *reliquia*, s. f. *quello che avanza de' corpi, e cose de' santi*.

He keeps it like a relick, *lo conserva come una reliquia, come una cosa santa*.

Relick, s. *cadavere o cadavero*.

RE'LICT, s. [widow] *una vedova*.

RE'LICKS, s. [remnants of meat] *reliquie, rilievi, rimasugli*.

RELI'EF, s. [comfort, alleviation] *sollievo, conforto, ristoro, alleggiamento, alleviamento*, s. m.

Relief [succour] *soccorso, rinforzo, ajuto*, s. m.

The relief of a hare [the place where she goes to feed in the evening] *il luogo dove la lepre pasce la sera*.

Relief [redress at law] *ricorso*, s. m.

Relief [in carved work] *v.* Relievo.

To RELI'EVE [to comfort, to alleviate] *confortare, alleggerire, alleviare il dolore altrui, ristorare*.

To relieve [to succour, to assist] *soccorrere, assistere, sovvenire, ajutare*, pret. *soccorsi, sovvenni*, pref. *sovvengo*.

To relieve a place, *soccorrere una piazza*.

To relieve one in his necessities, *assistere, o sovvenire altrui nelle sue necessità*.

To relieve a centry, or the guard, *rilevare una sentinella, o la guardia*.

RELI'EVED, adj. *confortato, alleggerito, alleviato, ristorato*, *v.* To relieve.

RELI'EVER, s. *confortatore*, s. m. *confortatrice*, s. f.

RELI'EVO, s. [imbossed work] *rilievo*, s. m. *tutto quello che s'alza dal suo piano, come in opere di scoltura e d'intaglio, o che pare s'alzi come in opere di pittura e di disegno*.

Basso relievo [when the work is but little raised] *basso rilievo, quando le figure non si sollevano tutte dal loro piano*.

Alto-relievo [when the work is much raised] *alto rilievo, quando le figure s' alzano dal loro piano*.

To RELI'GHT [to light anew] *riaccendere*.

RELI'GION, s. [the worship of a deity] *religione*, s. f. *pietà verso Iddio*.

Religion [piety, godliness, *religione, pietà*, s. f.

Religion [particular order of fryars or nuns] *religione, ordine, e regola di religiosi*.

RELI'GIONIST, s. [a bigot to any religious persuasion] *un uomo troppo tenare di alcun punto di religione, o piuttosto di qualche particolar opinione in fatto di religione*.

RELI'GIOUS, adj. [belonging to religion] *religioso, pio, di religione, di pietà, di devozione*.

Religious worship, *culto religioso*.

Religious debates, *dispute di religione, controversie*.

Religious exercises, *esercizi di pietà, o di devozione*.

Religious [pious, godly] *religioso, pio, divoto, che teme Iddio*.

A religious observer of his promise, *inviolabile osservatore della sua promessa*.

Religious [belonging to a religion or regular order] *religioso, appartenente ad un ordine di religiosi*.

A religious habit, *un abito di religioso*.

A religious order, *una religione, ordine e regola di religiosi*.

To be admitted into a religious order, *esser ammesso a qualche religione*.

Religious houses, *case de' religiosi, i conventi, i monasteri*.

A religious, s. *un religioso, un frate, un monaco, colui che milita sotto qualche particolare ordine*.

RELI'GIOUSLY, adv. [or piously] *religiosamente, piamente, con religione*.

Religiously [punctually] *religiosamente, puntualmente, inviolabilmente*.

RELI'GIOUSNESS, s. [godliness] *religione, pietà*, s. f.

To RE'LINQUISH [to forsake] *relinquere, abbandonare, lasciare*.

To relinquish [to yield up, to part with] *redere, dare*, pref. *do*, pret. *diedi*.

RELI'NQUISHED, adj. *lasciato, ceduto, dato*.

Reli'nquisher, s. quello, o quella che relinque, o abbandona.

Reliqui'ary, s. [a shrine or casket, in which the relicks of deceased saints are kept] reliquiario, reliquiere, vaso o altra custodia, dove si tengono e conservano le reliquie.

Re'lish, s. [taste] gusto, sapore, s. m.

To Re'lish [to give a relish or taste] dar buon gusto, o buon sapore.

To relish [to have a good savour] aver buon gusto, o buon sapore.

To relish [to like, to approve] gustare, trovar buono, di suo gusto, approvare.

No meat relishes with me, tutte le carni mi svogliano.

This relished so ill with him, that— questo gli dispiacque tanto, che—

I don't relish your opinion, la vostra opinione non mi quadra.

Re'lishable, adj. gustoso, saporoso, saporito.

Re'lished, adj. che ha buon gusto, gustato, approvato.

To Reli've [to revive, to live anew] rivivere, viver di nuovo.

To Relo've [to love in return] amare chi ama.

Relu'cent, adj. [shining, transparent] lucente, rilucente, trasparente.

To Relu'ct [to be averse to, to strive against] contendere, contrariare, esser contrario, o alieno, resistere, oppugnare, ripugnare, far resistenza, contrastare.

Relu'ctance, } s. [aversion, un-
Relu'ctancy, } willingness, averseness] ripugnanza, resistenza, violenza, avversione, s. f.

To do a thing with reluctancy, fare una cosa con ripugnanza, di mala voglia, a contro cuore, malvolentieri, violentarsi.

To Relu'me, } allumar di nuovo,
To Relu'mine, } illuminar un altra volta.

To Rely [to depend upon] fidarsi, aver fidanza, rimettersi, far capitale.

I depend upon you, mi fido in voi, mi rimetto in voi.

I'll do it, you may rely upon it, siate pur sicuro che lo farò.

Rely'd upon, adj. fidato, confidato, rimesso.

Relying upon, s. fidanza, confidenza, fiducia, s. f.

To Rema'in [to be left] restare, avanzare, rimanere, pref. rimango, pret. rimasi.

To remain behind, restare indietro.

It remains that I shift for myself, nel resto, bisogna che badi a' fatti miei.

Rema'inder, s. [that which remains, or is left] residuo, avanzo, rimasuglio, rilievo, resto, s. m. reliquia, s. f.

The remainder of the money, il residuo, il resto del danaro.

Rema'ining, s. restante, che resta.

Rema'ins, s. [remainer] residuo, avanzo, s. m. reliquie, s. f.

The remains of the army, le reliquie dell' esercito.

The sad remains of his fortune, i tristi avanzi della sua fortuna.

To Rema'ke [to make anew] rifare, far di nuovo.

To Rema'nd [to send back] rimandare, mandar indietro.

Rema'nded, adj. rimandato, mandato indietro.

Re'manent, s. [the part remaining] rimanente; la parte che rimane.

Rema'rk, s. [note, observation] nota, osservazione, s. f.

Remark [note, worth] nota, stima, s. f. conto, s. m.

A person of remark, una persona di nota, o di conto.

To Rema'rk [to observe, to take notice of] notare, por mente, considerare, osservare, far attenzione.

Rema'rkable, adj. [worthy of remark, notable] da notare, notabile, considerabile, segnalato.

Rema'rked, adj. notato, osservato.

Re'mediless, adj. [without or past remedy] irremediabile, irreparabile, senza rimedio.

Re'medyed, adj. rimediato, provveduto, riparato.

Not to be remedied, incurabile, irremediabile.

Re'medy, s. [medicine, physick] rimedio, s. m. tutto ciò che è atto e s'adopera per tor via qualunque male.

To use remedies, servirsi di rimedi, aver ricorso a' rimedi.

Past remedy, incurabile, dove non c' è rimedio.

Remedy [cure, help] rimedio, riparo, ripiego, s. m.

There is no remedy against jealousy, contro la gelosia non val rimedio.

Remedy [at law] ricorso.

Where will you have a remedy? a chi avrete voi ricorso.

To Re'medy [to help] rimediare, por rimedio o riparo, provvedere, riparare.

To Reme'mber [to call to mind] ricordarsi, rammentarsi, ridursi a memoria, sovvenire.

I do not remember his name, non mi ricordo o non mi sovviene del suo nome.

As far as I can remember, per quanto posso ricordarmi.

To remember [to be mindful of, to mind] ricordarsi, pensare, far riflessione, riflettere.

Remember your promise, ricordatevi della promessa vostra.

To remember [to put in mind of] ricordare, ridurre a memoria.

Remember me to him [present my service to him] salutatelo da mia parte, me lo riverisca da mia parte.

Reme'mbrance, s. [remembring, memory] rimembranza, memoria, ricordanza, s. f.

To come to remembrance, venire in memoria, ricordarsi, sovvenire.

To put in remembrance, ridurre a memoria, ricordare.

A remembrance book [a book of remembrance] libro di memorie.

Reme'mbrancer, s. [one who puts in mind] ammonitore, s. m.

The three remembrancers of the Exchequer, i tre segretari della tesoreria.

To Remi'nd [to put in mind] ricordare, rammemorare, ridurre a memoria.

Remi'nded, adj. ricordato, rammemorato.

Re'miniscence, s. [the faculty or power of remembering or calling to mind] reminiscenza, reminiscenzia, s. f. potenza di ritornarsi le cose nella memoria.

Re'miss, adj. [slack, careless] lento, pigro, tardo, infingardo, rimesso, trascurato, negligente.

Re'missible, adj. [pardonable] remissibile, perdonabile.

t Remi'ssion, s. [forgiveness, pardon] remissione, s. f. perdono, s. m.

Re'missly, adv. [negligently, carelessly] rimessamente, lentamente, pigramente, negligentemente.

Re'missness, s. [slackness, carelessness] negligenza, lentezza, infingardia, trascuraggine, freddezza, pigrizia, s. f.

To Remi't [to forgive] rimettere, perdonare, condonare, pret. rimisi.

To remit sins, rimettere o perdonare i peccati.

To remit a debt, perdonare un debito.

To remit [to abate] sminuire, scemare.

To remit something of one's right, cedere alquanto del suo diritto.

To remit [to send back] rimettere, rimandare.

To remit a sum of money by bills of exchange, rimettere una somma di danari per lettere di cambio.

To remit a thing to providence, rimettere, o commettere che che si sia alla provvidenza.

To remit [to abate] diminuirsi, scemarsi, mitigarsi.

The cold weather remits, il freddo diminuisce, si mitiga.

Remi'tment, } s. [return of mo-
Remi'ttance, } ney] rimessa, s. f.

Remi'tted, adj. rimesso, perdonato, v. To remit.

Re'mnant, s. [that which remains or is left of any thing] avanzo, resto, scampolo, s. m.

Re'monstrance, s. [complaint, expostulatory declaration] dichiarazione, dimostranza, s. f. manifesto, s. m.

To Re'monstrate [to show, to make appear] dimostrare, rappresentare, mostrare, far vedere, far palese, provare.

Re'mora, s. [a fabulous fish] remora, pesce favoloso.

Remora [obstacle] ostacolo, impedimento, intoppo, s. m.

To Re'morate [to retard] trattenere,

nere, ritardare, pref. *trattengo,* pret. *trattenni.*

REMO'RSE, s. [check, sting of conscience] *rimorso, rimordimento, riconoscimento d' errori,* s. m. *finderesi,* s. f.

REMO'RSELESS, adj. *senza rimorso.*

REMO'TE, adj. [far distant] *rimoto, remoto, lontano, distante.*

REMO'TENESS, s. [great distance] *lontananza, distanza,* s. f.

REMO'VEABLE, adj. [that may be removed] *che si può rimuovere.*

REMO'VAL, s. [the act of putting out of any place] *l' atto del rimuovere cosa da un luogo.*

Removal, s. [the act of putting away] *l' atto del porre via, del trar via, del buttare.*

Removal, s. [dismission from a post] *il togliere la carica o il posto, il rimuovere da un posto o carica.*

Removal, s. [the state of being removed] *lo essere rimosso.*

REMO'VE, s. [change of place] *cambiamento di luogo.*

Remove, s. [susceptibility of being removed] *attezza a esser rimosso.*

Remove, s. [translation of one to the place of another] *trasporto d' una cosa nel luogo d' un altra; il rimuovere.*

Remove, s. [state of being removed] *l' essere rimosso.*

Remove, s. [act of moving a chesman or draught] *mossa; il muovere una pedina al giuoco delle dame, o un pezzo a quello degli scacchi.*

Remove, s. [the act of changing place] *l' atto del rimuoversi.*

Remove, s. [departure; act of going away] *partenza, l' andar via.*

Remove, s. [a small distance] *poca distanza.*

To remove [to shift lodgings] *sgomberare, e per sincopa sgombrare, portar via masserizie da luogo a luogo, mutar domicilio.*

To remove [to set or take away] *muovere, levare, rimovere, e rimuovere.*

Remove that chair, *levate quella sedia.*

To remove one from all his suspicions, *levare, rimovere ad alcuno tutti i sospetti.*

Wormwood removes all obstructions, *l' assenzio rimove ogni ostruzione.*

To remove from one place to another, *rimovere, o trasportare da un luogo all' altro.*

To remove one out of the way [to kill him, to dispatch him] *disfarsi d' alcuno, spedirlo, ammazzarlo.*

REMO'VED, adj. *rimosso, v.* To remove.

He is removed from his place, *egli è levato dal suo impiego.*

To REMO'UNT [to mount again] *rimontare, montare di nuovo.*

REMO'UNTED, adj. *rimontato.*

To REMU'NERATE [to reward] *rimunerare, ricompensare, guiderdonare, rimeritare.*

REMU'NERATED, adj. *rimunerato, ricompensato, guiderdonato, rimeritato.*

REMUNERA'TION, s. [reward] *rimunerazione, ricompensa,* s. f. *guiderdone,* s. m.

To RENA'VIGATE [to sail again] *navigar di nuovo, di nuovo veleggiare, far vela di nuovo.*

RENCO'UNTER, s. [meeting] *rincontro, incontro,* s. m.

Rencounter [chance fight] *combattimento fatto nel rincontrarsi, sacramuccia.*

To RENCOUNTER [to meet] *scontrare, incontrare, rincontrare.*

To REND [to tear with violence] *squarciare, stracciare, mettere in pezzi, lacerare.*

To RE'NDER [to return] *rendere, restituire,* pret. *resi,* pref. *restituisco.*

To render thanks, *render grazie, ringraziare.*

To render like for like, *render la pariglia, render pan per focaccia.*

To render a place, *rendere una piazza.*

To render a good office, *fare qualche piacere ad uno, servirlo, favorirlo.*

He rendered his master all the offices of a faithful servant, *compì col suo padrone tutte le parti d' un fedel servidore.*

To render [to turn or translate] *traslatare, tradurre,* pref. *traduco,* pret. *tradussi.*

To render one's self considerable, *rendersi famoso, divenir famoso.*

RE'NDERED, *part. di* to render, *reso.*

RE'NDEVOUS } s. [a meeting place]
RE'NDEZVOUS } *posta, luogo prefisso e determinato.*

Rendevous } [a meeting place for
Rendezvous } an army] *piazza d' arme.*

To give a rendezvous, *dar la posta, fissar il luogo dove uno debba incontrarti.*

To RE'NDEVOUS } [to meet] *in-*
To RE'NDEZVOUS } *contrarsi, accozzarsi insieme in un certo luogo, trovarsi alla posta.*

RE'NDIBLE, adj. [that may be rendered] *che si può rendere.*

RENDS, s. [the seams between the planks of a ship] *le fessure d' un navilio le quali si calefatano.*

RENEGA'DE } s. [one who has deny-
RENEGA'DO } ed or renounc'd the christian religion] *un rinnegato, uno apostata,* s. m.

To RENEW [to begin a-new] *rinnovare, rinnuovare, tornar a fare di nuovo, ricominciare, ripigliare a fare, rinnovellare.*

To renew the fight, *rinnovar il combattimento.*

To renew an old friendship with one, *rinnovellare l' antica amicizia con uno.*

RENEW'AL, s. *rinnovamento,* s. m. *rinnovanza, rinnovazione, rinnovellazione,* s. f.

RENEW'ED, adj. *rinnovato, rinnuovato, ricominciato, rinnovellato.*

RENEW'ER, s. *rinnovatore,* s. m.

RENEW'ING, s. *rinnovamento, rinnovellamento,* s. m.

RE'NNET, s. [the maw of a calf] *raglio,* s. m. *materia colla quale si rappiglia il cacio.*

Rennet [a sort of pippin] *appiuola,* s. f. *sorta di mela.*

To RE'NOVATE [to renew, to restore to the first state] *rinnovare, rinnovellare.*

RENOVA'TION, s. [renewing] *rinnovazione, rinnovellazione,* s. f.

To RENO'UNCE [to forsake, to quit claim] *rinunziare, spontaneamente cedere la propria ragione o 'l dominio sopra che che si sia.*

To renounce [to disown] *rinnegare, rifiutare, rigettare.*

To renounce [at cards] *rifiutare, al giuoco delle carte.*

RENO'UNCED, adj. *rinunziato, v.* To renounce.

RENO'UNCING, s. *rinunziamento, rifiuto,* s. m. *rinunziazione, rinunzia,* s. f.

RENO'WN, s. [fame, great reputation] *rinomanza, fama, nominanza, rinomata, rinominanza,* s. f. *rinomo, nome,* s. m.

RENO'WNED, adj. [famous] *rinomato, famoso, illustre.*

RENT, s. [a sum of money issuing yearly out of lands and tenements] *rendita, entrata,* s. f. *facoltà che si traggono da' terreni o da altro.*

A yearly rent, *una rendita annuale.*

Rent service, *rendita feudale.*

Land-rent, *terratico.*

House-rent, *pigione di casa.*

Rent [from to rend] *squarcio, taglio,* s. m.

Rent in the church [schism] *scisma, divisione della chiesa.*

Rent, adj. [from to rend] *squarciato, stracciato.*

To RENT [to take by rent] *torre a pigione, appigionare.*

RE'NTABLE, adj. [that may be rented] *che si può torre a pigione.*

RE'NTAL, s. [an account of rents] *conto di rendite.*

RE'NTED, adj. *tolto a pigione.*

RE'NTER, s. [he that holds by paying rent] *colui che ha preso a pigione.*

RE'NVERSED, adj. [over-turned] *rovesciato.*

RENUNCIA'TION, s. [renouncing] *rinunzia, rinunziazione,* s. f. *rinunziamento,* s. m.

REPA'IR, s. [repairing, mending] *riparazione, ristaurazione, rinnovazione,* s. f.

To keep a house in repair, *fare le riparazioni d' una casa, riparar una casa.*

A house kept in good repair, *una casa ben tenuta, o ben riparata.*

The REPA'IR of a ship, *il racconciamento d' un vascello.*

To repair [to mend a building] *riparare,*

rare, rifare, riſtaurare, riſarcire un edificio, pref. *riſarciſco*.

To repair a figure of marble, *riſtaurare una figura di marmo*.

To repair an injury [to give ſatisfaction for it] *riparare un torto*.

To repair [to make up] a loſs, *riſarcire una perdita*.

To repair [to refit] a ſhattered ſhip, *racconciare un vaſcello ſdruſcito*.

To repair, verb neut. [to go] *andare, traſferirſi, renderſi, condurſi*.

He was ordered to repair to court, *ricevè ordine di traſferirſi alla corte*.

To repair to one for a thing, *ricorrere, o aver ricorſo ad uno per che che ſia*.

REPA'IRABLE, adj. *riparabile, rimediabile, che ſi può riparare, o rimediare*

REPA'IRED, adj. *riparato, rifatto, riſtaurato, riſarcito*, v. To repair.

Not to be repaired, *irreparabile, irremediabile*.

REPA'IRER, s. *riparatore*, s. m. *che ripara*.

Repairer [an artificer who chaſes figures and beautifies ſword hilts] *artefice che ſcolpiſce figure, e puliſce guardie di ſpade*.

REPARA'TION, s. [mending] *riparazione, riſtaurazione*, s. f. *riparo*, s. m.

Reparation [ſatisfaction] *riparazione, ſodisfazione*, s. f.

To make one a reparation for an injury, *dar ſodisfazione ad uno per qualche torto fattogli*.

RE'PARTEE, s. [a quick and witty reply, or anſwer] *riſpoſta pronta e acuta, una botta, una buona riſpoſta*.

REPARTI'TION, s. [ſubdiviſion] *ſpartizione, ſpartigione, diviſione*, s. f.

To REPA'SS [to paſs over again] *ripaſſare, di nuovo paſſare*.

To repaſs a river, *ripaſſare un fiume*.

REPA'ST, s. [meal] *paſto*, s. m.

To REPA'Y [to pay again] *pagare di nuovo, o una ſeconda volta*.

To repay [to pay back] *rimborſare, rendere*, pret. *reſi*.

To repay a benefit, *riconoſcere un beneficio, rendere un beneficio*.

REPAY'ED, adj. *pagato, rimborſato, reſo*.

REPA'YING, } s. *doppio pagamento*.
REPA'YMENT, }

REPE'AL, s. [a revoking] *rivocazione, e rivocagione*, s. f.

To REPE'AL [to revoke, to annul] *rivocare, aunullare, caſſare, cancellare, abolire*, pref. *aboliſco*.

REPE'ALABLE, adj. *rivocabile*.

REPE'ALED, adj. *rivocato, annullato, caſſato, cancellato, abolito*.

REPE'ALING, s. *rivocamento*, s. m. *rivocazione, rivocagione*, s. f.

To REPE'AT [to ſay the ſame thing over again] *ripetere, tornar a dire di nuovo, ridire, replicare*, pref. *ridico*, pret. *ridiſſi*.

REPE'ATED, adj. *ridetto, replicato, ripetuto*.

REPE'ATER, s. *ripetitore*, s. m.

Repeater, or repeating watch, *un oriuolo a ripetizione*.

REPE'ATING, s. *ripetizione*, s. f.

REPE'EK, s. [a term uſed at the game called picket] *ripicco*, s. m.

To REPE'EK, *far ripicco*.

To REPE'L [to beat back, to drive back] *ricacciare, rigittare, riſpignere, riſoſpignere, ſcacciare*, pref. *ripingo, riſoſpingo*, pret. *riſpinſi, riſoſpinſi*.

To repel an objection, *confutare un' obbiezione*.

RE'PELLED, adj. *ricacciato, rigittato, riſpinto, riſoſpinto, ſcacciato*.

REPE'LLER, s. *ſcacciatore*, s. m.

To REPE'NT [to be ſorry for what one has done or omitted] *pentirſi, dolèrſi*.

I don't at all repent it, *non me ne pento mica*.

REPE'NTANCE, s. [a ſorrow for paſt deeds or omiſſions] *pentimento*, s. m.

REPE'NTANT, } adj. [penitent, ſor-
REPE'NTING, } rowful] *penitente, che ſi pente*.

REPE'NTED of, adj. *pentito*.

To REPE'OPLE [to ſtock with people anew] *di nuovo popolare*.

REPEOPLED, adj. *di nuovo popolato*.

REPERCU'SSION, s. [the act of driving back, rebound] *ripercuſſione*, s. f. *ripercuotimento*, s. m.

REPERCU'SSIVE, adj. [which ſtrikes or rebounds back] *ripercuſſivo, che ripercuote, che rimanda indietro, che ribatte*.

RE'PERTORY, s. [a book in which things are methodically placed for the more ready finding] *repertorio*, s. m. *indice, tavola. per la quale ſi può facilmente ritrovare*.

REPETI'TION, s. [iteration of the ſame thing] *ripetizione, l' atto del ripetere e far di nuovo*.

Repetition [recital of the ſame words over again; rehearſal] *ripetizione, prova; e diceſi di coſe teatrali ſpecialmente*.

To REPI'NE [to grieve, to grudge at] *rincreſcere, aver diſpiacere, dolerſi, rimbrottare, rimproverare, invidiare*.

Envious men always repine at one's good fortune, *agli invidioſi rincreſce molto l' altrui buona fortuna; gl' invidioſi doglionſi dell' altrui felicità*.

He repines at every thing he gives, *rimprovera tutto quel che da; ſi pente di tutto quel che da*.

REPI'NING, s. *diſpiacere, travaglio, faſtidio, dolore*, s. m. *noja, moleſtia*, s. f.

A factious repining, *ammutinamento*, s. m. *ſedizione*, s. f.

To REPLA'NT [to plant again] *ripiantare, di nuovo piantare*.

REPLA'NTED, adj. *ripiantato, di nuovo piantato*.

To REPLE'AD [to plead again to that which was once before pleaded] *piatire o litigare di nuovo per quel che uno aveva prima piatito o litigato*.

To REPLE'NISH [to fill again] *riempiere, di nuovo empiere*.

REPLE'NISHED, adj. *riempito*.

REPLE'TE, adj. [full, filled] *pieno, riempito*.

REPLE'TION, s. *replezione*, s. f. *riempimento*, s. m.

REPLE'VIN, or REPLE'VY, s. [the releaſing of cattle or other goods diſtrained by virtue of a writ called Replegiare, upon ſurety to anſwer the diſtrainer's ſuit] *reintegrazione*, s. f.

REPLE'VY [bailing of a man] *malleveria, mallevadoria*, s. f.

To REPLE'VY [to recover] *ricuperare, riavere, riottenere*.

To replevy a diſtreſs [to recover goods diſtrained] *ricovrare quello del quale altri s' era impoſſeſſato*.

REPLE'VIED, adj. *ricovrato*.

REPLICA'TION, s. [the plaintiff's reply to the defendant's anſwer] *replica, riſpoſta*, s. f.

RE'PLY, s. [anſwer] *replica, riſpoſta*.

To RE'PLY [to anſwer] *replicare, tornar di nuovo a dire, ſoggiugnere*, pret. *ſoggiunſi*.

'Tis true, replied he, *è vero, ſoggiunſe egli*.

RE'PLYED, adj. *replicato, ſoggiunto*.

RE'PLYING, s. *replica*, s. f.

REPO'RT, s. [rumour, talk] *fama, voce*, s. f. *grido, biſbiglio, romore*, s. m.

There's a report of her being dead, *corre voce ch' ella ſia morta*.

There's ſuch a report, *corre un tal biſbiglio o romore; così ſi dice*.

By report, *per fama, per quel che ſi dice, o ſi diſcorre*.

Report [relation, account] *ragguaglio, rapporto, rapportamento*, s. m. *narrazione, relazione, narrativa*, s. f.

Report [a repetition of a caſe debated] *rapporto*.

To make a report of a cauſe, *fare il rapporto d' una cauſa o d' un proceſſo*.

Report [name, reputation] *riputazione, fama*, s. f. *nome, odòre, concètto*.

To have an ill report, *avere una cattiva riputazione o fama, eſſere in cattivo concetto*.

The report of a gun, *lo ſtrepito, lo ſcoppio d' un cannone, o altr' arme da fuoco*.

To REPO'RT [to tell, or relate] *rapportare, riferire, riportare, ragguagliare, raccontare*, pref. *riferiſco*.

To report [to give an account of] *rapportare, dar conto, eſporre, dichiarare*, pref. *eſpongo*, pret. *eſpoſi*.

To report a law ſuit, *rapportare, eſporre lo ſtato, e le particolarità d' un proceſſo*.

To report ill of one, *ſparlar d' uno, parlar male di lui*.

To report [to make a noiſe as a gun] *ſcoppiare, far romore come quello degli ar-*

archibusi, o di simili strumenti quando si scaricano.

REPO'RTED, adj. *rapportato, riferito, v.* To report.

It is reported, *corre voce, porta la fama, si dice.*

A man ill reported of, *un uomo di cattiva riputazione o fama; un uomo che è in cattivo concetto.*

I can't believe what is reported of him, *non posso credere quel che mi vien riferito di lui.*

REPO'RTER, s. *rapportatore,* s. m.

REPO'SE, s. [rest] *riposo,* s. m. *quiete,* s. f.

To take some repose, *prender un poco di riposo.*

To REPO'SE [to take some rest] *riposare, prender riposo.*

To repose [to commit or leave a thing to one's care] *riposarsi sopra uno, starsene a lui, lasciargliene tutta la cura, commettere, rimettere.*

To repose one's trust in one, *fidarsi o riposarsi sopra uno, mettere ogni confidenza in lui.*

To repose an entire confidence in one, *rimettersi intieramente nelle altrui mani; mettere ogni fiducia in alcuno.*

REPO'SED, adj. *riposato, v.* To repose.

He has acted contrary to the trust reposed in him, *egli ha operato contro la fiducia che s' aveva in lui.*

REPO'SEDLY, *riposatamente, quietamente, tranquillamente.*

REPOSI'TION, s. [a settling again] *stabilimento,* s. m.

The reposition of the forest [an act whereby several forest grounds made purlieu, were laid to the forest again] *stabilimento della foresta.*

REPO'SITORY, s. [a store-house or place where things are laid up and kept] *ripositorio, ripostiglio,* s. m. *luogo da riporvi che che si sia.*

To RE'POSESS [to put or go into possession again] *rimettere o rientrare in possesso.*

RE'POSSESSED, adj. *rimesso, o rientrato in possesso.*

To RE'PREHEND [to reprove, or rebuke] *riprendere, ammonire, correggere,* pret. *ripresi, corressi,* pres. *ammonisco.*

RE'PREHENDED, adj. *ripreso, ammonito, corretto.*

REPREHE'NSIBLE, adj. [that may be reprehended, reproveable] *riprensibile, riprendevole.*

REPREHE'NSION, s. [reproof, reprimand] *riprensione, correzione, ammonizione, ripassata,* s. f.

To RE'PRESENT [to make appear, to shew] *ripresentare, rappresentare, chiaramente mostrare, far vedere, far conoscere, significare, mettere avanti agli occhi.*

To represent [to describe] *rappresentare, figurare, esprimere, descrivere,* pret. *descrissi.*

To represent [to be in the room of one, to supply his place] *rappresentare, tener il luogo d'un altro.*

REPRESENTA'TION, s. [a representing, description] *rappresentazione, descrizione,* s. f.

REPRESE'NTATIVE, s. [one who represents the person of another] *un rappresentante, un rappresentatore.*

The members of the house of Commons are the representatives of the people, *i membri della camera bassa sono i rappresentanti del popolo.*

RE'PRESENTED, adj. *rappresentato, v.* To represent.

RE'PRESENTING, s. *rappresentamento,* s. m. *rappresentazione,* s. f. *il rappresentare.*

REPRESE'NTMENT, s. representation] *rappresentazione,* s. f. *rappresentamento,* s. m.

To REPRE'SS [to restrain, to keep back, to curb] *reprimere, raffrenare, rintuzzare, tenere a segno, moderare.*

REPRE'SSED, adj. *represso, raffrenato, rintuzzato.*

REPRE'SSER, s. *quello o quella che reprime.*

REPRE'SSING, s. *reprimento,* s. m. *il reprimere.*

REPRI'EVE, s. [a warrant for the suspending the execution of a malefactor] *sospensione, prolungazione, differimento di giustizia.*

To REPRI'EVE [to respite] a malefactor, *sospendere, prolongare, o differire l' esecuzione d' un reo condannato alla morte.*

RE'PRIMAND, s. [reproof, check, rebuke] *riprensione, ammonizione, ripassata, sbrigliatura, sbarbazzata,* s. f.

To RE'PRIMAND [to reprove sharply and with authority] *riprendere, ammonir biasimando, fare una ripassata,* pret. *ripresi.*

RE'PRIMANDED, adj. *ripreso, biasimato.*

To RE'PRINT [to print again] *ristampare, di nuovo stampare.*

RE'PRINTED, adj. *ristampato.*

RE'PRINTING, s. *il ristampare.*

REPRI'SAL } s [a seizing upon an REPRI'SALS } equivalent for the loss sustained upon another's account, or by another] *ripresaglia, rappresaglia,* s. f.

To make use of reprisals, *usar rappresaglie.*

RE'PRISE, s. [the act of taking something in retaliation of injury] *ripresaglia, rappresaglia.*

Reprises [a law word for charges and duties] *costo, e spese.*

Besides all reprises, *senza le spese.*

REPROACH, s. [upbraiding] *rimprovero,* s. m.

Reproach [infamy] *rimprovero, obbrobrio, vituperio,* s. m. *infamia, ignominia, villania,* s. f.

Reproach [injury, offence] *ingiuria, offesa,* s. f. *affronto, oltraggio,* s. m.

To REPRO'ACH [to upbraid, to cast in the teeth] *rimproverare, rinfacciare, rimprocciare.*

To reproach one with ingratitude, *rimproverare, rinfacciare ad alcuno la sua ingratitudine, tassarlo d' ingratitudine.*

To reproach with, *accusare, tassare.*

REPRO'ACHABLE, adj. [that deserves reproach] *biasimevole, degno di biasimo, vituperevole.*

REPRO'ACHED, adj. *rimproverato, rinfacciato, rimprocciato, accusato, tassato.*

REPRO'ACHFUL, adj. [abusive, injurious] *ingiurioso, oltraggioso, vituperoso.*

Reproachful language, *parole ingiuriose.*

To give one reproachful language, *ingiuriare, oltraggiare, maltrattare alcuno.*

REPRO'ACHFULLY, adv. *oltraggiosamente, ingiuriosamente, vituperosamente.*

REPRO'ACHING, s. *rimprovero, rimproccio,* s. m. *il rimproverare.*

RE'PROBATE, s. [one predestinated to damnation] *reprobo,* s. m.

Reprobate [a very wicked person] *un reprobo, un maligno, un malvagio.*

To RE'PROBATE [to cast off, to reject utterly] *reprobare, riprovare, dannare come malvagio.*

RE'PROBATED, adj. *reprobato, riprovato, condannato.*

REPROBA'TION, s. *reprobazione,* s. f. *l' esser reprobo.*

To RE'PRODUCE [to produce again, to produce anew] *riprodurre, produrre di nuovo.*

REPRODU'CTION, s. [the act of producing anew] *riproduzione, il produrre di nuovo.*

REPRO'OF, s. [check, reprimand] *riprensione, ammonizione, ripassata,* s. f. *rabuffo,* s. m.

REPRO'VEABLE, adj. [worthy of reproof] *riprensibile, riprendevole, degno di riprensione.*

To REPRO'VE [to check, to rebuke] *riprendere, ammonire biasimando,* pret. *ripresi.*

REPRO'VED, adj. *ripreso, ammonito aspramente.*

REPRO'VER, s. *riprenditore,* s. m. *riprenditrice,* s. f.

REPRO'VING, s. *riprendimento,* s. m. *il riprendere.*

To REPRU'NE [to prune a second time] *potar di nuovo le viti, ò cimar di nuovo gli alberi.*

RE'PTILE, s. [any thing that crawls upon his belly] *rettile,* s. m. *ogni animale, che va colle pancia per terra.*

REPU'BLICAN, s. [a commonwealth's man] *repubblichista, uno nato in repubblica.*

REPU'BLICK, s. [commonwealth, free state] *repubblica,* s. f.

REPU'DIABLE, adj. *degno d'esser ripudiato.*

To REPU'DIATE [to divorce, to put away] *ripudiare, rifiutare.*

REPU'DIATED, adj. *ripudiato, rifiutato.*

REPUDIA'TION, s. *ripudio,* s. m. *il ripudiare.*

To RE'PUGN [to refift, or be contrary] ripugnare, oftare, contradiare, opporfi, pref. oppongo.

REPU'GNANCE } s. [contrariety, REPU'GNANCY } contradiction] ripugnanza, contradizione, controverfia, contrarietà, s. f.

The repugnancy of two propofitions, la ripugnanza di due propofizioni.

Repugnancy [averfenefs] ripugnanza, avverfione, difficoltà nel fare che che fi fia.

REPU'GNANT, adj. [contrary] appofto, contrario, che ripugna.

REPU'GNANTLY, adv. con ripugnanza, con difficoltà, a mala pena, di mala voglia.

Repugnantly, adv. oppoftamente, in maniera oppofta, contradittoriamente.

REPU'LSE, s. [refufal, denial] ripulfa, negativa, s. f.

To meet with a repulfe, effer ripulfato.

To repulfe [to deny] ripulfare, far ripulfa, rifiutare.

REPU'LSED, adj. ripulfato, rifiutato.

REPU'LSING } s. ripulfa, s. f. rifiuto, REPU'LSION } s. m.

RE'PUTABLE, adj. [of good repute] onorato, che è in buona riputazione.

REPUTA'TION, s. [fame, credit, efteem] riputazione, fama, ftima, opinione, s. f. credito, onore, concetto, s. m.

She is ruined in her reputation, ella ha perduta la riputazione, o 'l concetto.

REPU'TE, s. [reputation] riputazione, ftima, opinione, fama, s. f. nome, credito, concetto, s. m.

To be in good repute, effer in buon concetto.

To REPU'TE [to count, to look upon] reputare, e riputare, giudicare, ftimare, credere, tenere in concetto.

They repute him a wife man, vien riputato uomo dabbene, è in concetto d' uomo dabbene.

REPU'TED, adj. riputato, giudicato, ftimato, creduto, tenuto.

REQUE'ST, s. [petition] richiefta, preghiera, domanda, fupplica, s. f. richiedimento, s. m.

At my requeft, a mia richiefta, a mia preghiera, o domanda.

A mafter of requefts, un maeftro delle fuppliche.

The court of requefts, la camera, o la corte delle fuppliche.

To make a requeft of one, fare una richiefta o una domanda ad uno, pregare o domandare uno di qualche cofa, richiedere qualche cofa ad uno.

Requeft [vogue] richiefta, fama, riputazione, s. f. credito, s. m.

They are in no requeft, non fono in alcun modo richiefti, non fono in neffun credito, non fono ricercati.

To REQUE'ST [to entreat, to defire] richiedere, domandare, chiedere pregando, fupplicare.

REQUE'STED, adj. richiefto, domandato, fupplicato.

REQUE'STER, s. [petitioner] richieditore, fupplicante.

RE'QUIEM, s. [a prayer for the reft of the fouls of deceafed perfons] orazione per li morti.

REQUI'RABLE, adj. [fit to be required] ricercabile, degno di effere ricercato.

To REQUI'RE [to afk, to demand] chiedere, richiedere, domandare, ricercare, efigere.

As far as neceffity fhall require, per quanto la neceffità lo richiederà.

As occafion fhall require, fecondo che il bifogno lo ricercherà.

That requires confideration, ciò domanda confiderazione.

To require fatisfaction, domandar foddisfazione.

REQUI'RED, adj. chiefto, richiefto, domandato, ricercato, efatto.

RE'QUISITE, adj. [neceffary, convenient] requifito, neceffario, conveniente, opportuno.

Requifite, s. [a thing requifite] un requifito, una circoftanza neceffaria.

RE'QUISITELY, adv. [neceffarily; in a requifite manner] neceffariamente, in modo neceffario.

RE'QUISITENESS, s. [neceffity, the ftate of being requifite] neceffità fecondo lo natura delle cofe.

REQUI'TAL, s. [reward, acknowledgment] ricompenfa, riconofcenza, ricompenfazione, s. f. contraccambio, s. m.

To REQUI'TE [to reward] compenfare, ricompenfare, rimunerare, contraccambiare, dare o rendere il contraccambio, riconofcere, rimeritare, pret. riconobbi.

REQUI'TED, adj. compenfato, ricompenfato, rimunerato, contraccambiato, riconofciuto, rimeritato.

REQUI'TER, s. rimuneratore, s. m. rimuneratrice, s. f.

REQUI'TING, s. ricompenfamento, s. m. ricompenfazione, s. f.

RE'REMOUSE, s. [bat] nottola, s. f. vifpiftrello, pipiftrello, s. m.

RE'REWARD, s. [the rear of an army] retroguardia, s. f. retroguardo, s. m.

To RE'SAIL [to fail back] veleggiare o navigare indietro, tornare navigando al luogo d' onde s' era partito.

RESALUTA'TION, s. il rifalutare.

To RESALU'TE [to falute again] rifalutare, di nuovo falutare.

RESALU'TED, adj. rifalutato.

To RESCI'ND [to repel, to difannul] annullare, caffare, cancellare, abolire, pref. abolifco.

RESCI'NDED, adj. annullato, caffato, cancellato, abolito.

RECI'SSION, s. [difannulling] annullazione, caffazione, s. f.

RE'SCISSORY, adj. [making void] che annulla.

To RE'SCRIBE [to write back] fcriver di nuovo a chi già t' è fcritto, o a chi ti fcrive.

To refcribe [to write over again] copiare, ricopiare, trafcrivere quello che già fi è fcritto.

RE'SCRIPT, s. [edict] editto, refcritto.

RE'SCUE, s. [deliverance] fcampo, ricovero, e ricovro, s. m. liberazione, s. f.

To RE'SCUE [to fave, to deliver, to free from an oppreffor] rifcuotere, levar d' impegno, liberare, campare, fcampare, ricoverare.

RE'SCUED, adj. rifcoffo, liberato, campato, fcampato, ricoverato.

RE'SCUER, s. liberatore, s. m. liberatrice, s. f.

RE'SCUING, s. rifcoffa, liberazione, s. f. campo, fcampo, s. m.

RESE'ARCH, s. [a ftrict enquiry] inchefta, inchiefta, s. f. ricercamento, s. m.

To RESE'ARCH [to make a ftrict enquiry] inchiedere, minutamente domandare.

RESE'MBLANCE, s. [likenefs] fomiglianza, e fimiglianza, s. f.

This bears no refemblance with that, quefto non ha veruna fomiglianza con quello.

To RESE'MBLE [to be like] fimigliare, o fomigliare, aver fimiglianza, effer fimile, raffomigliare, raffembrare.

He refembles his father, egli raffomiglia a fuo padre.

RESE'MBLED, adj. fimigliato, e fomigliato, raffomigliato, raffembrato.

RESE'MBLING, adj. raffomigliante, fimile, fimiglievole, fomigliante.

Refembling, s. fomiglianza, e fimiglianza, raffomiglianza, fimilitudine, s. f.

To RE'SEND [to fend back, to fend again] rimandare, mandar di nuovo, rimandar indietro, mandar indietro.

To RESE'NT [to take well or ill] pigliar in buona o mala parte.

To refent [to take ill, to confider as an injury or affront] rifentirfi, offenderfi, pigliar per ingiuria, pigliar per affronto e per offefa.

To refent an affront, rifentirfi, o far rifentimento d' un' ingiuria.

RESE'NTED, adj. rifentito.

RESE'NTING } s. [fenfible appre-RESE'NTMENT } henfion of an injury] rifentimento, s. m. il rifentirfi.

RESE'NTINGLY, adv. rifentitamente, con rifentimento.

RESERVA'TION, s. [a referving or keeping in ftore] rifervazione, rifervazione, riferbagione, rifervagione, riferba, riferva, s. f. riferbo, rifervo, s. m.

Refervation [reftriction] riferba, reftrizione, s. f.

RESE'RVE, s. [things kept in ftore, to be ufed as there fhall be occafion] riferba, riferva, s. f. riferbo, rifervo, s. m.

Referve of foldiers, corpo di riferba.

Re-

Reſerve [exception, limitation] *riſerba, eccezione, limitazione*, s. f.

I am your's without reſerve, *ſon tutto voſtro.*

Reſerve [diſcretion, warineſs] *riſerba, cautela, circoſpezione*, s. f.

To reſerve [to keep in ſtore, to ſave] *riſerbare, e riſervare, conſervare, ſerbare, ſalvare.*

RESE'RVED, adj. *riſerbato, riſervato, conſervato, ſerbato, ſalvato.*

Reſerved [grave, cloſe, wary] *riſerbato, cauto, circoſpetto, cauteloſo, prudente, ritenuto.*

RESE'RVEDLY, adv. *con avvertenza, con riguardo, cauteloſamente.*

RESE'RVEDNESS, s. [the being reſerved and cloſe] *riſerba, avvertenza, cautela, circoſpezione*, s. f. *riguardo*, s. m.

RESE'RVOIR, s. [a place where any thing is kept in ſtore] *ſerbatojo, luogo, dove checcheſſia è ſerbato.*

To RESE'TTLE [to ſettle again] *riſtabilire*, pref. *riſtabiliſco.*

RESE'TTLED, adj. *riſtabilito.*

To RESI'DE [to ſtay, to continue, to abide] *riſedere, ſtare fermamente, ſtanziare in un luogo, e diceſi per lo più di perſone pubbliche.*

RESI'DED, adj. *riſeduto, ſtato, ſtanziato.*

RE'SIDENCE, s. [dwelling place] *reſidenza, e riſidenza*, s. f. *riſedio*, s. m.

Reſidence [ſtay, ſojourning] *reſidenza, dimora, ſtanza*, s. f. *ſoggiorno*, s. m.

To make his reſidence in a place, *far reſidenza, dimorare in un luogo.*

To be bound to reſidence, *eſſer tenuto, o obbligato alla reſidenza.*

Reſidence [the employ of a reſident] *reſidenza, il carico di reſidente.*

RE'SIDENT, adj. [that reſides] *reſidente, che riſiede, che fa la ſua reſidenza.*

Reſident, s. [a prince's miniſter ſent to continue ſome time in the court of another prince] *un reſidente.*

RESIDE'NTIARY, adj. [belonging to a reſident] *di reſidente.*

Reſidentiary, s. [a reſident] *un reſidente.*

RE'SIDUE, s. [the reſt, the remainder] *reſiduo, avanzo, rimanente, reſto*, s. m.

To RESI'GN [to give up, to ſurrender] *raſſegnare, conſegnare, reſtituire, cedere*, pref. *reſtituiſco.*

To reſign one's place to one, *raſſegnare, o cedere il ſuo luogo ad uno.*

To reſign one's ſelf [to ſubmit wholly] to God's will, *raſſegnarſi, ſommetterſi alla volontà di Dio.*

RESIGNA'TION, s. [a voluntary giving up] *raſſegnazione, ceſſione, raſſegna*, s. f. *raſſegnamento*, s. m.

Reſignation to God's will, *raſſegnazione, raſſegnamento alla volontà di Dio.*

RESI'GNED, adj. *raſſegnato, conſegnato, reſtituito, ceduto.*

Reſigned, s. [the party to whom a thing is reſigned] *colui a chi ſi fa la raſſegna.*

RESI'GNER, s. [the party that reſigns] *raſſegnàtore*, s. m. *colui che raſſegna.*

RESI'GNING, } s. *raſſegna, raſſegnazione*, s. f. *raſ-*
RESI'GNMENT, } *ſegnamento*, s. m.

RESI'LIANCY, } s. [the ſtate or quality of that which
RESILIA'TION, } is reſilient] *zampillio*, s. m. *lo zampillare.*

RESI'LIENT, adj. [rebounding] *zampillante, che zampilla.*

RESINA'CIOUS, } adj. [that yields
RE'SINOUS, } roſin, full of roſin] *reſinoſo, ragioſo.*

RESI'PISCENCE, s. [repentence] *reſipiſcenza*, s. f. *pentimento*, s. m.

To RESI'ST [to withſtand or oppoſe] *reſiſtere, repugnare, contraſtare, oſtare, contrariare, far riſiſtenza, opporſi.*

To reſiſt ſtoutly, *reſiſtere vigoroſamente, fare una vigoroſa reſiſtenza.*

To reſiſt one's own reaſon, *oppugnare la ſua propria ragione, rinunciare, contrariare alla propria ragione.*

RESI'STANCE, s. [defence] *reſiſtenza*, s. f.

Reſiſtance [oppoſition] *reſiſtenza, oppoſizione*, s. f. *oſtacolo*, s. m.

RESI'STED, adj. *reſiſtito, repugnato, contraſtato, oſtato, contrariato, oppoſto.*

RESI'STER, s. *quello, o quella che reſiſte.*

RESI'STING, s. *reſiſtenza*, s. f. *il reſiſtere.*

RESI'STLESS, adj. [irreſiſtable, that cannot be oppoſed] *irreſiſtibile*; *che sforza in modo da vincere ogni reſiſtenza.*

RESO'LVABLE, adj. *ſolubile.*

RESO'LVE, s. [deliberation, deciſion] *deliberazione, deciſione, riſoluzione*, s. f.

Reſolve, s. [purpoſe, deſign, intention] *riſoluzione, intenzione*, s. f. *intento, diſegno, propoſito*, s. m.

To RESO'LVE [to clear a hard queſtion] *riſolvere, ſciorre, decidere, determinare una quiſtione, o un dubbio.*

To reſolve [to diſſolve, to ſoften, to melt] *riſolvere, conſumare, diſſipare, ammollire, liquefare.*

To reſolve into, *riſolvere, ridurre*, pref. *riduco*, pret. *riduſſi.*

To reſolve [to deſign, to purpoſe] *riſolvere, deliberare, determinare, ſtatuire*, pref. *ſtatuiſco.*

To reſolve itſelf [to turn, to change] *riſolverſi, ridurſi, mutarſi, cambiarſi.*

To reſolve into matter, *riſolverſi in marcia, marcire.*

The moral of the fable reſolves into this, *la moralità della favola ſi riduce in ciò.*

Reſolve me what it is, *ditemi quel che è.*

RESO'LVED, adj. *riſoluto*, v. To reſolve.

The war is reſolved upon, *la guerra è già ſtabilita.*

RESO'LVEDLY, adj. [with a reſolved mind] *reſolutamente, con riſoluzione, aſſertivamente.*

RESO'LVEDNESS, s. [firm diſpoſition] *reſoluzione, fermo propoſito.*

RESO'LVENTS, s. [machines which diſſolve and diſperſe] *rimedi diſſolutivi.*

RESO'LVING, s. *reſoluzione*, s. f.

The reſolving of a hard queſtion, *riſoluzione, o dichiarazione d' un dubbio.*

RE'SOLUTE, adj. [ſtout, bold] *riſoluto, ardito, coraggioſo, bravo, intrepido.*

RE'SOLUTELY, adv. [ſtoutly] *riſolutamente, arditamente, intrepidamente, coraggioſamente.*

RE'SOLUTENESS, s. [ſtoutneſs] *riſoluzione, fermezza, arditezza, intrepidezza*, s. f. *coraggio, animo*, s. m.

RESOLU'TION, s. [reſolve, determination] *reſoluzione, e riſoluzione, determinazione, ſoluzione, deciſione*, s. f.

Reſolution [deſign] *riſoluzione, deliberazione*, s. f. *diſegno*, s. m.

Reſolution [reſoluteneſs] *riſoluzione, fermezza, arditezza*, s. f. *ardire, coraggio*, s. m.

Reſolution [reduction] *analiſi, il riſolvere, il diſſolvere.*

The reſolution of a body into its principles, *la riſoluzione d'un corpo ne' ſuoi principi.*

RE'SONANT, adj. [reſounding] *riſonante, che riſuona.*

RESO'RT, s. [concourſe] *concorſo, concorrimento, ridotto*, s. m. *calca, moltitudine di gente concorſa.*

Reſort [refuge] *ricorſo, rifugio*, s. m.

Reſort [in law] *giuriſdizione, riſtretto, contado.*

To RESO'RT [to repair, to go to a place] *capitare, praticare, bazzicare, frequentare.*

To reſort to a place, *bazzicare, frequentare un luogo.*

'Tis a place where all ſtrangers reſort to, *è un luogo dove tutti i foreſtieri capitano.*

RESO'RTED, adj. *capitato, praticato, bazzicato, frequentato.*

RESO'RTER, s. *quello e quella che bazzica o frequenta un luogo.*

To RESO'UND [to eccho] *riſonare, rimbombare, echeggiare.*

His fame reſounds high in the ears of all the world, *la ſua fama riſuona per tutto il mondo*; *la ſua fama ſi fa ſentire da per tutto.*

RESO'UNDED, adj. *riſonato, rimbombato.*

RESO'UNDING, s. *riſonanza*, s. f. *il riſonare, rimbombo*, s. m.

Reſounding, adj. *riſonante, che riſuona.*

RESO'UNDINGLY, adv. *d'una maniera riſonante, riſonantemente.*

RESO'URCE, s. [ſomething to apply back to for ſuccours] *rimedio, ripiego*, s. m.

To,

To RE'SOW [to sow anew] *seminar di nuovo.*

To RE'SPEAK [to answer] *rispondere, ripigliare, far risposta.*

RESPE'CT, s. [esteem] *rispetto, riguardo,* s. m. *considerazione, stima,* s. f.

I have a great deal of respect for him, *ho gran rispetto per lui; fo grande stima di lui.*

Out of respect to you, *per rispetto vostro, per amor vostro.*

Respect [honour, reverence] *rispetto, onore,* s. m. *riverenza,* s. f.

To show a great respect to one, *mostrare rispetto grande ad alcuno; rispettarlo; onorarlo.*

To pay one's respect to one, *riverire, salutare uno.*

With respect be it spoken, *parlando con rispetto, o con riverenza.*

In respect of, *a rispetto, in rispetto, per rispetto, in comparazione, a petto, a paragone.*

In some respect, *in qualche modo.*

Respects [compliments] *complimenti, baciamani.*

Pray remember my respects to her, *vi prego di riverirla da mia parte, o farle i miei baciamani.*

To RESPE'CT [to honour] *rispettare, portar rispetto, avere in venerazione, riverire, onorare,* pres. *riverisco.*

To respect [to concern] *riguardare, concernere, spettare, appartenere, toccare.*

RESPE'CTED, adj. *rispettato,* v. To respect.

That will make you respected by all the world, *ciò vi farà rispettare da ognuno.*

RESPE'CTFUL, adj. *rispettoso, umile, pien di rispetto.*

RESPE'CTFULLY, adv. *rispettosamente, con rispetto, umilmente.*

RESPE'CTIVE, adj. [reciprocal] *rispettivo, che ha rispetto reciproco.*

Respective [relative, having relation] *rispettivo, relativo.*

RESPE'CTIVELY, adv. *rispettivamente, in rispetto, a rispetto, in riguardo.*

RESPIRA'TION, s. [breathing] *respirazione,* s. f. *il respirare.*

To RESPI'RE [to take breath] *respirare, e rispirare, attrarre l' aere esterna.*

To respire [to rest, to take rest from toil] *respirare, riposare dopo d'aver fatta cosa faticosa.*

RESPI'TE, s. [time, delay] *intervallo, indugio, tempo, respitto.*

To give a debtor some respite, *dar tempo ad un debitore di pagare.*

My business gives me no respite, *il mio negozio non patisce indugio, il mio negozio mi stringe.*

To RESPI'TE [to give some respite] *dar tempo.*

To respite the time of execution, *differire, o rimettere l' esecuzione d' una sentenza, d' una condanna.*

RESPLE'NDENCY, s. [brightness] *splendore,* s. m.

RESPLE'NDENT, adj. [bright] *risplendente, che risplende.*

RESPO'NDENT, s. in canon law [he who makes answer to such questions as are demanded of him] *rispondente, la parte che risponde alle interrogazioni.*

Respondent [a student in an university who answers in a disputation] *rispondente, colui che mantiene una tesi.*

RESPO'NSAL, s. [an answer made by the clerk and people during the time of divine service] *risponso,* s. m. *risposta,* s. f.

RESPO'NSIBLE, adj. [able to answer or to pay] *benestante, che è capace di pagare.*

Responsible [answerable, accountable] *mallevadore, obbligato.*

I shall be responsible for it, *io ne sarò mallevadore.*

REST, s. [quiet, peace] *riposo,* s. m. *resta, pace, quiete,* s. f.

To take some rest, *prender qualche riposo.*

To be at rest, *esser in pace.*

A day of rest, *un giorno di riposo.*

Rest [sleep] *riposo, sonno, il dormire.*

I had no rest all night, *non ho riposato, o dormito in tutta la notte.*

I had a very good night's rest, *ho riposato, o dormito molto bene.*

Rest [a pause in poetry] *pausa, fermata,* s. f.

The rest of a lance, *resta di lancia.*

The rest [residue, remnant] *resto, rimanente, avanzo, residuo, restante,* s. m.

All the rest went away, *tutti li altri andarono via.*

The rest of the money, *il resto del danaro.*

To REST [to take some rest] *riposare, prender riposo.*

To rest [to sleep] *riposare, dormire.*

To rest [to lean upon a thing] *appoggiarsi a che che si sia.*

To rest [to remain] *restare, stare.*

Rest yourself satisfied about that, *non vi pigliate fastidio di questo.*

The difficulty rests there, *quì sta la difficoltà.*

The fault must needs rest upon your misfortune, *bisogna attribuirne la colpa alla vostra cattiva fortuna.*

To rest, *dar pace.* God rest his soul, *Iddio dia pace alla sua anima.*

RESTAURA'TION, s. [restoring, reestablishment] *resturazione, o ristaurazione,* s. f. *il restaurare.*

RE'STFUL, adj. *che riposa, che dorme, o prende riposo.*

After he took the julep he was restful, *dopo che ebbe preso il giuleppe riposò.*

RE'STIFF, adj. [unwilling to stir; resolute against going forward; obstinate, stubborn] *restio, non volonteroso di andar innanzi, ostinato, capone.*

RE'STIFNESS, s. [obstinacy, reluctance] *ostinazione, caponeria.*

RE'STILY, adv. [frowardly] *ostinatamente, caparbiamente.*

RE'STINESS, s. [speaking of a horse] *restio,* s. m. *qualità d' un cavallo che è restio.*

Restiness [stubbornness, obstinacy] *restio,* s. m. *caparbietà, caparbierià, ostinazione, pertinacia, caponeria.*

RE'STING, s. [rest] *riposo,* s. m. *quiete,* s. f.

Resting, adj. ex. a resting place, *un luogo di riposo.*

RESTITU'TION, s. [the act of giving back again] *restituzione,* s. f. *restituimento,* s. m.

RE'STIVE, adv. [drawing back as a horse] *restio, parlando delle bestie da cavalcare, e da soma, quando non vogliono passare avanti,* v. Restiff.

RE'STLESS, adj. [that does not sleep] *che non dorme, che non riposa.*

Restless [impatient] *impaziente, inquieto.*

RE'STLESSLY, adv. *senza riposo, senza dormire.*

RE'STLESSNESS, s. [want of rest] *mancanza di riposo, inquietudine,* s. f.

Restlessness [impatience] *impazienza, inquietudine,* s. f.

RESTO'RATIVE, adj. [that is of a restoring or strengthening quality] *ristorativo, che ha virtù, e forza di ristorare, e confortare.*

Restorative, s. *ristorativo.*

To RESTO'RE [to re-establish, to settle again] *ristorare, restaurare, rinnovare.*

To restore one to his place, *ristabilire alcuno nel suo impiego.*

To restore one to favour, *rimettere in grazia.*

To restore one to life again, *ridare la vita ad uno, richiamarlo in vita, risuscitarlo.*

To restore one to liberty, *rimettere in libertà.*

To restore [to give up again, to return] *restituire, rendere, tornare in potere altrui quel che gli s' è tolto,* pres. *restituisco,* pret. *resi.*

RESTO'RED, adj. *ristorato, ristaurato, rinnovato, restituito, reso,* v. To restore.

RESTO'RER, s. *ristoratore,* s. m. *restauratrice,* s. f.

RESTO'RING, s. *restituzione,* s. f. *il restituire.*

Restoring [restauration] *restaurazione, e restaurazione,* s. f.

To RESTRA'IN [to keep in, to bridle or curb, to repress] *reprimere, raffrenare, rintuzzare, ritenere, impedire,* pres. *impedisco.*

To restrain one from a thing, *ritenere, impedire uno da qualche cosa.*

RESTRA'INED, adj. *represso, raffrenato, rintuzzato, impedito.*

RESTRA'INEDLY, adv. *con ritegno limitatamente.*

RESTRA'INER, s. *quello, o quella che reprime, che raffrena, che ritiene.*

RESTRA'INT, s. [curb] *freno, raffrenamento, morso,* s. m.

To

To be under some restraint, *esser in qualche modo raffrenato.*

To be under no restraint, *esser in piena libertà, aver potere di fare quel che ti aggrada.*

To RE'STRICT [to limit, to confine] *restringere, limitare.*

RESTRI'CTION, s. [limitation] *limitazione, riserva,* s. f.

To RESTRI'NGE [to bind] *ristrignere, strigner maggiormente,* pres. *ristringo,* pret. *ristrinsi.*

RESTRI'NGED, adj. *ristretto.*

RESTRI'NGENT, adj. [of a binding quality] *astringente.*

RE'STY, adj. [drawing back, as a horse does] *restio, ostinato.*

Resty [froward, headstrong, stubborn] *restio, caparbio, ostinato, testereccio, capone.*

To RE'SUBLIME [to sublime another time] *sublimare di nuovo.*

RE'SULT, s. [conclusion, upshot, to issue] *risultamento, esito, fine,* s. m. *conclusione, riuscita,* s. f.

To RESU'LT [to follow from, to arise from] *resultare, e risultare, nascere, derivare, venire, venire per conseguenza.*

To result [to fly back] *fuggir indietro.*

To RESU'ME [to take up again] *resumere, ripigliare.*

To resume a discourse, *resumere, ripigliare il discorso.*

Let us resume our former discourse, *ritorniamo al nostro primo discorso.*

RESURRE'CTION, s. [rising again from the dead] *risurrezione,* s. f. *il risuscitare dei morti.*

To RESU'SCITATE [to rise up again from the dead] *risuscitare.*

RETA'IL, s. [selling by parcels] *minuto, ritaglio.*

To sell by retail, *vendere a minuto, o a ritaglio.*

The retail trade, *vendita a minuto, o a ritaglio.*

To RETAI'L [to sell by retail] *vendere a minuto.*

RETAI'LED, adj. *venduto a minuto, o a ritaglio.*

RETA'ILER, s. *chi vende a minuto.*

RETA'ILING, s. *il vendere a minuto.*

To RETA'IN [to keep or hold back] *ritenere,* pres. *ritengo,* pret. *ritenni.*

I retained him for my council, *l' ho preso per mio avvocato.*

To retain [to keep in mind, to remember] *ritenere, tenere a mente.*

RETA'INED, adj. *ritenuto.*

RETA'INABLE, adj. [that may be retained] *che si può ritenere.*

RETA'INER, s. a servant attending upon some special occasions] *una persona salariata al servizio di qualcheduno, senza esser suo domestico.*

RETA'INING, s. *ritenimento, ritegno,* s. m. *il ritenere.*

To RE'TAKE [to take again] *pigliar di nuovo, ripigliare, pret.* retook, *part.* retaken.

To RETA'LIATE [to return, to do like for like] *rendere, render la pariglia, contraccambiare.*

To RETA'LIATE a kindness, *riconoscere o contraccambiare un beneficio.*

RETA'LIATED, adj. *reso.*

RETALIA'TION, s. [like for like] *pariglia,* s. f. *contraccambio.*

By way of retaliation, *in contraccambio, in vendetta.*

Retaliation of an injury, *vendetta d' una ingiuria.*

To RETA'RD [to delay] *ritardare, intertenere, fare indugiare,* pres. *intertengo,* pret. *intertenni.*

RETARDA'TION, s. the act of delaying] *indugio, ritardo.*

RETA'RDED, adj. *ritardato, intertenuto, indugiato.*

RETA'RDER, s. [hinderer, obstructor] *colui che cagiona ritardo o indugio, o la cosa che fa indugiare e ritardare.*

RETA'RDING, s. *il ritardare.*

To RE'TCH [to strain, to vomit] *aver voglia di recere, star per recere.*

RE'TCHLESS, adj. [lazy, careless] *infingardo, pigro, lento.*

RE'TCHLESSLY, adj. *negligentemente, da infingardo, pigramente, lentamente.*

RE'TCHLESSNESS, s. [laziness, carelessness] *infingardia, lentezza, pigrizia, infingardaggine,* s. f

RETE'NSION, s. [the act of retaining] *ritenzione,* s. f. *il ritenere.*

Retention of urine, *ritenzione d' urina.*

RETE'NTIVE, adj. [that retains] *ritenente, che ritiene.*

The retentive faculty, *la ritentiva, la virtù del tenere a mente.*

RE'TINUE, s. [a train of attendants] *comitiva,* s. f. *corteggio, accompagnamento,* s. m.

To RETI'RE [to withdraw, to depart] *ritirarsi, andarsene.*

To retire home, *ritirarsi a casa.*

To retire from business [to lay it aside] *ritirarsi dagli affari, tralasciare gli affari, desistere dagli affari.*

To retire, verb. act. *ritirare, tirare a se.*

Which forced him to retire his arms, *il che lo sforzò di ritirare le braccia.*

RETI'RED, adj. *ritirato.*

Retired [solitary] *ritirato, solitario.*

A retired life, *una vita ritirata, o solitaria.*

A very retired man, *un uomo molto ritirato, che non conversa molto con la gente.*

RETI'REDLY, adv. *privatamente, solitariamente.*

RETI'REDNESS, s. [solitariness] *ritiratezza,* s. f. *vita ritirata.*

REEI'REMENT, s. [solitude] *ritiratezza, solitudine.*

RETI'RING, *il ritirare.*

A retiring place, *un luogo ritirato.*

Nature's dark retiring place [the grave] *la sepoltura.*

RETI'RINGLY, adv. *addietro, indietro.*

RETO'RT, s. [a chymical vessel of a round figure] *storta,* s. f. *vaso da stillare.*

Retort, s. [a censure or incivility returned] *biasmo o inciviltà restituita e al biasimatore e allo incivile.*

To RETO'RT an argument, *ritorcere un argomento.*

RETO'RTED, adj. *ritorto.*

To RETO'SS [to toss back] *far balzar indietro.*

To RETRA'CT [to draw back] *ritirare indietro.*

To retract [to recant, to unsay] *ritrattare, ritrattarsi, disdirsi, dir contro a quel che s' è detto prima.*

RETRA'CTION, s. [recantation] *ritrattazione,* s. f.

RETRA'CTED, adj. *ritrattato, disdetto.*

RETRA'CTING, *ritrattazione, il ritrattarsi.*

RETRE'AT, s. [act of retiring before a superior force] *ritirata,* s. f. *il ritirarsi, e dicesi propriamente degli eserciti.*

To sound the retreat, *batter la ritirata.*

Retreat [a retiring place] *luogo ritirato.*

To RETRE'AT, to retire from a place] *ritirarsi, andar via, far la ritirata.*

RETRE'ATED, adj. *ritirato.*

To RETRE'NCH [to cut off, to abridge, to diminish] *levare, tagliare, sminuire, scemare, diminuire, menomare.*

To retrench one's expences, *menomare le spese.*

To retrench [to cast up a retrenchment] *trincerare, fortificare con trincee.*

To retrench, *trincerarsi.*

RETRE'NCHED, adj. *levato, tagliato,* v. To retrench.

RETRE'NCHMENT, s. *trincea,* s. f. *riparo militare, trinceramento,* s. m.

To RE'TRIBUTE [to recompence, to requite] *ricompensare, rimeritare, render la mercede, il contraccambio,* pres. *retribuisco.*

RE'TRIBUTED, adj. *ricompensato, rimeritato.*

RE'TRIBUTER, s. *che retribuisce.*

RETRIBU'TION, s. [requital] *retribuzione, ricompensa,* s. f.

RETRI'EVABLE, adj. [that may be retrieved] *che si può ricovrare.*

To RETRI'EVE [to recover, to get again, to repair] *ricuperare, ricovrare, racquistare.*

To retrieve one's honour, *ricovrare il suo onore.*

To retrieve a loss, *riparare una perdita, rifarsi d' un danno.*

To retrieve partridges, *far levare le pernici di nuovo.*

RETRI'EVED, adj. *ricovrato, racquistato, ricuperato.*

RETROCE'SSION, s. *il tornare indietro, il retrocedere.*

RE-

RETROGRADA'TION, s. [going back] *il retrogradare, il tornare indietro.*

RETRO'GRADE, adj. [that goes back] *retrógrado.*

To RETRO'GRADE [to turn back, or go back] *retrogradare, termine astrologico, tornare addietro.*

RETRO'GRADED, adj. *retrogradato.*

RETRO'GRADING, s. *il retrogradare.*

RETROGRE'SSION, s. [retrogradation] *il retrocedere.*

To RE'TROSPECT [to look backwards] *guardare indietro.*

RETROSPE'CTION, s. [a looking backwards] *il guardare indietro.*

To RETU'ND [to blunt] *rintuzzare.*

RETU'RN, s. [coming back] *ritorno,* s. m. *ritornata,* s. f.

Return [answer] *risposta,* s. f.

Return [acknowledgment] *riconoscenza, ricompensa,* s. f. *contraccambio,* s. m.

To make return of kindness, *riconoscere o rimeritare un beneficio.*

Return in love, *corrispondenza in amore.*

Return of money, *rimessa di danari.*

A commodity that yields a quick return, *una mercanzia di buono spaccio, che si vende bene.*

To RETU'RN [to come back] *ritornare, di nuovo tornare.*

To return [to render] *ritornare, restituire, rendere.*

To return a thing borrow'd, *ritornare, restituire, rendere una cosa prestata.*

To return thanks, *render grazie, ringraziare.*

To return [to send back] *rimandare, mandare indietro.*

To return an answer, *render risposta, rispondere,* pret. *risposi.*

To return [to repay, to requite] *ricompensare, rimeritare, contraccambiare.*

To return a sum of money, *rimettere una somma di danari.*

RETU'RNABLE, adj. *di rimando.*

A returnable commodity, *una mercanzia di rimando.*

RETU'RNED, adj. *ritornato, v.* To return.

To get a sum of money returned to one, *fare una rimessa di danari ad uno.*

RETU'RNER, s. [one who pays or remits money] *colui che paga o rimette danaro.*

RETU'RNING, s. *ritornamento,* s. m. *il ritornare.*

REVE, s. [the bailiff of a franchise or manor] *guardiano d' un feudo.*

To REVE'AL [to lay open, to disclose, to discover] *rivelare, scoprire, manifestare, pubblicare, far sapere.*

REVE'ALED, adj. *rivelato, scoperto, manifestato, pubblicato.*

REVE'ALER, s. *rivelatore,* s. m. *rivelatrice,* s. f.

REVE'ALING, s. *rivelamento, il rivelare.*

RE'VEL, s. [a feast with loose and noisy jollity] *gozzoviglia, festa romorosa.*

To RE'VEL [to make merry, especially in the night time] *festeggiare, divertirsi, stare allegramente, far baldoria, gozzovigliare.*

REVELA'TION, s. *rivelazione; scoperta.*

RE'VELLER, s. *che si divertisce gozzovigliando.*

RE'VELLING, s. *baldoria, allegrezza, gozzoviglia.*

RE'VEL-ROUT, s. [a mob, an unlawful assembly] *una festa o gozzoviglia romorosa e non permessa dalle leggi.*

RE'VELRY, s. *gozzoviglia, tresca; il trescare e far baldoria grande.*

REVE'NGE, s. [the taking satisfaction for an affront or injury done] *vendetta,* s. f. *onta, o danno, che si fa altrui in contraccambio d' offesa ricevuta.*

To take one's revenge upon one, *far le sue vendette d' uno, vendicarsi di lui.*

In revenge, *in contraccambio.*

Revenge [among gamesters] *rivinta,* s. f. *il riscattarsi al giuoco.*

You must give me my revenge, *bisogna darmi la mia rivinta.*

I will have my revenge, *voglio riscattarmi.*

To REVE'NGE [to take vengeance of] *vendicarsi, prender vendetta, vendicare, far vendetta.*

To revenge an affront, *vendicare, o vendicarsi d' un affronto.*

REVE'NCED, adj. *vendicato.*

I'll be revenged on him, *mi vendicherò di lui, me la pagherà.*

REVE'NGEFUL, adj. *vendicativo, inclinato alla vendetta.*

REVE'NGEFULLY, adv. *d' una maniera vendicativa.*

REVE'NGER, s. *vendicatore,* s. m. *vendicatrice,* s. f.

RE'VENUE, s. [income, rent] *entrata, rendita,* s. f.

To REVE'RBERATE [to strike, reflect, or beat back again] *riflettere, riverberare, ripercuotere, rimandare indietro, e dicesi propriamente de' raggi quando ribattuti da corpo non trasparente tornano indietro.*

To reverberate [among chymists, is the flame of a fire to beat back down on the metal] *riverberare, ripercuotere, termine chimico.*

REVE'RBERATED, adj. *riverberato, ripercosso, riflesso, ribàttuto.*

REVE'RBERATING, adj. *riverberante.*

Reverberating fire, *fuoco di riverbero.*

REVERBERA'TION, s. [a beating back] *riverberazione,* s. f. *riverberamento, riverbero,* s. m.

REVE'RBERATORY, s. a sort of strong furnace used for the calcination of minerals, by a reverberating fire] *riverberatorio,* s. m. *fornace di chimista che serve alla calcinazione de' metalli per mezzo del fuoco di riverbero.*

To REVE'RE [to respect, to honour] *reverire, riverire, portar reverenza, onorare, rispettare, portar rispetto,* pres. *reverisco, e riverisco.*

REVE'RED, adj. *riverito, ornato, rispettato.*

RE'VERENCE, s. [honour, respect] *reverenza, riverenza,* s. f. *rispetto, onore,* s. f.

To RE'VERENCE [to honour, to respect] *reverire, e riverire, onorare, rispettare, portar rispetto, reverenza,* pres. *reverisco, e riverisco.*

RE'VERENCED, adj. *reverito, riverito, onorato, rispettato.*

Reverenced, adj. *reverendo, riverendo, venerabile, degno di reverenza.*

RE'VEREND, adj. [worthy to be reverenced] *reverendo, riverendo, degno di reverenza, da esser riverito.*

Right reverend, or most reverend, *reverendissimo, riverendissimo.*

RE'VERENT, } adj. [respectful]
REVERE'NTIAL, } *reverente, riverente, rispettoso.*

To have a reverential regard to the authority of the church, *portar rispetto all' autorità della chiesa.*

RE'VERENTLY, adj. *reverentemente, riverentemente, con reverenza, con rispetto.*

REVE'RSE, s. [that is on the back or behind] *il rovescio, la parte opposta.*

The reverse of a medal, *il rovescio d' una medaglia.*

To REVE'RSE [to repeal, to make void] *annullare, cassare, rivocare, abolire,* pres. *abolisco.*

REVE'RSED, adj. *annullato, cassato, rivocato, abolito.*

REVE'RSIBLE, adj. [that may be reversed] *rivocabile, che si può rivocare.*

REVE'RSION, s. [is when the possession and estate, which was parted with for a time, returns to the donor or his heirs] *riversione,* s. f. *diritto di riversione.*

REVE'RSIONARY, adj. to be enjoyed in succession] *da godersi succedendo a un altro.*

REVE'RTED, adj. *ritornato, ricaduto.*

To REVE'RT [to return, as an estate or honour does to the crown] *ritornare, ricadere, come i beni livellari, fidecommissi, e titoli d' onori.*

RE'VESTIARY } s. the place where
RE'VESTRY } the church vestments are kept] *sagrestia, sacristia.*

To REVI'CTUAL, *vettovagliare di nuovo, e dicesi delle navi.*

REVI'CTUALLED, adj. *di nuovo vettovagliato.*

REVIE'W, s. [the act of looking over, examination] *rivista, riconsiderazione,* s. f. *esame,* s. m.

Review [muster of soldiers] *mostra, rassegna, e ordinanza d' eserciti.*

To pass an army in review, *far la mostra.*

To

To Revie'w [to view again] *rivedere, riconsiderare, esaminare di nuovo.*

Revie'wed, adj. *rivisto, riconsiderato.*

To Revi'le [to abuse, to rail at] *ingiuriare, dire parole ingiuriose, maltrattare, usar villania, svillaneggiare, oltraggiare.*

Revi'led, adj. *ingiuriato, maltrattato, svillaneggiato.*

Revi'ler, s. *ingiuriatore*, s. m.

Revi'ling, s. *ingiuria, villania*, s. f. *oltraggio*, s. m.

Revi'sal, s. [a second examination] *rivista*, s. f. *secondo esame.*

Upon revisal he found it otherwise, *nel rivedere dei conti trovò che la cosa andava altrimenti.*

Revi'se, s. [a second proof of a printed sheet] *una seconda prova, termine di stampatore.*

To Revi'se [to review] *rivedere, esaminare di nuovo, riconsiderare*, pret. *rividi.*

Revi'sed, adj. *rivisto, riconsiderato, riveduto.*

Revi'sor, s. [examiner, superintendant] *riveditore, revisore*, s. m.

Revi'sion, s. [review] *rivista, revisione, l' esaminar di nuovo, nuovo esame.*

To Revi'sit [to visit again] *rivisitare, visitar di nuovo, ritornar la visita.*

To Revi've [to bring to life again, to renew] *rivivere, ravvivare, ritornare in vita, riprender vita e vigore, avvivare.*

To revive the memory of great men, *ravvivare la memoria de' grandi uomini.*

To revive old quarrels, *rinnovare le gare antiche.*

To revive [to come to life again] *ravvivarsi, avvivarsi, riprender vita e vigore.*

He begins to revive, *comincia a ritornare a se, e a ricuperar gli spiriti.*

We shall see trade revive, *vedremo il commercio fiorire ancora.*

Revi'ved, adj. *ravvivato, avvivato*, v. To revive.

Reu'nion, s. [joining again] *riunimento*, s. m.

Reunion [reconciliation] *riconciliazione*, s. f.

To Reuni'te [to unite, to join together] *riunire, di nuovo unire*, pres. *riunisco, unisco.*

To reunite [to reconcile] *riunire, riconciliare, rappacificare, metter d' accordo.*

Reuni'ted, adj. *riunito*, v. To reunite.

Reuni'ting, s. *riunimento*, s. m.

Revo'cable, adj. [that may be revoked] *rivocabile, che si può rivocare.*

Revoca'tion, s. [repealing] *rivocazione, rivocagione*, s. f. *il rivocare.*

To Revo'ke [to repeal] *rivocare, cassare, annullare, abolire*, pres. *abolisco.*

To revoke at cards, *rinunciare, e dicesi a giuoco di carte.*

Revo'ked, adj. *rivocato, cassato, annullato, abolito*, v. To revoke.

That cannot be revoked, *irrevocabile, che non si può rivocare.*

Revo'kement, s. [revocation, repeal, recal] *il rivocare, il cassare, il render nullo.*

Revo'lt, s. [insurrection] *rivolta, ribellione, sollevazione*, s. f.

To Revo'lt [to rebel] *rivoltarsi, ribellarsi, sollevarsi.*

To revolt from one's religion, *mutar di religione, rinunciare alla religione, abbandonarla, apostatare.*

Revo'lted, adj. *rivoltato, ribellato, sollevato.*

Revo'lter, s. *un ribelle, un apostata.*

To Revo'lve [to cast about in one's mind, to ruminate] *rivolgere, esaminar colla mente, discorrer seco medesimo, ruminar nel pensiero*, pret. *rivolsi.*

Revo'lved, adj. *rivolto, esaminato, ruminato.*

Revolu'tion, s. [a notable turn of affairs, or change in government] *rivoluzione, e revoluzione*, s f.

To Revy [a term of a game at cards] *invitare di nuovo, termine usato al giuoco delle carte.*

Rewa'rd, s. [recompence] *rimunerazione, ricompensa, ricompensazione*, s. f. *contraccambio, ricompenso, rimerito, guiderdone*, s. m.

To Rewa'rd [to recompence] *ricompensare, rimunerare, dare o rendere il contraccambio, contraccambiare, rimunerare, guiderdonare, rimeritare.*

God reward you, *Iddio ve lo renda.*

Rewa'rdable, adj. [worthy of reward] *degno di ricompensa, di premio.*

Rewa'rded, adj. *ricompensato*, v. To reward.

Rewa'rder, s. *rimuneratore*, s. m. *rimuneratrice*, s. f.

Re'wet, s. [the lock of a gun] *la rotella d' un archibuso.*

To Rewo'rd [to repeat in the same words] *ripetere colle stesse parole.*

Rhaba'rbate, adj. [impregnated or tinctured with rhubarb] *immollato, infuso nel rabarbaro.*

Rha'psody, s. [a confused collection of poems] *rapsodia*, s. f. *collezione confusa di diversi poemi.*

Rhe'nish, s. [Rhenish wine] *vino del Reno.*

Rhe'tor, s. [he that teaches rhetorick] *un rettorico, uno che insegna la rettorica.*

Rheto'rical, adj. [belonging to rhetorick] *rettorico.*

Rheto'rically, adv. *rettoricamente.*

To Rheto'ricate [to use rhetorical figures, to speak like an orator] *fare il rettorico, parlar da rettorico.*

Rhetori'cian, s. [one skilled in, or a professor of rhetorick] *un rettorico, che sa rettorica, professore in rettorica.*

Rhe'torick, s. [the art of speaking well and eloquently] *rettorica*, s. f. *arte di ben parlare.*

Rheu'barb, v. Rhubarb.

Rhe'um, s. [a thin watery matter oozing through the glands] *reuma, rema, catarro.*

Rheuma'tick, adj. *rematico, reumatico, infermo di rema o reuma.*

Rhe'umatism, s. *rema, reuma, flussione, o catarro supposto procedere da umori acri.*

Rhe'umy, adj. *pieno d' umore acro, rematico, reumatico.*

Rhino'ceros, s. [a large beast in Africa and in India] *rinoceronte*, s m. *animali di grandezza quasi eguale all' elefante.*

Rhomb, s. [a parallelogram, that has all its sides equal, but not all its angles] *rombo*, s. m. *i matematici chiamano una figura di quattro lati uguali, e d'angoli obliqui.*

Rhombo'id, s. [a quadrilateral figure, whose opposite sides and angles are equal] *romboide*, s. f. *figura quadrilatera, prodotta dal rombo.*

Rhombo'idal, adj. [belonging to the rhomboides] *romboidale, di figura di romboide.*

Rhu'barb, s. [the root of a plant, good to purge choler and phlegm] *rabarbaro, reubarbaro*, s. f. *radice medicinale.*

Bastard rhubarb [an herb so called] *rapontico, e reupontico*, s. m.

Rhyme, s. [the consonance of verses; the correspondence of the last sounds of one verse, to the last sounds or syllables of another] *rima.*

Rhyme, s. *poesia, poema, rima.*

To Rhyme, *rimare, accordarsi nel suono.*

To rhyme, *rimare, far poesie, far versi.*

Rhy'mer, } s. [one who makes
Rhy'mister, } verse, a versifier] *rimatore, versificatore, un che fa rime o versi.*

Rhy'thmical, adj. *armonioso; pieno d' armoniosi numeri; di suoni che hanno buona vicendevole proporzione.*

Rib, s. [a side bone of the body] *costola*, s. f. *uno di quegli ossi che si partono dalla spina, e vengono al petto.*

Ri'bald, s. [a loose fellow] *un ribaldo, un rubaldo, uno sciagurato, uno scellerato, uno sgherano, un briccone.*

A great ribald, *un ribaldone, un ribaldonaccio.*

A little ribald, *un ribaldello.*

To play the ribald, *ribaldeggiare, far cose da ribaldi.*

A band of ribalds, *ribaldaglia, rubaldaglia*, s. f. *moltitudine, razza, masnada di ribaldi, canagliaccia iniqua.*

Ri'baldry, s. [debauchery] *ribalderia, sciagurataggine, oscenità*, s. f.

Ri'band, v. Ribbon.

Ri'bble-rabble, s. [ill or pitiful

tiful ftuff] *robaccia*, s. f. *roba cattiva.*

Ribble rabble [mob] *canaglia, plebe* s. f. *popolaccio*; s. m.

RI'BBON, s. [a narrow fort of filk] *naftro*, s. m. *fettuccia*, s. f.

To RI'B-ROST [to beat or bang foundly] *tartaffare, malmenare, batter ben bene.*

RI'BWORT, s. [an herb] *piantaggine*, s. f. *fpezie d' erba.*

RICE, s. [a fort of grain or pulfe] *rifo*, s. m.

RICH, adj. [wealthy] *ricco, che ha ricchezza, opulento, doviziofo.*

A rich man, *un uomo ricco.*

He married a rich fortune, *s' è ammogliato con una ricca donna.*

A rich ftone, *una pietra di gran prezzo*

A rich banquet, *un feftino lauto, un banchetto magnifico.*

Rich [plentiful] *ricco, abbondante, fertile.*

A rich country, *un paefe ricco.*

A rich language, *una lingua ricca, copiofa, abbondante in parole ed efpreffioni.*

Rich wine, *vino gagliardo, vino eccellente.*

Very rich, *ricchiffimo.*

The rich, *i ricchi.*

RICHES, s. [wealth] *ricchezza*, s. f. *abbondanza de' beni di fortuna.*

RI'CHLY, adv. *riccamente, funtuofamente, magnificamente, lautamente, pompofamente.*

Richly clad, *riccamente veftito.*

RI'CHNESS, s. [magnificence] *ricchezza, funtuofità, magnificenza, pompa*, s. f.

The richnefs of his attire, *la ricchezza de' fuoi arnefi.*

RICK, s. [a heap] *bica*, s. f.

A rick of hay or corn, *una bica di fieno, o di grano.*

The RI'CKETS, s. [a difeafe common to young children] *fpezie di malattia molto rara in Italia, e molto comune in Inghilterra, ed è una fpezie di nodi che vengono alle gambe ed alle braccia de' fanciulli, che le rende torte e le impedifce di crefcere.*

RI'CKETY, adj. *che è foggetto al malore, chiamato in Inghilterra*, RICKETS.

RID, adj. [freed] *liberato, fpacciato, sbrigato.*

To get rid, *liberarfi, sbrigarfi, disfarfi, fpedirfi, levarfi d' attorno, fvilupparfi, ufcire, ftrigarfi.*

I don't know how to get rid of that troublefome fellow, *non fo come levarmi d' attorno quefto importuno.*

To get rid of a diftemper, *liberarfi da qualche malattia.*

How fhall we get rid of thefe troubles? *Come faremo per ifvilupparci di quefti imbrogli.*

To RID [to free from, to difengage] *liberare, sbrigare, fviluppare.*

To rid one of all his troubles, *liberare, trarre uno d' impaccio*

To rid one's felf of a troublefome bufinefs, *ufcir di qualche impaccio o faftidiofa faccenda.*

To rid one of his money, *fcroccare ad uno il fuo danaro.*

To rid one's felf of all one has, *fcialacquare, mandare a male le fue foftanze.*

RI'DDANCE, s. [difpatch] *fpedizione*, s. f. *fpaccio*, s. m.

To make a clear riddance, *fpacciare un luogo, votarlo, lafciarlo libero.*

I made at laft a good riddance of him, *alla fine me ne fono sbrigato; me l' ho levato d' attorno.*

To make quick riddance of a commodity, *fpacciare una mercanzia.*

RI'DDEN, adj. [from to ride] *cavalcato.*

RI'DDLE, s. [a hard queftion, a dark faying] *indovinello*, s. m. *enigma*, s. f.

Riddle [fieve] *cribro, vaglio*, s. m.

To RI'DDLE [to folve, to unriddle] *fpiegare un enimma, un indovinello.*

To riddle, v. n. [to fpeak ambiguoufly or obfcurely] *parlare ambiguamente o ofcuramente.*

To riddle, *vagliare, cribrare.*

RI'DDLED, adj. *vagliato, cribrato, v.* To riddle.

To RIDE [to go on horfeback, coach, waggon, &c.] *cavalcare, andare a cavallo, in carozza, in un carro, e fimili.*

To ride on horfeback, *cavalcare, andare a cavallo.*

To ride upon a mule, *montare un mulo.*

To ride in a coach, *andare in carozza.*

To ride away, *andarfene, fuggire.*

To ride back, *ritornarfene.*

To ride about, *fare una girata, andar qua, e là.*

To ride [to manage a horfe] *maneggiare un cavallo.*

To learn to ride, *imparare a montare a cavallo.*

To ride [fpeaking of a fhip, a fhip is faid to ride, when fhe is held in fo faft by her anchors, that fhe does not drive away by wind or tide] *effere all' ancora.*

A fhip that rides at anchor, *un vafcello che è all' ancora, che ha dato fondo.*

To ride in triumph, *andare in trionfo.*

To ride a free horfe to death, *abufare della bontà, o pazienza altrui.*

RI'DER, s. *cavaliere, cavalcatore*, s. m.

RIDGE, s. [top] *cima, fommità*, s. f.

The ridge of a hill, *la cima d' un monte, il giogo d' un monte.*

The ridge of a houfe, *il tetto, la fommità d' una cafa.*

A ridge-tile, *tegola*, s. f.

Ridge, s. *quel terreno che il vomere taglia ed alza in folcando.*

RI'DGES [in architecture, the fpaces between the channels of timber or ftone wrought] *fcanalatura*, s. f.

A long ridge of hills, *giogaja*, s. f. *continuazione di monti.*

The ridge bone of the back, *la fpina del doffo.*

Ridge-band [that part of a draught-horfe's harnefs, which runs over crofs his back] *doffiere*, s. m.

To RI'DGE [to cover a houfe with tiles] *coprire di tegole.*

RI'DGED, adj. *coperto di tegole.*

Ridged [that has many ridges and channels] *fcanalato.*

RI'DGELING, } s. [a beaft that has
RI'DGEL, } loft one ftone] *il mafchio d' una beftia, al quale non è ftato tagliato che un tefticolo.*

RI'DICULE, s. [that which is ridiculous] *ridicolo*, s. m. *la cofa, che induce a rifo.*

To turn into ridicule, *fchernire, burlarfi d' alcuno, renderlo ridicolo, prenderlo a gabbo.*

To RI'DICULE [to render ridiculous] *render ridicolo, pigliare a gabbo, farfi gabbo, pigliare a giuoco, riderfi, burlarfi, beffarfi, fchernire*, pret. *fchernirfi.*

RI'DICULED, adj. *pigliato a gabbo, fatto gabbo, burlato, beffato, fchernito.*

RIDI'CULOUS, adj. [fit to be laught at] *ridicolo, atto a muovere il rifo, degno di rifo.*

A ridiculous man or woman, *un uomo ridicolo, una donna ridicola.*

RI'DICULOUSLY, adv. *con modo ridicolo.*

RI'DICULOUSNESS, s. [that which is ridiculous] *ridicolo*, s. m. *la cofa che induce a rifo.*

RI'DING, s. [from to ride] *l' andare a cavallo.*

Riding-habit, *abito da cavalcare.*

A riding hood, *vefte da donna a foggia di mantello da cavalcare.*

A riding coat, *un abito da cavalcare, gabbano.*

A riding rod, *una bacchetta, una verga.*

RI'DINGS [in Yorkfhire] *divifioni della provincia di York.*

RIDO'TTO, s. [a place of entertainment] *ridotto*, s. m. *luogo dove gente fi riduce per divertirfi.*

RIFE, adj. [common, frequent] *comune, frequente, che regna, che domina.*

The fmall-pox is very rife this year, *il vajuolo è molto comune quest' anno.*

The rain has been very rife this year, *queft' anno ha piovuto più frequentemente dell' ufato.*

RIFF-RAFF, s. [refufe, dregs, forry ftuff] *cofe di nullo pregio, robbaccia, feccia, cattive cofe.*

To RI'FLE [to pillage, to rob] *mettere a bottino, faccheggiare, predare, rubare, fvaligiare, fpogliare.*

RI'FLED, adj. *meffo a bottino, faccheggiato, predato, rubato, fvaligiato, fpogliato.*

RIFT,

RIPT, s. [cleft, chink] *feſſura, crepatura,* s. f.

To RIFT [to ſplit, to cleave] *ſpaccare, fendere.*

To rift [to belch] *ruttare, mandar fuora per la bocca il vento, che è nello ſtomaco.*

To rift, or to reef the ſails, *ammainare le vele.*

To RIG [to furniſh a ſhip with tackling] *ammannare, arredare, alleſtire,* pref. *alleſtiſco.*

To rig a ſhip, *alleſtire un vaſcello.*

To rig [to dreſs, to accoutre] *ornare, addobbare.*

RIG, s. [a wanton girl, a ſtrumpet] *una fanciulla laſciva, una puttanella.*

RI'GGED, adj. *ammannato, alleſtito.*

RI'GGING, s. *l' ammannare, ammannamento,* s. m.

The rigging of a ſhip [the ropes or cordage belonging to her] *ſartiame,* s. m. *nome generico di tutte le funi che ſi adoperano nelle navi, arredi di nave.*

RI'GGISH, adj. [wanton, whoriſh] *laſcivio, puttaneſco.*

To RI'GGLE about [to juggle about] *dimenarſi, agitarſi, muoverſi qua e là.*

RI'GGING, s. *il dimenarſi.*

RIGHT, adj. [in oppoſition to left] *dritto, diritto, deſtro, contrario di ſiniſtro.*

The right hand, *la mano diritta, o deſtra.*

Right [ſtreight] *diritto, che non piega da niuna banda, retto.*

A right line, *una linea diritta, o retta.*

The right way, *la ſtrada dritta.*

Right [honeſt, juſt] *diritto, retto, giuſto.*

Right [downright, true] *franco, vero, mero, puro.*

He is a right buffoon, *egli è un vero buffone.*

The right truth, *la pura verità.*

Right [true, proper] *vero, conveniente, opportuno.*

This is the right way, *queſto è il vero mezzo.*

This is his right name, *queſto è il ſuo proprio nome.*

To be in one's right ſenſes, *eſſere in buon ſenno.*

Right [in health] *bene, in buona ſalute.*

I am not right, *non iſto bene.*

Right, s. [claim] *diritto, e dritto,* s. m. *ragione, pretenſione.*

You have no right to, *voi non ci avete diritto alcuno.*

To maintain one's right, *mantenere il ſuo dritto.*

He aſks but that which is his right, *non domanda altro che il ſuo, non domanda ſe non il ſuo.*

Right [prerogative, privilege] *diritto, potere, privilegio,* s. m. *prerogativa, autorità,* s. f.

Right [juſtice, equity, reaſon] *diritto, ragione, giuſtizia, equità,* s. f.

To do one right, *render giuſtizia ad alcuno.*

To be in the right, *aver ragione.*

This belongs to me by right, *queſto m' appartiene per diritto.*

You ſhould not have it by right, *veramente voi non dovreſte averlo.*

I ſhould do it by right, *in giuſtizia toccherebbe a me di farlo.*

Right, adv. [well] *bene.*

I am not right, *non ſto bene.*

Very right, *molto bene.*

A right honeſt man, *un gran galantuomo, un vero uomo dabbene.*

A right learned man, *un uomo molto ſavio.*

You ſay right, *voi dite bene.*

I am in the right, *io ho ragione.*

Right over againſt, *in faccia, dirimpetto.*

Right or wrong, *bene o male, a dritta e a ſiniſtra.*

To RIGHT [to do juſtice] *fare, o render giuſtizia.*

To right one, *far giuſtizia, o diritto ad uno.*

To right one's ſelf, *farſi giuſtizia, vendicarſi.*

RI'GHTEOUS, adj. [juſt, upright, equitable] *diritto, giuſto, retto.*

RI'GHTEOUSLY, adj. *dirittamente, convenevolmente, giuſtamente.*

RI'GHTEOUSNESS, s. *giuſtizia, equità,* s. f.

RI'GHTFUL, adj. [lawful] *legitimo, ſecondo la legge.*

RI'GHTFULLY, adv. *legitimamente, raginevalmente.*

RI'GHTLY, adv. [well] *bene.*

He is ſerved rightly, *egli lo merita.*

RI'GHTS, ex. to ſet to rights [to redreſs, to rectify] *ravviare, avviare, indirizzare, metter in ordine, ordinare, aggiuſtare.*

To ſet two perſons to rights, *riconciliare, pacificare, appaciare due perſone.*

RI'GID, adj. [ſevere, ſtrict] *rigido, duro, aſpro, ſevero, auſtero.*

RIGI'DITY } s. [ſeverity] *rigidità, rigidezza, ſeverità, aſprezza, auſterità, durezza,* s. f.
RI'GIDNESS }

RI'GOL, s. [a circle] *un cerchio.*

Rigol [a diadem] *diadema,* s. m.

RI'GOUR, s. [ſeverity, roughneſs] *rigore,* s. m. *ſeverità, aſprezza, durezza,* s. f.

In the utmoſt rigour, *in tutto rigore.*

RI'GOROUS, adj. [full of rigour] *rigoroſo, ſevero, aſpro.*

Rigorous courſes, *vie rigoroſe.*

RIGO'ROUSLY, adv. *rigoroſamente, ſeveramente, aſpramente.*

RILL, s. [rivulet, ſtreamlet, brook] *ruſcello.*

To RILL [to run in ſmall ſtreams] *ſcorrere in piccioli ruſcelli.*

RI'LLET, s. [a ſmall ſtream] *ruſcelletto, rivoletto.*

RIM, s. [the border or edge of any thing] *orlo, margine di che che ſi ſia.*

The rim of the belly, *omento,* s. m. *rete,* s. f. *quel pannicolo, che cuopre gl' inteſtini degli animali.*

RIME, s. [a falling miſt] *brina, brinata, nebbia,* s. f.

Rime [the likeneſs of ſound at the end of words] *rima,* s. f. *conſonanza, o armonia procedente dalla medeſima deſinenza di parole, ſcriveſi meglio* rhyme.

Doggrel rime [paltry, pitiful rime] *rimaccie, rime baſtarde, rime cattive.*

To RIME [to make rimes] *mettere in rima, comporre delle rime.*

To make one verſe rime with another, *far che un verſo termini in rima.*

RI'MED, adj. *meſſo in rima.*

RI'MER, s. *dicitor in rima.*

RI'MING, s. *rima, il comporre in rima.*

RI'MY, adj. [foggy] *nebbioſo, brinoſo, umido.*

RIND, s. [bark, huſk] *ſcorza, corteccia, buccia,* s. f.

The rind or peel of an orange, *la corteccia d' un melangolo.*

The prickly rind of a cheſnut, *riccio,* s. m. *la ſcorza ſpinoſa della caſtagna.*

RI'NDED, adj. *che ha della corteccia.*

Thick-rinded, *che ha la corteccia groſſa.*

RING, s. [an ornament for the finger] *anello,* s. m.

Wedding ring, *anello matrimoniale.*

Diamond ring, *anello ni diamanti.*

Ring thimble, *anello di ſartore.*

Ring to run at, *anello.*

To run the ring, *correr l' anello.*

The ring of a door, *anello di porta, che ſerve in luogo di martello.*

The ring on a piece of coin, *cordoncino d' una moneta.*

A ring of people, *un cerchio di gente.*

The ring of a manage, *la volta del maneggio.*

A fine ring of bells, *un bell' accordo di campane.*

To give the bell a ring, *dar un tocco al campanello.*

An ear-ring, *orecchino,* s. m. *pendente, che ſi appicca agli orecchi delle donne.*

A ring-dove, *piccione torrajuolo.*

Ring-worm, *empitiggine, volatica,* s. f.

Ring-leader, *capo.*

Ring-tail [a kind of kite] *gheppio,* s. m.

To RING, *ſonare.*

To ring the bells, *ſonar le campane, ſcampanare.*

The bell rings, *la campana ſuona.*

To ring again, *riſonare.*

My ears ring, *le orecchie mi ſuonano.*

RI'NGER, s. *sonator di campane.*
RI'NGING, s. *il sonare le campane.*
Ringing of bells, *suono di campane, scampanata*, s. f. *scampanio*, s. m.
To RINSE [to wash] *sciacquare.*
To rinse a glass, *sciacquare un bicchiere.*
RI'NSED, adj. *sciacquato.*
RI'OT, s. [rout, excess, debauchery] *eccesso, stravizzo, disordine*, s. m. *gozzoviglia, sregolatezza*, s. f.
Riot [rout, tumult] *riotta, contesa*, s. f. *baccano, romore, fracasso, strepito, tumulto*, s. m.
Riot [in law, unlawful act, by three or more persons met together for that purpose] *violenza, disordine commesso da tre o più persone, riotta*, s. f.
To RIOT [to make a riot] *riottare, contendere, quistionare.*
To riot [to live riotously] *gozzovigliare, scialacquare, viver licenziosamente.*
To riot [to make a riot] *riottare, contendere, quistionare.*
RI'OTER, s. *uno scapestrato, uno sciagurato, uno sviato.*
RI'OTISE, s [dissoluteness, luxury] *dissolutezza, sfrenatezza.*
RI'OTOUS, adj. [given to luxury, lewd, disorderly] *licenzioso, dissoluto, sfrenato, sregolato.*
A riotous person, *una persona licenziosa.*
RI'OTOUSLY, adv. *licenziosamente, dissolutamente, sfrenatamente, sregolatamente.*
To live riotously, *viver licenziosamente, menare una vita licenziosa.*
RI'OTOUSNESS, s. [luxury, debauchery] *licenza, sfrenatezza, sregolatezza*, s. f.
To RIP [to tear; to lacerate; to cut asunder by a continued act of the knife] *stracciare; lacerare; tagliar in due con un moto continuato di strumento tagliente, scannare.*
To rip, or rip up [to unsew] *scucire.*
To rip up an old sore, *rinovellare una piaga vecchia.*
To rip, to rip open one's belly] *fendere il ventre ad uno.*
RIPE, adj. [come to maturity] *maturo, condotto alla perfezione.*
A ripe fruit, *un frutto maturo.*
Ripe years, *età matura.*
A design ripe for execution, *un disegno maturo, pronto ad essere eseguito.*
Soon ripe soon rotten, *cosa che matura con troppa fretta, presto marcisce.*
To RIPE [to ripen, to grow ripe, to be mature] *maturarsi, divenir maturo.*
To ripe, v. a. *maturare, render maturo.*
RI'PELY, adv. *maturamente.*
To RI'PEN [to grow to maturity] *maturare, venire a perfezione.*
To ripen [to bring to maturity] *maturare, dar fine, compimento.*
Time has ripen'd my designs, *il tempo ha maturato il mio disegno.*
Ripened, adj. *maturato, maturo.*
RI'PENESS, s. *maturità, maturezza, maturazione*, s. f.
RI'PENING, s. *maturamento*, s. m. *il maturare.*
Ripening, adj. [apt to ripen] *maturante, maturativo.*
RI'PIER, s. [one that brings fish from the sea-coasts to sell in the inland parts] *rivenditor di pesce.*
To RI'PLE [a sea term, to froth] *spumare, parlando del mare.*
RI'PPED } adj. [from to rip] *scu-*
RI'PPED up } *cito.*
RI'PPER, s. *quello o quella che scuce, che lacera o straccia.*
RISE, s. [the head or spring of a river] *l' origine, la scaturigine, la sorgente d' un fiume*
Rise [occasion, cause] *origine, causa, cagione*, s. f. *principio, cominciamento, nascimento.*
Rise [preferment] *aggrandimento, avanzamento, accrescimento*, s. m.
The rise of the sun, or the sun-rise, *il levar del sole, l' apparire, il nascer del sole.*
To RISE [to spring up, to come, to proceed] *scaturire, sorgere, aver la sua scaturigine.*
To rise from bed, *levarsi, uscir di letto.*
Why do you rise so soon? *perchè vi levate così a buon' ora?*
To rise from table, *levarsi di tavola.*
To rise [to begin to appear on the horizon, as the sun, the moon, and the stars do] *levarsi, cominciare ad apparire.*
The sun rises, *il sole si leva.*
To rise [to go upwards] *levarsi.*
The vapours rise from the water, *i vapori si levano dall' acqua.*
To rise [to make an insurrection] *levarsi in armi, rivoltarsi.*
To rise [to grow bigger, to swell] *gonfiarsi, ingrossare.*
Her belly begins to rise, *il suo ventre comincia a gonfiarsi.*
The waters begin to rise, *le acque cominciano a crescere, a gonfiarsi.*
To rise [to ferment, as dough does, lievitarsi, levitarsi.*
The corn begins to rise [to grow dear] *il grano comincia ad' incarire, a crescer di prezzo.*
To rise from the dead, *risuscitar da' morti.*
To rise up in arms, *prender le armi, sollevarsi, rivoltarsi.*
RI'SEN, adj. *levato*, v. To rise.
RI'SER, s. ex. [an early riser] *un uomo che si leva di buon' ora.*
RI'SIBLE, s. [capable of laughing] *risibile.*
RISIBI'LITY, s. [the being capable of laughing] *risibilità*, s. f.
RI'SING, s. [the appearing above the horizon] *il levare, il far del sole.*
The rising of a hill, *la scoscesa, il pendio d' una collina.*
A rising [or insurrection] *sollevazione, rivolta, ribellione*, s. f.
A rising of the skin, *tumore*, s. m. *gonfiagione*, s. f.
The rising from the dead, *la resurrezione della carne.*
Rising, adj. *levante, nascente.*
The rising sun, *il sol nascente.*
A rising passion, *una passione crescente.*
A rising ground, *un' altezza, un' eminenza.*
A rising man [a thriving man] *un uomo che s' avanza, e s' aggrandisce.*
RISK, s. [hazard, chance] *rischio, risico, pericolo, ripentaglio*, s. m.
To RISK [to venture, to hazard] *arrischiare, mettere in cimento, in pericolo, a ripentaglio.*
RISKER, s. *colui che arrischia, che mette a pericolo.*
RITE, s. [order observed on solemn occasions, a church ceremony] *rito, statuto*, s. m.
RITORNE'LLO, s. [repetition of some notes at the end of a song, or a couplet of verses at the end of a stanza] *ritornello*, s. m.
RI'TUAL, s. [a book containing the particular rights and ceremonies of a church] *rituale*, s. m. *libro nel quale si contengono i riti, o le cerimonie d' una chiesa.*
Ritual, adj. *rituale, solennemente fatto e secondo il rito religioso.*
RI'TUALIST, s. [a stickler for ceremonies in religious worship] *un difensore de' riti, e delle cerimonie della chiesa.*
RI'VAGE, s. *riva, ripa, sponda, costa, lito, lido.*
RI'VAL, s. [one who stands in competition with another, especially in love affairs] *rivale*, s. m. f. *concorrente d' amore nello stesso obbietto.*
Rival [competitor] *rivale, competitore.*
To RI'VAL one [to be his rival] *esser rivale, emulare.*
RI'VALRY } s. [competition] *ri-*
RI'VALSHIP } *valità, concorrenza*, s. f.
To RIVE [to cleave asunder] *spaccare, fendere.*
To rive asunder, verb neut. *spaccarsi, fendersi.*
To RI'VEL [to contract into wrinkles and corrugations] *aggrinzare.*
RI'VEN, adj. *spaccato, fesso.*
RI'VER, s. [a great stream of water running from its spring] *riviera*, s. f. *fiume*, s. m.
RI'VER-DRAGON, s. *coccodrillo*; e *figuratamente, nome dato al re d' egitto da Milton.*
RI'VER-GOD, s. *fiume*; *deità tutelare d' un fiume.*
RI'VER-HORSE, s. *caval marino, ippopotamo.*
RI'VER-WATER, *acqua di riviera.*
RI'VET, s. [a riveted nail] *chiodo o pezzo di ferro ribadito da' due lati.*

To

To Ri'vet [to clinch] *ribadire*, pres. *ribadisco*.
To rivet a nail, *ribadire un chiodo*.
To rivet a thing in one's mind, *imprimere, scolpire che che si sia nella memoria*.
Ri'veted, adj. *ribadito*.
Ri'vulet, s. [a little river, a small brook] *ruscello, rivoletto*, s. m.
Rix-dollar, s. [a German coin] *tollero*, s. m. *spezie di moneta d'Alemagna*.
Roach, s. [a sort of fish] *pesce d'acqua dolce*.
As sound as a roach, *sano come una lasca, d'intera sanità*.
Road, s. [high-way] *strada, via*, s. f. *cammino largo*, s. m.
Road [where ships ride at anchor] *piaggia*, s. f.
Road [inroad] *scorrimento*, s. m. *scorreria*, s. f.
Road [journey] *viaggio per terra*.
To Roam [to range and ramble up and down] *scorrere, correre attorno, andar ramingo, trascorrere, andar errando, vagare, vagabondare*, pret. *scorsi, trascorsi*.
Ro'amed, adj. *scorso, andato attorno, trascorso, vagato, vagabondato*.
Ro'amer, s. *vagabondo, errante*, s. m.
Roan, s. [a sort of colour in horses] *sagginato*.
A roan horse, *cavallo sagginato*.
Roar, s. *mugghio, ruggito, grida strepitose, mormorio orrendo*.
To Roar [to cry out like a lion] *ruggire*, pres. *ruggisco*.
The sea roars, *il mare rugge*.
To roar [to cry out hideously] *ruggire, gridare orrendamente*.
To roar [to sound as the wind or sea] *mugghiare come fa 'l mare, o il vento*.
Ro'ared, adj. *ruggito, gridato*.
Ro'aring, s. *ruggito, mugghio, mugghiamento*, s. m.
The roaring of the sea, *il ruggito, o mugghio del mare*.
Ro'ary, adj. [dewy] *rugiadoso*.
To Ro'ast, *arrostire, ardere in faccia al fuoco senza distruggere affatto la cosa così esposta*.
Roast, *in vece di* roasted.
To rule the roast, *governare a suo modo, commandar a bacchetta*.
Ro'asted, adj. *arrostito*.
Roast-meat, s. *carne arrostita*.
To Rob [to take away by force] *rubare, tor l'altrui o per inganno, o per violenza*.
To rob a house, *rubare una casa*.
I will not rob you of that pleasure, *non voglio privarvi di questo piacere*
To rob Peter to pay Paul, *scoprire un altare per ricoprirne un altro, fare un debito nuovo, per pagarne un vecchio*.
To rob upon the highway, *gittarsi alla strada, andare alla strada, rubar le strade*.

Ro'bbed, adj. *rubato*.
Ro'bber, s. *rubatore, ladro*, s. m. *rubatrice, ladra*, s. f.
A church-robber, *un sacrilego*.
A sea-robber, *un corsale, un pirata*.
Ro'bbery, s. *ruba, ruberia, rapina*, s. f. *rubamento, ladroneccio*, s. m.
Ro'bbing, s. *rubamento, ladroneccio*, s. m.
Robe, s. [a long vest or gown] *vesta, veste*, s. m.
The gentlemen of the long robe, *le persone togate*.
To Robe [to dress pompously] *vestire pomposamente, ornare di veste magnifica*.
Ro'bin } Ro'bin-red-erbast } *pettirosso*, s. m. *uccello che ha il petto rosso*.
Robin-good-fellow [a boon companion] *un buon compagnone*.
Robu'st } Robu'stous } adj. [strong, lusty] *robusto, forte, gagliardo*.
Robu'stness, s. [strength] *robustezza, gagliardia, fortezza di membra*.
Rocambo'le, s. [a sort of wild garlick] *sorta d'aglio salvatico*.
To rock, v. n. [to be violently agitated] *essere dimenato o agitato violentemente*.
Roche, s. [rock] *rocca, roccia, balza, scoscesa, rupe*, s. f.
Roche-alum [a sort of mineral] *allume di rocca*.
Ro'chet, s. [a kind of surplice worn by bishops,] &c. *rocchetto*, s. m. *sopravveste clericale di tela bianca*.
Rock, s. [a mass of stone] *rocca, roccia, balza, scoscesa, rupe*, s. f.
A rock of crystal, *cristallo di rocca*.
Rocks in the sea, *scogli*.
Rock [an instrument used in spinning] *rocca*, s. f. *strumento da filare*.
To Rock, verb act. *cullare, dimenar la culla*.
To rock a child, *cullare un bambino*.
To rock [to reel] *barcollare*.
Ro'cked, adj. *cullato*.
Ro'ckless, adj [without rocks] *senza rocche, senza scogli*.
Ro'ckwork, s. stones fixed in mortar in imitation of the asperities of rocks] *sassi fitti nella calce o cimento a imitazione d'un luogo scosceso*.
Ro'cky, adj. [full of rocks] *montagnoso, pieno di rocche, e di scogli*.
Rocky, adj. *duro, sassoso, aspro*.
Rod, s. [wand, long twig] *verga, bacchetta*, s. f.
Rod [to whip with] *frusta, sferza*, s. f.
Save the rod and spoil the child, *madre pietosa, figlio tignoso*.
Angling-rod, *canna da pescare*.
Rod-net [to catch blackbirds and wood-cocks] *ragna*, s. f.

Ro'domontade, s. [a vain-glorious bragging or boasting] *giattanza, millanteria*, s. f.
Rof, s. [a kind of deer] *capriuolo*, s. m. *spezie di damma*.
A roe buck, *caprio*, s. m. *damma*, s. f.
The hard roe of fish, *uova di pesce*.
The soft roe of fish, *latte di pesce*.
Roga'tion, s. ex. the rogation week [the next but one before Whitsunday] *le rogazioni*.
Rogue, s. [villain, knave, cheat] *un furbo, un furfante, un barattiere, un mariuolo*.
Rogue [thief] *un ladro*.
Rogue [being used in a familiar way, is sometimes a word of kindness] *cattivello, cattivella, bricconcello, bricconcella, furfantello, furfantella*.
To play the rogue [to jest] *scherzare, burlare*.
Ro'guery, s. [knavery] *furberia, furfanteria, mariuoleria, baratteria*; s. f.
Roguery [banter, raillery] *burla*, s. f. *scherzo, giuoco*, s. m.
Ro'guish, adj. [knavish] *furbesco, da furbo, da briccone*.
Roguish tricks, *atti furberschi, azioni da furfante, tratti da briccone, bricconerie, furfanterie*.
Roguish eyes, *occhi assassini*.
Ro'guishly, adv. *furbescamente, da briccone*.
Ro'guishness, s. *furfanteria, bricconeria, mariuoleria*, s. f.
Roguishness [bantering] *burla*, s. f. *scherzo, giuoco*, s. m.
To Ro'ist } To Ro'ister } [to behave turbulently, to act : t discretion, to be at free quarter, to bluster] *far il bravaccio e il cattivo, esser turbolento, violento, o soverchiatore, bravare*.
Ro'ster, s. [a turbulent, brutal, lawless, blustering fellow] *un uomo violento, torbido, e minacciante; un gradassaccio*.
Roke, s. [sweat] *sudore*, s. m.
To make one's self all in a roke, *sudar da capo a' piedi*.
Roll, s. [a bundle of any thing rolled up] *involglio, ruolo*, s. m.
A roll of parchment, *un ruolo di pergamena*.
A roll of tobacco, *un ruolo di tabacco*.
A roll [to strike any thing even] *rullo*, s. m.
A roll [a list of names] *ruolo*, s. m.
To Roll [to make up into a roll] *invogliare, avviluppare, inviluppare*.
To roll [to turn] *rotolare, ruotolare, voltolare*.
To roll one's eyes, *girar gli occhi*.
To roll land [to break the clods with a roller] *rullar il terreno*.
To roll in money, *esser danajoso, essere ricchissimo*.

To

To roll down, verb neut. *voltolarsi, rivolgersi in giro per terra.*

ROʹLLED, adj. *invogliato, inviluppato, avviluppato, v.* To roll.

ROʹLLER, s. [a round piece of wood to break clods] *rullo, s. f. strumento di legname, che spiana e trita il terreno.*

Roller, s. [a swathing band for young children] *fascia, s. f.*

ROʹLLING, s. *rotolamento, voltolamento, s. m.*

Rolling, adj. ex. a rolling pin, *spianatojo.*

Rolling eyes, *occhi stralunati.*

A rolling stone gathers no moss, *pietra che rotola non fa muffa.*

ROʹMAN, adj. [belonging to the city or church of Rome] *Romano.*

Roman church, *chiesa Romana.*

Roman letter, *lettera Romana, lettera tonda.*

Roman-like, *alla Romana.*

ROMAʹNCE [a feigned story] *romanzo, s. m.*

A romance, *una favola, una menzogna, una fola.*

To ROʹMANCE [to tell lies] *contar favole.*

ROMAʹNCER, s. *romanziere, s. m. che compone romanzi.*

ROʹMANIST, s. [papist] *un cattolico Romano.*

ROMAʹNTICK, adj. [belonging to romance] *favoloso, vano, chimerico.*

Romantick [improbable, false] *improbabile, inverisimile, falso.*

Romantick [fanciful; full of wild scenery] *scenico, solitario, romitico, romitano, selvaggio, capriccioso; e dicesi per lo più d' un luogo vagamente campestre.*

ROʹMESCOT, s. [a certain tribute formerly paid to Rome] *certo tributo che si pagava anticamente alla corte di Roma dagl' Inglesi.*

ROʹMISH, adj. [popish] *Romano.*

Romish-church, *chiesa Romana.*

ROMP, s. [a rude, awkward, boisterous, untaught girl] *ragazzaccia di contado, che è malcreata, rumorosa, balorda, e amante di trescare.*

Romp, *giuoco da villano, tresche contadinesche.*

To ROMP, *trescare come fanno i contadini.*

ROOD, s. [the fourth part of an acre] *la quarta parte d' una bifolca.*

Rood [a cross] *una croce.*

The holy-rood days, *il giorno di santa croce.*

A rood loft [a shrine on which a crucifix was placed] *cassetta che conteneva un crocifisso.*

ROOF, s. [the top of a house] *il tetto d' una casa.*

Roof-tile, *tegola, s. f.*

The roof of the mouth, *il palato.*

The roof of a coach, *il cielo d' una carrozza.*

ROOK, s. [a fowl] *spezie di cornacchia, s. f.*

Rook [one of the chess-men] *rocco, s. m. torre, s. f. una di quelle figure, colle quali si giuoca agli scacchi.*

A rook [a cheat, a sharper] *un furfante, un barattiere, un mariuolo.*

A rook [a cunning man] *un uomo fine, astuto, sagace, un volpone.*

To ROOK [to cheat, to bubble] *ingannare, mariuolare, truffare, acchiappare.*

ROʹOKED, adj. *ingannatò, mariuolato, truffato, acchiappato.*

ROʹOKERY, s. [a nursery of rooks] *luogo pieno di cornacchie.*

ROʹOKING, s. *mariuoleria, truffa, s. f. inganno, s. m.*

ROʹOKY, adj. [inhabited by rooks] *pieno di cornacchie.*

ROOM, s. [an apartment in a house] *camera, stanza.*

A small room, *una camerella, una cameretta.*

A dining room, *sala da mangiare.*

Room [place] *luogo, spazio, s. m.*

He is come in my room, *egli deve entrare in mio luogo.*

Here is not room for all, *qui non c' è spazio per tutti.*

I will make room for you, *io vi farò luogo.*

Room [occasion reason] *luogo, soggetto, s. m. occasione, ragione, cagione.*

You have no room to complain, *voi non avete cagione di lamentarvi.*

There is no room to doubt of it, *non v' è luogo da dubitarne.*

ROʹOMY, adj. [spacious] *largo, ampio, spazioso.*

ROOST, s. [a place where fowls rest] *pollajo, s. m. luogo dove i polli stanno a dormire.*

To ROOST [to rest as fowls do] *appollajarsi, l' andare che fanno i polli a dormire.*

The hens go to roost, *le galline vanno ad appollajarsi.*

The ROOT, s. [that part of a plant which grows downward] *radice, barba, s. f.*

To take root, *radicarsi, appigliarsi alla terra colle radici, abbarbicarsi.*

The root of the nails, of hair, of corn, &c. *la radice dell' unghie, de' capelli, del grano, e simili.*

Root [rise, beginning] *radici, cagione, origine, s. f. principio.*

Covetousness is the root of all evils, *l' avarizia è la radice d' ogni male.*

Root [in grammar, original word] *una parola primitiva.*

Square root [in arithmetick, number, which being multiplied by itself, produces a power called a square] *radice quadra, termine aritmetico.*

Cube root [number, which being multiply'd twice by itself, produces a power called a cube] *radice cuba.*

To ROOT up, or root out, *sradicare, sbarbare, sbarbicare, sveller dalle radici.*

To root up a tree, *sradicare un albero.*

To root out a vice, *sradicare, sbarbicare un vizio.*

To root [to rout, as swine do] *scavare la terra col grifo, come fanno i porci.*

ROʹOTED in, adj. *radicato, abarbicato.*

Rooted up, or rooted out, *sradicato, sbarbicato.*

ROʹOTING out } ROʹOTING up } *sradicamento, diradicamento, lo sbarbicare.*

ROʹOTY, adj. [full of roots] *che ha molte radici.*

ROPE, s. [cord] *corda, fune, s. f.*

Rope-girt, *la punta d' una corda.*

A small rope, *corda piccola.*

The ropes [or cordages] of a ship, *sartiame di vascello.*

Name not a rope where one has hanged himself, *non bisogna parlar di corda in casa dell' impiccato.*

A rope of onions, *una resta di cipolle.*

A rope of pearls, *un filo, un vezzo di perle.*

Rope-ripe, adj. *che merita la forca, impiccatojo.*

Rope-yard, *il luogo dove si fanno le corde.*

Rope-maker, *funajo, funajuolo.*

Rope-dancer, *ballerino di corda.*

To ROPE [to run thick, as some liquors do] *filare.*

ROʹPERY, s. [rogue's-tricks] *bricconeria, furfanteria.*

ROʹPETRICK, s. [trick that deserves the halter] *bricconeria, tiro che merita la corda.*

ROPY, adj. [clammy, slimy] *viscoso, tenace.*

ROʹQUELAURE, s. [a cloak for men] *sorta di ferrajuolo con maniche.*

ROʹRID, adj. [dewy] *rugiadoso, pieno di rugiada.*

ROʹSARY, s. a set of beads called fifteens, containing fifteen pater-nosters, and an hundred and fifty ave-maria's] *rosario, s. m. il recitamento di avemarie e paternostri in numero particolare, ad onor della santissima Vergine, e la filza delle pallottole sù cui si stanno contando mentre si ricitano.*

ROSA-SOLIS, s. [an herb] *sorta d' erba.*

ROSE, s. [a flower] *rosa, s. f.*

No rose without a thorn, *non v' è rosa senza spine.*

Oil of roses, *olio rosato.*

Honey of roses, *mele rosato.*

A rose-bud, *un bottone di rosa.*

Rose-water, *acqua rosata, o acqua rosa.*

The rose of a musical instrument, *la rosa d' uno strumento musicale.*

The golden rose [a rose which the Pope usually blesses at mass, upon a Sunday in Lent] *rosa d' oro che benedice il Papa per mandare a' principi.*

Under the rose [privately, secretly] *privatamente, segretamente.*

Be it spoken under the rose [between you and I] *che la cosa non vada*

più

più avanti, che ciò sia detto fra me a voi.

Rose-tree, *rosajo*, s. m. *pianta che produce la rosa.*

Rose, *è un preterito del verbo* To rise.

RO'SEMARY, s. [a plant well known] *rosmarino, ramerino*, s. m. *pianta nota.*

ROSICRU'CIANS, s. [chymists who call themselves brothers of the rosy cross] *frati della croce rossa, chimici che si facevano così chiamare.*

RO'SIER, s. [rosebush] *roseto*, s. m. *luogo pieno di rosai.*

RO'SIN, s. [an oily juice that runs out of some trees] *ragia*, s. f.

RO'SINED, adj. [full of rosin] *resinoso, ragioso.*

RO'STRATED, adj. [adorned with beaks of ships] *rostrato, adorno di timoni di vascelli.*

RO'STRUM, s. [the beak of a bird] *il becco d' un uccello; rostro.*

Rostrum [the beak of a ship] *timone d' uno nave.*

Rostrum [the scaffold where orators harangued] *il rostro dove li antichi romani arringavano.*

Rostrum [the pipe which conveys the distilling liquor into its receiver in the common alembicks] *becco di lambicco.*

RO'SY, adj. *rosèo, di color di rose.*

Rosy lips, *labbra vermiglie; labbra di rose.*

ROT, s. [disease in sheep] *moria*, s. f. *mortalità pestilenziale fra le pecore.*

Rot, s. *putrefazione, putridezza*, s. f.

To ROT [to putrefy] *infracidare, infradiciare, putrefare, marcire*, pres. *marcisco.*

To rot [to grow rotten] *infracidarsi, infradiciarsi, putrefarsi.*

To rot in a jail, *marcire in prigione.*

ROTA, s. [the chief jurisdiction of the court of Rome] *rota*, s. f. *la principale giurisdizione della corte di Roma.*

ROTA'TION, s. [the act of turning round like a wheel] *rotazione*, s. f. *il rotare.*

Rotation [vicissitude] *ruota, rivoluzione*, s. f. *cambiamento*, s. m.

ROTE, s. *pratica.*

To learn by rote, *imparar per pratica.*

To ROTE [to fix in the memory without informing the understanding] *imparar per pratica; fissar nella memoria senza esame dell' intelletto.*

RO'TCUT, s. *birra cattiva, birra che marcisce le budella.*

RO'THER-BEASTS, s. [horned beasts] *bestiame grosso.*

Rother-soil [the dung of horned beasts] *lo sterco del bestiame cornuto.*

RO'TTEN, adj. *infracidato, infradiciato, putrefatto, marcio, marcito, fracido.*

A rotten apple, *una mela fracida, o fradicia.*

Rotten flesh, *carne putrefatta.*

A rotten egg, *uovo imputridito.*

Rotten wood, *legno fracido.*

He is dead and rotten, *è morto e ridotto in polve.*

A man rotten at the core [not of sound principles] *un uomo cattivo, di mala coscienza, di principi scellerati.*

RO'TTENNESS, s. *fracidezza, fradicezza, fracidume, putrefazione*, s. f.

ROTU'NDITY, s. [roundness] *rotondità*, s. f.

To ROVE [to ramble, to range, to wander] *andar ramingo, vagare, andar attorno, correr qua e la.*

RO'VER, s. [pirate] *corsale, pirata*, s. m.

At rovers, adv. [at random] *inconsideratamente, a caso, a vanvera, disavvedutamente, temerariamente, a tastone.*

To shoot at rovers [to do things at random] *fare che che si sia all' ciera, inconsideratamente, a ventura, a caso.*

ROUGH, adj. [harsh, uneven, rugged] *ruvido, rozzo, aspro, scabro, scabroso.*

Rough skin, *pelle ruvida.*

Rough wine, *vino ruvido.*

Rough way, *strada scabrosa.*

Rough [harsh, severe, grim] *ruvido, rozzo, scortese, villano, zotico.*

Rough stile, *stile rozzo.*

A rough diamond [neither cut nor polished] *un diamante greggio o grezzo, tal quale si ritrova nella miniera, rozzo, non pulito.*

Rough [hairy, bristly] *rozzo, ispido, irsuto.*

Rough [homely] *rustico, villano, grossolano.*

Rough [proud] *superbo, fiero, arrogante, insolente.*

A rough sea, *mar tempestoso.*

A rough-draught, *uno schizzo, un abbozzo.*

The rough draught of a deed, *il primo abbozzo d' un contratto.*

RO'UGH-CAST, adj. *arricciato.*

To RO'UGH-CAST a wall, *arricciare un muro, dargli la prima crosta rozza della calcina.*

To RO'UGH-HEW, *abbozzare, schizzare.*

RO'UGH-HEWN, adj. *abbozzato, schizzato.*

RO'UGHLY, adv. *rozzamente, aspramente, zoticamente, scortesemente, incivilmente, grossolanamente.*

RO'UGHNESS, s. [ruggedness] *rozzezza, ruvidezza, asprezza*, s. f.

Roughness of stile, *ruvidezza di stile.*

Roughness [harshness, severity] *rozzezza, zotichezza, scortesia, villania, severità, austerità*, s. f.

RO'UGHT, *antico preterito del verbo* To reach.

RO'UNCE, s. [the handle of a printing press] *manovella di torchio di stampatore.*

RO'UNCEVAL-PEAS [a kind of large peas, from Rounceval, a place at the foot of the Pyrenean hills] *piselli di Roncisvalle.*

ROUND, adj. [in form of a circle or ball] *rotondo, ritondo, tondo.*

To have a round delivery [or clear utterance] *esprimersi, parlar facilmente, e speditamente.*

A good round trot [a quick troting pace] *un bel trotto.*

Round house, *carrere.*

To make round, *ridurre in forma tonda.*

A round sum of money, *una buona somma di danari.*

To drink round, *bere in giro.*

To look round, *guardar attorno.*

Round, s. *giro, cerchio*, s. m.

To take a round, *fare un giro, una girata.*

The sun having made his round, *il sole avendo finito il suo corso.*

To walk the round, or the rounds [among soldiers] *far la ronda.*

In the whole round of my life, *in tutto il corso della mia vita.*

Round, adv. *in giro, all' intorno.*

To turn round, *voltarsi in giro.*

My head turns round, *la testa mi gira.*

The sun goes round the world, *il sole fa il giro del mondo.*

A river that goes round the walls, *un fiume che attornia le mura, che va attorno le mura.*

All the year round, *tutto l' anno.*

Ten miles round, *dieci miglia all' intorno.*

Round about, *tutt' all' intorno, da ogni parte.*

I took a view of the countries round about, *visitai tutto 'l paese circonvicino.*

You must go round about, *bisogna che voi facciate il giro.*

To ROUND [to make or cut round] *ridurre in forma tonda.*

To round one in the ear [to whisper something in his ear] *soffiare che che si sia negli orecchi ad uno.*

RO'UNDED, adj. *fatto tondo.*

RO'UNDEL, } s. [a song beginning and ending
RO'UNDELAY, } with the same sentence] *strambotto*, s. m.

RO'UNDEL, s. [circumference, enclosure] *chiuso, circonferenza.*

RO'UNDHEAD, s. [a puritan; so named from the practice once prevalent among them of cropping their hair round] *testa tonda, soprannome dato a certa razza di Calvinisti in Inghilterra che avevano in costume di tagliarsi i capelli corti.*

RO'UNDISH, adj. *ritondetto, alquanto tondo.*

RO'UNDLY, adv. *ritondamente.*

Roundly [honestly, sincerely] *schiettamente, apertamente, sinceramente, onestamente, fedelmente.*

To go roundly to work, *operare schiettamente, sinceramente, in buona fede, entrar per l' uscio, tener la linea retta, incamminarsi al fine co' mezzi debiti.*

Roundly [boldly, freely] *francamente, rettamente, schiettamente, liberamente.*

I tell you roundly, *vi dico francamente.*

To take one up roundly [to rebuke one sharply] *fare una ripassata ad alcuno, sgridarlo.*

RO'UNDNESS, s. *rotondità, ritondità, ritondezza,* s. f.

ROUNDS, *v.* Round.

ROUSE, s. *dose di liquore un po' troppo forte.*

To ROUSE, *v.* To rouze.

RO'USSELET, s. [a kind of pear] *spezie de pero.*

ROUT, s. [a multitude or throng of people] *folla, calca, pressa,* s. f. *concorso di popolo.*

Rout [squabble, noise] *sciarra, contesa,* s. f. *disturbo, fracasso, strepito,* s. m.

Rout [the way which the soldiers are to march] *sfilata,* s. f. *passo di soldati.*

Rout [defeat of an army] *rotta, sconfitta d' esercito.*

The rout of a deer, *la traccia d' un cervo.*

To ROUT [to put to the rout, to defeat an army] *mettere in rotta, sconfiggere.*

To rout one [to put him out of his measures] *imbarrazzare, confondere, imbrogliare alcuno.*

ROUTE, s. [road, way] *strada, via, cammino.*

Row, s. [order, rank] *filare,* s. m. *fila,* s. f.

A row of houses, or of trees, *un filare di case, o d' alberi.*

A row of teeth, *un ordine di denti.*

To set in a row, *ordinare, mettere in fila.*

Criss cross-row, or Christ-cross-row, *abbicì, saltero, alfabeto.*

ROW-BARGE, *barca che va a vele, e a remi.*

To Row [to tug at the oar] *remare, spignere la nave per l' arqua co' remi, vogare.*

To row against the stream, *remare a ritroso, andar contro la corrente.*

To look one way, and row another, *accennare in coppe, e dare in bastoni, mostrare di voler fare una cosa, e farne un' altra.*

They don't row together [or don't agree] *eglino non vanno d' accordo; uno tira da una banda e l' altro dall' altra.*

RO'WEL, s. [the goad or pricks of a spur] *stella,* s. f. *quella parte dello sprone, fatta a uso di stella, che pugne.*

RO'WER, s. [one that rows] *rematore,* s. m.

The rower that rows with the first oar in a galley, *spalliere, colui che voga alla spalliera della galea.*

The fore rower, or chief rower in a galley, *portolatto,* s. m. *colui che nella galea è il primo a vogare, e che da il tempo egli altri che vogano dopo di lui.*

RO'WING, s. *il remare, il vogare.*

To ROWZE [to awake] *svegliare, destare, rompere il sonno.*

To rowze one, to rowze him up, *svegliare, destare alcuno.*

He rowzed me out of my first sleep, *egli m' ha rotto il primo sonno.*

To rowze a deer, *levare un daino.*

To rowze up one's spirits, *animarsi, prender animo.*

To rowze in [a sea term, to haul or pull in] *tirare coll' alzana.*

RO'WZED, adj. *svegliato, destato.*

RO'WZING, s. *lo svegliare, destamento,* s. m.

Rowzing, adv. ex. a rowzing lie, *una gran menzogna.*

RO'YAL, adj. [belonging to a king] *reale, regale, da Re; attenente e convenіente a Rè.*

The royal society, *la società reale.*

The royal family, *la famiglia reale.*

Royal [noble, magnificent] *reale, nobile, magnifico, superbo.*

RO'YALIST, s. [one who is of the King's party] *colui che tiene pel Re.*

RO'YALLY, s. adv. *realmente, regalmente, da Re, nobilmente, magnificamente, superbamente.*

RO'YALTY, s. [royal dignity, kingship] *realtà,* s. f. *dignità reale.*

The ensigns of royalty, *le insegne della realtà.*

The RO'YALTIES, s. [or royal rights] *le prerogative regali d' un Rè.*

To RO'YNE [to gnaw, to bite] *rodere, rosicchiare, morsicchiare,* obs.

RO'YNISH, adj. [paltry, sorry, mean] *povero, meschino, vile, abjetto.*

RUB, s. [obstacle, hindrance] *intoppo, ostacolo, impedimento,* s. m.

Rub [banter] *bottone, scherzo aruto e mordace.*

To give one a dry rub, *sbottonare, sbottoneggiare alcuno, dire alcun motto contr' uno.*

To rub [to wipe hard] *stropicciare, fregare, strofinare.*

To rub shoes, *stroppicciare le scarpe.*

To rub a thing against another, *fregare una cosa contro ad un' altra.*

To rub one's head against a thing, *dar della testa contro a qualche cosa.*

To rub [to scratch] *grattare.*

To rub a horse, *strofinare un cavallo.*

To rub off a spot, *levare una macchia fregando.*

Things rub on bravely, *le cose vanno a seconda.*

I make shift to rub on, *m' ingegno di guadagnarmi il pane bel bello; mi sforzo di tirare innanzi.*

To rub one up, *dare un bottone ad uno, sbottoneggiarlo.*

To rub up one's memory [to rub up the remembrance of a thing] *rinfrescar la memoria di qualche cosa, rimettersela nella memoria.*

RU'BARB, *v.* Rhubarb.

RU'BBED, adj. *stropicciato, fregato, strofinato.*

RU'BBER, s. [or rubbing cloth] *strofinaccio, strofinácciolo,* s. m.

RU'BBING, s. *strofinamento, stropicciamento,* s. m. *stropicciagione, stropicciatura,* s. f.

A rubbing cloth, *strofinaccio, strofinacciolo,* s. m.

A rubbing brush, *spázzola fatta di setole di porco per uso di nettare.*

RU'BBISH, s. [the refuse of buildings, as brick, mortar, dirt, &c.] *calcinaccio,* s. m.

Rubbish [old tatter'd cloaths] *stracci, cenci, robe vecchie.*

Rubbish [sorry stuff] *robaccia, roba cattiva.*

RU'BBLE, *v.* Rubbish.

RU'BICUND, adj. [blood-red] *rubicondo, rosseggiante.*

RU'BIED, adj. *del colore del rubino, rosseggiante.*

RUBI'FICK, adj. *che fa rosseggiare.*

To RU'BIFY [to make red] *tinger in rosso, far rosso.*

RU'BIOUS, adj. *rosso, rosseggiante, non è in uso.*

RU'BRICK, adj. [red] *rosso.*

Rubrick, s. [the directions given in the liturgy, so called because formerly written or printed in red] *rubrica.*

RUBY, s. [a precious stone] *rubino,* s. m. *pietra preziosa di color rosso.*

Ruby, adj. [red] *rosso.*

To RUD [to make red] *far rosso, tinger in rosso.*

RU'DDER, s [a piece of timber which serves to direct the course of a ship] *timone,* s. m. *quel legno, col quale si regge la nave.*

RU'DDLE, s. [a sort of red earth] *sinopia,* s. f. *spezie di terra di color rosso.*

RU'DDOCK, s. [a robin-red-breast] *pettirosso,* s. m. *uccelletto col petto rosso.*

RU'DDY, adj. [red, rubicund] *rubicondo, rosso, rosseggiante.*

RU'DE, adj. [rough] *rozzo, grossolano, materiale, mal fatto.*

A rudedraught, *un abbozzo grossolano, uno schizzo mal fatto.*

Rude [clownish] *rozzo, ruvido, zotico, villano, rustico.*

Rude [insolent, saucy] *incivile, scortese, malcreato, insolente, impertinente.*

Rude [ignorant] *ignorante, grossolano.*

The rude multitude [the vulgar] *la canaglia, il popolaccio, la plebe.*

To give one rude language, *parlare incivilmente ad uno, maltrattarlo con parole, svillaneggiarlo, dirgli villania.*

RU'DELY, adv. [coarſely] *groſſolanamente, alla peggio.*

Rudely [uncivilly] *incivilmente, inſolentemente, villanamente, da villano.*

RU'DENESS, s. [clowniſhneſs] *rozzezza, zotichezza, ignoranza, ruſtichezza, ſalvatichezza, ruſticità,* s. f.

Rudeneſs [incivility, inſolence] *incivilità, brutalità, inſolenza, impertinenza, malacreanza,* s. f.

RU'DIMENTS, s. [the firſt principles or grounds of any art or ſcience] *rudimenti, primi principi.*

RUE, s. [an herb well known] *ruta,* s. f. *pianta nota.*

Of rue, *rutato, di ruta.*

To RUE [to repent] *pentirſi.*

You ſhall rue it as long as you live, *ve ne pentirete mentre avrete vita.*

I'll make him rue the time that ever he did it, *gli farò beſtemmiare il giorno, che fece queſto.*

RU'EFUL, adj. [ſad, pitiful] *povero, meſchino, miſerabile, compaſſionevole, degno di pietà.*

Rueful [dreadful] *terribile.*

RU'EFULLY, adv. ex. He looks ruefully, *ha una triſta cera.*

RUE'LLE, s. [an aſſembly at a private houſe] *aſſemblea in una caſa privata.*

RUFF, s. [an old faſhioned ornament for the neck] *lattuga, gorgiera,* s. f.

Ruff [a kind of fiſh] *ſorta di peſce.*

To RUFF [to trump at cards] *pigliare una carta col trionfo.*

RU'FFIAN, s. [aſſaſſin, deſperate villian] *un maſnadiere, un furfante, un aſſaſſino, uno ſcellerato.*

Ruffian, adj. [brutal; ſavagely boiſterous] *brutale, ſanguinario.*

To RU'FFIAN [to rage, to raiſe tumults; to play the ruffian] *operare da ſcellerato, da ribelle, da crudele, da aſſaſſino.*

RU'FFLE, s. *manichino,* s. m.

Laced ruffles, *manichini di merletto.*

RU'FFLE, s. *diſturbo, conteſa, tumulto.*

To RU'FFLE [to fold into ruffles] *increſpare.*

To ruffle a napkin [to fold it into ruffles] *increſpare una ſalvietta.*

To ruffle [to rumple] *ſcompigliare, diſordinare, confondere,* pret. *confuſi.*

To ruffle [to diſorder, or diſcompoſe] *diſturbare, inquietare, diſordinare, ſturbare.*

Anger ruffles the mind, *la collera diſturba la mente.*

To ruffle [to anger, to make one angry] *crucciare, fare adirare, metter in collera, muover la bile.*

RU'FFLED, adj. *increſpato,* v. To ruffle.

RUG, s. [a ſhaggy coverlet for a bed] *coperta da letto con peli lunghi.*

Rug, s. *cane groſſo, peloſo, e cattivo.*

RU'GGED, adj. [rough, uneven] *rozzo, ruvido, aſpro, alpeſtre, ſalvatico.*

Rugged ſkin, *pelle ruvida.*

A rugged ſtile, *uno ſtile rozzo.*

A rugged man, *uno zotico, un uomo rozzo, un villano.*

A rugged anſwer, *una riſpoſta incivile, bruſca, aſpra.*

To give one a rugged anſwer, *riſponder bruſcamente, rigidamente ad uno.*

Rugged [rigid, ſevere] *rigido, ſevero, bruſco, auſtero, aſpro.*

RU'GGEDLY, adj. [roughly, ſeverely] *rozzamente, ruvidamente, aſpramente, ſeveramente, bruſcamente.*

RU'GGEDNESS, s. *rozzezza, aſprezza, ruvidezza, zotichezza, ſalvatichezza, rigidezza,* s. f.

RUIN, s. [deſtruction] *rovina, ruina, diſtruzione,* s. f. *danno, diſfacimento, ſterminio,* s. m.

He has been the ruin of me, *egli è ſtato la mia rovina.*

To build one's fortune upon another man's ruin, *aggrandirſi col danno e precipizio altrui.*

To bring one to ruin, *rovinare, perdere altrui.*

To come to ruin, *rovinare, rovinarſi.*

RUINS, s. [in the plural number] *rovine.*

The ruins of a building, *le rovine d' un edificio.*

The ruins of a good face, *i miſeri avanzi di fallita beltà.*

To RUIN [to deſtroy, to lay waſte, to bring to ruin] *rovinare, ruinare, diſtruggere, mandare a male, deſolare, perdere,* pret. *diſtruſſi.*

To ruin a country, *rovinare, diſtruggere un paeſe.*

To ruin a man's reputation, *macchiare, infamare l' altrui riputazione.*

To ruin one's ſelf, *rovinarſi.*

RU'INED, adj. *rovinato, ruinato, diſtrutto, deſolato.*

RU'INOUS, adj. [falling to decay, ready to fall] *rovinoſo, che minaccia rovina, cadevole.*

Ruinous [dangerous, that brings to ruin] *rovinoſo, precipitoſo, fatale, pericoloſo.*

RU'INOUSLY, adv. *rovinoſamente, con molta rovina.*

Ruinouſly [miſchievouſly; deſtructively] *cattivamente, ſcelleratamente.*

RULE, s. [an inſtrument to rule with] *régolo,* s. m. *ſtrumento di legno o di metallo, col quale ſi tiran le linee rette.*

A carpenter's rule or ſquare, *ſquadra,* s. m. *ſtrumento col quale ſi ſquadra, fatto di due régoli.*

Rule [model, exemplar] *régola,* s. f. *modello, eſempio,* s. m.

Rule [precept, principles to go by] *regola, norma,* s. f. *modo, ordine, precetto, dimoſtramento della via dell' operare,* s. m.

To learn a language by rules, *imparare una lingua per regole.*

Done according to rule, *fatto ſecondo le regole.*

The rules of the goſpel, *i precetti del vangelo.*

Rule [ſtatute, or conſtitution of a religious order] *regola, iſtituto, coſtituzione d' un ordine di religioſi.*

Rule [order] *regola, ordine.*

There's no rule in that houſe, *non c' è regola in quella caſa.*

Rule [cuſtom] *regola, coſtume, uſanza.*

Rule [ſway, command] *comando, potere, autorità.*

To bear rule, *aver il comando, comandare, governare.*

To RULE [to draw lines with a rule] *rigare, tirar le linee col regolo.*

To rule paper, *rigare della carta.*

To rule [ſquare, frame, or order] *regolare, ordinare, diriggere, guidare, dirizzare.*

To rule one's life by the dictates of reaſon, *regolare la ſua vita ſecondo i dettati della ragione, conformarla alle regole della ragione.*

To rule, to rule over, *dominare, ſignoreggiare, governare.*

To rule a ſtate, *dominare, governare uno ſtato.*

To rule unjuſtly, *governare ingiuſtamente.*

To rule [to command, to maſter] *domare, ſoggiogare, reprimere, rintuzzare, moderare, mortificare, umiliare, ammanſare.*

To rule one's affections, *domare le ſue paſſioni, mortificare gli affetti.*

RU'LED, adj. *rigato,* v. To rule.

Be ruled by me, *credete a me, pigliate il mio conſiglio.*

He would not be ruled by me, *egli non m' ha voluto credere, non s' è voluto laſciare guidar da me.*

RU'LER, s. [a rule] *regolo,* s. m.

Ruler [governor] *governatore, conduttore, guida, duce.*

RUM, s. [a ſort of brandy diſtilled from ſugar] *ſpezie d' acquavite diſtillata dal zucchero.*

RUMB, s. [one point of the mariner's compaſs] *quarta di vento.*

To RU'MBLE [to make a hollow noiſe] *rombare, ſtrepitare, romoreggiare, gorgogliare.*

My guts rumble, *il mio ventre gorgoglia.*

RU'MBLING, s. *rombo, rombazzo, ſtrepito, fracaſſo, fraſtuono, gorgogliamento,* s. m.

A rumbling of the belly, *gorgogliamento di ventre.*

RU'MINANT, adj. [chewing the cud] *ruminante, che rumina.*

Ruminant animals [ſuch as chew the cud, as oxen, ſheep, deer, &c.] *animali rumi-*

rumiánti, che ruminano, come buoi, pecore, cervi, e simili.

To RU'MINATE [to chew the cud] *rugumare, ruminare, far ritornare nella bocca il cibo mandato nello stomaco non masticato, per masticarlo, ed è proprio degli animali del piè fesso.*

To ruminate [to weigh in the mind, to study or think seriously upon] *rugumare, ruminare, riconsiderare, riandar col pensiero, pesare, riflettere.*

RUMINA'TION, s. *il rugumare, il ruminare delle bestie dal piè fesso.*

Rumination, s. [meditation, reflection] *il meditare, il riflettere, attentamente.*

To RU'MMAGE [to search, to plunder, to evacuate] *cercare, metter sottosopra, scompigliar cercando, saccheggiare.*

RU'MMER, s. [a large drinking glass] *pecchero,* s. m. *sorta di bicchier grande.*

Rummer [brimmer] *bichiero pieno.*

RU'MOUR, s. [report, fame, common talk] *romore, grido,* s. m *fama, voce,* s. f.

RU'MOURED, adj. ex. 'Tis rumoured abroad, *corre voce, è fama.*

RUMP, s. [the tail piece, especially of a bird, or of an ox, sheep, &c.] *groppone,* s. m. *e dicesi di tutti gli animali così quadrupedi, come bipedi.*

RU'MPLE, s. [a fold in a garment] *piega, crespa, grinza,* s. f.

To RU'MPLE [to make into rumples, to ruffle] *increspare, raggrinzare, rugare.*

RU'MPLED, adj. *increspato, raggrinzato, rugato.*

Rumpled skin, *pelle grinza, rugosa.*

RUN, *è un preterito del verbo* To run.

Run, s. ex. To put a man to the run [to make him run away] *far fuggire uno, metterlo in fuga.*

At a long run, *al lungo andare.*

To take a run, *prendere una corsa.*

Good or ill run at play, *detta o disdetta al giuoco.*

To have a good or ill run at play, *essere in detta, o disdetta al giuoco.*

To RUN [to move with a swift pace] *correre, andare con velocità,* pret. *corsi.*

To run before or after, *correr avanti, o dietro.*

To run post, *correr la posta.*

To run after one, *correr dietro ad uno.*

To run with full speed, to run apace, *correr velocemente.*

To run a full gallop, *correre a briglia sciolta, a tutta briglia, galloppare.*

To run about, to run up and down, *correr qua e là.*

To run at the ring, *correr l' anello.*

To run a race, *correre il palio.*

To run a hazard, *correr rischio.*

To run a hare, *correr la lepre.*

To run one through with the sword, *passar uno da banda a banda colla spada.*

To run a ribbon in a ring, *passare, infilzare un nastro in un anello.*

To run the gantlope [a military punishment] *passar per le bacchette.*

To run [to drop] *colare, gocciolare.*

His nose runs, *gli cola il naso.*

To run [to flow] *scorrere, passare.*

The river runs by the walls, *il fiume scorre, o passa per le mura.*

A verse that runs smooth, *un verso facile e dolre.*

Time runs away, *il tempo passa, scorre.*

To run from, *uscire,* pres. *esco.*

To run with matter [to suppurate] *render marcia, far capo.*

The sore runs, *la piaga corre, rende della marcia.*

To run against a post, *urtare rontro un palo.*

To run one's head against a wall, *dar della testa in un muro.*

To run to one's help, *risuggire, ricorrere, aver ricorso ad uno per ajuto.*

To run to seed [as plants do] *semenzire, andare in semenza.*

Her tongue runs perpetually, *ella parla incessantemente, o per sempre.*

Your tongue runs before your wit, *voi non pensate a quel che dite.*

His eyes run, *gli occhi gli colano, egli è cisposo.*

To run away, *fuggire, corsela, battersela.*

To run one's country, *abbandonare il paese.*

I will run with you for a wager, *scommetto che corro meglio di voi.*

To run mad, *impazzire, diventar matto,* pres. *impazzisco.*

That would make one run mad, *questo farebbe impazzire uno.*

It runs in their blood, *vien di razza.*

To run a division, *gorgheggiare, tirar di gorga.*

My head does not run that way, *io non penso, non bado a queste cose.*

To run a-ground, or to run on ground, *dare in secco, dar nelle secche.*

To run against a rock [as a ship does] *naufragare contro uno scoglio, urtare in uno scoglio.*

To run for't [to scamper away] *fuggire, corsela, battersela; darla a gambe, mettersi la via tra le gambe.*

That ever runs in my mind, *cio mi corre sempre nell' animo, o per la mente.*

To run away with a thing, *portar via che che si sia.*

To run away with a virgin, *trasugare una zitella.*

The horse ran away with him, *il cavallo lo portò via.*

To run away from one's text [to make a digression] *fare una digressione.*

To run back, *correr indietro.*

To run counter [to be contrary, to clash] *ripugnare, esser ripugnante, opposto, contrario.*

The accusations run high on both sides, *le accuse sono gagliarde d' ambe le parti.*

The sedition ran so high, *la sedizi ne divenne si grande.*

To run down a stag, *straccare un cervo, prenderlo dopò averlo cacciato un pezzo.*

To run down with arguments, *convincere alcuno a forza d' argomenti.*

To run a thing down [to despise or undervalue it] *vilipendere, disprezzare una cosa.*

To run down with blood, *stillare, gocciolare di sangue.*

To run from one thing to another, *scartarsi dal suo soggetto, fare una digressione.*

To run one's self into mischief, *esporsi a qualche pericolo.*

To run in debt, to run one's self in debt, *indebitarsi, fare o contrattar debiti.*

A thorn did run into my foot, *m' è entrata una spina nel piede.*

To run a pin into one's arm, *pugnere uno nel braccio con una spilla.*

To run on, *seguitare, continuare, andare avanti.*

He runs on still in his lewd courses, *continua sempre à vivere dissolutamente.*

If you run on at this rate you will quickly be a beggar, *se voi andate avanti nella medesima manierà di vivere, sarete ben presto ridotto alla mendirità.*

To run over to a place, *passare, andare in qualche luogo con fretta.*

To run over a book [to peruse it in haste] *trascorrer un libro, darli una scorsa, leggerlo superficialmente.*

To run over one's work again, *rivedere, emendare un' operá.*

The river runs over the banks; *il fiume ha soverchiate le sponde.*

The pot runs over, *la pignatta versa, o trabocca.*

To run out into excess, *andare all' eccesso.*

To run out in expences [to spend too high] *fare troppo grandi spese, eccedere nello spendere.*

To run one's self out of breath, *correr fino a perder il fiato.*

To run out one's race, *finire la sua corsa.*

To run out of one's wits, *perdér il senno, impazzire,* pres. *impazzisco.*

To run out in length, *stendérsi in lunghezza.*

To run through, *passare da banda, a banda, passar fuorfuora.*

To run through a hook [to read it over] *lèggere tutto un libro.*

To run through thick and thin, *esporsi ad ogni sorta d' inconvenienze.*

To

To run up, *montare, salire,* pres. *salgo.*
To run up a wall [to raise it] *alzare un muro.*
To run it up too high, *farlo troppo alto.*
To run upon, *gettarsi, lanciarsi sopra avventarsi.*
All his discourse runs upon that, *tutto 'l suo discorso batte, o consiste in ciò.*
A beam that runs upon the wall, *una trave, che posa sopra 'l muro.*
To run upon great dangers, *correr gran pericoli.*
RU'NAGATE, s. [renegado] *un rinnegato.*
Runagate [a rambling or roving fellow] *un vagabondo.*
RU'NAWAY, s. [deserter] *disertore, fuggitivo.*
RU'NDLE, s. [the figure of a round ball or bullet] *globo, corpo tondo per tutti i versi.*
RU'NDLET [a step of a ladder] *piuolo d'una scala.*
Rundlet, s. [a small cask for liquors] *bariletto, barlotto.*
RUNG, preterito *del verbo* To ring.
RU'NNER, s. [from to run] *corridore, corritore,* s. m.
The runner of a mill, *la mola di sopra del mulino.*
RU'NNET, s. *quaglio, coagulo.*
RU'NNING, s. *corrimento,* s. m. *il correre.*
The running of the reins, *gonorrea, scolazione,* s. f.
A running of the nose, *cimurro,* s. m.
A running place, *carriera,* s. f. *corso,* s. m.
A running-footman, *un lacchè.*
A running water, *acqua corrente.*
A running knot, *cappio, nodo scorsojo.*
A running sore, *una piaga che cola.*
The running-title of a book, *il titolo che si mette in cima ad ogni facciata d' un libro.*
RUNT, s. [a Scotch or Welch cow] *una vacca di Scozia o di Wales.*
A runt fellow, *un nano, un uomicciatto.*
An old runt, *una vecchiaccia.*
RU'PTORY, s. [a corrosive caustick] *rottorio, cauterio,* s. m.
RU'PTURE, s. [burstenness, or burst belly] *rottura, crepatura, allentatura, ernia,* s. f.
Rupture-wort, s. [an herb] *erniaria,* s. f. *sorta d' erba.*
Rupture [falling out] *rottura, rompimento, disunione.*
RU'RAL, adj. [belonging to the country] *rustico, campestre, campestro, di campo, villesco, villereccio.*
Rural life, *vita campestre.*
RUSH, s. [a plant] *giunco,* s. m. *pianta che cresce presso l' acqua.*
A rush-hill, *giuncheto,* s. m. *giuncaja.*
Full of rushes, *giuncoso, pieno di giunchi.*
A place where rushes grow, *giuncaja,* s. f. *giuncheto,* s. m.
To strew with rushes, *giuncare, coprire di giunchi.*
I value it not a rush, *non lo stimo un fico.*
I care not a rush for you, *mi burlo, mi rido di voi, non vi stimo un fico.*
It is not worth a rush, *non vale un frullo.*
I would not give a rush for't, *non ne darei un fico.*
He will never be worth a rush, *mentre che vive sarà un dappoco.*
Ruth, s. [violent course] *l' atto del correre, dello scagliarsi.*
To RUSH, *lanciarsi, scagliarsi, avventarsi*
He rushed among the naked swords, *si lanciò, si gettò fra le spade nude.*
To rush in, *entrare improvvisamente, è per forza.*
To rush in upon one [to take him napping] *sorprendere alcuno, corlo all' improvviso.*
To rush out of company, *svignare dalla campagnia.*
RU'SHY, adj. [full of rushes] *giuncoso, pien di giunchi.*
RUSK, s. [hard bread for stores] *biscotto, pezzo di pane cotto due volte.*
RU'SSET, adj. [dark brown] *rossetto, rossiccio, rossigno.*
A russet colour, *color rossetto.*
RU'SSETIN, s. [a kind of apple] *mela ruggine, spezie di mela.*
RUST, s. [a sort of crust with grows upon iron] *ruggine,* s. f. *quella materia che si genera in sul ferro.*
To RUST [to contract rust] *irruggire, arrugginire,* pret. *irrugginisco, arrugginisco.*
RU'STICAL, } adj. [country-like,
RUSTICK, } clownish] *rustico, rozzo, villesco, da contadino, zotico.*
RU'STICALLY, adv. *rusticamente, con modo rustico, villanamente, zoticamente.*
To RU'STICATE [to render rustical] *render rustico o zotico come un contadino.*
To rusticate, *andar in villa, starsene in villa.*
RU'STICATED, adj. [made or become clownish] *divenuto zotico, fatto rustico.*
RUSTI'CITY, s. [clownishness] *rusticità, rustichezza, rusticaggine, zotichezza, zoticaggine,* s. f.
RUSTICK, s. *contradino, rustico, abitante della campagna.*
Rustick, adj. *v.* Rustical.
RU'STINESS, s. [rust] *ruggine,* s. f.
The rustiness of iron, *la ruggine del ferro.*
The rustiness of bacon, *rancidezza del lardo.*
To RU'STLE [to make a noise as armour or new garments] *cigolare, romoreggiare, strepitare, ronzare.*
RU'STLING, s. *strepito, romore, ronzo.*
RU'STY, adj. [cover'd with rust] *rugginente, rugginoso.*
Rusty bacon, *lardo rancido.*
To grow rusty, *irrugginire arrugginire.*
RUT, s. *frega,* s. f.
Rut [the mark of a wheel in the road] *rotaja, ruotaja,* s. f. *il segno che fa in terra la ruota.*
To RUT, *andare in frega.*
RU'THFUL, adj. [compassionate] *misericordioso, compassionevole, pieno di tenerezza, pietoso.*
Ruthful [pitiful, that deserves pity] *miserabile, compassionevole, degno di compassione, deplorabile.*
RU'THFULLY, adv. *miserabilmente, miseramente.*
RU'THFULNESS, s. *pietà, compassione,* s. f.
RU'THLESS, adj. *spietato, crudele, inumano.*
RU'TTING, adj. ex. the rutting time, *frega, il tempo, nel quale le bestie vanno in frega.*
RU'TTISH, adj. [wanton, libidinous, salacious, lustful, lecherous] *lascivo, libidinoso.*
RYE, s. [a kind of corn] *segala,* s. f. *spezie di biada.*
Rye-bread, *pane di segala.*
RY'EGRASS, s. [a kind of strong grass] *sorta d' erba che ha il gambo duro.*

S.

S, *In Inglese si pronuncia come in Italiano. Non si pronunzia in* Isle *nè in* Island.

SA'BAOTH [the Lord God of Sabaoth] *sabaoth, l'Omnipotente Dio.*

SABBATA'RIANS, s. [a sort of hereticks, who about an age ago kept the Jewish sabbath instead of the Lord's day] *sabatariani, setta d' eretici.*

Sabhatarian, s. [a rigid observer of the sabbath] *un rigido osservatore del sabato.*

The SABBATH, s. [the seventh day of the week, observed as a day of rest among the Jews, which is Saturday among the Christians] *sabato,* s. m. *il giorno di riposo fra li Ebrei, che è la Domenica fra i Cristiani.*

The christian sabbath [the Lord's day or Sunday] *il sabato de cristiani, la Domenica.*

SABBA'TICAL, } adj. [belonging to
SABBA'TICK, } the sabbath] *attenente al sabato.*

SABE'ANS, s. [a sect, who patch'd up Christianism, Judaism, Mahometanism, and Heathenish superstition together] *sabei, setta d' eretici, la di cui credenza era un miscuglio di Cristianismo, Giudaismo, Maomettismo, e Paganismo.*

SABINE, s. *sabina, nome d' una pianta.*

SA'BLE, s. [a beast not unlike a polecat] *zibellino,* s. m. *animale assai simile alla martora.*

Sable [the fur of sable] *zibellino, la pelle del zibellino.*

Sable, adj. [black] *nero, bruno.*

SA'BRE, s. [a cymetar, a short sword with a convex edge, a faulchion] *sciabla, sciabola, scimitarra.*

SA'CCHARINE, adj. [having the taste or any other of the chief qualities of sugar] *zuccherino, di zucchero, rassomigliante il zucchero.*

SACERDO'TAL, adj. [belonging to a priest, priestly] *sacerdotale, di sacerdote.*

SA'CHELL, *v.* Satchel.

SACK, s. [a bag] *sacco,* s. m.

Sack [a measure of wool] *sacco, misura di lana.*

Sack [a wine called canary, brought from the Canary islands] *spezie di vin dolce, che viene dall Isole Canarie.*

Sack, s. *saccheggio, sacco, ruba.*

Sack, s. *sorta di gonna femminile.*

To SACK [to plunder, to pillage] *saccheggiare, dare il sacco, porre, o mettere a sacco.*

To sack up [to put in the sack] *insaccare, mettere in sacco.*

SA'CKBUT, s. [a musical instrument] *sambuca,* s. f. *strumento musicale.*

SACK-CLOTH, s. *tela da far sacca; tela grossolana.*

SA'CKED, adj. *saccheggiato, posto a sacco, messo a sacco.*

SA'CKER, s. *saccheggiante,* s. m. *che saccheggia.*

SA'CKFUL, adj. [topfull] *pieno affatto, ricolmo.*

SA'CKING, s. *saccheggiamento, sacco,* s. m. *il saccheggiare.*

The sacking of Troy, *il sacco di Troja.*

SA'CKPOSSET, s. *bevanda usata in Inghilterra, fatta di vino, zucchero, &c.*

SA'CRAMENT, s. [a visible sign of an invisible grace] *sacramento, sagramento,* s. m.

The sacrament [or communion] *il sagramento dell' altare.*

SACRAME'NTAL, adj. [belonging to a sacrament] *sacramentale, sagramentale, attenente a sacramento.*

SACRAME'NTALLY, adv. *sacramentalmente, sagramentalmente.*

SACRAMENTARIANS, s. [a name given by the papists to the protestants, and chiefly to the calvinists] *sagramentarj, nome che i cattolici Romani danno ai protestanti, e particolarmente ai calvinisti.*

SA'CRED, adj. [holy] *sacro, sacrato, santo.*

His sacred majesty, *la persona sacrata del rè, sua sacra maestà.*

The sacred writ [the books of holy scripture] *la scrittura sacra, la bibbia.*

Sacred [inviolable] *sacrato, inviolabile, sacrosanto, e sagrosanto.*

SA'CREDLY, adv. *santamente, religiosamente.*

SA'CREDNESS, s. *santità,* s. f.

SA'CRIFICE, s. [an offering made to God] *sacrificio, e sacrifizio,* s. m. *culto offerto a Dio.*

To offer up a sacrifice, *offerire, a fare un sacrificio.*

To SA'CRIFICE [to offer up in sacrifice] *sacrificare, far sacrificio.*

To sacrifice [to devote] *sacrificare, dicare, consagrare, consecrare.*

To sacrifice [to quit or leave a thing upon some consideration] *sacrificare, cedere, rinunziare.*

SACRIFICED, adj. *sacrificato, v.* To sacrifice.

I sacrificed to him all my resentments, *gli ho fatto un sacrificio di tutt' i miei risentimenti.*

SACRIFI'CER, s. *sacrificatore,* s. m.

SACRIFI'CIAL, } adj. [belonging to
SACRIFICAL, } sacrifices] *di sacrificio, attenente a sacrificio.*

SA'CRILEGE, s. [the stealing of sacred things] *sacrilegio,* s. m. *il furar le cose sacrate, in luogo sacrato.*

SACRILE'GIOUS, adj. [guilty of sacrilege] *che commette sacrilegio.*

A sacrilegious man or woman, *un sacrilego, una sacrilega.*

A sacrilegious act, *un sacrilegio.*

SACRILE'GIOUSLY, adv. *sacrilegamente.*

SAC'RIST, } s. [a sexton or vestry-keeper]
SACRI'STAN, } *sagrestano,* s. m. *colui che è proposto alla cura della sagrestia.*

SA'CRISTY, s. *sagrestia, sacristia.*

SAD, adj. [sorrowful, melancholy] *mesto, malcontento, maninconico, tristo.*

Sad [grievous] *tristo, infelice, dolente, meschino.*

It is a sad thing to be poor, *l' esser povero è una cattiva cosa.*

A very sad mischance, *una gran disgrazia.*

Sad news, *rie novelle.*

Sad [pitiful, sorry, bad] *cattivo, vile, abietto, meschino, tapino, povero.*

Sad verses, *cattivi versi*

A sad workman, *un cattivo lavoratore, un povero artefice.*

Sad weather, *cattivo tempo, tempo molto brutto.*

Sad

Sad colour, *coloré bruno, oscuro.*

To SA'DDEN [to look sad] *parer tristo, o dolente, avere una cera mesta.*

To sadden [to make sad] *render mesto, affliggere.*

A SA'DDLE, s. [a seat for horsemen] *sella,* s. f.

To put the saddle upon the right horse, *dar la colpa a chi ha torto.*

A saddle bow, *arcione di sella.*

The pommel of a saddle, *il pomo d' una sella.*

A saddle-cloth, *gualdrappa,* s. f.

A pack-saddle, *un basto.*

Saddle-back'd, *sellato, si dice del cavallo, quando ha la schiena troppo concava.*

To SA'DDLE, verb act. *sellare, metter la sella.*

To saddle a horse, *sellare un cavallo.*

To saddle with a pack-saddle, *imbastare, mettere il basto.*

SA'DDLE, adj. *sellato.*

SA'DDLE-MAKER } s. [a maker of
SA'DDLER } saddles] *sellajo,* s. m. *che fa le selle.*

A pack-saddler, *bastiere, bastajo,* s. m. *facitor di basti.*

SA'DDUCEES, s. [a sect among the Jews, who received only the five books of Moses, denied the being of angels and spirits, the immortality of the soul, and the resurrection of the body] *sadducei, setta d' eretici fra li Ebrei, che ricevevano solamente i cinque libri di Mosè, negavano l' essenza degli angeli e degli spiriti, l' immortalità dell' anima, e la resurrezione della carne.*

SA'DDUCISM, s. [the principles and doctrine of the sadducees] *l' eresia de' sadducei.*

SA'DLY, adv. [sorrily, pitifully, ill] *malamente, cattivamente, miserabilmente, meschinamente.*

SA'DNESS, s. [heaviness, melancholy] *tristezza, afflizion d' animo, malinconia,* s. f. *affanno, dolore,* s. m.

In sober sadness [seriously] *seriamente, in sul serio.*

SAFE, adj. [out of danger] *salvo, sicuro, fuor di pericolo.*

With a safe conscience, *in buona coscienza.*

A safe place, *un luogo sicuro.*

A safe remedy, *un rimedio sicuro.*

A safe man, *un uomo fidato.*

Safe [happy] *felice.*

A safe return, *un felice ritorno.*

I wish you safe home, *vi auguro un felice ritorno a casa.*

He is come home safe, *egli è arrivato a salvamento.*

This is a safe way, *questo è un mezzo sicuro.*

A safe conduct, *un salvocondotto.*

I do not think it safe for us to stay here, *non credo che noi siamo in sicurezza quì.*

Your money will be safe in his hands, *il vostro danaro sarà sicuro nelle sue mani.*

God keep you safe, *Iddio vi conservi.*

Safe, s. [a sort of cupboard to keep victuals in, contrived with holes to let in air] *uno stipo.*

SA'FEGUARD, s. [a protection] *salvaguardia, protezione,* s. f.

A woman's safe-guard [a kind of apron of colour'd stuff] *grembiule di lana che le donne portano per conservare gli abiti netti.*

SA'FELY, adv. [without danger] *salvamente, con salvezza, sicuramente.*

Safely [with a safe conscience] *salvamente, in buona coscienza.*

I can swear it safely, *posso giurarlo in coscienza.*

SA'FETY, s. [surety] *salvezza, sicurezza, salute,* s. f. *scampo,* s. m.

A place of safety, *un luogo di sicurezza, luogo sicuro.*

SA'FFRON, s. [a plant] *zafferano,* s. m.

Bastard, or mock saffron, *zafferano salvatico*

Saffron flower, *fior di zafferano, che nasce di cipolla.*

Saffron gold [among chymists, a chymical preparation of gold, that, fired, makes an explosion like gun-powder] *oro fulminante, il quale quando se li da fuoco, fa uno scoppio come la polvere da cannone.*

To SAG [to hang heavy] *pesare, esser pesante.*

SAGA'CIOUS, adj. [of a quick apprehension, subtle] *sagace, astuto, considerato, avveduto, accorto.*

SAGA'CITY, s. [sharpness of wit, quickness of apprehension] *sagacità, vivacità d' ingegno, perspicacia.*

SAGE, adj. [prudent, wise] *saggio, savio, accorto, prudente.*

Sage, s. [a wise man] *un saggio, un uomo savio.*

Sage, s. [a sweet smelling plant] *salvia,* s. f.

Sage of Jerusalem [a plant] *polmonaria,* s. f.

SA'GELY, adv. *sagiamente, saviamente.*

SA'GENESS, s. [wisdom] *savviezza,* s. f.

SAGITTA'RIUS } s. [the name of one
SA'GITTARY } of the twelve signs of the zodiack] *sagittario,* s. m. *uno de' dodici segni del zodiaco.*

Sagittary [a centaur] *centauro,* s. m.

SA'ICK, s. [a sort of merchant ship, used chiefly in the Mediterranean, as also among the Turks] *saira,* s. f. *spezie di navillo.*

SAID, *preterito e participio del verbo* To say.

I have said, *ho detto.*

Said I, *dissi io.*

SAIL, s. [a large piece of canvass, which catches the wind, and serves to give way to the ship] *vela,* s. f. *quella tela che legata e distesa all' albero della nave, riceve il vento.*

To set sail, *far vela, distender le vele, spiegar le vele.*

To be under sail, *esser alla vela, veleggiare.*

In a few days sail we arrived at Leghorn, *dopo pochi giorni di navigazione arrivammo a Livorno.*

A fleet of an hundred sail, *una flotta di cento vele, o di cento navi.*

The sails of a wind-mill, *le ali d' un mulino a vento.*

The main-sail, *la vela maestra.*

The top-sail, *trinchetto.*

The mizen-sail, *terzeruolo.*

The sail yard, *l' antenna.*

To hoise up sail, *far vela.*

To strike sail, *ammainare le vele.*

To SAIL [to set sail] *far vela, veleggiare, andare a vela.*

To sail northward, *veleggiare, far vela verso tramontana.*

To sail in the main, *veleggiare in alto mare.*

To sail along the coast, to coast along, *costeggiare, andar per mare lungo le coste.*

SA'ILING, s. *veleggiamento,* s. m. *navigazione,* s. f.

SA'ILOR, s. [or sea-man] *marinaro, navigante,* s. m.

Sailor [a fish] *nautilo, spezie di pesce.*

A very good sailor [a ship that sails well] *un vascello che veleggia bene, un vascello legiero alla vela, un buon veleggiatore.*

SAIM, s. [or lard] *saime, lardo, grasso strutto,* s. m.

SA'INFOIN, s. [a kind of grass, otherwise called holy grass, meddick fodder, trefoil] *trifoglio,* s. m.

SA'INT, s. [a holy person] *un santo, una santa.*

Saint Peter, *san Pietro.*

Saint Frances, *santa Francesca.*

Saint Anthony's fire [a disease growing to a scab, like a tetter] *volatica, fuoco salvatico.*

To SA'INT [to canonize] *canonizzare.*

To saint [to act with a show of piety] *far il santo.*

SA'INTED, adj. *canonizzato.*

Sainted [holy, pious, virtuous] *santo, pio, dabbene.*

Sainted [holy, sacred] *santo, sacro.*

SA'INT-LIKE, adj. *santo, come santo, a simiglianza di santo.*

SA'INTLY, adv. *santamente, da santo.*

SA'INTSHIP, s. *carattere o qualità di santo, santità.*

SAKE, s. [cause] *causa, cagione, rispetto, amore.*

For God's sake, *per l' amor di Dio.*

For your sake, *per l' amor vostro, per rispetto vostro.*

For peace sake, *per aver la pace, per esser in pace.*

For brevity's sake, *per brevità, per esser breve.*

Beasts are bred for man's sake, *le bestie sono create per uso dell' uomo.*

He is my name-sake, *egli porta il mio nome.*

SA'KER, s. [a kind of hawk] *sagro,* s. m. *spezie di falcone.*

Sake

Saker [a ſort of great gun] *ſagro ſorta di pezzo d' artiglieria.*

SAL, s. *ſale*; *vocabolo di farmacia.*

SA'LABLE, adj. [that ſells well] *vendibile, vendevole.*

SALA'CIOUS, adj. [luſtful, lecherous, wanton] *laſcivo, caldo, focoſo, luſſurioſo, ſalace.*

SALA'CITY, s. [lechery] *laſcivia, calore, luſſuria,*

SA'LAD, s. [or head-piece] *celata,* s. f. *cappelletto di ferro, che ſi porta in capo per difeſa.*

Salad, *inſalata.*

SALAMA'NDER, s. [a ſpotted creature like a lizard, which is ſuppoſed for ſome time to endure fire] *ſalamandra,* s. f. *ſpezie di lucertola, che ſi ſuppone viva per qualche ſpazio nelle fiamme.*

SA'LARY, s. [ſtipend, allowance of wages] *ſalario,* s. m. *mercede pattuita che ſi da a chi ſerve, ſtipendio,* s. m.

To give a ſalary, *ſalariare, dar ſalario, ſtipendiare.*

SALE, s. [from to ſell] *vendita,* s. f.

To expoſe any thing to ſale, *mettere in vendita, vendere.*

To make an open ſale by outcry, *vendere all' incanto.*

SA'LENDINE, s. [an herb] *celidonia minore.*

SA'LEABLE, adj. *vendibile, proprio per vendere.*

SA'LESMAN, s. *venditore di abiti fatti.*

SA'LEWORK, s. *roba fatta per vendere*; *roba fatta con negligenza e all' ingroſſo.*

SA'LICK } adj. *ſalica.*
SA'LIQUE }

The ſalick law [a French law, which excludes females from the crown] *la legge ſalica.*

SA'LIENT, adj. [leaping, bounding] *che ſalta, che balza.*

Salient [beating, panting] *palpitante, anſante.*

Salient, *che ſale con velocità.*

SA'LIGOT, s. [a plant] *ſaligaſtro, ſalicone,* s. m.

SALI'NE } adj [ſalt, briniſh] *ſalſo, ſalmaſtro, ſalato, che ha o produce ſale.*
SALI'NOUS }

Saline blood, *ſangue ſalſo.*

SA'LIVAL } adj. [belonging to the ſpittle] *appartenente alla ſciliva*; *ſalivale.*
SA'LIVARY }

To SA'LIVATE, *mandar fuora molta ſciliva dalla bocca.*

SALIVA'TION, s. *ſalivazione,* s. f.

SA'LLET, s. [a diſh of raw herbs] *inſalata,* s. f.

SA'LLET-OIL, *olio d' oliva.*

SA'LLETTING } s. *erbe, onde ſi fan l' inſalate.*
SA'LLADING }

SA'LLOW, adj. [pale] *pallido, ſmorto, malaticcio.*

Sallow or ſallow-tree, s. [a kind of willow-tree] *ſalcio, ſalce,* s. m. *albero, che creſce ne' luoghi umidi e paludoſi.*

SA'LLOWNESS, s. [yellowneſs, ſickly paleneſs] *paliore giallo*; *pallidezza procedente da malore.*

SA'LLY, s. [an irruption of the beſieged upon the beſiegers] *ſortità,* s. f. *termine militare, l' uſcir fuori che fanno i ſoldati da' lor ripari per aſſaltare i nemici.*

Sally [a tranſport or ſudden fit of paſſion] *furia,* s. f. *bollore, ſollevamento, infiammamento d' animo.*

To SA'LLY } verb act. *ſortire, termine militare, uſcir de' ripari, per aſſaltare il nemico.*
To SA'LLY forth }

SA'LLYPORT, s. [gate at which ſallies are made] *quella porta nella fortezza da cui ſi fanno le ſortite.*

SALMAGU'NDY, s. [a mixture of chopped meat and pickled herrings with oil, vinegar, pepper, and onions] *ſtrana vivanda uſata in Inghilterra fatta di carne cotta ſminuzzata, di aringhe ſalate con olio, aceto, pepe, e cipolle.*

SA'LMON, s. *ſalmone, ſorta di peſce groſſo molto buono a mangiare che parte dell' anno ſta nell' acqua dolce, e parte nella ſalata.*

SA'LMONTROUT, s. *ſorta di trota che ha la carne roſſigna.*

A ſalmon-pipe, s. [an engine to catch ſalmon in] *macchina da prender ſalmoni.*

Salmon-peel [a ſort of ſalmon] *ſpezie di ſalmone.*

Salmon-ſewſe [the young fry of ſalmons] *fregola di ſalmoni.*

SALSAPARI'LLA, s. [the rough bindweed of Peru] *ſalſapariglia,* s. f. *radice d' una pianta portata dall' Indie occidentali.*

SALT, s. *ſale,* s. m.

Salt made of ſea water, *ſale marino.*

Bay-ſalt, *ſale bigio.*

Mineral-ſalt, *ſalgemma,* s. f. *ſalgemmo,* s. m.

Salt-cellar, s. *ſaliera.*

Salt, adj. [or ſalted] *ſalato.*

Salt-beef, *bue ſalato.*

Salt-meat, *ſalato,* s. m. *carne ſecca, carne ſalata.*

Salt-bitch, *cagna che è in ſucchio.*

Salt marſh, or ſalt-pit, *ſalina,* s. f. *luogo d' onde ſi cava il ſale.*

Salt-houſe [wherein ſalt is made] *ſalina.*

Salt ſpring, *una ſorgente d' acqua ſalmaſtra.*

To SALT [to ſeaſon with ſalt] *ſalare, aſperger di ſale.*

SA'LTED, adj. *ſalato.*

SA'LTER, s. [one who deals in ſalt] *uno che vende del ſale.*

SALTI'RE, adj. [a term uſed in heraldry, one of the ordinaries in form of St. Andrew's croſs] ex. a ſaltire croſs, *croce di Sant' Andrea, termine araldeſco.*

SA'LTLESS, adj. *che non ha guſto veruno di ſale, dolce di ſale.*

SALTPE'TER, s. [a kind of mineral ſalt] *ſalnitro, nitro,* s. m.

SA'LVAGE, s. [in civil law, a recompence allowed to a ſhip that has ſaved or reſcued another from enemies or pirates] *guiderdone conceſſo dalla legge ad un vaſcello che abbia difeſo o ricoverato un altro vaſcello dalle mani de' nemici, o pirati.*

Salvage, wild, *v.* Savage.

SALVA'TION, s. *ſalvazione, ſalute,* s. f. *ſalvamento,* s. m.

That brings ſalvation, *ſalutare, ſalutevole, che apporta ſalute.*

SALU'BRIOUS, adj. [wholeſome, healthful] *ſalubre, ſano, ſalutifero.*

SALU'BRITY, s. [wholeſomneſs] *ſalubrità,* s. f.

The ſalubrity of the air, *la ſalubrità dell' aria.*

SALVE, s. [an unguent, or medicinal compoſition for plaſters] *unguento,* s. m.

An eye-ſalve, *un unguento per gli occhi.*

To SALVE [to ſave or preſerve] *ſalvare, conſervare, difendere,* pret. *difeſi.*

To ſave the matter [to come off well] *ſalvar la capra e i cavoli, ſtrigarſi d' un negozio con vantaggio.*

SA'LVED, adj. *ſalvato, conſervato, difeſo.*

SA'LVER, s. [one who has ſaved a ſhip or its merchandizes] *uno che ha ſalvato un vaſcello, o le ſue mercanzie.*

Salver [a piece of wrought plate, to ſet glaſſes of liquor upon] *ſottocoppa, coppa,* s. f.

SA'LVO [a come off] *ſcuſa,* s. f.

To find a ſalvo for every objection, *trovare una riſpoſta ad ogni obiezione*; *aver più faſci che un altro ritortole*; *trovar ſubito riparo a tutte le accuſe.*

SA'LUTARY, adj. [wholeſome] *ſalutare, ſalutevole.*

SALUTA'TION, s. [or greeting] *ſalutazione,* s. f. *ſaluto,* s. m.

SALU'TE, s. [a bow] *ſaluto,* s. m. *riverenza,* s. f.

To give a ſalute, *fare un ſaluto, ſalutare.*

Salute [kiſs] *un bacio.*

A ſalute [in military affairs, a diſcharge of guns] *una ſalva di cannonate.*

To SALU'TE [to ſhow reſpect and civility, either in words or ceremonies] *ſalutare, pregar ſalute e felicità altrui facendogli motto.*

To ſalute [to kiſs] *ſalutare, baciare, dare un bacio.*

SALU'TED, adj. *ſalutato.*

SALU'TER, s. *quello, o quella che ſaluta.*

SA'MAR, s. [a ſort of long robe] *una zimarra.*

SAME, adj. *medeſimo, ſteſſo.*

At the ſame time, *nel medeſimo tempo.*

In the ſame place, *nel medeſimo luogo.*

I am in good health, I hope you are the ſame, *io ſto bene di ſalute, il ſimile ſpero di voi.*

It is the very ſame, *queſto è deſſo.*

SA'MENESS, s. [a being the ſame] *medeſimezza*, s. f.

SA'MPHIRE, s. [a plant which generally grows upon rocky cliffs in the ſea, and it is uſually preſerved in pickle] *finocchio marino, eriſamo*, s. m.

SA'MPLE, s. [a pattern or model] *eſemplare, eſemplo, modello*, s. m.

SA'MPLER, s. [ſome part of a commodity given as a pattern to ſhew the quality or condition of it] *moſtra*, s. f. *ſaggio*, s. m.

SA'NABLE, adj. [that may be healed or cured] *ſanabile, atto a ſanarſi.*

SA'NATIVE, adj. [of a healing quality] *ſanativo, ehe ha virtù di ſanare.*

SANCE, prep. [a word borrowed from the French, for without] Ex. ſance ceremony, *ſenza ceremonie. Scriverſi anche* ſans.

The ſance bell, s. [a little bell uſed in churches] *campanello, che ſi ſonava altre volte nel ſacrificio della meſſa.*

SANCTIFICA'TION, s. [a making holy] *ſantificazione*, s. f.

SA'NCTIFIED, adj. *ſantificato.*

SA'NCTIFIER, s. *ſantificatore*, s. m.

To SA'NCTIFY [to make holy] *ſantificare, far ſanto.*

SA'NCTIFYING, s. *ſantificamento*, s. m. *il ſantificare.*

SANCTIMO'NIOUS, adj. [holy] *ſanto.*

SA'NCTIMONY, s. [holineſs] *ſantimonia, ſantità*, s. f.

SA'NCTION, s. [a decree, ordinance] *ordine, decreto, ſtatuto.*

The pragmatical ſanction, *la prammatica ſanzione.*

SA'NCTITY, s. [holineſs] *ſantità*, s. f.

SA'NCTUARY, s. [a holy and ſanctified place] *ſantuario*, s. m.

Sanctuary [church] *chieſa*, s. f. *ſantuario*, s. m.

Sanctuary [refuge] *aſilo, refugio*, s. m.

SAND, s. [fine gravel] *arena, rena, ſabbia*, s. f. *ſabbione*, s. m.

Sands, or ſhelves of ſand in the ſea, *maſſa di rena che ſi trova nel mare, ſecca*, s. f.

Sand-box, *polverino*, s. m.

Sand-pit, or ſand-bed, *cava di ſabbione.*

Sand-blind, or pur-blind, adj. *che ha diffetto negli occhi, e malore di marchiuzze come rena.*

SA'NDAL, s. [a kind of ſhoe, open at the top, and faſtened with latchets] *ſandalo*, s m.

Sandal [a kind of wood brought out of India] *ſandalo*, s. m. *albero di più ſpezie, e di differenti colori, che viene a noi dall' Indie:*

SA'NDARACK, s. [a mineral not much unlike red arſenick] *ſandaraca*, s. f. *minerale che naſce nelle miniere de' metalli di color roſſo, come cinabro.*

Sandarack [a ſort of gum] *ſandaraca*; *gomma di ginepro.*

SA'NDEL, } s. [a ſea-fiſh] *anguilla*
SA'ND-EEL, } *di ſabbia, peſciolino che ſi trova nella ſabbia ſul lido del mare in Inghilterra.*

SA'NDERS, s. [ſandal, an Indian wood] *ſandali.*

SA'NDEVER, s. [the droſs of glaſs] *fondiglio di vetro.*

SA'NDING, s. [a ſea-fiſh] *barbio*, s. m. *ſorta di peſce.*

SA'NDY, adj. [full of ſand] *ſabbioſo, arenoſo, pien di ſabbione.*

SA'NGUINARY, adj. [blood-thirſty, cruel] *ſanguinolente, vago di far ſangue, crudele, ſanguinario.*

SA'NGUINE, adj. [blood red] *ſanguigno, ſanguinoſo, di colore ſimile al ſangue.*

Sanguine [full, or abounding with blood] *ſanguigno, che abbonda di molto ſangue.*

Sanguine [warm, ardent, confident] *caldo, ardente, volonteroſo, ardito, veemente.*

SANGUI'NOLENT, adj. [bloody] *ſanguinolento, crudele.*

SA'NICLE, s. [the herb ſelf-heal] *rigalico*, s. m. *ſpezie d'erba.*

SA'NITY, s. [ſoundneſs of mind] *ſanità*, s. f. *e diceſi della mente.*

SANK, *preterito del verbo* To ſink.

SANS [without] *ſenza.*

To SA'NTER, or to ſanter about [to wander up and down] *vagare, vagabondare, andare attorno.*

SAP, s. [the juice of trees] *ſucchio, ſugo, umore*, s. m. *ed è proprio delle piante, per virtù del quale comincian no a muovere, generando le foglie e i fiori.*

The trees are in ſap, *gli alberi ſono in ſucchio.*

Sap [the white part of a tree, betwixt the bark and the wood] *la buccia delle piante, che è tra 'l legno e la corteccia.*

To SAP [to undermine] *zappare, rovinare dalli fondamenti.*

To ſap a wall, *zappare, rovinare un muro.*

SAPHE'NA, s. [the crural vein, which goes down under the ſkin of the thigh and leg] *ſafena*, s. f. *vena che è nel lato di fuori del tallone.*

SA'PPHIRE, s. [a precious ſtone] *zaffiro*, s. m. *pietra prezioſa di color purpurino.*

SA'PID, adj. [taſteful] *guſtoſo*; *contrario d'inſipido.*

SA'PIDNESS, } s. *ſapore, guſto*, s. m.
SAPI'DITY, } *contrario d'inſipidezza.*

SA'PIENCE, s. [wiſdom; ſageneſs; knowledge] *ſapienza, ſaviezza, ſapere, conoſcimento.*

SA'PIENT, adj. *ſavio, ſapiente.*

SA'PLESS, adj. [without ſap] *ſenza ſucchio, che non ha ſucchio.*

Sapleſs, *ſecco, vecchio, che non ha che una povera e ſerra burria.*

SA'PLING, s. [a young tree] *un arbuſcello.*

SA'PPY, adj. [full of ſap] *pieno di ſucchio.*

SA'RABAND, s. [a dance] *ſarabanda*, s. f. *ſpezie di ballo Spagnuolo.*

SA'RCASM, s. [a biting ſcoff or taunt] *ſarcaſmo, motto pungente e ſatirico, bottone.*

SARCA'STICAL, } adj. [ſcoffing, ſaty-
SARCA'STICK, } rical] *ſatirico, pungente, acuto maligno.*

SARCA'STICALLY, adv. *in maniera pungente o maligna, malignamente.*

To SA'RCLE [to weed corn] *ſarchiare.*

SA'RCLING, s. [or the ſarcling time] *ſarchiagione*, s. f. *il tempo del ſarchiare.*

SARCOCO'LLA, s. [a gum which drops from a tree in Perſia] *ſarcocolla*, s. f. *liquore d'un albero di Perſia.*

SARCO'TICKS, s. [medicines which fill up wounds or ulcers with fleſh] *rimedi ſarcotici, che riempiono le piaghe di carne dopo d'averle ben purgate.*

SA'RDEL, } s [a ſort of fiſh] *ſardi-*
SA'RDINE, } *na, ſardella*, s. f. *piccol peſce così detto.*

SARDO'NICK laughter [an immoderate and ſneering laughter] *cacchinno, riſo ſardonico.*

SARDO'NYX, s. [a precious ſtone; partly of the colour of a man's nail, and partly of a cornelian colour] *ſardonico*, s. m. *pietra prezioſa.*

SA'RP-CLOTH, } s. [canvas to wrap
SA'RPLIER, } wares in] *tela da ſarco.*

Sarplier, s. [half a ſack] *mezzo ſarco.*

Sarplier of wool, *mezzo ſarro di lana*

SA'RSA, } s. [a plant grow-
SARSAPARE'LLA, } ing in Peru and Virginia] *ſalſapariglia*, s. f. *radice d'una pianta portata dell' Indie occidentali.*

SARSE, s. [a ſieve] *ſtaccio.*

To SARSE [to ſift through a fine ſieve] *ſtacciare.*

SASH, s. [a ſort of ſilk-band] *cinto di ſeta, diſtintivo di officiale militare.*

Saſh [a window ſo formed as to be let up and down by pullies] *fineſtra fatta in modo che ſcorre in ſu e in giù.*

SASHO'ON, s [leather put about the ſmall of a leg under a boot] *cuojo che ſi porta ſotto lo ſtivale nella parte più ſottile della gamba.*

SA'SSAFRASS, s. [the bark of a tree growing in America, which has a ſweet ſmell like cinnamon] *ſaſſafraſſo*, s. m.

SASSE, s. [a ſluice or lock in a river] *quella chiuſura di legnami che ſi fa calare da alto a baſſo, per impedire il paſſaggio all' acque.*

SAT, *preterito del verbo* To ſit.

SA'TAN, s. [the devil] *ſatan, ſatana, ſatanaſſo, il diavolo, il demonio.*

SATA'NICAL, } adj. [deviliſh] *di*
SATANICK, } *ſatanaſſo, diabolico.*

SA'TCHEL, s. [a little ſack, or bag] *ſacca*, s. f. *ſacchetto*, s. m.

To

To SATE [to satiate, to glut, to pall, to feed beyond natural desire] *saziare, pascere più del bisogno, satollare, far satollo.*

SA'TED, adj. [glutted] *satollo, sazio, saziato.*

Sated with meat, *satollo di carne.*

SATE'LLITE, s. [the life guard or officers attending upon a prince] *satellite*, s. m.

The satellites of Jupiter [four little stars that are near that planet] *i satelliti di Giove.*

To SA'TIATE [to satisfy or glut] *satollare, saziare, soddisfare interamente all' appetito e al senso.*

SA'TIATED, adj. *satollato, satollo, saziato, soddisfatto.*

SA'TIATING, s. *saziamento, satollamento*, s. m. *il saziare, il satollare.*

SATI'ETY, s. [fulness] *satollezza, sazietà*, s. f.

SA'TIN, s. [a sort of silk] *raso*, s. m. *spezie di drappo liscio.*

Flowered satin, *raso fiorito.*

SA'TIR, s. *satira; poema in cui il mal costume o la sciocchezza d' una o più persone è rabbuffata o vilipesa. La satira maligna, ingiusta, e personale in Inglese si chiama* lampoon.

SATI'RICAL, } adj. *satirico, di satira,*
SATI'RICK, } *mordace, severo in parole.*

SATI'RICALLY, adj. *satiricamente, mordacemente.*

SA'TIRIST, s. *scrittore di satire.*

To SA'TIRIZE, *scrivere satire o mordere con parole amo' di satira.*

SATISFAC'TION, s. [content] *soddisfazione*, s. f. *contento*, s. m.

Satisfaction [amends] *soddisfazione, ragione, ristaurazione*, s. f.

She has full satisfaction for the wrong done to her, *ella è appieno vendicata del torto fattole.*

SATISFA'CTORILY, adv. *d'una maniera soddisfacente.*

SATISFA'CTORY, adj. [sufficient to satisfy] *soddisfacente, che soddisfà.*

The death of our Saviour is satisfactory, *la morte del nostro Salvatore è soddisfacente.*

A satisfactory reason, *una ragione soddisfacente, che appaga.*

To SA'TISFY [to fill with meat] *soddisfare, satollare, saziare*, pres. *soddisfaccio*, pret. *soddisfeci.*

To satisfy one's lust, *soddisfare al suo appetito.*

To satisfy one's passions, *contentare le sue passioni.*

To satisfy [to pay] *soddisfare, dar soddisfazione, pagare, contentare.*

To satisfy [to convince] *soddisfare, appagare, convincere, acquetare*, pret. *convinsi.*

SA'TISFIED, adj. *soddisfatto, satollato, saziato.*

Satisfied [pay'd] *soddisfatto, pagato, contentato.*

Satisfied [convinced] *soddisfatto, appagato, pago, convinto, acquetato.*

I am not satisfied with him, *non sono soddisfatto, o contento di lui.*

I am not satisfied whether it is so or no, *non son sicuro se la cosa vadia così, o no.*

Rest yourself satisfied as to that [never trouble yourself about it] *non vi pigliate fastidio intorno a questo.*

You ought to be satisfied that I warned you of it before, *dovrebbe bastarvi, che vi ne ho avvertito prima.*

SA'TRAP, s. [the chief governor of a province in Persia] *satrapo*, s. m. *governatore d' una provincia in Persia.*

SA'TTEN, }
SA'TTIN, } *v.* Satin.

To SA'TURATE [to fill or satisfy] *satollare, saziare.*

SA'TURATED, adj. *saturo, satollato, satollo.*

SA'TURDAY, s. [the seventh day of the week] *Sabato, e Sabbato*, s. m. *nome del settimo dì della settimana.*

SATU'RITY, s. [fulness, satiety] *satollezza, satollanza, sazietà*, s. f.

To feed to saturity, *satollarsi, saziarsi.*

SA'TURN, s. [the highest of the planets] *Saturno*, s. m. *nome d' un pianeta.*

Saturn [the most ancient of the heathen gods, held to be the son of Cœlus and Vesta, deposed by his son Jupiter] *Saturno.*

Saturn [among alchymists, lead] *saturno, o piombo.*

SATU'RNALS, } s [solemn feasts and
SATURNA'LIA, } sacrifices in honour of Saturn] *saturnali, feste e sacrifici in onore di Saturno.*

SA'TURNINE, } adj. [belonging to,
SATU'RNIAN, } or of the nature of the planet of Saturn] *saturnino, di Saturno.*

Saturnine [dull, melancholy] *saturnino, maninconico, tristo, mesto.*

A saturnine man, *un uomo saturnino.*

SA'TYR, s. [a fabulous demi-god among the heathens, half beast and half man, imagined to preside over forests] *satiro*, s. m. *dio boschereccio finto da' poeti, metà uomo, e metà bestia.*

SATY'RION, s. [or standlewort, an herb] *satirio, satirione*, s. m. *spezie d' erba.*

SA'VAGE, adj. [wild] *salvatico, di selva, non domestico.*

Savage [fierce] *salvatico, fiero, crudele.*

The savages, s. [wild Indians] *popoli salvatici delle Indie.*

SA'VAGELY, adv. *salvaticamente, alla salvatica, con modo, e costume salvatico.*

SA'VAGENESS, s. *salvatichezza, rozzezza, zotichezza, crudeltà, ferocia.*

SAVA'NA, s. [a Spanish word, used in America, to signify a clear piece of land without woods, and pasture ground for feeding deer and cattle] *prati in America, senza boschi, che servono di pascolo al bestiame, che li Spagnuoli chiamano savanas, vale a dire lenzuola.*

SA'UCE, s. *salsa*, s. f. *condimento di più maniere che si fa alle vivande.*

To dip in the sauce, *intigner nella salsa.*

SA'UCE-PAN, *un padellino*, s. m.

SA'UCE-BOX, *un impertinente, uno sfacciato, uno sfrontato, un arrogante.*

To have sweat meat and sour sauce, *aver del bene e del male.*

To give one sweat meat and sour sauce, *fare del bene e del male ad alcuno.*

I'll serve him the same sauce, *gli renderò pan per focaccia.*

It will cost him sauce, *caro li costerà.*

SA'UCED, adj *condito.*

Meat well sauced, *carne ben condita.*

SA'UCER, s. *piattello, scodellino.*

SA'UCILY, adv. *sfacciatamente, impudentemente, arrogantemente, insolentemente, con arroganza, con insolenza.*

To carry one's self saucily, *portarsi, arrogantemente.*

SA'UCINESS, s. *sfacciataggine, impudenza, arroganza, insolenza*, s. f.

SA'UCY, adj. [impertinent, malapert] *sfacciato, sfrontato, malcreato, impertinente, arrogante, insolente, prosuntuoso.*

To give one a saucy answer, *rispondere ad alcuno insolentemente, darli una risposta impertinente.*

SAVE, prep. [except, but] *salvo, eccettuato, fuorchè, se non.*

All, save you, *tutti, fuorchè voi.*

Save that, *eccettuato questo.*

Save only to you, *se non a voi.*

To SAVE [to deliver] *salvare, campare, conservare, difendere*, pret. *difesi.*

To save one from death, *sottrarre uno dalla morte.*

I saved his life, *li ho salvata la vita.*

To save [to lay up] *riserbare, riservare, serbare.*

To save [to spare] *risparmiare, sparagnare.*

That will save me charges, *questo mi risparmierà della spesa.*

I'll save you that trouble, *voglio esentarvi da questo incommodo.*

To save one's longing, *far passar la voglia di che che sia.*

To save quarrels, *prevenire, ovviare contese.*

God save the King, *viva il Re.*

God save him, *Iddio lo conservi.*

To save time, *per non perder tempo.*

I'll save him harmless [I'll indemnify him] *io gli farò buona ogni perdita, io gli ristorerò ogni perdita.*

SA'VE-ALL, s. [a prolonger] *ordigno d' argento o d' altro metallo, sul quale si posa la candela quando viene a finire,*

nire, per far che duri e non si strugga nel candeliere.

SA'VED, adj. *salvato, campato, v.* To save.

A penny saved is a penny got, *un soldo risparmiato è un soldo guadagnato.*

SA'VINE, s. [a plant] *savina,* s. f. *pianta nota.*

SA'VING, s. *salvamento,* s. m. *salvezza,* s. f.

Saving [sparing] *risparmio,* s. m.

Saving [exception] *eccezione, clausula,* s. f.

Saving, adj. [that saves] *che salva.*

A saving faith, *una fede che salva.*

Saving [thrifty] *economo, che risparmia, parco.*

To be saving, *usar economia, risparmiare.*

Saving, prep. [save] *salvo, eccettuato, fuorchè, se non.*

Saving that, *salvo questo.*

SA'VINGLY, adv. [sparingly] *frugalmente, con frugalità, con risparmio, parcamente.*

SA'VINGNESS, s. [sparingness] *frugalità, moderanza nel vivere, parcità, moderazione,* s. f.

SA'VIOUR, s. *salvatore, liberatore.*

Our Saviour Jesus Christ, *Gesù Cristo nostro Salvatore.*

To SAUNTER about [to go idling up and down] *batter le strade, vagare, vagabondare, andar ramingo, andare attorno.*

SA'VONET, s. [a wash-ball] *saponetto,* s. m.

SA'VOUR, s. [taste] *sapore, gusto,* s. m.

Savour [scent, or smell] *odore,* s. m.

Something has some savour, nothing has no taste, *un poco val meglio che niente.*

To SA'VOUR [to taste, or relish] *saporare, assaporare, assaggiare.*

To savour, verb neut. [to taste] *aver qualche gusto.*

To savour [or smell] *sentire.*

That opinion savours of heresy, *questa opinione sente dell' eresia.*

SA'VOURILY, adv. *saporitamente, gustosamente, saprosamente.*

SA'VOURY, adj. [that has good savour] *saporito, di buon sapore, saporoso.*

Savoury kisses, *baci saporiti.*

Savoury, s. [an herb] *satureja, santureggia, timbra,* s. f. *erba nota.*

SA'VOY, s. [a sort of cabbage] *cappuccio, cavolo cappuccio.*

SA'USAGE, s. [minced meat made into a sort of pudding in hog's guts] *salsiccia,* s. f.

A Bolonia sausage, *salcicciotto o mortadella di Bologna.*

SAW, s. [a tool to saw with] *sega,* s. f. *strumento di ferro dentato, col quale si segano i legni.*

Saw-dust, *segatura,* s. f.

HAND-SAW, *seghetta, sega piccola.*

SAW-FISH, *nome d'un pesce di mare.*

An old saw [from an old saying] *un proverbio antico.*

Saw, *è il preterito del verbo* to see.

To SAW [to cut with a saw] *segare.*

Good to saw, *segaticcio, buono per esser segato.*

SAWED, adj. *segato.*

SA'WING, s. *segamento,* s. m. *il segare.*

SA'WER, s. *segatore,* s. m. *che sega.*

SA'XIFRAGE, s. [the stone-breaker, an herb good for the stone or bladder] *sassifrogia,* s. f. *erba che nasce tra' sassi, si dice anche sassifraga.*

SAY. s. [a thin sort of stuff] *saja,* s. f. *spezie di panno lano sottile, e leggieri.*

Say [or sample, used by contraction from assay] *mostra,* s. f. *saggio,* s. m.

Say, s. [speech; what one has to say] *quello che uno ha da dire.*

He had no sooner said out his say [or what he had to say] *avendo appena detto quel che aveva a dire.*

To SAY [to speak, to tell, to relate] *dire, raccontare, ragionare, favellare, narrare,* pres. *dico,* pret. *dissi.*

What do you say? *che dite?*

That is to say, *cioè.*

To say mass, *dire la messa.*

Say you so, *sarebbe pur vero?*

To say no more, *per non dir altro.*

To say by heart, *recitare a mente.*

Don't say nay, *non mi dite di no.*

Say on, *proseguite il vostro discorso.*

To say over again, *ridire, dire di nuovo,* pres. *ridico,* pret. *ridissi.*

They say, *si dice.*

SA'YING, s. *dicimento,* s. m.

Saying [or sentence] *un detto, un motto.*

A common saying, an old saying, *un detto comune o antico.*

A true saying, *una verità.*

SCAB, s. [itch] *rogna, scabbia,* s. f.

A scab [a dry'd scurf of a wound, pimple, or sore] *scabbia,* s. f. *croste di piaga, rogna, e simili; schianza.*

Scab, s. [a paltry fellow, so named from the itch] *un birbone pien di rogna.*

SCA'BBARD, s. [the sheath of a sword] *fodero,* s. m.

The scabbard of a sword, *il fodero d' una spada.*

SCA'BBED, adj. *scabbioso, rognoso.*

One scabbed sheep mars a whole flock, *una pecora rognosa guasta tutta la mandra.*

SCA'BIOUS, s. [an herb so called from its virtue in curing the itch] *scabbiosa,* s. f. *spezie d' erba.*

SCA'BROUS, adj. [rough, rugged] *scabro, scabroso, ronchioso, rozzo.*

A scabrous verse, *un verso scabroso.*

SCA'BWORT, s. [a plant] *enula, enula campana,* s. f. *sorta d'erba.*

SCA'BBY, adj. [full of scabs] *scabbioso, rognoso.*

SCA'FFOLD, s. [a place raised higher than the ground floor, for the better prospect] *palco.*

SCA'FFOLDING, s. *struttura di palchi.*

SCALA'DE, } s. [the mounting of a
SCALA'DO, } wall of a fortify'd town or castle with scaling ladders] *scalata,* s. f. *scalamento,* s. m.

To SCALD [to burn with hot liquor] *scottare con liquore caldo.*

SCA'LDED, adj. *scottato con acqua calda.*

SCA'LDING, s. *scottatura,* s. f.

SCA'LE, s. [scales of fishes] *squama o scaglia di pesce.*

The scale of a map, *la scala d' una carta di geografia.*

The scales of iron, *scaglia di ferro, quella foglia che casca dal ferro quando col martello si percuote.*

Scales in the head, *forfora, forforaggine,* s. f. *escrementi bianchi, secchi, e sottili, che si adunano fra capegli.*

A scale or bason of a balance, *il guscio della bilancia, quella parte ove si pongono le cose da pesare.*

A pair of scales, *bilance.*

The scale [or handle] of a razor, *il manico d' un rasojo.*

To SCALE a fish [to take off the scales] *scagliare i pesci, levar le scaglie.*

To scale the walls of a town, *scalare le mura d' una città.*

SCA'LED, adj. *v.* To scale.

SCALE'NE, } triangle [one that
SCALE'NOUS, } has its three sides unequal to each other] *triangolo scaleno, dicono i geometri quello, i lati del quale sono disuguali tra loro.*

The two scalenous muscles, *i due muscoli scaleni che servono al moto del collo.*

SCA'LING, s. *lo scalare; lo scagliare.*

Scaling-ladders, *scale da scalar le mura.*

SCALL, s. [scurf] *tigna, lepra,* s. f.

Scall-pated or scalled, adj. *tignoso, infetto di tigna.*

SCA'LLED head, or scald head, *testa tignosa.*

SCA'LLION, s. [shalot] *scalogno,* s. m. *spezie d' agrume simile alla cipolla, ma di picciol capo.*

SCA'LLOP, s. *sorta di pesce.*

SCALP, s. [the skin that covers the skull-bone] *pericranio,* s. m.

SCA'LPER, } s. [an instru-
SCALPING-IRON, } ment to scrape corrupted flesh from the bones] *strumento di cerusico per uso di raschiare la carne putrefatta dall' osso.*

SCA'LY, adj. [full of scales] *scaglioso, squamoso.*

A scaly fish, *un pesce scaglioso.*

To SCA'MBLE [to be turbulent and rapacious; to scramble; to get by struggling with another] *essere torbido e rapace; rapire, guadagnare dopò aspra contesa.*

To scamble [to shift aukwardly] *approvecciarsi grossolanamente.*

To scamble [to mangle, to maul] *storpiare, guastare.*

SCA'MBLER, s. [a bold intruder upon one's generosity or table] *uno sfacciato leccapiatti; uno che si abusa dell' altrui generosità; uno che sfacciatamente si caccia innanzi e va a desinare dove non è invitato.*

SCA'MBLINGLY, s. *con romorosa sfacciatezza, sfacciatamente.*

SCAMMO'NIATE, adj. [made with scammony] *fatto di scamonea.*

SCA'MMONY, s. [a purging herb] *scamonea,* s. f. *pianta medicinale purgativa.*

To SCA'MPER, } [to run a-
To SCA'MPER AWAY, } way in a hur-

hurry] *fuggir via, corſela, battcrſela, andar via, ſcampare.*

To SCAN a verſe [to meaſure it according to the manner of its feet] *ſcandere un verſo.*

To ſcan a buſineſs, *eſaminare ponderare, peſare, diligentemente eſaminare un negozio.*

SCA'NDAL, s. [offence] *ſcandalo,* s. m.

To raiſe a ſcandal, *dare ſcandalo.*

Scandal [ſhame] *ſcandalo, danno,* s. m. *vergogna, ignominia, infamia,* s. f.

To lie under a ſcandal [to have an ill name] *avere cattiva riputazione, eſſere in cattivo concetto.*

To SCA'NDAL [to ſlander, to defame] *ſcandalezzare, ſcandolezzare, ſcandalizzare, diffamare, infamare, macchiar la fama altrui con maldicenza.*

To SCA'NDALIZE [to give offence] *ſcandalizzare, dare ſcandalo, offendere,* pret. *offeſi.*

SCA'NDALIZED, adj. *ſcandalezzato, ſcandalizzato, ſcandolezzato.*

SCANDALI'ZING, s. *lo ſcandalezzare.*

Scandalizing, adj. *ſcandalezzante, ſcandalizzante.*

SCA'NDALOUS, adj. [giving offence, defaming] *ſcandaloſo, infame, che apporta ſcandolo, diffamatorio.*

A ſcandalous life, *una vita ſcandaloſa.*

A ſcandalous libel, *un libello diffamatorio.*

SCA'NNED, adj. *ſcandito.*

Scanned [ſifted, examined] *eſaminato, ponderato, peſato.*

SCA'NSION, s. [the ſcanning of a verſe] *lo ſcandere un verſo.*

SCANT, adj. [leſs than is requiſite, ſcarce] *ſcarſo alquanto manchevole.*

Scant, adv. *appena, a pena.*

SCA'NTED, adv. ex. I was ſomething ſcanted in time, *appena ebbi tempo.*

SCA'NTINESS, or SCANTNESS, s. [ſcarcity] *ſcarſezza, ſcarſità,* s. f.

SCA'NTLING, s. [ſize, or meaſure] *grandezza, miſura,* s. f.

Scantling [little meaſure] *un pezzetto.*

SCA'NTLY, adv. *ſcarſamente, meſchinamente.*

SCA'NTY, adj. [ſhort or ſcarce, as proviſions] *ſcarſo, che manca, parlando delle provviſioni.*

Scanty [too ſtrait, that has not ſtuff enough, ſpeaking of garments] *ſcarſo, troppo ſtretto, che non è ampio abbaſtanza, parlando de' veſtimenti.*

A ſcanty dinner, *un picciolo pranzo.*

SCAPE, s. [eſcape; flight from hurt or danger] *fuga, ſcampo.*

Scape [looſe act of vice or lewdneſs] *atto laſcivo.*

To SCAPE [to eſcape, to avoid, to ſhun] *ſcampare, evitare, fuggire.*

SCA'PULAR, SCAPULARY, } s. [a long narrow piece of ſtuff worn by monks and nuns over the reſt of their habit] *ſcapolare,* s. m.

SCAR, s. [the ſeam or mark of a wound] *cicatrice,* s. f. *quel ſegno che rimane in ſulla carne della ferita.*

A ſcar in the face, *uno ſfregio, cicatrice che rimane d' uno ſfregio fatto nel viſo.*

Full of ſcars, *coperto di cicatrici.*

A ſcar [a ſea term] *uno ſcoglio ſcoſceſo.*

SCA'RE-WORT, s. [a plant] *lopidio,* s. m. *ſpezie di pianta.*

To SCAR [to help up to a ſcar] *formarſi in cicatrice.*

A SCA'RABEE, s. [beetle] *ſcarafaggio, ſcarabeo,* s. m.

SCA'RAMOUCH, s. [an Italian buffoon] *ſcaramuccia,* s. m. *buffone maſcherato nelle commedie Italiane.*

SCARCE, adj. [rare, uncommon] *ſcarſo, raro.*

Money is very ſcarce, *il danaro è molto ſcarſo.*

Scarce, SCARCELY, } adv. [hardly] *appena, a mala pena, a fatica, a ſtento.*

SCA'RCENESS, SCARCITY, } s. *ſcarſezza, ſcarſità,* s. f.

To SCARE [to put in fear, to fright] *atterrire, ſpaventare, far paura,* preſ. *atteriſco.*

To ſcare one out of his wits, *sbigottire uno, farli gran paura.*

SCA'RE-CROW, s. [a figure made of ſtraw or clouts, ſet up in gardens or fields to ſcare away the birds] *ſpaventacchio, ſpauracchio,* s. m. *cencio o ſtraccio che ſi mette ne' campi ſur una pertica per iſpaventare li uccelli.*

SCA'RED, adj. *atterrito, ſpaventato.*

To have a ſacred countenance, *aver gli occhi ſtralunati.*

SCA'REFIRE, s. [a fright by fire; or a fire breaking out ſo as to raiſe terrour] *ſubita paura cagionata da fuoco; o fuoco che improvviſamente ſcoppiando t' empie di terrore.*

SCARF, s. [an ornament of ſilk for women] *ciarpa,* s. f. *il taffetà che le donne portano in capo o ſulle ſpalle.*

A ſcarf [an ornament for military officers and divines] *ciarpa, quella banda che portano gli ufficiali di guerra, e i preti proteſtanti.*

Scarf-ſkin [the outward ſkin which ſerves to defend the body] *l' epidermia, la pelle eſteriore che cuopre tutto il corpo.*

To SCARF, *veſtirſi d' un abito che preſto ſi pone e preſto ſi leva.*

To ſcarf [a ſea term, to faſten or join two pieces of wood together] *commettere, incaſtrare, combaciare, congegnare,* pret. *commiſi.*

SCA'RFED, adj. *commeſſo, incaſtrato, combaciato, congegnato.*

Scarfed [covered or adorned with a ſcarf] *coperto, ornato di ciarpa.*

SCARIFICA'TION, s. *ſcarificazione,* s. f.

To SCA'RIFY [to cut or lance] *ſcarificare, ſcarnare, intaccare.*

SCA'RIFIED, adj. *ſcarificato, ſcarnato, intaccato.*

SCA'RIFYING, s. *ſcarificazione,* s. f.

SCA'RLET, or ſcarlet colour, s. *ſcarlattino, ſcarlatto, color roſſo.*

Scarlet, adj. [of the colour of ſcarlet; red deeply died] *ſcarlatto, del color dello ſcarlatto.*

Scarlet cloth, *ſcarlatto, panno roſſo di nobiliſſima tintura.*

A ſcarlet robe, *una veſta di ſcarlatto.*

The ſcarlet-oak, *elce,* s. f. *leccio,* s. m.

SCARP, s. [the ſlope of that ſide of the ditch which is next to the place, and looks towards the fields] *ſcarpa,* s. f. *quel pendio delle mura, che le fa ſporger in fuora più da piè che da capo.*

SCA'RRED, adj. [from to ſcar] *formato in cicatrice.*

SCATCH, s. [a ſort of a horſe's bit] *morſo di cavallo.*

SCA'TCHES [ſtilts] *trampani.*

SCATE, s. [a ſea fiſh] *ſquadro,* s. m. *ſpezie di peſce di mare.*

SCATES [a ſort of pattens to ſlide upon the ice] *zoccoli, ſtrumento di ferro, che ſi lega ſotto le piante de' piedi, ſul quale ſi ſdrucciola ſopra il ghiaccio.*

To SCATE, *ſdrucciolare ſopra il ghiaccio.*

SCATHE, s. [hurt] *male, danno,* s. m.

SCATHEFUL, adj. [or hurtful] *dannoſo.*

To SCA'TTER [to diſperſe] *ſparpagliare, ſpargere, diſpergere, conſumare, ſbaragliare,* pret. *ſparſi, diſperſi.*

SCA'TTERED, adj. *ſparpagliato, ſparſo, diſperſo conſumato, ſbaragliato.*

SCA'TTERING, s. *ſpargimento, di ſpergimento,* s. m.

SCA'TTERINGLY, adv. *ſpartamente, ſparſamente, diſunitamente, chi qua, chi là.*

SCA'TTERLING, s. [a vagabond; one that has no home or ſettled habitation] *un vagabondo; un cavalier errante, uno che non ha nè caſa nè bottega.*

SCA'VENGER, s. [a pariſh officer, annually choſen to ſee that the ſtreets be cleanſed from dirt] *ufficiale d' una parrocchia che ha la cura di far nettar le ſtrade.*

SCA'WRACK, s. [a ſort of ſea weed] *muſchio marino.*

SCENE, s. [the front or fore-part of a theatre on which plays are acted] *ſcena,* s. f. *luogo dove ſi rappreſentan commedie.*

Scene [the changing of perſons in every act or comedy] *ſcena, parte d' un atto d' un opera teatrale.*

SCE'NES [the pictures repreſenting land, ſhips, buildings, &c. round about the ſtage] *le ſcene, il paeſe e luogo finto ſul paleo del teatro.*

Scene [the place of any great action] *teatro, luogo dove ſia arrivata qualche coſa notabile.*

Flanders has been the ſcene of war for many years, *la Fiandra è ſtata il teatro della guerra per parecchi anni.*

SCE'NERY, s. *ſcena, ſcenario, diſpoſizione delle ſcene.*

SCE'NICK, SCE'NICAL, } adj. [belonging to a ſcene] *ſcenico di ſcena.*

SCENOGRA'PHICAL, SCENOGRA'PHICK, } adj. [belonging to ſcenography] *ſcenografico.*

SCENOGRAPHY, s. [the repreſentation

tion of a building or fortreſs, as they are repreſented in perſpective, with its ſhadows and dimenſions] *ſcenografia*, s. f.

SCENT, s. [the power of ſmelling; the ſmell] *facoltà di fiutare*; *odorato*.

Scent, s. [the object of ſmell; odour, good or bad] *l' oggetto dell' odorato*; *odore buono o cattivo*.

Scent, s. [chaſe followed by the ſmell] *fiuto*, s. m. *peſta*, s. f. *il ſeguire la fera in caccia fiutando*.

To SCENT [to ſmell, to perceive by the noſe] *odorare, fiutare*.

To ſcent [to perfume; or to imbue with odour, good or bad] *dar buono o cattivo odore a checcheſſia*.

SCE'PTER, s. [a royal ſtaff or battoon] *ſcettro*, s. m. *bacchetta reale, ſegno d' autorità, e dominio*.

Scepter-bearer, *colui che porta lo ſcettro*.

SCE'PTICAL, adj. [belonging to ſcepticiſm] *ſcettico*.

SCE'PTICISM, s. [the doctrine and opinion of the ſcepticks] *precetti, inſegnamenti, de' ſcettici*.

SCE'PTICKS, s. [a ſet of philoſophers, who conſidered and contemplated matters, but doubted of every thing, and would admit of no determination] *ſcettici, filoſofi, che ſecondo gl' inſegnamenti della loro ſetta, niente afferman per vero, e di tutto dubitano. Molto ſcrivono* ſkepticks.

SCE'PTICK, adj. *ſcettico*.

The ſceptick philoſophy, *la filoſofia ſcettica*.

SCHE'DULE, s. [a ſcroll of paper, or parchment] *cartuccia, ſcritta, polizza, cedola*, s. f.

SCHE'MATISM, s. *aſpetto, figura, forma de' corpi celeſti*.

SCHEME, s. [draught, model] *piano, modello*, s. f.

SCHIFF, s. [a ſhip boat] *ſchifo, paliſchelmo*, s. m.

SCHISM, s. [a diviſion in the church] *ſciſma*, s. f. *diviſione, e ſeparamento dall' unità della fede*.

SCHISMA'TICAL, } adj. [inclining
SCHISMA'TICK, } to, or guilty of ſchiſm] *ſciſmatico*.

SCHISMA'TICALLY, adv. *da ſciſmatico*.

SCHISMA'TICK, s. [one who ſeparates from the true church] *uno ſciſmatico*.

SCHO'LAR, s. [one who learns any thing at ſchool, or elſewhere] *uno ſcolare, uno ſcolaro, uno che va ad imparare*.

A ſcholar [a learned perſon] *un uomo dotto, un letterato*.

A ſcholar [or learned woman] *una donna dotta*.

To be bred a ſcholar, *eſſere allevato nelle belle lettere, ſtudiare*.

A great ſcholar, *un uomo dotto, un uomo verſato nelle ſcienze*.

A general ſcholar, *uomo verſato in tutte ſcienze*.

Scholar-like, *da ſcolare, dottamente*.

SCHO'LARSHIP, s. [the being a ſcholar] *la qualità d' uno ſcolare*.

Scholarſhip [learning] *dottrina, ſcienza*, s. f. *ſapere*, s. m.

SCHOLA'STICALLY, adv. *da ſcolaſtico, alla maniera degli ſcolaſtici*.

SCHOLA'STICAL, } adj. [belonging
SCHOLA'STICK, } to a ſcholar or ſchool] *ſcolaſtico, di ſcuola*.

Scholaſtick divinity, *teologia ſcolaſtica*.

SCHO'LIAST, s. [a commentator] *un commentatore*.

SCHO'LIUM, s. [a brief expoſition, ſhort comment] *breve eſpoſizone, breve commentario*.

SCHOOL, s. [a place where any art or ſcience is taught] *ſcuola*, s. f.

To go to ſchool, *andare alla ſcuola*.

To keep a ſchool, *tenere ſcuola*

A grammar ſchool, or a Latin ſchool, *una ſcuola Latina*.

A fencing ſchool, *una ſcuola di ſcherma*.

A dancing ſchool, *una ſcuola di ballo*.

A ſchool-maſter, *un maeſtro di ſcuola*.

A ſchool-dame, or a ſchool-miſtreſs, *una maeſtra di ſcuola*.

A ſchool-boy, *uno ſcolare, o uno ſcolajo*.

A ſchool-fellow, *un condiſcepolo, compagno nell' imparare*.

A ſchool-man, or a ſchool-divine, *uno ſcolaſtico, un teologo ſcolaſtico*.

School divinity, *la teologia ſcolaſtica*.

To SCHOOL [to check or chide ſeverely, to reprehend] *riprendere, ammonire, cenſurare, bravare*, pret. *ripreſi*.

To ſchool [to inſtruct, to train] *iſtruire, ammaeſtare*.

SCHO'OLED, adj. *ripreſo, ammonito, cenſurato, ſbravato*.

SCHO'OLING, s. [or ſchool hire] *la paga che ſi da al maeſtro o maeſtra di ſcuola*.

To pay for a child's ſchooling, *pagare il maeſtro di ſcuola*.

SCIA'TICA, } s. [the hip-gout] *ſci-*
SCIA'TICK, } *atica*, s. f. *male cagionato da umore fermatoſi verſo l' oſſo ſcio*.

He that is troubled with a ſciatick, *uno ſciatico, infermo di ſciatica*.

SCIA'TICK, adj. *ſciatico*, ex. The ſciatick vein, *la vena ſciatica*.

SCI'ENCE, s. [knowledge, learning] *ſcienza, e ſcienzia*, s. f. *notizia certa di che che ſi ſia, dependente da vera rognizione de' ſuoi principj, dottrina, letteratura*, s. f. *ſapere*, s. m.

Science [liberal art] *arte liberale*.

SCIENTI'FICAL, } adj. [that cauſeth
SCIENTI'FICK, } or promoteth knowledge, learned] *ſcientifico, ſcienziato*.

SCI'MITAR, s. *ſcimitarra, ſorta di ſciabla ritorta*, s. f.

To SCI'NTILLATE [to ſparkle or gliſter] *ſcintillare, ſfavillare*.

SCINTILLA'TION, s. [a ſparkling] *ſcintillazione*, s. f. *lo ſcintillare*.

SCI'OLIST, s. [a ſmatterer in any kind of knowledge or learning] *un ſaccentino, un ſaccentuzzo, un ſemidotto*.

SCION, s. [a graft or young ſhoot of a tree] *ramicello che s' inneſta ſur una pianta a cui non apparteneva*.

SCI'SSION, s. [the act of cutting] *l' atto del tagliare*; *taglio*.

SCI'SSOR, s. [a ſmall pair of ſheers or blades moveable on a pivot and intercepting the thing to be cut] *ceſoje, forbici*, s. f. plur.

To SCOAT [to ſtop a wheel by putting a ſtone or piece of wood under it] *fermare una ruota mettendole un ſaſſo o un legno ſotto*.

SCOFF, s. [a deriſion or mock] *burla, beffa, baja, deriſione*, s. f. *ſcherno*, s. m.

To SCOFF at one [to deride or mock at him] *burlare, beffare, deridere, ſcoccoveggiare, ſchernire alcuno*, pret. *deriſi*, preſ. *ſcherniſco*.

Scoffed at, adj. *burlato, beffato, deriſo, ſcoccoveggiato, ſchernito*.

SCO'FFER, s. *deriſore, irriſore, ſchernitore, beffardo, beffatore*, s. m. *beffatrice, ſchernitrice*, s. f.

SCO'FFING, s. *burla, beffa, baja*, s. f. *ſcherno*.

SCOLD, s. [a ſcolding woman] *una garritrice, una contenditrice, una donna riottoſa*.

To SCOLD [to quarrel, to uſe angry reproachful words] *brontolare, borbottare, lagnarſi, garrire, gridare, ſgridare, contendere, rimproverare*, preſ. *garriſco*.

To ſcold at one, *bravare alcuno, farli una bravata, ſgridarlo, rampognare, riprendere, imbrottare*.

SCO'LDED at, adj. *brontolato, borbottato, lagnato, garrito, gridato, ſgridato, rimproverato, bravato, rampognato*.

SCO'LDING, s. *conteſa*, s. f. *contendimento*, s. m.

Scolding, adj. ex. A ſcolding man, *un garritore, un contenditore, un uomo riottoſo*.

A ſcolding woman, *una contenditrice, una garritrice, una donna riottoſa*.

SCO'LLOP, s. [a kind of ſhelled fiſh] *ſpezie di conchiglia, petoncolo*.

Scollop-ſhell, *nicchio, guſcio, conchiglia di petoncolo*.

SCOLOPE'NDRA, s. [a venomous worm, having eight feet, and a forked tail] *ſcolopendra*, s. f. *ſpezie d' inſetto velenoſo*.

Scolopéndra, s. [an herb] *ſcolopendrica, nome d' erba*.

SCOMM, s. [a buffoon] *un buffone, un zanni*.

SCONCE, s. [a ſmall fort built for defence of ſome paſs, river, &c.] *un forte*.

SCONCE, s. [the head] *il capo*.

To build a ſconce [to run up a ſcore from one publick houſe to another] *mangiar a credito ora in un' oſteria or in un' altra*.

A ſconce [a ſort of branched candleſtick] *certo ſoſtegno quaſi braccio, che ſerve per ſoſtener* i *lumi*.

To SCONCE [in the univerſity of Oxford is to ſet up ſo much in the buttery-book upon one's head, to be paid as a puniſhment for ſome duty neglected, or ſome offence committed] *fare ammenda, o per aver traſcurato il ſuo debito, o per aver commeſſo qualche offeſa termine usato fra gli studenti nell' Università d' Oxford.*

SCO'NCED, adj. *condannato all' ammenda.*

SCOOP, s. [a sort of wooden shovel] *attignitojo*, s. m. *strumento di legno col quale s' attigne.*

Scoop for corn, *pala da grano.*

SCOPE, s. [aim, end, purpose] *scopo, fine, disegno*, s. m. *meta*, s. f.

To have a free scope [or latitude] *aver campo o libertà di fare che che si sia.*

SCORBU'TICAL, } adj. [belonging
SCORBU'TICK, } to, or troubled with the scurvy] *di scorbuto, afflitto di scorbuto.*

SCORCE, s. *voce usata in vece di discourse da Spenser.*

To SCORCH [to parch, to burn] *riardere, scottare, abbruciare, abbrustiare, ardere*, pret. *riarsi, arsi.*

To scorch in the sun, *abbronzare.*

SCO'RCHED, adj. *riarso, scottato, abbruciato, abbrustiato, arso, adusto, arficcio.*

Scorched to the sun, *abbronzato.*

SCO'RCHING, s. *adustione*, s. f. *riardimento*, s. m.

Scorching, adj. *adustivo, ardente.*

Scorching heat, *calore adustivo, bollore, gran caldo.*

SCO'RDIUM, s. [an herb] *spezie d' erba.*

SCORE, s. [account, reckoning] *conto, scotto*, s. m.

To quit scores, *saldare un conto.*

Score [tally] *taglia*, s. f.

Score [twenty] *venti, ventina.*

Four-score, *ottanta.*

Six-score, *cento venti.*

Three-score, *sessanta.*

Score [account, consideration] *conto, rispetto, risguardo*, s. m. *stima.*

I desire it upon the score of friendship, *ve lo domando in risguardo della nostra amicizia.*

Upon what score? *perchè? per che ragione? in virtù di che?*

Upon a new score, *da capo, di nuovo.*

To SCORE, verb act. *segnare, notare, metter in conto.*

To score a writing [to draw lines under it] *rigare, lineare una scrittura.*

To score out, *scancellare, cassare, cancellare.*

SCO'RED, or scored up, adj. *segnato, notato, rigato.*

Scored out, *scancellato, cassato, cancellato.*

SCORN, s. [contempt] *disprezzo, sdegno, scherno, scorno*, s. m.

To look upon one with scorn, *riguardare alcuno con disprezzo, o scorno.*

He thinks scorn to do it, *si crederebbe disonorato, se lo facesse.*

To SCORN [to despise] *dispregiare, disprezzare, avere o tenere a vile, sdegnare, avere o tenere a sdegno, schifare, vilipendere, recarsi a scorno.*

He scorns my company, *egli disprezza, o tiene a vile la mia compagnia.*

I scorn it, I scorn to do such a thing, *io non son da tale da far ciò, ho a sdegno di fare tal cosa.*

I scorn your words, *mi beffo, mi rido di quel che dite.*

SCO'RNED, adj. *dispregiato, disprezzato, sdegnato, schifato, vilipeso.*

SCO'RNER, s. *dispregiatore, disprezzatore*, s. m. *dispregiatrice.*

SCO'RNFUL, adj. [disdainful] *sdegnoso, disprezzante, orgoglioso, altiero, fiero.*

To look upon one with a scornful eye, *guatar alcuno con disprezzo.*

SCO'RNFULLY, adv. *dispregevolmente, disprezzevolmente, con dispregio, sdegnosamente, orgogliosamente, alteramente.*

SCO'RNING, s. *dispregiamento*, s. m. *il dispregiare.*

After scorning comes catching, *bene spesso desideriamo quel che una volta abbiamo dispregiato.*

SCO'RPION, s. [a venomous insect] *scorpione*, s. m. *insetto velenoso, scorpio, scorpione*, s. m.

Scorpion [a fish] *scorpione, pesce di mare.*

The scorpion [one of the twelve celestial signs] *scorpione, uno de' dodici segni celesti.*

Scorpion-wort, or scorpion-grass, *nome d' erba.*

Scorpion's-tail, *nome d' erba.*

SCOT, s. [a part, or portion] *parte, porzione*, s. f.

To pay scot and lot, *pagare i diriti della parrocchia.*

Scot-free [that pays nothing] *franco, che non paga niente, a bardotto.*

Scot-free [unpunished] *impunito, immune, esente.*

SCOTCH, s. [a slight cut, a shallow incision] *picciol taglio, tagliuzzo, incisioncella.*

To SCOTCH [to cut with a shallow incision] *fare un picciol taglio, tagliare ma appena la pelle o la superficie.*

SCOTCH-CO'LLOPS, s. [slices of veal fry'd] *braciuola di carne di vitella fritta.*

SCOTCH-HO'PPERS, s. *giuoco fanciullesco che si fa saltando sopra una cordicella.*

SCO'TOMY, s. [a dizziness or swimming of the head] *scotoma, vertigine*, s. f.

SCO'VEL, s. [an oven map] *spazzatojo*, s. m. *arnese per ispazzare il forno.*

To SCOUL, } to knit one's brow,
To SCOWL, } [to look gruff] *fare il grugno, arricciare il muso, guatar in cagnesco.*

SCO'UNDREL, s. [a very rogue, a rascally fellow] *un gaglioffo, un briccone, un ribaldo, un manigoldo, ur furfante, un mascalzone.*

To SCOUR [to rub hard with any thing rough] *fregare con qualche cosa di aspro.*

To scour [to cleanse or make clean] *forbire, nettare, pulire*, pres. *forbisco, pulisco.*

To scour pewter, *forbire stagno.*

To scour clothes, *nettare abiti.*

To scour the seas, *corseggiare, andare in corso, far il mestiere del corsale.*

I shall scour you, *ti gratterò la rogna*, ti batterò.

To scour away [to scamper away] *svignare, corsela, battersela, fuggir via.*

To scour about [to ramble, to run raking about] *vagabondare, vagare, andar attorno, correr la cavallina.*

SCO'URED, adj. *forbito, nettato, pulito*, v. To scowr.

SCO'URER, s. *che forbisce, che netta.*

Scourer of pewter, *donna che forbisce stagni.*

Scourer of cloaths, *un cavamacchie.*

Scourer [rambler] *un vagabondo, un perdigiorno, uno scioperato.*

SCO'URING, s. [in horses, a looseness] *uscita, soccorrenza, flusso ne' cavalli.*

SCOURGE, s. [whip] *sferza, frusta*, s. f.

Scourge [plague] *fragello, flagello, gastigo*, s. m. *disgrazia, avversità grande.*

To SCOURGE [to whip] *sferzare, frustare.*

To scourge [to punish, to chastise] *punire, gastigare, flagellare, mandar travagli, travagliare, affliggere*, pres. *punisco*, pret. *afflissi.*

SCO'URGED, adj. *frustato, sferzato*, v. To scourge.

SCOUT, s. [one that is sent to bring tidings of the enemies army] *corridore*, s. m. *soldato che scorre la campagna, termine militare.*

To send out scouts, *mandare corridori a far la scoperta.*

Scouts, or scout-watches, *vedetta, e veletta, soldato che sta sulle mura delle fortezze a far la guardia.*

To scout, to scout about, *batter le strade, scorrer qua e là a far la scoperta.*

To scout [to watch] *stare alle velette.*

To SCOUL, v. To scowl.

To scoul, v. n. [to frown, to pout, to look angry, sour or sullen] *aggrottare, mostrar una ciera, brusca, mostrar un viso arcigno, guardare in cagnesco o dispettosamente.*

SCOWL, s. [look of sullenness or discontent; gloom] *cipiglio, guardo arcigno.*

To SCRA'BBLE [to tear with the nails] *graffiare, stracciar la pelle coll' unghie.*

To SCRA'BBLE [to feel about with the hands] *tastare, brancolare, andar tastone, andar brancolando.*

SCRAG, s. [a lean body] *uno scheletro, un corpo magro, uno che non ha che la pelle e l' ossa.*

The scrag-end of a neck of mutton, *quella parte del collo d' un castrato che più s' avvicina al collo, la scannatura del collo del castrato.*

SCRA'GGILY, adj. ex. He looks scraggily, *pare molto magro, ha una ciera molto sparuta.*

SCRA'GGY, adj. [very lean] *sparuto, gramo, molto magro, che non ha che la pelle e l' ossa.*

To SCRALL, v To scrawl.

To scrall [to scribble] *scarabocchiare, schiccherare, scriver male.*

SCRA'LLED, adj. *ſcarabocchiato, ſchiccherato, maleſcritto.*

SCRA'LDER, s. *uno ſcrittoraccio, un cattivo ſcrittore.*

To SCRA'MRLE [to ſnatch eagerly] *ciuffare, acciuffare, aggrappare, ghermire, pigliar con violenza, arraffare, acchiappare,* pres. *ghermiſco.*

To SCRA'MBLE [to climb up] *rampicare.*

SCRA'MBLED, adj. *v.* To ſcramble.

To SCRANCH [to craſh with the teeth] *ſchiacciare, rompere co' denti.*

SCRA'NCHED, adj. *ſchiacciato, rotto co' denti.*

SCRAP, s. [ſmall bit] *rimaſuglio, avanzaticcio.*

To SCRAP, *raſchiare, raſtiare, grattare.*

To ſcrape a root, *raſchiare una radice.*

To ſcrape at the door, *raſchiare alla porta.*

To ſcrape a leg [to make an awkward bow] *fare una riverenza ſgraziatamente.*

To ſcrape up a ſum of money, *accumulare a poco a poco una ſomma di danari.*

To ſcrape upon a muſical inſtrument, *ſtrimpellare uno ſtrumento di muſica.*

To ſcrape [as a hen does] *razzolare, raſpare come fanno i polli.*

To ſcrape [to blot out] *cancellare.*

SCRA'PED, adj. *raſchiato, raſtiato, v.* To ſcrape.

SCRA'PE-GOOD
SCRA'PE-PENNY } s. *un taccagno, un ſpilorcio, un miſero, un avaro.*

SCRA'PER, s. [an inſtrument to ſcrape with] *raſchiatatojo,* s. m. *ſtrumento di raſchiare.*

Scraper [ſorry fidler] *un cattivo ſonator di violino.*

SCRA'PING, s. *raſchiatura, raſtiatura,* s. f. *il raſchiare.*

Scraping [the thing ſcraped] *raſchiatura, la materia che ſi leva in raſchiando.*

SCRAT, s. [hermaphrodite] *un ermafrodito, uomo dell' uno e dell altro ſeſſo.*

SCRATCH, s *ſgraffio, graffio,* s. m. *graffiatura,* s. f.

Scratches [in horſes, certain dry ſcabs, a diſeaſe] *malattia che viene ai cavalli.*

To ſcratch [to rub gently] *grattare.*

To ſcratch one's head, *grattarſi la teſta.*

To ſcratch one's ſeif, *grattarſi.*

To ſcratch [to tear with the nails] *graffiare, ſtracciar la pelle coll' unghie.*

To ſcratch one's eyes out, *cavar li occhi ad uno.*

To ſcratch out a writing, *cancellare una ſcrittura.*

SCRA'TCHED, adj. *grattato, v.* To ſcratch.

To SCRAWL [to write after a ſorry careleſs manner] *ſcarabocchiare, ſchiccherare, ſcriver male.*

SCRA'WLED, adj. *ſcarabocchiato, ſchiccherato.*

SCRA'WL, s. [bad writing] *piedi di moſche, lettere mal fatte, cattiva mano.*

SCRAY, s. [ſea-ſwallow] *rondine di mare.*

To SCREAK [to make a noiſe like a door whoſe hinges are ruſty, or a wheel that is not well greaſed] *cigolare, ſtridere, come fanno i ferramenti, o i legnami fregati inſieme quando s' adoperano.*

The wheel of that coach ſcreaks, *la ruota di quella carrozza cigola.*

SCRE'AKING, s. *cigolamento, cigolìò,* s. m,

To SCRE'AM
To SCRE'AM out } [to cry out, eſpecially as in a fright] *gridare, ſtrillare, ſtridere.*

SCRE'AMED, adj. *gridato, ſtrillato, ſtriduto.*

SCRE'AMING, or ſcreaming out, s. *ſtrido, ſtridore,* s. m.

To SCREECH [to hoot or howl as a ſcreech-owl] *ſquittire, interrottamente ſtridere, con voce acuta, e ſottile.*

A ſcreech-owl, s. *civetta,* s. f. *ſorta d' uccello notturno.*

To SCREEK
To SCREEK out } *gridare, ſtridere, ſtrillare.*

SCRE'EKING, or ſcreeking out, s. *ſtrido, ſtridore, grido,* s. m.

SCREEN, s. [a kind of fan to keep off the heat of the fire] *un parafuoco.*

A ſcreen, or folding ſcreen, *un paravento.*

A ſcreen [a frame for ſifting gravel, corn, &c.] *vaglio,* s. m.

To SCREEN [to ſhelter, protect, or defend] *ſpalleggiare, proteggere, coprire, difendere,* pret. *proteſſi, difeſi.*

To ſcreen [to ſift through a ſcreen] *vagliare.*

SCRE'ENED, adj. *ſpalleggiato, protetto, coperto, difeſo, vagliato.*

SCREW, s. [an inſtrument for ſeveral uſes] *vite.*

Cork-ſcrew, *ſtrumento da cavar il ſughero alle bottiglie.*

To SCREW
To SCREW in } verb act. *fare entrare girando.*

To ſcrew up, *ſtrignere, o ſerrare a vite.*

To ſcrew one's ſelf into one's favour, *inſinuarſi nella grazia di qualcheduno, cattivarſi l' altrui amicizia.*

To ſcrew one's ſelf into other people's matters, *ingerirſi, intrometterſi, impacciarſi negli altrui affari.*

To ſcrew a thing out of one [to pump it out of him] *ſcalzare alcuno, cavargli di bocca artatamente quello, che ſi vorrebbe ſapere.*

To ſcrew the barrel of a gun, *pertugiare la canna d' uno ſchioppo.*

SCRE'WED, adj. *ſtretto, o ſerrato a vite, v.* To ſcrew.

To SCRI'BBLE [to ſcrawl] *ſcarabocchiare, ſchiccherare, ſcriver male.*

SCRI'BBLER, s. *uno ſcrittoraccio, un cattivo autore.*

SCRI'BE, s. [an expounder of the law among the Jews] *ſcriba,* s. m. *dottore della legge fra li Ebrei.*

Scribe [a writer or ſcrivener] *ſcriba, ſcrivano, ſcrittore,* s. m.

SCRIP, s. [a budget or bag] *biſaccia, ſacca, taſca,* s. f.

A ſcrip [or little piece] of paper, *un pezzetto di carta.*

SCRI'PTURAL, adj. [belonging to the holy ſcripture] *ſcritturale, della ſcrittura ſacra.*

SCRI'PTURE, s. [the holy ſcrtpture, or the holy writ] *la ſcrittura, la ſcrittura ſacra.*

SCRI'PTURISTS, s. [thoſe who ground their faith on the ſcriptures only] *quelli che mettono ogni loro credenza ſolamente nella ſcrittura.*

SCRI'TCH-OWL, *v.* Screech-owl.

SCRI'TORY, s. [a ſort of large cabinet for the conveniency of writing] *ſcrittojo,* s. m.

SCRI'VENER, s. [one who draws up and engroſſes writings] *ſcrivano,* s. m. *che tiene ſcritture.*

SCROFULA'RIA, s. [a plant] *ſcrofolaria,* s. f. *pianta.*

SCRO'LL, s. [a ſlip or roll of parchment] *un ruolo di pergamena.*

SCRUB, s. [an old broom] *una ſcopa, o granata vecchia.*

Scrub [a ſorry fellow] *un uomo di niente, un cionno, un uomo dozzinale, un uomicciatto.*

To SCRUB [to rub hard] *ſtrofinare, fregar ben bene.*

SCRU'BBED
SCRU'BBY } adj. [mean, vile, worthleſs, dirty, ſorry] *vile, ſcabbioſo, tignoſo, ſpregevole, ſporco.*

SCRU'FF, s. [little ſticks, coals, &c. which poor people gather by the Thames for fewel] *ſtecchi, carboni, e ſimili, che la povera gente va cogliendo nel Tamigi quando la marea è baſſa, per accendere il fuoco.*

SCRU'PLE, s. [doubt of conſcience] *ſcrupolo, ſcrupulo,* s. m. *dubbio che perturba la coſcienza.*

Scruple [among apothecaries, the third part of a dram, or twenty grains in weight] *ſcropolo, fra i ſpeziali è la terza parte d' una dramma.*

To SCRU'PLE at ſome thing, *fare o avere ſcrupolo di che che ſia.*

SCRUPULO'SITY
SCRU'PULOUSNESS } s. [a ſcrupulous humour, nicety of conſcience] *umore ſcrupoloſo.*

SCRU'PULOUS, adj. [full of ſcruples, nice, preciſe] *ſcrupoloſo, che ſi ſa ſcrupolo agevolmente.*

SCRU'PULOUSLY, adv. *ſcrupoloſamente, con iſcrupolo.*

To SCRUSE [to preſs or thruſt hard, to crowd] *incalzare, premere, affollare, ſerrare.*

To ſcruſe out, *ſpremer fuora, fare uſcire, premendo.*

SCRU'SED, adj. *incalzato, premuto, affollato, ſerrato.*

To SCRU'TINIZE [to examine thoroughly

rough'y] *cercare, ricercare, frugare, investigare, accuratamente, esaminare, scrutinare.*

To scrutinize a business, or into a business, *investigare, frugare, diligentemente esaminare un negozio.*

SCRU'TINIZED, adj. *cercato, ricercato, inchiesto, frugato, investigato, accuratamente esaminato, scrutinato.*

SCRU'TINY, s. [strict search, diligent enquiry] *scrutinio, ricercamento, esame*, s. m.

Scrutiny [a perusal of suffrages or votes at the election of magistrates] *scrutinio, squittinio, o squittino.*

SCRU'TORE } s. *scrittojo, banco.*
SCRU'TORY }

SCRY, s. [a great flock of fowl] *una folla d' uccelli.*

SCUD, s. [a sudden shower of rain] *rovescio, scroscio*, s. m. *subita e veemente pioggia.*

To SCUD, or scuddle away [to run away all of a sudden] *svignare, corsela, battersela, fuggir via, mettersi la via fra le gambe.*

SCU'FFLE, s. [quarrel, fight, fray] *zuffa, riotta, sciarra, rissa, contesa*, s. f.

To SCU'FFLE [to quarrel] *contrastare, contendere, combattere, azzuffarsi, riottare.*

We have nothing to scuffle for, *noi non abbiamo che spartire insieme.*

SCULK, s. [company] *truppa, banda*, s. f.

A sculk of foxes, *una truppa di volpi.*

To SCULK [to hide one's self] *celarsi, nasconderfi, appiattarsi.*

To sculk for one, *codiare, alcuno, spiare, indagare i suoi andamenti.*

SCU'LKING, adj. ex. a sculking place, or a sculking hole, *un nascondiglio, un ripostiglio.*

SCULL, s. [the bone of the head] *cranio*, s. m. *osso del capo, che a foggia di volta cuopre, e difende il cervello dell' animale.*

A scull-cap, *cuffia di tela, che alcuni portano sotto la parrucca.*

An iron scull, *celata*, s. f. *morione*, s. m.

A scull of friers [company of friers] *confraternità di monaci.*

Scull [a small boat with one oar only] *barchetta a un remo solo.*

Scull [little oar] *piccol remo.*

SCU'LLER, s. [boat rowed with sculls] *battello con un barcajuolo solo.*

SCU'LLERY, s. [place to wash or scower the dishes in] *lavatojo*, s. m. *luogo nella cucina dove si lavano i piatti.*

SCU'LLION, s. [kitchen drudge] *guattero di cucina.*

Scullion wench, *una guattera di cucina, una sporca.*

SCULP, s. [cut, print] *stampa in rame.*

To SCULP [to carve, to engrave] *intagliare, scolpire.*

SCU'LPTILE, adj. [made by carving] *intagliato, fatto di scoltura.*

SCU'LPTOR, s. [carver, engraver] *scultore*, s. m.

SCU'LPTURE, s. [the art of carving figures in wood, stones, &c.] *scultura*, s. f. *l' arte dello scolpire.*

Sculpture [sculp, figure] *scultura, la cosa scolpita.*

To SCU'LPTURE [to cut, to engrave] *scolpire, intagliare.*

SCUM, s. [froth, dross] *schiuma*, s. f.

The scum of a pot, *la schiuma d' una pignatta.*

The scum of the people, *la feccia del popolo, la canaglia.*

The scum of metals, *la schiuma, o spuma de' metalli.*

Full of scum, *spumoso, schiumoso, pien di schiuma.*

To SCUM [to skim, to take off the scum] *schiumare, levare, e tor via la schiuma.*

SCU'MBER, s. [the dung of a fox] *sterco o cacherello di volpe.*

SCU'MMER, s. *una mestola.*

SCU'MMED, adj. *schiumato.*

SCU'RF, s. [a scall on the head] *tigna*, s. f. *ulcere sulla cotenna del capo.*

Scurf on the childrens heads, *escremento contratto nell' utero materno, dal bambino, mandato alla superficie del capo, per ispurgare, in particolare il cervello*; *forfora, forforaggine, scabbia, schianze.*

Scurf of a wound, *scabbia, o croste di piaga.*

SCU'RFINESS, s. [scabbiness] *tigna.*

SCU'RFY, adj. [full of scurf] *tignoso, scabbioso.*

SCURRI'LITY, s. [buffoonry, saucy jesting] *scurrilità, buffoneria, gaglioffería, giulleria, loquacità, disonestà*, s. f.

SCU'RRILOUS, adj. [railing, saucy, abusive] *buffonesco, giullaresco, ingiurioso, impertinente.*

SCU'RVILY, adv. *malamente, cattivamente, fellamente, bruttamente.*

To do a thing scurvily, *fare che che si sia malamente.*

SCU'RVINESS, s. *cattivezza, furfanteria, malignità, malvagità, malizia*, s. f.

SCU'RVY, adj. [bad, naughty, untoward] *cattivo, fello, furfante, ghiotto, maligno, malvagio, sciagurato, ribaldo, tristo.*

A scurvy fellow, *un fellone, un furfante, un ghiotto, un malvagio, uno sciagurato.*

A scurvy trick, *un tiro da bricone.*

A scurvy business, *un cattivo negozio.*

Scurvy, s. [a disease] *scorbuto*, s. m. *spezie di malattia.*

Scurvy-grass, *gramigna*, s. f.

SCUT, s. [the tail of a hair or coney] *la coda d' una lepre o d' un coniglio.*

SCU'TCHEON, s. [the ground on which a coat of arms is painted] *scudo*, s. m. *quel fondo ovato o tondo dove son dipinte l' insegne d' una famiglia.*

The scutcheon of a lock, *la toppa d' una serratura.*

Scutcheon [bud to be grafted] *scudicciuolo*, s. m. *l' occhio che s' innesta nella tagliatura del nesto.*

Scutcheon [the key or center stone in a building] *la chiave, o la pietra che è nel centro d' un edificio.*

SCU'TELLATED, adj. [divided into small surfaces] *tagliato a diamante, diviso in varie superficie.*

SCU'TIFORM, adj. [shaped like a shield] *fatto a mo' di scudo.*

SCU'TTLE, s. [a dust basket] *paniere, dove si pongon le immondizie.*

The scuttle of a mill, *tramoggia di mulino.*

Scuttle [the bowl on the top-mast of a ship] *gabbia*, s. f. *quello strumento che i marinari mettono in cima all' antenna, sul quale sta la veletta.*

Scuttles [in a ship, little windows which are cut out in cabins to let in the light] *finestrelle che sono nella camera di poppa, per dar lume.*

To SCU'TTLE here and there, *andar quà e là, andare e venire.*

SDE'IGNFUL, adj. [contracted for disdainful] *sdegnoso, sdegnato, pien di sdegno.*

SEA, s. [that general collection of waters which encompasses the earth] *il mare, universal congregamento dell' acque che circonda la terra.*

The billows of the sea, *cavalloni di mare.*

The roaring of the sea, *il fremito del mare.*

To go to sea, *andar sul mare.*

To put out to sea, *mettere a mare far vela.*

By sea and land, *per mare e per terra.*

A great sea [or stormy weather] *una barrasca, o fortuna, di mare.*

A sea [a sea gate, a wave or billow, a surge] *un' onda*, s. m. *flutto, cavallone*, s. m.

Sea-water, *acqua marina, o di mare.*

The main sea, *alto, o alto mare.*

A sea-captain, *capitano di naviglio.*

A sea-fight, *combattimento navale.*

A sea-man, *un marinajo.*

A sea-faring man, *persone che vanno per mare.*

Sea-sick, *mareggiato.*

To be sea-sick, *mareggiarsi.*

The sea-coast, *la costa, la spiaggia del mare.*

The sea-side, *il lido del mare, la marina.*

A narrow-sea, *uno stretto, un golfo.*

A sea-port, *porto di mare.*

A sea-port town, *terra marittima.*

A sea-card, or sea-map, *carta da navigare.*

A sea-voyage, *viaggio per mare.*

A sea-rover, *un corsale, un corsaro, un pirata.*

Sea-

Sea-gates, *onde, flutti, cavalloni di mare.*

Sea-lungs [the froth of the sea] *la spuma del mare.*

Sea-ward, or sea-board [towards the sea] *in alto mare.*

To sail sea-ward, *veleggiare in alto mare.*

Sea coal, *carbone di terra.*

Sea-green, *verdazzurro, sorta di colore.*

Sea-fan [a herb] *corallina, s. f. muschio marino.*

A sea-calf, *vitello marino.*

A sea-devil [a bird] *folaga, s. f. uccello aquatico*

A sea-pad [an insect] *stella di mare, spezie d' insetto.*

A sea-hog [porpoise] *porcello marino.*

Sea-onion } s. *squilla,* s. f.
Sea-leek }

Sea-lettice, *titimaglio,* s. m.

Sea-weed, or sea-ware [a plant] *alga,* s. f. *erba aquatica.*

SEAL, s. [a piece of metal, on which a coat of arms, or some other device is engraved] *sigillo, suggello,* s. m.

To tell a thing under the seal of secrecy, *dire che che si sia sotto sigillo di confessione.*

Agreement under hand and seal, *un contratto sottoscritto e sigillato.*

Seal [sea-calf] *vitello marino.*

A seal-ring, *anello con un sigillo scolpito.*

To SEAL, verb. act. *sigillare.*

To seal a letter, *sigillare una lettera.*

To seal hermetically [among chymists, is to stop the mouth or neck of a glass bottle, with a pair of pincers heated red-hot] *sigillare col sigillo d' ermete.*

SE'ALED, adj. *sigillato.*

SE'ALER, s. *colui che pone il suggello, ufficiale del suggello.*

SEAM, s. [a row of stitches with a needle] *cucitura,* s. f. *la congiuntura del cucito.*

Seam, s. [the juncture of planks in a ship] *commessura de' legni n' una nave.*

Seam, s. [cicatrix, scar] *cicatrice.*

Seam-rent, *scucitura,* s. f.

Seam [the fat of a hog fried] *saime, lardo, grasso, strutto,* s. m.

A seam of corn [eight bushels] *otto staja di grano.*

A seam of glass [that is 120 pounds] *cento venti libbre di vetro.*

SE'AMAN, s. *marinajo.*

SE'AMED, adj. [that hath seams] *cucito, che ha cuciture.*

SE'AMLESS, adj. [without seams] *senza cuciture, tutto d' un pezzo.*

SEAM [joint of stone in building] *commessura.*

SE'AMSTER, s. *cucitore di panni lini.*

SE'AMSTRESS, s. *cucitrice, donna che cuce panni lini.*

SE'AMY, adj. [having a seam; showing a seam] *che ha o mostra commessure.*

SEAN, s. [a sort of large fishing net] *sagena,* s. f. *rete da pescare.*

Sean-fish [fish taken with a sean] *spezie di pesce, che si pesca colla sagena.*

To SEAR [to burn with a hot iron] *arrossare con ferro rovente.*

To sear linen, *arrossare delle biancherie.*

To sear a stuff with a searing candle, *incerare del panno.*

SEARCE [a fine sieve] *staccio,* s. m.

To SEARCE [to sift] *abburattare, stacciare.*

SE'ARCED, adj. *abburattato, stacciato.*

SEARCH, s. [enquiry] *inchesta, inchiesta,* s. f. *ricerca,* s. f.

To SEARCH [to seek, to enquire after] *cercare, visitare.*

To search for a thing, *cercare che che sia.*

To search a house, *visitare una casa.*

To search one's pockets, *cercar le scarselle ad uno*

To search a wound, *tentare una ferita.*

To search into [to enquire into, to examine] *inchiedere, ricercare, esaminare, informarsi, penetrare.*

To search after, *ricercare, inchiedere.*

SE'ARCHED, adj. *cercato, visitato, v.* To search.

SE'ARCHER, s. [one who searches] *visitatore, cercatore, esaminatore,* s. m.

SE'ARCHING, s. *cerca,* s. f.

SEAR-CLOTH, s. [a plaster for pains, aches, &c.] *cerotto,* s. m. *composto medicinale, fatto di materia tenace perche s' appicchi.*

Sear-woods [dead boughs cut off from trees in a forest] *frasconi,* s. m. *vettoni di querciuoli o simil legname, chè si taglian per abbruciare.*

Sear leaves [leaves withered or dead] *foglia morta.*

Searing candle, *candela di cera per uso d' incerare.*

SE'ASON, s. [one of the four quarters of the year] *stagione,* s. f. *nome comune a tutte le quattro parti dell' anno, come primavera, state, autunno, e verno.*

The season [a proper time to do a thing] *stagione, tempo opportuno.*

A thing in season, *una cosa che è di stagione.*

To do every thing in its season, *fare che che si sia di stagione, in tempo opportuno, a suo tempo.*

In the mean season, *nulladimeno.*

To SE'ASON, [to salt, to give any thing a relish with salt, spice, &c.] *condire, stagionare,* pres. *condisco.*

To season meat, *condire o stagionare*

SE'ASONABLE, adj. [in its season] *che è di stagione.*

Seasonable [proper, convenient] *comodo, opportuno, conveniente, acconcio.*

SE'ASONABLENESS, s. [the being in season] *qualità di quel che è di stagione.*

Seasonableness [opportunity] *stagione, tempo opportuno, opportunità,* s. f.

SE'ASONABLY, adv. *acconciamente, opportunamente, a tempo debito.*

SE'ASONED, adj. *condito, stagionato.*

A seasoned cask, *una botte stagionata.*

Well seasoned timber, *legname secco, buono ad esser lavorato.*

SE'ASONER, s. *quello che stagiona, stagionatore.*

SE'ASONING, s. *stagionamento, condimento,* s. m.

The seasonings [in the West-Indies, an aguish distemper, which foreigners are subject to on their first coming] *spezie di febbre alla quale i forestieri sono soggetti arrivando nell' Indie occidentali.*

SEAT, s. [any thing to sit on] *sedia,* s. f. *seggio,* s. m. *ogni luogo da sedere.*

A bishop's seat, *sedia episcopale.*

Seat [scene, or theatre] *scena,* s. f. *teatro,* s. m.

The seat of a town, *la situazione d' una città.*

A fine seat [a fine country-house] *una bella villa.*

A judgment seat, *un tribunale.*

The heart is the seat of life, *il cuore è il seggio della vita.*

To SEAT [to place] *situare, collocare, posare.*

To seat [to settle] *stabilire,* pres. *stabilisco.*

To seat one's self in a good place, *stabilirsi in un buon luogo.*

SE'ATED, adj. *situato, v.* To seat.

A strongly seated place, *una piazza situata in luogo forte.*

A Cupid seated upon an eagle, *un Cupido assiso sopra un' aquila.*

SE'ATER, s. [an idol worshipped by the ancient Saxons on Saturday: the form of this idol was an old man on a pillar, standing on a fish, a pail of water in his right hand full of fruits, and a whale in his left] *nome d' Idolo che li antichi Sassoni adoravano il Sabato; la sua forma era un vecchio sopra un pilastro sopportato da un pesce, una secchia nella man dritta piena di frutti, e nella man sinistra una balena. Quindi il vocabolo* Saturday, *Sabato, di di Seater, e non di Saturno.*

SE'AWARDS, adv. [towards the sea] *verso il mare.*

SEAX } s. [a sword made like a
SEAXE } scythe, used by the old Saxons] *spezie di spada in forma di falce usata dagli antichi Sassoni.*

SE'CANT, s. [a term of geometry] *secante o linea che sega.*

To SECE'RN [to separate finer from grosser matter] *separare il sottile dal grossolano di qualsisia materia.*

SECE'SSION, s. *l' andare, o il ritirarsi a parte.*

The secession or adjournment of a par-

parliament, *ſeparazione del parlamento.*

SE'CLE, s. [century] *ſecolo.*

To SECLU'DE [to ſhut out] *eſcludere, eccettuare, ſeparare mettendo fuora*, pret. *eſcluſi.*

SECLU'DED, adj. *eſcluſo, eccettuato, ſeparato.*

SECLU'DING } s. *eſcluſione*, s. f.
SECLU'SION }

SE'COND, adj. *ſecondo.*

A ſecond hand ſuit, *un abito uſato.*

He is a ſecond Cicero, *egli è un altro Cicerone.*

The ſecond wheel of a watch, *la ruota mezzana d' un oriuolo.*

A ſecond hand dinner, *un pranzo riſcaldato.*

A ſecond, s. [one that backs or defends another] *un difenſore, un protettore.*

A ſecond [he that backs another in a duel] *patrino*, s. m. *quegli che aſſiſte il cavaliere in duello.*

A ſecond [the ſixtieth part of a minute] *la ſeſſanteſima parte d' un minuto.*

To SE'COND [to aid, to aſſiſt, to favour] *ſecondare, ajutare, favorire. proteggere, ſpalleggiare, aſſiſtere*, preſ. *favoriſco*, pret. *proteſſi.*

SE'CONDED, adj. *ſecondato, ajutato, favorito, protetto, ſpalleggiato, aſſiſtito.*

SE'CONDINE, s. [the after-birth, wherein the embryo is wrapped whilſt in the womb] *ſeconda, ſecondina*, s. f. *quella materia unita, o compatta, che eſce dopo il parto.*

SE'CONDLY, adv. *ſecondamente, ſecondariamente, in ſecondo luogo.*

SE'CRECY, s. [the keeping of a matter ſecret] *ſegretezza*, s. f.

To carry on a buſineſs with great ſecrecy, *maneggiare, trattare un negozio con grande ſegretezza*

SE'CRET, adj. [private, hidden] *ſegreto, privato, occulto.*

Secret dealing, *pratiche ſegrete.*

Secret [cloſe, that can keep a ſecret] *ſegreto, che ſa tacerſi, che guarda il ſegreto.*

Secret, s. [a ſecret thing] *ſegreto*, s. m. *coſa occulta, o coſa tenuta occulta.*

To tell one a ſecret, *dire o confidare un ſegreto ad uno.*

In ſecret, *in ſegreto, al ſegreto, ſegretamente.*

Secret [a thing which few people know] *ſegreto, ricetta, o modo ſaputo da pochi di far che che ſia.*

SE'CRETARY, s. [one who is employed in writing letters for his maſter] *ſegretario*, s. m. *colui che s' adopera negli affari ſegreti e ſcrive le lettere del ſuo padrone.*

The ſecretary's office, *ſegreteria*, s. f.

SE'CRETARYSHIP, s. *uſficio di ſegretario.*

SE'CRETLY, adv. [in ſecret] *ſegretamente, non ſegretezza.*

SE'CRETNESS, s. [ſecreſy] *ſegretezza*, s. f.

SECT, s. [a party profeſſing the ſame opinion] *ſetta*, s. f. *quantità di perſone, che aderiſcono a qualche particolare opinione, dottrina, o fazione.*

SECTA'RIAN, adj. [belonging to a ſect] *di ſetta, appartenente a qualche ſetta.*

SE'CTARY, s. [a follower of a particular ſect] *ſettario*, s. m. *ſeguace, di ſetta.*

SE'CTION, s. [a diviſion] *ſezione, diviſione*, s. f.

SE'CTOR, s. [an inſtrument uſed in all the practical parts of the mathematicks] *ſettore*, s. m. *compaſſo di proporzione.*

SE'CULAR, adj. [temporal] *ſecolare, ſecolareſco, temporale.*

A ſecular prieſt [not regular] *un prete ſecolare.*

Secular games [ſolemn feaſts, celebrated at the end of every hundred years] *giuochi ſecolari.*

SECULA'RITY, s. *lo ſtato di perſona ſecolare.*

SECULARIZA'TION, s. [a ſecularizing] *ſecolarizzazione*, s. f.

To SE'CULARIZE [to make ſecular] *ſecolarizzare.*

To ſecularize a monk, *ſecolarizzare un frate.*

SE'CULARIZED, adj. *ſecolarizzato.*

SE'CULARLY, adv. [in a worldly manner] *mondanamente, ſecolarmente.*

SE'CUNDARY, adj. [ſecond, next to chief] *ſecondario, che ſuccede dopo il primo.*

SE'CUNDI'NE, *v.* Secondine.

SECU'RE, adj. [that is out of danger, ſafe] *ſicuro, ſalvo, fuor di pericolo.*

Secure [fearleſs, careleſs] *ſicuro, ardito, certo, che può aſſicurarſi del ſuo ſapere e del ſuo potere.*

To SECU'RE [to ſave, to ſhelter, to protect] *ſalvare, campare, mettere in ſicuro, preſervare, difendere, proteggere*, pret. *difeſi, proteſſi.*

To ſecure one's ſelf, *ſalvarſi, metterſi in ſicuro.*

To ſecure, *aſſicurare, accertare, render ſicuro.*

To ſecure one, *arreſtare alcuno, prenderlo, acchiapparlo, imprigionarlo.*

To ſecure a place, *impadronirſi d' una piazza.*

SECU'RED, adj. *ſalvato*, *v.* To ſecure.

Secured of a truth, *aſſicurato, ſicuro d' una verità.*

SECU'RELY, adv. *ſicuramente, fermamente, con certezza.*

Securely [cautiouſly] *ſicuramente, in piena ſicurezza, tranquillamente.*

SECU'RITY, s. [or aſſurance] *ſicurezza, ſicurtà, franchezza.*

Security [bail] *ſicurtà, cauzione, malleveria*, s. f.

Security [unconcernedneſs] *ſicurezza, fiducia, baldanza, arditezza, fidanza*, s. f.

SE'DAN, s. [chair to carry any thing in] *ſedia.*

SEDA'TE, adj [quiet, compoſed, undiſturbed in mind] *ſedato, quieto, tranquillo, calmo, moderato.*

With a ſedate mind, *con mente tranquilla.*

SEDA'TENESS, s. [or tranquillity] *tranquillità, moderazione*, s. f.

SE'DENTARY, adj. [that is much given to ſitting] *ſedentario, che ama di ſtare aſſiſo.*

A ſedentary man, *uno che fa ſue faccende ſedendo.*

A ſedentary life, *una vita ſedentaria.*

Sedentary parliaments in France [are ſuch as are fixt and ſettled in a place] *parlamenti ſiſſi.*

SEDGE, s. [a kind of weed] *ſpezie d' erba.*

SE'DIMENT, s. [the ſettlement or dregs of any thing] *fondigliuolo, rimaſuglio*, s. m. *poſatura, feccia*, s. f.

SEDI'TION, s. [mutiny] *ſedizione*, s. f. *tumulto, ſcompiglio*, s. m.

SEDI'TIOUS, adj. [factious, mutinous] *ſedizioſo, riottoſo, vago di ſedizione, che cagiona ſedizione, ſcandaloſo.*

SEDI'TIOUSLY, adv. *ſedizioſamente, tumultuariamente, riottoſamente.*

SEDI'TIOUSNESS, s. turbulence, diſpoſition to ſedition] *tumulto, diſpoſtezza a ſedizione.*

To SEDU'CE [to miſlead or deceive] *ſedurre, diſtorre altrui con inganno dal bene, ſobillare*, pret. *ſeduſſi.*

To ſeduce [to corrupt or debauch] *ſedurre, corrompere, ſviare*, pret. *corruppi.*

SEDU'CED, adj. *ſedotto, ſobillato, corrotto, ſviato.*

To ſuffer one's ſelf to be ſeduced, *laſciarſi ſedurre.*

SEDU'CEMENT, s. *ſeduzione*, s. f. *il ſedurre.*

SEDU'CER [one who ſeduces] *ſeduttore*, s. m.

SEDU'CIBLE, adj. [corruptible, capable of being drawn aſide] *ſeducibile, che ſi può ſedurre.*

SEDU'CTION, s. [the act of ſeducing] *ſeduzione*, s. f. *ſviamento*, s. m.

SEDU'CING, ſeduction, s. *ſeduzione*, s. f. *il ſedurre.*

Seducing, adj. *che ſeduce.*

SEDU'LITY, s. [continual care, diligence] *accuratezza, diligenza, cura, aſſiduità*, s. f.

SE'DULOUS, adj. [very careful or diligent, induſtrious] *accurato, diligente, aſſiduo.*

SE'DULOUSLY, adv. *accuratamente, diligentemente, aſſiduamente.*

SEE, s. ex. a biſhop's ſee [or ſeat] *ſedia epiſcopale.*

See [epiſcopal dignity] *ſedia, o dignità epiſcopale.*

To SEE [to perceive with the eyes] *vedere, comprender coll' occhio l' obbietto che ci ſi para d' avanti, ſcorgere*, pret. *veddi, vidi, ſcorſi.*

I do not ſee him, *non lo vedo.*

He ſees nobody [he receives no viſits] *non*

non vede nessuno, non ammette nessuno, non riceve visite.

To go to see [to make a visit] *andare a vedere, visitare.*

To see [to enquire or ask] *vedere, domandare, informarsi.*

See who is at the door, *vedete chi picchia alla porta.*

See what he wants, *domandategli quel che vuole.*

To see [to conceive, to apprehend, to understand] *vedere, conoscere, comprendere,* pret *conobbi, compresi.*

I don't see how you can do it, *non vedo, non comprendo in che modo voi potrete farlo.*

See that all be ready, *sia vostra cura che il tutto sia in ordine.*

To see [to take heed] *avvertire, aver l' occhio, badare, stare in cervello.*

See you don't fall, *avvertite di non cascare.*

I shall see you home, *vi condurrò, v' accompagnerò a casa.*

I shall see you paid, *vi farò pagare, sarà mio pensiero che voi siate pagato.*

To let one see [to shew] *mostrare, far vedere, far conoscere.*

Let me see it, *mostratemelo, lasciatemelo vedere.*

I shall let you see that I am not a fool, *vi farò conoscere rhe io non sono un pazzo.*

To see for a thing, *cercare che che sia.*

See for your book, *ccreate il vostro libro.*

To see into a thing, *penetrare un negozio.*

A fine house to see, *una bella casa in apparenza.*

SEED, s. [the matter which in all plants and fruits is disposed by nature for the propogation of the kind] *seme,* s. m. *sementa, semente, semenza,* s. f. *sustanzia, nella quale è virtù di generare, e che genera cosa simile al suo subbietto.*

Every plant is known by its seed, *ogni erba si conosce per lo seme.*

To run to seed [as plants do] *tallire, fare il tallo.*

Seed [sperm of animals, that serves for their generation] *sperma,* s. f. *seme degli animali.*

Seed [a cause that produces some effects] *seme,* s. f. *sementa, cagione, origine,* s. f.

The seeds of virtue, *i semi della virtù.*

Seed-time [sowing-time] *sementa, il tempo del seminare.*

Seed-plot, *semenzajo,* s. m. *luogo dove si pongono, o si seminano i semi di piante o d' erbe per trapiantarle.*

SE'EDLING, s. [a young plant just risen from the bed] *pianticella appena uscita del terreno,*

SE'EDMAN, s. *mercante di semi.*

Seed pearl, *semenza di perla.*

To SEED [to run to seed] *tallire, semenzire, fare il tallo,* pres. *tallisco, semenzisco.*

SE'EDED, adj. *tallito.*

Seeded with stars [full of stars] *seminato di stelle, stellato, pieno di stelle.*

SE'EDNESS, s. [seed time; the time of sowing] *sementa; il tempo del seminare.*

SE'EDSMAN, s. [the sower, he that scatters the seed] *seminatore, colui che semina.*

SE'EDY, adj. [full of seeds] *pieno di semenza.*

SE'EING, s. *il vedere.*

Seeing is believing, *quando la cosa si vede si crede.*

The thing is not worth seeing, *non è cosa degna d' esser veduta, non è cosa che meriti d' esser vista.*

The sense of seeing [the sight] *la vista, il vedere.*

Seeing, or seeing that, conj. *poichè, mentre che.*

Seeing you will have it so, *piochè voi volete così.*

To SEEK } [to look or to see for]
To SEEK for } *cercare.*

What do you seek for? *che cercate?*

To seek for help or assistance, *domandar soccorso o ajuto.*

To seek for preferment, *cercar fortuna, andare appresso agli onori.*

To seek to serve one, *procurare, ingegnarsi di servir qualcheduno.*

To seek one's ruin, *macchinare, tramare l' altrui rovina.*

To seek out, *andar cercando.*

To seek after, *domandare, informarsi.*

To seek after an office, *cercare un impiego.*

I am further to seek than I was, *mi trovo più angustiato di prima.*

Whether that be true or no, I am as yet to seek, *non so ancora se ciò sia vero o no.*

SE'EKER, s. *cercatore,* s. m. *cercatrice,* s. f.

SE'EKING, s. *cerca,* s. f. *cercamento,* s. m.

SEEKSO'RROW, s. [one who continues to give himself vexation] *tormentator di se stesso; colui che trova modo di affliggersi senza cagione.*

To SEEL [a ship is said to seel, when she tumbles suddenly and violently, sometimes to one side, and sometimes to another] *barcollare, parlando d' un navilio.*

To seel a ship, *mettere un navilio alla banda per rattopparlo.*

To seel [to close the eyes. A term of falconry, the eyes of a wild or haggard hawk being for a time seeled] *accigliare un falcone.*

To seel, *fare il soffitto.*

To seel a room, *fare la soffitta o il cielo ad una camera.*

SE'ELED, adj. *barcollato, v.* To seel.

SE'ELING, s. [cieling] *la soffitta, il cielo d' una camera.*

SE'ELY, adj. [lucky, happy] *fortunato, avventuroso.*

Seely [silly, foolish, simple] *mentecatto, folle, sempliciaccio.*

To SEEM [to appear] *parere, sembrare, apparire,* pret. *parvi, apparvi.*

That seems reasonable, *questo pare ragionevole.*

It seems, verb imperf. *pare.*

It seems to me, *mi pare, son di parere.*

SE'EMING, adj. *apparente.*

He concealed his joy with a seeming grief, *celò la sua allegrezza sotto un apparente dolore.*

SE'EMINGLY, adv. *apparentemente, in apparenza, verisimilmente.*

SE'EMLINESS, s. *decenza,* s. f. *decoro,* s. m.

SEEN, adj. from to see, *veduto, visto.*

He is so little that he can hardly be seen, *egli è sì piccolo che si può vedere appena.*

His head alone was seen above the water, *la testa sola avanzava fuor dell' acqua.*

A man well seen in business, *un uomo versato o pratico negli affari.*

SEER, s. [prophet] *profeta.*

To SEE-SAW [to swing] *bilicarsi.*

To SEETH [to boil] *bollire, lessare.*

SE'ETHED, adj *bollito, lesso.*

SE'ETHING, s. *bollimento,* s. m. *lessatura,* s f.

Seething-pot, *pignatta, pentola.*

SE'GMENT, s. [piece cut off from something] *fetta,* s. f. *pezzo,* s. m.

SE'GNITY, s. [sluggishness, inactivity] *infingardia, infingardaggine.*

To SE'GREGATE [to separate] *disceverare, segregare, separare, sequestrare.*

To segregate, verb neut. *disceverarsi, separarsi.*

SE'GREGATED, adj. *disceverato, segregato, separato, sequestrato.*

SEGREGA'TION, s. *segregazione,* s. f.

SEIGNEU'RIAL, adj. [invested with large powers; independant] *sovrano, principesco, signorile, indipendente*

SE'IGNIOR, s [signior, lord, master] *signore.*

The Grand Seignior [the Emperor of the Turks] *il Gran Signore, il Gran Turco.*

Seignior, in law [lord of the mannor] *il signore, o padrone d' un feudo.*

SE'IGNORY, s. [lordship] *signoria,* s. f.

SE'IGNORAGE, s. [a prerogative of the King, whereby he challenges allowance of gold or silver brought in the mass to his exchange for coin] *signoraggio.*

SE'IZABLE, adj. [that may be seized] *che si può afferrare.*

To SE'IZE, to seize upon [to take, to lay hold of] *afferrare, pigliare, tener per forza, acchiappare.*

He seized him by the arm, *l' afferrò, lo prese per il braccio.*

To seize [to usurp] *usurpare, prender per forza.*

To ſeize, *ſtaggire, ſequeſtrare*, preſ. *ſtaggiſco.*

To ſeize upon again, *riprendere.*

To ſeize [as diſtempers do] *aſſalire, ſoprendere*, preſ. *aſſaliſco.*

He was ſeized with a violent pain in his ſide, *fu aſſalito da un gran dolore nel fianco.*

SEIZED, ſeized upon, adj. *afferrato, preſo, acchiappato, v.* To ſeize.

SE'IZURE, s. [attachment, diſtreſs] *ſtaggina*, s. f. *ſequeſtro*, s. m.

SE'LDOM, adv. [not often] *rado, di rado, radamente, rade volte.*

SE'LDOMNESS, s. *radezza, poca frequenza*, s. f. *Vocabolo poco in uſo.*

The ſeldomneſs of his appearing was taken notice of, *fu oſſervato ch' egli ſi faceva rade volte vedere.*

SE'LDSHOWN, adj. [ſeldom exhibited to view] *di rado eſpoſto alla viſta, moſtrato rare volte.*

SELE'CT, adj. [choice] *ſcelto.*

Select troops, *gente ſcelta.*

To SELE'CT [to pick out] *ſcegliere, e ſcerre, eleggere*, preſ. *ſcelgo*, pret. *ſcelſi.*

SELE'CTED, adj. *ſcelto, eletto.*

SELE'CTOR, s. [he who ſelects] *ſceglitore, colui che ſceglie.*

SELENO'GRAPHY, s. [deſcription of the moon] *deſcrizion della luna.*

SE'LERY, *v.* Celery.

SELF, pron. *medeſimo, ſteſſo.* Inſtead of *medeſmo* ſome ſay *medemo*, but 'tis a word not to be uſed: In poetry we ſay *medeſmo.*

Myſelf, thyſelf, himſelf, herſelf, *io medeſimo, tu medeſimo, egli medeſimo, ella medeſima.*

Ourſelves, yourſelves, themſelves, *noi medeſimi, voi medeſimi, eſſi medeſimi.*

I went thither by myſelf, *vi andai ſolo.*

You ſhall have it all to yourſelf, *l' averete tutto per voi.*

One's ſelf, *ſe ſteſſo, ſe, ſi.*

To look to one's ſelf, *badare a ſe, aver cura di ſe ſteſſo.*

To clear a man's ſelf, *giuſtificarſi.*

To live like one's ſelf, *viver ſecondo la ſua qualità.*

Your royal ſelf, [ſpeaking to the king or queen] *la voſtra perſona reale.*

To lay a thing by itſelf, *metter una coſa a parte, dapperſe.*

Self do ſelf have, *chi la fa la paga.*

Self-heal, or ſanicle [an herb] *rigaligo*, s. m. *ſpezie d' erba.*

SELF-SAME, *deſſo, quelle ſteſſo.*

I am the ſelf-ſame, *io ſon deſſo.*

The ſelf-ſame day, *l' iſteſſo giorno.*

Self-conceit, ſelf conceitedneſs, s. *proſunzione, vanità, vanagloria, arroganza, oſtentazione*, s. f.

Self-conceited, adj. *capriccioſo, vanaglorioſo, che ha buona opinione di ſe, borioſo, arrogante.*

Self-love, *amor proprio.*

Self-ends, ſelf-intereſt, *intereſſe proprio.*

Self-will, s. *oſtinazione, caparbieta*, s. f.

Self-willed, adj. *oſtinato, caparbio, di ſua teſta.*

Self-denial, s. *mortificazione*, s. f.

Self-dependent, adj. *che non dipende da neſſuno.*

Self-evident, adj. *chiaro, manifeſto, evidente, che non ha biſogno di pruova.*

Self-murder, s. *omicidio ch' uno commette nella ſua perſona propria.*

Self-murderer, *omicida di ſe ſteſſo.*

Self-excellency, *eccellenza naturale, o propria.*

SE'LFISH, adj. [own] *proprio, intereſſato.*

For ſelfiſh ends, *per i ſuoi propri fini.*

Selfiſh [that is all for himſelf] *intereſſato, che non riſguarda, che non ha mira che a' ſuoi propri intereſſi.*

A ſelfiſh man, *un uomo intereſſato, un taccagno, un tanghero.*

SE'LFISHNESS, s. *umore intereſſato.*

SELIA'NDER, or SELLANDER, s. [a dry ſcab growing in the very bent of the ham of a horſe's hinder leg] *giarda*, s. f. *giardone*, s. m. *galla che viene al cavallo nel garretto.*

SE'LION, s. [a ridge of land] *un tratto di terreno.*

To SELL, *vendere, ſpacciare.*

To ſell one's commodities, *vendere, o ſpacciare le ſue mercanzie.*

A commodity that ſells well, *una mercanzia che ha buono ſpaccio.*

SE'LLANDER. *v.* Seliander.

SE'LLER, s. [he that ſells] *venditore*, s. m. *venditrice*, s. f.

SE'LLING, s. f. *vendimento, ſpaccio*, s. m. *vendita*, s. f.

SE'LVAGE, s. [the ſkirt of linen cloth] *orlo, orliccio*, s. m.

To SE'LVAGE, *orlare, fare l' orlo.*

SE'LVAGING, s. *orlatura*, s. f. *l' orlare.*

SE'LVES, *è il plurale di* SELF.

SE'MBLABLE, adj. [like] *ſimile, ſimigliante.*

SE'MBLABLY, adv. *ſimilmente, ſimigliantemente.*

SE'MBLANCE, s. [appearance] *ſimiglianza, ſomiglianza, apparenza*, s. f.

Semblance of truth, *apparenza di verità.*

SE'MBLANT, adj. [like, reſembling; having the appearance of any thing] *ſimile, ſomiglievole, ſomigliante. Non è voce di troppo uſo.*

Semblant, s. [ſhow, figure, reſemblance] *ſomiglianza, figura, apparenza.*

SE'MBLATIVE, adj. [ſuitable, accomodate, fit, reſembling] *proprio, acconcio, atto, ſomigliante.*

SEME, *v.* Seam.

SE'MIBRIEF, s. [in muſick] *ſemibreve, termine muſicale.*

SEMICI'RCLE, s. [one half of a circle] *ſemicircolo*, s. m.

SEMICI'RCULAR, adj. [made in the ſhape of, or belonging to the ſemicircle] *ſemicircolare, di mezzocerchio.*

SEMICO'LON, s. [a ſtop or point in a ſentence between a comma and a colon, marked thus (;) *punto e virgola.*

SE'MINARY, s. [nurſery] *ſeminario, ſemenzajo*, s. m.

Seminary [where youth is educated] *ſeminario, luogo dove ſi tengono in educazione i fanciulli.*

SEMIQUA'VER, s. [a note half the quantity of a quaver] *mezzo trillo.*

SEMITO'NE, s. [half tone] *ſemituono*, s. m. *mezzo tuono.*

SEMI-VOWEL, s. [ſo are called certain conſonants, ſuch as f, l, m, n, s.] *mezza vocale.*

SE'MPERVIVE, adj. [ever-green] *ſempre verde, ſempre-vivo.*

SEMPITE'RNAL, adj. [continual, perpetual] *ſempiterno, che non ha avuto origine, ne può aver fine.*

SEMPITE'RNITY, s. [everlaſtingneſs] *ſempiternità*, s. f.

SENA, s. [the leaves of a ſhrub growing in India] *ſena*, s. f. *erba medicinale.*

SE'NATE, s. [the aſſembly or ſupreme council of the ſenators] *ſenato*, s. m.

Senate, ſenate-houſe, *ſenato, il luogo dove ſi tiene il ſenato.*

SE'NATOR, s. [a member of the ſenate] *ſenatore*, s. m.

SENATO'RIAN, adj. [belonging to a ſenator] *di ſenatore, ſenatorio.*

To SEND [to cauſe one to go, or a thing to be carried] *mandare, inviare.*

To ſend one on an errand, *mandare alcuno a fare un meſſaggio.*

To ſend a meſſenger, *ſpedire un meſſaggiero.*

To ſend a letter by the poſt, *mandare una lettera per la poſta.*

To ſend money, *rimetter del danaro.*

To ſend one word [to let one know] *mandare a dire.*

To ſend for one, *mandare a cercare una perſona.*

To ſend back, *rimandare, mandare indietro.*

To ſend in, *fare entrare.*

To ſend a letter away, *ſpedire una lettera.*

To ſend away a ſervant, *licenziare un ſervo.*

If God ſend me life, *ſe Iddio mi da vita.*

God ſend he be well, *Iddio voglia che si conſervi in buona ſalute.*

SE'NDAL, s. [a ſort of thin ſilk] *zendado*, s. m. *ſpezie di drappo ſottile.*

SE'NDING, s. *l' atto del mandare, v.* To ſend.

He will come without ſending for, *verra ſenza mandarlo a chiamare.*

SENE, *v.* Sena.

SE'NESCAL, } s. *ſiniſcalco*, s. m.
SENESCHAL, }

The lord high ſeneſchal of England, *il gran ſiniſcalco d' Inghilterra.*

SE'NGREEN, s. [the herb houſeleek] *ſempreviva*, s. f.

SE'NILE, adj. [belonging to old age] *ſenile, vecchio.*

SE'NNIGHT, s. [ſeven night] *ſette giorni e ſette notti, una ſettimana.*

This day ſe'nnight, *oggi otto.*

SE'NIOR, adj. [elder] *anziano.*

SENIO'RITY, s. *anzianità*, s. f.

SE'NNA, s. [a phyſical tree] *ſena, pianta medicinale che produce la ſena.*

SENSA'TION, s. [perception that the mind has when any object ſtrikes the ſenſes; the act of perceiving things by the ſenſes] *ſenſazione*, s. f. *ſenſo*, s. m.

SENSE, s. [the faculty of a living creature, whereby it receives the impreſpreſſion of outward objects] *ſenſo*, s. m. *potenzia dell' anima, per la quale ſi conoſcono le coſe corporee preſenti.*

The five natural ſenſes, *i cinque ſenſi della natura.*

Senſe [feeling] *ſentimento, ſenſo*, s. m. He has loſt his ſenſes, *ha perduto il ſentimento.*

Senſe [an affection or paſſion of the ſoul] *ſentimento, affetto*, s. m. *paſſione*, s. f.

He has no ſenſe of humanity, *egli non ha ſentimento d'umanità.*

Senſe [reaſon] *ſenno, ſenſo, ſentimento, intelletto, cervello, giudizio*, s. m.

To ſpeak good ſenſe, *parlar giudizioſamente, con giudizio, fondatamente.*

Senſe [wit] *ſenno, ſapere*, s. m. *ſapienza, prudenza*, s. f.

A man of great ſenſe, *un uomo di gran ſenno.*

Senſe [ſignification] *ſenſo, ſignificato*, s. m.

Senſe [opinion] *parere, ſentimento, giudicio*, s. m. *opinione*, s. f.

SENSELESSLY, adv. *ſenza giudicio, vanamente, ſcioccamente.*

SE'NSELESSNESS, s. *vanità, ſchiocchezza, pazzia*, s. f.

SE'NSELESS, adj. [that has no ſenſe or feeling] *che ha perduto l' uſo de' ſenſi, che è quaſi morto.*

Senſeleſs [fooliſh, impertinent] *inſenſato, ſenza ſenno, ſciocco, mentecatto, forſennato.*

SE'NSELESSLY, adv. [in a ſenſeleſs manner, ſtupidly, unreaſonably] *pazzamente, ſcioccamente, ſtupidamente, irragionevolmente.*

SE'NSELESSNESS, s. [folly, unreaſonableneſs, abſurdity, ſtupidity] *follia, mentecattaggine, irragionevolezza, aſſurdità, ſtupidezza.*

SENSIBI'LITY, s. [the quality of being ſenſible] *ſenſibilità*, s. f.

SE'NSIBLE, adj. [that falls within the compaſs of the ſenſes] *ſenſibile, atto a comprenderſi dal ſenſo.*

Senſible [grievous] *ſenſible, doloroſo, angoſcioſo.*

A ſenſible part, *una parte ſenſibile.*

To be ſenſible of pleaſure and pain, *eſſer ſenſibile di piacere e di dolori.*

I am very ſenſible of your kindneſs, *riconoſco con cuor grato i voſtri favori.*

To be ſenſible of a thing [to know it, to be perſuaded of it] *eſſer perſuaſo o convinto di che che ſia, ſaperlo, conoſcerlo.*

I am ſenſible I have done amiſs, *conoſco che ho mal fatto.*

Senſible [of good ſenſe, judicious] *di buon ſenno giudicioſo, di gran giudicio.*

SE'NSIBLLENESS, s. [ſenſibility] *ſenſibilità.*

Senſibleneſs [good ſenſe] *ſenno, giudicio, cervello, intelletto*, s. m.

SE'NSIBLY, adv. *ſenſibilmente.*

SE'NSITIVE, adj. [that has the faculty of feeling or perceiving] *ſenſitivo, che ha ſenſo.*

The ſenſitive ſoul, *l'anima ſenſitiva.*

The ſenſitive plant, *la ſenſitiva, ſpezie di pianta.*

The SE'NSORY, s. [the organ or inſtrument of ſenſe] *l'organo del ſenſo.*

SE'NSUAL, adj. [voluptuous, given to ſenſual pleaſure] *ſenſuale, laſcivo, voluttuoſo.*

Senſual pleaſures, *i piaceri ſenſuali o carnali.*

SENSUA'LITY, s. [ſtimulation of the ſenſes] *ſenſualità*, s. f. *forza e ſtimolo del ſenſo e dell' appetito; libidine.*

SENSUALLY, adv. *ſenſualmente, con ſenſualità, ſecondo 'l ſenſo.*

SCENT, s. [ſmell] *odore, ſentore, fiuto.* It has a good ſcent with it, *egli ha buon odore.*

A dog of a good ſcent, *un cane che ha buon fiuto.*

Sent, adj. [from to ſend] *mandato, inviato, v.* To ſend.

I ſcent him out [I have him in the wind] *ſo quel che vuol dire.*

To SCENT [to perfume] *profumare.*

To ſcent [or ſmell as a dog] *annaſare, fiutare.*

To ſcent, verb neut. [to ſmell] *ſentire, avere, odore.*

SCE'NTED, adj. *profumato, v.* To ſcent.

SE'NTENCE, s. [a certain number of words joined together] *ſentenza*, s. f. *periodo*, s. m.

Sentence [wiſe, or witty ſaying] *ſentenza, motto breve, e arguto.*

Sentence [a decree of a court of juſtice] *ſentenza, deciſion di lite pronunziata dal giudice, giudicamento, giudicio*, s. m.

To SE'NTENCE [to pronounce ſentence upon] *ſentenziare, dar ſentenzia, giudicare.*

SE'NTENCED, adj. *ſentenziato, condannato per ſentenzia.*

SENTE'NTIOUS, adj. [full of pithy ſentences] *ſentenzioſo, pien di ſentenzie.*

SENTE'NTIOUSLY, adv. *ſentenzioſamente, ſaviamente, giudizioſamente.*

SE'NTIMENT, s. [opinion] *ſentimento, concetto, penſiere, parere*, s. m. *opinione*, s. f.

SE'NTINEL, } s. [a private ſoldier
SE'NTRY, } upon guard in a convient poſt] *ſentinella*, s. f. *ſoldato che fa la guardia.*

SE'NVY, s. [the plant, of whoſe ſeed muſtard is made] *ſenapa, ſenape*, s. f. *erba nota, il cui ſeme è minutiſſimo e d'acutiſſimo ſapore.*

Senvy-ſeed [muſtard-ſeed] *ſeme di ſenape.*

SEPARABI'LITY, s. [the quality of that which is ſeparable] *qualità di quel che è ſeparabile, diviſibilità.*

SE'PARABLE, adj. [that may be ſeparated] *ſeparabile, che ſi può ſeparare, diviſibile.*

SE'PARABLENESS, s. [capableneſs of being ſeparable] *attezza ad eſſer ſeparato.*

SE'PARATE, adj. [diſtinct] *ſeparato, diſtinto, particolare, differente.*

To allow one's wife a ſeparate maintenance, *dare una penſione alla moglie in caſo di ſeparazione.*

To SE'PARATE [to part, to divide, to put aſunder] *ſeparare, diſgiugnere, ſpartire, diſunire*, pref. *diſgiungo, diſunisco*, pret. *diſgiunſi.*

To ſeparate, verb neut. *ſepararſi, diſgiugnerſi, ſpartirſi, diſunirſi.*

SEPARA'TED, adj. *ſeparato, diſgiunto, ſpartito, diſunito.*

SE'PARATELY, adv. *ſeparatamente, a parte.*

SE'PARATENESS, s. *ſtato di ſeparazione.*

I ſpeak of the ſeparateneſs of their function, *io parlo della funzione di ciaſcheduno in particolare.*

SE'PARATING, s. *ſeparamento, il ſeparare, diſgiugnimento*, s. m.

SEPARA'TION, s. [the act of ſeparating] *ſeparazione*, s. f. *ſeparamento.*

SE'PARATIST, s. [one who ſeparates himſelf from the church without any lawful cauſe] *uno ſciſmatico.*

SEPARA'TOR, s. [one who divides, a divider] *diviſore, un che ſepara, un che divide.*

SE'PARATORY, adj. [uſed in ſeparation] *dividente, che divide.*

SE'PIMENT, s. [a hedge, a fence] *ſiepe*, s. f.

SEPT, s. [clan, race, generation] *ſchiatta, razza, famiglia numeroſa.*

SEPTA'NGULAR, adj. [that has ſeven angles] *che ha ſette angoli.*

SEPTA'NGLE, s. [a figure having ſeven angles] *ſettangolo*, s. m. *figura di ſette angoli e ſette lati.*

SEPTE'MBER, s. [one of the twelve months of the year] *Settembre*, s. m. *uno de' dodici meſi dell' anno.*

SEPTENA'RIOUS, } adj. [belonging
SE'PTENARY, } to the number ſeven] *ſettenario, di ſette.*

Septenary, s. [ſeven years of one's life] *ſettenario*, s. m. *ſette anni di vita.*

SEPTE'NNIAL, adj. [of the ſpace or age of ſeven years] *ſettennio, che ha durato ſette anni, dell' età di ſette anni.*

SEPTE'NTRIONAL, adj. [northern] *ſettentrionale, di ſettentrione.*

SEPTI'EME, s. [a ſequence of ſeven cards at the game of picket] *ſettima, ſequela di ſette carte al giuoco di picchetto.*

SEPTIMA'RIAN, s. [a weekly officer in monaſteries] *ebdomadario*, s. m. *colui che in quella ſettimana deve celebrare e far l'altre funzioni.*

SE'PTUAGENARY, adj. [ſeventy years old] *ſettuagenario, che ha ſettanta anni.*

SEPTUAGE'SSIMA, s. [the third Sunday before the firſt Sunday in Lent] *Settuageſima*, s. f. *la terza domenica avanti la quareſima.*

SEPTUAGE'SIMAL, adj. [belonging to ſeptuageſima] *di ſettuageſima.*

SE'PTUAGINT, s. [the Greek tranſlation of the Bible, ſo called becauſe ſaid to have been tranſlated by ſeventy-two Jewiſh Rabbins, at the appointment of Ptolemy Philadelphus, king of Egypt] *la Bibbia, o la traduzione della Bibbia de' ſettanta, così nominata, per eſſere, come ſi dice, tradotta da ſettanta due Rabbini, per ordine di Tolomeo Piladelfo re d' Egitto.*

SE'PTUAGINT, s. [the ſeventy-two interpreters] *i ſettanta.*

SEPU'LCHRAL, adj. [belonging to a ſepulchre] *ſepolcrale, di ſepolcro.*

SE'PULCHRE, s. [grave, tomb] *ſepolcro, avello,* s. m. *ſepoltura, tomba,* s. f.

SE'PULTURE, s. [burial] *ſepoltura, eſequie,* s. f.

SEQUA'CIOUS, adj. [eaſily following] *ſeguace, che ſegue facilmente.*

SEQUA'CITY, s. [ductility] *facilità ad eſſer maneggiato.*

SE'QUEL, s. [conſequence, concluſion] *ſequela, conſeguenza,* s. f. *conſeguente, ſucceſſo,* s. m.

Sequel [continued ſucceſſion, ſeries] *ſequela, ſerie, ſeguenza,* s. f.

In the ſequel of the diſcourſe, *nella ſeguenza del diſcorſo.*

SE'QUENCE, s. [a ſuit of things in order] *ſeguenza,* s. f. *numero di coſe che ſeguono in ordine.*

It follows in ſequence, *ne ſiegue per conſeguenza.*

To SEQUE'STER [to ſeparate, ſever, to put aſunder] *ſequeſtrare, allontanare, ſeparare.*

To ſequeſter [in common law, to ſeparate a thing in diſpute from the poſſeſſion of the contending parties] *ſequeſtrare, ſtaggire,* pref. *ſtaggiſco.*

To ſequeſter [in civil law, when the widow diſclaims to have any thing to do with the eſtate of her deceaſed huſband] *rinunciare ai beni del marito defunto.*

To ſequeſter one's ſelf from the world] *allontanarſi dal mondo, rinunciare al mondo, ritirarſi dal mondo.*

SEQUESTRATION, s. *ſequeſtrazione,* s. f. *ſtaggimento, ſequeſtro,* s. m.

SEQUESTA'TOR, s. [the third perſon to whom the keeping of the things in controverſy is committed] *terza perſona che ha in cuſtodia le coſe ſequeſtrate.*

SEQUE'STRATED, } adj. *ſequeſtrato,*
SEQUE'STRED, } *ſtaggito.*

SEQUE'STREE, *v.* Sequeſtrator.

SERA'GLIO, s. [the place of the Grand Signior and other eaſtern princes, where their wives and concubines are kept] *ſerraglio,* s. m. *il luogo dove il Gran Signore e altri principi dell' oriente tengono ſerrate le loro donne.*

SE'RAPH, s. [one of the orders of angles] *ſerafino, uno dell' ordine degli angeli.*

SERA'PHICAL, } adj. [belonging to
SERA'PHICK, } ſeraphims] *ſerafico, di ſerafino.*

SE'RAPHIM, s. [the higheſt order of angles] *ſerafino,* s. m.

SE'RASQUIER, } s. [a general a-
SE'RASKIER, } mong the Turks] *ſeraſchiere,* s. m. *generale fra i Turchi*

SERE, adj. [dry, withered, no longer green] *ſecco, non più verde.*

SERENA'DE, s. [night muſick play'd by a lover at his miſtreſs's door, or under her window] *ſerenata,* s. f. *il cantare e 'l ſonare, che ſan gli amanti la notte al ſereno davanti alla caſa della dama.*

To SERENADE [to entertain with nocturnal muſick] *ſar una ſerenata; ſuonare o far ſuonare di notte tempo ſotto le fineſtre della innamorata.*

SERE'NE, adj. [clear, fair, without clouds] *ſereno, chiaro, ſenza nuvoli.*

A ſerene weather or ſky, *un tempo, o un cielo ſereno.*

Serene [calm, quiet] *ſereno, calmo, tranquillo.*

A ſerene mind, *una mente ſerena.*

A ſerene look, *una faccia allegra, un aſpetto giocondo.*

Moſt ſerene [a title of honour given to ſome princes] *ſereniſſimo,* titolo *di alcuni principi.*

SERE'NENESS, } s. [clearneſs of the
SERE'NITY, } ſky] *ſerenità, chiarezza,* s. f.

Serenity [calmneſs of mind] *ſerenità, tranquillità, calma,* s. f.

Serenity [a title given to ſome princes] *ſerenità,* titolo *di alcuni principi.*

SERGE, s. [a kind of woollen ſtuff] *ſargia,* s. m. *ſpezie di panno.*

SE'RGEANT, s. [an officer who arreſts people for debt] *ſergente, birro,* s. m.

Sergeant [an inferior officer in a company of foot or a troop of horſe] *ſergente, colui che ha rura dell' ordinanza della milizia.*

Sergeant at law, *dottor di legge, un avvocato.*

The king's ſergeant at law, *l' avvocato fiſcale.*

Sergeant [an officer of juſtice] *ſergente, miniſtro.*

Sergeant at arms, *ſergente d'armi.*

Sergeant of the mace, *mazzieri, ſervi di magiſtrato che portano avanti a' loro Signori la mazza in ſegno d' autorità.*

SE'RGEANTSHIP, s. *carico di ſergente.*

SE'RGENTY, s. [a ſervice which cannot be due to any lord from his tenant, but only to the king or queen] *ſergenteria,* s. f. *ſpezie di feudo.*

Grand ſergeanty [is where a man holds certain lands of the king by the perſonal ſervice of carrying his banner or lance, or leading his horſe, being his champion, carver, or butler, &c. at his coronation] *gran ſergenteria, ufficio d'una perſona, che poſſede feudi del re, d'aſſiſter perſonalmente alla ſua coronazione, portando la bandiera e la lancia, e menando per la briglia il ſuo cavallo, come ſuo campione, ſcalco, o cantiniere.*

Petty ſergeanty [is where a man becomes tenant to the king, by yielding him annually ſome ſmall thing towards his wars, as a buckler, bow, arrow, &c.] *picrola ſergenteria, quando una perſona poſſiede feudi del re, con obbligo di fornirgli in tempo di guerra qualche piccola coſa, come un cimiero, un arco, uno ſtrale, e ſimili.*

SE'RIES, s. [orderly proceſs or continuation of things one after another, order, courſe] *ſerie, ſeguenza, ſequela, e,* s. f.

SE'RIOUS, adj. [ſober, grave] *ſerioſo, ſerio, grave, conſiderato.*

A ſerious man, *un uomo ſerioſo, grave, compoſto.*

Serious [important] *ſerioſo, importante.*

Serious affair, *negozio ſerioſo, o importante.*

Serious [ſincere, true, earneſt] *ſerio, ſincero, franco, vero, non finto.*

Are you ſerious? [do you ſpeak in earneſt?] *ſiete in ſul ſerio? dite da vero?*

SE'RIOUSLY, adv. [gravely] *ſerioſamente, gravemente, in ſul ſerio, ſeriamente.*

Seriouſly [in earneſt] *ſeriamente, in ſul ſerio, in ſul ſodo, da ſenno, con ſerietà da vero.*

SE'RIOUSNESS, s. *ſerio, aria ſerioſa, gravità.*

SE'RMON, s. [a publick diſcourſe up on ſome text] *ſermone,* s. m. *predica,* s. f.

Funeral ſermon, *orazione funebre.*

To SE'RMON [to diſcourſe as in a ſermon] *far un ſermone, far un diſcorſo a mo' di predica.*

To ſermon [to tutor, to teach dogmatically, to leſſon] *inſegnare con ſeverità, riprendere come farebbe il predicatore, iſtruire con altura di parole, con aria di ſuperiorità.*

SE'RMOUNTAIN, s. [an herb] *fuſaggine,* s. f. *ſilio,* s. m.

SERO'SITY, s. [a watry matter] *ſeroſità,* s. f.

SE'ROTINE, adj. [late in the evening] *ſerotine, tardivo.*

SE'ROUS, adj. [watry] *ſieroſo, che ha in ſe del ſiero.*

SE'RPENT, s. [a venomous creature] *ſerpe, ſerpente,* s. m.

Serpent [ſnake] *ſcorzone,* s. m.

Little ſerpent, *ſerpentello.*

Serpent's tongue [an herb] *lingua di ſerpente,* s. f. *erba medicinale.*

Serpent [a ſort of ſquib] *razzo,* s. m.

Serpent-like, *ſerpentino, a guiſa di ſerpente.*

Breeding ſerpents, *ſerpentiſero, ſerpentoſo, che ha, e produce ſerpenti.*

The ſerpent [a northern conſtellation] *ſerpentario,* s. m. *coſtellazione celeſte.*

SE'RPENTARY, s. [the herb dragonwort] *ſerpentaria,* s. f. *erba medicinale.*

SERPENTI'NE, adj. [belonging to a ſerpent] *ſerpentino, di ſerpente, a guiſa di ſerpente.*

Serpentine [winding about] *ſerpeggiante, che ſerpeggia.*

Serpentine verſes [a ſort of verſes which begin and end with the ſame words, as *Ambo florentes ætatibus Arcades ambo*] *ſpezie di verſi, che principiano e finiſcono colla medeſime parole.*

Serpentine ſtone [a kind of marble] *ſerpentino,* s. m. *ſpezie di marmo finiſſimo di color nero, e verde.*

SE'RPET, s. [a kind a baſket] *corba,* s. f.

To SERR [to drive hard together; to croud into a little ſpace] *ſerrare, chiudere con forza.*

SE'RRED, adj. [cloſe] *ſerrato, fitto.*

To SE'RRY [to preſs cloſe, to drive

hard

hard together, to ferr] *ferrare, chiudere con molta forza.*

S'ERVANT, s. [menial fervant, domeftick in general] *fervente, fervidore, fervo, familiare,* s. m.

A fervant, or man fervant, *un fervo, un fervidore.*

A fervant, or a woman fervant, *una ferva.*

To be fervant to one [to ferve him as a fervant] *fervire una perfona, effer fuo fervidore.*

Servant [lover] *amante*

Your fervant [by way of compliment] *fervitor fuo.*

Servant like, *da fervidore.*

To SERVE [to attend, to wait upon] *fervire, far fervitù, miniftrare ad altrui.*

To ferve [to do fervice or kindnefs] *fervire, render fervizio, far piacere, ajutare, affiftere.*

To ferve in the war [to bear arms] *fervire in guerra, portar le armi, militare.*

To ferve God [to worfhip him] *fervire Iddio, rendergli il culto dovuto.*

To ferve meat up to the table, *portare le vivande in tavola.*

To ferve [to be of fome ufe] *fervire, ufare, adoperare.*

Fire ferves to warm, *il fuoco ferve a fcaldare.*

To ferve [to be inftead] *fervire, tener luogo, far ufficio.*

This will ferve for an example, *quefto fervirà d' efempio.*

Do you ferve me fo? *in quefta maniera mi trattate?*

You ferved him right, *voi avete fatto bene, l' ha ben meritato.*

I'll ferve him in his kind, I'll ferve him the fame fauce, *gli renderò la pariglia, gli renderò pan par focaccia, me la pagherà.*

To ferve [to laft] *durare.*

This won't ferve me long, *quefto non mi durerà molto.*

To ferve one a trick, *fare una burla ad uno, fargli la barba di ftoppa.*

When occafion fhall ferve, *quando fi prefenterà l' occafione.*

The wind ferves, *il vento è propizio, o favorevole.*

While the time ferves bethink your felf, *penfateci mentre avete il tempo.*

To ferve one's turn [to fuffice, to be enough] *baftare, effer baftante.*

That won't ferve my turn, *quefto non mi bafta.*

Here's as much as will ferve your turn, *ecco quanto vi farà a baftanza.*

There's as much as will ferve one three times, *quefto mi bafterà per tre volte.*

A little wine ferves my turn, *un poco di vino mi bafta.*

A little work ferves his turn, *non ama molto lavorare.*

And yet my heart will not ferve to fpeak it, *e pure non mi bafta l' animo di dirlo*

My fight ferves me not to read this print, *la mia vifta non è affai buona per leggere quefta ftampa.*

To ferve a warrant or a writ upon one, *arreftare una perfona giuridicamente.*

To ferve one's apprenticefhip, *effer garzone il tempo ch' un dev' effere.*

To ferve apprentice to a trade [to ferve one's time, *imparare un meftiere come garzone.*

To ferve out one's time, *finire il tempo che uno doveva fervire come garzone.*

To ferve out one's apprenticefhip, *finire il fuo fervizio di garzone.*

SERVED, adj. *fervito,* v. To ferve.

Firft come, firft ferved, *i primi venuti fono i primi ferviti.*

He is well enough ferved, *l' ha ben meritato.*

SE'RVICE, s. [the ftate or condition of a fervant] *fervigio, fervizio,* s. m. *il fervire.*

To be at one's fervice, *ftare all' altrui fervigio.*

To go to fervice, *metterfi al fervizio.*

Thefe fhoes will do you great fervice, *quefte fcarpe vi dureranno lungo tempo.*

Service [good turn, office] *fervizio, beneficio, piacere, comodo,* s. m.

I have done him a great piece of fervice, *gli ho fatto un gran fervizio.*

Service [ufe] *fervigio, ufo,* s. m.

A fhip not fit for fervice, *un vafcello che non può più fervire.*

What I have is at your fervice, *le cofe mie fono al voftro fervizio.*

Service [the employment of one that ferves the king] *fervigio, impiego di coloro che fervono al re.*

Service [courfe] *meffa,* s. f. *fervizio,* s. m.

Divine fervice, *ufficio divino.*

Remember my fervice to him, *fategli i miei baciamani, falutatelo da parte mia.*

My father gives his fervice to you, *mio padre la riverifce.*

Hard fervice, *fatica.*

Service [a fort of fruit, called alfo forb-apple] *forba,* s. f. *frutto noto.*

Service [at tennis] *mandata,* s. f. *termine del giuoco della balla.*

SE'RVICEABLE, adj. [ready to ferve one] *che volentieri fa fervizio.*

Serviceable [ufeful] *utile, comodo.*

SE'RVICEABLENESS, s. [officioufnefs] *maniera officiofa, cortefia,* s. f.

Serviceablenefs [ufefulnefs] *utilità,* s. f.

SE'RVICEABLY, adv. [officioufly] *officiofamente, cortefemente.*

SE'RVILE, adj. [flavifh, mean, bafe] *fervile, baffo, abbietto, vile.*

Servile foul, *anima fervile, animo abbietto.*

SE'RVILELY. adv. *fervilemente, fervilmente, a maniera di fervo.*

SE'RVILENESS, } s. [flavifhnefs] *fchiavitù,* s. f. *fervaggio,* s. m. *umore o maniera fervile.*
SERVI'LITY,

SE'RVING, s. *il fervire.*

Serving, adj. ex. a ferving man, *un uomo di fervizio, un fervo, un fervidore.*

SE'RVITOR, s. [in an univerfity, a fcholar who attends or waits upon others for his maintenance] *fervidore, un povero ftudente che fa i fervigi degli altri pel fuo vitto nelle univerfità Inglefi.*

Servitors of bills [fervants or meffengers, belonging to the marfhal of the king's bench, who are fent abroad with bills or writs to fummon men to that court, commonly called tipftaves] *fergenti, birri.*

SE'RVITUDE, s. [bondage, flavery] *fervitù, fchiavitù,* s. f. *fervaggio,* s. m.

SERUM, s. [the thin and watry part that feparates from the reft in any liquor] *fero, parte acquofa del fangue.*

SE'SAME, } s. [a fort of Indian corn] *fifamo, fefamo,* s. m. *feme di pianta che viene a noi di Sicilia, con altro nome detto* giuggiolena.
SE'SAMUM,

SE'SELI, s. [hart-wort] *fefeli,* s. m. *forta d' erba.*

SESQUIA'LTER, } adj. containing one and a half] *fefquialtero, che contiene una volta e mezza più.*
SESQUIA'LTERAL,

SE'SQUIPEDAL, } adj. [containing a foot and a half] *fequipedale, contenente un piede e mezzo.*
SESQUIPEDA'LIAN,

SE'SSION, s. [meeting of a council, affizes, &c.] *feffione,* s. f.

Seffion of parliament, *feffione di parlamento.*

The feffion of a general council, *feffione di concilio ecumenico.*

The quarter feffions, *le affife che fi tengono quattro volte l' anno in tutte le provincie del regno per giudicare caufe civili e criminali.*

The feffions-hall, *corte di giuftizia, luogo dove fiedono i giudici.*

To keep the feffions, *tenere le affife.*

SE'STERCE, s. [an old Roman coin] *fefterzio,* s. m. *antica moneta Romana.*

SET, adj. *meffo,* v. To fet.

Set meal, *pafto regolato.*

Set price, *prezzo ftabilito.*

Set hour, *ora fiffa.*

Set form of prayers, *formula di preghiere.*

Set vifit, *vifita formale.*

Set fpeech, *difcorfo ftudiato.*

A well fet body, *un corpo ben compleffo, formato, membruto.*

Set battle, *battaglia fchierata.*

To be fet out with merit and honour, *effer ornato di merito e d' onore.*

I am finely fet out [in an ironical fenfe] *i' fto frefco.*

Set refolution, *ferma rifoluzione.*

On fet purpofe, *a pofta, a bella pofta, a bello ftudio, deliberatamente.*

Set, s. [fetting dog] *can di ferma.*

Set [game] *partita di giuoco.*

Set [compleat fuit of any thing] *guernimento, guarnimento, affortimento,* s. m.

Set of diamonds, *guernimento di diamanti.*

Set of buttons, *guarnizione di bottoni.*

A fine fet of filver plate, *un bell' apparato d' argenteria.*

Set of trees, *un filare d' alberi.*

Set of teeth, *dentatura, filare o ordine di denti.*
A set of coach-horses, *un tiro di cavalli da carozza, una muta.*
A set of men, *una banda, una tavolata, un certo numero di persone.*
Set-foil [tormentil, ash-weed] *tormentilla, s. f. sorta d' erba.*
To SET [to put, to lay, to place] *mettere, porre, collocare.*
To set in order, *metter in ordine, ordinare.*
To set a thing before one [to propose a thing to one] *mettere che che sia avanti agli occhi ad uno, proporglielo.*
To set free [to set at liberty] *mettere in libertà.*
To set down, *mettere in iscritto, scrivere.*
To set a thing on foot, *mettere una cosa in piedi, stabilirla.*
To set on shore, *mettere a terra, sbarcare.*
To set on the pot [to set the pot on the fire] *mettere la pignatta al fuoco.*
To set one on horseback, *mettere alcuno a cavallo*
To set a house on fire, *dar fuoco ad una casa, incendiare una casa.*
To set to sale, *mettere all' incanto, esporre in vendita.*
Set your heart at rest, *quetatevi, non vi pigliate fastidio.*
To set the seal to a letter, *mettere il sigillo ad una lettera, sigillar una lettera.*
To set aside, *mettere da parte, por da banda.*
To set sail, *spiegar le vele, far vela, dar le vele ai venti.*
To set a stone in gold, *legare una pietra preziosa in oro.*
To set a page [to compose it, as printers do] *comporre una pagina.*
To set to musick, *mettere in musica.*
To set a song to musick, *mettere una canzone in musica.*
To set a price to a thing, *mettere il prezzo ad una cosa, apprezzarla, stimarla.*
To set a time, *determinare, stabilire il tempo.*
To set a watch by a sun-dial, *regolare un oriuolo al sole.*
To set a bone, *rimettere un osso slogato.*
To set a razor, *affilare un rasojo.*
To set one against another, *eccitare, stimolare, istigare, incitare uno contro ad un altro.*
To set a dog at one, *aizzare un cane contro ad alcuno.*
To set one his task, *assegnar ad uno la parte del lavoro che deve fare.*
To set meat before one, *dare a mangiare ad uno.*
To set nets, *tender reti.*
To set a step, *fare un passo.*
To set open the door, *aprire la porta.*
To set one a lesson to learn, *dare ad uno una lezione ad imparare.*
To set one a copy to write by, *dare un esempio ad uno.*
To set good examples to follow, *da buon esempio.*
To set one's hand to a thing, *sottoscrivere che che sia.*
To set one's name to a letter, *sottoscrivere una lettera*
To set [as the planets do] *tramontare.*
The sun sets, *il sole tramonta.*
To set a going, *far muovere.*
To set about a thing, *mettersi a fare una cosa.*
To set a story abroad, *divulgare una ciancia, dar fuora una cosa.*
To set again in its place, *rimettere nel suo luogo.*
To set against one, *opporsi ad alcuno.*
To set one thing against another, *mettere una cosa in paragone d' un' altra.*
To set forth [to show, to represent] *esporre, rappresentare, far vedere, dire.*
To set at nought, *dispregiare, avere o tenere a vile, non far conto.*
To set at defiance, *sfidare.*
To set one at work, *dar da lavorare ad uno.*
To set back, *rinculare, arretrare.*
To set forth a book, *pubblicare, dare alla luce un libro.*
To set forth God's praises, *annunciare le lodi di Dio.*
To set forth [to ordain] *ordinare, comandare, stabilire, pres. stabilisco.*
To set one forth [to praise him much] *lodare, vantare uno.*
To set one's self forth, *vantarsi.*
To set forth [to go away] *partire, andarsene.*
To set one forward [to encourage him] *animare, incoraggiare, inanimire, solecitare, assistere, spalleggiare.*
To set one's self forward, *avanzarsi, aggrandirsi.*
To set forward [to go away] *andar via, partire.*
To set off, *abbellare, abbellire, far bello, adornare.*
She had nothing to set off her beauty, *ella non aveva niente da fare spiccare la sua bellezza.*
To set on a lock, *mettere una serratura.*
To set the teeth on edge, *allegare i denti.*
To set one on, *animare alcuno, incitarlo, sollecitarlo, aizzarlo.*
To set one's affections on a woman, *metter amore ad una donna, divenirne amante.*
To set one to work, *dar da lavorare ad uno.*
To set to work, to set one's self to work, *mettersi a lavorare.*
To set up, *ergere, innalzare, rizzare.*
To set up a monument, *ergere un monumento.*
To set up a shop, or to set up one's self, *aprir bottega.*
To set up a tavern, *aprir taverna.*
To set up [to pretend to be] *spacciarsi, farsi, darsi.*
To set up for a physician, *spacciarsi o darsi per medico.*
To set up for a reformer, *fare il riformatore.*
To set up a flag, *innalberare la bandiera.*
To set up a may-pole, *piantare il majo.*
To set up a cry, *mettersi a gridare.*
To set up a laughter, *sganasciar delle risa.*
To set a bill upon a door, *affiggere, affissare un cartello ad una porta.*
To set one's heart upon a thing, *metter amore a che che sia, incaponirsi d' una cosa.*
To set upon one, *assaltare, assalire, avventarsi, attaccare, investire alcuno.*
To set a stamp upon paper, *bollare la carta.*
To set one's heart or mind upon a thing, *applicarsi a che che sia.*
To set one over a thing, *dar l' incombenza o la cura di che che sia ad uno.*
To set out, *mettere a parte, da parte, da banda.*
To set out [to set off] *ornare, adornare, parare, abbellare, abbellire.*
To set out a fleet, *allestire, ammanare una flotta.*
To set one out [to speak much to his praise] *lodare, vantare alcuno, commendarlo.*
To set out a child [to dress him] *abbigliare un fanciullo.*
To set out a book, *pubblicare, dare alla luce un libro.*
To set out [to go away] *partire, andarsene.*
To set out on a journey, *mettersi in cammino, mettersi in viaggio.*
SETA'CEOUS, adj. [bristly, set with strong-hairs] *setoloso, ispido, pien di dure setole.*
SETTE'E, s. [a large long seat with a back to it] *canapé, sorte di sedia da sedersi lunga, larga, piena di borra, e col dosso.*
SETTER, s. [spy] *spia, colui che in guerra è mandato ad osservare gli andamenti de' nemici.*
Setter [pimp] *ruffiano.*
Setter [follower or assistant to a bailiff or sergeant] *un cagnotto, un bravo.*
Setter [a companion of sharpers] *un furbo.*
Setter [setting dog] *can da ferma.*
SE'TTER-WORTH [a plant] *elleboro, nero, s. m. erba medicinale.*
SE'TTING, s. *il mettere, v.* To set.
Setting, adj. a setting or composing stick [a printer's tool] *regolo, s. m. strumento di stampatore.*
A setting stick [a gardener's tool] *strumento d' ortolano, e serve a far buchi nella terra.*
Setting dog, *can da ferma.*
SE'TTLE, or settle-bed, s. *lettieruolo.*
Settle [a wooden bench, or a seat with a back to it] *una panca.*
To SE'TTLE [to establish, to fix] *sta-*

ſtabilire, rendere ſtabile, fermare, preſ. *ſtabiliſco.*

To ſettle one's abode ſomewhere, *accaſarſi, aprir caſa, acconciarſi, ſtanziare in qualche luogo.*

To ſettle one's mind, *quietare la ſua mente.*

To ſettle one's ſpirits [after a ſudden paſſion] *achetarſi.*

To ſettle [to regulate, to fix, to determine] *regolare, ordinare, aggiuſtare, determinare.*

To ſettle the nation, *regolar lo ſtato.*

To ſettle the value of the coin, *regolar la moneta.*

To ſettle an accompt, *ſaldare un conto.*

To ſettle one's concerns, *regolare, ordinare, mettere in aſſetto, porre in ordine i ſuoi affari.*

To ſettle a yearly penſion upon one, *aſſegnare una penſione annuale ad uno.*

To ſettle one's eſtate upon one, *coſtituire uno ſuo erede.*

To ſettle, verb neut. [to reſt, as liquors do] *raſſettarſi, poſarſi, parlando de' liquori.*

To ſettle to the bottom, *andare a fondo.*

To ſettle on ſomething, *determinarſi a qualche coſa, appigliarſi a qualche coſa.*

The weather ſettles, *il tempo ſi mette al bello.*

Se'ttled, adj. *ſtabilito, v.* To ſettle.

Se'ttledeness, s. [firmneſs] *ſtabilezza, ſtabilità,* s. f.

Se'ttlement, s. [ſettling] *ſtabilimento,* s. m.

Settlement [habitation] *abituro, domicilio, ſoggiorno,* s. m. *caſa, abitazione,* s. f.

Settlement [ſettled revenue] *entrata fiſſa.*

To make a ſettlement upon, *aſſegnare ad uno un' entrata fiſſa.*

He has a ſettlement of a thouſand pounds a year, *egli ha un' aſſegnazione di mille lire ſterline all' anno.*

Settlement [that which ſticks to the bottom of liquors] *fondigliuolo, rimaſuglio, poſatura di coſe liquide, feccia.*

Settlement [agreement] *accordo, patto.*

Se'ttling, s. *ſtabilimento, lo ſtabilire.*

Settling of liquor [ſediment] *fondigliuolo, poſatura di qualche liquore, feccia.*

Se'twall, } s. [an herb] *valeriana,*
Se'twell, } s. f. *ſpezie d' erba.*

Se'twort [bear's-foot, an herb] *brancorſina,* s. f. *erba medicinale.*

Se'vantly, adv. [well] *bene,* obſ.

Seven, s. *ſette.*

Seven-fold, adj. *doppio ſette volte, a ſette doppi.*

Se'venscore, adj. [ſeven times twenty] *ſette volte venti, cenquaranteſimo.*

Se'venteen, adj. *diecisette, diciaſette.*

Sevente'enth, adj. *dieciſetteſimo, decimo ſettimo, diciaſetteſimo.*

Se'venth, adj. *ſettimo.*

Se'venthly, adj. *in ſettimo luogo.*

Se'ventieth, adj. *ſettanteſimo.*

Se'venty, adj. *ſettanta.*

To Se'ver [to part] *ſceevrare, ſceverare, ſeparare, partire, ſpartire, ſequeſtrare, dividere,* preſ. *partiſco, ſpartiſco,* pret. *diviſi.*

Se'veral, adj. [diverſe] *molti, diverſi, parecchi.*

Several perſons, *molte o diverſe perſone.*

Several times, *ſpeſſe fiate, parecchie volte, molte volte.*

In ſeveral places, *in diverſi luoghi.*

Several men, ſeveral minds, *quante teſte tanti cervelli.*

Se'verally, adv. [aſunder] *ſeparatamente, a parte, uno a uno, un dopo l' altro.*

To go out ſeverally [by ſeveral ways] *uſcire per diverſi luoghi, chi di quà chi di là.*

Se'verance, s. [a law word, uſed for ſingling or ſeparation] *ſeparazione, diviſione,* s. f. *ſceveramento,* s. m.

Severance of corn, *il mettere a parte la decima dal reſtante del grana.*

Seve're, adj. [rough, ſharp, hard, rigorous] *ſevero, rigido, aſpro, crudele, duro, auſtero.*

A ſevere judge, father, or maſter, *un giudice, un padre, un maeſtro ſevero.*

Severe winter, *inverno rigido, verno aſpro.*

Severe [auſtere, grave] *ſevero, auſtero, grave.*

Severe look, *cera ſevera, auſtero ſguardo.*

Se'verely, adv. *ſeveramente, rigidamente, aſpramente, crudelmente, duramente, auſteramente.*

Seve'rity, s. *ſeverità,* s. f. *rigore,* s. m.

Severity of life, *auſterità di vita.*

Sevoca'tion, s. [the act of calling aſide] *l' atto del chiamar chiccheſſia a parte.*

Sew, s. [a cow when her milk is gone] *varca che non ha più latte.*

To Sew [to ſtitch with a needle] *cucire, v.* To ſow.

To ſew [to ſue, to follow] *ſeguire, ſeguitare.*

To ſew [to drain] *ſeccare.*

To ſew a pond [to drain, to empty a pond] *ſerrare uno ſtagno.*

To ſew [a ſhip is ſaid to be ſewed, when ſhe comes to lie on the ground, or lies dry] *reſtare a ſecco, rimanere in ſerro.*

Sewed, adj. *cucito.*

Sewed, *rimaſto in ſerro.*

The ſhip is ſewed, *il navilio è a ſecco.*

Se'wer, s. [carver] *un trinciante, uno ſcalco.*

Sewer [common ſhore] *fogna,* s. f. *condotto ſotteraneo, per ricevere, immondizie.*

Common-ſewer, } [proſtitute] *ba-*
Common-ſhore, } *gaſcia, puttanaccia.*

Se'wet, s. [the fat of beaſts] *graſſo d' animale.*

Beef or mntton ſewet, *graſſo o di caſtrato, o di manzo.*

Sex, s. [the different nature of male and female] *ſeſſo,* s. m. *l' eſſer proprio del maſchio e della femmina, che diſtingue l' un dall' altro.*

The male and the female ſex, *il ſeſſo maſcolino e il femminino.*

Sexage'sima, s. [the Sexageſſima Sunday, the ſecond Sunday before Lent] *ſeſſageſima.*

Sexa'ngle, s. [a figure conſiſting of ſix angles] *ſeſſagono,* s. m. *figura geometrica di ſei lati e ſei angoli.*

Sexe'nnial, adj. [that is of ſix years continuance] *di ſei anni, che ha durato ſei anni.*

Se'xtain, s. [a ſtanza or ſtave, containing ſix verſes] *ſeſtina,* s. f. *ſei verſi.*

Se'xtary, s. [an ancient meaſure] *ſorta di miſura antica.*

Sexte, s. [one of the ſeven canonical hours] *ſeſta,* s. f. *nome d' una delle ſette ore canoniche.*

Se'xtile, s. [an aſtrological aſpect, when two planets are diſtant ſixty degrees or one ſixth part of the zodiack] *ſeſtile,* s. m. *termine aſtrologico.*

Se'xton, s. [an officer who has the care of the veſtry] *ſagriſtano.*

Se'xtry, s. [veſtry] *ſagreſtia,* s. f.

To Shab [to play mean tricks] *giuocar di ſotto mano, operare con aſtuta viltà. Vocabolo plebeo.*

Sha'bbily, adv. *mendicamente, da mendico, poveramente.*

Shabbily [meanly, reproachfully, deſpicably] *vilmente, vituperoſamente, ſpregievolmente.*

To go ſhabbily, *andar veſtito come un mendico, eſſer mal veſtito.*

Sha'bbiness, s. *mendicaggine, mendicità,* s. f.

Shabbineſs [meanneſs, paltrineſs] *viltà, coſa o atto vituperevole.*

Sha'bby, adj. [ragged, beggarly] *ſciammannato, ſcompoſto, ſtracciato, mal veſtito.*

Shabby fellow, *uno ſtracciato, un mendico.*

Shabby wench, *una pettegola.*

Shabby ſuit, *abito ſtracciato.*

Shabby doings [baſe, pitiful doings] *azioni baſſe, indegne d' un galantuomo.*

Sha'ckles, s. [fetters for malefactors in priſon] *ferri, ceppi,* s. m. *catene,* s. f.

Hand-ſhackles, *manette.*

To Sha'ckle, verb act. *mettere in ceppi, inceppare.*

Sha'ck.

SHA'CKLED, adj. *messo a' ferri, in ceppi*.

SHAD, s. [a sort of fish] *pesce di mare così detto*.

SHADE, s. *ombra*, s. f.

Night-shade [an herb] *morella*, s. f. *spezie d' erba*.

Shade [an ornament for a woman's head] *certo femminile ornamento di testa per donna*.

To SHADE, *ombrare, fare ombra*.

SHA'DED, adj. *ombrato*.

SHA'DINESS, s. [shade] *ombra*.

SHA'DOW, s. [the representation which any thing makes of itself, being interposed between the light, and any solid body] *ombra*, s. f.

The shadow of a man or house, *l' ombra d' un uomo o d' una casa*.

Shadow [dark colours in painting] *ombra nella pittura, quel colore scuro rappresentante l' ombra vera*.

To be afraid of one's shadow [to fear without a cause] *farsi paura coll' ombra, temere delle cose che non possan nuocere*.

Shadow [favour, protection] *ombra, protezione, difesa*, s. f.

Under the shadow of so powerful a master, *sotto l' ombra d' un sì potente padrone*.

Shadow [mark, sign] *ombra, apparenza, dimostrazione*, s. f. *segno*, s. m.

Shadow [type or sign of a thing to come] *ombra, figura*, s. f. *segno*, s. m.

Shadow-grass [an herb] *gramigna*, s. f.

To SHA'DOW [to shade] *ombrare, ombreggiare, fare ombra*.

To shadow a picture, *ombreggiare, abbozzare una pittura*.

SHA'DOWED, adj. *ombrato, ombreggiato*.

SHA'DOWY, } adj. [making a shade]
SHA'DY, } *ombroso*.

Shady woods, *boschi ombrosi*.

SHAFT, s. [a case of arrows] *faretra*, s. f.

Shaft [arrow] *freccia, saetta*, s. f. *dardo, strale, quadrello*, s. m.

The shaft of a pillar, *il fusto d' una colonna*.

The shaft of a chimney, *fummajuolo, e fumajuolo*, s. f. *la rocca del cammino d' onde esce il fumo*.

Shafts [holes like wells made by miners to free the works from the springs that arise in them] *buchi rotondi come pozzi che si fanno nelle miniere*.

SHAG, s. [a sort of hairy stuff] *felpa*, s. f. *drappo col pelo più lungo del velluto*.

Shag-breeches, *calzoni di felpa*.

A shag haired dog, *barbone*, s. m. *bracco d' arqua*.

Shag [a sea fowl] *spezie d' uccello di mare*.

SHA'GGED or SHA'GGY, adj. [rough with hair] *velloso, velluto, peloso, irsuto, ispido*.

A shagged dog, *un barbone*.

SHAGRE'EN, adj. [vexed, out of humour] *maninconico, pensieroso, nojoso, di cattivo umore*.

You look very shagreen, *voi sembrate tutto pensieroso o maninconico*.

Shagreen, s. [a sort of rough-grained leather] *zigrino*, s. m.

A shagreen case, *uno stucchio di zigrino*.

To SHAGRE'EN [to irritate, to provoke] *irritare, provocare, dar fastidio, far istizzire, muovere stizza*.

To SHAIL [to walk sidewise] *camminare inclinando da un lato. Vore bassa*.

SHAKE, s. [jerk, pull] *scossa*, s. f.

Shake [in musick] *trillo*, s. m.

To shake [to move violently] *scuotere, agitare con violenza, crollare*, pret. *scossi*.

To shake one's head, *scuoter la testa*.

To shake a tree, *far crollare un albero*.

The fear of death shakes the stoutest men alive, *il timor di morire fa tremare i più coraggiosi*.

To shake hands, *darsi la mano*.

To shake hands with one [to part with him] *lasciare alcuno*.

To shake off, *scuotere, levarsi d' addosso*.

To shake off one's yoke, *scuotere il giogo*.

To shake one off [to get rid of one] *strigarsi d' uno, levarselo d' attorno*.

To shake to pieces, *far cascare in pezzi*.

To shake, verb neut. *tremare*.

My hand shakes, *mi trema la mano*.

To shake [in musick] *gorgheggiare, termine de' musici*.

SHA'KED, adj. *scosso, mosso, agitato, crollato*, v. To shake.

SHA'KER, s. [the person or thing that shakes] *la persona che scuote o la cosa che crolla*.

SHA'KING, s. *scossa*, s. f. *crollo, crollamento*, s. m.

SHALE [corrupted for shell; husk; the case of seeds in siliquous plants] *scorza di baccello, e diceji di tutte le piante che hanno somiglianza colle fave, co' piselli, e simili*.

SHALL, *è il segno del tempo futuro de' verbi Inglesi*.

I shall see, *vedrò*.

I shall go, *anderò*.

In luogo di SHALL, *gl' Inglesi si servono anche di* WILL, *ma con questa differenza, che* SHALL *nelle prime persone dinota una dichiarazione di volontà, e nelle seconde e terze un comando Ma* WILL *dinota in tutte le persone una promessa, una risoluzione o intenzione di voler fare qualche cosa*.

Will you do it? I shall, *volete farlo? lo farò*.

He will have me go along with him, but I shall not, *egli vuole che io vada seco, ma io non v' anderò*.

To be at shill-I-shall-I [to be at a stand, or in suspence] *star sospeso, esser irresoluto, star bilanciando, vacillare, tempellare, stare tra 'l sì e 'l no*.

SHALLO'ON, s [a slight woollen stuff] *sorta di panno lano leggiero*.

SHA'LLOP, s. [a small vessel] *schiffo*.

SHA'LLOW, adj. [not deep] *di poco fondo, che non è profondo*.

A shallow river, *un fiume di poco fondo, che non è profondo*.

Shallow water, *acqua bassa*.

Shallow-pated, shallow-brained, shallow-witted, or a shallow man, a shallow wit, or shallow brains, *un nidiace, un pecorone, un fantoccio, uno scemo, uno scempiato, uno scempio, un uomo di poco cervello, un lavaceci*.

Shallow, s. [a flat in the sea] *serra, luogo nel mare che ha poco fondo*.

Shallow [ford in a river] *guado*.

To ford a shallow, *guadare*.

SHA'LLOWLY, adv. [with no great depth] *poco profondamente*.

Shallowly [simply, foolishly] *scempiatamente, da scemo*.

SHA'LLOWNESS, s. [the state of not being deep] *poco fondo, arqua bassa*.

Shallowness of wit, *poco cervello, sciocchezza, scimunitaggine*.

SHALM, s. [a sort of musical instrument] *sorta di strumento musicale da fiato*.

SHALO'ON, s. [a sort of woollen stuff] *rascia*, s. f. *spezie di panno di lana*.

SHA'LOT, s [a small sort of onion, used in sauces] *scalogno*, s. m. *spezie di cipolla di picciol capo*.

SHALT, *è la seconda persona di* shall.

SHAM, s. [flam] *baja, burla, beffa*, s. f.

To put a sham upon one, *dar la baja ad uno, beffarlo, burlarsi di lui*.

Sham [is used sometimes adjectively, for pretended, false] *preteso, supposto, falso*.

A sham business, *una cosa supposta*.

Sham sleeves, *mezze maniche*.

To SHAM one [to put a trick upon him] *dar la baja ad uno, burlarlo, schernirlo*.

To sham one thing for another upon one, *ingannare alcuno, darli una cosa per un' altra, dargliela a credere*.

SHAMA'DE, s. [beat of drum for a parley] *chiamata*, s. f.

To beat the shamade, *batter la chiamata*.

SHA'MBLES, s. [a place where butchers sell meat] *beccheria*, s. f.

SHA'MBLING, adj. [moving aukwardly and irregularly] *che si muove goffamente e con modo irregolare*.

SHAME, s. [reproach, disgrace] *vergogna, infamia, ignominia*, s. f. *vitupeio, biasimo*, s. m.

For

For ſhame [fy upon] *vergognatevi.*

Shame [baſhfulneſs] *vergogna, roſſore, pudore.*

To loſe all ſhame, *perder la vergogna.*

Every body cries ſhame on it, *ognuno biaſima queſta azione.*

To SHAME [to diſgrace] *ſvergognare, diſonorare.*

To ſhame one [to make him aſhamed] *far vergognare o arroſſire alcuno.*

SHAMED, adj. *ſvergognato, diſonorato.*

Shame faced, adj. [baſhful] *vergognoſo, tocco da vergogna.*

Shame-facedly, adv. *vergognoſamente, con vergogna, riſpettoſamente.*

Shame-facedneſs, s. *vergogna, modeſtia, timidità,* s. f. *roſſore, pudore,* s. m.

SHA'MEFUL, adj. [baſe, diſhoneſt] *vergognoſo, vituperevole, ignominioſo, infame.*

Shameful death, *morte ignominioſa.*

SHA'MEFULLY, adv. *vergognoſamente, ignominioſamente, con ignominia, con iſcorno.*

SHA'MEFULNESS, s. *vergogna, infamia, villania,* s. f. *vituperio, diſonore, biaſimo,* s. m.

Shamefulneſs, s. *sfacciataggine, impudenza,* s. f.

SHA'MELESS, adj. [impudent] *ſfacciato, ſfrontato.*

Shameleſs action, *azione ſfacciata.*

A ſhameleſs man, *uno ſfacciato, uno ſfrontato.*

A ſhameleſs woman, *una ſfacciata.*

SHA'MELESSLY, adv. *ſfacciatamente, con iſfacciatezza, ſfrontatamente.*

SHA'MELESSNESS, s. [impudence] *ſfacciatezza, ſfacciataggine.*

SHA'MMED, adj. *burlato, beffato, deriſo.*

SHA'MMER, s. [a cheat, an impoſtor] *un truffatore, un ingannatore, un impoſtore.*

SHA'MMING, s. *baja, burla,* s. f.

Shamming, adj. ex. a ſhamming trick, *una baja, una burla.*

SHAMO'IS, s. [a kind of wild goat] *camozza,* s. f. *capra ſalvatica*

Shamois or ſhamoy-leather, *camoſcio,* s. m. *pelle di camozza o d' altro ſimile animale.*

SHA'MPINION, s. [muſhroom] *fungo,* s. m.

SHA'MROCK, s. [the Iriſh name for three leaved graſs] *nome dato dagl' Irlandeſi al fieno che ſi taglia per la terza volta in una ſtagione.*

SHA'NK, s. [leg] *gamba,* s. f. *ſtinco,* s. m.

Small ſpindle ſhanks, *gambe di fuſo.*

The ſhank or ſtalk of a plant, *il fuſto, o il gambo d' un' erba.*

The ſhank of a chimney, *il fummajuolo o fumajuolo, quella parte del cammino per dove eſce il fummo.*

SHA'NKER, s. [a ſort of ulcer] *ſorta d' ulcera.*

SHAPE, s. [form, figure] *forma, figura,* s. f.

To come to ſome ſhape, *formarſi.*

Shape [ſtature, proportion of the body] *ſtatura, vita,* s. f.

Fine ſhape, *bella ſtatura, bella vita.*

To SHAPE [to form, to proportion] *dar forma, formare, proporzionare.*

To ſhape one's courſe towards a place at ſea [to ſteer] *far vela, poggiare, drizzare il corſo verſo qualche luogo.*

SHA'PED, adj. *formato, proporzionato.*

To be well ſhaped [to have a body well ſhaped] *avere una bella vita, eſſer ben fatto di corpo.*

SHA'PELESS, adj. [ill ſhaped] *ſformato, di brutta forma o ſtatura, mal fatto.*

SHARD, s. [a broken piece of tile or ſome earthen veſſel] *coccio,* s. m. *pezzo di vaſo di terra cotta quando è rotto.*

SHA'RDBORN, adj. [born or produced among broken ſtones or pots] *che è nato o prodotto in un terreno pieno di cocci e di rottame.*

SHA'RDED, adj. [inhabiting ſhards] *che mena ſua vita in luogo pieno di ſaſſi rotti e cocci di vaſi, credo ſia uno epiteto dato agli ſcorpioni e ſchifoſi inſetti.*

SHA'RE, s. [part] *parte, porzione,* s. f.

Share, or plough-ſhare, *coltro,* s. m. *ſorta di vomero che taglia da una parte ſola.*

Share [grein] *anguinaja,* s. f.

The ſhare-bone, *l'anca,* s. f.

Share-wort [an herb] *erba che guariſce il dolore dell' anguinaja.*

For my ſhare [as for me] *per me, in quanto a me, dal canto mio.*

It fell to his ſhare, *gli accadde in ſorte.*

Share and ſhare alike, *ugualmente.*

I'll have my ſhare to a farthing, *voglio la parte mia fino ad un quattrino.*

To SHARE [to divide into ſhares] *far parti, dividere, ſpartire, diſtribuire,* pref. *ſpartiſco, diſtribuiſco.*

To ſhare a thing with one [to make him partaker of it] *ſpartire una coſa con uno, fargliene parte.*

SHA'RED, adj. *diviſo, ſpartito, diſtribuito.*

SHA'RER, s. *ſpartitore,* s. m. *che fa le parti; che ha parte.*

SHA'RING, s. *ſpartimento,* s. m. *ſpartigione, diviſione,* s. f.

SHARK, s. [a kind of ſea wolf, the moſt ravenous of fiſhes, from whence comes the word ſharking-fellow] *ſpezie di lupo marino, il più vorace di tutti i peſci.*

Shark [ſharking-fellow, one who lives upon the catch] *un ſcrocco, uno ſcroccone, un paraſito.*

To ſhark up and down [to go ſhifting and ſhuffling about] *ſcroccare, fare ſcrocchi.*

SHA'RKING, s. *ſcrocco,* s. m. *lo ſcroccare.*

A ſharking trick, *un tiro di ſcroccone.*

A ſharking-fellow [a ſhark] *uno ſcroccone.*

SHARP, adj. [keen] *acuto, tagliente, affilato*

Sharp [pointed] *acuto, puntuto.*

Sharp knife, *coltello affilato, tagliente.*

Sharp voice, *voce acuta e ſottile.*

Sharp ſight, *viſta acuta.*

Sharp wit, *ingegno acuto, ſottile, penetrante, fine.*

Sharp [cunning] *aſtuto, fine, ſagace, ſcaltrito, ſottile.*

Sharp [ſmart] *agro, pugnente, mordente, mordace, acido.*

Sharp urnine, *urina agra, mordente.*

Sharp words, *parole agre o ſevere.*

Sharp [in taſte] *piccante, forte, agro.*

Sharp [acute or violent, as a diſeaſe or pain] *acuto, vivo, violento, grande.*

Sharp ſtomach, *gran fame, grande appetito.*

Sharp [bloody, cruel] *fiero, crudele, ſpietato.*

Sharp fight, *fiero o ſanguinoſo combattimento.*

Sharp winter, *inverno aſpro, rigoroſo, molto freddo.*

Sharp cold, *freddo acuto o rigido.*

Sharp reproof, *aſpra bravata, riprenſione auſtera.*

To be ſharp [to eat with a good ſtomach] *mangiare con buono appetito.*

To look ſharp [to be upon one's guard] *ſtar ſulle ſtoccate, ſtare attento, ſtar cogli occhi aperti, ſtar in cervello.*

Sharp-ſet [very hungry] *affamato, morto di fame, che ha gran fame.*

Sharp-ſet upon pleaſure, *abbandonato ai piaceri.*

Sharp-ſighted, *che ha la viſta buona, acuta, o ſottile.*

Sharp-witted, *d' ingegno acuto, perſpicace, di ſottile ingegno.*

Sharp, s. [a ſharp or acute ſound] *ſtrido.*

Sharp [pointed weapon, ſmall ſword, rapier] *arme colla punta, ſtocco.*

To SHARP [to cheat] *mariuolare, truffare, acchiappare, ingannare.*

To ſharp, } [to make ſharp] *aguzzare, affilare, arrotare.*
To SHA'RPEN, }

To ſharpen the ſtomach, *aguzzare, riſvegliare l' appetito.*

SHA'RPENED, adj. *aguzzato, affilato.*

SHA'RPER, s. [cunning man] *un furbone, un uomo aſtuto.*

Sharper [rook, cheat] *mariuolo, furfante, truffatore, truffiere, scroccone.*
SHA'RPLY, adv. [smartly, wittily] *sottilmente, ingegnosamente, spiritosamente.*
Sharply [severely] *agramente, acerbamente, severamente, aspramente.*
To tax one sharply, *sgridare, riprendere, bravare alcuno agramente.*
SHA'RPNER, s. *arrotino, quello che arrota.*
SHA'RPNESS, s. [keenness, point] *filo,* s. m. *punta,* s. f.
Sharpness of humours, *acrimonia degli umori.*
The sharpness of the air or weather, *l' intemperie dell' aria o del tempo.*
The sharpness of winter, *il rigor del verno.*
The sharpness of cold, *la rigidezza del freddo.*
Sharpness of sight, *perspicacità, acutezza di vista.*
Sharpness of wit, *sottigliezza d' ingegno.*
Sharpness of stomach, *buono appetito.*
SHASH, s. [the linen of which a Turkish turban is made] *quel panno lino del quale è fatto il turbante d' un Turco.*
Shash [sash] *cintura,* s. f.
SHA'TTER, s. [small piece] *scheggia,* s. f. *scheggio,* s. m.
To SHA'TTER [to damage, to impair] *sconquassare, scassinare, conquassare, sdrucire,* pres. *sdrucisco.*
SHA'TTERED, adj. *sconquassato, scassinato, conquassato, sdrucito.*
Shattered vessel, *vascello sdrucito.*
A shattered-pate [a shattered-pated fellow] *un mentecatto, uno scervellato.*
To SHAVE [to shear, to trim, to barb] *rádere, levar il pelo col rasojo, far la barba, tondere,* pret. *rasi, tosi.*
To shave [to pare close to the surface] *radere fin presso alla superficie.*
To shave [to skim by passing near or slightly touching] *toccare a malapena.*
To shave [to cut in thin slices] *tagliare in fette sottilissime.*
To shave [to strip, to oppress by extortion, to pillage] *spogliare, saccheggiare, opprimere con estorsioni.*
SHA'VED, adj. *raso, tonduto, toso.*
I am shaved three times a week, *mi fo la barba tre volte la settimana.*
Shave-grass [horse tail] *coda di cavallo, spezie d' erba.*
SHA'VELING, s. [shaven priest] *uno che ha ricevuta la prima tonsura.*
Shaveling [a man shaved, a friar] *un uomo tonduto, un frate che ha 'l capo raso.*
SHA'VEN, adj. *che ha ricevuto la prima tonsura.*
SHA'VER, s. [barber] *barbiere,* s. m.
SHA'VING, s. *tonditura,* s. f. *il radere, il tosare.*
Shavings of wood, *brúcioli, trucioli,* s. m. pl. *striscie sottilissime levate dal legno colla pialla.*
SHA'WM, s. [hautboy, cornet] *oboè, o altro simile strumento musicale usato dagli antichi Ebrei.*
SHE, pron. [the feminine of HE] *ella, essa.*
She walks, *ella cammina.*
She is a good woman, *ella è una buona donna.*
SHEAF, s. [a bundle of corn upon the straw] *covone di grano.*
Sheaf [a bundle of arrows] *un fascio di strali.*
To SHEAF corn [to bind corn up into sheaves] *accovonare il grano, fare i covoni.*
To SHEAR [to clip, to cut] *tondere, tosare,* pret. *tosi.*
To shear the sheep, *tonder le pecore.*
To shear cloth, *cimare il panno.*
SHE'ARED, adj. *tonduto, tosato.*
SHE'ARER, s. *tonditore,* s. m. *colui che tonde.*
Cloth shearer, *cimatore,* s. m.
SHE'ARING, s. *tonditura, tosatura, cimatura,* s. f.
Shearing time, *tonditura, il tempo del tondere le pecore.*
SHE'ARING, s. [what is shorn off] *tonditura, tosatura, cimatura,* s. f. *quel che in tondendo si leva.*
SHE'AR-MAN, s. [one who shears cloth] *cimatore,* s. m.
SHE'ARS, s. [large scissors for cutting and clipping] *forbici,* s. f.
SHE'ATS, s. [sheat ropes in a ship] *scotte,* s. f. *quelle funi che s' attaccano alle vele per tirarle a poppa.*
The sheat or sheat anchor [the biggest anchor] *l' áncora la più grossa.*
The sheat cable, *la gomena.*
The sheat fish, *salura,* s. f. *spezie di pesce del Nilo.*
SHE'ATH, s. [the case for a knife] *guaina,* s. f.
Sheath for a sword [scabbard] *fodero di spada.*
Sheath [a delicate Indian fish] *spezie di pescolino delicatissimo.*
To SHEATH a sword [to put the sword up in the sheath] *mettere la spada nel fodero.*
He sheathed his sword into her breast, *le immerse la spada nel petto.*
To sheath a ship [to cover that part of her which is under water, with something to keep the worms from eating into her planks] *ricoprire il fondo d' un navilio con panche per difenderlo da vermi che nel guastino rodendo.*
SHE'ATHED, adj. *rimesso nel fodero, immerso.*
SHE'ATH-WINGED, adj. [having hard cases which are folded over the wings] *aggiunto proprio di certi insetti che hanno una spezie di fodero all' ali.*
SHE'ATHY, adj. [forming a sheath] *che forma come un fodero, che ha forma o somiglianza di fodero.*
SHEAVES, *è il plurale di* Sheaf.
SHE'CK LATON, s. [gilded leather] *cuojo indorato.*
SHED, adj. *sparso, versato, disperso.*
Blood-shed, s. *effusione di sangue.*
Shed, s. [a little house adjoining to a great one] *casipola, casupula, casuccia,* s f. *casa piccola.*
To SHED [to send forth] *versare, spargere, spandere,* pret. *sparsi.*
To shed tears, *versare lagrime.*
He begins to shed teeth, *comincia a mutare i denti.*
To shed the horns [as deer do] *mutar le corna.*
SHE'DDING, s. *spargimento, spandimento,* s. m.
Shedding of blood, *effusione o spargimento di sangue.*
SHEEN, adj. [shining] *lucido, risplendente.* Obsolete.
SHEEP, s. [a creature well known] *una pecora.*
To cast a sheep's eye at one, *guardar uno sotto occhio o colla coda dell' occhio.*
Sheep skin [felt] *pelle di castrato o di pecora.*
Sheep's-head, *testa di pecora.*
A sheep's-head [a block-head] *un cionno, un pecorone, uno sciocco, uno scimunito.*
Sheep-hook, *verga di pastore.*
Sheep's pluck, *ocratella di perora o di castrato.*
Sheep-fold, *mandra,* s. f. *ovile,* s. m.
Sheep's coat, *parco di pecore o di castrati.*
SHE'EPISH, adj. [simple, silly] *semplice, inesperto, soro, sciocco.*
SHE'EPISHNESS, s. *semplicità, inesperienza, sciocchezza.*
SHEER, adv. [altogether, quite] *affatto, intieramente, del tutto.*
Sheer through, *da banda a banda.*
He carried sheer away, *lo portò via affatto.*
To SHEER [among sailors, a ship is said to sheer or to go sheering, when in her sailing she is not steadily steer'd] *andare alla banda, parlando d' un vascello.*
To sheer off, v. n. [to steal away, to slip off clandestinely] *involarsi, fuggir via di nascoso.*
SHE'ERING, adj. ex. a ship that goes sheering, *un vascello che va alla banda.*
SHEERS, s. [shears] *forbici.*
SHEET, s. [a large linen cloth to lay on a bed] *lenzuolo,* s. m. *lenzuola,* s. f. plur.
Sheet of paper, *foglio di carta.*
Book in sheets [book in quires, not bound] *un libro sciolto, non legato.*
To SHEET [to furnish with sheets] *porre le lenzuola.*
To sheet [to enfold in a sheet] *involgere in un lenzuolo, o in un foglio di carta.*
To sheet [to cover as with a sheet] *co-*

coprire leggermente, e con cosa sottile come un foglio di carta.

SHE'KEL, s. [an ancient Jewish coin] *conio Giudaico antico.*

SHELD, adj. [of different colours] *maculato, chiazzato.*

SHELDA'PPLE, s. [chaffinch] *pincione, fringuello,* s. m.

SHELF, s. [a board made fast to a wall to lay things on] *scaffale,* s. m. *scansia,* s. f.

Shelf [heap of sand in the sea] *secca,* s. f. *luogo in mare che per la poca acqua è pericoloso a' naviganti.*

SHELLS, s. [the crustaceous coverings of fishes] *conchiglia, conca,* s. f. *nicchio.*

Oister-shell, *conchiglia d' ostrica.*

Tortoise-shell, *scudo o guscio della testuggine.*

Egg-shell, *guscio d' uovo.*

Nut-shell, *scorsa o guscio di noce.*

Fish-shell, *nicchio di pesce.*

Shell-fish, *pesce di nicchio.*

The shells of pease or beans, *guscio di piselli o fave.*

The shell or rind of a pomegranate, *scorza di granato.*

Shell [bomb] *bomba.*

To throw shells, *gittar bombe.*

To SHELL [to take off the shell or husk] *digusciare, sgranare.*

To shell pease or beans, *sgranare piselli o fave.*

To shell wall-nuts, *digusciare delle noci.*

SHE'LLY, adj. *squamoso, coperto di conchiglie.*

SHE'LTER, s. [a safe place against bad weather] *coperto, riparo,* s. m. *copertura,* s. f.

To get a shelter while it rains, *mettersi a coperto mentre piove.*

Shelter [refuge, protection] *asilo, rifugio, ricovero,* s. m. *protezione, sicurtà, salvezza,* s. f.

To fly for a place to shelter, *rifuggire in qualche luogo, correre al coperto.*

He is fled to me for shelter, *egli è ricorso a me per sicurtà.*

To SHE'LTER one [to receive one into one's house] *ricevere alcuno a casa sua, dargli il coperto, proteggerlo.*

SHE'LTERLESS, adj. *che non ha ricovero alcuno, che non ha rifugio, che è esposto ad ogni pericolo.*

SHELVES, *è il plurale de* shelf.

SHE'LVING, adj. [that leans on one side] *pendente, che pende da una banda, più che dall' altra.*

To SHEND [to blame] *biasimare, sgridare, garrire.*

To shend [to disgrace] *svergognare disonorare.*

SHENT, adj. *biasimato, sgridato, ripreso, garrito, disonorato.*

SHE'PHERD, adj. [one who looks after sheep] *pastore, pecorajo,* s. m.

SHE'PHERDESS, s. *pastorella, pecoraja,* s. f.

Shepherd's purse [an herb] *borsa di pastore, spezie d' erba.*

SHE'RBET, s. [a sort of pleasant drink] *sorbetto,* s. m. *sorta di bevanda congelata.*

Sherbet [the mixture of water, lemons, and sugar, designed for punch] *la mistura dell' acqua, limoni, e zucchero per fare del puncio.*

SHE'RIFF, s. [a chief officer appointed by the king yearly in every shire or county] *sceriffe, ufficiale o magistrato creato dal re in chiascheduna provincia, il di cui officio è appresso a poco come quello del bargello.*

SHE'RIFFALTY, } s. [the office of a SHRI'EVALTY, } sheriff] *l' ufficio del sceriffe o bargello.*

SHE'RIFFWICK, s. *la giurisdizione d' un bargello.*

SHE'RMAN, s. [sheerman] *cimatore,* s. m.

SHE'RRY, s. [a sort of wine] *spezie di vin bianco.*

SHEW, s. [appearance, pretence, colour] *apparenza, mostra, vista,* s. f. *colore, mantello, pretesto,* s. m.

Gli antichi Inglesi probabilmente pronunciavano shew, *e perciò scrivevano* shew. *Oggi però che si pronuncia* show, *si dovrebbe anche scrivere* show, *come saggiamente avverte il signor Samuello Johnson nel suo Dizionario; e così il verbo* to show *co' suoi derivati.*

To make a shew [to make as if, to pretend] *far vista, far sembiante, fingere,* pret. *finsi.*

To make a shew of anger, *far vista o fingere d' esser in collera.*

Shew [spectacle] *pompa, festa,* s. f. *spettacolo,* s. m.

To make a shew of one's riches, *far pompa delle sue ricchezze.*

That was a fine shew indeed, *veramente fu un bello spettacolo.*

To make a fine shew, *far figura, vestir bene, sfoggiare.*

My lord mayor's shew, *la festa del governatore della città di Londra.*

To SHEW [to let see] *mostrare, manifestare, palesare.*

To shew [to prove, to make appear] *mostrare, far vedere, provare.*

To shew one a great deal of kindness, *accogliere uno favorevolmente, fargli molte carezze.*

To shew [to teach] *insegnare.*

To shew [to make known] *anunnciare, far sapere, pubblicare.*

To shew mercy to one, *far grazia ad uno, perdonargli, mostrargli misericordia.*

To shew tricks, *far giuochi di mano.*

To shew one a trick, *far una burla o un tiro ad uno.*

To shew respect and civility to one, *portar rispetto ad uno, rispettarlo, onorarlo.*

To shew cause [to shew reason why] *addurre ragioni.*

To shew one a pair of heels [to scamper away] *darla a gambe, voltar le calcagna ad uno, fuggirsene, svignare.*

To shew forth, *pubblicare, annunciare.*

To shew one's self a man, *dar prova del suo coraggio.*

To shew, verb neut. [to appear or look] *parere,* pret. *parvi.*

That shews black, *questo pare nero.*

To shew [to make shew as if] *far vista o mostra, mostrare, fingere, far credere, dare ad intendere.*

SHEWED, adj. *mostrato,* v. To shew.

SHE'WER, s. *colui che fa vedere.*

A shewer of tricks, *un ciarlatano.*

SHE'WING, s. *mostramento,* s. m. *mostranza, mostra, dimostrazione,* s. f.

SHEWN, v. Shewed.

SHIELD, s. [buckler] *scudo, brocchiero, brocchiere.*

Shield-bearer, *scudiere,* s. m.

Shield [defence, protection] *scudo, riparo, sostegno,* s. m. *difesa, protezione,* s. f.

To SHIELD [to protect, to defend] *difendere, proteggere, salvare.*

SHIE'LDED, adj. *difeso, protetto, salvato.*

SHI'ELDING, s. *protezione, difesa,* s. f.

SHI'FT, s. [smock] *camiscia da donna.*

Shift [after-game, remedy, expedient] *rimedio, spediente, mezzo termine, modo, scampo.*

A poor shift, *un povero rimedio.*

To find out some shift, *trovar qualche mezzo termine.*

Shift [subterfuge, evasion] *scusa,* s. f. *pretesto, rigiro, giro,* s. m.

He has a great many shifts and evasions, *egli ha molti giri e rigiri.*

Shift [cunning shift] *astuzia,* s. f.

To put one to his shifts [to puzzle] *imbarazzare alcuno, metterlo in confusione, confonderlo.*

To be put to one's shifts, or to one's last shift, *non saper che fare, esser imbrogliato, esser ridotto alle strette, non sapere da che lato voltarsi.*

I made shift to go thither a foot, *viaggiai a piedi al meglio che potei.*

I shall make shift to do it, *procurerò di farlo, m' ingegnerò di farlo.*

He makes shift to live, *vive alla giornata, si guadagna la vita con istento.*

I shall make shift with this for to day, *farò che questo mi serva per oggi.*

To SHIFT [to change] *cambiare, mutare.*

To shift one's cloaths, *cambiar d' abiti.*

To shift one's lodgings, *mutare la sua dimora, mutar di casa.*

To shift one's self [to put on a clean shirt or shift] *cambiar di camiscia, mutarsi.*

To shift the scene, *cambiar le scene.*

To shift from place to place, *trasportare da un luogo in un altro.*

To shift a liquor out of one vessel into another, *travasare qualche liquore da un vaso in un altro.*

To shift for one's self [to take care of one's self] *ingegnarsi, industriarsi, affaticarsi di vivere.*

To shift for one's self [to go away] *andarsene via, fuggirsene.*

To shift [to use shifts or evasions, to dodge] *trovar giri e rigiri, usare astuzie e furberie.*

To shift one off [to rid one's self of one] *strigarsi d' uno, levarselo d' attorno, disfarsene.*

To shift the sail, *far passar la vela dall' altra banda.*
SHI'FTED, adj. *cambiato, mutato, v.* To shift.
SHI'FTER, s. [a shifting fellow] *un mariuolo, un furfante, un truffatore, un truffiere.*
SHI'FTING, *cambiamento*, s. m.
Shifting, adj. ex. a shifting fellow, *un furbo, un mariuolo, un ingannatore, un truffiere.*
Shifting trick, *astuzia, arte, sagacità, furberia*, s. f. *scaltrimento*, s. m.
SHI'FTINGLY, adv. [cunningly] *astutamente, artatamente, con arte, finamente.*
SHI'FTLESS, adj. [wanting expedients; wanting means to act or live] *povero di spedienti o di mezzi per operare o per vivere.*
SHI'LLING, s. [a silver coin worth twelve-pence] *scellino*, s. m. *moneta d' argento che vale dodici soldi d' Inghilterra, equivalente di circa due paoli Romani.*
SHILL-I-SHALL-I [a corrupt reduplication of shall-I] *dubitazione, il dubitare, l' atto del rimaner sospeso.*
To STAND SHILL-I-SHALL-I [to continue hesitating] *stare in dubbio, star sospeso, non saper che risolvere.*
SHI'LY, adv. [reservedly] *con ritrosia, con peritanza, timidamente, vergognosamente.*
SHIN, } s. [the forepart of
SHI'N-BONE, } the leg] *stinco*, s. m. *osso della gamba dal ginocchio al collo del piede.*
SHINE, s. *chiarezza*, s. f. *splendore*, s. m.
The sun-shine, *la chiarezza o lo splendore del sole.*
The moon-shine, *il chiaro della luna.*
To shine [to look bright, to cast a light] *rilucere, risplendere, mandar fuori luce, brillare, scintillare.*
The sun or the moon shines, *il sole o la luna riluce.*
A diamond that shines, *un diamante che brilla.*
That verse shines more than the rest, *questo verso spicca più de gli altri.*
This is the unluckiest day to me that ever shone, *questo è il più fatale de' miei giorni.*
SHINESS, s. [reserve] *ritrosia, peritanza*, s. f.
SHI'NGLES, s. pl. [laths to cover houses with] *assicelle colle quali si cuoprono le case.*
The shingles [a kind of St. Anthony's fire] *fuoco salvatico.*
SHI'NGLER, s. [a maker of shingles] *facitor d' assicelle.*
SHI'NING, s. [light] *luce*, s. f. *splendore*, s. m.
Shining, adj. *risplendente, luminoso, scintillante.*
SHI'NINGLY, adv. ex. To look shiningly, *rilucere, risplendere*, pret. *rilussi.*
SHIP, s. [a sea vessel] *navilio, vascello*, s. m. *nave*, s. f.
To take ship, *imbarcarsi.*
Ship-boat, *schiffo, palischelmo*, s. m.
Ship-boy, *mozzo di nave.*
Ship board, *bordo di vascello.*
To go on ship-board, *andare a bordo, imbarcarsi.*
Ship-man, *marinajo.*
Ship-wright or ship-carpenter, *falegname di vascello.*
Ship money, *tassa che si esigeva un tempo in Inghilterra per la costruzione de' vascelli.*
To ship [to ship away] *imbarcare.*
To ship away commodities, *imbarcare delle mercanzie.*
SHI'PPED [shipped away] adj. *imbarcato.*
SHI'PPING, s. *imbarcamento*, s. m. *l' imbarcare.*
To take shipping [to go on shipboard] *imbarcarsi.*
Shipping [navy] *flotta*, s. f. *molte navi.*
SHI'PWRECK, s. *naufragio*, s. m.
To SHI'PWRECK [to suffer shipwreck] *naufragare.*
SHIRE, s. [county, province] *provincia, contea.*
SHIRT, s [linen garment worn by men next their skin] *camiscia*, s. f.
Shirt of mail, *giaco.*
SHI'TTLE, or shittle-headed, adj. [fickle] *leggiere, incostante, volubile, fantastico, bisbetico.*
Shittle, or shuttle, *v.* Shuttle.
A shittle-cock, *volante*, s. m.
To play at shittle-cock, *giuocare al volante.*
SHI'VER, s. [a piece or clift of wood] *scheggia*, s. f.
Shiver [in a ship, a little round wheel in which the rope of a block or pulley runs] *girella, carrucola.*
To SHI'VER [to shake for cold or fear] *termar di freddo, raccapricciarsi di paura.*
To shiver [to beat in pieces] *sminuzzare, spezzare, rompere in minuzzoli.*
SHI'VERED, adj. *tremato, raccapricciato, sminuzzato, rotto.*
SHI'VERING, s. [shivering fit] *capriccio, ribrezzo, brivido*, s. m.
SHI'VERY, adj. [loose of coherence, incompact, easily falling into many fragments] *non compatto, non sodo, che facilmente si scheggia.*
SHOAL, s. [croud, multitude, throng] *folla, campagnia f olta, moltitudine.*
Shoal, s. [shallow bank, a shallow] *secca, luogo in mare che ha poco fondo.*
Shoal, adj. [shallow, obstructed or uncumbered with banks] *poco profondo, pien di secche.*
To SHOAL [to croud, to throng] *affollarsi, affoltarsi, andare in folla, andare una moltitudine insieme.*
To shoal [to be shallow, to grow shallow] *esser poco profondo*
SHO'ALY, adj. [full of shoals] *pien di secche, poco profondo.*
SHOAR, *v.* Shore.
SHOCK, s. [encounter, brunt, fight] *urto, assalto, conflitto, scontro, combattimento*, s. m.
A shock of corn, *una bica di grano.*
To SHOCK [to clash with, to knock against] *urtare.*
SHOD, adj. [from shoe] *calzato.*
Horse well shod, *cavallo ben ferrato.*
SHOG, s. [shake, concussion] *scossa*, s. f. *scuotimento*, s. m.
To SHOG [to jog, to justle] *sbattere, scuotere, crollare.*
SHOLE, s. [shoal, company of fishes] *un banco di pesci.*
SHOLES [shoals, flats in the water] *secche nel mare.*
SHOE, s. [cover for the feet] *scarpa*, s. m. *il calzar del piede.*
Horse shoe, *ferro di cavallo.*
Wooden shoes, *zoccoli.*
Little shoe, *una scarpetta.*
The upper-leather of a shoe, *tomajo*, s. m.
SHOE-BOY, s. *ragazzo che netta le scarpe alla gente per le vie.*
Shoe-sole, *suolo di scarpa.*
Every shoe fits not every foot, *non tutti si calzano al medesimo punto, cioè tutti non gradiscono la medesima cosa.*
Shoe-string, *coreggiuolo di scarpe.*
To save shoe-leather, *risparmiare le scarpe.*
To SHOE a horse, *ferrare un cavallo.*
SHOE'ING, s. *il ferrare.*
Shoeing-hammer, *martello da ferrare i cavalli.*
Shoeing-horn, *calzatojo*, s. f.
SHOE-MAKER, s. *calzolajo*, s. m. *che fa le scarpe.*
Shoe-maker's shop, *bottega di calzolajo.*
Shoe-maker-row, or shoe-maker-street, *luogo dove si vendono le scarpe, strada abitata principalmente da' calzolai.*
To be in the shoe-maker's-stocks, *portar le scarpe troppo strette.*
SHOOK, *è un preterito del verbo* to shake.
SHOONE [shoes] *scarpe.* Obs.
SHOOT, s. [a young sprout or bud] *pollone, rampollo*, s. m.
SHOOT [young pig that has done sucking] *un porcastro.*
Shoot [a shooting with a gun or bow] *colpo, tiro*, s. m.
I shoot three shoots at him, *gli ho tirato tre colpi.*
To SHOOT [to discharge shot or arrows] *sparare, tirare, lanciare, scoccare.*
To shoot a gun, *sparare uno schioppo.*
To shoot an arrow, *scoccare un dardo.*
To shoot at one, *tirare ad uno.*
To shoot [to wound] *ferire*, pres. *ferisco.*
To shoot [as plants do] *pullulare, germogliare.*
To shoot out in ears [as corn does] *spigare, far le spighe.*
To shoot [as lightning does] *passare come un lampo, corruscare, lampeggiare, balenare.*
To shoot [as a star does] *cascare, parlando d' una stella.*

To shoot forth [to run swiftly forward] *lanciarsi, avventarsi.*
A cape that shoots forth into the sea, *un promontorio o capo che s' avanza nel mare.*
To shoot [as a pricking pain does] *battere, martellare, il tormentare che fa il dolor dell' ulcere quando generano la putredine.*
To shoot corn, coals, or the like out of a sack, *vuotare un sacco di grano, di carbone, e simili.*
To shoot one to death, *moschettare.*
To shoot a bridge [to go through it] *passare sotto un ponte.*
To shoot a gulf, *passare un golfo.*
To shoot a mast by the board, *abbattere un albero di vascello.*
To shoot in a bow, *tendere un arco.*
To shoot through, *passare da banda a banda.*
SHOOTER, s. *tiratore, s. m. che tira.*
SHOO'TING, s. [budding] *pullulamento, germogliamento.*
The shooting of plants, *il germogliar delle piante.*
A shooting of a gun, *un tiro di cannone.*
Shooting star, *stella errante, o erratica.*
SHOP, s. *bottega, s. f.*
Shop-book, *libro di conti, giornale di bottegajo.*
Shop-keeper, *bottegajo, s. m. bottegaja, s. f.*
Shop-lifter [one who, cheapening wares under pretence of buying, takes opportunity to steal] *un mariuolo, che sotto pretesto di comprare della roba cerca l' occasione di rubarla; e significa anche una che ruba una bottega rompendone la porta, o aprendola in alcun modo violento e furfantesco.*
SHO'RAGE, s. [a duty paid for goods brought on shore] *diritto che si paga per lo sbarco delle mercanzie.*
SHORE, s. [a coast or tract of land on the sea-side] *lido, lito, s. f. spiaggia, costa, s. f.*
To go on shore, *andare a terra, metter piede a terra.*
To come on shore, *sbarcare, approdare.*
Shore [prop] *puntello, rincalzo, sostegno, sostentamento, s. m.*
Common-shore [sewer] *fogna, s. f.*
To SHORE up [to under-prop] *appuntellare, puntellare, reggere, rincalzare, sorreggere, sostentare,* pret. *ressi, sorressi.*
SHO'RED up, adj. *appuntellato, puntellato, retto, rincalzato, sorretto, sostentato.*
SHO'RLING, s. [the sheep-skin after the fleece is shorn off] *pelle di pecora tonduta.*
SHORN, adj. [from to shear] *tonduto, tosato, toso.*
Shorn velvet, *velluto raso.*
SHORT, adj. [of small length] *corto, di poca lunghezza.*
Short sword, *spada corta.*
Short [not long in duration] *corto, di poca durata.*
The days are short in winter, *i giorni sono corti nel verno.*
Short [succinct, brief] *corto, succinto, breve.*
Short speech, *discorso breve.*
To be short [not to speak long] *esser breve, essere succinto.*
To make short work, *per finirla, in poche parole.*
To be short of money [to want money] *essere sprovvisto di danari.*
To be short, or cut short, in short, *per abbreviarla, per finirla, in breve, finalmente, in conclusione.*
Short-breath, *ambascia, s. f. difficoltà di respirare.*
Short-sight, *corta vista.*
Short man or woman, *uomo piccolo, uomicciatto, donna piccola, donnetta.*
Short-hand, *maniera di scrivere per abbreviature.*
Short-hand writing, *scritture per abbreviature.*
Some short time, *un giorno o l' altro.*
Short-while, *poco tempo.*
In a short time, *fra poco tempo, ben presto.*
Thing of short continuance, *cosa di poca durata.*
Short-bowl, *pallottola corta, che non arriva al segno essendo tratta.*
Short, adv. *corto.*
To come short of one's design [to miss one's aim] *mancare il colpo, non venire a fine del suo disegno.*
Our provisions fell short [failed us] *le provvisioni ci mancarono.*
To fall short of one's expectations [to be disappointed] *restar deluso nelle sue speranze.*
He comes short of no man in courage, *non la cede a nessuno in coraggio.*
To come, to be, to fall short [to be inferior, not to come near] *cedere, essere inferiore.*
The translation falls short of the original, *la traduzione non ha che fare coll' originale, la traduzione non è da paragonarsi all' originale.*
To cut short a discourse, *abbreviare un discorso.*
To speak short [to have a short way of speaking] *mangiar le parole, non parlare distintamente.*
To cut a thing shorter, *scorciare o scortare una cosa.*
To fetch one's breath short, *avere ambascia, respirare con difficoltà.*
To keep one short of money, *tener uno corto a danari, dargli poca cosa da spendere.*
I will know the short and the long of that business, *voglio sapere il come e'l quanto di questo negozio.*
Short-sighted, *di corta vista.*
Short-lived, *di corta vita.*
Short winded, *bolso, che con difficoltà respira.*
To SHO'RTEN [to make short] *accorriare, accortare, scorciare, abbreviare.*
And to shorten my discourse, *e per iscorciare, o abbreviare il mio discorso.*
To shorten [to grow short] *accorciarsi, accortarsi; scorciarsi.*
SHO'RTENED, *accorciato, abbreviato.*
SHO'RTER [the comparative of short] *più corto.*
To cut shorter, *scorciar di più.*
SHO'RTEST [the superlative of short] *il più corto.*
The shortest way, *la strada più corta, la più breve via.*
SHO'RTLY, adv. [in a short time] *in breve, fra breve, in poco tempo.*
Shortly after, *poco tempo dopo, non molto dopo.*
SHO'RTNED, adj. *accorciato, accortato, scorciato.*
SHO'RTNESS, s. *cortezza, brevità,* s. f.
Shortness of time, *brevità di tempo.*
Shortness of breath, *ambascia,* s. m. *difficoltà di respirare.*
SHO'RTNING, s. *accorciamento, scorciamento,* s. m.
SHO'RY, adj. [lying near the coast] *litorale, che è vicino al lido del mare.*
SHOT, adj. [from to shoot] *tirato, sparato,* v. To shoot.
He was shot in the thigh, *fu ferito con palla nella coscia, ricevè un colpo di palla nella coscia.*
Shot, s. [all sorts of bullets for fire arms] *palle d' arme da fuoco; pallini.*
Small shot [used to shoot with a birding piece] *pallini,* s. m. *treggea,* s. f.
Great shot, *palle di piombo.*
Great and small shot [great guns and muskets] *i cannoni e la moschetteria.*
A volley of shot, *una salva di moschettate.*
Cannon-shot, or bullet, *palla di cannone.*
Shot [reach] *tiro,* s. m.
To be within cannon shot, *essere a tiro di cannone.*
Within a musket-shot, *a tiro di moschetto.*
To make a shot of a business [to make an end of it] *terminare un negozio.*
Shot [scot, reckoning] *scotto,* s. m.
Shot-free, or scot-free, *franco, bardotto, che non paga*
To eat and drink shot-free, *mangiare e bere a bardotto.*
Shot-free [safe] *salvo, fuor di pericolo.*
Shot-free [unhurt] *senza esser ferito.*
Shot-free [proof] *di tutta botta.*
Shot, or shote [a young pig that has done sucking] *un porcastro.*
SHOTE, s. [a fish] *nome di pesce.*
SHOTTEN, adj. [speaking of fish that has spent the roe, spawned] *che è andato in frega, parlando de' pesci.*
Shotten-herring, *aringa che ha gettate l' uova.*
He looks like a shotten herring, *egli è molto scarno, egli è magro come un' aringa.*
Shotten milk, *latte grumoso o guasto.*
SHOVE, s. [thrust] *spinta,* s. f. *urto,* s. m.
Shove-net, *ritrosa,* s. f. *spezie di rete.*
To SHOVE [to push, to thrust] *spignere, spingere, urtare,* pret. *spinsi.*
To shove along or forward, *spignere avanti, fare avanzare.*
To shove back, *spingere indietro.*

SHO'VED, adj. *spinto, urtato.*
SHO'VEL, s. *pala, paletta,* s. f.
SHOVEL-BOARD [a kind of game] *spezie di giuoco che si fa spignendo un pezzo tondo di metallo sopra una lunga tavola.*
Little shovel, *paletta.*
Fire-shovel, *paletta da fuoco.*
SHOVELER, s. [pelican, a fowl] *pellicano,* s. m.
SHOUGH, s. [a species of shaggy dog, a shock] *sorta di cane peloso.*
SHOULD [ought] *questa parola che viene da* SHALL *serve per esprimere l' imperfetto del subjuntivo del verbo* Dovere.
I should do it, *dovrei farlo.*
It should be so, *dovrebbe esser così.*
Gl' Inglesi si servono di SHOULD, *come d' un segno dell' imperfetto del subjuntivo di qualsisia verbo.*
I should be very sorry for it, *me ne dispiacerebbe.*
SHO'ULDER, [a part of the body joining the arm to it] *spalla,* s. f. *omero,* s. m.
Broad shoulder, *spallaccia.*
To have good broad shoulders, *aver buone spalle.*
Over the left shoulder [the wrong way] *tutto 'l contrario.*
This horse's shoulder is out of joint, *questo cavallo è spallato.*
Shoulder-bone [shoulder-blade] *l' osso della spalla.*
Shoulder-piece, *spallaccio,* s. m. *armadura che cuopre la spalla.*
Shoulder-belt, *ciarpa.*
To SHO'ULDER [to lay on the shoulders] *mettere sopra la spalla.*
To shoulder up a burden, *mettere un fardello sopra le spalle.*
To shoulder one up [to bear him up] *spalleggiare alcuno, fargli spalla, ajutarlo.*
To shoulder-squat a horse [to sprain a horse's shoulder, to put it out of joint] *spallare un cavallo.*
SHOULDERCLAPPER, s. [one who affects familiarity] *uno che ti vuol essere familiare, che ti da della mano in sulla spalla in segno di familiarità.*
SHOULDERSHOTTEN, adj. [strained in the shoulder] *che ha una spalla dislocata.*
SHO'ULDERSLIP, s. [dislocation of the shoulder] *dislocamento di spalle.*
SHO'ULDERED, adj. ex. broad-shouldered, *che ha le spalle larghe.*
SHOUT, s. *clamore, grido,* s. m.
Shout for joy, *giubilo, giubbilo,* s. m. *allegrezza,* s. f.
To SHOUT [to make a shout or cry] *gridare, acclamare, far applauso.*
SHO'UTING, s. *grido d' acclamazione.*
SHOW, *v.* Shew, *e la nota che ho aggiunta sotto tal voce.*
To SHOW, *v.* To shew, *e la nota che ho aggiunta sotto la voce* shew.
SHOWER, s. *pioggia,* s. f. *scroscio,* s. m. *rovescio di pioggia.*
Great shower, *acquazzone.*

To SHOWER down, *scrosciare, piovere, piovere a rovescio, diluviare.*
They shower on his shield a rattling war, *gittano sopra il suo scudo un rovescio di strali.*
SHOWE'RY, adj. ex. showery weather, *tempo piovoso.*
SHO'WISH, } adj. [splendid, gaudy,
SHO'WY, } ostentatious] *splendido, vistoso, pomposo, pieno d' ostentazione.*
SHOWN, *pret. e particip. passato del verbo* to show.
SHRANK, *preterito del verbo* to shrink.
SHRED, adj. [cut small] *sminuzzato, tagliuzato.*
SHRED, s. [a small cutting of any thing] *ritaglio,* s. m. *pezzo di panno, drappo o simili, levato dalla pezza.*
Shreds of cloths, *ritagli di panno.*
Parchment shreds, *ritagli di pergamena.*
To SHRED [to cut small, *sminuzzare, tagliuzzare, tagliar minuto.*
To shred [to lop off] *potare.*
To shred boughs of trees, *diradare gli alberi, potare.*
SHRE'DDING, s. *sminuzzamento, potamento,* s. m. *lo sminuzzare.*
SHREW, s. [a scolding contentious woman] *una garritrice, una donna litigiosa o garrula, una diavola. Pron.* shrow.
Shrew-mouse [field-mouse] *spezie di topo campestre.*
SHREWD, adj. [cunning, subtle] *astuto, sagare, scaltrito, fine, arguto.*
He is a shrewd man, *egli un uomo astuto, un formicon di sorbo.*
Shrewd answer, *risposta arguta, mordace replica.*
Shrewd business, *negozio geloso, difficile a trattare.*
Shrewd turn, *tiro cattivo, cattiva azione.*
SHREWDLY, adv. [cunningly] *astutamente, sagacemente, finamente, scaltritamente, argutamente.*
SHREW'DNESS, s. *astuzia, sottigliezza, sagacità,* s. f.
SHRE'WISH, adj. [having the qualities of a shrew; froward, petulantly clamorous] *insolentemente garrulo; romoroso e petulante insieme.*
SHREIK, s. *grido,* s. m.
To SHREIK [to cry, to make a noise] *gridare, strillare.*
SHRI'EKING, s. *grido, stillo,* s. m.
SHRIFT, s. [a confession of sins made to a priest] *confessione,* s. f.
SHRILL, adj. [sharp] *squillante, acuto, chiaro, risonante, sottile.*
Shrill voice, *una voce squillante, acuto, chiaro, risonante, sottile.*
Shrill voice, *una voce squillante, acuta voce.*
SHRI'LLY, adv. to speak shrilly, *parlar forte, con voce risonante, strepitare.*
SHRI'LNESS, s. *voce squillante, acuta; acutezza di voce.*
SHRIMP, s. [a little sea-fish] *squilla,* s. f. *spezie di gamberetto marino.*
Shrimp [a little fellow, a dwarf] *un pigmeo, un nano, un uomicciatto.*
SHRINE, s. [a case to hold reliques]

reliquiario, s. m. *vaso o altra custodia dove si tengono o conservano le reliquie.*
To SHRINK [to contract, to lessen in length] *scorciare, scortare.*
To shrink, verb neut. *scorciarsi, ritirarsi.*
Stuff that shrinks, *panno che si ritira.*
My money begins to shrink, *il mio danaro comincia a mancare o a diminuire.*
To shrink with cold, *batter i denti, tremar di freddo.*
To shrink in the neck or shoulders, *ristrignersi nelle spalle.*
To shrink [to go back] *arretrare, rinculare, andare indietro.*
To shrink under the weight of misfortunes, *soccombere alle disgrazie, restar oppresso dalle disgrazie.*
Our spirits are apt to shrink at the thoughts of death, *noi non possiamo far di meno di non raccapricciarci al pensiero della morte.*
SHRI'NKING, adj. *che si ritira, che si scorcia.*
A shrinking of the sinews, *raggricchiamento di nervi.*
The shrinking shrub, *la sensitiva; pianta, di cui le foglie s' abbassano subito ch' è toccata.*
To SHRIVE [to confess] *confessarsi.*
SHRI'VING, s. *confessione,* s. f.
To SHRI'VLE [to wrinkle] *raggrinzarsi, empirsi di grinze.*
SHRIV'ELLED, adj. *raggrinzato.*
SHROUD, *v.* Shrowd.
SHRO'VETIDE, s. [carnaval] *carnasciale, carnesciale, carnovale,* s. m.
Shrove-Tuesday, *Martedì grasso.*
SHROWD, s. [a garment to wrap up a dead corpse] *vestimento lano nel quale s' inviluppano i corpi morti in Inghilterra.*
Shrowd [shelter] *coperto, coverto,* s. m. *luogo coperto.*
Shroud] [in fortification] *difese,* s. f.
Shrouds of a ship, *sartiame di vascello, nome generico di tutte le funi che si adoperano nelle navi, e che sono legate all' albero; sarte.*
The shrouds of trees, *i rami che sono stati taliati dagli alberi.*
To SHROWD [to cover] *coprire, e cuoprire.*
To shrowd the trees, *potare gli alberi.*
To shrowd [to shelter] *coprire, mettere al coperto.*
To shrowd one's self, *mettersi al coperto.*
SHROW'DED, adj. *coperto, v.* To shrowd.
SHRUB, s. [a dwarf tree] *arbuscello, arbusto,* s. m. *pianticelli,* s. f.
Shrub [shrimp] *pigmeo, pimmeo, nano, uomicciato.*
To SHRUB [to cudgel] *bastonare, percuotere, battere.*
SHRU'BBED, adj. *bastonato, battuto, percosso.*
To SHRUG [to shrink up the shoulders] *ritirarsi nelle spalle.*
SHRUNK, } adj. *scorciato, ritira-*
SHRUNK IN, } *to, diminuito, v.* To shrink.

My

My heart is shrunk with grief, *il mio cuore è oppresso dal dolore.*

SHRU'NKEN, *participio passivo del verbo* to shrink.

To SHUDDER [to shiver] *tremare.*

To shudder with cold, *tremar di freddo.*

SHU'FFLE, s. [the act of disordering things, or making them take confusedly the place of each other] *scompiglio, guazzabuglio, rimescolamento.*

Shuffle [trick, artifice] *truffa, furberia, astuzia.*

To SHU'FFLE [to mingle] *mescolare.*

To shuffle the cards, *mescolare le carte.*

To shuffle one off, *disfarsi d' uno, levarselo d' attorno.*

To shuffle off a business, *tergiversare, barcollare in un negozio, trovar mezzi termini per non venire a termine d'un negozio.*

SHU'FFLECAP, s. [a play at which money is shaken in a hat] *giuoco che si fa scuotendo e dibattendo i danari nel cappello, chiamato in alcuni luoghi d' Italia* Cappelletto.

SHU'FFLED, adj. *mescolato, v.* To shuffle.

SHU'FFLER, s. *un furbo, un uomo doppio.*

SHU'FFLING, s. *mescolamento,* s. m. *il mescolare.*

The shuffling of cards, *il mescolar le carte.*

Shuffling, adj. ex. a shuffling fellow *un furbo, un briccone.*

SHU'FFLINGLY, adv. [with an irregular gait] *sconciamente, e dicesi del muoversi colla persona.*

To SHUN [to avoid] *evitare, scansare, sfuggire.*

SHU'NNED, adj. *evitato, scansato, sfuggito.*

To SHUNT [to shove] *spignere,* pret. *spinsi.*

SHUT, adj. *serrato, fermato.*

To get shut of one, *disfarsi d' uno, levarselo d' attorno.*

To get shut of a business, *liberarsi d' un negozio.*

To SHUT, verb act. *chiudere.*

To shut the door, *chiudere la porta.*

He shut the door upon me, *mi chiuse la porta in faccia.*

To shut in, *rinchiudere,* pret. *rinchiusi.*

To shut one out, *chiuder la porta dietro ad uno, non lasciarlo entrare.*

SHU'TTER, s. *finestra,* s. f.

SHU'TTING, s. *il chiudere.*

The shutting in of the day-light, *il far della sera, l' imbrunir della sera.*

SHU'TTLE, s. [an instrument used by weavers] *spola, spuola,* s. f.

A shuttle, or shuttle-headed fellow, *uno sciocco, un cionno, un minchione.*

SHY, adj. [reserved, coy] *peritoso, ritroso, schifo, contegnoso.*

She is very shy, *ella è molto contegnosa, ella fa molto la ritrosa.*

To look shy upon one, *guardar uno freddamente.*

He is very shy of me, *egli mi fugge, egli si nasconde da me.*

SHY'NESS, *v.* Shiness.

SI'BILANT, adj. [hissing] *che fischia, che sibila.*

SIBILAT'ION, s. [hissing sound] *sibilo, fischio,* s. m.

SI'BIL, s. [a virgin prophetess among the ancients] *sibilla,* s. f.

SI'CAMORE, s. *sicamoro,* s. m.

To SI'CCATE [to dry] *seccare, render secco.*

SICCA'TION, s. [the act of drying] *il seccare.*

SICCI'FICK, adj. [causing dryness] *che secca, che rende arido.*

SI'CCITY, s. [driness] *siccità, secchezza, aridità,* s. f.

SICE, s. [at dice, the number six] *due sei, al giuoco de' dadi.*

SICH, adj. *v.* Such. Obs.

SICK, adj. [indisposed in the body] *ammalato, indisposto, che non ista bene, infermo.*

A sick man, *un ammalato.*

A sick woman, *un' ammalata.*

To be sick of a thing, *essere svogliato o fastidito di qualche cosa.*

His fancy fell so sick upon it, *questo pensiero ne lo svogliò o infastidì talmente.*

To be sick of the simpleness [to be silly] *esser molto semplice.*

The sick, s. *gli ammalati, gli infermi.*

To SICK, } [to fall sick] *ammalarsi, divenire infermo, infermarsi.*
To SI'CKEN, }

To sicken [to make sick, to disease] *render amalato, cagionar morbo.*

To sicken [to weaken, to impair] *render debole, indebolire.*

SI'CKISH, adj. *che è un poco ammalato o indisposto.*

SI'CKLE, s. [a hook for reaping corn] *falce,* s. f.

SI'CKLEMAN, } s. [reaper] *falciatore, colui che falcia il fieno.*
S'ICKLER, }

SI'CKLINESS, s. *poca sanità.*

SI'CKLY, adj. [unhealthy] *malaticcio, infermiccio.*

Sickly weather, *un tempo malsano.*

To SI'CKLY [to make diseased, to taint with the hue of disease] *ammorbare, cagionar malattia o morbo.*

SI'CKNESS, s. [disease] *malattia, infermità,* s. f.

The green-sickness, itterizia, s. f. *malattia che procede da spargimento di fiele.*

The falling-sickness, *l' epilessia, il mal caduco, il mal maestro.*

The sickness, the great sickness [the plague] *la peste, il contagio.*

SIDE, s. *lato, canto, fianco,* s. m.

To have a pain in the side, *aver male, o un dolore nel fianco.*

To walk by one's side, *camminare a lato di qualcheduno.*

Side [part of any thing] *lato, banda, parte.*

On that side, *da quella banda.*

The right side of a stuff, *il diritto d'un panno, d' un drappo.*

On the other side, *dall' altra parte, dall' altra banda, dall' altro canto.*

On the other side of the river, *dall' altra banda del fiume, di là dal fiume.*

On this side the Tiber, *di quà del Tevere.*

On both sides, *dalle due bande.*

The side of a river, *la sponda d' un fiume.*

The sea-side, *il lito del mare.*

The side of a bed, *la sponda d' un letto.*

The side of a hill, *il pendio d' un colle.*

Side [party] *parte, fazione, setta,* s. m.

I am of neither side, *non sono dalla parte di nessuno, non sono per nessuno.*

To take one's side, *pigliar le parti, o la difesa di qualcheduno.*

Side [page] *facciata,* s. f.

To speak on one's side, *parlare in favore di qualcheduno.*

I give it on your side, *io sono per voi, io vi do ragione.*

The trial will go on his side, *egli guadagnerà la causa, o il processo.*

To beat one's sides, *battere, bastonare alcuno.*

Side-saddle, *sella da donna.*

The side-boards of a tub, *le doghe d' un tino.*

The side beams of a printer's press, *gli alberi d' un torchio.*

Side-board, *buffetto,* s m.

Side-face, *testa di profilo.*

Side-wind, *vento in fianco.*

To sail with a side-wind, *bordeggiare.*

Side-bow, *rovescione.*

Side-ways, side-wise, side-long, adv. *a traverso, in traverso, per traverso, a sghembo, obliquamente, biecamente.*

To side with one, *parteggiare, pigliar la parte d' uno, tener da uno.*

Side-lays, s. [is when the dogs are set in the way to be let slip at a deer as he passes by] *rilascio.*

SI'DELONG, adv. [a thwart, sloping] *a traverso, per traverso, obliquamente, a sghembo.*

SI'DER, s. [cider] *sidro,* s. m.

SI'DERAL, adj. [starry, astral] *distella, d' astro, sidereo, stellato, astrale.*

SIDERA'TION, s. [a sudden mortification, a blast, a sudden deprivation of sense] *l' improvviso assiderare; privazione repentina dell' uso de' sensi.*

SI'DESADDLE, s. [a woman's seat on horseback] *sella da donna.*

SI'DESMAN, s. [assistant to the churchwarden] *assistente del sacristano, sottosacristano.*

SI'DEWAYS, } adv. [laterally, on one
SI'DEWISE } side] *da canto, lateralmente, da' lati.*

To SI'DLE, adv. ex. to go sidle-sadle [to waddle] *andar barcollone, barcollare.*

SI'EGE, s. the encamping of an army before a place, in order to take it either by force or famine] *assedio,* s. m.

To lay the siege before a town, *metter l' assedio ad una città, assediarla.*

SIEVE, s. [a tool for separating the coarser part of any thing from the finer] *buratello, crivello, vaglio, staccio,* s. m.

Meal-sieve, *staccio.*

Sieve-maker, *stacciajo,* s. m. *colui che fa o vende gli stacci.*

Bolting-sieve, *frullone.*

To SIFT [to separate the finer part of any thing pulverised by a sieve] *crivellare, stacciare, vagliare, cernere.*

To sift one, *scalzare uno, cavare altrui di bocca artatamente quello che si vorrebbe sapere, toccargli il polso.*

To sift a business, *discutere, esaminare, considerar sottilmente un negozio.*

To sift out a thing, *procurar di scoprire, penetrare o sapere che che sia.*

SI'FTED, adj. *crivellato, stacciato, vagliato,* v. To sift.

SI'FTER, s. *vagliatore,* s. m.

SI'FTING, s. *crivellare o stacciare.*

A sifting out, *esatta inchiesta.*

SI'FTINGS [that which is sifted out] *vagliatura, stacciatura,* s. f. *crusca,* s. f.

SICH, s. *sospiro,* s. m.

To fetch a sigh, *fare un sospiro, sospirare.*

To SIGH, verb neut. *sospirare.*

SI'GHING, s. *sospiro.*

Sighing, adj. *sospiroso.*

Sighing lover, *amante che sospira.*

SI'GHT, s. [the sense of seeing] *vista,* s. f. *uno de' cinque sensi.*

Sight, s. [the act or faculty of seeing] *vista, visione.*

Sight [the organs of the sight, the eyes] *la vista, gli occhi.*

Pleasant to the sight, *grato alla vista, agli occhi, al vedere.*

To lose sight of a thing [to see it no more] *perder che che sia di vista.*

Death is before my sight, *la morte è avanti gli occhi miei.*

In the sight of the whole world, *in presenza d' ognuno.*

To pay a bill of exchange at sight, *pagare una lettera di cambio a vista.*

To know one by sight, *conoscer alcuno di vista.*

Sight [shew] *vista, spettacolo, cosa notabile a vedere.*

The sight-hole of a cross-bow, or the sight of a gun, *la mira d' una balestra, o dell' archibuso.*

To come in sight, *apparire, farsi vedere,* pres. *apparisco,* pret. *apparvi.*

He never comes in my sight, *non lo vedo mai.*

I was never out of his sight, *non m' ha giammai perso di vista.*

At the first sight, *a prima vista, subito.*

Get you out of my sight, *sfrattate di qui, levatevi di qui, toglietemivi d' innanzi.*

To vanish out of sight, *svanire, sparire,* pres. *svanisco, sparisco.*

To have a thing in sight [to aim at it] *aver la mira a qualche cosa, volger il pensiero a qualche cosa.*

SI'GHTED, adj. ex. quick sighted, *perspicace, d' acuta vista.*

Quick-sighted [quick-witted] *perspicace, accorto, astuto, penetrante.*

Short-sighted, *di corta vista.*

Dim-sighted, *di poca vista e torbida.*

SI'GHTLESS, adj. [blind] *cieco.*

SI'GHTLY, adj. [handsome] *vistoso, di bella presenza.*

SI'GIL, s. [seal] *sigillo.*

SIGN [token, mark] *segno, cenno, contrassegno, indizio,* s. m.

To make signs to one, *far segno o cenno ad uno.*

Sign [foot-step] *traccia, pedata, orma,* s. f. *vestigio,* s. m.

The sign of the cross, *il segno della croce.*

Sign over a shop or door, *insegna,* s. f. *segno,* s. m.

The twelve signs of the zodiack, *i dodici segni del zodiaco.*

Sign manual, *segno, segnatura.*

To SIGN [to put a seal, or set a name or mark to any deed or writing] *segnare, mettere il segno, il suo nome, imprimere il suo suggello a qualche scrittura.*

To sign a letter, *sottoscrivere una lettera.*

To sign [to make signs] *accennare, far cenno, far segno.*

SI'GNAL, adj [notable, remarkable] *segnalato, egregio, illustre, nobile, eccellente, notabile.*

Signal, s. [sign or token given for the doing of a thing] *segnale, segno, contrassegno,* s. m.

To give the signal for the fight, *dare il segnale per la battaglia.*

SIGNA'LITY, s. [quality of something remarkable or memorable] *qualità d' uomo segnalato.*

T SI'GNALIZE, [to make famous by some notable action] *segnalare, render famoso, far segnalato.*

To signalize one's self, *segnalarsi.*

SI'GNALIZED, adj. *segnalato.*

SI'GNALLY, adv. [eminently, remarkably, memorably] *segnalatamente.*

SIGNA'TION, s. [sign given] *segno, segnale,* s. m.

SI'GNATURE, s. [the hand or mark set to a writing] *segnatura, segno, mano.*

Signature [among printers, the letters of the alphabet they set at the bottom of every printed sheet, as A, B, C, &c.] *segnatura, le lettere dell' alfabeto che gli stampatori mettono al margine di sotto d' ogni foglio stampato.*

SI'GNED, adj. *segnato.*

A blank signed, *un bianco segnato.*

SI'GNET, s. [a seal set in a ring] *suggello,* s. m.

The King's signet, *il suggello del Re.*

The privy signet [one of the King's seals with which his private letters are signed] *il suggello privato del Re.*

SIGNI'FICANCY, s. [the state of being significant] *significanza, importanza,* s. f.

SIGNI'FICANT, adj. [that expresses much, effectual, expressive] *significante, significativo, espressivo, enfatico, che esprime molto.*

SIGNIFICA'TION, s. [meaning] *significazione, significanza,* s. f. *senso,* s. m.

SIGNI'FICANTLY, adv. [with force of expression] *significantemente, con molta forza d' espressione.*

SIGNIFICA'TOR, s. [a planet which signifies something remarkable in nativities] *significatore,* s. m. *termine astrologico.*

To SI'GNIFY [to mean, to imply a certain sense] *significatore, esprimere, inferire,* pres. *inferisco.*

To signify [to notify, to give notice of] *significare, fare intendere, mandare a dire, avvisare.*

To signify [to presage, to be a sign of] *significare, denotare, presagire, notare, esser segno di qualche cosa.*

SI'GNIFIED, adj. *significato, espresso, inferito,* v. To signify.

SI'GNIFYING, s. *significamento,* s. m. *significazione,* s. f. *il significare.*

SI'GNING, *il segnare.*

To SIKE [to sigh] *sospirare.*

SI'KER, adj. [sure] *sicuro, certo.*

SI'KERLY, adv. *sicuramente, certamente.*

SI'KERNESS, s. [security] *sicurezza, certezza,* s. f.

SI'LENCE, s. [cessation of noise or speaking] *silenzio,* s m. *taciturnità,* s. f. *lo star cheto, il non parlare.*

Silence here, *silenzio, zitto.*

To break silence, *rompere il silenzio, cominciare a parlare.*

To put one to silence, *imporre silenzio ad uno, farlo tacere.*

To SI'LENCE [to impose or command silence] *imporre silenzio, far fare silenzio, far tacere.*

I silenced him, *lo feci tacere, lo confusi.*

To silence a church-minister, *sospendere, interdire un prete.*

To

To ſilence the play-houſe, *interdire la commedia.*

SI'LENCED, adj. *a chi è ſtato impoſto ſilenzio, ſoſpeſo, interdetto.*

SI'LENT, adj. [that holds his peace] *taciturno, cheto, che ſi tace, ſilente, tacito.*

Be ſilent, *tacete.*

Silent [huſht, peaceful] *taciturno, cheto, tranquillo, tacito, ſilente.*

By ſilent ſteps [inſenſibly] *inſenſibilmente, impercettibilmente, pian piano, a poco a poco.*

SILE'NTIARY, s. [a gentleman-uſher, who takes care that good order and ſilence be kept at court [*ufficiale di corte che ha la cura di far fare ſilenzio.*

SI'LENTLY, adv. [without noiſe] *tacitamente, pianpiano, ſenza ſtrepito.*

SILI'CIOUS, adj. [made of hair] *di cilicio, fatte di peli.*

SILI'CULOSE, adj. [huſky, full of huſk] *pien di ſilique, pien di baccelli, baccelluto.*

SI'LIQUA, s. [a carat, of which ſix make a ſcruple] *ſei ſcrupoli.*

Siliqua the ſeed-veſſel, huſk, cod, or ſhell of ſuch plants as are of the pulſe kind] *ſiliqua,* s. f. *baccello,* s. m.

SI'LIQUOSE, SI'LIQUOUS, } adj. *baccelluto.*

SILK, s. *ſeta,* s. f.

Raw or wrought ſilk, *ſeta cruda.*

Silk-ſtockings, *calzette di ſeta.*

Silk or ſilk ſtuff, *drappo o drappo di ſeta.*

Silks, ſilk-wares, *drapperia, mercanzie di ſeta.*

A ſilk-man, *un ſetajuolo, mercante di drappi di ſeta, o di ſete.*

Silk-weaver, *facitor di drappi.*

Silk-throwſters, *torcitori di ſeta.*

Silk-dyer, *tintore di ſeta.*

Silk-worm, *baco, vermicello che fa la ſeta.*

SI'LKEN, adj. [of ſilk] *di ſeta, ſetàceo.*

SILL, s. [threſhold] *limitare,* s. m. *ſoglia dell' uſcio.*

SI'LLABUB, SI'LLIBUB, } s. [a potable, made with milk, cyder, ſugar, ſpice, &c.] *mangiaretto che ſi fa col latte, vin dolce, e altri ingredienti e ſpezierie, e ſi mangia a belle curchiajate.*

SI'LLILY, adv. *ſcioccamente, goffamente.*

SI'LLINESS, s. *ſciocchezza, ſtoltizia, pazzia, goffaggine, gofferia, goffezza,* s. f.

SI'LLY, adj. [ſimple, fooliſh] *ſciocco, goffo, inetto, ſcimunito, ſtolto, cionno, ſemplice.*

A ſilly man, *uno ſciocco, un cionno, un minchione.*

A ſilly woman, *una ſciocca, una goffa.*

Silly thing, *ſchiocchezza, ſcempiaggine.*

SI'LVER, s. [a ſort of metal] *argento,* s. m.

Quick-ſilver [mercury] *argento vivo, mercurio.*

Silver [ſilver coin] *argento, moneta d' argento.*

Silver wire, *argento filato.*

To do a thing over with ſilver, *inargentare che che ſia, coprir con foglia d' argento.*

Silver-foam, *ſchiuma d' argento.*

Silver-buſh [a plant] *ſpezie di pianta, detta in Latino* Barba Jovis, *barba di Giove.*

Silver-thiſtle [a plant] *brancorſina,* s. f. *ſpezie di pianta.*

Silver-ſmith, *argentiere, orefire, orafo,* s. m.

Silver mine, *miniera d' argento.*

A ſilver-hilted ſword, *una ſpada con guardia d' argento.*

Silver lace, *gallone d' argento.*

Silver-ſpoon, *cucchiajo d' argento.*

Silver-weed [white tanſy] *argentina,* s. f. *ſorta di pianta.*

Of the colour of ſilver, *argentino, di color d' argento.*

Like ſilver, *argentale, ſimile all' argento.*

To SI'LVER over, *inargentare.*

He that ſilvers over, *inargentatore,* s. m.

SI'LVERED over, adj. *argentato, inargentato.*

SI'LVERLY, adv. [with the appearance of ſilver] *argentinamente.*

SI'LVERY, adj. [beſprinkled with ſilver] *ſparſo d' argento; argenteo.*

SI'MAR, s. [a woman's robe] *zimarra, veſte lunga da donna.*

SI'MILAR, adj. [of like nature] *omogeneo, della medeſima natura, ſomigliante.*

SI'MILE, s. [ſimilitude, parable] *ſimilitudine, ſimiglianza, comparazione, parabola,* s. f.

Simile [example] *eſempio,* s. m.

SI'MILITUDE, s. [compariſon] *ſimilitudine, comparazione, ſimiglianza,* s. f.

SIMILITU'DINARY, adj. [belonging to, or expreſſed by way of ſimilitude] *di ſimilitudine, che s' eſprime con qualche ſimilitudine.*

SI'MITAR, s. [a ſort of broad ſword] *ſcimitarra,* s. f.

SI'MNEL, s. [cake or bun made of fine flower] *una ciambella, chicca.*

SIMONI'ACAL, adj. [done by ſimony] *ſimoniale, ſimoniaco.*

SIMONI'ACALLY, adv. *per ſimonia.*

SI'MONIACK, SI'MONIST, } s. [one guilty of ſimony] *un ſimoniaco, che fa ſimonia.*

SI'MONY, s. [the buying and ſelling of church livings, or other ſpiritual things for money] *ſimonia,* s. f. *mercanzia delle coſe ſacre e ſpirituali.*

To commit ſimony, *ſimoneggiare, far ſimonia.*

SI'MPER, s. [ſmile, generally a fooliſh ſmile] *ſorriſo, e s' intende per lo più del ſorridere degli ſciocchi o de' ſemplici.*

To SI'MPER [to ſmile or look pleaſantly] *ſorridere,* pret. *ſorriſi.*

To ſimper at one [to look pleaſantly at him] *ſorridere a qualcheduno, riguardarlo con viſo lieto.*

To ſimper [to begin to boil as the pot does] *grillare, principiare a bollire.*

SI'MPERING, s. *ſorriſo,* s. m.

SI'MPLE, adj. [not compound] *ſemplice, puro; ſenza miſtura.*

Simple [ſingle, not double] *ſemplice, ſcempio, contrario di doppio.*

Simple [innocent, harmleſs] *ſemplice, ingenuo, innocente, ſenza malizia, puro, ſchietto.*

Simple [ſilly, fooliſh] *ſemplice, ſciocco, ineſperto, ſoro, goffo.*

Simple thing, *ſciocchezza, beſſaggine, ſcipitezza, babbuaſſaggine,* s. f.

A ſimple fellow, *un ſemplicione, uno ſciocco, un beſſo, un cionno, un lavaceci, un bue.*

The ſimple, s. [the weak ſort of people] *i ſemplici.*

SI'MPLENESS, s. [ſillineſs] *ſemplicità, ſemplicezza, beſſaggine, ſciocchezza,* s. f.

SI'MPLER, SI'MPLIST, } s. [one who has ſkill in, or a gatherer of ſimples] *ſempliciſta, botanico,* s. m. *quello, che conoſce la virtù dell' erbe dette ſemplici e le cuſtodiſce.*

SI'MPLES, s. pl. [phyſical herbs] *ſemplici, erbe che communemente s' uſan per medicina.*

SI'MPLETON, s. [a ſilly half-witted perſon] *un ſemplicione, un ſempliciotto, uno ſciocco, un ſoro, un cionno, un beſſo, un balordo.*

Simpleton [ſilly woman] *una ſemplicetta, una ſciocca.*

SIMPLI'CITY, s. [plainneſs, downright honeſty] *ſemplicità, ſchiettezza, purità, ingenuità,* s. f.

Simplicity [ſillineſs] *ſemplicità, ineſperienza, ſciocchezza, beſſaggine,* s. f.

SI'MPLING, adj. ex. [to go a ſimpling or gathering of ſimples] *andar cogliendo ſemplici.*

SI'MPLIST, *v.* Simpler.

SI'MPLY, adv. [ſillily] *ſemplicimente, ſciocamente.*

He looks ſimply upon it, *pare tutto confuſo, ſembra fuor di ſe ſteſſo.*

SI'MPTON, s. [a plant] *ſena,* s. f. *erba medicinale.*

SI'MULACRE, s. [image] *ſimulacro,* s. m. *ſtatua,* s. f.

SI'MULAR, s. [one that counterfeits] *ſimulatore, colui che ſimula o contraffà.*

SIMULA'TION, s. [the act of diſſembling] *ſimulazione,* s. f. *il ſimulare.*

To SI'MULATE [to diſſemble, to feign] *ſimulare, moſtrare il contrario di quello che ſi ha nell' animo.*

SIMULTA'NEOUS, adj. acting together; exiſting at the ſame time] *che opera inſieme; eſiſtente nello ſteſſo tempo.*

SIN, s. [offence, tranſgreſſion] *peccato, delitto,* s. m. *colpa,* s. f.

Sin [fault, crime] *peccato, fallo, difetto, mancamento,* s. m.

To commit a ſin, *commettere un peccato.*

To SIN [to tranſgreſs againſt God's law] *peccare, commettere peccato, traſgredire la legge di Dio.*

To ſin [to commit a fault] *peccare, errare, fallire,* pref. *falliſco.*

SI'NAPISM, s. [an outward medicine of muſtard-ſeed, to raiſe bliſters] *ſenapiſmo,* s. m. *ſorta d' impiaſtro nel quale entra la ſenapa.*

SINCE, prep. and adv. [from that time] *di poi, dopo.*

Since his death, *dopo la ſua morte.*

Since the beginning of the world, *ſin dal principio del mondo.*

That happened ſince, *cio accadde dopo, o dopo quel tempo.*

Some days ſince, *dopo non molti giorni.*

How long ſince was it done? *quanto tempo è che queſto è fatto?*

How long is it ſince? *quanto tempo è?*

Long ſince [long ago] *molto tempo fa, un pezzo fa.*

Not long ſince, *non è lungo tempo, ultimamente, poco fa, non ha guari.*

A while ſince, *poco fa.*

Many years ſince, *molti anni ſono.*

He died two years ſince, *ſono due anni che è morto.*

Is it not four days ſince? *non ſono quattro giorni?*

Since [ſeeing that] *poichè, poſciachè.*

Since it is ſo, *poichè è così.*

SINCE'RE, adj. [true, honeſt] *ſincero, puro, ſchietto, vero, franco, non finto.*

SINCE'RELY, adv. *ſinceramente, puramente, ſchiettamente, francamente.*

SINCE'RENESS, } s. [uprightneſs]
SINCE'RITY, } *ſincerità, purità, ſchiettezza, franchezza, integrità,* s. f.

To SINDGE, *abbruſtiare, abbronzare, leggermente avvampare, mettere alquanto alla fiamma li uccelli pelati per tor via quella peluria che rimane loro.* v. To ſinge.

To ſindge a capon, *abbruſtiare un cappone.*

SI'NDGED, adj. *abbruſtiato, abbronzato.*

SI'NDON, s. [a fold, a wrapper] *ſindone, panno da involgervi dentro che che ſia.*

SINE, s. [a right *ſine,* in geometry, is a right line drawn from one end of an arch perpendicularly upon the diameter drawn from the other end of that arch] *nome di una certa linea geometrica.*

SI'NE-CURE, s. [a benefice without cure of ſouls] *beneficio ſemplice, che non ha cura d' anime.*

SI'NEW, s. [nerve] *nervo,* s. m.

Money is the ſinew of war, *il danaro è il nervo della guerra.*

To SINEW [to knit as by ſinews] *unire, congiungere fortemente inſieme. E' vocabulo non uſato.*

SI'NEWY, adj. *nervoſo, nerboruto, forte.*

SI'NFUL, adj. [from ſin] *criminale, vizioſo, peccaminoſo, corrotto.*

Sinful actions, *azioni peccaminoſe.*

A ſinful nation, *una nazione corrotta, un popolo corrotto.*

Sinful pleaſures, *piaceri criminali.*

A ſinful man, *un peccatore.*

A ſinful woman, *una peccatrice.*

SI'NFULLY, adv. ex. to live ſinfully, *viver nel peccato, menare una vita peccaminoſa.*

SI'NFULNESS, s. *peccato,* s. m. *corruzione,* s. f.

To SING [to make melody with the voice] *cantare.*

To ſing an air, *cantare un' aria.*

To ſing [a poetical expreſſion for to praiſe] *cantare, poetare, lodare, celebrare, publicar le lodi.*

To SINGE, *malamente ſcritto da alcuni,* to ſindge [to ſcorch, to burn lightly or ſuperficially] *abbruciare leggermente, ardere a malapena la ſuperficie.*

SI'NGED, adj. [ſcorched, lightly or ſuperficially burnt] *leggermente arſo, a malapena abbruciato.*

SI'NGER, s. [he or ſhe that ſings] *cantatore, cantante, cantatrice.*

SI'NGING, s. *canto,* s. m. *il cantare.*

The ſinging of birds, *il canto degli uccelli.*

Singing [vocal muſick] *muſica di voce, concento, armonia.*

Singing, adj. *cantante.*

A ſinging man, *un cantante.*

A ſinging boy, *un zago.*

Singing maſter, s. [one who teaches to ſing] *uno che inſegna l' arte del cantare.*

SI'NGLE, adj. [ſimple, alone] *ſemplice, ſolo.*

A ſingle game, *una ſemplice partita.*

A ſingle man, *uno ſcapolo, uno ſmogliato.*

A ſingle woman, *una zitella, una donna non maritata, una giovane nubile.*

Single life, *celibato, la vita d' uno ſcapolo, o d' una donna nubile.*

To live a ſingle life, *viver nel celibato.*

Single combat [duel] *un duello.*

Single-hearted man, *uomo ſincero, oneſto, ſchietto, franco.*

Single, s. [the tail of a deer] *la coda d' un cervo.*

To SI'NGLE, } [to pick out, to ſet a-
To ſingle out, } part] *ſeparare, ſceverare, ſegnare.*

To ſingle out a deer, *ſegnare un cervo.*

SI'NGLED, adj. *ſeparato, ſceverato, ſegnato.*

SI'NGLENESS, s. *ſemplicità, purità, ſchiettezza, ingenuità; franchezza,* s. f.

SI'NGLY, adv. [one by one] *ad uno ad uno, l' un dopo l' altro, ſeparatamente.*

SI'NGULAR, adj. [in oppoſition to plural] *ſingolare.*

The ſingular number, *il numero ſingolare, il numero del meno.*

Singular [ſpecial, particular] *ſingolare, ſpeciale, particolare.*

Singular [rare, excellent] *ſingolare, eccellente, raro, unico.*

Singular [particular, odd, that affects ſingularity] *ſingolare, particolare, bizzarro, fantaſtico, che affetta di diſtinguerſi dagli altri.*

The ſingular, s. [or the ſingular number] *il numero ſingolare, o il numero del meno.*

SINGULA'RITY, s. [in oppoſition to plurality] *ſingolarità, il contrario di pluralità, particolarità.*

Singularity [uncommonneſs, excellence] *ſingolarità, rarità, eccellenza.*

Singularity [a particular way, affectedneſs] *ſingolarità, affettazione,* s. f. *azione per la quale uno vuol parere migliore delli altri.*

SI'NGULARLY, adv. [in a ſingular manner] *ſingolarmente, particolarmente, con ſingolarità.*

SI'NGULT, s. [a ſigh] *ſingulto, ſinghiozzo di dolore.*

SI'NISTER, adj. [diſhoneſt, unjuſt, unlawful] *diſoneſto, ingiuſto, cattivo, illegitimo, iniquo.*

Siniſter [ill] *maligno, malizioſo.*

Siniſter [unlucky, unfortunate] *ſiniſtro, infelice, funeſto, fatale.*

SINI'STROUS, adj. [abſurd, perverſe, wrong-headed] *aſſurdo, maligno, perverſo, che ha la mente a rovescio, capone, oſtinato.*

SINI'STROUSLY, adv. *ſiniſtramente, malamente.*

SINK, s. [to drain waters off a kitchen] *ſentina,* s. f.

Sink [to waſh diſhes in] *lavatojo,* s. m.

Common-ſink [common-ſewer] *cloaca, fogna.*

The ſink of a ſhip, *la ſentina d' un vaſcello.*

To SINK [to plunge under water] *affondare, mandare a fondo, ſommergere,* pret. *ſommerſi.*

To ſink [to go to the bottom] *ſprofondare, affondare, andare a fondo, ſommergerſi.*

To ſink a ſhip, *affondare, mandare a fondo un vaſcello.*

To ſink [to deſtroy, to undo] *diſtruggere, disfare, mandar a male, conare.*

To ſink [to keep part of a ſum of money] *guardare, cuſtodire parte d' una ſomma di danari.*

Eyes ſunk in one's head, *occhi incavernati.*

This paper ſinks [the ink ſinks through this paper] *queſta carta bee l' inchioſtro.*

His courage ſinks [his courage fails] *il coraggio gli manca, ſi perde d' animo.*

To ſink in ſorrow, *laſciarſi opprimere o vincere dal dolore, darſi in preda al dolore, abandonarſi al dolore, ſoccombere a' mali.*

To ſink into one's mind [to make an im-

impression] *scolpire, imprimere nell' altrui memoria, fare impressione.*

To sink [to perish, to be undone] *perire, perdersi.*

I had rather sink, *perirei più tosto.*

SI'NKING, s. *l' affondare, v.* To sink.

Sinking, adj. *che bee.*

Sinking paper, *carta che bee l' inchiostro.*

SI'NLESS, adj. [exempt from sin] *che non ha alcun peccato, immaculato, senza peccaminosa macchia.*

SI'NLESSNESS, s. [exemption from sin] *impeccabilità, esenzione da peccato.*

SI'NNED, *è un preterito del verbo.* To sin.

SI'NNER, s. *peccatore, s. m. peccatrice, s. f.*

SI'NNING, s. *il peccare.*

SI'NNET, s. [a line made of rope-yarn] *funicella, s. f.*

SIN-O'FFERING, s. [expiation or sacrifice for sin] *sacrificio o offerta fatta in espiazione di peccato.*

SI'NOPER, } s. [a mineral commonly
SI'NOPLE, } called ruddle, or red-lead, used by painters for a deep red or purple colour] *sinopia, senopia, s. f. spezie di terra di color rosso.*

SINUO'SITY, s. [the state of being full of turnings and windings] *sinuosità, s. f. seno, s. m.*

SI'NUOUS, adj. [full of turnings and windings] *sinuoso, che ha seno, che fa seno.*

SI'NUS, s. [a gulf or large bay] *seno, luogo stretto, golfo, s. m.*

SIP, s. [a small draught] *sorso, centellino, s. m.*

I had but two little sips, *non ne ho bevuto che due sorsi.*

A little sip, *un sorsetto, un sorsettino.*

To SIP [to drink but a little at a time] *bere a sorsi.*

SI'PPER, s. *colui che beve a piccoli sorsi, bevitorello.*

SI'PPET, s. [small slice of bread] *fetticella di pane.*

SI'QUIS, s. [a paper or bill set up in some open place to proclaim any thing that is lost] *cartello, s. m.*

SIR, s. [speaking to the king] *sire, titolo di maestà.*

Sir [a title of honour for a gentleman] *signore.*

Sir [before a christian name, is a proper title for a knight] SIR, *quando è accompagnato con nome di battesimo, è titolo cavalleresco, equivalente al titolo di cavaliere.*

Sir John Norris, *il Cavaliere Giovanni Norris.*

SIRE, s. [father] *padre.*

Grand-sire, *avolo.*

SI'REN, s. [mermaid] *sirena, s. f. ninfa del mare.*

SI'RINGE, *v.* Syringe.

SI'RIUS, s. [the dogstar] *sirio, la canicola.*

SI'RNAME, *v.* Surname.

SIRO'CCO, s. [the south-east or Syrian wind] *scirocco, scilocco, vento che spira tra occidente e mezzogiorno, e che viene dalle parti di Soria o Assiria.*

SI'RRAH, *termine di disprezzo o d' ingiuria, che vuol dire appresso poco, briccone, furfante, baroncello.*

SI'RROP, } s. *sciroppo, s. m.*
SI'RRUP, }

SI'RRUPED, adj. [sweet like sirrup, bedewed with sweets] *dolce come lo sciroppo.*

SI'RRUPY, adj. [resembling sirrup] *che s' assomiglia allo sciroppo.*

SI'SKIN, s. [a green finch, a bird] *lucherino, s. m. uccelletto di penne verdi e gialle.*

SI'STER, s. *sorella, sirocchia, suora, s f.*

Sister-in-law, *cognata.*

The nine-sisters ['the sacred nine, the nine muses] *le nove sorelle, le muse.*

SI'STERHOOD, s. *qualità, o grado di sorella.*

Sisterhood [a set of sisters] *un gruppo di sorelle.*

Sisterhood [a number of women of the same order] *un numero di donne che sieguono lo stesso ordine, li stessi statuti, le stesse regole.*

SI'STERLY, adj. [becoming a sister, like a sister] *sorellesco, sirocchievole.*

SI'STRUM, s. [a kind of musical instrument] *sistro, s. m. strumento musicale da corde.*

To SIT [to repose upon a seat] *sedere, stare a sedere, stare assiso, sedersi.*

To sit at table, *sedersi a tavola.*

To sit fast on horseback, *star fermo a cavallo.*

To sit in the sun, *stare al sole.*

Which way does the wind sit? *in che parte è il vento? da che parte viene il vento?*

A hen that sits upon the eggs, *una gallina che cova.*

To sit [to be assembled] *adunarsi, radunarsi.*

When will the parliament sit? *quando s' adunerà il parlamento?*

To sit waiting for one, *aspettare qualcheduno.*

To sit drinking, *passar il tempo a bere.*

To sit still [not to stir] *star fermo, non muoversi.*

Sit you still, *non vi movete.*

To sit still [to be idle] *stare ozioso, star con le mani a cintola.*

To sit at work, *lavorare.*

He sits at his work from morning till night, *egli lavora dalla mattina alla sera.*

To sit airing one's self under a tree, *prender il fresco sotto un albero.*

To sit for one's picture, *farsi dipignere, farsi fare il ritratto.*

To sit close to one's work, *lavorare assiduamente, applicarsi al suo lavoro.*

A coat that sits close to the body, *un abito attillato, un abito che va bene alla vita.*

This coat does not sit close enough, *questo abito è troppo largo.*

It sits too close, *è troppo stretto.*

A coat that sits well, *un abito attillato, ben fatto.*

That does not sit well, *mal fatto.*

To sit up at night, *vegliare, stare in piedi tutta la notte.*

To sit up with a sick body [to watch a sick person] *far la guardia ad un ammalato.*

To sit up the whole night at play, *passar la notte al giuoco, giuocare tutta notte.*

To sit up at work, *lavorar di notte.*

To sit up in one's bed, *sedersi, tenersi assiso sul letto.*

To sit up [to rise] *levarsi, levarsi in piedi.*

The doctors sate upon him, *i medici fecero consulta sulla sua malattia.*

To sit upon one, or upon a thing [to sit as a judge] *giudicare alcuno, o qualche cosa.*

The coroner sat upon the dead body, *i commissari hanno visitato il corpo morto.*

To sit down, *sedersi.*

Sit you down, *sedetevi, accomodatevi.*

To sit down at table, *sedere, o mettersi a tavola.*

To sit down before a place [to lay siege to a place] *assediare un luogo, metter l' assedio ad una piazza.*

SITE, s. [situation] *sito, s. m. situazione, s. f.*

SITH, conj. [for since] *poichè, posciachè.* Obs.

Sithe, s. [a tool to mow with] *falce, s. f.*

SI'THENCE, adv. *lo stesso che* since. Obsolete.

SI'TTER, s. [that sits] *uno che sta a sedere.*

Sitter [a bird that broods] *un uccello che cova.*

SI'TTING, s. *il sedere.*

Sitting [session of an assembly] *sessione, s. f.*

Sitting of the parliament, *sessione del parlamento.*

The sitting of the states, *l' assemblea degli stati.*

I lost fifty crowns in two sittings, *ho perduto cinquanta scudi in due volte.*

A sitting place, *un seggio, un luogo comodo per sedere.*

SI'TUATE, } adj. *situato, collocato.*
SI'TUATED, }

SITUA'TION, s. [site] *sito, s. m. situazione, s. f.*

The situation of a town, *la situazione d' una città, il sito d' una città.*

SIVE, *v.* Sieve.

SI'VET, *v.* Civet.

SI'VIL, adj. [a Seville orange] *un melangolo di Siviglia, un melangolo agro.*

SIX, adj. *sei.*

Six-hundred, *secento, nome numerale che contiene sei centinaja.*

Six-thousand, *semila, seimila.*

At sixes and sevens [at random,

 with-

without any order] *in abbandono, in confusione, in disordine.*

To leave all at sixes and sevens, *lasciare ogni cosa in abbandono, in confusione, in disordine.*

SIXTE'EN, *sedici.*

SIXTE'ENTH, *sedicesimo.*

A sixteenth [a sixteenth part] *una sedicesima parte.*

SIXTH, adj. *sesto.*

A sixth [in musick] *una sesta, termine musicale.*

SI'XTIETH, adj. *sessantesimo.*

SI'XTHLY, adv. *in sesto luogo.*

SI'XTY, adj. *sessanta.*

SI'ZEABLE, adj. [of a good size] *d' una buona grandezza, assai grande, ben proporzionato, di giusta proporzione.*

SIZE, s. [proportion, measure] *misura, grandezza, statura, grossezza, lunghezza, proporzione,* s. f.

My shoes must be of this size, *bisogna che le mie scarpe sieno di questa grandezza.*

These are of too large a size, *queste sono troppo grandi.*

A middle-sized man, *un uomo di mezzana statura.*

The size of the paper, *la grandezza della carta.*

What size are your shoes of? *di quanti punti sono le vostre scarpe?*

Size [a shoemaker's measure] *misura di calzolajo.*

A leg all of a size [an ill shaped leg] *un gamba di fuso, una gamba mal fatta.*

Size [a sort of paste used by shoemakers] *colla di calzolajo.*

Size [whiting] *latte di calcina per imbiancare i muri.*

To SIZE [to measure] *misurare.*

To size a wall [to wash it first in order to white it] *lavare un muro per imbiancarlo.*

To size [as taylors do seams] *incerare, termine di sartore.*

To size [in Cambridge, to score, as students do in the buttery-book; which at Oxford is called to battle] *scrivere nel libro delle spese quello che uno studente prende per il suo mantenimento, come pane, birra, butirro, e simili.*

To size the pieces for coining, *aggiustare la moneta col peso.*

SI'ZED, adj *misurato.*

SIZEABLE, adj. [reasonably bulky] *di conveniente grandezza, proporzionatamente grande*

SI'ZER, s. [at Cambridge, as servitor in Oxford] *un povero scolare che serve gli altri.*

SI'ZERS, s. [scissars] *forbici, cesoje.*

SI'ZIEME, s. [a sequence of six cards at the game of picket] *sesta, seguenza di sei carte al giuoco di picchetto*

SI'ZINESS, s. [glutinousness, viscosity] *viscosità, qualità appiccaticcia.*

SI'ZY, adj. [viscous, glutinous] *viscoso, appiccaticcio.*

SKA'DDLE, s. [hurt, damage] *danno, male, pregiudizio.*

SKA'DDONS, s. [the embrios of the bees] *gli embrioni delle pecchie.*

SKAIN, s. [a length of thread or yarn it is wound on the reel] *matassa,* s. f.

A skain of thread, *una matassa di refe.*

SKA'INSMATE, s. [messmate] *compagno di tinello, colui che mangia con un altro.*

To SKATCH, to stop [a wheel, by putting a stone or piece of wood under it] *appuntellare una ruota.*

SKATE, *v.* Scate.

SKE'GGER, s. [a kind of small salmon] *spezie di salmone.*

SKE'LETON, s. [the dry bones of a man or woman] *scheletro, carcame,* s. m. *tutte l' ossa d' un uomo o d' una donna tenute insieme da' nervi e scosse di carne.*

SKE'LLET, } s. [a small vessel for
SKI'LLET, } boiling] *pajuolo.*

SKE'LLUM, s. [a Dutch word, a rogue] *furfante, briccone.*

SKEP, s. [a vessel to put corn in] *vaso composto di cordoni di paglia per tenervi entro biade.*

SKETCH, *schizzo, abbozzo,* s. m.

To SKETCH, *schizzare, abbozzare, disegnare alla grossa, far il primo disegno.*

SKEW, *v.* Skue.

SKEW'ER, s. [a long slender wooden pin such as butchers use] *brocco, stecco,* s. m.

SKEIN, s. [an Irish short sword] *spezie di spada Irlandese.*

To SKID a wheel [to stop it at the descent of a hill] *incatenare o legare una ruota d' una carrozza o carro in luogo scosceso per far che non rotoli con troppa velocità.*

SKIE, *v.* Sky.

SKIFF, s. [a shallop, the lesser of the two ship boats] *schifo, palischelmo,* s. m.

SKI'LFUL, adj. [that has skill or is well versed in] *saccente, dotto, esperto, intendente, sperimentato, perito, scienziato, versato, pratico.*

SKI'LFULLY, adv. *dottamente, espertamente, saviamente.*

SKI'LL, s. [capacity, knowledge, experience] *perizia, esperienza, maestria, idoneità, sufficienza, arte, scienza, capacità, pratica,* s. f. *sapere, scaltrimento,* s. m.

To have skill in any thing, *intendersi di qualche cosa, avere sperienza, esser versato o pratico in qualche cosa.*

He has skill in all languages, *egli è versato in tutte le lingue.*

I have no skill in horses, *io non m' intendo di cavalli.*

He has great skill in mathematicks, *egli è molto intendente nella matematica, o nelle matematiche.*

It is past my skill, *queste non son cose della mia portata.*

To try one's skill [to give a trial of one's skill] *dar pruova del suo sapere.*

SKILLED, *v.* Skilful.

SKI'LLESS, adj. [wanting art] *ignorante, privo di cervello, privo d' arte, privo d' invenzione, senza garbo.*

Skillet, s. [kettle, boiler] *caldaja piccola.*

It SKILLETH, *importa,* it skilleth me, *egli m' importa;* Obs.

To SKIM [to scum] *schiumare, levare, tor via la schiuma.*

To skim, *toccare a malapena.*

To skim a thing over [to pass it over slightly] *scorrere, leggere, o trattare leggiermente una materia.*

SKIMBLE-SCAMBLE, adj [wandering, wild] *errante, vagante, impazzato.*

SKIMMED, adj. *schiumato, v.* To skim.

SKI'MMER, s. a shallow vessel with which the scum is taken off] *schiumatoja, romajuolo bucato che serve a togliere la schiuma di checchessia.*

SKIN, s. [the hide of an animal] *pelle,* s. f. *cuojo,* s. m.

A man's or woman's skin, *la pelle d' un uomo o d' una donna.*

The skin of a serpent, *la scoglia, o lo scoglio d' una serpe.*

The skin of some fruits, *buccia.*

He is afraid of his skin, *egli ha paura della sua pelle, d' essere bastonato, d' esser nuiso.*

He is ready to leap out of his skin for joy, *egli non cape nella pelle d' allegrezza.*

Between the skin and the flesh, *pelle pelle, poro addentro, nella superficie.*

I would not be in his skin, *non vorrei essere nella sua pelle, o nel suo luogo.*

He has nothing but skin and bones, *non ha che la pelle e l' ossa, è molto magro.*

Near is my shirt but nearer is my skin, *mi stringe più la camicia che non la gonnella.*

To SKIN [to take off the skin] *scorticare, tor via la pelle.*

SKINK, s. [a four-footed sepent, a kind of land crocodile] *serpe di quattro piedi, spezie di crocodrillo terrestre.*

To SKINK [to serve drink at table] *dare a bere in tavola.*

SKI'NNER, s. [cup-bearer] *coppiere,* s. m. *colui che serve di coppa.*

SKI'NNED, adj. *scorticato.*

Thick-skinned [that has a thick skin] *che ha la pelle grossa e dura.*

SKI'NKER, s. *pellicciajo,* s. m.

SKIP, s. [leap, jump] *salto, balzo,* s. m.

To give a skip, *fare un salto.*

By skips, *saltellone, saltelloni, a salti.*

A skip-jack [a pitiful fellow] *uno sciocco, un cionno, un uomo da niente.*

A skip-kennel [a foot-boy] *un lacchè.*

To SKIP [to leap or jump] *saltare, saltellare.*

To skip back, *saltare indietro.*

To skip over, *saltar sopra.*

To skip over in reading, *saltare leggendo, trascorrere qualche cosa senza leggerla.*

SKIPPED, adj. *saltato, saltellato.*

SKIPPER, s. *saltatore,* s. m. *che salta.*

A skipper of a Dutch ship, *padrone d' una barca Olandese.*

Skipper [common seaman] *un marinajo semplice.*

SKI'PPING, s. *il saltare, v.* To skip.

SKI'RMISH, s. [a small engagement with

with the enemy] *ſcaramuccia*, s. f. *leggier combattimento.*

To SKIRMISH [to fight without obſerving order]. *ſcaramucciare.*

SKI'RMISHER, s. *uno che ſcaramuccia.*

SKI'RMISHING, s. *ſcaramuccia*, s. f. *lo ſcaramucciare.*

To SKIRRE, v. n. [to ſcour, to ſcud, to run in haſte] *ſcorrere.*

SKI'RRET, s. [a ſort of root] *ſiſaro*, s. m.

SKIRT, s. [border, hem] *fimbria*, s. f. *fregio, gherone, orlo*, s. m.

The ſkirts of a garment, *il gherone, l' orlo d' un veſtimento.*

The ſkirt of a gown, *il lembo d' una gonna.*

The ſkirts of a country, *le frontiere, i confini d' un paeſe.*

To ſit upon one's ſkirts, *metterſi addoſſo ad uno, malmenarlo*, tormentarlo, *farlo arrabbiare.*

To SKIRT [to border, to run along the edge] *cingere intorno, ſcorrere ſul confine.*

SKITCH, s. [the firſt draught of a picture] *ſchizzo, abbozzo*, s. m.

To SKITCH, *ſchizzare, abbozzare, diſegnare alla groſſa.*

SKI'TTISH, adj. [jadiſh, reſty, as ſome horſes are] *reſtio, renitente, parlando delle beſtie da cavalcare quando non vogliono paſſare avanti.*

Skittiſh [ſhy, eaſily frighted] *ſchifo, che toſto e per poca coſa s' intimoriſce.*

Skittiſh [humourſome, fantaſtical, friſking] *fantaſtico, capriccioſo, bizzarro, biſbetico, umoriſta, volubile, ghiribizzoſo, incoſtante.*

SKI'TTISHLY, adv. *ſaltellone, ſaltelloni.*

SKI'TTISHNESS, s. *qualità d' un cavallo ch' è reſtio.*

Skittiſhneſs [capricious humour] *capriccio, ghiribizzo*, s. m. *fantaſia, bizzaria*, s. f.

SKREEN, s. [riddle or coarſe ſieve] *ſtaccio da ſtacciare coſe groſſolane, come ſabbia e ſimili.*

Skreen [any thing by which the ſun or weather is kept off] *paraſuoco, paraſole, paravento, e ogn' altra coſa che difende la perſona contro il calor del fuoco o del ſole, o dalla pioggia, dal vento e ſimili.*

Skreen [ſhelter, concealment] *coperto; naſcondiglio, aſilo.*

To SKREEN [to riddle, to ſift] *ſtacciare, paſſar per groſſolano ſtaccio coſe groſſolane.*

To ſkreen [to ſhade from ſun, light, or weather] *riparare dal ſole, dalla luce, dal tempo, e ſimili.*

To ſkreen [to ſhelter, to protect] *proteggere, difendere.*

SKREENED, adj. *dal verbo* To ſkreen.

SKUE, adv. *a traverſo, in traverſo, a ſghembo, a ſghimbeſcio.*

To look ſkue upon one [to look upon him with an evil eye] *guardare uno con occhio bieco, mirarlo di mal' occhio.*

To SKUE [to walk ſkuing] *camminare di traverſo.*

SKUTE, s. [a ſort of boat] *ſorta di battello.*

SKY, s. *il firmamento, il cielo.*

Sky-colour, *azzurro, turchino.*

Sky-lark, *allodola.*

Sky-rocket, *razzo*, s. m.

SLAB, s. [puddle] *fango, limo, loto*, s. m. *melma, belletta*, s. m.

To SLA'BBER [to dirt] *ſporcare, imbrattare.*

To ſlabber one's cloaths, *ſporcare i ſuoi abiti.*

To ſlabber [to drivel] *bavare.*

Slabber-chops, *un bavoſo.*

SLA'BBERED, adj. *ſporcato, imbrattato.*

SLA'BBERER, s. *un bavoſo, una bavoſa.*

SLA'BBERING, s. *lo ſporcare.*

See what ſlabbering you make in the room, *vedete un poco come ſporcate la camera.*

Slabbering, adj. *bavoſo, ſudicio, ſporco.*

A ſlabbering man, *un bavoſo.*

A ſlabbering woman, *un bavoſa, una ſporca.*

SLA'BBINESS, *lo ſtato d' una coſa ch' è fangoſa, o melmoſa.*

SLA'BBY, adj. [plaſhy, full of dirt] *fangoſo, melmoſo, ſporco.*

A ſlabby way, *un cammino fangoſo.*

Slabby weather, *tempo ſporco.*

SLACK, adj. [looſe, unbent] *lento, contrario di tirato.*

Slack [ſlow, careleſs] *tardo, pigro, lento, agiato, infingardo, negligente.*

Slack in payments, *lento nel pagare.*

Slack [ſmall coal, coal broken in ſmall parts] *carbone minuto.*

To SLACK [to grow remiſs] *allentarſi, rallentarſi, diminuirſi, ſcemarſi.*

His fever ſlacks, *la ſua febbre ſi rallenta, o diminuiſce.*

To ſlack [to looſen, to unbend] *allentare, rallentare, render lento.*

To ſlack [or retard] *tardare, ritardare.*

Slack no time, *non perdete tempo.*

To ſlack one's ſpeed, *rallentare i paſſi.*

To ſlack one's hand [in working] *rallentar l' animo, ricrearſi, prender qualche riposo.*

To SLA'CKEN [to looſen, to unbend] *allentare, rallentare, render lento.*

To ſlacken, verb neut. *allentarſi, rallentarſi.*

SLA'CKENED, adj. *allentato, rallentato.*

SLA'CKENING, s. *allentamento, rallentamento*, s. m.

SLA'CKLY, adv. *lentamente, freddamente, pigramente, tardamente.*

SLA'CKNESS, s. *lentezza, freddezza, negligenza, infingardaggine, pigrizia, pigrezza, tardezza*, s. f.

SLAG, s. [the droſs or recrement of metal] *la feccia d' ogni metallo quando è fuſo.*

SLAIE, s. [a weaver's reed] *la ſpola d' un teſſitore.*

SLAIN, adj. [from to ſlay] *ammazzato, ucciſo.*

SLAKE, s. [flake of ſnow] *un fiocco di neve.*

To SLAKE [to dilute] *ſtemperare, liquefare, far divenir quaſi liquido che che ſia disfacendolo con liquore.*

To ſlake one's thirſt, *ſmorzarſi la ſete.*

To ſlake one's deſires, *moderare i ſuoi deſiri.*

SLA'KING, s. *ſtemperamento*, s. m. *ſtemperanza*, s. f.

SLAM, s. [the winning of all the tricks at cards] *cappotto*, s. m. *termine di giuoco di carte.*

SLA'NDER, s. [backbiting] *calunnia, maledicenza*, s. f.

To SLA'NDER [to backbite, to ſpeak evil of] *calognare, calunniare, ſparlar d' uno.*

SLA'NDERER, s. *calunniatore, e calonniatore, maldicente*, s. m.

SLA'NDERING, s. *maldicenza, calunnia*, s. f.

SLA'NDERING, adj. *maldicente.*

SLA'NDEROUS, adj. [ſlandering, abuſive] *calunnioſo, maldicente.*

Slanderous tongue, *lingua maldicente.*

SLA'NDEROUSLY, adv. *calunnioſamente, oltraggioſamente, con calunnia.*

SLANK, adj. [ſlim, ſlender] *aſciutto, magro, macilente, ſtenuato, ſmunto, gramo, ſmilzo.*

Slank, s. [a ſort of ſea-weed] *ſala*, s. f. *ſorta d' erba che creſce nel mare.*

SLANT, } adj. [glancing, not
SLA'NTING, } ſtraight] *traverſo, obliquo, in pendio.*

Slanting blow, *roveſcione.*

To give a ſlanting blow, *dare un roveſcione.*

SLA'NTINGLY, adv. *obliquamente, di traverſo, a ſchimbeſcio, a ſchianci.*

SLAP, s. [buffet, blow] *colpo, percoſſa.*

To give one a ſlap, *dare un colpo o una percoſſa ad uno.*

A ſlap on the chops, or a ſlap over the face, *uno ſchiaffo, una guanciata.*

Slap [bad drink, bad potion] *lavatura, bevanda cattiva.*

Slap-ſauce [lick diſh] *un leccapiatti, un goloſo, un leccardo, un ghiottone.*

Slap-daſh, adv. [on the ſudden] *in un colpo, in un ſubito, di punto in bianco.*

To SLAP [to ſtrike] *battere, percuotere*, pret. *percoſſi.*

To ſlap one over the face, *ſchiaffeggiare uno, dargli uno ſchiaffo.*

To ſlap up, *inghiottire, ingojare.*

SLA'PPED, adj. *del verbo* To ſlap.

SLA'PPING, s. *il battere; percuotimento*, s. m. *percoſſa*, s. f.

SLA'PE-ALE [plain ale] *cervogia pura, ſenza miſtura.*

SLAPT, adj. *battuto, percoſſo.*

SLASH, s. [of a whip] *ſtaffilata.*

Slaſh [cut] *taglio, fendente, ſfregio, ſquarcio.*

To give one a great ſlaſh, *fare un taglio, uno ſfregio ad uno.*

To ſlaſh [to whip] *ſtaffilare, fruſtare, battere con uno ſtaffile o fruſta.*

To ſlaſh [to cut] *tagliare, ſfregiare, fare*

fare uno ſfregio, un taglio, uno ſquarcio.

SLA'SHED, adj. *dal, v.* To ſlaſh.

SLATCH, s. [the middle part of a rope or cable that hangs down looſe] *il mezzo d' una corda o gomena che pende ſciolta. Voce marinareſca.*

SLATE, s. [a ſcaly ſort of ſtony ſubſtance for roofing houſes and other things] *ſpezie di pietra piatta.*

To ſlate [to cover with ſlate] *coprir di pietre piatte.*

SLA'TED, adj. *coperto di pietre piatte.*

To SLA'TTER [to mind nothing, to leave all at random] *eſſere neghittoſo, non aver cura di nulla, laſciar ogni coſa in diſordine.*

SLA'TTERN, s. [a negligent woman] *una donna ſpenſierata, una donna neghittoſa, che laſcia tutto in diſordine.*

SLAVE [a bond man or woman] *uno ſchiavo, una ſchiava.*

To make a ſlave of one, *trattar uno da ſchiavo.*

To be a ſlave to one's paſſions, *eſſer ſchiavo alle ſue paſſioni, laſciarſi vincere dalle ſue paſſioni.*

Slave, *appellazione ingiurioſa, ed equivale a furfante, briccone, e ſimili.*

To SLAVE [to toil and moil like a ſlave] *tormentarſi, affaticarſi, lavorare come uno ſchiavo.*

SLA'VER, s. [drivel] *bava,* s. f.

To SLA'VER [to ſlabber, to drivel] *bavare.*

To ſlaver [to be ſmeared with ſpittle] *eſſere ſporco o imbrattato di bava.*

SLA'VERER, s. [one who cannot hold his ſpittle] *un bavoſo, un goffo, un idiota.*

SLA'VERY, s. [bondage] *ſchiavitù, ſervitù,* s. f.

SLA'UGHTER, s. [the act of ſlaying, the act of killing] *uccisione, ſtrage,* s. f. *macello,* s. m.

Slaughter-man [butcher] *un macellajo.*

Slaughter-houſe, *beccheria,* s. f. *macello,* s. m. *luogo dove s' uccidono le beſtie.*

To SLA'UGHTER, verb act. *ammazzare, trucidare, fare ſtrage.*

SLA'UGHTERED, adj. *ammazzato, trucidato, fatto ſtrage.*

SLA'UGHTEROUS, adj. [deſtructive, murderous] *micidiale, diſtruttivo, che fa ſtrage.*

SLA'VING, s [from to ſlave] *pena,* s. f. *travaglio, faſtidio,* s. m.

SLA'VISH, adj. *di ſchiavo, ſervile.*

A ſlaviſh life, *una vita di ſchiavo, ſervile e faticoſa vita.*

In a ſlaviſh condition, *in iſtato di ſchiavo, in iſchiavitù.*

SLA'VISHLY, adv. *da ſchiavo, ſervilmente.*

SLA'VISHNESS, s. *ſchiavitù, ſervitù, ſoggezione,* s. f.

SLAY, s. [an inſtrument belonging to a weaver's loom, having teeth like a comb] *pettine di teſſitore.*

To ſlay [to kill] *uccidere, ammazzare,* pret. *uccisi.*

SLA'YER, s. ex. A man-ſlayer, *un omicida.*

SLA'YING, s. *uccisione,* s. f. *ammazzamento,* s. m. *l' ammazzare.*

SLEAVE, s. [a kind of fiſh] *lolligine,* s. f. *peſce di mare.*

SLE'AVED, adj. *lavorato.*

Sleaved ſilk [wrought, fit for uſe] *ſeta lavorata.*

SLE'AZY, adj. [ſlight, thin, as ſome linen cloths are] *rado, ſottile, contrario di fitto.*

Sleazy ſtuff, *panno rado.*

Sleazy holland [a ſlight, thin holland cloth] *tela d' ollanda rada.*

SLED, *v.* ſledge.

SLEDDED, adj. [mounted on a ſled] *montato ſur una ſlitta.*

SLEDGE, s. [a ſort of carriage without wheels] *ſlitta,* s. f.

A ſmith's ſledge, *un martello di fabbro.*

SLEEK, adj. [ſmooth] *liſcio.*

A ſleek ſtick, *un brunitojo.*

To SLEEK [to ſmooth] *liſciare, ſtropicciare una coſa per farla pulita.*

SLE'EKED, adj. *liſciato, pulito.*

SLEEP, s. [reſt taken by ſleeping] *ſonno,* s. m.

To awake one out of his ſleep, *rompere il ſonno ad uno, ſvegliarlo.*

To ſleep a dog's ſleep, *far finta di dormire, far ſembiante di dormire.*

In his ſleep, *dormendo, mentre dormiva.*

To SLEEP [to take reſt by ſleeping] *dormire.*

He ſleeps like a pig, *dorme come un ghiro.*

SLEE'PER, s. *dormitore, dormiglione, dormiente,* s. m.

The ſeven ſleepers, *i ſette dormienti.*

SLEE'PILY, adv. *dormendo, freddamente, con freddezza.*

SLEE'PINESS, s. [drowzineſs] *ſonno, inclinazione o diſpozione a dormire, ripoſo,* s. m.

SLEE'PING, s. *il dormire, quiete,* s. f. *ſonno, ripoſo,* s. m.

Sleeping, adj. *dormendo.*

Sleeping place, *luogo opportuno a dormire.*

SLEE'PLESS, adj. *che non dorme, che paſſa la notte ſenza dormire.*

I got up ſleepleſs this morning, *mi ſono levato queſta mattina ſenza aver dormito tutta la notte.*

SLEE'PY, adj. [drowſy] *addormentato, ſonnaglioſo, ſonnacchioſo.*

The ſleepy diſeaſe [lethargy] *letargia,* s. f. *letargo,* s. m.

To SLEER [to leer, or peep] *guardar ſott' occhio, o colla coda dell occhio, occhieggiare, guardar ſottecchi.*

SLEE'RING, s. *il guardar ſottecchi, o ſott' occhi, l' occhieggiare.*

Sleering, adj. ex. A ſleering fellow, *una volpe vecchia, un furbo, un aſtuto, un furbacchiotto.*

SLEET, s. [rain and ſnow falling together] *pioggia meſcolata con neve.*

To SLEET, verb neut. *piover e nevicare inſieme, nevicar minutamente.*

SLEE'TY, adj. ex. ſleety weather, *un tempo piovoſo e nevoſo.*

SLEEVE, s. [that part of the garment which covers the arm] *manica,* s. f.

A ſhirt ſleeve, *una manica di camicia.*

To laugh in one's ſleeve, *ſogghignare.*

SLEEVE [calamary, a fiſh] *calamajo,* s. m. *ſpezie di peſce.*

Hanging ſleeve, *manicottolo,* s. m. *manica che ciondola, appiccata al veſtire.*

SLEE'VED, adj. *che ha delle maniche.*

SLEE'VELESS, adj. *ſenza maniche.*

Sleeveleſs errand, *un meſſaggio pazzeſco.*

SLEIGHT, s. [trick] *furberia, aſtuzia, burla,* s. f. *tiro,* s. m.

Sleight of hand, *giuoco di mano.*

Sleight, adj. [ſlight] *rado, ſottile, v.* Slight.

SLEI'GHTLY, adv. *finamente, aſtutamente, ſcaltritamente.*

SLE'NDER, adj. [ſlender, not thick, ſmall] *magro, ſmunto, aſciutto, ſottile, gramo, gretto.*

A ſlender woman, *una donna aſciutta, o ſecca.*

Slender dinner, *pranſo magro.*

Slender [ſmall, ſorrowful, pitiful] *povero, piccolo, mediocre, indifferente.*

Slender kindneſs, *piccolo, favore.*

He has a ſlender merit, *egli ha un merito ben mediocre.*

To have a ſlender eſtate, *avere una mediocre fortuna.*

SLE'NDERLY, adv. *poveramente, mediocremente.*

Slenderly lettered, *che ha poco ſapere.*

SLE'NDERNESS, s. *qualità magra, eſmunta, magrezza, grettitudine.*

SLEPT, *preterito del verbo* To ſleep.

SLEW, *preterito del verbo* To ſlay.

To SLEY, v. n. [to part or twiſt into threads] *dividerſi o attorcerſi in fila.*

SLICE, s. [a thin cut] *fetta,* s. f.

A printer's ink-ſlice, *paletta di ſtampatore.*

To SLICE [to cut into ſlices] *affettare, tagliare in fette.*

SLI'CED, adj. *affettato, tagliato in fette.*

SLICK, adj. [ſmooth] *liſcio, pulito, terſo.*

To SLI'CKEN [to ſmooth] *liſciare, far liſcio.*

SLID, *preterito del verbo* To ſlide.

SLI'DDEN, *participio paſſivo del verbo* To ſlide.

To SLI'DDER [to ſlide with interruption] *ſdrucciolare interrottamente, ſcorrere ſu coſa liſcia.*

To SLIDE [to glide along] *ſdrucciolare, ſcorrere,* pret. *ſcorſi.*

To ſlide upon the ice, *ſdrucciolare ſul ghiaccio.*

To ſlide one's hand into one's pocket, *metter pian piano la mano nella ſcarſella ad uno.*

Slide, s. [a place frozen to ſlide on] *ſdrucciolo, ſentiero dove ſi può ſdrucciolare.*

SLI'DER, s. *quello che ſdrucciola.*

SLI'D-

SLI'DING, s. lo sdrucciolare.
Sliding, adj. sdrucciolante, sdrucciolevole, sdrucciolo.
A sliding place, uno sdrucciolo.
A sliding knot, un nodo scorsojo.
SLIGHT, adj. [thin, light, sleazy] rado, sottile, che non è forte.
A slight basket, un panier rado, che non è fitto.
Slight paper, carta sottile.
Slight business [business of small consequence] negozio di poco importanza.
Slight excuse, scusa frivola.
Slight wound, leggiera ferita.
To make slight of a thing, far poco conto di che che sia, dispregiarlo, farne poca stima.
To SLIGHT [to take little notice of, to despise or neglect] dispregiare, disprezzare, non curare, avere o tenere a vile, far poco conto o stima.
To slight the fortifications of a place, smantellare una piazza.
SLI'GHTED, adj. dispregiato, disprezzato.
SLI'GHTING, s. dispregio, disprezzo, s. m.
SLI'GHTINGLY, } adv. dispregevolmente, disprezzevolmente, con dispregio, con isdegno.
SLI'GHTLY, }
Slightly, leggiermente, superficialmente.
Slightly [carelesly] alla peggio, negligentemente, con poca cura, leggiermente, alla leggiera.
SLI'GHTNESS, s. radezza, rarità, s. f. contrario di densità, leggerezza.
SLI'LY, adv. [craftily] astutamente, accortamente, destramente, sagacemente, scaltritamente, furbescamente.
SLIM, adj. [slender] smilzo, segalingo, magro, asciutto, secco.
A slim fellow, un perticone.
SLIME, s. [a clammy or glueish humour] vischio, umore, o materia viscosa e tenace.
Slime [soft mud] belletta, melma, melmetta, s. f. limo, s. m.
SLI'MINESS, s. viscosità, s. f. qualità viscosa e tenace, limosità, s. f.
SLI'MY, adj. viscoso e vischioso, tenace.
Slimy [muddy] limoso, limaccioso, melmoso.
SLI'NESS, s. [craftiness] destrezza, accortezza, astuzia, sagacità, s. f.
SLING, s. [an instrument to throw stones with], fromba, frombola, scaglia, s. f.
A brewer's sling, bastone grosso, con due uncini di ferro col quale si portano nella cantina i barili di birra.
Sling, s. [a throw, a stroke] colpo, s. m. botta, percossa, s. f.
To sling [to throw stones with a sling] scagliar pietre colla frombola.
To sling [to throw, to cast] tirare, dar un colpo.
To sling [to hang loosely by a string] penzolare da una fune.
SLI'NGER, s. fromboliere, s. m. che scaglia sassi colla frombola.
SLINK, s. [a cast calf] un vitello abortivo.

To SLINK [to steal away] scappare, corsela, battersela, svignare.
To sling aside, mettersi in disparte.
SLI'NKING [stealing away] scappata, s. f.
SLIP, s. [a fall in sliding] caduta che si fa sdrucciolando.
Slip [fault, mistake] errore, fallo, sbaglio, svario, svarione, s. m.
Slip [a branch to set in the ground] piantone, s. m. pollone spiccato dal ceppo della pianta per trapiantare.
Slip [stalk of a plant] pollone, rampollo d' una pianta.
A slip [silk string] cordone di seta.
A hempen slip, una corda.
A slip of paper, un pezzo di carta.
To give one the slip [to steal away] piantare uno, involarsi, scappare, salvarsi, svignare.
Slip shoes, scarpe che si portano come pianelle.
To SLIP [to slide] sdrucciolare, scorrere, frappare, guizzare.
The knife slipt out of my hand, il coltello mi scappò di mano.
The eel slipt out of her hand, l' anguilla le guizzò di mano.
To let slip a thing, lasciar cascare che che sia.
To slip away, corsela batterseła, scappare.
To slip away [as time] sdrucciolare, scorrere, passare.
To slip down, sdrucciolare, cascare.
To slip into a place, sottentrare, entrar pian piano in un luogo.
To slip out, uscire occultamente.
It will slip out of my memory, m' uscirà di mente me ne dimenticherò.
This word slipt out before I was aware, questa parola mi scappò di bocca senza pensarci.
To slip a fair opportunity, lasciarsi uscir di mano una bella occasione, lasciarsela scappare.
To slip out a word, lasciare andare una parola.
To slip one's neck out of the collar [to get out of a bad business] uscirsene pel rotto della cuffia, liberarsi da pericolo senza spesa o noja.
To slip one's neck out of the collar, lasciare in nasso, ricusare di fare quello che uno aveva promesso.
To slip a dog, lasciare un cane.
To slip one's clothes on, mettersi subito gli abiti in dosso.
To slip one's shoes, mettersi subito le scarpe.
To slip off a bough of a tree, sbrancare un ramo d' albero.
To slip off one's shoes, cavarsi le scarpe.
SLI'PPED, v. Slipt.
SLI'PPER, s. [a sort of loose shoe to be worn within doors] pianella, s. f.
SLI'PPERINESS, s. qualità sdrucciolevole.
SLI'PPERY, adj. [that one cannot stand upon] sdrucciolevole.
A slippery way, un cammino sdrucciolevole.
Slippery [that slips out of one's hands] guizzante.

A slippery eel, un anguilla guizzante.
A slippery tongue, una lingua troppo libera, che parla più del dovere.
She has a slippery tongue, ella è una linguacciuta, una linguarda.
A slippery woman [a woman too free] una donna troppo libera, una donna tenera di calcagno, che si lascia facilmente svolgere, inclinata a lascivia.
A slippery business, un negozio geloso.
SLI'PPING, s. lo sdrucciolare.
SLI'PPY, adj. lo stesso che Slippery.
SLI'PSHOD, adj. [having the shoes not pulled up at the heels, but barely slipped on] che ha le scarpe ne' piedi come si portan le pianelle senza tirarle su dalle calcagna.
SLI'PSLOP s. [bad liquor] cattivo liquore, vino o simil cosa di cattiva qualità e non buona a bere.
SLIPT, adj. sdrucciolato, v. To slip.
SLIT, adj. fesso, spaccato.
Slit, s. fenditura, fessura, crepatura, spaccatura, s. f.
To SLIT [to cut a thing according to the grain, as wood, whale-bone, &c.] fendere, spaccare.
To slit wood, fendere delle legna.
To slit, verb neut. fendersi, spaccarsi.
SLI'VER, s. [slice] una fetta.
To SLI'VER [to cut into slivers or slices] affettare, tagliare in fette.
To sliver a loaf, affettare un pane.
SLI'VERED, adj. affettato, tagliato in fette.
SLO'CKER, } s. [one that entices away another man's servant] uno che fa il mestiere di sviare gli altrui servi per porli al servizio d' un altro.
SLOCKSTER, }
SLOE, s. [a sort of wild plumb] prugnuola, s. f. susina selvatica.
Sloe-tree, s. prugnuolo, s. m.
Sloe-worm [an insect] cicigna, s. f.
SLOOP [a small sea vessel] schifo, palischelmo.
To SLOPE [to cut a slope] tagliare in pendio.
SLO'PENESS, s. [or obliquity] obliquità, s. f. pendio, s. m.
SLO'PING, adj. obliquo, pendente.
SLO'PINGLY, adv. obliquamente, in pendio.
SLOPS, s. [seamen's wide breeches] calzoni di marinari.
Slops [physical potions] sciroppi, bevande medicinali.
SLOT, s. [the view or print of a stag's foot in the ground] la traccia d' un cervo.
SLOTH, s. [idleness] accidia, infingardaggine, infingardia, pigrizia, s. f. ozio, s. m.
SLO'THFUL, adj [dronish, idle] ozioso, sfaccendato, infingardo, pigro, lento, scioperato.
A slothful man, uno scioperato, uno sfaccendato. un infingardo.
To grow slothful, infingardire, divenire infingardo, pres. infingardisco.
SLO'THFULLY, adv. pigramente, lentamente.

SLO'THFULNESS, s. [sloth] *pigrizia, infingardia, infingardaggine*, s. f.
SLOUCH, s. [a great lubberly fellow, a mere country bumkin] *un zotico, un villanaccio, un contadinaccio.*
SLO'VEN, s. [a nasty fellow] *uno sporco, un brodoloso, uno schifo, un lercio.*
SLO'VENLINESS, s. *schifezza, sporchezza, sporcizia*, s. f. *sucidume, sudiciume*, s. m.
SLO'VENLY, adj. *schifo, lordo, sporco, sucido, imbrattato, brodoloso.*
A slovenly woman, *una sporca, una donna sucida o brodolosa.*
Slovenly, adv. *sporcamente, schifamente, a' una maniera sucida, e schifa.*
SLO'VENLY, s. [dirtiness want of neatness] *sporcizia, mancanza di pulizia.*
SLOUCH, s. [a deep and muddy place] *pozza, lacuna, pozzánghera*, s. f. *pantano*, s. m. *luogo fangoso.*
The slough of a coal-pit, *l' umidità d' una miniera di carbone.*
The slough of a wild boar, *covile di cinghiale.*
The slough of a wound, *la crosta d' una piaga.*
The slough of a snake, *scoglia*, s. f. *scoglio di serpe, la pelle che getta ogni anno la serpe.*
SLO'UGHY, adj. [miry, boggy, muddy] *fangoso, melmoso, limaccioso.*
SLOUTH, s. [herd, company] *truppa, frotta*, s. f.
A slouth of bears, *una truppa o frotta d' orsi.*
SLOW, adj. [the contrary of quick] *pigro, lento, agiato, tardo.*
A slow animal, *un animale pigro o tardo.*
A slow pace, *passo lento.*
A slow poison, *un veleno lento, che fa il suo effetto lentamente.*
A very slow man, *un uomo molto agiato.*
A slow-back [one that hates work] *un uomo lento, tardo, pigro, infingardo.*
A slow wit, *un ingegno ottuso.*
He is slow, but sure, *egli è lento, ma sicuro.*
Slow, or slowly, adv. *lentamente, pigramente, adagiatamente.*
Great bodies move slowly, *le gran macchine si muovono lentamente.*
My watch goes slow, *il mio oriuolo va troppo tardi.*
SLO'WNESS, s. *lentezza, tardità, pigrizia, agiatezza*, s. f.
SLO'WORM, s. *sorta di réttile velenoso.*
To SLU'BBER [to do carelessly, or without application] *acciabattare, abborracciare, acciarpare, far che che si sia alla grossa e senza diligenza.*
To slubber [to stain, to daub] *macchiare, imbrattare, sporcare.*
To slubber [to cover coarsely or carelessly] *ricoprire stracuratamente o grossolanamente.*
SLUBBERDEGU'LLION, s. [a paltry, dirty, sorry wretch] *un birbante cencioso.*
SLU'BBERED over, adj. *acciabattato, abborracciato, acciarpato, fatto alla grossa, o alla peggio.*
SLUG, s. [a heavy sort of great gun] *spezie di cannone grosso.*
A slug [a ship that sails heavily] *un vascello che non veleggia bene, un vascello pesante.*
A slug, or slug-snail, *una lumaca.*
A slug-a-bed, *un dormiglione, un infingardo, che ama dormire.*
SLU'GGARD, s. [a slothful dronish person] *un dormiglione, un pigro, un infingardo.*
SLU'GGISH, adj. *dormiglioso, sonnacchioso, pigro, infingardo, lento.*
SLU'GGISHLY, adv. *lentamente, pigramente.*
SLU'GGISHNESS, s. *infingardaggine, infingardia, lentezza, pigrizia*, s. f.
SLU'ICE, s. [a frame of wood set in a river to keep out the water] *cateratta*, s. f.
To sluice, or sluice out, *inondare, romper le sponde.*
SLU'ICY, adj. [falling in streams as from a sluice or flood-gate] *inondante, e quasi vegnente giù da cateratta.*
SLU'MBER, s. *sonno, sonno leggiero.*
To fall into a slumber, *addormentarsi.*
To SLU'MBER [to doze] *dormicchiare, dormigliare, dormire leggiermente.*
SLU'MBERING, s. *sonno, il dormicchiare.*
SLUNG, } *part. del verbo* To fling.
SLUNK, }
SLUR, s. [trick] *burla*, s. f. *tiro*, s. m.
To put a slur upon, *fare una burla, far un tiro ad uno.*
To slur [to soil, to dawb] *sporcare, imbrattare.*
To slur one's clothes, *sporcarsi gli abiti.*
To slur one [to put a trick upon him] *fare una burla, o un tiro ad uno, acchiapparlo.*
To slur over a thing, *far vista di non badare a qualche cosa.*
SLUT, s. [a nasty, dirty woman] *una sporcaccia, una sporca, una donna sudicia.*
SLU'TTERY, s. [sluttishness] *sporcizia, porcheria, sucidezza, lordura*, s f.
SLU'TTISH, *sporco, sucido, imbrattato, unto, bisunto.*
SLU'TTISHLY, adv. *sporcamente, schifamente, lordamente.*
SLU'TTISHNESS, s. *sporcizia, porcheria, lordura*, s. f. *sucidume, sudiciume*, s. m.
SLY, adj. [crafty] *fino, astuto, scaltrito.*
A sly blade, *una volpe vecchia.*
SMACK, s. [taste, relish] *gusto, sapore*, s. f.
It has an ill smack with it, *ha un cattivo gusto.*
He has a smack of his country speech, *egli ha un accento del suo paese nel parlare.*
To have a little smack of learning, *aver qualche tintura, infarinatura, o leggiera conoscenza delle scienze.*
Smack [eager kiss with a noise made by the lips] *un bacio che scoppia o suona fra le labbra.*
To kiss a woman with a smack, *scoccare un bacio ad una donna, darle un bacio che scoppi.*
Smack [a small sea vessel with one mast, which attends men of war in carrying provisions on board] *palischelmo di nave da guerra.*
Smack-sail, *vela latina.*
To SMACK [to taste] *sapere, aver sapore.*
To smack [to make a noise in eating] *fare strepito colla bocca mangiando.*
To smack [to taste] *assaggiare.*
To smack a woman [to kiss her with a smack] *scoccare un bacio ad una donna, baciarla facendo scoccar le labbra.*
SMA'CKER, s. *assaggiatore*, s. m.
SMA'CKERING, s. [a longing or mind] *voglia, volontà, brama*, s. f. *desiderio, appetito*, s. m.
To have a smackering after a thing, *aver voglia o brama di qualche cosa; bramare eccessivamente una cosa.*
Smackering, adj. ex. well smackering, *che ha buon sapore, o gusto.*
SMALL, adj. [little] *piccolo, e piccinolo.*
A small number, *un piccolo numero.*
Small print, *piccola lettera, lettera minuta.*
To cut small, *tagliar minuto, o in piccole parti, tritare.*
Small [light, slight] *piccolo, leggiero.*
Small fault, *piccolo errore, erroruzzo, colpa leggiera.*
Small [not strong] *piccolo, che non è forte.*
Small wine, *vin piccolo, vinetto.*
A small supper, *una cena leggiera.*
A man of small learning, *un uomo di poco sapere.*
It is a small matter, *questa è piccola cosa, è una cosa di poca consèguenza, o importanza.*
At a small rate, *per poca cosa, a buon mercato.*
A man of small credit, *un uomo che non ha gran credito.*
Small arms, *armi corte da fuoco.*
The small cards, *la carte basse.*
The small-pox [a disease] *il vajuolo.*
The small, s. [the small of the leg] *la parte minuta della gamba.*
SMA'LLAGE, s. [an herb] *appio*, s. m. *erba di più forte,*
SMA'LLNESS, s *piccolezza, picciolezza, tenuità*, s. f.
SMA'LLY, adv. [in a little quantity, with minuteness, in a little or low degree] *pocamente, in poca quantità, minutamente,*
SMALT, s. [blue colour in powder] *smalto*, s. m.
SMART, adj. [sharp, quick, violent] *acuto, cocente, ardente, doloroso, frizzante.*
A smart remedy, *un rimedio cocente o frizzante.*
A smart pain, *un dolore acuto.*
Smart [sharp of taste] *piccante, agro, forte.*

A ſmart fight, *un aſpro combattimento.*

Smart [ſharp, biting in diſcourſe] *mordace, piccante, fine, arguto.*

A ſmart anſwer, *una riſpoſta arguta, e mordace.*

Smart [briſk, quick] *leſto, ſpiritoſo, vivace.*

A ſmart fellow, *un uomo vivace, vagamente veſtito.*

Smart, s. [ſmart pain] *cociore, ſpaſimo, dolore acuto.*

I feel a great ſmart in my wound, *ſento un gran cociore o ſpaſimo nella piaga.*

To SMART [to be painful, as a ſore] *frizzare, pizzicare, cuocere, far male, dar del dolore.*

My wound ſmarts, *la mia piaga mi frizza, o mi cuoce.*

You ſhall ſmart for it, *voi ne pagherete il fio, voi la pagherete.*

SMA'RTING, s. *cociore e cuociore, ſpaſimo, dolore acuto.*

SMA'RTLY, adv. *ſottilmente, vivamente, vigoroſamente, fortemente, argutamente.*

SMA'RTNESS of pain, *violenza del dolore.*

The ſmartneſs of a diſeaſe, *la forza, l' energia d' un diſcorſo.*

SMATCH, s. ex. to have a ſmatch of learning, *avere una tintura di ſcienza.*

Smatch, s. *nome d' uccelletto.*

To SMA'TTER [to have a ſlight taſte, to have a ſlight, ſuperficial, imperfect knowledge] *avere una poca di tintura, ſapere un pochino di checcheſſia.*

To ſmatter [to talk ſuperficially or ignorantly] *parlare o cianciare ſuperficialmente e da ignorante.*

SMA'TTER, s. [ſuperficial or light knowledge] *leggiera tintura di ſapere.*

SMA'TTERER, s. [one who has ſome ſmatch or tincture of learning] *un ſemidotto, un letteratuccio, uno che ha qualche tintura delle ſcienze.*

SMA'TTERING, s. [ſuperficial or ſlight knowledge] *tintura, infarinatura, mediocre cognizione in che che ſi ſia.*

He has a ſmattering of the Latin tongue, *egli è un poco infarinato nella lingua Latina, egli intende mediocremente il Latino.*

To SMEAR [to beſmear] *imbrattare, lordare, ſporcare.*

SMEA'RED, adj. *imbrattato, lordato, ſporcato.*

SMELL, s. *odore, ſentore,* s. m.

A good ſmell, *un buon odore.*

To have a good or ill ſmell, *aver buono o cattivo odore, ſentire bene o male.*

A ſmell-feaſt, *un paraſito, uno ſcrocco.*

To SMELL [to have or caſt a ſmell] *ſparger odore, aver odore, ſentire, fiutare.*

This flower ſmells ſweet, *queſto fiore ha buon odore.*

To ſmell, *putire.*

This meat ſmells rank, *queſta carne pute di rancido.*

I ſmell a great ſtink, *io ſento un gran puzzo.*

Smell this roſe, *odorate queſta roſa.*

I ſmell a rat [I miſtruſt ſomething] *mi diffido, o ſoſpetto di qualche coſa.*

To ſmell a thing out, *odorare, avere odore, preſentire qualche coſa, ſcoprirla.*

SME'LLER, s. [he who ſmells] *colui che fiuta.*

SME'LLFEAST [a paraſite; one who haunts good tables] *paraſito, uno che va in buſca di buoni deſinari.*

SME'LLING, s. [the ſenſe of ſmelling] *l' oderato.*

SMELT, adj. *odorato, ſentito.*

Smelt out, *odorato, preſentito, ſcoperto.*

Smelt, s. [a fiſh] *ſpezie di peſce, cefalo.*

To SMELT [to melt ore ſo as to extract the metal] *fondere o far liquefare un pezzo di miniera tanto che ſe n' eſtragga il metallo.*

SME'LTER, s. [one who melts ore] *colui che fa fondere metalli.*

To SMERK [to look pleaſantly] *aver una cera allegra, e giojoſa.*

To ſmerk upon one, *guardar uno con viſo allegro e ridente.*

SME'RKING, s. *aria, viſo, cera ridente.*

To SMI'CKER [to look amorouſly or wantonly] *vagheggiare, guardar con diletto, con compiacenza un oggetto, occhieggiare.*

To ſmicker at a woman, *vagheggiare una donna.*

SMI'CKERING, s. *vagheggiamento, ſguardo amoroſo.*

SMI'CKET, s. [the under garment of a woman] *gonnella che le donne portan ſotto la veſte, ſottana.*

SMILE, s. *ſorriſo.*

To ſmile [to look pleaſant, to ſimper] *ſorridere, fare un ſorriſo,* pret. *ſorriſi.*

She ſmiled upon me, *ella m' ha ſorriſo.*

Fortune SMILES upon you, every thing ſmiles upon you [every thing ſucceeds with you] *la fortuna vi arride, vi favoriſce, vi ride in ogni coſa.*

SMI'LING, s. *ſorriſo, il ſorridere.*

Smiling, adj. *ridente, giojoſo, feſtoſo, allegro.*

SMIT, *participio paſſivo del verbo* To ſmite.

To SMITE [to ſtrike] *percuotere, battere.*

She has ſmit me [I am ſmitten with her] *ella m' ha rapito il cuore.*

SMI'TER, s. *percuotitore, percotitore,* s. m.

SMITH, s. [blackſmith] *un fabbro.*

A ſmith's ſhop, *una fucina.*

A gold-ſmith, *un orefice, un oraſo.*

A ſilver-ſmith, *un argentiere.*

A gun-ſmith, *un armajuolo, uno che ſabbrica armi.*

A lock-ſmith, *un magnano, un che fa chiavi.*

SMI'THERY, s. [the ſhop of a ſmith] *bottega di fabbro ferrajo.*

SMI'THING, s. [an art manual by which iron is wrought into an intended ſhape] *arte del fabbro ferrajo.*

SMI'TING, s. *percuotimento,* s. m. *il percuotere.*

SMI'TTEN, adj. *percoſſo, battuto.*

To be ſmitten with a woman [to be paſſionately in love with her] *eſſer appaſſionatamente innamorato d' una donna, eſſerne incapricciato.*

Smitten with lunacy, *lunatico, matto.*

SMOAK, v. Smoke.

SMOCK, s. *una camicia da donna. Vocabolo plebeo.*

A ſmock-face, *un viſo effemminato.*

SMO'CKFACED, adj. [palefaced, maidenly] *pallido, da fanciulla.*

SMOKE, s. *fumo, fummo,* s. m.

Where there is ſmoke there is fire, *non c' è fumo ſenza fuoco.*

To SMOKE [to caſt forth ſmoke] *fumare, fummare, far fummo, fumicare.*

This room ſmokes, *queſta camera fuma.*

To ſmoke [to hang or dry in the ſmoke] *affumicare, ſeccare nel fummo.*

To ſmoke tobacco, *fumar del' tabacco.*

To ſmoke [to beſmoke, or trouble with ſmoke] *affumicare, far fumo, dar fumo ad una coſa.*

To ſmoke a buſineſs, *odorare, aver ſentore di qualche negozio, preſentirlo, indovinarlo, ſcoprirlo.*

I ſhall ſmoke you for it, *ve ne farò pentire, me la pagherete.*

SMO'KED, adj. *fumato,* v. To ſmoke.

SMO'KELESS, adj. [having no ſmoke] *ſenza fumo, che non fa fumo.*

SMO'KER, s. *fumatore,* s. m.

SMO'KINESS, s. *gran fumo.*

SMO'KING, s. *il fumare.*

He loves ſmoking, *egli ama fumare.*

SMO'KY, adj. *affumicato, macchiato o tinto di fumo, fumoſo, che fa fumo.*

SMOTE, *preterito del verbo* To ſmite.

SMOOTH, adj. [even, level] *piano, uguale, morbido.*

A ſmooth table, *una tavola piana.*

A ſmooth way, *un cammino piano.*

Smooth [ſoft or ſleek] *liſcio.*

Smooth [courteous] *dolce, affabile, umano, corteſe, civile.*

A ſmooth ſtile, *uno ſtile corrente, facile, dolce, eguale.*

A fine ſmooth file, *una lima ſorda.*

A ſmooth tongue, *una lingua melata, una lingua luſinghiera.*

He has a ſmooth way of painting, *egli ha una maniera delicata di pignere.*

To SMOOTH [to make ſmooth] *appianare, ſpianare, liſciare.*

To ſmooth one up, *piaggiare, adulare, luſingare, vezzeggiare alcuno.*

To SMOO'THEN [to make even and ſmooth] *liſciare, render uguale e liſcio.*

SMOO'THED, adj. *appianato, ſpianato, liſciato.*

SMOO'THFACED, adj. [mild-looking, having a ſoft air] *che ha l' aſpetto mite o molle.*

SMOO'THING, s. *l' appianare, il liſciare.*

SMOO'THLY, adv. *dolcemente, bel bello, pian piano, adagio, morbidamente.*

SMOO'THNESS, s. *dolcezza, morbidezza,* s. f.

Smoothneſs of temper, *umor piacevole e trattabile.*

Smoothneſs of ſtyle, *ſtile limato.*

To SMO'THER [to ſtifle or choak] *affogare, ſoffocare.*

To ſmother with ſmoke, *affumicare, incomodare moltiſſimo col fumo.*

To ſmother up [to conceal] *affogare, celare, ſopprimere.*

SMO'THERED, adj. *affogato, ſoffocato, celato, ſoppreſſo.*

SMO'THERER, s. *quello, o quella che affoga.*

SMO'THERING, s. *affogamento,* s. m. *l' affogare.*

To SMO'ULTER [to ſtifle] *affogare, ſoffocare.*

SMO'ULTRY, adj. *affogante.*

Smoultry heat, *un caldo eceſſivo.*

SMUG, adj. [ſpruce, neat] *pulito, leſto, attillato, lindo.*

To SMUG one's ſelf up [to trim, to ſet one's ſelf off to the beſt advantage] *aggiuſtarſi, adornarſi, pararſi, acconciarſi.*

SMU'GGED up, adj. *aggiuſtato, adornato, parato, acconcio.*

To SMU'GGLE [to run goods by ſtealth, without paying cuſtom] *fare il meſtiere di contrabbandiere, portare delle mercanzie naſcoſamente ſenza pagare la dogana.*

To ſmuggle the coal [to make people believe one has no money when the reckoning is to be paid] *dare ad intendere che uno non ha danari quando ſi viene a pagare lo ſcotto.*

SMU'GGLER, s. *contrabbandiere,* s. m.

SMU'GLY, adv. [neatly, ſprucely] *pulitamente, attillatamente.*

SMU'GNESS, *pulizia, lindezza, attillatura,* s. f.

SMUT, s. [dirt, naſtineſs] *ſporchezza, ſporcizia,* s. f.

Smut [diſcourſes] *oſcenità, diſoneſtà, ciance oſcene.*

To SMUT [to dawb with ſmut] *imbrattare, ſporcare.*

To SMUTCH [to black with ſmoke], *annerare col fumo.*

SMU'TTED, adj. *imbrattato, ſporcato, lordato.*

SMU'TTILY, adv. [blackly, ſmokily] *neramente, affumicatamente.*

Smuttily [obſcenely] *oſcenamente.*

SMU'TTINESS, s. [ſoil from ſmoke] *fuligine, nerezza di fumo.*

Smuttineſs [obſceneneſs] *oſcenità.*

SMU'TTY, adj. [obſcene] *diſoneſto, oſceno, licenzioſo, impuro, impudico.*

SNACK, s. [ſhare] *parte.*

To go ſnacks with one, *ſpartire con uno.*

To put in for a ſnack, *voler la parte ſua.*

SNA'COT, s. [a fiſh] *nome di peſce.*

SNA'KET, s [a ſort of haſp for a caſement] *ſbarra,* s. f.

SNA'FFLE, s. [a ſort of bit for a horſe] *filetto a morſo di cavallo.*

SNAG, s. [knot, knob, bunch] *nodo, bozzola, enfiato,* s. m. *bozza,* s. f.

Snag [ſnail] *lumaca,* s f.

SNA'GGED, } adj ex. a ſnagged
SNA'GGY, } tooth, or ſnaggy tooth [that does not ſtand even] *un dente che non è uguale, un ſopraddente.*

SNAIL, s. *lumaca,* s. f.

Snail-trefoil [a plant] *cedrangola,* s. f *ſpezie d' erba.*

SNAKE, s. [a ſort of ſerpent] *ſerpe, biſcia,* s. f.

A water-ſnake, *ſerpe acquatica.*

Snake weed, *biſtorta,* s. f.

SNA'KY, adj. [ſerpentine, belonging to a ſnake, reſembling a ſnake] *ſerpentino, di biſcia, appartenente a biſcia, ſimile a una biſcia.*

Snaky [having ſnakes] *che ha o produce biſcie.*

SNAP, s. [noiſe] *ſtrepito, romore, fracaſſo,* s. m.

Snap [morſel, bit] *un pezzo, un boccone.*

A cunning ſnap [a cunning blade] *un uomo aſtuto, una volpe, una volpe vecchia.*

A merry ſnap [a merry fellow] *un uomo gioviale, un buon compagnone.*

SNAP-HAUNCE [a fire-lock] *rotella d' archibuſo.*

SNAP-DRA'GON, s. [a plant] *nome di pianta.*

Snap-dragon [a kind of play, in which brandy is ſet on fire, and raiſins thrown into it, which thoſe who are unuſed to the ſport are afraid to take out, but which may be ſafely ſnatched by a quick motion and put blazing into the mouth, which being cloſed, the fire is at once extinguiſhed] *ſorta di giuoco fanciulleſco; e ſi fa mettendo dell' acquavite ſul fuoco, poi vi ſi gitta dentro de' grani d' uva paſſa, che chi non è avezzo al giuoco non ha coraggio di pigliare, comechè ſi poſſano ſenza pericolo di danno togliere e ſcagliarſeli nella bocca con deſtro e veloce modo, e con iſtantaneamente chiuderla eſtinguer la fiamma e mangiarſeli.*

To SNAP [to break] *rompere, frangere,* pret. *ruppi, franſi.*

To ſnap [to catch] *afferrare, pigliare, acchiappare.*

The dog ſnapt his leg, *il cane gli afferrò la gamba.*

He ſent out men to ſnap him, *mandò uomini per acchiapparlo.*

To ſnap one up, *ſgridare, riprendere, garrire, bravare, gridare alcuno.*

To ſnap one [to ſurprize him] *coglier uno all' improvviſo.*

To ſnap with the fingers, *ſcoppiettare colle dita.*

To ſnap a thing away, *ſtrappar via che che ſia.*

To ſnap [to break] *romperſi, fenderſi.*

To ſnap [to give a ſnap] *ſcoppiare, ſcoppiettare, fare ſtrepito.*

SNA'PPED, *v.* Snapt.

SNA'PPER, s. [one who ſnaps] *acchiappatore, colui che all' improvviſo acchiappa checcheſſia.*

SNA'PPERS, s. *caſtagnette,* s. f.

SNA'PPING, s. *il rompere, v.* To ſnap.

SNA'PPISH, adj. [rough, moroſe] *rozzo, zotico, brutale, incivile.*

A ſnappiſh man, *una zotico, un villano, un brutale.*

SNA'PPISHLY, adv. *rozzamente, zoticamente, incivilmente.*

SNA'PSACK, s. [a ſoldier's bag] *biſaccia di ſoldato.*

SNA'PT, adj. *rotto, franto, v.* To ſnap.

SNA'RE, s. [gin, trap to catch birds or beaſts] *galappio, trabocchello, trabocchetto,* s. m. *trappola, tagliuola, trama, ſchiaccia, ſtiaccia,* s. f.

To lay ſnares, *tender inſidie.*

To ſnare, *v.* To inſnare.

To SNA'RL [to intangle] *aggroppare, avviluppare, intrigare, raggruppare.*

To ſnarl ſilk or thread, *raggropparee avviluppare ſeta o refe.*

To ſnarl, v. n. [to grin like a dog] *ringhiare, come fanno i cani.*

SNA'RLED, adj. *aggroppato, avviluppato, intrigato, raggruppato, ringhiato.*

SNA'RLING, adj. ex. A ſnarling dog, *un can ringhioſo.*

SNATCH, s. [bit] *pezzo.*

A ſnatch and away, *mengiamo un boccone in piede e andiamocene.*

To do a thing by girds and ſnatches, *fare che che ſia a ſpilluzzico.*

To SNATCH, to ſnatch away [to wreſt, to take away] *abbrancare, afferrare, acchiappare, ſtrappare, arrappare, arraffare.*

SNA'TCHED, or ſnatched away, adj. *abbrancato, afferrato, acchiappato, ſtrappato, arrappato, arraffato.*

SNA'TCHER, s. *arrappatore, arraffatore,* s. m. *arraffatrice,* s. f.

SNA'TCHING, s. *l' arrappare, l' arraffare, lo ſtrappare.*

SNA'TCHINGLY, adv. [haſtily] *con modo ſubito violento, e ſtrappante.*

To SNEAK [to creep] *rampicare.*

To

To ſneak [to creep up and down pitifully] *andare colla teſta baſſa, col capo chino, peritare, vergognarſi, non avere ardire.*

To ſneak into corners, *celarſi, naſconderſi nei cantoni, non aver ardire di moſtrarſi.*

SNE'AKING, adj. [baſe, pitiful] *vile, abbietto, peritoſo.*

A ſneaking man [a pitiful fellow] *un uomo vile e abbietto.*

Sneaking doings, *azioni da facchino, azioni vili.*

Sneaking [poor, ſorry] *povero, tapino, meſchino, miſero.*

SNE'AKINGLY, adv. [baſely] *baſſamente, abbiettamente, infamamente, vilmente.*

Sneakingly [pitifully] *poveramente, tapinamente, meſchinamente, miſeramente.*

SNE'AKINGNESS, s. [baſeneſs] *baſſezza, viltà, miſeria, s. f.*

Sneakingneſs [niggardlineſs] *ſpilorceria, miſeria eſtrema, avarizia, s. f.*

A SNE'AKS, } s. [a ſneaking ſorry
A SNE'AKSBY, } fellow, who ſcarce dares to ſhew his head] *un tapino, un miſero, un vigliaccaccio.*

SNE'AKUP, s. [a cowardly, creeping, inſidious ſcoundrel] *un birbone umilmente ed inſidioſamente codardo.*

To SNE'AP [to reprimand, to check] *riprendere ſvillaneggiando, ſgridare, fare una ripaſſata.*

To ſneap [to nip] *guaſtare checcheſſia onde non creſca; e diceſi per lo più de' teneri germogli delle piante e de' fiori quando l' intemperie dell' aria, la mano dell' uomo, o altro ſimile accidente li rompe o ſecca.*

SNE'AP, s. [a reprimand, a check] *una ripaſſata, s. f. un rabbuffo, s. m.*

To SNEB [properly to ſnib or to ſneap] *ſgridare, fare un rabbuffo, riprendere aſpramente e ſvillaneggiando.*

To SNEER [to laugh ironically, to laugh at] *ghignare, ſogghignare.*

SNEE'RING, s. *ghignata, s. f. ſogghigno, s. m.*

To SNEEZE, *ſtarnutare, ſtarnutire, pref. ſtarnutiſco.*

SNEE'ZE-WORT [an herb ſo called from its faculty of cauſing ſneeze] *ſternutatoria, s. f.*

SNEE'ZING, s. *ſtarnuto, s. m. lo ſtarnutire.*

SNER, s. [a hunting term, the fat of all ſorts of deer] *graſſo di cervo.*

SNI'CK-UP, s. [a ſneezing] *ſtarnuto, s. m.*

To SNI'GGER [to laugh privately, to laugh in one's ſleeve] *ſorridere, ghignare.*

SNIP, s. [bit] *un pezzo, un beccone, un poco.*

Full of ſnips, *reperto di cenci.*

He has a ſnip of white on the noſe, *egli ha una macchia bianca ſul naſo.*

To go ſnips with one, *ſpartire con uno, far a metà con uno.*

To ſnip off [to cut off] *mozzare, troncare.*

SNIPE, s. [a ſort of fowl] *beccaccino, s. m.*

SNIPT off, adj. *mozzato, troncato, tronco.*

SNITE, s. [a bird called alſo a BAIL] *francolino, s. m.*

To SNITE one's noſe, *ſoffiarſi il naſo.*

SNI'VEL, s. [ſnot] *moccio, s. m.*

SNI'VELLING, adj. *moccioſo.*

Snivelling cold, *catarro.*

SNI'VELLY, adj. [full of ſnivel] *moccioſo.*

To SNOOK [to lie lurking for a thing] *ſtare giù in agguati per cercar d' acchiappare qualche coſa, acquattarſi.*

SNORE, s. [audible reſpiration of ſleepers through the noſe] *il ſuono del ruſſare.*

To SNORE [to make a noiſe through the noſtrils in ſleeping] *ruſſare, lo ſtrepitare che ſi fa nell' alitare dormendo.*

SNO'RER, s. *quello, o quella che ruſſa.*

SNO'RING, s. *il ruſſare.*

To SNORT [to blow through the noſe as a high mettled horſe] *sbuffare, ſoffiar forte, ed è proprio d' un cavallo che ha di molto fuoco e feroce.*

SNOT, s. *moccio, mucco.*

To ſnot one's noſe, *ſoffiarci il naſo.*

SNO'TTY, adj. *moccioſo.*

SNOUT, s. [the noſe of a beaſt] *grugno, grifo, muſo, s. m.*

The ſnout of an elephant, *la tromba, o la proboſcide d' un elefante.*

The ſnout of the bellows, *il cannello d' un ſoffietto.*

SNO'UTED, adj. [having a ſnout] *che ha il grugno in fuora come il porco.*

SNOW, s. *neve, s. f.*

To SNOW, *nevicare, fioccare.*

It ſnows, *nevica.*

SNO'WY, adj. *nevoſo, di neve.*

A ſnowy country, *un paeſe nevoſo.*

Snowy weather, *un tempo nevoſo, o di neve.*

This will be a ſnowy day, *noi averemo della neve oggi.*

To SNUB one [to take one up ſharply] *rabbuffare, bravare, garrire, ſgridare.*

To ſnub [to keep under] *reprimere, ritenere, raffrenare, tenere a freno.*

To ſnub [to ſob] *ſinghiozzare, ſoſpirare con pianto.*

SNU'BBED, adj. *rabbuffato, bravato, garrito, ſgridato, v. To ſnub.*

SNU'DGE, s. [an old curmudgeon, or cloſe-fiſted fellow] *un vecchio avaro, uno ſpilorcio, un taccagno, un tanghero.*

To ſnudge along [to walk looking downwards and poring, as though the head was full of buſineſs] *camminare come un muſorno coll' capo chino, andar muſando.*

SNUFF, s. [ſneezing powder] *tabacco in polvere.*

The ſnuff of a candle or lamp, *lucignolo d' una lucerna, ſtoppino d' una candela.*

Snuff [a little piece of a candle] *un moccolo, un pezzo di candela.*

Snuff-box, *tabacchiera, ſcatola da tabacco.*

Snuff-diſh, *piattello da mettervi dentro lo ſmoccolatojo.*

To take ſnuff, or to take a thing in ſnuff, *prendere che che ſi ſia in mala parte.*

To go away in ſnuff, *andarſene in collera, o mal ſoddisfatto.*

To SNUFF [to take ſnuff] *prender del tabacco.*

To ſnuff up a thing into one's noſe, *prender che che ſia pel naſo.*

To ſnuff the candle, *ſmoccolar la candela.*

To ſnuff out the candle, *ſpegner la candela nello ſmoccolarla.*

To ſnuff at a thing [to take it in dudgeon] *avere in uggia o in odio che che ſia, adirarſi, prender che che ſia in cattiva parte.*

To ſnuff at one [to be angry at him] *andare in collera contro uno.*

SNU'FFED, adj. *ſmoccolato, v. To ſnuff.*

SNU'FFER, s. [he that ſnuffs the candles] *colui che ſmoccola le candele.*

SNU'FFERS, s. *ſmoccolatojo, s. m.*

Snuffers-pan, *piattello da ſmoccolatojo.*

To SNU'FFLE [to ſpeak in the noſe] *parlar nel naſo.*

SNU'FFLER, s. *quello, o quella che parla nel naſo.*

SNUG, adj. [compact, cloſe] *comodo, commeſſo, ben fatto.*

A ſnug room, *una camera comoda.*

A ſnug ſhip, *un vaſcello ben rommeſſo, o ben fatto.*

To lie ſnug in a bed, *ſtrignerſi nel letto, avvilupparſi ſi nelle coperte.*

To SNUG, verb neut. *ſtrignerſi, accoſtarſi.*

To ſnug to one's bed-fellow, *ſtrignerſi, accoſtarſi al ſuo compagno di letto.*

To SNU'GGLE [to ſnuggle together] *ſtrignerſi, accoſtarſi, avvicinarſi.*

SO, adv. [thus] *così, in queſto modo, in queſta maniera.*

It is ſo, *è così.*

Suppoſe it be ſo, *ſuppoſto che ſia così.*

Why d'ye do ſo? *perchè fate ciò.*

Why ſo? *e perchè?*

So much, *tanto.*

I do ſo love him, *l' amo tanto.*

'Tis ſo good, *è così buono.*

This is not ſo good as the other, *queſto non è tanto buono quanto l' altro.*

So that, *di maniera che, talmente che.*

So [provided that] *purchè.*

So he do me no hurt, *purchè non mi faccia del male.*

That is not so, *la cosa non va così.*

If it be so, that ——, *se pur è vero, che* ——.

So we came to know it, *in questo modo ci pervenne a notizia.*

Do so, *fate come vi dico.*

So, as I was telling you, *ora, come vi dicevo.*

And so forth, *e così del resto.*

As the one was good, so the other was bad, *quanto l' uno era buono, tanto l' altro era cattivo.*

So long, *lungo così.*

So many, *tanti.*

So so [indifferently, not much amiss nor well] *così così, mediocremente, nè ben nè male.*

To SOAK, v. n. [to lie steeped in moisture] *essere in molle, essere tuffato in cosa liquida, inzupparsi.*

To soak [to enter by degrees into pores] *insinuarsi pianpiano ne' pori.*

To soak [to drink gluttonously and intemperately] *bere avida e smoderatamente, trincare a dismisura.*

To soak, v. a. [to macerate in any moisture, to steep, to keep wet till moisture is imbibed, to drench] *macerare checchessia tenendolo nell' acqua o in altro liquore, immerger velo finchè di quell' acqua o liquore sia bene imbevuto, tuffare, inzuppare.*

To soak [to drain, to exhaust] *inbevere, render esausto succiando, succiare.*

SOAP, s. [a substance used in washing, made of a lixivium of vegetable alkaline ashes and unctuous substance] *sapone.*

SOAP-BOILER, s. [one whose trade is to make soap] *colui che fa il sapone.*

SOAPWORT, s. [a kind of campion] *nome d' un' erba.*

To SOAR [to fly high] *sorare, volare a giuoco, e dicesi de' falconi che si lasciano volare senza avere avanti la preda.*

To soar [to aim high, to be aspiring] *aspirare a cose grandi, alzar la vista troppo in alto.*

To soar high after sublime notions, *andar investigando sublimi cose.*

SO'AR-HAWK, *un falcone soro.*

SO'ARING, adj. [sublime] *sublime, alto, eccelso.*

A high soaring style, *uno stile sublime.*

SOB, s. *singhiozzo,* s. m.

To SOB [to sigh in weeping or lamentation] *singhiozzare, sospirar con pianto.*

SO'BBING, s. *il singhiozzare, singhiozzo*

Sobbing, adj. *singhiozzoso.*

Sobbing words, *parole singhiozzose.*

SO'BER, adj. [moderate, temperate] *sobrio, parco, astinente, moderato, temperato.*

Sober [modest, grave, serious] *sobrio, grave, serio, composto.*

Sober [not drunk] *sobrio, che non è briaco.*

SO'BERLY, adv. *sobriamente, parcamente, moderatamente, temperatamente.*

SO'BERNESS, s. [sober look] *aria modesta, grave, o composta.*

SO'BERNESS, } s. moderation, temperance] *sobrietà,*
SO'BRIETY, }
parcità, moderazione, temperanza, s. f.

SO'CAGE, } s. [a tenure of lands by inferior services in husbandry, to be performed to the lord of the fee] *servizi ignobili che un fittuale è obbligato di fare al padrone del feudo.*
SO'CCAGE, }

SO'CAGER, } s. [a tenant, who holds lands and tenements by soccage] *fittuale, che è obbligato in virtù del feudo che possiede di rendere al suo signore alcuni servigi ignobili.*
SO'CCAGER, }

SO'CIABLE, adj. [that delights in, or is fit for company] *soriabile, sociale, compagnevole, che ama la compagnia.*

SO'CIABLENESS, s. *umore sociabile.*

SO'CIAL, adv. *d' una maniera sociabile, compagnevolmente.*

SOCI'ETY, s. [company, conversation, fellowship] *società, compagnia, conversazione,* s. f.

Society [company, body] *società, compagnia, corpo.*

The Royal Society of England [a fellowship of learned men, founded by King Charles II. for improving natural knowledge] *la Società Reale d' Inghilterra.*

SOCI'NIANS, s. [a sect so called from one Lelius Socinus, who asserted that Christ was mere man and had no existence before Mary; he denied the personality of the Holy Ghost, original sin, grace, and predestination, the sacraments, and immensity of God] *Sociniani, setta d' eretici.*

SOCI'NIANISM, s. [the opinions and principles of the Socinians] *Socinianismo,* s. m. *l' opinioni e principi de' Sociniani.*

SOCK, s. [a sort of shoe worn by the comedians of old] *socco,* s. m. *calzare usato dagli strioni antichi nella commedia.*

SO'CKET, s. [of a candlestick] *piattellino da porre sul candeliere, che si leva e pone.*

The sockets of the teeth, *le gengive, le gingie.*

Socket [the receptacle of the eye] *occhiaja, il buco in cui l' occhio è dalla natura locato.*

SO'CKETCHISSEL, s. [a strong sort of chissel] *scalpello forte.*

SO'CLE, s. [a flat square member under the bases of pedestals of statues and vases] *zoccolo, termine d' architettura.*

SOD, s. [turf] *gleba,* s. f. *zolla di terra che abbia secco l' erba.*

SOD, or SODDEN, adj. [from to seeth] *lesso, bollito.*

SODA'LITY, s. [fellowship] *compagnia, compagnevolezza,* s. f.

SO'DDY, adj. [full of sod] *pieno di zolle, di glebe.*

SO'DER, } s. a composition used by plumbers, silver-smiths, and other artificers, in the working and binding metals] *saldatura,* s. f. *la materia con che si salda.*
SO'LDER, }

To SO'DER, or to SO'LDER [to join or fasten with soder] *saldare, riunire, ricongiugnere con saldatura.*

SO'DERED, adj. *saldato.*

SO'DERING, s. *saldatura, il saldare.*

SOEVER, *è una particella che s' unisce a' pronomi* WHO, WHAT, WHICH.

Ex. WHOSOE'VER, *chiunque, qualunque.*

WHATSOE'VER, *che che sia.*

Which way soever, *in qualunque maniera.*

SO'FA, s. [a sort of stuffed chair much used in eastern countries] *sofà,* s. m.

SOFT, adj. [tender, not hard] *molle, tenero, morbido, delicato, molliccio.*

A soft bed, *un letto molle.*

Soft bread, *pan tenero.*

Soft stone, *pietra molliccia.*

Soft hands, *mani morbide.*

Soft [mild, gentle] *molle, benigno, piacevole, trattabile, umano, mite.*

To speak with a soft voice, *parlar sotto voce.*

Soft pace, *passo lento.*

To have a soft place in one's head [to be crazed] *aver dato le cervella a rimpedulare, aver poco giudizio, avere una vena di pazzo.*

Soft fire makes sweet malt, *si guadagna più colle buone che colla forza.*

Soft, adv. *mollemente, morbidamente.*

To lie soft, *dormire morbidamente.*

Soft [hold there] *piano, alto là.*

Soft, s. ex. The soft of the belly, *la parte molle del ventre, la ventresca.*

Soft-brained, *stolto, scimunito, goffo, scioco, scervellato.*

Soft-hearted, *misericordioso, pietoso, compassionevole.*

To SO'FTEN [to make soft] *ammorbidare, ammorbidire, far morbido, mollificare, ammollire.*

To soften [to lenify, to mollify, to alleviate] *addolcire, mitigare, allenire, disasprire, alleggerire, alleggiare, sgravare, sollevare,* pref. *addolcisco, allenisco, disasprisco, alleggerisco.*

To soften [to effeminate] *ammorbidare, ammollire, render effeminato.*

To soften iron, *ammollire il ferro.*

To

To ſoften [to grow ſoft] *ammorbidirſi, ammollirſi, raddolcirſi.*

SO'FTENED, adj. *ammorbidito, mollificato, ammollito, v.* To ſoften.

SO'FTENING, s. *il raddolcire, v.* To ſoften.

Softening, adj. [apt to ſoften] *ammollitivo, atto ad ammollire, atto a raddolcire, mollificativo.*

SO'FTISH, adj. *molliccio, alquanto molle.*

SO'FTLY, adv. [without noiſe] *piano, pian piano, bel bello.*

Softly [leiſurely, ſlowly] *con bel modo, piacevolmente, acconciamente, adagio, lentamente, paſſo paſſo.*

Softly [hold] *piano, alto là.*

Softly [not too loud] *piano, ſotto-vore.*

To ſpeak ſoftly, *parlar piano o ſotto-voce.*

Softly, adj. [ſlow] *lento, agiato, pigro.*

A ſoftly man, *un uomo lento o agiato.*

A ſoftly man [a ninny, a fool] *un minchione, un cionno, un gonzo, un lavaceci.*

SO'FTNED, *v.* Softened.

SO'FTNESS, s. [the ſtate or quality of being ſoft] *morbidezza, dilicatezza,* s. f.

Softneſs [effeminacy] *effeminatezza, dilicatezza, mollezza, mollizie,* s. f.

SO'HO, interj. [a form of calling from a diſtant place] *voce o grido uſato nel chiamar da lontano.*

SO'IL, s. [ground, conſidered with reſpect to its quality or ſituation] *ſuolo, terreno,* s. m.

This ſoil is good for corn, *queſto ſuolo, o queſto terreno è buono per il grano.*

Fruitful ſoil, *terreno fertile.*

Native ſoil [native country] *paeſe natio.*

Soil [dung] *letame, concio,* s. m.

The ſoil of a wild boar [the ſlough wherein he wallows] *il porcile d'un cinghiale.*

To take ſoil [a hunting term, to run into the water, as a deer when cloſely purſed] *tuffarſi nell' acqua, come fanno i cervi quando ſono ſeguitati dai cani.*

To SO'IL [or dung] *dar il concio, letamare.*

To ſoil one's clothes, *ſporcarſi i panni, imbrattarſi gli abiti.*

To ſoil a doubt, *chiarire, riſolvere un dubbio.*

To ſoil milk [to ſtrain milk] *colare il latte.*

SOI'LED, adj. *concio, letamato, v.* To ſoil.

To SO'JOURN [to tarry or ſtay a while in a place] *ſoggiornare, dimorare, intertenerſi in un luogo.*

SOJO'URNER, s. *foreſtiero, foreſtiere, ſtraniero,* s. m. *foreſtiera, ſtraniera,* s. f.

SOJO'URNING, s. [ſtay] *ſoggiorno,* s. m. *dimora,* s. f.

SOKE, s. ex. You need give it but one good ſoke, *baſta che l' immolliate bene una ſol volta.*

Soke [in law, the privilege of keeping a court] *il privilegio di tenere una corte.*

To SOKE [to ſteep] *immollare, iuzuppare.*

To let the ſoop ſoke upon the chafing-diſh, *laſciar iſtuſare la zuppa ſopra lo ſcaldavivande.*

To ſoke one's pockets, *vuotare la borſa ad uno.*

To ſoke in, *inzupparſi.*

To ſoke through, *penetrare.*

SO'KED, adj. *immollato, inzuppato.*

SO'KER, s. [toper] *beone, bevitore.*

SO'KING, adj. *immollamento,* s. m. *v.* To ſoke.

Soking paper, *carta che ſuccia o bee l' inchioſtro.*

To lay the ſoop a ſoking, *laſciar iſtuſare la zuppa.*

SOL, s. [the name of one of the notes in the gamut] *ſol, voce muſicale.*

Sol [the ſun] *il ſole; vore poetica.*

Sol [among chymiſts, gold] *oro.*

SO'LACE, s. [comfort, conſolation] *ſollazzo, conforto,* s. m. *conſolazione.*

To SO'LACE [to comfort] *confortare, conſolare.*

To ſolace one's ſelf, *ſollazzarſi, ricrearſi, pigliarſi piacere, ſpaſſarſi.*

SO'LAND-GOOSE [a bird] *pellicano.*

SO'LAR, adj. [of or belonging to the ſun] *ſolare, di ſole.*

Solar year, *anno ſolare.*

Solar, s. [upper room] *ſoffitta,* s. f. *ſtanza a tetto.*

SOLD, adj. [from to ſell] *venduto.*

A thing to be ſold, *una coſa da vendere.*

SO'LDAN, *v.* Sultan.

SO'LDER, *v.* Soder.

SO'LDIER, s. [a fighting man, a warrior] *ſoldato, guerriero,* s. m. *è generalmente uſato per ſoldato ſemplice,* e *non per ufficiale.*

SO'LDIER-LIKE, } adj. [martial, war-
SO'LDIERLY, } like, military, becoming a ſoldier] *ſoldateſco, militare, guerriero, valoroſo; da ſoldato.*

SO'LDIERSHIP, s. [military character; martial qualities; behaviour becoming a ſoldier] *carattere militare; qualità bellicoſe; bravura o coraggio ſoldateſco.*

SO'LDIERY, s. [body of military men] *ſoldateſca.*

Soldiery, s. [ſoldierſhip; martial ſkill] *carattere ſoldateſco.*

SOLE, adj. [only, alone] *ſolo, unico.*

This is the ſole reaſon that hinder'd me, *queſta è la ſola ragione che m' ha trattenuto.*

He is my ſole comfort, *egli è l' unico mio comforto.*

Sole, s. [of the foot] *la pianta del piede, il ſuolo del piede.*

The ſole of a ſhoe, *il ſuolo d' una ſcarpa.*

Sole [horſe's hoof] *ſuolo,* s. f. *ſuprema parte dell' unghia morta delle beſtie da ſoma e da traino.*

Sole [a ſort of flat fiſh] *ſogliola,* s. f. *ſorta di peſce di mare.*

To SOLE, verb act. *mettere i ſuoli alle ſcarpe.*

To ſole a pair of ſhoes, *mettere i ſuoli ad un pajo di ſcarpe*

SO'LECISM, s. [an impropriety of ſpeech contrary to the rules of grammar] *ſolecíſmo,* s. m. *error di gramatica.*

SO'LELY, adv. [only] *ſolamente, unicamente.*

To be a man's heir ſolely and wholly, *eſſer erede univerſale di qualcheduno.*

SO'LEMN, adj. [that is celebrated in due order at ſome ſtated time] *ſolenne, che ſi celebra in certi giorni dell' anno.*

Solemn [done with great pomp] *ſolenne, magnifico, grande ſplendido, eccellente, pomposo.*

Solemn [authentick] *ſolenne, autentico.*

Solemn promiſe, *promeſſa ſolenne.*

To take a ſolemn oath, *giurare ſolennemente.*

SOLE'MNIAL, adj. [ſolemn] *ſolenne, celebre.*

SOLE'MNITY, s. *ſolennità, pompa, magnificenza, gran cerimonia.*

Solemnity [the pomp of celebrating an anniverſary feaſt] *ſolennità, giorno di gran feſta ſolito di celebrarſi ogni anno.*

SOLEMNIZA'TION, s. [the act of ſolemnizing] *ſolennità,* s. f. *il ſolenneggiare.*

To SO'LEMNIZE [to celebrate] *ſolenneggiare, ſolennizzare, celebrar con ſolennità.*

SO'LEMNIZED, adj. *ſolenneggiato, ſolennizzato.*

SOLEMNI'ZING, s. *il ſolenneggiare.*

SO'LEMNLY, adv. *ſolennemente, con ſolennità.*

To SOLI'CIT, *ſollecitare, v.* To ſollicit, e tutti i *ſuoi derivativi; ſcrivi però ſempre con una* l *ſola che è più ſecondo l' etimologia Latina da cui gl' Ingleſi hanno queſta voce e non dal Toſcano ſollecitare; e con una ſola* l *lo pone* Johnſon *nel ſuo dizionario, come che l'* Altieri *abbia altramente uſato.*

SO'LID, adj. [that has length, breadth, and depth] *ſolido.*

Solid [hard, maſſy] *ſolido, duro, maſſiccio.*

Solid gold, *oro ſolido o maſſiccio.*

Solid [real, ſubſtantial, not vain or frivolous] *ſolido, ſodo, ſaldo, reale, effettivo, durabile.*

Solid, s. [a ſolid body] *un ſolido, un corpo ſolido.*

SOLI'DITY, s. [firmneſs, ſoundneſs] *ſolidità, ſolidezza, ſaldezza, durezza, fermezza,* s. f.

SO'LIDLY, adv. ſolidamente; con ſolidezza, ſoldamente.

SO'LIDO, s. ex. A bond in ſolido [a bond or writing obligatory for the whole] un' obbligazione in ſolido, ed è quando intervenendovi molti, ciaſcuno reſta obbligato dell' intero.

SOLIFI'DIAN, s. [one who holds that faith only, without works, is neceſſary to ſalvation] colui che crede poterſi ſalvare ſolamente colla fede ſenza l' opere.

SO'LILOQUY, s. [a diſcourſe of one that ſpeaks alone] ſoliloquio, s m.

SO'LING, s. [from to ſole] il mettere i ſuoli alle ſcarpe.

My ſhoes want ſoling, le mie ſcarpe hanno biſogno d' eſſer riſuolate.

SO'LITARILY, adv. [privately] ſolitariamente, ſolo a ſolo.

SOLITA'RINESS, s. [ſolitary life] vita ſolitaria, ritiratezza.

Solitarineſs [ſolitude] ſolitudine, qualità ſolitaria d' un luogo.

SO'LITARY, adj. [loneſome, retired, unfrequented] ſolitario, non frequentato, deſerto, romito.

Solitary [that loves to be retired, or alone] ſolitario, che fugge la compagnia, ritirato.

SO'LITUDE, s. [a retirement, a ſolitary life] ſolitudine, ritiratezza, vita ſolitaria, deſerto, luogo deſerto.

SO'LLAR [a garret] granajo, la più alta parte della caſa, e viene da ſolarium Latino, o dal Toſcano ſolajo.

To SOLLI'CITE [to proſecute] continuare, andare, avanti, v. To ſolicite, e la nota che ò ho fatta.

To ſollicite [to importune, to preſs, to egg on] ſollecitare, ſtimolare, fare iſtanzia, importunare, affrettare.

SOLLICITA'TION, s. [inducement, inſtance] ſollecitazione, inſtigazione, iſtanza, richieſta, perſuaſione, s. f.

SOLLI'CITED, adj. ſollecitato, v. To ſollicite.

SOLLI'CITING, s. ſollecitamento, s. m. ſollecitazione, s. f. il ſollecitare.

SOLLI'CITOR, s. [one who ſollicites] ſollecitatore, s. m.

SOLLI'CITOR [in law, a perſon employed to take care of, and follow ſuits in law] ſollecitatore.

SOLLI'CITOUS, adj. [much troubled or concerned about a buſineſs] ſollecito, curante.

SOLLI'CITUDE, s. [trouble, anxiety] ſollecitudine, cura, s. f. penſiero, affanno, s. m.

SOLO, s. [a tune played by a ſingle inſtrument] ſonata, ſolo.

SO'LOMON'S-LOAF, s. nome di pianta.

SO'LOMON'S-SEAL, s. nome di pianta.

SO'LSTICE, s. [the time when the ſun is come to either of the tropicks] ſolſtizio, s. m. il tempo che 'l ſole è ne' tropici.

SOLSTI'TIAL, adj. [belonging to the ſolſtice] ſolſtiziario, di ſolſtizio.

The ſolſtitial points, i punti del ſolſtizio.

SO'LVABLE, adj [that may be reſolved or explained] che ſi può ſolvere o dichiarare, ſolvibile.

SO'LVABLE [able to pay] beneſtante, ricco, che può pagare, ſolvente.

SO'LUBLE, adj. [looſe] ſolubile.

To keep the belly ſoluble, ſolvere, o muovere il ventre.

Soluble [that may be unlooſed or diſſolved] ſolubile, atto a ſciorſi.

To SOLVE [to reſolve, to decide] ſolvere, riſolvere, decidere, pret. deciſi.

SOLVED, adj. ſoluto, riſoluto, deciſo.

SO'LVENT, adj. [ſolvable] ſolvente, che può pagare.

SOLU'TION, s. ſoluzione, riſoluzione, deciſione.

SOLU'TIVE, adj [that looſens the belly] ſolutivo, che ſolve il ventre.

SOLUND-GOOSE, s. [a foul in bigneſs and feather very like a tame gooſe, but his bill and his wings longer] ſpezie d' oca ſalvatica.

SOME, pron. [a part of the whole] qualche.

In ſome meaſure, in ſome place, in qualche maniera, in qualche luogo.

Some times, qualche volta.

Some time or other, un giorno o l' altro.

Some [a little] un poco, un po.

Give me ſome bread, ſome meat, datemi del pane, della carne.

I have ſome, ne ho.

Some [ſome men] alcuni.

Some ſay, alcuni dirono.

Some one way, ſome another, chi di qua, chi di la.

Some ſay one thing, ſome another, chi dice una coſa, chi un' altra.

Some [certain] certi, alcuni, qualcheduni.

I won't do it for ſome reaſons beſt known to me, non voglio farlo, per certe ragione ch' io ſo.

Some will not believe it, alcuni non vogliono crederlo.

Some body, ſome body or other, qualcheduno.

Some body elſe, qualchedun' altro.

He will be look'd upon as ſome body, egli ſarà riſpettato.

Give me ſome of it, datemene un poco.

Some [about] da, incirca.

I was ſome twenty miles off, io n' ero diſtante da venti miglia.

Some thing, qualche coſa.

Do that, and I'll give you ſomething, fate ciò, e vi darò qualche coſa.

He is ſomething indiſpoſed, egli è un poco indiſpoſto.

Somewhat [ſomething] qualche coſa.

I have ſomewhat to tell you, ho qualche coſa a dirvi.

Somewhat [a little] un poco, alquanto.

Somewhere, adv. in qualche luogo.

Somewhere elſe, altrove.

From ſomewhere elſe, altronde.

SOMNI'FEROUS, adj. [bringing ſleep] ſonnifero, che induce ſonno.

SO'MNOLENCE, s. [drowſineſs, ſleepineſs] ſonnolenza.

SON, s. [a male child, in reſpect to the parents] figlio, figliuolo, s. m.

Son-in-law, figliaſtro genero.

Grandſon, un nipote.

God ſon, un figlioccio.

Every mother's ſon, ciaſcheduno, ognuno.

SONG, s. [a poetical piece to be ſung] canzona, canzone, s. f.

To give a thing for a ſong [for little or nothing] dar qualche coſa per un pezzo di pane, quaſi per nulla.

SO'NGSTER, s. un cantanta, una cantante.

SO'NNET, s. [a ſort of Italian poem conſiſting of fourteen verſes] un ſonetto.

Sonnet, s. [a ſhort compoſition in verſe] breve componimento in verſi.

SONO'ROUS, adj. [ſounding, or making a great ſound] ſonoro, che rende ſuono.

SONO'ROUSLY, adv. con ſonorità, ſonoramente.

SO'NSHIP, s. [from ſon] qualità di figlio, figliazione.

SOON, adv. [quickly] toſto, ben toſte, ſubito, quanto prima, preſto.

Too ſoon, troppo preſto.

As ſoon as I can, ſubito che potrò.

He will be here ſoon, verrà quanto prima, ſarà quì preſto.

Soon after, non molto dopo.

As ſoon as I ſaw him, ſubito che lo vidi, nel vederlo.

As ſoon as I have dined, pranſato ch' averò.

As ſoon as may be, quanto prima.

How ſoon will you come back, quanto tempo ſarete a venire, quando riternerete?

SO'ONER, adj. [the comparative of ſoon] più toſto, anzi, meglio.

I wou'd ſooner die than wrong you, vorrei più toſto morire che farvi torto.

I could come no ſooner, non ho potuto venire più preſto.

No ſooner I ſaw him, ſubito che lo vidi, appena vedutolo.

SO'ONEST, adv. [the ſuperlative of ſoon] il più preſto.

SOOP, s. [pottage] zuppa, mineſtra, s. f.

SOOT, s. [the black ſtuff that ſticks to the chimney] fuligine, filiggine, caligine, s. f.

To SOOTH up [to flatter] luſingare, accarezzare, piaggiare, adulare.

SO'OTHED up, adj. luſingato, accarezzato, piaggiato, adulato.

SO'OTHING, adj. luſinga, adulazione, carezza, s. f.

SOOTHSA'YER, v. Southſayer.

SOOTY, adj. [full of ſoot] filiginoſo, caliginoſo, pien di caligine, bujo.

SOP, s. [a ſlice of bread dipt in gravy] pan unto.

Wine ſop, pane inzuppato nel vino.

To SOP, verb act. inzuppare, intignere, preſ. intingo, pret. intinſi.

SOPE, s. ſapone, s. m. oggi ſi ſcrive più comunemente ſoap.

To waſh in ſope, inſaponare.

Sope-boiler, s. colui che fa o vende il ſapone.

Sope-wort [an herb] ſaponajo, s. f. ſpezie d' erba.

To SOPE [to ſoap, to daub with ſoap] inſaponare, impiaſtrar di ſapone.

SOPED, adj. inſaponato.

SOPH,

SOPH, s. [sophister] *sofista, sofistico*, s. m. *che fa sofismi.*

Soph [a young man who has been two years at the university] *un giovane che è stato due anni allo studio.*

SO'PHI, s. [a title of the supreme monarch of Persia] *il Sofì, il rè Persia.*

SO'PHISM, s. [a cunning shifting argument or speech] *sofisma*, e *sofismo* s. m. *argomento fallace.*

SO'PHIST, } s. [a subtle cavil-
SO'PHISTER, } ling disputer] *sofistico*, s. m.

Sofister [a student at the university of Cambridge] *studente nell' università di Cantabrigia.*

Sophister [a cunning sharp man] *una volpe, un volpone, un formicon di sorbo, un uomo astuto.*

SOPHI'STICAL, adj. [captious, deceitful] *sofistico, cavilloso.*

To **SOPHI'STICATE** [to mingle, to debase, to adulterate] *sofisticare, adulterare, falsificare.*

SOPHI'STICATED, adj. *sofisticato, adulterato, falsificato.*

SOPHI'STICATING, } s. *sofisticheria*,
SOPHISTICATION, } s. f. *il sofistirare, l' adulterare.*

SOPHISTICA'TOR, s. *colui che sofistica, che adultera, che falsifica.*

SO'PHISTRY, s. [the art of circumventing or deceiving by false arguments] *sofisticheria*, s. f.

To **SO'PORATE** [to bring sleep] *addormentare, far dormire.*

SO'PORATING, } adj. [bringing
SOPORI'FEROUS, } sleep] *soporifero, sonnifero, che fa dormire.*

SOPPED, adj. [from to sop] *inzuppato, intinto.*

SORB-APPLE, s. [service-berry] *sorba*, s. f. *sorta di frutto.*

Sorb apple-tree, *sorbo*, s. m. *sorta d' albero fruttifero.*

SO'RBONIST, s. [a divine belonging to the college of Sorbonne in Paris] *dottore o teologo del collegio della Sorbona in Parigi.*

SO'RCERER, s. [a wizzard] *uno stregone, un maliardo.*

SO'RCERESS, s. [a witch] *una strega, un stregona, una maga.*

SO'RCERY, s. [witchcraft] *stregoneria*, s. f. *stregoneccio, ammaliamento, affatturamento*, s. m. *fattura*, s. f.

SORD, s. [turf, grassy ground] *terreno che produce minuta, verde, e foltissima erba.*

SO'RDES, s. [foulness, dregs] *sporcizie, fece.*

SORDET, v. Sordine.

SO'RDID, adj. [dirty, filthy] *sozzo, sucido, sudicio, sporco.*

Sordid [base, niggardly, pitiful] *sordido, cacastecchi, misero, meccanico, spilorcio, stretto, taccagno, avaro.*

A sordid man, *un cacastecchi, un avaro, un misero, un tanghero, un taccagno.*

SO'RDIDLY, adv. *grettamente, schifamente, sordidamente.*

SO'RDIDNESS, s. *sordidezza, bruttezza, deformità, avarizia, miseria, spilorceria, strettezza*, s. f.

SO'RDINE, s. [a little pipe put into the mouth of a trumpet to make it sound lower] *sordina*, s. f.

SORE, adj. *dolente, doloroso, che fa male.*

A sore place, *una parte dolorosa, che fa male, che da del dolore.*

Sore eyes, *mal d' occhi.*

Sore [great, cruel] *grande crudele, atroce duro.*

A sore bout, *un duro conflitto.*

Sore enemy, *crudel nemico, nemico capitale.*

Sore, s. [sore place] *male*, s. m.

Here lies my sore, *qui è il mio male.*

Sore [ulcer, wound] *ulcera, ferita, piaga*, s. f.

Full of sores, *ulceroso, pieno d' ulcere.*

Sore [male deer four years old] *daino di quattr' anni.*

Sore, adj. [greatly, vehemently] *molto, grandemente, fieramente.*

I am sore afraid, *temo molto.*

I was sore afraid, *avevo gran paura, temevo molto.*

Sore wounded, *fieramente ferito.*

My heart is sore vexed with grief, *il mio cuore è trafitto dal dolore.*

Full sore against my will, *mio mal grado.*

SO'REL, s. [male fallow deer three years old] *daino di tre anni.*

SO'RELY, adv. *gravemente, grandemente, aspramente.*

SO'RENESS, s. *male.*

Soreness of the eyes, *mal d' orchi.*

SORI'TES, s. [an argument where one proposition is accumulated on another] *sorite, argomento in cui una proposizione s' appoggia sur un altro. E' termine logico.*

SO'RRAGE, s. [the blades of green wheat or barley] *il gambo del frumento o dell' orzo quando è verde anrora.*

SO'RREL, s. [an herb] *acetosa*, s. f. *erba che prende il nome dal suo sapore che è acetoso.*

Roman sorrel, *acetosa Romana.*

Petty sallet sorrel, or small sheep sorrel, *acetosa salvatica.*

Sorrel, adj. [a sort of colour amongst horses] *sauro, aggiunto, che si da a cavallo di pelo tra bianco e tanè.*

Sorrel horse, *un cavallo sauro.*

Burnt sorrel horse, *un cavallo sauro abbruciato.*

SO'RRILY, adv. [scurvily] *malamente, cattivamente, pessimamente, goffamente, meschinamente.*

SO'RRINESS, s. [meanness, wretchedness, despicableness, pitiableness] *meschinezza, tristizia, spregievolezza, povertà, fursanteria.*

SO'RROW, s. [misfortune] *sfortuna, disgrazia*, s. f. *malore*, s. m.

Sorrow [affliction, grief] *dolore, affanno, cordoglio, rincrescimento, travaglio, disgusto*, s m. *afflizione*, s. f.

To my great sorrow, *con mio gran cordoglio.*

The more my sorrow, *e più mi duole.*

Sorrow proof [insensible] *indolente, insensibile.*

To **SO'RROW** [to be sorry] *affliggersi, affannarsi, darsi pena, attristarsi.*

SO'RROWFUL, adj. *tristo, afflitto, dolente, sconsolato affannato.*

Sorrowful [pitiful, miserable] *misero, infelice, sgraziato.*

SO'RROWFULLY, adv. [sadly, with sorrow] *cordogliosamente, dogliosamente.*

Sorrowfully [miserably] *infelicemente, sfortunatamente, miseramente, meschinamente.*

SO'RRY, adj. [that grieves] *tristo, mesto, sconsolato, affannato, cordoglioso.*

I am sorry for it, *mi dispiace, ne sento gran dispiacere, mi rincresce.*

Sorry [bad, paultry, vile] *dispregevole, povero, meschino, da niente.*

A sorry fellow, *un uomo di niente, un vigliacco.*

SORT, s. [kind] *sorta, sorte, spezie, qualità*, s. f.

Sort [way, manner] *modo*, s. m. *maniera*, s. f.

This is another sort of wine, *questa è un' altra sorta di vino.*

After this sort, *in questo modo, in questa maniera.*

The common sort of people, *il volgo, la plebe, il popolo minuto.*

To be out of all sorts, or out of humour, *esser di cattivo umore, esser tristo, maninconico.*

To **SORT** [to match, to dispose things in their proper classes] *assortire, scerre, distinguere, scompartire*, pres. *assortisco, sceigo, scompartisco*, pret. *srelsi, distinsi.*

SO'RTABLE, adj *convenevole.*

SO'RTABLY, adv. *convenevolmente.*

SO'RTANCE, s. [suitableness, agreement] *convenevolezza, proporzione.*

SO'RTED, adj. *assortito, scelto, distinto, scomparito.*

SOT, s. [blockhead, dull fellow] *babbuasso, cionno, sciocco, minchione, scimunito*, s. m.

A drunken sot, *un imbriacone.*

To **SOT**, ex, to sot one's time away [to spend it foolishly] *gettar via il tempo, mettere stoppia in aja.*

SO'TTISH, adj. *sciocco, scimunito, scipito.*

A sottish fellow, *uno sciocco, uno scimunito.*

SO'TTISHLY, adv. *scioccamente, goffamente, balordamente.*

SO'TTISHNESS, s. *sciocchezza, scimunitaggine, pazzia, schioccheria.*

SOUCE, s. [pork souced] *porco marinato.*

To **SOUCE** pork, *marinare del porro.*

SOUCED, adj. *marinato.*

SO'VEREIGN, adj. [absolute, supreme] *sovrano, soprano, assoluto, superiore, principale.*

Sovereign [excellent; supreme] *sovrano, eccellente, singolare.*

Sovereign remedy, *rimedio sovrano.*

Sovereign felicity, *suprema felicità.*

Sovereign, s. [a sovereign prince] *sovrano*, s. m. *che ha sovranità, principe sovrano, signor assoluto.*

SO'VEREIGNLY, adv. *sovranamente, assolutamente, independentemente.*

Sovereignly [excellently] *sovranamente, eccellentemente, singolarmente.*

SOVEREIGNTY [supreme power] *sovranità, superiorità, maggioranz*

Sovereignty [a sovereign state] *sovranità, stato d' un principe sovrano.*
SOUGH, s. [a subterraneous drain] *fogna, cloaca sotteranea.*
SOUGHT, *è un preterito del verbo* To seek.
SOUGHT, adj. [from to seek] *cercato, v.* To seek.
SOUL, s. [the principle of life] *anima, s. f. vita degli animanti.*
Soul [mind, spirit] *anima, spirito.*
A great and generous soul, *un' anima grande, un animo generoso.*
The souls of the dead, *le anime de' morti.*
Soul [or person] *anima, persona.*
There is not a soul at home, *non v' è anima nata in casa.*
A good honest soul, *un uomo dabbene, una donna dabbene.*
Upon my soul, *su l' anima mia, in coscienza mia.*
With all my soul, *di tutto cuore.*
Soul [life, that which acts and animates any thing] *anima, vita.*
Charity is the soul of christian virtues, *la carità è l' anima delle virtù cristiane.*
All-souls day, *il Giorno de' Morti.*
Soul-saving [a Presbyterian expression] *salutare.*
SO'ULDIER, s. *soldato, scrivesi oggidì.* SOLDIER.
Foot-souldier, *soldato a piè, fantaccino, fante.*
The souldier's pay, *la paga, il soldo.*
Souldierly, adv. *alla soldatesca, da soldato.*
SO'ULDIERY, s. *la soldatesca, i soldati.*
SOULED, adj. [furnished with mind] *che ha anima.*
SO'ULLESS, adj. [mean, low, spiritless] *vile, dappoco, vigliacco, senz' anima, senza cuore, timido, pauroso.*
SOUND, s. [the object of hearing] *suono, rimbombo.*
To make or yield a sound, *render suono, risuonare.*
The Sound [the streights of the Baltick sea] *lo Stretto del mare Baltico.*
The sound of an organ, *cannone d' organo.*
The sound-post of a musical instrument, *l' anima d' uno strumento musicale.*
Sound, adj. [entire, whole] *intiero, al quale non manca niente, in buono stato, ben condizionato.*
Sound commodities, *mercanzie ben condizionate.*
Sound [healthful] *sano, gagliardo, che sta bene.*
I am as sound as a roach, *io sono sano come una lasca.*
Sound, [judicious, solid] *sano, solido, fondato, giudicioso, parlando d' un discorso.*
Sound doctrine, *dottrina sana.*
To be in a sound sleep, *esser in un profondo sonno.*
To give one a sound blow, *dare un gran colpo ad uno.*
Wood that is not sound [rotten wood] *legno fracido, legno fradicio.*

To have sound principles, *aver sentimenti d' onore, di probità retti.*
To SOUND, verb act. *sonare.*
To sound a trumpet, *sonar la tromba.*
To sound the retreat, *batter la ritirata.*
To sound forth, *risonare, rimbombare.*
To sound a letter, *pronunciare una lettera.*
To sound the depth of the sea, or of a river, *scandagliare il mare, o un fiume.*
To sound [to pump, to sift] *tentare, tastare, scalzare, spiar l' animo.*
To sound, verb neut. *suonare, risonare, rimbombare.*
The trumpet sounds, *la tromba suona.*
To sound like an echo, *risuonare come un eco.*
SO'UNDBOARD, s. [board which propagates the sound in organs] *tavola che propaga il suono dell' organo.*
SO'UNDED, adj. *sonato, v.* To sound.
SO'UNDER [herd, company] *truppa.*
Sounder of swine, *truppa di porci.*
Sounder [the comparative of sound] *più sano.*
SO'UNDING, s. *il suonare, v.* To sound.
Sounding lead, *scandaglio.*
Sounding, s. *sonante, risonante, che suona.*
Sounding voice, *voce sonora.*
SO'UNDLY, adv. *fortemente, gagliardamente.*
To beat one soundly, *battere uno malamente, tartassarlo, malmenarlo.*
To sleep soundly, *dormir profondamente.*
SOUNDNESS, s. *stato perfetto.*
Soundness [perfect health] *sanità, salute perfetta.*
SOUP, s. [strong decoction of flesh for the table] *brodo forte di carne con qualcosa mista in esso.*
SOUR, v. Sowr, *e i suoi derivativi scrivi però* sour *colla* u *semplice, e non con la doppia come fe' l' Altieri, che così usano i meglio scrittori moderni.*
SOURCE, s. [head spring] *sorgente, fonte, scaturigine.*
SOUS, s. [a French penny] *un soldo di Francia.*
SOUTH, s. *mezzogiorno, merigge mezzodì.*
South, adj. [southern] *meridionale, di mezzo dì.*
South wind, *vento di mezzogiorno.*
South countries, *paesi meridionali.*
South east wind, *scilocco.*
South west wind, *garbino, libeccio.*
SO'UTHERLY, SO'UTHERN, } adv. *di mezzogiorno.*
Southern, adj. [that lies south] *meridionale, meriggiano.*
Southern-wood [an ever-green plant] *abrotino, abruotino, s. m. abrotina, s. f.*
SO'UTHMOST, adj. [farthest towards the south] *il più lontano dal canto di mezzogiorno.*
SO'UTHSAY [*propriamente* soothsay, prediction] *predizione.*

To SO'UTHSAY, *indovinare, predire* pref. *predico*, pret. *predissi.*
SOUTHSA'YER, s. *indovino, s. m. indovina, s. f.*
SOUTHSA'YING, s. *l' indovinare, il predire.*
SO'UTHWARD, adv. [towards the south] *verso mezzogiorno, australmente.*
SO'UTHWEST, s. [point between the south and west] *punto tra il mezzogiorno e l' occidente.*
SO'UVENANCE, s. [remembrance, memory] *rimembranza, memoria.*
SOW, s. [the female of a hog] *troja, s. f. la femmina del bestiame porcino.*
To take a wrong sow by the ear [to mistake the person] *pigiare una persona in isrambio, ingannarsi a proprio danno.*
Sow of melted iron, *un grosso pezzo di ferro.*
Sow of lead, *massa di piombo.*
Sow-pig [little sow] *una porchetta.*
Sow-gelder, *un castraporci.*
Sow [an insect] *porcellino terrestre, spezie d' insetto.*
Sow-bread [truffle] *pan porcino.*
Sow-thistle [a plant] *cicerbita, s. f.*
To SOW [to cast, to sow seed] *seminare, sementare, gettare, o spargere il seme sopra la materia atta a produrre.*
To sow a field, *seminare un campo.*
To sow dissentions among friends, *seminar dissenzioni fra amici, metterli male, metter la divisione fra gli amici.*
To sow [to sew, to stitch] *cucire.*
SOWED, s. *seminato, v.* To sow.
Sowed field, *seminato, campo dove fu sparso il seme.*
Sowed [stitched] *cucito.*
SO'WER, s. *seminatore, s. m. seminatrire, s. f.*
SO'WING, s. *seminamento, s. m. il seminare.*
Sowing time [seed time] *sementa, s. f. il tempo del sementare.*
Sowing silk, *seta da cucire.*
SOWN, adj. *seminato, sementato.*
SOWR, adj. [sour] *agro, acido, acerbo, brusco, arcigno, v.* Sour *E' la nota che vi ho fatta.*
Sowr taste, *gusto argo, sapore acerbo.*
Sowr apple, *mela acerba.*
To turn sowr, *inforzarsi, divenir agro, inacerbirsi.*
A man of a sowr temper, *un uomo d' un temperamento rozzo, zotico, o severo.*
Sowr look, *cera brusca, rigida, burbera, austera, aspra, arcigna.*
To be tied to the sowr apple-tree [to have an ill husband] *esser mal maritato avere un cattivo marito.*
To sowr [to turn sour] *inforzarsi, inacetirsi, divenir argo,* pref. *inacetisco.*
To sowr [to make sowr, in a proper and figurative sense] *innasprire, innasprare,* pref. *innasprisco, innaspro.*
SOWRED, adj. *inforzato, inacetito, innasprito, innasprato.*
SO'WRISH, adj. [somewhat sower] *agretto, alquanto, argo, o afro.*
SO'WRLY, adv. [in a figurative sense] *agramente, aspramente, fieramente, crudelmente.*
To look sowrly upon one, *fare strano sembiante ad uno, guardarlo di mal' occhio,*

occhio, farli il viſo dell' armè, guardare con viſo arcigno.

SO'WRNESS, s. agrezza, acidezza, aſprezza, acerbezza, s. f.

Sowrneſs of look, viſta acerba; arcigno ſguardo, aſpetto bruſco.

SOWTER, s. [cobler, ſhoemaker] ciabattino.

To SOYL, v. To ſoil.

SPACE, s. [diſtance, of either time or place] ſpazio, s m. quel tempo o luogo, che è di mezzo tra due termini.

In a ſhort ſpace of time, in piccolo ſpazio di tempo.

Space between places, diſtanza.

For the ſpace of three months, per lo ſpazio di tre meſi.

Space between, intervallo.

SPA'CIOUS, adj. [great, large, broad] ſpazioſo, ampio.

SPA'CIOUSLY, adv. ſpazioſamente, ampiamente.

SPA'CIOUSNESS, s. ampiezza di luogo.

SPADE, s. [a tool to cut the ground] zappa, vanga, s. f.

Spades [a colour at cards] ſpade o picche; uno de' quattro pali delle carte da giuocare.

Spade [deer three years old] cervo o daino di tre anni.

To call a ſpade a ſpade, chiamar la gatta, gatta; dir le coſe com' elle ſtanno.

Spade [a gelded man or beaſt] un caſtrato.

SPADI'CEOUS, adj. [light red] roſſigno.

SPA'DIERS, s. [labourers who dig in the mines in Cornwall] zappatori, uomini che lavorano nelle miniere di ſtagno nella provincia di Cornovaglia.

SPADI'LLE, s. [the ace of ſpades at ombre] ſpadiglia, l' aſſo di ſpade o di picche al giuoco dell' ombre, del quadriglio, &c.

SPAIN, s. Spagna, monarchia di Spagna.

SPAKE, è un preterito del verbo To ſpeak.

SPAN, s. [a meaſure from the thumb's end to the top of the little finger] ſpanna, s. f. la lunghezza della mano aperta e diſteſa dalla ſtremità del dito mignolo a quella del groſſo.

Spick and ſpan new, nuovo di zecca.

To SPAN [to meaſure with the hand] miſurare a ſpanne.

SPAN, è un preterito del verbo To ſpan.

SPANCO'UNTER, } s. [a play at
SPANFA'RTHING, } which money is thrown within a ſpan or mark] nomi d'un giuoco fanciulleſco che ſi fa gittando i danari fra certi ſegni diſtanti circa una ſpanna l' un dall' altro.

SPA'NGLE [a ſmall round thin piece of gold or ſilver] foglia, pagliuola, s. f. minutiſſima parte d' oro, o d' argento.

Spangle, s. ogni coſa minuta e ſcintillante.

To SPA'NGLE [to beſprinkle with ſpangles or ſhining bodies] ſpargere di pagliuole o ſcagliuzze minutiſſime e ſcintillanti.

SPA'NGLED, adj. ornato di pagliuole.

SPA'NIARD, s. uno Spagnuolo.

SPA'NIEL, or SPANIEL-DOG, un bracco, un barbone.

SPA'NISH, adj. [belonging to the country of Spain] Spagnuolo, di Spagna.

Spaniſh brown, caſtagno,

Spaniſh-fly, canterella, s. f.

Spaniſh-wool, liſcio, s. m. pezzetta, s. f.

Spaniſh-pick tooth, nome d' erba.

Spaniſh-red, cinabro, s. m.

SPA'NKER, s. [a ſmall coin] moneta piccola e di poco valore.

SPA'NKING, adj. [ſpruce] leſto, lindo, pulito, zerbino.

SPA'NNER, s. [the lock of a carbine, or fuzee] il cane d' una carabina, o ſchioppo.

SPAR, s. [bar of wood] una ſbarra di legno.

The ſpars of a ſpining wheel, i raggi d' una ruota da filare.

Spar [Muſcovy glaſs] vetro di Moſcovia.

Spar [ſtones like gems found in lead mines] ſorta di marcaſſita, o pietra lucente, che ſi trova nelle miniere di piombo in Inghilterra, ed in Germania.

To SPAR [to ſhut with a ſpar] ſbarrare, chiudere con iſbarra.

To ſpar a door, ſbarrare una porta.

SPA'RABLES, s. [ſmall nails] chiodi piccoliſſimi.

SPA'RAGRASS, } s. aſparago, s. m.
SPARAGUS, } frutice noto

SPARE, adj. [lean, thin] magro, ſmunto, macilente, ſmilzo.

A ſpare man, un uomo magro.

Spare diet, vita parca, e frugale.

Spare thing, coſa di riſerva.

If I have ſpare time, ſe avrò 'l tempo.

Do it at your ſpare time, fatelo a voſtro agio.

Spare money, danaro d' avanzo.

Spare-deck [the innermoſt deck in ſome great ſhips, called alſo orlop] il terzo ponte in alcuni vaſcelli groſſi.

Spare ribs, coſtole di porco ſalate.

Spare horſe, cavallo di riſpetto.

To SPARE [to ſave, to huſband] riſparmiare, ſparagnare.

To ſpare money, riſparmiar danaro.

To ſpare for nothing, non iſparagnar niente.

To ſpare [to favour] riſparmiare, favorire, eſſer favorevole, pref. favoriſco.

He does not ſpare himſelf, non ha neſſun riguardo a ſe ſteſſo, non ſi riſparmia in nulla.

I'll ſpare you that trouble, voglio eſentarvi da queſto incomodo.

Can't you ſpare this book for a while, potete far di meno di queſto libro per poco tempo.

If I can ſpare any time [if I have any time to ſpare] ſe averò tempo, ſe mi verrà fatta.

I can't ſpare money to buy this thing, non ho danaro da ſpendere in queſta coſa.

I can ſpare you ſome money, poſſo accomodarvi di qualche ſomma di danari.

I have enough to ſpare, ne ho più che non biſogna, ne ho d' avanzo.

To ſpare [to lay up] riſerbare, metter da banda, conſervare.

To ſpare [to forbear] aſtenerſi ritenerſi.

To ſpare [to forgive] riſparmiare, perdonare.

I won't ſpare him in the leaſt thing, non voglio riſparmiargliene una.

SPARED, adj. riſparmiato, ſparagnato, v. To ſpare.

SPA'RER, s. [one who avoids expence] uno che fugge l' occaſione di ſpendere, un economo, un riſparmiatore, uno ſpilorcio, un tanghero, un avaro, un miſero, un taccagno.

SPAR-HAWK, ſparviere, s. m.

SPA'RING, s. riſparmio, ſparagno, s. m. economia, s. f.

Sparing, adj. riſparmiante, leſinante parco, riſtretto.

He is a very ſparing man, un uomo molto parco o moderato.

SPA'RINGLY, adv. parcamente, con parſimonia, moderatamente.

To live ſparingly, viver parcamente o moderatamente.

SPA'RINGNESS, s. riſparmio, s. m. economia, parſimonia.

SPARK, s. [a very ſmall part of fire] ſcintilla, favilla.

Spark [gallant, lover] drudo, amatore.

To SPARK [to emit particles of fire, to ſparkle] mandar fuora ſcintille di fuoco, ſcintillare.

SPA'RKLE, s. [ſpark] ſcintilla.

Sparkles of iron, pagliuole di ferro battuto.

To SPA'RKLE [to caſt ſparks] ſcintillare, sfavillare.

Wine that ſparkles, vino frizzante.

Her eyes ſparkle, i ſuoi occhi ſcintillano, o ſono ſcintillanti.

SPA'RKLING, adj. [that ſparkles] ſcintillante, sfavillante.

SPA'RROW, s. [a bird well known] paſſero.

Cock-ſparrow, paſſero.

Hen-ſparrow, paſſera.

Hedge-ſparrow, verdiero, s. m. ſpezie d' uccello.

Sparrow-mouth'd, che ha una gran bocca.

SPA'RROW-GRASS [corrotto da ASPARAGUS, che alcuni pronunciano e ſcrivono anche ſparagraſs] aſparago.

SPA'RRY, adj. abbondante di quella marcaſſita chiamata dagl' Ingleſi ſpar, v. l' ultimo ſignificato di ſpar.

SPASM, s. [convulſion; violent and involuntary contraction] ſpaſmo, ſpaſimo.

SPASMO'DICK, adj. [convulſive.] ſpaſmodico, convulſivo.

SPAT, preterito del verbo To ſpit.

Spat, s. [the ſpawn of oyſters] fregola d' oſtriche.

To SPA'TTER [to beſpatter] ſporcare, lordare, imbrattare.

SPHATTERDA'SHES [a ſort of light boots without ſoles] ſpezie di ſtivali o di ſopraccalze.

SPA'TTERED, adj. ſporcato, lordato, imbrattato.

SPA'TTLE, or SPA'TULE, s. [a tool

ufed by furgeons and apothecaries] *fpatola*, s. f. *piccolo ftrumento di legno o di qualche metallo a fimilitudine di fcalpello che adoperano i cerufici e gli fpeziali.*

SPA'VIN, s. [a difeafe in horfes when the feet fwell] *fpavenio*, s. m. *malattia di cavallo.*

To SPAWL [to fpit] *fputare, fornacchiare.*

SPA'WLING, s. *lo fputare, fputo, fornacchio*, s. m.

SPAWN, s. [the femen or milk of fifh] *uova di pefce, fregolo*, s. m.

Spawn [feed in general] *feme*, s. m. *fementa*, s. f.

To SPAWN, verb neut. *andare in frega, e dicefi de' pefci.*

SPA'WNER, s. [the female fifh] *pefce femmina*, *v.* Milter.

Spawner [young fifh] *pefciolino.*

SPA'WNING, s. *frega*, s. f.

Spawning-time, *il tempo che i pefci vanno in frega.*

To SPAY [to geld] *caftrare animali femmine.*

To fpay a mare, *caftrare una giumenta.*

SPAYED, adj. *caftrata.*

SPA'YING, s. *il caftrare.*

To SPEAK [to utter words, to talk] *parlare, proferire, pronunciare.*

To fpeak out, *parlar ad alta voce.*

To fpeak low or foftly, *parlar fottovoce, o pianpiano.*

To fpeak to one, *parlare ad uno.*

To fpeak for one, *parlare in favore di qualcheduno.*

To fpeak [to fay] *dire*, pref. *dico*, pret. *diffi.*

To fpeak the truth, *dire la verità.*

To fpeak one's mind, *dire il fuo fentimento.*

If I were to fpeak my mind, *fe ardiffi dire il mio fentimento.*

To fpeak without book, *ingannarfi a partito, tirare in arcata, giudicare alla groffa, e fenza fondamento.*

To fpeak not a word, *non dire una parola.*

To fpeak [to exprefs] *efprimere, moftrare, far vedere.*

To fpeak to one's fatisfaction about a thing, *moftrare la fua fatisfazione intorno qualche cofa.*

To fpeak fair to one, *far buona cera ad uno, adularlo, piaggiarlo, allettarlo con finte parolette.*

Speak fair, and think what you will, *penfieri ftretti e vifo fciolto.*

To fpeak the word, *dire nettamente, fchiettamente quel che altri ha in penfiero.*

His mein fpeaks him a gentleman, *dall' aria fi può vedere ch' egli è gentiluomo.*

The firft verfe fpeaks the book to be a copy, *il primo verfo chiaramente dimoftra che 'l libro non è che una copia.*

SPE'AKER, s. *oratore.*

The fpeaker of the houfe of commons, *l' oratore della camera de' comuni.*

SPE'AKING, s. *il parlare.*

Speaking, adj. ex. fpeaking trumpet, *tromba marina.*

SPEAR [lance] *lancia, afta*, s. f. *forta d' arme in afta.*

SPE'AR-HEAD, *quel ferro che è in cima alle lance.*

Spear-ftaff, *l' afta d' una lancia.*

Spear-man, *lancia, cavaliere armato di lancia.*

Little fpear, or fhort fpear [a javelin] *afta corta.*

A French fpear [a fort of dart] *un dardo.*

A boar-fpear, *uno fpiedo.*

King's-fpear [a plant] *afodillo*, s. m. *fpezie d' erba.*

Spear wort [a plant] *ranunculo, o ranuncolo*, s. m. *forta d' erba.*

To SPEAR, v. a. [to kill or pierce with a fpear] *uccidere o traffiggere con lancia o fpiedo.*

To fpear, v. n. [to fhoot, to fprout] *germogliare, pullulare.*

SPE'CIAL, adj [particular, fingular] *fpeciale e fpeziale, fingolare, particolare.*

Special [excellent, extraordinary] *eccellente, fquifito, eletto, ottimo, fingolare.*

This is fpecial wine, *quefto vino è eccellente o fquifito.*

A fpecial fervant, *un bravo fervitore.*

By his majefty's fpecial command, *per ordine efpreffo del re.*

SPE'CIALLY, adv. *fpezialmente, particolarmente, principalmente, fopra* tutto.

SPE'CIALTY, } s. [a bond, a bill; SPECIA'LITY, } or fuch like deed, under hand and feal] *ogni forta di ftrumento o atto pubblico, come obligazione, cedola.*

SPE'CIES, s. [kind, fort] *fpezie, fpecie, forta*, s. f. *che comprende fotto di fe più cofe differenti folamente di numero.*

The propagation of the fpecies, *la propagazione della fpezie.*

Species [fort of money] *fpecie, una forta di moneta.*

To pay a fum in fpecie, *pagare una fomma in ifpecie.*

Species [images and reprefentatives of objects] *fpezie, imagine.*

SPECI'FICAL, } adj. [fpecial, parti- SPECI'FICK, } cular] *fpecifico, che coftituifce fpezie.*

SPECI'FICALLY, adv. *fpecificamente, fpecificatamente.*

To SPECI'FICATE [to mark by notation or diftinguifhing particularities] *fpecificare, dichiarare pofitivamente.*

SPECIFICA'TION, s. [the act of fpecifying] *fpecificazione*, s. f. *lo fpecificare.*

SPECI'FICK, *v.* Specifical.

Specifick medicine, *rimedio fpecifico.*

To SPE'CIFY [to particularize, to exprefs in particular] *fpecificare, dichiarare in particolare.*

SPE'CIFIED, adj. *fpecificato.*

SPE'CIFYING, s. *fpecificazione*, s. f. *lo fpecificare.*

SPE'CIMEN, s. [effay, proof] *faggio, cimento*, s. m. *pruova, moftra*, s. f.

SPE'CIOUS, adj. [fair in appearance, plaufible, feemingly] *fpeziofo, colorito, apparente, plaufibile.*

SPE'CIOUSLY, adv. [with fair appearance] *apparentemente, plaufibilmente.*

SPECK, s. [fpot] *macchia, tacca*, s. f.

To SPECK [to fpot, to ftain in drops] *macchiare, chiazzare, cagionar macchie.*

SPE'CKLE, s. [fmall fpeck, little fpot] *macchiuzza, macchia piccola.*

To SPE'CKLE, *macchiare, maculare, taccare, chiazzare.*

SPE'CKLED, adj. *macchiato, maculato, chiazzato, taccato.*

SPECT, s. [fpeight woodpecker] *picchio, uccello così detto dal picchiare che e' fa col becco negli alberi per farne ufcir fuora le formiche, e fonne di diverfe grandezze e di diverfi colori.*

SPE'CTABLE, adj. [to be looked on] *fpettabile, riguardevole.*

SPE'CTACLE, s. [publick fhow or fight] *fpettacolo*, s. m. *giuoco, o fefta rapprefentata pubblicamente.*

Spectacles [glaffes to help the fight] *occhiali.*

A pair of fpectacles, *un pajo d' occhiali.*

Spectacle maker, *occhialajo*, s. m. *quegli che fa gli occhiali.*

SPE'CTACLED, adj. [furnifhed with fpectacles] *fornito d' occhiali.*

SPE'CTATIVE, adj. [fpeculative, contemplative] *fpeculativo, contemplativo.*

SPECTA'TOR, s. [looker on, beholder] *fpettatore*, s. m.

SPECTA'TRESS, s. [female beholder] *fpettatrice*, s. f.

SPE'CTER, s. [a frightful apparition, a ghoft, a fpirit] *fantafma, immagine fpaventevole, fpirito, fpettro*, s. m.

To SPE'CULATE [to contemplate, to obferve, to view] *fpeculare, fpecolare, contemplare.*

SPECU'LATION, s. [contemplation] *fpeculazione, fpecolazione, contemplazione*, s. f.

Speculation [the theory or ftudy of an art or fcience] *teorica fpeculativa*, s. f.

SPE'CULATIVE, adj. [contemplative] *fpecolativo, contemplativo.*

SPE'CULATIVELY, adv. *fpeculativamente, fpecolativamente, contemplativamente.*

SPE'CULATOR, s. [one that fpeculates] *fpeculatore, fpecolatore.*

SPE'CULATORY, adj. [belonging to fpeculation] *fpeculativo, contemplativo.*

SPE'CULUM, s. [a mirror, a looking glafs] *fpecchio.*

SPED, *preterito del verbo* To fpeed.

Sped, adj. ex. Thofe things are fped in the king's name, *quefte cofe fono fatte a nome del re.*

SPEECH, s. [the faculty of fpeaking] *favella, parola, facoltà di parlare.*

To lofe one's fpeech, *perder la favella.*

Speech [tongue, or language] *favella, lingua*, s. f. *linguaggio, idioma particolare.*

Vulgar fpeech, *lingua volgare.*

Speech [difcourfe, oration] *difcorfo, ragionamento*, s. m. *orazione*, s. f.

He

He made a ſpeech to the people, *egli fece un' orazione del popolo.*

The eight parts of ſpeech in grammar, *le otto parti dell' orazione.*

To be ſlow of ſpeech [to ſpeak ſlow] *parlar lentamente.*

The laſt ſpeech of a dying perſon, *l' ultime parole d' una perſona moribonda.*

How ſhall I come to the ſpeech of him? *in che modo potrò mai parlargli?*

SPE'ECHLESS, adj. *che ha perduto la favella, o la parola.*

He ſtood ſpeechleſs, *rimaſe fuor di ſe.*

SPEED, s. [haſte] *fretta, ſollecitudine, preſtezza, preſcia,* s. f.

To make ſpeed, *affrettarſi, ſpedirſi, uſar ſollecitudine.*

He will come with all ſpeed, *verrà quanto prima, verrà toſto.*

Go thither with all ſpeed, *andate preſto, affrettatevi d' andar colà.*

To run with all ſpeed, to run with full ſpeed, *correr frettoloſamente, con fretta grandiſſima.*

To gallop with full ſpeed, *galoppare a briglia ſciolta, a tutta briglia.*

To make more haſte than good ſpeed, *affrettarſi troppo, fare una coſa con troppa precipitazione.*

To SPEED [to meet with ſucceſs] *riuſcire, ſortire, avere effetto,* preſ. *rieſco, ſortiſco.*

To ſpeed [to proſper] *far riuſcire, dar buon ſucceſſo.*

God ſpeed you, *Iddio v' accompagni.*

SPE'EDILY, adv. *prontamente, ſpeditamente, frettoloſamente, preſto, ſubito.*

SPE'EDINESS, s. *prontezza, ſollecitudine, diligenza, fretta.*

SPE'EDWELL, s. [the herb fluellin] *veronica,* s. f.

Female ſpeedwell [a plant] *ſanguiſorba,* s. f.

SPE'EDY, adj. [quick] *pronto, ſpedito, ſollecito, ſnello, veloce.*

Let me have a ſpeedy anſwer, *datemi una pronta riſpoſta.*

SPEIGHT, s. [ſpeckt, woodpecker, ſort of bird] *picchio,* s. m. *uccello così detto dal picchiare, che fa col becco negli alberi, per farne uſcir fuora le formiche.*

SPELL, s. [charm] *incantamento, incanto, ſortilegio,* s. m.

To SPELL [to name or write down the letters of a ſyllable or word] *compitare, l' accoppiar delle lettere e delle ſyllabe che fanno i fanciulli quando comiciano ad imparare a leggere.*

To ſpell a word right, *ortografizzare una parola bene.*

To ſpell [to inchant] *incantare.*

SPE'LLED, *pret. è participio del verbo* to ſpell.

SPE'LLER, s. *quello, o quella che compita.*

A good or bad ſpeller, *una perſona che intende bene o male l' ortografia.*

SPE'LLING, s. *il compitare, l' ortografizzare.*

The art of ſpelling, *l' ortografia, l' arte di ſcrivere le parole correttamente.*

SPELT, adj. *compitato, ortografizzato.*

Spelt, s. [a ſort of corn] *ſpelda, e ſpelta,* s. f. *biada nota.*

SPE'LTER, s. [a ſort of imperfect metal, the ſame as zink] *ſpezie di metallo imperfetto che ſi trova nella miniere, e ſerve a polire lo ſtagno*

To SPEND [to lay out, to conſume] *ſpendere, conſumare, impiegare, mandar a male.*

To ſpend one's money in buying books, *ſpendere il ſuo danaro in libri.*

He has ſpent all his eſtate, egli *ha ſpregato o conſumato* tutte *'l ſuo avere.*

To ſpend one's time in reading, *paſſare, conſumare, impiegare il ſuo tempo a leggere.*

To ſpend one's ſelf, *conſumarſi.*

To ſpend your breath in vain, *voi parlate al vento, le voſtre parole ſono inutili.*

To ſpend one's verdict [to give one's opinion] *dire il ſuo parere, il ſuo ſentimento.*

A ſhip that has ſpent her maſt [that has loſt it] *un vaſcello che ha perduto l' albero.*

To ſpend pains upon a thing, *affaticarſi in qualche coſa.*

They ſpent themſelves upon it, *hanno ſudato ſangue in ciò.*

SPE'NDER, s. [that ſpends much] *ſpenditore, ſpendereccio,* s. m. *uno che ſpende aſſai.*

SPE'NDING, s. *lo ſpendere.*

This I keep for my own ſpending, *conſervo queſto per mio proprio uſo.*

SPE'NDTHRIFT, *uno ſpendereccio, un prodigo.*

SPENT, adj. *ſpeſo, conſumato, impiegato, ſpregato.*

Ill got, ill ſpent, *beni male acquiſtati non fanno pro; farina del diavolo va tutta in cruſca.*

Three days were ſpent in thoſe debates, *conſumarono* tre *giorni in tali conteſe.*

When the night was ſpent, *quando la notte fu paſſata.*

I am quite ſpent, *ſono ſtracco morto.*

Spent with cares, *oppreſſo da' penſieri.*

A horſe quite ſpent, *un cavallo ſtracco affatto.*

A bullet ſpent, *una palla morta, che ha perduta la ſua forza.*

A maſt that is ſpent by foul weather, *un albero di vaſcello ſpezzato in una tempeſta.*

SPE'RABLE, adj. [ſuch as may be hoped] *ſperabile, che ſi può ſperare.*

SPERM, s. [ſeed of animals] *ſperma,* s. f. *ſeme dell' animale.*

SPERMACE'TI, s. [*corrottamente pronunziato* ſparmaſitty] *cervello o graſſo di balena.*

SPERMA'TICAL, } adj. [belonging to
SPERMA'TICK, } ſperm] *ſpermatico.*

Spermatick veſſels, *vaſi ſpermatici.*

To SPERSE, [to diſperſe, to ſcatter] *ſpargere.*

To SPET [to bring or pour abundantly] *verſare in copia.*

To SPEW, v. a [to vomit, to eject from the ſtomach] *vomitare, recere, cacciar fuora dello ſtomaco.*

To ſpew [to eject, to caſt forth] *cacciar fuora, rigettare.*

To ſpew [to eject with loathing] *buttar fuora per iſtomachezza.*

To ſpew, v. n. [to vomit, to eaſe the ſtomach] *alleggerirſi lo ſtomaco recendo o vomitando.*

To SPHA'CELATE [to affect with a gangrene] *cagionar canchero.*

To ſphacelate, v. n. [to mortify, to ſuffer the gangrene] *incancherirſi, aver uno o più cancheri in una o più parti del corpo.*

SPHA'CELUS, s. [mortification, gangrene] *canchero,* s. m. *cancrena,* s. f.

SPHERE, s. [a ſolid round body] *sfera, ſpera,* s. f. *corpo ſolido rotondo.*

Sphere [a repreſentation of the world] *sfera;* tutto *l' aggregato o la rappreſentazione del mondo.*

The ſphere of a planet [the place wherein it is conceived to move] *la sfera d' un pianeta.*

Sphere [the compaſs or reach of one's power or knowledge] *sfera, portata.*

This is out of my ſphere, *queſto non è alla mia portata.*

SPHE'RICAL, adj. [round] *sferico.*

SPHE'RICALLY, adv. *sfericamente, d' una maniera sferica.*

SPHE'ROID, s. [a ſolid figure made by the plane of a ſemi-ellipſis, turned about one of its axes, and is always equal to two thirds of its circumſcribing cylinder] *sferoide,* s. f. *ſorta di figura geometrica.*

SPHEROI'DAL, adj. [belonging to a ſpheroid] *appartenente ad una sferoide.*

SPHINX, s. [a fabulous monſter] *sfinge,* s f. *moſtro favoloſo.*

SPICE, s. [aromatical drug] *ſpezie,* s. f *ſpezierie,* s. f. pl. *aromati,* s. m pl.

A ſpice of a diſtemper [the beginning or remains of it] *acceſſo o reſto di malattia.*

To SPICE [to ſeaſon with ſpices] *condire con iſpezierie.*

SPI'CED, adj. *condito con iſpezierie.*

SPI'CER, s. [grocer] *ſpeziale, droghiere,* s. m.

SPI'CERY, s. [a place where ſpices are kept] *ſpezieria,* s. f. *luogo dove ſi conſervano le ſpezierie.*

SPICK, ex. ſpick and ſpan new, *nuovo di zecca.*

SPI'CKNEL, s. [a plant] *pianta, che produce il gambo e le foglie simili all' aneto, ma è più grosso.*

SPI'DER, s. [a sort of insect] *ragno, ragnatelo*, s. m.

Spider's web, *ragnatelo*, s. m. *ragna*, s. f. *la tela che il ragno fabbrica.*

Spider-wort, *spezie d' erba buona contro la morsicatura del ragno.*

SPIGHT, *dispetto, astio.*

SPI'GNEL, *v.* Spicknel.

SPI'GOT, s. [stopple for a tap] *zipolo*, s. m. *legnetto col quale si tura la cannella della botte.*

SPIKE, s. [a pointed iron] *chiodo grosso.*

A door fenced with iron spikes, *una porta guernita di grossi chiodi.*

To SPIKE, verb act. *appuntare, aguzzare.*

To spike a gun, *inchiodare un cannone.*

To spike one's self [to fall upon spikes] *cascare sopra punte di ferro.*

SPI'KED, adj. *appuntato, aguzzato.*

A spiked gun, *un cannone inchiodato.*

SPI'KENARD, s. [a sweet smelling plant] *spiganardo, nardo*, s. m. *pianta odorifera.*

SPILL, s. [a spill of money] *un piccolo regalo in danari.*

To SPILL, [to spoil, to waste] *versare, spargere, spandere*, pret. *sparsi.*

SPILT, adj. *versato, sparso.*

To SPIN, *filare.*

To spin wool, *filare della lana.*

To spin gold in thread, *filare dell' oro.*

To spin out the time [to delay] *prolungare, procrastinare, mandare in lunga.*

To spin out the war, *prolungare, far durare la guerra.*

The top spins [or turns round on the same place] *la trottola dorme.*

The blood spins out of his nostrils, *il sangue gli zampilla per il naso.*

SPI'NAGE, s. [a pot-herb] *spinace*, s. f. *erba nota che s' usa cotta in cibo.*

SPI'NAL, adj. [belonging to the spine] *spinale.*

The spinal marrow, *midolla spinale, quella parte del cervello che scorre dentro tutta la spina fino all' osso sacro.*

SPI'NDLE, s. [an instrument used in spinning] *fuso*, s. m. *strumento da filare*, plur. *fusa*, s. f.

Spindle-leggs, *gambe di fuso.*

Spindle-tree [a shrub] *fusagine*, s. f. *filio*, s. m.

The spindle of a winding staircase, *il fuso d' una scala a chiocciola.*

The spindles of a capstan, *le lieve d' un argano di vascello.*

Spindle-maker, *fusajo, colui che fa le fusa.*

SPI'NGLE-SHANKED [having small legs] *che ha gambe di fuso, che ha gambe lunghe e sottili.*

SPINE, s. [the back bone] *la spina, l' arco dell' osso.*

The spine, s. [the back bone] *spina*, s. f. *l' osso del fil delle rene dove son commesse le costole.*

SPI'NET, s. [a sort of musical instrument] *spinetta*, s. f. *spezie di strumento musicale.*

SPI'NGARD, s. [a sort of brass gun] *spingarda*, s. f. *strumento bellico da trarre e rompere mura.*

SPINI'FEROUS, adj. [bearing thorns] *pien di spini, spinoso.*

SPINK, s. [chaffinch, a bird] *fringuello*, s. m.

SPI'NNER, s. [a sort of spider] *ragno*, s. m.

Spinner [he or she that spins] *filatore*, s. m. *filatrice*, s. f.

SPI'NNING, s. *il filare.*

Spinning-wheel, *filatojo*, s. m. *strumento di legno da filare, che ha una ruota colla quale si torce il filo.*

SPINO'SITY, s. [crabbedness, thorny or briary perplexity] *intrigo*, s. m. *perplessità*, s. f.

SPI'NSTER, s. [a woman that spins] *filatrice*, s. f.

Spinster [a title given in law to all unmarried women, from a viscount's daughter to the meanest] *titolo che si da in Inghilterra in tutti li atti pubblici, a tutte le zitelle, dalle figlie di visconte alle più infime.*

SPI'NY, adj. [thorny] *spinoso, pien di spine.*

SPI'RACLE, s. [a breathing hole, a vent, a small aperture] *spiraglio, spiracolo.*

SPI'RAL, adj. [turning round like a skrew] *spirale, fatto a spire.*

SPI'RALLY, adv. *spiralmente, colle spire.*

SPIRE, s. [steeple that rises tapering by degrees, and ends in a sharp point at top] *spiro, guglia, piramide*, s. f.

The spire of a church, *la guglia d' una chiesa.*

To SPIRE [to grow up into a spire, as corn does] *spigare, far la spiga.*

SPI'RIT, s. [substance distinct from matter] *spirito*, s. m. *sustanza immateriale o incorporea.*

God is a spirit, *Iddio è un spirito.*

Spirit [a virtue or supernatural power that enlivens the soul] *spirito, il senso vitale.*

Spirit [soul] *spirito, anima.*

Spirit [ghost of a dead body] *spirito, l' anima d' una persona morta.*

Spirit a term in chymistry, the subtlest substance extracted from mixt bodies] *spirito, la parte più sottile e ignea di tutti gli enti che si traggono dalle cose per distillazione o simile.*

Spirit of salt, *spirito di sale.*

Spirits [in an animal body are distinguished in two kinds, vital and natural] *spiriti.*

The vital and natural spirits, *gli spiriti vitali e naturali.*

The spirits of wine and other strong liquors, *gli spiriti del vino e d' altri liquori forti.*

Spirit [wit, liveliness] *spirito, intelletto, ingegno.*

Spirit [genius, humour, or nature] *spirito, genio, umore*, s. m. *natura, natural disposizione*, s. f.

That is the spirit of the people, *questo è il genio o l' umore del popolo.*

To do a thing out of a spirit of charity, *fare che che sia per motivo di carità.*

Spirit [courage] *spirito, animo.*

To have a high or great spirit, *esser altiero, fiero, orgoglioso.*

To put spirit into one, *animare, inanimire, incoraggiare alcuno.*

To recover one's spirits, *raccogliere, riprendere, ricuperar gli spiriti, rinvenire.*

To spirit [to encourage] *animare, incorraggiare, dar animo, inanimire.*

To spirit away [to kidnap] *menar via.*

SPI'RITED, adj. [encouraged] *animato, incoraggiato, inanimito.*

High-spirited, *fiero, orgoglioso, altiero.*

Mean-spirited, *di basso cuore, vile, abbietto, d' animo vile.*

Spirited away, *menato via.*

SPI'RITEDNESS, s. [disposition of mind] *spirito, disposizione d' animo.*

SPI'RITFULNESS, s. [sprightliness, liveliness] *spirito, vivacità.*

SPI'RITLESS, adj. [dejected, low, deprived of vigour, depressed] *scorato, abjetto, vile, privo di vigore, depresso.*

SPI'RITOUS, adj. [refined, defecated, advanced near to spirit] *spiritoso, raffinato, purgato dalla feccia, che ha dello spirito.*

Spiritous [fine, ardent, active] *sottile, ardente, attivo.*

SPI'RITOUSNESS, s. [fineness and activity of parts] *spirito, sottigliezza e attività di parti.*

SPI'RITUAL, adj. [that consists of spirit without matter] *spirituale, incorporeo, di spirito.*

Spiritual [ecclesiastical, in opposition to temporal] *spirituale, attenente a religione, contrario di temporale.*

Spiritual [devout, pious, religious] *spirituale, pio, divoto, dato allo spirito.*

SPIRITUA'LITY, s. [the contrary of temporality] *spiritualità, devozione; coltivamento di religione.*

The spiritualities of a bishop [the profits which a bishop receives from his spiritual livings; and not as a temporal lord, as from his visitations, the ordaining and instituting of priests, &c.], *lo spirituale d' un vescovato, cioè l' entrate d' un vescovo come vescovo, e non come pari del regno d' Inghilterra.*

SPIRITUALIZA'TION, s. [a chymical

cal term, the extraction of the moſt pure and ſubtle ſpirits out of natural bodies] *ſpiritualizzazione*, s. f. *termine chimico.*

To SPIRI'TUALIZE [to reduce a compact mixt body into the principle called ſpirit] *ſpiritualizzare, ridurre un corpo ſolido con eſtrarne gli ſpiriti.*

SPIRI'TUALIZED, adj. *ſpiritualizzato.*

SPIRI'TUALLY, adv. *ſpiritualmente.*

SPIRI'TUOUS, adj. [full of ſpirits] *ſpiritoſo, che ha vivacità di ſpirito.*

SPISS, adj. [cloſe, firm, thick] *groſſo, ſodo, ſpeſſo, compatto.*

SPI'SSITUDE, } s. [thickneſs] *ſpeſſezza, denſità*, s. f.
SPI'SSITY, }

SPIT, s. [an inſtrument for roaſting meat] *ſpiedo, ſchidione, ſtidione*, s. m.

Turn-ſpit, *menarroſto.*

Spit, *è un preterito del verbo* To ſpit.

Spit, adj. *ſputato.*

To SPIT [to put on the ſpit] *mettere nello ſpiedo.*

To ſpit [to evacuate ſpittle] *ſputare.*

To ſpit blood, *ſputar ſangue.*

SPI'TCHCOCK, } s. [a large ſort of eel] *ſpezie d' anguilla groſſa.*
SPI'TCHCOCK-EEL, }

SPI'TE, s. [ſpight, malice, grudge, ſpleen] *rancore, diſpetto, odio, maltalento*, s. m. *onta, malizia*, s. f.

He has a ſpite againſt me, *mi ha in odio, è pieno di maltalento verſo di me.*

In ſpite, *per diſpetto, a diſpetto, ad onta, malgrado.*

I will do it in ſpite of your teeth, *voglio farlo a diſpetto voſtro, malgrado voſtro.*

To SPITE, *diſpettare, far diſpetto, ſdegnare.*

SPI'TED, adj. *diſpettato, irritato.*

SPI'TEFUL, adj. *diſpettoſo, che ſi compiace di far diſpetto, di coſtumi ſcorteſi, malizioſo.*

SPI'TEFULLY, adv. *diſpettoſamente, con diſpetto, con rabbia, di mal talento, ſdegnoſamente, malizioſamente.*

SPI'TEFULNESS, s. *diſpetto, maltalento*, s. m. *malizia, ſtizza*, s. f.

SPI'TTED, adj. [from to ſpit] *meſſo nello ſpiedo.*

SPI'TTER, s. [one that ſpits often] *uno che ſputa ſpeſſo.*

The ſpitter of a deer, *le prime corna d' un cervo.*

Spitter [a red male deer above a year old] *cerviatto, che ha paſſato un anno.*

Spittle, s. [the moiſture of the mouth] *ſputo*, s. m. *ſcialiva*, s. f. *la materia che ſi ſputa.*

Spittle, *ſpedale*, s. m.

Spittle-beggar, *un mendico, un pezzente uſcito dallo ſpedale.*

To rob the ſpittle [a proverbial expreſſion] *rubar lo ſpedale, cioè rubare ad un povero uomo quel poco che ha.*

SPITVE'NOM, s. [poiſon ejected from the mouth] *veleno uſcito della bocca.*

SPLANCHNO'LOGY, s. [a treatiſe or deſcription of the bowels] *trattato ſulle budella; deſcrizione delle budella.*

SPLASH [of dirt] *zacchera*, s. f.

To SPLASH, verb act. *zaccherare, macchiar di zacchere.*

SPLA'SHED, adj. *zaccherato.*

SPLA'SHING, s. *zaccheramento*, s. m. *lo zaccherare.*

SPLA'SHY, adj. *zaccheroſo, ſporco, melmoſo.*

SPLA'TCHY, adj. [painted, counterfeit] *falſo, falſificato.*

To SPLAY a horſe [to put his ſhoulder out] *ſpallare un cavallo.*

Splay footed, *ſbilenco, ſtrambo, bilenco, che ha le gambe ſtorte*

SPLEEN, s. [the milt under the left ſhort-ribs] *milza*, s. f.

To be troubled with the ſpleen, *eſſer incomodato della milza.*

Spleen [ſpite, hatred, grudge] *odio, rancore, diſpetto, mal talento*, s. m. *ira, ſtizza, animoſità*, s. f.

To take a ſpleen againſt one, *avere in uggia o in odio qualcheduno, avere un calcio in gola altrui.*

Spleen-ſick [troubled with the ſpleen] *ſplenetico, che ha male di milza.*

Spleen-wort, *ſcolopendria*, s. f. *ſorta d' erba.*

SPLE'NDENT, adj. [ſhining, bright] *ſplendente, lucente.*

SPLE'NDID, adj. [great, magnificent] *ſplendido, magnifico, chiaro, ſuntuoſo, ragguardevole.*

SPLE'NDIDLY, adv. *ſplendidamente, magnificamente, ſuntuoſamente.*

SPLE'NDOR, s. [brightneſs] *ſplendore*, s. m.

Splendor [pomp, magnificence] *ſplendore, pompa, magnificenza.*

To live in great ſplendor, *vivere con grande ſplendore, molto ſplendidamente.*

SPLENE, v. Spleen.

SPLENE'TICK, adj. [ſpleen-ſick] *ſplenetico, che ha male di milza.*

The ſplenetick vein, *la vena ſplenetica.*

SPLENT } s. [a piece of broken bone] *ſcheggia d' oſſo.*
SPLINT }

Splent [a flat piece of wood for a broken bone] *aſſicella*, s. f.

Splent [a hard ſwelling on the bone of the leg] *ſpinella*, s. f. *malattia che viene al cavallo nell' oſſo della gamba.*

Splents [harneſs for the arms] *bracciale*, s. m.

To SPLICE a rope [to join one rope to another, by interweaving their ends, after opening their ſtrands] *congegnare due corde pe' due capi.*

SPLINT, v. Splent.

SPLI'NTER [a ſmall ſhiver of wood] *ſcheggia*, s. f. *ſtecco*, s. m.

To SPLIT [to cleave, to cut aſunder] *fendere, ſpaccare.*

To ſplit aſunder, *fendere in due parti, fenderſi in due parti.*

To ſplit upon a rock, *naufragare contro uno ſcoglio*

To ſplit one's ſides with laughing, *ſmaſcellarſi, ſganaſciarſi dalle riſa, morir delle riſa, ſcoppiar dalle riſa.*

SPLI'TTED, or ſplit, adj. *feſſo, ſpaccato, ſcoppiato, naufragato.*

SPOIL, s. [plunder] *ſpoglia, preda.*

Spoil [robbery] *ladroneccio, ladrocinio, furto.*

To commit ſpoils, *commetter un ladroneccio.*

To SPOIL [to rob, to plunder] *rubare, commetter ruberia, predare, ſaccheggiare.*

To ſpoil a country, *deſolare, rovinare, predare un paeſe.*

To ſpoil [to marr] *guaſtare, ſconciare, rovinare.*

To ſpoil one's work, *guaſtare, ſconciare il lavoro.*

Eating in the morning ſpoils my ſtomach, *il far colazione mi guaſta l' appetito.*

To ſpoil one's meaſures, *rompere l' altrui miſure, deludere gli altrui diſegni.*

SPO'ILED, adj. *guaſto, guaſtato, rubato, predato, ſaccheggiato.*

SPO'ILER, s. *guaſtatore*, s. m. *guaſtatrice*, s. f.

SPOKE, *è un preterito del verbo* To ſpeak.

SPOKES, s. [the rays of a wheel] *raggi*, s. m. pl. *que' legni della ruota, che partendoſi dal mezzo, ove è impoſtato, reggono e collegano il cerchio eſteriore.*

A weaver's ſpoke, *ſubbio di teſſitore.*

SPO'KEN, adj. [from to ſpeak] *parlato, detto.*

The things ſpoken of, *le coſe ſopraddette.*

Not to be ſpoken, *che non ſi può dire.*

A well ſpoken man, *un uomo che parla bene, un uomo eloquente.*

SPO'KESMAN, s. [one who ſpeaks in behalf of another] *oratore, avvocato, colui che parla in favor d' altri.*

To SPO'LIATE [to ſpoil, to rob] *ſpogliare, privare, rubare.*

SPOLIA'TION, s. [the act of ſpoiling or robbing] *ſpogliamento*, s. m. *ſpogliagione, privazione*, s. f.

SPO'NDEE, s. [a foot of Latin or Greek verſe conſiſting of two long ſyllables] *ſpondeo*, s. m. *piede di due ſyllabe ne' verſi Latini e Greci.*

SPO'NDYLE, s. [a knukle or turning joint of the back-bone] *congiuntura dove ſi collegano le coſtole alla ſpina.*

SPONGE, s. v. Spunge [a ſoft porous ſubſtance ſuppoſed by ſome the nidus of animals. It is remarkable for ſucking up water] *ſpugna*, s. f. *ſoſtanza molle e poroſa, ſuppoſta da alcuni un ricettacolo d' inſetti*

insetti, e rimarchevole per la qualità che ha di assorbire ogni corpo liquido.

To SPONGE [to blot, to wipe away as with a sponge] *forbir via come fareb be una spugna.*

To sponge [to suck in as a sponge, to gain by mean arts] *succ are come spugna; e dicesi metaforicamente di chi con male arti cava da altri quello che non gli appartiene.*

SPO'NGER, s. [one who hangs for a maintenance on others] *colui che cava il proprio mantinemento da un altro, colui che vive a spese d' altri.*

SPO'NGINESS, s. [softness and fulness of cavities like a sponge] *spugnosità.*

SPO'NGIOUS, } adj. [soft and full of
SPO'NGY, } small interstitial holes] *spugnoso.*

Spongy [wet, drenched, soaked] *bagnato, inzuppato.*

SPO'NSAL, adj. [belonging to a spouse or marriage] *sposereccio, matrimoniale.*

SPO'NSION, s. [promise, obligation] *promessa, obbligazione, s. f.*

SPO'NSOR, s. [an undertaker or surety for another] *mallevadore, s. m.*

Sponsor [godfather] *padrino, compare.*

SPONTA'NEOUS, adj. [free, that acts of its own accord] *spontaneo, volontario.*

SPONTA'NEOUSLY, adv. *spontaneamente, di propria volontà.*

SPOOL, s. *cannello, s. m. nel quale viene accannellata la trama, e si mette dentro della spola sostenuto da uno spoletto.*

SPO'OLING-WHEEL, *arcolajo, s. m. strumento rotondo sul quale si mette la matassa per incannarla nel cannello.*

SPOON, s. *cucchiajo, s. m.*

To be past the spoon [to be beyond the state of infancy] *esser fuor dell' infanzia, aver il bellico rasciutto.*

SPOON-FULL, *una cucchiajata.*

SPOON-MEAT, *tutte quelle vivande che si mangiano col cucchiajo.*

SPORT, s. [pastime, diversion] *diporto, passatempo, trastullo, sollazzo, spasso, s. m. ricreazione, s. f.*

For sport's sake, *per diporto.*

You shall see pretty sport, *voi vedrete qualche cosa di bello.*

She is used to see the sport, *ella fa il suo mestiere.*

Sport [hunting, fowling, fishing, &c.] *il piacer della caccia, della pesca, e simili.*

He is a great sportsman, *egli è un grand' amator della caccia o della pesca.*

To make sport [to divert] *divertire, ricreare, far ridere*

To make sport of one [to laugh at one] *ridersi, burlarsi, farsi beffe d' uno.*

I did it only to make sport, *l' ho fatto solamente per passatempo.*

Sport [basket used by mendicant friars] *sporta, s. f.*

To SPORT [to sport one's self, to divert one's self] *diportarsi, spassarsi, pigliarsi spasso, scherzare, trastullarsi.*

Fortune sports with men, *la fortuna si burla degli uomini.*

To sport with one [to make a fool of one] *burlarsi, beffarsi, farsi beffe d' uno.*

To sport with religion, *far poco conto della religione.*

SPO'RTED, adj. *diportato, spassato, scherzato, trastullato, v.* To sport.

SPO'RTER, s. *quello o quella che scherza volentieri.*

SPO'RTFUL, adj. [diverting] *gustoso, piacevole, che divertisce.*

Sportful [gamesome, full of play] *scherzoso, burlevole, scherzevole, scherzante.*

SPO'RTFULLY, adv. [sportingly] *per passatempo, per ischerzo, per divertimento.*

SPO'RTING, s. *diporto, passatempo, scherzo, trastullo, divertimento, s. m.*

SPOT, s. [blot, stain] *macchia, s. f.*

Spot of oil, *macchia d' olio.*

Spot of dirt, *zacchera, s. f.*

Spot of ink, *scorbio, e sgorbio, s. m. macchia d' inchiostro.*

The spot of sin, *la macchia del peccato.*

Spot [blur] in one's reputation, *taccia d' infamia.*

Spot [speck, mark] *macchia, chiazza.*

A fine spot of ground, *un bel pezzo di terra.*

I was upon the spot, *io era presente.*

He died upon the spot, *morì in quello stesso luogo.*

To pay money upon the spot, *pagare danari contanti.*

To SPOT [to stain] *macchiare, sporcare, imbrattare.*

To spot one's reputation, or honour, *macchiare l' altrui reputazione, l' altrui onore.*

To spot with ink, *sgorbiare, scorbiare, imbrattar con inchiostro.*

To spot [to speckle] *macchiare, maculare, schiazzare, indanajare.*

SPO'TLESS, adj. [without spot] *immacolato, senza macchia, senza mancamento, intero, buono.*

Spotless life, *vita immacolata, senza macchia.*

SPO'TTED, adj. *macchiato, sporcato, imbrattato.*

Spotted [speckled] *macchiato, maculato, chiazzato, danajato, pezzato.*

SPO'TTER, s. *ricamatrice.*

Spotter of hoods, *ricamatrice di cuffie.*

SPO'TTY, adj. [full of spots] *macchiato, imbrattato, sporcato, pieno di macchie, maculato.*

SPO'USAL, adj. [nuptial, matrimonial, conjugal, connubial, bridal] *nuziale, matrimoniale, conjugale.*

Spousal, s. [marriage, nuptial] *matrimonio, maritaggio, sposalizio, nozze.*

SPO'USE, s. [bridegroom, husband] *sposo, marito.*

Spouse [bride, wife] *sposa, moglie.*

SPO'USED, adj. [wedded, espoused, joined together in matrimony] *sposato, maritato, ammogliato, unito in matrimonio.*

SPOUT, } *s. zampillo, s. m. sottil*
Water spout, } *filo d' acqua che schizza fuori da picciol canaletto.*

Spout [a mass of water collected between a cloud and the surface of the sea, in shape of a pillar, and brings ships that are near them into danger, unless they be dispersed and broken by shot from the great guns] *nembo, nuvola oscura, la quale dopo aver attratta dall' una delle sue estremità una gran quantità d' acqua del mare, è seguitata da un turbine di vento che la dissolve, e fa che i vascelli che vi si trovano vicini pericolano d' esser sommersi, se non viene a tempo dispersa dai tiri de' cannoni.*

Rain-spout [a sudden fall of rain, like a torrent] *torrente di pioggia, acquazzone.*

Spout for rain, house-eaves, *gronda, s. f.*

The spout of a mill-hopper, *tramoggia, s. f.*

To spout, or to spout out, *gettare, riversare, spandere, spargere, traboccare, versare.*

To spout, or to spout out, verb neut. *docciare, sgorgare, zampillare, schizzar fuori, sboccare.*

To spout down, *diluviare, piovere strabocchevolmente.*

SPO'UTING out, s. *sgorgo, sgorgamento.*

Spouting out, adj. *zampillante, sgorgante.*

SPRAIN, s. [a contortion or wresting of the tendons of the muscles, by some accident] *storcimento, s. m. slogatura, s. f.*

To SPRAIN, verb act. *sconciare, dislogare, slogare, storcere,* pret. *storsi.*

To sprain one's foot, *dislogarsi, sconciarsi un piede.*

To sprain one's arm, *slogarsi un braccio.*

SPRAI'NED, adj. *sconciato, sconcio, dislogato, slogato, storto.*

SPRAINTS, s. [the dung of an otter] *lo sterco d' una lontra.*

SPRANG, *preterito del verbo* To spring.

SPRAT, s. [a fish] *spezie di sardina, s. f.*

To SPRAWL [to lie on the ground, to stretch out at length] *stendersi per terra.*

SPRAY, s. [bough, sprig] *frasca, s. f. ramicello, s. m.*

Spray - faggot, *fastello di frasche.*

Spread, adj. *teso, tirato, stirato, sparso, v.* To spread.

To spread [to stretch out] *tendere, distendere, slargare, stendere.*

To spread one's arms, *tendere, stendere le braccia.*

Spread your legs, *stendete, slargate le gambe.*

To spread the cloth, *metter la tovaglia, apparecchiar la tavola.*

To spread a net, *tender una rete.*

To spread sail, *spiegar le vele.*

To spread [to scatter] *spándere, spargere, sparpagliáre.*

To spread dung, *spandere del letame.*

To spread straw in a room, *sparpagliare della paglia in una camera.*

To spread, or to spread about a report, *spandere, sparger fama, divolgare, dar fuora.*

To spread, verb neut. *stendersi, spargersi.*

To spread [as a flower] *aprirsi, parlando d' un fiore.*

Spre'ader, s. *spargitore, che sparge; e metaf. che pubblica, che divulga, che dissemina.*

Sprent *participio* [sprinkled] *spruzzato.*

Sprig, s. [small twig, branch] *ramuscello, bronco, germoglio, virgulto, s. m.*

Sprig of rosemary, *ramuscello di ramerino.*

Spri'ggy, adj. *pieno di ramuscelli o germogli.*

Spright, s. [phantom, spirit, hobgoblin] *spirito, s. m. fantasima, s. f.*

To Spright [to haunt as a spright] *bazzicare come fanno gli spiriti.*

Sprights [a sort of short arrows formerly used in sea fights, which had wooden heads made sharp] *spezie di frecce corte, delle quali si servivano altre volte nelle battaglie di mare.*

Spri'ghtful, adj. *spiritoso, allegro, vivace.*

Spri'ghtlully, adv. [briskly, vigorously] *vivacemente, vigorosamente.*

Spri'ghtliness, s. *vivacità, allegria, s. f. brio, s. m.*

Spri'ghty, adj. [gay, brisk, lively, vigorous, airy, vivacious] *gajo, allegro, snello, vivace, vivido, vigoroso, lieve, leggiero.*

Spring, s. [source or fountain] *fonte, scaturigine, sorgente, s. f.*

Spring-water, *acqua sorgente.*

Spring [origin, cause] *fonte, origine, causa, principio.*

The spring of the day, *l' alba, il far del giorno.*

Spring [one of the four seasons of the year] *primavera, s. f. una delle quattro stagioni dell' anno.*

The spring of a lock, *molla di serratura.*

He sets all springs a going in order to get his aim, *egli impiega ogni mezzo per ottenere il suo intento.*

Spring in order to leap, *lancio.*

To take a spring in order to leap, *prender il lancio.*

To spring [to arise, to come, to sprout out, as water does] *sorgere, scaturire, scoppiare, uscire, sgorgare, sboccare, parlando dell' acqua.*

Where the river springs, *in quel luogo dove nasce il fiume.*

The water that springs out of the rock, *l' acqua che scaturisce dal sasso.*

To spring [to sprout or shoot forth like plants or flowers] *spuntare, germogliare, cominciare a nascere, gemmare, parlando delle piante e de' fiori.*

To spring [to arise, to proceed] *nascere, procedere, derivare, venire,* pret. *nacque, venne.*

Thence spring all our misfortunes, *da cotesto procedono tutte le nostre disgrazie.*

To spring [to leap] *saltare, lanciarsi.*

To spring a partridge, *far levare una pernice.*

To spring a mine, *far volare una mina, fare scoppiare una mina.*

To spring a leak [to begin to leak] *fare acqua, dar la nave l' entrata per le sue fessure all' acqua.*

To spring a well, *cavare un pozzo.*

To spring a mast [sea term, when a mast is only crack'd, but not broken, in any part of it] *fendere l' albero.*

The storm has sprung our mast, *l' albero s' è fesso nella tempesta.*

Spri'ngal, s. [a stripling or young man] *un fraschetta, un giovanotto.*

Springe, s. [snare made of twisted wire to catch birds or small beasts] *lacciuolo, galappio, s. m.*

Spri'nger, s. [the springer of an arched gate] *imposta, s. m.*

Spri'ngy, adj. ex. Springy bodies, *corpi elastici, che hanno molla.*

Spri'nkle, s. [a holy water sprinkle] *aspersorio, s m.*

To Spri'nkle [to bedew with some liquor, to wet with drops of liquor] *aspergere, bagnare, spruzzare, spruzzolare.*

To sprinkle with holywater, *aspergere con acqua santa.*

To sprinkle with salt, *aspergere di sale.*

Spri'nkled, adj. *asperso, bagnato, spruzzato, spruzzolato.*

Spri'nkling, s. *aspersione, s. f. spruzzolo, spruzzo.*

Small sprinkling rain, *spruzzaglia, acquicella, poca pioggia e leggiera.*

He has some small sprinkling of Italian, *egli ha una tintura, un' infarinatura d' Italiano.*

Sprit-sail [the sail which belongs to the bolt-sprit mast] *trinchetto.*

Sprouts, s. [a sort of young cole-worts] *broccoli, talli di cavolo.*

Sprout of a tree, *germoglio, pollone, tallo, sprocco d' albero.*

To Sprout [to put forth as plants] *cestire, germogliare, gettare, mettere.*

Spro'uting, adj. *germogliante, che germoglia, che getta.*

Spruce, adj [neat or fine in clothes] *attillato, galante, leccato, leggiadro, lindo, pulito, vago.*

Spruce leather [corrupted from Prussia leather] *cuojo di Prussia.*

Spruce fellow, *zerbinotto, damerino.*

To Spruce, *pararsi, adornarsi, star sulle attillatura, attillarsi.*

Spru'cely, adv. *adornatamente, contamente, vagamente, pulitamente, lindamente, adornamente.*

Spru'ceness, s. *acconcezza, attillatura, lindezza, pulizia, s. f.*

Sprung, *è un preterito del verbo* To spring.

Sprunt, adj. [very active, brisk, wonderful lively] *molto lesto e vivace.*

Sprunt, s. [any thing that is short and will not easily bend] *un pezzo di checchessia che è corto, e non si piega facilmente.*

Spud, s. [a short sorry knife] *coltellaccio, cattivo coltello.*

A spud [a despicable fellow] *un uomicciatto, un nano, un pigmeo.*

To Spue, or to spue up [to vomit] *vomitare.*

Spu'ing, s. *vomito, s. m.*

Spume, s. [scum] *spiuma, schiuma, spuma.*

To Spume [to foam, to froth] *spumare, cacciar fuora spuma.*

Spu'mid } adj. [foamy, frothy]
Spu'mous } *spumoso, pien di spuma.*

Spun, *preterito del verbo* To spin.

Spunge, s. *spugna, s. f. v.* sponge.

To Spunge [to wash or rub a thing with a spunge] *nettare o fregare che che si sia con una spugna.*

To spunge upon one [to eat and drink at his cost] *scroccare, mangiare e bere a spese d' un altro.*

Spu'nged, adj. *nettato, fregato con una spugna.*

Spunged, *scroccato.*

Spu'nger, s. *scroccone, parasito, s. m.*

Spu'nginess, s. *spugnosità, s. f.*

Spu'nging, s. *lo scroccare, scrocchio.*

A spunging house, *la casa d' un birro.*

Spu'ngious } adj. [like a spunge]
Spu'ngy } *spugnoso, bucherato a guisa di spugna.*

Spunk, s. [touchwood, half rotten wood] *esca, legno mezzo fracido.*

Spunk [match] *miccia, s. f.*

Spur, s. [a device to make a horse

go] *ſprone*, s. m. *ſtrumento col' quale ſi pugne il cavallo.*

Spur [encitement] *ſprone, incentivo.*

A cock's ſpur, *ſprone o unghione di un gallo.*

To be upon the ſpur [to be in great haſte] *eſſer in gran fretta.*

To come upon the ſpur, *venire a ſpron battuto, a briglia ſciolta, con grandiſſima fretta.*

To ſpur [to prick a horſe with a ſpur] *ſpronare, pugnere collo ſprone le beſtie da cavalcare.*

To ſpur one on [to egg him on, to quicken him forward] *ſpronare, ſollecitare, affrettare, eccitare, incitare.*

To ſpur-gall a horſe, *piagare un cavallo cogli ſproni.*

SPURGE, s. [a ſort of herb] *titimaglio, titimalo*, s. m. *ſorta d' erba.*

SPU'RIOUS, adj. [baſe born] *ſpurio, baſtardo, nato in adulterio.*

Spurious [not genuine, falſe, counterfeit] *falſo, corrotto, falſificato, ſuppoſto.*

SPURN, s. [kick and contemptuous treatment] *calcio, o trattare ſprezzante e pieno di vilipendio.*

To SPURN [to kick at] *calcitrare, tirar calci, dar de' calci.*

He ſpurn'd him away, *lo cacciò via a calci.*

SPU'RRED, adj. *ſpronato, ſollecitato, affrettato, incitato, eccitato.*

Spurred [having ſpurs] *ſpronato, che ha ſproni.*

A cock ſpurred, *un gallo ſpronato.*

SPU'RRER, s. *quello, o quella che ſprona, che ſollecita.*

SPU'RRIER, s. [maker of ſpurs] *facitor di ſproni.*

SPU'RRY, s. [a ſort of herb] *ſorta d' erba.*

SPURT, s. *capriccio, ghiribizzo*, s. m. *fantaſia.*

To be all for a ſpurt, or upon a ſpurt, *eſſer fatto a capriccio.*

To SPURT [to burſt out, as liquor out of a bottle] *ſchizzare, zampillare, ſaltar fuora, proprio de' liquidi quando ſcaturiſcono con impeto.*

SPU'RTED, adj. *zampillato, ſchizzato.*

SPU'TTER, s. [noiſe, buſtle] *ſtrepito, fracaſſo, romore.*

To SPU'TTER [to ſpit faſt] *ſputacchiare, ſputare poco e ſpeſſo.*

SPY, s. *ſpia, ſpione*, s. m.

To SPY [to obſerve, to watch] *ſpiare, oſſervare, inveſtigare.*

To ſpy [to ſee, to perceive] *vedere, ſcoprire, diſcernere.*

To ſpy out a fault, *trovare un fallo, ſcoprire un errore.*

SPY'D, adj. *ſpiato, oſſervato, inveſtigato, veduto, ſcoperto.*

SQUAB, s. [ſoft ſtuffed cuſhion or ſtool] *ſgabello ripieno di borra.*

Squab, adj. [thick and ſtout; fat; aukwardly bulky] *groſſo e forte; paffuto; groſſo ma ſenza bella forma.*

Squab, s. [a thick fat man] *un uomicciatto groſſo e tondo.*

SQUAB, adj. [little and fat] *paffuto, corto e groſſo.*

Squab rabbit [a rabbit ſo young as not to be fit to eat] *coniglio giovane tanto che non è buono a mangiare.*

Squab [unfeathered, newly hatched] *ſenza penne, appena nato, e diceſi d' ogni augello.*

Squab, adv. [with a heavy and ſudden fall] *con ſubita e peſante caduta; ſtrammazzatamente.*

To SQUAD [to beat, to maſh] *tartaſſare, malmenare, zombare.*

SQU'ABBED, adj. *tartaſſato, malmenato, zombato*

SQUA'BBISH, adj. [thick, heavy, fleſhy] *paffutetto, molto, carnuto.*

SQUA'BBLE, s. [quarrel, diſpute] *zuffa, riſſa, conteſa, ſcompiglio.*

To SQUA'BBLE [to quarrel] *contendere, diſputare, contraſtare*, litigare.

SQUA'BBLED, adj. *conteſo, diſputato, contraſtato, litigato.*

Squabbled [among printers, is when ſeveral lines are mix'd one among another in the form] *una forma di cui le righe ſono ſcompigliate.*

SQUA'BPIE, s. [a pie made of many ingredients] *paſticcio fatto di diverſi ingredienti.*

SQUA'DRON, s. [a certain number of horſe] *ſquadra, banda, ſchiera*, s. f. *ſquadrone*, s. m.

A ſquadron of men of war, *una ſquadra di vaſcelli da guerra.*

SQUA'DRONED, adj. [formed into ſquadrons] *ſchierato.*

SQUALL, s. [ſudden ſtorm of wind or rain] *burraſca, tempeſta*, turbine *di vento o di pioggia.*

To SQUALL, *v.* To ſquaul.

SQUA'LLID, adj. [foul, naſty] *ſporco, ſudicio, ſurido, imbrattato, ſquallido.*

SQUA'MOUS, adj. [ſcaly, covered with ſcales] *ſquamoſo, ricoperto di ſquame.*

To SQUA'NDER [to laviſh, to ſpend to waſte] *prodigalizzare, ſcialacquare, mandare a male, ſciupare, buttar via.*

SQUANDERED away, adj. *prodigalizzato, ſcialacquato, mandato a male, ſciupato, buttato via.*

SQUA'NDERER, s. *ſcialacquatore, prodigo*, s. m. *ſcialacquatrice, prodiga*, s. f.

SQUA'NDERING away, *ſcialacquo*, s. m. *prodigalità*, s. f.

SQUARE, adj. [conſiſting of four equal ſides and as many right angles] *quadro, di figura quadra.*

Square number [in arithmetick, a number multiplied by itſelf] *numero quadro.*

Square root, *radice quadra quella ſomma, che multiplicata in ſe ſteſſa produce il numero dato.*

Square [honeſt, juſt, fair] *oneſto, giuſto, leale, candido, ſchietto, ſincero.*

Square dealings, *maniere di* trattare *oneſte, giuſte, candide, ſchiette.*

Square, s. [ſquare figure] *quadro, figura quadra, che há li angoli e le facce eguali.*

Square [rule] *ſquadra*, s f. *ſtrumento col quale ſi ſquadra.*

To bring a thing into ſquare, to work it up ſquare, *ſquadrare che che ſia, ridurre in quadro.*

This is out of ſquare [this is irregular] *non è quadro, è irregolare.*

A ſquare [a ſquare open place in a town] *piazza*, s. f. *luogo aperto e quadrato dentro le mura di una città.*

Upon the ſquare [fairly, honeſtly, without diſſimulation] *francamente, ſchiettamente, ſinceramente, candidamente.*

To play upon the ſquare, *giuocar francamente, ſenza truffare.*

Upon the ſquare [without odds] *del pari, egualmente, ſenza vantaggio.*

How go ſquares? *come vanno gli affari?*

He told me how ſquares went, *mi raccontò lo ſtato delle coſe.*

That will break no ſquares, *queſto non è gran fatto, queſto non farà breccia, non guaſterà nulla.*

Square built, *fabbricato in quadro.*

To SQUARE [to make ſquare] *quadrare, ridurre in forma quadra.*

To ſquare [to quadrate or agree] *quadrare, accordarſi, convenire, ſtar bene.*

His converſation ſquares my humour very well, *la ſua converſazione quadra col mio umore, ſi confà col mio umore.*

SQUA'RED, adj. *quadrato.*

SQUA'RENESS, s. [the ſtate of being ſquare] *quadratezza, l' eſſer quadro, la forma quadra.*

SQUA'RING, s. *quadro*, s. m. *lo ſquadrare, quadratura.*

The ſquaring of the circle, *la quadratura del cerchio.*

SQUASH, s. [any thing ſoft and eaſily cruſhed] *checcheſſia molle e che facilmente s' ammacca, ſi ſchiaccia, s' infragne.*

Squaſh [any thing unripe, any thing ſoft] *checcheſſia molle per poca maturità.*

Squaſh, *nome di pianta chiamata in latino* Melopepo.

Squaſh [a ſudden fall] *caduta ſubita, improvviſa caſcata; ſtrammazzone.*

Squaſh [a ſhock of ſoft bodies] *urto di corpi molli.*

To SQUASH [to puſh, to bruiſe flat] *ſchiacciare, ammaccare, infragnere*, pret. *infranſi.*

SQUA'SHED, adj. *ſchiacciato, ammaccato, infranto.*

SQUAT, adj. [lying down] *quatto; quattone.*

To lie ſquat, *ſtar quatto o quattone.*

Squat [thick and ſhort] *paffuto, corto e groſſo.*

Squat houſe [well compacted] *una caſa ben fabbricata, ben commoda.*

Squat, s. [ſudden fall] *repentina e peſante caduta o caſcata; ſtrammazzone.*

Squat, s. [a ſort of mineral] *ſorta di minerale.*

To SQUAT [to lie ſquat] *appiattarſi, ſtar quatto.*

To SQUAL [to bawl out] *gridare, ſchiamazzare, ſtridere, ſtrillare.*

She is in labour, I hear her ſqual, *ella ha le doglie, la ſento gridare.*

SQUALER, s. *quello o quella che grida.*

SQUEAK, *grido, ſtrido, ſtrillo.*

To give a ſqueak, *gettar un grido.*

To SQUEAK out, *ſtridere, ſtrillare.*

SQUE'AK.

SQUE'AKING, s. *grido, ſtrillo*, s m.

To SQUEAL [to cry with a ſhrill ſharp voice; to cry with pain] *ſtrillare, ſtridere.*

SQUEAMISH, adj. weak-ſtomached] *ſvogliato, troppo delicato.*

A ſqueamiſh ſtomach, *uno ſtomaco ſvogliato.*

SQUE'AMISHNESS, s. *ſtomacaggine.*

SQUEEZE, s. [compreſſion, preſſure] *compreſſione, ſtretta.*

To SQUE'EZE [to preſs hard] *ſpremere, premere.*

SQUE'EZED, adj. *premuto, ſpremuto.*

SQUELCH, s. [heavy fall] *caſcata*, s. f. *ſtramazzone*, s. m.

SQUIB, s. [a ſort of fire-work] *razzo*, s. m. *ſorta di fuoco lavorato che ſi getta per l' aria.*

SQUILL, s. [or ſea-onion] *ſquilla, cipolla ſquilla.*

SQUI'NANCY, } SQUI'NCY, } s. [a diſeaſe which affects the throat, ſtops the breath, and hinders the ſwallowing of meat] *ſquinanzia*, s. f. *male che ſerra le fauci, e ſoffoca, che diciamo anche ſcheranzia, e ſchinanzia.*

Troubled with the ſquincy, *ſquinantico, che ha il male della ſquinanzia.*

SQUI'NANTH, s. [a medicinal ſweet ruſh] *ſquinante*, s. m. *giunco odorato.*

SQUINT, or ſquint-eyed [one that has ſquinting eyes] *un guercio, che ha gli occhi ſtorti, uno ſtralunato.*

To SQUINT [to look a ſquint] *ſbiecare, eſſer guercio, guardar di traverſo, ſtralunare.*

He or ſhe ſquints, *egli è guercio, o ella è guercia.*

SQUI'NTING, s. *l' eſſer guercio.*

SQUI'NTINGLY, adv. *biecamente, da guercio, ſtralunatamente.*

SQUIRE, s. [contracted from eſquire] *ſcudiero, titolo d' onore in Inghilterra, un grado al di ſotto di quello d' un cavaliere.*

A French ſquire [a ſpunger] *uno ſcroccone, un paraſito.*

Squire, for ſquare, *v.* To ſquare.

SQUI'RREL, s. [a ſort of wood weaſel] *ſcojattolo*, s. m. *animal ſalvatico della ſpezie de' topi, colla coda volpeſca.*

SQUIRT, s. [looſeneſs] *diarrea, ſoccorrenza*, s. f.

STAB, s. [wound with a dagger] *una ſtoccata, una pugnalata.*

To give one a ſtab, *dare una ſtoccata ad uno.*

To STAB [to wound by a thruſt with a dagger or ſword] *pugnalare, ferir di pugnale o di ſpada.*

STABBED, adj. *pugnalato, ferito di pugnale, o di ſpada.*

STABI'LITY, s. [firmneſs] *ſtabilità, fermezza.*

STA'BLE, adj. [conſtant, firm] *ſtabile, fermo, durabile, coſtante, permanente.*

Stable, s. [to keep horſes in] *ſtalla.*

Stable for ſwine [hog-ſty] *porcile.*

Stable for ſheep, *ovile, mandra.*

When the ſteed is ſtolen, ſhut the ſtable door, *ſerra la ſtalla perduti i buoi; cioè cerca de' rimedi ſeguito il danno.*

To STA'BLE [to houſe cattle in a ſtable] *alloggiar beſtie in una ſtalla.*

STA'BLED, adj. *alloggiato in una ſtalla.*

STA'BLING, s. [what they pay in an inn for horſes lying in the ſtable] *ſtallaggio*, s. m. *quel che ſi paga all' oſteria per l' alloggio delle beſtie.*

STABLE'NESS, s. [ſtability] *ſtabilità, fermezza*, s f.

To STA'BLISH [contracted from to eſtabliſh] *ſtabilire, confermare, ſtatuire, diliberare, ordinare*, pref. *ſtabiliſco, ſtatuiſco.*

STACCA'DO, s. [pale, fence] *ſteccato*, s. m.

STACK, s. [a pile of wood three foot long, as many broad, and twelve foot high] *cataſta di legna, lunga e larga tre piedi, e alta dodici.*

A ſtack of chimneys, *un filare di cammini.*

Stack of corn or hay, *bica di grano, o di fieno.*

STACTE, s. [an aromatick; the gum that diſtils from the tree that produces myrrh] *aromo, aromato; quella gomma che diſtilla dall' albero che produce la mirra.*

STA'DLE, s. [any thing which ſerves for ſupport to another] *coſa qualunque ſi ſia che ſerve di ſoſtegno a un altra.*

Stadle [a ſtaff, a crutch] *gruccia, baſtone ſu cui uom s' appoggia per tenerſi ritto ſtando o camminando.*

Stadle [a tree ſuffered to grow for coarſe and common uſes] *albero che ſi laſcia creſcere per adoperarne il legno in coſe groſſolane e comuni.*

STAFF, s. [ſtick] *baſtone.*

Quarter-ſtaff, *baſtone a due punte.*

Jacob's-ſtaff [a mathematical inſtrument] *aſtrolabio.*

Hunting-ſtaff [boar-ſpear] *ſpiedo*, s. m.

The ſtaff of an halberd, *l' aſta d' un' alabarda.*

The white ſtaff [or rod, ſuch as is worn by ſome of the king's officers] *la bacchetta bianca.*

A croſier ſtaff, or biſhop's ſtaff, *un paſtorale.*

Staff of verſes [ſtanza] *ſtanza*, s. f.

Staff of a pſalm, *verſetto d' un ſalmo in muſica.*

STAG [a red male deer five years old] *cervo di cinque anni.*

Stag beetle [an inſect] *cervo volante.*

STAGE, s. [a place where players act] *teatro, palco*, s. m.

To bring one upon the ſtage, *mettere una perſona in ballo.*

To go off the ſtage [in a proper ſenſe] *ritirarſi dopo aver fatto la ſua parte.*

To go off the ſtage [to die] *morire, andare a babboriveggoli.*

Stage-play, *opera teatrale, commedia, tragedia.*

Stage-writer, *quegli che ſcrive o compone commedie o tragedie.*

Stage [of a journey] *poſta.*

To come to the ſtage, *arrivare alla poſta.*

Stage-horſe, *cavallo di poſta.*

Stage coach, *carozza di viaggio.*

STA'GER, s. [a player] *commediante.*

Stager [one who has long acted on the ſtage of life] *uno che ha fatta lungamente la parte ſua ſul teatro della vita.*

STA'GGARD, s. [a young male deer four years old] *cervo di quattro anni.*

To STA'GGER [to trip, to reel] *barcollare, tentennare, traballare.*

To ſtagger [to waver, to be in doubt] *vacillare, ſtare ambiguo, ſtar dubbioſo, fluttuare, titubare.*

STA'GGERER, s. *quello o quella che barcolla, che títuba.*

STA'GGERING, adj. [in a proper and figurative ſenſe] *barcollante, vacillante, fluttuante, titubante.*

STA'GGERINGLY, adv. *barcollone.*

To walk ſtaggeringly, *camminar barcollone, andar barcollando.*

STA'GGERS, s. [a diſeaſe in horſes ſomewhat like the vertigo or dizzineſs in men and women] *vertigine di cavallo.*

STA'GNANCY, s. [the ſtate of being ſtagnant] *ſtato ſtagnante.*

STA'GNANT, adj. [ſtanding, as water of ponds or pools] *ſtagnante, che ſtagna, che non corre.*

To STA'GNATE [to ſtand ſtill as water, to want a free courſe] *ſtagnare, fermarſi l' acqua ſenza ſcorrere.*

Blood that ſtagnates, *ſangue che ſtagna, che non ha la debita circolazione.*

STAGNA'TION, s. [ſtop of courſe, ceſſation of motion] *ſtagnamento, quiete, ceſſazione di moto.*

STAID, *è un preterito del verbo* To ſtay.

STAID, adj. [ſober, grave, regular] *ſobrio, grave, regolare.*

STA'IDNESS, s. [ſobriety, gravity, regularity] *ſobrietà, gravità, metodo, ordine, regola.*

STAIN, s. [ſpot] *macchia, imbrattatura.*

To STAIN [to ſpot] *macchiare, bruttar con macchia.*

To ſtain one's reputation, *macchiare l' altrui riputazione.*

STA'INED, adj. *macchiato, imbrattato.*

STAIR, s. [ſtep] *grado, ſcaglione.*

Stairs, or ſtair-caſe, *ſcala.*

Private ſtair-caſe, *ſcala ſegreta.*

Winding ſtair caſe, *ſcala a lumaca, ſcala a chiocciola.*

One pair of ſtairs, *il primo piano, il primo appartamento.*

Two pair of ſtairs, *il ſecondo piano, o appartamento.*

To walk up ſtairs, *ſalir le ſcale, montare ſu.*

STAKE, s. [poſt] *ſteccone, palo*, s. m.

He goes to it like a bear to a ſtake, *vi va come la biſcia all' incanto.*

Pointed ſtakes about the walls of a town, *palificata.*

Stake [what every one lays down at play] *poſta.*

To ſweep ſtakes [in a proper ſenſe] *tirar la poſta.*

To ſweep ſtakes [to take all away] *portar tutto via.*

Our honour lies at ſtake [is concern- ed]

ed] *ci va dell' onore, ſi tratta dell' onore.*

To lay all at ſtake, *giuocar del reſto, mettere il tutto a ripentaglio.*

To STAKE [to lay down one's ſtake] *riſpondere alle poſte.*

STALE, adj. [that is not freſh, old] *vieto, ſtantio, vecchio.*

Stale bread, *pan duro.*

Stale beer, *birra vecchia.*

A ſtale maid, *una zittella attempata.*

To grow ſtale, *invecchiare, divenire ſtantio, o vecchio.*

Stale, s. [urine] *orina*, s. f.

Stale [a decoy fowl] *zimbello*, s. m. *uccello che ſi fa ſvolazzare per allettar gli altri uccelli.*

To make one a ſtale to one's deſign, *ſervirſi dell' opera altrui per compiere il ſuo diſegno; cavare i marroni dal fuoco colla zampa del gatto.*

To ſtale [to piſs as a horſe] *piſciare, parlando d' un cavallo.*

STA'LENESS, s. *vecchiezza.*

STALK, s. [the ſtem of a plant] *ſtelo, gambo*, s. m.

The ſtalk of a flower, *lo ſtelo o gambo d' un fiore.*

The ſtalk of corn or hemp, *ſtoppia di grano, gambo di canapa.*

The ſtalk of leaves or fruit, *picciuolo di foglia o di frutto.*

To STALK [to walk ſoftly, as fowlers do] *rodiare, camminar pian piano come fanno gli uccellatori.*

STALKERS, s. [a ſort of fiſhing-net] *ſpezie di rete da peſcare.*

STA'LKING, adj. ex. a ſtalking horſe, *cavallo per la caccia delle pernici.*

To make one a ſtalking-horſe [a mere tool to bring about a buſineſs] *ſervirſi dell' opera altrui come mezzo termine per compire i ſuoi diſegni.*

STALL, s. [ſtable for cattle] *ſtalla.*

Ox-ſtall, *ſtalla da buoi.*

Butcher's ſtall, *deſco di beccajo.*

Cobler's ſtall, *deſco di ciabattino.*

A ſtall in a fair or market, *bottega di fiera o di mercato.*

The ſtall of a ſhop, *moſtra di bottega, quel luogo delle botteghe dove ſi tengono le mercanzie, perchè ſien vedute.*

Stall in the choir of a church, *ſedia nel coro.*

Stall-money, ſtallage, *ſtallaggio*, s. m.

The head-ſtall of a bridle, *teſtiera di briglia.*

Stall boat [a kind of fiſher's boat] *ſpezie di barca da peſcatore.*

Stall-fed, *ſtallato, allevato nella ſtalla.*

To STALL [to put in a ſtable] *mettere nella ſtalla.*

STA'LLAGE, s. [money paid for pitching ſtalls in fairs or markets] *danaro che ſi paga per aprir bottega in una fiera, o mercato.*

Stallage [the right of ſtallage] *diritto di poter aprir bottega.*

STALLED, adj. *meſſo nella ſtalla.*

Stalled with a thing [weary of it] *ſtufo di qualche coſa.*

STA'LLION, s. [a ſtone horſe kept for covering mares] *ſtallone*, s. m. *cavallo deſtinato a far razza.*

To turn a ſtallion among mares, *dare lo ſtallone alle cavalle.*

A woman's ſtallion, *lo ſtallone, il drudo d' una donna.*

STA'MINA, s. [the firſt principle of any thing] *i primi principi, i primi ſtami di checcheſſia.*

Stamina [the ſolids of a human body] *le parti ſolide del corpo umano.*

Stamina [thoſe little fine threads or capillaments which grow up within the flowers of plants, encompaſſing round the ſtyle, and on which the apices grow at their extremities] *quegli ſtami, fili, o quaſi capelli e barbe che naſcono nel centro di ogni fiore.*

STA'MINE, s. [a light ſort of French ſtuff] *ſtamina.*

STA'MMEL, s. ex. a great ſtammel jade [a flouncing mare] *una cavallaccia.*

A great ſtammel jade [a bouncing woman] *una donna paffuta, una donnaccia.*

A ſtammel-colour horſe, *un cavallo bajo.*

To STA'MMER [to ſtutter] *tartagliare, balbettare.*

To ſtammer [to falter in one's ſpeech] *eſitare parlando.*

STA'MMERER, s. *tartaglione*, s. m. f. *colui o colei che tartaglia.*

STA'MMERING, s. *il tartagliare.*

STA'MMERINGLY, adv. *tartagliando.*

STAMP, s. [print] *ſtampa, imprenta, impronta.*

Stamp [print, mark] *ſegno*, s. m. *impreſſione*, s. f.

Stamp [to ſtamp money] *conio*, s. m. *con che s' improntano le monete.*

Of the ring ſtamp, *vero.*

With ſeveral other men of the ſame ſtamp, *con molt' altri uomini della medeſima tempra.*

To STAMP [to print, to mark] *ſtampare, imprimere, improntare.*

To ſtamp money, *improntare, batter moneta.*

To ſtamp a meaſure with the publick mark, *bollare le miſure pubbliche.*

To ſtamp [to pound] *peſtare.*

To ſtamp under foot, *calpeſtare, calcar col piede, ſcalpicciare, ſcalpitare.*

To ſtamp with one's foot, *batter col piede in terra fortemente.*

STA'MPED, adj. *ſtampato, impreſſo, improntato*, v. To ſtamp.

STA'MPER, s. [one that walks heavily] *colui che gravemente camminando pare voglia ſtampare il terreno co' piedi.*

STA'MPING, s. *ſcalpicciamento, calpeſtamento, calpeſtio, ſcalpiccio*, s. m.

STAN, [amongſt our forefathers was the termination of the ſuperlative degree; ſo ATHELSTAN, moſt noble, BETSTAN, the beſt, WISTAN, the wiſeſt] *voce che terminando uno adjettivo fra li antichi Ingleſi lo convertiva in ſuperlativo, come* Athelſtan, *il nobiliſſimo,* Betſtan, *l' ottimo,* Wiſtan, *il ſaviſſimo.*

STANCH, adj. [ſubſtantial, ſolid, good, ſound] *buono, ſolido, maſſiccio, ben condizionato.*

Stanch commodity, *mercanzia buona, ben condizionata.*

Stanch [downright] *franco, puro, pretto.*

A ſtanch knave, *un pretto furbo, un vero briccone.*

A ſtanch Preſbyterian, *un Preſbiteriano de' più bacchettoni.*

Stanch toper, *imbriaccone.*

To STANCH [to ſtop] *ſtagnare, riſtagnare.*

To ſtanch the blood, *ſtagnare il ſangue.*

To ſtanch, verb neut. *ſtagnarſi, riſtagnarſi.*

STA'NCHED, adj. *ſtagnato, riſtagnato.*

STA'NCHION, s. [ſupport] *puntello, ſoſtegno, rincalzo*, s. m.

STA'NCHLESS, adj. [not to be ſtopped] *che non ſi può ſtagnare o fermare, e diceſi di ſangue o d' altro liquore che ſcorra via fin che ve n' è.*

STA'NCHNESS of a commodity, *la bontà d' una mercanzia.*

STAND, s. [pauſe, ſtay] *alto.*

To make a ſtand, *fare alto, fermarſi.*

To make a ſtand [to ſtand the firſt brunt] *ſoſtenere il primo aſſalto.*

Stand [poſt, ſtanding place] *poſta*, s. f. *luogo prefiſſo, aſſegnato.*

To put one to a ſtand, *imbarazzare, intrigare, imbrogliare alcuno, metergli un cocomero in corpo, metterlo in penſiero.*

To be at a ſtand, *ſtar ſoſpeſo, irreſoluto, non ſaper che riſolverſi, avere un cocomero in corpo, rimanere in ſecco.*

Stand [a utenſil to ſet a candleſtick on] *lucerniere, ſtrumento di legno da poſarvi ſopra il candeliere.*

Stand [to ſet veſſels on in a cellar] *predella da poſarvi ſopra le botti in cantina.*

I am at a ſtand [I have no work to do] *io ſto ozioſo, io non ho niente a fare.*

The law ſuit is now at a ſtand [it does not go forward] *il proceſſo è pendente, non deriſo nè riſoluto.*

To STAND, verb neut. [to ſtop, not to go forward] *ſtare, fermarſi.*

Stand there, *ſtate lì.*

My watch ſtands [does not go] *il mio oriuolo non cammina, non va.*

To ſtand upon a thing, *inſiſtere, ſtar fermo e oſtinato in qualche coſa.*

To ſtand neuter, *eſſer neutrale, non tener per neſſuno.*

To ſtand ſtill [to do nothing] *non far niente, tenerſi le mani a cintola.*

To ſtand upon one's guard, *ſtare in guardia, ſtar ſulle ſue, ſtare in cervello.*

To ſtand to one's reſolution, *perſiſtere nella ſua riſoluzione, ſtar ſaldo, tener duro.*

To ſtand to an opinion, *appigliarſi ad una opinione.*

To ſtand to one's word, *mantenere la promeſſa, attender quel che s' è promeſſo.*

I ſhall ſtand to whatever you ſhall think fit, *me ne ſtarò alla voſtra deciſione.*

To ſtand [to ſubſiſt] *ſuſſiſtere.*

To ſtand for one [to be on one's ſide] *tener*

tener per alcuno, tener con alcuno, esser dalla sua parte, ajutarlo.

To stand upon one's legs, *stare in piede.*

I am scarce able to stand, *appena posso reggermi in piedi.*

My hair stands on end for fear, *mi s' arricciano i capelli di paura, mi sento tutto raccapricciar di paura.*

To stand centry, *stare in sentinella.*

To stand trifling [to loiter] *badalucare, stare a bada, intertenersi.*

To stand prating or talking, *stare a cicalare o parlare.*

To stand against [to hold out, to resist] *stare alla dura, star saldo, tener duro, resistere, oppugnare.*

To stand against an army, *far testa ad uno esercito, oppugnare un esercito.*

To stand the shock, *sostenere un assalto.*

To stand all hazards, *arrischiare, mettere il tutto a ripentaglio.*

To stand against one, *opporsi, far testa ad uno.*

To stand one's ground, *stare alla dura, tener duro, mantenersi saldo.*

To stand to a thing [to maintain or affirm it] *mantenere, difendere, sostentare, affermare.*

To stand upon a trifle in a bargain, *contestare, differire per poca cosa in un negozio fatto insieme.*

I won't stand upon a trifle with you, *non voglio che noi differiamo per una bagattella.*

To stand [to be seated] *stare, sedere, dimorare.*

My house stands by the river side, *la mia casa siede sulla ripa del fiume.*

To stand shill-I-shall-I [in suspence] *star sospeso, vacillare bilanciando.*

The case stands thus, *il fatto va così.*

However the matter stands, *sia il fatto come si voglia.*

The fact stood thus, *la cosa andò così.*

To stand good in law, *esser valido.*

Do not stand arguing the case with me, *non istate tanto a parlare.*

To stand godfather or godmother to a child, *levare un bambino dal sacro fonte, tenerlo a battesimo.*

To stand by one [to bear him up] *tener per uno, esser dalla sua parte, seguir la sua fortuna, ajutarlo*

To stand for [to signify] *significare.*

F. stands for Francis, *F. significa Francesco.*

To stand forth, *avanzare, presentarsi.*

To stand off, *stare alla larga.*

We stood off the the cape of Good Hope, *noi erevamo all' altezza del capo di Buona Speranza.*

The ship stood two leagues off from the port, *il vascello era due leghe lontano dal porto.*

To stand off and on [at sea] *bordeggiare.*

To stand in [to cost] *costare, montare.*

This cloth stands me in ten pounds, *questo panno mi costa dieci lire sterline.*

To stand in the way, *impedire, fare ostacolo.*

To stand in need of a thing, *aver bisogno di qualche cosa.*

To stand in one's light, *fare ombra ad alcuno, impedirgli il lume.*

To stand in one's own defence, *star in atto di difesa.*

To stand in fear of one, *temere alcuno, aver paura d' alcuno.*

To stand out [to maintain, to affirm] *mantenere, affermare, avverare,* pret. *mantenni.*

To stand out against one, *opporsi, far testa ad uno.*

I'll stand the loss, or I'll stand to the loss [I'll bear the loss] *la perdita sarà mia, questo sarà a conto mio.*

To stand up [to rise] *levarsi, stare in piedi.*

My hair stood an end for fear, *mi s' arricciarono i capelli di paura, mi raccapricciai tutto di paura.*

To stand upon one's reputation, *mantenere la sua riputazione.*

To stand upon the point of honour, *piccarsi d' onore.*

To stand with [to be consistent, to agree with] *comportare, esser decente, convenirsi.*

It cannot stand with my honour, *l' onore non me' l comporta.*

It does not stand with reason, *ripugna alla ragione.*

When it shall stand with your conveniency, *quando vi sarà comodo*

STA'NDARD, s. [ensign of an army or fleet] *stendardo,* s. m. *insegna, bandiera,* s. f.

Standard-bearer, *colui che porta lo standardo, gonfaloniere, alfiere.*

The standard [the standing measure of the king or state to which all measures are framed] *misura che serve di modello a tutte le altre.*

To frame the measures according to the standard, *aggiustar le misure.*

Standard [the standing allay of gold or silver, as it is settled in the king's mint] *saggio, certa quantità di lega che entra nell' oro e nell' argento secondo che è determinata nella zecca.*

Standard [model, rule] *modello,* s.m. *regola, norma,* s. f.

STA'NDER, } s. [a tree left for
STA'NDIL, } growth] *arbuscello che si lascia perchè cresca senza trapiantarlo.*

Stander-by, *spettatore, auditore.*

Stander-grass, *satirio, satirione,* s. m.

STA'NDING, s. *il fermarsi, v.* To stand.

Standing, or standing place, *posta,* s. f. *posto, luogo,* s. m.

We are friends of an old standing, *noi siamo amici vecchi.*

A thing of four years standing, *una cosa di quattr' anni, che ha quattr' anni.*

Standing, adj. ex. standing water, *acqua stagnante.*

Standing corn, *biada,* s. f. *tutte le semente ancora in erba.*

A standing regiment, *un reggimento in piedi.*

Standing forces, *gente in piedi.*

To do a thing standing, *far che che sia in piedi.*

STA'NDISH, s. [a standing inkhorn for a table] *calamajo,* s. m.

STANG, s. [perch] *stanga, pertica, bastone lungo.*

STANK, adj. [weak, worn out] *stanco, debole, fiacco, spossato.*

Stank, preterito *del verbo* to stink.

STA'NNEL, s. [bird] *gheppio,* s. m. *spezie d' uccello.*

STA'NZA, s. [a stave of verse] *stanza,* s. f. *numero determinato di versi.*

STAPES, s. [in anatomy, a little bone in the inner part of the ear] *staffa,* s. f. *dagli anatomisti s' appella uno di quegli officini, che si trovano nella cavità dell' orecchio degli animali.*

STA'PLE, s. [a publick store-house, town, or city, where merchants jointly lay up their commodities for the better vending of them] *mercato pubblico o fondaro dove i mercanti conservano le loro mercanzie per venderle poi all' ingrosso.*

Staple commodities [good and saleable commodities] *mercanzie buone e ben condizionate.*

Staple of a door, *quel buco della porta nel quale entra il catenaccio.*

STAR, s. [a luminous globe in the heavens] *stella.*

The fixed stars, *le stelle fisse.*

The evening-star, *l' espero.*

The dog-star, *la canicola.*

The morning-star, *lucifero,* s. m. *la stella di venere quando è mattutina.*

A blazing-star, *una cometa.*

The seven stars, *le plejadi, le sette stelle che si veggono tra'l toro, e l' ariete.*

A wandering star, *un pianeta, una stella errante.*

A flying or shooting-star, *stella volante, meteora.*

The star in a horse's forehead, *stella nella fronte d' un cavallo.*

Star [that which is supposed to have influence on men's fortunes or actions] *astro, fato, destino, stella.*

To be born under an unlucky star, *esser nato sotto un astro maligno, sotto nemica stella.*

Star fish, *stella, animaletto marino.*

Star-hawk, *falcone laniero.*

A star-night, *una notte stellata.*

Star-wort, *astro, spezie di pianta.*

Star of Bethlehem, s. *pianta chiamata in Latino* orinthogalum.

Star-apple, s. [a plant] *nome di pianta.*

Star [in printing] *asterisco.*

STA'RBOARD [the right-hand side of a ship or boat] *poggia,* s. f. *lato destro della nave.*

STARCH [a sort of thin paste for stiffening linen] *amido,* s. m.

To STARCH [to stiffen with starch] *inamidare, saldar con amido.*

STARCHA'MBER, s. [a kind of criminal court of equity] *nome di magistratura o corte di equità che fu un tempo stabilita in Inghilterra.*

STA'RCHED, adj. *inamidato.*

A starched discourse, *un discorso affettato.*

A starched man, *un cacasodo, un uomo*

che procede con troppa gravità e apparenza di grandezza, un uomo albagioso.

STA'RCHING, s. *l' inamidare.*

STA'RCHNESS, s. *maniere affettate.*

STARE, s. [ſtarling, a ſort of bird] *ſtornello*, s. m.

Stare [fixed look] *guatatura, ſguardo fitto in un particolare oggetto.*

To STARE AT or UPON [to look ſtedfaſtly upon] *guardar fiſſamente, guatare.*

To ſtare at one in the face, *guardar uno fiſſamente.*

To ſtare [to have a wild look] *aver gli occhi ſtralunati, ſtralunare.*

To make the hair ſtare. *fare arricciare i capelli, fare raccapricciare.*

STARGA'ZER, s. [aſtronomer or aſtrologer] *aſtronomo o aſtrologo, uno che contempla le ſtelle per meſtiere.*

STARHAWK, s. *aſtore, falcon pellegrino.*

STA'RING, s. *il guardar, fiſſamente.*

STA'RINGLY, adv. ex. to look ſtaringly, *guardar fiſſamente.*

STARK, adj. [rigid, ſevere] *rigido, auſtero, ſevero.*

A ſtark preſbyterian, *un rigido preſbiteriano.*

Stark [thoroughly] *pretto, puro, ſpacciato.*

He is ſtark mad, *è un matto ſpacciato.*

A ſtark ſycophant, *un vero calunniatore.*

Stark naked, *tutto nudo*

A ſtark knave, *un pretto furbo.*

Stark-naught, *che non val niente affatto.*

Stark [ſtiff] *intirizzato, intirizzito.*

Stark with cold, *intirizzato di freddo.*

To be ſtark, *intirizzirſi, eſſere intirizzato.*

STA'RLING, s. [ſtare, a bird] *ſtornello*, s. m.

STA'RRED, adj. [with ſtars] *ſtellato.*

STA'RRY, adj. [full of ſtars] *ſtellato, pieno di ſtelle.*

The ſtarry ſky, *il cielo ſtellato.*

START, s. [a ſudden leap] *ſalto, ſopraſſalto, riſalto.*

To give a ſtart, *fare un ſalto.*

To get the ſtart of one [to be before hand with him] *vincerla della mano o del tratto; eſſer prima dell' altro in che che ſia.*

I have the ſtart of him, *i' l' ho vinto della mano.*

Start [ſpurt] *capriccio, ghiribizzo*, s. m. *fantaſia*, s. f.

By ſtarts, *a capriccio, capricciosamente.*

To START [to give a ſudden leap or ſtart] *ſaltare, dare un ſalto, ſcuoterſi, riſcuoterſi, commuoverſi per ſubita paura.*

A horſe that ſtarts aſide, *un cavallo che ombra, che ſalta al canto.*

To ſtart back, *ſaltare in dietro.*

To ſtart from one's ſubject, *uſcire del ſoggetto, fare una digreſſione, ſaltar di palo in fraſca.*

To ſtart [to begin to run] *ſpiccarſi da un luogo, partire.*

To ſtart up [to riſe, to begin to appear] *levarſi, ſpuntare.*

He ſtarts up a gentleman, *egli comincia a fare il gentiluomo.*

To ſtart a hare, *levar la lepre.*

To ſtart a new queſtion, *proporre, mettere in campo una nuova queſtione.*

To ſtart a truth, *ſcoprire una verità.*

To ſtart an opportunity, *far naſcere un' opportunità.*

STA'RTED, adj. *ſaltato, v.* To ſtart.

STA'RTER, s. [young coney] *un giovane coniglio.*

STA'RTING, s. *il ſaltare, ſcoſſa*, s. f. *ſcotimento*, s. m.

Starting, adj. ex. a ſtarting horſe, *un cavallo ombroſo.*

Starting-hole [come off, ſubter fuge] *ſotterfugio, ſcampo*, s. m. *ſcuſa*, s. f.

Starting-place [at horſe-races] *moſſe*, s. f. *il luogo donde ſi muovono a corſo i cavalli che corrono il palio.*

A ſtarting dinner [a ſnatch and away] *un pranzo di viaggiatore.*

STA'RTINGLY, adv. [by ſudden fits; with frequent intermiſſion] *a ſcoſſe, a ſalti interrottamente.*

STA'RTISH, adj. [ſpeaking of a horſe] *un poco ombroſo.*

STA'RTLE, s. *lo ſteſſo che* ſtart.

To STA'RTLE [to cauſe to ſtart, to ſurprize by fright] *atterrire, ſorprendere, iſtupidire, far paura, impaurare, impaurire*, pref. *atterriſco, iſtupidiſco, impauriſco*, pret. *ſorpreſi.*

You ſtartled me, *voi m' avete impaurito, o fatto paura.*

To ſtartle, verb neut. [to ſtart or tremble for fear] *ſtrabiliare, traſecolare, tremar di paura.*

STA'RTLED, adj. *ſorpreſo, atterrito, iſtupidito, impaurato, impaurito, v.* To ſtartle.

To STARVE [to famiſh] *affamare, indur fame, far morir della fame.*

To ſtarve, verb neut. [to be famiſhed] *affamare, aver fame, morir della fame, eſſer affamato.*

He is ready to ſtarve for hunger, *egli è quaſi affamato, quaſi morto di fame.*

To ſtarve with cold, *morir di freddo; eſſer gelato di freddo.*

STARVED, adj. [famiſhed] *affamato, che ha gran fame, morto di fame, famelico.*

Starved with cold, *gelato, morto di freddo.*

Starved to death, *morto di fame, o di freddo.*

STA'RVELING, adj. [almoſt ſtarved] *affamaticcio.*

Starveling, s. [an animal thin and weak for want of nouriſhment] *animale ſparuto, fiacco, rifinito, magro, ſpoſſato, e ſimili per mancanza di nutrimento.*

STATE, s. [condition, diſpoſition] *ſtato, grado, eſſere*, s. m. *condizione*, s. f.

State [the government of a people living under the dominion of a prince or of a commonwealth] *ſtato, dominio*, s. m. *ſignoria, potenza*, s. f.

Council of ſtate, *conſiglio di ſtato.*

State affairs, *affari di ſtato.*

State [pomp, magnificence, majeſty] *pompa, grandezza, ſplendidezza, magnificenza*, s. f. *ſplendore*, s. m.

A bed of ſtate, *un letto di riſpetto.*

To lie in ſtate [as a dead body] *eſſer poſto in un letto di riſpetto, parlando d' una perſona morta.*

To live in great ſtate, *vivere ſplendidamente.*

State [pride] *alterigia*, s. f. *orgoglio*, s. m.

To take ſtate upon one [to carry it high] *far il grande, ſputar tondo, ſtare in ſul grande, ſtare in ſul quamquam, ſtar ſulla ſua.*

State [rank, degree] *ſtato, grado*, s. m. *qualità, condizione*, s. f.

The three ſtates of the kingdom, *i tre ſtati del regno.*

The ſtates, or the ſtates of Holland, or the ſtates of the United Provinces, *gli ſtati, gli ſtati confederati, gli ſtati delle provincie unite, l' Olanda.*

To STATE [to regulate, to determine] *regolare, ordinare, ſtabilire, determinare*, pref. *ſtabiliſco.*

To ſtate an account, *preparare un conto, metterlo in chiaro.*

I ſhall ſtate the cauſe to you, *io v'eſporrò il fatto, io vi metterò in chiaro il fatto.*

STA'TED, adj. *regolato, ordinato, ſtabilito, determinato, preparato, meſſo in chiaro.*

STA'TELINESS, s. [greatneſs, magnificence] *pompa, grandezza, magnificenza, fontuoſità, ſplendidezza*, s. f. *ſplendore*, s. m.

Statelineſs [ſtately look, majeſty] *maeſtà, aria nobile e grande.*

Statelineſs [pride] *alterigia*, s. f. *orgoglio*, s. m.

STA'TELY, adj. [magnificent] *ſuperbo, magnifico, ſplendido, ſontuoſo, pomposo, grande.*

To be in a ſtately garb, *eſſer veſtito in gala, eſſer pomposamente veſtito.*

Stately coach, *carrozza magnifica.*

Stately [majeſtick] *maeſtoſo, nobile, grande.*

Stately [proud] *fiero, altiero, ſuperbo, orgoglioſo.*

Stately, adv. [magnificently] *ſuperbamente, pomposamente, magnificamente, ſontuoſamente, ſplendidamente.*

Stately [proudly] *fieramente, alteramente, ſuperbamente, orgoglioſamente.*

Stately [with majeſty, majeſtically] *maeſtoſamente, nobilmente, con maeſtà.*

STA'TER, s. [an ancient Greek coin of ſeveral ſorts] *uno ſtatero, moneta Greca.*

Stater [among apothecaries, a weight of an ounce and a half] *un oncia è mezza, termine di ſpeziale.*

STA'TESMAN, s. [politician] *un politico, miniſtro di ſtato.*

STATESWOMAN, *una politica.*

STA'TICKS, s. [the ſcience of weights and meaſures] *ſtatica.*

STA'TION, s. [a ſtanding place] *ſtazio, poſto, ſtaggio, ſtollo*, s. m. *poſta, ſtanza, ſtazione, abitazione*, s. f.

Station [among Roman Catholicks, the act of viſiting a church or chapel appointed to pray in] *ſtazione, appreſſo i Cat-*

i Cattolici Romani, viſita che ſi fa a qualche chieſa o cappella ſecondo l' ordinazione del Pontefice per guadagnare l' indulgenze.

Station [poſt, condition, rank] *ſtato, grado*, s. m. *condizione, qualità.*

To know the ſtation of the wind, *ſapere dove è il vento*

STA'TIONARY, adj. [ſettled in a place] *ſtazionario.*

Stationary planets, *i pianeti ſtazionarj.*

STA'TIONER, s. [ſeller of paper, books, ink, wax, &c.] *colui che vende carta, libri da ſcrivere, inchioſtro, ceralacca, e ſimili.*

Stationer [bookſeller] *librajo.*

STA'TUARY, s. [a carver of ſtatues or images] *ſtatuario*, s. m. *colui che fa le ſtatue, ſcultore.*

Statuary [the art of making ſtatues] *ſcultura.*

STA'TUE, s. [a ſtanding image of metal, ſtone, wood, &c.] *ſtatua*, s. f. *figura di rilievo, di getto, o ſcolpita.*

STA'TURE, s. natural height, ſize, pitch] *ſtatura*, s. f.

STA'TUTABLY, adv. *conforme agli ſtatuti.*

STA'TUTE, s. [law, ordinance] *ſtatuto, decreto*, s. m, *legge*, s. f.

STA'TUTES [acts of parliament] *ſtatuti, leggi parlamentarie.*

To STAVE [to beat to pieces, as a ſhip, barrels, caſks, &c.] *fendere, ſpaccare.*

To ſtave a ſhip, *ſdrucire o romperſi un vaſcello.*

To ſtave a caſk, *ſfondare un barile.*

STAVED, adj. *fracaſſato, aperto, feſſo, ſdrucito, ſpaccato.*

A ſhip ſtaved to pieces, *una nave ſpaccata, rotta in pezzi.*

STAVES, s. *doghe.*

The ſtaves of a hogſhead, *le doghe d' una botte.*

Staves-acre, s. [a herb] *ſtafiſagra, ſtrafizzeca*, s. f. *erba da uccidere i pidocchi.*

STAULK, *v.* Stalk.

STAY, s. [ſtop] *ſoggiorno, indugio*, s. m. *tardanza, dimora*, s. f.

There I ſhall make ſome ſtay, *farò qualche dimora quivi.*

Make no ſtay [do not tarry] *non tardate, non vi fermate.*

The buſineſs ſtood at a ſtay, *il negozio reſtò imperfetto.*

To keep at a ſtay, *tener in freno.*

Stay [prop] *puntello, rincalzo*, s. m.

Stay [ſupport] *appoggio, ſoſtegno, ſoſtentamento*, s. m.

The ſtay of a weaver's loom, *pettine di teſſitore.*

To STAY [to continue in a place, to ſtand, to wait] *ſtare, fermarſi, tratteners̄i, reſtare, aſpettare, indugiare.*

Stay there, *ſtate lì, fermatevi lì.*

Stay a little while, *aſpettate un poco.*

To ſtay for [to expect] *aſpettare.*

Stay for me, *aſpettatemi.*

To ſtay [to ſtop, to tarry] *fermarſi, tardare.*

Where did you ſtay ſo long? *dove ſiete ſtato tanto tempo?*

He never ſtays in any place, *non ſi ferma mai in neſſun luogo.*

To ſtay [to tarry, to ſojourn] *ſoggiornare, dimoràre, interteners̄i.*

To ſtay [to make one ſtay] *fermare, ritenere, intertenere*, pret. *ritenni, intertenni.*

To ſtay bleeding, *ſtagnare il ſangue.*

To ſtay one's fury, *placare, rallentar l' altrui furore.*

To ſtay one's ſtomach, *levar la fame.*

To ſtay [to prop] *appuntellare, puntellare, por ſoſtegno, appoggiare.*

To ſtay to lean upon] *appoggiarſi.*

STAYED, adj. [grave, ſober, ſerious] *grave, ſerio, ritenuto, compoſto, moderato.*

STA'YEDLY, adv. *gravemente, con gravità, ſeriamente, compoſtamente, moderatamente.*

STAYS, s. [woman's ſtays] *buſto da donna.*

STEAD, s. [place] *luogo, vece.*

In his ſtead, *in ſuo luogo, in ſua vece.*

In ſtead of that, *in luogo di queſto.*

To ſtand in good ſtead, *ſervire, render ſervizio.*

To be of no ſtead, to ſerve in no ſtead, *non ſervire a nulla.*

To STEAD [to do ſervice] *ſervire, render ſervizio, eſſer utile.*

To ſtead, *ſoſtenere, aſſiſtere, ſpalleggiare.*

STE'ADFAST, adj. [faſt in place, firm, fixed] *fermo, ſodo, ben fitto.*

Steadfaſt conſtant, reſolute] *coſtante, fermo, riſoluto.*

STE'ADFASTLY, adv. firmly, conſtantly] *fermamente, coſtantemente, riſolutamente.*

STE'ADFASTNESS, s. [immutability, fixedneſs] *immutabilità, fermezza.*

Steadfaſtneſs [firmneſs, conſtancy, reſolution] *fermezza, coſtanza, riſolutezza.*

STE'ADILY, *con fermezza, con ſicurezza, coſtantemente, ſaldamente.*

STE'ADINESS, s. *fermezza, ſicurezza, ſaldezza, ſtabilità.*

STE'ADY, adj. firm, conſtant, ſure] *fermo, ſaldo, coſtante, ſicuro, ſtabile.*

Steady hand, *mano ferma.*

Steady reſolution, *ferma riſoluzione.*

Steady, ſteady [a word of command in a ſhip, when the commander would have the ſteerſman to keep the ſhip conſtant in her courſe] *orza, orza.*

STEAKS, s. [ſlices of meat to fry or broil] *braziuóla*, s. f.

Mutton or beaf ſteaks, *braciuole di caſtrato o di manzo.*

To STEAL [to take unlawfully and privately] *rubare, involare, imbolare.*

He ſtole my purſe, *egli m' ha rubata la borſa.*

To ſteal a marriage, *maritarſi clandeſtinamente.*

To ſteal away, verb neut. [to go away by ſtealth or unſeen] *involarſi, ſcantonarſi, andarſene naſcoſamente e alla ſfuggita, ſvignare.*

To ſteal into one's favour, *inſinuarſi a poco a poco nella grazia di qualcheduno, cattivarſi l' altrui amorevolezza pian piano.*

STE'ALER, s. *ladro, rubatore*, s. m. *ladra, rubatrice*, s. f.

STE'ALING, s. *rubamento*, s. m. *il rubare.*

STE'ALINGLY, adv. [by ſtealth] *ſegretamente, naſcoſamente, alla ſfuggita.*

By STEALTH, adv. ex. to do a thing by ſtealth, *fare che che ſi ſia ſegretamente, naſcoſamente, alla ſfuggita.*

To ſell or buy any thing by ſtealth, *vendere o comprar che che ſi ſia per iſcarriera.*

STEAM, s. [the vapour of any thing] *vapore, fumo, ſvaporamento*, s. m. *eſalazione*, s. f.

The ſteam of meat, *tanſo della carne.*

To STEAM [to ſend forth a vapour] *fumare, eſalare, mandar fuora fumo; come fa l' acqua o altro liquore che bolle.*

STE'DFAST, adj. [firm, conſtant] *fermo, ſaldo, coſtante, ſicuro, ſtabile.*

STE'DFASTLY, adv. *fermamente, ſaldamente, coſtantemente, con coſtanza.*

To look ſtedfaſtly, *guardar fiſſamente.*

STE'DFASTNESS, s. *fermezza, ſaldezza, coſtanza*, s. f.

STEED, s. [horſe] *cavallo, corſiero, deſtriero, corridore.*

It is to no purpoſe when the ſteed is ſtolen to ſhut the ſtable door, *non occorre chiuder la ſtalla perduti i buoj.*

STEEL, s. *acciajo*, s. m.

Steel ſword, *ſpada d' acciajo.*

Steel [to ſtrike fire with] *fucile*, s. m.

Steel-yard [a hand-ſcale] *una ſtadera.*

To STEEL [to harden] *indurire, indurare*, preſ. *induriſco, induro.*

To ſteel one's ſelf in ſin, *indurirſi nel peccato.*

To ſteel one againſt another, *animar l' uno contro l' altro.*

STE'ELED, adj. *indurito, indurato.*

Steeled in impudence, *ſfacciatiſſimo, ſfrontatiſſimo, che ha perduto ogni pudóre.*

STEEP, adj. [of difficult aſcent] *erto, ſcoſceſo, dirupato.*

Steep mountain, *montagna ſcoſceſa.*

Steep, s. [aſcent or deſcent approaching to perpendicularity; precipice] *aſceſa o diſceſa ripida, e quaſi perpendicolare; precipizio.*

To STEEP [to ſoak] *immollare, mettere in molle, tuffar in coſa liquida.*

STE'EPED, adj. *immollato, tuffato.*

STE'EPLE, s. *campanile*, s. m.

STE'EPNESS, s. [from ſteep] *pendio, ſcoſcendimento*, s. m. *diſceſa, ſceſa, china*, s. f.

The ſteepneſs of a hill, *il pendio, la diſceſa d' una collina.*

STEER, s. [bullock] *giovenco*, s. m. *bue giovane.*

To STEER [to guide a ſhip] *guidare, reggere, governare*, pret. *reſſi.*

To ſteer a ſhip, *guidare o reggere una nave.*

To steer northward, to steer one's course northward, *poggiare o far vela verso tramontana.*

Which way do you steer your course? *dove siete incamminato, dove andate?*

STE'ERAGE, s. [a place in a ship, where the steersman stands and lodges] *quel luogo del naviglio dove sta il timoniere o piloto.*

STE'ERAGE, } s. *governo, guida,*
STEERING, } *condotta; il governare, il guidare.*

STE'ERED, adj. *retto, guidato, governato.*

STE'ERSMAN, s. [he who steers or guides a ship] *timoniere, timonista, piloto,* s. m.

STE'LLAR, adj. [starry] *stellato.*

STE'LLIONATE, s. [in civil law, all kind of cousenage and knavish practice in bargaining] *stellionato.*

STEM, s. [the stalk of an herb, flower, or fruit] *stelo, gambo di fiore, d' erba, o frutto.*

The stem of a tree, *tronco d' albero.*

Noble stem [noble progeny or race] *casato, famiglia, schiatta, o razza nobile.*

The stem of a ship [great piece of timber which is wrought, compassing from the keel below, and serves to guide the ship's rake] *lo sprone d' un naviglio.*

To STEM [to stop, to put a stop] *fermare, arrestare, soprattenere.*

To stem a thing [to put a stop to it] *opporsi a qualche cosa, mettervi ostacolo.*

To stem the tide, *veleggiare a ritroso, o contro marea.*

STENCH, s. [stink] *puzza,* s. f. *puzzo, fetore,* s. m.

STEP, s. [pace] *passo,* s. m.

Step by step, *a passo a passo.*

Step [footstep] *traccia, pedata, orma,* s. f. *vestigio,* s. m.

To follow one's steps, *seguitar l' altrui pedate, pigliar il suo esempio, imitarlo.*

The step of a door, *la soglia o il limitare della porta.*

The steps of a staircase, *gli scalini d' una scala.*

Step [in one's conduct, way of proceeding] *passo, procedere, andamento,* s. m.

To make a false step, *fare un passo cattivo.*

Step-father, *patrigno, marito della madre di colui a chi sia morto il padre.*

Step-mother, *matrigna, moglie del padre di colui a chi sia morto la madre.*

Step-son, *figliastro.*

Step-daughter, *figliastra.*

To STEP [to make a step] *andare, fare un passo, fare una girata.*

Will you step thither with me? *volete andarvi meco, volete che vi andiamo a fare un passo?*

To step to one, *andare verso alcuno, andarlo a trovare.*

To step after, *seguitare, andare appresso.*

To step aside, *mettersi in disparte, farsi in disparte.*

To step back, *tornare indietro.*

To step in, *entrare.*

To step down, *scendere, andar giù.*

To step up, *salire, ascendere,* pret. *ascesi.*

To step out, *uscire,* pres. *esco.*

To step over, *passare, attraversare.*

To step into an estate, *entrare in possesso d' un bene.*

STE'PPINGSTONE, s. [stone laid to catch the foot and save it from wet or dirt] *sasso messo o fitto in luogo dove la gente passa, onde mettendovi su il piede non si bagni o imbratti.*

STEPT, *proterito del verbo* To step.

Well stept in years, *avanzato in età.*

STE'RIL, adj. [barren, unfruitful] *sterile, che non genera, che non produce, che non fruttifica, che non frutta.*

To grow steril, *sterilire, divenire sterile,* pref. *sterilisco.*

STERI'LITY, s. [barrenness] *sterilità,* s. f.

STE'RLING, s. a name given to English money, *sterlino.*

A pound sterling, or twenty shillings, *una lira sterlina, venti scellini.*

STERN, adj. [severe, crabbed] *torvo, austero, severo, brusco, burbero.*

Stern look, *cera torva o austera.*

A stern man, a man that looks stern, *un uomo austero o brusco.*

Stern, s. [the hindermost part of a ship] *la poppa d' un naviglio.*

The stern of a grey-hound, *la coda d' un levriere.*

STE'RNLY, adv. *con aria torva, o burbera, biecamente, stortamente, travoltamente.*

STE'RNNESS, s. [stern look] *aria, o cera torva, occhi biechi, cipiglio,* s. m. *guardatura d' adirato.*

STE'RNUM, s. [breast-bone] *cassero, casso,* s. m. *la parte concava del petto circondata dalle costole.*

STERNUTA'TION, s. [sneezing] *starnutazione,* s. f. *starnuto,* s. m.

STE'RNUTATORY, s. [sneezing powder] *starnutatorio,* s. m. *medicamento che fa starnutire.*

STEW, s. [a place to keep fish in alive for present use] *vivajo,* s. m *ricetto d' acqua da tenervi pesci.*

Stew [hot-house] *stufa,* s. f. *stanza riscaldata da fuoco che le si fa sotto o accanto.*

To STEW [to boil gently and a considerable time] *stufare.*

To stew meat, *stufare della carne.*

Stew-pan, *padella, tegame da stufare.*

STEW'ARD, s. [in a nobleman's family or gentleman's house] *maggiordomo, maestro di casa, dispensiere, dispensiero,* s. m.

The steward of a ship, *dispensiero d'un vascello.*

A country steward, or the steward of a manor, *fattore, castaldo,* s. m. *quello che ha cura del podere.*

The lord steward of the king's household, *il primo maggiordomo del re.*

STEW'ARDSHIP, s. *la carica d' un maggiordomo, fattoria,* s. f.

To give an account of one's stewardship, *render conto della sua amministrazione.*

STEW'ED, adj. [from to stew] *stufato.*

STEW'ED MEAT, s. *stufato,* s. m.

STEW'ING, s. *lo stufare.*

STEW, s. [bawdy-house] *bordello, chiasso, lupanare, postribolo,* s. m.

STI'BIAL, adj. [antimonial] *d' antimonio.*

STICHA'DOS, s. [a plant] *spezie d' erba.*

STICK, s. [a piece of bough, a staff] *bastone.*

Faggot-stick, *stecco di fastello.*

Stick of wax, *bastoncello di cera lacca.*

A printer's composing-stick, *il compositorio.*

Small sticks [to kindle fire with] *stecchi,* s. m.

To STICK [to cleave to] *attaccare, appiccare.*

To stick [to thrust a pointed weapon into] *ficcare, cacciare, spignere,* pret. *spinsi.*

To stick a nail into the wall, *ficcare, cacciare un chiodo nel muro.*

To stick with wax, *attaccare, appiccare con cera.*

To stick, verb neut. *appiccarsi.*

To stick like bird-lime, *appiccarsi come vischio.*

It sticks too fast, *è troppo fitto, è appiccato troppo.*

To stick to one, *appigliarsi ad uno.*

They stick close together, *sono strettamente legati insieme, v' è fra loro stretta unione.*

This nick name will stick by him as long as he lives, *questo sopranonme gli rimarrà tutta la sua vita.*

I fear this commodity will stick by me, or stick upon my hands, *temo che questa mercanzia non mi resti nelle mani; temo di non potermene disfare.*

He sticks at nothing for lucre's sake, *non v' è cosa che non faccia quando si tratta di guadagnare.*

He does not stick to say, *non si fa scrupolo di dire.*

Meat that sticks to the stomach, *carne che lo stomaco non può digerire.*

A thing that sticks in one's stomach, *risentimento conservato nel cuore; cosa che non si può digerire, in significato metaforico.*

To

To ſtick by one, *tener per uno, ajutarlo, ſpalleggiarlo.*

To ſtick in the mire, *eſſer immerſo nel fango.*

To ſtick a dagger in one's breaſt, *immergere un pugnale nell' altrui ſeno, trafiggere altrui il petto con un pugnale.*

To ſtick out, *ſporgere in fuori.*

Eyes that ſtick out of one's head, *occhi che eſcono in fuori della teſta.*

To ſtick to, *inſiſtere, fare iſtanza, pretendere,* pret. *preteſi.*

To ſtick to, *aderire, favorire, ſeguitare una parte, accoſtarſi a quella, inchinarvi.*

To ſtick through, *paſſar da banda a banda.*

To STI'CKE, ex. to ſtickle hard in a buſineſs, *adoperarſi, impiegarſi, affaticarſi in qualche coſa.*

STI'CKLEBAG, s. properly Stickleback [the ſmalleſt of freſh water fiſh] *il più minuto de' peſci d' acqua dolce.*

STI'CKLER, s. [a buſy body in others affairs, a zealous perſon] *un affannone, un arciſanſano, un fer faccenda, un uomo che volentieri s' intriga in ogni coſa.*

Stickler [a ſideſman to fencers, a ſecond to a dueliſt] *garzone di ſchermitore, colui che fa le veci ſue nella ſcuola di ſcherma; e colui anco che ſerve di ſecondo a un altro in un duello.*

Stickler [an obſtinate contender about any thing] *colui che oſtinatamente contende per checcheſſia.*

STI'CKLY, adj. [viſcous, adheſive, glutinous] *attaccaticcio, viſcoſo, aderente.*

STIFF, adj. [not pliable, hard] *duro, intirizzito, intirizzato.*

To grow ſtiff, *intirizzire, intirizzare,* preſ. *intirizziſco.*

Stiff [ſtarched, affected] *intirizzato, affettato, troppo intero della perſona.*

Stiff [reſolute, conſtant, obſtinate] *duro, fermo, coſtante, riſoluto, oſtinato, infleſſibile.*

Stiff [not free, ſpeaking of ſtyle] *duro, che non è naturale, parlando di ſtile.*

Stiff [not free, in painting] *ſtentato, parlando di pittura.*

Stiff gale [at ſea] *vento freſco, vento di terra.*

Stiff-necked [obſtinate] *oſtinato, duro, fermo caparbio.*

To STI'FFEN [to make ſtiff] *indurare, indurire, ſaldare.*

To ſtiffen with ſtarch, *inamidare, dàr l' amido.*

To ſtiffen [to benumb] *aſſiderare, agghiacciare, agghiadare, intormentire,* preſ. *intormentiſco.*

To ſtiffen, verb neut. *intirizzare, intirizzire, aſſiderarſi, agghiadarſi, intormentirſi,* preſ. *intirizziſco.*

STI'FFENED, adj. *indurato, indurito,* v. To ſtiffen.

STI'FFLY, adv. *fermamente, oſtinatamente.*

STI'FFNESS, s. [the ſtate of being ſtiff] *durezza, ſaldezza.*

Stiffneſs [numbneſs] *intirizzamento,* s. m. *aſſiderazione,* s. f.

Stiffneſs of opinion, *oſtinazione, caparbietà, pertinacia in qualche opinione.*

To STI'FLE [to ſuffocate] *ſtrangolare, ſoffocare.*

STI'FLED, adj. *ſtrangolato, ſoffocato.*

STI'FLING, adj. *che ſoffóca, che ſtrángola.*

Stifling, s. *ſoffocamento,* s. m. *ſoffocazione,* s. f.

STIGMA'TICK, } adj. [branded with
STIGMA'TICAL, } infamy or diſgrace] *infame, diſonorato.*

To STI'GMATIZE [to brand or mark with a hot iron] *ſtimatizzare, improntare con ferro caldo.*

To ſtigmatize [to brand with infamy] *diffamare, infamare, macchiare la fama altrui.*

STI'GMATIZED, adj. *ſtimatizzato, infamato, diffamato.*

STILB, s. [an entrance made with ſteps] *cancello,* s. m.

A ſtile [in dialing] *ſtilo,* s. m.

Stile, v. Style.

STILE'TTO [a ſmall dagger, of which the blade is not edged but round, with a ſharp point] *ſtiletto, ſtile, daga.*

STILL, adj. [calm, quiet] *calmo, tranquillo, quieto, che non è agitato.*

Still water, *acqua ſtagnante, acqua che dorme.*

The wind is ſtill, *il vento è abbattuto.*

Still [alembeck] *lambicco, limbicco,* s. m.

Still, adv. [always] *ſempre.*

They ſtill deſire more, *eglino deſiderano ſempre più.*

Still [yet] *ancora.*

Are you here ſtill? *ſiete ancora quì?*

Still [quiet, without motion] *quieto, ſenza moto.*

Stand ſtill, *ſtate quieto, non vi movete.*

To ſit ſtill, *ſedere in pace, ſeder tranquillo.*

Sit you ſtill, *non vi movete, reſtate aſſiſo.*

Hold ſtill [hold your tongue] *tacete, zitto, ſtate zitto.*

Still-born, *morto nato.*

To STILL [to diſtil] *lambiccare, ſtillare, diſtillare.*

To ſtill waters, *ſtillare acque.*

To ſtill [to quiet, to calm, to make quiet] *calmare, tranquillare, abbonacciare, quietare, acquetare.*

To ſtill a noiſe, *far ceſſare uno ſtrepito.*

I ſhall ſtill your din [I ſhall make you hold your tongue] *vi farò tacer io.*

STILLATI'TIOUS oils [oils drawn from mixed bodies by force of fire] *olj diſtillati.*

STI'LLATORY, s. [ſtill] *lambicco.*

STI'LLED, adj. *lambiccato, ſtillato, diſtillato.*

STILLE'TTO, s. [a dagger] *ſtiletto, ſtilo,* s. m. *ſpezie d' arme corta da offendere.*

STI'LLING, s. [from to ſtill] *diſtillazione,* s. f.

Stilling [wooden frame to ſet a veſſel on in a cellar] *predella,* s. f.

STI'LLNESS, s. [ſilence] *ſilenzio.*

The ſtillneſs of the night, *il ſilenzio della notte.*

Stillneſs [calmneſs, in a proper and figurative ſenſe] *calma, bonaccia, tranquillità, quiete,* s. f. *riposo,* s. m.

STILTS, s. [a device made of two ſticks on which to go through dirty places] *trampoli, trampani,* s. m. pl.

To go upon ſtilts, *camminare ſopra i trampoli.*

To STI'MULATE [to move, to ſtir up] *ſtimolare, incitare, ſpronare, animare.*

STI'MULATED, adj. *ſtimolato, incitato, ſpronato, animato.*

STIMULA'TION, s [the act of puſhing or egging on] *ſtimolazione,* s. f. *lo ſtimolare.*

STING, s. *ſpina,* s. f. *ago, pungiglione,* s. m.

The ſting of a fly, &c. *l' ago d' una moſca, &c.*

To STING [to wound with a ſting] *pungere, pugnere,* pret. *punſi.*

That ſtung me to the heart, *queſto mi traſiſſe il cuore.*

STI'NGED, v. Stung.

STI'NGINESS s. [from ſtingy] *grettezza, miſéria, pidocchieria, ſordidézza ſpilorceria, avarizia,* s. f.

STI'NGING, s. [from to ſting] *puntura, morſicatura.*

STI'NGLESS, adj. [having no ſting] *che non ha pungiglione.*

STI'NGO, s. [a ſort of drink made in Yorkſhire] *ſorta di bevanda che ſi fa nella provincia di York.*

STI'NGY, adj. [niggardly, covetous] *ſordido, ſpilòrcio, ſtretto, taccagno.*

A ſtingy man, *un cacaſtecchi, uno ſpilorcio, un taccágno, un tánghero.*

STINK, s. [ill ſmell] *puzza,* s. f. *puzzo, fetore,* s. m.

To STINK [to ſend forth an ill ſmell], *puzzare, putire, fetere.*

To ſtink of garlick, *puzzar d' aglio.*

STI'NKARD, s. [a mean, ſtinking, paltry fellow] *un taccagno, uno ſpilorcio, un tanghero.*

STI'NKER, s. [ſomething intended to offend by the ſmell] *coſa che pute.*

STI'NKING, adj. *puzzolente, fetido.*

Stinking fellow, *uomo vile, uomo da niente.*

STI'NKINGLY, adv. [with a ſtink] *puzzolentemente.*

STI'NKPOT, s. [an artificial compoſition

ſtion

fition offenfive to the fmell] *compoſto che pute.*

STINT, s. [bound, limit] *limite, confine*, s. m.

To go beyond the ftint, *paſſare i limiti preſcritti.*

To fet a ftint to a thing, *regolare, ordinare, metter ordine a qualche coſa.*

To ftint [to limit] *limitare, riſtrignere, por termine*, pret. *riſtrinſi.*

To ftint [to conftrain] *reprimere, frenare, raffrenare, rintuzzare.*

To ftint one in his victuals, *limitare ad uno il ſuo mangiare.*

We muft ftint ourfelves in our pleafures, *ci biſogna andare un poco più ritenuti ne' divertimenti.*

To ftint one's anger, *raffrenare, rintuzzare la ſua collera.*

To ftint [to ceafe] *ceſſare, deſiſtere, tralaſciare.*

STI'NTED, adj. *limitato, terminato, riſtretto, v.* To ftint.

STI'PEND, s. [pay, falary] *ſtipendio, ſalario*, s. m. *paga*, s. f.

STIPE'NDIARY, s. [that ferves for hire or wages] *ſtipendiario*, s. m. *che riceve ſtipendio.*

STI'PTICAL, } adj. [binding] *aſtrin-*
STI'PTICK, } *gente, coſtipativo, atto a coſtipare.*

Stiptick water [that ftanches blood] *acqua che ſtagna il ſangue.*

A ftiptick, s. *un rimedio aſtringente.*

To STI'PULATE [to covenant, to bargain, to agree] *ſtipulare, convenire, fare una ſtipulazione.*

STI'PULATED, adj. *ſtipulato, convenuto.*

STIPULA'TION, s. *ſtipulazione, convenzione*, s. f. *contratto*, s m.

STIR, s. [noife, buftle] *ſtrepito, fracaſſo, romore, fraſtuono*, s. m.

Stir [commotion, troubles] *diſturbo, ſcompiglio*, s. m. *commozione, conturbazione*, s. f.

To STIR [to move] *muovere, agitare, ſcuotere.*

To ftir a table, *muovere una tavola.*

To ftir the humours, *provocare gli umori.*

To ftir the corn, *voltare il grano.*

I cannot ftir it, *non poſſo muoverlo.*

To ftir the lees, *muover le feccie.*

To ftir, verb neut. [to move, to wag] *muoverſi, agitarſi, ſcuoterſi, dimenarſi.*

He cannot ftir, *non può muoverſi.*

Money does not ftir, *il danaro non corre, la gente non iſpende.*

To ftir up [to rife, to caufe a rifing in a ftate] *ſuſcitare, deſtare, eccitare diſturbi e commozioni nello ſtato.*

I cannot ftir abroad or out [I cannot go out] *io non poſſo uſcire.*

To ftir out of one's bed [to rife] *levarſi di letto.*

To ftir about, *camminare, ſpaſſeggiare, andare attorno.*

To ftir about [to be ftirring in a bufinefs] *imbrigarſi, brigarſi, ingegnarſi, induſtriarſi.*

To ftir up [to caufe] *eccitare, ſuſcitare, cauſare.*

To ftir up a rebellion, *ſuſcitare una ribellione.*

To ftir up [to move, to excite] *muovere, deſtare, eccitare.*

To ftir up the paffions, *muover le paſſioni.*

To ftir up devotion, *eccitare alla devozione.*

To ftir up the appetite, *aguzzar l' appetito.*

To ftir up one's anger, *provocar l'ira altrui, provocar uno, irritarlo.*

You muft ftir him up, *biſogna eccitarlo, animarlo, ſpronarlo.*

To ftir the fire, *attizzare il fuoco.*

STI'RRED, adj. *moſſo, v.* To ftir.

STI'RRER, s. [one who is in motion] *colui che è in moto.*

Stirrer [one who puts in motion] *colui che mette in moto.*

Stirrer [a rifer in the morning] *colui che ſi leva di letto la mattina per tempo.*

Stirrer [an inticer, an inftigator] *colui che ſtimola, che iſtiga.*

STIRRER UP, s. [inciter, inftigator] *ſtimolatore, uno che iſtiga.*

STI'RRING, s. *muovimento, il muovere, v.* To ftir.

Stirring [infurrection] *ſollevazione, ribellione.*

Stirring, adj. ex. to be ftirring, *levarſi di letto la mattina.*

To be always ftirring, *eſſere ſempre in moto.*

A ftirring man, *un uomo ſedizioſo.*

A ftirring man [a man fit for bufinefs] *un uomo attivo, intrigante, affaccendato.*

There's no wind ftirring, *non fa punto di vento ; l' aria tace.*

There's no money ftirring, *il danaro non corre.*

There's no news ftirring, *non v' è nulla di nuovo,*

STI'RRUP, s. *ſtaffa*, s. f.

The ftirrup-leather, *ſtriſcia di cuojo, alla quale ſta appiccata la ſtaffa.*

To lengthen the ftirrups, *allungar le ſtaffe.*

To fhorten the ftirrups, *accorciar le ſtaffe.*

To loofen the ftirrups, *ſtaffeggiare, cavare diſavvedutamente il piede della ſtaffa.*

To give one fome ftirrup-oil, *dare delle ſtaffilate ad uno.*

Stirrup ftockings, *calze a ſtaffa, calze a ſtaffetta.*

The ftirrup-cup, *la benandata.*

STITCH, s. [the fewing with a needle] *punto*, s. m.

To make a ftitch, *fare un punto.*

Stitch [fharp pricking pain] *fitta*, s. f. *dolore pungente, che pur quaſi che ſia data una ferita.*

Stitch [in knitting] *maglia.*

To take up a ftitch, *pigliare una maglia.*

To go through ftitch with a thing [to make an end of it] *venire a capo d' una coſa.*

A ftitch'd book, *un libro cucito.*

Stitch-wort, *camomilla*, s. f. *erba nota.*

To STITCH [to fow with a needle] *appuntare, cucire.*

To ftitch a book, *cucire un libro.*

STI'TCHED, adj. *appuntato, cucito.*

STI'TCHING, s. *l' appuntare, il cucire.*

Stitching filk, *ſeta groſſa.*

STI'THY, s. [anvil] *incudine*, s. f.

STI'VER, s. [a Dutch penny] *un ſoldo d' Olanda.*

STO'AKED, adj. [a fea term for ftopped] *turato*, ex. the pump is ftoaked, *la tromba è turata.*

STOCA'DO, s. [a thruft with a weapon, ftab] *una ſtoccata.*

STOCK, s. [ftem of a tree] *tronco d' albero.*

Stock [race, family] *ſchiatta, razza, progenie, famiglia*, s. f.

The ftock of an anvil, *il pedale d' un' incudine.*

The ftock of a gun or piftol, *la caſſa d' uno ſchioppo o piſtola.*

Stock [fet on the ground to graft on] *piantone.*

Stock [fund of money] *fondo, capitale*, s. m.

To be in ftock [to have money] *eſſer bene in fondo, aver danari.*

A merchant's ftock, *il fondo, il capitale d' un mercante.*

Good or great ftock [abundance] *quantità, molto.*

To have a good ftock of commodities, *eſſer ben fornito di mercanzie.*

He has a good ftock of learning, *egli è ſcienziatiſſimo, egli è dotto molto.*

The ftock [the cards not dealt at picket] *il monte.*

Leaning-ftock, *appoggio, ſoſtegno.*

Laughing-ftock, *zimbello, ludibrio.*

To be made a laughing-ftock, *eſſer lo zimbello, ſervir di ludibrio.*

A ftock of bees, *un arnia di api.*

Stocks [a pair of ftocks for malefactors] *ceppi.*

To be in the fhoemaker's ftocks, *aver i piedi alla tortura.*

Stocks [pofts framed to build a fhip or boat upon] *caſſo*, s. m.

A fhip upon ftocks, *un vaſcello in caſſo.*

Stock-fifh, *ſtoccofiſſo*, s. m. *ſorta di peſce che ſi mangia affumicato.*

Stock-dove, *colombaccio.*

Stock-

Stock-jobber, *ſenſale di fonde.*

To STOCK [to furniſh, to ſupply] *fornire, provvedere,* preſ. *forniſco,* pret. *provvidi.*

I am well ſtocked with clothes, *io ſon ben fornito d' abiti.*

To ſtock a ſhop, *fornire una bottega.*

To STOCK UP [to extirpate] *eſtirpare, ſbarbare, ſradicare, ſvellere.*

STOC'KDOVE, s. [ring-dove] *ſpezie di tortorella, o di colombo ſalvatico.*

STO'CKED, adj. *fornito, provviſto.*

I am ſtocked with every thing, *ſono ben provviſto di tutto.*

STO'CKING, s. [hoſe] *calzetta, calza,* s. f.

Silk ſtockings, *calze di ſeta.*

STO'CKSTILL, adj. [motionleſs] *immobile, affatto privo di moto.*

STOI'CAL, adj. [of the ſtoicks] *ſtoico.*

Stoical gravity, *gravità ſtoica.*

Stoical maxim, *maſſima ſtoica.*

STOI'CALLY, adv. [ſtoick-like] *ſtoicamente, da ſtoico, alla ſtoica.*

STO'ICISM, s. *la ſetta degli ſtoici.*

STO'ICK, s. [a porch diſciple of Zeno at Athens] *uno ſtoico, filoſofo della ſetta di Zenone.*

STOLE, s. [an ornament for the neck uſed by Roman Catholick prieſts] *ſtola,* s. f. *quella ſtriſcia di drappo che ſi pone il ſacerdote al collo.*

Stole [royal robe, long garment] *ſtola, veſta, abito.*

Groom of the ſtole [the head officer belonging to a prince's bed-chamber] *gentiluomo della guardaroba.*

Stole, *preterito del verbo* To ſteal.

STOLEN, adj. [from to ſteal] *rubato,* v. To ſteal.

STO'MACH } s. [that part of the body which receives and
STO'MACK } digeſts the food] *ſtomaco,* s. m. *quella parte del corpo dell' animale, dove è ricevuto il cibo, e dove ſi fa la prima concozione.*

To turn one's ſtomach, *ſtomacare, ſvogliare, perturbare lo ſtomaco.*

Fat meat turns my ſtomach, *la carne graſſa mi ſtomaca.*

To be ſick in the ſtomach, *aver male allo ſtomaco.*

Stomach [appetite, hunger] *appetito,* s. m. *fame.*

To have a good ſtomach, *avere buono appetito.*

That goes againſt my ſtomach [I have an averſion for it] *odio, aborriſco ciò.*

To ſtomach, or to ſtomach at [to be angry at, to reſent a thing] *ſtomacarſi, ſdegnarſi, offenderſi.*

STO'MACHER, s. [that women wear on their breaſt] *pettorina,* s f. *ornamento che le donne portan ſul petto.*

Stomacher [any piece of cloth to put over one's breaſt] *ogni pezzo di panno o drappo che ſi porta ſu lo ſtomaco.*

STO'MACHFUL, adj [that has pride, dogged, peeviſh, loath to ſubmit] *fiero, altiero, orgoglioſo, ritroſo, caparbio, oſtinato, capone.*

STO'MACHFULNESS, s. [ſtubbornneſs, ſullenneſs, obſtinacy] *pertinacia, oſtinatezza, oſtinazione, caponeria.*

STOMA'CHICK, adj. [good for the ſtomach] *ſtomacale, grato allo ſtomaco, che ſi confà collo ſtomaco.*

STO'MACHLESS, adj. [that has no ſtomach] *ſtomacato, ſvogliato, ſtuſo, ſtucco, che non ha appetito.*

STOMACHO'SITY, s. [anger, indignation] *fierezza, alterigia,* s. f. *orgoglio, ſdegno,* s. m.

STO'MACHOUS, adj. [ſoon angry, diſdainful] *ſtizzoſo, collerico, fiero, orgoglioſo, ſdegnoſo.*

STONE, s. *pietra,* s. f. *ſaſſo,* s. m.

Free-ſtone, *pietra viva, macigno.*

Pumice-ſtone, *pietra pumice.*

Precious ſtone, *pietra prezioſa.*

To kill two birds with one ſtone, *batter due chiodi ad una çalda; pigliar due colombi a una fava.*

A flint ſtone, *pietra focaja, ſelce.*

A touch-ſtone, *pietra di paragone.*

I don't love to walk upon the ſtones, *non amo di camminare ſopra pavimento di pietre.*

The ſtone [a diſeaſe] *pietra, quella rena petrificata, che ſi genera nelle reni.*

To be troubled with the ſtone, *aver la pietra.*

Stone [teſticle] *teſticolo.*

Stone-horſe, *cavallo intiero.*

Stone [in ſome ſort of fruits] *nocciolo, oſſo,* s. m. ex. cherry, olive, plum, peach ſtone, *nocciolo, oſſo di ciriege, ulive, ſuſine, peſche.*

Stones of grapes, *granelli, vinacciuoli, che ſon negli acini dell' uva.*

Stone [a weight containing fourteen pounds] *peſo di quattordici libbre.*

Stone-pitch, *pece ſecca, o indurita.*

Stone-break [or ſaxifrage] *ſaſſifraga, ſaſſifragia.*

Stone-throw, *tiro di pietra.*

Stone wall, *muro di pietra.*

Stone cutter, *taglia pietre.*

Stone-work, *lavoro di muratore.*

Stone-dead, *morto affatto.*

Stone buck, *rupicapra,* s. f.

Stone-bow, *una baleſtra.*

The ſtone-cray [a diſtemper in hawks] *calcolo; malore ne' falconi.*

Blood-ſtone, *ematite,* s. f.

To STONE [to throw ſtones at] *lapidare, percuotere con pietre o ſaſſi.*

STO'NEBREAK, s. [an herb] *nome d' erba.*

STONECHA'TTER, s. [a bird] *nome d' uccello.*

STO'NECROP, s. [a ſort of tree] *nome d' albero.*

STONECU'TTER, s. [one whoſe trade is to hew ſtones] *tagliapietra.*

STO'NED, adj. *lapidato.*

STO'NEFERN, s. [a plant] *nome d' erba.*

STO'NEFLY, s. [an inſect] *nome d' inſetto.*

STO'NEFRUIT, s. [fruit of which the ſeed is covered with a hard ſhell enveloped in the pulp] *frutto che ha il nocciolo duriſſimo.*

STO'NEHAWK, s. [a kind of hawk] *ſpezie di falcone.*

STO'NEHORSE, s. [a horſe not caſtrated] *ſtallone, cavallo intiero.*

STO'NEPIT, s. [a quarry, a pit where ſtones are dug] *maniera d' onde ſi cavano ſaſſi.*

STO'NER, s. *lapidatore,* s. m.

STO'NING, s. *lapidazione.*

STO'NY, adj. [full of ſtones] *ſaſſoſo, pietroſo, petroſo, pien di pietre.*

Stony heart, *cuor di pietra, cuor duro come pietra.*

Stony fruit, *frutto petroſo.*

STOOD, *preterito del verbo* To ſtand.

STOOL, s. [a thing to ſit upon] *ſcanno, ſeggio, ſgabello,* s. m.

Stool, or cloſe-ſtool, *predella, ſeggetta.*

To give one a ſtool, *fare andare alla ſeggetta.*

He had ſix good ſtools, *egli è andata ſei volte del corpo.*

Joint-ſtool, *ſgabello.*

STOOK, s. [a ſhock of corn containing twelve ſheaves] *bica,* s. f. *mucchio che contiene dodici covoni di grano.*

To STOOP [to bow, to bend downwards] *abbaſſare, chinare, piegare.*

To ſtoop, verb neut. *abbaſſarſi, chinarſi, piegarſi*

To ſtoop to the ground, *abbaſſarſi fino a terra.*

To ſtoop [to cringe, to ſubmit] *abbaſſarſi, umiliarſi, ſottometterſi, indurſi, calarſi.*

I can't ſtoop to that, *non poſſo indurmi a queſto.*

He makes his reaſon ſtoop to the exorbitancies of his paſſion, *egli ſommette la ragione al talento delle ſue paſſioni.*

To ſtoop [to bend down as a hawk does to ſtrike a fowl] *calare, parlando d' un falcone.*

STO'OPING, *abbaſſamento,* v. To ſtoop.

STOP [ſtay, delay] *indugio, ritegno,* s. m. *tardanza,* s. f.

Stop [rub, obſtacle] *intoppo, rincontro, oſtacolo, impedimento.*

To put a ſtop to a buſineſs, *apportar oſtacolo a che che ſia, impedirlo.*

This put a ſtop to my journey, *queſto ritardò il mio viaggio.*

Put a ſtop to your grief, *ceſſate d' affliggervi.*

To put a ſtop to complaints, *acquetare le doglianze.*

To put a ſtop to the war, *terminare*

minare la guerra, metter fine alla guerra.

Stop [used in writing] *punto.*

Full ſtop, *punto finale.*

Stop of a muſical inſtrument, *taſto di ſtrumento muſicale.*

Full ſtop in walking, *pauſa, dimora.*

To STOP [to ſtay, to hinder, to keep from going farther] *fermare, arreſtare, trattenere,* preſ. *trattengo,* pret. *trattenni.*

To ſtop a thief, *fermare un ladro.*

Stop thief, ſtop thief, *al ladro, al ladro.*

To ſtop the blood [to ſtanch it] *ſtagnare il ſangue.*

To ſtop [to ſuſpend, to cauſe to ceaſe] *arreſtare, ſoſpendere, far ceſſare.*

To ſtop [to retard, to hinder] *arreſtare, indugiare, ritardare, intertenere, impedire, fare indugiare,* preſ. *intertengo, impediſco,* pret. *intertenni.*

To ſtop, verb neut. *arreſtarſi, fermarſi, dimorare, fare alto, ceſſar d' andare.*

We ſtopped at his houſe, *noi ci fermammo in caſa ſua.*

To ſtop [to ſtop up, to ſhut] *chiudere, turare.*

To ſtop one's mouth, *chiudere altrui la bocca.*

To ſtop a bottle, *turare un fiaſco.*

To ſtop a paſſage, *chiudere un paſſaggio.*

To ſtop two gaps with one buſh, *batter due chiodi ad una calda.*

To ſtop one's breath [to choak, to ſtrangle, to ſtifle] *affogare, ſoffocare alcuno.*

STO'PPAGE, s. *ſoffocazione, oppilazione,* s. f.

STO'PPED, adj. *fermato, arreſtato, trattenuto,* v. To ſtop.

STO'PPING, adj. [cauſing a ſtop] *reſtringente, ſtagnante.*

STO'PPLE, s. *turaccio,* s. m.

STOPT, v Stopped.

STO'RAX, s. [gum of a Syrian tree, that is very ſweet ſcented] *ſtorace,* s. f. *ragia d' albero odorifero che naſce in Soria.*

STO'RAX-TREE, s. [a tree that produces a roſinous and odoriferous gum] *ſtorace, albero che produce una ragia odorifera e attaccaticcia.*

STORE, s. [abundance, plenty, much, many] *abbondanza, quantità, copia, dovizia, molto, numero grande.*

A great ſtore of proviſions, *grand' abbondanza, quantità grande di viveri o vettovaglia.*

We have ſtore of all things, *noi abbiamo copia o dovizia d' ogni coſa.*

Store is no ſore, *l' abbondanza non fa mai male.*

Store of money, *molti danari.*

Great ſtore of ſhips, *gran numero di vaſcelli.*

Store [proviſions, victuals] *viveri, vettovaglie.*

To lay in ſtore of proviſion, *far provviſione.*

STORES [for an army, or town] *munizioni, viveri.*

Store-houſe [magazine] *magazzino,* s. m.

To STORE [to furniſh with ſtores or proviſions] *munire, provvedere delle coſe neceſſarie.*

To ſtore a town with proviſions, *munire una piazza di viveri.*

To ſtore a ſhip, *alleſtire, vettovagliare un navilio.*

To ſtore [to lay up in ſtore] *riſerbare, conſervare.*

STORED, adj. *munito,* v. To ſtore.

STORIES, pl. *di* Story.

STORK, s. [a fowl] *cicogna,* s. f.

STORM, s. [bluſtering weather, tempeſt] *tempeſta, burraſca, fortuna, procella,* s. f.

To raiſe a ſtorm, *ſuſcitare una tempeſta.*

A ſtorm of rain, *acquazzone, diluvio d' acqua.*

After a ſtorm comes a calm, *dopò il cattivo tempo viene il buono.*

Storm [buſtle, noiſe] *fracaſſo, fraſtuono, romore.*

Storm [trouble, perſecution, ſedition] *turbolenza, confuſione, ſedizione, perſecuzione,* s. f. *tumulto, diſordine,* s. m.

Storm [aſſault, or ſudden attack] *aſſalto.*

To take a town by ſtorm, *eſpugnare una piazza per aſſalto.*

A ſtorm of muſket-ſhot, *una ſalva di moſchettate.*

To STORM [to chafe, to fume] *tempeſtare, imperverſare, ſtrepitare, ſaltare, infuriare, furiare.*

To ſtorm a town [to attack it furiouſly] *aſſaltare, attaccare una piazza, dare un fiero aſſalto ad una piazza.*

STO'RMED, adj. *tempeſtato, imperverſato,* v. To ſtorm.

STO'RMY, adj. [tempeſtuous] *tempeſtoſo, procelloſo, burraſcoſo, fortunoſo.*

STO'RY, s. [hiſtory] *iſtoria, ſtoria,* s. f.

Story [tale] *novella,* s. f.

Story [a recital of any particular adventure] *ſtoria, ſucceſſo, avvenimento,* s. m.

He told me all the ſtory, *mi raccontò tutta la ſtoria, tutto 'l ſucceſſo.*

An old woman's ſtory, *fanfaluca, la favola dell' uccellino.*

The ſtory goes, *ſi dice.*

Story [fable, flam] *una favola, una paſtocchia, una finzione.*

Story [in building] *piano.*

A houſe three ſtories high, *una caſa di tre piani.*

To STO'RY [to report, to relate] *narrare, raccontare, ragguagliare, dire,* preſ. *dico,* pret. *diſſi.*

STORYTE'LLER, s. [one who relates tales] *novelliſta, uno che narra novelle o ſtorie.*

STOTE, s. [a ſort of ſtinking ferret] *puzzola,* s. f. *ſorta di animale ſimile alla faina.*

STOVE, s. [a ſort of furnace to warm a room] *ſtufa.*

Stove [hot bath] *ſtufa, bagno caldo.*

To STOUND [to be in pain or ſorrow] *ſoffrir dolore, eſſer addolorato.*

To ſtound [to ſtune] *ſtuonare, non ſuonare o non cantare in tuono*

STOUND, s. [ſorrow, grief, miſhap] *dolore, affanno, ſventura.*

Stound [aſtoniſhment, amazement] *ſtupore.*

Stound [hour, time, ſeaſon] *ora, tempo, ſtagione.*

STOUR, s. [aſſault, incurſion, tumult] *aſſalto, tumulto, ſcompiglio.*

STOUT, adj. [couragious] *gagliardo, forte, valoroſo, prode, bravo, valente, ardito.*

Stout [luſty] *rigoglioſo, vigoroſo, forte, robuſto.*

To make a ſtout reſiſtance, *fare una vigoroſa reſiſtenza.*

Stout, s. [ſtrong ale] *cervogia forte.*

STO'UTLY, adv. [couragiouſly] *gagliardamente, valoroſamente, bravamente, valentemente, arditamente, con molto vigore, con bravura grande.*

Stoutly [vigorouſly] *vigoroſamente.*

To hold out ſtoutly, *tener fermo.*

To drink ſtoutly, *trincare, bere profuſamente.*

STO'UTNESS, s. [courage] *bravura, valenteria, valorìa, fermezza,* s. f. *valore, animo, coraggio,* s. m.

Stoutneſs [pride] *fierezza, arroganza,* s. f. *orgoglio,* s. m.

Stoutneſs [ſtiffneſs, ſturdineſs] *caparbietà, oſtinazione.*

To STOW [to place wares, proviſion, &c. in a ware-houſe, or in the hold of a ſhip] *ſtivare, ordinare, allogare, abbicare, ammucchiare, accataſtare.*

To ſtow goods in a ware-houſe, *ſtivare, aſſettare delle mercanzie in un magazzino.*

STO'WED, adj. *ſtivato, ordinato, allogato, abbicato, ammucchiato, accataſtato.*

STO'WAGE, s. [money paid for laying up goods] *magazzinaggio,* s. m. *termine mercantile; quel danaro che ſi paga pel conſervar della roba in un magazzino, affitto del magazzino.*

STOWR, s. [the round of a ladder] *ſcaglione di ſcala a piuòli.*

To STRA'DDLE [to ſpread the legs wide] *allargar le gambe camminando.*

STRA'DDLING, adj. ex. to ride ſtraddling, as men do, *andare a cavalcioni, con una gamba da una banda, e l altra dall' altra.*

To go ſtraddling, *camminare colle gambe allargate.*

To STRA'GGLE [to go from one's company, to wander] *ſcompagnarſi, non andar in compagnia, errare, vagare.*

STRA'GGLER, s. [straggling soldier] *un soldato ramingo, che non va in compagnia.*

STRA'GGLING, s. *lo scompagnarsi.*

Straggling, adj. ex. a straggling soldier, *un soldato che s' è sviato dagli altri.*

STRAIGHT, *v.* Strait.

STRAIN, s. [vehement effort] *forza, possibilità,* s. f. *sforzo, potere,* s. m.

Strain [a violent contortion of the sinews, sprain] *storcimento, lo slogarsi qualche membro.*

Strain [a breed of horses] *razza di cavalli.*

Strain [tune] *aria,* s. f.

A strain of musick, *un aria di musica.*

Melodious strains, *concenti armoniosi.*

A high strain of speech, *stile sublime e alto.*

A high strain of verses, *versi sublimi.*

He is too much upon the high strain, *egli è un poco troppo ampolloso nel suo dire.*

The strain of deer, *la pesta d' un cervo.*

To strain or strain through [to press any liquor through a sieve or cloth] *colare, far passar cosa liquida in panno o altro.*

To strain [to press, to wring, to squeeze] *spremere, premere.*

To strain out the juice of any fruit, *spremere il sugo da qualche frutto.*

To strain [to bind hard] *strignere, legar fortemente.*

To strain one's voice [to raise or force the voice] *alzare, sforzar la voce.*

To strain [to force, to wrest, to offer violence] *sforzare, far forza, violentare, far violenza.*

To strain too high [to over-do] *stiracchiare.*

To strain [among falconers, a hawk is said to strain when she catches at any thing] *il calarsi che fa il falcone ad ogni sorta di preda.*

To strain one's self, *sforzarsi.*

To strain an arm, *storcersi, slogarsi, dislogarsi un braccio.*

To strain [to endeavour greatly] *sforzarsi, fare ogni sforzo, cercare, procurare, ingegnarsi.*

STRA'INED, adj. *colato, v.* To strain.

STRA'INER, s. *colatojo,* s. m.

STRA'INING, s. *colamento,* s. m. *il colare.*

Without any straining, *senza forza, senza violenza alcuna.*

STAIT, STRAIGHT, STREIGHT, adj. [tight] *diritto, e dritto, che non piega da niuna banda, che non è torto.*

To make strait, *dirizzare, drizzare.*

Strait [narrow] *stretto, angusto.*

Strait-handed [close fisted] *stretto, abbietto, tapino, avaro, taccagno.*

Strait, adv. [presently] *subito, adesso, appunto, in questo punto.*

Go strait along, *andate dritto.*

Strait [a narrow arm of the sea] *stretto di mare.*

Straits, or streits [a sort of narrow cloth] *spezie di panno stretto.*

Straits [want, penury] *stretto, penuria, angustia, necessità, bisogno.*

To be in great straits, *trovarsi in grandi strette, in grande angustia, in gran bisogno.*

To be in great straits, *esser molto travagliato, molto perplesso.*

To STRA'ITEN [to make strait or right] *dirizzare, drizzare, far tornar dritto il torto o il piegato.*

To straiten [to make strait, or less wide] *strignere, ristrignere, far più stretto.*

To straiten [to press hard, to put hard to] *serrare, incalzare, violentare, serrar il basto ad uno.*

STRA'ITENED, adj. *dirizzato, drizzato, v.* To straiten.

STRAITLA'CED, adj. [stiff, constrained, without freedom] *allacciato, stretto, duro, costretto, sforzato, senza libertà.*

STRA'ITLY, adv. [narrowly] *strettamente.*

Straitly [streightly] *strettamente, caldamente, espressamente.*

STRA'ITNED, adj. *dirizzato, drizzato, v.* To straiten.

To be straitned [pinched, reduced to straits] *esser nelle strette, esser ridotto in miseria, esser angustiato, trovarsi in angustie.*

STRA'ITNESS, s. *strettezza,* s. f. *essere stretto.*

STRA'ITWAY, adv. [forthwith] *subito, incontanente, in un punto, adesso.*

STRAKE, *antico preterito del verbo* to strike.

STRAND [a high shore or bank of the sea or of a great river] *piaggia, sponda.*

Stand [twist of a rope] *filo di corda.*

STRA'NDBO, adj. [run aground] *naufragato sulla piaggia.*

STRANGE, adj. [surprising, uncommon, wonderful] *strano, nuovo, insitato, straordinario, stravagante.*

Strange [odd] *strano, bizzarro, fantastico.*

Strange [foreign] *strano, forestiero, straniero.*

Strange notions, *strane immaginazioni, idee strane.*

Strange countries, *paesi stranieri.*

Strange Gods, *Iddij falsi, falsi Dei.*

To look strange upon one, *far cattiva cera ad uno, guardarlo con una cera arcigna o burbera, guardarlo di mal' occhio, fargli il viso dell' arme.*

Oh strange! *oh meraviglia, oh maraviglia!*

To STRANGE [to wonder, to be astonished] *maravigliarsi, stupirsi.*

STRA'NGELY, adv. *stranamente, grandemente, smisuratamente, fuor di misura.*

STRA'NGENESS, s. *stranezza, rarità, singolarità,* s. f.

STRA'NGER, s. [one of another country, family, or society] *forestiero, straniero,* s. m. *forestiera, straniera,* s. f.

To make a stranger of one, *trattar uno da forestiero, star troppo sulle cerimonie.*

To make one's self a stranger, *fare il forestiero, usar troppe cerimonie, esser troppo cerimonioso.*

I am altogether a stranger to him, *non sa chi io mi sia, non mi conosce punto.*

I am a stranger to that business [I know nothing of it] *non so nulla di quest' affare.*

You are a great stranger [you seldom come] *voi non vi fate mai vedere.*

To STRA'NGER [to strange, to alienate] *alienare, distorre.*

To STRA'NGLE [to throttle] *strangolare, strozzare, affogare.*

STRA'NGLED, s. *strangolato, strozzato, affogato.*

STRA'NGLER, s. [one who strangles] *uno che strangola, che strozza.*

STRA'NGLES, s. [horse's disease] *stranguglioni,* s. m. *malattia di cavallo.*

Strangle-weed, s. *orobanche, (pianta.)*

STRANGU'LION, STRA'NGURY, s. [stoppage of the urine] *stranguria,* s. f. *infermità, che fa orinare a goccia a goccia.*

STRAP, s. [thong of leather] *coreggia,* s. f. *coreggiuolo,* s. m. *striscia di cuojo a guisa di nastro.*

To STRAP [to beat with a strap] *scoreggiare, percuotere colla coreggia.*

STRA'PPADO, s. [a kind of rack, a punishment inflicted on criminals, by drawing them high with their arms tied backwards] *strappata,* s. f. *tratto di corda.*

STRA'PPING, adj. ex. a strapping lass, *una ragazzaccia, una giovinastra.*

STRATA, s. [beds, layers] *suoli, e dicesi de' differenti letti di materia che si trovano scavando il terreno uno sotto l' altro è distinti l' un dall' altro.*

STRA'TAGEM, s. [politick device, subtle invention] *strattagemma, inganno,* s. m. *astuzia, furberia,* s. f.

STRAW, s. [stubble] *paglia,* s. f.

A straw, *un filo di paglia.*

I do not care a straw for him, *non lo stimo un fico.*

A stack of straw, *un pagliajo.*

A man of straw [an insignificant fellow] *un uomo di paglia, un uomo di poca considerazione.*

I would not give a straw for it, *non ne darei un frullo.*

To be in the straw [to lie-in] *aver partorito.*

Straw-hat, *cappello di paglia.*

Sraw bed, *pagliariccio, un ſaccone.*

STRA'WBERRY, s. [a ſort of fruit] *fragola*, s. f. *frutta nota.*

Strawberry plant, *pianta di fragola.*

STRAY, adj. [ſtrayed] *ſviato, traviato, perduto.*

To STRAY [to go a-ſtray] *ſviare, traviare, uſcir di via.*

STREAK, s. [line or track that any thing leaves behind it] *ſtriſcia*, s. f.

Streak [a ſeam between two planks in a ſhip] *le feſſure che ſi vedono fra le aſſe d' un vaſcello.*

The ſtreaks of a wheel, *i cerchi d' una ruota.*

To STREAK [to make lines or ſtreaks] *ſtriſciare, rigare, vergare.*

To mark with ſtreaks of ſeveral colours, *vergare di varj colori.*

STRE'AKED, adj. *ſtriſciato, rigato, vergato.*

STREAM, s. [running water] *ruſcello, rivo, rivolo*, s. m. *corrente*, s. f. *acqua che corre.*

The ſtream of a river, *la corrente d' un fiume.*

To go with the ſtream, *andar colla corrente, andare a ſeconda.*

Stream of eloquence, *fiume d' eloquenza.*

Streams of fire ſeen in the air, *raggi di fuoco che appariſcono nell' aria.*

To STREAM [to ſtream out, to run out] *colare, ſgorgare, uſcire, ſorgere, zampillare.*

STRE'AMER, s. [in a ſhip] *pennoncello*, s. m. *banderuola*, s. f.

STREET, s. *ſtrada, via, contrada.*

To run up and down the ſtreets, *andar per le ſtrade, ſcorrer la cavallina, andar ramingo.*

Street-walker [common ſtrumpet] *una bagaſcia, una puttanaccia.*

STREICHT, s. [narrow arm of the ſea] *ſtretto, golfo.*

The ſtreights of Gibraltar, *lo ſtretto di Gibilterra.*

STRENGTH, s. [vigour of body] *forza, poſſanza*, s. f. *potere, vigore*, s. m.

To gather ſtrength, *fortificarſi, rimetterſi, ripigliar le forze, riaverſi.*

The ſtrength of a town, *le fortificazioni d' una piazza*

Strength of mind, *forza d' ingegno, penetrazione*, s. f.

The ſtrength of a word, *la forza, l' energia, l' enfaſi d' una parola.*

Strength [power, ability] *forza, potere.*

To STRE'NGTHEN [to fortify to give ſtrength, in a proper and figurative ſenſe] *fortificare, afforzare, dar forza, dar vigore, invigorire, rinforzare.*

To ſtrengthen a town, *fortificare una città, munire una piazza.*

To ſtrengthen the body, *fortificare il corpo.*

To ſtrengthen the garriſon, *rinforzare la guarnigione.*

STRE'NGTHENED, adj. *fortificato, munito*, v. To ſtrengthen.

STRE'NGTHNER, } s. [that which STRE'NGTHENER, } gives ſtrength, that which makes ſtrong] *coſa che da forza, che rende forte.*

STRE'NGTHENER [that which adds to the bulk and firmneſs of the ſolids] *rimedio che fortifica.*

STRE'NGTHENING, s. *fortificamento*, s. m. *il fortificare.*

STRE'NGTHLESS, adj. [wanting ſtrength, deprived of ſtrength] *ſpoſſato, che non ha forza, privo di forza.*

Strengthleſs [wanting potency, weak] *che non ha virtù, che non ha potere, debole.*

STRE'NUOUS, adj. [bold, valiant, ſtout] *ſtrenuo, bravo, gagliardo, valoroſo, coraggioſo, ſodo.*

STRE'NUOUSLY, adv. *ſtrenuamente, gagliardamente, valoroſamente, di forza.*

STRE'NUOUSNESS, s. *bravura, gagliardia, arditezza, forza*, s. f. *valore, coraggio*, s. m.

STRESS, [the main point in buſineſs] *punto principale, fondamento, importanza, forza.*

Herein lies the ſtreſs of the whole matter, *qui ſta il punto principale, qui ſta l' importanza di tutto il negozio, queſto è il fondamento dell' affare.*

The ſtreſs of the war, *il nervo della guerra.*

To lay ſtreſs upon [to inſiſt] *fondarſi, inſiſtere, fare iſtanza, chiedere iſtantemente.*

To lay the ſtreſs upon a letter, *appoggiare ſopra una lettera.*

To lay too much ſtreſs upon ceremonies, *ſtare troppo ſulle ceremonie.*

Streſs of weather [ſtorm] *tempeſta, burraſca, fortuna.*

To STRESS [to diſtreſs, to put to hardſhips] *involgere in difficoltà, in affanni.*

STRETCH, s. [extent] *tratto, ſpazio*, s. m. *diſtanza*, s. f.

To put one's thoughts and wits upon the ſtretch, *ſtillarſi il cervello, lambiccarſelo.*

To STRETCH [to reach out, to draw into a length] *ſtendere, diſtendere, eſtendere, allargare, ſtiracchiare*, pret. *ſteſi, diſteſi, eſteſi.*

To ſtretch one's arms or hands, *ſtender le braccia o le mani.*

To ſtretch out a cord, *tendere una corda*

To ſtretch out in length, *allungare.*

To ſtretch one's ſelf, *diſtenderſi, diſtender le membra, come ſà chi diſtandoſi o ſtato a ſedere ſi rizza, e aprendo le braccia ſ' allunga.*

To ſtretch, or ſtretch out, verb neut. *ſtenderſi, diſtenderſi.*

To ſtretch [to make the matter more than it is] *ſtiracchiare, cavillare, ſofiſticare.*

To ſtretch [to ſtrain] *ſforzarſi, fare ogni ſforzo, ſbracciarſi.*

STRE'TCHED, adj. *ſteſo, diſteſo, eſteſo, allargato, ſtirato*, v. To ſtretch.

STRE'TCHER, s. [any thing uſed for extenſion] *coſa adoperata per ſortemente eſtenderne un altra.*

Stretcher [the timber againſt which the rower plants his feet] *legno contro al quale il rematore punta i piedi onde poſſa far forza colle braccia e colla perſona remando.*

STRE'TCHING, s. *ſtendimento, diſtendimento*, s. m.

To STREW [to ſpread] *ſpandere, ſpargere, ſeminare.*

To ſtrew flowers, *ſpander fiori.*

To ſtrew the ground with flowers, *coprir la terra di fiori.*

To ſtrew with flour or ſugar, *aſperger di farina o di zucchero, infarinare, inzuccherare.*

STRE'WED, adj. *ſparſo, coſperſo, ſeminato, coperto.*

STRE'WING, s. *ſpandimento.*

STE'WED [ſcattered here and there] *parpagliato, ſparſo quà e là.*

STREW'MENT, s. [any thing ſcattered in decoration] *checcheſſia ſparſo per ornamento in ſul terreno.*

STRIÆ, s. [ſmall channels in the ſhells of cockles and ſcollops] *ſtrie; canaletti nelle conchiglie.*

STRI'ATED, adj. [Lat.] *ſcanalato, parlando di conchiglie e di colonne.*

STRI'CKEN, adj. [advanced] *avanzato.*

Stricken in years, *avanzato in età, attempato.*

STRI'CKLE, s. [a thing to ſtrike off the over meaſures of corn] *picciol baſtone ritondo per uſo di levar via dello ſtajo il colmo che ſopravanza alla miſura.*

STRICT, adj. [cloſe] *ſtretto, intrinſeco.*

Strict alliance, *ſtretta alleanza.*

Strict familiarity, *ſtretta familiarità, amicizia intrinſeca.*

Strict [exact, punctual] *eſatto, puntuale.*

Strict [preciſe] *ſtretto, preciſo, formale.*

Strict [rigid, rigorous] *ſtretto, rigido, ſevero, rigoroſo, auſtero.*

Strict conſcience, *coſcienza rigida.*

Strict way of living, *vita auſtera.*

Strict maſter, *maeſtro ſevero.*

Strict [exact, done with exactneſs] *eſatto, accurato, fatto con eſattezza, con accuratezza.*

To have a ſtrict eye upon one, *oſſervare attentamente gli altrui andamenti.*

To keep a ſtrict hand over, *tener uno corto, tenerlo in freno.*

STRI'CTLY, adv. [cloſely] *ſtrettamente.*

Strictly united, *ſtrettamente uniti.*

Strictly [exactly, punctually] *ſtrettamente, puntualmente, eſattamente, rigoroſamente.*

Strictly [expreſsly, poſitively] *ſtrettamente, caldamente, eſpreſſamente.*

I forbid you ſtrictly to do it, *vi proibiſco eſpreſſamente di farlo.*

He charged me ſtrictly to ſpeak to you about it, *mi commiſe caldamente di parlarvi di ciò.*

STRI'CTNESS, s. [rigour, exactneſs] *ſtrettezza, rigidezza, auſterità, eſattezza,* s. f. *rigore,* s. m.

The ſtrictneſs of the laws, *la ſeverità delle leggi.*

STRI'CTURE, s. [ſpark from a red-hot-iron] *ſcintilla, favilla,* s. f.

Brutes have ſome ſtrictures of ratiocination, *gli animali bruti hanno qualche barlume di ragione.*

STRIDE, s. *paſſo lungo.*

Cock's ſtride [the tread of a cock in an egg] *il ſeme del gallo nell' uovo.*

To STRIDE [to ſtep wide] *camminare a paſſi lunghi.*

STRI'DINGLY, adv. *a gran paſſo.*

STRI'DULOUS, adj. [making a ſmall noiſe] *ſtridulo, che ſquittiſce.*

STRIFE, s. [diſpute, quarrel] *conteſa, diſputa, lite, zuffa, riſſa,* s. f.

STRI'FEFUL, adj. [contentious, diſcordant] *che contende, diſcordante.*

STRIKE, [a meaſure containing four buſhels] *miſura che contiene quattro ſtaja di grano.*

To STRIKE [to beat, to hit] *battere, percuotere, ferire, colpire,* preſ. *colpiſco, feriſco,* pret. *percoſſi.*

He ſtruck me on the head, *egli m' ha percoſſo ſulla teſta.*

To ſtrike fire, *batter il fuoco, percuoter la pietra per appiccare il fuoco.*

Strike the iron whilſt it is hot, *batti il ferro mentre è caldo.*

To ſtrike to the very heart, *trafiggere il cuore.*

The clock ſtrikes, *l' orologio ſuona.*

It ſtruck twelve o' clock, *ſono ſonate le dodici.*

To ſtrike corn [to make meaſure even with a ſtick] *radere il grano nel miſurarlo.*

To ſtrike ſail, *ammainar le vele, abbaſſar le vele, piegar le vele.*

To ſtrike the flag, *abbaſſar lo ſtendardo.*

To ſtrike the ſands, or to ſtrike [to run a-ground] *dar in un banco, dar nelle ſecche.*

To ſtrike one's hand againſt the wall, *batter la teſta contro 'l muro ; dar la teſta nel muro.*

He ſtrikes at every thing, *tira ad un fringuello ; s' appiglia ad ogni coſa.*

To ſtrike blind, *acciecare, render cieco.*

To ſtrike aſunder, *far caſcare in due pezzi.*

To ſtrike againſt [to claſh with] *contrariare, eſſer contrario, non confarſi.*

To ſtrike down, *ſtramazzare, batter per terra.*

To ſtrike a nail into a board, *ficcare un chiodo in una panca.*

To ſtrike battle, *dare o preſentar la battaglia.*

To ſtrike off, *tagliare, mozzare, ſpiccare.*

To ſtrike off the hand, *tagliar la teſta, mozzar il capo.*

To ſtrike out, *cancellare.*

To ſtrike the drum, *batter il tamburo, ſuonar il tamburo.*

To ſtrike up one's heels, *dare il gambetto ad uno, farlo caſcare.*

To ſtrike up a bargain, *conchiudere un mercato.*

To ſtrike with the heels, *calcitare, tirar calci.*

STRI'KER, s. *battitore,* s. m.

STRI'KING, s. *battimento,* s. m. *il battere.*

Without ſtriking a ſtroke, *ſenza dare un colpo.*

STRING, s. [any thing to tye with] *cordicella,* s. f.

The ſtrings of a muſical inſtrument, *le corde d' uno ſtrumento muſicale.*

The ſmall ſtrings of roots, *le barbe delle radici.*

The heart ſtrings, *le fibre del cuore.*

To have two ſtrings to one's bow, *tenere il piede in due ſtaffe, navigar per più venti.*

You have the world in a ſtring, *ogni coſa v' arride, ogni coſa vi va a seconda.*

To STRING a muſical inſtrument, *metter le corde ad uno ſtrumento muſicale.*

To ſtring pearls, *infilzare delle perle.*

To ſtring [to make tenſe] *tendere, ſtirare, render teſo.*

STRI'NGED, adj. *dal verbo* To ſtring.

STRI'NGENT, adj. [binding, contracting] *che ſtringe, che contrae.*

STRI'NGLESS, adj. [having no fibres] *ſenza corde, privo di corde.*

STRI'NGY, adj. [full of ſtrings or ſtrings] *fibroſo.*

String-root, *radice fibroſa.*

STRIP, s. [of cloth] *una ſtriſcia di panno.*

To make ſtrip and waſte, *ſcialacquare, mandare a male, buttar via.*

To STRIP [to ſtrip naked] *ſpogliare ignudo, nudare.*

To ſtrip one of his money, *vincere altrui tutti i ſuoi danari.*

To ſtrip one's ſelf, *nudarſi, ſpogliarſi.*

STRIPE, s. [blow] *colpo,* s. m. *percoſſa,* s. f.

Stripe [a ſtreak in ſilk, cloth, or ſtuff] *ſtriſcia o liſta di drappo.*

To make white or yellow ſtripes, *liſtare, rigare di bianco e di giallo.*

To ſtripe a ſtuff, *vergare drappi o panni*

STRIPED, adj. *vergato, liſtato.*

STRI'PLING, s. [a young man, a youth] *un giovanotto.*

STRI'PPED, *v.* Stript.

STRI'PPER, s. *ſpogliatore,* s. m.

STRI'PPING, s. *ſpogliamento,* s. m. *ſpogliatura,* s. f.

STRIPT, adj. *ſpogliato, nudato.*

To STRIVE [to endeavour] *procurare, cercare, procacciare, ingegnarſi d' avere.*

To ſtrive [to ſtruggle] *dimenarſi, agitarſi, ſcuoterſi,* pret. *ſcoſſi.*

To ſtrive [to contend] *contraſtare, contendere, diſputare, fare a gara.*

To ſtrive againſt, *oſtare, opporſi, reſiſtere.*

To ſtrive who ſhall run beſt, *fare a gara nel correre.*

All ſtrove who ſhould have the beſt horſe, *tutti contendevano fra di loro per avere il miglior cavallo.*

To ſtrive againſt the ſtream, *nuotare ritroſo.*

STRI'VER, s. *colui che procura, che s' ajuta, che ſi procaccia, v.* To ſtrive.

STRI'VINGLY, adv. *a gara.*

STRO'KAL, s. [an inſtrument uſed by glaſs-makers] *ſtrumento adoperato da coloro che fanno il vetro.*

STROKE, s. [blow] *colpo,* s. m. *percoſſa, battitura,* s. m.

A ſtroke with a ſtick, *una baſtonata.*

To come under the ſtroke of juſtice, *eſſer punito.*

The clock is upon the ſtroke of eleven, *ſono quaſi le undici, ſono per ſonare le undici.*

The ſtroke of a pen or pencil, *una pennata, una pennellata.*

Maſter-ſtroke, *colpo da maeſtro.*

STROKE, } *antichi preteriti del verbo* To ſtrike.
STROOK, }

To STROKE [to rub, to feel gently with the hands] *piaggiare, accarezzare, paſſar la mano bel bello ſopra qualche coſa.*

To ſtroke a horſe, *accarezzare un cavallo ſtrofinandolo.*

STROKED, adj. *piaggiato, accarezzato.*

To STROLL [to rove, to ramble about] *vagare, vagabondare, andare attorno.*

STRO'LLER, s. [ſtrolling player] *commediante, ciarlatano.*

STRO'LLING, adj. *vagabondo.*

STROND, s. [the beach, the bank] *piaggia, lido, lito, coſta, riva, ripa, ſponda, e s' intende d' un gran fiume o del mare.*

STRONG, adj. [robuſt, luſty, vigorous] *forte, gagliardo, robuſto, vigoroſo.*

Strong [mighty, powerful] *forte, poderoſo, potente, conſiderabile.*

Strong army, *poderoſo eſercito.*

A ſtrong place, *una piazza forte.*

Strong [thick] *forte, groſſo, ſpeſſo.*

Strong cloth, *panno forte.*

Strong box, *forziere,* s. f.

Strong liquors, *liquori forti.*

I will not play with you, you are too ſtrong for me, *non voglio giuocare con voi, voi ſiete troppo forte.*

Strong wind, *vento forte.*

Strong inclination or paſſion, *grande inclinazione o paſſione.*

Strong expreſſion, *eſpreſſione enfatica, energica.*

Strong [ſharp to taſte or ſmell] *forte, agro, acerbo, aſpro, piccante.*

Strong vinegar, *aceto forte.*

Strong breath, *fiato puzzente.*

Strong water, *acquavite.*

I have a ſtrong opinion of it, *ne concepiſco una grande opinione.*

It ſmells too ſtrong of the pepper, *ſa troppo di pepe.*

They were but ten thouſand men ſtrong, *le loro forze non aſcendevano che a dieci mila uomini.*

To be ſtrong in the purſe, *aver molti danari, aver la borſa ben fornita.*

STRO'NGFISTED, adj. [ſtronghanded] *che ha molta forza nelle mani o nelle pugna.*

Strong-limb'd, *nerboruto, forte, robuſto, rubeſto.*

A ſtrong-bodied man, *un uomo gagliardo, un uomo forte.*

Strong bodied wine, *vino gagliardo, vino ſpiritoſo.*

STRO'NGHAND, s. [force, violence] *forza, violenza.*

STRO'NGLY, adv. *fortemente, forte, gagliardamente, grandemente, vigoroſamente.*

A ſtrong-ſeated town, *una città ſituata in luogo forte.*

STROOK, *preterito del verbo* To ſtrike, *che poeticamente ſi uſa in vere di* STRUCK.

STRO'PHE, s. [ſtanza] *ſtrofa, ſtanza.*

STRÔVE, *è un preterito del verbo* To ſtrive.

To STROUT [to ſwell with an appearance of greatneſs, to walk with affected dignity] *camminar tronfio, paoneggiarſi, far il grande.*

To STROW [to ſtrew, to ſpread by being ſcattered] *ſpargere.*

To ſtrow [to beſprinkle] *ſpruzzare.*

To ſtrow [to ſcatter, to throw at random] *ſpargere, gittar a caſo quà e là.*

To STROWL [to range, to wander] *vagabondare, andar errando.*

To STROY [to deſtroy] *diſtruggere.*

STRUCK, adj. [from to ſtrike] *percoſſo, v,* To ſtrike.

STRU'CKEN, *l' antico preterito paſſivo del verbo* To ſtrike.

STRU'CTURE, s. [fabrick] *ſtruttura, fabbrica,* s. f.

STRU'GGLE, s. [reſiſtance, effort] *conteſa, reſiſtenza, diſputa.*

To STRU'GGLE [to beſtir one's ſelf violently] *ſcuoterſi, muoverſi, agitarſi.*

To ſtruggle [to wreſtle, to fight, to contend] *contendere, contraſtare, lottare, combattere, azzuffarſi.*

To ſtruggle with or againſt death, *combatter colla morte.*

When one ſtruggles with death, *nell' avvicinarſi della morte.*

He did ſo ſtruggle that he got away, *tanto fece che ſcampò.*

STRU'GGLER, s. *contenditore,* s. m. *contenditrice,* s. f.

STRU'GGLING, s. *ſcoſſa, agitazione.*

There is no ſtruggling with neceſſity, *biſogna cedere alla neceſſità.*

STRU'MA, s. *quel male che chiamiamo ſcrofole.*

STRU'MOUS, adj. *ſcrofoloſo.*

STRU'MPET, s. [a common whore] *una bagaſcia, una ſgualdrina, una puttana vile.*

To STRU'MPET [to make a whore, to debauch] *ſedurre una donna e renderla puttana.*

STRUNG, adj. [from to ſtring] *guarnito di corde, infilzato.*

To STRUT, } [to walk af-
To STRUT ALONG, } ter a proud and ſtately manner] *paoneggiarſi, paoneggiarſi, ringalluzzarſi, vagheggiarſi da ſe ſteſſo.*

STRUT, s. [an affectation of ſtatelineſs in the walk] *l' atto del paoneggiarſi camminando.*

STUB, s. [a ſtump or ſtock of a tree] *tronco, ceppo,* s. m.

A ſtub-nail, *un chiodo uſato.*

To pay money upon the ſtub, *pagar danari contanti.*

To STUB up, *ſradicare, eſtirpare.*

STU'BBED, adj. [ſtout, well ſet] *robuſto, membruto.*

A ſtubbed fellow, *un uomo paffuto.*

STU'BBLE, s. [ſhort ſtraw left after the corn is reaped] *ſtoppia,* s. f. *quella paglia, che riman nel campo ſulle barbe delle biade ſegate.*

A ſtubble-gooſe, *un' oca d' autunno.*

STU'BBORN, adj. [headſtrong, obſtinate] *caparbio, oſtinato, ritroſo, pertinace, capone, teſtuto, teſtereccio.*

STU'BBORNESS, s *caparbietà, oſtinazione, ritroſia, pertinacia.*

STU'BBORNLY, adve *caparbiamente, oſtinatamente, pertinacemente.*

STU'BBY, adj. [ſhort and thick; ſhort and ſtrong] *corto e groſſo, paffuto, corto e forte.*

STU'BNAIL, s. [a nail broken off] *chiodo rotto.*

STU'CCO, s. [a kind of fine plaiſter for walls] *ſtucco.*

STUCK, adj. [from to ſtick] *appiccato, ficcato, v.* To ſtick.

STUD, s. [a nail imboſſed in any thing] *borchia,* s. f. *ſcudetto che ſerve per ornamento.*

Stud [a poſt, a ſtake] *un palo, un pezzaccio di legno corto e groſſo.*

Stud [a collection of breeding horſes and mares] *una razza di cavalli.*

A ſtud of mares [a ſtock of breeding mares] *una razza di cavalle.*

To STUD, *guarnire di borchie.*

STU'DDED, adj. *guarnito di borchie.*

Studded with gems, *tempeſtato di gemme.*

STU'DENT, s. [ſcholar] *uno ſtudente, uno ſcolare.*

A great ſtudent [a ſtudious man] *un uomo molto ſtudioſo, applicato allo ſtudio.*

STU'DIED, adj. *dal verbo* To ſtudy.

STU'DIER, s. [one who ſtudies, *ſtudiante, uno che ſtudia.*

STU'DIOUS, adj. [given to ſtudy] *ſtudioſo, applicato, dedito allo ſtudio.*

To live a ſtudious life, *paſſar la vita ſtudiando.*

He is very ſtudious to pleaſe him, *egli è molto ſollecito in compiacerlo.*

STU'DIOUSLY, adv. *ſtudioſamente, con iſtudio, a ſtudio, ſollecitamente, con ſollecitudine.*

STU'DIOUSNESS, s. *applicazione allo ſtudio.*

STU'DY, adj. [application of mind to learn] *ſtudio,* s. m.

To be in a courſe of ſtudy, *fare i ſuoi ſtudj, eſſere a ſtudio.*

Study, s. [cloſet to ſtudy in] *ſtudio, luogo dove ſi ſtudia.*

A little ſtudy, *uno ſtudiuolo.*

Study [application of mind to do any thing] *ſtudio, applicazione, diligenza, induſtria.*

I will make it my ſtudy to pleaſe, *m' ingegnerò, porrò ogni mio ſtudio in compiacervi.*

To be in a brown ſtudy [to be dull or melancholy] *ſtar penſieroſo, o penſoſo.*

To STUDY [to apply the mind to] *ſtudiare, dare opera alle ſcienze.*

To ſtudy hard, *ſtudiar molto, applicarſi molto allo ſtudio.*

To ſtudy [to prepare, or meditate before hand] *ſtudiare, meditare, preparare, comporre,* pret. *compoſi.*

To ſtudy a ſermon, *ſtudiare una predica.*

To ſtudy [to obſerve in order to know] *ſtudiare, oſſervare per conoſcere.*

To ſtudy one's humour, *ſtudiare l' umore di qualcheduno.*

To ſtudy one's brains about a thing, *ſtillarſi il cervello in qualche coſa.*

To ſtudy, verb neut. [to endeavour] *ſtudiarſi, affaticarſi, induſtriarſi, ingegnarſi, porre ogni ingegno.*

He ſtudies to pleaſe all the world, *ſi ſtudia, pone ogni ingegno per compiacere ad ognuno.*

He does nothing but ſtudy miſchief, *non penſa che a far del male.*

STU'DYED, adj. *ſtudiato; ſcrivi* ſtudied.

Studyed [done with much ſtudy] *ſtudiato, meditato, preparato, accurato.*

STU'DYING, s. *ſtudiamento, ſtudio,* s. m. *lo ſtudiare.*

STUFF, s. [thin clothes] *panno, drappo.*

Woollen or ſilk ſtuff, *panno, drappo.*

Houſhould ſtuff, *mobili, maſſerizie.*

Stuff [matter] *materia, roba,* s. f.

The ſtuff that runs out of a ſore, *la materia che eſce d' una piaga.*

What naſty ſtuff is this? *che porcheria è queſta?*

Bad ſtuff, *cattiva roba.*

To STUFF [to cram, to fill] *ſtivare, riempire.*

To ſtuff veal with herbs, *fare il ripieno ad un pezzo di vitella.*

To ſtuff a chair, *riempire una ſedia di borra.*

To ſtuff a ſaddle, *imbottire una ſella.*

STU'FFED, adj. *ſtivato, riempito.*

My head is ſtuffed up with cold, *ho una grande infreddatura nella teſta.*

STU'FFING, s. f. *ſtivamento,* s. m.

STUKE, s. [plaiſter of paris] *ſtucco,* s. m.

STULTI'LOQUENCE, s. [fooliſh talk] *pazzo cianciare, ſciocco ragionare.*

STUM, s. [wine yet unfermented] *moſto.*

Stum [new wine uſed to raiſe fermentation in dead and vapid wines] *moſto, o vin nuovo adoperato per muovere a fermento vin vecchio ſpoſſato.*

Stum [wine revived by a new termentation] *vino acconcio è ravvivato con nuova fermentazione.*

To STUM [to put certain ingredients into decayed wine, to revive it and make it briſk] *meſcolare il vino che ha preſo la punta con certi ingredienti per farlo piccante.*

STUM-

STU'MBLE, s. [a trip in walking] *l' inciampare camminando.*

Stumble [a blunder, a failure] *un granchio, un granciporro, uno sproposito massiccio.*

To STU'MBLE [to falter, to fall] *inciampare, porre il piede in in fallo, intoppare.*

STU'MBLED, adj. *inciampato, intoppato.*

STU'MBLER, s. *quello, a quella che inciampa, che s' intoppa.*

STU'MBLING, s. *inciampo,* s. m. *l' inciampare, intoppo, l' intoppare.*

Stumbling, adj. ex. a stumbling block, *impaccio, pericolo, difficoltà, ostacolo, scoglio.*

A stumbling horse, *cavallo che inciampa.*

STUMP, s. [a broken piece of tree] *tronco,* s. m.

The stump of a tree, *il tronco o ceppo d' un albero.*

The stump of a tooth, *pezzo di dente, dente rotto.*

Stump-footed, *che ha il piede tondo.*

To STUN [to render stupid by a blow, or noise] *intronare, stordire, offendere con colpo o soverchio romore la testa.*

Do not stun my head with your prating, *non mi state a romper la testa colle vostre chiacchiere.*

STUNG, adj. [from to sting] *morso, morduto, v.* To sting.

STU'NNED, adj. *intronato, stordito.*

STU'NNING, s. *intronamento,* s. m.

STUPEFA'CTION, s. [benumming] *intormentimento,* s. m.

Stupefaction [astonishing] *stupefazione, stupidezza,* s. f. *stupore,* s. m.

STUPEFA'CTIVE, adj. [that is of a stupifying quality] *che stupefà, narcotico, che addormenta.*

A stupefactive medicine, *una medicina narcotica, che addormenta.*

STUPE'NDOUS, adj. [prodigious, wonderful] *stupendo, maraviglioso, miracoloso, da indurre stupore.*

STU'PID, adj. [blockish, dull] *stupido, insensato, melenso, scimunito, sciocco, scempiato.*

Stupid [dismay'd] *stupido, stupito, attonito.*

STUPI'DITY, s. *stupidità, stupidezza, beffaggine,* s. f.

STU'PIDLY, adv. *da stupido.*

To STU'PIFY [to benumb, to make insensible] *stupefare, intormentire, privar di sentimento,* pres. *stupefaccio, intormentisco,* pret. *stupefeci.*

To stupify [to make stupid or dull] *istupidire, rendere stupido,* pres. *istupidisco.*

To stupify [to astonish] *stupefare, stupidire, stupire, empir di stupore.*

STU'PIFIED, adj. *stupefatto, intormentito, stupidito, stupito.*

STU'PIFYING, s. *stupefazione, stupidezza,* s. f.

STU'POR, s. [numbness] *stupore, intormentimento,* s. m.

STUPRA'TION, s. [the crime of deflowering, rape] *stupro, strupo,* s. m.

STU'RDILY, adv. [bluntly] *bruscamente, con modo brusco, rigidamente, stizzosamente.*

Sturdily [saucily] *insolentemente, con modo insolente.*

STU'RDINESS, s. [bluntness] *rigidezza, zotichezza,* s f.

Sturdiness [sauciness] *insolenza, audacia,* s. f.

Sturdiness [lustiness] *forza, robustezza,* s. f.

STU'RDY, adj. [strong, lusty, resolute] *robusto, gagliardo, vigoroso, forte.*

Sturdy [blunt] *brusco, insolente, zotico.*

STU'RGEON, s. [a sea-fish] *storione,* s. m. *pesce marino.*

STURK, s. [young ox, heifer] *un giovenco, una giovenca.*

To STU'TTER [to stammer] *tartagliare, scilinguare, balbettare.*

STU'TTERER, s. *tartaglione, balbo, scilinguato,* s. m.

STU'TTERING, s. *il tartagliare, il balbettare.*

STY, s. [a place for keeping and fattening swine] *porcile,* s. m.

Sty [any place of bestial debauchery] *nome generale d' ogni luogo dove si commettono cose sozze.*

To STY [to shut up in a sty] *chiudere nel porcile.*

STY'GIAN, adj. [hellish, infernal; pertaining to styx, one of the poetical rivers] *stigio, tartareo, infernale, appartenente a stige o alla palude stigia.*

STYLE, s. [manner of writing with regard to language] *stile, particolar maniera di scrivere una lingua.*

Style [manner of speaking appropriated to particular characters] *stile, modo di esprimersi proprio d' una tal persona.*

Style [title, appellation] *titolo, nome.*

The king gave them in his commission the style and appellation which belonged to them. *Il re nella patente diede loro il titolo e 'l nome che loro apparteneva.*

Style [course of writing] *stile, discorso.*

Style [a pointed iron used anciently in writing on tables of wax] *stile, stromento puntuto col quale gli antichi scrivevano sulle tavolette loro.*

Style [any thing with a sharp point, as a graver, the pin of a dial, &c.] *stile, stiletto, bulino, il ferro che mostra l' ore nell' orologio solare, e in generale ogni cosa lunga, sottile, e aguzza.*

Style [the stalk which rises from amid the leaves of a flower] *stile, o stilo; e dicesi di quelle quasi fila, o barbe, o raggi che spuntano dal centro della più parte de' fiori.*

Style of court [properly the practice observed by any court in its way of proceeding] *pratica, modo, particolarità, ceremoniale.*

Style [the way of reckoning the beginning of the year] *stile; modo di contare il tempo*—old style, new stile; *vecchio stile, nuovo stile, o stile Gregoriano.*

To style [to call, to term, to name] *chiamare, nominare, appellare.*

SUA'SION, s. [persuasion] *persuasione,* s. f.

SUA'SORY, adj. [tending to persuade] *persuasivo.*

SUA'VITY, s. [sweetness] *soavità, dolcezza,* s. f.

SUB-A'LMONER, s. *sotto elemosinario.*

SUBA'LTERN, adj. [plac'd under another] *subalterno, inferiore.*

A subaltern, s. [an inferior officer] *un subalterno, un ufficiale subalterno.*

Sub deacon, s. *sottodiacono,* s. m.

Sub-deaconship, s. *sottodiaconato,* s. m.

Sub-dean, s. *sotto decano.*

Sub-delegate, s. *un deputato, un sostituto.*

SUBDITITIOUS, adj [put in another's room] *supposto, messo in luogo d' un altro.*

To SU'BDIVIDE [to divide a division] *suddividere;* pret. *suddivisi.*

SUBDIVI'DED, adj. *suddiviso.*

SUBDIVI'SION, s. *suddivisione,* s. f.

SUBDO'LOUS, adj. [deceitful] *doloso, fraudolente.*

To SUBDU'E [to conquer, to master; in a proper and figurative sense] *soggiogare, vincere, superare, metter sotto la sua podestà,* pret. *vinsi.*

To subdue one's flesh, *mortificare la carne.*

SUBDU'ED, adj. *soggiogato, vinto, superato.*

SUBDU'ER, s. *soggiogatore,* s. m. *soggiogatrice,* s. f.

SUBDU'ING, s. *il soggiogare, soggiogazione,* s. f.

SU'BJECT, adj. [tied, obliged to dependance] *soggetto, sottomesso, suddito, sottoposto.*

Subject [apt, wont] *atto, portato, dedito, inclinato, soggetto.*

Subject to swear, *dedito a giurare.*

Subject to several diseases, *soggetto a molte infermità.*

The subject matter, *il soggetto, la materia della quale si tratta.*

Subject, s. [one who is under the dominion of a sovereign, prince, or state] *soggetto, suddito,* s. m. *soggetta, suddita,* s. f.

Subject [the matter treated of] *soggetto, materia alla quale si tratta.*

Subject [with philosophers, the substance to which qualities are joined] *soggetto, termine filosofico; sostanza alla quale le qualità sono apposte.*

To SUBJE'CT, [to make subject, to bring under] *soggettare, e suggettare, soggiogare.*

To subject [to make liable, to oblige] *soggettare, costrignere, obbligare.*

SUBJE'CTED, adj. *soggettato, soggiogato.*

SUBJE'CTION, s. [dependance, ſlavery] *ſoggezione, dipendenza, ſervitù*, s. f.

Subjection [obligation, neceſſity] *ſoggezione, obbligazione, ſervitù*, s. f.

Subjection [the ſtate of being a ſubject] *ſoggezione, condizione o ſtato d' un ſoggetto.*

To bring under ſubjection, *ſoggettare, ſottomettere*, pret. *ſottomiſi.*

To SU'BJOIN [to add] *aggiugnere, ſoggiugnere*, pret. *aggiunſi, ſoggiunſi.*

SU'BJOINED, adj. *aggiunto*

SUBITA'NEOUS, adj. [ſudden] *ſubitaneo, ſubitano, improvviſo, repentino.*

To SU'BJUGATE [to ſubdue] *ſoggiogare, vincere, ſuperare, metter ſotto la ſua autorità*, pret. *vinſi.*

SU'BJUNCTIVE, adj. *ſoggiuntivo*, ex. the ſubjunctive mood, *il modo ſoggiuntivo, termine gramaticale.*

To SU'BLIMATE [to raiſe any volatile or light matter by means of fire] *ſublimare, raffinare per diſtillazione.*

SU'BLIMATED, adj. *ſublimato.*

SU'BLIMATING, s. *il ſublimare, ſublimamento*, s. m.

SU'BLIMATORY, s. [an inſtrument or veſſel of ſublimation] *vaſo da ſublimare.*

SUBLIMA'TUM, s. [white mercury] *ſublimato, mercurio ſublimato.*

SUBLIMA'TION, s. *ſublimazione*, s. f.

SU'BLIME, adj. [high, lofty] *ſublime, alto, eccelſo.*

Sublime genius, *ingegno ſublime.*

Sublime ſtyle, *uno ſtile ſublime.*

To SU'BLIME [to raiſe, to refine] *raffinare, purificare, ſollevare, ſublimare.*

SU'BLIMED, adj. *raffinato, purificato, ſollevato, ſublimato.*

SUBLI'MENESS, } s. [height, loftineſs]
SU'BLIMITY, } *ſublimità, altezza, eccellenza, grandezza*, s. f.

SUBLU'NARY, adj. [under the moon] *ſublunare.*

SUBME'RSION [drowning] *ſommerſione*, s. f. *annegamento*, s. m.

To SUBMINI'STER [to ſupply with] *ſomminiſtrare, dare, porgere*, pret. *diedi, porſi.*

SUBMINI'STERED, adj. *ſomminiſtrato, dato.*

SU'BMISS, v. Submiſſive.

SUBMI'SSION, s. [reſpect, humbleneſs] *ſommiſſione, umiliazione, umiltà, obbedienza*, s. f.

SUBMI'SSIVE, adj. [humble, reſpectful] *ſommeſſo, umile, riſpettoſo, pieno di riſpetto.*

SUBMI'SSIVELY, adv. *ſommeſſamente, d' una maniera ſommeſſa, umilmente.*

SUBMI'SSIVENESS, s. [humility; confeſſion of fault or inferiority] *umiltà, ſommeſſione, confeſſione di fallo o d' inferiorità.*

SUBMI'SSLY, adv. [humbly, with ſubmiſſion] *con ſommeſſione, umilmente.*

To SUBMI'T [to bring under, to ſubject] *ſommettere, e ſottomettere, ſoggettare*, pret. *ſommiſi, ſottomiſi.*

To ſubmit one's ſelf, *ſommetterſi, ſottometterſi.*

To ſubmit [to leave, to refer] *ſommettere, rimettere, ſtarſene.*

To ſubmit [to yield] *ſottometterſi, cedere, piegarſi, conformarſi.*

You muſt ſubmit to that, *biſogna vi ſottomettiate o conformiate a queſto, vi biſogna piegare il collo.*

SUBMI'TTED, adj. *ſommeſſo, ſottomeſſo*, v. To ſubmit.

SUBO'RDINACY, } s. [the ſtate of
SUBO'RDINANCY, } being ſubject] *ſubordinazione, lo eſſere ſubordinato.*

SUBO'RDINATE, adj. [inferior] *ſubordinato.*

To SUBO'RDINATE [to place or ſet under another] *ſubordinare, coſtituir dipendente d' alcun ſuperiore.*

SUBO'RDINATED, adj. *ſubordinato.*

SUBORDINA'TION, s. *ſubordinazione.*

To SUBO'RN [to ſeduce, to put one on ſome miſchievous deſign, to inſtruct one privately what to do or ſay] *ſubornare, ſedurre, imbecherare, iſtruire di naſcoſo.*

SUBORNA'TION, s. *ſubornazione*, s. f.

SUBO'RNED, adj. *ſubornato, imbecherato, ſedotto.*

SUBO'RNER, s. [one that procures a bad action to be done] *ſeduttore, colui che induce altri a far coſa mala.*

SUBRE'CTOR, s. [the rector's vicegerent] *ſottorettore, colui che fa le veci del* rettore.

SU'BROGATE, v. Surrogate.

To SUBSCRI'BE [to ſign, to ſet one's hand to a writing] *ſoſcrivere, ſottoſcrivere, ſottoſcriverſi, metter la mano a qualche ſcritura*, pret. *ſottoſcriſſi, ſoſcriſſi.*

To ſubſcribe a letter of attorney, *ſottomerſi.*

SUBSCRI'BED, adj. *ſottoſcritto*, v. To ſubſcribe.

SUBSCRI'BER, s. *quello o quella che ſoſcrive, ſottoſcrivente.*

Subſcriber to a book, *ſottoſcrivente a un libro.*

SUBSCRI'BING, s. *il ſottoſcrivere.*

SUBSCRI'PTION, s. [ſign manual] *ſoſcrizione, e ſottoſcrizione*, s. f.

To put out a book by way of ſubſcription, *pubblicare un libro per ſoſcrizione.*

SU'BSEQUENCE, s. [the ſtate of following, not precedence] *l' andar dietro, contrario di precedenza.*

SU'BSEQUENT, adj. [immediately following] *ſuſſeguente, che ſeguita immantinente.*

SU'BSEQUENTLY, adv. *ſuſſeguentemente, dopo, poi.*

To SUBSE'RVE [to promote, to help forward] *ſervire, favorire, ajutare, ſecondare, appoggiare, ſpalleggiare, promovere*, pret. *favoriſco*, pret *promoſſi.*

SUBSERVIENCE, } s. [the act of
SUBSE'RVIENCY, } being ſubſervient] *utilità*, s. f. *ſervizio*, s. m.

SUBSE'RVIENT, adj. [ſerviceable, helpful] *utile, profittevole, vantaggioſo.*

To make all things ſubſervient to one's private intereſt, *non aver mira che al ſuo privato comodo.*

To SU'BSIDE [to ſink, to lower] *abbaſſarſi, ſcemarſi, andare a fondo.*

The ſtreams ſubſide from their banks, *i ruſcelli abbaſſan le loro acque nelle ſponde.*

SU'BSIDENCE, } s. [ſettlement]
SU'BSIDENCY, } *fondigliuolo*, s. m. *feccia.*

SUBSI'DIARY, adj. [auxiliary, helping] *auſiliario, che ajuta, che da ſuſſidio.*

SU'BSIDY, s. [aid] *ſuſſidio, ajuto nella neceſſità, ſoccorſo.*

Subſidy [ſupply of money] *ſuſſidio, ſoccorſo di danari.*

To SUBSI'GN [to ſign under] *ſegnar ſotto.*

To SUBSI'ST [to exiſt, to continue, to be] *ſoſſiſtere, eſſere, eſiſtere, mantenerſi, continuar in eſſere.*

To ſubſiſt [to live] *ſuſſiſtere, vivere, mantenerſi*, pret. *viſſi, mantenni.*

SUBSI'STENCE, s. *ſuſſiſtenza, eſiſtenza, eſſenza*, s. f. *ſtato, eſſere*, s. m.

Subſiſtence [food, livelihood] *ſuſſiſtenza, mantenimento, vitto*, s. m.

Subſiſtence money [half pay given to ſoldiers] *ſuſſiſtenza, mezza paga che ſi da alle truppe.*

SUBSI'STENT, adj. [having real being] *ſuſſiſtente, eſiſtente.*

SU'BSISTANCE, s. [eſſence, being] *ſoſtanza, ſuſtanza, quel che ſi ſoſtenta per ſe medeſimo, eſſenza, quiddità*, s. f. *eſſere*, s. m.

Subſtance [the beſt, the nouriſhing part of a thing] *ſuſtanza, quello che ſi trova di migliore, di nutritivo in qualunge coſa.*

Subſtance [the moſt material part of a diſcourſe] *ſuſtanza, ſomma*, s. f. *contenuto, riſtretto*, s. m.

Subſtance [reality] *ſuſtanza, realità.*

Subſtance [eſtate, goods] *ſuſtanza, eſſenziale.*

SUBSTA'NTIAL, adj. [eſſential] *ſoſtanziale, ſuſtanziale, che ha ſuſtanza, eſſenziale.*

The ſubſtantial part of a diſcourſe, *la parte ſuſtanziale o eſſenziale d' un diſcorſo.*

Subſtantial food, *vivanda ſuſtanzioſa.*

Subſtantial cloth, *panno forte.*

Subſtantial man, *un uomo beneſtante, ricco, comodo.*

Subſtantial [real, ſolid] *ſuſtanziale, reale, ſolido.*

SUBSTA'NTIALS, s. plur. [eſſential parts] *parti eſſenziali.*

SUBSTA'NTIALLY, adv. *ſuſtanzialmente, ſoſtanzialmente, eſſenzialmente.*

SU'BSTANTIVE, adj. [a term of grammar] *ſuſtantivo, che ha ſuſtanza, o ſuſſiſtenza.*

A noun ſubſtantive, a ſubſtantive, *un nome ſuſtantivo, un ſuſtantivo.*

SU'BSTANTIVELY, adv. *ſuſtantivamente, a modo di ſuſtantivo.*

SU'BSTITUTE, s. [deputy] *ſoſtituto, ſuſtituto*, s. m. *che tiene la vece altrui*

To SU'BSTITUTE [to appoint in the room of another] *ſoſtituire, ſuſtituire, mettere in luogo ſuo*, pref. *ſoſtituiſco; ſuſtituiſco.*

Subſtitute s. [one placed by another to act with delegated power] *un ſoſtituto, colui che è ſoſtituito da un altro.*

SU'BSTITUTED, adj. *ſoſtituito, ſuſtituito.*

SUBSTITU'TION, s. *ſoſtituzione*, s. f. *il ſoſtituire.*

To SU'BSTRACT [to deduct, to take off] *ſottrarre, cavare d' una ſomma maggiore altra minore, levare*, pref. *ſottraggo*, pret. *ſottraſſi.*

SUBSTRA'CTED, adj. *ſottratto, levato.*

SUBSTRA'CTING, s. *ſottraggimento*, s. m. *il ſottrarre.*

SUBSTRA'CTION, s. *ſottrazione*, s. f.

Subſtraction, or the rule of ſubſtraction [in arithmetick] *la ſottrazione, o la regola di ſottrazione, termine aritmetico.*

SU'BTERFUGE, s. [ſhift, evaſion] *ſutterfugio, ſcampo, ripiego, mezzo termine*, s. m.

SUBTERRA'NEAL, SUBTERRA'NEAN, SUBTERRA'NEOUS, } adj. [under ground] *ſotterraneo, ſotterranno, che è ſotto terra.*

SU'BTILE, v. Subtle.

SUBTILIZA'TION, s. [the art of ſubtilizing] *aſſottigliamento.*

To SU'BTILIZE [to make ſubtle, to rarify] *aſſottigliare, render ſottile.*

To ſubtilize [to uſe ſubtilities, ſhifts] *ſottilizzare, aguzzar l' ingegno, ghiribizzare, fantaſticare.*

SU'BTILIZED, adj. *aſſottigliato, ſottilizzato.*

SU'BTILTY, s. *ſottigliezza, tanto in ſenſo proprio quanto metaforicamente.*

SU'BTLE, SU'BTIL, } adj. [thin, penetrating, piercing] *ſottile, penetrativo, penetrante, acuto.*

Subtle [cunning] *ſottile, fine, acuto, ingegnoſo, aſtuto.*

Subtle trick, *ſottigliezza, tiro molto furbeſco.*

SU'BTLETY, s. *ſottigliezza.*

Subtlety, s. [craft, cunning fetch, quirk] *ſottigliezza, acutezza d' ingegno, aſtuzia*, s. f.

SU'BTLY, adv. [cunningly] *ſottilmente, con ſottigliezza, ſagacemente, malizioſamente, aſtutamente.*

To SU'BTRACT, *ſottrarre.*

SUBTRA'CTION, v. Subſtraction.

To SUBVE'RSE [to ſubvert] *ſovvertire, mandar ſozzopra.*

SUBVE'RSION, s. [overthrow] *ſovverſione*, s. f. *il ſovvertere, rovina*, s. f.

To SUBVE'RT [to overturn, to overthrow, to ruin] *ſovvertere, ſovvertire, rovinare, mandar ſozzopra, guaſtare, diſtruggere*, pret. *diſtruſſi.*

SUBVE'RTED, adj. *ſovvertito, rovinato, mandato ſoſſopra, guaſtato, diſtrutto.*

SUBVE'RTER, s. *quello o quella che ſovverte, diſtruggitore.*

SUBVE'RTING, s. *ſovvertimento*, s. m. *il ſovvertere, ſovverſione*, s. f.

SUB-VI'CAR, s. *ſotto vicario.*

SUB-VICARSHIP, s. *ſotto vicariato.*

SU'BURB, s. [that part of the city or town which lies without the walls] *borgo*, s. m. *lo accreſcimento di caſe fuor delle mura delle terre murate.*

SUBU'RBAN, adj. [inhabiting the ſuburb] *ſuburbano, che abita nel borgo d' una terra murata.*

SUBWO'RKER, s. *operajo ſubordinato ad un altro operajo.*

To SUCCE'ED [to come after] *ſuccedere, ſeguire, venir dopo*, pret. *ſucceſſi.*

To ſucceed one [to be his heir] *ſuccedere a qualcheduno, ereditare de' ſuoi beni, divenir ſuo erede, venire nella ſua eredità.*

To ſucceed [to ſpeed well, to proſper] *riuſcire, ſortire, avere effetto.*

To ſucceed [to fall out] *ſuccedere, avvenire, accadere*, pret. *ſucceſſe, avvenne, accadde.*

SUCCE'EDED, adj. *ſucceduto, ſucceſſo, ſeguito*, v. To ſucceed.

SUCCE'EDER, s. [one who follows] *colui che viene immediatamente dietro a un altro.*

Succeeder [one who comes into the place of another] *colui che viene nel luogo d' un altro ſucceſſore.*

SUCCE'EDING, s. *ſuccedimento, ſucceſſo*, s. m.

Succeeding, adj. [following] *ſuccedente, ſeguente.*

SUCCE'SS, s. [event] *ſucceſſo, evento.*

Succeſs [proſperous event, happy iſſue] *ſucceſſo, buon ſucceſſo, buona riuſcita.*

To have ſucceſs [to ſucceed well] *riuſcire bene, ſortir buon' effetto.*

SUCCE'SSFUL, adj. [fortunate] *avventuroſo, felice, fortunato.*

He has been ſucceſsful in his undertaking, *la ſua impreſa ha ſortito buono effetto, l' impreſa gli è ben riuſcita.*

SUCCE'SSFULLY, adv. *avventuroſamente, felicemente, fortunatamente.*

SUCCE'SSFULNESS, s. [happy concluſion, deſired event, ſeries of good fortune] *felicità, buon ſucceſſo, evento fortunato.*

SUCCE'SSION, s. [the act of ſucceeding another, inheritance] *ſucceſſione, eredità*, s. f.

Succeſſion of time, *progreſſo di tempo, ſerie d' anni.*

For many ſucceſſions of years, *per lunga ſerie d' anni.*

SUCCE'SSIVE, adj. [that ſucceeds or follows one after another] *ſucceſſivo, che viene l' un dopo l' alto.*

SUCCE'SSIVELY, adv. *ſucceſſivamente, l' un dopo l' altro.*

SUCCE'SSIVENESS, s. [the ſtate of being ſucceſſive] *progreſſione.*

SUCCE'SSLESS, adj. *infelice, ſgraziato, ſfortunato.*

SUCCE'SSOR, s. [one who ſucceeds another in place or ſtate] *ſucceſſore*, s. m. *che ſuccede.*

SUCCI'NCT, adj. [ſhort, brief] *ſuccinto, corto, breve, compendioſo.*

SUCCI'NCTLY, adv. *ſuccintamente, con brevità, compendioſamente.*

SUCCI'NCTNESS, s. *brevità*, s. f.

SU'CCORY, s. [an herb] *cicoréa, e cicoria*, s. f. *radicchio*, s. m.

SU'CCOUR, s. [help, relief] *ſoccorſo, ajuto, ſuſſidio*, s. m.

To SU'CCOUR [to aſſiſt, to help, to relieve] *ſoccorrere, ajutare, porger ajuto, dar ſuſſidio.*

SU'CCOURED, adj. *ſoccorſo, ajutato.*

SU'CCOURING, s. *ſoccorrimento*, s. m. *il ſoccorrere.*

SU'CCOURLESS, adj. *privo di ſoccorſo.*

SU'CCUBUS, s. [a devil which aſſumes a woman's ſhape to lie with a man] *un ſuccubo.*

SU'CCULENCY, s. [the quality of being ſucculent] *ſugoſità*, s. f.

SU'CCULENT, adj. [juicy] *ſugoſo, e ſucoſo, pien di ſugo, pien di ſucco.*

To SUCCU'MB [to yield, to ſink under any difficulty] *ſoccombere, rimaner ſoverchiato.*

SUCH, adj. [ſame, like, of the ſame manner] *tale, ſimile.*

Such as it is, *tale quale è.*

I have no ſuch thing, *non ho tal coſa.*

For ſuch a ſmall matter, *per sì poca coſa.*

I am not ſuch a fool, *non ſono così ſciocco.*

He made ſuch a progreſs that one can hardly believe it, *fece un sì gran progreſſo che appena è credibile.*

Such as [thoſe that] *quelli, quelle, che*, ex. Such as govern the ſtate, *quelli o quei tali che governano lo ſtato.*

For ſuch a man as I, *per un uomo della mia fatta.*

I am not ſuch a man as to go back from my word, *io non ſon uomo da mançar di parola.*

It is not fit for ſuch a man as you to do ſuch a thing, *non conviene ad un uomo come voi di fare ſimile coſa.*

There's no ſuch a thing, *non v' è tal coſa.*

And ſuch like, *e altri ſimili.*

I love all fruits that grow in hot countries, ſuch as figs, grapes, and the like, *amo tutte quelle ſorte di frutta che naſcono in paeſi caldi, come ſarebbe a dire fichi, uva, e ſimili,*

SUCK, s. ex. to give ſuck, *allattare, nutrir con latte.*

Suck-ſtone [a fiſh called alſo a ſea lamprey] *lampreda di mare.*

To SUCK [to draw in with the mouth any liquor] *ſucciare, attrarre a ſe l' umore, e 'l ſugo.*

To ſuck the breaſt [as children do] *poppare.*

A child that ſucks, *un bambino alla mammella.*

To ſuck one's ſubſtance, *ſucciare l' altrui ſangue.*

To ſuck in, *ſucciare, poppare.*

To ſuck in an error with on's mother's milk, *ſucciare o poppare un errore dalla mammella, eſſerne imbevuto a buon'ora.*

To ſuck out, *ſucciare, fare uſcire ſucciando.*

To ſuck out the air, *ſucciar ſu l' aria.*

SU'CKER, s. [one that ſucks] *quello che ſuccia o poppa.*

The fucker of a pump, *il cannoncello della tromba.*

SU'CKETS, s. [a fort of fweetmeats] *zuccherini, confetti*, s. m.

SU'CKING, s. *fucciamento*, s. m. *il fucciare.*

Sucking, adj. *fucciante, lattante.*

Sucking lamb, *agnello lattante, o di latte.*

Sucking bottle, *vafetto col becco che ferve a dare a bere a' bambini.*

He is not well paft his fucking bottle, *gli puzza ancora la bocca di latte.*

To SU'CKLE [to give fuck] *allattare, nutrir con latte.*

SU'CKLED, adj. *allattato.*

SU'CKLING, s. *l' allattare.*

Suckling, s. [a young creature yet fed by the pap] *creatura che ancora poppa la madre o la nutrice.*

A fuckling [a lamb that fucks the dam] *agnello lattante, o di latte.*

SU'CTION, s. [lat.] *fucciamento, l' atto del fucciare.*

SU'DDEN, adj. [coming unexpected, hafty, quick] *fubitaneo, fubitano, che viene in un fubito, repentino, improvvifo.*

To die a fudden death, *morir di morte fubitana, morire fubitanamente.*

Upon the fudden; on a fudden; all of a fudden; or SU'DDENLY, adv. *fubitamente, fubitanamente, fubito, in un fubito, improvvifamente, repentinamente.*

He died fuddenly, *morì fubitanamente.*

SU'DDENNESS, s. *prontezza.*

SUDORI'FICK, adj. [provoking or caufing fweat] *fudorifico, che fa fudare.*

Sudorifick, s. *medicamento fudorifico, che fa fudare, che provoca il fudore.*

SUDS, s. [a lixivium of foap and water] *lifciva di fapone e acqua.*

To be in the fuds, *frafe familiare, e vale effere fitto in qualche difficoltà, effere imbrogliato o perpleffo.*

To SUE [to profecute by law] *citar in giudicio, richiamarfi in giudicio d' uno.*

To fue, *litigare, effer in lite.*

To fue [to entreat earneftly] *pregare, fupplicare, domandar con iftanza, fcongiurare.*

To fue to one for a thing, *ricorrere, aver ricorfo, rifuggire ad alcuno per che che fia.*

SUED at law, adj. *citato in giudicio, richiamato in giudicio.*

Sued for, *follecitato, procurato.*

SU'ET, s. [a hard fat, particularly that about the kidneys] *graffo di carne duro, e fpecialmente quello che è intorno agli arnioni.*

SU'ETY, adj. [confifting of fuet, refembling fuet] *graffo, che confifte di graffo duro, che s' affomiglia a quel graffo duro che circonda gli arnioni.*

To SU'FFER [to undergo, to endure] *fofferire, foffrire, patire, fopportare, comportare, tollerare.*

I fuffer a great pain, *io foffro un gran dolore.*

All religions are fuffered in Holland, *tutte le religioni fono tollerate in Olanda.*

To fuffer a great lofs, *fare una gran perdita.*

To fuffer fhipwreck, *far naufragio, naufragare.*

To fuffer [to be punifhed, to bear the punifhment] *foffrire, patire, portar la pena, effer punito.*

You fhall fuffer for all your imprudent actions, *voi porterete la pena, voi pagherete il fio delle voftre imprudenze.*

To day the prifoners fuffer [are to be executed] *i prigionieri faranno giuftiziati oggi.*

To fuffer [to give leave, to permit] *comportare, lafciare, permettere.*

My heart won't fuffer me to leave you, *non mi comporta il cuore, non mi bafta l' animo di lafciarvi.*

I fhall not fuffer you to go away without me, *non vi lafcerò andare fenza me.*

Why do you fuffer him to do fuch things? *perchè permettete che faccia fimili cofe?*

SU'FFERABLE, adj. [that may be endured] *fopportevole, atto a fopportarfi, comportevole.*

SU'FFERABLY, adj. [tolerably; fo as to be endured] *tollerabilmente; così che fi può foffrire.*

SU'FFERANCE, s. [allowance, permiffion, leave] *fofferenza, permiffione, licenza, tolleranza*, s. f.

SU'FFERED, adj. *fofferto*, v. To fuffer.

This is not to be fuffered, *quefta non è cofa da fopportarfi.*

SU'FFERER, s. *quello o quella che foffre, che patifce, che ha fofferto o patito, fofferitore.*

Sufferer [lofer] *perditore*, s. m. *perditrice*, s. f.

SU'FFERING, s. *fofferenza*, s. f. *fofferimento*, s. m. *il fofferire.*

To SUFFI'CE [to be enough] *baftare, effer baftante, effere abbaftanza.*

SUFFI'CIENCY, s. [ability] *fofficienza, fufficienza*, s. f.

Sufficiency [capacity] *fofficienza, dottrina, capacità*, s. f.

Sufficiency [pride, prefumption] *orgoglio*, s. m.

SUFFI'CIENT, adj. [that fuffices] *fufficiente, fofficente, baftevole, che bafta.*

Sufficient bail, *malleveria fufficiente, che è folvente.*

Sufficient [able] *fofficiente, fufficiente, capace, idoneo.*

SUFFI'CIENTLY, adv. [enough] *fofficientemente, a baftanza.*

SU'FFISANCE, s. [excefs, plenty] *eccesso, abbondanza.*

To SU'FFOCATE [to choak by exclufion or interception of air] *foffocare.*

SUFFOCATION, s. [the act of choaking; the ftate of being choaked] *foffocazione, foffocamento.*

SU'FFOCATIVE, adj. [having the power to choak] *foffocativo, che ha poffa di fuffocare.*

SU'FFRAGAN, s. [a bifhop who is fubordinate to an archbifhop] *fuffraganeo, foffraganeo*, s. m. *vefcovo, fottopofto al metropolitano.*

SU'FFRAGE, s. [a vote given in elections in favour of any perfon] *fuffragio, voto*, s. m.

Suffrage [approbation] *fuffragio, approvazione.*

To SUFFU'MIGATE [to fmoak underneath] *fuffumigare, dare il fumo.*

SUFFUMIGA'TION, s. [an external remedy by ufing of fmoak] *fuffumigazione*, s. f. *fuffumigamento*, s. m.

SU'FFUMIGE, s. [a medicine fume] *fuffumigio ordinato da' medici per certi mali.*

To SUFFU'SE [to fpread over with fomething expanfible, as with a vapour or a tincture] *fpandere, come verbigrazia con un vapore o con una tintura.*

SUFFU'SION, s. [a difeafe in the eye] *fuffufione*, s. f. *forta di malattia che viene agli occhi e impedifce il vedere.*

SUG, s. [an infect call'd a fea-flea] *pulce di mare.*

SU'GAR, s. *zucchero*, s. m.

To fweeten with fugar, *inzuccherare.*

Sugar-loaf, *pan di zucchero.*

To SU'GAR [to put fuger in] *inzuccherare, metter del zucchero, condire con zucchero.*

SU'GARED, adj. *inzuccherato, zuccherato, condito di zucchero dolce.*

Sugared words, *parole inzuccherate, piene d' affetto.*

SU'GARY, adj. *zuccherofo, che ha in fe del zucchero, dolce, dolciato.*

To SUGGE'ST [to prompt, to put into one's mind] *fuggerire, mettere in confiderazione, proporre*, pref. *fuggerifco, propongo*, pret. *propofi.*

SUGGE'STED, adj. *fuggerito, propofto.*

SUGGE'STER, s. *fuggeritore*, s. m. *che fuggerifce.*

SUGGE'STING, } s. [a prompting, a
SUGGE'STION, } putting into one's mind] *fuggeftione, infinuazione, iftigazione, follecitazione*, s. f. *fuggerimento*, s. m.

To SU'GGILLATE [to beat black and blue; to make livid by a bruife] *ammarcare con percoffe la carne, battere qualcuno onde ne fia livido.*

SU'ICIDE, s. [felf-murder; the horrid crime of deftroying one's felf] *fuicidio, l' orrido delitto di diftrugger fe fteffo.*

SU'ILLAGE, s. [drain of filth] *fugo di letame, fporcizia.*

SU'ING, s. [from to fue] *lite*, s. f.

SUIT at law, or in law, s. *processo*, s. m.

To have a suit against one, *aver un processo con uno, esser in processo con uno.*

Suit [petition among lawyers] *memoriale*, s. m. *supplica*, s. f.

Suit [request, petition] *richiesta, domanda, preghiera, sollecitazione, istanza*, s. f.

Suit [a set; a number of things corresponding to one another] *numero di cose corrispondenti fra se stesse.*

Suit [cloaths made one part to answer another] *abito intero da uomo.*

Suit [consecution, series, regular order] *seguenza, serie, ordine regolare.*

Suit [retinue, company] *séguito, compagnia, corteggio.*

Suit [courtship] *amoreggiare con intenzione di matrimonio, far all' amore.*

To SUIT [to fit, to adapt to something else] *adattare.*

To suit [to be fitted to, to become] *adattarsi, esser proprio.*

To suit [to dress, to clothe] *far un abito, vestire.*

To suit [to agree, to accord] *accordarsi, porsi d' accordo.*

SU'ITER } s. [a candidate for an office] *supplicante, candidato*, s. m.
SU'ITOR }

Suitor [for marriage] *amante.*

SU'ITRESS, s. [a female supplicant] *supplicatrice*, s. f.

SULL, s. [a western word for a plough] *aratro.*

SU'LLEN, adj. [peevish] *ritroso, arcigno, burbero, torvo.*

Sullen look, *viso arcigno, cera burbera.*

Sullen [stubborn] *ostinato, capone, caparbio.*

SU'LLENLY, adv. *ritrosamente, con viso arcigno.*

Sullenly [stubbornly] *ostinatamente, caparbiamente, caponescamente.*

SU'LLENNESS, s. [peevishness] *umore ritroso, cattivo umore.*

Sullenness [stubbornness] *ostinazione, caparbietà, caponeria.*

SU'LLEN, s. [morose temper] *caparbietà, caponeria.*

SU'LLY, s. [oil, tarnish, spot] *macchia, bruttura.*

To SU'LLY [to defile, to dirty] *sporcare, imbrattare, macchiare.*

To sully a man's reputation, *macchiare l' altrui riputazione.*

SU'LLYED, adj. *sporcato, imbrattato, macchiato.*

SU'LPHUR, s. [brimstone] *zolfo, solfo*, s. m. *minerale che tosto s' accende.*

Sulphur pit, *zolfatara*, s. f. *luogo d' onde si cava, e dove si lavora il zolfo.*

Sulphur-wort [a plant] *finocchio porcino, peucedano*, s. m.

SU'LPHURY } adj. [belonging to, or full of sulphur] *sulfureo, di qualità di zolfo.*
SULPHU'REOUS }

Sulphury waters, *acque sulfuree.*

SU'LTAN, s. [grand signior] *il sultano, il gran signore, il gran Turco.*

Sultan [a Mahometan prince] *sultano, principe Maomettano.*

SULTA'NA } s. [the grand signior's wife] *la sultana, la regina sultana.*
SU'LTANESS }

Sultana [a Turkish man of war] *sultana, nave da guerra Turchesca.*

SU'LTANARY, s. [an eastern empire] *un impero orientale.*

SU'LTRY, adj. [excessive hot] *eccessivo, fervido, fervoroso.*

Sultry heat, *afa, caldo soverchio di state.*

SUM, s. [a certain quantity] *somma*, s. f.

A sum of money, *una somma di danari.*

The sum of a discourse, *la somma, la sustanza, il ristretto d' un discorso.*

The sum of a book, *il sommario, il compendio, l' argomento, d' un libro.*

To SUM up [to cast up] *sommare, raccore i numeri.*

To sum up all, *in somma, finalmente, in conclusione.*

SU'MAGE } s. [load, horse-load] *soma*, s. f.
SU'MMAGE }

Sumage [a toll for carriage on horseback] *diritto che si paga per ogni soma d' un cavallo.*

SU'MACH, s. [a shrub] *sommaco, e sommacco*, s. m.

SU'MLESS, adj. [not to be computed] *infinito, che non si può computare.*

SU'MMARILY, adv. *sommariamente, in sommario, compendiosamente.*

SU'MMARY, adj. [short, brief] *sommario, fatto sommariamente e senza solennità di giudicio, breve, succinto, corto.*

Summary, s. *sommario, breve ristretto, compendio.*

SU'MMED up, adj. *sommato, calcolato.*

SU'MMER, s. [one of the four seasons of the year] *state, estate*, s. f. *una delle quattro stagioni dell' anno.*

One swallow does not make the summer, *un fiore non fa primavera.*

Summer-weather, *tempo di state, tempo estivo.*

Summer-house, *gabinetto di verdura.*

Summer-suit, *abito di state.*

Summer-quarters, *quartieri di state.*

Summer [or main beam in a building] *la trave principale d' un edificio.*

To SU'MMER [to pass the summer] *passar la state.*

To summer in the country, *villeggiare, passar la state in villa.*

SU'MMIT } s. [top] *cima, sommità, vetta*, s. f.
SU'MMITY }

The summit of a hill, *la cima d' un monte.*

The summit of a plant, *la vetta d' una pianta.*

To SU'MMON [to call one to appear before a judge or magistrate] *citare, chiamare in giudicio.*

To summon [to bid, to command] *comandare, significare, intimare, far sapere.*

SU'MMONED, adj. *citato*, v. To summon.

SU'MMONER, s. *sergente, ministro della giustizia.*

SU'MMONING, s. *citazione* s. f.

SU'MMONS, s. [a citing to a court of judicature] *citazione.* s. f. *comandamento*, s. m.

SU'MPTER, s. ex. a sumpter-horse [a horse which carries necessaries and provisions for a journey] *somiere*, s. m. *somiera*, s. f. *giumento, cavallo da soma.*

Sumpter-saddle, *basto*, s. m.

SU'MPTION, s. [the act of taking] *l' atto del togliere.*

SU'MPTUARY, adj. [belonging to expences] *suntuario, che riguarda la moderazione delle spese.*

Sumptuary laws, *leggi suntuarie, che moderano le spese.*

SU'MPTUOUS, adj. [rich, costly, magnificent] *sontuoso, suntuoso, di grande spesa, ricco, splendido, magnifico, superbo.*

SU'MPTUOUSLY, adv. *sontuosamente, suntuosamente, splendidamente, magnificamente.*

SUMPTUO'SITY, s. [costliness, magnificence] *sontuosità, suntuosità, magnificenza, splendidezza*, s. f.

SUN, s. [a luminous planet, the spring of light and heat] *sole*, s. m. *pianta che illumina il mondo.*

The sun of righteousness [a scripture-phrase for JESUS CHRIST] *il sol di giustizia.*

Sun-shine, *la chiarezza, il lume, lo splendore del sole.*

The sun-beams, *i raggi del sole, i raggi solari.*

Sun-rising, *il levar del sole.*

Sun-set, *il tramontar del sole.*

Sun-burning, *l' abbronzare.*

Sun burnt, *abbronzato.*

To SUN [to set or dry in the sun] *soleggiare, porre qualsisia cosa al sole ad oggetto d' asciugarla.*

SU'NBEAM, s. [ray of the sun] *raggio di sole.*

SU'NBEAT, adj. [shone on by the sun] *esposto al sole, battuto dal sole.*

SU'NBRIGHT, adj. [resembling the sun in brightness] *lucente come il sole.*

SU'NCLAD, adj. [clothed in radiance] *vestito di raggi, lucentissimo.*

SU'NDAY, s. [the first day of the week] *Domenica*, s. f.

Palm-Sunday, *la Domenica delle palme.*

To SU'NDER [to part, to separate, to divide] *separare, dividere.*

SU'NDER, s. [two, two parts] *due, due parti.*

SU'NDRY, adj. [divers, several] *diversi, parecchi, molti.*
In sundry places, *in diversi luoghi.*
Sundry ways, *molte maniere.*
SUNG, adj. [from to sing] *cantato,* v. To sing.
SUNK, adj. [from to sink] *affondato, andato a fondo, sommerso,* v. To sink.
Sunk in his credit, *screditato, che ha perduto il credito.*
Sunk, *è anche un preterito del verbo* To sink.
SU'NLESS, adj. [wanting sun] *privo di sole, privo di calore.*
SU'NLIKE, adj. [resembling the sun] *simile al sole.*
SU'NNED, adj. *soleggiato.*
SU'NNY, adj. *aprico, esposto al sole o a solatio.*
A sunny place, *un luogo aprico posto a solatio.*
SUP, s. *sorso, centellino,* s. m.
To take a sup, *prender un sorso.*
To SUP [to eat one's supper] *cenare.*
To sup [to drink by little and little] *sorbire, centellare, bere a centellini o a sorsi.*
SU'PERABLE, adj. [that may be conquered] *superabile, che si può superare.*
To SU'PERABOUND [to be over and above]. *soprabbondare, sommamente abbondare, sopravanzare.*
SUPERABU'NDANCE, s. *soprabbondanza,* s. f. *soverchia abbondanza.*
SUPERABU'NDANTLY, adv. *soprabbondantemente, con soprabbondanza.*
To SU'PERADD [to add over and above] *aggiugner di più o troppo.*
SUPERA'DDED, adj. *aggiunto.*
SUPERA'NNUATED, adj. [worn out, grown out of date, worn out with age] *stantio, vecchio, troppo vecchio.*
A superannuated beauty, *una bellezza stantia.*
A superannuated soldier, *un soldato vecchio, incapace di servire, affatto invalido.*
SUPERCI'LIOUS, adj. [that is of a sour countenance, proudly severe, too grave] *severo, grave, sostenuto, austero, fiero, arrogante, burbero.*
SUPERCI'LIOUSLY, adv. *severamente, gravemente, fieramente, altieramente, con sostenutezza, burbantemente.*
SUPERCI'LIOUSNESS, s. *sussiego, orgoglio,* s. m. *gravità, sostenutezza, arroganza,* s. f.
SUPRE'MINENCE, s. [excellency, prerogative] *preminenza.*
SUPERE'MINENT, adj. [excelling, above] *eminente, eccellente.*
SUPERE'MINENTLY, adv. *eminentemente, eccellentemente.*
To SUPERE'ROGATE [to give or to do more than is required] *dare o fare più di quel che uno è obbligato, strafare.*
SUPERERÓGA'TION, s. [doing or giving more than is required] *il dare, o il fare più di quel che uno è tenuto.*
SUPERFI'CIAL, adj. [outward] *superficiale, che è nella superficie, esteriore.*
SUPERFI'CIALLY, adv. *superficialmente, in superficie, esteriormente.*
SUPERFI'CIES, s. [surface] *superficie,* s. f. *il di fuori di ciascuna cosa.*
The superficies of the earth, *la superficie della terra.*
SU'PERFINE, adj. [very fine] *finissimo, sopraffino.*
Superfine cloth, *panno sopraffino.*
SUPERFLU'ITY, s. [over-plus, excess] *superfluità, soprabbondanza,* s. f.
SUPE'RFLUOUS, adj. [over much, more than need] *superfluo, soperchio, inutile, soverchio.*
SUPE'RFLUOUSLY, adv. *soverchiamente, superfluamente, con superfluità, di soverchio.*
SUPERHU'MAN, adj. [more than human] *soprumano, sopra la condizione umana.*
To SUPERINTE'ND [to oversee, to have the chief management of affairs] *soprantendere, aver la soprantendenza, vegliare, invigilare.*
SUPERINTE'NDENCY, s. *soprantendenza, ispezione,* s. f.
SUPERINTE'NDENT [overseer or surveyor] *soprantendente,* s. m. *quegli, che ha autorità primaria sopra qualche uffizio o opera.*
Superintendent, adj. [that over-rules and governs] *soprantendente, che governa.*
SUPERIO'RITY, s. [pre-eminence, excellence above others] *superiorità, preminenza, eccellenza,* s. f.
SUPE'RIOUR, adj. [that is above, upper] *superiore, che soprasta, contrario d' inferiore.*
Superiour [that is above others in authority, power, &c.] *superiore.*
The superior father [in a monastery] *il padre superiore.*
The superiour mother, *la madre superiora, la madre badessa.*
Their forces were much superiour to ours, *le loro forze erano molto superiori alle nostre.*
Superiour, s. *superiore, principale, capo,* s. m.
SUPE'RLATIVE, adj. [of the highest degree] *superlativo, più superiore di tutti, il più sublime.*
The superlative degree, *il grado superlativo.*
SUPE'RLATIVELY, adv. *superlativamente, in superlativo grado.*
SUPE'RNAL, adj. [that comes from above] *supernale, superiore, di sopra.*
SUPE'RNALLY, adv. *supernalmente, con potenza supernale, divinamente.*
SUPERNA'TURAL, adj. [that is above the course, strength, or reach of nature] *soprannaturale, che è sopra la natura.*
SUPERNA'TURALLY, adv. *soprannaturalmente, con modo soprannaturale.*
SUPERNU'MERARY, adj. [that is above the limited or usual number] *soprannumerario.*
To SUPERSCRI'BE [to write over, or on the outside of any thing] *soprascrivere,* pret. *soprascrissi.*
SUPERSCRI'BED, adj. *soprascritto.*
SUPERSCRI'BER, s. *quello o quella che soprascrive.*
SUPERSCRI'PTION, s. *soprascrizione, soprascritta,* s. f. *soprascritto,* s. m.
To SUPERSE'DE [to suspend, to put off, to stop, to forbear] *soprassedere, tralasciare per qualche tempo, differire,* pres. *differisco,* pret. *soprassi.*
SUPERSE'DED, adj. *soprasseso, tralasciato, differito, rimesso.*
SU'PERSE'SSION, s. *intermissione, il soprassedere.*
SUPERSTI'TION, s. [mistaken devotion] *superstizione,* s. f.
SUPERSTI'TIOUS, adj. [addicted to superstition, bigotted] *superstizioso, pien di superstizione.*
A superstitious man, *un uomo superstizioso.*
A superstitious woman, *una donna superstiziosa.*
SUPERSTI'TIOUSLY, adv. *superstiziosamente, con superstizione.*
To SUPERSTRU'CT [to build upon] *fabbricare, edificar sopra.*
SUPERSTRU'CTED, adj. *fabbricato, edificato sopra.*
SUPERSTRU'CTURE, s. *edificio, o altra fabbrica che s' alza sopra qualche fondamento.*
SUPERVACA'NEOUS, adj. [superfluous] *superfluo, inutile, soperchievole, soperchio, soverchio.*
To SUPERVE'NE [to come unlooked for, to come upon a sudden] *sopraggiugnere, sopravvenire,* pret. *sopraggiungo, sopravvengo,* pret. *sopraggiunse, sopravvenne.*
To SUPERVI'SE [to over-see] *soprantendere, aver l' ispezione o soprantendenza di che che si sia.*
He is to supervise the business, *egli ha l' inspezione del negozio.*
To supervise [to revise, to examine] *rivedere, esaminar di nuovo,* pret. *rividi.*
To supervise a will, *vedere se la volontà del testatore è ben eseguita secondo il tenore del testamento.*
SUPERVI'SED, adj. *soprantesο, riviſto, esaminato.*
SUPERVI'SOR, s. [over-seer] *soprantendente, direttore, ispettore,* s. m.
To SU'PERVIVE [to overlive, to outlive] *sopravvivere.*
SUPI'NE, adj. [idle, careless, negligent] *supino, negligente, ozioso, infingardo, pigro, trascurato.*
Supine, s. [a term of grammar] *supino, termine grammaticale.*

SUPI'NELY, adv. [carelesly] *supinamente, supino, negligentemente, oziosamente, infingardamente, pigramente, trascuratamente.*

SU'PINENESS, } SUPI'NITY, } [sloth, negligence] *negligenza, trascuraggine, infingardia, infingarderia, lentezza, pigrizia, trascurataggine, infingardaggine,* s. f.

SU'PPED, *preterito del verbo* To sup.

To SUPPE'DITATE [to find to furnish] *suppeditare, amministrare, ministrare, somministrare.*

SU'PPER, s. *cena,* s. f.

To bring in supper, *servir la cena.*

To eat one's supper [to sup] *cenare.*

To go to supper, *andare a cena, andar a cenare.*

The Lord's supper, *la santa cena, la comunione.*

A supper man, *colui che è accostumato a renare.*

Supper-time, *tempo il cenare.*

SU'PPERLESS, adj. *senza cena, che non ha cenato.*

To SUPPLA'NT [to trip on one's heels] *dare il gambetto ad uno, farlo cascare, e s' usa per lo più in senso metaforico.*

To supplant [to deceive or beguile, to undermine] *dare il gambetto, ingannare, giuntare.*

SU'PPLE, adj. [soft, limber] *flessibile, pieghevole, arrendevole, che facilmente si piega.*

Supple [humble, pliant] *umile, cortese, sommesso.*

To SU'PPLE [to make supple] *render flessibile, pieghevole, o arrendevole.*

SU'PPLEMENT, s. [addition made to supply something deficient before] *supplemento,* s. m.

SU'PPLENESS, s. [the state or quality of being supple] *flessibilità,* s. f.

Suppleness [compliance, submission] *umiltà, sommissione,* s. f.

SU'PPLETORY, adj. [that which is to fill up deficiencies] *che supplisce, che dee supplire.*

SU'PPLIANT, } SU'PPLICANT, } s. [petitioner] *supplicante,* s. m. f. *che supplica.*

To SU'PPLICATE [to make humble request, to beg, to intreat] *supplicare, pregare umilmente, pregare affettuosamente, far istanza, chiedere istantemente.*

SUPPLICA'TION, s. [petition] *supplica,* s. f. *memoriale,* s. m.

SU'PPLY, s. [relief] *soccorso, rinforzo.*

A supply of men or money, *un soccorso, un rinforzo di gente o di danaro.*

To SU'PPLY [to make up what was wanting] *supplire, sovvenire al difetto,* pres. *supplisco.*

To supply [to fill up] one's place, *occupare, empiere il luogo d' un altro.*

SUPPLI'ED, adj. *supplito.*

SUPPO'RT, s. [help, prop, protection] *sostenimento, sostegno, soccorso, sovvenimento, appoggio, patrocinio,* s. m.

To SUPPO'RT [to bear up] *sopportare, portare, sostenere, appoggiare, puntellare, appuntellare,* pres. *sostengo,* pret. *sostenni.*

To support [to maintain] *sopportare, sostentare, mantenere,* pres. *mantengo,* pret. *mantenni.*

To support [to help] *assistere, ajutare, sovvenire,* pres. *sovvengo,* pret. *sovvenni.*

To support [to favour, to back] *portare, proteggere, appoggiare, favorire, spalleggiare,* pret. *protessi,* pres. *favorisco.*

To support [to maintain, to feed] *sostenare, alimentare, pascere.*

SUPPO'RTABLE, adj. *sopportevole, comportevole, tollerabile.*

SUPPO'RTANCE } SUPPORTA'TION } s. [maintenance, support] *mantenimento, sostegno.*

SUPPO'RTED, adj. *sopportato, portato, sostenuto, appoggiato, puntellato, appuntellato,* v. To support.

SUPPO'RTER, s. [support, protector] *appoggio, sostegno, protettore, fautore, mantenitore, sostenitore, sostentatore.*

Supporter of a table, *un piede di tavola.*

SUPPO'SABLE, adj. [that may be supposed] *che si può supporre.*

SUPPO'SAL, v. Supposition.

SUPPO'SE, s. v. Supposition.

To SUPPO'SE [to imagine, to think] *supporre, pensare, credere, imaginarsi,* pres. *suppongo,* pret. *supposi.*

To suppose [to grant, or to take for granted] *supporre, presupporre, concedere,* pret. *concessi.*

To suppose [to produce a false thing instead of the true] *supporre.*

SUPPO'SED, adj. *supposto,* v. To suppose.

It is to be supposed, *bisogna credere.*

His supposed father, *suo padre putativo.*

SUPPO'SER, s. [one that supposes] *colui che suppone.*

SUPPO'SING, s. *il supporre.*

SUPPOSI'TION, s. [case put] *supposizione, presupposizione,* s. f. *supposto,* s. m.

Supposition [the putting of one thing instead of another] *supposizione.*

SUPPOSITI'TIOUS, adj. [false] *supposto, falso.*

To SUPPRE'SS [to keep under, to put a stop to, to smother] *sopprimere, togliere, levare, impedire, far cessare,* pres. *tolgo, impedisco,* pret. *tolsi.*

To suppress an office, *abolire un uffizio.*

SUPPRE'SSED, adj. *soppresso, tolto, levato, impedito, restato.*

SUPPRE'SSING, } SUPPRE'SSION, } s. *soppressione, abolizione,* s. f. *il sopprimere.*

SUPPRE'SSOR, s. *colui che sopprime.*

To SU'PPURATE [to run, as a sore does] *far capo, marcire, suppurare.*

SUPPURA'TION, s. *il marcire.*

SUPPUTA'TION, s. [reckoning] *computo, calcolo,* s. m.

To SUPPU'TE [to reckon] *computare, calcolare.*

SUPPU'TED, adj. *computato, calcolato.*

SUPPU'TING, s. *computamento, computo, calcolo.*

SUPRE'AM, v. Supreme.

SUPRE'MACY, s. [the supreme or chief power of the King or Queen of England in ecclesiastical affairs] *primato,* s. m.

SUPRE'ME, adj. [highest] *supremo, il più alto, il più eminente.*

SUPRE'MELY, adv. [in the highest degree] *altissimamente, eccellentemente, perfettamente.*

SU'RAL, adj. [being in the calf of the leg] *che è nella polpa della gamba.*

SURBA'TE, s. [a bruise under a horse's foot, often occasioned by travelling unshod] *malattia che rende i cavalli spedati, e nasce generalmente dall' aver camminato troppo sferrati.*

To SURBA'TE a horse, *spedare un cavallo.*

To SURCE'ASE [to give over] *cessare, tralasciare.*

Surcease from any further trouble, *non vi pigliate più fastidio.*

SUFCE'ASED, adj. *cessato, tralasciato.*

SURCHA'RGE, s. [charge upon charge] *sopraccarico,* s. m. *soverchio carico.*

To SURCHA'RGE [to overload] *sopraccaricare, caricar troppo.*

SURCHA'RGED, adj. *sopraccaricato.*

SURCI'NGLE, s. [a girdle, with which the clergymen of the church of England usually tye their cassocks] *cintola, cintura,* s. f.

SU'RCLE, s. [shoot, twig, sucker] *germoglio, rampollo, ramicello.*

SURCO'AT, s. [a sort of upper garment] *saltambarco, saltamindosso,* s. m. *sopravvesta,* s. f.

SURD, adj. [a term used in matheticks] *sordo.*

A surd number, *numero sordo.*

SU'RDITY, s. [deafness] *sordità, sordaggine,* s. f.

SURE, adj. [assured, certain] *sicuro, certo, assicurato.*

I am sure of the contrary, *sono sicuro che la cosa non va così.*

We are sure of victory, *noi siam certi della vittoria, la vittoria è in man nostra.*

Sure [true, undoubted] *sicuro, indubitato.*

Sure [infallible] *sicuro, infallibile, che non può mancare.*

Sure [true, faithful] *sicuro, sincero, fedele.*

Sure [safe] *sicuro, fuor di pericolo.*

A sure pay-master, *un buon pagatore, un uomo che paga bene.*

Sure [firm] *sicuro, sodo, fermo, solido, stabile.*

To make sure of one, *assicurarsi d' una persona.*

To make sure of a thing [to seize a thing] *impadronirsi di qualche cosa.*

Be sure to do it, *son mercante di farlo.*

As sure as I am alive, *così come io son vivo.*

To be sure [surely] *certamente, indubitatamente, senza dubbio.*

Yes sure, *sicuramente, certamente.*

No sure, *eh via.*

SUREFO'OTED, adj. [treading firmly, not stumbling] *che cammina con sicurezza di piede, che non inciampa, che non intoppa.*

SU'RELY, adv. [certainly] *sicuramente, certamente, veramente, per certo.*

Surely [securely] *sicuramente, con sicurezza.*

SU'RENESS, s. [certainty] *sicurezza, certezza, s. f.*

SU'RETISHIP, s. [the quality of being a surety] *malleveria, s. f.*

SU'RETY, s. [bail] *mallevadore.*

To be surety for one, *mallevare alcuno, esser suo mallevadore.*

SU'RFACE, s. [outside] *superficie, s. f.*

The surface of the water, *la superficie dell' acqua.*

SU'RFEIT [excess in eating and drinking] *crapula, s. f. eccesso nel mangiare e nel bere.*

To take a surfeit, *avere un' indigestione.*

Surfeit water, *acqua distillata con erbe buone contro l' indigestione.*

Surfeit [satiety] *stucchevolezza, noja, nausea, s. f. rincrescimento, fastidio, s. m.*

To SU'RFEIT one's self with a thing, *saziarsi di qualche cosa, essere stufo di qualche cosa.*

SU'RFEITER, s. [one who riots, a glutton] *un mangione, un ghiottone.*

SU'RFEITING, s. *stucchevolezza, s. f.*

SURFEITWA'TER, s. [water that cures surfeits] *acqua che guarisce della troppa ripienezza di stomaco.*

SU'RGE, s. [a billow or wave of the sea] *onda, s. f. cavallone, flutto, s. m.*

To SU'RGE [to rise up in waves] *ondeggiare, gonfiarsi, far cavalloni, parlando del mare.*

SU'RGEON, s. [one that is skilled in, or professes surgery] *cerusico, chirurgo, s. m. colui che è versato, o che esercita la cirugia.*

SU'RGEONRY, } s. [an art which
SU'RGERY, } teaches how to cure the outward diseases of a human body by the help of the hands] *cirugia, chirurgia, s. f. quella parte di medicina, che cura manualmente.*

SU'RGY, adj. [raising in billows] *gonfio, altamente ondeggiante, procelloso; e dicesi del mare.*

SU'RLILY, adv. *fastidiosamente, fantasticamente, increscevolmente, fieramente, orgogliosamente, burberamente.*

SU'RLINESS, s. [a being surly] *noja, sdegnosità, caponeria, fastidiosaggine, s. f.*

SU'RLING, s. [a sour morose fellow] *un caparbio, uno che sempre guarda altrui in cagnesco.*

SU'RLY, adj. [morose, crabbed, dogged] *arcigno, burbero, dispettoso, aromatico, fastidioso, sdegnoso, ritroso, ombroso, caparbio, capone.*

SU'RMISE, s. [imagination, supposition, suspicion] *immaginazione, opinione, supposizione, s. f. pensiero, s. m.*

To SU'RMISE [to think, to imagine, to suppose] *pensare, credere, immaginarsi, mettersi in testa, darsi a credere, supporre,* pres. *suppongo,* pret. *supposi.*

SURMI'SED, adj. *pensato, creduto, immaginato, supposto.*

SU'RMISING, s. *pensiero, sospetto,* s. m. *immaginazione, s. f.*

To SURMO'UNT [to overcome, to get the better] *sormontare, superare, vincere.*

To surmount all difficulties, *sormontare tutte le difficoltà.*

To surmount [to exceed, to excel] *sormontare, avanzare, soprafare,* pret. *soprafeci.*

SURMO'UNTABLE, adj. [conquerable, superable] *che si può vincere, che si può sormontare.*

SURMO'UNTED, adj. *sormontato, superato, vinto, avanzato, soprafatto.*

SU'RMULET, s. [a sea fish] *triglia, s. f. pesce di mare.*

SURNA'ME, s. [name of family] *soprannome, rognome, s. m.*

To SURNA'ME [to give a surname] *soprannomare, cognominare.*

SURNA'MED, adj. *soprannomato, cognominato.*

To SURPA'SS [to exceed, to excel, to go beyond] *superare, avanzare, eccedere, soprastare, sormontare, sovranzare, vantaggiare.*

SURPA'SSABLE, adj. *che si può superare o avanzare.*

SURPA'SSED, adj. *superato, avanzato, ecceduto, sormontato, vantaggiato.*

SURPA'SSING, adj. [excellent in a high degree] *che eccede, che è eccellente di molto.*

SURPA'SSINGLY, adv. *straordinariamente, d' una maniera straordinaria.*

SU'RPLICE, s. [a linen garment worn by clergymen, when they officiate at divine service] *cotta, s. f. quella sopravvesta di panno lino bianco che portano nell' esercitare i divini uffici gli ecclesiastici.*

SU'RPLUS, } s. [that which is o-
SURPLU'SAGE, } ver and above] *soprappiù, il soverchio.*

SURPRI'SAL, } s. [a sudden assault,
SURPRI'SE, } or coming upon a man unawares] *sorpresa, s. f.*

Surprise [amazement, astonishment] *sorpresa, maraviglia, stupore.*

To SURPRI'SE [to take unawares] *soprapprendere, sorprendere, corre all' improvviso,* pret. *soprappresi, sorpresi.*

To surprise [to amaze] *sorprendere, maravigliare, stupire.*

You surprise me, *voi mi fate stupire.*

SURPRI'SED, adj. *soprappreso, sorpreso, colto all' improvviso, maravigliato, stupito.*

SURPRI'SING, adj. [strange] *stupendo, maraviglioso, strano.*

SURPRI'SINGLY, adv. *con istupore, con maraviglia, stranamente.*

SU'RQUEDRY, s. [pride, presumption] *fierezza, arroganza, alterigia,* s. f. *orgoglio,* s. m.

SU'RRENDRY, } s. [the act of resign-
SURRE'NDER, } ing or giving up] *resa,* s. f. *il rendere.*

The surrender of a town, *la resa d' una città.*

To SURRE'NDER [to yield, to give up] *rendere, consegnare, dare in mano,* pret. *resi.*

To surrender one's place, *rassegnare il suo ufficio.*

To surrender one's self a prisoner, *rendersi prigione.*

To surrender, verb neut. [to yield] *rendersi, arrendersi,* pret. *resi, arresi.*

SURRE'NDERED, adj. *reso, consegnato, rissegnato, arreso.*

SURRE'PTION, s. [the act of doing any thing by stealth] *sorpresa.*

SURREPTI'TIOUS, adj. [done by stealth] *surrettizio.*

SURREPTI'TIOUSLY, adv. *segretamente, sotto mano, di soppiatto.*

SU'RROGATE, s. [one substituted to supply the place of another] *sostituto, sustituto,* s. m. *che tiene la vece altrui.*

Surrogate, adj. *sustituito, sostituto.*

To SU'RROGATE [to appoint in the room of another] *sustituire, sostituire, mettere uno in luogo suo o d' altrui,* pres. *sustituisco, sostituisco.*

SURROGA'TION, s. [the act of appointing a deputy] *il sostituire.*

To SURRO'UND [to incompass] *circondare, chiudere, strignere intorno.*

SURRO'UNDED, adj. *circondato, chiuso, stretto intorno.*

SU'RTOUT, s. [a large coat worn over all the rest] *abito che ricopre tutti i panni che un porta indosso.*

To SURVE'NE [to come as an addition] *venire per aggiunta.*

SURVE'Y, s. [general review] *rivista, s. f.*

To take a survey of one's lands, *fare la pianta delle sue terre,*

He writes the survey of the country, *egli*

egli fa la descrizione generale di tutto 'l paese.

To SURVE'Y [to look about on all sides] *vedere, osservare, esaminare attentamente da ogni banda.*

To survey land, *misurare terreno.*

To survey [to oversee] *aver la soprantendenza o ispezione, invigilare.*

SURVE'YED, adj. *visto, v.* To survey.

SURVE'YOR, s. [overseer] *soprantendente, intendente.*

Surveyor [measurer of land] *misuratore di terra, agrimensore.*

SURVE'YORSHIP, s. [the office of a surveyor] *l' officio del soprantendente o dell' agrimensore.*

To SURVIE'W [to overlook, to have in view] *sopravvedere, dare un occhiata.*

SURVI'VANCE, s. [the state of outliving another] *il sopravvivere ad un altro, sopravvivenza.*

To SURVI'VE [to outlive] *sopravvivere, viver più.*

SURVI'VED, adj. *sopravvissuto, sopravvisso.*

SURVI'VOR, s. [one who out-lives another] *sopravvivente.*

SURVI'VORSHIP, s. [out-living] *sopravvivenza.*

SUSCE'PTIBLE, adj. [apt to take impression] *suscettibile.*

SUSCE'PTION, s. [act of taking] *suscettibilità.*

SUSCE'PTIVE, adj. *suscettibile.*

To SU'SCITATE [to raise] *suscitare, eccitare, far nascere.*

SU'SCITATED, adj. *suscitato, eccitato.*

SUSCITA'TION, s. *suscitamento,* s. m. *il suscitare.*

SU'SKIN, s. [a sort of old coin] *spezie di moneta antica.*

SUSPE'CT, participle adjective [doubtful] *dubbioso.*

Suspect, s. [suspicion] *sospetto.*

To SUSPE'CT [to fear, to misturst] *sospettare, aver sospetto, diffidarsi.*

To suspect one's own strength, *diffidarsi delle sue proprie forze.*

To suspect [to surmise, to think] *sospettare, credere, pensare, immaginarsi.*

SUSPE'CTED, adj. *sospettato, diffidato, v.* To suspect.

SUSPE'CTFUL, adj. [distrustful] *sospettoso, diffidente.*

SUSPE'CTING, s. *il sospettare.*

SUSPE'NCE, s. [doubt] *dubbio,* s. m. *ambiguità, incertezza,* s. f.

To be in suspence, *star sospeso, star ambiguo, non sapere a che risolversi.*

To SUSPE'ND [to hang up] *sospendere, appiccare, sostenere in aria,* pret. *sospesi.*

To supend' [to keep in doubt] *sospendere, tener sospeso, render dubbioso.*

To suspend [to defer, to delay, to stop] *sospendere, prolungare, differire,* pres. *differisco.*

To suspend one from his office, *sospendere alcuno dal suo uffizio.*

SUSPE'NDED, adj. *sospeso, v.* To suspend.

SUSPE'NDING, s. *sospensione,* s. f. *il sospendere.*

SUSPE'NSE, s. *incertezza.*

Suspense, adj. *sospeso, dubbioso.*

SUSPE'NSION, s. [the lesser excommunication] *sospensione, censura ecclesiastica.*

SUSPE'NSORY, adj. [by which a thing hangs] *che tien sospeso, che tiene appeso.*

SUSPI'CABLE, adj. [liable to suspicion] *sospetto, che sospetta.*

SUSPI'CION, s. [jealousy, fear, distrust] *diffidenza,* s. f. *sospetto,* s. m.

To entertain suspicion of one, *prender sospetto, prender ombra d'uno.*

SUSPI'CIOUS, adj. [suspicable] *sospettoso, che arreca sospetto.*

Suspicious, [jealous, distrustful] *sospettoso, pien di sospetto, diffidente.*

SUSPI'CIOUSLY, adv. *sospettamente, con sospetto, sospettosamente.*

SUSPI'RAL, s. [breathing-hole] *spiraglio,* s. m.

SUSPIRA'TION, s. [sigh; act of fetching the breath deep] *il sospirare.*

To SUSTA'IN [to give strength, to maintain, to feed] *sostenere, mantenere, reggere, nutrire, sostentare,* pres. *sostengo, mantengo, nutrisco;* pret. *sostenni, mantenni, ressi.*

To SUSTA'IN [to support, to bear up] *sostenere, appoggiare, puntellare, appuntellare.*

To sustain [to suffer] *sostenere, sofferire, comportare, patire,* pres. *sofferisco, patisco.*

To sustain a loss, *fare una perdita.*

SUSTA'INABLE, adj. *che si può sostenere.*

SUSTA'INED, adj. *sostenuto, v.* To sustain.

SUSTA'INER, s. [one that props, one that supports] *sostenitore, spalleggiatore, puntellatore, colui o la cosa che serve di sostegno.*

Sustainer [one that suffers, a sufferer] *paziente; colui che soffre.*

SUSTA'INING, s. *sostenimento,* s. m. *il sostenere.*

SU'STENANCE, s. [nourishment, food] *alimento, sostentamento, uso de' cibi, cibo.*

SUSTENTA'TION, s. [support, preservation from falling] *sostegno, puntello, cosa che ti sostiene, che t' impedisce di cadere.*

Sustentation [support of life, use of victuals] *alimento, cibo, uso de' cibi.*

Sustentation [maintenance] *mantenimento, sostegno.*

SU'TABLE, adj. [agreeable] *conveniente, convenevole, conforme, proporzionato, oggi scriversi,* suitable.

SU'TABLENESS, s. [suitableness] *convenenza, conformità,* s. f.

SU'TABLY, adv. [suitably] *conformemente, convenevolmente, d' una maniera convenevole.*

SUTE [suit of cloaths] *abito, vestito.*

Sute [set of things] *assortimento.*

Sute of hangings, *assortimento di tapezzerie.*

Sute of cards, *una seguenza di carte.*

To SUTE [to suit, to fit, to agree] *accordarsi accomodarsi, convenire, esser buono, addirsi, confarsi.*

To sute [to match] *accoppiare, appajare.*

To sute cards [to put the sutes together] *assortire, distinguere, scompartire le carte.*

SU'TLER, s. [one that follows an army to sell victuals] *vivandiere,* s. m.

SU'TURE [seam] *cucitura,* s. f.

SWAB, s. [a kind of mop to clean floors] *sorta di scopa non cui si scopano i pavimenti delle stanze.*

To SWAB [to clean with a mop] *scopare.*

SWA'BBER, s. [drudge of a ship, sweeper of the deck] *mozzo di vascello che scopa i ponti.*

SWA'DDLE, s. [cloath bound round the body] *fascia,* pl. *fasce.*

To SWA'DDLE [to wrap up in swathing-bands] *fasciare, circondare, intorniar con fascia.*

To swaddle [to bang, to cudgel, to drub] *battere, bastonare, tartassare.*

SWA'DDLED, adj. *fasciato, battuto, bastonato, tartassato.*

SWA'DDLING-BAND,
SWA'DDLING-CLOATH,
SWA'DDLING-CLOUT, } s. [cloath wrapped round a new born child] *fascia o panno in cui è avvolto il bambino quando nasce.*

To SWAG [to hang on one side] *pendere inverso una delle parti, esser volto o inchinare per troppo peso.*

The coach swags on one side, *la carrozza pende da una parte.*

To swag, or to swag down, *pendere, ciondolare, dondolare.*

His belly swags down, *la pancia gli ciondola.*

A swag belly, *una panciaccia, una trippaccia.*

To SWAGE, *v.* To asswage.

To SWA'GGER [to play the hector, to boast] *vantarsi, gloriarsi, vanagloriarsi, bravare, braveggiare, fare il bravo.*

Swagger huff,
Swaggerer, } *un bravo, un tagliacantoni, un mangiaferro, uno sgherro, un gradasso, uno smargiasso.*

SWA'GGING, adj. [from to swag] *dondolone.*

Swagging breast, *poppe a dondolone.*

SWA'GGY, adj. [dependent by its weight] *che pende per soverchio peso.*

SWAIN, s. [a country man, a clown] *un contadina, un bifolco.*

Swain, or shepherd swain, *un pastore, un pastorello.*

Swain [a young man] *un giovane, un giovinetto.*

SWAL-

SWA'LLOW, s. [a bird] *rondine, rondinella.*
One swallow does not make a summer, *una rondine non fa primavera.*
Swallow [a flying-fish] *rondine, sorta di pesce alato.*
Water-swallow [a bird] *coditremola, s. f. spezie d' uccello.*
Swallow tail, *coda di rondine.*
Swallow [a whirlpool or gulph] *gorgo, inghiottimento, s. m. voragine, s. f.*
Swallow-wort, *celidonia, s. f. spezie d' erba.*
Swallow, s. [the throat, voracity] *la gola, il vizio della gola, voracità.*
To SWA'LLOW [to pass or let down the throat] *inghiottire, trangugiare,* pres. *inghiottisco.*
To swallow down one's victuals, *inghiottire il cibo.*
He has swallow'd a spider [he is bankrupt] *egli è fallito.*
To swallow [to receive without examination] *mandar giù senza esaminare.*
To swallow [to engross, to appropriate] *tirar tutto a se.*
To swallow [to absorb, to take in, to sink in any abyss, to engulf] *assorbire, tirar d n'ro, abbissare, ingolfare.*
To swallow [to devour, to destroy] *divorare, distruggere.*
To swallow [to be lost in any thing, to be given up] *essere perduto in checchessia, esser butato vi i.*
To swallow one's words, *disdirsi.*
SWA'LLOWED, adj. *inghiottito, trangugiato, v.* To swallow.
SWA'LLOWING, s. *inghiottimento, s. m. l' inghiottire.*
SWAM, *è un preterito del verbo* To swim.
SWAMP, s. [bog, fen, marshy-place] *pantano, palude, padule.*
SWA'MPY, adj. [marshy] *pantanoso, paludoso.*
SWAN, s. [a sort of bird] *cigno, s. m.*
Wild swan, *pellicano.*
Swan's skin, *pelle di cigno.*
SWA'NSKIN, s. [a kind of soft flannel] *sorta di flanella fine.*
SWAP, adv. [hastily, with hasty violence] *prestamente con violenta prestezza.*
He did it swap, *e' lo fece a un tratto.*
To SWAP [to exchange] *cambiare.*
SWARD, s. [a rind of bacon] *cotenna, s. f.*
The great sward of the earth, *la superficie della terra.*
SWARM, s. [of bees] *sciame d' api o di pecchie.*
Swarm of ants, *formicajo.*
Swarm [great number] *moltitudine, copia, gran quantità.*
Swarm of lice, *gran quantità di pidocchi.*
Swarm of people, *calca, folla, gran moltitudine di gente, sciame di gente.*
To SWARM [as bees do] *far lo sciame, parlando delle api.*
To swarm [to be full of] *abbondare, esser pieno, traboccare.*
The town swarms with rogues, *la città abbonda, è piena di malandrini.*
The streets swarm with people, *le strade sono piene di gente.*
SWART, adj. [swarth, black, darkly brown, tawney] *nero, bruno, ghezzo, moro, di color pendente più al nero che ad altro.*
Swart [gloomy, malignant] *maligno, tristo, cattivo, pien di nero veleno.*
To SWART [to blacken, to dusk] *annerare, render nero.*
SWARTH, *lo stesso che* swart *in ogni significato.*
SWARTHILY, adv. [blackly, duskily, tawnily] *neramente.*
SWA'RTHINESS, s. [swarthy complexion] *carnagione abbronzata, nerezza.*
SWA'RTHISH, s. [a little swarthy] *arsiccio, nericcio.*
SWARTHY, adj. [sun-burnt, tawny, blackish] *ghezzo, nero, v.* swart, e swarth.
To SWASH [to make fly about as water] *spruzzare, sprazzare.*
To swash [to make a noise with swords] *strepitar colle spade.*
SWASH, s. [stream of water] *ruscello, torrente, s. m.*
A swash-buckler, s. [a braggadocio, a vapouring fellow] *uno sgherro, un cagnotto, un bravo, un tagliacantoni, un mangiaferro.*
SWA'SHER, s. [one who makes a show of valour or force] *colui che fa mostra o pompa di valore o di forza.*
SWATCH, s. [swathe] *fascia.*
SWATH, s. ex. A swath of grass, barley, &c. *un ciglione d' erba tagliata, d' orzo, e simili.*
SWATHE, *v.* Swathes.
To SWATHE [to bind up with swathes] *fasciare.*
To swathe a child, *fasciare un bambino.*
SWA'THED, adj. *fasciato.*
SWA'THING, s. *il fasciare.*
SWA'THES [swathing-cloaths] *fasce.*
A swathing band, *una fascia.*
A child in swathing cloaths, *un bambino in fasce.*
SWAY, s. [power, rule, command] *potere, dominio, comando, imperio, s. m. autorità, s. f.*
To SWAY [to bear sway] *dominare, reggere, signoreggiare, comandare, aver il comando, il potere, l' autorità, aver imperio assoluto.*
To sway with one, *aver autorità sopra alcuno.*
To sway the scepter, *portar lo scettro, aver lo scettro in mano, regnare, dominare.*
SWA'YED, adj. *dominato.*
To SWEAL [to melt away] *fondersi, liquefarsi.*
The candle sweals, *la candela si liquefà.*
SWEAP, *v.* Swipe.
To SWEAR [to affirm, to confirm, to promise with an oath] *giurare, affermare, prometter con giuramento.*
To swear [to curse, to blaspheme] *giurare, bestemmiare.*
To swear one [to give or tender one his oath] *far giurare alcuno, prestar il giuramento.*
SWE'ARER, s. *giuratore, s. m. che giura.*
SWE'ARING, s. *giuramento, s. m. il giurare.*
SWEAT, s. *sudore, s. m.*
To cause sweat, *far sudare.*
To be all in a sweat, *esser molle di sudore.*
To SWEAT [to perspire through the pores of the body by reason of heat] *sudare, mandar fuor il sudore.*
To sweat blood and water, *sudar sangue e acqua.*
He sweats for fear, *egli suda di paura.*
To Sweat [to cause sweat] *far sudare*
SWE'ATED, adj *sudato.*
SWE'ATER, s. *uno che è suggetto a sudare.*
SWE'ATING, s. *sudore, il sudare.*
SWE'ATING, } adj. *sudato, bagnato,*
SWE'ATY, } *molle di sudore.*
SWEEP, s. [the act of sweeping] *lo scopare, scopatura.*
Sweep [the compass of any violent or continued motion] *l' estensione d' un moto violento o continuato.*
Sweep [violent destruction] *distruggimento violento.*
Sweep [direction of any motion not rectilinear] *direzione di moto non rettilineo.*
To SWEEP [to cleanse with a broom, brush, &c] *scopare, spazzare, nettare.*
To sweep the chimney, *spazzar il cammino.*
Sweep before your own door [meddle with your own business] *badate a' fatti vostri.*
To sweep away [to destroy] *rovinare, distruggere,* pret. *distrussi.*
SWE'EPER, s. *quello o quella che spazza.*
Chimney-sweeper, *uno spazzacammino.*
SWE'EPING, s. *lo spazzare, lo scopare.*
SWE'EPINGS, s. [filth, or dust swept out] *spazzatura, immodizia, che si toglie via nello spazzare, scopatura.*
Sweep-net [a sort of fishing-net] *vangajuola, s. f. spezie di rete da pescare.*
SWE'EPSTAKES, s. [a man that wins all] *colui che vince tutto il danaro degli altri.*
SWE'EPY, adj. [passing with great speed and violence] *che passa con molta prestezza e violenza.*
SWEET, adj. [pleasant in taste, as honey, &c.] *dolce.*
Sweet to the smell, *dolce, grato all' odorato, odorifero.*
Sweet breath, *fiato dolce.*
A very sweet flower, *un fiore odorifero, che ha buon odore.*
Sweet look, *cera amena e grata, guardatura piacevole.*
Sweet smile, *dolce sorriso.*
Sweet-temper, *umor allegro e gioviale, tempra mansueta.*
Sweet smell, *odor soave.*
Sweet child, *fanciullo amabile.*
To be sweet upon a woman [to look amor-

amorously upon her] *guardar con compiacenza una donna, amoreggiarla.*

Sweet [that does not stink] *che non puzza, che non ha cattivo odore.*

Sweet meat, *carne che non puzza.*

This meat is not sweet, *questa carne puzza.*

To keep one's self sweet and clean, *conservarsi pulito e netto.*

Sweet-meats, *confetture, confetti.*

Life is sweet when one wants for nothing, *la vita è dolce quando non ci manca nulla.*

Sweet, s. [pleasure, comfort] *dolcezza,* s. f. *conforto, piacere,* s. m.

The sweets of peace, *le dolcezze della pace.*

No sweet without some sweat, *non c' è rosa senza spine, non si può avere il mele senza le pecchie.*

Sweet-smelling, *odorifero, odoroso, soave.*

Sweet scented, *profumato.*

Sweet natured, *affabile, cortese, benigno, di buona pasta.*

The sweet bread of a breast of veal, *animella di vitella.*

Sweet-heart, s. *amante,* s. m. *innamorata,* s. f.

To SWE'ETEN [to make sweet] *addolcire, far dolce.*

To sweeten with sugar, *inzuccherare.*

Have you sweetened your coffee? *avete messo del zucchero nel vostro caffè?*

To sweeten [to soften, to alleviate] *addolcire, mitigare, placare, allentare.*

To sweeten pain, *addolcire il dolore.*

To sweeten anger, *allentare, placare lo sdegno.*

SWE'ETENED, adj. *addolcito.*

SWE'ETENER, s. [one that palliates, one that represents things tenderly] *colui che narrando o rappresentando un fallo o delitto suo o d' altrui lo sminuisce quanto può.*

Sweetner [that which contemperates acrimony] *cosa che tempra l'acrimonia d' altra cosa.*

SWE'ETISH, adj. [somewhat sweet] *alquanto dolce, dolcigno.*

SWE'ETLY, adv. [pleasantly] *dolcemente, con dolcezza, affettuosamente, piacevolmente, soavemente.*

She sings sweetly, *ella canta dolcemente o soavemente.*

SWE'ETNESS, s. *dolcezza,* s. f.

Sweetness [pleasantness] *dolcezza, soavità,* s. f. *gusto, contento,* s. m.

SWELL, s. *gonfiamento,* s. m. *gonfiezza,* s. f.

The swell of the sea, *i gonfiamenti, i cavalloni, l' onde del mare.*

To SWELL [to puff, to fill up] *gonfiare, empir di fiato o di vento che che sia.*

To swell [to swell up, to increase, to make bigger] *gonfiare, enfiare, ingrossare, agumentare, crescere.*

The rain has swelled up the river, *le piogge hanno gonfiato o fatto crescere il fiume.*

To swell up a volume, *ingrossare un volume.*

To swell, *gonfiarsi, crescere.*

The river swells, *il fiume si gonfia, le acque del fiume crescono.*

To swell out [as a wall does] *far sacco, parlando d' un muro quando sporge in fuori.*

SWE'LLING, s. *gonfiamento, enfiato, gonfio,* s. m. *gonfiatura, gonfiezza,* s. f.

Swelling in the groin, *tincone,* s. m.

To SWELT [to puff in sweat] *sbuffare quando un suda.*

To SWE'LTER, *affogare.*

To swelter with heat, *affogare, morir di raldo.*

SWE'LTRY, adj. ex. sweltry heat, or sweltry weather, *un caldo eccessivo, un tempo molto caldo.*

SWEPT, adj. [from to sweep] *spazzato, scopato.*

To SWERVE [to go from] *stornarsi, sviarsi, traviare.*

SWIFT, adj. [quick, nimble, rapid] *veloce, presto, spedito, ratto, pronto, rapido, lesto, leggiero, snello.*

Swift horse, *cavallo veloce, leggiero al corso.*

Swift river, *fiume rapido.*

To go a swift pace, *andar di buon passo.*

SWI'FTLY, adv. *velocemente, prestamente, speditamente,* ratto, *rapidamente, leggiermente.*

SWI'FTNESS, s. *velocità, prestezza, leggerezza nell' andare, rapidità,* s. f.

To SWIG [to drink by large draughts] *bere a gran sorsi, tracannare.*

SWILL, s. [hog's wash] *broda,* s. f.

Swill. [drink luxuriously poured down] *bevanda traccannata con grandissimo diletto.*

To SWILL [to gulp, to swallow] *inghiottire,* trangugiare.

To swill [to drink hard] *bere molto o avidamente,* trinrare, *imbriacarsi.*

Swill-belly'd, *panciuto, che ha la pancia grossa.*

Swill-bowl, swiller, or swill-pot, s. [drunkard] *bevitore, imbriacone.*

SWI'LLING, s. *crapula, imbriachezza,* s. f.

To SWIM [to float on the water] *nuotare, andare a nuoto.*

To swim over a river, *passare un fiume a nuoto.*

To swim away, *salvarsi, o scampare nuotando.*

The oil swims on the top of all other liquors, *l' olio nuota sopra* tutti *gli altri liquori.*

SWI'MMER, s. *nuotatore,* s. m.

SWI'MMING, s. *nuoto,* s. m. *il nuotare.*

A swimming of the head [dizziness] *vertigine,* s. f. *capogirlo,* s. m.

SWINE, s. [hog, pig] *porco,* s. m.

Swine herd, *porcaro,* s. m.

Swine bread [truffle] *tartufo,* s. m. *spezie di fungo.*

Sea-swine, *porcello di mare.*

Wild-swine, *cinghiale,* s. m.

Swine hull, or swine-sty, *porcile,* s. m.

Swine-like, adv. *da porco, come un porco.*

SWING, s. [jerk] *spinta, dondolata,* s. m.

To give one a swing, *dare un spinta ad uno, spignerlo.*

Swing, *altalena,* s. f.

He may have a swing for it [he may be hanged] *egli potrebbe dar de' calci a rovajo per questo, egli porebbe esser impiccato.*

To take one's swing, *cavarsi la voglia di qualche cosa.*

To SWING [to move to and fro hanging] *dondolare, mandare in qua e'n là la cosa sospesa.*

To swing about, *girare, andare attorno.*

To SWINGE, or to swinge off [to whip, to bang, to maul] *scopare, frustare, sferzare, battere, tartassare, bastonare.*

SWI'NGED off, adj. *scopato, frustato, sferzato,* battuto, *tartassato, bastonato.*

SWI'NGING, adj. [great] *grande, molto grande, molto grosso.*

SWI'NGINGLY, adv. [hugely] *vastamente, colossescamente.*

To SWI'NGLE [to dress flax] *scotolare,* battere *colla scotola il lino, maciullare.*

Swingle staff, s. [a staff to bent flax with] *scotola, maciulla,* s. f. *strumento di legno a guisa di coltello, col quale si batte il lino avanti che si pettini.*

SWINK, s. [labour] *travaglio,* s. m. *fatica.*

SWI'NKER, s. *artigiano,* s. m.

SWIPE, s. [an engine for drawing up water] *altaleno,* s. m.

SWITCH, s. *bacchetta,* s. f.

To SWITCH, *battere con bacchetta.*

SWI'VEL, s. [something fixed in another body so as to turn round it] *perno.*

SWO'LING, s. [as much land as one plough can till in a year] *tanta terra quanto con un aratro si può lavorare in un anno.*

SWO'LLEN, } adj. [from to swell]
SWOLN, } *gonfiato, gonfio, tumido.*

Swoln style, *stile gonfio.*

SWOM, *è un preterito del verbo* To swim.

SWOON, s. [a fainting fit] *svenimento,* s. m.

To SWOON [to faint away] *svenire, venir meno, tramortire,* pres. *svengo, tramortisco,* pret. *svenni.*

SWO'ONING away, s. *svenimento, sfinimento,* s. m.

SWOOP, s. [a fall of a bird of prey upon his quarry] *il piombare che fa un uccello rapace sulla sua preda.*

To SWOOP [to catch up with the talons, as birds of prey do] *afferrare cogli artigli, come fanno gli uccelli di rapina.*

To SWOP [to change, to barter] *barattare.*

SWO'PPING, s. *baratto,* s. m. *il barattare.*

SWORD, s. [a known weapon] *spada,* s. f.

To wear a sword, *portare spada.*

To draw the sword, *sfoderar la spada, metter mano alla spada.*

To put all to the sword, *metter tutti a fil di spada.*

To put all to fire and ſword, *metter ogni coſa a fuoco e a ſangue.*

By dint of ſword, *colla punta della ſpada, per forza d'arme.*

The King's ſword bearer, *colui che porta la ſpada avanti al Re.*

Sword-player, *un gladiatore.*

Sword-fiſh, *peſce ſpada.*

Sword-graſs [gladder] *ghiacciuolo,* s. m. *ſorta di pianta, le cui barbe ſono odorifere.*

SWO'RDED, adj. [girt with a ſword] *che ha la ſpada cinta al fianco.*

SWO'RDER, s. [a cut-throat, a ſoldier] *un ammazzatore, un ſoldato.*

SWO'RDKNOT, s. [ribband tied to the hilt of the ſword] *nodo di ſpada, fiocco di ſpada, naſtro che ſi porta legato all' elſe della ſpada.*

SWO'RDLAW, s. [violence] *violenza.*

SWO'RDMAN, s. [ſoldier, fighting-man] *ſoldato, combattitore.*

SWORE, *è un preterito del verbo* To ſwear.

SWORN, adj. [from to ſwear] *giurato, che ha preſtato il giuramento.*

He was ſworn a privy counſellor, *egli preſtò giuramento in qualità di conſigliere privato,*

SWUM, *preterito e participio paſſivo del verbo* To ſwim.

SWUNG, adj. [from to ſwing] *dondolato, v.* To ſwing.

SYB, adj. *propiamente* Sib [related by blood] *che ha parentela, parente.*

SY'CAMINE, } s. [the mulberry fig-
SY'CAMORE, } tree] *ficomoro,* s. m. *ſpezie di fico.*

SY'COPHANT, s. [pick-thank, flatterer] *un adulatore, un luſinghiero, un paraſito, uno ſcroccone,* s. m.

To SY'COPHANT, [to play the ſycophant] *far il meſtier del paraſito.*

SY'DER, s. [cider] *ſidro,* s. m. *ſorta di bevanda.*

SY'LLABAR, } s. [boore ating of
SY'LLABARY, } ſyllables] *libro che tratta delle ſillabe.*

SYLLA'BICAL, adj. *di ſillaba.*

SYLLABICA'TION, s. [the forming of ſyllables] *formazione delle ſillabe*

SYLLA'BICK, *v.* Syllabical.

SY'LLABLE, s. [an articular or compleat ſound made of one or ſeveral letters] *ſillaba,* s. f.

To SY'LLABLE [to utter, to pronounce, to articulate] *articolare, pronunciare.*

SY'LLOGISM, s [an argument of logick, conſiſting of three propoſitions] *ſillogiſmo,* s. m.

SYLLOGI'STICAL, } adj. *ſillogiſtico,*
SYLLOGI'STICK, } *fatto in forma di ſillogiſmo.*

SYLLOGI'STICALLY, adv. [in the form of a ſyllogiſm] *in forma di ſillogiſmo.*

To SYLLOGI'ZE [to argue by ſyllogiſms] *ſillogizzare, argomentare in ſillogiſmo.*

SY'LVAN, adj. [belonging to woods or foreſts] *ſilvano, di ſelva.*

SY'LVAN, s. [a wood-god, a ſatyr] *un ſilvano, un Dio de' boſchi, un ſatiro.*

SYLVA'TIC, adj. *ſilveſtro, ſilveſtre, ſalvatico.*

SY'MBOL, s. [ſign, token] *ſimbolo, ſegno,* s. m.

The apoſtolick ſymbol [the Creed] *il ſimbolo degli apoſtoli, il Credo.*

SYMBO'LICAL, adj. *ſimbolico, miſtico.*

SYMBO'LICALLY, adv. *miſticamente.*

To SY'MBOLIZE [to ſignify by certain outward ſigns] *ſimbolizzare, ſignificare con ſimboli.*

To ſymbolize with one [to agree in any thing with him] *ſimbolizzare con uno, aver qualche raſſomiglianza con lui.*

SYMBOLI'ZED, adj. *ſimbolizzato.*

SYMBOLI'ZING, s. *il ſimbolizzare.*

SYMME'TRIAN, s. [one eminently ſtudious of proportion] *colui che ſtudia di fare una coſa colle più eſatte proporzioni.*

SYMME'TRICAL, adj. *fatto con ſimmetria.*

SY'MMETRIST, *lo ſteſſo che* ſymmetrian.

SY'MMETRY, s. [due proportion or uniformity of each part in reſpect to the whole] *ſimmetria, proporzione,* s. f. *ordine,* s. m.

SYMPATHE'TICAL, } adj. [pertain-
SYMPATHE'TICK } ing to, or partaking of ſympathy] *ſimpatico, di ſimpatia.*

SYMPATHE'TICALLY, adv. *ſimpaticamente.*

To SY'MPATHIZE [to agree] *ſimpatizzare, andare a ſangue, aver ſimpatia.*

SY'MPATHY, s. [conformity in nature, paſſions, diſpoſitions, or affections] *ſimpatia,* s. f. *conformità naturale.*

Sympathy [fellow-feeling] *compaſſione,* s. f.

SYMPHO'NIOUS, adj. [harmonious, agreeing in ſound] *armonioſo.*

SY'MPHONY, s. [a melodious harmony, or muſical concert] *ſinfonia,* s. f. *armonia, conſonanza di ſtrumenti muſicali.*

SY'MPTOM, s. [a token that diſcovers what the diſtemper is, or indicates what will be the iſſue of it] *ſintoma,* s. m. *accidenti di malattia.*

Symptom [ſign]. *ſegno, indizio,* s. m.

SYMPTOMA'TICAL, } adj. [belong-
SYMPTOMA'TICK, } ing to, or attended with ſymptoms] *di ſintoma, cagionato da qualche ſintoma.*

SYNAGO'GICAL, adj [pertaining to a ſynagogue] *appartenente a ſinagoga.*

SY'NAGOGUE, s. [Jewiſh church] *ſinagoga,* s. f. *tempio e adunanza degli Ebrei.*

To SY'NCOPATE [to ſwoon] *ſvenire, venir meno, tramortire,* pref. *ſvengo, tramortiſco,* pret. *ſvenni.*

To ſyncopate [to make an eliſion or ſyncope] *torre qualche ſillaba, o una lettera da una parola.*

SY'NCOPE, s. [a figure in grammar, whereby one or more letters are taken out of a word] *ſincope,* s. f. *figura grammaticale, per la quale ſi tolgiono lettere da una parola,*

Syncope [in phyſick, a ſudden fainting or ſwooning away] *ſincope, ſincopa, ſfinimento, ſvenimento.*

SY'NCOPIST, s. [contractor of words] *colui che taglia le parole e le accorcia togliendo qualche lettera.*

SY'NDICK, s. [a perſon deputed to act for any corporation, or community] *ſindaco,* s. m. *procurator di comunità.*

SY'NDICABLE, adj. [ſubject to cenſure] *che merita d'eſſere ſindacato, o cenſurato.*

To SY'NDICATE [to judge, to paſs judgment on, to cenſure] *ſindacare, giudicare, biaſimare.*

SY'NDICATE, } s. [the place or
SY'NDICKSHIP, } dignity of a ſyndick, or the time of being in that office] *ſindacato,* s. m.

SY'NOD [a meeting or aſſembly of eccleſiaſtical perſons to conſult about religion and church affairs] *ſinodo,* s. m. *congregazione eccleſiaſtica.*

National ſynod [where the biſhops of one nation only meet] *ſinodo nazionale.*

Provincial ſynod [where thoſe of one province only meet] *ſinodo provinciale.*

Dioceſan ſynod [where thoſe of but one dioceſe only meet] *ſinodo dioceſano.*

General ſynod [where biſhops, &c. of all nations meet] *ſinodo ecumenico o generale.*

SY'NODAL, } adj. [belonging to,
SYNO'DICAL, } or done in a ſy-
SYNO'DICK, } nod] *ſinodale, di ſinodo.*

SYNO'DICALLY, adv. [by the authority of a ſynod or publick aſſembly] *ſinodicamente, coll' autorità d' un ſinodo o aſſemblea pubblica.*

SY'NONYM, s. [a word of the ſame ſignification] *ſinonimo, nome ſinonimo, che ha la ſteſſa ſignificazione.*

SYNO'NYMAL } adj. [of the ſame
SYNO'NYMOUS, } ſignification] *ſinonimo, che ha la ſteſſa ſignificazione.*

SYNO'PSIS, s. [epitome, abſtract, abridgment] *compendio, riſtretto, ſommario,* s. m.

Synopſis [a general view; all the parts brought under one view] *ſinopſi, viſta del tutto inſieme.*

SYNO'PTICAL, adj. [affording a view of many parts at once] *offerente una viſta di molte parti a un tratto.*

SY'NTAX, s. [order, conſtruction, that part of grammar which teaches how re-

regularly to join words and sentences together] *sintassi, costruzione*, s. f. *termine gramaticale.*

SYNTE'RESIS, s. [remorse of conscience] *sindéresi*, s. f. *rimordimento, rimorso di coscienza.*

SY'PHON, s. [tube, pipe] *sifone, tubo, canna.*

SY'RINGE, s. [an instrument used in injecting] *siringa*, s. f.

To SY'RINGE, *adoperar la siringa, siringare.*

SY'RINGED, adj. *siringato.*

SY'RTIS, s. [quicksand, bog] *sirte, secca*, s. f. *scoglio*, s. m.

SY'STEM, s. [a compleat treatise or body of any art or science] *sistema*, s. m.

T.

T *Questa lettera si pronuncia come in Italiano, eccettuato quando precede la I seguita da vorale, come in* nation, salvation, *e simili; che allora* T *ha anzi un suono avvicinantesi al nostro* SC *nelle voci* sciocco, scilinguato, scienza; *e simili; notando anche che se è preceduta nel suddetto caso dalla lettera* S, *ritiene il naturale Italico suone, come in* christian, question, *e simili.*

TA'BARD, s. [herald's coat] *sopravvesta d'araldo.*

TA'BBY, s. [a silk stuff] *tabì*, s. m. *sorta di drappo.*

TA'BBY } adj. *ondato, fatto*
TA'BBY-LIKE } *a foggia di tabì.*

TA'BERNACLE, s. [a place of worship] *tabernacolo*, s. m.

Tabernacle [among Roman Catholicks, a little vessel in which the pix is put on the altar] *tabernacolo, quella parte dell' altare dove si ripone la pisside.*

TA'BID, adj. [dry, lean] *magro, smunto, macilente.*

TA'BLATURE, s. [a kind of musick-book, directing to play on the lute, violin, &c.] *intavolatura*, s. f. *quella scrittura composta di note e di numeri che insegnano le vori del canto e del suono.*

TA'BLE, s. [a piece of houshold-stuff well known] *tavola*, s. f. *arnese composto d' uno o di più asse, che serve per diversi usi.*

Table to eat upon, *tavolà, mensa*, s. f.

Table to write upon, *tavolino.*

To rise from table, *levarsi di tavola.*

To keep a good table [to live well] *far buona tavola, trattarsi bene.*

To keep an open table, *tener tavola aperta.*

To come to the Lord's table [to receive the communion] *avvicinarsi all' altare, ricevere la communione.*

Table [wherein the ancients used to write their laws] *tavola.*

Table [index of a book] *tavola, indice d' un libro.*

Tables [to play at] *tavoliere*, s. m. *tavoletta sopra la quale si giuoca a tavole.*

To play at tables, *giuocare a tutte tavole.*

Table-cloth, *tovaglia*, s. f.

Table-plate, *vasellame, vasellamento da tavola d' oro o d' argento.*

Table-beer [small beer] *piccola birra.*

Side table, *buffetto*, s. m.

To TA'BLE, v. n. [to board] *stare a scotto, stare a dozzina.*

To table one [to entertain him at one's table] *spesare alcuno, dargli la tavola.*

To table, v. a. [to make into a catalogue, to set down] *far a modo d' indire o catalogo, registrare per ordine.*

TA'BLE-BEER, s. [beer used at victuals, small beer] *birra piccola.*

TA'BLEBOOK, s. [a book on which any thing is written or graved without ink] *libro in cui i caratteri non sono fatti coll' inchiostro, ma incisi.*

TA'BLET, s. [little table] *tavoletta*, s. f.

TA'BLE-TALK, s. [conversation at meals or entertainments] *conversazione che si fa a tavola.*

TA'BOR, s. [tabret] *tamburino, cimbalo*, s. m. *cerchio d' asse sottile, col fondo di cartapecora a guisa di tamburo, intorniato di sonagli e di girelline di lama d' ottone, e si suona picchiandolo con mano.*

To TA'BOR [to play upon the tabor] *suonare il cimbalo.*

TA'BORER, s. *colui che suona il cimbalo.*

TA'BOURET, s. [low stool] *sgabello*, s. m.

TA'BRERE, s. [tabourer] *colui che suona il cimbalo.*

TA'BRET, v. Tabor.

TA'CES, s. [an armour for the thighs] *cosciale*, s. m. *armadura che cuopre la coscia.*

TACH, s. [hook, buckle, clasp] *affibbiaglio, fermaglio*, s. m. *fibbia*, s. f.

TA'CIT, adj. [implied, meant] *tacito, implicito, non espresso, sottinteso.*

TA'CITLY, adv. *tacitamente, implicitamente.*

TACITU'RNITY, s. [close reserved humour] *taciturnità*, s. f.

TACK, s. [a small nail with a head] *agutello*, s. m.

To hold tack, *tener fermo.*

TACKS [ropes for carrying forward the clews of the sails] *armadure di vascello.*

To TACK [to fasten] *attaccare, appiccare, inchiodare.*

To tack together, *unire, accozzare insieme, cucire.*

To tack the ship [to bring the head of a ship so as to lie a contrary way] *dar la volta al vascello, girarlo.*

To tack about [to take other measures] *trovar altri mezzitermini, pigliar altre misure, cangiar di nota.*

TA'CKED, adj. *attaccato, appiccato*, v. To tack.

TA'CKLE-ROPES, } s. [small ropes
TA'CKLES, } of a ship] *funicelle di vascello, sartiame.*

TA'CKLING, s. [the ropes of a ship, whereby she is fitted for sailing] *sartiame di vascello, sarte.*

Tackling [things, goods] *robe, masserizie.*

Kitchen tackling, *arnesi di cucina.*

To look well to one's tackling, *badare a' fatti suoi, stare in cervello.*

To stand to one's tackling, *star sodo, tener duro, star sulla sua.*

TA'CTICAL, } adj. [relating to the
TA'CTICK, } art of ranging in battle] *appartenente all' arte dello schierare in battaglia.*

TA'CTICKS, s. [the art of ranging men in the field of battle] *l' arte dello schierare le truppe.*

TA'CTILE, adj. [that may be felt] *tangibile, che si può toccare, che cade sotto il senso del tatto.*

TA'CTION, s. [feeling, a word used in philosophy] *il tatto.*

TA'DPOLE, s. [young frog] *ranocchio, s. m. botta, s. f.*

TA'FFETA, } s. [a sort of silk] *taf-*
TA'FFETY, } *fettà, s. m. tela di seta leggerissima.*

TAG, s. [a point of lace] *puntale, s. m.*

The tag of a lace, *il puntale d' una stringa.*

A tag rag fellow, *un pezzente, un mendico, uno stracciato.*

To TAG, *metter il puntale.*

To tag a lace, *metter il puntale ad una stringa.*

TA'GTAIL, s. [a worm which has the tail of another colour] *verme che ha la coda di color differente da quello del corpo.*

TAIL, s. [the train of a beast, fowl, fish, &c.] *coda, s f.*

A fox's, dog's, or cat's tail, *la coda d' una volpe, d' un cane, d' un gatto.*

The tail of a letter, *il gambo d' una lettera.*

The plow tail, *il manico dell aratro.*

The tail of a gown, *la coda o lo strascico d' una gonna.*

Tail, s. *il deretano.*

To TAIL [to pull by the tail] *tirar per la coda.*

TA'ILED, adj. [that has a tail] *codato, che ha coda.*

TA'ILOR, *sarto, sartore.*

TAINT, s. [conviction] *prova di delitto.*

Taint [blur, spot] *macchia, taccia, infamia, s. f. disonore, s. m.*

To TAINT [to corrupt, to spoil] *putrefare, corrompere, guastare, pres. putrefò, pret. putrefeci, corruppi.*

Hot water taints the meat, *l' acqua calda putrefà la carne.*

To taint the blood, *corrompere il sangue.*

To taint [to corrupt, to bribe] *corrompere, guadagnar con donativi.*

TA'INTED, adj. [attainted, convicted of a crime] *convinto di qualche delitto.*

TA'INTED, adj. *putrefatto, corrotto, guastato, guasto.*

TA'INTLESS, adj. [free from infection] *non infetto, puro, immacolato, intemerato, incorrotto, incorruttibile.*

TA'INTURE, s. [taint, tinge, defilement] *macchia, bruttura, sporcizia, corruttela, immondizia, infezione.*

To TAKE [to lay hold on] *prendere, pigliare, pret. presi.*

To take physick, *prender medicina.*

To take upon tick [to take upon trust] *prendere a credito, pigliar a credenza.*

To take one's part, *pigliar la parte d' uno, tener per lui.*

I take him for my arbitrator, *io lo prendo per mio arbitro.*

To take one in the deed doing, *cogliere uno sul fatto, sorprenderlo.*

Whom do you take me to be? *con chi credete di trattare?*

Take my advice, *pigliate il mio consiglio, credete a me, fate come io vi dico.*

To take to heart, *prendere a cuore.*

To take a thing in good or ill part, *prender che che sia in buona o cattiva parte.*

You don't take it in a right sense, *voi l' intendete male.*

To take a town, *espugnare una città.*

To take heed, *aver cura, badare, stare in cervello, guardarsi.*

To take of one, *aver compassione d' uno, muoversi a pietà, muoversi a compassione.*

To take root, *radicare, abbarbicarsi.*

To take fire, *accendersi, appiccarsi il fuoco.*

The house took fire, *il fuoco s' appiecò alla casa.*

To take in marriage, *pigliar per moglie, sposare.*

She took a great affection to him, *ella concepì grande amore per lui.*

To take away one's life, *privar uno di vita.*

To take in writing, *mettere in iscritto.*

To take in pieces, *mettere in pezzi.*

I shall take it as a great favour, *lo terrò a gran favore.*

To take [to succeed] *riuscire, fare buona riuscita, aver buon successo.*

A book that takes, *un libro che ha buon successo, che si vende, che piace.*

This won't take with me [this pleases me not] *questo non mi quadra, non mi piace.*

To take towards a place, *incamminarsi verso qualche luogo.*

To take a turn, to take a walk, *fare una girata, una passeggiata.*

What course shall I take now? *che mi bisogna fare adesso?*

Let him take his swing, *farcia a modo suo.*

Take you no care of that, *non vi pigliate fastidio di questo.*

It took me a whole day to do it, *ho speso un giorno intero in farlo.*

To take hold of a thing, *prendere, afferrare una cosa, dar di mano ad una cosa.*

To take hold of an opportunity, *abbracciare un' opportunità.*

To take coach, *pigliare una carrozza.*

To take horse, *montare a cavallo.*

To take shipping, *imbarcarsi.*

To take one's chance, *rimettersi alla fortuna.*

To take offence at something, *tenersi offeso di qualche cosa.*

To take a thing into debate, *metter che che sia in consulta.*

To take a pride in a thing, *gloriarsi, vanagloriarsi, vantarsi di qualche cosa.*

Take my word for it, *statevene alla mia parola.*

He will take my word before your oath, *darà più credito alla mia semplice parola, che non al vostro giuramento.*

To take [to believe] *pensare, credere, imaginarsi, stimare.*

I take it to be the best way, *credo che questo sia il miglior modo.*

I take him for an honest man, *lo stimo un galantuomo.*

As I take it, *a mio parere, a mio giudizio*

What will you take for it? *quanto ne volete?*

I won't take under a guinea, *non voglio darlo per meno d' una ghinea.*

To take bad courses, *pigliar mala piega camminare al male.*

To take one's pleasure, *divertirsi, darsi bel tempo.*

To take one a box on the ear, *dare uno schiaffo ad uno.*

To take breath, *respirare, rifiatare.*

Take your choice, *scegliete.*

To take a disease in time, *rimediare di buon' ora ad una malattia.*

To take a thing kindly of one, *saper grado ad uno di qualche cosa.*

I take it very ill of you to use me in such a manner, *non è ben fatto di trattarmi in questo modo.*

To take the law of one [to go to law with him] *muover lite ad uno.*

To take the field, *uscire in campagna, accamparsi.*

To take effect, *aver effetto, riuscire.*

To take flesh, *incarnarsi.*

To take [to conceive, as a woman does] *concepire, divenir gravida.*

To take for granted, *supporre, presupporre, pres. suppongo, presuppongo, pret. supposi, presupposi.*

To take a thing into consideration, *considerare una cosa, esaminarla bene, farci riflessione su.*

To take a fancy to a thing, *metter amore a qualche cosa.*

To take a thing to pieces, *metter che che sia in pezzi, disfarlo.*

To take again, *riprendere, ripigliare.*

To take after one, *rassomigliare a qualcheduno.*

To take after the father, *padreggiare, esser ne' costumi simile al padre.*

To take after the mother, *madreggiare.*

To take asunder, *separare, mettere in pezzi.*

To take away [to clear the table] *sparecchiare.*

To

To take a thing down, *calare, abbassare, scendere che che sia.*

To take down one [to humble one] *abbassare, deprimere, umilare alcuno.*

To take in, *prendere*, pret. *presi.*

Take in some milk, *prendete del latte.*

To take in fresh water, *fare acqua, termine marinaresco.*

To take in hand, *intraprendere, pigliar a fare.*

To take one in [to admit one] *ammettor qualcheduno, riceverlo.*

To take off, *levare, toglier via.*

To take off one's hat, *levarsi il cappello.*

To take off the mask, *smascherarsi.*

To take off, *portar via.*

To take one off from his work, *distrarre, distorre alcuno dal suo lavoro.*

To take off the edge of a knife, *rintuzzare un coltello, ripiegare il taglio d' un coltello, togliergli il filo.*

To take off the skin, *levar la pelle, scorticare.*

To take one off from an ill course, *stornare alcuno da qualche vizio*

To take one off by death, *far morire alcuno.*

To take out, *tirare o cavar fuori.*

To take up arms, *prender le armi.*

This will take up a great deal of time, *questo richiederà gran tempo.*

To take state upon one's self, *sputar tondo, star sulla sua.*

To take up [to help to rise] *levare, alzare.*

To take one up sharply [to check, to reprimand one] *riprendere, sgridare alcuno acerbamente.*

To take up a sum of money, *pigliare in prestito una somma di danari.*

To take up [to busy, to keep employed] *impiegare, dar dell' impiego.*

To take up a trade, *intraprendere un negozio o un mestiere.*

To take up a quarrel [to adjust it] *aggiustare, accomodare una differenza, riconciliare, rappaciare.*

To take up a challenge, *accettare una disfida.*

To take a thing upon one's self [to undertake it] *intraprendere, addossarsi un negozio, prender l' incombenza.*

To take upon one the command of an army, *prender il comando d' un esercito*

He takes upon him to teach what he does not know, *s' ingerisce di voler insegnare quel che non sa.*

TAKEN, adj. *preso, v.* To take.

He was taken very ill, *egli s' ammalò gravemente.*

I am very much taken with her, *ella mi piace molto, ella mi va propio in verso.*

I am very much taken up, *sono molto affaccendato.*

TA'KER, s. *prenditore*, s. m. *prenditrice*, s. f.

TA'KING, s. *prendimento*, s. m. *il prendere, presa*, s. f.

Taking, adj. [pleasing] *piacevole, grato, cortese, avvenente.*

TA'LBOT, s. a dog with a turned up tail] *cane, che ha la coda inarcata, levriere.*

TALE, s. [story, fable] *novella, favola, baja*, s f.

An old woman's tale [a tale of a tub] *cosa da dire a vegghia, cose senza sustanza, cose vane.*

To tell tales, *novellare.*

To tell tales of one, *sparlar d' uno, dir delle bugie d' uno.*

Tale-bearer, } *un novellista, un novellatore, un che dice i fatti altrui, una spia.*
Tale-teller, }

Tale [number, reckoning] *conto, numero, calcolo, computo*, s. m.

TA'LENT, s. *talento*, s. m. *somma di moneta fra gli antichi.*

Talent [good parts, endowments] *talento*, s. m. *dono di natura, capacità, abilità*, s. f.

Talent [desire, inclination] *talento, desiderio, voglia, volontà.*

TA'LISMAN, s. [magical character] *talismanno, segno o carattere magico.*

TALISMA'NICK, adj. [magical] *magico, negromantesco.*

TALK, s. [discourse] *parlare, discorso, ragionamento.*

To be made a common talk, *far parlar di se.*

She is all the town talk, *non si parla d' altro per la città che di lei.*

I must have a little talk with you, *bisogna ch' io vi parli un poco.*

She is full of talk, *ella è una cicalona.*

Talk [a sort of mineral] *talco*, s. m.

To TALK [to speak, to discourse] *parlare, ragionare, discorrere.*

Let us talk of other things, *parliamo d' altro.*

To talk one out of his dinner, *impedire alcuno di pranzare col parlargli a tavola.*

TAKLATIVE, adj. [full of talk] *ciarliero.*

A talkative man, *un ciarliero, un ciarlatore.*

A talkative woman, *una ciarliera, una ciarlàtrice.*

TA'LKATIVENESS, s. *ciarla, ciarleria*, s. f. *cicaleccio, cicalio*, s. m.

TA'LKED, adj. *parlato, ragionato, discorso.*

A thing much talked of, *una cosa di cui si fa gran romore, della quale si parla molto.*

TA'LKER, s. *parlatore, ciarlatore, ciarlone, ciarliero*, s. m. *parlatrice, ciarliera, ciarlona*, s. f.

Talker, *uno che parla.*

Talker [a boaster, a bragging fellow] *un millantatore, un gradasso, uno smargiasso.*

The greatest talkers are always the least doers, *can ch' abbaja non morde.*

TA'LKING, s. *il parlare, discorso, ragionamento*, s. m.

Much talking, *cicaleccio, cicalio*, s. m. *ciarla, vana loquacità, ciarleria.*

TA'LKY, adj. [consisting of talk] *che è fatto di talco.*

TALL, adj. [high in stature] *alto, grande.*

Tall man, tall woman, *uomo alto, donna alta.*

TA'LLAGE, s. [custom, impost] *tassa, taglia, imposizione, gravezza*, s. f.

TA'LLEY, } s. [a cleft piece of wood
TA'LLY, } to score up an account upon the notches] *taglia, tacca, tessera*, s. f. *legnetto diviso per lo lungo in due parti, sulle quali si fanno certe tacche per memoria di coloro che danno e ricevono roba a credenza.*

TA'LLON, s. [a claw of a bird of prey] *artiglio*, s. m.

TA'LLOW, s. [the fat of beasts melted] *sevo, sego*, s. m.

A tallow-chandler, *candelajo*, s. m. *colui che fa o vende candele di sevo.*

To TA'LLOW [to do over with tallow] *insevare, coprir di sego.*

TA'LLOWED, adj *insevato.*

TA'LLOWISH, adj. *pieno di sevo.*

To TA'LLY [to score upon a talley] *segnare sopra una taglia, tagliare.*

Tally the sheets [a word of command, when the sheets of the main sail are to be haled off] *ammaina, voce di comando sul mare.*

TA'LNESS, s. [the state of being tall] *altezza, grandezza, statura grande*, s. f.

TA'LWOOD, s. [fire-wood cleft and cut in billets] *legna*, s. f.

TA'MARIND, s. [a sort of Indian tree] *tamarindo*, s. m.

TA'MARISK, s. [a sort of shrub] *tamarisco*, s. m. *tamerice, e tamerigia*, s. f. *arbuscello noto.*

TAME, adj. [gentle, not wild] *domato, domo, ammansato, domestico, dimestico, addimesticato, mansueto.*

Tame beasts, *animali domestici.*

A tame lion, *un lione addomesticato.*

A tame horse, *un cavallo domato.*

Tame [humble] *umile, sommesso, docile, trattabile.*

To grow tame, *addomesticarsi, dimesticarsi.*

To tame [to make tame] *domare, rendere mansueto* e trattabile, *addimesticare, dimesticare, ammansare.*

To tame [to humble, to conquer] *domare, rintuzzare, mortificare, umiliare, ammansare.*

To tame one's own passions, *domare, rintuzzare le proprie passioni.*

TAMED, adj. *domato, rintuzzato, mortificato, umiliato, ammansato, addomesticato, dimesticato.*

TA'MEABLE, adj. [susceptible of taming] *domabile.*

TA'MELY, adv. *mansuetamente, umilmente, sommessamente.*

Tamely [cowardly] *vilmente, da vile, vigliaccamente, da vigliacco.*

TA'MENESS, s. *domestichezza, mansuetudine*, s. f.

TA'MER, s. *domatore*, s. m. *domatrice*, s. f.

To TA'MPER [to practise upon, to endeavour, to draw in, or bring over] *tener pratica con alcuno, sollecitarlo, tirarlo dalla sua, tastargli il polso.*

To tamper with a disease, *usar vari medicamenti nella cura d' una malattia.*

TA'MPERED with, *praticato, sollecitato.*

TA'MPIN, } s. [a stopple made for
TAMPING, } the mouth of a great gun] *turacciolo col quale si tura la bocca del cannone.*

TA'MY, s. [a sort of stuff] *spezie di pannina.*

TAN, s. [the bark of a young oak beaten small, and used by curriers] *concia,* s. f. *materia, onde si concian le pelli.*

To TAN [to dress hides with tan] *conciare.*

To tan [to burn as the sun does] *abbronzare, abbrustiare.*

Tan-vat, tan pit, *concia,* s. f. *calcinajo,* s. m. *luogo dove si metton le cuoja per conciarle.*

TANE, adj. *è participio del verbo* to take, *ed è capricciosamente o per me' dire seconda la più plebea pronuncia detto invece di* ta'en, *abbreviatura di* taken.

TANG, s. [rank taste] *tanfo,* s. m.

Tang, s. [a strong taste, a taste left in the mouth] *gusto forte, gusto lasciato nella bocca da cose forti, come le medicinali, e simili.*

Tang [taste, relish] *gusto, sapore.*

Tang, *cosa che lascia un po' di coeiore o dolore dietro di se.*

Tang [sound, tone] *suono, tintinno.*

To TANG, v. n. [to ring with] *tintinnare, suonare, e dicesi delle campane e simili.*

TA'NGENT, s. [right line drawn without a circle, perpendicular to some radius or semi-diameter] *tangente,* s. f.

TANGIBI'LITY, s. *qualità tangibile.*

TA'NGIBLE, adj. [that may be touched] *tangibile, che si può torcare, che cade sotto il tatto, toccabile.*

TAN-HOUSE, s. *concia,* s. f. *luogo, dove si concian le pelli.*

TANK, s. [cistern to keep water in] *cisterna da tenervi acqua.*

TA'NKARD, s. [a drinking pot with a hinged cover] *boccale.*

A silver tankard, *un boccale d' argento.*

TA'NNED, adj. [from to tan] *conciato.*

Tanned [tawny] *abbronzato, abbrustiato.*

TA'NNER, s. *conciatore, pelacane,* s. m. *quegli che concia le pelli.*

TA'NSY, s. [an herb] *tanceto,* s. m. *spezie d' erba.*

To TA'NTALIZE [to make one eager for a thing and yet not suffer him to enjoy it] *allettare, invitare, chiamare, incitare con piacevolezza e lusinghe a qualche cosa e poi deludere.*

TA'NTAMOUNT, adj. [equivalent] *equivalente, che vale altrettanto.*

TANTI'VY, s. [full gallop] *gran galoppo.*

To ride tantivy, *galoppare a briglia sciolta.*

Tantivy [nick-name given to a worldly minded churchman, who bestirs himself for preferment] *un ecclesiastico che corre dietro a' beneficj.*

TAP, s. [a faucet to draw liquor out of a vessel] *cannella,* s. f. *quel legno bucato per lo quale s' attigne il vino nella botte.*

Tap-house [ale-house] *taverna da birra.*

Tap [blow] *botta, percossa, bussa,* s. f.

To TAP [to broach a vessel] *spillare una botte, metter mano ad una botte.*

To tap [to give a blow] *battere, percuotere,* pret. *percossi.*

To tap a tree [to open it round about the root] *scalzare un albero, levar la terra intorno alla barbe d' un albero.*

TAPE, s. [a sort of ribbon] *fettuccia di filo; usasi per lo più ad effetto di orlare.*

TA'PER, s. [torch, large wax-candle] *cero,* s. m. *candela grande di cera.*

Taper or tapering, adj. [broad beneath, and sharp towards the top] *conico, piramidale.*

TA'PESTRY, s. [manufacture in worsted, silk, silver and gold thread, to adorn a room by covering its walls] *tappezzeria,* s. f. *arazzo,* s. m. *paramento da stanza.*

To hang a room with tapestry, *tappezzare una stanza.*

Tapestry-maker, *quello che lavora di tappezzeria.*

TA'PPED, adj. [from to tap] *spillato.*

To TA'PPY [to lie hid] *appiattarsi, nascondersi.*

TA'PSTER, s. [drawer of drink at an inn or ale-house] *colui che tira da bere in una osteria, o cantina.*

TA'PTOW, *ritirata,* s. f.

To beat the taptow, *batter la ritirata.*

TAR, s. [a sort of liquid pitch] *pece liquida.*

To do over with pitch and tar, *spalmare.*

To TAR [to do over with tar] *spalmare, impeciare.*

TARA'NTULA, s. [a kind of spider, speckled with white and black, whose bite is of such a nature, that it is to be cured only by music] *tarantola,* s. f. *insetto simile al ragno, di color bianchiccio, chiazzato, quasi come di lentiggine, la di cui morsicatura è di tal natura che non si guarisce se non col suono.*

Bitten by a tarantula, *tarantolato, morso dalla tarantola.*

TA'RDILY, adv. [slowly] *tardamente, lentamente, pigramente.*

TA'RDINESS, s. [slowness] *tardezza, tardanza, lentezza,* s. f.

TA'RDY, adj. [dull, slow] *tardo, pigro, lento, negligente.*

A tardy wit, *un ingegno ottuso.*

To TA'RDY, [to delay, to hinder] *ritardare, impedire.*

TARE, s. [the weight or allowance made to the buyer for the weight of the cask, chest, bag, &c. in which any goods are put or packed up, or a consideration in the weight for waste in emptying and selling goods] *tara,* s. f.

TARE, *è un preterito del verbo* to tear.

To TARE, verb act. *tarare.*

Tares, s. pl. [a sort of vetches] *loglio,* s. m. *erba che nasce tra le biade.*

TA'RGET, s. [a great shield or buckler] *targa,* s. f. *spezie da scudo.*

A wooden target, *un tavolaccio.*

TA'RIFF, s. [a book of rates agreed upon between princes or states, for duties to be laid upon their respective merchandizes] *tariffa,* s. f.

To TA'RNISH [to lose its lustre or brightness, to grow dull] *appannarsi, scolorirsi, perder il lustro.*

To tarnish [speaking of gold or silver wire] *rugginirsi, irrugginirsi.*

To tarnish [speaking of a glass] *appannarsi.*

To tarnish, *oscurare, scolorire.*

To tarnish one's reputation, *macchiare, oscurare l' altrui reputazione, appannarla.*

TA'RNISHED, adj. *appannato, oscurato, scolorito.*

TARPA'WLING, s. [a tarred canvass laid on the deck of a ship to keep the rain out] *tela incerata la quale si spande sopra il ponte del vascello per di fenderlo dalla pioggia.*

A tarpawling [a downright seaman] *un vero marinajo.*

TA'RRED, adj. *spalmato, impeciato.*

TA'RRAGON, s. [dragon-wort] *targone,* s. m. *erba odorifera e di sapore acuto.*

To TA'RRY [to stay, to lag, to loiter] *tardare, indugiare, trattenersi, fermarsi.*

Do not tarry, *non tardate, non indugiate a venire.*

We tarried there three days, *noi ci fermammo quivi tre giorni.*

Tarry for me here, *aspettatemi qui.*

TART, adj. [sharp, eager in taste] *agro, brusco, aspro, acerbo.*

Tart fruit, *frutto agro o acerbo.*

Tart wine, *vino piccante.*

Tart words, *parole aspre.*

To be tart with one, *aspreggiare alcuno, proceder con asprezza verso lui, trattarlo con asprezza.*

To give one a tart answer, *rispondere bruscamente ad uno.*

TART, s. [a pie made of fruit] *torta,* s. f.

Apple-tart, *torta di pomi.*

Tart-pan, *tortiera.*

TA'RTANE, s. [a vessel used in the Mediterranean sea] *tartana,* s. f. *barca grossa, in uso nel mar Mediterraneo.*

TA'RTAR, s. [a sort of salt arising from reaking wines, that hardens into a crust, and sticks to the sides of the vessel] *tartaro,* s. m. *gromma di botte.*

To catch a Tartar [to meet one's match] *trovar carne pe' suoi denti.*

To catch a Tartar [to be disappointed] *restar con un palmo di naso.*

TARTA'REAN, adj. [hellish] *tartareo, infernale.*

TA'RTAROUS, adj. [full of tartar] *pieno di tartaro.*

TA'RTLY, adv. [sharply] *agramente, aspramente, bruscamente, mordacemente.*

TA'RTNESS, s. [sharpness] *asprezza, acerbità, agrezza*, s. f.

TA'RTISH, adj. [somewhat tart] *agretto, bruschetto, aspretto.*

TASK, s. [a determinate portion of work laid upon or required of a person] *carico, parte.*

Hard task, *cosa malagevole a fare.*

To take one to task for a thing, *sgridare alcuno per qualche cosa, farli una ripassata, riprenderlo.*

TA'SSEL, s [a male hawk] *terzuolo*, s. m. *il maschio dell' astore.*

Tassel, s. [an ornamental bunch of silk or glittering substances] *fiocco, o frangia di seta, d' oro, o d' argento.*

Tassel, s. [a small ribbon or silk sewed to a book, to put between the leaves] *nastro che si cuce al libro, per aprirlo facilmente.*

The tassels of a coach, *fiocchi di carrozza.*

Tassel [a kind of hard bur used by clothworkers in dressing cloth] *cardo col quale si cava fuori il pelo a' panni.*

TA'SSELLED, adj. [adorned with tassels] *ornato di fiocchi, frangie, e simili.*

TA'SSES, s. [armour for the thighs] *cosciali, armatura delle coscie.*

TA'STABLE, adj. [that may be tasted, savoury] *che può esser assaggiato, saporoso.*

TASTE, s. [savour, relish] *gusto, sapore*, s. m.

To be out of taste, *essere svogliato.*

This has put my mouth out of taste, *questa cosa mi ha guasto il palato.*

Taste [discerning faculty] *gusto.*

To have a good taste for painting, *aver buon gusto in pittura, esser intelligente nella pittura.*

To have a taste of a thing, *aver una vena di qualche cosa.*

This wine has a little taste of the wood, *questo vino ha una vena del legno.*

To TASTE [to try the taste of a thing by the palate or tongue] *gustare, assaggiare.*

Taste that wine, *assaggiate questo vino.*

To taste, verb neut. *aver qualche gusto.*

This wine tastes well, *questo vino ha buon gusto.*

TA'STED, adj. *gustato, assaggiato.*

Well tasted, *gustoso, che ha buon gusto, gustevole.*

Ill tasted, *ingrato, che ha cattivo gusto.*

TA'STER, s. *gustatore*, s. m.

The king's taster, *colui che assaggia le vivande del re.*

Taster [a litle cup to taste a liquor with] *saggiuolo*, s. m.

TA'STING, s. *gustamento*, s. m. *il gustare.*

The sense of tasting, *il gusto.*

TA'STELESS, adj. *che non ha verun gusto, insipido.*

TA'TOUS, s. [an American wild beast, covered with scales like armour] *sorta d' animale in America, di grandezza come un porcelletto, che ha la pelle coperta di scaglie.*

TA'TTER, s. [rag] *cencio, straccio*, s. m.

TATTER-DE-MA'LLION [a ragged shabby fellow] *uno stracciato, un mendico, un pezzente, un cencioso.*

TA'TTERED, adj. *stracciato, cencioso, coperto di renci.*

Tattered cloaths, *abiti stracciati, o cenciosi.*

To TA'TLLE [to chate, to prate] *ciarlare, cornacchiare, cicalare, cinguettare, chiacchierare.*

Tattle-basket [a tattling man or woman] *un chiacchierone, un ciarliero, un ciarlone, un cicalone; una ciarlatrice, una ciarliera, una chiacchierona.*

TA'TTLER, s. *un cicalone, un chiacchierone, un ciarliero.*

TA'TTLING, s. *cicaleria, cicalata, ciarleria*, s. f. *cicaleccio, cicalio*, s. m.

TA'TTLING, adj. *ciarliero.*

TATTO'O, s. [the beat of drum by which soldiers are warned to their quarters] *quel suonar di tamburo che avverte i soldati di ritirarsi a' loro quartieri.*

TA'UDRY, adj. [ridiculously gay] *sfoggiato, troppo pomposo.*

TAUDRY cloaths, *abiti sfoggiati.*

A taudry woman, *una donna che veste sfoggiatamente.*

TA'VERN, s. [a house where wine is sold] *taverna, osteria*, s. f.

Tavern-haunter, *quegli che frequenta le taverne.*

Tavern keeper, *un tavernajo*, s. m. *quegli che tien taverna.*

TAUGHT, adj. [from to teach] *insegnato*, v. To teach.

You are better fed than taught, *voi avete più danari che buoni costumi.*

Taught [a sea term, tight, stiff] *steso, duro.*

TAUNT, s. [reproachful biting jest] *motto, detto pungente, bottone*, s. m.

To TAUNT [to joke sharply upon] *motteggiare, burlare, sbottonare, sbottoneggiare.*

Taunt-masted [speaking of a ship, when she has the mast too tall for her] *che ha l' albero troppo grande, parlando d' un vascello.*

TA'UNTED, adj. *motteggiato, burlato, sbottonato, sbottoneggiato*

TA'UNTER, s. *motteggiatore, burlone.*

TA'UNTING, s. *motteggio*, s. m. *burla*, s. f.

TA'UNTINGLY, adv. *in burla, da scherzo.*

TA'URUS, s. [one of the twelve celestial signs] *tauro*, s. m. *uno de' dodici segni celesti.*

To TAUTO'LOGIZE [to use tautology] *usar soverchieria di parole, ridire le medesime cose.*

TAUTO'LOGY, s. [repetition of something over again] *soverchieria di parole, ripetizione di parole.*

TAW, s. [a marble to play with] *pezzo di marmo con cui si giuoca.*

To TAW [to tan, to dress leather] *conriare, e dicesi solo del conciar con allume e render la pelle bianca, che quando vuoi* CONCIARE *colla concia solita e grossolana di scorza d' albero o simili allora si dice* to tan.

TAWNED, adj *conciato.*

TA'WNER, s. *conciatore, pelacane*, s. m. *quegli che concia le pelli.*

TA'WNY, adj. [that is of a tanned yellowish colour] *bruno, fosco, abbronzato.*

Tawny complexion, *carnagione bruna, abbronzata.*

TAX, s. [tribute, duty] *tassa, imposizione, gabella*, s. f.

Land-tax, *tassa sopra i beni stabili.*

Tax-gatherer, *collettore delle tasse.*

To tax [to lay a tax] *tassare, ordinare le tasse.*

To tax one with a thing, *tassare, tacciare, accusare alcuno di qualche cosa.*

To tax [to blame] *biasimare.*

TA'XABLE, adj [liable to taxes] *soggetto alle tasse.*

TAXA'TION, s. *tassagione, tassazione*, s. f *il tassare, tassa.*

TA'XED, adj. *tassato*, v. To tax.

TA'XING, s. *tassagione, tassa, il tassare.*

TAYL, v. Tail.

TA'YLOR, s. [one that makes cloaths] *sartore, sarto*, s. m.

Man's taylor, *sartore da uomo.*

Woman's taylor, *sartore da donna.*

TA'ZEL, s. [a kind of hard bur used by cloath-makers] *cardo*, s. m.

TEA, s. [an Indian shrub, or the leaf of it] *tè*, s. m. *arbuscello Indiano, o le sue foglie.*

Tea [a known liquor, made of the leaves of the tea-shrub] *tè, bevanda fatta colle foglie del tè.*

To TEACH [to instruct in literature, trade, art, or science] *insegnare, ammaestrare, istruire*, pres. *istruisco.*

To teach one to read and write, *insegnare a leggere e a scrivere ad alcuno.*

Teach me how to do it, *mostratemi come devo farlo.*

To teach one's grandam to grope ducks, or teach one's grandam to suck, *i paperi voglion menar a bere l' oche, gl' ignoranti vogliono insegnare a' dotti.*

TEACHABLE, adj. [apt to learn] *insegnevole, docile, atto ad apprendere insegnamento.*

TE'ACHER, s. [he that teaches] *insegnatore, che insegna, maestro*, s. m.

Teacher [preacher] *predicatore.*

Teacher [in a school] *sottomaestro.*

TE'ACHING, s. *insegnamento, documento, ammaestramento, l' insegnare*, s. m.

TEAD or TEDE, s. [a torch, a flambeau] *torcia o torchio. Noi diciamo poeticamente le nuziali* Tede.

TEAL, s. [a wild fowl] *farchetola*, s. f. *uccello d' acqua.*

TEAM, s. [a certain number of horses for drawing] *tiro*, s. m.

A team of horses, *una tiro di cavalli.*

A team of oxen [to draw the plough] *una pajo di buoi.*

A team of ducks, *una covata d' anitre.*

TEAR, s. *lagrima*, s. f. *pianto*, s. m.

To shed tears, *versar lagrime, lagrimare, piangere, piagnere.*

Full of tears, *lagrimoso, piangente.*

To TEAR [to rend, to pull in pieces] *stracciare, squarciare, sbranare.*

To tear one to pieces, *ſtranare alcuno, metterlo in pezzi.*

To tear, verb neut. *ſtracciarſi.*

TE'ARING, s. *ſtracciamento,* s. m. *lo ſtracciare.*

Tearing [a thing torn] *ſtracciatura,* s. f. *rottura che riman nella coſa ſtracciata.*

Tearing, adj. *forte, acuto,* ex. a tearing voice, *voce forte, acuta, ſottile.*

A tearing laſs, *una fanciulla tutta brio.*

Tearing, adj. ex. ſhe goes tearing fine, *ella è ſempre attillatiſſima.*

TEAT, s. [dug] *mammella, tetta, poppa,* s. f.

To TEAZE [to diſquiet, to vex] *affannare, affliggere, tormentare, penare, angoſciare, cruciare.*

TE'AZED, adj. *affannato, afflitto, tormentato, penato, angoſciato, cruciato.*

TE'ASIL, v. Taſſel.

TE'CHINESS, s. [frowardneſs] *fantaſticaggine, ſdegnoſità,* s. f. *faſtidiomodo di proceder faſtidioſo.*

TE'CHNICAL, adj. [belonging to the terms and rules of arts and ſciences] *appartenente a qualche arte o ſcienza.*

Technical word, *termine d' arte.*

TE'CHY, adj. [forward, apt to find fault with every thing] *aromatico, diſpettoſo, fantaſtico, ſdegnoſo, faſtidioſo, oſtico, ſpiacevole, ritroſo.*

To TED [to turn or ſpread new mown graſs] *voltare o ſpandere l'erba freſcamente mietuta.*

TE'DDER, v. Tether.

TE'DIOUS, adj. [irkſome, weariſome] *tedioſo, nojoſo, faſtidioſo, ſpiacevole, rincreſcevole.*

Tedious [over long] *tedioſo, lungo.*

Tedious preacher, *predicatore tedioſo.*

Tedious diſcourſe, *diſcorſo tedioſo, nojoſo.*

TE'DIOUSLY, adv. *nojoſamente, faſtidioſamente, ſpiacevolmente.*

TE'DIOUSNESS, s. *tedio, faſtidio, annojamento, rincreſcimento,* s. f. *increſcenza, ſpiacevolezza, noja,* s. f.

To TEEM [to be pregnant] *eſſer gravido.*

TE'EMING, adj. *fertile, fecondo, parlando d' una donna.*

Teeming [fruitful] *fertile, fecondo, abbondante, copioſo.*

TE'EMLESS, adj. [unfruitful, not prolifick] *infruttuoſo, non prolifico.*

TEEN, s. [ſorrow, grief] *dolore, affanno.*

To TEEN [to excite, to provoke to do a thing] *eccitare, incoraggire a fare.*

TEENS, s. *gli anni quando contati dalle terminazioni in* teen, *che ſono* thirteen, fourteen, fifteen, ſixteen, ſeventeen, eighteen, *e* nineteen, *e quando ſi dice una Giovane è ne' ſuoi* teens, *s' intende generalmente che la è da marito.*

TIER, s. *batteria di cannoni ſopra un vaſcello.*

TEETH, *denti, è il numero del più di* Tooth.

TEIL-TREE, s. [linden-tree] *tiglio,* s. m. *albero noto.*

TE'LESCOPE, s. [a perſpective glaſs] *teleſcopio,* s. m.

To TELL [to ſay, to declare] *dire, dichiarare.*

To tell one's opinion, *dire la ſua opinione.*

To tell [to ſhow] *moſtrare, far vedere.*

That very thing tells us who you are, *queſto ci fa vedere chi voi ſiete.*

To tell [to count, to compute] *contare, numerare.*

To tell [to recount, to relate] *dire, raccontare, narrare, recitare.*

To tell news, *dire delle novelle.*

To tell a ſtory, *narrare, racontare una ſtorietta.*

To tell ſtories of one, *dire, raccontar coſe falſe di qualcheduno.*

To tell one what he ſhall write, *dettare a qualcheduno quel che deve ſcrivere.*

My conſcience tells me quite contrary, *la coſcienza mi detta tutto 'l contrario.*

To tell one of his faults, *avvertire, ammonire alcuno de' ſuoi* errori.

I cannot tell what I muſt do, *non ſo che farmi.*

No body can tell, *neſſuno ſa.*

I cannot tell, *non ſo.*

Tell tale, s. *quegli che parlando teco dice mal del tuo avverſario, e all' incontro al tuo avverſario dire male di te.*

TE'LLER, s. *dicitore,* s. m.

A fortune-teller, *un aſtrolago, uno ſtrolago.*

A teller of money, *un che conta de' danari.*

Tellers of the exchequer, *i pagatori e ricevitori dell' erario pubblico.*

Tale-teller, *novelliſta.*

TE'LLING, s. *dicimento,* s. m. *dicitura,* s. f.

TEMERA'RIOUS, adj. [raſh] *temerario, troppo ardito, imprudente, inconſiderato.*

TEME'RITY, s. [raſhneſs] *temerità, ardir ſoverchio, inconſiderazione, audacia,* s. f.

TE'MPER, s. [conſtitution] *tempera, tempra,* s. f. *temperamento* s. m.

To be in good temper, *eſſer in buona tempra.*

Temper [nature, humour, genius] *tempra, diſpoſizione, natura,* s. f. *umore,* s. m.

To be of a good temper, *eſſer di buona tempra, di buon umore.*

To be out of temper, *eſſer di cattivo umore, crucccioſo, crucciato.*

The temper of iron or ſteel, *tempera di ferro o d' acciajo.*

To TEMPER [to moderate] *temperare, temprare, moderare, raffrenare.*

To temper [to qualify] *temprare,* correggere, *adequare il ſoverchio di che che ſia colla forza del ſuo contrario.*

To temper iron or ſteel, *temprar del ferro o del' acciajo.*

To temper [to ſeaſon] *condire, ſtagionare,* pref. *condiſco.*

To temper colours [as painters do] *ſtemperare* i *colori.*

TEMPE'RAMENT, s. [habitude or natural conſtitution of the body] *temperamento,* s. m. *compleſſione,* s. f.

Temperament [proportionable mixture of any thing] *temperamento,* s. m. *tempra, tempera,* s. f.

Temperament [means found out in a buſineſs or controverſy] *temperamento, accomodamento, mezzo, mezzo termine, modo,* s. m. *via,* s. f.

TE'MPERANCE, s. [moderation, ſoberneſs, reſtraint of affections or paſſions] *temperanza, virtù morale che è ſtrignimento del diſordinato appetito nella potenza concupiſcibile, moderazione,* s. f.

TE'MPERATE, adj. [neither too hot nor too cold] *temperato, nè troppo caldo, nè troppo freddo.*

Temperate country, *paeſe temperato.*

Temperate weather, *tempo temporato.*

Temperate [ſober] *temperato, ſobrio, moderato.*

TE'MPERATELY, adv. *temperatamente, con tempramento, moderatamente.*

TE'MPERATENESS, s. [temperance of the air] *temperie,* s. f. *temperamento d' aria.*

TEMPE'RATURE, s. [conſtitution of nature; degree of any qualities] *tempera o tempra, grado di qualſiſia qualità.*

Temperature [mediocrity, due ballance of contrarieties] *mediocrità, tempra, bilanciamento proporzionato di coſe fra di loro contrarie.*

Temperature [moderation, freedom from predominant paſſion] *tempra, moderazion d' animo.*

TE'MPERED, adj. *temperato, temprato, v.* To temper.

TE'MPERING, s. *temperatura, tempera,* s. f. *il temperare.*

TE'MPEST, s. [ſtorm] *tempeſta, burraſca, procella,* s. f.

To raiſe a tempeſt, *ſuſcitare una tempeſta.*

A tempeſt of rain, *tempeſta, gragnuola,* s. f. *nembo,* s. m.

A tempeſt of wind, *procella,* s. f. *turbine,* s. m.

TEMPE'STUOUS, adj. [ſtormy] *tempeſtoſo, procelloſo.*

Tempeſtuous ſea, *mar tempeſtoſo, procelloſo, burraſcoſo.*

TE'MPLAR, s. [a knight templar] *templare,* s. m. *ſorta di cavaliere religioſo ne' di delle crociate.*

TE'MPLE, s. [church] *tempio, templo,* s. m. *chieſa,* s. f.

The temple of Jeruſalem, *il tempio di Geruſalemme.*

Temporal [a lateral part of the ſkull in the middle between the ears and the eyes] *tempia,* s. f. *parte della teſta poſta tra l' occhio, e l' orecchio.*

TE'MPORAL, adj. [that continues for a certain time] *temporale, che dura a tempo, non perpetuo.*

Temporal [ſecular, in oppoſition to ſpiritual] *temporale, ſecorale.*

Temporal [worldly] *temporale, caduco, mondano.*

TEMPORA'LITIES, s. [the temporal eſtate of the church or churchmen] *temporalità, il temporale, i beni temporali,* *entra-*

entrata temporale di chiese o d' ecclesiastici.

TEMPORALLY, adv. *temporalmente, a tempo, non eternamente, secolarmente, mondanamente.*

TEMPORA'NEOUS, } adj. [that lasts TE'MPORARY, } but for some time] *temporale, che dura a tempo, non perpetuo.*

To TE'MPORIZE [to comply with times] *temporeggiare, secondare il tempo, governarsi secondo l' opportunità, navigar secondo il vento.*

TEMPORI'ZER, s. [time-server] *colui che temporeggia, che seconda il tempo.*

TEMPORI'ZING, s. *il temporeggiare.*

To TEMPT [to allure, to entice] *tentare, importunare, istigare, sollecitare.*

To TEMPT [to invite] *tentare, invitare, eccitare, provocare.*

TEMPTA'TION, s. [tempting] *tentazione, s. f. il tentare.*

To yield to temptation, *soccombere alla tentazione.*

TE'MPTED, adj. *tentato, v.* To tempt.

TE'MPTER, s. *tentatore, s. f. che tenta.*

The tempter [the devil] *il tentatore, il diavolo.*

TE'MPTING, s. *tentamento, il tentare.*

Tempting, adj. [inviting] *tentante, che invita, che alletta, che piace.*

TEN, adj. *dieci.*

Ten times, *dieci volte.*

TE'NABLE, adj. [that may be held or maintained] *che si può tenere o conservare.*

Tenable place, *piazza che si può mantenere, che può far resistenza.*

This opinion is not tenable, *questa non è opinione da sostenere.*

TENA'CIOUS, adj. [that holds fast] *tenace, viscoso, tegnente, che agevolmente s' attacca.*

Tenacious of his liberty [that keeps it with might and main] *tenace, geloso della sua libertà.*

Tenacious [close fisted, covetous] *tenace, stretto, avaro, tanghero.*

TENA'CIOUSLY, adv. *tenacemente, con tenacità.*

TENA'CITY, s. [the state of being tenacious] *tenacità, viscosità, s. f.*

Tenacity [nigardliness] *tenacità, strettezza, avarizia.*

TE'NANCY, s. [a dwelling-house held of another] *casa che teniamo d' un altro.*

TE'NANT, s. [one who holds or possesses lands by any kind of right] *ogni persona che possiede terre o case, sia per diritto d' eredità, sia per dono, o per compra.*

Tenant [that holds land for a certain rent he pays to the landlord] *fittuario, fittajuolo, s. m. quegli, che tiene l' altrui possessione a fitto.*

Tenant [that holds by homage] *feudatario, vassallo.*

Tenant [that holds a house] *pigionale, s. m. che tiene casa a pigione.*

TENCH, s. [a fresh water fish] *tinca, s. f. spezie di pesce d' acqua dolce.*

To TEND [to incline, to draw to, to aim at] *tendere, aver la mira.*

I know not what your discourse tends to, *non so dove il vostro discorso vada a parare.*

To tend [to take care of, to look to] *attendere, badare, curare, aver cura.*

To tend a sick body, *aver cura d'un ammalato, curarlo, servirlo.*

To tend the cattle, *guardare il bestiame.*

TE'NDANCE, s. [attendance, state of expectation] *aspettativa.*

Tendance [person, attendant] *colui che sta intorno a un altro per corteggiarlo o per servirlo.*

Tendance [act of waiting] *lo stare aspettando.*

Tendance [care, act of waiting] *cura, sollecitudine usata intorno a qualcuno.*

TE'NDENCE, } [inclination, aim, TE'NDENCY, } drift] *inclinazione, propensione, s. f.*

TE'NDER, adj. [soft] *tenero, che non è duro.*

Tender age, tender years, *tenera età, la gioventù, l' età giovanile.*

Tender [nice, the contrary of hardy] *tenero, delicato, morbido.*

Tender [kind, good-natured] *tenero amorevole.*

He has a tender heart, *egli ha un cuor tenero.*

She has a tender love for her children, *ella ama teneramente i suoi figliuoli.*

Tender words, *parole tenere.*

I have a tender regard for your reputation, *io sono molto geloso della vostra fama.*

Tender conscience, *coscienza tenera o delicata.*

Tender eyed, *che ha gli occhi teneri o delicati.*

Tender-hearted, *sensibile, pietoso, che ha il cuor tenero, compassionevole, affettuoso.*

Tender-heartedness, *tenerezza, compassione, affetto.*

To make tender, *intenerire, ammollire,* pref. *intenerisco, ammollisco.*

Somewhat tender, *tenerello.*

Tender, s. [nurse of sick people] *persona che attende agli ammalati.*

Tender [offer] *offerta, s. f.*

To TE'NDER [to offer] *offrire, presentare.*

To tender an averment in law, *proferire le prove in giudicio.*

To render [to indulge] *trattar teneramente, con tenerezza.*

To tender [to love] *amare, portar amore, aver della tenerezza.*

As you tender your life do not do it, *per vita vostra non fate ciò.*

As they tender his majesty's displeasure, *sotto pena d' incorrere l' indignazione o la disgrazia di sua maestà.*

TE'NDERED, adj. *offerto.*

TE'NDERLING, s. [the first horns of a deer] *le corna tenere che prima spuntano ad un cervo o daino.*

TE'NDERLY, adv. *teneramente, con tenerezza, affettuosamente.*

TE'NDERNESS, s. [softness] *tenerezza, delicatezza.*

Tenderness [indearingness] *tenerezza, compassione, s. f. affetto, s. m.*

Tenderness of conscience, *delicatezza di coscienza.*

TE'NDON, s. [the extremity of a muscle where its fibres run into a strong springy chord] *téndine, s. m. termine anatomico.*

TE'NDRIL, s. [young shoot or sprig of a tree] *tenerume, s. m. ramo tenero degli alberi.*

Tendril [the clasp of a vine or other climbing plant] *pámpino di vite o d' altra pianta serpeggiante all' insù.*

TENEBRO'SITY, s. [darkness] *tenebre, s. f. pl. bujo, s. m.*

TE'NEBROUS, adj. [dark] *tenebroso, pien di tenebre, bujo, oscuro.*

TE'NEMENT, s. [the house or land which a man holds of another] *case, possessioni che uno tiene d' un altro.*

TENET, s. [doctrine, opinion] *dottrina, opinione, s. f.*

TE'NNIS, } s. *pallacorda.* TE'NNIS BALL, }

Tennis-play, *giuoco di pallacorda.*

Tennis-court, *il luogo dove si giuoca alla pallacorda.*

TE'NON, s. [that part of a post or rafter which is put into a mortise-hole] *arpione, s. m.*

TE'NOUR, s. [intent, meaning] *tenore, suggetto, contenuto, s. m.*

Tenour [order, fashion] *tenore, forma, maniera.*

The tenour of his words, *il senso delle sue parole.*

Tenour [in musick, that part next to the bass] *tenore, quella parte che si canta dalla voce che è in mezzo tra il basso, e il soprano.*

TENSE, s. [a term of grammar] *tempo, s. m. termine gramaticale.*

Tense, adj. *esteso, teso.*

TE'NSIBLE, adj. [capable of being extended] *suscettibile di tensione.*

TE'NSION, s. [bending or stretching out] *tensione, s. f.*

TENT, s. [pavilion] *tenda, s. f. padiglione, s. m.*

Tent-cloth, *foltero, s f.*

Tent [for a wound] *tasta, s. f.*

Tent [a sort of Spanish wine, of a deep red] *sorta di vino dolcissimo che viene d' Alicante.*

Tent-wort [a plant] *rapelvenere, s. m. spezie d' erba.*

TENTA'TION, s. [tryal] *saggio*, s. m. *prova*, *tentativa*, s. m.

TE'NTER, } *uncino*, *rampino*.
TE'NTER-HOOK, }

TENTH, adj. *decimo*.

TE'NTHLY, adv. *in decimo luogo*.

TENTHS, s. [that yearly portion or tribute that all ecclesiastick livings pay to the King] *decime*, s. f. plur.

TENU'ITY, s. [smallness, slenderness] *tenuità*, s. f.

TE'NUOUS, adj. [slender, thin] *tenue*, *scarso*.

TE'NURE, s. [the manner whereby lands or tenements are held of their respective lords] *titolo*, *in virtù del quale si possiede qualche possessione sotto* certe *condizioni*.

TE'PID, adj. [lukewarm] *tiepido*, *tepido*.

Tepid [indifferent] *tiepido*, *freddo*, *pigro*, *lento*.

TEPI'DITY, s. [lukewarmness] *tepidezza*, s. f.

Tepidity [indifferency] *tiepidezza*, *indifferenza*, *freddezza*, *pigrizia*, *lentezza*, s. f.

TERCE, s. [a measure of liquids] *misura di liquidi*.

TE'RCET, s. [a third in musick] *mezzana*, s. f.

TE'REBINTH, s. [turpentine] *trementina*, s. f.

TERGIVERSA'TION, s. [fetch, shift] *tergiversazione*, s. f. *storcimento*.

TERM, s. [word] *termine*, s. m. *parola*, s. f. *locuzion propria e particolare di scienze o d' arti*.

Term [bound, limit] *termine*, *confine*, s. m.

Term [set time] *termine*, *spazio di tempo*.

The term of ten years, *il termine di dieci anni*.

The four terms of the year [fixed times when courts of judicature are open for all law suits] *i quattro termini dell' anno ne' quali s' agitano liti nelle curie*.

Term-time, *giorni curiali*.

Terms [in the plural; conditions] *termine*, *condizione*.

The terms of a capitulation, *le condizioni d' una capitolazione*.

To make good terms with one, *vantaggiarsi in qualche aggiustamento*.

To be upon even terms with one, *esser del pari con uno*, *non cedergli in nulla*.

I shall make him come to my own terms, *lo farò ben io stare a partito*.

Not upon any terms [by no means] *in alcuna maniera*, *in conto alcuno*, *in nessun modo*.

To TERM [to call, to name] *nomare*, *nominare*, *chiamare*.

TE'RMAGANCY, s. [turbulence, tumultuousness] *torbidezza d' animo*.

TE'RMAGANT, s. [a ranting, lusty, bold woman] *campionessa*, *donacc a*.

Termagant, adj. [tumultuous, turbulent] *torbido*, *turbolente*, *tumultuante*.

Termagant [quarrelsome, scolding, furious] *litigioso*, *che sgrida e fa romore per ira mal fondata*, *infuriato*.

TE'RMED, adj. *nomato*, *nominato*, *chiamato*.

To TE'RMINATE [to limit, to bound] *terminare*, *limitare*, *por termini o confini*, *tra l' una possessione e l' altra*.

To terminate [to end] *terminare*, *finire*, *metter fine*, pref. *finisco*.

To terminate a difference, *terminare una differenza*, *decidere una contesa*.

To terminate, verb neut. *terminarsi*, *finirsi*.

TE'RMINATED, adj. *terminato*, *finito*, *limitato*.

TERMINA'TION, s. [bound] *terminazione*, s. f. *termine*, s. m. *il terminare*.

Termination [conclusion] *terminazione*, *conclusione*, *fine*, s. f.

The termination of a word, *la terminazione d' una parola*.

TE'RMLESS, adj. [unlimited, boundless] *che non ha limiti*, *che non ha confine*.

TE'RNARY, } adj. [belonging to
TE'RNARIOUS, } a ternion] *ternario*.

TE'RNION, s. [three in number] *tre*, *numero di tre*, *numero ternario*.

TERRA'QUEOUS, adj. [belonging to the earth and water mixed] *terracqueo*.

The terraqueous globe, *il globo terracqueo*.

TE'RRAS, } *terrazzo*, s. m. *terrazza*, s. f.
TERRAS-WALK, }

TERRE'STRIAL, adj. [earthly] *terrestre*, *di terra*, *che ha qualità di terra*.

TE'RRIBLE, adj. [frightful, dreadful] *terribile*, *spaventevole*, *orrendo*, *orribile*.

TE'RRIBLENESS, s. *terribilità*, s. f. *terrore*, *spavento*, s. m.

TE'RRIBLY, adv. *terribilmente*, *orribilmente*, *spaventevolmente*.

TE'RRIER, s. [a kind of hunting dog] *can bassetto*.

Terrier [anger] *succhiello*, s. m.

TERRI'FICK, adj. [frightful] *terribile*, *spaventevole*, *spaventoso*.

To TE'RRIFY [to fright, to make afraid] *atterrire*, *spaventare*, *far paura*, *impaurire*, pref. *atterrisco*, *impaurisco*.

TE'RRIFIED, adj. *atterrito*, *spaventato*, *impaurito*.

TE'RRITORY, s. [a certain compass of land belonging to the jurisdiction of any state, city, or town] *territorio*, s. m.

TE'RROUR [dread, great fear, fright] *terrore*, *spavento*, s. m.

TERSE, adj. [neat] *terso*, *pulito*, *netto*.

Terse style, *stile*, *terso*, *netto*.

TE'RTAIN, adj. ex. a tertain ague which returns again every third day, *una febbre terzana*, *una terzana*.

To TE'RTIATE [to till ground a third time] *interzare*, *lavorar la terra per la terza volta*.

TE'SSELLATED, adj. [variegated by squares] *commesso a scacchi*, *fatto a scacchi*; *e dicesi per lo più d' un pavimento*.

TEST, s. [an instrument made of bone ashes, hooped with iron, for purifying gold and silver] *coppella*, s. f. *picciol vasetto fatto di raschiatura di corna*, *nel quale si cimenta l' oro e l' argento*.

Test [trial] *saggio*, *rimento*, s. m. *prova*, *coppella*, s f.

To put one to the test, *far prova d' uno*, *metterlo in prova*.

To stand the test, *star a coppella*, *resistere al martello*.

TESTA'CEOUS, adj. [shelly, that has a shell] *testaceo*.

TE'STAMENT, s. [the last will of a person] *testamento*, s. m. *ultima volontà*, *nelle quale l' uomo costituisce l' erede*.

Testament [in a scriptural sense, a covenant] *testamento*, *la scrittura sarra*, *così vecchia*, *come nuova*.

TESTAMENTA'RIOUS, } adj. [be-
TESTAME'NTARY, } longing to a testament] *testamentario*.

TE'STATE, adj. [having made a will] *che ha fatto testamento*.

TESTA'TOR, s. [he that makes, or has made a testament] *testatore*, s. m.

TESTA'TRIX, s. [a woman who makes a will] *testatrice*.

TE'STER, s. [the value of six pence] *sei soldi*.

Tester or TESTERN of a bed, *cielo del letto*.

TE'STICLE, s. *testicolo*, s. m. *parte genitale dell' animale*.

TESTIFICA'TION, s. [proof by witnesses] *testificazione*, *testimonianza*, s. f.

To TE'STIFY [to witness, to certify, to make appear] *testificare*, *far testimonianza*, *testimoniare*, *assicurare*, *certificare*.

TE'STIFIED, adj. *testificato*, *assicurato*, *certificato*.

TE'STILY, adv. [fretfully, peevishly, morosely] *caparbiamente*, *con caponeria*, *con mal umore*.

TESTIMO'NIAL, adj. [belonging to testimony] *testimoniale*, *di testimonianza*.

Testimonial, s. [certificate of an ecclesiastical superiour] *testimoniale*, *lettera testimoniale*.

TE'STIMONY, s. [witness] *testimonio*, *testimone*, s. m. *quegli*, *che fa testimonianza*.

Testimony [proof] *testimonio*, *prova*, *fede*, *sicurtà*.

In testimony whereof, *in fede di che*.

Tes-

Teſtimony [quotation from an author] *teſtimonio, citazione.*

Teſtimony [in the holy ſcriptures ſignifies a law or an ordinance] *teſtimonio, teſtimonianza, legge, ordine.*

TE'STINESS, s. [peeviſhneſs] *fantaſticaggine, noja, ſdegnoſità, caparbieta, caponeria, oſtinatezza, ſtitichezza,* s. f. *faſtidio, modo di proceder faſtidioſo.*

TE'STON, s. [a ſilver coin] *teſtone,* s. m.

TE'STY, adj. [peeviſh, apt to take pet, moroſe] *aromatico, diſpettoſo, fantaſtico, faſtidioſo, ſdegnoſo, ſtitico, oſtico, ritroſo, caparbio, capone, oſtinato, teſtereccio, pertinace.*

TE'THER, s. [a rope to tie a horſe's leg with] *paſtojo,* s. f.

To be brought to a tether [under ſubjection] *venire in ſoggezione.*

To hold one to his tether, *tener uno in freno, tenerlo a ſtecco.*

To keep within one's tether, *reſtar entro i limiti.*

To TE'THER, *impaſtojare, mettar le paſtoje.*

TE'THERED, adj. *impaſtojato.*

TE'TRAGON, s. [a ſquare] *tetragono,* s. m.

TETRAPHA'RMACUM, s. [a medicine conſiſting of four ingredients] *tetrafarmaco,* s. m. *unguento compoſto di quattro ingredienti.*

TE'TRARCH, s. [a governor of the fourth part of a country] *tetrarca,* s. m.

TE'TRARCHY, s. government of a tetrarch] *tetrarchia,* s. f.

TETRA'STICH, s. [ſentence or epigram compriſed in four verſes] *ſentenza o epigramma compreſo in quattro verſi.*

TE'TTER, s. [ring-worm] *pitigine, empitigine, volatica,* s. f.

TEUTO'NICK, adj. [belonging to the Germans, anciently called Teutones] *Teutonico, Germanico, Tedeſco, Alemanno.*

The Teutonick order, *l' ordine Teutonico.*

The old Teutonick language, *l' antico Teutonico, il Tedeſco antico, l' antica lingua Tedeſca.*

TEW, s. [materials for any thing] *materiali per che chè ſia.*

TEW [an iron chain] *una catena di ferro.*

To TEW [to tug, to pull] *tirare, ſtrappare.*

To tew mortar, *ſbattere la calcina.*

To tew [to work] *lavorare, far un lavoro.*

TEXT, s. [the very words of an author, without any expoſition] *teſto,* s. m.

The text of the law, *il teſto della legge.*

The text of a ſermon, *il teſto d' una predica.*

TE'XTUARY [a book which contains only the bare text without any gloſs or comment upon it] *libro, nel quale ſi contiene il puro teſto ſenza veruna eſpoſizone o commento*

Textuary [one ſkilled in texts of ſcripture] *uomo intendente de' teſti della ſcrittura.*

TE'XTURE, s. [the ordering or framing of a diſcourſe] *teſtura, teſſitura,* s. f. *il teſſuto.*

THAN [a conjunction uſed to make a compariſon] *più che non, anzi che.*

Gold is more precious than ſilver, *l' oro è più prezioſo dell' argento.*

My houſe is larger than yours, *la mia caſa è più grande della voſtra.*

I am more contented with my ſmall fortune than others with their great riches, *ſono più contento della mia mediocre fortuna che non gli altri che poſſiedono ricchezze grandi.*

I know it better than you, *lo ſo meglio di voi.*

THANK, v. Thanks.

To THANK [to give thanks] *ringraziare, render grazie.*

He may thank me for it, *deve ringraziarmene.*

He is ruined, and he may thank himſelf, *egli è rovinato, e n' è la cauſa egli ſteſſo.*

THA'NKED, adj. *ringraziato.*

God be thanked, *ringraziato Iddio, grazie a Dio.*

THA'NKFUL, adj. [grateful] *grato, riconoſcente, ricordevole de' beneficj.*

THA'NKFULLY, adv. *gratamente, con gratitudine, con riconoſcenza, con ringraziamenti.*

THA'NKFULNESS, s. *gratitudine, riconoſcenza,* s. f. *ringraziamento,* s. m.

THA'NKLESS, adj. [ungrateful] *ingrato, ſconoſcente.*

THA'NKLESSNESS, s. *ingratitudine, ſconoſcenza.*

THANKS, s. *grazie,* s. f. *ringraziamenti,* s m.

Give God thanks, *rendete grazie a Dio.*

Thank-offering, *ſacrificio di rendimento di grazie.*

Thanks-giving, *ringraziamento, rendimento di grazie.*

THAT [a pronoun demonſtrative] *quello, quella.*

That book, *quel libro.*

That woman, *quella donna.*

What man is that? *che uomo è quello?*

That is [that is to ſay] *cioè, cioè a dire.*

With that, *con ciò.*

So that, *di modo che, di maniera che, ſicchè.*

That [to the end that] *affinchè, acciocchè.*

The ſame day that I came, *il medeſimo giorno che io venni.*

They ſay that we ſhall have a war, *ſi dice che avremo la guerra.*

At that time, *in quel tempo, allora.*

That way, *per là, per quella via.*

That [which] *chi, che.*

He that does good, good ſhall come to him, *chi fa bene, bene aſpetti.*

The book that you promiſed me, *il libro che mi avete promeſſo.*

He that ſpeaks, *colui che parla.*

Seeing that, *poichè, poſciachè.*

I will take care that you may be acquainted with it, *ſarà mia cura d' informarvi del tutto.*

That I may be ſhort, *per finirla in poche parole.*

Not that I know of, *no per quel che ne ſo.*

THATCH, s. [ſtubble] *ſtoppia, paglia,* s. f.

To THATCH, verb act. *coprire di ſtoppia, o paglia.*

THA'TCHED, adj. *coperto di ſtoppia, o paglia.*

Thatched houſe, *caſa col tetto di ſtoppia, o di paglia.*

THA'TCHER, s. *uno il cui meſtiero è coprir caſe di paglia o di ſtoppia.*

THAUGHTS, s. [a ſea-term] *banchi ſopra i quali i rematori ſono aſſiſi.*

THAW, s. *il dighiacciare.*

To THAW [to melt after froſt] *dighiacciare, disfarci il ghiaccio.*

It thaws, *dighiaccia.*

THAWED, adj. *dighiacciato.*

THA'WING, s. *il dighiacciare.*

THE [an article called definite] *il, lo, la, i, gli, le.*

The time, *il tempo.*

The ſcholar, *lo ſcolare.*

The woman, *la donna.*

The richer we are the prouder we grow, *più ſiamo ricchi più ſuperbi diveniamo.*

THEAM, } s. [a ſubject to write or
THEME, } ſpeak upon] *tema, ſoggetto,* s. m. *materia,* s. f.

THE'ATRE [play-houſe] *teatro,* s. m. *edificio dove ſi rappreſentano li ſpettacoli.*

Theatre [ſtage] *palco,* s. m.

The theatre of war, *il teatro della guerra.*

THE'ATRAL, } adj. [belonging to
THEA'TRICAL, } a theatre or ſtage]
THEA'TRICK, } *teatrale, di teatro.*

THEE, *caſo obliquo del pronome* Thou.

THEEF, v. Thief.

THEFT, s. [the act of ſtealing] *latrocinio, ladroneccio, furto,* s. m. *ruberia,* s. f.

THEIR [*è il plurale del pronome poſſeſſivo* his *e* her] *loro.*

Their father, *il padre loro.*

Their pride, *la loro ſuperbia.*

This is theirs, *queſto è il loro.*

THEM [the pronoun *they* in an oblique caſe] *li, le, loro, gli.*

I love them, *li amo o le amo.*

I was with them, *io era con loro.*

I told them, *diſſi loro.*

THEME, s. a ſubject on which one ſpeaks

ſpeaks or writes] *tema, ſoggetto, ſubbjetto ſu cui uom parla o ſcrive.*

Theme [a ſhort diſſertation written by boys on any topick] *tema, lezione, ſoggetto, ſul quale i ragazzi devono ſcrivere alla ſcuola.*

Theme [the original word whence others are derived] *la voce originale da cui altre dirivano.*

THEMSE'LVES, *plurale di* himſelf or herſelf. *Eſſi, deſſi, eſſi, ſteſſi, églino.*

THEN [at that time] *allora, in quel tempo.*

Then he told me, *allora mi diſſe.*

Now and then [ſometime] *di quando in quando, qualche volta.*

Then [afterwards] *poi, dopo.*

Let us ſtay till it has done raining and then we will go, *aſpettiamo che ſia reſſata la pioggia e poi ce n' andremo.*

Then [therefore] *dunque.*

What ſhall I do then? *che farò dunque?*

I have done it, and what then? *io l' ho fatto, e che volete dire per cio?*

THENCE, adv. [from thence, from that place] *di là, indi.*

He is gone from thence, *egli è partito di là.*

Thence is that, *da queſto procede, queſta è la ragione che.*

THE'NCEFORTH [from thenceforth] *da quel tempo in quà, da indi in quà.*

THEO'GONY, s. [the genealogy of the gods] *teogonia, la genealogia degli dei.*

THEO'LOGER, } s. [divine, pro-
THEOLO'GIAN, } feſſor of divinity] *teologo,* s. m. *profeſſore, dottore in teologia.*

THEOLO'GICAL, adj. [belonging to divinity] *teologale, teologico, di teologia.*

Faith, hope, and charity, are the theological virtues, *le virtù teologali ſono fede, ſperanza, e carità.*

THEOLO'GICALLY, adv. *teologicamente, ſecondo la teologia.*

THEO'LOGY, s. [divinity] *teologia,* s. f.

THEO'RBO, s. [a kind of muſical inſtrument] *tiorba,* s. f. *ſtrumento muſicale.*

THE'OREM, s. [a demonſtrable rule in any art or ſcience] *teorema,* s. f. *dimoſtrazione e prova evidente in qualche arte o ſcienza.*

THEOREMA'TICK, } adj. [conſiſting
THEOREMA'TICAL, } of theorems] *teorematico, che conſiſte in teoremi.*

THEORE'TICK, } adj. [belonging to
THEO'RICAL, } theory, ſpecula-
THEO'RICK, } tive] *teorico, ſpeculativo.*

THE'ORY, s. [the contemplation or ſtudy of any art or ſcience without practice] *teorica,* s. f. *ſcienza ſpeculativa.*

THERE, adv. *lì, là.*

Who is there? *chi è là?*

There he is, *eccolo lì.*

In there, *là entro.*

Here and there, *quà e là.*

There is, there are, *vi è, vi ſono.*

There is a man that wants to ſpeak with you, *v' è un uomo che vorrebbe parlarvi.*

There are ſome who think that ———, *vi ſono alcuni che credono che* ———

There is none, *non ve n' è.*

THE'REABOUT, adv. [about that number] *incirca, circa, intorno.*

Thereabout [about it] *intorno a queſto, concernente queſta materia.*

Thereabouts, adv. [about that place] *là intorno.*

It is ſomewhere thereabouts, *è in qualche luogo là intorno.*

Ten pounds or thereabouts, *dieci lire in circa.*

The country thereabouts, *il paeſe circonvicino.*

THE'REFORE, conj. [for that cauſe] *perciò, perilchè, laonde, onde.*

Therefore [then] *dunque.*

THE'REIN, *in ciò.*

THE'REOF, *di ciò.*

THE'RIACAL, adj. [belonging to treacle] *triacale, di triaca.*

THERMO'METER, s. [an inſtrument to meaſure or ſhow the ſeveral degrees of heat and cold] *termometro,* s. m. *ſtrumento per miſura del caldo, e del freddo.*

To THE'SAURIZE [to gather or lay up treaſure] *teſaurizzare, ammaſſare, accumular teſoro.*

THESE [is the plural of the pronoun demonſtrative *this*] *queſti, queſte.*

THE'SIS, s. [a ſubject to diſpute upon] *teſe,* s. f.

THEY [is the plural of the pronoun perſonal *he, ſhe*] *eglino, elleno, loro.*

They who, *coloro che.*

THICK, adj. [contrary to thin] *ſerrato, ſpeſſo, groſſo, groſſolano.*

Thick cloth, *panno ſerrato.*

Thick wood, *boſco folto.*

Thick board, *panca groſſa.*

Thick man, *uomo groſſo.*

Thick air, *aria ſpeſſa,*

Thick water, *acqua torbida o melmoſa.*

To lie very thick, *eſſer molto ſerrati.*

An inch thick, *groſſo un dito.*

To ſpeak thick, *aver la lingua groſſa.*

Thick of hearing, *ſordaſtro, quaſi ſordo.*

Thick ſet, *ſpeſſo, folto.*

A thick-ſet hedge, *una ſiepe folta.*

Thick-ſkinned, *che ha la pelle dura.*

Thick-ſculled, *che ha la teſta dura.*

Thick, adv. *in folla.*

To THI'CKEN [to make thick] *ſpeſſare, ſpeſſire.*

To thicken a ſauce, *ſpeſſare una ſalſa.*

To thicken [to grow thick] *ſpeſſarſi, ſpeſſirſi.*

THI'CKENED, v. Thickned.

THI'CKET, s. [a place full of buſhes] *boſchetto folto,* s. m.

A thicket of trees, *un boſchetto.*

THI'CKLY, adv. *ſpeſſamente, foltamente.*

THI'CKNED, adj. *ſpeſſato, ſpeſſito.*

THI'CKNESS, s. *ſpeſſezza, denſità, groſſezza,* s. f.

THIEF, s. [one that ſteals] *ladro, rubatore,* s. m. *ladra, rubatrice,* s. f.

Opportunity makes a thief, *la comodità fa l' uomo ladro; all' arca operta il giuſto vi pecca.*

To play the thief, *far il meſtiero di ladro, rubare.*

Thief catcher, *birro.*

To THIEVE [to ſteal] *rubare.*

THI'EVERY, s. [the practice of ſtealing] *il rubare.*

Thievery [that which is ſtolen] *la coſa rubata.*

THIEVES, *plurale di* thief.

THI'EVING, s. *ladroneccio, furto,* s. m. *ruberia,* s. f.

Given to thieving, *dedito a rubare.*

THI'EVISH, adj. [apt to ſteal] *inclinato a rubare.*

THI'EVISHLY, adv. *da ladro.*

THI'EVISHNESS, *inclinazione a rubare.*

THIGH, s. [a member of the body from the knee to the groin] *coſcia,* s. f.

THILK, pron. [that ſame] *quello ſteſſo, lo ſteſſo.*

THILL, s. [the beam or draught-tree of a cart] *timone di carro.*

THI'LLER, } s. [that horſe that
Thill-horſe, } is put under the thill] *il cavallo che ſta al timone.*

THI'MBLE, s. *ditale,* s. m.

THIME, s. [a fragrant herb] *timo, erba di gratiſſimo odore.*

THIN, adj. [not thick] *ſottile, rado.*

Thin cloth, *panno ſottile, rado.*

Thin broth, *brodo lungo, brodo leggiero.*

The corn is very thin here, *il grano è molto rado quì.*

Thin body, *corpo ſmilzo.*

A thin ſuit of cloaths, *un abito leggiero.*

To go in thin cloaths, *andar leggiermente veſtito.*

Thin [little, ſmall] *piccolo, minuto.*

Thin congregation, *una piccola aſſemblea.*

Thin air, *aria ſottile.*

Thin [lean] *magro, ſmunto, macilente, ſmilzo, ſparuto.*

To go through thick and thin, *eſporſi ad ogni pericolo.*

Thin city, *città ſpopolata, dove c' è poca gente.*

To grow thin, *ſmagrire, divenir magro.*

Thin-bodied, *smilzo*.

To THIN [to make thin] *diradare, allargare, tor via la spessezza*.

To thin a wood, *diradare un bosco*.

To thin a tree, *diramare un albero, troncarli una parte de' rami*.

THINE [belonging to thee] *il tuo, la tua, i tuoi, le tue*.

Thine uncle, *tuo zio*.

Thine aunt, *tua zia*.

Thine friends, *i tuoi amici*.

This is thine, *questo è tuo*.

Here is thine, *ecco il tuo*.

THING, s. [a matter, substance, accident, &c.] *cosa*, s. f. *nome di termine generalissimo, e si dice di tutto quel che è*.

A fine thing, *una bella cosa*.

Above all things, *più che qualsivoglia cosa, sopra modo, molto, principalmente*.

It is an usual thing with us, *questa è nostra usanza, gliè nostro costume*.

She is a little scornful thing, *ella è una ritrosetta, una sdegnosetta*.

Where are my things? *dove sono le mie robe?*

To THINK [to meditate] *pensare, meditare, discorrer nella mente*.

What do you think? *che pensate?*

To think well or ill, *pensar bene o male*.

To think of or upon [to muse upon] *pensare, considerare, riflettere, far riflessione, ruminare*.

To think of what one has to say, *pensare a quel che uno deve dire*.

That made me think of it, *questo me ne ha fatto ricordare*.

He thinks of some great matter, *qualche gran cosa gli va per testa, sta pensando a qualche cosa d' importanza*.

To think [to suppose, to imagine, to be of opinion, to believe] *pensare, stimare, darsi ad intendere, immaginarsi, credere*.

He thinks himself an able man, *egli si stima un valente uomo*.

I think so, *credo di sì, credo così*.

As you think fit, *come voi giudicherete meglio, come meglio vi parrà, come vi piacerà*.

To think well or ill of one, *pensar bene o male d' una persona, averne buona o cattiva opinione*.

You must not think to be above us, *non bisogna che voi vi stimiate da più di noi*.

I shall think it no disgrace, *non piglierei cio a disonore*.

What think you of it? *che ne dite, che ve ne pare?*

I know not what to think of it, *io non so che mi dire di cio*.

I think this fits you very well, *mi pare che questo vi stia molto bene*.

He thinks much to go thither, *far gran difficoltà d' andarvi*.

To think light of a thing [to have an ill opinion of it] *far poco conto, o poca stima di qualche cosa, dispregiarla*.

I cannot think of his name, *non posso ricordarmi del suo nome*.

Without you think otherwise, *a meno che voi non siate di contrario parere*.

One would think that you have done it on purpose, *pare che l' abbiate fatto a posta*.

I think it long till I see him, *mi par mill' anni di vederlo*.

To think well of one's self, *stimarsi, aver buona opinione di se stesso, presumer di se stesso*.

But I began to think, that—, *ma mi venne nell' animo, che—*

THI'NKER, s. [one who thinks in a certain manner] *uno che pensa in un certo modo, un che pensa assai*.

THI'NKING, s. *pensamento, pensiero*, s. m.

To my thinking, *a mio parere o giudizio, in quanto a me*.

Thinking, adj. [judicious, reasonable] *giudizioso, ragionevole, prudente, accorto*.

THI'NLY, adv. *radamente, rado*.

Thinly inhabited, *poco abitato*.

THI'NNESS, s. *radezza, rarità*, s. f.

THIRD, adj. *terzo*.

The third day, *il terzo giorno*.

To put a thing in a third hand, *metter che che sia nelle mani d' un terzo*.

Every third day, *di tre in tre giorni*.

A third, s. *un terzo, una terza parte*.

THI'RDLY, adv. [in the third place] *in terzo luogo*.

To THIRL [to pierce, to perforate] *forare, succhiellare*.

THIRST, s. *sete*, s. f.

His thirst after riches, *la sete che ha per le ricchezze*.

To THIRST, verb neut. *aver sete*.

To thirst after a thing, *aver sete di qualche cosa, desiderarla, ambirla grandemente*.

THI'RSTINESS, s. [the state of being thirsty] *sete, lo stato di chi ha sete*.

THI'RSTY, adj. [troubled with thirst] *assetato, sitibondo, che ha sete*.

Blood-thirsty, *sanguinolente, sitibondo di sangue*.

THIRTE'EN, adj. *tredici*.

THIRTE'ENTH, adj. *tredicesimo*.

THI'RTIETH, adj. *trentesimo*

THI'RTY, adj. *trenta*.

THIS [a pronoun demonstrative] *questo, questa*.

This book, *questo libro*.

This house, *questa casa*.

This I am for, *questo mi piace*.

Give me this, *datemi questo*.

What does this mean? *che vuol dir questo? questo che significa?*

This is the book I look for, *ecco il libro che io vo cercando*.

By this way, *per quì*.

From this place, *da quì*.

To this place, *fin quì*.

As they were talking of this and that, *mentre stavano ragionando d' una e d' un altra cosa*.

THI'STLE, s. [weed] *cardo, cardone*, s. f.

Blessed thistle [a plant] *cardo benedetto, cardo santo*.

The star-thistle, *cardone stellato*.

The sow-thistle, *titimaglio, titimalo*, s. m

Fuller's-thistle, *cardo da cardare i panni*.

The order of the thistle [in Scotland] *l' ordine del cardone o l' ordine di sant Andrea, in Iscozia*.

Thistle-down, *cottone di cardone*.

THI'THER, adv. *lì, là*.

Go thither, *andate là*.

We are but half way thither, *noi non siamo che a mezza strada*.

THI'THERTO, adv. [to that place] *fin là*.

THI'THERWARDS, adv. *verso là, verso quella parte*.

THO', v. Though.

THOKES, s. [fish with broken bellies] *pesce sventrato*.

To THOLE [to wait a while] *aspettar un poco*.

THO'MISTS, s. [divines who follow the doctrine of Thomas Aquinus] *tomisti, quelli che seguitano la dottrina di san Tomaso d' Aquino*.

THONG, s. [a strap of leather] *striscia di cuojo, correggia*.

The thong of a wallet, *le corregge d' una bisaccia*.

THO'NGED, adj. [tied with thongs] *legato con istrisce di cuojo*.

THORN, s. [a prickle of a bush] *spina*, s. f. *spino, pruno*, s. m.

White-thorn or haw-thorn, *spinalba*, s. f. *prun bianco*.

Thorn-apple, s. *nome di pianta*.

Thorn-bush, *spineto*, s. m.

Thorn back [a sea fish] *razza*, s. f. *sorta di pesce*.

THO'RNY, adj. [full of thorns] *spinoso, pien di spine*.

THO'ROUGH } prep. *per traverso, a*
THO'ROW } *traverso*.

Thorough-fare, *passaggio, strada per cui si passa*.

Thorough change, *intiero cangiamento*.

THORP, s. [village, country-town] *villaggio, terricciuola*.

THOSE [the plural of *that*] *quelli, quegli, que', quelle*.

Those men, *quegli uomini*.

What books are those? *che libri son quelli?*

Those that say such a thing, *coloro che dicono tal cosa*.

THOU [a pronoun personal] *tu*.

Thou art my friend, *tu sei mio amico*.

To thou, *dar del tu ad uno*.

The Quakers thou every body, *i quaccheri danno del tu ad ognuno*.

THOUGH, or THO', conj. *benchè, ancorchè, quantunque*.

Though

Though you be older than he, *benchè siate più vecchio di lui.*

Though it were so, *supposto che fosse così.*

To make as though, *far le vista, far sembiante, fingere.*

THOUGHT, adj. [from to think] *pensato, v.* To think.

It is well thought of you, *voi dite bene.*

Marriage is a thing seriously to be thought of, *il matrimonio è una cosa alla quale si deve maturamente pensare.*

It is thought there will be a peace, *si crede che avremo la pace.*

I would not have it thought, *non vorrei che si credesse.*

A thing not thought of, *una cosa impensata, improvvisa, inaspettata.*

Thought, s. [the act of thinking] *pensiero*, s. m. *il pensare.*

That thought came into my head, *questo pensiero mi venne in capo.*

Thought [consideration] *pensiero, considerazione, riflessione.*

Thought [care] *pensiero, cura, fastidio.*

Take no thought for to-morrow, *non vi pigliate pensiero per domani.*

Thought [opinion, mind] *pensiero, parere, sentimento*, s. m. *opinione*, s. f.

I will speak my thought, *voglio dire il mio pensiero, il mio sentimento.*

To entertain ill thoughts of one, *aver cattiva opinione d' una persona, averla in cattivo concetto.*

Thought [design, aim] *pensiero, disegno*, s. m. *intenzione*, s. f.

I have other thoughts in my head, *ho altri pensieri in testa, penso ad altre cose.*

It has been a long time in my thoughts, *è un pezzo che l' ho avuto in pensiero, che ne ho formato il disegno.*

It came into my thoughts, *mi venne in pensiero, nella mente.*

THO'UGHTFUL, adj. *pensoso, pensieroso, pien di pensieri.*

THO'UGHTFULLY, adv. *con viso pensoso, in atto pensoso.*

THO'UGHTFULNESS, s. *umor pensieroso, pensier profondo.*

THO'UGHTLESS, adj. [without thoughts, careless] *spensierato, trascurato, senza pensieri, negligente.*

THO'UGHTLESSLY, adv. [without thought, carelessly, stupidly] *spensieratamente alla spensierata, straccuratamente, negligentemente, stupidamente.*

THO'USAND, adj. *mille.*

Thousand times, *mille volte.*

Two thousand, *duemila.*

THOU'SANDTH, adj. *millesimo.*

The thousandth part, *la millesima parte.*

THRA'LDOM, s. [servitude, bondage] *servitù, schiavitù.*

THRALL, s. [a slave] *uno schiavo.*

To THRASH [to beat corn, to free it from the chaff] *trebbiare.*

To thrash [to beat, to drub] *battere, percuotere, spianar le costole, bastonare.*

To thrash [to labour, to drudge] *affaticarsi, lavorar come cane.*

THRA'SHER, s. [one who thrashes corn] *trebbiatore.*

THRA'SHING-FLOOR, s. [an area on which corn is beaten] *aja.*

THRASO'NICAL, adj. [full of ostentation] *vanaglorioso, pien d' albagia.*

THRAVE, s. [two stocks, or twenty-four sheaves of corn] *ventiquattro covoni di grano.*

THREAD, s. *filo*, s. m.

Thread to sew with, *refe*, s. m. *accia*, s. f. *per uso di cucire.*

Thread by thread, *filo a filo, l' un dopo l' altro.*

A bottom of thread, *un gomitolo di filo.*

To reassume the thread of one's discourse, *ripigliare il filo del suo discorso.*

Thread-bare, *usato, spelato, logoro.*

The thread of a razor, knife, &c. *il filo d' un rasojo, d' un coltello, e simili.*

To THREAD, or thread a needle, *infilare un ago.*

THRE'ADEN, adj. [made of thread] *fatto di filo.*

To THREAP, or to threap down [to affirm positively] *affermare, mantenere, sostenere, avverare*, pref. *mantengo, sostengo*, pret. *mantenni, sostenni. Non in uso.*

THREAT, s. *minaccia*, s. f.

Full of threats, *minaccevole, minacciante, minaccioso.*

To THREAT }
To THRE'ATEN } [use threats] *minacciare.*

THRE'ATENED, or THREATNED, adj. *minacciato.*

Threatened folks live long, *di minacce non temere, di promesse non godere.*

THRE'ATENER, s. *minacciatore*, s. m.

THRE'ATENINGLY, adv. [with menace, in a threatening manner] *minaccevolmente.*

THRE'ATENINGS }
THRE'ATNINGS } s. *minacce.*

Threatening, adj. *minaccevole, minacciante, minaccioso.*

Threatening words, *parole minaccevoli*

THRE'ATENINGLY, adv. *minaccevolmeate, con minacce.*

THREE, adj. *tre.*

Three times, *tre volte.*

THREE-LEAFED-GRASS, *trifoglio*, s. m.

THREE-FO'OTED, adj. *che ha tre piedi.*

THREE FORKED, adj. *triforcato, triforcuto, con tre punte.*

THREE-CORNERED, adj. *triangolare, di tre angoli.*

THREE'-FOLD, adj. [treble] *triplice, triplicato.*

Threefold [divided into three] *tripartito, partito in tre.*

THREESCORE, adj. *sessanta.*

THRE'NODY, s. [a funeral song] *una canzone funebre, treno.*

THRE'EPENNY, adj. [vulgar, mean] *volgare, vile, di poco valore.*

THRE'EPILE, s. [an old name for good velvet] *velluto buono, velluto in tre peli. Voce antica.*

To THRESH [to beat the grain of corn out from the ear] *trebbiare.*

To thresh corn, *trebbiare il grano.*

To thresh one, or to thresh one's coat [to beat him soundly] *battere, tartassare alcuno, spianargli le costure, bastonarlo.*

THRE'SHED, adj. *trebbiato, battuto, tartassato, bastonato.*

THRE'SHER, s. *trebbiatore*, s. m.

THRE'SHING, s. *trebbiatura*, s. f. *il trebbiare.*

THRE'SHOLD, s. [the ground timber of a door] *limitare*, s. m. *soglia*, s. f.

THREW, *è un preterito del verbo* To throw, *v.* To throw.

THRICE, adv. [three times] *tre volte.*

I shall do it in a thrice, *lo farò in un momento, in un batter d' occhio.*

THRIFT, s. [savingness, sparingness] *parsimonia, frugalità, economia*, s. f. *risparmio*, s. m.

SPEND-THRIFT, *un prodigo, un scialacquone.*

THRI'FTILY, adv. [savingly] *assegnatamente, moderatamente, parcamente, con frugalità.*

THRI'FTINESS, s. [thrift] *economia, parsimonia, frugalità*, s. f. *risparmio*, s. m.

THRI'FTY, adv. [saving] *parco, moderato, frugale, economico.*

A thrifty man, *un massajo.*

A thrifty woman, *una massaja.*

THRILL, s. [drill, boring tool] *succhiello, succhio, trapano*, s. m.

To THRILL [to bore] *succhiare, succhiellare, trapanare.*

THRI'LLED, adj. *succhiato, succhiellato, trapanato.*

To THRIVE [to grow, to encrease mightily, to prosper, to grow rich] *prosperare, profittare, avanzarsi, andar di bene in meglio, approdare, acquistare, arricchirsi, riuscire*, pref. *arricchisco, riesco.*

To thrive [to grow as a child does] *crescere, venire innanzi, profittare, parlando d' un fanciullo.*

To thrive [as a plant or tree] *attecchire, venire innanzi, avanzare, acquistare, crescere, allignare, parlando d' una pianta o d' un albero.*

To thrive [in health] *star bene migliorare, ingrassare.*

To thrive in learning, *profittare, far profitto, avanzare, far progresso nelle scienze.*

THRI'V-

THRI'VER, s. [one that prospers, one that grows rich] *uno che va prosperando, che va diventando ricco.*

THRI'VING, s. [prosperity] *felicità, prosperità*, s. f. *avanzamento, profitto*, s. m.

Thriving, adj. ex. A thriving man, *un uomo prospero nelle sue imprese, che s' avanza, un uomo fortunato, che riesce ne' suoi negozi.*

THRI'VINGLY, adv. *prosperamente, felicemente, con buon successo.*

He goes on thrivingly, *egli tira innanzi di bene in meglio.*

THROAT, s. [the wind-pipe] *gola, strozza*, s. f. *gorgozzule*, s. m. *la canna della gola.*

To have a sore throat, *aver male alla gola.*

To cut one's throat, *scannare, tagliare la canna della gola.*

The throat band of a bridle, *il soggolo della briglia.*

THRO'AT PIPE, s. [the weason, the windpipe] *lo strozza, il gorgozzule, la canna della gola.*

THRO'ATWORT, s. *nome di pianta.*

THROB, s. [heave, beat, palpitation] *palpito*, s. m. *palpitazione*, s. f.

To THROB [to beat, to pant] *palpitare.*

My heart throbs, *mi palpita il cuore.*

THRO'BBING, s. *palpitamento*, s. m. *palpitazione*, s. f.

THROE, s. [the pain of travail, the anguish of bringing children] *doglia di parto, dolore del partorire.*

To THROE [to put in agonies] *angosciare, cagionar angoscia, dare smisurato dolore.*

THRONE, s. [royal seat] *trono*, s m.

To sit upon the throne [to reign] *seder sul trono, regnare.*

To THRONE [to enthrone, to set on a royal throne] *porre in trono.*

THRONG, s. [croud, press of people] *calca, frotta, folla*, s. f. *gran concorso, di gente.*

To THRONG, } *andare o*
To THRONG together, } *venire in frotta, concorrere, formeggiare, fare flormo, adunarsi.*

To throng [to croud, to press close] *affollare.*

THRO'NGED, adj. *flormeggiato, affollato.*

THRO'STER, s. [silk throster] *torritore di seta.*

THRO'STLE, s. [thrush] *tordo*, s. m.

THRO'TTLE, s. *strozza, canna della gola.*

To THRO'TTLE [to choak] *strangolare.*

THRO'TTLED, adj. *strangolato.*

THROVE, *preterito del verbo* to thrive.

THROUGH, prep. *a traverso, per.*

To walk through the fields, *rammmnare pe' campi.*

To go through a town, *passare per una città.*

To look through a grate, *guardare a traverso una gelosia.*

To run one through with a sword, *passar uno da banda a banda con una spada.*

I am wet through, *sono bagnato fino alla pelle.*

Through him [by his means] *per mezzo suo.*

Through and through, *da banda a banda, fuorfuora.*

THRO'UGH-BRED, adj. [compleatly educated, compleatly taught] *compiutamente educato, perfettamente istrutto.*

THRO'UGHLIGHTED, adj. [lighted on both sides] *illuminato tutto, rischiarato da entrambi i lati.*

THRO'UGHLY, adv. [perfectly] *perfettamente, intieramente, affatto.*

THRO'UGHOUT, prep. [quite through, in every part of] *fuorfuora, da banda a banda, in ogni sua parte.*

Throughout, adv. [every where, in every part] *dappertutto, in ogni luogo, e il Salvini disse anche per ogni dove.*

THRO'UGHPACED, adj. [perfect, compleated] *perfetto, compiuto.*

THROW, s. [cast] *tiro, tratto, colpo*, s. m.

A stone throw, *un tiro di pietra.*

The throws of a woman in labour, *le doglie, i dolori del parto in questo senso è meglio scrivere* throes, *v.* Throe.

To THROW [to cast] *gettare, tirare, lanciare, scagliare.*

To throw a stone, *gettare una pietra.*

To throw a man down, *stramazzare uno, gettarlo a terra.*

To throw headlong, *precipitare, buttar capitomboli.*

To throw away, *gettar via.*

To throw away one's money, *gettar via, il suo danaro.*

To throw one's self away, *esporsi, cimentarsi, mettersi a cimento, porsi a pericolo.*

To throw off one's cloak, *levarsi il mantello.*

To throw one off, *disfarsi, brigarsi d' uno, levarselo d' attorno.*

To throw up the cards, *gettar le carte, tralasciare di giuocare.*

To throw the house out of the windows, *metter ogni cosa sossopra.*

To throw a thing into one's dish [to twit him in the teeth with it] *rinfacciare, improverare che che sia ad uno.*

To throw silk, *torcer della seta.*

THRO'WER, s. ex. A silk thrower, *torcitore di seta.*

THROWN, adj. *gettato, tirato, tratto, lanciato, scagliato.*

Thrown silk, *seta torta.*

A stone was thrown to him from a window, *gli fu tratta una sassata da una finestra.*

THRUM, s. [the ends of a weaver's threads] *la frangia dello stame.*

To THRUM [to beat] *battere, bastonare, tartassare.*

To thrum [to grate, to play coarsely] *strimpellare, suonare sgarbatamente e da ignorante.*

THRU'MMED, adj. *battuto, bastonato, tartassato.*

Thrummed, adj. *strimpellato, suonato sgarbatamente e ignorantemente.*

THRUSH, s. [a bird] *tordo*, s. m. *uccello noto.*

Thrush [small, round, and superficial ulceration in the mouth] *ulceretta che viene nella bocca.*

THRUST, adj. *spinto, v.* To thrust.

Thrust, s. [push] *spinta*, s. f. *urto*, s. f.

Thrust [pass in fencing] *botta*, s. f.

To falsify a thrust, *fare una finta.*

To THRUST [to push] *spignere, spingere, urtare, carciare*, pret. *spinsi, pinsi.*

To thrust back, *rispignere, spignere indietro.*

To thrust in, *cacciare, ficcare.*

To thrust one into prison, *mettere alcuno in prigione.*

To thrust one forward, *spignere alcuno avanti.*

To thrust one's self into a business [to intermeddle in it] *ingerirsi, impacciarsi in qualche affare.*

To thrust through, *passar da banda a banda, passar fuorfuora.*

To thrust together, *serrare, legare insieme, strignere*, pref. *stringo*, pret. *strinsi.*

To thrust out, *scacciare.*

To thrust one out of doors, *scacciare, mettere uno fuor di casa.*

To thrust a thing upon one, *dare che che sia ad uno per forza.*

THRU'STER, s. [he that trusts] *colui che fida a un altro, colui che si fida d' altrui.*

To THRYFA'LLOW [to give the third plowing in summer] *dare la terza aratura al terreno la state.*

THUMB, s. [the largest finger] *pollice*, s. m. *il dito grosso.*

The thumb's breadth, *un pollice, la larghezza d'un pollice.*

To THUMB a book, *squadernare, leggere un libro.*

To thumb [to hand aukwardly] *maneggiare con poca grazia o destrezza.*

THUMP, s. [a blow with the hand] *colpo, pugno*, s. m. *percossa, botta*, s. f.

To THUMP [to knock, to beat] *battere, bastonare, tartassare, perruotere*, pret. *percossi.*

To thump at the door, *picchiare alla porta.*

THU'MPED, adj. *battuto, bastonato, tartassato, percosso.*

THU'MPING, s. *il battere; percuotimento*, s. m.

Thumping, adj [big] *grosso*

A thumping child, *un fanciullo grosso.*

THU'NDER, s. *tuono.*

A clap of thunder, *uno scoppio di tuono*

Thunder-bolt, *folgore, fulmine.*

To THU'NDER; verb neut. *tuonare.*

It thunders, *tuona.*

THU'NDERING, s. *tuonamento, tuono*, s. m. *il tuonare.*

Thundering, adj. *tonante, terribile.*

Thundering [great, very loud] *grande, strepitoso.*

A thundering noise, *un gran romore, uno strepito, un fracasso.*

A thundering voice, *una voce strepitosa.*

THURI'FEROUS, adj. [bringing forth frankincenſe] *che porta, o produce dell' incenſo.*

THU'RSDAY, s. [the fourth day of the week] *Giovedì*, s. m.

Maundy-Thurſday, *il Giovedì Santo.*

THUS, adv. [ſo, after this manner] *così, in queſto modo, in queſta maniera, in queſta forma.*

Do it thus, *fatelo così, fatelo in queſta maniera.*

Having thus ſpoken, *avendo parlato in queſto modo, avendo detto queſte parole.*

Thus far [hitherto] *ſin quì, ſin adeſſo.*

Thus far you are in the right, *in quanto a queſto voi avete ragione.*

Thus much, *tanto.*

Thus much for that, *tanto baſti intorno a cio.*

I value you not this much, *non vi ſtimo un fico.*

THWACK, s. *fruſta, sferza*, s. f.

To THWACK, v. [to beat] *sferzare, fruſtare, battere, percuotere*, pret. *percoſſi.*

THWA'CKED, adj. *sferzato, fruſtato, battuto, percoſſo.*

THWART, adj. [a-croſs] *bieco, bistorto, indiretto, obbliquo, ſchimbeſcio, ſghembo, traſverſo.*

To THWART [to croſs] *attraverſare, contradiare, contrariare, contraſtare, opporſi, ovviare, contendere*, preſ. *oppongo*, pret. *oppoſi, conteſi.*

To thwart one's deſigns, *attraverſare, deludere gli altrui diſegni.*

THWA'RTED, adj. *attraverſato, contradiato, contrariato, contraſtato, oppoſto, ovviato, conteſo.*

THWA'RTING, s. *contraddizione, contrarietà, oppoſizione*, s. f.

Thwarting, adj. *contrario, avverſo, oppoſto*, s. f.

THY [the pronoun poſſeſſive, from *thou*] *il tuo, la tua, i tuoi, le tue.*

Thy ſervant, *il tuo ſervo.*

Thy maid, *la tua ſerva.*

Thy children, *i tuoi figli.*

Thy daughters, *le tue figliuole.*

THYME, s. [a ſweet herb] *timo*, s. m. *erba odorifera.*

Wild or creeping thyme, *ſermollino*, s. m.

TIA'RA, s. [the pope's triple crown] *tiara.*

TICK, s. [ſcore, truſt] *conto, credito.*

Tick [the caſe which holds the feathers of a bed] *coperta o fodera di piumaccio o materaſſo di piume.*

The tick of a pillow, *la fodera d' un guanciale.*

Tick [a ſmall blackiſh inſect] *zecca*, s. f.

Tick [a horſe diſeaſe] *tiro*, s. m. *malattia di cavallo.*

To go upon tick, *pigliare a credito, o a credenza.*

To TICK [to go upon tick] *pigliare a credenza.*

TI'CKET, s. [a ſmall note for ſeeing a play, payment of ſeamen's wages, quartering of ſoldiers, &c.] *bulletta*, s. f. *bullettino*, s. m.

To TI'CKLE, *ſolleticare, dilettare.*

To tickle [to pleaſe, to flatter] *ſolleticare, luſingare, piacere.*

TI'CKLED, adj. *ſolleticato.*

TI'CKLING, s. *ſolletico*, s. m.

TI'CKLISH, adj. [eaſily tickled] *ſolleticoſo, che è ſoggetto al ſolletico.*

Ticklish [touchy, captious] *diſcolo, litigioſo, riottoſo.*

Ticklish [nice, dangerous] *delicato, pericoloſo, geloſo.*

A ticklish buſineſs, *un negozio delicato, un affare geloſo.*

TID, adj. [dainty] *delicato, lezioſo, ſchifo.*

A tid bit, *un boccone delicato.*

To TI'DDLE, ex. to tiddle one up in his humour [to humour one] *ſecondare l' altrui umore, accomodarſi all' altrui umore, compiacere uno.*

TIDE, s. [the ebbing and flowing of the ſea] *fluſſo del mare, marea*, s. f.

The tide of ebb, *rifluſſo.*

The tide of flood, *rifluſſo.*

Windward tide [the tide againſt the wind] *marea contro vento.*

Leeward tide, *vento e marea.*

To go with the tide, *andar a ſeconda della marea, andar colla marea.*

Tide-man [a cuſtom-houſe officer, appointed to guard ſhips till the cuſtom be paid] *doganiere che è deſtinato alla guardia d' un vaſcello che arriva nel porto, affinchè non ſi fraudi la dogana.*

Tide [water, ſea] *l' acqua, il mare, l' onde.*

Tide [time, ſeaſon] *tempo*, s. m. *ſtagione.*

Whitſun-tide, *la Pentecoſte, la ſtagione della Pentecoſte.*

Martinmaſs-tide, *la feſta di ſan Martino, la ſtagione della feſta di ſan Martino.*

Evening-tide, *la ſera.*

To TIDE [to drive with the ſtream] *ſoſpingere col flutto, ſpigner coll' onde.*

TI'DING, s. [news] *novelle.*

TI'DY, adj. [handy] *deſtro, attivo, arconcio, accomodato ad operare.*

TIE, s. [bond] *legame, nodo*, s. m.

Marriage is a ſacred tie, *il matrimonio è un nodo ſacrato.*

To TIE [to bind] *legare, ſtrigner con fune o altro, attaccare.*

To tie one thing to another, *legare una coſa ad un' altra.*

To tie [to bind, to oblige] *legare, impegnare, obbligare, coſtrignere*, preſ. *coſtringo*, pret. *coſtrinſi.*

To tie a knot, or to tie in a knot, *annodare, fare un nodo.*

To tie up [to tie] *legare, attaccare.*

He tied himſelf by a vow to do it, *egli s' obbligò con voto a farlo.*

TIED, adj. *legato, attaccato, annodato.*

TIER, s. [a row, a rank] *un fila, un filare, un numero alla fila.*

TIERCE, s. [one of the ſeven canonical hours] *terza*, s. f. *una delle ore canoniche.*

Tierce [a thruſt in fencing] *terza, termine di ſcherma.*

Tierce [a veſſel holding the third part of a pipe] *ſorte di tino o di botte.*

TI'ERCEL, s. [a male hawk] *terzuolo*, s. m. *il maſchio dell' aſtore.*

TI'ERCET, s. [a ſong of three ſtanzas, or a ſtave of three verſes] *terzetto*, s. m.

TIFF, s. [anger] *collera, ſtizza*, s. f.

Tiff, s. [liquor, drink] *bevanda, liquore.*

TIFFANY, s. [a ſort of thin ſilk] *ſpezie di taffettà.*

TIGER, s. [a fierce wild beaſt] *tigre*, s. m.

TIGH, s. [cloſe, incloſure] *chiuſo*, s. m. *chiuſura*, s. f.

TIGHT, adj. [neat] *pulito, aggiuſtato, affettato, attillato.*

A tight woman, *una donna pulita, aggiuſtata, attillata.*

A tight caſk [one that will not leak] *un barile ben commeſſo, che non cola.*

Tight [ſpoken of a rope, ſtraight] *tiràto, diſteſo.*

To tie a thing tight, *legare che che ſia bene ſtretto.*

TI'GHTLY, adv. [cloſely, not looſely] *ſtrettamente.*

Tightly [neatly] *attillatamente.*

TI'GHTNESS, s. [cloſeneſs, not looſeneſs] *affettatezza, ſtrettezza, attillatura.*

TI'GRESS, s. [a female tiger] *tigre*, s. f.

TIKE, s. [the louſe of dogs or ſheep] *pidochi che vengono a' cani o alle pecore.*

Tike, in Shakeſpeare, *è nome d' un cane.*

TILE, s. [a ſquare earthen plate for covering houſes] *tegola*, s. f. *tegolo*, s. m. *lavoro di terra cotta per coprire i tetti.*

Little tile, *tegoletta*, s. f. *tegoletto*, s. m. *picciol tegolo.*

Gutter or roof tile, *embrice*, s. m.

Tile of wood, *aſſicella*, s. f.

Tile kiln, *fornace da tegole.*

Tile-ſheard, *coccio*, s. m. *pezzo di tegolo.*

Little tile [to pave with] *mattone*, s. m.

To TILE [to cover with tiles] *coprir con tegole.*

TI'LED, adj. *coperto di tegole.*

TI'LER, s. [tile-maker] *facitor di tegole.*

TI'LING, s. [the roof covered with tiles] *tetto coperto di tegole.*

TILL, s. [a ſmall drawer in a deſk] *piccolo tiratojo.*

The till of a printer's preſs, *tavoletta di ſtampatore.*

Till [a money box] *caſſettina in cui ſi ripongono i danari.*

Till, adv. [until] *fino, infino.*

Till now, *fin adeſſo.*

Till then, *fin allora.*

Till ten o'clock, *fino alle dieci.*

He never left intreating till he prevailed, *tanto pregò che ottenne la ſua richieſta.*

To TILL the ground [to dig or turn it up with a ſpade, to plough] *zappare*

lavo-

lavorare, arare coltivare la terra.

Ti'llage, s. [husbandry] *agricoltura, coltura,* s. f.

Land fit for tillage, *terra arabile, buona ad esser lavorata.*

Ti'ller, s. [ploughman] *lavoratore, agricoltore,* s. m.

Tiller [a small tree left to grow till it is fellable] *piccolo albero che si lascia in piedi fino a tanto che sia buono a tagliare.*

Tiller [that which serves for a helm in a boat] *timone d' una barca.*

Ti'lling, s. *coltura, agricoltura,* s. f.

Tillyfa'lly, } adj. [trifling,
Tillyva'lley, } impertinent] *sciocco e fuor di tempo.*

Tilman, s. [husbandman, one who tills] *agricoltore, bifolco.*

Tilt, s. [cloth or tent to cover a boat] *tenda,* s. f.

Tilt-boat, *barca coperta.*

Tilts [an exercise, when two armed persons on horseback run against one another with spears or lances] *giostra,* s. f.

To run at tilts, *giostrare.*

To run a-tilt at one, *correr impetuosamente contro ad uno, urtarlo.*

A tilt-yard, *luogo destinato alla giostra.*

To Tilt [to run at tilts] *giostrare, torneare.*

To tilt with swords or foils, *armeggiare.*

To tilt beer [to raise a cask of beer that is near out, to set it stooping] *alzar una botte di birra, quando comincia ad esser vuota.*

Ti'lted, adj. *alzato, v.* To tilt.

Ti'lter, s. [one who tilts, one who fights]. *giostratore, giostrante; combattitore.*

Tilth, s. [tilling or manuring land] *coltura, agricoltura,* s. f.

A field out of tilth, *un campo inculto, che non è coltivato.*

Tilth, adj. [arable, tilled] *arabile, coltivabile, coltivato.*

Ti'lting, s. *torneamento, e torniamento, torneo,* s. m *giostra,* s. f.

Tilting-staff, *lancia.*

Ti'mber, s. [wood for building] *legname,* s. m. *nome universale de' legni grossi che tagliati si lavorano; legnami.*

Timber-merchant, *mercante di legname.*

Timber-work, *lavoro di legname.*

Timber-wood, *legname grosso.*

Timber-tree, *un albero che produce legname grosso, come la quercia, e simili.*

Belly-timber, [eatables] *viveri, provvisioni, robe da mangiare.*

A timber of skins [forty skins] *quaranta pelli.*

To Ti'mber [to nestle, to make a nest as birds of prey do] *annidarsi, fare il nido.*

Ti'mbersow, s. [a worm in wood] *verme che si genera nel legno.*

Ti'mbrel, s. [tabor] *cembalo, tamburello,* s. m.

Time, s. [a certain measure by which the distance and duration of things are measured] *tempo,* s. m.

The time past, present, and to come, *il tempo passato, presente, e futuro.*

Time out of mind, *tempo immemorabile.*

In time, *col tempo, dopo.*

From time to time, *di tempo in tempo, di quando in quando.*

A mouse in time may bite a cable in two, *col tempo e colla paglia si maturano le nespole.*

Time [age] *tempo, secolo,* s. m. *età,* s. f.

The primitive times of the church, *i tempi della primitiva chiesa.*

Time [season, occasion] *tempo, opportunità, occasione.*

To take a seasonable time, *prender il tempo o l' opportunità.*

To watch a time, *spiar l' occasione.*

All in good time, *ogni cosa col tempo.*

It is high time for me to go, *è tempo d' andarmene.*

Time [leisure] *tempo, comodo.*

If I can spare time, *se avrò tempo.*

Prayer-time, *tempo d' andare alle preghiere, tempo consecrato o destinato a pregar Dio.*

Church-time, *tempo d' andare alla chiesa.*

One time or other, *un giorno o' l' altro.*

The time past, *l' ora è passata, non è più tempo.*

What time of the day is it? *che ora è?*

Time [set or prefixed time, term of time] *tempo, termine.*

The time is expired, *il termine è scorso.*

To give one time for payment, *dar del tempo ad uno per pagare.*

Time in music, *tempo, battuta,* s. m. *quella misura di tempo, che da il maestro della musica in battendo a' cantori, o suonatori.*

To beat the time, *portar la battuta.*

Time [bout] *volta.*

This is not the first time, *questa non è la prima volta.*

Every time, *ogni volta.*

Some times, *qualche volta.*

To come time enough, *venire a tempo, o in tempo.*

In good time [well and good] *alla buon' ora.*

In times past, *tempo fu, per l' addietro, già, altre volte.*

Long before this time, *molto tempo prima.*

At that time, *allora.*

At this time, *adesso, a quest' ora.*

From this time forth, *d' or' in avanti, da qui innanzi, d' ora in poi.*

In time coming, or in time to come, *per l' avvenire, in avvenire.*

I'll do it at any time for you, *farò questo per voi ogni volta che vorrete.*

If at any time you chance to go thither, *se mai vi andaste.*

At no time [never] *giammai, mai.*

Mean time, in the mean time, *frattanto, in questo mentre.*

I shall be with you by the time you have dined, *sarò da voi subito che avrete pranzato.*

It shall be ready by the time you come back, *sarà in ordine quando ritornerete.*

To hinder one's time, *stornare, interrompere alcuno, fargli perdere il tempo.*

In a day's time, *in un giorno, fra un giorno.*

In an hour's time, *fra un' ora.*

In the day time, *di giorno.*

In the night time, *di notte.*

He lived long after their time, *visse molto tempo dopo loro.*

To Time, *prender il tempo, prender un tempo favorevole.*

To time a business well, *fare un affare in tempo opportuno.*

To time [to measure harmonically] *porre in tuono, accordare, e dicesi delli stromenti musicali.*

Ti'meful, adj. [seasonable, timely, early] *opportuno, primaticcio.*

Ti'meless, adj. [unseasonable, done at an improper time] *inopportuno, fatto fuor di tempo.*

Timeless [untimely, immature, done before the proper time] *immaturo, fatto prima del debito tempo.*

Ti'mely, adv. [opportunely] *a tempo, opportunamente, maturamente.*

Timely [soon] *di buon' ora, per tempo.*

Timely, adv [seasonable] *opportuno, fatto al tempo debito.*

To give timely notice, *avvertire in tempo.*

Ti'mid, adj. *v.* Timorous.

Timi'dity, s. [fearfulness] *timidezza, timidità, paura,* s. f.

Ti'morous, adj. [fearful] *timido, pauroso.*

To make timorous, *render timido.*

Ti'morously, adv. *timidamente, con timore, paurosamente.*

Ti'morousness, s. [timidity] *timidità, timidezza, paura.*

Ti'mous, adj. [early, timely] *opportuno, fatto per tempo.*

Tin, s. [metal] *stagno,* s. m.

Tin [iron tinned over] *latta,* s. f.

A tin candlestick, *un candeliere di latta.*

To tin over, *stagnare, coprir di stagno.*

Ti'ncel, s. [a kind of glittering stuff made of silk and copper] *orpello,* s. m.

Tinct, s. [a colouring] *tintura,* s. f.

To Tinct [to die] *tignere.*

Ti'ncture, s. [colour, dye] *tintura, tinta,* s. f. *il color della cosa tinta.*

Tincture [impression] *tintura, impressione, idea,* s. f.

Tincture [smack, smattering] *tintura, infarinatura, leggiera conoscenza, barlume.*

To Ti'ncture, *dare una tintura, tiguere.*

Ti'nctured, adj. *che ha qualche tintura, tinto.*

He is tinctured with that opinion, *egli è imbevuto di questa opinione.*

To TIND [to light] *accendere,* pret. *accesi.*

To tind a candle, fire, &c. *accendere una candela, il fuoco, e simili.*

TI'NDER, s. *esca,* s. f.

TI'NDERBOX, s. *scatola in cui si tiene il fucile e l' esca da batter fuoco.*

TING, s. [the sound of a bell] *tintinno di campana.*

TI'NGED, adj. [coloured or dyed lightly] *colorito, tinto leggiermente, che non ha che una picciola tintura.*

To TI'NGLE, [as a bell or vessel of metal] *tintinnire, risonare.*

My ears tingle, *mi risonan gli orecchi.*

TI'NGLING, s. [the noise of a little bell] *tintinno,* s. m. *voce fatta per esprimere il suono del campanuzzo.*

Tingling in the ears, *bucinamento, zufolio d' orecchi.*

TI'NKER, s. a maker or mender of vessels of brass, copper, &c.] *calderajo,* s. m.

TI'NNED, adj. *stagnato.*

TI'NSEL, s. [a kind of shining cloth] *drappo tessuto con orpello.*

Tinsel [any thing shining with false lustre] *orpello; ogni cosa che luce con luce falsa.*

To TI'NSEL [to decorate with cheap ornaments; to adorn with lustre that has no value] *coprire o adornare d' oro o d' argento falso.*

TI'NTAMAR, s. [confused noise] *strepito, fracasso, romore, frastuono,* s. m.

TI'NY, adj. [small, slender] *piccolo magro, smunto, macilente, minuto, sottile.*

TIP, s. [the outmost point of any thing] *punta, cima,* s. f.

The tip of the nose, *la punta del naso.*

The tip of the finger, *la punta del dito.*

Tip-toe, *punta del piede.*

Tip-staff, s. [one of the wardens of the Fleet's men] *tavolaccino, sergente,* s. m.

To TIP [with iron] *munire di ferro.*

To tip a rod with silver, *munire la punta d' una bacchetta con argento.*

To tip one the wink, *dare un' occhiata ad uno, occheggiarlo, guardarlo sottecchi.*

To tip down, *abbattere, stramazzare, gettar per terra.*

To tip one's hand [to give one a bribe] *ugner le mani ad uno, corromperlo con donativi.*

To tip [to fall] *cascare.*

To tip off, to tip over the perch [to die] *tirar le calze, morire.*

TI'PLE, s. *bevanda,* s. f.

To TI'PLE [to drink often or much] *bere poco e frequente.*

TI'PLER, s. *bevitore.*

TI'PLING, s. *imbriachezza,* s. f.

Tipling house, *taverna, osteria.*

The tipling philosophers, *i filosofi briachi, i filosofi beoni.*

TI'PPET, s. [a long scarf, which doctors of divinity wear over their gowns] *ciarpa,* s. f. *striscia di seta che i dottori di teologia e i capellani de' signori portano al collo in Inghilterra.*

A woman's tippet [a kind of handkerchief for women's necks, commonly of fur] *collare di pelle, che le donne portano al collo.*

TI'PSY, adj. [a little in drink] *mezzo cotto, mezzo imbriaco.*

TIPT, adj. ex. A rod tipt with silver, *una bachetta con punta d' argento.*

TIRE, s. [attire] *ornamento, abigliamento,* s. m. *acconciatura,* s. f.

A tire woman, *una cameriera.*

A tire of guns in a ship, *una fila di cannoni in un vascello.*

To TIRE [to dress] *ornare, adornare, abbigliare, acconciare.*

To tire [to weary] *faticare, lassare, stancare, straccare.*

To tire [to weary, to be tedious] *faticare, tediare, annojare, apportar noja, infastidire,* pres. *infastidisco.*

I fear I shall tire you, *temo d' esservi nojoso, ho paura d' infastidirvi.*

To tire [to be, or grow tired] *lassarsi, straccarsi, stancarsi, tediarsi.*

TI'RED, adj. *affaticato, stanco, stracco, lasso.*

I am tired with walking, *sono stanco di camminare.*

I am quite tired of meat, *sono stufo di carne.*

TI'RESOM, adj. *tedioso, nojoso, molesto, fastidioso, importuno, incomodo.*

TI'RWHIT, s. [a bird] *sorta d' uccello.*

'TIS [it is] *egli è.*

'Tis so, *gli è così.*

TISA'NE, v. Ptisane.

TI'SICK, s. [an ulceration of the lungs, accompanied with a hectic fever that causes a consumption] *tischezza,* s. f. *infermità di polmoni ulcerati.*

TI'SICAL, adj. *tisico.*

TI'SSUE, s. [a rich stuff made of silk and silver or gold, woven together] *drappo d' oro o d' argento; rircio.*

TIT, s. [a little bird] *lui,* s. m. *cingallegra,* s. f. *uccello picciolo di più colori.*

Tit [little horse], *cavalluccio cavallino, bidetto,* s. m.

Tit, s. *una donna; ed è voce di disprezzo.*

TI'TBIT, s. properly tidbit [nice bit] *boccone, delicato, cibo delicato.*

TI'THEABLE, adj. [liable to yield tithes] *soggetto alla decima,*

TITHE, s. [the tenth part of all fruits that is due to the parson of the parish] *decima,* s. f.

To TITHE [to take the tenth part] *decimare, riscuotere e pigliar le decime.*

TI'THED, adj. *decimato.*

TI'THER, s. [tithe-gatherer] *riscuotitor di decime.*

TI'THYMAL, s. *titimalo, nome d' erba.*

TI'THING, s. *il decimare.*

Tithing [a company of ten men with their families all bound to the king for the peaceable behaviour of each other] *una decina, una società o numero di dieci uomini colle loro famiglie.*

Tithing man [the chief of a tithing] *il capo d' una decina o d' una famiglia.*

To TI'TILLATE [to tickle] *titillare, solleticare.*

TITILLA'TION, s. [tickling] *dileti-co, solletico,* s. m.

TI'TLARK, s. *sorte d' allodola.*

TI'TLE, s. [inscription of a book or act] *titolo,* s. m. *iscrizione, denominazione,* s. f.

The title-page of a book, *il titolo d' un libro.*

Title [name of honour, given to persons according to their rank or quality] *titolo, grado, nome,* s. m. *dignità,* s. f.

A title of honour, *un titolo d' onore.*

Title [right, claim] *titolo, ragione.*

By a good title, *à buono titolo.*

To give up one's title or right, *ceder il suo titolo o la sua ragione.*

To TI'TLE [to give a title] *titolare, intitolare.*

To title a book, *titolare o intitolare un libro.*

TI'TLED, adj. *titolato, intitolato.*

To TI'TTER, v. To twittter.

TI'TTLE, s. *quel punto che si mette sopra la lettera* i.

Not a tittle, *non una parola, neppure un ette.*

I will not part with a tittle of my right, *non voglio cedere un punto della mia ragione.*

TI'TTLE TATTLE [twittle-twattle] *cicalio, cicalamento,* s. m.

A tittle-tattle [a prattler] *un cicalone, un gracchiatore.*

To TI'TTLE-TATTLE [to prattle] *cicalare, chiacchierare, gracchiare.*

TI'TULAR, adj. [that bears a title] *titolare, che non ha che il titolo.*

Titular bishop, *vescovo titolare.*

To, prep. [unto] *a, al, allo, alla.*

To every one, *a ciascheduno.*

He is gone to Rome, *egli è andato a Roma.*

To go to school, *andare alla scuola.*

He is very much given to study, *egli è molto dedito allo studio.*

He sent to me, *mi mandò, mandò a me.*

I spoke to him, *gli parlai.*

I said to them, *dissi loro.*

He made love to her, *le fece l' amore.*

To go to France, *andare in Francia.*

To, before a verb, is the sign of the infinitive mood, ex: to love to read, *amare leggere.*

To commend one to his face, *lodare alcuno in faccia, in sua presenza.*

I will maintain it to his face, *glielo manterrò in faccia.*

From top to toe, *da capo a piedi.*

From door to door, *di porta in porta.*

From hand to hand, *di mano in mano.*

To have a title to a thing, *aver ragione sopra qualche cosa.*

He is always to his work, *egli è sempre a lavorare.*

To [towards] *verso.*

He went ſtrait to the place, *egli ſen' andò a dirittura verſo quel luogo.*
To be ungrateful to one, *eſſer ingrato verſo qualcheduno.*
I did wait on him to his houſe, *l' accompagnai fino a caſa ſua.*
I am unpaid to this day, *non ſono ancora pagato.*
To the beſt of my power, *per quanto per me ſi portà, per quanto ſarà in poter mio.*
My love to you, *l' amor che vi porto.*
That is loſt to me, *queſto è perduto per me.*
To drink to exceſs, *bere eceſſivamente, ſmoderatamente.*
To [in compariſon] *a petto, in paragone, in comparazione.*
You are but a fool to him, *voi ſiete uno ſciocco a petto a lui.*
This is nothing to what I have ſeen, *queſto è nulla a paragone di quel che ho veduto.*
Men's wiſdom is folly to God, *la ſaviezza degli uomini e ſciochezza innanzi a Dio.*
This is no prejudice to you, *queſto non vi fa torto.*
He lived to a great age, *viſſe molto vecchio.*
It is nothing to me, *ciò poco m' importa.*
Not to my knowledge, *non per quel che ne ſo.*
I am glad to ſee you, *godo di vedervi.*
As to this, *in quanto a queſto.*
According to, *ſecondo.*
He grew to that pride, *divenne sì ſuperbo.*
He has a kind man to his father, *egli ha un padre molto benigno.*
He was like to die, *egli fu per morire.*
To-day, *oggi.*
To-morrow, *domani, dimani, domane.*
To-night, *ſtaſera.*
After to-morrow, *poſdomane, doman l' altro.*
To and fro, *quà e là, ſu e giù.*
As to that, *in quanto a ciò.*
I will do it to oblige you, *lo farò per compiacervi.*
To the end that, *affinchè.*
He loves to read, *egli ama a leggere.*
I am grieved to think of it, *ſono trafitto di dolore al penſarci.*
TOAD, s. [a venomous reptile] *botta*, s. f. *roſpo*, s. m. *animal velenoſo, ſimile al ranocchio.*
Toad-ſtool, *ſpezie di fungo.*
Toad-flax [a plant] *linaria*, s. f. *pianta.*
Toad-ſtone, *chelonite*, s. m. *ſorta di pietra.*
TOAST, s. [bread dried before the fire] *fetta di pane arroſtita al fuoco, fetta di pan toſtato.*
Toaſt, s. *fetta di pane che dopo d' eſſere ſtata arroſtita al fuoco è ſparſa di butirro ed eſpoſta al fuoco di nuovo.*
Toaſt, s. [bread dried and put into liquor] *fetta di pan toſtato inzuppata in vino, acqua, o altro liquore.*
Toaſt, s. [a celebrated woman, whoſe health is often drunk] *donna celebre o per bellezza o per altro, alla ſalute di cui ſi beve da tutti i commenſali un dopo l' altro.*
Your toaſt Sir. *Datemi un Brindiſi, Signore; cioè ditemi quel è la Dama alla di cui ſalute io deggio bere; ſi dice anche*, give me your toaſt.
TO'ASTER, s. [he who toaſts] *colui che bee alla ſalute di qualche donna.*
TOBA'CCO, s. [a plant well known] *tabacco*, s. m.
Tobacco in ſtalks, or in the leaf, *tabacco in foglia.*
To ſmoke tobacco, *fumar del tabacco.*
Tobacco pipe, *pipa per fumar del tabacco.*
Tobacco-box, *tabacchiera, ſcatola da tabacco.*
TOBA'CCONIST, s. *mercante o venditor di tabacco.*
TOD, s. [28 pounds, or two ſtones] *peſo de 28 libbre.*
A tod of wool, *ventotto libbre di lana.*
Tod [a buſh, a thick ſhrub] *fratta, ceſpuglio, arbuſto foltiſſimo.*
TOE, s. [a finger of the foot] *dito del piede.*
The great toe, *il dito groſſo del piede.*
The little toe, *il dito mignolo del piede.*
From top to toe, *da capo a' piedi.*
To turn one's toes out, *voltare i piedi in fuori.*
To turn one's toes in, *voltare i piedi in dentro.*
To kiſs the Pope's toe, *baciare i piedi del Papa.*
TO'FORE, adv. [before] *prima, innanzi, avanti.*
TOFT, s. [grove of trees] *un boſchetto.*
Toft, s. [a law term, a place where a houſe or meſſuage has been] *il luogo dove altre volte era una caſa.*
TO'GED, adj. [gowned] *togato, che ha la toga indoſſo.*
TO'GETHER, adv. *inſieme, unitamente, in compagnia, di brigata.*
To walk together, *paſſeggiare inſieme.*
Let us go together, *andiamo in copagnia, andiamo inſieme.*
Three days together, *tre giorni alla fila, tre giorni continui.*
To mix together, *tramiſchiare, meſcolare inſieme.*
To gather together, *raccogliere, aſſembrare, adunare.*
Together with [in union with] *in compagnia.*
TOIL, s. [pains, trouble] *pena, fatica*, s. f. *affanno*, s. m.
It was a great toil to me, *durai molta fatica.*
Toils [a kind of net] *lungajuola*, s. f. *ſorta di rete lunga e baſſa, che ſi tende agli animali terreſtri.*
To TOIL [to labour, to drudge] *lavorare, faticare, penare, affannarſi, durar fatica, ſtentare, affaticarſi.*
TO'ILER, s. *quello o quella che dura fatica.*
TOILET, s. [a dreſſing table] *tavolino a cui le donne s' acconciano, da' moderni con voce franciosa chiamato* toeletta.
TO'ILING, s. *fatica, pena, malagevolezza*, s. f. *lavoro, travaglio, ſtento*, s. m.
TO'ILSOME, adj. *fatichevole, laborioſo, faticoſo, malagevole, travagliante, penoſo.*
TO'ILSOMENESS, s. *pena, fatica, affanno, ſtento.*
TO'KEN, s. [ſign, mark] *ſegno, contraſſegno.*
In token of my gratitude, *in ſegno della mia gratitudine.*
Token of ill luck, *funeſto preſagio.*
Token [gift, preſent] *preſente, regalo.*
Token, or plague-token, *carbone, carbonchio*, s. m. *enfiato peſtilenziale, bolla*, s. f. *gavocciolo*, s. m.
Token [farthing] *quattrino.*
To TO'KEN [to make known] *far conoſcere per mezzo d' un ſegnale.*
TOLD, adj. [from to tell] *detto*, v. To tell.
I am told, *mi vien detto, m' è ſtato detto.*
To TOLE [to drain, to draw by degrees] *ſeccare, trarre a poco a poco, e diceſi dell' acqua da' luoghi paludoſi e ſimili.*
TO'LERABLE, adj. [ſufferable] *tollerabile, comportabile, comportevole.*
Tolerable [indifferent] *medicore, così così.*
TO'LERABLENESS, s. *mediocrità*, s. f.
TO'LERABLY, adv. *tollerabilmente, mediocremente, così così.*
TO'LERANCE, s. [power of enduring, act of enduring] *tolleranza.*
To TO'LERATE [to bear] *tollerare, comportare, ſupportare.*
TO'LERATED, adj. *tollerato, comportato, ſopportato.*
TO'LERATING, } s. *tolleranza*, s. f.
TOLERA'TION, } *il tollerare.*
TOLL, s. [tribute or cuſtom paid for paſſage] *pedaggio*, s. m. *dazio, che ſi paga per paſſare a piede in qualche luogo.*
To pay the toll, *pagare il pedaggio.*
A toll-gatherer, *collettore del pedaggio.*
Toll-money, *pedaggio.*
Toll-free, *franco di pedaggio.*
Toll-booth, *il luogo dove ſi paga il pedaggio.*
Toll [liberty to buy and ſell within the precincts of a manour] *privilegio di vendere e di comprare in una ſignoria.*
To TOLL a bell [to ring it after a particular manner] *rintoccare una campana, ſonare una compana a tocchi.*
To toll one [to intice] *adeſcare, incitare, ſpronare, ſpignere, incoraggiare*, pref. *ſpingo*, pret. *ſpinſi.*

TOLLBOOTH, s. [a prison] *prigione.*

To TO'LLBOOTH [to imprison in a tolbooth] *imprigionare, chiuder su.*

TO'LLED, adj. *rintoccato.*

Tolled on, *adescato, incitato, spronato, spinto, incorraggiato.*

TOMB, s. [sepulchre of stone] *tomba, sepoltura,* s. f. *sepolcro,* s. m.

Tomb-stone, *lapide, lapida,* s. f. *pietra che cuopre la sepoltura.*

To TOMB [to bury, to entomb] *chiuder nella tomba, seppellire.*

TO'MBLESS, adj. [wanting a tomb, wanting sepulchral monument] *privo di tomba, privo di monumento sepolcrale.*

TO'MBOY, s. [a wanton frolicksome young woman] *una spavalda, una giovane spavalda.*

TOME, s. [separate part or distinct volume of a book] *tomo,* s. m. *col primo o aperto, volume, parte.*

TO'MKIN, } s. [stopple of a great
TO'MPION, } gun or mortar] *turaccio,* s. m.

TO'MTIT, s. [titmouse, a small bird] *lui, cinciallegra, o simil altro uccelletto.*

TON, *v.* Tun.

TONE, s. [a certain degree of elevation or depression of the voice] *tuono, accento,* s m.

Doleful tone, *tuono flebile.*

One may know by his tone that he is an Italian, *si può conoscere dall' accento ch' egli è un Italiano.*

TONG, s. [the catch of a buckle] *ardiglione di fibbia.*

TONGS, s. [an instrument belonging to a fire hearth] *molle,* s. m.

TONGUE, s. [the instrument of speech] *lingua,* s. f. *membro che è nella bocca dell' animale, col quale si forma la voce.*

His tongue runs upon wheels, *gli ha messo la lingua in molle; non fa altro che cicalare.*

He speaks what comes next to his tongue's end, *gli ha sempre la bocca aperta; gli è molto largo di bocca.*

Your tongue runs before your wit, *voi non pensate a quel che dite.*

He has lost his tongue [he can't speak] *gli ha perduta la favella; non può parlare.*

To find one's tongue again, *ricominciare a parlare.*

To have a thing at one's tongue's end, *aver qualche cosa in sulla punta della lingua.*

What the heart thinks, the tongue speaks, *la lingua batte dove il dente duole.*

A neat's tongue, *lingua di bue.*

Dog's tongue [an herb] *lingua di cane, spezie d' erba.*

Tongue [language] *lingua, idioma, linguaggio, favella.*

The English tongue, *la lingua Inglese.*

The gift of tongues, *il dono delle lingue.*

The tongue of a ballance, *la lingua o l' ago d' una bilancia.*

The tongue of a razor, *il manico d' un rasojo.*

To hold one's tongue, *tacersi.*

His tongue failed him, *gli mancò la parola.*

Keep your tongue in your hand, *parlate colla lingua fra' denti, parlate come si deve.*

Tongue-tyed, *mezzo muto, che ha la lingua legata, che non può ben parlare.*

To TONGUE [to talk, to prate] *cicanciare; ciarlare.*

TONGUED, adj. ex. Long-tongued, *linguardo, linguacciuto.*

An ill tongued man or woman, *un linguardo, un linguacciuto, un maldicente, una linguarda, una linguacciuta, una maldicente.*

Double-tongued man [dissembler] *uomo doppio, che dice una cosa quando ne pensa un' altra.*

TO'NGUELESS, adj. [wanting a tongue, speechless] *che non ha lingua, che non ha parole.*

Tongueless [unnamed, not spoken of] *non nominato, di cui non si son fatte parole.*

TO'NNAGE, *v.* Tunnage.

TO'NSILS, s. [the almonds of the ear, two glands at the root of the tongue] *gavigne, gavine,* s. f.

TO'NSURE, s. [the act of clipping the hair] *tonsura, il tagliar i capelli.*

TOO, adv. [also] *anche, anco, ancora, parimente, altresì, eziandio.*

I know it too, *lo so anch' io.*

Too [over-much] *troppo.*

Too big, *troppo grande.*

Too little, *troppo piccolo.*

Too well, *troppo bene, pur troppo.*

I love you too well, *v' amo pur troppo.*

Too much of any thing is good for nothing, *il soverchio rompe il coperchio.*

TOOK, *è un preterito del verbo* To take.

TOOL, s. [instrument of any sort] *stromento, ordigno,* s. m.

He made him the tool of his revenge, *si servì di lui come di stromento per effettuare la sua vendetta.*

He is a sad tool, *egli è un povero uomo che non val niente.*

TOOTH, s. *dente,* s. m. *plur.* Teeth.

To have a sweet tooth [to love dainties] *esser ghiotto o leccardo, amar i buoni bocconi.*

To have an aking tooth, *perseguitare, contrariare per odio o stizza.*

To breed teeth, *spuntare i denti.*

I shall do it in spite of your teeth, *la farò mal grado vostro, ad onta vostra, a vostro marcio dispetto, alla barba vostra.*

To go to it tooth and nail [with might and main] *sbracciarsi, adoperarsi in che che sia con ogni forza e sapere.*

The teeth of a saw, rake, comb, &c. *i denti d' una sega, d' un rastrello, d' un pettine, e simili.*

To laugh from the teeth outward, *ridere contro voglia, ridere colle labbra.*

To make one's teeth water, to set one's teeth a watering [to make one long for any thing] *far venire l' acqua in bocca ad uno.*

To the teeth [in opposition] *in faccia, sulla faccia.*

To cast in the teeth [to insult by open exprobation] *rinfacciare, insultare in presenza.*

TO'OTH-AKE, *mal di denti.*

Tooth-drawer, *cavadenti.*

Tooth-wrest [an instrument to draw teeth with] *cane,* s. m. *ferro col quale si cavano i denti.*

Tooth-picker, *stuzzicadenti, piccol fuscello o altra cosa con che si cava il cibo rimaso fra' denti.*

A row or set of tooth, *dentatura,* s. f. *ordine e componimento de' denti.*

To set one's tooth on edge, *allegare i denti.*

To cast the teeth, *mutare i denti.*

To crash with the teeth, *stridere co' denti.*

The crashing of the teeth, *stridor di denti.*

To TOOTH [to furnish with teeth, to indent] *fornir di denti, lasciar delle morse onde una cosa si possa conficcar nell' altra.*

To tooth [to lock in each other] *chiudere o conficcare una cosa dentata in un altra pur dentata.*

TO'OTHED, adj. *dentato, che ha denti.*

TO'OTHING, s. [a corner-stone left for more buildings] *morse,* plur. *di morsa,* s. f. *pietre o mattoni i quali sporgono in fuori da' lati de' muri, lasciativi a fine di potervi collegar nuovo muro.*

TO'OTHLESS, adj. *sdentato, che non ha denti, senza denti.*

Toothless mouth, *bocca sdentata.*

TO'OTHSOME, adj. [pleasant to the tooth] *gustoso, delicato, piacevole al palato.*

TO'OTHWORT, s. [a plant] *nome di pianta.*

TOP, s. [height, uppermost end of a thing] *sommità, cima, punta,* s. f. *sommo,* s. m. *l' estremità dell' altezza.*

The top of a hill, *la sommità, la cima d' un monte.*

The top of a rock, *la cima, la punta d' una roccia, d' un sasso, d' una rupe.*

The top of the head, *il cocuzzolo del capo.*

The top of a tree, *la cima d' un albero.*

The top of a house, *comigno, comignolo,* s. m. *la parte più alta de' tetti.*

The top of the bed, *il cielo del letto.*

The top of the water, *la superficie dell' acqua.*

From top to bottom, *da alto a basso.*

From top to toe, *da capo a piedi.*

The top of glory, happiness, *il colmo della gloria, della felicità.*

Top knot, *nastro che le donne portano sulla testa.*

Top-

Top-heavy [so heavy at the top that the weight of it sways it one way or other] *troppo pesante in cima.*

Top-heavy [so drunk that he cannot hold up his head] *talmente briaco che non può regger la testa.*

The round-top of a ship mast, *gabbia*, s. f. *quello strumento che i marinai mettono in cima dell' antenna, sul quale sta la veletta.*

Top-mast, top-gallant-mast, *trinchetto*, s. m. *la cima dell' albero del vascello.*

Top-gallant gale, *vento fresco, vento di terra.*

Top-gallant spark, *damerino, vago, zerbino, zerbinetto, parigino, milordino.*

Top-sail, *vela di trinchetto.*

Top, adj. [chief] *primo, principale.*

He is the top man of all, *egli è il primo, il migliore di tutti.*

Top, s. [a play-thing for boys] *fattore, paleo*, s. m. *trottola*, s. f.

To Top [to strike off the top] *tagliare la cima.*

To top trees, *tagliare la cima degli alberi, cimar gli alberi.*

To top [to cover] *coprire, cuoprire.*

To top a candle, *smoccolare una candela.*

To top upon one [to brag over one, to out-do one] *pigliar superiorità sopra qualcheduno.*

Topa'ze, s. [precious stone] *topazo*, s. m.

To Tope [to drink lustily] *trincare, bere assai.*

To'per, s. [hard drinker] *bevitore, beone, trincatore*, s. m.

To'pful, adj. [full to the top, full to the brim] *pieno sino alla cima, pieno fino all' orlo, colmo.*

To'pless, adj. [having no top] *privo di cima.*

To'phet, s. [hell; a scriptural name] *inferno, abbisso.*

To'p-proud, adj. [proud in the highest degree] *orgogliosissimo, d' ogni orgoglio in cima.*

To'pical, adj. [belonging to, or applied to a particular place] *topico, appartenente a qualche luogo comune.*

Topical logick, *logica topica.*

To'pick [subject] *soggetto*, s. m. *materia*, s. f.

Topicks [that part of logick which treats of the invention of arguments] *topici*, s. m. pl. *capi principali, dai quali si ne tirano gli argomenti probabili.*

Topo'grapher, s. *colui che fa la descrizione d' un luogo particolare.*

Topogra'phical, adj. [belonging to topography] *topografico.*

Topo'graphy, s. [a description of a place or of some small quantity of land] *topografia, descrizione di qualche luogo particolare.*

To'pped, adj. [from to top] *spuntato, v.* To top.

Sharp topped, *puntuto.*

To'pping, adj. [first, chief] *primo, principale, del primo grado.*

A topping man, *un uomo considerabile, un uomo de' più principali, un uomo di grido.*

Topsy-turvy, adv. [upside-down] *sottosopra, sozzopra.*

To lay all topsy-turvy, *voltare, mettere ogni cosa sottosopra, in confusione, in iscompiglio.*

Torch, s. [taper] *torcia*, s. f. *torchio, doppiere*, s. m.

A little torch, *un torchietto.*

Torch-weed or torches [an herb] *tassobarbasso, verbasco*, s. m. *spezie d' erba.*

Torchbe'arer, s. *colui il cui officio è di portare la torcia innanzi a chicchessia.*

To'rch-light, s. *lume di torcia, lume di doppiere.*

To'rcher, s. [one that gives light] *colui che fa lume colla torcia.*

Tore, *preterito del verbo* To tear.

To'rment, s. [violent pain] *tormento, travaglio*, s. m. *pena, afflizione*, s. f.

To Torme'nt [to put to great pain] *tormentare, dar tormenti.*

To torment [to afflict, to disquiet] *tormentare, affliggere, travagliar l' animo, angustiare.*

Torme'nted, adj. *tormentato, afflitto, travagliato, angustiato.*

Torme'nter, } s. [one that torments] *tormentatore*, s. m. *che tormenta.*
Torme'ntor,

To'rmentil, s. [the herb set foil] *tormentilla*, s. f. *sorta d' erba.*

Torme'nting, *tormentagione*, s. f. *tormento*, s. m. *il tormentare.*

Tormenting, adj. *tormentoso, pien di tormento, che apporta tormento.*

Torme'ntor, s. [hangman] *boja, carnefice*, s. m.

Torn, adj. [from to tear] *stracciato, v.* To tear.

Torna'do, s. [sudden and violent storm at sea] *burrasca, fortuna, tempesta*, s. f.

To'rpent, } adj. [benumbed] *intormentito, assiderato, agghiadato, intorpidito.*
To'rpid,

To'rrent, s. [strong stream, violent land-flood] *torrente*, s. m. *corso rapido d' acque che impetuosamente cresce e scema.*

To'rrid, adj. [burning hot] *torrido.*

The torrid zone, *la zona torrida.*

Tort, s. [a law term, injury, wrong] *torto*, s. m. *ingiustizia, ingiuria*, s. f.

Tort feasor, s. [a law term, trespasser] *malfattore.*

To'rtious, adj. [injurious, doing wrong] *pregiudiziale, dannoso, che fa torto.*

To'rtive, adj. [twisted, wreathed] *attorcigliato, tortuoso, serpeggiante, che s' avvolge intorno.*

To'rtoise, s. [an amphibious creature] *testuggine*, s. f. *animal terrestre e aquatico.*

Land-tortoise, *testuggine terrestre.*

Sea-tortoise, *testuggine di mare.*

Tortoise-shell, *tartaruca, scaglia di testuggine.*

To'rtuous, adj. [winding, turning in and out] *tortuoso, torto, che va serpeggiando.*

To'rturable, adj. [capable of being tortured] *capace di tortura.*

To'rture, s. [rack, exquisite pain or torment] *tortura*, s. f. *tormento, travaglio*, s. m.

To To'rture, [to put to great pain] *dar la tortura, tormentare.*

To'rtured, adj. *tormentato.*

To'rturer, s. *ministro di giustizia che da la tortura a' pretesi rei.*

To'rturing, s. *tortura*, s. f.

To'rvity, s. [sourness, severity of countenance] *il guardar torvo, aspetto burbero.*

To'rvous, adj. [sour of aspect, stern, severe of countenance] *torvo, burbero, arcigno.*

To'ry, s. *colui che in Inghilterra aderisce o pretende aderire alle antiche leggi e all' apostolica Gerarchia della chiesa Anglicana. Il suo opposto chiamasi* Whig.

To Tose [to comb wool] *scardassare o pettinar lana.*

Toss, s. [pull, jerk] *scossa*, s. f. *sbalzo*, s. m.

To be in a toss, *esser in pena, esser in gran perplessità.*

To Toss [to shake, to move up and down] *scuotere, agitare, dimenare, sbalzare, trabalzare, balzare.*

To toss one in a blanket, *sbalzare alcuno in una schiavina, dare la copertaccia.*

To toss a matter, *discutere, esaminare, crivellare una materia.*

To toss a thing in one's hand, *ruminare, riandar nel pensiero qualche cosa.*

To toss a thing about, *gettare una cosa qua e la.*

To toss a ball, *rimandare una palla.*

To toss [a term used in a tennis-court] *pallare, palleggiare.*

To toss [to vex, to disquiet] *affannare, travagliare, affliggere, tormentare, penare.*

To'ssed, adj. *scosso, sbalzato, balzato, v.* To toss.

To toss from post to pillar, *sbalzare d' un luogo ad un altro.*

To'ssing, s. *scossa, agitazione*, s. f. *sbalzo, balzo*, s. m.

The continual tossing of the sea, *il continuo moto del mare.*

Tost, *pret. e part. pass. del verbo* To toss.

To'tal, adj. [wholly, intire] *totale, intero.*

The total sum, *la somma totale.*

Tota'lity, s. [the total or whole

whole sum] *il totale, la somma totale.*

TO'TALLY, adv. [utterly, intirely] *totalmente, interamente, affatto, in tutto e per tutto.*

T'OTHER [the other] *l' altro.*

T'other day, *l' altro giorno.*

To TO'TTER [to shake, to stagger, to reel] *vacillare, andare a onde, traballare, barcollare.*

He totters like a drunken man, *egli va a onde, o barcolla, come un imbriaco.*

TO'TTERING, s. *vacillamento, barcollo.*

Tottering, adj. *vacillante, che barcolla.*

A tottering crown, *una corona vacillante.*

A tottering house, *una casa mal fondata.*

TO'TTERINGLY, adv. *a onde, vacillando.*

TO'TTERY, } adj. [shaking, unsteady, dizzy] *vacillante, vertiginoso.*
TO'TTY, }

TOUCH, s. [feeling] *tatto,* s. m. *il toccare.*

To give one a touch [to touch one] *toccare alcuno.*

Touch [stroke in painting] *tratto di pennello, pennellata.*

Touch [witty expression] *detto arguto, scherzo mordace.*

Touch [tincture, smattering] *tintura, infarinatura, leggiera conoscenza.*

Touch [assay of gold or silver] *saggio, paragone, cimento,* s. m. *pruova,* s. f.

Touch-stone, *paragone,* s. m. *pietra sulla quale fregando l' oro o l' argento si fa prova della sua qualità.*

To bring gold to the touch [to try gold by the touch-stone] *provar l' oro al paragone.*

Touch [trial] *prova, cimento, paragone, esame.*

He fears to come to the touch, *teme di venire alle prove.*

This will never stand the touch, *questo non può resistere all' esame.*

Touch [gentle wipe] *bottone, motto acuto e pungente, tratto.*

To give one a touch by the by, *sbottonare, sbottoneggiare alcuno.*

A touch of a disease, *attacco di malattia.*

It has a touch of purple, *egli tira un poco al color di porpora.*

I must have a touch with him [he and I must fight] *bisogna ci diamo quattro botte.*

To give a short touch to a thing, *toccare, discorrere brevemente sopra qualche cosa.*

I have a mind to have another touch, *ho gran voglia di provare un' altra volta.*

To keep touch with one [to be as good as one's word with one] *mantener la parola ad uno, attener la promessa ad uno.*

Touch-hole of a gun, *spiraglio d' un' arma da fuoco.*

The touch-pan of a gun, *il focone d' un' arma da fuoco.*

Touch-wood, *esca,* s. f.

To TOUCH [to feel] *toccare.*

To touch one's hand, *toccare la mano ad uno.*

To touch one another, *toccarsi.*

To touch [to be contiguous or next to] *toccare, esser vicino o contiguo.*

To touch a thing [to take some of it] *toccare una cosa, prenderne, levarne.*

To touch a musical instrument [to play upon it] *toccare uno strumento musicale, sonar qualche strumento musicale.*

To touch [to cast anchor, to go ashore] *toccare, approdare, fare scala, pigliar porto, dar fondo.*

We touched at Leghorn, *noi femmo la scala di Livorno, noi femmo scala in Livorno.*

To touch upon a thing [to speak of it by the by] *toccare una cosa, parlarne brevemente.*

To touch or touch upon [to concern] *toccare, appartenere, aspettarsi,* pres. *appartengo, appartenni.*

It nearly touches me, *ciò mi tocca sul vivo.*

To touch [to affect, to move] *toccare, compugnere,* pres. *compungo,* pret. *compunsi.*

TO'UCHABLE, adj. *che si può toccare.*

TO'UCHED, adj. *toccato, v.* To touch.

God has touched his heart, *Iddio gli ha toccato il cuore.*

I touched him to the quick, *io l' ho toccato sul vivo.*

A little touched [tainted a little] *che ha un poco del tanfo.*

TO'UCH-HOLE, s. [the hole through which the fire is conveyed to the powder in the gun] *focone, spiraglio d' un arma da fuoco.*

TO'UCHINESS, s. [peevishness, irascibility] *mal umore, stizza.*

TO'UCHING, s. *toccamento,* s. m. *il toccare.*

Touching, adj. [moving] *compassionevole, penetrante, che tocca, che muove a compassione.*

Touching [near] *contiguo, vicino.*

Touching, adv. [concerning] *intorno, circa, sopra, concernente.*

TO'UCHINGLY, adv. [with feeling emotion; in a pathetick manner] *pateticamente, in modo patetico.*

TO'UCHSTONE, s. [stone by which metals are examined] *pietra di paragone.*

Touchstone [any test or criterion] *esame, criterio, paragone.*

TO'UCHWOOD, s. [rotten wood used to catch the fire struck from the flint] *legno putrido e secco che s' usa come esca.*

TO'UCHY, adj. [exceptious] *litigioso, riottoso, aromatico, dispettoso, ostico, sdegnoso, ritroso, stizzoso.*

TOUGH, adj. [hard, not tender] *tiglioso, duro.*

This meat is tough, *questa carne è tigliosa o dura.*

Tough [stout] *robusto, vigoroso, forte.*

He is a tough fellow, *egli è un uomo robusto o vigoroso.*

Tough [hard, cruel] *duro, crudele, spietato.*

Tough [hard difficult] *difficile.*

A tough difficulty, *una gran difficoltà.*

TO'UGHNESS, s. *durezza, tigliosità,* s. f. *v.* Tough.

TOUR, s. a tour of hair, *una treccia di capelli.*

Tour [travel about a country] *giro, scorsa, spasseggiata.*

To make the tour of Italy, *fare il giro dell' Italia.*

Let us go to make a tour in the park, *andiamo a fare una girata, una passeggiata nel parco.*

TOW, s. [the hard or coarser part of hemp or flax] *stoppa,* s. f.

Tow, *canape, o fune che serve a rimurchiare i vascelli, alzana,* s. f.

Tow [a small boat in a ship] *schiffo,* s. m.

To TOW a ship [to hale her along the water] *rimburchiare e rimurchiare un vascello.*

TO'WAGE, s. *rimurchio,* s. m. *il rimurchiare.*

TO'WARD, adj. [inclining to] *dédito, inclinato, prono.*

He has a toward genius to vice, *egli è dedito o prono al vizio.*

TO'WARD, } prep. *verso, inverso.*
TOWARDS, }

Towards the fields, *verso i campi.*

Toward the end of the week, *verso il fine della settimana.*

It grows towards night, *si fa notte, annotta, la notte avanza.*

Towards the right-hand, *a man dritta.*

Towards the left-hand, *a man manca.*

Towards his last, *verso il fine.*

Charitable towards the poor, *caritatevole verso i poveri.*

His love towards her, *l' amore che le porta.*

Look towards me, *voltatevi a me, voltate gli occhi inverso me.*

Towards what place, *verso dove.*

I want some money towards the finishing my business, *ho bisogno di danari per finire il mio negozio.*

TO'WARDLINESS, s. [the quality of being towardly] *docilità, dispostezza, attitudine, disposizione ad imparare.*

TO'WARDLY, adj. [gentle, good-natured] *affabile, cortese, umano, trattabile.*

Towardly [orderly, obedient] *obbediente, che obbedisce, trattabile.*

Towardly [docile] *docile, disposto ad imparare.*

Towardly, adv. *destramente, con destrezza.*

TO'W-

TO'WED, adj. [from to tow] *rimburchiato, rimurchiato.*

TO'WEL, s. [a cloth to wipe hands on] *tovaglia, salvietta,* s. f. *tovagliuolo, tovagliuolino,* s. m.

TO'WER, s. *torre,* s. f.

The tower of London, *la torre di Londra.*

Tower [from to tow] *colui che rimurchia un vascello, alzaniere.*

To TO'WER [to soar, to fly or rise high] *volare, alzarsi alto, torreggiare,* v. to towre.

TO'WERED, adj. *dal verbo* To tower.

Towered, adj. [adorned or defended by towers] *ornato di torri o difeso da torri.*

TO'WREY, adj. *ornato di torri, difeso da torri.*

TO'WING, s. [from to tow] *rimurchio,* s. m. *il rimurchiare.*

TOWN, s. *città, piazza.*

A country town, *una terra.*

Sea town, *città maritima.*

An inland town, *una città mediterranea.*

A well-traded town, *una città mercantile.*

Walled-town, *terra murata.*

Strong or fortify'd town, *piazza forte.*

A sea-port town, *un porto di mare.*

A woman of the town [a lady of pleasure, a whore] *una femmina del mondo, una donna di partito, una meretrice, una puttana.*

A man of the town [a lewd man] *un puttaniere, uno scapestrato.*

TOWN'S-MEN [the inhabitants of a town] *borghesi, cittadini, abitatori d' una città.*

He is my town's-man, *noi siamo della medesima città.*

Town walls, *mura della città.*

The town-house, *la casa della città.*

Town-talk, *romore, bisbiglio.*

This is the town-talk, *così si dice per la città.*

She was the town-talk, *non si parlava che di lei per la città.*

Town-cress [a plant] *crescione,* s. m. *spezie d' erba buona a mangiare.*

TO'WNSHIP, s. [the extent of a town's jurisdiction] *la giurisdizione o il territorio d' una città.*

To TO'WRE [to fly high] *prender il volo in alto, poggiare, innalzarsi volando, oggi scrivesi* to tower.

To towre aloft, to towre too high in thoughts [to soar high] *innalzarsi, aver pensieri sublimi.*

TO'WRING, adj. [high, in a proper and figurative sense] *alto, eccelso, sublime, rilevato.*

Towring structure, *alto edificio.*

A man of a towring spirit, *un uomo ambizioso, altiero, orgoglioso.*

Towring thoughts, *pensieri ambiziosi.*

TO'WRY, adj. [set with towers] *circondato di torri.*

To TOWZE [to tug, to pull about, to rumple] *scompigliare, disordinare, confondere, ingarbugliare, abbaruffare,* pret. *confusi.*

To towze wool, *scardassare della lana.*

TO'WSED, adj. *scompigliato, disordinato, confuso, ingarbugliato, abbaruffato.*

TO'WZER, s. [one that makes a bustle] *un uomo torbido o turbolento, un ciarpone.*

TOY, s. [play-thing for children] *bagatella, ciappoleria, coserella, cosellina,* s. f.

Toy [pretty little thing] *giojello,* s. m. *giojetta,* s. f. *ornamento di poco valore.*

Toy [silly thing] *una bagatella, una frascheria, una giammengola.*

Toy-shop, *bottega dove si vendono delle bagatelle.*

To TOY, verb neut. *cianciare, scherzare, burlare, chiacchierare, vaneggiare, trastullare.*

TO'YER, s. *cianciatore, uomo che volentieri ciancia.*

TO'YING, s. *ciancia, beffa, burla,* s. f. *scherzo,* s. m.

TO'YISH, adj. [trifling, wanton] *amante di bagatelle, lascivetto.*

To TOZE [to towse, to pull by violence or impetuosity] *strappare, tirare con violenza o con impeto.*

TRACE, s. [footstep, track, print] *traccia, pedata, orma,* s. f.

The trace of wild beasts, *traccia, pedata, orma di fiere.*

To TRACE [to follow by the footing] *tracciare, seguitar la traccia.*

To trace [to find out by the footsteps] *rintracciare, trovare col seguire la traccia.*

To trace [to make a draught of an edifice, upon paper] *delineare la pianta d' un edificio sulla carta.*

To trace a thing to its original, *ripigliare il principio o l' origine di che che sia da lontano.*

To trace premisses into consequences, *tirare delle conseguenze dalle premesse.*

To trace out [to find out] *rintracciare, trovare, scoprire.*

To trace out [to follow] *seguitare.*

To trace out the author of a pamphlet, *scoprire l' autore d' un libello.*

TRA'CED, adj. *tracciare,* v. To trace.

TRA'CER, s. [one that traces] *un che trova la traccia.*

TRACK, s. [footstep] *traccia, orma, pedata, pesta, vestigio.*

To follow one by the track, *seguitare uno alla pesta.*

Track [mark remaining of any thing] *traccia, vestigio, segno, tratto.*

A great track of hills, *una giogaja di monti.*

The track of a coach or cart-wheel, *carreggiata.*

To TRACK [to follow by the footsteps or marks left in the way] *seguir la traccia.*

TRA'CKLESS, adj. [without track] *senza traccia, senza via.*

TRACT, s. [extent] *tratto, spazio, distanza.*

A great tract of land, *un lungo tratto di terra*

Tract of time, *tratto o spazio di tempo.*

In tract of time, *col tempo, alla lunga, in processo di tempo.*

The tract of a boar, *la traccia, la pesta d' un cinghiale.*

Tract [treatise] *trattato, discorso compilato e messo in iscrittura.*

To TRACT [to prolong the time] *prolungare, allungare, differire, prorogare, mandare in lungo il tempo.*

TRA'CTABLE, adj. [gentle] *trattabile, benigno, pieghevole, flessibile, affabile, facile a governare.*

TRA'CTABLENESS, s. [gentleness] *trattabilità, affabilità, benignità,* s f.

TRA'CTABLY, adv. [gently] *trattabilmente, affabilmente, benignamente.*

TRA'CTATE, s. [treatise] *trattato,* s. m.

TRA'CTION, s. [the act of drawing; the state of being drawn] *l' atto del tirare, o lo esser tirato.*

TRA'CTILE, adj. [ductile] *tirabile, estensibile, estendibile, maneggevole.*

TRACTI'LITY, s. [the quality of being tractile] *attezza ad esser esteso o tirato per lo lungo.*

TRADE, s. [mechanick art] *mestiere,* s. m. *arte meccanica.*

To drive a trade of a thing, *far mestiere di qualche cosa.*

Trade [profession, employment] *mestiere, professione, impiego.*

The trade of war, *l' arte della guerra, il mestiere dell' armi.*

The trade of a poet, *il mestiere di poeta, l' arte del poetare.*

Trade [tools] *ordigni.*

Trade [traffick] *negozio, commercio, traffico,* s m.

Trade [life, way of living] *vita, maniera di vivere.*

Will you always drive on this trade? *vorrete sempre menar questa vita?*

What trade is this? *che strepito, che romore è questo?*

Trade-wind [a wind which at certain seasons blows regularly at sea] *vento eolisco, vento regolato che in alcune stagioni soffia per qualche tempo da una banda.*

To TRADE [to merchandize, to traffick] *trafficare, negoziare, far commercio, mercatare, mercatantare, mercanteggiare.*

TRA'DED, adj. *trafficato, negoziato, mercatato.*

A well traded town, *una città mercantile.*

TRA'DER, s. *mercatante, negoziante, mercante.*

Trader [merchant-man] *vascello mercantile, nave da carico.*

TRA'DESFOLK, s. [people employed in trade] *gente data al mercantaggiare; gente vile, canaglia, sciocca al vil guadagno intenta.*

TRA'DES-

TRA'DESMAN, s. [mechanick] *artefice, artigiano, uomo di mestiere.*

Tradesman [citizen] *mercante, borghese, cittadino.*

Belonging to a tradesman, *artigianesco, d' artigiano.*

TRADESWO'MAN, s. *donna di mestiere, artigiana, mercantessa.*

TRA'DING, s. *negozio, traffico, commercio,* s. m. *mercatura,* s. f.

TRADI'TION, s. [the successive delivering or transmitting of doctrines or opinions to posterity] *tradizione,* s. f. *memoria cavata non da scrittura, ma da racconto de' vecchi.*

TRADI'TIONAL } adj. [belonging
TRADI'TIONARY } to or grounded upon tradition] *di tradizione, fondato sopra tradizione.*

TRADI'TIONALLY, adv. *per tradizione.*

TRADI'TIONIST, s. [one who stands for or follows tradition] *colui che va dietro alle tradizioni.*

TRA'DITIVE, adj. *trasmesso o che può trasmettersi a' posteri.*

To TRADU'CE [to defame, to speak ill of, to slander] *diffamare, infamare, calunniare, macchiar la fama altrui con maldicenza, sparlar d' uno, dir male, mormorare.*

You traduce him without subject, *voi sparlate di lui senza cagione.*

To traduce [to accuse] *accusare.*

TRADU'CED, adj. *diffamato, infamato, calunniato, sparlato.*

TRADU'CEMENT, s. [censure, obloquy] *diffamazione, detrazione, maldicenza, biasimo, critica ingiusta.*

TRADU'CER, s. *diffamatore, infamatore, detrattore, maldicente, mormoratore,* s. m.

TRADU'CING, s. *diffamamento, mormoramento, biasimo,* s. m. *maldicenza, diffamazione, mormorazione,* s. f.

TRADU'CTION, s. [defamation] *calunnia, maldicenza,* s. f.

Traduction [derivation from one of the same kind, propagation] *cosa procedente da cosa della stessa specie o natura, derivazione, propagazione.*

Traduction [tradition; transmission from one to another] *tradizione, il trasmettere da uno a un altro.*

Traduction [conveyance] *mezzo, passaggio, condotto, canale.*

Traduction [transition] *l' atto del far passaggio da luogo a luogo.*

TRA'FFICK, s. [trading] *traffico, negozio, commercio,* s. m. *mercatura,* s. f.

To TRA'FFICK [to trade] *trafficare, negoziare, far mercatura, mercanteggiare.*

TRA'FFICKER, s. [trader, merchant] *mercante, trafficante, negoziante.*

TRA'GACANTH, s. [a sort of gum] *dragante,* s. f. *spezie di gomma.*

TRAGE'DIAN, s. [a writer of tragedies] *componitor di tragedie, autore tragico.*

Tragedian [an actor of tragedies] *attore tragico.*

TRA'GEDY, s. [play in which great persons are brought upon the stage] *tragedia,* s. f.

To act a tragedy, *rappresentare una tragedia.*

Tragedy [fatal event] *tragedia, accidente violente e deplorabile.*

TRA'GICAL } adj. [belonging to
TRA'GICK } tragedies] *tragico, di tragedia.*

A tragick poet, *un poeta tragico.*

A tragical style, *uno stile tragico, sublime, grave.*

Tragical [sad, tragick, fatal] *tragico, mesto, doloroso, fatale.*

TRA'GICALLY, adv. [in a tragical manner] *tragicamente, d' una maniera tragica.*

TRA'GICALNESS, s. [mournfulness, calamitousness] *miseria, infortunio dolorosissimo, calamità terribile.*

TRAGICOMEDY, s. [a play partly tragedy and partly comedy] *tragicomedia,* s. f.

TRAGICO'MICAL, adj. *tragicomico, misto di commedia e di tragedia.*

TRAGICO'MICALLY, adv. [in a tragicomical manner] *tragicomicamente.*

TRA'JECT, s. [a ferry; a passage for a water carriage] *tragitto, luogo dove si passa la riviera sur una barra.*

To TRAJE'CT [to cast, to throw] *trarre, tirare, scagliare.*

TRAJE'CTION, s. [the act of darting through] *l' atto dello scagliar per mezzo.*

To TRAIL [to drag, to draw along] *strascinare, tirare per terra, strascicare.*

To trail upon the ground, *strascinare per terra.*

TRA'ILING, s. *strascino, strascio, lo strascinare, strascinamento.*

Trailing, adj. *che strascica.*

TRAIN, s. [retinue] *seguito, accompagnamento, corteggio,* s. m. *comitiva,* s. f.

He has a noble train, *egli ha nobil corteggio o accompagnamento.*

Train of artillery, *tremo, traino, equipaggio d' artiglieria.*

Train of powder, *traccia di polvere.*

Train [trail] *coda, strascico.*

The train of a bird, *la coda d'un uccello.*

The train of a gown, *lo strascico d' una veste.*

Train [trap, wheedle] *rete, trappola, insidia.*

To lay a train for one, *tender insidie ad uno, insidiare qualcheduno.*

The train bands, *la milizia.*

To TRAIN } to bring up, or in-
To TRAIN UP } struct] *allevare, educare, istruire, disciplinare.*

To train one up to a thing, *allevare uno a qualche cosa.*

To train up soldiers, *disciplinare, agguerrire i soldati.*

TRAINED } adj. *allevato, educa-*
TRAINED UP } *to, istruito, disciplinato, agguerrito.*

TRA'INER, s. ex. a trainer of soldiers, *ufficiale che ha la cura di disciplinare i soldati.*

TRA'INOIL, s. [oil drawn by coction from the fat of the whale] *olio di balena cotto.*

TRA'INY, adj. [belonging to train-oil] *appartenente ad olio di balena.*

To TRAIPSE [to walk in a careless or sluttish manner] *camminare con molto negligente e svenevole.*

TRAIT, s. [a stroke, a touch] *colpo, tocco, tratto.*

TRA'ITOR, s. [one who being trusted betrays] *traditore, giuda, gaino, ganellone.*

TRA'ITORLY, adj [treacherous, perfidious] *traditore, perfido.*

TRA'ITOROUS, adj. [treacherous] *traditore, traditoresco, perfido, proditorio.*

TRAI'TOROUSLY, adv. *traditoriamente, da traditore, traditorescamente.*

TRA'ITRESS, s. [a woman who betrays] *traditrice, traditora.*

TRA'MMEL, s. [drag-net, a sort of fishing-net] *tramaglio,* s. m. *foggia di rete da pescare.*

To TRA'MMEL [to catch, to intercept] *acchiappare, pigliare alla rete.*

To TRA'MPLE upon, or under foot, [to tread under foot] *calpestare, calcar co' piedi, disprezzare, far poco conto, conculcare, oppressare.*

TRA'MPLED, adj. *calpestato, calcato co' piedi, disprezzato, conculcato, oppressato.*

TRA'MPLING, s. *calpestamento, conculcamento,* s. m.

Trampling, adj. ex. a trampling noise, *calpestio.*

TRANCE, s. [rapture, extasy, transport of mind] *estasi, elevazion dell' anima.*

To fall into a trance or to be in a trance, *esser rapito in estasi, esser in estasi.*

TRA'NCED, adj. [lying in a trance or extasy] *estatico, rapito in estasi.*

TRANE-OIL, *olio di pesce.*

TRA'NGRAM, s. [an odd intricately contrived thing] *cosa strana e intricata.*

To TRA'NQUILIZE [to cause tranquillity] *tranquillare, render tranquillo, calmare, abbonacciare.*

TRA'NQUILLIZED, adj. *tranquillato, calmato, abbonacciato.*

TRANQUI'LLITY, s. [calmness, stillness, quietness of mind] *tranquillità, bonaccia, quiete, giocondità,* s. f.

To TRANSA'CT [to manage an affair] *negoziare, maneggiare, trattare.*

To transact a business, *maneggiare un negozio, trattar un affare.*

TRANSA'CTED, adj. *negoziato, maneggiato, trattato.*

TRANSA'CTION, s. [negotiation, thing in hand] *transazione, negoziazione, quel che si tratta, che si maneggia.*

Let me know all the transactions, *fatemi sapere tutto quel che si maneggia.*

While these transactions were on foot, *in questo mentre, intanto che si trattava questo.*

The philosophical transactions of the Royal Society, *l' esperienze filosofiche della Società Reale.*

Trans-

Tranfaction [convention] *tranfazi-one, convenzione.*

Transa'ctor, s. *quello che negozia, o che fa qualche cofa.*

Tra'nsalpine, adj. [that lies or lives on the other fide of the Alps] *tranfalpino, di là dalle Alpi.*

The tranfalpine Gaul, *la Gallia tran-falpina.*

The tranfalpine countries, *i paefi che fono di là dalle A'pi.*

To Transce'nd [to furpafs, to go beyond] *trafcendere, fopravanzare, fu-perare, eccedere.*

Trance'ndency, s. [excellency] *eccellenza,* s. f.

Transce'ndent, adj. [excellent, extraordinary] *trafcendente, ftraordina-rio, eccellente, fublime.*

Tranfcendent [among logicians, paf-fing the predicaments] *trafcendente, ter-mine logico.*

Transce'ndently, adv. [in a tranfcendent manner] *perfettamente, ftraordinariamente, d' una maniera traf-rendente.*

To Tra'nscolate [to ftrain through] *colare, paffare.*

To Transcri'be [to write or co-py out] *trafcrivere, copiare,* pret. *traf-criffi.*

Transcri'bed, adj. *trafcritto, co-piato.*

Transcri'ber, s. *copifta,* s. m. *co-lui che trafcrive, o copia.*

Tra'nscript, s. [the copy of an o-riginal writing] *copia,* s. f.

To Transcu'r [to go from one place to another] *trafcorrere, fcor-rere, paffare, andare da un luogo all' altro.*

Transcu'rrence, } s. *fcorrimento,*
Transcu'rsion, } s. m. *fcorfa,* s. f.

To Transfe'r [to convey from one place to another] *trasferire, trafpor-tare.*

He transferred the Roman empire into Germany, *egli trasferì l' imperio Romano in Alemagna.*

To transfer a bufinefs to another man, *rimettere un negozio nelle mani d' un altro.*

Transfe'rred, adj. *trasferito, trafportato, v.* To transfer.

Transfe'rring, s. *il trasferire.*

Transfigura'tion, s [the chang-ing of one fhape or figure into another] *trasfigurazione,* s. f.

The day of our Saviour's tranf-figuration, *il giorno della trasfigurazi-one di noftro Signore, la trasfigurazione.*

To Transfi'gure [to change the form or fhape] *trasfigurare, mutare ef-figie o figura.*

Transfi'gured, adj. *trasfigurato.*

To Transfi'x [to run thro'] *tra-paffare, trafiggere,* pret. *trafiffi.*

Transfi'xed, adj. *trapaffato, tra-fitto.*

To Transfo'rm [to change from one form to another] *trasformare, can-giar in altra forma, mutar forma e fi-gura.*

Vol. II.

Transforma'tion, s. *trasforma-zione,* s. f. *mutamento di forma, il traf-formare.*

Transfo'rmed, adj. *trasformato, cangiato, mutato in altra forma, e fi-gura.*

Transfo'rmer, s. *quello, o quella, che trasforma.*

Transfo'rming, s. *trasformamen-to,* s. m. *trasformanza, trasformazione,* s. f. *il trasformare.*

To Transfu'se [to pour out of one veffel into another] *trasfondere, trava-fare, infondere d' un vafo in un altro,* pret. *trasfufi, infufi.*

Transfu'sed, adj. *trasfufo, trava-fato, infufo.*

Transfu'sion, s. *trasfondimento,* s. m. *il trasfondere.*

To Transgre'ss [to trefpafs upon a law or order] *trafgredire, ufcir di co-mandamento, difubbidire, violare una legge o comandamento.*

Transgre'ssed, adj. *trafgredito, difubbidito, violato.*

Transgre'ssing, } s. *trafgredimen-*
Transgre'ssion, } *to,* s. m. *il traf-gredire, trafgreffione,* s. f.

Transgre'ssive, adj. [faulty, cul-pahle, apt to break laws] *trafgreffivo, reo, atto a trafgredir leggi.*

Transgre'ssor, s. *trafgreffore,* s. m. *colui che trafgredifce.*

Tra'nsient, adj. [tranfitory] *tran-fitorio, paffeggiero, che ha fine, che paffa, che vien meno.*

Tra'nsiently, adv. *tranfitoria-mente, di paffaggio.*

Transi'lience, } s. [leaps from
Transili'ency, } thing to thing] *paffaggio, o falto di cofa in cofa.*

Tra'nsit, s. [pafs, liberty to pafs] *tranfito, libertà di paffare.*

Transi'tion, s. [removal, paffage] *paffaggio, il paffare da un luogo all' al-tro.*

Tranfition [change] *cambiamento, mutamento.*

Tranfition [paffage in writing or con-verfation from one fubject to another] *tranfizione, o paffaggio che fi fa d' uno in altro fubbietto fcrivendo, o conver-fando.*

Tra'nsitive, adj. [having the power of paffing] *tranfitivo; paffeg-giero; che paffa; che ha facoltà di paf-fare.*

A *Verb Tranfitive,* in grammar, is that which fignifies an action conceived as having an effect upon fome object; as, *I ftrike the earth. Verbo Tranfitivo chi-amano i grammatici quello che efprime un atto il cui effetto fi concepe cadente fur un qualche oggetto; efempligrazia,* Io per-cuoto il terreno.

Tra'nsitory, adj. [foon paffing a-way, fading] *tranfitorio, che paffa, paf-feggiero.*

The tranfitory pleafures of the world, *i piaceri tranfitori del mondo.*

To Transla'te [to turn out of one language into another] *traflatare, tradurre, volgarizzare, ridurre le fcrit-ture ed i componimenti d'una lingua in un' altra,* pret. *traduffi.*

To tranflate word for word, *tradurre parola per parola.*

To tranflate [to transfer, to remove] *traflatare, trafportare, trasferire di lu-ogo a luogo.*

To tranflate a bifhop to another bi-fhoprick, *trasferire un vefcovo in un altro vefcovato.*

Transla'ted, adj. *traflatato, tra-dotto, volgarizzato, trafportato, trasfe-rito.*

Transla'ting, } s. *traflazione, tra-*
Translation, } *duzione,* s. f. *il traflatare, il tradurre.*

Transla'tor, s. *tradúttore,* s. m.

Translu'cid, adj [tranfparent, fhining through] *trafparente.*

Tra'nsmarine, adj. [that comes from, or is of the parts beyond the fea] *oltramarino, d' oltremare.*

To Tra'nsmigrate [to pafs from one place or body to another] *trafmi-grare, paffare da un luogo, o da un corpo all' altro.*

They fay the foul tranfmigrates out of one body into another, *fi dice che l' anima paffa da un corpo all' altro.*

Tra'nsmigrated, adj. *trafmigra-to, paffato da un luogo, o da un corpo all' altro.*

Transmigra'tion, s. [paffage] *trafmigrazione,* s. f. *il trafmigrare, il paffare da un luogo, o da un corpo all' al-tro.*

The tranfmigration of fouls, *la traf-migrazione delle anime.*

Transmi'ssion, s. [conveying] *trafmiffione,* s. f. *trasfondimento,* s. m.

To Transmi't [to convey, to deliver, to make over] *trafmettere, trasfondere, far paffare,* pret. *trafmifi, trasfufi.*

Transmi'tted, adj. *trafmeffo, traf-fufo.*

Transmi'tting, s. *il trafmet-tere.*

Transmu'table, adj. [capable of being changed] *trafmutabile, atto a traf-mutarfi.*

Transmuta'tion, s. *trafmutazi-one, il trafmutare, trasformazione,* s. f. *trafmutamento,* s. m.

To Transmu'te [to change one matter or fubftance into another] *traf-mutare, trasformare, cambiare, mutare una materia, o foftanza in un' altra.*

To tranfmute a metal, *trafmutare un metallo.*

Transmu'ted, adj. *trafmutato, trasformato, cambiato, mutato.*

Tra'nsom, s. [over-thwart beam] *traverfa,* s. f. *pezzo di legno, o trave meffa a traverfo.*

Tranfom [lintel over a door] *impofta di porta.*

Tranfom window, *telojo,* s. m.

The tranfom piece of a fhip [a piece of timber that lies a-thwart the ftern] *traverfa di vafcello.*

Transpa'rency, s. [the quality of being tranfparent] *trafparenza, diafa-nità,* s. f.

Transpa'rent, adj. [that may be feen through] *trafparente, diafano.*

To be tranſparent, *traſparire, tralucere.*

TRANSPI'CUOUS, adj. [tranſparent pervious to the ſight] *traſparente, diafano, per cui la viſta paſſa ſenza oſtacolo.*

To TRANSPI'ERCE [to pierce, or run through] *trapaſſare, trafiggere,* pret. *trafiſſi, paſſar ſuorſuora.*

TRANSPIE'RCED, adj. *trapaſſato, trafitto, paſſato ſuorſuora.*

TRANSPIRA'TION, s. [the breathing of vapours through the pores of the ſkin] *traſpirazione, perſpirazione,* s. f.

To TRANSPI'RE [to come forth by perſpiration] *perſpirare, eſalare, mandar ſuori per i pori del corpo.*

TRANSPI'RED, adj. *traſpirato, eſalato.*

TRANSPI'RING, s. *traſpirazione,* s. f. *il traſpirare.*

To TRA'NSPLACE [to remove, to put into a new place] *rimuovere, porre in un altro luogo.*

To TRANSPLA'NT [to plant in another place] *traſpiantare, trapiantare, cavar la pianta d' un luogo e piantarla in un altro.*

TRANSPLANTA'TION, s. *traſpiantamento,* s. m. *il traſpiantare.*

TRANSPLA'NTED, adj. *traſpiantato, trapiantato.*

TRANSPLANTER, s. *quello, o quella che trapianta.*

TRANSPLA'NTING, s. *traſpiantamento,* s. m. *il traſpiantare.*

TRA'NSPORT, s. [extaſy, rapture] *eſtaſi, ſoverchia allegrezza, eccesſo di gioja.*

Tranſport [a violent motion of the paſſions, a ſudden ſally] *eccesſo di collera, ira, ſtizza.*

Tranſport-ſhip, *vaſcello di traſporto, nave da carico.*

To TRANSPO'RT [to convey or to carry over to another place] *traſportare, traſferire, portare da un luogo ad un altro.*

To tranſport malefactors, *traſportare de' malfattori, mandarli in iſchiavitù nelle Indie.*

To tranſport [to put beſides one's ſelf] *traſportare, metter fuor di ſe*

Anger tranſports him, *la collera lo traſporta.*

TRANSPORTABLE, adj. [that may be tranſported] *che ſi può traſportare.*

TRANSPO'RTANCE, s. [conveyance, carriage, removal] *traſportazione, l' atto del rimuovere, o traſportar altrove.*

TRANSPORTA'TION, s. [carriage from one place to another] *traſportazione,* s. f. *traſporto,* s. m.

TRANSPORTED, adj. *traſportato, traſferito.*

Tranſported with pleaſure, *traſportato dal piacere.*

TRANSPO'RTING, s. *traſporto,* s. m. *il traſportare.*

To TRANSPO'SE [to put out of its place] *traſporre, traſportare, traſpiantare,* pref. *traſpongo,* pref. *traſpoſi.*

TRANSPO'SED, adj. *traſpoſto, traſportato, traſpiantato.*

TRANSPO'SING } s. *traſponimento,*
TRANSPOSI'TION } s. m. *traſpoſizione,* s. f. *il traſporre.*

To TRA'NSSHAPE [to transform, to bring into another ſhape] *traſformare, dare un altra forma o figura a checcheſſia.*

To TRANSUBSTA'NTIATE [to change out of one ſubſtance into another] *tranſuſtanziare, mutar ſoſtanza, cangiare in altra ſoſtanza.*

TRANSUBSTA'NTIATED, adj. *tranſuſtanziato.*

TRANSUBSTANTIA'TION, s. [the change of the ſacramental bread and wine, according to the church of Rome, into Chriſt's body and blood] *tranſuſtanziazione,* s. f.

TRANSUBSTANTIA'TOR [one who holds the doctrine of tranſubſtantiation] *difenſore della tranſuſtanziazione.*

To TRA'NSVASSATE [to pour from one veſſel to another] *traſvaſare, travaſare, mutare il liquore o altra coſa di vaſo in vaſo.*

TRANSVASA'TION, s. [the act of pouring from veſſel to veſſel] *il traſvaſare.*

TRA'NSVERSE, adj. [a-croſs] *traſverſale, traſverſo, che attraverſa, obbliquo.*

TRAP, s. [a device to catch wild beaſts, fowls, &c.] *trappola.*

To ſet a trap, *tendere una trappola.*

Mouſe-trap, *trappola da ſorci.*

Trap [ſnare, train] *trappola, inſidia, trama,* s. f.

You do not underſtand trap, *voi non ſiete troppo aſtuto.*

Trap-door, *trappola, porta fatta a modo di trappola, trabocchello, trabocchetto, ſchiaccia, ſtiaccia.*

Trap [a play at which a ball is driven with a ſtick] *giuoco in cui una palla è percoſſa e riſpinta con una mazza o baſtone.*

To TRAP [to ſet out with trappings] *fornire d' arneſi, mettere gli arneſi.*

To trap [to catch in a ſnare, to enſnare] *attrappare, trappolare, ingannare, inſidiare.*

To trap one [to deceive one] *attrappare, acchiappare alcuno, ingannarlo.*

TREPAN, v. Trepan.

To TRAPE [to go idly up and down] *vagare, vagabondare, correr le ſtrade, andar ramingo.*

A TRA'PES, s. [a dirty ſlut] *una donna ſporca, una femmina ſudicia, una donnaccia.*

TRA'PPINGS, s. [the harneſs of a ſaddle horſe] *gualdrappe,* s. f. pl. *arneſi da cavallo.*

TRASH, s. [trumpery, bad commodity] *trappole da quattrini, coſe vaghe all' occhio e di niuna utilità, robaccia.*

Traſh [bad fruit] *frutti cattivi.*

Traſh [a worthleſs perſon] *una perſona vile o ſpregievole.*

To TRASH [to lop, to crop] *tagliar via la ſommità come buona a nulla.*

To traſh [to cruſh, to humble] *domar l' orgoglio altrui, umiliare altrui.*

TRA'SHY, adj. [worthleſs, vile, uſeleſs] *vile, ſpregèvole, da nulla.*

To TRA'VAIL [to labour, to toil] *lavorare, affaticarſi.*

To travail [to be in labour, to ſuffer the pains of childbirth] *eſſere ne' dolori del parto, ſtar gemendo per doglie di parto.*

To travail [to haraſs, to tire] *tormentare, affannare, affaticare altrui.*

TRA'VAIL [labour, toil, fatigue] *lavoro, fatica, ſforzo, affanno.*

Travail [labour in childbirth] *dolori del parto, doglie del partorire.*

TRAVE, s. [traviſe; a place encloſed with rails for ſhoeing unruly horſes] *ordigno nel quale ſi mettono i cavalli, o altre beſtie faſtidioſe per medicarle, o ferrarle.*

TRA'VEL [pains] *travaglio, affanno,* s. m. *perturbazione, moleſtia, ſollecitudine,* s. f.

Travel [the pangs or labour of a woman with child] *doglie di parto.*

Travel [journey, voyage] *viaggio, giornata.*

To TRA'VEL [to labour, to take pains] *travagliare, travagliarſi, affaticarſi, darſi affanno, affannarſi.*

To travail with child, *aver le doglie del parto.*

To travel [to go upon a journey] *viaggiare, far viaggio.*

He has travelled all over France, *egli ha viaggiato per tutta la Francia.*

After I had travelled ſeveral countries, *dopo che ebbi viaggiato per molti paeſi*

TRA'VELLED, adj. *travagliato, affatirato, affannato; viaggiato.*

TRA'VELLER, *viaggiatore, viaggiante,* s. m.

Traveller's joy [a plant] *viburno,* s. m. *ſorta di pianta.*

TRA'VELLING, s. *il viaggiare, viaggio.*

To go a travelling, *andare a viaggiare.*

Travelling, adj. *vierècrio, paſſeggiero.*

A travelling bird, *un uccéllo di paſſaggio.*

Whither are you travelling? *dove andate?*

Travelling with child, *doglie di parto.*

TRAVELTA'INTED, ad. [harraſſed, fatigued with travel] *ſtanco e conſumato dal lungo viaggiare; fruſto e logoro dal lungo viaggio.*

TRA'VERSE, s. [the way of a ſhip, when ſhe makes angles in and out, and cannot keep directly to her true courſe] *bordeggio,* s. m. *il bordeggiare d' un vaſcello.*

To ſail by traverſe, *bordeggiare, ſtar ſulle volte; termine marinareſco, e diceſi d' un vaſcello allora, che ſenza ven-*

to favorevole pur cerca d' acquistar cammino.

Traverse [in fortification, a trench with a little parapet on each side, which the besiegers make quite a-cross the moat of the place] *traversa*, s. f. *termine di fortificazione.*

Traverse [in heraldry, a partition made cross an escutcheon] *sbarra*, s. f.

Traverses [crosses, troubles] *traverse, traversie, avversità.*

The traverses of fortune, *le traversie di fortuna.*

To TRA'VERSE [to cross, to go cross] *traversare, attraversare, passare attraverso.*

To traverse a country, *traversare un paese.*

To traverse [to cross, to thwart] *attraversare, guastare, impedire, ovviare, deludere*, pret. *delusi*, pres. *impedisco.*

To traverse one's designs, *attraversare, deludere li altrui disegni.*

To traverse an action at law, *opporsi, ostare, mettere ostarolo ad un' azione in giustizia.*

To traverse an indictment [to contradict or deny some part of it] *negare qualche capo dell' arrusa dataci in giustizia.*

TRA'VERSED, adj. *traversato, attraversato*, v. To traverse.

TRA'VESTED, adj. [disguised] *travestito.*

Virgil or Ovid travested, *Virgilio o Ovidio travestito.*

TRAY, s. [a sort of trough, cut and hollowed out of a piece of wood] *truogo, truogolo*, s. m.

A mason's tray, *truogolo di muratore.*

A tray-man, *manovale*, s. m. *quegli che serve al muratore per portargli le materie per murare.*

Tray-trip, s. [a kind of play] *sorta di giuoco.*

TRA'YTEROUS, adj. *traditore, traditoresco, di traditore, perfido, proditorio.*

Trayterous act, *azione traditoresca, di traditore.*

TRA'YTEROUSLY, adv. *da traditore.*

To act trayterously, *trattar da traditore.*

TRA'YTOR, s. *un traditore.*

Traytor-like, *da traditore.*

TRA'YTORESS, s. [a woman traytor] *traditrice.*

TREA, s. [three at dice] *un tre a' dadi.*

TRE'ACHEROUS, adj. [perfidious] *traditore, perfido, disleale, infedele, infido, proditorio, traditoresco.*

A treacherous man or woman, *un traditore, un disleale, un perfido; una traditrice, una disleale, una perfida, un' ingannatrice.*

Treacherous memory, *memoria corta.*

Treacherous doings, *azioni da traditore, disleali, perfide.*

Treacherous hopes, *speranze fallaci, ingannatrici.*

TRE'ACHEROUSLY, adv. *da traditore, perfidamente.*

TRE'ACHERY, s. [perfidiousness] *tradimento*, s. m. *perfidia, dislealtà*, s. f.

TREA'CHETOR, } s. [a traitor] *traditore*, *violator di sua fede, dal Francese* tricher, tricheur.
TRE'CHOUR, }

TRE'ACLE, s. [a physical composition made of many ingredients] *teriaca, triara, tiriaca*, s. f.

Venice treacle, *teriaca di Venezia.*

Treacle [molosses; the spume of sugar] *la schiuma del zucchero tratta quando bolle e si raffina.*

TREAD, s. *camminatura, andatura*, s. f. *andare, passo*, s. m. *il modo dell' andare.*

Tread [way, track, path] *via, traccia, sentiero.*

Tread [the cocks part in the egg] *l' atto del gallo nel coito.*

To TREAD [to go] *andare, camminare.*

To tread upon one's toes, *camminare sulla punta de' piedi.*

To tread softly, *camminar sopra l' uova, pian piano.*

To tread handsomely, *camminar bene, andar bene sulla vita.*

To tread outward or inward, *camminare colla punta de' piedi infuori, o indentro.*

To tread in the footsteps of the ancients, *seguitar le pedate, o la traccia degli antichi.*

To tread upon a thing [to trample it under foot] *calpestare che che sia, non farne conto, vilipendere una cosa.*

He is as honest a man as ever trod upon a shoe of leather, *egli è un galantuomo se ve ne fu mai nel mondo.*

The cock treads the hen, *il gallo galla la gallina.*

To tread the grapes, *calpestar l'uva, calcarla, pigiarla.*

To tread upon one's heels [to follow one close] *seguitare uno d' appresso, incalzarlo.*

To tread one's shoes down at the heels, *scalcagnare le scarpe, cavare il tallone della scarpa.*

TRE'ADER, s. *calcatore, che calca, o pigia.*

TRE'ADLE, s. ex. the treadle of a weaver's loom, *calcole*, s. f. *regoli appiccati con funirelle a' licci del pettine, in su i quali il tessitor tiene i piedi.*

Treadle [the sperm of the cock] *sperma del gallo, o d' altro augello maschio.*

Treadles of sheep, *sterco di pecora.*

TRE'ASON, s [treachery, perfidiousness] *tradimento*, s. m. *dislealtà, perfidia, malvagità*, s. f.

High treason [offence against the security of the prince or state] *delitto di lesa maestà.*

Petty-treason [is when a servant kills his master, a wife her husband, a secular or religious man his prelate or superior] *il delitto d'un servitore chè ammazza il suo padrone, d' una moglie suo marito, d' una persona religiosa il suo superiore.*

TRE'ASONABLE, adj. [trayterous] *traditore, traditoresco, di traditore.*

TRE'ASONABLY, adv. [traytor-like] *da traditore.*

TRE'ASONOUS, adj. *traditoresco.*

TRE'ASURE, s. [store of gold, silver, jewels, riches hoarded up] *tesoro*, s. m.

To heap up treasures, *tesaurizzare, tesorizzare, ammassare ricchezze, accumular tesori.*

The King's treasure, *il tesoro del Re.*

Treasure [a thing of great value] *tesoro, cosa preziosa, di grande stima, di gran prezzo.*

Treasure-house, *la tesoreria.*

To TRE'ASURE up [to hoard up riches] *tesaurizzare, tesorizzare, ammassare ricchezze, accumular tesori.*

TRE'ASURED up, adj. *tesaurizzato, tesorizzato.*

TRE'ASURER, s. [an officer that keeps or lays out the treasure of another] *tesoriere*, s. m. *ministro, o custode del tesoro.*

Lord-treasurer of England, *gran tesoriere d'Inghilterra.*

Treasurer of war, *tesoriere di guerra.*

TRE'ASURERSHIP, s. *la carica d' un tesoriere.*

TRE'ASUREHOUSE, } s. [treasure] *luogo del tesoro.*
TRE'ASURY, }

The royal treasury, *il tesoro reale.*

The publick treasury, *il tesoro pubblico, la tesoreria, il luogo dove si tiene il tesoro pubblico.*

The treasury or treasure-office, *la tesoreria.*

TREAT, s. [entertainment] *pasto che si da a qualcheduno, convito.*

To give a treat, *dar un gran pasto.*

Treat or treate [a law word, used for withdrawn or taken out] *eccettuato, levato del numero.*

To TREAT [to give a treat or entertainment] *dar un pasto.*

To treat [to deal with] *trattare.*

To treat one kindly, *trattare uno cortesemente.*

I will treat you no better than—— *non ho più rispetto per voi, che per——*

To treat of a thing, *trattare, ragionare, discorrere d' una cosa*, pret. *discorsi.*

To treat [to be upon a treaty or bargain] *trattare, praticare, adoperarsi per conchiudere qualche negozio.*

To treat with one about a business, *trattare qualche negozio con alcuno, negoziar un affare con alcuno.*

To treat about a peace, to treat of peace with the enemy, *trattar la pace col nemico, trattar di pace.*

TRE'ATABLE, adj. [tractable] *trattabile, pieghevole, ragionevole, moderato.*

TRE'ATABLY, adv. *moderatamente.*

TRE'ATED, adj. *regalato, trattato*, v. To treat.

TRE'ATING, s. *trattamento*, s. m. *il trattare.*

Treating-house [ordinary] *bettola, osteria.*

TRE'ATISE, s. [discourse upon some particular subject] *tratto, discorso compilato sopra qualche soggetto particolare.*

TRE'ATMENT, s. [usage] *trattamento,* s. m. *maniera di trattare.*

TRE'ATY, s. [a covenant or agreement between two or more parties, for peace, commerce, navigation, &c.] *trattato, accordo, accomodamento,* s. m. *convenzione,* s. f.

There is a treaty on foot, *v' è un trattato in piedi.*

To be upon a treaty with one concerning a business, *essere in trattato di che che sia con alcuno, sopra qualche negozio.*

TRE'BLE, adj. [three fold] *triplicato, triplice, tre volte più.*

We were treble their number, *noi eravamo tre volte più di loro.*

Treble, s. [a sharp sound] *suono acuto, trillo.*

The treble, s. [a treble part in musick] *il soprano, termine musicale.*

The first and second treble, *il primo e il secondo soprano.*

To TRE'BLE, *triplicare, rinterzare, far tre volte tanto.*

TRE'BLED, adj. *triplicato, rinterzato.*

TRE'BLENESS, [the state of being treble] *triplicità.*

TRE'BLY, adv. *triplicemente, con triplicità.*

TREE, s. [a great woody plant] *albero, arbore,* s. m.

Fruit-tree, or fruit bearing-tree, *albero pomifero, pianta fruttifera.*

Apple-tree, *melo,* s. m. *albero che produce mele.*

Pear-tree, *un pero.*

Tree [a long and thick piece of timber] *albero, pezzo di legno grosso e lungo.*

The tree of a saddle, *l' arcione della sella.*

The tree-ivy, *ellera,* s. f.

TREEN, *era anticamente il plurale di tree.*

Treen, adj. [wooden, made of wood] *di legno, fatto di legno.*

TRE'FOIL, s. [the herb commonly called three leaved grass] *trifoglio,* s.m. *spezie d' erba.*

The shrub trefoil [honey-suckle] *madreselva, succiamiele.*

Sweet-trefoil [a plant] *meliloto,* s. m. *spezie di pianta.*

TRE'LLIS, s. [lattice, grate] *gelosia,* s. f. *ingraticolato di legno, il quale si tiene alle finestre per vedere e non esser veduto.*

Trellis [a sort of stiff linen cloth] *traliccio,* s. m. *spezie di tela.*

TRE'LLISED, adj. [latticed, grated with wood] *che ha gelosia, con gelosia.*

To TREMBLE [to shake, to quake] *tremare.*

To tremble for fear or cold, *tremar di paura o di freddo.*

To tremble [to fear] *tremare, aver paura, temere.*

TRE'MBLED, adj. *tremato.*

TRE'MBLING, s. [quaking] *il tremare.*

To cause a trembling, *far tremare.*

Trembling, adj. *tremante, che trema.*

TRE'MBLINGLY, adv. *tutto tremante.*

TREME'NDOUS, adj. [dreadful] *tremendo, terribile, spaventevole.*

TRE'MOUR, s. [the state of trembling] *brivido, tremore, lo stato di chi trema.*

Tremour [quivering or vibratory motion] *moto tremulo, moto di vibrazione.*

TRE'MULOUS, adj. [trembling, fearful] *tremante, che abbrivida per paura.*

Tremulous [quivering, vibratory] *tremulo, vibrante, tremolante per iscossa ricevuta.*

TRE'MULOUSNESS, s. [the state of quivering] *il tremolare, o la vibrazione di checchessia.*

TREN, s. [an instrument wherewith mariners strike a fish at sea] *pettinella, fiocina,* s. f.

TRENCH, s. [a ditch or cut made in the earth] *fosso,* s. m. *fossa, fossata,* s. f.

A trench to drain a pond, *chiassajuola,* s. f. *fosso, per seccare uno stagno.*

To make a trench about a house, *affossare una casa, circondarla con fosso.*

Trench [made before a town, in order to attack it, as also such lines as are cut to defend and cover an army incamped in the field] *trincea,* s. f. *riparo militare.*

To open the trenches, *aprir le trincere.*

To TRENCH about [to fence with trenches] *circondar con trincee, trincierare.*

TRE'NCHANT, adj. [cutting, sharp] *tagliente, affilato.*

TRE'NCHED about, adj. *trincierato.*

TRE'NCHER, s. [a sort of wooden plate to eat victuals on] *tagliere e tagliero,* s. m. *legno piano e ritondo a guisa di piattello, su cui si taglian le vivande.*

A good trencher-man [a great eater] *un gran mangiatore.*

Trencher-friend [belly friend] *scroccone, un parasito.*

TRE'NCHER-FLY [one that hunts tables; parasite] *parasito, scroccone.*

TRE'NCHERMATE [a table companion, a parasite] *compagno di tavola, scroccone, parasito.*

To TREND [to tend, to lie in any particular direction] *tendere ad una qualche determinata parte.*

TRE'NDEL, } s. [a sort of weight
TRE'NDLE, } or post in a mill] *il perno sul quale gira la macina d' un mulino.*

TRE'NELS, s. [long wooden pins, with which the planks are fastened into the timbers of a ship] *cavicchie, o cavicchi i quali servono a congegnare le panche d' un vascello.*

TRE'NTAL, s. [among the Roman Catholicks, is an office for the dead, which lasts thirty days or consists of thirty masses] *servizio per i morti, che dura trenta giorni, o che consiste in trenta messe.*

TRE'PAN, s. [a surgeon's instrument with which they open a broken skull] *trapano,* s. m.

Trepan [sharper, cheat] *furbo, truffatore.*

To TRE'PAN, ex. To trepan a skull, *trapanare un cranio.*

To trepan [to ensnare, to decoy] *adescare, allettare, lusingare, invitare, tirare alle sue voglie con alleitamenti ed inganni, acchiappare.*

To trepan one into a premunire, *fare una burla, o un tiro ad uno.*

TRE'PANNED, adj. *trapanato,* v. To trepan.

TREPA'NNER, s. *furbo, guidone, furfante, ingannatore.*

TRE'PHINE, s. [a small trepan] *trapanetto; stromento di chirurgo*

TREPIDA'TION, s. [trembling] *trepidazione,* s. f. *il trepidare.*

TRE'SPASS, s. [offence, crime] *misfatto, fallo, delitto, peccato,* s. m. *offesa, trasgressione,* s. f.

Forgive us our trespasses, *perdonaci le nostre offese.*

To TRE'SPASS against [to offend] *offendere,* pret. *offesi.*

To trespass upon [to transgress] *trasgredire, violare, infringere, fallire,* pres. *trasgredisco.*

To trespass upon the law, *violare, trasgredire la legge.*

I fear to trespass upon you, or upon your patience, *temo d' abusare della pazienza vostra.*

TRE'SPASSER, s. *trasgressore, violatore, offenditore,* s. m.

TRESS, s. [lock of hair] *treccia di capelli.*

Her golden tresses, *le sue trecce d' oro, le sue bionde trecce.*

TRE'SSED, adj. [knotted or curled] *annodato in treccia.*

TRE'SSES, *plurale di tress, ed è molto più in uso che il singolare.*

TRE'STLE, s. [a three-footed stool] *tripode, treppiede.*

Trestle [a stool to set a table or any thing upon] *trespolo,* s. m. *strumento di tre piedi sopra 'l quale si posan le mense, o altro.*

TRET, s. [an allowance made by merchants to retailers] *basso accordato da' mercanti all' ingrosso a que' che rivendono al minuto, ed è di quattro libbre per cento.*

TRE'TLESS, s. [the dung of a rabbet] *sterco di coniglio.*

TRE'THINGS, s. [taxes, imposts] *tasse, dazi.*

TRE'VET, s. [an iron instrument with three feet, to set a pot or saucepan over the fire] *treppiede e treppiè,* s. m. *strumento triangolare di ferro con tre piedi, per uso di cucina.*

TREY, *un tre quando è un segno nelle carte, o ne' dadi.*

TRIAD, s. [three united] *triade, unità di tre.*

TRIAL, s. [essay, experiment] *prova, esperienza,* s. f. *saggio, cimento,* s. m.

To make a trial of a thing, *far prova di che che si sia, provarla, esperimentarla, farne l' esperienza.*

To

To give a trial of one's skill, *dar prova di quel che l' uom sa fare.*

Trial [endeavour] *sforzo, attentato,* s. m.

Trial at law, *lite,* s. f. *processo,* s. m.

To bring a prisoner to his trial, *fare il processo ad un criminale.*

When are you to have a trial? *quando sarà giudicata la vostra causa?*

TRIA'NGLE, s. [a figure with three angles] *triangolo, un figura di tre angoli.*

TRIA'NGULAR, adj. [three-cornered] *triangolare, di tre angoli.*

TRIA'RIANS, } s. [the Roman soldiers in the rear] *triarij, soldati Romani che alloggiavano vicino alla cavalleria.*
TRIA'RII, }

TRIBE, s. [company of people dwelling together in the same ward or liberty] *tribù,* s. f. *una delle parti, nelle quali anticamente si dividevano le nazioni, o le città, par distinguere le schiatte e le famiglie.*

He is one of the tribe, *egli è della razza.*

Tribe, *razza, stirpe, famiglia. E' talora voce di dispregio.*

TRI'BLET, } s. [a gold-smith's tool for making rings] *ordigno che l' orafo adopera quando fa anella.*
TRI'BOULET, }

TRIBULA'TION, s. [great trouble, affliction] *tribulazione, afflizione, molestia,* s. f. *affanno,* s. m.

TRIBU'NAL, s. [judgment-seat] *tribunale,* s. m. *luogo dove seggono i giudici a render ragione.*

TRIBU'NE, s. [a magistrate among the Romans] *tribuno,* s. m. *nome di magistrato della republica Romana.*

The office of a Roman tribune, *il grado e l' ufficio del tribunato.*

TRIBUNI'TIAL, } adj. [suiting a tribune, relating to a tribune] *tribunizio, di tribuno, appartenente al tribuno.*
TRIBUNI'TIOUS, }

TRIBUTARY, adj. [that pays tribute] *tributario, obbligato a pagar tributo.*

TRI'BUTE, s. [what a prince or state pays to another as a token of dependance, *tributo,* s. m. *censo che si paga da un principe, o da uno stato ad un altro, in segno di dipendenza.*

Tribute [tax] *tributo, tassa, censo che si paga dal vassallo, o dal suddito al suo signore.*

To pay tribute to nature [to die] *pagare il tributo alla natura, morire.*

TRICE, s. ex. in a trice, *in un punto, in un momento, in un attimo, in un batter d' occhio.*

TRICK, s. [a sly fraud] *tiro, tratto, giro, rigiro,* s. m. *burla, furberia, invenzione, sottiglieza,* s. f.

I know none of your tricks, *io non intendo i vostri rigiri, o le vostre sottigliezze.*

To play one a trick, to serve him a trick, to put a trick upon him, *fare una burla, o un tiro ad uno, acchiapparlo, ingannarlo.*

Base trick, knavish trick, *azione indegna, furberia, furfanteria.*

Simple trick, *schiocchezza.*

To play one a slippery trick [to fail of one's promise to him] *mancar di parola ad uno.*

He is full of tricks, *egli è pieno di maliziette.*

Trick [lift at cards] *mano, e dicesi giuocando alle carte.*

To TRICK [to put a trick upon, to humble, to cheat] *burlare, fare una burla, acchiappare, giuntare, moriuolare, ingannare, gabbare.*

To TRICK, v. n. [to live by fraud] *procacciarsi la vita gabbando.*

To TRICK [in painting] *abbozzare, dar la prima forma così alla grossa.*

To trick up [to set out] *parare, ornare, abbigliare.*

To trick one's self up, *pararsi, abbigliarsi.*

TRI'CKED, adj. *acchiappato,* v. To trick.

TRI'CKER, s. [of a gun] *il grillo d' uno schioppo.*

TRI'CKING, s. [dress, ornament] *abbigliamento, ornamento della persona.*

TRI'CKISH, adj. [knavishly, artful, fraudulently cunning, mischievously subtle] *che gabba bricconescamente, che sottilmente inganna o procaccia danneggiarti; furfantesco, cattivamente artificioso.*

TRI'CKLE, s. [drop] *gocciola,* s. f.

A trickle of water, *una gocciola d' acqua.*

To TRI'CKLE, } [to run down by drops] *gocciolare, cascar a gocciole.*
To trickle down, }

TRICLED, adj. *gocciolato.*

TRI'CKING, adj. *gocciolante, che gocciola.*

TRI'CKY, adj. [pretty] *vago, avvenente, piacevole, galante.*

TRI'DENT, s. [three-forked mace] *tridente,* s. m.

Neptune's trident, *il tridente di Nettuno.*

Trident, adj. [having three teeth] *tridentato, tridentuto, che ha tre denti.*

TRI'DING, s. *la tenza parte d' una contea o provincia d' Inghilterra.*

TRI'DUAN, adj. [lasting three days] *che dura tre giorni, che dura un triduo.*

Triduan, adj. [happening every third day] *che accade ogni terzo dì.*

TRIE'NNIAL, adj. [that continues three years, that happens every third year] *triennio, che dura tre anni, che arriva ogni tre anni.*

Triennial parliament, *parlamento di tre anni.*

Triennial meeting, *assemblea che si fa di tre in tre anni.*

TRI'ER, s. *saggiatore,* s. m. *colui che saggia.*

To TRIFA'LLOW [to till or plough land the third time] *terzare, termine d' agricoltura, arare la terza volta.*

TRI'FFLE, s. [a whiffling silly thing] *bagattella, baja, ciancia, cosa di poco valore, frasca, frascheria, giammengola,* s. f.

It is a mere trifle, *è una pera bagattella.*

To stand upon trifles, *arrestarsi, badare, dare orecchio a cose frivole.*

To TRI'FLE [to toy] *cianciare, scherzare, burlare, far bagattelle, chiacchierare, vaneggiare, fraschegiare, sciocchegiare.*

To trifle away one's time, *spender il tempo in vano, stare a bada.*

TRI'FLER, s. *bagattelliere, bajone,* s. m.

TRI'FLING, s. *ciancia, baja, burla, bagattella,* s. f. *scherzo, badalucco, trastullo,* s. m.

TRI'FLING, adj. [of no moment, whiffling] *da nulla, di poco momento, di poca importanza, frivolo, vano.*

Trifling business, *affare di nulla, di poco momento, bagattella.*

TRI'FLINGLY, adv. [without weight, without dignity, without importance] *di nessun peso, dignità, o importanza; scioccamente, vanamente, frivolamente.*

TRI'FORM, adj. [having a triple shape] *triforme che ha triplice forma o figura.*

To TRIG [to catch or stop a wheel] *incatenare una ruota.*

To trig [to set a mark to stand at, in playing at nine-pins] *segnare a qualcheduno il luogo donde deve giuocare nel giuoco degli sbrigli.*

TRI'GAMY, s. [the having three husbands, or three wives] *lo stato di colui che ha tre mogli, o di colei che ha tre mariti.*

TRI'GGED, adj. *fermato, incatenato.*

TRI'GGER, s. [an iron to trig a wheel] *pezzo di ferro col quale si fermano le ruote d' un carro, o carrozza in un luogo scosceso.*

Trigger, s. [a hook which holds the spring of a gun-lock] *grillo d' uno schioppo.*

TRI'GINTALS, s. [a number of masses to the tale of thirty] *trenta messe celebrate una dopo l' altra.*

TRI'GLYPH, s. *triglifo; termine d' architettura; ed è nome d' un membro del fregio dell' ordine Dorico posto direttamente sopra ogni colonna o pilastro, e in certi spazi degl' intercolunni.*

TRI'GON, s. [triangle] *triangolo,* s. m. *figura di tre angoli.*

TRI'GONAL, adj. [triangular] *triangolare, di tre angoli.*

TRIGONO'METRY, s. [the art of measuring triangles] *trigonometria,* s. f. *arte di misurare i triangoli.*

TRILA'TERAL, adj. [that has three sides] *che ha tre lati.*

TRILL, s. [a quivering or shaking, with voice or instrument] *trillo,* s. m.

To TRILL [to quaver] *gorgheggiare, trillare cantando o suonando.*

To trill [to drop, to trickle down] *gocciolare, cascare a gocciola.*

TRI'LLION, s. *un milione di milioni di milioni.*

TRIM, adj. [neat in clothes, spruce, fine] *pulito, attillato affettato ben alla vita.*

Trim [neat, snug, handsome] *bello, pulito, ben fatto.*

Trim, s. [dress, ornament] *abbigliamento,*

mento, ornamento, s. m. *attillatura*, s. f. *abito o vestire ornato ed attillato.*

The trim of a ship [the proportion of ballast, which is most apt to her good failing] *stiva, zavorra che si mette nella sentina d' un vascello acciochè stia pari e non barcolli.*

To TRIM [to furnish] *guernire, e guarnire, fornire*, pref. *guernisco, guarnisco, fornisco.*

To trim a suit of clothes with ribbon, *guernire un abito di nastri.*

To trim with silver or gold lace, *gallonare d' argento, o d' oro.*

To trim one, *radere uno, fargli la barba.*

To trim a boat [to set her so even on both sides as to balance her, so that she may not swag one way more than the other] *mettere una barca in istiva, pareggiarla in modo che non barcolli.*

To trim [to carry it fair between two parties] *star di mezzo, temporeggiare, navigar secondo il vento.*

To trim up, *aggiustare, accomodare, parare, ornare.*

To trim old clothes, *accomodare, rappezzare abiti vecchi.*

To trim up a tree, *diramare un albero, potarlo.*

TRI'MLY, adv. [neatly] *pulitamente.*

TRI'MMED, adj *guernito, guarnito, fornito. v.* To trim.

TRI'MMER, s. [one that trims, or carries fair with both parties] *un che tiene dalle due bande, un voltacasacca.*

TRI'MMING, s. *il guarnire.*

The trimming of a suit, *guarnimento, fornimento d' abito.*

TRI'MNESS, s. *pulizia, garbatezza, aggiustatezza, galanteria*, s. f.

TRI'NAL, adj. [threefold] *a tre doppi.*

TRINE, adj. [belonging to the number of three] *trino, di tre.*

The trine aspect of two planets [when they are distant from one another 120 degrees, or a third part of the zodiack] *trino aspetto di due pianeti, quella linea o raggio che comprende la terza parte del zodiaco.*

TRI'NITY, s. [one only God in three persons] *trinità, uno Dio in tre persone.*

Trinity-Sunday [the first Sunday after Whit Sunday] *Domenica della Trinità.*

TRI'NKET, s. [the top gallant, or the highest sail of any mast in a ship] *trinchetto*, s m.

Trinkets, s. [gewgaws, toys] *bagattelle, ciancie, cianciafruscole, giammengole*, s. f. pl.

TRIO'BOLAR, adj. [mean, vile, worthless] *da tre soldi, vile, dappoco, spregievole.*

A triobolar strumpet, *una vil puttanella, una femminazza da tre soldi.*

TRIP, s. [a stumble, a false step] *urto, inciampo.*

A trip of goats, *un truppa di capre.*

Trip [short journey or voyage] *scorsa, piccolo viaggio, giro.*

To TRIP [to stumble] *inciampare, intoppare, porre il piede in fallo in andando.*

To trip [to walk nimbly upon the toes] *camminare sulla punta de' piedi.*

To trip [to hop] *saltellare, arrancare.*

He trips with his tongue, *egli non sa quel che dice.*

To trip one up [to trip up one's heels] *dare il gambetto, o dar cella gamba ad uno, farlo cascare.*

TRI'PARTITE, adj. [divided into three parts] *tripartito, partito in tre.*

TRIPE, s. [part of the entrails of neat-cattle, parboiled and cleansed for eating, *trippa*, s. f.

Tripe woman, *donna che vende delle trippe.*

TRI'PERY, s. *mercato, dove si vendon le trippe.*

TRIPE'TALOUS, adj. ex. tripetalous plants, [those plants whose flowers consist of three leaves] *piante, di cui i fiori son composti di tre foglie.*

TRI'PTHONG, s. [three vowels joined together and making one sound] *trittongo, tre vocali che formano un solo suono.*

TRI'PLE, adj. [three-fold] *triplice, triplicato.*

The pope's triple crown, *la triplice corona del papa, la tiara del papa.*

The triple-tree [the gallows] *le forche.*

To TRI'PLE [to fold three times] *triplicare, rinterzare.*

TRI'PLET, s. [three of a kind] *tre d' una sorta.*

Triplet [three verses rhyming together] *terzetto, tre versi che rimano insieme.*

TRI'PLICATE, adj. [tripled] *triplicato, rinterzato.*

TRIPLICA'TION, s. *il triplicare.*

TRIPLI'CITY, s. [the quality of that which is triple] *triplicità*, s. f. *trino*, s. m.

TRI'POD, s. [a three-footed stool, used by the priestess of Apollo at Delphos] *tripode*, s. m.

TRI'POLY, s. [a stone used by lapidarics to polish their jewels] *tripoli, spezie di pietra da pulire.*

To TRISE } [to haul up any
To TRISE UP, } thing by a dead rope, that is, one not running in a pulley] *tirar su a bordo d' un vascello con fune.*

TRI'STFUL, adj. [sad, melancholy, gloomy] *triste, maninconoso, pien di tristezza, pieno di malinconia.*

TRISY'LLABLE, s. [a word consisting of three syllables] *trisillabo, vere composta di tre silabe.*

TRITE, adj. [threadbare, common] *trito, comune, usitato.*

Trite saying, *detto comune, proverbio.*

TRI'TON, s. [a fabulous sea-deity, Neptune's trumpeter] *Tritone, Dio marino favoloso, che è il trombettiere di Nettunno.*

Triton [vane, weather-cock] *girella, bandaruola*, s. f.

TRI'TONE [in musick, a greater fourth] *trituono*, s. m. *vore musicale.*

TRI'TURABLE, adj. that may be triturated] *che si può tritare.*

To TRI'TURATE [a chemical expression, for to pulverize] *tritare, stritolare.*

TRI'TURATED, adj. *tritato.*

TRITURA'TION, s. *il tritare, lo stritolare.*

TRI'VIAL, adj. [common, ordinary] *triviale, comune, ordinario, volgare.*

TRI'VIALLY, adv. *trivialmente, comunemente, ordinariamente.*

TRIUMPH, s. [a solemn pomp or show at the return of a victorious general from the wars, used by the antient Romans] *trionfo*, s. m. *festa pubblica che si faceva in Roma in onor de' capitani quando ritornavan coll' esercito vincitore.*

A triumph [victory] *trionfo, vittoria.*

To TRI'UMPH [to make a solemn and pompous entry] *trionfare, ricever l' onor del trionfo.*

To triumph over [to vanquish, to overcome] *trionfare, vincere, soggiogare, aver la vittoria.*

To triumph over one's enemies, *trionfar de' suoi nemici.*

To triumph [to subdue, to master] *vincere, domare.*

To triumph [to glory, to take pride in] *trionfare, festeggiare, vantarsi, pregiarsi.*

TRI'UMPHAL, adj. [belonging to a triumph] *trionfale, di trionfo.*

Triumphal chariot, *carro trionfale.*

TRI'UMPHANT, adj. [triumphing, victorious] *trionfante, che trionfa, trionfale, vittorioso.*

Triumphant chariot, *carro trionfale.*

TRI'UMPHANTLY, adv. [in a triumphant manner] *trionfalmente, con trionfo, a guisa di trionfo.*

TRI'UMPHED, adj. *trionfato, vinto, soggiogato.*

TRIU'MPHER, s. *trionfatore*, s. m. *che trionfa.*

TRIU'MPHING, s. *il trionfare.*

TRIU'MVIR, s. [one of the three magistrates that governed the Roman empire in chief] *triumviro*, s. m. *uno de' tre del triumvirato.*

TRIU'MVIRATE, s. [the office of a triumvir] *triumvirato*, s m.

TRIU'NE, adj. ex. the triune God, *un solo Dio in tre persone.*

To TROAT [to cry as a buck does at rutting time] *urlare e braveggiare come fa il cervo, o il daino quando va in amore.*

TRO'CHISK, s. [a physical composition] *trocisco*, s. m. *spezie di medicamento.*

TROD, } adj. *calpestato, v.* To
TRO'DDEN, } tread.

Trodden road, *cammino battuto, strada battutà.*

TRO'GLODYTE, s. [one who inhabits caves of the earth] *abitator di caverne, un che vive in un antro; troglodita.*

To TROLE about [to ramble up and down] *correre, vagabondare, andar qua e là par le strade, scorrer la cavallina.*

To troll away [to make haste with one's

one's business] *spacciarsi, sbrigarsi, affrettarsi, far presto che che sia.*

To troll for fish, *pescar del pesce coll' amo.*

To troll along with one's words, *parlar presto.*

Troll-madam, s. [a game which is also called pigeon's-holes] *giuoco che si fa con pallottole.*

TRO'LLOP, s. [a nasty slut, a slatternly woman] *una schifa, una donna sporca, una porcaccia.*

TRO'NAGE, s. [custom or toll taken for the weighing of wool] *diritto che si paga per pesare la lana.*

TRONA'TOR, s. [officer whose business it was to weigh wool brought into the city of London] *ufficiale, il di cui officio era di pesare la lana portata nella città di Londra.*

TROOP, s. [a multitude of people] *truppa, frotta, s. f. stormo, stuolo, s. f.*

Troop of soldiers, *truppa di soldati.*

Troop of horse, *campagnia di cavalleria.*

Troops [forces] *truppe, forze, gente di guerra, esercito.*

To TROOP [to flock together] *adunarsi, ragunarsi.*

To troop away, or troop off [to get away, or run away] *campare, salvarsi, fuggire*, pret. *fuggo.*

TRO'OPER, s. [horse-soldier] *un cavaliere, un soldato a cavallo.*

TROPE, s. [a term in rhetorick, signifying the turn of a word from its proper and genuine signification to another] *tropo*, s. m. *termine rettorico.*

TRO'PHYED, adj. [adorned with trophies] *ornato di trofei.*

TRO'PHY, s. [a monument set up in a place where enemies were vanquished, with their ensigns, warlike harnesses, and other spoils of war hanging on it] *trofeo*, s. m.

Trophy-money [a duty of 6*d.* paid annually by house keepers to the trainbands, for the drums, colours, &c. for their respective companies] *tassa di sei soldi che ogni capo di famiglia paga ogn' anno per le spese de' tamburi, stendardi, &c. della compagnia.*

TRO'PICAL, adj. [belonging to the tropick] *tropico.*

Tropical [rhetorically changed from the original meaning] *figurativo, metaforico, allontanato rettoricamente dal suo significato originale, o primario.*

The TRO'PICKS, s. [two circles of the sphere, parallel to the equinoctial line or equator, and equally distant from it about 23 degrees, 30 minutes] *tropici*, s. m. *due circoli della sfera paralelli all' equatore.*

TROPO'LOGICAL, adj. [belonging to tropology, moral] *tropologico, morale.*

The tropological sense, *il senso tropologico, il senso morale.*

TROPO'LOGY, s. [figurative or moral discourse] *discorso tropologico, discorso morale.*

TROT, s. [a horse's, or saddle-beast's going between a pace and a gallop] *trotto*, s. m. *spezie d' andare tra 'l passo communale e' l galoppo.*

An old trot [an old woman] *una verchia.*

Trot town [gadder] *un perdigiorno, uno scioperato, un vagabondo.*

To TROT [to go a jolting pace, as a horse] *trottare, andar di trotto.*

To trot up and down, *trottare, correr qua e la, andar su e giù.*

TROTH, s. [truth] *vero, fede.*

By my troth, *da vero, per mia fe.*

TRO'TTER, s. [trotting horse] *un trottatore, un cavallo che trotta.*

Trotters [sheeps feet] *peducci*, s. m.

TRO'TTING, s. *trotto*, s. m. *il trottare.*

Trotting, adj. ex. a trotting horse, *un cavallo che trotta, che va di trotto.*

TRO'UBLE, s. [inconveniency, pain] *pena, fatica, incomodità*, s. f. *fastidio, incomodo, travaglio, affanno, impaccio*, s. m.

To be a trouble to, *incomodare, infastidire, importunare.*

His old age is no trouble to him, *la sua vecchiezza non l' incomoda.*

Without any trouble, *senza veruna pena, senza alcuno incomodo.*

With little trouble, *senza molta fatica.*

Trouble [misfortune, cross accident, sorrow, disquiet of mind, disturbance] *disgrazia, disavventura, traversia, afflizione*, s. f. *disturbo, infortunio*, s. m.

It is a great trouble to me to see him in that condition, *mi duol molto di vederlo in tale stato*

To be in trouble, *essere in pena, esser travagliato.*

To bring into troubles, *travagliare, angustiare alcuno, darli travaglio o afflizione.*

You brought me into all these troubles, *voi siete la cagione di tutti questi miei disturbi.*

To bring one's self into troubles, *tirarsi addosso disgrazie procacciarsi delle disgrazie.*

To get one out of trouble, *cavar uno d' impaccio.*

Trouble [confusion, disturbance] *disturbo, disordine, imbroglio*, s. m. *confusione, turbolenza*, s. f.

The troubles of a state, *le turbolenze d' uno stato.*

Trouble [vexation, anxiety] *cura molesta, sollecitudine, tribolazione, angustia*, s. f. *affanno, pensiero, travaglio*, s. m.

A trouble-feast, *un importuno, un uomo fastidioso.*

To TRO'UBLE [to make any liquor thick or muddy] *intorbidare, far devenir torbido.*

To trouble the water of a spring, *intorbidar l' acqua d' una fontana.*

To trouble [to be troublesome to, to importune] *disturbare, incomodare, molestarr, importunare.*

To trouble one's rest, *disturbare l' altrui riposo.*

To trouble the publick peace, *disturbare la pubblica tranquillità.*

To trouble the state, *causar turbolenze nello stato.*

Why do you trouble yourself with such a man? *perchè volete voi impacciarvi con un tale uomo?*

Do not trouble yourself, *non vi pigliate fastidio.*

To trouble [to disturb, to interrupt] *sturbare, interrompere, impacciare, intrigare, impedire, dar noja, stornare.*

To trouble one's conversation, *sturbare l' altrui conversazione.*

To trouble one at work, *stornare uno del suo lavoro.*

To trouble [to vex, to disquiet, to afflict] *inquietare, travagliare, dare affanno, affannare, affliggere.*

That news troubles me much, *questa novella m' affligge, mi da affanno.*

Nothing troubles him, *non si prende fastidio di nulla.*

What need you trouble yourself? *che v' importa questo? di che v' ingerite?*

Nothing troubles me more, *questo è quel che più m' affligge, nulla mi da più affanno.*

To trouble [to cause pain, to give torment] *affliggere, tormentare, penare, incomodare, molestare.*

The gout troubles me much, *la gotta m' affligge, mi tormenta molto.*

It troubles me, *mi rincresce, mi dispiace.*

Do not trouble my head with your nonsense, *non istate a rompermi la testa co' vostri spropositi.*

TRO'UBLED, adj. *disturbato, sturbato, incomodato, molestato, importunato, afflitto.*

Troubled with a distemper, *afflitto da qualche malatria.*

Troubled with various thoughts, *combattuto da vari pensieri.*

I am troubled at it, *me ne dispiace, me ne rincresce.*

Troubled water, *acqua torbida.*

To fish in troubled water, *pescare in acqua torbida, pescar nel torbido.*

TRO'UBLER, s. *perturbatore, sturbatore*, s. m. *sturbatrice*, s. f.

TRO'UBLESOME, adj. [that causes trouble] *affannoso, angoscioso, duro, nojoso, fastidioso, gravoso, importuno, penoso, tormentoso, cattivo, increscevole, molesto.*

A troublesome business, *un cattivo negozio, un affare imbrogliato.*

A troublesome man, *un importuno, un uomo nojoso, o fastidioso.*

Troublesome times, *tempi calamitosi.*

To be troublesome, *esser incomodo, importuno, nojoso, molesto.*

A troublesome man at law, *un breccalite.*

This is a troublesome world we live in, *questo mondo è pieno d' affanni.*

TRO'UBLE-STATE, s. [disturber of a community; publick make-bate] *disturbatore dello stato, del comune, della società.*

TRO'UBLOUS, adj. [tumultuous, confused, disordered, put into commotion] *torbido, pien di tumulto, confuso, scompigliato, in disordine, violentemente, commosso. Non è voce in uso.*

TROUGH, s. [any thing hollowed and open longitudinally on the upper side] *ogni cosa incavata e longitudinalmente aperta di sopravia.*

TROUGH, s. [for hogs to feed in] *truogo, truogolo,* s. m.

Kneading trough, *madia,* s. f.

Smith's trough, *truologo di fabro.*

A trough of the sea [among sailors, the hollow made between any two waves in a rowling sea] *una valle fra due onde.*

To TROUL [to move volubly] *muoversi volubilmente.*

To troul [to utter volubly] *parlare con volubilità di lingua.*

To TROUNCE [to abuse] *maltrattare, strapazzare.*

To trounce one of his money, *scroccar ad uno i danari.*

TRO'UNCED, adj. *maltrattato, strapazzato,* v. To trounce.

TROUP, v. Troop.

TROUT, s. [a delicate fish] *trota,* s. f. *pesce noto per la sua dilicatezza.*

A trout [a confident fellow] *un uomo tanto ardito, che vuol essere tuo familiare a tuo dispetto.*

To TROW [to believe] *credere.*

TRO'WEL, s. [a mason's tool to spread mortar with] *cazzuola,* s. f. *mestola di ferro colla quale i muratori pigliano le calcina.*

To TROWL, v. To troul.

TROY-WEIGHT [a weight of 12 ounces to the pound] *sorta di peso di dodiri once la libbra.*

TRU'ANT, s. [a vagabond, a loitering fellow] *un vagabondo, un perdigiorno, un infingardo.*

To play the truant [to absent from school] *fuggire la scuola.*

TRU'B-TAIL, s. [a little squat woman] *una femminuccia, una donnicciuola.*

TRUCE, s. [a cessation of arms] *tregua,* s. f. *sospendimento d' arme.*

TRU'CHMAN, s. [interpreter] *interprete, turcimanno.*

TRUCIDA'TION, s. [a cruel murdering] *trucidazione,* s. f. *trucidamento,* s.m.

TRUCK, s. [exchange, bartering] *baratto,* s. m.

To TRUCK [to barter, to exchange] *barattare, cambiar cosa per cosa.*

TRU'CKED, adj. *barattato.*

TRU'CKER, s. *barattierre,* s. m. *che fa baratte.*

TRU'CKING, s. *baratto, cambio,* s. m. *il barattare.*

TRU'CKLE, s. [a little running wheel] *girella,* s. f. *picciola ruota, per lo più di legno.*

Truckle bed, *carriuola; letto che in vere di piedi ha quattro girelle, e tiensi sotto altri letti.*

To TRU'CKLE [to submit, to yield, to buckle to] *sommettersi, cedere, rendersi, arrendersi,* pret. *resi, arresi.*

To truckle to one, *sommettersi a qualcheduno,*

TRU'CKLING, s. *sommissione,* s. f. *il sommettersi.*

TRUCKS, s. [a kind of billiards] *trucco,* s. m. *sorta di giuoco di palle.*

The truck-table, *tavola dove si giuoca al trucco.*

TRU'CULENT, adj. [of a cruel, fierce look or disposition] *feroce, barbero, arcigno, crudele, spietato, fiero.*

To TRUDGE [or trot up and down] *trottare, andar su e giù, o qua e la, andare attorno.*

To trudge a-foot, *andare a piedi.*

To trudge [to toil and moil] *affaticarsi, affannarsi, darsi pena, darsi affanno.*

TRU'DGING, s. *pena, travaglio, affanno.*

TRUE, adj. [certain, sure] *vero, certo, sicuro.*

His account is true, *il suo racconto è vero.*

He does not speak a true word, *non dire una parola di vero.*

A true diamond, *un vero diamante.*

That's the true meaning of the author, *questo è il vero senso dell' autore.*

True [faithful, trusty] *vero, sincero, svisceràto, fedele, leale.*

A true friend, *un vero amico, un amico sincero, o leale.*

A true knave, *un pretto furbo.*

To be true to one, *esser fedele ad uno, servargli fede.*

True [exact] *esatto.*

True justice, *esatta giustizia.*

To speak true English, *parlar buon Inglese, parlar Inglese correttamente.*

To speak true, *dire la verità, dire il vero.*

'Tis likely enough to be true, *la cosa è molto verisimile.*

He guessed true, *l' ha indovinata.*

True hearted, adj. *franco, sincero, schietto, libero, leale, fedele, di buona fede, vero.*

True-heartedness, s. *lealtà, sincerità, buona fede, schiettezza, franchezza,* s. f.

True-love, s. [a plant] *uva di volpe.*

TRU'ENESS, s. [sincerity] *sincerità, schiettezza, franchezza,* s. f. *candore,* s. m.

TRUG [a hod to carry mortar in] *truògolo di muratore.*

TRULL, s. [harlot] *una bagascia, una sgualdrina, una puttana vile.*

TRU'LY, adv. [in truth, sincerely] *veramente, in verità, in vero, sinceramente.*

TRUMP, s. [a winning card] *trionfo.*

To have trumps, *aver trionfi.*

The trump card, *il trionfo.*

To be put to one's trumps, *trovarsi alle strette, esser ridotto all' estremità.*

Trump [trumpet] *tromba,* s. f.

The trump of an elephant, *la proboscide d' un elefante.*

To TRUMP, *prendere con un trionfo, trionfare, giuocar trionfo.*

To trump [to cry up] *esaltare, magnificare.*

TRU'MPERY, s. [trash, old paltry stuff] *cenci, ciabatte, ciarpe, robe vecchie.*

TRU'MPET, s. [a warlike musical instrument] *tromba,* s. f. *strumento da fiato proprio della milizia.*

To sound the trumpet, *suonar la tromba.*

To proclaim by sound of trumpet, *proclamare a suon di tromba.*

Trumpet-marine, *tromba marina.*

Little-trumpet, *una trombetta.*

TRU'MPET-FLOWER, s. [a tubulous flower] *bignonia, sorta di fiore tuboloso.*

To TRU'MPET, [to sound a trumpet] *suonar la tromba.*

To trumpet [to publish, to spread abroad, to proclaim] *pubblicare manifestare, divulgare, proclamare.*

Homer trumpets for Achilles in his praises, *Omero è la tromba delle lodi d' Achille.*

TRU'MPETER, s. [he that sounds the trumpet] *trombettiere,* s. m. *sonator di tromba.*

TRU'MPET-TONGUED, adj. [having a tongue vociferous as a trumpet] *che ha lingua sonora, romorosa, o risonante come tromba; e credo Shakespeare dia questo epiteto alla fama.*

TRU'NCHEON, t. [a short club] *un bastone.*

TRU'NDLE, s. [a carriage with low wheels, to draw heavy burdens on] *carriuola,* s. f. *strumento di legname con quattro girelle, e serve per tirare gravi pesi.*

To trundle [to roll along] *rotolare, e ruotolare.*

Trundle-tail [a wench which runs up and down with a draggle-tail] *una berghinella che scorre le strade spazzando la terra collo strascico della gonna.*

TRUNK, s. [chest] *cofano,* s. m. *cassa,* s. f.

A trunk covered with leather, *un baule, un forziere.*

An iron trunk, *un forziere di ferro.*

Trunk-maker, *un baulajo.*

The trunk of a tree, *il tronco d' un albero.*

The trunk of a man's body, *il busto.*

The trunk of a figure, *il busto, il torso d' una statua.*

Trunk, *cerbottana,* s. f. *mezza lunga e vota dentro a guisa di canna, per la quale con forza di fiato si spigne fuora colla bocca una palla di terra.*

Trunk [wooden pipe for the conveyance of water] *cannone da condotti, doccia,* s. f. *canaletto di legno, per la quale si fa correre unitamente l' acqua.*

An elephant's trunk, *la tromba, o la proboscide d' un elefante.*

Trunk-breeches, *brache.*

TRU'NKED, adj. *formato dal sostantivo* trunk.

TRU'NKHOSE, s. [large breeches formerly worn] *brache large usate anticamente.*

TRU'NNIONS, s. [those knots or bunches of a gun, which bear her up upon the cheeks of the carriage] *orecchioni di cannone.*

TRUSS, s. [a bundle] *fardello, fascio, fastello,* s. m.

Truss of hay, *fastello o fascio di fieno.*

Truss [a kind of bandage for persons that are bursten] *brachiere,* s. m. *fasciatura di ferro o di cuojo per sostener gl' intestini che cascan per crepatura.*

To TRUSS up [to tie up] *legare, annodare, attaccare.*
To truss up one's hair, *legarsi, annodarsi i capelli.*
To truss a fowl, *accomodare un pollastro.*
To truss [to make a fardel] *imballare, far fardello.*
To truss [to snatch up] *levar su, portar via.*
An eagle trusses a leveret, *un aquila leva su un lepratto.*
To truss upon a tree, *appiccare ad un albero.*
To truss up one's cloaths, *succignersi, levar su i vestimenti,* pref. *succingo,* pret. *succinsi.*
Trussed up, adj. *legato, annodato, attaccato, v.* To truss.
A horse well trussed, *un cavallo raccolto.*
TRUST, s. [confidence, assurance] *confidenza, fede, fiducia,* s. f.
To put one's trust in God, *metter la sua confidenza in Dio, confidare in Dio.*
There's no trust to be put in him, *non è da por fede in lui; non è persona da potersi fidare.*
Trust [*depositum*] *deposito,* s. m.
To put one in trust with a thing, *confidare che che sia ad uno, depositarlo nelle sue mani.*
A feoffee of trust, *un fidecomissario.*
Place of great trust, *carica importante, di grande importanza.*
A man of great trust, *un uomo fedelissimo, d' incorrotta fede.*
Trust [credit, tick] *credenza,* s. f.
To take upon trust, *pigliare a credenza.*
To give upon trust, *dare a credenza.*
To TRUST [to put in trust with] *fidare, confidare, commettere alla fede altrui.*
To trust one with a secret, *confidare un segreto ad uno.*
I trust you with this diamond, *vi confido questo diamante.*
To trust [to depend on, to rely upon] *confidare, confidarsi, fidarsi, assicurarsi, far capitale.*
I won't trust him, *non voglio fidarmi di lui.*
To trust one [to give one credit] *far credenza ad uno, dargli qualche cosa a credenza.*
Who will trust one word he says? *chi vorrà mai prestar fede a quel che dice?*
To trust in God, *confidare, metter la sua confidenza in Dio.*
To trust too much to one's self, *presumer troppo di se, fidarsi troppo delle proprie forze.*
To have something to trust to, *aver di che vivere.*
'Tis all I have to trust to, *questo è tutto quel che ho nel mondo.*
To trust [to hope] *sperare.*
I trust in God he will recover his health, *spero che Iddio gli farà la grazia di ricuperar la sanità.*
TRU'STED, adj. *fidato, confidato, v.* To trust.

He is not to be trusted, *egli non è uomo da fidarsi.*
TRUSTE'E, s. [one that keeps a trust] *depositario, fidecommissario.*
Trustee [one who has an estate or money put into his hands for the use of another, a guardian] *curatore.*
TRU'STER, s. [one who trusts] *colui che si fida d' altrui, o che si confida in altrui.*
TRUSTILY, adv. [faithfully] *fedelmente, lealmente.*
TRU'STINESS, *fedeltà, lealtà,* s. f.
TRU'STLESS, adj. [unfaithful, unconstant, not to be trusted] *sleale, infedele, incostante, da non potersene o doversene fidare.*
TRU'STY, adv. [faithful] *fidato, fedele, leale.*
Trusty friend, *amico fidato.*
TRUTH, s. [certainty, fidelity] *verità,* s. f. *vero,* s. m.
To speak or tell the truth, *dire la verità.*
To tell you the truth of the matter, *a dirvi il vero, a dirvela come sta.*
The naked truth, *la pura verità, la schietta verità.*
All truths are not to be spoken at all times, *non ogni verità si deve dire in ogni tempo.*
To preach the truths of the gospel, *predicare le verità evangeliche.*
There's no truth in any thing, *non v' è niente di sicuro sotto 'l cielo.*
Speak the truth and shame the devil, *piscia chiaro e fatti beffe del medico; cioè abbi netta la coscienza e non temere.*
In truth [seriously, without jesting] *da vero, su' l serio, seriamente, per certo.*
You shall know the whole truth of the matter, *voi saprete tutto il negozio.*
There is no truth in him, *egli non dice il vero.*
TRUTINA'TION, s. [the act of weighing; examination by the scales] *il pesare, l' atto del pesare, lo esaminare colla bilancia quanto una cosa pesi.*
To try [to essay, to prove] *fare il saggio, far la prova, sperimentare, fare sperienza, cimentare, tentare.*
To try a suit of cloaths, a pair of shoes, *provare un vestimento, un pajo di scarpe.*
To try a friend, *sperimentare un amico.*
To try a medicine, *fare sperimento d' una medicina.*
To try a gun, *provare un arme da fuoco.*
To try gold by the touch stone, *cimentar l' oro col paragone.*
To try the chance of war, *tentar la fortuna della guerra.*
To try out a matter, *esaminare, discutere, crivellare, considerare una materia.*
To try by weight, *pesare.*
To try one [to feel his pulse] *tastare, scalzare alcuno, riconoscer l' animo di qualcheduno.*
To try a quarrel by dint of sword, *decidere, terminare una contesa colla punta della spada.*
To try one for his life [to bring one to his tryal] *fare il processo ad uno, giudicarlo, sentenziarlo.*
To try [to refine, to purify] *raffinare, purificare.*
To try metals, *raffinare metalli.*
To try a liquor, *purificare un liquore.*
To try by experiments, *fare sperimenti.*
To try conclusions, *cimentare, metter a cimento.*
To try one's skill, *far prova delle proprie forze.*
To try [to endeavour] *cercare, provare, tentare, sforzarsi, fare ogni sforzo.*
TRY'AL, *v.* Trial.
TRYED, adj. *saggiato, v.* To try.
TRY'ING, s. *saggio,* s. m. *il saggiare.*
'Tis but trying, *il tentare non nuoce.*
TUB, s. [a wooden vessel] *tina,* s. f. *tino,* s. m.
Bucking tub, *tinaccio da bucato.*
Kneading-tub, *madia.*
Salting or powdering tub, *tinello.*
A tale of a tub [an idle tale] *novella da dire a vegghia, novella vana, la favola dell' uccellino.*
Tub, s. [a state of salivation] *lo scilivare.*
TUBE, s. [a pipe, a syphon, a long body] *tubo, sifone, corpo lungo e vuoto.*
TUBE'RCLE, s. [a small swelling or excrescence on the body; a pimple] *tubercolo, bitorzolo, tumoretto, porro, bernoccolo,* s. m. *verruca,* s. f. *picciola escrescenza o gonfiamento cagionato da malore sulla superficie del corpo umano.*
TU'BEROSE, s. [a white fragrant flower] *tuberoso,* s. f. *spezie di fiore odorifero.*
TUBERO'SITY, s. [a bunching out] *tuberosità,* s. f. *bitorozolo, bernoccolo,* s. m.
TU'BEROUS, adj. [full of bunches or knots] *tuberoso, pieno di bitorzoli o di bernoccoli.*
TUCK, s. [a rapier, a narrow long sword] *sorta di spada di lama stretta e lunga.*
Tuck [a kind of net] *sorta di rete.*
To TUCK [to turn, to gather up] *succignere, alzare, levar su.*
To tuck up one's gown, *succignersi la gonnella.*
To tuck in the bed cloaths, *fare entrare l' estremità delle coperte sotto le coltrici.*
To tuck [to crush together, to hinder from spreading] *schiacciare, opprimere, impedire dal crescere e diramarsi.*
To tuck, v. n. [to contract] *raggrinzarsi, restringersi.*
TU'CKED, adj. *succinto, alzato, levato su, v.* To tuck.
TU'CKER, s. [a slip of fine linen or lace pinned along the top of women's stays] *gala,* s. f. *ornamento, che portan le donne sul petto alquanto fuor del busto, ed è una striscia di panno lino o merletto.*

Tucker [a fuller of cloth] *follone*, s. m.
Tucker's mill, *gualchiera*, s. f.
TU'CKSELS, s. [the teeth called grinders] *i mascellari.*
TU'ESDAY, s. [the third day of the week] *Martedì.*
Shrove Tuesday, *Martedì grasso.*
TU'FFET } s. [lock of hair] *ciuffetto di capelli.*
TUFT }
Tuft of silk, *fiocco di seta.*
Tuft of feathers, *mazzo di piume.*
The tuft of a tree, *la cima d' un albero.*
A tuft of rushes, *un cesto di giunchi.*
A tuft of trees, *un bosco d' alberi.*
A tuft of grass, *zolla che abbia seco l' erba.*
Tuft [crest of a bird] *la cresta d' un uccello.*
Tuft, adj. *velluto, velloso.*
Tuft ribbond, *nastro velluto o velloso.*
TU'FFED, adj. *velluto o velloso.*
Tufted flower, *fiore velluto o velloso.*
Tufted lark, *allodola crestata.*
TU'FTY, adj. *velluto o velloso.*
TUG, s. [pull] *tirata, strappata,* s. f.
To give a tug, *dare una tirata, strappare.*
Tug [a waggon to carry timber] *carro per carreggiare legnami.*
To tug [to pull] *tirare, trarre, strappare.*
To tug at the oar, *tirar il remo.*
To tug hard for a thing, *darsi molta pena, affannarsi, sudare per ottenere che che sia.*
TU'GGED, adj. *tirato, tratto, strappato.*
TU'GGER, s. *quello, o quella che tira o che strappa.*
TU'GGING, s. *tiramento,* s. m. *il tirare, lo strappare.*
Tugging, adj. ex. a tugging horse, *un cavallo da traino.*
TUI'TION, s. [care] *cura, condotta,* s. f.
Tuition [protection, patronage] *protezione, difesa,* s. f.
TU'LIP, s. [a flower] *tulipano,* s. m. *spezie di fiore.*
TU'MBLE, s. [fall] *cascata,* s. f. *capitombolo,* s. m.
To TU'MBLE [to roll] *rotolare, ruotolare, spignere una cosa per terra facendola girare.*
To tumble stones down a hill, *rotolare delle pietre dall' alto d' una montagna.*
To tumble one upon a bed, *gettare, rovesciare uno sopra un letto.*
To tumble a bed, *sconvolgere, metter sossopra un letto, disfarlo.*
To tumble one's cloaths, *scompigliare, spiegazzare un abito.*
To tumble down [to make fall] *far cascare, gettare per terra.*
To tumble over books, *squadernar libri.*
To tumble [to tumble down, to fall down] *cascare, cadere,* pret. *caddi.*
To tumble [to wallow one's self] *voltolarsi, rivoltarsi, gettarsi, stendersi, dimenarsi.*
To tumble upon the bed, *voltolarsi gettarsi, dimenarsi su' l letto.*
A ship that tumbles [that rolls or labours at sea] *un vascello che barcolla, che bordeggia.*
To tumble [to play tumbling tricks] *capitombolare, far capitomboli.*
TU'MBLED, adj. *rotolato,* v. To tumble.
TU'MBLER, s. *saltatore che fa capitomboli, che capitombola.*
A tumbler dog, *un bassetto.*
TU'MBLING, s. *il rotolare,* v. To tumble.
Tumbling, adj. ex. To play tumbling tricks, *far capitomboli, capitombolare.*
TU'MBREL, s. [dung cart] *carretta,* s. f. *carro,* s. m.
TUMEFA'CTION, s. [swelling] *tumore, enfiamento,* s. m *gonfiatura,* s. f.
To TU'MEFY [to swell] *enfiare, gonfiare.*
TU'MEFYED, adj. *enfiato, gonfiato.*
TU'MID, adj. [swelling] *tumido, gonfiato.*
A tumid style, *uno stile gonfio.*
TU'MOUR, s. [swelling] *tumore, enfiamento,* s. m. *enfiatura,* s. f.
Tumour in the groin, *tinçone,* s. m.
TU'MULT, s. [bustle, uproar, hurly-burly] *tumulto, romore, fracasso di popolo sollevato.*
TUMU'LTUARILY, adv. *tumultuariamente, con tumulto.*
TUMU'LTUARINESS, s. [turbulence, inclination or disposition to tumults and commotion] *turbolenza, inclinazione o disposizione a tumultuare.*
TUMU'LTUARY, adj. [done in a tumult] *tumultuario, fatto senza ordine, confuso, pien di tumulto.*
To TUMU'LTUATE [to make a tumult] *tumultuare, alzar confusione e tumulto.*
TUMULTUA'TION, s. [irregular and confused agitation] *tumulto, il tumultuare; agitazione violenta, irregolare, e confusa.*
TUMU'LTUOUS, adj. [riotous] *tumultuoso, confuso, riottoso, sedizioso.*
TUMU'LTUOUSLY, adv. *tumultuosamente, con tumulto, tumultuariamente.*
TUN, s. [pipe] *botte,* s. f.
Tun [a measure of liquids] *misura d' oglio, di vino, e altri liquidi.*
Tun [the weight of two thousand pounds] *tonellata,* s. f. *termine mercantile, peso di due mila libbre.*
A ship of 200 tons, *una nave di dugento tonellate.*
A tun of timber [a measure of forty solid feet] *misura di quaranta piedi di legname.*
Tun [a drunkard] *un beone, un briaco. E' voce burlesca.*
Tun-belly'd, *panciuto, che ha la pancia grossa.*
To TUN [to put into a tun] *imbottare, mettere nella botte.*
TU'NA, s. [an American tree in the leaves of which the cochineal are bred] *tuna,* s. f.
TU'NABLE, adj. [harmonious, that is agreeable to the rules of musick] *armonioso.*
Tunable voice, *voce armoniosa.*
TU'NABLY, adj. *armoniosamente, con armonia.*
TUNE, s. [agreement in sound] *tuono,* s. m. *accordo, consonanza di voce.*
Melodious tunes, *tuoni o concenti armoniosi.*
To sing in tune, *cantare in tuono.*
To sing out of tune, *cantar fuor di tuono.*
Tune [air, way of singing or playing] *aria, tuono, spezialità di canto o di suono.*
The tune of a song, *l' aria d' una canzone.*
To sing another tune, *cangiar di nota, cambiar discorso.*
To be out of tune [to be out of humour] *non esser di buon umore.*
To rattle one to some tune, *lavar la testa ad uno, sgridarlo, farli una ripassata.*
To TUNE [to put in tune] *accordare.*
To tune a musical instrument, *accordare uno strumento musicale.*
To tune [to sing harmoniously] *cantare armoniosamente.*
TU'NED, adj. *accordato.*
TU'NEFUL, adj. [musical, harmonious] *musicale, armonioso.*
TU'NELESS, adj. [without tune, or out of tune] *discordante, scordante.*
TU'NER, s. [one who tunes] *colui che accorda uno strumento.*
TU'NICK, s. [a sort of sleeveless coat] *tunica, tonaca,* s. f.
Tunick, or tunicle [a little skin covering any part of the body] *tunica, burcia, membrana, integumento.*
The tunicle of the eye, *la tunica dell' occhio.*
TU'NING, s. *accordo,* s. m. *accordatura,* s. f.
TU'NNAGE, s. [an impost for every tun of merchandize exported or imported in ships] *dazio che si paga per ogni tonellata di mercanzia, che si trasporta dentro o fuori d' Inghilterra per via di vascelli.*
TU'NNED, adj. *imbottato.*
TU'NNEL, s. [or funnel through which liquors are poured into a vessel] *imbuto,* s. m. *pevera,* s. f.
Tunnel [a sort of net to catch partridges] *spezie di rete da prender pernici.*
The tunnel of a chimney, *il fummajuolo, la rocca del cammino.*
To TU'NNEL [to form like a tunnel] *far a modo d' imbuto.*
To tunnel [to catch birds in a net] *pigliar uccelli col tramaglio.*
TU'NNELLER, s. [one that takes partridges with a tunnel] *colui che piglia le pernici colla rete.*
TU'NNY, s. [a sea-fish] *tonno,* s. m. *pesce di mare così detto.*
Pickled tunny, *tonnina,* s. f.
The place where they fish for tunny, *tonnaja,* s. f. *seno di mare ove si pescano i tonni.*
TUP, s. [a ram] *montone non castrato.*

to, ariete. E voce ancora in uſo in Staffordſhire.

To TUP [to but like a ram] *cozzare come fa il montone.*

TU'RBAN, TU'RBAND, TU'RBANT, } s. [a ſort of cap worn by the Turks, and moſt of the eaſtern people, *turbante*, s. m.

TU'RBANED, adj. [wearing a turband] *che porta il turbante.*

TU'RBARY, s. [a right to dig turfs in the ground of another] *diritto o privilegio di prender delle piote nella terra d' un altro.*

TU'RBOT, s. [a ſea-fiſh] *rombo*, s. m.

TU'RBULENCY, s. [troubleſomeneſs] *turbolenza, perturbazione.*

TU'RBULENT, adj. [boiſterous, bluſtering] *turbulento, impetuoſo.*

Turbulent [ſeditious] *turbolento, ſedizioſo, riottoſo.*

TU'RBULENTLY, adj. *con turbolenza, d' una maniera turbolente.*

TU'RCISM, s. [religion, principles, or opinions of the Turks] *religione de' Turchi, Maomettiſmo.*

TURCO'ISE, s. [a precious ſtone of azure colour] *turchina*, s. f. *pietra prezioſa di color azzurro.*

TURD, s. [excrement] *ſterco umano.*

TURF, s. [clod] *pezzo di terra coperto d' erba.*

TU'RGENT, adj. [ſwelling, protuberant, tumid] *gonfio, turgido, tumido.*

TURGE'SCENCE, s. [a ſwelling] *tumore, enfiato*, s. m. *enfiatura*, s. f.

TU'RGID, adj. [ſwollen] *turgido, gonfiato.*

TURK, s. [a native of Turkey] *un Turco.*

Turk [the Turkiſh language] *il Turco, la lingua Turca.*

TU'RKISH, adj. *Turco, Turcheſco.*

The Turkiſh language, *la lingua Turca.*

The Turkiſh empire, *l' imperio de' Turchi, l' imperio Ottomano.*

TU'RKEY, s. [a country in Europe and Aſia] *Turchia.*

Turkey merchant, *uno che mercanteggia con gente in Turchia.*

Turkey, *gallo d' India, gallinaccio.*

Turkey-hen, *una gallina d' India.*

Turkey-wheat, *grano d' India, meliga.*

TU'RMERICK, s. [the root of an herb growing in India and Arabia, good for the yellow jaundice] *turtumaglio*, s. m.

TU'RMOIL, s. [tumult, buſtle, ſtir] *tumulto, ſtrepito, fracaſſo, romore*, s. m.

To TU'RMOIL [to make a buſtle] *ſtrepitare, far grande ſtrepito, ſchiamazzare.*

TURN, s. [a turner's lathe] *tornio, e torno*, s. m. *ordigno ſul quale ſi fanno diverſi lavori.*

Turn [walk] *girata, paſſeggiata*, s. f.

To take a turn, *fare una girata, una paſſeggiata.*

Will you take a turn with me thither? *volete far colà una ſcorſa meco?*

Turn [courſe] *giro*, s. m. *vicenda*, s. f.

Every one in his turn, *ognuno in giro, ognuno a vicenda.*

When it comes to my turn, *quando ſarà il mio giro, quando toccherà a me.*

By turns, *in giro, a vicenda, vicendevolmente.*

At every turn, *ad ogni tratto, ad ogni momento.*

A turn [change] *rivoluzione, mutazione*, s. f. *cangiamento*, s. m.

Turn [a good or bad office] *ufficio, ſervizio*, s. m.

To do one a good turn, *render un buon ufficio ad uno, fargli qualche buon ſervizio.*

To do one an ill turn, *render ad uno un cattivo ufficio, farli un mal tiro.*

One good turn deſerves another, *amore con amor ſi paga.*

A friendly turn, *un tiro d' amico.*

Turn [turning] *volta*, s. f. *il voltare.*

Give it a turn, *voltatelo.*

In the turn of a hand [in a moment] *in un batter d' occhio.*

'Twas within the turn of a die, *non tenne che ad un capello ; poco mancò.*

He is not fit for my turn, *egli non fa per me.*

This will ſerve my turn very well, *queſto farà per me.*

I ſhall do you as good a turn another time, *un' altra volta vi renderò pan per focaccia, vi renderò la pariglia.*

I don't know what turn to give this phraſe, *non ſo in che modo eſprimere queſta fraſe.*

Turn-coat [one that goes over to another party] *volta caſacca.*

Turn-coat [in religion] *rinnegato, apoſtata.*

A turn-back [a coward] *un codardo, un vigliacco, un poltrone.*

Turnſole [a ſort of flower] *giraſole*, s. m.

To gallop a horſe two or three turns, *far fare due o tre giri ad un cavallo.*

Turn-broach, turn-ſpit, *un menarroſto.*

Turn-pipe, *cavallo di friſa.*

Turn-pike, *cancello*, s. m.

Turn-ſtile, *girandola.*

To TURN [to move round] *voltare, volgere*, pret. *volſi.*

To turn a wheel, *volgere una ruota.*

To turn one's back, *voltar le ſpalle.*

To turn the ſpit, *girar lo ſpiedo.*

To turn the leaves of a book, *voltar i fogli d' un libro.*

To turn the toes in or out, *voltar le punte de' piedi in dentro o in fuori.*

To turn head [to make head] againſt, *voltar faccia, far teſta.*

To turn tail [to ſhuffle, to ſhift] *girare, rigirare, trovar giri e rigiri.*

To turn back [to forſake] *voltar le ſpalle, laſciare, abbandonare.*

To turn back [to fly] *voltar le ſpalle, fuggire, pigliar la fuga.*

He does not know which way to turn [he is put to his laſt ſhifts] *egli non ſa che partito pigliare.*

To turn [to turn the inſide out] *rivoltare.*

To turn a ſuit of clothes, *rivoltare un abito.*

To turn the ſcale, *dar il trabocco alla bilancia.*

To turn the milk, *guaſtare il latte.*

To turn, *torniare, lavorare al tornio.*

To turn one's thoughts to ſomething, or upon ſomething, *volgere il penſiero a qualche coſa.*

To turn out of one language into another [to tranſlate] *tradurre, volgarizzare, ridurre da una lingua in un' altra.*

To turn every thing to one's advantage, *volgere ogni coſa a proprio vantaggio.*

To turn into ridicule [to make a jeſt] *beffarſi, farſi beffe.*

To turn one into ridicule [to make a fool of him] *beffare, uccellare alcuno, ſchernirlo.*

I turn and wind him as I pleaſe, *io fo di lui tutto quel che mi piace.*

To turn a buſineſs well or ill, *maneggiare o condurre un negozio bene o male.*

To turn [to move or to go round] *girare, andare in giro.*

There's a diſpute whether the ſun turns round the earth, or the earth round the ſun, *ſi diſputa ſe il ſole gira intorno alla terra, o ſe la terra intorno al ſole.*

To turn [to move this way or that way] *moverſi e muoverſi.*

To turn upon the enemy, *voltar faccia, far teſta al nemico.*

My head turns round [I am giddy] *la teſta mi gira.*

To turn to all winds [to be inconſtant] *voltarſi ad ogni vento, eſſere incoſtante, eſſer volubile.*

To turn [to incline, to end, to have a certain iſſue] *tornare, riſultare, ridondare.*

That will turn to account, *queſto tornerà a conto, queſto ſarà vantaggioſo.*

That will turn to your honour, *ciò ridonderà in voſtro onore.*

That will turn to your ſhame, *queſto tornerà in voſtro diſonore.*

To turn [as milk does] *guaſtarſi.*

To turn [to bend another way] *ſtornare, fraſtornare.*

To turn the courſe of a river, *fraſtornare il corſo d' un fiume.*

To turn one's eyes from one object to another, *rivolger gli occhi da un oggetto ad un altro.*

To turn one thing into another, *cangiare, convertire una coſa in un' altra.*

To turn wine into water, *cangiar il vino in acqua.*

I pray God to turn his heart, *prego Iddio che lo converta.*

To turn from one's religion, *cangiar religione, farſi d' un' altra religione, convertirſi ad un' altra religione, pervertire.*

To turn one [to make him turn his religion] *far cangiar religione ad uno, convertirlo, pervertirlo.*

To turn [to be changed or converted, to become] *cambiarsi, cangiarsi, convertirsi, divenire, farsi*, pres. *divengo*, pret. *divénni.*

To turn into stone, *cangiarsi o cambiarsi in pietra, impeitrarsi.*

Turn unto the Lord your God, *convertitevi al signor vostro Dio.*

To turn sour, *divenir agro, inacetirsi.*

To turn sour [speaking of wine] *inforconarsi, divenir cerrone.*

To turn physician, *farsi medico.*

The wind turns, *il vento si cangia.*

To turn a horse to grass, *metter un cavallo all' erba.*

That's enough to turn his brain, *questo è capace di voltargli il cervello, di farlo impazzire.*

That turns my stomach, *questo mi sconvolge lo stomaco.*

To turn to one, *abbracciare il partito d' un altro, andar dalla sua banda.*

To turn a stallion amongst mares, *dare lo stallone alle cavalle.*

To turn about [to move round] *girare, muoversi in giro.*

To turn about, *voltarsi, voltar faccia.*

The room is so little that one can hardly turn about, *la camera è sì piccola che appena un si può movere.*

To turn away a servant, *licenziare un servo, mandarlo via, metterlo fuor di casa.*

To turn back, *tornare, ritornare.*

To turn down, *piegare.*

To turn one off, *liberarsi da uno, levarselo d' attorno.*

To turn off [to avert] *stornare, liberare.*

To turn off a malefactor, *impiccar un malfattore per la gola.*

To turn in, *piegare, raddoppiare.*

To turn in and out, *serpere, andar torto a guisa di serpe, serpeggiare, volteggiare.*

To turn a thing over to one, *rimettere una cosa ad uno, metterla nelle sue mani.*

Turn him over to me, *mandatelo da me.*

To turn over books, *leggere, squadernare, volgere, rivolgere libri.*

To turn over every leaf of a book, *squadernare un libro.*

To turn over a new leaf [to take another course] *pigliar altre misure, trovar altri mezzi termini.*

To turn over a new leaf [to change one's course of life] *cangiar vita, mutar costumi.*

To turn out of doors, *scacciare fuor di casa.*

To turn one out of his office, *levare uno dalla sua cari a, dal suo impiego, dal suo uffic.o.*

To turn up, *voltare, alzare, sucrignere, piegare.*

To turn up one's sleeves, *alzarsi le maniche.*

To turn up one's mask, *alzarsi la maschera.*

To turn up the ground, *vangare, zappare la terra, smuovere la terra.*

To turn upside down, *rovesciare, metter sossopra, sconvolgere*, pret. *sconvolsi.*

To turn one out of his way, *travviare uno, metterlo fuor della via.*

TU'RNAMENT, s. [a justing or tilting] *torniamento, e torniamento*, s. m. *giostra*, s. f.

TU'RNBENCH, s. *nome d' un ordigno o strumento da torniajo.*

TU'RNCOAT, s. [one who forsakes his party or principles; a renegado] *voltacásacca, colui che dà un partito si lieva e vassene al partito contrario; colui che avendo professato sempre una cosa, a un tratto se ne stacca, e alla contraria s' appiglia: un apostata, un rinnegato.*

TU'RNED, adj. *v* To turn.

My stomach is turned against it, *questo mi stomaca.*

TU'RNEP, s. [a well known root] *rapa*, s. f.

TU'RNER, s. [one who turns vessels or instruments in wood or metal] *torniajo*, s. m. *maestro di tornio.*

TU'RNING, s. *giro*, s. m.

In the turning of a hand [in a trice] *in un voltar di mano, in un batter d' occhio, in un attimo.*

The turnings and windings of a river, *giravolte, serpeggiamenti d' un fiume.*

Turning, adj. ex. a turning joint, *vertebra*, s. f. *l' osso della spina del dosso.*

TU'RNINGNESS, s. [quality of turning, subterfuge] *l' aggirarsi; sutterfugio; abbindolamento.*

TU'RNIP, s. [a white esculent root] *rapa. Alcuni scrivono meno propriamente*, turnep.

TU'RNPIKE, s. *sbarra; steccato; luego sbarrato onde non passino cavalli o carriaggi senza pagare pedaggio.*

TU'RPENTINE, s. [a clear gum or resin issuing from several sorts of trees] *trementina*, s. f.

The turpentine tree, *terebinto*, s. m.

TU'RPITUDE, s. [filthiness, baseness] *turpitudine, deformità, bruttura*, s. f.

TU'RREL, s. [a sort of tool used by coopers] *succhiello, succhio*, s. m. *strumento da bucare.*

TU'RRET, s. [a little tower] *torricciuola, torricella*, s. f.

TU'RRETED, adj. [formed like a tower; rising like a tower] *che è fatto o s' alza a mo' di picciola torre.*

TU'RTLE, s. [tortoise] *testuggine di mare.*

Turtle } *tórtora, tértola, tortorélla*, s. f.
Turtle-dove }

TU'SCAN, adj. [of Tuscany] *Tosco, Toscano, di Toscana.*

The Tuscan language, *la favella Toscana, il parlar Toscano, la lingua Toscana.*

The Tuscan order [in architecture, so called because it was invented in Tuscany; here the columns together with base and capital are to be seven modules in length, and to have the upper part of the pillar one fourth less in diameter than the bottom] *l' ordine Toscano, termine d' architettura.*

TUSH [an interjection of slighting or displeasure] *oibò!*

TU'SHES of a horse [four particular teeth] *certi denti del cavallo.*

Tushes } of a boar [the great teeth
TUSKS } that stand out] *zanne*, s. f.

TU'SKED } adj. *zannuto, che ha zanne.*
TU'SKY }

TUT, s. [an Imperial ensign of a golden globe with a cross on it] *pomo*, s. m. *quella palla, che ha sopra una crocetta, che si porta in mano dagl' Imperadori e da' Re.*

Tut, interj. [a particle noting contempt] *voce di disprezzo.*

TU'TANAG, s. [a Chinese name for spelter] *sorta di metallo imperfetto.*

TU'TELAGE, s. [guardianship] *tutela*, s. f. *protezione del pupillo, la quale ha il tutore d' esso pupillo.*

TU'TELAR } adj. [that protects] *tutelare, guardiano, che protegge, che difende.*
TU'TELARY }

A tutelary angel, *angelo tutelare o custode.*

TURMO'UTHED, adj. [that has the chin and nether jaw standing further than the upper] *che ha il mento, e 'l labbro di sotto che sporge in fuori più di quello di sopra.*

TU'TOR, s. [private master, preceptor, governor] *precettore, maestro, ajo*, s. m.

Tutor [guardian] *tutore*, s. m. *quegli che ha la cura del pupillo.*

To TU'TOR [to teach manners, to chide] *ammaestrare, addottrinare, disciplinare, insegnare, riprendere, correggere*, pret. *ripresi, corressi.*

TU'TORED, adj. *ammaestrato, addottrinato, disciplinato, insegnato, ripreso, corretto.*

TU'TORESS [she guardian] *tutrice*, s. f.

TU'TORSHIP, s. [a tutor's office] *tutela*, s. f.

TU'TSAN, s. [a plant] *spezie d' erba.*

TU'TTY } [a nosegay] *un mazzetto di fiori. Voci non in uso.*
TU'ZZIMUZZY }

Tutty s. [a sublimate of zinc or calamine collected in the furnace] *sorta di sublimato; tuzia.*

TUZ, s. [a lock or tuft of hair] *ciuffo o ciuffetto di capelli.*

TWAIN, adj. [two] *due.*

TWANG, s. [a sharp sound] *suono acuto.*

Twang [hogoe, ill taste] *cattivo sapore, tanfo.*

Twang [ill sound in one's pronunciation] *cattivo accento, cattiva pronuncia.*

To speak with a twang [to speak through the nose] *parlar col naso.*

To TWANG [to sound like the string of an instrument] *render un suono acuto*

TWA'NGLING, adj. [contemptibly, noisy] *che ha suono acuto, senza artificio, e spregievole.*

To TWANK [to make a sound] *render suono.*

'Twas, *è contratto da it was, ciò era, questo era, ciò fu, questo fu.*

To TWATTLE [to prittle prattle] *cicalare, ciarlare, chiacchierare, cornacchiare.*

Twattle-basket [one that does nothing but twattle] *un ciarlone un ciarlatore, un ciarliero, una ciarlatrice.*

TWA'TTLING, s. *ciarleria,* s. f. *cicaleccio, cicalamento,* s. m.

Twattling, adj. ex. A twattling housewife, *una ciarlatrice, una cicalona.*

TWAY [twain] *due.*

TWA'YBLADE, s. [an herb] *due foglie, spezie d' erba.*

TWEAG, } s. [perplexity, trouble]
TWEAK, } *imbroglio, intrigo,* s. m. *perplessità,* s. f.

To be in a sad tweak, *esser in un grand' intrigo.*

To TWEAK [to pinch] *pizzicare.*

To tweak by the nose, *tirare per il naso.*

To TWE'EDLE [to play on the fiddle or bag-pipe] *sonare violino o il la cornamusa.*

To tweedle [to handle lightly] *maneggiar checchessia pian piano o con leggerezza.*

TWE'EZERS, s. [nippers] *mollette,* s. f. *molle piccole che servono a strappare i peli.*

TWELFTH, adj. *duodecimo.*

Twelfth-day, } [epiphany feast] *l'*
Twelfth-tide, } *Epifania, giorno festivo, la di cui solennità si celebra a' sei di gennajo, e dicesi con vocabolo corrotto befania o befana.*

TWELVE, adj. *dodici, nome numerale.*

A book in twelves, *un libro in duodecimo.*

A twelve month [a year] *un anno.*

TWE'LVEPENCE, s. [a shilling] *uno scellino, moneta Inglese, che in quest' anno 1757 vale una lira di Savoja o due paoli d' argento.*

TWELVEPE'NNY, adj. *venduto per dodici denari o per uno scellino.*

TWE'LVESCORE, s. *dodici ventine, dodici volte venti, dugento quaranta.*

TWE'NTIETH, adj. *ventesimo.*

Twenty, adj. *venti.*

One and twenty, *ventuno.*

Two and twenty, *ventidue.*

Five and twenty, *venticinque.*

TWI'BILL, s. [an iron tool used by paviors] *piccone,* s. m.

TWICE, adv. [two times] *due volte.*

If things were to be done twice, all would be wise, *ognuno impara a sue spese.*

Twice-fold, *doppiamente.*

Twice as much, *il doppio, una volta più.*

To TWIDLE [to touch lightly] *leggermente toccare, maneggiar con delicatezza e riguardo, lo stesso che* To tweedle.

To TWIFA'LLOW ground [to till or plough it a second time] *lavorare un campo la seconda volta.*

TWIG, s. [a small sprout of a tree] *vermena,* s. f. *vimine,* s. m. *sottile e giovine ramicello di pianta.*

A lime-twig, *panione, paniuzzo, uccellare,* s. m. *paniuzzola, uccelliera,* s. f.

To set lime twigs, *uccellare coll' uccelliera.*

TWI'GGEN, adj. [made of twigs] *fatto di vimini, contesto di vimini.*

TWI'GGY, adj. [full of twigs] *pien di vimini.*

TWI'LIGHT, s. [that dubious or half light which shines in the dawn of the morning, just before the sun rising, and in the dusk of the evening a little after the sun setting] *crepuscolo, barlume,* s. m *l' ora nella quale apparisce il giorno, o se ne va.*

Twilight, adj. [not clearly or brightly illuminated; obscure; deeply shaded] *non chiaramente illuminato; oscuro, molto coperto d' ombra.*

Twilight, adj. [seen by twilight] *veduto tra 'l lume e 'l bujo.*

TWIN, s. [two children born at one birth] *gemello,* s. m. *quegli che è nato con un altro ad un medesimo parto.*

They are twins, *eglino sono gemelli.*

TWINE, s. [small twisted thread] *filo ritorto, spago.*

To TWINE [to twist] *torcere, avviticchiare.*

To twine thread, *torcere il filo.*

To twine about, *abbracciare, avviticchiare, avvinghiare.*

TWI'NED, adj. *torto, abbracciato, avviticchiato avvinghiato.*

TWI'NER, s. torcitore, s. f.

TWI'NING, s. torcimento, s. m. *torcitura,* s. f. *il torcere.*

TWINGE, s. [a violent pain] *dolore acuto.*

The gout gives him many a shrewd twinge, *la gotta lo tormenta terribilmente.*

Twinge [torment] *tormento, crucio,* s. m.

The gripes of avarice, and the twinges of ambition, *le cure mordaci degli avari, e i tormenti degli ambiziosi.*

To TWINGE [to torment] *tormentare, cruciare, dolere.*

TWI'NGED, adj. *tormentato, cruciato, doluto.*

TWI'NKLE, s. [the twinkling of an eye] *batter d'occhio, occhiata.*

To give one a twinkle, *dare un' occhiata ad uno, fargli cenno cogli occhi*

To twingle [to sparkle as stars do] *sfavillare, scintillare.*

To twinkle with one's eyes, *ammiccare, occhieggiare, far d' occhio, dar d' occhio.*

TWI'NKLING, s. *lo scintillare.*

In the twinkling of an eye [in a moment] *in un batter d' occhio, in un momento, in un subito.*

Twinkling, adj. *scintillante, sfavillante.*

To TWIRL, *voltare.*

Twirl it, *voltatelo.*

To twirl [to turn round about] *girare intorno, cignere intorno.*

TWI'RLED, adj. *voltato, girato, cinto.*

TWIST, s. *filo.*

A rope with three twists, *una corda a tre fila.*

The twist [the hollow of the thigh] *il didentro della coscia.*

Twist [a piece of timber, otherwise called a girder] *travicello,* s. m.

To TWIST [to twine] *torcere, rattorcere, attorcigliare, attorcere, avvolgere, avviticchiare,* pret. *torsi, rattorsi, attorsi, avvolsi.*

To twist two things together, *avvolgere due cose insieme.*

To twist thread, *torcere del filo.*

To twist hair, *intrecciare capelli.*

To twist the cord with the ball at tennis, *tagliare la corda colla palla.*

TWI'STED, adj. *torto, rattorto, attorcigliato, attorto, avvolto, avviticchiato, avvinto.*

TWI'STER, s. *torcitore, cordajo,* s. m.

Twister [an instrument to twist with] *torcitojo,* s. m. *ordigno col quale si torce la lana o la seta; strettojo,* s m.

To TWIT [to upbraid with, to hit in the teeth] *rimproverare, rimprocciare, rimbrottare, rinfacciare, buttar in occhio.*

TWITCH [pinch] *pizzico.*

Twitch with hot pincers, *il tormento d' esser attanagliato.*

To TWITCH [to pinch] *pizzicare.*

To twitch with hot pincers, *attanagliare, tormentare i condannati strignendo loro le carni con tanaglie infocate.*

TWI'TCHED, adj. *pizzicato.*

Twitched with hot pinchers, *attanagliato.*

TWI'TCHING, s. *pizzicore,* s. m. *il pizzicare, l' attanagliare.*

TWI'TCHGRASS, s. [a plant] *nome di pianta.*

TWI'TTED in the teeth, adj. *rimproverato, rimprocciato, rimbrottato, rinfacciato.*

TWI'TTER, s. [any motion or disorder of passion] *moto d' affetto sregolato.*

To TWI'TTER [to quake, to shiver with cold] *tremar di freddo.*

To twitter [to sneer, to laugh at one scornfully] *beffare, schernire, fare scherno, ridersi.*

To twitter [to be suddenly moved with any inclination] *volgere di subito l' affetto a checchessia.*

TWI'TTLE-TWA'TTLE, s. *cicaleccio, cicalio,* s. m.

To TWI'TTLE-TWA'TTLE [to prate] *cicalare, chiacchierare, cianciare.*

TWIXT, *lo stesso che* betwixt.

TWO, adj. *due.*

Two and two, *due a due.*

Two to one is odds, *due contro uno è troppo.*

To kill two birds with one stone, *batter due chiodi ad una calda, pigliar due colombi a una fava.*

TWO-E'DGED, adj. [having an edge on either side] *a due tagli, che ha due tagli, che taglia da due bande.*

TWO-FOLD, *doppio.*

Two-fold, adv. *al doppio, due volte più.*

TWO-HEADED, adj. [large, bulky, enormous of magnitude] *estremamente grosso, paffutissimo.*

TWO'-PENCE, s. [a small coin] *due soldi.*

TWO'-PENNY GRASS, s. [a plant] *spezie di pianta.*

To TYE, *v.* To tie.

TYGER,

TYGER, *v.* Tiger.

TYKE, s. [a dog, or one as contemptible as a dog] *cane, ed è anche appellativo di spregio.*

TY'MBAL, s. [a kind of kettle-drum] *taballo, stromento musicale militare.*

TY'MPAN, s. [a drum] *timpano, tamburo, tamburino.*

The tympan of the ear, *il timpano dell' orecchio.*

A printer's tympan [a frame belonging to a printing press, covered with parchment, on which every sheet is placed, in order to be printed off] *timpano di stampatore.*

TY'MPANIST, s. [one troubled wirh the tympany] *idropico, che ha il ventre teso come un tamburo.*

TY'MPA'NUM, s. *v.* Tympan.

TY'MPANY, s. [a hard swelling of the belly with wind] *spezie d' idropisia che gonfia il ventre come un tamburo.*

TY'NY, adj. [small] *piccolo, piccino.*

TYPE, s. [the figure or mystical shadow of a thing] *simbolo, segno,* s. m. *figura, rappresentazione, ombra,* s. f.

Type [model, pattern] *modello,* s. m.

TY'PICK, } adj. *figurativo, rappresentativo.*
TY'PICAL, }

TY'PICALLY, adv. *figurativamente, in senso figurativo.*

To TY'PIFY [to figure, to show in emblem] *figurare, mostrare emblematicamente.*

TYPO'GRAPHER, s. [printer] *stampatore,* s. m.

TYPOGRA'PHICAL, adj. *di stampatore.*

TYPOGRAPHY, s. [the art of printing] *stampa,* s. f. *l' arte dello stampare.*

TY'RANNESS, s. [a she tyrant] *una tiranna.*

TYRANNICAL, adj. [cruel, unjust] *tirannico, crudele, di tiranno.*

Tyrannical power, *potere tirannico.*

Tyrannical man, *tiranno.*

Tyrannical woman, *tiranna.*

TYRA'NNICALLY, adv. *tirannicamente, con modo tirannico.*

TYRA'NNICIDE, s. [one that has killed a tyrant] *tirannicida, colui che ha ammazzato un tiranno.*

TYRA'NNICK, *v.* Tyrannical.

To TY'RANNIZE [to oppress, to use tyrannically] *tiranneggiare, tirannicamente, dominare, usar tirannia.*

TY'RANNIZED, adj. *tiranneggiato.*

TY'RANNOUS, *v.* Tyrannical.

TY'RANNOUSLY, *v.* Tyrannically.

TY RANNY, s. [the government of a tyrant] *tirannia, tirannide, tiranneria,* s. f. *dominio tirannico.*

TY'RANT, s. [one who has usurped the sovereign power of a state] *tiranno,* s. m. *colui che s' è usurpato il sovrano potere d' uno stato.*

Tyrant [a prince, though lawful, that abuses the royal power in oppressing his subjects] *tiranno, signore crudele, amatore solamente dell' util proprio.*

A tyrant [any one that abuses his authority] *tiranno, colui che abusa della propria autorità.*

Petty tyrant, *un tirannello, o tiranneto.*

TY'RO, s. *colui che non possiede ancor bene la sua* arte. *Sarebbe meglio scriverlo* Tiro.

TYTHE, *v.* Tithe.

V.

V, *Ventesima lettera dell' alfabeto Inglese.*

VA'CANCY, s. [empty space] *vuoto,* s. m. *spazio vuoto.*

Vacancy [empty place or dignity] *vacanza,* s. f. *dignità vacante.*

The vacancy of an episcopal see, *la vacanza d' una sedia episcopale.*

Vacancy of time [leisure] *vacazione, vacanza, intermissione,* s. f. *cessamento, riposo,* s. m.

VA'CANT, adj. [void, empty] *vacante, voto, che vaca.*

Vacant time [leisure] *vacanza, vacazione,* s. f. *agio, riposo,* s. m.

To VA'CATE [to empty] *votare.*

To vacate [to annul, to make void] *annullare, cassare, scancellare.*

VA'CATED, adj. *votato, annullato, cassato, scancellato.*

VACA'TION, s. [cessation from ordinary business] *vacazione, vacanza, intermissione,* s. f. *cessamento, riposo,* s. m.

Vacation [in common law, the time between the end of one term and the beginning of another] *vacanze, vacazioni.*

Vacation [vacancy of a living] *vacazione d' un beneficio.*

VA'CCARY, s. [cow-house] *stalla da vacche.*

Vaccary [cow-pasture] *pascolo o pastura da vacche.*

VACI'LLANCY, s. [a state of wavering; fluctuation, inconstancy] *vacillamento, il vacillare.*

VA'CILLANT, adj. [tottering, wavering] *vacillante, che vacilla.*

To VA'CILLATE [to reel, to stagger] *vacillare, vagillare, barcollare.*

VACILLA'TION, s. *vagillazione,* s. f. *vacillamento,* s. m.

VA'CUIST, s. [a philosopher that holds a vacuum] *filosofo che ammette il voto, che sostiene che v' è vacuo.*

VACU'ITY, s. [emptiness, void space] *vacuità,* s. f. *spazio voto; vacuo,* s. m.

VA'CUOUS, adj. [empty, unfilled] *vuoto, vacuo.*

VA'CUUM, s. *vacuo; spazio non occupato da materia.*

To VADE [to vanish, to pass away] *svanirsi, sparire.*

VA'FROUS, adj. [subtle, crafty, sly] *fine, astuto, sagace, scaltrito.*

VA'GABOND, s. [a wandering idle person] *un vagabondo, un perdigiorno.*

VA'GARY, s. [freaks, pranks] *fantasia, stravaganza,* s. f. *capriccio, ghiribizzo,* s. m.

VA'GRANCY, s. [a vagrant or ill life] *vita vagabonda.*

VA'GRANT, adj. [wandering, strolling, roving up and down] *vagabondo, che vagabonda.*

Vagrant lust, *desiderio sfrenato.*

Vagrant, s. [vagabond] *un vagabondo, un perdigiorno, uno scioperato.*

VAGUE, adj. [wandering, vagrant, vagabond] errante, *vagante, vagabondo.*

Vague,

Vague [unfixed, unsettled, undetermined] *incerto, non determinato*.

VAIL, s. [a piece of stuff, silk, &c. that covers or hides any thing from being seen] *velo*, s. m. *scrivesi con più proprietà* veil.

Vail [money given to servants] *parte di salario d' un servo*, v. vale.

To VAIL [to cover with a vail] *veláre, coprir con velo*.

To vail one's bonnet [to put off one's hat, to show any sign of respect] *levar il cappello ad uno, salutarlo*.

VA'ILED, adj. *velato*.

VA'ILING, s. *velamento*, s. m. *il velare*.

VAILS, s. [profits that arise to officers or servants, besides salary or wages] *mancia, strenna*, s. f. *profitti*, s. m.

VAIN, adj. [useless, frivolous, idle] *vano, inutile, frivolo, di poca importanza, di poca utilità*.

Vain [proud] *vano, orgoglioso, vanaglorioso, borioso, superbo, altiero*.

Vain glory, *vanagloria, orgoglio, superbia, boria, alterigia*.

Vain-glorious, adj. [full of vain-glory] *vanaglorioso, pieno di vanagloria, orgoglioso, superbo, borioso*.

In vain, } adv. *vanamente, in vano*,
Vainly, } *inutilmente*.

VA'INNESS, s. *vanità, inutilità*, s. f.

VAIRE, s. [a sort of fur in heraldry] *vajo*, s. m. *termine araldesco*.

VALE, s. [valley] *valle*, s. f.

Vale, s. [money given to servants] *danaro dato a un servo*.

VALEDI'CTION, s. [farewel] *licenza*, s. f. *comiato*, s m.

He made his valediction, *prese licenza o comiato, s' accomiatò*.

VALEDI'CTORY, adj. *di licenza, di comiato*.

VA'LENCE, s. [short curtains for the upper part of the furniture belonging to a bed, window, &c.] *cortine che si metton pendenti da' cieli de' letti, finestre, &c. cortinaggi*.

VALE'RIAN, s. [an herb] *valeriana*, s. f. *erba così chiamata*.

VA'LET, s. [servitor, man-servant] *servo, servitore*, s. m.

Valet-de chamber, *cameriero*.

VALETUDINA'RIAN, } adj. [sickly]
VALETU'DINARY, } *infermiccio, infermuccio, malatticcio*.

Valetudinary, s. [hospital] *infermeria*, s f. *spedale*, s. m.

VA'LIANCE, s [valour, personal puissance, bravery] *valore, forza della persona, coraggio, animo*.

VA'LIANT, adj. [stout, brave] *valoroso, bravo, coraggioso, prode, magnanimo, valente*.

VA'LIANTLY, adv. *valorosamente, bravamente, con bravura, coraggiosamente*.

VA'LIANTNESS, s. *valore, bravura*.

VA'LID, adj. [authentick, binding, good in law] *valido, legittimo, autorevole*.

To VA'LIDATE [to make valid] *corrobare, render valido*.

VA'LIDATED, adj. *corroborato*.

VA'LIDATING, } s. *corroborazione*,
VALIDA'TION, } s. f.

VALI'DITY, s. [strength, force of a deed or instrument] *validità*, s. f.

VA'LLEY, s. [a space of ground surrounded with hills] *valle*, s. f. *quello spazio di terreno che è racchiuso tra monti o colli*.

Little valley, *valletta*, s. f. *piccola valle*.

Large valley, *vallone*, s. m.

VA'LLANCY, s. [a large wig that shades the face] *parruccone, parrucca che copre parte della faccia*.

VA'LOROUS, adj. [valiant] *valoroso, coraggioso, prode*.

VA'LOUR, s. [courage, stoutness, bravery] *valore, coraggio, animo*, s. m. *prodezza, virtù, valenzia*, s. f.

VA'LUABLE, adj. [that is of great value] *prezioso, di gran prezzo, considerabile, di gran valuta*.

Valuable [weighty, important] *importante, considerabile, di grande importanza o momento*.

VALUA'TION, s. [estimate] *valuta, stima*, s f. *valsente, prezzo*, s. m.

VALUA'TOR, s. [an appraiser] *stimatore*.

VA'LUE, s. [price] *valore, prezzo*, s. m. *valuta*, s. f.

A thing of value [of great price] *una cosa di valore, o di valuta*.

Value [esteem] *stima, considerazione*, s. f. *conto, pensiero*, s. m.

To set a great value upon a thing, *far grande stima o conto di che che sia*.

Thing of no value, *cosa di nessun valore, cosa da niente*.

To be of some value, *valer qualche cosa*.

To be of no value, *non valer niente*.

I have a great value for him, *lo stimo molto, fo grande stima di lui*.

To value [to prize, to rate] *valutare, dar la valuta, stimare*.

To value [to esteem, to set much on] *stimare apprezzare, pregiare, avere in pregio, fare stima, far conto*.

He values himself much upon his learning, *egli si stima molto per la sua dottrina*.

I do not value it a rush, *non lo stimo un fico*.

I do not value you, *non fo conto di voi, mi rido di voi*.

VA'LUED, adj. *valutato, stimato, pregiato*.

A thing not to be valued, *una cosa inestimabile, che non si può stimare*.

VA'LUELESS, adj. [being of no value] *spregevole, di nessun valore*.

VALVE, s. [a folding door] *una porta a due imposte*.

Valve [any thing that opens over the mouth of a vessel] *ogni cosa che serve di coperchio a un vaso*.

Valve [a kind of membrane which opens in certain vessels to admit the blood and shuts to prevent its regress] *valva; sorta di membrana che serve per ammettere o escludere gli umori ne' vasi del corpo umano*.

VA'LUING, s. *valuta, stima*, s. f. *prezzo, valore*, s. m.

VA'MBRACE, s. [armour for the arm] *bracciale*, s. m. *quella parte dell' armadura che arma il braccio*.

VAMP, s. [the upper leather of a shoe] *tomaja*, s. f. *la parte di sopra della scarpa*.

To VAMP [to mend, to furbish up] *accomodare, aggiustare, rappezzare*.

VA'MPED, adj. *accomodato, aggiustato, rappezzato*.

VA'MPLATE, s. [gauntlet, iron glove] *guanto di ferro*.

VAN } s. [the fore-part of an
VA'NGUARD } army] *vanguardia*, s. f.

Van [winnowing fan, cribble] *vaglio*, s. m. *strumento da vagliare*.

To VAN [to winnow corn] *vagliare, sceverare col vaglio il mal seme o altra mondiglia dal grano*.

To VA'NISH, } [to disappear,
To VA'NISH away, } to go out of sight] *svanire, sparire*, pret. *svanisco, sparisco*.

VA'NISHED, adj. *svanito, sparito*.

VA'NITY, s. [vainness, emptiness, unprofitableness] *vanità, inutilità*, s. f.

Vanity [vain-glory, pride] *vanità, vanagloria, alterigia, boria, presunzione*, s. f. *orgoglio*, s. m.

To VA'NQUISH [to overcome, to subdue, to conquer] *vincere, superare, soggiogare, domare*, pret *vinsi*.

VA'NQUISHED, adj. *vinto, superato, soggiogato, domato*.

VA'NQUISHER, s. *vincitore, vittorioso*.

VA'NTAGE, s. [that which is given over and above just weight or measure] *vantaggio*, s. m. *aggiunta, giunta*, s. f.

Vantage, v. Advantage.

To VA'NTAGE [to profit] *aver vantaggio, aver profitto, avvantaggiare, approfittare*.

VA'NTGUARD, v. Van.

VA'PID, adj. [palled, dead] *svaporato*.

Vapid wine, *vin cercone*.

To grow vapid, *incerconire, diventar cercone, svaporare*.

VAPORA'TION, s. [a sending forth of vapours] *vaporazione*, s. f. *il vaporare*.

VA'POROUS, adj. [full of vapours, that sends forth vapours] *pien di vapori*.

VA'POUR, s. [an exhalation, raised by the heat of the sun or any other heat] *vapore*, s. m. *fumo aqueo, caldo o umido*, tratto *dal calor del sole o da altro calore*.

Vapours of the stomach, *vapori di stomaco*.

To VA'POUR [to huff, to crack, to brag] *far il bravo, bravare*.

To vapour away [to evaporate] *svaporare, vaporarsi*.

VA'POURISH, adj. [vaporous, splenetick, humoursome] *lunatico, di mal umore, fastidioso, bizzarro*.

VA'POURING, s. *fierezza, bravura*, s. f.

Vapouring, adj. ex. a vapouring fellow, *un bravo, un millantatore, un arcifanfano*.

Va'riable, adj. [subject to variation, changeable] *variabile, incostante, atto a mutarsi, mutabile, instabile.*

Va'riableness, s. *variazione, incostanza, instabilità*, s. f.

Va'riably, adv. [changeably, mutably, inconstantly, uncertainly] *variamente, mutabilmente, incostantemente, incertamente.*

Vari'ance, s. [difference, dispute, quarrel] *differenza, lite, controversia, dissenzione*, s. f.

To set at variance, *metter male insieme, disunire.*

Variance [a law term] *variazione, alterazione*, s. f.

Va'riation, s. [alteration] *variazione*, s. f. *cangiamento*, s. m.

A variation of notes in musick, *cangiamento di note nella musica.*

Varico'loured, adj. [of many colours] *variato, divisato, pezzato di varj colori.*

Va'ricous, adj. [diseased with dilatation] *varicoso, malato per dilatazione. Termine medico.*

To **Va'riegate** [to diversify, to make of different colours] *variare, screziare, divisare, differenziare con diversi colori.*

Va'riegated, adj. *variato, screziato, divisato, differenziato.*

Variega'tion, s. *variazione, diversità di colori.*

Vari'ety, s. [diversity, change] *varietà, diversità*, s. f. *cangiamento*, s. m.

Va'rious, adj. pl. [several, diverse] *varj, parecchi, diversi.*

Various persons, *varie o diverse persone.*

Va'riously, adv. *variamente, diversamente, differentemente.*

Va'rlet, s. [rogue, rascal] *briccone, furfante, guidone, barone, birbante.*

Va'rnish [a compound of gums, and other ingredients for setting a gloss upon pictures, &c] *vernice*, s. f. *composto di ragia e d' altri ingredienti che serve a dare il lustro alle pitture e simile.*

To **Va'rnish** [to do over with varnish] *dar la vernice, inverniciare.*

To varnish a picture, *inverniciare una pittura.*

Va'rnished, adj. *inverniciato.*

Va'rnisher, s. *colui che fa o da la vernice.*

Va'rnishing, s. *il dar la vernice.*

Va'rvels, s. [small silver rings about the leg of a hawk, having the name of the owner engraven on them] *geti, cerchietti d' argento legati a' piedi d' un falcone, ne quali è intagliato il nome di colui a chi appartiene.*

Va'ried, adj. *variato, mutato, diversificato, cangiato.*

To **Va'ry** [to diversify, to change] *variare, mutare, diversificare, cangiare.*

They varied among themselves, *erano in contrasto fra di loro.*

Va'ry, s. [change, alteration] *variazione, cambiamento, alterazione.*

Vase, s. [a sort of flower-pot set in a garden] *testo, o vaso in cui si ponzon le piante in un giardino.*

Va'ssal, s. [one who holds lands of another by homage and fealty] *vassallo*, s. m.

A she vassal, *una vassalla.*

Va'ssalage, s. [the condition of a vassal] *vassallaggio*, s. m. *servitù dovuta dal vassallo al signore.*

Vast, adj. [large, huge, great] *vasto, grande, immenso, smisurato.*

Vast genius, *ingegno vasto.*

Vast country, *paese vasto o ampio.*

Vast quantity, *gran numero, gran quantità.*

Vast power, *potere immenso.*

Vast, adv. *molto, eccessivamente, vastamente.*

Vast, s. [an empty waste] *terreno, luogo, o spazio vasto non occupato da cosa alcuna, o solo pieno di desolazione.*

Vasta'tion, e. [a destroying] *desolazione, rovina*, s. f. *guasto*, s. m.

Va'stity [largeness, greatness] *vastità, ampiezza, grandezza*, s f.

Va'stly, adv. *molto, grandemente, eccessivamente.*

Va'stness, s. *vastità, grandezza, ampiezza, larghezza*, s. f.

Va'sty, adj. [large] *vasto, ampio, largo.*

Vat, s. [a kind of vessel to hold ale, beer, cyder, or any other liquor in brewing or other preparation] *tino*, s. m.

Little vat, *tina, tinozza*, s. f.

Dyer's vat, *vagello*, s. m.

Cheese vat, *fiscella*, s. f. *castella, o zana tessuta di vinchi, nella quale si fa il formaggio.*

Va'ticide, s. [a murderer of poets] *vaticida, ucciditor di poeti.*

To **Vati'cinate** [to prophesy, to practise prediction] *vaticinare, profeteggiare, predire.*

Vault, s. [arched building] *volta*, s. f.

Vault, s. [a vaulted cellar for wine] *cantina.*

To **Vault** [to cover arch-ways] *voltare, fare o coprire a volta.*

To vault upon a horse [a term of horsemanship] *volteggiare un cavallo.*

Va'ultage, s. [arched cellar] *cantina fatta a volta.*

Va'ulted, adj. *voltato, fatto a volta.*

The vaulted sky, *la volta celeste, il cielo.*

Va'unmure, s. [a false wall] *antimuro.*

Va'ulty, adj. *voltato, fatto a volta.*

Vaunt [boasting] *vanto, vantamento*, s. m.

To make a vaunt of a thing, *vantarsi, pregiarsi, gloriarsi, darsi vanto di qualche cosa.*

Vaunt, s. [the first part] *la prima parte.*

To **Vaunt**, } [to boast, to brag,
To **Vaunt** of, } to glory] *vantarsi, gloriarsi, pregiarsi, darsi vanto, millantarsi.*

Va'unted, adj. *vantato, gloriato, pregiato, millantato.*

Va'unter, s. [boaster] *vantatore*, s. m. *che si vanta; bravaccio.*

Va'untful, adj. [boastful, ostentatious] *che si da troppo vanto, che millanta.*

Va'unting, s. *vantamento, vanto*, s. m. *il vantarsi, il millantare.*

Va'untingly, adv. *con vanto, col vantarsi millantando.*

Vaward, s. [van-guard] *vanguardia.* Obs.

Va'yvode, s. [a prince or chief ruler of Transilvania, Valachia, or Moldavia, who are tributary to the Grand Seignor] *vaivode, principe, o governatore di Transilvania, Valachia, o Moldavia, ora tributarj del Gran Signore.*

Ubero'sity, } s. [plentifulness] *u-*
Ube'rty, } *bertà, dovizia, abbondanza*, s. f.

U'berous, adj. [plentiful] *ubertoso, abbondante, copioso.*

Ubi'quity, s. [omnipresence, existence at the same time in all places] *ubiquità, lo esser dappertutto a un tempo stesso.*

U'dder, s. [dug] *tetta, poppa, mammella*, s. f. *e dicesi delle vacche e d' altri animali grandi.*

Veal, s. [the flesh of a calf] *vitella*, s. f. *carne di vitella.*

Ve'cture, s. [carriage] *carriaggio, vettura.*

To **Veer** [to turn] *girare, voltare.*

To veer the sails, *voltare le vele.*

To veer [to chop about as the wind does, sometimes to one point, sometimes to another] *cangiarsi, passare da un canto all' altro, termine marinaresco.*

To veer out a rope [to let it go by hand, or to let it run out of itself] *mollare una gomena.*

Ve'ering, [a sea term, a ship is said to go loft veering, when the sails at large with the sheet veered out] *volteggiare, termine marinaresco.*

Vegetabi'lity, s. [vegetable nature] *natura vegetabile.*

Ve'getable, adj. [capable of growing] *vegetabile, vegetativo.*

The vegetables, *i vegetabili, le piante.*

To **Ve'getate** [to grow as plants, to shoot out, to grow without sensation] *vegetare.*

Vegeta'tion [growth] *vegetazione*, s. f. *il vegetare.*

V'egetative, adj. [growing] *vegetativo, che ha facultà di vegetare.*

Ve'gete, adj. [that has a growing life] *che vegeta, che vive, che cresce come fanno le piante.*

Ve'getive, adj. [lively, strong] *vigoroso, forte.*

Vehe'mence, } s. [passion, heat, vi-
Vehe'mency, } olence] *veemenza, impetuosità, forza, violenza*, s. f. *ardere*, s. m.

Vehe'ment, adj. [violent, impetuous, fierce] *veemente, violento, impetuoso.*

Vehe'mently, adv. *veementemente, con veemenza, impetuosamente.*

Ve'hicle, s. [a general name for that which serves to carry any thing along] *veicolo*, s. m.

Vein, s. [a vessel containing the blood in human bodies] *vena, s. f. canale per cui negli animali viventi corre il sangue.*

To open a vein [to let blood] *aprir la vena, cavar sangue.*

A vein of gold, silver, or water, *vena d' oro, d' argento, o d' acqua.*

A vein in wood or in a stone, tiglio, s. m. *vena, s. f. quei segni che vanno serpendo ne' legni e nelle pietre a guisa delle vene nel corpo.*

Wood full of veins, *legno tiglioso.*

Poetical vein, *vena poetica.*

Ve'ined, } adj. [full of veins] *venoso, pien de vene.*
Ve'iny, }

Ve'llam, s. [the finest sort of parchment] *cartapecora, s. f.*

Velle'ity, s. [the lowest degree of desire] *velleità; desiderio che è a mala pena desiderio.*

To Vellicate [to twitch] *pizzicare.*

To vellicate [to rail at] *sbottonare, sbottoneggiare, dire alcun motto pungente contro alcuno.*

Vellica'tion, s. [twitching] *pizzico, s. m. il pizzicare.*

Ve'llum, *v.* Vellam.

Velo'city [swiftness, nimbleness] *velocità, prestezza, celerità, s. f.*

Ve'lvet, s. [a sort of fine shagged silk manufacture] *velluto, s. m. drappo di seta col pelo.*

Velvet-like, *vellutato, fatto a guisa di velluto.*

Velvet, adj. *di velluto, vellutato.*

A velvet coat, cap, or purse, *un abito, una berretta, una borsa di velluto.*

Velvet, adj. [soft, delicate] *molle, delicato.*

To Ve'lvet [to paint velvet] *dipingere i panneggiamenti come se fossero di velluto.*

Velu're, s. [velvet] *velluto.*

Ve'nal, adj. [that is to be sold] *venale, vendereccio, da vendersi.*

A venal employment, *un impiego venale.*

Venal [mercenary, prostitute] *venale, mercenario, prostituito.*

Vena'lity, s. [the quality of being venal] *venalità, s. f.*

To Vend [to sell, to put off] *vendere, spacciare.*

Vende'e, s. [the person to whom any thing is sold] *compratore, s. m.*

Ve'nder, s. [seller] *venditore.*

Ve'ndible, adj. [to be sold] *vendibile, vendevole, vendereccio, che si vende facilmente, che ha buono spaccio.*

Ve'nding, s. *vendita, s. f. spaccio, s. m. il vendere, lo spacciare.*

Vendi'tion, s. [the act of selling or putting off] *vendita, vendimento.*

Ve'ndor, s. [law term; seller] *venditore, s. m. venditrice, s. f.*

Vene'fical, } adj. [poisonous] *venenoso, velenoso.*
Venefi'cial, }

Ve'nefice, s. *venenamento, s. m. il venenare.*

Ve'nemous }
Ve'nene } adj. [poisonous] *venenoso, velenoso, venenifero.*
Ve'nenose }
Ve'nenous }

Ve'nerable, adj. [worthy of reverence or respect] *venerabile, da esser venerato, degno di venerazione.*

Ve'nerably, adv. [in a manner that excites reverence] *venerabilmente; in modo da eccitar venerazione.*

To Ve'nerate [to respect, to honour] *venerare, portare onore, riverire, onorare, rispettare, portar rispetto,* pres. *riverisco.*

Ve'nerated, adj. *venerato, riverito, onorato, rispettato.*

Venera'tion, s. *venerazione, riverenza, s. f. gran rispetto, onore, s. m.*

Vene'real, } adj. [belonging to Venus the goddess of lust] *venereo, lussurioso, libidinoso.*
Vene'reous, }

Venereal pleasures, *piaceri venerei o libidinosi.*

Venereal disease [a virulent distemper, commonly called the French pox] *mal Francese.*

Ve'nery, s. [lustfulness, carnal lust] *piacere venereo, libidine, lussuria, s. f.*

Venery [hunting] *caccia, s. f.*

Ve'new, *v.* Venue.

Ve'ngeance, s. [revenge] *vendetta, s. f. il vendicarsi.*

To take vengeance, *far vendetta, vendicarsi.*

With a vengeance [a sort of curse] *alla mal' ora, in tanta mal' ora.*

Where vice goes before, vengeance follows after, *ad ogni santo viene la sua festa, domeneddio non paga il sabato, cioè il gastigo può differirsi ma non si toglie.*

Ve'ngeful, adj. [a poetical word for revengeful] *vendicativo.*

Ve'nial, adj. [pardonable, which may be forgiven] *veniale, degno di perdono.*

Venial sin, *peccato veniale.*

Ve'nison, s. [the flesh of a buck or other wild beast of chace] *salvaticina, salvaggina, s. f. carne d' animal salvatico buona a mangiare.*

Venison pasty, *pasticcio di salvaggina.*

Ve'nom, s. [poison] *veneno, veleno, tossico, s. m.*

Ve'nomous, adj. [poisonous] *venenoso, velenoso.*

Venomous [virulent, abusive] *velenoso, mordace, mordente, maledico.*

Venomous tongue, *lingua mordace o maledica.*

Ve'nomousness, s. *velenosità, s. f.*

Ve'nous, adj. [veiny] *venoso, pien di vene.*

Vent, s. [air, wind] *aria, s. f. vento, s. m.*

To give vent to a cask of wine, *dar vento, sventare, aprire una botte di vino.*

Vent, s. [vent-hole] *sfogatojo, spiraglio.*

Vent [rime, chink] *fessura, s. f. pelo, s. m.*

To give vent [to ease] *sfogare, esalare.*

Vent [sale of commodities] *vendita, s. f. spaccio, s. m.*

To Vent [to give vent, to air] *sventare, dar del vento o dell' aria.*

To vent [to wind as a spaniel does] *fiutare.*

To vent [to take breath as an otter does] *respirare, rifiatare.*

To vent a secret, *scoprire, palesare, pubblicare, divulgare un segreto.*

To vent one's thoughts, *dire il suo pensiero liberamente.*

To vent one's passion, *sfogare, esalare la sua passione.*

They vented their fury upon him, *sfogarono la loro rabbia sopra di lui.*

To vent [to sell commodities] *vendere, spacciare.*

To vent [among glass-plate workers, is to crack in working] *creparsi, crepolarsi.*

Ve'nted, adj. *sventato, v.* To vent.

Ve'nter, s. ex. brother by the same venter, *fratello uterino.*

Ve'ntiduct, s. [a conveyance of wind by pipe or otherwise] *condotto di vento.*

To Ve'ntilate [to fan, to winnow] *ventolare, sventolare, ventilare.*

To ventilate [to give vent] *sventare, dar vento o aria.*

Ve'ntilated, adj. *ventolato, ventilato, sventolato.*

Ventila'tion, s. *ventilazione, s. f. il ventilare.*

Ventila'tor, s. [an instrument contrived by Dr. Hale to supply close places with fresh air] *ventilatore, ventilatojo; strumento inventato dal Dottor Hale per introdurre aria fresca in luoghi chiusi.*

Vento'sity, s. [windiness] *ventosità, s. f. vento, s. m.*

Ve'ntricle, s. [the stomach] *ventricolo, ventre, s. m.*

Ventricle [any cavity in the body] *ventricolo.*

The ventricles of the brains, *i ventricoli del cerebro.*

The ventricles of the heart, *i ventricoli del cuore.*

Ve'nture, s. [hazard] *ventura, sorte, s. f. risico, rischio, s. m.*

At a venture, *alla ventura, per sorte.*

To put a thing to a venture, *mettere che che sia alla ventura.*

Venture [goods that a man ventures at sea] *mercanzie che uno avventura in mare.*

To Ve'nture [to hazard] *venturare, avventurare, arrischiare, arrisicare, mettere in cimento.*

Nothing venture nothing have, *chi non arrischia non guadagna.*

To venture a wager, *scommettere, fare una scommessa.*

To venture, verb neut. *venturarsi, avventurarsi, arrischiarsi, arrisicarsi, porsi a cimento.*

He ventured too far, *egli s' è troppo avventurato.*

To venture upon a thing, *intraprendere una cosa.*

They durst not venture out of the harbour, *egli non ardirono uscire dal porto.*

Ve'ntured, adj. *venturato, avventurato, arrischiato, arrisicato.*

'Tis not a thing to be ventured upon, *è cosa troppo pericolosa.*

VE'NTURER, s. *venturiere*, s. m. *colui che arrischia.*

VE'NTUROUS, adj. [that ventures too much] *arrischiante, ardito, che s' arrischia troppo.*

VE'NTUROUSLY, adv. *alla ventura.*

VE'NTUROUSNESS, s. [boldness, willingness to hazard] *audacia, ardire, lo arrischiare.*

VE'NUE, s. [a word used in law for a neighbouring place] *vicinato, contorno, luogo circonvicino.*

VE'NUS, s. [the goddess of love and beauty] *Venere*, s. f. *la dea d' amore e della bellezza.*

Venus [the morning and evening star] *venere, nome di stella.*

Venus's bason [a plant] *cardo*, s. m.

Venus's comb [a plant] *pettine di Venere, spezie di pianta.*

Venus's hair [a plant] *capelvenere*, s. m.

Venus's navel-wort [a plant] *umbelico di Venere*, s. m. *spezie di pianta.*

Venus's shell, *sorta di conchiglia.*

VE'NUST, adj. [beautiful] *venusto, bello, grazioso.*

VERA'CITY, s. [truth] *veracità, verità*, s. f.

VERA'CIOUS, adj. [observant of truth] *verace, veridico, veritiero.*

VERB, s. [one of the eight parts of speech] *verbo*, s. m. *una delle otto parti dell' orazione.*

VE'RBAL, adj. [derived from a verb] *verbale, dependente dal verbo.*

Verbal [delivered in words, by word of mouth] *verbale, di bocca, di viva voce, che non è scritto.*

Verbal [verbose, full of words] *verboso, parolajo, consistente di sole parole senza sustanza.*

Verbal [litteral; having word answering to word] *verbale, che corrisponde parola per parola.*

Verbal, s. [a verbal noun] *un verbale, un nome verbale.*

VE'RBALLY, adv. *verbalmente, di bocca, a bocca, in parole.*

VERBA'LITY, s [the quality of being verbal] *qualità di quel' che è verbale.*

VERBA'TIM, adv. [word for word] *parola per parola, verbo a verbo.*

VERBERA'TION, s. [the act of heating or striking back] *riverberazione*, s. f. *riverberamento*, s. m.

VERBO'SE, adj. [full of words, talkative] *verboso, che parla assai, parabolano, ciarlatore, loquace, parolajo.*

VERBO'SITY, s. [the quality of being verbose] *loquacità*, s. f. *cicaleccio, cicalio*, s. m.

VE'RDANT, adj. [green] *verdeggiante, verde.*

VERDE'E, } s. [a sort of white wine
VERDE'A, } made in Florence] *verdèa*, s. f. *spezie di vin bianco.*

VE'RDEGREASE, s. [the rust of brass] *verderame*, s. m. *quella gromma verde che si genera nel rame per umidezza.*

VE'RDICT, s. [the jury's answer upon any cause committed to their examination by a court of judicature] *giudizio o opinione de giurati sopra una causa civile o criminale, che la legge ha commessa al loro esame.*

The jury have brought in their verdict, *i giurati hanno dato il loro giudizio.*

Verdict [judgment, opinion] *parere, sentimento*, s. m. *opinione*, s. f.

To give one's verdict upon something [to put in one's verdict] *dire il suo sentimento sopra qualche cosa, dichiarare la sua opinione.*

VE'RDIGRISE, s. v. verdegrease.

VER'DITURE, s. [one of the three green colours generally used by painters] *verdeporro*, s. m.

VE'RDURE, s. [the greenness of trees, herbs, leaves, &c.] *verdura, verzura*, s. f.

VE'RDUROUS, adj. [green, covered with green; decked with green] *verde, verdeggiante, ricoperto di verde, ornato di verdura.*

VERGE, s. [wand, a sergeant's mace] *verga, mazza, bacchetta*, s. f.

Verge [compass of power] *giuridizione, giurisdizione*, s. f.

VE'RGER, s. [tip-staff, one who carries a white wand before the justices of either bench] *mazziere*, s. m. *bidello di magistrato che porta avanti a' suoi signori la mazza in segno d' autorità.*

Verger of a cathedral, *bidello*, s. m.

VERI'DICAL, adj. [speaking the truth] *veridico, che dice il vero, veritiero.*

VE'RIEST, adj. [the superlative of very] ex. he is the veriest rogue that ever lived, *egli è il più gran briccone che mai sia stato al mondo.*

VERIFICA'TION, s. [verifying] *verificazione, prova*, s. f.

To VE'RIFY [to prove, to make good] *verificare, dimostrar vero, certificare, provare.*

VE'RIFIED, adj. *verificato, dimostrato, certificato, provato.*

VERIFI'ER, s. *quello o quella che verifica.*

VERIFYING, s. *il verificare, prova.*

VE'RILY, adv. [truly] *veramente, in verità, in vero, realmente.*

VERISI'MILAR, adj. [likely] *verisimigliante, verisimile.*

VERISIMI'LITUDE } [likelihood] *verisimile*, s. m.
VERISIMI'LITY } *verisimilitudine*, s. f.

VE'RITY, s [truth] *verità*, s. f.

VE'RJUICE, s. [the juice of sour and unripe grapes] *agresto*, s. m. *il liquore, che si cava dell' agresto o dell' uva acerba.*

VERMICE'LLI, s. [an Italian thin paste like small worms] *vermicelli*, s. m. *certe fila di pasta fatte alla somiglianza di vermicelli, e mangiansi cotti nel brodo o col butirro.*

VERMI'CULATED, adj. [wrought with chequer-work or small pieces of divers colours] *vermicolato.*

VERMI'LLION, s. [lively deep red colour] *vermiglio*, s. m *rosso acceso.*

VE'RMINE, s. [any kind of hurtful creatures or insects] *vermi, vèrmini*, s. m. *ogni sorta d' animalucci o insetti nocivi, come pidocchi, cimici, pulci, scorpioni, centopiedi, e simili.*

Vermine [rogues] *canaglia, gente di mal' affare, furbi, mariuoli, guidoni.*

VERNA'CCIA, s. [a sort of Italian wine] *vernaccia*, s. f. *sorta di vino.*

VERNA'CULAR, adj. [proper and peculiar to the country one lives or was born in] *vernacolo, del paese.*

The vernacular tongue, *il volgare, il linguaggio, l' idioma vivo che si favella in un paese.*

VE'RNAL, adj. [belonging to the spring] *di primavera, appartenente a primavera.*

The vernal season [the spring] *la primavera.*

VE'RNISH, v. Varnish.

VE'RRIL, s. [a little brass or iron ring at the end of a cane or handle of a tool] *anelletto o cerchietto di ferro, o d' altro metallo, appiccato al manico d' un bastone o d' altro strumento.*

VERSE, s. [a number of words, having a certain cadence, and measured by a determinate number of syllables or feet] *verso*, s. m. *membro di scrittura poetica, certa misura di piedi o di sillabe.*

To make verses, *verseggiare, far versi.*

Verse-maker, *versificatore, un che fa versi.*

Verse of a chapter, *versetto.*

To VERSE [to tell in verse, to relate poetically] *cantare, dir in versi, narrar poetando, verseggiare.*

To be VERSED, v. n. [to be skilled in, to be acquainted with] *sapere molto di checchessia, esser versato in checchessia.*

VE'RSICLE, s. [a little verse] *versetto*, s. m. *piccol verso.*

VERSIFICA'TION, s. [the act of making verses] *versificazione*, s. f. *il versificare.*

VERSIFI'ER, s. [maker of verses, a poet] *versificatore, rimatore*, s. m.

To VE'RSIFY [to make verses] *verseggiare, versificare, far versi.*

VE'RSION, s. [a translation out of one language into another] *versione, traduzione, traslazione*, s. f.

VERT, s. [every thing that grows or bears a green leaf in a forest and is capable of affording shelter to deer] *gli alberi d' una foresta.*

VERTE'BRE, s. [the joints of the neck and back bone of an animal] *vertebre*, s. f. *nodi*, s. m.

VE'RTEX, s. [the top of any thing] *vertice*, s. m. *cima*, s. f.

VE'RTICAL, adj. [belonging to the vertex] *verticale, di vertice, che appartiene a vertice, che passa per il vertice.*

Vertical angles [those angles, which being opposite one to another, touch only in the angular point] *angoli verticali.*

Vertical circles [great circles of the heavens, intersecting one another in the ZENITH and NADIR, and consequently at right angles with the horizon] *circoli verticali.*

VER-

Vertı'ginous, adj. [giddy] *vertiginoſo.*

Vertigo, s. [giddineſs, dizzineſs, ſwimming in the head] *vertigine,* s. f. *capogiro,* s. m.

Ve'rtue, *v.* Virtue.

Verva'ine, } s. [an herb] *verbena,* s. f. *ſorta d' erba.*
Ve'rvine, }

Ve'rvise, s. [a ſort of coarſe woollen cloth] *ſorta di panno groſſolano.*

Ve'ry, adj. [true, perfect] *vero.*

He is the very picture of his father, *è il vero ritratto di ſuo padre, è ſuo padre ſputato.*

Very [true, arrant] *mero, pretto, ſchietto, ſchietto.*

He is a very knave, *egli è un pretto furbo.*

Very [ſelf, himſelf, herſelf, itſelf] *medeſimo, ſteſſo, medeſima, ſteſſa.*

This is the very ſame man that betray'd you, *queſto ſteſſo è l' uomo che vi tradì.*

The very name of it turns my ſtomach, *il nome ſolo mi ſconvolge lo ſtomaco.*

It is the very ſame, *egli è deſſo.*

Very, adj. *molto.*

Very faithful, *molto fedele, fedeliſſimo.*

Very hot, *molto caldo.*

Very little, *quaſi niente.*

Very well, *molto bene, beniſſimo.*

I am not very well, *non iſtò molto bene.*

Very ill, *molto male, maliſſimo.*

Your very humble ſervant, *umiliſſimo ſervo.*

Very much, *molto.*

It is the very ſelf ſame, *egli è deſſo.*

Very fain, *bene, pure, volentieri.*

I would very fain ſee him, *vorrei ben vederlo, vorrei pur vederlo.*

Very lately, *teſtè, poco fa, non ha guari.*

Very ſpeedily, *fra poco, in poco tempo, ben preſto, ben toſto.*

I ſtand in very great need of, *ne ho grandiſſimo biſogno.*

I am very much afraid of it, *ne temo moltiſſimo.*

He enquired into the very leaſt faults, *egli eſaminò le colpe le più minute.*

In the very middle of the ſtreet, *nel bel mezzo della ſtrada.*

To Ve'sicate [to bliſter] *porre veſcicatorio, appiccar veſcicante ſulla pelle propria o altrui.*

Ve'sicatory, s. [a medicine which ſerves to raiſe bliſters on the ſkin] *veſcicatorio, veſcicante,* s. m. *impiaſtro che appiccato alla carne vi fa naſcere d lle veſciche.*

eVe'sicle, s. [a ſmall cuticle filled or enflated] *veſcichetta,* s. f. *piccola veſcica.*

The veſicle of the gall, *la veſcichetta del fiele.*

Ve'sper, s. [the evening ſtar, the evening] *veſpro; la ſtella della ſera; la ſera.*

Ve'spers, s. [evening prayers] *veſpero e veſpro,* s. m. *una della ſette ore canoniche.*

Sicilian veſpers [a general maſſacre of the French by the inhabitants of the iſland of Sicily] *veſpro Siciliano, ucciſione celebre de' Franceſi da' Siciliani.*

Ve'spertine, adj. [happening or coming in the evening] *che accade la ſera, che vien la ſera; veſpertino.*

Ve'ssel, s. [a general name of many utenſils to put any thing in] *vaſo,* s. m. *nome generale di tutti gli ſtrumenti fatti per ricevere e per ritenere in ſe quache coſa, e più particolarmente liquore.*

To pour out of one veſſel into another, *travaſare.*

A veſſel of election or reprobation [a ſcripture expreſſion, for an elect or a reprobate] *un vaſo di elezione o di reprobazione, un eletto o un reprobo.*

Veſſel [a ſhip] *vaſcello, legno,* s. m. *nave, barca,* s. f.

Veſſel [conduit for blood or humours in animal bodies] *vaſo.*

Spermatick veſſels, *vaſi ſpermatici.*

To Ve'ssel [to put into a veſſel, to barrel] *imbottare, porre o verſare n' una botte, n' un barile, o altro ſimil vaſo.*

Ve'sset, s. [a ſort of woollen cloth commonly made in Suffolk] *ſpezie di panno groſſolano che ſi fabbrica comunemente nella provincia di Suffolk.*

Vest, s. [waiſtcoat] *camiciuola,* s. f.

To Vest [to beſtow upon, to admit to the poſſeſſion of] *inveſtire, porre in poſſeſſo.*

To veſt one with ſupream power, *inveſtire uno d' un ſovrano potere.*

To veſt [to dreſs, to deck, to enrobe] *veſtire, porre altrui l' abito indoſſo, ornare.*

To veſt [to dreſs in a long garment] *porre la toga o altra gonna lunga indoſſo altrui.*

Ve'sta, s. [a heathen goddeſs of the earth or nature] *Veſta,* s. f. *la dea della terra o della natura.*

Ve'stal, adj. ex. a veſtal virgin, or a veſtal, s. [a virgin conſecrated for thirty years to the ſervice of Veſta] *una veſtale, una vergine veſtale.*

Veſtal, s. [a pure virgin] *vergine, verginella, pura vergine.*

Ve'sted, adj. *veſtito, riveſtito.*

The prieſt is veſted [ſpeaking of a Roman prieſt when he is going to ſay maſs] *il prete è veſtito.*

Ve'stiary, s. [a place in a monaſtery where the monks clothes are laid up] *veſtiaria,* s. f.

Ve'stibule, s. [porch, entry into a houſe] *veſtibulo,* s. m. *primo luogo degli edificj.*

Ve'stige, s. [foot-ſtep, trace] *veſtigio,* s. m. *orma, pedata, traccia,* s. f.

Ve'stment, s. [raiment, garment] *veſtimento, abito.*

A prieſt's veſtment [garment, which a prieſt wears when he ſays maſs] *paramento da prete, pianeta.*

Ve'stry, s. [a room adjoining to a church, where the prieſts garments and ſacred utenſils are kept] *ſagreſtia,* s. f. *luogo nel quale ſi ripongono e conſervano le coſe ſacre e li arredi della chieſa.*

Veſtry-keeper, *ſagreſtano, colui che è prepoſto alla cura della ſagreſtia.*

Veſtry [aſſembly of the heads of the pariſh uſually held in that place] *aſſemblea, adunanza de' principali parrocchiani nella ſagreſtia.*

To call a veſtry, *fare adunare i principali della parrocchia nella ſagreſtia.*

Veſtry-men, *quelli che compongono l' aſſemblea della ſagreſtia.*

Ve'sture, s. [or garment] *veſtimento,* s. m.

Veſture [poſſeſſion, admittance to a poſſeſſion] *inveſtitura,* s. f.

The veſture [of an acre of land] *la rendita d' una bubulca di terra.*

Vetch, s. [chich-peas, a kind of pulſe] *veccia,* s. f. *ſpezie di biada nota.*

Bitter vetch, *ſorta di veccia amara.*

Kidney-vetch [a plant] *vulneraria,* s. f. *ſpezie di pianta.*

Full of vetch, *vecciſo.*

Ve'tchy, adj. [made of vetch, abounding in vetches] *vecciſo, fatto di veccia, abbondante in veccia.*

Ve'teran, adj [that has ſerved long in war] *veterano, che ha eſercitato la milizia molto tempo.*

Veteran ſoldier, *ſoldato veterano.*

Veteran, adj. [that has ſerved long in a place or office] *veterano, che ha ſervito lungo tempo in qualche impiego o ufficio.*

Veteran, s. [an old ſoldier, a man long practiſed] *un ſoldato che ha fatto il ſuo meſtiere lungamente, e per traſlato, un uomo che ha fatto un certo meſtiere lungo tempo.*

To Vex [to teaſe, to trouble, to torment] *angoſciare, affannare, travagliare, dare affanno, moleſtare, dar faſtidio, infaſtidire, inquietare, affliggere,* pret. *afflſſi.*

It vexes me to the very heart, *mi diſpiace fino all' anima.*

What vexes me more is that — *quel che più m' affanna è, che* —

To vex [to anger] *ſtizzare, iſtizzire, fare adirare, fare andare in collera, fare arrabbiare, far dare nelle ſmanie.*

This will vex him, *queſto la farà arrabbiare, gli farà perder la pazienza.*

To vex one's ſelf, *affliggerſi, affannarſi, pigliarſi affanno, inquietarſi, angoſciarſi.*

Vexa'tion, s. [diſquiet, trouble of mind] *affanno, travaglio, crucio, faſtidio,* s. m. *moleſtia, ſollecitudine, angoſcia, afflizione, noja,* s. f.

Vexa'tious, adj. [that cauſes trouble or grief; troubleſome] *faſtidioſo, affannoſo, angoſcioſo, diſpiacevole, duro, increſcevole, moleſto, nojoſo, gravoſo, incomodo.*

Vexa'tiously, adv. [troubleſomely, uneaſily] *affannoſamente, moleſtamente.*

Ve'xed, adj. *angoſciato, affannato, travagliato, moleſtato, inquietato, afflitto, infaſtidito.*

Ve'xer, s. *un moleſto, un nojoſo, che moleſta, che affligge.*

U'glily, adv. *bruttamente, ſozzamente, laidamente.*

U'gliness, s. [homelineſs] *bruttezza,*

tezza, laidezza, deformità, sozzezza, s. f.

The uglinefs of vice, *la bruttezza del vizio.*

The uglinefs of a crime, *l' enormità d' un delitto.*

UGLY, adj. [homely] *brutto, deforme, malfatto, svenevole, laido, sozzo.*

An ugly woman, *una donna brutta.*

To grow ugly, *diventar brutto.*

Ugly [unbecoming] *sconcio, indegno, vergognoso, vituperoso.*

Ugly [naughty] *cattivo.*

Ugly action, *cattiva azione, azione indegna, cosa vituperosa.*

VIAL, s. [a fmall thin glafs bottle] *caraffina, guastadetta, fiala,* s. f.

VI'AND, s. [meat, food, victuals] *cibo, vivanda.*

VIA'TICUM, s. [the facrament given to dying perfons] *viatico, il sagramento dell' altare che si da a' moribondi.*

To VI'BRATE [to brandifh, to move to and fro with a quick motion] *vibrare, brandire con moto celere, render tremolo.*

To vibrate, v. n. *vibrarsi.*

VIBRA'TION, s. [motion to and fro] *vibrazione,* s. f.

VI'CAR, s. [deputy] *vicario,* s. m. *che tiene il luogo o la vece altrui.*

Vicar, s. [the parfon of a parifh where the tithes are impropriated] *vicario, piovano, curato d' una parrocchia.*

VI'CARAGE, s. [the fpiritual cure or benefice of a vicar] *cura o beneficio di vicario.*

VICA'RIOUS, adj. [belonging to a vicar] *di vicario.*

Vicarious power, *potere di vicario.*

VI'CARSHIP, s. *vicariato,* s. m.

VICE, s. [a habit contrary to virtue] *vizio,* s. m. *abito elettivo che consiste nel troppo o nel poco, contrario di virtù.*

Reigning vice, *vizio dominante.*

Vice [jefter in a play] *zanni,* s. m. *personnaggio vile e buffonesco introdotto nelle commedie.*

Vice [in compofition implies a fubordination, or the fupplying of another's place] *vice; vocabolo che unito a certe parole denota inferiorità, o lo stato d' una persona che tiene il luogo d' un altro, come negli esempi seguenti.*

Vice-admiral, *vice ammiraglio.*

Vice-chancellor, *vicecancelliere.*

Vice-commiffary, *vire commissario.*

Vice-doge, *vire doge.*

Vice-regent, s. [deputy] *vicereggente, che sostien la vere, che opera in vere.*

Vice [a fort of inftrument ufed by fmiths, and other artificers, to hold iron or any thing faft, while they file or work it] *vite, morsa, tanaglia,* s. f. *strumento col quale i fabbri e altri artefici stringono, e tengon fermo il lavoro ch' egli hanno tra mano per lavorarlo.*

The vice-pin, *la chiave d'una morsa.*

The vice of a prefs, *la vite d' un torchio.*

To VICE [to draw] *stringer con una vite o con una morsa.*

VI'CED, adj. [corrupt, vitiated] *corrotto, vizioso, viziato.*

VI'CEROY, s. [or deputy king] *vicerè,* s. m. *che tiene il luogo del rè.*

VICERO'YALTY, s. [the place and dignity of a viceroy] *carica e dignità di vicerè.*

VI'CETY, s. [nicety, exactnefs] *dilicatezza, esattezza.*

To VI'CIATE [to corrupt, to fpoil] *viziare, guastare, corrompere, magagnare,* pret. *corruppi.*

To viciate a virgin, *corrompere una zittella.*

VI'CIATED, adj. *viziato, guastato, corrotto, magagnato.*

VI'CINAGE, } s. [neighbourhood, VI'CINITY, } nearnefs] *vicinanza, vicinità, prossimità, propinquità,* s. f.

VI'CINAL, } adj. [near, neighbour- VI'CINE, } ing] *vicino, prossimo.*

VI'CIOUS, adj. [given to vice] *vizioso, pien di vizj.*

Vicious man, *uomo vizioso.*

To lead a vicious life, *menare una vita viziosa, viver licenziosamente.*

VI'CIOUSLY, adv. *viziosamente, licenziosamente, malamente.*

Vicioufly writ, *male scritto, ove sono molti errori, scorretto.*

VICI'SSITUDE, s. [change, turn] *vicissitudine, vicenda, mutazione,* s. f. *scambiamento,* s. m.

Viciffitudes of fortune, *vicende della fortuna.*

VI'COUNT, *v.* Vifcount.

VI'CTIM, s. [a beaft killed in facrifice] *vittima, bestia offerta in sacrificio.*

VI'CTOR, s. [conqueror] *vincitore,* s. m.

VICTO'RIOUS, adj. [that has got a victory] *vittorioso, che ha vinto, che ha ottenuto vittoria.*

VICTO'RIOUSLY, adv. *vittoriosamente, con vittoria.*

VI'CTORY, s. [overthrow or defeat of an enemy] *vittoria,* s. f. *il vincere, il restar vincitore.*

To get the victory, *ottenere la vittoria.*

To get the victory of one's paffions, *trionfare delle proprie passioni.*

VI'CTRESS, s. [a female that conquers] *vincitrice.*

To VI'CTUAL [to furnifh with victuals or provifions] *vettovagliare, provvedere di vettovaglia.*

To victual a fhip, *vettovagliare un vascello.*

VI'CTUALLED, adj. *vettovagliato.*

VICTUA'LLER [one who furnifhes or provides victuals] *oste che da a mangiare.*

Victualler [a fmall fhip or veffel that carries provifions for a fleet] *piccolo vascello, che porta le vettovaglie d' un' armata.*

VICTUA'LLING, s. *il vettovagliare.*

Victualling-houfe, *taverna, osteria, bettola.*

VI'CTUALS, s. [provifions, food, things neceffary for life] *vettovaglie, vittuaglie, provvisioni,* s. f. pl. *tutto quello che è necessario al nutrirsi.*

Victuals for an army, *viveri, vettovaglie per un esercito.*

I eat my victuals very well, *io mangio molto bene, io ho buon appetito.*

He has no victuals, *egli non ha da mangiare.*

VI'DAME, s. [in France, the judge of a bifhop's temporal jurifdiction] *giudice temporale d' un vescovo.*

VIDE'LICET, adv. [to wit; that is] *cioè. Gl' Inglesi scrivono per lo più viz.*

VIDU'ITY, s. [the ftate or condition of a widow, widowhood] *vedovità, vedovaggio,* s. m.

VIE, s. [at cards] *invito.*

To VIE [term of games at cards] *invitare, fare un invito, termine di giuocò alle carte.*

To vie [to contend, to ftand in competition] *contestare, contendere, disputare, gareggiare, sfidare, fare a gara.*

To vie cunning with one, *fare a chi sarà più astuto.*

I'll vie with him for all his ftrength, *lo disfido non ostante la sua forza.*

VIEW, s. [fight, act of feeing] *vista,* s. f. *il vedere.*

To judge of a thing at the firft view, *giudicare d' una cosa a prima vista.*

At one view, *alla prima, ad un' occhiata.*

To take a view of, *vedere, riguardare, esaminare, riconoscere.*

View [profpect] *vista, aspetto, prospettiva.*

The view of a building, *la facciata, la prospettiva d' un edificio.*

View of foldiers, *mostra, rassegna di soldati.*

At firft view, at the firft view [at firft] *a prima vista, alla prima, subito.*

View [the print of the feet of a fallow deer on the ground] *traccia di cervo.*

To VIEW [to take a view of, to look upon, to examine] *vedere, riguardare, esaminare, rinconoscere,* pret. *vidi, riconobbi.*

To view foldiers, *rassegnare o far la rassegna de' soldati.*

VIEW'ED, adj. *visto, riguardato, esaminato, riconosciuto.*

VIEW'ER, s. *quello o quella che vede, che riguarda.*

VIEW'ERS [fuch perfons who are fent by a court to view any place or perfon] *esperti, persone esperte.*

VIEW'LESS, adj. [unfeen, not difcernible by the fight] *non visto; non discernibile colla vista.*

VI'GIL, s. [the eve or day next before any holy-day] *vigilia,* s. f. *il giorno avanti a qualche giorno festivo.*

Vigil [a man or woman who watches at nights] *vigilia.*

VI'GILANCE, } s. [watchfulnefs, VI'GILANCY, } good heed] *vigilanza, attenzione, cura, diligenza, accortezza,* s. f.

VI'GILANT, adj. [watchful, diligent, careful] *vigilante, sollecito, accurato, attento, accorto, diligente,* s. f.

VI'GILANTLY, adv. *vigilantemente, attentamente, con attenzione, accuratamente,*

mente, con cura, con diligenza, con accortezza.

VI'GONE, s. [a sort of Spanish wool] *vigogna*, s. f. *spezie di lana di Spagna.*

Vigone [a hat made of that wool] *capello di vigogna.*

VI'GOR, *v.* Vigour.

VI'GOROUS, adj. [stout, brisk] *vigoroso, che ha vigore, rigoglioso, forte, gagliardo, robusto.*

VI'GOROUSLY, adv. *vigorosamente, con vigore, rigogliosamente, gagliardamente.*

VI'GOROUSNESS, } s. [strength, VI'GOUR, } stoutness] *vigore*, s. m. *robustezza, forza, gagliardia*, s. f.

To give vigour, *invigorire, dar vigore.*

VILE, adj. [of no account, despicable, mean] *vile, di poco pregio, di poca stima, abjetto, povero, basso.*

Vile condition, *una vile condizione.*

Vile mercenary soul, *anima vile, briccone venale.*

Vile wretch, *uomo abbietto, uomo da niente, bricconaccio.*

Vile commodity, *mercanzia di vil prezzo, di poca stima, affatto cattiva.*

VI'LED, adj. [abusive, scurrilous] *oltraggioso, che vilipende.*

VI'LELY, adv. [wickedly] *male, malamente, da briccone.*

VI'LENESS, s. [vile condition] *viltà, bassezza, vile condizione.*

To VI'LIFY [to run down, to despise] *vilificare, avvilire, vilipendere, dispregiare, sprezzare, non fare stima, non tener conto*, pres. *avvilisco*, pret. *vilipesi.*

To vilify one's friend, *sparlare o dir male del proprio amico.*

VI'LIFIED, adj. *vilificato, avvilito, vilipeso, dispregiato, sprezzato.*

VILE, s. [a law word, sometimes taken for a parish or part of it, and sometimes for a manor] *parrocchia, parte di parocchia, signoria. E' voce del foro.*

VI'LLA, s. [a country seat] *villa, casa di rampagna; cioè la casa che un signore ha per andare a passar la state.*

VI'LLAGE, s. [a number of country houses or cottages without any wall or inclosure] *villaggio*, s. m. *mucchio di case in villa senza cinto di mura.*

VI'LLAGER, s. [inhabitant of a village] *abitator di villaggio, villanzone, villano, contadino.*

VI'LLAGERY, s. [district of villages] *territorio di villaggi.*

VI'LLAIN, s. [formerly a country farmer, a man of low and servile condition, a man to the lord of the manor] *villano, uom della villa, lavoratore contadino.*

Villain [rogue] *briccone, guidone, furfante, traditore, assassino.*

VI'LLANAGE, s. [the state of a villain, base servitude] *lo stato d' un villano, condizion di contadino.*

Villanage [baseness, infamy] *villania, infamia.*

To VI'LLANIZE [to debase, to degrade] *degradare, avvilire.*

VI'LLANOUS, adj. [base, shameful, pitiful] *villano, infame, basso, indegno, scellerato, tristo.*

Villanous act, *atto villano, azione infame o bassa, villania.*

VI'LLANOUSLY, adv. *villanamente, bruttamente, infamemente, indegnamente.*

VI'LLANY, s. [baseness, wickedness] *villania, infamità, bassezza, indegnità, scortesia, mala creanza*, s. f.

VILLA'TICK, adj. [belonging to villages] *villereccio, villesco, campestre.*

VI'LLI, s. pl. [in anatomy, are the same as fibres; in botany, small hairs like the grain of plush or shag] *velli, peli, peluzzi.*

VI'LLOUS, adj. [shaggy, rough] *velloso, setoloso, pien di peli, pien di setole.*

VIMI'NEOUS, adj. [made of twigs] *vimineo, fatto di vimini, contesto di vimini.*

VI'NCIBLE, adj. [that may be overcome] *vincibile, vincevole, atto ad esser vinto.*

VI'NCTURE, s. [binding] *legatura*, s. f.

VINDE'MIAL, adj. [belonging to a vintage] *di vendemmia.*

To VINDE'MIATE [to gather grapes or other ripe fruits] *vendemmiare, cor l' uva dalla vite per farne il vino.*

VINDE'MIATORY, adj. [belonging to a vintage] *di vendemmia.*

To VI'NDICATE [to defend, to maintain] *difendere, mantenere, sostenere*, pres. *mantengo, sostengo*, pret. *difesi, mantenni, sostenni.*

To vindicate [to clear, to justify, to make an apology for] *giustificare, purgare, lavare.*

To vindicate [to revenge] *vendicare.*

VI'NDICATED, adj. *difeso*, v. To vindicate.

VINDICA'TION [defence] *difesa, protezione*, s. f.

Vindication [apology] *giustificazione, apologia*, s. f.

Vindication [revenge] *vendetta*, s. f.

VI'NDICATIVE, adj. [revengeful, given to revenge] *vendicativo.*

VINDICA'TOR [defender, asserter] *difensore, protettore, colui che difende, che protegge.*

Vindicator [avenger] *vendicatore*, s. m.

VI'NDICATORY, adj. [punitory, performing the office of vengeance] *che punisce, che vendica.*

Vindicatory [defensory, justificatory] *che vendica, che difende, che giustifica.*

VINDI'CATIVE, adj. [revengeful] *vendicativo.*

VINE, s. [the plant that bears the grape] *vite, vigna*, s. f.

Vine-yard, *vigneto*, s. m. *luogo coltivato a vigne.*

Vine-dresser, *vignajo, vignajuolo.*

Vine-reaper, *vendemmiatore*, s. m.

Vine fretter or vine-grub, *bruco*, s. m.

VI'NEGAR, s. [wine or other liquors made sour] *aceto*, s. m.

VI'NNET, s. [a kind of border, flower or flourish in the beginning, end, or any other part of a book] *fogliame, o altro ornamento che gli stampatori mettono ne' libri.*

VI'NNEW, s. [mouldings] *muffa*, s. f. *tanfo*, s. m.

VI'NNEWED, adj. [mouldy] *muffato, mucido.*

To grow vinnewed, *muffarsi, divenir muffato.*

VINO'SITY, s. [the quality or state of being vinous] *qualità vinosa.*

VI'NOUS, adj. [that has the taste or smell of wine] *vinoso, che ha l' odore o il gusto di vino.*

VI'NTAGE, s. [vine-harvest] *vendemmia*, s. f.

Vintage [the time wherein the grapes are gathered] *le vendemmie.*

VI'NTAGER, s. [vine reaper] *vendemmiatore*, s. m.

VI'NTNER, s. [tavern-keeper] *tavernajo*, s. m.

Vintner's wife, *tavernaja.*

VI'NTRY, s. [wine-cellar, place for the selling of wine] *luogo dove si vende vino.*

VI'OL, s. [a musical instrument] *viola*, s. f. *sorta di strumento musicale.*

VI'OLABLE, adj. [such as may be violated or hurt] *violabile, che può essere violato o offeso.*

VIOLA'CEOUS, adj. [resembling violets] *violaceo, paonazzo, pavonazzo, pagonazzo, del colore delle viole che s' assomiglia alle violette.*

To VI'OLATE [to break, to transgress] *violare, trasgredire, rompere*, pres. *trasgredisco*, pret. *ruppi.*

To violate a law, *violare, trasgredire una legge.*

To violate a virgin, *violare una zitella.*

VI'OLATED, adj. *violato, trasgredito, rotto*, v. To violate.

VIOLA'TION, s. *violazione*, s. f. *il violare.*

VIOLA'TOR, s. *violatore*, s. m.

VI'OLENCE, s. [fierceness, vehemency] *violenza, impetuosità, veemenza, rapidità*, s. f.

Violence [force, constraint used unlawfully] *violenza, forza*, s. f.

To offer violence to one, *far violenza ad uno, violentarlo.*

VI'OLENT, adj. [fierce, vehement, forcible] *violento, che fa violenza, impetuoso, veemente.*

You are a little too violent [too hasty, too passionate] *voi siete un poco troppo violento e collerico.*

Violent pain, *dolore acerbo o acuto.*

They laid violent hands upon him, *l' hanno violentemente assalito.*

To lay violent hands upon one's self, *ammazzarsi, darsi la morte.*

VI'OLENTLY, adv. *violentemente, con violenza, sforzatamente, per forza, impetuosamente.*

VI'OLET, s. [a flower] *viola, violetta*, s. f.

Syrup of violets, *sciroppo violato.*

Violet, adj. [of violet or purple colour] *violato, di color di viole, paonazzo.*

VI'OLIN, s. [a musical instrument] *violino*, s. m. *strumento musicale.*

A player upon the violin, *un sonator di violino.*

VI'OLIST, s. [a player upon the viol] *sonator di viola.*

VI'PER, s. [a kind of serpent] *vipera*, s. f.

A young or little viper, *un viperino*, *una viperetta.*

A catcher of vipers, *viperajo*, s. m. *cacciator di vipere.*

Viper-grass [a plant] *scorzonera*, s. f. *spezie di pianta.*

VI'PERINE, adj. [of or belonging to a viper] *viperino, vipereo, di vipera.*

VI'PEROUS, adj. [having the quality of a viper] *vipereo, che ha qualità di vipera.*

VIRA'GO, s. [a stout manly woman] *gigantessa, amazzone, donna grande, un donnone*, s. m. *una donna feroce.*

VI'RELAY, s. [a sort of comical song] *frambotto*, s. m.

VI'RENT, adj. [green, not faded] *virente, verde, verdeggiante.*

VIRGE, s. [a dean's mace] *la mazza che va innanzi al decano portata sulla spalla dal bidello del capitolo in segno d' autorità.*

VI'RGIN, s. [maid] *vergine, zittella, fanciulla.*

She is a virgin still, *ella è ancora vergine.*

To keep herself a virgin, *conservare la sua virginità.*

Virgin, adj. [befitting a virgin; suitable to a virgin; maidenly] *virgineo, virginale, proprio di vergine.*

Virgin-honey, *miele vergine.*

Virgin-wax, *cera vergine.*

To VI'RGIN [to play the virgin] *far la verginella, la ritrosa, la modesta, la schifalpoco.*

VIRGIN-LIKE, } adj. [belonging to
VI'RGINAL } a virgin] *verginale, virginale.*

Virginal milk [benjamin water] *latte virginale.*

Virginal, s. [a musical instrument, touched after the same manner with the harpsichord] *spezie di spinetta.*

To VI'RGINAL [to put, to strike as on a virginal] *torcar con tutte le dita come si farebbe sulla spinetta, sul gravicembalo, e simili.*

VIRGI'NIA, s. [a province of northern America] *Virginia*, s. f. *provincia nella parte settentrionale d' America.*

Virginia tobacco, *tabacco di Virginia.*

VIRGI'NITY, s. [maidenhead] *virginità, verginità*, s. f. *pulcellagione*, s. m.

VI'RGO, s. [one of the twelve signs of the Zodiack] *vergine*, s. f. *uno de' dodici segni del Zodiaco.*

VI'RILE, adj. [manly, stout] *virile, valoroso, di gran forza.*

Virile courage, *animo virile.*

Virile endeavours, *sforzi degni d' un uomo.*

VIRI'LITY, s. [manhood] *virilità*, s. f. *quel che distingue l' uomo dalla donna.*

Virility [manhood, stoutness] *virilità, cuore, animo, coraggio.*

VI'RTUAL, adj. [equivalent, effectual] *virtuale, equivalente, effettivo.*

VI'RTUALLY, adv. *virtualmente, in virtù, potenzialmente.*

VI'RTUE, s. [efficacy, power, force, propriety] *virtù, possanza, forza, qualità naturale, efficacia*, s. f. *vigore*, s. m.

Virtue [an habit of the soul, whereby a man is inclined to do good and to shun evil] *virtù.* s. f. *buona qualità di mente o abito dell' animo, per lo quale si fa il bene e si fugge il male.*

To make virtue of necessity, *far della necessità virtù.*

Cardinal virtues are prudence, temperance, justice, fortitude, *le virtù cardinali sono, prudenza, temperanza, giustizia, fortezza.*

VIRTUO'SO, s. [a man skilled in antique or natural curiosities; a man studious of painting, statuary or architecture] *uno che s' intende d' antichità, di cose naturali, o di pittura, scultura, e architettura.*

VI'RTUOUS, adj. [endowed with, or inclined to virtue] *virtuoso, che ha virtù.*

VI'RTUOUSLY, adv. *virtuosamente, con virtù.*

VI'RTUOUSNESS, s. *stato, o carattere di persona virtuosa.*

VI'RULENCY, s. [poisonous or venomous quality] *marcia, veleno de' mali venerei.*

Virulency [poison, venom] *veleno*, s. m. *in senso metaforico.*

VI'RULENT, adj. [venomous, infectious] *velenoso.*

A virulent ulcer, *un' ulcera velenosa.*

Virulent [sharp, biting] *velenoso, mordente, mordace, maldicente, maledico, satirico.*

A virulent tongue, *una lingua maldicente o maledica.*

VI'RULENTLY, adv. *d' una maniera mordace, mordacemente.*

VI'SAGE, s. [face] *visaggio, viso, volto*, s. m. *faccia, ciera*, s. f.

VI'SARD, v. Vizard.

VI'SCERAL, adj. [belonging to the bowels] *delle viscere.*

VI'SCID, adj. [glutinous, tenacious] *viscido, viscoso, tenace, attaccaticcio.*

VISCO'SITY, s. [clamminess, gluish quality] *viscosità*, s. f. *qualità viscosa.*

VI'SCOUNT, s. [a nobleman next in degree to a count or earl] *visconte*, s m. *nome di dignità o grado.*

VI'SCOUNTESS, s. [a viscount's wife] *viscontessa*, s. f. *moglie di visconte.*

VI'SCOUNTY, s. [the territory of a viscount] *viscontado*, s. m. *viscontea*, s. f. *giurisdizione o territorio del visconte.*

VI'SCOUS, adj. [clammy, slimy] *viscoso, vischioso, tenace, di qualità di vischio.*

VI'SER, s. [the sight of a headpiece] *visiera*, s. f. *parte dell' elmo che cuo il viso.*

VISIBI'LITY, s. [the state or quality of being visible] *qualità visibile*

VI'SIBLE, adj. [that may be seen or discerned] *visibile, che può vedersi, che si vede.*

VI'SIBLY, adv. *visibilmente, in modo visibile, apertamente, palesemente, chiaramente.*

VI'SION, s. [faculty of seeing, sight] *visione, il vedere.*

Vision [apparition] *visione, immagine, apparizione.*

VI'SIONARY, } s. [a fantastical pre-
VI'SIONIST, } tender to visions] *uno che s' imagina aver delle visioni.*

Visionary, adj. [belonging to visions] *che appartiene alle visioni.*

VI'SIT, s. *visita*, s. f.

To make, to pay, to give one a visit, *fare o rendere visita a qualcheduno, visitarlo.*

To VI'SIT [to go to see] *visitare, andare a vedere altrui per ufficio di carità, d' affezione, o di ceremonia.*

To visit one's friends, *visitare i suoi amici.*

To visit [to go about to see whether things be as they should] *visitare, far la visita.*

To visit [to afflict, to try] *visitare, affliggere, provare.*

If God should visit us with any disease, *se Iddio ci visitasse con qualche malattia.*

VI'SITABLE, adj. [liable to be visited] *visitabile, che può esser visitato.*

VI'SITANT, s. [one who goes to see another] *celui che va a visitare altrui.*

VISITA'TION, s. [the act of visiting] *visitazione*, s. f. *il visitare.*

The visitation which afflicted this nation during two years, *la gran peste che regnò in Inghilterra nell' anno* 1665 e 1666.

Visitation [among the clergy, the office or act performed by the bishop once in three years, or by the archdeacon once a year, in each diocese] *visitazione, visita*, s. f.

The feast of the Visitation of our Lady, *la festa della Visitazione della Madonna.*

VI'SITED, adj. *visitato, afflitto, provato.*

VI'SITER, s. *visitatore*, s. m. *che visita.*

VI'SITING, s. *visitamento*, s. m. *visita*, s. f. *il visitare.*

To go a visiting, *andare in visita.*

A visiting day, *giorno di visite.*

VI'STOR, s. [one who visits a monastery or religious house] *visitatore*, s. m.

VISNOMY, s. [*corrotto da* physiognomy. Face, countenance] *fisonomia, faccia, aspetto, sguardo.*

VI'SOR, s. [a mask used to disfigure or disguise] *maschera.*

VI'SORED, adj. *mascherato.*

VISO'RIUM, s [among printers, an instrument to which a leaf of copy is fixed for the compositor's more convenient seeing thereof] *visorio*, s. m. *strumento di stampatore.*

VI'STO, s. [a corruption of the Italian

ian word VISTA, a profpect] *vifta, pro- pettiva*, s. f.

VI'SUAL, adj. [belonging to the fight] *vifuale, della vifta, vifivo.*

The vifual point [in perfpective, is a point in the horizontal line, wherein all the ocular rays unite and all others that are parallel to it] *punto vifuale, o vifivo.*

VI'TAL, adj. [of life, that has life in it] *vitale, di vita, che conferva la vita, che da vita.*

The vital fpirits, *gli fpiriti vitali.*

Vitals, s. [vital parts, the parts of the body which chiefly conduce to the prefervation of life, *viz.* the heart, brain, lungs, and liver] *le parti vitali.*

To VI'TIATE, *v.* To viciate.

VI'TREAN, VI'TREAL, VI'TREOUS } adj. [glaffy, belonging to glafs] *vitreo, di vetro.*

The vitreal humour [one of the three humours of the eye, fo called from its refemblance to melted glafs] *umore vitreo.*

VITRI'FICABLE, adj. [that may be vitrified] *che fi può convertire in vetro.*

VITRIFICA'TION, s. [vitrifying] *il convertire in vetro.*

To VI'TRIFY [to turn into glafs] *convertire o ridurre in vetro.*

VI'TRIFIED, adj. *convertito o ridotto in vetro.*

VI'TRIOL, s. [a kind of mineral] *vetriolo, e vitriolo,* s. m. *forta di minerale.*

VITRIO'LICK, VI'TRIOLOUS } adj. [belonging to or partaking of the nature of vitriol] *vitriolato, di vitriolo.*

VITU'PERABLE, adj. [blame-worthy] *vituperabile, da effer vituperato, degno di biafimo.*

To VITU'PERATE [to blame] *vituperare, infamare, fvergognare, biafimare, difonorare.*

VITU'PERATED, adj. *vituperato, infamato, fvergognato, biafimato, difonorato.*

VITUPERA'TION, s. *vituperazione,* s. f. *vituperio,* s. m.

VIVA'CIOUS, adj. [lively, brifk] *vivace, fvegliato, pieno di vivacità, fpiritofo.*

VIVA'CITY, s. [livelinefs, brifknefs] *vivacità, attività;* s. f. *fpirito,* s. m.

VI'VARY, s. [in a law fenfe; a park, warren, or fifh-pond] *un parco, una conigliera, un vivajo.*

VI'VER, s. [fea-dragon, a fifh] *drago di mare; fpezie di pefce.*

VIVES, s. [a horfe difeafe] *vivole,* s. f. *male che viene a' cavalli.*

VI'VID, adj. [lively] *vivace, allegro, fpiritofo.*

VIVI'FICAL, adj. [that vivifies] *vivificante, che vivifica.*

To VIVI'FICATE [to vivify; to quicken or to give life] *vivificare, dar vita o vigore.*

VIVIFICA'TION, s. *vivificazione,* s. f.

VI'XEN, s. [a ranting woman] *una donna crucciofa, una garritrice.*

Vixen [froward child] *un ragazzo che non fa altro che gridare e piagnere.*

Vixen, s. [a fox's cub] *un volpicino.*

VIZ. [to wit, that is] *cioè.*

VI'ZARD, s. [a mafk] *mafchera.*

To put on a vizard, *metterfi una mafchera, mafcherarfi.*

To VI'ZARD [to mafk] *mafcherare, coprir con mafchera.*

U'LCER, s. [a running fore] *ulcera,* s. f.

To U'LCERATE [to caufe or break out into an ulcer] *ulcerare, ulcerarfi, pervenire ad ulcera.*

U'LCERATED, adj. *ulcerato.*

U'LCERATING, adj. *che ulcera.*

ULCERA'TION, s. [a breaking out into ulcers] *ulcezarione, ulceragione,* s. f.

U'LCEROUS, adj. [full of ulcers] *ulcerofo, pien d' ulcere.*

U'LCERED, adj. [grown by time from a fore to an ulcer] *ulcerato, che di femplice piaga s' è fatto ulcera.*

ULTE'RIOR, adj. [on the further fide] *ulteriore.*

U'LTIMATE, adj. [final, laft] *ultimo, finale.*

U'LTIMATELY, adv. *ultimamente, finalmente.*

They ultimately refolved upon the bufinefs, *eglino hanno prefa l' ultima rifoluzione.*

U'LTION, s. [revenge] *vendetta,* s. f.

ULTRA-MARI'NE, adj. [from beyond fea] *oltramarino, d' oltre mare.*

Ultra-marine, s. [the fineft fort of blue colour] *azzuro, oltramarino.*

ULTRA-MONTA'NE, adj. [dwelling on the other fide the mountains] *oltramontano, d' oltre i monti.*

To U'LULATE [to howl] *ululare.*

U'MBER, s. [a fort of trout-fifh] *ombrina,* s. f. *pefce di delicato fapore.*

Umber [a dark yellowifh colour] *terra d' ombra.*

U'MBERED, adj. [fhaded, clouded] *ombreggiato, ofcurato, quafi ofcurato o offufcato da' nugoli.*

UMBI'LICAL, adj. [belonging to the navel] *d' umbilico; pertinente al bellico.*

U'MBLES [part of the intrails of a deer] *coratella di cervo o daino.*

U'MBO, s. [the point or prominent part of a buckler] *la punta che è rilevata nel centro d' uno fcudo o brocchieri.*

U'MBRAGE, s. [fhade] *ombra,* s. f.

Umbrage [jealoufy, fufpicion] *ombra, gelofia,* s. f. *fofpetto,* s. m.

Umbrage [pretence, colour] *ombra, pretefto, colore, fcufa, coperchio.*

UMBRE'LLA, s. [a fort of fkreen that is held over the head for preferving from the fun or rain] *ombrella,* s. f. *ombrello,* s. m. *ftrumento per parare il fole, o la pioggia, al quale diciamo anche parafole.*

U'MPIRAGE, s. [the office or judgment of an umpire] *arbitrato,* s. m. *giudicio d' arbitri, arbitrazione,* s. f.

U'MPIRE [arbitrator] *arbitro,* s. m. *giudice eletto dalle parti.*

UNABI'LITY, *incapacità, inabilità,* s. f.

UNA'BLE, adj. *incapace, inabile.*

UNA'BLENESS, s. *inabilità, incapacità,* s. f.

UNACCE'PTABLE, adj. *ingrato, difpiacente, non accetto.*

UNACCO'UNTABLE, adj. [not to be juftified] *ftrano, bizzarro.*

UNACCO'UNTABLY, adv. *ftranamente, d' una ftrana maniera.*

UNACCU'STOMED, adj. [unufual] *infolito, non comune.*

UNACQUA'INTED, adj. *che non fa, che non conofce, ignorante, non verfato.*

UNACQUA'INTEDNESS, s. *ignoranza, poca conofcenza,* s. f.

UNA'CTIVE, adj. *lento, pigro, infingardo.*

UNADDI'CTED, adj. *che non è dedito.*

UNADVI'SABLE, adj. *che non fi deve configliare, che non è prudente di fare.*

UNADVI'SED, adj. *malavvifato, mal configliato, fconfigliato, imprudente, indifcreto, inconfiderato.*

UNADVI'SEDLY, adv. *imprudentemente, indifcretamente, inconfideratamente.*

UNADVI'SEDNESS, s. *imprudenza, indifcrezione, inconfiderazione, inavvertenza,* s. f.

UNAFFECTA'TION, *v.* Unaffectednefs.

UNAFFE'CTED, adj. [natural] *fenza affettazione; femplice, fchietto, naturale.*

UNAFFE'CTEDLY, adv. *fenza affettazione, fchiettamente. naturalmente.*

UNAFFE'CTEDNESS, s. [plainnefs] *femplicità, fchiettezza, purità, maniera di parlare o di trattare fenza affettazione.*

UNAGREE'ING, adj. *difcordante, fcordante, che difcorda.*

UNA'LIENABLE, adj. *inalienabile, che non fi può alienare.*

UNA'LIENATED, adj. *che non è alienato.*

UNALLO'WABLE, adj. *che non fi deve permettere.*

UNALLOW'ED, adj. *che non è permeffo, illecito.*

UNA'LTERABLE, adj. *che non fi può alterare.*

UNA'LTERED, adj. *che non è alterato o cangiato.*

UNAMA'ZED, adj. *intrepido, che non teme, fenza fpaventarfi o atterrirfi.*

UNAMA'ZEDLY, adv. *intrepidamente; fenza fpaventarfi.*

UNAMA'ZEDNESS, s. *intrepidità,* s. f.

UNAME'NDABLE, adj. *incorreggibile.*

UNA'MIABLE, adj. *che non è amabile, ingrato, fpiacevole.*

UNANI'MITY, s. *unanimità, conformità, unione di parere, di volontà.*

UNA'NIMOUS, adj. [of one mind, of one accord] *d' un comune accordo, che è del medefimo fentimento o parere, della medefima volontà, unanime.*

UNA'NIMOUSLY, adv. [with one accord] *unanimamente, d' un animo concorde; concordemente, d' un comun confenfo.*

To act unanimoufly, *operare unanimamente.*

It was unanimoufly refolved, *fu rifoluto d' un comun confenfo.*

UNANO'INTED, adj. [not anointed] *non unto, non facrato, non ancora coftituito Re coll' unzione de' facri oli.*

Unanointed [not prepared for death by extreme unction] *non unto ancora coll' olio fanto in articulo mortis.*

UNA'NSWERABLE, adj. *a che non fi può rifpondere o replicare, inconteftabile.*

UNA'NSWERABLY, adv. *d' una maniera inconteftabile.*

UNA'NSWERED, adj. *al che non s' è potuto rifpondere.*

UNAPPE'ASABLE, adj. *implacabile, che non fi può placare.*

UNAPPREHE'NSIBLE, adj. *incomprenfibile, che non fi può comprendere, o concepire.*

UNAPPRO'ACHABLE, adj. [inacceffible] *inacceffibile.*

UNA'PT, adj. *incapace, mal atto, che non è capace, che non è atto, che non ha della capacità o della difpofizione.*

UNA'PTLY, adv. [untowardly] *male.*

UNA'PTNESS, s. *incapacità, poca difpofizione,* s. f.

To UNA'RM, *difarmare, toglier le armi.*

UNA'RMED, adj. *difarmato.*

UNA'SKED, adj. *fenza domandarlo, non richiefto.*

UNASSU'RED, adj. *che non è ficuro, incerto.*

UNATTA'INABLE, adj. *che non fi può ottenere.*

UNATTA'INED, adj. *che non s' è potuto ottenere.*

UNATTE'MPTED, adj. *che non s' è tentato o provato.*

UNATTE'NDING, adj. *che neglige.*

UNAVA'ILABLE, adj. *che non giova.*

UNAUGME'NTED, adj. *che non è aumentato.*

UNAVO'IDABLE, adj. *inevitabile.*

UNAVO'IDABLY, adv. *inevitabilmente.*

UNAWA'KED, adj. *che non è fvegliato fenza effere fvegliato o defto, dormendo.*

UNAWA'RE } adv. [fuddenly, unex-
UNAWA'RES } pectedly] *difavvedutamente, all' improvvifo, improvvifamente, impenfatamente, fubitamente, repentinamente.*

To take one unawares, *corre uno all' improvvifo.*

Unawares [through overfight or miftake] *fenza penfarci, per inavvertenza, inavvertentemente.*

UNA'WED, adj. [unreftrained by fear or reverence] *non trattenuto da timore o riverenza.*

UNBA'CKED, adj. [not tamed; not taught to bear the rider] *non domo; non avvezzo a effere cavalcato, e diceft de' puledri principalmente.*

Unbacked [not countenanced, not aided] *non ifpalleggiato, non affiftito, non ajutato, non protetto.*

To UNBA'R, *levar la sbarra.*

UNBECO'MING, adj. *indecente, fconvenevole, difdicevole.*

UNBECO'MINGNESS, *indecenza, fconvenenza, fconvenevolezza,* s. f.

UNBEFI'TTING, adj. *indecente, che non conviene.*

UNBEGO'TTEN, adj. *non generato.*

UNBELI'EF, s. *incredulità, mifcredenza,* s. f.

To UNBE'ND [to loofen, to flacken] *rallentare, allentare, render lento.*

To unbend one's mind, *ricrearfi, riftorarfi, ripofarfi, prender ripofo o riftoro.*

UNBE'NT, adj. *rallentato, allentato.*

To UNBENU'M, *il contrario d' affiderare o agghiadare; rifcaldare, ravvivare.*

UNBENU'MMED, adj *rifcaldato, ravvivato, contrario d' affiderato o agghiadato.*

To UNBESE'EM, verb neut. *difdirfi, non convenire, effer difdicevole,* pref. *difdiro,* pret. *difdiffi.*

It may not unbefeem me fo to do, *forfe che non averei torto di far così.*

UNBESE'EMING, adj. [unbecoming] *difdicevole, fconvenevole, indecente.*

UNBESE'EMINGNESS, *indecenza, fconvenevolezza,* s. f.

UNBESE'EMINGLY, adv. *indecentemente, fconvenevolmente.*

To UNBESO'T, *fcozzonare, dirozzare, impratichire,* pref. *impratichifco.*

UNBESO'TTED, adj. *fcozzonato, dirozzato, impratichito.*

UNBESO'UGHT, adj. [not intreated] *non pregato, non fupplicato.*

UNBEWA'ILED, adj. [not lamented] *non compianto.*

To UNBEWI'TCH, *contrario d' ammaliare, romper la malìa.*

UNBI'ASSED, adj. [impartial] *che non s' è lafciato guadagnare con doni o corrompere, che non è parziale, incorrotto.*

UNBI'DDEN, adj. *che non è comandato, che non è invitato.*

To UNBI'ND [to unty] *fciogliere, e fciorre, flegare,* pref. *fciolgo,* pret. *fciolfi.*

UNBLA'MEABLE, adj. *innocente, irreprenfibile, incolpabile.*

UNBLA'MEABLENESS, s. *innocenza, qualità irreprenfibile.*

UNBLA'MEABLY, adv. *innocentemente, d' una maniera innocente o irreprenfibile.*

UNBLE'ST, adj. *che non è benedetto, fenza effer benedetto.*

To UNBLI'ND, *sbendare, render la vifta.*

UNBLI'NDED, adj. *sbendato, che ha ricovrata la vifta.*

UNBLO'ODY, adj. *fenza fpargimento di fangue, non fanguinofo.*

The unbloody facrifice of the mafs, *il facrificio non fanguinofo della meffa.*

UNBLO'WN, adj. [having the bud yet unexpanded] *non ifbocciato, che non ha ancora aperta, la borria.*

UNBO'DIED, adj. *incorporeo.*

UNBO'ILED, adj. *che non è bollito.*

To UNBO'LT, *fcatenacciare.*

UNBO'LTED, adj. *fcatenacciato.*

To UNBO'NE, *difoffare.*

UNBO'NED, adj. *difoffato.*

UNBO'NNETED, adj. [wanting a cap or a bonnet] *sberrettato, che non ha berretta in capo.*

UNBO'OKISH, adj. [not ftudious] *non iftudiofo, non amante di libri.*

Unbookifh [not cultivated by erudition] *non dotto, di poca o nulla erudizione.*

UNBO'OTED, adj. *fenza ftivali.*

To UNBO'RDER, *inondare, trabboccare.*

UNBO'RDERED, adj. *inondato, trabboccato.*

UNBO'RN, adj. *che non è ancora nato.*

To UNBO'SOM, *sfogarfi, aprire il fuo cuore, comunicare i più relati penfieri.*

UNBO'UGHT, adj. *che non è ancora comprato.*

UNBO'UND, adj. [from to unbind] *fciolto, flegato, che è in libertà.*

UNBO'UNDED, adj. [without bounds] *illimitato, infinito immenfo.*

To UNBO'WEL [to draw the guts] *fmentare, sbudellare.*

UNBO'WELLED, adj. *fventrato, sbudellato.*

To U'NBRACE, *sfibbiare.*

U'NBRACED, adj. *sfibbiato.*

UNBRI'BED, adj. *che non è corrotto o guadagnato con donativi.*

To UNBRI'DLE, *sbrigliare, cavare la briglia.*

UNBRI'DLED, adj. *sbrigliato.*

An unbridled luft, *appetito fmoderato.*

UNBRI'DLENESS, s. *sfrenatezza, licenza sfrenata.*

UNBRO'KEN, adj. *che non è rotto.*

An unbroken horfe, *un cavallo indomito.*

To UNBU'CKLE, verb act. *sfibbiare.*

UNBU'CKLED, adj. *sfibbiato.*

UNBU'ILT, adj. *che non è edificato.*

To UNBU'NG, *levar il cocchiume.*

To UNBU'RDEN, *fcaricare, alleggerire,* pref. *alleggerifco.*

UNBU'RDENED, adj. *fcaricato, alleggerito.*

UNBU'RIED, adj. *che non è feppellito, fenza fepoltura.*

UNBU'RNT, adj. *che non è abbruciato.*

To UNBU'RY, *fterrare, difotterrare.*

To UNBU'TTON, *sbottonare.*

To unbutton one's bofom, *sbottonarfi il petto.*

UNBU'TTONED, adj. *sbottonato.*

UNCA'LLED, adj. *che non è chiamato, fenza effer chiamato.*

UNCANO'NICAL, adj. *che non è canonico, che non è fecondo i canoni.*

UNCA'PABLE, adj. [incapable] *incapace.*

UNCA'PABLENESS, s. *incapacità,* s. f.

To UNCA'SE, *tirar fuora dallo ftucchio.*

To uncafe a man, *nudare, fpogliare alcuno, levargli li abiti.*

UNCA'UGHT, adj. *che non è prefo.*

UNCE'NSURED, adj. *che non è cenfurato, criticato, o biafimato.*

UNCE'RTAIN, adj. [not certain, not fure] *incerto, dubbiofo, che non è certo.*

Uncertain [changeable, fickle] *incerto, variabile, incoftante, volubile.*

To be in an uncertain condition, *effer nell' incertezza, ftare in dubbio.*

To

To be uncertain whether, *esser incerto, non sapere.*

Uncertain [indefinite, unlimited] *incerto, indefinito, indeterminato.*

An uncertain number, *un numero incerto.*

UNCE'RTAINLY, adv. *incertamente, con incertezza, d' una maniera incerta.*

UNCE'RTAINNESS, } s. [doubtfulness]
UNCE'RTAINTY, } *incertezza, irresoluzione,* s. f. *dubbio,* s. m.

UNCE'SSANT, adj. *continuo.*

UNCE'SSANTLY, adv. *incessantemente, senza cessare, continuamente.*

To UNCHA'IN, *scatenare.*

UNCHA'INED, adj. *scatenato.*

UNCHA'NGEABLE, adj. *immutabile, che non cangia, costante, fermo, sodo.*

UNCHA'NGEABLENESS, s. *immutabilità, fermezza, costanza,* s. f.

UNCHA'NGEABLY, adv. *fermamente, costantemente.*

UNCHA'RITABLE, adj. *che non ha carità, che non è caritatevole.*

UNCHA'RITABLENESS, s. *mancanza di carità.*

UNCHA'RITABLY, adv. *senza carità.*

UNCHA'RITY, *v.* Uncharitableness.

To UNCHA'RM, *romper la malia.*

UNCHA'RY, adj. [not wary, not cautious] *non circospetto, incauto.*

UNCHA'STE, adj. [not chaste, lecherous] *che non è casto, incontinente, impudico, lascivo.*

Unchaste [smutty, bawdy] *impuro, impudico, osceno, disonesto.*

UNCHA'STLY, adv. *incontinentemente, impudicamente, lascivamente.*

UNCHA'STNESS, s. *incontinenza, lascivia, impudicizia,* s. f.

UNCHE'ERFULNESS, s. [melancholy; gloominess of temper] *malinconia; tristezza; il contrario della naturale allegria.*

UNCHE'WED, adj. *che non è masticato, senza esser masticato.*

UNCHRI'STENED, adj. *sbattezzato.*

UNCHRI'STIAN, adj. *indegno d' un cristiano.*

To unchristian, *sbattezare.*

UNCHRI'STIANLY, adv. *d' una maniera poco cristiana, indegno d' un cristiano.*

To UNCHU'RCH, *scomunicare.*

UNCHU'RCHED, adj. *scomunicato.*

UNCI'RCUMCISED, adj. *incirconciso, non circoncisо.*

A man uncircumcised, *un incirconciso.*

UNCIRCUMCI'SION, s. *lo stato d' un uomo incirconciso.*

UNCI'RCUMSPECT, adj. [unwary] *imprudente, indiscreto, inavvertito, sconsiderato.*

UNCIRCUMSPE'CTLY, adv. *imprudentemente, indiscretamente, inavvertentemente, sconsideratamente.*

UNCI'VIL, adj. *incivile, rozzo.*

UNCLA'D, adj. *spogliato, privo di veste.*

To UNCLA'SP, *sfibbiare.*

UNCLA'SPED, adj. *sfibbiato.*

U'NCLE, s. [the father or mother's brother] *zio,* s. m. *fratello del padre o della madre.*

UNCLE'AN, adj. [filthy] *immondo, sporco, bruttato, lordo, impudiro, osceno.*

Unclean discourses, *discorsi impudici, o osceni.*

Unclean spirit, *spirito immondo.*

UNCLE'ANLINESS, s. [want of cleanliness] *bruttura, sporcizia, schifezza, immondizia, schifezza; e metaforicamente, impudicizia.*

UNCLE'ANLY, adv. *sporcamente, impudicamente.*

UNCLE'ANNESS, s. *immondizia, sporcizia, bruttura, schifezza, impudicità, impudicizia,* s. f.

UNCLE'ANSED, adj. *che non è nettato.*

UNCLE'FT, adj. *che non è fesso o spaccato.*

To UNCLO'ATH, *spogliare, svestire.*

UNCLO'ATHED, adj. *spogliato, svestito.*

To UNCLO'SE, *schiudere, aprire.*

To U'NCOIF a woman [to pull off her head-gear] *strappare la cuffia dalla testa d' una donna.*

UNCO'MBED, adj. *che non è pettinato, senza essere pettinato.*

UNCO'MELINESS, s. *indecenza, sconvenevolezza,* s. f.

UNCO'MELY, adv. *indecentemente, disdicevolmente, sconvenevolmente.*

UNCO'MFORTABLE, adj. [sad, grievous, troublesome] *inconsolabile, miserabile, infelice, tristo, malcontento, sconsolato, travagliato.*

UNCO'MFORTABLENESS, s. *miseria, scontentezza, infelicità, tristizia.*

UNCO'MFORTABLY, s. *miseramente, infelicemente, sconsolatamente.*

UNCOMMO'DIOUS, *v.* Incommodious.

UNCO'MMON, adj. *che non è comune, raro, straordinario.*

UNCO'MMONNESS, s. *rarità.*

UNCOMMU'NICABLE, adj. *incomunicabile, che non si romunica.*

UNCOMPA'CT, adj. [not compact, not closely cohering] *non sodo, non incorporato fittamente insieme, non compatto, non fermo, non duro.*

UNCO'MPANIED, adj. [having no companion] *scompagnato, privo di compagno, che non ha compagnia.*

UNCOMPE'LLED, adj. *che non è sforzato, senza essere sforzato, volontario.*

UNCOMPO'UNDED, adj. *che non è misto, semplice, schietto.*

UNCOMPO'UNDEDNESS, s. *semplicità, schiettezza,* s. f.

UNCONCE'IVABLE, adj. *che non si può concepire o comprendere, incomprensibile.*

UNCONCE'IVABLENESS, s. *incomprensibilità,* s. f.

UNCONCERN, s. [negligence; want of interest; freedom from anxiety; freedom from perturbation] *indifferenza; negligenza; freddezza; spassionatezza; disamore; il non soffrire ansietà o turbamento d' animo.*

UNCONCE'RNED, adj *spassioniato, che non è tocco o mosso, indifferente.*

UNCONCE'RNEDLY, adv. *spassionatamente, indifferentemente, d' una maniera indifferente.*

UNCONCE'RNEDNESS, s. *indifferenza,* s. f. *v.* Unconcern.

UNCONCE'RNING, adj. [not interesting, not affecting] *che non torra, che non muove l' animo, che è indifferente, che ti lascia indifferente.*

UNCONCLU'DING, } adj *che non conchiude.*
UNCONCLU'SIVE, }

An unconcluding argument, *un argomento che non conchiude.*

UNCONCO'CTED, adj. *crudo, che non è concotto, indigesto.*

UNCONDE'MNED, adj. *che non è condannato, senza esser condannato, assoluto.*

UNCONFI'NED, adj. [unlimited] *che non è limitato, senza limite.*

Unconfined [free] *libero.*

UNCONFI'RMED, adj. *che non è confirmato.*

UNCONFO'RMABLE, adj. *che non è conforme.*

UNCONFO'RMED, adj. *che non si conforma o che non s' è conformato.*

UNCONFO'RMITY, s. *differenza, contrarietà* s. f.

UNCO'NQUERABLE, adj. *invincibile, insuperabile.*

UNCO'NQUERED, adj. *invitto, non vinto.*

UNCO'NSCIONABLE, adj. *irragionevole, rhe non ha coscienza, ingiusto.*

UNCO'NSCIONABLY, adv. *senza coscienza, irragionevolmente.*

UNCO'NSCIONABLENESS, s. *mancanza di coscienza.*

UNCO'NSECRATED, adj. *che non è consagrato.*

UNCONSTRA'INED, adj. *che non è costretto o sforzato, senza essere sforzato.*

UNCONSTRAI'NEDLY, adv. *senza forza, volontariamente.*

UNCONSU'MABLE, adj. *rhe non può esser consumato.*

UNCONSU'MED, adj. *che non è consumato, senza esser consumato.*

UNCONTE'MNED, adj. *che non è disprezzato.*

UNCONTE'STED, adj. *indubitato, del quale non si dubita.*

UNCONTROULABLE, adj. *che non si deve contraddire.*

Uncontroulable, adj. [not to be disputed] *incontestabile, indubitabile.*

UNCONTRO'ULED, adj. *che non è contraddetto.*

Uncontrouled [undisputed] *che non si disputa o contesta.*

UNCONVE'RSABLE [not to be conversed with] *insociabile, impraticabile.*

To UNCO'RD, *sciorre, slegare quel che è legato con rorde.*

UNCO'RDED, adj. *sciolto, slegato.*

UNCORRE'CT, adj. *scorretto, che non è corretto.*

UNCORRE'CTED, adj. *che non è corretto, senza esser corretto.*

UNCORRU'PT, } adj. *incorrotto.*
UNCORRU'PTED, }

UNCORRU'PTIBLE, adj. *incorruttibile.*

UNCORRU'PTLY, adv. *con integrità, incorrottamente.*

To UNCOVER, *scoprire, scovrire.*

UNCO'VERED, adj. *scoperto, scoverto.*

To UNCO'UPLE, *scioglicre, spajare.*

UNCO'UPLED, adj. *spajato.*

UNCO'URTEOUS, adj. *scortese.*

UNCO'UTH, adj. [rough, harsh, unpolished] *rozzo, goffo.*

An uncouth expression, *un' espressione goffa.*

UNCO'UTHNESS, s. *rozzezza, goffaggine,* s. f.

UNCREA'TED, adj. *increato.*

To UNCRO'WN, *levar la corona.*

UNCRO'WNED, adj. *a cui è stata levata la corona, deposto.*

U'NCTION, s. [anointing] *unzione,* s. f.

UNCTUO'SITY, s. [the quality of being unctuous] *untuosità,* s. f.

U'NCTUOUS, adj. [oily, fat] *untuoso, che ha in se dell' unto.*

UNCU'LTIVABLE, adj. [not to be cultivated] *che non si può coltivare, indocile.*

An uncultivable nature, *una natura indocile.*

UNCU'LTIVATED, adj. *inculto.*

UNCU'RABLE, adj. [incurable] *incurabile, da non poterſi curare.*

UNCU'RED, adj. *che non è guarito, senza esser guarito.*

UNCU'RIOUS, adj. *che non è curioso.*

UNCU'RSED, adj. *che non è maledetto.*

UNCU'T, adj. *intero, che non è tagliato, che non è tronco.*

To UNDA'M [to open, to free from the restraint of mounds] *aprire, toglier via i ritegni che impedivano il corso.*

UNDA'MAGED, adj. [not made worse, not impaired] *non danneggiato, non guasto.*

UNDA'UNTED, adj. *intrepido, senza paura, fermo, risoluto.*

UNDAU'NTEDLY, adv. *intrepidamente, con coraggio, con intrepidità.*

UNDAU'NTEDNESS, s. *intrepidità, intrepidezza.* s. f.

UNDECEI'VABLE, adj. *che non si può sgannare.*

To UNDECE'IVE, *sgannare, cavar altrui d' inganno.*

UNDECE'IVED, adj. *sgannato, ravato d' inganno.*

UNDE'CENT, adj. *indecente.*

UNDECI'DED, adj. *indeciso, indeterminato.*

UNDECLI'NABLE, adj. *indeclinabile, che non si declina.*

UNDECKED, adj. *mal adorno, sciancio, senza ornamenti, disadorno.*

UNDE'E, adj. [like waves, in heraldry] *ondato, termine araldico.*

UNDEFA'CEABLE, adj. *indelebile.*

UNDEFA'CEABLE, adj. *indelebile.*

UNDEFE'NDED, adj. *che non è difeso, senza difesa.*

UNDEFI'LED, adj. *puro, senza macchia, intemerato, intatto, immaculato.*

UNDEFI'NED, adj. [not circumscribed; not explained by a definition] *non definito, non circoscritto, non spiegato con propria definizione.*

UNDEFI'NABLE, adj. [not to be marked out or circumscribed by a definition] *non definibile, da non essere rirroscritto o particolarmente caratterizzato con definizione.*

UNDEFO'RMED, adj. [not deformed, not disfigured] *non reso deforme, non guasto nella persona.*

UNDEFI'ED, adj. [not set at defiance, not challenged] *non isfidato, non provocato da disfida.*

UNDEJE'CTED, adj. *che non è sgomentato, fermo, intrepido, senza paura.*

UNDENI'ABLE, adj. [undisputable] *incontestabile, che non si può negare.*

UNDENI'ABLY, adv. *incontestabilmente.*

U'NDER, prep. *sotto.*

Under the bed, *sotto il letto.*

Under colour, *sotto colore, sotto pretesto.*

From under ground, *di sotto terra.*

To go under, *andar di sotto.*

Under fifteen years of age, *meno di quindici anni.*

Over or under, *più ò meno.*

I cannot sell it under, *non posso venderlo per meno.*

All the country lies under water, *tutto 'l paese è inondato, o sotto acqua.*

To swim under water, *nuotar sott' acqua.*

To be under age, *esser minore.*

To under some restraint, *star soggetto, esser in qualche soggezione.*

To be under an oath, *esser obbligato sotto giuramento.*

To be under an obligation, *esser obbligato, esser tenuto.*

To give a note under one's hand, *dare una polizza sottoscritta di sua mano.*

Under hand and seal, *sottoscritto e sigillato.*

A ship under sail, *un vascello alla vela.*

To lie under a distemper, *esser afflitto da qualche malattia.*

To bring under, *sommettere, sottomettere, soggiogare.*

To keep under, *tener corto, tener sotto.*

To tread under foot, *calpestare.*

All under one, *tutto alla volta, tutto insieme.*

Under favour, under correction, *con vostra licenza, con vostra pace.*

Under-age [non-age] *minorità.*

To UNDER-BID [to offer less for a thing than it is worth] *offrir meno che la rosa non vale.*

To under-bid one, *offrir meno d' un altro.*

To UNDER-BIND, *legar per di sotto.*

Under-bound, adj. *legato per di sotto.*

Under-Brigadier, s. *sotto brigadiere.*

Under-butler, s. *sotto bottigliere.*

Under caterer, s. *sotto dispensiere.*

Under - chamberlain, *vice-ciambellano.*

Under-cook, s. *sotto cuoco.*

To UNDER-FEEL, *presentire,* pref. *presento.*

To UNDER-FLOW, *scorrere per di sotto.*

To UNDER-GIRD, *cigner per di sotto.*

Under-girdle, s. *cintura di sotto.*

UNDER-GIRT, adj. *cinto per di sotto.*

To U'NDERGO, *soffrire, patire, sottomettersi.*

To undergo a punishment, *esser punito.*

U'NDERGONE, adj. *sofferto, patito.*

Under-governor, s. *sotto governatore.*

U'NDER-HAND, adv. *sottomano, di soppiatto.*

Under-hand dealings, *pratiche segrete.*

UNDERI'VED, adj. *che non è derivato.*

UNDERLA'YER [a piece of wood to bear up any thing] *puntello,* s. m.

Under-leather, s. *cuojo di sotto, suolo,* s. m.

Under - lieutenant, s. *sotto luogotenente.*

U'NDERLING [one that acts under another] *un inferiore, colui che è sotto la direzione d' un altro.*

U'NDERLIP, s. *il labbro di sotto.*

To UNDERMI'NE, verb, *minare, contramminare, sottominare.*

To undermine [to waste, to consume, to destroy by degrees] *consumare, distruggere poco a poco.*

To undermine one [to endeavour to supplant him] *cercare di spiantare, o di nuocere ad alcuno.*

U'NDERMOST, adj. *che è in fondo.*

The undermost, *il più basso, il più sotto.*

UNDERNE'ATH, adv. *di sotto, sotto.*

UNDER-PRI'OR, s. *sotto priore.*

To UNDER-PRO'P, *puntellare, porre un puntello.*

UNDER-PRO'PPED, adj. *puntellato.*

UNDER-RA'TE, *vil prezzo, basso prezzo.*

To UNDER-RA'TE [to under-value] *disprezzare, avvilire, stimar meno che la rosa non vale.*

UNDER-SE'CRETARY, s. *sotto segretario.*

To UNDERSE'LL [to sell for less than the thing is worth] *vender per meno che la cosa non vale.*

To undersell [to sell cheaper] *vender a miglior mercato.*

UNDER - SE'RVANT, s. *servidore basso.*

To UNDERSE'T, s. *metter di sotto.*

UNDER-SO'RT, adj. ex. [the under sort of people] *il popolaccio, il popolazzo, la plebe, la feccia del popolo, il popol minuto.*

To UNDERSTA'ND [to apprehend, to conceive] *intendere, comprendere, capire,* pret. *intesi, compresi,* pref. *capisco.*

To give to understand, *dare ad intendere.*

To

To underſtand an art or a ſcience, *intendere un' arte o una ſcienza.*

He underſtands a horſe, *egli s'intende i cavalli.*

To underſtand [to hear, to be told] *intendere, eſſer informato, avere avviſo.*

I underſtand that he is come to town, *mi vien detto che egli è venuto in città.*

To underſtand [to think, to believe] *credere, penſare.*

I underſtood quite contrary, *credevo tutto 'l contrario, credevo altrimente.*

To underſtand one's ſelf [to know how to carry one's ſelf] *conoſcerſi, comportarſi bene.*

UNDERST'ANDER, s. [one ſkilled in any thing] *conoſcitore,* s. m. *conoſcitrice,* s. f.

UNDERSTA'NDING, s. [intellect] *intendimento, intelletto.*

Underſtanding [knowledge] *intendimento, ſapere, intelligenza,* s. f.

He is a man of underſtanding, *egli è un uomo d' intendimento, di ſapere.*

Underſtanding [intelligence, correſpondence] *intelligenza, corriſpondenza, familiarità, amicizia,* s. f.

There's a good underſtanding betwixt them, *paſſa buona intelligenza fra loro.*

Ill underſtanding, *cattiva intelligenza, inimicizia.*

Underſtanding, adj. [knowing] *intelligente, ſaputo, che ha intelletto.*

UNDERSTA'NDINGLY, adv. *giudicioſamente, con giudicio. Vore cattiva.*

UNDERSTO'OD, adj. *inteſo, compreſo, capito,* v. To underſtand.

Eaſy to be underſtood, *intelligibile, facile ad intenderſi.*

'Tis rare to ſee merit underſtood at court, *rare volte ſi riconoſce il merito in corte.*

UNDERSTRA'PPER, s. [a petty fellow, an inferior agent] *un uomo da poco, un piccolo agente d'un altro.*

To UNDERTA'KE [to take upon one] *intraprendere, prendere a fare, impegnarſi,* pret. *intrapreſi.*

To undertake a building, *intraprendere un edificio.*

I'll undertake to do it, *m' impegno di farlo.*

To undertake an employment, *prendere, abbracciare un impiego.*

To undertake for one [to bail him] *mallevare alcuno, eſſer ſuo mallevadore.*

To undertake [to meddle] *ingerirſi, impacciarſi, intrometterſi,* preſ. *ingeriſco,* pret. *intromiſi.*

It is not for private perſons to undertake matters of publick concernment, *le perſone private non devono ingerirſi in materie ſpettanti al pubblico.*

UNDERTA'KEN, adj. *intrapreſo,* v. To undertake.

UNDERTA'KER, s. *intraprenditore,* s. m.

Undertaker for another, *mallevadore.*

UNDERTA'KING, s. [a thing undertaken, or deſign] *impreſa,* s. f. *diſegno,* s. m.

UNDER-TEETH, s. *i denti di ſotto.*

UNDERTOO'K, *è un preterito del verbo* To undertake.

UNDER-TRE'ASURER, s. *vice teſoriere.*

UNDERVALUA'TION, s. [rate not equal to the worth] *ſtima non eguale al vero o intrinſeco valore.*

UNDERVA'LUE, s. *diſonore, biaſimo* s. m.

This is no undervalue at all to you, *queſto non vi fa diſonore alcuno.*

To UNDERVA'LUE [to ſlight] *diſprezzare, vilipendere, avvilire.*

UNDERVA'LUED, adj. *diſprezzato, avviliſto, vilipeſo.*

UNDERVA'LUER, s. [one who eſteems lightly] *ſpregiatore, diſprezzatore, colui che poco ſtima altrui, o che poco pregia checcheſſia.*

UNDERWE'NT, *è il preterito del verbo* To undergo.

UNDER-WHE'ELS, s. *ruote di ſotto.*

UNDER-WO'OD, s. [coppice, or any other wood that is not counted timber] *alberi piccoli.*

To UNDER-WO'RK [to undermine, to endeavour to ſupplant] *cercar di ſpiantare, procurar di diſtruggere.*

To UNDER-WRI'TE, *ſottoſcrivere,* pret. *ſottoſcriſſi.*

UNDER-WRI'TTEN, adj. *ſottoſcritto.*

UNDESE'RVED, adj. *immeritevole, che non ha merito.*

UNDESE'RVEDLY, adv. *immeritamente.*

UNDESERVING, adj. *immeritevole, indegno, non meritevole.*

UNDESIGNING, adj. *buono, ſincero, ſchietto.*

UNDESI'RABLE, adj. *che non è da deſiderarſi.*

UNDETE'RMINABLE, adj. *che non ſi può terminare, o limitare.*

UNDETE'RMINATE, adj. *non determinato, irreſoluto.*

UNDETE'RMINED, adj. [uncertain, irreſolute] *indeterminato, incerto, irreſoluto.*

Undetermined [undecided] *indeterminato, indeciſo.*

UNDEVO'UT, adj. *non divoto.*

UNDEVO'UTLY, adv. *indivotamente.*

UNDI'ED, adj. *che non è tinto.*

UNDIGE'STED, adj. *non digerito.*

UNDI'LIGENT, adj [negligent] *negligente, neghittoſo, che non è diligente.*

UNDIMI'NISHABLE, adj. *che non ſi può diminuire.*

UNDIMI'NISHED, adj. *che non è diminuito, intero.*

UNDI'PPED, adj. [not dipped, not plunged] *non tuffato, non intinto.*

UNDIRE'CTED, adj. [not directed] *non diretto, non regolato.*

UNDISCE'RNED, adj. [not obſerved, not diſcovered, not deſcried] *non oſſervato, non ſcoperto, non viſto, non veduto, che non s' è potuto diſcernere.*

UNDISCE'RNABLE, adj. *che non ſi può diſcernere.*

UNDISCE'RNING, adj. *che non ha diſcernimento.*

UNDISCHA'RGED, adj. *che non è ſcaricato.*

UNDISCI'PLINED, adj. *che non è diſciplinato, ignorante.*

UNDISPO'SED of, adj. *del quale non s' è ancora diſpoſto.*

UNDISPRO'VABLE, adj. [not to be excepted againſt] *che non ſi può diſapprovare.*

UNDISPU'TABLE, adj. *che non è da diſputare.*

UNDISPU'TED, adj. *che non è diſputato o conteſtato.*

UNDISSO'LVED, adj. *che non è ſciolto.*

UNDISTA'INED, adj. *puro, ſenza macchia.*

UNDISTI'NGUISHABLE, adj. *che non ſi può diſtinguere.*

UNDISTI'NGUISHED, adj. *che non è diſtinto.*

UNDISTU'RBED, adj. *che non è interrotto o diſturbato, che è tranquillo, placido.*

UNDISTU'RBEDLY, adv. [without being diſturbed] *ſenza diſturbo, tranquillamente, pacificamente.*

UNDIVI'DABLE, adj. *indiviſible, che non ſi può dividere.*

UNDIVI'DABLY, adv. *indiviſibilmente, indiviſamente.*

UNDIVI'DED, adj. *indiviſo, non diviſo.*

To UNDO' [to untie] *ſciorre, ſcioglie-re, ſlegare,* preſ. *ſciolgo,* pret. *ſciolſi.*

To undo a knot, *ſciorre un nodo.*

To undo a thing [to take it pieces] *disfare, mettere in pezzi.*

To undo a match, *rompere un matrimonio.*

To undo one, *rovinare alcuno.*

UNDO'ER, s. *disfacitore,* s. m. *che disfà, che rovina, che guaſta.*

UNDO'ING, s. *disfacimento, perdita, rovina, guaſtamento.*

This was the undoing of him, *queſto è ſtato la ſua rovina.*

UNDO'NE, adj. *disfatto, rovinato,* v. To undo.

To leave a thing undone, *laſciare una coſa imperfetta.*

UNDO'UBTED, adj. *indubitato, certo, che non ha dubbio, indubitabile.*

UNDO'UBTEDLY, adv. *indubitatamente, ſenza dubbio, certamente, di ſicuro.*

UNDRA'INABLE, adj. *che non ſi può ſeccare, o ridurre a ſecco.*

To UNDRA'W, verb act. *tirare.*

To undraw the curtains, *tirare le cortine.*

UNDRE'SS, s. *abito della mattina.*

To be in an undreſs, *eſſer in veſte da camera.*

To UNDRE'SS, verb act. *ſpogliare,*

To undreſs one's ſelf, *ſpogliarſi.*

UNDRE'SSED, } adj. *ſpogliato.*
UNDRE'ST, }

UNDRI'ED, adj. *che non è ſecco.*

UNDU'E, adj. *indebito, ingiuſto, inconvenevole.*

Undue hour, *ora indebita.*

UNDU'ELY, adv. *indebitamente.*

U'NDULATE, or U'NDULATED, adj.

 [made

[made like waves] *ondeggiato, ondato, fatto ad onde.*

UNDULA'TION, s. [a motion like that of the waves] *ondeggiamento*, s. m.

UNDU'TIFUL, adj. *disubbidiente.*

Undutiful child, *fanciullo disubbidiente, figlio disobbediente.*

UNDU'TIFULLY, adv. *disubbidientemente.*

To carry one's self undutifully, *esser disubbidiente.*

UNDU'TIFULNESS, *disubbidienza*, s. f.

UNE'ASILY, adv. *disagiatamente, disagiosamente, incomodamente, inquietamente.*

UNEA'SINESS, s. [inconveniency] *disagio, scomodo*, s. m. *incomodità, inconvenienza.*

Uneasiness [trouble, disquiet] *inquietudine, passione, tribolazione*, s. f. *travaglio*, s. m.

UNEASY, adj. [difficult] *difficile.*

Uneasy [troublesome, inconvenient] *incomodo, disagiato, disagioso.*

This chair is very uneasy, *questa sedia è molto incomoda.*

Uneasy [not at his ease] *che non ista a suo comodo.*

To lie uneasy, *non esser coricato comodamente.*

Uneasy [disturbed, disquieted, concerned] *inquieto, travagliato, commosso, tribolato, addolorato.*

UNE'ATABLE, adj. *che non si può mangiare, che non è buono a mangiare.*

UNE'ATEN, adj. [not devoured] *non mangiato, non divorato.*

UNE'ATH, adv. [not easily] *senza facilità, difficilmente.*

Uneath, *pare che* Spenser *abbia usato questo avverbio in vece di* beneath *sotto, di sottovia.*

UNEDIFY'ING, adj. [not improving in good life] *che non edifica, che non è edificante.*

UNE'FFECTUAL, adj. *inefficace, non efficace.*

UNELE'CTED, adj. [not chosen] *non iscelto, non eletto.*

UNE'LIGIBLE, adj. [not worthy to be chosen] *non eligibile, non meritevole d' esser scelto o eletto.*

UNE'LOQUENT, adj. *che non è eloquente; rozzo.*

UNE'LOQUENTLY, adv. *d' una maniera non eloquente, rozzamente.*

UNE'NDOWED, adj. *che non è dotato.*

UNE'QUAL, adj. *ineguale.*

UNE'QUALLY, adv. *inegualmente.*

UNE'RRING, adj. [that cannot err] *infallibile, che non può fallire o peccare.*

UNESTI'MABLE, adj. *inestimabile, imprezzabile.*

UNE'VANGELICAL, adj. *che non è secondo il vangelo, che non è compreso nel vangelo.*

UNE'VEN, adj. [not even] *ineguale.*

Uneven ground, *terreno ineguale.*

Uneven temper, *umore capriccioso, umor bisbetico.*

UNE'VENLY, adv. *inegualmente.*

UNE'VENNESS, s. *inegualità*, s. f.

UNE'VITABLE, adj. [inevitable] *inevitabile.*

UNEXA'MPLED, adj. *che non ha esempio, senza esempio.*

UNEXCE'PTIONABLE, adj. [speaking of a witness] *d' intera fede.*

UNE'XECUTED, adj. *che non è stato eseguito o mandato ad effetto.*

UNEXHA'USTED, adj. *che non è esausto.*

UNEXPE'CTED, adj. *non previsto, inopinato, non pensato, non immaginato, impensato, improvviso.*

UNEXPE'CTEDLY, adv. *improvvisamente, inopinatamente, impensatamente.*

UNEXPE'RIENCED, adj. *che non è sperimentato, versato, o pratico; soro, inesperto.*

UNEXPE'RT, adj. [unskilful] *inesperto, soro, che non ha pratica, che non è esercitato.*

UNEXPE'RTLY, adv. *da ignorante, da novizio.*

UNE'XPLICABLE, *v.* Inexplicable.

UNEXPO'UNDABLE, adj. *inesplicabile.*

UNEXPRE'SSIBLE, *v.* Inexpressible.

UNE'XPUNGABLE, adj. *inespugnabile.*

UNEXTE'NDED, adj. *che non si stende.*

UNEXTE'RMINABLE, adj. *che non si può sterminare o sradicare.*

UNEXTI'NGUISHABLE, adj. *inestinguibile, da non potersi estinguere.*

UNEXTI'NGUISHED, adj. *che non è estinto.*

UNEXTI'RPATED, adj. *che non è estirpato.*

UNPA'INED, *v.* Unfeigned.

UNFA'ITHFUL, adj. [not faithful, treacherous, false] *infedele, sleale, perfido, traditore, disleale.*

Unfaithful [uncredulous] *infedele, incredulo.*

The unfaithful, s. [the unbelievers] *gl' infedeli.*

UNFAI'THFULLY, adv. *infedelmente, dislealmente.*

UNFAI'THFULNESS, s. *infedeltà, dislealtà, perfidia*, s. f. *tradimento*, s. m.

UNFA'LSIFIED, adj. *che non è falsificato, vero.*

UNFA'SHIONABLE, adj. *che non è alla moda.*

UNFA'SHIONED, adj. *informe, sformato.*

To UNFA'STEN, verb act. *sciorre, scioglière, slegare, disunire, disfare.*

UNFA'STENED, adj. *sciolto, slegato, disunito, disfatto.*

UNFA'THOMABLE, adj. *che non si può scandagliare.*

UNFA'THOMABLY, adj. *d' una maniera da non potersi scandagliare.*

UNFA'THOMED, adj. *che non è scandagliato.*

UNFE'ASABLE, adj. *che non è fattibile, che non si può fare.*

UNFE'ATHERED, adj. *spiumato, senza piume.*

UNFE'D, adj. *che non ha mangiato niente, non pasciuto.*

UNFE'ELING, adj. [insensible, void of mental sensibility] *insensibile, di cuor duro, d' animo indifferente.*

UNFE'IGNED, adj. *sincero, leale, schietto, non finto, non simulato.*

UNFE'IGNEDLY, adv. *sinceramente, lealmente, schiettamente.*

UNFE'IGNEDNESS, s. *sincerità, lealtà, schiettezza*, s. f.

UNFE'LT, adj. *insensibile, che non si sente; di cui uom non s' accorge.*

UNFE'NCED, adj. *che non è difeso o fortificato, senza difese, senza fortificazioni.*

UNFERME'NTED, adj. [not fermented] *che non la fermentato.*

UNFERTILE, adj. [not fruitful, not prolifick] *sterile, che non da frutto, che non è prolifico.*

To UNFE'TTER, verb act. *sferrare, levare i ferri, togliere i ceppi, porre in libertà.*

UNFE'TTERED, adj. *sferrato, messo in libertà, uscito de' ceppi, tolto de' ceppi.*

UNFI'NISHED, adj. *che non è finito, imperfetto.*

UNFI'T, adj. [not fit, unapt, incapable] *inetto, non atto, incapace, disadatto, insufficiente.*

Unfit [not fit, not convenient] *che non è decente o buono, indecente, sconvenevole, disdicevole, improprio.*

That's a thing unfit to be spoken, *questa non è cosa decente a dire, questa non è cosa che si debba dire.*

It is unfit, *non conviene, non stà bene, non è decente, non è proprio, non è adatto.*

Unfit for service, *che non può servire, non atto a servire.*

UNFI'TLY, adv. *male, malamente, sconvenevolmente, disadattamente, impropriamente.*

That is very unfitly applied, *questo è molto male adattato.*

UNFI'TNESS, s. *incapacità*, s. f.

UNFI'TTING, adj. *che non è conveniente, disdicevole, sconvenevole.*

UNFI'XED, or UNFI'XT, adj. *che non è fitto.*

UNFLE'DGED, adj. *che non è coperto di piume, che non può volare; parlando degli uccelli.*

UNFO'ILED, adj. [unsubdued, not put to the worst] *non sottommesso, non ridotto al peggio.*

To UNFO'LD, *spiegare, sviluppare.*

To unfold a napkin, *spiegare una salvietta.*

To unfold a mystery, *sviluppare, spiegare un mistero, un arcano.*

To unfold sheep, *fare uscire le pecore dell' ovile.*

UNFO'LDED, adj. *spiegato, sviluppato.*

To UNFO'OL [to restore from folly] *guarire della pazzia, render savio chi prima era fuor del senno.*

UNFO'RCED, adj. *che non è sforzato, senza essere sforzato, libero, volontario.*

UNFO'RCEDLY, adv. [freely] *liberamente, volontariamente, di sua propria volontà.*

UNFO'RCIBLE, adj. *inispugnabile, che non si può espugnare.*

UNFO'RESEEN, adj. *inopinato, non previsto, improvviso.*

UNFO'RMED, adj. [without form] *informe, sformato, che non ha forma.*

UNFO'RTIFIED, adj. *che non è fortificato.*

UNFO'RTUNATE, adj. [unhappy] *sfor-*

ſfortunato, ſventurato, infelice, ſciagurato.

UNFO'RTUNATELY, adv. *ſfortunatamente, ſventuratamente, infelicemente, ſciaguramente.*

UNFO'RTUNATENESS, s. *ſfortuna, ſventura, ſciagura, infelicità*, s. f. *infortunio*, s. m.

UNFO'UND, adj. *che non è trovato.*

UNFRE'E, adj. *che non è libero.*

UNFRE'QUENCY, s. *rarità*, s. f.

UNFRE'QUENT, adj. [rare] *raro, che arriva rare volte, non frequente, non comune.*

UNFREQUE'NTED, adj. *non frequentato, deſerto.*

UNFRE'QUENTLY, adv. [ſeldom] *radamente, raramente, di rado, rade volte.*

UNFRIE'NDLINESS, s. *poca amicizia.*

UNFRIE'NDLY, adj. *ſcorteſe, indegno d' un amico, non amichevole.*

UNFRIE'NDLY, adv. *ſcorteſemente.*

UNFRU'ITEFUL, adj. [barren] *infruttifero, infruttuoſo, ſterile, inutile.*

UNFRU'ITFULLY, adv. *infruttuoſamente, ſenza frutto.*

UNFRUITFULNESS, s. *ſterilità*, s. f.

UNFULFI'LLED, adj. [not fulfilled] *non ripieno, non colmo, non mantenuto ancora come s' era promeſſo ; non avvenuto ancora.*

To UNFU'RNISH, *ſfornire, tor via i fornimenti.*

UNFU'RNISHED, adj. *ſfornito.*

To UNGA'GE, *diſimpegnare, riſcuotere un pegno.*

UNGA'GED, adj. [not meaſured] *che non è ſcandagliato o miſurato.*

UNGA'INED, adj. [odd, ſtrange] *ſtrano, bizzaro, biſbetico.*

He is an ungained fellow, *egli è un uomo ſtrano.*

UNGAI'NFUL, adj. *che non è lucrativo.*

UNGAINLY, adj [aukward] *ſgarbato, ſenza garbo, ſvenevole, ſconcio, ſciamannato, ſgraziato.*

Ungainly, adv. *diſacconciamente, ſconciamente, ſvenevolmente, ſciamannatamente, ſgraziatamente.*

UNGUA'RDED, adj. *che non è guardato.*

UNGA'RNISHED, adj. *ſfornito.*

UNGA'THERED, adj. *che non è colto.*

UNGENTE'EL, adj. [clowniſh] *groſſolano, rozzo, materiale, zotico.*

Ungenteel [not gentleman like] *ſcorteſe, indegno d' un gentiluomo.*

UNGENTE'ELNESS, s. [clowniſhneſs] *rozzezza, zotichezza*, s. f.

UNGENTE'ELY, adv. *groſſolanamente, rozzamente, zoticamente, ſcorteſemente.*

UNGE'NTLE, adj. [untractable] *indocile, intrattabile.*

Ungentle [ſevere, hard] *ſevero, aſpro, rigoroſo, duro.*

UNGE'NTLEMANLIKE, adj. *incivile, indegno d' un galantuomo.*

UNGENTLENESS, s. [untractableneſs] *indocilità, zotichezza*, s f.

Ungentleneſs [ſeverity] *ſeverità, rigidezza, durezza*, s. f. *rigore*, s. m.

UNGE'NTLY, adv. *rozzamente, aſpramente, ſeveramente, rigoroſamente.*

UNGE'NEROUS, adj. *non generoſo.*

To UNGI'LD, *levar l' oro.*

To UNGILT, adj. *che non è dorato.*

To UNGI'RD, *levar le cinghie, ſciogliere la cintura.*

To UNGLU'E, *ſcollare.*

UNGLU'ED, adj. *ſcollato.*

UNGO'DLILY, adv. *ſenza religione, empiamente.*

UNGO'DLINESS, s. *empietà, irreligione.*

UNGO'DLY, adj. *empio, irreligioſo.*

An ungodly man, *un empio.*

An ungodly act, *un' azione empia.*

UNGO'VERNABLE, adj. [unruly] *ſfrenato, indomito, indomabile, ritroſo.*

UNGO'VERNABLENESS, s. *ſfrenatezza*, s. f. *umore indomito.*

UNGRA'CEFUL, adj. *ſgraziato, ſenza grazia, ſenza avvenenza, ſvenevole.*

UNGRA'CEFULLY, adv. *ſgraziatamente, ſvenevolmente, ſenza grazia, con iſgraziataggine.*

UNGRA'CEFULNESS, s. *ſgraziataggine, ſvenevolezza.*

UNGRA'CIOUS, adj. [unlucky, untoward] *ſgraziato, cattivo, ſiniſtro, infelice.*

UNGRA'CIOUS, *ſcorteſe, villano.*

UNGRA'CIOUSLY, adv. [unluckily] *malamente, ſgraziatamente, ſiniſtramente.*

Ungraciouſly [ungenteely] *ſcorteſemente, d' una maniera ſcorteſe.*

UNGRA'CIOUSNESS, s. [ungracious carriage] *ſcorteſia, ſgarbatezza, inciviltà*, s. f.

UNGRA'FTED, adj. *che non è inneſtato.*

UNGRAMMA'TICAL, adj. *contrario alle regole grammaticali.*

UNGRA'TEFUL, adj. [unthankful] *ingrato, ſconoſcente.*

An ungrateful man or woman, *un ingrato, un' ingrata.*

Ungrateful ſoil, terra *ingrata, ſterile, infruttuoſa.*

Ungrateful [unpleaſant] *ingrato, nojoſo, ſpiacevole, faſtidioſo.*

UNGRA'TEFULLY, adv. [unthankfully] *ingratamente, con ingratitudine, ſconoſcentemente.*

Ungratefully [unpleaſantly] *ingratamente, nojoſamente, ſpiacevolmente.*

UNGRA'TEFULNESS, s. *ingratitudine, ſconoſcenza*, s. f.

Ungratefulneſs [unpleaſantneſs] *ſpiacevolezza*, s. f.

To UNGRA'VEL, *levar la ghiaja. Queſta è la propria ſignificazione di queſto verbo, ma figuratamente ſignifica levar gli ſcrupoli, rimovere gli ſcrupoli.*

To UNGRE'ASE, *levar il graſſo, toglier l' unto.*

UNGROUNDED, adj. [having no foundation] *malfondato, privo di fondamento.*

UNGRU'DGINGLY, adv. [without ill-will ; heartily ; cheerfully] *ſenza 'nvidia, ſenza mal volere, volonteroſamente, di buon cuore, lietamente.*

U'NGUENT, s. [ointment] *unguento*, s. m.

UNGUI'LTINESS, s. *innocenza.*

UNGUI'LTY, adj. [innocent] *innocente, non reo, non colpevole.*

UNHA'BITABLE, adj. [not fit to be inhabited] *inabitabile.*

UNHA'BITABLENESS, s. *lo ſtato d' un luogo inabitabile.*

To UNHA'FT, *levar il manico.*

UNHA'FTED, adj. *ſenza manico, ſmanicato.*

UNHA'LLOW [to profane] *profanare.*

UNHA'LLOWED, adj. *profanato.*

UNHA'LLOWING, s. *profanazione*, s. f. *il profanare.*

To UNHA'LTER, *levar a cavezza.*

To UNHA'ND, *laſciar andare* [unhand me, let me go] *laſciami andare.*

UNHA'NDSOME, adj. [ugly] *brutto, laido, deforme.*

Unhandſome [ugly, ungenteel] *ſcorteſe, incivile, ſgarbato.*

To give one unhandſome language, *maltrattare uno di parole, ingiuriarlo.*

UNHA'NDSOMELY, adv. *bruttamente, malamente, incivilmente, ſcorteſemente, ſgarbatamente.*

UNHA'NDSOMENESS, s. *bruttezza, laidezza, deformità.*

To UNHA'NG, *ſpiccare una coſa che è appiccata.*

To unhang a room, *ſpiccare le tapezzerie d' una camera.*

UNHA'PPILY, s. [unfortunately] *infelicemente, ſfortunatamente, ſgraziatamente.*

UNHA'PPINESS, s. *infelicità, ſfortuna, ſventura, diſgrazia*, s. f. *diſaſtro infortunio*, s. m.

UNHA'PPY, adj. [unlucky, unfortunate] *infelice, ſfortunato, ſgraziato.*

Unhappy [unlucky, full of malice] *cattivo, malizioſo.*

To UNHA'RBOUR [to rouze] *fare uſcire della tana, levare.*

To unharbour a deer, *levare un cervo.*

UNHA'RMFUL, adj. *innocente, che non è nocivo, che non può far male.*

UNHA'RMONIOUS, adj. *diſcordante, ſcordante, diſſonante.*

To UNHA'RNESS, *levar gli arneſi.*

To UNHA'SP, *ſfibbiare.*

UNHA'SPED, adj. *ſfibbiato.*

UNHE'ALABLE, adj. *incurabile.*

UNHE'ALED, adj. *che non è guarito.*

UNHE'ALTHFUL, adj. [ſickly] *malſano, malaticcio, infermiccio.*

Unhealthful [unwholſeſome] *malſano, contrario alla ſalute.*

Unhealthful place, *luogo malſano.*

UNHE'ALTHFULLY, adv. ex. He lives very unhealthfully, *egli è molto malaticcio.*

UNHE'ALTHFULNESS, s. [ſickneſs] *mala ſanità*, s. f.

The unhealthineſs of a place, *l' aria cattiva d' un luogo.*

UNHE'ALTHY, v. Unhealthful.

UNHE'ARD, adj. *inudito, inaudito, non più udito.*

UNHE'EDED, adj. [not minded] *non curato, non badato.*

UNHE'EDILY, adv. *negligentemente.*

UNHE'EDINESS, s. *negligenza, trascuraggine*, s. f.

UNHEEDING, adj [negligent, careless] *negligente, trascurato, che non bada, mentecatto, che non pon mente.*

UNHEE'DY, adj. [negligent] *negligente, trascurato.*

Unheedy, adj. [precipitate, sudden] *subito, precipitoso.*

To UNHELE [to uncover, to expose to view] *scoprire, esporre alla vista.*

UNHE'LPED, adj. [unassisted, having no auxiliary, unsupported] *non spalleggiato, non ajutato, non assistito, non soccorso.*

UNHI'DEBOUND, adj. [lax of maw, capacious] *che ha lo stomaco ampio, che è grande e capace.*

To UNHI'NGE, verb act. *sgangherare, cavar de gangheri, sconmettere*, pret. *scommessi.*

UNHI'NGED, adj. *sgangherato, scommesso.*

UNHO'LY, adj. *profano, empio.*

UNHO'NEST, adj. *disonesto, non onesto.*

To UNHO'ODWINK, verb act. *sbendare li occhi.*

To UNHO'OK, verb act. *spiccare dall' uncino.*

UNHO'OKED, adj. *spiccato dall' uncino.*

UNHO'PED for, adj. *non sperato, inaspettato.*

UNHOPE'FUL, adj. *che non da buona speranza.*

To UNHO'RSE, *scavalcare, levar di sella, buttar da cavallo.*

UNHO'RSED, adj. *scavalcato, smontato.*

UNHO'SPITABLE, *v.* Inhospitable.

UNHURT, adj. *illeso, che non è stato ferito, che non s' è fatto male.*

UNHU'SBANDED, adj. *incalto, che non è coltivato.*

To UNHU'SK, verb act. *sgranare, levare i legumi del guscio.*

UNHU'SKED, adj. *sgranato.*

UNICORN, s. [a beast said to have but one horn] *liccorno*, s. m. *animale che dicesi abbia un corno in fronte.*

UNI'FORM, adj. [regular, even] *uniforme, conforme, regolare, uguale, eguale.*

UNIFO'RMITY, s. *uniformità, conformità, uguaglianza*, s. f.

UNIFORMLY, adv. *uniformemente, con uniformità, conformemente, egualmente.*

UNIMA'GINABLE, adj. *che non si può immaginare.*

UNI'MITABLE, *v.* Inimitable.

UNIMPLO'YED, adj. [not used] *non usato, non adoperato.*

Unimployed [having nothing to do, idle] *ozioso, neghittoso, che non ha che fare, disimpiegato, senza impiego.*

UNINDE'BTED, adj. *che non ha debiti, che non è indebitato.*

UNINHA'BITED, adj. *disabitato, deserto.*

UNINSTITU'TED, adj. *che non è istituito.*

UNINTE'LLIGIBLE, adj. [not to be understood] *che non è intelligibile, oscuro.*

UNINTERE'STED, adj. *disinteressato.*

UNINTERMI'TTED, adj. *continuo, senza intermissione.*

UNINTERRUPTED, adj. *che non è interrotto.*

UNINTHRA'LLED, adj. *che è libero, che è padron di se stesso, che non è schiavo di nessuno.*

UNINTRE'ATABLE, adj. *inesorabile.*

UNINVITED, adj. *che non è invitato.*

U'NION, s. [the act of joining together, or the state of being joined together] *unione*, s. f. *accoppiamento*, s. m.

Union [concord] *unione, concordia*, s. f.

To UNJOI'N, verb, *disgiugnere, separare, disunire, spartire*, pret. *disgiunsi*, pres. *disunisco.*

UNJO'INED, adj. *disgiunto, separato, disunito, spartito.*

To UNJOINT [to cut at the joint] *tagliar le giunture.*

To unjoint [to put out of joint] *dislogare, sconciare, storcere.*

UNJO'INTED, adj. *dislogato, slogato, sconciato, storto.*

U'NISON, s. [a term of musick, the agreement of two notes in one] *unisono*, s. m. *termine musicale.*

U'NIT, s. [a term in arithmetick signifying one] *unità*, s. f. *il principio di tutti i numeri.*

Units, tens, hundreds, thousands, &c. *numero, decina, centinaja, migliaja, &c.*

UNI'TABLE, adj. *che si può unire.*

To UNI'TE [to join, to make one] *unire, congiugnere*, pres. *unisco*, pret. *congiunsi.*

UNI'TED, adj. *unito, congiunto.*

UNI'TING, s. *unione, congiunzione*, s. f. *congiugnimento*, s. m.

U'NITIVE, adj. [having the power of uniting] *che ha possa di unire; che ha virtù di congiungere; unitivo.*

U'NITY, s. *unità*, s. f.

Unity [union, concord] *unità, concordia, unione*, s. f.

UNIVE'RSAL, adj. [general] *universale, generale.*

To be an universal scholar, to have an universal knowledge, *avere una conoscenza universale di tutte le cose.*

Universal, s. [in logick, is that which is common to several things; a predicable] *un universale, un predicamento, termine di logica.*

UNIVERSA'LITY, s. *universalità, generalità*, s. f.

UNIVE'RSALLY, adv. *universalmente, in universale, comunemente, da per tutto.*

UNI'VERSE [the whole world] *universo, il mondo tutto.*

The universe [the earth] *l' universo, la terra.*

UNIVE'RSITY, s. [the whole in general] *universitá.*

University [in law, a body politick, corporation] *università, il comune, tutto'l popolo d' una città.*

University [a society of learned men established by public authority to learn languages, arts and sciences] *università, studio.*

An university-man, *un membro dell' università.*

UNI'VOCAL, adj. [consisting of one voice, sound, or name] *univoco.*

Univocal terms [in logick, are such whose name and nature is the same] *termini univoci.*

UNI'VOCALLY, adv. *d' una maniera univoca.*

UNJU'ST, adv. *ingiusto.*

An unjust act, *un' azione ingiusta.*

UN'JUSTICE, *v.* Injustice.

UNJUSTIFI'ABLE, adj. *illecito, che non si può giustificare.*

UNJUSTIFIA'BLENESS, s. *qualità, o stato d' una cosa illecita.*

UNJU'STLY, adv. *ingiustamente, a torto.*

To UNKE'NNEL, *far uscire*: to unkennel a fox, to force a fox from his hole, *fare uscire una volpe della sua tana.*

UNKI'ND, adj. [not kind] *scortese, rozzo, crudele, rigoroso, inumano.*

You are very unkind, *voi siete molto scortese.*

He is very unkind to me, *egli mi tratta malamente.*

A husband unkind to his wife, *un marito che non tratta bene sua moglie.*

Unkind usage, *cattivo trattamento.*

Why are you so unkind to me? *perchè mi trattate sì malamente.*

UNKI'NDLY, adv. *male, malamente, scortesemente, d' una maniera scortese.*

To take a thing unkindly, *prender a male che che sia.*

UNKI'NDNESS, s. *scortesia*, s. f. *cattivo trattamento.*

UNKI'ST, adj. *che non è baciato.*

U'NKLE, *v.* Uncle.

To UNKNI'T, *disfare, snodare.*

UNKNI'TTED, adj. *disfatto, snodato.*

UNKNO'WABLE, adj. [not to be known] *che non si può sapere.*

UNKNO'WING, adj. [ignorant] *ignorante.*

UNKNO'WINGLY, adv. *ignorantemente, senza saperlo.*

UNKNO'WN, adj. *incognito, sconsciuto, che non si sa chi sia, che non si conosce.*

He is unknown to me, *non lo conosco.*

It is unknown to me, *questo m' è nuovo, non lo so.*

To speak in an unknown tongue, *parlare in una lingua non intesa.*

Unknown to me, to you, to him, to us [without my, yours, his, or our knowledge] *senza mia, vostra, sua, o nostra saputa.*

Unknown to him [without his perceiving it] *senza accorgersene, inavvedutamente.*

UNLA'BOURED, adj. [untilled] *che non è coltivato, senza esser coltivato.*

Unlaboured [not elaborate] *non fatto con fatica e con attenzione.*

Unlaboured [spontaneous, voluntary] *spontaneo, volontario.*

To UNLA'CE, *slacciare, sciogliere cosa allacciata.*

UNLA'CED, adj. *slacciato, sciolto.*

To UNLA'DE [to disburden] *scaricare, alleggerir dal peso.*

To unlade [to lade out] *vuotare, votare.*

UNLA'DEN, adj. *scaricato, vuotato, votato.*

UNLA'ID, adj. [not placed; not fixed] *non collocato, non posto in determinato luogo.*

Unlaid [not pacified; not stilled] *non acquietato, non pacificato, non tranquillo.*

UNLAME'NTED, adj. [not deplored] *senza essere compianto, non compianto.*

To UNLA'TCH [to open by lifting up the latch] *aprire tirando su o alzando il saliscendo.*

UNLA'UDABLE, adj. [not commendable] *che non è lodevole, vituperevole.*

UNLA'WFUL, adj. *illecito, illegitimo, proibito dalla legge.*

UNLA'WFULLY, adv. *illecitamente, illegittimamente.*

UNLA'WFULNESS, s. *lo stato d' una cosa illecita.*

To UNLE'ARN [to forget what one has learned] *disapparare, disapprendere, scordarsi, dimenticarsi,* pret. *disappresi.*

UNLE'ARNED, adj. *disapparato, disappreso, scordato dimenticato.*

Unlearned [illiterate, ignorant] *non letterato, ignorante, idiota.*

An unlearned man, *un idiota, un ignorante.*

UNLE'ARNEDLY, adv. *da ignorante, da idiota, ignorantemente.*

UNLE'ARNT, adj. [unlearned] *disapparato, disappreso, scordato, dimenticato.*

To UNLE'ASH [to let go] *sciorre, e dicesi de' i cani.*

To UNLE'AVE [to pluck off the leaves] *sbrucare, levar via le foglie, sfrondare.*

UNLE'AVED, adj. *sbrucato, sfrondato.*

UNLE'AVENED, adj. *senza fermento, senza lievito, azzimo.*

UNLE'SS, conjunct. [except; if not; supposing that not] *a meno; se non; eccetto; eccettuato che; supponendo che non; supposto che non.*

UNLE'SSONED, adj. [not taught] *senza aver avuto insegnamento o suggerimento.*

UNLE'TTERED, adj. [illiterate] *idiota, ignorante, senza lettere.*

UNLIBI'DINOUS, adj. [not lustful] *non libidinoso, non lascivo.*

UNLI'CENSED, adj. *stampato o fatto senza licenza.*

UNLI'KE, adj. *differente, dissimigliante, dissimile, vario, diverso.*

They are very unlike, *sono molto differenti, sono assai dissimili.*

This is so unlike a gentleman, *questa condotta è tanto indegna d' un gentiluomo.*

UNLI'KENESS, s. *dissimiglianza, differenza, disagguaglianza.*

UNLI'KELY, adj. *che non è verisimile, improbabile.*

Unlikely, adv. *non verisimilmente, improbabilmente.*

UNLI'KENESS, s. *differenza, disagguaglianza, dissimiglianza.*

UNLI'MITED, adj. *che non è limitato, illimitato.*

To UNLI'NE [to take off the lining] *levar via la fodera, sfoderare.*

UNLI'NED, adj. *sfoderato, senza fodera.*

To UNLO'AD, *scaricare, alleggerir del peso.*

UNLO'ADED, adj. *scaricato, alleggerito.*

To UNLO'CK, *schiavare, aprire.*

To unlock one's bosom to a friend, *sfogarsi, dire i suoi segreti, guai ad un amico.*

UNLO'CKT, } adj. *schiavato, aperto.*
UNLO'CKED, }

UNLO'OKED for, adj. *non previsto, inopinato, subito.*

To UNLO'OSE, *disfare, slegare, sciorre.*

To unloose a question, *spiegare una quistione.*

UNLO'OSED, adj. *disfatto, slegato, sciolto.*

UNLO'VELY, adj. *che non è amabile, sgraziato, svenevole, sguajato.*

UNLU'CK, s. [ill luck] *disgrazia, disavventura.*

UNLU'CKILY, adv. *per mala fortuna, disgraziatamente, per disgrazia.*

UNLU'CKINESS, s. [misfortune] *disgrazia, disavventura,* s. f. *infortunio,* s. m.

UNLU'CKY [untoward] *sinistro, malaguroso.*

Unlucky [mischievous] *maligno, cattivo, malizioso.*

UNLU'STROUS, adj. [wanting splendour, wanting lustre] *privo di splendore, che non è lucido.*

To UNLU'TE [to open vessels closed with chymical cement] *aprire vasi che eran chiusi chimicamente.*

UNMA'DE, adj. *che non è fatto, che non è finito.*

To UNMA'N [to geld] *castrare.*

To unman [to soften] *effeminare, far divenire effeminato.*

To unman [to degrade] *degradare.*

To unman a ship, *disarmare un vascello.*

To unman [to enfeeble, to soften] *indebolire, intenerire.*

UNMA'NAGEABLE, adj. [hard to be managed] *che non si può maneggiare, difficile a maneggiare o governare.*

A unmanageable affair, *un negozio difficile a maneggiare.*

UNMA'NAGED, adj. [not broken by horsemanship] *non addestrato dal cavalerizzo; e dicesi d' un cavallo.*

Unmanaged [not tutored, not educated] *non educato, che non ha avuto insegnamenti.*

UNMA'NLINESS, s. *condotta indegna d' un uomo.*

UNMA'NLY, adj. *indegno d' un uomo.*

UNMA'NNED, adj. *castrato, effeminato, degradato, disarmato.*

UNMA'NNERLINESS, s. *inciviltà, rozzezza, rusticità, mala creanza, scostumatezza,* s. f.

UNMA'NNERLY, adj. *malcreato, scostumato, incivile, rozzo, rustico.*

Unmannerly, adv. *incivilmente.*

UNMANU'RED, adj. *che non è coltivato, non coltivato, incolto.*

To UNMA'RRY, *rompere il matrimonio.*

UNMA'RRIED, adj. [single] *scapolo, smogliato, nubile, senza marito.*

To UNMA'SK, *smascherare, levar la maschera.*

UNMA'SKED, adj. *smascherato, senza maschera.*

To UNMA'ST, *levar l' albero del vascello.*

UNMA'STED, adj *senza albero.*

To UNMA'TCH, *spajare.*

UNMA'TCHED, adj. *spajato.*

UNME'ASURABLE, adj *che non si può misurare, immenso, eccessivo, smisurato.*

UNME'ASURABLENESS, s. *immensità, smisuratezza,* s. f.

UNME'ASURABLY, adv. *smisuratamente, senza misura, eccessivamente.*

UNME'ASURED, adj. *smisurato, immenso.*

UNME'ET, adj. *che non è conveniente, che non è convenevole.*

UNME'LLOWED, adj. [not fully ripened] *non affatto maturo.*

UUME'RCIFUL, adj. [cruel] *spietato, crudele, barbaro, inumano.*

UNME'RCIFULLY, adv. *spietatamente, crudelmente, barbaramente, inumanamente.*

UNME'RCIFULNESS, s. *crudeltà, inumanità, barbarie,* s. f.

UNME'RITED, adj. [not deserved, not obtained otherwise than by favour] *non meritato, non ottenuto che per favore.*

UNME'RITABLE, adj. [having no desert] *immeritevole, che non ha alcun merito.*

UNMI'NDED, adj. *negletto, non osservato.*

UNMI'NDFUL, adj. *negligente, trascurato.*

UNMI'NDFULNESS, s. *negligenza, trascurataggine, trascuraggine,* s. f.

UNMI'NGLED, } adj. *semplice, schietto, puro, che non è composto, mescolato, o misto.*
UNMI'XT, }

UNMOLE'STED, adj. *che non è molestato, senza esser molestato.*

To UNMO'OR a ship [a sea phrase, to weigh anchor] *salpare, sarpare, levar l' ancore.*

UNMO'ORED, adj. *salpato, sarpato.*

UNMO'VABLE, adj *fermo, immobile, stabile.*

UNMO'VEABLENESS, s. *fermezza, stabilità, immobilità* s. f.

UNMO'VEABLY, adv. *fermamente, stabilmente, immobilmente.*

UNMO'VED, adj. *immobile.*

Unmoved [not affected] *che non è tocco.*

To UNNA'IL, *schiodare.*

UNNA'ILED, adj. *schiodato.*

UNNA'TURAL, adj. [preternatural, against nature] *sopranaturale, che è contra natura, che non è conforme alla natura, che non è naturale.*

Unnatural [void of natural affection] *inumano, barbaro, snaturato, crudele, spietato.*

UNNATURALLY, adv. [against nature].

ture] *contra natura, soprannaturalmente, contro le regole della natura.*

Unnaturally [without natural affection] *inumanamente, barbaramente.*

UNNATURALNESS, s. *inumanità, barbarie*, s. f.

UNNA'VIGABLE, adj. *che non è navigabile*

UNNE'CESSARILY, adv. *senza veruna necessità.*

UNNE'CESSARY, adj. *inutile, che non è necessario.*

UNNE'EDFUL, adj. [needless, unnecessary] *inutile, che non è necessario.*

UNNO'BLE, v. Ignoble.

UNNUMBERED, adj. *che non è numerato o contato.*

UNNU'MERABLE, v. Innumerable.

UNOBE'DIENT, adj. *disubbidiente.*

UNO'CCUPIED, adj. *che non è occupato.*

UNOFFI'CIOUS, v. Inofficious.

UNO'RDERLY, v. Disorderly.

UNO'RDINARY, adv. [uncommon] *raro,*

UNO'RGANISED, adj. *che non è organizzato.*

To UNPA'CK, *sballare, aprire o disfare le balle.*

UNPA'ID, adj. *che non è pagato.*

I am upaid to this day, *non sono ancora pagato.*

UNPA'INED, adj. [suffering no pain] *che non soffre pena o dolore.*

UNPA'INFUL, adj. [giving no pain] *non doloroso, che non da dolore.*

UNPA'INTED, adj. *che non è dipinto.*

UNPA'LATABLE, adj. [nauseous, disgustful] *nauseoso, che disgusta il palato, spiacevole al palato.*

UNPA'RALLELLED, adj. *incomparabile, che non ha simile.*

UNPA'RDONABLE, adj. *irremissibile, che non è degno di perdono, che non si deve perdonare.*

UNPA'RED, adj. *che non è mondato.*

UNPA'RTABLE, adj. *inseparabile, indivisibile.*

UNPA'RTABLY, adv. *inseparabilmente indivisibilmente.*

UNPA'RTED, adj. *che non è separato, che non è diviso, indiviso.*

UNPA'STURED, adj. *a chi non s' è dato pascolo, che non ha avuto di che pascere,*

UNPA'TIENT, v. Impatient.

UNPA'TTERNED, adj. *senza esempio.*

To UNPA'VE, *disfare il selciato.*

UNPE'ACEABLE, adj. *che non è pacifico o tranquillo, torbido, agitato.*

UNPE'ACEABLY, adv. *in disordine, torbidamente.*

To UNPE'OPLE, *spopolare.*

UNPE'OPLED, adj. *spopolato.*

UNPERCE'IVABLE, adj. *impercettibilmente, d' una maniera impercettibile.*

UNPERCE'IVED, adj. *del quale uno non s' è accorto.*

UNPERCE'IVEDLY, adv. [so as not to be perceived] *impercettibilmente, senza essere visto.*

UNPE'RFECT, v. Imperfect.

UNPERFO'RMED, adj. *che non è stato messo in esecuzione.*

UNPE'RISHABLE, adj. *incorruttibile.*

To UNPE'STER, *sviluppare, sgombrare.*

UNPE'STERED, adj. *sviluppato, sgombrato.*

To UNPI'N, *toglier via le spille.*

UNPI'TIED, adj. *del quale non s' ha pietà, che non è compianto.*

To UNPLA'IT, *spiegare, togliere o aprir le pieghe.*

UNPLA'ITED, adj. *spiegato.*

UNPLEA'SANT, adj. *ingrato, spiacevole, nojoso che dispiace.*

UNPLE'ASANTLY, adv. *ingratamente, spiacevolmente, nojosamente.*

He looked very unpleasantly upon me, *mi guarda di mal occhio.*

UNPLE'ASANTNESS, s. *spiacevolezza*, s. f.

UNPLI'ANT, adj. *inflessibile, che non si può piegare.*

UNPLI'ANTNESS, s. *inflessibilità*, s. f.

UNPLO'WED, adj *che non è arato, che non è lavorato, che è inculto.*

UNPO'LISHED, adj. *rozzo, non ripulito, ruvido.*

A rude unpolished person, *una persona rozza o zotica.*

UNPO'LLUTED, adj. *intemerato, puro, che non è polluto.*

UNPRA'CTISED, adj. [not practised, not used] *non praticato, non usato, che non è in uso.*

UNPRAC'TISED, [unskilful] *inesperto, soro, che non è versato.*

UNPREFE'RRED, adj. *che non è preferito o avanzato.*

UNPRE'GNABLE, adj. *inespugnabile.*

UNPREJU'DICATED, adj. *che non è preoccupato o prevenuto.*

UNPRE'JUDICED, adj. *che non è prevenuto o preoccupato.*

UNPREME'DITATED, adj. *che non è premeditato, senza essere premeditato, improvviso.*

UNPREPA'RED, adj. *che non è preparato, senza esser preparato.*

UNPREPA'REDNESS, s. *lo stato d' una persona che non è preparata.*

UNPREPOSSE'SSED, adj. *che non è preoccupato o prevenuto.*

UNPRE'SSED, adj. *che non è stato spremuto.*

UNPRETE'NDED, adj. *non preteso.*

UNPRI'SABLE, adj. [unvaluable] *inestimabile.*

UNPRO'FITABLE, adj. [vain, useless] *inutile, vano.*

Unprofitable [of no profit] *che non è profittevole o vantaggiojo.*

UNPRO'FITABLENESS, s. *inutilità*, s. f.

UNPRO'FITABLY, adv. *inutilmente, in vano.*

UNPRONO'UNCED, adj. *che non si pronuncia.*

A vowel unpronounced, *una vocale che non si pronuncia.*

UNPROPO'RTIONABLE } adj. *sproporzionato.*
UNPROPO'RTIONED, }

UNPROPORTIONABLY, adv. *sproporzionatamente.*

UNPRO'SPEROUS, adj. *infelice, che non prospera.*

UNPRO'SPEROUSLY, adv. *infelicemente.*

UNPRO'VED, adj. *che non è provato, o esperimentato.*

UNPRO'VIDED, adj. *sprovvisto.*

To take one unprovided, *corre alcuno improvvisamente, all' improvviso.*

UNPROVIDENT, adj. *imprudente.*

UNPRO'VIDENTLY, adv. *imprudentem nte.*

UNPROVO'KED, adj. *non provocato, senza esser provocato.*

UNPRU'NED, adj. [not cut, not lopped] *non potato, non cimato, non tagliato.*

UNPU'NISHED, adj *impunito.*

UNQUA'LIFIED, adj. *che non è atto, che non è capace, che non ha le qualità necessarie.*

UNQU'ENCHABLE, adj. *inestinguibile, che non si può estinguere.*

UNQUE'NCHED, adj. *che non è estinto.*

UNQUE'STIONABLY, adj. *indubitabile, incontestabile.*

A man of unquestionable reputation, *un uomo d' intera fede.*

UNQUE'STIONABLENESS, s. *certezza*, s. f.

UNQUE'STIONABLY, adv. *indubitatamente, certamente, senza dubbio.*

UNQUI'ET, adj. [not quiet, uneasy] *inquieto, senza quiete, travagliato, commosso, tribolato.*

To have an unquiet mind, *aver la mente inquieta.*

UNQUI'ETLY, adv. *inquietamente, senza quiete.*

UNQUI'ETNESS, s. [restlessness] *inquietudine, passione, tribolazione*, s. f. *travaglio, affanno*, s. m.

UNRA'CKED, adj. [not poured from the lees] *non torchiato, non ispremuto dalle fecce col torchio.*

Unracked [not thrown together and covered] *non ammucchiato e coperto, non ammassato col rastrello.*

UNRANSA'CKED, adj. [not pillaged] *non saccheggiato, non posto a sarcomanno; non ricercato minutamente; non violato, non deflorato.*

To UNRA'VEL [to clear] *sviluppare, schiarire.*

UNRA'VELLED, adj. *sviluppato, schiarito.*

UNRA'ZORED, adj. [unshaven] *che non ha la barba fatta, che non ha avuta la faccia tocca ancora dal rasojo.*

UNRE'ADINESS, s. *lo stato d' una cosa o d' una persona che non è in ordine. Non in uso.*

UNRE'ADY, adj. [not ready] *che non è in ordine.*

Unready [not drest] *che non è vestito.*

An unready horse, *un cavallo restio.*

UNRE'ASONABLE, adj. *irragionevole, senza ragione, che non ha ragione.*

Unreasonably [unjust] *irragionevole, ingiusto.*

UNRE'ASONABLENESS, s. [folly] *poca ragione, follia, pazzia*, s. f.

Unreasonableness [injustice] *ingiustizia*, s. f.

UNRE'ASONABLY, adv. [without reason] *d' una maniera irragionevole, irragionevolmente, senza ragione.*

Unrea-

Unreasonably [unjustly] *irragionevolmente, ingiustamente.*

Unreasonably [excessively] *troppo, eccessivamente.*

UNREBU'KABLE, adj. *irreprensibile.*

UNREBU'KED, adj. *che non è stato ripreso, censurato, o biasimato.*

UNRECA'LLABLE, adj. *irrevocabile.*

UNRECA'LLABLY, adv. *irrevocabilmente.*

UNRECLA'IMED, adj. *che non è ridotto o messo alla ragione.*

UNRECO'NCILEABLE, adj. *irreconciliabile, implacabile.*

UNRECONCI'LED, adj. *che non è riconciliato.*

UNRECO'VERED, adj. *che non è ricuperato.*

UNREDE'EMABLE, adj. *che non si può redimere, che non possi riscattare.*

UNREDE'EMED, adj. *che non è riscattato.*

UNREFO'RMABLE, adj. *che non si può riformare, incorreggibile.*

UNREFO'RMED, adj. *che non è riformato, che è sregolato.*

UNREGA'RDED, adj. [slighted] *negletto, disprezzato.*

UNREGA'RDFUL, adj. *negligente, pigro.*

UNRELE'NTING, adj. *inflessibile, inesorabile, che non si lascia piegare.*

An unrelenting heart, *un cuore inflessibile, un cuor duro.*

UNRELI'EVED, adj. *che non è soccorso.*

UNRE'PARABLE, adj. *irreparabile.*

UNREPA'IRED, adj. *che non è riparato, non risarcito.*

UNREPE'ALED, adj. *che non è abolito, che è ancora in forza, in vigore.*

UNREPE'NTED, adj. [not regarded with penitential sorrow] *non pentito di peccato.*

UNREPE'NTING, } adj. [not repent-
UNREPE'NTANT } ing, not penitent] *che non si pente; che non s' è pentito; che non è penitente; che non è venuto o non viene ancora a penitenza; impenitente.*

UNREPRO'VABLE, adj. *irriprensibile.*

UNREPRO'VED, adj. *che non è ripreso, che non è sgridato, non è corretto.*

UNREQUI'TED, adj. *irremunerato, non rimunerato.*

UNRESI'STABLE, adj. *al quale non si può resistere, irresistibile.*

UNRESI'STED, adj. *al quale non s' è fatta resistenza.*

UNRESPE'CTFUL, adj. *che manca di rispetto, malcreato, screanzato, incivile, irriverente.*

UNRESPE'CTFULLY, adv. *d' una maniera poco rispettosa, incivilmente, irriverentemente.*

UNRESPE'CTFULNESS, s. *mala creanza, inciviltà, irriverenza.*

UNRE'ST, s. [disquietedness] *inquietudine, s. f.*

UNRESTORE'D, adj. *non restituito.*

UNRETU'RNABLE, adj. *che non può ritornare.*

UNREVE'ALED, adj. *che non è stato rivelato.*

UNREVE'NGED, adj. *invendicato, inulto.*

UNREWA'RDED, adj. *non rimunerato, non premiato.*

To UNRI'DDLE, *spiegare, sviluppare, scoprire, dichiarare, palesare.*

UNRI'DDLED, adj. *spiegato, sviluppato, scoperto, dichiarato, palesato.*

To UNRI'G [a sea term] *toglier le sarte*, ex. To unrig a ship, *toglier le sarte d' un vascello.*

UNRI'GHTEOUS, adj. *iniquo, ingiusto, empio.*

UNRI'GHTEOUSLY, adv. *iniquamente, ingiustamente, empiamente.*

UNRI'GHTEOUSNESS, s. *iniquità, ingiustizia, empietà.*

To UNRI'P, *scucire, squarciare.*

UNRI'PE, adj. *immaturo, che non è maturo.*

UNRI'PENESS, s. *lo stato d' una cosa che è immatura.*

UNRI'PT, adj. *scucito, squarciato.*

UNRI'VALLED, adj. *che non ha rivale.*

To UNRO'LL, *sviluppare.*

UNRO'LLED, adj. *sviluppato.*

To UNRO'OST, *snidare.*

UNRO'OSTED, adj. *snidato.*

To UNRO'OT, *sradicare, svellere, sbarbare, sbarbicare, strappar dalle radici.*

UNRO'OTED, adv. *sradicato.*

UNRU'LILY, adv. *sregolatamente, disordinatamente, sfrenatamente.*

UNRU'LINESS, s. *sregolatezza, sfrenatezza, irregolarità, s. f. disordine.*

UNRU'LY, adj. *indomito, sregolato, sfrenato, licenzioso, scapestrato.*

An unruly horse, *un cavallo indomito, sfrenato.*

An unruly passion, *una passione sregolata, una passione violenta.*

To UNSA'DDLE, *levar la sella.*

UNSA'DDLED, adj. *senza sella.*

UNSA'FE, adj. *pericoloso, che non è sicuro.*

UNSA'FELY, adv. *pericolosamente, con pericolo.*

UNSA'ID, adj. [from to unsay] *disdetto.*

UNSA'LTED, adj. *non salato.*

UNSALU'TED, adj. *non salutato, senza esser salutato.*

UNSA'NCTIFIED, adj. *che non è santificato, profano.*

UNSATISFA'CTORY, adj. *imperfetto, che non sodisfà.*

An unsatisfactory answer, *una risposta imperfetta, ambigua, che non sodisfà.*

UNSATISFI'ABLE, adj. *insaziabile, che non si può saziare o contentare.*

UNSA'TISFIED, adj. *mal sodisfatto, mal contento, che non è sodisfatto.*

UNSA'VOURILY, adv. *d' una maniera insipida, insipidamente.*

UNSA'VOURINESS, s. *insipidezza, scipitezza, s. f.*

UNSA'VOURY, adj. [tasteless] *insipido, sciapito, senza gusto.*

To UNSA'Y [to recant] *disdirsi, ritrattarsi, negar la cosa detta.*

To unsay a thing, *disdirsi d' una cosa.*

To UNSCA'LE, *scagliare, levar le scaglie a' pesci.*

UNSCA'LED, adj. *scagliato.*

UNSCRI'PTURAL, adj. [not prescribed in the holy scripture] *che non è fondato nella scrittura sacra.*

To UNSE'AL, *levare il sigillo.*

To unseal a letter, *aprire una lettera.*

UNSEA'RCHABLE, adj. *imperscrutabile, impenetrabile, che non si può intenere, nè ricercare.*

UNSE'ARCHABLENESS, s. *qualità imperscrutabile.*

UNSE'ASONABLE, adj. *fuor di stagione, che non è di stagione, intempestivo.*

Unseasonable weather, *un tempo che non è di stagione.*

To keep unseasonable hours, *ritirarsi a casa a ore indebite.*

UNSE'ASONABLENESS, s. *lo stato d' una cosa che è fuor di stagione.*

UNSE'ASONABLY, adv. *fuor di stagione, intempestivamente.*

UNSE'ASONED, adj. [unseasonable, untimely, ill-timed, out of use] *fuor di stagione, intempestivo, inopportuno, mal a proposito, fuor d' uso.*

Unseasoned [unformed, not qualified for use] *di mala forma, non approvato dalla gente.*

Unseasoned [irregular, inordinate] *irregolare, sregolato, disordinato, in mal ordine.*

Unseasoned [not salted] *non condito con sale, insipido, che non ha sale.*

UNSECO'NDED, adj. [not supported] *non assistito, non spalleggiato.*

Unseconded [not exemplified a second time] *che non ha esempio dopo.*

UNSECU'RE, adj. *che non è sicuro, che è in pericolo, che corre richio.*

UNSE'EMLINESS, s. *indecenza, s. f.*

UNSE'EMLY, adj. *indecente, disdicevole, sconvenevole.*

UNSE'EN, adj. *invisibile, che non si vede, che non s' è veduto, senza esser veduto.*

UNSE'NT for, adj. *che non s' è mandato a cercare.*

UNSE'RVICEABLE, adj. [of no use] *inutile, che non serve a niente, che non può servire.*

UNSE'RVICEABLENESS, s. *inutilità, s. f.*

UNSE'T, adj. *che non è piantato, senza esser piantato.*

UNSE'TTLED, adj [not settled, speaking of liquors] *che non è riposato, parlando de' liquori.*

Unsettled [inconstant, fickle] *incostante, volubile.*

Unsettled [that has no settlement in the world] *che non è stabilito, che non ha stabilimento alcuno.*

UNSE'TTLEDNESS, s. *lo stato d' una cosa che non è riposata, incostanza, volubilità.*

To UNSHA'CKLE, *scatenare.*

UNSHA'CKLED, adj. *scatenato.*

UNSHA'DED, adj. *scoperto, aprico, che non è ombrato.*

UNSHA'KEN, adj. [not shaken, not moved

moved] *che non è smosso.*

Unshaken [not to be shaken] *immobile, costante, fermo.*

A man of an unshaken fidelity, *un uomo d' una costante fedeltà.*

UNSHAMEFA'CED, adj. *sfacciato, sfrontato.*

UNSHAMEFA'CEDNESS, s. *sfacciataggine, sfacciatezza.*

UNSHA'PEN, adj. *deforme, sproporzionato, malfatto.*

UNSHA'VED or UNSHA'VEN, adj. *che non è raso, che non è sbarbato.*

To UNSHEA'TH, *sguainare, cavar dalla guaina.*

UNSHE'ATHED, adj. *sguainato.*

UNSHO'D, adj. [without shoes] *scalzo, a piedi nudi, senza scarpe.*

Unshod [as a horse] *sferrato.*

To U'NSHOE a horse, *sferrare un cavallo.*

UNSHO'RN, adj. *che non è tonduto.*

UNSI'GHT UNSE'EN, adv *alla cieca, cogli occhi chiusi.*

To buy a thing unsight unseen, *comprare una cosa senza vederla.*

UNSI'LVERED, adj. *che non è inargentato.*

UNSINCE'RE, adj. *che non è sincero, finto, dissimulato.*

UNSI'NNING, adj [perfect] *perfetto, senza peccato.*

UNSKI'LFUL, adj. *che non è versato, inesperto, inabile, ignorante, insufficiente.*

UNSKI'LFULLY, adv. *male, malamente, da ignorante.*

UNSKI'LFULNESS, s. *ignoranza, inesperienza, insufficienza.*

To UNSLO'UGH, ex. To unslough a wild boar, *lanciare un cinghiale, farlo uscire del suo covo.*

UNSO'CIABLE, adj. *che non ama la compagnia, solitario.*

UNSOCIA'BLENESS, s. *umore solitario.*

UNSO'DDEN, *non bollito.*

UNSO'LD, adj. *non venduto.*

UNSOI'LED, adj. *non isporco, netto, pulito.*

To UNSO'LDER, *levare la saldatura.*

To UNSO'LE, *levar le suola.*

To unsole a shoe, *levar le suola d'una scarpa.*

UNSO'LD, adj *non solido.*

UNSOLLI'CITED, adj. *non sollecitato, senza esser sollecitato.*

UNSO'UGHT, adj. *non ricercato.*

UNSO'UND, adj. [unhealthy] *malsano, malatticcio.*

Unsound [corrupt, rotten] *corrotto, guasto, putrefatto.*

Unsound wood, *legno fracido.*

To UNSO'W, *scucire.*

UNSO'WED, adj. *scucito.*

UNSPE'AKABLE. adj. *ineffabile, indicibile, che non si può con parole esprimere.*

UNSPE'AKABLY, adv. *ineffabilmente, indicibilmente.*

UNSPE'CIFIED, adj. [not particularly mentioned] *non mentovato distintamente, non menzionato particolarmente.*

UNSPE'D, adj. [not dispatched, not performed] *non ispedito, non ispacciato, non fatto.*

UNSPE'NT, adj. *che non è speso o consumato.*

To UNSPHE'RE [to remove from its orb] *rimuovere dalla sua sfera, togliere del suo orbe.*

UNSPI'ED, adj. [not discovered, not seen] *non ispiato, non visto, non iscoperto.*

UNSPI'LT, adj. [not shed] *non versato fuora; e dicesi de' liquori dal verbo versare.*

Unspilt [not spoiled] *non guasto, intatto.*

To UNSPI'RIT [to dispirit, to depress, to deject] *scoraggire, far perder l' animo altrui.*

UNSPO'ILED, adj. [not plundered, not pillaged] *non saccheggiato, non posto a saccomanno.*

Unspoiled [not spoiled] *non guasto, intatto.*

UNSPO'KEN of, adj. *del quale non s' è parlato.*

UNSPO'TTED, adj. *puro, senza macchia, immaculato, intatto.*

UNSTABI'LITY, s. [instability] *istabilità, inconstanza.*

UNSTA'BLE, adj. [instable] *istabile, volubile, inconstante.*

U'NSTABLY, } adv. *istabilmente,*
UNSTA'BLELY, } *leggiermente.*

UNSTA'INED, adj. *senza macchia, puro, netto, immaculato.*

UNSTA'YED, adj. *volubile, leggiero, incostante.*

UNSTA'YEDNESS, s. *leggerezza, volubilità, inconstanza.*

UNSTE'ADILY, adv. *leggiermente, volubilmente.*

UNSTE'ADINESS, s. *leggerezza, incostanza, volubilitá.*

UNSTE'ADY, adj. [not steady, fickle, uncertain] *non fermo, leggiero, incostante, debole, che non ha fermezza.*

Unsteady motion, *moto irregolare.*

UNSTE'DFAST, adj. *volubile, incostante, leggiero.*

UNSTE'DFASTLY, adv. *senza fermezza.*

UNSTE'DFASTNESS, s. *inconstanza, leggerezza, volubilità.*

UNSTI'RRED, adj. *non mosso.*

To UNSTI'TCH, *scucire.*

UNSTI'TCHED, adj. *scucito.*

To UNSTO'CK a gun [to take its stock off] *smontare uno schioppo.*

To UNSTO'P [to open] *sturare.*

UNSTO'PPED, } adj. *sturato.*
UNSTO'PT, }

UNSTRI'CKEN, adj. *che non è stato battuto*

UNSTRU'NG, adj. *che non ha corde, scordato.*

UNSTU'FFED, adj. *che non ha ripieno.*

UNSUBDU'ED, adj. *che non è vinto o soggiogato.*

UNSUCCE'SSFUL, adj. *che non è riuscito, che non ha avuto buon successo, sventurato, malaguroso, infelice.*

UNSUCCE'SSFULLY, adv. *senza successo, senza riuscita.*

UNSUCCE'SSFULNESS, s. *sventura, infelicità, mal successo.*

UNSU'FFERABLE, adj. *insopportabile, intollerabile.*

UNSU'FFERABLY, adv. *insopportabilmente, intollerabilmente.*

UNSU'LLIED, adj. *non isporco, puro, netto, immaculato.*

UNSU'RE, adj. *incerto, non sicuro.*

UNSU'RELY, adv. *incertamente, d' una maniera incerta.*

UNSU'RENESS, s. *incertezza.*

UNSURMO'UNTABLE } adj. *insuper-*
UNPA'SSABLE } *abile, invincibile.*

UNSU'TEABLE, adj. *inconveniente, indecente, sconvenevole, che non conviene.*

UNSU'TEABLENESS, s. *inconvenienza, indecenza, sconvenevolezza, incongruità*

To UNSWA'THE, } *sfasciare.*
To UNSWA'DDLE, }

To unswathe a child, *sfasciare un bambino.*

To UNSWE'LL, *sgonfiare, sgonfiarsi.*

UNSWO'RN, adj. *che non ha prestato giuramento.*

UNTA'INTED, adj. [not tainted, sweet] *che non è corrotto, che non ha cattivo odore.*

UNTA'INTED [unspotted] *netto, puro, immaculato, senza marchia.*

UNTA'KEN, adj. *che non è preso.*

UNTA'MEABLE, adj. *indomabile, da non potersi domare.*

UNTA'MEABLENESS, s. *qualità indomabile.*

UNTA'MED, adj. *indomito, non domato, terribile, fiero, non domo.*

To UNTA'NGLE, *distrigare, strigare, dichiarare, avviare.*

UNTA'NGLED, adj. *distrigato, strigato, dichiarato, avviato.*

UNTA'STED, adj. *che non è stato assaggiato o gustato.*

UNTA'UGHT, adj. *che non è stato insegnato, senza maestro.*

To UNTE'ACH, *fare scordare, insegnare il contrario di quello che uno ha imparato, far disimparare.*

UNTE'ACHABLE, adj. *che non vuole imparare, indocile.*

To UNTE'AM [to unteam horses] *levare i cavalli dalla carrozza o dal carro.*

UNTE'MPTED, adj. [not embarrassed by temptation] *che non è tentato, che non soffre tentazione peccaminosa.*

Untempted [not invited by any thing alluring] *non allettato, non invitato da cosa che alletti o che dia speranza di vantaggio o di diletto.*

UNTE'RRIFIED, adj. *intrepido, coraggioso, che non teme.*

UNTE'STATE, adj. [without making a will] *intestato, senza testamento.*

UNTHA'NKFUL, adj. *ingrato, sconoscente.*

An unthankful man, *un ingrato.*

UNTHA'NKFULLY, adv. *ingratamente, sconoscentemente.*

UNTHA'NKFULLNESS, s. *ingratitudine, sconoscenza,* s. f.

UNTHA'WED, adj. *che non è dighiacciato.*

To

To UNTHI'CKEN, *render meno ſpeſſo, rarificare.*

To Unthicken, *rarificarſi.*

UNTHI'CKENED, adj. *rarificato.*

UNTHI'NKING, adj. *indiſcreto, imprudente, ſenza penſiero, ſpenſierato.*

UNTHO'UGHT of, adj. *impenſato, inopinato, non penſato.*

To UNTHRE'AD, ex. to unthread a needle, *sfilare un ago.*

UNTHRI'FT, adj. *prodigo, ſcialaquone, ſviato, ſpendereccio.*

UNTHRI'FTILY, adv. *prodigamente, ſcialacquatamente.*

UNTHRI'FTINESS, s. *prodigalità*, s.f. *ſcialacquo*, s. m.

UNTHRI'FTY, adj. *prodigo, ſcialacquante.*

UNTHRI'VING, adj. *che non creſce, che non va innanzi.*

To UNTHRO'NE, *levar dal trono, toglier la corona, privar del regnò.*

To UNTI'E, *ſlegare, ſciogliere, ſnodare*, pret. *ſciolſi.*

UNTI'ED, adj. *ſlegato, ſciolto, ſnodato.*

To UNTI'LE a houſe, *ſcoprire il tetto d' una caſa.*

UNTI'LED, adj. *ſcoperto.*

UNTI'L, adv. *lo ſteſſo che* Till.

UNTI'LLED, adj. *inculto, non coltivato.*

UNTI'MBERED, adj. [not furniſhed with timber; weak] *non ſoſtenuto da groſſi o forti pezzi di legno o travi; debole.*

UNTI'MED, adj. *fatto fuor di tempo.*

UNTI'MELINESS, s. *lo ſtato d' una coſa che ſi fa fuor di tempo o in tempo indebito.*

UNTI'MELY, adv. [unſeaſonably] *intempeſtivo, fuor di tempo.*

Untimely death, *morte intempeſtiva.*

Untimely [haſty, before the time] *primaticcio.*

Untimely fruit, *frutto primaticcio.*

An untimely birth, *ſconciatura.*

UNTI'REABLE, adj. *infaticabile, indefeſſo.*

UNTO, prep. [to]

And he ſaid unto him, *ed egli gli diſſe.*

UNTO'LD, adj. [not ſaid] *non detto.*

Untold [not counted] *non contato, non numerato.*

He took the money untold, *egli preſe il danaro ſenza contarlo.*

UNTO'OTHSOME, adj. *che non è grato al guſto.*

UNTO'UCHABLE, adj. *che non ſi può toccare.*

UNTO'UCHED, adj. *intatto, non toccato, non tocco.*

UNTO'WARD, adj. [unruly, ſtubborn] *cattivo, malvagio, oſtinato, caparbio.*

Untoward [unlucky, ſcurvy; ſad] *cattivo, perverſo, maligno, ſiniſtro.*

This is an untoward buſineſs, *queſto è un cattivo negozio.*

To paſs an untoward judgment upon one, *giudicare ſiniſtramente d' uno.*

UNTO'WARD [aukward] *ſcioperato, diſadatto, ſgarbato.*

UNTO'WARDLY, adj. [ſtubbornly] *oſtinatamente.*

Untowardly [unluckily] *ſiniſtramente, cattivamente, infelicemente.*

Untowardly [aukwardly] *ſgarbatamente, ſcioperatamente.*

Untowardly [againſt the grain, unwillingly] *contro voglia, mal volentieri.*

UNTO'WARDNESS, s. [ſtubbornneſs] *oſtinazione, caparbietà, perverſità, caponeria.*

UNTRA'CTABLE, *v.* Intractable.

To UNTRA'P, *levar gli arneſi.*

UNTRI'MMED, adj. [not adorned] *che non è ornato o abbellito.*

Untrimmed [unſhaved] *che non è raſo.*

UNTRO'D, } adj. *che non è calpeſtato.*
UNTRO'DDEN, }

UNTRO'UBLED, adj. *che non è intorbidato, che non è reſo torbido.*

UNTRU'E, adj. [not true, falſe] *che non è vero, falſo.*

Untrue [falſe, treacherous] *infedele, infido, ſleale, traditore, perfido.*

UNTRU'ELY, adv. *falſamente.*

To UNTRU'SS, *ſciogliere.*

UNTRU'SSED, adj. *ſciolto.*

UNTRU'STINESS, *perfidia, ſlealtà, infedeltà*, s. f.

UNTRU'STY, adj. *perfido, traditore, malvagio, ſleale.*

UNTRU'TH, s. [lie] *falſità, menzogna, bugia*, s. f.

To UNTU'CK, verb act. *calare.*

UNTU'CKED, adj. *calato.*

UNTU'NEABLE, adj. *ſcordante, che ſcorda.*

UNTU'RNED, adj. *che non è voltato.*

To leave no ſtone unturned [to uſe all poſſible means] *fare ogni sforzo, porre ogni ingegno o ſtudio.*

UNTU'TORED, adj. *che non è ſtato ripreſo.*

To UNTWI'NE, } *ſtorcere*, pret. *ſtorſi.*
To UNTWI'ST, }

To untwine, or untwiſt, *ſtorcerſi.*

UNTWI'NED, } adj. *ſtorto.*
UNTWI'STED, }

To U'NTY, *v.* To untie.

To UNVA'IL, verb act. *ſvelare, levar il velo, ſcoprire.*

UNVA'ILED, adj. *ſvelato, ſcoperto.*

UNVA'LUABLE, adj. *ineſtimabile, ſenza prezzo.*

UNVA'LUED, adj. [not prized, neglected] *negletto, non curato, diſprezzato.*

Unvalued [ineſtimable, above price] *ineſtimabile, ſenza prezzo, maggior d' ogni valore.*

UNVA'NQUISHED, adj. *invitto, indomito.*

UNVA'RIABLE, adj *invariabile, non variabile.*

UNVA'RIABLENESS, s. *qualità invariabile, immutabilità.*

UNVA'RIABLY, adv. *d' una maniera invariabile, immutabilmente.*

UNVA'RIED, adj. *che non ha variato.*

UNVE'RSED, adj. *che non è verſato, ineſperto.*

UNU'SEFUL, adj. *inutile.*

UNU'SUAL, adj. [uncommon, extraordinary] *inuſitato, inſolito, ſtraordinario.*

UNU'SUALLY, adv. *inuſitatamente, raramente, di rado.*

UNU'SUALNESS, s. *rarità*, s. f.

UNU'TTERABLE, adj. *ineffabile, indicibile, inenarrabile.*

UNWA'LLED, adj. *ſenza mura, che non ha mura.*

A town unwalled, *una città ſenza mura.*

UNWA'RILY, adv. *imprudentemente, inaccortamente, inconſideratamente.*

UNWA'RINESS, s. *imprudenza, inaccortezza, ſconſideratezza.*

UNWA'RRANTABLE, adj. *che non ſi può giuſtificare.*

UNWA'RY, adj. *imprudente, ſconſiderato, ſenza conſiderazione.*

UNWA'SHED, adj. *ſporco, lordo, che non è lavato, ſenza eſſer lavato.*

UNWA'STED, adj. *che non è conſumato.*

UNWA'TERED, adj. *che non è adacquato.*

UNWA'VERING, adj. *fermo, ſodo, che non vacilla.*

UNWE'ARIED, adj. [refreſhed] *riposato.*

Unwearied [indefatigable] *infaticabile, indefeſſo.*

UNWE'ARIEDLY, adv. *infaticabilmente.*

UNWE'ARINESS. } s. *diligenza infaticabile.*
UNWE'ARIEDNESS }

To UNWE'AVE, *sfilare.*

To unweave linen, *sfilare della tela.*

UNWE'DDED, adj. *che non è maritato, che è ſcapolo, che è nubile.*

UNWE'LCOME, adj. *che non è ben venuto.*

Unwelcome [unpleaſant] *ſpiacevole, rincreſcevole, nojoſo, faſtidioſo.*

Unwelcome news, *cattive novelle, ſpiacevoli nuove.*

UNWE'PT, adj. [not lamented, not bemoaned] *non pianto, non compianto.*

UNWHI'PT, adj. [not puniſhed, not corrected] *non punito, non corretto, non fruſtato.*

UNWHO'LSOME, adj. *malſano, contrario alla ſanità.*

UNWIE'LDINESS, s. *lenta, grave, groſſa e penſante coſa.*

UNWIE'LDILY, adv. *lentamente, pigramente, con poca o nulla attezza.*

UNWIE'LDY, adj. [over heavy] *peſante, lento, che non ſi può maneggiar bene.*

UNWI'LLING, adj. *che non ha inclinazione di fare una coſa, che non ha voglia.*

He is very unwilling to come, *non ha buona volontà di venire.*

I am very unwilling to trouble you, *m' increſce incomodarvi.*

Willing or unwilling you muſt do it, *biſogna farlo, vogliate o non vogliate.*

I found him very unwilling to do it, *l' ho trovato mal diſpoſto a farlo.*

UNWI'LLINGLY, adj. *mal volentieri, contro voglia, contro la inclinazione, di mala voglia.*

UNWI'LLINGNESS, s. *ripugnanza, mancanza di volontà, ritroſia.*

To Unwi'nd [to get out, to disintangle] *distrigare, strigare.*

Unwi'se, adj. *imprudente, mal' accorto, poco cauto, sciocco, insensato.*

Unwi'sely, adv. *imprudentemente, malaccortamente, scioccamente.*

Unwi'shed, adj. *che non si desidera, non desiderato, non bramato.*

To Unwi't [to deprive of understanding] *cavar del senno, toglier la mente, privar d' intelletto.*

Unwi'therable, adj. *che non può appassire, immarcescibile, incorruttibile.*

Unwi'thered, adj. *che non è appassito, incorrotto.*

Unwi'tting, adj. *che non sa, che ignora.*

Unwitting to me, *senza la mia saputa.*

Unwi'ttingly, adv. *senza saperlo, inavvertentemente, per inavvertenza.*

Unwi'ttily, adv. *pazzamente, scioccamente.*

Unwi'tty, adj. *sciocco, scioperato, insensato.*

Unwo'nted, adj *insolito, che non è solito o comune, raro.*

Unwo'ntedness, s. *rarità, novità.*

Unwo'rn, *che non è usato, che non è stato portato addosso.*

Unwo'rthily, adv. *indegnamente.*

Unwo'rthiness, s. [want of merit] *indegnità, mancanza di merito.*

Unworthiness [indignity, baseness] *indegnità, viltà, infamia.*

Unwo'rthy, adj. [not worthy, not deserving] *indegno, immeritevole, che non è degno.*

I am unworthy of these favours, *non son degno di questi favori, non merito queste grazie.*

'Tis a thing unworthy of you, *è una cosa indegna d' un par vostro.*

Unworthy [ill, base] *indegno, cattivo, vile, infame.*

Unworthy action, *azione indegna, indegnità, viltà.*

Unwo'ven, adj. [unravelled] *sfilato.*

Unwoven [not woven] *che non è tessuto.*

To Unwra'p [to unfold] *sviluppare.*

Unwra'ped, adj. *sviluppato.*

To Unwre'ath, verb act. *storcere, contrario di torcere, pret. storsi.*

To Unwri'ng, *storcere, contrario di torcere.*

To unwring, verb neut. *storcersi.*

To Unwri'nkle, *levar via le rughe.*

Unwri'tten, adj. *non iscritto, che non è scritto.*

Unwro'ught, adj. *crudo, che non è lavorato*, ex. Unwrought silk, *seta cruda.*

Unyi'elded, adj [not given up] *non rinunciato, non ceduto.*

Unyi'elding, adj. *inflessibile, che non cede.*

Unyielding rigour, *rigore inflessibile.*

To Unyo'ke, *levar dal giogo, disgiogare, sciorre dal giogo.*

To unyoke oxen, *levare i buoi dal giogo, togliere il giogo a' buoi.*

To unyoke one's self out of bondage or slavery, *scuotere il giogo, mettersi in libertà.*

Voca'bulary, s. [dictionary, word-book] *vocabolario, s. m. raccolta di vocaboli, dizionario.*

Vo'cal, adj. [belonging to the voice] *vocale, di voce.*

Vocal and instrumental musick, *musica vocale, e istrumentale.*

Vocal prayer, *preghiera vocale.*

Voca'lity, s. *qualità di quel che è vocale.*

Voca'tion, s. [call, employ] *vocazione, s. f. arte, mestiere, impiego, esercizio, s. m.*

Vo'cative, adj. ex. The vocative case, or the vocative, s. [in grammar] *il caso vocativo o il vocativo.*

Vocifera'tion, s. [bawling, crying] *vociferazione, s. f.*

Voci'ferous, adj. [clamorous, noisy] *remoroso, che fa troppo romore.*

Vogue [esteem, credit] *voga, stima, riputazione, s. f. credito, concetto. s. m.*

To be in vogue, *esser in voga, in istima, in credito.*

A thing in vogue [a thing in fashion] *una cosa alla moda.*

Vo'ice, s. [a sound that comes out of the mouth] *voce, s. f.*

With a loud voice, *ad alta voce.*

With a low voice, *sotto voce, con voce sommessa.*

The voice of God [a scripture expression, for the command of God] *la voce di Dio, la parola, il comandamento di Dio.*

The inward voice of the spirit, *l' ispirazione dello spirito santo.*

Voice [vote, suffrage] *voce, voto, suffragio.*

To give one's voice, *dar il voto.*

Voice [approbation] *voce, approvazione.*

To Vo'ice [to proclaim] *pubblicare, gridare.*

To voice it high and loud, *pubblicarlo ad alta voce.*

Vo'iced, adj. *pubblicato, gridato.*

Void, adj. [empty] *voto, col primo O aperto.*

A void space or place, *spazio, o luogo voto.*

Void [vacant] *vacante, vacuo, voto.*

Void [deprived of] *voto, sprovvisto, manchevole, privo.*

A man void of sense, *un uomo privo di senno.*

A discourse void of sense, *un discorso vano.*

Void [of no effect] *nullo, invalido.*

The contract is void, *il contratto è nullo.*

To make void a law, *annullare una legge.*

Void, s. [empty space] *il voto, il vano, la concavità vacua, il vacuo.*

To Void [to go out, to depart from] *votare, lasciare, partirsi, abbandonare.*

To void the town, *votar la terra.*

To void the kingdom, *partirsi dal regno.*

To void, *mandar fuor gli escrementi, scaricar il ventre.*

Voida'ble, adj. [such as may be annulled] *da poter essere annullato o reso nullo.*

Vo'idance, s. [want of an incumbent or clerk in possession of a benefice] *vacanza di beneficio.*

Vo'ided, adj. *votato, v.* To void.

Vo'ider, s. [table basket] *canestro.*

Vo'iding, s. *votamento, il votare.*

Vo'iture, s. [carriage] *vettura, cocchio, calesse, e simili.*

Vola'cious, adj. [with philosophers, apt to fly] *volatile, atto a volare.*

Vo'lant, adj. *volante, che vola.*

The volant animals, *i pennuti, gli uccelli, tutti gli animali che volano.*

A camp volant, *un campo volante.*

Vola'tica, s. [tetter] *volatica, empitiggine, s. f.*

Vo'latile, adj. [in chemistry, apt to evaporate or resolve itself into air] *volatile.*

Volatile salt, *sale volatile.*

Vo'latiles, s. [living creatures which fly in the air as birds do] *i volatili, gli uccelli.*

Volati'lity, s. *volatilità.*

Vo'lery, s. [a great bird-cage where there is room for them to fly up and down] *uccelliera, s. f.*

To Vo'litate [to fly, to flutter up and down] *svolazzare.*

Voli'tion, s. [the act of willing] *volontà, velleità.*

Vo'lley, s. [shout] *acclamazione, s. f. grido, s. m.*

A volley of musket shot, *una salva di moschettate.*

A volley [at random] *inconsideratamente, a tastone.*

Vo'lta, s. [in horsemanship, a bounding turn] *volta.*

Volubi'lity, s. [aptness to roll] *volubilità, facilità a voltarsi.*

The volubility of a wheel, *la volubilità d' una ruota.*

Volubility of tongue, *volubilità, prestezza di lingua.*

Vo'luble, adj. [easily rolled, or nimble in speech] *volubile, leggiero, presto.*

Vo'lume, s. [part of a book] *volume, s. m. parte distinta di libro.*

Volume [a poetical expression for wave] *onda.*

Volu'minous, adj. [bulky] *voluminoso, grosso, parlando d'un libro.*

Volu'ntarily, adv. *volontariamente, di proprio volere, spontaneamente.*

Volu'ntary, adj. [free, that is done without compulsion] *volontario, spontaneo.*

Voluntary, s. [a voluntary action] *azione volontaria.*

Voluntary [in musick, that which a musician plays extempore] *capriccio, termine musicale.*

Vo'lunteer, s. [one who serves voluntarily in wars] *volontario, s. m.*

VOLU'PTUARY, s. [a voluptuous man] *uomo voluttuoso.*

VOLU'PTUOUS, adj. [sensual] *voluttuoso, sensuale.*

VOLU'PTUOUSLY, adv. *voluttuosamente, sensualmente.*

VOLU'PTUOUSNESS, s. [sensual pleasures] *voluttà, sensualità,* s. f. *piaceri sensuali.*

VO'MIT, s. [a potion to cause vomit] *vomitivo,* s. m.

Vomit [vomiting] *vomito,* s. m. *il vomitare.*

To VO'MIT [to cast up] *vomitare, rerere.*

VO'MITED, adj. *vomitato.*

VO'MITING, s. *vomito, il vomitare.*

VO'MITORY, adj. [that causes or provokes vomit] *vomitivo, che ha virtù di far vomitare.*

Vomitory, s. *vomitivo.*

VORA'CIOUS, adj. [ravenous, greedy] *vorace, ingordo, goloso, avido, rapare.*

Voracious beast, *bestia rapace.*

Voracious man, *uomo vorace.*

Voracious stomach, *stomaco vorace, ingordo.*

VORA'CIOUSLY, adv. *voracemente, ingordamente, golosamente, avidamente, rapacemente.*

VORA'CIOUSNESS, } s. [greediness,
VORA'CITY, } gluttony] *voracità, ingordigia, golosità, ghiottornia, rapacità,* s. f.

VO'RTEX, *plurale* vortices [any thing whirled round] *vortice.*

VO'RTICAL, adj. [having a whirling motion] *che s' aggira impetuosamente come vortice.*

VO'TARIST, s. [one devoted to any person or thing] *colui che tiene ostinatamente o religiosamente da una persona o da una cosa.*

VO'TARY, s. [one who has bound himself to the performance of a religious vow] *un devoto, una devota, un religioso, una religiosa, qualunque persona, che abbia fatto voto di religione.*

A votary of love, *un' amante, un' amanza.*

A votary of learning, *una persona del tutto dedita alle lettere.*

Votary, adj. [consequent to a vow] *fatto in conseguenza d' un voto.*

VOTE, s. [voice, suffrage] *voto, col primo O stretto, suffragio,* s. m. *voce,* s. f.

Vote [advice, opinion, deliberation] *voto, opinione,* s. f. *sentimento, parere,* s. m.

VOTES [the things voted for, the resolutions of an assembly] *le risoluzioni, le deliberazioni d' una assemblea che decide le cose per la pluralità delle voci.*

To VOTE [to give one's vote] *dar la sua voce o suffragio, dire la sua opinione, il suo parere.*

To vote [to resolve by the majority of votes] *stabilire, risolvere, conchiudere per pluralità di voci.*

VO'TED, adj. [resolved] *risoluto, stabilito, conchiuso.*

Voted for, *per chi s' è data la voce.*

Voted against, *contro chi s' è dato il suffragio.*

To VOUCH [to avouch, to affirm, to maintain] *affermare, mantenere, accertare, asserire,* pres. *mantengo, asserisco.*

I'll vouch this horse for a good horse, *vi mantengo questo cavallo per buono.*

To vouch one [in law, to call him to court to make good his warrant] *citare o chiamare uno in giudicio, per rispondere alla sua malleveria.*

To vouch for one [to certify in one's behalf, to pass his word for him] *comprommettersi per qualcheduno, entrar mallevadore per lui.*

VOU'CHED, adj. *affermato, mantenuto, accertato, asserito,* v. To vouch.

VOUCHE'E, s. [a person vouched for] *colui che è citato o chiamato in giudizio per far buona la sua malleveria.*

VO'UCHER, s. [he that vouches one at law] *colui che chiama un altro in giudicio per far buona la sua malleveria.*

To VO'UCHSAFE [to condescend, to be pleased to] *degnarsi, compiacersi,* pret. *mi compiacqui.*

To vouchsafe [to grant] *concedere, dare, accordare.*

Vouchsafe us the grace of the Holy Spirit, *concedici la grazia dello Spirito Santo.*

VOUCHSA'FEMENT, } *condescendenza, il degnarsi.*
VOUCHSA'FING; }

Vow [religious promise] *voto, boto,* s. f. *promessa solenne fatta a Dio.*

To make a vow, *fare un voto, votare, botare.*

To Vow [to make a vow] *botare, e votare, fare un volto.*

To vow chastity, *far voto di castità.*

To vow a temple to God, *dedicare un tempio a Dio.*

To vow [to swear, to protest, to assure] *giurare, protestare, assicurare, promettere.*

I vow 'tis very good, *vi giuro che è molto buono.*

I vow I am in the wrong, *ho torto sicuramente.*

VO'WED, adj. *botato, votato.*

VO'WEL, s. [a single sounding letter] *una vocale.*

VOWFE'LLOW, s. [one bound by the same vow] *colui che ha fatto lo stesso voto che tu.*

VO'YAGE, s. [a passage by sea] *viaggio,* s. m. *l' andare e il venire per mare, l' andar per terra si dice travel.*

To go a long voyage, *fare un lungo viaggio per mare.*

To VO'YAGE [to go by sea] *fare viaggio per mare.*

VO'YAGER, s. *viaggiatore per mare.*

UP, adv. *su, in su.*

To look up, *guardare in su.*

Up there, *la su.*

Up [not sitting] *in piedi, ritto.*

To stand up, *stare in piedi, rizzarsi, levarsi.*

Up on end, *in piedi ritto.*

It makes my hair stand up on end, *mi fa inorridire, mi fa arricciare i capelli.*

To be up [to be risen from bed] *essere in piedi, esser levato del letto.*

To be up [to sit no longer] *essere finito.*

The parliament is up, *il parlamento è finito.*

How many games up? *a quanti giuochi va la partita?* five up, *a cinque giuochi.*

I am up [at play] *ho guadagnato.*

To get up, *salire, montare.*

To get up a tree, *salire sur un albero.*

To get up stairs, *andar su, salir le scale, montar le scale.*

To be in the water up to the chin, *esser nell' acqua fin al mento.*

Up one pair of stairs, *al primo appartamento.*

To run up and down, *andar qua e la, su e giu.*

To follow one up and down, *seguitare alcuno per tutto.*

To go up hill, *montare, salire una collina.*

Up hill, *in su.*

My blood is up, *il sangue mi bolle nelle vene.*

Drink it up, *bevetelo tutto.*

To come up to town, *ritornare in città.*

The river is frozen up, *il fiume è tutto gelato.*

To do up a letter, *piegare una lettera.*

To rise up, *levarsi, rizzarsi.*

Up, interj. [a word exhorting to rise from bed] *su. Voce con cui si esorta uno a uscir di letto, a non dormir di più.*

Up [a word of exhortation, exciting or rousing to action] *su. Voce con cui si esorta o eccita altrui ad operare o a mostrar valore e coraggio.*

To UPBE'AR [to sustain aloft, to support in elevation] *sostenere in alto, tener sospeso in atto.*

To upbear [to raise aloft] *alzare, mandar in alto.*

To upbear [to support from falling] *sostener uomo o cosa onde non caschi.*

To UPBRA'ID [to charge contemptuously with any thing disgraceful] *svillaneggiare; accusar uno in dispregevole atto di cosa vituperosa da lui commessa; vilipendere.*

To upbraid [to reproach] *rimproverare, rinfacciare, buttare in occhio.*

UPHE'LD, adj. [from to uphold] *sostenuto, mantenuto, favorito, appoggiato, spalleggiato.*

To UPHO'LD [to support, to maintain, to favour] *sostenere, mantenere, favorire, spalleggiare, proteggere,* pres. *sostengo, mantengo, favorisco,* pret. *sostenni, mantenni, protessi.*

UPHO'LDER, s. *fautore, che tien su.*

UPHO'LDING, s. *mantenimento, protezione.*

The upholding of a ballad [the burden of it] *ritornello.*

UPHO'LSTERER, s. *tapezziere, colui che fa e vende paramenti da camere, e che fa i letti.*

Upla'nd, s. [high-ground] *montagne, paese montagnoso.*

Upla'nder, s. *montanaro*, s. m.

Upmost, *v.* Uppermost.

Upo'n, prep. *su, sopra.*

Upon the bed, *su 'l letto.*

Upon the table, *sopra la tavola.*

Upon [next, near] *vicino, a canto, a lato.*

London is seated upon the Thames, *Londra siede sul Tamigi.*

Upon [about, towards] *per, presso, incirca.*

She is upon her departure, *ella sta per partire, ella è in procinto di partire.*

Upon the news of his coming, *alla novella della sua venuta.*

Upon a mere suspicion, *per un semplice sospetto.*

Upon my word, *sopra la mia parola.*

Upon my conscience, *in coscienza mia.*

Upon pain of death, *sotto pena della vita.*

To send message upon message, *mandar messaggi sopra messaggi.*

A bill upon a merchant, *una lettera di cambio sopra un mercante.*

Upon the first opportunity, *per la prima opportunità.*

Upon his coming, *al suo arrivò.*

Upon the right or left hand, *a man dritta, a man sinistra.*

I did it upon his motion, *l' ho fatto a sua richiesta.*

Resolved upon a thing, *risoluto a qualche cosa.*

To make war upon one, *far la guerra ad uno.*

Upon any occasion, *in ogni occasione.*

To be upon a journey, *esser in viaggio.*

Come upon a Sunday, *venite una Domenica.*

Upon that very day, *quell' istesso giorno.*

He could not prove it upon me, *non l' ha potuto provare contro di me.*

To depend upon one, *far capitale d'uno.*

He grew fat upon it, *questo l' ingrassò.*

To take a servant upon trial, *prender un servo a prova.*

Upon a full perusal of my writing, *esaminate ch' ebbi le mie scritture.*

Upon the whole matter, or upon the whole, *del resto, in fine.*

He has been upon an embassy to the king of France, *egli è stato in ambasciata appresso il re di Francia.*

To call upon, *invocare.*

I shall call upon you tomorrow, *io sarò da voi domani.*

To look upon, *riguardare, mirare.*

Questa preposizione unita con un verbo partecipa della significazione di detto verbo.

To fall upon the enemies, *assalire i nemici.*

To fall upon one, *avventarsi sopra uno.*

To think upon, *considerare, riflettere, pensare.*

U'pper, adj. *alto, superiore.*

Upper room, *camera alta.*

The upper Germany, *la Germania superiore.*

The upper lip, *il labbro di sopra.*

The upper teeth, *i denti di sopra.*

The upper-hand [advantage] *vantaggio, superiorità.*

U'ppermost, adj. *il più alto, il più elevato.*

To be uppermost [to prevail, to have the advantage] *restar superiore, vincere, superare.*

The uppermost seats, *i primi luoghi.*

Upri'ght, adj. [in opposition to lying or sitting] *ritto, in piedi.*

Upright [honest, sincere] *onesto, giusto, sincero, leale, schietto, candido, diritto.*

Upri'ghtly, adv *dirittamente, e drittamente, convenevolmente, giustamente, onestamente, sinceramente, lealmente, schiettamente, condidamente, con candore.*

Upri'ghtness, s. *dirittura, drittura, lealtà, sincerità, candidezza, equità, schiettezza*, s. f. *candore*, s. m.

U'prise, s. [appearance above the horizon] *il sorgere l' apparire, il mostrarsi, o l' alzarsi all' orizzonte.*

To U'prise [to rise from decumbiture] *alzarsi, sorgere, torsi da giacere.*

To uprise [to rise from below the horizon] *apparire all' orizzonte, mostarsi all' orizzonte, sorgere, alzarsi.*

Upro'ar, s. [great noise, great bustle] *tumulto, strepito, romore, fracasso, frastuono, rombazzo*, s. m.

To Uproar [to throw into confusion] *metter in confusione, mandar sozzopra*

To U'prouse [to weaken from sleep; to excite to action] *svegliar altrui dal sonno, eccitare, incoraggire, incorraggiare.*

U'pshot, s. [issue, end, success] *esito, fine, evento, successo*, s. m.

Upon the upshot, *in fine, alla fine de' fini.*

Up'side down, adv. *sotto sopra, sossopra, sozzopra.*

Upsi'tting, s. [a woman's upsitting that laid in of a child] *il tempo che una donna si leva di parto.*

U'pspring, s. [a man suddenly exalted] *uomo diventato gran cosa repentinamente.*

To U'pstart [to spring up suddenly] *saltar sù repentinamente.*

U'pstart, } s. *villan rifatto.*
Upsta'rt-man, }

To U'pstay [to sustain, to support] *sostenere, tener dritto in piedi, spalleggiare.*

To U'pswarm [to raise in a swarm] *alzarsi in folla come uno sciame d' api.*

To U'ptake [to take into the hands] *pigliare nelle mani.*

To U'ptrain [to bring up, to educate] *allevare, educare.*

To U'pturn [to throw up, to furrow] *gittar sù, svolgere, formar solco.*

Upwa'rd, } adv. *in su.*
Upwa'rds, }

To fly upward, *volare in su.*

Upwards and downwards, *per di sopra e per di sotto.*

It amounts to ten pounds and upwards, *monta a dieci lire e più.*

Upward, s. [the top] *la punta, la cima, il sommo, la sommità.*

Urba'nity, s. [civility] *urbanità, gentilezza, civiltà*, s. f.

U'rchin, s. [hedge-hog] *riccio*, s. m.

Urchin [dwarf] *nano.*

Ure, s. [use, custom] *uso, costume*, s. m. ex. to put one's self in ure [to accustom one's self] *accostumarsi, avvezzarsi, assuefarsi.*

Brought in ure, *accostumato, avvezzato, avvezzo, assuefatto.*

To keep in ure, *esercitare.*

To keep one's self in ure, *esercitarsi.*

Ure ox [a kind of wild ox] *spezie di bufalo.*

U'reter, s. [a membranous vessel, which conveys the urine from the reins to the bladder] *uretra, canale dell' urina.*

To Urge [to press, to sollicit] *sollecitare, fare istanza, stimolare, strignere, rincalzare, instigare*, pres. *stringo*, pret. *strinsi.*

To urge [to incense, to provoke, to exasperate] *incitare, eccitare, irritare, inasprire, provocare*, pres. *inasprisco.*

U'rged, adj. *sollecitato, stimolato*, *v.* To urge.

U'rgency, s. [pressure of difficulty] *urgenza, stimolo, strignimento*

U'rgent, adj. [pressing] *urgente, che preme.*

Upon urgent occasions, *nelle urgenti necessità.*

U'rgently, adv. *istantemente, con istanza, ardentemente, strettamente.*

Urgewo'nder, s. [a sort of grain] *sorta di grano.*

U'rging, adj. *urgente.*

U'rinal, s. *orinale*, s m.

U'rinary, adj. *dell' orina*, ex. the urinary passage, *il canale dell' orina.*

Urina'tor, s. [a diver] *pescatore, colui che si tuffa nel mare per pescare qualche cosa.*

U'rine, s. [the animal water] *orina*, s. f.

To provoke urine, *fare orinare.*

To U'rine [to make water] *orinare.*

Urn, s. [a sort of pitcher in use among the ancients to preserve the ashes and bones of the dead] *urna.*

U'rsulines, s. pl. [a sort of nuns] *orsoline*, s. f. pl.

Us, *è un caso del pronome personale* we, *noi.*

He told us, *ci disse.*

This is for us, *questo è per noi.*

With us, *con noi.*

U'sage, s. [use, practice, custom] *uso, costume*, s. m. *usanza*, s. f.

Use [habit] *costume, abito.*

Usage [treatment] *trattamento, maniera di trattare.*

Kind or unkind usage, *buono o cattivo trattamento.*

What usage did you find? *come siete stato trattato?*

U'SAGER, s. [one who has the use of any thing in trust for another] *colui a cui è permesso l' uso di cosa confidatagli da altri.*

U'SANCE, s. [a term used among merchants, for the space of time between any day of the month and the same day of the next following, which time is generally allowed for payment of a bill of exchange] *uso.*

To pay a bill of exchange at double usance, *pagare una lettera di cambio a due usi.*

USE, s. *uso, serviglio.*

This is for my use, *questo è per mio proprio uso.*

To make a good use of a thing, *servirsi a bene d' una cosa, profittarne, prevalersene.*

I gave him good advice, but he did not make good use of it, *gli ho dato buoni consigli, ma egli non ha saputo valersene.*

Your book has been of great use to me, *il vostro libro mi è stato d' un gran giovamento.*

To make an ill use of a thing, *servirsi male d' una cosa, abusare d' una cosa.*

To make use of [to employ, to use] *mettere in uso, servirsi.*

Charitable uses, *usi pij.*

Use [employment of a thing for a while] *uso.*

Use [usage, custom] *uso, costume,* s. m. *usanza,* s. f.

'Twas the use of those times, *era l' uso, era il costume di quei tempi.*

A word received into use, or a word in use, *una parola usata.*

Use [practice, exercise] *usanza, pratica,* s. f. *esercizio, uso,* s. m.

To put a thing into use, *mettere che che sia in uso o in pratica.*

Use [habit, custom] *costume, abito.*

Use [interest of money] *uso, interesse.*

To put one's money to use, *mettere il suo danaro ad uso, ad interesse.*

Use-money, *interesse.*

Use [usefulness, utility, service] *uso, vantaggio, servizio, utilità.*

It will be of great use, *questo sarà di grande utilità, questo sarà molto utile.*

A thing of no use, *una cosa inutile, di nessuno giovamento.*

To make use of [to improve] *servirsi, prevalersi.*

Make use of my service, *servitevi dell' opera mia.*

To USE [to make use of] *usare, servirsi, mettere in uso, adoperare.*

To use remedies, *usare rimedi.*

To use a word, *usare una parola, servirsene, metterla in uso.*

To use exercise, *fare esercizio.*

To use one well or ill, *trattare uno bene o male.*

To use one ill, *maltrattare uno, trattarlo male.*

I'll use you as you were my own brother, *vi tratterò da fratello.*

To use one to a thing, *avvezzare uno a qualche cosa.*

To use a place, *usare, praticare, frequentare, bazzicare in un luogo.*

To use the sea, *frequentare il mare.*

To use [to be wonted, to be accustomed] *solere, esser solito.*

Do as you used to do, *fate come solete, fate come siete solito di fare.*

I don't use to do so, *io non sono solito di far così.*

It is but what you used to do, *è il vostro costume.*

U'SED, adj. *solito, accostumato, avvezzato, avezzo.*

A word that is used, *una parola usata, che è in uso.*

U'SEFUL, adj. [profitable] *utile, vantaggioso, profittevole.*

Useful [necessary] *utile, necessario.*

To make one's self useful, *rendersi utile, rendersi necessario.*

U'SEFULLY, adv. *utilmente, necessariamente, profittevolmente, d' una maniera utile, vantaggiosamente.*

U'SEFULNESS, *utilità, profitto, vantaggio, comodo.*

U'SELESS, adj. [answering no purpose; having no end] *inutile, di nessun uso, buono a nulla.*

U'SELESSLY, adv. [without the quality of answering any purpose] *inutilmente, senza utilitade alcuna.*

U'SELESSNESS, s. [unfitness to any end] *inutilità.*

U'SER, s. [one who uses] *uno che fa uso di cosa.*

U'SHER, s. [a lady's gentleman-usher] *bracciere d' una dama.*

Usher [under-master in a school] *sotto maestro.*

Usher [the door-keeper of a court] *portinajo, usciere.*

To U'SHER in [to introduce] *introdurre,* pref. *introduco,* pret. *introdussi.*

To usher one in, *introdurre alcuno, farlo entrare.*

To usher in a new doctrine, *introdurre una nuova dottrina.*

U'SHERED in, adj. *introdotto.*

U'SEQUEBAUGH, s. [a strong cordial] *sorta di liquor forte, o d' acquavite.*

USTO'RIOUS, adj. [having the quality of burning] *ustorio, che ha virtù d' ardere.*

U'SUAL, adj. [common, ordinary, accustomed] *ordinario, comune, frequente, solito, consueto, usato.*

In the usual manner, *al solito.*

U'SUALLY, adv. *communemente, ordinariamente, generalmente, d' ordinario, per la maggior parte del tempo.*

U'SUALNESS, *il frequente uso di che che sia.*

The usualness of the danger has made him lose the fear of it, *è talmente usato a' pericoli che non li teme più.*

U'SUFRUCT, s. [enjoyment of the profits without power to alienate] *usufrutto.*

USUFRU'CTUARY, s. [one who has the use and profit of a thing, but not the property and right] *usufruttuario, colui che ha l' usufrutto.*

To U'SURE [to practise usury; to take interest for money] *dar a usura.*

U'SURER, s. [one who lends upon usury] *usurajo, che da o presta ad usura.*

USU'RIOUS, adj. [belonging to usury] *che contiene usura.*

An usurious contract, *un contratto usurajo.*

To USU'RP [to take wrongfully] *usurpare, occupare ingiustamente l' altrui.*

USURPA'TION, s. *usurpazione,* s. f.

USU'RPED, adj. *usurpato.*

USU'RPER, s. *usurpatore,* s. m. *usurpatrice,* s. f.

USU'RPING, s. *usurpamento,* s. m. *l' usurpare, usurpazione,* s. f.

USU'RPINGLY, adv. [without just claim] *senza dritto, senza avervi su ragione.*

U'SURY, s. [an unreasonable and unlawful profit] *usura,* s. f.

To lend upon usury, *usureggiare, fare usura, dar ad usura.*

I shall pay you with usury, *ve la renderò, o la pagherete con usura.*

UT, s. [one of the chief musical notes] *ut, nota musicale.*

U'TAS, s. [a word used in the return of writs, and signifies the eighth day following any term or festival] *l' ottava, l' ottavo giorno.*

U'TENSIL, s [any thing that serves for use, a necessary implement or tool] *ordigno, strumento, arnese.*

U'TERINE, adj. [of the same mother] *uterino.*

UTI'LITY, s. [use, benefit, profit] *utilità,* s. f. *pro, comodo, giovamento, utile, profitto,* s. m.

UTLA'RY, } *v.* Outlawry.
UTLAWRY, }

UTMO'ST, adj. *il più remoto, l' ultimo.*

The utmost parts of the earth, *le parti più remote della terra.*

I'll do my utmost endeavours, *farò ogni mio sforzo.*

I'll serve him to the utmost of my power, *vi servirò in tutto quel che potrò.*

Utmost, s. ex. I shall do my utmost, *farò ogni possibile, opererò con ogni mio sforzo.*

U'TTER, adj. [total] *totale, intero.*

To U'TTER [to speak forth] *proferire, pronunciare.*

To utter [to tell, discover, or express] *manifestare, esprimere, scoprire, palesare, dire.*

To utter one's mind or thoughts, *dire il suo sentimento, manifestare la propria mente.*

To utter [to vend, to sell] *vendere, spacciare.*

U'TTERANCE, s. [delivery, manner of speaking] *maniera di parlare o di fare un discorso.*

A man of good utterance, *un uomo che parla bene, un uomo elegante.*

Utterance [sale] *vendita,* s. f. *spaccio,* s. m.

U'TTERED, adj. *proferito, pronunciato, v.* To utter.

U'TTERER, s. [a divulger, a discloser] *divolgatore, scopritore.*

U'TTERLY, adv. [totally, entirely] *totalmente, interamente, affatto, del tutto.*

U'TTERMOST, s. [the greatest degree] *il più estremo grado.*

Ut-

Uttermoſt, adj. [extreme, being in the higheſt degree] *eſtremo, che è in eſtremo grado.*

Uttermoſt [moſt remote] *eſtremamente remoto, il più remotamente diſtante.*

VU'LCAN, s. [the God of ſubterranean fire] *Vulcano.*

VULCA'NO, s. [a burning mountain that throws forth fire] *vulcano, mongibello, monte che butta fuoco dalla vetta.*

VU'LGAR, adj. [common] *volgare, di volgo, comunale.*

'Tis the vulgar opinion, *è il ſentimento comune.*

Vulgar [ordinary, mean] *volgare, comune, triviale, baſſo, vile.*

A vulgar ſoul, *un' anima vile.*

A vulgar ſtyle, *uno ſtile volgare, triviale.*

Vulgar arts, *arti volgari, arti meccaniche.*

The vulgar, s. [the common people] *il volgo, la plebe, il popolo minuto, il popolaccio.*

VU'LGARLY, adv. [commonly] *volgarmente, comunalmente.*

Vulgarly [meanly] *volgarmente, d' una maniera volgare, trivialmente.*

VU'LNERABLE, adj. [ſuſceptive of wounds; liable to external injuries] *vulnerabile, che può ricever ferita, che può eſſer ferito, che non è invulnerabile che non è fatato.*

VU'LNERARY, adj. [curing wounds] *vulnerario, che guariſce le ferite.*

VU'LTURE, [a great bird of prey] *avvoltojo, s. m.*

VU'LTURINE, adj. [of or like a vulture] *d' avvoltojo.*

U'VULA, s. [that little piece of red ſpungy fleſh, that hangs down from the palate between the glandules called amygdalæ] *ugola, s. f. parte carnoſa pendente tra le fauci dell' animale.*

UXO'RIOUS, adj. [over-fond, doting upon his wife] *che ama troppo la propria moglie che ſi laſcia governare dalla moglie.*

UXO'RIOUSLY, adv. [with fond ſubmiſſion to a wife] *con amor ſommeſſo alla moglie.*

UXO'RIOUSNESS, s. connubial dotage; fond ſubmiſſion to a wife] *amore o tenerezza ſoverchia per propria moglie.*

W.

W. *Il ſuono di queſta lettera, è così particolare, che non credo poſſibile ſe ne poſſa dar idea che a viva voce.*

To WA'BBLE [to wriggle about, as an arrow ſometimes does in the air] *volteggiare, ondeggiare.*

WAD, s. [a bundle of ſtraw, or peaſe] *un faſcio di paglia o di piſelli.*

Wad [a ſort of flocks of ſilk, cotton] *fiocchi di ſeta.*

Wad [a ſtopple of paper, hay, ſtraw, old clouts, &c. which is forced into a gun upon the powder, to keep it cloſe in the chamber] *ſtoppaglio. s. m. quella ſtoppa o altra coſa che ſi mette nella canna dell' archibuſo, onde la polvere vi ſtia dentro calcata.*

Wad-hook [a rod or ſtaff, with an iron turned ſerpent-wiſe or like a ſcrew, to draw the wad or okam out of a gun when it is to be unloaded] *cava ſtoppa.*

Wad [black lead] *nome di minerale che ſi trova nelle miniere di piombo, e di cui ſi formano le matite.*

WA'DABLE, adj. [that may be wadded] *guadoſo, che ſi può guadare.*

To WA'DDLE [to go ſidelong as a duck does] *dimenarſi, come fa l' anitra camminando.*

To WADE [to go or paſs over or through the water] *guadare, paſſare fiumi da una ripa all' altra o a cavallo o a piedi.*

To wade over a river, *guadare un fiume.*

To wade in the water, *andare nell' acqua.*

To wade very deep, *andare o penetrare molto indentro.*

To wade into a buſineſs, *ingolfarſi in un negozio.*

WA'DED, adj. *guadato, v.* To wade.

Waded into, *penetrato, ingolfato.*

WA'FER, s. [a thin ſort of paſte for ſealing letters] *cialda, oſtia, s. f.*

Wafer-maker, *cialdonajo, s. m.*

Wafer-iron, *ferro da cialde.*

WAFT, s. [a ſign made to ſhips or boats to come on board in caſe of danger] *ſegnale che ſi da ſul mare a' vaſcelli o barche, per venire a bordo in caſo di pericolo.*

To WAFT [to convey or guard any ſhip or fleet at ſea] *convogliare, accompagnare vaſcelli per ſicurezza.*

To waft [to float] *andar ſull' acqua a galla.*

To waft [to carry through the air or on the water] *condurre per aria o ſull' acqua.*

To waft [to beckon, to inform by a ſign of any thing moving] *far cenno, avviſare con qualche ſegnale da una nave que' che ſono in un altra nave di qualche coſa.*

WA'FTAGE, s. [carriage by water or air] *coſa che ſerve ad attraverſar l' aria o l'acqua.*

WA'FTED, adj. *convogliato.*

WA'FTER, s. [a frigate to convey merchant-men] *fregata di convoglio, che ſerve a convogliare navi da carico.*

Wafter [a paſſage boat] *barca da attraverſar acque.*

WA'FTURE, s. [the act of waving] *l' atto d' ondeggiare.*

WAG, s. [a merry fellow] *un traſtullatore, un giocoſo, un uomo gioviale.*

WA'G-TAIL [a bird] *cutrettola.*

Wag halter, *una forca, un impiccato, un capeſtro, cioè uno quaſi degno della forca, della gogna, o del capeſtro.*

To WAG [to move, to ſtir, to ſhake] *ſcuotere, muovere, agitare, dimenare leggiermente,* pret. *ſcoſſi, moſſi.*

To wag the tail, *muover la coda.*

To wag the head, *accennare, far ſegno colla teſta.*

To wag, verb neut. *muoverſi, ſcuoterſi, agitarſi dimenarſi.*

WAGE, s. *pegno*, s. m.

To WAGE [to lay a wager] *scommettere, fare una scommessa*.

To wage war [to enter upon, to begin a war] *fare o muover guerra*.

To wage [to give security for the performance of a thing] *dar malleveria per l' esecuzione di qualche trattato*.

To wage law [to prosecute or carry on a suit at law] *litigare, piatire, processare, fare il processo, proseguire in giustizia*.

WA'GER, s. [bett] *scommessa*, s. f.

To lay a wager, *scommettere, fare scommessa*.

A wager of law [an offer to take an oath on a book, that he does not owe any thing to the plaintiff, nor detain his goods in the manner and form as he has declared] *offerta di far giuramento, che uno non deve niente all' attore e che non possiede niente del suo*.

WA'GES, s. [salary] *salario, stipendio*, s. m. *paga, mercede*, s. f.

Soldiers wages, *soldo o paga di soldato*.

WA'GGISH, adj. *scherzevole, sollazzevole, gajo, giocoso, giocondo, lascivetto*.

WA'GGERY, } s. *scherzo, trastullo, sollazzo*.
WA'GGISHNESS, }

To WA'GGLE [to be always in motion] *dimenarsi, muoversi, esser sempre in moto*.

To waggle [to joggle, to move up and down] *dimenare, scuotere, agitare*.

WA'GGON, s. [a long sort of cart with four wheels] *sorta di carro a quattro ruote, carretta*, s. f.

Covered waggon, *carro coperto*.

WA'GGONER, s. *carrettajo, carrettiere*, s. m.

The waggoner [a northern constellation called Charles's wain] *l' orsa maggiore*.

WAIF, s. [goods lost, that are found and claimed by no body, which belong to the king, or lord of the manor if upon proclamation made they are not challenged in a year and a day] *qualunque cosa perduta la quale appartiene al re, se nel proclamarla non è domandata da nessuno*.

To WAIL, *v.* To bewail.

WA'ILING, s. *lamento*, s. m.

WAIN, s. [cart] *carro*, s. m. *carretta*, s. f.

Wain-driver, *un carrettiajo, un carrettiere*.

Wain load, *carrettata*.

Charles's wain [a northern constellation] *orsa maggiore, costellazione che è vicina al polo artico*.

WA'INABLE, adj. [that may be manured or ploughed] *arabile, acconcio ad essere arato*.

WA'INSCOT, s. [a lining of walls, made of boards, within-side of a room] *tavolato*, s. m.

To wainscot [to line walls with wainscot] *coprir le mura delle stanze di tavole*.

WA'INSCOTTED, adj. *coperto di tavole*.

WAIR, s. [a piece of timber two yards long and a foot broad] *pezzo di legname lungo due braccia e largo un piede*.

WAIST, s. [the smallest part of the body; the part below the ribs] *cintura; le parte più stretta del corpo; la parte del corpo che è sotto le coste*.

Waist, s. [the middle deck of a ship] *il ponte di mezzo d' un vascello*.

WAIT, s. *aguato, agguato, inganno*, s. m. *insidia, imboscata*, s. f.

To lay wait for one, or to lie in wait for one, *mettere agguato ad uno, tendere insidie a qualcheduno*.

To WAIT [to stay for, to expect] *attendere, aspettare*.

I wait your leisure, *aspetto la vostra comodità*.

We only wait for a good wind, *noi non aspettiamo che un vento favorevole*.

To wait, to wait on, to wait upon [to serve] *servire*.

To wait at table, *servire a tavola*.

Who waits? *olà, chi è la?*

To wait on, to wait upon [to accompany, to go along with] *accompagnare, condurre*.

To wait upon to the door, *accompagnare, o condurre fino alla porta*.

To wait on, to wait upon [to go to visit, to pay one's respect to] *andare a vedere, a visitare, a riverire*.

To wait on a friend, *visitare, andare a vedere un amico*.

I will wait on him to-morrow morning, *anderò domattina a riverirlo*.

I will wait on you presently, *io sarò con voi adesso adesso*.

WA'ITED, adj. *atteso, aspettato, v.* To wait.

WA'ITER, s *servo, quello o quella che serve*.

WA'ITING, s. *aspettamento*, s. m. *l' aspettare*.

To be in waiting [as an officer at court] *esser di guardia*.

WAITING-GENTLEWO'MAN, } s. [an upper servant, who attends on a lady in her chamber] *cameriera d' una dama, damigella d' una signora*.
WAITING-WOMAN, }
WA'ITING-MAID, }

WAITS [a sort of hautboy] *spezie di piva*.

To WAIVE [to quit, to forsake] *lasciare, abbandonare*.

Waive [a woman outlawed for contemptuously refusing to appear when sued in law] *donna condannata per contumaria*.

WA'IVED, adj. *lasciato, abbandonato*.

WA'IWARD, *v.* Wayward.

WAKE, s. [that smooth water which a ship leaves a-stern when under sail] *solco*, s. m. *il fendimento dell' acqua che fa la nave quando veleggia*.

Wake, s. *festa, v.* Wakes.

Wake, s. [vigil, state of forbearing sleep] *vigilia, il vigilare, l' astenersi dal dormire*.

To WAKE [to awake, to rouze from sleep] *destare, svegliare*.

To wake, verb neut. *destarsi, svegliarsi*.

To wake [to watch] *vegliare, vegghiare, non dormire*.

WA'KEFUL, adj. [that does not sleep] *svegliato, che non dorme*.

WA'KEFULLY, adv. ex. he lay wakefully all night, *egli è stato svegliato tutta notte*.

WA'KEFULNESS, s. *poca disposizione a dormire*.

WA'KE-MEN, s. [a title given to the chief magistrates of Rippon in Yorkshire] *titolo che si da al primo magistrato di Rippon nella provincia di York*.

To WA'KEN, v. n. *svegliarsi*.

To waken, v. a. *svegliare, eccitare, produrre*.

Wake-robin, s. [a plant] *spezie di pianta*.

WA'KES, s. [country feasts celebrated for some days after the saint's day, to whom the parish was dedicated, which are still observed in some parts of England] *certe feste rusticane, ancora in uso in alcune parti d' Inghilterra*.

WALE, s. [those outward timbers in a ship's side, on which men set their feet when they clamber up] *pezzi di legno attaccati alle bande d' un vascello, che servono di gradini a quelli che montano*.

Wale-knot [a round knot of a rope] *nodo rotondo fatto in una fune*.

WALK, s. [a place to walk in] *viale*, s. m. *viottolo*, s. m. *camminata*, s. f.

Walk [walking] *passeggiata*, s. f. *spasso*, s. m.

To take a walk, *fare una passeggiata, andare a spasso*.

To WALK about, *spasseggiare, passeggiare, portar quà e là*.

To walk, verb neut. [to go about for pleasure or exercise] *spasseggiare, passeggiare, andare a spasso*.

To walk [to go, to march] *andare, camminare*.

To walk in the streets, *andare o camminare per le strade*.

Let us walk thither, *andiamo là*.

To walk after, *camminare appresso, seguitare*.

To walk the rounds, *far la ronda*.

To walk in, *entrare*.

To walk out, *uscire*, pres. *esco*.

WA'LKER, *camminatore*, s. m. *che cammina*.

Night-walker [common trull] *una bagascia, una sgualdrina, una puttana vile che va intorno la notte*.

Walkers [foresters] *guardiani di foresta*.

WA'LKING, s. *spasseggiata, passeggiata*, s. f.

To go a walking, *andare a spasso, andare a passeggiare*.

Walking-staff, *bastone*.

WALL, s. *un muro*, s. m. *i muri*, s. m. pl. *le mura*, s. f. pl.

Little wall, *muricciuolo*, s. m. *piccol muro*.

Partition-wall, *parete*.

Brick-wall, *muro di mattoni*.

Dry-wall, *muro secco*.

Dead-wall, *muro in luogo appartato.*

Of or belonging to a wall, adj. *murale, di muro.*

To give one the wall, *dar la dritta ad uno.*

To live within the walls, *dimorare nella città, dentro le mura, dentro il circuito delle mura.*

Wall-wort (an herb] *parietaria*, s. f.

Wall-tree, *spalliera*, s. f.

Wall-loufe [a kind of bug] *sorta di cimice*, s. m.

Wall-creeper. [a fort of bird] *sorta d'uccello piccolissimo.*

To WALL [to enclofe with a wall] *murare, circondar con muro.*

To wall a town, *murare una città.*

To wall up a window, *murare una finestra.*

WALL-CREEPER, s. *nome d'uccelletto.*

WA'LLED, adj. *murato, circondato di muro.*

WA'LLET, s. [a fort of bag with two pouches in it] *valigia, bisaccia*, s. f.

Wallet, s. [any thing protuberant and fwagging] *ogni cosa gonfia o paffuta.*

To WA'LLOW [to roll, to tumble] *voltolare, rivoltare.*

To wallow, verb neut. *voltolarsi, rivoltolarsi.*

WA'LLOWING, s. *voltolamento*, s. m. *il voltolare.*

Wallowing place, *luogo fangoso.*

WA'LLOWISH, adj. [unfavory, infipid] *insipido, scipito.*

WA'LLOWISHNESS, s. *scipidezza, scipitezza*, s. f.

WALM, s. [a fhort boiling over the fire] *bollitura*, s. f.

Three or four walms are enough to boil herbs, *bastano tre o quattro bolliture per bollire dell'erbe.*

WA'LLNUT, s. [a large fort of nut well known] *noce*, s. f.

Wallnut-tree, *noce, albero che produce le noci.*

Wallnut-fhell, *scorza di noce.*

WALT, adj. a fea term [a fhip is faid to walt when fhe has not her due ballaft, *i. e.* not enough to enable her to bear her fails, or keep her ftiff] *non bene stivata, che non ha zavorra a bastanza per far che non barcolli, e dicesi d'una nave.*

To WALT, *barcollare*; e *dicesi d'una nave o vascello che non ha bastevole o proporzionata zavorra per tenerlo bene in equilibrio.*

To WA'MBLE [to move or ftir, as the guts fometimes do with wind] *gorgogliare, romoreggiare, come fanno gl' intestini per vento o per altra cagione.*

To wamble [to rife up, as boiling water does] *bollire.*

To wamble to and fro, *vacillare, vagillare, barcollare.*

WA'MBLING, s. [a wambling in the belly] *gorgogliamento, gorgoglio*, s. m.

WAN, adj. [pale] *pallido, smorto, macilente.*

Wan, *è un preterito antico del verbo* to win, *vinsi*, v. To win.

WAND, s. [rod] *verga, bacchetta, bacchetta magica.*

Mercury's wand, *il caduceo di Mercurio.*

To WA'NDER [to go up and down] *errare, vagare, vagabondare, andare errando, trascorrere*, pret. *trascorsi.*

To wander out of the way, *smarrirsi, errar la strada*, pref. *smarrisco.*

WA'NDERED, adj. *errato, vagato, vagabondato, trascorso.*

WA'NDERER, s. [one that wanders] *un vagabondo, un uomo errante.*

WA'NDERING, adj. [that wanders] *errante, vagabondo.*

Wandering rumor, *voce o fama che corre.*

Wandering mind, *spirito errante, di poca stabilità.*

WANE, s. [the decreafe of the moon] *scemo della luna.*

To WANE [to decreafe, to grow lefs] *scemarsi, diminuirsi, ridursi a meno*, pref. *diminuisco.*

WANG, s. [field] *campo, prato*, s. m.

Wangs, or wang-teeth [jaw-teeth] *i mascellari.*

WA'NNED, adj. [turned pale and faint-coloured] *pallido, di poco colore.*

WA'NNESS, s. [from wan] *macilenza, stenuatezza, magrezza, pallidezza, sparutezza*, s. f.

WANT, s. [deficiency, lack, need] *mancanza, povertà, deficienza, necessità, carestia*, s. f. *biosogno, mancamento*, s. m.

For want of money, *per mancanza di danaro.*

I fhall fupply your wants, *io provvederò a' vostri bisogni.*

I have no want of it, *io non ne ho bisogno.*

We have no want of any thing, *non ci manca niente.*

Want [mole] *talpa*, s. f.

Want-hill [mole-hill] *mucchio di terra che fanno le talpe in iscavando il terreno.*

To WANT [to lack] *mancare, aver bisogno, abbisognare, bisognare, faltare, patire*, pref. *patisco.*

What do you want? *che vi manca? che v' abbisogna? che volete? che cercate?*

I want ftrength, *le forze mi mancano.*

You fhall want for nothing, *non vi mancherà niente.*

I want words to exprefs my love, *l' amor ch' io vi porto è indicibile.*

To want wherewithal to fuftain one's life, *non aver di che mantenersi.*

An army that wants a head, *un esercito senza capitano.*

The enemy wanted provifions, *il nemico patisce di vettovaglie.*

This news wants confirmation, *questa novella merita confermazione.*

It wants a quarter of an hour of five, *sono cinque ore meno un quarto.*

Here wants a crown, *ci manca uno scudo.*

It wants a great deal of it, *ce ne manca molto.*

There wanted little but he had been drowned, *poco mancò che non s' annegasse.*

There WA'NTED not fome that faid —*vi furono di quelli che dissero*—

Wanted, adj. *mancato*, v. To want.

WA'NTING, adj. *manchevole, che manca.*

He was not wanting in generofity towards every body, *la sua generosità non fu mai scarsa verso nessuno.*

His bounty is never wanting to our needs, *la sua liberalità supplisce sempre a' nostri bisogni.*

Though there was not wanting fome turbulent men in the affembly, *benchè vi fussero nell' assemblea uomini turbolenti.*

It fhall never be wanting on my part, *per me non istarà che la cosa non si faccia.*

Wanting, s. *bisogno, mancamento*, s. m. *indigenza, necessità, mancanza*, s. f.

WA'NTON, adj. [gamefome, full of play] *scherzevole, lascivetto.*

A wanton girl, *una lascivetta, una ragazza gioviale.*

Wanton [lafcivious] *lascivo, impudico.*

Wanton difcourfes, *discorsi disonesti, impudici.*

Wanton eyes, *occhi lascivi.*

Wanton look, *sguardo amoroso.*

Wanton palate, *un palato delicato.*

Wanton tricks, *scherzi, trastulli.*

Wanton, s. [a lafcivious perfon; a ftrumpet; a whoremonger] *una persona lasciva, una puttana, un puttaniere*

To play the wanton, *scherzare, trastullare, operar lascivamente.*

To make a wanton of, *accarezzare, vezzeggiare.*

To WA'NTON [to play lafcivioufly] *scherzare lascivamente.*

To wanton [to revel, to play] *bagordare, gozzovigliare, far tempone.*

WA'NTONLY, adv. [waggifhly] *scherzevolmente, da scherzo.*

Wantonly [lewdly] *lascivamente, impudicamente.*

To talk wantonly, *parlar lascivamente.*

To look wantonly upon, *guardar con occhi amorosi o lascivi.*

WA'NTONNESS, s. [waggifhnefs] *scherzo, giuoco, trastullo.*

Wantonnefs [lafcivioufnefs] *lascivia, impudicizia, disonestà*, s. f.

Wantonnefs [nicety] *delicatezza*, s. f.

WA'NTWIT, s. [a fool, an idiot] *un baccello, uno sciocco, un donzellone.*

WA'PENTAKE, s. [hundred, divifion of a fhire or county] *cantone o divisione di certe provincie in Inghilterra.*

WAR, s. [ftate of hoftility between two or more nations] *guerra*, s. f.

To make war, *fare o muover guerra.*

Man of war [foldier] *uomo di guerra, soldato.*

Man of war, *nave da guerra.*

War-faring, *guerriero, di guerra.*

War-faring man, *uomo di guerra.*

To War [to make war] *guerreggiare, far guerra, andare alla guerra.*

To Wa'rble [to sing as birds do] *cantare, come fanno gli uccelli.*

To warble [to sing in a trilling or quavering voice] *gorgheggiare.*

Wa'rbler, s. [a singster, a songster] *un canterino, un che canta, un che gorgheggia, un che trilla.*

Wa'rbling, s. [of birds] *canto d' uccelli.*

Warbling [quavering] *trillo*, s. m.

Ward, s. [district or portion of the city of London, committed to the special charge of one of the aldermen] *una delle parti nelle quali si divide Londra.*

Ward of a forest, *parte d' una foresta.*

Watch and ward, *agguato.*

Ward [prison] *prigione, carrere*, s. f.

Ward of a prison [apartment of it] *appartamento d' una prigione.*

The wards of a lock, *le guardie d' una toppa o serratura.*

To Ward [to keep watch or ward] *far la guardia.*

To ward [to parry, to keep off] *parare, schivare.*

Wa'rden, s. [guardian, keeper] *guardiano, custode.*

Warden of the mint, *guardiano della zecca.*

The warden of a college in a university, *il rettore d' un collegio in una università.*

Warden of the Fleet, *il carceriere della prigione chiamata Fleet in Londra.*

Warden [in a religious house] *custode.*

Warden pear [a large sort of baking pear] *spezie di pera.*

Wa'rders, s. [guards] *guardie.*

The warders of the Tower, *le guardie della Torre di Londra.*

Wa'rdmote, or wardmote-court [a court kept in every ward of London] *sorta di magistrato Inglese.*

Wa'rdrobe, s. [place where a prince's or nobleman's robes are kept] *guardaroba*, s. f. *stanza, dove si conservan gli arnesi.*

Ware, s. [commodity, merchandize] *mercanzia, roba*, s. f.

Ware-house, *magazzino*, s. m. *stanza dove si riponzon le mercanzie.*

Ware-house-keeper, *magazziniere*, s. m.

Ware, or earthen ware, *vasellame, vasellamento di terra.*

Dutch-ware, *majolica.*

China-ware, *porcellana.*

Small wares, *merceria*, s. f.

Haberdasher of small wares, *merciajo*, s. m.

To Ware [to take heed of, to beware] *guardarsi, andar cauto.*

Wa'reful, adj. *cauto, circospetto.*

Wa'refulness, s. *cautela, circospezione.*

Wa'reless, adj. [uncautious, unwary] *incauto, non circospetto.*

Wa'rely, *v.* Warily.

Wa'rfare, s [the state of war] *la guerra, la vita militare.*

Wa'rily, adv. [wisely] *accortamente, sagacemente, prudentemente, con circospezione, savièzza, cautela, timidezza*, s. f. *timore*, s. m.

Wariness [savingness] *economia*, s. f. *risparmio*, s. m.

Wa'rlike, adj. [belonging to the art or affairs of war] *bellico, guerriero, militare, che appartiene alla guerra.*

Warlike exploits, *fatti militari.*

Warlike [that loves war, stout, valiant] *béllico, bellicoso, armigero, guerriero, belligero.*

Warlike nation, *nazione bellicosa.*

Warlike man, *guerriero, soldato, uomo d' arme, uomo prode.*

Warm, adj. [not cold] *caldo.*

Warm weather, *tempo caldo.*

Warm room, *camera calda.*

To be warm, *aver caldo.*

To make warm, *scaldare, far caldo.*

To grow warm, *divenir caldo, scaldarsi.*

When they come once to be warm in their drink, *quando sono un tratto scaldati dal vino.*

To grow warm in a dispute, *scaldarsi in una disputa.*

Warm [passionate] *caldo, veemente, foroso, stizzoso, collerico.*

Warm [eager] *caldo, ardente, focoso, avido.*

Luke-warm, *tiepido, tepido.*

Warm, adv. *caldamente.*

To be warm clad, *esser caldamente vestito.*

To Warm [to make warm] *scaldare.*

To warm one's self, *scaldarsi.*

The sun warms the earth, *il sole scalda la terra.*

To warm again, *riscaldare.*

Wa'rmed, adj. *scaldato.*

Wa'rming, s. *lo scaldare.*

Warming-pan, *scaldaletto.*

Wa'rmly, adv. *caldamente, con caldezza, efficacemente, vigorosamente.*

Wa'rmness, } s. *caldezza*, s. f.
Warmth, } *caldo, caldore*, s. m.

To Warn [to tell, to give notice of a thing before-hand, to admonish] *avvertire, dar avvertimento, ammonire, avvisare*, pres. *avvertisco, ammonisco.*

To warn one of a thing, *avvertire uno di qualche cosa.*

To warn [in law, to summon, to appear in a court of justice] *citare, chiamare a' magistrati per mezzo de' ministri pubblici o in voce o in iscritto.*

To warn one away, *licenziare alcuno, dargli congedo.*

Wa'rned, adj. *avvertito, ammonito.*

Wa'rner, s. *avvisatore, ammonitore*, s. m.

Wa'rning, s. *avvertimento, avvisamento, avviso*, s. m.

To give one warning, *avvertire qualcheduno.*

To give one's tenant warning, *avvertire il suo fittuale di provvedersi altrove, dargli congedo.*

To take warning, *pigliar esempio, stare avvertito.*

Take this for a warning, *osservate quel che vi dico.*

Warp [the thread at length, into which the woof is woven] *ordito*, s. m. *il filo messo per lungo in sull' orditojo, per farne la tela.*

To Warp [to cast, or bend as boards do when they are not dry] *piegarsi.*

To warp a ship [to hale her to a place when the wind is wanting] *rimurchiare un vascello.*

Warps [a hawser, or any rope used in the warping of a ship] *alzana*, s. f. *ogni sorta di fune che serve a rimurchiare un vascello.*

Wa'rped, adj. *piegato.*

Wa'rping, s. [bending] *piegamento*, s. m. *il piegare.*

A weaver's warping loom, *orditojo*, s. m.

Wa'rrant, s. [an order, authentick permission, power] *ordine, permissione autentica, autorità, potere.*

To have a warrant against one to arrest him, *aver un ordine o permissione d' arrestare alcuno.*

Warrant [for a place at court] *patente.*

A warrant of attorney [a letter of attorney] *procura.*

By divine warrant, *per divina permissione.*

To Wa'rrant [to secure, to maintain] *assicurare, mantenere, far buono*, pres. *mantengo*, pret. *mantenni.*

I warrant it good, *ve lo mantengo, ve lo do per buono.*

To warrant [to assure, to promise] *assicurare, accertare, promettere*, pret. *promissi.*

He has done it I warrant you, *v' assicuro, credetelo a me, sopra la mia parola, egli è lui che l' ha fatto.*

I shall find him out I warrant you, *vi prometto di trovarlo, lasciate pur fare a me, lo troverò ben io.*

To warrant [in law] *mallevare, dar malleveria.*

Wa'rranted, adj. *assicurato, mantenuto*, v. To warrant.

Wa'rranter, s. *mallevadore*, s. m. *sicurtà*, s. f.

Wa'rrantise, } s. [a covenant to
Wa'rranty, } secure a bargain] *malleveria, sicurtà, obbligazione*, s. f.

Wa'rren, s. [a place to keep conies, hares, patridges, and pheasants] *conigliera*, s. f.

Wa'rrenner, s. [a keeper of a warren] *guardiano di conigliera.*

Wa'rrior, } s. [a warlike man,
Wa'rriour, } one skilled in military affairs] *guerriero*, s. m. *uno ammaestrato nell' arte delle guerra.*

Wa'rring, s. *il guerreggiare.*

Wart, s. [a kind of small liard swelling] *porro*, s. m. *piccolo bitorzolino calloso e rotondo che nasce sopra la pelle senza dolore; verruca*, s. f.

Wa'rt-wort, *erba buona contro i porri.*

Wa'rty, adj. [full of warts] *pieno di porri.*

WA'RWORN, adj. [worn with war] *consumato o distrutto dalla guerra.*

WA'RY, adj. [prudent, provident, cautious] *prudente, circospetto, ritenuto, cantelloso, accorto, provvido, timido.*

Wary [thrifty] *parco, frugale.*

WAS, preterito del verbo I am, v. To be.

I was there, *vi ero, vi fui, vi sono stato.*

WASE, s. [a wreath of cloth to be laid under any vessel or burden that is borne on the head] *cercine,* s. m. *un ravvolto di panno a foggia di cerchio, usato da chi porta de' pesi in capo per salvarlo da offesa.*

WASH [hogs-wash] *imbratto,* s. m. *broda,* s. f.

Wash [a lotion to wash with] *acqua artificiale che serve a conservare il viso.*

A wash of oysters [ten strikes] *misura d' ostriche, che contiene dieci di quelle misure che si chiamano* strikes.

The washes in Norfolk [so called because it is washed by the tides dashing against it] *i pantani, o le paludi della provincia di Norfolk.*

Wash-house, *lavatojo, luogo dove si lavan le biancherie.*

Wash-pot, *bacino da lavare.*

Wash-tub, *tino da lavar biancherie.*

Wash-ball, *palla di sapone.*

To WASH [to cleanse with water or any other liquor] *lavare, far pulita e netta una cosa, levandone la sporcizia con acqua.*

To wash one's hands, *lavarsi le mani.*

To wash foul linnen, *lavare delle biancherie.*

To wash a glass, *lavare, o sciacquare un bicchiere.*

To wash [to bathe, to water, to lave] *lavare, bagnare.*

The river washes the walls of the town, *il fiume lava, o bagna le mura della città.*

To wash away, off, or out, *lavare, nettare, purgare, cancellare.*

WA'SHED, adj. *lavato,* v. To wash.

WA'SHER-WOMAN, *lavandaja,* s. f. *donna, che lava panni a prezzo.*

WA'SHING, s. *lavamento,* s. m. *il lavare.*

Washing tub, *uno tino da lavarvi le biancherie.*

I pay so much for my washing, *io pago tanto per l' imbiancatura de' miei panni.*

WA'SHY, adj. [watry, damp] *umido, inumidito, bagnato, inaffiato.*

Washy [weak, not solid] *debole, non solido.*

WASP, s. [a sort of flinging fly] *vespa,* s. f. *insetto volatile simile alla pecchia.*

WA'SPISH, adj. [fretful, peevish] *dispettoso, fastidioso, fantastico, sdegnoso, ostico, strano.*

WA'SPISHLY, adv. *fantasticamente, fastidiosamente, increscevolmente.*

WA'SPISHNESS, s. *fantasticaggine, noja, sdegnosità,* s. f. *fastidio,* s. m.

WASSA'ILER, s. [toper, drunkard] *beone, briacone.*

WA'SSEL, s. [an ancient custom, still used in some places on Twelfth-day at night, of going about with a great bowl of ale, drinking of healths] *costume antico, ancora in uso in altruni luoghi d' Inghilterra, d' andare attorno per le case la sera dell' Epifania, con una gran tazza di cervogia, bevendo alla salute di qualcheduno.*

A wassel bowl [a large cup or bowl] *una gran tazza.*

WA'SSELLERS, s. [company of people who make merry and drink together] *tavolata di gente che bevono e si divertono insieme.*

WAST, *seconda persona di* was *dal verbo* to be. *Eri, fosti.*

WASTE, adj. [good for nothing] *inutile, che non serve a niente, che non val niente.*

Waste-paper, *carta straccia.*

Waste-ground, *terra inutile e inculta.*

To lay a country waste, *desolare, distruggere, rovinare, predare un paese.*

Waste, s. [spoil, havock, destroying] *preda, strage, rovina, distruzione, desolazione,* s. f. *danno, guasto.*

To make a waste of a thing, *menare a guasto, guastare, dissipare una cosa.*

To make waste in houses, *lasciar andar una cosa in rovina.*

Wastes [waste ground] Those lands which are not in any man's possession, but lie common] *terra deserta che non appartiene a nessuno o a tutti.*

Waste [the middle of a man's body] *cintura,* s. f. *il mezzo dalla persona.*

To take one about the waste, *prendere, o abbracciare alcuno per la cintura.*

He is not taller than my waste, *egli non mi arriva ch' alla cintura.*

To have a long waste, *aver la vita lunga.*

Waste-coat, *camiciuola.*

Waste-belt, *cinturino,* s. m.

The waste of a ship [that part of her which lies between the main-mast and fore-mast] *il mezzo d' un vascello.*

Waste cloaths, sea term [certain clothes hung about the cage-work of a ship's hull, to shadow the men from the enemy in a fight] *pavese,* s. m. *striscia di tela che si stende intorno al bordo d' una nave da guerra, per impedire al nemico nella battaglia di vedere gli uomini, e quel che si fa nella nave.*

A waste-goods [spend all] *un prodigo, uno spendereccio.*

To WASTE [to spoil, spend or consume] *guastare, scialacquare, consumare, spendere.*

To waste [to lay waste] *desolare, rovinare, distruggere, dare il guasto.*

To waste, verb neut. [to decoy] *scemare, diminuire, consumarsi, scemarsi.*

The day wastes, *il giorno s' abbassa, si fa notte.*

WA'STED, adj. *guastato, dissipato,* v. To waste.

WA'STEL-BREAD [the finest sort of white-bread] *pane il più bianco.*

WA'STER, s. [from to waste] *distruggitore, distruttore, consumatore,* s. m.

WA'STEFUL, adj. *prodigo, spendereccio, scialacquatore, consumatore.*

WA'STEFULLY, adv. *prodigamente.*

WA'STEFULNESS, s. *prodigalità, consumazione,* s. f. *consumamento, scialacquo,* s. m.

WA'STECS, s. [a sort of thieves and robbers *spezie di ladri o malandrini.*

WATCH [guard] *guardia,* s. f.

To be upon the watch, *far la guardia.*

Watchman, *un uomo che fa la guardia la notte per le strade.*

Watch [the fourth part of the night] *vegghia,* s. f.

Watch-light [at sea] *fanale.*

To have a watch upon a man's actions [to watch one] *codiare alcuno, osservare i suoi andamenti.*

To be upon the watch, *stare alle vedette.*

Watch [a pocket clock] *un oriuolo.*

Alarm-watch, *sveglia, la squilla degli oriuoli, che suona a tempo determinato per destare.*

Watch-case, *rassa d' oriuolo.*

Watch-maker, *un orologiajo.*

To WATCH [to sit up] *vegghiare, vegliare, star desto, non dormire.*

To watch [to look to, to be upon one's guard] *vegliare, prender guardia, badare, stare attento, star sulle sue, stare alle vedette, stare in cervello.*

To watch [to watch and guard] *far la guardia.*

To watch a sick body [to sit up with him] *vegliare un ammalato, passar la notte con lui per averne cura.*

To watch one, *codiare alcuno; spiare, osservare i suoi andamenti.*

To watch one's motions, *osservare l' altrui azioni.*

To watch an opportunity, or for an opportunity, *spiare l' occasione, guatare, appostare, corre il tempo.*

WA'TCHED, adj. *vegghiato, vegliato,* v. To watch.

Watch-glass [a glass whose sand is four hours in running out, us'd by sailors] *oriuolo da sabbia o da polvere.*

WA'TCHER, s. [one who watches] *uno che veglia, che sta in guardia.*

Watcher [diligent overlooker or observer] *osservatore accurato e diligente.*

WA'TCHET-COLOUR, s. [a kind of pale blue colour] *spezie di color turchino pallido.*

WA'TCHFUL, adj. [vigilant] *vigilante, diligente, attento, accurato, applicato.*

To have a watchful eye over one, *appostare, osservar cautamente alcuno, codiarlo, aver l' occhio sopra di lui.*

To be watchful over a man's failings, *esaminare gli altrui difetti.*

WA'TCHFULLY, adv. *vigilantemente, con vigilanza, con accuratezza.*

WA'TCHFULNESS, s. *vigilanza, accuratezza, diligenza, attenzione,* s. f.

WA'TCH-HOUSE, s. [place where the watch is set] *luogo dove si pone gente a guardare ed osservare.*

WA'TER, s. [one of the four elements] *acqua,* s. f. *uno de' quattro elementi.*

Spring,

Spring, rock, pump, river, rain, ſea-water, *arqua di fonte, di rocca, di pozzo, di fiume, piovana, di mare.*

Running water, *arqua corrente.*

Standing water, *arqua morta, o ſtagnante.*

Mineral waters, *arque minerali.*

Artificial or diſtilled waters, *arque artificiali o diſtillate.*

Cordial waters, *arque cordiali.*

Roſe water, *arqua roſa, arqua nanſa.*

Holy water, *acqua ſanta.*

Water [urine] *arqua, urina.*

To make water, *far dell' arqua.*

Water [rain] *arqua, piova, pioggia.*

We have had a great deal of water, *noi abbiamo avuto molt' arqua, o molta pioggia.*

To be all in water [in a ſweat] *eſſer tutto molle di ſudore, ſudare.*

Water [luſtre of pearls, diamonds, and the like] *arqua, ſplendore di perle, diamanti, e ſimili.*

A diamond of a very good water, *diamante d' una bell' arqua.*

Water [river, lake, pond] *arqua, fiume, lago, ſtagno.*

On the water ſide, *alla ripa dell' acqua, o del fiume.*

To ſwim under water, *nuotar ſott' arqua.*

To take water, *prender barra, imbarcarſi.*

To go by water, *andar per arqua.*

Water [tide] *marea.*

High water, low water, *marea alta, marea baſſa.*

To take in water [a ſea phraſe] *fare arqua.*

To watch one's water [to watch him] *appoſtare, ſpiare, codiare alcuno, oſſervare i ſuoi andamenti.*

To fiſh in troubled water [to make a benefit of others troubles] *peſcare in arqua torbida.*

Water-archer [a plant] *ſagittaria,* s. f. *ſpezie di pianta, che raſſomiglia ad una ſaetta.*

Water-man, *un barcaruolo.*

Water-fowls, *uccelli aquatici o d' acqua.*

Water-dog, *bracco da arqua.*

Water-trough, *abbeveratojo.*

Water pot, *vaſo da arqua.*

Holy water-pot, *acquaſantajo.*

Water-mill, *mulino a arqua.*

Water-works, *giuochi d' acqua.*

Water-ſpring, *ſorgente, fontana, fonte.*

Water-ſpout, *getto d' acqua.*

Water-fall, *caſcata.*

Water-colours, *acquerella.*

To paint in water colours, *dipignere in acquerella.*

Water-gold, *oro macinato.*

Water-borne, adj. [a-float, as a ſhip] *galleggiante, rhe galleggia, che ſta a galla.*

Water-page [a ſea wall or bank to keep off the current or overflowing of the water] *muro, o argine per impedire l' impeto dell' arque.*

Water-gage [an inſtrument to meaſure the depth or quantity of any water] *ſtrumento da miſurare la profondità e la quantità delle arque.*

Water houſe, *conſervatojo o mulino, dal quale ſi diſtribuiſce l' arqua per tutte le caſe di Londra.*

To WA'TER [to bathe, to ſprinkle with water] *adacquare, annaffiare, innaffiare, bagnare.*

To water a garden, *adacquare un giardino.*

The Thames waters the walls of London, *il Tamigi bagna le mura di Londra.*

To water a horſe, *bagnare un cavallo.*

To water [to give water to drink] *abbeverare.*

To water a horſe, *abbeverare un cavallo.*

To water herrings, *diſſolare delle aringhe.*

To make one's mouth water, *far venir l' arqua alla borra, far appetire grandemente che che ſia.*

To water, a ſea term [to take in freſh water] *fare arqua, provvederſi d' acqua freſca.*

WA'TERED, adj. *adacquato, inaffiato, bagnato, abbeverato.*

Watered [as ſtuffs made like waves] *ondato.*

Watered camlet, *ciambellotto ondato.*

WA'TERFAL, s. [cataract, caſcade] *cataratta, caſcata d' arque.*

WA'TERFOWL, s. *uccello rhe vive o ſi nutre nell' acque.*

WA'TERINESS, s. [humidity, moiſture] *umidità, umidezza.*

WA'TERING, adj. *adacquamento, inaffiamento,* s. m.

Watering place, *abbeveratojo.*

Watering-pot, *annaffiatojo,* s. m. *vaſo con che s' annaffia.*

WA'TERISH, adj. *acquoſo, aqueo, pieno d' arqua.*

Wateriſh matter, *materia acquoſa.*

To taſte wateriſh, *ſaper d' arqua.*

WA'TERISHNESS, s. *umore acqueo.*

Wateriſhneſs of the blood, *ſeroſità,* s. f.

Water-man, s. *barcaruolo,* s. m.

WA'TERY, } adj. [full of water] *ac-*
WA'TRY, } *quoſo, pieno, d' arqua, umido.*

Watery ground, *terreno acquoſo, pieno d' acqua.*

Watery eyes, *occhi bagnati di lagrime.*

WA'TTLE, s. *filo, che compone una fune.*

WA'TTLES, *v.* Waddles.

To WA'TTLE [to cover with hurdles, grates] *coprire o chiudere con graticci, ingraticolare.*

WA'TTLED, adj. *roperto, o chiuſo con grattirci, ingraticolato.*

A wattled wall, *muro fatto di gratirri.*

WAVE, s. [ſurge] *onda,* s. m. *flutto,* s. m.

A ſhip toſſed by the waves, *un vaſcello combattuto dall' onde.*

To WAVE [to riſe and fall like waves] *ondeggiare, muoverſi in onde, fluttuare.*

To wave [to make like the waves of the ſeu] *ondeggiare, fare a onde.*

To wave [to run to and fro] *voltare, rivoltare.*

To wave [to paſs by] *paſſare, ometterr, laſciare, tralaſciare.*

To wave one's privilege, *cedere, o rinunciare al ſuo privilegio.*

To wave a buſineſs, *ſchivare, evitare, ſcanſare un negozio.*

To wave a diſcourſe, *cangiar diſcorſo.*

To wave, among ſailors [to make ſigns for a ſhip or boat to come near, or keep off] *chiamare o far ſegno ad un vaſcello d' accoſtarſi, o d' allontanarſi.*

To wave the wings, *batter l' ali, parlando degli uccelli.*

WAVED, adj. *ondeggiato, fluttuato,* v. To wave.

To WA'VER [to be irreſolute, or uncertain what to do] *ondeggiare, fluttuare, vacillare, ſtare in dubbio o irreſoluto, titubare, tentennare, traballare.*

WA'VERER, s. [one unſettled and irreſolute] *un che titubà; che è irreſoluto; che ondeggia fra più penſieri e non ſa a qual partito s' appigli.*

WA'VERING, s. *dubbio,* s. m. *incertezza, irreſolutezza,* s. f.

Wavering, adj. [fickle, uncertain] *vacillante, titubante, incoſtante, irreſoluto, incerto.*

WA'VERINGLY, adv. *in bilancio, in dubbio, incertamente.*

WA'VY, adj. [in the manner of waves] *ondato, fatto a onde, ondeggiante.*

WAWES, or waes, for WAVES.

To WAWL [to howl as cats do in the night] *gridare, come fanno i gatti la notte o quando ſi battono, gnaulare.*

The wawling of the cats, *il gnaulare de' gatti.*

WAX, s. [a glewy and bituminous ſubſtance well known] *rera,* s. f.

Sealing-wax, *ceralacca,* s. f. *rera ad uſo di ſigillare.*

Wax-candle, *candela di rera.*

Wax-taper, *rero, candela grande di rera, torria.*

Wax-maker, *colui che fa la rera.*

Wax chandler, *cerajuolo,* s. m. *arteſice che lavora di cera.*

To WAX [to do over with wax] *incerare.*

To wax, verb neut. pret. wox, waxed, part. paſſ. waxed, waxen [to grow or become] *divenire, diventare, farſi,* pret. *divenni.*

WA'XED, } adj. *incerato.*
WA'XEN, }

WAY, s. [road, ſpace to go from one place to another] *ſtrada, via,* s. f. *cammino,* s. m.

High-way, *ſtrada maeſtra, ſtrada battuta.*

Deep way, *ſtrada rotta.*

Covered way [in fortification] *ſtrada coperta, termine di fortificazione.*

To go the ſame way, *pigliare la medeſima ſtrada.*

To go out of one's way, *ſmarrire la ſtrada perder la ſtrada.*

Which is the way to London? *che cammino biſogna tenere per andare a Londra?*

To

The way of a ship, *la corsìa d'un vascello.*

To make or give way, *far luogo, scostarsi.*

Way [side] *parte, banda.*

I know not which way to turn myself, *non so da che parte voltarmi.*

Every way, *da ogni banda.*

Which way do you go? *per dove andate?*

This way, *per qui, per questa parte.*

That way, *per la, per quella parte.*

The wrong way, *a rovescio.*

To do a thing the wrong way, *fare che che sia a rovescio.*

You take it the wrong way, *voi non lo pigliate per la buona parte.*

To turn this way, that way, *voltare in quà, in là.*

Way [means, expedient, course] *modo, maniera, mezzo, espediente.*

I will show you the way to obtain it, *vi mostrerò io il modo d' ottenerlo.*

To make way for one's self, *farsi strada.*

To be in the way of salvation, *esser nella via di salute.*

You must find out a way for that, *bisogna, che voi troviate qualche spediente o mezzo termine per questo.*

Is this your way? *questa è dunque la vostra maniera di trattare?*

Is this his way of dealing with friends? *così dunque egli tratta gli amici?*

Any way, *in qualunque modo.*

No way, no manner of way, *in alcuna maniera, in conto alcuno.*

I will do it my own way, *voglio farlo a mio modo, a mio genio, a mia fantasia.*

Well, use your own way, *e bene, fate a modo vostro, fate come v' aggrada.*

Which way? *come? in che modo? in che maniera?*

Way [custom, use] *maniera, uso, costume.*

The ways of a country, *le maniere, i costumi d'un paese.*

Way [condition, pass] *stato, condizione.*

He is in a fair way to raise his fortune, *egli è in istato di far la sua fortuna.*

It was never in my way to grow rich, *non è stato mai in poter mio d' arricchirmi.*

To show one the way [to give him an example] *mostrar la via ad uno, dargli esempio.*

To lead the way [to go before] *condurre, mostrar la strada.*

Over the way, or cross the way, *dirimpetto, opposto, all' incontro.*

To cross the way, *traversare la strada.*

By the way, *di passaggio.*

Go your ways, *andate pe' fatti vostri.*

Go your ways home, *andatevene a casa.*

'Tis a long way thither, *c' è un gran pezzo di strada.*

We are but a little way from the town, *noi non siamo molto lontani dalla città.*

A good word goes a great way with him, *una buona parola ha molta forza in lui.*

If it falls in my way, *se mi vien fatta, se avrò l' opportunità.*

To be in the way [to be near at hand] *esser a mano, esser vicino.*

To be in the way [to be in readiness] *stare in ordine, stare apparecchiato.*

To stand in one's way, *impedire qualcheduno di passare.*

To stand in one's way [to be a hindrance to him] *servir d' ostacolo a qualcheduno, impedirlo, nuocergli, fargli torto.*

To go out of the way [to lose one's way] *smarrirsi, perder la strada.*

To go out of the way [to absent one's self] *assentarsi, allontanarsi.*

To be out of the way, *essere assente.*

You are always out of the way when I want you, *non c' è modo di trovarvi, quando ho bisogno di voi.*

This is a thing out of my way [it is not in my power] *queste non son cose che dipendano da me, non è in mio potere di fare queste cose.*

'Tis much out of my way, *questo mi fa gran torto, ho perduto molto per questo.*

His absence is a hundred pounds out of my way, *la sua assenza m' ha fatto perdere ben cento lire sterline.*

I think it not out of my way, *stimo che non sarà fuor di proposito.*

To be out of the way [to be in error] *ingannarsi, sbagliare.*

To keep one out of the way [to conceal him] *nascondere, celare, occultare alcuno.*

To keep out of the way [to abscond] *nascondersi, celarsi, occultarsi.*

To get out of the way [to be gone] *andarsene, ritirarsi, salvarsi, prender la fuga.*

To get out of the way [to remove] *allontanare mandar via.*

To dispatch one out of the way [to kill one] *spacciare, spedire alcuno, ammazzarlo.*

To ask out of the way [to ask too much] *soprassare, domandare troppo.*

To gave way [to make room for] *far luogo.*

To gave way [to yield] *cedere, dar luogo.*

If it lie in my way to do you any kindness, *se s' offrirà l' occasione di farvi qualche servizio.*

If it lie in my way I'll do it, *la farò se mi verrà fatta, o se mi sarà possibile.*

An army that gives way, *un esercito che piega, che da indietro, che cede.*

To give way to the times, *acconciarsi al tempo, temporeggiare, navigar secondo il vento.*

To give way to a thing, *dar luogo a qualche cosa.*

To give way to a thing, *soffrire, tollerare, permettere qualche cosa.*

I am inclined that way, *io sono portato a questo, inclinato a questo.*

I know which way he stands affected, *io so la sua inclinazione, il suo genio.*

Is there no way with you but you must speak? *c' è modo da farvi tacere?*

He is no way fitted for that, *egli non è punto atto a ciò.*

He has a great gift that way, *egli ha un gran talento in ciò.*

To make one's way through the croud, *farsi strada fra la calca.*

This is to make way for all manner of vices, *questo sarebbe un dar campo ad ogni sorta di vizi.*

He is very singular in his way [he has peculiar ways with him] *egli è molto singolare in alcune cose.*

A way through [a passage] *un passo, o passaggio.*

A way in [entry] *entrata,* s. f.

A way out, *uscita,* s. f.

To WAY a horse [to teach him to travel in the way] *incamminare un cavallo.*

WA'YED, adj. *incamminato*

That horse is not well wayed, *quel cavallo non è bene incamminato.*

Way-bred [an herb] *piantaggine,* s. f.

Way-faring, adj. ex. A way-faring man, *un viandante, un viaggiatore.*

Way-faring tree [wild vine] *viburno,* s. m.

Way-laid, adj. *insidiato.*

To way-lay one, *insidiare, tendere insidie ad uno.*

Way laying, s. *l' insidiare.*

WA'YLESS, adj. [pathless, untracked] *che non ha via, che non ha sentiero.*

WA'YMARK, s. [mark to guide in travelling] *segno che si mette nel cammino onde il viaggiatore riconosca il luogo dove egli è.*

To WA'YMENT [to lament, to grieve] *compiangere, addolorarsi.*

WA'YWARD, adj [froward, peevish] *fantastico, capriccioso, ostinato, protervo, aromatico, dispettoso, fastidioso, ostico, strano, ritroso.*

The wayward sisters [the witches, the fates] *le streghe; le parche.*

WA'YWARDLY, adv. [frowardly, perversely] *ostinatamente, con mal garbo, con mal umore, dispettosamente.*

WA'YWARDNESS, s. [peevishness, frowardness] *fantasticaggine, caparbietà, ostinatezza, dispettosaggine.*

WE [the plural of I] *noi.*

We have, *noi abbiamo.*

WEAK, adj. [feeble, infirm, that has no strength, faint] *debole, debile, di poca forza, di poca possa, fievole, fiacco, infermo, impotente, spossato.*

Weak body, *corpo debole, corpo infermo.*

Weak stomach, *stomaco debole, che non può digerire.*

Weak [simple] *debole, dappoco, di basso ingegno, semplice, inesperto, soro.*

A weak man or woman, *un uomo, o una donna debole, semplice, di poco giudizio, un dappoco, una dappoca.*

A weak remembrance, *una debole memoria.*

To WE'AKEN [to make weak] *debilitare, affievolire, far divenir debole, scemar le forze, infiaccare, infiebolire, sforzare, snervare, infiacchire.*

To weaken, verb neut. [to grow weak

weak] *debilitarsi, affievolirsi, divenir debole, perder le forze.*

WE'AKENED } adj. *debilitato, affievolito, divenuto debole, v.* To weaken.
WE'AKNED }

WE'AKENING } s. *debilitamento,* s. m. *il debilitare.*
WE'AKNING }

A WE'AKLING, s. [a child that has little or no strength] *un deboletto, uno sparuto.*

WE'AKLY, adv. *debolmente, e debilmente, infermamente, còn debolezza.*

Weakly, adj. [weak, crazy] *debole, dilicato, fievole, impotente, spossato, tenero.*

WE'AKNESS, s. [want of strength] *debolezza, fievolezza, debilità, mancamento di forze, fiacchezza.*

WE'AKSIDE, s. [foible, deficience, infirmity] *il debole, la parte desirata.*

WEAL, s. *bene*; ex. the common weal, *il ben pubblico.*

Weal, s. [the mark of a stripe] *il segno che lascia una percossa ricevuta con una correggia o altra simil cosa.*

WE'ALAWAY, interj. [alas] *ohimé, meschino a me!*

WEALD, s. [the woody part of a country] *le foreste, i boschi d' un paese.*

The weald of Kent, *i boschi della provincia di Kent.*

WEALTH, s. [riches] *beni, ricchezze, dovizie, opulenza, facoltà.*

Commonwealth, *repubblica.*

Commonwealth-man, *un repubblichista.*

WE'ALTAINESS, s. *opulenza, ricchezza,* s. f.

WE'ALTHY, adj. [rich] *opulente, ricco, facoltoso.*

To WEAN [to take a child from the breast] *svezzare, spoppare.*

To wean a child, *svezzare un bambino.*

To wean one's self from a pleasure [to abstain from it] *svezzarsi di qualche piacere, rimanersene, astenersene.*

WE'ANED, adj. *svezzato, spoppato.*

WE'ANEL } s. [a young beast newly taken off from sucking his dam] *una bestiuola novellamente spoppata.*
WE'ANCE }

WE'ANLING, s. [a young creature fit to be weaned] *creaturina d' età da essere spoppata.*

WE'APON, s. *arma,* s. f.

Weapon salve, *unguento simpatico.*

WE'APONED, adj. *armato.*

Well or ill weaponed, *bene, o male armato.*

WE'APONLESS, adj. *disarmato, senz' arme.*

WEAR, s. [any thing that is worn for clothing] *ogni sorta d' arnesi che si pertan per vestimenti.*

This is all the wear now, *non si porta altro addosso.*

This is good enough for my wear, *questo è assai buono per me.*

Cloth of good wear, *panno di buon servizio, di buona durata.*

Wear, or weir [a dam in a river for taking fish] *ordigno che serve a pigliare i pesci ne fiumi.*

To WEAR [to have on or about] *portare, avere addosso.*

To wear a suit of clothes, *portare un abito.*

To wear a sword, *portar la spada.*

To wear out a suit of clothes, *usare un abito.*

To wear land out of heart, *sfruttare, indebolire una terra, renderla sterile.*

To wear out a man's patience, *fare scappar la pazienza ad uno.*

This cloth wears very well, *questo panno è di buona durata.*

Night wears apace, *la notte è molto avanzata.*

To wear out, *consumarsi.*

To wear away [to decay] *consumarsi, scemarsi, diminuire,* pret. *diminuisco.*

WE'ARABLE, adj. *portabile, da potersi portare.*

WE'ARER, s. *portatore,* s. m. *un che porta addosso.*

WE'ARIED, adj. [tired] *lasso, stracco, faticato.*

WE'ARINESS, s. [the state of being weary] *stanchezza, stracchezza,* s. f.

WE'ARING, s. *il portare.*

Every thing is worse for wearing, *ogni cosa si consuma portandola.*

Wearing apparel, *abiti, vestimenti arnesi.*

WE'ARISH, adj. [boggy, watery] *pantanoso, melmoso, limaccioso.*

WE'ARISOME, adj. [tiresome] *nojoso, molesto, importuno, increscevole, rincrescevole, penoso, tedioso, tormentoso, grave.*

WE'ARISOMENESS, s. *ambascia, angoscia, noja, gravezza, molestia,* s. f. *travaglio, fastidio,* s. m.

WE'ARY, adj. [tired] *lasso, affaticato, stanco, stracco.*

Weary of walking, *lasso di camminare.*

Weary [tired, or disgusted with] *lasso, tediato, stucco, infastidito, sazio, nojoso, stufo.*

I am weary of my life, *la vita m' è divenuta nojosa.*

I am never weary of the country, *non sono mai sazio della campagna; la campagna non mi vien mai a noja.*

To grow weary, *stufarsi, lassarsi, straccarsi, faticarsi, tediarsi.*

To WE'ARY [to tire] *stufare, fiaccare, straccare, lassare, stancare.*

To weary [to incommode] *tediare, fastidire, rincrescere, nojare.*

To weary one with one's discourses, *tediare alcuno con discorsi.*

To weary out with toil, *fiaccare, straccare, consumare, logorare le forze colla fatira.*

WE'ASAND, *v.* WE'SAND.

WE'ASEL, s. [a small animal that eats corn and kills mice] *donnola.*

To WEAT the head [to look for lice] *cercare i pidocchi nella testa.*

WE'ATHER, s. [the disposition of the air] *tempo,* s. m. *disposizione dell' aria.*

Fine weather, *bel tempo.*

Bad weather, *cattivo tempo.*

Rainy weather, *tempo piovoso.*

What weather is it? *che tempo fa?*

Dirty weather, *tempo sporco.*

Weather glass, *termometro.*

Weather cock, *agnolo di badia, girandola.*

Weather wise [skilled in foretelling the change of weather] *che sa prevedere il tempo che farà.*

A hare is more weather-wise than the best astrologer, *la lepre conosce meglio il tempo che non il migliore astrologo.*

Weather-gage, *vantaggio del vento.*

To get the weather-gage [to come up with the wind] *aver il vento in poppa.*

To lose the weather-gage, *essere sotto vento, avere lo svantaggio del vento.*

Weather, or weather sheep [a male sheep gelt] *un castrato.*

Weather-mutton, *carne di castrato.*

Bell-weather, *castrato che porta il campanaccio.*

To WE'ATHER [to double, to go to the windward of a place] *trapassare.*

To weather a point, *trapassare una punta.*

To weather a point [to overcome a difficulty] *superare, vincere una difficoltà.*

To weather a hawk [to set her abroad to take the air] *svolazzare un falcone.*

WEATHERBE'ATEN, adj. [harrassed and seasoned by hard weather] *sbattuto dal mal tempo, consumato dall' intemperie del tempo.*

WEATHERDRI'VEN, *participio* [forced by storms or contrary winds] *spinto suo malgrado da burrasca o venti contrari.*

WE'ATHERED, adj. *trapassato.*

To WEAVE [to make cloth, silk, &c. in a loom] *tessere.*

To weave cloth, *tessere del panno.*

To weave hair for a perriwig, *intrecciar capelli per fare una parrucca.*

WE'AVED, *v.* Woven.

WE'AVER, *tessitore,* s. m. *tessitrice,* s. f.

A weaver's beam, *un subbio.*

A weaver's loom, *un telajo.*

WE'AVING, s. *tessitura,* s. f. *il tessere.*

WEB, s. [the cloth that is weaving] *tela, che è sul telajo.*

Cob-web, *ragnatelo,* s. m. *tela di ragna.*

A web of lead, *un foglio di piombo.*

A web [a spot or pearl in the eye] *maglia, macchia nell' occhio.*

WE'BSTER, s. [weaver] *tessitore,* s. m. *tessitrice,* s. f.

To WED [to marry] *sposare, ammogliarsi, maritare.*

To wed a wife, *ammogliarsi.*

WE'DDED, adj. *sposato, ammogliato, maritato.*

Wedded to his own opinion, *caparbio, rapone, ostinato, fermo nella sua opinione.*

Wedded to his interest, *interessato.*

WE'DDING, s. [the celebration of marriage] *sposalizio,* s. m. *nozze,* s. f.

I was at the wedding, *io fui alle nozze.*

Wedding garment, *vesta nuziale, vesti sposereccie.*

WEDGE, s. [a tool to cleave wood]

conio,

conio, s. m. *strumento di metallo, o di legno che percosso ha forza di fendere*.

Wedge-wise, *in forma di conio*.

A wedge of gold or silver, *verga d' oro o d' argento*.

WE'DLOCK, s. [matrimony, marriage] *matrimonio*, s. m.

Joined in wedlock, *maritato, ammogliato*.

WE'DNESDAY, s. [the fourth day of the week] *Mercoledì*, s. m. *nome del quarto giorno della settimana*.

WEED, s. [any wild herb that grows of itself] *erba salvatica, mal' erba*.

Ill weeds grow apace, *le mal' erbe crescono il più*.

Weed, s. [a garment, or suit of clothes] *abito, vestimento*.

Black weeds, *bruno*, s. m. *gramaglie, abito lugubre che si porta in onoranza de' morti*.

A friar's weed, *un abito monacale*.

Choke-weed, *roda-cavallina*, s. f. *spezie d' erba*.

Rope-weed [a plant] *vilucchio*, s. m. *spezie d' erba*.

Sea-weed [a plant] *alga*, s. f. *erba aquatica*.

To WEED [to pluck up or to root out weeds] *sarchiare, tagliar col sarchio l' erbe salvatiche*.

WE'EDED, adj. *sarchiato*.

WE'EDER, s. *sarchiatore*.

WE'EDHOOK, s. [a hook by which weeds are cut away or extirpated] *ferro incurvato per uso di sarchiare*.

WE'EDING, s. *sarchiamento*, s. m. *sarchiagione, sarchiatura*, s. f.

Weeding hook, *sarchio*, s. m. *piccola marra per uso di sarchiare*.

WE'EDLESS, adj. [free from weeds; free from any thing useless or noxious] *libero dalle gramigne, senza mal' erba; libero da ogni cosa inutile o nociva*.

WE'EDY, adj. [consisting of weeds] *pien di male erbe, abbondante di gramigne*.

WE'EK, s. [the cotton match in a candle] *stoppino, lucignolo di candela*.

Week [the space of seven days] *settimana*, s. f.

So much a week, *un tanto la settimana*.

The next week, *la settimana prossima*.

WE'EKDAY, s. [any day not Sunday] *ogni giorno non Domenica, giorno di lavoro*.

WE'EKLY, adj. *ogni settimana, d'ogni settimana*.

WE'EL, s. [bow net to take fishes in] *nassa*, s. f. *sorta di rete che ha 'l ritroso*.

Weel [whirl pool] *voragine*, s. f.

To WEEN [to think, to be of opinion] *pensare, credere, giudicare, esser di parere, stimare*.

WE'ENING, s. *pensiero, parere*, s. m. *opinione, credenza*, s. f.

To WEEP [to shed tears] *piangere, e piagnere, lagrimare*, pret. *piansi*.

To weep for the death of a relation, *pianger la morte d' un parente*.

WE'EPER, s. *piangitore, piagnitore, piagnone*, s. m.

WE'EPING, s. *piangimento e piagnimento*, s. m. *il piangere*.

He fell a weeping, *egli cominciò a piagnere*.

WE'EPINGLY, adv. *piangevolmente, o piagnevolmente, con pianto*.

WE'ESEL, s. [a little wild creature like a mouse] *donnola*, s. f. *bestiuola piccola simile al topo*.

Weesel red, *rossiccio, del colore della donnola*.

To WEET, v. n. pret. wot or wote [know, to have knowledge, to be informed] *sapere, esser conscio, esser informato*. Obs.

WE'EVIL, s. [a small black worm that eats corn in the loft] *gorgoglione, tonchio*, s. m. *baco, che è ne' legumi e li vota*.

WEFT, s. [a thing woven] *un tessuto*.

A weft of hair, *una treccia di capelli*.

WEIGH, s. *peso*.

To WEIGH [to ponderate, to poise, to try the weight of a thing] *pesare, gravitare, ponderare*.

To weigh gold, silver, bread, meat, *pesare oro, argento, pane, carne*.

To weigh [to examine, judge, or consider] *pesare, esaminare, ponderare, considerare*.

You must weigh all these reasons, *voi dovete pesare tutte queste ragioni*.

To weigh every word, *ponderare ogni parola*.

To weigh all accounts by pleasures and sorrows, *giudicare d' ogni cosa per i piaceri e i disgusti che se n' hanno*.

To weigh, or to weigh anchor, *salpare, sarpare, sciogliere l' ancora*.

To weigh down, *pesar più, far traboccar la bilancia*.

That weighs down all objections, *questo supera ogni objezione*.

To weigh, verb neut. [to be of weight, to have a certain weight] *pesare, esser di peso, esser pesante*.

How many pounds do you think I weigh without my clothes? *quanto credete che io pesi senza gli abiti?*

This weighs 20 pounds, *questo pesa venti libbre*.

A pistole that weighs, *una doppia di peso*.

A pistole that does not weigh, *una doppia scarsa, che non è di peso*.

To weigh [to be of weight, to be considerable, important] *esser di peso, esser importante, esser di momento*.

His authority weighs more than his arguments, *la sua autorità è di più gran peso che non i suoi argomenti*.

That reason does not weigh with me, *questa ragione è di niun peso, è molto frivola per me*.

WEIGHED, adj. *pesato*, v. To weigh.

WE'IGHER, s. *pesatore*, s. m. *che pesa*.

WE'IGHING, s. *il pesare*.

WEIGHT, s. [the heaviness of a thing] *peso*, s. m. *pesanza, gravezza*, s. f.

The weight of afflictions, *il peso delle afflizioni*.

Weights [pieces of metal or stone to weigh with] *pesi, alcuni pezzi i quali contrapposti sulla bilancia alla cosa che si pesa distinguono la sua gravezza*.

To sell things by weight, *vendere che che sia a peso*.

To do every thing with weight and measure [with deliberation] *fare ogni cosa a peso e misura, pesatamente, con giudicio, accortamente*.

To make good weight, *far buon peso*.

He is worth his weight in gold, *val tant' oro quanto pesa; è una coppa d' oro*.

A pistole of weight [that bears down the weight] *una doppia traboccante*.

That pistole is not of weight, *questa doppia è scarsa, non è di peso*.

A hundred pound weight, *cento libbre, un cantáro*.

Weight [importance, consequence] *peso, momento*, s. m. *importanza*, s. f.

The weights of a clock, *i contrappesi di un orologio*.

WEIGHTS or a pair of weights, *una bilancia*.

WE'IGHTINESS, s. [the being weighty] *peso*, s. m. *pesanza, gravezza*, s. f.

Weightiness [weight, importance] *peso, momento, importanza*.

WE'IGHTLESS, adj. [light, having no gravity] *leggiero, che non è grave, non pesante*.

WE'IGHTY, adj. [ponderous, heavy] *pesante, che pesa, grave*.

Weighty [of great moment, of concern, important] *pesante, di gran considerazione o momento, importante*.

For weighty reasons, *per ragioni importanti*.

This reason is very weighty, *questa ragione è di gran peso*.

WELAWAY, interj. [alas!] *ohimè, misero me!*

WE'LCOME, adj. [a salutation used to a grateful guest, visitant, or customer] *ben venuto*.

You are welcome, *voi siete il ben venuto*.

You are welcome, gentlemen, *ben venuti, signori*.

If you like it you are welcome to it, *se vi aggrada è al vostro comando, ne siete il padrone*.

Your letters are always welcome to me, *le vostre lettere mi sono sempre grate*.

To bid or make one welcome, *ricevere, accogliere alcuno con amorevolezza, fargli buona accoglienza*.

Welcome coming, *benvenutezza, felice arrivo*.

To WE'LCOME [to bid welcome] *accogliere, fare accoglienza, ricever con amorevolezza*, pret. *accolsi*.

WE'LCOMED, adj. *accolto*.

WE'LCOMNESS, s. [gratefulness] *piacevolezza, accettatezza, lo essere o riuscire grato o accetto*.

WE'LCOMER, s. [the saluter or receiver of a new comer] *colui che primo saluta, o accarezzando riceve un che giunge*.

WE'LCOMING, s. *accoglienza, amore-*

morevolezza, s. f. *affetto*, s. m.

To WELD [among smiths, to forge iron] *battere il ferro caldo.*

WE'LFARE, s. [prosperity, health] *salute, sanità, prosperità, bene, bene stare, conservazione.*

WELK, s. [a sort of shell fish] *petoncolo*, s. m. *spezie di conchiglia.*

To WELK [to clould, to obscure] *adombrare, oscurare, offuscare.*

WE'LKED, adj. [wrinkled, wreathed] *rugoso, pien di rughe.*

WE'LKIN, s. [firmament, sky] *l' etere, il cielo, il firmamento.*

WELL, s. [a pit of spring water] *pozzo.*

Well-water, *acqua di pozzo.*

WELL, adv. *bene.*

I am very well, *io sto molto bene.*

Well [much] *bene, molto.*

Well beloved, *molto amato, carissimo.*

He lives very well, *egli vive molto comodamente.*

To grow well again, *ricuperar la salute.*

And well it might, *e con ragione.*

It is well for you that I was not there, *ben per voi che io non mi trovai presente.*

It happened as well as could be, *la cosa non poteva riuscir meglio.*

To think well of one's own self, *aver buona opinione di se stesso, presumer molto di se.*

To take a thing well, *pigliare una cosa in buona parte.*

To take a thing well of one, *restare obbligato ad uno per qualche cosa.*

I love you too well, *io v' amo pur troppo.*

I wish you well, *vi desidero ogni bene.*

He spends more than he is well able, *spende più, che non comporta il suo avere.*

Well and good *alla buon ora.*

Well near, well nigh, *appresso a poco, quasi.*

Well born, well descended, *ben nato, di buona nascita.*

Well-favoured, well-featured, *bello, vago, ben fatto.*

Well-affected, well-minded, *ben affetto, ben intenzionato.*

Well-mannered, *civile, cortese, ben creato.*

Well-wisher, *amico, che desidera bene.*

Well-bottomed, *ben fondato.*

Well-disposed [charitable] *caritatévole.*

Well-meant, *ben intenzionato, ben affetto.*

Well-meaning, *buona intenzione.*

A well-meaning man, *un galantuomo, un uomo onorato, un uomo dabbene.*

Well tasted, *che ha buon gusto.*

Well-traded, *mercantile, di gran traffico.*

Well-doing, *buone azioni.*

To WELL [to spring, to issue as from a spring] *zampillare, scaturire, mandar fuori acqua come fa la sorgente.*

WE'LLADAY! interj. *cappita! capperi!*

WELT, s. [fold, doubling down of cloth in making of a garment] *orlo*, s. m.

To WELT [to double] *orlare.*

WE'LTED, adj. *orlato.*

To WE'LTER [to wallow] *voltolarsi.*

To welter in one's own blood, *voltolarsi nel proprio sangue.*

WEM, s. [small blemish in cloth] *macchia*, s. f.

Wem, s. [belly, guts] *pancia.*

WEN, s. [hard swelling, bunch] *lupa*, s. f.

Wen in the throat, *gozzo*, s. m. *enfiamento di gola.*

WENCH, s. [a familiar or a contemptuous word for a maid or girl] *una zittella, una ragazza, una berghinella.*

A pretty wench, *una bella zittella.*

Wench [whore, crack] *baldracca, bagascia, puttana, puttanella.*

A man given to wenches, *un puttaniere, che va dietro alle puttane.*

To WENCH [to whore] *puttaneggiare, andar dietro alle puttane.*

WE'NCHER, } s. *puttaniere, che*
WE'NCHING-man, } *attende a puttane.*

Wenching, s. *puttaneggio*, s. m. *il puttaneggiare.*

To go a wenching, *puttaneggiare, andare a puttane.*

WEND, s. [a tract of land] *tratto di terra d' una certa misura Inglese.*

To WEND [to go] *andare.* Obsolete.

WE'NNEL, s. [an animal newly taken from the dam] *animale tolto di fresco dalla madre.*

WE'NNY, adj. [having the nature of a wen] *gozzuto, pieno di gonfiamenti; gonfio.*

WENT, s. [the only time in use of the obsolete verb To wend] *è un preterito in uso del verbo inusiato*, To wend.

I went, *andai.*

The business went thus, *la cosa passò in questo modo.*

Went, s. [way] *cammino*, s. m.

WEPT, *preterito del verbo* To weep, *pianfi.*

Wept for, adj. *pianto, lagrimato.*

WERE [the plural of was, in the verb, To be] *è il plurale di* was, *nel verbo* To be

We were, *noi eramo, noi eravamo*, you were, *voi erate, voi eravate*, they were, *eglino erano.*

Were is also a singular, as in the following examples, *usano gl' Inglesi* were *anche nel numero del meno, come si vede ne' seguenti esempi.*

If I were rich, *s' io fossi ricco.*

Were you a man of your word, *se voi foste uomo di parola.*

Were it not for his good conduct, *se non fosse per la sua buona condotta.*

I were a great knave to do it, *sarei un gran briccone, se facessi questo.*

I wish he were gone, *vorrei che fosse partito.*

I would to God you were as happy, *volesse Dio che voi foste così contente.*

You were better to go, *voi fareste meglio d' andarvene.*

Were it but for your own honour, *quando non fosse che per vostro onore.*

As it were, *per così dire, in qualche maniera.*

WE'RE-WOLF, s. [a man wolf] *un lupo uomo, creatura immaginata.*

WE'RRISH, adj. [unsavoury] *insipido, scipito, senza sapore.*

WERT, s. *la seconda persona singolare del preterito del verbo* To be.

WE'SAND, } s. [wesand-pipe] *stroz-*
WE'SIL, } *za, la canna della gola, il gorgozzule.*

WEST, s. [the quarter of the world where the sun sets] *ponente, occidente*, s. m. *la parte del mondo dove il sole tramonta.*

The west, or western parts, *il ponente, l' orridente, le parti occidentali.*

West, adj. *occidentale, d' occidente.*

The west countries, *i paesi occidentali.*

The West-Indies, *le Indie occidentali.*

WE'STERLY, } adj. *occidentale, d' oc-*
WE'STERN, } *cidente.*

Westerly or western wind, *vento occidentale o d' occidente, il vento di ponente.*

The western churches, *le chiese d' occidente.*

The western world, *il mondo nuovo, l' America occidentale.*

WE'STWARD, } adv. *verso po-*
WE'STWARDLY, } *nente, all' occidente, o ponente.*

WET, adj. [moist with liquor] *bagnato, molle, umido.*

My clothes are all wet, *i miei abiti sono bagnati.*

Wet room, *camera umida.*

Her eyes are wet with tears, *i suoi occhi sono molli di lagrime.*

To make wet, *bagnare.*

Wet-shoo'd *che ha i piedi bagnati.*

Wet-nurse, *balia.*

Wet sweetmeats, *confetture liquide.*

Wet weather, *tempo piovoso.*

The ground is wet with dew, *la rugiada ha bagnata la terra.*

To do a thing with a wet finger, *fare che che sia facilmente, con facilità.*

Wet, s. [moisture] *umidità, mollezza*, s. f.

To WET [to make wet, to moist] *bagnare.*

To wet one's hand, *bagnarsi le mani.*

To wet the ground, *adacquare la terra.*

WE'THER, s. [a ram castrated] *un montone castrato.*

WE'TNESS, s. [moisture] *umidità, mollezza*, s. f.

WO'TTED, adj. *bagnato.*

WE'TTING, *bagnamento*, s. m. *bagnatura*, s. f. *il bagnare.*

To WEX [to grow, to encrease] *crescere, farsi grande.*

WEY, s. [the greatest measure of dry things, containing five chaldrons] *la più*

più gran misura Inglese dolle cose secche.

WE'ZAND, *v.* Wesand.

WHALE, s. [the greatest of fishes] *balena*, s f.

Whale-bone, *balena, osso di balena.*

WHARF, s. [a broad plain place near a creek or hithe, to land or lay wares on that are brought from or on the water] *molo, porto di fiume,*

WHA'RFAGE, s. [the fee due for laying goods on a wharf] *diritto che si paga per sbarcare robe sopra il molo.*

WHA'RFINGER, s. [the owner or keeper of a wharf] *padrone o guardiano d' un molo.*

To WHARL [to stutter in pronouncing the letter R] *balbettare nel pronunciare la lettera R.*

WHAT? [an interrogative pronoun] *che? quale?*

What say you? *che dite?*

What, *che, cosa, qualunque.*

I do not know what, *non so che.*

In what condition soever, *in qualunque stato sia.*

Mind well what I say to you, *badate bene a quel che vi dico.*

I speak nothing but what is true, *non dico che il vero; tutto è vero quel che dico.*

What do you ask for it? *quanto ne volete?*

What if I should go? *dato il caso che io andassi?*

Well, and what of all this? *e bene, che volete dire per ciò?*

What is your name? *come vi chiamate?*

What with his conduct, what with his courage, *tanto per la sua condotta, che per il suo coraggio.*

WHATE'VER [a pronoun] *qualunque, che che, quel che.*

Whatever thing happens, *accada quel che si voglia.*

Whatever it be, *sia come si voglia, in qualunque modo sia.*

Whatever he be, *sia chi si voglia, chiunque egli sia.*

Whatever you will, *tutto quel che vorrete.*

WHATSOE'VER, *v.* Whatever.

In what condition soever I be, *in qualunque stato che io mi trovi.*

WHAY, s. *siero*, s. m. *v.* Whey.

WHA'YINESS, s. *sierosità*, s. f.

WHEAL, s. [push, pimple] *ciccione, cosso*, s. m, *bolla, bollicella, pustula*, s. f.

Wheal-worm, s. [an insect] *baco*, s. m.

WHEAT, s. [that grain of which the finest bread is made] *grano*, s. m. *quella biada, della quella comunemente facciamo il pane.*

No wheat without its chaff, *non si trova nessuno senza difetto.*

Wheat-ear [a bird] *spezie d' uccelletto.*

WHE'ATEN, adj. *di grano.*

Wheaten flour, *fior di farina di grano.*

WHE'ATEAR, s. *nome d' uccelletto.*

WHE'ATPLUM, s. *sorta di susina.*

WHE'EDLE, s. [a subtle drawing of one in] *allettamento, lacciuólo, vezzo*, s. m. *lusinga, lusingheria*, s. f.

To WHE'EDLE [to draw in craftily, to sooth] *lusingare, allettare, indurre con belle parole, ingannare, zimbellare, piaggiare.*

WHE'EDLED, adj. *lusingato, allettato, indotto con belle parole, ingannato, zimbellato.*

WHE'EDLER, s. *lusingatore, piaggiatore*, s. m.

WHE'EDLING, s. *blandimento, lusingamento, zimbello*, s. m. *lusinghe*, s. f.

Wheedling, adj. *lusinghevole.*

A wheedling man or woman, *un lusingatore, una lusingatrice, una lusinghiera.*

WHEEL, s. *ruota*, s. f.

The wheels of a coach or cart, *le ruote d' una carrozza o d' un carro.*

Water-wheel, *ruota di pozzo.*

Wheel to break malefactors upon, *ruota da romper vivi i malfattori.*

To break upon the wheel, *romper vivo sopra una ruota.*

Wheel, or spinning-wheel, *filatojo*, s. m. *strumento di legno da filare, che ha una ruota, colla quale girandola si torce il filo.*

A chair that goes upon wheels, *una sedia a carrucole.*

A turner's wheel, *un tornio.*

To set the chief wheels a-going, *adoperare i mezzi i più efficaci.*

Wheel-wright [wheeler] *facitor di ruote.*

Wheel-barrow, *carriuola.*

To WHEEL about [to turn about] *voltar faccia, voltarsi.*

Time wheels about, *il tempo passa.*

To wheel salt out of a pit, *tirar su del sale d' una salina.*

WHE'ELAGE, s. [duty paid for carts and waggons] *tassa che pagano i carri.*

WHE'ELER, s. [a maker of wheels] *un che fa ruote.*

To WHEEZE [to squeak as one that has a cold] *parlare, come fa una persona che è infreddata.*

WHELK, s. [an inequality, a protuberance] *bitórzolo.*

Whelk [a pustule] *pustula, ciccione, cosso, bolla, bollicella.*

WHELP, s. [puppy, young dog] *un cagnuollno.*

Whelp [the young cub of any wild beast] *piccino di tutti li animali terrestri salvatici.*

Lion's whelp, *lioncino.*

Wolf's whelp, *lupacchino, lupicino.*

Viper's whelp, *una viperetta.*

Whelp [an injurious word for a young rogue] *baroncello, bricconcello.*

To WHELP [to bring forth puppies as a bitch does] *figliare, fare i cagnuolini.*

The bitch has whelped, *la cagna ha figliato, ha fatto i cagnolini.*

WHE'LPISH, adj. [currish, ill] *tristo, cattivo.*

Whelpish trick, *cattiva burla.*

WHEN [at what time] *quando.*

When [at, or in the time that] *quando, allora che, nel tempo che, nel mentre.*

When will you go? *quando volete andare?*

When it is time for it, *quando sarà tempo.*

Last year when I was in France, *l' anno passato mentre ero in Francia.*

And when all is said, *in somma.*

WHENCE, from whence, *donde.*

Whence, or from whence come you? *donde venite?*

From whence I conclude, *dal che io conchiudo.*

WHENE'VER, } adv. *quando, ogni*
WHENSOE'VER, } *volta che.*

WHERE, adv. *dove, in che luogo.*

Where is he? *dov' è?*

I do not know where I am, *non so dove mi sia, non so dove sto colla testa.*

Every where, *dapertutto, pertutto.*

Any where, *ovunque, in qualunque luogo si sia.*

I will go any where rather than stay here, *vo' andare in qualsisia luogo piuttosto che star qui.*

Let us go any where, *andiamo ovunque volete.*

WHE'REABOUT, } adv. *dove, in che*
WHE'REABOUTS, } *luogo.*

I know whereabouts you are, *v' intendo, so quel che volete dire.*

WHE'REAS, adv. [because] *perchè, stante che.*

Whereas, *in luogo che.*

WHE'REAT, adv. [at which] *al che, del che.*

Whereat I was much surprised, *del che io restai molto sorpreso.*

WHE'REBY, adv. [by which] *per il quale.*

The means whereby he compassed it, *il mezzo per il quale egli l' ha ottenuto.*

WHERE'VER, adv. *ovunque, in qualunque luogo.*

WHE'REFORE, adv. [why] *per che causa.*

Wherefore did you do it? *perchè l' avete fatto?*

Wherefore [therefore] *perciò.*

WHE'REFROM [from whence] *donde.*

WHE'REIN [in which] *in che, nel quale, dove, nella quale.*

That's wherein you failed, *questo è il punto nel quale voi avete mancato.*

A letter wherein he complains, *una lettera nella quale si duole.*

WHEREI'NTO, adv. *nel quale, nella quale.*

The house whereinto he went, *la casa nella quale egli andò.*

WHE'REOF, adv. [of which] *del quale, della quale, de' quali, delle quali.*

The thing whereof I spoke to you, *la cosa della quale io v' ho parlato.*

WHERESOE'VER, adv. *ovunque, in qualunque luogo.*

WHERE'VER, adv. [at whatsoever place] *ovunque, in qualunque luogo.*

WHE'RETO, } [to which] *al*
WHE'REUNTO, } *che.*

Whereto he answered, *al che egli rispose.*

WHE'REUPON, adv. [upon which] *nel che, in questo mentre.*
WHEREWITH, adv. [with which] *con che, col quale, colla quale.*
WHE'REWITHAL, adv. *di che.*
I have not wherewithal to do it, *io non ho il modo di farlo.*
WHE'RRET, s. [a box on the ear] *uno schiaffo, una guanciata.*
To give one a wherret on the ear, *dare uno schiaffo ad uno.*
To WHE'RRET, *schiaffeggiare, dare uno schiaffo.*
WHE'RRY, s. [a small boat to go over a river] *barchetta da passar un fiume.*
Wherry-man, *barcaruolo.*
WHET, s. ex. to take a whet in the morning, *incantar la nebbia, bever la mattina a buon' ora.*
I must have a whet first, *bisogna ch' io beva prima.*
WHET-STONE [a stone for whetting] *cote,* s. f. *pietra da affilar ferri, da aguzzarli.*
That's a whet-stone to wit, *questo aguzza l' ingegno.*
To WHET [to sharpen] *affilare, arrotare, arruotare, assottigliar il taglio a' ferri taglienti.*
WHE'THER, pronoun [which] *quale, quale de' due.*
Whether it be true or no, *che la cosa sia vera o no.*
Whether [if] *se.*
I'll see whether he be at home, *voglio vedere s' egli è in casa.*
'Tis all one to me whether he comes or no, *che venga o non venga non m' importa.*
Whether had you rather live here or in the country? *dove amereste meglio dimorare? quì o in campagna?*
Whether he will or no, *voglia o non voglia, suo malgrado.*
WHE'TTED, adj. *affilato, arrotato, e arruotato.*
WHE'TTER, s. *affilatore, arrotino.*
WHE'TTING, s. *l' affilare.*
WHEY, s. [the thin or serous part of the milk, from which the oleose or grumous part is separated] *siero; parte sottile o sierosa del latte.*
Whey [it is used of any thing white or thin] *siero; così chiamano pure gl' Inglesi ogni cosa liquida che è sottile e bianca.*
WHE'YEY, WHE'YISH, adj. [partaking of whey; resembling whey] *sieroso, che ha del siero, che s' assomiglia al siero.*
WHICH [pronoun relative] *che, il quale, la quale.*
The book which you had promised me, *il libro che m' avevate promesso.*
Take which you please, *prendete quale volete.*
I know not which it is, *non so quale de' due sia.*
Which [pronoun interrogative] *quale,*
Which is the best? *quale è il migliore?*
Which do you like best? *quale de' due amate meglio?*
Which way? *per dove?*
Which way? [how?] *come? in che modo?*
WHICHSOE'VER [a pronoun] *qualunque.*
Whichsoever of those two, *qualunque de' due.*
WHIFF, s. [a breath] *alito, fiato,* s. m.
A whiff of tobacco, *un soffio di tabacco.*
To WHI'FFLE [to move inconstantly as if driven by a puff of wind] *muoversi ondeggiando; non si tener fermo come se spinto da un soffio di vento.*
To whiffle [to trick one out of a thing] *truffare, mariuolare.*
To whiffle [to stand trifling] *stare a bada, dondolarsi, consumare il tempo senza far nulla.*
WHI'FFLED, adj. *dal, v.* To whiffle.
WHI'FFLER, s. [a piper in a company of soldiers] *un piffero, un sonator di piffero.*
A whiffler or whiffling fellow [a pitiful, mean, sorry fellow] *un dappocco, un uomo da niente.*
Whiffling, adj. [mean, inconsiderable] *di niun valore, di poca considerazione, frivolo.*
WHIG, s. [whey] *siero,* s. m. *parte sierosa del latte.*
Whig, s. *setta di politici in Inghilterra, i di cui principj sono dannati da i tory loro nemici che li dipingono come gente per lo più di mala morale, di nulla religione, e d' inclinazioni repubblichesche.*
WHI'GGISM, s. m. *la pretesa filosofia d' un* whig.
WHILE, s [time] *tempo, volta, fiata.*
You made me stay a long while, *voi m' avete fatto aspettare lungo tempo, un gran pezzo.*
A while after, *qualche tempo dopo.*
For a while, for some while, *per qualche tempo.*
Between whiles [from time to time] *di quando in quando.*
But a while since, *poco fa, non ha guari, testè.*
One while he flatters, another while he threatens me, *ora mi lusinga, ed ora mi minaccia.*
'Tis not worth my, your, or his while, 'tis not worth the while, *non vale la pena.*
Mean while, in the mean while, *frattanto, in questo mentre.*
While, conj. [during the time] *mentre, tanto che.*
While you do that, I do this, *mentre voi farete quello, io farò questo.*
While I remember, *intanto che me ne ricordo, mentre me ne ricordo.*
To WHILE off [to put off] *procrastinare, indugiare, differire, mandare in lunga.*
To while away one's time, *perder il tempo, dondolarsela, consumare il tempo in vano.*
To WHILK [to yelp, to bark as a little dog] *squittire, stridere come fanno i cagnolini.*
WHILST, or whilst that, adv. *mentre, mentre che.*
WHIM, or WHIMSEY, s. [maggot, fancy, conceit, freakish humour] *capriccio, ghiribizzo,* s. f. *fantasia,* s. f.
Whim-wham [toy] *bagattella, baja, cianciafruscola.*
WHI'MMISH, *v.* Whimsical.
To WHI'MPER [to begin to cry as a young child does] *gagnolare, dolersi, lamentarsi, rammaricarsi.*
WHI'MPERING, s. *lamento, rammarico, rammarichio, piagnisteo,* s. m.
WHI'MSEY, *v.* Whim.
WHI'MSICAL, adj. [freakish, fantastical] *capriccioso, ghiribizzoso, bisbètico, fantastico.*
A whimsical man or woman, *un capriccioso, un fantastico, una capricciosa, una fantastica.*
WHI'MSICALLY, adv. *capricciosamente, fantasticamente, a capriccio.*
WHI'MSY, *v.* Whim.
WHIN, s. [a shrub] *pruno, pugnitopo,* s. m.
To WHINE [to make a mournful noise] *gagnolare, dolersi, rammaricarsi, querelarsi, lamentarsi, mugolare.*
WHI'NING, s. *dolore, rammarico, lamento, mugolio,* s. m.
Whining, adj. *dolente, querulo, lamentevole.*
To WHI'NNY [to neigh] *nitrire,* pres. *nitrisco.*
WHI'NYARD, s. [a sword, in contempt] *spada; è voce di disprezzo.*
WHIP [lash, scourge] *frusta, sferza, ferza,* s. f.
Coachman's whip, *frusta di cocchiere.*
A whip to whip a top, *sferza da percuoter la trottola.*
To have the whip hand, *aver l' avvantaggio, esser superiore.*
WHIP, s. [a sort of round stitch] *sovraggiunto.*
Whip-saw, *pialla,* s. f.
Whip, or whip-staff [a piece of timber fastened in the helm thereby to move the helm and steer the ship] *manovella,* s. f.
To WHIP [to scourge, to lash with a whip] *frustare, battere, e percuotere con frusta, sferzare.*
To whip a child, *frustare un fanciullo.*
To whip a top, *sferzare una trottola.*
To whip out one's sword, *metter mano alla spada, sfoderare la spada*
To whip [to sew round] *trapuntare.*
To whip up, to whip off [to take suddenly] *afferrare, acchiappare, strappare.*
He whipt up the money in his pocket, *egli acchiappò il danaro, e se lo cacciò in tasca.*
To whip off a thing [to make short work with it] *spedire, sbrigare un negozio.*
To whip up and down, *frustare, andar vagando, andar qua e la.*
To whip out, *uscir subitamente, corsela.*
To whip up, *salir prontamente.*
To whip down, *scender prontamente.*

WHI'PPING, s. *frustatura*, s. f. *il frustare.*

It will cost you a whipping, *voi sarete frustato per questo.*

WHI'PSTER, s. *frustatore*, s. m.

Whipster [sharper] *furbo, mariuolo.*

WHIPT, adj. *frustato, sferzato.*

WHIRL, s. [vortex] *turbine*, s. m.

Whirl [a round piece of wood put on the spindle to spin with] *pezzo di legno tondo, bucato nel mezzo, il quale si mette nel fuso acciocchè aggravato giri più unitamente e meglio.*

WHIRLBAT, s. [any thing moved rapidly round to give a blow] *checchessia che aggiriamo con impeto per dare un gran colpo.*

The whirl-bone [the knee-pan, the round bone of the knee] *la padella del ginocchio.*

Whirl-pool, *una voragine.*

Whirl-pool [a kind of sea fish] *spezie di mostro marino.*

Whirl-wind, *un turbine.*

Whirl worm, *spezie di vermicello che s' avviticchia alle radici delle piante, e si chiama in Latino* Spondyle.

To WHIRL, or to whirl about [to turn swiftly about] *girare con impeto.*

Whirled about, adj. *girato con impeto.*

WHI'RLING, s. *girata, giro impetuoso*, s. f.

Whirling, or whirl-gig [a plaything to turn round] *un zurlo.*

WHISK [a brush made of osier twigs] *spazzola*, s. f. *granata di filo di saggina, colla quale si nettano i panni.*

Whisk [a game at cards] *sorta di giuoco di carte, v.* Whist.

To WHISK [to brush, to cleanse with a whisk] *spazzolare, nettar colla spazzola.*

To whisk away [to make haste] *spedirsi, spacciarsi, sbrigarsi.*

WHI'SKER [a tuft of hair on the upper lip of a man] *mustacchio*, s. m. *basetta*, s. f.

WHI'SKING, adj. [great] *grande. E' vocabolo burlesco, e non molto usato.*

Whisking lie, *una gran bugia.*

WHI'SPER, s. *mormorio, bisbiglio*, s.m.

There's a whisper of such news about the town, *si bisbiglia una tal novella per la città.*

To WHI'SPER [to speak softly] *parlar sotto voce, parlare o zufolar nell' orecchio, bisbigliare pian piano.*

Such a news is whispered about the town, *si buccina, si bisbiglia, corre voce per la città.*

WHI'SPERED, adj. *bisbigliato, burrinato.*

'Tis whispered about, *si buccina, si dice, corre voce.*

WHI'SPERING, s. *bisbiglio*, s. m.

I hear a whispering, *odo un bisbiglio.*

WHIST [an interjection of silence] *silenzio, zitto.*

Whist, s. *altri scrivono* whisk, *giuoco di carte molto usato e credo inventato dagl' Inglesi che lo giuocano con gran silenzio d' onde forse ha avuto il nome.*

To WHIST, *tacersi, non dir niente.*

WHI'STLE, s. [a little pipe to whistle with] *un fischio, strumento da fischiare.*

The whistle [the wind-pipe, or wesand pipe] *la strozza, la canna della gola.*

To wet one's whistle [to drink] *bere*, pres. *bevo, beo.*

To WHI'STLE [to make musical sounds with the lips and breath, without any vocal sounds] *zufolare, fischiare.*

The birds whistle, *gli uccelli fischiano.*

Do you hear how the wind whistles? *sentite come il vento fischia?*

WHI'STLER, s. *quello o quella che fischia.*

WHI'STLING, s. *fischio, zufolio, fibilo*, s. m.

The whistling of a thrush, *voce acuta o tronca del tordo.*

WHI'STLING, adj. *che fischia.*

Whistling wind, *vento che fischia.*

WHIT, s. [some small part] *un poco, un tantino.*

Not a whit [never a bit] *niente affatto, punto.*

He does not see a whit, *non vede punto, è affatto cieco.*

You are every whit as bad as he, *voi siete cattivo quanto lui, voi non siete punto meno cattivo di lui.*

WHITE, adj. [the contrary of black] *bianco, il contrario del nero, candido.*

As white as snow, *bianco come la neve.*

White-lime, *calcina bianca.*

White, s. [white colour] *bianco, color bianco.*

He was clad in white, *era vestito di bianco.*

The white of the eye, *il bianco dell' occhio.*

White of an egg, *bianco d' uovo, albume, chiara d' uovo.*

White [white paint] *sbelletto bianco.*

White [aim to shoot at] *bersaglio, e berzaglio*, s. m. *segno bianco, dove gli arcieri o altri tiratori dirizzan la mira per aggiustare il tiro.*

To hit the white, *dar nel bersaglio, dar nel segno.*

White-wort [an herb] *marticale*, s.f. *erba nota.*

White-pot [milk with herbs, fine bread, sugar, and spice, baked in an earthen pot] *latte cotto nel forno in un vaso di terra con uova, pane, zucchero, e spezierie.*

To WHITE [to whiten] *imbiancare, far divenir bianco*, pres. *imbianco.*

WHI'TEWASH, s. [wash to make the skin seem fair] *liscio, sbelletto, acqua di cui le donne fanno uso per imbiancarsi il muso.*

To WHITEWASH, *intonicare.*

WHI'TED,
WHI'TENED, } adj. *imbiancato.*

WHI'TELY, adj. [pale, wan] *pallido, macilente.*

WHI'TENESS, *bianchezza*, s. f.

WHI'TENING, s. *l' imbiancare.*

WHI'THER, adv. *dove.*

Whither do you go? *dove andate?*

WHI'TING, s. *l' imbiancare.*

WHI'TING, s. [to whiten walls with] *bianco*, s. m. *quella materia di color bianco, colla quale s' imbiancan le mura.*

Whiting [a fish] *merluzzo*, s. m. *spezie di pesce.*

To let go a whiting [to let go an opportunity] *lasciarsi scappar di mano un' occasione.*

WHI'TISH, adj. [somewhat white] *bianchetto, biancastro, bianchiccio, che tende al bianco.*

WHI'TISHNESS, s. *bianchezza*, s. f.

WHI'TLOW, s. [a preternatural swelling at the fingers ends] *panereccio*, s.m. *postema che viene nelle dita delle mani, alle radici dell' unghie.*

Whitlow-glass, s. [a certain herb of great efficacy against felons and whitlows] *spezie d' erba buona alla guarigione de' panerecci, e chiamasi in Latino* Paronychia.

WHI'TSOUR, s. [a kind of apple] *sorta di mela.*

WHI'TSTER, s. [one who whitens linen cloth] *imbiancatore*, s. m.

WHI'TSUN, adj. *Pentecoste.*

Whitsun holy-days, *le feste della Pentecoste.*

WHI'TSUNDAY, s. [a solemn festival, otherwise called Pentecost] *Pentecoste, il giorno della Pentecoste, Pasqua rosata.*

WHITSU'NTIDE, s. [the season of that festival] *la Pentecoste, la stagione delle Pentecoste, Pasqua rosata.*

WHI'TTAIL, s. [a bird] *lui*, s. m. *spezie d' uccellino.*

WHI'TTEN-TREE, s. *oppi*, s. m. *albero così chiamato.*

WHI'TTLE, s. [a little knife] *un coltellino.*

Whittle [a small blanket worn over the shoulders by women] *mantellina*, s.f.

To WHI'TTLE [to cut sticks into small pieces] *tagliuzzare, minutamente tagliare.*

WHI'TTLED, adj. [cup-shot] *cotto, briaco, avvinazzato.*

To WHIZZE [to make a noise as liquor does when poured over the fire] *fare uno ronzio come un liquore che si versa sopra il fuoco.*

WHO, pron. [which] *chi.*

Who is there? *chi è là?*

WHOE'VER [a pronoun] *chiunque, qualunque.*

WHOLE, adj. [all, entire] *tutto, intero.*

The whole world, *tutto 'l mondo.*

A whole year, *un anno intero.*

The whole sum, *tutta la somma, la somma totale.*

Whole and sound, *bello e buono.*

To make one whole, *sanare, guarire alcuno.*

To swallow one's meat whole, *inghiottire il cibo senza masticarlo.*

To sleep in a whole skin, *dormire a suo agio, senza paura.*

The whole, s. *il tutto.*

To divide the whole into its parts, *dividere il tutto nelle sue parti.*

In the whole, *in tutto e per tutto.*

To sell by the whole, *vendere all' ingrosso.*

Who'lesale, *vendita all' ingrosso.*

A wholesale man, *un mercante che vende all' ingrosso.*

Whole-chase-boots [large riding boots] *stivali da cavalcare.*

Who'leness, s. *integrità*, s. f. *lo stato d' una cosa che è intera.*

Who'lesome, adj. [healthful, good, sound] *sano, salubre, salutifero, che contribuisce alla salute.*

A wholesome place or air, *un luogo salubre, un' aria salubre.*

Wholesome waters, *acque salutifere.*

Wholesome [good, true] *sano, vero, salutare.*

Wholesome doctrine, *dottrina sana, o salutare.*

Wholesome advice, *sano consiglio.*

Who'lesomely, adv. *sanamente.*

To look wholesomely, *aver buona cera.*

Who'lesomeness, s. *sanità, salubrità*, s. f.

Who'lly, adv. [entirely] *interamente, affatto, compiutamente, perfettamente.*

He gives himself wholly to pleasures, *è interamente dedito a' piaceri.*

Whom, *è un caso del pronome* [who] *che, il quale, al quale, a chi, chi.*

The man whom I love, *l' uomo che amo.*

The person whom I spoke to, *la persona, alla quale ho parlato.*

With whom, for whom, *con chi, da chi.*

Whomsoe'ver, *chiunque.*

Whoo'bub, s. [hubbub] *tumulto, rissa.*

Whoop, s. [pewet, a sort of bird *pupa*, s. f.

Whoop, s. [a sort of malignity] *acclamazione o applauso fatto per beffa e dettato dalla malignità.*

To Whoop [to shout with malignity] *acclamare per malignità, far applauso per beffa.*

To whoop [to insult with shouts] *insultare con maligno applauso e befardo.*

Whore, s. [a prostitute, a strumpet] *puttana, meretrice, zambracca, bagascia, sgualdrina cantoniera.*

To play the whore, *far la puttana.*

Whore-master, } *puttaniere, bor-*
Whore-monger, } *delliere, fornicatore.*

Whore-house [bawdy-house] *chiasso, bordello, lupanare*, s. m.

To Whore [to go a whoring] *puttaneggiare, andare a puttane.*

To whore away one's estate, *consumare il suo avere colle puttane.*

Who'redom, s. *puttaneggio*, s. m. *puttaneria, puttania*, s. f.

To commit whoredom, *fornicare.*

Who'ring, s. *puttaneggio.*

To go a whoring, *puttaneggiare, andare a puttane.*

Who'rish, adj. *di puttana.*

Whorish look, *cera di puttana, faccia di bagascia, viso di meretrice.*

Who'rishly, adj. *da puttana.*

To be whorishly inclined, *esser dedito alle puttane.*

Who'rson [whoreson] *figlio di puttana, bastardo.*

Whose [a pronoun signifying of whom, from whom, of which, from which] *di cui, di chi, a chi, da chi.*

A woman whose virtue is known every where, *una donna di cui la virtù è celebre dappertutto.*

Whose book is this? *di chi è questo libro?*

Whosesoe'ver [a pronoun] *di chiunque, a chiunque.*

Whosoever [whoever] *chiunque, qualunque.*

To Whur [to snarl as a dog does] *ringhiare, digrignare i denti come il cane.*

Why, adv. [for what cause or reason] *perchè, per che causa, per che ragione.*

Why don't you come? *perchè non venite?*

Why so? *perchè? per che ragione?*

Is there any reason why he should not do it? *e perchè non lo farebbe?*

Why not? *e perchè non?*

Wick [borough, village] *borgo, villaggio, terra.* It is never used but at the end of some names of towns, as Berwick.

Wi'cked, adj. [bad, vile] *cattivo, tristo, iniquo, vizioso, scellerato, malvagio.*

A wicked man or woman, *un uomo cattivo, una donna malvagia.*

A wicked action, *una cattiva azione.*

The wicked, s. *gli empi, i cattivi.*

Wickedly, adv. *male, malamente, cattivamente, tristamente, iniquamente, empiamente, malvagiamente.*

Wi'ckedness, s. *cattivanza, ribalderia, tristizia, malvagità*, s. f.

Wi'cker, s. *vinco*, s. m.

Wicker chair, *sedia di vinchi.*

Wi'cket, s. [a little door within a gate] *portello, sportello*, s. m. *piccolo uscio di alcune porte grandi.*

Widdle-waddle, adj. ex. to go widdle-waddle [to go sideling, first to one side, then to another] *camminar barcollando.*

Wide, adj. [large, broad] *largo, ampio.*

Wipe street, *una strada larga.*

How wide is this cloth? *quanto ampio è questo panno?*

Wide difference? *gran differenza.*

To be left to the wide world, *essere abbandonato da ognuno.*

Wide, adv. ex. to set a door wide open, *spalancare una porta.*

To leave it wide open, *lasciarla tutta aperta.*

Far and wide, *da ogni banda, dappertutto.*

Your fame will spread far and wide, *la vostra fama si spanderà dappertutto.*

To shoot wide from the mark, *andar largo dal segno o dal berzaglio.*

You throw wide, *voi sbagliate, voi v' ingannate di molto.*

That's wide for my purpose, *questo è tutto lontano dal mio pensiero.*

Wi'dely, adv. *largamente, ampiamente.*

He discovered widely from the matter, *egli s' è molto discostato dal soggetto.*

To Wi'den [to make wide] *slargare, allargare.*

Wi'deness, s. *larghezza, ampiezza*, s. f.

Wi'dgeon, } s. [a sort of bird]
Wi'dgin, } *spezie d' uccello.*

Widgin [simpleton, silly fellow] *uno sciocco, un dappoco, uno sciatto, un gonzo.*

Wi'dow, s. [a woman whose husband is dead] *vedova.*

To Wi'dow [to deprive of a husband] *privar del marito.*

To widow [to endow with a widowright] *investire una vedova de' suoi diritti.*

To widow [to strip of any thing good] *privare di checchessia che è bene.*

Wi'dowed, adj. *che ha perduta la moglie, parlando d' un uomo; che ha perduto il marito, parlando d' una donna.*

Wi'dower, s. [a man who survives his wife] *un vedovo.*

Wi'dowhood [the state of a widow or widower] *vedovaggio, vedovatico*, s. m. *vedovanza*, s. f. *stato vedovile.*

Of or belonging to a widow or widower, *vedovile, di vedovo, di vedova.*

Widowhu'nter, s. [one who courts widows for a jointure] *uno che amoreggia vedove per la dote, un Irlandese.*

Widowma'ker, s. [one who deprives women of their husbands] *un che toglie alle mogli i mariti loro.*

Width, adj. [breadth, wideness] *larghezza, ampiezza.*

Widow-wail [a plant] *camedrio*, s. m.

To Wield [to handle, to manage] *maneggiare, trattare.*

He is able to wield a sword, *egli è capace di maneggiare una spada.*

To wield the scepter, *portar lo scettro, governare uno stato.*

Wi'elding, s. *maneggio*, s. m. *il maneggiare.*

Wi'eldy, adj. *attivo, intrigante.*

Wife, s. [married woman] *moglie, mogliera.*

A good wife, *una buona moglie.*

A son's wife, *una nuora.*

A brother's wife, *una cognata.*

A wife's father, *suocero.*

To marry a wife, *ammogliarsi.*

Wig, s. [a sort of cake] *ciambella, chicca*, s. f.

Wig [perriwig] *parrucca*, s. f.

Wight, s. [a living creature, either man or woman] *una creatura, un uomo o una donna.*

Wild, adj. [untamed, savage, fierce] *salvatico, selvaggio, indomito, feroce.*

Wild beast, *fera selvaggia, animale salvatico.*

Wild goose, *oca salvatica.*

To lead one a wild goose chace [to amuse one with fair hopes] *tenere a bada.*

bada uno con belle promesse; pascerlo di vento.

Wild country, paese salvatico o deserto.

Wild look, occhi stralunati, cera feroce, viso burbero.

I think he is wild, credo ch' egli sia matto.

A wild youth, un giovane sventato, privo di senno, senza giudizio.

Wild fire [a plant] epatica, s. f. sorta d erba.

Wild-fire [running worm; a kind of St. Anthony's fire] fuoco salvatico, spezie di malattia.

The wild holm-tree [a shrub] bosso, s. m.

Wild [extravagant, impertinent] salvatico, zotico, rozzo, intrattabile, stravagante, fuor di stagione.

Wild conceits, stravaganze.

WILDS, s. [wild regions] paesi campestri, salvatici, deserti.

WI'LDERNESS, s. [a large uncultivated place] deserto.

Wilderness [a little wood] salvatice, s. m. luogo pieno d' alberi posticci per delizia.

WI'LDING, s [the fruit of a wilding tree] corbézzola, s. f. il frutto del corbézzolo.

The wilding-tree, corbézzolo, s. m.

WI'LDINGS, s. [wild fruits] frutti salvatici.

WI'LDLY, adv. salvaticamente, alla salvatica, con modo e costume salvatico, zoticamente.

WI'LDNESS, salvatichezza, ferocia, rozzezza, zotichezza, s. f.

WILE, s. [cunning, or craft, a subtil trick] furberia, astuzia, sottigliezza, s. f.

WI'LFUL, adj. [obstinate, unruly] ostinato, caparbio, capone, di sua testa.

A wilful man, un caparbio.

A wilful negligence, una negligenza affettata.

Wilful [premediated] premeditato, fatto a posta, con proposito deliberato.

Wilful sin, peccato premeditato commesso volontariamente.

Wilful murder, omicidio premeditato commesso con proposito deliberato.

WI'LFULLY, adv. [obstinately] ostinatamente, caparbiamente, con ostinazione.

Wilfully [on set purpose] con proposito deliberato, premeditatamente.

WI'LFULNESS, s. ostinazione, caparbietà, caponeria, s. f.

WI'LILY, adv. fraudolosamente, astutamente, accortamente, ingannevolmente.

WI'LINESS, s. [cunning, guile] astuzia, furberia, fraude.

WILK, v. Welk.

WILL, s. [a particular faculty of the soul] volontà, s. f. facoltà particolare dell' anima.

Will [mind, pleasure] volontà, piacere, inclinazione, modo.

To submit to God's will, sottomettersi alla volontà di Dio.

For such is our will and pleasure, perchè tale è il nostro piacere, perchè così ci piace.

To do one's will with a thing, far d' un cosa a nostro modo.

Use your own will, fate a modo vostro.

To do a thing with a good will, fare una cosa di buona voglia, volentiermente.

To do a thing with an ill will, far che che sia di mala voglia, di male gambe, malvolentieri.

He did it of his own good will, lo fece spontaneamente, di sua spontanea volontà, di proprio moto, lo fece da se.

WILL, or last will [testament] testamento, s. m.

Will parole [a will only by word of mouth] un testamento di viva voce.

To make one's will, fare il suo testamento.

Good will [kindness] buona volontà, bontà, amorevolezza, benevolenza, s. f.

Against one's will, malgrado, malvolentieri.

To bear good-will to one, voler bene ad uno, amarlo.

To bear ill-will to one, voler male ad uno, odiarlo.

To let one have his will, lasciar fare uno a suo modo, quel che li piace.

If I might have my will, s'io fossi padrone della mia volontà, se fosse in poter mio.

Will [a diminutive of William] diminutivo del nome Guglielmo.

To WILL [to be willing] volere, aver la volontà di fare che che sia.

What you will, come volete, come vi piace.

He that will not when he may, when fain he would he shall have nay, chi non vuole quel che può, quel che vorrà poi non avrà.

Will he, nill he, buon grado malgrado, a suo dispetto, ad onta sua.

Let him be who he will, sia chiunque si voglia.

La parola will, sovente è il segno' del futuro dell' Indicativo.

I will tell you, vi dirò.

To WILL [to desire] pregare, supplicare, chiedere in grazia.

I willed him to do that for me, l'ho pregato di far questo per me.

To will [to command] ordinare, comandare.

WI'LLED, adj. ex. ill-willed, avverso, contrario.

Self-willed, ostinato, caparbio, capone.

WI'LLIAMS, or SWEET-WILLIAMS, s. [a flower] fiorellino così chiamato.

WI'LLING, adj. vogliente, pronto a fare, volonteroso.

I am willing to do it, voglio farlo, sono pronto a farlo.

To do a thing with a willing mind, fare che che sia di buon grado, volentiermente.

Nothing is impossible to a willing mind, chi vuole non trova niente difficile.

Willing or unwilling he must go, bisogna che vada, buon grado o mal grado suo.

God willing, se piace a Dio.

WI'LLINGLY, adv. [readily] volentiermente, volentieri, con pronta volontà.

I'll do it willingly, lo farò volentieri, di buona voglia.

WI'LLINGNESS, s. disposizione o prontezza a fare qualche cosa; buona volontà.

WI'LLOW, } s. salce, salcio, s.
Willow-tree, } m.

Spiked willow [a shrub] viburno, s. m. arbuscello.

Willow-weed [a plant] lisimacchia, s. f.

Willow plot, or willow-bed, salceto, s. m. luogo pieno di salci.

WI'LLOWISH, adj. che ha colore di foglia di salce.

WI'LY, adv. [full of wiles, cunning] fine, astuto, viziato, scaltrito, sagace.

WI'MBLE [a sort of piercer] foratojo, succhio, succhiello, s. m.

WI'MBLE, adj. [active, nimble] agile, destro, disinvolto, snello.

To WI'MPLE [to make a hole with a wimble] succhiare, bucar col succhiello, succhiellare.

WIMO'TE, s. [a plant] bismalva, s. f.

WI'MPLE, s. [the linen cloth which nuns wear about their neck] soggolo, s. m. velo che le monache portano sotto la gola.

Whimple [streamer, flag] banderuola, s. f. pennoncello, s. m.

To WI'MBLE [to draw down as a hood or veil] calar giù come si calerebbe sulla faccia il velo che le monache portano in capo ripiegato.

To WIN [to get, to gain] vincere, guadagnare; pret. vinsi.

To win money of one, vincere del danaro ad uno.

To win [to get the better, to obtain, to carry] guadagnare, riportare, acquistare, ottenere, pres. ottengo, pret. ottenni.

To win the prize, riportare il premio.

To win a wager, guadagnare una scommessa.

To win the day [to win the battle] ottenere la vittoria, vincer la giornata o la battaglia.

To win [to carry, to make one's self master of] guadagnare, impadronirsi, espugnare.

To win the counterscarp, guadagnare la contrascarpa.

To win a place by assault, espugnare una città per assalto.

To win [to bribe, to prevail] guadagnare, corrompere farsi uno amico con presenti.

To win [to acquire] cattivarsi l' altrui amicizia o benevolenza, rendersi uno amico.

To win [to persuade] guadagnare, prevalere, persuadere, indurre a fare.

To WINCE [to kick, to spurn] calcitrare, tirar de' calci.

WIN-

WI'NCING, s. *calcio*, s. m.

Wincing, adj. *che tira calci.*

A wincing horſe, *un cavallo che tira calci.*

WINCH, s. [an iron inſtrument to turn ſcrews with] *vite, chiocciola*, s. f. *ſtrumento meccanico per uſo di ſtringere inſieme.*

To WINCH [to wind round with a winch] *attorcere, contorcere con vite.*

WINCOPI'PE, s. [a ſmall red flower in the ſtubble fields] *fioretto roſſo che frequentemente ſi trova ne' campi fra le ſtoppie.*

WIND, s. [the current or ſtream of the air] *vento*, s. m. *dibattimento d' aria.*

The four principal winds, *i quattro venti principali.*

Cold wind, *vento freddo, brezza*, s. f.

Great or high wind, *vento grande, gran vento.*

The wind blows, *fa vento, il vento tira.*

Wind that blows from the land or ſea, *vento di terra o di mare.*

To ſail againſt the wind, *navigare contra 'l vento, aver il vento a prua, aver il vento contrario.*

To ſail before the wind, *aver il vento in poppa.*

Wind [vanity] *vento*, s. m. *vanità*, s. f.

A man that turns with every wind [a fickle or uncertain man] *un uomo che ſi volge ad ogni vento, un uomo leggiero, incoſtante.*

Wind [breath, reſpiration] *vento, fiato, ſoffio, aura.*

To fetch wind [to fetch one's breath] *fiatare, reſpirare, pigliar fiato.*

To recover one's wind, *ripigliar fiato.*

Wind [air retained in the body of an animal] *vento, flato nel corpo d' un animale.*

To be troubled with wind, *aver venti o flati.*

To break wind upwards, *ruttare, mandar fuor per bocca il vento che è nello ſtomaco.*

To have a thing in the wind [to have a hint of it] *aver indizio o ſentore di che che ſia.*

I had it in the wind preſently, *me ne accorſi ſubito.*

To go down the wind, *ſcadere, declinare, venire in peggiore ſtato.*

Between wind and water, *a fior d' acqua.*

Wind-mill, *mulino a vento.*

The wind pipe, *la canna della gola.*

They are quite gone down the wind, *hanno dato l' ultimo tuffo.*

Wind-fall, *accidente proſpero, buona fortuna.*

Wind-falls [fruit blown off the tree by the wind] *frutti che il vento ha fatti cadere.*

Wind-flower, *anémone* s. f.

A wind beam of a houſe, *colonna di legno che ſoſtiene una caſa.*

Wind-bound [kept back by contrary winds] *trattenuto dal vento.*

Wind-egg, *un uovo vuoto.*

Wind-gall, in horſes [a ſoft ſwelling on the joint of the leg] *tumore acqueo che viene alle gambe de' cavalli.*

Wind-raunet [a bird] *gheppio*, s. m. *uccello di rapina.*

To WIND [to turn, to twiſt, to roll about] *girare, volgere*, pret. *volſi.*

To wind a ſhip, *girare un vaſcello.*

How winds the ſhip? *da qual parte del vaſcello ſoffia il vento?*

To wind ſilk or thread, *aggomitolare della ſeta o del refe.*

To wind [to ſcent as dogs do] *fiutare, annaſare.*

To wind off a bottom, *annaſpare un gomitolo, avvolgere il filo in ſul naſpo per formarne la mataſſa.*

To wind into bottoms, *aggomitolare.*

To wind a horn, *ſonare il corno.*

To wind, verb neut. [ſpeaking of a ſerpent] *attorcigliarſi, parlando d' un ſerpente.*

To wind one in by craft [to enſnare him] *tendere inſidie ad uno, inſidiarlo, coglierlo nella rete.*

To wind one's ſelf into one's favour, *cattivarſi l' altrui benevolenza, inſinuarſi nell' altrui favore.*

To wind one's ſelf into an amour, *innamorarſi.*

To wind one's ſelf out, *ſtrigarſi, liberarſi, ſvilupparſi.*

To wind up a watch or clock, *tirar ſu un oriuolo o un orologio.*

To wind up a thing in a piece of paper, *avvolgere, inviluppare che che ſia in un pezzo di carta.*

To wind up a diſcourſe, *finire, terminare, conchiudere un diſcorſo.*

And to wind up all in one word, *e per finirla in una parola.*

To wind up [ſpeaking of a ſhip being at anchor] *eſſere all' áncora.*

WI'NDED, adj. *girato, volto*, v. To wind.

Short winded, *aſmatico, che patiſce d' aſma.*

Broken winded, *bolſo, che con difficoltà reſpira.*

Long-winded [tedious] *lungo, tedioſo.*

A long-winded preacher, *un predicatore tedioſo.*

A long winded diſcourſe, *un diſcorſo lungo, o tedioſo.*

Winded [as thread] *aggomitolato.*

WI'NDER, s. *aggomitolatore*, s. m.

WI'NDINESS, s. [windineſs of the ſtomach] *ventoſità*, s. f.

WI'NDING, s. *giramento*, s. m. *il girare*, v. To wind.

Windings and turnings, *ſerpeggiamenti, ſinuoſità, giravolte.*

The windings of a river, *i ſerpeggiamenti, i giri d' un fiume.*

Winding, adj. ex. a winding ſheet, *palio di morto.*

Winding-ſtairs or winding ſtair-caſe, *ſcala a chiocciola.*

Winding river, *fiume che ſerpeggia.*

WI'NDLASS, } s. [a draw-beam in
WI'NDLESS, } ſmall ſhips placed upon the deck, juſt abaft the foremaſt] *ſpezie d' argano.*

WI'NDLESS [blades to wind yarn on] *naſpo*, s. m. *ſtrumento ſopra 'l quale ſi forma la mataſſa.*

WI'NDOW, s. [caſement] *fineſtra*, s. f.

To throw the houſe out at the window, *mandare ogni coſa in rovina.*

Little window, *fineſtrella, fineſtretta.*

Glaſs window, *vetriata.*

Paper-window, *impannata, chiuſura di carta che ſi fa alle fineſtre.*

WI'NDWARD, or windward tide [a tide which runs againſt the wind] *marea contro vento.*

WI'NDY, adj. [ſubject or expoſed to the wind] *ventoſo, che patiſce di vento, eſpoſto al vento.*

Windy [that cauſes wind in the body, or that is cauſed by winds] *ventoſo, che genera ventoſità.*

Windy meat, *cibi ventoſi.*

Windy expreſſions, *eſpreſſioni ventoſe, piene di vento, gonfie, ſtravaganti, ampolloſe.*

WINE, s. [liquor made of the juice of grapes] *vino*, s. m. *bevanda tratta dal frutto della vite.*

Small wine, *vinello, vinetto, vini di poca forza.*

Sour wine, *vino bruſco.*

Flat or dead wine, *vino ſventato.*

French wine, *vino di Francia.*

Wine [a liquor made of other fruits beſides the grapes] *vino, liquore tratto da' altri frutti che le uve.*

Raſberry-wine, *vino di more di rovo.*

Cherry-wine, *vino di ciriege.*

Wine-cellar, *cantina.*

A wine pot, *un vaſo di vino.*

Wine-glaſs, *bicchiere.*

Wine-preſs, *ſtrettojo, torchio.*

Wine bibber, *bevitore, beone, ſoverchio amatore del vino.*

Wine-merchant, *mercante di vino.*

Wine-cooper, *bottajo, cantiniere, che traffica in vino.*

WING, s. [that part of a bird which is uſed in flying] *ala, alia*, s. f. *membro col quale volano gli uccelli.*

The wings of an eagle, pigeon, or partridge, *le ali d' un aquila, d' un colombo, d' una pernice.*

The wing of a rabbit, *la ſpalla d' un coniglio.*

One cannot fly without wings, *non ſi può volare ſenza ali.*

To take wing [to fly away] *volare.*

To be upon the wing [to be flying] *volare.*

To be upon the wing [to be ready to go] *ſtare in ſull' ale, eſſer in punto o in procinto di partire.*

To clip the wings to one [to diminiſh his power or credit] *tarpare le ali ad uno, diminuire il ſuo potere o'l ſuo credito.*

The wings of love or fame, *le ali dell' amore, della fama.*

The wings of the Lord [God Almighty's protection] *le ali dei Signore, la protezione di Dio.*

Wing [ſide] *ala, corno, late.*

The wings of an army, *le ali d' un eſercito, il corno d' un eſercito.*

The

The wings of a great house, *le ali d' una casa.*

To WING [to raise] *muover l' ali, levare in alto.*

To wing away, *volar via.*

WI'NGED, adj. *alato, che ha ale.*

Winged horse, *cavallo alato.*

WI'NGSHELL, s. [the shell that covers the wing of insects] *quello quasi astuccio in cui è avvolta l' ala di qualche insetto.*

WI'NGY, adj. [having wings] *alato, che ha ale, che ha vanni.*

WINK, s. [twinkle] *batter d' occhio, cenno.*

To give one the wing, or to tip one the wink, *far cenno ad uno, accennargli cogli occhi.*

I did not sleep a wink all night, *non ho dormito punto in tutta la notte, non ho chiusi gli occhi in tutta la notte.*

To wink [to close or shut the eyes] *serrare o chiuder gli occhi.*

To WINK [to tip the wink] *dare un' occhiata, occhieggiare, far cenno cogli occhi.*

To wink [to connive at] *usar connivenza, chiuder gli occhi, tollerare, simulare, permettere, dissimulare.*

WI'NKED at, adj. *tollerato, simulato, permesso.*

WI'NKER, s. *quello o quella che fa cenno cogli occhi.*

WI'NKING, s. *cenno.*

Winking at, *connivenza, dissimulazione.*

WI'NNER, s. [he that wins] *guadagnatore, s. m. guadagnatrice, s. f.*

WI'NNING, s. *il guadagnare.*

Winnings [that which one has won] *guadagno, quel che uno ha guadagnato.*

Winning, adj. ex. the winning side, *la parte che guadagna.*

To WI'NNOW [to fan or separate corn from chaff by the wind] *spagliare, ventilare, sventolare, vagliare.*

To winnow corn, *spagliare, ventilare il grano, vagliare il grano.*

WI'NNOWED, adj. *spagliato, ventilato, sventolato, vagliato.*

WI'NNOWER, s. *ventilatore, s. m. che ventila, che vaglia.*

WI'NNOWING, s. *ventilamento, s. m. ventilatura, ventilazione, s. f. il ventilare.*

Winnowing sieve, *un vaglio.*

Winnowings, *lolla, loppa, s. m.*

WI'NTER, s. [one of the four seasons of the year] *verno, inverno, s. m. una delle quattro stagioni dell' anno.*

The winter season, *il verno, la stagione dell' inverno, una vernata, un invernata.*

A winter night, *una notte d' inverno.*

Winter weather, *tempo d' inverno.*

Winter quarters, *quartieri d' inverno.*

To WI'NTER [to abide in a place during the winter] *invernare, svernare, dimorare il verno in un luogo.*

To winter [to feed in the winter] *nutrire o dar pascolo in tempo d' inverno.*

WINTERBE'ATEN, adj. [harrassed by severe weather] *maltrattato o malconcio dal rigido freddo.*

WI'NTERED, adj. *invernato, svernato.*

WI'NTERING, s. *svernamento, s. m. lo svernare.*

WI'NTERLY, or WINTERISH, adj. *d' inverno, invernale, vernale.*

Winterly weather, *un tempo d' inverno, un tempo freddo.*

To WI'NTER-RIG [to fallow or till land in winter] *arare la terra nell' inverno.*

WI'NTRY, adj. [brumal, hyemal] *d' inverno, gelato.*

WI'NY, adj. [from wine] *vinoso, di vino.*

Winy smell, *odore di vino.*

WIPE, s. [jeer] *bottone, s. m. motto pungente.*

To give one a wipe, *sbottoneggiare alcuno.*

Wipe [deceit] *fraude, s. f. inganno, s. m.*

Wipe [a sort of bird] *pavoncella, s. f. sorta d' uccello.*

To WIPE [to rub gently off] *asciugare, spazzare, nettare, strofinare.*

Wipe your hands, *asciugatevi le mani.*

To wipe one's shoes, *spazzarsi, o nettarsi le scarpe.*

To wipe one's nose, *soffiarsi il naso.*

To wipe one of his money, *truffare alcuno del suo danaro.*

To wipe off the dust, *spolverare, levar la polvere.*

To wipe off one's tears, *asciugar le lagrime.*

To wipe out, *cancellare.*

WI'PED, adj. *asciugato, v.* To wipe.

WI'PER, s. *quello, o quella che asciuga.*

WI'PING, s. *asciugamento, s. m. l' asciugare.*

Wiping clout, *asciugatojo, sciugatojo, strofinaccio, strofinacciolo.*

WIRE, s. [metal drawn out into slender threads] *filo fatto d' alcun metallo*

Copper wire, *fil di rame.*

Iron wire, *fil di ferro.*

Gold wire, *filo d' oro.*

Silver wire, *filo d' argento.*

Wire strings [such as are used for some musical instruments] *corde d' ottone.*

To WIRE-DRAW [to draw out any metal into long threads] *filare un metallo.*

To wire-draw gold or silver, *filare o tirare dell' oro o dell' argento.*

To wire-draw a business [to spin it out] *tirare a lungo un negozio, mandare in lunga, allungare un negozio.*

To wire draw one [to get what one can out of him] *tirar d' uno quel che si può scroccare, acchiappare.*

WIRE-DRA'WER, s [one who spins wire] *colui che fa filo di qualche metallo.*

WIRE-DRAWN, adj. *filato, tirato.*

WIRES, s. [for a woman's head] *orecchini, s. m.*

To WIS, pret. and part. pass. wist [to know] *sapere.* Obs.

WI'SDOM, s. [the knowledge of high things] *sapienza, s. f. scienza, che contempla la cagione di tutte le cose.*

The wisdom of God is infinite, *la sapienza di Dio è infinita.*

Wisdom [prudence, discretion] *sapienza, savièzza, accortezza, prudenza, circospezione, s. f. avvedimento, avviso, s. m.*

WISE, adj. [prudent, discreet] *saggio, savio, accorto, avveduto, prudente, circospetto.*

A wise man [a sage, a philosopher] *un uomo savio, un savio, un filosofo.*

Wise [learned, skilled, witty] *savio, dotto, abile, intelligente, intendente, saputo.*

As wise as you are, *per savio che voi siate; savio come siete.*

Wise, s. *saputo.*

A word is enough to the wise, *a buono intenditor poche parole.*

Wise, s. [manner] *modo, maniera, guisa.*

In this wise, *in questo modo, in questa maniera, in questa guisa.*

In any wise, *ad ogni modo.*

In no wise, *in conto alcuno, in modo veruno.*

WI'SEACRE, s. [a nickname for a silly fellow] *uno sciocco, uno scimunito, un cionno, un balordo, un minchione.*

WI'SELY, adv. [discreetly] *saviamente, cautamente, saggiamente, discretamente, prudentemente.*

WI'SENESS, s. [wisdom, sapience] *sapienza, dottrina, sapere.*

WI'SER [the comparative of wise] *più saggio, più savio.*

He is wiser than you, *egli è più savio di voi.*

WI'SEST [the superlative of wise] *il più savio.*

WISH [desire] *desiderio, disidero, voto, s. m. voglia, brama, s. f.*

According to my wish, *secondo il mio desiderio.*

To have one's wish, *avere quel che si desideria.*

To WISH [to desire] *desiderare, disiderare, bramare, aver voglia, nutrir brama.*

I could wish he should live, *io bramerei pur che vivesse*

I have what I wished, *ho quel che desiderava.*

I wish you a happy voyage, *vi auguro un felice viaggio.*

To wish one well, *desiderare ad uno ogni bene.*

To wish one dead, *desiderare la morte di qualcheduno.*

To wish one joy, *congratularsi, rallegrarsi delle felicità dell' amico con esso lui; dire ad uno mi rallegro.*

I wish to God he would come, *volesse Dio che venisse.*

WI'SHED, or wished for, adj. *desiderato, disiderato, bramato, v.* To wish.

A thing to be wished, *una cosa desiderabile.*

WI'SH-

WI'SHFUL, adj. [longing, showing desire] *ansante per desiderio, desideroso, avido.*

WELL-WISHER, *un buon amico di qualcheduno, una persona che gli desidera bene.*

WI'SHING, s. *il desiderare.*

WI'SHLY, adj. *amoroso*, ex. To cast a wishly look upon a woman, *vagheggiare una donna, guardarla con occhi amorosi.*

WI'SKET, s. [basket] *canestro, cestello.*

WISP [a handful of straw or hay to rub horses with] *strofinaccio, stronfinacciolo; tantà paglia o fieno quanta si può tenere in mano da strofinar un cavallo.*

Wisp [a wreath to carry any thing upon the head] *cercine*, s. m.

To wisp a horse with straw, *strofinare un cavallo con uno strofinaccio di paglia.*

WIST, adj. ex. Had I wist [had I known] *se avessi saputo.*

To wist [to know] *sapere.* Obsolete.

WI'STLY, adv. [fixedly] *fissamente.*

To look wistly on one, *guardar alcuno fissamente.*

WIT, s. [one of the faculties of the soul] *ingegno, intelletto, senno, spirito*, s. m.

A great wit, *un grande ingegno.*

She has a great deal of wit, *ella ha un grande ingegno, molto spirito.*

A man of good wit, *un uomo di spirito, un uomo di grande ingegno.*

Wit [wisdom, judgment] *senno, giudizio, sapere*, s. m. *savìezza, prudenza*, s. f.

Wit [cunning] *sottigliezza d' ingegno, acutezza, astuzia, sagacità.*

To teach one wit, *scozzonare, dirozzare, impratichire alcuno.*

We must try our wit, *bisogna inventare qualche astuzia.*

To learn wit, *imparar senno.*

His poem is full of wit, *il suo poema è pieno di belli pensieri, di lampi bellissimi.*

Where did you learn so much wit? *dove avete imparato tante belle cose?*

Your tongue runs before your wit, *voi sbalestrate, voi strafalciate, voi non pensate a quel che dite.*

A wit [a man of wit] *un bell' ingegno.*

To have one's wits about one, *essere in senno.*

To be out of one's wits, *non essere in senno, uscir del senno, impazzire, esser pazzo.*

He makes me out of my wits, *mi trae del senno, mi fa uscir di senno, mi fa impazzare.*

To live by one's wits, *industriarsi, ingegnatsi, viver d' industria.*

To be at one's wits end, *non saper che fare, essere imbrogliato.*

To wit, adv. *cioè.*

To WIT [to know] *sapere.*

WITCH [sorcerer, sorceress] *stregone, maliardo*, s. m. *strega, maga*, s. f.

To WITCH [to bewitch] *stregare, ammaliare, affatturare.*

WI'TCHERY, s. [enchantment] *stregoneccio, incantamento, opera di mago, di stregone, d' incantatore, o di negromante.*

WI'TCHCRAFT, s. *stregoneccio, ammaliamento, affatturamento*, s. m. *stregoneria, malia, fattura*, s. f.

Witch hazel tree, *appio*, s. m.

To WITE [to blame, to reproach] *biasimare, rimproverare.*

WITH [a conjunctive preposition] *con, col, colla, col, colle.*

With me, *meco, con me.*

With thee, *teco, con te.*

With him, *seco, con lui, con esso.*

Come along with me, *venite meco.*

To cut with a knife, *tagliare con un coltello.*

With my own hand, *colla mia propria mano.*

With all my heart, *di tutto cuore, con tutto 'l mio cuore.*

Paved with stones, *lastricato di pietre.*

What shall I do with it? *che ne farò?*

What will you do with this man? *che volete fare di quest' uomo?*

With a good or evil eye, *di buono o di mal' occhio.*

To cure a disease with fasting, *guarire una malattia coll' astinenza.*

I'll begin with that, *comincerò di quì.*

To be in hand with a thing, *aver qualche cosa fra le mani, esser attorno a qualche cosa.*

To speak with one, *parlare ad uno.*

With a loud voice, *ad alta voce.*

With much ado, *a gran pena, a mala pena, a grande stento, appena, difficilmente, con difficoltà.*

To compare one thing with another, *comparare una cosa ad un' altra.*

To be angry with one, *esser in collera, sdegnato, stizzato con uno.*

I am contented with it, *ne sono contento.*

He is very well pleased with him, *egli n' è molto sodisfatto.*

He hurt himself with a fall, *s' è fatto male cascando.*

That's of little availment with me, *ciò nulla mi giova.*

He finds fault with it, *egli vi trova a ridire.*

To meet with one, *incontrare qualcheduno.*

I shall meet with him [I shall be even with him] *gli renderò la pariglia, gli renderò pan per focaccia.*

Give me leave to speak a word with you, *mi permetta ch' io le dica una parola.*

What would you have with me? *che volete da me?*

Did that business succeed with him? *ha egli riuscito in quel negozio?*

We had the wind with us, *noi avevamo il vento propizio, favorevole.*

To agree with one another, *accordarsi, restar d' accordo insieme.*

To contend one with another, *contendere, esser in contesa.*

'Tis a usual thing with him, *questa è una cosa che gli è molto comune.*

It has a good smell with it, *ha un buon odore.*

It has an ill smell with it, *puzza, ha un cattivo odore.*

I don't get a crown one with another, *in tutto e per tutto non guadagno uno scudo.*

With child, *gravida.*

Withe, s. *giunco.*

WITHA'L, prep. [with] *con, da, per.*

What shall I do it withal? *con che lo farò.*

An instrument to cut withal, *uno strumento da tagliare.*

I have nothing to do it withal, *non ho mente per farlo.*

Withal, adv. [also, besides] *anche, ancora, oltre che, di più.*

To WITHDRA'W [to draw away or back] *ritirare, ritrarre, trar fuori, levare.*

To withdrew his forces, *egli ritirò, o fece ritirare le sue forze.*

To withdraw one's mind from one, *alienare la mente da qualcheduno.*

To withdraw [to retire or go away] *ritirarsi tirarsi indietro, andarsene, partire, uscire*, pref. *esco.*

WITHDRA'WING, *ritirata*, s. f. *il ritirarsi.*

Withdrawing-room, *retrocamera.*

WITHDRA'WMENT, s. *ritirata.*

WITHDRE'W, *è un preterito del verbo* To withdraw.

WITHE, s. [a willow-twig] *un ramicello di salcio.*

Withe [a bond; properly a band of twigs] *legatura fatta di rami teneri e pieghevoli.*

To WI'THER [to fade, to grow dry] *sfiorire, appassarsi, appassirsi, seccarsi*, pref. *sfiorisco, appassisco.*

WI'THERED, adj. *sfiorito, appassato, appassito, vizzo, passo.*

WI'THEREDNESS, s. *lo stato d' una cosa che è vizza e quasi marcia.*

WI'THERING, adj. *che appassa, che sfiorisce, che secca.*

Withering, s. *aridezza*, s. f.

WITH-HE'LD, adj. *ritenuto, impedito, fermato, arrestato.*

To WITH-HO'LD [to keep back, to stop] *ritenere, impedire, fermare, arrestare*, pref. *ritengo, impedisco.*

To with-hold [to keep that which is another's] *ritenere, serbare, tenere.*

To with-hold one's estate, *ritenere l' altrui beni.*

WITH-HO'LDEN, *participio passivo del verbo* To with-hold.

WITH-HO'LDER, s. *ritenitore*, s. m. *ritenitrice*, s. f.

WITH-HO'LDING, s. *ritenimento, ritegno*, s. m. *il ritenere.*

WITHI'N, prep. [in] *in, fra dentro, indentro.*

Within a few days, *fra pochi giorni.*

Within-ward, *indentro, internamente.*

From within, *di dentro.*

Within [at home] *a casa.*

Is he within? *è in casa?*

To keep within doors, *restare in casa.*

Within a musket-shot, *a tiro di moschetto.*

Within an inch of the ground, *a un dito da terrà.*

This crime is within that ſtatute, *a queſto delitto provvede queſta legge.*

That's not within my reach, *queſto non è alla mia portata.*

Within a while after, *qualche tempo dopo.*

Within a ſmall matter, *appreſſo a poco.*

He was within a little of being killed, *poco mancò che non foſſe ammazzato, che non foſſe ucciſo.*

WITHI'NSIDE, adv. [in the interiour parts] *interiormente, nelle parti interiori.*

WITHO'UT, adv. [out, abroad] *fuori, fuora, fuore.*

He is without, *egli è fuora.*

A fine houſe without, *una bella caſa al di fuori.*

Without, prep. [out] *fuor, fuori.*

Without the town, *fuori della città.*

Without [an exceſſive propoſition, the contrary of with] *ſenza, fuori.*

Without the King's order, *ſenza l' ordine del Re.*

Without much ado, *ſenza ſoverchia difficoltà.*

Without doubt, *ſenza dubbio.*

I cannot live without a wife, *non poſſo vivere ſenza moglie.*

To learn a thing without book, *imparare che che ſia a mente.*

No body is without his follies, *ognuno ha le ſue pazzie.*

WITHO'UTEN, prep. [without] *ſenza.*

To WITHSA'Y [to deny] *negare, contraddire.*

To WITHSTA'ND [to ſtand againſt, to reſiſt] *reſiſtere, far reſiſtenza, oſtare, contrariare, rintuzzare, ripugnare, reprimere, contraſtare, opporſi,* preſ. *oppongo.*

To withſtand God's grace, *reſiſtere alla grazia di Dio.*

To withſtand reaſon, *opporſi, ripugnare alla ragione.*

You withſtand your own good fortune, *voi v' opponete alla voſtra fortuna.*

WITHSTA'NDER, s. *quello o quella che reſiſte, che ripugna.*

WITHSTA'NDING, s. *reſiſtenza, oppoſizione,* s. f. *contraſto,* s. m.

WITHSTO'OD, *preterito del verbo* To withſtand.

WI'THY, s. [ozier] *vinco,* s. m.

WI'TLESS, adj. [without wit] *balorde, ſciocco, ſcimunito, mentecatto, ſcipito, ſenza cervello.*

WI'TNESS, s. [one who teſtifies a thing] *teſtimonio, teſtimone,* s. m. *quegli che fa teſtimonianza.*

Eye-witneſs, *teſtimonio oculare, di veduta, di viſta.*

Ear-witneſs, *teſtimonio che teſtifica per aver ſentito dire.*

To call to witneſs, *chiamare in teſtimonio.*

I call God to witneſs, *chiamo Iddio in teſtimonio, Iddio mi è teſtimonio.*

To be witneſs [or godfather] to a child, *eſſer padrino d' un bambino.*

Witneſs my hand, *teſtimonio ne ſia la mia mano.*

To WI'TNESS [to bear witneſs] *teſtificare, far teſtimonianza, eſſer teſtimonio.*

To witneſs a writing, *teſtificare una ſcrittura.*

WI'TNESSED, adj. *teſtificato.*

WI'TNESSING, s. *teſtimonianza,* s. f.

WITSNA'PPER, s. [one who affects rapartee] *uno che con affettazione ſtudia di dar belle ed ingegnoſe riſpoſte.*

WI'TTED, adj. ex. Quick witted, *che è d' acuto ingegno.*

Dull-witted, *ſtupido, inſenſato.*

Half-witted, *ſciocco, ſemplice, eionno.*

WI'TTICISM, s. [a witty ſaying] *concetto ſpiritoſo.*

WI'TTILY, adv. [ingeniouſly] *ingegnoſamente.*

WI'TTINESS, s. [the quality of being witty] *lo aver ingegno o acutezza naturale d' ingegno.*

WI'TTINGLY, adv. *a poſta, a bello ſtudio, a poſta fatta, a caſo penſato.*

WI'TTOL, s. [a man who knows the falſhood of his wife and ſeems contented] *berco contento; infame marito che ſa l' infedeltà della mogliera e ſe ne contenta.*

WI'TTOLY, adj. [cuckoldly] *che è berro contento; appartenente a berro contento.*

WI'TTY, adj. [full of wit] *ſpiritoſo, ingegnoſo, arguto.*

WI'TWAL, s. [a bird] *picchio.* s. m.

To WIVE [to marry a wife] *ammogliarſi, prender moglie.*

WI'VELY, adj. [belonging to a wife] *moglierecio, muliebre, moglieſco, appartenente alla moglie.*

WIVES, *è numero del più di* wife.

WI'VING, s. [marrying] *l' ammogliarſi, matrimonio.* Obſolete.

WI'ZARD, s. [cunning man, ſorcerer] *indovino, mago, ſtregone.*

WI'ZARDY, s. *malia, ſtregoneria,* s. f. *ſtregoneccio,* s. m.

WO, } s. grief, trouble, ſorrow]
WOE, } *guajo, dolore, infortunio, malore,* s. m. *diſgrazia, ſventura, miſeria, avverſa fortuna,* s. f.

Wo, interj. *guai.*

Wo to you, *guai a voi.*

Wo is me, or wo's me, *guai a me, povero me, infelice, ſventurato me.*

WOAD, s. [an herb much uſed in the dying of cloth] *guado,* s. m. *erba colla quale ſi tingono i panni.*

To WOAD [to die with wood] *tigner con guado.*

WO'ADED, adj. *tinto con guado.*

WO'BEGONE, adj. [loſt in woe] *addoloratiſſimo, immerſo in guai.*

WO'FUL, adj. [ſad, doleful] *triſto, dolente, afflitto, addolorato, meſto.*

Woful. [ſad, unhappy] *triſto, infelice, miſero.*

A woful man, *un uomo ſtrano, bizzarro, biſbetico.*

WO'FULLY, adv. *miſeramente, cordoglioſamente, doglioſamente.*

WOLD, s. [a down, ground hilly and void of wood] *una campagna aprica e montagnoſa, ſenza alberi.*

WOLF, s. [a kind of wild dog] *lupo,* s. m.

To hold a wolf by the ears, *tenere il lupo per gli orecchi, aver per le mani impreſa difficile a ſeguitare e pericoloſiſſima a tralaſciare.*

She wolf, *lupa.*

Young wolf, *lupicino.*

Sea-wolf, *lupo marino.*

Wolf [a ſort of eating ulcer] *ulcera, che viene nelle gambe.*

Wolves-teeth [two teeth in the upper jaw of a horſe, ſharp pointed] *ſopraddenti di cavallo.*

Wolf's milk [a ſort of herb] *titimalo, titimaglio,* s. m.

Wolf's-bane [a plant] *aconito,* s. m.

Wolves, *è 'l numero del più di* wolf.

Wolviſh, adj. [greedy] *vorare, goloſo.*

A wolviſh perſon, *un goloſo.*

WO'MAN, s. [the female of the human race] *donna, femmina.*

Young woman, *donna giovane, una giovane.*

Old woman, *donna vecchia, una vecchia.*

To love women, *donneare, far all' amore colle donne.*

To be given to women, *eſſer dedito alle donne, ai piaceri carnali.*

A lady's woman, or waiting woman, *una cameriera d' una dama.*

A woman of the town [a courtezan, a crack] *una donna di partito, una puttana.*

To WO'MAN [to make pliant like a woman] *render molle o pieghevole come donna.*

WO'MANED, adj. [united with a woman] *unito o accompagnato con donna.*

WO'MAN-LIKE, adj. *donneſco, di donna.*

WO'MANHOOD, s. *lo ſtato, la condizione d' una donna.*

WO'MANISH, adj. [of a woman, effeminate] *donneſco, di donna, femminile, effeminato.*

Womaniſh face, *viſo donneſco o di donna, viſo femminile.*

To WO'MANIZE, verb neut. *prender maniere o coſtumi donneſchi.*

WO'MAN KIND, s. [the female ſex, the race of women] *il femmineo ſeſſo, le donne.*

WO'MANLY, adj. *muliebre, femminino, feminineo, donneſco, da donna, debole.*

Womanly, adv. *muliebremente, donneſcamente; femminilmente, effeminatamente, debolmente.*

WOMB, s. [matrix] *utero,* s. m. *matrice,* s. f. *fianco,* s. m.

WO'MEN, *è 'l numero del più di* woman, *donne, femmine.*

WON, *è preterito del verbo* To win, *vinſi, v.* To win.

Won, adj. [from to win] *guadagnato, vinto, v.* To win.

WO'NDER, s. [marvel, prodigy, thing to be wondered at] *maraviglia, coſa maraviglioſa,* s. f. *ſtupore,* s. m.

To perform wonders, *far maraviglie.*

To make a wonder of a thing, *maravigliarſi, ſtupirſi di che che ſia.*

Wonder-working, *maraviglioso, stupendo.*

To Wo'nder [to admire, to be in admiration] *maravigliarsi, prendersi maraviglia, stupirsi*, pref. *stupisco.*

I wonder at it, *me ne maraviglio, ne resto maravigliato.*

I wonder you should think otherwise, *mi maraviglio che voi crediate altrimente.*

I wonder what this is? *vorrei ben sapere che cosa è questa?*

What's that, I wonder? *di grazia, che rosa è questa?*

Wo'ndered, adj. *maravigliato.*

Wo'nderer, s. *ammiratore*, s. m. *ammiratrice*, s. f.

Wo'nderful, adj. [strange and surprising] *maraviglioso, che apporta maraviglia, ammirabile, stupendo.*

Wonderful, adv. ex. wonderful well, *benissimamente, molto bene, a maraviglia.*

Wonderful rich, *ricco fuor di modo, ricchissimo.*

Wo'nderfully, adv. *maravigliosamente, a maraviglia, fuor di modo.*

Wo'nderfulness, s. *qualità maravigliosa.*

Wo'ndering, s. [admiration] *maraviglia, ammirazione*, s. f. *stupore*, s. m.

Wo'nderment, s. [wondering, surprize] *stupore*, s. m. *ammirazione, sorpresa, maraviglia*, s. f.

He made great wonderment at it, *egli ne restò molto maravigliato.*

Wo'nderstruck, adj. [amazed] *istupidito, stupido, maravigliato, percosso dallo stupore, stupefatto.*

Wo'ndrous, adv. *maraviglioso, stupendo, ammirabile, mirabile.*

Wondrous, } adv. [wonderful-
Wo'ndrously, } ly] *maravigliosamente, a maraviglia, mirabilmente.*

Wong, s. [wang] *rampo, prato*, s. m.

Wont [an abbreviation of will not] I won't, *non voglio.*

Wont, adj. [used, accustomed] *avvezzo, avvezzato, solito, accostumato.*

I am wont to do so, *sono avvezzo a far così.*

He was wont to come every day, *egli soleva venire ogni giorno.*

As I am wont, *al solito.*

Wont, s. [custom] *uso, costume*, s. m. *usanza*, s. f.

After my wont, *secondo 'l mio costume.*

To Wont, } [to be used or accusto-
To be wont, } med] *solere, esser solito, costumare, usare, esser consueto di fare.*

To wont [to be usually at a place] *frequentare, bazzicare.*

Wo'nted, adj. *solito, accostumato.*

To Woo [to court, to make love to] *amoreggiare, far l' amore.*

I Wooed him to do it, *lo pregai, lo scongiurai di farlo.*

Wood, s. [a large space of ground beset with trees and shrubs] *bosco*, s. m. *selva*, s. f.

Wood [timber, substance of trees] *legno*, s. m. plur. *legna*, s. f.

Wood-bine [honey-suckle] *madreselva*, s. f. *succiamiele*, s. m.

Wood-pecker, s. [a bird] *picchio*, s. m.

Wood-cock, s. [a wild fowl] *beccaccia*, s. f. *uccello salvatico.*

Wood-culver [wood-pigeon] *colombarrio, colombo salvatico.*

Wood-louse, *centogambe*, s. m.

Wood-fretter, *gorgoglio, gorgoglione, tonchio*, s. m. *baco che è ne' legni e gli vota.*

Wood-sorrel, *acetosa salvatica.*

Wood-house, *luogo dove si tengon le legna.*

Wood pile, *catasta di legna.*

Wood yard, *cortile dove si tengon le legna.*

Wood-land, *paese boscoso.*

Wood-monger, *venditore o mercante di legna.*

Wood-men [officers who have the charge especially of looking after the King's woods] *guardiani de' boschi del Re.*

Wood-ward [a forest officer] *ufficiale di foresta.*

Wood and wood; a sea term [is when two pieces of timber are so let into each other, that the wood of the one joins close to the other] *due pezzi di legno incastrati e commessi insieme.*

Wood, adj. [mad] *insano, furibondo.*

Wo'oded, adj. [supplied with wood] *fornito di legna.*

Wo'od-drink, s. [decoction or infusion of medicinal woods, as sassafras] *decozione o infusione di legni medicinali, come sassofrasso e simili.*

Wo'oden, adj. *di legno, fatto di legno.*

Wooden shoes, *scarpe di legno, zoccoli.*

Wooden [clumsy, aukward] *goffo, pesante, mal atto, mal destro.*

Woodfre'tter, s. *nome d' insetto, che rode il legno.*

Wo'odland, s. [woods; ground covered with woods] *boschi; terreno coperto di boschi.*

Wo'odlark, s. *sorta d' allodola.*

Wo'odlouse, s. *sorta d' insetto.*

Wo'ody, adj. [full of woods] *boscoso, pien di boschi.*

Wo'oed, adj. [from to woo] *amoreggiato.*

Wo'oer, s. [sweet-heart] *amante, amatore.*

Woof, s. [thread woven cross the warp in a weaver's loom] *trama*, s. f. *le fila da riempir la tela.*

Wool, s. *lana*, s. f.

Wool-driver, *colui che compra la lana in campagna e la rivende nel mercato.*

Wood-staple, s. [a place where wool is used to be sold] *luogo dove suole vender la lana.*

Wool-comb [a comb for wool] *scardasso, strumento con denti di ferro col quale si scardassa la lana.*

Wool-blade [a plant] *tassobarbasso, verbasco*, s. m.

Wool-gathering, ex. Your wits are a wool-gathering, *voi avete dato le cervella a rimpedulare; voi non sapete dove state colla testa, voi non badate a quel che fate.*

Wo'ollen, adj. *di lana.*

Woollen-stockings, *calzette di lana.*

Woollen-cloth, *panno*, s. m.

Woollen, s. *pannina*, s. f. *ogni sorta di panni lani.*

Woollen-draper, *pannajuolo*, s. m. *mercante di panni.*

Wo'olly, adv. *lanoso, pien di lana, che ha della lana.*

Wo'olpack, } s. [a bag of wool, a
Wo'olsack, } pack of wool] *sacco di lana, balla o fascio di lana. È così chiamansi anco i sedili de' Lordi Inglesi nel parlamento, forse perchè dapprima tali balle o sacca piene di lana usarono in vece di sedie. E per metafora dicesi d' ogni cosa grossa e di grande apparifcenza, ma di poco peso.*

Wo'osted, s. [yarn] *lana filata, stame*, s. m.

Woosted stockings, *calzette di stame, calzette di lana.*

Word, s. [that one speaks or writes] *parola*, s. f. *termine*, s. m.

A word used, a word in use, *una parola usata.*

Word for word, *parola per parola.*

Proper word, *termini proprj.*

I want to speak a word with you, *vorrei dirvi una parola.*

Not to say a word, *non dire una parola.*

At a word, or in a word, *in una parola.*

In few words, *in poche parole.*

He had not a word to say for himself, *non disse la minima parola, non seppe che dire in sua difesa.*

Pray make no words on't [say not a word of that] *di grazia non ne fate motto, non ne parlate.*

Soft words, *parole amorevoli o melate.*

Words of course, *parole di complimento o di civiltà, maniere di parlare.*

Empty words, *parole da vegghia, chiacchiere, frasi di collegio.*

Good or fair words, *buone o belle parole.*

Ill words, *parole oltraggiose, villanie.*

To give ill words, *maltrattar di parole, oltraggiare, ingiuriare.*

There passed some words betwixt them, *ebbero che dire insieme.*

The word, or the watch-word, *nome*, s. m. *segno, o motto, che si da negli eserciti per riconoscersi.*

To bring the word, *portare il nome.*

To take the word, *ricever il nome.*

Word [offer in bargain] *parola, prezzo che si offre.*

I have but one word, *io non so molte parole.*

Is that your last word? *è questo l' ultimo prezzo?*

I take you at your word, *piglio la vostra parola.*

Word [promise] *parola, promessa.*

To pass one's word, *dar parola, obbligarsi con parole.*

A man of his word, a man as good as his word, *un uomo di parola.*

To keep one's word, to be as good as one's word, *mantener la parola, esser uomo di parola.*

To fail of one's word, to go back from one's word, *mancar di parola, non mantener la promessa, disdirsi.*

Words, vain words, *parole da veglia, parole vane.*

A word is enough to the wise, *a buon intenditor porhe parole.*

Many words will not fill a bushel, *le parole non empiono il corpo.*

If you will take my word, *se volete creder a me.*

Take my word for't, *credetelo a me.*

To send word, *mandare a dire, far sapere, avvisare.*

A man of few words, *un uomo di poche parole.*

A man of many words *un parolajo, un ciarlone.*

To make many words about a trifle, *disputare di lana caprina, disputar dell' ombra dell' asino, disputar di cose che non importano nulla*

I left word that he should do it, *ho lasciato ordine che lo facesse.*

He left word at home that he should come again within an hour, *ha lasciato detto a casa, che sarebbe di ritorno fra un' ora.*

By word of mouth, *di bocca.*

Word-book, *nomenclatore, vocabolario.*

To Word [to express, to indite] *scrivere, mettere in iscritto.*

To word a thing well, *esprimere bene una cosa.*

Wo'rded, adj. *espresso, scritto.*

A letter well worded, *una lettera bene scritta, dettata in termini eleganti.*

Wore, *è un preterito del verbo* To wear.

Work, s. [labour, pain in doing any thing] *travaglio, affanno, s. m. pena, fatica, s. f.*

Work [business] *lavoro, lavorio, opera.*

To love work, *amare il lavoro, lavorare.*

To be at work, *esser al suo lavoro, esser occupato a lavorare.*

To set to one's work, *mettersi a lavorare.*

To mind work, *esser assiduo a' lavoro.*

The work of the brain, *opera dell' intelletto, opera d' ingegno.*

To reward work, *ricompensare l' altrui fatica.*

There's a twelve month's work, *v' è da lavorare per un anno.*

To have no work to do, *non aver che fare.*

The works of God and Nature, *le opere di Dio e della Natura.*

A fine piece of work, *un bel lavorio, una bell' opera.*

An ingenious piece of work, *un' opera ingegnosa.*

You have made a fine work of it [in an ironical sense; that is, you have spoiled all] *voi avete fatto un bel negozio, cioè, voi avete fatto un grande sproposito.*

An author's work, *le opere d' un autore.*

Work [deed, action] *opera, azione.*

Good works, *buone opere.*

Work [business, trouble] *affare, pena, disturbo, disordine, imbarazzo.*

You make yourself more work than you need, *voi v' affaticate più che non bisogna.*

You'll find yourself work enough, *voi avrete molto da fare.*

A woman's work is never at an end, *al mulino ed alla sposa sempre manca qualche cosa.*

He has made a good day's work [he has got a great deal to-day] *egli ha guadagnato molto oggi.*

To be hard at work, *lavorare assiduamente.*

I will go another way to work, *io terrò un altro modo, tenterò un' altra via.*

A work day, *un giorno di lavoro.*

Work-house, *lavoratojo, s. m. luogo dove si fanno i lavori.*

To work [to labour] *lavorare, operare.*

To work hard, *lavorare gagliardamente, lavorare a mazza stanca.*

To work one's self weary, *affaticarsi lavorando, lavorar troppo.*

To work a man's ruin, *tramare, macchinare l' altrui rovina.*

To work iron, *lavorare del ferro.*

To work wool or silk, *lavorare lana o seta.*

To work a gown with gold, *ricamare o tessere una gonna con oro.*

To work [to operate, to do, to have effect] *operare, fare, effettuare, produrre qualche effetto.*

The physick has worked very well, *la medicina ha operato molto bene.*

The Holy Spirit works in our soul, *lo Spirito Santo opera nelle nostre anime.*

To work [to be in a fermentation, as wine and other liquors] *fermentare, bollire, proprio del vino o d' altri liquori.*

The sea begins to work, *il mare comincia a gonfiarsi, ad agitarsi.*

To work deceit, *tramar inganni.*

To work one's self into one's favour, *insinuarsi nell' altrui grazia, cattivarsi l' altrui benevolenza.*

To work one's self into credit, *acquistarsi credito.*

To work out one's task, *finire il dovuto lavoro.*

To work out one's design, *venire a capo del suo disegno.*

To work one out of error [to undeceive one] *disingannare uno, sgannare alcuno.*

To work one out of his place [to undermine him] *scavallare uno dal suo posto.*

To work one's self out, *sforzarsi d' uscire.*

Time will work it out, *il tempo lo metterà in chiaro, si scoprirà col tempo.*

To work upon the humours, *muovere gli umori.*

This sad example wrought upon him, *questo tristo esempio fece grand impressione nell' animo suo.*

To work one's self off, *trarsi d' impaccio, strigarsi, liberarsi.*

Wo'rker, s. *lavoratore, artigiano, operajo, s. m.*

Work fe'llow, s. [one engaged in the same work with another] *compagno nella fatica, nel lavoro, o nel' opera.*

Wo'rking, *lavoro, lavorio, operare.*

The working of physic, *l' effetto, l' operazione d' una medicina.*

The working of the sea, *l' agitazione del mare.*

Wo'rkingday, s. [day on which labour is permitted; not the Sabbath.] *Dì di lavoro, giorno di lavoro.*

Wo'rked, the preter tense and participle of the verb To work, *v.* To work.

Wo'rkman, s. [an artificer a maker of any thing] *operajo, artista, artefice, artigiano, lavoratore, garzone.*

Wo'rkmanly, adj. [skilful, well performed, workmanlike] *ben fatto, da perito artefice, ben lavorato; e dicesi di qualsisia lavoro che è tale.*

Workmanly, adv. *cortigianamente, da perito artefice.*

Wo'rkmanship, s. [manufacture; something made by any one] *manifattura; cosa fatta da artigiano o da operajo.*

Workmanship [the skill of a worker] *lavoro che mostra che il lavoratore avea ingegno.*

Workmanship [the art of working] *l' arte dell' artigiano.*

Wo'rky, adj. ex. worky day, *giorno di lavoro.*

World, s. [the universe, the heaven and earth] *mondo, universo, cielo e terra insieme e ciò che si racchiude in essi.*

The world [the earth] *il mondo, la terra, il globo terracqueo.*

To come into the world [to be born] *venire al mondo, nascere,* pret. *nacqui.*

To go out of the world, to leave this world [to die] *uscire da questo mondo, uscir di vita, morire.*

He is known all the world over, *egli è conosciuto per tutto 'l mondo.*

The new world [the West Indies, America] *il mondo nuovo, le Indie occidentali, l' America.*

He is the best man in the world, *egli è il miglior uomo del mondo.*

To live in the great world, *frequentare persone grandi.*

He has seen the world, *egli ha praticato; ha gran pratica del mondo.*

All the world knows it, *ognuno lo sa.*

To know the world, to understand the world, *saper vivere, saper comportarsi.*

So goes the world, *così va il mondo.*

World [secular life, in opposition to religious life] *mondo, secolo.*

To

To renounce the world, *rinunciare al mondo.*
To love the world, *amare il mondo.*
To think of the next world [of a future life] *pensare all' altro mondo, alla vita futura, all' altra vita.*
To begin the world, *mettersi in istato di vivere; stabilirsi; cominciare ad avanzarsi nel mondo.*
World [an expletive term] *mondo.*
He says the finest things in the world, *dice le più belle cose del mondo.*
Nothing in the world pleases more, *niente al mondo mi piace più.*
He minds nothing in the world, *egli non bada a nulla.*
I know not what in the world to do, *io non so quel che mi fare.*
No where in the world, *in nessun luogo.*
I know not which way in the world to hide it, *non so come nasconderlo.*
A world [a great number, a great quantity] *un mondo, un gran numero, una gran quantità.*
A world of people, *un mondo di gente, una gran calca di gente.*
A world of money, *una gran quantità di danari.*
World without end [an expression only used in the Common Prayer, for ever] *ne' secoli de' secoli, eternamente.*
To be beforehand in the world, *aver qualche cosa, aver qualche capitale, aver qualche somma di danaro oltre il necessario.*
To have the world in a string [to drive the world before him] *aver la pera mezza, esser in fortuna, aver il vento in poppa.*
To be behind in the world, *far male i fatti suoi.*
I am for the woods against the world, *io preferisco i boschi ad ogni altra cosa.*
To leave one to the wide world [to leave him to his shifts] *lasciare uno in nasso, lasciarlo in abbandono.*
To recommend a thing to the world, *raccomandare una cosa al pubblico.*
What says the world of me? *che dice la gente di me? che si dice di me?*
The world says that ——, *si dice che* ——.
The world will not always be at one stay, *le cose non andranno sempre in un modo.*
WO'RDLINESS, s. [wordly vanity] *vanità mondana, cose mondane.*
WO'RLDLING, s. [a mortal set upon profits] *uno che principalmente pensa a guadagnare e a far roba senza troppo curarsi della vita avvenire, un mondano.*
WO'RLDLY, adj. [of the world] *mondano, di mondo, dedito alle vanità del mondo.*
Wordly pleasures, *piaceri mondani.*
A worldly-minded man, *un uomo mondano.*
WO'RLDLING, s. [a worldly-minded man] *un mondano.*
WORM, s. [a creeping insect] *un verme, vermo, baco, s. m. insetto che va colla pancia per terra.*

Belly-worm, *verme, baco.*
Book-worm, *tignuola, s. f.*
Chur-worm, *grillotalpa, s. m.*
Glow-worm, *lucciola, s. f.*
Earth-worm, *lombrico, s. m.*
Gold-worm, *crisalide, s. f.*
Hand-worm, *setola, s. f.*
Ring-worm, *empitiggine, s. f.*
Silk-worm, *baco da seta, s. m.*
Slow-worm, *cicigna, s. f.*
Wood-worm, *tarlo, s. m.*
Worm [a wretched creature] *un verme di terra, un niente, una misera creatura.*
Tread on a worm and it will turn, *ogni serpe ha il suo veleno.*
He has got a worm in his head, *egli ha grilli in testa, egli ha capricci in capo.*
A worm [for a gun] *un cavastoppa.*
The worm of a screw, *la chiocciola d' una vite.*
Worm [among distillers, a long winding pewter pipe to cool and thicken the vapours in the distillation of spirits] *storta*
WORM-E'ATEN, adj. [old, worthless] *vecchio, buono a nulla.*
Worm-eaten, *bacato, mangiato da' vermi, tarlato, magagnato.*
To grow worm-eaten, *tarlarsi, magagnarsi.*
Worm wood, *assenzio, s. m. erba nota.*
Worm wood wine, *vino assenziato.*
To WORM, verb neut. *bacarsi, inverminarsi.*
To worm one out of a place, *scavallare alcuno dal suo impiego.*
To worm a cable, a sea phrase [to strengthen it by winding a small rope all along between the strands] *foderare una gomona di cordicelle per moglio conservarla.*
WO'RMED, adj. *tarlato, magagnato, bacato.*
WO'RMY, adj. *verminoso, pien di vermi, bacato.*
WORN, adj. [from to wear] *portato,* v. To wear.
To WO'RRY [to pull or tear in pieces as wild beasts do] *sbranare, rompere in brani, stracciare.*
WORRIED, adj. *sbranato, stracciato.*
WORSE [the comparative of bad] *più cattivo, più tristo, peggiore, peggio.*
He is worse than ever he was, *egli è più cattivo che mai; egli è peggio che mai.*
To make one's condition worse, *peggiorare la sua condizione.*
There's nothing worse than that, *non v' è cosa peggiore di questa.*
You are worse than your word, *voi non siete uomo di parola, voi non mantenete la vostra promessa.*
'Tis worse and worse, *è peggio che mai; è di male in peggio.*
To grow worse and worse, *peggiorare, andar di cattivo stato in peggiore*
He can't do worse by me, *non saprebbe farmi peggio, non può trattarmi peggio.*

He is worse than ever [in point of health] *egli sta peggio che mai.*
To take one for better for worse [to marry] *ammogliarsi maritarsi.*
The worse, s. [the loss, not the advantage, not the better] *il peggio, il disavvantaggio, il contrario del meglio.*
The worse, s. [something less good] *cosa men buona d' altra cosa.*
To WORSE [to put to disadvantage] *cagionare svantaggio.*
Every thing is the worse for wearing, *ogni cosa si consuma col portarla.*
I shall not value him a hair the worse, *non lo stimerò punto meno.*
WO'RSHIPFUL, adj. [claiming respect by any character or dignity] *rispettabile per carattere o dignità.*
Worshipful, *rispettabile in senso ironico.*
WO'RSHIPUULLY, adv. *in rispettosa maniera, rispettosamente.*
WO'RSHIP [adoration] *adorazione, culto religioso, onore, riverenza, servizio divino.*
The divine worship, *il culto, o 'l servizio divino.*
Your worship [a title given to the gentry] *vossignoria.*
To WO'RSHIP [to adore, to do reverence] *adorare, onorare, portare onore e riverenza.*
To worship God, *adorare Iddio, rendergli un culto religioso.*
To worship one [in the scripture phrase, to fall down before him] *prostrarsi innanzi ad uno.*
WO'RSHIPPED, adj. *adorato, onorato.*
Worthy to be worshipped, *adorabile.*
WO'RSHIPPER, s. *adoratore, s. m. adoratrice, s. f.*
WO'RSHIPPING, s. *adorazione, s. f. l' adorare.*
WORST [the superlative of bad] *il più cattivo, il peggiore.*
'Tis the worst that can befall him, *è la più gran disgrazia che possa accadergli.*
He is the worst of men, *è 'l più vile uomo del mondo, è il peggiore di tutti gli uomini.*
Worst, s. [the worst thing] *il peggiore, il peggio.*
To chuse or take the worst, *scegliere il peggiore, appigliarsi al peggiore.*
I fear we shall come by the worst of it, *temo che noi avremo la peggio.*
Let the worst come to the worst, *al peggio de' peggi; il peggio che possa arrivare.*
He had the worst of it, *egli restò sopraffatto.*
Do your worst, I don't fear you, *rincaratemi il fitto, fatemi il peggio che potete, non vi temo.*
To WORST one [to have the better of one] *sopraffare, soperchiare, vantaggiare alcuno.*
WO'RSTED, adj. *sopraffatto, soperchiato, vantaggiato.*
WORT, s. [new drink, either ale or beer] *birra novella.*
Wort, s. [a plant of the cabbage kind] *sorta di cavolo.*
Wort [herb] *erba, e in questo senso non*

non si mette da se, ma si trova alla fine de' nomi di certe erbe, come sarebbe a dire, colewort, liverwort, *&c.*

WORTH, adj. [of a certain piece, or value] *che vale, di valore.*

To be worth, *valere, essere d'un certo prezzo o valore.*

He is worth a thousand pounds a year, *egli ha mille doppie d' entrata.*

It is little worth, *non val molto.*

A thing not worth minding, *una cosa che non è degna di notare.*

'Tis not worth while, *non val la pena.*

A diamond worth a thousand pounds, *un diamante che val mille lire sterline.*

Worth, s. [price, value] *prezzo, valore, valsente,* s. m. *valsuta, valuta,* s. f.

A thing of little worth, *una cosa di poco valore.*

I'll give you the worth of it, *ve lo pagherò quel che vale.*

Worth [desert, merit] *merito.*

A man of great worth, *un uomo di gran merito.*

To WORTH, or Wurth, v. n. [to be] *essere, esistere.*

WO'RTHILY, adv. *degnamente, meritamente.*

WO'RTHINESS, s. *merito, dignità, importanza.*

WO'RTHLESS, adj. *vile, di nessun valore, indegno, immeritevole.*

WO'RTHLESSNESS, s. *viltà, indegnità,* s. f.

WO'RTHIES, s. [men of great worth, illustrious personages] *uomini grandi, personaggi grandi, uomini illustri.*

WO'RTHY, adj. [deserving, that deserves any thing] *degno, meritevole, che merita qualunque cosa.*

Worthy of reward, *degno di guiderdone, che merita ricompensa.*

Praise-worthy, *degno di lode, lodevole.*

A worthy man [a man of worth] *un uomo di merito.*

A worthy action, *un' azione onorata.*

A worthy friend, *un amico degno di stima.*

To WO'RTHY [to render worthy, to aggrandize, to exalt] *render degno, ingrandire, esaltare.*

WOT, *è un preterito del verbo inusitato.* To wot, ex. God wot [for God knows] *Iddio sa.*

WOVE } adj. [from the verb, To WO'VEN, } weave] *tessuto.*

WOULD [from the verb to will] *voleva, volli, ho voluto, vorrei, volessi.*

I could do it if I would, *potrei farlo se volessi.*

I would not do it before he desired me, *non ho voluto farlo prima che me ne pregasse.*

I would not do it for all the world, *non vorrei farlo per qualsivoglia cosa el mondo.*

Would, *è sovente usato per segno del secondo futuro.*

I would have done it if I had been able, *l' avrei fatto se avessi potuto.*

I would have you know that ——, *voglio che sappiate* ——.

As luck would have it, *per buona fortuna.*

He went along with me whether I would or no, *volle venir meco mio malgrado.*

Would to God, *volesse Dio.*

WO'ULDING, s. [motion of desire; disposition to any thing, propension, inclination, incipient purpose] *propensione, inclinazione, desiderio cominciante, desio non ancor maturo o perfetto.*

WOUND, adj. [from to wind] *voltato.*

Wound up [wrapt up] *inviluppato.*

Wound, s. *ferita,* s. f.

To give one a wound, *ferire alcuno.*

To give him a mortal wound, *ferirlo a morte.*

Love wound, *ferita amorosa.*

To WOUND [to give a wound] *ferire,* pref. *ferisco.*

To wound to death, *ferire a morte.*

To wound [to offend, to wrong] *offendere, far torto.*

To wound one's own conscience, *offendere la propria coscienza.*

To wound a man's reputation, *far torto all' altrui riputazione.*

WO'UNDED, adj. *ferito.*

WO'UNDLESS, adj. [exempt from wounds] *fatato, invulnerabile, esente da ferite.*

WO'UNDY, adj. [or prodigious] *grande.* Obsol.

A woundy deal, *una gran quantità.*

Woundy, adv. *molto.* Obsol.

WOX } *preterito del verbo* to wax, WOXE } *divenire.* Obs.

WO'XEN, *participio del verbo* to wax, *divenire.* Obs.

WRACK, s. [ship-wrack, the casting away of a ship] *naufragio.*

To suffer ship-wrack, *far naufragio.*

To go to wrack, *andare in rovina, rovinare.*

Sea-wrack [a sea weed] *alga,* s. f. *erba aquatica.*

Wrack [the part of a ship that is perished and cast a-shore belonging to the King] *quella parte del vascello che rimane dopo fatto naufragio e che appartiene al Re.*

To WRACK [to suffer shipwrack] *naufragare, far naufragio.*

WRA'NGLANDS, s. [misgrown trees, that will never prove timber] *alberi intristiti che non son buoni da far legname.*

To WRA'NGLE [to brawl, to scold, to quarrel] *contrastare, contendere, contraddire, quistionare, disputare, rissare, competere, garrire,* pret. *contesi, contraddissi,* pref. *contraddico, garrisco.*

WRA'NGLER, s. *un contenditore, un riottoso, un garritore,* s. m. *una contenditrice, una riottosa, una garritrice,* s. f.

WRA'NGLING, s. *contesa, disputa, querela, rissa,* s. f. *contendimento, contrasto,* s. f.

Wrangling, adj. *riottoso.*

Wrangling fellow, *uomo riottoso, un contenditore.*

To WRAP [to infold, to inclose] *inviluppare, avviluppare, involgere, ravviluppare, rinvolgere, rinviluppare.*

To wrap [to wind about, to twist] *avvinghiare, avvincere, attorcigliare, attortigliare, cignere intorno,* pret. *cinsi.*

To wrap one's self up in one's own cloak, *avvilupparsi nel proprio mantello.*

WRA'PPER, s. *colui che avviluppa, o la cosa che avviluppa.*

WRAPT, adj. *inviluppato, avviluppato, avvinghiato, avvinto.*

Wrapt up in admiration of ecstasy, *rapito in estasi.*

To be wrapt up in one's mother's smock, *esser nato vestito, esser avventurato.*

I am so wrapt up in him, *l' amo talmente, ne sono talmente incapricciato.*

WRATH, s. [extreme anger, indignation] *collera, ira, stizza, indegnazione,* s. f. *sdegno, corruccio, cruccio,* s. m.

The wrath of God, *la collera, l' ira di Dio.*

WRA'THFUL, adj. *iracondo, collerico, stizzoso, corruccioso, sdegnoso, rabbioso, arrabbiato.*

WRA'THFULLY, adv. *bruscamente, iracondamente, stizzosamente, velenosamente.*

WRA'THLESS, adj. [free from anger] *che non ha rabbia, che non ha più o non può avere stizza, veleno, collera, e simili.*

WREAK, s. [revenge, vengeance] *vendetta.*

Wreak [passion, furious fit] *furore, veleno, momento rabbioso.*

To WREAK [to discharge, to vent] *sfogare.*

To wreak one's anger upon one, *sfogar la collera contra qualcheduno.*

WRE'AKFUL, adj. [revengeful, angry] *bramoso di vendetta, invelenito.*

WREATH, s. [a roll such as women wear on their heads in carrying a pail] *cereine,* s. m.

Wreath [garland] *ghirlanda,* s. f. *serto,* s. m.

Laurel wreath, *ghirlanda d' alloro.*

Wreath [in architecture, the torce or twisted work] *cordone,* s. m. *termine d' architettura.*

Wreath [among hunters, a boar's tail] *la coda d' un cinghiale.*

To WREATH [to twist, to twine about] *torcere, attorcigliare, attortigliare, avvinghiare,* pret. *torsi.*

To wreath a thing about one's arm, *attorcigliarsi che che sia intorno al braccio.*

To wreath [to crown] *coronare.*

WRE'ATHED, } adj. *torto, attorcigliato,* WRE'ATHEN, } *attortigliato, avvinghiato, coronato, cinto di serto, inghirlandato.*

WRECK, s. [wrack, destruction by being driven on rocks or shallows at sea] *distruzione cagionata da naufragio urtando contro uno scoglio o secca.*

Wreck [dissolution of violence] *dissoluzione violenta.*

Wreck [ruin, destruction] *rovina, distruzione.*

To Wreck [to wrack] *naufragare, far naufragio.*

Wren, s. [one of the leaſt ſort of birds] *luì*, s. m. *uccello piccoliſſimo.*

Wrench, s. [ſprain] *ſtorcimento*, s. m. *ſlogatura*, s. f.

To Wrench [to ſprain] *ſtorcere, ſlogare, diſlogare.*

To wrench one's foot, *ſtorcerſi, ſlogarſi un piede.*

To wrench a door, *rompere o ſpalancare una porta.*

Wre'nched, adj. *ſtorto, ſlogato, diſlogato, rotto, ſpalancato.*

Wrest, s. [a ſort of bow to tune muſical inſtruments with] *quello ſtrumento, col quale ſi accordano gli ſtrumenti muſicali.*

To Wrest [to wreath, to twiſt, to turn about] *torcere, attorcigliare, attortigliare, avvinghiare.*

To wreſt [to wring, to pull, to ſnatch] *ſtrappare, ſpiccare, levar via con violenza.*

To wreſt the ſenſe of an author or paſſage, *torcere, ſtravolgere il ſenſo d' un autore o d' un paſſo di qualche ſcrittura.*

Wre'sted, adj. *torto, v.* To wreſt.

To Wre'stle [to uſe the exerciſe of wreſtling] *lottare, giuocare alla lotta.*

To wreſtle [to contend, to ſtruggle] *contendere, contraſtare.*

Wre'stled, adj. *lottato.*

Wre'stler, s. *lottatore*, s. m.

Wre'stling, s. *lotta, lutta*, s. f.

To practiſe wreſtling, *eſercitarſi alla lotta.*

To have ſkill in wreſtling, *ſaper lottare.*

A wreſtling place, *una paleſtra, il luogo dove ſi lotta.*

Wretch, s. [an unfortunate forlorn creature] *un miſero, un meſchino.*

A wretch [a ſcoundrel, a raſcal, a worthleſs dog] *un furfante, un briccone, un birbone, un goglioffo, uno ſcellerato.*

An ungrateful wretch, *un ingrato.*

Wre'tched, adj. [pitiful, miſerable, unfortunate] *povero, miſero, meſchino, ſgraziato, ſventurato, infelice.*

He is a wretched man, *egli è un cattivo uomo.*

A wretched action, *una cattiva azione.*

Wre'tched [pitiful, ſorry, ſcurvy] *vile, indegno, da niente.*

Wretched fellow, *uomo vile, uomo da niente.*

Wre'tchedly, adv. *infelicemente, miſeramente, meſchinamente, poveramente, ſventuratamente, ſgraziatamente.*

To live wretchedly, *viver meſchinamente.*

Wretchedly [pitifully, ſadly, ſorrily] *vilmente, malamente, groſſolanamente, alla peggio.*

To do a thing wretchedly, *fare che che ſia malamente, groſſolanamente, alla peggio.*

To be wretchedly clad, *eſſer malamente veſtito, eſſer male in arneſe.*

Wre'tchedness, s. [miſery] *meſchinità, miſeria*, s. f.

Wretchedneſs [wickedneſs] *colpa, cattiva azione.*

To Wri'ggle [to turn here and there as a ſnake does] *piegarſi, torcerſi, ſtorcerſi, ſcontorcerſi come un ſerpente, ſerpeggiare.*

To wriggle [to thruſt] *ficcare, cacciare.*

He made a hard ſhift to wriggle his body into a hen-rooſt, *a gran pena ſi ficcò in un pollajo.*

To wriggle one's ſelf into favour, *inſinuarſi, introdurſi nella buona grazia di qualcheduno, cattivarſi la ſua benevolenza.*

To wriggle away from one, *ſbrigarſi, liberarſi da qualcheduno.*

Wri'ggling, s. [of a ſnake] *ſerpeggiamento*, s. m.

Wright, s. [artificer, workman] *artigiano.*

Cart-wright, *carrettajo*, s. m.

Ship-wright, *legnajuolo di vaſcelli.*

Wheel-wright, *facitor di ruote.*

To Wring [to wreſt, to turn about] *torcere, ſtorcere*, pret. *torſi, ſtorſi.*

To wring one's arm, *ſtorcere il braccio ad uno.*

To wring a thing from one, *ſtrappar che che ſia di mano ad uno.*

To wring [to preſs, to ſqueeze hard] *ſpremere, premere.*

To wring out the juice of an orange, *ſpremere il ſugo d' un melangolo*

This ſhoe wrings me, *queſta ſcarpa mi ſtringe troppo il piede.*

To wring [to pinch, to gripe] *pizzicare con tormento.*

The cholick wrings me, *la colica mi tormenta, la colica mi fa ſofferire dolori grandi.*

Wri'nger, s. [one who ſqueezes the water out of clothes] *colui che torcendo ſpreme l' acqua da' panni.*

Wri'nging, s. *torcimento.*

The wringing of the guts, *dolori colici.*

The wringing of the conſcience, *i rimorſi, la ſindereſi della coſcienza.*

Wri'nkle, s. [fold, as in garments, ſkin, &c.] *piega, ruga, grinza.*

Her face is full of wrinkles, *il ſuo viſo è pieno di rughe, è tutto rugoſo.*

To wrinkle [to cauſe wrinkles] *piegare, rugare, grinzare.*

To wrinkle [to have wrinkles] *grinzarſi, eſſer rugoſo, o grinzo.*

Wri'nkled, adj. *rugoſo, grinzo, piegato.*

Wrist, s. [the part of the arm adjoining to the hand] *quella parte del braccio cha più s' avvicina alla mano.*

Wri'stband, s. *quella liſta di tela che circonda il braccio all' eſtremità della manica della camicia e ſerraſi co' bottoni.*

Writ, s. [a written order or precept from the king or court of judicature, by which any thing is commanded to be done relating to a ſuit or action, as a defendant to be ſummoned or a diſtreſs to be taken] *ordine in iſcritto, citazione.*

To iſſue out a writ, *dare ordine.*

To ſend out a writ, *mandare una citazione.*

The holy writ [the ſcripture] *la ſcrittura ſacra, la ſcrittura.*

Writ, adj [from to write] *ſcritto.*

To Write, *ſcrivere, mettere in iſcritto.*

To write a book, *ſcrivere, comporre un libro.*

Write me word how it is, *ſcrivetemi, datemi avviſo, avviſatemi, fatemi ſapere la coſa come ſta.*

To write back or back again, *riſpondere, far riſpoſta.*

To write a thing over again, *riſcrivere, di nuovo ſcrivere.*

To write a thing down, *mettere che che ſia in iſcritto.*

To write out, *traſcrivere, copiare*, pret. *traſcriſſi.*

To write out, to write all out, *ſcriver tutto, ſcrivere da una parte all' altra.*

Wri'ter, s. [one that writes] *ſcrittore, copiſta*, s. m.

Writer [pen-man, author] *ſcrittore, autore*, s. m.

To Wri'the [to wring, to twiſt, to wreſt] *torcere, ſtorcere, piegare, attorcigliare, attortigliare, avvinghiare*, pret. *ſtorſi.*

To writhe a man's neck, *torcere il collo ad uno.*

To writhe the mouth, *torcere il muſo.*

To writhe a thing out of one's hands, *ſtrappare che che ſia di mano ad uno.*

Wri'then, adj. *torto, ſtorto, attorcigliato, attortigliato, avvinghiato.*

Wri'thing, s. *torcimento.*

To Wri'thle [to wrinkle, to corrugate] *cagionar rughe o grinze; raggrinzare.*

Wri'ting, s. [from to write] *ſcrittura*, s. f.

The art of writing, *l' arte dello ſcrivere.*

One's writing, or his hand-writing, *la ſcrittura, la mano d' una perſona.*

Short hand writing, *ſcrittura per abbreviazione.*

To put down in writing, *mettere in iſcritto.*

A writting [a written paper or note] *uno ſcritto.*

Writings [or papers of a ſuit at law] *ſcritture.*

The writings of an author, *gli ſcritti, le opere d' un autore.*

Writing-maſter, *maeſtro di ſcrivere, maeſtro di ſcrittura.*

Writing-deſk, *deſco da ſcrivervi ſù.*

Wri'tten, adj. *ſcritto, v.* To write.

Written news, *avviſi ſcritti a mano.*

Wro'ken, *participio paſſivo del verbo* to wreak.

Wrong, adj. *falſo, indiretto.*

To take wrong meaſures, *prendere mezzi indiretti o cattive miſure.*

I took the wrong glove, *ho preso un guanto per l' altro.*

The wrong side of the cloth, *il rovescio del panno.*

The wrong side outward, *alla rovescia.*

To be in the wrong box [to be in an error] *ingannarsi, sbagliare.*

Wrong s. [injury, injustice] *torto,* s. m. *ingiustizia, ingiuria,* s. f.

You do me wrong, *voi mi fate torto.*

To be in the wrong, *aver torto.*

Wrong, adv. *male, a torto.*

You understand it wrong, *voi l' intendete male.*

Right or wrong, *a diritto o a torto, bene o male.*

To WRONG [to do injustice] *far torto, fare ingiustizia, oltraggiare, ingiuriare.*

WRONG-DO'ER, s. *uomo ingiusto, uno che fa torto altrui.*

WRO'NGED, adj. *che ha ricevuto torto, oltraggiato.*

WRO'NGER, s. [wrong-doer] *quello o quella che fa torto; oltraggiatore, oltraggiatrice.*

WRO'NGFUL, adj. *ingiusto.*

WRO'NGFULLY, adv. *a torto, ingiustamente, senza ragione.*

WRO'NGHEAD, } adj. [having
WRONGHE'ADED, } a perverse understanding] *che ha la mente storta, di cervello stravolto.*

WRO'NGLY, adv. [unjustly, amiss] *ingiustamente, a torto, male.*

WRO'NGLESSLY, adv. [without injury to any] *senza recar danno o fare ingiuria ad alcuno.*

WROTE [*preterito del verbo* to write] *scrissi.*

WROTH, adj. [from wrath] *irritato, stizzato, in collera, corrucciato.*

WROUGHT, adj. [from to work] *lavorato, operato, v.* To work.

Wrought silver, *argento lavorato.*

WRUNG, adj. [from to wring] *torto, attorcigliato, attortigliato, avvinghiato.*

WRY, adj. [on one side, not straight] *bieco, bistorto, indiretto, obliquo, schimbescio, sghembo.*

A wry face, *grugno, muso storto.*

To make wry faces, *fare il grugno, arricciare il viso.*

Wry-legged, *che ha le gambe storte.*

Wry-mouthed, *che torce la bocca.*

Wry-necked, *che ha il collo storto:*

Wry-neck [a little bird] *torcicollo,* s. m. *sorta d' uccelletto, detto così dal frequente torcere il collo.*

To WRY, *torcere.*

To wry the neck, *torcere il collo.*

To wry, v. n. *torcersi, non andar dritto.*

WRY'ED, adj. *torto, storto, bieco.*

WRY'LY, adv. *a traverso, biecamente, obbliquamente, tortamente, a sghembo.*

WYCH-HO'USE [a house in which salt is boiled] *salina,* s. f. *luogo dove si fa il sale.*

X.

X, *Questa lettera non si trova mai la prima nelle voci della lingua Inglese, quando è in mezzo o in fine pronunciasi come dagl' Italiani la X Latina.*

Y.

Y, *Vigesima terza lettera dell' alfabeto Inglese.*

YACHT, s. [a small sort of sea-vessel] *una saettia, sorta di nave picciola,* s. f.

YAP, s. [a little dog] *cagnolino.*

YARD, s. [a measure of length] *misura Inglese di lunghezza, che presso noi si direbbe canna, braccio, o cosa simile.*

Yard [the timber cross the mast of a ship, on which the sails hang] *antenna,* s. f. *quello stile, che s' attraversa all' albero del navilio, al quale si lega la vela.*

The main yard, *l' antenna grande.*

Yard

Yard [inclosed ground adjoining to a house] *cortile, corte*, s. m.

Yard land, s. [a certain quantity of land, containing from twenty to forty acres] *un certo numero di pertiche di terra.*

YARE [eager] *avido, ardente.*

Yare, among sailors [nimble, quick, expeditious] *agile, snello, destro, leggieri, sciolto di membra.*

YA'RELY, adv. [skilfully, dexterously] *destramente, agilmente, bravamente.*

YARN, s. [spun wool] *stame, lana filata.*

Yarn-beam of a weaver, *subito*, s. m.

To YARR [as a dog] *ringhiare, broncolare.*

YA'RRING, s. *ringhio*, s. m. *ringhiare.*

YA'RRISH, adj. *ringhiosa, che ringhia.*

YA'RROW, s. [the herb milfoil] *millefoglie, spezie d' erba.*

To YAW [a ship is said to yaw, when, through the fault of the steersman, she is not kept steady in her course, but makes angles in and out] *barcollare, come fa un vascello.*

YAWLE } s. *piatta*, s. f. *spezie di barca con fondo piano.*
YAWL }

To YAWL [to bawl] *gridare, sgridare, miagolare, gagnolare, strillare.*

YA'WLING, s. *grido, strillo*, s. m.

YAWN, s. [gape, gaping] *sbadigliamento, sbadiglio*, s. m.

To YAWN [to gape] *sbadigliare, e sbavigliare.*

YA'WNING, s. *sbadigliamento e sbavigliamento, sbadiglio*, s. m. *lo sbadigliare.*

Yawning, adj. *sbadigliante, sbavigliante, che sbadiglia.*

Yawning is catching, *un che sbadiglia ne fa sbadigliar due.*

Y'CLAD, *participio usato in vere di* clad [clothed] *vestito.*

Y'CLEPED, adj. [called, termed, named] *chiamato, detto, nomato, nominato.*

Y'DREAD, *antico preterito del verbo* to dread.

YE, *voi*; *ed è nominativo plurale di* thou, *tu.*

YEA, adv. [yes] *sì, particola affirmativa.*

Say yea or nay, *dite sì, o no.*

To YEAD } v. n. *preterito* yode [to
To YEDE } go, to march] *andarsene, marciare, incamminarsi.*

To YEAN [to bring young] *figliare, e dicesi delle pecore.*

YE'ANLING, s. [the young of sheep] *pecorino, pecorella.*

YEAR, s. [the time the sun takes up in going through the twelve signs of the zodiack] *anno*, s. m.

Solar or lunar year, *anno solare o lunare.*

New year, *anno nuovo.*

The new year's day, *il primo giorno dell' anno.*

Once a year, *una volta l' anno.*

Every other year, *di due in due anni, un anno sì, un anno no.*

Every third year, *di tre in tre anni.*

Years [age] *anni, età.*

To be full of years, *esser aggravato dagli anni.*

Years of discretion, *gli anni della discrezione.*

To be in years, *esser avanzato in età, esser vecchio.*

To grow in years, *invecchiare, diventar vecchio.*

The more thy years, the nearer thy grave, *più uno invecchia più s' avvicina alla sepoltura.*

YE'ARLING, s. [of a year old] *che non ha che un anno.*

YE'ARLY, adj. [that happens every year] *annuale, che si rinnuova ogni anno.*

Yearly, adv. *annualmente, ogni anno, d' anno in anno.*

To YEARN [to feel great internal uneasiness] *essere molto turbato nell' interno, essere moltissimo affannato.*

To yearn [to be moved with compassion] *muoversi a pietà, a compassione.*

My bowels yearn, *il cuore mi si muove a compassione.*

To yearn to bark as beagles or hunting dogs do at their prey] *abbajare, squittire, come fanno i bracchi che seguitano la fera.*

YE'ARNED, adj. *mosso a compassione*; v. To yearn.

YE'ARNING, s. *commiserazione, compassione, pietà*, s. f.

YE'ARNFULLY, adv. *compassionevolmente, pietosamente.*

To YEDE, v. To read.

YELK, s. [yolk] *tuorlo*, s. m. *rosso d' uovo.*

To YELL [to make a dreadful howling noise] *urlare, gagnolare, mugolare.*

YE'LLED, adj. *urlato, gagnolato, mugolato.*

The dog yelled all night long, *il cane ha gagnolato tutta la notte.*

YE'LLING, s. [dismal howling] *ululo, urlamento, urlo, mugolamento, mugolio*, s. m.

YE'LLOW, adj. *giallo.*

To grow or become yellow, *divenir giallo.*

Yellow bay, *dorè, aurino, rancio.*

Yellow, s. *giallo, color giallo.*

To dye yellow, *tingere in giallo.*

Yellows [jaundice] *itterizia*, s. f.

YE'LLOWISH, adj. *gialliccio, gialletto, giallognolo.*

To be yellowish, *gialleggiare, tendere al giallo.*

YE'LLOWNESS, s. *giallezza*, s. f. *giallume giallore*, s. m.

YE'LPING, s. *lo squittire.*

YE'OMAN, s. [countryman or freeholder, who has lands of his own and lives upon good husbandry] *contadino ricco, che vive del suo.*

Yeomen of the guards [a sort of foot guards] *guardie a piedi che sono alla corte del Re d' Inghiterra, come gli Svizzeri nella corte del Papa e d' altri Principi.*

To YERK [to wince] *calcitrare, tirar de' calci.*

YES, adv. *sì.*

Yes truly, *veramente sì.*

I say yes, *dico di sì.*

One yes may make me happy, *un sì può farmi felice.*

YEST, s. [the sediments of ale, generally made use of in England to make the dough rise] *fermento o feccia di cervogia.*

YE'STERDAY, adv. *jeri.*

The day before yesterday, *avanti jeri, jer l' altro.*

Yesterday morning, *jermattina.*

Yesterday night, or yesternight, *jersera.*

YE'STY, adj. [frothy, spumy] *spumoso, pien di spuma.*

YET, adv. [still, at this time] *ancora.*

He is not gone yet, *egli non è ancora partito.*

Yet [notwithstanding] *però, nientedimeno, nulladimeno.*

Though you deny it yet I know it, *con tutto che voi lo negate io però lo so.*

She is ugly and yet he knows her, *ella è brutta e nientedimeno egli l' ama.*

YE'VEN, *usato in vece di* given.

YEW, s. [female sheep] *pecora*, v. Ewe.

Yew [yew tree] *tasso, nasso*, s. m.

To YEX [to hiccup, to sob] *singhiozzare, avere il singhiozzo.*

To YIELD [to give over, to give up] *cedere, dar luogo.*

To yield the victory, *cedar la vittoria.*

To yield one's self to another's mercy, *rendersi, abbondonarsi all' altrui misericordia.*

To yield [to give, to grant] *dare, concedere.*

To yield reasons for some thing, *allegare ragioni per qualche cosa.*

You must needs yield me this, *bisogna che voi mi cediate questo.*

To yield [to produce, to bring forth] *produrre, rendere, fruttare.*

His place yields him a thousand pounds a year, *il suo impiego gli rende mille lire sterline l' anno.*

The rose yields a sweet smell, *la rosa ha buon odore.*

That tree yields very good fruit, *quel' albero produce buoni frutti.*

To yield up [to make over] *cedere, far cessione.*

To yield up the ghost, *render l' anima, render lo spirito.*

To yield [to submit, to surrender] *rendersi, cedere, sottomettersi, soccombere, darsi per vinto.*

To yield to the times, *cedere al tempo, temporeggiare.*

All things yield to the force of arms, *ogni cosa cede alla forza delle armi.*

To yield to the temptation, *soccombere alla tentazione.*

I will not yield to these terms, *non voglio sottomettermi a queste condizioni.*

To yield to a thing, *concedere una cosa, darsi per vinto.*

To yield, to give [as stones do in wet weather] *sudare, trapelare, distillare, stillare.*

To yield [to grant, to confeſſes] *concedere, confeſſare, darla vinta.*

YI'ELDED, adj. *ceduto, v.* To yield.

YI'ELDER, s. [one who yields] *quella perſona che cede, che non tien ſaldo, che non reſiſte, che ſi ritira in vece di far fronte.*

YI'ELDING, s. *ceſſione, s. f. il cedere.*

Yielding, adj. *facile, comodo, condeſcendente, condiſcendente.*

She is a little too yielding, *ella è un poco troppo facile, ella è un poco troppo condeſcendente, ella ſi laſcia andare troppo facilmente.*

YI'ELDINGLY, adv. [freely] *liberamente, francamente, ſchiettamente.*

To crry one's ſelf yieldingly, *aver della condeſcendenza, eſſer condeſcendente.*

YI'ELDINGNESS, *facilità, compiacenza, condeſcendenza.*

YOKE, s. [a frame of wood to couple oxen together] *giogo,* s. m.

To put the oxen to the yoke, *mettere i buoi al giogo, accoppiare inſieme i buoi.*

Yoke [ſubjection, bondage, ſlavery] *giogo, ſervitù, ſoggezzione,* s. f.

To hring under the yoke, *ſoggiogare, metter ſotto il giogo.*

To ſhake off the yoke, *ſcuotere il giogo.*

To be under the yoke, *eſſer ſotto 'l giogo, ſoggiogato.*

Tye yoke of matrimony, *il giogo maritale.*

Yoke of oxen, *coppia di buoi.*

Yoke-elm [a ſort of tree] *ſorta d'arbore.*

To YOKE, *accoppiare al giogo, mettere il giogo.*

To yoke the oxen, *mettere i buoi al giogo, accoppiare i buoi.*

To yoke [to join or couple with another] *unire con un altro.*

To yoke [to enſlave, to ſubdue] *ſoggiogare, ſottomettere, impadronirſi.*

To yoke [to reſtrain, to confine] *raffrenare, limitare, riſtringere in limiti.*

YOKED, adj. *accoppiato, meſſo al giogo.*

YOKEFE'LLOW, YO'KEMATE, s. [companion in labour] *compagno nelle fatiche, nel lavoro.*

YOLD, *uſato in vece di* yielded.

YOLK, s. [yelk, the fellow part of an egg] *roſſo d'uovo.*

YON, YOND, adv. *là.*

Do you ſee yon fellow? *vedete quell' uomo là.*

Yond, adj. [mad, furious] *impazzato, matto, furioſo, furibondo.*

YO'NDER, adv. [there] *là, più in là.*

Yonder he is, *eccolo là.*

Yonder is my brother, *ecco là il mio fratello.*

YORE, of yore, adv. [heretofore, anciently] *già, per lo paſſato, anticamente.*

In the days of yore, *già, tempo fa, per l'addietro, anticamente.*

YOU, *voi; caſo obliquo di* ye, *ed è ſpeſſo uſato nel nominativo; come* you have, *voi avete;* you do *voi fate;* you ſay *voi dite, e ſimili; in vere della ſeconda perſona ſingolare gl' Ingleſi uſano il* you *come noi l'*ella *e il* lei.

YOUNG, adj. [not old] *giovane, giovanile.*

A young boy, a young girl, *un giovane, una giovane.*

A young horſe, *un cavallo giovane.*

Youug age, *età giovanile.*

To grow young again, *ringiovanire, ritornar giovane.*

Young [not ripe in judgment] *ſoro, novizio, ineſperto.*

Young [freſh, vigorous] *giovane, gagliardo, vigoroſo.*

Young, s. ex. the young-ones of a bitch, *i cagnolini.*

To bring forth young-ones, *figliare.*

To bear young, *portare, eſſer pregna.*

The bitch is with young, *la cagna è pregna.*

YO'UNGER [the comparative of young] *più giovane.*

The younger brother or ſiſter, *il fratel minore, la ſorella minore, il più giovane, o la più giovane.*

To be the younger hand [at play] *eſſer l'ultimo nel giuoco.*

YO'UNGEST [the ſuperlative of young] *il più giovane.*

The youngeſt brother of all, *il più giovane di tutti i fratelli.*

YO'UNGISH, adj. *alquanto giovine.*

YO'UNGLING, s. *creatura che è ne' primi anni di ſua vita.*

YO'UNGLY, adv. *giovenilmente; ignorantemente, ineſpertamente.*

YO'UNGSTER, s. [airy briſk young man] *giovanaſtro, giovanotto, giovane gagliardo e robuſto.*

YOUR [a poſſeſſive pronoun from YOU] *voſtro, voſtra.*

Your father, your mother, *voſtro padre, voſtra madre.*

Your houſe, your horſe, *la voſtra caſa, il voſtro cavallo.*

It is your own fault, *è voſtra colpa.*

Yourſelf, you yourſelf, your own ſelf, *voi ſteſſo, voi medeſimo.*

Your ſelves, your own ſelves, *voi ſteſſi, voi medeſimi.*

Yours [pron. poſſ.] *voſtro.*

This is yours, *queſto è voſtro, è il voſtro.*

YOUTH, s. [tender age] *giovanezza, gioventù,* s. f.

From my youth, *dalla mia giovanezza, dalla mia gioventù.*

Youth [youth people] *la gioventù, i giovani.*

A youth [a young man, a boy] *un giovanotto.*

YO'UTHFUL, adj. [young] *giovane, giovanile.*

In my youthful days, *nella mia gioventù.*

YO'UTHFULLY, adv. *giovanilmente, da giovane.*

YO'UTHFULNESS, *gioventù, giovanezza,* s. f.

YO'UTHLY, adj. *giovane, giovenile.*

YUCK, s. [itch] *rogna, ſcabbia.*

YULE, s. [a north country word for Chriſtmas] *natale, voce uſata in alcune parti ſettentrionali d' Inghilterra.*

YUX, s. [the hiccough] *il ſinghiozzo, il ſinghiozzire, il ſinghiozzare.*

Z.

Z, *Ultima lettera dell' alfabeto Inglese.*

ZA'FFAR, } s. *sorta di minerale fatto*
ZA'FFIR, } *artificiosamente.*

ZA'NY, s. [buffoon, merry-andrew] *zanni, buffone.*

ZEAL, s. [an earnest passion for any thing, but especially for one's religion and the welfare of one's country] *zelo, amore, affetto, desiderio, stimolo dell' altrui o del proprio bene.*

ZE'ALOT, s. [zealous person, great stickler] *zelatore, zelante, e per lo più dicesi della religione.*

ZE'ALOUS, adj. [full of zeal] *zelanto, che ha zelo.*

ZE'ALOUSLY, adv. *zelantemente, con zelo.*

ZECHI'N, s. [a Venetian coin] *zecchino,* s. m. *moneta d' oro Veneziana.*

ZED, *nome della lettera da noi chiamata zeta.*

ZE'DOARY, s. [a root not unlike ginger] *zedoaria,* s. f. *zettoario,* s. m.

ZE'NITH, s. [that point in the heavens which is directly over our head] *zenitte,* s. m. *punto verticale.*

ZE'PHYR, } s. [the west wind]
ZE'PHYRUS, } *zeffiro, zefiro,* s. m. *nome di vento occidentale che particolarmente spira la primavera.*

ZE'RO, s. [cypher, nought] *zero, niente*

ZEST [part of the peel of an orange] *un po' di scorza di arancio.*

ZO'DIACK, s. [the track of the sun through the twelve signs; a great circle of the sphere containing the twelve signs] *zodiaco.*

ZONE, s. [belt, girdle] *zona, fascia,* s. f.

Zones [in astronomy, are spaces contained between two parellels or divisions of the heavens or earth] *zone.*

There are five zones, one torrid, two temperate, and two frigid, *vi sono cinque zone, una torrida, due temperate, e due frigide.*

ZOOPHY'TES, s. [certain substances which partake of the nature of plants and living creatures, as spunges, &c.] *zoofito,* s. m.

F I N I S.

Lightning Source UK Ltd.
Milton Keynes UK
UKHW051051301118
332889UK00009BA/874/P

9 780666 190161